HARRIS, O'BOYLE & WARBRICK: LAW OF THE
EUROPEAN CONVENTION ON HUMAN RIGHTS

HARRIS, O'BOYLE & WARBRICK
LAW OF THE EUROPEAN CONVENTION ON HUMAN RIGHTS

Third edition

DAVID HARRIS LLM, PHD, CMG
Emeritus Professor in Residence, and Co-Director, Human Rights Law Centre, University of Nottingham

MICHAEL O'BOYLE LLB, LLM
Deputy Registrar, European Court of Human Rights

ED BATES LLB, LLM, PHD
Senior Lecturer in Law, University of Leicester

CARLA BUCKLEY LLB, LLM
Research Fellow, Human Rights Law Centre, University of Nottingham

Chapter 2 by
PAUL HARVEY LLB, PHD
Registry Lawyer, European Court of Human Rights

Chapter 12 by
MICHELLE LAFFERTY LLB, LLM, MA
Registry Lawyer, European Court of Human Rights

Chapter 13 by
PETER CUMPER LLB, LLM
Professor of Law, University of Leicester

Chapter 14 by
YUTAKA ARAI LLM, PHD
Senior Lecturer in International Law, University of Kent

Chapter 23 by
HEATHER GREEN LLB, PHD
Senior Lecturer, University of Aberdeen

OXFORD
UNIVERSITY PRESS

OXFORD
UNIVERSITY PRESS

Great Clarendon Street, Oxford, OX2 6DP,
United Kingdom

Oxford University Press is a department of the University of Oxford.
It furthers the University's objective of excellence in research, scholarship,
and education by publishing worldwide. Oxford is a registered trade mark of
Oxford University Press in the UK and in certain other countries

© Oxford University Press 2014

The moral rights of the authors have been asserted

First edition published 1994
Second edition published 2009

Impression: 1

Public sector information reproduced under Open Government Licence v1.0
(http://www.nationalarchives.gov.uk/doc/open-government-licence/open-government-licence.htm)

Crown Copyright material reproduced with the permission of the
Controller, HMSO (under the terms of the Click Use licence)

Published in the United States of America by Oxford University Press
198 Madison Avenue, New York, NY 10016, United States of America

British Library Cataloguing in Publication Data
Data available

Library of Congress Control Number: 2014933296

ISBN 978-0-19-960639-9

Printed in Great Britain by
Ashford Colour Press Ltd, Gosport, Hampshire

PREFACE

Much has happened since the last edition of this book in 2009. Notably, the Court's jurisprudence has grown apace, the reform of the enforcement system has been taken further and, disturbingly, discontent with the Court has increased in the UK.

The Court's judgments in the last five years have extended the reach of the Convention and further spelt out the meaning of its guarantee. Developments have included the continued expansion of the positive obligation in Article 2 to protect life (including protection against natural disasters: *Budayeva and Others v Russia*) and a requirement in Article 3 that whole life sentences be subject to review and the possible release of offenders (*Vinter v UK*). Human trafficking has been brought within the scope of Article 4 (*Rantsev v Cyprus and Russia*) and the crowd control technique known as 'kettling' has been held not to be detention within Article 5 (*Austin v UK*, on the facts of that case). In other Article 5 cases the Court has required more of states in relation to prisoner rehabilitation (*James, Well and Lee v UK*) and the regimes governing social care homes (*Stanev v Bulgaria*). On the right to a fair trial, the Court has adopted positions of particular interest to common law jurisdictions on whether juries must give reasons for their decisions (*Taxquet v Belgium*) and on the admissibility of hearsay evidence (*Al-Khawaja and Tahery v UK*). Article 8 jurisprudence has been considerable and wide-ranging. The Court has sought to exercise its review jurisdiction in harmony with the sensitive ethical and moral questions posed in areas of medical and scientific development (*Hristozov and Others v Bulgaria, SH v Austria, Costa and Pavan v Italy, Ternovszky v Hungary*), and has taken account of societal changes in the context of abortion (*A, B and C v Ireland, R.R. v Poland*). In some cases, the Court has responded to criticisms that it has tended to take the place of national decision-makers by a greater emphasis on subsidiarity in its case-law on immigration/deportation issues and in Article 8/10 privacy v. press freedom cases. The Court has also shown increasing recognition of a right of access to information arising under Article 8, the contours of which are as yet not clearly defined (*KH and Others v Slovakia, Haralambie v Romania, Joanna Szulc v Poland, Antoneta Tudor v Romania*). Generally, the case law has shown a continued expansion of the remit of Article 8 and emphasis on keeping its guarantees relevant in a changing society, to a certain extent at the expense of coherence in the case law, particularly where Article 8 rights overlap with rights afforded under other Articles (e.g. physical integrity cases, notably domestic violence and rape cases). Under Article 9, the Court has taken important decisions on freedom of religion in employment (*Eweida and Others v UK*) and on conscientious objection to military service (*Bayatyan v Armenia*). There have been many judgments on freedom of expression, including those in *Centro Europa 7 Srl and Di Stefano v Italy* (licensing of terrestrial television), *Mouvement Raelien Suisse v Switzerland* (prohibition of bill board posters) and *Animal Defenders International v UK* (ban on political advertising). The special relevance of freedom of expression on the internet is highlighted in cases concerning comments on internet news portals (*Delfi AS v Estonia*), and the publication of photographs on websites in breach of copyright (*Ashby Donald and Others v France*). Of great importance under Article 11 have been rulings on freedom of assembly concerning 'gay

pride' parades (*Alekseyev v Russia*) and on freedom of association for trade unions and
their members in cases concerning collective bargaining (*Demir and Baykara v Turkey*)
and the right to strike (*Enerji Yaoi-Yol Sen v Turkey*). The right to education in Article 2,
Protocol 1 was an issue in a highly controversial case on the presence of crucifixes in the
classroom (*Lautsi v Italy*). The right to free elections has generated much case law. The
leading case was *Scoppola v Italy (No 3)*, in which the Grand Chamber refined its doctrine
on prisoner disenfranchisement, an issue which continues to raise Convention challenges
from a number of states. It is a sensitive issue that poses a challenge for the Court given
the lack of European consensus, the domestic political will in some states (like the UK) to
maintain a ban, and the conflicting principle that restrictions on the right to vote should
be minimised to respect the concept of universal suffrage. The Court's recent case law also
develops the core principle of 'free elections' by strengthening the guarantees of Article 3,
Protocol 1 to embrace rights to secure impartial voting systems and election administration regimes. Another notable development is the Court's decision in *Communist Party of
Russia v Russia* that Article 3 applies to state regulation of broadcast election coverage, the
first time this issue has been recognized as falling within the scope of Article 3, Protocol
1. Important cases on other issues have been *Al-Saadoon and Mufdhi v UK* on the death
penalty, *El Masri v the Former Yugoslav Republic of Macedonia* on extraordinary rendition and *Al-Skeini and Others v UK* on the extra-territorial application of the Convention.

Paralleling these developments in the Court's jurisprudence have been further steps
to reform the Court and to reduce its backlog of cases. Protocol 14 has entered into force.
The reforms that it introduces, together with internal reforms such as the provisions for
pilot judgments and the prioritisation of important cases, have started to ease the Court's
workload. At the Court's annual press Conference in January 2014, it was announced that
the number of pending cases stood at 99,900—a considerable reduction from a figure in
excess of 160,000 of some two years before. These steps are taken into account in Part II
of the book.

In the Preface to the first edition in 1995 it was noted that the growth of support for a
bill of rights in the UK created the possibility that the provisions of the Convention could
be directly applicable in UK courts. It was also noted that 'if this were to come about,
the law of the Convention would be thrust to the fore of university legal curricula and
would achieve an immediacy and relevance that would dynamise, if not revolutionize,
the United Kingdom's constitutional system'. All of this has come true since the entry into
force of the Human Rights Act 1998, although in ways that could not have been imagined
in 1995. No student of law in the UK can emerge from university today without having
been exposed to the law of the ECHR or without having a basic understanding of what the
ECHR stands for and how it operates. The judicial interpretation of the Human Rights
Act 1998 has given rise to a home grown corpus of human rights law developed first by the
House of Lords and, subsequently, the Supreme Court. Both of these courts have based
themselves on the case law of the European Court of Human Rights and have not been
fearful of pointing to inconsistencies and lack of clarity in Strasbourg law when this was
called for. Strasbourg, for its part, has welcomed this new form of 'dialogue' *inter alia*
with the Supreme Court and looks with admiration at the manner in which Convention
principles have been applied and interpreted in an impressive body of national case law.
The relationship has run into episodic difficulties in cases like *Al-Khawaja and Tahery
v UK* and *Taxquet v Belgium* (where the UK was an intervenor) but the Court's Grand
Chamber has listened carefully to the arguments of the UK and adjusted its case law to
take into account the specificities of the UK legal system as pointed out by the Supreme
Court in keeping with the principle of subsidiarity. As has been noted by many commentators, there has developed over the years a healthy cross fertilisation between the

two courts and their respective judgments are eagerly and expertly parsed and dissected by each other. The same can be said for the Court's relationship with the superior courts of other countries—Germany and France being prime examples. The importance of this form of judicial dialogue for the orderly development of the law cannot be overstated. But it has also given rise to a realization that while the Strasbourg Court may not be able, as a judicial institution, to defend itself against the buffetings and criticisms it regularly receives from political figures, as in the UK, it can intensify its relationships with the national superior courts through the medium of 'dialogue' as a more appropriate and more adapted response to such criticisms. For it must not be forgotten that the essence of the notion of subsidiarity resides in the daily application by the national courts of Convention law.

We had also noted in 1995 that many of the issues examined in Strasbourg touch on highly sensitive subjects such as prisons, immigration and the administration of justice, and that political figures and media commentators in the UK frequently complain, in 'strident tones of indignation, of interference in the domestic affairs of the state by uninformed and ill-qualified foreign jurists'. This has not diminished. On the contrary it has intensified considerably. As a result of judgments of the Court against the UK in cases such as *Hirst (No 2)* (prisoners' votes), *Vinter* (whole life sentences) and *Othman* (*Abu Qatada*) (deportation to Jordan), the level of criticism in the UK against the Court has developed far beyond what had previously been observed and to the point where certain Government ministers have suggested that UK withdrawal from the Convention system should be considered, even going so far as to challenge the Court's legitimacy as an institution.

The Preface had also asked the rhetorical question in 1995 whether the system had developed to the point where no European state could seriously contemplate withdrawing from the Convention. It is a measure of the continued success of the Convention system that this remains a valid question today for the large majority of the treaty's 47 High Contracting Parties. The UK debate about the sovereignty of Parliament and the legitimacy of the Court is not replicated in other countries, as the Brighton reform conference illustrated, even though the Court may come in for occasional criticism also in these jurisdictions. Nevertheless it is difficult to imagine that one of the leading founders of the system could turn its back on the Convention without inflicting serious damage on the entire edifice by inspiring other states, beset by more fundamental problems of human rights, to follow suit. As the Secretary General of the Council of Europe has argued before the Parliamentary Joint Committee examining the prisoner voting issue, the UK's withdrawal from the Convention would imperil not just the Convention but the Council of Europe as a whole. While this is an issue that has come to the fore in UK politics in recent years it cannot be predicted with any certainty what the outcome will be. We would argue that the particular constitutional difficulties encountered by the UK in recent years are simply outweighed by the advantages of being a party to the Convention and the important role played by the ECHR in developing human rights standards throughout Europe and beyond as part of a collective guarantee of human rights—a role that is intimately bound up with peace and security in the region as recognized in the Convention's Preamble. To put in jeopardy what has been patiently built up over more than 60 years would be a disservice to Europe, the rule of law and to the peaceful settlement of disputes.

On a more positive note such difficulties have reinforced the determination of the Contracting Parties to reform the system, and to overcome the challenges resulting from the overloading of the Court that were addressed in the preface to the second edition of this book. The reform conferences held in Interlaken, Izmir and Brighton reveal a strong political will to put the European system on a more solid footing to give it the tools to deal more effectively with its worrying backlog of cases without seeking, at the same time, to clip the Court's wings or to weaken the level of protection it provides. Overall there is a clear political attachment to the ECHR amongst Council of Europe states and an endorsement of the Court's contribution to the development of human rights law and democratic standards. The reform agenda has placed the focus on the issues *inter alia* of delay in the examination of applications, the margin of appreciation and the notion of subsidiarity, interim measures, the election of judges and the vexed problem of the enforcement of the Court's judgments (where serious compliance problems have arisen since the first edition of this book). In the meantime two new Protocols have been opened for signature (Protocols 15 and 16), the latter providing for the possibility for a national superior court to request an advisory opinion from the Court on issues relating to the interpretation of the Convention. This has been dubbed the 'Dialogue Protocol' because it offers the prospect of another form of adjudication in Strasbourg, distinct from individual and inter-state complaints, involving the superior courts as willing partners in the elucidation and development of the case law rather than as the often irritated subjects of violation verdicts.

We also noted in the first edition that there was 'the possibility that the European Union might decide to adhere to the Convention'—a possibility that has now become a very real one. The project of the EU adhering to the Convention has taken a major step forward with the drafting of an Accession Agreement whose compatibility with EU law is currently being scrutinized by the European Court of Justice. It seems clear that while accession will eventually come about, as provided for in the Lisbon Treaty, the technical journey of permitting a legal space such as the EU to join a treaty designed essentially for state parties will be much longer than expected.

Fortunately nearly all of the team of authors for the second edition have been available to contribute to the third edition. Reluctantly, we acceded to the request of one of original authors, Colin Warbrick, to 'retire' from the book. We would like to place on record our sincere thanks for his large contribution to its success. Colin played a key role in shaping the original conception of the book and an invaluable part in bringing the project to fruition. Much of the text of his chapters remains in place, and his influence on the character of those chapters and the book as a whole remains fully and beneficially apparent. There are two new authors. Paul Harvey and Michelle Lafferty, both lawyers in the Registry of the European Court of Human Rights, who updated Chapters 2 and 12 respectively. We are very grateful to them and the other authors of particular chapters for taking part, sometimes under considerable time pressure, in what has been a most challenging endeavour given the immense number of cases to be covered.

We would like to thank Ms Zoe Bryanston-Cross, member of the Secretariat of the Directorate of Legal Affairs and Human Rights of the Council of Europe, for her helpful comments on Chapter 4 and Mikail Lobov, formerly of the Court's registry for his comments on the same chapter. We would also like to thank Stuart Wallace, PhD student in the School of Law, University of Nottingham, and Romana Lemishka, LLM student in the School of Law, University of Nottingham, for their research and editorial assistance in the preparation of some of the chapters in the book. Finally we would like to thank our colleagues at Oxford University Press for their assistance and understanding during the preparation of this new edition.

The views expressed in the book are personal to the authors and do not represent the views of any institution.

The book takes into account European Court cases and other developments as far as October 31 2013. It has been possible to note some later developments at the proof stage.

David Harris
Michael O'Boyle
Ed Bates
Carla Buckley
May 2014

TABLE OF CONTENTS

Preface   v

Note on the citation of Strasbourg cases   xix

*List of European Court of Human Rights and European Commission of
Human Rights cases*   xxi

Numerical list of Unnamed European Commission of Human Rights cases   lxvi

List of National Court cases   lxvii

List of International Court of Justice cases   lxviii

List of UN Human Rights Committee cases   lxviii

List of European Court of Justice cases   lxix

List of European Committee of Social Rights cases   lxix

List of I-ACtHR cases   lxix

PART I THE EUROPEAN CONVENTION ON
HUMAN RIGHTS IN CONTEXT

1 THE EUROPEAN CONVENTION ON HUMAN RIGHTS
   IN CONTEXT   3

   1 Background   3
   2 The Substantive Guarantee   5
   3 The Strasbourg Enforcement Machinery   6
   4 The Interpretation of the Convention   7
   5 Negative and Positive Obligations and *Drittwirkung*   21
   6 Reservations   24
   7 The Convention in National Law   26
   8 The Convention and the European Union   31
   9 Achievements and Prospects   34

PART II ENFORCEMENT MACHINERY

2 ADMISSIBILITY OF APPLICATIONS   43

   1 The General Approach to Admissibility   43
   2 Application of Admissibility Requirements to Inter-state Cases   45
   3 Exhaustion of Domestic Remedies   47
   4 The Six-month Rule   61
   5 No Significant Disadvantage (Article 35(3))   67
   6 Other Grounds of Inadmissibility   72
   7 Incompatibility and the Competence of the Court   81

3 THE EUROPEAN COURT OF HUMAN RIGHTS: ORGANIZATION, PRACTICE, AND PROCEDURE   103

   1 The Organization of the Court   103

   2 Procedure before the Court (I): From the Initial Application to Judgment   113

   3 Procedure before the Court (II): Additional Procedural Matters   136

   4 Article 41: Just Satisfaction   155

   5 Article 46   162

   6 Protocol 14   165

   7 Reform of the Court   166

   8 The Future   176

4 THE EXECUTION OF THE COURT'S JUDGMENTS   180

   1 The Role of the Committee of Ministers   181

   2 Procedure   181

   3 The Court and Execution of its Judgments   191

   4 The Parliamentary Assembly and Execution of Judgments   194

   5 Protocol 14   196

   6 Conclusion   198

PART III THE RIGHTS GUARANTEED

5 ARTICLE 2: THE RIGHT TO LIFE   203

   1 The Obligation to Protect the Right to Life by Law   203

   2 Preventive Action   207

   3 Health Care and Other Social Services   212

   4 The Procedural Obligation to Investigate   214

   5 Application of the Obligation to Protect Life to Non-fatal Cases   218

   6 Protection of the Unborn Child   219

   7 The Prohibition of the Taking of Life by the Use of Force   221

   8 Conclusion   233

6 ARTICLE 3: FREEDOM FROM TORTURE OR INHUMAN OR DEGRADING TREATMENT OR PUNISHMENT   235

   1 Introduction   235

   2 Torture   238

   3 Inhuman Treatment   241

   4 Inhuman Punishment   259

   5 Degrading Treatment   261

   6 Degrading Punishment   271

   7 The Obligation to Protect Individuals from Proscribed Ill-Treatment   274

   8 Conclusion   277

7   ARTICLE 4: FREEDOM FROM SLAVERY, SERVITUDE,
    OR FORCED OR COMPULSORY LABOUR 279

    1   Freedom from Slavery and Servitude 279
    2   Freedom from Forced or Compulsory Labour 280
    3   Human Trafficking 284
    4   Positive Obligations 284
    5   Deportation or Extradition to Another State 286
    6   Conclusion 286

8   ARTICLE 5: THE RIGHT TO LIBERTY AND SECURITY OF
    THE PERSON 287

    1   Article 5: Generally 288
    2   The Meaning of Arrest or Detention (ie Loss of 'Liberty') 289
    3   Loss of Liberty: Further Issues 297
    4   Overarching Principles: 'Lawfulness' of Detention and Protection
        from Arbitrary Detention 301
    5   Article 5(1)(a)–(f): Grounds for Detention 306
    6   Article 5(2): Reasons for Arrest to be Given Promptly 334
    7   Article 5(3): Accountability during Pre-trial Detention and Trial within
        a Reasonable Time 338
    8   Article 5(4): Remedy to Challenge the Legality of Detention 352
    9   Article 5(5): Right to Compensation for Illegal Detention 366
    10 Conclusion 368

9   ARTICLE 6: THE RIGHT TO A FAIR TRIAL 370

    1   Article 6: Generally 370
    2   Field of Application 373
    3   Article 6(1): Guarantees in Criminal and Non-criminal Cases ... 398
    4   Article 6(2): The Right to be Presumed Innocent in Criminal Cases ... 460
    5   Article 6(3): Further Guarantees in Criminal Cases 467
    6   Conclusion 491

10 ARTICLE 7: FREEDOM FROM RETROACTIVE CRIMINAL
    OFFENCES AND PUNISHMENT 493

    1   Ex Post Facto Criminal Offences 494
    2   Ex Post Facto Criminal Penalties 499
    3   General Principles of Law Exception 501

11 ARTICLES 8–11: GENERAL CONSIDERATIONS 503

    1   Introduction 503
    2   Negative and Positive Obligations 504
    3   Limitations 505
    4   Conclusion 521

12 ARTICLE 8: THE RIGHT TO RESPECT FOR PRIVATE AND FAMILY LIFE, HOME, AND CORRESPONDENCE   522

  1 Introduction   522

  2 The Four Interests Protected by Article 8(1)   524

  3 Negative, Positive, and Procedural Obligations   531

  4 Subject Areas   536

  5 Conclusion   590

13 ARTICLE 9: FREEDOM OF THOUGHT, CONSCIENCE, AND RELIGION   592

  1 The Scope of Article 9   592

  2 Freedom of Thought, Conscience, and Religion: The Right to Believe 594

  3 Freedom of Thought, Conscience, and Religion: The Individual, the Group, and the State   597

  4 Manifesting Religion or Belief in Worship, Teaching, Practice, and Observance   602

  5 Justifiable Interferences   605

  6 Conclusion   611

14 ARTICLE 10: FREEDOM OF EXPRESSION   613

  1 Introduction   613

  2 The Scope of Protection   614

  3 Different Categories of Expression   629

  4 Different Means of Expression   639

  5 Prescribed by Law   649

  6 Legitimate Aims   652

  7 Duties and Responsibilities under Article 10(2)   683

  8 Distinct Methodologies and Principles Developed to Examine Issues of Defamation   691

  9 Conclusion   707

15 ARTICLE 11: FREEDOM OF ASSEMBLY AND ASSOCIATION   710

  1 Introduction   710

  2 Freedom of Peaceful Assembly   711

  3 Freedom of Association   724

  4 Freedom to Form and Join Trade Unions   740

  5 Restrictions on Public Service Employees   750

  6 Conclusion   752

16 ARTICLE 12: THE RIGHT TO MARRY AND TO FOUND A FAMILY   754

  1 Introduction   754

  2 The Right to Marry   755

3   The Right to Found a Family   760

4   Non-married Persons   762

5   Conclusion   762

17 ARTICLE 13: THE RIGHT TO AN EFFECTIVE NATIONAL REMEDY   764

1   Introduction   764

2   Article 13 within the General Scheme of the Convention   765

3   Article 13: General Principles/Requirements of an 'Effective Remedy'   768

4   Article 13: General Principles/Requirements in Specific Contexts   774

5   Conclusion   782

18 ARTICLE 14 (FREEDOM FROM DISCRIMINATION IN RESPECT
    OF PROTECTED CONVENTION RIGHTS) AND PROTOCOL 12
    (NON-DISCRIMINATION IN RESPECT OF 'ANY RIGHT SET
    FORTH BY LAW')   783

1   Introduction   783

2   Overview of the Application of Article 14   785

3   Protection for Guaranteed Rights Only and the Ambit Test   786

4   Differential Treatment on a Prohibited Ground   788

5   Differential Treatment May Be Justified on Objective and
    Reasonable Grounds   792

6   Intensive Scrutiny of Differential Treatment for 'Suspect Categories'   796

7   Article 14, the Burden of Proof and the Protection of Minorities   809

8   Article 14 and Violence Motivated by Discrimination   811

9   Indirect Discrimination   815

10 Positive Obligations to Protect against Discrimination and Reverse
    Discrimination   817

11 Protocol 12   819

12 Conclusion   821

19 ARTICLE 15: DEROGATION IN TIME OF WAR OR OTHER PUBLIC
    EMERGENCY THREATENING THE LIFE OF THE NATION   823

1   Introduction   823

2   The Need to Resort to Article 15 (Some Comments on the Court's
    General Approach to 'Terrorism Cases')   825

3   The General Pattern of Article 15   829

4   'In Time of War or Other Public Emergency Threatening the Life of
    the Nation'   829

5   'Measures ... to the Extent Strictly Required by the Exigencies of
    the Situation ...'   837

6   Other International Law Obligations   843

7   Article 15(2): The Non-derogable Provisions   844

8   Article 15(3): The Procedural Requirements   846

    9 Proposals for Reform   847
   10 Conclusion   848

20 ARTICLES 16–18: OTHER RESTRICTIONS UPON THE RIGHTS
   PROTECTED   851
    1 Article 16: Restrictions on the Political Rights of Aliens   851
    2 Article 17: Restrictions on Activities Subversive of Convention Rights   852
    3 Article 18: Prohibition of the Use of Restrictions for an
       Improper Purpose   857
    4 Conclusion   861

21 ARTICLE 1, FIRST PROTOCOL: THE RIGHT TO PROPERTY   862
    1 Introduction   862
    2 The Structure of Article 1, First Protocol, and the Inter-relationship
       of its Provisions   872
    3 Article 1/1/1: Interference with the Peaceful Enjoyment of Possessions   880
    4 Article 1/1/2: Deprivation of Property   885
    5 Article 1/2: Control of Use   895
    6 Conclusion   903

22 ARTICLE 2, FIRST PROTOCOL: THE RIGHT TO EDUCATION   906
    1 Introduction   906
    2 No Denial of the Right to Education   909
    3 Respect for Parents' Religious and Philosophical Convictions   912
    4 Discrimination and Minority Rights   916
    5 Conclusion   918

23 ARTICLE 3, FIRST PROTOCOL: THE RIGHT TO FREE ELECTIONS   920
    1 Introduction   920
    2 General Principles Governing Article 3, First Protocol Jurisprudence   921
    3 The Scope of Electoral Rights: Legislative and Other Elections   924
    4 The Right to Vote   926
    5 The Right to Stand for Election   933
    6 Election Administration and Post-Electoral Rights   943
    7 Electoral Systems   946
    8 Media Reporting of Election Campaigns   949
    9 Conclusion   950

24 THE FOURTH, SIXTH, SEVENTH, AND THIRTEENTH
   PROTOCOLS   952
    1 Article 1, Fourth Protocol: Freedom from Imprisonment for
       Non-fulfilment of a Contractual Obligation   952

2 Article 2, Fourth Protocol: Freedom of Movement within a State and Freedom to Leave its Territory   953

3 Article 3, Fourth Protocol: The Right of a National not to be Expelled from and to Enter a State's Territory   959

4 Article 4, Fourth Protocol: Freedom of Aliens from Collective Expulsion   960

5 The Sixth and Thirteenth Protocols: The Death Penalty   963

6 Article 1, Seventh Protocol: Freedom from Expulsion of Individual Aliens   965

7 Article 2, Seventh Protocol: The Right to Review in Criminal Cases   966

8 Article 3, Seventh Protocol: Right to Compensation for Miscarriages of Justice   968

9 Article 4, Seventh Protocol: *Ne Bis In Idem*   969

10 Article 5, Seventh Protocol: Equality of Rights of Spouses   974

Index   977

NOTE ON THE CITATION OF
STRASBOURG CASES

The footnote references to Strasbourg cases in this book cite (i) the official reports of the European Commission of Human Rights and the European Court of Human Rights, and (ii) the European Human Rights Reports.

Official Reports

Until 1996, there were two series of publications of the judgments of the Court by way of official reports, in English and French: Series A (Judgments and Decisions) and Series B (Pleadings, Oral Arguments and Documents). Series B was incomplete, ceasing with volume 104, published in 1995. Series A reports are cited as follows: *Soering v UK* A 161 (1989).

In 1996, the Series A volumes, which were for individual cases, were replaced by annual volumes of the *Reports of Judgments and Decisions*, containing Court judgments, or extracts from them, plus some decisions as to admissibility or extracts from them. Most of the Court's judgments and most decisions as to admissibility are not published in the official reports, but are accessible in HUDOC (see below).

From 1996 to 1998 these official reports covered both the Commission and the Court; from 1999 they cover only the Court, following the demise of the Commission. The annual volumes are published in separate parts. The judgments and decisions are published in English and French. Citations indicate the volume and part, but not the page number within the volume, for example, *Khan v UK* 2000-V. There is no equivalent to the Series B reports.

Of great importance is the Court's HUDOC database, to be found on the Council of Europe website: http://www.echr.coe.int/echr/. HUDOC has all the recent Court judgments and admissibility decisions, whether they are printed later in the official reports or not. Judgments in HUDOC are cited as follows: *Ploski v Poland* hudoc (2002). Decisions as to admissibility are cited as follows: *Gonzalez v Spain No 43544/98* hudoc (1999) DA. DA is added to assist in finding the case in HUDOC. HUDOC judgments are in English and French or, in the case of less important cases, English *or* French.

Some report series are specific to the former European Commission of Human Rights:

Collection of Decisions of the European Commission of Human Rights

This series (volumes 1–46, 1959–1974) was published by the Council of Europe in English and French. These are cited as follows: *X v Norway No 867/60* 6 CD 24 1961.

Decisions and Reports of the European Commission of Human Rights

This series (volumes 1–94, 1975–1998) was published by the Council of Europe. It contains in English and French selected Commission decisions as to admissibility; Commission friendly settlement reports; and Commission reports on the merits under the former Article 31 of the Convention when the case was not referred to the Court. In the case of an Article 31 report, the Committee of Ministers resolution is also printed. As of volume 76, the volumes are published as volumes 76-A and 76-B, etc, with volume A containing the original language of the decision, etc, and volume B containing the translation.

Digest of Strasbourg Case-Law Relating to the European Convention on Human Rights

Volumes 1–5 and an index (vol 6), published 1984–1985, plus eleven looseleaf supplements published to 1997. Although linked to the Council of Europe, the *Digest* is not strictly an official source. It contains extracts from some Commission cases not reported elsewhere. These are cited as follows: *No 7126/75 (1977)* 1 Digest 87.

European Court of Human Rights Reports

This commercial series publishes in English only the judgments of the European Court of Human Rights and certain Commission reports and decisions as to admissibility. Cases are cited as follows: *Soering v UK* A 161 (1989); 11 EHRR 439.

LIST OF EUROPEAN COURT OF HUMAN RIGHTS AND EUROPEAN COMMISSION OF HUMAN RIGHTS CASES

000 Neste St Petersburg et al. v Russia (2004) ... 375

3 A.CZ s.r.o. v Czech Republic (2011)...69

97 Members of the Gladani Congregation of Jehovah's Witnesses v Georgia (2007) ... 275, 276, 599, 786, 814, 815

A

A v Croatia (2010) ... 541, 542

A v Denmark (1982) ... 335

A v Finland (2004) ... 391

A v Germany (1986) ... 423

A v Netherlands (2010) ... 252

A v Norway (2009) ... 553, 554

A v Spain (1990) ... 724

A v Sweden (1983) ... 607

A v UK (1998) ... 237, 273, 274

A v UK (2002) ... 10, 401, 405, 765

A and KBF v Turkey (1991) ... 246

A and Others v UK (2009) ... 47, 126, 159, 161, 289, 304, 328, 331, 332, 352, 356, 357, 358, 359, 367, 368, 824, 826, 828, 831, 832, 833, 834, 835, 836, 837, 839, 843, 844, 849

A, B and C v Ireland (2010) ... 55, 57, 154, 199, 219, 220, 524, 528, 533, 535, 546

AA v UK (2011) ... 577

AB v Netherlands (2002) ... 60, 589

AB v Slovakia (2003) ... 401, 414

AB Kurt Kellermann v Sweden (2003) ... 384, 743

AB Kurt Kellermann v Sweden (2004) ... 455

Abdi v UK (2013) ... 332

Abdoella v Netherlands (1992) ... 350, 442

Abdolkhani and Karimnia v Turkey (2009) ... 247, 774

Abdulaziz, Cabales and Balkandali v UK (1982) ... 92

Abdulaziz, Cabales and Balkandali v UK (1985) ... 15, 22, 28, 269, 526, 533, 576, 765, 787, 794, 796, 798

Abdulkhakov v Russia (2012) ... 140, 141, 249, 252

Abdullah Yạsa and Others v Turkey (2013) ... 243

Abdulrahman v Netherlands (2013) ... 66

Abdulsamet Yaman v Turkey (2004) ... 239

Abeberry v France (2004) ... 553

Abil v Azerbaijan (2012) ... 922, 936, 946

Abuyeva v Russia (2010) ... 160, 163

Abuyeva v Russia (2011) ... 187

Academy Trading Ltd v Greece (2000) ... 455

Acar v Turkey (2005) ... 222

Accardi v Italy (2005) ... 421

Achour v France (2004) ... 91

Achour v France (2006) ... 501

Aćimović v Croatia (2003) ... 401

Ackerl et al v Austria (1994) ... 281

Acmanne and Others v Belgium (1984) ... 544

AD v Netherlands (1994) ... 74

AD and OD v UK (2010) ... 570, 571

ADA and Others v Italy (2008) ... 86

Adali v Turkey (2005) ... 153, 271, 716

Adamkiewicz v Poland (2010) ... 453, 474

Adamov v Switzerland (2011) ... 304

Adams v Romania (2011) ... 158

Adams and Benn v UK (1997) ... 652

Adams and Others v Germany (2005) ... 67

Adamson v UK (1999) ... 499

Ādamsons v Latvia (2008) ... 935, 940

Aden Ahmed v Malta (2013) ... 65

Adetoro v UK (2010) ... 424

Adırbelli and Others v Yuteky (2008) ... 317

Adolf v Austria (1980) ... 483

Adolf v Austria (1982) ... 459, 460, 461, 464, 467, 468

Adrian Mihai Ionescu v Romania (2010) ... 71

ADT v UK (2000) ... 534, 549, 550, 803

Advisory Opinion on Certain Legal Questions Concerning the Lists of Candidates for the Election of Judges to the European Court of Human Rights (2008) ... 108, 109, 135

Advisory Opinion (no 2) on Certain Legal Questions Concerning the Lists of Candidates Submitted with a view to the Election of Judges to the European Court of Human Rights (2010) ... 109, 135

Adzi-Spirkoska and Others v the Former Yugoslav Republic of Macedonia (2011) ... 51

AEPI SA v Greece (2002) ... 404

Aerts v Belgium (1998) ... 267, 327, 353, 382, 384, 400

Afanasyev v Ukraine (2005) ... 242

Agbovi v Germany (2006) ... 50

Ağdaş v Turkey (2004) ... 148, 227

Agee v UK (1976) ... 851

Ageyevy v Russia (2013) ... 528

Agneessens v Belgium (1988) . . . 865
Agnelet v France (2013) . . . 430
Agrotexim, Vesela and Loyka v Greece
  (1995) . . . 90, 863, 869
Aguilera Jimenez and Others v Spain
  (2009) . . . 618
Ahlskog v Finland (2010) . . . 51
Ahmad v UK (1981) . . . 604, 802
Ahmed v Austria (1996) . . . 245, 252, 253
Ahmed v Sweden (2007) . . . 127
Ahmed and Others v UK (1998) . . . 685, 938
Ahmed Ali v Netherlands and Greece
  (2012) . . . 144
Ahmet Arslan and Others v Turkey
  (2010) . . . 609, 611
Ahmet Sadik v Greece (1996) . . . 630
Ahmet Özkan and Others v Turkey
  (2004) . . . 211, 231
Ahorugeze v Sweden (2011) . . . 246
Ahrens v Germany (2012) . . . 527
Air Canada v UK (1995) . . . 373, 382, 394, 879,
  880, 886, 896, 897, 900
Airey v Ireland (1977) 310Airey v Ireland
  (1979) . . . 18, 22, 380, 399, 400, 401, 443, 480,
  504, 523, 542, 564, 760, 784, 791, 810, 819
Ait-Mouhoub v France (1998) . . . 382, 403
Aizpurua Ortiz and Others v Spain
  (2010) . . . 92, 94, 883
Ajdarić v Croatia (2011) . . . 430
AK and L v Croatia (2013) . . . 570, 572
Akçiçek v Turkey (2011) . . . 55
Akdeniz and Others v Turkey (2001) . . . 224
Akdivar v Turkey (1996) . . . 47, 59, 60, 61, 79,
  114, 580
AK and L v Croatia (2013) . . . 528
Akgöl and Göl v Turkey (2011) . . . 719, 723
Akin v Netherlands (1998) . . . 761
Akkoç v Turkey (2000) . . . 210, 218, 223, 238,
  239, 240, 243
Akkum and Others v Turkey (2005) . . . 146, 215,
  222, 223, 270
Akkuş v Turkey (1997) . . . 868, 871, 881
Akman v Turkey (2001) . . . 129, 131
Akpinar and Altun v Turkey (2007) . . . 217, 270
Aksoy v Turkey (1996) . . . 59, 239, 339, 769, 779,
  825, 827, 833, 835, 839, 841, 848
Aksu v Turkey (2012) . . . 553, 784
Aktas v France (2009) . . . 610
Al Adsani v UK (2001) . . . 11, 275, 406
Al Jedda v UK (2011) . . . 84, 289, 306
Al Nashiri v Poland (2013) . . . 144
Alajos Kiss v Hungary (2010) . . . 796, 924, 929,
  930
Alapatu Israilova and Others v Russia
  (2013) . . . 160
Alatulkkila v Finland (2005) . . . 393, 791, 896
Alaverdyan v Armenia (2010) . . . 384
Albert and Le Compte v Belgium (1983) . . . 375,
  378, 390, 392, 393, 394, 395, 463, 471
Alberti v Italy (1989) . . . 420

Alboize-Barthes and Alboize-Montzume
  v France (2008) . . . 801
Albu v Romania (2010) . . . 432
Al-Dabbagh v Sweden (1997) . . . 966
Aldo and Jean-Baptiste Zanatta v France
  (2000) . . . 381
Aleksandr Zaichenko v Russia (2010) . . . 377,
  422, 474
Aleksanyan v Russia (2008) . . . 79, 114, 141
Alekseyev v Russia (2010) . . . 711, 712, 713, 717,
  718, 719
Alexandridis v Greece (2008) . . . 595
Alexseyev v Russia (2010) . . . 806
Algür v Turkey (2002) . . . 243
Ali v UK (2011) . . . 909
Ali and Ayşe Duran v Turkey (2008) . . . 218
Ali Erol v Turkey (2002) . . . 127
Ali Gedi and Others v Austria (2011) . . . 144
Ali Güneş v Turkey (2012) . . . 243
Ali Sahmo v Turkey (2003) . . . 64
Aliev v Ukraine (2003) . . . 585, 586, 587, 588, 589,
  761
Alikaj and Others v Italy (2011) . . . 231
Alimena v Italy (1991) . . . 480
Alinak v Turkey (2005) . . . 633, 635
Alkaya v Turkey (2012) . . . 551, 552
Al-Khawaja and Tahery v UK (2009) . . . 28
Al-Khawaja and Tahery v UK (2011) . . . 170,
  484, 485, 486, 487, 488
Alkin v Turkey (2009) . . . 208
Allan v UK (2002) . . . 423, 556
Allan v UK (2004) . . . 67
Allan Jacobsson v Sweden (No 1) (1989) . . . 382,
  389, 875, 895, 896, 900
Allan Jacobsson v Sweden (No 2) (1998) . . . 436
Allaoui v Germany (1999) . . . 57
Allard v Sweden (2003) . . . 899
Allen v UK (2002) . . . 424, 426
Allen v UK (2010) . . . 360
Allen v UK (2013) . . . 464, 465
Allen and Others v UK (2009) . . . 582
Allegemeine Gold -und Silberscheideanstalt
  (AGOSI) v UK (1986) . . . 373, 885, 886, 896,
  897, 899, 900
Allenet de Ribemont v France (1995) . . . 162, 466
Allenet de Ribemont v France (1996) . . . 133
Allianz-Slovenska Poistovna and Others v
  Slovakia (2010) . . . 883, 902
Almeida Ferreira and Melo Ferreira v Portugal
  (2010) . . . 898
Almeida Garrett, Mascarenhas Falcão v
  Portugal (2000) . . . 871
Al-Moayad v Germany (2007) . . . 248, 250, 299, 373
Al-Nashif v Bulgaria (2002) . . . 357, 358, 509,
  517, 536, 578, 776, 777, 828
Alpatu Israilova v Russia (2013) . . . 160
Al-Saadoon and Mufdhi v UK (2010) . . . 19, 96,
  140, 163, 225, 246, 259, 260, 277, 372, 964, 965
Al-Skeini and Others v UK (2011) . . . 11, 99, 101,
  126, 215

Alsterlund v Sweden (1988) . . . 396
Altay v Turkey (2001) . . . 242
Althoff and Others v Germany (2011) . . . 885
Altinay v Turkey (2013) . . . 795
Altuğ Taner Akçam v Turkey (2011) . . . 651
Altun v Germany (1983) . . . 245, 246
Altun v Turkey (2004) . . . 580
Altunay v Turkey (2012) . . . 51
Alves da Silva v Portugal (2009) . . . 615
Alvarez Sanchez v Spain (2001) . . . 481,
Amann v Switzerland (2000) . . . 559, 560–1, 776
Ambruosi v Italy (2000) . . . 867, 877
Amie and Others v Bulgaria (2013) . . . 578
Amihalachioaie v Moldova (2004) . . . 678, 693,
  698, 701
Aminoff v Sweden (1985) . . . 912
AMM v Romania (2012) . . . 566
Amrollahi v Denmark (2001) . . . 973
Amuur v France (1996) . . . 87, 90, 291, 292, 303,
  328, 333
Anagnostopoulos v Greece (2003) . . . 399
Ananyev and Others v Russia (2012) . . . 150
Anchugov and Gladkov v Russia (2013) . . . 924,
  930, 933
Andelković v Serbia (2103) . . . 18, 371
Anderson and Nine Others v UK (1997) . . . 713
Anderson v UK (1999) . . . 371
Andersson v Sweden (2010) . . . 436
Andersson (M&R) v Sweden (1992) . . . 12, 571,
  770, 771
Andersson and Kullman v Sweden (1986) . . .
  568, 761
Andorka and Vavra v Hungary (2006) . . . 63
Andrasik v Slovakia (2002) . . . 51
Andreas Wabl v Austria (2000) . . . 668, 669
Andrejeva v Latvia (2006) . . . 155
Andrejeva v Latvia (2009) . . . 786, 787, 790, 795,
  798
Andreou v Turkey (2009) . . . 232
Andrews v UK (2002) . . . 896
Andric v Sweden (1999) . . . 961
Andrl v Czech Republic (2011) . . . 799
Andronicou and Constantinou v Cyprus
  (1997) . . . 92, 230, 401
Angeleni v Sweden (1986) . . . 595, 906
Angelo Giuseppe Guerrera v Italy (2002) . . . 446
Angelov and Angelova v Bulgaria (2010) . . . 94,
  95
Angelucci v Italy (1991) . . . 377
Anghel v Italy (2013) . . . 536
Anguelov v Bulgaria (2004) . . . 211, 466
Anguelova v Bulgaria (2002) . . . 223, 300, 784,
  812
Anheuser-Busch Inc v Portugal (2007) . . . 672,
  863, 863, 864, 865, 885, 903
Animal Defenders International v UK
  (2013) . . . 12, 82, 169, 520, 646, 647, 512, 513,
  646, 647, 648, 649
Ankarcrona v Sweden (2000) . . . 863
Ankerl v Switzerland (1996) . . . 415

Anne-Marie Andersson v Sweden (1997) . . . 389
Annoni di Gussola v France (2000) . . . 403
Anokhin v Russia (2007) . . . 871
Antonenkov v Ukraine (2006) . . . 956
Antoneta Tudor v Romania (2013) . . . 564
Antonetto v Italy (2000) . . . 397
Antonov v Russia (2005) . . . 281
Aoulmi v France (2006) . . . 96, 141
AP, MP and TP v Switzerland (1997) . . . 462
APEH Üldözötteinek Szövetsége v Hungary
  (2000) . . . 384
Apostol v Georgia (2006) . . . 52, 58, 397
Apostolakis v Greece (2009) . . . 882
Appel-Irrgang and Others v Germany
  (2009) . . . 600, 915
Appleby v UK (2003) . . . 617, 619, 713
Aquilina v Malta (1999) . . . 54, 338, 339, 340, 342
Aquilina and Others v Malta (2011) . . . 707
Aras v Italy (2012) . . . 416
Arat v Turkey (2009) . . . 88
Arcuri v Italy (2001) . . . 901
Aresti Charalambous v Cyprus (2007) . . . 760
Arioglu and Others v Turkey (2012) . . . 51
Arma v France (2007) . . . 403
Armani da Silva v UK (De Menezes case . . . 232
Armonienė v Lithuania (2008) . . . 93, 552
Arnarsson v Iceland see Sigurdór Arnarsson
  v Iceland
Aronica v Germany (2002) . . . 247
Arras and Others v Italy (2012) . . . 429
Arrigo and Vella v Malta (2005) . . . 467
Arrondelle v UK (1980) . . . 583
Arrowsmith v UK (1978) . . . 593, 602, 603, 653
Arslan v Turkey (1999) . . . 653
Arslan v Turkey (2002) . . . 66
Arslan v Turkey (2006) . . . 910
Artemi and Gregory v 22 Member States of the
  European Union (2010) . . . 111
Artico v Italy (1980) . . . 18, 409, 468, 471, 480, 481
Artyomov v Russia (2006) . . . 732
Arutyunyan v Russia (2012) . . . 263
Arvanitaki-Roboti v Greece (2006) . . . 124, 864
Arvanitaki-Roboti v Greece (2008) . . . 124, 156
Asadbeyli and Others v Azerbaijan
  (2012) . . . 972
Asadov v Azerbaijan (2002) . . . 448
Ásatrúarfélagio v Iceland (2012) . . . 598
Asch v Austria (1991) . . . 485, 487, 488
Asci v Austria (2006) . . . 971
Asensio Serqueda v Spain (1994) . . . 385
Ashby Donald and Others v France (2013) . . .
  615, 672
Ashendon and Jones v UK (2011) . . . 464
Ashingdane v UK (1985) . . . 13, 294, 298, 307,
  327, 388, 402, 403, 405, 407
Ashot Harutyunyan v Armenia (2010) . . . 413
Ashworth v UK (2004) . . . 869
Aslakhanova and Others v Russia (2012) . . . 218
Assanidze v Georgia (2004) . . . 25, 29, 44, 164,
  288, 302, 378, 396

Asselbourg and Others v Luxembourg
(1999) . . . 582
Assenov v Bulgaria (1998) . . . 53, 276, 338, 341,
343, 350, 354, 356, 359, 365, 382, 779, 784
Associated Newspapers Ltd, Steven and
Wolman v UK (1994) . . . 680
Associated Society of Locomotive Engineers and
Firemen (ASLEF) v UK (2007) . . . 89, 158,
159, 738, 742
Association 21 December 1989 v Romania
(2011) . . . 206, 217
Association de defense des interêts du sport
v France (2007) . . . 89
Association des Chevaliers du Lotus d'Or
v France (2013) . . . 606
Association Ekin v France (2001) . . . 86, 654
Association for European Integration and
Human Rights and Ekimdzhiev v Bulgaria
(2007) . . . 509, 524, 530, 532, 555, 556
Association Les Témoins de Jéhovah v France
(2010) . . . 48
Association Les Témoins de Jéhovah v France
(2011) . . . 606
Association of Citizens Radko & Paunkovski v
the Former Yugoslav Republic of Macedonia
(2009) . . . 731, 736
Association of Real Property Owners in Łódź v
Poland (2011) . . . 131
Association Rhino and Others v Switzerland
(2012) . . . 736
Association Solidarité des Français v France
(2009) . . . 716
Association SOS Attentats and De Boëry v
France (2006) . . . 131, 153
Association X v Sweden (1977) . . . 738
Assunção Chavez v Portugal (2012) . . . 402
Aswat v UK (2013) . . . 255
Atakishi v Azerbaijan (2012) . . . 922, 936, 946
Atanasiu and Others v Romania (2010) . . . 150
Atanasova v Bulgaria (2008) . . . 408
Athanassoglu v Switzerland (2000) . . . 384, 391
Atkinson, Crook and The Independent v UK
(1990) . . . 675
Atmaca v Germany (2012) . . . 132
Attard v Malta (2000) . . . 368
August v UK (2003) . . . 383
Augusto v France (2007) . . . 56, 57, 418
Aune v Norway (2010) . . . 571
Austin v UK (2012) . . . 289, 292, 293, 294, 313,
368, 954
Austria v Italy (1961) . . . 8, 46, 115, 116, 117, 461
Austria v Italy (1963) . . . 422, 463, 466, 467
Autronic AG v Switzerland (1990) . . . 507, 509,
644, 649
AV v Bulgaria (1999) . . . 91, 92
Avsar v Turkey (2001) . . . 221
Averill v UK (1999) . . . 81
Averill v UK (2000) . . . 474
Avilkina and Others v Russia (2013) . . . 562
Avkhadova and Others v Russia (2013) . . . 159

AW Khan v UK (2010) . . . 575, 577
Axel Springer AG v Germany (2012) . . . 515,
523, 551, 660, 662, 663, 681
Aydan v Turkey (2013) . . . 230
Aydin v Germany (2011) . . . 654
Aydin v Turkey (1997) . . . 236, 237, 239, 240,
278, 779
Aydin v Turkey (2000) . . . 59, 63
Aydin Tatlav v Turkey (2006) . . . 670
Aygun v Sweden (1989) . . . 290
Aytaş and Others v Turkey (2009) . . . 719
Aytekin v Turkey (1998) . . . 67, 231
Axen v Germany (1981) . . . 433
Axen v Germany (1983) . . . 437, 438
Azimov v Russia (2013) . . . 331
Azinas v Cyprus (2004) . . . 44, 49, 125
Aziz v Cyprus (2004) . . . 784, 785, 926, 929, 948

B
B v Austria (1990) . . . 307, 343, 344, 348, 350,
443, 444
B v Belgium (2012) . . . 142, 575
B v Denmark . . . 677
B v France (No 10179/82) (1987) . . . 311, 337
B v France (1992) . . . 537
B v Moldova (2013) . . . 274, 541, 542
B v UK (1981) . . . 267
B v UK (1983) . . . 550
B v UK (1984) . . . 387
B v UK (1985) . . . 653
B v UK (1987) . . . 570
B and L v UK (2005) . . . 755, 756
B and P v UK (2001) . . . 434, 435, 439
B, R and J v Germany (1984) . . . 762
Babar Ahmad and Others v UK (2010) . . . 250,
255, 256, 965
Bachmann, Hofreiter and Gulyn v Austria
(1995) . . . 907
Bachowski v Poland (1959) . . . 968, 969
Bäck v Finland (2004) . . . 877, 881, 882
Backstrom and Andersson v Sweden
(2006) . . . 471
Bączkowski v Poland (2007) . . . 715, 716, 788,
805, 806
Bader and Kanbor v Sweden (2005) . . . 226, 372
Baegen v Netherlands (1995) . . . 488
Baggetta v Italy (1987) . . . 442
Baggs v UK (1985) . . . 583
Bagheri and Maliki v Netherlands (2007) . . . 79
Baghli v France (1999) . . . 63, 577
Bahaddar v Netherlands (1998) . . . 54
Bajrami v Albania (2007) . . . 134
Bakarić v Croatia (2001) . . . 392
Baklanov v Russia (2005) . . . 879
Balakchiev and Others v Bulgaria (2013) . . . 51, 178
Balakin v Russia (2013) . . . 96
Balan v Moldova (2012) . . . 51
Balçik v Turkey (2007) . . . 714, 715, 719
Balmer-Schafroth v Switzerland (1997) . . . 391
Balogh v Hungary (2004) . . . 242, 382

Balsyte-Lideikiene v Lithuania (2008) . . . 421
Banel v Lithuania (2013) . . . 206, 208
Banér v Sweden (1989) . . . 886
Banfield v UK (2005) . . . 882
Bankovic v Belgium and 16 other Contracting
　States (2001) . . . 99, 111
Bannikov v Latvia (2013) . . . 69
Bannikova v Russia (2010) . . . 427, 428
Barać and Others v Montenegro (2011) . . . 371
Barankevich v Russia (2007) . . . 599, 611, 711,
　712, 717–8
Baranowski v Poland (2000) . . . 302, 303, 319,
　362
Baraona v Portugal (1987) . . . 382
Barberà, Messegué and Jabardo v Spain
　(1988) . . . 409, 416, 421, 433, 448, 461
Barberà, Messegué and Jabardo v Spain
　(1994) . . . 157
Barborski v Belgium (2013) . . . 161
Barfod v Denmark (1989) . . . 17, 510, 676, 677
Barfuss v Czech Republic (2000) . . . 347
Barraco v France (2009) . . . 714, 716
Barrett v UK (1997) . . . 208
Barsom and Varli v Sweden (2008) . . . 479
Barthold v Germany (1985) . . . 380, 506, 508,
　512, 639, 649, 650
Bartik v Russia (2006) . . . 956, 957
Bashir and Others v Bulgaria (2007) . . . 578, 625
Baškauskaitė v Lithuania (1998) . . . 579, 924
Başkaya and Okçuoğlu v Turkey (1999) . . . 493,
　497, 628, 629, 653
Başpinar v Turkey (2002) . . . 604
Bassani v Italy (2003) . . . 957
Bastone v Italy (2005) . . . 586
Basyte-Lideikiene v Lithuania (2008) . . . 489
Bati and Others v Turkey (2004) . . . 240
Baumann v Austria (2005) . . . 134
Baumann v France (2001) . . . 958
Bauquel v France (2004) . . . 865
Bayatyan v Armenia (2011) . . . 283, 593, 601,
　602, 603
Bayrak v France (2009) . . . 610
Bayram and Yilirim v Turkey (2002) . . . 62, 63
Bayramov v Azerbaijan (2006) . . . 863
Baysayeva v Russia (2007) . . . 216, 224
Baytüre v Turkey (2013) . . . 545
Bazelyuk v Ukraine (2012) . . . 70
Bazorkina v Russia (2006) . . . 257
BB v France (1998) . . . 254
BB v UK (2004) . . . 550, 803
BB and FB v Germany (2013) . . . 571
BBC v UK (1996) . . . 387, 675
Beard v UK (2001) . . . 581
Beaumartin v France (1994) . . . 382, 447, 448,
　449, 866, 887
Becciev v Moldova (2005) . . . 347
Beck v Norway (2001) . . . 87
Beck, Copp and Bazeley v UK (2002) . . . 550, 579
Beckles v UK (2002) . . . 424
Beer v Austria (2001) . . . 413

Beer and Regan v Germany (1999) . . . 406
Behrami and Behrami v France (2007) . . . 33,
　84, 111, 153, 155
Beiere v Latvia (2011) . . . 310
Bekauri v Georgia (Preliminary Objection)
　(2012) . . . 79
Bekir-Ousta v Greece (2007) . . . 732
Bekos and Koutropoulos v Greece
　(2005) . . . 276, 812, 814
Belaousof v Greece (2004) . . . 44, 62
Belchikova v Russia (2010) . . . 582
Beldjoudi v France (1992) . . . 520, 576, 761
Bêlês v Czech Rep (2002) . . . 404
Belgian Linguistics case (No 2) (1968) . . . 7, 13,
　14, 16, 17, 524, 784, 787, 792, 793, 794, 795,
　811, 817, 818, 874, 906, 907, 909, 911, 912, 913,
　917, 918
Belilos v Switzerland (1988) . . . 24, 25, 26, 375,
　446–7, 448, 906
Bellet v France (1995) . . . 402
Belukha v Ukraine (2006) . . . 456
Belvedere Alberghiera srl v Italy (2000) . . . 879
Belziuk v Poland (1998) . . . 437
Ben Khemais v Italy (2009) . . . 141, 249
Ben Salah Adraqui and Dhaime v Spain
　(2000) . . . 50
Ben Yaacoub v Belgium (1987) . . . 453
Bendenoun v France (1994) . . . 375, 415
Benderskiy v Ukraine (2007) . . . 545
Beneficio Cappella Paolini v San Marino
　(2004) . . . 402
Benes v Austria (1992) . . . 526
BENet Praha, spol. s r.o. v Czech Republic
　(2011) . . . 69
Benham v UK (1996) . . . 302, 375, 409, 479
Benjamin and Wilson v UK (2002) . . . 354, 356,
　365
Bensaid v UK (2001) . . . 254
Benthem v Netherlands (1983) . . . 388
Benthem v Netherlands (1985) . . . 379, 381, 382,
　390, 392, 447
Berdzenishvili v Russia (2004) . . . 62
Bergens Tidende v Norway (2000) . . . 661, 663,
　664, 666
Berger-Krall v Slovenia (2013) . . . 98
Bergman v Estonia (2008) . . . 338
Berisha v Switzerland (2013) . . . 576
Berisha and Haljiti v the Former Yugoslav
　Republic of Macedonia (2005) . . . 961
Berktay v Turkey (2001) . . . 317
Berladir and Others v Russia (2012) . . . 71, 619, 721
Berlin v Luxembourg (2003) . . . 442
Berlinski v Poland (2002) . . . 243, 471, 474, 475
Berrehab v Netherlands (1988) . . . 527, 528, 576
Bertuzzi v France (2002) . . . 53
Bertuzzi v France (2003) . . . 401
Beru v Turkey (2011) . . . 208
Betayev and Betayeva v Russia (2008) . . . 224
Beyeler v Italy (2000) . . . 865, 876, 877, 878, 883,
　884, 886, 888, 891, 903, 905

Beyeler v Italy (2002) . . . 158, 160
Beygo v 46 Member States of the Council of
    Europe (2009) . . . 83
Bezicheri v Italy (1989) . . . 342, 343, 355, 360,
    363, 364, 365
Bhandari v UK (2007) . . . 159
Bianchi v Switzerland (2006) . . . 506
Biç v Turkey (2006) . . . 93
Bideault v France (1986) . . . 491
Big Brother Watch and Others v UK
    (2014) . . . 556
Bigaeva v Greece (2009) . . . 798
Bilgin v Turkey (2000) . . . 114, 224, 241
Bilgin (Irfan) v Turkey (2001) . . . 217
Biondo v Italy (1983) . . . 480, 483
Biriuk v Lithuania (2008) . . . 550
Birou v France (1992) . . . 351
Birutis and Others v Lithuania (2002) . . . 488
Biryukov v Russia (2004) . . . 443
Biserica Adevărat Ortodoxă din Moldova v
    Moldova (2007) . . . 598, 606
Bitiyeva and X v Russia (2007) . . . 160
Bizzotto v Greece (1996) . . . 298
Bjedov v Croatia (2012) . . . 528, 529, 582
Björk Eiðósdóttir v Iceland (2012) . . . 661, 688
Blackstock v UK (2004) . . . 365
Blackstock v UK (2005) . . . 365, 367
Bladet Tromsø and Stensaas v Norway
    (1999) . . . 663, 683, 687, 689, 690, 691, 693
Blake v UK (2005) . . . 81, 673, 683, 684
Bland v UK (2002) . . . 799
Blastland v UK (1987) . . . 415, 486
Blečić v Croatia (2006) . . . 44, 81, 97
Blokker v Netherlands (2000) . . . 375, 970
'Blondje' v Netherlands (2009) . . . 73
Blumberga v Latvia (2008) . . . 401
Bochan v Ukraine (2007) . . . 452
Bock v Germany (1989) . . . 441, 442
Bock v Germany (2010) . . . 80
Bocos-Cuesta v Netherlands (2005) . . . 488
Boddaert v Belgium (1992) . . . 377, 440
Bodrožić and Vujin v Serbia (2009) . . . 512
Boeckmans v Belgium (1965) . . . 451
Boffa and Others v San Marino (1998) . . . 544
Bogumil v Portugal (2008) . . . 268, 482, 545
Böhmer v Germany (2002) . . . 461
Boicenco v Moldova (2006) . . . 114, 266, 276
Bojinov v France (2004) . . . 319
Bok v Netherlands (2011) . . . 461
Bolat v Russia (2006) . . . 955, 965, 966
Bollan v UK (2000) . . . 264
Bompard v France (2006) . . . 924, 947
Bonazzi v Italy (1978) . . . 301
Boner v UK (1994) . . . 479, 480
Bönisch v Austria (1985) . . . 415, 484
Bönisch v Austria (1986) . . . 160
Bonnechaux v Switzerland (1979) . . . 267
Boofzheim v France (2002) . . . 375
Booth-Clibborn v UK (1985) . . . 925
Bordovskiy v Russia (2005) . . . 302

Borgers v Belgium (1991) . . . 414, 415
Borges De Brito v Netherlands (2013) . . . 49
Borisova v Bulgaria (2006) . . . 471
Boskoski v the Former Yugoslav Republic of
    Macedonia (2004) . . . 922, 924
Boso v Italy (2002) . . . 219, 220, 755, 760
Bosphorus Airways v Ireland (2005) . . . 31, 33,
    83, 84, 153, 172, 506, 876, 878, 896, 899
Bosphorus Hava Yollari Turizm ve Ticaret
    Anonim Sirketi v Ireland see Bosphorus
    Airways v Ireland (2005)
Botmeh and Alami v UK (2007) . . . 417
Botta v Italy (1998) . . . 525, 808
Bottaro v Italy (2002) . . . 51,
Bottaro v Italy (2003) . . . 957
Bottazzi v Italy (1999) . . . 445
Botten v Norway (1996) . . . 437
Bouamar v Belgium (1988) . . . 22, 301, 306, 320,
    321, 359, 360, 363, 364, 369
Bouchacourt v France (2009) . . . 560
Bouchelkia v France (1997) . . . 575
Boughanemi v France (1996) . . . 527, 577
Bouglame v Belgium (2010) . . . 88
Boujlifa v France (1997) . . . 575, 577
Boulois v Luxembourg (2012) . . . 373, 384, 389
Boultif v Switzerland (2001) . . . 531, 577
Bousarra v France (2010) . . . 575
Bove v Italy (2005) . . . 186
Bowler International Unit v France (2009) . . . 885
Bowman v UK (1998) . . . 629, 630, 631
Boyajyan v Armenia (2011) . . . 872
Boyce v Ireland (2012) . . . 57
Boychev and Others v Bulgaria (2011) . . . 606
Boyle v UK (1994) . . . 528, 589
Boyle and Rice v UK (1988) . . . 767, 768
Bozano v France (1984) . . . 61, 368, 369
Bozano v France (1986) . . . 229, 301, 304, 330
Bozano v France (1987) . . . 65
Bozcaada Kimisis Teodoku Rum Ortodoks
    Kilisesi Vakfi v Turkey (No 2) (2009) . . . 864
Bozgan v Romania (2007) . . . 731, 732
Bozinovksi v FYRM (2005) . . . 67
Bramelid and Malmström v Sweden
    (1982) . . . 863, 877, 882
Bramelid and Malmström v Sweden
    (1983) . . . 380, 399
Brand v Netherlands (2004) . . . 327
Brandstetter v Austria (1991) . . . 414, 415, 418,
    476, 484
Brânduşe v Romania (2009) . . . 529, 584
Branko Tomašić and Others v Croatia
    (2009) . . . 210
Brannigan and McBride v UK (1993) . . . 30, 154,
    340, 342, 825, 833, 834, 835, 836, 837, 838, 839,
    840, 841, 842, 844, 845, 846, 849
Brasilier v France (2006) . . . 694, 701
Bratří Zátkové, a.s., v Czech Republic
    (2011) . . . 69
Brauer v Germany (2009) . . . 801
Brega v Moldova (2012) . . . 292

Brennan v UK (2001) . . . 474, 475, 482
Brežec v Croatia (2013) . . . 582
Bricmont v Belgium (1986) . . . 459
Bricmont v Belgium (1989) . . . 485
Brigandi v Italy (1991) . . . 440
Brincat v Italy (1992) . . . 342
Brind v UK (1994) . . . 653, 655, 826
British-American Tobacco Co Ltd v
    Netherlands (1995) . . . 381, 447
Brogan v UK (1988) . . . 7, 15, 30, 35, 315, 316,
    338, 339, 340, 353, 367, 368, 369, 582, 826, 828,
    835, 842
Bromiley v UK (1999) . . . 209
Broniowski v Poland (2002) . . . 98
Broniowski v Poland (2004) . . . 16, 22, 29, 149,
    151, 157, 865, 867, 872, 874, 877, 878, 883, 884,
    891, 892
Broniowski v Poland (2005) . . . 198
Bronk v Poland . . . 586
Brown v UK (1998) . . . 375, 495
Brozicek v Italy (1989) . . . 58, 411, 468, 469, 470
Brualla Gómez de la Torre v Spain (1997) . . . 404
Brudnicka v Poland (2005) . . . 448
Brückmann v Germany (1974) . . . 960
Brüggemann and Scheuten v Germany
    (1978) . . . 220
Brumărescu v Romania (1999) . . . 29, 84, 431,
    432, 447, 887
Brumărescu v Romania (2001) . . . 29, 160, 163
Bruncrona v Finland (2004) . . . 875, 882
Brusco v France (2010) . . . 423, 475
Brusco v Italy (2001) . . . 51
Bryan v UK (1995) . . . 11, 392, 393, 394
BS v Spain (2012) . . . 814
Bubbins v UK (2005) . . . 215, 217, 228, 230, 767
Buchberger v Austria (2001) . . . 572
Buchholz v Germany (1980) . . . 20
Buchholz v Germany (1981) . . . 380, 442, 444
Buck v Germany (2005) . . . 530, 557
Buckland v UK (2012) . . . 581, 582
Buckley v UK (1996) . . . 521, 528, 529
Bucur and Toma v Romania (2013) . . . 96, 674
Budayeva v Russia (2008) . . . 208, 218
Budina v Russia (2009) . . . 270
Bugajny and Others v Poland (2009) . . . 134
Buijen v Germany (2010) . . . 373
Bujnița v Moldova (2007) . . . 164
Bukharatyan v Armenia (2012) . . . 601
Bukta and Others v Hungary (2007) . . . 715,
    719, 720
Bulai v Moldova . . . 546
Buldakov v Russia (2011) . . . 114
Bulgakov v Ukraine (2007) . . . 539, 540
Bulinwar OOD and Hrusanov v Bulgaria
    (2007) . . . 66
Bullock v UK (1996) . . . 463
Bulski v Poland (2004) . . . 913
Bulut v Austria (1996) . . . 414, 446, 458
Bulut v Turkey (1993) . . . 608
Bunate Bunkate v Netherlands (1993) . . . 443

Burden v UK (2008) . . . 794, 795, 807
Burden and Burden v UK (2006) . . . 47, 55, 86,
    789
Burdov v Russia (2002) . . . 90, 131, 387, 396, 397,
    863, 871, 876
Burdov v Russia (No 2) (2009) . . . 150, 157, 397
Burghartz v Switzerland (1994) . . . 539, 799
Burke v UK (2006) . . . 204
Burov v Moldova (2011) . . . 69, 70
Bursuc v Romania (2004) . . . 239
Buscarini and Others v San Marino (1999) . . .
    594–5, 597, 943
Buscarini v San Marino (2000) . . . 458
Buscemi v Italy (1999) . . . 454, 466
Busuioc v Moldova (2004) . . . 696, 698
Butkevicius v Lithuania (2002) . . . 466
Butler v UK (2002) . . . 896, 901
Buzescu v Romania (2005) . . . 420, 429, 430, 865
Bykov v Russia (2009) . . . 346, 423, 556
Byrzkykowski v Poland (2007) . . . 217

C
C v Belgium (1996) . . . 577, 798
C v Finland (2006) . . . 573
C v Italy (1988) . . . 468, 470
C v UK (1983) . . . 602
C Ltd v UK (1989) . . . 676, 679
Cabellero v UK (2000) . . . 345, 348
Çaçan v Turkey (2004) . . . 531, 580
Cahıt Demırel v Turkey (2009) . . . 163
Çakici v Turkey (1999) . . . 92, 146, 147, 159, 214,
    223, 240, 257, 300
Cakir v Turkey (2007) . . . 814
Calabro v Italy and Germany (2002) . . . 427, 485
Calcerrada Fornieles v Spain (1992) . . . 74, 76
Callaghan v UK (1989) . . . 377, 378, 432, 461
Calmanovici v Romania (2008) . . . 578, 931
Caloc v France (2000) . . . 242, 243
Calvelli and Ciglio v Italy (2002) . . . 204, 206,
    207, 213, 214, 215, 545
Camberrow MM5 AD v Bulgaria (2004) . . . 90
Camenzind v Switzerland (1997) . . . 557
Camilleri v Malta (2000) . . . 371, 421
Camilleri v Malta (2013) . . . 496
Camp and Bourimi v Netherlands (2000) . . .
    568, 801
Campagnano v Italy (2006) . . . 929
Campbell v UK (1978) . . . 587
Campbell v UK (1988) . . . 413
Campbell v UK (1992) . . . 482, 509, 512, 519,
    531, 588
Campbell and Cosans v UK (1980) . . . 914
Campbell and Cosans v UK (1982) . . . 163, 240,
    241, 273, 593, 906, 908, 910, 913, 915
Campbell and Fell v UK (1984) . . . 307, 399, 434,
    435, 436, 438, 447, 448, 449, 458, 469, 471, 472,
    477, 768, 770, 772
Campmany y Diez de Revenga and Lopez
    Galiacho Perona v Spain (2000) . . . 662
Campos Dâmaso v Portugal (2008) . . . 675

Can v Austria (1985) . . . 470, 472, 482, 483

Canea Catholic Church v Greece (1997) . . . 403, 612, 802

Cañete de Goñi v Spain (2002) . . . 404

Cantoni v France (1996) . . . 33, 497

Caraher v UK (2001) . . . 91

Carbonara and Ventura v Italy (2000) . . . 878, 879, 887

Cardona Serrat v Spain (2010) . . . 453

Cardot v France (1991) . . . 43, 47, 48, 50, 59, 61, 484

Carnduff v UK (2004) . . . 403

Carrillo and Burgoa v Spain (1986) . . . 618

Carson and Others v UK (2010) . . . 786, 789, 791, 795, 796, 822, 863, 866

CAS and CS v Romania (2012) . . . 277

Casado Coca v Spain (1994) . . . 638, 649

Casciaroli v Italy (1992) . . . 440

Casse v Luxembourg (2006) . . . 469

Castelli v Italy (1998) . . . 924

Castells v Spain (1992) . . . 48, 49, 57, 630, 707

Castillo Algar v Spain (1998) . . . 453

Castravet v Moldova (2007) . . . 361, 482

Catal v Turkey (2012) . . . 359

Catan and Others v Moldova and Russia (2012) . . . 100, 908, 909, 911, 912, 913

Čavajda v Czech Republic (2011) . . . 69

CC v Spain (2009) . . . 562

CD v France (2003) . . . 380

CDI Holding v Slovakia (2001) . . . 90

Cebotari v Moldova (2007) . . . 857

Celik v Netherlands (2013) . . . 72

Celik v Turkey (2004) . . . 63

Çelikateş v Turkey (2000) . . . 495

Celikbilek v Turkey (1999) . . . 91

Celikbilek v Turkey (2005) . . . 222

Celniku v Greece (2007) . . . 76

Cemalettin Canlt v Turkey (2008) . . . 560

Cengiz Kiliç v Turkey (2011) . . . 574

Central Mediterranean Development Corp v Malta (No 2) (2011) . . . 396

Centro Europa 7 Srl and Di Stefano v Italy (2012) . . . 79, 161, 645

Cereceda Martin and Others v Spain (1992) . . . 76, 77

Cernecki v Austria (2000) . . . 974, 975

Český v Czech Republic (2000) . . . 347

Cēsnieks v Latvia (2012) . . . 129

Çetin v Turkey (2003) . . . 652, 826

Çetinkaya v Turkey (2006) . . . 714, 715

Ceylan v Turkey (1999) . . . 628, 629, 630, 654

Ceylan v Turkey (2005) . . . 450

CG v Bulgaria (2007) . . . 74

CG v Bulgaria (2008) . . . 578, 776, 966

CG v UK (2001) . . . 433

CGIL and Cofferati v Italy (No 2) (2009) . . . 405

CGP v Netherlands (1997) . . . 472

Cha'are Shalom Ve Tsedek v France (2000) . . . 597, 605, 607, 608, 802

Chagos Islanders v UK (2012) . . . 99, 100, 101, 131

Chahal v UK (1996) . . . 96, 236, 244, 249, 252, 253, 277, 330, 331, 332, 333, 352, 353, 356, 357, 358, 360, 771, 772, 776, 825, 828, 954

Chalkley v UK (2002) . . . 66

Chapman v Belgium (2013) . . . 56, 406

Chapman v UK (2001) . . . 381, 393, 580, 581, 790, 810, 811, 818

Chappell v UK (1987) . . . 597, 602, 607

Chappell v UK (1989) . . . 530, 558

Chare née Jullien v France (1991) . . . 560

Chartier v Italy (1982) . . . 267

Charzynski v Poland (2005) . . . 51

Chassagnou and Others v France (1999) . . . 593, 724, 725, 784, 785, 791, 794, 869, 877, 895, 898

Chauvy v France (2003) . . . 497

Chauvy v France (2004) . . . 553, 624, 625, 626, 660, 671

Cheall v UK (1985) . . . 724, 741, 742, 743, 753

Chember v Russia (2008) . . . 259

Cheminade v France (1999) . . . 949

Chen v Netherlands (2007) . . . 96

Cherepkov v Russia (2000) . . . 925

Chernitsyn v Russia (2006) . . . 79

Chesne v France (2010) . . . 453

Chevrol v France (2003) . . . 90, 448

Chichlian and Ekindjian v France (1989) . . . 469

Chiragov and Others v Armenia (2011) . . . 63, 65, 869

Chiumiento v Italy (2006) . . . 929

Choreftakis and Choreftaki v Greece (2012) . . . 212

Chorherr v Austria (1993) . . . 24, 25, 615, 632

Chmelíř v Czech Republic (2005) . . . 453, 454

Chraidi v Germany (2006) . . . 346, 347, 351, 369, 827

Christian Democratic People's Party v Moldova (2006) . . . 717, 726, 736

Christian Federation of Jehovah's Witnesses in France v France (2001) . . . 86

Christians against Racism and Fascism v UK (1980) . . . 711, 712, 715, 717

Christie v UK (1994) . . . 555

Christinet v Switzerland (1979) . . . 363

Chrysostomos, Papachrysostomos and Loizidou v Turkey (1991) . . . 8, 65

Church of Scientology v Sweden (1979) . . . 636

Church of Scientology Moscow v Russia (2007) . . . 593, 598, 732, 733, 738

Ciancimino v Italy (1991) . . . 956

Cianetti v Italy (2004) . . . 453

Çiçek v Turkey (2001) . . . 224, 257

Cichopek and Others v Poland (2013) . . . 883

Ciechońska v Poland (2011) . . . 206

Çiftçi v Turkey (2004) . . . 912

Ciliz v Netherlands (2000) . . . 527, 577

Çiloğlu v Turkey (2007) . . . 243, 721

Cinar v Turkey (2003) . . . 54

Ciobanu v Romania and Italy (2013) . . . 303

Ciok v Poland (2012) . . . 308

Ciorap v Moldova (2007) . . . 268, 585, 586

Ciorap v Moldova (No 2) (2010) . . . 88

Cissé v France (2001) . . . 797

Cissé v France (2002) . . . 711, 716, 721, 752

Ciubotaru v Moldova (2010) . . . 540

Ciulla v Italy (1989) . . . 311, 315, 338, 367

Civet v France (1999) . . . 52

Claes v Belgium (2013) . . . 267

Clarke v UK (2005) . . . 449

Clift v UK (2010) . . . 789, 791

Clooth v Belgium (1991) . . . 347, 348

Clunis v UK (2001) . . . 403

CN v UK (2012) . . . 285

CN and V v France (2012) . . . 280

Cobzaru v Romania (2007) . . . 578073, 606, 814

Cocchiarella v Italy (2004) . . . 91

Cocchiarella v Italy (2006) . . . 89, 397

Codarcea v Romania (2009) . . . 546

Coëme v Belgium (2000) . . . 415, 458, 494

Cohen v UK (1996) . . . 909

Colak v Germany (1988) . . . 433

Collins and Akaziebie v Sweden (2007) . . . 257

Colman v UK (1993) . . . 638, 652

Colombani and Others v France (2002) . . . 666,
    691, 693, 707

Colon v Netherlands (2012) . . . 292, 559

Colozza and Rubinat v Italy (1985) . . . 410, 411,
    412

Comingersoll SA v Portugal (2000) . . . 89, 161,
    443

Communist Party of Russia and Others v
    Russia (2012) . . . 921, 922, 949, 950, 951

Condron v UK (2000) . . . 423, 424

Cone v Romania (2008) . . . 64

Conka v Belgium (2002) . . . 331, 333, 335, 336,
    354, 361, 768, 770, 774, 961

Conka v Belgium (2001) . . . 89, 797

Connors v UK (2004) . . . 518, 529, 535, 581, 810,
    811

Conscientious Objectors v Denmark
    (1978) . . . 601

Consorts Richet et Le Ber v France (2010) . . . 864

Constantinescu v Romania (2000) . . . 87, 437

Contrada v Italy (1998) . . . 347

Cooper v UK (2003) . . . 446, 447, 448, 449

Coorplan-Jenni GmbH and Elvir Hascic v
    Austria (2005) . . . 96

Copland v UK (2007) . . . 530, 556

Cordova v Italy (No 1) (2003) . . . 405, 630

Cordova v Italy (No 2) (2003) . . . 405, 630

Corigliano v Italy (1982) . . . 376, 377, 441

Cornelis v Netherlands (2004) . . . 420

Correia de Matos v Portugal (2001) . . . 77, 88,
    476, 478, 480

Corsacov v Moldova (2006) . . . 238

Coşcodar v Romania (2010) . . . 589

Çöşelav v Turkey (2012) . . . 211

Ćosić v Croatia (2009) . . . 582

Cossey v UK (1990) . . . 10, 21, 537

Costa and Pavan v Italy (2012) . . . 524, 548

Costache v Romania (2012) . . . 580

Costello-Roberts v UK (1993) . . . 24, 272, 273,
    526, 541, 907

Costică Moldovan and Others v Romania (2011)
    . . . 194

Cotleţ v Romania (2003) . . . 589

Cottin v Belgium (2005) . . . 418

Couillard Maugery v France (2004) . . . 570

Council of Civil Service Unions v UK
    (1987) . . . 77, 750

Covezzi and Morselli v Italy (2002) . . . 92

CR v UK (1995) . . . 497, 498, 878

Craxi v Italy (2002) . . . 467, 471, 484

Craxi v Italy (No 2) (2003) . . . 561

Creangă v Romania (2012) . . . 288, 290, 292,
    302, 303, 304

Credit and Industrial Bank v Czech Republic
    (2003) . . . 90

Crémieux v France (1993) . . . 557

Crociani v Italy (1980) . . . 307, 438, 447, 448,
    451, 458, 473

Croissant v Germany (1987) . . . 16, 476, 477,
    479, 480

Crompton v UK (2009) . . . 393, 395

Crook and National Union of Journalists v
    UK (1988) . . . 680

Crowther v UK (2005) . . . 445

Cruz Varas v Sweden (1991) . . . 20, 139, 247, 248, 250

CS v Germany (1989) . . . 716

Csikos v Hungary (2006) . . . 50, 58

Csoma v Romania (2013) . . . 524, 545

Csoszanszki v Sweden (2006) . . . 308

Csüllög v Hungary (2011) . . . 265

Cucu v Romania (2012) . . . 931

Cudak v Lithuania (2010) . . . 405, 406

Cumber v UK (1996) . . . 368

Cumhuriyet Vakfı and Others v Turkey
    (2013) . . . 640

Cummins v UK (2005) . . . 214

Cumpănă and Mazăre v Romania (2004) . . . 125, 640

Curley v UK (2000) . . . 260

Cuscani v UK (2002) . . . 490, 491

Custers, Devaux and Turk v Denmark
    (2007) . . . 496, 497

Cuvillers and Da Luz v France (2003) . . . 463

Cvetkovic v Serbia (2008) . . . 51

Cvijetic v Croatia (2004) . . . 529

Cyprus v Turkey (1982) . . . 847

Cyprus v Turkey (First and Second
    Applications) (1975) . . . 73, 115, 116, 117, 847

Cyprus v Turkey (First and Second
    Applications) (1976) . . . 116, 117, 237, 290,
    291, 846, 847

Cyprus v Turkey (Third Application) (1978) . . .
    45, 46, 115, 116, 117

Cyprus v Turkey (Third Application) (1983) . . . 290

Cyprus v Turkey (Fourth Application)
    (2001) . . . 61, 111, 116, 117, 185, 191, 198, 199,
    212, 213, 214, 224, 257, 265, 269, 270, 278, 297,
    300, 307, 446, 458, 599, 847, 869, 911

Czekalla v Portugal (2002) . . . 481, 482

D

D v Austria (1990) . . . 482

D v France (1983) . . . 593

D v Ireland (1986) . . . 455

D v Ireland (2006) . . . 57, 546

D v UK (1997) . . . 142, 236, 254, 256, 277

DA and BN and SN v Sweden (1993) . . . 909

Da Conceição Mateus and Santos Januário v
    Portugal (2013) . . . 883

Dąbrowski v Poland (2006) . . . 694, 701

Dacia SRL v Moldova (2008) . . . 416

Dacosta Silva v Spain (2006) . . . 25

Dadouch v Malta (2010) . . . 756

Dağtekin v Turkey (2005) . . . 635

Dağtekin and Others v Turkey (2007) . . . 418

Dahlab v Switzerland (2001) . . . 538, 608, 609,
    788, 802

Daktaras v Lithuania (2000) . . . 449, 466

Dalban v Romania (1999) . . . 90, 94, 131, 694

Dalea v France (2010) . . . 386

Dalia v France (1998) . . . 52

Dallos v Hungary (2001) . . . 469

Dammann v Switzerland (2006) . . . 614, 640,
    641, 652, 674

Danilenkov and Others v Russia (2009) . . . 749

Daniliuc v Romania (2012) . . . 589

Danini v Italy (1996) . . . 209

Daiudi v France (2009) . . . 247

Danev v Bulgaria (2010) . . . 367

Darby v Sweden (1990) . . . 594, 793, 902

Darren Omoregie and Others v Norwau
    (2008) . . . 577

Daud v Portugal (1998) . . . 481

Davison v UK (2010) . . . 589

Davran v Turkey (2009) . . . 402

Davydov and Others v Ukraine (2010) . . . 96

Dayanan v Turkey (2009) . . . 474

DB v Turkey (2010) . . . 114

DD v Lithuania (2012) . . . 295, 296, 355, 403

De Becker v Belgium (1962) . . . 841, 847

De Clerck v Belgium (2007) . . . 442

De Cubber v Belgium (1984) . . . 453, 459

De Diego Nafria v Spain (2002) . . . 685, 692, 700

De Donder and De Clippel v Belgium
    (2011) . . . 92, 93, 211

De Geouffre de la Pradelle v France
    (1992) . . . 402, 408

De Haan v Netherlands (1997) . . . 453

De Haes and Gijsels v Belgium (1997) . . . 416,
    677, 698

De Jong, Baljet and Van den Brink v
    Netherlands (1984) . . . 315, 339, 341, 342, 352,
    362, 363, 366, 768

De Jorio v Italy (2003) . . . 58

De Jorio v Italy (2004) . . . 405

De La Cierva Osorio de Moscovo v Spain
    (1999) . . . 863

De Luca v Italy (2013) . . . 882

De Moor v Belgium (1994) . . . 382, 429, 430

De Napoles Pacheco v Belgium (1979) . . . 868

De Pace v Italy (2008) . . . 75

De Parias Merry v Spain (1999) . . . 49

De Saedeleer v Belgium (2007) . . . 81

De Salvador Torres v Spain (1996) . . . 469

De Schepper v Belgium (2009) . . . 327

De Souza Ribeiro v France (2012) . . . 54, 769,
    771, 772, 774

De Varga-Hirsch v France (1993) . . . 221, 267

De Wilde, Ooms and Versyp v Belgium (Merits)
    (Vagrancy cases) (1971) . . . 56, 282, 322, 353,
    355, 356, 494

Deés v Hungary (2010) . . . 583

Del Latte v Netherlands (2004) . . . 464

Del Rio Prada v Spain (2013) . . . 133, 161, 163,
    180, 288, 306, 500, 501

Del Sol v France (2002) . . . 400

Delcourt v Belgium (1967) . . . 335

Delcourt v Belgium (1970) . . . 8, 414, 459, 787

Delfi AS v Estonia (2013) . . . 615

Delgado v France (1998) . . . 74

Demades v Turkey (2003) . . . 529

Dembele v Switzerland (2013) . . . 243

Demebukov v Bulgaria (2008) . . . 412, 436

Demicoli v Malta (1991) . . . 374, 447, 455

Demir v Turkey (1998) . . . 827, 840

Demir and Baykara v Turkey (2008) . . . 11, 22,
    514, 740, 741, 748, 749, 750, 751, 752

Demirel and Ateş v Turkey (2007) . . . 629

Demirbaş and Others v Turkey (2010) . . . 82

Demiray v Turkey (2000) . . . 223

Democracy and Change Party v Turkey
    (2005) . . . 726, 727

Demopoulos v Turkey (2010) . . . 47, 51

Demuth v Switzerland (2002) . . . 644, 645

Denev v Sweden (1989) . . . 896

Denimark Ltd v UK (2000) . . . 867, 896

Denis Vasilyev v Russia (2009) . . . 266

Denizci v Cyprus (2001) . . . 209, 238, 241, 276,
    302, 955

Denmark v Turkey (1999) . . . 45, 46

Denmark v Turkey (2000) . . . 117, 127

Denmark, Norway, Sweden v Greece (Second
    Greek case) (1970) . . . 46, 116

Denmark, Norway, Sweden and Netherlands
    v Greece (Greek case) (1969) . . . 45, 46, 116,
    238, 240, 242, 246, 263, 449, 458, 517, 716, 825,
    829, 830, 834, 846, 847, 856

Dennis and Others v UK (2002) . . . 62

Depalle v France (2010) . . . 865, 896

Depauw v Belgium (2007) . . . 51

Deschomets v France (2006) . . . 612

Desjardin v France (2007) . . . 696, 705

Desmeules v France (1990) . . . 937

Deumeland v Germany (1986) . . . 379, 380, 383,
    441, 443

Devenney v UK (2002) . . . 406

Devlin v UK (2001) . . . 406

Deweer v Belgium (1980) . . . 52, 375, 376, 377,
    399, 408, 461

DG v Ireland (2002) . . . 295, 320, 321

DH and Others v Czech Republic (2007) ... 50, 60, 145, 148, 786, 797, 809, 810, 812, 815, 816, 817, 822, 917

D'Haese, Le CompteVan Leuven and De Meyere v Belgium (1983) ... 271, 452

Dhoest v Belgium (1987) ... 307, 360, 500

Di Belmonte v Italy (2010) ... 902

Di Lazzaro v Italy (1997) ... 567, 761

Di Salvo v Italy (2007) ... 79

Di Sarno and Others v Italy (2012) ... 583, 585

Diaceno v Romania (2012) ... 70

Diallo v Sweden (2010) ... 490

Diamantides v Greece (No 2) (2005) ... 465

Dichand v Austria (2002) ... 703

Dickson v UK (2007) ... 11, 14, 16, 21, 158, 511, 528, 535, 547, 548, 564, 585, 589, 590, 755, 761, 763

Dicle on behalf of the DEP (Democratic Party) of Turkey v Turkey (2002) ... 726, 736

Didier v France (2002) ... 967

Dikme v Turkey (2000) ... 240, 336, 337, 827

Dimitras v Greece (2010) ... 595, 596

Dimitrios Georgiadis v Greece (2000) ... 382

Dimitrov and Hamanov v Bulgaria (2011) ... 163

Dimitrov-Kazakov v Bulgaria (2011) ... 560

Dimitrovska v the Former Yugoslav Republic of Macedonia (2008) ... 93

Dinc v Turkey (2001) ... 74

Dink and Others v Turkey (2010) ... 210, 617

Direkçi and Direkçi v Turkey (2006) ... 93, 95

Dirioz v Turkey (2012) ... 415

Disk and Kesk v Turkey (2012) ... 715, 719

Djavit An v Turkey (2003) ... 711, 715, 716

Djokaba Lambi Longa v Netherlands ... 84

DMD Group v Slovakia (2010) ... 458

DMT and DKI v Bulgaria (2012) ... 578

DN v Switzerland (2001) ... 355

Dobbie v UK (1996) ... 404

Dobrev v Bulgaria (2006) ... 44

Dobri v Romania (2010) ... 262

Dochnal v Poland (2012) ... 130

Dodov v Bulgaria (2008) ... 207, 209, 224

Doğan and Others v Turkey (2004) ... 865, 870, 878

Dogru v France (2008) ... 607, 609

Dojan and Others v Germany (2011) ... 600, 915

Dokić v Bosnia and Herzegovina (2010) ... 883

Dombo Beheer v Netherlands (1993) ... 409, 413, 414, 415

Domenichini v Italy (1996) ... 472, 587

Donnelly v UK (1975) ... 46, 59

Doorson v Netherlands (1996) ... 485, 486, 488, 561

Đorđević v Croatia (2012) ... 543

Dorigo v Italy (2007) ... 187

Döry v Sweden (2002) ... 437

Döşemealtı Belediyesi v Turkey (2010) ... 82

Douglas-Williams v UK (2002) ... 211, 215, 231, 243

Dougoz v Greece (2001) ... 262

Douiyeb v Netherlands (1999) ... 366

Dowsett v UK (2003) ... 417

Dowsett v UK (No 2) (2011) ... 96

Doyle v UK (2006) ... 926, 927

DP and JC v UK (2002) ... 275, 407

Dragotoniu and Militaru-Pidhorni v Romania (2007) ... 498

Draon v France (2005) ... 864, 882, 889

Draper v UK (1980) ... 756, 757

Drieman v Norway (2000) ... 716, 723

Drijfhout v Netherlands (2011) ... 79

Dritsas v Italy (2011) ... 961

Driza v Albania (2007) ... 165, 432, 451

Drozd and Janousek v France and Spain (1992) ... 307

Drozdowski v Poland (2005) ... 114

Družstevni Záložna Pria v Czech Republic (2008) ... 863, 878, 880

Dubenko v Ukraine (2005) ... 397

Dubetska and Others v Ukraine (2011) ... 582

Dubinskaya v Russia (2006) ... 402

Duclos v France (1996) ... 383

Dudek v Germany (2010) ... 72, 80

Dudgeon v UK (1981) ... 8, 9, 10, 16, 30, 86, 512, 513, 514, 516, 518, 531, 532, 534, 549, 784, 785, 791, 803

Duhs v Sweden (1990) ... 464

Duinhof and Dujff v Netherlands (1984) ... 341

Dujardin v France (1991) ... 205

Dulaş v Turkey (2001) ... 241, 580

Dulaurans v France (2000) ... 429

Dumitru Popescu v Romania (No 2) (2007) ... 556

Dunayev v Russia (2007) ... 401

Dupuis v Belgium (1988) ... 448

Dupuis and Others v France (2007) ... 668, 675

Đurđević v Croatia (2011) ... 543

Duringer and Grunge v France (2003) ... 79

Durini v Italy (1994) ... 82

Du Roy and Malaurie v France (2000) ... 682

Dvořáček and Dvořáčkova v Slovakia (2009) ... 207

Dybeku v Albania (2007) ... 165, 266, 267

Dyuldin and Kislov v Russia (2007) ... 692, 700

Dzieciak v Poland (2008) ... 211

E

E v Norway (1990) ... 352, 356, 362, 364

E and Others v UK (2002) ... 275

Earl and Countess Spencer v UK (1998) ... 551, 553

East African Asians v UK (1973) ... 269, 300, 959

Eastaway v UK (2004) ... 442

Easterbrook v UK (2003) ... 365, 378

EB v France (2008) ... 10, 524, 528, 550, 564, 567, 568, 761, 784, 787, 788, 804, 806, 822

EB and Others v Austria (2013) ... 803

Ebcin v Turkey (2011) ... 542, 543

Eberhard and M v Slovenia (2009) ... 47, 574

Ebibomi v UK (1995) . . . 910
Eccles, McPhillips and McShane v Ireland
   (1988) . . . 449
Ecer and Zeyrek v Turkey (2001) . . . 497, 501
Eckle v Germany (1982) . . . 84, 377, 378, 440,
   441, 442, 443
Edificaciones March Gallego SA v Spain
   (1998) . . . 404
Editions Périscope v France (1992) . . . 381, 382
Edition Plon v France (2004) . . . 640, 666, 667,
   668, 683
Editorial Board of Pravoye Delo and Shkteke v
   Ukraine (2011) . . . 615, 649
Edwards v UK (1991) . . . 45
Edwards v UK (1992) . . . 121, 409, 417, 459, 473
Edwards v UK (2002) . . . 211, 216, 217, 218
Edwards (Paul and Audrey) v UK (2001) . . . 62,
   63
Edwards (Paul and Audrey) v UK (2002) . . . 769,
   781
Edwards and Lewis v UK (2004) . . . 416, 417, 428
Efstathiou and Michailidis and Co Motel
   Amerika v Greece (2003) . . . 890
Efstratiou v Greece (1996) . . . 603
Ege v Turkey (2004) . . . 64
Egeland and Hanseid v Norway (2009) . . . 660, 681
Eğinlioğlu v Turkey (1998) . . . 88
Eğitim ve Bilim Emekçileri Sendikası v Turkey
   (2012) . . . 77, 616, 733
Eglise Evangélique Missionnaire et Salaun
   v France (2013) . . . 606
Egmez v Cyprus (2000) . . . 238, 240, 241
Egmez v Cyprus (2012) . . . 96
Egue v France (1988) . . . 363, 482
Einhorn v France (2001) . . . 412
Eisenstecken v Austria (2000) . . . 24, 25
EK v Turkey (2002) . . . 493
Ekbatani v Sweden (1988) . . . 19, 436, 437, 459
Ekeberg and Others v Norway (2007) . . . 456
Ekholm v Finland (2006) . . . 74
Ekoglasnost v Bulgaria (2012) . . . 923
Ekşi and Ocak v Turkey (2010) . . . 719
El Boujaidi v France (1997) . . . 577
El Majjaoui and Stichting Touba Moskee v
   Netherlands (2007) . . . 131
ElMasri v the Former Yugoslav Republic of
   Macedonia (2012) . . . 145, 146, 147, 153, 240,
   256, 276, 288, 297, 299, 300, 779, 827
El Morsli v France (2008) . . . 610
El Shennawy v France (2011) . . . 263
Elberte v Latvia (2010) . . . 545
Elci and Others v Turkey (2003) . . . 557
Elefteriadis v Romania (2011) . . . 262
ELH and PBH v UK (1997) . . . 589, 761
Elias v UK (2001) . . . 457
Eliazer v Netherlands (2001) . . . 408
Elli Poluhas Dödsbo v Sweden (2006) . . . 569
Elo v Finland (2004) . . . 430
Elsholz v Germany (2000) . . . 421, 437, 489, 806
Emesa Sugar NV v Netherlands (2005) . . . 385

Emine Arac v Turkey (2008) . . . 384
Emre v Switzerland (2008) . . . 577
Emre v Switzerland (No 2) (2011) . . . 96, 163, 194
Enea v Italy (2009) . . . 373, 384, 586, 587
Enerji Yapi-Yol Sen v Turkey (2009) . . . 749, 751,
   752
Enhorn v Sweden (2005) . . . 321, 322
Engel v Netherlands (1976) . . . 16, 226, 288, 292,
   306, 307, 311, 313, 353, 373, 374, 375, 376, 437,
   447, 448, 449, 461, 478, 483, 484, 488, 495, 856
Englert v Germany (1987) . . . 461
Englund v Sweden (1994) . . . 744
Ensslin, Baader and Raspe v Germany
   (1978) . . . 141, 264, 265, 412, 467, 474, 477
Eon v France (2013) . . . 70, 635, 698
EP v Italy (2001) . . . 134
EP v Slovak Republic (1998) . . . 974
Epple v Germany (2005) . . . 312
Epners-Gefners v Latvia (2012) . . . 585, 589
Epstein and Others v Belgium (2008) . . . 797
Er and Others v Turkey (2012) . . . 63, 300
Erbakan v Turkey (2006) . . . 622, 654
Erçep v Turkey (2011) . . . 601
Erdal Taş v Turkey (No 3) (2007) . . . 628
Erdal Taş v Turkey (No 4) (2007) . . . 628, 629
Erdem v Germany (2001) . . . 588, 826
Erdogan v Turkey(1992) . . . 470
Erdoğan v Turkey (2006) . . . 143, 148, 215
Erdoğan Yağiz v Turkey (2007) . . . 268
Erdoğdu and İnce v Turkey (1999) . . . 628, 629, 640
Eremia v Moldova (2013) . . . 274, 542, 798, 799
Ergi v Turkey (1995) . . . 44
Ergi v Turkey (1998) . . . 216, 222, 223, 227, 228,
   233
Ergin v Turkey (No 6) (2006) . . . 450
Eriksen v Norway (1997) . . . 309
Eriksson v Sweden (1989) . . . 384, 569
Eriksson v Sweden (2012) . . . 55
Erkapić v Croatia (2013) . . . 418
Erkner and Hofhauer v Austria (1987) . . . 396,
   868, 881, 882, 884
Ernst and Others v Belgium (2003) . . . 408, 434,
   614, 642, 643
Escoubet v Belgium (1999) . . . 375
Eski v Austria (2007) . . . 573
Esmukhambetov and Others v Russia
   (2011) . . . 258, 558
Esposito v Italy (1997) . . . 405
Estamirov and Others v Russia (2006) . . . 223
Estevez v Spain (2001) . . . 806
Etienne Tête v France (1987) . . . 947
Ettl v Austria (1987) . . . 12, 447
Eugenia Michaelidou Developments Ltd and
   Michael Tymvios v Turkey (2003) . . . 152,
   863, 869
Eurofinacom v France (2004) . . . 428
Europapress Holding DOO v Croatia
   (2009) . . . 688, 689
Éva Molnár v Hungary (2008) . . . 714, 715, 719,
   720

Evadsson and Others v Sweden (2006) . . . 77

Evaldsson v Sweden (2006) . . . 743

Evans v UK (2007) . . . 12, 16, 125, 142, 220, 505, 513, 514, 520, 524, 528, 534, 547, 548, 564, 590

Evrim Öktem v Turkey (2008) . . . 222, 227

Eweida and Others v UK (2013) . . . 538, 603, 604, 605, 607, 784, 802

Ewing v UK (1986) . . . 377

Ezeh and Connors v UK (2003) . . . 306, 373, 374, 477

Ezelin v France (1991) . . . 616, 715, 716, 721

F

F v Switzerland (1987) . . . 13, 755, 756, 760

F v UK (1986) . . . 473

F v UK (1992) . . . 489

F v UK (2004) . . . 257

F Santos Lda and Fachadas v Portugal (2000) . . . 90

Fáber v Hungary (2012) . . . 615, 625

Fabris v France (2013) . . . 787, 792, 793, 796, 801

Fadele v UK (1991) . . . 244

Fadeyeva v Russia (2005) . . . 188, 582, 584

Fägerskiöld v Sweden (2008) . . . 529, 583

Fahri v France (2007) . . . 456

Fahriye Calişkan v Turkey (2007) . . . 243

Faimblat v Romania (2009) . . . 163

Fairfield v UK (2005) . . . 93

Fakhretdinov and Others v Russia (2010) . . . 51

Falakaoğlu and Saygili v Turkey (2006) . . . 628

Falakaoğlu and Saygili v Turkey (2007) . . . 628

Falk v Netherlands (2004) . . . 462

Falter Zeitschriften GmbH v Austria . . . 677

Family H v UK (1984) . . . 909, 913

Farbtuhs v Latvia (2004) . . . 267

Farcas v Romania (2010) . . . 413

Farmakopoulos v Belgium (1992) . . . 361

Farragut v France (1984) . . . 465

Faruk Temel v Turkey (2011) . . . 630

Fashanu v UK (1998) . . . 464

Fatma Kacar v Turkey (2005) . . . 215

Fatullayev v Azerbaijan (2010) . . . 453, 466

Faulkner v UK (1999) . . . 400

Fawsie v Greece (2010) . . . 798

Fayed v UK (1994) . . . 13, 14, 389, 390, 405, 407

Fazliyski v Bulgaria (2013) . . . 386, 438

FCB v Italy (1991) . . . 410, 411, 477

FE v France (1998) . . . 402

Fedele v Germany (1987) . . . 490

Federación nacionalista Canaria v Spain (2001) . . . 947

Fédération hellénique des syndicats des employés du secteur bancaire v Greece (2011) . . . 76

Federation of Offshore Workers' Trade Unions v Norway (2002) . . . 750

Fedorov and Federova v Russia (2005) . . . 956, 957

Fedotov v Moldova (2011) . . . 70, 71

Fedotov v Russia (2005) . . . 241, 244, 262, 385

Fedotova v Russia (2006) . . . 113, 458

Feldbrugge v Netherlands (1986) . . . 379, 380, 383, 410, 416, 418, 866

Feldek v Slovakia (2001) . . . 693, 699, 700

Féret v Belgium (2009) . . . 622

Ferla v Poland (2008) . . . 586

Fernandez v France (2012) . . . 68

Fernandez Martinez v Spain (2012) . . . 579, 600

Fernandez-Molina Gonzalez and 370 other applications v Spain (2002) . . . 49

Fernie v UK (2006) . . . 62, 65

Ferrantelli and Santangelo v Italy (1996) . . . 420, 453, 485

Ferraro v Italy (1991) . . . 442

Ferraro-Bravo v Italy (1984) . . . 483

Ferrazzini v Italy (2001) . . . 379, 381, 384, 385, 386, 388, 902

Ferreira Alves v Portugal (2007) . . . 418

Feti Demirtaş v Turkey (2012) . . . 271, 601

Fey v Austria (1993) . . . 451, 452, 453, 676

Fidan v Turkey (2000) . . . 92

Filip v Romania (2006) . . . 266

Filipovic v Serbia (2007) . . . 97

Filippini v San Marino (2003) . . . 448

Filiz Uyan v Turkey (2009) . . . 263

Financial Times Ltd v UK (2009) . . . 48, 640, 641

Findlay v UK (1997) . . . 161, 449, 459

Finger v Bulgaria (2011) . . . 68, 70, 72, 163

Finogenov v Russia (2011) . . . 15, 227, 228

Finucane v UK (2003) . . . 216

Firth and 2,353 Others v UK (2013) . . . 931

Fischer v Austria (1995) . . . 25, 395

Fischer v Austria (2003) . . . 377

Fitt v UK (2000) . . . 417

Flamenbaum and Others v France (2012) . . . 583

Flamînzeanu v Romania (2011) . . . 266

Flinkkilä and Others v Finland (2010) . . . 660

Flisar v Slovenia (2011) . . . 68, 72

Floarea Pop v Romania (2010) . . . 88

Florea v Romania (2010) . . . 262

Floroiu v Romania (2013) . . . 282

Flux v Moldova (2007) . . . 689, 698

Flux v Moldova (No 2) . . . 691

Flux v Moldova (No 3) (2007) . . . 688

Flux v Moldova (No 4) (2008) . . . 688. 689, 698

Flux v Moldova (No 5) (2008) . . . 688

Flux v Moldova (No 6) (2008) . . . 688, 689

Flux v Moldova (No 7) (2009) . . . 688

Fociac v Romania (2005) . . . 397

Fogarty v UK (2001) . . . 152, 405

Foka v Turkey (2008) . . . 292

Földes and Földesné Hajlik v Hungary (2007) . . . 957

Foley v UK (2002) . . . 441, 445

Folgerø v Norway (2007) . . . 595, 600, 915, 916, 919

Folgerø and Others v Norway (2006) . . . 76, 77

Folgia v Switzerland (2007) . . . 678

Fomin v Moldova (2011) . . . 72

Former King of Greece and Others v Greece (2000) . . . 160, 864, 877, 894

Former King of Greece v Greece and Others
    (2002) . . . 160, 163, 889, 894, 905
Forrer-Niedenthal v Germany (2003) . . . 429
Foti v Italy (1982) . . . 52, 377, 440, 441, 442, 444
Foucher v France (1997) . . . 472, 476
Fouquet v France (1996) . . . 429
Four Companies v Austria (1976) . . . 281, 284
Fournier v France . . . 949
Fox v UK (2012) . . . 56
Fox, Campbell and Hartley v UK (1990) . . . 301,
    305, 317, 318, 334, 335, 336, 363, 366, 367, 368,
    369, 826, 827
Foxley v UK (2000) . . . 506
FPJM Kleine Staarman v Netherlands
    (1985) . . . 758
France, Norway, Denmark, Sweden and
    Netherlands v Turkey (1983) . . . 45, 46, 115,
    116
France, Norway, Denmark, Sweden and
    Netherlands v Turkey (1985) . . . 127, 116
Francesco Sessa v Italy (2012) . . . 608
Franz Fischer v Austria (2001) . . . 971, 972
Frasik v Poland (2010) . . . 362, 757
Frăsilă and Ciocîrlan v Romania (2012) . . . 619
Frau v Italy (1991) . . . 377
Freda v Italy (1980) . . . 310, 337
Fredin v Sweden (No 1) (1991) . . . 880, 886, 896,
    904
Freedom and Democracy Party (ÖZDEP)
    v Turkey (1999) . . . 44, 126, 726, 727
Freimanis and Lidums v Lithuania
    (2006) . . . 90, 131
Frérot v France (2007) . . . 263
Fressoz and Roire v France (1999) . . . 48, 49,
    660, 663, 673, 674, 687
Fretté v France (2002) . . . 158, 415, 528, 550, 567,
    568, 761, 787, 804
Frexias v Spain (2000) . . . 483
Friedl v Austria (1995) . . . 560, 721
Friend and Others v UK (2009) . . . 78–9, 525,
    529, 885, 897
Frodl v Austria (2010) . . . 931
Fruni v Slovakia (2011) . . . 449
Frydlender v France (2000) . . . 442
Fuentes Bobo v Spain (2000) . . . 617, 618, 619,
    685, 692
Fuklev v Ukraine (2005) . . . 871
Funke v France (1993) . . . 374, 377, 422, 423,
    424, 425, 460, 557, 616, 902
Furdik v Slovakia (2008) . . . 208
Fürst von Thurn und Taxis v Germany
    (2013) . . . 98
Fusu Arcadie and Others v Moldova
    (2012) . . . 598, 606
Frydlender v France (2000) . . . 440

G
G v France (1995) . . . 494, 496
G v Germany (1989) . . . 711, 723
G v Malta (1991) . . . 462

G v Netherlands (1987) . . . 794
G v Netherlands (1993) . . . 527
G v UK (1983) . . . 420
G v UK (2011) . . . 462
G, S and M v Austria (1983) . . . 896
Gabarri Moreno v Spain (2003) . . . 501
Gabay v Turkey (2006) . . . 134
Gäfgen v Germany (2010) . . . 48, 50, 88, 236,
    240, 241, 276, 277, 420, 422
Gaftoniuc v Romania (2011) . . . 70, 71
Gagiu v Romania (2009) . . . 114
Gagliano Giorgi v Italy (2012) . . . 70
Gaglione and Others v Italy (2010) . . . 69
Gaillard v France (2000) . . . 66
Gakiyev and Gakiyeva v Russia (2009) . . . 93
Galic v Netherlands (2009) . . . 84
Galovic v Croatia (2013) . . . 72
Galstyan v Armenia (2007) . . . 55, 62, 470, 471,
    716, 721, 967
Gamaleddyn v France (2009) . . . 610
Ganci v Italy (2003) . . . 384, 387, 401
Ganea v Moldova (2011) . . . 368
Gani v Spain (2013) . . . 483, 485
Garabayev v Russia (2007) . . . 252
Garaudy v France (2003) . . . 518, 624, 625, 671,
    854
Garcia Alva v Germany (2001) . . . 356, 357
Garcia Ruiz v Spain (1999) . . . 17, 371, 430, 431
Gardel v France (2009) . . . 499
Garimpo v Portugal (2004) . . . 392
Garnaga v Ukraine (2013) . . . 540
Garner v UK (1999) . . . 497
Garyfallou v AEBE v Greece (1997) . . . 375, 376
Gas and Dubois v France (2010) . . . 52, 56
Gas and Dubois v France (2012) . . . 526, 527,
    550, 805, 806
Gąsior v Poland (2012) . . . 694
Gaskin v UK (1989) . . . 13, 528, 534, 535, 537,
    538, 563, 620
Gasparini v Italy and Belgium (2009) . . . 33
Gast and Popp v Germany (2000) . . . 377
Gasus Dosier und Fordertechnik GmbH v
    Netherlands (1995) . . . 863, 865, 888, 901, 902
Gatis Kovaļkovs v Latvia (2012) . . . 608
Gatt v Malta (2010) . . . 310, 311, 952, 953
Gauer and Others v France (2012) . . . 258
Gautrin and Others v France (1998) . . . 455
Gavrielidou and Others v Cyprus (2003) . . . 93
Gavrilovici v Moldova (2009) . . . 699
Gawęda v Poland (2002) . . . 640, 649
Gay News Ltd and Lemon v UK (1982) . . . 669
Gayduk and Others v Ukraine (2002) . . . 872
Gaygusuz v Austria (1996) . . . 383, 797, 822, 866
GB v Bulgaria (2004) . . . 246, 964
GB v France (2001) . . . 471, 473
GCP v Romania (2012) . . . 466, 467
Gea Catalan v Spain (1995) . . . 469
Gebremedhin v France (2007) . . . 333, 774
Geerings v Netherlands (2007) . . . 461, 464
Geerk v Switzerland (1978) . . . 669

Gelfmann v France (2004) . . . 267
Gençel v Turkey (2003) . . . 164
Genovese v Malta (2011) . . . 540, 801
Gentilhomme, Schaff-Benhadji, and Zerouki
  v France (2002) . . . 81
Georgel and Georgeta Stoicescu v Romania
  (2011) . . . 523, 542
Georgia v Russia (2007) . . . 117
Georgia v Russia (I) (2009) . . . 45, 46, 47, 144
Georgia v Russia (II) (2011) . . . 45, 46, 117
Georgia v Russia (III) (2010) . . . 117
Georgia Makri v Greece (2005) . . . 93
Georgiadis v Greece (1997) . . . 430
Georgiadis v Greece see Dimitrios Georgiadis
  v Greece
Georgian Labour Party v Georgia (2007) . . . 80
Georgian Labour Party v Georgia (2008) . . .
  924, 943, 944
Georgian Labour Party v Georgia (No 2)
  (2006) . . . 85
Georgieva v Bulgaria (2008) . . . 349
Georgiou v Greece (2000) . . . 588
Georgios Papageogiou v Greece (2003) . . . 416
Gerger v Turkey (1999) . . . 628, 629
Ghazal v France (2009) . . . 610
Gheorghe v Romania (2007) . . . 442
Ghigo v Malta (2006) . . . 898
Ghosh v Germany (2007) . . . 245
Giacomelli v Italy (2006) . . . 528, 583, 584, 585
Giancarlo Lombardo v Italy (1992) . . . 383
Giannangeli v Italy (2001) . . . 441
Gillan and Quinton v UK (2010) . . . 292,559
Gillberg v Sweden (2012) . . . 532, 616, 621
Gillies v UK (1989) . . . 501
Gillow v UK (1986) . . . 100, 163, 403, 453, 528,
  795, 875, 895, 956
Giniewski v France (2006) . . . 669, 670, 671
Giorgi Nikolaishvili v Georgia (2009) . . . 300,
  304
Gitonas v Greece (1997) . . . 933, 938
Giulia Manzoni v Italy (1997) . . . 319
Giuliani and Gaggio v Italy (2011) . . . 230
Giumarra v France (2001) . . . 53
Giusti v Italy (2011) . . . 68
Giusto, Bornacin and V v Italy (2007) . . . 257
Giza v Poland (2012) . . . 308
GJ v Luxembourg (2000) . . . 90, 152
GL v Italy (1994) . . . 431
Gladysheva v Russia (2011) . . . 529, 883
Glas Nadezhda Eood and Elenkov v Bulgaria
  (2007) . . . 612
Glasenapp v Germany (1986) . . . 616, 686, 786
Glaser v Czech Republic (2008) . . . 868
Glass v UK (2004) . . . 11, 544
Glässner v Germany (2001) . . . 495
Glimmerveen and Hagenbeek v Netherlands
  (1979) . . . 270, 624, 854, 941
Glinowieki v Poland (2010) . . . 586
Glor v Switzerland (2009) . . . 795, 808
Gluhaković v Croatia (2011) . . . 573

GN and Others v Italy (2009) . . . 808, 809
GN and Others v Italy (2011) . . . 808, 809
Gnahoré v France (2000) . . . 400, 571
Gobec v Slovania (2013) . . . 573
Göbel v Germany (2011) . . . 885
Göç v Turkey (2002) . . . 382, 416, 433, 436, 437,
  438
Gochev v Bulgaria (2009) . . . 955, 959
Göçmen v Turkey (2006) . . . 186, 187, 419
Goddi v Italy (1982) . . . 477
Goddi v Italy (1984) . . . 410, 471, 472, 473, 483
Godelli v Italy (2012) . . . 538
Godlevskiy v Russia (2004) . . . 411
Goffi v Italy (2005) . . . 957
Göktan v France (2002) . . . 952, 970, 971
Gökçeli v Turkey (2003) . . . 464
Golder v UK (1975) . . . 7, 8, 380, 395, 398, 399,
  402, 403, 408, 504, 523, 588, 772
Golubović v Croatia (2012) . . . 453
Gongadez v Ukraine (2005) . . . 210, 258
Gonzalez v Spain (1999) . . . 222
Goodwin v UK (1996) . . . 640, 641, 650, 675, 687
Goodwin (Christine) v UK (2002) . . . 10, 13, 16,
  21, 22, 514, 526, 537, 754, 758, 759, 760, 784
Gorelishvili v Georgia (2007) . . . 691, 694, 698
Görgülü v Germany (2004) . . . 186
Gorizdra v Moldova (2002) . . . 922, 925
Gorodnitchev v Russia (2007) . . . 266, 268
Gorou v Greece (No 2) (2009) . . . 431
Gorovenky and Bugara v Ukraine (2012) . . . 212
Gorraiz Lizarraga v Spain (2004) . . . 89, 391,
  392, 429
Gorzelik and Others v Poland (2004) . . . 509,
  724, 725, 726, 731, 732, 736, 752, 921
Goţia v Romania (2010) . . . 564
Gough v UK (pending . . . 532, 539
Gourguénidzé v Georgia (2006) . . . 660
Grabchuk v Ukraine (2006) . . . 464
Grace v UK (1987) . . . 589
Grace v UK (1988) . . . 399
Gradek v Poland (2010) . . . 586
Grădinar v Moldova (2008) . . . 93
Gradinger v Austria (1995) . . . 25, 971, 972
Graeme v UK (1990) . . . 911
Grande Oriente D'Italia Di Palazzo Guistiniani
  v Italy (2001) . . . 724, 731
Grande Oriente D'Italia Di Palazzo Guistiniani
  v Italy (No 2) (2007) . . . 724
Grandrath v Germany (1967) . . . 283, 601
Granger v UK (1990) . . . 475, 479
Granos Organicos Nationales SA v Germany
  (2012) . . . 400
Grant v UK (1988) . . . 454, 501
Grant v UK (2006) . . . 537
Grasser v Germany (2004) . . . 52
Gratzinger and Gratzinger ova v Czech Republic
  (2002) . . . 864, 868
Grauzinis v Lithuania (2000) . . . 365
Grava v Italy (2003) . . . 303, 306, 500
Graviano v Italy (2005) . . . 484

Grayson and Barnham v UK (2008) . . . 421
Graziani-Weiss v Austria (2011) . . . 281
Greece v UK (1957) . . . 46
Greece v UK (1958) . . . 116, 117, 127, 824, 829
Greek case *see* Denmark, Norway, Sweden
    and Netherlands v Greece (Greek case) (1969)
    and Denmark, Norway, Sweden v
    Greece (Second Greek case)
Green v UK (2005) . . . 222
Greens and MT v UK (2010) . . . 190, 931
Greenpeace EV and Others v Germany
    (2009) . . . 582
Gregory v UK (1997) . . . 457, 797
Grepne v UK (1990) . . . 403
Grice v UK (1994) . . . 212
Grieves v UK (2003) . . . 449
Grifhorst v France (2009) . . . 903
Grigoriades v Greece (1997) . . . 692
Grimailovs v Latvia (2013) . . . 264, 267
Grisankova and Grisankovs v Latvia
    (2003) . . . 49
Grishin v Russia (2007) . . . 262
Grof v Austria (1998) . . . 383
Gronuś v Poland (1999) . . . 582
Groppera Radio AG v Switzerland
    (1990) . . . 506, 509, 644, 649
Grori v Albania (2009) . . . 266
Grosaru v Romania (2010) . . . 771, 922, 923,
    944, 945, 947
Grosskopf v Germany (2010) . . . 307, 309, 310
Gross v Switzerland (2013) . . . 548
Grossi v Italy (2012) . . . 134
Grosz vFrance (2009) . . . 405
Grzelak v Poland (2010) . . . 592, 596
Grzinčič v Slovenia (2007) . . . 51
GS v Austria (1999) . . . 382
GSM v Austria (1983) . . . 335
Gubler v France (2006) . . . 667
Guchez v Belgium (1984) . . . 382
Guenoun v France (1990) . . . 434
Guerra and Others v Italy (1998) . . . 208, 535,
    563, 582, 584, 585, 620, 621
Guillemin v France (1997) . . . 889
Guillot v France (1996) . . . 539
Guincho v Portugal (1984) . . . 391, 395, 442,
    443, 444
Guiso-Gallisay v Italy (2009) . . . 160
Guisset v France (2000) . . . 87
Guja v Moldova (2008) . . . 678, 679
Gül v Switzerland (1996) . . . 576
Gül v Turkey (2000) . . . 216, 218, 230
Gülay Çetin v Turkey (2013) . . . 266
Güleç v Turkey (1998) . . . 217, 231, 232, 233
Guliyev v Azerbaijan (2004) . . . 385, 922, 924
Gülmez v Turkey (2008) . . . 436, 586
Gulub Atanasov v Bulgaria (2008) . . . 298
Gümüşten v Turkey (2004) . . . 443, 445
Gün and Others v Turkey (2013) . . . 711, 723
Gündem v Turkey (1998) . . . 531, 580
Gündüz v Turkey (2003) . . . 622, 669

Gunnarsson v Iceland (2005) . . . 553
Gürbüz v Turkey (2005) . . . 141
Gürdogan, Mustak, Mustak and Mustak v
    Turkey (1989) . . . 271
Gurepka v Ukraine (2005) . . . 55, 967
Gurgenidze v Georgia (2006) . . . 554
Gurguchiani v Spain (2009) . . . 501
Gurov v Moldova (2006) . . . 164, 458
Gururyan v Armenia (2012) . . . 70
Gusinskiy v Russia (2004) . . . 303, 304, 316, 317,
    857, 860
Gustafsson v Sweden (1996) . . . 505, 743, 744,
    747
Gutfreund v France (2003) . . . 373, 387, 389, 398,
    478, 479
Gütl v Austria (2009) . . . 602
Gutsanovi v Bulgaria (2013) . . . 339
Guvec v Turkey (2009) . . . 344, 481
Guzzardi v Italy (1977) . . . 290
Guzzardi v Italy (1980) . . . 289, 290, 293, 313,
    316, 321, 322, 373, 954
Gypsy Council v UK (2002) . . . 711

H
H v Belgium (1987) . . . 382, 438, 446, 447
Hamalainen v Finland (pending . . . 537
H v France (1989) . . . 382, 391, 398, 416, 440, 441
H v Norway (1992) . . . 219, 220
H v UK (1985) . . . 403
H v UK (1987) . . . 442
H v UK (1988) . . . 160
H v UK (1993) . . . 593
H and B v UK (2013) . . . 247
H, W, P and K v Austria (1989) . . . 622
Haas v Germany (2005) . . . 485
Haas v Switzerland (2011) . . . 547
Haas v Netherlands (2004) . . . 565, 568, 801
Haase v Germany (2004) . . . 570
Haase v Germany (2008) . . . 571
Habsburg-Lothringen v Austria (1990) . . . 924
Hachette Filipacchi Associés v France
    (2007) . . . 659, 666, 667, 693
Hachette Filipacchi Associés (ICI PARIS) v
    France (2009) . . . 551, 660, 662
Haci Özen v Turkey (2007) . . . 419
Hacisuleymanoglu v Italy (1994) . . . 586
Hadjianastassiou v Greece (1992) . . . 430, 473,
    653
Hadrabova v Czech Republic (2007) . . . 79, 80,
    128
Hadri-Vionnet v Switzerland (2008) . . . 568
Hadzhiyska v Bulgaria (2012) . . . 870
Haider v Austria (2004) . . . 381, 896
Hajduová v Slovakia (2010) . . . 541, 542
Hajibeyli v Azerbaijan (2008) . . . 959
Hajili v Azerbaijan (2012) . . . 945
Håkansson and Sturesson v Sweden
    (1990) . . . 437, 438, 683, 895, 904
Hakkar v France (1995) . . . 187, 195
HAL v Finland (2004) . . . 416

Halford v UK (1997) . . . 85, 86, 530, 555
Halis v Turkey (2002) . . . 628, 791
Halis Doğan v Turkey (No 3) (2006) . . . 628, 687
Halka and Others v Poland (2002) . . . 382
Hamaidi v France (2001) . . . 57
Hämäläinen v Finland (2004) . . . 418
Hamer v Belgium (2007) . . . 376
Hamer v UK (1979) . . . 754, 755, 756, 757
Hamidovic v Italy (2011) . . . 140
Hamiyet Kaplan v Turkey (2005) . . . 206
Hammern v Norway (2003) . . . 461
Handyside v UK (1976) . . . 8, 13, 15, 16, 17, 510,
    511, 513, 516, 518, 519, 614, 616, 632, 656, 657,
    658, 899
Hanif and Khan v UK (2012) . . . 456
Hannak v Austria (2004) . . . 445
Haran v Turkey (2002) . . . 130
Harabin v Slovakia (2004) . . . 617
Harabin v Slovakia (2012) . . . 386, 455
Haralambidis v Greece (2001) . . . 64
Haralambie v Romania (2009) . . . 563, 564
Hardiman v UK (1996) . . . 456
Hardy and Maile v UK (2012) . . . 582, 583, 584,
    585
Harkins and Edwards v UK (2012) . . . 245, 246,
    247, 250, 255, 259
Harkmann v Estonia (2006) . . . 367
Harman v UK (1984) . . . 495, 650
Harroudj v France (2012) . . . 568
Hartman v Czech Republic (2003) . . . 57
Harutyunyan v Armenia (2007) . . . 97, 419
Harutyunyan v Armenia see Ashot
    Harutyunyan v Armenia
Hasan v Bulgaria (2007) . . . 508
Hasan and Chaush v Bulgaria (2000) . . . 44, 126,
    593, 597, 599, 602, 606, 769
Hasan and Eylem Zengin v Turkey
    (2007) . . . 600, 913, 915
Hasan Uzun v Turkey (2013) . . . 58
Hasanbasic v Switzerland (2013) . . . 576
Hashman and Harrup v UK (1999) . . . 303, 509,
    632, 651
Hatton v UK (2003) . . . 16, 517, 520, 582, 583,
    767, 769, 770, 869
Hauschildt v Denmark (1989) . . . 450, 451, 453
Havelka v Czech Republic (2007) . . . 570, 581
Havelka v Czech Republic (2011) . . . 70
Hayward v Sweden (1991) . . . 490
Hazar and Açik v Turkey (1991) . . . 593
HB v Switzerland (2001) . . . 336
Headley v UK (2005) . . . 222
Heaney and McGuiness v Ireland (2000) . . .
    423, 424, 425, 460, 462
Heaney and McGuiness v Ireland (2001) . . . 377
Heckl v Austria (1999) . . . 974
Heglas v Czech Republic (2007) . . . 423
Heinisch v Germany (2011) . . . 617, 659, 674, 703
Heino v Finland (2011) . . . 557
Heinz v Contracting States Parties to the
    European Patent Convention (1994) 32

Helle v Finland (1997) . . . 24, 431
Helmers v Sweden (1991) . . . 373, 390, 392, 437
Hellig v Germany (2011) . . . 263
Helly and Others v France (2011) . . . 885, 890
Hempfing v Germany (1991) . . . 638, 639
Henaf v France (2003) . . . 267, 269
Hendriks v Netherlands (1982) . . . 271
Hennings v Germany (1992) . . . 402, 408
Henry Kismoun v France (2013) . . . 539
Henryk and Ryszard Urban v Poland (2010) . . . 449
Hentrich v France (1994) . . . 47, 416, 442, 444,
    466, 875, 877, 878, 879, 880, 883, 884, 885, 886,
    887, 889, 890, 891, 902
Hentrich v France (1997) . . . 133
Henworth v UK (2004) . . . 442
Herbecq and the Association 'Ligue des droits
    de l'homme' v Belgium (1988) . . . 560
Herczegfalvy v Austria (1992) . . . 267, 269, 350,
    365, 544
Hermi v Italy (2006) . . . 410, 411, 437, 470, 490
Herri Batasuna and Batasuna v Spain
    (2009) . . . 729, 730
Herrmann v Germany (2011) . . . 725
Herrmann v Germany (2012) . . . 785, 791, 899
Hertel v Switzerland (1998) . . . 639
Herz v Germany (2003) . . . 324
Hewitt and Harman v UK (1989) . . . 555
Hilbe v Lichtenstein (1999) . . . 926
Hibbert v Netherlands (1999) . . . 94, 465
Hickey v United Kingdom (2010) . . . 49
Hilal v UK (2001) . . . 251
Hilda Hafsteinsdóttir v Iceland (2004) . . . 322, 324
Hilton v UK (1976) . . . 270
Hingitaq 53 and Others v Denmark (2006) . . . 100
Hins and Hugenholtz v Netherlands (1996) . . .
    643, 644
Hiro Balani v Spain (1994) . . . 430
Hirschhorn v Romania (2007) . . . 449
Hirsi Jamaa v Italy (2012) . . . 20, 100, 119, 144,
    153, 249, 251, 774, 961, 962, 963
Hirst v UK (2001) . . . 365
Hirst v UK (2003) . . . 385
Hirst v UK (No 2) (2005) . . . 10, 12, 14, 29, 31,
    161, 190, 511, 585, 920, 921, 923, 924, 926, 929,
    930, 931, 932, 933, 946
Hirvisaari v Finland (2001) . . . 430
Hizb ut-Tahrir and Others v Germany
    (2012) . . . 854, 855
HK v Finland (2006) . . . 572
HL v UK (2004) . . . 294, 295, 296, 303, 304, 324,
    353
HLR v France (1997) . . . 253
HM v Switzerland (2002) . . . 291, 295, 296
Hoare v UK (1997) . . . 657
Hoare v UK (2011) . . . 878
Hobbs v UK (2002) . . . 55
Hode and Abdi v UK (2012) . . . 576
Hodgson, Woolf Productions Ltd, National
    Union of Journalists and Channel Four
    Television Co Ltd v UK (1987) . . . 676, 680

Hofbauer v Austria (2004) ... 436
Hoffman v Austria (1993) ... 612, 788, 801
Hoffman Karlskov v Denmark (2003) ... 744
Hogben v UK (1986) ... 500
Hokkanen v Finland (1994) ... 442, 533, 535, 573, 574
Holding and Barnes plc v UK (2002) ... 393
Holm v Sweden (1993) ... 456, 459
Holub v the Czech Republic (2010) ... 69
Holy Monasteries v Greece (1994) ... 403, 877, 885, 886, 889
Holy Synod of the Bulgarian Orthodox Church (Metropolitan Inokentiy) and Others v Bulgaria ... 157, 599
Hood v UK (1999) ... 315, 341, 342
Hoogendijk v Netherlands (2005) ... 810
Hoppe v Germany (2002) ... 536
Hornsby v Greece (1997) ... 378, 381, 396, 397
Horoz v Turkey (2009) ... 212, 268
Horvat v Croatia (2001) ... 55
Horváth and Kiss v Hungary (2013) ... 816, 817
Housing Association of War Disabled and Victims of War of Attica v Greece (2006) ... 895, 896, 897, 905
Houtman and Meeus v Belgium (2009) ... 92
Howard v UK (1987) ... 580
Hrico v Slovakia (2004) ... 694, 696, 698, 699
Hristozov v Bulgaria (2006) ... 349
Hristovi v Bulgaria (2011) ... 241
Hristozov and Others v Bulgaria (2012) ... 213, 257, 546
HS and Others v UK (2010) ... 587
Huber v Austria (1974) ... 471
Huber v Switzerland (1990) ... 341, 342
Hugh Jordan v UK (2001) ... 153, 215, 216, 217, 218, 809
Hughes v UK (1986) ... 204
Hukic v Sweden (2005) ... 254
Hulki Gunes v Turkey (2003) ... 186, 187
Hulki Gunes v Turkey (2013) ... 96
Humen v Poland (1999) ... 382
Hummatov v Azerbaijan (2007) ... 266, 435
Huohvanainen v Finland (2007) ... 230
Hurtado v Switzerland (1994) ... 243, 266
Hurter v Switzerland (2005) ... 433
Husayn (Abu Zubaydah) v Poland (2013) ... 144
Hussain v UK (1996) ... 260, 306, 359, 364
Hüseyin Esen v Turkey (2006) ... 779
Huseyin Kaplan v Turkey (2013) ... 868
Hutchinson Reid v UK (2003) ... 325, 327, 352, 355, 362
Hutten-Czapska v Poland (2003) ... 98
Hutten-Czapska v Poland (2006) ... 14, 149, 884, 886, 895, 896, 898, 899, 904
Hutten-Czapska v Poland (2008) ... 150, 151, 198
Huvig v France (1990) ... 507, 530, 555
HW v Germany (2013) ... 304, 309, 310
Hyde Park and Others v Moldova (Nos 5 & 6) (2010) ... 711, 715, 720

I
I v Finland (2008) ... 562
I v Sweden (2013) ... 143
I v UK (2002) ... 537
I and C v Switzerland (1985) ... 460
IA v France (1998) ... 346, 347
IA v Turkey (2005) ... 612, 669, 670, 671
IAA and Others v UK (2014) ... 576
Iacov Stanciu v Romania (2012) ... 145
Iatridis v Greece (1999) ... 54, 64, 865, 882
Iatridis v Greece (2000) ... 160
IB v Greece (2012) ... 818
IB v Greece (2013) ... 808
Ibrahim Gürkan v Turkey (2012) ... 449
Ichin and Others v Ukraine (2010) ... 321
Icyer v Turkey (2006) ... 50, 51
Idalov v Russia (2012) ... 65, 262, 344, 346, 350, 359, 360
IG v Moldova (2012) ... 541
Igdeli v Turkey (2002) ... 362
Iglesias Gil and AUI v Spain (2003) ... 506
Ignaccolo-Zenide v Romania (2000) ... 506, 574
Ignatenco v Moldova (2011) ... 319, 349
Igors Dmitrijevs v Latvia (2006) ... 606
IJL v UK (1999) ... 74
IJL, GMR and AKP v UK (2001) ... 159
IK v Austria (2013) ... 161
Il v Bulgaria (2005) ... 262
Ilaşcu v Moldova and Russia (2004) ... 29, 100, 102, 141, 144, 163, 193, 199, 236, 239, 240, 264, 265, 288, 297, 307, 964
Ilayeva and Others v Russia (2012) ... 160
Ilhan v Turkey (2000) ... 43, 222, 238, 239, 276, 779
Ilicak v Turkey (2007) ... 941
Ilijkov v Bulgaria (2001) ... 344, 345, 355, 356
Illich Sanchez Ramirez v France (1996) ... 265, 298
Illiu v Belgium (2009) ... 78
Ilowiecki v Poland (2001) ... 362
Imakayeva v Russia (2006) ... 96, 146, 159, 558
Imberechts v Belgium (1991) ... 434
Imbrioscia v Switzerland (1993) ... 468, 474, 475
Immobiliare Saffi v Italy (1999) ... 58, 397, 871, 875, 884, 896, 897, 898
Incal v Turkey (1998) ... 448, 450, 518, 628, 630, 694, 827
Indelicato v Italy (2001) ... 242
Indra v Slovakia (2005) ... 453
Informationsverein Lentia v Austria (1993) ... 613, 643, 644, 652
Ingrid Jordebo Foundation of Christian Schools and Ingrid Jordebo v Sweden (1987) ... 907
Inocencio v Portugal (2001) ... 375, 376
Inze v Austria (1987) ... 800, 801, 867, 896
Ionescu v Romania (2010) ... 44
Iordache v Romania (2008) ... 65
Iordachi and Others v Moldova (2009) ... 555, 556

Iordan Iordanov and Others v Bulgaria
(2009) . . . 402
Iordanovi v Bulgaria (2011) . . . 93
Iorga and Others v Romania (2011) . . . 211
Iorgov v Bulgaria (2004) . . . 267
Iorgov v Bulgaria (No 2) (2010) . . . 259
Iosub Caras v Romania (2006) . . . 974
Iovioni and Others v Romania (2012) . . . 863, 864
Ipek v Turkey (2010) . . . 62
İpek and Others v Turkey (2009) . . . 340
Ireland v UK (1972) . . . 46, 116, 494
Ireland v UK (1976) . . . 236
Ireland v UK (1978) . . . 8, 13, 16, 26, 45, 46, 115,
116, 117, 144, 147, 148, 162, 235, 236, 237, 238,
239, 240, 241, 242, 244, 261, 312, 315, 336, 341,
765, 809, 825, 827, 834, 835, 838, 839, 840, 841,
842, 844, 845, 846
Irene Wilson v UK (2012) . . . 541, 542
Irfan Temel and Others v Turkey (2009) . . . 910
Iribarren Pinillos v Spain (2009) . . . 442
Isaak v Turkey (2008) . . . 232
Isaksen v Norway (2003) . . . 971
Isayeva, Yusupova and Bazayeva v Russia (2005)
. . . 60, 187, 221, 222, 227, 231, 248, 824, 826
Isgrò v Italy (1991) . . . 16, 485, 488
Iskandarov v Russia (2010) . . . 330
ISKCON v UK (1994) . . . 393, 593, 607, 899
Islamic Republic of Iran Shipping Lines v
Turkey (2007) . . . 896, 897
Ismailova v Russia (2007) . . . 801
Ismoilov and Others v Russia (2008) . . . 248,
249, 250, 460
Istratii v Moldova (2007) . . . 361
Isyar v Bulgaria (2008) . . . 490
ITC Ltd v Malta (2007) . . . 389
Ivan Atanasov v Bulgaria (2010) . . . 384, 391, 582
Ivan Vasilev v Bulgaria (2007) . . . 243
Ivanov and Others v Bulgaria (2005) . . . 711, 717
Ivanov v Ukraine (2006) . . . 955, 956
Ivanova v Bulgaria (2007) . . . 594, 604
Ivanovski and Others v the Former Yugoslav
Republic of Macedonia (2009) . . . 93
Ivanţoc and Others v Moldova and Russia
(2011) . . . 264, 288
Ivanţoc and Popa v Moldova and Russia
(2012) . . . 193
Iversen v Norway (1963) . . . 281, 283
Iwańczuk v Poland (2001) . . . 263, 348
Izevbekhai and Others v Ireland (2011) . . . 253
İzci v Turkey (2013) . . . 715, 719, 720
İzmir Savaş Karşitlari Derneği v Turkey
(2006) . . . 723, 724

J
J v Germany (1994) . . . 652
J v Switzerland (1989) . . . 418
JA Pye (Oxford) Ltd and JA Pye (Oxford) Land
Ltd v UK (2007) . . . 877, 881, 885, 886, 889,
896, 897, 904
Jabari v Turkey (1999) . . . 54

Jabari v Turkey (2000) . . . 259, 260, 774
Jablonski v Poland (2000) . . . 347, 363
Jacubowski v Germany (1994) . . . 637, 638
Jäggi v Switzerland (2006) . . . 565
Jahn and Others v Germany (2005) . . . 877, 892,
893, 904
Jakóbski v Poland (2010) . . . 603
Jakupovic v Austria (2003) . . . 577
Jalloh v Germany (2006) . . . 236, 267, 268, 418,
419, 422, 425, 426, 463
James and Others v UK (1986) . . . 11, 13, 15, 16,
160, 389, 580, 765, 766, 795, 871, 873, 877, 882,
887, 889, 891, 904
James, Wells and Lee v UK (2012) . . . 304, 305,
309, 310
Jamil v France (1995) . . . 499
Jan-Ake Andersson v Sweden (1991) . . . 437
Jancev v the Former Yugoslav Republic of
Macedonia (2011) . . . 69, 70
Jankausas v Lithuania (2005) . . . 588
Janosevic v Sweden (2002) . . . 374, 375, 376, 462,
464
Janowiec and Others v Russia (2012) . . . 257, 276
Janowiec and Others v Russia (2013) . . . 98
Janowski v Poland (1999) . . . 615, 696, 697
Jantner v Slovakia (2003) . . . 868
Jarnea v Romania (2011) . . . 563
Jasar v FYRM (2006) . . . 54, 55
Jasinski v Poland (2005) . . . 453
Jasińska v Poland (2010) . . . 211
Jasinskis v Latvia (2010) . . . 54, 212
Jasiūnienė v Lithuania (2003) . . . 397
Jasper v UK (2000) . . . 417
Jasvir Singh v France (2009) . . . 610
JB v Switzerland (2001) . . . 422, 426
Ječius v Lithuania (2000) . . . 24, 64, 94, 95, 303,
319, 353
Jehovah's Witnesses of Moscow v Russia
(2010) . . . 597, 598, 599, 611, 732, 733, 736, 738
Jeličić v Bosnia and Herzegovina (2005) . . . 54,
75, 152
Jensen v Denmark (2001) . . . 88
Jersild v Denmark (1994) . . . 11, 616, 622, 640, 854
Jerusalem v Austria (2001) . . . 699, 700
Jespers v Belgium (1981) . . . 472, 473
Jeunesse v Netherlands . . . 578
Jian v Romania (2004) . . . 79
Jimenez and Jimenez Merino v Spain
(2000) . . . 914
Jirsák v Czech Republic (2012) . . . 69
JJ v Netherlands (1998) . . . 418
JL v Latvia (2012) . . . 275, 277
JLS v Spain (1999) . . . 863
Joanna Szulc v Poland (2012) . . . 563
Jobe v UK (2011) . . . 497
Johannische Kirche and Peters v Germany
(2001) . . . 599, 607
Johansen v Norway (1985) . . . 283, 311, 494
Johansen v Norway (1996) . . . 569, 570, 571
Johansson v Finland (2007) . . . 539

Johansson v Sweden (1990) . . . 743
Johnson v UK (1997) . . . 326, 327
Johnston and Others v Ireland (1986) . . . 7, 9, 20, 85, 96, 514, 527, 533, 564, 755, 760, 791, 800
Jokela v Finland (2002) . . . 429, 883, 885, 903
Jokitaipale and Others v Finland (2010) . . . 660
Jones v UK (2003) . . . 411, 412
Jones v UK (2005) . . . 791
Joos v Switzerland (2012) . . . 69
Jordan v UK see Hugh Jordan v UK
Jordan v UK (No 2) (2002) . . . 443
Jorgic v Germany (2007) . . . 458, 497, 498
Jovanovic v Croatia (2002) . . . 97
Jovanović v Serbia (2012) . . . 569
Jucys v Lithuania (2008) . . . 889
Judge v UK (2011) . . . 430
Juhas Duric v Serbia (2011) . . . 71
Juhnke v Turkey (2008) . . . 263, 532, 545
Julin v Estonia (2012) . . . 262
Julio Bou Gibert and El Hogar Y La Moda J.A. v Spain (2003) . . . 662
Julius Kloiber Schlachthof GmbH and Others v Austria (2013) . . . 375
Juozaitienè and Bikulčius v Lithuania (2008) . . . 232
Jurisic and Collegium Mehrerau v Austria (2006) . . . 393
Jussila v Finland (2006) . . . 375, 436

K
K v Austria (1993) . . . 310, 355, 360, 361, 616
K v Denmark (1993) . . . 477, 616
K v France (1983) . . . 491
K v Ireland (1984) . . . 61, 65
K, F and P v UK (1984) . . . 56
K and T v Finland (2000) . . . 138
K and T v Finland (2001) . . . 44, 531, 570, 571, 572
KA v Finland (2003) . . . 570, 572
KA and AD v Belgium (2005) . . . 549, 550
KAB v Spain (2012) . . . 527, 570
KAB v Sweden (2013) . . . 249
Kaburov v Bulgaria (2012) . . . 93
Kadikis v Latvia (No 2) (2003) . . . 44
Kadlec v Czech Rep (2004) . . . 404
Kafkaris v Cyprus (2008) . . . 259, 260, 493, 495, 496, 497, 500
Kafkaris v Cyprus (No 2) (2011) . . . 194, 363
Kaftailova v Latvia (2007) . . . 130
Kaijalainen v Finland (1996) . . . 974
Kaisti v Finland (2004) . . . 398
Kaja v Greece (2006) . . . 262
Kajanen and Tuomaala v Finland (2000) . . . 743
Kakabadze and Others v Georgia (2012) . . . 716, 968
Kakoulli v Finland (2005) . . . 221
Kakoulli v Turkey (2005) . . . 228, 230, 231, 232
Kalaç v Turkey (1997) . . . 604, 622
Kalantari v Germany (2001) . . . 245
Kalashnikov v Russia (2001) . . . 585, 586, 589

Kalashnikov v Russia (2002) . . . 236, 262, 278, 343, 350, 442
Kalderas Gipsies v Germany and Netherlands (1977) . . . 810
Kalender v Turkey (2009) . . . 206
Kalinowski v Poland . . . 586
Kalogeropoulou v Greece and Germany (2002) . . . 405
Kalucza v Hungary (2012) . . . 542
Kamasinski v Austria (1989) . . . 137, 418, 437, 469, 470, 473, 481, 490, 491
Kanagaratnam and Others v Belgium (2011) . . . 263, 275, 330, 334
Kanellopoulou v Greece (2007) . . . 664
Kanlibas v Turkey (2005) . . . 59
Kanthak v Germany (1988) . . . 529
Kantner v Austria (1999) . . . 971
Kaperzyński v Poland (2012) . . . 695
Kara v UK (1998) . . . 539, 788
Karaçay v Turkey (2011) . . . 749
Karademirci v Turkey (2005) . . . 615, 650, 651
Karaduman v Turkey (1993) . . . 608
Karadžić v Croatia (2005) . . . 533
Karakasis v Greece (2000) . . . 430
Karako v Hungary (2009) . . . 54, 553
Karakurt v Austria (1999) . . . 740
Karalevičius v Lithuania (2005) . . . 589
Karapanagiotou and Others v Greece (2010) . . . 48
Karassev and Family v Finland (1999) . . . 540, 960
Karataş v Turkey (1999) . . . 628, 629, 635
Karhuvaara and Iltalehti v Finland (2004) . . . 630, 660, 666
Karman v Russia (2006) . . . 699, 705
Karnell and Hardt v Sweden (1971) . . . 917
Karner v Austria (2003) . . . 95, 132, 793, 803, 806
Karni v Sweden (1988) . . . 896
Karpetas v Greece (2012) . . . 700
Karrer v Romania (2012) . . . 574
Karoussiotis v Portugal (2011) . . . 50, 76
Kart v Turkey (2009) . . . 408
Karus v Italy (1998) . . . 912
Kashavelov v Bulgaria (2011) . . . 269
Kasparov and Others v Russia (2013) . . . 715, 719, 720, 722
Kasymakhunov and Saybatalov v Russia (2013) . . . 853, 854, 855
Katamadze v Georgia (2006) . . . 641, 659, 661, 692, 698
Katić v Serbia (2009) . . . 128
Katikaridis v Greece (1996) . . . 890
Katrami v Greece (2007) . . . 698
Kats and Others v Ukraine (2008) . . . 92, 93
Katsoulis v Greece (2004) . . . 875
Katte Klitsche de la Grange v Italy (1994) . . . 875, 886, 895
Kaukonen v Finland (1997) . . . 382, 390
Kaur v Netherlands (2012) . . . 66
Kaushal and Others v Bulgaria (2010) . . . 966

Kavakçi v Turkey (2007) . . . 941
Kay and Others v UK (2010) . . . 523, 529, 582
Kaya v Turkey (1998) . . . 210, 780
Kaya v Turkey (2005) . . . 81
Kaya and Others v Turkey (2006) . . . 214
Kaya and Seyhan v Turkey (2009) . . . 749
Kaya (Mahmut) v Turkey (2000) . . . 210, 223, 224, 274, 275
Kayak v Turkey (2012) . . . 210
KDB v Netherlands (1998) . . . 418
Kearns v France (2008) . . . 527, 528, 569, 570
Keegan v Ireland (1994) . . . 15, 384, 527, 572
Keenan v UK (2001) . . . 211, 236, 259, 266, 769, 781, 782
Keles v Germany (2005) . . . 577
Keller v Hungary (2006) . . . 666
Kelly v UK (1993) . . . 227, 229, 232
Kelly (No 2) v UK (2011) . . . 115
Kemal Taşkin and Others v Turkey (2010) . . . 539, 540
Kemaloglu v Turkey (2012) . . . 208
Kemevuako v Netherlands (2010) . . . 66
Kemmache v France (1991) . . . 344, 348, 350
Kempers v Austria (1997) . . . 482
Kenedi v Hungary (2009) . . . 562, 621
Kennedy v UK (1998) . . . 485
Kennedy v UK (2008) . . . 651
Kennedy v UK (2010) . . . 387, 530, 531, 555, 556, 649
Keretchachvili v Georgia (2006) . . . 79
Kerimli and Alibeyli v Azerbaijan (2012) . . . 945, 946
Kerimova v Azerbaijan (2010) . . . 945
Kerimova and Others v Russia (2011) . . . 231
Kerkhoven, Hinke and Hinke v Netherlands (1992) . . . 526
Kerr v UK (1999) . . . 335, 336
Kervanci v France (2008) . . . 609
Kervoëlen v France (2001) . . . 390
Keser v Turkey (2006) . . . 95
Keus v Netherlands (1990) . . . 336, 354, 355, 359, 364, 365
Kezer v Turkey (2004) . . . 74
KF v Germany (1997) . . . 318, 319
KH and Others v Slovakia (2009) . . . 563
Khadzhialiyev v Russia (2008) . . . 80, 258
Khamidov v Russia (2007) . . . 271, 399, 429, 863
Khan v UK (1986) . . . 755
Khan v UK (2000) . . . 55, 418, 419, 555, 556, 772
Khanhuseyn Aliyev v Azerbaijan (2012) . . . 936
Kharchenko v Ukraine (2011) . . . 319, 368
Kharin v Russia (2011) . . . 322, 323
Khashiyev and Akayeva v Russia (2005) . . . 60, 187, 223, 780
Khelili v Switzerland (2011) . . . 561
Khider v France (2009) . . . 271
Khlyustov v Russia (2013) . . . 957, 958
Khmel v Russia (2013) . . . 560
Khodorkovskiy v Russia (No 1) (2011) . . . 163, 268, 302, 304, 312, 345, 348, 361, 858, 859, 860

Khodorkovskiy and Lebedev v Russia (2013) . . . 361, 362, 453, 472, 482, 484, 485, 497, 587, 858, 859, 860
Khudobin v Russia (2006) . . . 265, 266, 267, 428
Khudoyorov v Russia (2005) . . . 262, 268, 302
Khudyakova v Russia (2009) . . . 362
Khuzhin and Others v Russia (2008) . . . 410, 561
K-HW v Germany (2001) . . . 495, 496
Kienast v Austria (2003) . . . 390
Kikots and Kikota v Latvia (2002) . . . 97
Kilic v Switzerland (1986) . . . 246
Kilic v Turkey (2000) . . . 210, 224
Kiliçgedik and Others v Turkey (2010) . . . 940, 941
Kimlya and Others v Russia (2009) . . . 593, 598
King v UK (2004) . . . 159
Kingsley v UK (2002) . . . 381, 393, 394, 453
Kingston v UK (1997) . . . 497
Kiousi v Greece (2011) . . . 70
Kipritci v Turkey (2008) . . . 66
Kirk v UK (1996) . . . 66
Kiryanov v Russia (2005) . . . 390
Kiyutin v Russia (2011) . . . 789, 796, 808, 822
Kizilyaprak v Turkey (2003) . . . 628, 629, 635
Kjartan Asmundsson v Iceland (2004) . . . 866, 875
Kjeldsen, Busk Madsen and Pedersen v Denmark (1975) . . . 908
Kjeldsen, Busk Madsen and Pedersen v Denmark (1976) . . . 8, 791, 907, 908, 912, 913, 914, 915, 917, 918
Klass v Germany (1977) . . . 387
Klass v Germany (1979) . . . 766, 767, 771, 772, 773, 775
Klass v Germany (1993) . . . 243
Klass and Others v Germany (1978) . . . 18, 84, 85, 512, 524, 531, 555, 651, 826, 828
Klaus and Iouri Kiladzé v Georgia (2010) . . . 871
Klein v Austria (2011) . . . 882
Klein v Germany (2000) . . . 444
Klein v Russia (2010) . . . 246, 249
Klein v Slovakia (2006) . . . 616, 670, 671
Kleyn v Netherlands (2003) . . . 451, 452
Klamecki v Poland (No 2) (2003) . . . 586
Klimentyev v Russia (2006) . . . 485
Klip and Kruger v Netherlands (1997) . . . 756
Klöpper v Switzerland (1996) . . . 974
Klouvi v France (2011) . . . 463
KM v UK (1997) . . . 754, 756
Knecht v Romania (2012) . . . 558
Knudsen v Norway (1985) . . . 220, 593, 604
Kobenter and Standard Verlags GmbH v Austria (2006) . . . 701
Koç and Tambaş v Turkey (2005) . . . 90–1
Koc and Tosun v Turkey (2008) . . . 63
Koch v Germany (2012) . . . 93, 205, 548
Koendjbiharie v Netherlands (1990) . . . 302, 362, 363
Kohlhofer and Minarik v Czech Republic (2009) . . . 403

Kok v Netherlands (2000) . . . 488, 489
Kokkinakis v Greece (1993) . . . 497, 520, 592, 598, 606, 610, 611
Köksal v Netherlands (2001) . . . 127
Koku v Turkey (2005) . . . 210
Kolanis v UK (2005) . . . 326
Kolevi v Bulgaria (2009) . . . 216
Kolk and Kislyiy v Estonia (2006) . . . 501–2
Kolompar v Belgium (1992) . . . 332, 363
Kolosovskiy v Latvia (2004) . . . 79
Kolyadenko and Others v Russia (2012) . . . 208, 870
Komanický v Slovakia (2002) . . . 415
Komanicky v Slovakia (2005) . . . 29
Komatinovic v Serbia (2013) . . . 79
Koniarska v UK (2000) . . . 295, 321
König v Germany (1978) . . . 378, 379, 380, 381, 382, 396, 440, 441, 442, 445
Kononov v Latvia (2008) . . . 11
Kononov v Latvia (2010) . . . 498, 501, 502
Konrad v Germany (2006) . . . 600, 909, 918
Konstas v Greece (2011) . . . 461
Konstantin Markin v Russia (2010) . . . 974
Konstantin Markin v Russia (2012) . . . 789, 796, 800, 822
Kontakt-Information-Therapie and Hagen v Austria (1988) . . . 235
Kontrová v Slovakia (2007) . . . 210
Konttinen v Finland (1996) . . . 604, 802
Koottummel v Austria (2009) . . . 436
Kop v Turkey (2009) . . . 243
Kopecký v Slovakia (2004) . . . 65, 125, 864, 865, 867, 868
Köpke v Germany (2010) . . . 556
Koplinger v Austria (1966) . . . 483
Koplinger v Austria (1968) . . . 472, 473
Kopp v Switzerland (1998) . . . 556
Koppi v Austria (2009) . . . 602
Korbely v Hungary (2008) . . . 496, 498, 502
Korellis v Cyprus (2003) . . . 415, 471, 473
Korenjak v Slovenia (2007) . . . 51
Koretskyy v Ukraine (2008) . . . 731, 733
Korneykova v Ukraine (2012) . . . 344
Korolev v Russia (2010) . . . 68, 69, 70, 71
Kosaitė-Čypienė and Others v Lithuania (2012) . . . 546
Köse and Others v Turkey (2006) . . . 609
Kosiek v Germany (1986) . . . 616, 686, 786
Koster v Netherlands (1991) . . . 341
Kosteski v the Former Yugoslav Republic of Macedonia (2006) . . . 595
Kostovski v Netherlands (1989) . . . 484, 487
Kotov v Russia (2012) . . . 863, 871, 872
Kötterl and Schittily v Austria (2003) . . . 865
Koua Poirrez v France (2003) . . . 797
Koufaki and Adedy v Greece (2013) . . . 883
Kovach v Ukraine (2008) . . . 945
Kovacic v Slovenia (2004) . . . 75
Kovacic and Others v Slovenia (2008) . . . 130
Kovalev v Russia (2007) . . . 410

Kowal v Poland (2012) . . . 542
Kozacioğlu v Turkey (2009) . . . 48, 54, 889
Kozlov v Russia (2009) . . . 410
Kozlova and Smirnova v Latvia (2001) . . . 96
KPD v Germany (1957) . . . 622, 725, 853
Krafft and Rougeot v France (1990) . . . 392
Krajisnik v UK (2012) . . . 308
Kramelius v Sweden (1996) . . . 909
Kraska v Switzerland (1993) . . . 382, 390, 429, 492
Krasniki v Czech Republic (2006) . . . 164
Krasnov and Skuratov v Russia (2007) . . . 922, 936
Krasulya v Russia (2007) . . . 694, 701
Krasuski v Poland (2005) . . . 770, 778
Krause v Switzerland (1978) . . . 460
Krejzová and Dubská v Czech Republic (2012) . . . 546
Kremzow v Austria (1990) . . . 375, 437, 457
Kremzow v Austria (1993) . . . 411, 415, 468, 471, 473
Kress v France (2001) . . . 413, 415, 418
Kreuz v Poland (No 1) (2001) . . . 401
Krickl v Austria (1997) . . . 869
Kristiansen and Tyvik AS v Norway (2013) . . . 401
Kristinsson v Iceland (1990) . . . 452
Kröcher and Möller v Switzerland (1981) . . . 470
Kröcher and Möller v Switzerland (1982) . . . 236, 265, 472
Krombach v France (2001) . . . 152, 967
Krone Verlag GmbH & Co KG v Austria (2002) . . . 694
Krone Verlag GmbH & Co KG v Austria (No 3) (2003) . . . 635, 636, 638, 640
Krone Verlag GmbH & Co KG and MEDIAPRINT Zeitungs-und Zeitschrift enverlag GmbH & CoKG v Austria (2003) . . . 698, 699
Kronfeldner v Germany (2012) . . . 327
Kroon v Netherlands (1994) . . . 523, 565–6
KRS v UK (2008) . . . 255
Krušković v Croatia (2011) . . . 565
Kruslin v France (1990) . . . 507, 508, 555
KS v UK (2012) . . . 571
KU v Finland (2008) . . . 534, 542
Kučera v Slovakia (2007) . . . 586
Kucheruk v Ukraine (2007) . . . 269
Kudeshkina v Russia (No 2) (pending) . . . 194
Kudla v Poland (2000) . . . 20, 21, 236, 241, 261, 265, 266, 267, 347, 408, 443, 765, 766, 768, 769, 770, 777, 778
Kuharec alias Kuhareca v Latvia (2004) . . . 540
Kühnen v Germany (1988) . . . 855,
Kuijper v Netherlands (2005) . . . 573
Kulikowski v Poland (2009) . . . 402
Kuolelis, Bartosevicius, and Burokevicius v Lithuania (2008) . . . 496
Kuopila v Finland (2000) . . . 415
Kurdov and Ivanov v Bulgaria (2011) . . . 970
Kurić and Others v Slovenia (2010) . . . 93

Kurić and Others v Slovenia (2012) . . . 150, 164, 198, 540

Kurier Zeitungsverlag und Druckerei Gmbh v Austria (2012) . . . 659, 661

Kurkowski v Poland (2013) . . . 586

Kurochkin v Ukraine (2010) . . . 528, 570–1

Kurt v Turkey (1998) . . . 92, 147, 223, 224, 257, 288, 300, 780

Kurtulmuş v Turkey (2006) . . . 609

Kurup v Denmark (1985) . . . 472, 489

Kushoglu v Bulgaria (2007) . . . 879

Kutcherenko v Ukraine (1999) . . . 54

Kutepov and Anikeyenko v Russia (2005) . . . 867

Kutic v Croatia (2002) . . . 401

Kutzner v Germany (2002) . . . 570, 571

Kuzmin v Russia (2010) . . . 466

Kuzmina v Russia (2009) . . . 386

Kuznetsova v Russia (2006) . . . 73

Kuznetsov v Russia (2007) . . . 429, 430, 606

Kvasnica v Slovakia (2009) . . . 555

Kwiecień v Poland (2007) . . . 696

Kyprianou v Cyprus (2004) . . . 451, 469

Kyprianou v Cyprus (2005) . . . 153, 450, 451, 454, 465, 680

Kyrtatos v Greece (2003) . . . 397, 582, 583

L

L v Finland (2000) . . . 138

L v Germany (1984) . . . 960

L v Lithuania (2007) . . . 165, 537, 759

L v Netherlands (2004) . . . 527

L v Norway (1990) . . . 555

L v Sweden (1988) . . . 294, 366, 387

L v Switzerland (1991) . . . 489

L and V v Austria (2003) . . . 9, 518, 550, 794, 803

La Frazia v Italy (2006) . . . 929

Laakso v Finland (2013) . . . 566

Labita v Italy (2000) . . . 110, 148, 277, 316, 319, 344, 345, 587, 929, 954,956

Labsi v Slovakia (2012) . . . 141

Lacadena Calero v Spain (2011) . . . 93

Lacko v Slovakia (2002) . . . 956

Ladbrokes Worldwide Betting v Sweden (2008) . . . 389

Ladent v Poland (2008) . . . 315

Laduna v Slovakia (2011) . . . 789

Ladygin v Russia (2011) . . . 68, 72

Lagardère v France (2012) . . . 464

Lagerblom v Sweden (2003) . . . 480, 491

Laidin v France (2002) . . . 52

Laidin v France (No 2) (2003) . . . 384

Lakicevic and Others v Montenegro and Serbia (2011) . . . 882

Lala v Netherlands (1994) . . . 81, 477

Lallement v France (2002) . . . 889

Lamanna v Austria (2001) . . . 382, 438, 461

Landvreugd v Netherlands (2002) . . . 957

Lang v Austria (2009) . . . 602

Langborder v Sweden (1983) . . . 447, 448, 455

Lanz v Austria (2002) . . . 482

Larioshina v Russia (2002) . . . 270, 867

Larissis v Greece (1998) . . . 497, 606, 611

Larkos v Cyprus (1999) . . . 529, 793

Lashin v Russia (2013) . . . 543, 755–6

Laska and Lika v Albania (2010) . . . 56, 409

Laskey, Jaggard and Brown v UK (1995) . . . 497

Laskey, Jaggard and Brown v UK (1997) . . . 526, 534, 549, 550, 803

L'association et la ligue pour la protection des acheteurs d'automobiles, Abid and 646 Others v Romania (2001) . . . 89

L'association des amis de Saint-Raphaël et de Fréjus and Others v France (2000) . . . 89

Latak v Poland (2010) . . . 51

Latimer v UK (2005) . . . 420

Lauko v Slovakia (1998) . . . 374, 376

Laumont v France (2001) . . . 319

Lautsi and Others v Italy (2011) . . . 16, 593, 600, 908, 913, 916, 919

Lavents v Latvia (2002) . . . 454, 458, 465, 466, 556

Lavrechov v Czech Republic (2013) . . . 883

Lavric v Romania (2014) . . . 554

Lawless v Ireland (Merits) (1961) . . . 13, 15, 313, 316, 494, 824–5, 827, 829, 830, 831, 832, 833, 834, 835, 838, 841, 842, 844, 846, 853

Lawrence v UK (2002) . . . 455

Lawyer Partners AS v Slovakia (2009) . . . 401

LB v Belgium (2012) . . . 327

LCB v UK (1998) . . . 203, 207, 208, 209, 212, 213, 218, 523

Le Bihan v France (2004) . . . 390

Le Calvez v France (1998) . . . 389

Le comité des médecins à diplômes étrangers v France (1999) . . . 89

Le Compte, Van Leuven and De Meyere v Belgium (1981) . . . 390, 391, 392, 435, 433, 447, 455, 459, 513, 724, 738, 740

L'Erabliere v Belgium (2009) . . . 391

Leaf v Italy (2003) . . . 332

Leander v Sweden (1987) . . . 16, 55, 504, 508, 531, 556, 559, 561, 563, 620, 764, 766, 767, 770, 771, 772, 773, 775, 776

Lebedev v Russia (2004) . . . 863

Lebedev v Russia (2007) . . . 339, 342, 357, 359, 361

Lechner and Hess v Austria (1987) . . . 443

Ledyayeva v Russia (2006) . . . 188

Lee v UK (2001) . . . 908

Lee Davies v Belgium (2009) . . . 419

Leech v UK (1994) . . . 58

Leela Förderkreis eV and Others v Germany (2008) . . . 607

Leempoel & SA ED Ciné Revue v Belgium (2006) . . . 553, 660, 674, 683

Léger v France (2006) . . . 259

Léger v France (2009) . . . 95, 132

Legillon v France (2013) . . . 430

Legrand v France (2011) . . . 432

Lehideux and Isorni v France (1998) . . . 518, 623, 853, 855

Lehtinen v Finland (1999) . . . 55
Lehtinen v Finland (2006) . . . 440
Lelievre v Belgium (2007) . . . 346
Lenskaya v Russia (2009) . . . 432
Lenzing AG v UK (1998) . . . 863
Lepojic v Serbia (2007) . . . 97
Leroy v France (2008) . . . 616, 655, 687
Les Travaux du Midi v Germany (1991) . . . 374, 404, 431
Lešnik v Slovakia (2003) . . . 704
Letellier v France (1991) . . . 343, 344, 346, 347, 348, 362, 363
Leuffen v Germany (1992) . . . 909
Leva v Moldova (2009) . . . 334
Levages Prestations Services v France (1996) . . . 402
Levänen v Finland (2006) . . . 867
Levin v Sweden (2012) . . . 571
Leyla Şahin v Turkey (2005) . . . 508, 513, 603, 608, 609, 907, 908, 909, 910, 912, 918, 919
Liakopoulou v Greece (2006) . . . 404
Liberal Party, R and P v UK (1980) . . . 924, 946, 948
Liberty and Others v UK (2008) . . . 85, 556, 649
Liepājnieks v Latvia (2010) . . . 96
Liga Portuguesa de Futebol Profissional v Portugal (2012) . . . 69
Ligue des musulmans de Suisse and Others v Switzerland (2011) . . . 87
Ligue du monde islamique et al v France (2009) . . . 403
Liivik v Estonia (2009) . . . 496
Lind v Russia (2007) . . . 349
Lindner and Hammermayer v Romania (2002) . . . 431
Lindon, Otchakovsky-Laurens and July v France (2007) . . . 454, 633, 683, 692, 693, 700, 701, 702
Lindsay and Lindsay v UK (1986) . . . 758, 807, 808
Lindsay and Others v UK (1979) . . . 946
Lingens v Austria (1986) . . . 10, 503, 512, 513, 629, 640, 666, 694, 695
Lingens and Leitgeb v Austria (1981) . . . 461, 462
Lithgow and Others v UK (1986) . . . 20, 160, 402, 773, 856, 877, 886, 887, 889, 890, 891
Liu v Russia (No 2) (2011) . . . 194
Liu and Lui v Russia (2007) . . . 578
LL v France (2006) . . . 56, 562
LL v UK (2013) . . . 56
Lobo Machado v Portugal (1996) . . . 415, 418
Loewenguth v France (2000) . . . 968
Löffelmann v Austria (2009) . . . 602
Loiseau v France (2003) . . . 384
Loizidou v Turkey (Preliminary Objections) (1995) . . . 8, 9, 25, 73, 99, 102, 847
Loizidou v Turkey (Merits) (1996) . . . 99, 184, 867, 868, 869, 870, 882, 887
Loizidou v Turkey (Article 50) (1998) . . . 184
Lombardo v Malta (2007) . . . 630, 706

Lominski v Poland (2010) . . . 51
Lopata v Russia (2010) . . . 113
Lopes Gomes da Silva v Portugal (2000) . . . 694
López Ostra v Spain (1994) . . . 9, 271, 582, 584, 869
Lorenzi, Bernardini and Gritti v Italy (1992) . . . 396
LTC v Malta (2007) . . . 387
Luberti v Italy (1984) . . . 307, 325, 326, 362, 363
Luca v Italy (2001) . . . 484, 485
Lucas v UK (2003) . . . 723
Luchaninova v Ukraine (2011) . . . 69, 968
Luczak v Poland (2007) . . . 798, 866
Lüdi v Switzerland (1992) . . . 87, 90, 427, 485, 487
Luedicke, Belkacem and Koç v Germany (1978) . . . 7, 35, 409, 479, 489, 490
Lukach v Russia (1999) . . . 907, 911
Lukanov v Bulgaria (1995) . . . 75, 494
Lukanov v Bulgaria (1997) . . . 18, 319
Lukenda v Slovenia (2005) . . . 150, 151
Luksch v Germany (1997) . . . 926
Luluyev v Russia (2006) . . . 223, 257
Luordo v Italy (2003) . . . 403, 957
Lupsa v Romania (2006) . . . 966
Lustig-Prean and Beckett v UK (1999) . . . 517, 579
Lustig-Prean and Beckett v UK (2000) . . . 159
Lutsenko v Ukraine (2012) . . . 857, 858, 860
Lutz v France (2002) . . . 74
Lutz v Germany (1987) . . . 464
Lykourezos v Greece (2006) . . . 922, 923, 938, 942
Lynas v Switzerland (1976) . . . 332
Lynch v UK (2009) . . . 444
Lyons and Others v UK (2003) . . . 29, 194

M
M v Bulgaria (2011) . . . 330, 331
M v Germany (No 10272/83) (1984) . . . 307, 365
M v Germany (No 10307/83) (1984) . . . 221, 958
M v Germany (2009) . . . 306, 307, 309, 316, 499
M v Italy (1991) . . . 499, 900
M v Switzerland (2011) . . . 540
M v UK (No 9728/82) (1983) . . . 480
M v UK (No 9907/82) (1983) . . . 265
M v UK (1987) . . . 80
M and C v Romania (2011) . . . 277, 541, 542
M and Co v Germany (1990) . . . 31
M and Others v Italy and Bulgaria (2012) . . . 280, 284
MA v Cyprus (2013) . . . 292, 293, 767, 774, 961
Maaouia v France (2000) . . . 385, 386, 388, 966
McBride v UK (2001) . . . 723
McBride v UK (2006) . . . 215
McCallum v UK (1990) . . . 587, 770
McCann v UK (1995) . . . 91, 154, 161, 203, 207, 214, 215, 221, 222, 227, 228, 229, 230, 232, 233
McCann v UK (2008) . . . 529, 535, 581
McComb v UK (1986) . . . 472, 482

McDonald v UK (2012) . . . 546
McElhinney v Ireland (2001) . . . 405
McFarlene v Ireland (2010) . . . 52, 57, 778
McFeeley v UK (1980) . . . 56, 64, 236, 263, 265, 266, 387, 532, 538, 558, 724
McGinley and Egan v UK (1995) . . . 760
McGinley and Egan v UK (1998) . . . 383, 416, 563, 620
McGinley and Egan v UK (2000) . . . 134
McGlinchey v UK (2003) . . . 265, 266
McGonnell v UK (2000) . . . 381, 446, 451, 452
McGoff v Sweden (1982) . . . 339
McGoff v Sweden (1984) . . . 163
McGuiness v UK (1999) . . . 943
McIntyre v UK (1998) . . . 911
McKay v UK (2006) . . . 288, 289, 338, 339, 343, 344, 345, 351
McKenny v UK (1994) . . . 586
McKerr v UK (2001) . . . 92, 187, 217, 218
McLean and Cole (2013) . . . 924
McLeod v UK (1998) . . . 558
McMichael v UK (1995) . . . 389, 418, 571, 754, 807, 808
McShane v UK (2002) . . . 114, 227
McVeigh v UK (1981) . . . 560
McVeigh, O'Neill and Evans v UK (1981) . . . 311, 312, 315, 334, 335, 826
McVicar v UK (2002) . . . 401, 693, 688, 702, 703
Maciariello v Italy (1992) . . . 442
Mackay and BBC Scotland v UK (2010) . . . 83, 640
Maclean and Cole v UK (2013) . . . 190
Macovei and Others v Romania (2007) . . . 276
Macready v Czech Republic (2010) . . . 574
Mađer v Croatia (2011) . . . 244
Maestri v Italy (2004) . . . 733
Magalhães Pereira v Portugal (2002) . . . 360
Magee v UK (2000) . . . 474, 791
Maggio and Others v Italy (2011) . . . 429
Mahdid and Haddar v Austria (2006) . . . 292
Mahfaz v UK (1993) . . . 758
Maillard v France (1998) . . . 388
Maiorano and Others v Italy (2009) . . . 212
Maire v Portugal (2003) . . . 574
MAK and RK v UK (2010) . . . 544
Makaratzis v Greece (2004) . . . 204, 206, 222, 779, 780
Makharadze and Sikharulidze v Georgia (2011) . . . 141, 211
Makhfi v France (2004) . . . 415
Makhmudov v Russia (2007) . . . 716
Maksimov v Azerbaijan (2009) . . . 410
Maksym v Poland (2006) . . . 114
Maktouf and Damjanovic v Bosnia and Herzegovina (2013) . . . 56, 501, 821
Makuc v Slovenia (2007) . . . 926
Malahov Moldova (2007) . . . 164
Malhous v Czech Rep (2000) . . . 65, 94, 98, 867, 868
Malhous v Czech Rep (2001) . . . 433

Malige v France (1998) . . . 376
Malik v UK (2013) . . . 55, 559
Malininas v Lithuania (2008) . . . 427
Malone v UK (1984) . . . 506, 531, 532, 555, 764
Malone v UK (1996) . . . 808
Malsagova and Others v Russia (2008) . . . 76
Maltzan v Germany (2005) . . . 98
Mamatkulov and Abdurasulovic v Turkey (2003) . . . 124
Mamatkulov and Askarov v Turkey (2005) . . . 96, 113, 124, 139, 141, 248, 250, 372, 373, 386
Mamère v France (2006) . . . 696, 697
Mammadov v Azerbaijan (No 2) (2012) . . . 945, 946
Manasson v Sweden (2003) . . . 970
Mancel and Branquart v France (2010) . . . 453
Mancini v Italy (2001) . . . 298
Mandil v France (2011) . . . 80, 129
Mangouras v Spain (2010) . . . 348, 349, 350, 368
Mann Singh v France (2008) . . . 610
Mannai v Italy (2012) . . . 141
Manners v UK (1998) . . . 404
Manoilescu and Dobrescu v Romania and Russia (2005) . . . 405
Manole v Moldova (2004) and (2006) . . . 89
Manoussakis v Greece (1996) . . . 593, 599, 608
Manoussos v Czech Republic and Germany (2002) . . . 137
Mansell v UK (2003) . . . 417
Mansuroğlu v Turkey (2008) . . . 228
Mantovanelli v France (1997) . . . 418
Manzanas Martin v Spain (2012) . . . 802
MAR v UK (1997) . . . 226
Marcello Viola v Italy (2006) . . . 437
Marckx v Belgium (1979) . . . 9, 10, 11, 18, 22, 29, 30, 35, 85, 189, 238, 504, 513, 514, 519, 523, 527, 528, 533, 564, 568, 758, 760, 785, 793, 800, 801, 867, 895
Marguš v Croatia (2012) . . . 970, 973
Marie-Louise Loyen and Bruneel v France (2005) . . . 93
Marincola and Sestito v Italy (1999) . . . 588
Marini v Albania (2007) . . . 402
Marinkovic v Serbia (2013) . . . 57
Markass Car Hire v Cyprus (2001) . . . 398
Markovic v Italy (2006) . . . 152, 407
Markt intern Verlag GmbH and Klaus Beermann v Germany (1989) . . . 507, 508, 636, 637, 638, 639, 650
Marônek v Slovakia (2001) . . . 661
Marpa Zeeland v Netherlands (2004) . . . 408
Marshall v UK (2001) . . . 835, 836, 837, 838, 840, 841, 842, 844
Martin and Others v France (2012) . . . 640
Martin v UK (2006) . . . 450
Martinez and Manzano v Spain (2012) . . . 585
Martinie v France (2004) . . . 381
Martinie v France (2006) . . . 415, 436
Marturana v Italy (2008) . . . 302
Marzari v Italy (1999) . . . 580

Masaev v Moldova (2009) . . . 598
Maslov v Austria (2008) . . . 575, 577
Maslova and Nalbandov v Russia (2008) . . . 239
Massa v Italy (1993) . . . 389
Massey v UK (2004) . . . 445
Masson and Van Zon v Netherlands (1995) . . . 382, 389
Mastromatteo v Italy (2002) . . . 204, 207, 212
Mata Estevez v Spain (2001) . . . 526
Mateescu v Romania (2014) . . . 578
Mater v Turkey (2013) . . . 553
Matheus v France (2005) . . . 397
Mathew v Netherlands (2005) . . . 148, 264
Mathieu-Mohin and Clerfayt v Belgium (1987) . . . 12, 13, 15, 629, 851, 920, 922, 923, 924, 925, 926, 946
Matos e Silva, Lda v Portugal (1996) . . . 865, 876, 881, 882, 886
Matoušek v Czech Republic (2011) . . . 69
Matter v Slovakia (1999) . . . 543, 544
Matthews v UK (1999) . . . 32, 33, 83, 189, 190, 922, 925, 929
Matthews v UK (2002) . . . 799
Mattick v Germany (2005) . . . 471
Mattoccia v Italy (2000) . . . 469
Matveyev v Russia (2008) . . . 97, 968
Matyjek v Poland (2006) . . . 376
Matyjek v Poland (2007) . . . 413, 415
Matznetter v Austria (1969) . . . 347, 348
Maumousseau and Washington v France (2007) . . . 574
Maupas v France (2006) . . . 89
Maurice v France (2005) . . . 221, 864, 882, 889
Maxwell v UK (1994) . . . 479, 480
Mayali v France (2005) . . . 488
Mayeka v Belgium (2006) . . . 334
Mayer v Germany (1996) . . . 867
Mazurek v France (2000) . . . 801
Mazzotti v Italy (2000) . . . 445
MB and GB v UK (2001) . . . 267
MC v Bulgaria (2003) . . . 236, 239, 274, 276, 541
MD and Others v Malta (2012) . . . 188, 571
Medenica v Switzerland (2001) . . . 412
Medova v Russia (2009) . . . 224, 297
Medvedyev v France (2010) . . . 290, 292, 301, 303, 338, 340, 368, 827
Medya FM Reha Radyo ve İletişim Hizmetleri AŞ v Turkey (2006) . . . 622, 645, 652
Meftah v France (2002) . . . 475, 476, 477
Megadat.com SRL v Moldova (2008) . . . 865, 875, 884, 896, 899
Megadat.com SRL v Moldova (2011) . . . 129
Megyeri v Germany (1992) . . . 360
Mehemi v France (1997) . . . 87, 577
Mehemi v France (No 2) (2002) . . . 87, 194
Mehmet Nuri Özen and Others v Turkey (2011) . . . 587
Mehmet Şentürk and Bekir Şentürk v Turkey (2013) . . . 214
Melin v France (1993) . . . 476

Mellacher and Others v Austria (1989) . . . 863, 896, 898, 899
Mellors v UK (2003) . . . 421, 445, 452
Melnik v Ukraine (2006) . . . 266
Melnychenko v Ukraine (2004) . . . 921, 926, 934
Melnychuk v Ukraine (2005) . . . 863
Meltex LTD v Armenia (2008) . . . 65, 97
Menendez Garcia v Spain (2009) . . . 565
Menesheva v Russia (2006) . . . 240
Meng v Portugal (1995) . . . 226
Mennesson v France (2012) . . . 567
Mennitto v Italy (2000) . . . 383
Menson v UK (2003) . . . 214, 216
Menteş v Turkey (1997) . . . 238, 780
Mentzen alias Mencena v Latvia (2004) . . . 539, 540, 615
Mercieca and Others v Malta (2011) . . . 398
Merger and Cros v France (2004) . . . 50, 801
Meriakri v Moldova (2005) . . . 130
Mersch v Luxembourg (1985) . . . 555, 556
Messina v Italy (1999) . . . 264
Messina (No 2) v Italy (2000) . . . 585, 587, 588
Metalco BT v Hungary (2012) . . . 134
Metin Turan v Turkey (2006) . . . 751
Metropolitan Church of Bessarabia v Moldova (2001) . . . 598, 599, 602, 603, 604, 607
Meulendijks v Netherlands (2002) . . . 385
MGN v UK (2011) . . . 661, 662
Miailhe v France (1993) . . . 557
Miażdżyk v Poland (2012) . . . 958
Micallef v Malta (2009) . . . 54, 93, 398, 455
Michalak v Poland (2005) . . . 51
Michaud v France (2012) . . . 33, 83, 530
Miconi v Italy (2004) . . . 58, 62
Midro v Poland . . . 586
Migon v Poland (2002) . . . 357
Mihailov v Bulgaria (2005) . . . 446, 448
Mihailovs v Latvia (2013) . . . 294, 295, 296, 324, 326
Mika v Sweden (2009) . . . 488
Mikayail Mammadov v Azerbaijan (2009) . . . 209
Mikheyev v Russia (2006) . . . 53, 157, 160, 239
Mikolajová v Slovakia (2011) . . . 48, 52, 553, 554, 561
Mikolenko v Estonia (2006) . . . 76
Mikulic v Croatia (2002) . . . 565, 566
Mikulová v Slovakia (2005) . . . 371, 404
Milanović v Serbia (2010) . . . 275, 814
Mild and Virtanen v Finland (2005) . . . 485
Miler v Czech Republic (2012) . . . 587
Mileva and Others v Bulgaria (2010) . . . 583
Milinienė v Lithuania (2008) . . . 428
Miller v Sweden (2005) . . . 436
Milosevic v Netherlands (2002) . . . 55
Minelli v Switzerland (1983) . . . 461, 464, 465, 466
Minelli v Switzerland (2005) . . . 551, 552
Miragall Escolano v Spain (2000) . . . 50, 404
Mirazovic v Bosnia and Herzegovina (2006) . . . 57

Mirilashvili v Russia (2008) . . . 415
Mirolubovs v Latvia (2009) . . . 80, 129, 599
Miroshnik v Ukraine (2008) . . . 449
Misick v UK (2012) . . . 101, 579
Missenjov v Estonia (2009) . . . 130
Mitkus v Latvia (2012) . . . 551
Mitev v Bulgaria (2010) . . . 93
Mižigárová v Slovakia (2010) . . . 223
Mizzi v Malta (2006) . . . 380, 404, 566
MK v Austria (1997) . . . 488
MK v France (2013) . . . 560
Mkrtchyan v Armenia (2007) . . . 716
MM v Netherlands (2003) . . . 506
MM v UK (2012) . . . 508, 524, 560
MN v Bulgaria (2012) . . . 276, 523, 541
Mocarska v Poland (2007) . . . 327
Modarca v Moldova (2007) . . . 262
Modinos v Cyprus (1993) . . . 86, 532, 550, 803
Mogos and Krifka a v Germany (2003) . . . 57
Mogos v Romania (2004) . . . 959
Mohammed v Austria (2013) . . . 251, 255
Mohammed Hussein and Others v Netherlands
(2013) . . . 255
Moiseyev v Russia (2004) . . . 435
Moiseyev v Russia (2008) . . . 413, 415, 449, 472,
473, 497, 586, 588
Moisejevs v Latvia (2006) . . . 262
Mojsiejew v Poland (2009) . . . 223
Mokrani v France (2003) . . . 577
Moldovan and Others v Romania (No 2)
(2005) . . . 270, 580, 797, 811, 812
Mólka v Poland (2006) . . . 524, 525, 579
Mond v UK (2003) . . . 405
Monedero Angora v Spain (2008) . . . 373
Monnat v Switzerland (2006) . . . 84, 625, 626, 632
Monnell and Morris v UK (1987) . . . 289, 308,
377, 415, 437, 459, 476
Monnet v France (1993) . . . 441
Montcornet de Caumont v France (2003) . . . 377
Montion v France (1987) . . . 55
Mooren v Germany (2009) . . . 302, 362
Mor v France (2011) . . . 668
Morby v Luxembourg (2003) . . . 87
Moreira Barbosa v Portugal (2004) . . . 54
Moreira de Azevedo v Portugal (1990) . . . 390
Morel v France (2003) . . . 376
Moreno Gomez v Spain (2004) . . . 583
Moretti and Benedetti v Italy (2010) . . . 92, 528,
567
Morganti v France (No 1) (1995) . . . 344
Morley v UK (2004) . . . 364
Morris v UK (2002) . . . 478
Morsink v Netherlands (2004) . . . 327, 328
Mort v UK (2001) . . . 414
Mortier v France (2001) . . . 404
Mosbeux v Belgium (1990) . . . 373
Moscow Branch of the Salvation Army v Russia
(2006) . . . 510, 598, 599, 732, 733, 738
Mosendz v Ukraine (2013) . . . 211
Moser v Austria (2006) . . . 434

Moskal v Poland (2009) . . . 863, 886
Moskovets v Russia (2009) . . . 88
Mosley v UK (2011) . . . 523, 549, 550, 551, 552,
660
Mostafa and Others v Turkey (2008) . . . 141
Mosteanu and Others v Romania (2002) . . . 452
Moulin v France (2010) . . . 341
Moullet v France (2007) . . . 461
Mousiel v France (2002) . . . 119, 266, 267, 269
Moustaquim v Belgium (1991) . . . 494, 500, 528,
576, 798
Mouvement raëlien suisse v Switzerland
(2012) . . . 505, 512, 657, 658, 802
MP and Others v Bulgaria (2011) . . . 94, 95
MPP Golub v Ukraine (2005) . . . 55
Mrozowski v Poland (2009) . . . 242
MS v Croatia (2013) . . . 542, 543
MS v Sweden (1997) . . . 562
MS and PS v Switzerland (1985) . . . 555
MSS v Belgium and Greece (2011) . . . 119, 138,
139, 144, 153, 249, 251, 252, 255, 270, 774
MT and ST v Slovakia (2012) . . . 541, 542
Mubilanzil Mayeka and Kaniki Mitunga v
Belgium (2006) . . . 241, 244, 256, 263, 275,
319, 578
Müller v Czech Republic (2011) . . . 500
Müller and Others v Switzerland (1988) . . . 508,
511, 516, 517, 518, 616, 634, 649, 650, 656, 657,
658, 669, 895
Muminov v Russia (2008) . . . 141
Muminov v Russia (2010) . . . 157
Municipal Section of Antilly v France
(1999) . . . 82
Muñoz Díaz v Spain (2009) . . . 755
Munjaz v UK (2012) . . . 298
Munro v UK (1987) . . . 401
Muradi and Alieva v Switzerland (2013) . . . 576
Murillo Saldias v Spain (2006) . . . 91
Murphy v Ireland (2003) . . . 612, 619, 643, 646,
647, 670
Murphy v UK (1972) . . . 471, 483
Murray v UK (1994) . . . 317, 318, 335, 336, 337,
560, 770, 827
Murray (John) v UK (1996) . . . 422, 423, 424,
425, 461, 462, 474, 475
Mürsel Eren v Turkey (2006) . . . 911
Musa and Others v Bulgaria (2007) . . . 578
Musayevand Others v Russia (2007) . . . 146,
222, 781
Musial v Poland (1999) . . . 353, 362
Muskhadzhiyeva v Belgium (2010) . . . 334
Müslüm Gündüz v Turkey (2003) . . . 628
Mustafa v France (2003) . . . 384
Mustafa (Abu Hamza) v UK (2011) . . . 460, 466,
467
Mustafa and Armağan Akin v Turkey
(2010) . . . 528, 573
Musumecī v Italy (2005) . . . 401
Mutlag v Germany (2010) . . . 577
Muyldermans v Belgium (1991) . . . 379, 380, 410

MYH and Others v Sweden (2013) . . . 251
Mykhaylenky v Ukraine (2004) . . . 882
Myšáková v Czech Republic (2006) . . . 867

N
N v Finland (2005) . . . 147, 248
N v Sweden (2010) . . . 253
N v UK (2008) . . . 14, 96, 142, 213, 254, 255
NA v UK (2008) . . . 248
Nachova v Bulgaria (2004) . . . 811, 812, 813, 814
Nachova and Others v Bulgaria (2005) . . . 147,
    148, 206, 215, 216, 217, 222, 231, 811, 812, 813
Nada v Switzerland (2012) . . . 290, 293
Nagla v Latvia (2013) . . . 642
Nagovitsyn and Nalgiyev v Russia (2010) . . . 51
Naime Doğan v Turkey (2007) . . . 164
Najafli v Azerbaijan (2012) . . . 243
Nakov v the Former Yugoslav Republic of
    Macedonia (20002) . . . 968
Nalbantski v Bulgaria (2011) . . . 959
Naldi v Italy (1984) . . . 301
Namat Aliyev v Azerbaijan (2010) . . . 922, 944,
    945, 946
Napijalo v Croatia (2003) . . . 958
Narinen v Finland (2004) . . . 556
Nart v Turkey (2008) . . . 344, 350
Nasri v France (1995) . . . 157
Nasrulloyev v Russia (2007) . . . 303
Nassau Verzekering Maatschappij NV v
    Netherlands (2011) . . . 90
Nataliya Mikhaylenko v Ukraine (2013) . . . 403
National and Provincial Building Society, Leeds
    Permanent Building Society and Yorkshire
    Building Society v UK (1997) . . . 404, 429,
    795, 864, 882, 893, 902, 904
National Association of Teachers in Further and
    Higher Education v UK (1998) . . . 750
National Union of Belgian Police case
    (1975) . . . 22, 740, 747, 748, 752
Navarra v France (1993) . . . 362, 365
Naydyan v Ukraine (2010) . . . 114
NC v Italy (2002) . . . 44, 290, 367
Necdet Bulut v Turkey (2007) . . . 241, 242
Nee v Ireland (2003) . . . 66
Negrepontis-Giannisis v Greece (2011) . . . 568
Neilsen v Denmark (1959) . . . 469
Nejdet Şahin and Perihan Şahin v Turkey
    (2011) . . . 402, 432
Nencheva v Bulgaria (2013) . . . 208
Neshev v Bulgaria (2004) . . . 404
Neulinger and Shuruk v Switzerland
    (2010) . . . 142, 534, 535, 574, 575
Neumeister v Austria (1964) . . . 337
Neumeister v Austria (1968) . . . 343, 347, 349,
    350, 356, 360, 373, 378, 413, 440, 441, 445
Neves e Silva v Portugal (1989) . . . 382, 389
Nevmerzhitsky v Ukraine (2005) . . . 239, 268
News Verlags GmbH & CoKG v Austria
    (2000) . . . 640, 675, 682
NF v Italy (2001) . . . 508, 733

Ngendakumana v Netherlands (2013) . . . 66
Nibbio v Italy (1992) . . . 440
Nicol and Selvanayagam v UK (2001) . . . 716, 723
Nicoleta Gheorghe v Romania (2012) . . . 44, 71
Nicolò Santilli v Italy (2013) . . . 574
Nicolussi v Austria (1987) . . . 387
Niederöst-Huber v Switzerland (1997) . . . 409,
    417
Niedbala v Poland (2000) . . . 341, 356, 556, 587
Niedzwiecki v Germany (2005) . . . 568
Nielsen v Denmark (1959) . . . 335, 466
Nielsen v Denmark (1988) . . . 295
Niemietz v Germany (1992) . . . 525, 529, 530,
    557, 578, 895
Nikitin v Russia (2004) . . . 432, 972
Nikolova v Bulgaria (1999) . . . 44, 126, 161, 345,
    352, 356, 357
Nikolova v Bulgaria (No 2) (2004) . . . 290
Nikolova and Velichkola v Bulgaria
    (2007) . . . 231
Nikowitz and Verlagsgruppe News GmbH v
    Austria (2007) . . . 698
Nikula v Finland (2002) . . . 153, 692, 705
Nilsen and Johnsen v Norway (1999) . . . 615,
    684, 692, 697, 698, 701
Nilsson v Sweden (2005) . . . 971
Ninn-Hansen v Denmark (1999) . . . 412, 448, 466
Nitecki v Poland No 65653/01 (2002) . . . 213
Nivette v France (2001) . . . 227
Nizomkhom Dzhurayev v Russia (2012) . . . 153
NKM v Hungary (2013) . . . 863, 864, 883, 885
Nöel Narvii Tauira and 18 Others v France
    (1995) . . . 86
Nogolica v Croatia (2002) . . . 51
Nolan and K v Russia (2009) . . . 96, 291, 367,
    576, 606, 965, 966
Nölkenbockhoff v Germany (1987) . . . 93, 461
Norbert Sikorski v Poland (2009) . . . 52
Nordh v Sweden (1990) . . . 383
Nordisk Film & TV A/S v Denmark
    (2005) . . . 641, 642
Nordström-Janzon and Nordström-Lehtinen v
    Netherlands (1996) . . . 408
Norris v Ireland (1988) . . . 84, 86, 89, 189, 532,
    550, 803
Nortier v Netherlands (1993) . . . 372, 434, 453
Norwood v UK (2004) . . . 854
Novotka v Slovakia (2003) . . . 292, 313
Novotny v Czech Republic (1998) . . . 385
Nowak v Ukraine (2011) . . . 336
Nowicka v Poland (2002) . . . 311, 312
Nowicky v Austria (2005) . . . 382, 390
Noye v UK (2003) . . . 467
Nsona v Netherlands (1996) . . . 256, 577
Nunez v Norway (2011) . . . 576
Nuray Şen v Turkey (2003) . . . 839
Nur Radyo Ve Televizyon Yayinciliği AŞv
    Turkey . . . 645
Nurettin Aldemir and Others v Turkey
    (2007) . . . 715, 719

Nuri Kurt v Turkey (2005) . . . 531, 781
Nurmagomedov v Russia (2007) . . . 113
Nurminen v Finland (1997) . . . 924
NW v Luxembourg (1992) . . . 968
Nylund v Finland (1999) . . . 527, 807

O
OAO Neftyanaya Kompaniya Yukos v Russia
    (2011) . . . 78, 471, 858, 878, 895,901
Obasa v UK (2003) . . . 443
Obermeier v Austria (1990) . . . 395
Oberschlick v Austria (No 1) (1991) . . . 164, 453,
    694
Oberschlick v Austria (No 2) (1997) . . . 694, 695
Observer and Guardian v UK (1991) . . . 26, 508,
    510, 515, 517, 518, 520, 640, 654, 674
Obst v Germany (2010) . . . 579, 600
Öcalan v Turkey (2000) . . . 337
Öcalan v Turkey (2003) . . . 60, 124, 225, 298,
    299, 337, 360, 450, 964
Öcalan v Turkey (2005) . . . 29, 124, 141, 142,
    164, 226, 265, 268, 298, 299, 340, 354, 360,
    446, 468, 471, 472, 473, 474, 482, 964
Ocic v Croatia (1999) . . . 86
Odièvre v France (2003) . . . 14, 44, 125, 538,
    563, 567
O'Donoghue and Others v UK (2010) . . . 598,
    755, 756, 802
Oerlemans v Netherlands (1991) . . . 27, 390, 394
Oferta Plus SRL v Moldova (2006) . . . 113
Ofner v Austria (1960) . . . 468
Ofner and Hopfinger v Austria (1962) . . . 414
OGIS-Institut Stanislas, OGEC St Pie X and
    Blanche de Castille and Others v France
    (2004) . . . 429, 893
OGO v UK (2014) . . . 286
Ogur v Turkey (1999) . . . 217, 221, 227, 231
Ognyanova and Choban v Bulgaria (2006) . . . 812, 814
OH v Germany (2011) . . . 325, 499
O'Hallaran and Francis v UK (2007) . . . 425,
    426, 462
O'Hara v UK (2000) . . . 64
O'Hara v UK (2001) . . . 316, 317, 318, 336, 827
Ohlen v Denmark (2005) . . . 90, 131
Okyay v Turkey (2005) . . . 384, 391, 396
Okkali v Turkey (2006) . . . 275, 277
Olaechea Cahuas v Spain (2006) . . . 140
Olczak v Poland (2002) . . . 863
Oldham v UK (2000) . . . 365
Oleksandr Volkov v Ukraine (2013) . . . 451, 452,
    458, 579
Olesky v Poland (2009) . . . 88
Olexandr Volkov v Ukraine (2013) . . . 163
Oleynikov v Russia (2013) . . . 406
Oliveira v Switzerland (1998) . . . 971, 972
Olivieira v Netherlands (2002) . . . 955, 957
Öllinger v Austria (2006) . . . 712, 713, 715
Ölmez and Ölmez v Turkey (2005) . . . 45, 64, 121
Olsson v Sweden (No 1) (1988) . . . 192, 384, 510,
    523, 528, 564, 569, 570, 572

Olsson v Sweden (No 2) (1992) . . . 192, 569
Olujić v Croatia (2009) . . . 386, 434, 454
Omar v France (1998) . . . 408
Omeredo v Austria (2011) . . . 253
Omojudi v UK (2009) . . . 577
Omwenyeke v Germany (2007) . . . 954
Öneryildiz v Turkey (2004) . . . 11, 203, 204, 206,
    207, 208, 215, 218, 234, 584, 770, 779, 780, 781,
    782, 864, 865, 870, 871, 876, 883
Onur v UK (2009) . . . 575
Open Door and Dublin Well Woman v Ireland
    (1992) . . . 85, 137, 219, 508, 509, 510, 650, 651
Optim and Industerre v Belgium (2012) . . . 864
Opuz v Turkey (2009) . . . 23, 210, 274, 784, 798
Oral and Atabay v Turkey (2009) . . . 339
Orban v France (2005) . . . 855
Orchin v UK (1982) . . . 377, 441
Orchowski v Poland (2009) . . . 262
Orhan v Turkey (2002) . . . 93, 241, 257, 300
O'Rourke v UK (2001) . . . 529, 580
Oršuš and Others v Croatia (2010) . . . 384, 388,
    440, 442, 786, 793, 797, 810, 816, 817, 912
Orujov v Azerbaijan (2011) . . . 946
Orujov v Azerbaijan (2012) . . . 936
Osinger v Austria (2005) . . . 434
Osman v UK (1991) . . . 332
Osman v UK (1998) . . . 16, 23, 207, 209, 210, 211,
    212, 218, 285, 407
Osmani v the Former Yugoslav Republic of
    Macedonia (2001) . . . 714, 715, 717, 723
Osmanoglu v Turkey (2008) . . . 210, 224
Osmanov and Husseinov v Bulgaria
    (2003) . . . 88
Ospina Vargas v Italy (2004) . . . 587
Ostendorf v Germany (2013) . . . 294, 311, 313,
    314, 315, 316, 369
Österreichische Vereinigung zur Erhaltung
    Stärkung und Schaffung eines wirtschaftlich
    gesunden land-und forstwirt-schaftlichen
    Grundbesitzes v Austria (2013) . . . 562–3
Österreichischer Rundfunk v Austria
    (2006) . . . 695
Ostrovar v Moldova (2005) . . . 147, 509
Osypenko v Ukraine (2010) . . . 311
Otegi Mondragon v Spain (2011) . . . 630, 666,
    692, 707
Othman (Abu Qatada) v UK (2012) . . . 125, 142,
    299, 307, 372, 828
Otto v Germany (2005) . . . 617, 685, 686, 687
Otto v Germany (2009) . . . 62
Otto-Preminger-Institut v Austria (1994) . . .
    515, 517, 612, 634, 656, 657, 669, 670, 818
Ouardiri v Switzerland (2011) . . . 87
Ouinas v France (1990) . . . 586
Ould Barar v Sweden (1999) . . . 286
Ould Dah v France (2009) . . . 206, 238, 498
Ouranio Toxo and Others v Greece (2005) . . . 739
Ouzounis v Greece (2002) . . . 396
Oya Ataman v Turkey (2006) . . . 711, 714, 715,
    719

Oyal v Turkey (2010) ... 157, 159, 165, 207, 215
Oyston v UK (2002) ... 484
Özgür Gündem v Turkey (2000) ... 23, 617, 619, 620, 628, 629, 640
Özgür Radyo-Ses Radyo Televizyon Yapim Ve Tanitim AŞ v Turkey (2006) ... 640, 646
Özgürlük ve Dayanişma Partisi (ÖDP) v Turkey (2012) ... 949
Özpinar v Turkey (2010) ... 579
Öztürk v Germany (1984) ... 12, 375

P
P v Austria (1989) ... 377
P v UK (1987) ... 386
P and S v Poland (2012) ... 271, 274, 321, 546
P, C and S v UK (2002) ... 400, 570, 755
P4 Radio Hele Norge ASA v Norway (2003) ... 675, 681
Pabla Ky v Finland (2004) ... 451
Padin Gestoso v Spain (1999) ... 468, 469
Padovani v Italy (1993) ... 453
Păduraru v Romania (2005) ... 871
Paeffgen GmbH v Germany (2007) ... 863, 896
Paez v Sweden (1997) ... 159, 248
Pakelli v Germany (1983) ... 474, 477, 478
Paksas v Lithuania (2011) ... 56, 853, 854, 923, 941, 942
Paladi v Moldova (2007) ... 128, 266
Paladi v Moldova (2009) ... 96, 140, 141, 142
Palau-Martinez v France (2003) ... 612, 801
Palomo Sánchez and Others v Spain (2011) ... 617, 618, 619, 632
Pammel v Germany (1997) ... 444
Panaitescu v Romania (2012) ... 213
Panarisi v Italy (2007) ... 464, 484
Pancenko v Latvia (1999) ... 270
Pandjikidze and Others v Georgia (2009) ... 458
Panjeheighalehei v Denmark (2009) ... 385
Pannullo and Forte v France (2001) ... 569
Panovits v Cyprus (2008) ... 477
Pantčenko v Latvia (1999) ... 96
Panteleyenko v Ukraine (2006) ... 562
Pantelimon and Vasilica Savu v Romania (2011) ... 69
Papachelas v Greece (1999) ... 64, 889, 890
Papamichapoulos and Others v Greece (1993) ... 876, 886, 887
Papamichapoulos v Greece (Article 50) (1995) ... 29, 157, 160, 889, 891
Papastavrou and Others v Greece (2003) ... 889, 896
Papon v France (No 1) (2001) ... 266, 267
Papon v France (No 2) (2001) ... 430, 467, 501
Papon v France (2002) ... 408, 967
Papon v France (2005) ... 385
Papoulakos v Greece (1995) ... 389
Paradis v France (2007) ... 310
Paramanathan v Germany (1986) ... 954
Paraskeva Todorova v Bulgaria (2010) ... 797
Pardo v France (1993) ... 433

Pardo v France (1997) ... 134
Paritchi v Moldova (2005) ... 128
Parizov v the Former Yugoslav Republic of Macedonia (2008) ... 51
Parlov-Tkalcic v Croatia (2009) ... 455
Paroisse Gréco-Catholique Sambata Bihor v Romania (2004) ... 67
Parris v Cyprus (2002) ... 419
Parry v UK (2006) ... 759
Parti Nationaliste Basque-Organisation Régionale D'Iparralde v France (2007) ... 144, 735, 737
Partidul Comunistilor (Nepeceristi) and Ungureanu v Romania (2005) ... 727
Partija 'Jaunie Demokrati' and Partija 'Musu Zeme' v Latvia (2007) ... 947
Partington v UK (2003) ... 81
Parviz v Sweden (2012) ... 572
Pasa and Erkan Erol v Turkey (2006) ... 82, 212
Paschalidis, Koutmeridis, and Zaharakis v Greece (2008) ... 943
Pasculli v Italy (2007) ... 160
Paslawski v Poland (2002) ... 57
Patera v Czech Republic (2006) ... 75
Paton v UK (1980) ... 92
Patrianakos v Greece (2004) ... 441
Paturel v France (2005) ... 632, 699
Patyi v Hungary (2012) ... 715, 716
Pauger v Austria (1997) ... 383, 437
Paulić v Croatia (2009) ... 529, 582
Paulik v Slovakia (2006) ... 565, 566, 795
Pauliukiene and Pauliukas v Lithuania (2013) ... 553
Pauwels v Belgium (1988) ... 342
Pavel Ivanov v Russia (2007) ... 854
Pavlovic v Sweden (1999) ... 246
Pay v UK (2008) ... 550
Payot and Petit v Switzerland (1991) ... 489
PB and JS v Austria (2010) ... 526, 803
Peck v UK (2003) ... 550, 551, 555, 560, 770
Pedersen and Baadsgaard v Denmark (2004) ... 377, 440, 554, 660, 661, 691
Peers v Greece (2001) ... 114, 144, 262, 461, 589
Pekaslan v Turkey (2012) ... 723
Peker v Turkey (No 2) (2011) ... 222
Pelladoah v Netherlands (1994) ... 81
Pellegrin v France (1999) ... 386, 387
Pellegrini v Italy (2001) ... 372
Pellegriti v Italy (2005) ... 55
Pelli v Italy (2003) ... 382
Péllisier and Sassi v France (1999) ... 468, 469
Peltier v France (2002) ... 404
Peltonen v Finland (1995) ... 387, 958
Penart v Estonia (2006) ... 502
Pendragon v UK (1998) ... 711
Pentiacova v Moldova (2005) ... 213, 546
Pentidis v Greece (1997) ... 599
Peraldi v France (2009) ... 74, 76, 77
Perdigão v Portugal (2010) ... 892
Pereira Henriques v Luxembourg (2006) ... 206, 215

Perez v France (2004) . . . 96, 371, 380, 392
Perez de Rada Cavanilles v Spain (1998) . . . 404
Perez Mahia v Spain (1985) . . . 471
Perić v Croatia (2008) . . . 415
Perişan and Othersv Turkey (2010) . . . 206, 222, 233
Perk and Others v Turkey (2006) . . . 230
Perkins and R v UK (2002) . . . 550
Perks v UK (1999) . . . 160, 310
Perna v Italy (2003) . . . 153, 488, 693, 704
Perrin v UK (2005) . . . 649, 657
Perry v Latvia (2007) . . . 606
Perry v UK (2003) . . . 556, 560
Peruš v Slovenia (2012) . . . 453
Peruzzo and Martens v Germany (2013) . . . 561
Pescador Valero v Spain (2003) . . . 455
Pessino v France (2006) . . . 498
Pesti and Frodl v Austria (2000) . . . 967
Peta Deutschland v Germany (2012) . . . 659
Peters v Netherlands (1994) . . . 544
Petkov v Bulgaria (2007) . . . 65
Petkov and Others v Bulgaria (2009) . . . 769, 922, 945, 946
Petra v Romania (1998) . . . 113
Petrea v Romania (2008) . . . 266
Petrenco v Moldova (2010) . . . 554
Petri Sallinen and Others v Finland (2005) . . . 530
Petrina v Romania (2008) . . . 553, 554
Petrov v Bulgaria (2008) . . . 588, 808
Petrova v Latvia (2009) . . . 545
Petrovic v Austria (1998) . . . 793, 794, 795, 799, 800, 822
Petyo Petkov v Bulgaria (2010) . . . 271
PF and EF v UK (2010) . . . 275
Pfeifer and Plankl v Austria (1992) . . . 446, 453, 683
Pfeifer v Austria (2007) . . . 553
Pfeifer v Bulgaria (2011) . . . 660
Pfunders case see Austria v Italy (1961)
PG and JH v UK (2001) . . . 419, 556, 560, 772
Pham Hoang v France (1992) . . . 462, 479
Philis v Greece (1991) . . . 403
Phillips v UK (2001) . . . 378, 421, 461, 462, 903
Phinikaridou v Cyprus (2007) . . . 566
Phocas v France (1996) . . . 875, 877, 882
Phull v France (2005) . . . 610
Pialopoulos v Greece (2001) . . . 882
Pibernik v Croatia (2004) . . . 529
Pichkur v Ukraine (2013) . . . 789
Pichon and Sajous v France (2001) . . . 603
Piechowicz v Poland (2012) . . . 264, 585, 586
Pieniążek v Poland (2004) . . . 442
Piermont v France (1995) . . . 101, 630, 653, 851, 852, 953, 954
Pierre Marais v France (1996) . . . 624
Pierre-Bloch v France (1997) . . . 376, 385, 922
Piersack v Belgium (1982) . . . 450, 452, 492
Pietiläinen v Finland (2009) . . . 477
Pilčić v Croatia (2008) . . . 265
Pincová and Pinc v Czech Republic (2002) . . . 889, 892, 893

Pine Valley Developments Ltd v Ireland (1991) . . . 89, 863, 864, 895, 896, 904, 905
Pine Valley Developments Ltd v Ireland (1993) . . . 884
Pini and Others v Romania (2004) . . . 397, 528, 568
Pinnacle Meat Processors Company v UK (1998) . . . 896
Piroğlu and Karakaya v Turkey (2008) . . . 649, 651
Piruzyan v Aremnia (2012) . . . 346
Pisano v Italy (2002) . . . 125, 131, 159
Pishchalnikov v Russia (2009) . . . 478
Pitarque v Spain (1989) . . . 90
Pitkänen v Finland (2004) . . . 421, 869
Pitkevich v Russia (2001) . . . 617
PK v Finland (2002) . . . 421
PK, MK and BK v UK (1992) . . . 586
Pla and Puncernau v Andorra (2004) . . . 565, 568, 761, 784, 800, 801
Planka v Austria (1996) . . . 430
Platakou v Greece (2001) . . . 404, 881
Plattform 'Ärzte für das Leben' v Austria (1985) . . . 505, 711, 712, 713, 724, 764
Plattform 'Ärzte für das Leben' v Austria (1988) . . . 23, 503
Plaza v Poland (2011) . . . 574
Plechanow v Poland (2009) . . . 871
Plepi v Albania and Greece (2010) . . . 586
Pleso v Hungary (2013) . . . 325
Ploski v Poland (2002) . . . 587, 588
Plotnicova v Moldova (2012) . . . 145
PM v UK (2004) . . . 66
PM v UK (2005) . . . 765, 806
POA and Others v UK (2013) . . . 44, 76, 77
Podbielski and PPU Polpure v Poland (2005) . . . 403
Podbolotova v Russia (2005) . . . 128
Podkolzina v Latvia (2002) . . . 924, 933, 939
Podoreski v Croatia (2007) . . . 455
Poghosyan and Baghdasaryan v Armenia (2012) . . . 969
Poiss v Austria (1987) . . . 381, 442, 881, 882, 884
Poitrimol v France (1993) . . . 410, 477
Pokis v Latvia (2006) . . . 90
Polacek and Polackova v Czech Republic (2002) . . . 868
Polanco Torres and Movilla Polanco v Spain (2010) . . . 93, 553, 554, 660
Polat v Turkey (1999) . . . 628, 629
Poldtoratskiy v Ukraine (2003) . . . 246
Polednová v Czech Republic (2011) . . . 496
Polidario v Switzerland (2013) . . . 575
Poltorachenko v Ukraine (2005) . . . 432
Poltoratskiy v Ukraine (2003) . . . 22, 246, 262, 276, 277, 606
Poncelet v Belgium (2010) . . . 464
Ponomaryovi v Bulgaria (2011) . . . 909, 910
Ponsetti and Chesnel v France (1999) . . . 971
Popa v Romania (2013) . . . 539

Popenda v Poland (2012) . . . 586
Popov v France (2012) . . . 275, 331, 334
Popov v Moldova (No 1) (2005) . . . 79, 397
Popov v Russia (2006) . . . 489
Popov v Ukraine (2006) . . . 265
Popovski v the Former Yugoslav Republic of
    Macedonia (2013) . . . 554
Portmann v Switzerland (2011) . . . 268
Porter v UK (1987) . . . 398, 459
Porter v UK (2003) . . . 374, 376, 381
Portington v Greece (1998) . . . 442
Posokhov v Russia (2003) . . . 458
Posti and Rahko v Finland (2002) . . . 65, 381,
    390, 399, 896
Potocka v Poland (2001) . . . 393
Potomska and Potomski v Poland (2011) . . . 868
Powell and Rayner v UK (1990) . . . 389, 408,
    583, 768
Powell v UK (2000) . . . 207, 213, 215
Poznanski and Others v Germany (2007) . . . 79
Prado Bugallo v Spain (2003) . . . 556
Prager and Oberschlick v Austria (1995) . . . 663,
    676, 677, 693
Pravednaya v Russia (2004) . . . 432
Predescu v Romania (2008) . . . 79, 132
Predil Anstalt v Italy (2002) . . . 51
Prehn v Germany (2010) . . . 361
Prencepe v Monaco (2009) . . . 53, 130
Prescher v Bulgaria (2011) . . . 958
Pressos Compania Naviera SA and Others v
    Belgium (1995) . . . 864, 877, 882, 885
Pretto v Italy (1983) . . . 18, 380, 396, 438, 439, 443
Pretty v UK (2002) . . . 119, 125, 154, 205, 261,
    275, 505, 526, 547, 593, 790
Previti v Italy (2009) . . . 74
Previti (No 2) v Italy (2010) . . . 452
Prezec v Croatia (2008) . . . 142
Price v UK (1988) . . . 528
Price v UK (2001) . . . 261, 263, 266, 808, 818
Priebke v Italy (2001) . . . 466, 467
Prince Hans-Adam II of Liechtenstein v
    Germany (2001) . . . 33, 407
Priorello v Italy (1985) . . . 385
Prisma Presse v France (2003) . . . 662
Procedo Capital Corporation v Norway
    (2009) . . . 456
Procola v Luxembourg (1995) . . . 33, 381, 384,
    451
Prodan v Moldova (2004) . . . 871, 883, 898
Prokopovich v Russia (2004) . . . 528, 529
Pronina v Ukraine (2006) . . . 429, 430
Proshkin v Russia (2012) . . . 328
Prötsch v Austria (1996) . . . 877, 882
Prystavska v Ukraine (2002) . . . 54
Przemyk v Poland (2013) . . . 130
PS v Germany (2001) . . . 488
Pudas v Sweden (1987) . . . 381, 389
Pugliese v Italy (No 2) (1991) . . . 396
Puhk v Estonia (2004) . . . 497
Pulatli v Turkey (2011) . . . 292

Pullar v UK (1996) . . . 456, 488
Pullicino v Malta (2000) . . . 413, 467
Punzelt v Czech Republic (2000) . . . 347
Puolitaival v Pirttiaho v Finland (2004) . . . 454
Purcell v Ireland (1991) . . . 622, 655, 855
Purtonen v Finland (1998) . . . 974
Putintseva v Russia (2012) . . . 206
Putistin v Ukraine (2013) . . . 553
Putz v Austria (1996) . . . 374
Puzinas v Lithuania (2005) . . . 281
Puzinas (No 2) v Lithuania (2007) . . . 588
Py v France (2005) . . . 101, 925, 926
PZ and Others v Sweden (2012) . . . 64, 85

Q
Qama v Albania and Italy (2013) . . . 64, 575
Quadrelli v Italy (2000) . . . 429
Quaresma Afonso Palma v Portugal
    (2003) . . . 66
Quaranta v Switzerland (1991) . . . 474, 476, 479,
    480
Quinn v France (1995) . . . 319, 332

R
R v UK (2007) . . . 373
R and F v UK (2006) . . . 759
R and H v UK (2011) . . . 570, 571, 572
R, S, A and C v Portugal (1984) . . . 267
Rabus v Germany (2006) . . . 81
Radio ABC v Austria (1997) . . . 644
Radio France and Others v France (2004) . . .
    462, 497, 640, 688
RADIO TWIST AS v Slovakia (2006) . . . 667, 672
Radio X, S, W and A v Switzerland (1984) . . . 643
Radovanovic v Austria (2004) . . . 577
Radu v Germany (2013) . . . 325
Raf v Spain (2000) . . . 332
Rahimi v Greece (2011) . . . 270, 334
Raichinov v Bulgaria (2006) . . . 696
Raidl v Austria (1995) . . . 256
Rai, Allmond, and 'Negotiate Now' v UK
    (1995) . . . 716, 717, 721
Rai and Evans v UK (2009) . . . 711, 714, 715,
    720, 721, 723
Railean v Moldova (2010) . . . 204
Raimondo v Italy (1994) . . . 94, 291, 373, 381,
    900, 901, 954, 955, 956
Rainys and Gasparavičius v Lithuania
    (2005) . . . 791
Rajcoomar v UK (2004) . . . 428
Rajkowska v Poland (2007) . . . 204
Rakevich v Russia (2003) . . . 352, 354
Ramaer and Van Willigen v Netherlands
    (2012) . . . 864
Ramanauskas v Lithuania (2008) . . . 427, 428
Ramazanova v Azerbaijan (2007) . . . 738
Ramirez Sanchez v France (2006) . . . 262, 264,
    265, 765, 771
Ramishvili and Kokhreidze v Georgia
    (2009) . . . 355, 356

Ramsahai v Netherlands (2007) . . . 92, 215, 216, 217, 232, 780

Raninen v Finland (1997) . . . 261, 268

Ranjit Singh v France (2009) . . . 610

Ranson v UK (2003) . . . 454

Rantsev v Cyprus and Russia (2010) . . . 218, 284, 285, 286, 297

Rappaz v Switzerland (2013) . . . 212, 268

Rasmussen v Denmark (1984) . . . 16, 565, 785, 786, 795

Rassemblement Jurassien Unité Jurassienne v Switzerland (1979) . . . 711, 717

Ravnsborg v Sweden (1994) . . . 374, 375, 392

Ravon and Others v France (2008) . . . 384, 387

Rawa v Poland (2003) . . . 441

Rayner v UK (1986) . . . 869

Raza v Bulgaria (2010) . . . 523, 578

RC v Sweden (2010) . . . 247

RD v Poland (2001) . . . 478

Redfearn v UK (2012) . . . 739

Rees v UK (1986) . . . 13, 505, 536, 537, 754, 755, 758

Reeve v UK (1994) . . . 221

Refah Partisi (The Welfare Party) v Turkey (2003) . . . 89, 513, 622, 631, 725, 727, 728, 729, 732, 735, 736, 752, 835, 853, 921, 941

Rehbock v Slovenia (2000) . . . 242, 243, 589

Rehak v Czech Republic (2004) . . . 79

Reid v UK (1997) . . . 797

Reid v UK (2001) . . . 389

Reigado Ramos v Portugal (2005) . . . 186

Reinhardt and Slimane-Kaid v France (1998) . . . 418

Reinprecht v Austria (2005) . . . 352, 359, 360, 384

Reisz v Germany (1997) . . . 384, 385

Rekasi v Hungary (1996) . . . 392

Reklos and Davourlis v Greece (2009) . . . 660

Rekvényi v Hungary (1999) . . . 507, 653, 685

Religionsgemeinschaft der Zeugen Jehovas and Others v Austria (2008) . . . 598, 602, 802

Remetin v Croatia (2012) . . . 534, 542

Remli v France (1996) . . . 47, 456

Remuszko v Poland (2013) . . . 619

Renda Martins v Portugal (2002) . . . 401

Renolde v France (2008) . . . 92, 211

Republican Party of Russia v Russia (2011) . . . 730, 731, 737, 738

Ressegatti v Switzerland (2006) . . . 93

Ressiot and Others v France (2012) . . . 673

Resul Sadak v Turkey (2008) . . . 134

Reuther v Germany (2003) . . . 50

Reyntjens v Belgium (1992) . . . 311, 313

Rezette v Luxembourg (2004) . . . 442

Reznik v Russia (2013) . . . 693

Riad and Idiab v Belgium (2008) . . . 54, 263, 291, 329

Ribitsch v Austria (1995) . . . 17, 241, 242, 243

Ricci v Italy (2013) . . . 664

Riela v Italy (2001) . . . 901

Riener v Bulgaria (2006) . . . 957, 958

Riepan v Austria (2000) . . . 433, 435, 459, 460

Riera Blume v Spain (1999) . . . 297

Rigopoulos v Spain (1999) . . . 340

Ringeisen v Austria (1971) . . . 378, 379, 391, 392, 395, 447, 453

Ringeisen v Austria (1973) . . . 133

Ringvold v Norway (2003) . . . 465

Rinck v France (2010) . . . 71

Rivas v France (2004) . . . 242

Rivière v France (2006) . . . 266

RK and AK v UK (2008) . . . 571, 572

RL and M-JD v France (2004) . . . 318

RMD v Switzerland (1997) . . . 354

RMS v Spain (2013) . . . 570

Robathin v Austria (2012) . . . 557, 558

Roberts and Roberts v UK (2011) . . . 553, 554

Robineau v France (2013) . . . 211

Robins v UK (1997) . . . 396

Roche v UK (2005) . . . 407, 563, 620

Rock Ruby Hotels Ltd v Turkey (2010) . . . 161

Rodrigues da Silva and Hoogkamer v Netherlands (2006) . . . 577

Roemen and Schmit v Luxembourg (2003) . . . 614, 642, 643

Roepstorff v Denmark (2000) . . . 743

Roffey and Others v UK (2013) . . . 62

Rohde v Denmark (2005) . . . 264

Roldan Texeira v Italy (2000) . . . 959

Rolf Gustafson v Sweden (1997) . . . 383, 389

Romańczyk v France (2010) . . . 397

Rommelfanger v Germany (1989) . . . 618

Rosca and Others v Moldova (2005) . . . 431, 432

Rosca Stanescu and Ardeleanu v Romania (2002) . . . 86

Rosengren v Romania (2008) . . . 956

Rosenquist v Sweden (2004) . . . 970

Rosenzweig and Bonded Warehouses Ltd v Poland (2005) . . . 877

Roshka v Russia (2003) . . . 880

Ross v UK (1986) . . . 473

Rotaru v Romania (2000) . . . 87, 560, 766, 775, 776

Rothe v Austria (2012) . . . 551

Rousk v Sweden (2013) . . . 582

Rowe and Davis v UK (2000) . . . 417

Rowley v UK (2005) . . . 207

Różański v Poland (2006) . . . 565

Rozhin v Russia (2011) . . . 130

RP and Others v UK (2012) . . . 403, 536, 571

RPD v Poland (2004) . . . 442

Rrapo v Albania (2012) . . . 226–7, 965

RR and Others v Hungary (2012) . . . 209

RR v Poland (2011) . . . 129, 271, 528, 546

RR v Romania (2009) . . . 575

RT v Switzerland (2000) . . . 970

RTBF v Belgium (2011) . . . 398, 651

Rudan v Croatia (2001) . . . 398

Rudnichenko v Ukraine (2013) . . . 484, 485, 487

Ruis-Mateos v Spain (1993) . . . 415, 444

Ruiz Torija v Spain (1994) . . . 430
Ruminski v Sweden (2013) . . . 55, 178
Rumyana Ivanova v Bulgaria (2008) . . . 688
Runkee and White v UK (2007) . . . 866
Ruotolo v Italy (1992) . . . 443
Ruotsalainen v Finland (2009) . . . 972
Rushiti v Austria (2000) . . . 464
Russian Conservative Party of Entrepreneurs v
    Russia (2007) . . . 85, 926, 933, 937, 942
Rutecki v Poland (2009) . . . 586
Rutkowski v Poland (2000) . . . 481, 482
Rutten v Netherlands (2001) . . . 363
Růžičková v Czech Republic (2008) . . . 66
Ryabykh v Russia (2003) . . . 404, 431, 432
Ryabikin v Russia (2008) . . . 253
Ryakib Biryukov v Russia (2008) . . . 438

S
S v France (1988) . . . 332
S v France (1999) . . . 869
S v Germany (1983) . . . 485
S v Germany (No 9686/82) (1984) . . . 283, 284
S v Germany (No 10365/83) (1984) . . . 751
S v Germany (2012) . . . 316
S v Sweden (1985) . . . 958
S v Switzerland (1988) . . . 387
S v Switzerland (1991) . . . 360, 482, 483
S v UK (1986) . . . 526
S and Marper v UK (2008) . . . 11, 145, 190, 514,
    531, 560, 561, 660
SA Dangeville v France (2002) . . . 864, 876, 902
Saadi v Italy (2008) . . . 13, 138, 147, 153, 248,
    249, 252, 253, 828
Saadi v UK (2008) . . . 304, 305, 311, 328, 329,
    334, 335, 336
Saaristo and Others v Finland (2010) . . . 660
Sabanchiyeva and Others v Russia (2008) . . . 569
Sabanchiyeva and Others v Russia (2013) . . . 271, 547
Sabeh El Leil v France (2011) . . . 406
Sabri Gunes v Turkey (2012) . . . 61, 62
Sabri Taş v Turkey (2006) . . . 134
Sacchi v Italy (1976) . . . 644
Saccoccia v Austria (2007) . . . 500
Saccoccia v Austria (2008) . . . 397
Saccomanno and Others v Italy (2012) . . . 946
Sacilor-Lormines v France (2006) . . . 451
Sadak v Turkey (No 1) (2001) . . . 469, 471, 489
Sadak and Others v Turkey (No 2) (2002) . . .
    921, 933, 942
Saday v Turkey (2006) . . . 676
Sadegul Ozdemir v Turkey (2005) . . . 350
Saez Maeso v Spain (2004) . . . 404
Saghinadze and Others v Georgia (2010) . . . 50,
    863, 878, 880
Sahin v Germany (2001) . . . 796
Sahin v Germany (2003) . . . 158, 573, 806, 808
Said v Netherlands (2005) . . . 248
Saime Özcan v Turkey (2009) . . . 749
Saint-Paul Luxembourg SA v Luxembourg
    (2013) . . . 530, 557, 642

Sainte-Marie v France (1992) . . . 453
Sakhnovskiy v Russia (2010) . . . 482
Sakik v Turkey (1997) . . . 354, 367, 827, 833
Sakkapoulos v Greece (2004) . . . 431
Salabiaku v France (1988) . . . 375, 462, 463
Salah Sheekh v Netherlands (2007) . . . 56, 249,
    251
Salakhov and Islyamova v Ukraine
    (2013) . . . 142, 257
Salaman v UK (2000) . . . 455
Salapa v Poland (2002) . . . 589
Salduz v Turkey (2008) . . . 304, 474, 478
Salem v Portugal . . . 227
Salesi v Italy (1993) . . . 383, 866
Salgueiro da Silva Mouta v Portugal
    (1999) . . . 803, 821
Saliba v Malta (2005) . . . 896
Saliba and Others v Malta (2011) . . . 886
Saliyev v Russia (2010) . . . 619
Salleras Llinares v Spain (2000) . . . 925
Salman v Turkey (2000) . . . 92, 148, 211, 214, 216,
    222, 240
Salomonsson v Sweden (2002) . . . 159
Salonen v Finland (1997) . . . 539
Salontaji-Drobnjak v Serbia (2009) . . . 543
Salov v Ukraine (2005) . . . 614, 616, 703
Salvatore v Italy (2002) . . . 586
Salvatore (Manuele) v Italy (2005) . . . 587
Salvetti v Italy (2002) . . . 544
Şaman v Turkey (2011) . . . 490
Sâmbata Bihor Greco-Catholic Parish v
    Romania (2010) . . . 393, 403, 802
Sambor v Poland (2011) . . . 242, 243
Samer v Germany (1971) . . . 471
Samoilǎ and Cionca v Romania (2008) . . . 463
Sampanis v Greece (2008) . . . 786, 797, 809, 816
Samsonnikov v Estonia (2012) . . . 577
Samüt Karabulat v Turkey (2009) . . . 243, 715, 719
San Leonard Band Club v Malta (2004) . . . 453
Sanchez Cardenas v Norway (2007) . . . 554
Sanchez Navajas v Spain (2001) . . . 748
Sanchez-Reisse v Switzerland (1986) . . . 356,
    362, 363
Sancho Cruz and 14 other 'Agrarian Reform'
    cases v Portugal (2011) . . . 69
Sander v UK (2000) . . . 451, 457
Sanders v France (1996) . . . 756
Sanocki v Poland (2007) . . . 669
Sandru and Others v Romania (2009) . . . 206
Sanles Sanles v Spain (2000) . . . 87, 205
Sanles Sanles v Spain (2010) . . . 93
Sannino v Italy (2006) . . . 481
Sanoma Uitgevers BV v Netherlands
    (2010) . . . 641, 651
Santos Couto v Portugal (2010) . . . 550
Santos Nunes v Portugal (2012) . . . 574
Saoud v France (2007) . . . 211, 230, 231
Saoudi v Spain (2006) . . . 250
Sapan v Turkey (2010) . . . 660
Sapunarescu v Germany (2006) . . . 488

Sara Lind Eggertsdottir v Iceland (2007) . . . 416
Saramati v France, Germany, and Norway
  (2007) . . . 84, 111, 153, 155
Sarban v Moldova (2005) . . . 268
Sardin v Russia (2004) . . . 62, 867
Sardinas Alba v Italy (2004) . . . 490
Sargsyan v Azerbaijan (2011) . . . 63, 65
Sari and Colak v Turkey (2006) . . . 586
Saribek v Turkey (2004) . . . 63
Saric v Denmark (1999) . . . 430
Sarica and Dilaver v Turkey (2010) . . . 886
SARL de Parc d'activities de Blotzheim v France
  (2003) . . . 392
SAS v France (pending . . . 538
Saso Gorgiev v the Former Yugoslav Republic of
  Macedonia (2012) . . . 212
Satik v Turkey (2000) . . . 242, 277
Satka and Others v Greece (2003) . . . 397
Saucedo Gómez v Spain (1999) . . . 807
Saunders v UK (1996) . . . 422, 423, 426
Savasci v Germany (2013) . . . 577
Savda v Turkey (2012) . . . 601
Savez Crkava 'Riječživota' and Others v Croatia
  (2010) . . . 598, 821
Savino and Others v Italy (2009) . . . 386
Saviny v Ukraine (2008) . . . 570, 581
Savitchi v Moldova (2005) . . . 689
Savitskyy v Ukraine (2012) . . . 239
Savoia and Bounegru v Italy (2006) . . . 756, 758
Savovi v Bulgaria (2012) . . . 556
Savriddin Dzhurayev v Russia (2013) . . . 164, 211
Savu v Romania (2011) . . . 70
Sawoniuk v UK (2001) . . . 267, 431
Saya and Others v Turkey (2008) . . . 715
Saygili and Falakaoğlu v Turkey (2008) . . . 654
Sayoud v France (2006) . . . 87
SBC v UK (2001) . . . 345
SC v UK (2004) . . . 413
Schädler-Eberle v Liechtenstein (2013) . . . 96
Schalk and Kopf v Austria (2010) . . . 526, 564,
  759, 804, 806, 822
Scharsach and News VerlagsgesellschaS GmbH
  v Austria (2003) . . . 692, 699
Scarth v UK (1999) . . . 399
Scavuzzo-Hager v Switzerland (2004) . . . 52
Schaal v Luxembourg (2003) . . . 573
Schelling v Austria (2010) . . . 194
Schenk v Switzerland (1988) . . . 371, 418, 419, 463
Scherer v Switzerland (1994) . . . 656, 657
Schertenlieb v Switzerland (1979) . . . 483
Schiesser v Switzerland (1979) . . . 315, 335, 341,
  342, 449
Schimanek v Austria (2000) . . . 497, 854
Schlumpf v Switzerland (2009) . . . 421, 437, 537
Schmautzer v Austria (1995) . . . 375
Schmid v Austria (1985) . . . 956, 958
Schmidt v Germany (1994) . . . 283, 284, 788, 799
Schmidt v Germany (2006) . . . 268
Schmidt and Dahlstrom v Sweden (1976) . . . 747,
  749, 750

Schneider v France (2009) . . . 403
Schneider v Germany (2011) . . . 527
Schneider v Luxembourg (2007) . . . 899
Schober v Austria (1999) . . . 758
Schönenberger and Durmaz v Switzerland
  (1988) . . . 472
Schöpfer v Switzerland (1998) . . . 676
Schouten and Meldrum v Netherlands (1994) . . .
  379, 385, 387, 396, 442
Schreiber and Boetsch v France (2003) . . . 374,
  387, 398
Schuchter v Italy (2011) . . . 255
Schuitemaker v Netherlands (2010) . . . 281
Schuler-Zgraggen v Switzerland (1993) . . . 383,
  416, 436, 437, 438, 459
Schüssel v Austria (2002) . . . 552, 666
Schüth v Germany (2010) . . . 579, 600
Schwabe v Austria (1992) . . . 705, 706
Schwabe and MG v Germany (2011) . . . 311, 313,
  316, 711, 715
Schweizerische Radio-und Fernsehgesellschaft
  SRG v Switzerland (2012) . . . 681
Sciacca v Italy (2005) . . . 551, 561
Scialacqua v Italy (1998) . . . 213
Scollo v Italy (1995) . . . 898
Scoppola v Italy (No 2) (2009) . . . 19, 52, 494, 500
Scoppola v Italy (No 3) (2011) . . . 12, 648
Scoppola v Italy (No 3) (2012) . . . 920, 929, 930,
  931, 932, 933, 951
Scordino v Italy (No 1) (2006) . . . 51, 91, 150,
  429, 446, 778, 890
Scott v Spain (1996) . . . 350
Scozzari and Giunta v Italy (2000) . . . 84, 92,
  113, 157, 569
Šečić v Croatia (2007) . . . 814
Seckerson and Times Newspapers Ltd v UK
  (2012) . . . 456
Segerstedt-Wiberg v Sweden (2006) . . . 560, 649,
  770, 775, 776
Sejdić and Finci v Bosnia and Herzegovina
  (2009) . . . 44, 144, 152, 183, 199, 793, 797, 821,
  925, 926, 933
Sejdovic v Italy (2006) . . . 29, 44, 151, 164, 372,
  410, 411, 412
Sekanina v Austria (1993) . . . 461, 464
Selahattin Çetinkaya and Others v Turkey
  (2009) . . . 156
Selcuk v Turkey (2006) . . . 348
Selçuk and Asker v Turkey (1998) . . . 236, 241,
  257
Selim v Cyprus (2002) . . . 756
Selistö v Finland (2004) . . . 512, 663, 664, 665,
  666, 689, 691
Selmouni v France (1999) . . . 47, 51, 52, 59, 147,
  162, 236, 237, 238, 240, 242, 278
Sen v Netherlands (2001) . . . 576
Senator Lines GmbH v 15 member States
  (2004) . . . 91
Senator Lines GmbH v Austria and 14 Other
  Contracting States (2004) . . . 111

Sener v Turkey (2000) . . . 630
Sentges v Netherlands (2003) . . . 546
Sequeira v Italy (2003) . . . 428
Sereny v Romania (2013) . . . 70
Sergey Kuznetsov v Russia (2008) . . . 711, 714, 715, 717, 722
Sergey Smirnov v Russia (2006) . . . 58, 402
Sergey Solovyev v Russia (2012) . . . 361
Sergey Zolotukhin v Russia (2009) . . . 970, 971, 972, 973
Serghides and Christoforou v Cyprus (2002) . . . 402
Serif v Greece (1999) . . . 599
Şerife Yiğit v Turkey (2010) . . . 526, 755
Serves v France (1997) . . . 423
Servet Gunduz and Others v Turkey (2011) . . . 209
Seven Individuals v Sweden (1982) . . . 532
Sevinger and Eman v Netherlands (2007) . . . 926
Sevtap Veznedaroglu v Turkey (2000) . . . 276
Seyidzade v Azerbaijan (2009) . . . 923, 938
Sezen v Netherlands (2006) . . . 577
SF v Switzerland (1994) . . . 290
SF and Others v Sweden (2012) . . . 247
SH and Others v Austria (2007) . . . 761
SH and Others v Austria (2011) . . . 505, 524, 528, 548, 564, 784
Shabanov and Tren v Russia (2006) . . . 659, 693, 700
Shackell v UK (2000) . . . 807, 808
Shamayev and Others v Georgia and Russia (2003) . . . 73
Shamayev and Others v Georgia and Russia (2005) . . . 141, 225, 227, 248, 250, 335, 336, 964
Shamsa v Poland (2003) . . . 291
Shannon v UK (2005) . . . 426
Shannon v UK (2004) . . . 428
Shannon v UK (2005) . . . 424, 426, 427
Shapovalov v Ukraine (2012) . . . 387
Shavdarov v Bulgaria (2010) . . . 565, 566
Shchebet v Russia (2008) . . . 263
Shefer v Russia (2012) . . . 68
Sheffield and Horsham v UK (1998) . . . 10, 537
Shelley v UK (2008) . . . 546, 589
Shesti Mai Engineering OOD and Others v Bulgaria (2011) . . . 871
Shestjorkin v Estonia (2000) . . . 24
Shevanova v Latvia (2007) . . . 130
Shilbergs v Russia (2009) . . . 88
Shimovolos v Russia (2011) . . . 292, 316, 561
Shindler v UK (2013) . . . 922, 927, 928, 951
Shishkov v Bulgaria (2003) . . . 351
Shmalko v Ukraine (2004) . . . 397
Shofman v Russia (2005) . . . 566
Shopov v Bulgaria (2010) . . . 544
Shpakovskiy v Russia (2005) . . . 397
Shtukaturov v Russia (2008) . . . 114, 141, 296, 403, 543
Shulgin v Ukraine (2011) . . . 367
Sialkowska v Poland (2007) . . . 399
Sibgatullin v Russia (2009) . . . 411

Sibson v UK (1993) . . . 743, 746, 753
Sidabras and Džiautas v Lithuania (2004) . . . 532, 578, 791
Siddik Aslan (2005) . . . 59
Sidiropoulos and Others v Greece (1998) . . . 724, 731, 732, 738
Siebenhaar v Germany (2011) . . . 600
Sieminska v Poland (2001) . . . 215
Sigma Radio Television Ltd v Cyprus (2011) . . . 393, 394
Sigurdór Arnarsson v Iceland (2003) . . . 437
Sigurdsson v Iceland (2003) . . . 455
Sigurjónsson v Iceland (1993) . . . 9, 20, 725, 745, 817
Sijakova and Others v FYRM (2003) . . . 760
Sikić v Croatia (2010) . . . 464
Silay v Turkey (2007) . . . 941
Sildedzis v Poland (2005) . . . 896
Siliadin v France (2005) . . . 11, 279, 280, 285, 286
Silih v Slovenia (2009) . . . 98, 215, 217
Silva Pontes v Portugal (1994) . . . 396, 442
Silva Rocha v Portugal (1996) . . . 364
Silver v UK (1983) . . . 399, 506, 507, 508, 585, 587, 766, 767, 770, 772, 773
Silvius Magnago and Südtiroler Volkspartei v Italy (1996) . . . 947
Simaldone v Italy (2009) . . . 446, 892
Simons v Belgium (2012) . . . 304, 314, 335
Simpson v UK (1989) . . . 908
Simsek v Turkey (2005) . . . 232
Simsek v UK (2002) . . . 456
Simsic v Bosnia and Herzegovina (2012) . . . 498
Sinan Işik v Turkey (2010) . . . 163, 540, 596, 597
Sindicatul 'Păstorul Cel Bun' v Romania (2013) . . . 12, 600, 740
Singartiski and Others v Bulgaria (2012) . . . 717
Singh and Others v UK (2006) . . . 761
Sipavičius v Lithuania (2002) . . . 469
Sipoş v Romania (2011) . . . 534
Sîrbu v Moldova (2004) . . . 621
Şişman and Others v Turkey (2011) . . . 749
Sisojeva v Latvia (2005) . . . 954
Sisojeva v Latvia (2007) . . . 126, 114, 130, 131, 159
Sissanis v Romania (2007) . . . 958
Sitaropoulos and Giakoumopoulos v Greece (2012) . . . 20, 920, 926, 927, 951
Sitokhova v Russia (2004) . . . 62
Siveri and Chiellini v Italy (2008) . . . 724
Siwak v Poland (2004) . . . 375
Skalka v Poland (2003) . . . 618, 676, 678, 705
Skawińska v Poland (2001) . . . 268
Skender v the Former Yugoslav Republic of Macedonia (2001) . . . 787, 917
Skendžić and Krznarić v Croatia (2011) . . . 216
Skiba v Poland (2009) . . . 720
Skoogström v Sweden (1982) . . . 461
Skoogström v Sweden (1983) . . . 342
SL v Austria (2001) . . . 86
Slawomir Musial v Poland (2009) . . . 267
Slimani v France (2004) . . . 211

Slivenko v Latvia (2003) . . . 25, 152, 330, 506, 575, 867, 960
Slyusarev v Russia (2010) . . . 235, 271
Smirnov v Russia (2007) . . . 558
Smirnova v Russia (2003) . . . 317, 346, 351, 558
Smirnova and Smirnova v Russia (2002) . . . 74, 77
Smith v UK (1995) . . . 385
Smith v UK (2002) . . . 424
Smith and Grady v UK (1999) . . . 270, 394, 531, 550, 579, 605, 766, 769, 770, 776, 784, 803
Smith Kline and French Laboratories v Netherlands (1990) . . . 863
Smokovitis and Others v Greece (2002) . . . 864, 882
SN v Sweden (2002) . . . 485, 488
Šneersone and Kampanella v Italy (2011) . . . 574
Soare v Romania (2011) . . . 223, 271
Soare and Others v France (2011) . . . 206
Sobhani v Sweden (1998) . . . 226
Sobolewski (No 2) v Poland (2009) . . . 437
Socialist Party v Turkey (1998) . . . 631, 726, 727
Société Anonyme 'Sotiris et Nicos Koutas ATTEE' v Greece (2000) . . . 382, 404
Société Colas Est and Others v France (2002) . . . 530, 557
Société Stenuit v France (1992) . . . 207
Söderbäck v Sweden (1998) . . . 573
Söderman v Sweden (2013) . . . 534, 542
Soering v UK (1989) . . . 7, 9, 13, 18, 19, 35, 85, 139, 142, 225, 226, 227, 236, 237, 240, 245, 246, 247, 248, 253, 277, 286, 372, 468, 494, 766, 771, 963
Sofianopoulos and Others v Greece (2002) . . . 540
Sofri v Italy (2003) . . . 416
Sokolowski v Poland (2005) . . . 615, 616, 699, 700
Sokurenko and Strygun v Ukraine (2006) . . . 458
Solakov v the Former Yugoslav Republic of Macedonia (2001) . . . 488
Soldatenko v Ukraine (2008) . . . 253
Solmaz v Turkey (2006) . . . 350
Solmaz v Turkey (2007) . . . 65
Solodyuk v Russia (2005) . . . 871, 876
Solomou v Turkey (2008) . . . 232
Soltysyak v Russia (2011) . . . 957
Somjee v UK (2002) . . . 441
Sommerfeld v Germany (2003) . . . 421, 489, 573
Somogyi v Italy (2004) . . . 164, 412
Sorensen and Rasmussen v Denmark (2006) . . . 11, 741, 745, 746, 748
Sorrentino Prota v Italy (2004) . . . 898
Soto Sanchez v Spain (2003) . . . 44
Soumare v France (1998) . . . 364
Sovtransavto Holding v Ukraine (2002) . . . 432, 447, 452, 863
Sovtransavto Holding v Ukraine (2003) . . . 161
Söylemez v Turkey (2006) . . . 186, 187
Söyler v Turkey (2013) . . . 931
Soylu v Turkey (2007) . . . 781

SP v UK (1997) . . . 906, 911
Špaček sro v Czech Republic (1999) . . . 878
Spadea and Scalabrino v Italy (1995) . . . 898
Spampinato v Italy (2007) . . . 597
Spillman v Switzerland (1988) . . . 555
Sporrong and Lönnroth v Sweden (1982) . . . 14, 189, 381, 399, 856, 868, 872, 873, 874, 875, 880, 881, 882, 884, 885, 886, 895, 904
Spöttl v Austria (1996) . . . 799
Spyra and Kranczkowski v Poland (2012) . . . 546
Sramek v Austria (1984) . . . 447, 448, 449, 451
Stafford v UK (2002) . . . 9, 309, 364, 365
Staiku v Greece (1997) . . . 756
Stallinger and Kuso v Austria (1997) . . . 25
Stambuk v Germany (2002) . . . 638, 639, 652
Stamose v Bulgaria (2012) . . . 958
Stamoulakatos v Greece (No 1) (1993) . . . 440
Standard Verlags GmbH v Austria (No 2) (2007) . . . 689, 690, 691
Standard Verlags GmbH v Austria (No 2) (2009) . . . 660
Stanev v Bulgaria (2012) . . . 290, 294, 295, 296, 324, 325, 354, 369, 402, 403, 543
Stanford v UK (1994) . . . 412, 482
Stanford v UK (2002) . . . 259
Stankiewicz v Poland (2006) . . . 416
Stankov and the United Macedonian Organization Ilinden v Bulgaria (2001) . . . 629, 631, 711, 717, 718
Stapleton v Ireland (2010) . . . 80
Staroszczyk v Poland (2007) . . . 400
Stašaitis v Lithuania (2002) . . . 302
Stec and Others v UK (2005) . . . 96, 383, 787, 822, 866, 867, 903
Stec and Others v UK (2006) . . . 9, 18, 125, 786, 790, 794, 799, 818, 863
Steck-Risch and Others v Liechtenstein (2010) . . . 96, 194
Stedman v UK (1997) . . . 403, 593, 604, 802
Steel v UK (1998) . . . 303, 315, 318, 374, 509, 653
Steel and Morris v UK (2005) . . . 159, 400, 401, 413, 632, 684, 693, 703, 706
Stefan v UK (1997) . . . 392
Ştefănescu v Romania (2011) . . . 71
Ştefănică and Others v Romania (2010) . . . 402
Stegarescu and Bahrin v Portugal (2010) . . . 402
Steindel v Germany (2010) . . . 281
Steiner v Austria (1993) . . . 455
Stephens v Cyprus, Turkey and the United Nations (2008) . . . 84
Stephens v Malta (No 1) (2009) . . . 299, 366
Stepuleac v Moldova (2007) . . . 317
Stere and Others v Romania (2006) . . . 884, 902
Steur v Netherlands (2003) . . . 683, 696
Stevens v UK (1986) . . . 539, 910
Stewart v UK (1984) . . . 228, 229, 232, 233, 236
Stewart-Brady v UK (1997) . . . 400
Stichting Mothers of Srebrenica and Others v Netherlands (2013) . . . 78, 84, 406
Stjerna v Finland (1994) . . . 534, 535, 539

Stocké v Germany (1991) . . . 433
Stögmuller v Austria (1969) . . . 344, 346, 347, 349, 439, 440
Stoica v Romania (2008) . . . 243, 813, 814
Stoicescu v Romania (2004) . . . 134, 543
Stoichkov v Bulgaria (2005) . . . 307, 308, 412
Stojakovic v Austria (2006) . . . 447
Stojanov v the Former Yugoslav Republic of Macedonia (2007) . . . 94
Stoll v Switzerland (2007) . . . 640, 660, 672, 673, 674, 689
Storbråten v Norway (2007) . . . 970
Storck v Germany (2005) . . . 288, 291, 294, 295, 296, 297, 324, 371, 543, 544
Stran Greek Refineries and Stratis Andreadis v Greece (1994) . . . 183, 184, 381, 382, 416, 429, 863, 864, 875, 882, 886, 889, 905
Streletz, Kessler, and Krenz v Germany (2001) . . . 227, 493, 495, 498
Stretch v UK (2003) . . . 864, 875, 876
Strohal v Austria (1994) . . . 616
STS v Netherlands (2011) . . . 366
Stubbings and Others v UK (1996) . . . 404, 789, 795
Stübing v Germany (2012) . . . 549, 550
Stummer v Austria (2011) . . . 96, 280, 282, 787, 790, 791, 796
Sud Fondi SRL v Italy (2009) . . . 501, 879
Suda v Czech Republic (2010) . . . 399
Sufi and Elmi v UK (2011) . . . 248, 249, 251, 270
Suhadolc v Slovenia (2011) . . . 436
Süheyla Aydin v Turkey (2005) . . . 222
Sujeeun v UK (1996) . . . 400
Sukhorubchenko v Russia (2005) . . . 402
Sukhorukikh v Russia (2006) . . . 128
Sukhovetskyy v Ukraine (2006) . . . 924, 937, 938
Şükran Aydin and Others v Turkey (2013) . . . 615, 784, 821
Sulak v Turkey (1996) . . . 910
Sulaoja v Estonia (2005) . . . 347, 348
Sulejmanovic v Italy (2002) . . . 962
Sultani v France (2007) . . . 961
Sunday Times v UK (1986) . . . 650
Sunday Times v UK (No 1) (1979) . . . 16, 30, 89, 204, 229, 467, 506, 507, 508, 511, 516, 519, 605, 640, 649, 650, 679, 681, 682
Sunday Times v UK (No 2) (1991) . . . 640, 654
Sürek v Turkey (No 1) (1999) . . . 462, 627, 628, 629, 687
Sürek and Ozdemir v Turkey (1999) . . . 627, 683
Sürmeli v Germany (2004) . . . 74
Sürmeli v Germany (2006) . . . 440, 441, 442, 445, 773, 778
Surugiu v Romania (2004) . . . 580
Suso Musa v Malta (2013) . . . 329, 330, 332, 361
Sussmann v Germany (1996) . . . 383, 392, 440, 444
Sutherland v UK (1997) . . . 803
Sutherland v UK (2001) . . . 127
Sutter v Switzerland (1979) . . . 449, 538–9
Sutter v Switzerland (1984) . . . 439

SV and SV v Bosnia and Herzegovina (2012) . . . 49
Svarc and Kavnik v Slovenia (2007) . . . 454
Svenska Managementgruppen v Sweden (1985) . . . 902
Svetlana Naumenko v Ukraine (2004) . . . 451
Svetlana Orlova v Russia (2009) . . . 442
Svinarenko and Slyadnev v Russia (2012) . . . 268
Svyato-Mykhaylivska Parafiya v Ukraine (2007) . . . 598, 606
SW v UK (1995) . . . 497
Swedish Engine Drivers Union case (1976) . . . 26, 741, 747, 749
Sychev v Ukraine (2005) . . . 82
Sylvester v Austria (2003) . . . 186, 574
Sylvester v Austria (No 2) (2005) . . . 442
Syngelidis v Greece (2010) . . . 405
Synod College of the Evangelical Reformed Church of Lithuania v Lithuania (2002) . . . 865
Szabo v Sweden (2006) . . . 373
Szarapo v Poland (2002) . . . 445
Szima v Hungary (2012) . . . 700
Szuluk v UK (2009) . . . 588
Szypusz v UK (2010) . . . 456

T
T v Belgium (1983) . . . 622
T v Italy (1992) . . . 411
T v UK (1999) . . . 413
T and V v UK (1999) . . . 153, 154
Tabor v Poland (2006) . . . 400
Taheri Kandomabadi v Netherlands (2004) . . . 386
Tahir Duran v Turkey (2004) . . . 164
Tahirova v Azerbaijan (2013) . . . 719
Tahsin Acar v Turkey (2003) . . . 126, 129
Tahsin Acar v Turkey (2004) . . . 130
Tahsin Ipek v Turkey (2000) . . . 64
TAÏS v France (2006) . . . 211
Talmon v Netherlands (1997) . . . 281
Tammer v Estonia (2001) . . . 667, 694
Tamosius v UK (2002) . . . 557
Tănase v Moldova (2010) . . . 55, 510, 923, 934, 935, 936
Tănase and Chirtoacă v Moldova (2008) . . . 935
Taniş v Turkey (2005) . . . 146, 224, 257
Tanli v Turkey (2001) . . . 144, 222, 240
Tanribilir v Turkey (2000) . . . 211, 218, 258
Tanrikulu v Turkey (1999) . . . 114, 210, 216, 223
Tanrikulu, Cetin, Kaya v Turkey (2001) . . . 85, 89
Tapie v France (1997) . . . 385
Tara and Poliata v Moldova (2007) . . . 694, 695
Tarariyeva v Russia (2006) . . . 267, 269
Tarhan v Turkey (2012) . . . 601
Tarkoev v Estonia (2010) . . . 789
Tarantino and Others v Italy (2013) . . . 907, 908
Taron v Germany (2012) . . . 51
Társaság a Szabadságjogokért v Hungary (2009) . . . 562, 621
Taş v Turkey (2000) . . . 93, 217, 257, 300

Tase v Romania (2008) . . . 344, 345
Taşkin and Others v Turkey (2004) . . . 11, 208,
  583, 584, 585
Taştan v Turkey (2008) . . . 271
Tatar v Romania (2009) . . . 584
Tátar and Fáber v Hungary (2012) . . . 615
Tatishvili v Russia (2007) . . . 430, 954,955
Tavli v Turkey (2006) . . . 566
Taxquet v Belgium (2010) . . . 430, 432
Taylor v UK (2003) . . . 405
Taylor Family et al v UK (1994) . . . 213, 216, 217
Taylor-Sabori v UK (2002) . . . 530
Taziyeva and Others v Russia (2013) . . . 558
Tebieti Mühafize Cemiyyeti and Israfilov v
  Azerbaijan (2009) . . . 725, 731, 736, 737, 738
Tehrani and Others v Turkey (2010) . . . 142
Teixeira de Castro v Portugal (1998) . . . 427, 428
Tekin v Turkey (1998) . . . 262
Tekin Yilidiz v Turkey (2005) . . . 141, 212, 267
Tele 1 Privatfernsehgesellschaft mbH v Austria
  (2000) . . . 643, 644
Telegraaf Media Nederland Landelijke Media
  BV and Others v Netherlands (2012) . . . 556,
  641, 651
Telfner v Austria (2001) . . . 462
Temeltasch v Switzerland (1983) . . . 24
Teodor v Romania (2013) . . . 466
Tepe v Turkey (2003) . . . 96
Terazzi srl v Italy (2002) . . . 881
Terem Ltd Chechetkin and Olius v Ukraine
  (2005) . . . 90
Ternovszky v Hungary (2010) . . . 546
Terra Woningen v Netherlands (1996) . . . 395
Tete v France (1987) . . . 937
Teteriny v Russia (2005) . . . 396
Thaler v Austria (2005) . . . 455
Thévenon v France (2006) . . . 94
Thlimmenos v Greece (2000) . . . 96, 382, 578,
  601, 604, 786, 790, 815, 818, 822
Thoma v Luxembourg (2001) . . . 687, 692
Thomann v Switzerland (1996) . . . 453
Thompson v UK (2004) . . . 161, 342
Thomas v UK (2005) . . . 486
Thorgeir Thorgeirson v Iceland (1992) . . . 452,
  703
Thorkelsson v Iceland (2001) . . . 743
Thynne, Wilson and Gunnell v UK (1990) . . .
  353, 356, 364, 367
Tiğ v Turkey (2005) . . . 539
Tillack v Belgium (2007) . . . 642, 643
Timciuc v Romania (2010) . . . 660
Timergaliyev v Russia (2008) . . . 413, 480
Times Newspapers Ltd and Neil v UK (1991) . . . 672
Times Newspapers Ltd (Nos 1 and 2) v UK
  (2009) . . . 615, 620, 688
Timishev v Russia (2005) . . . 797, 811, 911, 955
Timofeyev v Russia (2003) . . . 188
Timperi v Finland (2004) . . . 455
Timpul Info-Magazin and Anghel v Moldova
  (2007) . . . 554, 620

Timtik v Turkey (2010) . . . 243
Timurtas v Turkey (2000) . . . 146, 223, 224, 300
Tinnelly and McElduff v UK (1998) . . . 406
Tirado Ortiz and Lozano Martin v Spain
  (1999) . . . 460
TK and SE v Finland (2004) . . . 377
Tocono et al v Moldova (2007) . . . 455
Toğcu v Turkey (2005) . . . 214
Tolstoy Miloslavsky v UK (1995) . . . 384, 403,
  661, 698
Toma v Romania (2009) . . . 551
Tomasi v France (1992) . . . 236, 242, 261, 278,
  345, 348, 351, 839
Tomic v UK (2003) . . . 247
Tonchev v Bulgaria (2009) . . . 273
Topčić-Rosenberg v Croatia (2013) . . . 791, 822
Toshev v Bulgaria (2006) . . . 349
Toteva v Bulgaria (2004) . . . 242
Toth v Austria (1991) . . . 348, 351, 356, 365
Tourancheau and July v France (2005) . . . 682
Touvier v France (1997) . . . 501
Tovsultanova v Russia (2010) . . . 146
Toyaksi v Turkey (2010) . . . 404
TP and KM v UK (2001) . . . 407, 569, 572
Trabelsi v Italy (2010) . . . 141
Trade Union of the Police in the Slovak Republic
  and Others v Slovakia (2013) . . . 751
Transpetrol as v Slovakia (2011) . . . 82
Tre Traktörer Aktiebolag v Sweden
  (1989) . . . 376, 381, 865, 875, 904
Tregubenko v Ukraine (2004) . . . 431, 432
Trepashkin v Russia (No 2) . . . 360, 366
Trevalec v Belgium (2011) . . . 222
Tricard v France (2001) . . . 404
Trijonis v Lithuania (2005) . . . 291, 954
Tripodi v Italy (1994) . . . 481, 482
Tripon v Romania (2012) . . . 466
Trivedi v UK (1997) . . . 486
Trocellier v France 92006) . . . 545
Trosin v Ukraine (2012) . . . 586
Trzaska v Poland (2000) . . . 343, 346
Tsaturyan v Armenia (2012) . . . 601
Tsfayo v UK (2006) . . . 393, 395
Tsirlis and Kouloumpas v Greece (1997) . . . 602
Tsironis v Greece (2001) . . . 404
Tsourlakis v Greece (2009) . . . 571
Tucka v UK (No 1) (2011) . . . 55, 62
Tum Haber Sen and Cinar v Turkey (2006) . . .
  748, 749, 750, 751
Tumilovich v Russia (1999) . . . 54
Tuquabo-Tekle and Others v Netherlands
  (2005) . . . 576
Turczanik v Poland (2005) . . . 397
Turgut and Others v Turkey (2013) . . . 51, 178
Turham v Turkey (2005) . . . 694, 695, 700
Türk Ticaret Bankasi Munzam Sosyal Güvenlik
  Emekli Ve Yardim Sandiği Vakfi v Turkey
  (2006) . . . 863
Turluyeva v Russia (2013) . . . 211, 224
TV v Finland (1994) . . . 561

TW v Malta (1999) . . . 54, 342
TW Computeranimation GmbH and Others v
    Austria (2005) . . . 863
Twalib v Greece (1998) . . . 471, 478, 479, 480
Twenty One Detained Persons v Germany
    (1968) . . . 282
Twomey, Cameron and Guthrie v UK (2013) . . . 432
Tymoshenko v Ukraine (2013) . . . 353, 857, 858,
    859, 860
Tyrer v UK (1978) . . . 7, 9, 10, 30, 31, 35, 100, 101,
    132, 236, 240, 260, 261, 271, 272, 541
Tysiac v Poland (2007) . . . 154, 528, 546

U
U v Luxembourg (1985) . . . 415
Ubach Mortes v Andorra (2000) . . . 489
Ucak v UK (2002) . . . 491
Ucar v Turkey (2006) . . . 214
Udeh v Switzerland (2013) . . . 577
Ugilt Hansen v Denmark (2006) . . . 50
Uhl v Germany (2005) . . . 443
UJ v Hungary (2011) . . . 659
Ukranian Media Group v Ukraine (2005) . . . 128
Ukuskauskas v Lithuania (2010) . . . 414
Ülke v Turkey (2004) . . . 64
Ülke v Turkey (2006) . . . 602
Ülkü Ekinci v Turkey (2002) . . . 257
Ullens de Schooten and Rezabek v Belgium
    (2011) . . . 175
Ulmarova and Others v Russia (2012) . . . 160
Umar Karatepe v Turkey (2010) . . . 242, 266
Umirov v Russia (2012) . . . 361
Unabhängige Initiative Informationsvielfalt v
    Austria (2002) . . . 705
Ünal Tekeli v Turkey (2004) . . . 10, 518, 799
Üner v Netherlands (2006) . . . 96, 153, 521, 577
Unēdic v France (2008) . . . 432
Unión Alimentaria Sanders SA v Spain
    (1989) . . . 441
UNISON v UK (2002) . . . 750
United Christian Broadcasters Ltd v UK
    (2000) . . . 644–5
United Communist Party of Turkey v Turkey
    (1998) . . . 8, 631, 725, 726, 727, 736, 827, 853,
    921, 941
United Macedonian Organization Ilinden and
    Ivanov v Bulgaria (2005) . . . 711, 712, 717, 727
United Macedonian Organization Ilinden and
    Ivanov and Others v Bulgaria (2006) . . . 726,
    732, 736, 737, 738
United Macedonian Organization
    Ilinden-PIRIN v Bulgaria (2005) . . . 728, 730,
    736
United Macedonian Organization
    Ilinden-PIRIN and Others v Bulgaria (No 2)
    (2011) . . . 736
Unterpertinger v Austria (1986) . . . 485
Uoti v Finland (2004) . . . 443
Urbanczyk v Poland (2002) . . . 52
Urbanek v Austria (2010) . . . 401

Urcan v Turkey (2008) . . . 749
UTE Saur Vallnet v Andorra (2012) . . . 50
Užukauskas v Lithuania (2010) . . . 384, 416
Uzun v Germany (2010) . . . 556, 560
Uzun v Turkey (2013) . . . 178

V
V v Denmark (1992) . . . 959
V v UK (1999) . . . 236, 258, 260, 261, 306, 364,
    372, 413, 434, 435
Vaari v Estonia (2008) . . . 94, 95
Vacher v France (1996) . . . 473
Vagrancy cases see De Wilde, Ooms and Versyp
    v Belgium (Merits) (Vagrancy cases)
Vajnai (II) v Hungary (2011) . . . 615
Vakhayeva v Russia (2012) . . . 160
Valasinas v Lithuania (2000) . . . 907
Valašinas v Lithuania (2001) . . . 144, 263, 559
Valcheva and Abrashev v Bulgaria (2013) . . . 51,
    178
Valenzuela Contreras v Spain (1998) . . . 555
Valiuliené v Lithuania (2013) . . . 130, 274
Valkov and Others v Bulgaria (2011) . . . 863, 883
Vallianatos and Others v Greece (2013) . . . 527,
    550, 564, 804, 805
Vallon v Italy (1983) . . . 74
Valová, Slezák, and Slezák v Slovakia
    (2004) . . . 436
Valsamis v Greece (1996) . . . 272, 603, 913, 914
Van Colle v UK (2012) . . . 209
Van de Hurk v Netherlands (1994) . . . 429, 430,
    447
Van de Vin v Netherlands (1992) . . . 956
Van der Heijden v Nethrlands (2012) . . . 526,
    569
Van der Leer v Netherlands (1990) . . . 301, 302,
    324, 334, 336, 362, 366
Van der Mussele v Belgium (1983) . . . 13, 24,
    281, 283, 788
Van der Putten v Netherlands (2013) . . . 72
Van der Sluijs, Zuiderveld and Klappe v
    Netherlands (1984) . . . 341
Van der Tang v Spain (1995) . . . 81
Van der Velden v Netherlands (2012) . . . 560
Van der Ven v Netherlands (2003) . . . 263, 264, 587
Van Anraat v Netherlands (2010) . . . 498
Van Droogenbroeck v Belgium (1982) . . . 280,
    282, 307, 308, 309, 352, 353, 354, 356, 364
Van Geyseghem v Belgium (1999) . . . 477
Van Houten v Netherlands (2005) . . . 130
Van Kück v Germany (2003) . . . 371, 429, 537
Van Marle v Netherlands (1986) . . . 390, 865
Van Mechelem v Netherlands (1997) . . . 485, 487
Van Melle and Others v Netherlands . . . 277
Van Oosterwijck v Belgium (1979) . . . 536
Van Oosterwijck v Belgium (1980) . . . 47, 56,
    59, 536
Van Orshoven v Belgium (1997) . . . 418
Van Raalte v Netherlands (1997) . . . 799
Van Thuil v Netherlands (2004) . . . 373

Van Velden v Netherlands (2011) . . . 69
Van Volsem v Belgium (1990) . . . 867
Van Vondel v Netherlands (2006) . . . 387
Vanjak v Croatia (2010) . . . 386
Vanyan v Russia (2005) . . . 427
Varbanov v Bulgaria (2000) . . . 79, 305, 324
Varela Geis v Spain (2013) . . . 469
Varnas v Lithuania (2013) . . . 789
Varnava and Others v Turkey (2009) . . . 63, 74, 93, 222, 257, 300
Varnava and Others v Turkey (1998) . . . 75
Varnima Corp International SA v Greece (2009) . . . 416
Vasil Sachov Petrov v Bulgaria (2010) . . . 222, 231
Vasilchenko v Russia (2010) . . . 70
Vasilescu v Romania (1998) . . . 887
Vasileva v Denmark (2003) . . . 137, 311, 312, 313, 426
Vasilkoski and Others v FRYOM (2010) . . . 56
Vasquez v Switzerland (2013) . . . 577
Vassilios Stravopoulos v Greece (2007) . . . 461
Vassiliy Ivashchenko v Ukraine (2012) . . . 114
Vassis v France (2013) . . . 340
Vasylenko v Ukraine (2001) . . . 80
Vaturi v France (2006) . . . 484
Vaudelle v France (2001) . . . 410, 470, 480
Vayic v Turkey (2006) . . . 441
VC v Slovakia (2011) . . . 242, 258, 545
VD v Romania (2010) . . . 271, 488
VDSO and Gubi v Austria (1994) . . . 766
Vejdeland and Others v Sweden (2009) . . . 622, 623
Veeber v Estonia (No 1) (2002) . . . 97, 282
Veeber v Estonia (No 2) (2003) . . . 497
Veermäe v Finland (2005) . . . 308
Velcea and Mazăre v Romania (2009) . . . 568
Velikova v Bulgaria (2000) . . . 44, 162, 187, 215, 223, 784, 812
Velikovi and Others v Bulgaria (2007) . . . 892
Vellutini and Michel v France (2011) . . . 694
Ven v Hungary (1993) . . . 58
Vendittelli v Italy (1994) . . . 900
Venema v Netherlands (2002) . . . 570, 572
Ventura v Italy (1980) . . . 441
Vera Fernández-Huidobro v Spain (2010) . . . 447
Verdam v Netherlands (1999) . . . 485
Verein Alternatives Lokalradio, Bern v Switzerland (1986) . . . 767
Verein der Freunde der Christengemeinschaft and Others v Austria (2009) . . . 598
Verein Gegen Tierfabriken Schweiz (Vgt) v Switzerland (2001) . . . 192, 504, 617, 646, 647
Verein Gegen Tierfabriken Schweiz (Vgt) v Switzerland (No 2) (2009) . . . 14, 30, 50, 74, 162, 164, 192, 193, 194
Vereinigung Bildender Kunstler v Austria (2007) . . . 509, 518, 615, 635, 702
Vereinigung Demokratischer Soldaten Österreichs and Gubi v Austria (1994) . . . 613, 653, 694

Vereiniging Weekblad Bluf! v Netherlands (1995) . . . 654
Vergos v Greece (2004) . . . 599, 607
Verités Santé Pratique Sarl v France (2005) . . . 652
Verlagsgruppe News GmbH v Austria (2006) . . . 687
Vermeire v Belgium (1991) . . . 27, 30, 189, 800
Vermeulen v Belgium (1996) . . . 415, 416, 418
Vernes v France (2011) . . . 433, 451
Vesela and Loyka v Slovakia (2005) . . . 90
Veselov and Others v Russia (2012) . . . 427, 428
Vertucci v Italy (2006) . . . 929
Veznedaroğlu v Turkey (1999) . . . 62
Veznedaroğlu v Turkey (2000) . . . 148
Vezon v France (2006) . . . 429
VF v France (2011) . . . 285
Vicenzo Taiani v Italy (2006) . . . 929
Vidakovic v Serbia (2011) . . . 89
Vidal v Belgium (1992) . . . 467, 484, 488, 489
Vides Aizsardzības Klubs v Lithuania (2004) . . . 630, 632, 640, 698, 706
Vidgen v Netherlands (2012) . . . 485
Vijayanathan and Pusparajah v France (1992) . . . 85
Vilborg Yrsa Sigurdardotir v Iceland (2000) . . . 463
Vilho Eskelinen v Finland (2007) . . . 11, 17, 21, 380, 384, 386, 387, 578
Vilnes and Others v Norway (2013) . . . 563
Vilvarajah v UK (1991) . . . 248, 766, 769
Vinčić and Others v Serbia (2009) . . . 57, 402
Vinter and Others v UK (2013) . . . 259, 260, 306, 363
Virabyan v Armenia (2011) . . . 466
Virabyan v Armenia (2012) . . . 239, 814
Visser v Netherlands (2002) . . . 485
Vistiņš and Perepjolkins v Latvia (2011) . . . 893
Vistiņš and Perepjolkins v Latvia (2012) . . . 157
Vito Sante Santoro v Italy (2004) . . . 925, 929, 955
VK v Croatia (2012) . . . 96, 760
Vladimir Romanov v Russia (2008) . . . 239
Vo v France (2004) . . . 12, 15, 16, 207, 219, 220, 545
Voggenreiter v Germany (2004) . . . 392
Vogt v Germany (1995) . . . 578, 605, 616, 685, 686, 687, 941
Vojnity v Austria (2013) . . . 801, 802
Vojtechova v Slovakia (2012) . . . 130
Volnyth v Russia (2009) . . . 397
Von Hannover v Germany (2004) . . . 23, 504, 512, 523, 534, 550, 551, 659, 662, 666, 687, 708
Von Hannover v Germany (No 2) (2012) . . . 515, 523, 551, 552, 660
Von Hannover v Germany (No 3) (2013) . . . 552
Von Maltzen v Germany (2005) . . . 867
Vona v Hungary (2013) . . . 733, 734, 735, 752, 855, 856
Vördur Ólafsson v Iceland (2010) . . . 746
Vorobyeva v Ukraine (2002) . . . 55

Voskuil v Netherlands (2007) . . . 641, 642
Voulfovitch and Oulianova v Sweden
    (1993) . . . 965
Vulakh and Others v Russia (2012) . . . 465
Vyerentsov v Ukraine (2013) . . . 130, 716

W
W v Germany (1985) . . . 400
W v Germany (1986) . . . 74
W v Sweden (1988) . . . 294
W v Switzerland (1983) . . . 82
W v Switzerland (1993) . . . 347, 351
W v UK (1983) . . . 209
W v UK (1987) . . . 390, 395, 408, 528, 535, 571
W & DM and M & HI v UK (1984) . . . 909, 913
W and K v Switzerland (1991) . . . 656
W and KL v Sweden (1985) . . . 907
W, X, Y and Z v UK (Boy Soldiers case)
    (1968) . . . 283
Wagner and JMWL v Luxembourg (2007) . . . 568
Wainwright v UK (2006) . . . 263, 559, 769
Waite v UK (2002) . . . 309, 352, 359, 360
Waite and Kennedy v Germany (1999) . . . 11,
    33, 406
Wakefield v UK (1990) . . . 526, 586
Walczak v Poland (2002) . . . 494
Waldberg v Turkey (1995) . . . 421
Walker v UK (2000) . . . 44, 61
Wallishauser v Austria (2012) . . . 405
Wallová and Walla v Czech Republic (2006)
    . . . 570, 580
Walston v Norway (2001) . . . 455
Walston (No 1) v Norway (2003) . . . 416
Warsicka v Poland (2007) . . . 453
Warwick v UK (1986) . . . 235, 273, 768, 914
Wasa Liv Omsesidigt v Sweden (1988) . . . 902
Wasilewska and Kalucka v Poland (2010) . . . 232
Wasilewski v Poland (1999) . . . 214
Wasmuth v Germany (2011) . . . 596, 597
Wassink v Netherlands (1990) . . . 301, 324, 367
Webb v UK (1983) . . . 400
Webb v UK (2004) . . . 895
Weber v Switzerland (1990) . . . 24, 25, 374, 376,
    516, 520
Weber and Saravia v Germany (2006) . . . 556,
    649, 651
Wedler v Poland (2007) . . . 267
Weeks v UK (1987) . . . 15, 259, 294, 306, 308,
    353, 354, 355, 356, 364
Weeks v UK (1988) . . . 160
Wegera v Poland (2010) . . . 586
Węgrzynowski and Smolczewski v Poland
    (2013) . . . 553, 554
Weh v Austria (2004) . . . 424, 426
Weissman v Romania (2006) . . . 401, 403
Wejrup v Denmark (2002) . . . 87
Welch v UK (1995) . . . 499, 501, 903
Weller v Hungary (2009) . . . 798
Wemhoff v Germany (1968) . . . 7, 8, 18, 20, 307,
    343, 344, 347, 351, 377, 440, 441

Werner v Austria (1997) . . . 382, 439
Werner v Poland (2001) . . . 384, 451
Wessels-Bergervoet v Netherlands (2002) . . .
    799
Wettstein v Switzerland (2000) . . . 454
White v Sweden (2006) . . . 551, 552
Whiteside v UK (1994) . . . 543
Whitfield v UK (2005) . . . 374, 449
Whitman v UK (1989) . . . 909
Wickramsinge v UK (1997) . . . 375
Widmer v Switzerland (1993) . . . 204
Wiechart v Germany (1964) . . . 489
Wieczorek v Poland (2009) . . . 883
Wierzbicki v Poland (2002) . . . 415, 416, 421
Wieser v Austria (2007) . . . 263
Wieser and Bicos Beteiligungen v Austria
    (2007) . . . 557
Wiesinger v Austria (1991) . . . 396, 442
Wiggins v UK (1978) . . . 863
Wiktorko v Poland (2009) . . . 263
Willcox and Hurford v UK (2013) . . . 255, 307, 308
Wille v Liechtenstein (1999) . . . 684, 687
Willem v France (2009) . . . 683, 684
Williams v UK (2009) . . . 55, 62
Willis v UK (2002) . . . 786, 799
Wilson v UK (1998) . . . 375, 382
Wilson, National Union of Journalists v UK
    (2002) . . . 748
Wimmer v Germany (2005) . . . 440
Windisch v Austria (1990) . . . 487
Winer v UK (1986) . . . 401, 553
Wingrove v UK (1996) . . . 612, 657, 669, 670
Wintersberger v Austria (2004) . . . 790
Winterstein and Others v France (2013) . . . 582
Winterwerp v Netherlands (1979) . . . 13, 15, 18,
    288, 289, 301, 302, 305, 324, 325, 327, 353, 355,
    359, 360, 363, 369, 381
Wirtschafts-Trend ZeitschriS en-Verlags
    GmbH v Austria (No 3) (2005) . . . 660, 701
Witold Litwa v Poland (2000) . . . 289, 321, 322,
    323, 369
Witzsch v Germany (2005) . . . 854
Wizerkaniuk v Poland (2011) . . . 666
Wloch v Poland (2000) . . . 318, 467
Wloch v Poland (No 2) (2011) . . . 368
WM v Denmark (1992) . . . 953
Wockel v Germany (1998) . . . 208
Wojtas-Kaleta v Poland (2009) . . . 669, 685,
    687
Wolkenberg v Poland (2007) . . . 149
Women on Waves and Others v Portugal (2009)
    . . . 615, 632
Woonbron Volkshuisvestingsgroep and Others
    v Netherlands (2002) . . . 387
Worm v Austria (1997) . . . 43, 63, 681, 683
Woś v Poland (2005) . . . 24, 82, 383
Woukam Moudefo v France (1988) . . . 360
WP v Poland (2004) . . . 726, 853, 854, 855
WR v Austria (1999) . . . 391
Wynne v UK (1994) . . . 364

X
X v Austria (1960) . . . 456
X v Austria (No 1135/61) (1963) . . . 472
X v Austria (No 1747/62) (1963) . . . 593
X v Austria (No 1753/63) (1965) . . . 603
X v Austria (No 1913/63) (1965) . . . 435
X v Austria (1966) . . . 463
X v Austria (No 2291/64) (1967) . . . 463
X v Austria (No 2370/64) (1967) . . . 471
X v Austria (No 2432/65) (1967) . . . 25
X v Austria (No 2676/65) (1967) . . . 420
X v Austria (1968) . . . 307
X v Austria (No 4161/69) (1970) . . . 307
X v Austria (No 4338/69) (1970) . . . 460
X v Austria (1973) . . . 284
X v Austria (No 6185/73) (1975) . . . 470, 472, 490
X v Austria (No 6317/73) (1975) . . . 65
X v Austria (No 7008/75) (1976) . . . 925
X v Austria (No 7045/75) (1976) . . . 87, 220
X v Austria (No 7720/76) (1978) . . . 494, 500
X v Austria (No 8141/78) (1978) . . . 497
X v Austria (No 8251/78) (1979) . . . 471
X v Austria (No 8278/78) (1979) . . . 221, 292,
    310, 544
X v Austria (1982) . . . 465
X v Austria (No 8893/80) (1983) . . . 410
X v Austria (No 8998/80) (1983) . . . 375
X v Austria (2013) . . . 180, 805, 806, 822
X v Austria and Germany (1974) . . . 959
X v Belgium (No 1028/61) (1961) . . . 920
X v Belgium (No 1065/61) (1961) . . . 920
X v Belgium (1969) . . . 229, 233
X v Belgium (1972) . . . 340
X v Belgium (1973) . . . 334
X v Belgium (1975) . . . 360
X v Belgium (1980) . . . 418
X v Belgium (No 8901/80) (1981) . . . 381, 956
X v Belgium (No 8988/80) (1981) . . . 494
X v Belgium and Netherlands (1975) . . . 567, 762
X v Croatia (2008) . . . 570, 572
X v Denmark (1978) . . . 90
X v Denmark (1981) . . . 489
X v Denmark (1982) . . . 336
X v Denmark (1983) . . . 258
X v Finland (2012) . . . 324, 544
X v France (No 9993/82) (1982) . . . 528
X v France (No 9587/81) (1982) . . . 61
X v France (1992) . . . 94, 95, 382, 442
X v Germany (No 448/59) (1960) . . . 494
X v Germany (No 509/59) (1960) . . . 478
X v Germany (No 530/59) (1960) . . . 920
X v Germany (No 770/60) (1960) . . . 282
X v Germany (No 599/59) (1961) . . . 480
X v Germany (No 914/60) (1961) . . . 461
X v Germany (1962) . . . 460
X v Germany (1963) . . . 410, 497
X v Germany (No 2413/65) (1966) . . . 553
X v Germany (No 2646/65) (1966) . . . 463
X v Germany (1969) . . . 960
X v Germany (No 3925/69) (1970) . . . 387

X v Germany (No 4260/69) (1970) . . . 408
X v Germany (No 5025/71) (1971) . . . 953
X v Germany (No 5207/71) (1971) . . . 214
X v Germany (No 6062/73) (1974) . . . 465
X v Germany (No 6566/74) (1974) . . . 473
X v Germany (No 5935/72) (1975) . . . 550
X v Germany (No 6659/74) (1975) . . . 310
X v Germany (No 7085/75) (1976) . . . 473
X v Germany (No 7175/75) (1976) . . . 758
X v Germany (1977) . . . 958
X v Germany (No 8098/77) (1978) . . . 336
X v Germany (No 8741/79) (1978) . . . 593
X v Germany (No 8410/78) (1979) . . . 281
X v Germany (No 8414/78) (1979) . . . 483
X v Germany (No 8744/79) (1979) . . . 463
X v Germany (1980) . . . 871
X v Germany (No 8334/78) (1981) . . . 525
X v Germany (No 8626/79) (1981) . . . 338
X v Germany (No 8682/79) (1981) . . . 281
X v Germany (No 8769/79) (1981) . . . 431
X v Germany (No 8770/79) (1981) . . . 473
X v Germany (No 1022/82) (1983) . . . 491
X v Germany (No 9546/81) (1983) . . . 310
X v Germany (No 9706/82) (1983) . . . 332
X v Germany (1987) . . . 485
X v Germany (1977) . . . 536
X v Germany (1981) . . . 268
X v Iceland (1976) . . . 525
X v Iceland (1981) . . . 946, 948
X v Ireland (1971) . . . 740, 743
X v Ireland (1973) . . . 209
X v Ireland (1976) . . . 213
X v Ireland (No 9429/81) (1983) . . . 377
X v Ireland (No 9742/82) (1983) . . . 80
X v Italy (1976) . . . 593
X v Latvia (2013) . . . 575
X v Netherlands (1962) . . . 334
X v Netherlands (1966) . . . 334
X v Netherlands (1967) . . . 608
X v Netherlands (1971) . . . 869
X v Netherlands (1974) . . . 926
X v Netherlands (1976) . . . 494
X v Netherlands (No 7721/76) (1977) . . . 497
X v Netherlands (1978) . . . 268
X v Netherlands (1981) . . . 761
X v Norway (1961) . . . 220
X v Sweden (1959) . . . 410
X v Sweden (1968) . . . 644
X v Sweden (1969) . . . 960
X v Sweden (1977) . . . 913
X v Switzerland (1979) . . . 282, 319, 321
X v Switzerland (No 8788/79) (1980) . . . 347
X v Switzerland (No 9012/80) (1980) . . . 270, 330
X v Switzerland (1981) . . . 756
X v Turkey (2012) . . . 264
X v UK (1969) . . . 467
X v UK (No 3898/68) (1970) . . . 755
X v UK (No 4042/69) (1970) . . . 471, 483
X v UK (1971) . . . 505
X v UK (No 4798/71) (1972) . . . 412

X v UK (No 5076/71) (1972) . . . 408, 463, 464
X v UK (No 5124/71) (1972) . . . 462
X v UK (No 5327/71) (1972) . . . 473
X v UK (No 4991/71) (1973) . . . 454
X v UK (No 5506/72) (1973) . . . 489
X v UK (No 5442/72) (1975) . . . 593
X v UK (No 5574/72) (1975) . . . 454
X v UK (No 6084/73) (1975) . . . 653
X v UK (No 6298/73) (1975) . . . 477
X v UK (No 6404/73) (1975) . . . 473
X v UK (No 6564/74) (1975) . . . 760, 761
X v UK (No 6679/74) (1975) . . . 501
X v UK (No 6683/74) (1975) . . . 494
X v UK (No 7096/75) (1975) . . . 924
X v UK (No 5155/71) (1976) . . . 925
X v UK (No 6886/75) (1976) . . . 607
X v UK (No 6956/75) (1976) . . . 82
X v UK (No 7379/76) (1976) . . . 65
X v UK (No 7566/76) (1976) . . . 926
X v UK (No 7366/76) (1977) . . . 434
X v UK (No 7626/76) (1977) . . . 912
X v UK (No 8081/77) (1977) . . . 332
X v UK (No 6728/74) (1978) . . . 377
X v UK (No 7782/77) (1978) . . . 917
X v UK (No 7992/77) (1978) . . . 607
X v UK (No 8208/78) (1978) . . . 387
X v UK (No 8266/78) (1978) . . . 643
X v UK (No 8295/78) (1978) . . . 477
X v UK (No 8010/77) (1979) . . . 334, 913
X v UK (No 8233/78) (1979) . . . 408
X v UK (1980) . . . 264, 362
X v UK (No 8416/78) (Paton case) (1980) . . . 219, 220
X v UK (No 8496/79) (1980) . . . 375
X v UK (1981) . . . 334, 335, 353, 355, 356, 361, 363, 364
X v UK (No 7977/77) (1981) . . . 307, 309, 325, 327
X v UK (No 8160/78) (1981) . . . 593, 595, 598, 810
X v UK (No 8231/78) (1982) . . . 264, 593, 607
X v UK (No 9702/82) (1982) . . . 559
X v UK (1983) . . . 484
X v UK (1992) . . . 487, 489
X v UK (1998) . . . 382, 394
X and Association Z v UK (1971) . . . 643, 645, 646
X and Church of Scientology v Sweden (1979) . . . 597, 603
X and Others v Austria (2013) . . . 526, 527, 550
X and Y v Austria (1978) . . . 471
X and Y v Belgium (1963) . . . 477
X and Y v Belgium (1964) . . . 92
X and Y v Belgium (1982) . . . 643
X and Y v Croatia (2011) . . . 403, 410, 543
X and Y v Germany (1972) . . . 477
X and Y v Ireland (1980) . . . 432, 458
X and Y v Netherlands (1985) . . . 18, 23, 271, 276, 504, 533, 534, 536, 541, 542, 820
X and Y v Sweden (1976) . . . 292
X and Y v Switzerland (1978) . . . 761
X and Y v UK (1977) . . . 761

X Company v UK (1983) . . . 656
X Ltd and Y v UK (1982) . . . 634
X SA v Netherlands (1994) . . . 643
X, Y and Z v Belgium (1977) . . . 656
X, Y and Z v Germany (1976) . . . 925
X, Y and Z v Germany (1982) . . . 909
X, Y and Z v UK (1997) . . . 82, 527, 567
Xenides-Arestis v Turkey (2005) . . . 150, 183, 185, 869
Xenodochiaki SA v Greece (2001) . . . 863, 867
Xiros v Greece (2010) . . . 266

Y
Y v Norway (2003) . . . 465
Y v Russia (2008) . . . 245
Y v UK (1992) . . . 273
Yagci and Sargin v Turkey (1995) . . . 346, 347
Yagmurdereli v Turkey (2001) . . . 76
Yagtzilar v Greece (2001) . . . 404
Yakovenko v Ukraine (2007) . . . 147
Yakovlev v Russia (2005) . . . 411
Yalçin Küçük v Turkey (2002) . . . 635
Yalçinkaya and Others v Turkey (2013) . . . 628
Yanasik v Turkey (1993) . . . 622
Yankov v Bulgaria (2003) . . . 261, 263, 692
Yankov and Others v Bulgaria (2010) . . . 377
Yaremenko v Ukraune (2008) . . . 477
Yaroslavtsev v Russia (2004) . . . 896
Yaşa v Turkey (1998) . . . 43, 91, 92, 214, 215, 218, 223
Yassar Hussain v UK (2006) . . . 464
Yavuz v Austria (2004) . . . 411
Yavuz v Turkey (2000) . . . 448
Yavuz v Turkey (2005) . . . 64
Yazar v Turkey (2002) . . . 631
Yazar, Karataş, Aksoy, and the People's Labour Party (HEP) v Turkey (2002) . . . 385
Yazgül Yilmaz v Turkey (2011) . . . 271
YC v UK (2012) . . . 523, 535, 569, 570, 571, 572
Yefimenko v Russia (2013) . . . 302, 307, 587, 588, 589
Yetiş and Others v Turkey (2010) . . . 163, 892
Yildirim v Italy (2003) . . . 896, 900
Yildirim v Italy (2012) . . . 651
Yildiz v Austria (2002) . . . 577
Yoh-Ekale Mwanje v Belgium (2011) . . . 254, 265
Yoh-Ekale Mwanje v Belgium (2012) . . . 334
Yoldas v Turkey (2010) . . . 478
Yonghong v Portugal (1999) . . . 101
Yordanova and Others v Bulgaria (2012) . . . 528, 529, 580, 582
Young v Ireland (1996) . . . 405
Young v UK (2007) . . . 53
Young, James and Webster v UK (1981) . . . 20, 23, 35, 155, 505, 605, 612, 724, 740, 741, 744, 745, 746, 752, 753, 817
Young, James and Webster v UK (1982) . . . 159
Younger v UK (2003) . . . 211
Youth Initiative for Human Rights v Serbia (2013) . . . 620

Yumak and Sadak v Turkey (2008) . . . 921, 923, 924, 946, 947, 948, 949
Yuri Nikolayevich Ivanov v Ukraine (2010) . . . 188, 190
Yuriy Nikolayevich Ivanov v Ukraine (2009) . . . 150, 397
Yuriy Volkov v Ukraine (2013) . . . 545
Yurttas v Turkey (2004) . . . 264, 475
Yvon v France (2003) . . . 416
YY v Turkey (2010) . . . 537

Z
Z v Austria (No 7950/77) (1980) . . . 466
Z v Finland (1997) . . . 138, 562
Z v Netherlands (1984) . . . 332
Z v Switzerland (1983) . . . 653, 673
Z v UK (1997) . . . 784
Z and Others v UK (2001) . . . 17, 23, 275, 382, 407, 523, 770, 771, 781
Zagaria v Italy (2007) . . . 482
Zaharievi v Bulgaria (2009) . . . 892
Zaicevs v Latvia (2007) . . . 967, 968
Zalli v Albania (2011) . . . 386
Zamir v UK (1983) . . . 362
Zammit Maempel v Malta (2011) . . . 583
Zana v Turkey (1997) . . . 97, 411, 627, 628, 653, 827
Zanatta v France see Aldo and Jean-Baptiste Zanatta v France
Zand v Austria (1978) . . . 458, 448
Zandbergs v Latvia (2011) . . . 350
Zannouti v France (2000) . . . 53
Zaprianov v Bulgaria (2003) . . . 500
Zaprianov v Bulgaria (2004) . . . 376
Zarb Adami v Malta (2006) . . . 283, 284, 786, 787, 788, 789, 792, 793, 799, 809, 815
Zarouali v Belgium (1994) . . . 457
Zarzycki v Poland (2013) . . . 264
Zaunegger v Germany (2009) . . . 801, 806, 807
Zborovsky v Slovakia (2012) . . . 72
Zdanoka v Latvia (2004) . . . 852
Ždanoka v Latvia (2006) . . . 513, 518, 852, 921, 922, 923, 924, 939, 940, 941, 942

Zehentner v Austria (2009) . . . 84, 529, 582, 885
Zehnalová and Zehnal v Czech Republic (2002) . . . 525, 546, 808
Zeïbek v Greece (2009) . . . 798, 868, 882
Zelisse v Netherlands (1989) . . . 387
Zemanová v Czech Rep (2006) . . . 404
ZH v Hungary (2012) . . . 263, 335
Zhechev v Bulgaria (2007) . . . 727, 731, 738
Zhigalev v Russia (2006) . . . 865
Zhovner v Ukraine (2004) . . . 188
Zhuk v Ukraine (2010) . . . 414
Žiačik v Slovakia (2003) . . . 444
Ziegler v Switzerland (2002) . . . 396
Zielinski and Pradal & Gonzalez v France (1999) . . . 429
Zigarella v Italy (2002) . . . 971
Ziliberberg v Moldova (2004) . . . 716
Ziliberberg v Moldova (2005) . . . 375, 410, 411
Ziliberberg v Moldova (2007) . . . 714
Ziliberberg v Moldova (2009) . . . 722
Zimmermann and Steiner v Switzerland (1983) . . . 444, 505
Živić v Serbia (2011) . . . 71
Znamenskaya v Russia (2005) . . . 565
Zolatas v Greece (2013) . . . 871
Zollmann v UK (2003) . . . 405
Zolotukhin v Russia (2009) . . . 373, 374, 376
Zontul v Greece (2012) . . . 239, 277
Zoon v Netherlands (2000) . . . 473
Zouhar v Czech Republic (2005) . . . 573
Zu Leiningen v Germany (2005) . . . 755
Zubayrayev v Russia (2008) . . . 146
Zuckerstatter and Reschenhofer v Austria (2004) . . . 377
Zumtobel v Austria (1993) . . . 393, 394, 438
Zuyev v Russia (2013) . . . 335
Zvolský and Zvolská v Czech Republic (2002) . . . 877, 893, 894
Związek Nauczycielstwa Polskiego v Poland (2004) . . . 403
Zylkov v Russia (2011) . . . 404

NUMERICAL LIST OF UNNAMED
EUROPEAN COMMISSION OF
HUMAN RIGHTS CASES

715/60) . . . 208
1287/61 . . . 221

48321/99) . . . 760
39678/09 . . . 58

LIST OF NATIONAL COURT CASES

A v B plc (2003) . . . 661
A (FC) v Secretary of State for the Home
    Department (2004) . . . 28, 831, 832, 844, 845

Baker v Carr (1962) . . . 684
Barrett v Enfield LBC (1999) . . . 407

Griggs v Duke Power Co (1971) . . . 815

JJ v SSHD (2006) . . . 291

Malone v Metropolitan Police Comr (1979) . . . 506
McCaughey and another, Re [2011] UKSC
    20 . . . 98
Mendoza v Ghaidan (2004) . . . 803
Minister of Home Affairs v Fisher (1980) . . . 35
Miranda v Arizona (1966) . . . 423, 475

New York Times v Sullivan (1964) . . . 694

P and Q (by their litigation friend, the Official
    Solicitor) (Appellants) v Surrey County
    Council (Respondent) (2014) . . . 294
Pratt v AG for Jamaica (1993) . . . 35
Preston v Wandsworth Borough Council and
    Lord President of the Council (2011) and
    (2012) . . . 928

R v Bieber (2009) . . . 260
R v Davis (2008) . . . 487

R v H and C (2004) . . . 417
R v Horncastle (2009) . . . 28, 170
R v Jones (2002) . . . 411
R v Radio Authority, ex p Bull (1998) . . . 646
R v Secretary of State for Work and Pensions, ex
    p Carson (2005) . . . 791, 796
R (Al-Skeini) v Secretary of State for Defence
    (2005) . . . 28
R (Amin) v Secretary of State for the Home
    Department (2003) . . . 215, 234
R (Anderson) v Secretary of State for the Home
    Department (2002) . . . 365
R (Chester) v Secretary of State for Justice &
    McGeoch v Lord President of the Council
    (2013) . . . 925
R (Hicks and Others) v Commissioner of Met
    Police (2014) . . . 316

Secretary of State for the Home Department v
    AF (2009) . . . 359
Secretary of State for the Home Department v
    AP (2010) . . . 290
Secretary of State for the Home Department v JJ
    (2007) . . . 290
State v Ncube (1992) . . . 35

Teare v O'Callaghan (1981) . . . 31

Wright v Secretary of State for Health
    (2006) . . . 522

LIST OF INTERNATIONAL COURT
OF JUSTICE CASES

ELSI case (US v Italy) (1989) . . . 887
Jurisdictional Immunities of the State case (Germany v Italy) (2012) . . . 406

LIST OF UN HUMAN RIGHTS
COMMITTEE CASES

Leirvag v Norway (2004) . . . 78, 915
Toonen v Australia (1994) . . . 803

LIST OF EUROPEAN COURT
OF JUSTICE CASES

ERT v DEP and Sotirios Kouvelas (1991) ... 32
Herbert Karner Industrie-Auktionen GmbH v
   Troostwijk GesmbH (2004) ... 635

Netherlands v Council (1996) ... 620
P v S and Cornwall CC (1996) ... 32
WWF UK v Commission (1997) ... 620

LIST OF EUROPEAN COMMITTEE OF
SOCIAL RIGHTS CASES

International Association of Autism-Europe v France (2004) ... 918

LIST OF I-ACTHR CASES

Claude Reyes v Chile (2006) ... 674

PART I

THE EUROPEAN CONVENTION ON HUMAN RIGHTS IN CONTEXT

1 The European Convention on Human Rights in Context 3

1

THE EUROPEAN CONVENTION ON HUMAN RIGHTS IN CONTEXT

1. BACKGROUND

The European Convention on Human Rights[1] was adopted in 1950. It was drafted within the Council of Europe, an international organization that was formed after the Second World War in the course of the first post-war attempt to unify Europe. The reason for the Convention was partly the need to elaborate upon the obligations of Council membership.[2] More generally, the Convention was a response to current and past events in Europe. It stemmed from the wish to provide a bulwark against communism, which had spread from the Soviet Union into European states behind the Iron Curtain after the Second World War. The Convention provided both a symbolic statement of the principles for which West European states stood and a remedy that might protect those states from communist subversion. It was also a reaction to the serious human rights violations that Europe had witnessed during the Second World War. It was believed that the Convention would serve as an alarm that would bring such large-scale violations of human rights to the attention of other West European states in time for action to be taken to suppress them. In practice, this last function of the Convention has remained largely dormant, playing a role so far in just a small number of inter-state applications and cases arising out

---

[1] 87 UNTS 103; ETS 5. See generally Caflisch, Callewaert, Liddell, Mahoney, Villiger, eds, *Liber Amicorum—Luzius Wildhaber: Human Rights—Strasbourg Views*, 2007; Christoffersen and Madsen, eds, *The European Court of Human Rights: Between Law and Politics*, 2007; Costa, *La Cour européene des droits de l'homme*, 2013; Greer, *The European Convention on Human Rights*, 2006 (hereafter *European Convention*); Leach, *Taking a Case to the European Court of Human Rights*, 3rd edn, 2011; Macdonald, Matscher, and Petzold, eds, *The European System for the Protection of Human Rights*, 1993 (hereafter *European System*); Mahoney, Matscher, Petzold, and Wildhaber, eds, *Protecting Human Rights: the European Perspective: Studies in honour of Rolv Ryssdal*, 2000 (hereafter *Ryssdal Mélanges*); Matscher and Petzold, eds, *Protecting Human Rights: the European Dimension: Studies in Honour of Gérard J Wiarda*, 1988 (hereafter *Wiarda Mélanges*); Reid, *A Practitioner's Guide to the European Convention on Human Rights*, 4th edn, 2011; Sharpe, ed, *The Conscience of Europe*, 2011 and addenda; Van Dijk and Van Hoof, *Theory and Practice of the European Convention on Human Rights*, 4th edn, 2006; White and Ovey, *Jacobs and White: The European Convention on Human Rights*, 5th edn, 2010. On the drafting of the Convention, see Bates, *The Evolution of the European Convention on Human Rights*, 2010; Simpson, *Human Rights and the End of Empire: Britain and the Genesis of the European Convention*, 2001; and Wicks, PL 438 (2000).

[2] Under Article 3, Statute of the Council of Europe 1949, 87 UNTS 103; ETS 1, a member state 'must accept the principles of the rule of law and of the enjoyment by all persons within its jurisdiction of human rights and fundamental freedoms'. The importance of the Convention's role in giving meaning to these obligations has been highlighted in recent years by the fact that becoming a party to the Convention is now a political obligation of membership of the Council: Parliamentary Assembly Resolution 1031 (1994), para 9.

of the state of emergency in Turkey.[3] The Convention has instead been used primarily to raise questions of particular violations of human rights in states that basically conform to its requirements and are representative of the 'common heritage of political traditions, ideals, freedoms and the rule of law' to which the Convention Preamble refers, or, in the case of post-communist member states, that, upon becoming Convention parties, committed themselves to move in this direction. Increasingly, it has evolved in the direction of being a European bill of rights, with the European Court of Human Rights having a role with some similarities to that of a constitutional court in a national legal system.[4]

The Convention entered into force in 1953 and has been ratified by all forty-seven member states of the Council of Europe,[5] whose total population of over 800 million people is protected by it. The number of contracting parties increased greatly following the fall of the Berlin Wall in 1989 and the disintegration of the Socialist Federal Republic of Yugoslavia in the early 1990s. As a consequence largely of the policy of admitting Russia and other post-communist states to the Council of Europe in the period that followed these changes, the number of states parties rose from twenty-two in 1989 to forty-seven in 2008. As will be seen, this development, while in other ways welcome, has introduced new problems of interpretation and application of the Convention for the Court and greatly increased its workload.[6]

The substantive guarantee in the Convention has been supplemented by the addition of further rights by the First,[7] Fourth,[8] Sixth,[9] Seventh,[10] Twelfth,[11] and Thirteenth[12] Protocols to the Convention that are binding upon those states that have ratified them. There have also been other Protocols that have amended the enforcement machinery. The most recent Protocols of this second kind are the Eleventh[13] and Fourteenth[14] Protocols, which introduced fundamental reforms to the enforcement machinery of the Convention. The Fifteenth[15] and Sixteenth[16] Protocols were adopted in 2013; they (mostly) amend the

---

[3] On the Convention and gross violations, see Kamminga, 12 NQHR 153 (1994); Reidy, Hampson, and Boyle, 15 NQHR 161 (1997) (Turkey); and Sardaro, 2003 EHRLR 601. On state applications, see Prebensen, 20 HRLJ 446 (1999).   [4] See section 9.III.

[5] These are Albania, Andorra, Armenia, Austria, Azerbaijan, Belgium, Bosnia and Herzegovina, Bulgaria, Croatia, Cyprus, Czech Republic, Denmark, Estonia, Finland, France, Georgia, Germany, Greece, Hungary, Iceland, Ireland, Italy, Latvia, Liechtenstein, Lithuania, Luxembourg, Malta, Moldova, Monaco, Montenegro, the Netherlands, Norway, Poland, Portugal, Romania, Russia, San Marino, Serbia, Slovakia, Slovenia, Spain, Sweden, Switzerland, the former Yugoslav Republic of Macedonia (FYRM), Turkey, Ukraine, and the UK. The European (or part European) states of Belarus, Kazakhstan, and the Vatican City are not Council of Europe members. On the application of the Convention to Kosovo, see Knoll, 68 ZaoRV 431 (2008).

[6] See Greer, *European Convention*, p 105 and Ch 3; Gross, 7 EJIL 89 (1996); Harmsen, 5 IJHR 18 (2001); and Schokkenbroek and Zeimele, 75 NJB 1914 (2000).

[7] 213 UNTS 262; ETS 9. Adopted 1952. In force 1954. Forty-five parties: all Convention parties except Monaco and Switzerland.

[8] 1469 UNTS 263; ETS 46. Adopted 1963. In force 1968. Forty-three parties: all Convention parties except Greece, Switzerland, Turkey, and the UK.

[9] ETS 114. Adopted 1983. In force 1985. Forty-six parties: all Convention parties except Russia.

[10] ETS 117. Adopted 1984. In force 1988. Forty-three parties: all Convention parties except Germany, Netherlands, Turkey, and the UK.

[11] ETS 177; 8 IHRR 300 (2000). Adopted 2000. In force 2005. Eighteen parties. The UK is not a party.

[12] ETS 187; 9 IHRR 884 (2002). Adopted 2002. In force 2003. Forty-three parties: all Convention parties except Armenia, Azerbaijan, Poland, and Russia.

[13] ETS 155; 1–3 IHRR 206 (1994). Adopted 1994. In force 1998. Ratified by all Convention parties. See Caflisch, 6 HRLR 403 (2006).

[14] ETS 194; 9 IHRR 884 (2002). Adopted 2004. In force 2010. Ratified by all Convention parties.

[15] ETS 213. Not in force. Ratification by all Convention parties required. Six ratifications so far.

[16] ETS 214. Not in force. Ten ratifications required. None so far.

enforcement machinery and provide for national courts to seek advisory opinions from the European Court respectively.

The Convention is a part of a network of international human rights treaties of universal or regional application. It is the regional counterpart to the International Covenant on Civil and Political Rights 1966 (ICCPR), to which all Convention parties are parties.[17] At the regional level, it is comparable with the American Convention on Human Rights 1969[18] and the African Charter on Human and Peoples' Rights 1981.[19] As with these treaties, the Convention protects rights first spelt out in the Universal Declaration of Human Rights 1948.[20]

2. THE SUBSTANTIVE GUARANTEE

The human rights in the Universal Declaration are commonly divided into civil and political rights, on the one hand, and economic, social, and cultural rights, on the other. Civil and political rights are those that derive from the natural rights philosophy of the late eighteenth century in Europe. Economic, social, and cultural rights[21] appeared with the emergence of socialist governments in the early twentieth century. The European Convention protects predominantly civil and political rights.[22] This was a matter of priorities and tactics. While it was not disputed that economic, social, and cultural rights required protection too, the immediate need was for a short, non-controversial text which governments could accept at once, while the tide for human rights was strong. Given the values dominant within Western Europe, this meant limiting the Convention for the most part to the civil and political rights that were 'essential for a democratic way of life';[23] economic, social, and cultural rights were too problematic and were left for separate and later treatment.[24] The Convention, including its Protocols, protects most civil and political rights, but not all. It does not directly guarantee the rights of members of minority groups,[25] freedom from racist or other propaganda or the right to recognition as a person

---

[17] 999 UNTS 171. The ICCPR provides for an optional right of individual communication. All Convention parties have accepted it except Monaco, Switzerland, and the UK.

[18] 1144 UNTS 123. In force 1978. Twenty-three parties.

[19] 1520 UNTS 143; 21 ILM 59 (1981). In force 1986. Fifty-three parties. The African Charter is not limited to civil and political rights.   [20] GA Res 217A (III), GAOR, 3rd Sess, Part 1, resns, p 71.

[21] Examples are the rights to work, to health, and to take part in cultural life respectively.

[22] The Convention strays into the field of economic, social, and cultural rights with its guarantees of the rights to property and education (Articles 1 and 2, First Protocol) and of equality between the spouses (Article 5, Seventh Protocol). There are also certain overlaps between the two categories in the case of freedom from forced labour (Article 4, Convention), the right to respect for family life (Article 8, Convention), and freedom of association (Article 11, Convention). The non-discrimination guarantee in the Twelfth Protocol applies generally. In *Airey v Ireland* A 32 (1979); 2 EHRR 305 para 26, the Court stated that there is no 'watertight division' separating Convention rights from economic and social rights. See Pellonpää, *European System*, Ch 37 and Warbrick, in Baderin and McCorquodale, eds, *Economic, Social and Cultural Rights in Action*, 2007, Ch 10.

[23] M Teitgen, CE Consult.Ass, Debates, 1st Session, p 408, 19 August 1949.

[24] Economic and social rights are now protected by the 1961 European Social Charter, 529 UNTS 89; ETS 35 and the 1996 Revised European Social Charter, 2151 UNTS 279; ETS 163; 3 IHRR 726 (1996). Forty-three Council members are parties to the Charter or the Revised Charter or both. The missing members are Liechtenstein, Monaco, San Marino, and Switzerland.

[25] These are the subject of the Council of Europe Framework Convention for the Protection of National Minorities 1995, 2151 UNTS 246; ETS 157; 2 IHRR 217 (1995). In force 1998. Thirty-nine parties, including the UK. See also the European Charter for Regional or Minority Languages 1992, 2044 UNTS 246; ETS 148. In force 1998. Twenty-five parties, including the UK. Neither of these Conventions has a right of petition. Some protection is indirectly afforded by the Convention to members of minority groups, through eg the non-discrimination guarantees in Article 14, Convention and the Twelfth Protocol to the Convention.

before the law. These rights are protected by the ICCPR, which also contains fuller guarantees of the rights to be treated with 'humanity' and 'dignity' while in detention,[26] to a fair trial,[27] and to participate in public life.[28] The ICCPR also prohibits derogation from its obligations in time of war or public emergency in the case of more rights than does the European Convention.[29] In addition, some Convention guarantees are found only in Optional Protocols which not all parties have accepted.[30] However, the generally worded guarantees in the Convention text have been interpreted purposively so as to remedy some, at least, of these defects.[31]

3. THE STRASBOURG ENFORCEMENT MACHINERY

Compared to most other international human rights treaties, the Convention has very strong enforcement mechanisms. It provides for both state and individual applications.[32] Under Article 33, any party may bring an application alleging a breach of the Convention by another party that has ratified it. In addition, and considerably more important in practice, under Article 34 all parties accept the right of 'any person, non-governmental organisation or group of individuals', regardless of nationality,[33] claiming to be a victim of a breach of the Convention to bring an application against it.[34] Under Protocol 11, both state and individual applications go to the European Court of Human Rights,[35] which is a permanent court composed of full-time judges. The Court decides whether the application should be admitted for consideration on the merits.[36] If it is admitted, the Court decides in a judgment that is binding in international law whether there has been a breach of the Convention.[37] The execution by parties of Court judgments against them

---

[26] Article 3, Convention covers the more extreme cases.

[27] Some Article 6 'fair trial' omissions are made good by the Seventh Protocol for the parties to it. Even with the Seventh Protocol, the Convention contains a less extensive guarantee for juveniles and of the right to appeal in criminal cases.

[28] Article 3, First Protocol is narrower than Article 25, ICCPR.

[29] See Article 4, ICCPR. The Article 4, ICCPR prohibitions may, however, apply under the Convention by virtue of Article 15(1), Convention.

[30] The most important of these is the free-standing non-discrimination guarantee in the Twelfth Protocol.

[31] Eg, freedom from self-incrimination (in Article 14(3)(g) ICCPR) has been read into Article 6 Convention.

[32] Article 52 also provides for occasional reports by states on their compliance with the Convention, as and when requested. This procedure has seldom been used. Most recently, in 2005 it provided the vehicle for requesting from parties information about rendition in torture cases. Before that, it had been used just five times requesting reports by all parties on compliance with the Convention generally and on two other occasions, requesting a report from Russia on Chechnya and from Moldova on the suspension of a political party. See http://www.coe.int.

[33] An application may be brought by both nationals and non-nationals of the respondent state.

[34] This right was made compulsory by the Eleventh Protocol as of 1998; before then, it was only applicable as against those parties that made a declaration accepting it.

[35] The Court has its seat at Strasbourg, France, and operates within the framework of the Council of Europe, which has its headquarters there. The Court is totally distinct from the European Court of Justice, which has its seat in Luxembourg and is the Court of the European Union.

[36] There is also provision for the friendly settlement of cases.

[37] Prior to the Eleventh Protocol, in force 1998, there was a second Strasbourg institution, the European Commission of Human Rights, composed of independent experts, which decided on the admissibility of state and individual applications and assisted with friendly settlements. It also adopted non-legally binding reports on the merits of admitted cases, which could, if the respondent state accepted the Court's jurisdiction, be referred to the Court by the Commission or a state with a recognized interest for a legally binding judgment, or—if the respondent state was a party to the Ninth Protocol—by the individual applicant. If no such reference was made, the case was decided by the Committee of Ministers of the Council of Europe. Both the Commission and the Court were part-time bodies before 1998.

is monitored by the Committee of Ministers of the Council of Europe, which is composed of government representatives of all of the member states.

4. THE INTERPRETATION OF THE CONVENTION

I. THE GENERAL APPROACH

As a treaty, the Convention must be interpreted according to the international law rules on the interpretation of treaties.[38] These are to be found in the Vienna Convention on the Law of Treaties 1969.[39] The basic rule is that a treaty 'shall be interpreted in good faith in accordance with the ordinary meaning to be given to the terms of the treaty in their context and in the light of its object and purpose'.[40] A good example of the use of this rule is the case of *Luedicke, Belkacem and Koç v Germany*.[41] There the Court adopted the 'ordinary meaning' of the words '*gratuitement*' and 'free' in the two authentic language texts[42] of Article 6(3)(e), which it found 'not contradicted by the context of the sub-paragraph' and 'confirmed by the object and purpose of Article 6'. The terms in the Convention have their 'ordinary' meaning. Accordingly, words such as 'degrading' (Article 3) have been understood in their dictionary sense.[43]

II. EMPHASIS UPON THE OBJECT AND PURPOSE OF THE CONVENTION

In accordance with the Vienna Convention, considerable emphasis has been placed on the interpretation of the Convention through a teleological approach, ie one that seeks to realize its 'object and purpose'. This has been identified in general terms as 'the protection of individual human rights'[44] and the maintenance and promotion of 'the ideals and values of a democratic society'.[45] As to the latter, it has been recognized that 'democracy' supposes 'pluralism,

---

[38] See eg, *Golder v UK* A 18 (1978); 1 EHRR 524 para 29 PC, and *Johnston v Ireland* A 112 (1986); 9 EHRR 203 para 51 PC. See Rosakis, in *Valticos Mélanges*, 487. On the interpretation of the Convention generally, see Golsong, *European System*, Ch 8; Greer, *European Convention*, Ch 4; Letsas, *A Theory of Interpretation of the European Convention on Human Rights*, 2007.   [39] 1155 UNTS 331. See Articles 31–3.

[40] Article 31(1), Vienna Convention. The 'context' of a treaty includes its preamble and any agreement or instrument relating to and made in connection with it: Article 31(2). The subsequent practice of the parties to a treaty and any relevant rules of international law shall be taken into account 'together with the context': Article 31(3). On the use of the *travaux préparatoires*, see section 4.XIII, 'Recourse to the *travaux préparatoires*'.   [41] A 29 (1978); 2 EHRR 149 para 46.

[42] Ie, the English and French texts. Where, as was not the case in the *Luedicke* case, the two authentic texts of the Convention differ in their meaning, they must be interpreted in such a way as to 'reconcile them as far as possible': Article 33(4), Vienna Convention. If they cannot be reconciled, the 'object and purpose' becomes decisive: see *Wemhoff v Germany* A 7 (1968); 1 EHRR 55 and *Brogan v UK* A 145-B (1988); 11 EHRR 117 PC.   [43] *Tyrer v UK* A 26 (1978); 2 EHRR 1.

[44] *Soering v UK* A 161 (1949); 11 EHRR 439 para 87 PC. Cf the '*Belgian Linguistics*' case A 6 (1968); 1 EHRR 241 PC.

[45] *Kjeldsen, Busk Madsen, and Pedersen v Denmark* A 23 (1976); 1 EHRR 711 para 53. Both of the considerations mentioned are confirmed by the Convention Preamble. The Preamble also identifies 'the achievement of greater unity between its Members' as the aim of the Council of Europe. See Gearty, 51 NILQ 381 (2000); Harvey, 29 ELR 407 (2004); Marks, 66 BYIL 209 (1995); and Mowbray, 1999 PL 703. The commitment to democracy was crucial in *United Communist Party of Turkey v Turkey* 1998-I; 26 EHRR 121.

tolerance and broadmindedness'.[46] The primary importance of the 'object and purpose' of the Convention was strikingly illustrated in *Golder v UK*.[47] There the Court read the right of access to a court into the fair trial guarantee in Article 6. It did so, in the absence of clear wording in the text to the contrary, mainly by reference to guidance as to the 'object and purpose' of the Convention to be found in its Preamble.[48] This indicated, *inter alia*, that the drafting states were resolved to 'take the first steps for the collective enforcement of certain of the rights stated in the Universal Declaration' in furtherance of the rule of law. As the Court stated, one could not suppose compliance with the rule of law without the possibility of taking legal disputes to court. What is remarkable is that the Court has extended the reach of the Convention in many other contexts, too, apparently by reference to its object and purpose. Article 8 is a striking example, with the right to privacy in particular having an almost limitless scope.

The Court also confirmed in the *Golder* case its earlier pronouncement in *Wemhoff v Germany*[49] that '[g]iven that it is a law-making treaty, it is also necessary to seek the interpretation that is most appropriate in order to realize the aim and achieve the object of the treaty, and not that which would restrict to the greatest possible degree the obligations undertaken by the parties'. This approach was forcefully opposed by Judge Fitzmaurice in his separate opinion in the *Golder* case. Judge Fitzmaurice argued, *inter alia*, that the 'heavy inroads' made by the Convention into an area previously within a state's domestic jurisdiction, namely the treatment of its own nationals, demanded 'a cautious and conservative interpretation'. Such an argument, which emphasizes the character of the Convention as a contract by which sovereign states agree to limitations upon their sovereignty, has now totally given way to an approach that focuses instead upon the Convention's law-making character and its role as a European human rights guarantee that must be interpreted so as to permit its development with time.

It is in this last connection that statements to the effect that the Convention is 'an instrument of European public order (ordre public)'[50] are relevant. They signify that in the interpretation and application of the Convention, the overriding consideration is not that the Convention creates 'reciprocal engagements between contracting states', but that it imposes 'objective obligations' upon them for the protection of human rights in Europe,[51] with the Convention evolving in the direction of becoming Europe's constitutional bill of rights.[52]

III. DYNAMIC OR EVOLUTIVE INTERPRETATION

It follows from the emphasis placed upon the 'object and purpose' of the Convention that it must be given a dynamic or evolutive interpretation.[53] Thus, in *Tyrer v UK*,[54] the Court

---

[46] *Handyside v UK* A 24 (1976); 1 EHRR 737 para 49 PC. Cf *Dudgeon v UK* A 45 (1981); 4 EHRR 149 para 53 PC.

[47] A 18 (1975); 1 EHRR 524 PC.

[48] The Court also referred to the emphasis on the rule of law in the Statute of the Council of Europe (Preamble, Article 3).

[49] A 7 (1968) p 23; 1 EHRR 55 at 75. Cf, *Delcourt v Belgium* A 11 (1970); 1 EHRR 355 para 25, concerning Article 6 in particular.

[50] *Loizidou v Turkey* (Preliminary Objections) A 310 (1995); 20 EHRR 99 para 93. Cf, *Austria v Italy No 788/60*, 4 YB 112 at 140 (1961) and *Chrysostomos, Papachrysostomou and Loizidou v Turkey Nos 15299/89, 15300/89 and 15318/89*, 68 DR 216 at 242 (1991).

[51] *Ireland v UK* A 25 (1978); 2 EHRR 25 para 239 PC. The 'objective' character of the obligations manifested itself in *Austria v Italy No 788/60*, 4 YB 112 (1961), in that Austria was permitted to question Italian conduct that occurred before Austria became a party to the Convention.

[52] See further below, section.

[53] The term 'evolutive', rather than 'dynamic', is sometimes used by the Court: see eg, *Johnston v Ireland* A 112 (1986); 9 EHRR 203 para 53 PC. On the interpretative and law-making role of the Court, and formerly the Commission, generally, see Gearty, 52 CLJ 89 (1993); Mahoney, 11 HRLJ 57 (1990); and Stavros, *The Guarantees for Accused Persons under Article 6 of the European Convention on Human Rights*, 1993, pp 340–50 (hereafter Stavros).

[54] A 26 (1978); 2 EHRR 1 para 31.

stated that the Convention is 'a living instrument which...must be interpreted in the light of present-day conditions'. Accordingly, the Court could not 'but be influenced by the developments and commonly accepted standards in the penal policy of the member states of the Council of Europe' when considering whether judicial corporal punishment was consistent with Article 3. What was determinative, the Court stated, were the standards currently accepted in European society, not those prevalent when the Convention was adopted. In terms of the intentions of the drafting states, the emphasis is therefore upon their general rather than their particular intentions in 1950.[55] Other decisions that follow the *Tyrer* approach have reflected changes in the policy of the law in European states resulting from changed social attitudes towards, for example, children born out of wedlock[56] and homosexuals,[57] and from other policy developments.[58] However, the Convention may not be interpreted in response to 'present-day conditions' so as to introduce into it a right that it was not intended to include when the Convention was drafted. For this reason, Article 12, which guarantees the right to marry, could not be interpreted as including a right to divorce, even though such a right is now generally recognized in Europe.[59] In this way, a line is sought to be drawn between judicial interpretation, which is permissible, and judicial legislation, which is not. Mahoney[60] has suggested that, with this distinction in mind, the Court tends to emphasize incremental, rather than sudden change. The closed shop cases[61] are good examples of this gradualist approach. However, as in national law, the line between judicial interpretation and legislation can be a difficult one to draw, particularly in the case of generally worded provisions. Decisions can be seen either as instances of judicial creativity that move the Convention into distinct areas beyond its intended domain, or as the elaboration of rights that are already protected. For example, the Court's finding of positive obligations for states throughout the Convention[62] and, more particularly, its application of Article 3 to cases of removal of individuals from a state's territory[63] and of Article 8 to environmental matters,[64] can either be seen as the discovery of obligations that were always implicit in the guarantees concerned or as the addition of new obligations for states.

When deciding a case by reference to the dynamic character of the Convention, the Court must make a judgment as to the point at which a change in the policy of the law has achieved sufficiently wide acceptance in European states to affect the meaning of the Convention. In the course of doing so, the Court has generally been cautious, preferring to follow state practice rather than to precipitate a new approach. But the Court does not necessarily wait until only the respondent state remains out of line before it recognizes a

---

[55] Cf Mahoney, 11 HRLJ 57 at 70 (1990). See also Nicol, 2000 PL 152.

[56] *Marckx v Belgium* A 31 (1979); 2 EHRR 330 PC.

[57] *Dudgeon v UK* A 45 (1981); 4 EHRR 149 PC. Cf, *L and V v Austria* 2003-I; 36 EHRR 1022.

[58] See eg, *Soering v UK* A 161 (1989); 11 EHRR 439 PC (death penalty); *Sigurjonsson v Iceland* A 264 (1993); 16 EHRR 462 (closed shops); *Stafford v UK* 2002-IV; 35 EHRR 1121 GC (life sentences). The Convention enforcement machinery provisions are also to be interpreted dynamically: *Loizidou v Turkey (Preliminary Objections)* A 310 (1995); 20 EHRR 99 para 71.

[59] *Johnston v Ireland* A 112 (1986); 9 EHRR 203 PC. *Quaere* whether the sensitive nature of the divorce question in Ireland at the time was another factor in the *Johnston* case.

[60] 11 HRLJ 57 at 60 (1990). Mahoney draws an analogy with the judicial activism and judicial restraint distinction found in the jurisprudence of the US Supreme Court.

[61] See Chapter 15, section 4.III. Cf, the gradual extension of Article 6(3) to pre-trial criminal proceedings. See also the Court's approach to different retirement ages for men and women in *Stec v UK* 2006-VI; 43 EHRR 1017 GC.

[62] See generally Mowbray, *The Development of Positive Obligations under the European Convention on Human Rights by the European Court of Human Rights*, 2004.

[63] See *Soering v UK* A 161 (1989); 11 EHRR 439 PC.

[64] See *Lopez Ostra v Spain* A 303-C (1994); 20 EHRR 227.

new approach.[65] For example, in *Marckx v Belgium*[66] the Court relied upon a new approach to the status of children born out of wedlock that had been adopted in the law of the 'great majority', but not all, of Council of Europe states by 1979. The Court adopted a somewhat different and less demanding approach than this in the case of *Goodwin (Christine) v UK*.[67] In a series of transsexual cases from the mid-1980s onwards, the Court had indicated that it was not satisfied that a common new European standard requiring the full recognition in law of the new sexual identity of post-operative transsexuals had emerged; standards were still in transition with 'little common ground between the contracting states'.[68] However, in the *Goodwin* case, while recognizing that there remained no 'common European approach' on the matter, the Court was persuaded to overturn its earlier rulings by 'clear and uncontested evidence of a continuing international trend', both in Europe and elsewhere, in the direction of 'legal recognition of the new sexual identity of post-operative transsexuals'. It thus referred to national standards around the world, as well as in Europe, and did not require that a 'great majority' of European states follow the new approach.[69]

IV. RELIANCE UPON EUROPEAN NATIONAL LAW AND INTERNATIONAL STANDARDS

The question whether the Court should be influenced by the law in European states in its interpretation of the Convention is relevant not only in contexts in which the policy of the law has changed. The question may arise when the Court has to decide how rigorously to interpret the requirements of the Convention in other circumstances also. Here, too, any European consensus that exists has had a considerable impact upon the Court's jurisprudence.[70] For example, the Court's ringing pronouncements on the importance of freedom of speech and of the press in a democratic society[71] stem from a confident conviction as to long-standing values that generally underpin European society. Equally clearly, the easy incorporation into Article 1, First Protocol of a compensation requirement for the taking of the property of nationals, followed from the 'legal systems of the contracting states'.[72] And in *S and Marper v UK*[73] the Court was strongly influenced by the fact that England, Wales and Northern Ireland appeared to be 'the only jurisdictions in the Council of Europe to allow the indefinite retention of fingerprints and DNA

---

[65] A state that is entirely on its own is particularly at risk of an adverse judgment if its practice offends common European standards relevant to human rights: see eg, the *Tyrer* case, mentioned earlier (corporal punishment) and *Unal Tekeli v Turkey* 2004-X; 42 EHRR 1185 (married women's surnames). For an exception, see *EB v France* hudoc (2008); 47 EHRR 509 GC.

[66] A 31 (1979); 2 EHRR 330 para 41 PC. Cf *Dudgeon v UK* A 45 (1981); 4 EHRR 149 PC and *Hirst v UK (No 2)* 2005-IX; 42 EHRR 849 GC.

[67] 2002-VI; 35 EHRR 447 para 85 GC.

[68] *Cossey v UK* A 184 (1990); 13 EHRR 622 para 40.

[69] A 'majority', but not the 'great majority', of member states provided for full legal recognition: *Sheffield and Horsham v UK* 1998-V; 27 EHRR 163 paras 35, 57 and *Goodwin (Christine) v UK* 2002-VI; 35 EHRR 447 GC.

[70] See Dzehistarou, Public Law (2011) 534; Dzehistarou, 2 German LJ 1730 (2011); Helfer, 26 Cornell ILJ 133 (1993); Heringa, 3 Maastricht JECL 108 (1996).

[71] See *Lingens v Austria* A 103 (1981); 8 EHRR 407 para 41 PC.

[72] *James v UK* A 98 (1986); 8 EHRR 123 para 54 PC. Other examples include *A v UK* 2002-X; 36 EHRR 917 (parliamentary immunity) and *Bryan v UK* A 335-A (1995); 21 EHRR 342 (judicial review of administrative action).

[73] 2008-; 48 EHRR 1169 GC. See also *Demir and Baykara v Turkey* 2008-; 48 EHRR 1272 para 151 GC ('vast majority' of European states recognized civil servants' right to collective bargaining).

material' of any criminal suspect: there was a 'strong consensus' to the contrary, with the 'great majority' of jurisdictions with DNA databases, including Scotland, requiring that they be destroyed. Former Judge Van der Meersch[74] has pointed to the paradox of taking standards in national law into account when interpreting an international treaty whose purpose is to control national law. The convincing justification that he provides is that there is a necessarily close relationship between the Convention standards and the European 'common law' by which they are inspired. Another reason may be that an interpretation of the Convention that deviated substantially from general European practice would undermine state confidence in the Convention system and thereby threaten its continued success or acceptance by states.[75] Generally, the Court's reliance upon any European consensus is acceptable in that it is likely to be in accordance with recognized human rights standards, as in the case of the emphasis placed upon freedom of speech. Even so, the Court needs to be aware that government and individual interests do not always coincide and that a practice may not be acceptable in human rights terms simply because it is generally followed.

The Court increasingly refers to other sources of international human rights standards when interpreting the Convention in its judgments. Thus the Court refers to other human rights treaties and other relevant instruments—both of the Council of Europe itself[76] and of other international institutions[77]—and decisions by bodies applying them.[78] A treaty may be referred to whether the respondent state is a party to it or not.[79] The Court also interprets the Convention, as a treaty, against the background of public international law generally.[80] This is all to be welcomed in ensuring a uniformity of approach where this is appropriate.

In the absence of a European or international consensus, the Court has tended to reflect national law by applying a lowest common denominator approach or to accommodate variations in state practice through the margin of appreciation doctrine[81] when deciding upon the meaning of a Convention guarantee. The result is that a state's law or conduct may well escape condemnation if it reflects a practice followed in a number of European states or where practice is widely varied. For example, the fact that members of a linguistic minority may not be able to vote in an election for candidates whose language is theirs[82] or that civil servants may sit as expert members of a tribunal[83] does not present problems for the rights to free elections (Article 3, First Protocol) and an independent

[74] 1 HRLJ 13 at 15 (1980).   [75] See Stavros, p 346.

[76] See eg, *Sorensen and Rasmussen v Denmark* 2006-I; 46 EHRR 572 GC (European Social Charter); *Dickson v UK* 2007-V; 46 EHRR 927 GC (European Prison Rules); *Oneryildiz v Turkey* 2004-XII; 41EHRR 325 GC (Committee of Ministers and Parliamentary Assembly recommendations).

[77] See eg, *Al Adsani v UK* 2001-XI; 34 EHRR 273 GC (UN Torture Convention); *Jersild v Denmark* A 298 (1994); 19 EHRR 1 (UN Racial Discrimination Convention); *Siliadin v France* 2005-VII; 43 EHRR 287 GC (ILO Conventions); and *Vilho Eskelinen and Others v Finland* 2007-XX; 45 EHRR 985 GC (EU Charter on Fundamental Rights).

[78] See Forowicz, *The Reception of International Law in the European Court of Human Rights*, 2010.

[79] See eg, *Marckx v Belgium* A 31 (1979); 2 EHRR 330 (Children Born Out of Wedlock Convention) and *Demir and Baykara v Turkey* 2008- ; 48 EHRR 1272 GC (European Social Charter).

[80] See eg, *Al-Skeini and Others v UK* 2011- GC (jurisdiction), and *Waite and Kennedy v Germany* 1999-I; 30 EHRR 261 (sovereign immunity). For references to non-human rights treaties, see *Glass v UK* 2004-II; 39 EHRR 341 and *Taskin v Turkey* 2004-X; 42 EHRR 250. 'International law' is directly incorporated into Article 7 of the Convention: see *Kononov v Latvia* hudoc (2008).

[81] As to this doctrine, see section 4.VII.

[82] *Mathieu-Mohin and Clerfayt v Belgium* A 113 (1987); 10 EHRR 1 para 57 PC ('a good many states').

[83] *Ettl v Austria* A 117 (1987); 10 EHRR 225 para 40 ('domestic legislation...of member states affords many examples').

and impartial tribunal (Article 6) respectively, given that such situations are common in European states. Widespread differences in practice in European states can lead to a similar tolerance, as in the case of laws governing abortion,[84] artificial insemination,[85] the right of prisoners to vote,[86] the regulation of political advertising,[87] and relations between church and state.[88] Other examples can be found in connection with the right to a fair trial, where there is much diversity of practice resulting, most clearly, from the differences between civil and common law systems of criminal justice. Thus, when interpreting the Article 6(1) requirement that judgments be 'pronounced in public', the Court has taken account of the fact that courts of cassation in civil law jurisdictions commonly do not deliver their judgments in public.[89] Similarly, the Court has been influenced in its approach to the 'trial within a reasonable time' guarantee in Article 6(1) by the characteristics of civil law criminal justice systems.[90]

It is encouraging, however, that, faced with a diversity of practice, the Court has sometimes acted positively in the interests of protecting human rights. This is the case, for example, in the Court's application of Article 6(1) to administrative justice, its strict reading of the requirement of an impartial tribunal that is found in the same provision, and its expansive interpretation of the residual 'fair hearing' guarantee.[91] More controversial, perhaps, is the balance that the Court has struck between the rights of parents and their children. The policy of some states of permitting their child care authorities to intervene to protect children at the expense of parental rights more than most European states do so has led to findings of breaches of the Convention in several cases.[92]

Finally, it is interesting to consider the evidence that the Court has available to it when it acts by reference to the standards in European national law or international law. After many years in which the Court lacked the time or resources to undertake research in relevant areas of law, it now has a research division which is asked to carry out studies on questions of comparative or international law that arise in cases, mostly cases before the Grand Chamber. This is an important new development in the practice of the Court that has taken place over the last decade or so.[93] The result is that today Grand Chambers and occasionally Chambers will have at their disposal in-house documents that provide extremely useful and detailed comparative and international law information.[94] Beyond such resources, the Court relies upon the collective knowledge of its members and its registry and upon the *amicus curiae* briefs of non-governmental organizations and others, which have been of great assistance on occasion.[95] The contribution of judges is obviously

---

[84] See *Vo v France* 2004-VIII; 40 EHRR 259 GC.

[85] See *Evans v UK* (2007); 46 EHRR 728.

[86] See *Scoppola v Italy (No 3)* hudoc (2011). In *Hirst v UK (No 2)* 2005-IX; 42 EHRR 849 GC the margin of appreciation was exceeded.

[87] *Animal Defenders International v UK* hudoc 2013- GC ('somewhat wider' margin).

[88] *Sindicatul 'Păstorul Cel Bun' v Romania* hudoc 2013- GC.   [89] See Chapter 9 section 3-III.

[90] See Chapter 9 section 3-IV. Note also the absence of any need for jury trial in criminal cases, which is not found generally across Europe. For other examples of differing practice concerning the law of evidence and trial *in absentia*, resulting in a 'low common denominator', see Stavros, pp 238 and 265–266.

[91] See Chapter 9 section 3-II.

[92] See eg, *Andersson (M & R) v Sweden* A 226-A (1992); 14 EHRR 615.

[93] For earlier doubts as to whether the Court made a thorough investigation of the law of European states when relying on common standards, see eg, the dissenting opinion of Judge Matscher in *Öztürk v Germany* A 73 (1984); 6 EHRR 409 PC and, among authors, Bernhardt, *European System*, p 35; Helfer, 26 Cornell ILJ 133 at 138–40 (1989); and Mahoney, 11 HRLJ 57 at 79 (1990).

[94] At present, research reports are not communicated to the parties to a case.

[95] See eg, the reliance on a study by the NGO Liberty in *Goodwin (Christine) v UK* 2002-VI; 35 EHRR 447 GC.

valuable but is curtailed by the Court's practice of hearing cases in chambers and the fact that judges are unlikely to claim expertise in all areas of their national law.

V. THE PRINCIPLE OF PROPORTIONALITY

The principle of proportionality[96] is a recurring theme in the interpretation of the Convention. Reliance on the principle is most evident in those areas in which the Convention expressly allows restrictions upon a right. Thus, under the second paragraphs of Articles 8–11, a state may restrict the protected right to the extent that this is 'necessary in a democratic society' for certain listed purposes. This formula has been interpreted as meaning that the restriction must be 'proportionate to the legitimate aim pursued'.[97] Similarly, proportionality has been invoked when setting the limits to an implied restriction that has been read into a Convention guarantee[98] and in some cases in determining whether a positive obligation has been satisfied.[99] The principle has also been introduced into the non-discrimination rule in Article 14, so that for its prohibition of discrimination to be infringed there must be 'no reasonable relationship of proportionality between the means employed and the aim sought to be pursued'.[100] Finally, the principle is relied upon when interpreting the requirement in Article 15 that measures taken in a public emergency in derogation of Convention rights must be 'strictly required by the exigencies of the situation'.[101] In general, the principle of proportionality is not applied under Article 3, which contains an absolute guarantee.[102] A limitation upon a right, or steps taken positively to protect or fulfil it, will not be proportionate, even allowing for a margin of appreciation, where there is no evidence that the state institutions have balanced the competing individual and public interests when deciding on the limitation or steps, or where the requirements to be met to avoid or benefit from its application in a particular case are so high as not to permit a meaningful balancing process.[103]

---

[96] See Christoffersen, *Fair Balance: Proportionality, Subsidiarity and Primarity in the European Convention on Human Rights*, 2009; McBride, in Ellis, ed, *The Principle of Proportionality in the Laws of Europe*, 1999; and Van Drooghenbroeck, *La proportionalité dans le droit de la Convention européenne des droits de l'homme*, 2001.

[97] *Handyside v UK* A 24 (1976) para 49; 1 EHRR 737 PC. See also the 'absolutely necessary' test in Article 2(2), where the test is one of 'strict proportionality'. The principle has also been applied to differently formulated restrictions in other Articles, eg, Article 5 (*Winterwerp v Netherlands* A 33 (1979); 2 EHRR 387 para 39); Article 12 (*F v Switzerland* A 128 (1987); 10 EHRR 411 PC); and Article 1, First Protocol (*James v UK* A 98 (1986); 8 EHRR 123 para 50 PC).

[98] *Mathieu-Mohin and Clerfayt v Belgium* A 113 (1987); 10 EHRR 1 para 52 PC (Article 1, First Protocol) and *Fayed v UK* A 294-B (1994); 18 EHRR 393 para 71 (Article 6(1)). In the former case the Court also stated that a restriction must not impair the 'essence' of the right. Cf, *Ashingdane v UK* A 93 (1985); 7 EHRR 528 para 57 (Article 6(1)). The Court not uncommonly uses this last idea when vetting a restriction under any of the headings discussed above, whether as an element of 'proportionality' or as a separate requirement.

[99] See eg, the Article 8 cases of *Rees v UK* A 106 (1986); 9 EHRR 56 para 37 PC and *Gaskin v UK* A 160 (1989); 12 EHRR 36 para 49 PC.

[100] *'Belgian Linguistics'* case A 6 (1968) p 34; 1 EHRR 241 at 284 PC. Cf, the recourse to proportionality when interpreting the term 'forced labour' in Article 4: *Van der Mussele v Belgium* A 70 (1983); 6 EHRR 163 para 37 PC.

[101] See *Lawless v Ireland* (Merits) A 3 (1961); 1 EHRR 15 and *Ireland v UK* A 25 (1978); 2 EHRR 25 PC. Although the term proportionality is not mentioned in these judgments, the principle is applied in fact.

[102] See *Saadi v Italy* hudoc (2008).

[103] *Hirst v UK (No 2)* 2005-IX; 42 EHRR 849 GC (absolute ban on prisoners' right to vote) and *Dickson v UK* 2007-V; 46 EHRR 927 GC (strict limits on prisoners' artificial insemination). See, however, *Odièvre v France* 2003-III; 38 EHRR 871 GC (no right to know one's biological parent) where the Court majority gave little heed to such considerations.

VI. A FAIR BALANCE

In *Soering v UK*,[104] the Court stated that 'inherent in the whole of the Convention is a search for a fair balance between the demands of the general interest of the community and the requirements of the protection of the individual's fundamental rights'. Mowbray states that the fair balance principle is used by the Court 'as a basis for assessing the proportionality of respondents' interferences with the Convention rights of applicants and for determining when states are subject to implied positive obligations under the Convention'.[105] As to proportionality, in *Hutten-Czapska v Poland*,[106] for example, the Court stated:

> there must be a reasonable relation of proportionality between the means employed and the aim sought to be realised [by any interference with the right to property in Article 1, Protocol 1]…That requirement is expressed by the notion of a 'fair balance' that must be struck between the demands of the general interest of the community and the requirements of the protection of the individual's fundamental rights.

As to positive obligations, in *Verein Gegen Tierfabriken Schweiz v Switzerland (No 2)*,[107] for example, when deciding whether the respondent state had a positive obligation under Article 10 of the Convention to act to allow a controversial television advertisement to be broadcast after the Strasbourg Court had held that its prohibition was a violation of freedom of expression, the Court similarly stated that 'regard must be had to the "fair balance" that has to be struck' between the community interest and individual rights.

VII. THE MARGIN OF APPRECIATION DOCTRINE

A doctrine that plays a crucial role in the interpretation of the Convention and that has been extensively commented upon is that of the margin of appreciation.[108] In general terms, it means that the state is allowed a certain measure of discretion, subject to European supervision, when it takes legislative, administrative, or judicial action in the area of a Convention right. The doctrine was first explained by the Court in *Handyside v UK*.[109] This was a case concerning a restriction upon a right within the Articles 8–11

---

[104] A 161 (1989); 11 EHRR 439 para 89 PC. Cf, *'Belgian Linguistics' case (No 2)* A 6 (1968); 1 EHRR 252 PC; *Sporrong and Lönnroth v Sweden* A 52 (1982); 5 EHRR 35 PC; and *Fayed v UK* A 294-B (1994); 18 EHRR 393. More recently, see eg, *N v UK* hudoc 2008-; 47 EHRR 885 GC.

[105] Mowbray, 10 HRLR 289 at 315 (2010).

[106] 2006-VIII; 45 EHRR 52 para 167 GC. The 'fair balance' concept is particularly prominent in right to property cases.   [107] Hudoc (2009); 52 EHRR 394 para 91 GC.

[108] From a large literature, see on the doctrine, Arai-Takahashi, *The Margin of Appreciation Doctrine and the Principle of Proportionality in the Jurisprudence of the ECHR*, 2002; Brauch, 11 Col J European Law 113 (2004); Greer, *The Margin of Appreciation: Interpretation and Discretion under the European Convention on Human Rights*, Council of Europe Human Rights File 17, 2000; id, *European Convention*, Ch 5; Legg, *The Margin of Appreciation in International Human Rights Law*, 2012; Letsas, 26 OJLS 705 (2006); Macdonald, in *European System*, Ch 6; articles by Mahoney *et al*, 19 HRLJ 1–36 (1999); Ostrovsky, Hanse LR 47 (2005); Sottiaux and Van Der Schyff, 31 Hastings I and C LR 115 (2008); and Yourow, *The Margin of Appreciation Doctrine in the Dynamics of European Human Rights Jurisprudence*, 1996. The doctrine is included in Protocol 15.

[109] A 24 (1976); 1 EHRR 737 paras 48–9 PC. It had in effect been relied upon by the Court earlier, following the Commission, in *Lawless v Ireland* (Merits) A 3 (1961); 1 EHRR 15 para 28, in the context of public emergencies (Article 15). On the use of the doctrine in Articles 8–11, see further, Ch 8.

group of rights. In the *Handyside* case, the Court had to consider whether a conviction for possessing an obscene article could be justified under Article 10(2) as a limitation upon freedom of expression that was necessary for the 'protection of morals'. The Court stated:

> By reason of their direct and continuous contact with the vital forces of their countries, state authorities are in principle in a better position than the international judge to give an opinion on the…'necessity' of a 'restriction' or 'penalty'…it is for the national authorities to make the initial assessment of the reality of the pressing social need implied by the notion of 'necessity' in this context.
>
> Consequently, Article 10(2) leaves to the contracting states a margin of appreciation. This margin is given both to the domestic legislator ('prescribed by law') and to the bodies, judicial amongst others, that are called upon to interpret and apply the laws in force.
>
> Nevertheless, Article 10(2) does not give the contracting states an unlimited power of appreciation. The Court, which, with the Commission, is responsible for ensuring the observance of those states' engagements, is empowered to give the final ruling on whether a 'restriction' or 'penalty' is reconcilable with freedom of expression. The domestic margin of appreciation thus goes hand in hand with a European supervision. Such supervision concerns both the aim of the measure challenged and its 'necessity'; it covers not only the basic legislation but also the decision applying it, even one given by an independent court…
>
> The Court must decide, on the basis of the different data available to it, whether the reasons given by the national authorities to justify the actual measures of 'interference' they take are relevant and sufficient.

The doctrine has since been applied in the above sense to other Convention articles. As well as Article 10, it has been relied upon when determining whether an interference with other rights in the Articles 8–11 group of rights is justifiable on any of the grounds permitted by paragraph (2) of the Article concerned. The doctrine is also used when assessing whether a state has done enough to comply with any positive obligations that it has under these[110] and other Articles[111] and when determining whether a state's interference with the right to property protected by Article 1, First Protocol is justified in the public interest.[112] A margin of appreciation is also allowed in the application of other guarantees where an element of judgment by the national authorities is involved, as in certain parts of Articles 5[113] and 6[114] and in Article 14.[115] It has been instrumental as well in the application of Article

---

[110] See eg, *Abdulaziz, Cabales and Balkandali v UK* A 94 (1985); 7 EHRR 741 para 67 PC and *Keegan v Ireland* A 290 (1994); 18 EHRR 342 para 49.

[111] See eg, *Mathieu-Mohin and Clerfayt v Belgium* A 113 (1987); 10 EHRR 1 PC (Article 3, First Protocol); and *Vo v France* 2004-VIII; 40 EHRR 259 GC (Article 2).

[112] See eg, *James v UK* A 98 (1986); 8 EHRR 123 PC.

[113] See *Winterwerp v Netherlands* A 33 (1979); 2 EHRR 387 (person of unsound mind); *Weeks v UK* A 114 (1987); 10 EHRR 293 PC (release on parole); *Brogan v UK* A 145-B (1988); 11 EHRR 117 PC (terrorist suspects). No margin of appreciation in Article 5(3). As to a margin of appreciation in connection with the 'absolutely necessary' test in Article 2: see *Finogenov v Russia* 2011-.

[114] See eg, *Osman v UK* 1998-VIII; 29 EHRR 245 (1998) (right of access), but no margin of appreciation on trial within a reasonable time.

[115] '*Belgian Linguistics' Case* A 6 (1968) p 35; 1 EHRR 24 at 284 PC and *Rasmussen v Denmark* A 87 (1984); 7 EHRR 371 para 40.

15 when deciding whether there is a 'public emergency' and, if so, whether the measures taken in response to it are 'strictly required by the exigencies of the situation'.[116] As will be apparent, these Articles largely coincide with those to which the principle of proportionality spelt out in the *Handyside* case applies, the point being that in assessing the proportionality of the state's acts, a certain degree of deference is given to the judgment of national authorities when they weigh competing public and individual interests in view of their special knowledge and overall responsibility under domestic law. Finally, it should be noted that national courts are allowed considerable discretion, either under an implied margin of appreciation doctrine or under the fourth instance doctrine (see section VIII), in the conduct of trials in respect of such matters as the admissibility or evaluation of evidence. Thus the Court has stated that Article 6(3)(d) generally 'leaves it to the competent authorities to decide upon the relevance of proposed evidence'[117] and that 'it is for the national courts to assess the evidence before them'.[118] An interference with a right that has been ordered or approved by the objective decision of a national court following a full examination of the facts will also benefit from a margin of appreciation in its favour.[119]

The margin of appreciation doctrine is applied differentially, with the degree of discretion allowed to the state varying according to the context. A state is allowed a considerable discretion in cases of public emergency arising under Article 15,[120] in some national security cases,[121] in cases involving the move from communist to free market economies,[122] and in the protection of public morals.[123] Similarly, the margin of appreciation 'available to the legislature in implementing social and economic policies should be a wide one'.[124] It will be wide, too, when 'there is a no consensus within the member states of the Council of Europe, either as to the relative importance of the interest at stake or as to the best means of protecting it, particularly where the case raises sensitive moral or ethical issues'.[125] A wide margin also usually applies 'if the state is required to strike a balance between competing interests or Convention rights'.[126] At the other extreme, the margin of appreciation is limited where 'a particularly important facet of an individual's identity or existence is at stake'[127] and is reduced almost to vanishing point in certain areas, as where the justification for a restriction is the protection of the authority of the judiciary.[128]

The margin of appreciation doctrine reflects the subsidiary role of the Convention in protecting human rights.[129] The overall scheme of the Convention is that the initial and

---

[116] *Ireland v UK* A 25 (1978); 2 EHRR 25 PC.   [117] *Engel v Netherlands* A 22 (1976); 1 EHRR 647 para 91 PC.

[118] *Isgro v Italy* A 194-A (1991) para 31. A state is also allowed a margin of appreciation under Article 6 in deciding whether an accused must be legally represented: *Croissant v Germany* A 237-B (1987); 16 EHRR 135 para 27.

[119] See eg, *Handyside v UK* A 24 (1976); 1 EHRR 737 PC.

[120] See Chapter 19.   [121] See eg, *Leander v Sweden* A 116 (1987); 9 EHRR 433 para 67.

[122] *Broniowski v Poland* 2004-V; 40 EHRR 559 para 182 GC.

[123] See eg, *Handyside v UK* A 24 (1976); 1 EHRR 737 PC.

[124] *Hatton v UK* 2003-VIII; 37 EHRR 611 para 97 GC (airport noise), citing *James v UK* A 98 (1986); 8 EHRR 123 PC (taking of property).

[125] *Evans v UK* hudoc 2007-I; 46 EHRR 728 para 77 GC. Cf, *Rasmussen v Denmark* A 87 (1984); 7 EHRR 371 (fathers' rights); *Vo v France* 2004-III; 40 EHRR 259 (abortion); *Lautsi and Others v Italy* 2011- GC(crucifixes in classrooms). Even so, a state's discretion is not unlimited: *Dickson v UK* 2007-V; 46 EHRR 927 GC.

[126] *Evans v UK* hudoc 2007-I.

[127] *Evans v UK* hudoc 2007-I. Cf *Dudgeon v UK* A 45 (1983); 4 EHRR 149 PC (homosexual acts) and *Christine Goodwin v UK* 2002-VI; 35 EHRR 447 PC (transsexuals).

[128] *Sunday Times v UK* A 30 (1979); 2 EHRR 245 PC. The Court may have been influenced by the disagreement within the relevant UK institutions as to the need for the restriction.

[129] See Matscher, *European System*, Ch 5 at p 76. On the principle of subsidiarity in the Convention generally, see Petzold, *European System*, Ch 4 and Rysdall, 1996 EHRLR 18 at 24ff. The principle will be added

primary responsibility for the protection of human rights lies with the contracting parties.[130] The Court is there to monitor their action, exercising a power of review that has some similarities with that of a federal constitutional court over conduct by democratically elected governments or legislatures within the federation.[131]

The margin of appreciation doctrine serves as a mechanism by which a tight or slack rein is kept on state conduct, depending upon the context. The doctrine is nonetheless a controversial one. When it is applied widely, so as to appear to give a state a blank cheque or to tolerate questionable national practices or decisions,[132] it may be argued that the Court has abdicated its responsibilities. However, the doctrine has its counterpart in the context of judicial review in national systems of administrative law and may be essential to retain state confidence in the operation of the Convention system. In its absence, Strasbourg might well be seen as imposing solutions from outside without paying proper regard to the knowledge and responsibilities of local decision-makers. Underlying the doctrine is the understanding that the legislative, executive, and judicial organs of a state party to the Convention basically operate in conformity with the rule of law and human rights and that their assessment and presentation of the national situation in cases that go to Strasbourg can be relied upon. Given this premise, the doctrine can probably be justified.[133] The difficulty lies not so much in allowing it as in deciding precisely how to apply it to the facts of particular cases.

VIII. THE FOURTH INSTANCE DOCTRINE

The Court, and formerly the Commission, has made it clear that it does not constitute a further court of appeal, ie a fourth instance ('*quatrième instance*'), from the decisions of national courts applying national law. In the words of the Court, 'it is not its function to deal with errors of fact or law allegedly committed by a national court unless and insofar as they may have infringed rights and freedoms protected by the Convention.'[134] An application that merely claims without more that a national court has made an error of fact or law will be declared inadmissible *ratione materiae*. A claim that such an error is a breach of the right to a fair hearing in Article 6 will not succeed, as Article 6 provides a procedural guarantee only; it does not guarantee that the outcome of the proceedings is fair. However, where the Court is called upon to determine the facts of a case in order to apply a Convention guarantee (eg whether there was inhuman treatment contrary to Article 3), it is not bound by the finding of facts at the national level.[135] Where an application alleges that national law violates the Convention, the Strasbourg authorities will not in principle question the interpretation of that law by the national courts.[136] However,

to the Convention Preamble by Protocol 15. On the principle in the Court's jurisprudence, see eg, *Z v UK* 2001-V; 34 EHRR 97 GC and *Vilho Eskelinen and Others v Finland* 2007-IV; 45 EHRR 985 GC.

[130] '*Belgian Linguistics' Case* A 6 (1968) p 34; 1 EHRR 241 at 284 PC and *Handyside v UK* A 24 (1978); 1 EHRR 737 para 48 PC. Thus Article 1 requires the contracting parties to 'secure' the rights' in the Convention. See also Articles 13 and 53, Convention.

[131] See Mahoney, 11 HRLJ 57 at 65 (1990), who compares the roles of the European Court and the US Supreme Court.

[132] See, eg, *Barfod v Denmark* A 149 (1989); 13 EHRR 493 paras 28–36.

[133] Note, however, that it is not used by UN human rights treaty monitoring bodies, and has only a modest presence in the inter-American and African human rights systems.

[134] *Garcia Ruiz v Spain* 1999-I; 31 EHRR 589 para 28.

[135] See eg, *Ribitsch v Austria* A 336 (1995); 21 EHRR 573.

[136] *X and Y v Netherlands* A 91 (1985); 8 EHRR 235 para 29.

it may do so where the interpretation by the national court is 'arbitrary or manifestly unreasonable',[137] or where it is a part of a Convention requirement that national law be complied with (eg that an arrest is 'lawful': Article 5(1)).[138] Even so, it is very exceptional for the Court to disagree with any decision by a national court on its interpretation and application of its own national law.[139]

IX. EFFECTIVE INTERPRETATION

An important consideration which lies at the heart of the Court's interpretation of the Convention, and which is key to realizing its 'object and purpose', is the need to ensure the effective protection of the rights guaranteed. In *Artico v Italy*,[140] the Court stated that 'the Convention is intended to guarantee not rights that are theoretical or illusory but rights that are practical and effective'. There the Court found a breach of the right to legal aid in Article 6(3)(c) because the legal aid lawyer appointed by the state proved totally ineffective. The Court has relied upon the principle of effectiveness in other cases when interpreting positive obligations.[141] In other contexts, the Court has emphasized the need to ensure the effectiveness of the Convention when interpreting the term 'victim' in Article 25[142] and when giving the Convention extra-territorial reach under Article 3.[143]

X. CONSISTENCY OF INTERPRETATION OF THE CONVENTION AS A WHOLE

In *Stec v UK*,[144] the Court stated that the 'Convention must be read as a whole, and interpreted in such a way as to promote internal consistency and harmony between its various provisions'. Accordingly, in that case a crucial factor for the Court in ruling that the right to property in Article 1, First Protocol extended to non-contributory as well as contributory benefits was that it had been held that rights to both kinds of benefit were protected by the right to a fair trial in Article 6 of the Convention.

XI. LIMITS RESULTING FROM THE CLEAR MEANING OF THE TEXT

Although the Strasbourg authorities rely heavily upon the 'object and purpose' of the Convention, they have occasionally found that their freedom to do so is limited by the clear meaning of the text. Thus in *Wemhoff v Germany*,[145] it was held that Article 5(3) does not apply to appeal proceedings because of the wording of Article 5(1)(a). Remarkably, in *Pretto v Italy*,[146] the Court went against the clear wording of the Convention text in order to achieve a *restrictive* result. There it held that the unqualified requirement in Article 6(1)

---

[137] See, eg, *Andelković v Serbia* hudoc (2013).
[138] See, eg, *Lukanov v Bulgaria* 1997-II; 24 EHRR 121.
[139] *Winterwerp v Netherlands* A 33 (1979); 2 EHRR 387 para 46.
[140] A 37 (1980); 3 EHRR 1 para 33. Cf *Airey v Ireland* A 32 (1979); 2 EHRR 305.
[141] See *Klass v Germany* A 28 (1978); 2 EHRR 214 para 34 PC.
[142] *Marckx v Belgium* A 31 (1979); 2 EHRR 330 PC.
[143] *Soering v UK* A 161 (1989); 11 EHRR 439 para 87 PC.
[144] 2006-V; 43 EHRR 1027 para 48 GC. Cf *Klass v Germany* A 28 (1978); 2 EHRR 214 PC.
[145] A 7 (1968); 1 EHRR 55.   [146] A 71 (1983); 6 EHRR 182 para 26 PC.

that judgments be 'pronounced publicly' (*rendu publiquement*) does not apply to a Court of Cassation. The Court considered that it must have been the intention of the drafting states (although there was no clear evidence in the *travaux préparatoires*) to respect the 'long-standing tradition' in many Council of Europe states to this effect.[147] For this reason, the Court did not 'feel bound to adopt a literal interpretation' and preferred a more flexible approach that it felt was not inconsistent with the basic 'object and purpose' of Article 6. Similarly, in *Scoppola v Italy (No 2)*,[148] there was a clear departure from the language of Article 7 to introduce the *lex motior*, this time to the benefit of the accused.

In a remarkable development, the Court has taken the position that the text of the Convention may be amended informally by state practice. In *Soering v UK*,[149] faced with wording in Article 2 which expressly permitted capital punishment, the Court stated that '[s]ubsequent practice in national penal policy, in the form of a generalized abolition of capital punishment, could be taken as establishing the agreement of the contracting states to abrogate the exception provided for under Article 2(1)'. While state practice had not reached this point by the time of the *Soering* case, in the *Al-Saadoon* case the Court later concluded that it had, so that the numbers of ratifications of the Thirteenth Protocol prohibiting capital punishment completely and other state practice were 'strongly indicative that Article 2 has been amended so as to prohibit the death penalty in all circumstances'.[150]

XII. THE AUTONOMOUS MEANING OF CONVENTION TERMS

Legal terms that might be considered as referring back to the meaning that they have in the national law of the state concerned have not been so interpreted.[151] Instead, they have been given an autonomous Convention meaning. They include terms such as 'criminal charge', 'civil rights and obligations', 'tribunal', and 'witness' in Article 6.[152] The words 'law' and 'lawful', however, have a mixed national law and Convention meaning. They both require that there be a national law basis for what is done and are imbued with a Convention idea of the essential qualities of law. As to the latter, a 'law' must not be arbitrary; it must also be publicly available, have a reasonably predictable effect and be consistent with the general principles of the Convention.[153]

XIII. RECOURSE TO THE *TRAVAUX PRÉPARATOIRES*

Recourse may be had to the *travaux préparatoires*, or preparatory work, of the Convention[154] in order to confirm its meaning as established in accordance with the rule in Article 31 of the Vienna Convention or where the application of that rule leaves its

---

[147] The Court's approach may have been influenced by the fact that the text of Article 6 was probably drafted with only trial proceedings in mind. [148] Hudoc (2009) GC.

[149] A 161 (1989); 11 EHRR 439 para 103 PC.

[150] *Al-Saadoon and Mufdhi v UK*, 2010- para 120. This illustrates the risk that an optional protocol to the Convention may, at least until widely ratified, foreclose the possibility of a broad interpretation of the original Convention. See, however, *Ekbatani v Sweden* A 134 (1988); 13 EHRR 504 para 26 PC, in which the Court stated that the addition of a right in a protocol was not to be taken as limiting the scope of the meaning of the original Convention guarantee.

[151] See Letsas, 15 EJIL 279 (2004); Matscher, *European System*, Ch 5 at pp 70–3, and Van der Meersch, *Wiarda Mélanges*, p 201.

[152] Cf, the autonomous meaning of the terms 'vagrant' and 'persons of unsound mind' in Article 5(1)(d).

[153] See Chapters 8 and 11 concerning Articles 5 and 8–10.

[154] For the *travaux préparatoires* of the Convention, see the *Collected Edition of the Travaux Préparatoires of the European Convention on Human Rights*, 8 vols, 1975–85 (hereafter *TP*).

meaning 'ambiguous or obscure' or 'leads to a result which is manifestly absurd or unreasonable'.[155] In practice, the Court, and formerly the Commission, has only made occasional use of the *travaux préparatoires*.[156] This is partly because the *travaux* are not always helpful[157] and partly because of the emphasis upon a dynamic and generally teleological interpretation of the Convention that focuses, where relevant, upon current European standards rather than the particular intentions of the drafting states.[158]

XIV. THE INTERPRETATIVE ROLE OF THE COURT

The interpretation of the Convention is the role of the Court. The Committee of Ministers makes no attempt to interpret the Convention when it monitors compliance with judgments under Article 46(2). Before its abolition in 1998, the Commission also played an important part in the interpretation of the Convention. The Commission gave reasoned decisions at the admissibility stage, particularly when it declared an application to be inadmissible.[159] In addition, the Commission's reports on the merits of admitted applications were fully reasoned.[160] However, it followed from the scheme of the Convention that in practice the 'last word'[161] as to its meaning rested with the Court. If the Court interpreted the Convention differently from the Commission, the Court's view prevailed and the Commission, if sometimes slowly, changed its mind.[162] Although the Court has, since 1998, developed its own jurisprudence on admissibility and has filled in many of the gaps in its interpretation of the Convention's substantive guarantee, some pre-1998 Commission interpretations remain of authority in the absence of Court pronouncements.

There is no common law distinction between *ratio decidendi* and *obiter dicta* in the practice of the European Court of Human Rights. Any statement by way of interpretation of the Convention by the Court, and formerly the Commission, is significant, although inevitably the level of generality at which it is expressed or its centrality to the decision on the material facts of the case will affect the weight and influence of any pronouncement. Clearly, a Grand Chamber ruling is more authoritative than one by a Court Chamber.

There is no doctrine of binding precedent in the sense that the Court is bound by its previous interpretations of the Convention (or those of the former Commission).[163] The

---

[155] Article 32, Vienna Convention.

[156] See, eg, *Johnston v Ireland* A 112 (1986); 9 EHRR 203 para 52 PC; *Lithgow v UK* A 102 (1986); 8 EHRR 329 para 117 PC; *Kudla v Poland* 2000-XI GC; *Hirsi Jamaa v Italy* 2012-; 55 EHRR 627 GC; *Sitaropoulos and Giakoumopoulos v Greece* 2012- GC. See also its extensive use under Article 1, First Protocol.

[157] See, eg, *Cruz Varas v Sweden* A 201 (1991); 14 EHRR 1 para 95 PC (*travaux préparatoires* 'silent').

[158] Remarkably, in *Young, James and Webster v UK* A 44 (1981); 4 EHRR 38 PC and *Sigurjonsson v Iceland* A 264 (1993); 16 EHRR 462, the Court resorted to the *travaux préparatoires* only to reject the evidence that it found.

[159] Applications are sometimes admitted (now by the Court) on the basis that they raise complex issues of fact and law that should be left to the merits; in such cases, there is little or no reasoning at the admissibility stage.

[160] In contrast, Commission reports (and now Court judgments) on friendly settlements contain little or no interpretation of the Convention.

[161] Mosler, in Kaldoven, Kuyper and Lammers, eds, *Essays on the Development of the International Legal Order, in Memory of Haro Van Panhuys*, 1980, p 152. In theory, the contracting parties to the Convention have the 'last word' as to the meaning of their treaty and could, if they were all agreed (either when meeting within the Committee of Ministers or otherwise), adopt an interpretation that would prevail over that of the Court.

[162] Eg, the Commission adopted (see eg, its Report, para 95 in *Buchholz v Germany* B 37 (1980)) the Court's approach to the interpretation of the reasonable time requirement in Article 5(3) following the Court's rejection of the Commission's approach in *Wemhoff v Germany* A 7 (1968); 1 EHRR 55.

[163] On precedent in the Court, see Mowbray, 9 HRLR 179 (2009) and Wildhaber, in *Ryssdal Mélanges*, p 1529.

rules concerning precedent have to be read in the context of a Court that sits in five separate Chambers of equal standing and a Grand Chamber to which certain cases may be relinquished by the Chamber for an initial decision on the merits or to which a case that has been decided initially by a Court Chamber may be referred for a re-hearing.[164] In *Cossey v UK*,[165] the Plenary Court (which was replaced by the Grand Chamber in 1998) stated that it 'is not bound by its previous judgments' but that 'it usually follows and applies its own precedents, such a course being in the interests of legal certainty and the orderly development of the Convention case-law'. However, the Court continued, it is free to depart from an earlier judgment if there are 'cogent reasons' for doing so, which might include the need to 'ensure that the interpretation of the Convention reflects societal changes and remains in line with present day conditions'. For example, in *Goodwin (Christine) v UK*,[166] the Grand Chamber reversed the ruling of the Plenary Court in the *Cossey* and other cases on the legal status of post-operative transsexuals in the light of changing trends. Reformulating the position taken by the Plenary Court in the *Cossey* case, in the *Christine Goodwin* case the Grand Chamber stated that 'it is in the interests of legal certainty, foreseeability and equality before the law that it should not depart, without good reason, from precedents laid down in previous cases'. This 'cogent' or 'good reason' approach applies to Grand Chamber reversals of its own or Plenary Court decisions; it will feel much freer to reverse previous Chamber decisions.[167] As to Chambers, it follows from this approach that a Chamber should follow an earlier decision of another Chamber unless there are 'cogent reasons' not to do so. All Chambers are expected to follow Grand Chamber judgments, regardless of 'cogent reasons', unless the case can be distinguished in some other manner.

5. NEGATIVE AND POSITIVE OBLIGATIONS AND *DRITTWIRKUNG*

Article 1 of the Convention requires the contracting parties to 'secure' the rights and freedoms included in it.[168] Together with the text of later articles dealing with particular rights, this wording in Article 1 has been interpreted as imposing both negative and positive obligations upon states. A negative obligation is one by which a state is required to abstain from interference with, and thereby respect, human rights. For example, it must refrain from torture (Article 3) and impermissible restrictions upon freedom of expression (Article 10). Since such obligations are typical of those that apply to civil and political rights, it is not surprising that most of the obligations that a state has under the Convention are of this character.

---

[164] Articles 30, 43, Convention.   [165] A 184 (1990); 13 EHRR 622 para 35 PC.

[166] 2002-VI; 35 EHRR 447 para 74 GC. As well as the need for a dynamic interpretation of the Convention, other 'cogent reasons' recognized by the Court are the needs to clarify the meaning of the Convention (*Vilho Eskelinen and Others v Finland* 2007-XX; 45 EHRR 985 GC) and to tackle the rise in application numbers (*Kudla v Poland* 2000-XI GC). See Mowbray, 9 HRLR 647 (2009).

[167] The Grand Chamber is, of course, totally free to reverse a decision of a Chamber in the same case: see eg, *Dickson v UK* 2007-V; 46 EHRR 927 GC.

[168] See Clapham, *Human Rights in the Private Sphere*, 1993, Ch 7; Cherednychenko, 13 Maastricht JECL 195 (2006); Conforti, 13 ItYIL 3 (2003); and Drzemczewski, *European Human Rights Convention in Domestic Law*, 1983, Ch 8.

A positive obligation is one whereby a state must take action to secure human rights.[169] Positive obligations are generally associated with economic, social, and cultural rights[170] and commonly have financial implications, as, for example, with an obligation to provide medical treatment in realization of the right to health. However, positive obligations can also be imposed in respect of civil and political rights and they are to be found the European Convention. Before considering those in the Convention, it should be noted that a different, tripartite typology of obligations to respect, protect, and fulfil human rights is now well established.[171] In this typology, obligations to respect are negative obligations. Obligations to protect and to fulfil are positive obligations, requiring respectively state protection from the acts of other persons, whether state agents or private persons, and other positive action by the state to fulfil a human right.

A number of positive obligations are expressly present in, or necessarily follow from, the text of the Convention. There are, for example, obligations to protect the right to life by law (Article 2(1)); to provide prison conditions that are not 'inhuman' (Article 3); to provide courts, legal aid in criminal cases, and translators in connection with the right to a fair trial (Article 6); and to hold free elections (Article 3, First Protocol).

Other positive obligations have been read into the Convention by the Court.[172] This process finds its source in the Court's jurisprudence in *Marckx v Belgium*.[173] There the Court stated, in the context of the right to 'respect for family life' in Article 8, that 'it does not merely compel the state to abstain from such interferences: in addition to this primary negative undertaking, there may be positive obligations inherent in an "effective respect" for family life'. In that case, a positive obligation had been infringed, *inter alia*, because Belgian family law did not recognize a child born out of wedlock as a member of the mother's family, thus not allowing the mother and child 'to lead a normal family life'. In *Airey v Ireland*,[174] the same approach was used to establish a positive obligation, this time one involving public expenditure,[175] under the same Article 8 guarantee to provide for effective access to a court in civil proceedings for an allegedly battered wife to obtain an order of judicial separation. Generally, the Court has justified its finding of positive obligations as being necessary to make a Convention right effective.[176]

In the *Marckx* and *Airey* cases, the state's positive obligations were to grant individuals the legal status, rights, and privileges needed to ensure that their Convention rights were 'secured' (Article 1). In terms of the tripartite typology referred to previously, they were obligations to use the power of the state to fulfil Convention rights. Other obligations of this kind of great importance that have been read into the Convention by the Court are

---

[169] The Court sometimes has difficulty in deciding whether a case involves a positive or a negative obligation, and may decide not to make the distinction: see eg *Broniowski v Poland* 2004-V; 43 EHRR 495 GC. Whichever approach is adopted, 'the applicable principles are broadly similar': *Demir and Baykara v Turkey* 2008- ; 48 EHRR 1272 para 111 GC.

[170] See Van Hoof, in Alston and Tomasevski, eds, *The Right to Food*, 1984, p 97.

[171] It was first formulated in UN Doc E/CN.4/Sub.2/1987/23 and is used by the UN Committee on Economic, Social, and Cultural Rights. See Koch, 5 HRLR 81 (2005).

[172] See generally Mowbray, *The Development of Positive Obligations under the European Convention on Human Rights by the European Court of Human Rights*, 2004.

[173] A 31 (1979); 2 EHRR 330 para 31 PC. Cf, *Abdulaziz, Cabales and Balkandali v UK* A 94 (1985); 7 EHRR 471 para 67 PC and *Goodwin (Christine) v UK* 2002-VI; 35 EHRR 447 GC. See also the '*National Union of Belgian Police*' case A 19 (1975); 1 EHRR 518 para 39.   [174] A 32 (1979); 2 EHRR 305 para 32.

[175] For other cases involving public expenditure, see eg, *Bouamar v Belgium* A 129 (1988); 11 EHRR 1 and *Poltoratskiy v Ukraine* 2003-V; 39 EHRR 916 para 148.

[176] See Mowbray, *The Development of Positive Obligations under the European Convention on Human Rights by the European Court of Human Rights*, 2004, p 221.

the obligations to investigate suspicious deaths (Article 2)[177] and allegations of torture (Article 3).

In other cases, following the same typology, the Court has established that there are positive obligations upon contracting parties to 'protect' Convention rights, by protecting persons' rights from the acts of others. The first clear indication of this came in *X and Y v Netherlands*,[178] where a state was held liable because its criminal law did not provide a means by which a sexual assault upon a mentally handicapped young woman could be the subject of a criminal prosecution. In the words of the Court, the Article 8 obligation to respect an individual's privacy imposed positive obligations that 'may involve the adoption of measures designed to secure respect for private life *even in the sphere of the relations of individuals themselves*'. The same formula was later used in *Plattform 'Ärzte für das Leben' v Austria*,[179] in which the Court held that a state must take reasonable and appropriate measures to protect demonstrators from interference by other private persons intent upon disrupting their demonstration in breach of the right to freedom of assembly protected by Article 11. More recently, the Court has found positive obligations to protect individuals from assault[180] and other ill-treatment[181] and from invasions of their privacy by private persons.[182]

The full extent to which the Convention places states under positive obligations to protect individuals against infringements of their rights by other private persons has yet to be fully established, with the Court continuing to add to their number. Domestic violence (Articles 3 and 8), and deprivation of liberty by terrorists or other kidnappers (Article 5) are obvious areas to which an obligation to protect individuals against interferences with their rights by other persons extend.

The question of the protection under the Convention of individuals against other private persons is sometimes spoken of, misleadingly, in terms of the concept of *drittwirkung*. This concept, which is most developed in German legal thinking and law,[183] supposes that an individual may rely upon a national bill of rights to bring a claim against a private person who has violated his rights under that instrument.[184] Given that this involves the liability of private individuals, or the horizontal application of law, it can have no application under the Convention at the international level,[185] because the Convention is a treaty that imposes obligations only upon states.[186]

Insofar as the Convention touches the conduct of private persons, it does so only indirectly through such positive obligations as it imposes upon a state. As noted earlier, the basis for the state's responsibility under the Convention in the case of such obligations is that, contrary to Article 1, it has failed to 'secure' to individuals within its jurisdiction

---

[177] This obligation includes investigation of alleged killings by both state and private actors.

[178] A 91 (1985); 8 EHRR 235 para 23. Italics added. See also *Young, James and Webster v UK* A 44 (1981); 4 EHRR 38 PC.   [179] A 139 (1988); 13 EHRR 204 para 32.

[180] *Osman v UK* 1998-VIII; 29 EHRR 245 (death threat); *Özgur Gündem v Turkey* 2000-III, 31 EHRR 1082 (protection of journalists from attack); *A v UK* 1998-VI; 27 EHRR 611 (parental corporal punishment); *Opuz v Turkey* hudoc (2009); 50 EHRR 695 (domestic violence).

[181] *Z v UK* 2001-V; 34 EHRR 97 GC.   [182] *Von Hannover v Germany* 2004-VI; 43 EHRR 139.

[183] For its meaning in German law, see Lewan, 17 ICLQ 571 (1968).

[184] This is the concept of direct *drittwirkung*. For indirect *drittwirkung*, which likewise does not refer to positive obligations of the kind that exist under the Convention, see Lewan, 17 ICLQ 571 (1968).

[185] What may happen, however, is that in a state in which the Convention is a part of national law, the Convention guarantee may be treated, like some national bills of rights, as generating rights vis-à-vis private persons: see Drzemczewski, *European Human Rights Convention in Domestic Law*, 1983, Ch 8, particularly concerning Germany (p 210).

[186] See Article 1. Accordingly, an application may not be brought under Article 34 against a private person and Article 33 supposes only inter-state applications.

the rights guaranteed in the Convention by not rendering unlawful the acts of private persons that infringe them.

The position may be different, however, where the private conduct falls within the area of a Convention right or is the result of 'privatization'. The first of these situations existed in *Costello-Roberts v UK*,[187] which was a case concerning corporal punishment in a private school. The Court noted that the case fell within the ambit of a right—the right to education—that was protected by the First Protocol to the Convention. It stated that 'the state cannot absolve itself from responsibility' to secure a Convention right 'by delegating its obligations to private bodies or individuals'.[188] Accordingly, the Court held that, although the act of a private person, the treatment complained of could engage the responsibility of the respondent state under Article 3. This approach was followed *mutatis mutandis* in *Woś v Poland*[189] in the situation where the respondent state had entrusted a private law foundation to administer a compensation scheme. The Court held that the 'exercise of state powers which affects Convention rights and freedoms raises an issue of state responsibility regardless' of the fact that their exercise may have been delegated by the state to a private actor. Consequently, given the need to protect rights effectively, the respondent state was accountable under the Convention for the acts of the foundation. It would be consistent with this reasoning for the state to be directly responsible under the Convention for the acts of private companies and other persons to whom powers that are traditionally state powers have been transferred by privatization, as in the case of private prisons.

6. RESERVATIONS

Article 57 (formerly Article 64) of the Convention allows a party on signature or ratification 'to make a reservation in respect of any particular provision of the Convention to the extent that any law then in force in its territory is not in conformity with the provision'.[190] Reservations have been made by over twenty of the forty-seven parties to the Convention.[191] They have been invoked successfully in several cases to prevent a claim being heard,[192] although some reservations have been held to be invalid.[193] Article 57 requires that a reservation must not be 'of a general character'. In *Belilos v Switzerland*,[194] the Court stated that a reservation falls within this prohibition if it is 'couched in terms that are too vague or broad for it to be possible to determine their exact meaning and scope'. In that case, having confirmed its competence to rule on the validity of reservations, the

---

[187] A 247-C (1993); 19 EHRR 112.

[188] A 247-C (1993); 19 EHRR 112 para 27. Cf, *Van der Mussele v Belgium* A 70 (1983); 6 EHRR 163 PC.

[189] *No 22860/02* hudoc (2005) para 72 DA.

[190] See Frowein, *Wiarda Mélanges*, p 193. The rules on reservations in Articles 2(1)(d) and 19–23 in the Vienna Convention on the Law of Treaties 1969 apply to the Convention as customary international law: *Temeltasch v Switzerland* 5 EHRR 417 at 432 (1983) Com Rep.

[191] For the text of reservations, see http://www.coe.int. A few reservations have been withdrawn (eg Finland: Article 6). Reservation may be for a limited time: see *Jecius v Lithuania* 2000-IX; 35 EHRR 400 (one year).

[192] See, eg, *Chorherr v Austria* A 266-B (1993); 17 EHRR 358; *Helle v Finland* 1997-VIII; 26 EHRR 159; and *Shestjorkin v Estonia No 49450/99* hudoc (2000) DA.

[193] See *Belilos v Switzerland* A 132 (1988); 10 EHRR 466; *Eisenstecken v Austria* 2000-X; 34 EHRR 860; and *Weber v Switzerland* A 177 (1990); 12 EHRR 508.

[194] A 132 (1988); 10 EHRR 466 para 55. See Bourguignon, 29 VJIL 347 (1989); Macdonald, 21 RBDI 429 (1988); and Marks, 39 ICLQ 300 (1990).

Court held that a Swiss reservation concerning the scope of Article 6 was invalid, *inter alia*, on the basis of this test.[195] Reservations that 'do not specify the relevant provisions of the national law or fail to indicate the Convention articles that might be affected by the application of those provisions' are reservations of a 'general character' and hence invalid.[196] A reservation is limited in its scope to the articles and national law to which it refers.[197] Moreover, it may only concern the extent to which a national law in force in a state's territory at the time of signature or ratification is consistent with the Convention; it cannot provide a shield for laws or amendments to laws that come into force later.[198] The text of Article 57 suggests that reservations may only be made to the Articles of the Convention that contain its substantive guarantees. Accordingly, reservations limiting the territorial scope of the Convention are not permitted[199] and a reservation to the right under Article 34 to make an application to the Court is almost certainly invalid.[200] A question that remains to be decided is whether a reservation to a provision such as Article 15 is invalid, either on this basis or as being of a 'general character'.[201]

In the *Belilos* case, the Court also held that a further requirement of a valid reservation in (now) Article 57(2) had not been satisfied, namely, that any reservation 'made under this Article shall contain a brief statement of the law concerned'.[202] Since this is 'not a purely formal requirement but a condition of substance',[203] non-compliance with it renders a reservation invalid without more.

The outcome of the Court's decision in the *Belilos* case was that Switzerland was bound by (and found in breach of) Article 6 without the shield of the reservation that was held to be invalid. In holding that this was the case, the Court noted that it was 'beyond doubt that Switzerland is, and regards itself as, bound by the Convention irrespective of the validity of the declaration' and that it had recognized the Court's competence to rule on the question of validity.[204] In later cases in which the Court has held a reservation to be invalid, the Court has not referred to such matters,[205] seemingly taking the view that severance is always the outcome, the state remaining a party to the Convention without

[195] The reservation read: 'The Swiss Federal Council considers that…Article 6 …is intended solely to ensure ultimate control by the judiciary over the acts or decisions of the public authorities'. A reservation must be interpreted in the language in which it is made, which need not be either the English or French authentic Convention languages: *X v Austria No 2432/65*, 22 CD 124 (1967).

[196] *Slivenko v Latvia No 48321/99* hudoc para 60 DA GC.

[197] *Gradinger v Austria* A 328-C (1995).

[198] *Fischer v Austria* A 312 (1995); 20 EHRR 349 and *Dacosta Silva v Spain* 2006-XIII.

[199] *Assanidze v Georgia* 2004-II; 39 EHRR 653 GC.

[200] Cf, *Loizidou v Turkey* A 310 (1995); 20 EHRR 99 (on restrictions to declarations accepting the former optional right of application). See Barratta, 11 EJIL 413 (2000).

[201] See the French reservation to Article 15 which restricts the competence of the Court to question the French government's judgment as to the need for emergency measures.

[202] In *Belilos*, there was no statement of the law at all. Cf *Stallinger and Kuso v Austria* 1997-II; 26 EHRR 81. The 'brief statement' need not include a summary of the law concerned; an indication of its subject matter and a reference to an official source in which the text may be found is sufficient: *Chorherr v Austria* A 266-B (1993); 17 EHRR 358 para 21.

[203] *Chorherr v Austria* A 266-B (1993); 17 EHRR 358, para 59. The requirement was 'both an evidential factor' and contributed to 'legal certainty'; generally it was intended to ensure that a 'reservation does not go beyond the provisions expressly excluded by the state concerned':para 59. Cf, *Weber v Switzerland* A 177 (1990); 12 EHRR 508 para 38 in which another Swiss reservation was held to be invalid for non-compliance with Article 64(2). See also *Eisenstecken v Austria* 2000-X; 34 EHRR 860.

[204] *Belilos v Switzerland* A 132 (1988); 10 EHRR 466 para 59.

[205] See *Eisensteken v Austria* 2000-X; 34 EHRR 860 and *Weber v Switzerland* A 177 (1990); 12 EHRR 508. On the severance of reservations to treaties generally, see Aust, *Modern Treaty Law and Practices*, 3rd edn, 2013, pp 131–4.

the benefit of the reservation regardless of its intention when making the reservation or the importance of the reservation to it.

In the *Belilos* case, the Court also held that an instrument deposited on signature or ratification may qualify as a reservation even though it is not described as such; it is sufficient that the state intended it to be a reservation. In that case, Switzerland had deposited on ratification what it described as two 'interpretative declarations', including the instrument in issue, and two 'reservations'. The Court held that the 'interpretative declaration' concerned was a reservation for the purposes of (now) Article 57 (although it proved not to be a valid one) in the light of the evidence in the Swiss *travaux* as to Switzerland's intentions. The Court's approach can be criticized as not taking account of the need for certainty in this regard and the reasonable expectation that a state knows the distinction in international law between a reservation and an interpretative declaration, particularly when it uses both terms in the instrument that it deposits.[206]

7. THE CONVENTION IN NATIONAL LAW

I. THE APPLICATION OF THE CONVENTION BY NATIONAL COURTS

International human rights guarantees are most valuable when they are enforceable in national law.[207] Even in the case of as successful an international guarantee as the European Convention on Human Rights, a remedy in a national court will usually be more convenient and efficient than recourse to an international procedure. Accordingly, if the Convention can be relied upon in a party's national courts, an important extra dimension is added to its effectiveness, particularly in a state that lacks its own national bill of rights.[208] Application through national courts is also consistent with the principle of subsidiarity which underlies the Convention, by which the primary responsibility to enforce the Convention falls upon the states parties.

Under Article 1 of the Convention, the parties undertake to 'secure' the rights and freedoms in the Convention to persons within their jurisdiction. This does not require a party to incorporate the Convention into its law.[209] While compliance with this obligation finds 'a particularly faithful reflection in those instances where the Convention has been incorporated into domestic law',[210] a party may satisfy Article 1 instead by ensuring, in whatever manner it chooses,[211] that its law and practice is such that Convention rights are guaranteed. In fact, the Convention has now been incorporated into the law of all the contracting parties.[212]

---

[206] Note, however, that Article 2(1)(d), Vienna Convention on the Law of Treaties defines a reservation as a 'unilateral statement, *however phrased or named*' (emphasis added).

[207] See Blackburn and Polakiewicz, eds, *Fundamental Rights in Europe*, 2001; Drzemczewski, *European Human Rights Convention in Domestic Law*, 1983; Gardner, ed, *Aspects of Incorporation of the European Convention of Human Rights into Domestic Law*, 1993; Greer, *European Convention*, Ch 2; Keller and Stone Sweet, *A Europe of Rights*, 2008; Polakiewicz, *2 All-European Human Rights Yearbook* (1992), 11, 147; Polakiewicz, 18 HRLJ 405 (1997).

[208] The UK is one such state.

[209] See, eg, *Observer and Guardian v UK* A 216 (1991); 14 EHRR 153 PC.

[210] *Ireland v UK* A 25 (1978); 2 EHRR 25 para 239 PC.

[211] '*Swedish Engine Drivers Union*' Case A 20 (1976); 1 EHRR 617.

[212] See Blackburn and Polakiewicz, eds, *Fundamental Rights in Europe*, 2001, Ch 2 and Keller and Stone Sweet, *A Europe of Rights*, 2008, p.683.

Although incorporation of the Convention into national law is desirable, it does not by itself ensure a remedy in a national court for a breach of the Convention. This will depend on the details of incorporation and the approach taken by the judiciary in response to it. Keller and Stone Sweet[213] summarize the position as follows: 'Other things being equal, the ECHR is most effective where Convention regimes, *de jure* and *de facto*: (1) bind all national officials in the exercise of public authority; (2) ... occupy a rank superior to that of [pre- and post-ratification] statutory law in the hierarchy of legal norms...; and (3) can be pleaded directly by individuals before judges who may directly enforce' the Convention. They give Austria, Belgium, the Netherlands, Spain, and Switzerland as examples of states in which these conditions are met. Austria and Spain go so far as to give the Convention the status of constitutional law,[214] and in the Netherlands the Convention even prevails over the Constitution.[215] Although the Convention has been strongly incorporated in Belgium, it provides an example of the difficulties that may arise in respect of positive Convention obligations. While the negative obligation in Article 8 not to interfere with family life was held to be self-executing, the positive obligation to create an appropriate legal status for children born out of wedlock required legislation.[216] Whereas formal incorporation of the Convention into national law is most easily achieved by states following the monist—as opposed to dualist—approach to the relationship between international and national law,[217] in practice the effectiveness of the incorporation for individuals will turn much upon the attitude of the judiciary. For example, 'the ECHR has had far more impact in Belgium [dualist] than in France [monist], precisely because Belgian judges chose to confer supra-legislative status [prevailing over later as well as earlier legislation] on Convention rights and to directly apply them, while French judges declined to do so.[218] Also relevant is that, in a state such as Germany, that has its own well-established national bill of rights, the Convention may be given only a limited role, with the local courts preferring to rely upon the bill of rights in the national constitution.[219]

Local factors may influence how a state incorporates the Convention into its law. For example, in recognition of the long-standing importance of parliamentary sovereignty in the United Kingdom constitution, the Human Rights Act 1998 provides only for the indirect incorporation of the rights of the Convention into UK law as 'Convention rights'.[220] The courts may not declare a parliamentary statute to be invalid. Instead, first, if primary UK legislation applicable in cases coming before the courts cannot, despite all efforts, be interpreted compatibly with the Convention, the competent court may make a 'declaration of incompatibility'. This does not affect the validity of the legislation, but alerts the government to the need to amend the law. Second, a victim has a public law right of action for damages or other relief against a public authority (but not a private person) which acts inconsistently with a 'Convention right'. The Human Rights Act has greatly increased the powers of the UK courts to provide a remedy nationally for a breach of the Convention, with the result that the numbers of both Strasbourg applications and adverse judgments against the United Kingdom has decreased.[221]

---

[213] Keller and Stone Sweet, *A Europe of Rights*, 2008, p 683.

[214] Keller and Stone Sweet, *A Europe of Rights*, 2008, Ch 6.

[215] See *Oerlemans v Netherlands* A 219 (1991); 15 EHRR 561.

[216] *Vermeire v Belgium* A 214-C (1991); 15 EHRR 488 para 11.

[217] On the monist and dualist approaches, see Crawford, *Brownlie's Principles of Public International Law*, 8th edn, 2012, pp 48–59. In a monist state, a treaty will become part of the national law upon ratification; in a dualist state, legislation will be required.

[218] Keller and Stone Sweet, *A Europe of Rights*, 2008, p 683. French judges have now changed their approach: ibid.   [219] See Ress, 40 Texas ILJ 359 at 360 (2005).

[220] Cf the Irish European Convention on Human Rights Act 2003.

[221] On the impact the Human Rights Act generally, see UK Department of Constitutional Affairs, *Review of the Implementation of the Human Rights Act*, 2006.

There has generally been a marked increase in reliance upon the Convention in national courts in recent years.[222] With the dramatic increase in the extent and impact of the European Court's jurisprudence, national courts have become all too aware that their decisions may find their way to Strasbourg to be scrutinized there by reference to Convention standards.[223] When the Convention is relied upon by a national court, the question arises whether, although not bound to do so, it will follow the interpretation of it that has been adopted at Strasbourg. In practice, national courts have usually done so, although there have been exceptions.[224] In *R v Horncastle*,[225] the Supreme Court declined to follow the Strasbourg Court Chamber judgment in *Al-Khawaja and Tahery v UK*[226] on whether the English hearsay rule of criminal evidence complied with the Convention. Lord Phillips stated that although the Human Rights Act obligation to 'take account' of Strasbourg jurisprudence 'will normally result in this Court applying principles that are clearly established by the Strasbourg Court', there will be:

> rare occasions where the Court has concerns as to whether a decision of the Strasbourg Court sufficiently appreciates or accommodates particular aspects of our domestic process. In such circumstance it is open to this Court to decline to follow the Strasbourg decision. This is likely to give the Strasbourg Court the opportunity to reconsider the particular aspect of the decision that is in use, so that there takes place what may prove to be a valuable dialogue between the Court and the Strasbourg Court.

Where a point of interpretation has not been ruled upon in a Strasbourg case, the national courts will have no choice but to adopt their own interpretation. Insofar as they do so, it is possible that courts in different legal systems may interpret the Convention differently, particularly as there is at present no procedure for the reference of a case to Strasbourg for a definitive ruling.[227]

Whether a state incorporates the Convention into its law or not, it is required by Article 13 to provide an 'effective remedy' under its national law for a person who has an arguable claim under the Convention. Thus, for example, a wife whose husband has been excluded from a state's territory because of an immigration law that may infringe the Convention must have an effective remedy under national law by which to challenge the legality of the husband's exclusion.[228] The Court's jurisprudence suggests that a state that does not make the Convention enforceable in its national law is especially at risk of being in breach of Article 13.[229]

---

[222] See Polakiewicz, in Blackburn and Polakiewicz, eds, *Fundamental Rights in Europe*, 2001, pp 50–2 and Keller and Stone Sweet, *A Europe of Rights*, 2008, pp 695–701. Many key UK human rights cases, eg *A (FC) v Secretary of State for the Home Department* [2004] UKHL 56 and *R (application of Al-Skeini) v Secretary of State for Defence* [2005] EWCA Civ 1609, would have lacked a legal basis without the Human Rights Act. But the Convention is far less known and used as yet by the courts in most post-communist states parties.

[223] Cf Polakiewicz and Jacob-Folzer, 12 HRLJ 136 at 141 (1997).

[224] Polakiewicz and Jacob-Folzer, 12 HRLJ 136 at 141 (1997), refer to rulings by Austrian, Belgian, and French courts on the scope of Article 6(1) as ones in which exceptionally the Court has been 'openly defied'.

[225] [2009] UKSC 14 *per* Lord Phillips, para 11.

[226] Hudoc (2009); 49 EHRR 1. The Grand Chamber reversed the Chamber judgment after *Horncastle*.

[227] Contrast the provision made under Article 234, Treaty of Rome for the reference by national courts of cases to the European Court of Justice for the interpretation of European Union law. Protocol 16 of the Convention will give the Strasbourg Court jurisdiction to give advisory opinions.

[228] *Abdulaziz, Cabales and Balkandali v UK* A 94 (1985); 7 EHRR 471 para 93 PC.

[229] The number of applications and adverse judgments against the UK under Article 13 has declined since the Human Rights Act.

II. THE EXECUTION OF STRASBOURG JUDGMENTS

A Court judgment is 'essentially declaratory'.[230] Article 41 of the Convention provides that the Court may award a victim 'just compensation'—a power which has been understood to permit the award of monetary compensation and legal costs.Otherwise, 'in principle, it is not for the Court to determine what remedial measures may be appropriate to satisfy the respondent state's obligations';[231] instead it is for that state 'to put an end to the breach and make reparation for its consequences in such a way as to restore as far as possible the situation existing before the breach'.[232] Whereas, in accordance with this approach, the Court used always to refrain from specifying action that should be taken to comply with its judgments, it has modified its position recently.[233] In some cases, although these remain the exception, it has indicated specific forms of restitution for the victim of a breach of the Convention. Thus it has required the return of the property concerned *as an alternative* to the payment of compensation for a breach of Article 1, Protocol 1.[234] In the case of the continued detention of an individual contrary to Article 5, the Court has found itself competent to specify, without in this context allowing any alternative, that the individual's release be secured, on the basis that the 'very nature' of the breach does not 'leave any real choice as to the measures required to remedy it'.[235] Finally, in cases in which a person has been convicted of a criminal offence in proceedings in breach of Article 6, the Court has stated that 'a retrial or reopening of the case, if requested, represents in principle an appropriate way of redressing the violation'.[236] However, the Court does not have jurisdiction to order a new trial or the quashing of a conviction.[237]

As well as specifying particular forms of restitution for the victim, the Court has also, but again exceptionally, moved in the direction of giving some indication in its judgments of the steps that a state found in breach of the Convention should take more generally to bring its law or practice into line with its Convention obligations. Whereas formerly the Court had left it entirely to the state concerned to decide what should be done, in *Broniowski v Poland*[238] the Court introduced the idea of 'pilot judgments'. These are appropriate where there is a breach of the Convention that results from a 'systematic defect' which may give rise to many claims. In such a case, the Court stated, some indication

---

[230] *Marckx v Belgium* A 31 (1979); 2 EHRR 330 para 58 PC. A judgment 'cannot of itself annul or repeal' inconsistent national court judgments or national law: *Marckx v Belgium*. For discussion of the execution of Strasbourg judgments, see Barkhuysen, van Emmerik, and van Kempen, *The Execution of Strasbourg and Geneva Human Rights Decisions in the National Legal Order*, 1999; Janis, 15 Conn JIL 39 (2000); Christou and Raymond, eds, *European Court of Human Rights, Remedies and Execution*, 2005; and Lambert-Abdelgawad, *The Execution of Judgments of the European Court of Human Rights*, CoE Human Rights File 19, 2nd edn, 2008.   [231] *Broniowski v Poland* 2004-V; 43 EHRR 495 para 193 GC.

[232] *Brumărescu v Romania* (Article 41) 1999-VII; 35 EHRR 887 para 19.

[233] See Leach, 2005 EHRLR 148.

[234] See eg, *Papamichalopoulos v Greece* (Article 50) A 330-B (1995); 21 EHRR 439 and *Brumărescu v Romania* (Article 41) 2001- I; 33 EHRR 887 GC.

[235] *Assanidze v Georgia* 2004-II; 39 EHRR 653 para 202 GC. See also *Ilaşcu and Others v Moldova and Russia* 2004-VII; 40 EHRR 1030 GC.

[236] *Sejdovic v Italy* 2006-II para 126 GC. See also *Öcalan v Turkey* 2005-IV; 41 EHRR 985 GC.

[237] *Lyons and Others v UK* No 15227/03 2003-IX; 37 EHRR CD 183 DA and *Komanický v Slovakia*, No 13677/03 hudoc (2005) DA (civil case). It did not do so in *Sejdovic* or *Öcalan*.

[238] 2004-V; 40 EHRR 563 para 193. A pilot judgment suspends the consideration by the Court of other applications deriving from the same defect pending measures being taken. In *Hirst v UK (No 2)* 2005-IX; 42 EHRR 849 GC, the Court declined a government request to give guidance on what restrictions were permissible on the right to vote in the absence of a systematic defect.

of the general measures that a state should adopt is in order 'so as not to overburden the Convention system with large numbers of applications deriving from the same cause'.

The judgments of the Court arising out of applications to Strasbourg are binding in international law upon the parties to the case.[239] However, a national court is not obliged under the Convention to give them direct effect; this is a matter for the national law of the respondent state, which is free to implement Strasbourg judgments in accordance with the rules of its national legal system.[240] Assessments of the record of states in complying with judgments has until recently been very positive. In 1996, the President of the Court stated that they had 'not only generally but always been complied with by the contracting states concerned. There have been delays, perhaps even examples of minimal compliance, but no instances of non-compliance'.[241] This was true of the payment of compensation and costs awarded by the Court under (now) Article 41, the steps by way of restitution taken to remedy a wrong done to an individual applicant and the amendment of legislative and administrative practices found contrary to the Convention. In a number of cases, a Strasbourg judgment has provided a government with a lever to help overcome local opposition to law reform, as with the change in the law on homosexuality in Northern Ireland following *Dudgeon v UK*.[242] But sometimes it is uncertain whether the steps taken by the defendant state go far enough.[243] In other cases, a state may be slow in putting the necessary measures in place because of constitutional difficulties.[244] Thus it took fifteen years before the Isle of Man Tynwald enacted the Criminal Justice (Penalties, etc) Act 1993 to abolish judicial corporal punishment, thereby bringing the United Kingdom fully into line with its obligations under Article 3 following the *Tyrer* case.[245] Prior to the 1993 legislation, in the context of the special constitutional position of the Isle of Man,[246] the UK government had informed the Manx government after the *Tyrer* case that judicial corporal punishment would be contrary to the Convention and the case was brought to the attention of the local courts by the Manx authorities. Although this was considered sufficient by the Committee of Ministers, acting under what is now Article 46(2), to

---

[239] See Article 46(1), Convention. On states' obligations under Article 46, see *Verein Gegen Tierfabriken Schweiz (Vgt) v Switzerland (No 2)* 2009-; 52 EHRR 394 GC.

[240] See eg, *Vermeire v Belgium* A 214-C (1991); 15 EHRR 488. Under Malta's European Convention Act 1987, its Constitutional Court is empowered to enforce judgments of the Strasbourg Court. In national legal systems generally, practice varies as to whether legislative or administrative action is required or whether the national courts are competent, where appropriate, to act, eg by quashing a national court decision, including a criminal conviction, found at Strasbourg to be in breach of the Convention. In Spain, the courts can so act; in Germany, they cannot: see Bernhardt, *European System*, Ch 3, at p 38. See generally *The European Convention on Human Rights: Institution of Relevant Proceedings at the National Level to Facilitate Compliance with Strasbourg Decisions*, Council of Europe Committee of Experts Study, 13 HRLJ 71 (1992).

[241] Ryssdal, in Bulterman and Kuijers, eds, *Compliance with Judgments of International Courts: Schermers Symposium Proceedings*, 1996, 49 at 67. Cf Leuprecht, *European System*, Ch 35 at p 798. For a case of minimal compliance, see the UK Contempt of Court Act 1981 implementing *Sunday Times v UK (No 1)* A 30 (1979); 2 EHRR 245 PC. A clear case in which a state refused point blank to change its (terrorism) law to comply with a judgment is *Brogan v UK* 145-B (1988); 11 EHRR 117 PC in which the UK made an Article 15 declaration instead. This was considered sufficient by the Committee of Ministers: see *Brannigan and McBride v UK* A 258-B (1993); 17 EHRR 539 PC.   [242] A 45 (1981); 4 EHRR 149 PC.

[243] As Churchill and Young, 62 BYIL 283 at 346 (1992) point out, it may be unclear what steps are required by a judgment or whether the legislation read *in abstracto* is sufficient.

[244] Delays in the payment of compensation or legislative or administrative change have many other causes, including the cost involved, political or public opposition, or the parliamentary timetable.

[245] A 26 (1978); 2 EHRR 1. There was much delay in complying with *Marckx v Belgium* A 31 (1979); 2 EHRR 330. See also Mahoney and Prebensen, *European Supervision*, Ch 26 at p 636.

[246] The Isle of Man is a Crown possession that by convention is not subject to the legislative powers of Westminster on most internal matters.

comply with the *Tyrer* judgment,[247] it would appear that the United Kingdom's obligation to 'secure' the rights and freedoms in the Convention required that it go further and for the relevant law to be amended.

While the record of state compliance with judgments remains generally good, commentators on the record of states have recently been more critical.[248] Central and East European states have found particular difficulty in complying with some judgments against them, although they have not been alone in this respect.[249] A result is that the role of the Committee of Ministers in supervising the execution of judgments has become more demanding and important.[250] Unfortunately, the Committee, being a political body composed of representatives of member states, is not the best equipped or motivated body to question whether the steps taken go far enough. The Parliamentary Assembly has also assumed a role. In its seventh report,[251] its Committee on Legal Affairs and Human Rights gave priority to the situation in states where major structural problems had led to many repeat violations. The main problems continued to be excessive length of judicial proceedings (endemic notably in Italy), chronic non-enforcement of domestic judicial decisions (widespread, in particular, in Russia and Ukraine), deaths and ill-treatment by law enforcement officials and lack of effective investigations into them (particularly in Russia and Moldova), and unlawful or over-long detention on remand (a problem notably in Moldova, Poland, Russia, and Ukraine).[252]

8. THE CONVENTION AND THE EUROPEAN UNION

The European Union (EU)[253] has legislative and executive jurisdiction by which it may act against member states[254] or private persons[255] in a way that impacts upon their Convention obligations and rights respectively.[256] When exercising jurisdiction in these ways, it is possible that EU institutions may infringe Convention rights. The question

---

[247] CM Res DH (78) 39. There was no case in which a sentence of judicial corporal punishment was executed prior to its abolition in 1993. In *Teare v O'Callaghan*, 4 EHRR 232 (1981), a post-*Tyrer* sentence of corporal punishment was quashed by the Isle of Man High Court on the ground that it was contrary to Isle of Man international obligations and should be imposed only if other forms of punishment are unsuitable.

[248] See Greer, *European Convention*, Ch 2; Lambert-Abdelgawad, *The Execution of Judgments of the European Court of Human Rights*, CoE Human Rights File 19, 2nd edn, 2008, pp 64–7; and Polakiewicz, in Blackburn and Polakiewiecz, eds, *Fundamental Rights in Europe*, 2001, pp 69ff.

[249] On Central and East European states and on the systemic problems in Italy, see Greer, *European Convention*, pp 103ff. The UK has yet to implement *Hirst v UK (No 2)* on prisoners' right to vote.

[250] On the role of the Committee of Ministers, see above, Chapter 4. See also Cali and Koch, 14 HRLR 000 (2014); Lambert-Abdelgawad, *The Execution of Judgments of the European Court of Human Rights*, pp 32–9; Leuprecht, *European System*, Ch 35; and Martens, in Bulterman and Kuijer, eds, *Compliance with Judgments of International Courts: Schermers Symposium*, 1996, p 77.

[251] Seventh Report on the 'Implementation of Judgments of the European Court of Human Rights', CE Doc. 12455 (2011), pp 1–2.   [252] On compliance with Court judgments, see further Ch 24.

[253] The term European Union is used to refer to the European Union generally and to the European Community in particular.

[254] Eg, by requiring them to take certain action: see the *Bosphorus Airways* case later in this chapter.

[255] Eg, by imposing a fine: see *M and Co v Germany No 13258/87*, 64 DR 138 (1990).

[256] See Craig and de Búrca, *EU Law*, 5th edn, 2011, ch 11, and see further, ch 23. For a comparison of the interpretation of the Convention by the Strasbourg and Luxembourg courts, see Spielmann, in Alston, ed, *The EU and Human Rights*, 1999, Ch 23, and Turner, 5 EPL 453 (1999).

therefore arises whether these institutions must comply with the Convention when they act. A related question is whether member states are responsible under the Convention for the effect on private persons of their national legislative or other public acts that are a consequence of EU membership.

As to the position of the EU, an application may not be made to Strasbourg against it under the Convention for any conduct on the part of its institutions because the EU is not a party thereto.[257] Following much debate and hesitation over many years, the Treaty on European Union (TEU), as amended by the Treaty of Lisbon, provides that the EU 'shall accede' to the Convention.[258] A draft agreement on EU accession has been drawn up and is now in the final stages of adoption.[259] The EU has its own Charter of Fundamental Rights, which was adopted in 2000 and became legally binding in 2009 under Article 6(1) TEU, as amended by the Treaty of Lisbon.[260]

Pending the EU's accession to it, the Convention controls EU conduct within its own legal order as the Convention has been incorporated into EU law. The TEU[261] reads:

> Fundamental rights, as guaranteed by the European Convention for the Protection of Human Rights and Fundamental Freedoms and as they result from the constitutional traditions common to the Member States, shall constitute general principles of the Union's law.

Accordingly, claims may succeed before the European Court of Justice (ECJ) on the basis that the challenged EU action is inconsistent with the Convention.[262] This way of indirectly subjecting EU institutions to the Convention is comparable to its incorporation into the national law of a state and falls short in its impact of Union accession to the Convention. In particular, as noted, it does not allow an individual to make an application to Strasbourg against the EU. Moreover, insofar as the Convention is applied as a part of EU law, the Convention would not prevail over a conflicting provision of Union primary (ie, treaty) law[263] and the interpretation and application of the Convention remains a matter for the ECJ, not the Convention's own Court.[264] Generally, the present situation is not satisfactory and EU accession to the Convention is clearly desirable.

With regard to the position of individual EU member states,[265] the following general rules apply. The Convention does not prohibit states parties from transferring sovereign power to an international (including supranational) organization such as the EU, but this will not in itself take away from their responsibility under the Convention for acts done as members of the organization. However, there is a presumption that a state party is not in breach of its obligations under the Convention by virtue of acts that are necessarily

---

[257] *Matthews v UK* 1999-I: 29 EHRR 361 GC. The same is true of other European institutions: *Heinz v Contracting States also Parties to the European Patent Convention No 21090/92*, 76A DR 125 (1994); 18 EHRR CD 168 (European Patent Office).

[258] Article 6(2). Article 17, Protocol 14, Convention amends Article 59, Convention to permit the EU to accede.

[259] See Council of Europe Press Release DCO 41 (2013).

[260] On the Charter, see Peers, Harvey, Kenner, and Ward, eds, *The EU Charter of Fundamental Rights*, 2014 and De Vries, Bernitz, and Weatherill, eds, *The Protection of Fundamental Rights in the EU After Lisbon*, 2013.

[261] Article 6(3), as amended by the Treaty of Lisbon. ECJ case law is to the same effect: see eg, *ERT v DEP and Sotirios Kouvelas*, Case C-260/89 [1991] ECR I-2925. See also the EU Charter of Fundamental Rights, Preamble and Article 52(3).   [262] See eg, *P v S and Cornwall CC*, Case C-13/94 [1996] ECR I-2143.

[263] See *Matthews v UK* 1999-I; 28 EHRR 361 GC. Secondary legislation (regulations, directives) must be read subject to the Convention.   [264] See Jacque, *European System*, Ch 39 at pp 894–5.

[265] All EU member states are parties to the Convention, though not to all of its Protocols.

undertaken by it in fulfilment of obligations as members of the organization so long as the organization concerned provides human rights protection that is 'equivalent' to that in the Convention 'as regards both the substantive guarantee offered and the mechanisms controlling their observance'.[266] But this presumption may be rebutted if the protection provided by the other organization is 'manifestly deficient' on the facts of the particular case.[267] These general rules were formulated by the Court in the leading case of *Bosphorus Airways v Ireland*.[268] There the Irish authorities impounded a civil aircraft leased by the applicant Turkish company from the Yugoslav national airline that had landed in Dublin. The authorities did this in compliance with a legal obligation imposed on EU member states by an EU regulation adopted in implementation of UN Security Council resolutions requiring economic sanctions against the Federal Republic of Yugoslavia in the context of the conflict in the Balkans. The Court rejected a claim that the impounding was a violation by Ireland of the right to property guarantee in Article 1, First Protocol to the Convention, for the reason that Ireland was carrying out an obligation of its membership of the EU and 'equivalent' human rights protection was provided for the applicant in the EU legal order on the facts of the case. The protection afforded by the EU was 'equivalent' substantively, because of the reliance on the Convention as a source of human rights protection in EU law, and, in terms of mechanisms, through the remedies provided to enforce the substantive guarantee before the European Court of Justice and national courts. The resulting presumption that Ireland had not infringed the Convention by impounding the aircraft was not rebutted as this protection was not 'manifestly deficient' on the facts: judicial review, through the national courts and a preliminary ruling at Luxembourg, had been available and had been used to challenge the interference with the Convention right to property.

The immunity allowed by the *Bosphorus* case does not apply where the state has some discretion in its application of EU law, in which case the state will be in breach of the Convention if it does not exercise its discretion consistently with it.[269] Nor does the immunity apply to an act of a member state that is in execution of a treaty or other EU primary law obligation that has, by definition, been freely entered into by the member state and that, as primary law, is not subject to judicial review within the EU legal order. This was the case in *Matthews v UK*,[270] where the EC Act on Direct Elections governing elections to the European Parliament, which was a EC treaty by which the UK was bound, excluded persons in Gibraltar from voting even though EC law applied to Gibraltar. The UK was held to be responsible for the resulting breach of Article 3, Protocol 1 of the Convention on free elections because it had freely agreed to the Act, which as primary law could not be challenged in the European Court of Justice.

---

[266] *Bosphorus Hava Yolları Turizm ve Ticaret Anonim Şirketi (Bosphorus Airways) v Ireland* 2005-VI; 42 EHRR 1 para 154 GC. Cf *Michaud v France* 2012-. 'Equivalent' means 'comparable', not 'identical': *Bosphorus*, para 155. Organizations other than the EU to which the general rule applies include the UN; see *Behrami and Behrami v France* and *Saramati v France, Germany and Norway, Nos 71412/01 and 78166/01* hudoc (2007). See also *Waite and Kennedy v Germany* 1999-I; 30 EHRR 261 GC (European Space Agency) and *Gasparini v Italy and Belgium* hudoc (2009) (NATO). And see *Prince Hans-Adam II of Liechtenstein v Germany* 2001-VIII GC (Convention prevails over any later inconsistent treaty obligation).

[267] 'Bosphorus Airways' case, para 156.

[268] 'Bosphorus Airways' case, para 156. See Costello, 6 HRLR 87 (2006).

[269] See eg, *Procola v Luxembourg* A 326 (1995); 22 EHRR 193 and *Cantoni v France* 1996-V. Costello, 6 HRLR 87 (2006), p 111, suggests that *Bosphorus Airways* was exceptional on its facts; there will normally be some discretion.

[270] 1999-I; 28 EHRR 361 GC. See Harmsen, 7 EPL 625 (2001) and Canor, 25 ELR 3 (2000).

9. ACHIEVEMENTS AND PROSPECTS

I. CONTRIBUTION TO THE INTERNATIONAL LAW OF HUMAN RIGHTS

The Convention was an important landmark in the development of the international law of human rights. For the first time, sovereign states accepted legal obligations to secure the classical human rights for all persons within their jurisdiction and to allow all individuals, including their nationals, to bring claims against them leading to a legally binding judgment by an international court finding them in breach. This was a revolutionary step in a law of nations that had been based for centuries on such deeply entrenched foundations as the ideas that the treatment of nationals was within the domestic jurisdiction of states and that individuals were not subjects of rights in international law. If it has since been joined by other regional and universal treaty-based guarantees of human rights, the Convention remains the most advanced instrument of this kind. It has generated the most sophisticated and detailed jurisprudence in international human rights law and its enforcement mechanisms are unrivalled in their effectiveness and achievements.[271] The Court has made a large contribution to the jurisprudence of international human rights law concerning the meaning of the particular rights it protects, the development of key concepts of general application, such as the principle of proportionality, and its strongly teleological approach to the interpretation of human rights norms. In addition, it has contributed to other areas of international law, particularly the law on state jurisdiction and state immunity, and on the functioning of international courts (eg the local remedies rule and interim measures).

II. IMPACT ON THE PROTECTION OF HUMAN RIGHTS IN EUROPE

a. Influence upon national law

The Convention has had a considerable effect upon the national law of the contracting parties. It has served as a catalyst for legal change that has furthered the protection of human rights at the national level and has, in so doing, assisted indirectly in the process of harmonizing law in Europe.[272] Changes in the law have occurred mostly following judgments on the merits[273] in cases to which the state amending its law has been a party. Insofar as a judgment involves a determination that a national law or administrative practice is inconsistent with the Convention,[274] the respondent state is required by international law to change its law or practice in order to comply with its treaty obligation in Article 1 of the Convention to 'secure' the rights and freedoms guaranteed. In compliance with this obligation, the parties to the Convention have made many legislative or other changes following decisions or judgments against them.[275] At a more general level,

---

[271] See Mowbray, 5 HRLR 57 (2005); O'Boyle, 2008 EHRLR 1; Greer, *European Convention*, ch 7;and Wildhaber, 40 CYIL 309 (2002).   [272] See Leonardo, 8 ERPL 1139 (1996).

[273] States have also undertaken to change their law or administrative practice in some friendly settlement cases.

[274] This will not always be the case. For example, the failure to try a person within a 'reasonable time' or to treat a prisoner humanely may result from inefficiency or misconduct respectively on the particular facts.

[275] See Greer, *European Convention*, Ch 5; Ress, in *European System*, pp 812ff; Ress, 40 Texas ILJ 395 (2005); Polakiewicz and Jacob-Foltzer, 12 HRLJ 65, 125 (1991); Blackburn and Polakiewicz, *Fundamental*

Frowein[276] has pointed to the considerable impact that the European Court's judgments have had on the constitutional traditions of contracting parties, involving, for example, the strengthening of the role of national courts in reviewing legislation and the introduction or increased importance of the principle of proportionality as a basis for overturning restrictions upon human rights.

In a number of cases, states have acted to amend their law or practice to bring it into line with the Convention following judgments in cases to which they have not been a party.[277] For example, the Netherlands amended its legislation on children born out of wedlock as a consequence of *Marckx v Belgium*.[278] There have also been instances of a state changing its law in order to comply with the Convention or a Protocol before becoming a party.[279]

The Convention's influence upon the law of states that are not parties to a case illustrates the following general point. The real achievement of the Convention system can be said to go beyond the statistical tally of cases and the provision of remedies for individuals. It resides in the deterrent effect of an operational system. States, confronted with a system that works, must keep their law and administrative practices under review. As happens in Whitehall, new legislation must, as far as foreseeable, be 'Strasbourg proofed'.[280] In this way the Convention radiates a constant pressure for the maintenance of human rights standards and for change throughout Europe. A judgment of the Court in a case brought by one person may have an impact on forty or more national jurisdictions.[281]

Finally, it may be noted that the Convention has also influenced national law outside of Europe. Its text is echoed in the bills of rights of a number of states that were formerly colonies of Convention parties[282] and the jurisprudence of the Court has been relied upon or cited in cases decided in the national courts of non-European states.[283]

b. A remedy for individuals

For individuals who claim to be victims of human rights violations, the primary effect of the Convention has been to provide a remedy before an international court of justice when all national remedies have failed. 'We will now take our case to Strasbourg' is a familiar refrain that may mean more than just 'blowing off steam'.

Rights in Europe, 2001, *passim*; Keller and Stone Sweet, *A Europe of Rights*, 2008, pp 695–701. As to the UK, see Churchill and Young, 62 BYIL 283 (1992).

[276] Lecture reprinted in *Dialogue between Judges*, published by the European Court of Human Rights, 2007, p 73.

[277] Although, as non-parties, they are not legally bound by the judgment, they are bound to 'secure' the rights guaranteed by the Convention.

[278] A 31 (1979); 2 EHRR 330 PC. The Netherlands also amended its law concerning the time limit within which a suspect must be brought before a court in the light of the *Brogan* case: see Myjer, NCJM-Bulletin 1989, p 459. The Danish law on the closed shop was amended following *Young, James, and Webster v UK* A 44 (1981); 4 EHRR 38 PC: see Bernhardt, *European System*, Ch 3 at p 39ff. France amended its law on interpretation costs because of *Luedicke, Belkacem, and Koç v Germany* A 29 (1978); 2 EHRR 149: see French Decree no 87–634 of 4 August 1987. For other examples, see Polakiewicz and Jacob-Foltzer, 12 HRLJ 125 (1991).

[279] See Polakiewicz and Jacob-Foltzer, 12 HRLJ 125 (1991) and Polakiewicz, in Blackburn and Polakiewicz, eds, *Fundamental Rights in Europe*, 2001, p 50.

[280] See now the statement of compatability required by s 19, Human Rights Act 1998.

[281] Cf Judge Ryssdal, *European System*, p xxvii.

[282] Eg, Nigeria: see Elias, *Nigeria: The Development of its Laws and Constitution*, 1967, p 142. Cf, *Minister of Home Affairs v Fisher* [1980] AC 319 at 328 PC (Caribbean states).

[283] See eg, *State v Ncube* 90 ILR 580 (1992) (a Zimbabwean case referring to the *Tyrer* case). See also *Pratt v AG for Jamaica* [1993] 4 All ER 769, a Privy Council case which cites *Soering v UK* A 161 (1989); 11 EHRR 439 PC. For other examples, see Mahoney and Prebensen, *European Supervision*, Ch 26 at p 637.

One measure of the undoubted value of the Convention remedy from the individual's point of view is the large number of admitted applications that have led to a favourable outcome for the applicant in a judgment of the Court or by way of a friendly settlement.[284] Another is the wide variety of cases in which breaches have been found.[285] Most violations have concerned the right to a fair trial. Cases under Article 6 have brought to light many delays in the hearing of cases in breach of the right to 'trial within a reasonable time'. Other common Article 6 infringements have concerned the right of access to a court and the requirements of an independent and impartial tribunal and of equality of arms. The next most problematic guarantee for states has been that of the right to property, particularly in recent years. Almost equally problematic has been the right to freedom of the person. Many breaches of Article 5 have been found concerning various aspects of defendants' rights, such as the right to pre-trial release, the length of detention on remand, and the need for a remedy to challenge detention. Other cases have involved the preventive detention of terrorists and the detention of the mentally disordered, vagrants, children, and deportees. Claims relying upon the right to respect for family life, privacy, etc, in Article 8 have been almost equally successful. In this context, the Court has made great use of its 'dynamic' approach to the interpretation of the Convention in the light of changed social values and the idea that there may be positive obligations upon states, requiring them, for example, to legislate so as to respect the rights of homosexuals, children born out of wedlock, and transsexuals.[286] Cases under Article 10 have confirmed the fundamental importance attached to freedom of expression, particularly freedom of the press. Violations of Article 3 have been found in such diverse areas as the ill-treatment of persons in detention, judicial corporal punishment, and extradition to face the death row phenomenon, with the concepts of 'inhuman and degrading treatment' being given a broad interpretation. At the other extreme, the guarantees of freedom from slavery and forced labour (Article 4), the right to marry (Article 12), the right to education (Article 2, Protocol 1), and the rights in the Fourth and Seventh Protocols have so far led to relatively few adverse rulings.

Analysing the Strasbourg case law from another perspective, the blind-spots revealed by the Convention have varied from one state to another. For example, in the United Kingdom the Convention has thrown a spotlight on prisons, causing an antiquated system of prison administration to be brought up to date. It has also provided checks upon state conduct in the same country in such diverse contexts as the Northern Ireland emergency, courts-martial, and discretionary life sentences. In the Netherlands and Sweden, the Convention has highlighted the absence of judicial control over executive action in such areas as the licensing of commercial activities. In Italy, it has uncovered repeated delays in the administration of justice. In Central and East European states it has revealed problems in the restitution of property and various weaknesses in the administration of justice left over from the former Soviet systems. The latter include the non-enforcement of judicial decisions in a number of such states and the re-opening of final judicial decisions by way of special supervisory procedures in Russia or as regard property decisions (Romania).

---

[284] A breach of at least one article of the Convention has been found by the Court in the great majority of cases (92% in cases decided on the merits between 1959 and 2012). However, less than 5% of applications are admitted. In 2012, 86,201 applications were declared inadmissible or struck out, a 70% increase over 2011 (50,677).

[285] See the table for the period 1959–2012 in the Court's 2012 Annual Report, pp 158–9.

[286] The concept of a positive obligation to 'secure' the rights to life and freedom from torture has also led to many findings of breaches of Articles 2 and 3 respectively.

If the Convention may thus provide a valuable remedy in respect of human rights violations over a wide range of subject areas, the Strasbourg procedures nonetheless have certain limitations or disadvantages from the applicant's standpoint. Some of these are inherent in all international remedies. Recourse to Strasbourg is inevitably less convenient than to a local court for obvious reasons, such as language, distance, and cost. Similarly, any international remedy will be less efficient because of procedural weaknesses, such as the absence of a power to subpoena witnesses or to enforce or execute properly interlocutory injunctions or judgments respectively.

Other limitations are particular to the Strasbourg system as it functions at present. By far the most serious of these is the length of proceedings at Strasbourg. Although this has always been a problem, the situation has been made worse by the huge backlog of cases that has developed in recent years. As has often been pointed out, it is somewhat ironic that the Court could well be considered to infringe the trial within a reasonable time guarantee which it enforces against others.

Given the importance now attached to the Convention system as providing a remedy for individuals, it is interesting to note how matters have progressed in this regard beyond the intentions of the drafting states. The original purpose of the Convention was not primarily to offer a remedy for particular individuals who had suffered violations of the Convention but to provide a collective, inter-state guarantee that would benefit individuals generally by requiring the national law of the contracting parties to be kept within certain bounds. An individual (as well as a state) application was envisaged as a mechanism for bringing to light a breach of an obligation owed by one state to others, not to provide a remedy for an individual victim. In accordance with this conception of the Convention, no provision was made for individuals to refer their case to the Court or to take part in proceedings before it. This, however, is not how the Convention has evolved. The individual has been brought more to the centre of the stage by allowing him a right of audience before the Court and also by making the right of individual petition to the Court compulsory. The Court's, and formerly the Commission's, constructive use of the friendly settlement procedure, which usually leads to an immediate remedy for the applicant (compensation, pardon, etc), and the Court's application of Article 41 to award an applicant compensation and costs have also enhanced the value of the Convention remedy from the standpoint of the individual. The situation that has thus developed by which Strasbourg provides an international remedy for all individual victims of violations of the Convention is, however, now under threat because of the great increase in the Court's workload.

III. PROSPECTS

As to the substance of the Convention's guarantee, the Court's future lies in the consolidation and further development of its jurisprudence, particularly in cases coming from post-communist states. The momentum of the Court's work has increased rapidly in recent years, with the Court giving detailed meaning to many different parts of the Convention guarantee. Reassuring examples of the Court's continued willingness to read the Convention in a positive, teleological way are its ruling that the Convention imposes positive obligations to secure various rights, such as the rights to life and privacy, and extends to protection from environmental pollution. Jurisprudence interpreting and applying the free-standing non-discrimination guarantee in the Twelfth Protocol, which entered into force in 2005, will add a new dimension to the Convention guarantee.[287]

---

[287] However, the more significant consequence of Protocol 12 so far has been the development of the Court's jurisprudence under the non-discrimination guarantee in Article 14 of the Convention.

While it is to be hoped that the Court will continue to conceive of its function as the guardian of human rights in a dynamic and probing way, it must at the same time take care to respect the rich diversity of law in the legal systems of the contracting parties and not lose touch with common European values.

There is much that the contracting parties themselves could do to improve the Convention's impact. They could immediately increase its effect by withdrawing such reservations as they have made and by ratifying the Protocols that they have not yet accepted. A Protocol bringing appropriate economic and social rights within the Convention system of individual petitions would also be valuable.[288] Although member states constantly acknowledge that economic and social rights are indivisible from and just as important as civil and political rights,[289] states lack the necessary conviction to establish rights of individual petition for the former, even though they are familiar with judicial remedies for the breach of obligations concerning economic and social rights in EU law and their own national law.[290] However, a move in this direction is now even less likely than formerly in view of the pressure upon the Court in coping with its workload under the existing Convention guarantee.

The immense difficulties besetting the Convention's enforcement machinery resulting from the overloading of the system by the great increase in the number of applications in recent years is by far the main problem facing the Court. Paradoxically, the large number of applications to the Court that are a testimony to the success of the Convention could also be its undoing. Reasons for the startling increase in applications include the greater awareness of the Convention on the part of individuals and non-governmental organizations, the adoption of more Convention protocols protecting rights, and the fact that the individual right of petition became compulsory for all contracting parties in 1998. But much the most important reason is the large increase since 1989 in the number of contracting parties (from twenty-two to forty-seven), including, most significantly, post-communist states.[291]

The number of applications, which was manageable in the early years, rose steadily in the 1980s and 90s[292] to the point where worries about the backlog of pending applications and the anticipated further growth in new applications led to the procedural reforms of the Eleventh Protocol, which came into effect in 1998. Despite Protocol 11, the number of applications continued to spiral upwards. However, the year 2012 marked an encouraging reduction in the Court's backlog of cases. 'The number of pending applications, which had topped 160,000 in September 2011 and stood at 151,000 on 1 January 2012, had been reduced to 128,000 by the end of the year'.[293] This reduction resulted partly from the changes brought about by Protocol 14—particularly the introduction of the single-judge

---

[288] On previously unsuccessful attempts to add a Convention protocol protecting economic, social, and cultural rights, see Berchtold, in Matscher, ed, *The Implementation of Economic and Social Rights*, 1991, p 355. There is a collective complaints mechanism under the European Social Charter.

[289] See eg, the Final Resolution of Council of Europe Ministerial Conference on the European Social Charter, Turin, 1991, para 2.

[290] See eg, the ECJ case law under Article 119 on sexual discrimination in employment and national law remedies before employment and social security courts or tribunals.

[291] Other factors were the large number of Turkish cases, resulting mainly from the response to the threat posed by the PKK, and the continuing number of repetitive Italian fair trial cases. For other reasons, see Greer, *European Convention*, pp 38ff. Of the 128,00 applications pending at the end of 2012, 70% were against just six states: Russia, Turkey, Italy, Ukraine, Serbia, and Romania, in decreasing order.

[292] Registered applications rose over tenfold, from 404 in 1981 to 4,750 in 1997.

[293] Foreword, European Court of Human Rights Annual Report 2012. 'Pending applications' include those waiting for a decision on admissibility.

formation for deciding on the admissibility of applications[294]—and from a levelling off of the number of new applications.[295] Nonetheless, the number of applications pending before the Court remains formidable. Whereas the backlog of applications waiting for a ruling on admissibility should be brought under control within the next few years, there remains a serious and continuing overload of admitted applications needing a ruling on the merits.[296] Using current procedures, the Court is not in a position to give enough judgments annually to bring its caseload of admitted cases down to acceptable proportions. The Convention parties have held conferences considering what further steps to take, leading to a series of Declarations, the latest and most significant of which was the 2012 Brighton Declaration.[297] The Brighton Declaration provided the impetus for Protocols 15 and 16, which were adopted in 2013. But these will do little to decrease the Court's backlog,[298] and the view of many commentators[299] is that, whatever procedural reforms can realistically be put in place, it will not be possible for the Court to cope with the numbers of individual applications generated by more than 800 million individuals across Europe in the case-by-case way that it has done to date. The argument runs that the Court must convert itself into a constitutional court.[300] By this is meant that, while continuing to take jurisdiction through the medium of individual applications, as the Convention provides, the Court should focus more upon making general rulings as to what the Convention requires in a particular context, rather than providing individual justice. Thus it might in a selected case make a ruling that a national law or practice is contrary to the Convention, spelling out the Convention requirements in the subject area for the benefit of states parties generally.[301] It would then not rule on other cases on the same point, at least from the same state, supposing that the state concerned will make the necessary changes to the benefit of others within its jurisdiction. Another approach would be to limit the Court's jurisdiction to 'serious' cases, as suggested by Greer and Wildhaber.[302] They also point

---

[294] As a result, in 2012, more than 80,000 applications were declared inadmissible or struck out, a 70% increase over 2011.

[295] Other factors were the increased implementation of the Court's case prioritization system and the introduction of a filtering section.

[296] At present, admitted cases take on average four-and-a-half years from registration to judgment: Court Registrar at annual press conference: http://www.echr.coe.int/ECHR/EN/Header/The+Court/The+President/Press+conferences/.

[297] For the Interlaken, Izmir, and Brighton Declarations, 2010, 2011, and 2012, see the European Court of Human Rights website (The Court: Reform of the Court).

[298] The reduction in the time limit to bring cases from six to four months will have an effect. Protocol 16 on advisory opinions will increase the Court's workload in the short term.

[299] But not the Court or states parties, which continue to see the Convention as providing a remedy for all individual complaints. See eg the Court's Preliminary Opinion in Preparation for the Brighton Conference, on the Court's website. In the Brighton Declaration, para 2, 'the states parties reaffirm their attachment to the right of individual application' and make no mention of a constitutional court. NGOs generally take the same view.

[300] See Greer, *European Convention*, pp 174ff; Greer and Wildhaber, 12 HRLR (2012); Sadurski, 9 HRLR 397 (2009); Harmsen, 5 IJHR 18 (2001); Wildhaber, 23 HRLJ 161 (2002). See also Alkema, *Ryssdal Mélanges*, p 50 and Warbrick, 10 MJIL 698 (1989) in the earlier literature.

[301] Cf the role of the US Supreme Court and the German Constitutional Court: see Greer, *European Convention*, pp 181ff. However the 2006 Report of the Group of Wise Persons, CM (2006) 203, para 42, opposed giving the Court the power to take a case at its discretion (cf the US Supreme Court's certiorari jurisdiction) as risking 'politicising the system'. But the Report stressed that the Court already had a constitutional role, viz to 'lay down common principles and standards of human rights', which it already exercises but could take further, para 24.

[302] 12 HRLR 655 at 686 (2012).

out that the Court has already moved towards becoming a constitutional court through its development of the concept of pilot judgments; the introduction by Protocol 14 of a 'no significant advantage' ground for inadmissibility;[303] the adoption of a 'priority policy' whereby the Court has regard to the importance and urgency of the issues raised in a case when deciding the order in which cases are dealt with;[304] and the practice of considering similar cases against the same state together in one judgment.[305] If these developments do not have the desired effect of reducing the backlog of admitted applications sufficiently, more radical steps in the direction of making the Court a constitutional court may be required.

States may themselves do a great deal to reduce the Court's difficulties. Above all, action to reduce the figure of over 60 per cent of judgments on the merits attributable to 'repetitive' violations resulting from structural problems that states have not rectified following judgments against them[306] would help greatly. More effective application of the Conventon at the national level, in accordance with the principle of subsidiarity, would also contribute greatly to reducing the burden upon the Strasbourg Court: the provision of local remedies by national courts applying the standards of the Convention would greatly reduce the need for recourse to Strasbourg.

The Convention's future is also bound up with that of the new Europe. Providing both a statement of European human rights values and the machinery for their enforcement, it can continue to have a key role in the process of European integration. This is a role that has taken on an extra dimension as cases are arriving from the new Council of Europe member states in Central and Eastern Europe. The Convention's relationship with the European Union is close to resolution. The fact that the member states of the European Union are subject to the Convention, but that the supranational institutions to which they have transferred certain of their powers are not, has long been a weakness in the arrangements for securing human rights in Europe that should be remedied by the accession of the European Union to the Convention. While the current situation remains, and while the Strasbourg Court continues to have severe workload problems, the European Union's Court of Justice in Luxembourg will, as it applies the EU Charter, have a considerable opportunity to develop a larger human rights role for itself vis-à-vis the Union and its member states.

---

[303] As yet this additional admissibility requirement has had little impact. See Buyse, in Haeck, McGonigle, Herrera, and Garduno, eds, *Liber Amicorum for Leo Zwaak*, 2014.

[304] Non-priority cases still remain to be decided in due course.

[305] In 2012, the Court gave 1,093 judgments, in which it disposed of 1,678 applications.

[306] Explanatory Report to the Fourteenth Protocol, para 7 (figure for 2003).

PART II

ENFORCEMENT MACHINERY

2 Admissibility of Applications 43

3 The European Court of Human Rights: Organization, Practice,
and Procedure 103

4 The Execution of the Court's Judgments 180

2

ADMISSIBILITY OF
APPLICATIONS

Over the years, the Court (and before it the Commission) has established an impressive body of case law interpreting and applying the various conditions of admissibility set out in Articles 34 and 35. The Court's case law, for example, on exhaustion of domestic remedies has made an important contribution to international law where the rule is of general application. Most of the admissibility requirements are procedural in nature, such as the six-month and exhaustion of domestic remedies rules; but some of the criteria, such as those of 'manifestly ill-founded' and, most recently, 'no significant disadvantage', require the Court to assess the merits of the case at this preliminary phase. As will be seen later, this process has involved the examination of many thousands of cases, most of which have been rejected as inadmissible.[1]

1. THE GENERAL APPROACH
TO ADMISSIBILITY

The Court has frequently stated that the rules on admissibility must be applied with some degree of flexibility and without excessive formalism[2] and that account also has to be taken of their object and purpose[3] and of those of the Convention in general, which, as a human rights treaty, must be interpreted and applied so as to make its safeguards practical and effective.[4] The Court has relied on those precepts to give a more favourable interpretation to rules such as the obligation to exhaust domestic remedies for the benefit of applicants. Similarly, those precepts have been relied on to reject objections by governments to the admissibility of applications which are not raised at the earliest possible stage of proceedings.

In applying the admissibility criteria, two phases must be distinguished. Before a respondent government is given notice of the application and asked for its observations (also known as 'communication' of the application), the Court may of its own motion

---

[1] While separate statistics on the different heads of admissibility are not available, in 2013, 89,738 applications were declared inadmissible or struck out of the list of cases by a single Judge, a Committee, or a Chamber. Of these, 80,583 were declared inadmissible by a single Judge. In the same year, judgments were delivered in respect of 3,659 applications (counted in this manner—rather than simply the number of judgments—because one judgment could cover more than one application). Of these judgments, 2,756 were delivered by Committees of three judges. See the Court's Analysis of Statistics 2013: http://www.echr.coe.int/Documents/Stats_analysis_2013_ENG.pdf.

[2] *Ilhan v Turkey* 2000-VII; 34 EHRR 869 at para 51 GC; *Cardot v France* A 200 (1991); 13 EHRR 853.

[3] *Worm v Austria* 1997-V; 25 EHRR 454.   [4] *Yaşa v Turkey* 1998-VI; 28 EHRR 408.

declare the application inadmissible on the basis of the criteria set out in Articles 34 and 35 of the Convention. After communication of an application, the Court will generally only examine admissibility questions if the respondent government raises any admissibility objections.[5] The exception to this rule is that the Court can, at any time in the proceedings, consider questions relating to incompatibility *ratione loci, materiae, personae,* and *temporis* on its own motion.[6] The justification for this is that these go to the heart of the Court's jurisdiction to hear complaints under the Convention. The six-month rule and the rule that cases should not have been submitted to another procedure of international investigation or settlement are also ones that the Court can always apply of its own motion for this reason.[7] After communication, the Court will not examine questions relating to non-exhaustion of domestic remedies unless explicitly raised by the government.[8] The Court has also considered the application of the new, no significant disadvantage criterion of its own motion, even though the criterion was not explicitly raised by the respondent government.[9] It must be doubted whether this approach is correct, given that the issue of significant disadvantage involves a substantive examination of the applicant's complaint and does not go to the heart of the Court's jurisdiction to hear complaints.

When cases are referred to the Grand Chamber under Article 43 of the Convention, the Grand Chamber may also reconsider admissibility objections raised by the government where these have already been addressed by the Chamber.[10] A government will be estopped from raising admissibility objections in proceedings before the Grand Chamber if it has not already raised them before the Chamber[11] or if the Chamber considered the same admissibility question on its own motion.[12]

There is no set order in which the admissibility criteria are applied. For example, the Court will frequently find that it is unnecessary for it to rule on preliminary objections as to the non-exhaustion of domestic remedies when it may be more expeditious to find that the complaint in question is clearly incompatible *ratione materiae* or is manifestly ill-founded.

---

[5] See Rule 55 of the Rules of Court. A doctrine of estoppel will normally also apply to government admissibility objections: while the Court may declare an application inadmissible at any stage of the proceedings in accordance with Article 35(4), this does not signify that a respondent state is able to raise an admissibility question at any stage of the proceedings if that question could have been raised earlier. See *Velikova v Bulgaria* 2000-VI para 57; *NC v Italy* 2002-X paras 42–7 GC.

[6] *Blečić v Croatia* 2006-III paras 63–9 GC; *Sejdic and Finci v Bosnia and Herzegovina* hudoc (2009) para 27.

[7] See *POA and others v UK No 59253/11* hudoc (2013) DA; *Assanidze v Georgia* 2004-II; 39 EHRR 653 para 160 GC; *Belaousof and Others v Greece* hudoc (2004); *Kadikis v Latvia (No 2) No 62393/00* hudoc (2003) p 22 DA; *Soto Sanchez v Spain No 66990/01* hudoc (2003) DA. Nor can the six-month rule be waived, regardless of whether the respondent government objects: *Walker v UK No 34979/97* hudoc (2000) DA.

[8] See *K and T v Finland* 2001-VII; 36 EHRR 255 para 145 GC; *NC v Italy* 2002-X para 44 GC; *Sejdovic v Italy* 2006-II paras 40–1 GC. This same principle has been applied where the respondent government has not submitted any observations at all. See *Ergi v Turkey No 23818/94,* 80 DR 157 at 160 (1995) and the judgment in the same case: 1998-IV paras 65–7; *Dobrev v Bulgaria* hudoc (2006), para 112.

[9] *Ionescu v Romania No 36659/04* hudoc (2010) DA; *Nicoleta Gheorghe v Romania* hudoc (2012).

[10] *Odièvre v France* 2003-III; 38 EHRR 871 para 22 GC; *Azinas v Cyprus* 2004-III; 40 EHRR 166 paras 32, 37 GC.

[11] See, *mutatis mutandis, Nikolova v Bulgaria* 1999-II; 31 EHRR 64 paras 41–4 GC; *Hasan and Chaush v Bulgaria* 2000-XI; 34 EHRR 1339 para 56 GC.

[12] *Mutatis mutandis, Freedom and Democracy (Özdep) v Turkey* 1999-VIII; 31 EHRR 674 para 23 GC (the Commission considering the admissibility question on its own motion being sufficient to allow the government to raise it before the Grand Chamber).

While the Rules of Court are silent on the question, in exceptional circumstances the Court will allow a request for revision of an admissibility decision under its inherent jurisdiction but only when there has been a clear error which has affected its original decision.[13]

2. APPLICATION OF ADMISSIBILITY REQUIREMENTS TO INTER-STATE CASES

It is clear from the terms of paragraphs (2) and (3) of Article 35 that apart from conditions *ratione materiae, personae, loci*, and *temporis*, the only admissibility requirements applicable to inter-state cases are those set out in Article 35(1), namely the requirement to exhaust domestic remedies and the six-month rule.[14] In its recent decision in *Georgia v Russia (II)*, the Court refused to reject the application on the grounds that it was substantially the same as the application lodged by Georgia at the International Court of Justice, on the ground that this criterion applied only to individual applications.[15]

The Commission and Court have consistently refused to assess the merits of an inter-state case at the admissibility stage. Thus an Article 33 application cannot be rejected under Article 35(3) as manifestly ill-founded.[16]

It has also been argued in various inter-state cases that the application should be rejected as 'abusive' on the grounds that it was politically inspired or that it consisted of accusations of a political nature designed to further a propaganda campaign. That has always been rejected, most recently in *Georgia v Russia (I)*,[17] the Court applying the settled case law of the Commission which had previously found that, even if allegations had a political element, it was not such as to render them 'abusive' in the general sense of the term.[18] It left open, however, the issue as to whether an Article 33 application could be rejected on the basis of a general principle of international law that proceedings before an international tribunal must not be abused.[19]

The sole condition for the Court's competence *ratione personae* to hear an inter-state case is that both the applicant and respondent states have ratified the Convention. An applicant state, unlike an individual applicant, does not have to claim to be a 'victim' in any way of the alleged breach. Nor does the applicant state have to justify a special interest in the subject matter of the complaint; in particular, it is not a condition that the matter complained of should have affected or prejudiced one of its nationals.[20] The

[13] *Ölmez and Ölmez v Turkey* hudoc (2005) (re-opening decision) at p 5 (see also references therein) and *Edwards v UK No 13071/87* hudoc (1991) DA.

[14] See *Denmark v Turkey No 34382/97* hudoc (1999) p 33 DA. In *Georgia v Russia (II) No 38263/08* hudoc (2011) DA, where Russia invited the Court to rule in its admissibility as to the compatibility *ratione loci* and *materiae* of the application, the Court decided that these issues were so closely connected to the merits of the case that they should not be decided at the admissibility stage and joined them to the merits of the case. See also Prebensen, in Alfredsson *et al*, eds, *International Human Rights Monitoring Mechanisms*, 2001, pp 533–59.

[15] *Georgia v Russia (II) No 38263/08* hudoc (2011) DA. See also the third *Cyprus v Turkey* case, *No 8007/77*, 13 DR 85 at 154–5 (1978) Com Rep; CM Res DH (92) 12 and *Ireland v UK* B 23-I at 670 Com Rep.

[16] *France, Norway, Denmark, Sweden and Netherlands v Turkey Nos 9940–9944/82*, 35 DR 143 at 160–2 (1983); *Denmark v Turkey No 34382/97* hudoc (1999) DA.   [17] Hudoc (2009) at para 43.

[18] *Denmark, Norway, Sweden and Netherlands v Greece* 11 YB 764 (1968) and the third *Cyprus v Turkey* case 11 YB 764 (1968).

[19] *Denmark, Norway, Sweden and Netherlands v Greece* and the third *Cyprus v Turkey* case.

[20] *Ireland v UK* A 25 (1978); 2 EHRR 25 para 239 PC.

application may concern not only a specific case but the broader allegation of an administrative practice[21] or where the alleged breach 'results from the mere existence of a law which introduces, directs or authorises measures incompatible with the rights and freedoms guaranteed'.[22] In the latter case, this is subject to the proviso that the impugned law has to be sufficiently clear and precise to make the breach immediately apparent; otherwise, an examination of the interpretation and application of the law *in concreto* has to be undertaken.

The exhaustion rule applies in inter-state cases: see *Austria v Italy*[23] and *Greece v UK*.[24] This is subject to two exceptions.

The first exception is that the rule on exhaustion of domestic remedies does not apply to inter-state complaints concerning legislative measures.[25] This exception 'must be seen as a consequence of the absence, in many countries, of legal remedies against legislation'.[26]

The second exception is that the rule will be waived where there is an administrative practice in the respondent state that would render any remedies ineffective. An administrative practice involves: (i) a repetition of acts; and (ii) official tolerance.[27] The Court in *Ireland v UK* described the first criterion as 'an accumulation of identical or analogous breaches which are sufficiently numerous and inter-connected to amount not merely to isolated incidents or exceptions but to a pattern or system'.[28] Official tolerance means that superiors, though cognizant of acts of ill-treatment, refuse to take action to punish those responsible or to prevent their repetition; or that a higher authority manifests indifference by refusing any adequate investigation of their truth or falsity; or that in judicial proceedings a fair hearing of such complaints is denied.[29]

At the admissibility stage, only *prima facie* evidence of an administrative practice is required: see *France, Norway, Denmark, Sweden and Netherlands v Turkey*[30] and *Denmark v Turkey*.[31] In the latter case, Denmark's application related to an alleged widespread practice of torture and ill-treatment in policy custody in Turkey and had the aim of preventing its continuation or recurrence. Since Denmark's complaint in this respect was of a general nature and was not 'wholly unsubstantiated', it followed that the rule as to the exhaustion of domestic remedies did not apply.

The approach taken in *Denmark v Turkey* was applied in *Georgia v Russia (I)* and *Georgia v Russia (II)*, where, in each case, the Court simply observed that the evidence before the Court meant Georgia's complaints were not 'wholly unsubstantiated' and all the other questions concerning the existence and scope of the alleged administrative practices, as well as its compatibility with the provisions of the Convention, related to the merits of each case and could not be examined by the Court at the admissibility stage (paragraphs 46 and 90 respectively).

Georgia v Russia (I) also confirmed the rule laid down in *Denmark v Turkey* that, if the administrative practices or situations ended six months before the date of the application,

---

[21] See *Denmark v Turkey No 34382/07* hudoc (1999) DA.
[22] *Ireland v UK* A 25 (1978); 2 EHRR 25 para 240 PC.
[23] *No 788/60*, 4 YB 116 (1961).   [24] *No 299/57*, 2 YB 186 (1957).
[25] *Greece v UK No 299/57*, 2 YB 186 at 192 (1957); the *Greek* case 11 YB-II 690 at 726 (1968); *Second Greek case No 4448/70*, 13 YB 109 at 134 (1970); *Ireland v UK Nos 5310/71 and 5451/72*, 41 CD 3 at 84 (1972); *Cyprus v Turkey No 8007/77 (Third Application)*, 13 DR 85 at 151–2 (1978); *France, Norway, Denmark, Sweden and Netherlands v Turkey Nos 9940–9944/82*, 35 DR 143 at 162 (1983).
[26] *France, Norway, Denmark, Sweden and Netherlands v Turkey*, p 163.
[27] *Donnelly v UK Nos 5577–83/72*, 4 DR 64 (1975).   [28] A 25 (1978); 2 EHRR 25 para 159.
[29] 12 YB (the *Greek* case) at 196 (1969) (report of the Commission).
[30] 35 DR 143 at 162–8 (1983).   [31] Hudoc (1999).

they would fall outside the scope of the Court's examination; however, if the situation was still continuing, the six months rule would not apply. In *Georgia v Russia (I)*, the Court found that the question of the application of the six-month rule and compliance with it were so closely related to that of the existence of an administrative practice that they had be considered jointly during an examination of the merits of the case (see paragraph 47 of the decision).

3. EXHAUSTION OF DOMESTIC REMEDIES

I. THE PURPOSE AND CRUX OF THE RULE

Article 35(1) provides that:

> The Court may only deal with the matter after all domestic remedies have been exhausted, according to the generally recognised rules of international law…

Article 35(1) can now be said to have three purposes. The first is to afford the contracting states the opportunity of preventing or putting right the violations alleged against them before those allegations are submitted to the Court.[32] Consequently, states are dispensed from answering for their acts before an international body before they have had an opportunity to put matters right through their own legal system.[33] The second purpose is to codify the presumption:

> reflected in Article 13 of the Convention—with which [Article 35(1)] has close affinity— that there is an effective remedy available in respect of the alleged breach in the domestic system. In this way, it is an important aspect of the principle that the machinery of protection established by the Convention is subsidiary to the national systems safeguarding human rights.[34]

The third purpose of the rule might be said to flow from the first two: if, despite the existence of national remedies, an application is nonetheless brought to Strasbourg, the Court should have the benefit of the views of the national courts before it rules on the matter.[35]

Thus, the crux of the rule on exhaustion is that the complaint made to the Court must first have been made: (a) at least in substance; (b) to the appropriate domestic body; (c) and in compliance with the formal requirements and time limits laid down in domestic law.[36] These basic requirements will be considered in section II 'The basic requirements of the rule'. The questions of the burden of proof and what remedies are considered adequate and effective will be considered in sections III and IV to VII.

---

[32] *Selmouni v France* 1999-V; 29 EHRR 403 para 74 GC; *Hentrich v France* A 296-A (1994) para 33; and *Remli v France* 1996-II; 22 EHRR 253 para 33.

[33] Thus the rule is founded on the principle of international law that states must first have the opportunity to redress the wrong alleged in their own legal system. See, *inter alia*, *Van Oosterwijck v Belgium* A 40 (1980); 3 EHRR 557 para 34 PC.

[34] *Selmouni v France* 1999-V; 29 EHRR 403 para 74 GC. See also *Akdivar v Turkey* 1996-IV; 23 EHRR 143 para 65; *Eberhard and M v Slovenia* hudoc (2009) at para 103 and *Demopoulos v Turkey Nos 46113/99 and others* hudoc (2010) DA, para 69.

[35] *A and Others v UK* hudoc (2009), para 154; *Burden v UK* hudoc (2008) para 42.

[36] See *Cardot v France* A 200 (1991); 13 EHRR 853 para 34.

It should be emphasized that, in common with the rest of the admissibility criteria, the rule on exhaustion has always been one which the Court has intended should apply with some degree of flexibility and without excessive formalism.[37] As such, the rule is neither absolute nor capable of being applied automatically, and thus when applying it, the Court must take realistic account, not only of the existence of formal remedies in the legal system of the Contracting Party concerned, but also of the context in which they operate and the personal circumstances of the applicant.[38] For instance, *Financial Times Ltd and others v UK*[39] concerned the hearing by the High Court of an application for an order requiring the *Financial Times* newspaper to deliver up within twenty-four hours a leaked document which it had obtained. It was alleged before the Strasbourg Court that the newspaper had failed to put its Article 10 complaint in substance in the course of the High Court hearing or on appeal. The Court found that, having regard to the haste with which the proceedings took place in the High Court and Court of Appeal, the applicants had satisfied the requirements of the exhaustion rule.

II. THE BASIC REQUIREMENTS OF THE RULE

a. In substance

For the requirement that the complaint be made in substance, it remains the position that this does not mean expressly invoking an Article of the Convention. That principle was established in *Fressoz and Roire v France*,[40] where the applicants were journalists who had been convicted of handling stolen goods, notably documents relating to the tax assessments of a third party which had formed the basis of an article they had written. The government had argued that the applicants had failed to exhaust domestic remedies since they had confined themselves to denying the charge that had been brought against them and had not argued before the trial court that there was a contradiction between that charge and their freedom of expression. The Court rejected that submission. In their cassation appeal, the applicants had made explicit reference to the domestic Freedom of the Press Act. They had also argued that they had improperly been charged with a general offence of handling stolen goods and that this had been done in order to circumvent the special provisions of French law governing the media. In the Court's view, by ruling on this point, the Court of Cassation had also ruled indirectly on the scope of the right of journalists to information. On that basis, the Strasbourg Court held that freedom of expression was in issue, if only impliedly, in the proceedings before the Court of Cassation such that an Article 10 complaint was raised at least in substance before that court.[41]

While *Fressoz and Roire* remains good law (and is regularly cited by the Court for rejecting pleas of non-exhaustion by the respondent government), it may be questioned whether, in countries where the Convention has been incorporated into domestic law

---

[37] A 200 (1991); 13 EHRR 853 para 34.
[38] *Kozacıoğlu v Turkey* hudoc (2009) para 40; *Mikolajová v Slovakia* hudoc (2011) para 30.
[39] Hudoc (2009) paras 42–4.   [40] 1999-I; 31 EHRR 28 paras 33–7 GC.
[41] See also *Castells v Spain* A 236 (1992); 14 EHRR 445 paras 24–32; *Gäfgen v Germany* hudoc (2010), para 44; and *Karapanagiotou and Others v Greece* hudoc (2010), para 29. For an example of a case where one of the complaints was raised explicitly before the domestic courts (and was thus admissible) and the other was not raised even implicitly (and was thus inadmissible), see *Association Les Témoins de Jéhovah v France No 8916/05* hudoc (2010) DA. In contrast to this line of cases, see *Cardot v France* A 200 (1991); 13 EHRR 853 paras 32–5, where the Court held that the applicant had failed to raise his Article 6(3)(d) complaint regarding witnesses against him in substance before the French courts. At trial he had not asked for the witnesses to be called and his pleadings to the Court of Cassation were too vague to draw that court's attention to his real complaint under Article 6(3)(d).

and is pleaded in domestic courts on a daily basis, the rule should now be stricter and applicants should be required expressly to invoke the Articles of the Convention in the domestic courts before applying to Strasbourg.

There are some indications that the Court may, in time, come to take this stricter approach. For instance, in *Azinas v Cyprus*,[42] concerning a domestic dispute over loss of pension rights, the applicant had withdrawn that part of his appeal to the Supreme Court of Cyprus that asserted that the loss of pension rights was contrary to his right to property. In finding that the applicant had not exhausted domestic remedies, the Grand Chamber relied, *inter alia*, on the fact that Convention was an integral part of the Cypriot legal system and Article 1 of Protocol 1 was directly applicable.[43] Other instances of non-exhaustion for failure to rely on specific Articles of the Convention (where the Convention is part of domestic law and thus there was nothing to prevent applicants from doing so) include: *Borges De Brito v Netherlands*,[44] *SV and SV v Bosnia and Herzegovina*,[45] and *Hickey v United Kingdom*.[46] In none of these cases was the Court expressly departing from or overruling *Fressoz and Roire*, but the time may have come for the Court to address the issue directly. In point of fact, at least for those countries which have incorporated the Convention, there may be some merit in a 'bright-line rule' which requires that the Convention complaint be made expressly before the domestic courts. This is not least because it would accord with Court's own view that, as stated earlier, one of the purposes of the rule on non-exhaustion is that the Court should have the benefit of the views of the national courts before it rules on the matter.

b. The appropriate domestic body

Whether a particular court is an 'appropriate domestic body' may depend more on the right in question than on the court itself. For example in Spanish cases, given the overlap between the Convention and the rights guaranteed by the Spanish constitution, applicants will normally be required to lodge *amparo* appeals with the Constitutional Court.[47] However, in *de Parias Merry v Spain*,[48] a case concerning property rights, the applicant had lodged such an *amparo* appeal with the Constitutional Court. This was dismissed on the ground that the right of property was not among those in respect of which such an appeal could be made. The inappropriateness of an *amparo* appeal to the Constitutional Court as regards this right therefore meant that the rejection by the Constitutional Court was not the final domestic decision in the applicant's case. Since the final domestic decision was therefore the earlier Administrative Court decision, and since this was given more than six months prior to the lodging of the application in Strasbourg, the application was declared inadmissible. The case is illustrative, therefore, of the care that should be taken in exhausting the appropriate domestic remedy for any given right and lodging an application promptly thereafter.[49]

---

[42] 2004-III; 40 EHRR 166.

[43] But see the joint dissenting opinion of Judges Costa and Garlicki to the effect that this ruling was unduly strict and formalistic, relying *inter alia* on the Court's ruling in *Fressoz and Roire*.

[44] *No 29388/11* hudoc (2013) DA, para 30.   [45] Hudoc (2012), paras 31–3.

[46] *No 39492/07* hudoc (2010) DA.

[47] *Castells v Spain* A 236 (1992); 14 EHRR 445 and *Grisankova and Grisankovs v Latvia No 36117/02* hudoc (2003) DA.   [48] *No 40177/98* hudoc (1999) DA.

[49] Though this decision should be read in the light of the later decision in *Fernandez-Molina Gonzalez and 370 other applications v Spain Nos 64359/01 and others* hudoc (2002) DA where the applicants had taken an *amparo* appeal to the Constitutional Court *inter alia* on the basis of Article 24 of the Constitution guaranteeing the principle of non-discrimination. In Strasbourg they complained, *inter alia*, of a breach of Article 1 of Protocol 1 taken together with Article 14 of the Convention. The Court took the view that it would be too formalistic to require the applicants to apply to the Court on two different dates in order for the Article 1 of

c. In compliance with formal requirements and time limits

Article 35(1) also operates with some deference to national procedural law, in that it normally requires compliance with the 'formal requirements and time limits laid down in domestic law' for exhausting remedies. In one sense, this has the same justification as the Court's own six-month time limit in fostering legal certainty.[50] Thus in ordinary legal proceedings where there are no special circumstances justifying a failure to abide by national procedures, the Court will frequently reject cases for non-exhaustion where the applicant had clearly sought to exhaust a remedy but through his own negligence failed to observe the requirements of domestic law.[51] This is most common in cases where there is a clear failure to lodge an appeal in time and will apply even where the appeal, if it had been properly lodged, would have had a reasonable prospect of success.[52] It will also be applicable to other procedural requirements, such as paying the applicable court fees.[53] One possible area of flexibility in this regard may be when, in the Court's view, the procedural rules for the hearing of domestic appeals have been interpreted too strictly by the domestic courts such as to prevent an applicant using an available remedy.[54] Another is when the applicant seeks to make reference to new case law of the Strasbourg Court in domestic proceedings when the relevant decision or judgment is delivered after the deadline for submissions in the domestic proceedings: new case law of the Court is a factor beyond the control of prospective applicants when they are still engaged in domestic proceedings.[55] Another exception is when, in spite of the applicant's failure to observe the forms prescribed by law, the competent court has nevertheless examined the substance of the appeal. In such cases, the rule on exhaustion of domestic remedies cannot be held against the applicant.[56] The same is true if the domestic court considered that the appeal was not admissible under its own procedures but nonetheless ruled on the substantive merits of the appeal.[57]

Finally, it was traditionally the case that the assessment of whether domestic remedies had been exhausted was normally carried out with reference to the date on which the application was lodged with the Court.[58] However, this rule has in recent years become subject to a number of exceptions.[59] Notably, if a new domestic remedy in respect of length of proceedings becomes available to the applicant after the introduction of the application but before the Court is called upon to decide on its admissibility, the applicant

Protocol 1 complaint and the Article 14 complaint to be compatible with the six-month rule. See, too, *DH and others v the Czech Republic* hudoc (2007), para 118, where the Court refused to apply the non-exhaustion rule in respect of the Roma applicants' failure to appeal the decision to place them in special schools, when the Czech Constitutional Court, in hearing their cases, had disregarded that omission and when, therefore, it would have been unduly formalistic to require the applicants to exercise a remedy which even the highest court of the country concerned had not obliged them to use.

[50] *Saghinadze and others v Georgia* hudoc (2010), paras 80–4.

[51] *Agbovi v Germany No 71759/01* hudoc (2006) DA with further references therein.

[52] *Ugilt Hansen v Denmark No 11968/04* hudoc (2006) DA; *Ben Salah Adraqui and Dhaime v Spain No 45023/98 DA* hudoc (2000) *Cardot v France* A 200 (1991); 13 EHRR 853 para 34.

[53] *Reuther v Germany No 74789/01* 2003-IX DA.

[54] *UTE Saur Vallnet v Andorra* hudoc (2012), paras 36-44 and *Miragall Escolano and others v Spain*, ECHR 2000-I, para 36.   [55] *Merger and Cros v France No 68864/01* hudoc (2004) DA.

[56] See *Gäfgen v Germany* hudoc (2010) para 143.

[57] *Verein Gegen Tierfabriken Schweiz (VgT) v Switzerland (No 2)* hudoc (2009) at paras 43–5 (see para 34 of the Chamber judgment which is quoted at para 43 of the Grand Chamber judgment and the references therein).

[58] *Csikos v Hungary* 2006-XIV para 17 and references therein. The Court will, however, accept the exhaustion of the final stage of remedies soon after the lodging of the application: *Karoussiotis v Portugal* hudoc (2011) at para 57.

[59] *Icyer v Turkey No 18888/02* hudoc (2006) para 72 DA and references therein.

must exhaust this new domestic remedy.[60] As concerns repetitive cases, if the government creates a new remedy, the Court will examine whether that remedy is effective in a leading case. If the remedy is found to be effective, the Court will hold that applicants in pending applications in similar cases are required to exhaust the new remedy, provided they are not time-barred from doing so. It will thus declare these applications inadmissible under Article 35(1), even when they were lodged before the creation of the new remedy. This has so far applied to cases involving interference with property rights, non-enforcement of domestic judgment, complaints of prison overcrowding, and length of proceedings, and, given the number of different remedies and contracting states to which it has applied, is quickly becoming the norm.[61] Perhaps its most controversial application came in the *Demopoulos* case, concerning the effectiveness of a new remedy for property claims in northern Cyprus. The Court found that this was a remedy Greek Cypriots were required to exhaust; and the applicant's and intervening Cypriot government's arguments to the effect that the remedy was not part of Turkish law, that there was an administrative practice of ongoing violations of human rights in northern Cyprus, that the remedy lent legitimacy to an illegal occupation, and that the applicants could not be required to use remedies in a jurisdiction to which they had not submitted, were all rejected by the Court.[62]

III. BURDEN OF PROOF

The Court has also stated that Article 35 provides for a distribution of the burden of proof.[63] In practice, the burden of proof operates as follows. Prior to the communication of an application to the respondent state for observations, the applicant must provide information to show that the requirements of Article 35 have been satisfied (Rule 47(f) of the Rules of Court). The Court will examine the matter on its own motion at this stage and will reject for non-exhaustion if it appears that an appropriate remedy has not been pursued. Where the case is formally communicated for observations, the burden is then on the respondent government. It is then incumbent on a government claiming non-exhaustion to satisfy the Court that the remedy was an effective one available

---

[60] *Fakhretdinov and others v Russia Nos 26716/09 and others* hudoc (2010) DA; *Grzinčič v Slovenia* ECHR 2007 (para 48); *Scordino v Italy (No 1)* 2006-V; 45 EHRR 207 paras 140–9 GC; *Korenjak v Slovenia No 463/03* hudoc (2007) DA, paras 66–71; *Michalak v Poland No 24549/03* hudoc (2005) DA, paras 41–4; *Charzynski v Poland No 15212/03* hudoc (2005) DA paras 40–3; *Predil Anstalt v Italy No 31993/96* hudoc (2002) DA; *Bottaro v Italy No 56298/00* hudoc (2002) DA; *Brusco v Italy* ECHR 2001-IX; *Andrasik and Others v Slovakia No 57984/00* hudoc (2002) DA; *Nogolica v Croatia* hudoc (2002) For a case where a new remedy was found to be ineffective, *inter alia*, because it made no provision for cases already pending before the Court, see *Parizov v the Former Yugoslav Republic of Macedonia* hudoc (2008) at para 45. As regards a new right of constitutional appeal, which might have been effective but for the fact that it would have had to have been filed over three years after the filing of the Strasbourg application, see *Cvetkovic v Serbia* hudoc (2008) at paras 42 and 43. That there was no requirement to avail oneself of a remedy introduced via new case law handed down over three years after the introduction of the Strasbourg application, see *Depauw v Belgium No 2115/04* hudoc (2007) DA.

[61] Property: *Demopoulos v Turkey Nos 46113/99 and others* hudoc (2010) DA, in particular paras 87 and 88; *Arioglu and others v Turkey No 11166/05* hudoc (2012) DA; *Altunay v Turkey No 42936/07* hudoc (2012) DA; *Icyer v Turkey* hudoc (2006) DA paras 74 *et seq.* Non-enforcement: *Nagovitsyn and Nalgiyev v Russia Nos 27451/09 and 60650/09* hudoc (2010) DA, paras 27–45; *Balan v Moldova No 44746/08* hudoc (2012) DA. Prison overcrowding: *Latak v Poland No 52070/08* hudoc (2010) DA, paras 79-87 and *Lominski v Poland No 33502/09* hudoc (2010) DA, paras 69–73. Length of criminal proceedings: *Ahlskog v Finland No 5238/07* hudoc (2010) DA, paras 68–80; *Turgut and others v Turkey No 4860/09* hudoc (2013) DA. Length of civil proceedings: *Adzi-Spirkoska and others v the Former Yugoslav Republic of Macedonia No 38914/05 and others* hudoc (2011) DA; *Taron v Germany No 53126/07* hudoc (2012) DA, paras 37–47; *Balakchiev and Others v Bulgaria No 65187/10* hudoc (2013) DA; *Valcheva and Abrashev v Bulgaria Nos 6194/11 and 34887/11* hudoc (2013) DA.

[62] *Demopoulos v Turkey*, paras 89–102.   [63] *Selmouni v France*, 1999-V; 29 EHRR 403 GC para 76.

in theory and in practice at the relevant time, that is to say, that it was accessible, was one which was capable of providing redress in respect of the applicant's complaints, and offered reasonable prospects of success.[64] However, once this burden of proof has been satisfied, it falls to the applicant to establish that the remedy advanced by the government was in fact exhausted or was for some reason inadequate and ineffective in the particular circumstances of the case or that there existed special circumstances absolving him or her from the requirement.[65] After communication, the respondent government may, of course, expressly waive the right to rely on the rule.[66]

Though the normal course is for it simply to state that the respondent government has not shown with a sufficient degree of certainty the existence of an available and effective remedy, the Court has occasionally explicitly stated that the respondent government has failed to discharge the burden of proof. For example in *Apostol v Georgia*,[67] the government had sought to argue that the right to enforcement of a judicial decision was a right guaranteed by the constitutional right of access to court. The Court noted that the government had not referred to any decisions or judgments of the Georgian Constitutional Court interpreting the right of access in this way. Equally, in *Mikolajova v Slovakia*,[68] the applicant complained that a police decision, which found she had committed a criminal offence without ever having interviewed her in relation to it, violated Article 8. The Court dismissed the government's preliminary objection as to non-exhaustion because it had failed to show, with reference to demonstrably established consistent case law in cases similar to the applicant's, that their interpretation of the scope of a civil action for protection of personal integrity was sufficiently certain, not only in theory but also in practice, and offered at least some prospects of success.

IV. ADEQUACY AND EFFECTIVENESS OF REMEDIES

The only remedies which Article 35 of the Convention requires to be exhausted are those that relate to the breaches alleged and, at the same time, are available and sufficient.[69] These remedies must be sufficiently certain not only in theory but also in practice, failing which they will lack the requisite accessibility and effectiveness. It falls to the respondent government to establish that these various conditions are satisfied. It is then for the Court, in any case where a plea of non-exhaustion is made by the government, to decide whether any given remedy is, in the light of its particular attributes and the applicant's particular circumstances, adequate and effective.[70] Although a certain overlap exists between the notions of the 'adequacy' and 'effectiveness' of a given remedy, appropriate distinctions

---

[64] See *Dalia v France* hudoc (1998) at para 38 and, as recent authorities, *Scoppola v Italy (No 2)* hudoc (2009) para 71 and *McFarlane v Ireland* hudoc (2010), para 107. This will also require a degree of precision from the government: it is not sufficient to refer to 'other remedies' without specifying what they are: *Deweer v Belgium* A 35 (1980); 2 EHRR 439 para 26. See also *Foti v Italy* A 56 (1982) 5 EHRR 313 para 48 (vague assertions as to the existence of remedies); *Scavuzzo-Hager v Switzerland No 41773/98* hudoc (2004) DA; and *Norbert Sikorski v Poland* hudoc (2009) at para 117 (insufficiently clear legal basis for the remedies suggested).

[65] See, for instance, *Grasser v Germany No 66491/01* hudoc (2004) DA with further references therein and *Gas and Dubois v France No 25951/07* hudoc (2010) DA. On special circumstances see the following section of this chapter.

[66] *Urbanczyk v Poland No 33777/96* hudoc (2002) DA. The Court has on one occasion applied the rule on its own motion after communication to the respondent government (in *Laidin v France No 43191/98* hudoc (2002)). However, this ruling has not been followed and it is to be queried whether the case is still good law.

[67] 2006-XIV para 39.   [68] Hudoc (2011) para 34.

[69] *Selmouni v France* 1999-V; 29 EHRR 403 para 75.

[70] *Civet v France* 1999-VI; 31 EHRR 871 para 41.

between the two concepts can be drawn. For example, a remedy may be adequate in the sense that it would in theory address the grievances but not be effective if it took too long or if the applicant was prevented from having recourse to it.[71] Thus in *Bertuzzi v France*,[72] the applicant had been granted legal aid to sue a lawyer. After the withdrawal of three lawyers appointed by the president of the bar to represent him, his legal aid entitlement lapsed. Among the remedies suggested by the government was the possibility of a disciplinary appeal against the president of the bar to the Prosecutor General at the Court of Appeal. The Court rejected this remedy on the ground that it was not an available remedy: the applicant could not be expected, unassisted by a lawyer, to know all the arcane judicial or disciplinary remedies against the president of the bar.

The availability, as opposed to the effectiveness, of a remedy will of course depend on the circumstances of the applicant's case and can often depend on when a remedy appears. In *Giumarra and Others v France*,[73] the applicants' complaints related to the length of criminal proceedings which they had joined as a civil party. Some months before the applicants introduced their application, a landmark judgment (*l'arrêt Gautier*) of the Paris Court of Appeal created a remedy for length of proceedings based on Article L 781–1 of the Judicial Code. The Court noted that the judgment had been followed by a number of other Appeal Courts and that the person who had obtained the judgment had not applied to the Strasbourg Court within six months of it. This meant it had acquired a sufficient degree of certainty such that it could and should be considered an available remedy for the purposes of Article 35(1) by the time the applicants introduced their application. Finally, in *Prencipe v Monaco*,[74] the Court found that the applicant could not be blamed for failing to lodge an appeal with the principality's Judicial Revision Court against a judgment of the Court of Appeal when the Criminal Code imposed a fine automatically on an appellant if the appeal was rejected. This, in the Court's view, effectively penalized recourse to the Judicial Revision Court, and imposing a fine based on the outcome of an appeal when no abuse of process was alleged rendered the appeal ineffective.

The domestic remedy which an applicant must exhaust will depend on the nature of the violation alleged. Generally, however, it may be said that legal procedures that involve the vindication of a personal right must be tried. Normally, these will be formal court proceedings, but they may also be—in the first instance at least—administrative procedures with later recourse to the courts should that prove necessary.[75]

There is, however, no absolute rule that an applicant will always be required to bring administrative, public, or constitutional claims. For example, if an applicant complains of police brutality, the rule could be complied with by bringing civil proceedings for damages against the police or, in some jurisdictions (eg France), criminal proceedings to which he could be joined as a civil party, since the lodging of a criminal complaint in such jurisdictions is regarded as an effective and sufficient remedy. Where there is no follow-up to the complaint, the victim is not required to bring additional civil proceedings for compensation or to challenge the decision not to pursue the complaint.[76]

Finally, in rare cases, where, through his application, the applicant is attempting to prevent an violation of the Convention, the question of whether a domestic remedy is effective

---

[71] *Mikheyev v Russia* hudoc (2006) para 86.   [72] Hudoc (2002).
[73] Hudoc (2001). See by contrast, *Zannouti v France No 42211/98* hudoc (2000) DA, where the same remedy had not been demonstrated as effective for length of pre-trial detention complaints and the relevant domestic judgments referred to by the government post-dated the lodging of the application to the Court.
[74] Hudoc (2009), paras 93–7.   [75] See eg *Young v UK* hudoc 2007; 45 EHRR 689.
[76] *Assenov and Others v Bulgaria* 1998-VIII; 28 EHRR 652 para 86.

(and thus requires to be exhausted before lodging the application) may depend on whether the remedy has suspensive effect. For instance, in asylum or immigration cases where an applicant alleges that, if removed from the contracting state, he or she will be subjected to ill-treatment contrary to Article 3, he or she will be expected to exhaust only those remedies which have suspensive effect.[77] However, this is peculiar to asylum and immigration cases, the justification being that any violation of Article 3 that arose after removal would be irreparable because the person would be outside the jurisdiction of the contracting state concerned. Outside Article 3, the rule is not one of general application.

V. SEVERAL REMEDIES

It is settled case law, confirmed by the Grand Chamber in *Micallef v Malta*[78] and *Kozacioğlu v Turkey*,[79] that where numerous remedies exist which are likely to be adequate and effective, it is enough that the applicant has had recourse to one of them.[80] This has been understood to mean two things. First, in the event of there being a number of remedies which an individual can pursue, that person is entitled to choose the remedy which addresses his or her essential grievance.[81] Second, when a remedy has been pursued, use of another remedy which has essentially the same objective is not required. Thus, for example, if a criminal complaint has been pursued, additional civil or administrative remedies need not be pursued.[82] This in turn also means that applicants are only expected to make normal use of domestic remedies, that is, those which arise in the context of the legal proceedings which might form the subject of their substantive complaint to the Court. Thus, for example, in a criminal length of proceedings cases, if the applicant has applied unsuccessfully to have the proceedings expedited, he or she will not then be required to begin separate proceedings against the state to establish liability on its part.[83]

VI. EXTRAORDINARY OR DISCRETIONARY REMEDIES

An applicant is only required to have recourse to remedies which are capable of providing an effective and sufficient means of redressing the alleged wrong. Extraordinary remedies, such as petitions for a re-opening of proceedings or for supervisory review, are not regarded as effective and sufficient remedies,[84] nor is requesting a court to review its decision.[85] The same principle will apply to remedies which depend on the discretionary powers of public officials such as, in the UK, an application to the relevant criminal cases review commission[86] or,

---

[77] *De Souza Ribeiro v France* hudoc (2012) and *Jabari v Turkey No 40035/98* hudoc (1999) DA. This will also be the case in countries where it is open to applicants to seek interim injunctions whilst they are pursuing remedies. If they do not pursue such remedies when interim injunctions are available, this may result in a finding of non-exhaustion: *Bahaddar v Netherlands* 1998-I; 26 EHRR 278 paras 47 and 48.

[78] ECHR 2009, para 58.   [79] Hudoc (2009), para 40.

[80] *Micallef v Malta* hudoc (2009) and *Kozacioglu v Turkey* hudoc (2009), confirming the rule as stated in *TW v Malta* hudoc (1999) and *Aquilina v Malta* hudoc (1999) that an applicant who has exhausted a remedy that is apparently effective and sufficient cannot be required also to have tried others that were available but probably no more likely to be successful. See also *Iatridis v Greece* 1999-II; 30 EHRR 97 para 47 GC; *Jasar v the Former Yugoslav Republic of Macedonia No 69908/01* hudoc (2006) DA and references therein.

[81] *Jeličić v Bosnia and Herzegovina* hudoc (2005); *Karako v Hungary* hudoc (2009), para 14.

[82] *Karako v Hungary* hudoc (2009); *Jasinskis v Latvia* hudoc (2010), paras 50–5.

[83] *Moreira Barbosa v Portugal*, no 65681/01, 2004-V DA, confirmed in *Riad and Idiab v Belgium* hudoc (2008), para 84.

[84] *Prystavska v Ukraine No 21287/02* hudoc (2002) DA; *Kutcherenko v Ukraine No 41974/98* hudoc (1999) DA; *Tumilovich v Russia No 47033/99* hudoc (1999) DA.

[85] *Cinar v Turkey No 28602/95* hudoc (2003) DA.

[86] *Tucka v UK (No 1) No 34586/10* hudoc (2011) DA, paras 14 and 15 with further references therein; *Gurepka v Ukraine* hudoc (2005) at para 60; *Horvat v Croatia* hudoc (2001), para 47.

in other countries, appeals to authorities such as presidents of courts or prosecutors.[87] The same principle applies to remedies which are not directly accessible to the applicant because they depend on the exercise of discretion by a private intermediary.[88] The principle also applies to remedies which have no precise time limits, as this would render the six-month rule nugatory.[89]

For the UK and in accordance with the Court's ruling in *Hobbs v UK*,[90] at present an application for a declaration of incompatibility under the Human Rights Act 1998 will not be an effective remedy, since the declaration will only provide the appropriate minister with the power and not the duty to amend the offending legislation.[91] In *Burden and Burden*,[92] the Court observed that it was possible that at some future date evidence of a long-standing practice of ministers giving effect to the courts' declarations of incompatibility might be sufficient to persuade it of the effectiveness of the procedure. The former President of the Court and former United Kingdom judge on the Court, Sir Nicolas Bratza, also indicated that there were signs the Court's attitude to declarations of incompatibility might soon be revisited.[93] However, this is unlikely to happen soon, not least because the government did not argue the point in the most recent case where the point arose, *Malik v UK*,[94] meaning the Court was reluctant to take the step itself.

Complaints to ombudsmen or other organs which supervise the administration have been regarded as inadequate,[95] as are administrative remedies which betray a lack of independence, such as internal police complaints procedures.[96] However, in light of the growing powers awarded to national ombudsmen and a strong custom of national authorities abiding by the decisions of ombudsmen, it may be that, in future case law, the Court will have occasion to allow exceptions to this general principle. One possible sign of a move in this direction is the Court's findings in *Eriksson* and *Ruminski* against Sweden that seeking compensation for violations of the Convention through the Chancellor of Justice was one remedy among others that applicants would be required to exhaust, particularly given the recent developments in the Chancellor's practice of awarding compensation for such cases.[97]

VII. APPEALS TO HIGHER COURTS

In principle, the applicant must appeal to the highest court of appeal against an unfavourable decision at first or second instance.[98] Mere doubts as to the prospects of success of national proceedings do not absolve the applicant from the obligation to exhaust.[99] It

---

[87] *Akçiçek v Turkey No 40965/10* hudoc (2011) DA.

[88] *Tanase v Moldova* hudoc (2010) at para 122.

[89] See *Tucka* and, *inter alia*, *Galstyan v Armenia* hudoc (2007), para 39; and *Williams v UK No 32567/06* hudoc (2009) DA.   [90] *No 63684/00* hudoc (2002) DA.

[91] The same is true for declarations of incompatibility under the Irish European Convention on Human Rights Act 2003: *A, B and C v Ireland* hudoc (2010) at para 150.   [92] Hudoc (2008) GC.

[93] See 'The Relationship between the UK Courts and Strasbourg' [2011] EHRLR 505.

[94] *No 32968/11* hudoc (2013) DA at para 28.

[95] *Lehtinen v Finland* 1999-VII; *Jasar v the Former Yugoslav Republic of Macedonia No 69908/01* hudoc (2006) DA; *Montion v France No 11192/84*, 52 DR 227 (1987); *Leander v Sweden* A 116 (1987) paras 80–4.

[96] *Khan v UK* 2000-V; 31 EHRR 1016; *Jasar v the Former Yugoslav Republic of Macedonia No 69908/01* hudoc (2006) DA.

[97] *Eriksson v Sweden* hudoc (2012) at para 51; *Ruminski v Sweden No 10404/10* hudoc (2013) DA, at paras 39 et seq.   [98] *Vorobyeva v Ukraine No 27517/02* hudoc (2002) DA.

[99] *Pellegriti v Italy No 77363/01* hudoc (2005) DA; *MPP Golub v Ukraine No 6778/05* hudoc (2005) DA; *Milosevic v Netherlands No 77631/01* hudoc (2002) DA.

is a different matter, however, if a remedy is bound to fail, for example because of recent negative case law by the appeal courts in cases which are factually or legally similar to the applicant's case[100] and where there is no likelihood of the appeal court reversing its own recent precedent.[101]

The most problematic aspect of this part of the rule is how it is to be applied to cases which fall between the two poles, that is, to cases where it might be said that there are more than just 'mere doubts' as to the prospect of success of a remedy but, at the same time, it cannot be said for certain that the remedy would be bound to fail. There are suggestions in the Court's recent case law that, if there are any doubts at all as to the prospect of success, the applicant will be penalized for not lodging an appeal and letting the domestic court resolve those doubts. For instance, it will be incumbent on the applicant to do so if the applicant him or herself believes there is the possibility of the court in question reversing its own case law in his or her case or, in subsequent case law, the court does in fact do so.[102] Equally, where an analysis of the national case law reveals a dispute in the domestic courts as to what the relevant legal rules are, the applicant will be required to bring proceedings in order to assert his version of the appropriate rule.[103]

An interesting aspect of this part of the rule is the extent to which the Court will accept the opinion of counsel that a remedy is or is not effective. In its early case law, the Court was prepared to find that applicants were not obliged to make use of remedies which, according to 'settled legal opinion' existing at the relevant time, did not provide redress for their complaints[104] and a well-reasoned opinion from counsel, which set out the position under national law, was evidence of 'settled legal opinion'.[105] That was confirmed recently in *Chapman v Belgium*,[106] where the Court found that an applicant was entitled not to lodge an appeal with the Court of Cassation after receiving legal advice from an advocate before that court who advised that an appeal would have no reasonable prospect of success. This was particularly because the assistance of an advocate before the Court of Cassation was compulsory, a rule which had a preventative effect, both for appellants and the court.

However, other cases have reached the opposite conclusion. In *Fox v UK*,[107] counsel's assessment that renewing a judicial review application from the High Court to the Court of Appeal stood no greater than a 50 per cent chance of success was insufficient reason for the applicant's failure.[108] Nor was the dismissal of the judicial review application evidence of 'settled legal opinion' justifying the applicant in not seeking to test the matter in the

---

[100] See, as recent authorities, *Maktouf and Damjanovic v Bosnia and Herzegovina* hudoc (2013), paras 59 and 60; *Gas and Dubois v France No 25951/07* hudoc (2010) DA; *Vasilkoski and Others v the Former Yugoslav Republic of Macedonia* hudoc (2010), paras 45–6; and *Laska and Lika v Albania* hudoc (2010), paras 45–8.

[101] *Paksas v Lithuania* hudoc (2011), para 76; *Salah Sheekh v Netherlands* hudoc (2007) 45 EHRR 1158 paras 121–3.

[102] *Augusto v France* hudoc (2007) para 42. However, where an applicant's request for legal aid has been refused on the absence of grounds for pursuing the appeal, an application will not be inadmissible for failure to pursue the appeal to the Court of Cassation: *L.L. v France* 2006-XI.

[103] *Van Oosterwijck v Belgium* A 40 (1980); 3 EHRR 557 paras 30–41 PC.

[104] *De Wilde, Ooms and Versyp v Belgium* (the *Vagrancy* cases) A 12 (1971) p 33; 1 EHRR 373, 401 PC.

[105] In *McFeeley v UK No 8317/98*, 20 DR 44 (1980), though cf *K, F and P v UK No 10789/84*, 40 DR 298 (1984).   [106] *No 39619/06* hudoc (2013) DA, paras 32 and 33.

[107] *No 61319/09* hudoc (2012) DA.

[108] See also *LL v UK No 39678/09* hudoc (2013) DA, where the Court, in finding that the applicant should have appealed to the Judicial Committee of the Privy Council, placed little reliance on the doubts on the part of the applicant's legal representatives as to her chances of success before the Privy Council, expressed in written form apparently only after the government raised the issue in the proceedings before the Court (para 27 of the decision).

Court of Appeal. It was also relevant that different judicial opinions had been expressed on the merits of the applicant's complaint in cases similar to his own. In *McFarlane*, concerning the question of remedies for length of criminal proceedings in Ireland, the Grand Chamber rejected the Irish government's reliance on an opinion by an 'experienced Irish constitutional lawyer and practitioner' who had concluded that an action for damages for a breach of a constitutional right to reasonable expedition was an effective remedy. However, the Court was not convinced, observing that this remedy has been available in theory for almost 25 years but has never been invoked, and recent judicial dicta indicated that the availability of this remedy remained an open question.

Notwithstanding its conclusions on that particular remedy, the *McFarlane* judgment confirmed the now well-established rule that in common law systems (and, indeed, now in many other, non-common law systems)[109] it is normally incumbent on an aggrieved individual to allow the domestic courts the opportunity to develop existing rights by way of interpretation.[110] The Court's reasoning in this respect can be difficult to predict and whether an applicant can be expected to do so in any given case will—it seems—depend *inter alia* on the nature of the domestic right, the likelihood of the domestic courts developing that right in the applicant's favour, and, as always, the practical realities of the applicant's situation.[111]

Subject to the above observations, applicants are ordinarily expected to appeal to the highest possible court of appeal in the contracting state. In legal systems with a written constitution and a constitutional bill of rights, the highest court of appeal will normally be the constitutional court, so that a constitutional action must be brought to challenge the law or administrative practice alleged to be in breach of the Convention. Thus, in Bosnia and Herzegovina, the Czech Republic, Germany, Poland, Serbia, and Spain, complaints must, where possible, be pursued to the constitutional court.[112] The same is now true for Turkey. However, in its decision finding that an individual application to the Turkish Constitutional Court (a new remedy which was created in 2010) was one that applicants now had to exhaust, the Court expressly reserved the right to examine the consistency of the Constitutional Court's case law with its own and went on to state that its decision was not therefore a ruling on the effectiveness of the remedy in question and

---

[109] See, eg, *Augusto v France* hudoc (2007), paras 37–46 and *Hamaidi v France No 39291/98* hudoc (2001) DA (that in France, a cassation appeal is in principle among the remedies which require to be exhausted).

[110] Paragraph 120.

[111] Contrast, for instance, *A, B and C v Ireland* hudoc (2010), paras 142–9 (a declaratory action based on Article 40.3.3 of the Constitution, which acknowledges the right to life of the unborn child and gives due regard to the equal right to life of the mother, not an effective remedy for three women challenging the prohibition on abortion in Ireland on health and well-being grounds) and *D v Ireland No 26499/02* hudoc (2006) DA (the same action is an effective remedy when seeking an abortion on grounds of a fatal foetal abnormality). See also *Boyce v Ireland No 8428/09* hudoc (2012) DA, an action based on the personal rights in Article 40.3.2 of the Constitution should have been pursued in order to challenge the taking, retention and use of the blood sample at a police station. However, given the fact that, in this latter case, the applicant had already raised the matter in substance in the criminal proceedings against him, it is not clear how the Court's conclusion can be reconciled with the general rule, discussed in section (v), that, where numerous remedies exist which are likely to be adequate and effective, it is enough that the applicant has had recourse to one of them.

[112] *Mirazovic v Bosnia and Herzegovina No 13628/03* hudoc (2006) DA; *Hartman v Czech Republic* 2003-VIII; 42 EHRR 587 (though finding that since the Constitutional Court could not take practical steps to expedite proceedings in lower courts, it was not a remedy that need be exhausted in length of proceedings cases); *Allaoui and Others v Germany No 44911/98* hudoc (1999) DA; *Mogos and Krifka v Germany No 78084/01* hudoc (2003) DA; *Paslawski v Poland No 38678/97* hudoc (2002) DA; *Vincic and others v Serbia* hudoc (2009) at para 51; *Marinkovic v Serbia No 5353/11* hudoc (2013) DA, para 59; and *Castells v Spain* A 236 (1992); 14 EHRR 445.

that it would be for the respondent government to prove that the remedy was effective, both in theory and in practice.[113]

Beyond these contracting states, the effectiveness of a constitutional complaint will depend on the nature of the constitutional remedy in each contracting state. For example, in Italy, where individuals cannot bring cases directly before the Constitutional Court but rely on lower courts to refer the case, this will not constitute a remedy that requires exhaustion.[114] In Hungary, the Hungarian Constitutional Court will be an ineffective remedy since it is only entitled to control the general constitutionality of laws and cannot quash or modify specific measures taken against an individual by the state.[115] In *Apostol v Georgia*,[116] the Court held that in Georgia the Constitutional Court is an ineffective remedy, since it cannot set aside decisions of public authorities or courts, and a finding of unconstitutionality of an act will not lead to the quashing of judicial decisions taken on the basis of that act. From the *Apostol* judgment, where the Court surveyed its case law on a number of constitutional courts, it would appear that the key factor is whether a constitutional complaint makes it possible to remedy violations of rights committed by public authorities or forbid authorities from continuing to infringe on the right in question. As concerns judicial decisions, the constitutional complaint must make it possible, where a law is found to be unconstitutional, to annul all final decisions made on the basis of the law and provide direct and speedy redress to the complainant.

Finally, for the UK, it remains an open question whether, in cases where appeal lies to the Supreme Court, applicants will be expected to seek permission to appeal to it, not least because to obtain permission to appeal, an appellant has to convince the court that the case raises an arguable point of law of general public importance and there may well be cases where the appellant's Convention complaint, even if well-founded, is not one of general public importance.[117] There are signs, however, that in any case where it is at least arguable that a point of general public importance arises, the Strasbourg Court will require prospective applicants to seek leave to the Supreme Court, not least given the high proportion of human rights appeals the Supreme Court hears every year. The likelihood of a change in the Court's approach in this direction can be seen in the fact that it recently faulted one applicant for failing to appeal to the Judicial Committee of the Privy Council, considering that the grounds of her appeal (on the absence of a youth detention facility for female minor offenders in Jersey) pointed to a miscarriage of justice going beyond the facts of her case.[118] Of particular note in that case was the Court's observation that the Judicial Committee of the Privy Council was principally composed of Justices from the Supreme Court of the United Kingdom, with extensive experience of Convention issues.

VIII. SPECIAL CIRCUMSTANCES AND EXEMPTION FROM OBLIGATION TO EXHAUST

It has been recognized by the Strasbourg organs that according to the 'generally recognised principles of international law', there may be special circumstances where an

---

[113] *Hasan Uzun v Turkey No 10755/13* hudoc (2013) DA.

[114] *Immobiliare Saffi v Italy* 1999-V; 30 EHRR 756 para 42 GC; *De Jorio v Italy No 73936/01* hudoc (2003) DA; *Brozicek v Italy* A 167 (1989); 12 EHRR 371 para 34 PC. See also *Miconi v Italy* hudoc (2004).

[115] *Ven v Hungary No 21495/93* hudoc (1993) DA; *Csikos v Hungary* 2006-XIV paras 18–19. See also *Sergey Smirnov v Russia* hudoc (2006) (no requirement to apply to Constitutional Court concerning domestic court's interpretation of statute when the applicant did not allege that the statute was unconstitutional).

[116] 2006-XIV.

[117] For Scottish appeals, where there is no requirement of leave to appeal, see the older authority *Leech v UK No 20075/92* hudoc (1994) DA.   [118] *No 39678/09* hudoc (2013) DA.

applicant is absolved from the requirement to exhaust even adequate and effective domestic remedies.[119] This flows from the understanding of the rule as one that must be applied 'with some degree of flexibility and without excessive formalism'.[120]

Where an applicant alleges that an administrative practice exists and is able to show that there is official tolerance at the highest level of the state, he or she will be absolved from exhausting remedies, since there will be an assumption that they will be ineffective in practice. Where the administrative practice involves official tolerance at the middle or lower levels of command, it will be a question of fact to be resolved in each case whether the remedies are still effective and sufficient.[121]

In *Akdivar and Others v Turkey*,[122] the Court was called upon to examine the destruction of the applicants' homes during security operations in south-east Turkey during a time of serious disturbance when most of the region was subject to emergency rule. The Turkish government had argued that, despite this, there was a range of civil, administrative, and criminal remedies available to the applicants. In rejecting this submission, the Court held, in determining whether special circumstances existed, that it had to take 'realistic account not only of the existence of formal remedies in the legal system of the Contracting Party concerned but also of the general legal and political context in which they operate'. The general context prevailing in south-east Turkey at the time was such that there were obstacles to the proper functioning of the system of the administration of justice, such as difficulties in securing probative evidence. Similarly, the severe civil strife in the region meant the prospects of success of civil proceedings based on allegations against the security forces had to be considered to be negligible in the absence of any official inquiry into their allegations, even assuming that the applicants would have been able to secure the services of lawyers willing to press their claims before the courts.[123] Despite the possible breadth of the Court's ruling in *Akdivar*, it would appear that the circumstances in this case were indeed exceptional and the Court in later cases has not been prepared to find the existence of special circumstances due to local conditions. In *Siddik Aslan and others*,[124] the applicants had alleged that their relatives had been unlawfully killed by security forces and that there had been a failure to investigate on the part of the authorities. While there had been attempts to recover the bodies, it appears that the applicants themselves had buried them without informing the authorities for fear of reprisals. The Court was not convinced that their fears were well-founded. Equally in *Kanlibas v Turkey*,[125] the applicant had alleged that his brother had been killed by security forces and the body mutilated. He had a medical report by a British forensic pathologist to this effect, which he alleged he did not submit to the Turkish authorities for fear of reprisals. The Court again found no verifiable evidence to support or corroborate that argument and found that the complaints made under Articles 2 and 3 in their substantive aspects to be inadmissible.

---

[119] See *Van Oosterwijck v Belgium* A 40 (1980); 3 EHRR 557 paras 36–40 PC and *Selmouni v France* 1999-V; 29 EHRR 403 paras 76–7.

[120] *Selmouni v France*, para 77; *Cardot v France* A 200 (1991); 13 EHRR 853 para 34.

[121] *Donnelly v UK Nos 5577–5583/72*, 4 DR 4 (1975). [122] 1996-IV; 23 EHRR 143 para 69.

[123] See also *Aksoy v Turkey* 1996-VI; 23 EHRR 553 paras 41–57 and *Aydin and Others v Turkey Nos 28293/95, 29494/95 and 30219/96*, 2000-III DA. In *Aksoy* (and subsequently in *Aydin*) the Court extended its ruling in *Akdivar* to allegations of torture on the part of the authorities. It found that after the public prosecutor, who had seen the injuries to the applicant, had taken no action, it was understandable if the applicant formed the belief that he could not hope to secure concern and satisfaction through national legal channels and this amounted to special circumstances absolving him of the need to exhaust domestic remedies (paras 56–7). [124] Hudoc (2005).

[125] *No 32444/96* hudoc (2005) DA.

The Court, however, applied its ruling in *Akdivar* in the first Chechen cases to come before it. In *Isayeva, Yusupova and Bazayeva v Russia*,[126] the applicants complained about the deaths of their relatives and their own injuries as a result of the bombing of Grozny in October 1999. The government had argued that both civil and criminal remedies remained open to the applicants. The Court noted that while these remedies were in principle available under Russian law, in respect of civil actions, Russian courts were unable to consider properly the merits of a claim relating to alleged serious criminal actions in the absence of any results from a criminal investigation. It further noted the practical difficulties cited by the applicants in bringing such an action and the fact that the law-enforcement bodies were not functioning properly in Chechnya at the time. It therefore found that special circumstances existed which affected the applicants' obligation to exhaust remedies. In respect of the possibility of criminal remedies, the Court considered that this limb of the government's preliminary objection on non-exhaustion raised issues concerning the effectiveness of the criminal investigation. Indeed it went on to find a violation of the procedural limb of Article 2 in this respect.

In a more peaceful general context, however, the plea of 'special circumstances' has been rarely accepted. *AB v Netherlands*[127] concerned the applicant's conditions of detention in the Netherlands Antilles, the authorities' interference with his correspondence, and the question of a lack of an effective remedy in respect of these complaints. The government had argued that the applicant could have pursued a civil claim in tort through summary proceedings where he could also have sought the necessary interim measures. The Court found that in assessing this remedy it had to take account of its existence in the legal system of the Netherlands Antilles and, on the basis of the *Akdivar* ruling, the general legal and political context in which it operated as well as the personal circumstances of the applicant. It referred to similar proceedings taken by six detainees of the same prison. It appeared that the authorities had remained totally passive for more than a year in complying with six injunctions granted by the court hearing that case. The absence of convincing explanations from the government as to the failure to remedy the situation and observe these injunctions meant there were special circumstances absolving the applicant from the obligation to exhaust the remedy suggested by the government. In *Öcalan v Turkey*,[128] the Chamber and Grand Chamber concurred in finding that the manner of the applicant's detention was a special circumstance absolving him from taking proceedings by which the lawfulness of it could be challenged. He had been kept in total isolation, possessed no legal training, and had no possibility of consulting a lawyer while in police custody. An additional factor was the unusual manner of the applicant's arrest (he had been arrested by security forces in Kenya after leaving the Greek embassy *en route* to Nairobi airport), which meant he was the principal source of direct information on his arrest. Finally, the movement of his lawyers had been obstructed by the police. Finally, in *DH and others v the Czech Republic* (concerning the placement of Roma children in schools for children with special needs), though it was not concerned with whether there were special circumstances absolving the applicants from exhausting domestic remedies altogether, the Court was prepared to state that 'in the special circumstances of the present case' certain of the applicants could not be faulted for failing to lodge constitutional appeals with the Czech Constitutional Court. It was not stated expressly what those special circumstances were, though from the judgment it would seem implicit that these

---

[126] Hudoc (2005); 41 EHRR 847. See also *Khashiyev and Akayeva v Russia* hudoc (2005) and *Isayeva v Russia* hudoc (2005); 41 EHRR 791, judgments of the same date.

[127] Hudoc (2002); 37 EHRR 928 at para 63–74.

[128] Hudoc (2003) paras 66–76; 37 EHRR 238 and 2005-IV; 41 EHRR 985 paras 62–71 GC.

were the general context and importance of the issue in the case, and the usual procedural history of the applicants' particular cases in the Czech legal system.

These rulings would seem to indicate that the threshold for a 'special circumstances' dispensation is an extremely high one. Special circumstances will only exist when it can be demonstrated that pursuing a remedy would have been dangerous or impossible rather than simply difficult or particularly onerous for the applicant in question.

This is indicative of a general trend in the case law that, as the Convention becomes an ever greater part of domestic law and as domestic remedies develop, the exhaustion rule will become stricter and the Court will be less likely to apply its *dicta* in *Cardot* and *Akdivar* that the rule should be applied with some degree of flexibility and without excessive formalism.

4. THE SIX-MONTH RULE

I. THE AIM OF THE RULE

Article 35(1) further provides that the Court 'may only deal with the matter...within a period of six months from the date on which the final decision was taken'.

Protocol 15, when ratified, will reduce the period from six months to four. A transitional provision accompanying the change, contained in Article 8(3) of the Protocol, is designed to allow potential applicants to become fully aware of the new deadline: it provides that the change shall enter into force following the expiration of a period of six months after the date of entry into force of the Protocol.[129] Article 8(3) also provides that the change will not have retroactive effect, since it specifies that the change does not apply to applications in respect of which the final decision within the meaning of Article 35(1) of the Convention was taken prior to the date of entry into force of the new rule.

The aims of rule (which will not change with the reduction from six to four months) were recently restated by the Grand Chamber in *Sabri Gunes v Turkey*.[130] These are: (i) to maintain legal certainty by ensuring that cases raising issues under the Convention are examined within a reasonable time, and to prevent the authorities and other persons concerned from being kept in a state of uncertainty for a long period of time; (ii) to afford the prospective applicant time to consider whether to lodge an application and, if so, to decide on the specific complaints and arguments to be raised; (iii) to facilitate the establishment of facts in a case, since with the passage of time, any fair examination of the issues raised is rendered problematic; and (iv) to mark out the temporal limit of the supervision exercised by the Court and to signal, both to individuals and state authorities, the period beyond which such supervision is no longer possible (this being justified by the wish of the High Contracting Parties to prevent past judgments being constantly called into question).[131]

As stated earlier, the rule applies to both inter-state and individual applications.[132] Given the importance of the provision in enabling the Court to avoid the examination of 'historic' complaints, it is not surprising that it has held that the respondent government cannot waive the application of the rule on its own authority,[133] nor can the Court set

---

[129] See para 22 of the Protocol's Explanatory Report: http://conventions.coe.int/Treaty/EN/Reports/Html/213.htm.   [130] Hudoc (2012).

[131] Paragraphs 39 and 40.

[132] Eg, *Cyprus v Turkey* (fourth inter-state case) 2001-IV; 35 EHRR 731.

[133] See *Walker v UK No 34979/97* hudoc (2000) DA. See also *X v France No 9587/81*, 29 DR 228 (1982); *K v Ireland* No 10416/83, 38 DR 158 (1984); *Bozano v France No 9990/82*, 39 DR 119 (1984).

aside the application of the rule (for example, in the absence of a preliminary objection by the respondent government in its observations).[134] When the government raises an objection based on the six-month rule, the Court is not bound by the date of the final decision as calculated by the government and may calculate for itself the appropriate date.[135] It is also immaterial to the Court's calculation of the six-month period the date upon which domestic authorities believe domestic remedies have been exhausted.[136]

The two main issues of interpretation that have arisen in respect of the rule are: (i) the calculation of the date of the final domestic decision (the start of the six-month period); and (ii) the date which is to be taken as the date of introduction of the application (the end of the six-month period). These points are considered further below. In all cases, six months means six calendar months, regardless of the actual duration of those months.[137] The six-month period is also calculated without regard for national rules on the calculation of time limits, such as when the time limit falls on a non-working day, prolonging it to the next working day.[138] It starts to run from the day after the date of the final decision.[139]

II. THE DATE OF THE FINAL DECISION

The 'final decision' for purposes of Article 35 will normally be the final domestic decision rejecting the applicant's claim.[140] The time limit only starts to run from the final decision resulting from the exhaustion of remedies which are adequate and effective to provide redress in respect of the matter complained of. The six-month rule and the exhaustion requirement are thus intertwined in this respect. It follows that the time limit will not run from the date of decisions resulting from extraordinary or discretionary remedies or remedies with imprecise time limits (see the examples given in section 3.VI below). Thus, the Court's case law is clear: if these remedies are pursued, the application is likely to be declared inadmissible as out of time.[141] The same will apply in respect of an appeal to a court to which, in the applicant's case, no appeal lies. In such a case, the final decision will be that of the lower court, not the date upon which the applicant is informed that he has no right of appeal to the higher court. Ignorance, through lack of legal assistance, for example, is no defence in this respect.[142]

Where no adequate and effective remedy is available, the 'final decision' will be the act or decision complained of and thus the six-month rule will apply strictly from this date.[143] In *Miconi v Italy*,[144] the alleged violation of the Convention (preventing full legal costs being awarded in a certain class of litigation involving pension rights) was held to be the automatic effect of the entry into force of two laws regulating the matter. There was no remedy through the courts against the laws in question since the courts were

---

[134] *Belaousof and others v Greece* hudoc (2004), para 38.

[135] *Ipek v Turkey* No 39706/98 hudoc (2010) DA.

[136] *Fernie v UK* No 14881/04 hudoc (2006) DA.

[137] *Otto v Germany* No 21425/06 hudoc (2009) DA.

[138] *Sabri Gunes v Turkey* hudoc (2012), at para 61 and the references therein.

[139] *Otto v Germany* No 21425/06 hudoc (2009) DA.

[140] *Paul and Audrey Edwards v UK* No 46477/99 hudoc (2001) DA.

[141] See, *inter alia*, *Tucka v UK (No 1)* No 34586/10 hudoc (2011) DA and *Galstyan v Armenia* hudoc (2007); *Williams v UK* No 32567/06 hudoc (2009) DA; *Berdzenishvili v Russia* No 31697/03 hudoc (2004) DA.

[142] See *Fernie v UK* No 14881/04 hudoc (2006) DA.

[143] *Roffey and others v UK* No 1278/11 hudoc (2013) DA; *Dennis and others v UK* No 76573/01 hudoc (2002) DA; *Bayram and Yildirim v Turkey* No 38587/97, 2002-III DA; *Veznedaroglu v Turkey* hudoc (1999). *Sardin v Russia* No 69582/01 hudoc (2004) DA; and *Sitokhova v Russia* No 55609/00 hudoc (2004) DA (the quashing of a final judgment in supervisory review proceedings being the final domestic decision).

[144] No 66432/01 hudoc (2004) DA.

bound by them and had no discretion in their implementation. In addition, although the Constitutional Court could rule on the compatibility of the laws with the constitution after their entry into force, since individuals were not entitled to apply directly to that court it was not a remedy that required to be exhausted. The six-month period was held to run from the entry into force of the relevant laws. However, the Court has also stated that special considerations could apply in exceptional cases where applicants first avail themselves of a domestic remedy and only at a later stage become aware, or should have become aware, of the circumstances which make that remedy ineffective. In such a situation, the six-month period might be calculated from the time when the applicant becomes aware, or should have become aware, of these circumstances. This has frequently arisen in cases involving disappearances where there has been some sporadic investigation of the circumstances of the disappearance. The question is how long relatives may wait before bringing a case before the Court. The Court has found, most notably in *Varnava and others v Turkey*,[145] that applications can be rejected as out of time where there has been excessive or unexplained delay once they have, or should have, become aware that no investigation has been instigated, that an investigation has lapsed into inaction or become ineffective, or there is no prospect of an effective investigation in the future. The Court has wisely avoided giving any precise indication of how long applicants may wait (stating that this will unavoidably depend on the case), but that once ten years have elapsed since the disappearance, applicants would generally have to show convincingly that there is some ongoing, and concrete, advance being achieved to justified further delay in coming to Strasbourg.[146]

There have been a number of problems with the application of the six-month rule in situations where the final domestic decision is not in dispute but the parties disagree as to what date to take for the purposes of the rule. This arises from different national practices in delivering judgments. Two situations must be distinguished. First, where a judgment is not pronounced in open court and the applicant is entitled to be served with a written copy of it, the time limit will be calculated from the date on which the judgment is actually served.[147] If the judgment is served on the applicant's lawyer, then the six-month period will run from this date, even if the applicant only became aware of the judgment later.[148] In this respect, an applicant's negligence in maintaining contact with a former lawyer may be a factor to be taken into account.[149] It is for the state that invokes the six-month

---

[145] Hudoc (2009), at para 157; *Er and others v Turkey* hudoc (2012), paras 48–69; *Paul and Aubrey Edwards v UK No 46477/99* hudoc (2001) DA; *Aydin v Turkey No 28293/95* hudoc (2000) DA. See also *Bayram and Yildirim v Turkey No 38587/97*, 2002-III DA.

[146] Paragraph 166 of the *Varnava* judgment. This approach was applied by the Grand Chamber to property and other complaints arising from the Nagorno-Karabakh conflict in *Chiragov and others v Armenia No 13216/05* hudoc (2011) DA, and *Sargsyan v Azerbaijan No 40167/06* hudoc (2011) DA, in each case finding that, having regard to the prevailing situation of conflict, the applicants had acted without undue delay in lodging their cases three and four years after the ratification of the Convention by Armenia and Azerbaijan respectively (*Chiragov* paras 134–47; *Sargsyan* paras 133–48).

[147] *Worm v Austria* 1997-V; 25 EHRR 454; *Sarıbek v Turkey No 41055/98* hudoc (2004) DA. In *Baghli v France* 1999-VIII; 33 EHRR 32 paras 29–31, an application concerning a deportation order imposed on a settled immigrant, the applicant had never been served with the full text of the final judgment dismissing his appeal against the deportation order. The Court rejected the government's preliminary objection to the effect that it would have been straightforward for the applicant or his lawyer to have established the tenor of the judgment against him. The Court held that the six-month period cannot start to run until the applicant has effective and sufficient knowledge of the final domestic decision. On this latter point, see also *Koc and Tosun v Turkey No 23852/04* hudoc (2008) DA.

[148] *Andorka and Vavra v Hungary Nos 25694/03 and 28338/03* hudoc (2006) DA.

[149] *Celik v Turkey No 52991/99* hudoc (2004) DA.

rule, however, to establish the date on which the applicant learned of the final decision.[150] Secondly, where the judgment is not served on the parties because domestic law does not provide for such service, the date taken will be the date on which the judgment is finalized, certified, and signed. This will be the date on which the parties are definitively able to find out the content of the judgment and obtain copies.[151] In legal systems where it is established practice that appeal judgments are not served or notified but deposited with the lower court's registry, applicants will be taken to be aware of this practice and thus under a duty to follow the appeal proceedings with due diligence.[152]

III. CONTINUING SITUATIONS

The six-month rule does not apply to continuing situations where the alleged violation takes the form of a state of affairs as opposed to a specific act or decision.[153] In *Ülke v Turkey*,[154] the applicant was a conscientious objector who was called up for military service. He was repeatedly convicted and imprisoned for refusing to wear uniform or deserting. Each time he was released he was sent back to his unit, refused again to wear uniform, and was convicted again. This series of prosecutions and convictions was found to amount to an 'ongoing state of affairs' against which he had no remedy in domestic law.

Nor will the six-month rule apply where there is a refusal of the executive to comply with a specific decision. In *Iatridis v Greece*,[155] the applicant had obtained a decision of the Athens Court of First Instance in his favour, quashing an eviction order against him concerning an open-air cinema which he had operated. The Minister of Finance had refused to comply with that decision. The Court found that this refusal meant that the six-month period did not run from the decision of the Athens Court of First Instance.[156]

This principle will also apply, by analogy, to prospective violations where the decision which would give rise to a violation has not been enforced. For instance, in *PZ and others v Sweden*,[157] the Court confirmed what had hitherto been implicit in its approach to asylum and immigration cases, namely that, if an order for removal from the contracting state has not been enforced and the individual remains on the territory of the state, the six-month period has not yet started to run. In the view of the Court, this situation, involving an 'ongoing potential violation of the Convention', thus resembles continuing situations.

The rule will start to apply, however, if the continuing situation comes to an end. This is a common ground for rejecting complaints relating to detention, a continuing situation, which are filed six months after the date of release from detention.[158] However, if proceedings challenging a deprivation of liberty commence after the detention has finished, the six-month period will run from the end of the proceedings, not the end of the detention.[159] The Court has also clarified that whereas multiple, consecutive periods of

---

[150] *Sahmo v Turkey No 37415/97* hudoc (2003) DA.

[151] *Haralambidis and Others v Greece* hudoc (2001); *Papachelas v Greece* 1999-II; 30 EHRR 923 GC.

[152] *Tahsin Ipek v Turkey No 39706/98* hudoc (2000) DA; *Yavuz and Others v Turkey No 48064/99* hudoc (2005) DA; *Olmez and Olmez v Turkey No 38464/08* hudoc (2005) DA.

[153] In states which have only recently ratified the Convention, this overlaps considerably with questions of compatibility *ratione temporis* considered later.

[154] Hudoc (2004). See also *McFeeley v UK No 8317/78*, 20 DR 44 (1980): repeated disciplinary punishments for persistent refusal to obey the prison rules was considered to amount to a continuing situation.

[155] 1999-II; 30 EHRR 97.

[156] See also *Cone v Romania* hudoc (2008), paras 22–7; and *Qama v Albania and Italy* hudoc (2013), para 68.   [157] *No 68194/10* hudoc (2012) DA.

[158] For example, *Ječius v Lithuania* 2000-IX; 35 EHRR 400 para 44; *Ege v Turkey No 47117/99* hudoc (2004) DA.   [159] *O'Hara v UK No 37555/97* hudoc (2000) DA.

detention should be regarded as a whole (and thus the six-month period should run from the end of the last period of detention),[160] non-consecutive periods of pre-trial detention should be treated as separate for the purposes of the six-month time limit.[161]

Normally, the Court has also been careful to emphasize that a continuing situation refers to a state of affairs which operates by continuous activities by or on the part of the state to render the applicants victims. By contrast, the fact that an event has significant consequences over time does not mean that the event has produced a 'continuing situation'.[162] This most commonly arises in property cases, where the Court has always found that acts of expropriation depriving a person of his property are not to be seen as involving a continuing situation of lack of property.[163] There are, however, exceptions to this rule, which have mainly arisen from the Court's case law on civil emergencies, conflicts, and disputed territories. From this case law, it is clear that there can be a continuing situation if, *inter alia*, the deprivation results from a legal act which is invalid or unlawful (such as in northern Cyprus) or it results from an ongoing *de facto* situation (such as eviction in a prolonged state of emergency).[164] One test applied by the Court in order to distinguish between an instantaneous act and a continuing situation is whether the applicant can still be regarded as the legal owner of the property or other right at issue.[165]

Other exceptions have arisen. For instance, in *Iordache v Romania*,[166] the Court was prepared to regard the automatic deprivation of parental rights of a prisoner in respect of his child as a continuing situation rather than as an instantaneous act. The Court reasoned that this was because the applicant had no effective remedy against this automatic deprivation and because it had led to a series of acts involving the child to which he had not consented. The Court's reasoning is unconvincing, not least because it is difficult to see the difference between the deprivation of parental rights in this case and any number of decisions that may be taken in the family law field, such as taking into care or adoption without a biological parent's consent, decisions which will, in turn, lead to further decisions being taken in respect of the child without the biological parent's consent. The judgment is also one which the Court has implicitly declined to follow in other cases.[167]

Finally, the running of the six-month period may be interrupted by 'special circumstances' which absolve the applicant from the strict application of the rule. The burden of establishing such circumstances falls on the applicant. In *K v Ireland*,[168] the applicant maintained that his mental state rendered him incapable of lodging a complaint within the time limit. The Commission rejected the claim, noting laconically that his state of mind did not appear to hinder the pursuit of numerous appeals before the Irish courts. Preventing a prisoner from writing to the Court will undoubtedly constitute a special circumstance; error or ignorance of the law will not.[169]

---

[160] *Solmaz v Turkey* hudoc (2007) paras 34–7.   [161] *Idalov v Russia* hudoc (2012).

[162] See *Posti and Rahko v Finland* ECHR 2002-VII paras 39 and 40; *Petkov v Bulgaria Nos 77568/01 and others* hudoc (2007) DA; and *Meltex LTD v Armenia No 37780/02* hudoc (2008) DA.

[163] *X v UK No 7379/76*, 8 DR 211 (1976). Cf, *Malhous v Czech Republic No 33071/96*, 2000-XII GC; *Kopecký v Slovakia* 2004-IX, 41 EHRR 944 para 35 GC; and *Chrysostomos v Turkey Nos 15299/89, 15300/89 and 15318/89*, 68 DR 216 (1991).

[164] See also *Chiragov and others v Armenia No 13216/05* hudoc (2011) DA, paras 96–100 and *Sargsyan v Azerbaijan No 40167/06* hudoc (2011) DA, paras 83–7.

[165] *Chiragov and others v Armenia*, at para 100; *Sargsyan v Azerbaijan*, at para 87.

[166] Hudoc (2008), paras 47–67.   [167] *Aden Ahmed v Malta* hudoc (2013), paras 67–72.

[168] *No 10416/83*, 38 DR 158 (1984). See also *X v Austria No 6317/73*, 2 DR 87 (1975).

[169] *Bozano v France* A 111 (1987); 9 EHRR 297 and *Fernie v UK No 14881/04* hudoc (2006) DA.

IV. THE DATE OF INTRODUCTION

The six-month period ends on the date of introduction of the application. The traditional rule was that the date of introduction was, as a general rule, the date of the first communication from the applicant setting out, even summarily, the objection of the application, provided that a duly completed application form had been submitted with the time limits laid down by the Court. Further to this rule, the traditional practice used to be that, if the first communication was not a fully completed application form, the Court's Registry would send the applicant an application form with a deadline for its completion and return of eight weeks.

This is no longer the case: now, a much stricter approach is taken. On 1 January 2014 a new version of the Rules of Court entered into force. Rule 47(6)(a) now provides that the date of introduction of the application for the purposes of Article 35(1) of the Convention will be the date on which an application form satisfying the requirements of Rule 47 is sent to the Court. The effect of this change is that first communications from applicants which are not properly completed application forms will not interrupt the running of the six-month time limit. Furthermore, in recent years, the Court has also become much stricter in what it considers to be a completed application form. The requirements of a completed application form are set out in Rule 47 of the Rules of Court and, under this stricter approach, forms which do not fulfil the requirements of Rule 47 risk being dismissed by the Registry without judicial examination. The consequence of this stricter approach when taken with the rule that improperly completed applications will not interrupt the six-month time limit means that if a subsequent, properly completed application form is submitted outside the six-month time limit, the second application will be inadmissible.[170] The same is true for the date on which a legal representative's authority form, properly completed by the representative and the applicant, is sent.[171]

To make due allowance for differences in postal systems, the date the application is lodged is always taken as the day it is sent, not the date it is received at the Court's Registry,[172] and this has not changed with the entry into force of the new Rule 47 (see Rule 47(6)(a)). Normally the date an application has been sent will prove uncontroversial and the date for these purposes will normally be taken as the postmark or the date the letter was written. Where there is a significant interval between the date on which the letter was written and the postmark, in the absence of explanations by the applicant, the Court will take the date of the postmark as the date of introduction.[173]

The Court is frequently faced with the problem of applications being registered following substantial periods of inaction on the part of applicants. Such applications may be rejected on the basis of the six-month rule.[174] The Court will normally require the applicant's representatives to maintain regular contact with it and to provide explanations for periods of inactivity.[175]

---

[170] *Kemevuako v Netherlands No 65938/09* hudoc (2010) DA; *Abdulrahman v Netherlands No 66994/12* hudoc (2013) DA.

[171] *Kaur v Netherlands No 35864/11* hudoc (2012) DA; *Ngendakumana v Netherlands No 16380/11* hudoc (2013) DA.

[172] *Kipritci v Turkey* hudoc (2008), para 18, unless it is impossible to tell the date of the postmark and the letter itself is dated before the postmark: *Bulinwar OOD and Hrusanov v Bulgaria* hudoc (2007) at para 30.

[173] *Arslan v Turkey No 36747/02* 2002-X DA; *Růžičková v the Czech Republic No 15630/05* hudoc (2008) DA.   [174] *PM v UK No 6638/03* hudoc (2004) DA.

[175] *Nee v Ireland No 52787/99* hudoc (2003) DA; *Chalkley v UK No 63831/00* hudoc (2002) DA; *Gaillard v France No 47337/99* hudoc (2000) DA; *Kirk v UK No 26299/95* hudoc (1996) DA; *Quaresma Afonso Palma v Portugal No 72496/01* hudoc (2003) DA.

As a general rule, delays in pursuing an application on the ground that the applicant is in the process of exhausting further domestic remedies will not be acceptable. However, one pragmatic exception to this rule is when the applicant wishes to pursue further or new domestic remedies and has reasonable doubts as to their effectiveness. An example from the UK might be seeking a declaration of incompatibility. In such a case, the applicant may run the risk on the one hand that the application will be rejected under the six-month rule (ineffective remedies not interrupting the six-month period), and on the other that the application will be rejected for non-exhaustion if the Court considers that the further or new domestic remedies are indeed effective and required to be exhausted. In such a case, the applicant should introduce an application before embarking on the further or new remedy, but the application should set out in detail the remedy being pursued. The Registry would then register the application subject to the condition that the applicant or his representative keep it regularly informed of the status of the domestic proceedings. This is part of a general duty applicants and their lawyers have towards the Court. In assessing whether domestic remedies have been exhausted, it will be a factor which weighs against applicants if they fail to inform the Court of domestic remedies which they are pursuing.[176]

V. AMENDING THE APPLICATION

Cases frequently arise when applicants seek to amend or amplify their application to the Court. Such amendments may be rejected for non-compliance with the six-month rule, even if the initial application is introduced within the time limit. For example, the Court has found that the mere fact that the original application invoked Article 6 of the Convention is not sufficient to constitute the introduction of all subsequent complaints made under that provision,[177] nor will it be sufficient to simply send documents from domestic proceedings and subsequently introduce complaints based on those proceedings.[178] Complaints raised after the end of the six-month period will not be examined unless they touch upon particular aspects of complaints initially raised within the period. However, it will be sufficient if the complaints are raised in substance or arise from the facts as submitted within the period.[179]

5. NO SIGNIFICANT DISADVANTAGE (ARTICLE 35(3))

Protocol 14 introduced the new admissibility criterion of no significant disadvantage into Article 35(3), thus enshrining the principle of *de minimis non curat praetor* in the Convention system. It took effect from 1 June 2010 (the date of entry into force of the Protocol) and, for the first two years of its life, was to be applied only by Chambers and the Grand Chamber (Article 20 of the Protocol). While perhaps necessary in order to resolve initial difficulties of interpretation, this created the unsatisfactory irony that, in order to establish clear case-law principles, the Court was required to devote valuable judicial

---

[176] *Aytekin v Turkey* 1998-VII; 32 EHRR 501 para 80.
[177] *Allan v UK No 48539/99* hudoc (2004) DA; *Adam and others v Germany No 290/03* hudoc (2005) DA.
[178] *Bozinovksi v FYRM No 68368/01* hudoc (2005) DA.
[179] See *Paroisse Gréco-Catholique Sambata Bihor v Romania No 48107/99* hudoc (2004) pp 14–16 DA and references therein.

time to deciding if a case should be declared inadmissible on the grounds that the case did not merit any judicial time at all.[180] Nonetheless, clear principles do emerge from the cases in which it has been applied. The provision currently has three limbs: (i) the absence of any significant disadvantage to the applicant; (ii) that respect for human rights does not require an examination on the merits; and (iii) that the case was duly considered by a domestic tribunal. All three grounds must be satisfied before an application can be declared inadmissible. The latter two limbs were introduced as 'safeguards' against an over-broad application of the criterion, although Protocol 15 will delete the third limb, the need for consideration by a domestic tribunal. Each limb will be considered further in the paragraphs that follow.

There is no strict hierarchy or order in which the Court will consider the limbs. In other words, it is not necessary to consider whether the applicant has suffered a significant disadvantage if, in any event, the remaining two limbs have not been fulfilled. For instance, in *Finger v Bulgaria*,[181] the Court did not consider whether the applicant had suffered a significant disadvantage on account of the allegedly excessive length of her domestic court proceedings because, in any event, the second and third limbs had not been met. Equally in *Flisar v Slovenia*,[182] no conclusion was reached on whether the applicant's criminal conviction had amounted to a significant disadvantage because the third limb, the need for due consideration by a domestic tribunal had not been met: it was precisely the applicant's complaint under Article 6 of the Convention that, in imposing a fine for a minor offence, the domestic courts had not properly examined the case.

I. WHAT CONSTITUTES NO SIGNIFICANT DISADVANTAGE

The first limb—whether there is a significant disadvantage—is 'at the core of the new criterion'.[183] Although the Court has wisely not attempted to provide an all-encompassing definition of what will constitute a significant disadvantage, it has stated that it hinges on the idea that the violation of a right, however, real from a purely legal point of view, should attain a minimum level of severity to warrant consideration by an international court, and violations which are purely technical and insignificant outside a formalistic framework do not merit European supervision.[184] As always, this will depend on all the circumstances of the case. This will include the nature of the right violated, the seriousness of the alleged violation and/or the potential consequences of the violation on the applicant's personal situation[185] and the applicant's conduct in any domestic proceedings.[186] The severity should also be assessed taking into account both the applicant's subjective perception and what is objectively at stake,[187] though the subjective perception is not enough and must be justified on objective grounds.[188] The most frequent type of case to be dismissed under the new criterion are money claims where the amount at stake is small. Examples where no significant disadvantage was found range from EUR 1 to

---

[180] Evocatively described in one publication as examining futilities through a magnifying glass: Spielmann and Chernishova (in Russian, translation from English), *Examiner à la loupe le dérisoire? To examine futilities through the magnifying glass? 'No Significant Disadvantage': Overview of the first two years' application.* published in Сравнительное Конституционное Обозрение (Comparative Constitutional Review), No 5, 2012, Moscow.   [181] Hudoc (2011), paras 74–7.

[182] Hudoc (2011).   [183] *Shefer v Russia No 45175/04* hudoc (2012) DA.

[184] *Shefer v Russia.*   [185] *Giusti v Italy* hudoc (2011); *Fernandez v France No 65421/10* (2012) DA.

[186] *Shefer v Russia No 45175/04* hudoc (2012) DA.

[187] *Korolev v Russia No 25551/05* hudoc (2010) DA.

[188] *Ladygin v Russia No 35365/05* hudoc (2011) DA.

EUR 228.[189] Examples where a significant disadvantage was found range from EUR 200[190] to expropriation cases where the amounts at stake were over EUR 30,000.[191]

However, it is not simply a question of money; the applicant will have suffered a significant disadvantage if, despite the low value of the claim, the dispute concerns a matter of principle for him. Thus in *Giuran*, concerning proceedings for the recovery of stolen goods worth EUR 350, there was a matter of principle at stake for the applicant because the goods had been stolen from his home.

Many cases considered under the new criterion have not concerned money at all. Here, the Court's focus has been on the nature of the prejudice suffered by the applicant. Thus, for example, in cases concerning matters of fairness in national proceedings, such as the non-communication of one party's observations to the other side, the Court has applied the new criterion to reject the cases, finding that no prejudice has been suffered either because the observations did not contain anything new or because the relevant court's decision was not based on them.[192] The same reasoning was applied to the non-pronouncement of a first-instance court decision in *Jancev v 'the former Yugoslav Republic of Macedonia'*.[193] Where, on the other hand, non-communicated observations could have contained new information and may have factored in the domestic court's reasoning, the criterion will not apply.[194] The effect of the alleged violation will also be relevant. For instance, in *Pantelimon and Vasilica Savu v Romania*,[195] where the complaint concerned the refusal of a mayor to issue a land ownership certificate, there was no significant disadvantage because ownership of the land had been recognized in a final judicial decision.

Rightly, the Court has been reluctant to apply the criterion to criminal cases. In *Luchaninova v Ukraine*,[196] the applicant was convicted of theft of labels worth less than a euro; however, the conviction had been the basis for her dismissal from her job and the criminal court's finding had been relied on by the civil courts before which she had unsuccessfully challenged her dismissal, leading the Court to find that she had suffered a significant disadvantage. In *Van Velden v Netherlands*,[197] the applicant had complained that he had been unable to take proceedings challenging the lawfulness of his pre-trial detention. The government had argued that no significant disadvantage had been suffered, since the period of pre-trial detention had been deducted from his prison sentence. The Court found that it was a feature of the criminal procedure of many contracting states, if not most, to deduct periods of detention prior to final conviction and sentencing from the eventual sentence; therefore, for the Court to hold that any harm resulting from pre-trial detention was nugatory for Convention purposes would remove a large proportion of potential complaints under Article 5 from the scope of its scrutiny. It therefore dismissed the government's preliminary objection. That reasoning was applied to a complaint made under Article 5(3) in *Bannikov v Latvia*:[198] see in particular the

---

[189] *Korolev v Russia No 25551/05* hudoc (2010) DA; *Burov v Moldova No 38875/08* hudoc (2011) DA.

[190] See the joined cases of *Gaglione and Others v Italy Nos 45867/07 and others* hudoc (2010), concerning non-enforcement of domestic judgments awarding compensation for length of proceedings, though the highest unpaid sum in that case was €13,750.

[191] *Sancho Cruz and 14 other 'Agrarian Reform' cases v Portugal* hudoc (2011), paras 32–5.

[192] *Holub v the Czech Republic No 24880/05* hudoc (2010) DA; *Bratři Zátkové, a.s., v Czech Republic No 20862/06* hudoc (2011) DA; *Matoušek v Czech Republic No 9965/08* hudoc (2011) DA; *Čavajda v Czech Republic No 17696/07* hudoc (2011) DA; *Jirsák v Czech Republic No 8968/08* hudoc (2012) DA; *Liga Portuguesa de Futebol Profissional v Portugal No 49639/09* hudoc (2012) DA.   [193] *No 18716/09* (2011) DA.

[194] *3A.CZ s.r.o. v Czech Republic* hudoc (2011); *BENet Praha, spol. s r.o. v Czech Republic* hudoc (2011); *Joos v Switzerland* hudoc (2012), paras 19 and 20.   [195] *No 29218/05* hudoc (2011).

[196] Hudoc (2011), paras 46–50.   [197] Hudoc (2011), paras 31–9.

[198] Hudoc (2013), paras 58 and 59.

spirited concurring opinion of Judges De Gaetano and Ziemele to the effect that the criterion should never apply to cases involving deprivation of liberty. Equally, in *Diaceno
v Romania*,[199] the fact that the complaint not only concerned criminal proceedings, in
which the applicant was ordered to pay over EUR 2000, but also concerned an alleged
breach of the presumption of innocence, was enough for the Court to find that there
had been a significant disadvantage. In *Eon v France*,[200] the conviction of the applicant
for insulting the French President and the imposition of a suspended fine of EUR 30
amounted to a significant disadvantage. He had challenged it right through the French
legal system (even though he had been refused legal aid), the case been a *cause célèbre*, and
raised the question of the continued criminalization of insulting the President, a subject
of regular debate in Parliament. A significant disadvantage was found in respect of the
length of criminal proceedings in *Sereny v Romania*,[201] given the matter of principle at
stake (the applicant's guilt or innocence) and the order for pecuniary damages which had
been made against him in the proceedings. However, the criterion was found to be met in
Gagliano Giorgi v Italy,[202] a complaint which also concerned length of criminal proceedings, where the fact that the applicant's sentence had been reduced was accepted as having
compensated or reduced the prejudice suffered by the applicant to the stage where there
was no longer any significant disadvantage.

II. WHETHER RESPECT FOR HUMAN RIGHTS REQUIRES AN EXAMINATION OF THE APPLICATION ON THE MERITS

This safeguard was taken from Article 37(1) of the Convention, which governs the striking out of applications. Understandably, therefore, much of the jurisprudence on this
limb of the no significant disadvantage criterion has drawn on the general principles
already laid down in the jurisprudence on Article 37(1). The Court has thus found that
the limb will not been satisfied if, notwithstanding the lack of a significant disadvantage
to the applicant, the case raises questions of a general character affecting the observance of the Convention. In *Korolev v Russia*,[203] the Court stated that such questions
of a general character would arise, for example, where there was a need to clarify states'
obligations under the Convention or to induce the respondent state to resolve a structural deficiency affecting other persons in the same position as the applicant. That would
lead the Court to verify whether the general problem raised by the case had been or was
being remedied and whether similar legal issues had been resolved by the Court in other
cases. That was not the case in *Korolev* itself, which concerned non-enforcement of a
final judgment and non-payment of a small sum of money to the applicant, the Court
finding that it had already examined this issue on numerous occasions and it and the
Committee of Ministers had addressed the systemic problem of non-enforcement.[204]
In *Finger, v Bulgaria*,[205] however, the Court found that respect for human rights did

---

[199] Hudoc (2012), paras 39–47.   [200] Hudoc (2013), para 34.   [201] Hudoc (2013), para 105.
[202] Hudoc (2012), paras 51–63.   [203] *No 25551/05* hudoc (2010) DA.

[204] See also on non-enforcement, *Fedotov v Moldova No 51838/07* hudoc (2011) DA; *Vasilchenko v Russia*
hudoc (2010), para 49; *Gaftoniuc v Romania No 30934/05* hudoc (2011) DA; *Savu v Romania No 29218/05* hudoc
(2011) DA; *Burov v Moldova No 38875/08* hudoc (2011) DA; and *Gururyan v Armenia No 11456/05* hudoc
(2012) DA. In respect of similar conclusions on length of proceedings see: *Kiousi v Greece No 52036/09*
hudoc (2011) DA; and *Havelka v the Czech Republic No 7332/10* hudoc (2011) DA. On public pronouncement
of judgments and lack of opportunity to comment on other parties' observations respectively see: *Jancev v
'the former Yugoslav Republic of Macedonia' No 18716/09* (2011) DA; and *Bazelyuk v Ukraine No 49275/08*
hudoc (2012) DA.   [205] Hudoc (2011).

require an examination on the merits of the applicant's complaint on the unreasonable length of the civil proceedings in her case. It observed that, in the case, it had considered addressing the issue of the potential systemic problem of the unreasonable length of civil proceedings in Bulgaria and the alleged lack of effective remedies for that problem through the 'pilot judgment' procedure. Indeed, in their observations to the Court, the government had stated that they would welcome any recommendations made by the Court with a view to overcoming the issues raised by the case. In *Živić v Serbia*,[206] concerning a complaint of inconsistent national case law on the payment of salary increases to police officers, the Court rejected the government's objection based on the criterion. Although not explicitly stated, it would seem clear from the Court's reasoning (and, in particular, references to the number of people affected by the inconsistent domestic case law and the reduced confidence in the judicial system caused by that inconsistency) that it considered the issue to be of general importance. As with the no significant disadvantage test itself, in cases involving criminal proceedings, the Court has been reluctant to conclude that respect for human rights does not require an examination on the merits. For example, in *Nicoleta Gheorghe v Romania*,[207] although the sanction was only a fine of EUR 17 (imposed on the spot by the police for breach of the peace), respect for human rights required an examination on the merits. This was because the case raised issues as to the applicability of Article 6 to this type of procedure, the compatibility of a change in national law and practice with Article 6, and because a decision of principle was necessary for the guidance of the national courts. In *Juhas Đurić v Serbia*,[208] the non-payment of legal fees to a lawyer for attending police stations as a duty solicitor deserved an examination on the merits, as it related to the functioning of the criminal justice system. In *Berladir and others v Russia*,[209] fines imposed for participating in a counter-demonstration were also found to deserve an examination on the merits, as raising an important matter of principle (though ultimately no violation was found on the merits). The second limb, however, was applied in *Rinck v France*,[210] a road traffic offence case, where, *inter alia*, the Court recalled that it had already found the applicable laws to be compatible with the Convention.

III. DULY CONSIDERED BY A DOMESTIC TRIBUNAL

Protocol 15, when ratified, will delete this limb. It was described as a 'second safeguard clause' by the drafters of Protocol 14,[211] and the Court, for its part, has added that the purpose of it has been to avoid a denial of justice and to ensure applicants have had the opportunity to submit their arguments to at least one level of domestic jurisdiction.[212] However, it has in practice had little effect: there are no cases where the Court has found that there was no significant disadvantage, and where it has been satisfied that respect for human rights did not require an examination on the merits, but where it has nonetheless considered that it should examine the case because it has not been duly considered by a domestic tribunal. The only cases where the limb has been mentioned as a reason for not rejecting the case have involved cases where the complaint was

---

[206] Hudoc (2011), paras 38–41.   [207] Hudoc (2012), paras 24–6.
[208] Hudoc (2011), paras 56–8.   [209] Hudoc (2012), para 34.
[210] *No 18774/09* hudoc (2010) DA.
[211] http://conventions.coe.int/Treaty/EN/Reports/Html/194.htm at para 82.
[212] See *Korolev v Russia No 25551/05* hudoc (2010) DA; *Gaftoniuc v Romania No 30934/05* hudoc (2011) DA; *Fedotov v Moldova No 51838/07* hudoc (2011) DA; *Adrian Mihai Ionescu v Romania No 36659/04* hudoc (2010) DA, para 35; and *Ştefănescu v Romania No 11774/04* hudoc (2011) DA.

precisely that the applicant's case was not heard by the national courts, either because of insufficient reasons on their part, or because there was no effective remedy for the complaint.[213] There have, however, been matters of interpretation of the word 'duly'. First, this is not synonymous with the requirements of a fair hearing under Article 6, although some defects by the domestic tribunal could be so serious as to mean the case was not duly considered. Second, 'duly examined' does not require the national courts to examine the merits of any claim brought before them, however frivolous it might be. Thus, if an applicant attempts to bring a claim which clearly has no basis in national law, the limb will be satisfied.[214] Third, the limb will not apply when the applicant alleges a violation of the Convention by highest instance court of the domestic legal system (ie the Constitutional Court or Supreme Court), since a contrary construction would prevent the Court from rejecting any case, however insignificant, relating to a violation imputable to that highest court.[215] This is consistent with the Court's case law on Article 13, which does not require an effective remedy in respect of a violation by the state's highest court.

If the aim of the no significant disadvantage criterion was to help the Court reduce its backlog of inadmissible cases, then it has been of only limited success, since proportionately very few cases are rejected on this ground: to date around forty in nearly three years by Chambers of the Court, as against 89,738 applications that were declared inadmissible or struck out by the various formations of the Court in 2013 alone.[216] This may change as single judges begin to apply the criterion, but given the enormous increase in the number of applications the Court now manages to dispose of each year, it does not seem that the Court needs the new criterion to tackle its backlog and it would appear that, rather than helping the Court, the new criterion has hindered it by forcing it to devote time to defining the scope of its application.

6. OTHER GROUNDS OF INADMISSIBILITY

Article 35(2) and (3) provide:

> 2. The Court shall not deal with any application submitted under Article 34 that
>   (a) is anonymous; or
>   (b) is substantially the same as a matter that has already been examined by the Court or has already been submitted to another procedure of international investigation or settlement and contains no relevant new information.
> 3. The Court shall declare inadmissible any individual application submitted under Article 34 if it considers that:
>   (a) the application is incompatible with the provisions of the Convention or the Protocols thereto, manifestly ill-founded, or an abuse of the right of individual application; or

---

[213] *Flisar v Slovenia* hudoc (2011); *Fomin v Moldova* hudoc (2011); *Finger v Bulgaria* hudoc (2011); *Dudek v Germany* hudoc (2010). See also *Zborovsky v Slovakia* hudoc (2012), paras 39 and 56, where the complaint concerned a lack of access to court and, for that reason, the government's preliminary objection on no significant disadvantage was joined to the merits and ultimately dismissed.

[214] *Ladygin v Russia* No 35365/05 hudoc (2011) DA.

[215] *Galovic v Croatia* No 54388/09 hudoc (2013) DA; *Celik v Netherlands* No 12810/13 hudoc (2013) DA; *Van der Putten v Netherlands* No 15909/13 hudoc (2013) DA.   [216] See n 1.

> (b) the applicant has not suffered a significant disadvantage, unless respect for human rights as defined in the Convention and the Protocols thereto requires an examination of the application on the merits and provided that no case may be rejected on this ground which has not been duly considered by a domestic tribunal.

Unlike the non-exhaustion and six-month rule, these requirements, as is clear from the wording of Article 35, do not apply to inter-state cases. The Court has, however, left it open that an inter-state complaint could be rejected as abusive in the light of general principles of international law.[217] The question of inadmissibility on the ground that the application is 'incompatible with the provisions of the Convention' (Article 35(3)) is considered separately later.

I. ANONYMITY (ARTICLE 35(2)(A))

In practice this is not an important ground of inadmissibility since applicants are required to disclose their identity when completing the application form.[218]

The matter did arise in *'Blondje' v Netherlands*,[219] where the applicant, a purported alien who had been arrested in the Netherlands, had refused to give his name to the Dutch authorities or courts and had then lodged a Strasbourg application challenging, *inter alia*, the lawfulness of his detention in the Netherlands. He did not provide his name to the Court and, as file did not contain any information enabling the Court to identify the applicant, it was declared inadmissible on this ground.

In *Shamayev and Others v Georgia and Russia*,[220] the Court, in very exceptional circumstances, accepted applications registered under pseudonyms where the applicants felt that they would have been at risk of serious ill-treatment if they had furnished their full names. The Court accepted the reasons for initially furnishing pseudonyms and accepted that the applicants were real and identifiable persons. It is, however, open to applicants to request that their identity not be made public but they are required to submit a statement of the reasons justifying this request. If this request is granted by the President of the Chamber,[221] anonymity will be ensured in any eventual judgment or decision in their case. However, the identity of the applicant is not concealed from the respondent government. The application and all documents relating to it are copied in full and sent to the representative of the government concerned. In an application brought by a Church, a political party, or other non-governmental organization concerning an infringement of its rights, it is not necessary to reveal the identity of members, though the application must provide the organization's full name, date of incorporation or registration, official registration number (if any), and official address: Rule 47(1)(a).

II. SUBSTANTIALLY THE SAME (ARTICLE 35(2)(B))

Article 35(2)(b) has two discrete limbs: (a) substantially the same as a matter that has already been examined by the Court; and (b) substantially the same as a matter which

---

[217] *Loizidou v Turkey (Preliminary Objections)* A 310 (1995); 20 EHRR 99. As did the Commission in *Cyprus v Turkey (first and second applications)*, 2 DR 125 at 138 (1975).

[218] See Rule 55 of the Rules of Court. As long as the form contains the applicant's personal details, an unsigned form does not make the application anonymous: *Kuznetsova v Russia No 67579/01* hudoc (2006) DA.

[219] *No 7245/09* hudoc (2009) DA.   [220] *No 36378/02* hudoc (2003) pp 36–8 DA.

[221] Rule 47 of the Rules of Court gives the President of the Chamber the power to authorize anonymity in 'exceptional and duly justified cases'.

has or has already been submitted to another procedure of international investigation or settlement.

a. A matter already examined by the Court

The Court will reject an application under this head if the factual basis of the new application is the same as that of an application that has previously been rejected by it[222] or has been the subject of a friendly settlement between the parties.[223] The key question is whether there is new information which gives rise to a fresh violation of the Convention;[224] it makes no difference if the second application contains new legal arguments.[225] However, if the applicant has previously made an application to the Court but has not pursued it or if no formal decision has been taken by the Court then the rule will not apply.[226] The situation is also different where new information is provided which alters the factual basis of the previous complaint. For example, an application which has been rejected for non-exhaustion of domestic remedies may be re-examined after the applicant has had recourse to the remedy.[227] Similarly, it is open to applicants complaining of the length of proceedings or of the length of detention on remand to bring a second application if the proceedings have still not terminated or if the detention continues.[228] In such cases, although the Convention complaint remains the same, the facts have evolved.[229] In applications raising more than one complaint, only those complaints which are substantially the same as those in a previous application will be rejected.[230]

The fact that an inter-state case has been delivered on a similar issue does not make an individual application under Article 34 'substantially the same' and does not deprive individual applicants of the possibility of introducing, or pursuing, their own claims.[231]

b. Another procedure of international investigation or settlement

The purpose of the second limb of Article 35(2)(b) is to prevent a duplication of examination by different international bodies.[232] It does not matter what stage the proceedings before the other international body have reached. Thus, if the application files his Strasbourg application first and seeks an adjournment of the procedure before the other international body, the case will be inadmissible. What counts is the situation that exists at the moment of examination of admissibility by the Strasbourg Court of the application before it. The fact that an identical case is pending before another procedure of international investigation and has not been withdrawn is enough for the rule to apply.[233] This

---

[222] See, eg, *Ekholm v Finland No 5952/03* hudoc (2006) DA.

[223] *Kezer and Others v Turkey No 58058/00* hudoc (2004) DA.

[224] *VgT Verein gegen Tierfabriken (No 2)* at para 63. See also *Previti v Italy No 45291/06* hudoc (2009) DA at para 293: 'a complaint is characterized by the facts alleged in it, not by the legal grounds or arguments relied on'.

[225] *Lutz v France No 49531/99* hudoc (2002) DA; *IJL v UK No 39029/97* hudoc (1999) DA.

[226] *Surmeli v Germany No 75529/01* hudoc (2004) DA.

[227] *AD v Netherlands No 21962/93*, 76 DR 157 (1994).

[228] *Delgado v France No 38437/97* hudoc (1998) DA; *W v Germany No 10785/84*, 48 DR 102 (1986); and *Vallon v Italy No 9621/81*, 33 DR 217 (1983).

[229] See *CG and Others v Bulgaria No 1365/07* hudoc (2007) DA.

[230] *Dinc v Turkey No 42437/98* hudoc (2001) DA.

[231] *Varnava and others v Turkey* hudoc (2009), para 118.

[232] *Smirnova and Smirnova v Russia Nos 46133/99 and 48183/99* hudoc (2002) DA.

[233] *Calcerrada Fornieles v Spain No 17512/90*, 73 DR 214 (1992). Cf *Peraldi v France No 2096/05* hudoc (2009) DA, that the rule applies notwithstanding the dates of introduction of the different procedures; the key element was the prior existence of a decision on the merits when the Court comes to examine the case.

was, however, slightly qualified in *Patera v Czech Republic*,[234] where the Court found that it was competent to hear that part of an application which concerned new facts that had occurred after the United Nations Human Rights Committee had given its views on a communication lodged by the applicant. That part of his Strasbourg application which pre-dated the Committee's view was inadmissible.

Three issues of interpretation have arisen under this rule: (i) what is a procedure of *international* investigation or settlement; (ii) what kind of 'procedure' the Article contemplates; and (iii) when is the application to the Court substantially the same as that submitted to another procedure?

For the first, the inclusion of the word 'international' in the phrase 'international investigation or settlement' means that it refers to international institutions and procedures set up by states and excludes non-governmental bodies. Thus in *Lukanov v Bulgaria*,[235] the Human Rights Committee of the Inter-Parliamentary Union, a non-governmental organization, was not considered to fall within the scope of the Article. Naturally, it also excludes bodies which are domestic in nature. This can be difficult to determine. In *Jelicic v Bosnia and Herzegovina*,[236] the Court was called upon to decide whether the Human Rights Chamber for Bosnia and Herzegovina was a domestic or an international body. It examined various aspects of the Chamber—the body's composition, its competence, its place (if any) in the legal system of Bosnia and Herzegovina, and its funding. While the Chamber had been set up pursuant to an international agreement, had a mixed composition of national and foreign members, and depended on international organizations for both part of its funding and the supervision of the execution of its decisions, many of these factors were related to the particular post-war context of its establishment and were of a transitional nature. The mandate of the Chamber was to assist only Bosnia and Herzegovina in honouring its own obligations under the Convention and other human rights treaties, and was finally terminated by Bosnia and Herzegovina and its entities in 2003 without the involvement of any other state. The Court was therefore able to conclude that the Chamber was part of the legal system of Bosnia and Herzegovina and of an essentially domestic character.

For the second kind of procedure contemplated by Article 35(2)(b), it is clear from the case law that the term refers to judicial or quasi-judicial proceedings similar to those set up by the Convention. It is therefore limited to procedures in which a matter is submitted by way of a petition lodged by an applicant. For example, in the first *Varnava and others* case against Turkey[237] the United Nations Committee on Missing Persons in Cyprus did not constitute another international investigation or settlement since it could not receive petitions, could not attribute responsibility for the deaths of any missing persons, and had limited investigative capacity. The reasoning applies to the Council of Europe's Committee for the Prevention of Torture.[238] Equally, the fact that the problem of foreign currency savings in the various successor states of the Socialist Federal Republic of Yugoslavia had been the subject of failed arbitration by the International Monetary Fund (IMF) and failed mediation by the Bank for International Settlements (BIS) was not a bar to the affected individuals filing an application with the Strasbourg Court.[239] The parties to the arbitration and mediation proceedings were different from those before the Court and, indeed, the IMF and BIS proceedings appear to have been entirely inter-governmental.

---

[234] *No 25326/03* hudoc (2006) DA.   [235] *No 21915/93*, 80-A DR 180 (1995).
[236] *No 41183/02* hudoc (2005) DA.   [237] *Nos 16064–66/90 and 16068–73/90*, 93-A DR 5 (1998).
[238] *De Pace v Italy No 22728/03* hudoc (2008) DA, paras 25-29.
[239] *Kovacic and Others v Slovenia Nos 44574/98, 45133/98 and 48316/9* hudoc (2004), DA.

The various organs of the United Nations system have caused difficulties. These are undoubtedly all international, but only some have been found to be judicial or quasi-judicial procedures. It is the settled case law of the Court that a communication lodged with the United Nations Human Rights Committee under the Optional Protocol to the International Covenant on Civil and Political Rights is such a procedure.[240] So, too, is a complaint to the Committee on Freedom of Association of the International Labour Organization.[241] However, a visit by a Special Rapporteur appointed by the then United Nations Commission on Human Rights to, among other detainees, the applicant, was clearly not such a procedure,[242] nor was a Working Group on disappearances established by the Commission.[243] The same was true for the Commission on Human Rights itself, since, in the view of the Court, this was essentially an inter-governmental organ composed of state representatives, which dealt with situations rather than individual complaints and which offered no redress to individual victims,[244] and whose '1503 procedure' for receiving complaints did not allow for individual participation but existed to enable it to identify gross and systemic human rights violations.[245] By contrast, in *Peraldi v France*,[246] the Court was satisfied that the United Nations Working Group on Arbitrary Detention was an international procedure. Although it came under the auspices of the Commission on Human Rights (and later its replacement, the Human Rights Council), its procedures were different from the '1503 procedure' of the Commission. In particular, it was composed of independent experts. It could accept individual applications, and the individuals submitting those applications were entitled to take part in the proceedings and to be informed of the opinions issued by it. Its recommendations made it possible to determine state liability in cases where arbitrary detention was found, and even to put an end to the impugned situations. Finally, there was a monitoring procedure to ensure its opinions and the recommendations in them were implemented. The Court therefore concluded that the Working Group's procedures bore many similarities to those of the United Nations Human Rights Committee, which, as stated previously, is an international procedure for the purposes of Article 35(2)(b).

The principles emerging from the Court's case law on the United Nations bodies were applied to proceedings before the European Commission in *Karoussiotis v Portugal*, concerning the unlawful removal of a child from Germany to Portugal.[247] The applicant had complained to the European Commission, asking it to initiate infringement proceedings against Portugal, alleging that it had infringed Regulation EC 2201/2003 (concerning jurisdiction and the recognition and enforcement of judgments in matrimonial matters and matters of parental responsibility). The Court found that it was the settled case law of the Court of Justice of the European Union that the European Commission had discretion to launch infringement proceedings before the Court of Justice, and this was preceded by several formal steps between the Commission and the Member State concerned. The sole purpose of 'infringement proceedings' or 'pre-litigation proceedings' was to secure voluntary compliance by the Member State concerned with the requirements of

---

[240] See *Calcerrada Fornieles v Spain No 17512/90*, 73 DR 214 (1992), and *Folgerø and others v Norway No 15472/02* hudoc (2006) DA, with further references therein.

[241] *POA and others v UK No 59253/11* hudoc (2013) DA; *Fédération hellénique des syndicats des employés du secteur bancaire v Greece No 72808/10* hudoc (2011) DA; *Cereceda Martin and Others v Spain No 16358/90*, 73 DR 134 (1992).   [242] *Yagmurdereli v Turkey No 29590/96* hudoc (2001) DA.

[243] *Malsagova and others v Russia No 27244/03* hudoc (2008) DA.

[244] *Mikolenko v Estonia No 16944/03* hudoc (2006) DA.

[245] *Celniku v Greece No 21449/04* hudoc (2007) DA, para 40.

[246] *No 2096/05* hudoc (2009) DA.   [247] *No 23205/08* hudoc (2011), paras 60–77.

European Union law and any judgment of the Court of Justice would have no effect on the complainant's rights, as it could not award individual compensation (a matter for the domestic courts). The complaint to the Commission was not, therefore, a 'procedure of international investigation or settlement' for the purposes of Article 35(2)(b) of the Convention.

For the third issue of interpretation, whether the application is substantially the same, the Court will look principally at the parties to the proceedings before it and their complaints and will compare them with those before the other international body. For instance, in *POA and others v UK*,[248] concerning the legislative prohibition on industrial action by prison officers, the Court found that certain of the applicants, prison officers, were individuals and could not therefore have joined the complaint against the prohibition which had been made by the first applicant, a trade union, to the ILO Committee. However, their applications were not unique, but simply exemplified the effects of the legislative prohibition. Permitting them to maintain their application would have been tantamount to circumventing Article 35(2)(b).[249]

However, if the application before the Court is significantly wider than the application before the other international body, then the rule will not apply. Thus in *Smirnova and Smirnova v Russia*,[250] the first applicant had lodged a petition before the Human Rights Committee concerning her arrest and detention on fraud charges. Further proceedings and arrests took place involving her and the second applicant, her sister. The first applicant's internal passport was also withdrawn. The Strasbourg application was brought by both sisters and covered various aspects of the proceedings since the first arrest as well as the circumstances surrounding the withdrawal of the internal passport. The Court noted that the petition before the Human Rights Committee concerned only the first applicant and its effects could not be extended to the second applicant. While the scope of the factual basis for the first applicant's application to the Court went back to the first arrest it was significantly wider than that. Therefore the application was not substantially the same. In *Peraldi v France*, it was the applicant's brother who applied to the United Nations Working Group on Arbitrary Detention but he had requested that it examine the applicant's situation rather than his own. In addition, the two applications concerned the applicant's pre-trial detention and its allegedly abusive nature. The Working Group had ruled on the issue of whether the applicant's detention was arbitrary on the basis of numerous elements, mainly that of the length of the pre-trial detention. Its examination had thus covered the complaints submitted by the application to the Court. It followed that the facts, parties, and complaints were identical.

Generally, though, the rule will not apply unless the complainants before the two institutions are identical. In *Folgerø and others v Norway*,[251] a group of parents and their

---

[248] No 59253/11 hudoc (2013) DA. Compare *Eğitim ve Bilim Emekçileri Sendikası v Turkey* hudoc (2012), para 38, where it had been a different trade union (albeit one to which the applicant trade union was affiliated) which had lodged an ILO complaint. See also *Evadsson and others v Sweden No 75252/01* hudoc (2006) DA, which was distinguished in *POA and others* on the grounds that a complaint had been brought the European Committee of Social Rights, not the individual worker applicants and had been of a general character, whereas the Strasbourg application had addressed the specific situation of the five individual applicants.

[249] For older authorities, see *Council of Civil Service Unions v UK No 11603/85*, 50 DR 228 (1987) and *Cereceda Martin and Others v Spain No 16358/90*, 73 DR 134 (1992).

[250] *Nos 46133/99 and 48183/99* hudoc (2002) DA, at 10–11.

[251] No 15472/02 hudoc (2006) DA. Unsuccessful applicants to Strasbourg are not prevented from then successfully taking their cases to the Human Rights Committee in Geneva. One example of this is *Correia de Matos v Portugal No 48188/99* 2001-XII DA, which before the Human Rights Committee became

children had unsuccessfully taken proceedings in Norway challenging the absence of an exemption from a religious education course in public schools. Some of the parents filed an application in Strasbourg, while four other sets of parents lodged a communication in Geneva.[252] Even though the applicants before the Court and the authors of the communication before the Human Rights Committee were complaining about the same question, if the complainants before the two institutions were not identical then the application to the Court was not substantially the same and could not be rejected. In *Illiu v Belgium*,[253] the application to the Court and a communication made to the Working Group on Arbitrary Detention were not substantially the same, as the latter had been made by a non-governmental organization and not the applicants themselves, and had been made in the context of the Working Group's urgent appeal procedure and therefore been much more limited than the complaints before the Court. Finally, in *OAO Neftyanaya Kompaniya Yukos v Russia*,[254] concerning an application brought by the liquidated Russian oil company, the Court considered that parallel arbitration proceedings brought by the company's majority shareholders against Russia before the Permanent Court of Arbitration in the Hague and similar proceedings brought by foreign minority shareholders under bilateral investment treaties were not substantially the same as the application before the Court. Despite certain similarities in the subject-matter of the case before the Court and that of the arbitration proceedings, the claimants in the arbitration proceedings were the applicant company's shareholders acting as investors, and not the applicant company itself, which was at the time still an independent legal entity. Although these shareholders could arguably be seen as having been affected by the events leading to the applicant company's liquidation, they had never taken part, either directly or indirectly, in the Strasbourg proceedings. This conclusion is surely correct, since it is entirely consistent with the Court's settled case law that majority shareholders cannot claim to be victims of an alleged violation of the company's rights under the Convention and that an exception will only be made to that rule when it is clearly established that it is impossible for the company to apply to the Court through the organs set up under its articles of incorporation or, in the event of liquidation, through its liquidators (see section 7.I.b).

III. MANIFESTLY ILL-FOUNDED (ARTICLE 35(3))

This provision requires the Court to make a preliminary examination of the merits of an application and decide whether it deserves further examination at the merits stage. The term has been broadly interpreted as encompassing cases which have no merit, because the applicant has failed to substantiate his allegations, to cases where the Court considers that no *prima facie* violation of the Convention has been made out. This spectrum of standards, ranging from totally unmeritorious to no *prima facie* breach, means in effect that the qualification 'manifestly' may not always be applied and that cases will be rejected on the grounds that the Court considers them to be 'ill-founded'. The question is asked how a case can be rejected as *manifestly* ill-founded after extensive legal argument and a lengthy fully reasoned decision of the Court with which not all may not the judges agree?[255] There is often a great deal of force in this criticism. However, there are two advantages to the current system. First, in single judge and Committee formations, it

---

Communication No 1123/2002, 28 March 2006; 13 IHRR 948 (2006). See O'Boyle, in *Liber Amicorum Luzius Wildhaber*, and Phong, 7 HRLR 385 (2007).

[252] *Leirvag v Norway*, decision of 23 November 2004; 4 IHRR 909.

[253] *No 14301/08* hudoc (2009) DA.   [254] Hudoc (2011), paras 519–26.

[255] Recent examples might include *Stichting Mothers of Srebrenica and others v Netherlands No 65542/12* hudoc (2013) DA (no liability of the Dutch State for the Srebrenica massacre) and *Friend and others v UK*

allows the Court summarily to declare cases inadmissible, thus freeing judicial time for more deserving cases. Second, it allows Chambers of the Court to dispose of cases where, even though the issues may be quite complex, nothing useful is to be gained from communicating the case and obtaining the views of the respondent government: so called 'de plano inadmissibility decisions'.

IV. ABUSE OF THE RIGHT OF PETITION (ARTICLE 35(3))

Dismissal on this ground is a rare but growing occurrence and is mostly reserved for applicants who file multiple complaints which have no foundation, particularly if they cause a waste of the Court's efforts.[256] The Court has emphasized that it is for it to police the procedural obligations imposed by the Convention and the Rules of Court on the parties, not the respondent government; any action taken by the respondent government to penalize a potential abuse of the right of individual petition by the applicant could raise a problem of hindering the right of individual petition.[257] There are a broadly four types of abusive applications.

The first type of abusive application is misleading the Court by knowingly basing an application on untrue facts. More blatant examples include the use of a false identity[258] and the falsification of documents.[259] More frequently, it involves failing to inform the Court of material facts, such as new developments after the lodging of the application which have a bearing on the Court's examination of the case.[260] This is usually a new domestic decision in the case which is in the applicant's favour, and the Court has been particular critical of lawyers who fail to inform the Court of such developments.[261] In both cases (knowingly basing an application on untrue facts and failing to inform the Court of new developments), an intention to mislead has to be established with sufficient certainty.[262]

The second type of abusive application is the use of offensive or threatening language, whether towards the Court, its Registry, or other parties to the proceedings, when that language exceeds the normal bounds of criticism and amounts to contempt of court,[263] and when the applicant has been warned of the possible consequences of such language.[264]

The third is disclosing the terms of friendly settlement negotiations (which are confidential). This was first mooted in *Popov v Moldova*[265] but, perhaps given that the applicant had alleged improper coercion on the part of the respondent government to agree

---

Nos. 16072/06 and 27809/08 hudoc (2009) DA (statutory bans on fox-hunting in Scotland and England and Wales).

[256] *Komatinovic v Serbia No 75381/10* hudoc (2013) DA.   [257] Hudoc (2009), paras 62–71.

[258] *Drijfhout v Netherlands No 51721/09* hudoc (2011) DA.

[259] *Jian v Romania No 46640/99* hudoc (2004) DA; *Bagheri and Maliki v Netherlands No 30164/06* hudoc (2007) DA; and *Poznanski and others v Germany No 25101/05* hudoc (2007) DA.

[260] See, among several authorities, *Akdivar and Others v Turkey* 1996-IV; 23 EHRR 553 GC; *Varbanov v Bulgaria* 2000-X; *Keretchachvili v Georgia No 5667/02* hudoc (2006) DA (with further references therein); *Hadrabova and others v the Czech Republic Nos 42165/02 and 466/03* hudoc (2007) DA; *Predescu v Romania* hudoc (2008).   [261] *Bekauri v Georgia (Preliminary Objection)* hudoc (2012), paras 21–5.

[262] *Centro Europa 7 Srl and Di Stefano v Italy* hudoc (2012), paras 96–100; *Komatinovic v Serbia No 75381/10* hudoc (2013) DA.

[263] *Rehak v Czech Republic No 67208/01* hudoc (2004) DA; *Di Salvo v Italy No 16098/05* hudoc (2007) DA. For emotional, irrelevant, or polemical language not reaching the threshold, see *Aleksanyan v Russia* hudoc (2008), paras 116–18; *Kolosovskiy v Latvia No 50183/99* hudoc (2004) DA. See also *Chernitsyn v Russia* hudoc (2006), paras 24–8, where withdrawing the language and apologizing counted in the applicant's favour.

[264] *Di Salvo v Italy No 16098/05* hudoc (2007) DA; *Duringer and Grunge v France Nos 61164/00 and 18589/02*, 2003-II DA.   [265] Hudoc (2005).

to a friendly settlement, the Court declined to declare the application inadmissible on this basis. There have, however, been cases where, given the absence of such coercion, and in the absence of a convincing explanation from the applicant as to why the terms of the negotiations were disclosed, an abuse of the right of petition was found.[266] Detailed guidance on the application of this principle was given in *Mirolubovs v Latvia*.[267] This concerned a complaint of unjustified interference by the respondent government in the affairs of an Old Orthodox community, and it appeared that a fellow parishioner of the applicants (rather than the applicants themselves or their representative) had send details of the friendly settlement negotiations to the Latvian Prime Minister. The Court found that a too wide and rigorous approach to the rules of confidentiality of friendly settlement negotiations would undermine an applicant's legitimate interest, for example in seeking advice on a case before the Court. The principle existed to prevent publicizing confidential negotiations through the media[268] or in communications liable to be read by a large number of people. The disclosure also had to be intentional, and this had to be established with sufficient certainty; mere suspicion was not enough.

The fourth type of abusive application is a vexatious application. This had traditionally involved an application—or a series of repeat applications containing no new information—which is querulous and creates unnecessary work for the Court.[269] Efforts were made before the entry into force of the no significant disadvantage criterion to develop this ground to include petty complaints, such as in *Bock v Germany*[270] and *Dudek v Germany*,[271] where the applicants complained of the unreasonable length of civil proceedings concerning, respectively, the sum of EUR 8 (in one set of proceedings) and just over EUR 900 (in four sets of proceedings).[272] However, since the entry into force of the no significant disadvantage criterion, the development of this type of abuse of the right of petition is not likely to continue. Indeed, it may be questioned whether this development was necessary, given the fact that such applications could be considered manifestly ill-founded (what is at stake for the applicant in the domestic proceedings is a relevant criterion in determining whether the proceedings are excessively lengthy) and further development would have required disproportionate amounts of judicial time to be spent on insignificant cases.

An application is not considered abusive merely by the fact that it is motivated by the desire for publicity or propaganda as long as it contains genuine grievances.[273] Media interviews on pending cases may amount to an abuse if they contain deliberately untrue statements of fact which are motivated by political considerations, or display an irresponsible and frivolous attitude to the Court and the application, and reach the level of offensive language (see the second type of abusive application described earlier).[274]

Finally, an application will not now be rejected as abusive by an applicant who has fled from domestic law enforcement. Although the Commission had rejected one case under this heading,[275] in *Stapleton v Ireland* (an extradition case where the applicant's

---

[266] For instance, *Hadrabova and others v the Czech Republic Nos 42165/02 and 466/03* hudoc (2007) DA and *Mandil v France No 67037/09* hudoc (2011) DA.   [267] Hudoc (2009), paras 67–71.

[268] As proved to be the case in *Mandil v France No 67037/09* hudoc (2011) DA.

[269] *M v UK No 13284/87*, 54 DR 214 (1987).   [270] *No 2205107* hudoc (2010) DA.

[271] *No 1297709* hudoc (2010) DA.

[272] See also the rejection of a complaint about the fairness of proceedings concerning a token fine of §3 as an abuse of the right of petition in *Vasylenko v Ukraine No 25129/03* hudoc (2001) DA.

[273] *Khadzhialiyev v Russia No 3013/14* hudoc (2008).

[274] *Georgian Labour Party v Georgia No 9103/04* hudoc (2007) DA.

[275] The Commission had rejected one case under this heading where the applicant, who had gone into hiding, complained about the length of extradition proceedings: *X v Ireland No 9742/82*, 32 DR 251 at 254 (1983).

whereabouts were unknown),[276] the Court confirmed its rulings in *Van Der Tang v Spain*,[277] and *Averill v UK*,[278] that, while absconding was wrongful, it did not render illegitimate the applicant's interest in obtaining from the Court a ruling on the alleged violation of the Convention which the applicant maintained took place beforehand. In a similar vein, the fact that the applicant was a convicted spy who had escaped from prison in the UK and fled to the Soviet Union was not a bar to his subsequently bringing an application against the UK in relation to the length of civil proceedings brought to prevent him profiting from publishing in the UK.[279]

7. INCOMPATIBILTY AND THE COMPETENCE OF THE COURT

This head of admissibility concerns the competence of the Court to examine individual or inter-state complaints. It is the practice of the Court to examine questions of competence as issues of admissibility under Article 35(3). Questions of competence are essentially concerned with the limits of the Court's jurisdiction and, as such, as stated previously, they must be examined by the Court on its own motion even if the respondent government fails to raise them.[280] They concern questions such as who is competent to bring a case and against whom (*ratione personae*), the subject matter of the application (*ratione materiae*), and the time and place of the alleged violation (*ratione temporis* and *ratione loci*).

I. COMPETENCE *RATIONE PERSONAE*

Competence *ratione personae* has two components: the application must be brought *against* a contracting state and *by* a legal or physical person with standing before the Court, in accordance with the terms of Article 34 (so called 'victim status').

a. The respondent state

Competence or compatibility *ratione personae* requires the alleged violation of the Convention to have been committed by a contracting state or to be in some way imputable to it.[281] Individual complaints against states which have not ratified the Convention (or its Protocols) will therefore be rejected on this ground, normally administratively by the Court's Registry. If the complaint involves a Protocol which the respondent state has not ratified, this will also be considered incompatible *ratione personae*.[282]

Complaints can only be brought against the state concerning actions of the state itself or of state bodies such as the courts, the security forces, or local government. An individual cannot complain of the actions of a private person or body such as a lawyer

---

[276] *No 56588/07* hudoc (2010) DA.   [277] A 321 (1995); 22 EHRR 363.
[278] *No 36408/97* hudoc (1999) DA. See also the reports of the Commission in *Lala v Netherlands* A 297-A (1994); 18 EHRR 586 and *Pelladoah v Netherlands* A 297-B (1994); 19 EHRR 81.
[279] *Blake v UK No 68890/01* 2005-XII (decision), and hudoc (2006) (judgment).
[280] *Blečić v Croatia* 2006-III para 67.
[281] *Gentilhomme, Schaff-Benhadji and Zerouki v France* hudoc (2002).
[282] *De Saedeleer v Belgium* hudoc (2007), paras 67–9; *Rabus v Germany No 43371/02* hudoc (2006) DA; *Kaya v Turkey No 43517/02* hudoc (2005) DA; *Partington v UK No 58853/00* hudoc (2003) DA.

or newspaper.[283] Acts by private individuals or bodies may, however, give rise to state responsibility in certain circumstances. The Court has repeatedly reiterated that the state cannot absolve itself from responsibility *ratione personae* by delegating its obligations to private bodies or individuals.[284]

Moreover, the state may have a positive obligation to secure particular Convention rights against possible violations of those rights by private individuals. It is impossible to set out precisely the extent of states' positive obligations under the Convention, since they cannot be divorced from an examination of the substance of the rights guaranteed.[285] Nor can those positive obligations ever be clearly distinguished from the primarily negative nature of states' obligations under the Convention, ie their obligation to refrain from committing any act which will violate an individual's Convention rights. Indeed the Court has often stated that the boundaries between states' negative and positive obligations do not always lend themselves to precise definition.[286]

The development of the positive obligations doctrine has somewhat solved the difficult questions of state responsibility under the Convention which may or may not arise in respect of the acts of public corporations or other public bodies. The key question is not the degree of autonomy a body has from the state or whether it is even a public body at all, but rather whether the act complained of is regulated by domestic law. Thus, for example, where applicants have complained of the refusal of private commercial television stations to show advertisements, it has been sufficient for the Court that the refusal has been based on domestic laws prohibiting political advertising rather than any direct action by the state.[287]

Complaints under the Convention can only be brought by a 'person, non-governmental organisation or group of individuals claiming to be the victim of a violation' of a Convention right (Article 34). While 'non-governmental organisations' and 'groups of individuals' are broad categories, they do not cover, for example, municipalities, other local government organizations, or semi-state bodies, particularly when the body's interests in bringing the application are concurrent with those of the respondent state.[288] The Court has refused to allow this rule to be circumvented by allowing public officials bringing the application in their personal capacities; such applications will be incompatible *ratione personae* if the right invoked was in fact attributable to the public body, and not the officials.[289] However, state broadcasters may be non-governmental organizations. Since they clearly do not exercise governmental powers but are, to an extent, public bodies, the Court will look to operational matters, such as how the broadcaster is financed, its management and how it is regulated, and the competitive environment in which it operates. In

---

[283] *X v UK No 6956/75*, 8 DR 103 (1976); *Durini v Italy No 19217/91*, 76-B DR 76 (1994). A lawyer, even if officially appointed, does not incur the liability of the state under the Convention: *W v Switzerland No 9022/80*, 33 DR 21 (1983).

[284] *Sychev v Ukraine* hudoc (2005), para 53; *Wos v Poland No 22860/02* hudoc (2005) DA.

[285] For an Article-by-Article analysis of the doctrine of positive obligations, see Mowbray, *The Development of Positive Obligations Under the European Convention on Human Rights by the European Court of Human Rights*, 2004; and, for a more critical analysis, Xenos, *The Positive Obligations of the State under the European Convention of Human Rights*, 2013.

[286] *X, Y and Z v UK* 1997-II; 24 EHRR 143 para 41.

[287] *Animal Defenders International v the United Kindom* hudoc (2013).

[288] *Döşemealtı Belediyesi v Turkey No 50108/06* hudoc (2010) DA; *Municipal Section of Antilly v France No 45129/98*, 1999-VIII DA. The same logic would appear to apply to local government officials to the extent that they may share responsibility for the impugned acts (*Pasa and Erkan Erol v Turkey* hudoc (2006), paras 19–22). On state-owned companies see, in particular, *Transpetrol as v Slovakia No 28502/08* hudoc (2011) DA, with further references therein.

[289] *Demirbaş and Others v Turkey Nos 1093/08 and others* hudoc (2010) DA.

applying this test to Radio France, Osterreichischer Rundfunk (the Austrian broadcasting corporation), and the BBC, the Court has found that they were non-governmental organizations capable of lodging applications.[290]

Complaints against the European Union as an international organization or which concern the acts of the Union will also be rejected as incompatible *ratione personae* until such time as the Union adheres to the Convention. In *Matthews v UK*,[291] concerning the failure of the UK to extend elections for the European Parliament to Gibraltar, the Court was quite clear that acts of the EC as such could not be challenged before the Court because the EC (as it then was) was not a contracting party. However, the Court in *Matthews* was just as clear that the UK, together with all the other parties to the (then) Maastricht Treaty, was responsible *ratione materiae* under Article 1 of the Convention for the consequences of that Treaty. In the particular circumstances of the case, the UK's responsibility derived from it having entered into treaty commitments after extending the applicability of Article 3 of Protocol 1 to Gibraltar. In *Bosphorus Airways v Ireland*,[292] the Court was more careful to distinguish jurisdiction from responsibility. The applicant had complained about the impounding of its leased aircraft by Ireland pursuant to an EC Regulation which in turn implemented a United Nations Security Council Resolution. It was not disputed that the impoundment of the aircraft was implemented by Ireland on its territory. In such circumstances the applicant company, as the addressee of the impugned act, fell within the 'jurisdiction' of Ireland, with the consequence that the complaint about that act was compatible *ratione loci*, *personae*, and *materiae* with the provisions of the Convention. The question of the scope of Ireland's responsibility (in question, given that the impoundment was in furtherance of its EC obligations) went to the merits of the complaint under Article 1 of Protocol 1. On the merits of the case, the Court held contracting states could not be absolved of their Convention responsibility by the transfer of sovereignty to an international organization. However, if equivalent protection of human rights was provided for in that international organization, then the presumption would be that a state had not departed from the requirements of the Convention when it did no more than implement legal obligations flowing from its membership of the organization. The Court then stated that any such presumption could be rebutted if it is considered that the protection of Convention rights was manifestly deficient. In such cases it held that 'the interest of international co-operation would be outweighed by the Convention's role as a "constitutional instrument of European public order" in the field of human rights'.[293]

Outside the European Union context, the Court has not applied this doctrine, preferring instead to ask whether the impugned act is be attributable under international law to the international organization or to one of the contracting states.[294] This doctrine was first

---

[290] *Mackay and BBC Scotland v UK No 10734/05* hudoc (2010), paras 18 and 19 with further references therein. [291] 1999-I; 28 EHRR 361 para 32 GC.

[292] *Bosphorus Hava Yollari Turizm ve Ticaret Anonim Sirketi (Bosphorus Airways) v Ireland* 2005-VI; 42 EHRR 1 para 137 GC.

[293] *Bosphorus Airways v Ireland*, para 156. See also *Michaud v France* hudoc (2012), paras 112–16, concerning France's implementation of EU Directives concerning money laundering and the compatibility reporting requirements placed on lawyers in respect of their clients by Article 8. There, the Court found that the presumption of equivalent protection did not apply because, first, in contrast to *Bosphorus*, the case concerned Directives and not Regulations (giving France a margin of manoeuvre not available to Ireland in *Bosphorus*), and second, in *Bosphorus* the control mechanism in EU law had been brought into play by the Irish Supreme Court's request for a preliminary ruling from the Court of Justice (which the French Conseil d'Etat had not done in the instant case).

[294] Complaints directly solely against the international organization will, of course, be inadmissible *ratione personae*: *Beygo v 46 Member States of the Council of Europe No 36099/06* hudoc (2009) DA.

applied in *Behrami and Behrami v France* and *Saramati v France, Germany and Norway*.[295] In *Behrami* the first applicant complained about the death of his son as a result of a mine, which he alleged French troops serving with KFOR[296] had negligently failed to clear. The second applicant complained about his injuries from the same mine. In *Saramati*, the applicant's complaint related to his detention by KFOR. The Court agreed that Saramati's detention fell within the mandate of KFOR but that in *Behrami*, the supervision of de-mining fell within the mandate of the United Nations Interim Administration in Kosovo (UMMIK). In any event, in both cases the Court found the impugned actions to be attributable to the United Nations. This was essentially different from the *Bosphorus* case because there the impugned act had been carried out by the respondent state authorities on its territory.[297]

In *Al Jedda v UK*,[298] this doctrine was developed by the Court, through its endorsement of the test of attribution set out by the International Law Commission in Article 5 of its draft Articles on the Responsibility of International Organizations, namely that the conduct of an organ of the state will be attributable to the international organization if the organization exercises effective control over that conduct. Applying that test to the internment of the applicant at a detention facility in Basrah City by British forces (acting as part of a multinational force) between 2004 and 2007, the Court found that, although the presence of the multinational force was authorized by a United Nations Security Council resolution, the Security Council had neither effective control nor ultimate authority and control over the acts and omissions of troops within the multinational force, and the internment had taken place within a detention facility controlled exclusively by British forces. The applicant's detention was therefore attributable to the UK and not the UN.

b. Victim status

Article 34 requires that the applicant claim to be a victim of a violation of one of the rights in the Convention. 'Victim' is an autonomous concept that the Court will interpret independently of any domestic law concepts, such as the capacity to take part in or bring proceedings, and irrespective of whether an applicant might require the approval of a guardian or other person to take domestic proceedings.[299] The essence of the rule is that the applicant claims to be directly affected in some way by the matter complained of,[300] even if the effects are only temporary.[301]

This provision has been characterized by the Court in *Klass v Germany*[302] as one of the keystones in the machinery of enforcement and at times it has been interpreted quite broadly by the Strasbourg organs. For example, in that case, the Court held that an

---

[295] Hudoc (2007) GC.

[296] KFOR is the Kosovo Force, the international security presence in Kosovo established under United Nations Security Council Resolution 1244. UNMIK is the United Nations Interim Administration in Kosovo.

[297] That approach was applied to the United Nations Peacekeeping Force in Cyprus (UNFICYP) and its actions within the buffer zone in Cyprus in *Stephens v Cyprus, Turkey and the United Nations No 45267/06* hudoc (2008) DA; to ICTY in *Galic v Netherlands No 22617/07* hudoc (2009) DA; and to the ICC in *Djokaba Lambi Longa v Netherlands No 33917/12* hudoc (2012) DA. For further cases, see *Stichting Mothers of Srebrenica and others v Netherlands No 65542/12* hudoc (2013) DA, para 150.

[298] *No 27021/08* hudoc (2011).

[299] *Norris v Ireland* A 142 (1988); 13 EHRR 186 para 31 PC; *Scozzari and Giunta v Italy* 2000 VIII; 35 EHRR 243 para 139 GC; *Zehentner v Austria No 20082/02* hudoc (2009).

[300] However, it is not necessary to show damage: this is more a question for just satisfaction under Article 41 and there is no *de minimis* principle (*Eckle v Germany* A 51 (1982); 5 EHRR 1; *Brumărescu v Romania* ECHR 1999-VII, para 50). In this respect, see the case law on potential victims described in this chapter, though if any damage has in fact been repaired by the state then the applicant may no longer be a victim; see the following section c.   [301] *Monnat v Switzerland No 73604/01* hudoc (2006) para 33.

[302] A 28 (1978); 2 EHRR 214 para 34 PC.

individual may, under certain conditions, claim to be the victim of a violation occasioned by the mere existence of secret measures or of legislation permitting secret measures, without having to allege that such measures were in fact applied to him. Since all users or potential users of the postal and telecommunication services in the state were directly affected by legislation which provided for secret surveillance, they fell into the category of victim.[303] In subsequent cases, however, the Strasbourg organs have narrowed the breadth of this ruling and in such situations the Court will now ask applicants to provide evidence sufficient to establish a 'reasonable likelihood' of such interference.[304]

Even beyond such instances of secret or undeterminable interferences, the category of persons affected by a particular issue may be very broad. Thus in *Open Door and Dublin Well Woman v Ireland*,[305] which concerned a Supreme Court injunction against the provision of information by the applicant companies concerning abortion facilities outside Ireland, the Commission and Court considered that women of child-bearing age could claim to be victims since they belonged to a class of women who may have been adversely affected by the restriction. In other areas the Court has been more circumspect. In *Russian Conservative Party of Entrepreneurs v Russia*,[306] in which an application was brought by a prohibited political party and some of its supporters, the Court refused to entertain the argument that not allowing the party to stand in elections had forced its supporters to change their voting preference or not to cast their vote at all. Accepting this argument would, in the Court's words, 'confer standing on a virtually unlimited number of individuals to claim that their right to vote had been interfered with'.

The position is more problematic in respect of applicants who complain as 'potential victims', normally where they argue there is a threat or risk of them being directly affected by a particular measure. Following the ruling in *Open Door*, this is possible in principle but the Strasbourg organs have been careful to draw a distinction between such applicants and those who simply seek to challenge domestic laws. An application of the latter kind, often referred to in the case law as an *actio popularis*, will be declared inadmissible as incompatible *ratione personae*.

As to the former, the Court will accept applications from persons who complain that there will be an interference with a Convention right if the state has already decided to take certain steps against them and the interference only requires the execution or implementation of that decision. The most common example of this is when an extradition or deportation order has been made but the applicant is waiting for the removal directions which will fix the date and time of his removal from the state.[307] Beyond immigration matters, there are numerous other examples of potential victims in the Court's case law. In *Johnston v Ireland*[308] and *Marckx v Belgium*,[309] the applicants risked

---

[303] Even though in the hearing before the Court, the agent of the government stated that none of the applicants had been subject to the surveillance measures in question: *Klass v Germany* A 28 (1978); 2 EHRR 214 para 37 PC.

[304] *Halford v UK* 1997-III, 24 EHRR 523 paras 47–8. See also *Liberty and others v UK* hudoc (2008), para 57, where the government were prepared to proceed on the basis that the applicants could claim to be victims of an interference with their communications sent to or from their offices in the UK and Ireland.

[305] A 246 (1992); 15 EHRR 44 para 41 PC.

[306] Hudoc (2007), 46 EHRR 863, para 78. See also *Georgian Labour Party v Georgia (No 2) No 9103/04* hudoc (2006) DA and (2007) DA. The same logic has been applied to readers of a newspaper seized by security forces complaining that this violated their right to receive information: *Tanrikulu, Cetin, Kaya and Others v Turkey Nos 40150/98, 40153/98 and 40160/98* hudoc (2001) DA.

[307] *Soering v UK* A 161 (1989), 11 EHRR 439 PC; *Vijayanathan and Pusparajah v France* A 241-B (1992), 15 EHRR 62. See also *PZ and others v Sweden No 68194/10* hudoc (2012) DA.

[308] A 112 (1986); 9 EHRR 203 para 42 PC.   [309] A 31 (1979); 2 EHRR 330 para 27 PC.

being directly affected by provisions of succession legislation concerning children born out of wedlock. In *Dudgeon v UK* and *Norris v Ireland*,[310] the Court considered that the very existence of legislation prohibiting private homosexual acts continuously and directly affected the applicants' private life—either they respected the law and refrained from the prohibited behaviour or they engaged in such acts and became liable to criminal prosecution. In *SL v Austria*,[311] the applicant, aged seventeen when he introduced his application, complained about a provision of the Criminal Code prohibiting homosexual acts between an adult male and a minor between fourteen and eighteen years of age. The applicant was directly affected by the legislation, even though there had been no prosecutions and, according to the Code, only his adult partner would have been prosecuted. It was sufficient that the applicant risked being involved in criminal investigations and having to testify on his sex life for him to be directly affected. However, the Court has also said that it is for the applicant to produce reasonable and convincing evidence of the likelihood that a violation affecting him personally will occur; mere suspicion or conjecture is insufficient in this respect.[312] For example, in *Burden and Burden v UK*,[313] two elderly sisters complained about the discriminatory nature of inheritance tax. One of the sisters would have to pay the tax upon the death of the other. The government raised a preliminary objection as to the sisters' victim status on the ground that their complaint was prospective and hypothetical. The Court dismissed the objection holding that it was virtually certain that one of the sisters would be required to pay the tax on the property inherited from the other sister.

By contrast, in *Christian Federation of Jehovah's Witnesses in France v France*,[314] the applicant organization complained that two parliamentary commissions had produced reports which were critical of them and which also recommended a series of general measures to be taken against sects. The Court took the view that the reports produced had no legal effect and could not serve as a basis for future proceedings against Jehovah's Witnesses or the applicant organization, so it was not a victim. By the same token, in *Rosca Stanescu and Ardeleanu v Romania*,[315] where the two journalists complained that provisions of the criminal code outlawing defamation of public servants put them at risk of conviction, the Court found that the domestic court had expressly found that the relevant provision did not apply to the press so the applicants were no longer at risk.[316] Finally, in *ADA and others v Italy*,[317] the Court rejected applications brought, *inter alios*, by the guardians of people with severe disabilities, regarding the authorization given by the Italian courts to stop the feeding of a woman in a persistent vegetative state. The Italian courts had based their authorization on evidence of the prior, clear wishes of the woman to that effect. The Court rejected the applicants' argument that the authorization set a precedent for their own cases, and would place them at risk of violations of Articles 2 and 3 of the Convention. It observed that if the competent national judicial authorities were called upon to rule on the question of whether the applicants' medical treatment should be continued, they could not disregard the wishes of the patients as expressed by their guardians, who had adopted a clear position in defence of the right to life of their relatives.

---

[310] A 45 (1981) para 41 PC and A 142 (1988) paras 28–34 PC. In both cases there had been no prosecution; but there was no stated policy *not* to enforce the law. There was thus a risk of prosecution. See also *Modinos v Cyprus* A 259 (1993) paras 17–24.   [311] *No 45330/99* hudoc (2001) DA.

[312] *Halford v UK* 1997-III; 24 EHRR 523; *Ocic v Croatia No 46306/99* hudoc (1999) DA; *Noël Narvii Tauira and 18 Others v France*, 83 DR 112 (1995).   [313] Hudoc (2006).

[314] *No 53430/99*, 2001-IX DA.   [315] *No 35441/97*, 2002-III DA.

[316] Cf *Association Ekin v France* 2001-VIII; 35 EHRR 1207 (the continued validity of law banning a book sufficient to maintain victim status).   [317] *No 55185/08 and others* hudoc (2008) DA.

By implication, the applicants had not produced reasonable and convincing evidence of the likelihood that a violation affecting them personally would occur.

As stated previously, where the applicant cannot demonstrate that he or she is directly affected, the Court may reiterate its time-honoured position that the Convention does not provide for applications in the form of an *actio popularis* nor may the Convention form the basis of a claim made *in abstracto* that a particular law or even constitutional provision contravenes the Convention. This principle was most recently applied in recent challenges to the Swiss constitutional prohibition on the construction of minarets: neither applicant in those cases could show that they had any intention of constructing a minaret nor had they shown that the ban had any other effect on their religious life, and it was clear that the Swiss courts would be able to review the compatibility with the Convention of any future refusal to allow the construction of a minaret.[318]

An applicant will be deprived of his victim status where the national authorities have acknowledged, either expressly or in substance, the breach of the Convention and then afforded appropriate redress for it.[319] A decision or measure that is merely favourable to the applicant is not in principle sufficient. This approach was confirmed in *Amuur v France*,[320] where the applicants had come to France seeking refugee status and had been detained in the international transit zone at Orly airport. A domestic court had ruled that holding them in the international transit zone was unlawful but this was twenty-two days after they had been detained and, more importantly, two days after they had been deported. Similarly in *Mehemi v France (No 2)*,[321] the applicant, an Algerian national, had been made the subject of a permanent exclusion order from France after a criminal conviction. He had filed an application with the Court (*Mehemi v France (No 1)*)[322] alleging that this violated Article 8 of the Convention. This had resulted in a finding of a violation by the Court, after which the permanent exclusion order was commuted to a ten-year order. Once this expired, he was given a series of six-month residence permits. In response to Mr Mehemi's second application, the government argued that the residence permits meant he was no longer a victim. This argument was rejected since there had still been periods after the Court's first judgment where the applicant could not return to France and the temporary residence permits with their accompanying limitations were not comparable to the status he had previously enjoyed in France.

This issue more commonly arises in criminal proceedings where compensation for possible violations of the Convention is made by a reduction in the applicant's sentence. For example, in *Lüdi v Switzerland*,[323] the applicant's sentence had been reduced to what his lawyer had suggested at the trial. He had complained, *inter alia*, under Article 8 of the activities of an undercover agent whose evidence had led to his conviction on drug charges. The Court rejected the argument that he was no longer a victim since the authorities, far from acknowledging a violation, had expressly decided that the actions of the undercover agent were in fact compatible with the Convention. By contrast, in *Morby v Luxembourg*,[324] the applicant was guilty of corruption, the maximum sentence being

---

[318] *Ouardiri v Switzerland No 65840/09* (2011) DA; *Ligue des musulmans de Suisse and Others v Switzerland No 66274/09* (2011) DA. The same rule has been applied in respect of prohibitions on abortion and assisted suicide: *Sanles Sanles v Spain No 48335/99* 2000-XI DA (assisted suicide); *X v Austria No 7045/75*, 7 DR 87 (1976) (abortion). [319] *Rotaru v Romania* 2000-V, paras 33–8 GC.

[320] 1996-III; 2 EHRR 533.

[321] *No 53470/99* hudoc (2002) DA, followed in *Sayoud v France No 70456/01* hudoc (2006) DA.

[322] 1997-VI, 30 EHRR 739.

[323] A 238 (1992) 15 EHRR 173, para 34. See also *Constantinescu v Romania* 2000-VIII, 33 EHRR 817; *Guisset v France* 2000-IX, 34 EHRR 1100; *Wejrup v Denmark No 49126/99* hudoc (2002) DA.

[324] *No 27156/02* hudoc (2003) DA. See also *Beck v Norway* hudoc (2001).

one year's imprisonment and a sizeable fine. He successfully argued before the trial court that the proceedings had exceeded the reasonable time provided for in Article 6(1). The trial court considered it appropriate to impose a suspended sentence of nine months and a much-reduced fine. The Court considered that the trial court had expressly recognized and then made reparation for the alleged violation of Article 6(1) such that the applicant could not claim to be a victim.[325] In the same manner, an acquitted defendant or a person against whom criminal proceedings have been discontinued cannot claim to be a victim of violations of the Convention which allegedly took place in the course of the proceedings.[326] However, this will only apply when the applicant is no longer affected at all by the proceedings in question. In *Correira de Matos v Portugal*,[327] the applicant had been charged with insulting a judge and had been denied the right to represent himself. He had later benefited from a general amnesty law but still had to pay damages to the judge in question. This was enough to maintain his victim status. The same conclusion was reached in *Arat v Turkey*,[328] concerning the fairness of criminal proceedings before the State Security Court, where the fact that, although the conviction was quashed, the applicant had served a substantial part of his sentence and had not been awarded or had any possibility of claiming compensation was sufficient to maintain his victim status.

The Court has also been required to consider whether the award of compensation, particularly in cases involving ill-treatment, satisfies the requirements of acknowledging a breach of the Convention and providing adequate redress. This will depend on the level of the award. In *Ciorap v Moldova (No 2)*,[329] an award of EUR 600 by the Moldovan Supreme Court in respect of substandard prison conditions and a denial of medical treatment was found not to deprive the applicant of victim status, given that the amount in question was considerably lower than the minimum generally awarded by the Court in comparable cases (the examples cited by the Court were cases where it had awarded EUR 6,000). Equally, in *Shilbergs v Russia*,[330] EUR 34 for three months' detention in unsanitary conditions was insufficient and manifestly unreasonable when considered against the Court's own awards. By contrast in *Floarea Pop v Romania*,[331] concerning the death of the applicant's son while in juvenile detention, the Romanian courts had awarded a sum of money which was lower than generally awarded by the Court. However, the Court found that the sum was not without any relationship of proportionality, bearing in mind that the domestic courts could not have awarded the applicant more than she had claimed in the domestic proceedings. The Court therefore accepted that the applicant no longer had victim status. It would have been a different matter if the ill-treatment in question was wilful. In *Gäfgen*,[332] the Grand Chamber was clear that, in such a case, the breach of Article 3 cannot be remedied only by an award of compensation to the victim, but also requires a thorough and effective investigation capable of leading to the identification and prosecution of those responsible. In that case, where the applicant had been threatened with ill-treatment in order to force him to reveal the whereabouts of a child he was suspected of kidnapping (and had in fact killed) the leniency of the criminal

---

[325] Contrast the lack of a clear recognition in *Jensen v Denmark No 48470/99* hudoc (2001) DA.

[326] *Bouglame v Belgium No 16147/08* hudoc (2010) DA; *Osmanov and Husseinov v Bulgaria No 54178/00* hudoc (2003) DA; *Eğinlioğlu v Turkey No 31312/96* hudoc (1998) DA. This line of case law has recently been applied, *mutatis mutandis*, to discontinued lustration proceedings: see *Olesky v Poland No 1379/06* hudoc (2009) DA.   [327] *No 48188/99* 2001-XII DA.

[328] Hudoc (2009), paras 46–8. For a similar conclusion in respect of unlawful detention, see *Moskovets v Russia No 14370/03* hudoc (2009) paras 48–52.   [329] Hudoc (2010).

[330] Hudoc (2009), paras 70–9.   [331] *No 63101/00* hudoc (2010).

[332] *Gäfgen v Germany* hudoc (2010).

and disciplinary sanctions imposed on the police officers responsible, and the failure promptly to determine the applicant's claim for compensation were sufficient to maintain his victim status under Article 3. Outside of Article 3, the issue most commonly arises in the context of non-pecuniary damage for unduly lengthy civil proceedings. The Court will tend accept lower awards of compensation as removing victim status, if the lower sum awarded is not unreasonable and is accompanied by a remedy which is designed to expedite proceedings.[333]

Professional associations and non-governmental organizations, to be regarded as victims, must show that they are in some way affected by the measure complained of. Normally, organizations will not be able to claim to be a victim of measures which affect the rights of their members; so, for example in *Norris*, discussed earlier, the Commission did not regard the National Gay Federation as a victim of the law prohibiting homosexual acts.[334] Similarly, in *Maupas and Others v France*,[335] the issue was the expropriation of property in order to build a motorway. The applicants were two home owners and a community association set up to defend the rights of those affected by the motorway building scheme. The Court rejected that part of the application brought by the association. In contrast, where an association set up to defend the rights of a group of people is party to domestic proceedings while its individual members are not, then both the association and the individual members can be victims of any violations arising from those domestic proceedings. The Court, in so finding in *Gorraiz Lizarriga and Others v Spain*,[336] observed that when citizens are confronted with particularly complex administrative decisions, recourse to collective bodies such as associations is sometimes the only means whereby they can defend their interests properly.

Churches, newspapers, political parties, and trade unions may of course be directly affected in their own right in relation to the freedom of religion, expression, and association.[337] Companies can also claim to be victims of violations of, for example, property rights or the right to have proceedings heard within a reasonable time.[338] Clearly, however, not all the rights in the Convention are of relevance to them. In *Pine Valley v Ireland*,[339] the Court upheld the status of victim of the two applicant companies, even though one had been struck off the register of companies and a receiver had been appointed for the

---

[333] See *Cocchiarella v Italy* hudoc (2006) and *Vidakovic v Serbia* no 1623107 hudoc (2011) DA.

[334] *No 10581/83*, 44 DR 132 (1985).

[335] Hudoc (2006). See also *Association de défense des interêts du sport v France No 36178/03* hudoc (2007) DA; *L'association et la ligue pour la protection des acheteurs d'automobiles, Abid and 646 others v Romania No 34746/97* hudoc (2001) DA; *Conka, la Ligue des droits de l'homme and others v Belgium No 51564/99* hudoc (2001) DA; *L'association des amis de Saint-Raphaël et de Frejus and others v France No 45053/98* hudoc (2000) DA; *Le comité des médecins à diplômes étrangers v France No 39527/98* hudoc (1999) DA.

[336] 2004-III para 38.

[337] For churches and other religious organizations, see Ch 13 and references therein. For newspapers, from many authorities, see *Sunday Times v UK* A 30 (1979); 2 EHRR 254 PC and more recently *Tanrikulu, Cetin, Kaya and Others v Turkey Nos 40150/98, 40153/98 and 40160/98* hudoc (2001) DA and references therein. For trade unions see most recently *Associated Society of Locomotive Engineers and Firemen (ASLEF) v UK* hudoc (2007); 45 EHRR 793. However, the Court has also found that *ad hoc* strike committees have no standing in this respect: *Manole v Moldova No 13936/02* hudoc (2004) and (2006). For political parties see *Refah Partisi (the Welfare Party) and Others v Turkey* 2003 II GC.

[338] *Comingersoll SA v Portugal* 2000-IV; 31 EHRR 722 GC. Whether a company or other association can receive pecuniary compensation for non-pecuniary damage will very much depend on the nature of the violation found. In *Comingersoll*, para 32, the Grand Chamber was prepared to make an award for non-pecuniary damage for a violation of Article 6 on account of length of proceedings and the 'considerable inconvenience and prolonged uncertainty' that these proceedings would have caused the company, its directors, and shareholders. For a survey of the applicability of the Convention to companies see Austin, 11 CL Pract 223 (2004). [339] A 222 (1991) paras 40–3.

other. The Court considered that the companies were no more than vehicles through which the third applicant (Mr Healy) had sought to implement a property development for which outline planning permission had been granted. To draw a distinction between the applicants was thus regarded as artificial. In addition, the company that had been dissolved had initiated the national proceedings and obtained the planning permission. This was considered sufficient to permit a claim to be made on its behalf. Insolvency was also considered immaterial to the Article 34 issue. It is now established that the shareholders of a company including the majority shareholders cannot claim to be victims of an alleged violation of the company's rights under the Convention.[340] An exception will only be made when it is clearly established that it is impossible for the company to apply to the Court through the organs set up under its articles of incorporation or, in the event of liquidation, through its liquidators.[341] The same principle will apply when the application is brought on behalf of a company in administration by a former president of the board or majority shareholder. In *Credit and Industrial Bank v Czech Republic*,[342] the essence of the complaint was the denial of effective access to court to oppose or appeal against the appointment of a compulsory administrator. The Court there stated that to hold that the administrator alone was authorized to represent the bank in lodging an application would be to render the right of individual petition theoretical and illusory. Aside from these special circumstances, it is now clear, however, that the right of individual petition is not a proprietary right that can be transferred from one company to another, whatever the validity of such a transaction in domestic law, and an application brought further to such a transfer will be inadmissible *ratione personae*.[343]

c. The loss of victim status after the lodging of an application

If the basis of the applicant's complaint is remedied while proceedings are pending before the Court, then the Court will frequently find that he or she can no longer claim to be a victim and it will strike the case out of the list. Early case law seemed to indicate that an applicant could cease to be a victim if a remedy was provided in the course of proceedings before the Court without an express recognition of a violation of the Convention by the contracting state.[344] This was problematic given that in such cases the applicant was deprived of a ruling on a complaint which raised important Convention issues of general interest. However, the Court's recent case law clearly indicates that recognition of a violation, either expressly or in substance, is required, together with adequate redress.[345] As with measures taken before an application is filed (*Amuur, Lüdi*, examined earlier), partial redress is not enough.[346] This is very much an individual assessment based on the particular facts of the case, but the general test applied by the Court is first whether the circumstances complained of by the applicant still obtain and secondly whether the effects of a possible violation of the Convention on account of those circumstances have also been redressed.[347] For example in *Koç and Tambaş*

---

[340] *Pokis v Latvia No 528/02* hudoc (2006) DA; *Terem Ltd Chechetkin and Olius v Ukraine* hudoc (2005), para 28; *Vesela and Loyka v Slovakia No 54811/00* hudoc (2005) DA; *F Santos Lda and Fachadas v Portugal* 2000-X; and *Agrotexim and Others v Greece* A 330-A (1995), paras 59–72.

[341] See *Agrotexim and Others v Greece* A 330-A (1995) and *Vesela and Loyka v Slovakia No 54811/00* hudoc (2005) DA; *CDI Holding and Others v Slovakia No 37398/97* hudoc (2001) DA; *Camberrow MM5 AD v Bulgaria No 50357/99* hudoc (2004) DA; and *GJ v Luxembourg* hudoc (2000), 36 EHRR 710 paras 22–5.

[342] 2003-XI, 39 EHRR 860, para 51.

[343] *Nassau Verzekering Maatschappij NV v Netherlands No 57602/09* hudoc (2011) DA.

[344] See, eg, *X v Denmark No 7658/76*, 15 DR 128 (1978) and *Pitarque v Spain No 13420/87*, 62 DR 258 (1989).

[345] *Dalban v Romania* 1999-VI, 31 EHRR 893 paras 41–5 GC; and *Burdov v Russia* 2002-III, 38 EHRR 639 paras 27–32.   [346] *Chevrol v France* 2003-III, paras 30–43.

[347] *Ohlen v Denmark* hudoc (2005) para 26. See also *Freimanis and Lidums v Lithuania*, hudoc (2006) paras 66–74 and references therein.

v Turkey,[348] the applicants had been convicted by a state security court, in apparent violation of Article 6(1) of the Convention. However, the sentences handed down by the Court had not been executed and, after changes to the Criminal Code, their criminal records had been erased. This meant that all the harmful consequences of the impartiality and independence of the state security court had been redressed and they could no longer be considered victims under Article 34.

Compensation or settlement of domestic claims will also be relevant to continued victim status.[349] In this connection, the Court has faced a number of difficulties in recent years where domestic remedies have been created specifically to redress systemic violations of the Convention, but the compensation awarded by the domestic courts under these new remedies has been substantially less than the Court itself would have awarded. While the Court may tolerate a situation in which the level of compensation awarded by the domestic authorities may be lower than that awarded by the Court, if it is significantly lower the applicant can still be said to be a victim. Conversely, it is difficult to draw conclusions from these cases as to what percentage of compensation the Court will accept as a reasonable amount. In the leading cases on the question, nine Grand Chamber judgments against Italy,[350] the amount of compensation given under the Italian remedy, the Pinto Law, was very small, as little as 10 per cent in one case, justifying the continuation of the applicants' victim status. The Court did make it clear that in general it will look to the nature of the remedy or remedies on offer. If the remedy only awards compensation, then the percentage will need to be higher than a remedy which awards compensation and also expedites pending proceedings. In such circumstances, lower compensation than the Court normally awards will be acceptable on the condition that the remedies are 'speedy, reasoned and executed very quickly'.[351]

d. Indirect victims

The Strasbourg organs have rendered Convention proceedings more effective by permitting applications not only by the person immediately affected (the direct victim) but also by an indirect victim. For example, in respect of alleged violations of the right to life (Article 2), close relatives such as spouses or parents will be regarded as indirectly affected and able to bring applications.[352] Whether the person bringing the application is the deceased's legal heir in domestic law is irrelevant: what matters is the closeness of the ties between the applicant and the deceased.[353] Similarly, for the purposes of Article 2 and complaints concerning the effectiveness of domestic investigations, it will be irrelevant if one close relative files a criminal complaint with the authorities but another relative brings the application to Strasbourg: the relative bringing the application will have victim status.[354]

Family members of those who have been detained or relatives of physically or mentally incapable victims such as young children, hospital patients, and persons of unsound

---

[348] *No 46947/99* hudoc (2005) DA. Cf *Achour v France No 67335/01* hudoc (2004) DA and *Senator Lines GmbH v 15 Member States No 56672/00*, 2004-IV GC.

[349] See, among many authorities, *Caraher v UK No 2452/94*, 2001-I DA and *Murillo Saldias v Spain* hudoc (2006).

[350] See the leading judgment of *Scordino v Italy (No 1)* 2006-V, 45 EHRR 207, paras 214 and 215 GC.

[351] See, eg, *Cocchiarella v Italy* hudoc (2004), para 97.

[352] *McCann v UK* A 324 (1995); 21 EHRR 97 GC. A nephew also has standing in respect of the murder of his uncle: *Yasa v Turkey No 22495/93* hudoc (1998), paras 61–6.

[353] *AV v Bulgaria No 41488/98* hudoc (1999) DA.

[354] *Celikbilek v Turkey No 27693/95* hudoc (1999) DA (the deceased's wife lodged the criminal complaint and his brother was the applicant in Strasbourg).

mind—may also be seen as indirect victims.[355] Broadly speaking the concept of indirect victims encompasses those who are also prejudiced by the violation, as well as those who may have a valid personal interest in having the violation established, such as parents or persons *in loco parentis*. In applications challenging decisions to take children into care, the parents will have standing to bring the application on their own behalf and on behalf of their children, since the nature of their complaint is precisely the fact that they have been deprived of the parental rights in domestic law.[356] Foster parents, however, will not necessarily have standing to bring an application in respect of children who have previously been in their care and when they do not currently exercise parental authority.[357]

A person may also be able to claim that he or she is directly affected as a consequence of a violation of the rights of someone else (eg, spouse or parents of a person liable to be deported, a wife complaining that damage to her husband's property also affected her own property, or someone suffering anguish in violation of Article 3 on account of the disappearance of a close relative).[358]

It is a quite different matter if the original victims die before they can bring an application and a relative or heir seeks to bring an application on their behalf.[359] The victim status of the relative or heirs will depend on whether the complaints in question can be considered to be transferable or whether the right concerned is so eminently personal that it cannot be transferred. This in turn depends very much on which Article of the Convention is invoked. The following broad lines can be discerned from the Court's case law.

For Articles 2 and 3, as stated earlier, if the complaint relates to the death or disappearance of a relative, a close relative will have victim status.[360] The same will apply if the ill-treatment was linked to the circumstances of the death of the relative, for example a case of suicide when in detention.[361] In the absence of any such link between the death and the ill-treatment, an applicant bringing the Article 3 complaint in respect of

[355] See *Houtman and Meeus v Belgium* hudoc (2009), paras 27–31 (husband challenging the inability of his wife to obtain compensation for her unlawful detention at a psychiatric hospital); *Paton v UK No 8416/78*, 19 DR 244 at 248 (1980) (a prospective father alleging a denial of the right to life on behalf of the foetus following the termination of his wife's pregnancy was considered to be so closely affected that he was a 'victim').

[356] *Scozzari and Giunta v Italy* 2000-VIII; 35 EHRR 243 GC paras 135–41; *Covezzi and Morselli v Italy No 52763/99* hudoc (2002) DA.

[357] *Moretti and Benedetti v Italy* hudoc (2010), paras 32–5.

[358] *Kurt v Turkey* 1998-III; 27 EHRR 373; *X and Y v Belgium No 1478/62*, 6 YB 591 at 618–20 (1964); *Abdulaziz, Cabales and Balkandali v UK Nos 9214/80, 9473/81 and 9474/81*, 29 DR 176 at 181–2 (1982). See also *Fidan v Turkey No 24209/04* hudoc (2000) DA, where the applicant complained of the forced gynaecological examination of his wife, found to be admissible. However, in the case of disappearances involving anguish and suffering on the part of a relative, see also *Cakici v Turkey* 1999-IV; 31 EHRR 133 GC, where the Court found no violation of Article 3 in respect of an applicant whose brother had disappeared. The Court distinguished *Kurt* on the grounds that, in that case, the applicant had been present at the time when the security forces took her son, whereas in *Cakici* the applicant had been in another town. In addition, the applicant in *Cakici* had not borne the brunt of making enquiries as to the whereabouts of his disappeared brother.

[359] A deceased person cannot lodge an application, even through a representative: *Aizpurua Ortiz and Others v Spain* hudoc (2010), para 30.

[360] This has been applied to: spouses (*Salman v Turkey* ECHR 2000 VII); unmarried partners (*AV v Bulgaria No 41488/98* hudoc (1999) DA); parents (*Ramsahai and Others v Netherlands* ECHR 2007 II); siblings (*Andronicou and Constantinou v Cyprus*, 9 October 1997, Reports of Judgments and Decisions 1997 VI); children (*McKerr v UK*, ECHR 2001 III); and nephews (*Yaşa v Turkey*, 2 September 1998, §§ 61–6, Reports of Judgments and Decisions 1998 VI).

[361] *De Donder and De Clippel v Belgium* hudoc (2011), paras 53–62; *Renolde v France*, ECHR 2008 (extracts); *Kats and Others v Ukraine* hudoc (2008).

ill-treatment of a relative will not have victim status.[362] Similar considerations apply in respect of Article 5 complaints: there must be a link to the death or disappearance of the applicant's relative while that relative was in state custody.[363] Different considerations may apply, however, if the application concerns Article 5(5) of the Convention (the right to compensation for unlawful detention), which is a pecuniary right and thus transferable to the heirs of the detainee, who can therefore bring an application after the detainee's death.[364]

As regards Article 6 complaints, the Court will look to whether the applicant/relative participated in the deceased person's domestic proceedings.[365] It will also consider the legitimacy of the applicant's interest in those proceedings and any effect it had on the applicant, including, for example, on his or her property rights either as heir or otherwise.[366] A wide approach has been taken to the idea of a legitimate interest: widows, for example, have been found to have standing to complain about the fairness of criminal proceedings against their husbands because of the legitimate interest in protecting the husbands' reputation.[367]

By contrast, Article 8 rights have been considered eminently personal and non-transferable and so relatives cannot bring complaints under this Article unless they are personally affected by the interference at issue.[368] A more flexible approach applies when the complaint relates to the reputation of the deceased person, which can affect the reputation of the family.[369] The general principle of non-transferability of Article 8 rights has applied, a fortiori, to complaints brought by relatives under Articles 9, 10, and 11 of the Convention, as well as under Article 3 of Protocol 1.[370] In respect of property claims brought under Article 1 of Protocol 1, two situations must be distinguished. First, it is clear that, if the applicants/close relatives are heirs to the estate of the deceased person and the complaint concerns property pertaining to that estate, they will be directly affected and thus will have a legitimate interest in making the application to the Court. Indeed, in such cases, they may be regarded as direct victims themselves.[371] However, if the complaint concerns a more personal property right which the applicants/close relatives

---

[362] *Kaburov v Bulgaria No 9035/06* hudoc (2012) DA, para 56, declared inadmissible because the ill-treatment of the applicant's father took place over two years before the father's death.

[363] *Taş v Turkey* hudoc (2000); *Orhan v Turkey* hudoc (2002); *Gakiyev and Gakiyeva v Russia* hudoc (2009), para 165; and *Varnava and others v Turkey* hudoc (2009), paras 112 and 208. This approach has also been applied to cases where the unlawful detention of the 'direct victim' was closely linked to the complaint under Article 2 concerning his or her death (see *Kats and Others v Ukraine* hudoc (2008), para 135, and implicitly in *De Donder and De Clippel v Belgium* hudoc (2011), para 101). See, conversely, *Iordanovi v Bulgaria* hudoc (2011), paras 88–9 (death of the applicants' son in police custody from a diabetes complication) and *Biç and Others v Turkey* hudoc (2006) (length of pre-trial detention no standing to widow and children of the man detained).   [364] *Marie-Louise Loyen and Bruneel v France* hudoc (2005).

[365] *Nölkenbockhoff v Germany*, 25 August 1987, Series A no 123 and *Micallef v Malta No 17056/06* hudoc (2009) (where there had been such participation) and *Georgia Makri and others v Greece No 5977/03* hudoc (2005) DA (where there had not). See also *Dimitrovska v the Former Yugoslav Republic of Macedonia No 21466/03* hudoc (2008) DA; and *Ivanovski and Others v the Former Yugoslav Republic of Macedonia*, hudoc (2009), paras 2 and 16.

[366] *Marie-Louise Loyen and Bruneel v France* hudoc (2005); and *Ressegatti v Switzerland* hudoc (2006).

[367] *Grădinar v Moldova* hudoc (2008), paras 90–104; *Lacadena Calero v Spain* hudoc (2011), paras 28–31.

[368] *Koch v Germany* hudoc (2012), paras 78–82; *Sanles Sanles v Spain No 48335/99* hudoc (2010) DA; *Kurić and Others v Slovenia* hudoc (2010), paras 277–8; *Mitev v Bulgaria No 42758/07* hudoc (2010) DA.

[369] *Armonienė v Lithuania* hudoc (2008), para 29; *Polanco Torres and Movilla Polanco v Spain* hudoc (2010), paras 30–3.

[370] *Fairfield and others v UK No 24790/04*, 2005-VI DA; *Direkçi and Direkçi v Turkey No 47826/99* hudoc (2006) DA. Article 3 of Protocol 1: *Gakiyev and Gakiyeva v Russia* hudoc (2009) paras 164–8.

[371] *Gavrielidou and Others v Cyprus No 73802/01* hudoc (2003) DA.

cannot inherit—such as a pension—then it is still an open question as to whether they will have victim status if they lodge an application.[372]

e. Death of the applicant

Conceptually, the indirect victim is to be distinguished from the continuation of Convention proceedings by an heir or personal representative, when the deceased has died after lodging the application him or herself. The death of the original applicant does not automatically mean that the Court will strike out the case under Article 37. The Court's approach—traditionally rather generous—is now more difficult to discern.

It appears the first condition is that the person continuing the case must be a close relative or heir. Thus, in *Ječius v Lithuania*,[373] the applicant's widow had a legitimate interest in pursuing the application in his place and continued with the examination of the case on the merits, whereas in *Thévenon v France*,[374] the applicant's sole legatee ('*légataire universel*') could not pursue the applicant's complaints after his death since she was neither his close relative nor, under French law, an heir. This condition is, however, not strictly applied. In *Malhous v Czech Republic*,[375] the person wishing to continue the application was the nephew of the original applicant. The original complaint had related to attempts to recover nationalized property from the state. At the time of the Court's examination of the case, the nephew was in the middle of an inheritance dispute with the original applicant's children. In finding that the nephew could continue the original application, the Court did not attach decisive importance to the fact that he was not the original applicant's heir or next of kin in national law; what was essential was that he could claim a legitimate interest in having the proceedings in the applicant's case being pursued before the Court. It was sufficient that the original applicant has designated him as his heir and that there were prospects of his eventually being recognized as such, in which case at least part of the original applicant's estate, including the property claims in issue in the case, would accrue to him.[376]

It is more difficult to state whether there is a second condition, namely whether the right in question is transferable in nature or not. As stated earlier, this condition applies to cases of 'indirect victims' whose relatives have died before the lodging of the application. It is, however, unclear whether this condition also applies to cases where the original applicant lodges an application then dies and the relatives wish to continue the application. The condition was applied to cases where the original applicant had died after lodging the application in *Angelov and Angelova v Bulgaria, Vääri v Estonia*, and *MP and Others v Bulgaria*,[377] meaning that complaints continued by the relatives were inadmissible. However, the condition was not even considered, still less applied, in *X v France, Raimondo v Italy, Jecius v Lithuania*, or *Stojkovic v the the Former Yugoslav Republic of Macedonia*,[378] and, in each of these cases and others, the Court continued its examination of the complaints originally

---

[372] *Aizpurua Ortiz and Others v Spain* hudoc (2010), para 30 *in fine*, when the Court preferred not to decide the question, finding that the applications concerned were, in any event, inadmissible under the six-month rule.

[373] 2000-IX; 35 EHRR IX. See also *Stojanov v the Former Yugoslav Republic of Macedonia* hudoc (2007), para 25 (wife and daughters); and *Hibbert v Netherlands* No 38087/97 hudoc (1999) DA (the deceased's mother being able to continue the application).

[374] No 2476/02 hudoc (2006) DA.   [375] 2000-XII GC.

[376] See also *Dalban v Romania* 1999-VI, 31 EHRR 893, where the applicant's widow was found to have a legitimate interest in obtaining a ruling that her late husband's conviction for libel constituted a breach of the right to freedom of expression.

[377] *Angelov and Angelova v Bulgaria* No 16510/06 hudoc (2010) DA; *Vaari v Estonia* No 8702/04 hudoc (2008) DA; *MP and Others v Bulgaria* hudoc (2011).

[378] Hudoc (1992); hudoc (1994); hudoc (2000); hudoc (2007) respectively.

submitted by the applicant and maintained by his or her relative after his or her death. The two lines of case law appear irreconcilable, since it would not appear, for example, that this question turns on the nature of the complaint (*Vääri* and *Jecius*, for example, both concerned Article 5 complaints). Although the line taken in *Angelov and Angelova*, *Vääri*, and *MP and Others* has the advantage of consistency with the Court's case law on indirect victims, it is suggested that the correct approach is that taken in *X v France* and subsequent, similar cases, for two reasons. First, in respect of indirect victims, the condition of transferability acts to prevent applications which should really have been lodged by the original victim while he or she was still alive; this consideration obviously does not apply to cases where the original applicant has died. Second, if the original applicant has died at a late stage in proceedings (for example after the parties' written submissions have been received) and his relatives wish to continue the application, it would appear unduly formalistic to consider whether the complaints are or are not transferable in nature. This is particularly so if there is an issue of general interest at stake in the case because, where a case raises such an issue, the Court can, in exceptional circumstances, continue to examine the case and can do so even where no heir can be found at all. For example, in *Karner v Austria*,[379] the original applicant had complained of his inability to succeed to the tenancy of his homosexual partner when a heterosexual partner would be able to. After the original applicant's death, his heir waived her right to succeed to his estate. The Court chose not to strike the application out of its list. It recalled that its judgments served not only to decide those cases before it but, more generally, to elucidate, safeguard, and develop the rules instituted by the Convention. Furthermore, although the primary purpose of the Convention system was to provide individual relief, its mission was also to determine issues on public policy grounds in the common interest, thereby raising the general standards of protection of human rights and extending human rights jurisprudence throughout the community of Convention states. It noted that the issue in the case was of general importance for Austria and other states, and thus respect for human rights required that it continue to examine the case.[380] It must be emphasized that this case is somewhat unusual and it has been far more common for the Court to strike out a case where no legitimate heirs have presented themselves.[381] For example, in *Leger v France*,[382] where the original applicant had challenged his life sentence for murder of a child as amounting in practice to a whole-life term but died—while on parole—in the course of the proceedings, the Court was not satisfied that a niece who had come forward had presented any evidence either of her status as an heir or close relative of the applicant, or of any legitimate interest and, accordingly, it struck the case out of the list. This was notwithstanding the dissenting opinion of four members of the Grand Chamber who considered that the importance of the issues raised in the case justified the continued examination of the case.

II. COMPETENCE *RATIONE MATERIAE*

The competence of the Court only extends to examining complaints concerning the rights and freedoms contained in the Convention and its Protocols. Complaints concerning rights not covered by the Convention are dismissed as incompatible *ratione materiae*.

---

[379] 2003-IX; 32 EHRR 528.

[380] *Karner v Austria*, paras 20–8. The Court did go on to find a violation and ordered that the awards made as just satisfaction be paid to the applicant's estate.

[381] *Direkçi and Direkçi v Turkey No 47826/99* hudoc (2006) DA; *Keser and Others v Turkey* hudoc (2006).

[382] Hudoc (2009).

Thus, for example, the Convention does not guarantee, as such, socio-economic rights,[383] a right to asylum,[384] the right of an alien to enter or to reside in a particular country,[385] the right to work or exercise a particular profession,[386] or the right to institute criminal proceedings against a third party.[387] Nor does it guarantee a right to divorce[388] or social security[389] where these are not provided in domestic law.

This list is far from exhaustive. However, the fact that a particular right is not contained in the Convention does not necessarily mean that all Convention protection is excluded. For example, while the right to asylum is not guaranteed, expulsion or extradition to a country where there are substantial reasons to fear that the person may be subjected to inhuman and degrading treatment may amount to a breach of Article 3 by the sending state.[390] Similarly, if a right is provided for in domestic law, this may engage the state's responsibility under Article 14 of the Convention not to discriminate in the provision of that right.[391]

Three further points are noteworthy. First, complaints that a respondent state has not properly executed a prior judgment of the Court finding a violation in the applicant's case will also be dismissed as incompatible *ratione materiae*, unless there are new facts giving rise to a fresh violation.[392] Second, it is now well-established in the Court's case law that individuals can complain of violations of rights set out in Section II of the Convention. In particular the Court has found violations of Article 34 (the undertaking not to hinder the right of individual petition)[393] and Article 38(1)(a) (the obligation to furnish all necessary facilities to enable the Court to examine the case),[394] and, where there are new facts giving rise to a fresh violation of the Convention after an initial judgment in the applicant's favour and a failure properly to execute that judgment, Article 46 taken together with the substantive Article of the Convention in question.[395] Third, complaints concerning rights in respect of which the state has filed a reservation under Article 57 will also be rejected as incompatible *ratione materiae*.[396] The Court is, however, competent to examine whether the reservation is in conformity with Article 57.[397]

---

[383] *Balakin v Russia* hudoc (2013), para 33; *N v UK* hudoc (2008); *Pančenko v Latvia No 40772/98* hudoc (1999) DA.   [384] *Chahal v UK* 1996-I; 23 EHRR 413 paras 73–4 GC.

[385] From many authorities see *Üner v Netherlands* 2006-XII; 45 EHRR 421, at para 54 GC with references.

[386] *Chen v Netherlands No 37075/06* hudoc (2007) DA; *Coorplan-Jenni GmbH and Elvir Hascic v Austria No 10523/02* hudoc (2005) DA; *Thlimmenos v Greece*, ECHR 2000-IV, para 41.

[387] *Perez v France* hudoc (2004), para 70.

[388] *VK v Croatia*, hudoc (2012), para 99; *Johnston v Ireland*, A 112 (1986); 9 EHRR 203 PC.

[389] *Stummer v Austria* hudoc (2011), para 82; *Stec and Others v UK Nos 65731/01 and 65900/01*, 2005-X, para 54 GC.   [390] See Ch 6.

[391] See, for instance, *Stummer v Austria* hudoc (2011), at para 83 with further references therein.

[392] *Hulki Güneş v Turkey No 17210/09* hudoc (2013) DA; *Egmez v Cyprus No 12214/07* hudoc (2012) DA; *Dowsett v UK (No 2) No 8559/08* hudoc (2011) DA; *Steck-Risch and Others v Liechtenstein No 29061/08* hudoc (2010) DA.

[393] Eg, *Paladi v Moldova No 39806/05* hudoc (2009); *Al-Saadoon and Mufdhi v UK* hudoc (2010); *Mamatkulov and Askarov v Turkey* 2005-I, 41 EHRR 494 GC. This is possible even where the Court finds no violation of the substantive rights that formed the subject of the original application: *Aoulmi v France* 2006-I, 46 EHRR 1.

[394] Usually as a result of a failure to submit investigative files or other documents requested by the Court or to cooperate with a fact-finding mission by the Court: see, eg, *Bucur and Toma v Romania* hudoc (2013); *Davydov and others v Ukraine* hudoc (2010); *Nolan and K v Russia* hudoc (2009); *Imakayeva v Russia* 2006-VIII; *Tepe v Turkey* hudoc (2003), 39 EHRR 584.

[395] *Emre v Switzerland (No 2)* hudoc (2011).

[396] See, eg, *Kozlova and Smirnova v Latvia No 57381/00* hudoc (2001) DA.

[397] *Schädler-Eberle v Liechtenstein* hudoc (2013); *Liepājnieks v Latvia No 37586/06* hudoc (2010) DA.

III. COMPETENCE *RATIONE TEMPORIS*

In consonance with the general principle of non-retroactivity of treaties, the Court has no competence to examine complaints concerning matters which took place before the entry into force of the Convention or the date of ratification by the respondent state.

This will, of course, be of decreasing importance with time, but cases still arise with great frequency from newer member states. In determining whether it has temporal jurisdiction, the Court considers: (a) whether the facts giving rise to the application occurred before or after the date of ratification; and (b) the scope of the Convention right alleged to have been violated.[398]

a. The facts giving rise to the application

For the first, clearly if the facts were instantaneous and were prior to ratification then the application is incompatible *ratione temporis*. However, many of the more difficult cases arise where either the act was prior to ratification but the applicant commenced proceedings to challenge it after that date, or, alternatively, where act was before ratification but the applicant alleges he still suffered adverse effects of the act after ratification. When the act is before ratification and the applicant takes proceedings challenging it after ratification, the application will be rejected as incompatible *ratione temporis*: thus, in cases concerning dismissal from a job, refusal of a broadcasting licence, police search and seizure, and the unauthorized taking of bodily tissues, it was immaterial that the applicants' unsuccessful court challenges to those actions took place after ratification.[399] However, it will be different (and properly so) if proceedings, especially criminal proceedings, are taken against the applicant in respect of acts which took place before ratification: there it is the date of conviction which is important and, if this is after the date of ratification, the case will not be rejected on this ground.[400]

As regards legal proceedings which begin before ratification and continue after it, the Grand Chamber attempted to provide some degree of clarification of the limits of its temporal jurisdiction in *Blecic v Croatia*.[401] There, the applicant had taken legal proceedings to recover property before the relevant date but had appealed unsuccessfully to the Constitutional Court after it. The Grand Chamber found that the interference with the applicant's property rights occurred with the Supreme Court's judgment before the relevant date. It was this judgment that was a definitive act which was by itself capable of violating the applicant's rights. The subsequent Constitutional Court decision only resulted in allowing the interference allegedly caused by that Supreme Court's judgment to subsist. While an application to the Croatian Constitutional Court was an effective remedy, it did not amount to a new or independent interference. The distinction between a judgment which is a definitive act amounting to an interference and a judgment which only allows an interference to subsist is not always easy to determine and, both before and after *Blecic*, the Court has found greater assistance in the notion of a continuing violation, especially in relation to complaints brought under Article 1 of Protocol 1 from former communist

---

[398] *Blečić v Croatia* ECHR 2006-III, para 82.
[399] *Jovanovic v Croatia No 59109/00* hudoc (2002) DA; *Meltex Ltd v Armenia No 37780/02* hudoc (2008) DA; *Veeber v Estonia (No 1) No 37571/97* hudoc (2002) DA, paras 54 and 55; *Kikots and Kikota v Latvia No 54715/00* hudoc (2002) DA.
[400] *Lepojic v Serbia* hudoc (2007), para 45; *Filipovic v Serbia* hudoc (2007), para 33; *Harutyunyan v Armenia*, hudoc (2007), para 50; *Zana v Turkey* 1997-VII; 27 EHRR 667. The same applies in respect of the *ne bis in idem* principle in Article 4 of Protocol 7 (if the second set of proceedings are after ratification) and to the right to compensation for wrongful conviction in Article 3 of the same Protocol (if the conviction is quashed after ratification): *Matveyev v Russia* hudoc (2008), para 38.   [401] 2006-III, para 82 GC.

countries. In cases of deprivation of property under communist regimes, the Court has distinguished nationalization and its continuing effects from the subsequent proceedings for restitution initiated after ratification of the Convention. For the former, deprivation of ownership or of another right *in rem* is in principle an instantaneous act and does not produce a continuing situation: thus applications complaining solely of nationalization by communist regimes are incompatible *ratione temporis*.[402] For the latter, the question of compatibility is less straightforward. The Court has been prepared to countenance the possibility that once a contracting state, having ratified the Convention including Protocol 1, enacts legislation providing for the full or partial restoration of property confiscated under a previous regime, such legislation may be regarded as generating a new property right protected by Article 1 of Protocol 1 for persons satisfying the requirements for entitlement. The same may apply in respect of arrangements for restitution or compensation established under pre-ratification legislation, if such legislation remained in force after the contracting state's ratification of Protocol 1.[403]

b. The scope of the Convention right

For the second criterion, the scope of the Convention right alleged to have been violated, the matter has proven controversial, principally as a result of the Grand Chamber's ruling in *Silih v Slovenia*[404] and subsequent case law that there is a requirement to carry out effective investigations for the purposes of Articles 2 and 3 of the Convention where the events giving rise to the substantive violation occurred before the date of ratification. In *Silih*, the Grand Chamber found that the procedural obligation under Article 2 was 'detachable' from the substantive obligation under that Article. The Grand Chamber qualified its ruling by stating, first, that only procedural acts or omissions after the date of ratification would fall within its temporal jurisdiction and, second, that there had to be a genuine connection between the death and the date of ratification. Thus it had to be established that a significant proportion of the procedural steps were or ought to have been carried out after ratification. Most controversially, the Court added that it would not exclude that in certain circumstances the connection could also be based on the need to ensure that the guarantees and the underlying values of the Convention were protected in a real and effective manner (the 'Convention values' test).[405]

The *Silih* test was sharply criticized as being difficult to apply and detrimental to legal certainty[406] and the Court revisited the issue in *Janowiec and others v Russia*,[407] concerning Russia's alleged failures properly to investigate the Katyn massacre. There, the Court recognized the uncertainty which *Silih* had caused and that further clarification was needed. It emphasized that its temporal jurisdiction extends to those procedural acts and omissions which took place or ought to have taken place in the period after the entry into force of the Convention in respect of the respondent state (paragraph 142 of the judgment). The Court held that for a 'genuine connection' to be established, both criteria must be satisfied: the period of time between the death as the triggering event and the entry into force of the Convention must have been reasonably short (and normally not

---

[402] From the many authorities see *Malhous v Czech Republic No 33071/96*, 2000-XII DA.

[403] *Broniowski v Poland No 31443/96*, 2002 X GC and *Hutten-Czapska v Poland No 35014/97* hudoc (2003) DA; *Maltzan and Others v Germany Nos 71916/01, 71917/01 and 10260/02* hudoc (2005) DA; *Fürst von Thurn und Taxis v Germany No 26367/10* hudoc (2013) DA, para 19. See also, on specially protected tenancies: *Berger-Krall v Slovenia* hudoc (2013), paras 113–15.   [404] Hudoc (2009).

[405] Paragraphs 161–3 of the judgment.

[406] See, eg, the judgment of the Supreme Court of the United Kingdom in *Re McCaughey and another* [2011] UKSC 20.   [407] *No 55508/07 and others* hudoc (2013).

longer than ten years), and a major part of the investigation must have been carried out, or ought to have been carried out, after the entry into force (paragraph 148). The Court further clarified the criteria for the application of the 'Convention values' test and held that the required connection may be found to exist if the triggering event was of a larger dimension than an ordinary criminal offence and amounted to the negation of the very foundations of the Convention. However, the 'Convention values' clause could not be applied to events which occurred prior to the adoption of the Convention, on 4 November 1950 (paragraph 151).

IV. COMPETENCE *RATIONE LOCI*

a. The concept of 'jurisdiction' in Article 1

The concept of competence *ratione loci*—the idea that the Convention does not apply to persons living or acts committed outside the legal territory of the contracting states—has all but been replaced by an examination as to whether an applicant is within the jurisdiction of a contracting state for the purposes of Article 1 of the Convention. It must therefore be doubted whether—save perhaps for Article 56 cases considered later—incompatibility *ratione loci* can be properly be said to remain a separate ground for inadmissibility, since any case where the applicant is found not to be within the jurisdiction will simply be rejected as 'incompatible with the provisions of the Convention'.[408] The concept of jurisdiction has been the subject of a long evolution in the case law of the Strasbourg organs, dating primarily from the Court's consideration as to whether the Convention applied to northern Cyprus.[409] However, the Court's previous case law in this field was rationalized and comprehensively re-stated in *Al-Skeini and others v UK*.[410] The case concerned the relatives of six Iraqis who had died either in British army custody or in the course of security operations carried out by British soldiers in south-east Iraq in 2003. The principles laid down by the Grand Chamber in *Al-Skeini* were later said by the Court (in *Chagos Islanders*[411]) to be the following six:

(i) A state's jurisdictional competence under Article 1 is primarily territorial.

(ii) Only exceptional circumstances give rise to exercise of jurisdiction by a state outside its own territorial boundaries.

(iii) Whether there is an exercise of jurisdiction is a question of fact.

(iv) There are two principal exceptions to territoriality: circumstances of 'State agent authority and control' and 'effective control over an area'.

(v) The 'State agent authority and control' exception applies to the acts of diplomatic and consular agents present on foreign territory; to circumstances where a contracting state, through custom, treaty, or agreement, exercises executive public powers or carries out judicial or executive functions on the territory of another state; and to circumstances where the state through its agents exercises control and authority over an individual outside its territory, such as using force to take a person into custody or exerting full physical control over a person through apprehension or detention.

---

[408] See, eg, *Banković and Others v Belgium and Others* ECHR 2001-XII, para 70.

[409] See the four inter-state cases involving Cyprus and Turkey as well as *Loizidou v Turkey (preliminary objections)* A 310 (1995) and *Loizidou v Turkey (merits)*, 1996-VI.   [410] Hudoc (2011).

[411] *No 35622/04* hudoc (2012) DA, para 70.

(vi) The 'effective control over an area' exception applies where through military action, lawful or unlawful, the state exerts effective control of an area outside its national territory.

On the facts of the case before it the Grand Chamber found that the UK had assumed authority and responsibility for the maintenance of security in south-east Iraq. Through its soldiers, who had been engaged in security operations in Basrah, the UK had exercised authority and control over individuals killed in the course of such security operations. This established a jurisdictional link between the deceased and the UK for the purposes of Article 1 of the Convention.

The Grand Chamber's re-statement of the general principles on jurisdiction has since been applied to the interception of vessels carrying asylum-seekers by the Italian police and coastguard, and the asylum-seekers' subsequent transfer to military ships and thence to Libya in *Hirsi Jamaa and Others v Italy* (where the applicants were found to be under the authority and control of the Italian authorities)[412] and *Catan and others v Moldova and Russia* (where Russia was found to be exercising effective control over Transdniestria).[413]

b. Article 56

Article 56(1), commonly referred to as the 'colonial clause', provides that a state may declare that 'the present Convention shall extend to all or any of the territories of whose international relations it is responsible'.[414] Article 56(3) provides: ' The provisions of this Convention shall be applied in such territories with due regard…to local requirements'. Though attacked by one set of applicants as a colonial relic, the Court has said that, anachronistic as colonial remnants may be, the meaning of Article 56 is plain on its face and it cannot be ignored; it remains a provision of the Convention which is in force and cannot be abrogated at will by the Court in order to reach a purportedly desirable result.[415] Rather, the essential questions for Article 56 are whether the contracting state is responsible for the international relations of the territory and whether it has made a valid declaration. If these conditions are not fulfilled, then the application will be rejected as incompatible *ratione loci* or, more recently, simply incompatible with the provisions of the Convention. Conversely, if the territory is not regarded as an overseas territory but rather as a overseas department (a *départements d'outre mer*) on the same footing as a department of the metropolitan state, then no declaration is necessary.[416] It is immaterial where the dependent territory is situated: the Court has accepted, for instance, declarations by the UK extending the Convention to the Isle of Man and Guernsey.[417] A statement that the respondent state is responsible for the territory's international relations is sufficient for the purposes of the Article 56 declaration.[418] The

---

[412] Hudoc (2012), paras 70–82.

[413] Hudoc (2012), paras 111–23. Jurisdiction in respect of Moldova was found, as in the earlier case of *Ilaşcu and Others v Moldova and Russia* ECHR 2004-VII, paras 322–352 on the basis that, although Moldova had no effective control over the acts of the regime in Transdniestria, the fact that the region was recognized under public international law as part of Moldova's territory gave rise to an obligation, under Article 1 of the Convention, to use all legal and diplomatic means available to it to continue to guarantee the enjoyment of the rights and freedoms defined in the Convention to those living there (paras 109 and 110).

[414] On the background and history of Article 56, see Simpson, *Human Rights and the End of Empire*, 2004, ch 16.   [415] *Chagos Islanders No 35622/04* hudoc (2012) DA, at para 74.

[416] See, by implication, *Hingitaq 53 and Others v Denmark No 18584/04* hudoc (2006) DA.

[417] *Tyrer v UK* A 26 (1978); 2 EHRR 1 and *Gillow v UK* A 109 (1986); 11 EHRR 335 paras 60–2.

[418] See, for instance, a 1950 statement made in respect of Guernsey in *Gillow*. In *Chagos Islanders No 35622/04* hudoc (2012) DA, though the Court preferred not to decide the case on the basis of jurisdiction, it did refuse to accept the applicants' argument that, because the British Indian Ocean Territory was under the control of the UK government, it had to be regarded as part of the metropolitan territory and no Article 56

declarations may be made on a temporary or permanent basis[419] and may be withdrawn and later re-made.[420] A separate declaration is, however, required in order for Protocol 1 to apply to the territory.[421] It is not possible for responsibility under the Convention or the Protocol to arise through the exercise of 'jurisdiction' in respect of a territory which has not been the subject of an Article 56 declaration.[422]

The 'local requirements' referred to in paragraph 3 of Article 56 may permit a lower standard of compliance with the Convention's requirements in dependent territories. There are, however, limits. Thus, the Court held in the *Tyrer* case that no requirement relative to the maintenance of law and order would entitle any contracting state, under Article 56, to make use of an 'inhuman or degrading punishment' (Article 3) in any territory, whatever its state of development. It is also difficult to see how a European self-governing territory such as the Isle of Man could have any 'local requirements' allowing for a different application of the Convention from the rest of Europe. In addition, there must be proof of 'local requirements'; beliefs and local public opinion do not on their own constitute such proof.[423] The Court did accept 'local requirements' in *Py v France*,[424] concerning the restriction of voting rights to individuals in New Caledonia. The Court found those restrictions to be appropriately linked to a series of transitional measures aimed at alleviating the bloody conflict there and reflecting the territory's transition to the acquisition of full sovereignty.

The clear purpose of Article 56 was facilitative: to allow for contracting states with overseas territories to extend the application of the Convention to those territories as they saw fit. However, the provisions of the Article have also been considered in a negative sense, where states have sought to argue that its provision can operate to exclude liability for certain territories for which they may otherwise be responsible. Also relevant is Article 57(1) which allows for a state, when signing or depositing its instrument of ratification, to make a reservation in respect of any particular provision of the Convention to the extent that forbids any reservations of a general character. Three states, Azerbaijan, Georgia, and Moldova, currently have entered open-ended declarations to the Convention in relation to areas which nominally fall within their national territory but would appear to be outside their *de facto* control. In the case of Moldova, the declaration states:

> The Republic of Moldova declares that it will be unable to guarantee compliance with the provisions of the Convention in respect of omissions and acts committed by the organs

declaration was thus necessary: the constitutional status had been set out in the domestic courts' judgments; it was a overseas Crown territory and not part of the UK itself (para 64 of the decision). Nor could jurisdiction attach simply because decisions regarding the territory had been taken in the UK (para 65).

[419] The UK declaration used to distinguish between classes of acceptance: territorial extension renewed for a period of five years and territorial extension on a permanent basis. As of 22 November 2010 acceptance is on a permanent basis for all territories concerned.

[420] As an example of such a withdrawal in respect of Article 3 of Protocol 1 and the Turks and Caicos Islands (though one where the applicant did not challenge the withdrawal of the declaration), see *Misick v UK No 10781/10* hudoc (2012) DA. The declaration was re-made on 19 December 2012 after elections in the territory.   [421] *No 15305/06* hudoc (2006) DA.

[422] *Yonghong v Portugal, No 50887/99*, 1999-IX DA. Nor can the system of declarations be replaced by the 'effective control' or the 'State authority and control' basis for jurisdiction set out in *Al-Skeini and others* (*Chagos Islanders No 35622/04* hudoc (2012) DA, at para 75).

[423] *Yonghong v Portugal*. In *Piermont v France* Series A 314 (1995); 20 EHRR 301, the Court did not consider a 'tense local political' atmosphere in French Polynesia during an election campaign to be 'local requirements' justifying an interference with Article 10 rights. These were thought to be 'circumstances and conditions' rather than 'requirements' (see paras 55–9).   [424] 2005-I; 42 EHRR 548.

of the self-proclaimed Trans-Dniester republic [Transdniestria] within the territory actually controlled by such organs, until the conflict in the region is finally settled.[425]

At the admissibility stage of the *Ilascu* case,[426] which concerned illegal detention in Transdniestria, the Moldovan government argued that Articles 56 and 57 applied together. While it conceded that the purpose of Article 56 was to enable a state to extend the application of the Convention, it argued for a broader interpretation of Article 56 to cover also the novel situation where a state has agreed to be bound by the Convention although *de facto* part of its territory is not under its control. The Court rejected this reasoning, saying that neither the spirit nor the terms of Article 56 could permit a negative interpretation. In respect of Article 57, it went on to hold that this declaration did not amount to a reservation within the meaning of the Convention since it was of a general character. Its effect was 'unlimited as to the provisions of the Convention but limited in space and time, whose effect would be that persons on that 'territory' would be wholly deprived of the protection of the Convention for an indefinite period'.[427]

The issue also arose in relation to northern Cyprus, in the opposite sense, as it were, in relation to Turkey's attempt to evade responsibility for territory outside its national territory but under its control. In *Loizidou v Turkey*,[428] the Court struck down Turkey's declarations made in relation to the then optional clauses on the right of individual petition and the compulsory jurisdiction of the Court, which declared that these only extended to acts performed within the boundaries of the national territory of the Republic of Turkey.[429] The Court stated:

If, as contended by the respondent Government, substantive or territorial restrictions were permissible under these provisions, Contracting Parties would be free to subscribe to separate regimes of enforcement of Convention obligations depending on the scope of their acceptances. Such a system, which would enable States to qualify their consent under the optional clauses, would not only seriously weaken the role of the Commission and Court in the discharge of their functions but would also diminish the effectiveness of the Convention as a constitutional instrument of European public order (*ordre public*).

---

[425] See also the Azerbaijan declaration (stating it is 'unable to guarantee the application of the provisions of the Convention in the territories occupied by the Republic of Armenia') and the Georgian declaration (stating that it is unable to undertake its Convention commitments in Abkhazi and Tskinvali and declines responsibility for the 'organs of self-proclaimed illegal forces' there). The Cyprus declaration was a little different, declining responsibility for 'the acts or omissions relat[ing] to measures taken by the Government of the Republic of Cyprus to meet the needs resulting from the situation created by the continuing invasion and military occupation of part of the territory of the Republic of Cyprus by Turkey'.

[426] Hudoc (2001), p 20. [427] *Ilascu* hudoc (2001), p 20.

[428] A 310 (1995); 20 EHRR 99 GC. [429] *Loizidou v Turkey*, paras 18 and 25–7.

3

THE EUROPEAN COURT
OF HUMAN RIGHTS:
ORGANIZATION, PRACTICE,
AND PROCEDURE

1. THE ORGANIZATION OF THE COURT

I. THE SETTING UP OF THE NEW COURT

The European Court of Human Rights is a unique body in the history of international law. More than 800 million people have direct access to the Court to complain of violations of their fundamental rights. The Court has established standards which permeate the legal order of the forty-seven contracting parties and has made a major contribution to the shaping of domestic law and practice in almost every area of law—the administration of criminal justice, civil and criminal law, family law, and the law of property, to name but a few. This is a notable achievement for an international tribunal that was set up in 1959 with the role of providing an early warning system against the decline of democratic standards and the growth of dictatorships. This essentially political mandate was to be achieved through the operation of law, in particular through the exercise of the right of individual petition.

The present permanent Court, which started its work on 1 November 1998 on the entry into force of Protocol 11, is the product of the fusion of two separate, part-time enforcement bodies, the now defunct European Commission of Human Rights and the former European Court of Human Rights.[1] Under Protocol 11, the existing Commission and Court were replaced by a single full-time institution composed of one judge in respect of each contracting party to the Convention. Judges would be permanently based in Strasbourg and would not be permitted to engage in any activity incompatible with the demands of a full-time office. The present Court's role goes far beyond that of ruling on the substantive issues raised by a case. It is an all-purpose Court, which has inherited from the Commission the essential tasks of filtering applications, fact-finding, determining admissibility, and negotiating friendly settlement, in addition to providing binding rulings in admissible cases.[2]

---

[1] For the operation of the former Commission and Court of Human Rights see Chs 22 and 24 of the first edition of this book.

[2] See, for an insider's view of how the Court operates in practice with special reference to the role of the Court's President, Costa, *La Cour européenne des droits de l'homme: Des judges pour la liberté*, 2013. Judge

The constant growth in the number of cases being brought to the Court since 1998 has required it to change its working methods continuously in order to find ways of rejecting obviously inadmissible cases with an economy of procedure.[3] It was soon realized that Protocol 11 was not sufficient and that further structural change was needed (the reform of the reform) to enable the Court to operate effectively. This led to the drafting of Protocol 14, which was opened for signature on 13 May 2004 and took more than six years to come into effect, due to Russia's reluctance to ratify the Protocol.[4] It was also recognized that the continuous growth of cases by 12 per cent every year was steadily asphyxiating the Court and undermining its authority.[5] In 2005 the Committee of Ministers set up a group of Wise Persons to examine the future of the Court and to set out a blueprint for its future long-term development. The Group reported in November 2006 and made a number of far-reaching proposals.[6] However, it was clear that the Group's thinking was predicated on the assumption that the changes brought about by Protocol 14 would be in place soon and that the future discussion on their proposals would be enriched by information as to the operation of the changes brought about by that Protocol. The process of reform had thus stalled, pending a final decision by Russia as to whether it would ratify the Protocol. The Protocol finally came into force in 2010. Three reform conferences were held over the next three years—in Interlaken (2010), in Izmir (2011) and in Brighton (2012)—leading to agreement on a blueprint for the Court's development over the next decade.[7]

II. COMPOSITION OF THE COURT

Section II of the Convention governs the operation of the Court and its procedures.[8] Article 20 provides that the number of judges shall equal the number of contracting

Costa was President of the Court from 2007 to 2011. On reform of the Court generally, see Wildhaber, *The European Court of Human Rights 1998–2006: History, Achievements, Reform*, 2006; also Benoît-Rohmer, 73 RTDH 3 (2008) and Reform of the European Human Rights System: Proceedings of the High-level Seminar, Oslo, 2004, Directorate General of Human Rights, Strasbourg: Council of Europe, 2004.

[3] On 1 November 2013 there were 107,600 cases pending before a judicial formation. Six countries gave rise to 72.1% of all applications: Russia (17.5%); Italy (13.6%); Ukraine (12.5%); Turkey (11.6%); Serbia (11%); Romania (5.9%). On 1 November 2013 there were 47,225 repetitive cases on the Court's docket. 87% of these were brought against just six states (Italy, Serbia, Turkey, Ukraine, Romania, and Russia). For detailed statistical information on the work of the Court and types of cases brought see *Survey of Activities 2012*, Registry of the European Court of Human Rights (2013). In the early years of the Convention, the number of applications lodged with the Commission was comparatively small, and the number of cases decided by the Court was much lower again. This changed in the 1980s, by which time the steady growth in the number of cases brought before the Convention institutions made it increasingly difficult to keep the length of proceedings within acceptable limits. Adding to the problem was the rapid increase in the number of Contracting States from 1990 onwards, rising from twenty-two to the current total of forty-seven. The number of applications registered annually with the Commission increased from 404 in 1981 to 4,750 in 1997, the last full year of operation of the original supervisory mechanism. By that same date, the number of unregistered or provisional files opened each year in the Commission had risen to over 12,000. Although on a much lower scale, the former Court's statistics reflected a similar story, with the number of cases referred annually rising from 7 in 1981 to 119 in 1997.

[4] For a description of Protocol 14, see section 6 of this chapter.

[5] Since the setting up of the new Court the number of cases has consistently increased. In 1999, 8,400 cases were allocated to a judicial formation; in 2000 the figure was 10,500; by 2008 the number had gone up to 49,816; in 2009, 57,101 cases were allocated, rising to 65,200 in 2012.

[6] Final Report of the Group of Wise Persons to the Committee of Ministers, Council of Europe, November 2006 (available at http://www.echr.coe.int). See also Future Developments of the European Court of Human Rights in the Light of the Wise Persons Report: proceedings of the colloquy, San Marino, 22–23 March, Council of Europe, 2007.   [7] See section 7 on reform later in this chapter.

[8] For details of the current composition of the Court, see the Court's website http://www.echr.coe.int.

parties; currently, therefore, there are forty-seven judges.[9] The judges are elected to a single, non-renewable term of nine years.[10] Judges' terms of office expire when they reach seventy years of age.[11] However, when read with the provision in Article 23(3) ('judges shall hold office until replaced'), a certain ambiguity appears. The practice has been that judges over the age of seventy have continued to sit until replaced.[12] Protocol 15, however, will replace the age limit with a requirement that candidates should be less than sixty-five years of age at the date by which the list of three candidates has been requested by the Parliamentary Assembly, thus effectively increasing the age limit to seventy-four.[13]

The criteria for office are set out in Article 21 of the Convention, which specifies that judges shall be of 'high moral character' and must possess the qualifications required for appointment to high judicial office or be jurisconsults of recognized competence. The latter term, taken to mean 'experts in law', considerably expands the pool of eligible candidates. The result is a Strasbourg judiciary of diverse professional backgrounds: the current Court includes former supreme and constitutional court judges, academics, prosecutors, and those recruited from the practising bar in contracting parties.[14]

In keeping with the nature of any full-time court, Article 21(3) requires that judges shall not engage in activity which is incompatible with their independence or impartiality or the demands of a full-time office. Rule 4 of the Rules of Court supplements this by making it clear that they shall not engage in any political or administrative activity which is incompatible with their independence or impartiality. Judges are expected to work full time in Strasbourg. All new judges are informed of this by the President of the Court and it is further reinforced both by the oath they swear upon taking up office[15] and the election procedures of the Parliamentary Assembly of the Council of Europe (PACE) considered in the following section. Rule 4 also provides that judges must declare any additional activity to the President and that in the event of a disagreement between the President and the judge concerned, any question arising shall be decided by the plenary Court.

Article 51 of the Convention entitles judges to privileges and immunities in the exercise of their functions, thus reinforcing the independence of the Court. These are today governed by the 1996 Sixth Protocol to the General Agreement on Privileges and Immunities of the Council of Europe,[16] ratified by nearly all of the contracting parties. The Protocol applies to both permanent and ad hoc judges.[17] This entitles judges, as well as their spouses and minor children, to the privileges and immunities accorded to diplomatic envoys, and

---

[9] As of January 2014, eighteen judges are women.

[10] See section 6 of this chapter on Protocol 14.

[11] Article 23(6) of the Convention. There is no provision or procedure for the formal impeachment of sitting judges. The matter is instead regulated by Article 24 of the Convention and Rule 7 of the Rules of Court, which allow for dismissal by a two-thirds majority of the plenary Court. It has never happened.

[12] On this point and the election of judges in general, see Hedigan, in Kohen, ed, *Liber Amicorum Lucius Caflisch*, 2007, pp 235–53. See further, Krüger, 1996 RUDH, 113; Valticos, in *Liber Amicorum M-A Eissen*, 1995; Carrillo-Salcedo, 1997 RUDH 1; and *'Judicial Independence: The Law and Practice of Appointments to the European Court of Human Rights'* Interights, May 2003, available at: http://www.interights.org/jud-ind-en/index.html.

[13] This modification aims at enabling highly qualified judges to serve the full nine-year term of office and thereby reinforce the consistency of the membership of the Court.

[14] See the Court's website for the judges' *curricula vitae*.

[15] The text of which is set out in Rule 3 of the Rules of Court.

[16] ETS 162; available from the Treaty Office online at: http://conventions.coe.int/. In force since 1998. Azerbaijan, Portugal, and San Marino have not yet ratified the Protocol.

[17] Article 2; also Committee of Ministers' Resolution 'On the Status and Conditions of Service of Judges of the European Court of Human Rights and of the Commissioner of Human Rights' (2009)5, Article 2, https://wcd.coe.int/ViewDoc.jsp?id=1508697&Site=CM.

guarantees judges' immunity from legal process in respect of words or acts done in the discharge of their duties.[18] The immunity continues in respect of such words or acts even when they are no longer involved in the discharge of such duties.[19] It also guarantees the inviolability of their papers and correspondence as well as that of the Court and the Registry 'in so far as they relate to the business of the Court'.[20] By Article 4 of the Protocol, privileges and immunities are accorded to judges 'not for the personal benefit of the individuals themselves but in order to safeguard the independent exercise of their functions'. Immunity can only be waived by the plenary Court. According to Article 4 it 'is under a duty to waive the immunity of a judge in any case where, in its opinion, the immunity would impede the course of justice, and where it can be waived without prejudice to the purpose for which the immunity is accorded'.[21]

The President of the Court is assisted by two Vice-Presidents, who are also Presidents of Sections, and three further Section Presidents, all of whom are elected by the plenary Court for a three-year term which may be renewed once.[22] The Convention itself is silent on many of the duties now assumed by the President, save for stating that he or she (with the Vice-Presidents and Presidents of the Chambers) will automatically be a member of the Grand Chamber.

Rule 9 of the Rules of Court elucidates the President's role in greater detail.[23] The first paragraph specifies that the President shall direct the work and administration of the Court and represent it, with particular responsibility for its relations with the authorities of the Council of Europe. He or she also has power to issue practice directions (Article 32).[24] These are wide-ranging duties and will involve managing the Court's relationship with its Registry, establishing and maintaining relations with national courts and governments (including protocol matters such as receiving delegations and visiting dignitaries to the Court), and relations with the Committee of Ministers and the Secretariat of the Council of Europe, encompassing, most importantly, budgetary matters.[25] The proper relationship between the Court and other parts of the Council of Europe can be a difficult one, not least because the President must ensure that the Court is fully independent in judicial matters whilst also accepting that, at least administratively, the Court and its Registry are an autonomous part of the wider Council of Europe system. For the judicial functions of the President, Rule 9(2) makes explicit what the Convention assumes: he or she will

---

[18] Articles 1 and 3.

[19] Article 3. Article 5 extends the privileges and immunities to the Registrar and Deputy Registrar of the Court.

[20] Article 6. Official correspondence and other communications of the Court, judges, or the registry may not be held up or subjected to censorship; Article 6(2).

[21] The Court rejected a request from the Romanian government to waive the immunity of Judge Birsan, but allowed the request to waive the immunity in respect of his wife who was being investigated for suspected criminal offences. In its Decision on the matter, the Court considered that Romania had violated the immunity of Judge Birsan and his wife by carrying out a search of his home on 6 October 2011. The Decision also emphasized that the waiving of immunity does not have retroactive effect; see Press Release issued by the Registrar annexing the Court's Decision (29 November 2011).

[22] By Article 26 of the Convention. Though that Article simply provides that they may be re-elected, Rule 8(3) of the Rules of Court limits this to one re-election. Rule 8(5) sets out elaborate procedures for their election.

[23] Note also the role of the Bureau which assists the President in directing the work and administration of the Court. It is composed of the President, the Vice-Presidents, the three Section Presidents, the Registrar, and the Deputy Registrar—Rule 9A of the Rules of Court.

[24] See the Court's website for, *inter alia*, practice directions issued by the President on interim measures, just satisfaction, and written pleadings.

[25] The Court's budget for 2012–2013 amounts to €61.5 million. Budgetary decisions are taken by the Committee of Ministers of the Council of Europe.

preside at plenary meetings of the Court, meetings of the Grand Chamber, and meetings of the panel of five judges which considers requests for referral to the Grand Chamber.

III. THE ELECTION OF JUDGES AND THE ADVISORY PANEL

Article 22 entrusts election of judges to the Parliamentary Assembly of the Council of Europe (PACE) from a list of three candidates nominated by the contracting party.[26] The lists submitted by contracting parties have at times proved controversial and PACE has rejected them on various occasions. The contracting parties have stressed the importance attached to the independence, impartiality, and quality of the judges in the Interlaken, Izmir, and Brighton Declarations, as well as the need to encourage applications by good candidates.[27] It is crucial to the fulfilment of the Court's mission that candidates should be put forward by the states for their juridical competence alone. Unfortunately, there are well-documented instances where unsuitable candidates have been put forward.[28] To ensure highly qualified candidates, the Committee of Ministers set up an Advisory Panel in 2010 composed of seven judges of the highest courts (including former judges of international courts) to advise the contracting parties on whether candidates satisfy the criteria set out in Article 21 of the Convention, as a specialized pre-examination to that carried out by the sub-committee on legal and political affairs of the Assembly. They scrutinize the lists and inform the contracting parties, on a confidential basis, whether there are any shortcomings, although it has no power to hear the candidates. They will also submit their views to PACE, again on a confidential basis.[29] The central idea of the Panel is that its members will be able to avail themselves of their judicial experience and wide contacts to make an informed assessment of the quality of the candidates on the list. The Panel's role is to ensure that only competent and qualified candidates are placed on the list to be assessed by PACE. The scheme will only work if the contracting parties and PACE comply with the observations made by the Panel. It is not an encouraging sign that in several cases the contracting party forwarded their lists to the Assembly without waiting for the Panel's view, and that the elections took place without PACE having obtained the views of the Panel on the candidates concerned.[30] On the other hand there are early signs that the system has indeed made a difference to the quality of candidates being put

---

[26] See, for a critical view of the system with proposals for reform, *Judicial Independence: The Law and Practice of Appointments to the European Court of Human Rights*, Interights, 2003, http://www.interights. org/jud-ind-en/index.html ; Drzemczewski, 'Election of Judges to the Strasbourg Court: An Overview', 4 EHRLR 377 (2010); and 'Procedure for electing judges to the European Court of Human Rights', Information document issued by the Committee on legal and political affairs, AS/Jur/inf (2013)02.

[27] See section 7 of this chapter.

[28] See Engel, 'More Transparency and Governmental Loyalty for Maintaining Professional Quality in the Election of Judges to the European Court of Human Rights', 32 HRLJ No 7-12, (2013) pp 448–55.

[29] See ResCM/Res (2010)26 *On the establishment of an Advisory Panel of experts on Candidates for Election as Judge to the European Court of Human Right*. Seven judges have been appointed by the Committee of Ministers following consultation with the President of the Court: Katarzyna Gonera (Poland); Renate Jaeger (Germany); John L Murray (Ireland); Matti Pellonpää (Finland); Professor Sami Selçuk (Turkey); Professor Luzius Wildhaber (Switzerland); Valery D Zorkin (Russia). The Panel is chaired by Luzius Wildhaber. Valery Zorkin resigned in 2013 and has been replaced by the former judge Nina Vajić (Croatia). Further changes are due in 2014.

[30] See the Panel's *Report of Activities for the attention of the Steering Committee for Human Rights* (15 May 2013) GT-GDR-E (2013)004 and proposals to enable the Panel to carry out its tasks effectively. For example, that the PACE sub-committee should not accept any list containing names of candidates who were not considered qualified by the Panel or that the Sub-Committee should not proceed with an election until it has received the Panel's comments; at section 15. See also the Panel's elucidation of the requirements of Article 21 § 1 of the Convention; section 5.

forward for election in 2012 and 2013, but not without a certain institutional friction with the sub-committee on legal and political affairs responsible for interviewing the candidates and making proposals to the Assembly. This body has made it clear that the role of the panel is to vet the lists before they are submitted to the Assembly and that it is the Assembly that has the sole responsibility for the election of the judges thereafter. It is clear that to be effective the Panel must be given more teeth and a *modus vivendi* needs to be established between the Panel and PACE. One commentator has suggested, *inter alia*, that the Panel should forward its proposals to all forty-seven governments; that the proposals of the sub-committee on its choice after interviewing the candidates be accessible to the press and made public; and that the interviews with the sub-committee should not take place if Governments omit to consult the Panel.[31]

While the election is a matter for PACE, it is not clear what, if any, conditions it may impose on candidates. Pursuant to its Resolutions 1366 (2004) and 1436 (2005), the Parliamentary Assembly's practice is that it will not vote on a list until it is satisfied that certain conditions are met, such as all three nominees being qualified to serve as judges, demonstrating sufficient independence from the nominating state, being capable of working in at least one of the Court's official languages, being willing to take up permanent residence in Strasbourg, and, in the interests of the gender balance of the Court, that the list contain at least one man and one woman.[32] Lists which have not met these criteria have been regularly rejected, as have lists which are not considered to offer the Assembly a real choice because of wide disparities in the qualifications and experience of the candidates. However, in such circumstances, the contracting party retains the right to nominate candidates. Therefore if a state were to insist on submitting the same list that has previously been unfavourably reviewed by the Advisory Panel or rejected by the Parliamentary Assembly, there would be an impasse.

Such a stand-off occurred in relation to the Maltese list, which was rejected by the Parliamentary Assembly because there were no female candidates on it. In the ensuing impasse, Malta prevailed upon the Committee of Ministers to ask the Court for an advisory opinion on two questions: first, whether a list which satisfied the criteria listed in Article 21 (described earlier) could be rejected on gender grounds; and second, whether the relevant resolutions of the Parliamentary Assembly adopting the requirement of both genders being represented on a list were in breach of the Assembly's responsibilities under Article 22. The Court in its Advisory Opinion of 12 February 2008[33] found it not necessary to answer the second question and answered the first by stating that, while there was no implicit link between the criteria laid down in Article 21 and mixed sex lists, a gender equality policy could, in principle, constitute grounds for rejection of a list by the Assembly. However, there were boundaries that the Assembly could not overstep in its pursuit of that policy. In particular, it should not have the effect of making it more difficult for contracting parties to put forward candidates who satisfied all the requirements of Article 21. Accordingly, provision had to be made for some exceptions to enable states

---

[31] See Engel, 'More Transparency and Governmental Loyalty for Maintaining Professional Quality in the Election of Judges to the European Court of Human Rights', 32 HRLJ No 7-12, (2013), p 449.

[32] See also the report of the Assembly's Committee on Legal Affairs and Human Rights on Resolution 1366 (Doc 9963 of 7 October 2003), which further outlines the general qualities it will look for in a candidate; also the *Guidelines of the Committee of Ministers on the selection of candidates for the post of judge* CM (2012)40, and the Explanatory Memorandum (29 March 2012), which are concerned with the national selection process.

[33] *Advisory Opinion on Certain Legal Questions Concerning the Lists of Candidates for the Election of Judges to the European Court of Human Rights* hudoc (2008) GC. See Mowbray, 8 HRLR 549 (2008).

to choose national candidates who satisfied the requirements of Article 21, especially for states where the legal profession was small. The practice of the Parliamentary Assembly in not allowing such exceptions was thus considered incompatible with the Convention.[34]

Another issue that has given rise to controversy arose in 2007, when Ukraine sought to withdraw its list on the grounds that there had been irregularities in the selection process in respect of one member. The Assembly requested Ukraine to replace the member, but not to submit a new list, as there were no 'exceptional circumstances' under its rules that would justify this.[35] The issue was important because it concerned the fate of the list against the background of changing local politics.

The Court was asked for an advisory opinion. It ruled that the states were authorized to withdraw a list, but only within certain limits. That limit was the deadline set by the Assembly for the submission of the list. Once that time had passed, it would no longer be open to the state to withdraw its list. Any later possibility of withdrawal was considered to hinder the normal course and timing of the procedure for the election. Where the states withdrew their list before the expiry of this time limit, it was open to them to submit a new list which would have to be considered by the Assembly.[36]

The Assembly has also made efforts to reform the way in which states select their lists of candidates. For example, its Resolution 1646 (2009) requires states to issue public and open calls for candidatures, to describe how candidates are selected, to put forward candidates with knowledge of the official languages, to consult, and to submit the lists in alphabetical order so as not to betray preferences for candidates. These efforts have had mixed success.

IV. INELIGIBILITY TO SIT AND WITHDRAWAL

As noted earlier, Article 21(3) states that the judges shall not engage in any activity which is incompatible with their independence, impartiality, or with the demands of a full-time office. Occasionally judges have had to withdraw from hearing individual cases because of inevitable conflicts of interest, most commonly when the judge, who may previously have held high judicial office in his or her home state, has already heard a case at the national level or been involved in a case as an advocate. In the early years of the new Court, judges who had previously been members of the Commission frequently had to withdraw because they had previously heard the case at the Commission. Similarly, judges who have previously been agents of their government or ambassadors involved, even remotely, in dealing with cases before the Court will not be able to hear cases which were communicated to the government when they acted in these capacities. Rule 28(2) sets out situations where the judge may not take part in the consideration of any case, including having a personal interest in the case or where the judge has expressed opinions publicly concerning the case that 'are objectively capable of adversely affecting his or her impartiality'. The mere fact that a judge has written an academic article concerning the interpretation of a provision of the Convention and has expressed a general opinion on the case law, unrelated to the facts of the case being considered, would not normally disqualify him or her from sitting. But, as with any court, difficult questions of judgment can arise in this context. Normally, the judge concerned will simply notify the President

---

[34] Following the *Advisory Opinion*, the Assembly changed its rules to permit exceptions to the gender requirement', Resolution 1627 (2008).

[35] For the relevant rules of the Assembly see Appendix to Resolution 1432 (2005).

[36] *Advisory Opinion (no 2) on certain legal questions concerning the lists of candidates submitted with a view to the election of judges to the European Court of Human Rights* hudoc (2010) GC, paras 45–9.

of the Section or the Grand Chamber, as the case may be, that he or she cannot sit, and Rule 28(1) places the burden on the judge to notify the President if he or she is prevented from sitting. If there is any doubt on the part of the judge or the President as to the existence of any grounds for ineligibility to sit, then, by Rule 28(4), the issue is decided by the Chamber (or, as appropriate, the Grand Chamber) without the presence of the judge concerned but after the judge has had an opportunity to express his views on the matter.[37]

V. *AD HOC* AND COMMON INTEREST JUDGES

In the event that a judge withdraws from a case, if it is not a case in which he or she is the national judge, then his or her place will simply be taken by one of the substitute judges in the Chamber or Grand Chamber. If he or she is the national judge, then this necessitates the appointment of another judge, since Article 28 requires the presence of the national judge. In accordance with an arrangement that was introduced to facilitate the Court's work and accepted by the government agents, the President will invite the respondent government to decide whether to appoint another elected judge to sit in the case or an *ad hoc* judge.[38] Where the Chamber seeks to reject a case *de limine* without communicating it to the government for observations, the Chamber will not ask for an *ad hoc* judge to be appointed.

Protocol 14 has altered the rules concerning the nomination of *ad hoc* judges.[39] Each contracting party is required to draw up a reserve list of *ad hoc* judges from which the President of the Court will choose when the need arises to make an appointment. The Explanatory Report to the Protocol explains that the reform was a response to criticism of the former system, which allowed a contracting state to choose an *ad hoc* judge after the beginning of proceedings. The Convention provides in Article 27(2) that for Chambers and Grand Chambers, the judge elected in respect of the state party concerned shall sit *ex officio* and, if there is none or he or she is unable to sit, a person of its choice shall sit in the capacity of judge. This is fleshed out by Rule 29 of the Rules of Court, which provides that the list of *ad hoc* judges submitted to the President shall contain the names of persons of both sexes and be valid for a renewable period of two years. The judges must satisfy the qualifications set out for judges in Article 21(1) of the Convention and they must also meet the demands of availability and attendance. If no list is provided or if less than three persons satisfy the conditions for appointment, the President may appoint one of the sitting judges.[40] For the duration of their appointment an *ad hoc* judge is not permitted to represent any party or third party in proceedings before the Court in order to avoid a situation where an *ad hoc* judge is both judge and advocate at the same time. It is open to the President to appoint another elected judge to sit as the *ad hoc* judge where he finds, *inter alia*, that the state has not supplied a list or where the judges on the list do not satisfy the qualifications indicated above.[41]

---

[37] See also the Court's Resolution on Judicial Ethics (23 June 2008)—available on the Court's website www.echr.coe.int.

[38] See, eg, the appointment of the judge elected in respect of San Marino to replace the judge elected in respect of Italy in *Labita v Italy* 2000-IV; 46 EHRR 1228 para 4 GC.

[39] Article 26(4) as amended by Protocol 14.   [40] Rule 29(2).

[41] See Rule 29 paras 1(a), (c) and 2(a) and (b). See also 'Ad Hoc Judges at the European Court of Human Rights: An Overview' (PACE Information report, by Mrs Marie-Louise Bemelmans-Videc), 19 October 2011, Doc 12827, available at http://assembly.coe.int/ASP/Doc/XrefViewHTML.asp?FileID=13035&Language=EN.

Neither the Convention nor the Rules of Court provide for the possibility of challenging a judge or *ad hoc* judge, although it is open to an applicant, a contracting party, or a third party intervener to request a judge's withdrawal to the President of the Chamber, setting out the reasons for any objection. It would then be a matter for the President to decide after having consulted the Chamber. Moreover, since the Rules do not provide for any consultation of the applicant before the appointment of an *ad hoc* judge, no right of veto can be inferred and thus the matter is wholly at the discretion of the Chamber.[42]

Finally when two or more applicant or respondent contracting states have a common interest in a particular case, for example when the application is brought against more than one contracting state, it is possible for the states to nominate a common interest judge. This occurred, for example, in the case of *Behrami and Saramati v France, Germany and Norway*,[43] concerning the actions of UNMIK in Kosovo, where the three respondent governments agreed to the appointment of Judge Costa, the judge elected in respect of France and then President of the Court, as common interest judge.

VI. COURT'S FORMATIONS: PLENARY, SINGLE JUDGES, COMMITTEES, SECTIONS, GRAND CHAMBER

The administrative and judicial work of the Court takes place in a number of formations. For administrative work, the most significant decisions are taken by the plenary Court, composed of all of the Court judges. Article 26 provides that it is the plenary Court that elects the President and Vice-Presidents of the Court as well as the Presidents of the Chambers.[44] It also sets up the Chambers, adopts the rules of court, and elects the Court's Registrar and Deputy Registrar. Apart from elections it votes by a show of hands.[45]

For judicial work, the Court is divided into Sections, currently five, of nine or ten judges. The Sections are changed every three years to ensure a rotation of judges across the Sections, a time frame that will correspond with the election or re-election of the President, Vice-Presidents, and Section Presidents. The composition of each Section is geographically and gender-balanced and is designed to reflect the different legal systems among the contracting parties.[46] Decisions as to admissibility are taken by Chambers of seven judges or, in clearly inadmissible cases, by single judges or Committees of three judges. Decisions on the merits of admitted cases are taken by Chambers or the Grand Chamber. Committees have been empowered by Protocol 14 to adopt judgments in

---

[42] The matter arose in the fourth *Cyprus v Turkey* inter-state case 2001-IV; 35 EHRR 731 para 8 GC, where both the respondent and applicant governments objected to a series of *ad hoc* judges appointed by the others after the judge elected in respect of Turkey withdrew from sitting on the case and the Turkish government objected to the judge elected in respect of Cyprus. It appears that, in each case, the decision on whether the national or *ad hoc* judges were eligible to sit was finally decided by the Grand Chamber in accordance with Rule 28(4). While not expressly provided for by the Convention or Rules of Court, a third party could also object to an *ad hoc* judge, particularly if it is a state exercising its right to intervene.

[43] *Behrami and Behrami v France and Saramati v France, Germany and Norway* Nos 71412/01 and 78166/01 hudoc (2007) DA. See also *Banković and Others v Belgium and 16 Other Contracting States No 52207/99*, 2001-XII GC and *Senator Lines GmbH v Austria and 14 Other Contracting States No 56672/00*, 2004-IV GC; also *Artemi and Gregory v 22 Member States of the European Union* hudoc (2010) DA.

[44] While Article 26 speaks of electing Presidents of Chambers, in practice the plenary Court elects Presidents of Sections, who will in most cases (except when they are the national judge) preside in the chambers of seven judges which are drawn from that Section.

[45] Rule 23(3) of the Rules of Court.

[46] See Rule 25(2). Each section itself elects its Vice-President who presides when the President cannot. For example, a President will not preside when a case against his or her state is being considered.

cases concerning issues of well-established case law (so-called WECL cases). Normally, any given Chamber or Committee formation is composed of judges from within the same Section. The Grand Chamber of seventeen judges is drawn by lot from across the Sections.[47]

The procedures followed by Single judges, Committees, Chambers, and the Grand Chamber are set out separately in the later sections of this chapter, but in essence the formation that will make the final decision or judgment on an application will depend entirely on the case's relative merit and importance.

VII. THE COURT'S REGISTRY

Article 24 of the Convention provides: 'The Court shall have a registry, the functions and organisation of which shall be laid down in the Rules of Court.' Article 24(2) provides that when dealing with single judge cases (ie inadmissible *de plano*) the court shall be assisted by non-judicial rapporteurs forming part of the registry appointed by and acting under the authority of the President. The task of the Registry is to provide legal and administrative support to the Court in the exercise of its judicial functions. It is therefore composed of lawyers, administrative and technical staff, and translators.[48] It also has a Research Division operating under the authority of the Court's Jurisconsult and a Filtering Division responsible for single judge decisions and the development of best practices throughout the registry in the handling of inadmissible cases and interim measures. The Court elects its Registrar and Deputy Registrar—the head and deputy head of the Registry respectively.[49] Each of the Court's five judicial Sections is assisted by a Section Registrar and a Deputy Section Registrar. The principal function of the Registry is to process and prepare for adjudication applications lodged by individuals and states with the Court.[50] The lawyers prepare files and analytical notes for the judge rapporteurs. They are also responsible for drafting decisions and judgments under the supervision of the judge rapporteur and the Registrar, responding to inquiries and investigating issues of national or international law relevant to the Court's work. Their legal work is subject to different layers of review: first within the Registry itself by Heads of Division and the Registrars; then by the judge rapporteur (in Chamber or Grand Chamber cases); and

---

[47] See Rule 24 of the Rules of Court.

[48] At time of writing (August 2013) there are more than 650 officials in the Registry including 270 lawyers and support staff. Registry employees are staff members of the Council of Europe, the Court's parent organization, and are subject to the Council of Europe's Staff Regulations concerning conditions of work and pension entitlement. Approximately half the Registry is employed on contracts of unlimited duration and may be expected to pursue a career in the Registry or in other parts of the Council of Europe. They are recruited on the basis of open competitions. All members of the Registry are required to adhere to strict conditions as to their independence and impartiality and are answerable in practice to the President of the Court rather than to the Secretary General of the Council of Europe. Following the Interlaken Declaration, states parties were asked to consider the possibility of seconding national judges and other officials to the Registry. The Court selects the candidates from lists supplied by the governments. There are around forty-four seconded officials working for the Court who are either judges/prosecutors or court officials. There are also seven judicial trainees working in the Court as part of a specially funded scheme. The rationale underlying the scheme is that they will assist the Registry in its work and will then return to their countries after one or two years with a greater knowledge of the workings of the court and its case law.

[49] Article 26(e) of the Convention and Rules 15 and 16 of the Rules of Court.

[50] The Registry's lawyers are divided into thirty-one case-processing divisions, each of which is assisted by an administrative team. Cases are assigned to the different divisions on the basis of knowledge of the language and legal system concerned. The documents prepared by the Registry for the Court are all drafted in one of its two official languages (English and French).

ultimately by the Court itself. They also correspond with the parties on procedural matters.[51] The Registry is recruited by the Council of Europe but is necessarily autonomous in the performance of its functions in order to preserve the independence of the Court and ultimately answerable only to the President of the Court. As a matter of convention, this autonomy has been more or less respected in practice by successive Secretaries General of the Council of Europe, and in 2012 was officially recognized by the Council of Europe by the delegation of various administrative powers to the Court's Registrar.[52]

2. PROCEDURE BEFORE THE COURT (I): FROM THE INITIAL APPLICATION TO JUDGMENT

I. INDIVIDUAL COMPLAINTS

As the statistics of individual complaints indicate, it is almost entirely through the exercise of the right of individual petition (Article 34) that the Court functions.[53] It is considered by the Court as 'a key component of the machinery' for the protection of human rights.[54]

II. HINDERING THE EFFECTIVE EXERCISE OF THE RIGHT OF INDIVIDUAL PETITION

Article 34, last sentence, indicates that the contracting parties must not 'hinder in any way the effective exercise of this right'. The Court has emphasized, in its case law on the scope of this obligation, that it is of the utmost importance for the effective operation of the system of individual petition that applicants or potential applicants are able to communicate freely with the Court without being subjected to any form of pressure from the authorities to withdraw or modify their complaints.[55] The right is an absolute one and admits of no hindrance. The word 'pressure' is understood as covering not only direct coercion and flagrant acts of intimidation of applicants or their families or legal representatives, but also other improper indirect acts or contacts designed to dissuade or discourage them from pursuing a Convention remedy.[56] In making its assessment

---

[51] In addition to its case-processing divisions, the Registry has divisions dealing with the following sectors of activity: information technology; case law information and publications; research and the library; just satisfaction; press and public relations; and internal administration. It has a central office, which handles mail, files, and archives. The Court also has a Jurisconsult who heads the Research Division and keeps the consistency of the case law of the Sections under review. There are two language divisions, whose main work is translating the Court's judgments into the second official language.

[52] CM Res (2011) 9 amending the Staff Regulations with regard to delegation of staff management powers to the Registrar of the European Court of Human Rights.   [53] See n 3.

[54] See *Mamatkulov and Askarov v Turkey* 2005-I; 41 EHRR 494 paras 100 and 122 GC. Individual complaints can be brought by any natural person or legal entity, regardless of nationality, place of residence, civil status, or capacity to possess rights and to be bound by obligations; *Scozzari and Giunta v Italy* 2000-VIII; 35 EHRR 243 para 138 GC. See also section 2.II of this chapter.

[55] See also, in this context, interference with communications with lawyers in respect of applications before the Court, Ch 12, section XVI on prisoners.

[56] See *Lopata v Russia* hudoc (2010); *Fedotova v Russia* hudoc (2006) (police questioning of the applicant's lawyer and translator concerning the claim for just satisfaction); *Oferta Plus SRL v Moldova* hudoc (2006) (failure to respect the confidentiality of lawyer–applicant discussions in a meeting room); *Petra v Romania* 1998-VII; 33 EHRR 105 (threats by the prison authorities); *Nurmagomedov v Russia* hudoc (2007) (refusal by the prison authorities to forward an application to the Court on the grounds that the applicant was not

of whether improper pressure has been imposed on an applicant, the circumstances of each case will be examined and the Court will have particular regard to the vulnerability of the complainant and his or her susceptibility to influence exerted by the authorities.[57] Interference with an applicant's letters to a lawyer or to the Court concerning the filing of an application or the carrying out of reprisals on an applicant would also give rise to an issue under Article 34.[58] In *Buldakov v Russia*, the Court found a violation after it was established that the prison authorities had not posted 900 pages of irreplaceable documents and had lost them.[59] Refusal to allow the applicant to make copies of medical documents essential for his claim or a requirement that a prisoner with no resources pay for copies of documents have been considered to violate this provision.[60] Refusals by the authorities to allow applicants to meet with their lawyers with a view to bringing proceedings, despite interim measures by the Court requiring the authorities to facilitate such contacts, have also led to violations.[61] In *McShane v UK*,[62] the Court found a violation under this head after the lawyer was reported by the police to the Law Society for breaching confidentiality by disclosing documents to the applicant for purposes of the application before the Court. Although no action was taken against him by the Law Society, the Court found a violation on the basis that the initiation of disciplinary proceedings could have a 'chilling effect' on the exercise of the right of individual petition by both lawyers and applicants. The context in which alleged interference takes place is also of importance. Putting pressure on villagers from south-east Turkey, who feared reprisals, to withdraw their applications and filming an interview by state authorities with them about their application was considered improper behaviour.[63] So was questioning by the very gendarmes whose behaviour was the subject of the application in Strasbourg.[64] The Court has also stressed that it is unacceptable to question an applicant where doubts have arisen concerning the authenticity of the power of attorney of the person acting for him; where a government believes that the right of petition is being abused, the correct course of action is to inform the Court and not bring the applicant in for questioning.[65] Not all questioning by the authorities, though frowned upon by the Court, leads to a finding of a breach of this provision. In *Sisojeva v Latvia*,[66] in an immigration context, the applicant was questioned by the security police about

considered to have exhausted his domestic remedies); *Boicenko v Moldova* hudoc (2006) (preventing a lawyer from having access to a client's medical file which was considered to be essential for the purposes of the application).

[57] *Sisojeva and Others v Latvia* hudoc (2007); 45 EHRR 753 para 116 GC, and the many authorities cited therein.

[58] *Maksym v Poland* hudoc (2006) (delaying the posting of a prisoner's letter to lawyer); *Drozdowski v Poland* hudoc (2005) (opening letters to a prisoner sent by the ECtHR); also *Peers v Greece* 2001-III; 33 EHRR 1192. See, in this connection, the European Agreement relating to persons participating in proceedings of the European Court of Human Rights, ETS 161.   [59] Hudoc (2011).

[60] *Vassiliy Ivashchenko v Ukraine* hudoc (2012); *Naydyan v Ukraine* hudoc (2010).

[61] *Shtukaturov v Russia* hudoc (2008); *Gagiu v Romania* hudoc (2009); and *DB v Turkey* hudoc (2010) (the applicant was an asylum seeker). Also *Aleksanyan v Russia* hudoc (2008), refusal, despite an interim measure, to allow examination of the applicant who was HIV positive, by a mixed medical commission. The Court considered that this was part of a strategy to hinder the applicant's complaint to Strasbourg.

[62] Hudoc (2002); 35 EHRR 593 para 151.

[63] *Akdivar and Others v Turkey* 1996-IV; 23 EHRR 143 paras 104–5.

[64] *Bilgin v Turkey* hudoc (2000); 36 EHRR 879 paras 132–6.

[65] *Tanrıkulu v Turkey* 1999-IV; 30 EHRR 950 paras 129–32 GC.

[66] Hudoc (2007); 45 EHRR 753 paras 121–4 GC; the Court attached weight to the 'wider context' of the interrogation when compared to the very different and more intimidatory contexts examined in the Turkish cases.

her application. However, the Court, while sceptical about the supposed reasons for the interrogation, emphasized that there was no evidence of pressure or intimidation, and that there were no legal consequences when she refused to answer the questions. Refusing to comply with the Court's interim measures is also considered as a hindrance in breach of this provision.[67] In addition, account should be taken of specific requirements on the parties to cooperate fully in the conduct of proceedings, to comply with orders of the Court, and to provide all information requested by the Court.[68] A failure to comply with these provisions is a relevant factor in determining compliance with this elementary but crucial obligation.[69]

III. INTER-STATE COMPLAINTS

Article 33 (formerly Article 24) provides that any contracting party may refer to the Court any alleged breach of the Convention and the Protocols thereto by another contracting party.[70] The right to bring a case flows directly from the ratification of the Convention and is not subject to any other conditions. In bringing an application, the state is fulfilling its role as one of the collective guarantors of Convention rights. As the former Commission indicated in *Austria v Italy*,[71] Convention obligations are essentially of an objective character being designed to protect 'the fundamental rights of individual human beings from infringement by any of the High Contracting Parties rather than to create subjective and reciprocal rights for themselves'. From this characterization of the nature of the Convention, the former Commission deduced that a contracting party could refer to the Commission any alleged breach of the Convention, regardless of whether the victims were its nationals or whether its own interests were at stake. It is not exercising a right of action for the purpose of enforcing its own rights, but rather to bring before the Commission an alleged violation of the public order of Europe.[72] The complaint under Article 33 forms part of the collective enforcement of human rights referred to in the Preamble.[73] It follows from this notion of the collective guarantee of the Convention that the principle of reciprocity is subordinated to the states' right to take enforcement action. Thus in *Austria v Italy*, the Commission accepted that Austria could file a complaint against Italy concerning matters arising before Austria became a party to the Convention. It appears to follow that an applicant state would not be prevented from complaining under Article 33 because it had entered a reservation to the provision allegedly violated by the respondent state or because the right concerned is protected by a Protocol which the applicant state has not ratified.[74] Nor is it relevant that the applicant government has not been recognized

---

[67] See section 3.V of this chapter on interim measures.   [68] Rules 44 A–C of the Rules of Court.

[69] See *Kelly (No 2) v United Kingdom No 28833/06* hudoc (2011) DA (strike-out for failure to comply with Rule 44 C).

[70] See Rogge, in Hartig, ed, *Études à la mémoire de Wolfgang Strasser*, 2007; Prebensen, in Gudmundur Alfredsson *et al*, eds, *International Human Rights Monitoring Mechanisms: Essays in Honour of Jakob Th Möller*, 2001, pp 533–59; and Greer, *European Convention*, pp 24–8; Kamminga, 12 NQHR 153 (1994).

[71] *No 788/60*, 4 YB 112, 140 (1961).

[72] *Austria v Italy No 788/60*, 4 YB 112, 140 (1961). See also *Ireland v UK* A 25 (1978) pp 90–1; 2 EHRR 25 at 104 PC and *Cyprus v Turkey No 8007/77 (Third Application)*, 13 DR 85 (1978).

[73] *Ireland v UK*, para 239.

[74] These specific issues have not yet arisen in an inter-state case. However, in *France, Norway, Denmark, Sweden and Netherlands v Turkey Nos 9940–9944/82*, 35 DR 143 at 168–9 (1983), the Commission found, with reference to the objective character of the Convention system, that France was not barred from bringing a case against Turkey which gave rise to a consideration of issues under Article 15 to which France has entered a reservation.

by the respondent government.[75] Inter-state complaints under Article 33 differ from individual complaints in the following respects.

(i) Under Article 33, states may refer 'any alleged breach' of the Convention to the Court while individual applicants can only complain under Article 34 of a violation of the rights and freedoms in the Convention. Thus allegations can be made of breaches of procedural as well as substantive provisions of the Convention. However the significance of this difference has been diminished by the Court's recognition that the individual can complain of breaches of Articles 34 §1 (*in fine*), 38 and 46 (see sections 3.V, 5 and 3.V1 of this chapter).

(ii) The state can challenge a legislative measure *in abstracto* where the law is couched in terms sufficiently clear and precise to make the breach apparent or with reference to the manner in which it is interpreted and applied *in concreto*.[76] In contrast, the individual must show that he is a 'victim' of the measure complained of.

(iii) The only formal admissibility requirements are the local remedies and six-month rule (Article 35). The requirements contained in Article 35(2) and (3) apply to individual complaints only.

(iv) An inter-state application is automatically communicated to the respondent government for observations on admissibility. The Court has no discretion in this respect. Moreover, unlike the procedure in individual cases, there are separate proceedings on questions of admissibility and the merits (Rules 48 and 58 of the Rules of Court).

In practice there have been few inter-state complaints.[77] In many of the cases that have been brought, the applicant state has had a political interest to assert in the proceedings,

[75] *Cyprus v Turkey* No 8007/77 *(Third Application)*, 13 DR 85 (1978). The constitutional propriety of the state's right to bring the complaint was discussed in the first two *Cyprus v Turkey* cases, *Nos 6780/74 and 6950/75*, 2 DR 125 (1975). The Commission, in finding that the applicant state had *locus standi*, based itself on the fact that the government was and continued to be internationally recognized by States and international organizations as the government of the Republic of Cyprus.

[76] *Ireland v UK* A 25 (1978); 2 EHRR 25 paras 239–40 PC and *Denmark, Norway, Sweden and Netherlands v Greece*, 12 YB (the *Greek* case) 134 (1969).

[77] So far, a variety of inter-state applications (referred to by application number) have been brought (relating to nine separate inter-state conflicts, some of them enduring today), many of them before the former Commission and four before the new Court: *Greece v UK Nos 176/56 and 299/57* 2 YB 186 (1958) Com Rep; CM Res (59) 12 and (59) 32 (two applications relating to the United Kingdom; it was alleged that various emergency laws and regulations were not compatible with the Convention and that there had been torture; the cases were settled after the Zurich agreement on Cypriot independence); *Austria v Italy No 788/60* 4 YB 113 (1961) Com Rep; CM Res (63) DH 3 (Articles 6 and 14; criminal trial connected with the prosecution of members of the German-speaking minority in South Tyrol); *Denmark, Norway, Sweden and Netherlands v Greece, Nos 3321–3/67, 3344/67*, 11 YB-II 691 (1968) and 12 YB (the *Greek* case) (1969) Com Rep; CM Res DH (70) 1 (wide-scale violations of human rights under the Greek dictatorship and abolition of democratic institutions); *Denmark, Norway, Sweden v Greece No 4448/70*, 13 YB 109 (1970) *(Second Greek* case: trial of thirty-four persons before a court-martial in Athens; withdrawn after Greece re-entered the Council of Europe); *Ireland v UK No 5451/72*, 41 CD 82 (1972) (allegations of violation of Article 7 withdrawn after UK undertaking); *Ireland v UK* A 25 (1978); 2 EHRR 25 PC (interrogation techniques involving alleged use of torture and detention of suspects under emergency powers in Northern Ireland; the first inter-state case to have been referred to the Court); *Cyprus v Turkey Nos 6780/74 and 6950/75 (First and Second Applications)* 2 DR 125 (1975); 4 EHRR 482 (1976); Com Rep; CM Res DH (79) 1 (consequences of the Turkish military intervention in northern Cyprus in 1974); *Cyprus v Turkey No 8007/77 (Third Application)*, 13 DR 85 (1978); 13 HRLJ 154 (1992) Com Rep; CM Res (92) 12; *No 25781/94 (Fourth Application*; referred to the Court), Com Rep, 4 June 1999; 2001-V; 35 EHRR 731 GC; *France, Norway, Denmark, Sweden and Netherlands v Turkey Nos 9940–9944/82*, 35 DR 143 (1983) and 44 DR 31 (1985) friendly settlement (the *Turkish* case; consequences of the military takeover in Turkey in 1980 with allegations of wide-scale violations of human

often connected to a long-standing political dispute between the two states concerned.[78] Often they have concerned allegations of violations of human rights on a large scale involving no national interest but evoking a concern for the 'public order of Europe'. The reality is that states will be reluctant to have recourse to legal action under the Convention to resolve their disputes. In the close-knit community of like-minded states in the Council of Europe, contracting states will be reluctant to jeopardize their good diplomatic relationships with other states and undoubtedly prefer negotiation to a legal process which may be lengthy, counterproductive, and ultimately ineffective.[79]

While the Court has jurisdiction to hear inter-state cases and, under more restricted conditions, to give advisory opinions, the vast majority of its work is based on individual applications lodged under Article 34.[80] The Convention itself does not provide for any different procedures to be followed for inter-state cases though Rule 58 of the Rules of Court provides for automatic notification to the respondent government and separation of the admissibility and merits phases of the procedure. There is, for example, no express requirement that such a case be heard by the Grand Chamber, though such cases are potential candidates for Grand Chamber examination following relinquishment if no friendly settlement takes place before the Chamber.[81]

IV. THE APPLICATION

The official languages of the Court are English and French but an application may be sent in the language of any of the contracting parties.[82] However, if the case is communicated for observations, all communications (including oral and written submissions) shall be in one of the official languages unless a special exemption is granted by the President.

---

rights and abolition of democratic institutions); *Denmark v Turkey* 2000-IV (alleged ill-treatment of a Danish national; case ended in a friendly settlement); *Georgia v Russia No 13255/07*, press release of 27 March 2007 (allegations of harassment of the Georgian immigrant population in the Russian Federation—alleged violations, *inter alia*, of Articles 3, 5, 8, 13, 14, and 18). Declared admissible on 30 June 2009; *Georgia v Russia (No 2)* (arising out of the armed conflict between the two states in 2008 with allegations of indiscriminate and disproportionate use of force). Declared admissible 12 December 2011. See also press release of 12 August 2008 concerning the application of interim measures; *Georgia v Russia (No 3)* (request by Georgia that the Court ask the Russian Federation to comply with their obligations under the Convention and to release four named Georgian boys being detained in South Ossetia). Struck out of the list on 16 March 2010. See also *Ukraine v Russia* - Press Release 13 March 2014.

[78] Rogge, in Hartig, ed, *Études à la mémoire de Wolfgang Strasser*, 2007, places nine of the cases in this category: *Greece v UK, Austria v Italy, Ireland v UK, Cyprus v Turkey*; to which can be added the *Georgia v Russia* cases.

[79] Consider, eg, the *Cyprus v Turkey* dispute. The Commission's report in the first two applications was forwarded to the Committee of Ministers in 1976. The Committee took formal note of the report as well as a memorial of the Turkish government, urged the parties to resume inter-communal talks, and 'found that events which occurred in Cyprus constitute violations of the Convention' without attaching direct responsibility. It took until 31 August 1979 for the case documentation (including the Commission's report) to be declassified (Resolution DH (79) 1 of 20 January 1979). In the third case the Commission's report of 4 October 1983 remained pending before the Committee of Ministers until 2 April 1992, when it was decided to publish it. The Committee of Ministers resolved that the decision to publish completed its consideration of the case under Article 32 (Resolution DH (92) 12).

[80] The conditions set out in Article 34 are considered in Ch 2. See also Protocol 16 in section 7.II of this chapter which provides for the possibility of advisory opinions requested by national superior courts.

[81] This is a requirement for any advisory opinion (see Article 31(b)). The procedure governing advisory opinions is considered separately in section 2.XV of this chapter. *Denmark v Turkey* was the subject of a settlement adopted by a Chamber (n 77).

[82] See, generally, the Practice Direction on the Institution of Proceedings, annexed to the Rules of Court (1 November 2003). Applicants should be diligent in conducting correspondence with the Registry.

When a case is communicated, accompanying Annexes to the observations need not be translated into the official languages and can be sent in the language in which they were lodged.[83]

Save in exceptional circumstances (such as an imminent expulsion or deportation), the Registry will take no immediate action on a simple letter setting out the complaints of the applicant. The application will be registered provisionally and prospective applicants will be sent an application form which they will be asked to complete. If no response is received within six months, the file will be destroyed.[84]

V. HOW TO PRESENT AN APPLICATION—A NEW POLICY BASED ON RULE 47 AS FROM 1 JANUARY 2014

Rule 47 of the current Rules of Court sets out what the application form should contain, as of course does the form itself.[85] Failure to comply with the requirements of Rule 47 often results in the application not being examined by the Court, and applicants will be warned if they do not.[86] A legal representative must provide a form of authority signed by the applicant authorizing him to act in proceedings before the Court. In response to the growing number of individual cases, the Court has decided to tighten its procedure under Rule 47. The new policy entered into force on 1 January 2014.[87] It requires applicants to follow to the letter the instructions provided for filing an application. Its purpose is to achieve greater efficiency in the way applications are dealt with at the initial stage of the process before the Court and to facilitate the filtering of cases. There are two main changes. Both represent an important break from past practices.

The first is that applicants must provide the Court with sufficient information in the application form itself to allow it to conduct an initial analysis of the application. Each application form submitted to the Court should contain all the essential information about the complaints made, and be accompanied by the necessary supporting documents (in particular copies of the relevant domestic decisions).[88] As the new Rule 47 indicates, the application form will be self-contained in the sense that it should be possible for the Court to see from the form alone what the applicant is complaining about and under what heads of the Convention.[89] This will allow the Registry to determine the nature and scope of the case at the outset. In this way, high priority cases can be identified at the initial stage. Similarly, applications with obvious problems of admissibility will be submitted rapidly to a single judge for decision. Applicants must provide the Court with a concise and legible statement of facts, and be clear in the way they formulate and argue their complaints. Recognizing that there are cases which are factually and legally complex, additional pages will be accepted, up to a maximum of twenty. If more pages are used, the Registry may instruct the applicant to re-submit the application in a shorter form. Crucially, unlike the

---

[83] Rule 34 regulates the use of languages in the procedure before the Court.

[84] See Ch 2, section 4 on the six-month rule.

[85] Details such as personal identification information; a brief statement of facts and complaints; an explanation as to compliance with the six-month rule and the rule of exhaustion of domestic remedies; the object of the application; and all supporting documents, especially national court decisions proving that domestic remedies have been tried.   [86] Rule 47(4) of the Rules of Court.

[87] See the Court's press release of 9 January 2014 setting out the details of the changes. See also the Rules of Court of 1 July 2013, which set out the amended version of Rule 47 that came into force on 1 January 2014.

[88] A new application form has been prepared. Some of the points in the current form will simply be deleted, such as asking the applicant to specify their gender or their occupation.

[89] See new Rule 47 2(a): 'All of the information referred to…should be sufficient to enable the Court to determine the nature and scope of the application without recourse to any other document'.

previous practice under Rule 47, if an applicant fails to comply with the formal require-ments, the application will be rejected *de plano* as being non-compliant. The Court retains, however, a general discretion to accept an application in certain circumstances.[90]

The second reform concerns the six-month time limit.[91] Under previous practice, the time limit could be interrupted by an incomplete application or a simple letter. Under the amended rule, only an application satisfying the formal requirements (submission of completed application form plus supporting documentation) will interrupt the running of the time limit, the relevant date being that of the postmark on the envelope. Registry staff have been instructed to examine all new applications promptly, so as to allow appli-cants a second chance to introduce their application, where possible.[92] If the applicant re-submits their application outside of the six-month period, it will be referred to the single judge for rejection as inadmissible. Where justified, the Court may consider that the time limit was interrupted on a different date, so as to permit the further examination of the application. This could apply, for example, in case of administrative error by the Registry, or if the submission of the form to the Court was unduly delayed through no fault of the applicant.

VI. PRIORITY POLICY FOR DEALING WITH CASES

The Court introduced a priority policy to deal with cases in 2009.[93] Faced with a constant increase in cases, it decided to abandon the general rule that cases would be dealt with in the order in which they were lodged in the Court. The aim is to ensure that the most serious cases and the cases which disclose the existence of widespread problems capable of generating large numbers of additional cases are dealt with more rapidly. Low priority is given to cases (the so-called clone or repetitive cases) which follow a pilot judgment establishing a structural problem. The lowest categories of priority are cases which are identified as clearly failing to satisfy the admissibility conditions.[94] The Court will deal with applications in the following order:

(1) urgent applications (in particular where there is a risk to the life or health of the applicant, other circumstances linked to the personal or family situation of the applicant, particularly where the well-being of a child is at issue; application of Rule 39 of the Rules of Court);

(2) applications raising questions capable of having an impact on the effectiveness of the Convention system (in particular a structural or endemic situation that the

---

[90] It will not apply where there is an adequate explanation for the failure to present the application in the required form. For example, an applicant who is in detention may not be able to obtain the necessary sup-porting documentation. A specific exception is made for applicants seeking interim measures. Lastly, the Court retains an overriding discretion to accept an application even if not presented in the correct form. These three exceptions, framed in light of real and recurring situations in the Court practice, are designed to ensure that the rule does not operate harshly or unjustly. This will concern a minority of new applications. For the great majority, the Registry has been instructed to systematically apply the new rule.

[91] Protocol 15 will reduce the six-month period to four months; see section 7.I of this chapter.

[92] It would be advisable for applicants to submit their application forms and supporting documents well within the six-month period to allow for the possibility of submitting later amendments to comply with Rule 47.

[93] See the Court's website www.echr.coe.int for further details. For cases dealt with on an urgent basis, see, eg, *Pretty v United Kingdom* hudoc (2002); *Hirsi Jamaa and others v Italy* (GC) hudoc (2012); *MSS v Belgium and Greece* (GC) hudoc (2011); *Mousiel v France* hudoc (2002).

[94] Though with a filtering policy that is based on the principle of 'one-in-one-out', it is these obviously hopeless cases that will be dealt with first by the single judge before cases belonging to a higher category.

Court has not yet examined, pilot-judgment procedure) or applications raising an important question of general interest (in particular a serious question capable of having major implications for domestic legal systems or for the European system), inter-State cases;

(3) applications which, on their face, raise as main complaints issues under Articles 2, 3, 4 or 5(1) of the Convention ('core rights'), irrespective of whether they are repetitive, and which have given rise to direct threats to the physical integrity and dignity of human beings;

(4) potentially well-founded applications based on other Articles;

(5) Applications raising issues already dealt with in a pilot/leading judgment ('repetitive cases');

(6) applications identified as giving rise to a problem of admissibility;

(7) applications which are manifestly inadmissible.

In principle, cases in a higher category will be eligible for examination before those beneath it, although it remains open to the President to decide to give priority to a particular case.[95]

VII. THE SINGLE JUDGE PROCEDURE

Cases which are obviously inadmissible or clearly hopeless, even though they may sometimes concern important questions and are supported by detailed written submissions, will be rejected by a single judge in a brief decision.[96]

The single judge is assisted by a non-judicial rapporteur appointed by the President from amongst the senior lawyers in the registry. The non-judicial rapporteur will in practice prepare a number of cases to be rejected by the single judge in this way. Most of the judges in the Court can act as single judges for this purpose, thereby enabling a large number of such decisions to be taken rapidly. The Court, in a short space of time, has come to rely on this procedure for reducing the continuously increasing number of misconceived cases which have clogged the Court's docket.[97] The results have been impressive and the procedure has become an important part of the Court's armoury. The single judge cannot take decisions concerning his own country. He or she can only reject a case as inadmissible. They have no power to communicate a case to the government or to declare cases admissible. They may, however, refer the case to a three-judge Committee or to a Chamber. The decisions of the single judge are final and no further correspondence will be entered into. However, in very exceptional cases where the Court itself has made

---

[95] The policy is being kept under review within the Court. One consequence is that cases raising important issues concerning Article 10 of the Convention are not generally accorded priority. It still remains open to lawyers to submit that there are particular reasons why their case should be afforded priority treatment.

[96] The single judge procedure was introduced by Protocol 14, which came into force on 1 June 2010. For the text of the Protocol and Explanatory Report, see 'Guaranteeing the effectiveness of the European Convention on Human Rights—Collected Texts', Council of Europe, 2004. For commentary, see Eaton and Schokkenbroek, 26 HRLJ 1 (2005) and Greer, PL 83 (2005).

[97] See Rule 27A. The single-judge formation decided 81,764 cases in 2012, an increase of 74% compared with 2011 (46,930). The increase is due to the introduction of new working methods and to the fact that in 2012 more judges were appointed single judges. For the first time since 1998, the stock of allocated applications pending before the Court decreased over the year, by 16% from 151,600 to 128,100. By January 2014 there were 99,000 pending cases; Analysis of Statistics (January 2013 and January 2014) report available on the Court's website.

a factual or legal mistake in the course of its examination—such as the date of the final decision for purposes of the six-month rule—it has an inherent power to re-open the case and restore it to the list.[98] This power would not, however, be used where the source of the error lies with the lawyer in the presentation of the case.[99]

VIII. COMMITTEE PROCEDURE

In accordance with Article 28 of the Convention, Committees of three judges can either declare cases inadmissible, strike cases out of the list, or consider the merits of repetitive cases with powers to declare admissible or adopt judgments.[100] The first category of cases are normally those that will be sent to the Committee by a single judge who considers that the case merits consideration by three of his colleagues or by a judge rapporteur who considers that the case does not merit examination by a Chamber. The decision must be unanimous and the Committee can only declare such applications inadmissible.[101] Its decision is final. If the Committee fails to reach agreement, the case will be sent to a Chamber for decision. Although national judges do not necessarily sit in the Committee dealing with cases concerning their countries, they will be provided with the copies of draft decisions concerning them and can make their views known.

But Protocol 14 also conferred on the Committee the power to declare cases admissible and adopt final judgments in cases where the underlying issue concerns an issue of well-established case law.[102] This was the Protocol's answer to the recurring problem of repetitive or clone cases concerning the same subject-matter that make up a large part of the Court's docket. In order to placate certain contracting parties who were uneasy about conferring such powers on only three judges, and who may have contested the use of the procedure in the particular case, Article 28 provides that the national judge may be invited to take the place of one of the three judges 'having regard to all relevant factors', including whether the contracting party has contested the application of the procedure. The Explanatory Report to Protocol 14 indicates that the presence of the national judge may be useful to the Committee where the state has contested the procedure because of the judge's familiarity with national law and practice, which will enable the Committee to better assess the objection. When an objection has been made by a contracting party, the decision to continue with the procedure will be taken by the Committee. The state may contest the applicability of the WECL procedure but it does not have a veto over the procedure. Where the Committee fails to reach a unanimous decision on the case it will be sent to a Chamber for decision. It also remains open to the Committee to reject the case as inadmissible, for example, if it considered that domestic remedies have not been exhausted. Although simple and accelerated, the new procedure will 'preserve the adversarial character of proceedings and the principle of judicial and collegial decision-making

---

[98] *Ölmez and Ölmez v Turkey No 39464/98* hudoc (2005) (re-opening decision) and the authorities cited therein; also *Edwards v UK* A 247-B; 35 EHRR 487 para 26. The re-opening decision will be taken by the formation that took the original decision.   [99] *Ölmez and Ölmez v Turkey.*

[100] See Article 28 of the Convention and Rule 27.   [101] Article 28(1).

[102] While the concept of 'well-established case law' (WECL cases) appears to refer to repetitive or clone cases, Article 28 does not limit it to such cases. There are other categories of cases that can be so described, relating, eg, to issues under many articles of the Convention where the questions of interpretation are the subject of extensive jurisprudence (eg Article 10 cases or cases concerning prison conditions). The Court is currently considering whether it can or whether it is appropriate to apply the accelerated WECL procedure to such cases, which are in many ways different from the traditional repetitive case concerning length of procedure or non-enforcement of a court judgment.

on the merits'.[103] Each of the five Sections constitutes a number of Committees for a period of twelve months and each Section generally has three.

The Committees have adopted an accelerated procedure for dealing with obviously well-founded repetitive cases. The cases are communicated to the government by the President of the Section (often in groups) on the basis of a very succinct statement of facts with a view to reaching a friendly settlement. The Court does not ask for observations in such cases, but governments retain the right to file observations in appropriate cases. Where observations are received, they are submitted to the applicant for information only. If no friendly settlement is reached or there is no unilateral declaration admitting liability, the Court will ask the applicant to submit just satisfaction claims. In such cases, applicants are not required to be represented by a lawyer and are not eligible for legal aid if they are. The judgment adopted by the Committee where there is no settlement will be brief.

Such judgments are final and thus may not be referred to the Grand Chamber (Article 28(2)). The procedure has proved itself to be particularly efficient. For example, 2,153 cases concerning non-execution of court judgments have been communicated to Ukraine, leading to 1,468 judgments or decisions.

IX. CHAMBER PROCEDURE: COMMUNICATION AND THE JOINT PROCEDURE

Cases which are not clearly inadmissible or which raise a *prima facie* issue will initially be assigned to a Chamber of seven judges, which can take a number of steps from declaring the application inadmissible to declaring it admissible and subsequently adopting a judgment on its merits. If an application is assigned to a Chamber, a judge rapporteur will be nominated by the President of the Section. He or she has the task of presenting the application to the Chamber and formally proposing the various procedural steps that the Chamber may take. The rapporteur may propose that the President communicate the case to the Government for observations on the admissibility and merits. Most cases are communicated in this way in current practice although it remains open to the Chamber to take the decision to communicate the case if it sees fit. If the case has not been communicated, then the Chamber, on the proposal of the judge rapporteur, may immediately adopt an inadmissibility decision, which is published on the website,[104] though this, too, is final and not subject to appeal. Where the application is communicated to the respondent government, this will involve sending a copy of the application to the government with all relevant documents, a statement of facts prepared by the Registry, and a question or series of questions that their observations should address.[105] Once the observations are received, the applicant will be given an opportunity to submit observations in reply with any claims for just satisfaction under Article 41 of the Convention. The government will be given a final opportunity to make further submissions in reply, after which the case is considered by the Chamber.[106] If any further observations are received at this stage, they

---

[103] Article 28 as amended and Explanatory Report, paras 68–72.

[104] If the decision is deemed sufficiently important it may be published in the official reports. This follows a decision by the Bureau of the Court. All judgments and decisions, apart from single judge decisions, are available on the Court's Hudoc site.

[105] Both the statement of facts and the questions are now available online on the Court's website (Hudoc, statement of facts collection) http://www.echr.coe.int.

[106] The Chamber can, however, ask for further observations, clarifications, and factual information from either party as it sees fit.

will be considered as unsolicited and, unless the President of the Chamber decides otherwise, they will be returned to the party and not admitted to the file.

It became the rule in recent years, due to the large number of pending cases, and for reasons of economy of process, for the Court, by expressly invoking former Article 29(3) of the Convention, to examine jointly the admissibility and merits of the application.[107] This practice is reflected in Article 29(1), which makes joint examination the norm, though leaves open the possibility that a separate decision on admissibility be taken in a particular case. It is open to the parties to request the Court to take a separate decision, but this would require special reasons for doing so. Such decisions are increasingly rare. A separate admissibility decision is final and cannot be referred to the Grand Chamber, whereas a judgment which considers admissibility and merits together can be so referred.[108]

X. THE GRAND CHAMBER

While the vast majority of the Court's work takes place in Committees and Chambers, the Grand Chamber is the constitutional formation of the Court. It consists of seventeen judges and has the task of hearing and giving judgment on the most important cases.[109] It also has the central function of ensuring overall coherence and consistency of the Court's case law. Cases come before the Grand Chamber by two means: relinquishment by a Chamber before it renders its judgment (Article 30) and, after a Chamber gives judgment, if one of the parties requests referral (Article 43). In the former case, the simple decision to relinquish is enough to seize the Grand Chamber of the case, provided one of the parties does not object.[110] In the latter case, the Convention provides for a panel of five judges of the Grand Chamber, which decides whether to accept or reject the party's request.[111]

Strangely, the criteria as to when a Chamber should relinquish (Article 30) and when the panel should accept a referral request (Article 43) are slightly different.[112] The drafting history of Protocol 11 does not shed any light on the difference of wording.

[107] See Article 29(1) which assumes that admissibility and the merits will be considered together (amendment introduced by Protocol 14). See also Rule 54A on the joint examination of admissibility and merits. Inter-state cases cannot be the subject of the joint procedure since admissibility must be examined separately; Rules 48 and 54A. [108] See n 116 and section 2.X of this chapter.

[109] See Rule 24 for the regime governing the composition of the Grand Chamber. The President, Vice-Presidents, and Presidents of Sections sit as *ex officio* members of the Grand Chamber. In a referral case under Article 43, the remaining members are drawn by lot by the President. The members of the Chamber which gave the original judgment are not eligible, apart from the President of the Section and the national judge. It often happens in a referral case that the President of the Section (unless he is also the national judge) will not exercise his right to sit in the Grand Chamber for reasons of conscience; having already given judgment in the case, it may be considered inappropriate to sit a second time. In a relinquishment case (Article 30), the full members of the relinquishing Chamber are automatically members of the Grand Chamber. The modalities for drawing lots to complete the formations have been worked out 'with due regard to the need for a geographically balanced composition reflecting the different legal systems among the Contracting Parties' (Rule 24(3)).

[110] The parties have a month following notification of the intention to relinquish to file a 'duly reasoned objection'; Rule 72(2). Cf, Article 30 of the Convention. Protocol 15 will remove this veto; see section 7.I of this chapter.

[111] See Court document '*The general practice followed by the Panel of the Grand Chamber when deciding on requests for referral in accordance with Article 43 of the Convention*' (October 2011); available at http://echr.coe.int/Documents/Note_GC_ENG.pdf.

[112] The difference in wording suggests that relinquishment should be limited to cases raising difficult issues of interpretation only. However, this has not been the practice of the Court to date. The Explanatory Report states that the wording was taken from the Rules of Court of the former Court (para 79) but gives no further explanation for the different wording. Relinquishment cases are described as 'cases with specified serious implications' (para 46)—a wording which is not limitative.

In relation to Article 30, the normal procedure is for the Chamber in question to notify the parties of its intention to relinquish and to give them one month to object. If no objection is received (and silence is taken as tacit consent to relinquishment) then the Chamber will formally relinquish. Rule 72(1) indicates that reasons need not be given for the decision to relinquish. However, the objection to relinquishment by one of the parties must be 'duly reasoned'. In practice, it is sufficient for one of the parties to indicate that it wishes to have the case examined by a Chamber with the possibility of re-examination by the Grand Chamber. It has occurred that a state objects to relinquishment under Article 43(2) and then subsequently seeks to refer the case to the Grand Chamber once the Chamber judgment has been handed down. In the practice of the panel, this is not seen as a reason for refusing a referral if there are important issues of law raised in the case.[113] No principle of estoppel is applied. It is not always clear why a party would object to relinquishment, since in the event of the objecting party obtaining a favourable result before the Chamber, it remains open to the other party to request referral under Article 43(2), and the same reasons why the Chamber contemplated relinquishment may also lead the panel to accept the referral request. An interest in delaying the proceedings may be one reason. Another may be the conviction, based on the drafting history of Protocol 11 and the famous historic compromise between states that were in favour of a two-tier system and those that were not, that the state has a right to an examination of the case by two instances.[114]

The composition of the panel that considers requests for referral under Article 43(2) is not provided for in the Convention (though the matter is governed by Rule 24(5) of the Rules of Court).[115] Following a recent change in the Court's practice, requesting parties are now told the names of the judges who considered their request. However, they are not given reasons for the decision to accept or reject their request.[116] This has been consistently refused by the Court on the grounds that it was not a Convention requirement and would give rise to an unacceptable increase in its work.[117]

All parts of the judgment can be grounds for referral, including the level or means of calculating just satisfaction under Article 41.[118] It therefore sometimes occurs that both parties request referral.[119] The request for referral must be received by the Registry within three months of the date of the judgment, failing which the panel will not examine the request, even though it may have been posted within the three-month period.[120] This

---

[113] See eg, *Mamatkulov and Askarov v Turkey* 2005-I; 41 EHRR 494 para 6 GC, where the government requested referral to the Grand Chamber, and *Mamatkulov and Abdurasulovic v Turkey* hudoc (2003) (the Chamber judgment in the same case where they objected to relinquishment). The same happened in *Öcalan v Turkey* 2005-IV; 41 EHRR 985 GC and *Öcalan v Turkey* hudoc (2003); 37 EHRR 238 para 6.

[114] See Ch 26 of the first edition of this book for the drafting history of Protocol 11.

[115] Which Rule provides that it shall be composed of the President of the Court, two Presidents of Sections designated by rotation, two other judges designated by rotation from the remaining sections, and two further substitute judges, save that it will not include any judge who took part in the consideration of the admissibility and merits of the case and any judge who is elected in respect of or who is a national of the contracting party concerned.

[116] In response to demands by states that reasons be given by the Panel, the Court has issued a report which sets out how the Panel procedure operates in practice and the criteria that are employed in its decision-making; see *The General Practice Followed by the Panel of the Grand Chamber when deciding on requests for referral in accordance with Article 43 of the Convention*, available on the Court's website.

[117] *The General Practice Followed by the Panel of the Grand Chamber*, p 4.

[118] See *Arvanitaki-Roboti and Others v Greece* hudoc (2006) and hudoc (2008) GC.

[119] *Öcalan v Turkey* 2005-IV; 41 EHRR 985 para 9 GC.

[120] The three months start to run from the day which follows the delivery date of the Chamber judgment: thus for a judgment delivered on 10 January the time limit expires at midnight on 10 April; see *The General Practice Followed by the Panel of the Grand Chamber*, available on the Court's website, p 12. The issue gave rise to a very public dispute with the UK Ministry of the Interior in connection with the last-minute

is different from the application of the six-month rule in respect of new applications, where the date will normally be taken as the postmark or the date the letter was written, rather than the date of registration at the Court's Registry.[121] The difference with referral requests is that judgments automatically become final three months after their delivery, unless the parties request referral, so there is a greater interest in legal certainty. The Court and the outside world have a stronger interest in knowing when its judgments acquire the status of *res judicata*. In most cases, faxing a copy of the request within the three-month period will prevent any problems arising. The panel accepts very few requests for referral and the fact that the Chamber may have been divided is not necessarily an indication that the case will be accepted. While Article 43 does not explicitly mention departure from previous case law as a ground on which the panel of five judges may accept a case, a 'serious issue affecting the interpretation' of the Convention could arise if a Chamber gave a judgment which significantly develops the case law. This would be an indication that an issue of consistency was involved which might require an authoritative interpretation by the Grand Chamber.[122] New issues on which there is no established case law or high-profile cases are also likely candidates for acceptance.[123] In cases where there is more than one applicant, a request for referral by one applicant can be taken as a request on behalf of all applicants. In *Cumpana and Mazare v Romania*,[124] two applicants brought a single application. Following an adverse finding by the Chamber, the first applicant lodged and signed a referral request on behalf of both applicants. A Panel of the Grand Chamber accepted that request. The respondent government, in its observations in the Grand Chamber, submitted that the scope of the Grand Chamber's jurisdiction was limited to the first applicant's complaints and requested the Grand Chamber not to examine the second applicant's complaints. The Grand Chamber rejected that submission, holding that the 'case' referred to the Grand Chamber necessarily embraces all aspects of the application previously examined by the Chamber in its judgment, there being no basis for a merely partial referral.[125]

It is not open to the parties to contest the decision of the panel on the question of referral to the Grand Chamber.[126] When a case is referred by the panel, the scope of the case before the Grand Chamber is not limited to the grounds set out in the referral request: instead, it embraces all aspects of the application declared admissible and examined by the Chamber. The Grand Chamber may also reconsider admissibility objections raised by the government where these have already been addressed by the Chamber, and thus it is entitled to come to a different conclusion from that of the Chamber.[127] However, subject to the above, a government will be estopped from raising admissibility objections in proceedings before the Grand Chamber if it has not already raised them before the

reference by the applicant's lawyers of the *Othman (Abu Qatada) v United Kingdom* case hudoc (2012); see the Court's press release concerning the Panel's refusal of the request on its merits (9 May 2012).

[121] See Ch 2, section 4.IV.

[122] See eg *Stec and Others v UK* 2006-VI GC (whether a non-contributory social security benefits came within Article 1 of Protocol 1) and *Kopecký v Slovakia* 2004-IX; 41 EHRR 944 GC (concerning the meaning of legitimate expectation in the area of property rights).

[123] See *The General Practice Followed by the Panel of the Grand Chamber*, available on the Court's website, pp 6–10; eg *Pretty v UK* 2002-III; 35 EHRR 1 (concerning refusal of euthanasia to a seriously ill person) and *Evans v UK* hudoc (2007); 46 EHRR 728 (concerning the implantation of embryos and the issue of consent).

[124] 2004-XI; 41 EHRR 200 paras 62–9 GC.

[125] *Cumpana and Mazare v Romania*, para 66 and references therein.

[126] *Pisano v Italy* hudoc (2002) paras 24–9 GC.

[127] *Odièvre v France* 2003-III; 38 EHRR 871 para 22 GC; *Azinas v Cyprus* 2004-III; 40 EHRR 166 paras 32, 37 GC.

Chamber,[128] but will not be estopped if the Chamber had considered the same admissibility question on its own motion.[129] It would not be open to a government to put arguments which are inconsistent with those raised before the national courts. Thus a government could not argue before the national courts that there existed a national emergency but contend the opposite before the Strasbourg court,[130] or to argue that persons had not been killed by the security forces if that point had not been contested before the national courts.[131]

In *Pisano v Italy*, the Grand Chamber stated that once a case is referred, it may 'employ the full range of judicial powers conferred on the Court'.[132] Hence it may approve friendly settlements, strike out cases, and form its own assessment of the facts of the case even where the original Chamber has already addressed such issues. Equally, after it accepts a referral request, it remains open to the Grand Chamber to limit the scope of its examination of a case at any stage in the proceedings and to adopt a judgment on a preliminary issue of admissibility.[133] Finally, after it accepts a referral request, the Grand Chamber may also strike out part of a case and at the same time give judgment on the merits of other complaints.[134]

XI. INTERNAL MECHANISMS FOR ENSURING CONSISTENCY OF CASE LAW

The Court is aware that with five Sections operating on a weekly basis and each Section adopting hundreds of judgments every year there is a risk of divergent approaches or inconsistent application of the case law to the facts of new cases.[135] The issue was the subject of much comment and exhortation during the Interlaken, Izmir, and Brighton conferences.[136] Apart from the role of the Grand Chamber Panel in deciding on requests for referral, the Court has responded to this risk by creating a variety of structures to address the problem at an earlier stage in the procedure. The first stage is the scrutiny of the draft judgments and decisions as soon as the file is distributed to judges. This is done by a group of registry lawyers under the authority of the Jurisconsult collectively known as the CLCP—Case Law Conflict Prevention unit. Such scrutiny is of a continuous nature and must be completed within a tight deadline, since there is usually only one week between distribution of the files and the meetings of the Sections. Where a potential conflict is noted, the CLCP will draw it to the attention of the relevant President and Section Registrar. The Court's registrars also discuss issues of consistency at the weekly

---

[128] See, *mutatis mutandis, Nikolova v Bulgaria* 1999-II; 31 EHRR 64 paras 41–4 GC; *Hasan and Chaush v Bulgaria* 2000-XI; 34 EHRR 1339 para 56 GC (in both cases, the government having failed to raise the question in proceedings before the old Commission, meaning it was estopped from raising it before the Grand Chamber of the new Court).

[129] *Mutatis mutandis, Freedom and Democracy (ÖZDEP) v Turkey* 1999-VII; 31 EHRR 674 para 25 GC (the old Commission have considered the admissibility question on its own motion being sufficient to allow the government to raise it before the Grand Chamber).

[130] *A and others v United Kingdom* GC hudoc (2011) paras 154–8; but the Court accepted that it was open to the government to challenge before the Grand Chamber the finding by the House of Lords that the derogation was invalid.

[131] *Al-Skeini and Others v United Kingdom* hudoc (2011) paras 98–100 GC.

[132] Hudoc (2002) GC.   [133] *Tahsin Acar v Turkey* ECHR 2003-VI paras 63–4 GC.

[134] *Sisojeva and Others v Latvia* hudoc (2007); 45 EHRR 753 GC.

[135] See the speech by the President of the Court, J-P Costa, to Leiden University on 30 May 2008 obtainable on the Court's website http://www.echr.coe.int.

[136] See, eg, the Izmir Declaration F (a) and the Brighton Declaration para 23.

meetings, flagging areas of dispute between the Sections. If the matter is not resolved in this manner, the issue may be referred to the Court's Bureau, which is composed of the President, the five Section Presidents, the Registrar, and Deputy Registrar. This may be done by the Section Presidents themselves or by the Court's Jurisconsult. As a measure to promote consistency, during the Brighton reform process the Court argued that governments should no longer have a veto over relinquishment since it prevented the Grand Chamber from examining issues of consistency. This has resulted in a provision in Draft Protocol 15 removing the right of states to object to relinquishment in favour of the Grand Chamber.[137] As a companion to this provision, the Court has amended the rules of court to make relinquishment obligatory where the chamber would reach a result inconsistent with the case law of the Court.

XII. FRIENDLY SETTLEMENT AND UNILATERAL DECLARATIONS

Article 39 of the Convention provides that at any stage of the proceedings the Court may place itself at the disposal of the parties concerned with a view to securing a friendly settlement.[138] Accordingly the parties may, at any stage of the procedure, make proposals for the friendly settlement of the case. Indeed, they are invited to make any proposals when they submit their observations. A friendly settlement proposal will generally involve the offer of a sum of money by the respondent government to the applicant which the applicant may choose to accept. Occasionally, other terms will also appear, such as in *Köksal v Netherlands*[139] (which concerned a death in police custody), where, in addition to the *ex gratia* payment of a sum of money, the Dutch government expressed its 'deepest regret' at the death. Another common term of a friendly settlement in immigration cases is for the applicant to be given a residence permit or for the state to give some equivalent undertaking not to deport the applicant.[140] States may also promise to make legislative or policy changes. For example, in *Sutherland v UK*,[141] a challenge to the difference between the heterosexual and homosexual age of consent, the application was struck out after the government abolished the difference in new legislation. In *Ali Erol v Turkey*,[142] a newspaper editor had been convicted of incitement to hatred and hostility on the basis of race or religion. The Court accepted a friendly settlement by which Turkey undertook urgently to bring its laws into conformity with Article 10 of the Convention and abide by the terms of Committee of Ministers resolution on the same matter.[143]

The Court 'placing itself at the disposal of the parties' in practice means that the Registry acts as a conduit for such proposals and can also suggest appropriate terms of settlement based on comparable previous settlements. It does this on a regular basis in

---

[137] See section 7.I of this chapter.

[138] See, for an overview of the Court's practice, Keller, Forowicz, and Engi, *Friendly Settlements before the European Court of Human Rights: Theory and Practice*, 2010. On unilateral declarations, see Rozakis, in Kohen, ed, *Promoting Justice, Human Rights and Conflict Resolution through International Law: Liber Amicorum Lucius Caflisch*, 2007. Also Myjer, in Caflisch *et al*, eds, *Liber Amicorum Luzius Wildhaber*, 2007, pp 309–27; Bychawska-Siniarska, 6 EHRLR 673–8.   [139] Hudoc (2001) para 14.

[140] *Ahmed v Sweden* hudoc (2007).   [141] Hudoc (2001) GC.   [142] Hudoc (2002).

[143] The inter-state case of *Denmark v Turkey* was one of the most constructive settlements reached before the Court in terms of the scope of the measures agreed to by the parties; 2000-IV para 2. Also the friendly settlement of *France, Norway, Denmark, Sweden and Netherlands v Turkey* Nos 9940–44/82, 44 DR 31 (1985) outlining the terms of a settlement whereby Turkey agreed to submit a series of reports on its implementation of Article 3 which would form the basis for a series of dialogues between Turkey and the Commission. See also *Greece v United Kingdom*; see n 77.

repetitive cases (eg length of proceedings/non-enforcement of domestic judgments) in order to secure a 'money settlement'. In the practice of the former Commission, there were frequent friendly settlement meetings organized by its Secretary. While there has been a substantial increase in the number of friendly settlements in the new Court,[144] repetitive cases account for the majority of these, and friendly settlement negotiations between the parties are not so frequent any longer, a casualty of the increased workload and time pressures upon the Registry. Where a settlement is reached, the parties will inform the Court of the terms of the settlement through the Registry. The Court will decide whether the matter has been resolved such that the case can be struck off its list. The criterion for doing so is set out in Article 39(1) and (3) of the Convention, namely if the Court is satisfied that the matter has been resolved and that the settlement has been reached on the basis of respect for human rights as defined in the Convention and its Protocols. When it is so satisfied, the Court will strike the case out of its list by means of a decision. Article 39(3) states that this shall be confined to a brief statement of the facts and of the solution reached. When the Court is not satisfied that the matter has been resolved, it can refuse to accept the terms of the settlement and, if special circumstances regarding respect for human rights as defined in the Convention and its Protocols require the examination of the application to be continued, it will do so. Such instances are extremely rare, and will either be when the Court is concerned about the manner in which a settlement has been reached, if the terms of the settlement are not commensurate to the seriousness of the alleged violation, or if the Court is of the view that the case raises important issues that call for an examination on the merits. For example, in *Paladi v Moldova*,[145] the applicant and government agreed to settle the case for a small sum but the applicant later asked the Court to continue its examination of the case. The Court agreed on the ground that the amount of compensation bore no reasonable relationship to the alleged violations of the Convention and had been accepted by the applicant while in a poor state of health and without the benefit of legal advice. In contrast, applicants who have simply changed their minds about accepting a settlement in the hope of further compensation will be given short shrift by the Court.[146] In *Ukranian Media Group v Ukraine*,[147] the Court refused to accept the settlement on the grounds of the serious nature of the complaints made under Article 10 and proceeded to find a violation of that article. Article 39(4) provides that the Committee of Ministers shall supervise the execution of the terms of the settlement. The Court may also restore to the list cases where the Government has not complied with the settlement.[148]

While the terms of the settlement are usually set out in the decision striking the case out of the list, under Article 39(2), the negotiations leading up to such a settlement are strictly confidential, whether or not the settlement process is successful. Under Rule 33(1), friendly settlement documents are also not accessible to the public, and by Rule 62(2) no offer or concession made during negotiations may be referred to in the contentious proceedings. Pleadings in the contentious proceedings which do so will be sent back to the relevant party, and when breach of confidentiality is established by revealing details to third parties or the press, the Court will reject the case for abuse. In *Hadrabova and Others v Czech Republic*,[149] the Court found that disclosing the terms of these negotiations

---

[144] Following the entry into force of Protocol 14, friendly settlements are now adopted by way of a decision striking the case off the list. In 2011, there were 606 friendly settlements and 1303 in 2012; see Analysis of Statistics (2012), Court's website.   [145] Hudoc (2007), see notes 215, 219 and 221.

[146] See, eg, *Sukhorukikh v Russia No 37548/04* hudoc (2006); *Paritchi v Moldova No 54396/00* (2005); and *Podbolotova v Russia No 26091/02* hudoc (2005).   [147] Hudoc (2005).

[148] *Katić v Serbia* (dec) hudoc (2009).   [149] Hudoc (2007).

(the amount of compensation proposed by the registry) in ancillary domestic proceedings amounted to an abuse of the right of petition. In *Mandil v France*, the applicants and their lawyers informed the press of the ongoing negotiations with the French authorities. The Court considered that the act was disloyal and was designed to discredit the government. It rejected the case for abuse.[150] On the other hand the Court requires that the divulgation by the applicant or his lawyer be an intentional act. In one case it accepted that a simple suspicion was not enough to reject a case for abuse where the disclosure was made by a person who was not involved in the case but by a member of the same religious community.[151] Protocol 14 has changed the friendly settlement procedure under the Convention in several important respects.[152]

When the parties have been unable to agree a friendly settlement, or when the applicant has unreasonably refused a settlement offer, it is still open to the Court to strike a case out when the government submits a unilateral declaration acknowledging liability and undertaking to pay compensation, even though the applicant wishes the Court to continue to examine the case.[153] This will also be possible at the Article 41 stage of the procedure where the matter has been resolved and the applicant has refused an equitable settlement offer.[154] Since the *Akman* judgment, the practice of submitting unilateral declarations leading to a strike-off decision has become almost as important as that of friendly settlement, particularly in repetitive cases that have not led to a settlement because the applicant has refused the offer made by the Registrar calculated on the basis of the Court's case law.[155] The requirement of acknowledging responsibility has not always been insisted on in such clone cases, but it has been a requirement in other more serious cases. The practice has developed because the Court considers that it should not necessarily be for the applicant to determine whether it is to carry out an examination of the merits of the case by withholding consent to the terms of a settlement.

In principle, a unilateral declaration is preceded by a friendly settlement offer. It is only when this has been refused by an applicant that the possibility of filing a declaration arises. However, there are limits to the readiness of the Court to accept such declarations. In *Tahsin Acar v Turkey*,[156] the Grand Chamber sought to define when such a unilateral declaration would be acceptable in a case which concerned a disappearance at the hands of the security forces. A non-exhaustive list of factors to be taken into account included the nature of the complaints made, whether the issues raised were comparable to issues already

---

[150] Dec hudoc (2011). The Court has not allowed a contracting party to refer to the applicant's failure to agree to a settlement as a reason for losing victim status; *RR v Poland* hudoc (2011).

[151] *Mirolubovs and others v Latvia* hudoc (2000) paras 66–70; see also the separate opinion of Judge Myjer on this point.   [152] See new Article 39.

[153] See eg *Akman v Turkey* 2001-VI, the first unilateral declaration adopted by the Court. The government had *inter alia* admitted liability in respect of a killing by the security forces and offered to pay £85,000 in compensation. The Court took into account not only the admissions and undertakings made by the government, but also the fact that it had previously specified in numerous cases the nature and extent of the obligations which arise for states concerning killings by the security forces. Criticism has focused on the fact that the compensation was paid *ex gratia* (notwithstanding the admission) and that no proper investigation had been carried out by the authorities. For critical comment on such decisions, see Sardaro, 6 EHRLR 601 (2003). Where the applicant expresses his agreement to a unilateral declaration, this will be considered a friendly settlement; *Cēsnieks v Latvia* hudoc (2012). The Court will no longer accept undertakings to pay *ex gratia* and requires that this term no longer appear in declarations.

[154] *Megadat.com SRL v Moldova* hudoc (2011).

[155] In 2011 there were 703 unilateral declarations and 606 in 2012; Analysis of Statistics (2012) Court's website; see n 3.

[156] 2003-VI para 76 GC. See also the dissenting opinion of Judge Loucaides in the Chamber judgment in this case; judgment of 9 April 2002 for criticism of unilateral declarations in disappearance cases.

determined by the Court in previous cases, and the nature and scope of any measures taken by the respondent government in the context of the execution of judgments delivered by the Court in any such previous cases. It would also be material whether the facts were in dispute between the parties. Other relevant factors included whether the unilateral declaration made any admission in relation to the alleged violations of the Convention and, if so, the scope of such admissions and the manner in which they intended to provide redress to the applicant. As to the latter, in cases in which it was possible to eliminate the effects of an alleged violation, the intended redress was more likely to be regarded as appropriate for the purposes of striking out the application. Finally, the Court emphasized that in this assessment it always retained the power to restore the application to its list.[157] In the *Tahsin Acar* case, the declaration did not contain any admission of liability. The Court accepted that a full admission of liability could not always be regarded as a condition *sine qua non* for striking an application out on the basis of a unilateral declaration by a respondent government, but since the declaration contained neither an admission of liability nor an undertaking to conduct an investigation into the disappearance, it fell short of what was required. Respect for human rights thus required the continued examination of the case.[158] However, it is clear that an assessment will be made on the specific facts of each case where the nature of the violation alleged and the existence of previous case law against the state concerned will play a role. Thus in *Prencepe v Monaco*,[159] the Court considered that an acknowledgement that there had been a violation of Article 5 (3) or some concession 'along those lines' was required before it would accept the unilateral declaration. In *Vyerentsov v Ukraine*,[160] the Court rejected the declaration and took into account that the case raised issues under Articles 7 and 11 that had not been previously examined by the Court in respect of Ukraine. A declaration was also refused by the Court in *Rozhin v Russia*,[161] on the grounds that its terms did not go far enough.

XIII. STRIKING OUT CASES–ARTICLE 37

In addition to cases where the government has submitted a unilateral declaration, the Court enjoys the power, granted under Article 37, to strike out cases from its list at any stage of the proceedings. 'Any stage of the proceedings' has been given a wide meaning and may even be applied after the parties' observations have been received and even by the Grand Chamber when a Chamber has already given judgment on the matter.[162] The

---

[157] As provided in Article 37(2) of the Convention and Rule 43(5) of the Rules of Court.

[158] The Court eventually gave judgment in the case, finding no substantive violation of Article 2 but a procedural violation of that Article; *Tahsin Acar v Turkey* 2004-III GC para 84. Other cases struck out on this basis include *Haran v Turkey* hudoc (2002); *Meriakri v Moldova* hudoc (2005); and *Van Houten v Netherlands* 2005-IX.

[159] Hudoc (2009). In an intentional killing or disappearance case, an admission of responsibility would be required: *Tahsin Acar*, para 84; also concurring opinion of Judge Ress.

[160] Hudoc (2013).

[161] Hudoc (2011). See also *Missenjov v Estonia* hudoc (2009) (refusal because the declaration did not encompass an Article 13 complaint); *Vojtechova v Slovakia* hudoc (2012) (refusal because the declaration did not provide the possibility of a re-opening of the proceedings); also *Dochnal v Poland* hudoc (2012), *Valiulienė v Lithuania* hudoc (2013), and *Przemyk v Poland* hudoc (2013).

[162] See eg, *Kovacic and others v Slovenia* hudoc (2008) GC; *Sisojeva and Others v Latvia* hudoc (2007); 45 EHRR 753 GC; also *Shevanova v Latvia* hudoc (2007) GC and *Kaftailova v Latvia* hudoc (2007) GC, where the Grand Chamber, taking a different view from the Chamber, found that the applicants, long-term immigrants who did not benefit from resident status in Latvia, could avail themselves of options outlined by the Latvian authorities to regularize their status, thus considering the matter to be 'resolved' within the meaning of Article 37(1)(b).

Court (Chamber or Grand Chamber) can also strike out part of an application whilst in the same judgment examining the applicant's remaining complaints on their merits.[163]

There are three conditions for striking out applications in Article 37(1): when the applicant does not intend to pursue his application; when the matter has been resolved; or when, for any other reason established by the Court, it is no longer justified to continue the examination of the application (sub-paragraphs (a)–(c) of the Article). For the first, a clear indication that the applicant intends to pursue the application will render the provision inapplicable, but the applicant's consent is not required for the other two conditions.[164] For the second, in assessing whether the matter has been resolved, the Court will ask two questions: first, whether the circumstances complained of directly by the applicants still obtain; and second, whether the effects of a possible violation of the Convention on account of those circumstances have also been redressed.[165] The first is plainly a factual assessment that will turn on the circumstances of each case. The second is similar to the Court's assessment of whether the applicant is still a victim at the time of its examination of the case,[166] namely whether there has been recognition of a violation, either expressly or in substance and whether adequate redress has been provided.[167]

The Court will attempt to focus on what the 'matter' of the case actually is, ie the question in dispute which brings the applicant and respondent state before it. Thus in *Association SOS Attentats and De Boëry v France*,[168] concerning the refusal of France to allow the victims of an explosion on board a passenger plane to sue the Libyan head of state, Colonel Gaddafi, and the applicants' complaint that this violated their right of access to court under Article 6 of the Convention, it was irrelevant to the matter in dispute that an agreement to compensate the victims of the attack had been reached between Libya and the applicants. This agreement did not enable the applicants to sue Colonel Gaddafi and thus a key aspect of the applicants' direct complaint persisted, which sufficed to conclude that Article 37(1)(b) did not apply.

The Grand Chamber, in *SOS Attentats*, also considered the application of Article 37(1)(c). It identified broadly five reasons for striking out an application this way: on the basis of a unilateral declaration by the government when the applicants had reached a settlement with domestic authorities which largely satisfied their demands under the Convention and they had thus lost their victim status; when the applicant had died in the course of the proceedings before the Court and no heir had come forward (or one had but had no legitimate interest); a lack of diligence by the applicant or his lawyer; and a failure to abide by the Rules of Court (such as failing to appoint a lawyer). This was not considered to be an exhaustive list, since the Grand Chamber emphasized that the Court 'enjoys a wide discretion in identifying grounds capable of being relied upon in striking out an application on this basis'.[169]

---

[163] See *Sisojeva*, paras 104 and 105 *et seq* (striking out the application insofar as it related to Article 8 and continuing its examination in relation to the Article 34 complaint).

[164] See *Akman v Turkey* 2001-VI; *Pisano v Italy* hudoc (2002) para 41; and *Ohlen v Denmark* hudoc (2005) para 25.

[165] *El Majjaoui and Stichting Touba Moskee v Netherlands* hudoc (2007) para 30 GC.

[166] See Ch 2, section 7.I on victim status.

[167] Matter considered resolved following a lead pilot judgment: *Association of Real Property Owners in Łódź v Poland* hudoc (2011); *Dalban v Romania* 1999-VI; 31 EHRR 39 paras 41–5 GC; *Burdov v Russia* 2002-III paras 27–32; *Ohlen v Denmark* hudoc (2005) para 26. See also *Freimanis and Lidums v Lithuania* hudoc (2006) paras 66–74 and references therein. However the requirement of a recognition of a violation is not a requirement in deportation cases; see *Sisojeva and Others v Latvia* hudoc (2007); 45 EHRR 753 para 93 GC.   [168] 2006-XIV GC.

[169] *Association SOS Attentats and De Boëry v France*, para 37 and the extensive authorities cited therein. See also *Chagos Islanders v United Kingdom* (dec) hudoc (2012), where the applicants were considered to have lost their victim status as a result of a settlement reached in national proceedings.

Article 37 provides the caveat that even where one of the three conditions mentioned has been satisfied, the Court shall continue the examination of the application if respect for human rights as defined in the Convention and protocols thereto so requires. Such continuance is a rare occurrence and the Court risks accusations of judicial activism if it proceeds to examine an application and finds a violation of the Convention where there is no longer a live dispute between the parties. Nonetheless, there have been instances where this has occurred. In *Karner v Austria*,[170] the original applicant had complained of his inability to succeed to the tenancy of his homosexual partner when a heterosexual partner would be able to do so. After the original applicant's death, his heir (the applicant's mother) waived her right to succeed to his estate. The Court chose not to strike the application out of its list. It recalled that its judgments served not only to decide those cases before it, but, more generally, to elucidate, safeguard, and develop the rules instituted by the Convention.[171] However in *Léger v France*,[172] the Grand Chamber struck out the applicant's case under Article 3 on the grounds that continued examination was no longer justified after he died and neither an heir nor a close relative nor a person with any other legitimate interest had sought to continue the proceedings.

XIV. REQUESTS FOR RECTIFICATION, INTERPRETATION, AND REVISION

Article 44 directs that Grand Chamber judgments shall be final. According to the same provision, Chamber judgments become final either (i) when the parties declare that they will not seek referral to the Grand Chamber; or (ii) three months after the date of the judgment when neither party seeks referral; or (iii) when the panel of the Grand Chamber rejects any request for referral. However, even when judgments do become final, while not provided for in the Convention, the Rules of Court allow for three types of requests for reconsideration of judgments: requests for interpretation (Rule 79); requests for revision (Rule 80); and requests for rectification of errors (Rule 81). These Rules reflect the Court's inherent jurisdiction to review the judgment in certain circumstances. Protocol 14 also introduced the possibility of a request for interpretation of a judgment being made by the Committee of Ministers.[173] The Explanatory Report stresses that it is not the intention of this new provision to ask the Court to give an opinion on the compatibility of proposed amendments to national law introduced pursuant to the judgment.[174]

Rule 81 is straightforward and allows the Court, of its own motion or at the request of a party made within one month of the delivery of a decision or judgment, to rectify clerical errors, errors in calculation, or obvious mistakes. The errors, however, must be patent mistakes. The Court will not accept proposals to alter the text of a judgment with a view to rephrasing or to striking out an argument. It will correct obvious

---

[170] 2003-IX; 38 EHRR 528. See also *Atmaca v Germany* hudoc (2012), struck out under Article 37(1)(c) (continued examination not justified) on the grounds that he no longer faced a real and imminent threat of extradition to Turkey following his release pending the outcome of extradition proceedings.

[171] See the discussion of the *Karner* case, in Ch 2, section 7.I. Also *Tyrer v United Kingdom* A 26 (1978) paras 24–7.

[172] Hudoc GC (2009), the person who sought to continue the case was unable to demonstrate any link with the applicant's family; see also *Predescu v Romania* hudoc (2008), struck out for abuse in respect of one applicant but not in respect of the other.   [173] Article 46(3).

[174] See section 6 of this chapter.

mistakes, for example, as regards the text of legislative provisions or the professional qualifications of those appearing before it. However, nothing that might affect the substance of the decision reached could be dealt with under this head. The Court need not wait for such a request and can correct such basic mistakes itself by way of its editorial revision of judgments. This possibility is noted in the preface to all Court judgments.

Rule 79 allows either party to request interpretation within a period of one year following the delivery of the judgment. The request must state the point or points in the operative provisions of the judgment on which interpretation is required. The Chamber may of its own motion refuse the request. If it does not do so, the request is communicated to the other party or parties who have the opportunity to submit comments. An oral hearing can also be held before the Chamber gives its decision by way of a judgment. Requests for interpretation of judgments have been rare and have related to issues concerning the payment of compensation. In the first such request the Court held in *Ringeisen v Austria*[175] that damages awarded under the head of non-pecuniary damage in respect of a violation of Article 5(3) were to be paid directly to the applicant, who was then living in Germany, free from attachment. The Commission had explicitly requested this in view of the applicant's needy circumstances. The Austrian authorities had paid the money into court, since it had been claimed by various creditors. The government had challenged the Court's jurisdiction to examine the issue on the basis that the Convention did not provide for requests for interpretation and that the matter was only governed by a Rule of Court. The Court held that it was a matter of its inherent jurisdiction and that such proceedings did not involve an appeal against the original judgment. The Court's role was limited to clarifying the meaning and scope which it intended to give to a previous decision. The Court has stressed in subsequent cases that the clarification of a judgment does not involve modification in respect of issues which the Court has already decided with binding force. Thus in *Allenet de Ribemont v France*,[176] where the Court had awarded a global sum to the applicant without making any distinction between pecuniary and non-pecuniary damage, the Court pointed out that it had not provided in its judgment that the sums awarded to the applicant were to be free from attachment, as requested by the applicant, and the matter had been left to the national authorities in accordance with national law. Nor was it prepared to rule, as requested by the Commission, that awards in respect of compensation were to be free from attachment, since it did not have jurisdiction under Article 50 (now Article 41) to issue orders to a contracting party.[177] In a similar vein, in the case of *Hentrich v France*,[178] the Court rejected a request for interpretation that the state should pay default interest in respect of delay in payments. This was not considered to be a matter of interpretation as such. The requirement to pay default interest was later introduced by the Court in January 1996.

The procedure is similar under Rule 80 as regards requests for revision of a judgment. This Rule provides for revision of the judgment when a party discovers 'a fact which might by its nature have a decisive influence and which, when a judgment was delivered, was unknown to the Court and could not reasonably have been known to that

---

[175] A 16 (1973).

[176] 1996-III; 20 EHRR 557. Note also the Committee of Ministers' decision in *Del Rio Prada v Spain* hudoc (2013) to accept Spain's decision not to pay sums awarded for non-pecuniary damage on the grounds that the applicant owed considerable amounts to the state in respect of unpaid damages to her victims.

[177] Attachment is discussed further in the following section 4 on Article 41.

[178] 1997-IV; 18 EHRR 440.

party'. The party has six months from when it acquired knowledge of the fact to make the request. This time limit is interpreted strictly by the Court. In *Grossi and others v Italy*,[179] the government's revision request was rejected for being submitted too late. They had known about the new facts relating to the considerably smaller acreage of the applicant's property since December 2010, but had waited until October 2011 to make a revision request. Under Rule 79, the Chamber may of its own motion refuse the request. If it does not, the request is communicated to the other party or parties who have the opportunity to submit comments. Exceptionally, an oral hearing can also be held before the Chamber gives its decision by way of a judgment.

The Court has shown that it is willing to accept revision of a judgment as regards issues relating to Article 41, for example, when information is submitted after the delivery of judgment that the applicant has died beforehand and the Court has been unaware of this fact. Thus in *Resul Sadak and Others v Turkey*,[180] where one of the applicants had died before judgment was given, the Court was prepared to revise the judgment to provide that the applicant's heirs should be awarded the amounts awarded to the deceased under Article 41. The applicant had been one of twelve applicants and it appears that no blame could be attached to either the lawyer who was unaware of the death or the heirs who may not have been aware of the proceedings.

The case of *Stoicescu v Romania*[181] was subsequently declared inadmissible on revision when the Court learned that the applicant in an expropriation case had previously lost his status of heir to the property in question following court proceedings in Romania and had not drawn the Court's attention to this crucial fact, which had removed his victim status. The government could not have been aware of this development owing to the absence of a database of pending cases at the relevant time.

While these cases demonstrate a relatively liberal practice on the revision of matters concerning Article 41, the Court has shown itself extremely reticent to revise its determination of whether or not there has been a violation of the Convention—apart from circumstances where vital facts have been withheld from it, as in *Stoicescu*. The Court's approach is one of strict scrutiny coupled with a clear reluctance to re-open a final judgment on the merits. A heavy burden thus rests with the party seeking to overturn the Court's original judgment.[182] In *McGinley and Egan v UK*,[183] it observed:

> The Court notes the embodiment of the principle of the finality of judgments in the present Article 44 of the Convention and recalls that, insofar as it calls into question the final character of judgments of the Court, the possibility of revision is considered to be an exceptional procedure. Requests for revision of judgments are therefore to be subjected to strict scrutiny.

---

[179] Hudoc (2012).

[180] Hudoc (2008). In the same vein, see *Bajrami v Albania* (Revision) hudoc (2007), where judgment was revised for the same reason but at the government's request, since it could not execute the judgment. For revision of costs and expenses, see *Baumann v Austria (Revision)* hudoc (2005). See also *Gabay v Turkey* hudoc (2006); *Sabri Taş v Turkey* hudoc (2006); *EP v Italy* hudoc (2001).

[181] Hudoc (2004).

[182] See, eg, *Bugajny and others v Poland* (Revision) hudoc (2009), where the government was unable to show that it could not reasonably have known the existence of the new fact; also *Metalco BT v Hungary* (Revision) hudoc (2012) where the Court rejected a request to revise the judgment on the basis that the company had gone into liquidation before the date of the Court's judgment. It held that the liquidator had not indicated that he had lost interest in the case. If he did not wish to pursue it he should have informed the Court.

[183] 2000-I para 36; see the dissenting opinions of Judges Casadevall and Maruste. Also *Pardo v France* 1996-III and 1997-III; 22 EHRR 563.

XV. ADVISORY OPINIONS REQUESTED BY THE COMMITTEE OF MINISTERS

Under Article 47, the Committee of Ministers may request an advisory opinion[184] concerning the interpretation of the Convention and its protocols.[185] This is subject to two important and constraining caveats: by paragraph two of the same article, such opinions may not deal with the content and scope of the rights or freedoms defined in Section I of the Convention and the Protocols or any other question the Court or Committee of Ministers may have to consider in consequence of any such proceedings as could be instituted in accordance with the Convention. Given the limited scope for advisory opinions under this provision, it is not surprising that there have only been three requests for opinions.[186] In the first, the Committee of Ministers sought an opinion on whether the Commonwealth of Independent States (CIS) Convention was another procedure of international investigation or settlement in the sense of Article 35(2)(b) of the European Convention on Human Rights (ECHR).[187] The Court ruled that it was not competent to give an advisory opinion.[188]

The Court gave its first advisory opinion on the merits on 12 February 2008.[189] The Court considered that it was confronted with a proper 'legal' (as opposed to political) question that did not result from any 'contentious proceedings', namely whether it was lawful for the Parliamentary Assembly to reject a list on the grounds that it was not gender-balanced. The Court examined a further criterion—not explicitly stated in Article 47—namely, whether it would be expedient for the Court to give an opinion. It held that it was appropriate to give a ruling on this question in the interests of the proper functioning of the Convention system, as there was a need to ensure that the situation which gave rise to the request for the opinion—that is, the disagreement between the Committee of Ministers and the Parliamentary Assembly on this issue—did not cause a blockage in the election system. The Court delivered its second opinion on the question whether it was open to a government to withdraw its list of candidates for election as judge after it had been submitted to the Parliamentary Assembly. The question was an important one for the integrity of the electoral process, which would be clearly undermined if governments had free rein to withdraw their lists at any stage of the process.[190]

Article 49 of the Convention provides that advisory opinions shall be reasoned, that judges are entitled to deliver separate opinions, and that the opinion shall be communicated to the Committee of Ministers. Chapter IX of the Rules of Court regulates the Court's procedure in dealing with advisory opinions. In particular, all requests for an opinion shall be considered by the Grand Chamber of the Court. In addition, under

---

[184] See generally, Costa and Titiun, *Les avis consultatifs devant la CEDH*, Mélanges Tavernier, 2013, pp 605–15.   [185] By Article 31, such requests are considered by the Grand Chamber.

[186] Provision is being made in a new Protocol 16 for advisory opinions to be sought by superior national courts; see section 7.II.

[187] The Court's 'reasoned' decision can be found at: http://www.echr.coe.int.

[188] Article 48 provides that is for the Court to decide whether a request for an advisory opinion is within its competence as defined in Article 47. Rules 87, 88, and 89 of the Court refer to the concept of a 'reasoned decision' for decisions taken pursuant to Article 48 on whether a request for an advisory opinion is within the Court's competence. This was the first such decision.

[189] *Advisory Opinion on Certain Legal Questions Concerning the Lists of Candidates for the Election of Judges to the European Court of Human Rights* hudoc (2008).

[190] *Advisory Opinion (no 2) on certain legal questions concerning the lists of candidates submitted with a view to the election of judges to the European Court of Human Rights* hudoc (2010). The Court also found that it had no jurisdiction to consider the compatibility with the Convention of provisions of a PACE resolution; see n 206, para 36.

Rule 84(2), contracting parties are given the right to submit written comments which, under Rule 86, may be developed at an oral hearing if the President decides to hold one.[191]

3. PROCEDURE BEFORE THE COURT (II): ADDITIONAL PROCEDURAL MATTERS

Regardless of the judicial formation which finally gives a decision or judgment in a particular case, there are a variety of procedural issues that may arise in a case and which are considered in the following sections.

I. PUBLICITY

The name of an applicant is public unless the President of the Chamber grants anonymity for good cause shown.[192] Anonymity would usually be granted in cases concerning issues of private health, custody, or sex abuse or divorce issues, and it is open to the President to grant anonymity in such cases even though it may not be asked for by the applicant. A mere desire to avoid publicity is not in itself a sufficient reason for anonymity. A request should be made when completing the application form.[193] There is also the possibility for applicants to be granted anonymity retrospectively. This was introduced by the Court in response to concerns voiced by applicants who complained that many years after they had brought proceedings details concerning their cases—and perhaps offences that they had committed—remained visible on the internet.[194]

II. LEGAL REPRESENTATION

If the application is introduced by a legal representative, he or she will be required to submit a power of attorney. The Court's website provides a suitable authority form which requires the signatures of both the applicant and his or her designated representative. It is, of course, possible for the applicant later to revoke that authority and appoint different representatives. There is some flexibility in the initial stages of proceedings as to who can actually be a representative. A legal qualification is not required at the outset of proceedings but only after an application is communicated to the respondent government. Rule 36(2) requires the applicant to be represented by an 'advocate' authorized to practise in

---

[191] No oral hearing has yet been held. The opinion of 12 February 2008 involved a written procedure in which each contracting party, as well as PACE, were given an opportunity to file written observations. It does not appear that the Convention makes any provision for third party interventions by NGOs in advisory opinion proceedings. Article 36 of the Convention covering such interventions speaks only of 'cases' and so appears only to contemplate inter-state cases and individual applications. However, support for the right to seek leave to intervene may be found in Rule 82, which allows the Court to apply other provisions of the Rules of Court to the extent it considers this to be appropriate and this may allow for such interventions in application of Rule 44.

[192] Rule 33. In keeping with the philosophy of transparency underlying Protocol 11 setting up the new Court, all documents will also be accessible to the public unless the President decides otherwise for good cause; Rule 33(2). Arrangements can be made at the Registry for the public or journalists to inspect such documents—see the Court's website for details. It is the Court's policy that documents must be consulted at the seat of the Court.

[193] See para 3 of *Practice Direction of 14 January 2010 on Requests for Anonymity* (Rules 33 and 47).

[194] *Practice Direction of 14 January 2010 on Requests for Anonymity*, paras 4 and 5.

any of the contracting parties and resident in the territory of one of them, or any other person approved by the President of the Chamber.[195] For the United Kingdom and Ireland, this can be a solicitor or a barrister/advocate. A number of non-governmental organizations (NGOs) have sought and obtained the President's leave to represent applicants where they have qualified lawyers on their staff who may not have fulfilled all the formalities for private legal practice. Lawyers may be refused permission to act in Court proceedings if the President of the Chamber considers that their behaviour warrants such a decision or if they have no longer the right to practise.[196] It is open to a lawyer practising in a non-contracting party, such as an American attorney or Canadian barrister/avocat, to seek leave to appear.[197] Permission may be given by the President of the Chamber to allow an applicant to represent himself. However, the Court would normally insist on the applicant being legally represented or assisted by an advocate if there was to be an oral hearing.[198] An applicant who represents himself would only be reimbursed expenses and would not be eligible to receive legal aid.

III. LEGAL AID

Legal aid is available to applicants when it is necessary for the proper conduct of the case and the applicant has insufficient means to meet all or part of the costs entailed,[199] but only after an application has been communicated to the government and only at the request of the applicant or his representatives.[200] For any request received before communication, the representative will be informed by the Registry that the request is premature, although if legal aid is subsequently granted, the offer will cover the initial preparatory phase of an application. On communication, the applicant is requested to submit a declaration of means, which must be certified by the appropriate domestic authority. It is no longer the rule that governments will be asked to comment on the declaration of means, although the President of the Chamber may request comments if necessary.[201] Offers of legal aid will be sent at each stage of the procedure: communication, oral hearings before the Chamber and Grand Chamber, and participation in friendly settlement discussions.[202] The amounts offered are small in comparison to legal costs in many western legal systems, but more reasonable when compared with costs in Central and East European countries. They are seen as a contribution to legal costs and it is open to the applicant to recoup the real cost of legal representation under Article 41 if he wins his case.

IV. ORAL HEARINGS

The parties can request an oral hearing at any stage of the proceedings, though it is for the Court to decide if a hearing is necessary. It might decide to do so if some novel point of law is involved. The Court can also on its own motion decide to have a hearing, which will

---

[195] See generally, Rule 36(1)–(5).

[196] Rule 36(4)(b). For a decision to refuse a lawyer permission to appear, see *Manoussos v Czech Republic and Germany* hudoc (2002). Even if a lawyer is no longer able to practise in his or her own country he or she could still be authorized by the President, who has full discretion to evaluate all the circumstances to represent an applicant.

[197] See, eg, *Open Door and Dublin Well Woman v Ireland* A 246-A (1992); 15 EHRR 44 PC and *Kamasinski v Austria* A 168 (1989); 13 EHRR 36.

[198] Rule 36(3).   [199] Rule 101.

[200] National legal aid schemes rarely offer legal aid for Strasbourg proceedings. The Danish Legal Aid Act (1999) is an exception; see *Vasileva v Denmark* hudoc (2003); 40 EHRR 681 para 50.

[201] Rule 102(2).   [202] The payment of legal aid is regulated by Chapter X of the Rules of Court.

usually take place in public.[203] Since 2007, hearings are usually webcast a few hours after the hearing unless the Chamber decides otherwise.[204] It is not open to the parties to object if the Court schedules a hearing. When an oral hearing is set, the parties will be sent a list of questions to be addressed which reflect what the Court considers to be the main questions in the case. These may cover both factual and legal issues. At the end of the hearing, the parties may be given an opportunity to submit supplementary information within a prescribed time limit.

Normally hearings are the exception at Section level. Most Grand Chamber cases will involve a hearing, but each of the five Sections of the Court will only hold one or two hearings each per year.[205] Apart from the bilingual nature of the proceedings, the oral procedure does not differ significantly from similar hearings at the appellate level in national courts, though it may be rather short by comparison. The parties are requested to provide the interpreters with a copy of their submissions at least one day in advance in order to facilitate their work. Each party is given a set time for their intervention (usually half an hour), questions may be put by the judges, and the President may permit a short adjournment to allow the parties to prepare their answers. There follows a brief second round when the parties are given an opportunity to respond to those questions and to the principal arguments of the other side. Non-governmental organizations intervening as third parties will not normally be permitted to make oral submissions, but contracting parties exercising their rights on behalf of a national under Article 36(1) have a right to appear at the hearing. Contracting parties which have intervened for other reasons may also be authorized to make further submissions at a hearing.[206] Under Protocol 14, the Council of Europe Commissioner for Human Rights was granted a right to make written submissions and to appear before the Court.[207]

V. INTERIM MEASURES

Requests for interim measures[208] are made under Rule 39 of the Rules of Court. Applications before the Court do not have suspensive effect. Consequently it is not normally open to the Court to issue an injunction to restrain a state from enforcing a particular measure. However, in some situations, as where life or death may be at stake, most commonly in a case of expulsion or extradition to a state where ill-treatment is feared,

---

[203] Rule 63. The public may be excluded 'in the interests of morals, public order or national security in a democratic society, where the interest of juveniles or the protection of the private life of the parties so require'; see Rule 63(2). *In camera* hearings have been rare but have taken place in a number of cases where the rights of children were at stake: *Z v Finland* 1997-I; 25 EHRR 371; before the Chamber in *K and T v Finland* hudoc (2000); 31 EHRR 484; and *L v Finland* hudoc (2000); 31 EHRR 737.

[204] ee the Court's website for an archive of oral hearing webcasts. Webcasting of hearings is not live and will take place in the afternoon of the hearing following a favourable decision of the Chamber.

[205] In 2011, the Grand Chamber held twenty-one hearings and eleven in 2012. Chamber hearings took place in nine cases in 2011 and seven cases in 2012 (see *Survey of Activities* for 2011 and 2012, available on the Court's website).

[206] For example, the United Kingdom's oral submissions in *Saadi v Italy* hudoc (2008).

[207] Article 36(3). His written and oral interventions have been very few and this for reasons of policy and staff resources. See, eg, *MSS v Belgium and Greece* GC hudoc (2011). For further details of third party interventions by the Commissioner, see his website at http://www.coe.int/en/web/commissioner; see section 3.IX of this chapter.

[208] See Rieter, *Preventing Irreparable Harm—Provisional Measures in International Human Rights Adjudication*, 2010; Caflisch, in Dupuy *et al*, eds, *Common Values in International Law: Essays in Honour of Christian Tomuschat*, 2006, pp 493–515; Garry, 17 EPL 399 (2001); Rozakis, in Pintens *et al*, eds, *Feestbundel voor Hugo Vandenberghe*, 2007; and Vajić, in Kohen, ed, *Liber Amicorum Lucius Caflisch* 2007.

an injunctive power is necessary if the right of individual petition is to be effective. If this were not the case, the Court could only carry out its examination of the complaint when the feared harm had actually materialized or where the individual had been exposed to the risk of such harm. Accordingly, the object of an interim measure is to preserve and protect the interests of the parties to the dispute pending the Court's determination of the compatibility of the impugned decision with the Convention, or, simply put, to preserve the *status quo*. Most of the cases where an interim measure is requested concern expulsion or extradition from the territory of a contracting party. The Court will only issue an interim measure against a state where, having reviewed all the relevant information, it considers that the applicant faces a real risk of serious, irreversible harm if the measure is not granted. The measure may be limited in time or for an indefinite period depending on the evidence adduced in support of it.

The number of such requests has increased exponentially in recent years, with increased migration to Europe and the development of firm exclusionary policies by many states. This has created a certain tension with the contracting parties who expressed concern at the growth in the number of measures that were being granted and the length of time it subsequently took the Court to examine the merits of such cases. For example, in 2010 the Court granted more than 1,443 requests (mainly in respect of expulsions to Iraq and Somalia). In that year more than 3,775 requests had been made. By 2012 the number of requests granted had been reduced to 103.[209] Concerned at the growing number of requests, the then President of the Court (Jean-Paul Costa) issued a Practice Statement indicating the Court's alarm at the sheer number of requests and that the Court was not to be seen as a fourth instance appeal body against decisions of national immigration tribunals. Interim measures were to be seen as 'exceptional'. He called on applicants and their representatives to respect the Court's Practice Direction, which provided guidance on the procedures for applying for a measure and for states to ensure that suspensive remedies existed under national law to enable domestic courts to examine the issue of risk.[210] As more failed asylum seekers are being sent back to their countries of origin, a last-minute application to the Court for a stay against removal is seen as the final bid for asylum. Despite this trend, interim measures are not a new feature of the permanent Court. The old Commission and Court had similar provisions under Rule 36 of their respective rules,[211] although the old Court had famously held the Commission's power to indicate interim measures not to be binding, in part because the Commission had no power to give binding judgments and the Convention lacked a specific interim measures provision.[212] What is distinctive about the new Court's practice on interim measures is that, as a result of the Grand Chamber's judgment in *Mamatkulov and Askarov v Turkey*,[213] they are now considered binding on contracting parties in that failure to abide by them will in most cases (see later) lead to a violation of Article 34 *in fine* which obliges states not to

---

[209] See the Izmir and Brighton Declaration, referred to in section 7 of this chapter. See, for statistics concerning interim measures, http://www.echr.coe.int/Pages/home.aspx?p=reports&c=#n1347956700110_pointer. Expulsion under the Dublin Regulations also gave rise to large numbers of requests being made during this period; see *MSS v Belgium and Greece*, n 224. To ensure consistency, the handling of requests has been centralized within the Court and decisions are taken by a duty judge specially appointed by the President: Rule 39(4).

[210] See the *Statement on requests for interim measures* issued by the President on 11 February 2011, doc GT-GDR-C(2012)005.

[211] See, for an early example, the indication of the old Court that extradition be deferred while Strasbourg proceedings were pending in *Soering v UK* A 161 (1989); 11 EHRR 439 PC.

[212] *Cruz Varas and Others v Sweden* A 201 (1991) PC.

[213] 2005-I; 41 EHRR 494 GC. See Tams, 63 ZAORV 681 (2003).

'hinder the effective exercise of the right of individual petition'. In reaching this conclusion the Court attached weight to developments in other international tribunals, such as the International Court of Justice and the Inter-American Court of Human Rights, as well as the fact that the Court's judgments, unlike the opinions of the old Commission, are binding by virtue of Article 46.

In *Olaechea Cahuas v Spain*,[214] the government did not comply with the indication made under Rule 39 that it should not remove the applicant (a suspected leader of the Sendero Luminosa) to Peru, having received assurances from the Peruvian authorities that he would not be subjected to torture or other ill-treatment. The risk of ill-treatment, in the event, did not materialize after his return and the Spanish government argued that in such circumstances the Court should not find a breach of its obligations under Article 34. The Court held that a state's decision as to whether to comply with the measure could not be deferred pending the hypothetical confirmation of the existence of a risk. Non-compliance with an interim measure on the basis of the existence of a risk was, in itself, a serious hindrance at that precise point in time of the effective exercise of the right of individual petition. In short, and crucial to the effectiveness of the Court's system of interim measures, the obligation of compliance took effect at the moment the measure was indicated, irrespective of whether the risk which motivated the Rule 39 decision later materialized. This approach has been endorsed by the Grand Chamber in *Paladi v Moldova*,[215] where the issue concerned a delay in implementing an interim measure requesting urgent medical treatment for a detainee by means of a transfer to a more appropriate hospital. The Court stressed that it was not open to a contracting state to substitute its own judgment for that of the Court in verifying whether or not there existed a real risk of immediate and irreparable damage to an applicant at the time when the interim measure was indicated. Neither was it for the domestic authorities to decide on the time limits for complying with an interim measure or on the extent to which it should be complied with. It was thus not relevant for the Court's assessment whether the feared damage actually occurred. It was always open to the state to make an application to the Court to annul the measure by submitting evidence that called into question its validity. In *Abdulkhakov v Russia*,[216] the Court noted that Russia had complied with a request not to extradite the applicant to Uzbekistan. However, it found that the Russia authorities had been involved in his subsequent kidnapping and secret transfer to Tajikistan five months later outside of any legal framework and in breach of the rule of law. In *Hamidovic v Italy*,[217] on the other hand, the Court found no breach of Article 34 where the failure to comply was the result of an error of transmission by the Italian authorities in Strasbourg to the relevant government department which had not received the request in good time. However that case concerned Article 8 and the Court underlined that the consequences had not been irremediable since the applicant had been brought back to Italy once the mistake had been recognized. Also in *Al-Saadoon and Mufdhi v United Kingdom*,[218] the Court rejected the government's plea that they were unable to comply with Rule 39 because of their international obligations and found a violation of Article 34 on the basis that the authorities had not done all that could reasonably be expected of them to ensure that the applicants would not receive the death penalty after they had been handed back to the Iraqi authorities.

Despite such episodic instances of non-compliance which have, to some extent, increased in recent years, there has always been a good record of compliance with interim

---

[214] 2006-X.   [215] GC hudoc (2009).   [216] Hudoc (2012).
[217] Inadmissibility decision—hudoc (2011)   [218] Hudoc (2010) paras 151–66. Reports 2010.

measures, even when they were considered non-binding. Refusals to comply are always taken seriously by the Court because of their rule of law implications but, given the large number of requests granted, remain relatively infrequent.[219] This can probably be explained by a certain apprehension that the Court could subsequently find a violation on the merits of the case. However, an inherent respect for the rule of law and the proper administration of justice are also factors which arguably weigh heavily with most of the contracting parties in such cases. Where the state has refused to comply, it has often invoked national security reasons for doing so.[220]

a. Scope

Interim measures can be both positive and negative in character. The majority will be negative (asking states to delay removals) but occasionally the Court will indicate positive measures, such as asking states to provide urgent or emergency medical treatment to detained persons,[221] or to meet with a lawyer to prepare a case before the Court[222] or to ensure that the death penalty would not be carried out.[223] It has also used Rule 39 to request hunger strikers to give up their protest to enable the Court to examine their complaints. In *Ilascu and Others v Moldova and Russia*,[224] the President of the Grand Chamber requested the respondent governments, under Rule 39, to take all necessary steps to ensure that one of the applicants who had been on hunger strike since 2003 'was detained in conditions which were consistent with respect for his rights under the Convention'. Several days later the President called on the applicant, under Rule 39, to call off his hunger strike. He complied with the request on the same day.

Interim measures are granted in cases involving '"an imminent risk of irreparable damage'.[225] In practice, the vast majority of cases have concerned deportation or extradition proceedings where there are substantial reasons to believe that there exists a real risk of death or ill-treatment in the country of destination. However, where the complaint concerns expulsion to one of the contracting parties, the Court will operate a

---

[219] Two prominent examples, in addition to *Mamatkulov*, are *Conka and Others v Belgium No 51564/99* hudoc (2001) DA (where there was allegedly a breakdown in communication) and *Aoulmi v France* 2006-I; 46 EHRR 1, though it must be added that, in each case, the failure to abide by the interim measure took place before the Court's ruling in *Mamatkulov*. For other examples of non-compliance in deportation/extradition cases leading to a violation of Article 34, see *Shamayev and Others v Georgia and Russia* 2005-III, concerning the extradition of Chechen applicants from Georgia to Russia; *Mostafa and others v Turkey* hudoc (2008), *Muminov v Russia* (no violation) hudoc (2008); *Ben Khemais v Italy*, ECHR 2009; *Trabelsi v Italy* hudoc (2010); *Mannai v Italy* hudoc (2012); *Labsi v Slovakia* (expulsion to Algeria) hudoc (2012); *Abdulkhakov v Russia* (kidnapping and secret transfer to Tajikistan) hudoc (2012). Instances of non-compliance in areas other than removal cases include *Paladi v Moldova* GC hudoc (2009); *Aleksanyan v Russia* hudoc (2008); *Shtukaturov v Russia* hudoc (2008); *Makharadze and Sikharulidze v Georgia* hudoc (2011).

[220] For example, *Mannai v Italy* and *Labsi v Sklovakia*, cited in the previous footnote.

[221] As in the *Paladi* case mentioned previously. The Court took the further step of asking the Turkish authorities to delay the detention of a number of applicants who had Wernicke-Korsakoff syndrome, at least until they had been examined by a team of medical experts and a delegation of judges sent by the Court: *Gürbüz v Turkey* hudoc (2005) and *Tekin Yilidiz v Turkey* hudoc (2005). In *Ensslin, Baader, and Raspe v Germany No 7572/76*, 14 DR 91 (1978), the former Commission also invoked Rule 36 (as it then was) to send a delegation prior to admissibility to Stammheim prison, Stuttgart, to investigate the alleged suicides of the applicants. In admissible cases, such a step would now be taken pursuant to Article 38 of the Convention—see fact-finding, section 3.VI of this chapter.

[222] *Aleksanyan v Russia* hudoc (2008); the Court requested the authorities to secure treatment in a specialized hospital for an inmate suffering from AIDS; also *Makharadze and Sikharulidze v Georgia* hudoc (2011). [223] *Öcalan v Turkey* 2005- IV GC; see press release of 30/11/1999.

[224] 2004-VII; 40 EHRR 1030 paras 10 and 11 GC.

[225] *Mamatkulov and Askorov v Turkey* 2005-I; 41 EHRR 494 para 6 GC, 108.

rebuttable presumption that the guarantees of the Convention will be respected. But the Court has also applied Rule 39 in cases concerning conditions of detention considered dangerous to health or, as in *Paladi v Moldova*, to provide appropriate medical treatment to detainees,[226] or, exceptionally, in Article 5 and 6 cases, where there is a risk of a flagrant denial of fair trial in the country of destination.[227] In the case of *D v UK*,[228] interim measures were granted in the case of a patient who was suffering from full blown AIDS and whose expulsion to St Kitts had been ordered. Similarly, interim measures were directed in the case of *N v UK*,[229] in which the applicant submitted that her expulsion to Uganda, where she would not have access to life-sustaining medicine for AIDS, would be tantamount to the imposition of a death sentence. It has also applied Rule 39 in certain Article 8 cases involving the returning of abducted children pursuant to the Hague Convention to countries where it is alleged that the interests of the child will be irreparably prejudiced.[230]

However, the Court has, from time to time, applied Rule 39 in cases concerning specific issues arising within contracting parties. In *Öcalan v Turkey*,[231] for example, where the applicant risked the death penalty before the State Security Court, the Court requested, *inter alia*, that Turkey ensure that the requirements of Article 6 were complied with and that the applicant was able to exercise the right of individual petition to the Court through lawyers of his own choosing. Subsequently, the Court requested the government to take all necessary steps to ensure that the death penalty was not carried out so that it could carry out an effective examination of the applicant's complaints under the Convention. Requests for interim measures in respect of other Convention complaints are unlikely to succeed unless, as illustrated by the *Öcalan* case, there are special elements linked to the notion of irreparable or irreversible harm.

After Articles 2 and 3, the highest number of Rule 39 requests concern Article 8 of the Convention, especially from parents who seek to prevent the adoption or taking into care of their children. Another category is when immigrants are to be deported from a contracting party and allege only that the deportation will violate their private and family life, the rest of the family residing in the contracting party concerned. Rule 39 will only be applied exceptionally in such cases (indeed there would be a presumption that it would not be applied), since it is rare that the 'irreparable damage' test will be met. Rule 39 was applied in *Evans v UK*,[232] where the Court indicated that the government should take appropriate measures to preserve frozen embryos belonging to the applicant until it could rule on whether she could use them over the objections of her ex-boyfriend with whom she had created them. The Chamber subsequently indicated in the operative part of its judgment that the Rule 39 measure was to continue until the judgment became final or until 'further order' in order to ensure that the embryos were protected in the event of the case being referred to the Grand Chamber.

---

[226] GC hudoc (2009); *Prezec v Croatia* (unilateral declaration by the government) hudoc (2008); *Tehrani and others v Turkey* hudoc (2010); see also *Salakhov Islyamova v Ukraine* hudoc (2013).

[227] *Othman (Abu Qatada) v United Kingdom* hudoc (2012); allegation that the applicant would be tried on the basis of statements by co-accused adduced through torture and that he would thus be subject to a flagrant violation of Article 6; see *Soering v United Kingdom* hudoc (1989) para 113.

[228] 1997-III; 24 EHRR 423.   [229] Hudoc (2008) GC.

[230] Hague Convention on International Child Abduction (1980); *Neulinger and Schuruk v Switzerland* GC hudoc (2010); *B v Belgium* hudoc (2012).

[231] 2005-IV; 41 EHRR 985 GC. See also Ch 9, section 5.IV.

[232] 2007-I GC; 46 EHRR 72 (the relevant British law required the continued consent of both gamete providers for the storage of the embryos (see para 38 of the judgment).

b. Procedure

Rule 39 requests are dealt with on an urgent basis. The procedures for handling them within the registry have been revised following the Izmir and Brighton Conferences. All requests are now supervised by a special section within the Court (the Filtering Section). Decisions are taken by one of duty judges of the Court appointed by the President to deal with such requests. Owing to the large numbers of complaints being submitted at the last moment, the President of the Court has issued a *Practice Direction on interim measures*, which sets out the proper procedures to be followed by applicants and their lawyers seeking Rule 39 measures.[233] Applicants are warned, *inter alia*, that a failure to make a request expeditiously or to submit all supporting documents—in particular domestic court decisions—may result in the Court being unable to examine the request properly or in good time. Normally, domestic remedies will have to be exhausted, especially where these have suspensive effect.[234] Where domestic remedies have been exhausted, it is certainly advisable for an application to be brought as soon as possible after an unfavourable decision has been obtained or even earlier where it is apprehended that there may be a risk of immediate removal in the event of an adverse decision on appeal to ensure that the request can be dealt with in good time. Normally the state of which the applicant is a national will be informed of the request in accordance with Rule 44 paras 1(a) and (b) of the Rules. That state has the right to submit comments under Article 36. However, the Court has recently decided not to apply this provision in cases where the reason for applying to the Court is based on a fear of return to that state.[235]

VI. INVESTIGATIONS AND FACT-FINDING

In most cases the facts of the case are undisputed and can be determined on the basis of the facts as found by the national courts.[236] The Court will normally accept the facts as established and has indicated that it would require cogent elements to lead it to depart from reasoned findings of fact reached by the national judicial authorities which have had the benefit of seeing and examining the relevant witnesses. Such cogent elements have been found to be present where the fact-finding by the national courts presented serious deficiencies. Thus in a criminal prosecution against Turkish police officers arising out of the killing of five suspects in four separate arrest operations, the Court noted that there were serious deficiencies in the manner in which the national court established the facts. These related to the absence of any effective investigation of the planning of the arrest operations; the absence of any photograph or sketch plans of the scenes of the incidents; the lack of any fingerprint, ballistics, or other forensic evidence; and the lack of contemporary individual statements by the police officers who participated in the operations. In these circumstances, the Court held that it must treat the findings of fact by the criminal court with some caution.[237] It went on to find a violation of both the substantive and procedural obligations under Article 2.

---

[233] http://echr.coe.int/Documents/PD_interim_measures_ENG.pdf.

[234] http://echr.coe.int/Documents/PD_interim_measures_ENG.pdf.

[235] *I v Sweden* hudoc (2013) paras 40–6. The case concerned the return of a person of Chechen origin to Russia.

[236] See O'Boyle and Brady, *Liber Amicorum, Anatoly Kovler*, 2012 and 4 EHRLR 378–91 (2013). Leach *et al*, Report by the Human Rights and Social Justice Research Institute, London Metropolitan University, *On Fact-Finding by the ECHR*, 2009; Costa, in *Mélanges en l'honneur de JP Puissochet*, 2008, pp 47–56. Chernishova and Vajić, *Mélanges Christos L Rozakis*, 2011, pp 47–79; Erdal and Bakirci, Article 3 of the ECHR: A Practitioner's Handbook, OMCT Handbook Series, 2006, pp 237–65.

[237] *Erdoğan v Turkey* hudoc (2006) paras 71–3.

The Court has powers to conduct fact-findings on the spot, although these are rather sparingly used, *inter alia* because of the amount of resources needed for such missions. Fact-findings by the Court, like those of the former Commission, have concerned many cases against Turkey regarding killings or disappearances or allegations of torture. Other on-the-spot missions have also concerned allegations relating to inhuman and degrading prison conditions.[238] In *Ireland v UK*,[239] the Commission heard over a hundred witnesses in Strasbourg, Norway, and the United Kingdom. In *Ilaşcu and Others v Moldova and Russia*,[240] a delegation of four judges took evidence from forty-three witnesses in Tiraspol and Chişinău. The witness hearings took place in different locations (a prison, an OSCE office, the headquarters of the Russian army in Transdniestria) and various political figures were heard. In *Georgia v Russia (No 1)*, the Court held fact-finding hearings in Strasbourg on the basis of witnesses put forward by both parties and the Court.[241] The number of fact-findings by the Court has steadily diminished over the years.[242] This is explicable in part by the development of case law of the Court concerning the drawing of adverse presumptions in certain circumstances when the government fails to cooperate as requested, as well as a policy to determine even Article 2 cases solely on the basis of a detailed case file, particularly if the facts relate to events that occurred many years ago when the usefulness of hearing witnesses may be in doubt.[243] In short, the Court has emphasized the states' obligation to carry out an investigation into the facts.

The Court has at its disposal other methods of elucidating the facts, such as the appointment of experts, the power to request third-party interventions, and the seeking of reports and opinions by other competent international bodies, primarily within the Council of Europe, but also on occasion from outside. It has also taken the initiative to request third-party interventions from the United Nations High Commissioner for Refugees,[244] who accepted and filed submissions before the Court. Another institution of the Council of Europe, the Venice Commission (the European Commission for Democracy through Law), has on many occasions contributed to the proceedings either as a third party[245] or by preparing, at the Court's request, expert opinions relevant to cases being examined by the Court.[246] The Grand Chamber case of *MSS v Belgium and Greece* is a good example of the role played by both the United High Commissioner for Refugees and the Council of Europe Commissioner for Human Rights, as well as the NGOs Amnesty International and *Médecins sans frontières*, in providing key factual information concerning the conditions of asylum seekers in Greece and the operation of asylum law there.[247]

---

[238] See eg, *Peers v Greece* 2001-III; 33 EHRR 1192 and *Valašinas v Lithuania* 2001-VIII.

[239] A 25 (1978); 2 EHRR 25 PC.   [240] 2004-VII; 40 EHRR 1030.   [241] Hudoc (2009) (dec).

[242] Since the Convention institutions were set up there have been around ninety-five fact-finding missions. The Court has become a reluctant *in situ* fact-finder. See, for discussion of the reasons for this, O'Boyle and Brady, *Liber Amicorum, Anatoly Kovler*, 2012, pp 387–9. Chernishova and Vajić note that remarkably there has not yet been a fact-finding in any Russian case concerning the events in the Northern Caucasus region of Russia, notwithstanding the seriousness of the allegations being examined and the large number of judgments in Article 2 and 3 cases against Russia: Chernishova and Vajić, *Mélanges Christos L Rozakis*, 2011, pp 64–5. The most recent fact-finding took place in Strasbourg in the 'secret rendition' cases of *Al Nashiri v Poland* and *Husayn (Abu Zubaydah) v Poland*, press release of 3 December 2013.

[243] See, as regard both points, *Tanlı v Turkey* 2001-III. The Court usually asks for the national investigation file to be forwarded in such cases. See Leach *et al*, Report by the Human Rights and Social Justice Research Institute, London Metropolitan University, *On Fact-Finding by the ECHR*, 2009.

[244] *Ahmed Ali v Netherlands and Greece* (dec) hudoc (2012); *Ali Gedi and others v Austria* (dec) hudoc (2011).   [245] *Sejdić and Finci v Bosnia and Herzegovina* hudoc (2009) para 44 GC.

[246] *Basque Nationalist Party—Iparralde Regional Organisation v France*, 2007-VII.

[247] *MSS v Belgium and Greece* hudoc (2011) GC; also *Hirsi Jamaa and others v Italy* hudoc (2012) GC.

It should also be noted that the Court has frequent recourse to the fact-finding capacities of other Council of Europe bodies, such as the Committee for the Prevention of Torture (CPT), the Parliamentary Assembly of the Council of Europe (PACE), and the European Commission against Racism and Intolerance (ECRI). It has relied in many cases on the reports of the CPT to establish the conditions of detention.[248] In *DH and others v the Czech Republic*,[249] it relied on the report of ECRI to establish, *inter alia*, the number of Roma children in special schools. PACE resolutions and recommendations are also used by the Court as a source of information concerning the plight of particular minorities or the typical problems of European society, such as terrorism or media concentrations or misuse of data. Finally, there are cases where the applicant's account of the facts is so well corroborated by other sources that the Court is prepared to consider that the allegations are substantiated to the appropriate standard of proof without the need for a fact-finding.[250]

The Chamber may appoint one or more of its members to carry out an on-site investigation.[251] The applicant and 'any Contracting Party concerned' are required by the Rules of Court to 'assist the Court as necessary'.[252] The relevant contracting party shall extend to the delegation the facilities and cooperation necessary for the proper conduct of the proceedings. These shall include freedom of movement and all adequate security arrangements for the delegation, the applicant, witnesses, and experts.[253] It is provided in the Rules that 'it shall be the responsibility of the Contracting Party—to take steps to ensure that no adverse consequences are suffered by any person or organisation on account of any evidence given, or any assistance provided, to the delegation'. Since investigations may take place in trouble zones, this obligation to protect witnesses from reprisals is primordial. It has happened that applicants and witnesses have been intimidated or harmed and even killed in suspicious circumstances.[254] Both parties are asked to nominate witnesses and the delegation decides in advance of the mission those witnesses it wishes to hear. The head of the delegation may decide to hold a preparatory meeting with the parties prior to any proceedings taking place,[255] which will greatly assist in the organization of the mission. The rules also make provision for the issuing of summonses and the relevant contracting party has the responsibility for servicing any summons sent to it by the Chamber for service. The contracting party is also required 'to take all reasonable steps to ensure the attendance of persons summoned who are under its authority or control'. The hearing of witnesses is *in camera*[256] and is inquisitorial in style, with the delegates and the representatives of the parties being able to question the witnesses.[257] Questions of procedure and objections to lines of questioning are dealt with by the head of the delegation.[258] Witnesses are normally not admitted to the hearing room before they give evidence, so that their testimony is not tainted by what other witnesses have said.[259] Following the hearing, a verbatim record of the proceedings is drawn up and

---

[248] See, *inter alia, Iacov Stanciu v Romania* hudoc (2012) and *Plotnicova v Moldova* hudoc (2012).

[249] Hudoc (2007) GC; also, amongst many authorities, *S and Marper v UK* hudoc (2008) GC.

[250] *El-Masri v 'the former Yugoslav Republic of Macedonia'* hudoc (2012), paras 154–67 GC.

[251] For the investigation procedure, see the Annex to the Rules of Court (concerning investigations).

[252] Rule A2(1). The President of the Chamber may grant leave to third parties to take part in an investigative measure, although this has not yet occurred (Rule A(6)).

[253] Rule A2(2). This rule should be read in conjunction with Rule 44A, which imposes a general duty on the parties to cooperate fully with the Court. See also Rules 44B and C.

[254] For a detailed account of such instances see the Report of the Committee on Legal Affairs and Human Rights of the Assembly on *Member States' Duty to Co-operate with the European of Human Rights*, by C Pourgourides, paras 18 *et seq*, 9 February 2007.   [255] Rule A4(2).

[256] Rule A1(5).   [257] Rule A7(1–5).   [258] Rule A7(5).   [259] Rule A7(3).

circulated to the parties for corrections.[260] Interpretation is organized by the Registry of the Court, and the costs of the hearing, including reasonable witness expenses, are paid from the Court's budget.

The weakness of the Court's fact-finding machinery lies in the inability of the Court to compel the attendance of witnesses and the production of documents.[261] The Convention does not explicitly impose these obligations on contracting parties. However, the failure to ensure the attendance of witnesses or to produce documentation which is considered important to the case can lead to a finding that the state has violated Article 38(1)(a), which requires that states furnish all necessary facilities for the effective conduct of the investigation. The Court has not been shy of recording violations of this provision where the state has failed to cooperate. Equally importantly, the Court has held that in certain instances it is only the government that has access to information capable of corroborating or refuting the applicant's allegations and that a failure to submit such information which is in its hands without a satisfactory explanation may not only give rise to a possible breach of Article 38(1)(a) but may also give rise to the drawing of inferences as to the well-foundedness of the applicant's allegations.[262] The same approach will apply where the state fails to secure the attendance of witnesses at a hearing, thereby making it more difficult to establish the facts. In the case of *Akkum and Others v Turkey*,[263] the Court went a step further and, drawing a parallel with the approach employed by the Court in cases concerning injuries inflicted during detention, held that the withholding of vital documents concerning the killings of the applicants' relatives had the effect of shifting the burden of proof to the government to disprove the applicants' allegations:

> It is appropriate, therefore, that in cases such as the present one, where it is the non-disclosure by the Government of crucial documents in their exclusive possession which is preventing the Court from establishing the facts, it is for the Government either to argue conclusively why the documents in question cannot serve to corroborate the allegations made by the applicants, or to provide a satisfactory and convincing explanation of how the events in question occurred, failing which an issue under Article 2 and/or Article 3 of the Convention will arise.

VII. BURDEN AND STANDARD OF PROOF

Evidence is presented to the Court in a variety of forms—the decisions of national courts on issues of fact, affidavit evidence of witnesses, medical reports and testimony, official investigation reports, and other documentary evidence, such as video or photographic

---

[260] Rule A8. Corrections may be made by the parties but in no case may such corrections affect the sense and bearing of what was said; Rule A8(3).

[261] See eg *Tanis and Others v Turkey* 2005-VIII para 160, where the Commanding Officer would not appear to give evidence in a disappearance case before the delegates and the authorities would not submit an unexpurgated version of the investigation file. The Court drew adverse inferences in this case as well as finding a breach of Article 38(1)(a). Cf, *Musayeva and Others v Russia* hudoc (2007) paras 121–4.

[262] See, *Timurtaş v Turkey*, ECHR 2000-VI para 89; *Taniş and Others v Turkey*, ECHR 2005–VIII para 164; *Çakıcı v Turkey* [GC], ECHR 1999-IV para 76; and *Imakayeva v Russia*, ECHR 2006-XIII paras 117–19. Cf *Zubayrayev v Russia* hudoc (2008) (no violation despite recourse to presumptions) and *Tovsultanova v Russia* hudoc (2010).

[263] 2005-II; 43 EHRR 526 para 211. See also *El-Masri v 'the former Yugoslav Republic of Macedonia'* hudoc (2012) paras152–3 GC; *Imakayeva v Russia* 2006-XIII.

evidence.[264] In many complaints under Article 3 about prison conditions, the Court has relied on reports of the Committee for the Prevention of Torture to corroborate allegations about prison conditions or facilities.[265] There is no prohibition of hearsay evidence and no fixed rules concerning illegally obtained evidence, privileged documents, or perjury. Such evidential issues will be decided on a case-by-case basis, having regard to all the facts established in the case and the nature of the allegations. The proceedings are governed by the principle of the free admission and assessment of evidence.[266] The case law reveals, however, a distinct approach to the burden of proof, both as regards admissibility issues and issues of fact.[267]

At the admissibility stage, the applicant must present facts which are supportive (albeit not conclusive) of his allegations by way of a 'beginning of proof' (*commencement de preuve*), although the practice of the Court today is to examine issues of admissibility and the merits together in cases which satisfy this threshold test and are not rejected *de limine*. Thus there should be enough factual elements to enable the Court, at this initial stage, to conclude that the allegations are not completely groundless. As regards issues of domestic remedies, there is a distribution of the burden of proof. The burden is on the state to demonstrate the existence of adequate and effective remedies, but then shifts to the applicant to demonstrate that the remedies adduced by the state are, in fact, inadequate and ineffective. It then remains to the state to rebut the arguments submitted by the applicant under this head.[268]

At the merits stage, the approach to the burden of proof is subtle and context dependent. The level of persuasion necessary for reaching a particular conclusion and the distribution of the burden of proof are linked to the specific circumstances of the case, the nature of the allegation made, and the Convention right at stake. The Court may also be attentive to the seriousness that attaches to a ruling that a contracting party has violated fundamental rights.[269] For example, as regards expulsion cases raising Article 3 issues, it is for the applicant to adduce evidence capable of proving that there are substantial grounds for believing that, if removed to the country of destination, he or she would be exposed to a real risk of being subjected to treatment contrary to Article 3. Where such evidence is adduced, it is for the government to dispel any doubts about it.[270] In cases concerning torture or ill-treatment of a detainee, the Court has consistently applied the rule that where a person is detained in good health but is found to be injured on release, it is incumbent on the state to provide a plausible explanation of how the injury occurred.[271]

The same principle has been applied to the disappearance of a person who had been in custody.[272] In cases concerning the use of lethal force by the security forces, the case law

---

[264] See, on the burden of proof generally, Erdal, 26 ELR, Human Rights Survey 68 (2001) and Kokott, *The Burden of Proof in Comparative and International Human Rights Law: Civil and Common Law Approaches with Special Reference to the American and German Legal Systems*, 1998.

[265] Eg, *Yakovenko v Ukraine* hudoc (2007) para 83 and *Ostrovar v Moldova* hudoc (2005) para 80.

[266] *Nachova v Bulgaria* 2005-VII; 42 EHRR 933 para 157 GC.

[267] In *Ireland v UK* A 25 (1978); 2 EHRR 25 para 160 PC, the former Court made it clear that it would not rely on the concept that the burden of proof is borne by one of the two governments appearing before it and that its approach was to examine all the material before it, including material obtained *proprio motu*. Since under the former system the fact-finding had been carried out by the Commission, this approach is understandable. But it was inevitable that the new Court, which must establish the facts for itself, would develop a different approach to the burden of proof.

[268] *Selmouni v France* 1999-V; 29 EHRR 403 para 87 and the authorities cited therein. See also Ch 2, section 3.III.　　　[269] *Nachova and Others v Bulgaria* 2005-VII; 42 EHRR 933 para 147 GC.

[270] *Saadi v Italy* hudoc (2008) para 129 GC and *N v Finland* hudoc (2005) para 167; 43 EHRR 195.

[271] For a good summary of the case law, see *El-Masri v the former Yugoslav Republic of Macedonia'* GC hudoc (2012), paras 154–67; also Ch 6, section I.

[272] *Kurt v Turkey* 1998-III; 27 EHRR 373 para 124 and *Çakıcı v Turkey* 1999-IV; 31 EHRR 133 GC. See also Ch 5, section 7.I.a.

conveys the impression that it is incumbent on the applicant to establish a violation of Article 2. As pointed out by Judge Bratza in a dissenting opinion, the wording of Article 2 strongly suggests that it falls to the state to demonstrate that the force used was 'no more than absolutely necessary'.[273]

Generally, it is for the state to demonstrate the 'necessity' of an interference with a Convention right under the second paragraph of Articles 8–11. For example, in freedom of speech cases, it will fall to the state, once an applicant has demonstrated that there has been an interference with his Article 10 rights, to prove the necessity for the interference with reference to reasons that are considered by the Court to be both relevant and sufficient.[274] However, the Court has refused to reverse the burden of proof in a discrimination case under Article 14 where the authorities had not carried out an adequate investigation into the question of whether unlawful killings were racially motivated on the basis that such an approach went too far, since it would require the authorities to disprove a subjective attitude by the person concerned.[275] Nevertheless, the Court recognizes that discrimination is notoriously difficult to prove and that less strict evidential rules may be justified in certain circumstances. In *DH and Others v Czech Republic*,[276] concerning allegations of discrimination against the Roma community, the Court considered that once the applicants had shown, with reference to statistical information, evidence of indirect discrimination against them as a group, the burden of proof shifted to the respondent government to show that the difference in treatment was not discriminatory. Finally, as noted in the preceding section on fact-finding, there are many instances where the Court will reverse the burden or draw adverse inferences from a state's refusal to cooperate or to provide information in respect of matters within their particular knowledge.

The standard of proof is that of 'beyond reasonable doubt'. This is regularly employed by the Court in allegations of violations of Articles 2 and 3. For the Court, such proof may follow 'from the coexistence of sufficiently strong, clear and concordant inferences or of similar unrebutted presumptions of fact', as well as from the conduct of the parties when evidence is being taken.[277] A reasonable doubt is a doubt for which reasons can be drawn from the facts presented and not a doubt raised on the basis of a mere theoretical possibility or to avoid a disagreeable conclusion.[278] It has been stressed that it has never been the Court's purpose to borrow the approach of the national systems which use that standard and that the Court's role is not to establish criminal or civil liability, but to determine the contracting parties' responsibility under the Convention.[279] Thus the fact that police officers may have been acquitted in criminal proceedings of the use of unlawful force cannot be decisive of the issue that arises under the Convention, namely whether the force used has been more than absolutely necessary in the circumstances.[280] Accordingly, the standard does not correspond with the high criminal law standard that is employed in many legal systems, although it does nevertheless connote a high standard of proof as regards the facts that are alleged to have occurred. The standard has been criticized in various dissenting opinions as inadequate, possibly illogical, and unworkable when trying to determine whether a person in custody has been ill-treated.[281]

---

[273] *Ağdaş v Turkey* hudoc (2004).   [274] See Ch 11, section III.

[275] *Nachova v Bulgaria* 2005-VII; 42 EHRR 933 para 157 GC.

[276] Hudoc (2007) paras 186–9 GC.

[277] First employed in *Ireland v UK* A 25 (1978) PC; 2 EHRR 25. See also, *inter alia, Salman v Turkey* 2000-VII; 34 EHRR 425 para 100 GC.   [278] *Ireland v UK*, para 30.

[279] *Nachova v Bulgaria* 2005-VII; 42 EHRR 933 para 147 GC; *Mathew v Netherlands* ECHR 2005-IX, para 156.   [280] *Erdogan v Turkey* hudoc (2006) para 71.

[281] See, eg, the dissenting opinion of eight judges in *Labita v Italy* 2000-IV; 46 EHRR 1228 GC and the dissent of Judge Bonnello in *Veznedaroğlu v Turkey* hudoc 2000; 33 EHRR 1412.

VIII. PILOT JUDGMENTS

A pilot judgment[282] is the Court's response to the recurring problem of repetitive or 'clone cases', ie large numbers of cases raising essentially the same issue of which there are some 47,000 in the Court's current docket.[283] In the 1980s, the problem was reflected in the large number of cases brought against Italy concerning length of procedure. Since the establishment of the new Court in 1998, a large volume of repetitive cases have been brought against many different countries concerning not only length of civil and criminal proceedings but many other issues, including non-enforcement of domestic judgments, delays in payment following expropriation, and access to property in northern Cyprus.

The Court itself proposed the introduction of a 'pilot judgment procedure' in cases which were related to a systemic or structural problem in the country concerned.[284] It was envisaged that the pilot judgment would give rise to an accelerated execution procedure before the Committee of Ministers and would impose on the state an obligation to address the structural problem and thereby provide domestic redress in respect of applications pending in Strasbourg. In the Court's view, applicants will gain redress more speedily if an effective remedy is established at national level than if their cases are processed on an individual basis by the Court.[285]

The 'pilot judgment procedure' was applied for the first time in the case of *Bronowski v Poland*.[286] In the operative part of the judgment, the Court held that the violation of Article 1 of Protocol 1 found in the case originated 'in a systemic problem connected with the malfunctioning of domestic legislation and practice caused by the failure to set up an effective mechanism to implement the "right to credit" of Bug River claimants'. The Court enjoined the state to secure the implementation of the property right in question in respect not only of the applicant but also of the remaining Bug River claimants. In the judgment the Court had noted that some 80,000 people were affected by the systemic problem. Following a friendly settlement concerning the setting-up of a compensation scheme for all those affected, the case was eventually struck off the Court's list. The compensation scheme later set up by the Polish authorities was subsequently accepted by the Court as providing a remedy which satisfied the principal *Broniowski* judgment.[287] A further pilot judgment was adopted by the Court in the case of *Hutten-Czapska v Poland*,[288]

---

[282] See Leach, Hardman, Stephenson, Blitz, *Responding to Systematic Human Rights Violations—An Anaylsis of Pilot Judgments of the European Court of Human Rights and their Impact at National Level*, 2010; Pilot Judgment Procedure in the European Court of Human Rights, 3rd Informal Seminar for Government Agents, Warsaw (2009); Colendra, 7 HRLR 397 (2007); Garlicki, in Caflisch *et al*, eds, *Liber Amicorum Luzius Wildhaber*, 2007, pp 177–92; Leach, 2005 EHRLR 148. See also section 3.VIII of this chapter.

[283] The procedure is governed by Rule 61 of the Rules of Court which provides, *inter alia*, that the parties will be consulted on the suitability of the case for the pilot procedure; that pilot judgments will be granted priority treatment, that the Court will identify both the nature of the structural or systemic problem and the type of remedial measures that should be taken, subject to possible time limits, and that the Court may adjourn the examination of all similar applications, although it reserves the right to examine any adjourned case where it is in 'the interests of the proper administration of justice' to do so; see also *The Pilot Judgment Procedure*, Information Note issued by the Registrar, available on the Court's website. Repetitive complaints amount to around 35% of the Court's docket.

[284] Position Paper of the European Court of Human Rights on proposals for reform of the ECHR and other measures, CDDH GDR (2003)024, 26 September 2003, paras 43–6.

[285] See Information Note, n 283, para 6.

[286] 2004-V; 40 EHRR 495 GC. See Degener and Mahoney, in Hartig, ed, *Recueil à la mémoire de Wolfgang Strasser*, 2007, pp 173–209.

[287] *Wolkenberg and Others v Poland No 50003/99* (dec) hudoc (2007).

[288] 2006-VIII; 45 EHRR 52 GC. Since the *Broniowski* judgment the procedure has developed gradually. During the first five years (2004–2009) only five pilot judgments were delivered. Thereafter, as the procedure gained wide acceptance, the Court has had more frequent recourse to it; see n 290.

which concerned failure of Polish law to secure a 'decent profit' for landlords. In its judgment on the merits, the Grand Chamber held that 'in order to put an end to the systemic violation identified in the present case, the respondent Government must through appropriate legal and/or other measures, secure in its domestic legal order a mechanism maintaining a fair balance between the interests of landlords and the general interests of the community, in accordance with the standards of protection of property rights under the Convention'. This case was also struck out following a friendly settlement concerning the general measures adopted by Poland in response to the Court's judgment.[289]

In the case of *Lukenda v Slovenia*,[290] the Court noted there were some 500 Slovenian length of proceedings cases pending before it. This was identified as a systemic problem resulting from inadequate legislation and inefficiency in the administration of justice. The Court urged the Slovenian government to amend the existing range of legal remedies in order to secure genuinely effective redress for such violations. The introduction of a remedy in Slovenia for length of proceedings subsequently enabled the Court to dispose of large numbers of such cases.

The category of pilot judgments also includes judgments which stop short of requiring the state to introduce corrective measures in the operative part of the judgment but nevertheless relate to structural problems and propose that measures be taken by the state to address them.[291]

The pilot judgment procedure has been endorsed by the Committee of Ministers,[292] the Woolf Report,[293] and the Wise Persons Group,[294] and in the recent intergovernmental conferences on reform.[295] The Court itself has set up a sub-committee to examine how the procedure can best be utilized in the future, as well as the types of cases that may be appropriately dealt with by this procedure. They have most significantly concerned specific structural problems arising in the area of property rights. The question arises whether such judgments can also be used to deal with common endemic problems in many contracting parties, such as non-enforcement of judgments or cases concerning length of civil and criminal procedure, detention on remand, and prison conditions. Some commentators have suggested that a measure of circumspection in resorting to the procedure may be desirable and that an inflation of pilot judgments would be counter-productive.[296]

---

[289] *Hutten-Czapska v Poland* hudoc (2008) GC and the separate opinions of Judges Zagrebelsky, Jaeger, and Ziemele for critical remarks on the settlement.

[290] 2005-X. As of 1 November 2013, the Court has adopted 32 such judgments with provisions in the operative part of the judgment requiring the state to introduce remedies (the 'full' pilot judgment). See, eg, *Burdov v Russia (No 2)* hudoc (2009) (non-enforcement of court judgments in Russia); *Yuri Nikolayevich Ivanov v Ukraine* hudoc (2009) (non-enforcement of court judgments); *Atanasiu and Others v Romania* hudoc (2010) (property restitution claims); *Ananyev and others v Russia* hudoc (2012) (conditions of detention); *Kuric and others v Slovenia* hudoc (2012) GC (the problem of the 'erased' people in Slovenia). Three thousand similar Romanian restitution complaints have been adjourned, as have 1,200 non-enforcement cases against Ukraine and 150 cases against Russia concerning prison condition. See the 'fact sheet' on pilot judgments available on the Court's website.

[291] See eg, *Xenides-Arestis v Turkey* hudoc (2005) and *Scordino v Italy (No 1)* 2006-V; 45 EHRR 207 GC. On the proposals made by the Court under Article 46, see section 5 of this chapter.

[292] Committee of Ministers' Resolution (2004) 3 on *Judgments Revealing an Underlying Systemic Problem*.

[293] Review of the Working Methods of the European Court of Human Rights, December 2005, pp 37–8.

[294] Report of the Group of Wise Persons to the Committee of Ministers, Council of Europe, November 2006 at paras 100–5.

[295] See, eg, The Brighton Declaration (19–20 April 2012), paras 20 (c) and 27.

[296] Garlicki, in Caflisch *et al*, eds, *Liber Amicorum Luzius Wildhaber*, 2007, p 191.

This is undoubtedly the case, since such a judgment requires the state to remedy often deeply-entrenched legal or socio-economic problems in its national system that may not admit of an easy legislative resolution.[297] While the procedure offers a useful tool to bring about such structural change, an excessive recourse to the procedure could lead to judgments that were not complied with. This in turn would undermine the usefulness of the procedure. Nevertheless, there has been a general acceptance by governments of the utility of the procedure as a sensible method of dealing with repetitive complaints and only one government so far has actually challenged the legal basis of such a procedure under the Convention.[298]

The pilot judgment procedure reflects the view of the Court that its role should not be to act as a claims commission examining large numbers of repetitive cases and, further, that states must assume their responsibilities to tackle the root problems underlying repetitive complaints.[299] It also reflects the reality that the Court is not capable of dealing with such large numbers of frequently well-founded complaints. The essential challenge facing the Court is to ensure that the root problems are addressed by the state within a reasonable time frame and that pending cases that have been adjourned pending the outcome of the pilot procedure can be repatriated following the introduction of satisfactory corrective measures. The procedure thus pursues the aim of restoring the balance in the relationship between the international and the domestic protection of human rights by emphasizing the importance of providing a national remedy. To date, the negotiation of friendly settlements in *Broniowski* and *Hutten-Czapska*, whereby agreement is reached on a series of general measures which seek to tackle the structural problems underlying the case, have essentially relieved the Committee of Ministers of the thorny problem of implementation. However, such 'pilot' settlements, brokered with the assistance of the Court's registry, have been reached only in these two leading cases. In the subsequent thirty pilot judgments, enforcement has been left to the Committee of Ministers. It may be questioned whether friendly settlement is, in all circumstances, the most appropriate manner of implementing such judgments and whether the Committee should be deprived of the opportunity of expressing a view on the nature of the general measures adopted.[300] Be that as it may, the future of this procedure is ultimately in the hands of the Committee of Ministers, since it is the successful enforcement of such judgments that will validate the Court's continued recourse to them.[301]

---

[297] See, in this context, Judge Zagrebelsky's dissenting opinion in *Lukenda v Slovenia* hudoc (2005).

[298] See the arguments of the Italian government in *Sejdovic v Italy* 2006-II GC.

[299] The Court has proposed to go even further in tackling repetitive complaints. It 'envisages a practice whereby in relation to clearly repetitive cases the Registry would simply refer a list of cases directly to the Government to be settled in an appropriate way. In the absence of any justified objections from the Government, failure to provide redress within a fixed period of time would lead to a "default judgment" awarding compensation to the applicant'. *Preliminary Opinion of the Court in preparation for the Brighton Conference* (20 February 2012) para 21, available on the Court's website.

[300] Is it appropriate, for example, that the discussion about general measures in friendly settlement meetings take place only between the applicant and the government—without the presence of other interested parties such as NGOs or other groups directly affected by the proposed legislation?

[301] 'The Committee of Ministers should pay particular attention to violations disclosing a systemic issue at national level, and should ensure that States Parties quickly and effectively implement pilot judgments.' Brighton Declaration, para 27.

IX. THIRD PARTY INTERVENTIONS

Article 36 of the Convention makes provision for third parties to intervene in proceedings.[302] Indeed, this is a frequent occurrence in the Court's higher profile cases where there may be points of general importance at stake. According to Rule 44 of the Rules of Court, requests should be submitted within twelve weeks of the communication of an application to the respondent government.[303] In Article 36, two types of intervention must be distinguished. First, when the application is brought by the national of one state against another contracting party, the state of which the applicant is a national has the right to intervene under Article 36(1), reflecting the traditional right of diplomatic protection.[304] Second, under Article 36(2), the President of the Court may, in the interests of the proper administration of justice, invite or grant leave to any other contracting party or any other person concerned to submit written comments.

In respect of the first, this right also extends to appearing before the Court in oral hearings. Accordingly, states in this category are in a considerably stronger legal position than an NGO seeking leave to intervene. They can, for example, insist on having access to the entire case file. However, the Court has decided that they cannot insist on the right to appoint an *ad hoc* judge since they are not parties to the case *stricto sensu*; nor do they have a right to comment on the terms of any friendly settlement that has been reached, although they will usually be sent the settlement for information. It must be stressed that this is a right but not a duty, and states can and do decline to take part in the proceedings, especially when there is no wider principle at stake or the national link between applicant and state is wholly incidental.[305]

In relation to the latter type (interventions that require leave from the Court), one can further distinguish three types of interveners: first, interventions by governments other than the respondent government that have a specific interest in the subject matter of the case; second, persons other than the applicant who are directly implicated in the facts of the case may also intervene with leave;[306] finally, and most commonly, NGOs with

---

[302] For a survey of third party interventions before the Court, see Mahoney and Sicilianos, in Ruiz Fabri and Sorel, eds, *La tiers à l'instance devant les juridictions internationales*, 2005; Cichowski, in Christofferson and Madsen, eds, *The European Court of Human Rights between law and politics*, 2011, pp 77–97.

[303] This is made easier by the Court's decision to publish details of most communicated cases on its website, as well as cases accepted for reference to the Grand Chamber by the panel and cases where jurisdiction has been relinquished to the Grand Chamber. See 'Communicated Cases Collection' at http://www.echr.coe.int/echr/en/hudoc.

[304] See, eg, the Russian government's intervention in *Slivenko v Latvia* 2003-XI; 39 EHRR 490 GC (concerning the rights of Russian-speaking settled immigrants to regular residence status); or the Cypriot government's intervention in *Eugenia Michaelidou Developments Ltd and Michael Tymvios v Turkey* hudoc (2003); 39 EHRR 772 (concerning access to property in northern Cyprus); and the intervention by the government of Serbia and Montenegro (as it then was) in *Markovic v Italy* 2006-XIV; 44 EHRR 1045 GC (concerning the unsuccessful attempts of Serbian nationals to obtain compensation through the Italian courts for an air strike by NATO).

[305] See, eg, *GJ v Luxembourg* hudoc (2000); 30 EHRR 710; *Krombach v France* 2001-II; and *Fogarty v UK* 2001-IX; 34 EHRR 302 GC, where, respectively, the Danish, German, and Irish governments declined to intervene.

[306] The Court has given a wide meaning to the notion of 'any person concerned who is not the applicant' in Rule 44(2). It encompasses not only individuals and NGOs, but also government-appointed human rights bodies, such as the Northern Ireland Human Rights Commission. The Council of Europe's Venice Commission has also been given leave on various occasions (*Sedić and Finci v Bosnia and Herzegovina* GC hudoc (2009); *Jeličić v Bosnia and Herzegovina* (dec) hudoc (2005)). Article 36(3) confers on the Commissioner of Human Rights a right to intervene. If the Commissioner has so far exercised this power sparingly, it can be explained by a certain tension between his traditional statutory role and involvement in cases brought against countries on whose cooperation he depends. See the Commissioner's website http://www.coe.int/en/web/commissioner for cases where he has intervened. A judicious use of the Commissioner's right to

particular experience in the area of law or practice being examined (such as Amnesty International, the AIRE Centre, International Commission of Jurists, Redress, Interights) frequently seek (and are granted) leave to intervene.

In respect of the first category, governments asserting an interest will almost always be given leave to intervene.[307] This frequently occurs in cases where a point of general public international law is being considered such as in *Behrami and Saramati*, discussed earlier, where five states intervened.[308] It has also occurred when the issue under consideration will have implications for their legal system or immigration policy.[309] Equally in *Üner v Netherlands*,[310] concerning the deportation of a settled immigrant with young children with a series of criminal convictions, the German government intervened, given the similarity of its policy on deportation to that of the Dutch government. It is extremely unusual for a contracting party whose nationals are not applicants to intervene in support of the finding of a violation, though it has occurred in one case involving the death of a journalist in northern Cyprus.[311]

With regard to the second category, interventions by persons directly concerned or affected by the facts, there are fewer examples. In *T and V v UK*,[312] concerning the right to a fair trial of two boys who had been convicted of murdering a toddler, the parents of the victim were given leave to intervene. In *Perna v Italy*,[313] where the applicant had been convicted of defaming a judge, the judge was also given leave to intervene.

More common is the third category, where an interested party intervenes because of the legal importance of a case in an area where it has special expertise. Non-governmental organizations are frequent interveners on this basis. Thus, to give just a few examples, in *Nikula v Finland*,[314] Interights submitted a comparative law survey concerning restrictions on speech imposed on lawyers. In *Hugh Jordan v UK*,[315] the Northern Ireland Human

intervene under the Protocol has been already shown to be beneficial to the Court since his specific knowledge of the human rights situation in particular countries, nourished by his contacts with national human rights institutions, place him in a strategic position especially in pilot cases relating to systemic problems. See *MSS v Belgium and Greece* hudoc (2011) GC. Permission has also been granted to the UN Commissioner for Human Rights (*El-Masri v the Former Yugoslav Republic of Macedonia* hudoc (2012) GC) and the United Nations High Commissioner for Refugees (*Hirsi Jamaa and others v Italy* hudoc (2012) GC). The Court has not yet decided the general question whether it would be open to a non-state party to intervene in proceedings. In *Nizomkhom Dzhurayev v Russia* (Article 3 case concerning forcible transfer, communicated in 2012) Tajikistan was refused permission by the Section to intervene. It remains to be seen whether permission would be given, for example, to the Council of Europe monitoring bodies such as ECRI or the Social Charter Expert Committee or the CPT. It can be argued that the Court is able to have recourse to their reports when examining cases so intervention is not necessary. PACE has not yet sought to intervene, but in the *El-Masri* case the President refused permission to the Rapporteur on extraordinary renditions (Dick Marty), whose reports were eventually used by the Court to establish the facts in the case.

[307] The United Kingdom has been a frequent intervener on this ground. See, eg, its interventions in *Association SOS Attentats and De Boëry v France* 2006-XIV GC (in support of the contention that heads of state in office enjoyed immunity *ratione personae* from civil and criminal proceedings); *Kyprianou v Cyprus* 2005-XIII; 44 EHRR 565 GC (contempt of court); *Bosphorus Hava Yollari Turizm ve Ticaret Anonim Sirketi (Bosphorus Airways) v Ireland* 2005-VI; 42 EHRR 1 GC (concerning the appropriate level of review to be applied by the Court when the alleged violation results from a state's legal obligations flowing from membership in another international organization, in this case the European Union).

[308] Denmark, Estonia, Poland, Portugal, and the United Kingdom.

[309] *Saadi v Italy* hudoc (2008) GC, where the UK government intervened to argue that the Court should overturn its view in *Chahal* that, in expulsion cases under Article 3, considerations relating to national security were not to be taken into account once a substantial risk of ill-treatment was established.

[310] 2006-XII; 45 EHRR 421 GC.

[311] *Adali v Turkey* hudoc (2005). The applicant, the widow of the deceased, was a Turkish national and the Cypriot government intervened in support of her.   [312] 1999-IX; 30 EHRR 121 GC.

[313] 2003-V; 39 EHRR 563 GC.   [314] 2002-II; 38 EHRR 944.   [315] 2001-III; 37 EHRR 52.

Rights Commission (a government-appointed Commission) was given leave to comment on the right to life in international jurisprudence with reference to UN principles and the case law of the Inter-American Court. In *Pretty v UK*,[316] the Voluntary Euthanasia Society submitted a comparative law survey of relevant legal principles concerning euthanasia as well as ethical arguments in support of its position. The Catholic Bishops' Conference of England was also authorized to make written submissions on the moral issues underlying the case.[317] Frequently, such interventions will involve comparative law studies across different states, which may point to a practice in the respondent state that is out of step with that in other contracting parties.

In general, the Court has a liberal policy as regards interventions generally and leave to intervene will normally be granted by the President if the party submits a request outlining the nature of the proposed intervention and the reasons why it will further the proper administration of justice (Rule 44). If the case is subsequently heard by the Grand Chamber, it is not necessary to ask for permission a second time. There are, however, limitations attached to any authorization, since the intervener is not considered as a party. It is usually stipulated in the letter permitting intervention that it should not address directly the admissibility or merits of the case, but provide information based on the expertise or experience of the interveners.[318] Interventions which do not conform to this condition may be refused or only accepted in part (Rule 44(4)). Requests may also be refused when they are submitted out of time or too close to the hearing of the case or where the Court has already granted permission to other organizations. The Court has on occasions requested interveners to group their submissions.[319] Because of the increasing interest of NGOs in the work of the Court leading to a greater number of requests, the Court may refuse permission if it considers that it has a sufficient number of interveners. On moral or sensitive social issues, the Court is careful to grant permission to organizations on different sides of the issue if requests have been made, as, for example in the *Pretty* case discussed earlier,[320] or *A B and C v Ireland*,[321] which concerned an abortion issue. Finally, it should be noted that intervention by organizations is usually limited to written submissions. The Court would not normally grant permission for an intervener to appear before it, although in exceptional situations where the intervener has a direct interest in the outcome of the case this has been authorized (as was the case in *T and V v UK*). The Rules of Court also provide that the President may invite or grant leave to a third party to participate in an investigative measure, such as a fact-finding (Rule A1(6) of the Annex to the Rules of Court concerning investigations).[322] The Court is, however, strict about the length of third party interventions, normally restricting them to ten pages, excluding appendices. The respondent government and applicant are always given an opportunity to comment on the third party's observations, as they may open up new lines of argument to be addressed by the parties.[323]

---

[316] 2002-III; 35 EHRR 1.

[317] See further Mahoney and Sicilianos, in Ruiz Fabri and Sorel, eds, *La tiers à l'instance devant les juridictions internationales*, 2005; and Leach, *Taking a Case to the European Court of Human Rights*, 2nd edn, 2005, pp 57–61, for further examples. See also the many interventions by both governments and NGOs in *Lautsi v Italy* hudoc (2010) GC (concerning the display of the crucifix in public schools) and in *AB and C v Ireland* hudoc (2010) GC (concerning abortion).

[318] There may be occasional exceptions to this approach, eg, where the Court seeks information in an expulsion case about conditions in another country.

[319] Eg, *McCann and Others v UK* A 324 (1995); 21 EHRR 97 para 5 GC.

[320] See also the five interventions in *Tysiac v Poland* hudoc (2007), concerning the inability of a woman to obtain an abortion in circumstances where, it was held, domestic law provided for that possibility.

[321] Hudoc (2010) GC.   [322] This has not yet happened.

[323] See, eg, the verbatim record of the hearing of 24 November 1992 in *Brannigan and McBride v UK*, p 16, where the government complained that the interveners had widened the scope of the case.

Though it is unusual, the Court may also invite interventions of its own motion. This occurred in *Young, James and Webster v UK*,[324] where the Court of its own motion invited the TUC to submit comments and to appear as a witness on certain factual matters, which it did, albeit in support of the argument that the closed shop was compatible with the Convention. It also requested the UN to intervene in *Behrami and Saramati v France, Germany and Norway*,[325] which concerned the actions of a UN peacekeeping force.

There is no doubt that the Court has been greatly assisted over the years by third party interventions, particularly by NGOs that have been able to provide much relevant information concerning comparative and international law and practice. Such a contribution not only brings to the Court's attention relevant judicial authorities, but also greatly assists the Court in determining whether a common ground exists between the contracting parties on particular issues. The practice that the new Court has developed over the years is thus based on its own desire to have as much relevant information at its disposal as possible when deciding a case.

4. ARTICLE 41: JUST SATISFACTION

Article 41[326] reads:

> If the Court finds that there has been a violation of the Convention or the Protocols thereto, and if the internal law of the High Contracting Party concerned allows only partial reparation to be made, the Court shall, if necessary, afford just satisfaction to the injured party.

The case law under Article 41 (which replaces Article 50) is characterized by the lack of a consistently applied law of damages at the level of detail which one would find in national systems and which permit specific calculations to be made on the basis of precedent for injury, loss of life, unlawful imprisonment, and loss of property. The Court applies a series of general principles—as set out later—to the facts of each case when a violation has been found.[327] Given the existence of five Sections and a Grand Chamber all taking decisions on just satisfaction, problems of consistency of awards have inevitably crept in, especially in the area of non-pecuniary awards. The Court's response has been to set up an Article 41 Unit with the Registry of the Court to advise the Chambers on the appropriate level of awards in similar cases and to adopt a series of detailed tables setting out a method of calculation of non-pecuniary damage in respect of each article of the

---

[324] A 44 (1981) para 8. The Chamber in *Andrejeva v Latvia No 55707/00* hudoc (2006) (currently pending before the Grand Chamber following relinquishment of jurisdiction) invited the Russian and Ukrainian governments to intervene, the applicant having worked in both countries. The issue concerns a pension dispute. The invitation was not accepted. [325] Hudoc (2007) GC.

[326] See the Court's Practice Direction on just satisfaction claims (28 March 2007) for a summary of the principles that govern its awards http://echr.coe.int/Documents/PD_satisfaction_claims_ENG.pdf.

[327] For commentaries on the Court's practice, see Shelton, *Remedies in International Human Rights Law*, 2005, pp 294 *et seq*; Bernhardt, *Schachter Collection*, p. 243; Costa, in Fairgrieve *et al*, eds, *Tort Liability of Public Authorities in Comparative Perspective*, 2002; Myjer, in Vandenberghe *et al*, eds, *Property and Human Rights*. 2006; Leach, *Taking a Case to the European Court of Human Rights*, 2nd edn, 2005, p 397 *et seq*; and Loucaides, 2 EHRLR 182 (2008); Reid, *A Practitioners Guide to the ECHR*, 4th edn, 2012, pp 841–7 and 850. For a highly critical view of the case law on Article 41, see Tavernier, 72 RDH 945 (2007).

Convention. The concern was not only to ensure consistency of awards as between the Court's five Sections, but also to ensure consistency as between the different articles of the Convention that have been violated since it had been observed that on occasions the awards for very serious breaches (loss of life or torture) were lower than awards for lesser breaches (loss of liberty or freedom of expression). The approach in respect of each Article is to indicate a minimum award and a maximum, bearing in mind the type of violation found. Thus, for example, the award for a substantive breach of Articles 2 and 3 will be higher than the award for a procedural violation of these provisions. The seriousness of the facts, particularly where breaches of Articles 2 and 3 are concerned, and the degree of relationship between the applicant and the victim are also factors to take into account. The resulting amounts awarded under each article will also be adjusted with reference to adjustment tables to take into account the standard of living in the country. Thus awards concerning countries such as Switzerland or the United Kingdom will be considerably higher than awards concerning poorer countries such as Albania, Bulgaria or Azerbaijan. The Court has also adopted tables in respect of non-pecuniary awards concerning length of judicial proceedings for breaches of Article 6(1), which take into account the length of the proceedings and the number of levels of jurisdiction with possibilities for increase and decrease having regard to the subject matter of the proceedings and the number of applicants.[328] A similar table has also been drawn up in respect of complaints concerning the non-enforcement of domestic judgments. It should be stressed that the Court considers that the purpose of the tables is to provide guidance for the different sections and the Grand Chamber. The tables are thus not written in stone. Moreover, the award of compensation remains a discretionary one and the Court may consider that the finding of a breach is sufficient vindication of the applicant's rights on the facts of the particular case. The tables mentioned earlier are also internal documents for the use of the Court with a view to ensuring greater consistency in awards. They have not yet been made public, although government agents have called on the Court to do so in order to guide national courts when they make awards for breaches of convention rights and generally make the sums awarded more predictable.[329] To date, the Court has been reluctant to do so on the basis that it risks adding a new level of dispute between the parties if the sums awarded are not seen as conforming to the tables—something that is perfectly possible given the inherent discretionary nature of the award coupled with the Court's appreciation of the seriousness of the facts. The matter is the subject of continuing discussion within the Court. In any event, it is open to the parties to study the Court's awards in its copious case law concerning each jurisdiction in order to determine the level of damages, if any, that might be awarded in respect of specific breaches concerning a particular country.

Despite the wording of Article 41 (that the Court shall afford just satisfaction 'if the internal law of the High Contracting Party concerned allows only partial reparation'), the Court does not require an applicant who has won his case to avail of national procedures to secure compensation even if these were available. The Court has indicated that it would

[328] Generally where there are multiple applicants, the Court has indicated that the awards to each applicant should be lower, although it has also indicated that in a particular case there might also be elements that justified a higher award. For the Court, the fact that a single set of proceedings with a shared objective had been brought alleviated the inconvenience and uncertainty experienced on account of the delay and so meant a reduction in the amount of the award: *Arvanitaki-Roboti and others v Greece* hudoc (2008) GC, 91 applicants complaining of length of civil proceedings; paras 29–32. Also *Selahattin Çetinkaya and others v Turkey* hudoc (2009), where a joint sum was awarded to a large number of applicants who were heirs to the original party to the national proceedings.

[329] This was also recommended by the Woolf Report (the Review of the Working Methods of the European Court of Human Rights, December 2005). See p 41 of the report, available at http://www.echr.coe.int.

not be compatible with the effective protection of human rights to require an applicant who has already exhausted domestic remedies to initiate further proceedings.[330] Nor does the fact that the applicant might later obtain damages before a domestic court prevent the Court from making an award.[331] The Court will not award punitive damages, but it has shown itself willing to take into account elements that militate in favour of an enhanced award.[332]

When it finds one or more violations of the Convention, it will, in the same judgment, consider what, if any, just satisfaction to award the applicant under Article 41 of the Convention. The award of just satisfaction, as previously indicated, is not a right when a violation has been found. It is a matter entirely within the Court's discretion. Part of the explanation for this is that Article 46 requires states to abide by the final judgments of the Court in any case to which they are parties, execution being supervised by the Committee of Ministers. A judgment in which the Court finds a breach imposes on the respondent state a legal obligation not just to pay those concerned the sums awarded by way of just satisfaction, but also to choose, subject to supervision by the Committee of Ministers, the general and/or, if appropriate, individual measures to be adopted in their domestic legal order to put an end to the violation found by the Court and to redress so far as possible its effects.[333] Hence the purpose of awarding sums by way of just satisfaction is to provide reparation solely for damage suffered by those concerned to the extent that such events constitute a consequence of the violation that cannot otherwise be remedied.[334] Thus the Court may and frequently does decide to hold that the finding of a violation is, in itself, sufficient vindication of the applicant's rights and limit its award to costs and expenses. The Court will not make an award of its own motion where no claim has been made or where a claim is made out of time.[335] In a minority of cases and in accordance with Rule 75 of the Rules of Court, the Court may decide that the question of just satisfaction is not ready for decision and reserve its decision in whole or in part on the question. This occurs most frequently in cases concerning Article 1 of Protocol 1, when the calculation of pecuniary loss may be complex and require further deliberation.[336] When it does so, and when the matter is ready for decision (usually after further observations from the parties), it will render a separate judgment if the parties have not managed to settle the issue themselves. If there is a settlement, the Court will verify the 'equitable nature' of the agreement and, if satisfied, strike the case out of its list.[337] It has been the practice of the Court occasionally to reserve Article 41 when it indicates general measures under Article 46.[338]

The Court makes awards under three headings: costs and expenses; awards for pecuniary damage; and awards for non-pecuniary damage. Since 2002, the awards have all been made in euros, to enable the Court to facilitate consistency between different countries. Awards are usually payable to the applicant, although the Court may provide that they be held for the applicant's benefit where minors or mentally incapacitated persons are involved, or where the applicant can no longer be located.[339] It may also in certain circumstances indicate particular individual or general measures contracting parties must

---

[330] *Barberà, Messegué and Jabardo v Spain* A 285-C (1994) para 17 PC.

[331] *Mikheyev v Russia* hudoc (2006) para 155.

[332] *Burdov v Russia* hudoc (2009) para 156; *Oyal v Turkey* hudoc (2010); *Mikheyev v Russia*, para 155.

[333] *Papamichalopoulos and Others v Greece* A 330-B (1995) para 34.

[334] *Scozzari and Giunta v Italy* 2000-VIII; 35 EHRR 243 paras 248–50 GC.

[335] Eg, *Nasri v France* A 320-B (1995) para 49. See rule 60 of the Rules of Court.

[336] Eg, *Vistiņš and Perepjolkins v Latvia* hudoc (2012) GC and, as regards just satisfaction, see hudoc (2014).

[337] Rule 75(4). See section on friendly settlement in section 2.XIII of this chapter.

[338] See *Broniowski v Poland* 2004-V; 40 EHRR 495 GC.

[339] *Holy Synod of the Bulgarian Orthodox Church (Metropolitan Inokentiy) and Others v Bulgaria* hudoc (2009); *Muminov v Russia* hudoc (2010).

take in order to remedy the violation found,[340] although in general these stop short of specific consequential measures, for example, that the state is required to take penal or administrative action in regard to the persons responsible for the infringement.[341] In the operative provisions of the judgment, the Court will provide that just satisfaction is to be paid within three months, failing which default interest is payable at a particular rate.

The process of considering the application of Article 41 will start when the Court sends the government's observations to the applicant's legal representative for comment. At the same time, the representative will be invited to submit his claims for just satisfaction. Where the joint procedure is used under Article 29(3) (ie in most cases), the Article 41 claims must be submitted with the observations in reply on both the admissibility and merits of the application. The representative will be reminded of Rule 60 of the Rules of Court, which provides that an applicant who wishes to obtain an award of just satisfaction under Article 41 must make a specific claim to that effect. The same rule states that the applicant must submit itemized particulars of all claims, together with any relevant supporting documents.[342] The claims are then sent to the respondent government for comment. The procedure in WECL cases is set out above in section 2.VIII.

I. COSTS AND EXPENSES

As regards costs and expenses, the Court is normally strict with representatives and frequently finds that they have either failed to itemize their costs properly, or that the number of hours billed is excessive, or that the hourly rate is excessive. Time limits for the submission of claims should be respected and the Court will not usually grant extensions of time limits in respect of Article 41 submissions unless good cause is shown for the delay. As it frequently states, an applicant is entitled to reimbursement of his costs and expenses only insofar as it has been shown that these relate to the violation(s) found, have been actually and necessarily incurred, and are reasonable as to quantum.[343] Any sums paid under the Court's legal aid scheme will be deducted from the award. Nonetheless, the costs of a full legal team can be claimed provided each of the representatives' costs are within these bounds and are properly itemized. Thus for a complex case, there will be no bar on claiming the costs of an instructing solicitor and both senior and junior counsel, though this must not involve an unnecessary duplication of work.[344] Additionally, the Court may award a lump sum to the applicant, which may prove problematic when this is a percentage of what is claimed and there are several legal representatives seeking to recover their fees. The Court is not bound by the scale of fees applied in national law, but these may be used by the Court as a benchmark for its calculation. Costs will not be awarded where a lawyer has acted free of charge. The applicant must have paid them or be bound to pay them pursuant to a legal or contractual obligation. Expenses will be considered under the same rubric, save for when the applicant obtains leave to represent himself,

---

[340] See section 5 of this chapter.

[341] For example, in *Dickson v UK* hudoc (2007); 46 EHRR 927 para 88 GC, the Court refused to order the government to provide artificial insemination facilities to a prisoner, despite having found that the failure of the UK prison authorities was a breach of his and his wife's Article 8 rights.

[342] Rule 60 is supplemented by the Practice Direction on just satisfaction claims (28 March 2007).

[343] Eg, in *Sahin v Germany* 2003-VIII para 105 GC and *Adams v Romania* hudoc (2011). They are also only recoverable insofar as they relate to the violation found: see *Beyeler v Italy* hudoc (2002) GC; *Adams v Romania* hudoc (2011).

[344] *Associated Society of Locomotive Engineers and Firemen (ASLEF) v UK* hudoc (2007); 45 EHRR 793 para 60.

in which case he may claim expenses but not costs for the time he or she has spent working on the case.[345] Expenses incurred in respect of translation costs, photocopies, and the use of expert testimony may be recoverable if such expenses have been actually and reasonably incurred.[346] It is in principle open to applicants to seek recovery of costs and expenses incurred before the domestic courts; the Court will only make such an award where these proceedings were concerned with preventing or seeking redress for the alleged violation of the Convention.[347] Where the Court finds that there is only a violation as regards part of the case presented, this may result in the Court reducing the amount awarded for costs and expenses.[348] Finally, Rule 43(4) provides that an award of costs may be made by the Court in respect of an application that has been struck out. This provision was added to the Rules in recognition of the work done by a legal representative in a case which may be struck out because the proceedings have led to some form of redress being given.[349]

II. PECUNIARY AND NON-PECUNIARY DAMAGE

Pecuniary damage encompasses losses of a pecuniary nature that are directly linked to the violation found.[350] This may include, for example, loss of earnings or reduction in the value of property, fines, and taxes imposed or inadequate levels of compensation for expropriated property. For an award of pecuniary damage to be made, the applicant must demonstrate, to the Court's satisfaction, that there is causal link between the violation and any financial loss alleged. This is seen as a matter of proof rather than speculation. It is easily established when there has been a taking of property, but significantly more difficult in other contexts. For example, a finding of a violation of Article 6 in the context of a criminal trial will not allow the applicant to claim lost earnings for any time he has spent in prison. However, the Court has been prepared to compensate for lost earnings in other situations, notably in right to life cases when the applicant is the widow or another dependent of the deceased,[351] or where there have been lost earnings flowing from the Convention breach.[352] In *Oyal v Turkey* (negligence by medical staff leading to the applicant contracting AIDS) the Court awarded the applicant a substantial sum for both pecuniary and non-pecuniary damage in addition to full and free medical care for the rest of the applicant's life.[353]

---

[345] *Steel and Morris v UK* 2005-II; 41 EHRR 403 para 112 (and references therein) and *Bhandari v UK* hudoc (2007) paras 28–30.

[346] Eg, *Salomonsson v Sweden* hudoc (2002); *Fretté v France* 2002-I; 38 EHRR 438 para 56; *Avkhadova and Others v Russia* hudoc (2013).

[347] *King v UK* hudoc (2004); 41 EHRR 11 para 52; *Associated Society of Locomotive Engineers and Firemen (ASLEF) v UK* hudoc (2007); 45 EHRR 793, para 58; *IJL, GMR and AKP v UK* hudoc (2001).

[348] *A and others v UK* GC hudoc (2009) para 256.

[349] *Pisano v Italy* hudoc (2002) paras 51–6 GC, although the same rules on submitting specific claims and schedules of costs applies: also *Sisojeva and Others v Latvia* hudoc (2007); 45 EHRR 753 paras 133 and 134 GC. Cf, *Paez v Sweden* 1997-VII, where the former Court struck out an Article 3 case concerning expulsion to Peru after the applicant had been allowed to stay in Sweden and after extensive examination of the case by the Commission which expressed the view that there would be no violation in sending him back. At that time the rules did not allow an award in such circumstances.

[350] See Reid, *A Practitioners Guide to the ECHR*, 4th edn, 2012, for detailed tables of awards made by the Court for pecuniary and non-pecuniary loss.

[351] *Imakayeva v Russia* 2006-XIII para 213; *Çakıcı v Turkey* 1999-IV para 127; 31 EHRR 133 GC.

[352] *Lustig-Prean and Beckett v UK* hudoc (2000); 31 EHRR 601; *Young, James and Webster v UK* A 55 (1982) para 11.

[353] Hudoc (2010) (€300.000 pecuniary damages and €78,000 non-pecuniary damages).

Claims for pecuniary damage will normally arise in cases involving property under Article 1 of Protocol 1.[354] Where the Court has found a violation, this can often give rise to complex calculations of how much to award, especially when the property in question is of significant value.[355] The amount awarded in these cases is rarely the market value. In the *Former King of Greece* case, the Court found that less than full compensation could be justified where the taking of property had been intended to complete 'such fundamental changes of a country's constitutional system as the transition from monarchy to republic'.[356] However the Court will normally order full compensation in the face of unlawful dispossession or *de facto* expropriation, as in the case of *Guiso-Gallisay v Italy*, where the authorities commenced construction on the applicant's land without formal expropriation.[357] The Court, in a change of its case law, clarified that the amount payable in compensation was the value of the property at the moment of its loss—adjusted by inflation and increased by interest up to the date of judgment.

In deciding how much to award, the Court will follow a number of steps. First, it will decide whether *restitutio in integrum* is possible. If it is not or if national law only allows partial reparation, the Court will consider making an award.[358] In property cases, it will then consider whether the parties can agree on the value of the property and, if so, whether they can agree to a settlement of the matter. If they cannot agree to either, the Court may place the valuation in the hands of an independent expert and then, basing itself on the expert's report, award pecuniary damages on the usual equitable basis.[359]

The Court will award non-pecuniary damages (or moral damages) on the basis of equitable considerations more readily than it awards pecuniary damages, although there is usually little explanation as to how it reaches the sums awarded. This head of damage covers such matters as pain and suffering, anguish and distress, inconvenience, and loss of opportunity.[360] For the most part, the amount awarded under this head will be in proportion to the seriousness of the violation (or violations) and its effect on the applicant. The highest awards will therefore tend to be made in relation to violations of Articles 2 and 3 of the Convention.[361] However, given that the Court always rules on an equitable basis and that there is some adjustment according to the cost of living in each member state, past awards are not always reliable predictors of future awards. This is especially so when

---

[354] For example, *Beyeler v Italy* hudoc (2002) GC; *Brumărescu v Romania* 2001-I; 33 EHRR 36 GC; *Iatridis v Greece* 2000-XI GC; *James and Others v UK* A 98 (1986); 8 EHRR 123; *Lithgow and Others v UK* A 102 (1986); 8 EHRR 329; *Papamichalopoulos and Others v Greece* A 330-B (1995).

[355] Eg, in *Former King of Greece and Others v Greece* hudoc (2002) GC (see also the principal judgment 2000-XII; 33 EHRR 516), about the expropriation of the former king's properties after his deposition, the final award ran to over €13 million.   [356] *Former King of Greece and Others v Greece*, para 87.

[357] GC hudoc (2009) paras 98–107.

[358] *Former King of Greece and Others v Greece* hudoc (2002) GC, para 73; *Beyeler v Italy* hudoc (2002) GC (just satisfaction).   [359] *Pasculli v Italy* hudoc (2007).

[360] The case law for loss of opportunity is not always consistent, eg, *Bönisch v Austria* A 103 (1986); 13 EHRR 409, and *Weeks v UK* A 145-A (1988); 13 EHRR 435 para 13 PC; *H v UK* A 136-B (1988) PC, where awards under this head were made. In other cases the Court has refused to speculate whether there were such losses: see eg, *Perks and Others v UK* hudoc (1999); 30 EHRR 33, where the applicant was unrepresented before a magistrates' court which sentenced him to a prison term.

[361] Awards today, in Russian cases, for a substantive violation of Article 2 (disappearance) coupled with violations of Articles 5 and 13 are around €60,000: *Alpatu Israilova v Russia* hudoc (2013); *Vakhayeva v Russia* hudic (2012); *Ilayeva and others* v Russia hudoc (2012); *Ulmarova and others* v Russia hudoc (2012); also *Bitiyeva and X v Russia* hudoc (2007), the death of four family members gave rise to an award of €85,000. In *Mikheyev v Russia* hudoc (2006), the Court awarded €120,000 in respect of a brutal torture which left the applicant paralysed. In *Abuyeva v Russia* hudoc (2010), which concerned the deaths of twenty-four relatives caused by the shelling of a village in Chechnya, the Court awarded €1.72 million.

the violation turns on the particular facts of the application, as is frequently the case with Articles 8, 9, 10, and 11 of the Convention. Nonetheless, thanks to the Court's internal tables, there is greater consistency in such awards as regards most repetitive cases, whether they are particular types of applications from one country (such as non-enforcement of court judgments) or the Court's most common type of application, the length of civil or criminal proceedings. For instance, for the latter, the Court will normally make an award based on the number of years the proceedings lasted, as against the number of instances (levels of jurisdiction) before which they took place.

As to who can claim non-pecuniary damages, this now appears to be virtually commensurate with victim status under Article 34. There were indications that only individuals and not, say, companies or other legal persons, were eligible for non-pecuniary damages. However, in *Comingersoll SA v Portugal*,[362] a length of proceedings case, the Court found that this possibility could not be excluded. The unreasonable length of the proceedings had caused inconvenience and prolonged uncertainty to the company, its directors, and shareholders, justifying an award of damages.[363] This has subsequently been confirmed in *Centro Europa 7 SRL and Di Stefano*,[364] where an award was made to cover disruption of the management of the company and anxiety and inconvenience caused to the management team.

It is always open to the Court to hold that the finding of a violation is sufficient just satisfaction.[365] This has happened regularly in the context of the due process rights set out in Articles 5 and 6 of the Convention, where the Court has stated that it would not make an award on the speculative basis that the applicant would not have been convicted if he had had the benefit of the guarantees of Article 5 or 6 of the Convention.[366] It will also take this approach when the focus of the application is having one's rights vindicated rather than seeking damages *per se*. For example, in *Hirst v UK (No 2)*,[367] in finding a violation stemming from legislation prohibiting prisoners from voting in elections, the Grand Chamber found that the government would be required to secure the right to vote in compliance with its judgment. In the circumstances, it considered that this could be regarded as providing the applicant with just satisfaction.

It is also open to the Court, in the exercise of its discretion, to decline to make an award on public policy grounds. This happens rarely, but did occur in *McCann and Others v UK*,[368] concerning the shooting of three terrorist suspects in Gibraltar by British special

[362] 2000-IV; 31 EHRR 772 paras 32–7 GC. In assessing this issue, 'account should be taken of the company's reputation, uncertainty in decision-planning, disruption in the management of the company (for which there is no precise method of calculating the consequences) and lastly, albeit to a lesser degree, the anxiety and inconvenience caused to the members of the management team'; para 35. See also Emberland, 74 BYIL 409 (2003).

[363] Confirmed in *Sovtransavto Holding v Ukraine* hudoc (2003) paras 78–82.

[364] Hudoc (2012) (violation of Article 10): also *Rock Ruby Hotels Ltd v Turkey (just satisfaction)* hudoc (2010) (violation of Article 1 Protocol 1).

[365] For example, *IK v Austria* hudoc (2013); *Barborski v Belgium* hudoc (2013), where period of detention found unlawful by the Court had been deducted from the remainder of the sentence. This approach is now uncommon. It can be said that there is almost a presumption that an award will be made even in cases involving terrorism: *A and others v United Kingdom* hudoc (2009) GC. Making no award has come in for robust criticism by some of the judges, eg, Judge Bonello's partly dissenting opinion in *Nikolova v Bulgaria* 1999-II; 31 EHRR 64 GC.

[366] For Article 5, see *Thompson v UK* hudoc (2004); 40 EHRR 245 para 50. For Article 6, the standard formula is to state that it is impossible speculate as to the outcome of the criminal trial had the violation of Article 6(1) of the Convention not occurred (see eg, *Findlay v UK* 1997-I; 24 EHRR 221 paras 85 and 88).

[367] 2005-IX; 42 EHRR 849 para 60 GC.

[368] A 324 (1995); 21 EHRR 97 para 219 GC. Cf, *Del Rio Prada v Spain* hudoc (2013) GC, where considerable damages were awarded to a convicted terrorist for breaches of Articles 5 and 7.

forces. The Court had regard to the fact that the deceased had been intending to plant a bomb in Gibraltar and so stated that it did not consider it appropriate to make an award under this head.

The Court has also had to consider whether the sums of money it awards under Article 41 can be accompanied by orders or directions that the money should be freely enjoyed by the applicant without attachment or other consequences for the applicant's existing financial situation. The matter first arose in *Allenet de Ribemont v France*,[369] where the applicant asked that any sums awarded to him be free from attachment to avoid enforcement of an outstanding French civil judgment. The Court declined this request, holding that it had no jurisdiction to issue such an order to a state. In *Velikova v Bulgaria*,[370] concerning the death of the applicant's husband in police custody, the applicant requested the Court to order that there should be no negative consequences for her, such as reduction in social benefits due to her, as a result of the receipt of any non-pecuniary damages. The Court noted that it would be incongruous to award the applicant an amount in compensation for, *inter alia*, deprivation of life constituting a violation of Article 2 of the Convention if the state itself were then allowed to attach this amount. The purpose of compensation for non-pecuniary damage would inevitably be frustrated and the Article 41 system perverted if such a situation were to be deemed satisfactory. However, the Court again found it had no power to make such an order and left the matter to the discretion of the Bulgarian authorities.[371]

5. ARTICLE 46

Article 46(1) provides: 'The High Contracting Parties undertake to abide by the final judgment of the Court in any case where they are parties.' A Contracting Party is under an obligation to give effect to the judgment of the Court and a complete or partial failure to do so can engage the state's international responsibility. The state party is:

> 'under an obligation not just to pay those concerned the sums awarded by way of just satis-faction, but also to take individual and/or, if appropriate, general measures in its domestic legal order to put an end to the violation found by the Court and to redress the effects, the aim being to put the applicant, as far as possible, in the position he would have been in had the requirements of the Convention not been disregarded.'[372]

The Court has in the past traditionally been reluctant to make 'consequential orders' in the form of directions or recommendations to the state to take a particular course of action. Thus, for example, in *Ireland v UK*,[373] it refused the request by the Irish government to order that criminal prosecutions be brought against those responsible for ill-treatment in breach of Article 3. On other occasions it has rejected invitations to require the state to undertake that children will not be corporally punished or to take steps to prevent such

---

[369] *Allenet de Ribemont v France* A 308 (1995) para 65.   [370] 2000-VI para 96.
[371] See also the earlier case of *Selmouni v France* 1999-V; 29 EHRR 403 paras 132 and 133 GC, where the Court made a similar observation and finding in respect of sums awarded in respect of a violation of Article 3.
[372] *Vgt Verein gegen Tierfabriken (VgT) v Switzerland (No 2)* hudoc (2009) GC paras 85–6. See Ch 4, section 3.   [373] Series A25 (1978); 2 EHRR 25 para 187.

breaches in the future.[374] This approach was based on the view that the Court only possesses powers to make an award of compensation.

However, in response to criticism that the Court should give more guidance to the states and to the Committee of Ministers in its judgments as to what corrective measures would be appropriate in the light of any violations found, the Court may also in exceptional cases indicate under the rubric of Article 46 what would be the most appropriate individual and general measures needed to provide redress. The most common instance has been in expropriation cases, where the Court has given states the choice to return the property or to pay the value of it in compensation to the applicant.[375] In *Assandize v Georgia*,[376] the Court, having found the applicant's detention to be illegal, held that Georgia had to secure his release at the earliest possible date. It was considered that the nature of the violation was such as to leave no real choice as to the measures required to remedy it. A similar direction was made in the case of *Illascu and Others v Moldova and Russia*.[377] Both directions in these cases were set out in the operative part of the judgment and were thus binding on the state.

It is now an established practice—although one that is exercised cautiously and in exceptional circumstances—for the Court to indicate general measures in judgments which reveal problems or gaps in legislation, administrative practices, and judicial remedies or a lack of other essential safeguards. Thus it has indicated under Article 46 that the state is required to take general measures to remedy depreciation in compensation for expropriated property;[378] to remove details of religious affiliation from identity cards;[379] to eliminate structural problems of length of pre-trial detention;[380] to remedy systemic defects in legislation on the restitution of land;[381] to reform the system of judicial discipline,[382] to give but a few examples. It also indicates what individual measures may be required. For example, that the state take all possible steps to obtain assurance from Iraqi authorities that applicants would not be subjected to death penalty;[383] that an independent investigation be carried out into the proportionality of the use of lethal force;[384] that a disproportionate exclusion order be revoked;[385] to secure the applicant's re-instatement as a Supreme Court judge (in the operative part of the judgment).[386]

The Court has indicated in *Khodorkovskiy v Russia*[387] that it will only issue such indications on an exceptional basis to put an end to a systemic problem, or a continuous situation in breach of the Convention, or to indicate the remedy required when the nature of the violation left no real choice. In that case it was not prepared to request that an independent expert be allowed to examine the applicant's prison conditions or that the authorities not keep him in a cage during criminal proceedings—judging that such requests did not

---

[374] *Campbell and Cosans v UK* A 48 (1982) para 16; *McGoff v Sweden* A 83 (1984) para 31; 8 EHRR 246; *Gillow v UK* A 109 (1986) para 9.

[375] See eg, *Former King of Greece and Others v Greece* hudoc (2002) GC para 77; *Brumărescu v Romania* 2001-I; 33 EHRR 36 GC, at points 1 and 2 of the operative part.

[376] 2004-II; 39 EHRR 653. For a recent example of similar directions in the operative part of the judgment, see *Del Rio Prada v Spain* hudoc (2013), where the Court (GC) required Spain to release the applicant from prison (the applicant was released within several days of the Court's judgment); and *Olexandr Volkov v Ukraine* hudoc (2013), where the Court ordered the applicant's re-instatement as a judge.

[377] 2004-VII; 40 EHRR 1030 GC, at point 22 of the operative part.

[378] *Yetiş and Others v Turkey* hudoc (2010). 　　[379] *Sinan Işık v Turkey* hudoc (2010).

[380] *Cahıt Demırel v Turkey* hudoc (2009); also *Dimitrov and Hamanov v Bulgaria* and *Finger v Bulgaria* hudoc (2011) (to introduce remedies for length of civil and criminal proceedings).

[381] *Faimblat v Romania* hudoc (2009). 　　[382] *Oleksandr Volkov v Ukraine* hudoc (2013).

[383] *Al-Saadoon and Mufdhi v UK* hudoc (2010).

[384] *Abuyeva and Others v Russia* hudoc (2010). 　　[385] *Emre v Switzerland* hudoc (2011).

[386] *Oleksandr Volkov v Ukraine* hudoc (2013). 　　[387] Hudoc (2011) paras 250–61.

fall into the categories where indications would be made. It should be stressed that such indications are not binding, as such, on the state, unless they appear in the operative part of the Court's judgment, as in *Assanidze v Georgia*[388] or the Court's pilot judgments.[389] In most cases they will appear in a part of the judgment devoted to Article 46 and will not appear in the operative part unless the judgment deals with an exceptional situation calling for immediate action.[390] It still remains to the national authorities to determine how to give effect to the Court's judgment when such non-binding suggestions are made.[391] However, they give a clear indication to the Committee of Ministers of the steps that the Court considers to be legally appropriate to respond to the violation found and, as such, have become essential to the proper execution of the judgment.

As we have seen, the Court has gone even further in various pilot judgments.[392] In *Gurov v Moldova*,[393] the Court found the applicant's Article 6 rights had been violated by the hearing of her civil claim by a tribunal that was not established by law (the term of office of one of the judges having expired). The Court noted the most appropriate form of relief would be to ensure that the applicant was granted in due course a re-hearing of the case by an independent and impartial tribunal. This was aided by the fact that the possibility existed under Moldovan law for the applicant, if she so requested, to obtain a re-hearing of her civil case in the light of the Court's finding that the proceedings did not comply with Article 6 guarantees. It was content, therefore, to make no award of damages and let the case take this course.[394]

The Court has stated that it does not have jurisdiction in general to order the re-opening of judicial proceedings.[395] However, it has made an exception in criminal proceedings, and where it has found there to be an unfair trial it often indicates that the applicants be given a re-trial if they so request.[396] It considers that this is the most effective way of remedying an unfair trial, although it has indicated there may be specific circumstances where such an option may not be feasible.[397] However, the Court has not been prepared to order the quashing of criminal convictions.[398] Where proceedings are still pending, the Court may make indications in respect of them. In *Naime Doğan and Others v Turkey*,[399] after finding a violation of Article 6(1) in respect of the length of civil proceedings that were ongoing, the Court indicated that the subsequent expedition and resolution of those proceedings within the shortest possible period of time offered appropriate redress for the violation.

---

[388] 2004-II; 39 EHRR 653.

[389] See, eg, *Kurić and Others v Slovenia* hudoc (2012) GC.

[390] See, eg, *Savriddin Dzhurayev v Russia* hudoc (2013) and the examples set out in n 376.

[391] 'Admittedly, subject to monitoring by the Committee of Ministers, the respondent State in principle remains free to choose the means by which it will discharge its obligations under Article 46 § 1 of the Convention, provided that such means are compatible with the conclusions set out in the Court's judgment': *Verein gegen Tierfabriken Schweiz (VGT) v Switzerland (No 2)* hudoc (2009) para 89 GC; also *Sedjovic v Italy* 2006-II GC.   [392] For these judgments, see section 3.VIII of this chapter.

[393] Hudoc (2006) paras 41–4.

[394] Other examples include *Malahov v Moldova* hudoc (2007) para 47 (that the applicant's appeal should be heard) and *Bujniţa v Moldova* hudoc (2007) para 29 (that the applicant's final acquittal be confirmed by the authorities and his conviction in breach of the Convention to be erased).

[395] *Verein gegen Tierfabriken Schweiz (VGT) v Switzerland (No 2)* hudoc (2009) para 89 GC.

[396] *Krasniki v Czech Republic* hudoc (2006) para 93. For instances where it has been done under Article 46, see *Sejdovic v Italy* 2006-II paras 119 *et seq* GC; *Öcalan v Turkey* 2005-IV; 41 EHRR 985 para 210 GC. Prior to such cases, such indications were only noted under Article 41: *Gençel v Turkey* hudoc (2003) para 27; *Tahir Duran v Turkey* hudoc (2004) para 23; *Somogyi v Italy* 2004-IV para 86.

[397] For example, *Öcalan v Turkey*, para 21.   [398] *Oberschlick v Austria* A 204 para 65 (1991).

[399] Hudoc (2007) para 34.

In *L v Lithuania*,[400] the applicant had started gender reassignment surgery but could not complete the surgery because there was no domestic law enabling him to do so. The Court found a violation of Article 8. Turning to Article 41, the Court considered that the applicant's claim for pecuniary damage would be satisfied by the enactment of the legislation within three months of the judgment becoming final. If that proved impossible, the Court was of the view that the applicant could have the final stages of the necessary surgery performed abroad and financed, at least in part, by the state. Consequently, as an alternative in the absence of any such subsidiary legislation, the Court awarded the applicant €40,000 for pecuniary damage. In *Oyal v Turkey*,[401] the Court found that there had been medical negligence resulting in the applicant contracting AIDS. It required the state in the operative part of the judgment to provide costly medical treatment to the applicant for life.

6. PROTOCOL 14

Protocol 14 was the result of more than four years' reflection by the Council of Europe's Steering Committee for Human Rights on the need for urgent measures to be taken to assist the Court to carry out its functions in the light of the ever-increasing number of applications being brought to the Court.[402] As we have seen earlier, it has made important changes to the functioning of the Court to enable it to dispose more rapidly of clearly inadmissible and repetitive cases and to concentrate its resources on more deserving cases by the introduction of the single judge procedure,[403] the Committee of three judges empowered to deal with WECL cases,[404] and a new inadmissibility criterion enabling the Court to reject cases where 'the applicant has not suffered a significant disadvantage',[405] although the Protocol provided that the single judge and the Committees would not be able to apply this new criterion for two years.[406] These changes operated with retrospective effect since the entering into force of the Protocol on 1 June 2010.[407]

The Protocol also introduced a number of other significant changes to the Convention. It provided that judges will be elected for a single term of nine years and that they may not be re-elected;[408] that at the request of the plenary Court, the Committee of Ministers may for a fixed period reduce the number of judges in a Chamber to five;[409] that *ad hoc* judges shall be chosen by the President from a list of candidates submitted in advance by

---

[400] Hudoc (2007) para 74, as well as points 5 and 6 of the operative part of the judgment.

[401] Hudoc (2010). For an indication of both individual and general measures see *Driza v Albania* hudoc (2007) and *Dybeku v Albania* hudoc (2007).

[402] The Explanatory Report, paras 20–33, charts the work on the Protocol from the Rome Ministerial Conference on Human Rights in 2000, which took stock of the Court's growing case load, until the opening for signature of the Protocol on 13 May 2004.

[403] Article 27 and Explanatory Report, paras 6–67; see section 2.VII of this chapter.

[404] Article 28 and Explanatory Report, paras 68–72; see section 2.VIII.

[405] Article 35(3)(b) and Explanatory Report, paras 77–85; see Ch 2, section 5.I.

[406] Article 20 para 2 of the Protocol. The two-year period ended on 1 June 2012.

[407] Article 20 of the Protocol and Explanatory Report, para 105. The lengthy delay in Russia's ratification (2010) gave rise to an agreement amongst certain states to provisionally apply the single-judge and Committee procedure (the Madrid Agreement, 2009) and a Protocol 14 bis (2009), also enabling provisional application of these provisions (CETS 204). Both instruments ceased to have effect when Protocol 14 entered into force; see also the Court's website for further information.   [408] Article 23(2).

[409] Article 26(2).

the contracting party;[410] that the Court shall, in principle, decide on admissibility decisions and the merits in the same decision (apart from inter-state cases);[411] that the Court may explore the possibility of friendly settlement at any stage of the proceedings and that the resulting agreement shall be in the form of a decision whose execution is to be supervised by the Committee of Ministers.[412] The Protocol also confers a right on the Council of Europe Commissioner for Human Rights to submit written comments and take part in hearings[413] and on the Committee of Ministers to submit a request to the Court for interpretation of a judgment (for the purpose of supervision of execution of judgments), as well as the possibility of initiating infringement proceedings in respect of a contracting party which refuses to abide by a final judgment.[414] Finally, the Protocol provides that the European Union may accede to the Convention.[415]

The Committee of Ministers has also adopted a series of recommendations and resolutions concerning, *inter alia*, the use of pilot judgments, the practice of friendly settlements, the screening of draft laws for compatibility with the Convention, the improvement of domestic remedies, and the dissemination of Convention case law in the member states and university education and professional training in the Convention.[416]

7. REFORM OF THE COURT

The reform process[417] began with the preparation of Protocol 14 which was designed to give the Court more tools to deal with its constantly increasing case load. The failure of Russia to ratify the Protocol by 2009, having been opened for signature in 2004, led the then President of the Court (Jean-Paul Costa) to prepare a Memorandum drawing attention to the Court's increasing difficulties (continuing increase in new cases, widening gap between decisions delivered and the number of incoming applications, the increase

---

[410] Article 26(4). This provision responds to the criticism that under the current system the state is asked to nominate an *ad hoc* judge after the proceedings have commenced in full knowledge of the issues involved. See Explanatory Report, para 64.

[411] Article 29(1) and (2). In fact the current practice of the Court has evolved in this direction independently, with issues of admissibility and the merits being decided jointly in one judgment (except for inter-state cases); see section 2.XIX of this chapter.

[412] Article 39. The present practice of the Court has also evolved in this sense. Friendly settlement proceedings can be pursued at any stage of the procedure and, if agreement is reached prior to admissibility, the case will be struck out, with the solution reached being signalled to the Committee of Ministers. However, the provision providing for execution of the terms of the agreement to be supervised by the Committee of Ministers is an important new safeguard.

[413] Article 36(3); see section 3.IX of this chapter.

[414] Article 46(3), (4), and (5). Both procedures require a majority of two-thirds of the representatives entitled to sit on the Committee. The Report makes it clear that the request for interpretation should be used where difficulties arise on issues of interpretation of the judgment and not to examine the measures taken by a state in compliance with the judgment (para 97). It is also clear that infringement proceedings should only be taken in exceptional circumstances (paras 99–100). While it increases the powers available to the Committee where there has been non-compliance, it is doubted that transferring what is essentially a political problem back to the Court will help resolve matters. It may, however, buy time for the political issues to be resolved amicably.   [415] Article 59(2).

[416] See the Explanatory Report, at pp 52–81 for the texts of these instruments.

[417] On reform of the Court generally see n 2; also Reform of the European Human Rights System: Proceedings of the High-level Seminar, Oslo, 2004, Directorate General of Human Rights, Strasbourg: Council of Europe, 2004; *Guaranteeing the Effectiveness of the European Convention on Human Rights—Collected Texts*, 2004; Leach, 6 EHRLR 725 (2009); O'Boyle and Darcy, 52 GYIL 139 (2009).

in repetitive complaints) and calling for the holding of an inter-governmental confer-ence to take political decisions concerning the long-term future of the Court.[418] At the Conference, the states were expected to outline how they saw the Court in 2020 and to indicate the amendments to the system that would, in consequence, be required. They were also invited to set out the short- to medium-term proposals for change that did not require amendment of the Convention.[419] The Conference took place at Interlaken (Switzerland) in 2010 and led to the adoption of the Interlaken Declaration, whereby the states set out for the first time an all-important road map for the reform process, lead-ing towards the long-term effectiveness of the Convention system.[420] The Conference reaffirmed the fundamental importance of the right of individual petition, called on the states to guarantee and implement the Convention at national level, and addressed a vari-ety of crucial issues for the Court, such as the need for more effective filtering of cases, the problem of repetitive cases, the need to maintain the independence of judges and to preserve the impartiality and quality of the Court, the need for the supervision of judg-ments of the Court to be more effective, and a simplified procedure for amending the Convention (a Court Statute). The Conference also prepared an action plan requiring the Committee of Ministers to issue terms of reference in respect of specific proposals and to evaluate in the course of 2012–2015 the extent to which the implementation of Protocol 14 and the action plan had improved the situation of the Court.[421]

Two further Conferences on reform were held in Izmir (Turkey) in 2011 and in Brighton (2012), leading to the Izmir and Brighton Declarations which advanced the reform agenda in a more critical and often over-directive manner.[422] These conferences sustained and developed the process of reform begun at Interlaken, but also addressed additional issues of particular concern to the states, such as the increase in the number of interim measures and the need for the Court to deliver judgments that were clear and consistent and to observe the principle of subsidiarity. All three Declarations stressed the shared responsibility between the Court and the States to ensure the viability of the Convention system. So far, they have led to renewed support for the work of the Court and a determination to protect the effective functioning of what has been built up over the last

---

[418] Memorandum of the President of the Court with a view to preparing the Interlaken Conference 3 July 2009, available at www.echr.coe.int.   [419] Memorandum of the President of the Court.

[420] The Interlaken Declaration of 19 February 2010, available at www.echr.coe.int.

[421] The Interlaken Declaration of 19 February 2010, *in fine*.

[422] The Izmir Declaration (2011) and the Brighton Declaration (2012). The issue arises as to whether it is in keeping with the rule of law to seek to give directions to an independent court, even in the course of a generally beneficial reform process. For example, the Izmir Declaration summoned the Court to 'a. Apply fully, con-sistently and foreseeably all admissibility criteria and the rules regarding the scope of its jurisdiction, *ratione temporis, ratione loci, ratione personae* and *ratione materiae*; b. Give full effect to the new admissibility criterion in accordance with the principle, according to which the Court is not concerned by trivial matters (*de minimis non curat praetor*); c. Confirm in its case law that it is not a fourth-instance court, thus avoiding the re-examination of issues of fact and law decided by national courts; d. Establish and make public rules foreseeable for all the parties concerning the application of Article 41 of the Convention, including the level of just satisfaction which might be expected in different circumstances; e. Consider that decisions of the pan-els of five judges to reject requests for referral of cases to the Grand Chamber are clearly reasoned, thereby avoiding repetitive requests and ensuring better understanding of Chamber judgments'; Declaration point F (2); also, but less controversially, in the Brighton Declaration, 'Judgments of the Court need to be clear and consistent. This promotes legal certainty. It helps national courts apply the Convention more precisely, and helps potential applicants assess whether they have a well-founded application. Clarity and consistency are particularly important when the Court addresses issues of general principle. Consistency in the application of the Convention does not require that States Parties implement the Convention uniformly. The Court has indicated that it is considering an amendment to the Rules of Court making it obligatory for a Chamber to relinquish jurisdiction where it envisages departing from settled case law': para 23.

fifty years, and to the drafting of two important Protocols (15 and 16) and have given an extra impetus to the project of accession of the EU to the Convention system. They have also led to important changes within the Court itself.[423]

I. PROTOCOL 15

The new Protocol was drafted in the wake of the Brighton Declaration and gives effect to certain of its proposals.[424] Its most important provision is to insert into the Preamble of the Convention a reference to the margin of appreciation. This follows the discussion during the Brighton process when a majority of the states were unable to accept the UK's proposal that the reference to the margin should be contained in the text of the Convention. The resulting compromise is set out in Article 1:

> Affirming that the High Contracting Parties, in accordance with the principle of subsidiarity, have the primary responsibility to secure the rights and freedoms defined in this Convention and the Protocols thereto, and that in doing so they enjoy a margin of appreciation, subject to the supervisory jurisdiction of the European Court of Human Rights established by this Convention.

The Explanatory Report makes it clear that the reference is to the concept of the margin of appreciation as developed by the Court in its case law.[425] The question arises as to the future impact of this reference on the Court's decision-making. It is submitted that this is not a passing preambular reference which will have no effect. The Preamble to an international treaty is an important part of the treaty and it can be foreseen that this reference to the margin will now be regularly invoked by governments in future litigation challenging state actions or policies. The reference also suggests that the margin applies in respect of every article in the Convention, whereas it is clear from the case law that it does not apply in certain key areas, such as Article 2 and 3. It is also clear from the case law that the breadth of the margin varies according to the context of the case and the issues being examined.[426] The provision in the Explanatory Report is thus important, since it provides a clear indication that the reference in the Preamble does not purport to add anything that has not been developed by the Court in its case law. So why add it in the Preamble if that is the case? As the Explanatory Report states:

> A new recital has been added at the end of the Preamble of the Convention containing a reference to the principle of subsidiarity and the doctrine of the margin of appreciation. It is intended to enhance the transparency and accessibility of these characteristics of the Convention system and to be consistent with the doctrine of the margin of appreciation as developed by the Court in its case law.

---

[423] For reports of the practical measures taken by the Court as a result of the Interlaken process, see *The Interlaken Process and the Court*, 16 October 2012 and 28 August 2013, available at http://echr.coe.int/Documents/2012_Interlaken_Process_ENG.pdf.

[424] Opened for signature on 24 June 2013. CETS No 213. The text of the Protocol 15 and the Explanatory Report are available at http://www.echr.coe.int/Pages/home.aspx?p=court/reform.

[425] See para 7; also at para 9, 'The jurisprudence of the Court makes clear that the States Parties enjoy a margin of appreciation in how they apply and implement the Convention, depending on the circumstances of the case and the rights and freedoms engaged.' The Court in its opinion on the Protocol has also emphasized this point; para 4, available on the Court's website.   [426] See Ch 1, section 4.VII.

Against such a legislative background, it seems clear that the states have generally respected the Court's wish that the margin of appreciation should be left exclusively to the Court itself to determine, although it can safely be predicted, given the important role that the concept plays in adjudication, particularly in cases concerning general issues,[427] that the often heated discussion with the states as to how and when it should be applied by the Court is far from over.

An important change is also made to the six-month rule. The Protocol amends Article 35(1) by reducing the six-month rule to four months. This is justified in the Explanatory Report with reference to swifter communications technology and the existence of a similar time limit in many member states.[428] It was requested by the Court itself in its opinion for the Brighton Conference.[429] The Protocol also removes the veto of the parties over relinquishment,[430] simplifies the new admissibility criterion in Article 35(3) by amending that provision,[431] and amends Article 21 by providing that candidates for election shall be less than 65 'at the date by which the list has been requested by the Parliamentary Assembly'.[432]

II. REQUESTS FOR ADVISORY OPINIONS (PROTOCOL 16)

Provision is made in Protocol 16[433] for the 'highest courts and tribunals' of a High Contracting Party to request the Court for an advisory opinion 'on questions of principle relating to the interpretation or application of the rights and freedoms defined in the Convention or the Protocols thereto'.[434] This can only be done by the national court in the context of a case pending before it. Reasons shall be given for the request, and details of the legal and factual background of the pending case shall be provided.[435] A panel of five judges of the Grand Chamber shall decide whether to accept the request.[436] Reasons must be given if the Panel refuses. If accepted, it shall be dealt with by the Grand Chamber.[437] The advisory opinion, for which reasons must be given, will

[427] See, eg, the Court's judgment concerning the general issue relating to political advertising in the United Kingdom: *Animal Defenders International v United Kingdom* hudoc (2013) GC.

[428] Paragraphs 22 and 23 (transitional provisions). [429] Available on the Court's website.

[430] Article 3 amending Article 30 of the Convention, see section 1. XIX of this chapter. This is a welcome provision since the parties will no longer be able to thwart the intention of the Court to send a case to the Grand Chamber. However the states expect the Chamber to consult the parties on its intentions and to narrow down the case as far as possible, including by finding inadmissible any relevant parts of the case before relinquishing it. The Chamber is also invited to give specific indication to the parties of the potential departure from existing case law or serious question of interpretation of the Convention or the Protocols motivating the relinquishment: Explanatory Report, paras 17–19.

[431] Article 5 amends Article 35(3) by deleting the words 'and provided that no case may be rejected on this ground which has not been duly considered by a domestic tribunal'. This had also been requested by the Court in order to make it easier to apply the new admissibility criterion created by Protocol 14 but effectively stymied by an overly complex formulation, see section 6 of this chapter.

[432] Article 2(1) and Article 8 (transitional provisions). This effectively extends the retirement age to 74. see section 1.II of this chapter.

[433] Opened for signature on 2 October 2013, CETS No 214. Text and Explanatory Report available at http://www.echr.coe.int/Pages/home.aspx?p=basictexts&c=; See O'Boyle and Darcy, 52 GYIL 139 (2009), 178–9. Also the Izmir Declaration, para 13 and the Brighton Declaration, para 12(d).

[434] Article 1(1). The Protocol is an optional protocol, which will enter into force after it has been ratified by ten Contracting Parties; Article 8(1). No reservations are permitted: Article 9.

[435] Article 1(2) and (3). Requests for *in abstracto* review of legislation are excluded. Explanatory Report para 10. [436] Article 2(1) and (2).

[437] Article 2(2) and (3). The Panel shall include *ex officio* the judge elected in respect of the relevant Contracting Party.

be communicated by the Court to the requesting court or tribunal and the respective High Contracting Party. It is not binding.[438] The proceedings before the Court would not be adversarial in nature, as in a contentious case, but nevertheless the parties in the domestic proceedings and the relevant contracting party would be able to take part on an equal footing, and the Court has made it clear that this would be provided for in the rules of court.[439]

The question of advisory opinions was discussed at length during the preparation of the Brighton Conference on the future of the Court, to which the Court contributed a detailed reflection paper.[440] Advisory opinions had also been recommended in the Wise Persons Report.[441] As indicated in the Preamble to the Protocol, its purpose is to create a framework for dialogue between the highest national courts and the European Court.[442] However, its successful implementation presupposes that the Court's leading judgments are translated into the national languages. Under the Court's contentious jurisdiction, national courts are frequently presented with binding court judgments in sensitive areas, giving rise on occasions to disagreement, irritation, and confrontation.[443] The advisory jurisdiction seeks to involve the national court in a non-confrontational manner by providing it with an opportunity to seek the non-binding views of the Strasbourg Court on issues of compatibility of laws and practices with the provisions of the Convention. In this way the national court becomes effectively part of the European decision-making

---

[438] Article 4(1) and (3) and Article 5. Judges can deliver separate opinion if there is no unanimous view: Article 4(2). Obviously the value of such an opinion would be seriously undermined were the Court to express its views by a vote of 9/8. Doubtless for this reason the Court has referred to its practice of seeking to speak with one voice when issuing advisory opinions requested by the Committee of Ministers. See section 2.XV of this chapter and *Opinion of the Court on Protocol 16*, para 11.

http://www.echr.coe.int/Documents/2013_Protocol_16_Court_Opinion_ENG.pdf.

[439] Article 3 confers a right to intervene on the Council of Europe Commissioner for Human Rights and the relevant Contracting Party. Other Contracting Parties may also apply or be given leave to take part in the proceedings. Although this provision does not say so explicitly, the individual parties involved in the domestic proceedings would be invited to take part in the proceedings as a matter of course. This is a question of equal treatment and has been made clear by the Court in its *Opinion on Protocol No 16*, para 10, n 472. See also paras 19–21 of the Explanatory Report, where it is noted that it is expected that the parties to the domestic case would be invited to take part in the proceedings.

[440] Reflection Paper on the proposal to extend the Court's advisory jurisdiction http://www.echr.coe.int/Documents/2013_Courts_advisory_jurisdiction_ENG.pdf. The report considers the advantages and disadvantages of introducing such an advisory opinion system, how it would work in practice side-by-side with the Court's contentious jurisdiction and its implications for the work load of the Court. There are important differences with the ECJ's preliminary ruling procedure and this procedure. For example, states may choose not to ratify the Protocol unlike the situation under EU law. In addition, requests will be entirely at the discretion of the national courts which are free to choose whether they wish to avail of the procedure. There is no equivalent of the EU obligation under Article 267 of the TFEU to bring the matter before the ECJ, where no appeal lies against the judgment of the superior national court. Also the Strasbourg Court may choose not to accept a request from a national court. In its Reflection Paper, the Court indicated that it could draw inspiration from the case law of the ECJ in relation to the preliminary reference procedure on that point (relevance of the question, the doctrine of *acte clair*). Lastly, under EU law the CJEU judgment falls to be applied to the facts of the case from which it has sprung. Under the advisory procedure the Court's opinion is only advisory in nature.

[441] Final Report of the Group of Wise Persons to the Committee of Ministers, Council of Europe, para 81, November 2006 https://wcd.coe.int/ViewDoc.jsp?Ref=CM(2006)203&Sector=secCM&Language=lanEnglish&Ver=original&BackColorInternet=9999CC&BackColorIntranet=FFBB55&BackColorLogged=FFAC75.

[442] 'Considering that the extension of the Court's competence to give advisory opinions will further enhance the interaction between the Court and the national authorities and thereby reinforce implementation of the Convention, in accordance with the principle of subsidiarity', para 3 of the Preamble.

[443] See, eg, *Al-Khawaja and Tahery v United Kingdom* GC hudoc (2011) paras 51–62, referring to the domestic judgments in *R v Horncastle and others*.

process itself, with freedom to follow or not to follow the views of the Court. However, those views, though not binding, would have 'undeniable legal effects', as the experience of the International Court of Justice and the Inter-American Court of Human Rights demonstrates. The practice of these courts shows that they draw upon their reasoning in advisory opinions in the same way as upon their case law in contentious cases. It also reflects the contribution to the development of the case law that an advisory opinion has the potential to make.[444] As the Court has made clear in its Reflection Paper, the right of individual application to the Court would not be undermined and the individual would retain a right to file an application where the domestic court did not follow the non-binding opinion.[445] This will undoubtedly create a certain pressure to follow the Court's opinion. The Court is likely to make it clear that when its Grand Chamber issues an advisory opinion on a particular matter, it will apply the same principles to individual cases subsequently filed with it or pending before it. Equally, where the domestic court implements the terms of the opinion, any subsequent individual case presented by an individual is likely to be dismissed *in limine*, unless there are valid grounds for distinguishing the case.[446]

Since the Protocol is an optional one, it remains to be seen how many states will welcome this new form of dialogue. Given the size of the Court's docket today, the Court sees this important development as part of the long-term thinking on the reform of the Court's future role and has expressed moderate concern at the implications of an increase in its workload. As it has noted, it sees advisory opinions as allowing it to hand down more important rulings on questions of principle or of general interest relating to the interpretation and application of the Convention,[447] and at the same time reinforce its relations with domestic courts and their role in implementing the Convention.[448] It is envisaged that it will take some time before the Protocol comes into force, that the number of requests would be manageable, and that in high-profile cases raising important issues other states will intervene as third parties.[449] Indeed for the Wise Persons, it was in this way that the Court's constitutional role, as the decider of important convention issues having had the benefit of submissions from many states, was to be enhanced.[450]

III. ACCESSION OF THE EU TO THE CONVENTION (THE ACCESSION AGREEMENT)

One of the anomalies of the protection of human rights in Europe is that the individual is not able to bring a complaint against the European Union directly in the same way that he or she would be able to bring a complaint against a contracting state, since the EU is not

---

[444] Pasqualucci, *The Practice and Procedure of the Inter-American Court of Human Rights*, 2003, pp 29–80; Buergenthal, 79 AJIL 1 (1985).

[445] Paras 45–6. The Court also considered that it was 'rather unlikely' that a domestic court asking for the Court's advice would subsequently not follow it; para 7. Of course, the goal of enhancing dialogue would be set back were the national court not to follow the opinion, although its reasons for not doing so would be considered and answered by the Court in any future individual case raising the same issue. In this way 'dialogue' between the courts would be continued.

[446] Especially, if the party has participated in the advisory opinion proceedings before the Court.

[447] Examples of such case are given in paras 29–31 of the Reflection Paper. They cover the types of cases that are typically examined by the Grand Chamber. Reference for an *in abstracto* review of legislation is given as an example of a request that would be refused. See also the Court's concern about the translation of the relevant documents: *Opinion of the Court*, para 13.   [448] *Opinion of the Court*, para 16.

[449] Reflection Paper, n 439.

[450] Wise Persons Report n 440, paras 76–86.

a party to the Convention.[451] This lack of external control of the compatibility of EU law and practice with the Convention has been the subject of growing concern within Europe. The Court has been able to examine complaints against individual states in respect of the implementation of EU law but has no jurisdiction to examine complaints concerning the acts or omissions of EU bodies or agencies or to examine complaints against the EU directly concerning some aspect of EU primary or secondary law.[452] Given the constantly increasing competencies conferred by member states on the EU and the impressive out-pouring of EU directives and regulations, imposing obligations on member states touch-ing on a very large number of important areas of law, such a lack of external control by the European Court of Human Rights can no longer be justified. Of course, the coming into force of the EU Charter on Human Rights and Fundamental Freedoms and the bur-geoning case law of the EU Court of Justice (CJEU) in the area of human rights has meant that human rights issues are being litigated more frequently within the EU.[453] What was lacking, however, was the outer level of human rights control exercised by the Strasbourg Court to which all EU member states are subject. Such control is necessary to provide those whose rights are adversely affected by EU law with the possibility of a direct rem-edy in Strasbourg and to protect against the emergence of divergent interpretations of European human rights law. Accession thus seeks to close a gap in human rights protec-tion and enhance consistency between the Strasbourg and the Luxembourg human rights systems. It will also afford citizens protection against the action of the Union similar to that which they already enjoy against action by all the member states, thereby improving judicial protection of fundamental rights in Europe generally.[454]

The political decision for the EU to accede to the ECHR system was reflected in the Lisbon Treaty (2009). Article 6(2) of the Treaty on the European Union (Lisbon Treaty), which came into force on 1 December 2009, provides that 'the Union shall accede to the Convention. Such accession shall not affect the Union's competencies as defined in the Treaties'. Article 59 of the Convention had already been amended by Protocol 14 to pro-vide for EU accession to the Convention.

A draft Accession Agreement has now been drawn up by legal experts drawn from the Council of Europe's Committee of Legal Experts (CDDH), together with representatives of the Legal Service of the EU Commission.[455] The Agreement is not final and may be

---

[451] See, for a detailed overview, Johan Callewaert, *Accession of the European Union to the European Convention on Human Rights*, Council of Europe, 2014; Craig, 36 Fordham Int'l LJ 1114 (2013); Groussot, Lock, and Pech, 218 European Issues 7 (2011), available at www.robert-schuman.eu.

[452] See, eg, *Bosphorus Airlines v Ireland* 2005-VI GC and the cases mentioned in Ch 1, section 8.

[453] See Gráinne de Búrca, *After the Charter of Fundamental Rights: The Court of Justice as a Human Rights Adjudicator?* Available at http://www.maastrichtjournal.eu/pdf_file/ITS/MJ_20_02_0168.pdf.

[454] Accession will also enhance the human rights credibility of the EU in the eyes of third countries which regularly call upon it to respect the ECHR.

[455] See the Draft Accession Agreement (*Agreement on the Accession of the European Union to the Convention for the Protection of Human Rights and Fundamental Freedoms*) and the Draft Explanatory Report to the Agreement. Hereinafter 'Accession agreement and Explanatory Report' www.coe.int/t/dghl/standardsetting/hrpolicy/Accession/Meeting_reports_en.asp. For the drafting history of the Agreement, see Explanatory Report, paras 8–16. The Agreement has already been submitted in July 2013 to the CJEU for an opinion as to its compatibility with EU law. This opinion is estimated to take between 18 months and two years. Were the Opinion to be adverse the Agreement would have to be revised. The procedure for ratification is especially complex. The Agreement will have to be approved by the European Parliament, the EU Council (unanimously), the EU member states and the non-EU member states in accordance with their constitutional traditions, see Article 218 (1)–(11) of TFEU (2008). The EU would then become the 48th Party to the Convention. The process of review, consultation, and ratification will therefore take several years and perhaps even longer.

subject to amendment in the light of the opinion of the CJEU on its compatibility with EU law. The originality of the agreement lies in the adaptation of the Convention to enable a party that is not a state to become a contracting party on an equal footing with the other contracting parties and with the same rights and obligations. As the Explanatory Report points out, 'with the accession of the EU, there can arise a unique situation in the Convention system in which a legal act is enacted by one high contracting party and implemented by another'.[456]

The general philosophy of the Accession Agreement is to:

> preserve the equal rights of all individuals under the Convention, the rights of applicants in the Convention procedures, and the equality of all High Contracting Parties. The current control mechanism of the Convention should, as far as possible, be preserved and applied to the EU in the same way as to other High Contracting Parties, by making only those adaptations that are strictly necessary. The EU should, as a matter of principle, accede to the Convention on an equal footing with the other Contracting Parties, that is, with the same rights and obligations. It was, however acknowledged that, because the EU is not a State, some adaptations would be necessary. It is also understood that the existing rights and obligations of the States Parties to the Convention, whether or not members of the EU, should be unaffected by the accession, and that the distribution of competences between the EU and its member States and the EU institutions shall be respected. [457]

The following salient elements of the Accession Agreement are of particular note:

1. Accession imposes on the European Union obligations with regard only to 'acts, measures or omissions of its institutions, bodies, offices or agencies, or of persons acting on their behalf. Nothing in the Convention or the Protocols shall require the European Union to perform an act or adopt a measure for which it has no competence under European Union Law.'[458]

2. The European Union may make reservations under Article 57 of the Convention under the same conditions as any other contracting party, including the right to make reservations when acceding to existing or future additional protocols. Any reservations must be consistent with the relevant rules of international law.[459]

3. A new mechanism has been created to allow the EU to become a co-respondent to proceedings instituted against one or more of its member states and, also, to allow the EU member states to become co-respondents to proceedings instituted against the EU. This mechanism is considered necessary to accommodate the specific situation of the EU as a non-state entity with an autonomous legal system where acts of the EU may be implemented by its member states and, conversely, where the provisions of the EU founding treaties may be implemented by institutions, bodies, or agencies of the EU.[460]

---

[456] Explanatory Report, para 38.

[457] Explanatory Report, para 7. See also the Protocol relating to Article 6 (2) of the TEU on the accession of the Union to the ECHR (annexed to the Lisbon Treaty).

[458] Article 1(3) of the Agreement. See also Article 1(4) for specific rules of attribution as between the EU and an EU member state: Explanatory Report, paras 23–4. For issues of attribution and responsibility relating to the exercise of EU common foreign and security policy: see Explanatory Report, paras 24–6.

[459] Article 2 of the Agreement and Explanatory Report paras 33-36. The EU enjoys the same possibilities to make reservations, declarations and derogations on an equal footing with other contracting parties.

[460] Article 3 of the Agreement and paras 37–69 of the Explanatory Report.

A co-respondent has the status of a party to the case. Thus if the Court finds a violation of the Convention, the co-respondent will be bound by the obligation under Article 46 of the Convention.[461] The mechanism would allow the EU to become a co-respondent to cases in which the applicant has brought an application only against one or more EU member states. Similarly, the mechanism would allow member states to become co-respondents to cases brought only against the EU. Where an application was directed against both the EU and an EU member state, the mechanism would also be applied if the EU or its member state was not the party that acted or omitted to act in respect of the applicant but was instead the party that provided the legal basis for that act or omission.[462] In cases where the applicant alleges different violations by the EU and one or more of its member states separately, the co-respondent mechanism will not apply. Applicants will be able to make submissions to the Court in each case before a decision on joining a co-respondent is taken.[463]

The Accession Agreement provides that the admissibility of an application shall be assessed without regard to the participation of the co-respondent in the proceedings. This provision ensures that an application will not be considered inadmissible as a result of the participation of the co-respondent, notably with regard to the exhaustion of domestic remedies.

A contracting party can become a co-respondent either by accepting an invitation by the Court or by a decision by the Court upon the request of that contracting party.[464] When inviting a contracting party to become a co-respondent, the Court shall seek the views of all the parties to the proceedings[465] and decide whether 'it is plausible' that the conditions set out in Article 3(1) and (2) have been met.[466] These provisions indicate specific triggering criteria as to when the European Union or a European Union member state may become co-respondents.[467] It is important to note, however, that the Court cannot oblige either the EU or another contracting party to become a co-respondent.[468]

---

[461] See Explanatory Report, para 38, for the reasons underlying the introduction of the mechanism. 'If the Court finds a violation of the Convention, the co-respondent will be bound by the obligations under Article 46 of the Convention. The co-respondent mechanism is therefore not a procedural privilege for the EU or its member states, but a way to avoid gaps in participation, accountability and enforceability in the Convention system.' Explanatory Report, para 39.

[462] In such a situation it is open to either of the respondents to apply to the Court to be made a co-respondent as opposed to a respondent: Explanatory Report, para 56. For termination of the co-respondent status on the basis of a joint representation by the EU and the member state that the criteria are no longer satisfied: see Explanatory Report, para 59.

[463] The tests for triggering the co-respondent mechanism are set out in Article 3(2) and (3) of the Agreement; also Explanatory Report, paras 47–50. The authors of the report envisage that the mechanism may be applied in only a limited number of cases, para 48.

[464] Article 3(5) of the Agreement.   [465] Article 3(5).

[466] For the procedure before the Court concerning the co-respondent mechanism, see Explanatory Report, paras 51–9. The mechanism will only be applied to cases which have been notified to a contracting party. For the differences between third party intervention and the co-respondent mechanism, see Explanatory Report, paras 45–6. The effect of being a co-respondent is that the party becomes a full party to the case and is bound by the judgment, unlike an intervening third party. The third party procedure 'may often be the most appropriate way to involve the EU in a case', para 46.

[467] For example, ' Where an application is directed against one or more member States of the European Union, the European Union may become a co-respondent to the proceedings in respect of an alleged violation notified by the Court if it appears that such allegation calls into question the compatibility with the Convention rights at issue of a provision of European Union law, including decisions taken under the TEU and under the TFEU, notably where that violation could have been avoided only by disregarding an obligation under European Union law.' Article 3(2) of the Agreement and Explanatory Report, paras 47–55.

[468] This follows from Article 3(5) of the Agreement, see also Explanatory Report, paras 51 and 56. However in Annex II (a) the EU attach a declaration that will be made at the time of the signing of the

Where the Court finds that there has been a violation of the Convention, the respondent and the co-respondent shall be jointly responsible unless the Court decides otherwise.[469]

4. When a case is brought against the EU, the applicant will first have to exhaust domestic remedies available in the national courts of the respondent member state. Those courts have the possibility of referring a question to the CJEU for a preliminary ruling on the interpretation or validity of the EU act at issue. However, this is not considered to be a domestic remedy that the applicant must exhaust before making an application to the Court, since the parties to the proceedings before the national courts can only suggest such a reference.[470] A situation could thus arise where the Court could be required to adjudicate on the conformity of an EU act without the CJEU having first had the opportunity to examine the validity of a provision of secondary law or the interpretation of a provision of primary law from the standpoint of EU law. To ensure that such a situation would be avoided, the Accession Agreement provides a procedure of 'prior involvement' of the CJEU in cases in which the EU is a co-respondent. In such cases the CJEU will have the opportunity to assess the compatibility with convention rights at issue of the provision of EU law. Such an assessment would take place before the Court decides on the merits of the application. The parties involved, including the applicant, will have the opportunity to make observations in the procedure before the CJEU. The applicant would be eligible for legal aid in such an eventuality.[471]

5. Once the EU is a party to the Convention, all states' parties will be able to bring a case against the EU and vice-versa under Article 33 of the Convention as amended. The inter-state case will be re-named the inter-party case.[472]

Agreement saying that it will ensure that 'it will request to become a co-respondent to the proceedings before the European Court of Human Rights or accept an invitation by that Court to that effect, where the conditions set out in Article 3 (2) of the Accession Agreement are met'. This is not a legal obligation to become a co-respondent if the Court believes that the conditions are met. The EU still retains the right to make that determination for itself. It is rather a statement that it will make its determination on the basis of good will. Nonetheless, it is surprising that the Court, after having received the parties' observations on the issue, does not have the final word in the applicability of the legal test contained in Article 3(2). The legal position in the Agreement thus reflects the determination of the EU to exercise control over the application of the co-respondent mechanism to avoid being held responsible for human rights violations which it considers not to be its responsibility. The Declaration in Annex II reveals that this point must have given considerable difficulty to the drafters of the Agreement and in particular the non-EU states.

[469] Article 3 (7) of the Agreement, after having sought the views of the parties. For friendly settlements and unilateral declarations, see Explanatory Report, paras 59–60.

[470] Explanatory Report, para 57; also *Ullens de Schooten and Rezabek v Belgium* hudoc (2011).

[471] Article 3(6) of the Agreement and Explanatory Report, paras 65–9. 'The EU shall ensure that such assessment is made quickly so that proceedings before the Court are not unduly delayed': Article 3(6). 'Assessing the compatibility with the Convention shall mean to rule on the validity of a legal provision contained in acts of the EU institutions, bodies, offices or agencies, or on the interpretation of a provision of the TEU, the TFEU or any other provision having the same legal value pursuant to those instruments. Such assessment would take place before the Court rules on the merits of the application. The CJEU will not assess the act or omission complained of by the applicant but the EU legal basis for it'; paras 66–7. See also Appendix II (b) to the Agreement which confers rights on contracting parties other than EU member states to submit statements of case or written observations to the CJEU in the Article 3(6) procedure. However, this only applies to those 'contracting parties which in a procedure under Article 267 of the TFEU are [already] entitled to submit statements of case or written observations to the CJEU'. This was considered important for several states in the drafting process as an example of 'equal footing' treatment between EU and non-EU states.

[472] Article 4 of the Agreement and Explanatory Report, paras 70–2. Once the EU is a party to the Convention all states parties will be able to bring a case against the EU and vice-versa under Article 33 of the Convention. However, Article 344 of the TFEU states that EU member states 'undertake not to submit

6. A delegation of the European Parliament will be entitled to participate with the right to vote in the sittings of the Parliamentary Assembly of the Council of Europe when it elects a judge under Article 22 of the Convention. The judge elected in respect of the EU shall participate equally with the other judges in the work of the Court and have the same status and duties.[473]

7. The EU shall be entitled to participate in the Committee of Ministers with the right to vote when the Committee of Ministers takes decisions concerning the provision of the execution of the Court's judgments (Article 46) and of the terms of friendly settlement (Article 39), the request for an Advisory Opinion of the Court on certain legal questions (Article 47), and the reduction at the request of the Plenary of the Court of the number of judges of the Chambers (Article 26(2)).[474] Under EU law, the EU and its member states are obliged to act in a coordinated manner when expressing positions in voting in certain circumstances. There is thus the theoretical possibility that the EU group comprising twenty-eight contracting parties could effectively block the exercise by the Committee of Ministers (composed of forty-eight contracting parties) of its supervisory functions under Article 46 of the Convention when considering an application against the EU or one or more of its member states jointly. It was therefore necessary to introduce specific provisions about the participation of the EU when the Committee of Ministers exercises these functions (Article 39 and 46 of the Convention). Article 7(4) of the Agreement provides that the 'exercise of the right to vote by the European Union and its member states shall not prejudice the effective exercise by the Committee of Ministers of its supervisory functions under Articles 39 and 46 of the Convention'. The voting rules of the Committee of Ministers have accordingly been adjusted by altering the majorities required for certain types of votes to ensure that in cases concerning the European Union the Committee of Ministers will be able to carry out its functions effectively.[475]

8. THE FUTURE

The new Court has had to confront major challenges since it was set up in 1998.[476] First, it had the difficult task of ensuring the continuity of the Convention system as it had been

---

a dispute concerning the interpretation or application of the EU treaties to any method of settlement other than that provided for therein'.

[473] Article 6 of the Agreement and Explanatory Report, paras 75–7. The modalities of the election are left to the PACE in cooperation with the European Parliament.

[474] For participation as regards functions not explicitly foreseen in the Convention (eg, adoption of texts such as recommendations, resolutions which are directly related to CM work by virtue of the Convention). The EU will be 'consulted'; see Article 7(3) and Explanatory Report 80–81.

[475] Article 7(4) of the Agreement and Explanatory Report, paras 84–90. The obligation for EU states to vote in a coordinated manner under EU law does not arise when voting in respect of cases against non-EU states or cases against EU member states concerning non-EU issues. The new voting rules will apply to all decisions in respect of obligations upon the EU alone and one or more of its member states jointly. They are set out in Appendix III of the Agreement. It remains to be seen whether these rules are sufficient to ensure that the supervisory system is not blocked by the EU states when voting, for example, on an interim resolution concerning the EU or an EU state relating to an EU issue (see Ch 4, section 2) where no provision is made for a special majority.

[476] See O'Boyle, *The Conscience of Europe*, ch 15, pp 190–201; PACE report of 3 December 2012, '*The future of the ECtHR and the Brighton Declaration*' AS/Jur (2012)42.

developed by the former Commission and Court for more than forty years. Building on and consolidating the case law of the Convention institutions in such a manner that it retained the confidence of both the international legal community and the contracting parties was a daunting challenge for a newly restructured Court and one that has been increasingly called into question by the states throughout the recent reform process. They have openly (and often unfairly) challenged the Court for, *inter alia*, its failure to respect the principle of subsidiarity, its over-willingness to grant interim measures, its inconsistent application of admissibility criteria, and the consistency and clarity of its case-law developments.[477] The states have used the opportunity of reform to caution the Court that it risked forfeiting their support if it did nothing to address such short-comings and seek to rebuild confidence by changing its approach to interpreting and applying the Convention.[478] At the same time, the states parties have demonstrated their attachment to the right of individual petition, to the need for a more effective system of supervising the enforcement of Court judgments, to improving national measures to provide effective domestic remedies for human rights violations, and, most impor-tantly, to the political and legal importance of the role played by the Court in today's Europe. However, notwithstanding the critical edge to the reform conferences, the cen-tral question throughout this process was how to preserve and consolidate the outstand-ing achievements of the Court over the last fifty years and create a structure that could endure in both the short and long term. How will this be done? It involves three essential developments.

The first concerns the development of more effective procedures by the Court itself to enable it to deal with the vast number of cases in its case docket. The recent results, vis-ible from the Court's statistics, have been promising.[479] The Court has constantly sought to make its procedures more efficient and has exhibited considerable ingenuity in doing so. It has developed the pilot judgment procedure as an effective legal technique for bringing about structural change and dealing with the difficult problem of repetitive or clone complaints. Where the contracting party is reluctant to introduce corrective meas-ures, the Court is likely to explore the possibility of introducing a brief default judgment system enabling it to record violations in such cases. It has introduced a system for grant-ing priority to certain categories of urgent or important cases to ensure that the impor-tant cases are dealt with more speedily than before.[480] It has demonstrated convincingly how the single judge procedure can be used to dismiss large numbers of cases with an economy of procedure that harnesses the decision-making capacity of most of the judges in the Court. It has exploited productively the three-judge committees empowered to give judgments in WECL cases, and will consider in the future a broader definition of the notion of 'well-established case law'. It has invented the unilateral declaration for rejecting cases where agreement to settle is unreasonably withheld by the applicant.[481] In keeping with the advice of Lord Woolf, it has sought to impose greater discipline on the way in which applications are brought to the Court by requiring applicants to complete the application form as required by the rules of court (Rule 47), with the sanction of not dealing with the case in the event of non-compliance.[482] There is the prospect that the Court will be in a position to considerably reduce, if not eliminate, its backlog by 2015.

---

[477] For a critical examination of these claims, see Bratza, 5 EHRLR (2011), 505–12.

[478] See section 7 of this chapter on reform of the Court.   [479] See n 3.

[480] Section 2.VI of this chapter.   [481] Section 2.XII of this chapter.

[482] Review of the Working Methods of the European Court of Human Rights (the Woolf Report) December 2005. For developments concerning Rule 47, see section 2.V of this chapter.

The second development concerns the realization, based on the notion of shared responsibility between the states and the Court, that more needs to be done at national level to provide remedies for human rights violations and for developing the role of national human rights structures. The Interlaken, Izmir, and Brighton Declarations have devoted considerable space to stressing the importance of effective national measures as an obvious method of reducing the need for applicants to complain to Strasbourg.[483] First among such measures is the effective implementation of Convention rights by national courts. This is clearly a long-term strategy which is unlikely to have much impact in the Court's docket in the short term. However, the application of the Court's case law by national courts and national judges on a routine basis is one of the fundamental goals of the Convention system and one that offers considerable promise as a method of enhancing the standard of human rights protection nationally and reducing the Court's docket, in the both the long and short terms. There are some promising signs that states are willing to introduce improved domestic remedies. Turkey, for example, has introduced a remedy for length of proceedings complaints, as well as a general remedy before the Constitutional Court for alleged human rights violations. Both have been considered by the Court to be effective remedies to be exhausted.[484] Bulgaria has also introduced effective remedies in respect of length of proceedings.[485]

The third development relates to the strengthening of the Court's constitutional role, ie its role in providing authoritative and binding judgments on the major human rights issues of the day, and in this way consolidating and furthering developing the *acquis conventionnel*. It is clear from the reform process that the Court will continue to develop its role of individual supervision and that the right of individual petition will be safeguarded to facilitate this. However, important developments such as the accession of the EU to the Convention and the introduction under Protocol 16 of a system of advisory opinions at the request of national courts will lead, gradually but surely, to the further growth and development of the Court's constitutional role.[486] In this respect it must be remembered that Convention principles as developed in the Court's case law have not only been received into national law and practice, but have also guided the pace and direction of law reform in many areas of law, aided and abetted by national courts and external Council of Europe bodies such as the CPT, ECRI, the European Social Charter, the Venice Commission, and the European Commissioner for Human Rights. These impressive accomplishments of the Convention system can only be enhanced in the future by furthering the dialogue with national courts by way of advisory opinions and enabling individuals to bring complaints directly against the EU.

All three developments, coupled with the changes brought about by the Interlaken process, mark out the development of the Court for the foreseeable future. It can be safely predicted that new challenges (and controversial disagreements with the states) will emerge over the course of the next decade that will require further initiatives. The shadow of UK withdrawal from the ECHR threatens the serenity that is needed to ensure further reform. The vital question is whether the Court, given the burdensome case docket that it is expected to bear, will be in a position during this period of intense change to continue

---

[483] For the impressive raft of national measures proposed during the reform process, see Interlaken Declaration, paras 4–5; Izmir Declaration, point B; Brighton Declaration, para 9(c).

[484] See *Turgut and others v Turkey* (dec) hudoc (2013) and *Uzun v Turkey* (dec) hudoc (2013); also *Ruminski v Sweden* (dec) hudoc (2013).

[485] *Valcheva and Abrashev v Bulgaria* and *Balakchiev and Others v Bulgaria* (decs) hudoc (2013).

[486] On this point see the Wise Persons Report (n 440) paras 76–86 (15 November 2006).

to perform its function effectively as Europe's leading human rights court. Following the blueprint for reform that has been developed by the states in the course of the reform process, it is certainly arguable that its prospects are better than they have been for some time. It remains to be seen whether the existing challenge to the Court's legitimacy in the UK derails this process or strengthens it.

4

THE EXECUTION OF THE COURT'S JUDGMENTS

If the Court finds in its judgment[1] that there has been a violation of one or more provisions of the Convention, it is self-evident that further steps will be called for to ensure that the judgment is properly implemented at national level.[2] As with any court, whether national, supranational, or international, judgments of the Court are not self-executing. Nor does the Court have the power to enforce its own judgments.[3] While the Court itself has made strides in recent years towards indicating individual and general measures in its judgments,[4] which will aid enforcement at the national level, at least for the time being, such indications lack the full force of consequential orders of national courts. Instead, by virtue of Article 46(2) of the Convention,[5] the task of execution and enforcement of its judgments falls to the Committee of Ministers of the Council of Europe (Committee of Ministers). The process is not an adversarial one. It is based essentially on peer pressure and political persuasion exercised within a forum where there is a genuine commitment to effective enforcement of judgments, but also on a commonality of political interest and often a self-interested tolerance of the practical problems associated with execution. The role of the Committee of Ministers, its procedures and common features, and recent developments in the execution process will be considered in the following sections of this chapter.

---

[1] See the proceedings of the Court's annual seminar, *Implementation of the judgments of the ECtHR: a shared judicial responsibility?*, 31 January (2014), available at the Court's website; also the Proceedings of the Gottingen Conference (21–23 September 2013) on *Judgments of the ECtHR—Effects and Implementation* (to be published by Luxembourg Max Planck Institute, 2014); Lambert-Abdelgawad, *The Execution of Judgments of the European Court of Human Rights*, 2nd edn, 2008; Leach, *The Effectiveness of the Committee of Ministers in Supervising the Enforcement of Judgments of the European Court of Human Rights*, 2006, pp 443–56; Polakiewicz, in Blackburn and Polakiewicz, eds, *Fundamental Rights in Europe*, 2001, pp 55–76.

[2] Some judgments have been executed with commendable speed. See *Del Rio Prada v Spain* hudoc (2013) GC, where the applicant was released several days after the judgment, and *X v Austria* hudoc (2013) GC, where amending legislation was introduced within several months –see, for discussion of the latter, Ch 18, section 6.VI.

[3] However, with the pilot judgment procedure the Court may require the state, in the operative part of the judgment, to introduce corrective measures in respect of a systemic or structural defect. See Ch 3, section 3.VI.

[4] See Ch 3, section 5. More directive Court judgments have the advantage of making implementation easier to monitor by both the Committee of Ministers and outside bodies especially the applicant. It also means that compliance is less open to political negotiation in the Committee of Ministers. See Greer, *The European Convention on Human Rights: Achievements, Problems and Prospects*, 2006, pp 160–1. However, there are limits to how far the Court is prepared to go in keeping with the general scheme of the Convention that leaves to the states the choice of appropriate corrective measures.

[5] 'The final judgment of the Court shall be transmitted to the Committee of Ministers, which shall supervise its execution.'

1. THE ROLE OF THE COMMITTEE
OF MINISTERS

To the extent that the Statute of the Council of Europe and the Convention provide for a separation of powers, the Committee of Ministers is the executive organ of the Council of Europe, with a role distinct from the Court's judicial role. According to Article 15 of the Statute of the Council of Europe, the general role of the Committee is to consider the action required to further the Council's aim, including the conclusion of conventions or agreements and the adoption by governments of a common policy with regard to particular matters. It is notionally composed of the Ministers of Foreign Affairs of all member states. In practice, however, it only meets once a year at ministerial level. Most of the Committee's business is carried out by Ministers' Deputies who are the permanent representatives of member states at the Council of Europe, ie career diplomats, who are in permanent session in Strasbourg. The role of the Committee in the Convention system has evolved with the system itself and there has been an overall trend towards less direct involvement in the judicial process. For example, the Committee originally elected members of the old Commission (former Article 21 of the Convention) and had the important task of deciding whether or not there had been a violation of the Convention in cases which had not been referred to the old Court (former Article 32). Currently, in addition to the supervision of the execution of judgments of the Court (current Article 46(2) of the Convention), the main tasks of the Committee are to receive and forward the lists of candidates for the election of judges to the Parliamentary Assembly of the Council of Europe (PACE), to request advisory opinions of the Court (Article 47),[6] and to set the Court's annual budget.[7]

2. PROCEDURE

In the exercise of its responsibilities for the execution of judgments under Article 46, the Committee of Ministers meets in four three-day sessions each year.[8] The workload is a heavy one (in reflection of the increasing number of judgments delivered by the Court).[9] Since January 2011, the Committee has operated a system of continuous supervision of all cases, and it only debates around twenty to thirty cases at one of its quarterly meetings. It

---

[6] It may also file a request for the interpretation of the judgment (Article 46(3)) and initiate infringement proceedings (Article 46(4)).

[7] To the extent that the Committee regulates personnel matters in the Council (including the staff of the Registry), this administrative aspect of its work might also be said to have an indirect impact on the work of the Court. Article 54 of the Convention also provides that 'Nothing in this Convention shall prejudice the powers conferred on the Committee of Ministers by the Statute...'

[8] A change introduced at the end of 2007; the previous practice was to hold six two-day meetings. This was to allow more time for the Secretariat and states to prepare cases, especially given the high level of bilateral contact between the states and the Secretariat. See the first Annual Report on supervision of the execution of judgments of the European Court of Human Rights, March 2008. Annual Reports can be found at http://www.coe.int/t/dghl/monitoring/execution/Documents/Publications_en.asp.

[9] At the end of 2012, there were 10,407 cases pending before the Committee of Ministers, although many of these are repetitive cases. Cases which raise new structural or general problems requiring general measures ('reference cases') are listed separately; see http://www.coe.int/t/dghl/monitoring/execution/Reports/Stats/Docs_Stats_2012_en.pdf.

also adopts decisions in around the same number of cases in a purely written procedure at the meeting.[10] The continuous supervision of such a large number of cases necessarily places a heavy burden on the Department for the Execution of Judgments of the European Court of Human Rights in the Council of Europe's Directorate General of Human Rights and Legal Affairs (the Execution Department), whose task it is to assist the Committee in managing the continuous supervision work and prepare the cases for examination at the quarterly meetings. The Committee adopted a series of Rules which provide an overarching guide to its procedures, the latest revision having been adopted in May 2006.[11] More recently, the Committee decided to apply new working methods[12] in implementation of the Interlaken Action plan and partly to address its heavy workload. These working methods set out the Committee's procedures in detail.

The meetings of the Committee take place *in camera*, though greater efforts have been made in recent years to make the process more transparent through the provision of considerably more information through the Council of Europe's website.[13] Virtually all the information submitted by the States in respect of execution is now public. After each meeting, an annotated agenda and all decisions taken will be made public unless the Committee decides otherwise (Rule 8(4)). The individual applicant and his legal representative are excluded from the Committee's deliberations, in stark contrast to the right of the respondent state to play a full part in the proceedings. However, this has been mitigated (if only slightly) by the Committee being entitled to consider any communication from the applicant with regard to the payment of just satisfaction or the taking of individual measures (Rule 9(1)) and any communication from non-governmental organizations (NGOs) and national human rights institutions (Rule 9(2)). The latter possibility opens up the process to NGOs and national human rights institutions, providing them with a precious opportunity to comment on the issues before the Committee of Ministers, although it has been noted that some of them are not yet fully aware of how to engage effectively in the process.[14] However, applicants are still not permitted to address comments on the issue of general measures.[15]

In addition to the decisions it adopts in each case examined at its meetings, the Committee can also act by means of resolutions. There are two types it may adopt, each

---

[10] In order to avoid having to debate every single case on its agenda at every meeting, the Committee has adopted a series of guidelines (adopted at the Committee's 879th DH meeting (April 2004)), as to when a case will be proposed for debate. This will occur if: the applicant's situation because of the violation warrants special supervision; it marks a new departure in case law by the European Court; it discloses a potential systemic problem which could give rise to similar cases in future; there is a difference of appreciation between the Secretariat and the respondent state concerning the measures to be taken; there is a delay in execution with reference to the timetable; or a government delegation or the Secretariat requests it.

[11] Rules adopted by the Committee of Ministers for the application of Article 46, para 2, of the European Convention on Human Rights, adopted on 10 May 2006 at the 964th meeting of the Ministers' Deputies. The Rules and all other public documents are available from http://www.coe.int/t/dghl/monitoring/execution/Documents/Doc_ref_en.asp. They are discussed in Lambert-Abdelgawad, *The Execution of Judgments of the European Court of Human Rights*, 2nd edn, 2008.

[12] See CM/Inf/DH(2010)37 6 September 2010 and CM/Inf/DH(2010)45 final 7 December 2010.

[13] http://www.coe.int/t/dghl/monitoring/execution/Default_en.asp. For the wide range of information available on the site, see Appendix 6 to the Annual Report (2012), available at http://www.coe.int/t/dghl/monitoring/execution/Source/Publications/CM_annreport2012_en.pdf.

[14] Leach, 6 EHRLR 732 (2009). Nevertheless, fifty NGO submissions were received by the Committee of Ministers in 2011 and 2012; Annual Report 2012, p 19.

[15] Rule 9(1) limits comments to just satisfaction and individual measures. Such a limitation is difficult to justify today, post the reform conferences, and comes in for criticism by the Director-General in the Annual Report 2012, p 19.

by a two-thirds majority of the representatives casting a vote and of a majority of the representatives entitled to sit on the Committee. Final resolutions are adopted when the Committee has established that the state concerned has taken all the necessary measures to abide by the judgment or that the terms of the friendly settlement have been executed (Rule 17). Interim resolutions may also be adopted (though need not be) in the course of the Committee's supervision in order to provide information on the state of progress of the execution of a judgment or, where appropriate, to express concern and/or to make suggestions with respect to execution (Rule 16). Interim resolutions may therefore have a useful role to play when the execution process has not been speedily concluded, whether as a result of the complexity of the case or the unwillingness of the state to hasten execution.[16] It is sometimes by way of such a resolution that the Committee of Ministers will express its concern that just satisfaction has not yet been paid or that the general measures required by the judgment have not yet been passed. The resolution will indicate that the matter will be reconsidered at a later date if the Committee is not satisfied.[17] This insistence of coming back to the issue will continue until a result has been achieved.

The Committee has the competence to supervise the execution of both full judgments on the merits and friendly settlements.[18] All judgments and decisions which are transmitted to the Committee are inscribed on its agenda (Rule 3).[19] The Committee will then take a decision to place a case in the enhanced or the standard supervision procedure.[20] The point of departure is that all cases are examined in the standard procedure unless the case meets one of the objective criteria for supervision in the enhanced procedure. As suggested by its title, the enhanced procedure is designed to enable the Committee to prioritize certain cases and increase their visibility. When a case is dealt with under the enhanced procedure, the Secretariat will engage in more intensive or pro-active discussion with the state. This may involve assistance in the preparation or implementation of action plans, or expert assistance in their preparation, or the organization of round tables or seminars to discuss the underlying issues more broadly. The Committee has identified a number of objective indicators for placing a case in the enhanced supervision procedure, which are:[21]

- judgments requiring urgent individual measures;
- pilot judgments;
- judgments disclosing *major* structural and/or complex problems as identified by the Court and/or the Committee of Ministers;
- inter-state cases.

---

[16] A collection of both Interim Resolutions and Final Resolutions is available on the Court's Hudoc database and on the website of the Council of Europe's Execution Department, http://www.coe.int/t/dghl/monitoring/execution/Source/Documents/IntRes2012_en.pdf.

[17] See, eg, the numerous interim resolutions in *Xenides-Arestis v Turkey* hudoc (2005); *Sedić and Finci v Bosnia and Herzegovina* GC hudoc (2009); *Loizidou v Turkey* and *Stran Greek Refineries and Stratis Andreadis v Greece* hudoc (1994), http://www.coe.int/t/dghl/monitoring/execution/Source/Documents/IntRes2012_en.pdf.

[18] The Rules applicable to friendly settlements (Rules 12–15) mirror those applicable to judgments and thus are not separately enumerated here.

[19] Cases remain on the Committee's agenda until it decides otherwise: Rule 7.

[20] The twin-track procedure was introduced following the Interlaken Conference on reform of the Court.

[21] See CM/Inf/DH(2010)45 final 7 December 2010, https://wcd.coe.int/ViewDoc.jsp?Ref=CM/Inf/DH(2010)45&Language=lanEnglish&Ver=final&Site=CM&BackColorInternet=C3C3C3&BackColorIntranet=EDB021&BackColorLogged=F5D383-P10_103 (section 10).

The Committee of Ministers may decide to examine any case under the enhanced procedure following an initiative of a member state or the Secretariat. States have six months from the date that a judgment becomes final to submit an action plan or action report indicating the steps they plan to take or have taken to execute the judgment. If no information is submitted within this period, the case will be automatically transferred to the enhanced procedure. All the action plans and reports submitted are published,[22] except when there is a reasoned request for confidentiality from a state.[23]

I. JUST SATISFACTION

Verifying whether any just satisfaction awarded by the Court under Article 41[24] has been paid will rarely prove problematic, since the government agent will often arrange for payment without waiting for the Committee to begin its examination.[25] After that, the state simply confirms to the Committee that payment has been made via a standard form available on its website. The Committee will only become more actively involved in the payment of just satisfaction where an applicant contests payment. If the applicant has not contested payment within two months of the judgment becoming final, then the Committee will usually automatically consider the just satisfaction paid. The question of payment of the just satisfaction has no bearing on the Committee's ability to proceed with the substantive examination of a case. The Annual Report for 2012 records that the ratio of payments of just satisfaction was 81 per cent during 2012.[26]

However, issues concerning payment of just satisfaction do arise, as in the *Stran Greek* case. Another case of serious delay in payment was *Loizidou v Turkey (Article 50)*,[27] where the Court awarded considerable sums of just satisfaction arising from its finding of a violation of Article 1 of Protocol 1 because the applicant had been denied access to her property in northern Cyprus.[28] The Turkish government took the position that sums awarded by the Court could only be paid to the applicant in the context of a global settlement of all property cases in Cyprus. In a series of strongly worded interim resolutions adopted between October 1999 and November 2003, the Committee rejected

---

[22] See the website of the Department for the Execution of Judgments of the European Court http://www.coe.int/t/dghl/monitoring/execution/Default_en.asp.

[23] See paragraph 5 of the decision of the Committee of Ministers from their 1100th meeting as set out in CM/Inf/DH(2010)45 final 7 December 2010.   [24] On Article 41, see Ch 3, section 4.

[25] See, for an informative overview of some of the practical difficulties the Committee of Ministers has faced in this area, Committee of Ministers Information Document, 'Monitoring of the payment of sums awarded by way of just satisfaction: an overview of the Committee of Ministers present practice', Memorandum prepared by the Department for the Execution of Judgments of the European Court of Human Rights, 11 March 2008, CM/Inf/DH(2008)7 revised. See also Annual Report 2012, p 27 for details concerning a new simplified procedure that has been introduced. One problematic case was *Stran Greek Refineries and Stratis Andreadis v Greece* A 301-B (1994); 19 EHRR 293, where the Court awarded considerable sums of just satisfaction. The Greek government, relying on the size of the award and economic problems in Greece, stated that it was unable to make immediate full payment and sought to pay in instalments. The Committee, in Interim Resolution DH (96) 251 of 15 May 1996, rejected this course, concluding that the modalities of payment envisaged by the Greek government could not be considered to be in conformity with the obligations following from the Court's judgment and urged it to pay without delay. When the final sums of over US$30 million were paid, the Committee closed its examination of the case: Final Resolution DH (97) 184 of 20 March 1997.

[26] The payment problems were mostly technical (eg unable to locate the applicant or bank account details). The total amount of just satisfaction awarded by the Court in 2012 was high—€178.8 million compared with €72.3 million in 2011; see Annual Report 2012, p 12.

[27] 1998-IV; *Stran Greek and Stratis Andreadis v Greece* A 301-B (1994); 19 EHRR 293.

[28] See the principal judgment in the case, 1996-VI; 22 EHRR 513.

this position, stating, *inter alia*, that the refusal of Turkey to execute the judgment of the Court demonstrated 'a manifest disregard for its international obligations, both as a High Contracting Party to the Convention and as a member state of the Council of Europe'.[29] Turkey finally agreed to pay the sums required, prompting the Committee, in Resolution DH(2003)190 of December 2003, to declare that it had 'exercised its functions under Article 46, paragraph 2, of the Convention' in respect of the 1998 just satisfaction judgment.[30] The examination of the merits of the case was resumed in November 2005 and has been pursued regularly by the Committee since then.[31] Both this case and the *Stran Greek* case are paradigm examples of a strong collective political will overcoming the states' refusal to comply with the judgments.

II. INDIVIDUAL MEASURES

The second step taken by the Committee in the execution of a judgment is governed by Rule 6(2)(b) of its Rules. This states that the Committee will take into account the discretion of the contracting state to choose the means necessary to comply with the judgment, but that the Committee should examine whether individual measures have been taken to ensure that the violation has ceased and that the injured party is put, as far as possible, in the same situation as it enjoyed prior to the violation of the Convention— *restituto in integrum*. The Rules themselves give examples of what individual measures may be required, including the striking out of an unjustified criminal conviction from the criminal records, the granting of a residence permit (if the Court finds removal of a non-national would breach the Convention), the re-opening of impugned domestic proceedings, or the release of those found to have been held illegally. Clearly, where the Court itself indicates (which it does increasingly, albeit in exceptional circumstances) what individual measures should be taken, the Committee will take its lead from the terms of the Court's judgment.[32]

The Committee's task has also been helped by its own willingness to adopt recommendations to member states on the steps they should take at the national level to facilitate execution. The best example is Recommendation (2000)2 'on the re-examination or reopening of certain cases at domestic level following judgments of the European Court of Human Rights'.[33] In this the Committee noted, *inter alia*, that its practice in supervising the execution of the Court's judgments showed that in exceptional circumstances the re-examination of a case or a re-opening of judicial proceedings had proved the most efficient, if not the only, means of achieving *restitutio in integrum*.[34] This step has greatly

---

[29] Interim resolutions DH (99) 680, DH (2000) 105, DH(2001)80 and DH(2003)174.

[30] Turkey finally paid the required sums in 2003. However, the question of payment remains outstanding in relation to around thirty other similar cases for which *Xenides-Arestis v Turkey* hudoc (2005) is the lead case. Overall, the Committee examines the issue in the context of the inter-state case of *Cyprus v Turkey* (25781/94).

[31] For the Committee's assessment of the individual measures in the case, see Information Document CM/Inf/DH(2010)21 and CM/Inf/DH(2010)36.

[32] Under Article 46: see Ch 3, section 5.

[33] Adopted on 19 January 2000 at the 694th meeting of the Ministers' Deputies. Other key recommendations are available online, see the website of the Execution Department (CM Recommendations) http://www.coe.int/t/dghl/monitoring/executionuments/CMRec_en.asp.

[34] See Lobov, in Chernishova and Lobov, eds, *Essays in Honour of Anatoly Kovler*, 2013, pp 77–105. It also said that *restitutio* should apply especially where the injured party continues to suffer very serious negative consequences because of the outcome of the domestic decision at issue, which are not adequately remedied by just satisfaction and cannot be rectified except by re-examination or re-opening, and the judgment of the Court leads to the conclusion that (i) the impugned domestic decision is on the merits contrary to the

enhanced the execution process, especially when one considers that unfair proceedings cases (whether criminal or civil) are one of the largest categories of cases considered by the Court. At the time of writing, most of the member states of the Council of Europe now expressly provide for the re-opening of a case after a Court judgment.[35] Other notable recommendations include Rec (2008)2, calling on member states to designate a coordinator of execution of judgments at the national level who would have powers to liaise with the different national authorities involved and initiate measures to accelerate execution, or Rec (2010)3, requesting states to have effective national remedies for excessive length of proceedings.[36]

By their nature, the individual measures to be taken will vary from case to case. However, there are a number of areas where similar problems occur repeatedly, perhaps because of intrinsic problems of execution of court judgments in certain subject areas. One such problematic area is the sensitive question of parental visiting rights, for instance where one or both parents have been deprived of access to their child, especially when one parent has started another relationship or the child has been taken into care. Understandably, the social services of member states may encounter some difficulties in re-establishing visitation rights when that depends on the cooperation of the child and those responsible for his or her care. It may also require that they seek leave from the family law courts, which may be reluctant to revisit the case, and that they act in accordance with any duties they have to give paramount consideration to the welfare of the child. In such cases, however, in order to establish that the required individual measures have been taken, the Committee may continue with its examination of the case to verify the steps taken by the domestic authorities towards re-establishing contact between the parent and child. It will note whether those steps have in fact been taken and are going in the right direction.[37] However, while this could raise questions as to whether it is appropriate for the highest level authority of the Council of Europe to micromanage such individual matters as ensuring weekly contact visits between a parent and his or her child, it should be noted that the Committee's usual practice is rather to consider information provided by the respondent state that those rights are protected or being observed at the national level by, for example, a local body which is closer to the parties (such as a national human rights ombudsman).[38]

A second common group of cases is, as suggested earlier, where the Court has found that domestic judicial proceedings have been unfair and where the obvious individual measure to be taken is the re-opening of those proceedings but domestic law does not provide for the possibility. The Committee, pursuant to its Recommendation (2000) 2 (mentioned earlier) on the matter, may ask the state to adopt such legislation. Where there is such legislation but it is inapplicable in the instant case, the Committee will explore whether *ad hoc* measures can be taken which will have the same effect of erasing the consequences of the violations found.[39] One case which reflected badly on both

---

Convention; or (ii) the violation found is based on procedural errors or shortcomings of such gravity that a serious doubt is cast on the outcome of the domestic proceedings complained of.

[35] See 'Reopening of proceedings before domestic courts following findings of violation by the European Court of Human Rights—Draft survey of existing legislation and case-law', DH-PR(2005)2. See also the documents on re-opening available at http://www.coe.int/t/dghl/monitoring/execution/Documents/Reopening_en.asp.

[36] Texts available at https://wcd.coe.int/ViewDoc.jsp?id=1246081&Site=COE.

[37] Examples of such cases include the execution of *Görgülü v Germany*, hudoc (2004); *Reigado Ramo v Portugal* hudoc (2005); and *Bove v Italy* hudoc (2005).

[38] See, eg, Resolution CM/ResDH(2010)84 in *Sylvester v Austria* (Application No 36812/97).

[39] See, eg, the cases of *Hulki Güneş v Turkey* 2003-VII; 43 EHRR 263, the subject of the Committee's interim resolutions ResDH(2005)113, ResDH(2007)26, and ResDH(2007)150; *Göçmen v Turkey* hudoc (2006); and *Söylemez v Turkey* hudoc (2006). In all three, the Court found violations in respect of the fairness of criminal

the Committee of Ministers and the respondent state, Italy, was the *Dorigo* case. There, the applicant was convicted in 1994 for his part in a terrorist attack on a NATO military base and sentenced to over thirteen years' imprisonment. The original complaint was that he had been unable to examine witnesses against him at his trial and the then Commission and Committee of Ministers found a violation of Article 6(1) and (3)(d) of the Convention. It took several interim resolutions of the Committee, two resolutions of the Parliamentary Assembly, a lengthy enquiry into the possibility of a presidential pardon, failed legislation in the Italian parliament, and two separate sets of legal proceedings (one on the initiative of a local prosecutor) before the Italian judiciary finally concluded that the applicant's continued detention was illegal, by virtue of the need to give direct effect to the Convention, and ordered his release in 2006. It was not until 2007, more than eight years after the former Commission's finding of a violation and thirteen years after the initial trial, that the Committee of Ministers closed its examination of the case by which point the applicant had served virtually his entire sentence.[40]

A third group of cases where difficulties have arisen (and continue to do so) in different contracting parties concern Article 2 judgments where the Court has found that the state failed to conduct an effective investigation in breach of its positive obligation under that Article. The Committee has taken the position that the authorities of the state have a continuing obligation to carry out an effective investigation and that this is part of their obligation to take appropriate individual measures to execute the Court's judgment. The assessment of whether an effective investigation can be carried out can be a difficult one. First, domestic authorities may have to amend their procedures for investigations if these were found to be at fault in the Court's judgment; and second, there are likely to be practical difficulties in performing such an investigation years after the Court's judgment and many more years after the events which gave rise to the need for such an investigation in the first place.[41]

proceedings at the conclusion of which the applicants were sentenced to lengthy terms of imprisonment. The relevant Turkish legislation on re-opening did not apply to the Court judgments which became final before 4 February 2003 or judgments rendered in applications lodged with the Court after that date. The applicants, having lodged their applications in 1995, 1999, and 2002 respectively, were not covered by the law. In adopting the last-mentioned interim resolution in the *Hulki Güneş* case (ResDH(2007)150) (and taking note of the *Göçmen* and *Söylemez* cases), the Committee found that the continuation of the present situation would amount to a manifest breach of Turkey's obligations and strongly urged the Turkish authorities 'to remove promptly the legal lacuna preventing the reopening of domestic proceedings'. In June 2013, the Committee's efforts finally paid off with the adoption of a new law which permitted re-opening for all of the cases pending before the Committee of Ministers. The case of *Hulki Güneş* was finally re-opened and heard by the domestic courts enabling, the case to be transferred to the standard procedure; see the order of business from the Committee's 1172nd meeting, http://www.coe.int/t/dghl/monitoring/execution/WCD/DHMeetings_en.asp.

[40] *Dorigo v Italy*, Final Resolution CM/ResDH(2007)83, 20 June 2007; also *Hakkar v France*, Commission Report of 27 June 1995, for similar difficulties; see n 92.

[41] The problem has arisen in several contexts. First, in six judgments on the action of security forces in Northern Ireland: *McKerr v UK* 2001-III; 34 EHRR 553, and others, see, *inter alia*, Interim Resolution CM/ResDH(2007)73 and Committee of Ministers Information Document CM/Inf/DH(2008)2, 22 February 2008, 'Cases concerning the action of security forces in Northern Ireland' (a memorandum prepared by the Secretariat). Second, in Bulgaria with the execution of *Velikova v Bulgaria* 2000-VI and ten other cases, see Interim Resolution CM/Res/DH(2007)107. In the Chechen disappearance cases, *Khashiyev and Akayeva v Russia* hudoc (2005); 42 EHRR 397 and others, considered in Committee of Ministers Information Document, 'Violations of the ECHR in the Chechen Republic: Russia's compliance with the European Court's judgments', 12 June 2007, CM/Inf/Dh(2006)32 revised 2; see also Interim Resolution CM (ResDH/2011)292 concerning the failure of the Russian Federation to carry out an effective investigation as required by the judgments in *Khashiyev and Akayayeva v Russia* hudoc (2005), *Isayeva v Russia* hudoc (2005), and *Abuyeva v Russia* hudoc (2011). See the Annual Reports 2007–2012 for further details, http://www.coe.int/t/dghl/monitoring/execution/Documents/Publications_en.asp.

Repetitive groups of cases may also pose logistical problems for the Committee's supervision of individual measures. One such problem area at present includes cases brought against a number of East European states concerning the failure or serious delay of the domestic authorities or state companies to implement final decisions of domestic courts, which can often involve substantial assets.[42] After the Court's judgments in these cases (which can number in the hundreds), the Committee may have to examine whether any further steps have been taken at the domestic level, such as whether writs of execution have been issued, whether debtor's assets can be found and transferred to successful litigants, and so on.

Not all the Committee's work on individual measures concerns such repetitive and mundane matters. New human rights problems will bring new problems for execution. Environmental rights, for example, have become more prominent in the Court's case law and the individual measures needed may be of some scale and complexity. They may also be closely related to the general measures the state must take. For example, in *Fadeyeva v Russia*[43] and *Ledyayeva and others v Russia*,[44] the Court found violations of Article 8 because of the impact of pollution from a steelworks on the applicants' private and family life. The individual measures currently under examination include rehousing the applicants outside the area affected by the pollution, but also, and this is related to the general measures simultaneously under examination, measures that would prevent or minimize the pollution, which appears to affect the entire town, Cherepovets, where the steelworks are based.[45]

III. GENERAL MEASURES

The third and most important step in execution is that the Committee will examine whether general measures have been adopted, preventing new violations or putting an end to continuing violations (Rule 6(2)(b)(ii)). Although the Committee will examine the question of general measures from the outset, it does not wait for individual measures to be adopted. It is sometimes the case that general measures must first be adopted to allow individual measures to be taken, for example, where a new remedy is created as a general measure which the applicant can then use.[46] The need for such measures follows from the general public international law requirement that the parties to a treaty, such as the Convention, have an obligation to ensure that their law and practice conforms to it. The Rules give examples: legislative or regulatory amendments, changes of case law or administrative practice, or publication of the Court's judgment in the language of the respondent state and its dissemination to the authorities concerned. The Annual Reports (2007–2012) of the Committee of Ministers also provide details concerning the measures called for in specific cases.[47] Training of state officials and other awareness-raising measures have also been considered in recent years. The assessment of whether general measures have been

---

[42] See eg, *Timofeyev v Russia* hudoc (2003); 40 EHRR 901 (and ninety-seven similar cases) and *Zhovner v Ukraine* hudoc (2004) (and 231 similar cases). The problems arising from the execution of both groups of cases are regularly examined by the Committee. Concerning *Zhovner*, see information document CM/Inf/DH(2013)11, which reflects the examination of the issue in light of the pilot judgment of October 2009 in the *Yuri Nikolayevich Ivanov* case.   [43] 2005-IV; 49 EHRR 295.

[44] Hudoc (2006).

[45] For an outline of the case and the measures taken and to be taken, see the Committee of Ministers Information Document CM/Inf/DH(2007)7, 13 February 2007, 'Industrial pollution in breach of the European Convention: Measures required by a European Court judgment' (a memorandum prepared by the Secretariat), available at the execution of judgments website.

[46] For example *MD and Others v Malta* hudoc (2012).   [47] See n 8.

taken is often the principal reason for a case remaining on the Committee's agenda for some time after any just satisfaction has been afforded and individual measures taken. Questions remain, however, as to what extent the Committee is qualified, as a political body composed of diplomatic representatives, to assess the legal issue of whether reme-dial legislation or amendments to administrative practices are sufficient to comply with the terms of the Court's judgment, even if in practice they are acting on the basis of legal advice from experts in their capitals.[48] As Peter Leuprecht has pointed out, the practical application of this aspect of Article 46 places a heavy responsibility on the shoulders of the Directorate General of Human Rights and Legal Affairs, whose duty it is to 'assist and advise' the Committee. As he states:

> Indeed, when there is reason to doubt whether the measures taken by the state as a con-sequence of a Court judgment are pertinent and sufficient, there is little chance of such doubt being expressed by the representatives of other states.... This uncomfortable task is usually left to the [Execution Department].[49]

In the light of the numerous administrative and legislative changes that are recorded in Article 46 resolutions, it is evident that the quiet influence brought to bear by the Execution Department has become an essential and effective part of the process. This may take the form of bilateral exchanges with governments, visits to particular coun-tries to provide advice and assistance on draft laws, or the preparation of memoranda on specific issues for the guidance of the Committee of Ministers.[50] Nevertheless, it is recognized that while there is an excellent compliance rate with the payment of just satisfaction, there are serious problems of delay in implementing the general meas-ures required by key judgments in certain states and, in a smaller number of cases, an unwillingness to comply with the judgment for political reasons. These problems have not yet been satisfactorily resolved. The problem of delay is openly acknowledged by the Committee of Ministers itself[51] and has been the object of investigation by the PACE Committee on Legal Affairs and Human Rights (CLAHR) in many of its reports over the years.[52] For example, it took the Belgian authorities almost eight years to introduce legislation amending 'various legal provisions relating to affiliation' in response to the *Marckx* judgment.[53] In the meantime, a further application based on the previous leg-islation was lodged with the Commission culminating in the Court's judgment in the case of *Vermeire v Belgium* in which a further violation was found.[54] Important delays also occurred in the enforcement of the *Sporrong and Lönnroth v Sweden* judgment (six years) and that of *Norris v Ireland* (four years).[55] It also took the United Kingdom seven years to execute the *Matthews* judgment, where the Grand Chamber had found a viola-tion of Article 3 of Protocol 1 because Gibraltarians could not vote in elections to the

---

[48] As can be seen from the Committee's order of business, some states also choose to send government lawyers or other legal experts to represent or advise them during the Committee's meetings; see the website of the Execution Department.   [49] Leuprecht, *European System*, p 798.

[50] See, eg, the Memoranda concerning the issues of property nationalized during the commu-nist regime in Albania and the issue of restitution and compensation for nationalized properties in Romania; H/Exec (2013) 1 and 2, http://www.coe.int/t/dghl/monitoring/execution/Source/Documents/Docs_exec/H-Exec(2013)1_Strain_en.pdf.   [51] See the Annual Report 2012, para 16.

[52] For details see Drzemczewski, 28(2) Netherlands Quarterly of Human Rights (2010) 164–78.

[53] *Marckx v Belgium* A 31 (1979); 2 EHRR 330 PC.

[54] *Vermeire v Belgium* A 214-C (1991); 15 EHRR 488.

[55] *Sporrong and Lönnroth v Sweden* A 52 (1982); 5 EHRR 35 PC; and *Norris v Ireland* A 142 (1988); 13 EHRR 186 PC.

European Parliament, although this delay was because of a Spanish veto to the United Kingdom's proposed change to the relevant EC provisions, causing it to remedy the situation by including Gibraltar in a metropolitan constituency in the United Kingdom.[56] Given the continuing dispute in the UK over prisoners' voting rights, neither the *Hirst (No 2)* nor the *Greens* judgment has been fully implemented.[57] Nor has the judgment in *S and Marper* concerning the indefinite retention of DNA and fingerprint evidence of persons acquitted of an offence,[58] although draft legislation has been prepared and is likely to be adopted. The latest PACE report identifies nine states as having difficulties with the implementation of judgments: Italy, Turkey, Russia, Ukraine, Moldova, Poland, Romania, Greece, Bulgaria.[59] Aside from difficulties with delay in general, the Committee is also faced with the question of a state failing to comply with the deadline set out in a pilot judgment affecting a large group of cases (see *Yuriy Nikolayevich Ivanov v Ukraine* (40450/04)) and resulting in the adoption of repeated interim resolutions by the Committee and high-level contacts with the authorities.[60]

The issue of delay in execution raises several important questions of principle. In the first place, while it must be recognized that the amendment of national legislation may take some time and may be subject to the vagaries of national politics and busy legislative agendas, proper 'supervision' of execution of the Court judgments presupposes that the Committee take firm and resolute action with recalcitrant states. The absence at present of a more effective procedure to cajole states into making speedier legislative or administrative changes casts a shadow over the integrity of the enforcement system. The Committee has recently acquired some new powers under Protocol 14, but whether it is prepared to give full effect to these powers remains to be seen (see Chapter 2, section 6). The Committee of Ministers has responded to this problem by using more Interim Resolutions, as well as detailed decisions supporting the pursuit of reforms and setting out the concerns of the Committee of Ministers.[61] The adoption of new working methods in 2011 was also aimed at addressing these concerns and the 2012 statistics show a decrease in the number of leading cases before the Committee for less than two years.[62] However, the overall case load is still increasing. Following the Interlaken, Izmir, and Brighton reform Conferences (see Chapter 2, section 7) there is a determination by the states and the Committee of Ministers to address these shortcomings and to make the system more effective.[63]

Taking general measures can be much more problematic for a contracting party when the problem relates to settled domestic case law, in spite of the growing trend towards the

---

[56] *Matthews v UK* 1999-I; 28 EHRR 361 GC; Final Resolution Res DH (2006) 57, 2 November 2006.

[57] As of date of writing, July 2013. Hudoc (2005) GC and hudoc (2010) respectively; see Ch 23, section 4 and the decision taken at its 1157th meeting (December 2012); see also the inadmissibility decision in *Maclean and Cole v United Kingdom* hudoc (2013).

[58] Hudoc GC (2008). Following the adoption of the Protection of Freedoms Act on 1 May 2012, the Committee transferred the case from the enhanced to the standard supervision track pending the entry into force of the legislation.

[59] *The Pourgourides Report on implementation of judgments of the Court*, 20 December 2010. The report provides ample details concerning the problem areas in respect of each state, available at http://assembly.coe.int/ASP/XRef/X2H-DW-XSL.asp?fileid=12589&lang=EN.   [60] Hudoc (2009).

[61] See, on the subject of delays in execution, secretariat proposals CM/Inf (2003) 37, CM/Inf/DH (2006)18, as well as proposals made by the Steering Committee (CDDH), CDDH (2006) 008; CDDH (2006) 008; CDDH (2008) 014.

[62] Showing that the 'younger' cases before the Committee are being more rapidly executed than the 'older' cases; see the remarks by the Director-General in the 6th Annual Report (2012), n 15.

[63] See CM/Rec (2008) 2, a recommendation proposing a variety of practical national measures to ensure rapid execution of judgments.

direct effect of the Convention in national legal systems. In such cases, Ministry of Justice circulars informing courts or officials of the Strasbourg Court judgment are unlikely to suffice for the Committee to close its examination; the Committee may prefer to wait until it has clear evidence that the domestic courts have adopted a more Convention-compliant approach. For example, the matter has arisen in the context of the Committee's execution of the Court's judgments on freedom of expression in Turkey, especially convictions by state security courts for insulting the state or nation, which until recently were consistently upheld by the Turkish Court of Cassation. The Committee observed that following judgments of the European Court, several provisions at the origin of the violations were amended with the coming into force of the Criminal Code in June 2005. Information provided by the government indicated that, while the practice of the courts and prosecutors had improved, it could not be said that the Turkish superior courts had fully aligned their practice with the Court's judgments. The matter was recently addressed in a high-level conference in Ankara organized by the Department for the Execution of Judgments in cooperation with the Turkish Ministry of Justice in February 2013, where both the Secretary General of the Council of Europe and the Turkish Minister of Justice spoke about the need for action to bring Turkish legislation in line with Council of Europe standards.[64]

The problem of ensuring that general measures are taken is almost inevitably more acute in inter-state cases. Perhaps because of the extent and number of violations, the Court found in *Cyprus v Turkey*,[65] after many years and various interim resolutions, a number of issues remain unresolved, in particular the plight of missing persons in northern Cyprus and the home and property of displaced persons. Indeed, while progress has been made in some areas,[66] it seems unlikely that the Committee will be able to close its examination of the entire case soon, not least because of its legal and factual complexity which goes to the roots of the political dispute between the two countries. It seems clear that the final resolution of the human rights dimension to the Cypriot conflict is inextricable from the resolution of the conflict itself.

3. THE COURT AND EXECUTION OF ITS JUDGMENTS

Does the Committee of Ministers possess exclusive competence in the field of enforcement?[67] Is it open, for example, to the applicant to complain that the state is in breach of its obligations under Article 46 to abide by the Court's judgment, and would the Court

---

[64] See, the Execution Department's website for more details concerning the conference at: http://www.coe.int/t/dghl/monitoring/execution/themes/hrtf/tables_rondes/conf_ankara_2013_EN.asp.

[65] (*Fourth inter-state case*) 2001-IV; 35 EHRR 731 GC. In 2012, Cyprus requested the Court to make an award of just satisfaction in respect of this judgment on the grounds that Turkey is no longer cooperating in the enforcement procedure. The issue had been adjourned in the 2001 judgment. The request is currently pending before the Grand Chamber.

[66] The Committee has so far closed its examination of the issues raised in the judgment concerning military courts, the living conditions of Greek Cypriots in northern Cyprus, as regards secondary education, the censorship of schoolbooks, and freedom of religion (see document CM/Inf/DH(2011)32 of 14 June 2011, setting out the state of play in relation to the examination of the case).

[67] See sections 4 and 6 of this chapter for the other Council of Europe actors that play a role in the execution process.

have competence to examine such a claim in proceedings instituted by an individual? The legal position has evolved considerably in recent years.[68]

The issue came before the former Court in *Olsson v Sweden (No 2)*,[69] in which it declined to become involved in the execution process. The applicants complained that despite the Court's judgment in the first *Olsson* case (where a violation had been found concerning the implementation of a care order), the Swedish authorities had continued to prevent their reunion with their children.[70] The Court considered that no separate issue arose under former Article 53 (now Article 46), since the fresh complaint raised a new issue which had not been determined by the *Olsson* judgment. Writing extra-judicially, Judge Martens forcefully argued that complaints under former Article 53 should not be decided by the Committee of Ministers but by the Court since: (i) the interpretation of its own judgments was better left to the Court than to a gathering of professional diplomats who were not necessarily trained lawyers possessing the qualifications required for judicial office; and (ii) the Committee could not be regarded as a 'tribunal': its members were under the direct authority of their internal administration; the representative of the state concerned was not excluded from the deliberations and could even vote; the Committee might be unable to reach a decision because of the requirements of a two-thirds majority; it sat in private; and applicants were excluded from participation in its proceedings.[71] Those arguments remain valid under the present system.[72]

The matter arose again in *Verein gegen Tierfabriken Schweiz (VgT) v Switzerland (No 2)*,[73] where the Court considered the second application of an animal rights group which had been prevented from showing a television commercial. In its first judgment of 28 June 2001,[74] the Court had held that the Swiss authorities' refusal to broadcast the commercial in question was in violation of Article 10 of the Convention. On 1 December 2001, on the basis of that judgment, the applicant association applied to the Federal Court for revision of the final domestic judgment prohibiting the commercial from being broadcast. On 29 April 2002, the Federal Court refused that request, stating that the association had not shown that it had a sufficient interest in broadcasting the original commercial given the amount of time that had passed. The Committee of Ministers was not informed that the Federal Court had refused the request for revision and had accordingly ended its examination of the first judgment by adopting a resolution in July 2003. However, that resolution noted the possibility of lodging a request for revision with the Federal Court. The applicant association therefore brought a second application in July 2002, complaining about the continued prohibition on broadcasting the television commercial in question.[75] The Swiss government argued that the application was incompatible *ratione materiae* with the Convention since the Federal Court's judgment did not raise any new issue that had not been determined in the Strasbourg Court's judgment, and the Committee of Ministers had discharged its duty in adopting its resolution. The execution of the Court's judgment, it was argued, falls solely within the jurisdiction of the Committee of Ministers. The Court rejected that argument. The Committee of Minister's role in this sphere did not exclude

---

[68] For a general survey of the Court's own role in execution, see Wildhaber, in Dupuy *et al*, eds, *Völkrrecht als Wertordnung/Common Values in International Law: Festschrift für/Essays in Honour of Christian Tomuschat*, 2006.   [69] A 250 (1992); 17 EHRR 134.

[70] *Olsson v Sweden (No 1)* A 130 (1988); 11 EHRR 259 PC.

[71] Martens, *Schermers Collection*, Vol III, 1994, pp 253–92.

[72] For a defence of the Court's approach, see Judge Rolv Ryssdal, *Schermers Symposium Proceedings*, 1996, pp 49–69.   [73] Hudoc (2009) GC.

[74] *Vgt Verein gegen Tierfabriken v Switzerland* 2001-VI; 34 EHRR 159.

[75] *Vgt Verein gegen Tierfabriken (VgT) v Switzerland (No 2)* GC hudoc (2009).

that steps taken by a state to remedy a violation cannot raise a new issue undecided by the judgment and form the subject of a new application before the Court. The test was to examine whether the applications relate to essentially the same persons, the same facts, and the same complaints. The Court held that in dismissing the application to re-open the proceedings, the Federal Court had mainly relied upon new grounds, namely that because of the time that had elapsed, the applicant association had lost all interest in having the commercial broadcast. For the Court, this constituted new information capable of giving rise to a fresh violation of Article 10. If the Court were unable to examine this new fact, it would escape all scrutiny under the Convention.[76] The Grand Chamber went to find a fresh violation of Article 10.

In reaching its conclusion the Court examined at length the nature of the state's obligation under Article 46. It held that the state is under an international obligation to take individual and/or general measures in order to put to an end the violation and to redress its effects, 'its aim being to put the applicant, as far as possible, in the position he would have been had the requirements of the Convention not been disregarded'. As was noted in Vgt (No 2), it remains free to choose the means by which it will discharge its obligations under Article 46, 'provided such means are compatible with the conclusions set out in the Court's judgment'.[77]

The issue of the Court encroaching upon the jurisdiction of the Committee of Ministers has also arisen in a situation where the Court had previously indicated both individual and general measures which were not complied with. The issue arose in Ivanţoc, Popa and others v Moldova and Russia,[78] a follow-up application to the Grand Chamber judgment in Ilaşcu, Ivanţoc, Leşco and Petrov-Popa v Moldova and Russia.[79] In its Ilaşcu judgment, the Court found a number of violations of the Convention arising from the trial, conviction, and continuing detention of the applicants in Transdniestria, held Moldova and Russia to be responsible, and stated that they were to take all necessary measures to put an end to the arbitrary detention of the applicants still imprisoned and secure their immediate release. Russia, however, did not comply, and in a series of interim resolutions the Committee of Ministers deplored the lack of progress made by Russia in securing the release of the applicants, whilst commending Moldova on the efforts it had made. The applicants, still in detention, brought a second application alleging that their detention was still unlawful and that the failure of both states to comply with their obligations to secure their release was a breach of Article 46.[80] The Court, following the approach developed by the Grand Chamber in VgT (No 2), considered that it was confronted with a new situation in that the two applicants continued to be detained after 8 July 2004 until June 2007. Those complaints (and the complaint concerning the absence of an effective remedy) had not been previously examined by the Court. It made no difference that the detention was a continuation of the detention found to have been in violation of the Convention in the Ilaşcu judgment. Again, it weighed heavily with the Court that if it were not able to examine the complaint, it would escape all scrutiny and the applicants would be deprived of an award of just satisfaction in respect of the fresh violation.[81]

It must be right that the Court is able to examine and rule on a claim that a contracting party is in violation of its obligations under Article 46 by failing to give effect to the

---

[76] VgT v Switzerland (No 2) paras 61–8.
[77] VgT v Switzerland (No 2), para 88. However, see the Court's practice concerning pilot-judgments and Article 46 directions: Ch 3, sections 3.VII and 5.   [78] Hudoc (2012).
[79] 2004-VII; 40 EHRR 1030 GC.   [80] Hudoc (2012) paras 1–3.   [81] Id, paras 90–6.

Court's judgment where this has the effect of giving rise to a fresh or continuing viola-tion.[82] However, a 'new' element or fact is required and in many cases of non-compliance, which do not involve a continuing situation, this may not be present.[83] Thus it may be argued that where the breach of Article 46 resides in a clear-cut refusal to comply (eg to introduce individual and/or general measures in a case concerning the taking of prop-erty), it would fall, under the scheme of the Convention, to the Committee of Ministers under Article 46 to take cognizance of such refusal. It seems that the Court will not exam-ine such non-compliance, even when it has become clear, for example, from a persistent refusal, that there has been a *déni de justice*. Nevertheless, where the case concerns a continuing situation (as in detention cases or access, custody, or other child care cases or disappearances), where the facts continue to evolve after the Court has given judgment, the Court has shown itself willing to examine the new situation on its merits and to make an award under Article 41. As indicated by the Court in the *Vgt (No 2)* judgment, it does so on the basis that new violations of the applicant's rights should not be able to escape the Court's scrutiny.[84]

As noted earlier, despite the possibility of a finding of a breach of Article 46, no sanc-tions against a respondent state for non-execution are specifically provided for under the Convention. But the Statute of the Council of Europe provides that a serious violation of the principles of the rule of law and human rights may lead to a state having its right of representation suspended and/or being requested by the Committee of Ministers to withdraw from the Council of Europe (Articles 8 and 3 of the Statute).[85] The likelihood, however, of such a severe sanction being employed for non-compliance with a judgment of the Court is remote.

4. THE PARLIAMENTARY ASSEMBLY AND EXECUTION OF JUDGMENTS

The Parliamentary Assembly has become a key actor in the execution of the Court's judgments through the work of the Committee on Legal Affairs and Human Rights (CLAHR).[86] Since 2000, the Assembly has adopted seven reports and resolutions and

---

[82] But not that corrective measures introduced by the state are insufficient. The Court considered that it had no jurisdiction to 'review the general and/or individual measures, if any, adopted by the respondent States to secure the rights of the applicants which the Court found to be violated in its [*Ilaşcu*] judgment', hudoc (2012), para 91. Note also the possibility of the Committee of Ministers to initiate infringement pro-ceedings under Article 46(4) of the Convention where there is non-compliance.

[83] See, for requests that have been rejected, *Lyons and Others v the United Kingdom* (dec), no 15227/03, ECHR 2003-IX; *Steck-Risch and Others v Liechtenstein* (dec), no 29061/08, hudoc (2010); *Schelling v Austria* (dec), no 46128/07, hudoc (2010); *Kafkaris v Cyprus (No 2)* (dec), no 9644/09, hudoc (2011), and *Costică Moldovan and Others v Romania* (dec), no 8229/04 and other applications, § 127, hudoc (2011).

[84] See, eg, *Mehemi v France (No 2)*, ECHR 2003-IV; *Liu v Russia (No 2)* hudoc (2011); *Emre v Switzerland (No 2)* hudoc (2011); also *Kudeshkina v Russia (No 2)* pending.

[85] The only relevant instance is the case of Greece, which, after the military *coup d'état* in 1967, dra-matically withdrew from the organization when it was evident that the Committee would vote to expel it. It returned in 1974 after the restoration of civilian rule. See Magliveras, *Exclusion from Participation in International Organisations: the Law and Practice Behind Member States' Expulsion and Suspension of Membership*, 1999, pp 79–87.

[86] See Drzemczewski, 28(2) NQHR (2010) 164–78 and *Recent Parliamentary Initiatives to Ensure Compliance with Strasbourg Court Judgments* in Mélanges Flauss (2012). Leach, *The Effectiveness of the Committee of Ministers in Supervising the Enforcement of Judgments of the European Court of Human Rights*, 2006, pp 443–56.

six recommendations on the subject of execution identifying states responsible for dila-tory implementation or non-implementation and calling on them to give effect to Court judgments.[87] The Assembly has a number of useful tools in its armoury. It can carry out state visits, make general recommendations aimed at improving the system of execu-tion, or raise individual cases for special examination. It may also seek explanations from national delegates for a failure to comply or make a recommendation to the Committee of Ministers.[88] The three Rapporteurs who have been involved in this activity since 2000 have adopted a pro-active approach and have visited many of the states' parties where there are particular problems of execution in engaging with national parliamentarians but also with government representatives on how to speed up the introduction of the required individual or general measures.[89] The focus has been on problematic instances of non-execution especially cases revealing systemic problems. The Assembly sees its role in this area as complementary to that of the Committee of Ministers. It is based on the conviction that many of the difficult issues could be resolved through the active involve-ment of PACE in close cooperation with national parliamentarians working with national PACE delegations. The CLAHR has stressed, in particular, the role of national parlia-mentarians in systematically verifying the compatibility of draft (and existing) legisla-tion with Convention standards and setting up parliamentary bodies to scrutinize the faithful implementation of judgments by the executive branch, as well as ensuring the existence of domestic remedies. There is, however, much progress to be made in this area, as only six parliaments in the contracting parties have such a special body for supervis-ing implementation of judgments. In the absence of such parliamentary bodies, CLAHR has encouraged the existence of parliamentary procedures to ensure that MPs are at least informed of adverse findings by the Court. However, so far only twelve states have indi-cated that they possess such information procedures.[90]

It is difficult to gauge whether the energetic work of the Assembly has improved the speed or diligence with which states comply with judgments. There have certainly been instances where, due to its privileged relations with national legislators, measures of implementation have been adopted or speeded up.[91] One clear effect is that the activities of PACE have placed in the public domain a large amount of useful information con-cerning the states responsible for delayed enforcement, and the specific cases involved in a manner that is more pointed and critical than the data available from the Execution Department. This has the effect of identifying the worst offenders in the system and

---

[87] CLAHR Reports on the execution/implementation of judgments of the European Court of Human Rights: (Erik Jurgens as Rapporteur) PACE Doc 8808, 12 July 2000; PACE Doc 9307, 21 December 2001; PACE Doc 9537, 5 September 2002; PACE Doc 10192 (concerning Turkey), 1 June 2004; PACE Doc 10351, 21 October 2004; PACE Doc 11020, 18 September 2006; also AS/JUR(2010) 36, CLAHR Rapporteur: Mr Christos Pourgourides, 9 November 2010. All of these texts are available on the Assembly website http://assembly.coe.int/defaultE.asp.

[88] See Leach, *The Effectiveness of the Committee of Ministers in Supervising the Enforcement of Judgments of the European Court of Human Rights*, 2006, at pp 449–50.

[89] Mr Jurgens, Mr Pourgourides, and Mr Klaas de Vries (Rapporteur for the 8th report), see AS/JUR (2013)14; CLAHR, *Preparation of the 8th report—Stock-taking and proposals by the Rapporteur.*

[90] See Drzemczewski, 28(2) NQHR (2010), 173–6. The six are Croatia, Finland, Hungary, Romania, Ukraine, and the United Kingdom. The twelve are Austria, Bosnia and Herzegovina, Croatia, Cyprus, Germany, Hungary, Italy, the Netherlands, Norway, Sweden, Switzerland, and the United Kingdom. The UK's Joint Committee on Human Rights is singled out as a rare example (and best practice) of a special parliamentary body with a specific mandate to verify and monitor the compatibility of a country's law and practice with the ECHR (p 174).

[91] See eg *Hakkar v France* (Commission Report of 27 June 1995) discussed in Lobov, in Chernishova and Lobov, eds, *Essays in Honour of Anatoly Kovler*, 2013, pp 91–4.

increasing the pressure on them to remedy the situation. But, as Andrew Drzemczewski has pointed out, the political impact of this work is not limited to 'naming and shaming', since the Assembly has a greater freedom of action than the Committee of Ministers through, for example, its country visits and its recognition of the strategic power of national parliamentarians to hold governments to account for their inaction. Indeed the strength of this activity lies in harnessing the dual role of parliamentarians as members of PACE and national parliaments.[92] It has become clear since the first PACE report in 2000 and the developments thereafter that the CLAHR has become an essential dimension in the complex exercise of ensuring that the states are held to high standards of compliance.

5. PROTOCOL 14

Protocol 14 came into force on 1 June 2010. The Protocol has an important impact on the work of the Committee of Ministers.[93] Two particularly important aspects are the extension of the Committee of Ministers supervision to all friendly settlements (not just those in the form of a judgment) and the possibility to refer questions back to the Court, either where the Committee has a question concerning the interpretation of a judgment or where a state failed to fulfil its obligation to abide by the judgment. The Explanatory Report to the Protocol states:

> Rapid and adequate execution has, of course, an effect on the influx of new cases: the more rapidly general measures are taken by states Parties to execute judgments which point to a structural problem, the fewer repetitive applications there will be.[94]

The Protocol takes two concrete steps to this end through the addition of three more paragraphs to Article 46 (paragraphs (3)–(5)). First, Article 46(3) empowers the Committee of Ministers to ask the Court to interpret a final judgment, for the purpose of facilitating the supervision of its execution. The justification for this is, as stated in the Explanatory Report,[95] that execution difficulties are sometimes encountered due to disagreement as to the interpretation of judgments. An interpretation by the Court would settle 'any argument' concerning a judgment's exact meaning.[96] The Explanatory Report also makes clear that the aim of the new Article 46(3) is to enable the Court to give an interpretation of a judgment, not to pronounce on the measures taken by a High Contracting Party to comply with that judgment.[97] Subject to that, the Court would also be free to decide on the manner and form in which it wished to reply to the request.[98] Secondly, Article 46(4)

---

[92] Lobov, p 177–8.

[93] A detailed analysis of the impact can be found in a document prepared by the Department for the Execution of judgments (Memorandum DH-DD (2010)278 of 25 May 2010).

[94] Explanatory Report, http://conventions.coe.int/Treaty/EN/Reports/Html/194.htm at para 16. See Ch 3, section 6.

[95] Explanatory Report, para 96. The decision to refer the matter to the Court would require a majority vote of two-thirds of the representatives entitled to sit on the Committee; this requirement is said by the explanatory report to show that the Committee of Ministers should 'use this possibility sparingly, to avoid over-burdening the Court'.   [96] Explanatory Report.

[97] Nor would there be any time limit for making such a request since the question of interpretation could arise at any time during the Committee of Ministers' examination of the execution of the judgment.

[98] It would normally be for the formation of the Court which delivered the original judgment to rule on the question of interpretation.

empowers the Committee, if it considered that a High Contracting Party had refused to abide by a final judgment, to refer to the Court the question whether that Party had failed to fulfil its obligation under Article 46(1) to abide by the judgment.[99] This is a controversial change, not least because the Court itself, in its comments on the final drafts of the Protocol, did not support it; its argument was that significant legal and practical questions were unanswered by the change.[100] Nonetheless, the change was adopted and the explanation for it is that the parties to the Convention have a collective duty to preserve the Court's authority.[101] The 'infringement proceedings' would be heard by the Grand Chamber, but would not re-open the question of the violation found in the initial judgment or lead to the award of further compensation. The political pressure of such proceedings was thought to suffice, and the final sanction remains suspension of voting rights in the Committee or expulsion from the Council under Article 8 of the Statute. In the event that the Court were to find a violation of Article 46(1), it would refer the case to the Committee of Ministers 'for consideration of the measures to be taken', pursuant to Article 46(5). In the event that the Court found no violation, it is to refer the case to the Committee of Ministers, 'which shall close its examination of the case'.

It is unlikely, but not inconceivable, that the Committee would ever make use of this new power, not least because under new Article 46(4), the decision to do so would require a two-thirds majority in the Committee. In a given case it may be easier to obtain a majority for a request for interpretation as a lesser alternative. To some extent there is an overlap between the two types of request, since the Court may have to address how its judgment should be interpreted in infringement proceedings. However, the instances of lengthy non-compliance set out previously make it at least possible that the Committee would consider this option in an egregious case. There are, of course, difficulties with asking the Court to undertake an assessment of whether a judgment has been executed. Clearly, the Court's task would be easier if in the original judgment it had itself indicated under Article 46 what measures (either individual or general) might be required of a state. But the task is more complicated if the Court is asked to assess whether general measures taken by a state are sufficient to meet its obligation under Article 46(1), since this is inevitably a more open-ended and prospective analysis, though, as Judge Martens has pointed out,[102] one which a court is better equipped to take. Both interpretation and infringement proceedings could be of crucial importance for pilot judgments. By definition, pilot judgments require states to take general measures of a structural nature, and in addition, these cases tend to be high profile so the Committee is likely to take a greater interest in ensuring prompt execution. If there is a dispute between the Committee and the state as to the measures that should be adopted in order to remedy any systemic problem the Court has found, then the Committee may be more inclined to refer the question to the Court. It is thought that it is more likely that the Committee would first bring interpretation proceedings, but if a state is dilatory in complying, in respect of a judgment that could affect hundreds of applicants, infringement proceedings may be a useful tool for the Committee to employ as a way of assisting or encouraging the state to introduce key reforms. Under the current system, the nature of a pilot judgment gives the Court a greater stake in the

---

[99] The Committee is required to serve formal notice on the state in question of the intention to make the reference.

[100] See the 'Response of the European Court of Human Rights to the CDDH Interim Activity Report prepared following the 46th Plenary Administrative Session on 2 February 2004', CDDH-GDR (2004)001 at paras 29 and 30.

[101] 'Response of the European Court of Human Rights to the CDDH Interim Activity Report', para 98.

[102] See n 71.

execution process, since if there are many follow-up applications already registered when it delivers a pilot judgment, it will only strike out all those follow-up cases when it is satisfied that the state has created a national remedy to address the problem and the follow-up applications can be 'repatriated'.[103]

6. CONCLUSION

The criticisms of the role of the Committee of Ministers under Article 46 have, at times, been strident. Commentators have expressed their dissatisfaction with a system which entrusts an essentially political body with the task of taking quasi-judicial decisions under Article 46. Some regard the Committee of Ministers as the 'Achilles heel' of the system for this reason.[104] Nevertheless, it is reflective of the maturing of the Convention system that the role of the Committee has been progressively limited by successive amending protocols to the Convention. In its favour, the overall record of the Committee of Ministers under Article 46, judged by the wealth of legal reform that it has presided over, can be seen as praiseworthy notwithstanding the growing problem of delayed execution or persistent refusal to execute by some states.[105] It must also be recognized that some of the problems that it has been asked to resolve are intractable (eg *Cyprus v Turkey*, the Italian and Ukranian justice systems, Russian actions in the Caucasus), and demonstrate perhaps the limits of what can be achieved through an international judicial system. It is thus too easy to lay the blame for the failure to resolve such problems at the door of the Committee of Ministers. The fact that its own authority as a political institution is involved in this process may, in fact, make it well suited to perform such a role. This perhaps provides an important insight into how it operates as well as its limitations. Peer pressure and persuasion have managed over the years to bring about results, but it has not been enough to deal with states that persistently refuse to comply or delay execution. As a result other actors such as the PACE (through the CLAHR) but (to a lesser extent) also the Commissioner for Human Rights,[106] the Venice Commission,[107] and the Court itself have become involved in the process of execution in different ways, reflecting the complexities involved in the process. This has given rise to creative synergies that are welcomed by the Committee of Ministers itself.[108] As the former PACE Rapporteur Erik Jurgens has noted:

> The ECHR's mechanism does not operate in a legal vacuum: the Court's judgments are implemented and translated into real life through a complex legal and political process, which involves a number of domestic and international institutions.[109]

However, as recognized in the reform process, further consideration should be given to the establishment of procedures which deal with the episodic problem of delay in introducing remedial legislation, as well as the often complex issues concerning the adequacy

---

[103] See *Broniowski v Poland* 2005-IX; 43 EHRR 1 GC and *Hutten-Czapska v Poland* GC hudoc (2008); *Kuric v Slovenia* GC hudoc (2012). Corr in FN 105 cant update.   [104] Greer, 83 PL 92 (2005).

[105] See the Annual Reports (section 2.III of this chapter) and the collection of interim and final resolutions, http://www.coe.int/t/dghl/monitoring/execution/Source/Documents/IntRes2012_en.pdf.

[106] See the Commissioner's activity report at http://www.coe.int/t/commissioner/Default_en.asp.

[107] See generally http://www.venice.coe.int/WebForms/documents/by_topic.aspx.

[108] See Annual Report 2012, pp 17–19.

[109] Cited by Leach, *The Effectiveness of the Committee of Ministers in Supervising the Enforcement of Judgments of the European Court of Human Rights*, 2006, p 455.

and sufficiency of such measures when measured against the judgment of the Court that has provoked them.[110] The Brighton Conference, in particular, has set out a comprehensive agenda for future change.[111]

Consideration should also be given to the manner in which the Committee seeks to enforce pilot judgments (as well as its more complex non-pilot cases[112]), since the implementation of such far-reaching judgments often raises more difficult problems concerning necessary reform than other more straightforward judgments. The use of national human rights institutions or the good offices of the Council's Commissioner for Human Rights or even outside legal experts to engage the state authorities in discussion as to the nature of the legal reforms required, are ideas which reflect the important 'execution' dimension of the pilot judgment procedure and which merit further reflection.[113]

Equally, the handling of the *Cyprus v Turkey* case, and the *Ilascu v Moldova and Russia* cases, as well as the on-going confrontation over the UK's refusal to implement the prisoners' voting judgments, demonstrate the limits of a system of execution that is, in the final analysis, inter-governmental and thus dependent on the will of sovereign states. There is perhaps also a tendency in such politically sensitive cases to deal with them as political questions and not, as they should be seen, as legal or rule of law questions relating to the execution of a binding court judgment. This is the natural gravitation of a political body and may also be inevitable given the intractable nature of the underlying political problems reflected in some cases. Unfortunately, apart from raising questions concerning compliance with Article 46, it reveals the limits of the concept of collective enforcement under the Convention in disputes concerning allegations of widespread violations, damages the reputation of the Committee, and undermines the integrity of the Convention system as a whole. The Brighton proposals reflect a keen awareness of these problems, as well as a determination to tackle them.[114]

---

[110] The Interlaken, Izmir, and Brighton reform conferences highlighted the problems associated with execution of judgments; see the Interlaken Declaration (19 February 2010) para 11; the Izmir Declaration (26/27 April 2011) Section H paras 1–63; the Brighton Declaration (18–20 April 2012) Section F paras 26–29.

[111] See Section F of the Brighton Declaration encouraging states to adopt domestic capacities and mechanisms to ensure rapid execution, and Annual Report (2012), pp 17–19.

[112] For example *Sejdić and Finci v Bosnia and Herzegovina* (GC) ECHR 2009;Insertion mark given here but no text found, check and update. *A, B and C v Ireland* (GC) hudoc (2010).

[113] See Fribergh, '*Pilot judgments from the Court's perspective*', Colloquy 'Towards stronger implementation of the European Convention on Human Rights at national level' Stockholm, 9–10 June 2008 and O'Boyle, 2008 EHRLR 1.

[114] Civil society is engaged in examining how the execution process can be made more effective. See the Open Society Justice Initiative Background Paper, *Supervision of Execution of ECHR Judgments*, November 2012; also the Open Society paper, *National Implementation of the Interlaken Declaration*, available at http://www.opensocietyfoundations.org/sites/default/files/echr-reform-implementation-10232012.pdf.

PART III
THE RIGHTS GUARANTEED

5   Article 2: The Right to Life 203

6   Article 3: Freedom from Torture or Inhuman or Degrading
Treatment or Punishment 235

7   Article 4: Freedom from Slavery, Servitude, or Forced or
Compulsory Labour 279

8   Article 5: The Right to Liberty and Security of the Person 287

9   Article 6: The Right to a Fair Trial 370

10   Article 7: Freedom from Retroactive Criminal Offences and
Punishment 493

11   Articles 8–11: General Considerations 503

12   Article 8: The Right to Respect for Private and Family Life, Home,
and Correspondence 522

13   Article 9: Freedom of Thought, Conscience, and Religion 592

14   Article 10: Freedom of Expression 613

15   Article 11: Freedom of Assembly and Association 710

16   Article 12: The Right to Marry and to Found a Family 754

17   Article 13: The Right to an Effective National Remedy 764

18   Article 14 (Freedom from Discrimination in Respect of Protected
Convention Rights) and Protocol 12 (Non-discrimination in Respect
of 'any Right Set Forth by Law') 783

19   Article 15: Derogation in Time of War or Other Public Emergency
Threatening the Life of the Nation 823

20   Articles 16–18: Other Restrictions upon the Rights Protected 851

21 Article 1, First Protocol: The Right to Property 862

22 Article 2, First Protocol: The Right to Education 906

23 Article 3, First Protocol: The Right to Free Elections 920

24 The Fourth, Sixth, Seventh, and Thirteenth Protocols 952

5

ARTICLE 2:
THE RIGHT TO LIFE

> **Article 2**
>
> 1. Everyone's right to life shall be protected by law. No one shall be deprived of his life intentionally save in the execution of a sentence of a court following his conviction of a crime for which this penalty is provided by law.
> 2. Deprivation of life shall not be regarded as inflicted in contravention of this article when it results from the use of force which is no more than absolutely necessary:
>   (a) in defence of any person from unlawful violence;
>   (b) in order to effect a lawful arrest or to prevent the escape of a person lawfully detained;
>   (c) in action lawfully taken for the purpose of quelling a riot or insurrection.

The first right guaranteed in the Convention, in Article 2, is the right to life, the most basic human right of all.[1] The fundamental nature of this right is recognized by the fact that Article 2 is one of the few Convention Articles that cannot be derogated from in time of war or other public emergency.[2] Together with the prohibition of torture and other proscribed ill-treatment in Article 3, it 'enshrines one of the basic values of the democratic societies making up the Council of Europe'.[3] For these reasons, the circumstances in which the deprivation of life may be justified under Article 2 (eg in self-defence) must be 'strictly construed'.[4] As well as a negative obligation not to take life, Article 2 places upon states a positive obligation to protect the right to life. This positive obligation must be interpreted and applied so that it is 'practical and effective'.[5] Where relevant, Article 2 applies to unintentional as well as intentional killings.[6]

1. THE OBLIGATION TO PROTECT
THE RIGHT TO LIFE BY LAW

The first sentence of Article 2(1) states that 'everyone's right to life shall be protected by law'. In *LCB v UK*,[7] the Court held that this establishes a positive obligation for states to

---

[1] On the right to life in Article 2, see Buckley, 1 HRLR 35 (2001); Korff, *The Right to Life: A Guide to the Implementation of Article 2 of the European Convention on Human Rights*, Council of Europe Human Rights Handbook No 8, 2006; Mathieu, *The Right to Life in European Constitutional Law and Conventional Caselaw*, 2006; Ni Aolain, 19 NQHR 21 (2001); Opsahl, in McDonald, Matscher, and Petzold, eds, *The European System for the Protection of Human Rights*, 1993, Ch 11.

[2] See Article 15(2), Convention. Exceptionally, derogation may be made from Article 2 'in respect of deaths resulting from lawful acts of war': Article 15(2).

[3] *McCann v UK* A 324 (1995); 21 EHRR 97 para 147 GC.   [4] *McCann v UK*, para 147.

[5] *McCann v UK*, para 146. Cf *Oneryildiz v Turkey* 2004-XII; 41 EHRR 325 GC.

[6] *McCann v UK*.   [7] 1998-III; 27 EHRR 212 para 36.

take 'appropriate steps to safeguard the lives of those within their jurisdiction'. From this flows a 'primary duty on the state to secure the right to life by putting in place an appropriate legal and administrative framework to deter the commission of offences against the person, backed up by law enforcement machinery for the prevention, suppression and punishment of breaches of such provisions'[8] and/or, in some cases, the provision of civil remedies.[9] The 'legal and administrative framework' referred to requires the adoption of (usually criminal) laws prohibiting the taking of life, and calls for the regulation of the conduct of the police and other state agents and private persons, as well as of activities or situations that might involve a risk to life. The 'law enforcement machinery' includes the police, the criminal prosecution services, and the courts.

I. LEGAL AND ADMINISTRATIVE FRAMEWORK

a. Laws prohibiting the taking of life

Effective criminal laws to deter the commission of life-threatening acts are generally required to protect life.[10] The principle of proportionality suggests that the degree of criminal liability (murder, manslaughter, etc) and the sentence may vary with the circumstances.[11] There must be criminal liability for gross negligence resulting in death in respect of dangerous activities.[12] Civil liability may be sufficient in some cases of unintentional killing.[13] In any case, the 'law' that protects the right to life should be 'formulated with sufficient precision to enable the citizen to regulate his conduct'.[14] Liability for the taking of life must extend under a state's law to the acts of private persons, as well as persons acting for the state.[15]

A state need not make every taking of life illegal. Certain permissible exceptions are indicated in or may be inferred from the text of Article 2. There are other cases in which the taking of life does not usually give rise to liability under European national law and which, accordingly, are not required by Article 2 to be made illegal. Examples are killings in self-defence by private persons[16] and accidental deaths in sporting contests.

b. Euthanasia

A controversial case in national law is euthanasia. Article 2 does not require that passive euthanasia, by which a patient is allowed to die by not being given treatment when the patient is not competent to give consent, be a crime provided that the guidelines followed by doctors are based on a ' a presumption…strongly in favour of prolonging life'; 'such a presumption accords with the spirit of the Convention'.[17] In *Burke v UK*, action based upon guidelines that stressed the best interests of the patient and that required

---

[8] *Makaratzis v Greece* 2004-XI; 41 EHRR 1092 para 57 GC.

[9] *Calvelli and Ciglio v Italy* 2002-I GC.   [10] *Osman v UK* 1998-VIII; 29 EHRR 245 para 115 GC.

[11] A system of prison leave in preparation for final release may comply with Article 2: *Mastromatteo v Italy* 2002-VIII GC.

[12] *Oneryildiz v Turkey* 2004-XII; 41 EHRR 325 GC. As to the need for criminal liability in road accident cases, see *Railean v Moldova* hudoc (2010) and *Rajkowska v Poland No 37393/02* hudoc (2007) DA.

[13] *Calvelli and Ciglio v Italy* 2002-I para 49 GC (medical negligence).

[14] *Sunday Times v UK (No 1)* A 30 (1979); 2 EHRR 245 para 49 PC, interpreting the word 'law' in Article 10, Convention.

[15] *Osman v UK* 1998-VIII; 29 EHRR 245 para 115 GC. *Quaere* whether members of the public must be obliged to assist in a medical emergency: see *Hughes v UK No 11590/85*, 48 DR 258 (1986).

[16] These do not fall within Article 2(2)(a).

[17] *Burke v UK No 19807/06* hudoc (2006) DA. See also *Widmer v Switzerland No 20527/92* hudoc (1993) DA.

that, before withdrawing life support, 'a doctor would be obliged to take account of the applicant's previously expressed wishes and those of the persons close to him, as well as the opinions of other medical personnel and, if there was any conflict or doubt as to the applicant's best interests, then to approach a court', were consistent with Article 2.

There may be a different answer in the case of active euthanasia, where the person's death is brought about by the positive act of another. Article 2 can be taken to require that euthanasia without the consent of the person concerned (involuntary euthanasia) must be a crime, even in the case of the 'mercy killing' of a person with an incurable or painful illness. Article 2 also clearly requires that the involuntary killing of the mentally or physically disabled is criminal. Less clear is the case of assisted suicide.[18] It is permitted, subject to stringent safeguards, in a small number of European states.[19] Although the great majority of European states make assisted suicide a crime, it is unlikely that Article 2 requires that this be so. In the light of European practice generally, it can be supposed that Article 2 does not require that suicide itself be a crime.

As yet, there has been very little Strasbourg jurisprudence under Article 2 on these difficult legal and moral questions. As in the case of abortion, it is likely that a wide margin of appreciation applies where national practice varied greatly.

c. No right to die

In *Pretty v UK*,[20] it was held that Article 2 does not guarantee a 'right to die'. In that case, there was no breach of Article 2 because the husband of the applicant, who was terminally ill and not able to commit suicide by herself, would be subject to prosecution for a criminal offence under English law if he assisted her to die. Whereas the *Pretty* case concerned assisted suicide on its facts, it is clear that Article 2 does not guarantee a right to voluntary euthanasia or to commit suicide by one's own hand. Nonetheless such rights could be guaranteed by another Convention right, particularly Article 8.

d. Amnesties

In *Dujardin v France*,[21] the Commission stated that an amnesty for murder is not a breach of Article 2 'unless it can be seen to form part of a general practice aimed at the systematic prevention of prosecution of the perpetrators of such crimes'. In that case, an amnesty was provided for some fifty individuals who were being prosecuted for murdering gendarmes during a political disturbance. The Commission held that the amnesty, as a part of a process of resolving conflict between rival communities in a French overseas territory, was consistent with Article 2 because it maintained a proper 'balance between the legitimate interests of the state and the interests of individual members of the public in having the right to life protected by law'.

Given the current move in public international law towards bringing persons guilty of war crimes, genocide, and crimes against humanity to justice rather than approving amnesties in a post-conflict situation,[22] it is not surprising that the Court has adopted a

---

[18] The question was not answered in *Pretty v UK* 2002-III; 35 EHRR 1. On assisted suicide, see Morris, 2003 EHRLR 65.

[19] It is not a crime in Sweden and Estonia. Belgium, Luxembourg, the Netherlands, and Switzerland permit medical practitioners to prescribe lethal drugs; 38 states make it a criminal offence: results of survey in *Koch v Germany No 479/09* (2012); 56 EHRR 195.

[20] 2002-III; 35 EHRR 1 para 39. See also *Sanles Sanles v Spain No 48335/99* hudoc (2000) DA.

[21] *No 16734/90*, 72 DR 236 at 243–4 (1991). An amnesty that prevented civil (but not criminal) proceedings against the perpetrator might infringe the right of access to a court in Article 6.

[22] See Cassese, Gaeta, and Jones, eds, *The Rome Statute of the International Criminal Court: A Commentary*, 2002, Vol 1, p 18.

more rigorous approach than the Commission to the compatibility of amnesties in post-conflict situations with the Convention, including Article 2. In *Association 21 December 1989 and Others v Romania*,[23] the Court held that the positive obligation in Article 2 to investigate the deaths of the applicants' son had been violated. He had been killed when government forces had used force against anti-government demonstrators at the time of the fall of the Head of State, Nicolae Ceausescu, resulting in over 1,000 deaths. In response to a draft Romanian law mentioned in the pleadings that proposed an amnesty for military personnel for their participation in the events of the 1989 revolution, the Court repeated its statement in the *Ould Dah* case[24] (concerning amnesties for torture) that 'an amnesty is generally incompatible with the duty incumbent on the states to investigate acts of torture', impliedly extending its application to acts in violation of the right to life.

e. Regulation of activities and situations that may pose a risk to life

Article 2 requires that activities and situations that may pose a threat to life be the subject of an appropriate regulatory regime to reduce the risk of a fatal injury as far as possible. Thus, given that the police and other state agents may use deadly force in circumstances falling within Article 2(2), the obligation to protect the right to life requires that 'a legal and administrative framework should define the limited circumstances in which law enforcement officials may use force and firearms, in the light of international standards' and provide for their proper training in accordance with those standards.[25] In *Nachova v Bulgaria*,[26] it was held that the required 'framework' was missing, in breach of Article 2, when the relevant regulations effectively permitted lethal force to be used by the military police when arresting a member of the armed forces 'for even the most minor offence'; under the regulations it was lawful to shoot any fugitive who ignored an oral warning and after a shot had been fired over his head.

A regulatory regime must also be provided in the 'public health sphere', 'compelling hospitals, whether public or private, to adopt measures for the protection of their patients' lives'.[27] Other dangerous activities must be subject to regulations geared to the particular activity and governing the licensing, operation, and monitoring of the activity.[28] Health and safety or similar regulations are required, with criminal sanctions for non-compliance, for building sites,[29] public places,[30] railways,[31] and other places and contexts in which there may be danger to life.

II. LAW ENFORCEMENT MACHINERY

The 'law enforcement machinery' needed to protect the right to life consists centrally of 'an effective judicial system' to enforce the criminal or other laws required by Article 2.[32] This will entail criminal investigation and prosecution in the criminal courts, or, in some

---

[23] Hudoc (2011) para 144. Cf *Sandru and Others v Romania* hudoc (2009).

[24] No 13113/03 hudoc (2009) DA.

[25] *Makaratzis v Greece* 2004-XI; 41 EHRR 1092 para 59 GC. The Court referred to the UN Basic Rules on the Use of Force and Firearms by Law Enforcement Officials 1990. See also *Hamiyet Kaplan and Others v Turkey* hudoc (2005) and *Soare and Others v France* hudoc (2011).

[26] 2005-VII; 42 EHRR 933 para 99 GC. See also *Perişan and Others v Turkey* hudoc (2010) and *Putintseva v Russia* hudoc (2012).   [27] *Calvelli and Ciglio v Italy* 2002-I para 49 GC.

[28] *Oneryildiz v Turkey* 2004-XII; 41 EHRR 325 GC.

[29] *Pereira Henriques v Luxembourg No 60255/00* hudoc (2006) DA.

[30] *Ciechońska v Poland* hudoc (2011) (public parks) and *Banel v Lithuania* hudoc (2013) (derelict buildings).   [31] *Kalender v Turkey* hudoc (2009).

[32] *Oneryildiz v Turkey* 2004-XII; 41 EHRR 325 GC para 92.

cases, the availability of civil and administrative courts to which victims have access. Disciplinary procedures may also be relevant. Although criminal law remedies will normally be required, a civil remedy may be sufficient where the taking of life is unintentional. In *Calvelli and Ciglio v Italy*,[33] a baby had died shortly after birth in a private clinic, allegedly as a result of medical negligence. Criminal proceedings for involuntary manslaughter against the doctor were commenced but became time-barred because of delays during the police inquiry and the judicial investigation. The Court found it unnecessary to decide whether the failure of the criminal proceedings because of delays for which the state was responsible gave rise to a breach of Article 2. It did so because the applicants had the possibility of an action for damages in the civil courts, which could be followed by disciplinary proceedings. In its judgment, the Court confirmed that the positive obligation under Article 2 to 'take steps' to protect life applied to the 'public health sphere', requiring 'an effective independent judicial system to be set up so that the cause of death of patients in the care of the medical profession, whether in the public or the private sector, can be determined and those responsible made accountable'. As to the kind of 'accountability' required, the Court stated that in 'the specific sphere of medical negligence the obligation may...be satisfied if the legal system affords victims a remedy in the civil courts, either alone or in conjunction with a remedy in the criminal courts...Disciplinary measures may also be envisaged'. The same approach was followed in *Vo v France*,[34] in which an involuntary abortion had resulted from medical negligence. Criminal proceedings for two possible offences were brought against the doctor, but were unsuccessful because one offence did not apply to the 20- to 21-week-old foetus and an amnesty applied to the other. There was, however, no breach of Article 2 because the applicant could have brought a claim for damages in the administrative courts (but failed to do so).[35] This civil remedy was sufficient: no mention was made of disciplinary proceedings.[36] The remedy must offer 'appropriate civil redress' and be provided within a reasonable time.[37]

In some cases, the positive obligation in Article 2 requires that the applicant must have a civil remedy against the state for compensation *in addition to* there being a criminal sanction. The Court left this question open in the *McCann* and *Osman* cases on the ground that any claim to such a remedy was more appropriately considered under Articles 6 and 13. Later, in *Mastromatteo v Italy*,[38] on the basis that the applicant had not invoked Article 13,[39] the Court indicated that Article 2 required a civil remedy against the state, as well as a criminal sanction, in a case of murder in which the state had been at fault.

2. PREVENTIVE ACTION

In *LCB v UK*,[40] the Court held that the obligation in Article 2(1) to take 'appropriate steps' to protect life may also require the state to take preventive action. The *LCB* obligation

---

[33] 2002-I paras 49, 51 GC. See also *Powell v UK No 45305/99* hudoc (2000) DA; and *Rowley v UK No 31914/03* hudoc (2005) DA.　　　　　　　　　　　　　　　　　　　　[34] 2004-VIII; 40 EHRR 259 GC.

[35] The Court has stressed the need to pursue available remedies: *Calvelli and Ciglio* and *Powell* cases.

[36] It has been suggested that 'civil, administrative *or* even disciplinary' remedies may be sufficient: *Oneryildiz v Turkey* 2004-XII; 41 EHRR 325 para 92 GC (emphasis added).

[37] *Oyal v Turkey* hudoc (2010); 51 EHRR 713. For other 'reasonable time' cases, see *Dvořáček and Dvořáčkova v Slovakia* hudoc (2009) and *Dodov v Bulgaria* hudoc (2008). Reasonable time cases are sometimes considered under the Article 2 procedural obligation.

[38] 2002-VIII GC. Those responsible had been convicted of murder.

[39] This was also the case in *McCann*.　　　　[40] 1998-III; 27 EHRR 212.

applies to the loss of life resulting from any life-threatening activity or situation. In *Oneryildiz v Turkey*,[41] the Court stated that 'this obligation must be construed as applying in the context of any activity, whether public or private, in which the right to life may be at stake, and *a fortiori* in the case of industrial activities, which by their very nature are dangerous, such as the operation of waste-collection sites'. In that case, a methane explosion occurred at a municipal refuse tip. A landslide of waste material engulfed ten slum dwellings, including that of the applicant, killing thirty-nine people, including nine of his close relatives. The public authorities had allowed the tip to operate in breach of health and environmental regulations, despite an expert report highlighting the serious operational risks involved, and had not prevented the unauthorized construction and occupation of slum dwellings adjacent to it. In addition, they had taken insufficient steps to inform the inhabitants of the risks they ran.[42] The Court found that the authorities knew or ought to have known that there was a real risk from explosion to the lives of the persons living near the tip. As a result, they had infringed their obligation under Article 2 to take such preventive measures as were necessary to protect them.[43] In a different context, the obligation to take preventive measures was violated in *Nencheva and Others v Bulgaria*,[44] in which fifteen children and young adults died in a home for severely physically and mentally disabled young persons during the winter when the state authorities failed to provide adequate food, medicines, and other basic necessities in a time of serious economic crisis.

The approach in *Oneryildiz* applies to natural disasters. In *Budayeva and Others v Russia*,[45] a mudslide engulfed a town, killing one person and injuring others. The area was prone to mudslides, but the authorities had not taken steps that should have been taken after the previous mudslide to prevent a re-occurrence. The Court held that 'there was no justification for the authorities' omissions in implementation of the land-planning and emergency relief policies in the hazardous area of Tyrnauz regarding the foreseeable exposure of residents, including all applicants, to mortal risk.' In *Furdik v Slovakia*,[46] the *Oneryildiz* obligation was extended further again, to provide protection by 'the provision of emergency services where it has been brought to the notice of the authorities that the life or health of an individual is at risk' on account of an accident.

The preventive obligation deriving from the *LCB* case can be seen to provide the basis for Strasbourg rulings in other areas. Thus the Commission held that the state is required to take preventive measures to protect individuals from the risk to life caused to an individual by smoking in public by other individuals.[47] However, there is a margin of appreciation left to the state in balancing the competing interest of smokers and non-smokers: a complete ban on smoking in public places to protect non-smokers would not appear to

---

[41] 2004-XII; 41 EHRR 325 para 71 GC. See also *Kolyadenko and Others v Russia* hudoc (2012) (failure to act to prevent flooding). And see *Alkin v Turkey* hudoc (2009) (injury from landmine).

[42] The public's right to information about the danger to life resulting from dangerous activities was held to fall within Article 2 as well as Article 8, as to which, see *Guerra v Italy* 1998-I; 26 EHRR 357.

[43] Cases of severe environmental pollution may also raise an issue under Article 8 concerning the right to respect for one's family life and home: see *Taskin v Turkey* 2004-X; 42 EHRR 1127 (dangerous gold mine). On the question whether nuclear testing and the disposal of radioactive waste could give rise to liability under Article 2, see also *No 715/60* (1960), cited in Fawcett, *The Application of the European Convention on Human Rights*, 1987, p 37.

[44] Hudoc (2013). See also *Banel v Lithuania* hudoc (2013) (derelict buildings: regulations not enforced: violation); *Kemaloglu v Turkey* hudoc (2012) (school pupil died in blizzard: violation); *Berü v Turkey* hudoc (2011) (death caused by stray dogs: no violation).   [45] Hudoc (2008).

[46] Hudoc (2008) DA, 48 EHRR SE9 146 (mountain climbing accident).

[47] *Wockel v Germany No 32165/96*, 93-A DR 82 (1998). The case was considered under Articles 2 and 8. See also *Barrett v UK No 30402/96*, 23 EHRR CD 185 (1997) (control of excessive alcoholism in army).

be required; a state that limits cigarette advertising, prohibits smoking in certain public areas, and campaigns to inform the public of the injurious effect of smoking complies with Article 2.

The *LCB* obligation applies more commonly to the situation where an individual's life is threatened by the criminal acts of another person. In *Osman v UK*,[48] it was held that it arises where the following conditions are met:

> ...the authorities knew or ought to have known at the time of the existence of a real and immediate risk to the life of an identified individual or individuals from the criminal acts of a third party and...failed to take measures within the scope of their powers which, judged reasonably, might have been expected to avoid that risk.[49]

The Court acknowledged two further limitations upon the obligation. First, in view of 'the operational choices which must be made in terms of priorities and resources', it 'must be interpreted in a way which does not impose an impossible or disproportionate burden on the authorities'.[50] Second, the police must respect due process and other human rights guarantees, such as those in Articles 5 and 8.[51] In *Osman*, a schoolteacher had developed an unhealthy attachment to a teenage schoolboy. After various incidents, the schoolteacher shot and injured the schoolboy and killed his father. A claim that the duty of protection under Article 2 had been infringed was rejected. Although the police had been alerted to general statements by the schoolteacher that he intended to commit a murder and to other indications of a disturbed mind, the Court held that it could not be said that they knew or ought to have known on the facts that the lives of the Osman family were at 'real and immediate risk'. Moreover, there were no measures which, 'judged reasonably', could have been taken to neutralize the threat from the schoolteacher or lead to his detention following court proceedings. The police could not 'be criticised for attaching weight to the presumption of innocence or failing to use powers of arrest, search and seizure having regard to their reasonably held view that they lacked at relevant times the required standard of suspicion to use those powers or that any action taken would in fact have produced concrete results.' [52] The Court did not respond in terms to the applicants' claim that the police should have kept a watch on the Osmans' home. It can be supposed, however, that the *Osman* obligation might extend to such a requirement in extreme cases, within the limits of 'priorities and resources'.[53] Priorities and resources were also taken into account in *Dodov v Bulgaria*,[54] when it was ruled that the steps taken by the police to search for an elderly resident of a state-run nursing home with Alzheimer's disease who had disappeared had been sufficient. In *Mikayil Mammadov v Azerbaijan*,[55] the Court

---

[48] 1998-VIII; 29 EHRR 245 para 115 GC. See also *Bromiley v UK No 33747/962* hudoc (1999); 29 EHRR CD 11; *Danini v Italy No 22998/93*, 87-B DR 24 (1996); *Van Colle v UK* hudoc (2012), 56 EHRR 839 (prosecution witness murdered by accused); and *RR and Others v Hungary* hudoc (2012), 56 EHRR 1113 (inadequate witness protection).

[49] 1998-VIII; 29 EHRR 245 para 116 GC. See also *Denizci v Cyprus* 2001-V para 375.

[50] 1998-VIII; 29 EHRR 245 para 116 GC. See also *W v UK No 9348/81*, 32 DR 190 (1983).

[51] 1998-VIII; 29 EHRR 245 para 116 GC. Thus preventive detention is not permitted and there are limits on powers of surveillance. [52] 1998-VIII; 29 EHRR 245 para 121.

[53] See *X v Ireland No 6040/73*, 16 YB 388, 392 (1973) (no duty to provide special protection for a person at risk from the IRA, 'at least not for an indefinite nature').

[54] Hudoc (2008), 47 EHRR 932 (her death was presumed after eleven years disappearance).

[55] Hudoc (2009) (self-immolation because of eviction from home). See also *Servet Gündüz and Others v Turkey* hudoc (2011) (suicide of soldier with mental problems).

accepted that where there was a real and immediate risk of a person committing suicide, the state was obliged to take all reasonable measures to prevent it.

The *Osman* obligation to take preventive operational measures was infringed in *Gongadze v Ukraine*,[56] in which the decapitated body of a political journalist who had criticized the government was found a month or so after his disappearance. Some two months before his disappearance, at a time when eighteen other journalists had been killed in Ukraine, the journalist had informed the Prosecutor General, whose Office was responsible for supervising police conduct, that the police were questioning his relatives and had him under surveillance, and had requested both an investigation and protection. No such action was taken despite a newspaper article identifying the police officers responsible for the disappearance. The Court held that the authorities had been at best 'blatantly negligent', a conclusion underlined by the fact that the identified police officers were arrested and convicted of the journalist's murder shortly after a change of government.

In an important ruling, the *Osman* obligation was applied to domestic violence in *Opuz v Turkey*.[57] In this case, the applicant's mother had been killed by the applicant's husband. The Court held that the authorities had not met their obligation of 'due diligence' which required them to take 'reasonable measures' to protect the applicant's mother's life. The authorities knew of the husband's long history of serious physical attacks on his wife and her mother, who had told the authorities shortly before her death that she was in immediate danger. Although action had been taken earlier, leading to the husband's conviction for offences against the applicant and her mother, the authorities could have pursued other criminal charges against the husband more forcefully or taken further protective action, such as keeping the husband away from the house where the applicant and her mother lived. The Court rejected an argument that further intervention by the state would have interfered with the right to family life in violation of Article 8 of the Convention: '[t]he seriousness of the risk to the applicant's mother rendered such intervention by the authorities necessary in the present case.'

The *Osman* obligation has also been held to have been infringed in a number of Turkish cases in which persons allegedly associated with the Kurdish cause in the emergency situation and who were known to be at risk were killed by persons unknown.[58] In these cases, the Court focused not on the limited protective measures taken, but on deficiencies in the criminal justice system in south-east Turkey which took away its effectiveness as a deterrent and generally sent the wrong signal to wrongdoers. The cases amount to a strong condemnation of the Turkish criminal justice system as it operated at the time in south-east Turkey[59] and one that demonstrates the inter-relationship between the obligation to protect persons at risk and the obligation to investigate killings that occur.[60]

---

[56] 2005-XI; 43 EHRR 967. Cf *Dink v Turkey* hudoc (2010). See also *Kontrová v Slovakia* hudoc (2007), in which there was a breach of Article 2 when the police took no action against a man who killed his children and himself, despite emergency calls and knowledge of his prior record of physical and mental abuse and threats with a shotgun. And see *Kayak v Turkey* hudoc (2012) (failure to supervise school premises where a child was murdered).

[57] Hudoc (2009); 50 EHRR 695 paras 131, 126, 144. See Londono, 9 HRLR 657 (2009). See also *Branko Tomašić and Others v Croatia* hudoc (2009).

[58] See *Akkoc v Turkey* 2000-X; 34 EHRR 1173. See also *Kaya (Mahmut) v Turkey* 2000-III; *Kilic v Turkey* 2000-III; 33 EHRR 1357; and *Koku v Turkey* hudoc (2005). In *Osmanoglu v Turkey* hudoc (2008); 53 EHRR 557 para 84, having found insufficient evidence that the men who abducted the applicant's 'disappeared' son were state agents, the Court found a violation of the *Osman* obligation, as the authorities had not taken 'reasonable measures' in a life-threatening situation to find him.

[59] Cf Mowbray, 1 HRLR 127, 129 (2001).

[60] The Court has sometimes not pursued a 'protection' claim if it has found a breach of the 'investigation' obligation: see, eg, *Kaya v Turkey* 1998-I; 28 EHRR 1 and *Tanrikulu v Turkey* 1999 IV; 30 EHRR 950 GC.

The approach followed in these Turkish cases was taken further in an important development in the Chechnyan case of *Turluyeva v Russia*,[61] in which the Court held that a state has a duty to make an 'effective and rapid response' in a disappearance case in which there is a 'real and immediate' threat to a person's life. The Court stated that this 'is true for any criminal abduction and disappearance, but is especially so in the context of relatively widespread unresolved disappearances, as in the Chechen Republic'. In such a situation, 'one could reasonably expect that in view of numerous previous similar crimes in the region an adequate system would have been set up by the time of the events in question', but this was not the case.

The *Osman* obligation applies to persons in detention.[62] The state must take reasonable measures to protect detained persons in real and immediate danger of life-threatening attacks from other detainees of which the authorities knew or ought to have known.[63] Given the vulnerable position of detainees and the special knowledge that the state will have of the circumstances, the state must account for the death of a detainee and is subject to a 'particularly stringent obligation' to show that it had done what it could to provide protection.[64] In *Edwards v UK*,[65] a vulnerable remand prisoner was killed by a dangerous, mentally ill remand prisoner with whom he was made to share a cell. A breach of Article 2 was found because of the failure of those acting earlier in the case (doctors, police, courts) to pass on to the prison authorities information relevant to the murderer's condition and of the inadequate nature of the screening process when he was admitted to prison.

In *Keenan v UK*,[66] the *Osman* obligation was extended in principle to cases of suicide in which state officials knew or ought to have known that the detainee posed a real and immediate risk of suicide. However, there was no breach of Article 2 on the facts, as the prison authorities had done all that could reasonably have been expected of them to counter the risk of suicide by placing him in hospital care and under watch when he showed suicidal tendencies.[67]

A failure to protect a detainee from other risks to their health by monitoring their condition or providing medical care resulting in death may be a breach of Article 2 also. A breach may result from the conduct of law enforcement officers in the immediate aftermath of an arrest[68] or from medical malpractice later in prison.[69] The use of police restraining techniques at the time of an arrest were in issue in *Saoud v France*.[70] In that case, police were called to the home of a mentally disabled young man who was holding his sister captive. Following his arrest, he was pinioned to the ground for some thirty

---

[61] Hudoc (2013) para 99. Cf *Savriddin Dzhurayev v Russia* hudoc 2013- (preventive operational measures required when the Russian authorities should have known that there was a risk that a person might be abducted to Takjikistan to face torture).

[62] It applies also to members of the armed forces: *Mosendz v Ukraine* hudoc (2013) (inadequate safeguards against bullying, leading to suicide).

[63] The state is also directly responsible for deaths caused by its agents: see *Salman v Turkey* 2000-VII; 34 EHRR 425 GC.   [64] *Edwards v UK* 2002-II; 35 EHRR 487 para 56.

[65] 2002-II; 35 EHRR 487 para 56. See also *Iorga and Others v Romania* hudoc (2011).

[66] 2001-III; 33 EHRR 913. See also *Tanribilir v Turkey* hudoc (2000) and *Younger v UK No 57420/00* hudoc (2003) DA.

[67] For cases of breach, see *Renolde v France* 2008-; 48 EHRR 969; *Jasińska v Poland* hudoc (2010); *De Donder and De Clippel v Belgium* hudoc (2011); and *Çoşelav v Turkey* hudoc (2012). See also *Robineau v France No 58497/11* hudoc DA (2013) (no breach).

[68] *Anguelova v Bulgaria* 2002-IV; 38 EHRR 659; *Douglas-Williams v UK No 56413/00* hudoc (2002) DA; *TAÏS v France* hudoc (2006).

[69] *Slimani v France* 2004-IX, 43 EHRR 1068; *Ahmet Özkan v Turkey* hudoc (2004); *Dzieciak v Poland* hudoc (2008); and *Makharadze and Sikharulidze v Georgia* hudoc (2011). Article 3 may also apply.

[70] Hudoc (2007). See also *Douglas-Williams v UK No 56413/00* hudoc (2002) DA.

minutes or so, which unintentionally caused his death by slow asphyxiation. Finding a breach of Article 2, the Court 'deplored' the fact that no medical examination of the deceased was conducted during the period of restraint, despite it being established that his mental state and the dangerous nature of the restraining technique that was used were known and that a doctor was available at the scene. Where a person with disabilities is detained, the authorities must 'demonstrate special care in guaranteeing such conditions as correspond to his special needs resulting from his disability.'[71] A refusal to release a sick prisoner that results in a reduction of his or her life expectancy may also raise an issue under the obligation to protect life.[72]

A difficult question is whether a state must forcibly feed a prisoner on hunger strike to save his life. The Court has taken the view that if a prisoner goes on hunger strike there will not be a violation of Article 2 if the authorities monitor the situation satisfactorily and provide medical treatment and attention so as to make the prisoner's situation as comfortable as possible should he maintain his decision to refuse nourishment: there is no obligation to force feed a prisoner who is capable of taking a decision on matters of life and death.[73]

The *Osman* obligation extends in principle beyond the protection of particular individuals to the protection of the public at large. Thus, when operating a system of leave or relaxed custody for prisoners in preparation for their release at the end of their prison term, the state owes a duty of care to members of the public in respect of any risk to their lives that may reasonably be anticipated.[74] In a different kind of case, in *Pasa and Erkan Erol v Turkey*,[75] there was a violation of Article 2 when a young boy was seriously injured by an anti-personnel mine while grazing his sheep when entry into the mined area had not been adequately prevented. Finally, in *Gorovenky and Bugara v Ukraine*,[76] the state was in breach of Article 2 when an off duty policeman murdered others in a private altercation, using a gun with which he had been issued in breach of regulations and without a personality check, despite incidents suggesting that one was called for.

3. HEALTH CARE AND OTHER SOCIAL SERVICES

The general Article 2 obligation in the *LCB* case to 'take appropriate steps' to protect life may have a further meaning relating to the provision of health care. Its possible application in this context was in issue in *Cyprus v Turkey*,[77] in which it was claimed that Greek Cypriots and Maronites in northern Cyprus had been denied access to available or adequate medical services there or, because of restrictions on freedom of movement, in southern Cyprus. The Court appeared to accept that in principle Article 2 could extend to the provision of health care. It stated, first, that there may be liability under Article 2 where a state places an individual's life at risk by denying him or her medical care that

---

[71] *Jasinskis v Latvia* hudoc (2010) (deaf and mute detainee not medically examined and not given pen and paper to communicate).

[72] *Grice v UK* No 22564/93, 77-A DR 90 (1994) (life expectancy of prisoner with AIDS).

[73] See *Horoz v Turkey* hudoc (2009) and *Rappaz v Switzerland* hudoc (2013) DA. And see *Tekin Yildiz v Turkey* hudoc (2005).

[74] *Mastromatteo v Italy* 2002-VIII GC. Cf *Maiorano and Others v Italy* hudoc (2009) and *Choreftakis and Choreftaki v Greece* hudoc (2012).   [75] Hudoc (2006).

[76] Hudoc (2012). Cf *Saso Gorgiev v the Former Yugoslav Republic of Macedonia* 2012.

[77] 2001-IV; 35 EHRR 731 GC.

is available to the general public, but rejected the claim on the facts. Second, in response to the applicant state's criticisms of the level of health care provided to the general public in northern Cyprus, the Court stated that it did not 'consider it necessary to examine in this case the *extent* to which Article 2 of the Convention may impose an obligation on a Contracting State to make available a certain standard of health care'.[78] It is reasonable to infer from the word 'extent' that the Court accepts that such an obligation exists to some undefined degree. Confirmation of such an interpretation of Article 2 would extend the guarantee of the Article 2 obligation to protect life in a way that would be in accord with national health care standards in European states and indirectly provide a partial, but welcome guarantee of the right to health, which is an established human right[79] that is not otherwise protected by the Convention, except through the prohibition of inhuman or degrading treatment in Article 3, which has been applied to health care in a few situations.[80] As far as Article 2 is concerned, although most European states are in a better position to comply with an obligation to make available life-saving health care for individuals, both nationals and non-nationals, within their jurisdiction than are most other states, the obligation must be one that is to some extent limited by financial considerations.[81] Although a European state may be expected to provide basic or emergency health care at public expense, any Article 2 obligation to ensure more extensive health care is likely to be held to be subject to 'available resources', as is commonly the case in European national law.[82] The role of the Court in such cases would be one of reviewing whether the failure to provide health care—for example, for an expensive drug or operation[83]—needed to protect life was a reasonable use of limited financial resources, with the state being allowed a margin of appreciation in its allocation of resources, and did not infringe fundamental human rights norms, such as non-discrimination and due process.

A separate question concerns the obligations that the state has under Article 2 for medical negligence. In *Calvelli and Ciglio v Italy*,[84] the Court established that the *LCB* positive obligation under Article 2 to take steps to protect life applies to health care and requires the State to provide both 'regulations compelling hospitals, whether public or private, to adopt appropriate measures for the protection of their patients' lives' and 'an effective independent judicial system...so that the cause of death of patients in the care of the medical profession, whether in the public or the private sector, can be determined and those responsible made accountable'. However, the state is not directly liable under Article 2 for deaths resulting from medical negligence by state health care personnel, except for deaths in prison.[85] In *Powell v UK*,[86] the Court stated that although a state must make 'adequate provision for securing high professional standards among health

---

[78] *Cyprus v Turkey*, para 219 (emphasis added).

[79] See Article 11, Revised European Social Charter and Article 12, ICESCR.

[80] Cf Opsahl, in *European System*, p 212.

[81] See *Nitecki v Poland No 65653/01* hudoc (2002) DA and *Pentiacova v Moldova No 14462/03* hudoc (2005) DA. The question whether medical care should be free was raised but not answered in *X v Ireland No 6839/74*, 7 DR 78 (1976) and *Scialacqua v Italy No 34151/96* hudoc (1998) DA.

[82] Cf *N v UK* 2008- GC, on the cost of medical care and Article 3. In *Panaitescu v Romania* hudoc (2012), Article 3 was infringed when a cancer patient was not given the drugs to which he was legally entitled.

[83] See *Hristozov and Others v Bulgaria* hudoc (2012) (no obligation to allow terminally ill cancer patients access to as yet unauthorized drugs).   [84] 2002-I paras 49, 51 GC.

[85] As to medical care in detention, see below, Ch 3, section 5-II.d.

[86] Although this statement was made in terms of the *LCB* positive obligation, it must also apply to the negative state obligation not to take life. The state would be liable for the intentional murder by a state health carer: see the facts of the *Taylor Family et al v UK* A 23412/94 DA (1994) (nurse serial killer).

professionals...it cannot accept that matters such as error of judgment on the part of a health professional or negligent coordination between health professionals in the treatment of a particular patient are sufficient in themselves to call a contracting state to account'. However, the state was liable under Article 2 when a woman died after medical staff in a state hospital had refused her treatment in an emergency, life-threatening situation because she could not pay a deposit in advance for the operation.[87]

Social services other than health care which may have a bearing on the right to life in Article 2 include social assistance and housing, which are both the subject of recognized social rights.[88] However, it has been held that neither Article 2 nor any other Convention provision guarantees a right for a person in need to financial assistance from the state.[89] As to housing, there has been scarcely any Strasbourg jurisprudence on the question whether the failure to provide housing might raise an issue under Article 2.[90] There is no reason in principle why states should not be obliged under Article 2 to 'take appropriate steps' to protect life in the context of such rights on the basis of the same approach as that suggested in respect of health care, ie taking into account 'available resources' where relevant. A reading of Article 2(1) that developed the positive obligation to protect life in the direction suggested and that respected standards in the national law of the contracting parties generally would be consistent with the object and purpose of the Convention and would be in step with the evolving interpretation of equivalent 'right to life' guarantees.

4. THE PROCEDURAL OBLIGATION TO INVESTIGATE

The preceding paragraphs have concerned the substantive element of the obligation in Article 2(1) to take 'appropriate steps' to protect life. When read in conjunction with the general obligation in Article 1 to 'secure' Convention rights, the obligation in Article 2 to protect the right to life also imposes a procedural obligation upon the state[91] to investigate deaths, whether they occur at the hands of state agents,[92] private persons,[93] or persons unknown.[94] The obligation extends beyond violent deaths,[95] to all cases of death other than from natural causes.[96] It may arise in some cases even though the victim of the attack has not died. These may include cases of disappeared persons whose fate is unknown.[97]

---

[87] *Mehmet Şentürk and Bekir Şentürk v Turkey* hudoc 2013-.

[88] See respectively Articles 13 and 31 Revised European Social Charter and Articles 9 and 11 ICESCR.

[89] *Wasilewski v Poland No 32734/96* hudoc (1999) DA.

[90] In *X v Germany No 5207/71*, 14 YB 698 (1971), a complaint that the forced eviction of an elderly woman endangered her life was admitted, but later rejected as an abuse of the right of petition on the facts.

[91] A contracting party to which a suspect has fled must cooperate with the state conducting the inquiry: *Cummins v UK No 27306/05* hudoc (2005) DA.

[92] *McCann v UK* A324 (1995); 21 EHRR 97 GC.   [93] *Menson v UK No 47916/99* hudoc (2003) DA.

[94] *Toğcu v Turkey* hudoc (2005); *Kaya v Turkey* hudoc (2006); and *Yasa v Turkey* 1998-VI; 28 EHRR 408. Deaths in or out of custody must be investigated: *Salman v Turkey* 2000-VII; 34 EHRR 425. On the obligation to investigate generally, see Mowbray, 51 ICLQ 437 (2002).

[95] *McCann v UK* A 324 (1995); 21 EHRR 97 GC and *Çakici v Turkey* 1999-IV; 31 EHRR 133 GC.

[96] *Calvelli and Ciglio v Italy* 2002-I para 49 GC (medical negligence) and *Ucar v Turkey* hudoc (2006) (suicide).

[97] *Cyprus v Turkey* 2001-IV; 35 EHRR 731 para 132 GC. Cf *Kaya v Turkey* hudoc (2006). For a non-disappearance case, see *Yasa v Turkey* 1998-VI; 28 EHRR 408.

The 'essential purpose' of the investigation is to 'secure the effective implementation of the domestic laws which protect the right to life' and to ensure the accountability of those responsible.[98] It also enables 'the facts to become known to the public and in particular the relatives of any victims'.[99] The obligation is for the state authorities to initiate an investigation once the matter has come to their attention; it is not dependent upon the lodging of a formal complaint by the next of kin or their suggesting a particular line of inquiry or investigative procedure.[100] The precise form that the investigation takes may vary according to the circumstances and national practice, so long as it meets the requirement of effectiveness.[101] Some allowance may be made for the difficulty of conducting an investigation in states of emergency and other 'difficult security conditions', but the authorities are required to take 'all reasonable steps' in the circumstances.[102]

The nature of the procedural obligation will vary according to whether or not the substantive obligation to protect the right to life in Article 2 requires a criminal sanction.[103] This distinction was spelt out in *Oneryildiz v Turkey*.[104] In that case, in the context of deaths caused unintentionally by an explosion at a municipal refuse tip, it was held that an investigation leading to possible criminal proceedings is required in cases involving dangerous activities where it is established that there has been gross negligence by public authorities. This was so because, as evidenced by developments in European law, criminal sanctions in such cases—to which an investigation was a necessary prelude—are required by the substantive obligation in Article 2. In cases in which Article 2 requires a criminal sanction, a criminal investigation followed, where justified, by a criminal prosecution and trial that results in a conviction and an appropriate sentence may satisfy the procedural obligation, as may a trial that results in an acquittal, although there are a number of acquittal cases in which the criminal proceedings have been considered not to satisfy the investigation obligation in Article 2.[105] Other procedures, such as an inquest in common law jurisdictions, may do so also when no case to take forward to prosecution is established.[106]

In contrast, in cases in which the substantive obligation in Article 2 requires only that there be a civil or other non-criminal remedy of which the victims might avail themselves,[107] the procedural obligation in Article 2 may be satisfied by the opportunities provided by these remedies to establish the cause of death and to make those responsible accountable in civil law. However, the civil remedy must be an effective one: in particular, delay in civil proceedings may violate the procedural obligation: the 'prompt examination' of cases of hospital deaths is 'important for the safety of users of all health services'.[108]

---

[98] *Nachova v Bulgaria* 2005-VII; 42 EHRR 933 para 110 GC. Cf *Ramsahai v Netherlands* hudoc 2007-II; 46 EHRR 983 GC.   [99] *Sieminska v Poland No 37602/97* hudoc (2001) DA.

[100] *Nachova v Bulgaria* 2005-VII; 42 EHRR 933 GC.

[101] *Hugh Jordan v UK* 2001-III; 37 EHRR 52 and *Velikova v Bulgaria* 2000-VI.

[102] *Al-Skeini and Others v UK* 2011-; 53 EHRR 589 para 164 GC. Cf *Yasa v Turkey* 1998-VI; 28 EHRR 408.

[103] As to which, see section 1.II.

[104] 2004-XII; 41 EHRR 325 para 93 GC. Cf *Pereira Henriques v Luxembourg* hudoc (2006) (building site accident).

[105] See, eg, *Akkum v Turkey* 2005-II; 43 EHRR 526; *Fatma Kaçar v Turkey* hudoc (2005); and *Erdoğan v Turkey* hudoc (2006). Disciplinary proceedings as well as prosecution are not required: *McBride v UK No 1396/06* hudoc (2006) DA.

[106] *McCann v UK* A 324 (1995); 21 EHRR 97 GC. See also *Douglas-Williams v UK No 56413/00* hudoc (2002) DA and *Bubbins v UK* 2005-II; 41 EHRR 458. In *Bubbins*, remarkably, the Court held that an inquest complied with Article 2 on its facts, discounting UK judicial decisions to the contrary in other cases, eg *R (Amin) v Secretary of State for the Home Dept* [2003] UKHL 51, HL.

[107] See *Calvelli and Ciglio v Italy* 2002-I para 49 GC and *Powell v UK No 43505/99* hudoc (2000) DA.

[108] *Šilih v Slovenia* hudoc (2009), 49 EHRR 996 para 196 GC. Cf *Oyal v Turkey* hudoc (2010); 51 EHRR 713. Non-'reasonable time' claims are sometimes dealt with under the substantive obligation to provide a civil remedy.

The requirement of effectiveness contains a number of elements. First, the persons who are responsible for the investigation and who conduct it must be 'independent and impartial, in law and in practice'.[109] In the case of deaths by state agents, what 'is at stake here is nothing less than public confidence in the state's monopoly on the use of force'.[110] In *Ergi v Turkey*,[111] there was no independence in practice where the prosecutor relied totally on the evidence of gendarmes implicated in the death, without interviewing other persons. Nor is the investigation of a death by police officers who are colleagues of other implicated officers acceptable.[112] Similarly, Article 2 was not satisfied where those conducting the investigation were for all practical purposes under the control of the Chief Public Prosecutor, who had been in dispute with the victim and was even alleged at one stage to have been his murderer.[113] The fact that an investigation by police officers of a death implicating other police officers was supervised by an independent body did not satisfy the requirement of independence in the absence of other sufficient safeguards.[114] The investigation must be conducted with particular 'vigour and impartiality' where an attack is racially motivated.[115]

Second, the investigation must be adequate in the sense that it must be capable of leading to a decision as to the cause and circumstances of the death, as to whether any use of force was justified under Article 2, and as to the 'identification and punishment of those responsible'.[116] This element of the obligation was explained by the Court in *Hugh Jordan v UK*[117] as follows:

> This is not an obligation of result, but one of means. The authorities must have taken the reasonable steps available to them to secure the evidence concerning the incident, including *inter alia* eyewitness testimony, forensic evidence and, where appropriate, an autopsy which provides a complete and accurate record of injury and an objective analysis of clinical findings, including the cause of death (see concerning autopsies, eg *Salman v Turkey*…para 106; concerning witnesses eg *Tannrikulu v Turkey*… ECHR 1999-IV para 109; concerning forensic evidence eg *Gul v Turkey*… para 89). Any deficiency in the investigation which undermines its ability to establish the cause of the death or the person or persons responsible will risk falling foul of this standard.

The absence of a power to compel testimony by eyewitnesses or other witnesses with material evidence may prevent an investigation from being effective,[118] as may a

---

[109] *Nachova v Bulgaria* 2005-VII; 42 EHRR 933 para 112 GC. The obligation is both a subjective and objective one: *Jordan v UK* hudoc 2001-III; 37 EHRR 52.

[110] *Ramsahai v Netherlands* hudoc 2007-II; 46 EHRR 983 para 325 GC.

[111] 1998-IV; 32 EHRR 388.

[112] *Ramsahai v Netherlands* 2007-II; 46 EHRR 983 GC. Cf *Skendžić and Krznarić v Croatia* hudoc (2011).   [113] *Kolevi v Bulgaria* hudoc (2009).

[114] *Hugh Jordan v UK* hudoc 2001-III; 37 EHRR 52. Supervision by a public prosecutor who decided on prosecution and who was hierarchically independent of the police was sufficient: *Ramsahai v Netherlands* 2007-II; 46 EHRR 983 para 325 GC.   [115] *Menson v UK No 47916/99* hudoc (2003) DA.

[116] *Nachova v Bulgaria* 2005-VII; 42 EHRR 933 para 113 GC. Article 2 does not require an inquiry into broader policy issues that a case may raise: *Taylor et al v UK No 23412/94*, 79-A DR 127(1994).

[117] 2001-III; 37 EHRR 52 para 107. Cf *Nachova v Bulgaria* 2005-VII; 42 EHRR 933 para 113 GC. See also *Baysayeva v Russia* hudoc (2007), 48 EHRR 771. In *Finucane v UK* 2003-VIII; 37 EHRR 656, there was a failure to investigate sufficiently allegations of collusion by security personnel.

[118] *Hugh Jordan v UK* 2001-III; 37 EHRR 52 para 105; *Edwards v UK* 2002-II; 35 EHRR 487. No breach if requests to examine witnesses (or see documents) are allowed in fact: *Taylor v UK No 23412/94*, 79-A DR 127 (1994).

culture within which it is understood that police conduct may not be investigated.[119] Public interest immunity certificates which prevent the disclosure of official documents may also do so.[120] However, the grant of anonymity to prosecution witnesses or the non-disclosure of police documents is permissible if the rights of the defence are not prejudiced.[121] Generally, the 'investigation's conclusions must be based on a thorough, objective and impartial analysis of all the relevant elements and must apply a standard comparable to the "no more than absolutely necessary" standard required by Article 2(2)' when determining the facts and deciding that a breach of Article 2 has occurred.[122]

The adequacy of an investigation was in issue in *Ramsahai v Netherlands*.[123] In that case, a suspected robber was shot dead by a policeman after pulling out a gun when confronted in the street. Following an investigation, the prosecutor decided not to prosecute the policeman because he had acted in self-defence. Reversing the Chamber judgment, the Grand Chamber held, by thirteen votes to four, that the investigation had not been adequate because of various deficiencies, including the failure to conduct certain forensic tests, to conduct a reconstruction of the incident, and to follow good practice in the questioning of the two key police officers. In a joint dissenting opinion, Judges Rozakis, Bratza, Lorenzen, and Vajic argued that a deficiency or deficiencies in an investigation should only give rise to a breach of the procedural obligation if the result is to undermine the investigation as a whole and concluded, persuasively, that this was not the case on the facts.

Third, the investigation must be initiated promptly and conducted with 'reasonable expedition'.[124] A prompt response by the authorities is needed 'to ensure public confidence in their maintenance of the rule of law and in preventing any appearance of collusion in or tolerance of unlawful acts'.[125] Fourth, there must be a 'sufficient element of public scrutiny of the investigation or its results to secure accountability in practice as well as in theory' and, again, to maintain public confidence.[126] Although the degree of public scrutiny may vary with the facts, in all cases 'the next of kin of the victim must be involved in the procedure to the extent necessary to safeguard his or her legitimate interests'.[127] It may be sufficient in some cases that the investigation takes place in private, provided that the report is made public.[128] In other cases, the circumstances of the case may be such that the public interest in state accountability requires that the investigation

[119] *Bilgin (Irfan) v Turkey* 2001-VIII; 35 EHRR 1291.

[120] *McKerr v UK* 2001-III; 34 EHRR 553. Lack of public scrutiny of police reports and other investigative material may be justified on confidentiality grounds: *Hugh Jordan v UK* 2001-III; 37 EHRR 52.

[121] *Bubbins v UK* 2005-II; 41 EHRR 458.

[122] *Nachova v Bulgaria* 2005-VII; 42 EHRR 933 para 113 GC.

[123] 2007-II; 46 EHRR 983 GC.

[124] *Hugh Jordan v UK* hudoc (2001); 37 EHRR 52 para 108 (inquest); *McKerr v UK* 2001-III; 34 EHRR 553 (police investigation): both breaches. See also *Tas v Turkey* 2000-XI; 33 EHRR 325; *Edwards v UK* 2002-II; 35 EHRR 487; *Byrzkykowski v Poland* hudoc (2006); 46 EHRR 675; *Silih v Slovenia* hudoc (2009) GC; and *Association 21 December 1989 v Romania* hudoc (2011).

[125] *Akpinar and Altun v Turkey* hudoc (2007) para 58 and *McKerr v UK* 2001-III.

[126] *McKerr v UK*.

[127] *Hugh Jordan v UK* 2001-III; 37 EHRR 52 para 109. This will include sufficient participation in an inquiry *in camera* (*Edwards v UK* 2002-II; 35 EHRR 487) and the disclosure to the next of kin of documents (*Ogur v Turkey* 1999-III; 31 EHRR 912 and *Hugh Jordan v UK* 2001-III; 37 EHRR 52 para 133). See also *Gulec v Turkey* 1998-IV; 28 EHRR 121 (victim's father not informed of decision not to prosecute).

[128] *Taylor et al v UK* No 2341/94, 79-A DR 127 (1994).

be conducted in public.[129] Fourthly, legal aid may be required where this is necessary for the family's effective participation.[130] Finally, where relevant, the authorities must take such steps as are necessary and available to obtain evidence from other states.[131]

Where more than one investigation procedure is used, the deficiencies of one procedure may be made good by the merits of another.[132] A failure to conduct an effective pre-trial investigation may be overcome by the establishment of the facts at the criminal trial of the murderer,[133] but this will not be the case where witnesses are not called because the accused pleads guilty[134] or not all of the relevant witnesses and material evidence is before the court.[135]

In *Oneryildiz v Turkey*,[136] the procedural obligation was extended beyond the investigation to the trial stage. The Court held both that the investigation must result in a prosecution where this is called for on the facts and that the national courts must treat the case with the appropriate seriousness, giving it the 'careful scrutiny' and imposing a sentence that will deter others. In that case, this last requirement was not met when the Turkish courts gave two local mayors, who were the only persons prosecuted, suspended sentences of the minimum possible statutory fine (about §9.70) for the negligent performance of their duties resulting in the loss of many lives.

In a number of cases, the procedural obligation to investigate has led to a finding of a breach of Article 2 when no breach of the substantive guarantee has been found because the Court has not been satisfied beyond a reasonable doubt that a death was attributable to state agents.[137] In *Aslakhanova and Others v Russia*,[138] the Court noted that it had found violations of Article 2 in cases of disappearances in Chechnya in more than 120 cases and that there was a systematic problem of non-investigation of disappearances in such cases. In this situation, the Court indicated certain general measures to be taken by Russia to deal with the problem.

5. APPLICATION OF THE OBLIGATION TO PROTECT LIFE TO NON-FATAL CASES

Where relevant, both the substantive and procedural obligations in Article 2 to take steps to protect life may apply even though the person at risk has not died. Thus the substantive obligation was held to apply in the *LCB* case,[139] so as to require the state to do all that could be reasonably required of it to prevent the applicant's life being avoidably put at risk from her father's exposure to radiation. It also applied in the *Osman* case[140] to the obligation to protect both a son and his father from a real and immediate risk to their lives posed by a private person, even though only the father was killed. The procedural obligation to conduct an investigation was held to apply in *Yasa v Turkey*,[141] where the applicant had survived an attack by an unknown gunman.

---

[129] *Edwards v UK*; 2002-II; 35 EHRR 487 (issues involved in prison death required public hearing).
[130] *Hugh Jordan v UK* 2001-III; 37 EHRR 52.
[131] *Rantsev v Cyprus and Russia* 2010-; 51 EHRR 1.
[132] *Rantsev v Cyprus and Russia*, and *Tanribilir v Turkey* hudoc (2000).
[133] *McKerr v UK* 2001-III; 34 EHRR 553.   [134] *Edwards v UK* 2002-II; 35 EHRR 487.
[135] *Gül v Turkey* hudoc (2000); 34 EHRR 719.
[136] 2004-XII; 41 EHRR 325 para 96 GC. Cf *Ali and Ayşe Duran v Turkey* hudoc (2008) (police never served their sentences).   [137] See eg *Akkoc v Turkey* 2000-X; 34 EHRR 1173.
[138] Hudoc (2012).   [139] *LCB v UK* 1998-III; 27 EHRR 212 para 36. Cf *Budayeva v Russia* hudoc (2008).
[140] *Osman v UK* 1998-VIII; 29 EHRR 245 para 115 GC.   [141] 1998-VI; 28 EHRR 408.

6. PROTECTION OF THE UNBORN CHILD

The first sentence of Article 2 states that 'everyone's right to life must be protected'. The question whether the word 'everyone' includes an unborn child—and if so from what point in its development and the extent to which protection is offered—has yet to be fully decided.

I. VOLUNTARY ABORTION

The question has arisen mostly in the context of voluntary abortion.[142] In *X v UK*,[143] the Commission ruled that the abortion of a ten-week-old foetus under British law to protect the physical or mental health of a pregnant woman was not in breach of Article 2. In doing so, it stated that Article 2 does not recognize an *absolute* right to life of an unborn child. However, the Commission left open the controversial question whether Article 2 does not protect the unborn child at all[144] or whether the foetus has a right to life under it subject to certain implied limitations. It was able to do so because, even if the latter were the position, the facts of the case came within one such limitation, namely the protection of the pregnant woman's health. TheCommission's position was further developed in *H v Norway*.[145] There a lawful abortion of a fourteen-week-old foetus on the statutory ground that the 'pregnancy, birth or care for the child may place the woman in a difficult situation of life'[146] was held not to be contrary to Article 2. This goes beyond the *X* case, in that the abortion was later in time and for social, rather than health, reasons. The key to the Commission's decision in *H v Norway* was its understanding that 'national laws on abortion differ considerably' within the states parties to the Convention.[147] In view of this, it considered that 'in such a delicate area the contracting states must have a certain discretion'. It then held that the respondent state's law, as it was applied to the facts of the case, did not exceed this 'discretion'. Whether the Commission would have reached the same conclusion if the case had involved that part of the respondent state's law that gave the pregnant woman an unlimited right to abortion during the first twelve weeks of pregnancy is not clear.

The Commission's approach in the *X* and *H* cases was followed by the Court in *Boso v Italy*.[148] In that case, the Court held that an abortion that was performed under Italian law within the first twelve weeks of pregnancy because of a risk to the woman's physical or mental health was not a breach of Article 2. Such a law struck 'a fair balance between, on the one hand, the need to ensure protection of the foetus and, on the other, the women's interests'. The Grand Chamber reviewed, without criticizing, the *X, H,* and *Boso* cases in the involuntary abortion case of *Vo v France* (examined in section II that follows).

---

[142] Other 'right to life' issues concerning the unborn child include those arising out of embryonic and foetal research and the taking of hazardous drugs by pregnant women. See Byk, *Medical and Biological Progress and the European Convention on Human Rights*, 1994.

[143] *No 8416/78*, 19 DR 244 (1980) (the *Paton* case).

[144] As the Commission noted, the textual evidence supports a negative interpretation. Thus the wording of Article 2 beyond the first sentence of Article 2(1) can only apply to persons already born and in most other Convention articles in which the word 'everyone' appears it has the same limited meaning.

[145] *No 17004/90*, 73 DR 155 (1992).

[146] English translation of the Norwegian abortion statute in the Commission's decision.

[147] See Plomer, 5 HRLR 311 at 335 (2005).

[148] *No 50490/99* hudoc (2002) DA. The question was not directly in issue and the Court found no need to consider it in *Open Door Counselling and Dublin Well Woman v Ireland* A 246-A (1993); 15 EHRR 244 PC or in *A, B and C v Ireland* 2010-; 53 EHRR 429 GC.

The limitations upon any right to life that the unborn child may have that the juris-prudence of the Court and the former Commission allows are, as they have been applied nationally, capable of covering most cases in which a voluntary abortion is sought and are likely to remain consistent with Article 2.[149]

A claim alleging that a voluntary abortion is in breach of Article 2 may only be brought by a 'victim' in the sense of Article 34, who must be someone personally affected. The 'potential father' qualifies as a 'victim' for this purpose so that he can bring a claim where the woman seeks or obtains an abortion without his consent.[150] An ordinary member of the public who opposes legislation permitting abortion is not so affected.[151] Nor is a church minister, even though he loses his office for refusal to carry out his functions as a result of his opposition to abortion.[152] Cases involving voluntary abortion issues may well be brought not by someone seeking to prevent an abortion under Article 2, but by a pregnant woman arguing for an abortion as a part of her right to privacy under Article 8.[153] Insofar as such cases are successful, there are inevitable ramifications for Article 2, since an abortion that is protected by Article 8 cannot at the same time be contrary to Article 2. In contrast, an unsuccessful claim to a 'right to an abortion' under Article 8 on the basis of respect for private life[154] does not necessarily have consequences for Article 2.

II. INVOLUNTARY ABORTION

In *Vo v France*,[155] the applicant went to hospital for her regular pregnancy examination, but, having been mistaken for another woman with the same name, was subjected with-out medical examination to a procedure that caused her to lose her baby. The question for the Grand Chamber was whether Article 2 required a criminal sanction for the medical negligence that had led to the involuntary abortion of the applicant's 20- to 21-week-old foetus against her wishes, or whether the civil remedy for damages that French law pro-vided on the facts was sufficient. Deciding that the latter was the case, the Court, as in the voluntary abortion cases, found no need to decide whether an unborn child qualified for protection under Article 2 and, if so, at what stage in its development (eg, nidation, viabil-ity) this occurred. The Court did, however, state that, given the absence of a European legal, medical, ethical, or religious consensus as to when life begins, a margin of apprecia-tion applies, even to the point where the Court doubted whether it was 'desirable, or even possible as matters stand, to answer in the abstract the question whether the unborn child is a person for the purposes of Article 2'.

In *Evans v UK*,[156] the Court followed the same margin of appreciation approach to embryos created by *in vitro* fertilization (IVF). In that case, the applicant and her partner

---

[149] In *A, B and C v Ireland* hudoc, para 112, the Court stated: 'Abortion is available on request (accord-ing to certain criteria including gestational limits) in some 30 Contracting States. An abortion justified on health grounds is available in some 40 Contracting States and justified on well-being grounds in some 35 such States. Three Contracting States prohibit abortion in all circumstances (Andorra, Malta and San Marino).' Ireland permits an abortion to safeguard the life of the mother, but not on grounds of the mother's health or for eugenic reasons or in cases of rape. See Wicks, 11 HRLR 556 (2011).

[150] *H v Norway No 17004/90* hudoc (1992) DA (partner) and *Boso v Italy No 50490/99* hudoc (2002) DA.

[151] *X v Austria No 7045/75*, 7 DR 87 (1976). Cf, *X v Norway No 867/60*, 6 CD 34 (1961).

[152] *Knudsen v Norway No 11045/84*, 42 DR 247 (1985).

[153] See, in particular, *Bruggemann and Scheuten v Germany No 6959/75*, 10 DR 100 (1978).

[154] In *X v UK*, the husband's claim to respect for family life under Article 8 failed because of the 'rights of others' restriction in Article 8(2) (the wife's rights).

[155] 2004-XIII; 40 EHRR 259 para 85 GC. See Plomer, 5 HRLR 311 (2005).

[156] Hudoc (2007); 46 EHRR 728 para 54 GC.

underwent IVF treatment, resulting in embryos that later could be implanted into the applicant's womb. But when the relationship broke down, the partner withdrew his consent to the use of the embryos in this way, which meant under English law that they had to be destroyed. The Grand Chamber rejected the applicant's claim that their destruction would be a breach of Article 2 on the basis that the position in English law, by which an embryo did not have a right to life, fell within the margin of appreciation that states had on this matter, given 'the absence of any European consensus on the scientific and legal definition of the beginning of life'.

A question that has not been considered directly is whether the state must provide adequate protection against acts (eg the pregnant woman's taking of drugs harmful to the foetus) that may reduce the 'quality of life' of a child once born without actually causing loss of life.[157] The Commission has in other contexts required that there be evidence of a danger to life, not just of ill-health, for Article 2 to apply.[158]

III. OTHER HARMFUL ACTS

In an early case,[159] the Commission expressed the opinion that in certain circumstances a sterilization operation might be contrary to Article 2, presumably by denying a person the possibility even of conception. The application was refused on its facts because the operation was for medical reasons and the sterilized person had given her consent.[160] The question has not arisen since under Article 2 and would seem to come more properly within Articles 3 and 8.

7. THE PROHIBITION OF THE TAKING OF LIFE BY THE USE OF FORCE

I. THE GENERAL RULE

Article 2 prohibits the taking of life where this is not justified by any of the exceptions permitted by its text. The prohibition extends to the use of force resulting in the unintentional, as well as to the intentional, taking of life.[161] It applies to the taking of life by the police,[162] soldiers,[163] and other state agents.[164] It does not make a state directly responsible for the taking of life by private individuals; a state's obligation in such cases is limited to the provision of protection in accordance with the first sentence of Article 2(1). A state may be liable under Article 2 not only for the conduct of its agents who actually kill an individual, but also for those who are responsible for an operation that may threaten life

---

[157] The Convention does not require a 'wrongful life' remedy for being born disabled by medical negligence: *Reeve v UK No 24844/94*, 79 DR 146 (1994). But see *Maurice v France* 2005-IX; 42 EHRR 885 GC.

[158] *De Varga-Hirsch v France No 9559/81*, 33 DR 158 (1993) and *M v Germany No 10307/83*, 37 DR 113 (1984). Cf *X v Austria No 8278/78*, 18 DR 154 (1979).

[159] *No 1287/61*, cited in Fawcett, *The Application of the European Convention on Human Rights*, 1987, p 36.

[160] The applicant was the husband who had not given his consent.

[161] *McCann v UK* A 324 (1995); 21 EHRR 97 GC and *Ogur v Turkey* 1999-III; 31 EHRR 912 GC.

[162] See, eg, *Hugh Jordan v UK* 2001-III; *37 EHRR* 52.

[163] See, eg, *Isayeva, Yusupova and Bazayeva v Russia* hudoc (2005); 41 EHRR 847.

[164] Village guards or security officers who hold themselves out as acting for the state are state agents: *Avşar v Turkey* 2001-; 37 EHRR 1014.

if it is not planned or managed by the authorities 'so as to minimise, to the greatest extent possible, recourse to lethal force'.[165]

Physical assault by a state agent that does not result in death will 'almost always' be examined under Article 3, not Article 2.[166] But Article 2 may apply in the absence of death in 'exceptional circumstances': relevant factors are the 'degree and type of force used and the intention or aim' underlying it.[167] In *Makaratzis v Greece*,[168] there were 'exceptional circumstances' that brought Article 2 into play (and led to its breach) when the applicant was seriously injured after thirty or so police fired many bullets into his car during a chaotic car chase. Although there was no intention to kill the applicant, the use of force was 'potentially lethal' and it was only 'fortuitous' that he was not killed; the applicant was 'the victim of conduct which, by its very nature, put his life at risk'. Article 2 has since been held to apply in several other cases where the applicant suffered life-threatening injuries, but did not die.[169] In *Trévalec v Belgium*,[170] the field of application of Article 2 was extended further when it was held to apply to the non-life-threatening injuries of a television journalist who was accidentally shot during a police operation.

Killings will be in breach of Article 2 even though they are in accordance with national rules governing the use of firearms by law enforcement agencies where those rules do not satisfy the Article 2 strict proportionality test.[171]

A state may be responsible under Article 2 for deporting or extraditing an individual to another state when there are substantial grounds for believing that this would involve a real risk to his or her life from the acts of state agents or private individuals,[172] although in practice such cases are usually treated under Article 3.

For the state to be liable under Article 2 for the killing of any individual, it must first be shown beyond a reasonable doubt that the individual was killed by one of its agents.[173] This requirement has presented considerable problems of proof. These problems have been eased for the applicant where an individual dies in custody or 'in an area within the exclusive control of the authorities of the state'.[174] In these situations, given the vulnerability of the detainee and the state's special access to information about what happened, the burden of proof shifts to the state to 'provide a satisfactory and convincing explanation'.[175] As to the standard of proof, 'strong presumptions of fact will arise in respect of injuries and death occurring' in detention.[176] The burden of proof upon the state was not satisfied in cases in which the victim was in good health on being taken into detention and there was no post mortem or other evidence to confirm the state's claim that he had died from a heart attack[177]

---

[165] *McCann v UK* A 324 (1995); 21 EHRR 97 para 194 GC. Cf *Ergi v Turkey* 1998-IV; 32 EHRR 388; and *Isayeva v Russia* hudoc (2005); 41 EHRR 791.

[166] *Ilhan v Turkey* 2000-VII; 34 EHRR 869 para 76 GC.   [167] *Ilhan v* Turkey, para 76.

[168] 2004-XI; 41 EHRR 1092 paras 52, 54 GC. Cf *Acar v Turkey* hudoc (2005) and *Green v UK No 28079/04* hudoc (2005) DA.

[169] See, eg, *Evrim Öktem v Turkey* hudoc (2008); *Perişan and Others v Turkey* hudoc (2010); *Vasil Sachov Petrov v Bulgaria* hudoc (2010); and *Peker v Turkey (No 2)* hudoc (2011).   [170] Hudoc (2011).

[171] *Nachova v Bulgaria* 2005-VII; 42 EHRR 933 GC and *Makaratkis v Greece* 2004-XI; 41 EHRR 1092 GC.

[172] *Gonzalez v Spain No 43544/98* hudoc (1999) DA and *Headley v UK No 39642/03* hudoc (2005) DA.

[173] If the perpetrator is shown to be a state agent, it will then be for the state to show that the killing falls within one of the permitted exceptions in Article 2: see *McCann v UK* A 324 (1995); 21 EHRR 97 para 194 GC.

[174] *Varnava and Others v Turkey* hudoc 2009- GC (Northern Cyprus under Turkish control) and *Akkum v Turkey* 2005-II; 43 EHRR 526 (army barracks).

[175] *Salman v Turkey* 2000-VII; 34 EHRR 425 para 100 GC. Cf *Musayev and Others v Russia* hudoc (2007). As to proof that an individual has been detained, see *Celikbilek v Turkey* hudoc (2005). The state must prove the release of a detained person: *Süheyla Aydin v Turkey* hudoc (2005).   [176] *Salman v Turkey*.

[177] *Salman v Turkey*. Cf *Tanli v Turkey* 2001-III; 38 EHRR 31.

or to explain injuries to the body satisfactorily.[178] Nor was it met when a prisoner was killed by an explosion when the authorities were not able to explain why he had been put in a place where he was at risk.[179]

The difficulty of proving beyond a reasonable doubt that a state agent is responsible for a non-custodial killing is in some cases, such as a killing on the street with no witnesses,[180] increased where the state fails to cooperate in establishing the facts. In this situation, too, the Court is prepared to assist, again on the basis of the exclusive knowledge of the authorities. In particular, it has held that where the applicant has made out a *prima facie* case that the killing was by a state agent and the respondent state refuses to produce relevant evidence, the burden of proof shifts to that state to show that the refusal is for a good reason or to provide a satisfactory explanation of the killing.[181] In *Soare and Others v Romania*,[182] a claim of self-defence was rejected when the respondent government failed to produce evidence to support its contention that the person killed in an 'on the street' incident was armed.

Although a breach of the state's substantive obligation not to take life by force may be impossible to establish in some cases, Article 2 has sometimes been found to have been infringed in them because the state has failed to comply with its procedural obligation to investigate the killing.[183] A breach of Article 2 may also be found in some cases on the basis that an unattributable death which results from a state operation, for example against terrorists, has not been planned or conducted by the authorities so as to minimize the risk of loss of life of innocent bystanders.[184]

a. Disappeared persons

There may be liability for a breach of the state's substantive obligation under Article 2 not to take life where a person has disappeared, but no body has been found. There may be a taking of life in breach of Article 2 in such a case (i) where it is established beyond reasonable doubt that the disappeared person has been detained by the state; and (ii) there is 'sufficient circumstantial evidence, based on concrete elements, on which it may be concluded beyond reasonable doubt' that the person is dead.[185] When these two requirements are met, the burden of proof is transferred to the state to account for the death of a person in its custody.[186] Breaches of the substantive obligation in Article 2 not to take life have been found on this basis in a series of cases involving disappeared persons in Turkey. In *Timurtas v Turkey*,[187] the Court found that the applicant's son had been arrested by gendarmes and taken to an identifiable place of detention. There was documentary evidence

---

[178] *Velikova v Bulgaria* 2000-VI; *Anguelova v Bulgaria* 2002-IV; 38 EHRR 659; *Mojsiejew v Poland* hudoc (2009); and *Mižigárová v Slovakia* hudoc (2010).   [179] *Demiray v Turkey* 2000-XII.

[180] See, eg, *Akkoc v Turkey* 2000-X; 34 EHRR 1173; *Yasa v Turkey* 1998-I; 28 EHRR 408; and *Kaya (Mahmut) v Turkey* 2000-III.

[181] *Estamirov and Others v Russia* hudoc (2006); 46 EHRR 696; *Khashiyev and Akayeva v Russia* hudoc (2005); 42 EHRR 397; and *Luluyev v Russia* 2006-VIII; 48 EHRR 1039. Failure to provide evidence may also involve a breach of the state's obligation to provide 'all necessary facilities' (Article 38(1)(a), Convention): *Akkum v Turkey* 2005-II; 43 EHRR 526. For a (now exceptional) case in which the Court held that inferences could not be drawn on the facts from a state's lack of cooperation, see *Tanrikulu v Turkey* 1999-IV; 30 EHRR 950 GC.

[182] Hudoc (2011).

[183] See *Akkoc v Turkey* 2000-X; 34 EHRR 1173; *Yasa v Turkey* 1998-I; 28 EHRR 408; and *Kaya (Mahmut) v Turkey* 2000-III.   [184] *Ergi v Turkey* 1998-IV; 32 EHRR 388.

[185] *Çakici v Turkey* 1999-IV; 31 EHRR 133 para 85 GC.   [186] *Çakici v Turkey*.

[187] 2000-VI; 33 EHRR 121. The more cautious approach that the Court had taken in *Kurt v Turkey* 1998-III; 27 EHRR 373 no longer applies.

to this effect[188] and credible evidence that two fellow detainees had seen the son in a place of detention in the month or so after his arrest, but he had not otherwise been seen during the six-and-a-half years following his arrest: further enquires had been discouraged by state officials. Finding that in this case there was sufficient concrete circumstantial evidence of death[189] and no explanation of the son's fate by the respondent state (which claimed not to have detained him), the Court found a breach of Article 2.

The Court noted the length of time since the son's disappearance; the credible evidence of his presence in a place of detention after the arrest; and the strong evidence that the son was wanted by the state in connection with PKK activities, a fact that made his unacknowledged detention life-threatening in the context of south-east Turkey where, the Court had decided in other cases,[190] the security forces were not held accountable for their actions. Breaches of the substantive obligation have been found in other similar cases from Turkey,[191] which have generally involved disappearances for five years or longer.[192] *Kurt* has been expressly distinguished in some cases; in others it has not.[193]

In a number of recent Russian cases the Court has also been willing to presume death. In *Baysayeva v Russia*,[194] the applicant's husband was, the Court found, arrested along with others by military servicemen when a security operation was being conducted in his village, since when there had been no news of him for some six years. The respondent state denied that he had been arrested by the state and had no custody records for him. The Court accepted the applicant's contention that when, in the context of the conflict in Chechnya, a person was arrested by unidentified servicemen without any subsequent acknowledgment of detention, the arrest could be considered life-threatening. In these circumstances, and noting also that the authorities had not taken the necessary early steps to open an investigation, the Court held that it could be presumed that the husband was dead. In *Turluyeva v Russia*,[195] the Court took matters further, presuming death in a life-threatening situation after disappearance for just three years and nine months. The Court noted that in the context of disappearances in the North Caucasus, there was 'enough evidence to suggest that the victims of disappearances often do not survive for very long after the abductions'.

Article 2 may apply to disappearances that are not the responsibility of the state. Thus the obligations to provide a legal system with satisfactory enforcement machinery and to take preventive or investigative action extends to a disappearance in life-threatening situations that is not proven to be caused by state agents, as, for example, where it results from abduction by unidentified armed men[196] or where a nursing home resident wanders off.[197]

---

[188] This was a photocopy of a post-operation report; the government challenged its authenticity, but the Court inferred otherwise when the government declined on security grounds to produce supporting evidence.

[189] The longer the period of disappearance, the less other circumstantial evidence is needed: *Timurtas v Turkey* 2000-VI; 33 EHRR 121 para 83.

[190] See *Kilic v Turkey* 2000-III; 33 EHRR 1357 and *Kaya (Mahmut) v Turkey* 2000-III.

[191] See, eg, *Çiçek v Turkey* hudoc (2001); 37 EHRR 464; *Bilgin v Turkey* hudoc (2000) 36 EHRR 879; and *Akdeniz v Turkey* hudoc (2001). See also *Cyprus v Turkey* 2001-IV; 35 EHRR 731 GC.

[192] See also *Tanis v Turkey* 2005-VIII; 46 EHRR 211 (four and a half years).

[193] See, eg, *Bilgin v Turkey* hudoc (2000); 36 EHRR 879 and *Akdeniz and Others v Turkey* hudoc (2001). See also *Cyprus v Turkey* 2001-V; 35 EHRR 731 GC.   [194] Hudoc (2007); 48 EHRR 771.

[195] Hudoc (2013) para 87. See also *Betayev and Betayeva v Russia* hudoc (2008) (five years); and *Medova v Russia* hudoc (2009) (four years).

[196] *Medova v Russia* hudoc (2009). See also *Osmanoğlu v Turkey* hudoc (2008), 53 EHRR 557.

[197] *Dodov v Bulgaria* hudoc (2008); 47 EHRR 932.

II. PERMITTED EXCEPTIONS

a. Capital punishment

The first exception concerns the death penalty, which is expressly permitted by the original text of Article 2(1). The use of the death penalty had to be allowed when the Convention was drafted because it was then generally provided for and applied in West European states. Practice has changed radically since, to the point where provision for the death penalty is almost entirely absent in the law of Council of Europe states or, where it is available, is not carried out.[198] Accordingly, the Sixth Protocol to the Convention[199] requires the abolition of the death penalty in peacetime by the parties to it. This partial prohibition was made total by the Thirteenth Protocol,[200] which requires the abolition of the death penalty in time of war also. Article 2 remains the governing provision for the parties to the Convention insofar as they are not parties to the two Protocols.

In *Soering v UK*,[201] the Plenary Court stated that it would have been possible for the parties to the Convention to have 'abrogated' the exception provided for in Article 2(1) by the 'generalised abolition of capital punishment' in their national law. However, given the adoption of the Sixth Protocol as recently as 1983, the Court considered that this had not occurred, despite the considerable move towards the abolition of the death penalty that had taken place by the time the case was decided in 1989, so that the Article 2 exception continued in being. The position was reviewed again in *Öcalan v Turkey*[202] in which it was noted by the Court Chamber that there had been 'a considerable evolution' in state practice concerning the death penalty since the *Soering* case. When the *Öcalan* case was decided, all but one of the then forty-four Convention parties had abolished the death penalty in peacetime, with the remaining state, Russia, applying a moratorium, and new Council of Europe member states undertaking to abolish the death penalty as a condition of membership. The result was that the territory of Council of Europe states constituted a 'zone free of capital punishment'. In consequence, it could 'be said that capital punishment in peacetime has come to be regarded as an unacceptable, if not inhuman, form of punishment which is no longer permissible under Article 2'. The Grand Chamber agreed with this conclusion.[203] No such conclusion was drawn in respect of the death penalty in time of war, given that a large number of states were not then parties to the Thirteenth Protocol.

The matter was considered again in *Al-Saadoon and Mufdhi v UK*,[204] where it was noted that the position of the contracting parties on the death penalty had developed to the point where forty-two of the forty-seven members of the Council of Europe were parties to the Thirteenth Protocol and three others had signed it. The Court Chamber concluded that '[t]hese figures, together with consistent State practice in observing the moratorium on capital punishment, are strongly indicative that Article 2 has been amended so as to prohibit the death penalty in all circumstances'. On the basis of this conclusion, the Court stated that it did not consider that the wording of Article 2(1) 'continues to act as a bar to its interpreting the words "inhuman or degrading

---

[198] Russia is the only Convention party that retains the death penalty in law in either peacetime or war; it has operated a moratorium in practice since 1996, although Amnesty International reported some executions in Chechnya between 1996 and 1999.

[199] All Convention parties are parties to the Protocol except Russia.

[200] The Thirteen Protocol now has forty-three parties and two other signatories.

[201] A 161 (1989); 11 EHRR 439 PC.

[202] Hudoc (2003); 37 EHRR 238 paras 195–8 (emphasis added). See also *Shamayev and Others v Georgia and Russia* 2005-III.

[203] 2005-IV; 41 EHRR 985 para 163.   [204] 2010-; 51 EHRR 212 para 120.

treatment or punishment" in Article 3 as including the death penalty'. Although the Court found it unnecessary to consider whether Article 2 would be violated by the respondent state if the applicants were returned to Iraq, it appears from the Court Chamber's judgment that the Article 2 exception has, as postulated in the *Soering* case, been abrogated by state practice so that the death penalty may not be carried out consistently with Article 2 in any circumstances, either in peacetime or in war. On a separate point, whereas the two Protocols prohibit the re-introduction of the death penalty,[205] Article 2 does not expressly do so. However, it is predictable that the Court would read such a prohibition into it if the question arose for any of the few states not parties to the Protocols.

Quite apart from capital punishment now in itself being a breach of Article 2, a state may infringe Article 2 if its provisions regulating the use of the death penalty are not complied with. The wording of Article 2 permits the death penalty only where it is imposed as 'a sentence of a court following... conviction of a crime for which this penalty is provided by law'. On its face, Article 2 permits the death penalty for any 'crime'. However, the principle of proportionality must apply, so that it should be permissible only for 'the most serious crimes'.[206] It is likely that the word 'crime' has an autonomous meaning in Article 2, as it has in Article 6.[207] The death penalty must be 'provided by law'. This means not only that there is a basis for it in national law, but also that this basis is 'accessible' and 'foreseeable', as these requirements have been interpreted in other Convention articles.[208] A death sentence must be imposed by a 'court', which means an 'independent and impartial tribunal' in the sense of Article 6.[209] Beyond that, it has been held that Article 2 will be infringed unless 'the most rigorous standards of fairness' are observed in the criminal proceedings leading to a death sentence, both at first instance and on appeal.[210] Thus the imposition of the death penalty in breach of the fair trial guarantee in Article 6[211] is a breach of Article 2, as must be its imposition in breach of the prohibition of retroactive criminal punishment in Article 7 and for an offence involving conduct protected by the Convention.[212] Discrimination contrary to Article 14 in the imposition of the death penalty would be a breach of Articles 2 and 14 taken together.

There will also be a breach of Article 2 where the deportation or extradition of an individual occurs when there are substantial grounds for believing that there is a real risk that he or she will be subjected to the death penalty[213] or in circumstances in which the provisions in Article 2 regulating the use of the death penalty will not be complied with, as when there would not be a fair trial.[214] The same considerations as those indicated earlier when discussing the use of the death penalty by a contracting party within its own jurisdiction, apply to deportation or extradition cases too.[215] For example, in *Rrapo*

---

[205] Cf Article 4, American Convention on Human Rights.

[206] Cf *Soering v UK* A 161 (1989); 11 EHRR 439 para 104 PC. And see *Meng v Portugal No 25862/94*, 83-B DR 88 (1995) (death penalty for multiple car thefts: case settled) and *MAR v UK No 28038/95*, 23 EHRR CD 120; (1997) Com Rep, F Sett (drugs possession offences).

[207] See *Engel v Netherlands* A 22 (1976); 1 EHRR 647 PC.

[208] *Öcalan v Turkey* 2005-IV; 41 EHRR 985 para 166 GC.   [209] *Öcalan v Turkey.*

[210] *Öcalan v Turkey.*

[211] *Öcalan v Turkey* and *Bader and Kandor v Sweden* 2005-XI; 46 EHRR 197. Whereas *Bader and Kanbor* refers to a 'fair trial' generally, *Öcalan*, paras 173–4, refers to Article 6.

[212] See *Sobhani v Sweden No 32999/06*, unreported (1998) DA (sexual orientation (Article 8): case settled).

[213] *Rrapo v Albania* hudoc (2012) DA.   [214] *Bader and Kanbor v Sweden* 2005-XI; 46 EHRR 197.

[215] Deportation or extradition by a party to the Sixth or Thirteenth Protocol to face a real risk of the death penalty would be a breach of those Protocols.

v Albania,[216] diplomatic assurances given by the US that the death penalty would not be sought or imposed were sufficient to dispel the risk. In practice, cases of deportation or extradition involving the death penalty are considered by the Court under either Article 2 or 3, or both.[217]

b. Deaths resulting from the use of force for permitted purposes

Article 2(2) lists three other situations in which the taking of life by the state is justified. These are when it results from the use of force[218] which is no more than absolutely necessary:

 (i)   in self-defence or the defence of another;

 (ii) to effect a lawful arrest or prevent an escape from lawful detention; and

 (iii) to quell a riot or insurrection.

This list is exhaustive. There have been a number of cases of the arbitrary use of lethal force by the police or other state agents in violation of Article 2 that clearly do not fall within the permitted exceptions in Article 2(2).[219] At one stage in the drafting, a fourth exception was permitted:[220] where force is used to prohibit 'entry to a clearly defined place to which access is forbidden on grounds of national security'. This wording was finally omitted so that the taking of life on this basis is not allowed. The taking of life to prevent crime[221] or escape from a state's territory[222] is also not permitted. Action against terrorists resulting in the loss of life has to be justified within Article 2(2)(a)–(c).[223] Article 2(2) regulates the unintentional as well as the intentional taking of life by the use of force.[224]

Article 2(2) permits the taking of life only when it results from the use of force which is 'no more than absolutely necessary' for one or more of the authorized purposes. The burden of proof is upon the state to show that the force used meets this requirement.[225] Force is 'absolutely necessary' only if it is 'strictly proportionate' to the achievement of a permitted purpose.[226] In this respect, Article 2(2) imposes a more rigorous test of necessity than that which applies under paragraphs (2) of Articles 8–11 of the Convention where the requirement is simply one of proportionality. Another crucial difference is that states are generally allowed no 'margin of appreciation' under Article 2(2); the Court makes its own objective assessment of the strict proportionality of the force used.[227]

However, in *Finogenov v Russia*,[228] a Court Chamber held that it may 'occasionally depart' from its 'rigorous standard' of 'absolute necessity' in circumstances in which 'its application may be simply impossible where certain aspects of the situation lie far beyond

---

[216] Hudoc (2012). Cf *Salem v Portugal No 26844/04* hudoc (2006) (diplomatic assurances that the death penalty would not be imposed sufficient). See also *Soering v UK* A 161 (1989); 11 EHRR 439 para 104 PC; and *Nivette v France No 44190/98* hudoc (2001) DA.

[217] See, eg, *Shamayev and Others v Georgia and Russia* 2005-III.

[218] Force includes using a vehicle to clear barricades: *McShane v UK* hudoc (2002); 35 EHRR 593.

[219] See eg *Evrim Öktem v Turkey* hudoc (2008).   [220] See 3 TP 82 and 4 id 58.

[221] *Kelly v UK No 17579/90*, 74 DR 139 (1993).

[222] *Streletz, Kessler, and Krenz v Germany* 2001-II; 33 EHRR 751 GC.

[223] *McCann v UK* A324 (1995); 21 EHRR 97 GC; *Ergi v Turkey* 1998-IV; 32 EHRR 388; and *Isayeva v Russia* hudoc (2005); 41 EHRR 791.

[224] *McCann v UK* A 324 (1995); 21 EHRR 97 para 148 GC and *Ogur v Turkey* 1999-III; 31 EHRR 912 GC.

[225] *McCann v UK* A 324 (1995); 21 EHRR 97 para 148 GC. Cf dissenting opinion of Judge Bratza in *Ağdaş v Turkey* hudoc (2004).

[226] *McCann v UK*, para 149 GC. The requirement in national law need not be expressed in terms of 'absolute necessity', so long as it is essentially the same in substance, as applied in practice: paras 152–5.

[227] There is no reference to a margin of appreciation in *McCann*.

[228] Hudoc (2011), paras 211, 243.

the Court's expertise and where the authorities had to act under tremendous time pressure and where their control of the situation was minimal'. In such circumstances, the Court added, a margin of appreciation may also be allowed. In that case, the Russian authorities had to deal with a situation in which 950 hostages, whose lives were at real and immediate risk, were being held in a theatre by Chechen terrorists. Given that the situation was such that the authorities had to act 'very quickly and in full secrecy' to save lives and were not in control of the building, the Court was 'prepared to grant them a margin of appreciation, at least in so far as the military and technical aspects of the situation were concerned'. In contrast, 'the organisation of the medical aid to the victims and their evacuation', when there were no time constraints and the authorities were in control of the building, could 'be subjected to a more thorough scrutiny than the "political" and military aspects of the operation'.[229] The Court held that the obligation to organize and conduct an operation that could be justified under Article 2(2)[230] with the least possible risk to life had been infringed in that, although the decision to storm the theatre was justified and the use of gas was not disproportionate, the rescue operation had not been adequately planned or implemented, with, *inter alia*, no centralized coordination and inadequate arrangements for medical assistance. In reaching this conclusion, the Court was influenced in its ruling by the fact that the gas must, despite claims by the respondent government that it was harmless (the government never revealed what gas it was), have been 'dangerous' to have killed 125 people.

'Strict proportionality' may require a verbal warning and a warning shot aimed in the air before potentially lethal force is used.[231] Also to be taken into account is whether the lives of innocent bystanders are placed at risk and the time available to assess the situation.[232] As to the latter, the Court has drawn a distinction between planned police and unplanned operations or actions, with a stricter test being applied in the case of the former.[233] The Court has also accepted that 'the use of force by agents of the state in pursuit of one of the aims delineated in Article 2(2) of the Convention may be justified under this provision where it is based on an honest belief which is perceived, for good reasons, to be valid at the time but which subsequently turns out to be mistaken',[234] as for example where a person shot is honestly and reasonably believed to have a gun which later proves to be a replica.[235] There may be liability for the actual disproportionate use of force or for the planning or control of an operation involving the use of force for a purpose permitted by Article 2(2) that does not minimize the risk to life as far as possible.[236]

For the taking of life to be justified under Article 2(2), the action taken must be 'lawful'. This is expressly stated in respect of Article 2(2)(b) and (c) and can be supposed to be the case in respect of Article 2(2)(a). This means that the action must be lawful under national law, so that the use of force in the particular circumstances must be authorized

---

[229] *Quaere* whether the Court should have fully retained the 'absolute necessity' test but allowed a margin of appreciation in applying it.

[230] The Court assumed that 'the authorities were pursuing simultaneously all three legitimate aims specified in Article 2(2) of the Convention, and that the "defence of any person from unlawful violence" was the predominant one': *Finogenov v Russia* hudoc (2011) para 218.

[231] *Kakoulli v Turkey* hudoc (2005); 45 EHRR 355.

[232] See *Stewart v UK* No 10044/82, 39 DR 162 (1984); *McCann v UK* A 324 (1995); 21 EHRR 97 para 148 GC; and *Ergi v Turkey* 1998-IV; 32 EHRR 388. For other considerations to be taken into account, see O'Boyle, *The Use of Lethal Force under Article 2 of the European Convention on Human Rights*, CE Doc DH-Ed-COLL (90), p 5.   [233] See *Bubbins v UK* ECHR 2005-II para 79 and *Mansuroğlu v Turkey* hudoc (2008).

[234] *McCann v UK* A 324 (1995); 21 EHRR 97 para 200 GC.   [235] *Bubbins v UK* hudoc (2005).

[236] See the *McCann* and *Ergi* cases, below, pp 63 and 65.

by national law.[237] It also means that it must be consistent with the requirements of the Convention.[238] These include the rule of law requirement that the national law is 'formulated with sufficient precision to enable the citizen to regulate his conduct'[239] and, for the purposes of Article 2(2)(b), the prohibition of arbitrary arrest in Article 5.

c. In self-defence or the defence of another

Article 2(2)(a) allows the use of force by state agents in self-defence or the defence of another; it does not permit it in defence of property. It justifies the use of force in self-defence only if it is 'absolutely necessary'. This test was found not to have been complied with in *McCann v UK*.[240] In that case, three members of the Provisional IRA were shot dead on the street by SAS soldiers in Gibraltar. The persons killed, whom the British authorities had allowed to cross the border from Spain, were suspected of having on them a remote control device to be used to explode a bomb that was believed to be in a car parked in a public place, the explosion of which would have caused a devastating loss of life. In fact, the suspects did not have such a device on them and there was no bomb in the car. Instead, they were on a reconnaissance visit to Gibraltar and the car had been left to save a parking space for a later bombing mission. The Court found unanimously that the actual killings were not in breach of Article 2, because the four soldiers had an honest and reasonable belief when they shot to kill that the suspects had made movements to activate remote control devices on them that would have exploded the bomb, causing serious loss of life. However, the Court held, by ten votes to nine, that Article 2 had been infringed because the use of force had not been 'strictly proportionate' to the attainment of its objective, namely the saving of lives, as the operation could have been planned and controlled so as to achieve that objective without the need to kill the suspects. It based this decision on three considerations. First, the authorities could have stopped the suspects from entering Gibraltar at the border, thereby eliminating any risk of loss of innocent lives. The Court rejected the respondent state's argument that it was justified in not doing this because there would probably then not have been enough evidence to detain and try the suspects for any offence, leaving them or others free to try again later. Secondly, the authorities had made insufficient allowance for the possibility that their intelligence assessments might be incorrect. In particular, they had passed their possible, but mistaken, suspicions as to the device and the bomb to the soldiers as facts, so that the use of lethal force by the latter was made 'almost unavoidable'. Thirdly, in accordance with their training, the soldiers had shot to kill, not wound, the suspects on the basis that this was necessary in order to save the lives of others. In the view of the majority, this lacked 'the degree of caution in the use of firearms to be expected from law enforcement personnel in a democratic society, even when dealing with dangerous terrorist suspects'.[241] In their joint opinion, the dissenting judges disagreed with the Court's conclusions on each of these three points. More generally, they cautioned against 'the temptations offered by the benefit of hindsight'[242] and stressed the large number of innocent lives at risk.

---

[237] See *Kelly v UK No 1759/90*, 74 DR 139 (1993); *Stewart v UK No 1004/82*, 39 DR 162 (1984); and *X v Belgium No 2758/66*, 12 YB 174 (1969).

[238] Cf the interpretation of 'lawful' in Article 5: see eg, *Bozano v France* A 111 (1986); 9 EHRR 297.

[239] *Sunday Times v UK (No 1)* A 30 (1979); 2 EHRR 245 para 49 PC.

[240] A 324 (1995); 21 EHRR 97 GC. See Joseph, 14 NHRQ 5 (1994).

[241] A 324 (1995); 21 EHRR 97 para 212 GC. However, the Court unanimously rejected a claim that there had from the outset been a plan to kill rather than arrest the suspects: para 178.

[242] A 324 (1995); 21 EHRR 97 para 212 GC, dissenting opinion para 8.

The approach in the *McCann* case was followed shortly afterwards in *Andronicou and Constantinou v Cyprus*,[243] but in that case the Court found in favour of the respondent state on the facts. There, Cypriot police special forces were called in to deal with a situation in which a young man was holding his fiancée hostage with a gun in their flat. When the police stormed the flat to rescue the fiancée, they killed them both in the course of using lethal force in defence of themselves and the fiancée. The Court held that the actual killings were 'strictly proportionate' on the facts and, by five votes to four, that the planning and control of the operation was 'strictly proportionate' too. The *McCann* and *Andronicou and Constantinou* cases are both to be contrasted on the facts with *Gül v Turkey*,[244] in which the massive force used by the police as they stormed the flat of a suspected terrorist was held to be 'grossly disproportionate' to what was needed by the police in self-defence. Different again was the case of *Giuliani and Gaggio v Italy*,[245] in which large 'anti-globalization' demonstrations at the G8 summit in Genoa had led to very violent clashes between demonstrators and law enforcement agencies. There was no substantive breach of Article 2 when, after giving a warning that he was about to do so, a policeman in a jeep that had been isolated and was being subjected to an extremely violent attack, fired shots, seemingly not aiming in any particular direction, and killed a demonstrator. The Grand Chamber held, by thirteen to four, that, in an 'extremely tense situation', and with a demonstrator about to throw a fire extinguisher into the jeep, the soldier had acted in self-defence in honest and reasonable fear for his life. In another case that turned upon an assessment of the facts, in *Perk and Others v Turkey*,[246] no substantive breach of Article 2 was found when the police returned fire from suspected terrorists in self-defence in an anti-terrorist operation even though they did not first resort to less deadly means, such as tear gas.

Article 2(2)(a) has been relied upon unsuccessfully in the context of measures taken by the state in response to armed insurrection in a number of cases. In particular, cases in which civilian lives were lost in the course of the Russian military response to the emergency in Chechnya have led to findings of breaches of Article 2 because of planning inadequacies or of a disproportionate use of armed force. In *Isayeva v Russia*,[247] a large group of rebel fighters had entered the applicant's village, which had a population of about 20,000. In response, the Russian armed forces implemented a plan involving an air and artillery attack upon the village, using high explosion aviation bombs and missile strikes. A bomb which was dropped from a Russian military plane exploded near the applicant's family's mini-van while they were trying to leave the village, killing the applicant's son and three nieces and injuring the applicant. The Court considered that using the kinds of weapons that were deployed 'in a populated area, outside wartime and without prior evacuation of the civilians, is impossible to reconcile with the degree of caution expected from a law enforcement body in a democratic society'.[248] While accepting that Article 2(2)(a) allows the state to use force to protect lives when faced with a situation in which the population of a village is held hostage by well-equipped and trained fighters, 'the massive use of indiscriminate weapons stands in flagrant contrast with this aim and

---

[243] 1997-VI; 25 EHRR 491. See also *Bubbins v UK* 2005-II; 41 EHRR 458; *Huohvanainen v Finland* hudoc (2007); *Kakoulli v Turkey* hudoc (2005); 45 EHRR 355; and *Saoud v France* hudoc (2007).

[244] Hudoc (2000); 34 EHRR 719. Fifty or more shots were fired at the door as the suspect unlocked it, killing him.

[245] 2011-; 54 EHRR 278 para 191. GC. See also *Aydan v Turkey* hudoc (2013).

[246] Hudoc (2006).   [247] Hudoc (2005).

[248] *Isayeva v Russia*, para 190. Steps taken to inform the inhabitants of a safe passage out of the village were found inadequate.

cannot be considered compatible with the standard of care prerequisite to an operation of this kind'.[249] Although accepting that the operation had a legitimate aim, the Court did not consider that it was 'planned and executed with the requisite care for the lives of the civilian population', and hence was in breach of Article 2.[250] A similar lack of planning and proportionality in execution was found in *Isayeva, Yusupova and Bazayeva v Russia*,[251] in which Russian military planes, engaged in a counter-terrorism operation in the area, bombed a large convoy of civilian vehicles escaping the armed conflict in Grozny on an open stretch of road, killing, among others, two children of the applicant. The pilots claimed that, having obtained permission from their air controller, they were defending themselves against machine gun fire from two trucks carrying Chechen rebel fighters, and that they were not aware of the convoy. The Court, which did not accept that the pilots had not seen the convoy, found that the counter-terrorism operation had not been planned with sufficient attention to possible civilian casualties and that the use of extremely powerful air to ground missiles was disproportionate in the circumstances.[252] In contrast, in *Ahmet Özkan and Others v Turkey*,[253] intense firing by security forces at a village using missiles and grenades in reaction to shots fired from the village in an area of known PKK terrorist activity was justified as being 'absolutely necessary' to protect life.

d. To effect an arrest or prevent an escape

The use of force is justified under Article 2(2)(b) if it is 'absolutely necessary' to effect an arrest or to prevent an escape. The use of excessive physical force for either of these purposes will not be 'absolutely necessary'.[254] Most cases under Article 2(2)(b) have concerned the use of firearms, which are particularly life threatening.[255] Where relevant, prior verbal warnings and warning shots in the air are taken into account by the Court when assessing the facts, although they will not in themselves render subsequent shots 'absolutely necessary'.[256] In *Nachova v Bulgaria*,[257] it was held that 'potentially deadly force cannot be considered absolutely necessary where it is known that the person to be arrested poses no threat to life or limb and is not suspected of having committed a violent offence', and that this is so even though 'a failure to use lethal force may result in the opportunity to arrest the fugitive being lost'. Thus, in the *Nachova* case there was a breach of Article 2 when the applicants, known to be unarmed and not otherwise dangerous, were shot and killed by the police when, despite being ordered by the police to stop or be fired upon, they ran away to avoid arrest in connection with an offence of unauthorized absence from work. It is submitted that the fact that it is the only way to stop an individual from avoiding arrest cannot justify the use of 'potentially deadly force', particularly by

---

[249] *Isayeva v Russia*, para 191. The number of civilian deaths may have been 'significantly higher' than the forty-six identified by the state: para 197.

[250] *Isayeva v Russia*, para 200. Cf *Kerimova and Others v Russia* hudoc (2011).

[251] Hudoc (2005); 41 EHRR 847.

[252] As noted in the argument in these cases, questions of liability under international humanitarian law also arose.

[253] Hudoc (2004). However, the 'callous' failure upon entry to the village to check whether there were civilian casualties was a violation of the obligation to protect life: para 306.

[254] *Nikolova and Velichkola v Bulgaria* hudoc (2007); 48 EHRR 915 (unjustified assaults). See also *Douglas-Williams v UK* No 56413/00 hudoc (2002) DA and *Saoud v France* hudoc (2007).

[255] The use of tazers has also caused deaths in the UK.

[256] See, eg, *Ogur v Turkey* 1999-III and *Kakoulli v Turkey* hudoc (2005); 45 EHRR 355. Cf *Gulec v Turkey* 1998-IV; 28 EHRR 121.

[257] 2005-VII; 42 EHRR 933 paras 95, 107 GC. Cf *Aytekin v Turkey* 1998-VII; 32 EHRR 501; *Alikaj and Others v Italy* hudoc (2011); 45 EHRR 355; and *Vasil Sachov Petrov v Bulgaria* hudoc (2010).

firearms, even where the individual to be arrested is honestly and reasonably thought to be dangerous. A contrary view is inconsistent with the purpose of arrest under the Convention, which is to bring an arrested person before the appropriate authorities in accordance with Article 5, and ignores the possibility of a later arrest.[258] Whether firing at just the tyres of a car or resorting to some other less life-threatening use of force (eg firing at a person's legs) that nonetheless causes death could on the facts be justified is not clear.[259] However, the use of firearms in such a case may be permissible, depending on the facts, on the ground of self-defence.[260] In such cases, the Court will consider whether the facts indicate a lack of the caution in the use of firearms to be expected of law enforcement officials.[261]

These considerations also apply to the use of force against a person who is already under arrest or in detention to prevent his or her escape (Article 2(2)(b)).

e. To quell a riot or insurrection

The terms 'riot' and 'insurrection' in Article 2(2)(c) have autonomous Convention meanings. This was held in *Stewart v UK*[262] in respect of the term 'riot' and can be taken to be true of 'insurrection' also. In the *Stewart* case, the Commission declined to define the term 'riot', deciding only on the facts of the case that 'an assembly of 150 persons throwing missiles at a patrol of soldiers to the point that they risked serious injury must be considered, by any standard, to constitute a riot'.[263] Similarly, without defining the term, in *Gulec v Turkey*,[264] the Commission found that 'a crowd of several thousand people, throwing projectiles at members of the security forces so that the latter were at risk of being injured, and breaking windows of public buildings' constituted a 'riot'.

In the *Stewart* case, the Commission established that there is no obligation to retreat when quelling a riot. But, as in the case of the other exceptions permitted by Article 2(2), the 'strict proportionality' interpretation of the 'absolutely necessary' requirement adopted in the *McCann* case is important in ensuring caution on the part of law enforcement officers when dealing with large crowds at public meetings and demonstrations that get out of control. The requirement was infringed in two cases which resulted from the deaths of Greek Cypriots who had entered the UN buffer zone in Cyprus as participants in a demonstration against the Turkish occupation of Northern Turkey. Violence had ensued as a crowd of Turkish Cypriots had counter-demonstrated. In *Isaak v Turkey*,[265] a demonstrator had been beaten and killed in the buffer zone by a group of persons who included Turkish soldiers, and in *Solomou v Turkey*,[266] a demonstrator who had crossed over the Turkish cease fire line from the buffer zone had been shot and killed by Turkish

---

[258] But see the different approach in *Kelly v UK No 1759/90*, 74 DR 139 (1993), as to which see Smith, 144 NLJ 354 (1994).

[259] See *Wasilewska and Kalucka v Poland* hudoc (2010) (Court not convinced shots fired at tyres).

[260] *Ramsahai v Netherlands* 2007-II; 46 EHRR 983 GC (deceased drew a gun). In both *Juozaitienė and Bikulčius v Lithuania* hudoc (2008); 47 EHRR 1194 and *Wasilewska and Kalucka v Poland* hudoc (2010), shooting at an escaping car was not justified as self-defence or to effect an arrest. See also *Armani da Silva v UK* (the De Menezes case), communicated to the UK government in October 2010. The level of threat to life posed by the person shot is relevant: *Juozaitiene and Bikulcius* case and *Kakoulli v Turkey* hudoc (2005); 45 EHRR 355.

[261] See, eg, *Juozaitiene and Bikulcius v Lithuania* hudoc (2008); 47 EHRR 1194. Adequate regulations governing police conduct and training are required: *Wasilewska and Kalucka v Poland* hudoc (2010).

[262] *No 10044/82*, 39 DR 162 (1984). [263] *Stewart v UK*, at 172.

[264] 1998-IV; 28 EHRR 121 para 232. The Court accepted the Commission's findings. See also *Simsek v Turkey* hudoc (2005) on the need for proper police training and centralized command.

[265] Hudoc (2008). [266] Hudoc (2008). See also *Andreou v Turkey* hudoc (2009).

soldiers while climbing a flagpole that displayed the Turkish flag. The Court held that these killings, resulting from action taken against two unarmed demonstrators, could not be justified as being 'absolutely necessary' to quell a riot. A violation of Article 2 was also found in *Perişan and Others v Turkey*,[267] in which the force used to quell a prison riot involving some thirty prisoners was not 'absolutely necessary'. Eight prisoners had died from multiple injuries, including fractured skulls, inflicted by security forces with truncheons and other implements, and others were seriously injured. The Court rejected claims that the prisoners were armed with dangerous implements justifying the degree of force used. It also stressed the lack of a system of adequate and effective safeguards against arbitrary and abusive use of force by state agents.

In accordance with *McCann*, the requirement of 'strict proportionality' applies not only to the conduct of the state agents who use force to quell a riot or insurrection, but to the planning and control of an operation as well. Thus in *Ergi v Turkey*,[268] there was a breach of Article 2 when an innocent villager was killed in cross-fire in a security forces ambush of terrorists which had not been planned in such a way as to minimize the possible risk to the lives of third parties. The 'strict proportionality' requirement was also held to have been infringed on this basis in the *Güleç* case. There the applicant's son and another person were killed as security forces fired live bullets in order to disperse 3,000 villagers who had become very disorderly while demonstrating against the destruction of a neighbouring village in the fight against terrorism. The Court found that, contrary to the government's submission, the demonstrators were unarmed and the security forces had fired not above their heads but at the ground in front of them, with an obvious risk of ricocheting bullets. The Court held that the force used had not been 'absolutely necessary'. The Court reached its decision on the *McCann* basis that the operation had not been planned so as to minimize the risk of life, stressing that the security forces had resorted to live bullets because they had not been provided with other less powerful weapons, such as truncheons, riot shields, water cannon, rubber bullets, or tear gas—despite the fact that the area was one in which a state of emergency had been declared and disorder could be expected. It might be that the Court would have reached the same conclusion on the basis that live bullets should never be planned to be used to quell a riot, even by firing above the head of the crowd in view of the risk of accident or mistake.[269]

The use of force must be 'lawful'. In *X v Belgium*,[270] the shooting of an innocent bystander by a policeman acting to quell a riot was not excused as being within Article 2(2)(e) because his use of firearms had not been 'lawful' under Belgian law for the reason that the required authorization had not been given.

8. CONCLUSION

It was not until 1995 that the European Court of Human Rights was called upon to take its first decision on the merits under Article 2, in the Northern Irish case of *McCann v UK*.[271] Since then, it has decided many more Article 2 cases, with the result that the meaning of Article 2 has become much clearer. The most striking consequence is the very extensive

---

[267] Hudoc (2010).   [268] 1998-IV; 32 EHRR 388.
[269] On the use of plastic bullets, see Jason-Lloyd, 140 NLJ 1492 (1990) and Robertson, 141 NLJ 340 (1991). On the use of CS gas, see *No 7126/75* (1977) 1 Digest 87.
[270] *No 2758/66*, 12 YB 174 (1969). See also *Stewart v UK No 10044/82*, 32 DR 162 (1984).
[271] A 324 (1995); 21 EHRR 97 GC.

meaning that has been given to the obligation to take steps to protect the right to life. The state must have appropriate laws prohibiting the taking of life and judicial machinery to enforce them. This obligation requires the regulation of activities and situations that may pose a threat to life, such as the use of firearms by the police. The state must also take preventive operational measures in some circumstances to protect an individual whose life is at risk. This includes police protection of members of the public and protection in places of detention. There may also be an obligation to provide health care and social services to safeguard life, although the Court has yet to explore the issue fully. In addition to these substantive obligations, there is a procedural obligation to protect the right to life by investigating suspicious deaths in accordance with strict standards that have been spelt out by the Court, leading in appropriate cases to criminal proceedings. The development of this procedural obligation has seen it become a rigorous one that has utterly transformed Article 2, not infrequently providing the basis for a breach of Article 2 when no breach of the substantive obligation not to take life has been found. The case law is extensive and is often the focus of national court decisions applying Article 2, as in the case of the United Kingdom.[272] In a striking development, the obligation was extended to the fields of health and safety and environmental law in the *Oneryildiz* case.[273]

The meaning of the state's negative obligation not to take life arbitrarily has also been clarified. The capital punishment exception has become redundant in peacetime in what has become death penalty free zone in Council of Europe states. The parameters of the exceptions allowed by Article 2(2) have been set. Some of the cases have concerned the disproportionate use of force by the police or security forces in safeguarding life or public order or in effecting arrests in non-emergency circumstances. But a high proportion of them have concerned the emergencies in Northern Ireland, south-east Turkey, and more recently in Chechnya. The cases arising out of the last two of these situations especially have raised issues previously more familiar to the Inter-American human rights system[274] than its European counterpart, involving responsibility for the disappearance of insurgents and other opponents of government and killings by unknown perpetrators, as well as the failure to investigate such incidents. These cases, in some of which human rights law overlaps with international humanitarian law, have presented considerable fact-finding problems. In the absence of reliable findings of fact in such cases by national courts, the Commission (now the Court) has made its own factual determinations, sometimes, in the case mainly of Turkey, after time-consuming on-the-spot hearings of witnesses. In determining the facts, after early hesitations, the Court has been prepared to draw inferences from the lack of state cooperation in generally life-threatening situations when determining whether state involvement in killings that do not by any stretch of the imagination fall within the exceptions allowed by Article 2(2) has been proved beyond a reasonable doubt.[275]

Finally, some progress has been made in resolving the question whether the obligation to protect the right to life applies to the unborn child. Treading cautiously in the light of the different approaches across Europe, the Court has, in the absence of consensus and on such a contentious issue, allowed states a wide margin of appreciation, which would seem to accommodate the practice of most European states.

---

[272] See, eg, *R (Amin) v Secretary of State for the Home Department* [2003] UKHL 51; [2004] 1 AC 653.

[273] *Oneryildiz v Turkey* 2004-XII; 41 EHRR 325 para 96 GC.

[274] See Harris and Livingstone, eds, *The Inter-American System of Human Rights*, 1998, p 2.

[275] On the Court's 'evolving response to states' failure to cooperate', seeChernishova and Vajic, in Spielmann, Tsirli, and Voyatzis, eds, *The European Convention on Human Rights: A Living Instrument*, 2011.

6

ARTICLE 3: FREEDOM FROM TORTURE OR INHUMAN OR DEGRADING TREATMENT OR PUNISHMENT

Article 3

No one shall be subjected to torture or to inhuman or degrading treatment or punishment.

1. INTRODUCTION

Article 3,[1] which applies to human beings but not to legal persons,[2] contains an absolute guarantee of the rights it protects.[3] It does so in two senses.[4] First, it cannot be derogated from in time of war or other public emergency.[5] It is this, as well as the historical background to the Convention, that has led to the argument that Article 3 should not be trivialized, ie understood to prohibit other than the most serious forms of ill-treatment.[6] But, as Judge Fitzmaurice pointed out, the temptation to lower the threshold of Article 3 is great since 'the Convention contains no prohibition covering intermediate forms of maltreatment... [so] that, if they are not actually caught by the strict language of the Convention, they deserve to be... because... they are nevertheless irreconcilable with the high ideal of human rights'.[7] In practice, the 'threshold' has been lowered to cover certain intermediate forms of maltreatment, and other particular instances of ill-treatment that would not have been in the minds of the Convention drafters are now covered.[8]

Second, Article 3, unlike most Convention articles, is expressed in unqualified terms. This has been understood as meaning that ill-treatment within the terms of Article 3

---

[1] On Article 3 generally, see Addo and Grief, 20 ELR 178 (1995); Cassese, *European System*, 1993, Ch 11; and Reidy, *A Guide to the Implementation of Article 3 of the European Convention on Human Rights*, Council of Europe Human Rights Handbook No 6, 2003.

[2] *Kontakt-Information-Therapie and Hagen v Austria No 11921/86*, 57 DR 81 (1988).

[3] See Addo and Grief, 9 EJIL 510 (1998); Addo and Grief, 23 ELR 17 (1998); Mavronicola, 12 HRLR 723 (2012); and McBride, 25 ELR 31 (2000).   [4] *Ireland v UK* A 25 (1978); 2 EHRR 25 para 163 PC.

[5] Article 15(2), Convention.

[6] See, eg, the joint partially dissenting opinion of Messrs Schermers, Batliner, Vandenberghe, and Hall in *Warwick v UK No 9471/81*, 60 DR 5 at 20 (1986) Com Rep; CM Res DH (89) 5.

[7] *Ireland v UK* A 25 (1978); 2 EHRR 25 PC.

[8] See, eg, *Slyusarev v Russia* hudoc (2010) (spectacles taken from prisoner).

is never permitted, even for the highest reasons of public interest. On this basis, it has been held that the need to fight terrorism[9] or organized crime[10] or to save someone's life[11] cannot justify state conduct that would otherwise be in breach of Article 3. Nor does it permit the return of an individual to another state on the ground of protecting the returning state's national security, where the return would involve a real risk of ill-treatment contrary to Article 3 in the receiving state.[12] However, there are recognized exceptions to the absolute nature of Article 3 in this second sense. If the taking of life by the state is not contrary to Article 2 of the Convention in certain circumstances (eg, on grounds of self-defence or to effect an arrest), 'it must follow a fortiori that severe wounding is in such circumstances justifiable'.[13] Similarly, conditions of detention that might otherwise be in breach of Article 3 may be justified by reference to the need to prevent escape or suicide.[14] In addition, considerations of penal policy may lead to the different treatment of conduct causing the same level of suffering. For example, whereas judicial corporal punishment is degrading punishment contrary to Article 3,[15] imprisonment in normal prison conditions, which may be just as or more degrading, is not. More generally, the 'suffering or humiliation involved must in any event go beyond that inevitable element of suffering or humiliation connected with a given form of legitimate treatment or punishment'.[16] Finally, the absolute nature of the guarantee in Article 3 is qualified by the fact that consent may negate liability under Article 3, at least in some cases concerning medical treatment.[17]

As Article 3 provides an absolute guarantee, there is no room for a margin of appreciation doctrine in the way that there might be if the text allowed certain exceptions to the negative obligation that it contains,[18] although the Court has been influenced by the presence or absence of uniformity of practice in European states when deciding whether state conduct is consistent with Article 3.[19]

Ill-treatment 'must attain a minimum level of severity' if it is to fall within Article 3.[20] The threshold level is a relative one:

> it depends on all the circumstances of the case, such as the nature and context of the treatment, the manner and method of its execution, its duration, its physical or mental effects and, in some cases, the sex, age and state of health of the victim.[21]

---

[9] *Tomasi v France* A 241-A (1992); 15 EHRR 1 para 115.

[10] *Selmouni v France* 1999-V; 29 EHRR 403 GC. Generally, the 'reprehensible nature' of the applicant's conduct is irrelevant: *D v UK* 1997-III; 23 EHRR 423 para 47.

[11] *Gäfgen v Germany* hudoc (2010); 52 EHRR 1 GC. See Greer, 11 HRLR 67 (2011).

[12] *Chahal v UK* 1996-V; 23 EHRR 413 GC.

[13] Mr Fawcett, separate opinion in *Ireland v UK* B 23-I, p 502 Com Rep (1976). Cf *Stewart v UK No 10044/82*, 39 DR 162 (1984).

[14] See *Kröcher and Möller v Switzerland No 8463/78*, 34 DR 24 (1982) Com Rep; CM Res DH (83) 15.

[15] *Tyrer v UK* A 26 (1978); 2 EHRR 1.

[16] *Kalashnikov v Russia* 2002-VI; 36 EHRR 587 para 95. Cf *Ilaşcu and Others v Moldova and Russia* 2004-VII; 40 EHRR 1030 GC.

[17] On self-inflicted conditions of detention, contrast *McFeeley and Others v UK No 8317/78*, 20 DR 44 (1980) ('dirty protest') and *Soering v UK* A 161 (1989); 11 EHRR 439 PC (prolongation of time on death row by appeals).

[18] See Callewaert, 19 HRLJ 6 (1998).

[19] See eg, *V v UK* 1999-IX; 30 EHRR 121 para 74 GC; *MC v Bulgaria* 2003-XII; 40 EHRR 459 para 185; and *Jalloh v Germany* 2006-IX; 44 EHRR 667 para 77 GC.

[20] *Kudla v Poland* 2000-XI; 35 EHRR 198 para 91 GC.

[21] *Kudla v Poland*, para 91. Cf *Ireland v UK* A 25 (1978); 2 EHRR 25 para 162 PC. As to duration, see eg, *Kalashnikov v Russia* 2002-VI; 36 EHRR 587 para 95. As to age and sex, see eg, *Aydin v Turkey* 1997-VI; 25 EHRR 251 GC. As to health, see eg, *Keenan v UK* 2001-III; 33 EHRR 913 (mental health). As to other personal circumstances, see eg, *Selçuk and Asker v Turkey* 1998-II; 26 EHRR 477.

These factors are relevant both when determining whether the suffering or humiliation caused is sufficient to amount to inhuman or degrading treatment or punishment and when distinguishing between these lesser kinds of ill-treatment proscribed by Article 3 and torture. In an important ruling, in *Selmouni v France*,[22] the Court established that the categorization of ill-treatment may change over time, so that 'acts which were classified in the past as "inhuman and degrading treatment" as opposed to "torture" could be classified differently in the future'. This followed from the dynamic character of the Convention and the Court's view that 'the increasingly high standard being required in the area of the protection of human rights and fundamental liberties correspondingly and inevitably requires greater firmness in assessing breaches of the fundamental values of democratic societies'. Similarly, the 'minimum level of severity' has been reduced by the Court in recent years, most notably concerning prison conditions and treatment, as the Court has become more demanding of states under Article 3.

Where the facts of a case warrant this, the Court may distinguish between the different categories of ill-treatment listed in Article 3. In some cases, the Court does not do this, simply finding a breach of Article 3 as a whole.[23] Although there is no need to draw such distinctions in the sense that Article 3 is infringed whatever the precise category of ill-treatment concerned, the boundary between torture and other forms of ill-treatment is relevant both to the question of compensation that may be awarded under Article 41 and to a state's reputation. With regard to the latter, the United Kingdom's concession before the Court in *Ireland v UK*[24] that the 'five techniques' were torture, not just inhuman or degrading treatment, proved to be ill-conceived when the Court held that only the latter had occurred.

When considering whether there has been ill-treatment in breach of Article 3, the Court examines all the evidence presented to it, whether emanating from the applicant, the respondent state, or other sources,[25] or which it obtains *proprio motu*.[26] The rules concerning the burden of proof, applicable to Convention claims generally, are explained later in Chapter 3, section VII. When weighing the evidence before it, the Court applies the high standard of proof of 'beyond a reasonable doubt'; 'such proof may follow from the coexistence of sufficiently strong, clear and concordant inferences or of similar unrebutted presumptions of fact'.[27]

A state may be responsible under Article 3 for the acts of its servants or agents that are *ultra vires*. In *Ireland v UK*,[28] the Court considered whether a state might claim not to be responsible on the basis of ignorance of the conduct of its servants or agents. It stated that where the conduct in breach of Article 3 amounted to a practice incompatible with the Convention, it was 'inconceivable that the higher authorities of a state should be, or at least be entitled to be, unaware of the existence of such a practice'. Moreover, 'under the Convention those authorities are strictly liable for the conduct of their subordinates; they are under a duty to impose their will on subordinates and cannot shelter behind their inability to ensure that it is respected'. In *Cyprus v Turkey*,[29] the Commission found

---

[22] 1999-V; 29 EHRR 403 para 101.

[23] See, eg, *Soering v UK* A 161 (1989); 11 EHRR 439 PC and *A v UK* 1998-VI; 27 EHRR 611.

[24] A 25 (1978); 2 EHRR 25 PC.

[25] These include the European Committee for the Prevention of Torture and Inhuman or Degrading Treatment or Punishment, UNHCR, and non-governmental organizations such as Amnesty International.

[26] *Ireland v UK* A 25 (1978); 2 EHRR 25 para 160 PC.

[27] *Ireland v UK* A 25 (1978); 2 EHRR 25 para 161 PC. The Court may draw inferences from the state's failure to produce evidence: *Aydin v Turkey* 1997-V; 25 EHRR 251 GC.

[28] A 25 (1978); 2 EHRR 25 para 159 PC.

[29] *Nos 6780/74 and 6950/75* (First and Second Applications) 4 EHRR 482 at 537 (1976) Com Rep; CM Res DH (79) 1.

the respondent state to be responsible for rapes committed by its soldiers on the 'positive obligation' basis that adequate measures had not been taken to prevent them or to effect disciplinary measures after the event.

A claim under Article 3 may raise an issue under another article of the Convention as well. In practice, this overlap has occurred mostly in the areas covered by Articles 3 and 8, particularly in connection with the rights to respect for family and private life. In such cases, the Court has in the past not considered the Article 8 claim unless a violation of Article 3 has not been found.[30] However, more recently the Court has found breaches of both Articles.

2. TORTURE

In *Ireland v UK*,[31] the Court defined torture as 'deliberate inhuman treatment causing very serious and cruel suffering'. Applying this test, it held that neither the use in interrogation of the 'five techniques' nor the physical assaults that had occurred in that case were torture. By 'deliberate' the Court meant that suffering must be inflicted intentionally. Suffering must also be inflicted for a purpose, such as obtaining evidence, punishment, or intimidation.[32] In *Denizci and Others v Cyprus*,[33] the applicants were Turkish Cypriots who were detained by the police in Cyprus before being returned to northern Cyprus. The Court held that they had been subjected by the police to intentionally inflicted inhuman treatment contrary to Article 3, but had not been tortured, partly because it had not been established that there had been any particular aim underlying the assaults, such as obtaining information. Because of the absolute nature of Article 3, the causing of 'very serious and cruel suffering' cannot be saved from being torture on public interest grounds, such as that its purpose is to extract information from terrorists that will protect innocent lives.[34] Similarly, an amnesty will not be effective to prevent prosecution for acts of torture.[35]

The first Strasbourg case in which torture was held to have occurred as a matter of final decision was the *Greek* case,[36] in which the Commission's finding was confirmed by the Committee of Ministers. In that case, the Commission concluded that political detainees had been subjected by the Athens security police to an administrative practice of 'torture and ill-treatment' contrary to Article 3. This had most often taken the form of *falaka*[37] or of severe beatings of all parts of the body with a view to extracting a confession or other information as to the political activities of subversive individuals. In *Ireland v UK*, the Court held that torture had not occurred because the intensity of the suffering inflicted

---

[30] See eg, *Marckx v Belgium* A 31 (1979); 2 EHRR 330 PC and *Mentes and Others v Turkey* 1997-VIII; 26 EHRR 595 GC.

[31] A 25 (1978); 2 EHRR 25 para 167 PC. On *Ireland v UK*, see Bonner, 27 ICLQ 897 (1978); Cohn 11 CWRJIL 159 (1979); Martin, 83 RGDIP 104 (1979); Mertens, 13 RBDI 10 (1977); O'Boyle, 71 AJIL 674 (1977); Pelloux, 24 AFDL 379 (1978); and Spjut, 73 AJIL 267 (1979).

[32] *Ilhan v Turkey* 2000-VII; 34 EHRR 869 para 85 GC. Cf *Akkoç v Turkey* 2000-X; 34 EHRR 1173 and *Ireland v UK* A 25 (1978); 2 EHRR 25 para 167 PC. In *Ireland v UK*, Judge Matscher supposed that sadistic pleasure would be purposive. In the same case, Judge Sir Gerald Fitzmaurice opposed any purpose requirement.   [33] 2001-V. Cf *Egmez v Cyprus* 2000-XII; 34 EHRR 753.

[34] *Selmouni v France* 1999-V; 29 EHRR 403 GC.

[35] *Ould Dah v France* No 13113/03 hudoc (2009) DA.

[36] 12 YB (the *Greek* case) 1 at 504 (1969) Com Rep; CM Res DH (70) 1.

[37] Beating of the feet causing excruciating pain and leaving no marks. See also *Corsacov v Moldova* hudoc (2006).

was insufficient. Remarkably, the unanimous opinion of the Commission in that case that the use in combination of the 'five techniques' of interrogation had amounted to torture was rejected by the Court by a large majority. The Court would appear to have applied a more rigorous test for suffering to amount to torture; it is also possible that it was less impressed than the Commission by the effects of psychological methods of interrogation. Nonetheless, as has been pointed out, the Court's ruling was surprising 'given that the Commission had found convincing evidence of weight loss, mental disorientation, and acute psychiatric symptoms during interrogation in some of the 14 suspects subjected to these techniques'.[38] Both the Commission and the Court considered that the physical assaults of detainees in the same case caused insufficient suffering to amount to torture, although, like the use of the 'five techniques', they did constitute inhuman treatment.

Since *Ireland v UK*, the Court has found that torture has occurred in a disturbing number of cases involving physical (and sometimes mental) ill-treatment by state agents. The first was *Aksoy v Turkey*,[39] in which the applicant's arms were paralysed after he had been stripped naked and suspended by his arms, which were tied behind his back ('Palestinian hanging'). In *Aydin v Turkey*,[40] it was established that a single act of rape by a state agent may constitute torture.[41] In that case, a seventeen-year-old girl was detained at gendarmerie headquarters for three days. While there, she was raped by an unidentified person. She was also subjected to other 'terrifying and humiliating experiences' by the security forces, being kept blindfolded, beaten during questioning, spun in a tyre under water pressure, and paraded naked. The Court held that the 'accumulation of acts of physical and mental violence inflicted on the applicant and the especially cruel act of rape' gave rise to suffering amounting to torture. The Court stated that it would have reached this conclusion on the basis of just the rape (or just the other instances of ill-treatment). In *Zontul v Greece*,[42] the Court held that the forced penetration of a male detainee's anus by a truncheon was an act of rape amounting to torture. In these cases the Court has stressed that they involved the 'rape of a detainee by an official of the state', which was 'an especially grave and abhorrent form of ill-treatment'.[43] States also have a positive obligation to protect individuals from rape by private persons by enacting and enforcing criminal law provisions punishing rape.[44]

Various other forms of ill-treatment of prisoners have been found to amount to torture. Forced feeding of a prisoner on hunger strike amounted to torture because of the manner of its administration in *Nevmerzhitsky v Ukraine*,[45] as did an extreme regime of solitary confinement in *Ilaşcu and Others v Moldova and Russia*.[46] In *Virabyan v Armenia*,[47] there was a finding of torture when the applicant in custody was beaten by police officers, who kicked him and hit his scrotum with metal objects, causing him to become unconscious and later to have a testicle removed. The use of electric shock treatment to obtain a confession was torture in breach of Article 3 in *Mikheyev v Russia*.[48]

---

[38] Amnesty International, *Torture in the Eighties*, 1984, p 15.   [39] 1996-VI; 23 EHRR 553.

[40] 1997-VI; 25 EHRR 251 GC. See also *Maslova and Nalbandov v Russia* hudoc (2008); 48 EHRR 851 (repeated rapes by police and other acts of physical violence were torture).

[41] Rape is also a crime against humanity and a war crime contrary to international humanitarian law: see Schabas, *An Introduction to the International Criminal Court*, 4th edn, 2011, pp 115, 126.

[42] Hudoc (2012).   [43] *Aydin v Turkey* 1997-VI; 25 EHRR 251 para 83 GC.

[44] *MC v Bulgaria* 2003-XII; 40 EHRR 459.   [45] 2005-II; 43 EHRR 645.

[46] 2004-VII; 40 EHRR 1030 GC.

[47] Hudoc (2012). Cf *Vladimir Romanov v Russia* hudoc (2008); and *Savitskyy v Ukraine* hudoc (2012). Other torture cases include *Akkoç v Turkey* 2000-X; 34 EHRR 1173; *Abdülsamet Yaman v Turkey* hudoc (2004); 40 EHRR 1199; *Bursuc v Romania* hudoc (2004); and *Ilhan v Turkey* 2000-VII; 34 EHRR 869 GC.

[48] Hudoc (2006).

In *El Masri v The Former Yugoslav Republic of Macedonia*,[49] the steps taken at Skopje Airport to effect the extraordinary rendition of the applicant to Kabul amounted to torture.

Of great importance was the ruling in *Selmouni v France*[50] that, as a result of the increasingly high standard being applied in the protection of human rights, ill-treatment that might previously have been regarded by the Court as causing suffering falling short of 'torture' (though still in breach of Article 3), could now be classified as 'torture'. In that case, the applicant had, in police custody, been beaten, called upon to perform oral sex with a police officer, urinated upon by the officer when he refused to do so, and threatened with a blow lamp and a syringe. The Court held that his treatment constituted torture, when, by inference, the Court would only have found 'inhuman' or 'degrading' ill-treatment if it had applied the standard of suffering that it had used earlier in *Ireland v UK*.

It is implicit in *Ireland v UK*[51] that mental suffering may constitute torture provided that it is sufficiently serious; suffering caused by bodily injury is not essential.[52] In the *Greek* case,[53] the Commission referred to 'non-physical torture', which it described as 'the infliction of mental suffering by creating a state of anguish and stress by means other than bodily assault'. In *Gäfgen v Germany*,[54] the Court confirmed that 'a threat of torture can amount to torture', as 'the fear of physical torture may itself constitute mental torture'. Mental suffering, when combined with physical suffering, has contributed to a finding by the Court of torture in a number of cases. These have included mental suffering resulting from the psychological pressure imposed by incommunicado detention,[55] being kept blindfolded,[56] threats of harm to one's family[57] or of rape,[58] the humiliation of being paraded naked,[59] mock executions,[60] and fear of execution while waiting on death row.[61] In *Menesheva v Russia*,[62] there was torture when the applicant, who, as a young woman being questioned by several policemen was 'particularly vulnerable', was twice beaten up and subjected to other kinds of physical and mental pressure, including the threat of rape.

The fact that the suffering is inflicted only for 'a short period of heightened tension and emotions' may weigh against a finding of torture.[63] It may also be difficult to prove torture in the case of a person who dies in custody: any such allegation must be substantiated by medical evidence of traumatic injury to the deceased's body; eye-witness evidence of such injury is not sufficient.[64]

---

[49] 2012- GC.   [50] 1999-V; 29 EHRR 403 GC.

[51] See also *Tyrer v UK* A 26 (1978); 2 EHRR 1; *Campbell and Cosans v UK* A 48 (1982); 4 EHRR 293; and *Soering v UK* A 161 (1989); 11 EHRR 439 PC.

[52] Cf the definition of torture in the UN Torture Convention 1984, Article 1.

[53] 12 YB (the *Greek* case) 1 at 461 (1969) Com Rep; CM Res DH (70) 1.

[54] 2010-; 52 EHRR 1 para 108 GC.   [55] *Dikme v Turkey* 2000-VIII.

[56] *Aydin v Turkey* 1997-VI; 25 EHRR 251 GC and *Dikme v Turkey* 2000-VIII.

[57] *Akkoç v Turkey* 2000-X; 34 EHRR 1173.   [58] *Menesheva v Russia* 2006-III; 44 EHRR 1162.

[59] *Aydin v Turkey* 1997-VI; 25 EHRR 251 GC.

[60] Eg, *Ilaşcu and Others v Moldova and Russia* 2004-VII; 40 EHRR 1030 GC.

[61] *Ilaşcu and Others v Moldova and Russia.*

[62] 2006-III; 44 EHRR 1162. See also *Bati and Others v Turkey* 2004-IV; 42 EHRR 736.

[63] *Egmez v Cyprus* 2000-XII; 34 EHRR 753 para 78 (assault during arrest and transportation to a police station: inhuman treatment, not torture).

[64] *Tanli v Turkey* 2001-III; 38 EHRR 31. See also *Salman v Turkey* 2000-VII; 34 EHRR 425 GC. Reliable eye-witness evidence may be sufficient to prove torture in the case of a disappeared person: *Çakici v Turkey* 1999-IV; 31 EHRR 133 GC.

3. INHUMAN TREATMENT

Ill-treatment 'must attain a minimum level of severity' if it is to amount to inhuman treatment contrary to Article 3. In particular, it must cause 'either actual bodily injury or intense physical or mental suffering'.[65] Where relevant the suffering caused must 'go beyond that inevitable element of suffering' that results from a 'given form of legitimate treatment or punishment'.[66] In contrast with torture, inhuman treatment need not be intended to cause suffering[67] and there is no need for the suffering to be inflicted for a purpose for it to be inhuman.[68] Otherwise, as the Court has emphasized,[69] the crucial distinction between torture and inhuman treatment lies in the degree of suffering caused. Clearly, less intense suffering is required than in the case of torture. A threat of torture, provided that it is 'sufficiently real and immediate', may generate enough mental suffering to be inhuman treatment.[70] Mental, or psychological, suffering by itself has been found sufficient in several contexts. For example, in *Selçuk and Asker v Turkey*,[71] there was inhuman treatment when, as a part of a security operation, the security forces destroyed the elderly applicants' home and property in a contemptuous manner in their presence, without regard to their safety or welfare and depriving them of their livelihood and shelter, causing them great distress. In a different context, in *Gäfgen v Germany*,[72] there was inhuman treatment when the applicant was threatened with 'intolerable pain', amounting to torture, if he refused to disclose the whereabouts of a young boy whom he had kidnapped. In several cases, the Court has stated that the 'terrifying experience' of those present when armed and masked police officers burst into their home may be disproportionate to the point of being inhuman treatment.[73] The mental suffering caused to an individual by the ill-treatment of a close family member may also be a breach of Article 3.[74] Finally, the anguish caused to an individual by being detained illegally by the state may contribute to a finding that the conditions of their detention are inhuman treatment.[75]

Conduct giving rise to inhuman treatment may take a number of forms, some of which are considered in the following sections.

I. ASSAULTS

Cases of assault are variously characterized by the Court as inhuman or degrading treatment or both,[76] or simply as a violation of Article 3.[77] Most cases of assault

---

[65] *Kudla v Poland* 2000-XI; 35 EHRR 198 para 92 GC.   [66] *Kudla v Poland.*

[67] *Ireland v UK* A 25 (1978); 2 EHRR 25 PC. Premeditation is taken into account when deciding whether treatment is inhuman, but it is not required: para 167.

[68] *Denizci v Cyprus* 2001-V and *Egmez v Cyprus* 2000-XII; 34 EHRR 753.

[69] *Ireland v UK* A 25 (1978); 2 EHRR para 167 PC.

[70] *Campbell and Cosans v UK* A 48 (1982); 4 EHRR 293 para 26 and *Gäfgen v Germany* 2010-; 52 EHRR 1 para 108 GC.

[71] 1998-II; 26 EHRR 477. Cf *Bilgin v Turkey* hudoc (2000); 36 EHRR 879 and *Dulaş v Turkey* hudoc (2001). In the absence of 'distinctive elements', such as those in *Selçuk and Asker*, the destruction of homes in a security operation will not be a breach of Article 3, but may infringe Article 8: *Orhan v Turkey* hudoc (2002) para 362.   [72] 2010-; 52 EHRR 1 GC.

[73] See, eg, *Hristovi v Bulgaria* hudoc (2011) para 80.

[74] *Mubilanzila Mayeka and Kaniki Mitunga v Belgium* 2006-XI; 46 EHRR 449.

[75] *Fedotov v Russia* hudoc (2005); 44 EHRR 544.

[76] In *Ribitsch v Austria* A 336 (1995); 21 EHRR 573, there was both inhuman and degrading treatment.

[77] Eg, *Necdet Bulut v Turkey* hudoc (2007).

reaching Strasbourg have occurred in detention or during arrest by the police. Assaults that amounted to inhuman treatment were unanimously held to have occurred in *Ireland v UK*. In that case, four detainees were found by a prison doctor to have contusions and bruising which were caused by severe beatings by members of the security forces in Northern Ireland during interrogation at Palace Barracks.[78] In the *Greek* case,[79] assaults by Greek security police upon political detainees in the course of interrogation during the Regime of the Colonels were 'torture or ill-treatment' contrary to Article 3.

The level of suffering in the cases just described was clearly high. In *VC v Slovakia*,[80] the Court expressed the threshold level for a violation of Article 3 as being 'bodily harm of a certain degree of severity', giving as examples the pain and suffering caused by gunshot wounds,[81] a broken jaw,[82] and other facial injuries.[83] In *Ribitsch v Austria*,[84] the Court stated that 'any recourse to physical force which has not been made strictly necessary by his own conduct diminishes human dignity and is in principle an infringement' of Article 3. In practice, when deciding whether Article 3 has been infringed in cases of physical force, the Court looks for evidence of physical injuries to the required level of 'bodily harm'.[85]

In cases of assault, the applicant must first provide reliable medical or other[86] evidence as to the injuries claimed to have been sustained. For example, in *Tomasi v France*,[87] medical certificates and reports by four different doctors that attested to the 'large number of blows inflicted upon Mr Tomasi and their intensity' were found to be sufficient. The Court also noted that the applicant had at once drawn attention to the bruises on his body when he was brought before a judge following his release from police custody.

A use of force that results in the required degree of 'bodily harm' may nonetheless not be in breach of Article 3 where it is not excessive in the circumstances. In the case of proven injuries that occur in police custody, it is for the state to show that no force was used by the police or that the force used by them was not excessive.[88] This runs counter to the normal rule in cases at Strasbourg, by which each party must prove what it alleges. In *Selmouni v France*,[89] the Court stated that 'where an individual is taken into police custody in good health but is found to be injured at the time of release, it is incumbent upon the State to provide a plausible explanation of how these injuries were caused'. When deciding whether such an explanation has been provided, the Court takes into account whether the detained individual was medically examined (or allowed to see a lawyer or family member who might serve as a witness) at intervals during the detention, and not

---

[78] The Court focused upon this group of cases to establish that there had been an administrative practice contrary to Article 3. It also drew attention to, but did not rule upon, other assaults during transit or interrogation that 'must have been individual violations of Article 3': *Ireland v UK* A 25 (1978); 2 EHRR 25 para 182 PC.   [79] 12 YB (the *Greek* case) 1 (1969) Com Rep; CM Res DH (70) 1.

[80] Hudoc (2011) para 102.

[81] *Sambor v Poland* hudoc (2011) (leg amputated) and *Necdet Bulut v Turkey* hudoc (2007) (knee injured).

[82] *Rehbock v Slovenia* 2000-XII. See also *Umar Karatepe v Turkey* hudoc (2010).

[83] *Mrozowski v Poland* hudoc (2009) (stitches, loss of teeth) and *Afanasyev v Ukraine* hudoc (2005); 42 EHRR 1171 (damaged ear).

[84] A 336 (1995); 21 EHRR 573 para 38. Cf *Caloc v France* 2000-IX; 35 EHRR 346. See also the dissenting opinion of Judge De Meyer in *Tomasi v France* A 241-A (1992); 15 EHRR 1.

[85] See, eg, the facts of *Ribitsch v Austria* A 336 (1995); 21 EHRR 573 para 38. See also *Toteva v Bulgaria* hudoc (2004); *Balogh v Hungary* hudoc (2004); and *Rivas v France* hudoc (2004).

[86] Eg, the evidence of witnesses at the time of release: *Ribitsch v Austria* A 336 (1995); 21 EHRR 573. For a case in which insufficient evidence was provided, see *Indelicato v Italy* hudoc (2001); 35 EHRR 1330.

[87] A 241-A (1992); 15 EHRR 1 para 115.

[88] The same applies to injuries that occur in prison: see eg, *Satik and Others v Turkey* hudoc (2000).

[89] 1999-V; 29 EHRR 403 para 87 GC. Cf *Altay v Turkey* hudoc (2001).

only upon being released.[90] The Court also pays great attention to any relevant findings of fact in national court proceedings, but these are not always conclusive.[91]

Similarly, where injuries are sustained not in police custody but in the course of an arrest or other action by the police, 'the burden rests on the Government to demonstrate with convincing arguments that the use of force was not excessive'[92] and was 'indispensable'.[93] This burden was not met by the state in *Rehbock v Slovenia*.[94] There the applicant suffered a broken jaw and facial contusions when, with two others, he was arrested as a suspected drug dealer at a border crossing by a team of thirteen policemen. Given that the police had time to plan the arrest; that the applicant had not resisted arrest; that the government's claim that the applicant's injuries had been caused when he fell against a car was not credible; and that there had been no national court proceedings in which the force used might have been found to have been justified, the Strasbourg Court held that there was a breach of Article 3, the state having failed to furnish 'convincing and credible arguments which would provide a basis to explain or justify the degree of force used'.[95] The argument for placing the burden of proof upon the state is that it is always difficult to marshal evidence sufficient to convince a court of police misconduct. Such an argument, which applies whether the applicant is under arrest or not, is not supported by the law of European states, in which there is commonly no such general reversal of the burden of proof in civil proceedings for assault against the police.[96]

As well as in cases of the use of force against detainees and during an arrest, Article 3 has been found to have been infringed when the police have used unnecessary force against an individual in the course of dispersing a demonstration. Thus in *Najafli v Azerbaijan*,[97] the applicant, a journalist, was beaten with truncheons by the police as they sought to end an unauthorized political demonstration, causing him physical and mental suffering that reached the minimum level of severity required by Article 3. The applicant had told the police he was a journalist and had not used violence against them or otherwise acted so as to justify the use of force against him. The use of tear gas or pepper gas by the police is, despite the potential health risks, not contrary to Article 3, where it can be justified for the purpose of law enforcement, whether in the context of demonstrations or otherwise, provided that clearly defined safeguards, including immediate access to a doctor, are in place[98] and the gas is not aimed directly at an individual.[99] However, the use of tear gas or pepper gas against an individual who is under police control cannot be justified and may amount to ill-treatment contrary to Article 3.[100]

---

[90] *Algür v Turkey* hudoc (2002) (no examination at the beginning or during fifteen days' detention). See also *Akkoç v Turkey* 2000-X; 34 EHRR 1173 para 118, in which, in the context of an Article 3 complaint, the Court endorsed the CPT view that 'proper medical examinations are an essential safeguard against ill-treatment of persons in custody'.

[91] See *Ribitsch v Austria* A 336 (1995); 21 EHRR 573. And see *Caloc v France* 2000-IX; 35 EHRR 346.

[92] *Rehbock v Slovenia* 2000-XII para 72. Cf *Stoica v Romania* hudoc (2008); 52 EHRR 918.

[93] *Ivan Vasilev v Bulgaria* hudoc (2007) para 63.

[94] 2000-XII. Cf *Samüt Karabulut v Turkey* hudoc (2009). For cases in which the force used was not excessive, see *Berliński v Poland* hudoc (2002); *Hurtado v Switzerland* A 280-A (1994) (F Sett before Court); *Douglas-Williams v UK No 56413/00* hudoc (2002) DA; and *Sambor v Poland* hudoc (2011).

[95] For other cases of excessive force, see eg, *Ivan Vasilev v Bulgaria* hudoc (2007) and *Fahriye Çaliṣkan v Turkey* hudoc (2007). The Court does not generally question national court decisions as to whether excessive force has been used: see *Klass v Germany* A 269 (1993); 18 EHRR 305.

[96] As to English law, eg, see Clayton and Tomlinson, *Civil Actions against the Police*, 3rd edn, 2004, Ch 4.

[97] Hudoc (2012). See also *Kop v Turkey* hudoc (2009) and *Timtik v Turkey* hudoc (2010). And see *Dembele v Switzerland* hudoc (2013) (unnecessary force during identity check).

[98] *Ali Güneṣ v Turkey* hudoc (2012); 57 EHRR 596. The Court concurred with CPT recommendations on the use of pepper gas. See also *Çiloğlu and Others v Turkey* hudoc (2007).

[99] *Abdullah Yȧsa and Others v Turkey* hudoc (2013).   [100] *Ali Güneṣ v Turkey* hudoc (2012).

II. USE OF PSYCHOLOGICAL INTERROGATION TECHNIQUES

Intense suffering not resulting from physical assaults of an old-fashioned 'beating up' kind was found to have been caused in *Ireland v UK*[101] by the use of 'five techniques' during the interrogation of persons placed in preventive detention in connection with acts of terrorism.[102] The techniques were described by the Court as wall standing; hooding; subjection to noise; deprivation of sleep; and deprivation of food and drink.

These methods 'were applied in combination, with premeditation and for hours at a stretch; they caused, if not actual bodily injury, at least intense physical and mental suffering to the persons subjected thereto and also led to acute psychiatric disturbances during interrogation'.[103] They were accordingly inhuman treatment contrary to Article 3.[104]

III. CONDITIONS OF DETENTION AND TREATMENT OF DETAINEES

In their early jurisprudence under Article 3, the Commission and the Court generally considered cases concerning the conditions of detention and the treatment of detainees under the heading of inhuman treatment, emphasizing the suffering caused to the detainee. Although some detention cases continue to be considered by the Court under that heading,[105] such cases are now more commonly decided by it as a matter of degrading treatment, emphasizing the humiliation involved.[106] For convenience, in this chapter the application of Article 3 to conditions of detention and the treatment of detainees is considered wholly in section 5 on degrading treatment.

IV. EXTRADITION AND DEPORTATION

A state's right in international law to refuse to admit an alien to its territory[107] is not affected by the Convention.[108] Nor do aliens who have been admitted have a right under the Convention not to be extradited or deported.[109] However, the fact that an individual is illegally present on a state's territory does not affect their Article 3 rights.[110] With regard to extradition, it is not *per se* contrary to Article 3 to extradite a fugitive offender in breach of an extradition treaty or of national extradition law: it is not the function of the Strasbourg authorities in this context 'to supervise the correct application of extradition

---

[101] A 25 (1978); 2 EHRR 25 para 96 PC. The techniques had previously been used by the UK authorities against terrorists in colonial situations.

[102] Several of the techniques did, however, involve illegal assault.

[103] *Ireland v UK* A 25 (1978); 2 EHRR 25 para 167 PC.

[104] The ruling was by sixteen votes to one. For Judge Fitzmaurice, who dissented, the evidence of the effects of the use of the 'five techniques' did not show sufficient suffering.

[105] For example, some cases of medical assistance or solitary confinement. In *Mader v Croatia* hudoc (2011), there was inhuman treatment when a detainee was deprived of sleep and required to sit on a chair without food or drink for nearly three days. Cf *Fedotov v Russia* hudoc (2005); 44 EHRR 544.

[106] In some cases the Court simply refers to Article 3 generally or, where the facts warrant this, to both inhuman and degrading treatment.

[107] See Alleweldt, 4 EJIL 360 (1993); Arai-Takahashi, 20 NQHR 5 (2002); and Vogler, in Matscher and Petzold, eds, *Protecting Human Rights: the European Dimension* (*Studies in Honour of Gérard J Wiarda*), 1988, p 663.

[108] *Chahal v UK* 1996-V; 23 EHRR 413 GC. But discriminatory exclusion may be degrading treatment. See also *Fadele v UK No 13078/87*, 70 DR 159 (1991) F Sett.   [109] *Chahal v UK*.

[110] *Mubilanzila Mayeka and Kaniki Mitunga v Belgium* 2006-XI; 46 EHRR 449.

law'.[111] Nor is it contrary to Article 3 to extradite a person for a political offence.[112] As to deportation,[113] the exercise of the state's sovereign power to deport aliens is not generally in breach of Article 3.[114]

Nonetheless, extradition or deportation, may be in breach of Article 3 in certain exceptional cases.[115] In the leading case of *Soering v UK*,[116] the Court held that it would be a breach of Article 3 for a party to the Convention to send an individual to another state 'where substantial grounds have been shown for believing that the individual concerned, if extradited, faces a real risk of being subjected to torture or to inhuman or degrading treatment or punishment in the requesting country'.[117] Although the rule, which has since been extended to deportation, applies to a risk of all kinds of breaches of Article 3, it is considered for convenience here under the heading of inhuman treatment.[118]

In the *Soering* case, which is one of the most important cases that the Court has decided, the UK Home Secretary signed a warrant for the extradition of the applicant, a West German national, to face capital murder charges in the state of Virginia in the United States, where he was accused of killing the parents of his girlfriend. The Court held unanimously that the return of the applicant would be a breach of Article 3.[119] The Court first held that there was a real risk of the death penalty being imposed if the applicant were extradited. This was so despite mitigating factors that the trial court might take into account[120] and the fact that, in satisfaction of the terms of the applicable UK–US extradition treaty, the United Kingdom had been given an undertaking that the prosecuting attorney in Virginia would make a representation to the trial court that the British government did not want the death penalty imposed. The Court gave little weight to this last point because the attorney had indicated that he would nonetheless press for the death penalty.

The Court's reasoning was not that the imposition of the death penalty *per se* would result in a breach of Article 3. This could not have been so because of the presence in

---

[111] *Altun v Germany No 10308/83*, 36 DR 209 at 231 (1983). This applies to treaty obligations to extradite nationals as well as aliens.   [112] *Altun v Germany*.

[113] The term 'deportation' is used to include the removal of asylum seekers who are deemed not to qualify for asylum. The fact that the UNHCR has declared someone to be a refugee does not necessarily mean that his or her deportation will breach Article 3, as the scope of Article 3 and the Refugee Convention are not identical: *Y v Russia* hudoc (2008); 51 EHRR 531.

[114] Exceptionally, Article 4, Fourth Protocol prohibits the collective expulsion of aliens and Article 8 may apply.

[115] See *Ghosh v Germany No 24017/03* hudoc (2007) DA. Article 3 ceases to apply if a deportation order is annulled (*Kalantari v Germany* 2001-X), but not if it is just suspended (*Ahmed v Austria* 1996-VI; 24 EHRR 278).

[116] A 161 (1989); 11 EHRR 439 PC. On the *Soering* case, see Breitenmoser and Wilms, 11 MJIL 845 (1990); Gappa, 20 GJICL 463 (1990); O'Boyle, in O'Reilly, ed, *Human Rights and Constitutional Law: Essays in Honour of Brian Walsh*, 1992, p 93; Quigley and Shank, 30 VJTL 241 (1989); Schabas, 43 ICLQ 913 (1994); Shea, 17 YJIL 85 (1992); Warbrick, 11 MJIL 1073 (1990); Wyngaert, 39 ICLQ 757 (1990); and Yorke, 29 ELR 546 (2004).

[117] *Soering v UK*, para 91. Cf the prohibitions on return in the Refugee Convention 1951, Article 33 and the UN Torture Convention 1984, Article 3.

[118] In the *Soering* case, there was a finding of a breach of Article 3 generally. In *Harkins and Edwards v UK* hudoc (2012); 55 EHRR 561, the Court held that it makes no distinction between torture and other forms of ill-treatment contrary to Article 3 in extradition and deportation cases.

[119] Remarkably, the case was decided only twelve months after the application was lodged. After the Court's judgment, the UK refused extradition on the charges of capital murder but surrendered the applicant on charges of non-capital murder: see CM Res DH (90) 8. The applicant was then convicted in Virginia of the two murders and given two life terms.

[120] These included the applicant's youth, lack of criminal record, and mental state.

Article 2 of the Convention of a provision permitting the death penalty.[121] However, the extradition of a fugitive offender could involve a breach of Article 3 in the particular circumstances of a case. In the applicant's case these were the seven or eight years that the applicant would be likely to face on death row in extreme conditions of detention[122] and his young age (18 years) and mental state at the time of the offence. As to the time spent on death row, the Court discounted the fact that much of this time resulted from the convicted individual's resort to the appeal procedures available because it was 'part of human nature that the person will cling to life by exploiting those safeguards to the full'.[123]

It is probable that the *Soering* case would now be decided in favour of the applicant on different grounds, as the position concerning return to face the death penalty has changed. In *Al Saadoon and Mufdhi v UK*,[124] a Chamber of the Court held that the return of an individual to another jurisdiction when there were substantial grounds to believe that there was a real risk that they would be subjected to the death penalty was a violation of Article 3. This was because, '[w]hatever the method of execution, the extinction of life involves some physical pain' and, '[i]n addition, the foreknowledge of death at the hands of the state must inevitably give rise to intense psychological suffering'.[125] The Chamber found itself able to reach this conclusion despite the express authorization of the death penalty in Article 2(1) because the number of Convention parties that had ratified Protocol 13, 'together with consistent state practice in observing the moratorium on capital punishment', were 'strongly indicative that Article 2 has been amended so as to prohibit the death penalty in all circumstances'. This being so, the wording in Article 2(1) no longer 'continues to act as a bar' to interpreting 'inhuman or degrading treatment or punishment' in Article 3 as including the death penalty.[126]

However, the general ruling in the *Soering* case prohibiting the sending of an individual to another state to face a real risk of torture or other proscribed ill-treatment remains intact. Considerations such as the risk of ill-treatment while in police custody or in prison remain applicable. Thus in *Klein v Russia*,[127] it was held that extradition to Colombia would be contrary to Article 3 when its Vice-President had said that the applicant should 'rot in jail' if returned. It may also be 'inhuman treatment' to extradite an individual where there is good reason to believe that the extradition process is being abused by the requesting state in order to prosecute him, contrary to the principle of speciality, for a political offence 'or even simply because of his political opinions'.[128] However, the mere fact that an individual extradited to another state may on his return face prosecution for a criminal offence that carries a severe sentence or one that is more severe than would apply in other European states does not in itself amount to a breach of Article 3. 'Due regard must be had for the fact that sentencing practices vary greatly between states and that there will often be legitimate and reasonable differences between states as to the length of sentences which are imposed, even for similar offences.'[129] Exceptionally, return to face

---

[121] But see now *Al-Saadoon and Mufdhi v UK* 2010-; 51 EHRR 212.
[122] Cf *Poltoratskiy v Ukraine* 2003-V; 39 EHRR 916 and *GB v Bulgaria* hudoc (2004).
[123] *Soering v UK* A 161 (1989); 11 EHRR 439 para 106 PC.   [124] 2010-; 51 EHRR 212.
[125] *Al-Saadoon and Mufdhi v UK*, para 115. See also *Poldtoratskiy v Ukraine* 2003-V; 39 EHRR 148.
[126] *Al-Saadoon and Mufdhi v UK*, para 120.
[127] Hudoc (2010). See also *Ahorugeze v Sweden* hudoc (2011); 55 EHRR 87.
[128] *Altun v Germany* No 10308/83, 36 DR 209 at 232–3 (1983).
[129] *Harkins and Edwards v UK* hudoc (2012); 55 EHRR 561 para 134. See also *Pavlovic v Sweden No 45920/99* hudoc (1999) DA (five years' imprisonment for desertion: not a breach). And see *Kilic v Switzerland No 12364/86*, 50 DR 280 (1986). Return to face military service is not inhuman treatment: *A and KBF v Turkey No 14401/88*, 68 DR 188 (1991).

a real risk of a sentence of life imprisonment without the possibility of release may be a breach of Article 3.[130]

The basis for liability under the rule in the *Soering* case is that the extraditing state has 'taken action which has as a direct consequence the exposure of an individual to proscribed ill-treatment'.[131] The returning state is 'not being held directly responsible for the acts of another state but for the facilitation, through the process of extradition, of a denial of the applicant's rights by that other state'.[132] On the basis of this approach, a state could be liable under the Convention if an individual's extradition presented a real risk of the infringement of any Convention Article, not just Article 3. As the Court noted in the *Soering* case, the situation is an unusual one in that liability normally arises under the Convention only where a violation has in fact occurred; the prospect of a breach, however probable, is normally not sufficient. The Court explained its extension of liability to a case involving only the risk of a violation on the basis that 'where an applicant claims that a decision to extradite him would, if implemented, be contrary to Article 3 by reason of its foreseeable consequences in the requesting country, a departure from this principle is necessary in view of the serious and irreparable nature of the alleged suffering risked, in order to ensure the effectiveness of the safeguard provided by that Article'.[133] This reasoning carries most weight in a case where the receiving state is not a party to the Convention; in other cases, it is possible if necessary to bring a claim under the Convention against the receiving state itself.[134] As far as a receiving state is concerned, although it cannot be held liable under the Convention for infringing Article 3 in proceedings to which it is not a party, there is no doubt, as the Court acknowledged in the *Soering* case,[135] that the Court's approach 'inevitably involves an assessment of conditions' in that state against the standards of the Convention, whether that state is a party to the Convention or not. But, as the Court also noted, 'there is no question of adjudicating on or establishing the responsibility of the receiving country, whether under general international law, under the Convention or otherwise'.[136]

A final point that emerges from a consideration of the *Soering* case is that insofar as Article 3 prohibits the extradition of a person when this is required by an extradition treaty, the requested state is placed in a position to which the rules as to inconsistent treaty obligations apply.[137]

The rule in the *Soering* case applies equally to deportation as well as to extradition. For example, in *SF and Others v Sweden*,[138] the Court held that to deport the applicants to Iran would be in breach of Article 3 because of the risk that they would be punished for having criticized the Iranian government while living in Sweden.

Cruz Varas and Others v Sweden[139] addressed the question of the evidence to be taken into account when assessing liability in cases of extradition or deportation in which, as in

---

[130] See *Harkins and Edwards v UK* hudoc (2012); 55 EHRR 561.

[131] *Soering v UK* A 161 (1989); 11 EHRR 439 para 91 PC.

[132] O'Boyle, in O'Reilly, ed, *Human Rights and Constitutional Law: Essays in Honour of Brian Walsh*, 1992, at p 97.   [133] *Soering v UK* A 161 (1989); 11 EHRR 439 para 90 PC.

[134] The Court does take into account that the receiving state is a Convention party when ruling on Article 3 cases: *Aronica v Germany No 72032/01* hudoc (2002) DA (extradition) and *Tomic v UK No 17837/03* hudoc (2003) DA (deportation).   [135] *Soering v UK* A 161 (1989); 11 EHRR 439 para 91 PC.

[136] *Soering v* UK, para 91.

[137] Article 30, Vienna Convention on the Law of Treaties 1969. The UK was not in this position in the *Soering* case: see s 11, Extradition Act 1870 and Articles IV and V(2), UK–US Extradition Treaty 1972.

[138] Hudoc (2012). See also *RC v Sweden* hudoc (2010) and *H and B v UK* Hudoc (2013); 57 EHRR 498 (risk of torture in Iran and Afghanistan respectively). And see *Daoudi v France* hudoc (2009) and *Abdolkhani and Karimnia v Turkey* hudoc (2009).   [139] A 201 (1991); 14 EHRR 1.

the *Cruz Varas* case, the applicant has already been returned when the case is decided at Strasbourg. The Court stated that in such a case the presence of a real risk of ill-treatment is to be judged 'primarily' by reference to what the respondent state knew or ought to have known at the time of the return. The Court may take into account, however, information that comes to light subsequently when judging whether the risk to the applicant has been rightly or wrongly assessed by the respondent state. Thus in the *Cruz Varas* case, account was taken of the fact that following his deportation the applicant had been unable to produce witnesses or other evidence in support of his claim of prior ill-treatment. The Court did not mention the fact that the applicant had not been ill-treated following his return. In later cases, the Court has increasingly placed reliance upon evidence of post-return treatment when judging whether the risk to the applicant has been rightly or wrongly assessed by the respondent state.[140] In cases in which the respondent state has not yet removed the applicant to another state, the Court decides whether his removal would infringe Article 3 by reference to the facts as they are known to the Court at the time of the Court's decision.[141] In all cases, the Court assesses the situation 'in the light of the evidence put before it or, if necessary, material obtained *proprio motu*'.[142]

As indicated earlier, for there to be a breach of Article 3, the risk of ill-treatment must be a 'real risk', not just a 'mere possibility'. In *Vilvarajah and Others v UK*,[143] the five applicants were Sri Lankan Tamils who claimed to be at risk of ill-treatment from state security forces in the conflict between the Sri Lankan government and the Tamil liberation movement. The applicants were refused asylum by the respondent state and returned to their national state. The Court held that their return was not a breach of Article 3. Earlier there had been considerable government violence against the Tamil community as a whole, triggered by the activities of the liberation movement, so that it might then have been accepted that there would be a real risk that any member of the community would have been ill-treated upon his return. However, the position had improved. Whereas there remained the 'possibility' that the applicants, as Tamils, might be detained and ill-treated, this was not sufficient to establish a breach of Article 3:[144] it was necessary to show that the applicants were especially at risk, which was not the case.[145] The Court was not influenced in its decision by the fact that three of the applicants were in fact subjected to ill-treatment on their return since 'there existed no special distinguishing features in their cases that could or ought to have enabled the Secretary of State to foresee that they would be treated in this way'.[146]

In *Sufi and Elmi v UK*,[147] the Court confirmed its earlier ruling that the general situation of violence in the place to which an individual was to be returned might be of such

---

[140] See eg, the *Shamayev*, *Al-Moayad*, and *Mamatkulov* cases, discussed later in this section.

[141] Eg, *Soering v UK* A 161 (1989); 11 EHRR 439 PC and *Ismoilov and Others v Russia* hudoc (2008); 49 EHRR 1128. In some cases, the non-removal is in response to Court interim measures.

[142] *Saadi v Italy* 2008-; 49 EHRR 730 GC. The Court attaches importance to Amnesty International and similar country reports: para 131. In *N v Finland* hudoc (2005); 43 EHRR 195, a Court fact-finding mission interviewed the applicant and others in the sending state to assess the applicant's claims.

[143] A 215 (1991); 14 EHRR 248 para 111. Cf *Said v Netherlands* 2005-VI; 43 EHRR 248 (real risk that the applicant would be subjected to extra-judicial punishments amounting to inhuman treatment as a military deserter if expelled to Eritrea).

[144] In *Salah Sheekh v Netherlands* hudoc (2007); 45 EHRR 1158 para 141, discussed later in this section, it was sufficient to show that members of the applicant's clan, as opposed to the whole population or the applicant in particular, were at risk. Cf *Saadi v Italy* hudoc (2008); 49 EHRR 730 para 132 GC. And see *Paez v Sweden* 1997-VII (links to terrorist organization).

[145] Where the 'general situation' evidence before the Court is not sufficient, it is for the applicant to produce other evidence corroborating his allegations: *Saadi v Italy* hudoc 2008-; 49 EHRR 730 GC.

[146] *Vilvarajah and Others v UK* A 215 (1991); 14 EHRR 248 para 112.

[147] Hudoc (2011); 54 EHRR 209. Cf *NA v UK* hudoc (2008); 48 EHRR 337 GC.

an intensity that it would be in violation of Article 3 to return a person there without the need to show that he or she was especially at risk, but added that this would be so only in 'the most extreme cases'.[148] In that case, the violence in Mogadishu, which was the city in Somalia to which the applicants were to be returned, was of 'such a level of intensity that anyone in the city, except possibly those who are exceptionally well-connected to "powerful actors" [which the applicants were not], would be at real risk of treatment prohibited by Article 3'.[149] In reaching this conclusion, the Court 'had regard to the indiscriminate bombardments and military offensives carried out by all parties to the conflict, the unacceptable number of civilian casualties, the substantial number of persons displaced within and from the city, and the unpredictable and widespread nature of the conflict'.[150]

Assurances given by the receiving state to the returning state about the treatment that the applicant will receive on return are taken into account when assessing the risk of ill-treatment, but in most cases they have not proved decisive: they have been inadequate in themselves or outweighed by other contrary evidence. In *Chahal v UK*,[151] in which there were fears for the safety of the applicant if he were deported to India, the Indian government gave the United Kingdom a general assurance that the applicant 'would enjoy the same legal protection as any other Indian citizen' and 'would have no reason to expect to suffer mistreatment of any kind at the hands of the Indian authorities'. Nonetheless, in view of reliable evidence from Indian and international sources of extra-judicial killings by the Punjab police, who had a particular reason to seek out the applicant as a leading Sikh separatist, the assurance, although accepted by the Court as genuine, did not prevent there being a 'real risk' of ill-treatment in breach of Article 3. In *Saadi v Italy*,[152] the Grand Chamber reached a similar conclusion in respect of a more limited government statement. Asked by the respondent government to give a diplomatic assurance that the applicant would not be ill-treated contrary to Article 3, the Tunisian government simply responded that Tunisian laws guaranteed prisoners' rights and that Tunisia had acceded to the relevant international treaties. The Court stated that such laws and accessions 'in principle are not in themselves sufficient to ensure adequate protection against the risk of ill-treatment where, as in the present case, reliable sources have reported practices resorted to or tolerated by the authorities which are manifestly contrary to the principles of the Convention', to which the applicant, as a convicted terrorist in the Tunisian courts, would be liable to be subjected.[153] Similarly, in *Ismoilov and Others v Russia*,[154] a general assurance of 'humane treatment' by the Uzbekistan government was not sufficient to counter the evidence from a number of objective sources (eg, the UN Special Rapporteur on Torture) that there was systematic torture of prisoners generally and that persons, such as the applicants, who were wanted in connection with a serious disturbance aimed at the government, would be particularly at risk of torture. In all of these cases, the assurances were very general or limited.[155] Whether the Court would take the same negative view of

---

[148] *Sufi and Elmi v UK*, para 218.

[149] *Sufi and Elmi v UK*, para 250. The situation had improved later: *KAB v Sweden* hudoc (2013).

[150] *Sufi and Elmi v UK*, para 248.

[151] 1996-V; 23 EHRR 413 GC. See Lester and Beattie, EHRLR 565 (2005).

[152] 2008-; 49 EHRR 730 GC. The 'reliable sources' included Amnesty International and US Department of State reports. See also *Ben Khemais v Italy* hudoc (2009).

[153] *Saadi v Italy*, para 147.

[154] Hudoc (2008); 49 EHRR 1128. See also *Abdulkhakov v Russia* hudoc (2012) and *Klein v Russia* hudoc (2010) (extradition to Uzbekistan and Colombia respectively). And see *Hirsi Jamaa and Others v Italy* 2012-; 55 EHRR 627 GC (Italian reliance on a bilateral treaty made with Libya committing the latter to comply with its human rights treaty obligations insufficient in view of evidence of Libya's poor human rights record).

[155] Cf those in *MSS v Belgium and Greece* 2011-; 53 EHRR 28 GC.

assurances with more detailed substantive, procedural, and monitoring safeguards[156] has yet to be tested. The likelihood that states that tolerate or engage in ill-treatment in breach of Article 3 would not respect their 'paper' undertakings suggests that the same negative view should prevail.[157]

In contrast, in cases concerning extradition to 'a requesting state which has a long history of respect for democracy, human rights and the rule of law, and which has longstanding extradition arrangements with contracting states', a presumption of good faith applies, so that an assurance will be accepted, provided that the assurance is confirmed by relevant evidence of the past practice of the state giving it. This was stated in *Babar Ahmad and Others v UK*,[158] in which the Court accepted on this basis assurances by the US government that the applicants would not be designated as enemy combatants, or subjected to extraordinary rendition or to the death penalty.

In all of the assurance cases just discussed, the Court has been called upon to make decisions before an individual is returned. In post-return cases in which assurances have been given, the Court, although judging the respondent state by reference to what it knew or ought to have known at the time of return,[159] has had knowledge of the applicant's fate on his return—knowledge which would seem in fact to have contributed to rulings that no breach of Article 3 has occurred. In *Shamayev and Others v Georgia and Russia*,[160] Georgia extradited to Russia five Russian nationals who had escaped across the border from Chechnya on charges of mainly terrorist-related offences. It did so on the basis of letters of guarantee from the Russian Acting Procurator General that the applicants would not be sentenced to death or subjected to torture or treatment or punishment that was cruel, inhuman, or contrary to human dignity. The Court noted that these guarantees were given by the highest official responsible for criminal prosecutions and for the treatment of prisoners in Russia and that there was no evidence that could otherwise reasonably have given the Georgian authorities cause to doubt their credibility. In finding no breach of Article 3, the Court also attached importance to the fact that information and evidence obtained subsequent to the applicants' extradition did not indicate that the applicants had been treated contrary to Article 3. Similarly, in *Al-Moayad v Germany*,[161] the applicant Yemeni citizen was extradited to the United States to face charges in an ordinary criminal court of providing money and equipment to Al-Qaeda and Hamas. The United States Embassy gave assurances to the German authorities that the applicant would not be prosecuted before a military or other extra-ordinary court. The German executive authorities and courts at the highest level understood these assurances to mean that the applicant would not be detained in Guantanamo Bay or a third state, places in respect of which the Court stated it was 'gravely concerned' by 'worrying reports' about the interrogation methods at variance with Article 3 used by the US authorities on individuals, such as the applicant, suspected of involvement in international terrorism. In assessing the effectiveness of the assurances, and finding no breach of Article 3, the Court noted that Germany had previously found that assurances given by the United States in

---

[156] See the UK memoranda of understanding with several states; for details, see Moeckli, 8 HRLR 534 (2008).   [157] But see *Ismoilov and Others v Russia* hudoc (2008); 49 EHRR 1128.
[158] *Nos 24027/07, 11949/08 and 36742/08* hudoc (2010) DA. Cf *Harkins and Edwards v UK* hudoc (2012); 55 EHRR 561. Assurances that the death penalty or irreducible life imprisonment would not be imposed have been held to be sufficient to permit return in other cases: see eg, *Saoudi v Spain No 22871/06* hudoc (2006) DA.   [159] See *Cruz Varas* A 201 (1991); 14 EHRR 1, discussed earlier in this section.
[160] 2005-III. See also *Mamatkulov and Askarov v Turkey* 2005-I; 41 EHRR 494 GC, in which assurances by Uzbekistan that the applicant would not be subjected to torture or capital punishment contributed to a finding of no violation of Article 3, but in which the absence of evidence of post-extradition ill-treatment in medical reports and other sources was important.   [161] *No 35865/03* hudoc (2007) DA.

the context of extradition had been fully respected and that the post-extradition evidence indicated that the assurances in the applicant's case, which were binding in international law, had been respected and that he had not been ill-treated.

Article 3 permits the sending of an individual to a particular part of a state where he would not be at risk of ill-treatment, even though there is such a risk elsewhere in the state. But, as held in *Salah Sheekh v Netherlands*,[162] he must be able to 'travel to the area concerned, gain admittance and settle there'. Where this is not so, his return to the state will be a breach of Article 3 if there is a 'real chance of his being removed, or of his having no alternative but to go to areas of the country' where there is a 'real risk' of ill-treatment.[163] In the *Salah Sheekh* case, the applicant was a Somali national whom the Dutch authorities sought to return to a safe area of Somalia after refusing him asylum. On the facts, the Court held that whereas there was good evidence from the UN High Commissioner for Refugees (UNHCR) that the area concerned was safe for members of the clans who resided there, it was unlikely that the applicant, as a member of a different clan, would be allowed to settle and that, as a member of his particular Ashraf clan, there was a 'real risk' that he would be ill-treated elsewhere in Somalia, so that his return would infringe Article 3. In contrast, in *MYH and Others v Sweden*,[164] the Court rejected the applications of Iraqi nationals who feared persecution because of their Christian religion if they were returned to Iraq; it did so because they could relocate to the Kurdish region of Iraq where they would not be at risk.

Similarly, state A may be in breach of Article 3 if it removes an individual to state B where there is a real risk that they will be expelled by that state to state C in which there is a real risk that they will be subjected to proscribed ill-treatment. Thus in *MSS v Belgium and Greece*,[165] the Grand Chamber held that, before removing an asylum seeker to an intermediary state, state A 'must make sure that the intermediary country's asylum procedure affords sufficient guarantees to avoid an asylum seeker being removed, directly or indirectly, to his country of origin [in this case Afghanistan] without any evaluation of the risks he faces from the standpoint of Article 3'. The case concerned the return of an asylum seeker by Belgium to Greece, another Convention party, in accordance with its obligations under EU law, but the Grand Chamber's statement can be taken to apply generally, to all asylum and non-asylum cases, and especially, but not only, to removals to intermediaries that are non-Convention parties. In *Hirsi Jamaa and Others v Italy*,[166] the respondent state had infringed Article 3 when it returned to Libya, whence they had come, Somali and Eritrean nationals, captured at sea, who were planning to obtain refuge in Italy, when it should have known that there was a real risk that they would be repatriated to their countries of origin, which were non-Convention parties, where there was a real risk that they would be subjected to torture or inhuman treatment for having left the country irregularly.

In all cases, where the authorities have information indicating that there is a real risk of ill-treatment in the receiving state, they must conduct a 'proper assessment' of the situation and must not remove the person unless they have taken steps that are sufficient to counter

---

[162] Hudoc (2007); 45 EHRR 1158 para 141. Cf *Hilal v UK* 2001-II; 33 EHRR 31. In *Sufi and Elmi v UK* hudoc (2011); 54 EHRR 209, the Court held that the applicants' internal transfer, which was possible, would still be a violation of Article 3 because of the human rights situation in the area to which they would be transferred, which was one in which the al-Shabaab enforced a particularly strict version of Shariah law.

[163] *Salah Sheekh v Netherlands*, para 143.   [164] Hudoc (2013).

[165] Hudoc (2011); 53 EHRR 28 para 342 GC. See Clayton, 11 HRLR 758 (2011). See also *Mohammed v Austria* hudoc (2013) (return to Hungary not a breach).

[166] 2012-; 55 EHRR 627 GC. See Moreno-Lax, 12 HRLR 574 (2012).

the risk. This was stated in *Garabayev v Russia*,[167] in which the applicant had informed the respondent state of his fears of torture and persecution if extradited to Turkmenistan and, in the view of the Court, the respondent state had, in the light of the evidence available to it, been put on notice that there was a real risk of ill-treatment. Finding that the state had extradited the applicant without making a 'proper assessment' of the situation and without taking steps such as obtaining assurances from the requesting state's government or arranging for medical reports or visits by independent experts to counter the risk, the Court found a breach of Article 3.

Where there remains a real risk of ill-treatment in another state, the obligation not to send an individual to that state is an absolute one; it is not open to the respondent state to claim that its own public interest reasons for deporting or extraditing the individual outweigh the risk of ill-treatment on his return, regardless of his offence or conduct. Thus in *Chahal v UK*,[168] there was a real risk that, as a well-known supporter of Sikh separatism, the applicant Indian citizen would, wherever he was deported to in India, be sought and killed by the Punjab police, who were out of lawful control. Given this real risk of a breach of Article 3, the United Kingdom could not argue that, on balance, the applicant could nonetheless be deported to India because of the threat to its national security that his activities in the United Kingdom posed.

The absolute nature of the guarantee established in *Chahal* was confirmed in *Saadi v Italy*.[169] In that case, the applicant was a Tunisian national against whom the respondent state had issued an order deporting him to Tunisia on the grounds that his conduct was disturbing public order and threatening national security in Italy because of his active role in supporting fundamentalist Islamist cells engaged in international terrorism. The order was made upon his release after serving a prison sentence resulting from his conviction in the Italian courts for offences the facts of which provided evidence of such a role. The applicant claimed that if he were returned to Tunisia he would be tortured, seemingly in connection with the investigation of terrorist activities which had led to charges against him in Italy.[170] Confirming the applicant's claims, the Court had before it reports, which it had no doubt were reliable, from Amnesty International, Human Rights Watch, and the US Department of State indicating that persons accused of terrorist offences were regularly tortured by the state in Tunisia to obtain confessions and other information. In these circumstances, the Court concluded that there was a 'real risk' of treatment contrary to Article 3 in Tunisia if the applicant were deported there. A unanimous Grand Chamber was not prepared to accept that the values underlying the European Convention that were articulated in Article 3 were open to compromise, however compelling the public interest justification. While acknowledging that 'states face immense difficulties in modern times in protecting their communities from terrorist violence' and that the 'scale of the danger of terrorism today' and the threat it poses to the community cannot be underestimated, the Court nonetheless rejected arguments, presented by the United Kingdom, intervening, and supported by the respondent state, that there were reasons to qualify the absolute

---

[167] Hudoc (2007); 49 EHRR 260. See also *Abdulkhakov v Russia* hudoc (2012). Cf *MSS v Belgium and Greece* 2011-; 53 EHRR 28 GC.

[168] 1996-V; 23 EHRR 413 GC. See also *Ahmed v Austria* 1996-VI; 24 EHRR 278 (deportation because of criminal conviction).

[169] 2008-; 49 EHRR 730 GC. See Moeckli, 8 HRLR 534 (2008). Cf *A v Netherlands* hudoc (2010).

[170] While serving his sentence in Italy, the applicant had been convicted by a Tunisian military court *in absentia* of membership of an international terrorist organization and incitement to terrorism and sentenced to twenty years' imprisonment. Presumably the risk was of ill-treatment in connection with the investigation of other terrorist activities or links while in prison serving this sentence.

nature of the guarantee spelt out in the *Chahal* case. The United Kingdom first argued that, whereas a rule of absolute liability should apply under Article 3 in cases where the ill-treatment was inflicted by the respondent state itself, in cases in which the risk was of ill-treatment by the authorities of another state, it should be balanced against 'the dangerousness he or she represents to the community' in the respondent state. Essentially, the United Kingdom was arguing that the feared harm to the individual, which might range within Article 3 from torture to inhuman or degrading treatment, should be weighed against the danger to the community in the returning state, which might range from the most serious 'ticking bomb' scenario to lesser degrees or kinds of danger. The Court characterized this argument as 'misconceived', on the basis that the 'concepts of "risk" and "dangerousness" in this context do not lend themselves to a balancing test because they are notions that can only be assessed independently of each other'.[171] The Court then rejected a second, related UK argument to the effect that stronger evidence of a risk of ill-treatment in the receiving state must be adduced where the applicant poses a threat to national security in the respondent state than in cases in which the public interest risk is of a less vital kind. In doing so, the Court stressed that it already requires 'substantial grounds' for believing that a real risk exists: that it 'applies rigorous criteria and exercises close scrutiny' when it decides upon the existence of a real risk of ill treatment, as evidenced by the fact that it had only 'rarely' decided that such a risk existed.[172]

Although most decided cases concerning extradition or deportation involve claims that the applicant will be ill-treated at the hands of the public authorities of the receiving state, the responsibility of the sending state also may be engaged where the risk is of ill-treatment by private groups or individuals. For example, a state may be in breach of Article 3 if it sends an individual to another state where there is a real risk of that individual being subjected there to ill-treatment by private drug traffickers[173] or by warring clans in a civil war situation,[174] or that a woman would be subjected to female genital mutilation.[175] The treatment of women by society was in issue in *N v Sweden*.[176] There the authorities had rejected applications by the applicant and her husband, both Afghan nationals, for asylum. The applicant had appealed unsuccessfully against this decision on the ground that if she were returned to Afghanistan, she risked ill-treatment contrary to Article 3, as she had now left her husband and had attempted to divorce him. The Court noted that Afghan women who do not conform to the gender roles ascribed to them may be subjected to 'domestic violence and other forms of punishment ranging from isolation and stigmatisation to honour crimes for those accused of bringing shame to their families, communities or tribes', and do not receive protection from the state. As the applicant's conduct was not in accordance with her 'gender role', and she had no family or other 'social network or adequate protection in Afghanistan', there were, 'in these special circumstances', substantial grounds for believing that, if deported to Afghanistan, the applicant would face 'various cumulative risks of reprisals [in breach of Article 3] ... from her husband, his family, her own family and from the Afghan society'. For the returning state to be liable in cases of private ill-treatment on a *Soering* basis, it must be shown that the public authorities in the receiving state are unable to provide protection against the private actors concerned, whether this failure is the fault of the receiving state or not.[177]

---

[171] *Saadi v Italy* 2008-; 49 EHRR 730 para 139 GC.
[172] See, eg *Soldatenko v Ukraine* hudoc (2008) para 72 and *Ryabikin v Russia* hudoc (2008); 48 EHRR 1322.
[173] *HLR v France* 1997-III; 26 EHRR 29 GC.
[174] *Ahmed v Austria* 1996-VI; 24 EHRR 278 (Somalia).
[175] *Izevbekhai and Others v Ireland* No 43408/08 hudoc (2011) DA and *Omeredo v Austria* No 8969/10 hudoc (2011) DA (no real risk on facts of both cases). [176] Hudoc (2010) paras 55, 61–2.
[177] *HLR v France* 1997-III; 26 EHRR 29 GC.

In very exceptional cases of serious illness, humanitarian considerations may prohibit the return of an individual to another state. In *D v UK*,[178] the applicant, who had AIDS, was ordered to be returned to his national state of St Kitts after he had completed his prison sentence for drug smuggling. Pending his removal and the outcome of his case at Strasbourg, the applicant had been placed in a hospice and was in the terminal stages of his illness when the European Court ruled that his return would be inhuman treatment in breach of Article 3. This was because the 'sophisticated treatment and medication' being given to him in the United Kingdom would not be available in St Kitts and he would not have family or other moral or social support there. Although the absence in St Kitts of the specialist treatment and medication available in London did not mean that his return would fall short of the standards in Article 3, the 'abrupt withdrawal' of his current treatment and medication, with the inevitable hastening of the applicant's death, would cause 'acute mental and physical suffering' and would 'expose him to a real risk of dying under most distressing circumstances'. In these 'very exceptional circumstances', involving 'compelling humanitarian considerations', the Court found a breach of Article 3. The Court stressed that Article 3 did not provide generally for an alien who is subject to expulsion any entitlement to remain in a Convention state in order to benefit from medical, social, or other forms of assistance that would not be available in the state to which he was to be sent, and that in a case of this kind it would examine very carefully the circumstances of the case, *inter alia* comparing the applicant's medical and other conditions that would pertain if he were not removed with those that would apply if he was. The *D* case has been relied upon in a number of cases[179] since it was decided, all cases involving physical or mental health, but in none has the Court found the humanitarian considerations to be sufficiently compelling to find a breach, underlining the point that the combination of circumstances in the *D* case was very exceptional. In these cases, the Court has stressed that it is not sufficient to show that medical treatment will be less good in the receiving state and emphasized that in the *D* case the applicant was both near to death and would lack family as well as medical support.

The 'very high threshold' established in the *D* case was confirmed by the Grand Chamber in *N v UK*.[180] In that case, the applicant was a Ugandan national who was to be returned to Uganda after her asylum claim had been rejected. She had been diagnosed with AIDS on her arrival in the United Kingdom, but, as a result of the free medication she had been given during the nine years of her asylum application, she was in a stable medical condition, with the prospect of many years of life. If she was deprived of this medication, she would die within a few years. The required medication was available, highly subsidized, in Uganda, but the applicant claimed that she would not be able to afford it and that it would not be available in her home rural area. While accepting that the quality of the applicant's life and her life expectancy would be affected if she were returned to Uganda, the Grand Chamber noted that, in contrast with the *D* case, the applicant was not yet critically ill and that the 'rapidity of the deterioration which she would suffer and the extent to which she would be able to obtain access to medical treatment, support and care, including help from relatives, must involve a certain degree of

---

[178] 1997-III; 24 EHRR 423 paras 51–4.

[179] See, eg, *Bensaid v UK* 2001-I; 33 EHRR 205 (mental illness); *Hukic v Sweden* No 17416/05 hudoc (2005) DA (Downs syndrome); and *Yoh-Ekale Mwanje v Belgium* hudoc (2011); 56 EHRR 1140 (AIDS). But see *BB v France* 1998-VI (F Sett).

[180] 2008-; 47 EHRR 885 GC. *N v UK* applies beyond AIDS to physical and mental illness generally: para 45.

speculation', particularly as AIDS treatment was evolving worldwide.[181] In doing so, it made the following important general comment:

> Although many of the rights it contains have implications of a social or economic nature, the Convention is essentially directed at the protection of civil and political rights...Advances in medical science, together with social and economic differences between countries, entail that the level of treatment available in the contracting state and the country of origin may vary considerably...Article 3 does not place an obligation on the contracting state to alleviate such disparities through the provision of free and unlimited health care to all aliens without a right to stay within its jurisdiction. A finding to the contrary would place too great a burden on the contracting states.[182]

N v UK was cited in *Harkins and Edwards v UK*,[183] in which the different standards of treatment to be expected in returning and receiving states was again in issue, but this time in a non-medical context. Here the Court accepted that, although the guarantee in Article 3 is an absolute one, treatment which might violate Article 3 when it is that of the Convention party which is extraditing or deporting an individual might not do so when it is that of the receiving state.[184] To rule otherwise, the Court stated, might be to 'impose Convention standards on other States'. The *Harkins and Edwards* case concerned the extradition of the two applicants to the United States to face homicide charges that might lead respectively to the imposition of mandatory or discretionary life sentences. On the facts of the case, the Court held that, in terms of a violation of Article 3, such sentences would not be 'grossly disproportionate' and that, at this stage in the proceedings (ie before the applicants had even been convicted), it could not be said that their imprisonment 'would not serve any legitimate penological purpose'. As the *Harkins and Edwards* case thus makes clear, the 'legitimate penological purpose' test, which is meaningful for the purposes of Article 3 in the case of a life sentence that is carried out in a contracting party, has little application in cases of extradition.[185]

The removal of an individual to another state has raised Article 3 issues in various other contexts also. In *Aswat v UK*,[186] it was held that extradition of a seriously mentally ill person to the US to face trial for terrorist offences would be a violation of Article 3 because there was a risk that, if convicted, he would serve his sentence in a prison (ADX Florence) that operated the strictest possible security regime, devised for terrorists and other very serious offenders, which would be inappropriate for a person in his mental condition. In a different kind of case, *MSS v Belgium and Greece*,[187] Belgium was found to be in breach of Article 3 when, applying EU asylum law, it removed an asylum seeker to Greece when it ought to have known that there was a real risk that the living conditions

---

[181] *N v UK*, para 50.

[182] *N v UK*, para 44. But see the strong joint dissenting opinion of Judges Tulkens, Bonello, and Spielmann.

[183] Hudoc (2012); 55 EHRR 561 para 134. See also *Schuchter v Italy* No 68476/10 hudoc (2011) DA.

[184] See also *Willcox and Hurford v UK* Nos 43759/10 and 43771/12 hudoc (2013) DA, in which the applicants had been transferred from Thailand to the UK to serve their drug-trafficking sentences. The Court rejected a claim that their sentences, which were normal for Thailand, were 'grossly disproportionate' as they would have been much lower in the UK.

[185] Cf *Babar Ahmad and Others v UK* hudoc (2012); 56 EHRR 1.   [186] Hudoc (2013).

[187] 2011-; 53 EHRR 28 GC. See also *Mohammed Hussein and Others v Netherlands and Italy* No 27725/10 hudoc (2013) DA and *Mohammed v Austria* hudoc (2013). In the earlier case of *KRS v UK No 32733/08* hudoc (2008) DA, return to Greece had not breached Article 3 as no evidence had been adduced to suggest that Greece would not comply with EU law.

that the applicant would face in Greece would be contrary to Article 3, and that he might be returned to Afghanistan.

Where an individual physically resists deportation or extradition, reasonable force, including the use of sedatives, may be used to effect the return.[188] But an individual should not be returned where he or she is not medically fit to travel.[189] Moreover, humanitarian considerations are relevant to the manner of return. In *Mubilanzila Mayeka and Kaniki Mitunga v Belgium*,[190] the return of an unaccompanied five-year-old girl without proper arrangements for her care in transit or on arrival caused her such 'extreme anxiety and demonstrated such a total lack of humanity' as to be inhuman treatment.

V. EXTRAORDINARY RENDITION

Extraordinary rendition was defined by the Grand Chamber in *El Masri v The Former Yugoslav Republic of Macedonia*[191] as 'an extra-judicial transfer of persons from one juris-diction or state to another, for the purposes of detention and interrogation outside the normal legal system, where there is a real risk of torture or cruel, inhuman or degrading treatment'. In the *El-Masri* case, the applicant, a German national, was arrested while travelling on a bus at the Serbian-Macedonian border and held incommunicado for twenty-three days by Macedonian security agents in a hotel room in Skopje where he was questioned about possible links with Islamic organizations. When he declared his intention to leave the hotel, he was threatened with a gun. The applicant was then taken, handcuffed and blindfolded, to Skopje airport where he was handed over to a CIA rendi-tion team. In the presence of Macedonian personnel, he was severely beaten by men wear-ing masks, forcibly undressed, sodomized with an object, given a suppository, and had a nappy and tracksuit put on him. 'Shackled and hooded, and subjected to total sensory deprivation', the applicant was forcibly placed on a CIA aircraft, which was surrounded on the tarmac by armed Macedonian security guards. On the aircraft, he was chained and tranquillized and flown, mostly unconscious, to Afghanistan, where he was detained in a CIA facility for five months in rudimentary conditions, during which time he was interrogated and force-fed when he went on hunger strike, before being flown to Albania, where he was left on the roadside. The Grand Chamber held unanimously that the appli-cant had been subjected in the hotel to inhuman and degrading treatment; although no physical force had been used, the mental suffering caused by the applicant's uncertainty as to his fate in lengthy solitary confinement, plus the threat that he might be shot, was in violation of Article 3. The Grand Chamber also held unanimously that the applicant's treatment at the airport amounted cumulatively to torture. The respondent state was responsible for these violations because its agents had committed them (at the hotel) or had 'actively facilitated the treatment and then had failed to take any measures that might have been necessary in the circumstances of the case to prevent it from occurring' (at the airport).[192] The Grand Chamber finally unanimously held the respondent state in violation of Article 3 for transferring the applicant into the custody of the US authorities when it knew, or ought to have known, that there was a real risk that he would, by way of extraordinary rendition to another state, be subjected to proscribed ill-treatment.

---

[188] *Raidl v Austria No 25342/94*, 82-A DR 134 (1995).

[189] See *D v UK* 1997-III; 24 EHRR 423 para 53.

[190] 2006-XI; 46 EHRR 449 para 69. Cf *Nsona v Netherlands* 1996-V; 32 EHRR 170.

[191] 2012- para 221 GC. The Grand Chamber adopted the definition in *Babar Ahmad and Others v UK* Nos 24027/07, 11949/08 and 36742/08 hudoc (2010) DA. On the *El Masri* case, see Fabbrini, 14 HRLR 85 (2014).

[192] *El Masri v The Former Yugoslav Republic of Macedonia*, para 211.

VI. DISAPPEARED PERSONS

Claims have been made that Article 3 has been infringed in a number of cases involving disappeared persons. Insofar as a claim is brought on behalf of a disappeared person, in the absence of the required evidence of proscribed ill-treatment, the case falls to be considered under Article 5 (freedom of the person), not Article 3.[193] However, in *Çakici v Turkey*,[194] it was held that there may be a breach of Article 3 in relation to a family member of the disappeared person where there are 'special factors' which give the applicant's suffering 'a dimension and character distinct from the emotional distress which may be regarded as inevitably caused to relatives of a victim of a serious human rights violation'.[195] Relevant considerations include 'the proximity of the family tie—in that context, a certain weight will attach to the parent-child bond, the particular circumstances of the relationship, the extent to which the family member witnessed the events in question, the involvement of the family member in the attempts to obtain information about the disappeared person and the way in which the authorities responded to those enquiries'.[196] The essence of the violation in respect of a family member lies not in the fact of the disappearance, but the 'reactions and attitudes' of the state authorities.[197] Taking this into account, in *Çakici* the Court held that a disappeared person's brother was not a victim of a breach of Article 3.[198] He had not been present at the arrest or played the leading role in complaining to the authorities, and there had been no 'aggravating features' in their response. In contrast, there was a breach in *Kurt v Turkey*[199] in relation to the disappeared person's mother, who had witnessed his detention, led the complaints against it, and suffered 'the authorities' complacency in the face of her anguish and distress'.[200] There was also a breach of Article 3 in *Cyprus v Turkey*,[201] in which Greek Cypriots had had to seek refuge in the south of Cyprus, which, together with the continued division of Cyprus and the lack of cooperation of the authorities, presented them with 'very serious obstacles' in their quest for information, thereby contributing to their mental suffering.

VII. OTHER KINDS OF INHUMAN TREATMENT

Various other instances of inhuman treatment have been found or postulated, of which the following are examples. Ill-treatment for being a homosexual may be inhuman treatment,[202] as may child abuse,[203] female genital mutilation,[204] or the destruction of a person's home.[205] However, the failure to give cancer patients access to an unauthorized experimental drug was not inhuman or degrading.[206]

---

[193] *Kurt v Turkey* 1998-III; 27 EHRR 373 para 115; *Çiçek v Turkey* hudoc (2001); 37 EHRR 464 para 154; and *Orhan v Turkey* hudoc (2002) para 354.

[194] 1999-IV; 31 EHRR 133 GC.

[195] *Çakici v Turkey*, para 98.   [196] *Çakici v* Turkey, para 98.

[197] *Çakici v Turkey*, para 98. Cf *Taş v Turkey* hudoc (2000); 33 EHRR 325 and *Janowiec and Others v Russia* 2013- GC.

[198] Cf *Ülkü Ekinci v Turkey* hudoc (2002).

[199] 1998-III; 27 EHRR 373. For other breaches see eg, *Taniş and Others v Turkey* 2005-VIII; 46 EHRR 211. For Chechnya cases, see *Bazorkina v Russia* hudoc (2006); 46 EHRR 261 and *Luluyev and Others v Russia* 2006-XIII; 48 EHRR 1039.

[200] *Çakici v Turkey* 1999-IV; 31 EHRR 133 para 98 GC. See also *Salakhov and Islyamova v Ukraine* hudoc (2013).

[201] 2001-IV; 35 EHRR 731 para 157 GC. See also *Varnava and Others v Turkey* hudoc 2009- GC.

[202] *F v UK No 17341/03* hudoc (2004) DA.

[203] *Giusto, Bornacin and V v Italy No 38972/06* hudoc (2007) DA.

[204] *Collins and Akaziebie v Sweden No 23944/05* hudoc (2007) DA.

[205] See *Selçuk and Asker v Turkey* 1998-II; 26 EHRR 477.

[206] *Hristozov and Others v Bulgaria* 2012-.

Experimental medical treatment may be inhuman treatment, if not torture, in the absence of consent.[207] Compulsory sterilization was understood to be contrary to the Convention during its drafting.[208] However, sterilization may be performed consistently with Article 3 'as a method of contraception, or for therapeutic purposes where the medical necessity has been convincingly established', but only, as was held in *VC v Slovakia*,[209] if it is done (i) with the informed consent of a 'mentally competent adult patient' and in accordance with satisfactory procedural guarantees; or (ii) in 'emergency situations in which medical treatment cannot be delayed and the appropriate consent cannot be obtained'. In *VC v Slovakia*, the applicant, while in labour and in pain, was asked by medical staff in a public hospital to sign a form requesting sterilization after being told that in any future pregnancy she or her baby would die. The Court held that there was a violation of Article 3 as (i) the applicant was not in a condition to give informed consent or in an emergency situation; and (ii) the serious medical and psychological suffering that she experienced following the sterilization reached the threshold required by Article 3.

As noted earlier the mental suffering caused to a family member of a 'disappeared person' may amount to a breach of Article 3 if there are 'special factors'. Although the Court has stated that the same approach does not apply where a person who is taken into custody is later found dead (the natural suffering resulting from the death of a close relative does not qualify),[210] recent cases have made this distinction less significant. The Court has accepted that where there has been a long period of disappearance before a person is found dead, there may be a breach of Article 3.[211] A further exception was made on the shocking facts of *Khadzhialiyev and Others v Russia*,[212] in which two men were kidnapped in Chechnya by Russian soldiers. Four days later, human remains were found, but the heads and other body parts were missing, the bodies having been blown up by an explosive. The Court held that in the 'specific circumstances' of the case, the 'moral suffering' endured by the parents and son of the deceased had, in violation of Article 3, 'reached a dimension and character distinct from the emotional distress which may be regarded as inevitably caused to relatives of a victim of a serious human rights violation'. An exception may also be allowed where the applicant witnesses the deaths of members of his family.[213]

In contrast, in *V v UK*,[214] it was held that the attribution of criminal responsibility at the age of ten years was not in breach of Article 3.[215] Crucial to the Court's decision was that there was no consensus as to the minimum age of responsibility among member states of the Council of Europe and that, although most of them set a higher limit, the age of ten was not so young as to differ 'disproportionately' from European states generally, and some states[216] had a lower age limit. In the same case, it was also held that the trial of a juvenile in public in an adult court (though with some modifications) was not in breach of Article 3: the suffering caused did not go significantly beyond that which would inevitably be present in any procedure that the authorities might adopt.

---

[207] See *X v Denmark No 9974/82*, 32 DR 282 (1983).   [208] 1 TP 116–17.

[209] 2011- paras 103, 106–8. See also *Gauer and Others v France* No 61521/08 hudoc (2012) DA (sterilization of mentally disabled young women: inadmissible, six months rule).

[210] *Tanli v Turkey* 2001-III; 38 EHRR 31.   [211] *Gongadze v Ukraine* 2005-XI; 43 EHRR 967.

[212] Hudoc (2008) para 121.

[213] *Esmukhambetov and Others v Russia* hudoc (2011) (wife and two sons killed by aircraft fire in applicant's presence).   [214] 1999-IX; 30 EHRR 121 para 74 GC.

[215] The Court's judgment is in terms of a breach of Article 3 as a whole.

[216] Eg, Cyprus, Ireland, and Switzerland.

4. INHUMAN PUNISHMENT

Although there has been little jurisprudence specifically on inhuman punishment, its meaning may be gauged from cases concerning other elements of Article 3, as the same general considerations apply. In cases involving punishment, the Court often does not distinguish between inhuman treatment and punishment, commonly finding both, or just a breach of Article 3 generally.[217] *Chember v Russia*[218] was one case in which the Court did find 'inhuman punishment'. There a soldier, as a disciplinary punishment for not cleaning army barracks adequately, had been made to do 350 knee bends even though it was known that he had a knee condition. He collapsed, was hospitalized, and was later discharged from military service on medical grounds and had been classified as a disabled person who could no longer walk properly.

Generally, a sentence imposed upon an individual convicted of a criminal offence will not be reviewed under Article 3. Instead the kind of sentence imposed for a particular offence or the length of a term of imprisonment is left to national courts. However, in *Vinter and Others v UK*,[219] the Grand Chamber stated that 'a grossly disproportionate sentence' would violate Article 3. The Grand Chamber added that 'gross disproportionality' is a strict test that will only be met on 'rare and unique' occasions. In *Harkins and Edwards v UK*,[220] the Court speculated that a mandatory life sentence without the possibility of release that was imposed upon someone below the age of 18 at the time of the offence might be 'grossly disproportionate', as might a mandatory life sentence without the possibility of release under the felony murder rule where there was no real culpability on the part of the convicted person. The principle of proportionality might also indicate a breach of Article 3 in some kinds of extreme cases other than those mentioned in *Harkins and Edwards*. For example, in *Weeks v UK*,[221] an indeterminate life sentence for a seventeen-year-old for robbery of 35 pence, not surprisingly, raised 'serious doubts', but was held not to infringe Article 3 because of the very special circumstances of the case. In *Jabari v Turkey*,[222] the Court found a breach of Article 3 when it accepted that there was a real risk that if the applicant were returned to her national state of Iran she would be punished, seemingly after criminal proceedings, for adultery by stoning to death, a finding that goes both to the manner of execution[223] and the proportionality requirement.

Distinct from 'gross disproportionality', in *Kafkaris v Cyprus*,[224] the Grand Chamber held that a mandatory sentence of life imprisonment without any 'prospect of release'—termed an 'irreducible' or 'whole life' sentence[225]—will be contrary to Article 3, if there is no possibility of review. In contrast, there is no breach of Article 3 where 'national law affords the possibility of review of a life sentence with a view to its commutation, remission, termination or the conditional release of a prisoner'.[226] In *Kafkaris*, the discretionary

---

[217] See eg, *Keenan v UK* 2001-III; 33 EHRR 913.   [218] 2008-.

[219] 2013- para 102 GC. As the applicants did not argue that their life sentences were grossly disproportionate, their cases were decided by reference to their irreducibility instead.

[220] Hudoc (2012); 55 EHRR 561. This was a case of extradition to face possible life sentences.

[221] A 114 (1987); 10 EHRR 293 para 47 PC. See the dissenting opinion of Judge De Meyer.

[222] 2000-VIII (deportation case).

[223] Return to face the death penalty would now be a breach of Article 3, regardless of the manner of execution and considerations of proportionality: see *Al-Saadoon and Mufdhi v UK* 2010-; 51 EHRR 212.

[224] 2008-; 49 EHRR 877 para 97 GC. See also *Léger v France* hudoc (2006) and *Iorgov v Bulgaria (No 2)* hudoc (2010). And see *Stanford v UK No 73299/01* hudoc (2002) DA.

[225] An 'irreducible' or 'whole life sentence' is one for which the court does not set a minimum term of imprisonment after which the prisoner is eligible for parole.

[226] *Kafkaris v Cyprus* 2008-; 49 EHRR 877 para 98 GC.

power of the President of Cyprus, on the recommendation of the Attorney General, to commute a life sentence meant that the applicant's sentence was not in breach of Article 3, given that there was evidence that the power was used in fact. This decision was taken by ten votes to seven, with the dissenting judges considering the President's limited power to be insufficient. The approach in the *Kafkaris* case was confirmed in *Vinter and Others v UK*,[227] in which the Grand Chamber explained why a 'whole life' sentence that cannot be reviewed is contrary to Article 3. Primarily, it is 'axiomatic that a prisoner cannot be detained unless there are legitimate penological grounds for that detention'.[228] Such grounds include punishment, deterrence, public protection, and rehabilitation, which may cease to justify the continued detention of a prisoner over time. Other considerations are that a prisoner should have the possibility to atone for his offence and that a 'whole life' sentence is incompatible both with respect for human dignity and the aim of rehabilitation. For these reasons, the Grand Chamber held that Article 3 required 'a dedicated mechanism guaranteeing a review no later than twenty five years after the imposition of a life sentence, with further periodic reviews thereafter'.[229] Moreover, the prisoner must be told at the outset of his sentence what he must do to qualify for release and when he may apply. In the *Vinter* case, there was held to be a violation of Article 3 because the scope of the power of review was, unlike that in the *Kafkaris* case, insufficient. The Secretary of State had interpreted his statutory power as authorizing him to order a 'whole life' prisoner's release only if the prisoner was terminally ill or physically incapacitated, and certain other conditions (as to the risk of re-offending, etc) were met. The Grand Chamber stated that if the Secretary of State's statutory power were instead interpreted 'as imposing a duty on him to exercise that power and to release a prisoner if it can be shown that his or her continued detention has become incompatible with Article 3, for example, when it can no longer be justified on legitimate penological grounds',[230] this would be compliant with Article 3.

As to this latter possible interpretation, in earlier cases the Court had already established that an indeterminate life sentence, by which a person may be detained beyond a punitive period for such time as he or she remains a danger to society, is not *per se* a breach of Article 3, but it may be such if account is not properly taken of the detained person's development when considering detention beyond the tariff period[231] or if there is an 'unjustifiable and persistent' delay in fixing the tariff period, leaving the detainee in uncertainty as to his or her future.[232]

In other kinds of cases, the level of pain and suffering caused may be a violation of Article 3 regardless of proportionality. In *Tyrer v UK*,[233] the Court considered whether the suffering resulting from a sentence of corporal punishment reached the threshold level of inhuman punishment, but concluded that 'on the facts of the case' (three strokes of the birch) it did not.[234] Some more severe sentences of corporal punishment might be regarded differently.[235] In *Al-Saadoon and Mufdhi v UK*,[236] the pain and suffering caused by the death penalty was held to be sufficient.

---

[227] 2013- GC.   [228] *Vinter and Others v UK*, para 111.

[229] *Vinter and Others v UK*, para 120.

[230] *Vinter and Others v UK*, para 125. The English Court of Appeal had interpreted the statutory power in this way in *R v Bieber* [2009] 1 WLR 223, but this interpretation had not been adopted by the Secretary of State.   [231] *Hussain v UK* 1996-I; 22 EHRR 1.

[232] *V v UK* 1999-IX; 30 EHRR 121 para 100 GC. As to inadequate review in the post-tariff period, see *Curley v UK* hudoc (2000); 31 EHRR 401.   [233] A 26 (1978); 2 EHRR 1 para 30.

[234] It was a degrading punishment: see section 5 of this chapter.

[235] See *Jabari v Turkey* (stoning to death for adultery) 2000-VIII, discussed earlier.

[236] 2010-; 51 EHRR 212, discussed earlier.

5. DEGRADING TREATMENT

Treatment is degrading if it 'is such as to arouse in the victims feelings of fear, anguish and inferiority capable of humiliating and debasing them'.[237] Or, in the language of an alternative formula that the Court sometimes adopts, treatment is degrading if it 'humiliates or debases an individual, showing a lack of respect for, or diminishing, his or her human dignity, or arouses feelings of fear, anguish or inferiority capable of breaking an individual's moral and physical resistance'.[238] In contrast with inhuman treatment, the emphasis is upon humiliation or debasement, rather than physical or mental suffering, although clearly the two overlap. As with other kinds of ill-treatment proscribed by Article 3, the test is a relative one, depending upon all the circumstances of the case.[239] Moreover, the humiliation involved must be more than that which follows inevitably from accepted forms of treatment, such as imprisonment.[240] The public nature of any treatment is relevant to its degrading character, although it may be sufficient that a person is humiliated in his or her own eyes.[241]

It is not essential that there be an intention to humiliate or debase for treatment to be degrading. The presence of such an intention is one of the factors that the Court will take into account, 'but the absence of any such purpose cannot conclusively rule out' a finding of a breach of Article 3.[242] In *Price v UK*,[243] the treatment of a disabled person in prison was degrading despite the absence of any evidence of an intention to humiliate or debase.

The same treatment may be both degrading and inhuman, as in the case of resort to the 'five techniques' of interrogation used in *Ireland v UK*[244] or to physical assault in *Tomasi v France*.[245] In those cases, it was relevant that it is humiliating to oblige a person by force to answer questions (or otherwise act) against his will or to violate his physical integrity. In the *Greek* case,[246] the Commission supposed that 'all torture must be inhuman and degrading treatment, and inhuman treatment also degrading'. However, all degrading treatment or punishment is not necessarily inhuman as well.[247]

I. CONDITIONS OF DETENTION AND THE TREATMENT OF DETAINEES

a. Generally

The conditions of detention or treatment of individuals in a place of detention may amount to inhuman treatment or degrading treatment or both, depending upon the presence of the required suffering or humiliation or both on the part of the detainee. In recent years, the Court has tended to consider Article 3 issues arising out of detention under degrading, rather than inhuman, treatment, although some decisions are still based upon a finding of the latter.[248] For convenience, such issues are considered in this chapter wholly under the heading of degrading treatment.

---

[237] *Kudla v Poland* 2000-XI; 35 EHRR 198 para 92 GC. On degrading treatment or punishment, see Arai-Yokoi, 21 NQHR 385 (2003).   [238] *Pretty v UK* 2002-III; 35 EHRR 1 para 52.

[239] See further Ch 6.   [240] *Kudla v Poland* 2000-XI; 35 EHRR 198 GC.

[241] See *Tyrer v UK* A 26 (1978); 2 EHRR 1 (punishment case).

[242] *V v UK* 1999-IX; 30 EHRR 121 para 71 GC.

[243] 2001-VII; 34 EHRR 1285. Cf *Yankov v Bulgaria* 2003-XII; 40 EHRR 854.

[244] A 25 (1978); 2 EHRR 25 PC.   [245] A 241-A (1992); 15 EHRR 1.

[246] 12 YB (the *Greek* case) 1 at 186 (1969) Com Rep; CM Res DH (70) 1.

[247] *Raninen v Finland* 1997-VIII; 26 EHRR 563.   [248] Cf Ch 6.

b. Conditions of detention and treatment of detainees

Conditions of detention have been found to amount to inhuman or degrading treatment in a variety of contexts. When examining conditions in a place of detention, the Court gives weight to the conclusions of the European Committee for the Prevention of Torture and Inhuman or Degrading Treatment or Punishment (CPT) when the latter has reported on them.[249] When assessing the conditions, the Court takes into account their cumulative effect as well as particular allegations made by the applicant. It also looks to the length of time during which the conditions prevailed.[250] Both of these considerations were relevant in *Kalashnikov v Russia*,[251] in which both the applicant's prison conditions and the cramped conditions in which he was transported from prison to the court were held to infringe Article 3. The applicant had been detained on remand for nearly five years in a detention facility that was recognized by the Russian government as falling short of European standards. He was one of normally at least fourteen prisoners in a cell that had a space per prisoner well below CPT guidelines even for the eight prisoners for whom it was designed. Because of the over-crowding, the applicant shared a bed with sometimes two other prisoners on an eight hour a day shift basis. The 'filthy, dilapidated cell' had one toilet, with no screen to ensure privacy, and inadequate ventilation; it was also infested with pests. The applicant contracted skin diseases and fungal infections while in detention.[252] The Court found that the conditions, 'in particular the severely overcrowded and insanitary environment and its detrimental effect on the applicant's health and well-being', combined with the length of the period of deten-tion, amounted to degrading treatment. The respondent government argued that the condi-tions, which it had taken steps to improve, as the Court acknowledged, were no worse than those of most detainees in Russia and were the result of financial constraints. The Court was not prepared to make any allowance for such considerations, applying the European stand-ard built into Article 3 for all states that have become parties to the Convention, regardless of their economic and other local circumstances.[253] In a series of subsequent cases, the Court has found violations of Article 3 in Russian remand prisons through overcrowding, as in *Kalashnikov.*[254]

Detention conditions have been found to amount to inhuman and/or degrading treat-ment in a large variety of cases from a number of states in the Court's recent jurispru-dence. For example, in *Modarca v Moldova*,[255] there was a breach of Article 3 when the applicant was detained for almost nine months 'in extremely overcrowded conditions with little access to daylight, limited availability of running water, especially during the night and in the presence of heavy smells from the toilet, while being given insufficient quantity and quality of food or bed linen'. Article 3 was also violated when a prisoner with chronic pulmonary disease was detained in a cell with two prisoners who smoked.[256]

---

[249] *Dougoz v Greece* 2001-II; 34 EHRR 1480. But see *Peers v Greece* 2001-III; 33 EHRR 1192. Compliance with the European Prison Rules 2006 is likely to mean compliance with Article 3: see *Ramirez Sanchez v France* 2006-IX; 45 EHRR 1099 para 130 GC.

[250] This may be quite short: twenty-two hours' detention in terrible conditions in a police cell was inhu-man treatment: *Fedotov v Russia* hudoc (2005); 44 EHRR 544. See also *Kaja v Greece* hudoc (2006).

[251] 2002-VI; 36 EHRR 587 paras 101–2.

[252] Several breaches have resulted from applicants contracting tuberculosis in detention: see eg, *Dobri v Romania* hudoc (2010).   [253] Cf *Poltoratskiy v Ukraine* 2003-V; 39 EHRR 916.

[254] See, eg, *Idalov v Russia* hudoc (2012) GC; *Khudoyorov v Russia* 2005-X; 45 EHRR 144; and *Grishin v Russia* hudoc (2007).

[255] Hudoc (2007); 48 EHRR 889 para 68. For other examples, see *Tekin v Turkey* 1998-IV; 31 EHRR 95; *II v Bulgaria* hudoc (2005); *Moisejevs v Latvia* hudoc (2006); *Orchowski v Poland* hudoc (2009); and *Julin v Estonia* hudoc (2012).

[256] *Elefteriadis v Romania* hudoc (2011). Cf *Florea v Romania* hudoc (2010).

There was inhuman and degrading treatment in *Shchebet v Russia*,[257] in which the applicant was kept for thirty-four days in a tiny cell in an airport transit zone that was designed
for detention for no more than three hours. In *Kanagaratnam and Others v Belgium*,[258]
the detention of young children (with their mother) for several months in a detention
camp for illegal immigrants in conditions that must have instilled feelings of anxiety
and inferiority and hindered their development was found to be inhuman and degrading
treatment.

Strip searches of prisoners may amount to degrading treatment. They may be justified on security or public order grounds, but must be conducted in an appropriate manner with due respect for the individual's dignity. In *Iwańczuk v Poland*,[259] a remand
prisoner who sought to cast his vote in a parliamentary election and who posed no
security or other threat was forced to strip to his underclothes before prison guards and
ridiculed by them. When he refused a further order to strip naked and undergo a body
search, he was not allowed to vote. The Court found that there was degrading treatment, the search not being justified or conducted in an appropriate manner.[260] In other
more borderline cases, the Court has had difficult decisions to make when assessing the
justification for strip searching. In *Wieser v Austria*,[261] the Court held, by a majority
of four to three, that the police were not justified in strip searching a handcuffed and
dangerous man for weapons in his home on arrest. Inhuman and degrading treatment
were found in *Van der Ven v Netherlands*[262] because of routine, weekly strip searches
for over three years, for which insufficient justification was provided by the respondent
government, coupled with other aspects of a strict security regime in a high security
remand facility.

In *Yankov v Bulgaria*,[263] the Court stated that the forced shaving off of a prisoner's hair
may 'in principle' be degrading treatment. In that case, the applicant's hair was shaven
off when he was placed in seven days' solitary confinement as a punishment. The Court
held that this was likely to humiliate him, in view of his age, 55 years, and the fact he was
shortly to appear in court. In an even more striking case, in *Hellig v Germany*,[264] it was
held that detaining a prisoner naked for seven days in a security cell was inhuman and
degrading treatment.

In contrast, insistence that a prisoner wear a prison uniform is not degrading treatment.[265] In a different kind of case, in *Price v UK*,[266] the applicant was a four-limb deficient
thalidomide victim who was sent to prison for civil contempt. She was kept overnight in a
police cell in which she was 'dangerously cold' and then moved to a prison for two nights
where she was unable to use the toilet without the assistance of male officers and where
conditions otherwise were unsuitable for a severely disabled individual. This was held to

---

[257] Hudoc (2008). Cf *Riad and Idiab v Belgium* hudoc (2008).

[258] Hudoc (2011); 55 EHRR 800. See also *Mubilanzila Mayeka and Kaniki Mitunga v Belgium* 2006-XI;
46 EHRR 449.

[259] Hudoc (2001); 38 EHRR 148. See also *McFeeley and Others v UK No 8317/78*, 20 DR 44 at 81 (1980) and
the *Greek* case 12 YB (the *Greek* case) 1 at 461, 463 and 465 (1969) Com Rep; CM Res DH (70) 1.

[260] Cf *Valasinas v Lithuania* 2001-VIII. Cf *Wiktorko v Poland* hudoc (2009); 56 EHRR 1018 and *Filiz Uyan
v Turkey* hudoc (2009). See also *Juhnke v Turkey* hudoc (2008); 49 EHRR 534 (consent to gynaecological
examination: no breach). On the strip searching of visitors, see *Wainwright v UK* 2006-X; 44 EHRR 809
(breach of Article 8, not Article 3).   [261] Hudoc (2007); 45 EHRR 1017.

[262] 2003-II; 38 EHRR 967. See also *Frérot v France* hudoc (2007) and *El Shennawy v France* hudoc (2011).

[263] 2003-XII; 40 EHRR 854.   [264] Hudoc (2011).

[265] *McFeeley and Others v UK No 8317/78*, 20 DR 44 at 81 (1980).

[266] 2001-VII; 34 EHRR 1285. For other cases of inadequate provision for disabled persons, see *ZH v
Hungary* hudoc (2012) and *Arutyunyan v Russia* hudoc (2012).

be degrading treatment. Generally, if the state places a disabled person in detention, it must ensure that the place of detention is suitable.[267]

c. Solitary confinement

Solitary confinement, or segregation, of persons in detention[268] is not in itself a breach of Article 3; it is permissible for reasons of security or discipline or to protect the segregated prisoner from other prisoners or *vice versa*.[269] It may also be justified in the interests of the administration of justice, eg to prevent collusion in respect of pending proceedings,[270] or to prevent a prisoner from making external criminal contacts.[271] In each case, 'regard must be had to the particular conditions, the stringency of the measure, its duration, the objective pursued and its effects on the person concerned'.[272] Generally, prolonged solitary confinement is undesirable, especially where the person is detained on remand.[273] As the Court has indicated, 'complete sensory isolation, coupled with total social isolation can destroy the personality and constitutes a form of inhuman treatment which cannot be justified by the requirements of security or any other reason'.[274]

Applying this approach, the Court, and formerly the Commission, has found arrangements for the solitary confinement of prisoners of the kind typically found in European criminal justice systems not to be in breach of Article 3.[275] But in some extreme cases, the Court has found a breach of Article 3, most notably in the *Ilaşcu* case,[276] in which the Court found that the conditions amounted even to torture. There the applicant was detained for eight years 'in very strict isolation' before his conviction and sentence to death for terrorist-related offences was quashed. He 'had no contact with other prisoners, no news from the outside—since he was not permitted to send or receive mail—and no right to contact his lawyer or receive regular visits from his family. His cell was unheated, even in severe winter conditions, and had no natural light source or ventilation'. He was also deprived of food as a punishment. These conditions and a lack of medical care caused his health to deteriorate. Taken together, they amounted to torture in breach of Article 3, a finding in which the stringency and length of the solitary confinement regime were prominent.

---

[267] *Grimailovs v Latvia* hudoc (2013). See also *Zarzycki v Poland* hudoc (2013).

[268] Most of the case law on solitary confinement concerns remand or convicted prisoners. The following section also applies *mutatis mutandis* to other persons in detention, such as mental patients and persons in preventive detention.

[269] *Ilaşcu and Others v Moldova and Russia* 2004-VII; 40 EHRR 1030 para 432 GC.

[270] *Rohde v Denmark* hudoc (2005); 43 EHRR 325.

[271] *Messina v Italy* No 25498/94 1999-V DA.

[272] *Ensslin, Baader and Raspe v Germany* No 7572/76, 14 DR 64 at 109 (1978), cited by the Court in *Ramirez Sanchez v France* 2006-IX; 45 EHRR 1099 para 120 GC.

[273] *Ensslin, Baader and Raspe v Germany*. As to duration, confining a prisoner to her cell for under two hours was not degrading treatment: *Bollan v UK* No 42117/98 hudoc (2000) DA.

[274] *Ilaşcu and Others v Moldova and Russia* 2004-VII; 40 EHRR 1030 para 432 GC. Sensory isolation results from restrictions on access to natural light, sound, etc: *Ensslin, Baader and Raspe v Germany No 7572/76*, 14 DR 64 at 110 (1978).

[275] See *Rohde v Denmark* hudoc (2005); 43 EHRR 325. For UK cases, see eg, *X v UK No 8158/78*, 21 DR 95 (1980) and *X v UK No 8231/78*, 28 DR 5 (1982). See also *Yurttas v Turkey* hudoc (2004).

[276] *Ilaşcu and Others v Moldova and Russia* 2004-VII; 40 EHRR 1030 para 438 GC. For the follow-up case to *Ilaşcu*, see *Ivanţoc and Others v Moldova and Russia* hudoc (2011). For other breaches of Article 3, see *Van der Ven v Netherlands* 2003-II; 38 EHRR 967 (limited contact with others); *Mathew v Netherlands* 2005-IX; 43 EHRR 444 (disruptive remand prisoner); *X v Turkey* hudoc (2012) (solitary confinement of homosexual for eight months to protect him from others); and *Piechowicz v Poland* hudoc (2012) ('dangerous detainee' regime).

In several other extreme cases, involving prolonged segregation but lesser degrees of sensory or social isolation than in *Ilaşcu*, the Court has not found a breach of Article 3. For example, *Ramirez Sanchez v France*[277] concerned the detention of a notorious international terrorist ('Carlos the Jackal') in solitary confinement for eight years following his conviction for terrorist-related offences. Although segregated from other prisoners, he had access to television and newspapers and generally was detained in conditions that complied with the European Prison Rules. Arrangements for visits by his priest, lawyers, and family were satisfactory, and the applicant was in good health. The Court was concerned, however, by the duration of the applicant's solitary confinement. While accepting that dangerous prisoners may, as is common in European prison systems, be segregated to prevent their escape or to preserve order and security within the prison, the Court stated that in cases of prolonged segregation the Court was required, under Article 3, to conduct a 'rigorous examination to determine whether the measures taken were necessary and proportionate compared to the available alternatives, what safeguards were afforded to the applicant and what measures were taken by the authorities to ensure that the applicant's physical and mental condition was compatible with his continued solitary confinement'. In this connection, the state must, following periodic review, give reasons for any decision to continue segregation and ensure regular monitoring of the detainee's physical and mental condition. Judicial review must be available to challenge continued prolonged segregation. The Court's approach was coloured by its awareness of the psychological dangers of prolonged segregation and that solitary confinement, 'even in cases entailing only relative isolation, cannot be imposed on a prisoner indefinitely'.[278] Applying its approach to the facts of the case, the Court held, by twelve votes to five, that Article 3 had not been infringed. In particular, the Court was responsive to the efforts made by the respondent state and the fact that, some months before the Court's judgment, it had ended the applicant's solitary confinement—a position which the Court stated 'should not in principle be changed'.[279]

d. Medical assistance

Article 3 requires that detainees are provided with the 'requisite medical assistance'.[280] This follows from the obligation that Article 3 imposes upon states to 'protect the physical well-being of persons deprived of their liberty'.[281] Where the lack of the 'requisite medical assistance' gives rise to a medical emergency or otherwise exposes the applicant to 'severe or prolonged pain', the breach of Article 3 takes the form of inhuman treatment.[282]

---

[277] 2006-IX; 45 EHRR 1099 GC. See also *Csüllög v Hungary* hudoc (2011). Cf *Öcalan v Turkey* 2005-IV; 41 EHRR 985 GC. For terrorist cases in which the Commission found no breach of Article 3 despite considerable sensory and social isolation, see *Ensslin, Baader and Raspe v Germany* No 7572/76, 14 DR 64 (1978); *McFeeley and Others v UK* No 8317/78, 20 DR 44 (1980) (IRA hunger strikers; 760 days' solitary confinement); and *Kröcher and Möller v Switzerland* No 8463/78, 34 DR 24 (1982) Com Rep; CM Res DH (83) 15. See also *M v UK* No 9907/82, 35 DR 130 (1983) (convicted murderer who killed two prisoners segregated in specially adapted cell for six years: no breach).   [278] *Ramirez Sanchez v France*, para 136, 145 GC.

[279] *Ramirez Sanchez v France*, para 150.

[280] *Kudla v Poland* 2000-XI; 35 EHRR 198 para 94 GC. Cf *Cyprus v Turkey* 2001-IV; 35 EHRR 731 GC. The required standard is adequacy, not the best available to the public outside prison: *Khudobin v Russia* 2006-XII; 48 EHRR 523.

[281] *Khudobin v Russia*, para 93. See also *Yoh-Ekale Mwanje v Belgium* hudoc (2011); 56 EHRR 1140 (HIV positive; no medication).

[282] *McGlinchey and Others v UK* 2003-V; 37 EHRR 821. Cf *Pilčić v Croatia* hudoc (2008) (failure to organize kidney stone operation: inhuman and degrading) and *Popov v Ukraine* hudoc (2006) (no regular check-ups for cancer victim).

Where it does not, a breach of Article 3 may nonetheless be found if the humiliation caused to the applicant by the stress and anxiety that he suffers because of the absence of medical assistance may reach the threshold level of 'degrading' treatment in the sense of Article 3.[283] In *Hummatov v Azerbaijan*,[284] the lack of medical treatment for the applicant's various illnesses, including tuberculosis contracted in prison, was 'degrading' because it caused considerable mental suffering diminishing his human dignity. In *Umar Karatepe v Turkey*,[285] it was 'inhuman and degrading' when a prisoner was refused medical treatment because he could not pay for it.

The obligation to provide medical assistance includes a requirement to have an effective medical care system in place.[286] In some cases, the required regime of assistance has been put in place, but has proved inadequate in particular circumstances.[287] In other cases, little or no regime has been put in place at all. In *Khudobin v Russia*,[288] a remand prisoner had epilepsy and other serious medical conditions that required regular medical care; he was also HIV positive and suffered from a serious mental disorder. Although he was treated in the prison hospital when he became ill, no regular monitoring of his condition or medication to prevent illnesses and emergencies was provided.

Ordinary medical negligence that does not cause the level of suffering or of anxiety or stress generating the necessary humiliation does not involve a breach of Article 3.[289] However, breaches of Article 3 have sometimes been found because of the delay in providing assistance.[290] The failure to act to prevent harm to life or limb in a non-arrest situation but where such prevention is dependent upon action by the state may also be a breach of Article 3.[291]

A number of cases have concerned the provision of psychiatric care. In *Keenan v UK*,[292] a convicted prisoner committed suicide the day after he was awarded seven days' solitary confinement and twenty-eight additional days of imprisonment as a disciplinary punishment just nine days before his expected release. The Court found that the imposition of this punishment in circumstances in which the prisoner, who was a known suicide risk, had not been adequately monitored or, as the Court emphasized, given the requisite psychiatric care, was inhuman and degrading treatment and punishment.

In *Dybeku v Albania*,[293] the Court held that certain categories of prisoners require a place of detention that offer conditions of detention and treatment suited to their particular medical and other needs, rather than a place that is aimed at 'ordinary' prisoners. It identified the mentally disabled; persons with a serious physical illness;[294] the physically disabled;[295] the elderly;[296] and drug addicts suffering from withdrawal symptoms[297] as

---

[283] *Khudobin v Russia* 2006-XII; 48 EHRR 523; *Paladi v Moldova* hudoc (2009); 47 EHRR 380; and *Xiros v Greece* hudoc (2010).   [284] Hudoc (2007); 49 EHRR 960. Cf *Grori v Albania* hudoc (2009).

[285] Hudoc (2010).

[286] *Gülay Çetin v Turkey* hudoc (2013). See also *McFeeley and Others v UK* No 8317/78, 20 DR 44 (1980).

[287] *McGlinchey and Others v UK* 2003-V; 37 EHRR 821. See also *Melnik v Ukraine* hudoc (2006) (failure to diagnose and adequately treat tuberculosis).

[288] 2006-XII; 48 EHRR 523. See also *Gorodnichev v Russia* hudoc (2007); *Boicenco v Moldova* hudoc (2006); and *Paladi v Moldova* hudoc 2009.

[289] See eg, *Filip v Romania* hudoc (2006).

[290] *Hurtado v Switzerland* A 280-A (1994) Com Rep (F Sett before Court).

[291] *Denis Vasilyev v Russia* hudoc (2009) (police delay in obtaining assistance for injured man).

[292] 2001-III; 33 EHRR 913. See also *Kudla v Poland* 2000-XI; 35 EHRR 198 GC; *Rivière v France* hudoc (2006); and *Petrea v Romania* hudoc (2008).   [293] Hudoc (2007).

[294] Eg, *Mouisel v France* 2002-IX; 38 EHRR 735.

[295] Eg, *Price v UK* 2001-VII; 34 EHRR 1285, discussed earlier, and *Flamînzeanu v Romania* hudoc (2011).

[296] Eg, *Papon v France (No 1)* No 64666/01 2001-VI DA.

[297] Eg, *McGlinchey and Others v UK* 2003-V; 37 EHRR 821.

falling within these categories. In the *Dybeku* case, the Court held that the regime in the general prison in which the applicant was detained was 'entirely inappropriate' for a person with mental health problems.[298] In *Grimailovs v Latvia*,[299] there was a breach of Article 3 when prison buildings were not adapted to meet the needs of a disabled prisoner confined to a wheelchair.

The fact that imprisonment is not in the best interests of a prisoner's health is not of itself sufficient to require his or her release to avoid liability under Article 3, since imprisonment following, for example, conviction or on remand is obviously permissible.[300] In most cases, while sometimes calling for humanitarian measures,[301] the Court has found that adequate medical assistance has been available in prison[302] or made available by way of visits from prison to outside hospitals for treatment.[303] As stated in *Wedler v Poland*,[304] however, should a prisoner's state of health become such that adequate medical or nursing assistance cannot be provided in detention, Article 3 requires that a prisoner be released, subject to conditions that the state reasonably imposes in the public interest.[305] The detention over a lengthy period of an elderly person with serious problems of health or infirmity may be in breach of Article 3, although cases in which this has been raised as an issue have generally been unsuccessful on their facts.[306]

When determining compliance with Article 3, account may be taken of the applicant's refusal of prison treatment[307] or to permit a medical examination,[308] but treatment may not be refused because of the prisoner's ill-conduct.[309]

e. Compulsory medical intervention

There is no obligation under Article 3 to provide medical assistance to a person in detention against that person's will. At the same time, the giving of such assistance, by force if necessary, will in principle not be in breach of Article 3 where it is 'of therapeutic necessity from the point of view of established principles of medicine' in the interests of the person's physical or mental health.[310] In such cases, the medical necessity must be 'convincingly shown' and appropriate procedural guarantees must apply. In addition, the manner in which the assistance is given must not exceed the minimum level of suffering or humiliation in order to avoid a breach of Article 3. In *Herczegfalvy v Austria*,[311] the Court held that the forcible administration of food and drugs to a violent, mentally ill patient on hunger strike, which was in accordance with established principles of medicine, was not in

---

[298] Cf *Aerts v Belgium* 1998-V; 29 EHRR 50; *Slawomir Musial v Poland* hudoc (2009); and *Claes v Belgium* hudoc (2013). [299] Hudoc (2013).

[300] See Article 5(1)(a) and (c).

[301] *Chartier v Italy No 9044/80*, 33 DR 41(1982) Com Rep; CM Res DH 83 (12).

[302] See *Chartier v Italy*. Cf *Bonnechaux v Switzerland No 8224/78*, 18 DR 100 (1979) Com Rep; CM Res DH 83 (12) and *Kudla v Poland* 2000-XI; 35 EHRR 198 GC. Claims that prisoners with AIDS should be released have been rejected in several cases: see eg, *Gelfmann v France* hudoc (2004); 42 EHRR 81.

[303] See *Henaf v France* 2003-XI; 40 EHRR 990. See also *Tarariyeva v Russia* 2006-XV (taken to hospital in unsuitable van: inhuman treatment). [304] Hudoc (2007).

[305] *Mouisel v France* 2002-IX; 38 EHRR 735. See also *Tekin Yildiz v Turkey* hudoc (2005) (neurological syndrome: unfit for prison) and *Khudobin v Russia* 2006-XII; 48 EHRR 523.

[306] *Papon v France (No 1) No 64666/01* 2001-VI DA and *Farbtuhs v Latvia* hudoc (2004) (imprisonment of a 90-year-old with a heart problem not inhuman: medical treatment available and his general health good). See also *Sawoniuk v UK No 63716/00* 2001-VI DA.

[307] *De Varga-Hirsch v France No 9559/81*, 33 DR 158 (1983).

[308] *R, S, A and C v Portugal Nos 9911/82 and 9945/82*, 36 DR 200 (1984).

[309] *Iorgov v Bulgaria* hudoc (2004); 40 EHRR 145.

[310] *Jalloh v Germany* 2006-IX; 44 EHRR 667 para 69 GC.

[311] A 244 (1992); 15 EHRR 437 para 82. Cf *MB and GB v UK No 35724/97* hudoc (2001) DA. But see *Henaf v France* 2003-XI; 40 EHRR 990. See also *B v UK No 6870/75*, 32 DR 5 (1981)

breach of Article 3. In contrast, in *Nevmerzhitsky v Ukraine*,[312] there was a breach of Article 3 where the applicant was subjected to forced feeding while on hunger strike. The Court found that the medical necessity to force feed the applicant in order to save his life had not been shown and that the applicable procedural safeguards had not been complied with. Beyond this, and most strikingly, the Court found that the manner of forced feeding—involving handcuffs, a mouth widener, and a special rubber tube inserted forcibly—gave rise to suffering at the level of torture, not just inhuman treatment.

The use of a medical procedure against a suspect's will to obtain evidence of a crime is not in breach of Article 3 if certain conditions or safeguards similar to those applicable to forced feeding are satisfied. In *Jalloh v Germany*,[313] an emetic was forcibly administered to the applicant, causing him to regurgitate a drug bubble which was then used as the main evidence against him in proceedings leading to his conviction and sentence to six months' imprisonment for a minor drug dealing offence. As to whether the medical intervention was necessary, the Court recognized the public interest in controlling drug trafficking, but noted that the applicant was not a major drug dealer and that anyway the police could have waited for nature to take its course, as was the approach in many other European states. The procedure also posed a health risk and the emetic was administered forcibly by a tube which must have caused pain and anxiety. The Court held, by ten votes to seven, that the applicant had been subjected to inhuman and degrading treatment contrary to Article 3. In *Bogumil v Portugal*,[314] the applicant underwent surgery to recover a packet of cocaine that he was smuggling. The case differed from the *Jalloh* case in that it was not clear whether he had or had not consented and because the operation was to avoid risk to the applicant's life, not to obtain evidence. The Court held that in these circumstances, the operation could be justified, regardless of consent, on grounds of medical necessity.

A requirement that an accused person submit to a psychiatric examination in connection with the investigation of his case is not degrading.[315]

f. Handcuffing and other restraints

The handcuffing of a prisoner is not degrading contrary to Article 3 provided that it is reasonably necessary in the circumstances.[316] Relevant considerations are the danger of escape or violence or the suppression of evidence, the degree of force used to effect the handcuffing, and the extent of any exposure to the public.[317] In *Erdoğan Yağiz v Turkey*,[318] the applicant, a doctor, was subjected to treatment that, in the absence of a good public interest reason, was degrading when he was placed in handcuffs on arrest in a public car parking area at his place of work and later taken in the course of investigation to his place of work and home in handcuffs, all in the sight of his work colleagues, family, and neighbours. It is degrading contrary to Article 3 for an accused to be kept in handcuffs[319] or in a cage[320] at public hearings in

---

[312] 2005-II; 43 EHRR 645. Cf *Ciorap v Moldova* hudoc (2007); *Horoz v Turkey* hudoc (2009); and *Rappaz v Switzerland No 73175/10* hudoc (2013) DA.

[313] 2006-IX; 44 EHRR 667 para 76 GC. The Court noted that the taking of compulsory blood and saliva samples had been held not to violate Article 3: *X v Netherlands No 8239/78*, 16 DR 187 (1978) and *Schmidt v Germany No 32352/02* hudoc (2006) DA.   [314] Hudoc (2008).

[315] *X v Germany No 8334/78*, 24 DR 103 (1981). Cf *Skawińska v Poland No 42096/98* hudoc (2001) DA.

[316] *Raninen v Finland* 1997-VIII; 26 EHRR 563 and *Öcalan v Turkey* 2005-IV; 41 EHRR 985 GC. In *Portmann v Switzerland* hudoc (2011), the handcuffing, hooding, and leg shackling for two hours of an especially dangerous suspect during arrest and in transit was not a breach of Article 3. On the transport of prisoners generally, see *Khudoyorov v Russia* 2005-X; 45 EHRR 144.   [317] *Raninen v Finland*.

[318] Hudoc (2007).   [319] *Gorodnitchev v Russia* hudoc (2007).

[320] *Sarban v Moldova* hudoc (2005); *Khodorkovskiy v Russia* hudoc (2011); 53 EHRR 1103; and *Svinarenko and Slyadnev v Russia* hudoc (2012), referred to Grand Chamber.

court when there is no good security or other public interest reason to justify it. The routine handcuffing of a convicted prisoner over many years every time he left his cell was degrading,[321] as was the handcuffing of a prisoner seriously ill with cancer while being taken to hospital outside of prison.[322] In *Henaf v France*,[323] the shackling to his bed overnight of a seventy-five-year-old prisoner who had been taken to hospital for an operation, which made sleeping difficult, was inhuman treatment in breach of Article 3. In contrast, 'although worrying', the handcuffing and strapping of the applicant by his ankles for two weeks because of the 'danger of aggression and the death threats' that he was making did not lead to a breach of Article 3 in *Herczegfalvy v Austria*.[324]

II. DISCRIMINATION

Discrimination may constitute degrading treatment under Article 3.[325] Such an interpretation is consistent with the probability that the drafters of the Convention had anti-Semitism in mind when prohibiting degrading treatment. Racial discrimination was found to be degrading treatment contrary to Article 3 in the *East African Asians* cases.[326] In those cases, in order to control immigration from Kenya and Uganda, legislation was enacted at Westminster terminating the right of entry of UK citizens lacking ancestral or 'place of birth' connections with the United Kingdom. The Commission considered in its opinion on the merits that this legislation was racially discriminatory and that the applicants' subjection to it, with the attendant publicity and in the special circumstances of their cases, was an affront to their dignity to the point of being 'degrading treatment' in breach of Article 3.[327] Further to its opinion in the *East African Asians* cases, in *Abdulaziz, Cabales and Balkandali v UK*,[328] the Commission stated that by virtue of Article 3 'the state's discretion in immigration matters is not of an unfettered character, for a state may not implement policies of a purely racist nature, such as a policy prohibiting the entry of any person of a particular skin colour'. Confirming the Commission's approach, in *Cyprus v Turkey*,[329] the Court found that there was discrimination by the government of the Turkish Republic of Northern Cyprus (TRNC)[330] against the Karpas Greek Cypriot minority living in northern Cyprus that amounted to degrading treatment in breach of Article 3. This discrimination was motivated by the different 'ethnic origin, race and religion' of the Greek Cypriot minority and was a consequence of the 'bi-zonal' policy of the TRNC government and would inevitably result in the community dying out. In particular, the members of the minority were not allowed to bequeath immovable property to relatives who did not live in the North; there were no secondary school facilities in the North; and Greek Cypriot children who went to school in the South were not allowed to reside in the North later as adults. There were also further freedom of movement and other limitations upon the Greek Cypriot minority that significantly restricted its members' rights to privacy and family life and to practise their religion. The result was

---

[321] *Kashavelov v Bulgaria* hudoc (2011). [322] *Mouisel v France* 2002-IX; 38 EHRR 735.
[323] 2003-XI; 40 EHRR 990. See also *Tarariyeva v Russia* 2006-XV and *Kucheruk v Ukraine* hudoc (2007); 52 EHRR 878. [324] A 244 (1992); 15 EHRR 437.
[325] *Cyprus v Turkey* 2001-IV; 35 EHRR 731 para 305 GC.
[326] 3 EHRR 76 (1973) Com Rep; CM Res DH (77) 2.
[327] The Committee of Ministers did not rule on the question of a breach. After much delay and all of the applicants had been admitted to the UK, it decided that no further action was called for: CM Res DH (77) 2.
[328] A 94 (1985); 7 EHRR 471 para 113. [329] 2001-IV; 35 EHRR 731 paras 307–11 GC.
[330] Turkey was responsible for the TRNC's acts: *Cyprus v Turkey*, para 77.

that the 'conditions under which that population is condemned to live are debasing and violate the very notion of respect for the human dignity of its members'.

Racial discrimination also contributed to the finding by the Court of a breach of Article 3 in *Moldovan and Others v Romania (No 2)*.[331] That case arose out of the death of a non-Roma villager after a fight with three Roma. In reprisal, a non-Roma crowd, including two police officers, destroyed the applicants' homes, following which destruction they were forced to live in appalling living conditions in cellars, hen houses, and stables, etc. This, together with the generally hostile attitude of the judicial and executive authorities when considering the applicants' claims, generated mental suffering and degradation to the level of a breach of Article 3. An 'aggravating factor' were the gratuitous remarks made by the courts and the mayor about the applicants' 'honesty and way of life', which, in the absence of any substantiation, were 'purely discriminatory'.

It can be supposed that other individual cases of racial discrimination may raise issues under Article 3.[332] If Article 3 did not apply to such cases of racial discrimination they would not be in breach of any part of the Convention unless Article 14 or Protocol 12 of the Convention could be invoked.[333] In the case of discrimination by private persons (eg employers, landlords), state responsibility under Article 3 would be based upon a positive obligation upon the state to ensure that private individuals do not lawfully infringe other individuals' rights.

A further question is whether discrimination on grounds other than race is subject to Article 3. It is likely that discrimination on any of the grounds that are recognized as having special protection under Article 14 may be degrading contrary to Article 3. In *Smith and Grady v UK*,[334] the Court did 'not exclude' the possibility that discrimination against homosexuals 'could, in principle, fall within the scope of Article 3'.

III. OTHER KINDS OF DEGRADING TREATMENT

Claims of degrading treatment have been considered in diverse other contexts. In *MSS v Belgium and Greece*,[335] Greece was held in breach of Article 3 for its failure to provide for the basic needs of an asylum seeker during the long period that his claim was under consideration. In the Court's words, 'the Greek authorities have not had due regard to the applicant's vulnerability as an asylum seeker and must be held responsible, because of their inaction, for the situation in which he has found himself for several months, living in the street, with no resources or access to sanitary facilities, and without any means of providing for his essential needs'. In similar vein, a wholly insufficient amount of pension and other social benefits might amount to inhuman and degrading treatment.[336]

In other cases, the mutilation of a son's body was degrading for a near relative,[337] and allegations of the smearing of the lips of Kurdish villagers with human excrement by

---

[331] 2005-VII; 44 EHRR 302 para 111.

[332] *Hilton v UK No 5613/72*, 4 DR 177 (1976) (alleged racial abuse in prison but no breach on the facts: 3 EHRR 104 Com Rep; CM Res DH (79) 3). See also *Glimmerveen and Hagenbeek v Netherlands Nos 8348/78 and 8406/78*, 18 DR 187 at 195 (1979) and *X v Switzerland No 9012/80*, 24 DR 205 (1980).

[333] Article 3 may apply in discrimination cases whether or not Article 14 applies: *Cyprus v Turkey* 2001-IV; 35 EHRR 731 GC.   [334] 1999-VI; 29 EHRR 493 para 121. No violation on the facts.

[335] 2011-; 53 EHRR 28 para 263 GC. Cf *Rahimi v Greece* hudoc (2011). See also *Sufi and Elmi v UK* hudoc (2011); 54 EHRR 209 para 292 ('dire humanitarian conditions' in refugee or IDP camps).

[336] *Larioshina v Russia No 56869/00* hudoc (2002) DA, *Budina v Russia No 45603/05* hudoc (2009) DA and *Pancenko v Latvia No 40772/98* hudoc (1999) DA. On the application of Article 3 to socio-economic conditions generally, see Cassese, 2 EJIL 141 (1991).

[337] *Akkum and Others v Turkey* 2005-II; 43 EHRR 526 (return of son's body with ears cut off). Cf *Akpinar and Altun v Turkey* hudoc (2007).

Turkish security forces were admitted for consideration on the merits under Article 3.[338] The conditions in which the bodies of terrorists were kept following their deaths was not inhuman treatment of their relatives in the circumstances.[339] Ill-treatment of a Jehovah's Witness while in prison for refusal to perform military service was inhuman and degrading treatment,[340] as was the harassment of a young woman to force her to have an abortion.[341] Constant surveillance by the police could also, exceptionally, be degrading.[342] Requiring a seventy-one-year-old man to do military service, subjecting him to training designed for much younger persons, was degrading treatment.[343] Other instances of degrading treatment include keeping witnesses to a killing at a police station overnight without food or drink;[344] requiring a remand prisoner to wear a balaclava for a year pending trial;[345] failure to provide a prisoner with dentures;[346] and repeated transfers from one prison to another without good security reason.[347]

As with claims of inhuman treatment, claims concerning private or family life that involve allegations of degrading treatment are more likely to succeed under Article 8. For example, the omission by a state to provide adequate criminal sanctions in the case of a sexual assault by a private person was not considered under Article 3 in respect of the humiliation suffered by the victim because liability had been established under Article 8.[348] Similarly, in *López Ostra v Spain*,[349] the noise and smells from a waste treatment plant near the applicant's family home infringed Article 8, but did not give rise to degrading treatment. However, in *RR v Poland*,[350] there was a violation of both Articles 3 and 8 when the applicant was unable to obtain access to genetic testing through the procrastination of the health officials for six weeks after she was alerted to the possibility that her baby might have a foetal abnormality, with the result that it was too late for her legally to have an abortion when the abnormality was confirmed. As far as Article 3 was concerned, the applicant had been humiliated in breach of Article 3. There was also 'degrading treatment' when an unaccompanied sixteen-year-old girl in police custody was given a gynaecological examination without her consent.[351]

6. DEGRADING PUNISHMENT

'Degrading' has the same meaning that it has in connection with degrading treatment. In *Tyrer v UK*,[352] the Court held that a judicial sentence of three strokes of the birch imposed by an Isle of Man juvenile court on a fifteen-year-old boy for assault and executed by a police constable at a police station in private was a degrading punishment contrary to

---

[338] *Gürdogan and Others v Turkey Nos 15202–5/89*, 76 A DR 9 (1989) F Sett.

[339] *Sabanchiyeva and Others v Russia* 2013-.

[340] *Feti Demirtaş v Turkey* hudoc (2012) (forced to wear military uniform, handcuffed to a bed, beaten up).

[341] *P and S v Poland* hudoc (2012).

[342] See *Adali v Turkey* hudoc (2005). See also *D'Haese, Le Compte and Others v Belgium No 8930/80*, 6 EHRR CD 114 (1984). [343] *Taştan v Turkey* hudoc (2008).

[344] *Soare and Others v Romania* hudoc (2011). [345] *Petyo Petkov v Bulgaria* hudoc (2010).

[346] *VD v Romania* hudoc (2010). Cf *Slyusarev v Russia* hudoc (2010) (taking away spectacles).

[347] *Khider v France* hudoc (2009) (transferred fourteen times in seven years).

[348] *X and Y v Netherlands* A 91 (1985); 8 EHRR 235. See also *Hendriks v Netherlands No 8427/78*, 29 DR 5 (1982) Com Rep; CM Res DH (82) 4.

[349] A 303-C (1994); 20 EHRR 277. Claim under Article 8 succeeded.

[350] 2011-; 53 EHRR 1047. [351] *Yazgül Yilmaz v Turkey* hudoc (2011).

[352] A 26 (1978); 2 EHRR 1 para 30. See Zellick, 27 ICLQ 665 (1978). On corporal punishment under Article 3 generally, see Phillips, 43 ICLQ 153 (1994).

Article 3. As to the private character of the birching, the Court stated that whereas publicity 'may be a relevant factor' in assessing whether a punishment is degrading, it did not consider that 'the absence of publicity will necessarily prevent a given punishment from falling into that category: it may well suffice that the victim is humiliated in his own eyes, even if not in the eyes of others'.[353] Also relevant was the three-week delay in administering the punishment pending an appeal and the fact that the birching was effected by a stranger. Finally, the 'indignity of having the punishment administered over the bare posterior aggravated to some extent the degrading character of the applicant's punishment', although 'it was not the only or determining factor'.[354]

What was crucial in deciding the case were considerations concerning the 'nature and context' of judicial corporal punishment generally. The Court emphasized that such punishment was 'institutionalised violence' imposed by one individual upon another in the name of the state, the individual being 'treated as an object in the power of the authorities'; it was 'an assault on precisely that which it is one of the main purposes of Article 3 to protect, namely a person's dignity and physical integrity'.[355] Moreover, it was irrelevant that Manx public opinion favoured the birch on grounds of deterrence; a punishment did not cease to be degrading because it was or was believed to be effective, and Manx public opinion was in any event out of step with 'commonly accepted standards in the penal policy' in Council of Europe states.[356] Adopting its 'dynamic' approach to the interpretation of the Convention, by which the Convention is to be interpreted in 'the light of present day conditions',[357] the Court considered that such standards were to be taken into account.

Although the *Tyrer* case did not in terms declare judicial corporal punishment to be degrading *per se*, it is unlikely, given present day European penal policy, to pass muster, however administered. The case also makes the point that the Convention contains a distinction between acceptable and unacceptable *kinds*, as well as *degrees*, of degradation. In the case of imprisonment, which is obviously not in itself in breach of Article 3, the fact of incarceration and the conditions that necessarily go with it mean that the level of humiliation must be at least as high as that which accompanies the use of the birch on a single occasion in circumstances such as those in the *Tyrer* case.

There have also been several cases concerning disciplinary corporal punishment in schools.[358] In *Costello-Roberts v UK*,[359] the Court held, by five votes to four, that a disciplinary measure at a private boarding school by which a seven-year-old boy was given three 'whacks' on the bottom with a gym shoe over his trousers by the headmaster with no one else present was not a degrading punishment. The Court distinguished the *Tyrer* case by reference to the fact that the applicant in the *Costello-Roberts* case was much younger; the punishment was not administered to the boy's bare bottom; and the delay in executing it (three days) was much shorter.[360] The Court also distinguished between the official state violence involved in the execution in a police station of a judicial sentence

---

[353] *Tyrer v UK* A 26 (1978); 2 EHRR 1 para 32.   [354] *Tyrer v UK*, para 35.

[355] *Tyrer v UK*, para 33. The Court added, somewhat inconclusively, that it could not 'be excluded that the punishment may have had adverse psychological effects': *Tyrer v UK*.   [356] *Tyrer v UK*, para 31.

[357] *Tyrer v UK*.

[358] As to other, non-corporal forms of school disciplinary punishment, see *Valsamis v Greece* 1996-VI; 24 EHRR 294 (one day's suspension: not degrading).   [359] A 247-C (1993); 19 EHRR 112.

[360] The Court noted further that in the *Tyrer* case the applicant was 'held by two policemen whilst a third administered the punishment, pieces of the birch breaking at the first stroke': *Costello-Roberts v UK*, para 31.

and the informal administration of a private school disciplinary code. The four dissenting judges[361] gave the following reasons for disagreeing: 'After a three-day gap, the headmaster of the school "whacked" a lonely and insecure seven-year-old boy. A spanking on the spur of the moment might have been permissible, but, in our view, the official and formalized nature of the punishment meted out, without the adequate consent of the mother, was degrading.' In the one other case on school corporal punishment that has reached the Court,[362] it was held in *Campbell and Cosans v UK*[363] that the *threat* of corporal punishment (resulting from its availability in a state school) did not cause sufficient suffering or degradation to be 'inhuman' or 'degrading' *treatment.*

Generally, the conclusion to be drawn from the jurisprudence of the Court and the Commission is that the imposition of disciplinary corporal punishment in state or private schools is suspect from the standpoint of Article 3, particularly where physical harm is inflicted or where the manner of its administration is humiliating. Bearing in mind that the problem would appear to be uniquely British, it should be noted that UK disciplinary corporal punishment cases should cease following legislative changes.[364]

Disciplinary corporal punishment by parents is also subject to Article 3. In *A v UK*,[365] it was held that English law failed to provide adequate protection for children against such punishment. In that case, a step-father had caned his 'difficult' nine-year-old step-son several times, causing bruising and suffering contrary to Article 3. He was prosecuted for assault occasioning actual bodily harm, but acquitted by a jury by a majority verdict. As the Strasbourg Court noted, under English law the step-father had a defence of lawful punishment, ie punishment that was moderate and reasonable in the circumstances, and the burden of proof was upon the prosecution to show beyond reasonable doubt that the assault had exceeded this limit. The Court held that, although the state had prosecuted the step-father, there was a breach of Article 3 because the law did not provide adequate protection, as the respondent government acknowledged in argument. It remains to be seen whether Article 3 will be interpreted as requiring the prohibition of all parental corporal punishment or as permitting some use of force within *stricter* limits than those that existed on the facts of *A v UK*. It is submitted that the best approach would be one similar to that in *Costello-Roberts*, by which a law that permitted a modest and proportionate use of force—unlike that used in the *A* case—would not be in breach of Article 3, particularly when a significant number of European states do not totally prohibit parental corporal punishment.[366] Presumably, disciplinary corporal punishment by child-minders is subject to the same rule as that applicable to parents, although there have been no cases as yet.[367]

---

[361] Judges Ryssdal, Vilhjálmsson, Matscher, and Wildhaber. As to 'adequate consent', in *Costello-Roberts* the school prospectus stated that a high standard of discipline was maintained, but did not mention corporal punishment.

[362] For Commission cases, see *Warwick v UK No 9471/81*, 60 DR 5 (1986) Com Rep; CM Res DH (89) 5 and *Y v UK* A 247-A (1992); 17 EHRR 238 Com Rep. F Sett. Violations found in both.

[363] A 48 (1982); 4 EHRR 293. There was a breach of Article 2, First Protocol.

[364] Corporal punishment is now prohibited in the United Kingdom in both state and independent schools: see the School Standards and Framework Act 1998, s 131.

[365] 1998-VI; 27 EHRR 611. See Ghandi and James, 3 IJHL 97 (1999).

[366] In 2013, 23 Convention parties had totally prohibited it: http://www.endcorporalpunishment.org/pages/pdfs/charts/Chart-Europe-CentralAsia.pdf.

[367] In *Tonchev v Bulgaria* hudoc (2009), a child was subjected to insufficient suffering to bring Article 3 into play when he was hit by an object thrown at him by a neighbour in retaliation for his mischievous conduct.

7. THE OBLIGATION TO PROTECT INDIVIDUALS FROM PROSCRIBED ILL-TREATMENT

In addition to the negative obligation not to subject an individual to torture or inhuman or degrading treatment or punishment, Article 3 contains a positive obligation to take appropriate steps to protect individuals from such ill-treatment or punishment. This implied obligation echoes that which the Court has read into Article 2 on the right to life. The obligation has both a preventative and an investigative dimension.

I. THE OBLIGATION TO PREVENT PROSCRIBED ILL-TREATMENT

A state must have a 'framework of law' of a preventative kind that provides 'adequate protection' against ill-treatment by state agents or private persons.[368] In the corporal punishment case of *A v UK*,[369] the Court ruled that the Article 1 obligation to 'secure' the rights in the Convention requires that states 'take measures designed to ensure that individuals within their jurisdiction are not subjected to' treatment proscribed by Article 3, 'including such treatment administered by private individuals'. 'Children and other vulnerable individuals', the Court said, 'are entitled to protection, in the form of effective deterrence, against such serious breaches of personal integrity'. Applying this approach, the Court held that the United Kingdom had infringed Article 3 because its law did not adequately protect a child against the infliction by a parent of suffering that reached the threshold of Article 3. The same obligation of protection applies to other private acts that result in suffering at the level required by Article 3, as in the case of some acts of racial discrimination.

An important development has been the extension of the obligation of protection to domestic violence.[370] In *Opuz v Turkey*[371] there was a violation of Article 3 when the state authorities had failed to take reasonable protective measures to prevent further serious physical violence by a husband against his wife. The fact that the law did not allow the authorities to prosecute the husband when the wife had withdrawn her complaint, the small fine imposed in earlier proceedings, and the lack of state action in providing shelter or other kinds of protection for the wife suggested a 'degree of tolerance' that fell short of the protection required by Article 3. In *Valiulienė v Lithuania*,[372] there was a breach of Article 3 when the prosecution of the applicant's husband for acts of physical violence causing suffering, including psychological suffering, at the level required by Article 3, had become statute barred as a result of the inefficiency of the state authorities. Given that one purpose of the prosecution was to deter the husband from further acts of violence, inadequate protection had been afforded to the applicant. Some cases involving domestic violence are expressed more in terms of the positive obligation to investigate and punish past violent acts, rather than the prevention of future violence,[373] though the two obligations overlap.

---

[368] *Mahmut Kaya v Turkey* 2000-III para 115 and *MC v Bulgaria* 2003-XII; 40 EHRR 459. See also *P and S v Poland* hudoc (2012).   [369] 1998-VI; 27 EHRR 611 para 22.

[370] Some cases of domestic violence are decided under Article 8 where the suffering does not reach the level required by Article 3.

[371] 2009-; 50 EHRR 695. Cf *B v Moldova* hudoc (2013). See also the breach of the same obligation in Article 2 in the *Opuz* case.

[372] Hudoc (2013).

[373] See, eg, *Eremia v Moldova* hudoc (2013) (suspension of prosecution on condition of non-repetition).

The obligation to prevent ill-treatment by private persons was infringed in *97 Members of the Gldani Congregation of Jehovah's Witnesses and 4 Others v Georgia*,[374] when the police failed to act when Jehovah's Witnesses attending a religious meeting were physically attacked by members of the Orthodox Church. In *PF and EF v UK*,[375] a seven-year-old schoolgirl and her mother were subject to sectarian abuse and intimidation that reached the threshold level for Article 3 as they walked daily to school. However, the Court held that action taken by the police to interpose police officers between the protesters and the applicants were sufficient to meet the state's positive obligation to protect the applicants. But there was a breach of Article 3 in *Milanović v Serbia*,[376] when the authorities did not take 'reasonable and effective steps' (such as video or other surveillance) when it was obvious that members of a religious minority were being systematically attacked.

In a different context, in *Z and Others v UK*,[377] the Court found a breach of Article 3 because there was a failure within the state's social services system to take reasonable steps to provide the applicant children with protection from 'serious, long-term neglect and abuse' by their parents of which the services had or ought to have known. There was also a breach of the duty of protection in *Mubilanzila Mayeka and Kaniki Mitunga v Belgium*,[378] when, in the absence of any other more suitable accommodation, an unaccompanied five-year-old girl was kept by the state for two months in a detention centre for *adult* illegal immigrants, with no one being assigned to her to provide counselling or educational assistance.

In *Pretty v UK*,[379] it was held that a state is not under an obligation under Article 3 to provide in its law or practice for a spouse of an individual in the final stages of an incurable illness to assist in the individual's suicide in order to avoid a distressing death. Although a state may be liable for acts or omissions on its part that exacerbate suffering or humiliation caused by a naturally occurring illness,[380] it has no obligation to protect an individual from a distressing death, involving suffering or humiliation, by authorizing or facilitating suicide in such a case: such an interpretation of Article 3 would require a state to sanction actions intended to end life, which would be inconsistent with the values underlying the right to life in Article 2.

Finally, in terms of protection, Article 3 does not require state A to provide a civil remedy for torture that has occurred in state B where state A has no causal connection, through its agents or otherwise, with the act in question.[381]

II. THE OBLIGATION TO INVESTIGATE AND TO ENFORCE THE LAW

Article 3 also imposes a procedural obligation to conduct a 'thorough and effective investigation' where an individual raises an 'arguable claim' of ill-treatment in breach

---

[374] Hudoc (2007); 46 EHRR 613. The obligation to investigate was also infringed. See also *Mahmut Kaya v Turkey* 2000-III (failure to protect from security forces) and *JL v Latvia* hudoc (2012) (attacks by other prisoners).

[375] *No 28326/09* hudoc (2010) DA.   [376] Hudoc (2010) para 90.

[377] 2001-V; 34 EHRR 97 para 74 GC. See also *E and Others v UK* hudoc (2002) (failure to protect children from sexual abuse) and *Okkali v Turkey* 2006-XII (failure to assign lawyer to child accused). And see *DP and JC v UK* hudoc (2002).

[378] 2006-XI; 46 EHRR 449. The Court also seemed to see the case as involving a breach of the negative obligation prohibiting inhuman treatment. See also *Popov v France* hudoc (2012) and *Kanagaratnam and Others v Belgium* Hudoc (2011); 55 EHRR 800, discussed earlier.

[379] 2002-III; 35 EHRR 1 para 52.   [380] Eg, deportation or failure to provide medical care.

[381] *Al-Adsani v UK* 2001-XI; 34 EHRR 273 GC.

of Article 3.[382] After at one point adopting a more limited approach,[383] the Court has now established that this obligation has the same scope and meaning as the procedural obligation in Article 2. The Article 3 obligation was first identified in *Assenov and Others v Bulgaria*,[384] in which a Chamber of the Court expressly derived it from the Article 2 obligation and justified it on the basis that it was necessary to make the substantive obligation in Article 3 effective, by preventing the abuse of power by state agents with impunity.[385]

As in the case of Article 2, the procedural obligation in Article 3 to investigate extends to allegations of ill-treatment by private persons as well as state officials. Thus in *MC v Bulgaria*,[386] there was a breach of Article 3 when the authorities did not investigate all of the circumstances of the case in a prosecution for rape before deciding not to prosecute. The case was one of 'date rape', in which the authorities focused unduly on the lack of physical resistance, not checking other evidence indicating lack of consent. The Court had considerable evidence before it indicating that European states generally now made lack of consent, not lack of physical resistance, the constituent element of the crime of rape. Since it was not clear whether Bulgarian law followed this approach or not, the Court did not find a breach of Article 3 on the preventative basis that the proper framework of law had not been put in place. Instead, it did so on the basis that in any event the investigation had not focused on lack of consent, whether shown by resistance or in other ways, as European standards required.[387] *Macovei and Others v Romania*[388] was another case of ill-treatment by private persons. There the applicants were seriously injured following an altercation with neighbours. The Court held that there was a breach of Article 3 when there was no possibility of appealing against the prosecutor's decision not to bring criminal proceedings.

The procedural obligation in Article 3 requires a 'thorough and effective official investigation' 'capable of leading to the identification and punishment of those responsible'.[389] Such an investigation must be launched *ex officio*, in the absence of a complaint, if there are sufficiently clear indications that torture or other ill-treatment has occurred.[390] In *Boicenco v Moldova*,[391] the Court stated that this meant that the person conducting the investigation must be independent of those implicated in the alleged ill-treatment, both institutionally and in practice. There was a breach of the latter requirement in the *Boicenco* case on this ground because the investigation was conducted by the prosecutor who had filed criminal charges against the applicant and had applied for his remand in custody. In the same case it was stated that all reasonable steps must be taken to obtain relevant evidence, including forensic[392] and eye-witness evidence. The available witnesses[393] and

---

[382] *Gäfgen v Germany* 2010-; 52 EHRR 1 para 117 GC. See generally, Mowbray, 51 ICLQ 437 (2002). If it finds a breach of the substantive obligation, the Court may decide not to rule on the procedural obligation: see *Denizci and Others v Cyprus* 2001-V.

[383] See *Ilhan v Turkey* 2000-VII; 34 EHRR 869 GC.   [384] 1998-VIII; 28 EHRR 652.

[385] For an alternative reason for the obligation, see *Janowiec and Others v Russia* hudoc (2012), referred to the Grand Chamber. In *El Masri v The Former Yugoslav Republic of Macedonia* 2012- para 193 GC, the Court stated that 'establishing the truth' of what had happened, in the interests of the victims and society, was a further reason for an effective investigation. On the 'right to truth' and Article 13, see Chap. 17.

[386] 2003-XII; 40 EHRR 459. Cf *MN v Bulgaria* hudoc (2012). See Pitea, 3 JICJ 447 (2005).

[387] The Court also found a breach of Article 8. In the earlier case of *X and Y v Netherlands* A 91 (1985); 8 EHRR 235, the Court had only found a breach of Article 8.   [388] Hudoc (2007).

[389] *Gäfgen v Germany* 2010-; 52 EHRR 1 para 116 GC. Cf *Veznedaroğlu v Turkey* hudoc (2000); 33 EHRR 1412 (no investigation at all). A failure to investigate possible racial motives for ill-treatment may infringe Articles 3 and 14: *Bekos and Koutropoulos v Greece* 2005-XIII; 43 EHRR 22.

[390] *97 Members of the Gldani Congregation of Jehovah's Witnesses and 4 Others v Georgia* hudoc (2007); 46 EHRR 613.   [391] Hudoc (2006).

[392] See also *Poltoratskiy v Ukraine* 2003-V; 39 EHRR 916 (medical examination unduly delayed).

[393] *Assenov and Others v Bulgaria* 1998-VIII; 28 EHRR 652. See also *MC v Bulgaria* 2003-XII; 40 EHRR 459 (confrontation of witnesses required).

possible suspects[394] must be questioned and the investigation generally must be conducted diligently.[395] It must also be conducted with reasonable expedition.[396] Cases of child abuse must be investigated with particular care.[397] Reasons must be given for rejecting a complaint,[398] and the applicant informed of the results.[399]

The procedural obligation also requires that, where the facts warrant this, the investigation leads to effective criminal, disciplinary, or other appropriate proceedings for the enforcement of the law against those responsible for the ill-treatment.[400] This requirement was not met when criminal proceedings against police officers for serious physical ill-treatment of a child suspect resulted in the clearly inadequate imposition of only minimum sentences that would anyway not be enforced if no further offences were committed within five years.[401]

As well as requiring an investigation and punishment of those responsible, the procedural obligation also requires an 'effective, adequate and accessible remedy' by which the victim may be awarded of compensation where appropriate.[402] In *Gäfgen v Germany*,[403] the remedy available to the victim was not effective, as more than three years had passed without a hearing.

8. CONCLUSION

Article 3 has proved a difficult provision to interpret because of the generality of its text. The terms 'inhuman' and 'degrading' especially have no clear legal meaning and tend to be over-used in ordinary speech. As a result, Article 3 has led to an extraordinary variety of complaints. Correspondingly, it offers a considerable opportunity for judicial creativity and in some respects the Court, and formerly the Commission, has not disappointed.

Most striking has been the adoption of the *Soering* principle, so that Article 3 prohibits extradition or deportation to face ill-treatment abroad, whether at the hands of state agents or private individuals. After some early disappointing decisions, the principle has come to be of value in asylum as well as other kinds of cases. The humanitarian potential of the *Soering* principle was graphically illustrated in the AIDS victim case of *D v UK*. Of great importance is the ruling in the *Chahal* and *Saadi* cases that the principle is an absolute one, in the sense that a person may not be returned to face ill-treatment, however compelling the public interest reason that the returning state may have to remove the person from its territory.

A remarkable, indeed unique, development was the ruling in the *Al-Saadoon* case that capital punishment is now contrary to Article 3 in the light of state practice which had moved to the point where capital punishment is no longer permitted by Article 2.

Another development that might also not have been anticipated is that Article 3 has been interpreted so as to impose a positive obligation upon the state to protect individuals from ill-treatment in breach of it. The obligation contains both preventative and

---

[394] *Satik and Others v Turkey* hudoc (2000).   [395] *M and C v Romania* hudoc (2011).
[396] *Labita v Italy* 2000-IV; 46 EHRR 1228 GC and *CAS and CS v Romania* hudoc (2012).
[397] *CAS and CS v Romania* hudoc (2012).   [398] *Poltoratskiy v Ukraine* 2003-V; 39 EHRR 916.
[399] *JL v Latvia* hudoc (2012).
[400] For a case in which criminal prosecution was not required, see *Van Melle and Others v Netherlands* No 19221/08 hudoc (2009) DA.
[401] *Okkali v Turkey* 2006-XII; 50 EHRR 1067. See also *Zontul v Greece* hudoc (2012) and *Gäfgen v Germany* hudoc (2010); 52 EHRR 1 GC.   [402] *Gäfgen v Germany*, para 127.
[403] 2010-; 52 EHRR 1 GC, para 127.

investigatory elements and follows the example of the positive obligation of protection in Article 2. The preventative obligation requires a state to take appropriate steps to protect individuals against other private persons, so that, most significantly, there is a duty to protect children from physical and sexual abuse by parents and others and to protect against domestic violence generally.

More predictably, though after a hesitant start, Article 3 has been interpreted as applying to conditions and treatment in prisons, on the basis that they are inhuman or degrading or both. In this connection, the Court is increasingly making use of the findings of the CPT in its reports on prison visits. In the *Kalashnikov* case, the Court confirmed that, in accordance with its general approach, lack of funds is not a defence to a claim of bad prison conditions.

On a related matter, the decision in the *Tomasi* and later cases reversing the burden of proof in cases of physical assault in police stations or in prisons is an important development that reflects evolving international human rights standards.

The continuing need for a human rights guarantee for Council of Europe states prohibiting torture has been confirmed by findings of torture by state agents in an increasing number of cases at Strasbourg, not all of which have involved the ill-treatment of suspected terrorists in an emergency context. The Court signalled its concern in this regard by its ruling in the *Selmouni* case that the threshold for torture should be lowered in order to underline the firmness that is needed to protect the fundamental values of democratic societies. Also of importance in the Court's interpretation of Article 3 is its ruling in the *Aydin* and later cases that rape constitutes torture.

Of potential importance for members of minority groups is the ruling by the Court in *Cyprus v Turkey* (2001) that discrimination on grounds of ethnic origin, race, or religion may be in breach of Article 3. Coupled with the positive obligation upon states to control private conduct, this may cause Article 3 to become a valuable remedy for members of such groups in discrimination cases.

Although the dynamic or broad interpretation of Article 3 adopted by the Court in several of the contexts described would scarcely have been anticipated by its drafters, they are nonetheless in tune with present day European standards.

7

ARTICLE 4: FREEDOM FROM SLAVERY, SERVITUDE, OR FORCED OR COMPULSORY LABOUR

Article 4

1. No one shall be held in slavery or servitude.
2. No one shall be required to perform forced or compulsory labour.
3. For the purpose of this Article the term 'forced or compulsory labour' shall not include:
   (a) any work required to be done in the ordinary course of detention imposed according to the provisions of Article 5 of the Convention or during conditional release from such detention;
   (b) any service of a military character or, in case of conscientious objectors in countries where they are recognised, service exacted instead of compulsory military service;
   (c) any service exacted in case of an emergency or calamity threatening the life or well-being of the community;
   (d) any work or service which forms part of normal civic obligations.

Article 4, which 'enshrines one of the fundamental values of democratic societies',[1] has generated very little case law. But in an important development, the Court has extended the scope of Article 4 to cover 'domestic slavery' and human trafficking respectively, both of which are serious problems in present day Europe. In particular, states have positive obligations to act against conduct by private employers or persons involved in trafficking.

1. FREEDOM FROM SLAVERY AND SERVITUDE

Article 4(1) requires that no one 'shall be held in slavery or servitude'. Its importance is underlined by the fact that it contains an absolute guarantee and cannot be derogated from in time of war or public emergency.[2]

---

[1] *Siliadin v France* 2005-VII; 43 EHRR 287 para 112. See Cullen, 6 HRLR 585 (2006).
[2] See Article 15(2), Convention.

In *Siliadin v France*,[3] the Court adopted the 'classic meaning' of slavery that is found in Article 1 of the Slavery Convention 1926.[4] There, slavery is defined as 'the status or condition of a person over whom any or all of the powers attaching to the right of ownership are exercised'. In the *Siliadin* case, the applicant was found not to have been held in slavery, as the couple who employed and exercised control over her did not have 'a genuine right of legal right ownership over her, thus reducing her to the status of an "object"'.[5]

In the same case, the Court stated that servitude in Article 4 means 'an obligation to provide one's services that is imposed by the use of coercion'.[6] Although distinct from slavery in that it does not involve legal ownership, servitude is linked to it in that servitude involves 'a particularly serious form of deprivation of liberty' and control over the person concerned. In distinguishing servitude from forced or compulsory labour, the Court adopted the statement by the Commission in *Van Droogenbroeck v Belgium*[7] that the status of servitude includes 'in addition to the obligation to provide certain services...the obligation on the "'serf" to live on another's property and the impossibility of altering his condition'.

In the *Siliadin* case,[8] the Court found that the applicant had been held in servitude. She was brought when a fifteen-year-old to France on a tourist visa from her home country, Togo, by a Mrs D with the consent of the applicant's family. She was 'lent' by Mrs D to Mr and Mrs B, and required to work for them for several years as a general housemaid and to look after their four children fifteen hours a day, seven days a week, and without pay. Her passport was confiscated, she was not allowed to leave the house without the children, and she was encouraged by her employers to fear that she was under threat of being arrested as an illegal immigrant. Thus she had no free time or freedom of movement and, as a vulnerable minor with no resources or friends, was completely dependent on Mr and Mrs B, and had no expectation that her situation would improve. As the *Silidian* case shows, the prohibitions of servitude and forced or compulsory labour in Article 4 overlap, in that the 'work' or 'service' required of a person in servitude in breach of Article 4(1) may also be forced or compulsory labour contrary to Article 4(2) (see section 2 that follows).

2. FREEDOM FROM FORCED OR COMPULSORY LABOUR

I. MEANING OF FORCED OR COMPULSORY LABOUR

Under Article 4(2), no one 'shall be required to perform forced or compulsory labour'. In the absence of any definition of these terms in the Convention, the Court has taken 'as a starting point'[9] the meaning of 'forced or compulsory labour' found in the International Labour Organization (ILO) Forced Labour Convention 1930,[10] Article 2 of which defines it as 'all work or service which is exacted from any person under the menace of any penalty and for which the said person has not offered himself voluntarily'. Applying this definition, in the *Siliadin* case,[11] the Court found that the applicant was subjected to forced

---

[3] 2005-VII; 43 EHRR 287.   [4] 60 LNTS 253; UKTS 161 (1927), Cmd 2910.
[5] *Siliadin v France* 2005-VII; 43 EHRR 287 para 122. Cf *M and Others v Italy and Bulgaria* hudoc (2012).
[6] *Siliadin v France*, para 124.   [7] B 44 Com Rep para 79.
[8] Cf *CN and V v France* hudoc (2012) with similar facts.
[9] *Stummer v Austria* 2011- para 118 GC.   [10] 39 LNTS 55; 134 BFSP 449; Cmd 3693.
[11] Cf *CN and V v France* hudoc (2012).

labour (as well as servitude). The fear of arrest, which was encouraged by Mr and Mrs B, amounted to the menace of a penalty, and the applicant's work was not voluntary as she had no choice but to work for them.

Forced or compulsory labour does not include a requirement that a lawyer or other professional person without their consent offer their services to others provided the requirement is not excessive or disproportionate. In *Van der Mussele v Belgium*,[12] the applicant, a pupil advocate, was called upon to provide such services. The Court held that the work required of the applicant was labour within Article 4(2). Labour ('*travail*' in the French text) extended beyond physical work to all kinds of 'work or service', as became clear from the wording of Article 4(3). The Court then held that the labour was forced or compulsory in the sense of the Forced Labour Convention 1930 definition. Although the applicant had committed no criminal offence by not participating, he would have run the risk of being struck off the roll of pupils. This was sufficient to amount to a 'penalty' for the purposes of Article 4(2). As to whether the applicant had 'offered himself voluntarily', the fact that he had given his prior consent when he became a pupil advocate was not conclusive. However, in a case of prior consent, it required a 'considerable and unreasonable imbalance between the aim pursued'[13]—here entry to the legal profession—and the obligations accepted as a condition of achieving that aim for there to be forced labour. In determining whether that imbalance existed, it was necessary to look at 'all the circumstances of the case'. In the present case, the question was whether the service imposed a 'burden which was so excessive or disproportionate to the advantages attached to the future exercise of [the legal] profession that the service could not be treated as having been voluntarily accepted'.[14] In answering this question in the negative, the Court took into account, *inter alia*, the fact that the required service was not unconnected with the profession in question; that, in return for it, advocates generally received certain advantages, including the exclusive right of audience in the courts; that the work contributed to a pupil advocate's professional training; and that the burden imposed upon the applicant, involving in particular work without remuneration, was not such as to leave him without sufficient time for paid work.

In the small number of other cases in which Article 4(2) has been applied, it has, *inter alia*, been held that it was not forced or compulsory labour to require an employer to deduct social security payments or income tax from an employee's salary,[15] to require an unemployed person to accept suitable employment as a condition of receiving unemployment benefit,[16] or for an employer to require an employee to move to another job.[17]

---

[12] A 70 (1983); 6 EHRR 163. Cf cases in which qualified professionals have been required to provide services without violating Article 4: see, eg, *Graziani-Weiss v Austria* 2011 (lawyer); *Steindel v Germany* No 29878/07 hudoc (2010) DA (doctor). See also *Iversen v Norway* No 1468/62, 6 YB 278 (1963) (dentist). And see *X v Germany* No 8682/79, 26 DR 97 (1981) (not forced or compulsory labour for lawyers to receive less for legal aid work). See also *X v Germany* No 8410/78, 18 DR 216 (1979). Lack of remuneration is a factor relevant to proportionality: *Van der Mussele* case, para 40.

[13] *Van der Mussele v Belgium*, para 40.

[14] *Van der Mussele v Belgium*, para 37. See also *Ackerl et al v Austria*, 78-A DR 116 (1994).

[15] *Four Companies v Austria* No 7427/76, 7 DR 148 (1976). The question whether Article 4 could protect a company was left open. See also *Puzinas v Lithuania* No 63767/00 hudoc (2005) DA (deductions from prison wage to cover board).

[16] *Schuitemaker v Netherlands* No 15906/08 hudoc (2010) DA. Cf, *Talmon v Netherlands* No 30300/96 hudoc (1997) DA.

[17] *Antonov v Russia* No 38020/03 hudoc (2005) DA.

II. PERMITTED WORK OR SERVICES

Article 4(3) excludes certain kinds of work or service from the prohibition of forced or compulsory labour in Article 4(2). These are not restrictions on the exercise of the right protected by Article 4(2), in which case they would be interpreted narrowly; instead they are part of the definition of forced or compulsory labour in Article 4(2) and so serve as an aid to interpretation of that paragraph.[18]

III. WORK DURING DETENTION

Article 4(3)(a) excludes from the prohibition of forced or compulsory labour 'work required to be done in the ordinary course of detention imposed according to the provisions of Article 5' or 'during conditional release from such detention'. This exception includes work required in the course of any kind of detention that is permitted by Article 5(1) of the Convention. It includes, therefore, not only work during detention following conviction by a court of law,[19] which will be the most common case, but also work required of a detained minor[20] or vagrant.[21] The fact that a person whose detention is permitted by Article 5(1) is, in breach of Article 5(4), not provided with a remedy to challenge the legality of his detention does not thereby render any work required of him in detention forced or compulsory labour.[22] Article 4(3)(a) refers to 'work required to be done in the ordinary course of detention'. This wording refers not only to the work that the state concerned ordinarily requires of a detained person; it also incorporates a European standard by which a particular state's practice can be measured. Such scrutiny relates to the purpose of the work required, as well as its nature and extent.[23] Thus in the *Vagrancy* cases,[24] work in a vagrancy centre had not exceeded the limits set by Article 4(3)(a) because it was aimed at the rehabilitation of vagrants and was comparable to that in several other Council of Europe member states.

In *Floroiu v Romania*,[25] the Court stated that non-payment for work done in prison does not prevent the work from falling within the Article 4(3)(a) exception. Similarly, in *Stummer v Austria*,[26] the Grand Chamber rejected the applicant's claim that the fact that prisoners did not benefit from the respondent state's national old age pension scheme meant that their work did not fall within Article 4(3)(a), and hence was forced or compulsory labour. The Court noted that, although there was an 'evolving trend' in this direction, only a 'small majority' of contracting parties affiliated working prisoners to their old age pension schemes, so that there was not a 'sufficient consensus' to require such affilation for the purposes of Article 4(3)(a) in application of the Convention's character as a 'living instrument'.[27] However, the Court noted that 'an

---

[18]   *Stummer v Austria* 2011- GC.

[19]   See *Van Droogenbroeck v Belgium* A 50 (1982); 4 EHRR 443. This includes work done by a convicted prisoner for a private firm as well as work done in prison: *Twenty One Detained Persons v Germany No 3134/67 et al*, 11 YB 528 (1968).   [20]   *X v Switzerland* No 8500/79, 18 DR 238 (1979).

[21]   *X v Germany* No 770/60, 6 CD 1 (1960).

[22]   *De Wilde, Ooms and Versyp v Belgium* (*Vagrancy cases*) A 12 (1971); 1 EHRR 373 para 89. Cf, *Van Droogenbroeck v Belgium* A 50 (1982); 4 EHRR 443.

[23]   *X v Switzerland* No 8500/79, 18 DR 238 (1979) (work not abnormally long or arduous for a juvenile).

[24]   A 12 (1971); 1 EHRR 373, para 90. Cf *Van Droogenbroeck v Belgium* A 50 (1982); 4 EHRR 443.

[25]   Hudoc (2013) DA. However, the Court referred to the European Prison Rules, Rule 26.10, which provides that 'in all instances there shall be equitable remuneraton of the work of prisoners' and noted that the applicant had received a reduced sentence for his work and so was 'not entirely unpaid'.

[26]   2011- GC, para 131.

[27]   The Court referred to the European Prison Rules 2006, Rule 26.17 which provides that 'as far as possible, prisoners who work shall be included in national social security systems'.

absolute majority' of states parties did affiliate prisoners 'in some way' to the national social security system or provide them with some specific insurance scheme, suggesting that this might be required for a prisoner's work not to be forced or compulsory labour.

IV. MILITARY SERVICE OR SUBSTITUTE CIVILIAN SERVICE

Article 4(3)(b) excludes 'any service of a military character or, in case of conscientious objectors in countries where they are recognised, service exacted instead of compulsory military service'. There has been no case in which the length or conditions of compulsory military service, in those European states that retain it,[28] has been considered. 'Service of a military character' includes voluntary enlistment in the armed forces as well as compulsory military service.[29] Article 4(3)(b) also excludes from the definition of 'forced labour' compulsory civilian work in substitution for conscription. A conscientious objector who refuses to do such work may be kept in detention for the period of military service. Since the Convention recognizes in Article 4(3)(b) that a conscientious objector may be required to do substitute civilian work, a state may take measures to ensure that such work is done or impose sanctions for non-compliance.[30] In *Bayatyan v Armenia*,[31] it was held that it was not to be inferred from Article 4(3)(b) that Article 9 of the Convention did not recognize a right to conscientious objection.

V. COMMUNITY SERVICE IN A PUBLIC EMERGENCY

Article 4(3)(c) excludes 'any service exacted in case of an emergency or calamity threatening the life or well-being of the community'. It was on this basis that two members of the majority of the Commission in the *Iversen* case[32] were of the opinion that the requirement that the applicant serve a year in the public dental service in northern Norway was not forced or compulsory labour. Noting that the Norwegian government had enacted the law imposing the requirement because, in the government's opinion, the shortage of volunteer dentists had created an emergency that threatened the well-being of the community in northern Norway, the two members, applying the margin of appreciation doctrine, accepted the government's assessment of the situation. In another case, the Commission decided that a requirement that a person holding shooting rights over land take part in the gassing of foxholes as a measure of control over rabies was within Article 4(3)(c).[33]

VI. NORMAL CIVIC OBLIGATIONS

Finally, Article 4(3)(d) excludes from the prohibition in Article 4(2) 'any work or service which forms part of normal civil obligations'. This includes compulsory jury service[34] and fire service.[35] Having held that it did not amount to forced or compulsory labour, the Court found it unnecessary in the *Van der Mussele* case to decide whether unpaid

---

[28] Thirteen Convention parties retain it; the number is declining. See www.swissinfo.ch.

[29] *W, X, Y and Z v UK* (*The Boy Soldiers case*) Nos 3435/67–3438/67, 28 CD 109 (1968).

[30] *Johansen v Norway* No 10600/83, 44 DR 155 (1985). See also *Grandrath v Germany*, No 2299/64 10 YB 626 (1967) Com Rep; CM Res DH (67) 1 (Jehovah's Witness refusal to do military or substitute civilian service).

[31] 2011- GC.   [32] No 1468/62, 6 YB 278 (1963).

[33] *S v Germany* No 9686/82, 39 DR 90 (1984).   [34] *Zarb Adami v Malta* 2006-VIII; 44 EHRR 49.

[35] *Schmidt v Germany* A 291-B (1994); 18 EHRR 513 para 22.

legal aid work required of pupil advocates came within Article 4(3)(d). In other cases, the Commission ruled the following to be 'normal civic obligations': obligations imposed by the state upon a lessor to arrange for the maintenance of his building,[36] upon a holder of shooting rights to participate in the gassing of foxholes,[37] and upon an employer to deduct taxes from an employee's income.[38] Discrimination between men and women in the imposition of a civil obligation may be a breach of Article 4 and Article 14, as successfully claimed by male applicants in the *Zarb Adami* and *Schmidt* cases for discrimination in respect of jury and fire service respectively.[39]

3. HUMAN TRAFFICKING

In *Rantsev v Cyprus and Russia*,[40] the Court held that human trafficking as defined in the Palermo Protocol[41] and the Anti-Trafficking Convention[42] was within the scope of Article 4. It did so without finding it necessary to decide whether it was slavery, servitude, or forced or compulsory labour. The Court stated that although there was no express mention of trafficking in its text, circumstances had changed since its adoption and the Convention was 'a living instrument which must be interpreted in the light of present-day conditions'.[43] The Court stated:[44]

> trafficking in human beings as a global phenomenon has increased significantly in recent years...In Europe its growth has been facilitated in part by the collapse of former Communist bloc...The Court considers that trafficking in human beings, by its very nature and aim of exploitation, is based on the exercise of powers of ownership. It treats human beings as commodities to be bought and sold and put to forced labour, often for little or no payment, usually in the sex industry but also elsewhere...It is...the modern form of the old worldwide slave trade...[and takes] place 'under a regime of modern slavery'.

The extension of Article 4 to cover human trafficking is an important development that extends the reach of the Convention to a present day source of human rights violations of a sadly common and serious kind.

4. POSITIVE OBLIGATIONS

As well as imposing upon states parties a negative obligation not to subject persons to slavery, servitude, or forced or compulsory labour, Article 4 also contains positive obligations. First, states must put in place a 'legal and administrative framework' to prohibit and

---

[36] *X v Austria No 5593/72*, 45 CD 113 (1973).   [37] *S v Germany No 9686/82*, 39 DR 90 (1984).

[38] *Four Companies v Austria No 7427/76*, 7 DR 148 (1976).

[39] *Zarb Adami v Malta* 2006-VIII; 44 EHRR 49; *Schmidt v Germany* A 291-B (1994); 18 EHRR 513 para 22.

[40] 2010-. See also *M and Others v Italy and Bulgaria* hudoc (2012).

[41] Protocol to Prevent, Suppress and Punish Trafficking in Persons, Especially Women and Children to the UN Convention Against Transnational Organized Crime 2000.

[42] Council of Europe Convention against Trafficking in Human Beings 2005.

[43] *Rantsev v Cyprus and Russia* 2010- para 277. Allain, 10 HRLR 546 (2010), argues that this extension of the scope of Article 4 takes the Court's dynamic approach too far.

[44] *Rantsev v Cyprus and Russia*, paras 278–81.

punish violations of Article 4.[45] In *Siliadin v France*,[46] the Court stated that this required states to adopt criminal law provisions which penalize the practices referred to in Article 4 and to apply them in practice. In the *Siliadin* case, the applicant's employers' convictions for relevant offences had been quashed on appeal. A court order of compensation for the applicant had been made, but the Court held that this civil remedy was insufficient. Given that a breach of Article 4 involved a breach of a fundamental value of democratic societies and the particular vulnerability of children, the criminal law legislation in place, which had been interpreted and applied so as not to punish those responsible for subjecting the applicant to servitude and forced or compulsory labour, did not afford her the effective protection that Article 4 demanded in the light of contemporary international standards and trends.[47] There was a breach of the same obligation in *CN v UK*,[48] in which the absence at the relevant time of a specific criminal offence of domestic servitude meant that the investigation into the applicant's complaints were ineffective. There were other offences that covered some of the ground, but there were gaps in the law, and the focus of the investigation was necessarily not on the question of servitude.

Second, in *Rantsev v Cyprus and Russia*,[49] the Court stated that where the state authorities 'were aware, or ought to have been aware, of circumstances giving rise to a credible suspicion that an identified individual has been, or was at real and immediate risk of being, trafficked or exploited', the state is required to take 'operational measures' to remove the risk, so far as they do not impose 'an impossible or disproportionate burden' on the state.[50] Third, Article 4 'entails a procedural obligation to investigate' violations of Article 4 and to punish offenders. In the *Rantsev case*, the applicant's Russian daughter, R, had left Russia to work in X's cabaret in Nicosia, with an 'artiste visa' and work permit issued by the Cypriot authorities. When R abandoned her work after three days, X took her to the police requesting her arrest and deportation. The police returned R to X later the same night and told him to take her to the immigration authorities the next morning. However, R fell to her death from the balcony of the flat in which X had arranged for her to spend the night as she tried to escape. The Court held that Cyprus had violated its positive obligation under Article 4 to 'put in place a legislative and administrative framework to prohibit and punish trafficking'.[51] In particular, the regime of 'artiste visas', which was well known to be a vehicle for bringing foreigners into the country for prostitution, was deficient and had not provided R with 'practical and effective protection against trafficking'.[52] Cyprus had also violated its positive obligation under Article 4 to take 'operational measures' to protect R, who the authorities had a 'credible suspicion' to be at real and immediate risk of being a victim of trafficking: although put on notice, it had left it to X to resolve the situation.[53] The Court finally held that there was no need for it to consider whether Cyprus's procedural obligation under Article 4 to investigate the applicant's claim that his daughter was being trafficked, as it had been subsumed under the equivalent obligation to investigate R's death under Article 2. The Court did, however,

---

[45] *Rantsev v Cyprus and Russia* 2010-.   [46] 2005-VII; 43 EHRR 287.
[47] The Court referred, *inter alia*, to the Convention on the Rights of the Child 1989, Article 32.
[48] Hudoc (2012).
[49] 2010- paras 286–7. The *Rantsev* judgment was expressed in terms of trafficking but can be taken to apply to all violations of Article 4.
[50] The Court here applied the Article 2 obligation in *Osman v UK* 1998-VIII; 29 EHRR 245 GC.
[51] *Rantsev v Cyprus and Russia* 2010- para 385.   [52] *Rantsev v Cyprus and Russia*, para 293.
[53] See also *VF v France No 7196/10* hudoc (2011) DA (police unaware of trafficking: no breach).

rule that Russia had violated its obligation to investigate whether R was being trafficked in Russia.[54]

5. DEPORTATION OR EXTRADITION TO ANOTHER STATE

The *Soering* principle applies to Article 4, so that the deportation or extradition of an individual to another state where there are substantial grounds for believing that the individual would face a real risk of being subjected to slavery or other situation in the receiving state would be in breach of Article 4.[55]

6. CONCLUSION

For many years, Article 4 had little impact. This has changed as a result of the *Siliadin* and *Rantsev* cases, which have signalled the application of Article 4 to what are sometimes called modern forms of slavery. These currently present much more serious human rights issues in European states than the traditional forms of ill-treatment that are associated with slavery, servitude, and forced or compulsory labour in response to which Article 4 was drafted.[56] In the light of these cases, it is clear that Article 4 can be applied to cases both of domestic service amounting to servitude or forced labour and of human trafficking for sexual and other purposes. Equally important is the establishment of positive obligations, comparable to those in Articles 2 and 3, to have a satisfactory legislative and administrative regime in place to tackle the problems of domestic labour and human trafficking and to take the necessary steps to protect individuals at risk and investigate alleged offences.

---

[54] The Court did not find that Russia had violated its positive obligations to have a satisfactory legislative and administrative framework in place or to take operational measures of protection.

[55] See *OGO v UK No 13950/12* hudoc (2014). In some cases the return may violate Article 3: *Ould Barar v Sweden No 42367/98* hudoc (1999) DA.

[56] See Salt, 38 Int Migration 31 (2000) and Kelly, 43 id 235.

8

ARTICLE 5: THE RIGHT TO LIBERTY AND SECURITY OF THE PERSON

Article 5

5 (1) Everyone has the right to liberty and security of person. No one shall be deprived of his liberty save in the following cases and in accordance with a procedure prescribed by law:

(a) the lawful detention of a person after conviction by a competent court;

(b) the lawful arrest or detention of a person for non-compliance with the lawful order of a court or in order to secure the fulfilment of any obligation prescribed by law;

(c) the lawful arrest or detention of a person effected for the purpose of bringing him before the competent legal authority on reasonable suspicion of having committed an offence or when it is reasonably considered necessary to prevent his committing an offence or fleeing after having done so;

(d) the detention of a minor by lawful order for the purpose of educational supervision or his lawful detention for the purpose of bringing him before the competent legal authority;

(e) the lawful detention of persons for the prevention of the spreading of infectious diseases, of persons of unsound mind, alcoholics or drug addicts or vagrants;

(f) the lawful arrest or detention of a person to prevent his effecting an unauthorised entry into the country or of a person against whom action is being taken with a view to deportation or extradition.

(2) Everyone who is arrested shall be informed promptly, in a language which he understands, of the reasons for his arrest and of any charge against him.

(3) Everyone arrested or detained in accordance with the provisions of paragraph 1(c) of this article shall be brought promptly before a judge or other officer authorised by law to exercise judicial power and shall be entitled to trial within a reasonable time or to release pending trial. Release may be conditioned by guarantees to appear for trial.

(4) Everyone who is deprived of his liberty by arrest or detention shall be entitled to take proceedings by which the lawfulness of his detention shall be decided speedily by a court and his release ordered if the detention is not lawful.

(5) Everyone who has been the victim of arrest or detention in contravention of the provisions of this article shall have an enforceable right to compensation.

1. ARTICLE 5: GENERALLY

Article 5(1)[1] protects the 'right to liberty and security of person'. The notion of 'liberty' here covers the physical liberty of the person,[2] which the Court views alongside Articles 2, 3, and 4 as 'in the first rank of the fundamental rights that protect the physical security of an individual'.[3] All kinds of detention by the state are controlled by Article 5, the right applying to 'everyone'. Most cases that have arisen have concerned arrest and detention in the context of criminal proceedings, but there have been many other important cases on such matters as the detention of minors, the mentally disordered, and persons being deported or extradited. In cases where there has been a clear violation of Article 5, the Court has taken the exceptional measure of ruling that the state concerned should take appropriate steps to secure the release of the individual concerned.[4]

The Strasbourg jurisprudence underlines the paramount importance of the right to liberty in a democratic society,[5] its relationship with the principle of legal certainty and the rule of law, and that the overall purpose of Article 5 is to ensure that no one should be dispossessed of his liberty in an 'arbitrary fashion'.[6] Consistent with this, the jurisprudence on the specific grounds for detention under Article 5(1)(a)–(f) emphasizes the procedural and substantive lawfulness of detention (in this connection see section 4 of this chapter). Similarly Article 5(2)–(5) guarantee 'a corpus of substantive rights which are intended to minimize the risks of arbitrariness by allowing the act of deprivation of liberty to be amenable to independent judicial scrutiny and by securing the accountability of the authorities for that act'.[7] In particular, Article 5(2) (see section 6) requires that reasons be given to a detainee for his arrest. Article 5(3) (see section 7) requires prompt judicial control over detainees facing criminal charges (Article 5(1)(c)) and for there to be a trial within a reasonable time. It requires the state to justify detention at all stages, and to release the detainee, on bail if necessary, unless there is a good reason to continue holding him. Article 5(4) (see section 8) applies to all categories of detainee and requires a remedy by which the detainee can challenge the legality of his detention (at reasonable intervals for some categories of detainee). By Article 5(5) (see section 9) an applicant should have an enforceable right to compensation in domestic law if there has been a breach of Article 5(1)–(4).

The student undertaking an examination of Article 5 would do well to first consider the structure of Article 5(1) and how it reflects the non-absolute nature of the right. It stipulates that deprivations of liberty can only be justified ('save in the following cases') under sub-paragraphs (a)–(f). This may be compared[8] to Articles 8 and Article 2, Fourth

---

[1] See Trechsel, *Human Rights in Criminal Proceedings*, 2005, Chs 17–19 and European Court of Human Rights, *Guide on Article 5*, (2012) available at http://www.echr.coe.int.

[2] *Engel v Netherlands* A 22 (1976); 1 EHRR 706 para 58 PC. *Creangă v Romania* hudoc (2012); 56 EHRR 361 para 84 GC.   [3] *McKay v UK* 2006-X; 44 EHRR 41 para 30 GC.

[4] *Assanidze v Georgia* 2004-II; 39 EHRR 653 para 203 GC (detention in defiance of domestic court order for release); *Ilaşcu v Moldova* 2004-VII; 40 EHRR 1030 para 490 GC (detention ordered by a court of a regime not recognized in international law; also *Ivanţoc v Moldova and Russia* hudoc (2011) para 144 (a 'particularly grave' violation of Article 5 following the continuing detention of the applicants despite Strasbourg's order to release (*Ilaşcu*)) and *Del Rio Prada v Spain* hudoc (2013) GC (see Joint partly dissenting opinion of Judge Mahoney).

[5] See, eg, *Winterwerp v Netherlands* A 33 (1979); 2 EHRR 387 para 37; *Storck v Germany* 2005-V; 43 EHRR 96 para 102.

[6] See, eg, *Engel v Netherlands* A 22 (1976); 1 EHRR 706 PC para 58; and *El-Masri v the Former Yugoslav Republic of Macedonia* ECHR-2012; 57 EHRR 25 paras 230–233 GC.

[7] *Kurt v Turkey* 1998-III; 27 EHRR 373 para 123.

[8] Cf Article 9(1) ICCPR, which has no equivalent Article 5(1)(a)–(f) 'list'.

Protocol to the Convention, provisions which have often been held to apply in cases when no deprivation of liberty has been found, ie when Article 5(1) has not been engaged. Both provide for a potentially much broader range of public interest restrictions justifying interference with the right in issue.[9]

As to the individual Article 5(1)(a)–(f) (public interest) restrictions or grounds for detention—see section 5 of this chapter—the Court has insisted that they comprise an exhaustive[10] list and that each individual ground must be given a 'narrow interpretation'.[11] It has insisted that its established jurisprudence here will not be reconfigured in the light of the threat posed by terrorism, for example.[12] The Court also maintains that the question of whether there is a deprivation of liberty in fact is a separate and distinct matter to whether there is an underlying public interest motive for the measure in issue.[13] Whether the Court has always stuck to this principle can be debated.

The structure of Article 5(1) may have created dilemmas for the Strasbourg judges. Any deprivation of liberty that cannot be justified by reference to the closed list Article 5(1)(a)–(f) provides for will be a violation of Article 5(1) (unless there has been an appropriate derogation from the Convention);[14] but if a person has *not* been deprived of his or her liberty in the first place, the state will not be required to pinpoint an Article 5(1)(a)–(f) basis for its actions (other Convention Articles may apply, of course). So, the initial, threshold question of whether there has been a deprivation of liberty can be a crucial one. The jurisprudence has thrown up some fascinating issues here and so we start by examining the concept of 'liberty' within the meaning of Article 5 (see sections 2 and 3 below).

2. THE MEANING OF ARREST OR DETENTION (IE LOSS OF 'LIBERTY')

I. WHAT IS A 'DEPRIVATION OF LIBERTY'?

Arrest or detention in the sense of Article 5 is an extreme form of restriction upon freedom of movement, which is a separate right and generally protected by Article 2, Fourth Protocol to the Convention.[15] There have been several cases in different factual contexts in which the Strasbourg authorities have had to draw the line between these two provisions, the Court not being bound by the conclusions of the domestic authorities.

---

[9] Cf Judge Sir Gerald Fitzmaurice (dissenting) in *Guzzardi v Italy* A 39 (1980); 3 EHRR 333.

[10] *Al-Jedda v UK* ECHR-2011; 53 EHRR 789 para 99 GC (applicant interned in Iraq, no derogation; UK government unsuccessfully argued that obligations arising out of relevant UN Security Council Resolutions displaced its Convention obligations under Article 5(1); see paras 98–110).

[11] *Winterwerp v Netherlands* A 33 (1979); 2 EHRR 387 para 37. *Cf McKay v UK* 2006-X; 44 EHRR 827 para 30 GC. But see *Monnell and Morris v UK* A 115 (1987); 10 EHRR 205 and *Witold Litwa v Poland* 2000-III; 33 EHRR 1267, section 5.V.c.

[12] Cf the Court's position in *A v UK* ECHR-2009; 49 EHRR 625 GC, regarding Article 5(1)(f) on which see section 5.IV.b below and Article 5(4) on which see section 8.II.C below.

[13] *Austin v UK* ECHR-2012; 55 EHRR 359 para 58 GC.

[14] On derogations, see Ch 19.

[15] *Austin v UK*, paras 55 and 57 GC (see paras 53–60 GC for a summary of general principles as regards 'deprivation of liberty'). Greece, Switzerland, Turkey, and the United Kingdom have not ratified Protocol 4. See Ch 24.

The classic case of detention in the sense of Article 5 occurs when a person is kept securely in a closed prison. However, Article 5 is not confined to this situation. As the Court has put it, '[d]eprivation of liberty may... take numerous other forms. Their variety is being increased by developments in legal standards and in attitudes; and the Convention is to be interpreted in the light of the notions currently prevailing in democratic States'.[16] This was demonstrated by *Guzzardi v Italy*.[17] There the applicant was required by a judicial compulsory residence order to live for sixteen months on a remote island off the coast of Sardinia on suspicion of illegal Mafia activities. He was restricted to a hamlet in an area of the island of some 2.5 square kilometres that was occupied solely by persons subject to such orders, although the applicant's wife and child were allowed to live with him. While the applicant could move freely within the area and there was no perimeter fence, he could not visit other parts of the island. Islanders were allowed to enter the area, but seldom did so. The applicant had to report to officials twice daily and was subject to a curfew. Drawing an analogy with the conditions typically found in a modern-day open prison, the Court held, by eleven to seven, that the applicant's conditions involved a sufficient degree of deprivation of liberty to fall within Article 5. The ruling on this point was crucial as the Court held that there was no sub-paragraph of Article 5(1) that could justify the applicant's detention and Italy was not at the relevant time a party to the Fourth Protocol.

In the *Guzzardi* case, the Court gave some general guidance as to the approach that should be followed when setting the parameters of Article 5. It stated that the distinction between restrictions upon freedom of movement serious enough to fall within it and others subject only to the Fourth Protocol is 'merely one of degree or intensity, and not one of nature or substance'.[18] When assessing whether the required 'degree or intensity' of restriction exists, regard must be had to 'a whole range of criteria such as the type, duration, effects and manner of implementation of the measure in question'.[19] *Guzzardi* demonstrates that as the degree of physical constraint lessens (for example, from that in a prison cell to that in a hamlet), so considerations such as social isolation and the other circumstances of detention identified by the Court come into play.[20]

It is clear that house arrest for twenty-four hours a day is a deprivation of liberty.[21] However, in what circumstances might a home curfew, combined with other restrictions, amount to a deprivation of liberty within the meaning of Article 5?[22] In accordance with *Guzzardi*, one must look to the facts of the case and the concrete situation of the applicant in order to assess the degree of restriction upon freedom of movement applicable

---

[16] *Guzzardi v Italy* A 39 (1980); 3 EHRR 333 para 95 PC.   [17] *Guzzardi v Italy*.

[18] *Guzzardi v Italy*, para 93. *Stanev v Bulgaria* ECHR-2012; 55 EHRR 696 para 115 GC.

[19] *Guzzardi v Italy* A 39 (1980); 3 EHRR 333 para 92 and, recently, *Creangă v Romania* hudoc (2012); 56 EHRR 361 para 91 GC and *Medvedyev and Others v France* ECHR-2010; 51 EHRR 899 para 73 GC.

[20] See also *Nada v Switzerland* hudoc (2012); 56 EHRR 593 GC (applicant unable to leave Italian enclave of Campione d'Italia; Swiss authorities refused transit; no deprivation of liberty, the case differing 'radically' (para 229) from *Guzzardi*; Nada simply prohibited from travelling through Switzerland, but otherwise at liberty in chosen location; see paras 229–33). Also *Guzzardi v Italy No 7960/77* (1977) unreported (Article 5 inapplicable when 'Guzzardi' transferred to mainland and restricted to an inhabited village where living conditions were the same as those for other residents, except reporting obligation). Cf *Aygun v Sweden No 14102/88*, 63 DR 195 (1989) and *SF v Switzerland No 16360/90*, 76A DR 13 (1994).

[21] See *NC v Italy* 2002-X para 33 GC and *Nikolova v Bulgaria (No 2)* hudoc (2004) para 60. On compulsory confinement by Turkish troops see *Cyprus v Turkey (First and Second Applications) Nos 6780/74 and 6950/75*; 4 EHRR 482 at 529 (1976) Com Rep; CM Res DH (79) 1. Cf *Cyprus v Turkey (Third Application)* 15 EHRR 509 (1983) Com Rep; CM Res DH (92) 12.

[22] Cf *Secretary of State for the Home Department v JJ & Others* [2007] UKHL 45 and *Secretary of State for the Home Department v AP* [2010] UKSC 24 concering (UK) anti-terrorism 'control orders' (now Terrorism Prevention and Investigation Measures).

and the general extent to which the state regulates the day-to-day life of the individual. Whilst the period of confinement is clearly a key factor, the impact of other restrictions both during and outside the confinement period are critical too, notably those affecting isolation and social contact.[23] For example, *Raimondo v Italy*[24] concerned special police supervision whereby the applicant was not allowed to leave his home without telling the police, had to report to them on such days, and had to stay at home between 9pm and 7am unless there were valid reasons for not doing so and the authorities were informed of his absence first. There was no deprivation of liberty, but a mere restriction on the liberty of movement to which Article 2, Fourth Protocol applied.[25] Article 5 did not apply either to an applicant's 'home arrest' which operated between 7pm and 7am weekdays and at all hours during the weekend, for the applicant was 'allowed to spend time at work as well as at home' during the (almost) sixteen-month period during which the regime operated.[26] So this admissibility decision looked to the extent of the control imposed by the state outside the curfew period and also took into account that the applicant was restricted to his own home, rather than another place. It would seem then that if the individual can maintain a (relatively) normal daily life, going to work and living at home, albeit otherwise subject to a restrictive regime, then there may not be a deprivation of liberty.[27] It is implicit in this decision that an individual may be required to stay at his home for up to twelve hours a day, and even the whole weekend, without this being a loss of liberty under Article 5. Of course, other Convention rights may apply, notably Article 8 and Article 2, Fourth Protocol.

In exceptional circumstances, Article 5 may apply even though the authorities are not literally 'detaining' individuals as they are, technically, free to leave. *Amuur v France*[28] concerned individuals who were denied entry to France and spent twenty days in the international transit zone at Paris airport, this being the time it took for their asylum applications to be refused. They were then returned to Syria. Over the twenty days they had been closely monitored by the police but essentially left to their own devices. They had been free to exit France but in reality they were deprived of legal and social assistance and had nowhere else to go; indeed their return to Syria only became possible following Franco-Syrian negotiations which secured assurances that the applicants would not be shuttled back to Somalia (Syria was not bound by the Geneva Convention relating to the Status of Refugees).[29] Article 5 applied for the holding in the international zone of the airport was, on the facts, 'equivalent in practice, in view of the restrictions suffered, to a deprivation of liberty'.[30] Emphasis was placed upon the fact that the individuals concerned were asylum seekers and so likely to be in a vulnerable situation. In order to prevent Article 5 from applying, the 'restriction upon liberty' involved could only be brief, ie long enough to 'enable states to prevent unlawful immigration while complying with their international obligations [under the Refugee Convention and the ECHR]'.[31] In another case concerning asylum seekers in a transit zone, this time for over one month at Vienna

---

[23] *HM v Switzerland* 2002-II; 38 EHRR 314 para 45; *Storck v Germany* 2005-V; 43 EHRR 96 para 73.

[24] A 281-A (1994); 18 EHRR 237 para 39.

[25] See *Cyprus v Turkey* 4 EHRR 482 at 524 (1976) Com Rep (village confinement by troops was subject to Fourth Protocol, not Article 5). [26] *Trijonis v Lithuania No 2333/02* hudoc (2005) DA.

[27] See also *JJ & Others v SSHD* [2006] EWHC 1623 (Admin) *per* Sullivan J at para 77.

[28] 1996-III; 22 EHRR 533. Other 'transit zone cases': *Shamsa v Poland* hudoc (2003); *Riad and Idiab v Belgium* hudoc (2008); and *Nolan and K v Russia* hudoc (2009); 53 EHRR 977.

[29] *Amuur v France*, para 48.

[30] *Amuur v France*, para 49 (violation of Article 5(1); the Commission thought Article 5 inapplicable).

[31] *Amuur v France*, para 43.

airport, the Court considered that Article 5 did not apply.[32] Unlike in *Amuur*, the asylum applications were processed in three days and it was the applicants' choice to stay thereafter. Further, the applicants had declined an offer to be lodged in a specially equipped zone, were not generally kept under special police surveillance, so they could 'go about their daily lives and…correspond and make contact with third parties without interference or supervision by the Austrian authorities', and throughout legal and social assistance was provided by a humanitarian organization. The Court did not accept that the applicants' situation was 'in practice comparable with or equivalent to the situation of persons in detention'.

Regarding physical detention at the hands of the police or state officials the Court has stated that an 'element of coercion'[33] or compulsion is indicative of a loss of liberty, even if the period concerned is short. So a person who is taken away for a purpose (eg to verify his identity), handcuffed or physically restrained is likely to be deprived of his liberty even if the time-span is quite brief.[34] However, neither the purpose itself, nor the measures of constraint (such as handcuffing, being placed in a cell, or physically restrained) constitute a 'decisive factor' in establishing a deprivation of liberty, the coercive element being more important.[35] In *Gillan v UK*, the applicants were not arrested, but the case concerned broad-ranging stop and search powers under anti-terrorism legislation, the application of which by the police meant that the applicants were 'entirely deprived of any freedom of movement'[36] for up to thirty minutes since they were obliged to remain with the police whilst they were searched (otherwise they would have been liable to arrest, detention at a police station, and criminal charges). Rather unhelpfully, and because it found a violation of Article 8,[37] the Court avoided reaching a conclusion as to whether there had been a deprivation of liberty, but it saw the 'element of coercion' as 'indicative' of this.

As to the presence of individuals at police stations, or similar institutions, Strasbourg cases may give rise to a factual dispute between the parties as to whether the person concerned was actually being detained, or able to leave. If the applicant can provide *prima facie* concordant evidence establishing that he was under the exclusive control of the authorities, the burden will then be on the respondent state to provide an explanation of his or her presence, and thereby displace the presumption that there has been a deprivation of liberty.[38]

In its recent jurisprudence the Grand Chamber has indicated that when assessing whether there has been a deprivation of liberty it may have regard to the 'specific context[39]

---

[32] See *Mahdid and Haddar v Austria No 74762/01* hudoc (2006) DA.

[33] *Gillan and Quinton v UK* ECHR-2010; 50 EHRR 1105 para 57. On 'coercion', see *MA v Cyprus* hudoc (2013) para 190; *Foka v Turkey* hudoc (2008) para 78; *Shimovolos v Russia* hudoc (2011) para 50 and *Brega v Moldova* hudoc (2012) para 43. Also *Medvedyev v France* ECHR-2010; 51 EHRR 899 GC (ships' crew subjected to restrictions imposed by French special forces who had arrested vessel, paras 74–5). See also the joint dissent in *Austin v UK* ECHR-2012; 55 EHRR 359 para 13 GC.

[34] *Novotka v Slovakia No 47244/99* hudoc (2003) DA (taken against will and held in a cell; 'relatively short duration of the interference' (less than an hour) but still a deprivation of liberty). See also *X v Austria No 8278/78*, 18 DR 154 (1979) and *X and Y v Sweden No 7376/76*, 7 DR 123 (1976).

[35] *MA v Cyprus* hudoc (2013) paras 189–93 (police required protesters to board buses (3am) to police headquarters; an 'element of coercion', even though the applicants did not resist, para 193).

[36] *Gillan v UK* ECHR-2010; 50 EHRR 1105 para 57.

[37] See also *Colon v Netherlands No 49458/06* hudoc (2012) DA (stop and search powers; area designated as security risk; examined under Article 8).

[38] *Creangă v Romania* hudoc (2012); 56 EHRR 11 paras 90 and 94 GC (applicant summoned to prosecution service premises and entered building under their control), see paras 88–90 regarding burden of proof.

[39] As to restrictions upon the freedom of movement of members of the armed forces are concerned, see *Engel v Netherlands* A 22 (1976); 1 EHRR 706 para 59 PC (see the second edition of this book at p 125). See also *Pulatli v Turkey* hudoc (2011) para 32.

and circumstances surrounding types of restriction other than the paradigm of confinement in a cell'.[40] This statement was first made in *Austin v UK*, when the applicants—a
protester, and passers-by—were held against their will by the police in a side street off
Oxford Circus in central London for periods ranging from five-and-half to seven hours.
Their individual requests to leave were rejected, for they were subject to (or caught up
in) a crowd control or containment technique known as 'kettling'. Riot police cordoned
approximately 2,000 protesters on a day of anti-globalization demonstrations in central
London, there being legitimate fears (confirmed by the domestic courts) of rioting and
damage to property. The Court noted that the coercive nature of the containment, its
duration, and the discomfort suffered by the applicants (there were no toilet facilities, no
food, no shelter etc) all gave it the colouring of a deprivation of liberty, when seen in terms
of the criteria set out in earlier case law.[41] However, it held (by fourteen votes to three) that
Article 5(1) did *not* apply. *Guzzardi* directed the Court to take into account 'the "type"
and "manner of implementation"' of the measure in question',[42] and this enabled it to
have regard to the 'specific context and circumstances', as noted earlier. The Court took
the view that the 'context in which action is taken is an important factor to be taken into
account, since situations commonly occur in modern society where the public may be
called on to endure restrictions on freedom of movement or liberty in the interests of the
common good'.[43] Being 'kettled' apparently fell into this bracket. It should be stressed,
however, that Article 5 *can* apply to kettling: in *Austin* the Grand Chamber stated, '[h]ad
it not remained necessary for the police to impose and maintain the cordon in order to
prevent serious injury or damage, the "type" of the measure would have been different,
and its coercive and restrictive nature might have been sufficient to bring it within Article
5'.[44] It put emphasis upon the volatile and dangerous conditions occurring, the police's
aim being to isolate and contain a large crowd, to avoid 'more robust methods, which
might have given rise to a greater risk of injury to people within the crowd'.[45] It accepted
the domestic courts' assessment that, in the exceptional circumstances of the day, 'the
imposition of an absolute cordon was the least intrusive and most effective means to
be applied'.[46] As to the duration of the measure, various attempts at controlled release
were frustrated by circumstances (eg crowd violence), the Court accepting the domestic
judges'[47] evaluation that 'the police kept the situation constantly under close review', but
that 'substantially the same dangerous conditions' persisted through the duration of the
containment exercise. The Court emphasized that its finding that Article 5 had not been
engaged was 'based on the specific and exceptional facts of this case',[48] and that no complaint under Articles 10 or 11 had been raised. It was at pains to point out that 'measures
of crowd control should not be used by the national authorities directly or indirectly to
stifle or discourage protest, given the fundamental importance of freedom of expression
and assembly in all democratic societies'.

   Austin was controversial, and premised on the principle that Article 5(1) could not be
'interpreted in such a way as to make it impracticable for the police to fulfil their duties

---

[40] *Austin v UK* ECHR-2012; 55 EHRR 359 para 59 GC (cf the joint dissenting opinion) and *Nada v
Switzerland* hudoc (2012); 56 EHRR 593 para 226 GC.   [41] *Austin v UK*, para 64.

[42] *Austin v UK*, para 65, and see para 59.

[43] The Court appeared to approve the House of Lords' reasoning, citing examples of travel by public
transport or on the motorway, or attendance at a football match, as ones that restricted freedom of movement, but should not amount to a deprivation of liberty. See D Mead 71 CLJ 472.

[44] *Austin v UK* ECHR-2012; 55 EHRR 359 GC para 68 (see also para 59). Cf *MA v Cyprus* hudoc (2013)
para 192 (demonstration was mainly peaceful).   [45] *Austin v UK*, para 66.

[46] *Austin v UK*, para 66.   [47] *Austin v UK*, para 67.   [48] *Austin v UK*, para 68.

of maintaining order and protecting the public, provided that they comply with the underlying principle of Article 5, which is to protect the individual from arbitrariness'.[49] The minority were critical of the judgment precisely because they regarded it as implying that the public interest had been used to justify a coercive and restrictive measure.[50] Nevertheless, the majority were clear that the purpose of a measure, eg the public protection motive, had 'no bearing on the question whether that person has been deprived of his liberty',[51] although that could be of relevance 'to the subsequent inquiry whether the deprivation of liberty was justified under one of the subparagraphs of Article 5(1)'.

II. DETENTION IN THE CONTEXT OF SOCIAL CARE

The Grand Chamber in *Austin* also observed that the principle stated in the last sentence of the previous paragraph concerning underlying public interest motives and Article 5(1) applied equally to a person taken into confinement in order 'to protect, treat or care in some way' for them, 'unless that person has validly consented to what would otherwise be a deprivation of liberty'.[52] Here it will be noted that Article 5(1)(e) permits the detention of persons of 'unsound mind',[53] and that the jurisprudence relevant to this provision has stressed that for a loss of liberty there is both an 'objective element' ('confinement in a particular restricted space for a not negligible length of time'),[54] and 'an additional subjective element' in that a detainee must not have validly consented to the confinement in question.

In terms of the 'objective element', the cases illustrate that, for Article 5, what counts is not so much whether the person is held under 'locked' conditions, but the extent to which he or she is in fact subject to a regime of continuous supervision and control, plus whether in practice he or she would be free to leave were this to be an issue.[55] In *Ashingdane v UK*,[56] a person kept compulsorily in a mental hospital under a detention order was protected by Article 5, even though he was in an 'open' (ie unlocked) ward and was permitted to leave the hospital unaccompanied during the day and over the weekend. The position would probably have been different if, although still subject to a detention order, he had been provisionally released.[57] Article 5 also applied in the case of *HL v UK*,[58] which concerned a vulnerable incapacitated individual treated within a psychiatric institution as an 'informal patient' rather than one compulsorily detained under mental health legislation. Owing to his state of mental health, he had been compliant and unable to express his consent or objection to his admission and continued residence in the psychiatric institution,

---

[49] *Austin v UK*, para 56 (new challenges faced by police given 'advances in communications technology' made it possible to 'mobilise protesters rapidly and covertly on a hitherto unknown scale'; containment techniques were a response), and at para 60. Cf *Ostendorf v Germany* hudoc (2013) para 88.

[50] See the Joint Dissenting Opinion at paras 3–6.

[51] *Austin v UK* ECHR-2012; 55 EHRR 359 GC para 58.   [52] *Austin v UK*, para 58.

[53] See section 5.V.d. For deprivation of liberty on mental health grounds, see *Stanev v Bulgaria* ECHR-2012; 55 EHRR 696 paras 116–20 GC. See also the UK Supreme Court's judgment in *P and Q (by their litigation friend, the Official Solicitor) (Appellants) v Surrey County Council (Respondent)* [2014] UKSC 19.

[54] *Storck v Germany* 2005-V; 43 EHRR 96 para 74 and *Stanev v Bulgaria* ECHR-2012; 55 EHRR 22 para 117 GC. Duration should be sufficiently long for the individual to feel 'full adverse effects' of restrictions, *Stanev v Bulgaria*, para 129 and *Mihailovs v Latvia* hudoc (2013) para 133.

[55] Cf *HL v UK* 2004-IX; 40 EHRR 761 paras 91–2. See also *Stanev v Bulgaria*, paras 125–8 and 132 GC.

[56] A 93 (1985); 7 EHRR 528 para 42. See also *Stanev v Bulgaria*, paras 124–8, 132.

[57] *W v Sweden* No 12778/87, 59 DR 158 (1988) and *L v Sweden* No 10801/84, 61 DR 62 (1988). Cf *Weeks v UK* A 114 (1987); 13 EHRR 435 PC (applicant out on licence, ie 'free', when recalled to hospital; Article 5 applied at that point (the recall) as 'liberty' was a question of fact).   [58] 2004-IX; 40 EHRR 761.

which he had never attempted to leave. The evidence was not entirely clear whether he was or was not held in 'locked' conditions; however, either way, Article 5 applied as the reality of the 'concrete' situation facing the applicant was that the health care professionals had exercised 'complete and effective control over his care and movements'.[59] That level of control may be demonstrated by factors such as constant supervision, the requirement of permission to leave, and forcible return after attempts to do so.[60]

The 'subjective element' requires that the person concerned must not have validly consented to the confinement in question, as might be the case for the admission of an individual to a private institution to receive social care and protection. *Nielsen v Denmark*[61] may be mentioned here, as it concerned a state hospital placing a twelve-year-old boy in a closed psychiatric ward at the request of his mother, who had sole parental rights, for treatment for his neurotic condition. The son was not mentally ill and, acting through his father, claimed that the resulting detention was a deprivation of his liberty against his will contrary to Article 5, for which the state was responsible. The Court saw the case as one of the exercise of parental rights by the mother over a child who was not capable of expressing a valid opinion,[62] not one involving a restriction upon freedom of movement by the state. The mother *had consented* to her child's hospitalization for the protection of his health, not as a means of keeping him away from his father, as had been suggested. The Court concluded, therefore, that the hospitalization of the applicant did not bring Article 5 into play, as it 'was a responsible exercise by his mother of her custodial rights in the interest of the child'.[63] It noted, however, that in principle 'the rights of the holder of parental authority cannot be unlimited and that it is incumbent on the state to provide safeguards against abuse'.[64]

The Court drew a comparison with the *Nielsen* case in *HM v Switzerland*,[65] where a neglected pensioner was placed forcibly in a nursing home. It concluded that there had been no deprivation of liberty on the facts, and in subsequent case law the Grand Chamber has noted of this controversial case that the placement in the nursing home was 'purely in [the applicant's] interests and, after her arrival there, [she] had agreed to stay',[66] ie the (subjective) consent element *was* present, ultimately at least.

---

[59] *HL v UK*, para 91. See also *DD v Lithuania* hudoc (2012) para 146 and *Mihailovs v Latvia* hudoc (2013) para 131.

[60] *Storck v Germany* 2005-V; 43 EHRR 96 paras 76–8; *Stanev v Bulgaria* ECHR-2012; 55 EHRR 696 para 128 GC (applicant not at any health risk necessitating control and supervision, para 128) and *Mihailovs v Latvia* hudoc (2013) para 132.   [61] A 144 (1988); 11 EHRR 175 PC.

[62] The child was 'still of an age at which it would be normal for a decision to be made by the parent even against the wishes of the child', at para 72; parental rights in the law of the contracting parties to the Convention included parental competence 'to decide where the child must reside and also impose, or authorise others to impose, various restrictions on the child's liberty', para 61; such restrictions included rules with which a child must comply within 'a school or other educational or recreational institution' and decisions as to hospitalization for medical treatment. Article 5 was simply not intended to apply, provided restrictions were imposed for a 'proper purpose'.

[63] *Nielsen v Denmark* A 144 (1988); 11 EHRR 175 para 73 PC. Cf *HL v UK* 2004-IX; 40 EHRR 761 (discussed earlier) when the hospital did not have legal authority to act on the applicant's behalf in the same way as the mother in *Nielsen* (see para 93).

[64] *Nielsen v Denmark*, para 72 (twelve votes to seven; the dissenting judges, like the Commission, considered that there had been a sufficient restriction upon the son's freedom of movement for Article 5 to apply). Cf *Koniarska v UK* No 33670/96 hudoc (2000) DA (local authority care orders for seventeen-year-old child; Article 5 applied; order placing child in secure accommodation made by a court lacking parental rights). See also *DG v Ireland* 2002-III; 35 EHRR 1153 para 72.   [65] 2002-II; 28 EHRR 17.

[66] See *Stanev v Bulgaria* ECHR-2012; 55 EHRR 696 GC para 131; cf *HM v Switzerland* 2002-II; 28 EHRR 17 para 47.

As noted earlier, in its recent case law the Grand Chamber insists that public protection motives are a separate issue from the question of whether there has been a deprivation of liberty. The Court has also stated that 'the right to liberty is too important in a democratic society for a person to lose the benefit of Convention protection for the single reason that he may have given himself up to be taken into detention'. This applies 'especially when it is not disputed that that person is legally incapable of consenting to, or disagreeing with, the proposed action'.[67] Indeed, the fact that a person lacks *de jure* legal capacity to decide matters for him or herself should not be taken to mean that he or she is *de facto* unable to understand his or her situation and thereby unable to object to confinement.[68] Notwithstanding legal incapacity, then, the authorities should make genuine efforts to ascertain the true wishes (where possible) of individuals deprived of their liberty in an institutional context both at the time of committal and thereafter.

The issue of respect for the patient's views (if possible), and the need for safeguards against those claiming to protect his or her interests, are underlined by the Grand Chamber judgment in *Stanev v Bulgaria*.[69] The applicant had schizophrenia, and was unable to work as a result; he had no accommodation and had been abandoned by his relatives. Without consultation or consent he was forcibly placed in a decrepit social care home for 'adults with mental disorders', located in a remote mountain village hundreds of kilometres from his home. The duration was indefinite and it transpired that his stay lasted more than eight years. He had no say in his committal, indeed the decision to place him was taken by a state official (acting as his guardian) who never met the applicant, let alone consulted him. The applicant's life became wholly regulated by the care home's staff, with his identity papers and financial affairs in their hands, permission being required to leave the institution, where general conditions were so bad that they were condemned as inhuman and degrading by the Committee for the Prevention of Torture, which called for the closure of the home, and a violation of Article 3 by the Court. Article 5(1) had been engaged given the authorities' involvement in the decision to place the applicant in the home and its implementation, the rules on leave of absence, the duration of the placement (eight years), and the applicant's lack of consent. As to the latter, what occurred was not one of tacit agreement to stay, as in *HM v Switzerland*. Rather the Court accepted that the applicant had been able to understand his situation (despite the lack of legal capacity),[70] and so object, noting that he did so from an early stage by 'explicitly express[ing] his desire to leave...both to psychiatrists and through his applications to the authorities to have his legal capacity restored and to be released from guardianship'.[71] As Article 5 was engaged, the legal safeguards that it afforded applied. This proved to be of great significance, as the applicant lacked legal standing to challenge his confinement under a domestic legal regime that characterized his plight as a protective measure rather than a deprivation of liberty.

---

[67] *HL v UK* 2004-IX; 40 EHRR 761 para 90. See also *Storck v Germany* 2005-V; 43 EHRR 96 para 75 and *Stanev v Bulgaria* ECHR-2012; 55 EHRR 696 para 119 GC.

[68] *Shtukaturov v Russia* hudoc (2008); EHRR 926 paras 108-109; *Stanev v Bulgaria* ECHR-2012; 55 EHRR 696 para 130 GC and *DD v Lithuania* hudoc (2012), para 150.

[69] *Stanev v Bulgaria* ECHR-2012; 55 EHRR 696 GC. See Lewis, Human Rights Brief 19(2)(2012) 2.

[70] *Stanev v Bulgaria*, para 130 (the Court acknowledging the difficult practicalities; however, it 'appear[ed] that [the applicant in *Stanev*] was well aware of his situation').

[71] *Stanev v Bulgaria*, para 130. See also *Mihailovs v Latvia* hudoc (2013) paras 134 and 139.

3. LOSS OF LIBERTY: FURTHER ISSUES

I. ENGAGING THE RESPONSIBILITY OF THE STATE, AND POSITIVE OBLIGATIONS

Article 5 may be of relevance to various situations where the person(s) directly responsible for detention are private individual(s), as opposed to public authorities. *Storck v Germany*[72] concerned the detention, in confusing circumstances and against the background of family conflict, of an eighteen-year-old in a *private* psychiatric institution on the instructions of her father. Over the next two years she tried to escape a number of times and at least once was forcibly returned by the police. The Court stated that the first sentence of Article 5(1) lays down a positive obligation on the state to protect the liberty of its citizens. Such a conclusion, it noted, is in keeping with its case law on Articles 2, 3, and 8, reflects 'the importance of personal liberty in a democratic society', and plugs what would otherwise be a 'sizeable gap in the protection from arbitrary detention'.[73] Therefore, the state is 'obliged to take measures providing effective protection of vulnerable persons, including reasonable steps to prevent deprivation of liberty of which the authorities have or ought to have knowledge'.[74] Hence, private psychiatric institutions must not only be licensed but regularly supervised and controlled to check that confinement and medical treatment is justified.[75]

A deprivation of liberty effected by non-state authorities may be imputed to a respondent state in several ways.[76] First, the state might breach the positive obligation just identified. Secondly, the state authorities may become actively involved in private detention, as when an applicant flees from a private psychiatric unit and, despite express objections, the police forcefully return him or her. Such circumstances should prompt the police or another state authority to review the lawfulness of the private detention.[77]

Finally, state responsibility under the Convention for a private detention may occur when, in a subsequent legal action for compensation brought against the private 'detainer', the domestic courts fail to interpret domestic law 'in the spirit of Article 5'.[78]

---

[72] 2005-V; 43 EHRR 96.   [73] *Storck v Germany*, para 102.   [74] *Storck v Germany*, para 102.

[75] *Storck v Germany*, paras 103 and 108 (Article 5 breached as private detention would not have occurred if proper supervision had been in place).

[76] Cf *Cyprus v Turkey* 2001-IV; 35 EHRR 731 para 81 GC and *Ilaşcu v Moldova* 2004-VII; 40 EHRR 1030 para 318 GC (state responsibility may be engaged via authorities' 'acquiescence or connivance...in the acts of private individuals which violate the Convention rights of other individuals'). See also *El Masri v the Former Yugoslav Republic of Macedonia* ECHR-2012; 57 EHRR 783 GC.

[77] *Storck v Germany* 2005-V; 43 EHRR 96 paras 91 and 106. In *Riera Blume v Spain* (1999-VII; 30 EHRR 632) (adult applicants brainwashed by a religious sect; contrary to judicial instruction the police transported unwilling applicants to a location where relatives detained them for days of 'de-programming'; police were aware ('the national authorities at all times acquiesced in the applicants' loss of liberty'), Article 5(1) applied as 'the ultimate responsibility for the matters complained of...lay with the authorities in question' (*Riera Blume v Spain*, para 35). See also *Rantsev v Cyprus and Russia* ECHR-2010; 51 EHRR 1 paras 319-321 (Cypriot police responsibility that 'human trafficking' victim returned to traffickers; circumstances were such that they should have been aware) and *Medova v Russia* hudoc (2009) paras 123–5 (authorities' did not stop arbitrary deprivation of liberty when power to do so).

[78] *Storck v Germany*, paras 89 and 93 (domestic court's failure to interpret civil law in the spirit of Article 5, para 99).

II. CONDITIONS OF DETENTION

Article 5 is generally concerned only with the fact of detention, not the conditions in which a person is detained, which are a matter for Article 3.[79] Thus Article 5(1)(a) was not violated when a drug addict and smuggler was detained in an ordinary prison, not an appropriate centre to receive treatment for his addiction as stipulated by the convicting court. The dominant reason for detention was punishment for a crime under Article 5(1)(a). The detention was therefore 'lawful' even though an earlier release date might have been obtained if the applicant had benefited from medical treatment to aid his addiction.[80] However, as we shall see, 'lawfulness' under Article 5(1) requires that 'there must be some relationship between *the ground of permitted deprivation of liberty relied on* and the place and conditions of detention' (emphasis added).[81] So, in principle a mentally ill detainee must be held in an appropriate institution, not a regular prison.[82] Nonetheless, there was no breach of Article 5(1) in *Ashingdane* where there had been a nineteen-month-long failure to implement the applicant's transfer from the 'special' psychiatric hospital to an ordinary psychiatric hospital where there was in fact a different and more liberal regime of hospital detention. The Court determined that the place and conditions of detention that the applicant was subjected to remained capable of satisfying Article 5(1)(e) at all times.[83]

Curiously the Court has not excluded the possibility that there may be a violation of Article 5 in respect of a person who is *already* lawfully detained when, for example, he or she is subjected to solitary confinement or a seclusion regime. It has held that such additional restrictions on confinement do not as a general rule amount to a *further* deprivation of liberty, but it is prepared to look at the circumstances of individual cases, and their context.[84]

III. TRANSFER ACROSS BORDERS, EXTRADITION AND EXPULSION

Extradition or deportation of fugitive offenders must not interfere with any specific rights recognized in the Convention.[85] In *Öcalan v Turkey*,[86] the leader of a terrorist organization in Turkey had fled to Kenya and there was no extradition treaty in place between the two countries. The applicant was seized by Kenyan operatives who facilitated his handing over to Turkish operatives in the international zone of Nairobi Airport. The latter arrested him inside an aircraft under effective Turkish authority[87] and immediately flew

---

[79] *Ashingdane v UK* A 93 (1985); 7 EHRR 528 para 44. On the relevance of rehabilitation to detention under Article 5(1)(a), see section 5.I.a; as to a potential right to treatment under Article 5(1)(e), see section 5.V.d; and possible violations of Article 5(1)(f) (minors in adult institutions), see section, 5.VI.b.

[80] *Bizzotto v Greece* 1996-V (suitable facilities did not exist).

[81] *Ashingdane v UK* A 93 (1985); 7 EHRR 528 para 44.   [82] See section 5.V.d.

[83] See, however, *Mancini v Italy* 2001-IX (violation of Article 5, by four votes to three; applicant remained in prison for one week longer than required by a court order which required his transfer to house arrest; see para 19). See also *Gulub Atanasov v Bulgaria* hudoc (2008).

[84] *Munjaz v UK* hudoc (2012) para 65 (no violation; applicant subjected to seclusion regimes (eighteen, fourteen, and nine days); applicant already under tight regime; seclusion imposed to protect others (not punishment) and followed clinical assessment; above all, *Munjaz*, para 72, the seclusion regime was applied in a liberal and flexible way (own room, was contact with staff, opportunities for visits, had meals on the ward etc). Articles 3 and 8 may be relevant. An extension of the period of detention by virtue of a prison disciplinary sentence may raise a question under Article 5(1) and entail the application of Article 6, see Ch 9.

[85] *Öcalan v Turkey* 2005-IV; 41 EHRR 985 para 86 GC (concerned Article 5(1)(c), not Article 5(1)(f)).

[86] *Öcalan v Turkey* 2005-IV; 41 EHRR 985 para 86 GC, see also *Öcalan v Turkey* hudoc (2003); 37 EHRR 238 (Chamber judgment).

[87] Hence Article 1 ('jurisdiction') applied, see para 91. See also *Illich Sanchez Ramirez v France No 28780/95*, 86 DR 155 (1996) (French authorities not in control of aircraft).

him back to Turkey. The Court observed that the mere fact that a fugitive is handed over as a result of cooperation between states does not in itself make the arrest unlawful or, therefore, give rise to any problem under Article 5.[88] However, Article 5 might apply if there was a lack of consent on the part of the refuge state for this would affect the person concerned's 'individual rights to security under Article 5(1)'.[89] The critical issue would be whether the 'seizing' state acted extra-territorially in a manner that was 'inconsistent with the sovereignty of the host state and therefore contrary to international law'.[90] As this was not the case, and as the arrest complied with Turkish domestic law and so fell within Article 5(1)(c), there was no violation of Article 5 in Öcalan.

If, on the facts of Öcalan, there had been an extradition treaty in place between Turkey and Kenya the rules established by it would have been a relevant factor to be taken into account for determining whether the arrest that led to the subsequent complaint to the Court was 'lawful'.[91] Otherwise the Convention contains no provisions concerning the circumstances in which extradition may be granted, or the procedure to be followed. The Court has stated: '[s]ubject to it being the result of cooperation between the States concerned and provided that the legal basis for the order for the fugitive's arrest is an arrest warrant issued by the authorities of the fugitive's State of origin, even an atypical extradition cannot as such be regarded as being contrary to the Convention'.[92]

Article 5(1) may also be relevant to cases concerning the expulsion of an individual from a Convention State to one where there is a real risk that he or she will suffer a 'flagrant breach' of that Article.[93] As with Article 6(1),[94] a high threshold is imposed, it being envisaged that a flagrant breach of Article 5(1) 'would occur only if, for example, the receiving State arbitrarily detained an applicant for many years without any intention of bringing him or her to trial', or 'if an applicant would be at risk of being imprisoned for a substantial period in the receiving State, having previously been convicted after a flagrantly unfair trial'.[95] There was no violation in Othman, when it was contended that there may be incommunicado detention for up to fifty days, this falling 'far short of the length of detention required for a flagrant breach of Article 5'.[96] However, Article 5(1) was engaged in El-Masri v the Former Yugoslav Republic of Macedonia,[97] an 'extraordinary rendition' case in which the respondent state handed over the applicant to the CIA in circumstances when there was a real risk of a flagrant violation of the applicant's rights under Article 5 (the circumstances being such that the respondent state should have been aware). He had been abducted and was then detained in Afghanistan for several months.[98] The Court

---

[88] Öcalan v Turkey, para 87. Indeed the element of cooperation may help establish the lawfulness.

[89] Öcalan v Turkey, para 85.   [90] Öcalan v Turkey, para 90. As to burden of proof, see para 90.

[91] Öcalan v Turkey, para 87. See also Stephens v Malta No 1 hudoc (2009); 50 EHRR 144 (deprivation of liberty attributed to Malta, which had requested detention pending extradition, although detention by Spanish authorities; Malta had to ensure arrest warrant and extradition request were valid under Maltese law, paras 50–4).

[92] Öcalan v Turkey 2005-IV; 41 EHRR 985 para 89 GC. See also Al-Moayad v Germany No 35865/03 hudoc (2007) DA (applicant tricked into going to Germany from Yeman; subsequent extradition to USA).

[93] Othman v UK ECHR-2012; 55 EHRR 1 paras 231–3.   [94] See Ch 9 section I.

[95] Othman v UK ECHR-2012; 55 EHRR 1 para 233.   [96] Othman v UK, para 235.

[97] ECHR-2012; 57 EHRR 783 paras 239–40 GC.

[98] See also El-Masri, paras 236–7 for the Court's strong criticism of the unacknowledged detention of the applicant by the national authorities prior to the hand over to the CIA. For relevant Council of Europe inquiries and reports into extraordinary rendition, see El-Masri, paras 37–9, and the judgment generally. See also Opinion on the International Legal Obligations of Council of Europe Member States in Respect of Secret Detention Facilities and Inter-State Transport of Prisoners adopted by the Venice Commission at its 66th Plenary Session (17–18 March 2006), CDL-AD(2006)009.

held that the applicant had been subjected to an 'enforced disappearance' (albeit temporary) as defined by international law, the responsibility of the respondent state being engaged during the entire period of his captivity, ie including at the hands of the CIA. The Court's case law on disappearances is commented upon in the next section.

IV. THE RIGHT TO SECURITY OF PERSON, 'DISAPPEARANCES', AND IMPLIED PROCEDURAL SAFEGUARDS DERIVED FROM ARTICLE 5(1)

Article 5(1) guarantees the 'right to liberty *and security* of person' (emphasis added). 'Security of person' must be understood in the context of physical liberty,[99] so that Article 5(1) 'must be read as a single right', the 'security' element being 'understood in the context of "liberty"'.[100]

The notion of 'security of person' has been referred to in judgments where very serious violations of Article 5 have been in issue, such as cases of unacknowledged detention— 'disappearances'—in which allegations under Articles 2 and 3 have also been raised.[101] Here the Court has recapitulated some key aspects of Article 5:[102] it protects against abuse of power and addresses 'both the protection of the physical liberty of individuals as well as their personal security in a context which, in the absence of safeguards, could result in a subversion of the rule of law and place detainees beyond the reach of the most rudimentary forms of legal protection'. In cases when it is established that an individual has been taken into detention,[103] Article 5 places an obligation on the state to provide a plausible explanation of the whereabouts and fate of that individual. Flowing from this is a positive obligation to take certain procedural steps, which if not taken, may also entail a violation of Article 5. A state must conduct a prompt and effective investigation into an arguable claim that a person has been taken into custody and has not been seen since.[104] It must also take effective measures to safeguard against the risk of disappearances. Thus, 'the recording of accurate holding data concerning the date, time and location of detainees, as well as the grounds for the detention and the name of the persons effecting it, is necessary for the detention of an individual to be compatible with the requirements of lawfulness for the purposes of Article 5(1)'.[105]

---

[99] *East African Asians v UK* 3 EHRR 76 at 89 (1973) Com Rep; CM Res DH (77) 2. Cf Human Rights Committee, General Comment No 35 (Article 9: Liberty and security of person), (CCPR/C/107/R.3), para 8.

[100] *Giorgi Nikolaishvili v Georgia* hudoc (2009), para 53. For further analysis see the second edition of this book at p 132.

[101] See, eg, *Kurt v Turkey* 1998-III; 27 EHRR 373; *Timurtas v Turkey* 2000-VI; 33 EHRR 121; and *Er and Others v Turkey* hudoc (2012). See also *El Masri v the Former Yugoslav Republic of Macedonia* ECHR-2012; 57 EHRR 783 GC (an 'extraordinary rendition' case).

[102] *Kurt v Turkey* 1998-III; 27 EHRR 373 paras 122–4.

[103] In 'disappearances' cases it may be very difficult for relatives to establish incontrovertible evidence of state detention. Here a government's failure to submit information to which only it could have access may give rise to inferences that the applicant's charges are well-founded, see *Timurtas v Turkey* 2000-VI; 33 EHRR 121 para 66.

[104] *Kurt v Turkey* 1998-III; 27 EHRR 373 para 124; *Taş v Turkey* 2000-XI; 33 EHRR 325; *Cyprus v Turkey* 2001-IV; 35 EHRR731 para 150 GC and *Varnava v Turkey* ECHR-2009 para 208 GC.

[105] *Çakici v Turkey* 1999-IV; 31 EHRR 133 para 105 GC, also *Kurt v Turkey* 1998-III; 27 EHRR 373 para 124. Other 'custody records' cases include *Anguelova v Bulgaria* 2002-IV; 38 EHRR 659 and *Orhan v Turkey* hudoc (2002).

4. OVERARCHING PRINCIPLES: 'LAWFULNESS' OF DETENTION AND PROTECTION FROM ARBITRARY DETENTION

In a large large number of Article 5 cases, after a detailed examination of the domestic law in issue, or the broader regime applying, the Court has concluded that the detention in issue was 'unlawful' or not sufficiently free from 'arbitrariness'. Issues that are of relevance to this are examined in this section.

The notion of 'lawfulness' is based on the introductory wording of Article 5(1), which stipulates that any deprivation of liberty must be 'in accordance with a procedure prescribed by law';[106] moreover, the wording of each sub-paragraph of Article 5(1) supposes that any detention is 'lawful'. The two requirements overlap and in practice the Court sometimes merges their consideration, treating procedural as well as substantive regularity by reference to the single requirement that a deprivation of liberty be 'lawful'.[107]

These requirements entail that *any detention* must satisfy certain standards, or overarching principles, failing which there will be a violation of Article 5(1), the detention being *unlawful* and/ or arbitrary even if it apparently otherwise fits within an Article 5(1) (a)–(f) category. The overarching principles can be summarized as:

(i) the detention has a basis in, and is in conformity with the applicable domestic law; and

(ii) domestic law satisfies Convention standards as to the 'quality of the law' (it is sufficiently ascertainable and certain); and

(iii) the application of that domestic law is in conformity with the general principles of the Convention: the detention must properly be for one of the grounds covered by Article 5(1)(a)–(f) *as interpreted by the Court*, and the individual must be protected from arbitrariness.

I. REVIEW OF COMPLIANCE WITH RELEVANT DOMESTIC LAW

With regard to (i) as just identified, it is in the first place for the national authorities, particularly the courts, to decide whether the relevant municipal (or, where relevant, international[108]) law has been complied with.[109] If a national court rules,[110] or a defendant state concedes in argument[111] that the procedures required by municipal law have not been complied with, the Court is unlikely to disagree. In other cases it may accept the interpretation and application of municipal law suggested by the defendant state.[112] However, the

---

[106] The term 'procedure' includes the procedure followed by a court when ordering detention (*Van der Leer v Netherlands* A 170-A (1990); 12 EHRR 567) and rules governing the making of arrests (*Fox, Campbell and Hartley v UK* A 182 (1990); 13 EHRR 157 para 29).

[107] See, eg, *Van der Leer v Netherlands* A 170-A (1990); 12 EHRR 567. In *Bouamar v Belgium* A 129 (1988); 11 EHRR 1, they were considered separately.

[108] *Medvedyev v France* ECHR-2010; 51 EHRR 899 para 79 GC (diplomatic notes and arrest of foreign vessel on high seas; major drug trafficking investigations).

[109] *Winterwerp v Netherlands* A 33 (1979); 2 EHRR 387 para 46 and *Bozano v France* A 111 (1986); 9 EHRR 297 para 58. [110] See, eg, *Bonazzi v Italy* No 7975/77, 15 DR 169 (1978).

[111] See, eg, *Naldi v Italy No 9920/82*, 37 DR 75 (1984).

[112] See *Winterwerp v Netherlands* A 33 (1979); 2 EHRR 387 and *Wassink v Netherlands* A 185-A (1990).

Court will of necessity retain a supervisory role since, with Article 5(1), compliance with the national law is inextricably linked with legal justification for detention. As the Court has stated, it must, as a supervisory body, have this ultimate power to interpret and apply national law when, as with Article 5, the Convention requires that a state comply with its national law.[113] Hence where the national authorities can clearly be seen to have infringed municipal law, a violation of Article 5 will be found.[114] The same applies if an applicant is detained in defiance of a court order for his immediate release.[115] If the respondent state provides no reasons for the applicant's detention, the Court will find a violation of Article 5.[116]

In principle detention will be lawful if it is carried out pursuant to a court order, so a 'subsequent finding of a superior domestic court that a lower court erred under domestic law in making the order will not necessarily retrospectively affect the validity of the intervening period of detention'.[117] When deciding whether a fault subsequently discovered in a detention order makes the preceding detention unlawful, the Court makes a distinction between *ex facie* invalid detention orders and detention orders which are *prima facie* valid and effective unless and until they have been overturned by a higher court, the former being flawed by a 'gross and obvious irregularity'.[118]

II. 'QUALITY OF THE [DOMESTIC] LAW' ('LEGAL CERTAINTY')

It is not enough that there exists a specific basis in national law covering detention, that law must also meet the standard of 'lawfulness' set by the Convention ('in accordance with the law'/' "prescribed" ' by law', see Articles 8(2)–11(2)). This concerns the 'quality of the law' in question.[119] The Court links this to the central principle of legal certainty (itself linked to notions of the rule of law and non-arbitrariness) as regards the *application* of law, a recent Grand Chamber ruling stating that it is:

> essential that the conditions for deprivation of liberty under domestic and/or international law be clearly defined and that the law itself be foreseeable in its application, so that it meets

---

[113] *Winterwerp v Netherlands* A 33 (1979); 2 EHRR 387 para 46; *Baranowski v Poland* 2000-III para 50; and *Creangă v Romania* hudoc (2012); 56 EHRR 361 para 101 GC.

[114] See *Van der Leer v Netherlands* A 170-A (1990); 12 EHRR 567 and *Koendjbiharie v Netherlands* A 185-B (1990); 13 EHRR 820 Com Rep.   [115] *Assanidze v Georgia* 2004-II; 39 EHRR 653 GC.

[116] *Denizci v Cyprus* 2001-V paras 392–3.

[117] *Mooren v Germany* hudoc (2009); 50 EHRR 554 para 74 GC. *Benham v UK* 1996-III; 22 EHRR 293 para 42. Hence the Court rejects applications from persons convicted of criminal offences who complain that their convictions or sentences were found by the appellate courts to have been based on errors of fact or law.

[118] *Mooren v Germany* hudoc (2009); 50 EHRR 554 para 75 GC (Grand Chamber held (nine to eight) that the domestic court's failure to set out facts and evidence in sufficient detail, as required by domestic law, did not render the detention unlawful, being a formal requirement only. The joint dissent took a stronger approach to Article 5(1) in the context of the case). The concept of 'gross and obvious irregularity' is not clear, although it evidently requires a high threshold and suggests arbitrariness, if not a degree of flagrancy. For analysis see *Mooren v Germany* at para 75; *Khodorkovskiy v Russia* hudoc (2011); 53 EHRR 1103 para 157 (exclusion of the public from relevant hearings did not entail a violation of Article 5(1) even though it was contrary to domestic law); and *Yefimenko v Russia* hudoc (2013) paras 103–10. On excess of jurisdiction see *Marturana v Italy* hudoc (2008) para 78; *Khodorkovskiy v Russia*, para 156; *Khudoyorov v Russia* hudoc (2005) para 129; and *Benham v UK* 1996-III; 22 EHRR 293 para 46. On quality of the legal reasoning see *Stašaitis v Lithuania* hudoc (2002) paras 66–7.

[119] Cf *Bordovskiy v Russia* hudoc (2005) para 49 (test is 'not an end in itself' and is only relevant if the applicant's substantive Convention rights have been 'tangibly prejudiced' by the poor 'quality of the law' in issue).

> the standard of 'lawfulness' set by the Convention, a standard which requires that all law be sufficiently precise to avoid all risk of arbitrariness and to allow the citizen—if need be, with appropriate advice—to foresee, to a degree that is reasonable in the circumstances of the case, the consequences which a given action may entail.[120]

There is an obvious breach of Article 5(1) if no legal provision exists to justify detention,[121] and if an applicant is held beyond the period of his sentence.[122] A Code of Criminal Procedure might permit measures of restraint in 'exceptional circumstances', such as remanding the applicant in custody before being charged. However, the 'quality of law' requirement of Article 5 will not be met if the Code does not provide details of what constitutes 'exceptional circumstances' and the government cannot submit practice or case law which help to identify the same.[123] A deprivation of liberty will not be prescribed by law within the meaning of Article 5(1) when the legal provision used to justify it has been shown to be vague enough to cause confusion as to its practical effects even amongst the competent state authorities.[124] However, there is room for some flexibility, as in *Steel v UK*,[125] when the Court accepted that the concept of 'breach of the peace' was sufficiently clear, in principle, for Article 5 as it had been clarified by a series of domestic rulings. In the same case, an order to be bound over to keep the peace and be of good behaviour—which the applicants had breached, leading to their detention—satisfied (on the facts) the notion of 'lawful order of a court' (Article 5(1)(b)).[126] Whilst the relevant order was vague and general, with the expression 'to be of good behaviour' being particularly imprecise, it followed a finding that the applicants had committed a breach of the peace. So the Court considered that in the circumstances the order would have been sufficiently clear to the applicants themselves in that they should refrain from causing further, similar, breaches of the peace during the ensuing twelve months.[127]

---

[120] *Medvedyev v France* ECHR-2010; 51 EHRR 899 para 80 GC; also *Creangă v Romania* hudoc (2012); 56 EHRR 361 para 120 GC, and *Ciobanu v Romania and Italy* hudoc (2013). *Medvedyev* concerned the seizure of Cambodian-registered ship on the High Seas (despite importance of fighting international drug smuggling, the 'diplomatic notes' said to justify detention were not sufficiently clear/foreseeable or issued in a context appropriate to satisfy the general principle of legal certainty (ten votes to seven)). The majority called for a tightening of the relevant international law regime on drug trafficking, to bring it into line with that on piracy, para 101. A strong joint dissent argued for a more 'realistic' approach to the 'diplomatic notes' that had been in issue given the exceptional (multi-jurisdictional operations/ High Seas/ drug smuggling) circumstances of the case.

[121] *Baranowski v Poland* 2000-III (prosecutor's decision to continue detention once an indictment had been served as this was the habitual practice).

[122] *Grava v Italy* hudoc (2003) (detention exceeded period applicable under domestic law as applicant served a longer sentence than the one which would have resulted had he been granted remission and the decision on this was taken at too late a stage).

[123] *Gusinskiy v Russia* 2004-IV; 41 EHRR 281 paras 63–4. For other examples, see *Amuur v France* 1996-III; 22 EHRR 533 paras 53–4 (unpublished circular was too brief and lacking in appropriate guarantees); *HL v UK* 2004-IX; 40 EHRR 761 para 119 (doubts expressed whether, even with legal advice, detention on the basis of necessity satisfied the foreseeability aspects of the test of 'lawfulness') and *Nasrulloyev v Russia* hudoc (2007); 50 EHRR 400 (Russian law governing detention of persons with a view to extradition was neither precise nor foreseeable).

[124] *Ječius v Lithuania* 2000-IX; 35 EHRR 400 para 59 (leading domestic authorities presenting differing views as to the practical effect of the legal provision insofar as it permitted detention of applicant).

[125] 1998-VII; 29 EHRR 365.   [126] *Steel v UK*, para 76–8.

[127] *Steel v UK*, para 76; note, however, the joint partly dissenting opinion of Judges Valticos and Makarczyk. Cf, *Hashman and Harrup v UK* 1999-VIII; 30 EHRR 241 GC (hunt saboteurs bound over to be 'of good behaviour'—an imprecise formulation which breached the 'prescribed by law' requirement of Article 10(2)).

As noted previously, *HL v UK*[128] concerned an incapacitated but compliant person held in a mental health institution on what the Court considered to be an 'arbitrary' basis. He was detained under the common law doctrine of necessity, so there were no fixed legal rules as regards admission and detention, rather the applicant was held on the basis of his doctors' clinical assessments completed when necessary. There being no doubts as to the doctors' professionalism, the violation of Article 5(1) stemmed from the absence of procedural safeguards to protect individuals against any misjudgments and professional lapses.

III. PROTECTING THE INDIVIDUAL FROM ARBITRARINESS

Article 5(1) additionally requires that 'any deprivation of liberty should be in keeping with the purpose of protecting the individual from arbitrariness'.[129] This notion 'extends beyond lack of conformity with national law',[130] and may encompass aspects such as the speed with which domestic courts replace a detention order which had either expired or had been found to be defective.[131] It does not entail that any person deprived of liberty must have the possibility of being assisted by a lawyer from the beginning of his or her detention.[132]

Although the Court has not produced an all-encompassing definition of 'arbitrariness' for the purposes of Article 5(1), certain key principles have emerged from the case law.[133] It is broader than unlawfulness, concerning as it does avoidance of abuse of power and the requirement of compliance with the rule of law broadly defined. To take an obvious example, even if there is compliance with the letter of national law, a detention will be arbitrary if there has been 'an element of bad faith or deception on the part of the authorities'.[134] Acts of subterfuge and dishonesty when bringing a person into custody may raise issues from the perspective of arbitrariness. The authorities should not, in the normal course of events, 'consciously' hide the intention to deprive someone of or otherwise affect an individual's physical liberty. Thus detention will also be unlawful if its true or 'outer purpose' differs from its real one.[135] For example, a detention that is purportedly under Article 5(1)(b) on the basis that the person concerned was obliged to appear as a witness (fully in accordance in national law) would be unlawful if the real reason for detention was to charge the person concerned and/or for ulterior motives.

The Court has also held that 'both the order to detain and the execution of the detention must genuinely conform with the purpose of the restrictions permitted by the relevant

---

[128] 2004-IX; 40 EHRR 761 para 121, see section 2.II above.

[129] *Saadi v UK* ECHR 2008; 47 EHRR 427 para 67 GC (citing earlier case law).

[130] *Saadi v UK*, para 68 GC. See also *Creangă v Romania* hudoc (2012); 56 EHRR 361 para 84 GC; *A v UK* ECHR-2009; 49 EHRR 625 para 164 GC.   [131] See *HW v Germany* hudoc (2013) paras 64–73.

[132] *Simons v Belgium No 71407/10* hudoc (2012) DA (issues may arise under Article 6(3), see *Salduz v Turkey* ECHR-2008; (2009) 49 EHRR 19 GC, see Ch 9).

[133] *Saadi v UK* ECHR 2008; 47 EHRR 427 paras 67–74 GC; and see *James, Wells and Lee v UK* hudoc (2012); 56 EHRR 399 paras 187–95.

[134] *Saadi v UK* ECHR 2008; 47 EHRR 427 para 69 GC (citing earlier case law). For example, detention ostensibly for the purpose of deportation that is really aimed at illegal extradition would be 'arbitrary', see *Bozano v France* A111 (1986); 9 EHRR 297. See also *Giorgi Nikolaishvili v Georgia* hudoc (2009) (issues as to what legitimate strategies the authorities may employ to effectively counter criminal activities, see para 58; violation as applicant detained to exert pressure on the brother to give himself up). See also *Adamov v Switzerland* hudoc (2011) para 59. A violation of Article 18 of the Convention read with Article 5 may still be found if there exist additional, impermissible reasons for the detention, see *Gusinskiy v Russia* 2004-IV; 41 EHRR 281 paras 73–8.

[135] *Khodorkovskiy v Russia* hudoc (2011); 53 EHRR 1103 para 142 (arrested as a witness when real intention was to charge and so change venue of subsequent proceedings).

sub-paragraph of Article 5(1)'.[136] So, for example, in cases when the state purports to justify detention on the basis of Article 5(1)(c)—reasonable suspicion of having committed an offence—the Court is prepared to examine whether there existed a basis for such reasonable suspicion, according to standards set out in its case law.[137] Likewise, for detention of a person of unsound mind under Article 5(1)(e), the Court has set out various standards it requires to be satisfied before it is prepared to accept that this ground may be legitimately relied upon by the state.[138]

Closely related to this, the Court has also held that, 'the requirement that detention not be arbitrary implies the need for a relationship of proportionality between the ground of detention relied upon and the detention in question'. Here the Court notes that 'the scope of the proportionality test to be applied in a given case varies depending on the type of detention involved'.[139] For some categories of detention, the Court will scrutinize whether it was actually necessary to detain the individual to achieve the aim stated within the sub-paragraph.[140] The individual approaches adopted for each sub-paragraph of Article 5(1) are discussed in detail later. By way of overview, the stricter approach (whether detention is necessary to achieve the stated aim)[141] is generally taken for sub-paragraphs (b), (d), and (e). The principle here is that 'detention of an individual is such a serious measure that it is justified only as a last resort where other, less severe measures have been considered and found to be insufficient to safeguard the individual or public interest which might require that the person concerned be detained'.[142] The duration of the detention will also be of relevance here.

By contrast, no such approach is taken for Article 5(1)(f), which, at least as far as the detention of adults[143] is concerned, only requires good faith on the authorities' part: detention under this provision will not be arbitrary provided it can be said that it is for the immigration or deportation purpose identified in the Article. However, the importance of the right to liberty is reflected in the understanding that a detention may be rendered arbitrary under this heading if certain standards are not observed: the immigration detention might last an unreasonable time, for example, or deportation proceedings are not pursued with due diligence.[144] The least strict approach under Article 5(1) is taken for Article 5(1)(a).[145] Under this provision, the Court will not question the length of a sentence or, generally speaking,[146] the decision to impose it; instead the safeguard against arbitrariness is reflected in the notion that there must at least be a sufficient 'causal connection' between conviction and the ensuing detention.[147]

Finally, as noted earlier, 'there must in addition be some relationship between the ground of permitted deprivation of liberty relied on and the place and conditions of detention'.[148] For example, detention for the purposes of 'educational supervision' (Article 5(1)(d)) should be in an appropriate institutional context in terms of educational

---

[136] *Saadi v UK* ECHR 2008; 47 EHRR 427 para 69 GC (citing earlier case law).
[137] See section 5.III.c (*Fox, Campbell and Hartley*).   [138] See section 5.V.d (*Winterwerp* etc).
[139] *James, Wells and Lee v UK* hudoc (2012); 56 EHRR 399 para 195.
[140] Although the authorities may benefit from a certain discretion or 'margin of appreciation' in their assessment of the situation: see, eg, *Winterwerp v Netherlands* A 33 (1979); 2 EHRR 387 para 40 and many subsequent cases.   [141] *Saadi v UK* ECHR 2008; 47 EHRR 427 para 70 GC.
[142] *Saadi v UK* (citing earlier case law). See also *Varbanov v Bulgaria* 2000-X para 46.
[143] As to the detention of minors under this head, see section 5.VI.b.
[144] For full details, see section 5.VI.
[145] Article 5(1)(c) is complex. A strict test applies for detention on remand, but less so for the initial arrest stage. The Article should be read alongside the special guarantees afforded by Article 5(3), see section 7.
[146] See sections 3.III and 5.I.   [147] See section 5.I.
[148] *Saadi v UK* ECHR 2008; 47 EHRR 427 para 69 GC (citing earlier case law).

objectives.[149] Detention of a person of unsound mind (Article 5(1)(e)) should be effected in a hospital, clinic, or other appropriate institution.[150]

5. ARTICLE 5(1)(A)–(F): GROUNDS FOR DETENTION

As noted earlier, Article 5(1), sub-paragraphs (a) to (f), provides an 'exhaustive' list of circumstances in which the state may detain an individual in the public interest. These are examined in this section. The exceptions listed are not mutually exclusive: the detention of a person in a mental hospital as a result of a conviction by a court may, for example, come within both Article 5(1)(a) and (e).

As interpreted by the Court, the exceptions do not permit general preventive (security or internment-type) detention[151] of an individual based on the general threat he or she poses to the community, which would require derogation from the Convention.[152] However, the Court accepts that an individual may be detained for very short, preventive periods under strict conditions in accordance with Article 5(1)(b)[153] and Article 5(1)(c).[154] It is also prepared to tolerate a form of preventive detention (under Article 5(1)(a)) when ordered by a sentencing court in addition to or instead of a prison sentence.[155]

I. ARTICLE 5(1)(A): DETENTION FOLLOWING CONVICTION BY A COMPETENT COURT

The purpose of Article 5(1)(a) detention is the execution of the sentence of imprisonment imposed by a court judgment.[156]

Article 5(1)(a) cannot be relied upon to challenge the length or appropriateness of a sentence of imprisonment,[157] and, generally speaking, conditions of detention are irrelevant. Detention will not be rendered retroactively 'unlawful' for the purposes of Article 5(1)(a) because the conviction or sentence upon which it is based is overturned by a higher municipal court on appeal.[158] However, detention will no longer be 'lawful' if the authorities do not grant remission when they are bound to do so and as a result the applicant serves a sentence which was longer than that imposed, taking into account the remission.[159]

Several points may be made in connection with the word 'conviction' under Article 5(1)(a). Having an autonomous meaning,[160] it covers 'both a finding of guilt after it has been

---

[149] *Bouamar v Belgium* A 129 (1988); 11 EHRR 1.   [150] See section 5.V.d.
[151] *Al-Jedda v UK* ECHR-2011; 53 EHRR 789 para 100 GC   [152] See Ch 19.
[153] See section 5.II.c.   [154] See section 5.III.
[155] *M v Germany* hudoc (2009); 51 EHRR 976 para 93, and see section 5.I.a.
[156] For a recapitulation of relevant principles, see *M v Germany* hudoc (2009); 51 EHRR 976 para 87–8.
[157] *Weeks v UK* A 114 (1987); 10 EHRR 293 para 47 PC (Court referred to Article 3, not to Article 5, when referring to the harsh life imprisonment in that case). See also *V v UK* 1999-IX; 30 EHRR 121 GC; *Hussain v UK* 1996-I; 22 EHRR 1 para 53 (lifelong detention of a juvenile might raise an issue under Article 3); and *Vinter v UK* (hudoc) 2013 paras 119–22 GC.   [158] See section 4.I
[159] *Grava v Italy* hudoc (2003). See also *Del Rio Prada v Spain* hudoc (2013) GC (significant change in domestic case law on calculation of remission after applicant was sentenced, which entailed postponement of date of applicant's release: violation of Art 5(1)).
[160] *Engel v Netherlands* A 22 (1976); 1 EHRR 706 para 68 PC; cf, cases engaging Article 6(1) *Ezeh and Connors v UK* 2003-X; 39 EHRR 1 para 124 GC (prison governor's award of additional days to person already

established in accordance with the law that there has been an offence... and the imposition of a penalty or other measure involving deprivation of liberty'.[161] So the Article applies to 'convictions' for disciplinary, as well as criminal, offences under municipal law.[162] It will also cover cases in which a person is found guilty of an offence and is ordered to be detained in a mental institution for treatment as mentally disordered.[163] Sub-paragraphs (a) and (e) overlap in applying to such cases,[164] at least initially.[165] Where, however, an accused is acquitted of an offence and then ordered to be detained in a mental institution, only Article 5(1)(e) applies.[166]

Article 5(1)(a) requires 'conviction by a competent court' for detention to be lawful. A 'competent' court is one with jurisdiction to try the case,[167] and one that is properly constituted.[168] However, it is the detention that must be 'lawful', not the person's conviction. So the Court will not subject the proceedings leading to conviction to a comprehensive scrutiny and verify whether they have fully complied with all the requirements of Article 6.[169] Nonetheless, a deprivation of liberty will not be justified under Article 5(1)(a) if the 'conviction' is the result of proceedings which were a 'flagrant denial of justice', ie were 'manifestly contrary to the provisions of Article 6 or the principles embodied therein'.[170] A violation was found on this basis in *Stoichkov v Bulgaria*,[171] when the applicant had been convicted *in absentia* and was imprisoned on his return to the country. Initially

---

lawfully in prison and after a finding of culpability constituted fresh deprivations of liberty imposed for punitive reasons), and *Campbell and Fell v UK* A 80 (1984); 7 EHRR 165 (loss of remission).

[161] *M v Germany* hudoc (2009); 51 EHRR 976 para 87 and *Grosskopf v Germany* hudoc (2010); 53 EHRR 280 para 43. A 'conviction' is a conviction by a trial court, so detention pending appeal is justified by reference to Article 5(1)(a), not Article 5(1)(c) (permits detention pending appeal of an accused on bail before conviction); *Wemhoff v Germany* A 7 (1968); 1 EHRR 55 para 9. See also *B v Austria* A 175 (1990); 13 EHRR 20 para 39. A 'conviction' exists so as to justify any detention based upon it, even though the judgment, giving the reasons for the conviction, has not been delivered yet; *Crociani v Italy No 8603/79*, 22 DR 147 (1980).

[162] *Engel v Netherlands* A 22 (1976); 1 EHRR 706 para 68 PC.

[163] *X v UK* A 46 (1981); 4 EHRR 188 para 39.

[164] The claim in *Ashingdane v UK* A 93 (1985); 7 EHRR 528 was made and considered under Article 5(1)(e). The particular basis for the claim may dictate the sub-paragraph that is most appropriate. See *M v Germany No 10272/83*, 38 DR 104 (1984).

[165] Cf, *X v UK* A 46 (1981); 4 EHRR 188 para 39 (Court supposed both paragraphs applied to initial detention, but expressed doubt if Article 5(1)(a) continues to apply if a person ordered to be detained in a mental institution is released and then recalled to the institution by an administrative decision). *Van Droogenbroeck v Belgium* A 50 (1982); 4 EHRR 443 PC, suggests Article 5(1)(a) continues to apply provided that there is a 'sufficient connection' between the recall and the initial court sentence.

[166] *Luberti v Italy* A 75 (1984); 6 EHRR 440 para 25. Cf, *Dhoest v Belgium No 10448/83*, 55 DR 5 (1987) (Com Rep; CM Res DH (88) 1); 12 EHRR CD 135.

[167] *X v Austria No 2645/65*, 11 YB 322 at 348 (1968) and *X v Austria No 4161/69*, 13 YB 798 at 804 (1970). Complex questions arise if the court belongs to an entity not recognized under international law; see *Cyprus v Turkey* 2001-IV; 35 EHRR 731 paras 231 and 236–7 GC and *Ilaşcu v Moldova* 2004-VII; 40 EHRR 1030 para 460 GC.

[168] Cf, *Yefimenko v Russia* hudoc (2013) (trial court not 'competent'; two lay judges had no authority to sit).

[169] *Stoichkov v Bulgaria* hudoc (2005); 44 EHRR 276, para 51. As regards faults with detention orders, see section 4.I

[170] *Stoichkov v Bulgaria*. On 'flagrant denial of justice'/Article 5(1)(a), see: *Drozd and Janousek v France and Spain* A 240 (1992); 14 EHRR 745 para 110 PC (conviction may be that of a foreign court: applicants imprisoned in France after being convicted in Andorra; no violation (twelve votes to eleven)); and *Ilaşcu v Moldova* 2004-VII; 40 EHRR 1030 para 461–4 GC (violation of Article 5: 'flagrant denial of justice' (para 461), 'sentence had no legal basis or legitimacy for Convention purposes' (para 436), conviction was by a court of a regime not recognized in international law, para 436). On 'flagrant denial of justice', see Chapter 9, section I and *Othman v United Kingdom* ECHR-2012; 55 EHRR 1 para 259 and *Willcox and Hurford v United Kingdom No 43759/10* hudoc (2013) DA para 95 (UK–Thai prisoner transfer agreement).

[171] Hudoc (2005); 44 EHRR 276.

the detention, based on the original conviction, was lawful under Article 5(1)(a), but it became unlawful (being 'manifestly contrary' to Article 6 etc[172]) upon the denial of a request for the case to be re-opened.[173]

With respect to prisoner transfer treaties,[174] the possibility of a Convention state transferring to another state where there would be a longer period of imprisonment (for example, if parole was generally granted later on in the administering state, thereby postponing release) does not in itself render the deprivation of liberty arbitrary as long as the sentence to be served as a matter of law does not exceed the sentence imposed in the criminal proceedings.[175] However, it is possible that 'a flagrantly longer *de facto* sentence in the administering state could give rise to an issue under Article 5', so engaging the responsibility of the sentencing state under that Article.[176]

a. Detention 'after' conviction ('causal connection')

The reference to detention *'after'* conviction entails the need for there to be a causative link between on-going detention and a conviction for a particular offence, as opposed to merely a chronological requirement that detention follows conviction. In *Van Droogenbroeck v Belgium*,[177] the applicant had been sentenced by a court to two years' imprisonment for theft and, on grounds of recidivism, 'placed at the Government's disposal' for ten years thereafter. Under Belgian law the two parts of the sentence constituted 'an inseparable whole'.[178] The two-year sentence was completed and the applicant released from prison but then detained by administrative decision for much of the next few years on the basis of the original court sentence. The Court held that these further periods of detention fell within Article 5(1)(a). Although they occurred several years after the sentence, they were authorized by it and were intended to achieve its purpose. The connection with the sentence would have been broken, so that Article 5(1)(a) would not have applied, if the decision to recall the applicant had been 'based upon grounds that had no connection with the objectives of the legislature and the court or on an assessment that was unreasonable in terms of those objectives'.[179] In that case, a detention that was lawful at the outset would have become 'arbitrary' and hence incompatible with Article 5. In these cases the Strasbourg authorities may review the merits of an administrative decision ordering detention in such a case, but will allow the national authorities a 'margin of appreciation' in assessing the factual situation when doing so.

Van Droogenbroeck was applied in *Weeks v UK*[180] to the system of discretionary life sentences in English law. In that case, the applicant, aged seventeen, was given a life sentence for armed robbery. In fact, he had stolen 35 pence from a pet shop after threatening the owner with a starting pistol. As the European Court stated, on first impression the life sentence was extremely harsh and arguably an 'inhuman punishment' contrary to Article 3 of the Convention. However, it was given because the applicant, who was characterized

---

[172] *Stoichkov v Bulgaria*, para 56.   [173] *Stoichkov v Bulgaria*, para 58.

[174] As to a special agreement between a Convention state and an international criminal court, see *Krajisnik v United Kingdom No 6017/11* hudoc (2012) DA para 57.

[175] *Veermäe v Finland No 38704/03* hudoc (2005) DA (ECHR does not require the contracting parties to impose its standards on third states or territories). See also *Csoszánszki v Sweden No 22318/02* hudoc (2006) DA; *Ciok v Poland No 498/10* hudoc (2012) DA; *Giza v Poland No 1997/11* hudoc (2012) DA; and *Willcox and Hurford v United Kingdom No 43759/10* (hudoc) 2013 DA (UK–Thai prisoner transfer agreement, see para 91).   [176] See *Veermäe v Finland No 38704/03* hudoc (2005) DA.

[177] A 50 (1982); 4 EHRR 443 para 35 PC.   [178] *Van Droogenbroeck v Belgium*, para 35.

[179] *Van Droogenbroeck v Belgium*, para 40.

[180] A 114 (1987); 10 EHRR 293 PC. See also *Monnell and Morris v UK* A 115 (1987); 10 EHRR 205.

by the trial court judge as a 'very dangerous young man', could be released on licence when no longer a threat to the community or himself, which might be much sooner than would be the case if he were sentenced to a particular term of imprisonment appropriate to the offence. In fact, the applicant's condition remained such that he was not released on licence for nearly ten years. He was then recalled by the Home Secretary a year after his release, following incidents involving minor offences. The Court considered that the case was comparable to the *Van Droogenbroeck* case, in that here, too, the purpose of the recall, which was the act of detention in question, was the legitimate one of social protection and the rehabilitation of the offender. Moreover, despite the considerable time that had elapsed, the causal link between the recall and the original sentence had not been broken: the Home Secretary's intention in recalling the offender was consistent with the objectives of the sentencing court. As to the justification for recalling the applicant on the facts, the Court noted that there was evidence of unstable and aggressive behaviour such as to give the Home Secretary grounds to act and that national authorities were allowed a 'margin of appreciation' in assessing such evidence.[181]

As the examples mentioned suggest, the Court is prepared to tolerate a form of preventive detention under Article 5(1)(a), when it is ordered by the sentencing court in addition to or instead of a prison sentence.[182] The 'causal connection' requirement constitutes an important safeguard in this context.[183]

For an individual already serving a sentence, there must be a sufficient causal connection between the purpose of the original detention and the reasons subsequently given by a body with responsibility for assessing whether the individual should be released. In *Stafford v UK*,[184] the applicant was a mandatory life prisoner by virtue of his murder conviction in the 1960s. He had been let out on licence and, many years later, convicted and imprisoned for fraud. The Home Secretary, relying on the mandatory life status of the applicant, then prevented his release in 1997, citing perceived fears of future *non-violent* criminal conduct. This was contrary to 'the spirit of the Convention, with its emphasis on the rule of law and protection from arbitrariness'.[185] For the causative link with the life sentence to remain intact, presumably the continued detention would not require fear of an identical offence to the original one (murder) being committed, but offences bearing a resemblance to it (violent crime).[186] Evidently, fear of fraud did not suffice on the facts.

James, Well and Lee v UK[187] concerned prisoners serving indeterminate sentences for the public's protection. The main issue was not the causative link said to justify continued detention, but the prisoners' inability to arrive at a situation when it was broken, due to the inadequacy of the regimes or facilities put in place by the state. Each applicant was in the post-tariff phase of imprisonment, and needed to show they were no longer dangerous in order to be released from their indeterminate sentence. The Court did not question the permissibility of indeterminate sentences as such but, on the facts, required a strong

---

[181] On the application of Article 5(1)(a) to administrative recalls of mentally disordered offender patients, see *X v UK* A 46 (1981); 4 EHRR 188.

[182] *M v Germany* hudoc (2009); 51 EHRR 976 para 93 (see also para 100) and see C Michaelsen, 12(1) HRLR 148 (2012). See also *Eriksen v Norway* 1997-III; 29 EHRR 328 (Norwegian system of preventive detention imposed by way of a security measure).

[183] See *HW v Germany* hudoc (2013) (violation: failure to obtain fresh psychiatric reports before making order for *continued* preventive detention). [184] 2002-IV; 35 EHRR 32 GC.

[185] *Stafford v UK*, para 82. On *Stafford* and Article 5(4), see section 8.III.

[186] See the separate opinion of Judge Rozakis. See also *Waite v UK* hudoc (2002); 36 EHRR 1001 and *Grosskopf v Germany* hudoc (2010); 53 EHRR 280 (preventive detention regime could apply to the 'committing [of] further serious property offences such as burglaries', para 50).

[187] Hudoc (2012); 56 EHRR 399.

safeguard against arbitrariness. It concluded that (in the post-tariff phase) the detention had become arbitrary (and so unlawful), as offenders were not given reasonable opportunities to take (or had suffered long delays in accessing) courses that would lead to their release (for example, courses aimed at helping them to address their offending behaviour and the risks they posed). Those courses were integral to the overall design and scheme of detention when it had been established, but insufficient provision had been made due to lack of resources (which was no defence) and appropriate planning by the authorities. Significantly, the Court pointed to the importance of the state having regard to encouraging rehabilitation for individuals being detained solely on the basis of the risk posed to the public.[188] Recent jurisprudence indicates that for this category of detainee, there may be emerging certain positive obligations on the state as regards the provision of relevant treatment or facilities,[189] failing which a violation of Article 5(1)(a) may be found on the basis of the inappropriateness of conditions of detention (broadly defined). However, the Court recognizes[190] that issues may arise here as to the efficient management of public funds, such that it should not take an overly rigid approach.

II. ARTICLE 5(1)(B): DETENTION FOR NON-COMPLIANCE WITH A COURT ORDER OR AN OBLIGATION PRESCRIBED BY LAW

The concept of 'lawfulness' relevant to Article 5(1)(b) was relevant to *Steel v UK* which was discussed earlier.[191]

a. Non-compliance with the lawful order of a court

The first limb of Article 5(1)(b) presumes that the person arrested or detained has had an opportunity to comply with the 'order' in question (which has been already made, and the person concerned informed of it)[192] and has failed to do so.[193] It includes failure to pay a court fine[194] or maintenance order and refusal to undergo a psychiatric/medical examination ordered by a court.[195] A wilful refusal to pay a local (poll) tax may also lead to a detention under this provision.[196]

The principle of proportionality may apply to a period of detention imposed under this first limb (and the broader circumstances of its imposition). In *Gatt v Malta*,[197] the applicant

---

[188] *James, Wells and Lee v UK*, para 218; see also para 208, the Court citing Art 10, ICCPR.

[189] *James, Wells and Lee v UK*, para 194, and see *Grosskopf v Germany*, hudoc (2010); 53 EHRR 280 (German preventive detention regime; Court 'concern' that there were 'no special measures...aimed at reducing the danger [relevant detainees]...present[ed]', thereby limiting duration of detention to strictly necessary period, para 51) and *HW v Germany* hudoc (2013) para 112. See also section 5.V.d with respect to treatment and Article 5(1)(e).

[190] *James, Wells and Lee v UK* hudoc (2012); 56 EHRR 399 para 194.   [191] Section 4.II.

[192] *Beiere v Latvia* hudoc (2011) para 50.   [193] *Beiere v Latvia*, para 49.

[194] *Airey v Ireland No 6289/73*, 8 DR 42 (1977).

[195] *X v Germany No 6659/74*, 3 DR 92 (1975). See also *Paradis v France No 4065/04* hudoc (2007) DA and *No 6944/75*, 1 Digest 355 (1976) (failure to hand over property); *X v Austria No 8278/78*, 18 DR 154 (1979) (failure to take blood test); *Freda v Italy No 8916/80*, 21 DR 250 (1980) (failure to observe residence restriction); and *X v Germany No 9546/81*, 1 Digest Supp para 5.1.4.2. (1983) (failure to make a declaration of assets). Detention for non-compliance with a court order for the enforcement of a contractual obligation merely because the person has been unable to comply with the order (eg for lack of funds) would be a breach of Article 1, Fourth Protocol to the Convention, but not Article 5.

[196] *Perks v UK* hudoc (1999); 30 EHRR 33. See also *K v Austria* (A 255-B (1993) Com Rep F Sett before Court).   [197] ECHR-2010; 58 EHRR 32 para 40 (proportionality).

was granted bail on condition of a personal guarantee of €23,000 and subject to a curfew. Five years later he breached the curfew on one occasion, and was unable to pay, hence there was non-compliance with a lawful order by a court (the order to pay). The fine was converted into imprisonment based upon a fee per day, the outcome of which was a total detention period of five-and-a-half years. The Court found a breach of Article 5(1)(b). It looked to the lack of balance between the length of the prison sentence imposed, and the fact that it was triggered by a one-time breach of a curfew. The Court found this disproportionate in itself, on the basis that it was excessive,[198] noting that much shorter periods had been applicable in other case law. It also looked to the means available to the applicant when, ultimately, the bail sanctions took effect, as it proceeded on the assumption that, five years on, when he was indigent, the applicant's circumstances were such that he would have been unable to obtain work, and so lacked the means to pay the fine at the material time.

b. Fulfilment of any obligation prescribed by law

Examples[199] of 'obligation[s]' prescribed by law under Article 5(1)(b) include an obligation to do military, or substitute civilian, service;[200] to carry an identity card and submit to an identity check;[201] to make a customs or tax return;[202] to live in a designated locality;[203] to appear at a police station for questioning;[204] or the obligation to pay a fine if bail conditions are breached.[205]

A number of principles apply to this second limb of Article 5(1)(b),[206] restricting its potentially very broad application. Firstly, the provision may only be relied upon to detain a person 'to compel him to *fulfil* a *specific and concrete* obligation which he has *until then* failed to satisfy' (emphasis added),[207] the nature of which (obligation) must be compatible with the Convention.[208] Secondly, the arrest and detention 'must be for the purpose of securing [the] fulfilment [of the obligation] and not punitive in character'.[209] Indeed, and thirdly, a balance must be struck between the importance in a democratic society of securing the immediate fulfilment of the obligation in question, and the importance of the right to liberty.[210] The duration of any detention is a relevant factor in striking such a balance,[211] although detention itself must be a last resort measure,[212] not to be used if

---

[198] *Gatt v Malta*, paras 43 and 51–2.

[199] For a recent list see *Ostendorf v Germany* hudoc (2013) para 92.

[200] *Johansen v Norway* No 10600/83, 44 DR 155 (1985). Any work or service listed in Article 4(3) of the Convention that is required of a person presumably qualifies.

[201] *Reyntjens v Belgium* No 16810/90, 73 DR 136 (1992) and *B v France* No 10179/82, 52 DR 111 (1987).

[202] See *McVeigh O'Neill and Evans v UK* Nos 8022/77, 8025/77 and 8027/77 25 DR 15 (1981); 5 EHRR 71, para 185.   [203] *Ciulla v Italy* A 148 (1989); 13 EHRR 346 para 36 PC.

[204] *Osypenko v Ukraine* hudoc (2010) para 56.

[205] *Gatt v Malta* hudoc (2010). However, see para 48.

[206] See *Ostendorf v Germany* hudoc (2013) paras 69–73 and *Vasileva v Denmark* hudoc (2003); 40 EHRR 681 paras 36–7.

[207] *Engel v Netherlands* A 22 (1976); 1 EHRR 706 para 69 PC. See also *Schwabe and MG v Germany* hudoc (2011) para 73.

[208] *Ostendorf v Germany* hudoc (2013) para 72. For example, an obligation to complete a census return must be consistent with the right to respect for privacy in Article 8 of the Convention.

[209] *Ostendorf v Germany*, para 71; also *Nowicka v Poland* hudoc (2002) para 60; *Vasileva v Denmark* hudoc (2003); 40 EHRR 681 paras 36–7.

[210] See *Nowicka v Poland*, para 61 (psychiatric examination ordered by a court—violation of Article 5(1): applicant not released immediately following the examination, para 64; she was also held unnecessarily for several days prior to examination, so no balance between the importance of securing the immediate fulfilment of the obligation in question, and the importance of the right to liberty, para 63).

[211] *Vasileva v Denmark* hudoc (2003); 40 EHRR 681 paras 36–7. See also *Saadi v UK* hudoc (2008); 47 EHRR 427 para 70 GC.   [212] See *Saadi v UK* hudoc (2008); 47 EHRR 427 para 70 GC.

'milder means' of fulfilling the obligation are available.[213] Fourthly, the basis for detention under Article 5(1)(b) ceases to exist as soon as the obligation has been fulfilled.[214]

An obligation imposed in connection with the enforcement of the criminal law may come within Article 5(1)(b), when it is 'specific and concrete'. In *McVeigh, O'Neill and Evans v UK*,[215] under anti-terrorism legislation persons entering Great Britain were potentially obliged to submit to 'further examination' at the point of entry. This was so for the three applicants who were stopped when travelling from Ireland. They were questioned, searched, photographed, and fingerprinted, and released after nearly two days (forty-five hours). No charges were ever brought. The Commission accepted that Article 5(1)(b) applied,[216] the obligation in issue being sufficiently 'specific and concrete' in that it applied only upon entering and leaving Great Britain to check the particular matters set out in the relevant legislation. It aimed at controlling the well-recognized problem of terrorism in Northern Ireland, in which context there was a 'legitimate need to obtain immediate fulfilment of the obligation to submit to such checks'.[217] Noting that examinations were made as far as possible without resort to detention and that, to be effective, it was necessary for any 'further examination' to take place subject to a limited period of detention, the Commission found that the applicants' detention was justified by Article 5(1)(b).[218] *McVeigh* establishes that in certain 'limited circumstances of a pressing nature' Article 5(1)(b) extends not only to cases in which there has been a prior failure to comply with an obligation, but also to cases in which short-term detention is considered necessary to make the execution of an obligation effective at the time that it arises.[219] The safeguards noted immediately above, and which have been developed in subsequent case law, will be of particular relevance. For example, the length of detention may be crucial to assessing whether the fair balance required by Article 5(1)(b) has been respected, and on this the Court subsequently observed that *McVeigh* concerned the 'exceptional context'[220] of prevention of terrorism. By contrast, there was an obvious lack of balance in *Nowicka v Poland*,[221] which concerned an obligation under a court order to carry out a psychiatric examination which took an inordinate amount of time to carry out, the total period of detention being eighty-three days. In *Vasileva v Denmark*,[222] the detention period was thirteen-and-a-half hours, but this too violated Article 5(1)(b), as it was unreasonable on the facts. The police detained the sixty-seven-year-old applicant for the statutory offence of refusing to reveal her identity after a dispute had evolved regarding whether she had a valid travel ticket. What was initially Article 5(1)(b)-compliant detention became

[213] *Khodorkovskiy v Russia* hudoc (2011); 53 EHRR 1103 para 136.

[214] *Nowicka v Poland* hudoc (2002) para 60.

[215] Nos 8022/77, 8025/77 and 8027/77, 25 DR 15 (1981); 5 EHRR 71. See Warbrick, 32 ICLQ 757 (1983).

[216] It drew a distinction between the obligation in issue and that in Regulation 10, made under the Civil Authorities (Special Powers) Act (NI) 1922, that was relevant in *Ireland v UK*, A 25 (1978); 2 EHRR 25 para 195 PC. Article 15 applied to this case. Under Regulation 10, any person could be detained at any time in Northern Ireland for interrogation 'for the preservation of the peace and maintenance of order'. This was held (*Ireland v UK*) not to impose an obligation in the sense of Article 5(1)(b) and viewed by the Commission in *McVeigh* as an example of 'a general obligation to submit to questioning or interrogation on any occasion, or for any purpose'.

[217] *McVeigh* Nos 8022/77, 8025/77 and 8027/77, 25 DR 15 (1981); 5 EHRR 71, para 192.

[218] *McVeigh*. The Commission considered that the detention did not fall within Article 5(1)(c) or any other part of Article 5.   [219] For the test applied by the Commission see 25 DR 15 at 42 (1981).

[220] *Vasileva v Denmark* hudoc (2003); 40 EHRR 681 para 41.

[221] Hudoc (2002) para 61.

[222] Hudoc (2003); 40 EHRR 681. See also *Epple v Germany* hudoc (2005) (applicant validly arrested under Article 5(1)(b) for disobeying police order to leave an area proximate to a folk festival; but nineteen-hour delay until brought before a court was disproportional).

unlawful as the deprivation of liberty exceeded a period proportionate to the cause of her detention: the offence (refusal to disclose identity) was minor (according to domestic law it only carried a fine); the applicant was not in possession of any documentation, which could have revealed her identity; it was not acceptable that no efforts were made to get the applicant to identify herself between 11pm and 6.30am upon the basis that the applicant needed sleep. As regards identity checks generally, the Court accepts that it is a fundamental condition for the police in order to carry out their tasks, and thus ensure law enforcement, that they can establish the identity of citizens.[223] Detention for a reasonable period of time in the circumstances to effect this is permitted.[224] However, the *Vasileva* case should send a powerful message to domestic authorities in the Convention states that they must constantly justify the reasonableness of maintaining detention under Article 5(1)(b).

c. Fulfilment of any obligation prescribed by law—custody for preventive purposes

The examples mentioned regarding the second limb of Article 5(1)(b) concern specific acts an individual has been ordered to, or is required to *perform* by law. By contrast, in its recent case law the Court has addressed whether the state may rely on Article 5(1)(b) with respect to a duty to *refrain* from doing something, ie whether an individual can be detained for a short period in order to prevent a criminal offence occurring, even when there is no intention of prosecuting that individual (which would potentially permit detention under Article 5(1)(c) (reasonable suspicion of committing a criminal offence)). It has done so against the background of arguments that the interpretation of Article 5(1) needs to take into account the state's obligations to protect the public (which may be relevant to a state's positive obligations under Articles 2 and 3).[225]

In this context, the Court has held that Article 5(1)(b) preventive-type 'obligation[s]' must be 'very closely circumscribed'.[226] Preventive detention of the sort that a state might introduce in an emergency situation,[227] or in other contexts,[228] is not acceptable, being inconsistent with the rule of law.[229] Rather, the prohibited act needs to be 'specific and concrete' to the extent that 'the place and time of the imminent commission of the offence and its potential victim(s) [are] sufficiently specified'.[230] Thus, the 'duty not to commit a criminal offence in the imminent future' cannot be considered sufficiently 'concrete and specific' for Article 5(1)(b), unless 'specific measures have been ordered which have not been complied with'.[231]

---

[223] *Vasileva v Denmark*, para 39. See also *Reyntjens v Belgium No 16810/90*, 73 DR 136 (1992).

[224] See *Novotka v Slovakia No 47244/99* hudoc (2003) DA (detained for fifty-five minutes, no violation).

[225] *Ostendorf v Germany* hudoc (2013) para 87. Addressing the matter the Court has held, on the one hand, that the state's positive obligations under different Convention Articles 'do not…as such warrant for a different or wider interpretation of the permissible grounds for a deprivation of liberty exhaustively listed in Article 5(1)', para 87. On the other hand, however, it accepted that that provision 'cannot be interpreted in such a way as to make it impracticable for the police to fulfil their duties of maintaining order and protecting the public—provided that they comply with the underlying principle of Article 5, which is to protect the individual from arbitrariness', *Ostendorf v Germany*, para 88 (citing *Austin v UK* ECHR-2012; 55 EHRR 359 GC para 56).   [226] *Ostendorf v Germany*, para 93.

[227] *Lawless v Ireland* A 3 (1961); 1 EHRR 15. On the relevance of derogation from the Convention here, see Ch 19.   [228] *Guzzardi v Italy* A 39 (1980); 3 EHRR 333 para 101 PC.

[229] *Engel v Netherlands* A 22 (1976); 1 EHRR 706 para 69 PC.

[230] *Ostendorf v Germany* hudoc (2013) para 93.

[231] *Schwabe and MG v Germany* hudoc (2011) para 82, *Ostendorf v Germany* hudoc (2013) para 70.

The respondent government successfully relied on Article 5(1)(b) in *Ostendorf v Germany*, when the potential victim(s) were rival football supporters and the general public potentially caught up in hooliganism associated with a particular football match and its vicinity. The general background was one of organized football hooliganism, the case concerning the detention for four hours (covering the time of the match in question) of the leader of a football hooligan gang who had travelled to an away match. The general obligation to keep the peace and prevent bodily harm, namely by not organizing a fight between rival supporters, *became* sufficiently specific and concrete for the purposes of Article 5(1)(b) on the facts. This was because the person concerned had been 'made aware of the specific act which he or she was to refrain from committing and…showed himself…not to be willing to refrain from so doing'.[232] Along with other football fans, he had been escorted by the police to the football stadium in circumstances which made it clear that there was a duty to refrain from organizing or participating in violence. However, he tried to evade the police and was caught trying to contact (by mobile phone) a rival gang leader in order to arrange violence. The applicant had therefore taken 'clear and positive steps' indicating that he would not fulfil the specific and concrete obligation in issue.

Having found Article 5(1)(b) applicable,[233] the Court in *Ostendorf* applied the general safeguard principles noted earlier, underlining the cautious approach it intended to take to this new departure in its case law and conscious, no doubt, to avoid potential abuse of power by the authorities: the detention had been genuinely for the purpose of preventing a hooligan brawl (rather than being punitive), and the nature of the obligation was compatible with the Convention. Furthermore, release had followed soon after the end of the football match, when rivals fans had dispersed—ie at a stage when the obligation to refrain from organizing violence had lapsed.[234] A due balance had been struck between the importance in a democratic society of securing the immediate fulfilment of the obligation in question and the importance of the right to liberty: '[t]he obligation not to hinder the peaceful running of such a sports event involving large numbers of spectators and to protect the public from dangers notably to their physical integrity was…a weighty duty in the circumstances of the case'.[235]

III. ARTICLE 5(1)(C): DETENTION ON SUSPICION OF HAVING COMMITTED A (CRIMINAL) OFFENCE, ETC

Article 5(1)(c) governs the arrest or detention of suspects in the administration of criminal justice. It is the first of three provisions (see also Article 5(3) and Article 6) that trace the steps that are followed in the course of investigating and prosecuting a person for a criminal offence.[236]

---

[232] *Ostendorf v Germany* hudoc (2013) para 93.

[233] However, see the Concurring Opinion of Judges Lemmens and Jaderblom, arguing that Article 5(1)(b) did not apply, but that Article 5(1)(c) did (which would require a revision of the Court's case law on Article 5(1)(c)).

[234] See also para 100, indicating that early release might be required if the person concerned could demonstrate that he was no longer going to commit the offence (eg by leaving the area).

[235] *Ostendorf v Germany*, para 101.

[236] Article 5(1)(c) itself does not regulate the questioning of suspects, either before or after arrest, and nor does it require assistance from a lawyer from the beginning of his or her detention, see *Simons v Belgium No 71407/10* hudoc (2012) DA. However, Article 5(2) places certain positive obligations on the state, see section 6. Moreover, the actions of the authorities at the initial stage of detention covered by Article 5(1)(c) can have an impact on the fairness of a subsequent criminal trial (Article 6), see Ch 9. As regards access to others,

As will be seen in the paragraphs that follow, there are three main issues to be examined as regards Article 5(1)(c): firstly, the meaning of 'offence'; secondly the issue of the *purpose* of detention permissible under the Article; and finally the question of what is 'reasonable suspicion'.

a. 'Offence'

An 'offence' for the purposes of Article 5(1)(c) obviously includes one under domestic criminal law,[237] but the reach of Article 5(1)(c) is wider than this, reflecting the principle of autonomous interpretation. *Steel v UK*[238] concerned protesters at events such as a grouse shoot and an arms sales fair and who had committed a 'breach of the peace', which is not classed as a criminal offence under English law. However, the Court considered that an 'offence' within the meaning of Article 5(1)(c) was in issue, bearing in mind the nature of the proceedings in question (breach of the peace being a public duty and an arrestable offence) and the penalty at stake (imprisonment if an individual refused to be bound over the keep the peace).[239]

The term 'offence' was interpreted in *Brogan v UK*.[240] The case concerned a statutory power to arrest any person 'concerned in the commission, preparation or instigation of acts of terrorism', where the definition of 'terrorism' was the 'use of violence for political ends'. Although such involvement was not itself a criminal offence, the power of arrest was held to be justified under Article 5(1)(c). The definition of 'acts of terrorism' was 'well in keeping with the idea of an offence'[241] and, following their arrest, the applicants had at once been questioned about specific offences of which they were suspected. Whereas the first consideration mentioned by the Court might suggest that it was applying an autonomous Article 5 meaning of 'offence', it would seem from the second that the Court decided the point on the basis that involvement in 'acts of terrorism' indirectly meant the commission of specific criminal offences under Northern Irish law, which would appear to be the better approach on the facts.

b. Purpose of detention

The scheme of Article 5(1)(c) and (3), which must be read together,[242] make it clear that Article 5(1)(c) is limited to the arrest or detention of persons for the purpose of enforcing the criminal law. Detention under this provision is only permitted, therefore, when it is effected in connection with criminal proceedings.[243] The detention should be proportionate in the sense of being necessary[244] to secure the applicant's appearance before the 'competent legal authority'. That body is the same as that of 'judge or other officer authorised to exercise judicial power' in Article 5(3).[245] In terms of English law, the 'competent legal authority' would be a magistrate.

---

eg families, issues may arise under Article 8 see *McVeigh, O'Neill and Evans v UK* Nos 8022/77, 8025/77 and 8027/77, 25 DR 15 (1981); 5 EHRR 71 para 239.

[237] See, eg, *Ciulla v Italy* A 148 (1989); 13 EHRR 346 para 38 PC.   [238] 1998-VII; 29 EHRR 365.

[239] *Steel v UK*, para 49. See also *Hood v UK* 1999-I; 29 EHRR 365 para 51 GC. Military *criminal* proceedings fall within Article 5(1)(c), see *De Jong, Baljet and Van Den Brink v Netherlands* A 77 (1984); 8 EHRR 20.

[240] A 145-B (1988); 11 EHRR 117 PC.

[241] *Brogan v UK*, para 51. Cf *Ireland v UK* A 25 (1978); 2 EHRR 25 para 196 PC.

[242] *Ciulla v Italy* A 148 (1989); 13 EHRR 346 PC. See also *Ostendorf v Germany* hudoc (2013) para 67.

[243] *Ostendorf v Germany* hudoc (2013) para 68. Article 5(1)(b) may permit short-term preventive custody in very specific circumstances, even if there is no intention to prosecute, see section 5.II.c.

[244] *Ladent v Poland* hudoc (2008) para 55.

[245] *Schiesser v Switzerland* A 34 (1979); 2 EHRR 417 para 29.

The fact that Article 5(1)(c) concerns only detention in the enforcement of the criminal law is relevant to the interpretation of the three grounds for arrest that it permits. Whereas the scope of the *first* of these grounds—suspicion of having committed an offence—is clear from its text, that of the second and third is less certain. In fact, the *third* ground of Article 5(1)(c) appears redundant, since a person who is 'fleeing after having' committed an offence can in any event be arrested under the first limb. As to the *second* (prevention of an offence), at first sight it could be read as authorizing a general power of preventive detention. However, since its earliest case law,[246] the Court has held that this aspect of Article 5(1)(c) 'does not … permit a policy of general prevention directed against an individual or a category of individuals who are perceived by the authorities, rightly or wrongly, as being dangerous or having propensity to unlawful acts'.[247] It may only be employed as a means of preventing a 'concrete and specific offence … as regards, in particular, the place and time of its commission and victim(s)'[248] (to this extent the person concerned does not have to be suspected of having *already* committed a criminal offence).[249] Even then, the detention must be 'reasonably considered necessary' (Article 5(1)(c)) in order to avert the commission of the offence(s). For that overarching reason, the preventive aspect of Article 5(1)(c) did not cover the detention of individuals by police aiming to prevent them from participating in a demonstration, by carrying banners that would incite others to liberate some prisoners.[250] Not only were the individuals detained for five-and-a-half days (too long in the circumstances), but the inscriptions on their banners were ambiguous (in any case they could simply have been seized by the authorities), and they had not shown a violent intention to free the prisoners themselves.

c. Reasonable suspicion

Returning to the first ground for detention under Article 5(1)(c), it will be noticed that a person may be kept detained only when there is a 'reasonable suspicion' that he has committed an offence. The fact that a suspicion is merely held in good faith is insufficient.[251] However, provided that 'reasonable suspicion' exists, a person may be arrested in good faith for questioning with a view to establishing the evidence needed to bring a charge without the arrest falling foul of Article 5(1)(c) because such evidence is not forthcoming.[252] Put another way, it is not necessary that, ultimately at least, charges be brought against the detained individual, nor for the authorities to have obtained sufficient evidence to bring charges upon arrest or during detention.[253] Indeed, the object of the detention before charge is 'to further a criminal investigation by confirming or discontinuing

---

[246] *Lawless v Ireland* A 3 (1961); 1 EHRR 15 para 14. Cf *Guzzardi v Italy* A 39 (1980); 3 EHRR 333 para 102 PC. See also *M v Germany* hudoc (2009); 51 EHRR 976 paras 89 and 102.

[247] *Ostendorf v Germany* hudoc (2013) para 66; see, however, the Concurring Opinion of Judges Lemmens and Jaderblom.

[248] *Ostendorf v Germany*, para 66 (and see at para 93 as regards the test of 'specific and concrete' under Article 5(1)(b)). See also *Shimovolos v Russia* hudoc (2011) (government's vague reference to 'offences of an extremist nature' not specific enough, para 55) and *S v Germany* hudoc (2012) para 91 (a future offence would have been sufficiently concrete and specific if it was shown that applicant 'had planned and was about to commit further violent offences against his ex-wife' (thirteen years on from previous offences of that nature)).

[249] See the careful analysis of Article 5(1)(c) by the Court of Appeal: *R (Hicks and others) v Commissioner of Met Police* [2014] EWCA Civ 3.   [250] *Schwabe and MG v Germany* ECHR-2011 para 78.

[251] *Gusinskiy v Russia* 2004-IV; 41 EHRR 281 para 53. As to arrest on the basis of information from an anonymous source, see *O'Hara v UK* 2001-X; 34 EHRR 812 para 43.

[252] *Brogan v UK* A 145-B (1988); 11 EHRR 117 para 53 PC; *Labita v Italy* 2000-IV 99; 46 EHRR 1228 para 155 GC.   [253] *Gusinskiy v Russia* 2004-IV; 41 EHRR 281 para 53.

suspicions which provide the grounds for detention'.[254] Nonetheless, the clear condition that suspicion be based on reasonable grounds 'forms an essential part of the safeguard against arbitrary arrest and detention'.[255] The constraint provided by this provision, as well as Article 5(2), may be of great importance, since Article 5(1)(c) does not seem to set an absolute limit to the length of time that a person may be detained prior to being charged.

As the Court stated in *Fox, Campbell and Hartley v UK*,[256] 'reasonable suspicion' supposes 'the existence of facts or information which would satisfy an objective observer that the person concerned may have committed the offence'. What may be regarded as 'reasonable' will 'depend upon all of the circumstances'.[257] In this connection, it is permissible to take into account the fact that a case concerns the investigation of terrorist activities, so that allowance may be made for the need the police have to act urgently (on reliable information) and not to place their informants at risk. On the one hand, the Court accepts that states 'cannot be required to establish the reasonableness of the suspicion grounding the arrest of a suspected terrorist by disclosing confidential sources of information'. On the other hand, the Court insists that 'the exigencies of dealing with terrorist crime cannot justify stretching the notion of "reasonableness" to the point where the safeguard secured by Article 5(1)(c) is impaired'.[258] In such cases 'the respondent government has to furnish at least some facts or information capable of satisfying the Court that the arrested person was reasonably suspected of having committed the alleged offence'.[259]

In *Fox, Campbell and Hartley v UK*, the accused were arrested in Northern Ireland by a constable exercising a statutory power (since abolished) allowing him to arrest for up to seventy-two hours 'any person whom *he* suspects of being a terrorist' (emphasis added), ie if the individual policeman had an 'honestly held suspicion'. Although, therefore, the power of arrest was capable of permitting an arrest that did not comply with Article 5(1)(c), the question for the European Court was whether there had on the facts been a 'reasonable suspicion' in the sense of that sub-paragraph, not whether the statute concerned was invalid *in abstracto*. Here the only evidence produced by the defendant government was that the applicants had, some seven years previously, been convicted of terrorist offences and that they were, on arrest, questioned about specific terrorist acts, the government arguing that, as the information justifying the arrest had been from informants, it could provide no further information for fear of endangering the lives of others. While accepting that some allowance could be made for the difficulties faced by the police in the emergency situation, the Court concluded that the evidence that had been provided was insufficient to establish that there was a 'reasonable suspicion', objectively determined, as Article 5(1)(c) required. As a result, Article 5(1) had been infringed.[260]

The Court has acknowledged that there may be a 'fine line between those cases where the suspicion grounding the arrest is not sufficiently founded on objective facts and those which are',[261] and this is apparent from two further 'terrorist' cases from Northern Ireland when it was accepted that Article 5(1)(c) had not been breached: *Murray v UK*[262] and *O'Hara*

---

[254] *Gusinskiy v* Rússia, para 53.   [255] *Gusinskiy v Russia*, para 53.

[256] A 182 (1990); 13 EHRR 157 para 32 and see *Stepuleac v Moldova* hudoc (2007).

[257] *Fox, Campbell and Hartley*, para 32.

[258] *O'Hara v UK* 2001-X; 34 EHRR 812 para 35. See also *Adırbelli and Others v Turkey* hudoc (2008).

[259] *Fox, Campbell and Hartley v UK* A 182 (1990); 13 EHRR 157 para 34. See also *O'Hara v UK* 2001-X; 34 EHRR 812 para 35.

[260] See also *Berktay v Turkey* hudoc (2001) paras 199–201.

[261] *O'Hara v UK* 2001-X; 34 EHRR 812 para 41. See, however, *Smirnova v Russia* 2003-IX; 39 EHRR 450 for a clear violation.

[262] A 300-A (1994); 19 EHRR 193 paras 56, 61–2. There was evidence from national court proceedings in the case and corroborative evidence about terrorist activity by other family members. The fact that the

v UK.[263] In the latter case the applicant had been detained for over six days before being released without charge. The Court was faced with one version of events from the respondent government (essentially it referred to the quality of intelligence information it had received from four informers) and a completely different one from the applicant (claiming there was no intention to charge him, rather that he was simply targeted by the authorities as a prominent member of a political party supporting the Republican movement). However, unlike the *Fox* and *Murray* cases, the standard of suspicion set by domestic law for arrest was closer to Article 5(1)(c): honest suspicion on reasonable grounds. This was 'a significant safeguard against arbitrary arrest'[264] and, on the facts, the Court was influenced by this, together with the applicant's ensuing failure to pursue the issue of 'reasonable suspicion' before the domestic courts (where he had focused on claims of assault and ill-treatment) and where, on the limited materials before him, the judge had inferred the existence of reasonable grounds of suspicion. Overall the European Court stated that there was no basis in the material provided to it to reject the government's version of events that the arrest was a pre-planned operation, more akin to the earlier *Murray* case, and based on slightly more specific detail than *Fox, Campbell and Hartley*. As to whether reasonable suspicion had existed, it stated that the domestic courts' approach was not incompatible with the standard imposed by Article 5(1)(c), and that the domestic legal regime provided checks against arbitrary arrest plus did not confer any impunity with regard to arrests conducted on the basis of confidential information. In the Court's view (six votes to one), it could therefore be said that Article 5(1)(c) was satisfied.[265]

It will be appreciated from these cases that Article 5(1)(c) does not permit the detention of an individual for questioning merely as part of an intelligence-gathering exercise (there must be an intention, in principle at least, to bring charges, otherwise the person must be released). In practical terms, however, it will be very hard for an international court to ensure that Article 5(1)(c) is always applied in good faith by the national authorities.

Cases such as *Fox, Campbell and Hartley* and the others considered immediately above concerned Article 5(1)(c) in the context of an 'arrest' and in the period immediately thereafter. However, provided reasonable suspicion exists, this provision may provide the basis for detention for a significant period of time beyond arrest. During this time, the continuing need for detention may be subject to periodic review under Article 5(3).[266]

d. Lawfulness more generally

The Court is prepared to find a violation of Article 5(1) when it is clear from the facts that the grounds for arrest simply did not exist. An example is *Steel v UK*,[267] where the Court found that, for certain of the applicants, their protest had been entirely peaceful such that the criteria making up the offence of breach of the peace had not been applied at the time the applicants were detained.[268]

In *KF v Germany*,[269] where domestic law permitted detention of the applicant for a maximum of twelve hours, the Court indicated that it could find as non-'lawful' a detention

---

maximum length of detention in this case was only four hours was also 'material to the level of suspicion required'.

[263] 34 EHRR 812.   [264] *O'Hara v UK*, para 38.
[265] See, however, the strong dissent of Judge Loucaides.   [266] See section 7.II.
[267] 1998-VII; 29 EHRR 365. See also *RL and M-JD v France* hudoc (2004) (violation by four votes to three).
[268] *Steel v UK*, paras 62–4 (the legal question regarding whether there had been a breach of the peace had not been before the domestic court as the prosecution had dropped the charges, whilst no civil claim for false imprisonment against the police was brought). See also *Wloch v Poland* 2000-XI; 34 EHRR 229 paras 111–17.
[269] 1997-VII; 26 EHRR 390 para 68.

within that time span but which was unreasonable to the extent that it was not actually justified (for example, the police were no longer pursuing the matter). In principle, detention will not be 'lawful' under Article 5(1)(c) when the maximum period laid down by law for detaining the applicant is exceeded, as it was on the facts of the *KF* case. The Court will take a strict approach here when the maximum period is absolute, specifically laid down by law, and so known in advance. The authorities would then be under a duty to take all necessary precautions to ensure that the permitted duration was not exceeded and even a short period in excess will violate Article 5.[270] Where the period of detention is not laid down in advance by statute and ends as a result of a court order or the determination of the charge against an accused, in principle Article 5(1)(c) will be violated immediately after the point when a charge is determined.[271] However, the Court has accepted that there may be some limited delay before a detained person is released, when this is a result of '[p]ractical considerations relating to the running of the courts and the completion of special formalities'.[272] But the delay must be kept to a minimum.[273]

The principle of legal certainty, inherent in the concept of 'lawful' detention, is contravened when detention under Article 5(1)(c) is permitted for an unlimited and unpredictable time and without being based on a concrete legal provision or on any judicial decision.[274] Hence, 'detention which extends over a period of several months and which has not been ordered by a court or by a judge or any other person "authorised...to exercise judicial power" cannot be considered "lawful" in the sense of [Article 5(1)(c)]'.[275] In fact, such a requirement is not explicitly stipulated in Article 5(1), but the Court infers it from Article 5 read as a whole, in particular from Articles 5(1)(c), 5(3), and 5(4).[276] Ordering detention without fixing any time limit on it will also breach Article 5(1)(c).[277]

IV. ARTICLE 5(1)(D): DETENTION OF MINORS

Article 5(1)(d) creates a specific basis to detain minors, but its existence does not prevent the potential reliance on other Article 5(1) paragraphs to detain minors.[278]

As with other Article 5(1) terms, 'minor' has an autonomous Convention meaning.[279] In the light of European standards, all persons under eighteen can be taken to be minors. Whether a state with an age of majority higher than eighteen would find that its detention of a person of eighteen years or more was justified under Article 5(1)(d) is unclear. In the case of both grounds for detention allowed by Article 5(1)(d), the detention must be 'lawful', which, as elsewhere in Article 5(1),[280] requires compliance with municipal law

---

[270] *KF v Germany*, paras 71–2 (violation of Article 5(1) when individual held forty-five minutes over the twelve-hour maximum). [271] However, Article 5(1)(a) may then apply.

[272] *KF v Germany* 1997-VII; 26 EHRR 390 para 71. *Ignatenco v Moldova* hudoc (2011) was distinguished from *KF*, see para 68. See also *Quinn v France* A 311 (1995); 21 EHRR 529 (Article 5(1)(c) violated when detainee held for eleven hours beyond court order requiring immediate release); *Labita v Italy* 2000-IV; 46 EHRR 1228 GC (twelve-hour delay due, at least in part, to absence of appropriate staff required to complete release formalities); and *Bojinov v France* hudoc (2004) (administrative problems).

[273] *Giulia Manzoni v Italy* 1997-IV; 26 EHRR 691 para 25.

[274] *Baranowski v Poland* 2000-III para 56. See also *Ječius v Lithuania* 2000-IX; 35 EHRR 400; *Laumont v France* 2001-XI; 36 EHRR 625. See also *Lukanov v Bulgaria* 1997-II; 24 EHRR 121 (former Prime Minister of Bulgaria charged for actions which were not criminal under domestic law).

[275] *Baranowski v Poland*, para 57. [276] *Baranowski v Poland*.

[277] *Kharchenko v Ukraine* hudoc (2011) para 98.

[278] *Mubilanzila Mayeka and Kaniki Mitunga v Belgium* hudoc (2006); 46 EHRR 449 para 100.

[279] *X v Switzerland No 8500/79*, 18 DR 238 (1979). Cf the interpretation of 'vagrant', etc in Article 5(1)(e), section 5.V.b. [280] See section 4.

and the Convention and supposes that any deprivation of liberty is 'in keeping with the purpose of Article 5, namely to protect the individual from arbitrariness'.[281]

The first of the two permitted grounds, *viz* detention 'for the purpose of educational supervision', applies when the detention results from a 'lawful order', which may be made by an administrative authority or by a court. This ground for detention would appear to authorize the legal obligation normally found in state law requiring children to attend school. It may be noted, however, that Article 5(1)(d) authorizes the detention of 'minors', not persons of an age that are required to attend school. In other words, where the school leaving age is sixteen, a seventeen-year-old may still be detained under Article 5(1)(d).[282]

In *Bouamar v Belgium*,[283] it was held that Article 5(1)(d) authorized the detention of a minor in a reformatory 'for the purpose of educational supervision' or in a remand prison as a preliminary to his transfer 'speedily' to such an institution. In that case, the defendant state was held to be in breach of Article 5(1) when the applicant, a seriously disturbed and delinquent sixteen-year-old, was detained by court order in a remand prison, which provided no educational facilities, for periods amounting to 119 days' detention during most of one year. The orders were made under a 1965 Act, the policy of which was that juveniles who committed criminal offences should normally be placed in juvenile reformatories rather than be convicted by a criminal court. The orders for the applicant's detention were made under a provision of the Act that permitted a juvenile's detention in a remand prison for up to fifteen days when it was 'materially impossible' to place him in a reformatory immediately. In the applicant's case, the problem was that the open reformatories that provided the required educational facilities were not willing to take him because of his difficult behaviour and there were no closed reformatories with such facilities in his French-speaking region. The Court accepted that the applicant might be detained temporarily in a remand prison, though this should be 'speedily' followed by detention in an Article 5(1)(d) compatible institution.[284] On the facts, however, the period of prison detention was too long and was not for the permitted purpose as the applicant's detention was an expedient adopted by the authorities in the absence of 'appropriate institutional facilities which met the demands of security and the educational objectives of the 1965 Act'.[285] If, for commendable policy reasons, Belgium had decided not to dispose of seriously disturbed juveniles through the criminal courts (in which case their detention could be justified following conviction under Article 5(1)(a)), it could only detain them consistently with Article 5 in institutions that offered the necessary educational supervision required by Article 5(1)(d). Should this involve the building of appropriate reformatories, the resulting commitment was, the Court made clear,[286] one that Belgium would have to undertake despite the cost involved.

How comprehensive and 'school-like' the regime of 'educational supervision' provided by a reformatory for disturbed juveniles has to be is not entirely clear. In the context of a young person in local authority care, the Court has accepted that the words do not have to be 'equated rigidly with notions of classroom teaching' and that 'educational supervision

---

[281] *Bouamar v Belgium* A 129 (1988); 11 EHRR 1 para 47.

[282] *DG v Ireland* 2002-III; 35 EHRR 1153 para 76 (under domestic legislation a 'minor' was below the age of eighteen).   [283] A 129 (1988); 11 EHRR 1.

[284] *Bouamar v Belgium*, para 50. There was a violation in *DG v Ireland* 2002-III; 35 EHRR 1153 paras 84–5 (no secure education facilities available and then hastily prepared facilities proved to be inadequate).

[285] *Bouamar v Belgium*, para 52.   [286] *Bouamar v Belgium*, para 52.

must embrace many aspects of the exercise, by the local authority, of parental rights for the benefit and protection of the person concerned'.[287]

The second of the two permitted grounds for the detention of a minor is 'his lawful detention for the purpose of bringing him before the competent legal authority'. The *travaux préparatoires* indicate that this wording was intended to cover the situation where a minor is detained with a view to being brought before a court not on a criminal charge (so that Article 5(1)(c) would apply) but 'to secure his removal from harmful surroundings'.[288] Thus the detention of a minor accused of a crime during the preparation of a psychiatric report necessary to the taking of a decision in his case is permitted,[289] as is detention pending the making of a court order placing a child in care.[290]

V. ARTICLE 5(1)(E): DETENTION OF PERSONS OF UNSOUND MIND, ALCOHOLICS, VAGRANTS, ETC

Each term within Article 5(1)(e) has an autonomous Convention meaning. The categories of persons covered by this sub-paragraph may all be deprived of liberty 'either in order to be given medical treatment or because of considerations dictated by social policy', or both combined, the 'predominant reason' for allowing detention being that the persons concerned 'are dangerous for public safety but also that their own interests may necessitate their detention'.[291] The Court applies a necessity test to detention under this sub-paragraph.

a. Prevention of the spreading of infectious diseases

The Court has held that the criteria for determining the lawfulness of detention under Article 5(1)(e) in relation to 'infectious diseases' is, firstly, 'whether the spreading of the infectious disease is dangerous for public health or safety', and secondly, 'whether detention of the person infected is the last resort in order to prevent the spreading of the disease, because less severe measures have been considered and found to be insufficient to safeguard the public interest'.[292] A deprivation of liberty ceases to be lawful when these criteria are no longer fulfilled.

Enhorn v Sweden[293] concerned a person carrying the HIV virus, which the Court accepted satisfied the first test just identified ('dangerous for public health and safety'). The applicant had been placed involuntarily in a hospital for a period totalling approximately one-and-a-half years further to a court order enforcing public health legislation and after the apparent failure of voluntary measures created to protect other members of society, the

---

[287] *DG v Ireland* 2002-III; 35 EHRR 1153 para 80; *Ichin and Others v Ukraine* hudoc (2010) para 39 (juvenile holding facility unsuitable; no programme or education; nor, on the facts, an intention to bring before the competent legal authority, paras 38–9); Cf *Bouamar v Belgium* A 129 (1988); 11 EHRR 1 para 50. See also *Koniarska v UK No 33670/96* hudoc (2000) DA (seventeen-year-old held in a specialist residential facility; Article 5(1)(d) applied given the multi-disciplinary teaching provided, even though number of classes attended limited because of applicant's behaviour; underlying position was that extensive educational provision was made, and 'the applicant benefited from it to a certain extent'); and also *P and S v Poland* hudoc (2012) (violation: essential purpose was to prevent a minor from having recourse to abortion).

[288] 3 TP 724, quoted in Fawcett, p 90.   [289] *X v Switzerland No 8500/79*, 18 DR 238 (1979).

[290] Cf, *Bouamar v Belgium* A 129 (1988); 11 EHRR 1 para 46.

[291] *Enhorn v Sweden* 2005-I; 41 EHRR 633 para 43. See also *Guzzardi v Italy* A 39 (1980); 3 EHRR 333 para 98 PC and *Witold Litwa v Poland* 2000-III 289; 33 EHRR 1267 para 60.

[292] *Enhorn v Sweden* 2005-I; 41 EHRR 633 para 44.   [293] 2005-I; 41 EHRR 633, para 45.

reason for the detention apparently being to stop the applicant spreading the disease through sexual acts. The European Court accepted that there was a basis for the detention in domestic law in that, firstly, the national courts had considered that the applicant had not voluntarily complied with the measures needed to prevent the virus from spreading; and, secondly, although the relevant medical officer had formulated practical instructions for the applicant to regulate his conduct on release, it was reasonable on the facts to suggest that these would not be complied with, plus that this would entail a risk of the infection spreading.[294] However, Article 5(1)(e) had been violated as the second ('last resort') test identified previously was not satisfied. Certain measures that might have reduced the risk posed by the applicant (eg, psychiatric treatment to change the applicant's behaviour and effective treatment to help him control his abuse of alcohol) had not been made a condition of the voluntary regime required of him prior to the order to detain. Moreover, although one sexual partner had been infected prior to the applicant's knowledge that he himself carried the virus, there was no evidence to suggest that the applicant had ever spread HIV intentionally or through gross neglect, including during the period of over five years when the order for detention was in force but when, in fact, he had absconded.[295] More generally, the Court considered that the authorities had failed to strike a fair balance between the need to ensure that the HIV virus did not spread and the applicant's right to liberty.[296]

b. 'Vagrants'

The term 'vagrants' was examined in *De Wilde, Ooms and Versyp v Belgium* (the *Vagrancy* cases).[297] The Court noted that in the Belgian Criminal Code, 'vagrants' were defined as 'persons who have no fixed abode, no means of subsistence and no regular trade or profession'. It commented that a person who came within this definition was 'in principle' a 'vagrant' for the purposes of Article 5(1)(e). Although the Court did not expressly state that the Convention meaning was co-terminous with that in Belgian law, it is likely that the latter reflects the generally understood meaning of the term. In *Guzzardi v Italy*,[298] the Court rejected a government argument that suspected Mafia members who lacked any identifiable sources of income were vagrants.

c. 'Alcoholics' and 'drug addicts'

In *Witold Litwa v Poland*,[299] the Court held that a person does *not* have to be in a clinical state of 'alcoholism' to be an 'alcoholic' for the purposes of Article 5(1)(e). The term potentially applies to 'persons...whose conduct and behaviour under the influence of alcohol pose a threat to public order or themselves'. Such individuals could 'be taken into custody for the protection of the public or their own interests, such as their health or personal safety'.[300] In this way Article 5(1)(e) can be employed to facilitate the detention of the type of intoxicated individuals just referred to for temporary (sobering up)

---

[294] *Enhorn v Sweden*, paras 37–8.   [295] *Enhorn v Sweden*, para 54.

[296] *Enhorn v Sweden*, para 55. See the concurring opinion of Judge Costa (systematic confinement of persons capable of spreading infectious diseases would turn them into outcasts; only acceptable for limited periods ('quarantine'), where the disease is curable).   [297] A 12 (1971); 1 EHRR 373 PC.

[298] A 39 (1980); 3 EHRR 333 PC.

[299] 2000-III; 33 EHRR 1267 paras 57–63. See also *Hilda Hafsteinsdóttir v Iceland* hudoc (2004) and *Kharin v Russia* hudoc (2011) paras 33–5.

[300] 2000-III; 33 EHRR 1267, para 61. See also para 62, and *Kharin v Russia* hudoc (2011) para 42 (noting that the State might also rely on Article 5(1)(e), but only on condition that it be for the protection of the well-being of the individual or others around him). *Witold Litwa* suggests that the Court would be prepared to be flexible as regards the requirement of addiction to drugs despite the express wording 'drug *addict*' (Article 5(1)(e)).

periods either when the misdemeanour is not actually a criminal offence or, if so, when, for whatever reason, there is no real intention of progressing them through the criminal justice system.[301]

In *Witold Litwa*, the Court maintained that its interpretation of 'alcoholics' was in keeping with the original spirit of Article 5;[302] however, Judge Bonnello, the sole dissenter, took strong exception to the interpretation employed which, he insisted, went against the whole thrust of Article 5 jurisprudence and was a 'quantum leap backwards'.[303] Certainly the broad reading of 'alcoholic' places a heavy burden on the controlling requirement that any detention under Article 5(1) must be 'lawful'. The test to be satisfied here is whether the intoxicated person should be detained in order 'to limit the harm caused by alcohol to himself and the public', or even, 'to prevent dangerous behaviour after drinking'.[304] This seems to be worryingly vague, but it is notable that the Court applied the test quite stringently in *Witold Litwa* itself (and in subsequent case law it has added that Article 5(1) (e) 'does not permit detention of an individual merely because of his alcohol intake'[305]). The applicant was involved in a disagreement at the post office in which the staff claimed he was drunk and abusive. He was almost fifty years old and practically blind, but still taken by the police to the Krakow sobering-up centre and detained there for six hours and thirty minutes. The proper legal procedures had been followed, but the 'lawfulness' test was not met as, given apparent elements of arbitrariness in the detention, the Court did not accept that what actually occurred was 'the lawful detention' of an 'alcoholic'. 'Serious doubts' existed as to whether the applicant had indeed behaved, under the influence of alcohol, in such a way that he posed a threat to the public or himself, or that his own health, well-being, or personal safety was endangered. As other options had been available to the police, eg simply escorting the applicant off the premises and taking him home, and these seemed to be appropriate on the facts, the applicant's detention had not been 'lawful'. The Court stated that

> [t]he detention of an individual is such a serious measure that it is only justified where other, less severe measures have been considered and found to be insufficient to safeguard the individual or public interest which might require that the person concerned be detained. That means that it does not suffice that the deprivation of liberty is executed in conformity with national law but it must also be necessary in the circumstances.[306]

The test of 'necessity' is therefore a check against the authorities' readiness to detain individuals (perhaps in a pre-emptive way) without proper consideration of the alternatives. It must be hoped that the domestic authorities will interpret this 'necessity' test strictly, placing the onus on the police (and the national authorities more generally[307]) to explain what alternatives to detention were considered and why they were not appropriate.

---

[301] Cf the requirements of Article 5(1)(c).

[302] The majority referred to the Convention's preparatory work, see *Witold Litwa v Poland* 2000-III; 33 EHRR 1267 para 63.

[303] Separate opinion of Judge Bonnello in *Witold Litwa*, arguing that Article 5(1)(e) applied only 'to continuing or habitual states of socially dangerous conditions or attitudes', as opposed 'to one-off, transient manifestations'. The Court had 'for the first time ever, and with a vengeance, departed from a healthy tradition, so far nurtured with religious fervour, of not adding to the list of exceptions which justify deprivations of liberty'.   [304] *Witold Litwa*, para 62.

[305] *Kharin v Russia* hudoc (2011) para 34 (see also para 43) (detention justified given applicant's aggressive and offensive behaviour; caused disturbance in a public place and posed a danger to others; as to required evidence of drunkenness, see paras 38–9).   [306] *Witold Litwa*, para 78.

[307] See the four-to-three ruling in *Kharin v Russia* hudoc (2011) (minority were extremely critical of the domestic court's failure to examine the necessity aspect (or the applicant's behaviour) and Strasbourg's willingness to resolve these aspects).

Finally, sight should not be lost of the importance of a precise regulatory framework governing detention in this sphere. The 'quality of law' requirements for detention of 'alcoholics' has been stressed in the case law. In *Hilda Hafsteinsdóttir v Iceland*,[308] the Court found a violation of Article 5(1) as administrative practice alone governed the scope and the manner of exercise of the police's discretion as regards the duration of detention.

d. 'Persons of unsound mind'

When claiming reliance upon Article 5(1)(e)[309] the authorities must comply with the procedures set out in domestic law, in order for detention to be lawful.[310] For example, in *Van Der Leer v Netherlands*,[311] the Court held that a person had been detained 'unlawfully' contrary to Article 5(1)(e) when a court had ordered the applicant's detention on the basis of mental illness without hearing her in person, as required by Dutch law. As the Court stated in *Winterwerp v Netherlands*,[312] the detention must be in 'conformity with the purpose of the restrictions permitted by Article 5(1)(e)' and must also be warranted on the facts of the case, otherwise it will be arbitrary.

More generally, to avoid 'arbitrariness' the case law requires that these minimum conditions have to be satisfied:

(i) prior to the detention, the detainee must be 'reliably shown' by 'objective medical expertise'[313] to be of 'unsound mind' (unless emergency detention is required);[314] *and*

(ii) the individual's 'mental disorder must be of a kind or degree warranting compulsory confinement', ie the deprivation of liberty must be shown to have been 'necessary in the circumstances';[315] and

(iii) the mental disorder, verified by objective medical evidence, must persist throughout the period of detention.

Furthermore, the domestic legal regime should 'provide adequate safeguards against arbitrariness',[316] both with respect to the committal to the institution (which must show respect for the views of the patient[317]) and with respect to the assessment of whether the alleged disorder warranting confinement persists over time.[318]

---

[308] Hudoc (2004) paras 51 and 53–6. See, however, the partly dissenting opinion of Judge Garlicki and the dissenting opinion of Judges Casadevall and Maruste.

[309] See Bartlett, Lewis, and Thorold, *Mental Disability and the European Convention on Human Rights*, 2006. Article 8 issues (physical and moral integrity) also regularly arise in cases concerning Article 5(1)(e) and mental health, as do Article 6 and 3 issues. As regards what is required for deprivation of liberty under this head, see section 2.II, and see *Stanev v Bulgaria* ECHR-2012; 55 EHRR 625 paras 115–20 GC; for the legal standards applicable under Article 5(1)(e), see paras 143–7, and as regards Article 5(4), see para 171.

[310] For a state's positive obligations in respect of private psychiatric institutions, see *Storck v Germany* 2005-V; 43 EHRR 96, section 3.I   [311] A 170-A (1990); 12 EHRR 567 para 22.

[312] A 33 (1979); 2 EHRR 387 para 39.

[313] This will include a personal and up-to-date medical examination, other than in an emergency situation. See, further, *Wassink v Netherlands* (1990) A 185-A paras 33 and 34; *Varbanov v Bulgaria* 2000-X paras 47–49 and *Herz v Germany* hudoc (2003). See also *X v Finland* ECHR-2012.

[314] Such an opinion should be obtained immediately after the arrest, *Varbanov*, para 47.

[315] *Varbanov*, para 46.

[316] See section 4 regarding lawfulness of detention etc, and section 2.II concerning *HL v UK* 2004-IX; 40 EHRR 761. See also *X v Finland* ECHR-2012 (insufficient safeguards against arbitrariness on the facts; involuntary confinement involving forced administration of medication; see paras 169 and 170).

[317] See section 2.II.   [318] *Mihailovs v Latvia* hudoc (2013) paras 149–50.

As to (i) above, the meaning of 'persons of unsound mind' was considered in *Winterwerp v Netherlands*.[319] It is not a term that can be given a 'definitive interpretation' because the medical profession's understanding of mental disorder is still developing, but it is evident that a person cannot be detained under Article 5(1)(e) 'simply because his views or behaviour deviate from the norms prevailing in a particular society'.[320] He must be suffering from a 'true mental disorder'.[321] Beyond this, when determining whether a person is of 'unsound mind', it is a matter of referring to the relevant municipal law, which need not define or list the categories of mental disorder to which it extends, and its application in the particular case in the light of current psychiatric knowledge.[322] Although the Strasbourg authorities have the final word as to whether the person concerned is of 'unsound mind', the defendant state is allowed a certain 'margin of appreciation' when making its own initial assessment of the situation.[323]

The second condition noted above is important since it stipulates that being of 'unsound mind' is not on its own enough to justify detention; the mental disorder must warrant compulsory confinement, ie be necessary in the circumstances.[324] The necessity test may be satisfied in respect of a *mental disorder* where a person 'needs therapy, medication or other clinical treatment to cure or alleviate his condition, but also where [he/she] needs control and supervision to prevent [him/ her], for example, causing harm to himself or other persons'.[325] As to the former, in fact Article 5(1)(e) does not require that the illness or condition be of a nature or degree amenable to medical treatment.[326] It is therefore possible to detain someone suffering from a psychopathic personality disorder that cannot be treated in an appropriate hospital.[327] If so, the measure must be properly justified by reference to the second basis just noted, ie the seriousness of the condition in the interests of ensuring his or her own protection or that of others.[328] As to whether the need for therapy/clinical treatment alone can justify confinement, the Court has stressed that 'involuntary hospitalisation may... be used only as a last resort for want of a less invasive alternative, and only if it carries true health benefits without imposing a disproportionate burden on the person concerned'. [329]

---

[319] A 33 (1979); 2 EHRR 387 para 36. See also *X v UK* A 46 (1981); 4 EHRR 188.

[320] A 33 (1979); 2 EHRR 387 para 37.

[321] *Winterwerp v Netherlands*, para 39. See the separate opinion of Judges Villiger and Power-Forde in *Radu v Germany* hudoc (2013) (in the absence of any mental illness, a person with a personality disorder could not be categorized as a person 'of unsound mind'). See also *OH v Germany* hudoc (2011); 54 EHRR 1025, including dissenting opinion of Judge Zupančič.

[322] *Winterwerp v Netherlands* A 33 (1979); 2 EHRR 387 para 38.

[323] *Winterwerp v Netherlands*, para 40; *X v UK* A 46 (1981); 4 EHRR 188 para 43; and *Luberti v Italy* A 75 (1984); 6 EHRR 440 para 27. The Court's role is to ascertain ascertain 'whether the domestic courts, when taking the contested decision, had at their disposal sufficient evidence to justify the detention', *Pleso v Hungary* hudoc (2013) para 61.   [324] *Stanev v Bulgaria* ECHR-2012; 55 EHRR 625 para 143 GC.

[325] *Hutchison Reid v UK* 2003 IV; 37 EHRR 211 para 52; *Radu v Germany* hudoc (2013) para 91.

[326] *Hutchison Reid v UK*, para 52.   [327] *Hutchison Reid v UK*, paras 51–2.

[328] *Stanev v Bulgaria* ECHR-2012; 55 EHRR 625 GC para 157. This case concerned placement in a social care home, primarily, it seems, as a protective measure as the applicant was unable to look after himself properly, see section 2.II. The Grand Chamber observed that 'in certain circumstances, the welfare of a person with mental disorders might be a further factor to take into account, in addition to medical evidence, in assessing whether it is necessary to place the person in an institution', para 153. However, 'the objective need for accommodation and social assistance must not automatically lead to the imposition of measures involving deprivation of liberty', it being necessary that 'any protective measure... reflect as far as possible the wishes of persons capable of expressing their will'. Their opinion should be sought to help safeguard respect for the 'rights of vulnerable persons'.

[329] *Pleso v Hungary* hudoc (2013) para 66, a case of forced committal, the Court holding that the applicant's mental disorder was not of a kind or degree warranting compulsory confinement. There was no imminent danger to others or to the applicant's health, rather in issue for the domestic courts was whether

The third condition (validity of continued confinement depends upon the persistence of the disorder) entails that there is no lawful basis for detention once the person has recovered—he or she must be released at that point. In this regard the periodic review that Article 5(4) affords Article 5(1)(e) detainees constitutes a very important safeguard,[330] and especially so in cases when detention has been initiated without judicial involvement but by a private individual (for example under regimes which permit a legal guardian to do so) and confirmed by municipal and social care authorities.[331]

With respect to the third condition, practical problems may arise as professional decisions on matters such as recovery cannot always be made with absolute certainty. In that context, the Court accepts that, on the facts, the wider interest of the community might be balanced against the individual's right to immediate and unconditional release. For example, as regards immediate release, in *Luberti v Italy*,[332] even if the medical evidence pointed to his recovery, it was held that a responsible authority was entitled to proceed with caution and might need some time to consider whether to terminate an applicant's confinement.

Issues may arise when the applicant's release is subject to certain conditions which are not easily fulfilled. The applicant in *Kolanis v UK*[333] continued to suffer from schizophrenia and to require treatment (including medication) and medical supervision in order to control her illness. Her condition was such that compulsory confinement was no longer warranted—though only on the basis that she continued to have certain treatment once at liberty. However, appropriate measures for that treatment were not put in place and so the applicant remained detained. There was no violation of Article 5(1), for in the circumstances her detention was still necessary. The Court stated that there was no absolute obligation on the authorities to ensure that the conditions were fulfilled. No comment was made as to the level of obligation, if any, that might arise by way of provision of treatment in the community to ensure the due effectiveness of the decision to release, though the Court expressed reassurance with the existence of legal safeguards entailing that local authorities or doctors could not wilfully or arbitrarily block the discharge of patients into the community without proper grounds or excuse.[334]

The Court accepts that under Article 5(1)(e) a responsible authority, viewing the matter as a whole and wishing to proceed cautiously in good faith, may 'retain some measure of supervision over the progress of the person once he is released into the community and to that end make his discharge subject to conditions'.[335] But Article 5(1)(e) places curbs on the authorities' freedom of action here, it being of 'paramount importance' that firstly, 'appropriate safeguards are in place so as to ensure that any deferral of discharge is consonant with the purpose of Article 5(1) and with the aim of the restriction in sub-paragraph (e)'. Secondly, the discharge must 'not [be] unreasonably delayed'. These points were highly relevant to the

medical treatment would improve his condition or the absence of such treatment would lead to a deterioration in that condition. As such, it was 'incumbent on the authorities to strike a fair balance between the competing interests emanating, on the one hand, from society's responsibility to secure the best possible health care for those with diminished faculties (for example, because of lack of insight into their condition) and, on the other hand, from the individual's inalienable right to self-determination (including the right to refusal of hospitalisation or medical treatment, that is, his or her "right to be ill")', para 66. More weight should have been given to the applicant's non-consent (he had legal capacity). This balancing test is controversial, it being unfortunate that this matter was not heard by the Grand Chamber.

[330] See section 8.III.   [331] See, eg, *Mihailovs v Latvia* hudoc (2013) para 155.

[332] *Luberti v Italy* A 75 (1984); 6 EHRR 440 para 29. See also *Johnson v UK* 1997 VII; 27 EHRR 196.

[333] Hudoc (2005); 42 EHRR 206.

[334] *Kolanis v UK*, para 71. She could also rely on Article 5(4) to ensure that any continued detention was consonant with the purpose of Article 5(1).

[335] *Johnson v UK* 1997 VII; 27 EHRR 196 para 63 (phased conditional discharge possible on the facts, para 64).

applicant in *Johnson v UK*.[336] He had apparently recovered from mental illness and did not require any further medication or treatment. Release was, however, still made subject to conditions for his effective monitoring, it being feared that his mental illness might return. The applicant therefore had to undertake a period of rehabilitation in a hostel. Even after the decision to order conditional discharge had been taken, it had been repeatedly deferred owing to a combination of circumstances, including lack of available hostel places, but also the applicant's behaviour, which caused some hostels to reject his proposed transfer to them. Meanwhile, as the process dragged on, the applicant was kept in his original confinement location, a secure psychiatric hospital until, after four years, his unconditional discharge was granted. Whilst the Court indicated that it would be prepared to accept some delay in granting conditional discharge based on practical issues, there had been a breach of Article 5(1) given the unreasonable delay and a lack of safeguards available to the applicant to challenge that delay and his consequential confinement in the secure psychiatric hospital.[337] The Court did not therefore consider whether the proposed requirement that the applicant stay in a hostel was itself a violation of Article 5.[338]

The Court has consistently rejected applicants' arguments that Article 5(1)(e) carries with it an implied 'right to treatment' appropriate to the person's mental state during the period of detention.[339] However, as indicated in *Ashingdane v UK*,[340] there is a general rule that in the case of a 'person of unsound mind', in principle detention must be in a 'hospital, clinic or other appropriate institution authorised for' the detention of such persons.[341] *Aerts v Belgium*[342] indicates that this condition may give rise to a violation of Article 5. As a temporary measure pending placement in the proper institution, the applicant was held in the psychiatric wing of a prison and this proved harmful to him, as he did not benefit from a therapeutic environment or receive the treatment required by the condition that had given rise to his detention. The finding of a violation was based on the deficiency in '[t]he proper relationship between the aim of the detention and the conditions in which it took place'.[343] *Morsink v Netherlands*[344] was a similar case. It concerned

---

[336] 1997 VII; 27 EHRR 196.

[337] Having made the discharge conditional on finding suitable hostel accommodation, there was an onus on the authorities to secure it, but neither the tribunal nor the authorities possessed the necessary powers to ensure that the condition could be implemented within a reasonable time. Furthermore, the applicant had only very limited and very occasional opportunities to seek a review of the terms of his continued detention, and there was no proper regime in existence to monitor independently his plight given the evolving difficulties (there was no possibility to petition the tribunal in between annual reviews or seek judicial review of the terms of conditional discharge order). In practice, the terms of the conditional discharge were tantamount to an indefinite deferral of the release from the psychiatric hospital (for full details, see *Johnson v UK*, paras 66–7).   [338] *Johnson v UK*, para 68.

[339] *Winterwerp v Netherlands* A 33 (1979); 2 EHRR 387 para 51.

[340] A 93 (1985); 7 EHRR 528 para 44. See also *Aerts v Belgium* 1996-V; 29 EHRR 50 para 46 and *Hutchinson Reid v UK* 2003-IV; 37 EHRR 211 paras 48 and 54 ('[g]enerally,… it would be prima facie unacceptable not to detain a mentally ill person in a suitable therapeutic environment').

[341] On Article 5 and conditions of detention, see section 3.II.

[342] 1998-V; 29 EHRR 50. See also *LB v Belgium* hudoc (2012) (detention in prison psychiatric wing when placement in structure adapted to applicant's pathology was required).

[343] *Aerts v Belgium*, para 49. An applicant's 'conduct or attitude does not exempt the domestic authorities from providing persons detained (solely) as mental health patients with a medical and therapeutic environment appropriate for their condition', see *Kronfeldner v Germany* hudoc (2012) para 82 (and para 83). Article 5(4) must afford the possibility of reviewing compliance with the conditions to be satisfied if the detention of a person of unsound mind is to be regarded as 'lawful' for the purposes of paragraph 1(e), see *X v UK* A 46 (1981); 4 EHRR 188 para 58.

[344] Hudoc (2004) paras 65–70. See also *Brand v Netherlands* hudoc (2004), *Mocarska v Poland* hudoc (2007) and *De Schepper v Belgium* hudoc (2009).

detention in an ordinary remand centre for fifteen months pending transfer to a custodial clinic (where treatment could be provided), the delay chiefly being due to a structural lack of capacity in custodial clinics. The failure to transfer the applicant to a clinic automatically did not violate Article 5(1)[345] and the Court refused to pursue the 'unrealistic and too rigid' approach of expecting the state to place the detainee immediately after he had been assessed. It accepted that, 'for reasons linked to the efficient management of public funds, a certain friction between available and required capacity in custodial clinics is inevitable and must be regarded as acceptable'.[346] Yet a violation of Article 5(1) was still found given the failure of the authorities to strike a reasonable balance between the competing interests involved, due regard being had to the importance of the applicant's right to liberty. The Court emphasized that, on the facts, a 'significant delay' in admission to a custodial clinic risked prolonging the detention overall, since it entailed a delay in treatment and reduced the prospects of its success. Reference was also made to the fact that a structural lack of capacity in custodial clinics had been identified domestically for over a decade such that it could not be said that the authorities were faced with an exceptional and unforeseen situation.[347]

VI. ARTICLE 5(1)(F): DETENTION PENDING DEPORTATION OR EXTRADITION, ETC

Under Article 5(1)(f)[348] there is no requirement that the detention be reasonably considered necessary, at least for adults. Instead the safeguards that operate are as follows:[349] detention under Article 5(1)(f) must be:

[i] carried out in good faith; [ii] ... closely connected to the purpose of preventing unauthorised entry of the person to the country [this for the first part of Article 5(1)(f)]; [iii] the place and conditions of detention should be appropriate, bearing in mind that 'the measure is applicable not to those who have committed criminal offences but to aliens who, often fearing for their lives, have fled from their own country';[350] and [iv] the length of the detention should not exceed that reasonably required for the purpose pursued.

a. Preventing 'unauthorized entry'

Most Strasbourg cases have concerned detention pending deportation or extradition. The first limb of Article 5(1)(f) was nevertheless in issue in *Saadi v UK*.[351] The applicant had sought asylum on his arrival at Heathrow airport. He was granted temporary admission to the UK and three days passed during which he was at liberty. During this period he

---

[345] See, however, the strong arguments presented in the concurring opinion of Judge Loucaides.

[346] *Morsink v Netherlands*, para 67.

[347] The judgment was by five votes to two. See also *Proshkin v Russia* hudoc (2012).

[348] For EU member states, the following may also be of relevance: Directive 2008/115/EC of the European Parliament and of the Council of 16 December 2008 on common standards and procedures in Member States for returning illegally staying third-country nationals. See also, within the Council of Europe, 'Guidelines on human rights protection in the context of accelerated asylum procedures (Adopted by the Committee of Ministers on 1 July 2009 at the 1062nd meeting of the Ministers' Deputies)'.

[349] *Saadi v UK* ECHR-2008; 47 EHRR 427 para 74 GC (numbers added). See also *A v UK* ECHR-2009; 49 EHRR 625 para 164 GC.   [350] *Saadi* citing *Amuur v France* 1996-III; 22 EHRR 533 para 43.

[351] ECHR-2008; 47 EHRR 427 GC (Chamber judgment: hudoc (2006); 44 EHRR 1005, no violation of Article 5(1), by four votes to three).

dutifully returned to the airport each day for the processing of his asylum claim, and it was only after the third day that he was detained for seven days in a fast-track centre for the quick processing of his asylum application. By eleven votes to six, the Court held that Saadi's detention did not contravene Article 5(1).

There were two important and contentious aspects to the Court's reasoning. First, temporary admission to enter a country after applying for asylum did not amount to a lawful 'entry' for the purposes of Article 5(1)(f). Leave to stay was required for this. Accordingly asylum seekers like Saadi, who had, after all, presented himself to the immigration authorities on successive occasions, *remained* 'unauthorized' entrants, and so remained susceptible to being detained under Article 5(1)(f) on the basis that this was preventing an unauthorized entry.[352]

The second noteworthy aspect of the ruling was the rejection of the principle that detention under the first limb of Article 5(1)(f) had to be necessary in each instance. After all, there was no evidence to suggest that Saadi himself intended to effect an unlawful entry into the United Kingdom; indeed, the facts indicated that he did not. However, this did not matter because the Court merely required that an individual's detention under Article 5(1)(f) should not be 'arbitrary'.[353] It was not as the good faith test was satisfied, the detention centre in issue having been set up especially for speedy administration of asylum claims and Saadi had been selected to go there as his application seemed ripe for the fast-track process.[354] The second ([ii]) condition noted earlier was also satisfied, as was the third,[355] whilst seven days detention was reasonable in the circumstances.[356]

In reaching its conclusion, the Grand Chamber in *Saadi* specifically referred to 'the difficult administrative problems' with which the United Kingdom was confronted during the period in question, with an escalating flow of huge numbers of asylum seekers.[357] Evidently it sought to strike a balance between the competing interests of, on the one hand, effective immigration controls and, on the other, meaningful protection of asylum seekers' rights under the Convention.[358] The minority argued that the Court had given inappropriate weight to the latter. The heart of their argument was that detention under the first limb of Article 5(1)(f) should not be used for the state's administrative convenience. Rather it could only be employed if it was established that the individual concerned was actually seeking to evade immigration controls. This, they insisted, reflected the importance attached to the right to liberty and was in keeping with other international standards. The Court was also criticized for failing to take proper account of the plight of asylum seekers by categorizing them all as ordinary immigrants. Indeed the Court's reading of the first limb of Article 5(1)(f) boldly assumes that all those who have not been fully authorized to stay are seeking illegal entry. In this respect the Court prioritized the states' interest in effective immigration control.[359] However, it circumscribed the alarmingly wide power Article 5(1)(f) gives states to detain by insisting that detention

---

[352] *Saadi v UK*, para 65 GC. See, however, *Suso Musa v Malta* hudoc (2013) para 97 (GC referral request pending at time of writing), the Court suggesting that *Saadi* should not be interpreted as allowing detention if national law itself prohibits this, ie authorizes entry or stay pending an asylum application.

[353] *Saadi v UK*, para 66 GC.   [354] *Saadi v UK*, paras 76–7.

[355] *Saadi v UK*, para 78 (importance of having suitable legal assistance at the centre). See also *Riad and Idiab v Belgium* hudoc (2008) (airport transit zone).   [356] *Saadi v UK*, para 79.

[357] *Saadi v UK*, para 80.

[358] Cf, the arguments presented by the third party interveners: UNHCR (paras 54–7) and Liberty, ECRE, and AIRE Centre (jointly at paras 58–60). See also the joint partly dissenting opinion of Judges Rozakis, Tulkens, Kovler, Hajiyev, Speilmann, and Hirvela.

[359] See ECHR-2008; 47 EHRR 427 para 64 GC. See also para 65 (inappropriate to interpret Article 5(1)(f) as permitting detention only if person shown to be trying to evade entry restrictions) and para 80.

in this context could be rendered arbitrary in certain circumstances, most notably if the period of detention was too long. The Court has since held that detention for three months under the first limb of Article 5(1)(f) for the purposes of determining an asylum claim was unreasonably long given the inappropriate conditions of the detention.[360]

b. 'Action is being taken with a view to deportation or extradition'

Bozano v France[361] concerned this second limb of Article 5(1)(f). A French court refused to order the extradition to Italy of the applicant, an Italian national convicted of murder, because he had been tried *in absentia*. The French government then made a deportation order against him. Despite knowledge of his whereabouts, the order was not served upon the applicant until a month later, when he was arrested suddenly one night. Without being given an opportunity to contact his wife or a lawyer (who might have taken legal steps to challenge the deportation) or to nominate a country of deportation (Spain was by far the nearest), the applicant was forcibly taken the same night by police officers by car across France to the Swiss border, where he was transferred to Swiss police custody. He was later extradited from Switzerland to Italy to serve his life sentence, on the basis of an Italian request for extradition initiated in Switzerland before the applicant's deportation from France. Subsequently, the deportation order against the applicant was declared invalid by a French court as being, *inter alia*, an abuse of power contrary to French law. The French court determined that the circumstances of the deportation demonstrated that the order's purpose had not been to cause the applicant's removal for reasons of a kind associated with deportation, but to effect an illegal extradition. In the light of the order's invalidity and of indications that French law might have been infringed when the applicant was handed over, the European Court expressed the 'gravest doubts whether the contested deprivation of liberty satisfied the legal requirements in the respondent state'.[362] As to the question of 'arbitrariness', the Court 'attached great weight to the circumstances in which the applicant was forcibly conveyed to the Swiss border'.[363] Considering the facts as a whole, relating both to the indications of non-compliance with French law and, particularly, of 'arbitrary' executive action, the Court concluded that the applicant's detention had not been 'lawful' as required by Article 5(1)(f). It was instead an element in a process designed to achieve 'a disguised form of extradition',[364] intended to circumvent the earlier domestic judgment against deportation, and so which could not be legitimately regarded as 'action...taken with a view to deportation'.

The text of Article 5(1)(f) stipulates that '*action* is being taken with a view to deportation' (emphasis added).[365] Construing this strictly, the Court regards as irrelevant arguments to the effect that, on its facts, the underlying decision to expel the applicant cannot be justified as being necessary under national or Convention law.[366] So it is not necessary

---

[360] *Kanagaratnam v Belgium* hudoc (2011); 55 EHRR 800 and see also *Suso Musa v Malta* hudoc (2013) para 102. Cf Human Rights Committee, General Comment No. 35 (Article 9: Liberty and security of person) (CCPR/C/107/R.3), para 18, stating that asylum seekers who unlawfully enter may be detained for (only) 'a brief initial period in order to document their entry, record their claims, and determine their identity if it is in doubt', with comments as to the conditions of detention.

[361] A 111 (1986); 9 EHRR 297 (see also *Iskandarov v Russia* hudoc (2010) paras 148–51).

[362] *Bozano v France*, para 58.   [363] *Bozano v France*, para 59.

[364] *Bozano v France*, para 60.

[365] Detention may be justified by Article 5(1)(f) even though a formal request or an order for extradition has not been issued, provided that enquiries have been made, since the enquiries amount to 'action' being taken in the sense of that provision, *X v Switzerland No 9012/80*, 24 DR 205 (1980).

[366] *Chahal v UK* 1996-V; 23 EHRR 413 para 112; *Slivenko v Latvia* 2003-XI; 39 EHRR 490 para 146 GC. The Court will not use Article 5(1)(f) to examine arguments to the effect that the deportation breaches international refugee law, see *M v Bulgaria* hudoc (2011) para 63.

that the detention itself be warranted on its facts, for example to prevent the applicant fleeing or committing a further offence[367] (although different considerations may apply to detention of minors).[368] However, if there is no actual intention to deport or extradite the individual concerned, there will be a violation of Article 5(1); moreover, even if such an intention exists, there may be a violation if deportation is not possible for legal or other reasons, since the provision only permits detention when 'action is being taken' etc.[369] Hence continuing loss of liberty under Article 5(1)(f) will only be justified for as long as deportation or extradition proceedings are actively in progress, indefinite detention under that head not being permissible, even for national security reasons.

It was against this background that the UK derogated from Article 5(1)(f) in late 2001 in order to establish what was believed to be a Convention-compliant basis to detain the (foreign) terrorist suspects concerned, who were deemed to be a threat to national security, but whose deportation could not be secured without potentially violating Article 3 of the Convention (a non-derogable right). In the subsequent case of *A v UK*,[370] before it looked at the Article 15 issues involved, the Court examined Article 5(1)(f), the British government having pleaded[371] for a modification of the standards applied under that Article, at least in the context of cases such as *A v UK* (ie involving terrorist suspects). It submitted that Article 5(1)(f) should permit 'a balance to be struck between the individual's right to liberty and the state's interest in protecting its population from terrorist threat'.[372] In effect, it argued that, if deportation was not possible for Article 3 reasons, detention should be permitted under Article 5(1)(f) (on the one hand, the individual's rights would be respected by allowing him to stay, ie not deporting; on the other, the community's interest would be protected by that purportedly dangerous individual not being at liberty in the host state). The Court rejected this balancing argument, insisting that, 'if detention does not fit within the confines of the paragraphs as interpreted by the Court, it cannot be made to fit by an appeal to the need to balance the interests of the State against those of the detainee'.[373] The British arguments were regarded as an attempt, in effect, to extend the list of Article 5(1)(a)–(f) grounds for detention to include a scheme for the preventive detention of non-nationals who came with the protection of Article 3 (*Chahal*).[374] Indeed, the argument was inconsistent with the text of Article 5(1)(f), which only permitted detention if 'action is being taken with a view to deportation'. In that regard, the Court concluded that this test had not been satisfied on the facts, at least for those applicants who had not been deported within the first few months, but had been detained for periods of between two and four years on grounds of national security. The reality of their situation was that throughout the period of detention there had been no realistic prospect of their being expelled without this giving rise to a real risk of ill-treatment contrary to Article 3,[375] so in those circumstances the government's policy of keeping the possibility

---

[367] *Conka v Belgium* 2002-I; 34 EHRR 1298 para 38.

[368] See section 5.VI.b (*Popov v France* hudoc (2012)).

[369] *Chahal v UK* 1996-V; 23 EHRR 413 para 112 and see *M v Bulgaria* hudoc (2011) ('[w]here there are obstacles to deportation to a given country but other destinations are in principle possible, detention pending active efforts by the authorities to organise removal to a third country may fall within the scope of Article 5(1)(f)', para 73). On the relevance of a Rule 39 (interim) request from the Court, see *Azimov v Russia* hudoc (2013) paras 170–1.   [370] ECHR-2009; 49 EHRR 625 GC.

[371] *A v UK*, para 148 GC.   [372] *A v UK*, para 171 GC.

[373] *A v UK*, para 171 GC. Note, however, that the Court has confirmed that it is prepared to accept appropriately robust Memoranda of Understandings in the context of Article 3 and Article 6(1) deportation cases; see Ch 6.   [374] *A v UK*, para 171.

[375] *A v UK*, para 167 GC (one applicant was stateless and no other state would accept him; for the other applicants, only after two years did the UK start to seek assurances against ill-treatment from the destination state, and none were received until much later).

of deporting the applicants 'under active review' did not suffice. Their detention was not, therefore, covered by Article 5(1)(f), the Court suggesting that the predominant reason for their loss of liberty was based on security considerations.[376] The Court went on to conclude that the derogating measures adopted were disproportionate in that they discriminated unjustifiably between nationals and non-nationals, such that there was a violation of Article 5(1) for several applicants.[377]

The proceedings ('action') relevant to Article 5(1)(f) must be pursued with 'due diligence',[378] otherwise their duration may be considered 'excessive'.[379] Accordingly, the Court will examine the record of legal proceedings before the domestic authorities (looking at phases of detention individually but also in combination) in the light of a 'due diligence' test. Here the conduct of the applicant—who might delay proceedings[380]—as well as that of the authorities,[381] is taken into account and there is no absolute limit to the time that proceedings may last. The test is one of diligence appropriate to the circumstances,[382] although for long periods of detention the Court will consider whether there existed sufficient guarantees to safeguard against arbitrary executive decisions to keep an individual in detention.

These points and the rather basic approach taken by the Court were illustrated in *Chahal v UK*,[383] where the applicant had been detained under Article 5(1)(f) for over three-and-a-half years before domestic legal avenues had been exhausted (and he remained in Bedford prison for a further two years while the matter progressed at Strasbourg). The domestic delay was caused by the time it took for his application for judicial review and, above all, resolution of the legal problem of whether it was appropriate to deport him to India given the Article 3 harm he might suffer there. The refusal to release the applicant in the meantime was repeatedly justified by reference to the threat to national security that he was alleged to pose given his purported links to terrorist organizations. The Court expressed its serious concern over the 'extremely long period' of detention,[384] but there was no breach of Article 5(1) on this point. The test of due diligence had not been contravened, it being observed that this was no ordinary deportation matter since it had concerned several complex issues of fact and law, and it was in the applicant's own interest to have them thoroughly examined.[385]

---

[376] *A v UK*, para 171 GC, and see para 172 (condemnation of preventive detention).

[377] See Ch 19.

[378] *Quinn v France* A 311 (1995); 21 EHRR 529 para 48; and *Chahal v UK* 1996-V; 23 EHRR 413 para 113.

[379] *Chahal v UK* 1996-V; 23 EHRR 413 para 113, and *A v UK* ECHR-2009; 49 EHRR 625 para 164 GC. See also *Suso Musa v Malta* hudoc (2013). Time spent in detention by virtue of a conviction does not count, *Raf v Spain* 2000-XI para 64.

[380] See *Kolompar v Belgium* A 235-C (1992); 16 EHRR 197 (no breach of Article 5(1) since applicant had delayed proceedings or impliedly consented to their prolongation for nearly three years). See also *S v France* No 10965/84, 56 DR 62 (1988) and *Osman v UK No 15933/89* hudoc (1991) DA. The respondent State may argue that the person concerned is free to leave the country, and so end his detention, although the latter may insist that he will suffer harm if returned; see *Abdi v UK* hudoc (2013); 57 EHRR 477 paras 71–4.

[381] Cf *Quinn v France* A 311 (1995); 21 EHRR 529 (a period of almost two years disclosed an abuse of the extradition procedure and so violation of Article 5(1)). Cf *Leaf v Italy No 72794/01* hudoc (2003) DA (nine months' delay was reasonable).

[382] See *X v Germany No 9706/82*, 5 EHRR 512 (1983) (twenty-two months' detention during extradition proceedings justifiable as regular judicial review and delay resulted from attempts by the West German government to obtain Turkish government undertaking not to impose death penalty, also no evidence of dilatoriness by the West German authorities). Cf *X v UK No 8081/77*, 12 DR 207 (1977) (eleven months' delay attributable to the need to obtain evidence from Pakistan and the applicant's own conduct). For early Commission jurisprudence, see *Lynas v Switzerland No 7317/75*, 6 DR 141 (1976); *X v UK No 8081/77*, 12 DR 207 (1977); and *Z v Netherlands No 10400/83*, 38 DR 145 (1984).

[383] 1996-V; 23 EHRR 413 GC. Commented upon in *A v UK* ECHR-2009; 49 EHRR 625 GC para 169.

[384] *Chahal v UK*, para 123.   [385] *Chahal v UK*, para 117. The Commission disagreed.

However, in view of the 'extremely long period' involved, the Court found it 'necessary to consider whether there existed sufficient guarantees against [the] arbitrariness' of the executive's decision to keep the applicant in detention.[386] The background here was that the domestic courts were not in a position effectively to control whether the decisions taken by the executive to keep Chahal in detention were justified, because the full material on which these decisions were based was not made available to them. This was because the executive asserted that national security was involved and so full disclosure to the courts did not follow, given the sensitivity of certain information. However, a special advisory panel was in place, which included experienced judicial figures, and, even though its report was never disclosed, the Court was satisfied that it had fully reviewed the evidence relating to the national security threat represented by the applicant. The procedure in question 'provided an adequate guarantee that there were at least *prima facie* grounds for believing that if Mr Chahal were at liberty, national security would be put at risk and thus, that the executive had not acted arbitrarily when it ordered him to be kept in detention'.[387] The procedure in question, however, failed to satisfy the requirements of both Article 5(4)[388] and Article 13—an indication of the inferior standard required under Article 5(1)(f).

Different factual scenarios occurred in *Amuur v France*[389] and *Conka v Belgium*.[390] The first case was discussed earlier[391] and was notable for the finding that Article 5 applied, plus certain statements made by the Court regarding the need for national authorities to have due regard to the vulnerability of asylum seekers.[392] In *Conka*, the applicants had been part of a group of illegal immigrants who had attended a police station following a deliberately misleading communication to the effect that their presence was required to address aspects of their asylum application. In what was clearly a pre-planned operation, they were arrested upon arrival and deported soon after. In its judgment, the Court acknowledged that the ruse to get the applicants to the police station would not vitiate the entire arrest procedure, or warrant it being qualified as an abuse of power, but it indicated disapproval and reiterated the point that no loss of liberty can be arbitrary. Thus, although the Court 'by no means exclude[ed] its being legitimate for the police to use stratagems in order, for instance, to counter criminal activities more effectively', it warned that 'acts whereby the authorities seek to gain the trust of asylum seekers with a view to arresting and subsequently deporting them may be found to contravene the general principles stated or implicit in the Convention'.[393] The exceptions to Article 5 had to be interpreted restrictively and that requirement also had to be 'reflected in the reliability of communications such as those sent to the applicants, irrespective of whether the recipients are lawfully present in the country or not'. The Court then added that, 'even as regards overstayers, a conscious decision by the authorities to facilitate or improve the effectiveness of a planned operation for the expulsion of aliens by misleading them about the purpose of a notice so as to make it easier to deprive them of their liberty is not compatible with Article 5'.[394]

---

[386] *Chahal v UK*, para 119.

[387] *Chahal v UK*, para 122. There were some strong dissenting judgments.   [388] See section 8.II.c.

[389] 1996-III; 22 EHRR 533. See also *Gebremedhin v France* hudoc (2007).

[390] 2002-I; 34 EHRR 1298.   [391] See section 2.I.

[392] The Court was highly critical of the absence of any proper legal regulation of the applicants' detention, *Amuur v France* 1996-III; 22 EHRR 533 para 53 (see also para 50, emphasis on the 'quality of law').

[393] *Conka v Belgium* 2002-I; 34 EHRR 1298 para 41.

[394] *Conka v Belgium*, para 42 (detention was arbitrary; applicants' failure to exhaust domestic remedies was excusable because, in effect, they were ineffective given the timescale and circumstances within which the domestic authorities had acted, and which they had themselves induced, see paras 43–6).

Finally, the Court has repeatedly stated that the arbitrariness test may not be satisfied if 'the place and conditions of detention [are not] appropriate',[395] highlighting the importance of this in the context of Article 5(1)(f) as regards the detention of children. A violation was found in a case when a would-be immigrant and her three children were kept in a closed facility designed for adults,[396] and in a case concerning the automatic detention of a minor who was unaccompanied.[397] The necessity of detaining children in this context must be very carefully considered by the national authorities.[398]

6. ARTICLE 5(2): REASONS FOR ARREST
TO BE GIVEN PROMPTLY

I. GENERAL ISSUES

Article 5(2) applies to arrest on any ground under Article 5(1) (some of which do not employ the word 'arrest'),[399] and it extends to cases in which a person is recalled after release.[400] It provides 'the elementary safeguard that any person arrested should know why he is deprived of his liberty',[401] enabling him to deny the offence and hence obtain his release without resorting to court proceedings[402] or to make *habeas corpus* proceedings effective. The arrestee must be told 'in simple, non-technical language that he can understand, the essential legal and factual grounds for his arrest, so as to be able, if he sees fit, to apply to a court to challenge its lawfulness in accordance with' Article 5(4).[403] 'Lawfulness' means 'lawfulness' under both municipal law and the Convention so that the information required must address the legality of a person's detention in terms of Article 5(1) of the Convention as well as the applicable municipal law.[404]

Article 5(2) does not require that the reasons for an arrest be given in any particular way,[405] eg in the text of any warrant or other document authorizing the arrest[406] or in writing at all.[407] Nor does it guarantee a right of access to a lawyer for an arrested

---

[395] *Saadi v UK* ECHR-2008; 47 EHRR 427 para 69 GC.

[396] *Kanagaratnam v Belgium* hudoc (2011); 55 EHRR 800. See also *Mayeka v Belgium* hudoc (2006) paras 101–4 and *Muskhadzhiyeva v Belgium* hudoc (2010) (violation in respect of children (but not mother) even though detained with parent). Issues may also arise in respect of Article 3. Article 37(b) of the (UN) Convention on the Rights of the Child states that detention of children should be a 'measure of last resort and for the shortest appropriate period of time'.

[397] *Rahimi v Greece* hudoc (2011) (also violation of Article 3).

[398] See *Popov v France* hudoc (2012) (fifteen days' administrative detention of foreign parents and their young children, pending expulsion: violation of Article 5(1)(f) (in respect of children, *not* parents) as premises not adapted to the children's extreme vulnerability (para 91) and their particular situation not properly addressed, nor had alternatives to administrative detention been considered. Arguably, then, detention of children under Article 5(1)(f) must be reasonably considered necessary, see para 92). See also *Yoh-Ekale Mwanje v Belgium* hudoc (2012); 56 EHRR 1140.

[399] *Van der Leer v Netherlands* A 170-A (1990); 12 EHRR 567 para 27 (case concerned a 'person of unsound mind' on its facts, but the reasoning extends to all cases of arrest or detention).

[400] *X v Belgium* No 4741/71, 43 CD 14 at 19 (1973). Cf *X v UK* A 46 (1981); 4 EHRR 188 para 66.

[401] *Fox, Campbell and Hartley v UK* A 182 (1990); 13 EHRR 157 para 40.

[402] *X v UK* No 8010/77, 16 DR 101 at 114 (1979).

[403] *Fox, Campbell and Hartley v UK* A 182 (1990); 13 EHRR 157 para 40. The obligation applies to all charges if they are multiple, *Leva v Moldova* hudoc (2009) para 61.

[404] *McVeigh, O'Neill and Evans v UK* Nos 8022/77, 8025/77 and 8027/77, 25 DR 15 (1981); 5 EHRR 71.

[405] *X v Netherlands* No 2621/65, 9 YB 474 at 480 (1966).   [406] *X v Netherlands* No 2621/65.

[407] *X v Netherlands* No 1211/61, 5 YB 224 at 228 (1962).

person,[408] though the inability for a detainee to contact a close relative such as a wife may entail a violation of Article 8.[409]

The reasons must be given to the arrested person, or possibly his representative,[410] 'in a language which he understands'. In a case in which the arrest warrant for a French-speaking person was in Dutch, this requirement was held to be complied with on the basis that the subsequent interrogation, during which the reasons became apparent, was in French.[411] If translation is performed, it must be completed with requisite 'meticulousness and precision'.[412]

The requirement in Article 5(2) overlaps with that in Article 5(4) in that the proceedings provided for by the latter also require that a person be told 'promptly' the reasons for his detention.[413] In criminal cases, Article 5(2) also overlaps to some extent with the obligation in Article 6(3)(a) by which an accused person, whether detained pending trial or not, must be told promptly of the nature and cause of the accusation against him. For obvious reasons, the information required by Article 6(3)(a) will be 'more specific and more detailed' than that called for under Article 5(2).[414]

II. THE REQUIREMENT OF PROMPTNESS AND THE LEVEL OF INFORMATION REQUIRED

Two aspects to the application of Article 5(2) have been particularly notable: firstly, whether the *content* of the information conveyed to a detainee is sufficient; and, secondly, the issue of the *promptness* of that information provision. Both are assessed case by case according to the special features of the application before the Court.

As regards the requirement of promptness ('promptly'), this will always apply to the provision of reasons for arrest. Obviously it will only apply to information relating to the charges brought if the decision is made to bring such charges, it being noted that 'facts which raise a suspicion need not be of the same level as those necessary to justify a conviction or even the bringing of a charge'.[415]

As regards arrest, the Court has indicated that the reasons for arrest should be conveyed to the detainee 'within a few hours of his arrest',[416] unless there are 'exceptional circumstances, such as the serious incapacity of the arrested person to comprehend the reasons that might have been given'.[417] In *Fox, Campbell and Hartley v UK*,[418] the background

---

[408] *Schiesser v Switzerland* A34 (1979); 2 EHRR 417 at para 36. See also *A v Denmark No 8828/79*, 30 DR 93 at 94 (1982); 5 EHRR CD 278.

[409] *McVeigh, O'Neill and Evans v UK Nos 8022/77, 8025/77 and 8027/77* 25 DR 15 (1981); 5 EHRR 71. Lack of access to a lawyer during the initial stage of detention may raise Article 6 issues, see *Simons v Belgium No 71407/10* hudoc (2012) DA.

[410] See *Saadi v UK* ECHR-2008; 47 EHRR 427 paras 84–5 GC. See also *ZH v Hungary* hudoc (2012) (obligation on authorities to take reasonable steps to provide adequate assistance to applicant who was deaf and dumb, illiterate, and had an intellectual disability).

[411] *Delcourt v Belgium No 2689/65*, 10 YB 238 at 270 (1967). In *Conka v Belgium* 2002-I; 34 EHRR 1298 para 52, the provision of a Slovakian-speaking interpreter was viewed as important by the Court.

[412] *Shamayev and Others v Georgia and Russia* ECHR 2005-III para 425.

[413] *X v UK* A 46 (1981); 4 EHRR 188 para 66. In that case, the Court applied Article 5(4) only.

[414] *Nielsen v Denmark No 343/57*, 2 YB 412 at 462 (1959) and *GSM v Austria No 9614/81*, 34 DR 119 (1983).

[415] *Murray v UK* A 300-A (1994); 19 EHRR 193 para 55.

[416] *Kerr v UK No 40451/98* hudoc (1999) DA.

[417] *Zuyev v Russia* hudoc (2013) para 83 ('no more than a few hours should elapse, save in exceptional circumstances'). Cf Human Rights Committee, General Comment No 35 (Article 9: Liberty and security of person) (CCPR/C/107/R.3), para 27.   [418] A 182 (1990); 13 EHRR 157 para 40.

for which was terrorism in Northern Ireland, intervals of up to seven hours between the arrests and the giving of all of the information required by Article 5(2) were found to meet the requirement of 'promptness'.[419] As the Court noted, the information in question does not have to be given 'in its entirety by the arresting officer at the very moment of the arrest';[420] provided that the arrested person is informed of the required legal and factual grounds for his arrest, whether at one time or in stages, within a sufficient period following the arrest. Whether this has occurred is to be assessed by reference to the facts of the particular case.[421] Ten days delay is obviously too long.[422] A delay in informing a person of a court order for his detention is not attributable to a state where the person's whereabouts are not known; it is sufficient that he is informed 'promptly' of the order once he makes contact or, presumably, when his whereabouts otherwise have become known.[423]

In terms of the detail of information to be provided, the case law demonstrates that the Court has taken a flexible, and somewhat lax approach to the application of Article 5(2) as regards the reasons for initial detention. Arrest on suspicion of committing a crime does not require that information be given in a particular form, nor that it consist of a complete list of charges held against the arrested person.[424] A 'bare indication of the legal basis for an arrest'[425] does not suffice; however, on the facts of one particular case, the Court has been satisfied with what it described as a 'fairly precise indication of the suspicions' against the applicant such that he could promptly gain 'some idea of what he was suspected of'.[426] *Fox, Campbell and Hartley v UK*[427] concerned applicants arrested on suspicion of terrorist offences and told that they were being arrested under a named statutory provision. They were later interrogated about specific criminal acts. The Court, disagreeing with the Commission, held that although the information given at the time of arrest was insufficient because it was limited to the legal basis for the arrests, this deficiency was made good[428] by the indications as to the factual basis for the arrests that the

---

[419] See also *O'Hara v UK* 2001-X; 34 EHRR 812 (notification within six to eight hours acceptable).

[420] *Fox, Campbell and Hartley v UK* A 182 (1990); 13 EHRR 157 para 40. See also *Kerr v UK No 40451/98* hudoc (1999) DA (promptness could 'reasonably be inferred from the intense frequency of the interviews' after arrest). See also *Murray v UK* A 300-A (1994); 19 EHRR 193 (sufficiently prompt that arrested at 7am then questioned from 8.20am to 9.35am same day).

[421] Cf *X v Denmark No 8828/79*, 30 DR 93 (1982). See also *Dikme v Turkey* 2000-VIII para 56 (applicant to some extent contributed to the prolongation of the period in question by concealing his identity) and *HB v Switzerland* hudoc (2001); 37 EHRR 1000 para 49 (Court had in mind that the applicant had specialized knowledge of financial situation as he was a senior figure in the company he was accused of defrauding).

[422] *Van der Leer v Netherlands* A 170-A (1990); 12 EHRR 567 para 31. See also *Conka v Belgium* 2002-I; 34 EHRR 1298 (Article 5(1)(f) detention: no violation when broad reasons for detention were given upon detention and written reasons supplied two days later); *Saadi v UK* ECHR-2008; 47 EHRR 427 paras 84–5 GC (violation given seventy-two-hour delay); and *Shamayev and Others v Georgia and Russia* 2005-III (violation: four-day delay).

[423] *Keus v Netherlands* A 185-C (1990); 13 EHRR 700 para 22 (mentally disordered person absconded; sufficient that he was told when he telephoned the hospital).

[424] *X v Germany No 8098/77*, 16 DR 111 (1978). *Saadi v UK* hudoc (2006); 44 EHRR 1005 (chamber judgment) para 51 (the information given may be 'even less complete' for detention under Article 5(1)(f), although it must be sufficient to enable an application for review of lawfulness); and *Nowak v Ukraine* hudoc (2011) para 63 (violation as arrestee merely told he was an 'international thief' when, in fact, the basis for detention was deportation; the notice was also served after four days).

[425] *Fox, Campbell and Hartley v UK* A 182 (1990); 13 EHRR 157 para 41. See also *Kerr v UK No 40451/98* hudoc (1999) DA.

[426] *Dikme v Turkey* 2000-VIII para 56 (sufficient on the facts and given broader context that during questioning interrogator directly accused applicant of belonging to a well-known illegal organization).

[427] A 182 (1990); 13 EHRR 157 para 41. See Finnie, 54 MLR 288 (1991).

[428] Cf, *Murray v UK* A 300-A (1994); 19 EHRR 193 para 77 and *Kerr v UK No 40451/98* hudoc (1999) DA. Contrast *Ireland v UK* A 25 (1978); 2 EHRR 25 para 198 PC.

applicants could infer from the nature of the questions put to them by the police during the subsequent interrogation.

In fact, a person need not be *expressly* 'informed' of the reasons for his *arrest* insofar as these are apparent from the surrounding circumstances.[429] Indeed, as regards the initial arrest period at least, there may be instances when the applicant is simply assumed to know why he was being detained, given the criminal and intentional nature of the act which preceded his arrest.[430] In *Öcalan v Turkey,*[431] the facts of which were described earlier,[432] the applicant was deemed to have been sufficiently informed of the reasons for his arrest by the time he was arrested. He was a notorious figure who had been wanted by the police for a considerable time as the leader of an illegal terrorist organization. Warrants had been issued for his arrest by various prosecuting authorities, a 'red notice' had been issued by Interpol, and details of the charges against him were featured on the extradition request that had been made for him in Italy. He did not deny being aware of this documentation and the Article 5(2) aspect of his application was declared manifestly ill-founded.[433]

The application of Article 5(2) is one that, in the more borderline cases, is prone to cause significant division before the Court.[434] Strong arguments can be made to the effect that the application of that Article in *Fox* and some subsequent case law involves an unacceptable dilution of a basic guarantee. Article 5(2) expressly requires that an arrested person be 'informed' of the reason for his arrest, not that he be able to gather them from the drift of the interrogation, which may involve the putting of various alternative assertions and, possibly, even exaggerated accusations. Having made this point, it may be added that an assessment of the Court's general approach to Article 5(2) should have in mind the fact that key cases have concerned people suspected of terrorist crimes. This is an area where the Court, for some years now, has emphasized the need to strike a balance between the defence of institutions of democracy in the common interest and the protection of individual rights. On the one hand, one can readily appreciate the need to apply Article 5(2) in a flexible way. This is especially so in the context of genuine suspected terrorism scenarios, when it is clear that an arrest may be warranted even on vague information at first[435] and there would be a danger that an onerous information provision requirement might unduly hamper the authorities in very important and delicate areas of their duties. On the other hand, it will be appreciated that for a society that cherishes the concept of liberty, there are also dangers to be guarded against. As noted earlier, one aim of Article 5(2) is that the applicant quickly knows the essential legal and factual grounds for his arrest as a prerequisite for an effective resort to the safeguard provided by Article 5(4). Once an individual has been released, however, Article 5(4) may not be resorted to. Accordingly, if the information provision requirement of Article 5(2) is too indulgent of the needs of the authorities, the greater is their scope to arrest individuals on general grounds (assuming they are *prima facie* lawful) when the main intention is really to hold the individual for intensive questioning as part of an intelligence-gathering exercise, there being little

---

[429] Cf *Neumeister v Austria No 1936/63,* 7 YB 224 (1964); *Freda v Italy No 8916/80,* 21 DR 250 (1980); and *B v France No 10179/82,* 52 DR 111 (1987).

[430] *Dikme v Turkey* 2000-VIII para 54 (arrest as false papers produced during an identity check).

[431] Hudoc (2003); 37 EHRR 238.   [432] See section 3.III.

[433] *Öcalan v Turkey No 46221/99* hudoc (2000) DA.

[434] See, eg, *Murray v UK* A 300-A (1994); 19 EHRR 191 (no violation of Article 5(2), thirteen votes to five), note the strong dissent of Judge Misfud Bonnici arguing that the decision reduced the meaning of Article 5(2) to an unacceptable level.

[435] Cf the Court's jurisprudence on the 'reasonable suspicion' requirement for Article 5(1)(c) see section 5.III.c.

or no actual intention of bringing them before a court (as required for detention under Article 5(1)(c)).

7. ARTICLE 5(3): ACCOUNTABILITY DURING PRE-TRIAL DETENTION AND TRIAL WITHIN A REASONABLE TIME

Article 5(3) should be read with Article 5(1)(c), 'which forms a whole with it'.[436] It concerns the criminal process, and is 'intended to minimise the risk of arbitrariness' by providing, in accordance with the concept of the 'rule of law', '[j]udicial control of interferences by the executive with the individual's right to liberty'.[437] Such control concerns two separate phases of detention.[438]

Firstly (see section 7.I), there is the judicial control required 'promptly' after the initial arrest: a person arrested in accordance with Article 5(1)(c) on suspicion of having committed an offence must be brought 'promptly' before a judge or similar officer to determine the legality of his arrest. Article 5(3) therefore requires the 'judicial officer' to consider legal criteria relating to the merits of the detention and to order provisional release if it is unreasonable.[439] This is a vital safeguard in a democracy and should be seen alongside the procedural safeguards and positive obligations that the Court has read into Article 5(1)[440] to help provide a custodial regime that promotes the protection of the individual detainee.

Secondly (see section 7.II), there is the judicial control required *after* the stage just referred to, that is the period pending eventual trial. Here the Court has again interpreted Article 5(3) creatively so as to imply from it a qualified right to release pending trial, on bail if this is appropriate.

Finally, a third important aspect to Article 5(3) is that it requires that a person detained on remand be tried within a reasonable time (see section 7.III). [441]

I. RIGHT TO BE BROUGHT PROMPTLY BEFORE A JUDGE OR 'OTHER OFFICER' AFTER ARREST

a. Brought before a judge or other officer authorized to exercise judicial power

Article 5(3) underlines the sanctity of the right to liberty and the need to provide accountability against abuse of the broad power to detain that Article 5(1)(c) necessarily provides to the executive.[442] The detainee 'shall'[443] be brought automatically and 'promptly'

---

[436] *Ciulla v Italy* A 148 (1989); 13 EHRR 346 para 38 PC and *Aquilina v Malta* 1999-III; 29 EHRR 185 para 47 GC.

[437] *Brogan v UK* A 145-B (1988); 11 EHRR 117 para 58 PC. See *Assenov v Bulgaria* 1998-VIII; 28 EHRR 652 para 146.

[438] Cf *McKay v UK* 2006-X; 44 EHRR 827 para 31 GC and *Medvedyev v France* ECHR-2010; 51 EHRR 899 paras 117–26 GC (summary of main Article 5(3) principles).

[439] *Aquilina v Malta* 1999-III; 29 EHRR 185 para 47 GC.   [440] See section 3.I.

[441] Article 5(3) (particularly its trial within a reasonable time guarantee) does not extend to a person who, although subject to an order for detention on remand, is also serving a prison sentence following conviction for another offence: *X v Germany* No 8626/79, 25 DR 218 (1981).

[442] *McKay v UK* 2006-X; 44 EHRR 827 para 32 GC.

[443] No exceptions are possible, not even if there has been prior judicial involvement: *Bergman v Estonia* hudoc (2008) para 45.

before a judge or other comparable officer. He must have the power to release and the 'initial automatic review of arrest and detention' performed must be capable of examining whether the detention falls under Article 5(1)(c), ie it must address 'lawfulness issues and whether or not there is a reasonable suspicion that the arrested person ha[s] committed an offence'.[444] Beyond this *at this initial stage* it is not necessary for there to be an automatic review of the additional and distinct question of whether the applicant should be released on bail pending trial, ie whether continued detention is justified or necessary in the circumstances of the individual case.[445] However, this should follow in due course[446] and the Court has stated that it is 'good practice' and 'highly desirable', albeit not a strict requirement, that the judicial officer who conducts the first initial review also has competence to consider release on bail.[447] Perhaps surprisingly, there is no general rule to the effect that hearings on the lawfulness of detention must usually be held in public.[448]

Judicial control of the detention must be 'automatic'[449] (unlike for Article 5(4)); it is insufficient that Article 5(3) only operates if the detainee makes an application to this effect.[450] This is because vulnerable categories of arrested persons, such as the mentally weak or those who do not speak the local language, may not bring the appropriate application of their own accord.[451] Furthermore, as Trechsel[452] has pointed out, Article 5(3) is a guarantee that is 'particularly important in states in which there exists an actual danger of police brutality or torture', especially since methods of ill-treatment may be used that do not leave long-lasting marks. As the Court stressed in the very first case when it found 'torture' under Article 3, '[j]udicial control of interferences by the executive with the individual's right to liberty is an essential feature of the guarantee embodied in Article 5(3), which is intended to minimise the risk of arbitrariness and to ensure the rule of law...Furthermore, prompt judicial intervention may lead to the detection and prevention of serious ill-treatment, which..., is prohibited by the Convention in absolute and non-derogable terms.'[453]

b. Promptly

Article 5(3) requires that an arrested person is brought 'promptly' before a judge or other officer, the 'clock' beginning to tick at the point of arrest. In *McKay v UK*,[454] the Grand Chamber proceeded on the understanding that four days was the 'maximum' period of time that could elapse before Article 5(3) review. The plain meaning of the word 'promptly' and the purpose of Article 5(3), which is to minimize the risk of 'executive arbitrariness',[455] underline the view that four days is to be regarded as a maximum, not an acceptable deadline, and that Article 5(3) may still be breached before this time elapses, if there are no special circumstances.[456] For example, the provision was breached in a case

---

[444] *McKay v UK* 2006-X; 44 EHRR 827 para 40 GC.

[445] See *McKay v UK*, although Judges Rozakis, Tulkens, Botoucharova, Myjer, and Ziemele disagreed.

[446] See section 7.II below.   [447] *McKay v UK* 2006-X; 44 EHRR 827 para 47 GC.

[448] *Lebedev v Russia* hudoc (2007); 47 EHRR 771 para 82.

[449] *De Jong, Baljet, and Van Den Brink v Netherlands* A 77 (1984); 8 EHRR 20 para 51 and *Aquilina v Malta* 1999-III; 29 EHRR 185 para 49 GC.

[450] *Aquilina v Malta* 1999-III; 29 EHRR 185 para 49 GC; *McGoff v Sweden* No 9017/80, 31 DR 72 (1982); 6 EHRR CD 101(1984).   [451] *Aquilina v Malta.*   [452] Trechsel, *European System* (1993), p 333.

[453] *Aksoy v Turkey* 1996-VI; 23 EHRR 553 para 76.

[454] 2006-X; 44 EHRR 827 para 47 GC. See also *Oral and Atabay v Turkey* hudoc (2009) para 43.

[455] *Brogan v UK* A 145-B (1988); 11 EHRR 117 PC para 58.

[456] See, eg, *Gutsanovi v Bulgaria* hudoc (2013) (violation: three days, five hours, and thirty minutes/ psychological fragility of the applicant). Of course exceptional circumstances may exist, see, eg, cases concerning detention on the High Seas and consequential delays in bringing before an Article 5(3)

concerning minors (a point which the Court stressed) who had no legal representation and whose appearance before a judge took place three days and nine hours after arrest.[457] In its General Comment on Article 9 of the ICCPR, the Human Rights Committee states that for the equivalent provision of the ICCPR, 'any delay longer than forty-eight hours should be justified by exceptional circumstances'.[458]

In *Brogan v UK*,[459] the Court held that a delay of four days and six hours in bringing a person before a judge did not comply with Article 5(3). In that case, the four applicants were arrested by the police in Northern Ireland as persons reasonably suspected of involvement in acts of terrorism. After being questioned for periods ranging from four days and six hours to over six days, all four were released without being charged with any offence or being brought before a magistrate. When determining the meaning of 'promptly', the Court stated that the use in the equivalent French text of '*aussitôt*', which literally meant immediately, confirmed that 'the degree of flexibility attaching to the notion of "promptness" is limited'.[460] The Court continued:[461]

> Whereas promptness is to be assessed in each case according to its special features, the significance to be attached to those features can never be taken to the point of impairing the very essence of the right guaranteed by Article 5(3).

Applying this approach to the facts of the case, the Court accepted that, 'subject to adequate safeguards, the context of terrorism in Northern Ireland has the effect of prolonging the period during which the authorities may, without violating Article 5(3), keep a person suspected of serious terrorist offences in custody before bringing him before a judge or other judicial officer'.[462] However, even in the light of these 'special features', the Court held, by twelve votes to seven, that the requirement of 'promptness' could not properly be stretched so as to permit a delay of four days and six hours or more.[463] Implicit in the Court's reasoning is that, beyond a certain time, the appropriate course for a state faced with an emergency is to make a derogation under Article 15, rather than for Article 5(3) to be interpreted beyond its proper limits. In *Brannigan and McBride v UK*,[464] the defendant state conceded that the detention of IRA suspects under the same power as in the *Brogan* case and for longer periods was contrary to Article 5(3). However, there was no breach of

official on the mainland: *Medvedyev v France* ECHR-2010; 51 EHRR 899 GC (no violation, the Court noting that it did not take longer than necessary to bring the detainees to shore (thirteen days) and considered the actions of the French authorities to be reasonable (para 131); the finding was by nine votes to eight, with a strong dissent arguing that the majority had diluted standards in the field of personal liberty); *Rigopoulos v Spain* 1999-II (no violation of Article 5(3); sixteen-day delay, exceptional circumstances); but see *Vassis v France* hudoc (2013) (violation as forty-eight hours' police custody after eighteen days' deprivation of liberty on vessel). See also *X v Belgium* No 4960/71, 42 CD 49 at 55 (1972) (delay of nearly five days permissible because applicant had been ill in hospital during this period). Cf *Öcalan v Turkey* 2005-IV; 41 EHRR 985 GC (Court not convinced that delay of seven days was due to adverse weather conditions: violation).

[457] *İpek and Others v Turkey* hudoc (2009) paras 36–7.
[458] Human Rights Committee, General Comment No 35 (Article 9: Liberty and security of person) (CCPR/C/107/R.3), para 34.   [459] A 145-B (1988); 11 EHRR 117 PC.
[460] *Brogan v UK*, para 59.
[461] *Brogan v UK*, para 59. Cf *Aquilina v Malta* 1999-III; 29 EHRR 185 para 48 GC ('the scope of flexibility in interpreting and applying the notion of promptness is very limited').
[462] *Brogan v UK*, para 61.
[463] Whereas the Court found a breach in all four terrorist cases, the Commission found one only in respect of the two applicants detained for over five days.
[464] A 258-B (1993); 17 EHRR 539 PC. See the discussion of this case under Article 15 in Ch 19.

the Convention because the United Kingdom had made a valid emergency derogation under Article 15.[465] In another 'special features' context, *viz* that of military criminal law, the Court held that 'even taking into account the demands of military life and justice', a delay of five days was in breach of Article 5(3).[466]

c. Characteristics of the judicial officer

The wording 'judge or other judicial officer authorised by law' has the same meaning as 'competent legal authority' in Article 5(1)(c).[467] As in that provision, in English law the requirement is satisfied by bringing an accused before a magistrate. Whereas the meaning of 'judge' has not caused difficulty, the phrase 'other officer authorised by law to exercise judicial power' has given rise to some notable jurisprudence. Two qualities that this 'officer' must have are independence and impartiality.

In *Schiesser v Switzerland*,[468] the Court stated that the first characteristic of an Article 5(3) 'officer' is his 'independence of the executive and the parties'. The notion of independence requires that the 'officer' must be able to make a legally binding decision as to detention or release (it is not sufficient that his recommendations are invariably followed).[469] There will be a violation when the prosecutor, or another member of the executive, is able to overturn such decisions.[470] An 'officer' is not considered independent when he is subordinate to authority belonging to the executive.[471] The mere fact that under applicable laws a prosecutor, in addition to exercising a prosecutorial role, also acted as guardian of the public interest does not give him 'judicial status'.[472] Nor in such circumstances will a violation of Article 5(3) be prevented here because an individual could apply to a judge against the prosecutor's decision to detain (as opposed to such reference being automatic).

The notion of impartiality under Article 5(3) is usually seen in the context of a relationship between the detainee and the 'officer' and has been particularly relevant to cases where the 'officer' also plays a part later on in the prosecution of the case. An officer will not be impartial, as required by Article 5(3), if he is not only competent to decide on the accused's pre-trial detention, but if he is also *entitled to intervene* in the subsequent criminal proceedings as a representative of the prosecuting authority' (emphasis added).[473] Thus, it is not sufficient that the officer does not in fact intervene at a later stage, as long as it is possible for him to do so: 'impartiality' involves an objective, as well as a

---

[465] See Ch 19, section 5.I.

[466] *Koster v Netherlands* A 221 (1991); 14 EHRR 396 (delay caused by foreseeable military manoeuvres not a good excuse). Cf *De Jong, Baljet and Van Den Brink v Netherlands* A 77 (1984); 8 EHRR 20 para 53 and *Duinhof and Duijf v Netherlands* A 79 (1984); 13 EHRR 478. See also *Van Der Sluijs, Zuiderveld and Klappe v Netherlands* A 78 (1984); 13 EHRR 461.

[467] *Schiesser v Switzerland* A 34 (1979); 2 EHRR 417 para 29.

[468] A 34 (1979); 2 EHRR 417 para 29. See also *Moulin v France* hudoc (2010) (deputy public prosecutor, a representative of the ministère public, did not offer sufficient guarantees of independence).

[469] *Ireland v UK* A 25 (1978); 2 EHRR 25 para 199 PC (Advisory Committee on Internment did not qualify). Cf the military criminal cases of *De Jong, Baljet and Van Den Brink v Netherlands* A 77 (1984); 8 EHRR 20; *Van Der Sluijs, Zuiderveld and Klappe v Netherlands* A 78 (1984); 13 EHRR 461; and *Duinhof and Duijf v Netherlands* A 79 (1984); 13 EHRR 478.

[470] *Assenov v Bulgaria* 1998-VIII; 28 EHRR 652 para 148.

[471] *Niedbala v Poland* hudoc (2000); 33 EHRR 1137 para 52.

[472] *Niedbala v Poland*, para 53. It is not clear if, for Article 5(3), an officer must have any particular qualifications or training, see A 34 (1979); 2 EHRR 417, para 31 (Court declined to examine this in *Hood v UK* 1999-I; 29 EHRR 365 para 59 GC).

[473] *Huber v Switzerland* A 188 (1990) para 43 PC (the early case of *Schiesser v Switzerland* A 34 (1979); 2 EHRR 417 merely required that the 'officer' not take part later in the prosecution case).

subjective, element so that the 'officer's' impartiality must not be open to doubt. Objective appearances *at the time of the decision on detention* are material. This objective element, which brings Article 5(3) into line with the 'impartiality' requirements of Article 6(1),[474] was applied in *Hood v UK*,[475] a case concerning a military police investigation, where Article 5(3) was violated because a commanding officer (or his subordinate) was liable to play a central role in the subsequent prosecution of the case against the accused soldier. The Court also took the view that the commanding officer's concurrent responsibility for discipline and order provided an additional reason for an accused reasonably to doubt that officer's impartiality when deciding on the necessity of the pre-trial detention of an accused in his command.

d. Function of officer and procedure to be followed

The judge or similar officer must 'consider the merits of the detention',[476] that is issues going to its lawfulness and the existence of 'reasonable suspicion' (Article 5(1)(c)). As was first set out in the *Schiesser* case,[477] his role is that of 'reviewing the circumstances militating for and against detention, of deciding, by reference to legal criteria, whether there are reasons to justify detention and of ordering release if there are no such reasons'.[478] The officer is under an 'obligation of himself hearing the individual brought before him',[479] ie there should be an oral hearing. He is not obliged to allow the accused's lawyer to be present at the hearing.[480]

Article 5(3) review must be automatic, but the procedures envisaged are more modest than Article 5(4), where a procedure of a 'judicial character' must be provided.[481] However, proceedings held under Article 5(3) must be adversarial and ensure equality of arms between the parties, the detainee having access to the documents in the investigation file which are essential for assessing the lawfulness of his detention. He should also have an opportunity to comment on the arguments put forward by the prosecution.[482]

In many systems of law the body before which the applicant is brought under Article 5(3) may be a court. If so, by virtue of the 'incorporation rule', the requirement of judicial supervision imposed by Article 5(4)[483] will be satisfied at that hearing, but the stricter demands of due process required by that Article, as opposed to Article 5(3)—eg possible attendance of the detainee, equality of arms, and advanced disclosure of documentation if relevant—must also be attendant if it is to count for the purposes of Article 5(4).

Assuming that a person is detained under Article 5(1)(c), during his detention on remand by virtue of Article 5(4) he must be able to take proceedings at reasonable intervals to challenge the lawfulness of his detention.[484] In view of the assumption under the

---

[474] See Ch 9.

[475] 1999-I; 29 EHRR 365 GC. See also *Thompson v UK* hudoc (2004); 40 EHRR 245; *Brincat v Italy* A 249-A (1992); 17 EHRR 60. As regards the objective impartiality requirements in military proceedings elsewhere, see *De Jong, Baljet and Van Den Brink v Netherlands* A 77 (1984); 8 EHRR 20 and *Pauwels v Belgium* A 135 (1988); 11 EHRR 238 (both violations of Article 5(3)).

[476] *TW v Malta* hudoc (1999); 29 EHRR 185 para 41 GC; *Aquilina v Malta* 1999-III; 29 EHRR 185 para 47 GC.   [477] A 34 (1979); 2 EHRR 417.

[478] *Schiesser v Switzerland*, para 31. As to 'legal criteria', see *Skoogström v Sweden* B 68-A (1983) Com Rep.

[479] *Schiesser v Switzerland*.

[480] *Schiesser v Switzerland*, para 36. Although see *Lebedev v Russia* hudoc (2007); 47 EHRR 771 paras 83–91.

[481] See section 8.II.b. In *Brannigan and McBride v UK* A 258-B (1993); 17 EHRR 539 para 58 PC, the Court stated that a 'procedure that has a judicial character' must be followed (citing the *Schiesser* and *Huber* cases).

[482] *Lebedev v Russia* hudoc (2007); 47 EHRR 771 para 77.   [483] See section 8.I.

[484] *Bezicheri v Italy* A 164 (1989); 12 EHRR 210 paras 20–1.

Convention that such detention is to be of strictly limited duration, 'periodic review at short intervals is called for'.[485]

II. THE RIGHT TO RELEASE PENDING TRIAL IN REASONABLE CIRCUMSTANCES

As noted earlier, Article 5(3) continues to apply after the detainee's initial appearance before the judge or 'other officer'. During this phase of detention a decision must be taken whether it is appropriate to release the detainee, on conditions if necessary. The decision must be made by an official with the characteristics and functions of the judge or other officer under Article 5(3) as noted earlier, except, of course, he must have the power to award bail if necessary. The first decision whether to order conditional release must take place with 'due expedition' (if not 'promptly').[486] Further decisions should take place from time to time thereafter, the domestic courts being required to 'review the continued detention of persons pending trial with a view to ensuring release when circumstances no longer justify continued deprivation of liberty'.[487]

Before the qualified right to bail[488] is considered in detail, the following points should be noted. First, the different roles of the national courts and the Strasbourg authorities in the application of the right to bail in Article 5(3) have been explained by the Court as follows. When the national courts take their decision 'they must examine all the facts arguing for and against the existence of a genuine requirement of public interest justifying, with due regard to the principle of the presumption of innocence, a departure from the rule of respect for individual liberty and set them out in their decisions on the applications for release'.[489] It is then 'essentially on the basis of the reasons given in these decisions [plus, where relevant, appeals] and of the true facts mentioned by the applicant' when pursuing his remedies for release at the national level that the Strasbourg authorities must make their judgment.[490] So the reasons must be those relied upon by the domestic authorities at the time, not new arguments put forward belatedly at Strasbourg.[491] The Court is quite willing to disagree with the national court's assessment of the need for detention on remand.

Secondly, there is the matter of the stages of the criminal process to which Article 5(3) applies. In *Wemhoff v Germany*,[492] it was held that Article 5(3) covers the period from the arrest of the accused on suspicion of having committed a criminal offence to his acquittal or conviction by the trial court.[493]

---

[485] *Bezicheri v Italy*. See also *Assenov v Bulgaria* 1998-VIII; 28 EHRR 652 para 162.

[486] *McKay v UK* 2006-X; 44 EHRR 827 para 46 GC. This leading case implies that the 'bail hearing' does not need to be automatic; it may follow the detainee's application or the judge's order, see para 46.

[487] *McKay v UK*, para 45.

[488] The qualified right to release is not easily identified under Article 5(3); however, this was the approach adopted by the Court in *Wemhoff v Germany*, A 7 (1968); 1 EHRR 55 (see Harris, 44 BYIL 87 (1970)).

[489] *Letellier v France* A 207 (1991); 14 EHRR 83 para 35. The Court also emphasized that in a case in which the final decision is taken on appeal, the appeal court should state 'clear and specific' reasons for reversing a decision to release by a lower court that is in a better position to assess the facts and the personality of the accused: para 52.

[490] *Letellier v France*. Cf *Neumeister v Austria* A 8 (1968); 1 EHRR 91 para 5.

[491] *Trzaska v Poland* hudoc (2000) para 66.

[492] A 7 (1968); 1 EHRR 55 paras 6–9. See also *Kalashnikov v Russia* 2002-VI; 36 EHRR 587.

[493] *Wemhoff v Germany* A 7 (1968); 1 EHRR 55 para 9 and see *B v Austria* A 175 (1990); 13 EHRR 20. Hence Article 5(3) does not cover detention pending appeal, it is not possible under that provision to challenge the grounds for detaining a convicted person during his appeal or to question the 'diligence' with which appeal

Other considerations to be borne in mind when applying Article 5(3) are that if the accused is detained for two or more separate periods pending trial, they are to be cumulated when applying the reasonable time guarantee in Article 5(3).[494] If proceedings are still pending before the national trial court when an application claiming a breach of Article 5(3) is heard at Strasbourg, the period of detention after an Article 34 application is made may be taken into account by the Court.[495]

a. More than 'reasonable suspicion' required to sustain prolonged detention

Consistent with the importance of the right to liberty, the whole thrust of Article 5(3) as interpreted by the Court is against any rule that individuals (and even more so children[496]) awaiting trial should be held in detention.[497] Rather a detention effected under Article 5(1)(c) during the remand stage must actually be necessary in the individual circumstances of the case and a person must be released pending trial unless the state can show that there are 'relevant and sufficient' reasons to justify his continued detention.[498] Justification for any period of detention, no matter how short, must be convincingly demonstrated by the authorities.[499]

Obviously, the persistence of a reasonable suspicion (according to the legal standards required by Article 5(1)(c)) that the person arrested has committed an offence remains a condition of the accused's continued detention under Article 5(1)(c). For 'an initial period' that suspicion alone justifies detention, but the need to justify continues through the remand period and 'there comes a moment when [reasonable suspicion] is no longer enough'.[500] Then Article 5(3) supposes that there also are *other* 'relevant and sufficient' public interest reasons to justify *further* interference with the 'right to liberty' of a person who is presumed to be innocent under Article 6(2).[501] Domestic authorities must be alive to the fact that reasons which may justify detention at the outset may become weaker over time (especially if the subsequent investigation uncovers no new evidence),[502] perhaps leading to a situation where release becomes necessary.

To satisfy Article 5(3), what is required from the domestic authorities are 'specific indications of a genuine requirement of public interest which, notwithstanding the presumption of innocence, outweighs the rule of respect for individual liberty'.[503] A reasoned decision is necessary for public scrutiny of the administration of justice.[504] It follows that the actual seriousness of the charge facing the individual cannot be the *sole* basis for denying bail,[505] whilst 'the existence and persistence of serious

proceedings are conducted, which is scarcely consistent with the bias in Article 5 in favour of the 'right to liberty'; *B v Austria*, paras 36–40. However, release pending appeal will not normally be such an important issue as release pending trial. Moreover, the length of the appeal proceedings may be questioned under the 'reasonable time' guarantee in Article 6(1).

[494] *Kemmache v France* A 218 (1991); 14 EHRR 520 para 44.   [495] *Kemmache v France.*

[496] See *Nart v Turkey* hudoc (2008) para 31. See also *Guvec v Turkey* hudoc (2009) para 109 and *Korneykova v Ukraine* hudoc (2012) para 44.

[497] Cf the wording of Article 9(3) ICCPR, 'It shall not be the general rule that persons awaiting trial shall be detained in custody'.   [498] *Wemhoff v Germany* A 7 (1968); 1 EHRR 55 para 12.

[499] *Idalov v Russia* hudoc (2012) para 140 GC.

[500] *McKay v UK* 2006-X; 44 EHRR 827 para 45 GC (Court declined to detail a particular time frame). See also *Stögmuller v Austria* A 9 (1969); 1 EHRR 155 para 4 and *Letellier v France* A 207 (1991); 14 EHRR 83 para 35.

[501] *McKay v UK*, and *Letellier v France* A 207 (1991); 14 EHRR 83 para 35.

[502] *Labita v Italy* 2000-IV; 46 EHRR 1228 paras 159 and 163 GC.

[503] *Ilijkov v Bulgaria* hudoc (2001) para 84.   [504] *Tase v Romania* hudoc (2008) para 41.

[505] *Morganti v France (No 1)* A 320-C (1995); 21 EHRR 34 para 62, Com Rep.

indications of guilt' do not on their own justify 'long detention',[506] although this is clearly a relevant factor for the assessment of whether detention is justified. As a general principle, the longer a person is held in detention, the greater the level of 'reasonable suspicion' should be. An opportunity for legal challenge lies under Articles 5(3) and 5(4). Whilst the Court has indicated that a detention based on hearsay evidence or from a single source may *initially* be sufficient for Article 5(1)(c),[507] particularly in the context of the fight against organized crime or terrorism, it also notes that such a potentially unreliable basis for detention presents dangers that need to be guarded against.[508] It therefore requires that, with the passage of time, there will need to be further evidence (eg corroboration of the single source and/or objective evidence backing up the hearsay evidence) during the course of the investigation for 'reasonable suspicion' to be retained.

Any system of mandatory detention on remand is incompatible with Article 5(3) *per se*.[509] That provision will also be violated when legislation automatically removes the possibility of the judicial control of pre-trial detention in advance, as in *Cabellero v UK*.[510] If the law provides for a presumption in favour of continued detention (eg detention presumed when alleged offence was of a certain category such as murder), the existence of concrete facts outweighing the rule of respect for individual liberty must be convincingly demonstrated before the Court. It is incumbent on the authorities to establish those relevant facts; they may not place a burden of proof on the applicant such that detention will continue unless he can persuade the domestic court otherwise.[511] Similar considerations apply if legislation requires that, given his previous conduct and/or record, the detainee should be granted bail only if 'exceptional circumstances' exist. To the extent that the 'exceptional circumstances' proviso imposes a burden of proof on the applicant, there may be a violation of Article 5(3), as there clearly would be for Article 5(4).[512]

As regards the content of the reasons provided by a domestic court or body for maintaining detention following an Article 5(3) hearing, the Court's approach again emphasizes the need for an independent and proper, critical assessment by the judge or judicial officer.[513] Although it will not necessarily entail a violation of Article 5(3), the Court has been quick to criticize as inadequate reasoning that does not appear to be tailored to the

---

[506] *Tomasi v France* A-241-A (1992); 15 EHRR 1 para 89.

[507] See *Labita v Italy* 2000-IV; 46 EHRR 1228 para 158 GC (violation of Article 5(3) in a case concerning mafia crime and detention lasting two years and seven months only on the basis of an anonymous informant's evidence). See also *McKay v UK* 2006-X; 44 EHRR 827 para 45 GC.

[508] *Labita v Italy* 2000-IV; 46 EHRR 1228 paras 157–9 GC.

[509] *Ilijkov v Bulgaria* hudoc (2001) para 84.

[510] *Cabellero v UK* 2000-II; 30 EHRR 643 GC (domestic law requiring refusal for charges of murder and manslaughter etc when the accused had a prior conviction for such an offence). See also *SBC v UK* hudoc (2001); 34 EHRR 619. For criticism see Trechsel, *Human Rights in Criminal Proceedings*, 2005, p 511.

[511] *Ilijkov v Bulgaria* hudoc (2001) (Article 5(3) violated: authorities relied solely on a statutory presumption based on the gravity of the charges which shifted to the accused the burden of proving that there was not even a hypothetical danger of absconding, re-offending, or collusion, para 87). See also *Bykov v Russia* hudoc (2009) para 64 GC.

[512] See also *Nikolova v Bulgaria* 1999-II; 31 EHRR 64 para 59 GC and *Ilijkov v Bulgaria* hudoc (2001) para 99 (Article 5(4) violated; Court took into account imposition of a strong burden of proof on applicants held in detention on remand to show that there was no risk of absconding).

[513] See *Tase v Romania* (hudoc) 2008 ('Quasi-automatic prolongation of detention contravenes' Art 5(3), para 40). See also, eg, *Khodorkovskiy v Russia* hudoc (2011); 53 EHRR 1103 para 202 (proceedings 'flawed in many respects', including poorly reasoned decisions, reliance on material obtained by way of a violation of the lawyer–client privilege, and failure to consider other measures of restraint).

individual circumstances of a case, on the basis that it is 'abstract',[514] 'stereotyped',[515] or simply too terse and lacking in detail given the length of detention[516] (the implication being that the matter was not properly examined). The Court is not prepared simply to assume that a particular ground has been relied on by the domestic authorities as the basis for detention; it will require it to be expressly stated in the decision of the domestic authorities.[517]

b. Grounds for refusing bail

Four basic grounds[518] upon which the refusal of bail may be justified have been identified by the Court: the danger of flight, interference with the course of justice, the prevention of crime, and the preservation of public order.[519] These are discussed in turn in the paragraphs that follow, but it should be emphasized that these grounds of detention need to be viewed alongside the fact that bail conditions may be imposed, as well as other 'preventative measures' such as police supervision, electronic tagging etc. Thus, an individual should only be detained if (i) his release would lead to a real risk that harm identified under one of the grounds for detention will occur; *and* (ii) if the imposition of bail conditions or other reasonable preventative measures cannot stop that risk or reduce it to a level which would not justify detention.[520] Bail conditions are also discussed later.[521]

Danger of absconding

Absconding is, of course, a classic reason potentially justifying detention. Clearly, the severity of the sentence that the accused may expect if convicted is of relevance to the assessment of the risk that he or she might abscond or reoffend; however, 'the need to continue the deprivation of liberty cannot be assessed from a purely abstract point of view, taking into consideration only the gravity of the offence'.[522] The general test applied is found in the *Stögmuller* case:[523]

> [T]here must be a whole set of circumstances…which give reason to suppose that the consequences and hazards of flight will seem to [the applicant] to be a lesser evil than continued imprisonment.

Relevant factors are 'those relating to the character of the person involved, his morals, his home, his occupation, his assets, his family ties and all kinds of links with the country

---

[514] *Letellier v France* A 207 (1991); 14 EHRR 83 para 51.

[515] *Yagci and Sargin v Turkey* A 319-A (1995); 20 EHRR 505 para 52.

[516] *Smirnova v Russia* 2003-IX; 39 EHRR 450 para 70.

[517] *Trzaska v Poland* hudoc (2000) para 66. As to arguments to the effect that reasoning or explanation is not required in 'self evident' cases, see *Bykov v Russia* hudoc (2009) GC para 66.

[518] *Piruzyan v Armenia*, hudoc (2012) para 94. *IA v France* 1998-VII para 108 suggests that in exceptional cases the safety of a person under investigation may justify continued detention. However, the proposition was firmly rejected in *Lelievre v Belgium* hudoc (2007) para 104.

[519] Article 5(3) does not require a detainee to be released on account of his state of health (an issue potentially within the scope of Article 3), although ill-health may be relevant to the assessment of 'trial within a reasonable time', *Jablonski v Poland* hudoc (2000); 36 EHRR 455 para 82, where Article 5(3) was violated on the facts (paras 84–5). [520] See *Jablonski v Poland*, para 84.

[521] See section 7.II.C.

[522] *Idalov v Russia* hudoc (2012) para 145 GC (see also *Chraidi v Germany* hudoc (2006); 47 EHRR 47 para 40; *Letellier v France* A 207 (1991); 14 EHRR 83 para 43).

[523] A 9 (1969); 1 EHRR 155 para 15. See also *Smirnova v Russia* 2003-IX; 39 EHRR 450 para 60.

in which he is being prosecuted'.[524] For example, when assessing the risk of flight, it may be of relevance that the detainee has a permanent place of residence in the state in question and a stable family relationship there. Of relevance, too, would be previous abscondings[525] (or lack of them), the 'accused's particular distaste ior detention',[526] indications that he has links with another country that will enable him to escape or that he is actually planning to escape,[527] the threat of further proceedings,[528] and the fact that the applicant has significant creditors which he may want to evade.[529]

The danger of flight 'necessarily decreases as the time spent in detention passes by', it being assumed that 'the length of detention on remand will be deducted from the period of imprisonment which the person concerned may expect if convicted', which is 'likely to make the prospect seem less awesome to him and reduce his temptation to flee'.[530] In *Chraidi v Germany*,[531] it was acceptable that the national courts had regard to the length of potential sentence together with other relevant factors. These included the fact that he had been extradited to Germany on international terrorism charges and that he 'had neither a fixed dwelling nor social ties in Germany which might have prevented him from absconding if released'.[532] The Court accepted the domestic courts' finding that no other measures to secure his presence would have been appropriate.

Of course, the reasons for continued detention must *remain* relevant and sufficient. So in *Kudla v Poland*,[533] for example, even if the applicant's failure to provide his address and a medical certificate might have initially justified detention, it did not do so for two years and four months.

Interference with the course of justice

A justifiable fear that the accused will interfere with the course of justice is another permissible ground for detention.[534] This includes destroying documents,[535] warning or collusion with other possible suspects,[536] and bringing pressure to bear upon witnesses.[537] A general statement that the accused will interfere with the course of justice is not sufficient; supporting evidence must be provided.[538] The longer the detention continues and the more the investigation makes progress, the less likely that interference with justice will remain a good reason for detention.[539]

---

[524] *Stögmuller v Austria*, see also *Becciev v Moldova* hudoc (2005) para 58. In *Yagci and Sargin v Turkey* A 319-A (1995); 20 EHRR 505 para 52, when, finding a breach of the right to bail, the Court took into account that the accused had returned voluntarily to resume residence in Turkey.

[525] *Punzelt v Czech Republic* hudoc (2000); 33 EHRR 1159 para 76.

[526] *Stögmuller v Austria* A 9 (1969); 1 EHRR 155 para 15.

[527] *Matznetter v Austria* A 10 (1969); 1 EHRR 198 para 8. See also *Ceský v Czech Republic* hudoc (2000); 33 EHRR 181 (fear of absconding justified by fact that applicant had entrusted a significant sum of money to an acquaintance, bought a car using another person's identity card, and obtained a false passport, para 79).

[528] *X v Switzerland No 8788/79*, 21 DR 241 (1980).

[529] *Barfuss v Czech Republic* hudoc (2000); 34 EHRR 948 paras 69–70.

[530] See, eg, *Neumeister v Austria* A 8 (1968); 1 EHRR 91 para 10.

[531] Hudoc (2006); 47 EHRR 47 para 40.

[532] Though cf *Sulaoja v Estonia* hudoc (2005); 43 EHRR 722 ('mere absence of a fixed residence does not give rise to a danger of flight', para 62).   [533] 2000-XI; 35 EHRR 198 GC.

[534] *Wemhoff v Germany* A 7 (1968); 1 EHRR 55 paras 13–14. See also *Contrada v Italy* 1998-V and *IA v France* 1998-VII.   [535] *Wemhoff v Germany*. Cf *W v Switzerland* A 254-A (1993); 17 EHRR 60.

[536] *Wemhoff v Germany*.   [537] *Letellier v France* A 207 (1991); 14 EHRR 83.

[538] *Clooth v Belgium* A 225 (1991); 14 EHRR 717 para 44. Also *Becciev v Moldova* hudoc (2005) para 59.

[539] *Clooth v Belgium*, para 43 (1991).

Prevention of crime

In *Matznetter v Austria*,[540] and subsequent case law[541] the Court has held that the detention of the applicant on the basis of the prevention of crime was compatible with Article 5(3). Accordingly, public interest in the prevention of crime may justify detention on remand where there are good reasons to believe[542] that the accused, if released, will commit an offence or offences of the same serious kind with which he is already charged. It is not necessary that there be a reasonable suspicion that any particular, identifiable offence will be committed. Where, however, the ground for believing that an accused charged with murder may commit other offences of violence if released is his mental condition, his detention should not be continued without steps being taken to give the accused the necessary psychiatric care.[543] The fact that the applicant is unemployed and has no family does not mean that he is inclined to commit new offences.[544]

Public order

A further ground for detention recognized by the Court is the preservation of public order. In *Letellier v France*,[545] the Court accepted that, in exceptional circumstances, 'by reason of their particular gravity and public reaction to them, certain offences may give rise to a social disturbance capable of justifying pre-trial detention, at least for a time'; this is so provided that the municipal law concerned recognizes the ground and there is evidence that the accused's release 'will actually disturb public order'. This test is not satisfied where, as in the *Letellier* case, the decision to refuse bail on this ground takes into account only the gravity of the offence in the abstract. In that case, the French courts, whose law recognized that certain offences may lead to a risk of public disorder justifying pre-trial detention, had only taken into account the fact that the offence (accessory to murder) was a very serious one, without considering whether the accused's release would be likely to cause a public disturbance on the facts.

c. Conditions of bail (including amount)

Article 5(3) states that if an accused is released on bail, his release 'may be conditioned by guarantees to appear for trial'. Automatic denial of bail will be a violation of Article 5(3).[546] The accused must faithfully furnish sufficient information, that can be checked if need be, so as to allow the amount of bail to be fixed.[547]

In *Mangouras v Spain*,[548] the Grand Chamber collated the general principles derived from its case law in this area. It was noted that bail may 'only be required as long as

---

[540] A 10 (1969); 1 EHRR 198 para 7 (four votes to three).

[541] See *Toth v Austria* A 224 (1991); 14 EHRR 551; *B v Austria* A 175 (1990); 13 EHRR 20; and *Clooth v Belgium* A 225 (1991); 14 EHRR 717.

[542] In *Clooth*, para 40, the Court used a different, possibly less strict, formula, stating that the danger of repetition must be a 'plausible' one. Previous convictions will be of relevance, see *Selcuk v Turkey* hudoc (2006) para 34.   [543] *Clooth v Belgium*.

[544] *Sulaoja v Estonia* hudoc (2005); 43 EHRR 772 para 64.

[545] A 207 (1991); 14 EHRR 83 para 51. Cf *Kemmache v France* A 218 (1991); 14 EHRR 520 para 52 and *Tomasi v France* A-241 (1992); 15 EHRR 1.

[546] *Cabellero v UK* 2000-II; 30 EHRR 643 GC. See also *Iwanczuk v Poland* hudoc (2001); 38 EHRR 148 (inappropriate delay in organizing bail when release justified). The Court nevertheless recognizes that sometimes the 'unavailability of bail' can be 'self-evident' (as when the 'suspect allegedly belongs to a gang implicated in violent crimes, or, probably, in terrorist cases'), especially in the early stages, see *Khodorkovskiy v Russia* hudoc (2011); 53 EHRR 1103 para 196.

[547] *Iwanczuk v Poland* hudoc (2001); 38 EHRR 148 para 66.

[548] ECHR-2010; 54 EHRR 903 paras 78–81 GC.

reasons justifying detention prevail',[549] and so if bail or other guarantees[550] can avoid the risk of absconding, the accused must be released. Such an assessment must have in mind that 'where a lighter sentence could be anticipated' there would be a reduced incentive for the accused to abscond.[551] As much care must be taken 'in fixing appropriate bail as in deciding whether or not the accused's continued detention is indispensable'.[552] The amount set must therefore be 'duly justified in the decision fixing bail'[553] and it must 'take into account the accused's means'.[554] The Grand Chamber stated that Article 5(3) is 'designed to ensure not the reparation of loss but, in particular, the appearance of the accused at the hearing'.[555] Any bail amount therefore had to be 'assessed principally'[556] by reference to a list of factors, as set out in the *Neumeister* case,[557] ie 'the accused's assets and his relationship with the persons who are to provide the security, in other words to the degree of confidence that is possible that the prospect of loss of the security or of action against the guarantors in case of his non-appearance at the trial will act as a sufficient deterrent to dispel any wish on his part to abscond'.

However, in *Mangouras* the Grand Chamber qualified this, adding that it did not seem 'unreasonable, in certain circumstances, to take into account also the amount of the loss imputed to [the detainee]'.[558] This was so in *Mangouras* when, by ten votes to seven, the Grand Chamber found no violation of Article 5(3) in a case which concerned the detention for eighty-three days of the (Greek) Master of a ship, leakage from which had caused a major environmental disaster. Bail had been fixed at €3 million, well beyond the personal means of the Master, and he was only released when the ship's insurers paid this. The majority nevertheless accepted that the domestic authorities had taken sufficient account of the applicant's personal situation, which included his 'status as an employee of the ship's owner, his professional relationship with the persons who were to provide the security, his nationality and place of permanent residence and also his lack of ties in Spain and his age'.[559] Highlighting the exceptional, specific factual background to the case—ie in particular, the disastrous environmental and economic consequences of the oil spill,[560] and the 'very significant implications in terms of both criminal and civil liability'[561]—the Grand Chamber accepted that the domestic courts had been justified in taking into account 'the seriousness of the offences in question and the amount of the loss imputed to the applicant'.[562] The ruling, departing as it does from some established aspects of the

---

[549] *Mangouras v Spain*, para 79.

[550] In the *Stögmuller* case, the Court implied that the surrender of a passport may be justified to prevent absconding, A 9 (1969); 1 EHRR 155 para 15. See also *Lind v Russia* hudoc (2007) para 81 and *Ignatenco v Moldova* hudoc (2011) para 83. [551] *Mangouras v Spain* ECHR-2010; 54 EHRR 903 para 79 GC.

[552] *Mangouras v Spain.* [553] See also *Georgieva v Bulgaria* hudoc (2008) para 30–1.

[554] *Mangouras v Spain* ECHR-2010; 54 EHRR 903 para 80 GC. See also *Hristova v Bulgaria* hudoc (2006) para 111. Thus a failure to assess the applicant's capacity to pay the sum required by the domestic courts may be a reason to conclude that Article 5(3) has been violated: *Toshev v Bulgaria* hudoc (2006) para 69.

[555] As was noted in *Neumeister*, the purpose is to ensure that there is 'a sufficient deterrent to dispel any wish on his part to abscond', *Neumeister v Austria* A 8 (1968); 1 EHRR 91 para 14.

[556] *Mangouras v Spain* ECHR-2010; 54 EHRR 903 para 68 GC.

[557] *Neumeister v Austria* A 8 (1968); 1 EHRR 91 para 14.

[558] *Mangouras v Spain* ECHR-2010; 54 EHRR 903 para 81 GC.

[559] *Mangouras v Spain*, para 92.

[560] *Mangouras v Spain*, paras 86–7 (citing growing concern both in Europe and internationally in relation to environmental offences, 'new realities' which the Court would take into account in interpreting the requirements of Article 5(3)). [561] *Mangouras v Spain*, para 87.

[562] *Mangouras v Spain*, para 92. There was a strong joint dissent (see joint separate opinion of Judges Rozakis, Bratza, Bonello, Cabral Barreto, David Thór Björgvinsson, Nicolaou, and Bianku).

Article 5(3) jurisprudence, may be seen in the light of 'the growing and legitimate concern both in Europe and internationally in relation to environmental offences',[563] and the need to secure accountability in this regard.

III. TRIAL WITHIN A REASONABLE TIME (THE NEED FOR 'SPECIAL DILIGENCE IN THE CONDUCT OF THE PROCEEDINGS')

Even if detention is justified under Article 5(3), that provision may still be infringed if the accused's detention is prolonged beyond a 'reasonable time'[564] because the proceedings have not been conducted with the required expedition. The period to be considered here is from the day the accused is taken into custody until the charge is determined.[565]

The guarantee in Article 5(3), which overlaps with that in Article 6(1), requires that in respect of a detained person the authorities show 'special diligence in the conduct of the proceedings',[566] although this should not hinder the efforts of the judicial authorities to carry out their tasks with proper care.[567] The same, higher standard of diligence would appear to apply under Article 6(1) when the accused is in detention.[568] In practice, 'reasonable time' claims brought by persons remanded in custody that just concern the stages of the proceedings to which Article 5(3) apply, *viz* from arrest to conviction by the trial court,[569] are considered just under that provision, not under Article 6(1).[570] Reasonable time claims that extend in time beyond the accused's conviction to include appeal proceedings are either considered under both Article 5(3) (for the stages to which it applies) and Article 6(1)[571] or just under Article 6(1).[572]

As to the considerations to be taken into account in assessing whether trial within a reasonable time has occurred, the same ones apply for both Articles 5(3) and 6(1). Thus, as with Article 6(1), relevant factors are the complexity of the case, the conduct of the accused, and the efficiency of the national authorities.[573] In one case the Court's conclusion that Article 5(3) was violated was strongly influenced by the fact that the applicant was a minor detained in an adult facility.[574]

---

[563] *Mangouras v Spain*, para 86.

[564] For the relevant period to which 'reasonable time' applies, see section 7.II.

[565] *Kalashnikov v Russia* 2002-VI; 36 EHRR 587 para 110. There is no general obligation to take into account the length of a pre-trial detention suffered in a third state (*Zandbergs v Latvia* hudoc (2011) para 63). As regards the application of the six-month admissibility rule (Article 35(1)) to multiple non-consecutive periods of pre-trial detention separated by considerable time, see *Idalov v Russia* hudoc (2012) GC.

[566] *Herczegfalvy v Austria* A 244 (1992); 15 EHRR 437 para 71. The complexity and special characteristics of the investigation are relevant for the assessment of 'special diligence', *Scott v Spain* 1996-VI; 24 EHRR 391 para 74.   [567] *Sadegul Ozdemir v Turkey* hudoc (2005) para 44.

[568] *Abdoella v Netherlands* A 248-A (1992); 20 EHRR 585 para 24.   [569] See section 7.II.

[570] *Abdoella v Netherlands* A 248-A (1992); 20 EHRR 585 para 24, concerned appeal proceedings, to which Article 5(3) does not extend.

[571] *B v Austria* A 175 (1990); 13 EHRR 20 (no breach of Article 5(3), but a breach of Article 6(1) in respect of post-conviction proceedings). See also *Solmaz v Turkey* hudoc (2006).

[572] See *Assenov v Bulgaria* 1998-VIII; 28 EHRR 652 (virtually no activity on the case for approximately a year).

[573] See *Neumeister v Austria* A 8 (1968); 1 EHRR 91 and *Kemmache v France* A 218 (1991); 14 EHRR 520. In both cases, the Court had already found a breach of the right to bail in Article 5(3).

[574] *Nart v Turkey* hudoc (2008) para 34.

As with Article 6(1), the Court frequently has cause to find violations of Article 5(3) under this particular head for reasons stemming from the disorganization and ineffectiveness of the authorities, for example extended periods of inactivity on the handling of a case prior to trial.[575] For the purposes of Article 5(3) the fact that the context of the criminal proceedings is 'international terrorism' may be of relevance for the Court's determination of reasonableness as it has 'special consideration' of 'the difficulties intrinsic to the investigation of offences committed by criminal associations acting on a global scale'.[576]

As under Article 6(1), the reasonableness of the length of proceedings depends on the facts of the case.[577] However, even the shortest period of pre-trial detention will violate this provision if it is not convincingly demonstrated that it is justified, for Article 5(3) cannot authorize pre-trial detention unconditionally provided that it lasts no longer than a certain period.[578] Moreover, very long periods do not *automatically* violate Article 5(3).

In *W v Switzerland*,[579] the Court held, by five votes to four, that proceedings resulting in a four-year period of pre-trial detention were not in breach of Article 5(3). In a strong dissent, Judge Pettiti[580] suggested that there should be an absolute limit to the length of pre-trial detention and that, given European standards and expectations, very strong evidence indeed was necessary to justify both the refusal of bail and the time taken to investigate and try a case over a period lasting as long as four years. The finding in *W* was controversial, however, in *Chraidi v Germany*,[581] the Court unanimously held that there had been no violation of Article 5(3) when the relevant period was over five-and-a-half years. It indicated that normally such a period would breach Article 5(3),[582] but stressed the exceptional circumstances of the case before it, 'a particularly complex investigation and trial concerning serious offences of international terrorism which caused the death of three victims and serious suffering to more than one hundred'.[583]

---

[575] See Ch 9, section IV.

[576] *Chraidi v Germany* hudoc (2006); 47 EHRR 47 para 37 (although see the concurring opinion of Judge Borrego Borrego).

[577] See *Wemhoff v Germany* A 7 (1968); 1 EHRR 55 para 5 and *McKay v UK* 2006-X; 44 EHRR 827 para 45 GC. In *Toth v Austria* A 224 (1991); 14 EHRR 551 (two years and one month's detention on remand), there were periods of inactivity totalling eleven months resulting largely because of a disinclination to photocopy the official file. In *Tomasi v France* A-241 (1992); 15 EHRR 1 (five years and seven months), the public prosecutor admitted to long periods in which no progress was made. See also *Birou v France* A 232-B (1992); 14 EHRR 738 Com Rep (five years' delay unreasonable; F Sett before Court).

[578] *Shishkov v Bulgaria* 2003-I para 66 ('relatively short period in detention' of seven months and three weeks violated Article 5(3)). Article 5(3) can apply to multiple detention periods, if so the Court examines not only the reasonableness of the total time, but also 'whether the repetitiveness of the detention' complies with Article 5(3), *Smirnova v Russia* 2003-IX; 39 EHRR 450 para 67.

[579] *W v Switzerland* A 254-A (1993); 17 EHRR 60.

[580] See the joint dissenting opinions. The Commission had found a breach (nineteen votes to one), suggesting that Article 5(3) should set a maximum length of pre-trial detention.

[581] Hudoc (2006); 47 EHRR 47.   [582] *Chraidi v Germany*, para 46.

[583] *Chraidi v Germany*, para 47 (cf the concurring opinion of Judge Borrego Borrego).

8. ARTICLE 5(4): REMEDY TO CHALLENGE THE LEGALITY OF DETENTION

I. THE IMPORTANCE OF ARTICLE 5(4) (REVIEW OF THE LAWFULNESS OF DETENTION)

Article 5(4) is the *habeas corpus* provision of the Convention,[584] providing a 'cornerstone guarantee'[585] against arbitrary detention by the state. It is in essence a detainee's 'right actively to seek [a prompt] judicial review of his detention',[586] and to be released if there is no lawful basis for his or her loss of liberty.

The core rules require that a detainee must be able to seek Article 5(4) review as soon as he or she is detained, the decision must take place 'speedily'[587] thereafter, and release ordered if detention is unlawful. Potentially, therefore, Article 5(4), which is a fully independent provision, may come into play before Article 5(3) (which, in any case only applies to detention under Article 5(1)(c)).[588] There is no precondition to the application of Article 5(4) that an applicant 'show that on the facts of his case he stands any particular chance of success in obtaining his release'.[589]

The review[590] of detention is not an appeal but must properly examine the procedural and substantive conditions which are essential for the 'lawfulness', in Convention terms, of the deprivation of liberty. There is no obligation on a domestic judge to address every argument contained in the appellant's submissions, and Article 5(4) 'does not guarantee a right to judicial review of such a scope as to empower the court, on all aspects of the case including questions of pure expediency, to substitute its own discretion for that of the decision-making authority'.[591] However, the court must have regard to and properly address concrete facts invoked by the detainee and capable of putting in doubt the existence of the conditions essential for the 'lawfulness', in the sense of Article 5(1), of the deprivation of liberty.[592] That is, the detained person must have the opportunity to question whether his detention is consistent both with the applicable municipal law and the Convention, including its general principles, and is not arbitrary.[593]

Accordingly, there will be an obvious violation when, in relation to a detention under Article 5(1)(c), the review body merely verifies the charges against the applicant but does

---

[584] Note, however, that in certain circumstances *habeas corpus* under English law has not satisifed Article 5(4).

[585] *Rakevich v Russia* hudoc (2003) para 43. For a statement of the relevant general principles, see *A v UK* ECHR-2009; 49 EHRR 625 paras 202–11 GC.   [586] *Rakevich v Russia.*   [587] See section 8.II.c.

[588] See Trechsel, *Human Rights in Criminal Proceedings*, 2005, p 466. Both Article 5(3) and (4) guarantees call for remedies that may lead to the applicant's release (soon after arrest and at regular intervals thereafter), but the questions that may arise when considering the 'lawfulness' of the accused's detention under Article 5(4) are 'often of a more complex nature' (*E v Norway* A 181-A (1990); 17 EHRR 30 para 64) than those that arise under Article 5(3). Also the procedural guarantees required by Article 5(3) are less rigorous than those in Article 5(4). However, where the procedures in fact followed under Article 5(3) meet the requirements of Article 5(4), the judicial control required by the latter is 'incorporated in' any confirmation of an accused's detention made by a 'judge or other officer' made under the former, *De Jong, Baljet and Van Den Brink v Netherlands* A 77 (1984); 8 EHRR 20 para 57.

[589] *Waite v UK* hudoc (2002); 36 EHRR 1001 para 59.

[590] See *Reinprecht v Austria* 2005-XII; 44 EHRR 797 para 31.

[591] *A v UK* ECHR-2009; 49 EHRR 625 para 202 GC; *Chahal v UK* 1996-V; 23 EHRR 413 para 127.

[592] *Nikolova v Bulgaria* 1999-II; 31 EHRR 64 para 61 GC.

[593] *Van Droogenbroeck v Belgium* A 50 (1982); 4 EHRR 443 para 48 PC. The onus of proof is on the authorities in this regard; they must prove that an individual satisfies the conditions for compulsory detention, rather than the converse, *Hutchison Reid v UK* 2003 IV; 37 EHRR 211 para 71.

not examine the concrete facts concerning the soundness of the charges against him with a view to ordering release if it could not be said that the test of 'reasonable suspicion' had been met.[594] Similarly, the scope and nature of Article 5(4) review requires a proper assessment of whether bail has been denied legitimately.[595] Again, to the extent that conditions of detention have a bearing on the issue of lawfulness, as in *Aerts v Belgium*,[596] the court should be able to review these too. Consistent with the requirements of Article 5(1)(f) as interpreted by the Court,[597] Article 5(4) does not require that the domestic 'court' have the power to review the merits of the underlying decision to expel. However, there must be a proper review of whether the decision to detain the applicant and to keep him in detention was justified on the grounds given by the state. For the detention of a 'person of unsound mind', it must be possible for the 'court' to determine whether the detention is warranted on medical grounds, since compliance with Article 5(1)(e) requires that the person's detention as being of 'unsound mind' is medically justified.[598] It was because no such possibility existed that *habeas corpus* proceedings in English law were held not to provide a sufficient remedy in *X v UK*.[599] *Habeas corpus* did constitute a sufficient Article 5(4) remedy by which to challenge the detention of an accused person within Article 5(1)(c), since it allowed the reasonableness of the grounds for suspicion, as well as the procedural legality of the detention, to be reviewed.[600] Prior to the entry into force of the Human Rights Act 1998, a number of cases brought against the United Kingdom exposed the failings of judicial review in English administrative law[601] in that it provided insufficiently close scrutiny of the grounds of detention to satisfy Article 5(4).

As the theory underlying Article 5(4) is that a judicial remedy should be available to review the legality of an administrative act of detention, there is no need for separate Article 5(4) review if the detention has been made by the order of a 'court'[602] (the 'incorporation rule'). This is most clearly the case when a person has been 'convicted by a competent court' consistently with Article 5(1)(a).[603] However, even if the original basis for detention is a court order, an Article 5(4) review may also be required for an administrative decision to *continue* to detain someone, and Article 5(4) may require a review of detention after a certain time and at reasonable intervals thereafter.[604] Most forms of detention will not require this, but it is required for detainees on remand and when the grounds for detention are susceptible to change over time, as with mental illness or when a detainee is being held during a discretionary phase of his sentence on the basis of his continuing dangerousness.

---

[594] *Van Droogenbroeck v Belgium*. See also *Ječius v Lithuania* 2000-IX; 35 EHRR 400.

[595] *Tymoshenko v Ukraine* hudoc (2013) paras 279–82.   [596] See section 5.V.d.

[597] See section 5.VI.b.

[598] See *Winterwerp v Netherlands* A 33 (1979); 2 EHRR 387 para 51, see section 5.V.d. The lawfulness requirement will require that the medical report before the court is appropriately up to date; see *Musial v Poland* 1999-II; 31 EHRR 720 para 50 GC (eleven-month-old report).

[599] A 46 (1981); 4 EHRR 188 para 58. *Habeas corpus* would suffice for an emergency admission, para 58.

[600] *Brogan v UK* A 145-B (1988); 11 EHRR 117 para 65 PC.

[601] See, eg, *Weeks v UK* A 114 (1987); 13 EHRR 435 PC and *Thynne, Wilson and Gunnell v UK* A190-A (1990); 13 EHRR 666 PC, where Article 5(1)(a) was the basis for detention; and *HL v UK* 2004-IX; 40 EHRR 761 paras 136–42, where Article 5(1)(e) was in issue. In *Chahal v UK* 1996-V; 23 EHRR 413 GC, neither judicial review nor *habeas corpus* was an Article 5(4)-compliant basis for challenging a deportation order on the facts.

[602] *De Wilde, Ooms and Versyp v Belgium* A 12 (1971); 1 EHRR 373 para 76 PC. Cf, *Engel v Netherlands* A 22 (1976); 1 EHRR 706 para 77 PC. See Trechsel, *Human Rights in Criminal Proceedings*, 2005, pp 469–70.

[603] The rule applies equally, however, to other situations where detention is ordered by a 'court' (*Winterwerp v Netherlands* A 33 (1979); 2 EHRR 387).   [604] See section 8.III.

II. THE QUALITIES AND PROCEDURES REQUIRED OF AN ARTICLE 5(4) 'COURT'

As to the specific requirements of Article 5(4) review, these are set out in the paragraphs that follow. Essentially, the review, which must take place 'speedily',[605] should have a judicial character and provide guarantees appropriate to the kind of deprivation of liberty in question.[606] So there may be variations of procedure according to the nature of the detention in issue.

Article 5(4) may be complied with by the provision of two or more separate remedies that together allow the applicant to test all aspects of the legality of his detention.[607] It is also sufficient that a remedy exists; it does not matter that the applicant finds it inadvisable to use it in his particular circumstances.[608] However, the principle of accessibility and effectiveness derived from Article 5(4) does require that the existence of the remedy must be sufficiently certain, not only in theory but also in practice.[609] As regards the latter requirement, the onus is on the respondent state to furnish the Court with specific examples of judicial decisions which testify to the existence and effectiveness of the remedy.[610] There is no requirement that remedies that are neither adequate nor effective should be used by the applicant.[611]

a. Effective access to review

The right to apply for a remedy should be exercisable by the detainee on his own initiative; it should not be dependent on the initiative or goodwill of the authorities.[612] There should also be a realistic possibility of resort to the remedy in practical terms. In *Öcalan v Turkey*,[613] for example, the applicant detainee was not legally trained, had no access to a lawyer, and, by virtue of is imprisonment, was in effect cut off from the outside world and so it was impossible in practical terms for him to mount an Article 5(4) claim. In *Conka v Belgium*,[614] Article 5(4) was violated as the speed with which the authorities expedited the deportation of the applicants meant that their lawyer was unable to mount an Article 5(4) challenge before their actual deportation occurred.

The interests of persons who, on account of their mental disabilities, are not fully capable of acting for themselves, may call for special procedural safeguards.[615] A person detained in an institution under Article 5(1)(e) may be capable of expressing a view on his confinement, but lack legal capacity to bring an action under Article 5(4). He or she may be being deprived of liberty at his or her guardian's request (if the domestic legal regime so permits), or, for example, the institution holding the detainee may act as legal guardian. In such circumstances, and as a check against abuse of the guardian role, the

---

[605] See section 8.II.c.   [606] *Assenov v Bulgaria* 1998-VIII; 28 EHRR 652 para 162.

[607] *Weeks v UK* A 114 (1987); 13 EHRR 435 para 69. Cf *Benjamin and Wilson v UK* hudoc (2002); 36 EHRR 1 para 36.   [608] *Keus v Netherlands* A 185-C (1990); 13 EHRR 700 para 28.

[609] *Van Droogenbroeck v Belgium* A 50 (1982); 4 EHRR 443 para 54 PC; also *Sakık v Turkey* 1997-VII; 26 EHRR 662 para 53.

[610] See, eg, *Sakık v Turkey*, para 53 (violation as, despite submissions relating to the effectiveness of the remedy, the Court was provided with no example of a successful application at domestic level).

[611] *Sakık v Turkey*, para 55.   [612] *Rakevich v Russia* hudoc (2003) paras 43–7.

[613] 2005-IV; 41 EHRR 985 paras 70–2 GC. See also *RMD v Switzerland* 1997-VI; 28 EHRR 224 para 52 (Article 5(4) violated as the applicant was transferred successively from one canton to another such that, owing to the peculiarities of domestic law and the organization of the national court system, in no single canton was he able to make effective use of the sound Article 5(4) remedies that were available).

[614] 2002-I; 34 EHRR 1298 para 55.

[615] *Stanev v Bulgaria* ECHR-2012; 55 EHRR 625 para 171 GC.

individual must be accorded an opportunity of contesting his or her confinement before a court (Article 5(4)), with separate legal representation.[616]

b. Judicial character of review body

As the Court has put it:

> [t]he 'court' referred to in [Article 5(4)] does not necessarily have to be a court of law of the classic kind, integrated within the standard judicial machinery of the country. The term denotes 'bodies which exhibit not only common fundamental features, of which the most important is independence of the executive and the parties to the case[617] ... but also the guarantees'—'appropriate to the kind of deprivation of liberty in question'—'of a judicial procedure', the forms of which may vary but which must include the competence to 'decide' the 'lawfulness' of the detention and to order release if the detention is not lawful.[618]

Bodies that have predictably been held not to meet the requirement of being a 'court' are a public prosecutor,[619] the medical officer of a 'person of unsound mind',[620] and a government minister.[621] In *Weeks v UK*,[622] the English Parole Board was found to have the necessary judicial character; it was 'independent of the executive and impartial in the performance of their duties'.[623] The distinction being drawn was between 'independence' of the executive and 'impartiality' as between the parties.

To be of a 'judicial character', a body must also be impartial.[624] In *K v Austria*,[625] a court of law did not satisfy Article 5(4) because the judge who ruled on the applicant's detention for failing to pay a fine had earlier imposed the fine.

An investigating judge in a civil law system is a 'court'.[626] This decision has been criticized on the basis that, although 'independent', an investigating judge is not 'impartial' as between the parties since he has a responsibility to bring the investigation successfully to an end and hence has an incentive to detain the accused to avoid him absconding or tampering with evidence.[627] However, the Court has confirmed[628] that, other than in special circumstances, the mere fact that a trial judge makes decisions on detention on remand does not in itself taint that figure as being 'impartial' for the purposes of Article 5(4). It takes the view that suspicion and a formal finding of guilt are not to be treated as being the same and that normally questions which the judge has to answer when deciding on detention on remand are not the same as those which are decisive for his final judgment.

---

[616] *DD v Lithuania* hudoc (2012) para 166.

[617] See *De Wilde, Ooms and Versyp v Belgium* A 12 (1971); 1 EHRR 373 para 77 PC. The qualities of independence and impartiality were not met in *Ramishvili and Kokhreidze v Georgia* hudoc (2009) paras 134–5 (judge apparently helping the prosecution, court-room dominated by security police (raising questions as to court's 'independence')).   [618] *Hutchinson Reid v UK* 2003 IV; 37 EHRR 211 para 64.

[619] *Winterwerp v Netherlands* A 33 (1979); 2 EHRR 387 para 64.

[620] *X v UK* A 46 (1981); 4 EHRR 188 para 61.

[621] *X v UK*. Cf, *Keus v Netherlands* A 185-C (1990); 13 EHRR 700 para 28.

[622] A 114 (1987); 13 EHRR 435 para 62 PC.

[623] Cf the Court's change in approach in respect of the meaning of 'officer' in Article 5(3), section 7.I.c.

[624] *DN v Switzerland* 2001-III; 37 EHRR 510 para 42 GC (objective and subjective tests are applied, para 44; impartiality is presumed until there is proof to the contrary, para 45).

[625] A 255-B (1993) Com Rep F Sett before Court.

[626] *Bezicheri v Italy* A 164 (1989); 12 EHRR 210.   [627] Trechsel, *European System*, p 327.

[628] *Ilijkov v Bulgaria* hudoc (2001) para 97 (Bulgarian law at the time entrusted decisions relating to the accused's detention to the same trial judge who subsequently examined the merits of the criminal case).

The 'court' in question must also have a 'judicial character' in the sense of being competent to 'decide' the 'lawfulness' of the detention and to make a legally binding order for release if the detention is unlawful (merely advisory functions will not suffice).[629] Thus in *X v UK*,[630] a Mental Health Review Tribunal, although independent of the executive and the parties, did not qualify because it could only make advisory recommendations for release to the Home Secretary.

c. Procedural guarantees required at review

Even if the review is provided by what appears to be a regular court according to domestic law, this does not mean that there will be no violation of Article 5(4), for the procedural guarantees afforded by that court may fall short of that Article's requirements. This was the case in *De Wilde, Ooms and Versyp v Belgium*,[631] where the plenary Court held that Article 5(4) obliges a 'court' to provide 'guarantees of judicial procedure', it being later stated that Article 5(4) proceedings 'must have a judicial character and provide guarantees appropriate to the kind of deprivation of liberty in question'.[632] The procedural guarantee required may therefore vary depending on context, facts, and circumstances.

Adversarial proceedings, fairness, and use of secret evidence

Article 5(4) requires an adversarial procedure. The method chosen by the domestic system must ensure 'that the other party will be aware that observations have been filed and will have a real opportunity to comment thereon'.[633]

The relevant cases have mostly concerned 'equality of arms',[634] which is a distinct procedural right that can be subsumed within the general principle of adversarial proceedings. For example, a breach of Article 5(4) was found in *Toth v Austria*,[635] because the prosecuting authority was present during the appeal hearing on the question of the applicant's detention when the applicant was not.[636] Equality of arms is clearly not ensured if the applicant's lawyer is denied access to those documents in the investigation file which are essential in order effectively to challenge the lawfulness of his client's detention.[637] One of the contributing factors taken into account by the Court in concluding that Article 5(4) had been breached in *Chahal*

---

[629] *A v UK* ECHR-2009; 49 EHRR 625 para 202 GC.

[630] A 46 (1981); 4 EHRR 188. In *E v Norway* (A 181-A (1990); 17 EHRR 30) the Court was satisfied that, whereas the Norwegian courts would normally just declare an administrative decision to be illegal without ordering that any remedial steps be taken, they could go further and order a person's release in a case of illegal detention, as Article 5(4) requires. In *Van Droogenbroeck v Belgium* (A 50 (1982); 4 EHRR 443. Cf *Benjamin and Wilson v UK* hudoc (2002); 36 EHRR 1 para 36), it was insufficient that a court could convict the responsible government official for illegal detention but could not order the detained person's release.

[631] A 12 (1971); 1 EHRR 373 para 78 PC.

[632] See also *Assenov v Bulgaria* 1998-VIII; 28 EHRR 652 para 162. *Ramishvili and Kokhreidze v Georgia* hudoc (2009) offers a striking example of when procedures were so chaotic (see paras 128–32) that a sober judicial examination of the relevant issues was impossible.

[633] *Garcia Alva v Germany* hudoc (2001); 37 EHRR 335 para 39.

[634] The ruling in the *Neumeister v Austria* A 8 (1968); 1 EHRR 91 that 'equality of arms' was not required can be disregarded.

[635] A 224 (1991); 14 EHRR 551. See also, *Niedbala v Poland* hudoc (2000); 33 EHRR 1137; *Nikolova v Bulgaria* 1999-II; 31 EHRR 64 GC; and *Ilijkov v Bulgaria* hudoc (2001) para 104.

[636] Cf *Sanchez-Reisse v Switzerland* A 107 (1986); 9 EHRR 71, in which the Court held that the applicant should have been allowed an opportunity to respond to the opinion of the Police Office.

[637] *Garcia Alva v Germany* hudoc (2001); 37 EHRR 335 para 39. See also *Weeks v UK* A 114 (1987); 13 EHRR 435 para 66 PC (violation of Article 5(4) since prisoner seeking release was not entitled to full disclosure of adverse material in the Parole Board's possession). Cf *Thynne, Wilson, and Gunnell v UK* A190-A (1990); 13 EHRR 666 para 80 PC.

v UK[638] (detention under 5(1)(f)) was the fact that the applicant was merely provided with an outline of the grounds for the notice of intention to deport.

With respect to detention under Article 5(1)(c), the procedures for review 'should in principle...meet, to the largest extent possible under the circumstances of an on-going investigation, the basic requirements of a fair trial'.[639] This approach reflects the position that persistence of a reasonable suspicion that the accused person has committed an offence is a condition *sine qua non* for the lawfulness of the continued detention. It follows that in this context, 'the detainee must be given an opportunity effectively to challenge the basis of the allegations against him', it may also be necessary for 'the court to hear witnesses whose testimony appears prima facie to have a material bearing on the continuing lawfulness of the detention', and for there to be 'access to documents in the case-file which form the basis of the prosecution case against him'.[640] However, Article 5(4) proceedings must also strike a balance between the rights of defence and the imperatives of investigation. Criminal investigations must be conducted efficiently, so some information collected may in principle be kept secret 'in order to prevent suspects from tampering with evidence and undermining the course of justice'.[641] But 'this legitimate goal cannot be pursued at the expense of substantial restrictions on the rights of the defence'. Accordingly, 'information which is essential for the assessment of the lawfulness of a detention should be made available in an appropriate manner to the suspect's lawyer', and counsel must have access to documents in the investigation file which are 'essential in order effectively to challenge the lawfulness of his client's detention'.[642]

This last requirement, and the balance to be struck between liberty and security, has also been a crucial issue in the context of anti-terrorism measures, in particular when the state maintains that there are valid reasons for *not* disclosing information to a detainee (for example, jeopardizing the safety of an informant, or because the techniques employed by the security services will be revealed). Then again, there is a risk that the intelligence concerned is flawed in some way, not providing a legitimate basis for detention, or plainly wrong, and so providing no basis for detention at all. In such circumstances, if the detainee cannot contest the evidence against him or her and effectively expose its shortcomings, he or she will not be able to secure his or her freedom. The cases of *Chahal v UK*[643] and *A v UK*[644] are of great importance as regards the extent of procedural fairness that Strasbourg requires of a state in this context.

In *Chahal*, which concerned detention under Article 5(1)(f), a proper review was not possible since the full material on which the decision to detain was based was not made

---

[638] *Chahal v UK* 1996-V; 23 EHRR 413 para 130.

[639] *Garcia Alva v Germany* hudoc (2001); 37 EHRR 335 para 39. See also *Al-Nashif v Bulgaria* hudoc (2002); 36 EHRR 655 para 92 ('person concerned should have access to a court and the opportunity to be heard either in person or through some form of representation'); and *Lebedev v Russia* hudoc (2007); 47 EHRR 771 at paras 70–3 (see also paras 75–9).

[640] *A v UK* ECHR-2009; 49 EHRR 625 para 204 GC.

[641] *Garcia Alva v Germany* hudoc (2001); 37 EHRR 335 para 42.

[642] *Garcia Alva v Germany*, para 42 (detainee charged with major drug trafficking activities and denied access to investigation files and witness statements containing information upon which the decision to detain was primarily based, given fear that to do so would endanger on-going investigations). The accused should be given 'a sufficient opportunity to take cognisance of statements and other pieces of evidence underlying them, such as the results of the police and other investigations, irrespective of whether the accused is able to provide any indication as to the relevance for his defence of the pieces of evidence which he seeks to be given access to', para 41. See also *Nikolova v Bulgaria* 1999-II; 31 EHRR 64 para 63 GC and *Migon v Poland* hudoc (2002) para 79.   [643] 1996-V; 23 EHRR 413.

[644] ECHR-2009; 49 EHRR 625 GC.

available to the domestic courts given national security considerations.[645] The Court accepted that the use of confidential material may be unavoidable where national security and terrorism is involved, but it stated that this did not mean that in such circumstances the national authorities should be 'free from effective control by the domestic courts'.[646] The state had failed to strike a proper balance since, as Canadian experience illustrated, it was possible to employ techniques which both accommodated legitimate security concerns about the nature and sources of intelligence information and yet accord the individual a substantial measure of procedural justice.[647] In reaction to *Chahal*, the UK government established the Special Immigration Appeals Commission (SIAC). This was an attempt to provide a sufficient level of procedural fairness to a detainee whilst denying him access to material that, it was maintained, could not be disclosed for national security reasons (the detainee could receive 'open' evidence, but not 'closed' evidence). Proceedings took place *in camera* before a judge who had full sight of all the evidence upon which the Secretary of State relied. Evidence could be withheld (become 'closed') from the detainee and his lawyer if it was sensitive from a national security perspective, and neither could attend the hearing. Instead, the detainee was represented by a special, security-cleared counsel ('special advocate') who did have sight of all the relevant material. However, the special advocate and detainee could only meet to discuss the reasons for detention before (not after) the former had sight of the closed evidence against the latter (unless permission was granted by SIAC).

The compatibility of this regime with Article 5(4), or more particularly whether and in what circumstances it counterbalanced the procedural unfairness caused by a lack of full disclosure, was a central issue in the Grand Chamber judgment in *A v UK* (the so-called 'Belmarsh detainees' case).[648] Amongst other things, Strasbourg examined the Article 5(4) procedural fairness issues arising in that case (which had not been addressed by the House of Lords), and in respect of which there had been no derogation from the European Convention on Human Rights (ECHR).

Citing relevant jurisprudence on Article 6(1),[649] the Court did not hold that the detainees in *A v UK* had to have sight of *all* the material against them, including confidential material purportedly sustaining the case that they were reasonably suspected of international terrorism. Its approach[650] was, on the one hand, to recognize the strong public interest issues involved in the fight against terrorism (and the associated issue of the national security interests attached to certain evidence), even though there had been no derogation from Article 5(4), but, on the other, to insist upon an appropriate level of procedural fairness under that provision. With respect to the latter, the Court noted that the detainees were, or had been, detained for lengthy periods and in a position of potentially indefinite detention, based on mere suspicion of being international terrorists.[651] In such circumstances, the Court required that the level of procedural fairness should offer 'substantially the same fair trial guarantees'[652] as Article 6. On that basis:

> it was essential that as much information about the allegations and evidence against each applicant was disclosed as was possible without compromising national security or the safety of others. Where full disclosure was not possible, Article 5(4) required that the

---

[645] Nor was this deficiency made up for by other potential avenues of address, see para 130.

[646] *Chahal v UK*, para 131.

[647] *Chahal v UK*, see paras 131 and 144. See also *Al-Nashif v Bulgaria* hudoc (2002); 36 EHRR 655 paras 94–8.

[648] On the Article 5(1)(f) aspects see section 5.VI.b. On the Article 15 issues see Ch 19. See also Doswald-Beck, *Human Rights in Times of Conflict and Terrorism*, 2011 pp 274–6 and Shah, 9 HRLR 473 (2009) pp 483–6.   [649] *A v UK* ECHR-2009; 49 EHRR 625 paras 205–8 GC.

[650] *A v UK*, paras 216–17.   [651] *A v UK*, para 217.   [652] *A v UK*, para 217.

difficulties this caused were counterbalanced in such a way that each applicant still had the possibility effectively to challenge the allegations against him.[653]

A v UK held that the special advocate system did not necessarily guarantee sufficient fairness under Article 5(4). SIAC was a 'court' within the meaning of Article 5(4) and had the potential to ensure that no material was unnecessarily withheld from the detainee, and the special advocate system could probe the case for secrecy and press the judge for greater disclosure. Nonetheless, the possibility remained that Article 5(4) would be breached because, although the special advocate provided an important role counterbalancing lack of full disclosure and a full, open adversarial hearing, that role would be deficient, 'unless the detainee was provided with sufficient information about the allegations against him to enable him to give effective instructions to the special advocate'.[654] So, whether there had been compliance with Article 5(4) depended on an assessment of each case. Here the Court established that there would be a violation of Article 5(4) if the only material disclosed to a detainee amounted to general assertions, the decision to detain him being 'based solely or to a decisive degree on closed material'.[655] The ruling on this point had important implications for the 'control order' regime employed in the United Kingdom at the time.[656]

Oral hearing (and presence of detainee)

As we have just observed, the detainees in *A v UK* did not appear before SIAC themselves. However, the Court has ruled that some circumstances may be such that it is 'essential to the fairness of the proceedings that the applicant be present at an oral hearing',[657] as 'where questions arise involving, for example, an assessment of the applicant's character or mental state'.[658] This would apply to detention falling within the ambit of Article 5(1)(e) (unsound mind).[659] A minor detained under Article 5(1)(d) is entitled to be heard in person and provided with effective legal assistance.[660]

For detention under Article 5(1)(c), Article 5(4) requires a 'hearing',[661] the Court adding that '[t]he opportunity for a detainee to be heard either in person or through some

---

[653] *A v UK*, para 218.   [654] *A v UK*, para 220.

[655] *A v UK*, para 220. By contrast, as a general rule, it was unlikely that Article 5(4) would be breached if 'open material played a predominant role' in the determination to detain, or 'if the allegations contained in the open material were sufficiently specific' so as to enable the detainee to refute them (for example, if the allegation was that a detainee had attended a terrorist training camp on certain dates, this would have enabled him to submit evidence confirming he was elsewhere at the time), see para 220. The Court concluded that Article 5(4) had been breached in respect of four of the eleven applicants, see paras 222–4.

[656] The main principles were applied by the House of Lords to control orders and in relation to Article 6(1) in *Secretary of State for the Home Department v AF and others* [2009] UKHL 28.

[657] *Waite v UK* hudoc (2002); 36 EHRR 1001 para 59. See also *Lebedev v Russia* hudoc (2007); 47 EHRR 771 para 113. Note, however, that the Court has stated that it is not a requirement that a 'detained person be heard every time he lodges an appeal against a decision extending his detention but that it should be possible to exercise the right to be heard at reasonable intervals': *Catal v Turkey*, hudoc (2012) para 187.

[658] *Waite v UK* hudoc (2002); 36 EHRR 1001 para 59.

[659] *Winterwerp v Netherlands* A 33 (1979); 2 EHRR 387 para 60 (person who is detained as being of 'unsound mind' must be allowed 'to be heard either in person or, where necessary, through some form of representation'). Legal representation will be vital where a 'person of unsound mind' does not understand what is happening. Cf *Keus v Netherlands* A 185-C (1990); 13 EHRR 700.

[660] *Bouamar v Belgium* A 129 (1988); 11 EHRR 1 para 60. See also *Hussain v UK* 1996-I; 22 EHRR 1 para 60 (juveniles detained 'during her majesty's pleasure').

[661] *Idalov v Russia* hudoc (2012) para 161 GC. See also *Reinprecht v Austria* hudoc (2005); 44 EHRR 797 para 31, and *Assenov v Bulgaria* 1998-VIII; 28 EHRR 652 paras 162–3.

form of representation features among the fundamental guarantees of procedure applied in matters of deprivation of liberty'.[662] Surprisingly, it does not appear to be an automatic requirement that the detainee attend in person,[663] although the onus would seem to be on the state to justify why he or she cannot, and attendance is necessary if 'fairness'[664] requires it. The jurisprudence is not clear as to whether the hearing should be oral or public. Here the Court has stated that Article 5(4) does not 'as a general rule require [the review] hearing to be public'; then again, the Court 'would not exclude the possibility that a public hearing may be required in particular circumstances'.[665] The Court justified its general position by distinguishing between Article 6(1) and 5(4), accepting that there was 'some force' in the argument that a requirement for public hearings under the latter could have negative effects on the 'speediness' of review required.[666]

No public hearing is needed before a tribunal considering the release of a mental patient[667] and an investigating judge, taking his decision privately in his office, has been held to be a 'court' under Article 5(4).[668]

Legal assistance

Guarantees concerning access to a lawyer have been found to be applicable in *habeas corpus* proceedings,[669] legal assistance generally being required if this is necessary for Article 5(4) to be effective given the individual's circumstances.[670] Hence in *Chahal*,[671] one of the factors taken into account by the Court in reaching its conclusion that the body reviewing the applicant's detention was not a 'court' within the meaning of Article 5(4), was that the applicant was not entitled to legal representation. Similarly a minor was entitled to 'the effective assistance of his lawyer' at the hearing at which his detention under Article 5(1)(d) was challenged,[672] as was a person detained as being mentally disordered, absent special circumstances.[673] In the latter case it was held that the person concerned should not be required to take the initiative to obtain legal representation, a principle which should apply to minors too. In *Öcalan*,[674] the applicant was kept in total isolation with no possibility of consulting a lawyer. He was not legally trained and in the circumstances

---

[662] *Idalov v Russia* hudoc (2012) para 161 GC.

[663] Special circumstances may require the presence of the detainee, even though he or she was legally represented; see *Allen v UK* hudoc (2010); 51 EHRR 555 para 43.

[664] *Allen v UK* hudoc (2010) para 47. As to the use of video-links see *Trepashkin v Russia (No 2)* hudoc (2010).

[665] *Reinprecht v Austria* hudoc (2005); 44 EHRR 797 para 41, no public hearing was required on the facts (Article 5(1)(c) case).

[666] *Reinprecht v Austria* hudoc (2005); 44 EHRR 797 para 40 (noting that hearings are often held in remand prisons and other relevant practical issues).

[667] *Dhoest v Belgium No 10448/83*, 55 DR 5 at 26 (1987), Com Rep; CM Res DH (88); 12 EHRR CD 135. Cf *X v Belgium No 6859/74*, 3 DR 139 (1975).

[668] *Bezicheri v Italy* A 164 (1989); 12 EHRR 210 para 20. Cf, *Neumeister v Austria* A 8 (1968); 1 EHRR 91.

[669] *Winterwerp v Netherlands* A 33 (1979); 2 EHRR 387 para 60.

[670] In this connection see Commission Reports in *Woukam Moudefo v France* A 141-B (1988); 13 EHRR 549 paras 86–91 Com Rep F Sett before Court. Cf *K v Austria* A 255-B (1993) Com Rep F Sett before Court. See also *S v Switzerland* A 220 (1991); 14 EHRR 670 para 53.   [671] 1996-V; 23 EHRR 413 para 130.

[672] *Bouamar v Belgium* A 129 (1988); 11 EHRR 1 para 60.

[673] *Megyeri v Germany* A 237-A (1992); 15 EHRR 584. See also *Magalhães Pereira v Portugal* hudoc (2002); 36 EHRR 865 paras 56–7 and *Waite v UK* hudoc (2002); 36 EHRR 1001 para 59 (legal representation required 'where characteristics pertaining to the applicant's personality and level of maturity and reliability are of importance in deciding on his dangerousness').

[674] Hudoc (2003); 37 EHRR 238 (Chamber judgment, para 72) comments endorsed by the Grand Chamber (2005-IV; 41 EHRR 985 para 70 GC).

'could not reasonably be expected to be able to challenge the lawfulness and length of his detention without the assistance of his lawyer'.[675] The principle of the confidentiality of information exchanged between lawyer and client must be protected[676] in the context of Article 5(4).

As we have seen, the procedural requirements under Article 5(4) are more flexible than Article 6, but they are much more stringent as regards the need for speediness. On the basis of the latter consideration, the Court has stated that, 'as a rule, the [Article 5(4)] judge may decide not to wait until a detainee avails himself of legal assistance, and the authorities are not obliged to provide him with free legal aid in the context of the detention proceedings'.[677] However, the general rule mentioned in the first part of this sentence may be departed from in certain circumstances,[678] and the state has a duty not to hinder the effectiveness of legal assistance already engaged by the applicant.[679] The absence of legal aid may also raise an issue as to the accessibility of the Article 5(4) remedy, where legal representation is required,[680] the Court stating that 'the right to receive legal assistance, if necessary, is implicit in the very notion of an adversarial procedure'.[681]

Time and facilities to prepare an application

A detained person must be allowed the necessary time and facilities to prepare his case.[682] In *Farmakopoulos v Belgium*,[683] the Commission stated that any time limit upon resort to an Article 5(4) remedy 'must not be so short as to restrict the availability and tangibility of the remedy'. In the same case, the Commission indicated that although Article 5(4) does not require that a detained person be informed of the remedy available, the failure to give such information is relevant when assessing the acceptability of any time limit.

As to facilities, the applicant must be told the reasons for his detention because this is information which is essential in order to challenge its legality.[684] Several of the cases considered in the preceding section on the principle of adversarial proceedings could also be regarded as concerning the right to facilities to prepare one's case.

---

[675] Neither relatives nor lawyer were able to act effectively without contact with the applicant, *Öcalan*, para 73.

[676] *Castravet v Moldova* hudoc (2007) paras 48–51 (glass partition between lawyer and client was not justified by security considerations and was a real impediment to lawyer–client interchange). See also *Khodorkovskiy v Russia* hudoc (2011); 53 EHRR 1103 para 232 (lawyer–client conversations could be overheard).

[677] *Lebedev v Russia* hudoc (2007); 47 EHRR 771 para 84. See also *Sergey Solovyev v Russia* hudoc (2012) para 64.

[678] *Lebedev v Russia*, paras 85–6 (applicant was coming almost directly from hospital; he had already engaged lawyers, who were excluded from hearing by judge). Cf the partly dissenting opinion of Judges Kovler, Hajiyev, and Jebens.

[679] *Lebedev v Russia*, para 87. See also *Istratii v Moldova* hudoc (2007).

[680] *Suso Musa v Malta* hudoc (2013) para 61.

[681] *Umirov v Russia* hudoc (2012) para 147; however, the detainee's right to choose his own counsel is not absolute (cf Article 6(3)(c)). See *Prehn v Germany* hudoc (2010) DA (applicant's choice of counsel overridden by domestic courts, and this did not entail a violation of Article 5(4) on the specific facts).

[682] *K v Austria* A 255-B (1993) Com Rep F Sett before Court. Cf Article 6(3)(b), see Ch 9. See also *Conka v Belgium* 2002-I; 34 EHRR 1298 paras 53–5 (rapid execution of deportation order made meaningful resort to Article 5(4) impossible), and *Khodorkovskiy and Lebedev v Russia* hudoc (2013) paras 518–20.

[683] A 235-A (1992); 16 EHRR 187 Com Rep (twenty-four-hour limit too short on the facts). Case withdrawn by applicant before Court.

[684] *X v UK* A 46 (1981); 4 EHRR 188 para 66. This is also required under Article 5(2), with which Article 5(4) overlaps.

Decision must be taken 'speedily'

Article 5(4) requires that a decision be taken 'speedily'.[685] For this purpose, time normally begins to run when Article 5(4) proceedings are instituted.[686] The relevant period ends when the final decision as to the detention of the applicant is made; surprisingly, it is not, in the case of a person whose detention is found to be illegal by the national court, the date of his release.[687] There may be a breach of Article 5(4) where a detained person simply has to wait for a period of time before a remedy is available.[688] Where a state provides the possibility of an appeal, the time taken before the decision on appeal must be taken into account;[689] however, the standard of 'speediness' required for the appeal stage is less stringent.[690]

When considering whether a decision has been taken 'speedily', the approach to be followed is similar to that when assessing whether the 'trial within a reasonable time' guarantees in Articles 5(3) and 6(1) are satisfied,[691] although Article 5(4) will require 'particular expedition'.[692] There is no absolute limit to the time that a decision may take. The matter is to be determined 'in the light of the circumstances of each case'.[693] Consideration must be given to the diligence of the national authorities and any delays brought about by the conduct of the detained person,[694] as well as any other factors causing delay that cannot engage the state's responsibility. Where the length of time appears *prima facie* 'incompatible with the notion of speediness', it is for the state to explain the reason for any apparent delay.[695]

---

[685] For a summary of general principles, see *Khudyakova v Russia* hudoc (2009) paras 92–4.

[686] *Van der Leer v Netherlands* A 170-A (1990); 12 EHRR 567.

[687] *Luberti v Italy* A 75 (1984); 6 EHRR 440 (eleven days' gap).

[688] *Igdeli v Turkey* hudoc (2002) para 34. Similarly, where a soldier held on a charge of having committed a military penal offence could only appeal to a military court six days after his detention had begun, there was a breach of Article 5(4), even allowing for the 'exigencies of military life and military justice' (*De Jong, Baljet, and Van Den Brink v Netherlands* A 77 (1984); 8 EHRR 20 para 58). Likewise a remedy available to a mental patient before an English Mental Health Review Tribunal only after he had been recalled for six months was not a 'speedy' remedy (*X v UK* B 41 (1980) para 138 Com Rep). An application for legal aid in connection with Article 5(4) must also be conducted 'speedily' (*Zamir v UK No 9174/80*, 40 DR 42 (1983); 5 EHRR 242 (1983) (seven weeks to hear *habeas corpus* application a breach for this reason)).

[689] *Igdeli v Turkey*. See also *Letellier v France* A 207 (1991); 14 EHRR 83.

[690] *Khudyakova v Russia* hudoc (2009) para 93 (examples of acceptable time frames at para 94, likewise see *Khodorkovskiy and Lebedev v Russia* hudoc (2013) para 521). Where a decision is not delivered in public, the period ends when it is communicated to the detained person or his lawyer (*Koendjbiharie v Netherlands* A 185-B (1990); 13 EHRR 820 para 28). If a person has to exhaust an administrative remedy before having recourse to a 'court', the period of time to be considered runs from the time that the administrative authority is seized of the case (*Sanchez-Reisse v Switzerland* A 107 (1986); 9 EHRR 71 para 54).

[691] See section 7.III and Ch 9.IV. See *Mooren v Germany* hudoc (2009); 50 EHRR 554 para 106 GC.

[692] *Hutchison Reid v UK* 2003 IV; 37 EHRR 211 para 59.

[693] *Sanchez-Reisse v Switzerland* A 107 (1986); 9 EHRR 71 para 55. See also *Frasik v Poland* hudoc (2010) para 63.

[694] Eg, a state will not be responsible for any delay resulting from a detained person's disappearance (*Luberti v Italy* A 75 (1984); 6 EHRR 440) or delay in filing an appeal (*Navarra v France* A 273-B (1993); 17 EHRR 594).

[695] *Koendjbiharie v Netherlands* A 185-B (1990); 13 EHRR 820 paras 28–30. The usual principle is that the primary responsibility for delays resulting from the provision of expert opinions rests ultimately with the state, *Musial v Poland* 1999-II 31 EHRR 720 para 46 GC. In certain instances the complexity of medical—or other—issues involved in a determination of whether a person should be detained or released can be a factor which may be taken into account under this aspect of Article 5(4), but it is not a licence to avoid the essential obligation under that provision, see *Ilowiecki v Poland* hudoc (2001); 37 EHRR 546 para 75; *Baranowski v Poland* 2000-III para 72 (an Article 5(1)(c) case)); *Musial v Poland* 1999-II; 31 EHRR 720 para 47 GC. Delay because the responsible judge is on holiday is not a good explanation, see *E v Norway* A 181-A (1990); 17 EHRR 30 para 66 (delay of almost eight weeks unacceptable). Nor is the fact that a judge has an excessive

When determining whether the time taken to decide an application for release infringes Article 5(4), account may be taken of the fact that the detained person was able to make other applications that were disposed of with reasonable expedition.[696] In terms of the lengths of time that have been ruled upon in actual cases, a period of five days was permissible in an Article 5(1)(c) case,[697] which is subject to Article 5(3) protection. For this provision in particular (Article 5(1)(c)), the Court has referred to 'a special need for a swift decision determining the lawfulness of detention in cases where a trial is pending', this since the person concerned 'should benefit fully from the principle of the presumption of innocence'.[698] Periods of up to five months to decide on detention of a minor under Article 5(1)(d) were too long,[699] as was a delay of four months in the case of a 'person of unsound mind' under Article 5(1)(e).[700] Sixteen days to decide on the continued long-term detention of an habitual offender under Article 5(1)(a) was considered sufficiently 'speedy'.[701] Periods of thirty-one and forty-six days taken to rule on the release of a person detained pending extradition under Article 5(1)(f) were in breach of Article 5(4).[702]

III. A CONTINUING REMEDY AT REASONABLE INTERVALS

The fact that the initial decision to detain a person is taken by a 'court' (the 'incorporation rule'), or that an administrative detention is subsequently ratified by such a body, will not always suffice for Article 5(4). This is because there may be detention circumstances where 'the very nature of the deprivation of liberty under consideration would appear to require a review of lawfulness at reasonable intervals'.[703] Above all, those circumstances are when the basis in law for detention may cease to exist—whereupon the detainee is entitled to an Article 5(4) review, to decide 'speedily' on the continued lawfulness of his or her detention. Classic examples are a mental health detainee who recovers his health to the point at which it is inappropriate to detain him, and life prisoners who have served the relevant tariff but whose continued detention is dependent on elements of dangerousness and risk.[704] Other situations in which a continuing remedy may be required are cases of

workload, see *Bezicheri v Italy* A 164 (1989); 12 EHRR 210 para 25. Cf *Sanchez-Reisse v Switzerland* A 107 (1986); 9 EHRR 71 and *Jablonski v Poland* hudoc (2000); 36 EHRR 455 para 90.

[696]   *Letellier v France* A 207 (1991); 14 EHRR 83 para 56.

[697]   *Egue v France* No 11256/84, 57 DR 47 at 70 (1988). Six days was too long in the *De Jong, Baljet and Van Den Brink v Netherlands* A 77 (1984); 8 EHRR 20.

[698]   *Jablonski v Poland* hudoc (2000); 36 EHRR 455 para 93. In a case in which persons detained on suspicion of having committed terrorist offences under Article 5(1)(c) were released forty-four hours before their applications for *habeas corpus* were determined, there was also no breach of the 'speedy' decision requirement, *Fox, Campbell, and Hartley v UK* A 182 (1990); 13 EHRR 157 para 45.

[699]   *Bouamar v Belgium* A 129 (1988); 11 EHRR 1 para 63.

[700]   *Koendjbiharie v Netherlands* A 185-B (1990); 13 EHRR 820 paras 28–30. See, as other examples, *Luberti v Italy* A 75 (1984); 6 EHRR 440 (eighteen months too long) and *Rutten v Netherlands* hudoc (2001) para 51 (violation as first instance court took two months and seventeen days and appellate court took a further three months).   [701]   *Christinet v Switzerland* No 7648/76, 17 DR 35 (1979).

[702]   *Sanchez-Reisse v Switzerland* A 107 (1986); 9 EHRR 71 para 57. In extradition cases, the same considerations that are relevant to the 'due diligence' requirement of Article 5(1)(f) may apply to the 'speedy' remedy requirement of Article 5(4) (*Kolompar v Belgium* A 235-C (1992); 16 EHRR 197 para 46).

[703]   *Winterwerp v Netherlands* A 33 (1979); 2 EHRR 387 para 55 (1979). In other terms, a continuing remedy is required if 'new issues affecting the lawfulness of the detention might subsequently arise': *X v UK* A 46 (1981); 4 EHRR 188 para 51.

[704]   This is not so for mandatory life sentences which were purely punitive in nature because of the gravity of the offence, when review will have taken place by virtue of the 'incorporation rule', *Kafkaris v Cyprus* hudoc (2011) DA. However, see *Vinter v UK* hudoc (2013) paras 119–20 GC as regards Article 3.

the preventive detention of recidivists,[705] the detention of minors,[706] and the refusal of bail to an accused person.[707]

The requirement for an Article 5(4) remedy at reasonable intervals was applied in *X v UK*,[708] in which the applicant had been ordered by the trial court following his conviction to be detained at Broadmoor as a restricted offender patient on the statutory grounds that he was mentally disordered and a danger to the public. Although the initial judicial supervision required by Article 5(4) was 'incorporated in the decision' of the trial court, which was clearly a 'court' in the sense of that provision, the possibility that the applicant's mental condition might improve so as no longer to warrant detention meant that Article 5(4) required that he be provided with further possibilities, either by way of 'automatic periodic review of a judicial character' or by the opportunity for him to 'take proceedings at reasonable intervals before a court', to challenge the lawfulness of his continued detention.[709]

The remedy at reasonable intervals aspect of Article 5(4) has been successfully employed on a case-by-case basis to challenge the role played by the British Home Secretary in certain parts of the criminal justice system in the United Kingdom. Two early cases resulted in the erosion of the Home Secretary's powers in respect of discretionary life sentence prisoners.[710] It was established that an Article 5(4) 'court'—not the Home Secretary—was required to determine periodically the case for release of a discretionary 'lifer' during the discretionary phase of his detention. Likewise the decision to re-detain a 'discretionary lifer' who had been out on licence had to be taken by a 'court' within the meaning of Article 5(4). The same principle was applied to juvenile offenders,[711] who, after expiry of the tariff period (the part of the sentence said to reflect the requirements of retribution and deterrence), were also serving indeterminate sentences such as detention 'during Her Majesty's pleasure'. These rulings raised questions regarding the role that a member of the executive (ie the Home Secretary) should play at later stages of detention for mandatory life prisoners. Such prisoners served a determinate sentence which included a tariff period set by the Home Secretary, but when this expired, like the earlier cases, the basis for detention appeared in reality to be the nature of the risk the detainee posed to society, ie matters that appeared ripe for consideration by a 'court'. Ultimately in *Stafford v UK*,[712] a Grand Chamber of the Court overruled an earlier judgment[713] and relied on developments in domestic law in the United Kingdom to hold that the 'review at reasonable intervals' aspect of Article 5(4) applied for mandatory life sentence prisoners too, though only after the expiry of the tariff period, for in reality at that stage the grounds for continued detention were considerations of risk and dangerousness.[714] It followed that the applicant's continued

---

[705] *Van Droogenbroeck v Belgium* A 50 (1982); 4 EHRR 443 PC and *E v Norway* A 181-A (1990); 17 EHRR 30.   [706] *Bouamar v Belgium* A 129 (1988); 11 EHRR 1.

[707] *Bezicheri v Italy* A 164 (1989); 12 EHRR 210. See also *Soumare v France* 1998-V para 38 (applicant's solvency as a relevant factor).   [708] A 46 (1981); 4 EHRR 188.

[709] *X v UK*, para 52. For a case of 'automatic periodic review' see *Keus v Netherlands* A 185-C (1990); 13 EHRR 700 para 24. See also *Silva Rocha v Portugal* 1996-V; 32 EHRR 333, involving a homicide committed by a person who could not be held criminally responsible for his actions and who was at the same time dangerous. See also *Morley v UK* No 16084/03 hudoc (2004) DA.

[710] *Weeks v UK* A 114 (1987); 13 EHRR 435 PC and *Thynne, Wilson and Gunnell v UK* A190-A (1990); 13 EHRR 666 PC, see Richardson, PL 34 (1991).

[711] See *Hussain v UK and Singh v UK* 1996-I; 22 EHRR 1 and *V v UK* 1999-IX; 30 EHRR 121 GC.

[712] 2002-IV; 35 EHRR 1121 GC. See Hunt, 22 YEL 483 at 490–3 (2003).

[713] *Wynne v UK* A 294-A; 19 EHRR 333.

[714] The Court did not accept arguments to the effect that 'public acceptability of release' could be another basis for continuing detention of mandatory life offenders, para 80.

detention after 1997, as decided by the Secretary of State,[715] had not been reviewed by a body that satisfied the requirements of Article 5(4). The Court referred to 'the wider recognition of the need to develop and apply, in relation to mandatory life prisoners, judicial procedures reflecting standards of independence, fairness and openness' and recognized that the notion of separation of powers between the executive and the judiciary had 'assumed growing importance in the case-law of the Court'.[716] Although this jurisprudence did not have an impact on the Home Secretary's specific statutory power to fix the tariff for life sentence prisoners, the House of Lords, relying on Strasbourg jurisprudence, subsequently reached the conclusion that that power was incompatible with Article 6(1) of the Convention.[717]

Finally, what time periods apply to the notion of 'reasonable intervals'? Although an initial review should be taken 'speedily', the answer to this question depends on the kind of case in issue. A period of one month has been held to be a 'reasonable interval' in the context of detention on remand, the nature of which is such as to call for a remedy at 'short intervals',[718] and given the assumption under the Convention that such detention is to be of strictly limited duration. Although a longer interval may be acceptable in the case of a 'person of unsound mind', a period in excess of one year has been held to be in breach of Article 5(4).[719] Where there is clear evidence of a change in a person's mental condition, a hearing within a shorter period may be required.[720] Arrangements for 'automatic periodic review' do not necessarily contravene Article 5(4) but must follow the same standards as to frequency[721] (ie be at reasonable intervals). As regards discretionary life prisoners in the United Kingdom, the Court has stated that it will not attempt to rule as to the maximum period of time between reviews which should automatically apply given the need for flexibility in the system.[722] Generally periods of less than a year between reviews have been acceptable, whilst periods of more than one year have breached Article 5(4).[723]

It is perhaps surprising that Article 5(4) does not require the 'court' referred to therein to have the power to set the timing of subsequent reviews of detention.[724]

IV. THE SCOPE OF ARTICLE 5(4)'S APPLICATION

Although Article 5(4) only requires a remedy at one level of jurisdiction, in *Toth v Austria*,[725] the Court held that if a party provides a right of appeal against a decision by

---

[715] For the facts of *Stafford* see section 5.I.a.

[716] *Stafford v UK* 2002-IV; 35 EHRR 1121 para 78 GC. See also *Benjamin and Wilson v UK* hudoc (2002); 36 EHRR 1 (Home Secretary's declared practice of following the recommendations of the Mental Health Review Tribunal was not itself compliant with Article 5(4); para 36).

[717] *R (Anderson) v Secretary of State for the Home Department* [2002] UKHL 46. See also *Easterbrook v UK* hudoc (2003); 37 EHRR 812.

[718] *Bezicheri v Italy* A 164 (1989); 12 EHRR 210 para 21. See *Assenov v Bulgaria* 1998-VIII; 28 EHRR 652 para 165 (violation as law only allowed for one review of pre-trial detention).

[719] *Herczegfalvy v Austria* A 244 (1992); 15 EHRR 437.

[720] *M v Germany No 10272/83*, 38 DR 104 (1984). See also *Hirst v UK* hudoc (2001) para 44 (twenty-one-month delay between reviews; improvement in mental state of discretionary life prisoner).

[721] See *Keus v Netherlands* A 185-C (1990); 13 EHRR 700 para 24. See also *Oldham v UK* 2000-X; 31 EHRR 813 para 36 (two-year delay between reviews was unreasonable, especially as the applicant had addressed areas of concern within eight months).

[722] *Hirst v UK* hudoc (2001) para 38 (twenty-one-month and two-year delays between reviews not reasonable).   [723] See *Blackstock v UK* hudoc (2005); 42 EHRR 55 para 44.

[724] *Blackstock v UK No 59512/00* hudoc (2004) DA (Court would take into account the failure to observe a recommendation from a 'court' as to timing).

[725] A 224 (1991); 14 EHRR 551 para 84. See also *Grauzinis v Lithuania* hudoc (2000); 35 EHRR 144. Cf *Navarra v France* A 273-B (1993); 17 EHRR 594. However, as regards the need for a public hearing, for

a first instance 'court' rejecting a claim for release, the appellate body must 'in principle' comply with Article 5(4).

The mere fact that the Court has found no breach of Article 5(1) does not mean that it is excluded from carrying out a review of compliance with Article 5(4).[726] That Article is a *lex specialis* in relation to the 'less strict' general remedy required by Article 13 of the Convention; if the Court finds a breach of Article 5(4), it is unlikely to consider a claim by a detained person under Article 13.[727]

Article 5(4) is only applicable to persons deprived of their liberty. It therefore has no application 'for the purposes of obtaining, after release, a declaration that a previous detention or arrest was unlawful', and it cannot be invoked by a person who is lawfully released.[728] Even if the person is only out on licence, Article 5(4) no longer applies whilst the individual has liberty; instead, Article 13 applies, requiring that a remedy be provided by which the released person may challenge the consistency with the Convention of his earlier detention.[729] Where a person in detention is released 'speedily' while his application for release is pending, the question whether the remedy that he has sought complies with Article 5(4) will not be pursued by the Court on the ground that it serves no purpose.[730] Thus in *Fox, Campbell and Hartley v UK*,[731] two of the applicants sought *habeas corpus* the day after their arrest but were released within the next twenty-four hours, before their application was heard. Given that the applicants had already been released 'speedily', the Court declined to consider whether the *habeas corpus* proceedings would have complied with Article 5(4). As with Article 13, Article 5(4) is of great importance because a municipal law remedy will be of (near) immediate effect and more convenient to obtain than one via Strasbourg for a breach of the international guarantee in Article 5(1).[732]

9. ARTICLE 5(5): RIGHT TO COMPENSATION FOR ILLEGAL DETENTION

Article 5(5) is the only provision in the Convention that provides for a right to compensation at the national level for a breach of a particular Convention right.[733] There is, for

---

example, the procedural guarantees need not always be of the same level as in the proceedings before the first-instance court, see *Trepashkin v Russia (No 2)* hudoc (2010) para 149, drawing comparisons with the relevant Article 6(1) case law.

[726] *Douiyeb v Netherlands* hudoc (1999); 30 EHRR 790 para 57 GC.

[727] *De Jong, Baljet and Van Den Brink v Netherlands* A 77 (1984); 8 EHRR 20 para 60.

[728] *Stephens v Malta (No 1)* hudoc (2009); 50 EHRR 144 para 102. A person who absconds remains entitled to a remedy under Article 5(4) because he is still deprived of his liberty in law: *Van der Leer v Netherlands* A 170-A (1990); 12 EHRR 567.

[729] *L v Sweden No 10801/84*, 61 DR 62 at 73 (1988) Com Rep; CM Res DH (89) 16.

[730] Different considerations may apply at the domestic level when 'a former detainee may well have a legal interest in the determination of the lawfulness of his or her detention even after having been released', for example in exercising Article 5(5) rights: see *STS v Netherlands* hudoc (2011); 54 EHRR1229 para 61.

[731] A 182 (1990); 13 EHRR 157.

[732] Cf Trechsel, *European System*, p 319, who emphasizes the subsidiary character of the remedy under the Convention.

[733] Cf Article 3 of the Seventh Protocol (compensation for miscarriages of justice).

example, no comparable Convention obligation to provide compensation under national law for torture in breach of Article 3.[734]

Article 5(5) applies when any one or more of paragraphs (1) to (4) has been contravened[735] as determined by either a domestic authority or by the Court.[736] The Article's applicability is not dependent on a domestic finding of unlawfulness or proof that but for the breach the person would have been released.[737] Even if the arrest or detention is lawful under domestic law, it may breach Article 5 and so potentially engage Article 5(5).[738]

Where an applicant alleges in his application a violation of Article 5(5) at the same time as he claims a breach of some other part of Article 5, the Court will proceed to examine the Article 5(5) claim in the course of considering that application if it finds that another paragraph of Article 5 has been infringed.[739] It will do so without requiring the applicant to go back and exhaust local remedies to see whether he could in fact obtain the compensation that Article 5(5) requires under municipal law.[740] Instead, a state will be found to comply with Article 5(5) if it can show 'with a sufficient degree of certainty' that a remedy of the kind required by Article 5(5) is available to the applicant.[741] In this connection, where the Convention has been incorporated into the law of the defendant state and it can be shown with 'sufficient...certainty' that Article 5(5) can be directly relied upon in the national courts as the basis for a claim to compensation, this will suffice.[742] In other cases, the remedy must be shown with sufficient certainty to exist under national law by some other means.[743] The domestic courts should, when considering compensation claims, interpret and apply domestic law 'in the spirit of Article 5', and they should not be 'excessively formalistic'.[744]

The Court has stated, 'there can be no question of 'compensation' where there is no pecuniary or non-pecuniary damage to compensate'.[745] However, domestic courts should not adopt an excessively formalistic approach to this non-pecuniary aspect, as occurred in *Danev v Bulgaria*.[746] A breach of Article 5(5) was found in that case, given the very narrow approach adopted domestically, one which entailed that compensation awards were unlikely for short-term detention when there was no objectively perceptible deterioration in the detainee's physical or psychological condition.

---

[734] However, compensation may be called for under the general right to an effective remedy under Article 13.

[735] See, eg, *Wassink v Netherlands* A 185-A (1990).   [736] *NC v Italy* 2002-X para 49 GC.

[737] *Thynne, Wilson and Gunnell v UK* A 190-A (1990); 13 EHRR 666 para 82 PC; also *Blackstock v UK* hudoc (2005); 42 EHRR 55 para 51.

[738] *Harkmann v Estonia* hudoc (2006) para 50. In *Nolan and K v Russia* hudoc (2009); 53 EHRR 977, domestic law only allowed for compensation if the domestic courts, not Strasbourg, found a deprivation of liberty (which they had not), so there was a violation of Article 5(5). See also *A v UK* ECHR-2009; 49 EHRR 625 GC, para 229.   [739] *Ciulla v Italy* A 148 (1989); 13 EHRR 346 paras 43–5 PC.

[740] Note, however, Judge Valticos' dissenting opinion in the *Ciulla* case, with whom three other judges agreed.

[741] *Ciulla v Italy* A 148 (1989); 13 EHRR 346 paras 43–5 PC. As to when the remedy should be available, it suffices that the remedy exists 'either before or after the findings by the Court': *Brogan v UK* A 145-B (1988); 11 EHRR 117 para 67 PC. Cf *Fox, Campbell and Hartley v UK* A 182 (1990); 13 EHRR 157 para 46.

[742] *Ciulla v Italy* A 148 (1989); 13 EHRR 346 paras 43–5 PC. Cf *Sakık v Turkey* 1997-VII; 26 EHRR 662 paras 58–61 (no examples of successful employment of the remedy by individuals, whilst domestic law only provided for compensation if this was illegal under domestic law itself).

[743] *Brogan v UK* A 145-B (1988); 11 EHRR 117 para 67 PC.

[744] *Shulgin v Ukraine* hudoc (2011) para 46. See also *Danev v Bulgaria* hudoc (2010).

[745] *Wassink v Netherlands* A 185-A (1990) para 38. Non-pecuniary damage includes moral damage (pain, emotional distress, etc).   [746] Hudoc (2010).

The remedy that Article 5(5) requires is one before a court, leading to a legally binding award of compensation (usually financial).[747] Hence remedies before, for example, an ombudsman or an *ex gratia* payment by the government are insufficient. Although it 'may be broader in scope than mere financial compensation', compensation in the sense of Article 5(5) does not include the detained person's release, since this is provided for by Article 5(4).[748] As to the amount of compensation, it is likely that states are allowed a wide margin of appreciation;[749] however, this is something over which the Court has a power of review. A very low award of compensation might be 'entirely disproportionate to the duration of [an applicant's] detention',[750] entailing a violation of Article 5(5).

A final question is the relationship between the rights to 'compensation' in Article 5(5) for a breach of Article 5(1)–(4) and to 'just satisfaction' in Article 41 for a breach of the Convention, including any part of Article 5. If compensation for damage is not available nationally in respect of a breach of Article 5(1)–(4), so that Article 5(5) has been infringed, there is the possibility of compensation under Article 41 for that infringement.[751]

10. CONCLUSION

Article 5 remains the subject of a considerable amount of jurisprudence interpreting what can be a confusing text. A large number of judgments today concern basic Articles 5(1), 5(3) and 5(4) violations.[752] However, even in the 2010s, novel issues continue to reach the Court, as with recent case law concerning 'kettling', whilst there has been a further enriching of that in relation Article 5(1)(a) (for example, in relation, potentially, to prisoner rehabilitation), Article 5(1)(e) (the legal regime applicable to social care homes in certain central European countries, for example), and Article 5(1)(f) (deportation of terrorist suspects). New cases have also seen 'extraordinary rendition' come before the Court.

Some recent case law may prompt a debate as to whether the Court is adapting Article 5 to new contexts and circumstances in a realistic and appropriate way, or diluting the vitally important standards of protection it affords. The division of opinion on display in the (divided) Grand Chambers in *Austin v UK* ('kettling' and Article 5(1)), and *Mangouras v Spain* (bail conditions in the context of an environmental disaster) make very interesting reading in that regard.[753]

Looking at some of the post-'September 11th' cases that have reached the Court, notably *A v UK*, arguably Strasbourg has refused to water down the standards of protection Article 5(1)(f) and 5(4) afford, despite considerable pressure to do so. A number of the

---

[747] *Brogan v UK* A 145-B (1988); 11 EHRR 117 para 67 PC; *Fox, Campbell and Hartley v UK* A 182 (1990); 13 EHRR 157 para 46.

[748] *Bozano v France* No 9990/82, 39 DR 119 at 144 (1984). See also *Wloch v Poland (No 2)* hudoc (2011) para 32 (crediting a period of pre-trial detention towards a penalty insufficient for Art 5(5) as non-financial).

[749] See Trechsel, *European System*, p 344.

[750] *Attard v Malta* No 46750/99 hudoc (2000) DA (inadmissible). See also *Cumber v UK* No 28779/95 hudoc (1996) DA and *Ganea v Moldova* hudoc (2011) para 30 (€63 too small given detention of three days, the figure being inferior compared to what the Court had itself awarded in like cases).

[751] See *Brogan v UK* A 145-B (1988); 11 EHRR 117 para 67 PC, where the Court stated that its finding of a breach of Article 5(5) because compensation was not available was 'without prejudice' to its competence under Article 50 (now 41).

[752] Cf *Kharchenko v Ukraine* (hudoc) 2011 (Article 46 orders made by Court: structural problems relating to pre-trial detention).

[753] See also the division of opinion in *Medvedyev v France* ECHR-2010; 51 EHRR 899 GC.

(now) older cases concerning Northern Ireland presented the Strasbourg authorities with difficult questions concerning the application of Article 5 to terrorist situations. It remains arguable that the remedy within the Convention system for a state faced with the very real problems posed by a sufficiently serious terrorist threat is to derogate under Article 15 from its Convention obligations, rather than to argue that Article 5 be tempered to meet its needs. We have seen that the Court was prepared to make some allowance for the Northern Ireland situation in cases that have reached it under Article 5. If such an approach is to be followed, it is better for the rule that emerges to be expressly limited to the terrorist situation,[754] rather than to be stated in unqualified terms that might be applied to non-emergency situations also.[755]

The understandable wish of some of the drafting states to have express confirmation of all of the circumstances in which they might detain an individual, rather than just a general prohibition of 'arbitrary' detention,[756] has caused predictable problems. Whereas the list in Article 5(1) offers some degree of certainty, its wording does not easily accommodate all of the recognized cases of arrest and is curiously old-fashioned in other respects. However, in recent case law (*Ostendorf*), Article 5(1)(b) has been interpreted so as to allow short-term detention for such purposes as preventing hooliganism (in very defined circumstances). The *Winterwerp* case and other cases have introduced detailed controls as to proportionality that can be applied to the detention of those covered by Article 5(1)(e), including, for example, HIV sufferers. Those controls might go some way to mitigating the broad interpretation of 'alcoholics' in the *Witold Litwa* case.

The requirement in Article 5(1) that detention be 'lawful' has been interpreted in an imaginative way that is in harmony with the reading of similar wording elsewhere in the Convention. In particular, the inclusion of a requirement that detention must not be 'arbitrary' is very important. For example, it provided a basis for findings of breaches of Article 5 by reference to the purpose for which an individual was detained in the *Bozano* and *Bouamar* cases concerning the improper use of powers of deportation and short-term detention of juveniles respectively. Article 5(1) has also provided a mechanism for the setting of detailed and rigorous procedural standards concerning the detention of the mentally disordered, and the continuing relevance of this is evident in cases reaching Strasbourg such as *Stanev v Bulgaria* (concerning social care homes). Looking back, of great general importance, too, has been the interpretation of Article 5(4) in such a way as to impose an obligation upon states to provide a judicial remedy by which an individual may challenge the legality of his detention. One striking result of this has been that United Kingdom procedures concerning the release of mental patients and persons given certain forms of life sentences have been revised following Strasbourg cases so as to shift the decision-making power from the Home Secretary to a 'court' in several respects.

---

[754] See *Brogan v UK* A 145-B (1988); 11 EHRR 117 PC, section 7.I.b. See also the express references to terrorism in connection with the approach taken to Article 5(3) in *Chraidi v Germany* 2006-XII; 47 EHRR 47 paras 37 and 47.

[755] This was not done in the *Fox, Campbell and Hartley v UK* A 182 (1990); 13 EHRR 157, on the Article 5(2) point.   [756] Contrast Article 9(1), ICCPR.

9

ARTICLE 6: THE RIGHT
TO A FAIR TRIAL

Article 6

1. In the determination of his civil rights and obligations or of any criminal charge against him, everyone is entitled to a fair and public hearing within a reasonable time by an independent and impartial tribunal established by law. Judgment shall be pronounced publicly but the press and public may be excluded from all or part of the trial in the interest of morals, public order or national security in a democratic society, where the interests of juveniles or the protection of the private life of the parties so require, or to the extent strictly necessary in the opinion of the court in special circumstances where publicity would prejudice the interests of justice.

2. Everyone charged with a criminal offence shall be presumed innocent until proved guilty according to law.

3. Everyone charged with a criminal offence has the following minimum rights:
   (a) to be informed promptly, in a language which he understands and in detail, of the nature and cause of the accusation against him;
   (b) to have adequate time and facilities for the preparation of his defence;
   (c) to defend himself in person or through legal assistance of his own choosing or, if he has not sufficient means to pay for legal assistance, to be given it free when the interests of justice so require;
   (d) to examine or have examined witnesses against him and to obtain the attendance and examination of witnesses on his behalf under the same conditions as witnesses against him;
   (e) to have the free assistance of an interpreter if he cannot understand or speak the language used in court.

1. ARTICLE 6: GENERALLY

The right to a fair trial has a position of pre-eminence in the Convention, both because of the importance of the right involved and the great volume of applications and jurisprudence that it has attracted.[1] As to the former, the Court has stressed that 'the right to a fair

---

[1] On Article 6, see Grotian, *Article 6 of the European Convention on Human Rights: the Right to a Fair Trial*, Council of Europe Human Rights File No 13, 1994. On Article 6 in criminal cases, see Stavros, *The Guarantees for Accused Persons under Article 6 of the European Convention on Human Rights*, 1993 (hereafter Stavros) and Trechsel, *Human Rights in Criminal Proceedings*, 2005.

trial holds so prominent a place in a democratic society that there can be no justification for interpreting Article 6(1) of the Convention restrictively'.[2] As to the latter, more applications to Strasbourg concern Article 6 than any other provision. The cases relate mostly to criminal and civil litigation before the ordinary courts. They also involve, to an extent that could not have been predicted, proceedings before disciplinary and administrative tribunals and administrative decisions determining 'civil rights and obligations'.

The application of Article 6 has presented the Court, and formerly the Commission, with various problems. A delicate question is the closeness with which it should monitor the functioning of national courts. The Court has studiously and properly followed the 'fourth instance' doctrine, according to which, as the Court regularly states, 'it is not its function to deal with errors of fact or law allegedly committed by a national court *unless and in so far as they may have infringed rights and freedoms protected by the Convention'.*[3] The right to a fair hearing, which is one such Convention right, has, as its wording suggests, been interpreted as providing only a procedural, not a substantive, guarantee. Accordingly, the Court will intervene in respect to 'errors of fact or law' by a national court only insofar as they bear upon compliance with the procedural guarantees in Article 6: it does not intervene under Article 6 because such errors affect the national court decision on its merits.[4] However, this last statement must be read subject to a limitation that is to be found in some more recent Court jurisprudence to the effect that there may be a breach of Article 6 where a national court decision on the merits has been 'arbitrary or manifestly unreasonable'.[5] For example, in *Andelković v Serbia*,[6] the Court held that there was not a fair hearing when an appellate court overturned a judgment in favour of the applicant's claim to holiday pay without referring to the facts as found by the trial court or to the relevant law, which clearly supported the applicant's claim. The appellate court's reasoning 'had no legal foundation' and was based on assertions that were 'quite outside' any 'reasonable judicial discretion', resulting in an 'arbitrary' judgment. As to errors of fact, in *Khamidov v Russia*,[7] the Court found that a national court had rejected the applicant's claim for compensation for damage to his land by police units on the basis that it was unproven that the units had even entered upon the land when there was 'abundant evidence' to the contrary. In the Court's view, the 'unreasonableness of this conclusion is so striking and palpable on the face of it', that the national court's decisions were 'grossly arbitrary'. In both of these cases, there was an undefined breach of Article 6, presumably of the residual 'fair hearing' guarantee.

The Court also allows states a wide margin of appreciation as to the manner in which national courts operate, for example in the rules of evidence that they use. A consequence of this is that in certain contexts the provisions of Article 6 are as much obligations of result as of conduct, with national courts being allowed to follow whatever particular rules they choose so long as the end result can be seen to be a fair trial.[8]

Although Article 6 applies only to a contracting party's own judicial system, it extends beyond that in the sense that a court of a contracting party that is called upon to confirm or execute a judgment of a court of another state that is not a party to the Convention

---

[2] *Perez v France* 2004-I; 40 EHRR 909 para 64 GC. This can be taken to apply to Article 6 as a whole.
[3] *Garcia Ruiz v Spain* 1999-I; 31 EHRR 589 para 28 GC (emphasis added).
[4] See, eg, *Anderson v UK No 44958/98* hudoc (1999) DA.
[5] *Camilleri v Malta No 51760/99* hudoc (2000) DA.
[6] Hudoc (2013) para 27. Cf *Van Kück v Germany* 2003-VII; 37 EHRR 973; *Storck v Germany* 2005-V; 43 EHRR 96; and *Mikulová v Slovakia* hudoc (2005). See also *Barać and Others v Montenegro* hudoc (2011) (decision based on an unconstitutional law). [7] 2007- ; 49 EHRR 326 para 174.
[8] See, eg, *Schenk v Switzerland* A 140 (1988); 13 EHRR 242 PC

must ensure that the foreign judgment concerned is the result of a fair trial in accordance with Article 6.[9]

In criminal cases, the interpretation of Article 6 is complicated by the basic differences that exist between common law and civil law systems of criminal justice.[10] The adversarial and inquisitorial systems that these respectively entail, and the dissimilar methods of investigating crime and conducting a trial that they use, necessarily make for difficulties in the interpretation of a text that provides a framework for legal proceedings throughout Europe. It is a challenge to the Strasbourg Court to meet the needs and circumstances of very different legal systems and still set appropriately high standards for a human rights guarantee of a fair trial.

Another problem has resulted from the application of Article 6 to administrative justice. If the Court, and formerly the Commission, has commendably acted to fill a gap by reading Article 6 as requiring that administrative decisions that determine a person's right, for example, to practise as a doctor or to use his land, are subject to Article 6, they have yet to establish a coherent jurisprudence spelling out the nature of the resulting obligations for states.

These problems have been compounded in civil as well as criminal cases by the need to apply a text that was designed as a template for trial courts of the classical kind to both appellate courts and disciplinary and other special courts, where the same procedural guarantees may not have such full application.[11]

Finally, it should be noted that Article 6 has an extra-territorial application in that it is a breach of Article 6 to deport or extradite an individual to another state where there are 'substantial grounds for believing that...he would be exposed to a real risk of being subjected to a flagrant denial of justice'.[12] The Court defined a 'flagrant denial of justice' in *Othman (Abu Qatada) v UK*[13] as follows: 'A flagrant denial of justice goes beyond mere irregularities or lack of safeguards in the trial procedures such as might result in a breach of Article 6 if occurring within the contracting states itself. What is required is a breach of the principles of fair trial guaranteed by Article 6, which is so fundamental as to amount to a nullification, or destruction of the very essence, of the right guaranteed by that Article.' In the *Abu Qatada* case, which was the first case in which the Court found a breach of Article 6 on this basis, an order was made for the deportation of the applicant to Jordan where he would face a retrial for offences of which he had been convicted *in absentia*, resulting in sentences of life and fifteen years' imprisonment, in which there was a real risk that evidence obtained by the torture of other defendants would be admitted. The use of such evidence would, the Court stated, be a 'flagrant denial of justice'. The Court also referred to other 'forms of unfairness' that it had in earlier cases indicated 'could amount to a flagrant denial of justice'. These were conviction *in absentia* with no possibility of reopening the proceedings;[14] a trial which is 'summary in nature and conducted with a total disregard for the rights of the defence';[15] 'detention without any access to an independent

---

[9] See *Pellegrini v Italy* 2001-VIII;35 EHRR 44 (Vatican City court judgment).

[10] For example, there are differences in the rules of evidence, the use of a case file, the permissibility of trials *in absentia*, and plea bargaining.

[11] See Stavros, p 328. On the application of Article 6 to juvenile criminal proceedings, see *Nortier v Netherlands* A 267 (1993); 17 EHRR 273 para 38 and *V v UK* 1999-IX; 30 EHRR 121 GC.

[12] *Othman (Abu Qatada) v UK* 2012- ; 55 EHRR 78 para 261. See also *Soering v UK* A 161 (1989); 11 EHRR 439 para 113 PC and *Mamatkulov and Askarov v Turkey* 2005-I; 41 EHRR 494 GC. Where an individual has already been returned, the existence of a 'flagrant denial' is to be assessed in the light of what the sending state knew or ought to have known at the time of the return: *Al-Saadoon and Mufdhi v UK* 2010- ; 51 EHRR 212.

[13] 2012- ; 55 EHRR 78, para 260.   [14] *Sejdovic v Italy* 2006-II para 84 GC.

[15] *Bader and Kanbor v Sweden* 2005-XI; 46 EHRR 1497.

and impartial tribunal to have the legality of the detention reviewed';[16] and the 'deliberate and systematic refusal of access to a lawyer, especially for an individual detained in a foreign country'.[17]

2. FIELD OF APPLICATION

I. IN THE DETERMINATION OF A CRIMINAL CHARGE

The rights guaranteed by Article 6 apply, firstly, when a 'criminal charge' is being determined. Article 6 only begins to apply when a criminal investigation has reached the point where the applicant has been 'charged' with a criminal offence. It does not extend to ancillary proceedings that are not determinative of a pending 'charge' against the applicant,[18] such as proceedings concerning legal aid,[19] pre-trial detention,[20] or committal for trial.[21] Nor does it apply to cases in which the applicant brings a private prosecution[22] or because the applicant's property is subject to forfeiture by a criminal charge against a third party.[23] It also does not apply to proceedings that may result in the applicant being placed under police supervision for the prevention of crime[24] or to the giving by the police of a statutory warning.[25] Proceedings concerning the administration of the prison system are not included.[26]

Finally, extradition proceedings to face a criminal charge in another state are not subject to Article 6.[27] Nor are the transfer of a convicted prisoner abroad[28] or the execution of a European arrest warrant.[29]

a. The meaning of 'criminal'

'Criminal' has an autonomous Convention meaning.[30] Otherwise, if the classification of an offence in the law of the contracting parties were regarded as decisive, a state would be free to avoid the Convention obligation to ensure a fair trial (as well as the guarantee against retroactive offences in Article 7) in its discretion. It would also result, in this context, in an unacceptably uneven application of the Convention from one state to another.

In *Engel v Netherlands*,[31] it was established that, when deciding whether an offence is criminal in the sense of Article 6, three criteria apply: the classification of the offence in

---

[16] *Al-Moayad v Germany No 35865/03* hudoc (2007); 44 EHRR SE 276 para 101 DA.
[17] *Al-Moayad v Germany*. [18] It does apply to sentencing proceedings, including forfeiture.
[19] *Neumeister v Austria* A 8 (1968); 1 EHRR 91 para 23 and *Gutfreund v France* 2003-VII; 42 EHRR 1076.
[20] *Van Thuil v Netherlands No 20510/02* hudoc (2004) DA.
[21] *Mosbeux v Belgium No 17083/90*, 71 DR 269 (1990).
[22] *Helmers v Sweden* A 212-A (1991); 15 EHRR 285 PC.
[23] *AGOSI v UK* A 108 (1986); 9 EHRR 1 and *Air Canada v UK* A 316-A (1995); 20 EHRR 150.
[24] *Guzzardi v Italy* A 39 (1980); 3 EHRR 333 para 108 PC and *Raimondo v Italy* A 281-A (1994); 18 EHRR 237. But the preventative confiscation of property may concern 'civil rights and obligations': see the *Raimondo* case. [25] *R v UK No 33506/05* hudoc (2007) DA (young offender warning).
[26] *Enea v Italy* 2009- GC; 51 EHRR 103 GC (allocation to secure unit) and *Boulois v Luxembourg* hudoc (2012); 55 EHRR 32 GC (prison leave)
[27] *Mamatkulov and Askarov v Turkey* 2005-I; 41 EHRR 494 GC.
[28] *Szabo v Sweden No 28578/03* hudoc (2006) DA. For an exception, see *Buijen v Germany* hudoc (2010).
[29] *Monedero Angora v Spain No 41138/05* hudoc (2008) DA.
[30] *Engel v Netherlands* A 22 (1976); 1 EHRR 647 PC. 'Criminal' has the same meaning in Article 6 and Articles 2–4, 7th Protocol: *Sergey Zolotukhin v Russia* 2009-; 54 EHRR 502 GC.
[31] A 22 (1976); 1 EHRR 647 PC. See also *Ezeh and Connors v UK* 2003-X; 39 EHRR 1 GC.

the law of the respondent state; the nature of the offence; and the possible punishment. The first is crucial in that if the applicable national law classifies the offence as criminal, it is automatically such for the purposes of Article 6 too.[32] This is because the legal and social consequences of having a criminal conviction make it imperative that the accused has a fair trial. In cases in which the offence is not classified as criminal in national law, the other two criteria listed above come into play. These two criteria are 'alternative and not necessarily cumulative'; but a cumulative approach may be adopted where neither criteria by itself is conclusive.[33] In practice, there have been a number of cases of offences characterized as disciplinary or regulatory or that are otherwise analogous to criminal offences without being classified as such in national law in which the 'one way' autonomous meaning of 'criminal' in Article 6 has been important.

As to the 'nature' of the offence, the purpose of the offence must be deterrent and punitive, not compensatory, these being 'the customary distinguishing features of a criminal penalty'.[34] The offence should extend to the population at large,[35] although it may be limited to such general categories of persons as taxpayers and road users. The minor nature of an offence does not detract from its inherently criminal character.[36]

In the context of disciplinary offences, the Court distinguishes between offences focusing on the internal regulation of a group possessing a special status in society, such as the armed forces or prisoners, and offences committed by members of such a group that involve generally anti-social behaviour, with only the latter being subject to Article 6. In this connection, the fact that the conduct proscribed by the disciplinary offence is also a criminal offence under national law (a 'mixed offence') is relevant.[37] Some cases have concerned disciplinary or similar offences aimed at protecting proceedings in court or in a national parliament. In *Weber v Switzerland*,[38] the applicant was convicted of an offence under the code of criminal procedure by revealing at a press conference confidential information about the judicial investigation into a criminal prosecution by the state of another person which had resulted from the applicant's complaint. Although the offence was not criminal in Swiss law, it was held to be criminal in 'nature' because it applied not just to judges and lawyers—for whom it might be seen as a non-Article 6 disciplinary matter—but to the whole population. In contrast, there was no criminal offence in *Ravnsborg v Sweden*,[39] where the applicant was guilty of the offence of disturbing the good order of the court, which was not shown to be criminal under Swedish law, by statements in his written pleadings as a party to civil litigation. The Strasbourg Court distinguished the *Weber* case on the basis that the offence could only be committed by those, such as the applicant, participating in court proceedings, thus making it an internal court matter.

---

[32] See *Funke v France* A 256-A (1993); 16 EHRR 297. A state may make any conduct a criminal offence unless it is conduct protected by a Convention right: *Engel v Netherlands* A 22 (1976); 1 EHRR 647 PC.

[33] *Ezeh and Connors v UK* 2003-X; 39 EHRR 1 para 86 GC.

[34] *Janosevic v Sweden* 2002-VII; 38 EHRR 473 para 68. And see *Porter v UK No 15814/02* hudoc (2003) DA (local authority surcharge not punitive).   [35] *Lauko v Slovakia* 1998-VI; 33 EHRR 994.

[36] *Ezeh and Connors v UK* 2003-X; 39 EHRR 1 GC and *Lauko v Slovakia* 1998-VI; 33 EHRR 994. A 'breach of the peace' is a criminal offence by its 'nature': *Steel v UK* 1998-VII; 28 EHRR 603. Cf *Zolotukhin v Russia* 2009-; 54 EHRR 502 GC (minor disorderly acts 'criminal').

[37] *Engel v Netherlands* A 22 (1976); 1 EHRR 647 para 80 PC and *Ezeh and Connors v UK* 2003-X; 39 EHRR 1 GC. See also *Whitfield v UK* hudoc (2005); 41 EHRR 967.

[38] A 177 (1990); 12 EHRR 508. Cf *Les Travaux du Midi v Germany No 12275/86*, 70 DR 47 (1991) and *Demicoli v Malta* A 210 (1991); 14 EHRR 47.

[39] A 283-B (1994); 18 EHRR 38. See also *Putz v Austria* 1996-I; 32 EHRR 271 and *Schreiber and Boetsch v France No 58751/00* hudoc (2003) DA.

Disciplinary offences involving professional misconduct by members of the liberal professions are seen as an internal regulatory matter that does not fall within Article 6, even though a severe punishment—such as a heavy fine, suspension, or striking-off—may be imposed.[40] They may, however, in some cases fall within Article 6 as involving the determination of 'civil rights and obligations'.[41] Disciplinary offences by civil servants and the police are likewise not criminal, even though they may lead to dismissal.[42]

Apart from disciplinary or similar offences, the autonomous concept of a 'criminal' offence in Article 6 has been used to apply its fair trial guarantee to regulatory and certain other offences that, although not classified as criminal in national law, have deterrent and punitive objectives. The leading case on regulatory offences is *Öztürk v Germany*.[43] There the Court held that an offence of careless driving, which was classified under German law as regulatory, not criminal, was none the less 'criminal' for the purpose of Article 6. The offence had characteristics that were the hallmark of a criminal offence: it was of general application, applying to all road users, and carried with it a sanction of a deterrent and punitive kind. It was also relevant that although some West European states had taken steps to decriminalize road traffic offences, the great majority of Convention parties continued to treat minor road traffic offences as criminal.[44] The Court was not concerned by the 'relative lack of seriousness of the penalty at stake' (a modest fine as opposed to imprisonment) because the second element of the *Engel* test was very clearly satisfied.

Other offences that have been regarded as 'criminal' in the sense of Article 6 and that may, more or less convincingly, be placed within the category of regulatory offences, are ones governing trade and commerce,[45] hours of work,[46] or public demonstrations,[47] and offences under a customs code.[48] In *Jussila v Finland*,[49] the Court ruled that the imposition of a tax surcharge as a financial penalty for tax evasion involved a 'criminal' charge in the sense of Article 6. Proceedings for committal to prison for non-payment of the UK community charge are also criminal.[50] But an administrative fine for non-compliance with planning laws[51] and a disqualification from being a company director[52] are preventive, not criminal, in character.

---

[40] *Brown v UK No 38644/97* hudoc (1998) DA (solicitor); and *Wickramsinghe v UK No 31503/96* hudoc (1997) DA (doctor).		[41] *Albert and Le Compte v Belgium* A 58 (1983); 5 EHRR 533 PC.

[42] *X v UK No 8496/79*, 21 DR 168 (1980) (police) and *Kremzow v Austria No 16417/ 90*, 67 DR 307 (1990) (civil servants). Disciplinary offences by the police and some civil servants will also not concern 'civil rights and obligations'. This is an unsatisfactory gap in the Convention 'fair trial' guarantee.

[43] A 73 (1984); 6 EHRR 409 PC. For other road traffic cases, see, eg, *Schmautzer v Austria* A 328-A (1995); 21 EHRR 511; *Escoubet v Belgium* 1999-VII; 31 EHRR 1034 GC (temporary withdrawal of driving licence preventive, not criminal); *Blokker v Netherlands No 45282/99* hudoc (2000) DA; and *Siwak v Poland No 51018/99* hudoc (2004) DA.

[44] When deciding on the nature of an offence, the Court regularly takes account of 'common features' of the national law of the contracting parties: see, eg, *Ravnsborg v Sweden* A 283-B (1994); 18 EHRR 38.

[45] *Deweer v Belgium* A 35 (1980); 2 EHRR 439; *Société Stenuit v France* A 232-A (1992); 14 EHRR 509 Com Rep; and *Garyfallou AEBE v Greece* 1997-V; 28 EHRR 344. But see *000 Neste St Petersburg et al v Russia No 69042/01* hudoc (2004) DA.

[46] *X v Austria No 8998/80*, 32 DR 150 (1983) (young persons' hours).

[47] *Belilos v Switzerland* A 132 (1988); 10 EHRR 466 PC and *Ziliberberg v Moldova* hudoc (2005).

[48] *Salabiaku v France* A 141-A (1988); 13 EHRR 379.

[49] 2006-XIV; 45 EHRR 892 GC, See also *Bendenoun v France* A 284 (1994); 18 EHRR 54; *Janosevic v Sweden* 2002-VII; 38 EHRR 473; and *Julius Kloiber Schlachthof GmbH and Others v Austria* hudoc (2013). A fine for late payment is not 'criminal': *Boofzheim v France No 52938/99* 2002-X DA.

[50] *Benham v UK* 1996-III; 22 EHRR 293 GC.		[51] *Inocencio v Portugal No 43862/98* hudoc (2001) DA.

[52] *Wilson v UK No 36791/97* hudoc (1998); 26 EHRR CD 195.

As to the third criterion, the Court looks to the nature and severity of the possible, not the actual, punishment.[53] In *Engel v Netherlands*,[54] the Court held that a punishment of imprisonment belonged to the criminal sphere unless its 'nature, duration or manner of execution, was not such that its effect could be "appreciably detrimental"'. Applying both the second and third criteria, the Court then found that military disciplinary offences involving the publication of a periodical tending to undermine army discipline and the driving of a jeep irresponsibly that could lead to three or four months' imprisonment were 'criminal', but that offences of being absent without leave that carried possible penalties of just two days' strict arrest were not. A possible punishment of a modest fine that may be converted into imprisonment for more than a minimal period for non-payment may fall within Article 6,[55] as may a substantial fine that cannot be converted into imprisonment.[56] Even an offence that carries a modest fine as the only possible punishment and that will not be entered on the accused's criminal record may fall within Article 6 if it is inherently 'criminal' in its 'nature'.[57] Disqualification from holding public office[58] or the deduction of points that may lead cumulatively to the loss of a driving licence for road traffic offences[59] may be criminal punishments, as may the demolition of a building for lack of planning permission;[60] but the withdrawal of a liquor licence, although severe in its consequences, is not.[61] Nor is a penalty for exceeding election expenses limits of disqualification from standing for election plus an order to repay the excess.[62]

b. The meaning of 'charge'

For Article 6 to apply, a person must be subject to a criminal 'charge'. The point at which this begins to be the case has been developed mostly in connection with the 'trial within a reasonable time' guarantee, for which it will always need to be established,[63] although the precise date on which Article 6 begins to apply to that guarantee will not be crucial if the possible dates that may be chosen involve only a small difference.[64]

Like the word 'criminal', 'charge' has an autonomous Convention meaning.[65] It is 'the official notification given to an individual by the competent authority of an allegation that he has committed a criminal offence' or some other act which carries 'the implication of such an allegation and which likewise substantially affects the situation of the suspect'.[66] As stated in *Deweer v Belgium*,[67] 'charge' is to be given a 'substantive', not a 'formal', meaning, so that it is necessary 'to look behind the appearances and investigate

---

[53] *Engel v Netherlands* A 22 (1976); 1 EHRR 647 PC.

[54] A 22 (1976); 1 EHRR 647 PC, para 82. Cf *Zolotukhin v Russia* 2009-; 54 EHRR 502 GC.

[55] *Weber v Switzerland* A 177 (1990); 12 EHRR 508 (up to three months' imprisonment).

[56] *Janosevic v Sweden* 2002-VII; 38 EHRR 473. But non-payment of any fine will normally lead to enforcement measures resulting in imprisonment: see *Garyfallou AEBE v Greece* 1997-V; 28 EHRR 344.

[57] *Lauko v Slovakia* 1998-VI; 33 EHRR 994. But a small tax surcharge was not 'criminal': *Morel v France* No 54559/00 hudoc (2003) DA.

[58] *Matyjek v Poland* No 38184/03 hudoc (2006) DA (lustration proceedings).

[59] *Malige v France* 1998-VII; 28 EHRR 578.

[60] *Hamer v Belgium* 2007-V. A fine is not: *Inocencio v Portugal* No 43862/98 hudoc (2001) DA.

[61] *Tre Traktörer Aktiebolag v Sweden* A 159 (1989); 13 EHRR 309. But it may determine 'civil rights and obligations': *Tre Traktörer Aktiebolag v Sweden*.

[62] *Pierre-Bloch v France* 1997-VI; 26 EHRR 202. Cf *Porter v UK* No 15814/02 hudoc (2003) DA.

[63] It also has relevance for the right of access to a criminal court: see *Deweer v Belgium* A 35 (1980).

[64] See, eg, *Zaprianov v Bulgaria* hudoc (2004).

[65] *Deweer v Belgium* A 35 (1980); 2 EHRR 439 para 42.

[66] *Corigliano v Italy* A 57 (1982); 5 EHRR 334 para 34.

[67] A 35 (1980); 2 EHRR 439 paras 44, 46.

the realities of the procedure in question' to see whether the applicant is 'substantially affected' by the steps taken against him. In practice, a person has been found to be subject to a 'charge' when arrested for a criminal offence;[68] when notified that he is being charged with an offence;[69] when, in a civil law system, a preliminary investigation has been opened and, although not under arrest, the applicant has 'officially learnt of the investigation or begun to be affected by it';[70] when authorities investigating customs offences require a person to produce evidence and freeze his bank account;[71] or when the applicant's shop has been closed pending the outcome of criminal proceedings.[72] In the case of an MP with parliamentary immunity, the relevant date was that on which the prosecuting authorities requested Parliament to lift the immunity.[73] In some recent cases, the Court has held that a person is 'substantially affected' from the moment that there is a reasonable suspicion of guilt. Thus in *Yankov and Others v Bulgaria*,[74] Article 6 began to apply from the moment that an applicant was questioned by the police about stolen fruit and confessed, which occurred more than eight years before he was formally charged.

Most of the case law on the meaning of 'charge' has concerned civil law systems of criminal justice. With regard to common law jurisdictions, applicants have been held to be subject to a 'charge' when they have been arrested[75] or charged by the police.[76] Presumably, the issuing of a summons would be sufficient.

Although the Convention does not guarantee a right of appeal, Article 6 applies to any appeal proceedings against conviction or sentence that are in fact provided.[77] Constitutional court proceedings involving claims alleging a violation of constitutional rights are included insofar as they are decisive for the outcome of a criminal case.[78] Article 6 ceases to apply if criminal proceedings are discontinued.[79]

Nor does it apply to proceedings that concern a person who is already finally convicted of an offence, and hence is no longer 'charged' with it. Thus Article 6 does not apply to proceedings for an amnesty for a convicted person[80] or for an application for a re-trial or a plea of nullity.[81] However, any separate sentencing proceedings are included, the 'charge

---

[68] *Wemhoff v Germany* A 7 (1968); 1 EHRR 55.

[69] *Pedersen and Baadsgaard v Denmark* 2004-XI; 42 EHRR 486 GC. In *Foti v Italy* A 56 (1982); 5 EHRR 313, the date on which two of the applicants were formally charged was chosen, not that of their arrest two or three days earlier. Yet a person must be 'substantially affected' from the time of his arrest. In *Boddaert v Belgium* A 235-D (1992); 16 EHRR 242 para 10, the date that the arrest warrant was issued was chosen, not the later date when the applicant surrendered to the authorities.

[70] *Eckle v Germany* A 51 (1982); 5 EHRR 1 para 74. In accordance with the 'substantially affected' test, it is the date of notification or of otherwise first being affected by the investigation that is crucial, not the date on which the decision to open the investigation is taken: *Corigliano v Italy* A 57 (1982); 5 EHRR 334. See also *Angelucci v Italy* A 196-C (1991) para 13 and *P v Austria* No 13017/87, 71 DR 52 (1989) Com Rep; CM Res DH 91 (33).

[71] *Funke v France* A 256-A (1993). See also *TK and SE v Finland* No 38581/97 hudoc (2004) DA (seizure of documents).

[72] *Deweer v Belgium* A 35 (1980).   [73] *Frau v Italy* A 195-E (1991) para 14.

[74] Hudoc (2010). Cf *Aleksandr Zaichenko v Russia* hudoc (2010) (incriminating statements at road check).

[75] *Heaney and McGuinness v Ireland* 2001-XII; 33 EHRR 264. Cf *Ewing v UK* No 11224/84, 45 DR 269 (1986); 10 EHRR 141.

[76] *X v Ireland* No 9429/81, 32 DR 225 (1983). See also *X v UK* No 6728/74, 14 DR 26 (1978).

[77] *Eckle v Germany* A 51 (1982); 5 EHRR 1 para 76. Applications for leave to appeal are included: *Monnell and Morris v UK* A 115 (1987); 10 EHRR 205.

[78] *Gast and Popp v Germany* 2000-II; 33 EHRR 895.

[79] *Eckle v Germany* A 51 (1982); 5 EHRR 1 para 78; *Orchin v UK* No 8435/78, 26 DR 18 (1982); 6 EHRR 391. An appeal against discontinuance is within Article 6: *Zuckerstatter and Reschenhofer v Austria* No 76718/01 hudoc (2004) DA.   [80] *Montcornet de Caumont v France* No 59290/00, 2003-VII DA.

[81] *Fischer v Austria* No 27569/02 hudoc (2003) DA. Article 6 does not guarantee a right to a retrial: *Callaghan v UK* No 14739/89, 60 DR 296 (1989).

not being determined until the sentence has been fixed'.[82] Similarly, Article 6 also applies to the execution of final judgments in criminal cases. In *Assanidze v Georgia*,[83] there was a breach of Article 6 when the accused had not been released from detention some three years after his acquittal. The Grand Chamber in that case extended the principle in *Hornsby v Greece*[84] to criminal cases. Accordingly, Article 6 may also apply where a convicted person seeks the execution of some aspect of the judgment in his case, although the rationale of the *Hornsby* case (making the right to a fair trial effective) does not apply convincingly in that situation.[85]

II. IN THE DETERMINATION OF CIVIL RIGHTS AND OBLIGATIONS

Article 6 applies, secondly, when a person's 'civil rights and obligations' are being determined.[86]

a. The meaning of 'civil' rights and obligations

Private law meaning

According to its text, Article 6(1) applies 'in the determination' of a person's 'civil rights and obligations'. In their early jurisprudence, the Strasbourg authorities established that the phrase 'civil rights and obligations' incorporated, by the use of the word 'civil', the distinction between private and public law, with 'civil' rights and obligations being rights and obligations in private law.[87] This distinction has long been significant in civil law systems for jurisdictional and other purposes and has more recently become important in UK administrative law.[88] On the basis of it, rights and obligations in the relations of private persons *inter se* clearly fall within Article 6, but some rights and obligations at issue in the relations between the individual and the state (eg the right to nationality and the obligation to pay taxes) do not, the problem in the latter case being to know where to draw the line. Criminal law is in a special position. Decisions taken in the 'determination of…any criminal charge' are included by a separate part of the wording of Article 6(1).[89] Ancillary decisions relating to criminal proceedings are not subject to Article 6 on the criminal side and not otherwise subject to Article 6 as decisions determinative of 'civil rights and obligations'. They are excluded both because of the distinction between private and public law and also, as the Court has preferred to emphasize, because, if certain decisions in criminal proceedings are specifically covered by Article 6(1), others, by inference, are not.[90]

---

[82] *Eckle v Germany* A 51 (1982); 5 EHRR 1 para 77. Tariff fixing (*Easterbrook v UK* hudoc (2003); 37 EHRR 405) and proceeds of crime confiscation (*Phillips v UK* 2001-VII) proceedings are included as a part of sentencing. See also *Callaghan v UK* No 14739/89, 60 DR 296 (1989) (Criminal Cases Review Commission reference).
[83] 2004-II; 39 EHRR 653.   [84] 1997-II; 24 EHRR 250.
[85] See the joint partially dissenting opinion of Judges Costa, Bratza, and Thomassen in the *Assanidze* case, rejecting the extension of *Hornsby* to acquittal cases.
[86] See Van Dijk, *Wiarda Mélanges*, p 131, and *European Supervision*, chap 14.
[87] *Ringeisen v Austria* A 13 (1971); 1 EHRR 455 para 94 and *König v Germany* A 27 (1978); 2 EHRR 170 para 95 PC.   [88] See Wade and Forsyth, *Administrative Law*, 10th edn, 2009, p 566.
[89] A particular factual situation may concern both a criminal charge and civil rights and obligations, although the case will normally be dealt with under one head only: see *Albert and Le Compte v Belgium* A 58 (1983); 5 EHRR 533 para 30 PC. Criminal proceedings may be determinative of 'civil rights' in some jurisdictions in criminal defamation cases or if a victim is joined as a civil party.
[90] *Neumeister v Austria* A 8 (1968); 1 EHRR 91 (right to bail not a 'civil right' for this reason).

It therefore follows that the Convention does not guarantee a fair trial in the determination of all of the rights and obligations that a person may arguably have in national law. However, as will be seen, the gaps in the coverage of Article 6 have been significantly, if somewhat confusingly, reduced by interpretation. Indeed, whereas the Court occasionally still relies upon the public law/private law divide when excluding rights or obligations as not being 'civil',[91] more recent jurisprudence, by which more and more rights and obligations have been brought within Article 6, is not always easy to explain in terms of any distinction between private and public law that is found in European national law.

An autonomous Convention meaning

As with the parallel Article 6 concept of a 'criminal charge', the Court has held that 'civil' has an autonomous Convention meaning, so that the respondent state's classification is not decisive.[92] In a particular case, therefore, a right that is regarded as a matter of public law in the legal system of the respondent state may be treated as falling within Article 6[93] and *vice versa*. Although adopting an autonomous Convention meaning of 'civil' rights and obligations, the Court has refrained from formulating any abstract definition of the term, beyond distinguishing between private and public law.[94] It has instead preferred an inductive approach, ruling on the particular facts, or categories, of cases as they have arisen. Even so, there are certain general guidelines that emerge from the cases. First, 'only the character of the right at issue is relevant'.[95] The 'character of legislation which governs how the matter is to be determined (civil, commercial, administrative law, etc) and that of the authority which is invested with jurisdiction in the matter (ordinary court, administrative body, etc) are therefore of little consequence'.[96] This guideline has minimal significance for cases involving disputes between private persons which will invariably be governed by national private law and usually be within the jurisdiction of the 'ordinary courts'. It is, however, of critical importance in cases that involve the relations between a private person and the state. In national law systems that traditionally have made use of the distinction between private and public law, the classification of such cases generally turns upon whether the state is acting in a sovereign or non-sovereign capacity in its dealings with the private person concerned. For the purpose of Article 6, however, whether the state has 'acted as a private person or in its sovereign capacity is...not conclusive';[97] instead, the focus is entirely upon the 'character of the right'.

Secondly, when determining the 'character of the right', the existence of any 'uniform European notion' that can be found in the law of the contracting parties is influential. This inference can be drawn from the *Feldbrugge* and *Deumeland* cases.[98] There the Court found that there was no 'uniform European notion' (which by implication would have been followed) as to the private or public law character of the social security rights before

---

[91] See, eg, *Ferrazzini v Italy* 2001-VII; 34 EHRR 1068 para 27 GC.

[92] *König v Germany* A 27 (1978); 2 EHRR 170 para 88 PC.

[93] As in the *Feldbrugge* and *Deumeland* cases, in the next paragraph.

[94] In *Benthem v Netherlands* A 97 (1985); 8 EHRR 1 para 34 PC, the Court declined the Commission's invitation, para 91 Com Rep, to give guidance on the matter.

[95] *König v Germany* A 27 (1978); 2 EHRR 170 para 90 PC. The wording quoted is phrased only in terms of 'rights', omitting 'obligations'. This tends to happen because most of the cases under Article 6 are brought by claimants, not defendants. For 'obligations' cases, see, eg, *Muyldermans v Belgium* A 214-A (1991); 15 EHRR 204 Com Rep (F Sett before Court) and *Schouten and Meldrum v Netherlands* A 304 (1994); 19 EHRR 432.

[96] *Ringeisen v Austria* A 13 (1971); 1 EHRR 455 para 94, quoted in the *König* case, A 27 (1978); 2 EHRR 170 para 90 PC.   [97] *König v Germany* A 27 (1978); 2 EHRR 170 para 90 PC.

[98] *Feldbrugge v Netherlands* A 99 (1986); 8 EHRR 425 para 29 PC and *Deumeland v Germany* A 100 (1986); 8 EHRR 448 para 63 PC. Cf, *König v Germany* A 27 (1978); 2 EHRR 170 para 89 PC.

it and was forced to make a choice in respect of rights it considered to have a mixed private and public law character.[99]

Thirdly, although the classification of a right or obligation in the law of the respondent state is not decisive, that law is nonetheless relevant, in that it necessarily determines the content of the right or obligation to which the Convention concept of 'civil' rights and obligations is applied.[100] For this reason, despite the autonomous nature of 'civil' rights and obligations, it would be possible for the same right or obligation to be subject to Article 6 as it exists in one legal system but not as it is found in another.

Finally, the Court adopts a restrictive interpretation, in accordance with the object and purpose of the Convention, of the exceptions to the safeguards afforded by Article 6(1). This consideration was relevant in *Vilho Eskelinen v Finland*,[101] when the Court ruled that some disputes concerning employment in the public service fall within Article 6.

Rights and obligations in the relations between private persons

In accordance with the position uniformly found in European national law, the rights and obligations of private persons in their relations *inter se* are 'civil' rights and obligations. Thus cases concerning, for example, such relations in the law of contract,[102] the law of tort,[103] the law of succession,[104] family law,[105] employment law,[106] commercial law,[107] insurance law,[108] and the law of personal[109] and real[110] property have been regarded as falling within Article 6.

State action determining private law rights and obligations

The position is more complicated in cases involving the relations of private persons with the state. In accordance with its approach in the *König* case,[111] in such cases the Court looks solely to the character of the right or obligation that is the subject of the case when deciding whether Article 6 applies. If that right or obligation falls within private law, then any state action that is directly decisive for it must be either taken by a tribunal that complies with Article 6 or, if it is administrative action, challengeable before such a tribunal.[112] What is remarkable, and a tribute to the Court's creativity, is the identity and nature of the rights and obligations of private persons that the Court has recognized as private law rights and obligations in this context. Most significantly, it has recognized certain rights of a very general character, such as rights that have a pecuniary nature or consequences, as being 'civil' rights. When, as is common, state action is determinative of such rights, it is controlled by Article 6.

---

[99] Cf *Muyldermans v Belgium* A 214-A (1991); 15 EHRR 204 para 56 Com Rep (F Sett before Court).

[100] See, eg, *König v Germany* A 27 (1978); 2 EHRR 170 para 89 PC 9 (a doctor's services were contractual, not a public service, so 'civil'). See also *Perez v France* 2004-I; 40 EHRR 909 GC.

[101] 2007-XX; 45 EHRR 985 GC.   [102] See, eg, *Buchholz v Germany* A 42 (1981); 3 EHRR 597.

[103] See, eg, *Golder v UK* A 18 (1975); 1 EHRR 524 PC (defamation).

[104] See, eg, *CD v France* hudoc (2003).

[105] See, eg, *Airey v Ireland* A 32 (1979); 2 EHRR 305 (separation) and *Mizzi v Malta* 2006-I; 46 EHRR 529 (paternity).   [106] See, eg, *Buchholz v Germany* A 42 (1981); 3 EHRR 597 (unfair dismissal).

[107] See, eg, *Barthold v Germany* A 90 (1985); 7 EHRR 383 (unfair competition).

[108] Implied in *Feldbrugge v Netherlands* A 99 (1986); 8 EHRR 425 PC and *Deumeland v Germany* A 100 (1986); 8 EHRR 448 PC.

[109] See, eg, *Bramelid and Malmström v Sweden* Nos 8588/79 and 8589/79, 38 DR 18 (1983) (share valuation) Com Rep; CM Res DH (84) 4.   [110] See eg, *Pretto v Italy* A 71 (1983); 6 EHRR 182 PC (sale of land).

[111] *König v Germany* A 27 (1978); 2 EHRR 170 para 89 PC 9.

[112] As to the requirement that state administrative action be subject to judicial challenge, see section 2.e below.

Pecuniary rights

The key determinant in cases involving state action is often whether the right or obligation in question is pecuniary in nature or, if not, whether the state action that is decisive for the right nonetheless has pecuniary consequences for the applicant.[113] If so, the
case will generally fall within Article 6, unless the state is acting within one of the areas
that 'still form part of the hard core of public authority prerogatives',[114] such as taxation.
Although the Court commonly states that 'merely showing that a dispute is "pecuniary"
in nature is not in itself sufficient to attract the applicability of Article 6',[115] this is mainly
intended to allow for the 'public authority prerogative' exception: in cases to which that
exception does not extend, Article 6 will generally apply if a pecuniary dimension is present.[116] The paragraphs that immediately follow concern rights and obligations that are
sometimes classified as 'civil' under other headings by the Court but that all have a pecuniary dimension.

The right to property

The right to property is clearly a right with a pecuniary character. Thus decisions by the
state concerning the expropriation[117] or the regulation of the use[118] of private land have
been held to be subject to the right to a fair hearing. With regard to personal property,
decisions by the state as to a person's capacity to administer property,[119] or ones that are
otherwise decisive for personal property rights,[120] are controlled by Article 6.

The right to engage in a commercial activity or to practise a profession

The right to engage in a commercial activity, which similarly has a pecuniary character, is
also a civil right.[121] Hence state action by way of the withdrawal of a commercial licence
or other authorization to engage in a commercial activity is controlled by Article 6.[122] The

---

[113] See, eg, *Editions Périscope v France* A 234-B (1992); 14 EHRR 597 and *Stran Greek Refineries and Stratis Andreadis v Greece* A 301-B (1994); 19 EHRR 293.

[114] *Ferrazzini v Italy* 2001-VII; 34 EHRR 1068 para 29 GC.   [115] *Ferrazzini v Italy*, para 25.

[116] For example, the obligation of a French public accountant to repay public monies lost by his negligence is within Article 6, despite its public law dimensions, because of its pecuniary impact on the accountant: *Martinie v France No 58675/00* hudoc (2004) DA. On surcharges on UK local authority officers, see
Porter v UK No 15814/02 hudoc (2003); 37 EHRR CD8 DA.

[117] *Sporrong and Lönnroth v Sweden* A 52 (1982); 5 EHRR 35 PC and also *Aldo and Jean-Baptiste Zanatta
v France* hudoc (2000). See also *Raimondo v Italy* A 281-A (1994); 18 EHRR 237 para 43 (confiscation) and
Poiss v Austria A 117 (1987); 10 EHRR 231 (land consolidation).

[118] For planning or building permission cases, see, eg, *McGonnell v UK* 2000-II; 30 EHRR 289; *Chapman
v UK* 2001-I; 33 EHRR 399 GC; *Haider v Austria No 63413/00* hudoc (2004) DA. For other land use cases, see,
eg, *Posti and Rahko v Finland* 2002-VII; 37 EHRR 158 (fishing).

[119] *Winterwerp v Netherlands* A 33 (1979); 2 EHRR 387 (mentally disabled person).

[120] See, eg, *British-American Tobacco Co Ltd v Netherlands* A 331 (1995); 21 EHRR 409 (patent applications and rights) and *Procola v Luxembourg* A 326 (1995); 22 EHRR 193 (milk levy).

[121] There may be an overlap between this right and the right to property; eg, in *Benthem v Netherlands*
A 97 (1985); 8 EHRR 1 para 36 PC, the Court noted that the licence had a proprietary character (being
assignable) and that its grant was 'closely associated with the right to use one's possessions'.

[122] See, eg, *Tre Traktörer Aktiebolag v Sweden* A 159 (1989); 13 EHRR 309 (sale of alcohol); *Kingsley v UK*
2002-IV; 35 EHRR 177 GC (gaming); *Pudas v Sweden* A 125-A (1987); 10 EHRR 380 (transport); *König v
Germany* A 27 (1978); 2 EHRR 170 PC (medical clinic); *Benthem v Netherlands* A 97 (1985); 8 EHRR 1 PC
(liquid petroleum gas); *Hornsby v Greece* 1997-II; 24 EHRR 250 (private school). Where disqualification
from a commercial activity results from a criminal conviction, it suffices that Article 6 is complied with in
the criminal proceedings: *X v Belgium No 8901/80*, 23 DR 237 (1981).

same is true of the right to practise a liberal profession.[123] Article 6 applies to the *grant* of a licence or other authorization to undertake a commercial activity or practise a profession as well as a decision to withdraw it. Reversing its approach in *König v Germany*,[124] in which it had emphasized the legitimate expectation of a licence holder in its continuance, in the *Benthem* and later cases,[125] Article 6 has been applied to applications for new licences, provided that the grant of the licence is not a discretionary decision by the state.[126]

The right to compensation for illegal state action

The Court's jurisprudence also recognizes as 'civil' the right to compensation from the state for injury resulting from illegal state acts, again on the basis of its pecuniary nature. Thus, in *X v France*,[127] the Court held that a claim for damages in an administrative court for contracting AIDS from a blood transfusion because of government negligence fell within Article 6. Although the case concerned the exercise of a general regulatory power by a minister and hence was clearly a matter of public law in France, its outcome was 'decisive for private rights and obligations', namely those concerning pecuniary compensation for physical injury.[128]

The *X* case has been followed by other cases in which claims for compensation for illegal state acts have been held to be decisive for 'civil' rights. These have concerned claims for compensation for ill-treatment by the police;[129] unlawful detention;[130] unreasonable delay in judicial proceedings;[131] breach of contract;[132] the seizure of property;[133] and a miscellany of other claims.[134]

Statutory rights to compensation against the state for 'wrongful conviction and unjustified detention' in connection with criminal proceedings also fall within Article 6.[135] The cases have involved compensation for detention where the proceedings are discontinued,[136] the accused is acquitted,[137] or the conviction is quashed on appeal.[138] Such

---

[123] See, eg, *König v Germany* A 27 (1978) 2 EHRR 170 PC (medicine); *GS v Austria* hudoc (1999); 31 EHRR 576 (pharmacy); *H v Belgium* A 127-B (1987); 10 EHRR 339 (law); *Thlimmenos v Greece* 2000-IV; 31 EHRR 411 GC (accountancy); *Guchez v Belgium* No 10027/82, 40 DR 100 (1984) (architecture). And see *Wilson v UK* No 36791/97, 26 EHRR CD 195 (1998) and *X v UK* No 28530/95, 25 EHRR CD 88 (company director).

[124] A 27 (1978); 2 EHRR 170 PC.

[125] *Benthem v Netherlands* A 97 (1985); 8 EHRR 1 PC. Cf *Allan Jacobsson v Sweden* A 163 (1989); 12 EHRR 56; *Nowicky v Austria* hudoc (2005); *Kraska v Switzerland* A 254-B (1993); 18 EHRR 188; and *De Moor v Belgium* A 292-A (1994); 18 EHRR 372.

[126] Article 6 applies only where a person has an arguable legal right.

[127] A 234-C (1992); 14 EHRR 483. Cf *H v France* A 162-A (1989); 12 EHRR 74. See also *Z v UK* 2001-V; 34 EHRR 97 GC.   [128] Cf *Editions Périscope v France* A 234-B (1992); 14 EHRR 597 para 40.

[129] *Assenov v Bulgaria* 1998-VIII; 28 EHRR 652 and *Balogh v Hungary* hudoc (2004) (assault); *Baraona v Portugal* A 122 (1987); 13 EHRR 329 (illegal arrest); *Veeber v Estonia (No 1)* hudoc (2002) (illegal search and seizure); *Ait-Mouhoub v France* 1998-VIII; 30 EHRR 382 (police theft, forgery, etc); *Kaukonen v Finland* No 24738/94, 91-A DR 14 (1997) (malicious prosecution).

[130] *Aerts v Belgium* 1998-V; 29 EHRR 50 and *Göç v Turkey* 2002-V; 35 EHRR 134 GC.

[131] *Pelli v Italy* No 19537/02 hudoc (2003) DA ('Pinto law').

[132] *Stran Greek Refineries and Stratis Andreadis v Greece* A 301-B (1994); 19 EHRR 293.

[133] *Air Canada v UK* A 316-A (1995); 20 EHRR 150.

[134] See, eg, *Beaumartin v France* A 296-B (1994); 19 EHRR 485 (claim for compensation under a treaty); *Neves e Silva v Portugal* A 153-A (1989); 13 EHRR 535 (official malpractice); and *S A Sotiris and Nicos Koutas Attee v Greece* No 39442/98 hudoc (1999) DA (refusal of state subsidy).

[135] *Humen v Poland* hudoc (1999); 31 EHRR 1168 para 57 GC. The payment of compensation must be as of right, not discretionary: *Masson and Van Zon v Netherlands* A 327-A (1995); 22 EHRR 491.

[136] *Göç v Turkey* 2002-V; 35 EHRR 134 GC and *Werner v Austria* 1997-VII; 26 EHRR 310.

[137] *Lamanna v Austria* hudoc (2001).

[138] *Dimitrios Georgiadis v Greece* hudoc (2000); 33 EHRR 561 and *Humen v Poland* hudoc (1999); 31 EHRR 1168 GC. See also *Halka and Others v Poland* hudoc (2002).

cases concern a right to compensation provided by the state under national law where the detention is not necessarily in breach of Article 5 of the Convention, but the detainee is not finally convicted.

Although not involving an illegal act, a claim under a state's criminal injuries compensation scheme may, because of its pecuniary character, fall within Article 6 if the scheme provides for a legal right to compensation, and not an *ex gratia* payment.[139]

The right to social security and social assistance

One of the most remarkable developments in the Court's jurisprudence has concerned the classification of rights to social security and social assistance which the Court has held fall within Article 6. Initially, in the companion cases of *Feldbrugge v Netherlands*[140] and *Deumeland v Germany*,[141] the Court adopted a balancing approach, and in both cases found that the private law aspects of the social security rights concerned outweighed their public law aspects, so that Article 6 applied. However, the Court has since gone further and established that 'the development in the law that was initiated by those judgments and the principle of equality of treatment warrant taking the view that today the general rule is that Article 6(1) does apply in the field of social insurance, including even welfare assistance'.[142] In addition, the Court has stressed that such rights are of a pecuniary, or economic, nature.[143] Since the Court adopted this position, disputes concerning social security and social assistance rights have routinely been accepted as falling within Article 6, commonly without argument to the contrary by the respondent state.[144] The right need not be linked to a contract of employment[145] or depend upon contributory payments.[146] There must, however, be entitlement as a matter of legal right for those who qualify: disputes about benefits or assistance given by the state in its discretion are not included.[147] This is not to do with the civil or non-civil character of the benefit or assistance, but because Article 6 extends only to disputes about 'rights'.

Non-pecuniary civil rights and obligations

Although an important touchstone, the pecuniary dimension of a right or obligation is not the only test for a 'civil' right or obligation. Other rights or obligations of private persons may qualify, again by reference to the general perception of them in national law

---

[139] *Rolf Gustafson v Sweden* 1997-IV; 25 EHRR 623 (a legal right) and *August v UK No 36505/02* hudoc (2003); 36 EHRR CD 115 (*ex gratia* payment). Article 6 does not apply to discretionary state compensation for a natural disaster: *Nordh v Sweden No 14225/88*, 69 DR 223 (1990).

[140] A 99 (1986); 8 EHRR 425 PC (employment sickness benefit).

[141] A 100 (1986); 8 EHRR 448 PC (industrial injuries benefit).

[142] *Schuler-Zgraggen v Switzerland* A 263 (1993); 16 EHRR 405 para 46 (invalidity pension). See also *McGinley and Egan v UK* 1998-III; 27 EHRR 1 (disability pension); *Pauger v Austria* 1997-III; 25 EHRR 105 (widower's pension); *Grof v Austria No 25046/94*, 25 EHRR CD 39 (1998) (maternity benefit). For a case of welfare assistance, see *Salesi v Italy* A 257-E (1993); 26 EHRR 187 (disability allowance for destitute persons). And see *Wos v Poland No 22860/02* hudoc (2005) DA (forced labour compensation).

[143] *Schuler-Zgraggen v Switzerland* A 263 (1993); 16 EHRR 405 para 46 (the applicant 'suffered an interference with her means of subsistence' and was claiming an 'individual economic right').

[144] See, eg, *Duclos v France* 1996-VI; 32 EHRR 86. If the issue is raised, the Court typically notes the right's pecuniary nature when finding that it is a 'civil' right: see, eg, *Sussmann v Germany* 1996-IV; 25 EHRR 64 para 42.

[145] See, eg, *Giancarlo Lombardo v Italy* A 249-B (1992); 21 EHRR 188 (public service pension). The rights in the *Feldbrugge* and *Deumeland* cases were so linked.

[146] *Salesi v Italy* A 257-E (1993); 26 EHRR 187. See also *Stec v UK No 65731/01* hudoc (2005) DA.

[147] *Salesi v Italy* and *Mennitto v Italy* 2000-X; 34 EHRR 1122 GC. See also *Gaygusuz v Austria* 1996-IV; 23 EHRR 364.

as private law rights or obligations with which the state may not interfere without due process. One right of a non-pecuniary character to which Article 6 applies is the right to respect for family life. Thus state action that is directly decisive for this right, such as decisions placing children in care[148] and restricting the contact of prisoners with their families,[149] have been held to be regulated by Article 6.

Other non-pecuniary rights that have been recognized as 'civil rights' are the rights to life;[150] physical integrity;[151] liberty;[152] respect for private life;[153] access to administrative documents;[154] a reputation (and a remedy to protect it);[155] respect for one's home;[156] freedom of expression and assembly (unless used for political purposes);[157] freedom of association;[158] education;[159] freedom from discrimination;[160] and a healthy environment.[161] Most of the rights listed in this paragraph are human rights protected by the Convention, although no reference to this link is usually made in Court judgments.[162]

Public law rights and obligations

Following from the private law reading of the word 'civil', claims concerning a number of rights and obligations are not subject to Article 6 because of their public law character. However, their number is limited and in decline. The Court's parsimonious approach to the exclusion of rights and obligations on public law grounds is governed by two general considerations. First, in accordance with the object and purpose of the Convention, a 'restrictive interpretation' must be adopted when deciding whether a right or obligation is excluded from the safeguards of Article 6.[163] Second, the Convention is a living instrument that must be interpreted dynamically.[164] The significance of this second consideration was explained by the Court in *Ferrazzini v Italy*,[165] where the Court noted: 'Relations between the individual and the State have clearly developed in many spheres during the 50 years which have elapsed since the Convention was adopted, with State regulation increasingly intervening in private law relations.' However, the Court continued, 'rights and obligations existing for an individual are not necessarily civil in nature'.[166] Giving

---

[148] *Olsson v Sweden (No 1)* A 130 (1988); 11 EHRR 259 PC. See also *Keegan v Ireland* A 290 (1994); 18 EHRR 342 (adoption) and *Eriksson v Sweden* A 156 (1989); 12 EHRR 183 PC (fostering).

[149] *Ganci v Italy* 2003-XI; 41 EHRR 272 and *Enea v Italy* 2009-; 51 EHRR 50 GC. As to prison leave, see *Boulois v Luxembourg* 2012-; 55 EHRR 32 GC.

[150] *Athanassoglou v Switzerland* 2000-IV; 31 EHRR 372 GC.

[151] *Athanassoglou v Switzerland*; and *Okyay v Turkey* 2005-VII; 43 EHRR 788.

[152] *Laidin v France (No 2)* hudoc (2003) and *Aerts v Belgium* 1998-V; 29 EHRR 50. But Article 6 does not apply to pre-trial detention cases within Article 5(4): *Reinprecht v Austria* 2005-XII.

[153] *Mustafa v France* hudoc (2003) (choice of surname); *Užukauskas v Lithuania* hudoc (2010) (state file on an individual); *Alaverdyan v Armenia No 4523/04* hudoc (2010) DA (establishment of paternity).

[154] *Loiseau v France* 2003-XII DA.

[155] *Tolstoy Miloslavsky v UK* A 316-B (1995); 20 EHRR 442 and *Werner v Poland* hudoc (2001); 36 EHRR 491.   [156] *Ravon and Others v France* hudoc (2008) (search and seizure).

[157] *Reisz v Germany No 3201/96*, 91-A DR 53 (1997).

[158] *AB Kurt Kellermann v Sweden No 41579/98* hudoc (2003); 37 EHRR CD DA 161 and *APEH Üldözötteinek Szövetsége and Others v Hungary* 2000-X; 34 EHRR 849.

[159] *Oršuš v Croatia* hudoc (2010) GC (primary) and *Emine Arac v Turkey* hudoc (2008) (higher education).

[160] *Oršuš v Croatia* hudoc (2010) GC.   [161] *Ivan Atanasov v Bulgaria* hudoc (2010).

[162] Such a link was made in the case of the *pecuniary* right to property in Article 1, First Protocol to the Convention in *Procola v Luxembourg* A 326 (1995); 22 EHRR 193.

[163] *Vilho Eskelinen v Finland* 2007-XX; 45 EHRR 985 para 49 GC.

[164] *Ferrazzini v Italy* 2001-VII; 34 EHRR 1068 para 26 GC.

[165] *Ferrazzini v Italy*, para 27. Footnotes omitted. But in some contexts the tendency has more recently been for the withdrawal of the state, involving deregulation and privatization.

[166] *Ferrazzini v Italy*, para 28.

political rights and obligations, rights in some cases concerning public employment, the expulsion of aliens, and the obligation to pay taxes as examples, the Court stated that rights and obligations that relate to matters that 'still form part of the hard core of public authority prerogatives'[167] remain excluded. In the case of such rights or obligations, the fact that there may in some cases be a pecuniary dimension to the right or to the consequences of its infringement is outweighed or overridden by its fundamentally public law character.

The obligation to pay tax

On its facts, *Ferrazzini v Italy* concerned the obligation to pay taxes to the state, which is not subject to Article 6: although the obligation has pecuniary elements, 'the public nature of the relationship between the taxpayer and the tax authority' remains predominant'.[168] In contrast, in *Schouten and Meldrum v Netherlands*,[169] it was held that Article 6 does apply to the applicant's obligation to pay social security contributions: following the approach it had used in the *Feldbrugge* case in respect of social security benefits, the Court decided that the private law features of the obligation outweighed its public law features.

Political rights and obligations

As to political rights and obligations, in *Pierre-Bloch v France*,[170] it was held that the right to stand for election to a national parliament does not fall within Article 6, because 'such a right is a political and not a "civil" one'. There the applicant, who had been elected to the French National Assembly, was found to have exceeded the election expenses limit and as a penalty was disqualified from standing for election for a year, made to forfeit his seat, and required to pay a sum equal to the expenses excess. Despite the pecuniary consequences of the decision, Article 6 was held not to apply. Generally, the right to engage in political activities is not a 'civil' right, so that, for example, disputes concerning the right to vote[171] or the dissolution of a political party[172] also do not fall within Article 6. Disputes concerning the election of an officer of a non-governmental organization[173] or of an employees' council representative[174] are excluded on a similar basis.

Entry, conditions of stay, and removal of aliens

Disputes concerning the entry, conditions of stay, and removal of aliens also fall on the public law side of the line. In *Maaouia v France*,[175] the Court held that proceedings

---

[167] *Ferrazzini v Italy*, para 29.

[168] *Ferrazzini v Italy*. See Lopardi, 26 ELR Human Rights Survey 58 (2001). See also *Emesa Sugar NV v Netherlands No 62023/00* hudoc (2005) DA (customs duties) and *Smith v UK No 25373/94* hudoc (1995); 21 EHRR CD 74 (UK poll tax). Surcharges imposed for non-payment of tax may involve a 'criminal charge' within Article 6.

[169] A 304 (1994); 19 EHRR 432. Followed in *Meulendijks v Netherlands* hudoc (2002).

[170] 1997-VI; 26 EHRR 202. See also *Tapie v France No 32258/96*, 88-A DR 176 (1997); *Asensio Serqueda v Spain No 23151/94*, 77-A DR 122 (1994); and *Guliyev v Azerbaijan No 35584/02* hudoc (2004) DA. All kinds of election disputes fall outside Article 6: see, eg, *Priorello v Italy No 11068/84*, 43 DR 195 (1985) (challenge to local election).

[171] *Hirst v UK No 74025/01* hudoc (2003); 37 EHRR CD 176 DA (prisoner's right to vote).

[172] *Yazar, Karataş, Aksoy and the People's Labour Party (HEP) v Turkey* hudoc (2002); 36 EHRR 59. See also *Reisz v Germany No 32013/96* hudoc (1997) DA and *Papon v France No 344/04* hudoc (2005) DA.

[173] *Fedotov v Russia No 5140/02* hudoc (2005) DA.

[174] *Novotny v Czech Republic No 36542/97* hudoc (1998) DA.

[175] 2000-X; 33 EHRR 1037 GC. Cf *Panjeheighalehei v Denmark No 11230/07* hudoc (2009) DA.

concerning the rescinding of an exclusion order against an alien physically present in France did not concern his 'civil' rights. More generally, the Court stated that 'decisions regarding the entry, stay and deportation of aliens do not concern the determination of an applicant's civil rights or obligations', and that this is so even though, in the case of an exclusion order, the decision 'incidentally' has 'major repercussions on the applicant's private and family life or on his prospects of employment'.[176] The approach in the *Maaouia* case was applied to the extradition of aliens in *Mamatkulov and Askarov v Turkey*.[177]

In the *Maaouia* case, the Court reached its conclusion that Article 6 did not apply to the 'expulsion of aliens' on the basis that the Seventh Protocol to the European Convention on Human Rights (ECHR) provides procedural safeguards for aliens who are to be expelled, which would not have been necessary if the right to a fair hearing in Article 6 already applied. This reasoning cannot apply to the entry or conditions of stay of an alien, to which the Seventh Protocol does not apply. It is likely that the Court would here rely upon the fact that these matters are a 'part of the hard core of public authority prerogatives'.[178]

Employment in the public service

To some extent, rights and obligations arising out of employment in the public service are excluded from Article 6, although the extent of this exception is now more limited than formerly. In *Vilho Eskelinen v Finland*,[179] the Court introduced a new two-part test, with a different emphasis and starting from the presumption that Article 6 does apply. For it not to do so, first, 'the state in its national law must have expressly excluded access to a court for the post or category of staff in question'. Second, where this condition is met, Article 6 nonetheless still applies unless the national law exclusion is justified on 'objective grounds'. These 'grounds' must relate not to the nature of the public servant's employment but the 'subject matter of the dispute' between the public servant and the state, with the latter being required to show that the dispute 'is related to the exercise of state power or that it has called into question the special bond of trust and loyalty' between public servants and the state.[180] Thus, even though there is no right of access to a court in national law in respect of such disputes, Article 6 will apply—and access to a court compliant with it will be required—to 'ordinary labour disputes, such as those relating to salaries, allowance or similar entitlements', regardless of the nature of the employment or status of the public servant (as diplomat, judge, etc).[181] In the *Vilho Eskilenen* case, which concerned a salary dispute between the applicant policemen, who were civil servants, and the state, the government's defence fell at the first hurdle, as the applicants did have a right of access to a court to decide the dispute in national law. Even if this had not been the case, Article 6 would have applied because the dispute was an 'ordinary labour dispute'. Applying the two parts of the *Vilho Eskelinen* test, the Court has found Article 6 to be applicable to disputes concerning the employment of public prosecutors,[182] the dismissal of judges[183] and disciplinary proceedings against police officers,[184] and compensation claims by military servicemen.[185]

---

[176] *Maaouia v France*, paras 40 and 38. Article 6 does not apply to asylum cases: *P v UK No 13162/87*, 54 DR 211 (1987) and *Taheri Kandomabadi v Netherlands No 6276/03* hudoc (2004) DA. Or to Schengen cases: *Dalea v France No 964/07* hudoc (2010) DA.

[177] 2005-I; 41 EHRR 494 GC. The extradition of nationals is probably excluded also.

[178] *Ferrazzini v Italy* 2001-VII; 34 EHRR 1068 para 26 GC.

[179] 2007-XX; 45 EHRR 985 GC para 62. This test replaced the functional test in *Pellegrin v France* 1999-VIII; 31 EHRR 651.   [180] *Pellegrin v France*, para 65.

[181] *Pellegrin v France*. Cf *Fazliyski v Bulgaria* hudoc (2013). See also *Savino and Others v Italy* hudoc (2009) (parliamentary employees) and *Harabin v Slovakia* hudoc (2012) (judge).

[182] *Zalli v Albania No 5253/07* hudoc (2011) DA.   [183] *Olujić v Croatia* hudoc (2009).

[184] *Vanjak v Croatia* hudoc (2010).   [185] *Kuzmina v Russia* hudoc (2009).

In contrast, in *Suküt v Turkey*,[186] Article 6 was held not to apply to a dispute concerning the discharge of a soldier for breaches of discipline, the 'special bond of trust and loyalty' between the applicant and the state being central to the dispute.

Although the *Vilho Eskelinen* case is a welcome step in the right direction, the Court still needs to go further. An approach by which a dispute concerning employment in the public service in which the applicant has an arguable case under national law should be subject to Article 6 without exception. Such an approach was proposed in the joint dissenting opinion of Judges Tulkens, Fischbach, Casadevall, and Thomassen in *Pellegrin v France*,[187] who state that whereas civil servants have traditionally had a special status in the public law of many European states, 'that justification has now largely lost its significance' as 'most member states have "judicialised" civil service disputes, if not entirely then at least in part'.

Other public law rights and obligations

An obligation which is a part of 'normal civic duties in a democratic society' also falls outside Article 6.[188] Thus an obligation to pay a fine[189] or to give evidence in court proceedings[190] is not a 'civil' obligation to which Article 6 applies. Other kinds of public law cases that have been regarded as falling outside it include cases concerning the rights to nationality;[191] liability for military service;[192] certain matters relating to the administration of justice;[193] the interception by the state of mail and telephone calls;[194] medical treatment;[195] public housing;[196] and the award of administrative contracts.[197]

Concluding comments

As will be apparent, although the Court has maintained its private law meaning of 'civil' rights and obligations, its evolving jurisprudence has led to a position in which, in addition to disputes between private persons, Article 6 regulates more kinds of disputes between the individual and the state than that meaning might suggest. This results partly from the extensive interpretation given by the Court to the word 'determination' in Article 6(1), but also from the Court's dynamic understanding of what amounts to a private law right or obligation for the purposes of Article 6. The ingenious use of such all-embracing concepts as the rights to property or to engage in commercial activities,

---

[186] *No 59773/00* hudoc (2007) DA.   [187] 1999-VIII; 31 EHRR 651 GC.

[188] *Schouten and Meldrum v Netherlands* A 304 (1994); 19 EHRR 432 para 50.

[189] *Schouten and Meldrum v* Netherlands, para 50.

[190] *BBC v UK No 25798/94* hudoc (1996) DA. See also *Van Vondel v Netherlands No 38258/03* hudoc (2006) DA and *Burdov v Russia* 2002-III; 38 EHRR 639.

[191] *S v Switzerland No 13325/87*, 59 DR 257 (1988). See also *Peltonen v Finland No 19583/92*, 80-A DR 38 (1995) (passport); and *X v UK No 8208/78*, 16 DR 162 (1978) (peerage).

[192] *Nicolussi v Austria No 11734/85*, 52 DR 266 (1987) and *Zelisse v Netherlands No 12915/87*, 61 DR 230 (1989).

[193] *Schreiber and Boetsch v France No 58751/00* hudoc (2003) DA (challenge to a judge); *X v Germany No 3925/69*, 32 CD 56 (1970) (legal aid), but see *Gutfreund v France* 2003-VII; 42 EHRR 1076 paras 39–44; *B v UK No 10615/83*, 38 DR 213 (1984) (lawyers' costs); and *Shapovalov v Ukraine* hudoc (2012) (no civil right to report court proceedings). On the disciplining of prisoners (which may involve a 'criminal charge'), see *McFeeley v UK No 8317/78*, 20 DR 44 (1980), now subject to *Ganci v Italy* 2003-XII; 41 EHRR 272.

[194] *Klass v Germany* B 26 (1977) Com Rep. The question was left open by the Court in *Kennedy v UK* hudoc (2010). But see *Ravon and Others v France* hudoc (2008), ruling that the search and seizure of documents in the home concerned the right to respect for the home, which was a civil right.

[195] *L v Sweden No 10801/84*, 61 DR 62 (1988) Com Rep para 87; CM Res DH (89) 16.

[196] *Woonbron Volkshuisvestingsgroep and Others v Netherlands No 47122/99* hudoc (2002); 35 EHRR CD 161 DA.

[197] *LTC v Malta No 2629/06* hudoc (2007) DA.

and especially the emphasis upon the pecuniary dimension of a right or obligation, has engineered considerable inroads into the realms of public law and administrative justice—sometimes to the point where the Court's attempt to explain its decisions in terms of private and public law as these concepts are understood in national law appears artificial and unconvincing.

It is arguable that the Court might do better to reformulate its approach in terms of an abstract definition of 'civil' rights and obligations that starts from a different premise. The Court's attempt to rationalize its approach in the *Ferrazzini* case has some merit, but is not ultimately convincing or of comprehensive application. Given that European states now commonly provide, or can be expected to provide, judicial remedies in areas such as taxation, the control of aliens, and electoral matters, the dynamic approach to the interpretation of Article 6 that the Court properly adopts should lead it to a different conclusion from one which still seeks to exclude disputes in the area of 'public authority prerogatives'. Instead, 'civil' rights and obligations might be interpreted as referring to all legal rights and obligations that an individual arguably has under national law, regardless of the area of law concerned and the nature of any involvement by the state.[198] This would be in line both with human rights expectations and evolving national practice in administrative law in European states. The difficulty with such an approach, the Court has stated, is that the principle of dynamic interpretation 'does not give the Court the power to interpret Article 6(1) as though the adjective "civil"... were not present in the text'.[199] However, in view of its juxtaposition with 'criminal' in the wording of Article 6(1), the term 'civil' could—without doing violence to the text—be read as meaning any right or obligation in law that is not a criminal one. Short of that, some extension of the Court's present approach would be to emphasize the pecuniary character of the obligation to pay tax[200] and of some other public law rights and obligations, or of the pecuniary consequences of their breach. A further pragmatic extension of the Court's understanding of the scope of Article 6(1) would be to consider that insofar as states actually have courts or tribunals (including, for example, immigration or tax tribunals) with jurisdiction to determine cases concerning rights and obligations of whatever kind in national law, these should comply with Article 6.[201]

The satisfactory end result of such developments would be that a person would be guaranteed a 'right to a court' in the sense of Article 6, both to assert or question any arguable legal 'right or obligation' that the person has under national law[202] and to challenge by means of judicial review any administrative decision taken by the state that directly affects such rights or obligations. While it may not have been intended when the Convention was drafted that the right to a fair trial in Article 6 should have such a wide application, an extensive reading along these lines would be fully in line with the perception of the right to a fair trial as a human right.

---

[198] Cf the dissenting opinion of Judge Loucaides in *Maaouia v France* 2000-X; 33 EHRR 1037 GC. For other proposals, see Van Dijk, *Wiarda Mélanges*, p 131 and the dissenting opinion of Messrs Melchior and Frowein in *Benthem v Netherlands* B 80 (1983) para 10 Com Rep.

[199] *Ferrazzini v Italy* 2001-VII; 34 EHRR 1068 para 30 GC.

[200] See the dissenting opinion of Judge Lorenzen, joined by Judges Rozakis, Bonello, Stráznická, Bîrsan, and Fischbach, in the *Ferrazzini* case.

[201] See *Oršuš and Others v Croatia* hudoc (2010); 52 EHRR 300 para 105 GC. And see the dissenting opinion of Mr Alkema in *Maillard v France* 1998-III; 27 EHRR 232 GC. Cf the approach by which Article 6 applies to whatever appeal courts states have.

[202] Any restriction on the access to a court would have to be consistent with the approach in *Ashingdane v UK* A 93 (1985); 7 EHRR 528.

b. The meaning of 'rights and obligations'

By 'rights and obligations' in Article 6 are meant 'rights and obligations' 'which can be said, at least on arguable grounds, to be recognised under domestic law, irrespective of whether... [they are] protected under the Convention'.[203] The requirement is only that the applicant have a 'tenable' argument, not that he will necessarily win.[204] If the applicant has no arguable right under national law,[205] Article 6 does not apply.[206] The fact that the state has under national law a discretion in responding to an applicant's claim (eg when granting a licence) will not prevent Article 6 applying if 'it follows from generally recognised legal and administrative principles that the authorities' do 'not have an unfettered discretion' when taking their decision.[207] In such a case, the applicant must be allowed to question whether the state has complied with these principles before a tribunal that satisfies the requirements of Article 6. Apart from this limitation, a discretionary decision is not subject to Article 6.[208] A person tendering for a contract does not have a 'right' during the evaluation phase.[209]

Article 6 does not control the content of a state's national law; it is only a procedural guarantee of a right to a fair hearing in the determination of whatever legal rights and obligations a state chooses to provide in its law. For example, in *James v UK*,[210] the applicants had been deprived of their ownership of certain properties by the exercise by their tenants of a right to acquire the properties that had been given to them by statute. The applicants had no remedy in court by which to challenge the exercise of this right. Although the case concerned their right to property, which was a 'civil' right, Article 6 did not come into play because the applicants had no arguable right under English law that had been infringed.

However, a limit to this approach was set in *Fayed v UK*.[211] There the applicants wanted to bring a claim in defamation arising out of a government inspector's report under the Companies Act 1985 which found that they had been dishonest. Whereas the law of defamation extended to cover the facts of their claim, it would have been successfully met by a defence of privilege. After referring with approval to its approach in the *James* case, the Court drew a distinction between cases in which there was no 'legal basis' in national law for the claim and others in which there was such a basis but the claim could be met by a defence. In the 'no legal basis' kind of case, the reasoning in the *James* case continued to apply, but in the *Fayed* kind of case, the rule of law dictated some degree of Convention 'restraint or control'. The vehicle for providing this 'restraint or control' is, the Court

---

[203] *Boulois v Luxembourg* hudoc 2012-; 55 EHRR 32 para 90 GC.

[204] *Neves e Silva v Portugal* A 153-A (1989); 13 EHRR 535 para 37. The right need only be 'arguable' when proceedings are commenced; changes in the law while they are pending are immaterial: *Reid v UK No 33221/96* hudoc (2001) DA.

[205] National law includes EC law for member states: *Papoulakos v Greece No 24960/94* hudoc (1995) DA.

[206] In *Boulois v Luxembourg* hudoc 2012-; 55 EHRR 32 para 102 GC, the Court noted that the Convention did not have a right to prison leave, suggesting that Article 6 may apply where there is a Convention right in issue, whether it is recognized in national law or not. Cf *Gutfreund v France* 2003-VII; 42 EHRR 1076 para 39.

[207] *Pudas v Sweden* A 125-A (1987); 10 EHRR 380 para 34. Cf *Allan Jacobsson v Sweden (No 1)* A 163 (1989); 12 EHRR 56. And see *Rolf Gustafson v Sweden* 1997-VI; 25 EHRR 623.

[208] *Boulois v Luxembourg* hudoc 2012-; 55 EHRR 32 GC; *Masson and Van Zon v Netherlands* A 327-A (1995); 22 EHRR 491; *Anne-Marie Andersson v Sweden* 1997-IV; 25 EHRR 722 para 36; *Le Calvez v France* 1998-V; 32 EHRR 481; *Massa v Italy* A 265-B (1993); 18 EHRR 266; *Ladbrokes Worldwide Betting v Sweden No 27968/05* hudoc (2008) DA.　　　　　　　　　　　[209] *ITC Ltd v Malta No 2629/06* hudoc (2007) DA.

[210] A 98 (1986); 8 EHRR 123 para 81 PC. Cf *Powell and Rayner v UK* A 172 (1990); 12 EHRR 335 (statute excluded liability in tort for aircraft noise). See also *McMichael v UK* A 307-B (1995); 20 EHRR 205.

[211] A 294-B (1994); 18 EHRR 393 para 65.

indicated in the *Fayed* case, the right of access to a court that Article 6 guarantees. In that case the Court, acting on the basis that Article 6 otherwise applied, concluded that the restriction upon the right of access presented on the facts of that case by the privilege defence to the applicants' defamation claim could be justified as having a legitimate aim and as being in proportion to its attainment.

c. A 'contestation' or dispute concerning civil rights and obligations

For Article 6 to apply there must be a 'dispute' at the national level, between two private persons or between the applicant and the state, the outcome of which is determinative of the applicant's civil rights and obligations. The need for a 'dispute' follows from the use of the word 'contestation' in the French text of Article 6. Generally, the Court has interpreted the 'dispute' requirement in such a way that it is not a significant hurdle.[212] It has held that 'contestation' should not be 'construed too technically' and that it should be given a 'substantive rather than a formal meaning'.[213] This approach is adopted as being in accordance with the spirit of the Convention and because the term 'contestation' has no counterpart in the English text, a fact that has led to hesitation as to its importance.[214]

A dispute may concern a question of law or of fact.[215] It need not concern the actual existence of a right, but may relate instead to its 'scope... or the manner in which the beneficiary may avail himself of it'.[216] The dispute must be 'genuine and of a serious nature'.[217] This requirement may exclude a case of a hypothetical kind, such as a case raising the question whether proposed legislation would, if enacted, infringe the applicant's rights,[218] or a case in which the applicant does not pursue his claim seriously, for example by not presenting evidence.[219] For a dispute to be 'genuine and serious', there must also be something 'at stake' for the applicant.[220] It is not necessary that damages be claimed for a dispute to be 'genuine and serious'; a request for a declaratory judgment is sufficient.[221]

A 'dispute' must be justiciable, ie it must be one that inherently lends itself to judicial resolution. This was relevant in *Van Marle v Netherlands*.[222] There the Court held that Article 6 was not applicable to a dispute concerning the applicants' registration as accountants. According to the reasoning in the Court's judgment, this was because the dispute was concerned essentially with the assessment of the applicants' competence as accountants, which was more akin to school or university examining than judging, whereas Article 6 is aimed at regulating only the latter.

---

[212] See *Oerlemans v Netherlands* A 219 (1991); 15 EHRR 561.

[213] *Le Compte, Van Leuven and De Meyere v Belgium* A 43 (1981); 4 EHRR 1 para 45 PC.

[214] In *Moreira de Azevedo v Portugal* A 189 (1990); 13 EHRR 721, the Court cast some doubt upon the very existence of the requirement ('if indeed it does' exist). Cf the joint dissenting opinion of six judges in *W v UK* A 121 (1987); 10 EHRR 29 PC, and the dissenting opinion of Judge de Meyer in *Kraska v Switzerland* A 254-B (1993); 18 EHRR 188.

[215] *Albert and Le Compte v Belgium* A 58 (1983); 5 EHRR 533 PC.

[216] *Le Compte, Van Leuven and De Meyere v Belgium* A 43 (1981); 4 EHRR 1 para 49 PC.

[217] *Benthem v Netherlands* A 97 (1985); 8 EHRR 1 para 32 PC.

[218] But a claim based upon enacted legislation of general application that affects the applicant is subject to Article 6: *Posti and Rahko v Finland* 2002-VII; 37 EHRR 158.

[219] *Kaukonen v Finland* No 24738/94, 91-A DR 14 (1997). See also *Kiryanov v Russia* No 42212/02 hudoc (2005) DA.   [220] *Kienast v Austria* hudoc (2003).

[221] *Helmers v Sweden* A 212 (1991); 15 EHRR 285 PC.

[222] A 101 (1986); 8 EHRR 483 PC. Cf *Le Bihan v France* No 63054/00 hudoc (2004) DA; *Nowicky v Austria* hudoc (2005); and *Kervoëlen v France* hudoc (2001).

d. When are civil rights and obligations being determined?

Supposing that a dispute exists, it is still necessary to show that civil rights and obligations are being 'determined' by the decision to which it is sought to apply Article 6(1). This will be the case when the decision is 'directly decisive' for the civil rights or obligations concerned.[223] This requirement is clearly met where the determination of the applicant's civil rights and obligations is the primary purpose of the decision-making process. Thus Article 6 undoubtedly applies, for instance, to a personal injuries claim in tort between private individuals before the ordinary courts,[224] and to a claim before an administrative court for negligence by a state hospital.[225]

In addition, it was held in *Ringeisen v Austria*[226] that Article 6 extends to proceedings which do not have the determination of 'civil rights and obligations' as their purpose, but which nonetheless are decisive for them. In that case, the applicant had entered into a contract to buy land from third parties. The sale was subject to the approval of an administrative tribunal which refused permission because the land would be used for non-agricultural purposes. The object of the proceedings before the tribunal—the granting of permission by reference to the public interest—clearly pertained to public law. Nonetheless, the Court held that civil rights—contract rights—were being determined.

In *Ringeisen v Austria*, the Court stated only that for Article 6 to apply the proceedings must be 'decisive' for civil rights and obligations. It was in *Le Compte v Belgium*[227] that the Court established that they must be '*directly* decisive' and that a 'tenuous connection or remote consequences do not suffice'. In that case, the applicants were Belgian doctors who had been temporarily suspended from medical practice by the competent disciplinary bodies. The Court accepted that the primary purpose of the disciplinary proceedings was to decide whether breaches of the rules of professional conduct had occurred. Nonetheless, the proceedings were 'directly decisive' for the applicants' private law right to practise medicine because the suspension of the applicants' exercise of that right was a direct consequence of the decision that breaches of the rules had occurred.[228]

In contrast, the applicants 'civil rights' were not 'directly' being determined in *Athanassoglu v Switzerland*.[229] In that case, a decision to renew a licence for a nuclear power station was not subject to Article 6 because, despite the general public interest ramifications, it was not directly decisive for the rights to life, physical integrity, and property of applicants living nearby who were not able to produce evidence showing that the station's operation exposed them to a specific and imminent danger of an infringement of these rights. But civil rights were being determined in proceedings in which an association challenged the building of a dam because of its direct impact on the lifestyle and property of its members as well as on public interest environmental grounds.[230]

Article 6 does not apply where a decision being challenged is important for the applicant economically but does not determine his or her legal rights. Thus an application requesting a court to annul a presidential decree in favour of an airport runway as being

---

[223] *Ringeisen v Austria* A 13 (1971); 1 EHRR 455; *Le Compte, Van Leuven and De Meyere v Belgium* A 43 (1981); 4 EHRR 1 PC. [224] See, eg, *Guincho v Portugal* A 81 (1984); 7 EHRR 223.

[225] See, eg, *H v France* A 162-A (1989); 12 EHRR 74. [226] A 13 (1971); 1 EHRR 455.

[227] A 43 (1981); 4 EHRR 1, para 47 PC (emphasis added).

[228] Disciplinary proceedings that result in a lesser penalty than suspension (eg, a fine) fall within Article 6 provided that interference with the exercise of the right (by suspension or termination) is 'at stake': *A v Finland No 44998/98* hudoc (2004); 38 EHRR CD 223 DA and *WR v Austria* hudoc (1999); 31 EHRR 985.

[229] 2000-IV; 31 EHRR 372 GC, following *Balmer-Schafroth v Switzerland* 1997-IV; 25 EHRR 598 PC. See also *L'Erablière v Belgium* hudoc (2009-) and *Ivan Atanasov v Bulgaria* hudoc (2010). Contrast *Okay v Turkey* 2005-VII; 43 EHRR 788. [230] *Gorraiz Lizarraga v Spain* 2004-III; 45 EHRR 1031.

unconstitutional did not fall within Article 6. While it was prejudicial to their economic activities relating to adjacent land that they owned, it left their legal rights intact.[231]

Despite the limiting effect of the *Le Compte* case, the impact of the *Ringeisen* case in extending Article 6 to cases in which the 'determination' of civil rights and obligations is a consequence, but not the purpose, of the proceedings has been considerable. In particular, it has provided the basis upon which cases involving decisions by administrative tribunals and, most significantly, by the executive regulating private rights in the public interest are brought within the reach of Article 6.

Civil rights and obligations may be determined in criminal proceedings. This is so, for example, where a criminal prosecution is the remedy provided in national law for the enforcement of a civil right, as, for example, in some legal systems in connection with the right to a reputation.[232] Article 6 also applies when a legal system allows the victim of a crime to be joined as a civil party in criminal proceedings against the offender in order to obtain damages or otherwise protect his or her civil rights; however, it does not apply in such cases where the victim's purpose in being joined is to punish the offender or to intervene on an *actio popularis* basis, not to obtain a personal civil remedy.[233]

Finally, proceedings before a constitutional court involve the determination of civil rights and obligations where their outcome is capable of being decisive for those rights.[234]

e. The application of Article 6(1) in the context of administrative decisions

Many decisions that are determinative of a person's civil rights and obligations are taken by the executive or some other body that is not a tribunal in the sense of Article 6. What Article 6 requires in such cases is the possibility of judicial review, or in some cases an appeal on the merits, by a body that complies with Article 6. Although this is an approach that conforms to practice generally in most European states, it has presented serious problems for some such states, where the tradition had been of review or appeal that was technically within the executive branch of government, and not of recourse to the courts.[235]

The first cases in which the Court expressed a clear opinion on the matter concerned decisions by professional disciplinary bodies rather than public bodies. In *Albert and Le Compte v Belgium*,[236] in which the applicant doctors wished to challenge disciplinary decisions against them on their merits, the decisions themselves were taken by a professional association, with a right of appeal to another such body and finally to the Belgian Court of Cassation. The European Court stated that the Convention required either that such associations meet the requirements of Article 6 or 'they do not so comply but are subject to subsequent control by a judicial body that has full jurisdiction and does provide the guarantees of Article 6(1)'. Article 6(1) was not complied with in the case because

---

[231] *SARL de Parc d'activities de Blotzheim v France No 48897/99*, 2003-III DA. Cf *Krafft and Rougeot v France No 11543/85*, 65 DR 51 (1990).

[232] See, eg, *Helmers v Sweden* A 212-A (1991); 15 EHRR 285 PC. But Article 6 does not apply if the defamation prosecution is intended to punish: *Rekasi v Hungary No 315061/96*, 87-A DR 164 (1996).

[233] *Perez v France* 2004-I; 40 EHRR 909 GC. See also *Garimpo v Portugal No 66752/01* hudoc (2004) DA.

[234] *Sussman v Germany* 1996-IV; 25 EHRR 64; *Gorraiz Lizarraga v Spain* 2004-III; 45 EHRR 1031; *Voggenreiter v Germany* 2004-I; 42 EHRR 456. For a case in which the constitutional court proceedings were *not* decisive, see *Bakarić v Croatia No 48077/ 99*, 2001-IX DA.

[235] See eg, *Benthem v Netherlands* A 97 (1985); 8 EHRR 1 PC and *Ravnsborg v Sweden* A 283-B (1994); 18 EHRR 38.

[236] A 58 (1983); 5 EHRR 533 para 29 PC. In *Stefan v UK No 29149/95* hudoc (1997); 25 EHRR CD 130, the *Bryan* approach to 'full jurisdiction', which is considered later was applied to a UK professional medical association's decision on a doctor's fitness to practise.

the professional association, which could rule on the facts, did not sit in public as Article 6 requires and because the Court of Cassation, which met all of the procedural demands of Article 6(1), could only consider points of law.

This approach has since been applied to administrative decisions by public bodies. When determining whether the *Albert and Le Compte* requirement has been met in such cases, the Court speaks of control by a judicial body that has 'full jurisdiction' or provides 'sufficiency of review'.[237] When applying this test, the Court looks to the 'subject matter of the decision appealed against, the manner in which that decision was arrived at, and the content of the dispute, including the desired and actual grounds of appeal'.[238]

For the purpose of deciding whether the scope of a judicial body's supervisory powers is sufficient, the Court has drawn a distinction between two categories of administrative decisions. The first category consists of decisions which require 'a measure of professional knowledge or experience and the exercise of administrative discretion pursuant to wider policy aims'.[239] For these, which involve 'the classic exercise of administrative discretion',[240] the Court has accepted that policy considerations dictate that the final decision on the merits may rest with the executive, rather than a court, despite the impact upon a person's 'civil rights and obligations' that the decision may have. Decisions concerning the expropriation of land for a road or for public housing are obvious cases in which this can be argued. In addition, administrative decisions that require 'professional knowledge' or technical expertise— seemingly whether or not they are linked with matters of policy[241]—which are entrusted in the first instance to bodies other than ordinary courts or tribunals, whose members may lack the required knowledge or expertise, also fall within this category.

In the case of administrative decisions within this first category, 'full jurisdiction' or 'sufficiency of review' does not require a full right of appeal on the merits: judicial review in the sense commonly found in administrative law in European states is enough. This was established in *Bryan v UK*.[242] There the applicant challenged a planning decision against him that had been taken by a planning inspector who, the Court held, did not meet the requirement of objective independence in Article 6.[243] The Strasbourg Court held that the judicial review proceedings which the applicant was able to bring in the English High Court to challenge the decision were sufficient to satisfy Article 6 because, although the High Court could not re-hear the case on the facts,[244] it had jurisdiction to rule on errors of law, which was all that the applicant had wished to argue. However, the Court stated that, supposing the applicant had wanted to question the inspector's findings of fact, there would still have been no breach of Article 6 because when taking his decision the inspector had followed 'a quasi-judicial procedure governed by many of the safeguards required by Article 6(1)'.[245] In particular, the procedure the inspector

---

[237] *Tsfayo v UK* hudoc (2006); 48 EHRR 457 para 43, referring to *Bryan v UK* A 335-A (1995); 21 EHRR 342.

[238] *Bryan v UK*, para 45. [239] *Tsfayo v UK* hudoc (2006); 48 EHRR 177 para 46.

[240] *Kingsley v UK* 2002-IV; 35 EHRR 177 para 32 GC.

[241] In *Crompton v UK* hudoc (2009); 50 EHRR 905 para 77, the Court referred only to 'specialist knowledge'.

[242] A 335-A (1995); 21 EHRR 342 para 47. See also *Chapman v UK* 2001-I; 33 EHRR 399 GC; *Potocka v Poland* 2001-X; *Alatulkkila v Finland* hudoc (2005); 43 EHRR 737; *Jurisic and Collegium Mehrerau v Austria* hudoc (2006); and *Sambata Bihor Greco-Catholic Parish v Romania* No 48107/99 hudoc (2010) DA. For earlier cases in which the *Bryan* approach was taken, see *Zumtobel v Austria* A 268-A; 17 EHRR 116 and *ISKCON v UK* No 20490/92, 72-A DR 90 (1994).

[243] Lack of 'independence' has been the most common Article 6 deficiency in public bodies taking administrative decisions.

[244] The High Court could, as the Strasbourg Court noted, quash the decision only if the findings of fact were 'perverse or irrational'.

[245] *Bryan v UK* A 335-A (1995); 21 EHRR 342, para 47. Cf *Sigma Radio Television Ltd v Cyprus* hudoc (2011), para 162. See also *Holding and Barnes plc v UK* 2002-IV DA.

had followed was in accordance with the Article 6(1) residual obligation to ensure a 'fair hearing': the failure to comply with Article 6(1) was only that the inspector did not meet the requirement of objective independence. Such a procedure, which largely complied with Article 6(1), the Court noted, were 'frequently a feature in the systems of judicial control of administrative decisions found throughout the Council of Europe member states'.[246]

The Court's judgment in the *Bryan* case suggests that if the initial administrative decision in cases involving the 'classic exercise of administrative discretion' is not followed by a quasi-judicial procedure that sufficiently complies with Article 6—for example, in an extreme case, if it is taken by an official in his office without any hearing of the applicant—then Article 6 must require an appeal on the facts before a tribunal, if and to the extent that the applicant wishes to question the findings of fact.

This last comment goes to a separate, important point in the Court's jurisprudence that is confirmed in the *Bryan* case. Article 6 is complied with if the applicant who is challenging an administrative decision has an opportunity to have a ruling by a tribunal that complies with Article 6 on the arguments that he or she wishes to make.[247] If the applicant has this opportunity, as he had in the *Bryan* case, it does not matter that the tribunal lacks jurisdiction to consider other points of law or fact that some other applicant might wish to raise.

Article 6 also requires that the reviewing tribunal have competence to act to ensure a remedy is provided for the applicant if successful. This was crucial in *Kingsley v UK*.[248] In that case, the Gaming Board decided, after a hearing before a panel of three of its members, that the applicant was not a 'fit and proper' person to hold a management position in the gaming industry and revoked his certificate to do so. The applicant applied to the English High Court for judicial review of the decision, claiming that the panel had not been impartial. Although agreeing that the panel did not meet the requirement of objective impartiality, the High Court found itself unable to quash the Gaming Board's decision on this ground because of the English law 'doctrine of necessity', the Board having been expressly designated by legislation as the body with the authority to decide the matter. The Strasbourg Court held that there was a breach of the right of access in Article 6 because the concept of 'full jurisdiction' articulated in the *Albert and Le Compte* case meant that the reviewing court must not only be able to 'consider the complaint but has the ability to quash the impugned decision and to remit the case for a new decision', in this case by an impartial tribunal.[249]

A further question that arises is whether the judicial body to which recourse may be had should be competent to rule upon the proportionality of the decision. It has been established by the Court that the effective remedy concerning a violation of Convention rights required by Article 13 of the Convention must be one in which the individual may challenge the proportionality of the decision allegedly amounting to a violation of a Convention right.[250] There has been no case in which this question has been decided under Article 6 in respect of civil rights and obligations.[251] It seems likely and desirable,

---

[246] *Bryan v UK*, para 47.

[247] Cf *Oerlermans v Netherlands* A 219 (1991); 15 EHRR 561; *Zumtobel v Austria* A 268-A (1993); 17 EHRR 116; *X v UK No 28530/95* hudoc (1998); 25 EHRR CD 88; and *Sigma Radio Television Ltd v Cyprus* hudoc (2011). [248] 2002-IV; 35 EHRR 177 GC.

[249] *Kingsley v UK*, para 32. See also *Sigma Radio Television Ltd v Cyprus* hudoc (2011) para 167.

[250] *Smith and Grady v UK* 1999-VI; 29 EHRR 493.

[251] The point was raised in argument in *Air Canada v UK* A 316-A (1995); 20 EHRR 150 para 57. See also *Sigma Radio Television Ltd v Cyprus* hudoc (2011) para 167.

given the existing and developing position in European national law,[252] and the requirement of proportionality in the jurisprudence of the European Court of Justice,[253] that the
Strasbourg Court would require that a person be allowed to raise the question of proportionality in judicial review proceedings before an Article 6 tribunal.

With regard to decisions that fall within the second category of decisions identified by
the Court, *viz* decisions that do not involve 'the classic exercise of administrative discretion', more is demanded, in addition to the requirements already indicated. The supervisory judicial body must have 'full jurisdiction' or 'sufficiency of review' in the *Albert and
Le Compte* sense, ie full jurisdiction to rule on questions of fact as well as law. In *Tsfayo
v UK*,[254] a local authority had refused the applicant's claim for housing and council tax
benefits because she had failed to show 'good cause' why she had not applied for them
earlier. The authority's Review Board (composed of three councillors) rejected the applicant's appeal on the merits. Since the Board was not an 'independent' tribunal as required
by Article 6(1), there was need for recourse to a judicial body that provided 'full jurisdiction' or 'sufficiency of review'. An application to the High Court for judicial review was
unsuccessful as the Board's decision was neither perverse nor irrational, which was the
limit of the High Court's power of judicial review of the facts under English administrative law. The Strasbourg Court held that this power of review was insufficient. The Review
Board was deciding a 'simple question of fact'—*viz* whether there was 'good cause' for the
applicant's delay in applying for benefits. The question was whether it believed her explanation for the delay, which was a question of 'credibility' that did not require 'specialist
expertise' and could be decided by a non-specialist tribunal, such as the High Court. Thus
'the central issue' in the case, which also did not concern 'broader judgments of policy or
expediency', could not be determined 'by a tribunal that was independent of one of the
parties to the dispute'.[255]

The Court's interpretation of the requirements of Article 6 in respect of administrative
decisions largely resolves a problem that the Court had created for itself by its early ruling
in the *Ringeisen* case. At the same time, inventive though it is, it involves a very forced
reading of Article 6. The same text of Article 6 now has two different meanings according to the kind of case involved. This is in line with European national law and the end
result is to uphold the rule of law in cases of administrative action. It now remains for the
Court to complete the picture by extending further its interpretation of 'civil rights and
obligations' for the Convention to provide a full guarantee of administrative justice that
is appropriate to the present day.

f. The stages of proceedings covered by Article 6(1)

Article 6 normally begins to apply in cases involving the determination of a person's civil
rights and obligations when court proceedings are instituted.[256] But, just as in criminal
cases it may apply before the competent court is seized, so too in civil cases Article 6 may
begin to run before the writ is issued.[257] This has been held to be so in cases in which the

---

[252] See Schwarze, *European Administrative Law*, revised 1st edn, 2006, p 680. Proportionality has recently
'infiltrated British law': Wade and Forsyth, *Administrative Law*, 10th edn, 2009, p 305.

[253] See Craig and de Búrca, *EU Law: Text, Cases and Materials*, 5th edn, 2011, pp 526ff.

[254] Hudoc (2006); 48 EHRR 457 paras 42–8. For earlier cases within the second category to the same
effect, see *W v UK* A 121 (1987); 10 EHRR 293 PC; *Obermeier v Austria* A 179 (1990); 13 EHRR 290; *Fischer
v Austria* A 312 (1995); *Terra Wonigen v Netherlands* 1996-VI; 24 EHRR 456.

[255] Cf *Crompton v UK* hudoc (1989).

[256] See, eg, *Guincho v Portugal* A 81 (1984); 7 EHRR 223. As in criminal cases, the point at which Article 6
begins to apply in 'civil rights and obligation' cases is mostly relevant in 'trial within a reasonable time' cases.

[257] *Golder v UK* A 18 (1975); 1 EHRR 524 PC.

applicant must exhaust a preliminary administrative remedy under national law before having recourse to a court or tribunal[258] or cases in which the applicant objects to a draft plan for land consolidation prior to a tribunal hearing.[259] In the first situation, the Court emphasized that, since the applicant had to exhaust such a remedy, it was only fair to require that this occur expeditiously. In the second situation, the Court's reasoning was that a dispute or 'contestation' concerning civil rights and obligations arose when the objections to the draft plan were officially lodged, not later when the applicant instituted tribunal proceedings after being served with notice of the decision to take his or her land.

Article 6 applies not only to the proceedings in which liability is determined, but also to any separate court proceedings in which the amount of damages is assessed[260] or costs are allocated,[261] since these proceedings are a continuation of the substantive litigation. Article 6 also applies beyond the trial stage to appeal and judicial review proceedings concerning civil rights and obligations.[262] The reasonable time guarantee applies until the time for an appeal or application for judicial review by the parties expires and the judgment becomes final.[263]

Article 6 also applies to the execution of judgments in both civil and criminal cases;[264] in particular, the reasonable time guarantee will apply to any delays for which the state is responsible in their execution.[265] This has proved to be an important ruling, with a number of violations being found. The leading case is *Hornsby v Greece*,[266] in which the state authorities had for more than five years not taken the measures necessary to comply with a final judgment in the Greek courts entitling the applicants, who were UK nationals, to establish a private English school in Greece. The Court justified its extension of the 'right to a court' to the execution of judgments, which is not expressly mentioned in Article 6, on the basis that the 'right to a court' would be 'illusory' if a final judgment were allowed to remain inoperative to the detriment of one party and that 'to construe Article 6 as being concerned exclusively with access to a court and the conduct of proceedings would be likely to lead to situations incompatible with the principle of the rule of law which the Contracting States undertook to respect when they ratified the Convention'.

The cases have concerned such matters as the execution by the state of judgments requiring its authorities to pay compensation[267] or to provide public housing.[268] In *Okyay v Turkey*,[269] there was a breach of Article 6 where the administrative authorities failed to comply with court orders upheld by the Supreme Administrative Court for the closure of

---

[258] *König v Germany* A 27 (1978); 2 EHRR 170 PC. Cf *Schouten and Meldrum v Netherlands* A 304 (1994); 19 EHRR 432 para 62.

[259] *Erkner and Hofauer v Austria* A 117 (1987); 9 EHRR 464 para 64. Cf *Wiesinger v Austria* A 213 (1991); 16 EHRR 258.   [260] *Silva Pontes v Portugal* A 286-A (1994); 18 EHRR 156 para 33.

[261] *Robins v UK* 1997-V; 26 EHRR 527 and *Ziegler v Switzerland* hudoc (2002). Proceedings for the award of costs where the applicant had withdrawn her claim were held not to fall within Article 6 in *Alsterlund v Sweden* No 12446/86 56 DR 229 (1988).

[262] *König v Germany* A 27 (1978); 2 EHRR 170 para 98 PC. In *Pretto v Italy* A 71 (1983); 6 EHRR 182 para 30 PC the 'reasonable time' guarantee ran until the Court of Cassation judgment was deposited with the court registry, whereupon it became public.

[263] *Pugliese v Italy (No 2)* A 206-A (1991); para 16. See also *Lorenzi, Bernardini, and Gritti v Italy* A 231-G (1992).

[264] Although, nearly all execution cases concern 'civil rights and obligations', the execution of judgments in criminal cases is also within *Hornsby*: see *Assanidze v Georgia* 2004-II; 39 EHRR 653.

[265] *Hornsby v Greece* 1997-II; 24 EHRR 250 para 40. The *Hornsby* case only applies to final judgments; any appeal possibilities must be exhausted first: *Ouzounis v Greece* hudoc (2002). Article 6 applies to a request for a stay of execution: *Central Mediterranean Development Corp v Malta (No 2)* hudoc (2011).

[266] *Hornsby v Greece*, para 40.   [267] *Burdov v Russia* 2002-III; 38 EHRR 644.

[268] *Teteriny v Russia* hudoc (2005).   [269] 2005-VII; 43 EHRR 788 para 73.

state power plants, which were causing pollution. A Turkish Council of Ministers' decision that the plants should continue to operate despite the court orders was stated by the Strasbourg Court in a strongly worded judgment to be 'obviously unlawful under domestic law', resulting in a situation that 'adversely affects the principle of a law-based state, founded on the rule of law and the principle of legal certainty'.

Under the *Hornsby* case, the state must also ensure the execution of judgments against third parties who are not state actors, so that, for example, the state must take action to ensure that private persons comply with judgments against them[270] for the payment of compensation,[271] the payment of divorce maintenance,[272] the transfer of custody of an adopted child,[273] the eviction of tenants,[274] and the demolition of houses built without planning permission.[275] Police assistance must be provided for court bailiffs where this is needed.[276] In *Turczanik v Poland*,[277] the state was required to ensure that a bar association allocated a barrister to chambers as required by a court judgment. No particular procedure for execution is required; the Court looks only to see that the procedure followed by the state is adequate and effective.[278] Adopting an appropriately strict approach, the Court has held that lack of available state funds[279] or other resources[280] is not a good reason for the state's failure to execute a judgment against it. But a delay in the execution of a judgment may be justified 'in particular circumstances', provided that the delay does not 'impair the essence of the right protected under Article 6'.[281] The onus is on the state to act and to justify any delay.[282] Delays in the payment of a monetary award against the state of one year or more have been found to be excessive.[283] In *Jasiūnienė v Lithuania*,[284] the government's obstructive attitude led to the Court to characterize the non-execution as an 'aggravated' breach of Article 6(1). In *Burdov (No 2) v Russia*,[285] the Strasbourg Court held that the respondent government's failure to satisfy judgment debts for several years after the Court's first judgment in the case in 2002[286] reflected a 'persistent structural dysfunction'. Noting there were over 700 similar cases pending before it, the Court, following its pilot judgment procedure, required the respondent state to adopt measures to afford adequate and sufficient redress to victims of non-payment in these cases within one year of its 2009 judgment.

---

[270] *Hornsby* exends to the enforcement of foreign judgments: *Saccoccia v Austria* hudoc (2008)

[271] *Satka and Others v Greece* hudoc (2003); 38 EHRR 579. [272] *Romańczyk v France* hudoc (2010).

[273] *Pini v Romania* 2004-V; 40 EHRR 312.

[274] *Immobiliare Saffi v Italy* 1999-V; 30 EHRR 756 GC and *Kyrtatos v Greece* 2003-IV; 40 EHRR 390. See also *Popov v Moldova (No 1)* hudoc (2005) (return of house to pre-Soviet owners).

[275] *Antonetto v Italy* hudoc (2000); 36 EHRR 120.

[276] *Immobiliare Saffi v Italy* 1999-V; 30 EHRR 756 GC. Cf *Matheus v France* hudoc (2005).

[277] 2005-VI; 52 EHRR 432. [278] *Fociac v Romania* hudoc (2005).

[279] *Burdov v Russia* 2002-III; 38 EHRR 639. The failure to execute a judgment debt may be a breach of the right to property in Article 1, Protocol 1 also: *Burdov v Russia*. A requirement that a litigant pay the cost of enforcement violated the right of access to a court: *Apostol v Georgia* 2006-XIV.

[280] For example, public housing: *Shpakovskiy v Russia* hudoc (2005).

[281] *Burdov v Russia* 2002-III; 38 EHRR 639 para 35. The conduct of the parties may excuse some delay: *Jasiūnienė v Lithuania* hudoc (2003). Failure to provide the applicant with a flat when its construction had been delayed through no fault of the state was not a violation: *Volnyth v Russia* hudoc (2009).

[282] *Dubenko v Ukraine* hudoc (2005). The state's obligation to execute a judgment expeditiously increases with the applicant's need: *Dubenko v Ukraine* (money to avoid bankruptcy) and *Shmalko v Ukraine* hudoc (2004) (payment for medication).

[283] *Yuriy Nikolayevich Ivanov v Ukraine* hudoc (2009). Judgments requiring compensation as redress for earlier court delays should be executed within six months: *Cocchiarella v Italy* 2006-V GC.

[284] Hudoc (2003) para 30.

[285] 2009- para 134. Cf *Yuriv Nikolatevich Ivanov v Ukraine* hudoc (2009) (similar pilot judgment).

[286] *Burdov v Russia* 2002-III; 38 EHRR 639.

As well as the execution of final judgments, Article 6 may also apply to some preliminary proceedings. In *Micallef v Malta*,[287] reversing earlier case law, the Court held that Article 6 applies to requests for interim measures, such as injunctions, where the 'measure can be considered effectively to determine the civil right or obligation at stake, notwithstanding the length of time it is in force'. However, the Court accepted that 'in exceptional cases—where, for example, the effectiveness of the measure sought depends upon a rapid decision-making process—it may not be possible immediately to comply with all of the requirements of Article 6'. While the independence and impartiality of the tribunal was 'an indispensable and inalienable safeguard' which must always apply, 'other procedural safeguards may apply only to the extent compatible with the nature and purpose of the interim proceedings at issue'.[288] The ruling in the *Micallef* case is to be welcomed as being in accordance with a right of effective access to a court and a purposive, human rights reading of the Convention. Earlier Court rulings concerning preliminary proceedings that do not effectively determine a civil right or obligation, such as a challenge to the composition of a court,[289] would seem to remain intact. The reasonable time guarantee in Article 6 applies to interim measures proceedings within the *Micallef* case. The question whether the reasonable time guarantee applies to a pre-trial application for legal aid in respect of litigation concerning a 'civil' right or obligation was left open in *H v France*.[290]

3. ARTICLE 6(1): GUARANTEES IN CRIMINAL AND NON-CRIMINAL CASES

I. THE RIGHT OF ACCESS TO A COURT

a. The *Golder* case

One of the most creative steps taken by the European Court in its interpretation of any article of the Convention has been its ruling in *Golder v UK*[291] that Article 6(1) guarantees the right of access to a court. In that case, a convicted prisoner was refused permission by the Home Secretary to write to a solicitor with a view to instituting civil proceedings in libel against a prison officer. The Court held that the refusal raised an issue under Article 6(1) because that provision concerned not only the conduct of proceedings in court once they had been instituted, but also the right to institute them in the first place. Although there was no express mention of the right of access in Article 6, its protection could be inferred from the text.[292] It was also a key feature of the concept of the 'rule of law', which, as the preamble to the Convention stated, was a part of the 'common heritage' of Council

---

[287] 2009-; 50 EHRR 920 GC para 85. Cf *Mercieca and Others v Malta* hudoc (2011) and *RTBF v Belgium* 2011. The Court had earlier moved in this direction in *Markass Car Hire v Cyprus No 51591/99* hudoc (2001) DA.
[288] *Micallef v Malta*, para 86. It would be for the respondent state to show that a safeguard could be dispensed with: para 86.
[289] *Schreiber and Boetsch v France No 58751/00*, 2003-XII DA. Applications for leave to appeal (*Porter v UK No 12972/87*, 54 DR 207 (1987)) or to re-open a case (*Rudan v Croatia No 45943/99* hudoc (2001) DA) remain excluded. But Article 6 does apply to the re-opened proceedings: *Kaisti v Finland No 70313/01* hudoc (2004) DA.
[290] A 162-A (1989); 12 EHRR 74 para 49. See further *Gutfreund v France* 2003-VII; 42 EHRR 1076 paras 38–44.   [291] A 18 (1975); 1 EHRR 524 PC.
[292] The wording '*à ce que sa cause soit entendue*' in the French text provided the clearest textual indication.

of Europe states. Moreover, any other interpretation would contradict a universally recognized principle of law and would allow a state to close its courts without infringing the Convention.[293] Despite cogent arguments to the contrary by the dissenting judges,[294] the Court's judgment has long been unquestioned and provides a secure foundation for the full guarantee of the 'right to a court'.[295] The right of access applies to such appeal proceedings as exist, as well as to proceedings at first instance.[296]

The right was established and retains most of its significance in connection with the determination of 'civil rights and obligations'. Cases may concern private litigation, as in the *Golder* case, or claims against the state, including claims arising out of administrative decisions.[297] If the law compels the parties to a civil dispute to go to arbitration instead of the courts, the arbitration tribunal must comply with Article 6.[298]

But the right of access also applies to criminal cases, where it means that the accused is entitled to be tried on the charge against him in a court.[299] The right of access does not include the right to bring a private criminal prosecution, since Article 6 is concerned only with a criminal charge against an accused.

The right of access means access in fact, as well as in law. It was for this reason that there was a breach of Article 6(1) in the *Golder* case.[300] Whereas the applicant was able in law to institute libel proceedings in the High Court, the refusal to let him contact a solicitor impeded his access to the courts in fact. It did not matter that, strictly speaking, the applicant's complaint was of an interference with his right of access to a solicitor, not the courts;[301] that he might have made contact with his solicitor other than by correspondence; that after doing so he might never have instituted court proceedings at all; or that the applicant would have been able to have written to his solicitor before his claim became statute-barred after his release from prison. A partial or temporary hindrance may thus be a breach of the right of access to a court.

b. A right of effective access

As the ruling in the *Golder* case also indicates, the right is a right of effective access to the courts. This may entail legal assistance, as was established in *Airey v Ireland*.[302] In that

---

[293] See *Khamidov v Russia* 2007-XX;49 EHRR 284 (Chechen courts closed for fifteen months in the emergency).

[294] See the separate opinions of Judges Verdross, Fitzmaurice, and Zekia. The last two of these judges noted, *inter alia*, that in at least some other instruments in which it had been intended to include the right of access, a separate provision had been inserted in addition to the equivalent of Article 6.

[295] By this term is meant the right of access to a court and the guarantees in Article 6 once proceedings are instituted: *Golder v UK* A 18 (1975); 1 EHRR 524 para 36 PC.

[296] See, eg, *Sialkowska v Poland* hudoc (2007); 51 EHRR 473.

[297] See, eg, *Sporrong and Lönnroth v Sweden* A 52 (1982); 5 EHRR 35 PC (no appeal to a court against expropriation permit). A decree that has general application but that is decisive for particular persons' civil rights and obligations must be subject to challenge by them: *Posti and Rahko v Finland* 2002-VII; 37 EHRR 158.

[298] *Bramelid and Malstrom v Sweden* Nos 8588/79 and 8589/79, 38 DR 18 (1983). Cf *Scarth v UK* hudoc (1999); 27 EHRR CD 37. See also *Suda v Czech Republic* hudoc (2010). Article 6 does not apply in the case of voluntary arbitration where the parties choose to go outside the courts.

[299] *Deweer v Belgium* A 35 (1980); 2 EHRR 439. See also *Anagnostopoulos v Greece* hudoc (2003).

[300] Similar breaches of the right of access have been found in other UK prisoner cases involving restrictions on contact with solicitors: see, eg, *Silver v UK* A 61 (1983); 5 EHRR 347. See also *Grace v UK No 11523/85*, 62 DR 22 (1988); Com Rep; CM Res DH (89) 21. The 'prior ventilation rule', by which prisoners were required to exhaust prison complaints procedures before resorting to the courts, also infringed it: *Campbell and Fell v UK* A 80 (1984); 7 EHRR 165.

[301] As the Court noted, the applicant could institute court proceedings without recourse to a solicitor.

[302] A 32 (1979); 2 EHRR 305. See Thornberry, 29 ICLQ 250 (1980).

case, a wife who was indigent was refused legal aid to bring proceedings in the Irish High Court for an order of judicial separation. Given the particular nature of the proceedings,[303] the Court held that, for the applicant's access to the court to be effective, she required legal representation, which for an indigent person meant free legal representation.[304] The Court rejected the respondent government's argument that the right of access to a court does not impose positive obligations upon states, particularly ones with considerable economic consequences, such as that to provide free legal aid.[305]

The *Airey* case has been applied in a number of cases in which civil legal aid has been claimed as a part of the right of access in Article 6(1). In the *Airey* case, the Court stressed that it was not deciding that the right of access provided a full right to legal aid in civil litigation comparable to that specifically provided by Article 6(3)(c) in criminal cases, which extends to all cases in which 'the interests of justice so require'. Instead, 'Article 6(1) may sometimes compel the state to provide for the assistance of a lawyer when such assistance proves indispensable for an effective access to court'.[306] This will be certainly be the case where legal representation is required by national law.[307] In other situations, the need for legal assistance must, as stated in *Steel and Morris v UK*,[308] be determined by reference to the facts of each case and 'will depend *inter alia* upon the importance of what is at stake for the applicant in the proceedings, the complexity of the relevant law and procedure and the applicant's capacity to represent him or herself effectively'. Legal aid will not be required where there is no arguable case on the facts.[309] Nor does the right of access require the provision of legal aid where the claim by the applicant involves an abuse of the law[310] or of the legal aid system.[311] Legal aid for legal persons in civil cases would not appear to be required.[312]

In *Steel and Morris*, McDonald's, the fast food chain, successfully brought an action for defamation against the two applicants for criticism of McDonald's on environmental and social grounds in a leaflet that was part of a London Greenpeace campaign, and was awarded a total of £76,000 damages against them personally. The Court upheld the applicants' claim that the United Kingdom had infringed Article 6(1) by refusing legal aid to the applicants, who were indigent. First, there was a lot 'at stake' financially for the applicants, who were of very modest means, with McDonald's claiming £100,000 damages. Second, the facts and the law in the case were complicated, with voluminous documentation and over 300 days of court hearings, some 100 of which were on legal argument. Third, although the applicants, who represented themselves, were articulate and resourceful and had some *pro bono* help from lawyers, the 'disparity between the

---

[303] The Court emphasized the complexity of the proceedings, the need to examine expert witnesses, and the emotional involvement of the parties. Cf *P, C and S v UK* 2002-VI; 35 EHRR 1075 (child care and adoption proceedings; legal aid required). Contrast *Webb v UK No 9353/81*, 33 DR 133 (1983).

[304] Ireland had made a reservation concerning criminal legal aid, which is expressly provided for in Article 6(3)(c). It did not anticipate the *Airey* judgment.

[305] But it was recognized in *P, C and S v UK* 2002-VI; 35 EHRR 1075 para 90, that 'limited public funds' may require 'a procedure of selection'.   [306] *Airey v Ireland* A 32 (1979); 2 EHRR 305 para 26.

[307] *Airey v Ireland*. Cf *Aerts v Belgium* 1998-V; 29 EHRR 50 and *Staroszczyk v Poland* hudoc (2007); 50 EHRR 114; and *Tabor v Poland* hudoc (2006).

[308] 2005-II; 41 EHRR 403 para 61. In *Faulkner v UK* hudoc (1999) F Sett before the Court, Guernsey agreed to establish for the first time a civil legal aid system after the applicant was denied legal aid to bring proceedings for false imprisonment, etc.

[309] *Gnahore v France* 2000-IX; 34 EHRR 967. See also *Del Sol v France* 2002-II; 35 EHRR 1281 and *Stewart-Brady v UK Nos 27436/95 and 28406/95*, 90-A DR 45 (1997).

[310] *W v Germany No 11564/85*, 45 DR 291 (1985).

[311] *Sujeeun v UK No 27788/95* hudoc (1996) DA.

[312] *Granos Organicos Nationales SA v Germany* hudoc (2012).

respective levels of legal assistance enjoyed by the applicants and McDonald's . . . could not have failed, in this exceptionally demanding case, to have given rise to unfairness'.[313] The *Steel and Morris* case marks a departure from a series of earlier defamation cases, mostly brought by plaintiffs, not defendants, in which the Commission or the Court found that legal aid was not required.[314] Key to the decision in the *Steel and Morris* case were the particularly strong and sympathetic facts.

Where the right of access does require legal assistance to ensure a fair hearing, Article 6 leaves states 'a free choice of the means' to be used towards this end: 'a legal aid scheme' is only one possibility.[315] Thus an *ex gratia* offer of legal aid in the particular case may be sufficient,[316] or proceedings may be simplified to avoid the need for legal assistance at all.[317] In *A v UK*,[318] the Court held that the availability of two hours' free legal advice under the 'green form' scheme together with the possibility thereafter of engaging a solicitor on a conditional fee basis was sufficient to provide the applicant with effective access to a court in her defamation claim. Where the applicant qualifies for the assistance of a lawyer under the national system, the state has an obligation to appoint a legal aid lawyer who will actually take up the case. Thus in *Bertuzzi v France*,[319] the applicant was denied 'effective access' to a court where another legal aid lawyer was not appointed after three lawyers had refused to act because of their personal links with the lawyer whom the applicant was suing.

Apart from the position of indigent litigants, the high cost of civil proceedings may be such as to infringe the right to effective access to the courts for litigants paying for their own lawyers and for court costs; the amount of the charges by the state for taking a case to court must be related to the particular circumstances, including the applicant's ability to pay.[320]

The need for access to the courts to be effective has also been in issue in a variety of contexts other than legal assistance. Thus the right of access is infringed not only when the applicant is not allowed to commence proceedings, but also when proceedings are stayed by the state for an unduly long period of time. In such cases, the right of access to a court and the right to trial within a reasonable time may both apply.[321] In *Kutic v Croatia*,[322] a civil claim for damage to property was stayed by statute pending the enactment of legislation governing claims for damage resulting from terrorist acts. It was held that the right of effective access had been infringed because six years had passed without any legislation being enacted.[323] In a case of quite a different kind there was a violation of the right of effective access when the plaintiffs were not permitted to register their claims electronically when the documents presenting the claim amounted to 40 million pages and concerned many thousands of persons.[324] In other cases there has been a violation where a court has, without giving reasons or explanations, simply refused to receive a litigant's pleadings[325] or declined to hear the case as being improperly submitted.[326] A requirement

---

[313] *Steel and Morris v UK* 2005-II; 41 EHRR 403, para 69.

[314] See *McVicar v UK* 2002-III; 35 EHRR 566; *Munro v UK No 10594/83*, 52 DR 158 (1987); and *Winer v UK No 10871/84*, 48 DR 154 (1986).   [315] *A v UK* 2002-X; 36 EHRR 917 para 98.

[316] *Andronicou and Constantinou v Cyprus* 1997-VI; 25 EHRR 491.

[317] *Airey v Ireland* A 32 (1979); 2 EHRR 305 para 26.   [318] 2002-X; 36 EHRR 917.

[319] 2003-III para 32. See also *AB v Slovakia* hudoc (2003) and *Renda Martins v Portugal No 50085/99* hudoc (2002) DA (refusal for lack of cooperation permissible).

[320] *Weissman v Roumania* 2006-VII and *Kreuz v Poland (No 1)* 2001-VI. See also *Urbanek v Austria* hudoc (2010).

[321] See, eg, *Kristiansen and Tyvik AS v Norway* hudoc (2013) (case decided under right of access).

[322] 2002-II. Cf *Aćimović v Croatia* 2003-XI; 39 EHRR 555.

[323] See also *Ganci v Italy* 2003-XII; 41 EHRR 272 and *Musumeci v Italy* hudoc (2005).

[324] *Lawyer Partners AS v Slovakia* 2009-.   [325] *Dunayev v Russia* hudoc (2007).

[326] *Blumberga v Latvia* hudoc (2008).

that a litigant provide a residential address violated the right of access of an applicant who lacked any such address but who could provide an address for correspondence.[327] Finally, there was a breach of the right of access when the Albanian Constitutional Court was unable to reach agreement on a decision on the applicant's appeal, thereby depriving him of a final decision in his case.[328]

The right of effective access also supposes that there is a 'coherent system' governing recourse to the courts that is sufficiently certain in its requirements for litigants to have 'a clear, practical and effective opportunity' to go to court.[329] A number of cases in which uncertainty in the law or its application or procedures has led litigants to act in a way that has prejudiced their access to a court have been decided in their favour on this basis.[330] The right of access also requires that the state take reasonable steps to serve documents on the parties to proceedings and to inform them of the dates of hearings, and of decisions.[331]

Inconsistency in the interpretation of the law by different courts within a judicial system may also be in breach of the right of access to a court. While acknowledging that 'the possibility of conflicting court decisions is an inherent trait of any judicial system' and an acceptable feature of the development of the law, the Strasbourg Court has held that states have a responsibility to put in place effective systems of judicial appeal or other methods to resolve such inconsistencies.[332]

c. Restrictions upon the right of access

The right is not an absolute one. Restrictions may be imposed since the right of access 'by its very nature calls for regulation by the state, regulation which may vary in time and place according to the needs and resources of the community and of individuals'.[333] As indicated in *Ashingdane v UK*,[334] in imposing restrictions, the state is allowed a certain 'margin of appreciation' but any restriction must not be such that 'the very essence of the right is impaired'. In addition, a restriction must have a 'legitimate aim' and comply with the principle of proportionality, ie there must be 'a reasonable relationship of proportionality between the means employed and the aim sought to be achieved'.[335] In the *Ashingdane* case, the applicant instituted civil proceedings challenging the Secretary of State's decision under the Mental Health Act 1959, in effect to continue to detain him in a secure mental hospital. However, there was no liability under the Act for acts done under it in the absence of bad

---

[327] *Sergey Smirnov v Russia* hudoc (2009).

[328] *Marini v Albania* 2007-XX. See also *Dubinskaya v Russia* hudoc (2006) (case 'lost').

[329] *De Geouffre de la Pradelle v France* A 253-B (1992) para 34 (appeal out of time because of uncertainty as to the applicable procedure). See also *Davran v Turkey* hudoc (2009) and *Stegarescu and Bahrin v Portugal* hudoc (2010).

[330] See, eg, *FE v France* 1998-VIII; 29 EHRR 591 para 40. Cf *Bellet v France* A 333-B (1995). See also *Beneficio Cappella Paolini v San Marino* 2004-VIII (uncertainty as to competent court); *Levages Prestations Services v France* 1996-V; 24 EHRR 351 (alleged uncertainty as to required documents: no breach); *Serghides and Christoforou v Cyprus* hudoc (2002); 37 EHRR 873 (applicant not told of land expropriation, so could not meet time limit). Some time limit and other cases of procedural uncertainty are decided on a 'disproportionate restriction' basis instead.

[331] See *Sukhorubchenko v Russia* hudoc (2005); *Assunção Chavez v Portugal* hudoc 2012; and *Kulikowski v Poland* hudoc (2009). See also *Hennings v Germany* A 251-A (1992); 16 EHRR 83.

[332] *Nejdet Şahin and Perihan Şahin v Turkey* hudoc (2011); 54 EHRR 747 para 51 GC. See also *Vinčić v Serbia* hudoc (2009); *Iordan Iordanov and Others v Bulgaria* hudoc (2009); and *Ştefănică and Others v Romania* hudoc (2010).

[333] *Golder v UK* A 18 (1975); 1 EHRR 524 para 38 PC.

[334] A 93 (1985); 7 EHRR 528 para 57. Cf *Stanev v Bulgaria* 2012- GC para 230. The 'very essence' requirement overlaps with the 'effective' right requirement: see *De Geouffre de la Pradelle v France* A 253-B (1992), mentioned earlier, where the Court used both terms.

[335] *Ashingdane v UK*, para 57. Cf *Lithgow v UK* A 102 (1986); 8 EHRR 329 para 194 PC.

faith or reasonable care. Moreover, a claim in respect of such an act could not be brought unless the High Court gave leave, which it could do only if it were satisfied that there were 'substantial grounds' for believing that these conditions were met. The Court held that these limitations on the right of access to a court were not in breach of the right. The limitation of liability under the Act had the 'legitimate aim' of preventing those caring for mental patients from being unfairly harassed by litigation and the availability of a claim only in a case of bad faith or lack of reasonable care both left intact the essence of the right to institute proceedings and was consistent with the principle of proportionality.

In accordance with the *Ashingdane* approach, restrictions upon access to the courts by *certain categories of persons* have been allowed or countenanced in principle if they are proportionate.[336] Restrictions upon access to court by mentally incapacitated persons may be imposed, but in *Stanev v Bulgaria*,[337] the Grand Chamber noted that there was 'a trend at European level' to allow them direct access in proceedings for the restoration of their legal capacity. However, in *RP and Others v UK*,[338] it was held that representation of the applicant, who had learning disabilities, by the Official Solicitor in child care proceedings complied with Article 6, given that the applicant could challenge the decision to appoint him.

The limitation of the right to bring proceedings to particular interested parties, to the exclusion of others, may be a breach of the right of access. Thus a law that barred certain Greek monasteries from bringing legal proceedings in respect of their property, giving the right to the Greek Church instead, was a breach of the monasteries' right of access, depriving them of the 'very essence' of the right.[339] A *fortiori*, a judicial decision by which a church was deprived of its legal personality, which prevented it from bringing any civil proceedings, was a breach.[340] In a different context, restrictions imposed on a managing director or shareholders who seek to question the liquidation or winding up of a company were held to be disproportionate on the facts.[341] Likewise, a residential or other requirement imposed on a foreign company wishing to go to court may be such as to deprive it unjustifiably of the essence of the right.[342]

Restrictions on the bringing of claims by *all litigants*[343] are acceptable if proportionate. Thus requirements that an appeal be lodged by a lawyer[344] or that a litigant pay security for costs, provided that the amount is not disproportionate,[345] are permissible, as is a fine

---

[336] See *Golder v UK* A 18 (1975); 1 EHRR 524 (prisoners, minors) PC; *Luordo v Italy* 2003-IX; 41 EHRR 547 (bankrupts); *H v UK No 11559/85*, 45 DR 281 (1985) (vexatious litigants); *Carnduff v UK No 18905/02* hudoc (2004) DA (police informers).

[337] 2012- ; 55 EHRR 696 para 243 GC. Cf *Shtukaturov v Russia* 2008-; 54 EHRR 962; *DD v Lithuania* hudoc (2012); and *Nataliya Mikhaylenko v Ukraine* hudoc (2013). See also *X and Y v Croatia* hudoc (2011).

[338] Hudoc (2012).

[339] *Holy Monasteries v Greece* A 301-A (1994); 20 EHRR 1 para 83. See also *Sâmbata Bihor Greek Catholic Parish v Romania* hudoc (2010); *Philis v Greece* A 209 (1991); 13 EHRR 741; and *Związek Nauczycielstwa Polskiego v Poland* 2004-IX; 38 EHRR 122.

[340] *Canea Catholic Church v Greece* 1997-VIII; 27 EHRR 521.

[341] *Arma v France* hudoc (2007) and *Kohlhofer and Minarik v Czech Republic* hudoc (2009).

[342] *Ligue du monde islamique et al v France* hudoc (2009).

[343] *Stedman v UK No 29107/95*, 89-A DR 104 (1997); 23 EHRR CD 168 (two years' employment for unfair dismissal claims). See also *Clunis v UK No 45149/98* hudoc (2001) DA (*ex turpi causa* limitation).

[344] *Gillow v UK* A 109 (1986); 11 EHRR 335. A requirement that a litigant pay damages awarded at first instance before appealing is acceptable unless his or her means do not allow this: *Annoni di Gussola v France* 2000-XI. Cf *Schneider v France No 49852/06* hudoc (2009) DA.

[345] *Tolstoy Miloslavsky v UK* A 316-B (1995); 20 EHRR 442; *Ait-Mouhoub v France* 1998-VI; 1999 EHRLR 215; and *Grepne v UK No 17070/90*, 66 DR 268 (1990). See also *Podbielski and PPU Polpure v Poland* hudoc (2005) (appeal fee) and *Weissman v Romania* 2006-VII (stamp duty).

for an abusive appeal.[346] Restrictions on the level of damages available in civil claims are also permissible.[347]

In other lack of access cases, there was a breach of the right of access when the refusal of the applicant's request to have his fixed penalty speeding fine referred to a court was based upon an error of law.[348] And, in an unusual case, the applicant was held to have been deprived of the 'very essence' of his right of access when a court declined, without giving any plausible reasons, to hear his claim on the ground that it should be heard in the courts of another country.[349]

The right of access also requires that procedural requirements governing recourse to the courts that are open to more than one interpretation should not be given a 'particularly strict' interpretation[350] or application,[351] so as to prevent litigants making use of an available remedy. Most cases have concerned time limits for the bringing of first instance or appeal proceedings;[352] others have concerned factual or clerical errors by a litigant.[353] A time limit which the applicant could not reasonably have been expected to meet will be a breach of the right of access,[354] but clear and avoidable errors by a litigant will not.[355] Time limits in themselves are permissible if they meet the requirement of proportionality, with a margin of appreciation being justified because of the variation in practice in European states. In *Stubbings v UK*,[356] a time limit for civil claims of childhood sexual abuse of six years from attaining the age of eighteen was proportionate.

Positive state action in the form of legislation with retroactive application that is designed to defeat a litigant's claim in the courts is also in breach of the right of access, unless it can be justified as a proportionate limitation on 'compelling' public interest grounds.[357] Most such cases have, however, been treated as involving a breach of the 'principle of the rule of law and the notion of a fair trial enshrined in Article 6', rather than as a breach of the right of access. The overturning of a court judgment that is *res judicata* has sometimes been considered as infringing the right of access,[358] but has generally been regarded as being contrary to the right to a 'fair hearing' instead. In contrast, failure to execute a court judgment is a breach of Article 6 that is unequivocally based on the right of access.

---

[346] *Les Travaux du Midi v France No 12275/86*, 70 DR 47 (1991) and *Toyaksi and Others v Turkey Nos 435699/08 et al* hudoc (2010) DA.

[347] *Manners v UK No 37650/97* hudoc (1998); 26 EHRR CD 200 (Warsaw Convention limit).

[348] *Peltier v France* hudoc (2002); 37 EHRR 197. See also *Mortier v France* hudoc (2001); 35 EHRR 163 and *Liakopoulou v Greece* hudoc (2006).   [349] *Zylkov v Russia* hudoc (2011).

[350] *Bĕlĕs and Others v Czech Republic* 2002-X para 51.

[351] *Perez de Rada Cavanilles v Spain* 1998-VIII; 29 EHRR 109 para 49. See also *Yagtzilar and Others v Greece* hudoc 2001-XII.

[352] See, eg, *Miragall Escolano and Others v Spain* 2000-I; 34 EHRR 658; *Tricard v France* hudoc (2001); 37 EHRR 388; *Zemanová v Czech Republic* hudoc (2005); and *Mikulová v Slovakia* hudoc (2005).

[353] See, eg, *Kadlec and Others v Czech Republic* hudoc (2004); *Société Anonyme 'Sotiris et Nikos Koutras ATTEE' v Greece* 2000-XII; 36 EHRR 410; and *Saez Maeso v Spain* hudoc (2004). Clerical errors by the state must not disadvantage the applicant: *Platakou v Greece* 2001-I.

[354] *Neshev v Bulgaria* hudoc (2004) and *Tsironis v Greece* hudoc (2001); 37 EHRR 183. See also *Cañete de Goñi v Spain* 2002-VIII and *AEPI SA v Greece* hudoc (2002).

[355] *Edificaciones March Gallego SA v Spain* 1998-I; 33 EHRR 1105.

[356] 1996-IV; 23 EHRR 213. See also *Dobbie v UK No 28477/95* hudoc (1996) DA; and *Mizzi v Malta* 2006-I; 46 EHRR 529.

[357] *National and Provincial Building Society et al v UK* 1997-VII; 25 EHRR 127 para 112 (retroactive legislation to fill a tax loophole justified in the public interest). Procedural changes do not infringe the right of access as there is a 'generally recognized principle' that they apply to pending cases: *Brualla Gómez de la Torre v Spain* 1997-VIII; 33 EHRR 1341.

[358] See, eg, *Ryabykh v Russia* 2003-XI; 40 EHRR 615.

A procedural bar to the successful bringing of a claim that takes the form of a defence that may be pleaded by the defendant is another kind of restriction upon the right of access to a court—one that has given rise to some important rulings. Whether the defence is consistent with the right of access turns upon whether it meets the *Ashingdane* requirements indicated earlier. This approach was first adopted by the Court in *Fayed v UK*, as noted earlier, concerning an immunity defence in defamation proceedings.[359]

The same approach has been used to justify parliamentary and state immunity. As to parliamentary immunity, in *A v UK*,[360] it was held that absolute immunity for Westminster Members of Parliament from liability in defamation for their statements in proceedings in Parliament was not a breach of Article 6. It had the legitimate aims of securing the freedom of speech of MPs on matters of public interest—which is a matter of great importance in a democracy—and of maintaining the separation of powers of the legislature and the judiciary. Although absolute and extending to both civil and criminal proceedings, the immunity did not exceed the margin of appreciation: it could be justified as a proportionate restriction on the right of access to a court in order to achieve these aims, particularly as it extended only to statements *in* Parliament. Also relevant was the fact the immunity was 'consistent with and reflects generally recognised rules within signatory states, the Council of Europe and Members of the European Parliament'.[361] An immunity that extends to statements made by parliamentarians *outside* of Parliament is given closer scrutiny.[362] Similarly, the grant of parliamentary immunity in a dispute over child custody was a violation, as it had no relation to parliamentary activity.[363]

As to state immunity, the immunity of states from civil liability in the courts of other states that is granted in accordance with international law has been held to be a proportionate restriction on the right of access to a court, with the legitimate aim of promoting comity and good relations among states. Thus immunity from civil process in a tort claim for personal injury against a foreign state and one of its soldiers,[364] a claim against the German government for payment for forced labour during World War II,[365] and a claim, in *Fogarty v UK*,[366] concerning the recruitment of a local national for employment as a secretary in a foreign diplomatic mission were not in breach of the right of access.[367] In *Cudak v Lithuania*,[368] the *Fogarty* case was distinguished because the *Cudak* case concerned the dismissal, not the recruitment, of a local national embassy switchboard operator, and international law no longer allowed immunity from civil suit in cases of

---

[359] See also *Taylor v UK No 49589/99* hudoc (2003); 38 EHRR CD 25 DA; and *Mond v UK No 49606/99* hudoc (2003) DA.

[360] 2002-X; 36 EHRR 917. See also *Young v Ireland* hudoc (1996); 84 DR 122 (1996). Cf *Esposito v Italy* 1997-IV.

[361] *A v UK*, para 83. The Court also noted that there was an alternative contempt of parliament remedy, but this was not crucial to its decision: see *Zollmann v UK No 62902/00* hudoc (2003) DA.

[362] *Cordova v Italy (No 2)* 2003-I (senator's statement at election meeting). See also *Cordova v Italy (No 1)* 2003-I; *De Jorio v Italy* hudoc (2004); 40 EHRR 961; *CGIL and Cofferati v Italy* hudoc (2009).

[363] *Syngelidis v Greece* hudoc (2010).

[364] *McElhinney v Ireland* 2001-XI; 34 EHRR 322 GC (Irish policeman injured by British soldier in border incident). Judges Rozakis, Caflisch, Cabral Barreto, Vajic, and Loucaides dissented on the ground that international law no longer imposed a duty on states to grant immunity in tort cases. See also *Kalogeropoulou and Others v Greece and Germany* 2002-X DA. State immunity—again based on international law—extends to the *execution* of judgments against state property: *Manoilescu and Dobrescu v Romania and Russia* 2005-VI DA.

[365] *Grosz v France No 14717/06* hudoc (2009) DA.   [366] 2001-XI; 34 EHRR 302 GC.

[367] See also *Wallishauser v Austria* hudoc (2012) (state immunity rule on the service of documents).

[368] 2010-; 51 EHRR 418 GC.

dismissal.[369] Immunity from civil proceedings for international organizations, in accordance with international law, may also be permissible.[370]

In the controversial case of *Al-Adsani v UK*,[371] state immunity from civil liability in tort for acts amounting to torture was also held to be proportionate. In that case the applicant brought a claim in tort against the government of Kuwait in the English courts in respect of torture allegedly committed in Kuwait by government agents. However, the respondent state successfully pleaded state immunity, this being a defence available to states in English law, as required by long-established customary international law. The European Court, by just nine votes to eight, held that this restriction on the right of access was permissible. It held that a rule of state immunity in national civil proceedings had the legitimate aim of 'complying with international law to promote comity and good relations between states through the respect of another state's sovereignty'.[372] As to proportionality, measures taken by a state to comply with its obligations under the international law of state immunity could not 'in principle' be regarded as disproportionate.[373] As to these obligations, the Court noted that the prohibition of torture in customary international law had become a peremptory norm (*ius cogens*) and that there were judicial precedents suggesting that customary international law had been modified to the point where a claim of state immunity could not bar *criminal* proceedings against an individual for acts of torture. However, the Court could find no evidence of a similar development in the context of *civil* proceedings, so that a state retained its absolute immunity from civil suit in the courts of another state, at least, as on the facts of the case, for acts of torture committed outside of the forum state. The dissenting judges mostly rejected the majority's distinction between criminal and civil proceedings, arguing that the consequences of the prohibition of torture as *ius cogens* was that it was hierarchically superior in customary international law to the law of state immunity and should prevail over the latter generally, so as to remove all of its legal effects, in both civil and criminal cases.[374] The argument of the dissenting judges is persuasive. As suggested by Judge Ferraro Bravo, the Court 'had a golden opportunity to issue a clear and forceful condemnation of all acts of torture'.[375] However, in *Stichting Mothers of Srebrenica and Others v Netherlands*,[376] the Court followed the approach of the majority in *Al-Adsani* when ruling that the UN was immune from civil suit for genocide at Srebrenica.

A different kind of immunity, in the form of an executive certificate that was conclusive of an issue before the courts, was the subject of *Tinnelly and McElduff v UK*.[377] In that

---

[369] *Cudak v Lithuania*, para 57. Cf *Sabeh El Leil v France* hudoc (2011); 54 EHRR 449 GC; and *Oleynikov v Russia* hudoc (2013).

[370] *Waite and Kennedy v Germany* 1999-I; 30 EHRR 261 GC; and *Beer and Regan v Germany* hudoc (1999); 33 EHRR 54 GC. In these cases the existence of an alternative European Space Agency remedy was important. See also *Chapman v Belgium No 39619/06* hudoc (2013) DA (NATO immunity).

[371] 2001-XI; 34 EHRR 273 GC. See Bates, 3 HRLR (2003) and Voyakis, 52 ICLQ 279 (2003).

[372] *Al-Adsani v UK*, para 54.   [373] *Al-Adsani v UK*, para 54.

[374] See the dissenting opinion of Judges Rozakis and Caflisch, joined by Judges Wildhaber, Costa, Cabral Barreto, and Vajic. For further arguments, see the dissenting opinions of Judges Ferraro Bravo and Loucaides.

[375] But for a well-argued presentation of the problems, eg, of execution of judgments, that would have arisen were the dissenting judges to have prevailed, see the dissenting opinion of Judge Pellonpää, joined by Judge Bratza.

[376] 2013-. The Court referred to the *Jurisdictional Immunities of the State* case (*Germany v Italy*, ICJ Rep 2012), to the same effect.

[377] 1998-IV; 27 EHRR 249. Cf *Devlin v UK* hudoc (2001); 34 EHRR 1029 and *Devenney v UK* hudoc (2002); 35 EHRR 643.

case, a right of action for damages for discrimination in Northern Ireland did not extend to acts done to protect national security. Whereas this by itself did not present a problem, the Court held that the rule by which an executive certificate to the effect that the act was done for that purpose was conclusive was a disproportionate limitation upon the right of access; it would have been possible, as the United Kingdom had done in other contexts, to have made special arrangements to allow an independent judicial, rather than an executive, determination of the facts.

The distinction between the situation where there is no 'legal basis' under national law and that where there is a procedural limitation by way of a defence that may be invoked is sometimes difficult to draw.[378] In *Z v UK*,[379] the applicant children, who brought a civil claim for damages against a local authority for failing to prevent their being abused by their parents, were denied the chance to plead their case on the merits when their claim was struck out by the courts. This followed proceedings in which it was held, deciding a new point of law, that the local authority owed no duty of care in negligence and had no liability for breach of statutory duty in respect of their statutory child care duties. The Court held that the inability to sue the local authority was not an immunity under the applicable law, in which case questions of a legitimate aim and proportionality would have been relevant, but a case of the absence of a right within the bounds of the substantive law, so that Article 6 did not apply at all. In its judgment in the *Z* case, the Court took the opportunity to signal a reversal of its reasoning in its judgment in *Osman v UK*.[380] Whereas in *Osman* the Court had ruled that the absolute immunity in English law of police officers from civil liability in negligence in the course of their conduct in the investigation and prevention of crime was a disproportionate limitation upon the right of access to a court, in *Z v UK*, the Court stated that, in the light of clarifications made by the English judiciary in later cases,[381] it now understood this exclusion as deriving from the extent of the duty of care in the substantive law of negligence, not as going to an immunity. As a result, it can be taken that the Court's ruling in *Osman* that the police immunity from liability was in breach of the right of access as being disproportionate because of its absolute nature is no longer good law; instead Article 6 simply did not apply.

As well as in defence cases, the Court has applied the *Ashingdane* approach where the national courts' jurisdiction has been ousted by treaty. In *Prince Hans Adam II of Liechtenstein v Germany*,[382] the applicant brought a claim in Germany concerning the expropriation by the Czechoslovak authorities of a painting to which he claimed title that was kept in Czechoslovakia, but which was temporarily in Germany for exhibition. The German courts held that, under the Settlement Convention, which was binding upon Germany and the Western Allies, they had no jurisdiction to hear a claim concerning 'German external assets'. Applying *Ashingdane*, the European Court, unanimously, found against the applicant on the basis that the restriction on the German courts' jurisdiction had a legitimate aim—the realization of German sovereignty and unity—and was not disproportionate to that end, given that the natural and most likely forum for such a claim was where the painting was kept, and that a claim had earlier been brought unsuccessfully in the Czechoslovak courts.

---

[378] See, eg, *Markovic v Italy* 2006-XX; 44 EHRR 1045 GC ('act of government' doctrine) and *Roche v UK* 2005-X; 42 EHRR 599 GC. The Court has sometimes declined to make it in cases in which the restriction is disproportionate, so that the outcome does not depend upon it. See, eg, the *Ashingdane* and *Fayed* cases.

[379] 2001-V; 34 EHRR 97 GC. Cf *TP and KM v UK* 2001-V; 34 EHRR 42 GC and *DP and JC v UK* hudoc (2002) 36 EHRR 183.   [380] 1998-VIII; 29 EHRR 245 GC.

[381] See *Barrett v Enfield LBC* [1999] 3 WLR 79, in which members of the House of Lords expressed their surprise at the *Osman* judgment.   [382] 2001-VIII GC.

The right of access may be restricted in criminal, as well as non-criminal cases. Thus a decision may be taken not to prosecute, or proceedings may be discontinued without infringing Article 6.[383] A practice whereby there is no hearing as to guilt or innocence (only as to the sentence) if an accused pleads guilty at the beginning of his trial is consistent with Article 6(1) provided that adequate safeguards exist to prevent abuse.[384] It is also permissible to issue a penal order by which a person is convicted and sentenced in respect of a minor criminal offence without any court hearing, provided that the person has sufficient opportunity to request a hearing.[385] The immunity of an investigating judge from criminal prosecution has also been held to be justified.[386] However, a requirement that a convicted person who appeals on a point of law must surrender to custody pending a decision on the appeal is a disproportionate restriction that takes away the very essence of the right of access to a court on appeal.[387] A violation also occurs where a civil party whose claim is joined to criminal proceedings is unable to pursue the claim when the proceedings become time barred because of the prosecution's delay.[388]

d. Waiver of the right of access

A person may waive his right of access in civil and criminal cases.[389] In *Deweer v Belgium*,[390] the Court stated that a claim of waiver should be subjected to 'particularly careful review'. In that case, a butcher chose to pay an out-of-court fine for an 'over-pricing' offence rather than wait for trial. A waiver was found not to have occurred because his decision to waive his right to a trial was subject to constraint. In particular, the accused was faced with the provisional closure of his shop pending prosecution, with consequential economic loss, if he elected to go for trial. In *Kart v Turkey*,[391] it was held that the National Assembly's refusal to lift the applicant Member of Parliament's immunity from criminal prosecution was a justifiable limitation on the applicant's freedom to waive his right of access in order to protect the Assembly's integrity.

e. Relationship with Article 13

Finally, the right of access to a court overlaps with the right to an effective national remedy in respect of a breach of a Convention right that is guaranteed by Article 13.[392] The overlap exists insofar as the Convention right is also a 'civil right' in the sense of Article 6(1). The right of access provides a stricter guarantee than Article 13 in that it requires a remedy before a court.[393]

---

[383] *Deweer v Belgium* A 35 (1980); 2 EHRR 439 para 49. See also *X v UK No 8233/78*, 3 EHRR 271 (1979). Where the discontinuance of proceedings may imply guilt, there may be a breach of Article 6(2).

[384] *X v UK No 5076/71*, 40 CD 64 at 67 (1972).

[385] *Hennings v Germany* A 251-A (1992); 16 EHRR 83. Cf *X v Germany No 4260/69*, 35 CD 155 (1970).

[386] *Ernst and Others v Belgium* hudoc (2003); 39 EHRR 724.

[387] *Omar v France* 1998-V; 29 EHRR 210 GC and *Papon v France* 2002-VII; 39 EHRR 217. See also *Eliazer v Netherlands* 2001-X; 37 EHRR 892 (no breach).   [388] *Atanasova v Bulgaria* hudoc (2008).

[389] *Deweer v Belgium* A 36 (1980); 2 EHRR 439 para 49; and *Nordström-Janzon and Nordström-Lehtinen v Netherlands No 28101/95*, 87-A DR 112 (1996) (arbitration agreed, not court hearing).

[390] A 35 (1980); 2 EHRR 439 para 49. See also *Marpa Zeeland v Netherlands* 2004-X; 40 EHRR 817 (denial of effective access by persuasion not to appeal against conviction).

[391] 2009-I; 51 EHRR 941 GC.

[392] On the inter-relationship between the two guarantees, see *Golder v UK* A 18 (1975); 1 EHRR 524 para 33 PC and *Kudla v Poland* 2000-XI; 35 EHRR 198. See also *Powell and Rayner v UK* A 172 (1990); 12 EHRR 355 and the joint separate opinion of Judges Pinheiro Farinha and De Meyer in *W v UK* A 121 (1987); 10 EHRR 29.

[393] See *De Geouffre de la Pradelle v France* A 253-B (1992) para 37.

II. THE RIGHT TO A FAIR HEARING

In contrast with the other guarantees in Article 6(1), the right to a 'fair hearing' has an open-ended, residual quality. It provides an opportunity for adding other particular rights not listed in Article 6 that are considered essential to a 'fair hearing', and for deciding whether a 'fair hearing' has occurred when the proceedings in a particular case are looked at as a whole, whether or not a particular right has been infringed.

In criminal cases, the 'fair hearing' guarantee has to be read together with the specific guarantees in Article 6(2) and (3). Whereas the latter are subsumed within the former, the general guarantee of a 'fair hearing' in Article 6(1) has elements that supplement those specified in Article 6(2) and (3).[394] Where a case falls within one (or more) of the specific guarantees in Article 6(2) or (3), it may be considered by the Court under that guarantee alone,[395] or in conjunction with Article 6(1),[396] or just under Article 6(1). When the last of these options is chosen, it is on the basis that the complaint is essentially that the proceedings in their entirety, including any appeal proceedings, were unfair.[397]

Whereas the right to a 'fair hearing' applies to civil as well as criminal proceedings, 'the contracting states have a greater latitude when dealing with civil cases concerning civil rights and obligations than they have when dealing with criminal cases'.[398] Thus although certain of the guarantees listed in Article 6(3) (eg, the right to legal aid or to cross-examine witnesses) are inherent in a 'fair hearing' in civil as well as criminal cases, they may not apply with the same rigour or in precisely the same way under Article 6(1) in civil proceedings as they do in criminal ones.[399] The same is true of some of the rights that flow exclusively from Article 6(1), such as the right to be present at the hearing.[400]

A number of specific rights have been added to Article 6(1) through the medium of its 'fair hearing' guarantee. The first of these to be established were 'equality of arms' and the right to a hearing in one's presence. Others have been added since, such as the right to freedom from self-incrimination. A breach of such a specific right may itself amount to a breach of the right to a 'fair hearing' without any need to consider other aspects of the proceedings.

As noted, in cases not involving a breach of a specific right, the Court may nonetheless find a breach of the right to a 'fair hearing' on a 'hearing as a whole' basis. Thus in *Barberà, Messegué and Jabardo v Spain*,[401] involving the prosecution of alleged members of a Catalan organization for terrorist offences, the Court identified a number of features of the hearing that cumulatively led it to conclude that there had not been a 'fair hearing'. The Court referred to the fact that the accused had been driven over 300 miles to the court the night before the trial, the unexpected changes in the court's membership, the brevity of the trial, and above all the failure to adduce and discuss important evidence orally in the accused's presence as considerations that, 'taken as a whole', rendered the proceedings unfair contrary to Article 6(1).

---

[394] *Artico v Italy* A 37 (1980); 3 EHRR 1 para 32. Article 6(3) guarantees 'minimum' rights.

[395] See, eg, *Luedicke v Germany* A 29 (1978); 2 EHRR 149.

[396] See, eg, *Benham v UK* 1996-III; 22 EHRR 293 GC.

[397] *Edwards v UK* A 247-B (1992); 15 EHRR 417 paras 33–4.

[398] *Dombo Beheer v Netherlands* A 274 (1993); 18 EHRR 213 para 32.

[399] *Dombo Beheer v* Netherlands, para 32.

[400] In some cases, there are no such differences: see *Niderost-Huber v Switzerland* 1997-I; 25 EHRR 709 para 28 (right to an adversarial trial).

[401] A 146 (1988); 11 EHRR 360 para 89 PC. Cf *Laska and Lika v Albania* hudoc (2010).

a. A hearing in one's presence

Although not expressly provided for in Article 6, the right to a hearing in one's presence is a part of the right to a 'fair hearing' in Article 6(1).[402] Clearly a litigant has an interest in witnessing and monitoring proceedings that are of great importance to him. The right of a litigant to be present at the hearing is also implicit in his right to 'participate effectively' in the hearing, the right to an adversarial trial,[403] and, in criminal cases, his rights in Article 6(3)(c), (d), and (e).[404] Where, exceptionally, Article 6 does not require an oral hearing, there is by definition no right to be present.

Whereas there is a general right of the accused in a criminal case to attend the hearing,[405] the right of a litigant to be present has been held to extend to only certain kinds of non-criminal cases. These include cases where the 'personal character and manner of life' of the party concerned is directly relevant to the decision[406] or where the case involves an assessment of the applicant's 'conduct'.[407] Similarly, a court that is deciding on the legal capacity of a mentally incapacitated person should in principle have 'personal contact' with that person.[408] In other cases it will be sufficient that there is a hearing at which the party is represented by a lawyer. However, the recognition of the right to an adversarial trial suggests that the right of a party to civil proceedings to be present should be more generally recognized.[409] In *Khuzhin and Others v Russia*,[410] a court proceeded to hear and dismiss the applicants' civil claims in defamation after their lawyer had decided in protest not to participate further when the applicants were not be able to attend because they were in custody. The Strasbourg Court held that 'the fact that the applicants' civil claim was heard with them being neither present nor represented deprived them of the opportunity to present their case effectively before the court', in breach of Article 6.[411]

A party to a criminal or non-criminal case may waive his right to be present at the hearing, provided that the waiver is made 'of his own free will, either expressly or tacitly', is 'established in an unequivocal manner', is 'attended by minimum safeguards commensurate to its importance', and does 'not run counter to any important public interest'.[412] Waiver will depend upon the applicant having knowledge of the hearing.[413] In *Sejdovic v Italy*,[414] the Court indicated that, while appropriate official notice is normally required, it 'could not rule out the possibility that certain established facts might sufficiently provide

---

[402] *Colozza v Italy* A 89 (1985); 7 EHRR 516.   [403] *Ziliberberg v Moldova* hudoc (2005).

[404] *Sejdovic v Italy* 2006-II para 81 GC. There is also a public interest in an accused attending so that his evidence can be checked in person against that of others: para 92. For this reason, the legislature may discourage 'unjustified absences': para 92.

[405] See *Hermi v Italy* 2006-XII; 46 EHRR 1115 GC. Prison authorities must ensure that an accused attends a hearing in his case of which it has knowledge: see *Goddi v Italy* A 76 (1984); 6 EHRR 457.

[406] *X v Sweden No 434/58*, 2 YB 354 at 370 (1959). Child access cases fall within this category (*X v Sweden*), but see *X v Austria No 8893/80*, 31 DR 66 (1983). So may some commercial cases (*X v Germany No 1169/61*, 6 YB 520 at 572 (1963)).

[407] *Muyldermans v Belgium* A 214-A (1991); 15 EHRR 204 para 64 Com Rep.

[408] *X and Y v Croatia* hudoc (2011).

[409] Cf *Feldbrugge v Netherlands* A 99 (1986); 8 EHRR 425 PC.   [410] Hudoc (2008) para 108.

[411] A prisoner must be brought to a civil court when a fair hearing requires this: *Kovalev v Russia* hudoc (2007) and *Kozlov v Russia* hudoc (2009).

[412] *Sejdovic v Italy* 2006-II para 86 GC. This was a criminal case, but these statements must apply also to non-criminal litigation. The required 'procedural guarantees' will include representation by a lawyer: para 91. See also *Poitrimol v France* A 277-A (1993); 18 EHRR 130.

[413] In order to exercise his right to be present, a litigant must be properly informed of the hearing: *Kovalev v Russia* hudoc (2007) and *Maksimov v Azerbijan* hudoc (2009).

[414] 2006-II para 99 GC. This revises the approach in *FCB v Italy* A 208-B (1991); 14 EHRR 909. On notification to the mentally incapacitated, see *Vaudelle v France* 2001-I; 37 EHRR 397.

an unequivocal indication that the accused is aware' of the criminal proceedings against him and does not intend to appear at them. It gave as one example, relevant to waiver, the situation where the accused states publicly or in writing that he does not intend to respond to summonses which he has become aware of other than through official sources. However, the mere fact that, as in the *Sejdovic* case, the accused has left his place of residence and is untraceable is not sufficient to show that he knows of the hearing.

Waiver need not be expressly indicated. It may be inferred from conduct, for example by a litigant not attending the hearing, having the required knowledge of it; non-attendance by itself is not a waiver.[415] However, notice must make clear what the hearing concerns,[416] and be given in good time to allow the accused to attend[417] and in a language that he understands,[418] before waiver may be inferred. 'Particular diligence' is required where notice of the hearing is given via the applicant's lawyer.[419] Refusal to participate in a hearing other than in the accused's own language is not a waiver.[420] A waiver is also not 'unequivocally' established where an accused could not reasonably have foreseen the consequences of his failure to attend. Thus there was no waiver in *Jones v UK*,[421] when the applicant's trial commenced in his absence when the applicant, having been given bail, did not surrender on the date set for the trial. There was held not to be a waiver because at the time it was not clear in English law that a trial could proceed to a conclusion in the accused's absence and without his being legally represented, and the seemingly invariable practice was to adjourn the proceedings until the accused could be brought to court.

As well as in cases of waiver, trial *in absentia* is permitted without infringing Article 6 in two other situations. The first is where the state has acted diligently, but unsuccessfully, to give an accused notice of the hearing. In *Colozza v Italy*,[422] the Court stated that this is because the 'impossibility of holding a trial by default may paralyse the conduct of criminal proceedings, in that it may lead, for example, to the dispersal of evidence, expiry of the time-limit for prosecution or a miscarriage of justice'. On the facts of the *Colozza* case, the Court found a breach of Article 6(1) because the authorities had sought to serve documents upon the applicant at his previous address, even though the police and the public prosecutor knew of his current address. The Court found that the authorities had not been diligent in the steps they had taken to locate the applicant's new address and that trial *in absentia* was a disproportionate penalty for failure to report a change of address. The onus was upon the state to show diligence, not upon the accused to show that he was 'not seeking to evade justice or that his absence was due to *force majeure*'.[423]

The second situation is where the accused, having knowledge of the trial, intentionally absents himself from it with a view to escaping trial.[424] Such cases differ from waiver in that there is no express or implied acceptance that the trial may proceed in the accused's absence. As with waiver, knowledge of the trial normally means official knowledge, except that it may be inferred from conduct, such as evading an attempted arrest.[425]

---

[415] *Godlevskiy v Russia No 14888/03* hudoc (2004) DA and *Hermi v Italy* 2006-XII; 46 EHRR 1115 GC.

[416] *Sibgatullin v Russia* hudoc (2009).

[417] See *Yakovlev v Russia* hudoc (2005). See also *Ziliberberg v Moldova* hudoc (2005).

[418] *Brozicek v Italy* A 167 (1989); 12 EHRR 371 PC.   [419] *Yavuz v Austria* hudoc (2004).

[420] *Zana v Turkey* 1997-VII; 27 EHRR 667.

[421] *No 30900/02* hudoc (2003) DA. In *R v Jones* [2002] UKHL 5, it was later held that an accused could be tried *in absentia* where there was an 'unequivocal' waiver. Cf *Kremzow v Austria* A 268-B (1993); 17 EHRR 322 (failure to apply to attend not a waiver when the state was under an obligation to ensure attendance).

[422] A 89 (1985); 7 EHRR 517 para 29. Cf *FCB v Italy* A 208-B (1991); 14 EHRR 909 and *T v Italy* A 245-C (1992).   [423] *Colozza v Italy*, para 30.

[424] *Sejdovic v Italy* 2006-II para 82 GC.   [425] *Sejdovic v Italy*, para 99.

In a case in which a trial is permitted *in absentia* under the rule in the *Colozza* case, the accused must be able to obtain 'a fresh determination of the merits of the charge, in respect of both law and fact',[426] should he later learn of the proceedings. A re-hearing adequately overcomes the 'fair' trial problems that may result from the accused's absence at the original trial and failure to provide one would be a denial of justice.[427] The requirement of a re-hearing may be satisfied by a trial court hearing, or by an appeal that provides for a sufficient consideration of the merits of the case.[428]

There is, however, no right to a re-trial in a case when under the Convention a trial is permitted *in absentia*, where it is established that the right to be present at the trial was waived, or in which the applicant intended to escape justice, by absconding or otherwise.[429] In addition to the cases mentioned in which a trial may commence and be fully conducted in the absence of the accused, a trial that has already commenced may continue in the absence of the accused in the interests of the administration of justice in some cases of illness or obstructive behaviour.[430] Obviously an accused who seeks to delay proceedings by claiming unsubstantiated illness may be tried in his absence.[431] Similarly, an accused or other litigant who behaves in the courtroom in such as way as to seriously obstruct proceedings may be excluded from the court, at least temporarily.[432]

Although Article 6 applies to such appeal proceedings as a state chooses to provide, there are limits to the right of the accused to be present at an oral hearing on appeal. In some cases written proceedings will suffice, so that the question of the right to be present does not arise. The cases in which an oral hearing has been required by the Court have mostly been ones in which the justification for the hearing has been the need for the appellate court to hear the appellant as a witness, in which situations his right to be present is implied. These cases are considered in the section on the right to an oral hearing.

b. The right to participate effectively at the hearing

In *Stanford v UK*,[433] the Court held that Article 6 guarantees not only the right of an accused to be present at the hearing, but also the right to hear and follow the proceedings and generally to participate effectively in them. This followed from 'the very notion of an adversarial procedure' and the specific guarantees in Article 6(3)(c), (d), and (e). The right must also apply to civil cases. In the *Stanford* case, the applicant claimed that he was unable to hear the proceedings because of a combination of his hearing difficulties and the acoustics in the courtroom. While the right to participate effectively meant, *inter alia*, that

---

[426] *Sejdovic v Italy*, para 82.

[427] *Sejdovic v Italy*. The destruction of the case file is not a good reason for not having a re-hearing: *Stoichkov v Bulgaria* hudoc (2005); 44 EHRR 276.

[428] The possibility of introducing fresh evidence before the English Court of Appeal meets this requirement: *Jones v UK No 30900/02* hudoc (2003) DA. A reasonable period of time to appeal is required: *Sejdovic v Italy* 2006-II GC.

[429] *Sejdovic v Italy* 2006-II para 82 GC; *Einhorn v France No 71555/01* 2001-XI; *Demebukov v Bulgaria* hudoc (2008); 50 EHRR 1040; and *Medenica v Switzerland* 2001-VI. Cf the European standard suggested in the Council of Europe Criteria Governing Proceedings held in the Absence of the Accused, CM Res (75) 11. It is for the state to have effective procedures in place to establish a waiver or an intention not to appear. Thus there was a breach of Article 6 where the procedure for considering the applicant's claim that his signature acknowledging receipt of the hearing notice had been forged was inadequate: *Somogyi v Italy* 2004-IV; 46 EHRR 47.

[430] *Ensslin, Baader and Raspe v Germany Nos 7572/76, 7586/76 and 7587/76*, 14 DR 64 (1978). See also *Ninn-Hansen v Denmark No 28972/95* 1999-V; 28 EHRR CD 96 DA (absence because of illness).

[431] *X v UK No 4798/71*, 40 CD 31 (1972).

[432] See *Colozza v Italy*, Report of the Commission, para 117 (1983).

[433] A 282-A (1994) para 26.

the state must provide a courtroom in which the accused is able to hear and follow the proceedings, the Court found no breach of Article 6 on the facts of the case as a whole. While it was accepted that the accused had indeed not been able to hear all of the evidence, the trial court had not been informed of this and the complaint about the acoustics was unjustified. In addition, the accused had experienced lawyers with him with whom he had been able to communicate and who had clearly defended him well. In other cases, the Court has confirmed that an accused's hearing disability or other medical condition will raise issues of effective participation, with the participation of his lawyer being a relevant consideration.[434] Similarly, a physically disabled person must be able to have access to a court where this is necessary for a fair hearing.[435] But it is not a breach of Article 6 for an accused to be placed in a glass cage for security reasons provided that he is able to communicate freely and confidentially with his lawyer and with the court.[436] In a different kind of case, in *Pullicino v Malta*,[437] the confiscation of the accused's notes during the trial hearing raised an issue of effective participation, but did not amount to a breach on the facts.

The right to participate effectively was infringed in *V v UK*.[438] In that case, the applicant was one of two boys tried at the age of eleven years[439] for the murder of a two-year-old boy in a case that had attracted huge publicity in the national media. The trial took place in public over three weeks in a packed Crown Court. Although some special measures were taken in view of the accused's young age,[440] nevertheless 'the formality and ritual of the Crown Court must at times have seemed incomprehensible and intimidating for a child of 11'; and there was evidence that the raising of the dock in which the accused was placed, in order for him to see the proceedings, increased his discomfort by exposing him to the press and the public. There was also psychiatric evidence to suggest that the accused had been terrified and unable to pay attention to the proceedings. The Court held that in these circumstances, the applicant's right to participate effectively in the hearing had not been respected; although his lawyers sat close by him, he would have been in no state to consult with them or generally to follow what was going on.[441]

c. Equality of arms

The right to a fair hearing supposes compliance with the principle of equality of arms.[442] This principle, which applies to both civil and criminal proceedings,[443] 'requires each party to be given a reasonable opportunity to present his case under conditions that do not place him at a substantial disadvantage vis-à-vis his opponent'.[444] In general terms,

---

[434] *Timergaliyev v Russia* hudoc (2008). [435] *Farcaş v Romania* No 32596/04 hudoc (2010).

[436] *Ashot Harutyunyan v Armenia* hudoc (2010); 55 EHRR 320. See also *Campbell v UK* No 12323/86, 57 DR 148 (1988) (handcuffing).

[437] No 45441/99 hudoc (2000) DA. Pre-trial limitations on access to the case file and the applicant's notes may also raise issues of effective participation: *Moiseyev v Russia* hudoc (2008); 53 EHRR 306. Cf *Matyjek v Poland* hudoc (2007); 53 EHRR 370.

[438] 1999-IX; 30 EHRR 121 GC. Cf *SC v UK* 2004-IV; 40 EHRR 226.

[439] For the case of the other accused, see *T v UK* hudoc (1999); 30 EHRR 121 GC.

[440] The trial procedure was explained to him, he was shown the courtroom before the trial, and the hearings were shortened.

[441] A Practice Direction on the trial of children and young persons was issued in 2000 to take account of the *T* and *V* cases: see [2000] 2 All ER 205.

[442] *Neumeister v Austria* A 8 (1968); 1 EHRR 91.

[443] *Dombo Beheer v Netherlands* A 274 (1993); 18 EHRR 213 para 33.

[444] *Kress v France* 2001-VI para 72 GC. Total equality between the parties is not required so that publicly funded legal aid does not have to match that provided privately by the other party: *Steel and Morris v UK* 2005-II; 41 EHRR 403 GC. The principle extends to ancillary proceedings, eg, for costs: *Beer v Austria* hudoc (2001).

the principle incorporates the idea of a 'fair balance' between the parties.[445] When deciding whether it has been complied with, 'appearances' are relevant, as is the seriousness of what is at stake for the applicant.[446] In criminal cases, the principle of equality of arms in Article 6(1) overlaps with the specific guarantees in Article 6(3).[447] It has, however, a wider scope than these guarantees, applying to all aspects of the proceedings.[448] Non-compliance with the principle does not depend upon proof of unfairness on the facts: the procedural deficiency in itself is a breach of the right to a fair trial.[449]

The principle has been applied most strikingly in cases from civil law jurisdictions in which the role of the *avocat général* or similar officer in final appellate court proceedings has been called in question. The key case was *Borgers v Belgium*.[450] There the Court held that the lack of equal standing in criminal proceedings before the Court of Cassation between the *avocat général* within the Belgian *procureur général's* department and the appellant was in breach of equality of arms. In particular, the *avocat général* was entitled to state his opinion at the hearing as to whether the appellant's appeal should be allowed[451] and then retire with the Court and take part (without a vote) in its discussion of the appeal. The appellant did not have prior notice of the *avocat général's* opinion and could neither reply to it nor retire with the judges. The decision reversed the European Court's earlier ruling to the contrary in the much-criticized case of *Delcourt v Belgium*,[452] and invalidated a century-old Belgian practice. In its reasoning, the Court accepted that the *avocat général* was not a part of the prosecution and that his function was to give independent and impartial advice to the Court of Cassation on the legal issues raised in the case and on the consistency of its case law. However, once he had expressed an opinion on the merits of the appeal and where this opinion favoured its dismissal, the *avocat général* became the applicant's 'opponent', to whose arguments the applicant should have been able to respond. Similarly, and 'above all', the *avocat général's* participation in the Court's private deliberations 'could reasonably be thought' to have afforded him an opportunity to reinforce his view that the appeal should be dismissed. In reaching its conclusion, the European Court emphasized the importance of 'appearances' and 'the increased sensitivity of the public to the fair administration of justice'.[453] The emphasis upon 'appearances', which echoes the English law doctrine that 'justice must be seen to be done', follows the use of the same idea in the Court's jurisprudence on the requirement of an 'independent and impartial' tribunal.

In a number of similar cases since *Borgers*, concerning both Belgium and other civil law jurisdictions and in both civil and criminal cases, the Strasbourg Court has continued to find breaches of Article 6(1), but has modified its reasoning. In particular, it has treated cases of the lack of prior disclosure of the opinion of an *avocat général* or similar officer, and of an opportunity to comment on it, as a breach not of equality of arms, but of the right to an adversarial trial. This is appropriate in that such officers are not parties to the proceedings and the lack of prior disclosure, etc, affects the preparation of their

---

[445] *Dombo Beheer v Netherlands* A 274 (1993); 18 EHRR 213 para 33.

[446] *AB v Slovakia* hudoc (2003).

[447] There may also be an overlap with the right to an adversarial trial: see, eg, *Užukauskas v Lithuania* hudoc (2010).

[448] *Ofner and Hopfinger v Austria* 6 YB 676 (1962) Com Rep para 46; CM Res DH (63) 1.

[449] *Bulut v Austria* 1996-II; 24 EHRR 84.

[450] A 214-B (1991); 15 EHRR 92 PC. See Wauters, 69 RDIDC 125 (1992). In *Mort v UK No 44564/98* hudoc (2001) DA, it was held that the role of the magistrates' court's clerk was not contrary to equality of arms.

[451] Cf *Zhuk v Ukraine* hudoc (2010) (prosecutor, but not appellant, participated in at appeal hearing).

[452] A 11 (1970); 1 EHRR 355.

[453] *Borgers v Belgium* A 214-B (1991); 15 EHRR 92 para 24 PC. Cf the reasoning in *Brandstetter v Austria* A 211 (1991); 15 EHRR 378.

case equally by all parties.[454] In cases in which the *avocat général* has also retired with the court, the Strasbourg Court has regarded the breach of the right to an adversarial trial as 'aggravated' by this second feature of the proceedings, and not identified it as a separate breach of equality of arms.[455] In *Kress v France*,[456] the fact that the *commissaire du gouvernement* retired with the Conseil d'Etat, having made submissions adverse to a civil litigant's case, was held by the Grand Chamber, by ten votes to seven, to be a breach of Article 6(1) generally, not of equality of arms, although the Court did refer to a legitimate 'feeling of inequality' that the litigant might have.

In criminal cases, apart from the obvious requirement established in the *Borgers* line of cases that the defence is entitled to a right of audience substantially equal to that of the prosecution, a number of other particular rulings have been made. Thus the failure to lay down rules of criminal procedure by legislation may be a breach of equality of arms, since their purpose is 'to protect the defendant against any abuse of authority and it is therefore the defence which is most likely to suffer from omissions and lack of clarity in such rules'.[457] In *Moiseyev v Russia*,[458] there was a lack of equality of arms because the prosecution (i) had control over the detained applicant's access to his lawyer, each visit requiring prosecution permission; and (ii) saw all documents passing between them. In court, an expert witness appointed by the accused must be accorded equal treatment with one appointed by the trial court who has links with the prosecution.[459] Requiring the lawyer for the accused, but not the prosecution, to wait many hours before being heard by the court may also be a breach of equality of arms.[460] The failure by the prosecution to disclose all 'material evidence' to the defence may be a breach of equality of arms (as well as of the right to an adversarial trial),[461] as may limitations upon an accused's access to his case file or other documents on public interest grounds,[462] or the refusal to allow witnesses to be called on equal terms with the prosecution,[463] or to admit written defence testimony.[464] In *Dirioz v Turkey*,[465] the prosecutor's privileged location in the courtroom was not a breach of equality of arms as it did not adversely affect the accused's defence.

With regard to 'civil rights and obligations' cases, there is a breach of equality of arms if one party may attend the hearing when the other may not.[466] The parties to a case must also be treated equally when calling witnesses.[467] In *Dombo Beheer v Netherlands*,[468] in which it had to be proved that an oral agreement had been made by X and Y at a meeting

[454] Cf *Kress v France* 2001-VI para 73 GC. *Martinie v France* 2006-VI; 45 EHRR 433 GC, was decided on a 'fair hearing' rather than an adversarial trial or other basis.

[455] *Vermeulen v Belgium* 1996-I; 32 EHRR 313. Cf *Lobo Machado v Portugal* 1996-I; 23 EHRR 79. Both are civil cases.   [456] 2001-VI paras 81–2 GC. See also *Fretté v France* 2002-I; 38 EHRR 438.

[457] *Coëme v Belgium* 2000-VII para 102.   [458] Hudoc (2008); 53 EHRR 306.

[459] *Bönisch v Austria* A 92 (1985); 9 EHRR 191. A court-appointed expert must be neutral: *Brandstetter v Austria* A 211 (1991); 15 EHRR 378.

[460] *Makhfi v France* hudoc (2004); 41 EHRR 745. For other criminal cases on 'equality of arms' see *Blastland v UK No 12045/86*, 52 DR 273 (1987); *U v Luxembourg No 10140/82*, 42 DR 86 (1985); *Kremzow v Austria* A 268-B (1993); 17 EHRR 322; and *Monnell and Morris v UK* A 115 (1987); 10 EHRR 205.

[461] Non-disclosure is considered in the later section on the right to an adversarial trial. See also *Bendenoun v France* A 284 (1994); 18 EHRR 54; and *Kuopila v Finland* hudoc (2000); 33 EHRR 615. On the handing over of evidence for scientific testing, see *Korellis v Cyprus* hudoc (2003).

[462] *Matyjek v Poland* 2007-XX; 53 EHRR 370 (lustration proceedings).

[463] *Perić v Croatia* hudoc (2008)   [464] *Mirilashvili v Russia* hudoc (2008).   [465] Hudoc (2012).

[466] *Komanický v Slovakia* hudoc (2002).

[467] *Wierzbicki v Poland* hudoc (2002); 38 EHRR 805. But the Court will respect a national court's refusal to hear a witness, unless it is 'tainted by arbitrariness': para 45.

[468] A 274 (1993); 18 EHRR 213. See also *Ankerl v Switzerland* 1996-V; 32 EHRR 1; and *Ruis-Mateos v Spain* A 262 (1993); 16 EHRR 505 PC.

which only they attended, there was a breach of the principle because the applicant was not allowed to call X to give evidence when the other party was allowed to call Y. In other cases, the Court has indicated that equality of arms requires that a party to civil proceedings be permitted to have material evidence in support of his case admitted in court;[469] be allowed equal access to evidence;[470] and be informed of, and hence be able to challenge, the reasons for an administrative decision.[471] A court-appointed expert must be neutral,[472] and litigants must also be allowed access to facilities on equal terms.[473] Unequal time limits for the bringing of proceedings may also be a breach of equality of arms,[474] as may rules as to costs that unduly favour the state or other party.[475]

Finally, the Court has relied upon the principle of equality of arms in some cases in which a state has enacted legislation with retroactive effect that is intended to influence the outcome of pending civil litigation.[476] In other such cases, the Court has treated the legislation as falling foul of a separate Article 6(1) 'fair hearing' requirement, distinct from equality of arms.

d. The right to an adversarial trial

The right to an adversarial trial 'means in principle the opportunity for the parties to a civil or criminal trial to have knowledge of and comment on all evidence adduced or observations filed with a view to influencing the Court's decision'.[477] It is for the court to take the initiative to inform an accused or a party to civil proceedings of the existence of such evidence or observations; it is not sufficient that the material is on file at the court for the party to consult.[478] In criminal cases, the right requires that the 'prosecution authorities should disclose to the defence all material evidence in their possession for or against the accused',[479] whether or not they use it in the proceedings. In criminal cases, the right to an adversarial trial overlaps with the specific guarantees in Article 6(3), particularly those in Article 6(3)(b) and (d) to adequate facilities and to call and cross-examine witnesses respectively.[480] Generally, the approach of the Court is to decide the case under Article 6(1), after considering whether the trial as a whole has been 'fair'. It is not necessary to show actual prejudice: the essence of the right is that the parties should be in a position to decide whether they wish to respond to the material.[481]

---

[469] *De Haes and Gijsels v Belgium* 1997-I; 25 EHRR 1.

[470] *Užukauskas v Lithuania* hudoc (2010) (access to government file on applicant refused).

[471] *Hentrich v France* A 296-A (1994); 18 EHRR 440 para 56.

[472] *Sara Lind Eggertsdottir v Iceland* 2007-XX; 48EHRR 753.

[473] See *Schuler-Zgraggen v Switzerland* A 263 (1993); 16 EHRR 405. For other civil cases, see *H v France* A 162-A (1989); 12 EHRR 74; *Yvon v France* 2003-V; 40 EHRR 938.

[474] *Varnima Corp International SA v Greece* hudoc (2009) and *Dacia SRL v Moldova* hudoc (2008).

[475] *Stankiewicz v Poland* 2006-VI; 44 EHRR 938.

[476] See, eg, *Stran Greek Refineries v Greece* A 301-B (1994); 19 EHRR 293 and *Aras v Italy* hudoc (2012).

[477] *Vermeulen v Belgium* 1996-I; 32 EHRR 313 para 33 GC. Cf *Barberà, Messegué and Jabardo v Spain* A 146 (1988); 11 EHRR 360 para 78 PC. In the *Barberà* case, the Court found a breach of the fair hearing guarantee partly because various witness statements and documents on the investigation file were simply read into the record. See also *Feldbrugge v Netherlands* A 99 (1986); 8 EHRR 425 PC (access to case file); *Georgios Papageogiou v Greece* 2003-VI (forged cheques not adduced); and *Sofri v Italy No 37235/97* hudoc (2003) DA (evidence destroyed).

[478] *Göç v Turkey* 2002-V; 35 EHRR 134 GC. See also *HAL v Finland* hudoc (2004). However, a party must use all available procedures for obtaining disclosure: *McGinley and Egan v UK* 1998-III; 27 EHRR 1.

[479] *Edwards and Lewis v UK* 2004-X; 40 EHRR 593 para 46 GC. This is sometimes formulated as a separate fair hearing requirement.

[480] These guarantees apply to civil proceedings under the rights to an adversarial trial and equality of arms: see *Wierzbicki v Poland* hudoc (2002); 38 EHRR 805.

[481] *Walston (No 1) v Norway* hudoc (2003) para 58.

While the facts of a case may give rise to issues under both the right to an adversarial trial and the right to equality of arms, the two rights differ in that whereas the latter is satisfied if the parties are treated equally, the former requires access to all relevant material, whether the other party has access to it or not.[482] The Court applied both the rights to an adversarial trial and to equality of arms in a group of UK criminal cases[483] in which material in the possession of the prosecution was not made available to the defence on public interest immunity grounds. In these cases, the Court established that whereas, as indicated earlier, the prosecution must disclose 'all material evidence' to the defence, this is not an absolute requirement. It is permissible to withhold evidence if this is 'strictly necessary' 'to preserve the fundamental rights of another individual or to safeguard an important public interest': for example, non-disclosure might be justified to protect informers, police undercover activities, or national security.[484] Where public interest immunity is claimed, the Strasbourg Court's role is not to assess the necessity for withholding the evidence, which is the function of the national courts, but to ensure that the procedure followed when the non-disclosure decision is taken incorporates adequate safeguards to protect the interests of the accused. In *Jasper v UK*,[485] the Grand Chamber held that the public interest immunity procedure in English law complied with Article 6(1) as it applied on the facts of the case. Under that procedure, the decision on non-disclosure on public interest immunity grounds was taken by the trial judge after examining the non-disclosed evidence. The defence was not shown the evidence or even told of the kind of evidence it was, but was permitted to outline its case to the judge, who was competent to order disclosure of evidence relevant to it. In ruling, by a bare majority of nine votes to eight, that the judge's decision authorizing non-disclosure was not a breach of the rights to an adversarial trial or equality of arms, the Court was strongly influenced by the fact that the non-disclosed evidence formed no part of the prosecution case and was not put to the jury. In contrast, in *Edwards and Lewis v UK*,[486] the Grand Chamber unanimously held that the same English law procedure did not comply with the same rights on the facts of that case. In particular, the facts differed from those in *Jasper* in that the non-disclosed material in *Edwards and Lewis* was directly relevant to the trial, for the reason that it related to the applicants' possible entrapment by the police into committing the alleged offence which, if established, would have led to the discontinuance of the prosecution. In these circumstances, a procedure that did not permit the defence to have access to the material, and an opportunity then to argue its case for entrapment with full information, was a breach of Article 6(1).[487]

A breach of the right to an adversarial trial was also found in a series of cases from civil law jurisdictions in which an *avocat général* or similar officer presented an opinion in the

---

[482] See *Niederöst-Huber v Switzerland* 1997-I; 25 EHRR 709.

[483] *Rowe and Davis v UK* 2000-II; 30 EHRR 1 GC; *Jasper v UK* hudoc (2000); 30 EHRR 441 GC; *Fitt v UK* 2000-II; 30 EHRR 480 GC; *Dowsett v UK* 2003-VII; 38 EHRR 845; *Edwards and Lewis v UK* 2004-X; 40 EHRR 593 GC; and *Mansell v UK No 60590/00* hudoc (2003) DA. See also *Edwards v UK* A 247-B (1992); 15 EHRR 417, in which the police failed to inform the defence of material evidence (fingerprints, failure to identify the accused) where there was no public interest immunity claim: no breach as any possible unfairness was rectified on appeal. Cf *Botmeh and Alami v UK* hudoc (2007).

[484] *Edwards and Lewis v UK* 2004-X; 40 EHRR 593 para 46 GC.

[485] Hudoc (2000); 30 EHRR 441 GC. Cf *Fitt v UK* 2000-II; 30 EHRR 480 GC. The procedure was introduced after a breach of Article 6 was found in *Rowe and Davis v UK* 2000-II; 30 EHRR 1 GC, in which the prosecution withheld evidence that a key witness was a paid informer without informing the trial judge. In contrast with *Edwards and Lewis v UK* 2004-X; 40 EHRR 593 para 46 GC, mentioned earlier, the unfairness in *Rowe and Davis* could not be rectified on appeal.   [486] 2004-X; 40 EHRR 593 GC.

[487] On the possible use of special counsel to represent the interests of the accused in the light of *Edwards and Lewis*, see *R v H and C* [2004] 2 WLR 335; [2004] UKHL 3.

final appellate court proceedings to which the parties had not had prior access or upon which they had not been able to comment.[488]

A breach of the right to an adversarial trial has been found in various other contexts. For example, in *Kamasinski v Austria*,[489] there was a breach of Article 6(1) when the Supreme Court obtained, and relied upon, information obtained over the telephone from the presiding judge at the trial; this was without the accused being informed or having an opportunity to comment on the judge's response.[490] In *McMichael v UK*,[491] there was a breach where social reports on children in care, relevant to a dispute between their parents and the local authority, were not revealed to the parents. In *Mantovanelli v France*,[492] there was a breach when the applicants were not permitted to participate in the procedure for obtaining a medical expert's report.

e. Rules of evidence

The right to a fair hearing in Article 6(1) does not require that any particular rules of evidence are followed in national courts in either criminal or non-criminal cases; it is in principle for each state to lay down its own rules.[493] Such an approach is inevitable, given the wide variations in the rules of evidence in different European legal systems, with, for example, common law systems controlling the admissibility of evidence very tightly and civil law systems setting very few restrictions. However, the Strasbourg Court has set certain parameters within which a state must operate.

Admissibility of evidence

In *Schenk v Switzerland*,[494] the Court stated that Article 6 'does not lay down any rules on the admissibility of evidence as such, which is therefore primarily a matter for regulation under national law'. Accordingly, it 'is not the role of the Court to determine, as a matter of principle, whether particular types of evidence…may be admissible…The question for the Court instead is whether the proceedings as a whole, including the way in which the evidence was obtained, were fair.'[495]

Accordingly, evidence may be admitted even if illegally obtained if this does not render the proceedings unfair. In the *Schenk* case, there was no breach of Article 6(1) when a tape recording of a conversation between the applicant and another person, P, that was obtained in breach of Swiss criminal and other law, and that incriminated the applicant, was admitted in evidence. This was because the proceedings as a whole were not unfair, for the following reasons. First, the rights of the defence had not been disregarded. In particular, the defence

---

[488] See *Vermeulen v Belgium* 1996-I; 32 EHRR 313 GC; *Lobo Machado v Portugal* (civil case) 1996-I; 23 EHRR 79 GC; *JJ v Netherlands* 1998-II; 28 EHRR 168; *KDB v Netherlands* 1998-II; *Van Orshoven v Belgium* 1997-III; 26 EHRR 55. See also *Reinhardt and Slimane-Kaïd v France* 1998-II; 28 EHRR 59 GC and *Kress v France* 2001-VI GC.

[489] A 168 (1989); 13 EHRR 36 para 102. Cf *Brandstetter v Austria* A 211 (1991); 15 EHRR 398. See also *Ferreira Alves v Portugal* hudoc (2007).

[490] Cf the facts of *J v Switzerland No 13467/87* hudoc (1989) DA (F Sett) in which a conviction was based on reports obtained after the hearing unknown to the accused.

[491] A 307-B (1995); 20 EHRR 205. Cf *Feldbrugge v Netherlands* A 99 (1986); 8 EHRR 425 PC.

[492] 1997-II; 24 EHRR 370. Cf *Cottin v Belgium* hudoc (2005). And see *Augusto v France* 2007-XX (non-communication of expert's report) and *Dağtekin and Others v Turkey* hudoc (2007) (security report withheld).

[493] For example, the burden of proof in civil proceedings is in principle a matter for national courts: *Hämäläinen v Finland No 351/02* hudoc (2004) DA. See also *X v Belgium No 8876/80*, 20 DR 233 (1980).   [494] A 140 (1988); 13 EHRR 242 para 46 PC.

[495] *Khan v UK* 2000-V; 31 EHRR 1016 para 34. Cf *Jalloh v Germany* 2006-IX;44 EHRR 667 para 94 GC and *Erkapić v Croatia* hudoc (2013).

had the opportunity to challenge both the authenticity of the recording and its admission as evidence and to examine both P and the police officer who had instigated the recording. Secondly, the recording was not the only evidence on which the conviction was based.

The *Schenk* case was applied in *Khan v UK*,[496] in which again no breach of Article 6 was found. There, a conversation between the applicant and X on the latter's premises had been recorded by an electronic listening device secretly installed on the premises by the police. The recording was admitted in evidence at the applicant's trial for a drug trafficking offence. In contrast to the *Schenk* case, the installation and use of the device were not contrary to national criminal law, although it was obtained in breach of Article 8 of the Convention.[497] The recording was the only evidence on which the applicant's conviction was based, but this consideration was discounted by the Court on the basis that the recording was both 'very strong evidence' and undoubtedly reliable and that in *Schenk* the recording had in fact also been important, possibly decisive evidence. Moreover, the applicant had, as in the *Schenk* case, been able to challenge the authenticity and admissibility of the recording and the national courts at three levels of jurisdiction had rejected claims that it should be excluded as rendering the proceedings unfair.

As emerges from these cases, whether the use of evidence obtained in breach of Article 8 of the Convention renders a trial unfair in breach of Article 6 depends upon the circumstances, including whether the rights of the defence have been respected and the strength of the evidence. The position concerning the admissibility of evidence obtained in breach of the absolute guarantee in Article 3 of the Convention is more complicated. In *Jalloh v Germany*,[498] the accused was convicted of drug-trafficking and given a six months' suspended prison sentence. The decisive evidence against him consisted of drugs that he had swallowed and that he had been made to regurgitate by the use of an emetic, the forcible administration of which, whilst not in breach of German law, was held by the Strasbourg Court to have been 'inhuman and degrading treatment', but not torture, contrary to Article 3. Had the administration of the emetic amounted to torture contrary to Article 3, its admission as evidence would without question have been a breach of Article 6. The Court stated that 'incriminating evidence—whether in the form of a confession or real evidence—obtained as a result of acts of violence or brutality or other forms of treatment which can be characterized as torture—should never be relied on as proof of the victim's guilt, irrespective of its probative value'.[499] On the facts of the case, the Court held the applicant's trial had been rendered unfair in breach of Article 6 by the use of evidence obtained by 'inhuman and degrading treatment'. This was because the regurgitated drugs were the decisive evidence that secured the conviction and the public interest in the conviction was limited, given that the applicant was a small-time street dealer who received only a light sentence. The Court discounted the fact that the infliction of pain and suffering may not have been intended and that the applicant had been able to challenge the use of the evidence. The decision was particular to its facts. The Court left open the question whether the use of evidence obtained by 'inhuman or degrading treatment' in breach of Article 3 in all cases 'automatically renders a trial unfair', as in the case of torture.[500]

---

[496] *Khan v UK*, para 37. Cf *PG and JH v UK* 2001-IX; 46 EHRR 1272 and *Lee Davies v Belgium* hudoc (2009). See also *Parris v Cyprus No 56354/00* hudoc (2002) DA (illegal post-mortem: no breach).

[497] See Ch 12, section 4.VI.   [498] 2006-IX; 44 EHRR 667 GC.

[499] *Jalloh v Germany*, para 105. Real evidence is tangible evidence. The use of evidence obtained by torture rendered the trial unfair in *Harutyunyan v Armenia* 2007-III.

[500] *Jalloh v Germany*, para 107. See also *Göçmen v Turkey* hudoc (2006) and *Haci Özen v Turkey* hudoc (2007) (inhuman treatment evidence admitted: breach of Article 6).

In *Gafgen v Germany*,[501] the Grand Chamber, by eleven votes to six, answered this question in the negative. It held that the admission of real evidence obtained by inhuman or degrading treatment contrary to Article 3 is only in breach of the right to a fair trial in Article 6 'if it has been shown that the breach of Article 3 had a bearing on the outcome of the proceedings against the defendant, that is, had an impact on his or her conviction or sentence'. This was not so in the *Gafgen* case, so that there was no breach of Article 6. In that case, having been threatened by the police with force involving 'intolerable pain'—which threat amounted to inhuman treatment but not torture—if he did not reveal the whereabouts of an abducted child, the applicant revealed the location, as a result of which the child's body and other real evidence (including tyre tracks and clothes) were found and admitted in court. However, the Grand Chamber noted that the evidence that was 'decisive' for the applicant's conviction was the confession made by him at his trial, together with other 'untainted' corroborative evidence. The real evidence obtained by inhuman treatment in violation of Article 3 was relied on at the trial only to test the veracity of the confession, not to prove guilt. In their joint opinion, the dissenting judges argued that the admission of all evidence, both statements and real evidence, obtained in violation of Article 3 should always be regarded as in breach of Article 6. In their view, which is persuasive, the majority had failed to treat the proceedings as an 'organic whole', so that they had not taken into account the fact that the applicant's confession was influenced by the admission of the real evidence obtained in breach of Article 3, which he would have realized had substantially reduced his chances of mounting a successful defence. The dissenting judges also criticized the Court for introducing a distinction in the consequences of different types of conduct prohibited by Article 3 which was not envisaged in the Convention text. A 'strict application' of the exclusionary rule would also deprive state agents of any incentive to engage in inhuman treatment, which, like torture, was the subject of an absolute guarantee. Other important considerations mentioned by the dissenting judges were the need to maintain the rule of law and the integrity of the judicial process.

In other cases in which there has been an allegation that evidence has been obtained by coercion or oppression in which there has been no finding of a breach of Article 3, the Strasbourg Court has made it clear that it will not intervene where appropriate safeguards are in place.[502] These include the presence of the accused's lawyer during police questioning or, in the absence of this, satisfactory procedures followed by the court that ensure that the statement has been freely made.[503]

Certain other national rules as to admissibility of evidence that do not concern coercion or oppression or breaches of Article 3 have been found to be acceptable. The admission of evidence by an accomplice or other accused who has been promised immunity is not in itself contrary to Article 6.[504] Consistently with the practice in a number of European criminal justice systems, it has also been held that it is not in breach of Article 6 for the court to be informed of the accused's criminal record during the trial,[505] or for a conviction to be founded solely on circumstantial evidence.[506]

---

[501] 2010- para 178 GC.

[502] The Court's reluctance to intervene in such cases was apparent in *Ferranti and Santangelo v Italy* 1996-III; 23 EHRR 288.

[503] See *Latimer v UK No 12141/04* hudoc (2005) DA and *G v UK No 9370/81*, 35 DR 75 (1983).

[504] *Cornelis v Netherlands No 994/03*, 2004-V.   [505] *X v Austria No 2676/65*, 23 CD 31 (1967).

[506] *Alberti v Italy No 12013/86*, 59 DR 100 (1989). But the admission of photocopied evidence must be subjected to strict scrutiny: *Buzescu v Romania* hudoc (2005).

Assessment of evidence

Just as the Strasbourg Court regards the rules as to the admissibility of evidence as primarily a matter for national decision, so it will not generally review the assessment of evidence by a national court.[507] It will only do so where the national court has drawn 'arbitrary or grossly unfair conclusions from the facts submitted to it'.[508] The same general 'hands off' approach extends to the means used to ascertain the relevant facts, so that the Strasbourg Court will not generally question a national court decision as to the calling of a witness or an expert.[509]

Disclosure of evidence

The obligation to disclose all material evidence to the other party has been considered previously under the right to an adversarial trial.[510]

f. Presumption of innocence in criminal cases

The presumption of innocence in criminal cases is guaranteed by Article 6(2) and is considered under that provision.[511] However, the presumption of innocence is also a part of the 'general notion of a fair hearing' in Article 6(1). This is crucial where the applicant is subject to a criminal 'charge' but where Article 6(2) does not apply. This was the case in *Phillips v UK*,[512] in which the applicant had been convicted of a drug trafficking offence and sentenced to nine years' imprisonment. In separate proceedings, the Crown Court later made an order confiscating property believed to have been gained from drug trafficking. In those proceedings the court applied a rebuttable statutory assumption that property held by the applicant following his conviction or during a six-year period before it was obtained by drug trafficking. In response to the applicant's claim that the assumption infringed the presumption of innocence, the Strasbourg Court held that Article 6(2) did not govern the confiscation proceedings as it ceased to apply after conviction, but that the presumption of innocence in Article 6(1) did apply as Article 6(1) generally 'applies throughout the entirety of proceedings'. However, no breach of the presumption of innocence was found, as the application of the statutory assumption on the facts of the case was 'reasonable'.

g. The principle of immediacy

It is 'an important element of fair criminal proceedings' that the accused should be able to confront a witness in the presence of the judge who finally decides the case.[513] Thus normally a change in the composition of the trial court after the hearing of an important witness should lead to the re-hearing of that witness, although exceptions may be allowed where the facts as a whole suggest that the outcome of the case was not affected.[514] This principle of immediacy applies also to civil proceedings, although less strictly.[515]

---

[507] *Barberà, Messegué and Jabardo v Spain* A 146 (1988); 11 EHRR 360 para 68 PC. Cf *Wierzbicki v Poland* hudoc (2002); 38 EHRR 805.

[508] *Waldberg v Turkey* No 22909/93 hudoc (1995) DA. Cf *Camilleri v Malta* No 51760/99 hudoc (2000) DA.

[509] See *Sommerfeld v Germany* 2003-VIII; 36 EHRR 565 GC (Article 8 case). Cf *Accardi v Italy No 30598/02* 2005-II. For exceptions, see *Elsholz v Germany* 2000-VIII; 34 EHRR 1412; *Schlumpf v Switzerland* hudoc (2009); and *Balsytė-Lideikienė v Lithuania* hudoc (2008).   [510] See section 3.II.d.

[511] See section 4.

[512] 2001-VII para 39. Cf *Grayson and Barnham v UK* hudoc (2008); 48 EHRR 722.

[513] *PK v Finland* No 37442/97 hudoc (2002) DA. The principle overlaps with the right to confront witnesses, section 5.V.

[514] *PK v Finland*. See also *Mellors v UK* No 57836/00 hudoc (2003) DA.

[515] *Pitkänen v Finland* hudoc (2004).

h. Freedom from self-incrimination

The right to a fair hearing includes freedom from self-incrimination in criminal cases. In one sense, this is an unexpected reading of Article 6(1), in that when Council of Europe member states added to the rights of the accused in the Seventh Protocol to the Convention, they considered including freedom from self-incrimination but decided not to do so. Nonetheless, the Court's subsequent jurisprudence under Article 6 fills an obvious and unfortunate gap. As the Court stated in *Saunders v UK*,[516] 'the right to silence and the right not to incriminate oneself are generally recognized international standards which lie at the heart of the notion of a fair procedure under Article 6'.

Freedom from self-incrimination follows from the autonomy of the individual, the need to avoid miscarriages of justice, and the principle that the prosecution should prove its case without the assistance of the accused.[517] In Article 6 it is 'primarily concerned with respecting the will of an accused to remain silent'.[518] Accordingly, it does not include the obtaining of tangible evidence (eg blood, breath, urine samples) by the state's use of compulsory powers.[519]

With regard to statements, freedom from self-incrimination includes not only obviously incriminating statements but also statements which appear 'on... [their] face to be of a non-incriminating nature—such as exculpatory remarks or mere information on questions of fact' since these 'may later be deployed in criminal proceedings in support of the prosecution case'.[520] Article 6 is not limited totally to the refusal to answer questions or make a statement. It also applies to situations in which there is 'coercion to hand over real evidence to the authorities'.[521] Thus in *Funke v France*,[522] in which the applicant was required himself to produce documents, as opposed to being subjected to the execution by others of a search warrant for them, the evidence was not obtained independently of his will, so that his right to freedom from self-incrimination was in issue. In *Jalloh v Germany*,[523] the *Funke* case was extended to cover a situation in which the applicant was subjected to the forced administration of an emetic causing him to regurgitate real evidence (drugs) from his body. Finding a breach of freedom from self-incrimination, the Grand Chamber distinguished the examples of material given in *Saunders* that fall outside the guarantee of freedom from self-incrimination on the following grounds. It noted that the material obtained in *Jalloh* was 'real evidence', as opposed to material that was wanted for forensic examination; that the degree of force used to obtain it was much greater than that used in the conduct of blood tests, etc; and that the procedure used to recover the drugs involved a breach of Article 3.

Freedom from self-incrimination is not absolute; what is prohibited is 'improper compulsion'.[524] 'Compulsion' may take various forms. Clearly, the use of physical force against a person aimed at obtaining a confession or other evidence from him is compulsion,[525] as is

---

[516] 1996-VI; 23 EHRR 313 para 68 GC.

[517] *Saunders v UK*. It is also closely linked to the presumption of innocence: *Saunders v UK*.

[518] *Saunders v UK*, para 69. The right to silence is a part of the larger concept of freedom from self-incrimination, which includes incrimination by, eg, a breath test or a search (matters within Article 8 of the Convention). Although Article 6 is mostly only about the right to silence, the general term is used in this chapter.   [519] *Saunders v UK*.   [520] *Aleksandr Zaichenko v Russia* hudoc (2010).

[521] *Jalloh v Germany* 2006-IX; 44 EHRR 667 para 111 GC.

[522] A 256-A (1993); 16 EHRR 297. See also *JB v Switzerland* 2001-III, in which freedom from self-incrimination was infringed where the applicant was fined for failing to produce business documents relevant to a pending tax evasion charge.

[523] 2006-IX; 44 EHRR 667 GC. Cf *Gafgen v Germany* 2010- para 178 GC (no breach of freedom from self-incrimination).

[524] *Murray (John) v UK* 1996-I; 22 EHRR 29 para 46 GC.

[525] See *Jalloh v Germany* 2006-IX; 44 EHRR 667 GC. See also *Austria v Italy* 6 YB 740 at 784 (1963) Com Rep; CM Res DH (63) 3.

requiring an accused to give evidence at his trial by law.[526] The threat[527] or imposition[528] of a criminal sanction for failure to provide information is compulsion and may be a breach of freedom from self-incrimination, whether or not the person concerned is later prosecuted for,[529] or convicted of,[530] an offence. In *Brusco v France*,[531] it was held that requiring an accused to take an oath to tell the truth when answering police questions, on pain of being charged with perjury if he did not do so, is compulsion. Remarkably, the Court also held in the *Brusco* case that there was a breach of Article 6(1) because the accused was not informed by the police before they began questioning of his right to remain silent.[532] A rule permitting the drawing of adverse inferences from the exercise of the right to silence is also a form of compulsion, by bringing pressure to bear to answer questions.[533] Similarly, the use of an undercover agent to solicit information may involve compulsion. This was the case in *Allan v UK*,[534] where the applicant confessed to a murder to an undercover police informer who was placed in his remand cell for the purpose of eliciting information from him, their conversations being recorded. Having resisted police questioning, the psychological pressures upon the applicant, who was induced to confess by persistent questioning by someone with whom he shared his cell, meant that the confession was obtained 'in defiance of the will' of the applicant. In contrast, there was no violation of the accused's freedom from self-incrimination in *Bykov v Russia*.[535] In that case, V, an employee of the applicant, told the police that he had been ordered by the applicant to kill the applicant's business associate. The police had V visit the applicant's house pretending that he had committed the murder and incriminating statements by the applicant were obtained by recorded conversations at the house. The Grand Chamber distinguished *Allan* on the grounds that the applicant was at his own house and not otherwise under pressure to talk to V; moreover, the evidence obtained by the covert operation was not the main evidence at the trial.

Compulsion is 'improper' if the 'very essence of the right' not to incriminate oneself is destroyed. This test was articulated in *Murray (John) v UK*.[536] There the Court held that the possibility of drawing adverse inferences from the failure of a suspect or an accused to answer questions, either before or at his or her trial for a criminal offence, does not amount to 'improper compulsion', destroying the 'very essence of the right', provided that proper safeguards are in place. In that case, the applicant was arrested in a house in which a police informer was being questioned by the IRA. He was convicted of aiding and abetting the informer's false imprisonment. Under the legislation applicable to terrorist offences in Northern Ireland, the applicant was tried by an experienced judge without a jury who drew 'strong inferences' from the applicant's failure, exercising his right to silence, to explain his presence in the house when he was arrested and interrogated by the police and from his refusal to give evidence at his trial. The Court held, by fourteen votes to five, that there was no 'improper compulsion' upon the applicant to break his silence, because of the safeguards that applied. These were that adverse inferences could only be drawn (i) if the accused had been cautioned that this could follow from his exercise of the

---

[526] See *Murray (John) v UK* 1996-I; 22 EHRR 29 para 47 GC. See also *Serves v France* 1997-VI; 28 EHRR 265 (applicant obliged to give evidence in the preliminary investigation of a fellow suspect for the same murder).   [527] *Saunders v UK* 1996-VI; 23 EHRR 313 GC.

[528] *Funke v France* A 256-A (1993); 16 EHRR 297.   [529] *Funke v France*.

[530] *Heaney and McGuiness v Ireland* 2000-XII; 33 EHRR 264.   [531] Hudoc (2010).

[532] Cf the similar requirement in US constitutional law: *Miranda v Arizona* 384 US 436 (1966).

[533] *Condron v UK* 2000-V; 31 EHRR 1.

[534] 2002-IX; 36 EHRR 143. The Court stressed that the informer could be seen as a state agent whose questioning was the equivalent of interrogation. Contrast *A v Germany No 12127/86* hudoc (1986) DA.

[535] Hudoc (2009) GC. Cf *Heglas v Czech Republic* hudoc (2007); 48 EHRR 1018.

[536] 1996-I; 22 EHRR 29 PC.

right to silence; (ii) there was a *prima facie* case against the accused that could lead to his conviction if unanswered; and (iii) that the judge both had a discretion as to whether it was appropriate to draw inferences from silence and had to give reasons should he do so. Given these safeguards and the 'formidable' case against the applicant, the Court concluded that the drawing of adverse inferences on the facts was 'a matter of common sense' and could not be regarded as 'unfair or unreasonable'; whereas it was contrary to the right to freedom of self-incrimination to base a conviction 'solely or mainly' on the accused's silence, this should not prevent that silence being taken into account in situations 'which clearly call for an explanation', provided that satisfactory safeguards apply. As the Court noted, the UK legislation providing for the drawing of inferences simply placed upon a 'formalized' basis the practice of criminal courts in 'a considerable number of countries' in Europe.

In the *Murray (John)* case, the Court distinguished *Funke v France* (mentioned earlier). In *Funke*, the applicant was convicted and fined for an offence of refusing to produce bank statements, which it was believed existed, at the request of the customs authorities who suspected him of having committed offences concerning financial dealings abroad.[537] The 'degree of compulsion' to which the applicant was subjected in *Funke* destroyed the 'very essence' of his freedom from self-incrimination.[538]

Adverse inferences were also at issue in *Condron v UK*.[539] There it was held that where adverse inferences may be drawn not by a judge, as happened in the *Murray* case, but by a jury, a necessary additional safeguard that is required to prevent an infringement of the right to freedom from self-incrimination is that the jury is directed that 'if it was satisfied that the applicants' silence at the police interview could not sensibly be attributed to their having no answer or none that would stand up to cross-examination it should not draw an adverse inference'. In the *Condron* case, the applicants, who were heroin addicts, were suspected of drug dealing. They exercised their right to silence during police questioning on the advice of their solicitor, who was present during the interview and was concerned that they would not be able to follow the questions because of the influence of drugs. In contrast with the *Murray* case, they did give evidence later at the trial. Applying legislation that contained the safeguards present in the *Murray* case, the judge directed the jury that they might draw adverse inferences from the accused's silence, but did not draw their attention to the possibility that there might have been a good reason for their remaining silent (following their solicitor's advice) other than that they had no satisfactory answers to give.

The 'very essence' of the right was also destroyed in *Heaney and McGuiness v Ireland*.[540] In that case, the applicants were arrested in a house on suspicion of membership of the IRA, and of involvement in a suspected terrorist bombing that had occurred nearby hours

[537] Although not arrested, the applicant in *Funke* was considered to be 'charged' as being 'substantially affected' by the allegation made against him: see *Weh v Austria* hudoc (2004); 40 EHRR 890 para 52. The applicant's death forestalled his prosecution for the substantive offence. For criticism of the *Funke* case, see Naismith, 3 EHRLR 229 (1997) and Stressens, ELR Human Rights Survey 45 (1996).

[538] *Murray (John) v UK* 1996-I; 22 EHRR 29 para 49 GC. The Court had not used 'very essence' language in *Funke*. The severity of the sanction is a relevant factor in deciding whether the 'very essence' of the right is destroyed: *Allen v UK No 76574/01* hudoc (2002) DA (a small fine: no breach). In *Heaney and McGuiness v Ireland* 2000-XII; 33 EHRR 264, no distinction was drawn between accumulated fines (*Funke*) and a six-month prison sentence (*Heaney and McGuiness*).

[539] 2000-V; 31 EHRR 1 para 61. *Condron* has been applied in, eg, *Beckles v UK* hudoc (2002); 36 EHRR 162; *Smith v UK No 64714/01* hudoc (2002) DA; and *Adetoro v UK* hudoc (2010).

[540] 2000-XII; 33 EHRR 264 para 48. See Ashworth, [2001] Crim LR 482. See also *Shannon v UK* hudoc (2005); 42 EHRR 660.

earlier. When they refused to answer questions about the bombing or their presence in the house, the applicants were requested to provide an account of their movements during the relevant period under a statute that made failure to give such an account a criminal offence, but they refused to do so. They were later acquitted of an offence involving membership of the IRA, but convicted of the offence of failing to provide the requested account of their movements. The latter convictions, resulting in sentences of six months' imprisonment, were held to be a violation of freedom from self-incrimination. Article 6 applied, as the applicants were 'substantially affected' by being arrested on the basis of their suspected criminal activities, and there was, as in the *Funke* case, 'improper compulsion' in breach of that Article, because the 'degree of compulsion' applied through the imposition of a criminal sanction for failure to supply the requested information destroyed the 'very essence' of the right to freedom from self-incrimination.

In the *Murray (John)* and *Heaney and McGuiness* cases, the Court adopted a 'degree of compulsion' criterion to be applied when deciding whether the compulsion was 'improper' so that the 'very essence' of the right to freedom from self-incrimination had been destroyed. In *Jalloh v Germany*,[541] the Court revised and added to this criterion. The Court stated that it would have regard to the following three criteria: 'the nature and degree of the compulsion, the existence of any relevant procedural safeguards, and the use to which any material so obtained is put'. Applying these three criteria to the facts, the Court noted that the 'nature and degree' of the compulsion in *Jalloh* had interfered with the applicant's physical and mental integrity to the point where it was 'inhuman and degrading treatment'; that while there were generally sufficient procedures to prevent the arbitrary or improper use of compulsion, the applicant's ability to withstand the force used had not been fully established because of his poor German; and that the evidence obtained was the decisive evidence in the case. The Court also introduced a fourth criterion later in its judgment in the *Jalloh* case, namely the weight of public interest in the investigation, but concluded that this could not on the facts justify such a grave interference with the applicant's physical and mental integrity. The use of this fourth criterion was not apparent in the earlier case of *Heaney and McGuiness v Ireland*.[542] There the Court rejected the defendant government's argument that it could require the applicants to give an account of their movements or face a criminal sanction of up to six months' imprisonment as a 'proportionate response' to a terrorist and security threat: such public interest considerations could not justify the imposition of a criminal sanction for remaining silent that destroyed the 'very essence' of the right.

In *O'Halloran and Francis v UK*,[543] the Grand Chamber confirmed and applied the criteria in the *Jalloh* case. In that case, each of the two applicants had been required, on pain of criminal sanction, to identify to the police the driver of his car in connection with a speeding offence. The first applicant revealed that he was the driver and was convicted of the speeding offence. The second did not reveal who the driver was, and was convicted of a different criminal offence of failing to identify the driver and fined for not doing so. The Grand Chamber held, by fifteen votes to two, that neither the threat nor the imposition of the criminal sanction for not identifying the driver destroyed the 'essence' of the right to freedom from self-incrimination. It did so on the basis of the 'special nature of the regulatory regime at issue and the limited nature of the information sought', both of which considerations the Court addressed under the first of the *Jalloh* criteria. As to the former, the Court stressed that the regulatory regime for motor vehicles was motivated

---

[541] 2006-IX; 44 EHRR 667 para 101 GC. For the facts, see earlier in this section.
[542] 2000-XII; 33 EHRR 264 paras 55–8.   [543] 2007-III; 46 EHRR 397 para 62 GC.

by their 'potential for grave injury'.[544] As to the latter, the Court noted that only the name of the driver was required, which in itself was not incriminating. The Court also noted, in terms of the third *Jalloh* criterion, that many other elements beyond the identification of the driver were needed to prove guilt.[545] Although the Court did not expressly refer to the fourth, public interest *Jalloh* criterion, it can be seen to underlie the Court's reference to the motivation for the regulatory regime, as can its comment that 'those who choose to keep and drive motor cars can be taken to have accepted certain responsibilities and obligations',[546] including informing the authorities of the drivers of their vehicles.

Public interest considerations were also relevant in *Allen v UK*.[547] In that case, after being pressured, the applicant eventually made the required declaration of his assets for tax purposes, but was convicted of making false statements in it. This was held not to be a breach of freedom from self-incrimination because the applicant did not allege that he was being forced to reveal prior acts or omissions that might contribute to his conviction for some other offence:[548] instead the offence of which he was convicted was committed only by the false statements in his declaration. In any event, as the Court stated, an obligation to declare income and capital for the assessment of tax is 'a common feature of the taxation systems of contracting states and it would be difficult to envisage them functioning effectively without it'.[549] Hence, it would seem that even an accurate return of income or capital (that is required for tax purposes on pain of criminal sanction) that reveals prior tax evasion would not be a breach of freedom from self-incrimination.

In *Weh v Austria*[550] it was pointed out that there are two different kinds of cases in which breaches of the right to freedom of self-incrimination have been found by the European Court. First, there are cases in which compulsion is used 'for the purpose of obtaining information which might incriminate the person concerned in pending or anticipated criminal proceedings against him, or—in other words—in respect of an offence with which that person has been "charged" within the autonomous meaning of Article 6(1)'.[551] Second, there are cases of 'incriminating information compulsorily obtained outside of the context of criminal proceedings' that is later used in criminal proceedings against the person concerned.[552] Most cases that raise freedom from self-incrimination issues are of the first kind. Cases of the second kind include cases such as *Saunders v UK*.[553] In that case, the applicant, on pain of criminal sanction (a fine or two years' maximum imprisonment), was required by law to answer (and did answer) questions put to him by Department of Trade and Industry inspectors in the course of their administrative investigation under company law into the conduct of a company takeover. Although this requirement did not *per se* raise an issue of freedom of self-incrimination, the use to which the information was put might do. In the *Saunders* case, the answers that the applicant gave, although not directly self-incriminating, were introduced by the prosecution to great effect in the later successful prosecution of the applicant for offences involving fraud. This was held to be 'improper compulsion' in violation of Article 6.

---

[544] *O'Halloran and Francis v UK*, para 57.
[545] As to the second criterion, there were sufficient procedural safeguards.
[546] *O'Halloran and Francis v UK* 2007-III; 46 EHRR 397 para 62 GC.
[547] *No 76574/01* hudoc DA. Contrast *JB v Switzerland* 2001-III, mentioned earlier.
[548] Contrast the *Saunders* case, in the next paragraph.
[549] For other possible examples, see *Vasileva v Denmark* hudoc (2003); 40 EHRR 681 (giving one's name in some circumstances) and *Shannon v UK* hudoc (2005); 42 EHRR 660 para 38 (requirement to attend an interview).   [550] Hudoc (2004); 40 EHRR 890.
[551] *Weh v Austria*, para 42.   [552] *Weh v Austria*, para 43.   [553] 1996-IV; 23 EHRR 313 GC.

i. Entrapment

Entrapment is conduct inciting the commission of a criminal offence by a person who would otherwise not have committed it. The use in a criminal trial of evidence obtained by police incitement may render the trial unfair in breach of Article 6. 'While the Court accepts the use of undercover agents as a legitimate investigative technique for combating serious crimes, it requires that adequate safeguards against abuse be provided for, as the public interest cannot justify the use of evidence obtained as a result of police incitement'.[554]

The Court has drawn a distinction between police incitement, which is unacceptable, and the investigation of criminal activity in an 'essentially passive manner', which is permissible.[555] In *Ramanauskas v Lithuania*,[556] the Grand Chamber stated: 'Police incitement occurs when the officers involved—whether members of the security forces or forces or persons acting on their instructions—do not confine themselves to investigating criminal activity in an essentially passive manner, but exert such an influence on the subject as to incite the commission of an offence that would otherwise not have been committed, in order to make it possible to establish the offence, that is, to provide evidence and institute a prosecution.'[557] The Grand Chamber added that the burden is on 'the prosecution to prove that there was no incitement, provided that the defendant's allegations are not wholly improbable'.[558] In the *Ramanauskas* case, the applicant was a prosecutor who, after repeated requests from members of the police anti-corruption unit, eventually accepted a bribe to secure the acquittal of a third person. The Grand Chamber held the applicant's subsequent conviction for a corruption offence, in which the key evidence was his taking of the bribe, was unfair in breach of Article 6(1). In reaching this decision, the Grand Chamber noted that there was no evidence that the applicant had committed any corruption or other offences beforehand and that all meetings between the police and the applicant had been initiated by the police. The police conduct went beyond the 'mere passive investigation of existing criminal activity' and incited the applicant to commit an offence which there was no objective indication (only rumours that he had taken bribes) that he would have committed without their intervention.[559]

The Grand Chamber in the *Ramanauskas* case followed the approach taken by a Court Chamber in *Teixeira de Castro v Portugal*,[560] in which the applicant was requested by undercover police officers to supply heroin. The trial leading to his conviction was held to have been unfair because the officers had not investigated the applicant's possible criminal activity in an 'essentially passive manner'. In reaching this conclusion the Court noted that there were no indications that the applicant was predisposed to commit drug-dealing offences: he had no criminal record and all the evidence suggested that he was essentially a drug user who was prepared to help others in need, rather than a person minded and equipped to deal in drugs. The Court also noted that, as in the *Ramanauskas* case, the evidence of the police officers had been the main evidence against him.[561] In contrast, there

---

[554] *Veselov and Others v Russia* hudoc (2012) para 89.

[555] The evidence of undercover agents who monitor or participate in an offence without inciting it may be admitted, even though they are excused from appearing as witnesses, subject to safeguards to protect the rights of the accused: *Ludi v Switzerland* A 238 (1992); 15 EHRR 173. See further, section 5.V.

[556] 2008-I; 51 EHRR 303 para 55 GC. Cf *Vanyan v Russia* hudoc (2005). As to wholly private incitement, see the *Shannon* case, later in this section, n 567.

[557] The 'influence' may be simply prompting the crime by, eg, a test purchase of drugs (the *Teixeira* case), or something more, such as pressure, threats or bribes: see *Bannikova v Russia* hudoc (2010) para 47.

[558] *Ramanauskas v Lithuania* 2008- para 70 GC.

[559] Cf *Malininas v Lithuania* hudoc (2008).   [560] 1998-IV; 28 EHRR 101 para 38.

[561] Contrast *Calabro v Italy and Germany No 59895/00* hudoc (2002) DA.

was no violation of Article 6 in *Milinienė v Lithuania*,[562] in which a private individual had approached the police complaining that the applicant, a judge, would require a bribe in order to decide a case in his favour. The police had then assisted the complainant by providing him with money for a bribe and recording equipment, facilitating his obtaining what became the main evidence leading to the judge's conviction for corruption. The Strasbourg Court found that there was not entrapment contrary to Article 6, as 'the police may be said to have "joined" the criminal activity rather than to have initiated it'.[563]

In these and later cases, the Court has elaborated upon the distinction between incitement to commit an offence and 'joining' an offence which is already planned or underway, with only the former being contrary to Article 6. For an undercover police operation to fall within this latter category, the police must have objective and verifiable evidence of pre-existing criminal intent.[564] Moreover, to ensure that the operation complies with this requirement and otherwise to safeguard the right to a fair hearing, the operation must be authorized and supervised by a judge or public prosecutor, or at least by a body that is separate from the police who conduct the operation.[565] In addition, an accused must have the possibility of claiming incitement in court proceedings which are 'adversarial, thorough, comprehensive and conclusive on the issue of entrapment', and in which the court's powers of judicial review extend to 'the reasons why the covert operation was mounted, the extent of the police's involvement in the offence and the nature of any incitement or pressure to which the applicant was subjected'.[566]

In *Shannon v UK*,[567] the question arose whether the use of entrapment evidence obtained not by the police or others acting for them, but by private persons acting on their own initiative, might give rise to unfairness in breach of Article 6. In that case, the applicant, a well-known TV actor, agreed to provide a *News of the World* journalist, disguised as a sheikh, with cocaine. The journalist revealed this in his newspaper story and handed over his audio and visual recordings to the police. The applicant was convicted of supplying drugs illegally, the recordings being a key part of the evidence. While noting that the *Teixeira de Castro* case was different in that it involved a direct 'misuse of state power', the Court nonetheless stated that the use by the prosecution as evidence in court of information handed over to the state by a third party may 'in certain circumstances' render the proceedings unfair. However, on the facts of the case the Court found no breach of Article 6, essentially because the applicant was, in contrast with the applicant of the *Teixeira de Castro* case, predisposed to supply drugs, responding readily in the manner of an experienced supplier. The Court also noted that the applicant had had the benefit of a five-day adversarial hearing by the trial judge who ruled that the admission of the evidence provided by the journalist would not have an adverse effect on the fairness of the trial.

j. Prejudicial media publicity

The Court has acknowledged that the state has a positive obligation to control the conduct of the media so to ensure a fair trial. Whereas Commission decisions to the this effect were expressed in terms of the residual 'fair hearing' guarantee in Article 6(1), in its jurisprudence the Court has considered this matter under the specific guarantee of the

---

[562] Hudoc (2008). Cf *Sequeira v Italy* No 73557/01 hudoc (2003) DA; *Eurofinacom v France* No 58753/00, 2004-VII DA.   [563] *Milinienė v Lithuania*, para 38.

[564] *Bannikova v Russia* hudoc (2010) para 40

[565] *Veselov and Others v Russia* hudoc (2012) para 105. Cf *Khudobin v Russia* 2006-XII; 48 EHRR 523.

[566] *Ramanauskas v Lithuania* 2008- paras 70–1 GC. Cf *Rajcoomar v UK* No 59457/00 hudoc (2004); 40 EHRR SE 20 DA. And see *Edwards and Lewis v UK* 2004-X; 40 EHRR 593 GC.

[567] No 67537/01 hudoc (2004) DA.

'presumption of innocence' in Article 6(2). Accordingly, the matter is examined under Article 6(2).[568]

k. Retroactive legislation designed to defeat a litigant's claim

Retroactive legislation that is designed to defeat a litigant's claim against the state in the courts in pending proceedings is in breach of the 'principle of the rule of law and the notion of a right to a fair trial enshrined in Article 6'.[569] In *Stran Greek Refineries and Stratis Andreadis v Greece*,[570] the state challenged in the courts an arbitration award against it arising out of a contract with the applicants. While the state's appeal to the Court of Cassation against lower court judgments was pending, the Greek Parliament, in breach of Article 6, enacted legislation that made it 'inevitable' that the arbitration award in the applicants' case was judicially declared void. While the *Stran* case and others have been ones in which the state has been a party to the proceedings, it has been held that the rule concerning retroactive legislation extends to cases in which this is not so, but in which legislative interference equally prevents a 'fair trial' between the parties.[571] Exceptionally, retroactive legislation that interferes with the administration of justice in pending cases is not in breach of Article 6 if it can be justified on 'compelling' public interest grounds.[572] In this connection, the state's financial needs are not in themselves sufficient.[573]

l. The right to have one's case properly examined

Given that Convention rights must be guaranteed 'effectively', Article 6 implies that the national court hearing a case has 'a duty effectively to examine the grounds, arguments and evidence adduced by the parties'.[574] There was a breach of Article 6(1) on this basis in *Dulaurans v France*.[575] There the Court of Cassation's sole reason for refusing an application to quash a lower court civil judgment was that it was based upon an argument that was new. The Strasbourg Court held that this was 'a clear error' on the part of the Court of Cassation. The records showed that the applicant had earlier raised the argument before both lower courts, so that the Court of Cassation had not properly examined the applicant's arguments, thereby denying her a fair hearing. In *Kuznetsov v Russia*,[576] there was a breach of Article 6 on a 'proper-examination' basis where their approach to the facts of the case 'permitted the domestic courts to avoid addressing the applicants' main complaint'. In *Pronina v Ukraine*,[577] the failure of a civil court to address an important argument by the applicant was also a breach of Article 6, although the Court relied upon the obligation to give reasons for a decision[578] more than the right to have one's arguments examined.

---

[568] See section 4.

[569] *Zielinski and Pradal & Gonzalez and Others v France* 1999-VII; 31 EHRR 532 para 57 GC.

[570] A 301-B (1994); 19 EHRR 293 paras 46, 49. The Court also relied upon 'equality of arms'. See also, eg, *Scordino v Italy (No 1)* 2006-V; 45 EHRR 207 GC. Some cases of interference have been decided on a right of access basis: see section 3.I.

[571] *Vezon v France* hudoc (2006) and *Arras and Others v Italy* hudoc (2012).

[572] *Forrer-Niedenthal v Germany* hudoc (2003) (furthering German reunification); *Gorraiz Lizarraga and Others v Spain* 2004-III (need for regional planning). See also *National and Provincial Building Society et al v UK* (public interest in clarifying tax law and securing tax payments) 1997-VII; 25 EHRR 127 and *OGIS-Institut Stanislas et al v France* hudoc (2004). [573] *Maggio and Others v Italy* hudoc (2011).

[574] *Dulaurans v France* hudoc (2000); 33 EHRR 1093 para 33. Cf *Van de Hurk v Netherlands* A 238 (1994); 18 EHRR 481. See also the *Van Kück* and *Khamidov* cases, mentioned earlier.

[575] Hudoc (2000). Cf *Kraska v Switzerland* A 254-B (1993); 18 EHRR 188 para 30 and *Fouquet v France* 1996-I; 22 EHRR 279 F Sett before the Court. See also *De Moor v Belgium* A 292-A (1994); 18 EHRR 372; *Quadrelli v Italy* hudoc (2000); 34 EHRR 215; and *Jokela v Finland* 2002-IV; 37 EHRR 581.

[576] 2007-XX; 49 EHRR 355 para 84.   [577] Hudoc (2006). Cf *Buzescu v Romania* hudoc (2005).

[578] On the obligation to give reasons, see section 3.II.m.

m. A reasoned judgment

The requirement of a 'fair' hearing also supposes that a court will give reasons for its judgment, in both criminal and non-criminal cases. Whereas national courts are allowed considerable discretion as to the structure and content of their judgments, they must 'indicate with sufficient clarity the grounds on which they base their decision' so as to allow a litigant usefully to exercise any available right of appeal.[579] Further justifications for the need for a reasoned judgment are the interest of a litigant in knowing that his or her arguments have been properly examined, and the interest of the public in a democratic society in knowing the reasons for judicial decisions given in its name.[580]

Precisely what is required will depend upon the nature and circumstances of each case.[581] It is not necessary for the court to deal with every point raised in argument.[582] If, however, a submission would, if accepted, be decisive for the outcome of the case, it may require a 'specific and express reply' by the court in its judgment, although an 'implied rejection' may be sufficient if clear.[583] Merely stating that a party has been grossly negligent where such negligence is crucial to the decision without explaining why this is so is unlikely to comply with Article 6.[584] Likewise, giving a reason for a decision that is not a good reason in law will not do so.[585] There was inadequate reasoning in breach of Article 6 where a court did not address inconsistencies in witness evidence and the mental condition of a key witness in its judgment.[586]

In *Taxquet v Belgium*,[587] the Grand Chamber held that a jury does not have to give reasons for its decision; Article 6 will be complied with provided that there are 'sufficient safeguards...to avoid any risk of arbitrariness and to enable the accused [and the public] to understand the reasons for his conviction'. The safeguards may include 'directions or guidance provided by the presiding judge to the jurors on the legal issues arising or the evidence adduced, and precise, unequivocal questions put to the jury by the judge, forming a framework on which the verdict is based or sufficiently offsetting the fact that no reasons are given for the jury's answers.' In addition, the existence of a right of appeal capable of remedying an improper verdict is relevant. In the *Taxquet* case, there was a breach of Article 6 in the absence of sufficient safeguards. Questions were put to the jury by the presiding judge, but the accused had been tried with seven co-defendants and the questions were identical for all of them, so that the applicant was unable to determine why he in particular was found guilty. There was also only a right of appeal on points of law, so that the reasons for the applicant's conviction might not emerge. In *Judge v UK*,[588] there were sufficient safeguards (details in the indictment, directions by the judge, and a

---

[579] *Hadjianastassiou v Greece* A 252 (1992); 16 EHRR 219. See also *Karakasis v Greece* hudoc (2000); 36 EHRR 507 and *Hirvisaari v Finland* hudoc (2001); 38 EHRR 139. In criminal cases, the Article 6(1) guarantee of a reasoned judgment overlaps with the Article 6(3)(b) 'facilities' guarantee in respect of appeals.

[580] *Tatishvili v Russia* hudoc (2007); 45 EHRR 1246.

[581] *Garcia Ruiz v Spain* 1999-I; 31 EHRR 589 GC.

[582] *Van de Hurk v Netherlands* A 288 (1994); 18 EHRR 481 para 61. But the applicant's 'main arguments' must be addressed: *Buzescu v Romania* hudoc (2005) and *Pronina v Ukraine* hudoc (2006).

[583] *Ruiz Torija v Spain* A 303-A (1994); 19 EHRR 553 para 30. Cf *Hiro Balani v Spain* A 303-B (1994); 19 EHRR 566 para 28; *Elo v Finland No 30742/02* hudoc (2004) DA; and *Kuznetsov v Russia* 2007-XX; 49 EHRR 355.   [584] *Georgiadis v Greece* 1997-III; 24 EHRR 606.

[585] *De Moor v Belgium* A 292-A (1994); 18 EHRR 372.   [586] *Ajdarić v Croatia* hudoc (2011).

[587] 2010-I; 54 EHRR 933 GC paras 90, 92. See Roberts, 11 HRLR 213 (2011). See also *Agnelet v France*; *Legillon v France* hudoc (2013) (insufficient indication why accused guilty in *Agnelet*, sufficient in *Legillon*).

[588] *No 35863/10* hudoc (2011) DA. For pre-*Taxquet* cases, see *Papon v France (No 2) No 54210/00* hudoc (2001) DA; *Saric v Denmark* hudoc (1999) DA; and *Planka v Austria No 25852/94* hudoc (1996) DA.

right to appeal for a 'miscarriage of justice') for the applicant to understand why he had been convicted so that the failure of the jury to give reasons did not render his trial unfair.

The right to a reasoned judgment applies to appellate, as well as lower court, decisions, although an appellate judgment may not have to be so fully reasoned. It may be sufficient for an appeal court that agrees with the reasoning of the trial or lower appeal court simply to incorporate that reasoning by reference, or otherwise indicate its agreement with it.[589] The essential requirement in such cases is that, in one way or another, the appeal court shows that it 'did in fact address the essential issues' in the appeal, and did not endorse without evaluation the decision of the lower court[590] or allow an appeal without addressing them.[591] In other cases, decisions by appeal courts rejecting appeals in very summary terms where there is clearly no merit in the appeal have been found not to be in breach of Article 6.[592] When refusing leave to appeal, there is no obligation to give detailed reasons or, in some cases, to give reasons at all.[593]

n. The principle of legal certainty

The right to a fair hearing also requires that the judgment by the final court that decides a case is *res judicata* and hence be irreversible, in accordance with the principle of legal certainty. In the leading case of *Brumarescu v Romania*,[594] a Court of First Instance held that the nationalization of the applicant's parents' house was invalid. In the absence of any appeal to a higher court, the decision became *res judicata* and the house was returned to the applicant. Later, the Procurator-General of Romania, who was not a party to the case, successfully applied to the Supreme Court of Justice for the decision to be quashed on the ground that the trial court had exceeded its jurisdiction. At Strasbourg, a Grand Chamber ruled in favour of the applicant on the following basis:

> The right to a fair hearing before a tribunal…must be interpreted in the light of the Preamble…which declares…the rule of law to be a part of the common heritage of the Contracting States. One of the fundamental aspects of the rule of law is the principle of legal certainty, which requires *inter alia* that where the courts have finally determined an issue, their ruling should not be called into question…In the present case the Court notes that…the exercise of that power by the Procurator-General was not subject to any time limit, so that judgments were liable to challenge indefinitely…The Court observes that, by allowing the application lodged under that power, the Supreme Court of Justice set at naught an entire judicial process which had ended in a judicial decision that was…'irreversible' and thus *res judicata*—and which moreover had been executed.

The power of the Prosecutor-General in issue in the *Brumarescu* case to initiate 'supervisory review' proceedings was a common feature in former Soviet-style legal systems, and was exercisable by a 'range of persons', including judges who were 'chairmen of the courts and their deputies'.[595]

---

[589] *Garcia Ruiz v Spain* 1999-I; 31 EHRR 589 GC.

[590] *Helle v Finland* 1997-VIII; 26 EHRR 159. Not shown in *Sakkapoulos v Greece* hudoc (2004).

[591] *Lindner and Hammermayer v Romania* hudoc (2002).

[592] See *X v Germany No 8769/79*, 25 DR 240 (1981). Fines for a vexatious appeal may not require detailed justification: *Les Travaux du Midi v France No 12275/86*, 70 DR 47 (1991) and *GL v Italy No 15384/89*, 77-A DR 5 (1994). [593] *Sawoniuk v UK* 2001-VI and *Gorou v Greece (No 2)* hudoc (2009) GC.

[594] 1999-VII; 33 EHRR 862 para 61.

[595] *Tregubenko v Ukraine* hudoc (2004); 43 EHRR 608 para 36 (deputy chairman, Supreme Court). See also *Ryabykh v Russia* 2003-IX; 40 EHRR 615 (regional court president) and *Rosca and Others v Moldova* hudoc (2005) (public prosecutor).

The *Brumarescu* ruling applies to the courts as well as to members of the executive, as the issue is one of legal certainty and not just of an interference by the executive.[596] Thus in *Driza v Albania*,[597] it was a violation of the principle of legal certainty for the Supreme Court to allow the President of that Court to quash a final decision of the Supreme Court (Administrative Division). A procedure for quashing a final judgment may, however, be consistent with the principle of legal certainty where it is 'made necessary by circumstances of a substantial and compelling character', which would include the need to correct a miscarriage of justice.[598] There is also no breach where earlier case law is overturned by the courts and applied retrospectively to the applicant's pending case:[599] 'case-law development is not, in itself, contrary to the proper administration of justice since a failure to maintain a dynamic and evolutive approach would risk hindering reform or improvement'.[600] Similarly, divergencies in the case law of the courts within a legal system are acceptable provided that there is a higher court or some other mechanism with competence to resolve 'profound and long standing differences'.[601]

Although the *Brumarescu* case was decided by the Grand Chamber on the basis of the residual right to a 'fair hearing' in Article 6(1), in their concurring opinions Judges Rozakis, Bratza, and Zupančič took the view, which has a lot to recommend it, that the situation is best considered as concerning the 'right of access to a court'. In their judgments in later cases, Chambers of the Court vary in their reasoning, referring to a 'fair hearing';[602] a 'fair hearing' and a 'right of access';[603] or generally to a 'right to a court'.[604]

o. Other fair hearing issues

A number of other particular 'fair hearing' issues have been resolved or raised in the jurisprudence of the Court, and formerly the Commission. One point that is clear is that a jury trial in criminal cases is not an element of the right to a 'fair hearing'.[605] Despite being highly prized in common law jurisdictions, the jury's lack of general use in European legal systems made this inevitable in view of the consensus approach to the interpretation of the Convention.[606] Where juries are used they must comply with the requirements of Article 6. This is particularly true of the requirement that a tribunal be 'impartial'.[607]

There is jurisprudence to suggest that the failure by a court to respect an undertaking or indication that it gives to a litigant, and that prejudices the presentation of his case,

---

[596] *Tregubenko v Ukraine*. Cf *Sovtransavto Holding v Ukraine* 2002-VII; 38 EHRR 911.

[597] 2007-V; 49 EHRR 779.

[598] *Pravednaya v Russia* hudoc (2004) para 25. See also *Nikitin v Russia* 2004-VIII and *Lenskaya v Russia* hudoc (2009). Miscarriage of justice procedures exist in European legal systems generally.

[599] *Unédec v France* hudoc (2008) and *Legrand v France* hudoc (2011).

[600] *Nejdet Şahin and Periham Şahin v Turkey* hudoc (2011) GC para 58.

[601] *Nejdet Şahin and Periham Şahin v Turkey*, paras 53, 54. Cf *Albu v Romania* hudoc (2010).

[602] *Rosca and Others v Moldova* hudoc (2005).

[603] *Ryabykh v Russia* hudoc (2003) and *Pravednaya v Russia* hudoc (2004).

[604] *Tregubenko v Ukraine* hudoc (2004). Cf *Poltorachenko v Ukraine* hudoc (2005).

[605] *X and Y v Ireland* No 8299/78, 22 DR 51 (1980) and *Callaghan v UK* No 14739/89, 60 DR 296 (1989). The same must be true in civil cases.

[606] In *Taxquet v Belgium* 2010-; 54 EHRR 933 GC, the Court noted, paras 45–7, that ten states parties, including Belgium, Russia, and the United Kingdom, had 'traditional' jury systems, with the presiding judge not participating in the deliberations of a lay jury. Fourteen states, including the Netherlands and Turkey, did not use juries at all; the remainder, including France and Germany, used a 'collaborative' system in which the judge and jury collectively decided the case.

[607] See section 3.V. As to the need to give reasons, see section 3.II.m. As to jury vetting and Article 6, see Gallivan and Warbrick, 5 HRR 176 (1980). As to trial by judge alone for fear of jury tampering, see *Twomey, Cameron and Guthrie v UK* No 67318/09 and No 22226/12 hudoc (2013) DA.

may render the hearing unfair, although there must be good evidence to show that the undertaking or indication was given.[608] In *CG v UK*,[609] it was implied that interventions or other conduct by the judge during the hearing that interferes with a litigant's freedom to plead his case may render the hearing unfair. In that case, the trial judge's interruptions during the defence's questioning of witnesses was 'excessive and undesirable' but were not, when the hearing was viewed as a whole, such as to render it unfair in breach of Article 6(1).

Certain other issues have been left open. For example, it is not established whether the trial of an accused who has been brought within the defendant state's territory following an abduction for which it is responsible infringes his right to a fair hearing.[610]

III. THE RIGHT TO A PUBLIC HEARING AND THE PUBLIC PRONOUNCEMENT OF JUDGMENT

a. The right to a public hearing

This guarantee has two elements:[611] it requires both that a hearing take place in public and by implication that there is in the first place an oral hearing, not just written proceedings. Focusing mainly on the first of these elements, the Court has explained the purpose of the guarantee as being to 'protect litigants against the administration of justice in secret with no public scrutiny', thereby contributing, through the resulting transparency, to a fair hearing and to the maintenance of confidence in the courts.[612] In this connection, the presence of the press, which includes reporters for the electronic media, is particularly important.[613] The guarantee applies in criminal and non-criminal cases.

The right to a public hearing has been a particular problem for administrative or disciplinary tribunals or other bodies that are not 'classic' courts within the ordinary court system, but that are competent to adjudicate upon either disciplinary or regulatory offences that qualify as 'criminal' for the purposes of Article 6[614] or a person's 'civil rights and obligations,' for example the right to practise a profession.[615] In the case of such a tribunal, its failure to provide a public hearing may be remedied if its decision is subject to review by a judicial body that does provide a public hearing, although the scope of the review that the judicial body must have may vary.[616] In the case of a court 'of the classic kind', this will not be sufficient: 'Given the possible detrimental effects that the lack of a public hearing before the trial court could have on the fairness of the proceedings, the absence of publicity could not in any event be remedied by anything other than a complete re-hearing before the appellate court'.[617]

---

[608] *Pardo v France* A 261-B (1993); 17 EHRR 383 para 28. See also *Colak v Germany* A 147 (1988); 11 EHRR 513.   [609] Hudoc (2001); 34 EHRR 789.

[610] See *Stocké v Germany* A 199 (1991); 13 EHRR 839 in which the Court was not satisfied, on the facts, that there had been state involvement.   [611] See Cremona, *Wiarda Mélanges*, p 107.

[612] *Malhous v Czech Republic* 2001-XII para 55 GC. Cf *Barberà, Messegué and Jabardo v Spain* A 146 (1988); 11 EHRR 360 para 89 PC, in which the right to a public hearing was breached because much of the evidence against the accused was made a part of the record without being adduced or read in court, and hence not subjected to 'the watchful eye of the public'.

[613] *Axen v Germany*, B 57 (1981) para 77 Com Rep. References to the 'public' in this section include the press.   [614] See, eg, *Vernes v France* hudoc (2011).

[615] See, eg, *Le Compte, Van Leuven and De Meyere v Belgium* A 43 (1981); 4 EHRR 1 PC; and *Hurter v Switzerland* hudoc (2005).

[616] *Riepan v Austria* 2000-XII para 39. On the scope of the required review, see section 2.II.e.

[617] *Riepan v Austria*, 2000-XII para 40. By a 'complete re-hearing' is meant one in which the court with the power of review hears the witnesses, etc, as if it were the trial court: *Göç v Turkey* 2002-V GC.

Whereas court hearings must generally be in public, the public may be excluded from an oral hearing on one or more of the grounds listed in Article 6(1). The list is an exhaustive one: a private hearing will be in breach of Article 6 if it is not justified on one or more of the listed grounds.[618]

In the interpretation of similar lists of restrictions to the rights guaranteed in Articles 8–11 of the Convention, the Court, and formerly the Commission, has required the restriction to be a proportionate response to a pressing social need.[619] This interpretation is based upon the wording 'necessary in a democratic society' in those Articles. Although the text of Article 6(1) does not contain this precise formula,[620] such a balancing approach seems generally appropriate. A proportionality test was used in *Campbell and Fell v UK*.[621] In that case, it was held that prison disciplinary proceedings could be conducted *in camera* on prison premises for 'reasons of public order and security'. The Court had in mind the problems of security that would result for the state in admitting the public to the prison or in transporting convicted prisoners to court.

In the interpretation of Articles 8 to 11 of the Convention, the Court has also applied a margin of appreciation doctrine, by which the state is allowed a certain discretion in its assessment of the need for a restriction in a particular factual situation.[622] However, there has been no case in which margin of appreciation language has been used in a Court judgment concerning restrictions on a public hearing:[623] instead the Court, and formerly the Commission, has made its own assessment of the need for a restriction without indicating that any discretion is left to the respondent state. The wording of the 'interests of justice' restriction ('in the opinion of the court') most clearly invites a margin of appreciation approach.[624]

As to the particular grounds on which a hearing *in camera* is permissible, in *B and P v UK*,[625] it was stated that proceedings in cases concerning the residence of children following the divorce or separation of the parents are 'prime examples' where private court hearings may be justified, in order to 'protect the privacy of the child and parties' and to 'avoid prejudicing the interests of justice'. In such cases, 'it is essential that the parents and other witnesses feel able to express themselves candidly on highly personal issues without fear of public curiosity or comment'. The exclusion of the public from divorce proceedings[626] and from medical disciplinary proceedings[627] is also permissible as being for the 'protection of the private life of the parties'. The 'interests of justice' may, even in criminal cases, justify the giving of evidence *in camera* 'to protect the safety or privacy of witnesses or to promote the free exchange of information and opinion in the pursuit of justice'.[628] The exclusion of the public from the trial of an accused for sexual offences

---

[618] For cases not falling within the listed exceptions, see *Osinger v Austria* hudoc (2005) (succession to property) and *Olujić v Croatia* hudoc (2009); 52 EHRR 839 (dignity of the accused and the judiciary).

[619] See Ch 8.

[620] As to the wording 'strictly necessary' in Article 6(1), see the standard set for 'absolutely necessary' in Article 2: section X.XX, p 000.

[621] A 80 (1984); 7 EHRR 165.   [622] See Ch 8.

[623] But see the separate opinions of Judge Morenilla in *Nortier v Netherlands* A 267 (1993); 17 EHRR 273 and Lord Reed in *V v UK* 1999-IX; 30 EHRR 121 GC, mentioned earlier, in the context of juvenile cases.

[624] But the wording *'strictly* necessary' suggests a limited margin.

[625] 2001-III; 34 EHRR 529 para 38. Cf *Moser v Austria* hudoc (2006) (child transfer to public care; public hearing required).   [626] *X v UK No 7366/76*, 2 Digest 452 (1977).

[627] *Guenoun v France No 13562/88*, 66 DR 181 (1990). See also *Imberechts v Belgium No 15561/89*, 69 DR 312 (1991) (private lives of patients).

[628] *B and P v UK* 2001-III; 34 EHRR 529 para 37. The private nature of pre-trial investigations is permissible in the interests of the privacy of those questioned and of justice: *Ernst and Others v Belgium* hudoc (2003); 37 EHRR 724.

against children was justified under Article 6(1) without specifying which particular ground of restriction was being applied.[629] As to the other grounds for private hearings permitted by Article 6(1), in *Campbell and Fell v UK*,[630] the Court relied upon the 'public order' restriction in Article 6(1), interpreting the term as having a wide public interest meaning, thereby including prison security, rather than one limited to public disorder.[631] A trial *in camera* may be justified on grounds of 'national security' in a prosecution for passing state secrets.[632]

More generally, the Court has accepted that it is permissible to exclude a whole class of cases from a public hearing by reference to one or more of the grounds listed in Article 6(1), subject to the Court deciding that the general exclusion of cases within the class falls within one of the grounds listed in Article 6(1). Thus in *B and P v UK*,[633] the Court found it acceptable that there was a rebuttable presumption in favour of a private hearing in all proceedings under the Children Act 1989.

Article 6(1) provides an entitlement to a 'public' hearing as an individual right which may be restricted on the initiative of the state on a permitted ground. However, there may be cases in which an accused or other litigant would prefer a private hearing. In such a case, the question will be whether a public hearing would be a violation of the right to a 'fair' hearing in Article 6(1), or of the right to privacy in Article 8. Thus in *V v UK*,[634] involving the trial of two young boys accused in a murder case that attracted great press attention, the issue was not whether the state *could* exclude the press and the public under Article 6(1), but what adaptations to the normal court procedures, including the public nature of the hearings, it was *obliged* to make in order to ensure that the accused had a 'fair' hearing in the sense of Article 6(1), free from the glare of publicity. In other cases in which an accused or private litigant has been refused a private hearing by a national court, a right to privacy claim under Article 8 may or may not be outweighed by a public interest justification allowed by Article 8(2).[635] Obviously, there is also an interest on the part of the public in knowing what is happening in the courts generally.

Court hearings must be open to the public in fact as well as in law. Accordingly, in *Riepan v Austria*,[636] the Court stated that Article 6 will only be complied with if the public is 'able to obtain information about its date and place and if this place is easily accessible to the public'. The latter requirement will normally be met by holding the hearing in a 'regular courtroom large enough to accommodate spectators'. In the *Riepan* case, there was not a 'public' hearing when, because of the risk of the applicant escaping, the hearing leading to the applicant's conviction for an ordinary criminal offence, for threatening prison officers, was held not in the criminal court building but in the prison where he was serving a sentence for murder. The hearing was open to the public and its prison location was on the weekly court list sent to the media and available to the public at the court's registry. But no particular measures were taken, such as directions to the prison, to facilitate attendance, and the hearing was held

---

[629] *X v Austria No 1913/63*, 2 Digest 438 (1965). Several grounds, including the 'interests of juveniles', could have applied. See also *V v UK* 1999-IX; 30 EHRR 121 GC.

[630] A 80 (1984); 7 EHRR 165, mentioned earlier. See also *Riepan v Austria* 2000-XII.

[631] Cf *Le Compte, Van Leuven and De Meyere v Belgium* A 43 (1981); 4 EHRR 1 para 59 PC. This public interest meaning is consistent with the French text of Article 6(1) which uses the term '*ordre public*'. Public disorder in the courtroom might be brought within the 'interests of justice' restriction.

[632] *Moiseyev v Russia No 62936/00* hudoc (2004) DA.   [633] 2001-III; 34 EHRR 529.

[634] 1999-IX; 30 EHRR 121 GC.

[635] In *B and P v UK* 2001-III; 34 EHRR 529, mentioned earlier, the wife had no need to bring an Article 8 claim, the court having rejected the applicant husband's claim to a public hearing.

[636] 2000-XII para 29. Cf *Hummatov v Azerbaijan* hudoc (2007); 49 EHRR 960.

in a small room early in the morning. In these circumstances, not enough had been done to counterbalance the detrimental effect for the public of holding the hearing in prison.[637]

An oral hearing

Although not expressly mentioned in the text of Article 6, an oral hearing 'constitutes a fundamental principle enshrined in Article 6(1)'. [638] This follows in criminal cases from the nature of the guarantees in Article 6(3)(c), (d), and (e) and has been held to be required in non-criminal cases also.[639] The right to an oral hearing has a general scope, applying both when a court sits in public and to hearings *in camera* in circumstances allowed by Article 6(1).[640]

The obligation to hold an oral hearing is not absolute. In *Jussila v Finland*,[641] the Grand Chamber characterized the position as follows. It stated that 'the character of the circumstances that may justify dispensing with an oral hearing essentially comes down to the nature of the issues to be decided', not their 'frequency', and that Article 6(1) did not 'mean that refusing to hold an oral hearing may be justified only in rare cases'. Prior to the *Jussila* case, the kinds of cases in which it had been established that the absence of an oral hearing is permissible had all been non-criminal cases. In these, the issues involved had been 'highly technical'[642] or concerned exclusively questions of law of 'no particular complexity'.[643] In these circumstances, in which the case could perfectly adequately be decided on the basis of written documents, the Court has recognized that 'it is understandable that the national authorities should have regard to the demands of efficiency and economy'.[644] However, in such cases the applicant should have the opportunity to request an oral hearing, either at first instance or, if applicable, on appeal, on the ground that the case presents special features, although the request may be rejected following proper consideration of it.[645]

In the *Jussila* case,[646] the Grand Chamber accepted that, although the right to an oral hearing 'is particularly important in the criminal context', it may also be dispensed with in some criminal cases. Generally, it distinguished between criminal cases that do not carry 'any significant degree of stigma', and others that form a part of the 'hard core of criminal law'. On the facts, the Grand Chamber held that an oral hearing was not required in a case involving the imposition of a tax surcharge. It also referred to cases involving administrative,[647] customs, competition, and other financial offences that fall

---

[637] The Court distinguished the *Campbell and Fell* case, A 80 (1984); 7 EHRR 165, p 272, because the latter concerned prison disciplinary offences. However, the *Campbell and Fell* offences were 'criminal' for the purposes of Article 6 and the conduct concerned would now be dealt with under English law as criminal offences in the ordinary courts.

[638] *Jussila v Finland* 2006-XIV; 45 EHRR 892 GC para 40. Cf *Göç v Turkey* 2002-V GC.

[639] *Demebulov v Bulgaria* hudoc (2008). Cf *Gülmez v Turkey* hudoc (2008) (prison disciplinary proceedings).

[640] The Court's jurisprudence has not always clearly distinguished between the requirements of a public hearing and an oral hearing: see, eg, *Ekbatani v Sweden* A 134 (1988); 13 EHRR 504 PC.

[641] 2006-XIV; 45 EHRR 892 GC para 42. Cf *Miller v Sweden* hudoc (2005).

[642] *Schuler-Zgraggen v Switzerland* A 263 (1993); 16 EHRR 405 para 58. The Court also stressed that there was no issue of 'public importance' involved: para 58. As in *Schuler-Zgraggen*, most cases have concerned social security benefit claims turning upon medical evidence: see, eg, *Miller v Sweden* hudoc; 42 EHRR 1155. See also *Martinie v France* 2006-VI; 45 EHRR 433 GC (judicial audit of accounts) and *Hofbauer v Austria No 68087/01* hudoc (2004) DA (whether door was fire-resistant).

[643] *Valová, Slezák and Slezák v Slovakia* hudoc (2004). See also *Allan Jacobson v Sweden (No 2)* 1998-I; 32 EHRR 463. [644] *Schuler-Zgraggen v Switzerland* A 263 (1993); 16 EHRR 405 para 58.

[645] *Martinie v France* 2006-VI GC; 45 EHRR 433; *Koottummel v Austria* HUDOC (2009); 52 EHRR 505 ; and *Andersson v Sweden* hudoc (2010). [646] 2006-XIV; 45 EHRR 892 GC paras 40, 43.

[647] See, eg, *Suhadolc v Slovenia* hudoc (2011) DA (road traffic offence).

within Article 6 under the *Engel* case but that do not strictly belong to the 'traditional categories of the criminal law' as being cases in which an oral hearing might not be required.

Clearly, where an oral hearing is required, a court of first instance must provide that hearing where there is no right of appeal.[648] In cases in which there has been an oral hearing at first instance, or in which one has been waived at that level,[649] there is no absolute right to an oral hearing in any appeal proceedings that are provided. Instead, whether this is required 'depends on the special features of the proceedings involved; account must be taken of the entirety of the proceedings in the domestic legal order and of the role of the appellate court therein'.[650] Where the proceedings involve an appeal only on points of law, an oral hearing is generally not required.[651] If an appeal court is called upon to decide questions of fact, an oral hearing may or may not be required, depending upon whether one is necessary to ensure a fair trial.[652] In practice, the cases have mostly concerned an oral hearing at which the applicant, as opposed to his lawyer, wished to be present in person to give evidence or otherwise assist the court.[653] In *Ekbatani v Sweden*,[654] an oral hearing was required on appeal where there was a dispute as to the facts in a criminal case that involved the accused's credibility: the accused's guilt or innocence 'could not, as a matter of a fair trial, have been properly determined without a direct assessment of the evidence given in person by the applicant'. In contrast, in *Jan-Ake Andersson v Sweden*,[655] an oral hearing was not required in the case of a minor road traffic offence in which the appeal did not raise 'any questions of fact or law which could not adequately be resolved on the basis of the case file'. What is at stake for the applicant is also relevant. Thus in *Helmers v Sweden*,[656] in a private criminal prosecution for defamation, it was relevant that the applicant's professional reputation and career were at stake.

Waiver of a public hearing

A person may waive his right to a public hearing, so long as the waiver is done of his own free will 'in an unequivocal manner' and there is no 'important public interest' consideration that requires a public hearing.[657] This possibility of waiver applies to the right to a public hearing in the sense of both a right to an oral hearing, and of access of the public thereto.[658] A waiver may be tacit, provided that it is clear from the facts that one is being made.[659] An 'unequivocal' waiver was found to have been made in *Håkansson*

---

[648] *Göç v Turkey* 2002-V GC.   [649] *Döry v Sweden* hudoc (2002).

[650] *Ekbatani v Sweden* A 134 (1988); 13 EHRR 504 para 27 PC. See also *Hermi v Italy* 2006-XII; 46 EHRR 1115 GC.

[651] *Axen v Germany* A 72 (1983); 6 EHRR 195. An oral hearing is not required for leave to appeal proceedings: *Monnell and Morris v UK* A 115 (1987); 10 EHRR 205.

[652] *Ekbatani v Sweden* A 134 (1988); 13 EHRR 504 PC. See also *Elsholz v Germany* 2000-VIII; 34 EHRR 1412 GC; *Sobolewski (No 2) v Poland* hudoc (2009); *Schlumpf v Switzerland* hudoc (2009).

[653] There is in such cases an overlap with the rights to be present at a hearing, section 3.II.a, and to participate effectively therein, section 3.II.g. On oral hearings at which the applicant must be represented by a lawyer, see section X.XX, p 000. A video-link may be sufficient on security grounds: see *Marcello Viola v Italy* 2006-XI.

[654] A 134 (1988); 13 EHRR 504 para 32 PC. See also *Kamasinski v Austria* A 168 (1989); 13 EHRR 36; *Botten v Norway* 1996-I; 32 EHRR 37; *Belziuk v Poland* 1998-II; 30 EHRR 614; *Schlumpf v Switzerland* hudoc (2009).

[655] A 212-B (1991); 15 EHRR 218 para 29.

[656] A 212-A (1991); 15 EHRR 285. See also *Kremzow v Austria* A 268-B (1993); 17 EHRR 322; *Constantinescu v Romania* 2000-VIII; and *Sigurdór Arnarsson v Iceland* hudoc (2003); 39 EHRR 426.

[657] *Håkansson and Sturesson v Sweden* A 171-A (1990); 13 EHRR 1 para 66. See also *Schuler-Zgraggen v Switzerland* A 263 (1993); 16 EHRR 405 para 58 and *Pauger v Austria* 1997-III; 25 EHRR 105 para 58.

[658] See the *Håkansson and Sturesson* and *Pauger* cases.

[659] See *Hermi v Italy* hudoc (2006); 46 EHRR 1115 GC.

and Sturesson v Sweden[660] when the applicant failed to ask for a public hearing before a court, which by law conducted its proceedings in private unless a public hearing was considered by it to be 'necessary'. The judgment can be criticized as requiring the applicant to take the initiative to request the application of an exception to a general rule, when the general rule should itself, consistently with Article 6(1), provide for a public hearing.[661] The cases in which a waiver has been established have concerned professional disciplinary proceedings or civil litigation; it is arguable that a stricter test should apply to criminal cases.

b. The right to the public pronouncement of judgment

In contrast with the right to a public hearing, the right to have judgment 'pronounced publicly' is not subject to any exceptions in the text of Article 6(1). However, the Court has applied the wording 'pronounced publicly' 'with some degree of flexibility'.[662] Whereas this wording appears to require that judgment be delivered orally in full in open court,[663] the Strasbourg Court has not taken this view. Instead it has established a number of limitations or exceptions.

First, it may be sufficient that delivery in court is not of the full text of the judgments at all levels of the proceedings. In *Lamanna v Austria*,[664] there was no breach of Article 6(1) when the Court of Appeal's judgment on a claim for compensation for detention was delivered by it in open court, but only contained a summary of the trial court's otherwise unpublished judgment. Further, it was not delivered until six years after its adoption, on the order of the Supreme Court after an application had been declared admissible at Strasbourg. In contrast, in *Ryakib Biryukov v Russia*,[665] it was held not sufficient just to read out the operative part of judgment in a civil case, without giving any reasons for the decision. Secondly, an exception may be allowed for reasons of security. In *Campbell and Fell v UK*,[666] in the special context of Boards of Visitors in the former English system of prison disciplinary proceedings, the Court accepted that a Board of Visitors award need not be delivered in the presence of 'press and public' in view of the problem of prison security, but found a breach of the 'pronounced publicly' requirement since no alternative arrangements had been made to publish the text of the award.[667]

Thirdly, noting that the publication of some kinds of judgments by making them available to the public in the court registry is a long-standing tradition in many Council of Europe member states, in *Pretto v Italy*,[668] the Strasbourg Court ruled that 'the form of publicity to be given to the "judgment"…must be assessed in the light of the special features of the proceedings in question and by reference to the object and purpose of Article 6(1)', with account being taken of the 'entirety of the proceedings', including the function of the court concerned and whether judgments have been pronounced in open court at any level in the case. Thus in the *Pretto* case, the Court held that Article 6(1)

---

[660] A 171-A (1990); 13 EHRR 1. Cf *H v Belgium* A 127–B (1987); 10 EHRR 339 PC. Failure to ask for a hearing by a court that lacks full jurisdiction in the case is not a waiver: *Göç v Turkey* 2002-V GC.

[661] Cf Judge Walsh's dissenting opinion.   [662] *Lamanna v Austria* hudoc (2001) para 31.

[663] The French text—'*rendu publiquement*'—suggests the same: *Pretto v Italy* A 71 (1983); 6 EHRR 182 PC.

[664] Hudoc (2001). See also *Crociani v Italy No 8603/79*, 22 DR 147 (1980).

[665] 2008-.

[666] A 80 (1984); 7 EHRR 165. The disciplinary function of Boards of Visitors has since been abolished.

[667] Following the judgment, arrangements were made for the publication of Boards of Visitors awards in the local press. See also *Fazliyski v Bulgaria* hudoc (2013) (one year delay in publishing judgment not justified).

[668] A 71 (1983); 6 EHRR 182 PC, paras 26–7. Cf *Axen v Germany* A 72 (1983); 6 EHRR 195 para 31 PC.

was complied with, even though the judgment of the Italian Court of Cassation rejecting the applicant's appeal in a civil claim was only made available to the public in the court registry without having been delivered orally in open court. The Strasbourg Court noted that the Court of Cassation had jurisdiction to consider only points of law and to reject an appeal or quash a judgment, and that it had given its judgment after a public hearing. Bearing in mind the purpose of the 'pronounced publicly' requirement, which is to contribute to a fair trial through public scrutiny,[669] publication via the registry was consistent with Article 6(1) on these facts.

The *Pretto* judgment concerned a state's highest court. The Court has applied the same dispensation to the publication of lower court judgments. In *Werner v Austria*,[670] the judgments of the trial court and the first court of appeal on the applicant's claim for compensation for detention after criminal proceedings against him had been discontinued were not delivered in court. They were served on the applicant but were otherwise only available from the registry to third parties who, in the court's opinion, could show a legitimate interest. Since it might be of importance to the person concerned that the public should know that any suspicion against him has been dispelled, the Strasbourg Court held that there was a breach of Article 6(1) because 'no judicial decision was pronounced publicly and...publicity was not sufficiently ensured by other appropriate means'. The second alternative allowed by the Court would seem to suggest that it is sufficient for judgments of lower courts to be made available to the public generally from the court registry. Involving the same deviation from the literal wording of Article 6(1), the Court's approach here again accords with the practice in a number of European legal systems.

Fourthly, the Court has accepted that the publication of orders or judgments concerning children's and parental rights may be restricted to interested persons, ie not made available to the public at large. Thus in *B and P v UK*,[671] it was sufficient that anyone who could establish an interest could consult or obtain a copy of the full text of the orders or judgments made by the court of first instance in child residence cases. Further, the publication of first instance and appeal court judgments in law reports in such cases sufficiently allowed the general public to study the approach taken by the courts. Interestingly, in the *B and P* case, the Court drew upon the 'interests of juveniles' and the 'administration of justice' exceptions to the requirement of a public hearing in the text of Article 6(1) when reaching this decision on the public pronouncement of judgment.

Whereas it is well established that the right to a public hearing may be waived, the Court, and formerly the Commission, has not ruled on the question whether this is the case with the right to public pronouncement of a judgment. There appears to be no good reason to distinguish between the two rights in this regard.

IV. THE RIGHT TO TRIAL WITHIN A REASONABLE TIME

The purpose of the 'reasonable time' guarantee, which applies to both criminal and non-criminal cases, is to protect 'all parties to court proceedings...against excessive procedural delays'[672] and 'underlines the importance of rendering justice without delays which

---

[669] See *Werner v Austria* 1996-VII; 26 EHRR 310.

[670] 1997-VII; 26 EHRR 310 para 60. Cf *Sutter v Switzerland* A 74 (1984); 6 EHRR 272 PC.

[671] 2001-III; 34 EHRR 529. The Court cited *Sutter v Switzerland* A 74 (1984); 6 EHRR 272 PC, in which there was no breach in military disciplinary proceedings when only a person who could establish an interest could consult or obtain a copy of a judgment from the court registry.

[672] *Stögmüller v Austria* A 9 (1969) p. 40; 1 EHRR 155, 191.

might jeopardize its effectiveness and credibility'.[673] In criminal cases, it is also 'designed to avoid that a person charged should remain too long in a state of uncertainty about his fate'.[674] In such cases, the effect that being an accused has upon a person's reputation is relevant too.

In criminal cases, the reasonable time guarantee runs from the moment that an accused is subject to a 'charge', by which is meant 'substantially affected'.[675] In non-criminal cases, it normally begins to apply from the initiation of court proceedings, but sometimes earlier.[676] In both kinds of case, the guarantee continues to apply until the case is finally determined.[677] If proceedings are still pending in the national courts when an application is under consideration at Strasbourg, the period covered by the reasonable time guarantee runs until the judgment is given in the case by the Court.[678] If the respondent state becomes a party to the Convention after Article 6 has begun to apply to a particular case, the guarantee will only begin to run as of the date of ratification.[679] Nonetheless, in assessing the reasonableness of the time that is taken to determine a case after that date, 'account must be taken of the then state of proceedings'.[680] Thus a decision as to whether a case has been treated with the necessary expedition after that date will be influenced by the fact that the case has already been pending for a long time.[681]

The obligation to decide cases within a reasonable time extends to constitutional courts, subject to the need to take account of their special role as guardian of the constitution.[682] In particular, they may delay consideration of a case to ensure that sufficient time is taken to rule on a matter of constitutional importance, possibly in combination with other similar cases.

The reasonableness of the length of proceedings in both criminal and non-criminal cases depends on the particular circumstances of the case.[683] There is no absolute time limit. Factors that are always considered are the complexity of the case, the conduct of the applicant, and the conduct of the competent administrative and judicial authorities.[684] The Court also takes into account what is 'at stake' for the applicant when applying the last of these criteria.[685] No margin of appreciation doctrine is applied, at least expressly, when determining the reasonableness of the time taken; the European Court simply makes its own assessment.[686] When it does so, it must bear in mind that Article 6 can only require such expedition as is consistent with the proper administration of justice.[687]

As to the first of the three factors listed in the previous paragraph, a case may be complicated for many reasons, such as the volume of evidence,[688] the number of defendants or

[673] H v France A 162-A (1989); 12 EHRR 74 para 58.
[674] Stögmüller v Austria A 9 (1969) p 40; 1 EHRR 155, 191. Cf Wemhoff v Germany A 7 (1968); 1 EHRR 55.
[675] See section 2.I.g.   [676] See section 2.II.f.
[677] See section 3.IV. A reasonable time claim subsists despite acquittal: Lehtinen v Finland hudoc (2006).
[678] Neumeister v Austria A 8 (1968); 1 EHRR 91 and Nibbio v Italy A 228-A (1992).
[679] Foti and others v Italy A 56 (1982); 5 EHRR 313.
[680] Foti and others v Italy A 56 (1982); 5 EHRR 313 para 53.
[681] Brigandi v Italy A 194-B (1991).
[682] Sussmann v Germany 1996-IV; 25 EHRR 64 GC. But see Wimmer v Germany hudoc (2005) and Oršuš v Croatia 2010-; 52 EHRR 300 GC.
[683] König v Germany A 27 (1978); 2 EHRR 170 PC and Pedersen and Baadsgaard v Denmark 2004-XI; 42 EHRR 486 GC.   [684] König v Germany A 27 (1978); 2 EHRR 170 PC.
[685] Frydlender v France 2000-VII; 31 EHRR 1152 GC. What is 'at stake' is sometimes treated as a separate fourth factor: see, eg, Sürmeli v Germany 2006-VII; 44 EHRR 438 GC.
[686] See, eg, Casciaroli v Italy A 229-C (1992), in which the Court disagreed with the defendant state's assessment of the complexity of the case.
[687] Boddaert v Belgium A 235-D (1992); 16 EHRR 242. The accused is entitled to reasonable time to prepare his defence: see Article 6(3)(b), section 5.III.
[688] Eckle v Germany A 51 (1982); 5 EHRR 1.

charges,[689] the need to obtain expert evidence[690] or evidence from abroad,[691] or the complexity of the legal issues involved.[692]

With regard to the second factor, the state is not responsible for delay that is attributable to the conduct of the applicant. While an applicant is entitled to make use of his procedural rights, any consequential lengthening of proceedings cannot be held against the state.[693] In a criminal case, although an accused is not required 'actively to co-operate with the judicial authorities',[694] if delay results, for example, from his refusal to appoint a defence lawyer, this is not the responsibility of the state.[695] But a state is responsible for its negligent delay in discontinuing proceedings against an accused: it cannot claim that the accused should have reminded it.[696] Where an accused flees from the jurisdiction or disappears while subject to a 'charge', the time during which he has absented himself from the proceedings is not to be taken into account in determining the length of proceedings, unless there is a 'sufficient reason' for the flight.[697]

In civil litigation, some municipal legal systems apply the principle that the parties are responsible for the progress of proceedings.[698] This does not, however, 'absolve the courts from ensuring compliance with the requirements of Article 6 concerning reasonable time'; the state must itself take appropriate steps to ensure that proceedings progress speedily.[699] Whether such a principle applies or not, the responsibilities of the applicant in civil cases are only to 'show diligence in carrying out the procedural steps relevant to him, to refrain from using delaying tactics, and to avail himself of the scope afforded by domestic law for shortening proceedings'.[700] Delay caused by the conduct of the applicant's legal aid lawyer in civil proceedings is not attributable to the state: although he is publicly appointed, such a lawyer acts for his client, not the state.[701] Nor is a state responsible for delay that results from the conduct of the defendant against whom the applicant brings a civil claim.[702]

As to the third factor, the state is responsible for delays that are attributable to its administrative or judicial authorities.[703] In criminal cases, breaches of Article 6(1) have been found because of unjustified delays in the conduct of the preliminary investigation in a civil law system,[704] entering a *nolle prosequi*,[705] appointing judges,[706] controlling expert witnesses,[707]

---

[689] *Neumeister v Austria* A 8 (1968); 1 EHRR 91.   [690] *Wemhoff v Germany* A 7 (1968); 1 EHRR 55.

[691] *Neumeister v Austria* A 8 (1968); 1 EHRR 91. The respondent state will not be responsible for another state's delays in supplying evidence: *Neumeister v Austria*.   [692] *Neumeister v Austria*.

[693] See, eg, *König v Germany* A 27 (1978); 2 EHRR 170 PC (changing lawyers, making appeals, calling new evidence).   [694] *Eckle v Germany* A 51 (1982); 5 EHRR 1 para 82.

[695] *Corigliano v Italy* A 57 (1982); 5 EHRR 334.

[696] *Orchin v UK No 8435/78*, 34 DR 5 (1982) Com Rep; CM Res DH (83) 14.

[697] *Vayic v Turkey* 2006-VIII, citing *Ventura v Italy No 7438/76*, 23 DR 5 at 91 (1980).

[698] See *Buchholz v Germany* A 42 (1981); 3 EHRR 597 para 50 and *Foley v UK* hudoc (2002).

[699] *Unión Alimentaria Sanders SA v Spain* A 157 (1989); 12 EHRR 24 para 35. Cf *Sürmeli v Germany* 2006-VII; 44 EHRR 438 GC.

[700] *Unión Alimentaria Sanders SA v Spain*. Cf *Deumeland v Germany* A 100 (1986); 8 EHRR 448 para 80 PC. For cases of litigant delay for which the state was not responsible, see *Monnet v France* A 273-A (1993); 18 EHRR 27 and *Patrianakos v Greece* hudoc (2004).

[701] *H v France* A 162-A (1989); 12 EHRR 74. But in a criminal case there is a duty to provide effective legal aid under Article 6(3)(c). The state is not responsible for delays caused by a lawyers' strike: *Giannangeli v Italy* hudoc (2001).

[702] *Bock v Germany* A 150 (1989); 12 EHRR 247 para 41.

[703] A private law reporter's delay is not attributable to the state: *Foley v UK* hudoc (2002). *Quaere* whether the UK is responsible for delays by its health authorities: see *Somjee v UK* hudoc (2002); 36 EHRR 228.

[704] *Eckle v Germany* A 51 (1982); 5 EHRR 1.

[705] *Orchin v UK No 8435/78*, 34 DR 5 (1982) Com Rep; CM Res DH (83) 14.

[706] *Georgiadis v Cyprus* hudoc (2002). See also *Foti and others v Italy* A 56 (1982); 5 EHRR 313 (transferring cases between courts).   [707] *Rawa v Poland* hudoc (2003).

communicating the judgment to the applicant,[708] and the commencement of appeals.[709] Whereas it may be sensible to hear cases against two or more accused persons together, this cannot 'justify substantial delay' in the bringing of a case against any one of them.[710] In appropriate circumstances, a court may be justified in permitting a delay in order to allow political or other passions to cool.[711]

Where applicable, the same considerations apply in non-criminal cases also. In such cases, states have been held responsible for delays in civil and administrative courts in performing routine registry tasks,[712] in the conduct of the hearing by the court,[713] in the presentation of evidence by the state,[714] for the adjournment of proceedings pending the outcome of another case,[715] and for delays caused by lack of coordination between administrative authorities.[716] As in criminal cases, the period of time to be considered continues until the judgment becomes final.[717]

As indicated, when assessing the reasonableness of the length of proceedings, the Court also takes into account what is 'at stake' for the applicant.[718] The Court has identified a large number of kinds of case in which particular expedition is required on this basis. These include cases concerning the applicant's employment;[719] civil status;[720] custody of children;[721] education;[722] health;[723] reputation;[724] title to land;[725] business interests;[726] and compensation for road accidents.[727] It may be relevant that the applicant has been charged interest on the sum in dispute while the case is pending.[728] In criminal cases, the likelihood of a life sentence or other heavy sentence is relevant.[729]

Criminal cases generally require more urgency than non-criminal ones[730] and a more rigorous standard applies where an accused is in detention.[731] In the latter case, the reasonable time guarantee in Article 6(1) overlaps with that in Article 5(3), under which 'special diligence' in the time taken in cases where the accused is in detention is also required.[732] However, since Article 5(3) ceases to apply once an accused is convicted, the

---

[708] *Eckle v Germany* A 51 (1982); 5 EHRR 1.

[709] *Eckle v Germany.* The reasonable time guarantee continues to apply until the time limit for an appeal is exhausted: *Ferraro v Italy* A 197-A (1991).

[710] *Hentrich v France* A 296-A (1994); 18 EHRR 440. See also *Rezette v Luxembourg* hudoc (2004).

[711] *Foti and others v Italy* A 51 (1982); 5 EHRR 313.

[712] *Guincho v Portugal* A 81 (1984); 7 EHRR 23.

[713] *König v Germany* A 27 (1978); 2 EHRR 170 PC.   [714] *H v UK* A 120 (1987); 10 EHRR 95 PC.

[715] *König v Germany* A 27 (1978); 2 EHRR 170 PC. See also *Iribarren Pinillos v Spain* hudoc (2009).

[716] *Wiesinger v Austria* A 213 (1991); 16 EHRR 258.   [717] *Maciariello v Italy* A 230-A (1992).

[718] See section X.XX, p 000.

[719] *Buchholz v Germany* A 42 (1981); 3 EHRR 597. Cf *Eastaway v UK* hudoc (2004); 40 EHRR 405 (company director) and *Svetlana Orlova v Russia* hudoc (2009) (pregnant employee).

[720] *Sylvester v Austria No 2* hudoc (2005). See also *Berlin v Luxembourg* hudoc (2003) (family life).

[721] *Hokkanen v Finland* A 299-A (1994); 19 EHRR 139. Cf *H v UK* A 120 (1987); 10 EHRR 95 PC (parental access).   [722] *Orsus v Croatia* hudoc (2010); 52 EHRR 300 GC

[723] *Bock v Germany* A 150 (1989); 12 EHRR 247; *RPD v Poland* hudoc (2004); *Gheorghe v Romania* 2007-XX; and *De Clerck v Belgium* hudoc (2007). 'Exceptional diligence' is required in claims of compensation for AIDS: *X v France* A 234-C (1992); 14 EHRR 483.   [724] *Pieniążek v Poland* hudoc (2004).

[725] *Poiss v Austria* A 117 (1987); 10 EHRR 231 and *Hentrich v France* A 296-A (1994); 18 EHRR 440.

[726] *De Clerck v Belgium* hudoc (2007).

[727] *Silva Pontes v Portugal* A 286-A (1994); 18 EHRR 156. But see *Sürmeli v Germany* 2006-VII; 44 EHRR 438 GC.   [728] *Schouten and Meldrum v Netherlands* A 304 (1994); 19 EHRR 432.

[729] *Henworth v UK* hudoc (2004); 40 EHRR 810 and *Portington v Greece* 1998-VI.

[730] *Baggetta v Italy* A 119 (1987); 10 EHRR 325. Special diligence is required in a re-trial: *Henworth v UK* hudoc (2004); 40 EHRR 810.

[731] *Abdoella v Netherlands* A 248-A (1992); 20 EHRR 585 and *Kalashnikov v Russia* 2002-VI; 36 EHRR 587.

[732] *Frydlender v France* hudoc (2000); 31 EHRR 1152.

reasonable time guarantee in Article 6(1) is the only one that protects a convicted person detained during subsequent appeal or other proceedings. Thus in *B v Austria*,[733] a breach of Article 6(1) was found when it took two years and nine months for an appeal court judge to draw up the court's judgment after the hearing of an appeal by a convicted person in detention. Another factor concerns the practice in criminal justice systems by which the time spent awaiting trial is taken into account when deciding upon the sentence in a criminal case. Any reduction in sentence, or other favourable outcome, may mean that the applicant is not a 'victim' who is competent to bring an application alleging a breach of the 'reasonable time' guarantee.[734]

When applying these factors, the Court has been prepared to tolerate some proven, but small, instances of delay as not involving a breach provided the overall length of the proceedings is not excessive given the number of stages of proceedings in the case. Thus in *Pretto v Italy*,[735] there were delays of several months in civil proceedings before an appeal was heard and before a judgment was filed with the court registry, but, 'although these delays could probably have been avoided, they are not sufficiently serious to warrant the conclusion that the total duration of the proceedings (of three years six months) was excessive'. But the Court has found breaches on the basis of a single instance of unexplained delay of sufficient duration regardless of the overall length of the proceedings. Thus in *Bunate Bunkate v Netherlands*,[736] there was a breach of the guarantee in a criminal case, lasting two years and ten months over three levels of proceedings, on the basis that there had been an unexplained delay of fifteen months in transferring the appeal from one appeal court to another.

In cases in which the overall length of time in criminal or non-criminal cases is on its face unreasonable for the kind of proceedings and the number of court levels, the Court will look at the explanation for any delays particularly closely.[737] Although the length of particular stages of proceedings may not seem unreasonable, the overall length of time taken to decide the case may be such that some action should have been taken to expedite proceedings.[738] For example, in *Obasa v UK*,[739] a claim of racial discrimination in employment took over seven years, during which time there were three appeal stages of one year or more each. While it was generally not unreasonable for an appeal stage to take a year, given the length of the proceedings as a whole the time taken for these appeals was unreasonable, in breach of Article 6(1). In some extreme cases, the Court would appear to decide the case essentially on the basis of the excessive total length, quite separately from particular instances of unjustified delay (even though these may exist), on the basis that no proceedings that took so long could have been conducted diligently.[740]

The discussion so far has supposed that the Court is considering whether the proceedings on the facts of a particular case have been conducted with sufficient expedition. There is, however, another dimension to the 'reasonable time' guarantee. The Convention places a duty on the contracting parties, which applies regardless of cost,[741] 'to organise their judicial systems in such a way that their courts can meet each of its requirements, including the

---

[733] A 175 (1990); 13 EHRR 87.			[734] *Eckle v Germany* A 51 (1982); 5 EHRR 1.

[735] A 71 (1983); 6 EHRR 182 para 37 PC. Cf *Biryukov v Russia No 63972/00* hudoc (2004) DA.

[736] A 248-B (1993); 19 EHRR 477. Cf *Kudla v Poland* 2000-XI; 25 EHRR 198 GC.

[737] See, eg, *Guincho v Portugal* A 81 (1984); 7 EHRR 223 para 30; *Deumeland v Germany* A 100 (1986); 8 EHRR 448 para 90 PC; and *Lechner and Hess v Austria* A 118 (1987); 9 EHRR 490 para 39.

[738] *Uhl v Germany* hudoc (2005).

[739] Hudoc (2003). See also *Jordan v UK (No 2)* hudoc (2002) and *Ruotolo v Italy* A 230-D (1992).

[740] See, eg, *Comingersoll SA v Portugal* 2000-IV; 31 EHRR 772 GC and *Gümüşten v Turkey* hudoc (2004). See also *Uoti v Finland No 20388/92* hudoc (2004) para 2 DA.

[741] *Airey v Ireland* A 32 (1979); 2 EHRR 305.

obligation to hear cases within a reasonable time'.[742] It follows that a state may be held liable not only for any delay in the handling of a particular case in the operation of a generally expeditious system for the administration of justice, but also for a failure to increase resources in response to a backlog of cases and for structural deficiencies in its system of justice that cause delays.

As to a backlog of cases, the Court has drawn a distinction between a situation of 'chronic overload', involving an ongoing problem, for which the state may be liable, and a sudden or 'temporary backlog', for which it will not be liable if it takes 'appropriate remedial action with the requisite promptness'.[743] In *Zimmermann and Steiner v Switzerland*,[744] the respondent state was held liable when administrative appeal proceedings of a straightforward kind, before the Swiss Federal Court, had taken nearly three-and-a-half years, during most of which time the applicants' case had remained stationary. The agreed reason for the delay was that the Court was overworked and had for that reason given priority to urgent or important cases,[745] within neither of which categories the applicants' case fell. The Court's caseload had built up over several years, and adequate steps to increase the number of judges and administrative staff or otherwise reorganize the court system to cope with what had become a permanent problem had not been taken to remedy the situation by the time that the applicants' appeal was heard. Similarly, a backlog defence was rejected in *Guincho v Portugal*,[746] in which delays in the civil courts were attributed to the increase in litigation that resulted from the return to democracy, the increase in litigation resulting from the impact of the new constitution, the repatriation of nationals from Portuguese colonies, and the 1970s economic recession. Portugal was found to be in breach of Article 6(1) because the resulting overloading had become a permanent problem by the time that the applicant's claim was brought and because it could, in some respects, have been foreseen. A situation of 'chronic overload' under which the German Constitutional Court had 'laboured since the end of the 1970s' was also a factor in finding a breach of the reasonable time guarantee in *Pammel v Germany*.[747]

However, in *Buchholz v Germany*,[748] the state was not liable for a delay that resulted from a backlog of cases that was not reasonably foreseeable where it had taken reasonably prompt remedial action. In that case, the delay in the consideration of the applicant's claim for unfair dismissal was attributable to a backlog of cases that had developed suddenly with the economic recession of the 1970s and because prompt steps had been taken to increase the number of judges when the problem became apparent. Although these steps did not benefit the applicant, they were all that could reasonably be expected of the respondent state in the circumstances. Similarly, no special measures were required to tackle a clearly temporary backlog in *Foti and Others v Italy*.[749] There, delays were caused when the competent regional courts were flooded by several hundred prosecutions as a result of large-scale public disorder. It was held that delays in certain of the cases concerned were acceptable simply by reference to the temporary overloading of the courts that had occurred.

---

[742] *Sussmann v Germany* 1996-IV; 25 EHRR 64 para 55.

[743] *Klein v Germany* hudoc (2000); 34 EHRR 415 para 43.

[744] A 66 (1983); 6 EHRR 17. See also *Žiačik v Slovakia* hudoc (2003).

[745] A system of priorities may be permissible as a short-term measure: *Sussmann v Germany* 1996-IV; 25 EHRR 64 para 60 GC (priority for German reunification cases permissible).

[746] A 81 (1984); 7 EHRR 223. Backlog arguments were also rejected in *B v Austria* A 175 (1990); 13 EHRR 87; *Ruiz-Mateos v Spain* A 262 (1993); 16 EHRR 505; and *Hentrich v France* A 296-A (1994); 18 EHRR 440 para 61.

[747] 1997-IV; 26 EHRR 100 para 69. Cf *Klein v Germany* hudoc (2000); 34 EHRR 415.

[748] A 42 (1981); 3 EHRR 597.

[749] A 56 (1982); 5 EHRR 313. Cf *Lynch v UK No 9504/06*, hudoc (2009) DA (temporary backlog of prisoners' cases using new remedy).

More delicate than the problem of delays resulting from a backlog of cases is the question whether a state can be required to restructure its administration of justice system to eliminate delays that are inherent in it. This question arose in *Neumeister v Austria*,[750] in which much of the delay had occurred at the preliminary investigation stage. Under some civil law systems of criminal justice, including that in Austria, a person may spend a considerable length of time waiting for a 'charge' against him in the sense of Article 6 to be fully examined by an investigating judge when much of that examination is a repetition of work already done by the police in its investigation. If such a system, which has advantages in other respects, were altered to eliminate this overlap of time, the period during which an accused had a charge hanging over him would generally be reduced. In the *Neumeister* case, the Court confirmed that preliminary investigation systems of the kind described are not in themselves contrary to Article 6; the requirement is only that they be administered efficiently. It could not have been the intention of the drafting states that such a fundamental change in the legal systems of many of their number would be required.

The same question arose again in *König v Germany*,[751] in the different context of the elaborate system of administrative courts in West Germany. Faced with one set of proceedings that had lasted nearly eleven years and were still pending, the Court first noted that it was not its function to comment on the structure of the courts concerned which, it conceded, was aimed at providing a full set of remedies for the individual's grievances. It added, however, that if efforts to this end 'resulted in a procedural maze, it is for the state alone to draw the conclusions and, if need be, to simplify the system with a view to complying with Article 6(1) of the Convention'. The implication is that if a case takes what is on the face of it an unreasonably long time, a state will not escape liability by providing that it has been dealt with efficiently within the limits of an unduly elaborate court structure.

What emerges generally from the case law of the Court on the reasonable time guarantee is the considerable length of time that both criminal[752] and civil[753] proceedings may take in European jurisdictions and the large number of cases in which the Court has found breaches of Article 6.[754] Either the Court is being too rigorous in its expectations, or—as is the more convincing alternative in the light of the facts of the Strasbourg cases— the 'law's delay' is a serious and pervasive problem in the legal systems of European states generally.[755]

Finally, in an important development by the Court in tackling its own caseload, it should be noted that in *Bottazzi v Italy*,[756] in response to the violations of the 'reasonable time' guarantee found at Strasbourg in many hundreds of cases coming from Italy, the Strasbourg Court noted that the 'frequency with which violations are found shows that there is an accumulation of identical breaches which are sufficiently numerous to amount not merely to isolated incidents'. This accumulation, the Court stated, 'accordingly

---

[750] A 8 (1968); 1 EHRR 91.   [751] A 27 (1978); 2 EHRR 170 para 100 PC.

[752] See, eg, *Gümüşten v Turkey* hudoc (2004) (seventeen years) and *Hannak v Austria* hudoc (2004) (fifteen years). Both cases involved appeals.

[753] See, eg, *Mazzotti v Italy* hudoc (2000) (twenty-four years, for one level of proceedings); *Szarapo v Poland* hudoc (2002) (nineteen years, with appeals); and *Surmeli v Germany* 2006-VIII; 44 EHRR 438 GC (sixteen years, with appeals and still pending).

[754] On tackling the problem through the Convention, see Kuijer, 13 HRLR 777 (2013).

[755] Whereas breaches of the 'reasonable time' guarantee were for a long time a problem mainly in cases coming from civil law jurisdictions, there has been a growing number of such breaches from common law jurisdictions: for UK cases, see, eg, civil cases: *Blake v UK* hudoc (2006) (nearly ten years) and *Foley v UK* hudoc (2003) (fourteen years); and criminal cases: *Massey v UK* hudoc (2004) (four years) and *Crowther v UK* hudoc (2005) (eight years), all more than one level. See also *Mellors v UK* hudoc (2003) (three years for one appeal level).   [756] 1999-V para 22 GC.

constitutes a practice that is incompatible with the Convention'. The consequence of this ruling has been that later 'reasonable time' cases from Italy have commonly been disposed in groups and after less detailed examination of the facts than would otherwise be the case.[757] In *Scordino v Italy (No 1)*,[758] it was held that while the Italian 'Pinto law', by which a person may claim compensation in an Italian court for breaches of the Article 6 reasonable time guarantee,[759] may constitute a domestic remedy for such a breach, it did not mean that a person who had suffered in that way could not bring a Strasbourg claim as a 'victim' of the breach: Italy still needed to reform its judicial system to prevent such violations.

V. THE RIGHT TO AN INDEPENDENT AND IMPARTIAL TRIBUNAL ESTABLISHED BY LAW

The right to a fair trial in Article 6(1) requires that cases be heard by an 'independent and impartial tribunal established by law'. The right applies equally to criminal cases and cases concerning 'civil rights and obligations'. There is a close inter-relation between the guarantees of an 'independent' and an 'impartial' tribunal. A tribunal that is not independent of the executive is likely to be in breach of the requirement of impartiality also in cases to which the executive is a party. Likewise, a tribunal member who has links with a private party to the case is likely to be in breach of both requirements. For this reason, the European Court commonly considers the two requirements together, using the same reasoning to decide whether the tribunal is 'independent and impartial'.[760] In respect of both requirements, there is a breach not only where there is proof of actual dependence or bias (subjective test), but also where the facts raise a 'legitimate doubt' that the requirement has been met (objective test).

An important question is whether the right to an independent and impartial tribunal may be waived. Although it is tempting to accept that an applicant should not be allowed at Strasbourg to claim against a state a right which he has earlier unequivocally, and without pressure, waived at the national level, it is arguable that the requirement that a case always be decided by an independent and impartial tribunal is crucial to the operation of the rule of law, and that an Article 6 application should always be available to maintain this value. However, such indications as have been given by the Court—and they are not clear, unequivocal pronouncements—appear to accept that waiver is permitted, subject to the usual conditions.[761]

a. A tribunal

A 'tribunal' was defined in *Belilos v Switzerland*[762] as follows:

> ...a 'tribunal' is characterized in the substantive sense of the term by its judicial function, that is to say determining matters within its competence on the basis of rules of law[[763]] and after proceedings conducted in a prescribed manner. It must also satisfy a series of further

---

[757] For criticism of this consequence, see Judge Ferrari Bravo's dissenting opinion in *Angelo Giuseppe Guerrera v Italy* hudoc (2002), pointing out that 133 Italian 'reasonable time' cases had been decided on this basis on one day.   [758] 2006-V; 45 EHRR 207 GC.

[759] 'Pinto' compensation must normally be paid within six months: *Simaldone v Italy* hudoc (2009).

[760] See, eg, *Cooper v UK* 2003-XII; 39 EHRR 171 GC.

[761] See *Pfeifer and Plankl v Austria* A 227(1992); 14 EHRR 692 para 37; *Öcalan v Turkey* hudoc; 37 EHRR 238; *McGonnell v UK* 2000-II; 30 EHRR 289 para 44; and *Bulut v Austria* 1996-II; 24 EHRR 84 para 34.

[762] A 132 (1988); 10 EHRR 466 para 64. See also *Cyprus v Turkey* 2001-IV; 35 EHRR 731 para 233 GC and *Mihailov v Bulgaria* hudoc (2005).

[763] Ed: A 'tribunal' requires a set of rules of procedure by which it operates: *H v Belgium* A 127-B (1987); 10 EHRR 339.

requirements—independence, in particular of the executive; impartiality; duration of its members' terms of office; guarantees afforded by its procedure—several of which appear in the text of Article 6(1) itself.

This definition is overly comprehensive insofar as it contains organizational and procedural elements that, as the Court notes, are included or may be subsumed under other guarantees in Article 6(1). As to the functional element, an important feature of a tribunal is that it must be competent to take legally binding decisions: the capacity to make recommendations or give advice (even if normally followed) is not enough.[764] A tribunal's decisions must also not be subject to being set aside by a non-judicial body;[765] and the government must not be empowered by law not to implement them, even though the power is never exercised.[766] The fact that a body has other functions (administrative, legislative, etc) does not in itself prevent it being a tribunal when exercising its judicial function.[767] The requirement of independence and impartiality applies in civil law systems to investigating judges and their equivalents, given the importance of their role.[768]

As to membership, although a tribunal will normally be composed of professional judges, this is not an absolute requirement. Lay assessors are a common feature of ordinary courts in European legal systems,[769] and a bench composed of lay magistrates, advised by a legally trained clerk (as in the English legal system), would appear to comply with Article 6. As to administrative and disciplinary tribunals, these may include persons who are not professional judges or qualified lawyers. Civil servants may be members of administrative tribunals,[770] and members of the armed forces may serve on military tribunals that try members of the armed forces for disciplinary[771] or criminal offences.[772] However, the participation of such members may raise issues on the facts of the case under the objective test.[773]

b. An independent tribunal

Many of the decided cases on the meaning of an 'independent' tribunal concern administrative or disciplinary tribunals, in which context the Strasbourg authorities have not imposed standards as high as might be applied to the ordinary, 'classic' courts of law. This is particularly true of such matters as the duration of office of tribunal members and their protection from outside pressures.

By 'independent' is meant 'independent of the executive and also of the parties'.[774] Clearly a government minister is not 'independent' of the executive, so that a decision taken by him does not comply with Article 6(1).[775] A tribunal that is otherwise separate

---

[764] *Benthem v Netherlands* A 97 (1985); 8 EHRR 1 PC.

[765] *Cooper v UK* 2003-XII; 39 EHRR 171 GC. See also *British-American Tobacco v Netherlands* A 331-A (1995); 21 EHRR 409; *Beaumartin v France* A 296-B (1994); 19 EHRR 485; and *Sovtransavto Holding v Ukraine* 2002-VII; 38 EHRR 911. As to the related Article 6 requirement of the finality of court judgments, see the *Brumarescu* case, 1999-VII; 33 EHRR 862 para 61, mentioned earlier.

[766] *Van de Hurk v Netherlands* A 288 (1994); 18 EHRR 481 para 45.

[767] *Campbell and Fell v UK* A 80 (1984); 7 EHRR 165; *H v Belgium* A 127-B (1987); 10 EHRR 339; and *Demicoli v Malta* A 210 (1991); 14 EHRR 47. However, it may raise issues of objective independence and impartiality on the facts. [768] *Vera Fernández-Huidobro v Spain* hudoc (2010).

[769] See, eg, *Langborder v Sweden*, A 155 (1983); 12 EHRR 416 PC.

[770] *Ettl and Others v Austria* A 117 (1987); 10 EHRR 225 and *Stojakovic v Austria* hudoc (2006).

[771] *Engel v Netherlands No 1* A 22 (1976); 1 EHRR 647 PC. Cf *Le Compte v Belgium* A 43 (1981); 4 EHRR 1 PC (medical disciplinary body). [772] *Cooper v UK* 2003-XII; 39 EHRR 171 GC.

[773] See, eg, *Sramek v Austria* A 84 (1984); 7 EHRR 351.

[774] *Ringeisen v Austria* A 13 (1971) para 95. It also means independence of Parliament: *Crociani v Italy No 8603/79*, 22 DR 147 at 221 (1980). [775] *Benthem v Netherlands* A 97 (1985); 8 EHRR 1 PC.

from the executive is not 'independent' where it seeks and accepts as binding Foreign Office advice on the meaning of a treaty that it has to apply; in such a case it has surrendered its judicial function to the executive.[776] With regard to other bodies, in *Campbell and Fell v UK*,[777] the Court indicated the considerations it takes into account when assessing independence:

> In determining whether a body can be considered to be 'independent'—notably of the executive and of the parties to the case—the Court has had regard to the manner of appointment of its members and the duration of their term of office, the existence of guarantees against outside pressures and the question whether the body presents an appearance of independence.

As far as 'manner of appointment' is concerned, appointment by the executive is permissible, indeed normal.[778] The arrangements for the selection or substitution of judges for a particular case from amongst the judiciary as a whole can give rise to questions of independence.[779] For a judge's independence to be challenged successfully by reference to his 'manner of appointment', it would have to be shown that the practice of appointment 'as a whole is unsatisfactory' or that 'at least the establishment of the particular court deciding a case was influenced by improper motives',[780] ie motives suggesting an attempt at influencing the outcome of the case.

With regard to the 'duration of their term of office', a short term of office has been accepted as permissible as far as members of administrative or disciplinary tribunals are concerned. In *Campbell and Fell v UK*,[781] appointment for a term of three years as a member of a prison Board of Visitors acting as a disciplinary tribunal was sufficient, the Court being influenced by the fact that members were unpaid and that it might be hard to find candidates for any longer period. With regard to ordinary courts, appointment of judges may be for life or a fixed term,[782] but a renewable four-year term has been questioned.[783]

As to 'guarantees against outside pressures', tribunal members must be protected from removal during their term of office, either by law or in practice.[784] The appointment of a judge for a fixed term, so as to prevent dismissal at will, is a relevant factor,[785] although apparently not in itself required. In *Engel v Netherlands*,[786] the military members of the Netherlands Supreme Military Court were removable by Ministers at will. The Court

---

[776] *Beaumartin v France* A 296-B (1994); 19 EHRR 485. Cf *Chevrol v France* 2003-III.

[777] A 80 (1984); 7 EHRR 165 para 78. Footnotes omitted. Cf *Langborger v Sweden* A 155 (1989); 12 EHRR 416 PC.

[778] *Campbell and Fell v UK* A 80 (1984); 7 EHRR 165; *Belilos v Switzerland* A 132 (1988); 10 EHRR 466; and *Asadov v Azerbaijan* No 138/03 hudoc (2002) DA. Appointment by Parliament is also permissible: *Filippini v San Marino* No 10526/02 hudoc (2003) DA and *Ninn-Hansen v Denmark* No 28972/95 1999-V; 28 EHRR CD 96 DA.

[779] See *Barberà, Messegué, and Jabardo v Spain* A 146 (1988); 11 EHRR 360 paras 53–9 (1988) (an impartiality case).

[780] *Zand v Austria* No 7360/76, 15 DR 70 at 81 (1978) Com Rep; CM Res DH (79) 6 (no breach). As to the appointment of judges for their political views, see *Crociani v Italy* No 8603/79, 22 DR 147 at 222 (1980) (question seen in terms of impartiality).

[781] A 80 (1984); 7 EHRR 165. Cf *Sramek v Austria* A 84 (1984); 7 EHRR 351. *Ad hoc* appointment of a military officer as a court-martial member for just one case was sufficient: *Cooper v UK* 2003-XII; 39 EHRR 171 GC. Cf *Dupuis v Belgium* No 12717/87, 57 DR 196 (1988). See also *Mihailov v Bulgaria* hudoc (2005) (no tenure).   [782] *Zand v Austria* No 7360/76, 15 DR 70 (1978) Com Rep; CM Res DH (79) 6.

[783] *Incal v Turkey* 1998-IV; 29 EHRR 449. But see *Yavuz v Turkey* No 29870/96 hudoc (2000) DA.

[784] *Engel v Netherlands* A 22 (1976); 1 EHRR 647 PC. See also *Zand v Austria* No 7360/76, 15 DR 70 at 82 (1978); *Sramek v Austria* A 84 (1984); 7 EHRR 351 para 38; and *Brudnicka v Poland* 2005-II; 51 EHRR 608.

[785] See *Crociani v Italy* No 8603/79, 22 DR 147 at 221 (1980).   [786] A 22 (1976); 1 EHRR 647 PC.

would appear to have considered, without discussion, that their independence was not an issue in fact. In the *Campbell and Fell* case, the Court did not require any 'formal recognition' in law of the irremovability of a prison Board of Visitors member during his term of office; it was sufficient that this was 'recognised in fact and that the other necessary guarantees are present'.[787] In both of the *Engels* and *Campbell and Fell* cases, the possibility of removal by the executive without procedures for judicial review was not questioned.[788] In other cases, the possibility of transferring tribunal members to other duties has also not been considered to present a problem.[789]

As far as other 'guarantees against outside pressure' are concerned, the Court requires that tribunal members are not subject to instructions from the executive, although here too it may be sufficient that this is the case in practice.[790] In the *Greek* case,[791] the extraordinary courts-martial during the regime of the Colonels were found not to be independent partly because their jurisdiction was to be exercised 'in accordance with decisions of the Minister of National Defence'. The secrecy of a tribunal's deliberations also affords protection against outside pressures.[792] Any authority given to the executive to grant an amnesty or a pardon must not be used so as to undermine the judicial function.[793]

Finally, the 'appearance of independence' requirement listed by the Court in the *Campbell and Fell* case relates to the objective test that has been developed by the Court in respect to the requirements of both independence and impartiality. A breach of the 'appearance of independence' requirement was found in *Findlay v UK*.[794] There it was held that there were 'fundamental flaws' in the UK court-martial system because of the role of the convening military officer. This officer decided which charges should be brought and was otherwise closely linked with the prosecuting authorities. He also appointed the court-martial members, who were below him in rank and in some cases under his command, and he could dissolve the court-martial. Finally, the convening officer had to confirm the court-martial decision for it to be valid and could vary the sentence. In these circumstances, an outside observer could legitimately doubt the court-martial's structural independence of the executive and its impartiality.[795] Applying the *Findlay* case, in *Daktaras v Lithuania*,[796] a legitimate doubt about possible outside pressure in breach of Article 6 was found when the President of the Criminal Division of the Supreme Court

---

[787] A 80 (1984) 7 EHRR 165 para 80. In practice, the Home Secretary would require the removal of a member 'only in the most exceptional circumstances': *Campbell and Fell*. See also *Clarke v UK* No 23695/02 2005-X DA (circuit judges). Cf *Fruni v Slovakia* hudoc (2011). But see *Henryk and Ryszard Urban v Poland* hudoc (2010). See also *Cooper v UK* 2003-XII; 39 EHRR 171 GC (sufficient safeguards against outside pressure on military officer court-martial members).

[788] Its availability was a relevant factor in *Eccles, McPhillips and McShane v Ireland* No 12839/87, 59 DR 212 (1988).

[789] See *Sutter v Switzerland* No 8209/78, 16 DR 166 (1979). See also *Clarke v UK* No 23695/02 hudoc (2005) DA. And see *Beaumartin v France* A 296-B (1994); 19 EHRR 485, mentioned earlier.

[790] See *Sramek v Austria* A 84 (1984); 7 EHRR 351 (law) and *Campbell and Fell v UK* A 80 (1984); 7 EHRR 165 (practice). Cf *Schiesser v Switzerland* A 34 (1979); 2 EHRR 417 (an Article 5(3) case).

[791] 12 YB (the *Greek* case) at 148 (1969); Com Rep CM Res DH (70) 1.

[792] *Sutter v Switzerland* No 8209/78, 16 DR 166 (1979).

[793] 12 YB (the *Greek* case) at 148 (1969) Com Rep; CM Res (70) 1.

[794] 1997-I; 24 EHRR 221 para 78. Cf *Hirschhorn v Romania* hudoc (2007) and *Ibrahim Gürkan v Turkey* hudoc (2012). See also *Miroshnik v Ukraine* hudoc (2008) (Ministry of Defence housing for military court judges who were servicemen: breach)

[795] A similar lack of 'structural independence' was found in internal prison disciplinary proceedings in *Whitfield v UK* hudoc (2005); 41 EHRR 967. As revised by the Armed Forces Act 1996, the UK court-martial system for the army and the RAF complies with Article 6 for the army and the RAF: *Cooper v UK* 2003-XII; 39 EHRR 171 GC. The naval system was amended by the Army Act 2006 to comply with *Grieves v UK* 2003-XII; 39 EHRR 51 GC.   [796] 2000-X. Cf *Moiseyev v Russia* hudoc (2008); 53 EHRR 306.

petitioned for the quashing of a court decision that was in favour of the applicant and then appointed the judges who would hear the petition.

The membership of military judges in ordinary criminal courts has been an issue in some Turkish cases. In *Incal v Turkey*,[797] the applicant was convicted of a criminal offence of inciting racial hatred, by distributing the leaflets of a Kurdish political party, by a National Security Court composed of two civilian judges and a military judge. The Strasbourg Court held the participation of the military judge in a civil (ie non-military) court was in breach of the requirements of independence and impartiality, since the civilian applicant 'could legitimately fear that because one of the judges of the Izmir National Security Court was a military judge it might allow itself to be unduly influenced by considerations which had nothing to do with the nature of the case'.[798] In *Öcalan v Turkey*,[799] it was held that the objective requirement had not been satisfied even though, following the *Incal* case, the military member of a State Security Court (a civil court) that tried the applicant had been replaced by a third civilian judge before judgment was given. In a persuasive joint dissenting opinion, President Wildhaber and five other judges took the view that the fact that the verdict and sentence were decided upon by a wholly civilian court was sufficient: to go further was 'to take the "theory" of appearances very far' and was neither 'realistic' nor 'fair'.[800]

The *Incal* and *Öcalan* cases involved the trial of civilians for criminal offences by civil courts that had a military judge as a member. In *Martin v UK*,[801] the Court held that the prosecution of civilians for criminal offences before *military* courts is a matter of even greater concern under Article 6. Although their jurisdiction over civilians was not 'absolutely' excluded by the Convention, it would be consistent with Article 6 'only in very exceptional circumstances'. In particular, it should not extend to civilians unless there was a 'clear and forseeable legal basis' and there were 'compelling reasons'. Moreover, the existence of such reasons 'must be substantiated in each specific case'; it was 'not sufficient for the law to allocate certain offences to military courts *in abstracto*'. In the *Martin* case, the applicant was a seventeen-year-old living with his family on a British military base in Germany, where his father was an army corporal. He was convicted in Germany by a British court-martial board of murder there. The Strasbourg Court found a breach of Article 6 on the basis that the court-martial board was not an independent and impartial tribunal. While it did not find it necessary to decide whether there was also a breach of Article 6 because the applicant had been tried by a military court, it expressed 'considerable doubts' as to whether there were 'compelling reasons' for him to be so tried.

c. An impartial tribunal

'Impartiality' means lack of prejudice or bias. To satisfy the requirement, the tribunal must comply with both a subjective and an objective test.[802] In *Kyprianou v Cyprus*,[803]

---

[797] 1998-IV; 29 EHRR 449 GC.

[798] *Incal v Turkey*, para 68. The Court took into account that the judge was subject to military discipline and appointed only for four years, and that the army took orders from the executive—considerations that outweighed certain guarantees of his independence and impartiality.

[799] 2005-IV; 41 EHRR 985 GC. But see *Ceylan v Turkey No 68953/01* hudoc (2005) DA in which a military judge's participation in interlocutory proceedings before his replacement by a civilian judge on the merits was not a breach.

[800] The fact that it was a death penalty case may have influenced the Court majority.

[801] Hudoc (2006); 44 EHRR 652 paras 44–5. For reasons for the Court's concern at the trial of civilians by military courts, see *Ergin v Turkey (No 6)* 2006-VI.

[802] *Hauschildt v Denmark* A 154 (1989); 12 EHRR 266 para 46. The test was first formulated in *Piersack v Belgium* A 53 (1982); 5 EHRR 169.   [803] 2005-XIII; 44 EHRR 565 para 122 GC.

the Court distinguished between two situations in which there might be a breach of the impartiality requirement, namely situations involving either 'functional or personal' partiality. In the case of the former, the issue was whether 'the exercise of different functions within the judicial process by the same person or hierarchical or other links with another actor in the proceedings' raised a legitimate doubt as to the court's objective impartiality. In the case of the latter, it was whether a judge's personal conduct raised such a doubt or indicated actual bias, thus going to both objective and subjective impartiality.

As to the *subjective* test, the question is whether it can be shown on the facts that a member of the court 'acted with personal bias' against the applicant.[804] In this connection, there is a presumption that a judge is impartial, 'until there is proof to the contrary'.[805] Given this presumption and the need to prove actual bias, it is not surprising that a breach of the subjective test is difficult to establish.[806] One case in which a breach was found was *Werner v Poland*.[807] There an insolvency judge who requested that the applicant be removed from his post as a judicial liquidator later sat as a member of the court that heard her request. The European Court held that it was 'only reasonable' to conclude that the insolvency judge held a personal conviction that her request was well founded and should be granted.

The *objective* test is comparable to the English law doctrine that 'justice must not only be done: it must also be seen to be done'. In this context, the Court emphasizes the importance of 'appearances'.[808] As the Court has stated, '[w]hat is at stake is the confidence which the courts in a democratic society must inspire in the public and, above all, as far as criminal proceedings are concerned, in the accused'.[809] In applying the objective test, the opinion of the party to the case who is alleging partiality is 'important but not decisive'; what is crucial is whether the doubt as to impartiality can be 'objectively justified'.[810] If there is a 'legitimate doubt' as to a judge's impartiality, he must withdraw from the case.[811] In this connection, the failure to disclose to the parties the identity of the judge/s in their case may raise a 'legitimate doubt'.[812]

There was such a 'doubt' in *McGonnell v UK*,[813] where the Guernsey Royal Court rejected the applicant's appeal against the refusal of his planning application by a development committee. The presiding judge in the applicant's appeal was the Bailiff of Guernsey, who, as Deputy Bailiff, had earlier presided over the Guernsey legislature (the States of Deliberation) when it adopted the development plan under which the applicant's planning application had been refused and which the Royal Court had to apply. As well as chairing the States of Deliberation, the Deputy Bailiff also had a casting vote in the event of a tie, although he was not called upon to exercise it in this case.

---

[804] *Hauschildt v Denmark* A 154 (1989); 12 EHRR 266, para 47.

[805] *Kyprianou v Cyprus* 2005-XIII; 44 EHRR 565 GC. The presumption applies to jury members: *Sander v UK* 2000-V; 31 EHRR 1003.   [806] Cf *Kyprianou v Cyprus* 2005-XIII; 44 EHRR 565 para 119 GC.

[807] Hudoc (2001); 36 EHRR 491. See also *Boeckmans v Belgium No 1727/62*, 8 YB 410 (1965) F Sett; *Kyprianou v Cyprus* hudoc (2004); *Driza v Albania* 2007-XX; 49 EHRR 779; and *Svetlana Naumenko v Ukraine* hudoc (2004). See also *Oleksdandr Volkov v Ukraine* 2013-. On the political sympathies of judges and their impartiality, see *Crociani, Palmiotti, Tanassi, Lefebvre, D'Ovidio v Italy No 8603/79*, 22 DR 147 at 222 (1980).

[808] *Sramek v Austria* A 84 (1984); 7 EHRR 351 para 42.

[809] *Fey v Austria* A 255-A (1993); 6 EHRR 387 para 30.

[810] *Hauschildt v Denmark* A 154 (1989); 12 EHRR 266 para 48.   [811] *Hauschildt v Denmark*.

[812] *Vernes v France* hudoc (2011).

[813] 2000-II; 30 EHRR 289 para 55. Cf *Procola v Luxembourg* A 326 (1995); 22 EHRR 193 (*Conseil d'État* members who had advised on legislation later applied it as judges: not impartial), distinguished in *Kleyn v Netherlands* 2003-VI; 38 EHRR 239 GC. See also *Sacilor-Lormines v France* 2006-XIII; 54 EHRR 1193. A member of parliament is not *per se* disqualified from being a judge: *Pabla Ky v Finland* 2004-V; 42 EHRR 688.

The European Court held that the 'mere fact' that the Deputy Bailiff presided over the legislature when the plan was adopted was sufficient to raise a 'legitimate doubt' as to his impartiality when he later served as the sole judge on the law when the applicant's planning appeal was rejected. More generally, the Court stated that 'any direct involvement in the passage of legislation, or of executive rules, is likely to be sufficient to cast doubt upon the judicial impartiality of a person subsequently called on to determine a dispute'[814] concerning its or their application. In considering such cases of overlapping roles, the Court has stated that the Convention does not suppose that contracting parties follow any particular constitutional theory concerning the separation of powers: the question is always whether there is a 'legitimate doubt' about impartiality (or independence) on the facts.[815]

Again in terms of the separation of powers, the objective test will be infringed where the executive intervenes in a case in the courts with a view to influencing the outcome. In *Sovtransavto Holding v Ukraine*,[816] while civil proceedings brought by the applicant Russian company in Ukraine were pending, the President of Ukraine drew the attention of the Supreme Arbitration Tribunal to the need to protect state interests. The Strasbourg Court held that, irrespective of whether it had influenced the outcome of the case, the President's intervention gave rise to a 'legitimate doubt' as to the Tribunal's independence and impartiality. In contrast, public remarks in another case by the Romanian President to the effect that judgments by the Romanian courts in decided cases for the restitution of property should not be implemented, which, it was claimed, might influence the courts, were not in breach of the objective test.[817] In *Bochan v Ukraine*,[818] the applicant successfully challenged the objective impartiality not of the executive but of the respondent state's Supreme Court, claiming that it had sought to influence the outcome of her case by reassigning it to a different regional court after judgments in her favour.

The Court has applied the objective test in many cases in which the trial judge in a criminal court has previously taken part in the proceedings at the pre-trial stage in a variety of different capacities. The Court has stated that 'the mere fact that a judge has also made pre-trial decisions in the case cannot be taken as in itself justifying fears as to his impartiality... What matters is the extent and nature of those decisions.'[819] In practice, the Court has found a 'legitimate doubt' in a number of cases, including some involving long-established national practices. In *Piersack v Belgium*,[820] the presiding trial court judge had earlier been the head of the section of the public prosecutor's department that had investigated the applicant's case and instituted proceedings against him. Although there was no evidence that the judge had actual knowledge of the investigation, the Court

---

[814] *McGonnell v UK* 2000-II;30 EHRR 289 para 55. In *Previti (No 2) v Italy No 45291/06* hudoc (2010) DA, participation in a case by members of the national legal service who had earlier criticized the law to be applied was not a breach.

[815] *Kleyn v Netherlands* 2003-VI; 38 EHRR 239 GC. Cf *Oleksandra Volkov v Ukraine* 2013-.

[816] 2002-VII; 38 EHRR 911. There was also a breach of the principle of legal certainty because all judicial decisions in the case were later quashed by the Supreme Administrative Tribunal following an objection by its President.   [817] *Mosteanu and Others v Romania* hudoc (2002).

[818] Hudoc (2007).   [819] *Fey v Austria* A 255-A (1993); 6 EHRR 387 para 30.

[820] A 53 (1982); 5 EHRR 169 para 30. A 'legitimate doubt' may also exist where the judge takes over the role of the prosecution during the trial: see *Thorgeir Thorgeirson v Iceland* A 239 (1992); 14 EHRR 843. See also *Kristinsson v Iceland* A 171-B (1990) Com Rep (F Sett before Court), in which the chief of police was also a criminal court judge. The Commission found a breach, the limited number of qualified persons in a small population being no excuse. See also *D'Haese, Le Compte, Van Leuven and De Meyere v Belgium No 8930/80*, 6 EHRR 114 (1983) and *Mellors v UK No 57836/00* hudoc (2003) DA.

held there had been a breach of the objective test. In *De Cubber v Belgium*,[821] the *Piersack* case was extended to the situation where a judge had earlier acted as an investigating judge. Although the investigating judge was, unlike a member of the public prosecutor's department, independent of the prosecution, he had links with that department and it could reasonably be supposed that he had already formed a view as to the accused's guilt before the trial, thereby giving rise to a 'legitimate doubt' as to his impartiality.

The position is normally different where pre-trial decisions are taken by a judge who is not linked to the investigation or prosecution of the case. In *Sainte-Marie v France*,[822] two members of an appeal court that sentenced the accused following his conviction on charges of possession of arms had earlier been members of a court that had refused his application for bail in criminal damage proceedings arising out of the same facts. Noting that the judges had played no part in the preparation of the case for trial, the Court stated that in such circumstances the 'mere fact that such a judge has already taken pre-trial decisions in the case, including decisions relating to detention on remand, cannot in itself justify fears as to his impartiality'.[823]

Another question is whether a judge can sit at more than one stage in the hearing of the merits of a case, or in both of two related cases. As to the former situation, in *Ringeisen v Austria*,[824] the Court indicated that 'it cannot be stated as a general rule resulting from the obligation to be impartial' that a case must be re-heard, having been referred back by an appellate court, by a tribunal with a totally different membership from that of the first hearing. In contrast, it has been held that a judge should not take part in two different appellate stages of the same case.[825] There was thus a lack of objective impartiality when most members of a court of cassation had sat in an earlier appeal hearing in the same case on the same facts.[826] Clearly, there is also a breach of the requirement of objective impartiality where a judge is the presiding judge of an appeals tribunal that hears an appeal from his own decision.[827]

As to a judge sitting in two related cases, the Court has sometimes held that a judge may participate in related civil and/or criminal cases concerning the applicant without this in itself raising a legitimate doubt as to his impartiality.[828] However, in other cases, depending on the facts, it has not.[829] In *Ferrantelli and Santangelo v Italy*,[830] there was a

---

[821] A 86 (1984); 7 EHRR 236. Cf *Pfeifer and Plankl v Austria* A 227 (1992); 14 EHRR 692 (breach of Article 6(1)—and national law—for an investigating judge to be the trial judge) and *Ben Yaacoub v Belgium* A 127-A (1987) Com Rep; F Sett before Court. Contrast *Fey v Austria* A 255-A (1993); 6 EHRR 387, in which the trial judge had played a marginal interrogating role at the pre-trial stage (no breach). See also *Adamkiewicz v Poland* hudoc (2010).

[822] A 253-A (1992); 16 EHRR 116 para 32. Cf *Padovani v Italy* A 257-B (1993); *Nortier v Netherlands* A 267 (1993); 17 EHRR 273; *Castillo Algar v Spain* 1998-VIII; 30 EHRR 27; and *Jasinski v Poland* hudoc (2005).

[823] There was a breach in the 'special circumstances' of *Hauschildt v Denmark* A 154 (1989); 12 EHRR 266 para 50 PC. See also *Cianetti v Italy* hudoc (2004) and *Cardona Serrat v Spain* hudoc (2010) (breaches).

[824] A 13 (1971); 1 EHRR 455 para 97. See also *Thomann v Switzerland* 1996-III; 24 EHRR 553.

[825] *Oberschlick v Austria* A 204 (1991); 19 EHRR 389. See also *Indra v Slovakia* hudoc (2005); 43 EHRR 388 and *Chesne v France* hudoc (2010).

[826] *Mancel and Branquart v France* hudoc (2010). Cf *Peruš v Slovenia* hudoc (2012).

[827] *De Haan v Netherlands* 1997-IV; 26 EHRR 417. See also *San Leonard Band Club v Malta* 2004-IX; 42 EHRR 473. And see *Kingsley v UK* 2002-IV; 35 EHRR 177 GC.

[828] *Gillow v UK* A 109 (1986); 11 EHRR 335 and *Khodorkovskiy and Lebedev v Russia* hudoc (2013). See also *Lindon et al v France* 2007-XX; 46 EHRR 761 GC.

[829] *Fatullayev v Azerbaijan* hudoc (2010); 52 EHRR 58; and *Golubović v Croatia* hudoc (2012).

[830] 1996-III; 23 EHRR 288. See also *Indra v Slovakia* hudoc (2005); 43 EHRR 388 and *Warsicka v Poland* hudoc (2007). There may also be a breach where a judge has been an opposing party to the applicant in an earlier case: *Chmelíř v Czech Republic* 2005-IV; 44 EHRR 404.

'legitimate doubt' where the President of the Court of Appeal that heard the applicants' appeal from their conviction for murder had earlier been the President of the Court of Appeal following the conviction of others for the same murder, when the Court of Appeal judgment in the earlier case contained passages referring to the applicants' involvement in the murder and the Court of Appeal's judgment in the applicants' case had cited these passages.

The procedures applicable in common law jurisdictions in cases of criminal contempt in the face of the court were in issue in *Kyprianou v Cyprus*.[831] There the applicant was a lawyer who had been convicted of criminal contempt in the face of the court for his offensive personal remarks and other behaviour during an exchange with the judges in a criminal case. After a short break in the proceedings, the same judges convicted him of contempt and sentenced him to five days' imprisonment. Finding a breach of the impartiality requirement, the Strasbourg Court held that the 'the confusion of roles between complainant, witness, prosecutor and judge could self-evidently prompt objectively justified fears as to the conformity of the proceedings with the time-honoured principle that no one should be a judge in his or her own cause and, consequently, as to the impartiality of the bench'. The correct course would have been for the court to have referred the matter to the prosecuting authorities with a view to trial before a differently composed court. The Court went on to find a breach of the subjective impartiality test also, on the basis of the statement made by the judges in their decision that they were 'deeply insulted', their generally 'emphatic language', the severe penalty imposed, and their statements in the exchanges with the applicant that he was guilty.

In view of the robust remarks sometimes made by English judges in court about defendants in criminal cases, it is noticeable that no English case of this kind has been admitted on the merits. In one such case,[832] in which the judge had indicated very clearly that the accused was guilty and expressed his concern at the cost of the case for the legal aid fund, the application was declared inadmissible, the Commission emphasizing that the trial had to be considered as a whole. In a civil case,[833] in which a judge was alleged by the applicant to have formed a prejudice against him in proceedings concerning his rights to his children, the Court found that although the judge had undoubtedly taken a strongly negative view of the applicant's character, this did not in itself indicate bias and that, in any event, any such defect had been rectified on appeal by the Court of Appeal.

There may also be a breach of the impartiality requirement where a judge makes extra-judicial pronouncements in the press or elsewhere that may raise a legitimate doubt about his impartiality in a case before him. In *Buscemi v Italy*,[834] the applicant had published a letter in the press complaining about the placing of his daughter in a children's home by court order. The President of the court in pending child custody proceedings concerning the child responded with a letter in the press in terms that, in the Strasbourg Court's view, 'implied that he had already formed an unfavourable view of the applicant's case' before deciding it, thereby raising a legitimate doubt as to his impartiality.

Breaches of the objective impartiality test may also arise where the judge has acted as a lawyer for the applicant's opponent in other proceedings. In *Wettstein v Switzerland*,[835]

---

[831] 2005-XIII; 44 EHRR 565 paras 127, 130 GC.

[832] *X v UK No 4991/71*, 45 CD 1 (1973). Cf *X v UK No 5574/72*, 3 DR 10 (1975) (accused had 'not a ghost of a chance'). See also *Grant v UK No 12002/86*, 55 DR 218 (1988).

[833] *Ranson v UK No 14180/03* hudoc (2003) DA.

[834] 1999-VI paras 67–8. See also *Lavents v Latvia* hudoc (2002) and *Olujić v Croatia* hudoc (2009); 52 EHRR 839.

[835] 2000-XII para 47. See also *Puolitaival and Pirttiaho v Finland* hudoc (2004); 43 EHRR 153; *Chmelíř v Czech Republic* 2005-IV. 44 EHRR 404; and *Svarc and Kavnik v Slovenia* hudoc (2007).

there was a breach of the objective test when the part-time judge in the applicant's civil case was at the same time acting as a lawyer for the applicant's opponent in that case, in other pending civil litigation. Although the two cases were unrelated on their facts, the applicant had a 'legitimate fear' that the judge might 'continue to see in him the opposing side'. In contrast, in *Walston v Norway*,[836] there was no such breach where the judge had acted as the lawyer for the applicant's opponent in an earlier case.

The objective test may also be infringed where the judge has a personal interest in the case. A financial interest will disqualify a judge as not being impartial,[837] although there will be no breach of Article 6(1) if the interest is disclosed and the applicant is given an opportunity to object.[838] Non-financial interests are also relevant. Thus in *Demicoli v Malta*,[839] the Maltese House of Representatives that tried the applicant for breach of parliamentary privilege was not impartial because two of its members who participated in the proceedings were the Members of Parliament who were criticized in the article that was the subject of the alleged offence.

The objective test was not satisfied in *Langborger v Sweden*,[840] which concerned lay assessors who were members of a Housing and Tenancy Court, whose function was to adjudicate upon the continuation of a clause in a tenancy agreement; they were nominated by, and had close links with, organizations that had an interest in the removal of the clause. It did not matter that the tribunal was composed of two judges as well as the two lay assessors, with the presiding judge having the casting vote. The *Langborger* case may be contrasted with the earlier case of *Le Compte, Van Leuven, and De Meyere v Belgium*,[841] in which the medical members of a professional tribunal had 'interests very close to' those of one of the doctors being disciplined.[842] This fact was counterbalanced by the presence of an equal number of judges, one of whom had the casting vote, so that there was no breach of Article 6(1).[843]

Personal links between a judge and a party to the case have been an issue in a variety of other particular contexts. In *Micallef v Malta*,[844] there was a lack of objective impartiality when one of the judges hearing an appeal was related (as uncle and brother) to two of the advocates appearing for the applicant's opponent. The fact that a judge is a freemason does not *per se* raise doubts as to his impartiality in a case in which a party to the case or a witness is also a freemason; the position may be different if the judge has personal knowledge of the freemason or his lodge.[845] In contrast, there was a 'legitimate doubt' where the judge was also a professor employed by the University that was the other party to the case,[846] and where a judge had threatened a reprisal after his son had been expelled from the school connected with the case.[847] The fact that a judge in a divorce case had a

---

[836] *No 37272/97* hudoc (2001) DA.   [837] *Sigurdsson v Iceland* 2003-IV; 40 EHRR 371.

[838] *D v Ireland No 11489/85*, 51 DR 117 (1986) (judge owned shares in defendant company).

[839] A 210 (1991); 14 EHRR 47.

[840] A 155 (1989); 12 EHRR 416 PC. Cf *Thaler v Austria* hudoc (2005); 41 EHRR 727. Contrast *AB Kurt Kellermann v Sweden* hudoc (2004) and *Timperi v Finland No 60963/00* hudoc (2004) DA (no breaches).

[841] A 43 (1981); 4 EHRR 1 para 58 PC.

[842] Report of the Commission in the *Le Compte* case, para 78.

[843] In contrast, see *Gautrin and Others v France* 1998-III; 28 EHRR 196 and *Harabin v Slovakia* hudoc (2012). See also *Thaler v Austria* hudoc (2005); 41 EHRR 727.   [844] 2009-; 50 EHRR 920 GC.

[845] *Salaman v UK No 43505/98* hudoc (2000) DA. For other cases in which personal links were not a breach, see *Steiner v Austria No 16445/90* hudoc (1993) DA; *Academy Trading Ltd and Others v Greece* hudoc (2000); 33 EHRR 1081; *Lawrence v UK No 74660/01* hudoc (2002) DA; and *Parlov-Tkalčić v Croatia* hudoc (2009).

[846] *Pescador Valero v Spain* 2003-VII. See also *Timperi v Finland No 60963/00* hudoc (2004) DA.

[847] *Tocono et al v Moldova* hudoc (2007). See also *Podoreški v Croatia* hudoc (2007) (F Sett) (judge close relative of plaintiffs).

conversation with the applicant's wife immediately after the hearing did not by itself raise a 'legitimate doubt'.[848] However, in *Belukha v Ukraine*,[849] there was a lack of impartiality when the employer against whom the applicant was claiming supplied the trial court with goods and services.

The requirement of impartiality applies to juries.[850] When assessing whether the facts give rise to 'legitimate doubts' in cases in which allegations of partiality are raised, the Court takes into account the safeguards that are in place, such as the oath that jury members take and directions given to them by the judge.[851] Whether a jury member's personal link with a party to the case or to a witness raises a 'legitimate doubt' depends in each case on 'whether the familiarity in question is of such a nature and degree as to indicate a lack of impartiality'.[852] There was no 'legitimate doubt' in *Simsek v UK*.[853] There a jury member was the sister-in-law of a prison officer, who worked in the house block of 180 prisoners in which the applicant had been detained on remand, but who had not escorted or worked with him. In contrast, in *Holm v Sweden*,[854] a breach of Article 6(1) was found because of the links between members of a jury and the defendants in an unsuccessful private prosecution brought by the applicant for libel in a book commenting on right-wing political parties. A majority of the jury were active members of a political party that owned the first defendant (the publisher) and that had been advised by the second defendant (the author), thereby giving rise to a 'legitimate doubt' as to the jury members' independence and impartiality. A breach was also found in *Hanif and Khan v UK*,[855] when a police officer was a jury member in a case in which the applicant's defence depended to a significant extent upon challenging police evidence, including that of a police officer with which the police officer jury member had worked. The Court left open the question whether a police officer could ever be a jury member consistently with the obligation of objective impartiality. It noted, however, that English law was very exceptional in allowing a police officer to be a jury member and appeared to hint that police officer jury membership would always be problematic. In contrast, there was no breach of the requirement of impartiality in *Szypusz v UK*,[856] when a police officer joined the jury to operate a video machine; although the police officer had been involved in the investigation of the case, the judge had made it clear that he should not talk with the jury, just show the video. No breach was also found in *Ekeberg and Others v Norway*,[857] where a jury member was discharged when it was discovered shortly after the trial began that she had earlier given a statement to the police about the case, there being no likelihood that she would have influenced the remaining jury members.

The question of impartiality has also arisen in cases alleging racial discrimination within juries. In *Remli v France*,[858] a certified statement by a third party was presented by

---

[848] *X v Austria No 556/59*, 4 CD 1 (1960).   [849] Hudoc (2006).
[850] So does the independence requirement, but impartiality will usually be most relevant: see *Pullar v UK* 1996-III; 22 EHRR 391.
[851] See, eg, *Pullar v UK*.   [852] *Pullar v UK*, para 83.
[853] *No 43471/98* hudoc (2002) DA. Cf *Pullar v UK* 1996-III; 22 EHRR 39, in which a juror was employed by a key prosecution witness's firm, but had no personal connection with the case: no 'legitimate doubt', taking into account, *inter alia*, that the jurors swore an oath—reinforced by the judge's directions—requiring impartiality. And see *Procedo Capital Corporation v Norway* hudoc (2009).
[854] A 279-A (1993); 18 EHRR 79. See also *Fahri v France* 2007-XX (*ministère public* private talk with jury: breach) and *Hardiman v UK* No 25935/94 hudoc (1996) DA (juryman invited barrister for a drink: no breach).
[855] Hudoc (2011); 55 EHRR 424. See Ashworth, 2012 Crim L R 295 and Hunderford-Welch, 2012 Crim L R 320.
[856] Hudoc (2010). On jury secrecy and Article 10, see *Seckerson and Times Newspapers Ltd v UK Nos 33844/10 and 33510/10* hudoc (2012) DA.
[857] Hudoc (2007).   [858] 1996-II; 22 EHRR 253.

the defence to a criminal court that was trying the applicant and another accused, who were both of North African origin. The statement indicated that the author had over-heard one of the jurors saying on entering the courtroom before the trial, 'What's more, I'm a racist.' Without considering its merits, the court refused a defence application that it should take formal note of the statement because it had no jurisdiction to take note of events occurring out of its presence. The trial proceeded and the applicant and his co-defendant were convicted of homicide. The Strasbourg Court held, by five votes to four, that the decision of the court to refuse the application without considering its sub-stance raised a 'legitimate doubt' as to the court's impartiality.

In contrast, no breach was found in *Gregory v UK*,[859] in which the applicant, who was black, was convicted of robbery by a jury, by ten votes to two, and sentenced to six years' imprisonment. While the jury was deliberating, a note was passed by the jury to the judge stating: 'Jury showing racial overtones. One member to be excused.' After consulting with both counsel, the judge gave a 'firmly worded' and 'forceful' redirection to the jury instructing them to put out of their minds 'any thoughts of prejudice of one form or another'. The Strasbourg Court held, by eight votes to one, that, in doing so, the judge had taken sufficient steps to 'dispel any objectively held fears or misgivings about the impartiality of the jury'.

The *Gregory* case was distinguished in *Sander v UK*,[860] in which the applicant, who was Asian, was convicted by a jury of conspiracy to defraud and sentenced to five years' imprisonment. During the hearing, a jury member passed a note to an usher stating that at least two jury members had been making 'openly racist remarks and jokes' and that he feared that they were going to convict the applicant because he was Asian. Rejecting defence counsel's application to dismiss the jury on grounds of bias, the judge told the jury of the note, reminded them of their oath, and asked them to consider overnight whether they could decide the case without prejudice. The following morning the judge was given a note signed by all of the jurors refuting the allegation and stating that they would reach a verdict according to the evidence and without prejudice. A second letter from a juror stated that although he might have made racist jokes, he apologized for any offence and was not racially biased. The Strasbourg Court held, by four votes to three, that there had been a breach of the requirement of objective impartiality.[861] The majority distinguished the *Gregory* case on the basis that in that case there had been no admission by a juror of racist comments; the complaint was vague and imprecise and its author unknown; and defence counsel had insisted throughout that the jury should be dismissed.[862] On the facts in *Sander*, the judge should, in the majority's view, have reacted in a 'more robust manner than merely seeking vague assurances', probably by dismissing the jury. Judge Bratza, in a dissenting opinion joined by Judges Costa and Fuhrmann, questioned the weight of the points of distinction between *Gregory* and *Sander* on their facts and considered that the judgment of an experienced judge as to what was necessary to dispel the perceived doubts as to racial bias should have been respected.

It has also been held that Article 6 does not require that the parties to a case be allowed to participate in the selection of the jury.[863]

---

[859] 1997-I; 25 EHRR 577 paras 47–8. See also *Elias v UK No 48905/99* hudoc (2001) DA (racial comment by counsel).   [860] 2000-V; 31 EHRR 1003.

[861] There was no breach of the subjective impartiality requirement, the judge not being in a position to inquire into the precise nature and context of the comments made in the jury room.

[862] There was some uncertainty in *Gregory* whether defence counsel had called for the jury to be dismissed.

[863] *Kremzow v Austria No 12350/86* (1990) DA. See also *Zarouali v Belgium No 20664/92* (1994) DA (denial of request for inquiry into political, religious, and moral beliefs of prospective jurors not a violation).

d. A tribunal established by law

Article 6(1) requires that the tribunal is 'established by law', a requirement that 'reflects the principle of the rule of law'.[864] The intention is that, with a view to ensuring its independence, 'the judicial organisation in a democratic society must not depend on the discretion of the Executive, but that it should be regulated by law emanating from Parliament'.[865] This does not mean that every detail of the court system must be spelt out in legislation: provided that the basic rules concerning its organization and jurisdiction are set out by legislation, particular matters may be left to the executive acting by way of delegated legislation and subject to judicial review to prevent illegal or arbitrary action.[866] The absence of any basis in law for a practice by which lay judges sat as court members meant that the court was not established by law.[867] Article 6(1) does not prohibit the establishment of special courts if they have a basis in legislation.[868]

But it is for the constitution and the legislature, not the judiciary, to provide for the organization of the judicial system and the jurisdiction of the courts. In *Coëme and Others v Belgium*,[869] the constitution gave the Court of Cassation, not the ordinary criminal courts, jurisdiction to try government ministers for certain criminal offences. When prosecutions were brought against both ministers and non-ministers for offences of fraud, the Court of Cassation decided to try all of the accused together because of the connection between the offences, even though it had no legislative authority to try the non-ministers. The Strasbourg Court held that because the 'connection rule' that the Court of Cassation applied to join the cases was its own rule, not one provided by legislation, the Court of Cassation was not 'established by law' vis-à-vis the applicant non-ministers. Similarly, there was a violation in *Sokurenko and Strygun v Ukraine*,[870] when the Supreme Court upheld a lower court decision when it had no authority in law to do so.

'Established by law' also means 'established in accordance with law', so that the requirement is infringed if a tribunal does not function in accordance with the particular rules that govern it.[871] Thus there was a violation of the requirement when the internal rules for the appointment of judges were not complied with.[872]

The courts in the Turkish Republic of Northern Cyprus were 'established by law' even though the laws which provided for them were not those of an internationally recognized state.[873]

---

[864] *DMD Group v Slovakia* hudoc (2010) para 58.

[865] *Zand v Austria* No 7360/76, 15 DR 70 at 80 (1978) Com Rep; CM Res DH (79) 6.

[866] *Zand v Austria.* Cf *Crociani v Italy* No 8603/79, 22 DR 147 at 219 (1980) and *Campbell and Fell v UK* A 80 (1984); 7 EHRR 165.

[867] *Pandjikidze and Others v Georgia* hudoc (2009). Cf *Oleksandr Volkov v Ukraine* 2013- and *Gurov v Moldova* hudoc (2006).

[868] See *X and Y v Ireland* No 8299/78, 22 DR 51 (1980) (special criminal court to deal with terrorist offences). See also the extraordinary courts-martial in the *Greek* case, 12 YB (the Greek case) at 148 (1969); Com Rep CM Res (70) 1.

[869] 2000-VII. The Strasbourg Court will not question the national courts interpretation of national law on these matters in the absence of a 'flagrant violation': *Jorgic v Germany* 2007-XX; 47 EHRR 207.

[870] Hudoc (2006).

[871] *Zand v Austria* No 7360/76, 15 DR 70 at 80 (1978) Com Rep; CM Res DH (79) 6 and *Buscarini and Others v San Marino* No 31657/96 hudoc (2000) DA.

[872] *Posokhov v Russia* 2003-V; 39 EHRR 441 and *Fedotova v Russia* hudoc (2006). See also *Lavents v Latvia* hudoc (2002) and *DMD Group v Slovakia* hudoc (2010). But waiver is permitted: *Bulut v Austria* 1996-II; 24 EHRR 84.

[873] *Cyprus v Turkey* 2001-IV; 35 EHRR 731 GC. For criticism, see Loucaides, 15 LJIL 225 at 235 (2002).

VI. THE APPLICATION OF ARTICLE 6(1) TO APPEAL PROCEEDINGS

Article 6(1) does not guarantee a right of appeal from a decision by a court complying with Article 6 in either criminal or non-criminal cases.[874] If, however, a state in its discretion provides a right of appeal, proceedings before the appellate court are governed by Article 6(1).[875] The extent to which Article 6(1) applies to appeal proceedings, however, depends upon the nature of the particular proceedings, including the function of the appeal court and the relationship of proceedings before it with those earlier in the case. For example, the requirement of a public hearing may not apply fully where the court hears an appeal on points of law only and where a public hearing has taken place on the merits in the trial court.The exercise of a right of appeal may be subjected to reasonable time limits.[876]

Where the initial determination of 'civil rights' within the meaning of Article 6 is made by an administrative or disciplinary tribunal or other body which does not comply with it, Article 6 is satisfied so long as its proceedings 'are subject to review by a judicial body that has full jurisdiction', on the law and the facts, that does comply with it.[877] This dispensation is a proper recognition of the 'demands of flexibility and efficiency'[878] that permit the use of such bodies.

As the Court established in *De Cubber v Belgium*,[879] the same is not true in respect of 'courts of the classic kind', ie courts that are 'integrated within the standard judicial machinery of the country'. In the case of such courts, Article 6 must be fully complied with both at the trial court stage and on any appeal. The fact that allowance may be made for special professional or disciplinary bodies 'cannot justify reducing the requirements of Article 6(1) in its traditional and natural sphere of application'. There is, however, a limit to this properly stringent rule. In a case in which the breach of Article 6 concerns the conduct of a first instance court, it may be that the appeal court can 'make reparation' for the breach, in which case Article 6 will be complied with. For example, in *Adolf v Austria*,[880] there was no breach of Article 6 when the appeal court corrected the impression given by the trial court that the accused was considered by it to be guilty, in breach of the presumption of innocence. Likewise, in *Edwards v UK*,[881] there was no breach of Article 6 when the implications of the police's failure to disclose relevant information to the defence at the trial were examined by the Court of Appeal, which was competent to overturn the conviction on the basis of the evidence of non-disclosure. However, where the earlier defect is or cannot be remedied on appeal, the position is different. This is particularly likely to be true where the defect concerns the organization of the trial court, rather than its conduct of the trial. Thus in *Findlay v UK*,[882] the role of the convening

---

[874] A right of appeal in criminal cases is provided by Article 2, Seventh Protocol. The interpretation of the Article 6 guarantee concerning appeal courts is not to be influenced by the content (particularly the limitations) of the guarantee in the Seventh Protocol: *Ekbatani v Sweden* A 134 (1988); 13 EHRR 504 PC.

[875] *Delcourt v Belgium* A 11 (1970); 1 EHRR 355. This includes leave to appeal proceedings in a criminal case: *Monnell and Morris v UK* A 115 (1987); 10 EHRR 205. But *semble* not in a civil case: *Porter v UK No 12972/87*, 54 DR 207 (1987).

[876] *Bricmont v Belgium No 10857/84*, 48 DR 106 (1986).

[877] *Riepan v Austria* 2000-XII para 39.

[878] *Le Compte, Van Leuven and De Meyer v Belgium* A 43 (1981); 4 EHRR 1PC para 51.

[879] A 86 (1984) para 32; 7 EHRR 236. Cf *Riepan v Austria* 2000-XII.

[880] A 49 (1982); 4 EHRR 313.

[881] A 247-B (1992); 15 EHRR 417. Cf *Schuler-Zgraggen v Switzerland* A 263 (1993); 16 EHRR 405.

[882] 1997-I; 24 EHRR 221 para 79. Cf the *De Cubber* case, in which the trial court was not impartial because the judge had taken part in an earlier stage of the case. See also *Holm v Sweden* A 279-A (1993); 15 EHRR 79

officer in military court-martial proceedings meant that the proceedings were neither independent nor impartial, which was a defect that could not be corrected by later review proceedings: as the Court stated, the applicant was entitled 'to a first instance tribunal which fully met the requirements of Article 6(1)'. Similarly, in *Riepan v Austria*,[883] the absence of a public hearing could not be rectified at a later stage: as with 'independence and impartiality', the requirement of a public hearing was a 'fundamental guarantee' upon which the applicant could insist at the trial stage, thus requiring a 'full re-hearing', with, for example, the hearing of witnesses.

4. ARTICLE 6(2): THE RIGHT TO BE PRESUMED INNOCENT IN CRIMINAL CASES

Article 6(2) provides that a person 'charged with a criminal offence shall be presumed innocent until proved guilty according to law'. It guarantees a right that is fundamental to both common law and, despite legend in the United Kingdom to the contrary,[884] civil law systems of criminal justice. The obligation in Article 6(2) is independent of those in other Article 6 guarantees, so that there may be a breach of it even though the rest of Article 6 is respected.[885]

Article 6(2) extends only to persons who are or have been subject to a 'criminal charge'.[886] Hence Article 6(2) does not benefit a person who is under suspicion of having committed an offence, but is not yet subject to a 'criminal charge'.[887] However, prejudicial statements at the pre-trial stage, as well as later, about an accused who is subject to a criminal charge are controlled by Article 6(2).[888] Although extradition decisions do not involve the determination of a criminal charge, they 'may raise an issue under Article 6 § 2 if supporting reasoning [for the decision to extradite] which cannot be dissociated from the operative provisions amounts in substance to the determination of the person's guilt'.[889]

In accordance with the general approach in the legal systems of contracting parties, Article 6 has been held not to apply to practices in the course of a criminal investigation such as the conduct of breath, blood, or urine tests,[890] or medical examinations,[891] or an order to produce documents.[892] By analogy, Article 6(2) also does not apply to fingerprinting and searches of the person and of property.[893] A conviction for an offence of failing to provide information is in some contexts considered to be in breach of the presumption of innocence, as well as freedom from self-incrimination.[894] Restrictions on

---

para 33 (defect stemming from jury system could not be cured by appeal court because it was bound by the jury's verdict).

[883] 2000-XII para 39.   [884] See Allen, *Legal Duties*, 1931, p 253.

[885] *I and C v Switzerland No 10107/82*, 48 DR 35 (1985) Com Rep; CM Res DH (86) 11.

[886] 'Criminal charge' has the same autonomous meaning as elsewhere in Article 6.

[887] See *Adolf v Austria* A 49 (1982); 4 EHRR 313 paras 30, 34. But it may be that pre-charge statements that bear upon the innocence of a person once charged are subject to Article 6(2): see *Mustafa (Abu Hamza) v UK* hudoc (2011) DA.   [888] *Krause v Switzerland No 7986/77*, 13 DR 73 (1978).

[889] *Ismoilov and Others v Russia* hudoc (2008); 49 EHRR 1128 para 167.

[890] *Tirado Ortiz and Lozano Martin v Spain No 43486/98* hudoc (1999) DA.

[891] *X v Germany No 986/61*, 5 YB 192 (1962).

[892] *Funke v France* A 256-A (1993); 16 EHRR 297 para 69 Com Rep.

[893] The seizure of the property of an arrested person as security for costs is not a breach of Article 6(2): *X v Austria No 4338/69*, 36 CD 79 (1970).

[894] See *Heaney and McGuiness v Ireland* 2000-XII; 33 EHRR 264.

pre-trial detention (eg as to clothing and correspondence[895] or cell conditions[896]) do not raise an issue under Article 6(2). Nor does it extend to the closure of a shop as a provisional measure or the offer of an 'out of court' fine.[897]

Article 6(2) continues to apply to the end of any appeal proceedings against conviction.[898] Where an appeal against conviction is pending, remarks that may influence the appeal hearing are subject to Article 6(2).[899] It does not apply to the consideration of a convicted person's character and conduct during his sentencing, as that person is then no longer subject to a 'charge'.[900] However, Article 6(2) does apply to accusations about a convicted person that are made during sentencing proceedings if they are of such a nature and degree as to amount to the bringing of a new 'criminal charge'.[901] Article 6(2) was held to apply on this basis and to have been infringed when a court revoked the suspension of the applicant's sentence for an earlier offence, because of the court's 'certainty' that the applicant was guilty of another offence for which he had not been tried.[902] Article 6(2) has been held to apply to proceedings concerning the discontinuance of a case against an accused[903] or the award of costs or compensation following discontinuance[904] or acquittal:[905] the test is whether they can be seen as sufficiently closely linked with the determination of the criminal charge. Similarly, statements about an acquittal in separate court proceedings related to the acquittal are subject to Article 6(2).[906] However, Article 6(2) does not apply to an application by a convicted person for a re-trial.[907]

Article 6(2) means, in common law terms, that the general burden of proof must lie with the prosecution,[908] or, in terms more appropriate for civil law systems, that the court, in its inquiry into the facts, must find for the accused in a case of doubt.[909]

The close link between the presumption of innocence and freedom from self-incrimination has been demonstrated in several cases. In *Murray (John) v UK*,[910] the accused's right to remain silent was limited to the extent that inferences could be (and were) drawn by the trial court from the accused's failure to explain his presence at the scene of the crime and to give evidence in court. The Strasbourg Court held that, having regard to the considerable weight of other evidence against the accused, the drawing of inferences from his failure to explain his presence was a matter of 'common sense and

---

[895] *Skoogström v Sweden No 8582/72*, 5 EHRR 278 (1982). Cf *Englert v Germany* A 123 (1987); 13 EHRR 392 para 47 Com Rep.

[896] *Peers v Greece* 2001-III; 33 EHRR 1192. Articles 5(1)(c) and 5(3) apply instead.

[897] *Deweer v Belgium* B 33 (1980) para 64 Com Rep.

[898] *Nölkenbockhoff v Germany* A 123 (1987); 10 EHRR 163 PC.

[899] *Konstas v Greece* hudoc (2011).

[900] *Engel v Netherlands* A 22 (1976); 1 EHRR 647 PC. But the presumption of innocence is also a part of the general fair hearing requirement in Article 6(1), which does apply to the sentencing stage: *Phillips v UK* 2001-VII.   [901] *Engel v Netherlands*. Cf *Geerings v Netherlands* 2007-XX; 46 EHRR 1212.

[902] *Böhmer v Germany* hudoc (2002); 38 EHRR 410.

[903] *Adolf v Austria* A 49 (1982); 4 EHRR 313.

[904] *Minelli v Switzerland* A 62 (1983); 5 EHRR 554.

[905] *Sekanina v Austria* A 266-A (1993); 17 EHRR 221; *Lamanna v Austria* hudoc (2001); *Hammern v Norway* hudoc (2003); *Bok v Netherlands* hudoc (2011). Article 6(2) does not apply to miscarriage of justice cases referred for judicial review: *Callaghan v UK No 14739/89*, 60 DR 296 (1989).

[906] *Vassilios Stravopoulos v Greece* hudoc (2007). But in *Moullet v France No 27521/04* hudoc (2007) DA disciplinary proceedings following the applicant's acquittal that arose out of the same facts were not subject to Article 6 (2) as they were not in French law a 'consequence and the concomitant of the criminal proceedings'.

[907] *X v Germany No 914/60*, 4 YB 372 (1961).

[908] *Barberà, Messegué and Jabardo v Spain* A 146 (1988); 11 EHRR 360 para 77 PC. See also *Austria v Italy* 6 YB 740 at 782–84 (1963) Com Rep; CM Res DH (63) 3.

[909] As to whether Article 6(2) incorporates the civil law principle *in dubio pro reo*, see *Lingens and Leitgeb v Austria No 8803/79*, 26 DR 171 (1981).   [910] A 300-A (1996); 22 EHRR 29 para 54 GC.

cannot be regarded as unfair or unreasonable in the circumstances'. Nor did it have 'the effect of shifting the burden of proof from the prosecution to the defence so as to infringe the principle of the presumption of innocence'. In contrast, there was such a shifting of the burden of proof in breach of Article 6(2) in *Telfner v Austria*,[911] when the accused, who refused to give evidence to the police or at the trial, was convicted of a road traffic accident offence on the basis that he was the driver of the car involved, when there was no direct evidence to show that he was. The conviction was based on the facts that, although registered in his mother's name, the accused was the main user of the car and that he had not been home that night, which facts required him, the national court determined, to show that he was not the driver. The Strasbourg Court distinguished the *Murray* case on Article 6(2) because in the *Telfner* case there was no *prima facie* case against the accused that justified the drawing of 'common sense' inferences in the absence of an explanation by the accused. There was also a breach of the presumption of innocence, as well as the freedom from self-incrimination in Article 6(1), in *Heaney and McGuiness v Ireland*,[912] because of certain legal consequences for the applicants of maintaining their right to silence.

Although the burden of proof must generally fall upon the prosecution, it may be transferred to the accused when he is seeking to establish a defence.[913] Similarly, Article 6(2) does not prohibit presumptions of fact or of law that may operate against the accused. However, it does require that states confine such presumptions 'within reasonable limits which take into account the importance of what is at stake and maintain the rights of the defence'. This was stated in the leading case of *Salabiaku v France*,[914] in which the applicant had been convicted of the strict liability customs offence of smuggling prohibited goods. The applicant had collected and taken through the 'green' customs exit at Paris airport a trunk that contained prohibited drugs, of which he claimed to have no knowledge. Under French law, a person who was in possession of prohibited goods in these circumstances was presumed to be guilty of smuggling them. Thus the case was not a straightforward one of strict liability for an act that the prosecution had proved that the accused had committed. Instead it was one in which the *actus reus* of smuggling had been presumed from the proven fact of possession. The Court found that, as applied to the applicant's case, this presumption of fact was not contrary to Article 6(2). Under French law, the applicant had a defence of *force majeure*, by which it was open to him to prove that it was impossible for him to have known of the contents of the trunk. This he failed to prove to the satisfaction of the trial court. The Court held that, having regard to the possibility of the *force majeure* defence, the Customs Code was not applied by the courts in a manner which conflicted with Article 6(2), despite what was 'at stake' (imprisonment and a substantial fine) for the applicant. In other cases it has been held that rebuttable presumptions, including that an accused was living knowingly off the earnings of a prostitute who was proved to be living with him or under his control,[915] that a company director was guilty of an offence committed by the company,[916] and that a dog was of a dangerous

---

[911] Hudoc (2001); 34 EHRR 207. But see now the approach to road traffic offences in *O'Hallaran and Francis v UK* 2007-III; 46 EHRR 397 para 62 GC.

[912] 2000-XII; 33 EHRR 264.

[913] *Lingens and Leitgeb v Austria* No 8803/79, 26 DR 171 (1983) (burden of proof on defence in criminal defamation proceedings to show that statement is true; no breach of Article 6(2)).

[914] A 141-A (1988); 13 EHRR 379 para 28. Cf *Pham Hoang v France* A 243 (1992) and *Janosevic v Sweden* 2002-VII; 38 EHRR 473. See also *AP, MP and TP v Switzerland* 1997-V; 26 EHRR 541; *Falk v Netherlands No 66273/01* hudoc (2004) DA; *Phillips v UK* 2001-VII (Article 6(1) case); and *G v UK No. 372204/08* (2011) DA.

[915] *X v UK No 5124/71*, 42 CD 135 (1972).

[916] *G v Malta No 16641/90* hudoc (1991) DA. Cf *Radio France v France* 2004-II; 40 EHRR 706.

breed,[917] were not inconsistent with Article 6(2). However, a statutory presumption that a ruling in a criminal case in which the applicant had been the complainant that there was no case to answer automatically meant that in later criminal proceedings against the complainant for malicious prosecution the allegations should be treated as false was contrary to the presumption of innocence.[918]

As the *Salabiaku* case also decided, Article 6(2) does not prohibit offences of strict liability, which are a common feature of the criminal law of the Convention parties. An offence may thus be committed, consistently with Article 6(2), on the basis that a certain act has been committed, without it being necessary to prove *mens rea*. Provided a state respects the rights protected by the Convention, it is free to punish any kind of activity as criminal and to establish the elements of the offence in its discretion, including any requirement of *mens rea*.

Although mainly concerned with the burden of proof, Article 6(2) extends to certain other evidential matters. As to the standard of proof, there is no clear statement that there is a requirement of proof of guilt beyond reasonable doubt; in *Austria v Italy*,[919] the Commission stated that Article 6(2) requires that a court find the accused guilty only on the basis of evidence 'sufficiently strong in the eyes of the law to establish his guilt'. What is clear is that, in accordance with their general policy of not acting as a 'fourth instance',the Strasbourg authorities do not regard themselves as competent to question findings of fact by the trial court that appear to be based upon probative evidence.[920] As to the kind of evidence that may be relied upon, this may be 'direct or indirect'.[921] A confession obtained by torture and, at least in some cases, inhuman or degrading treatment must not be admitted in evidence.[922] However, it is not contrary to Article 6(2) to reveal the accused's past criminal record to the court before his conviction.[923] But the accused must be allowed an opportunity to rebut the evidence presented against him.[924]

Various claims that the presumption of innocence has been infringed in the conduct of the trial other than in respect of the operation of the rules of evidence have been considered. The handcuffing of the accused in front of the jury was consistent with Article 6(2) as a necessary security measure.[925] Requiring convicted persons to wear their prison uniform when appearing in court on appeal was a breach of Article 6(2) as reinforcing the public impression of their guilt.[926] The arrest of a witness in the courtroom for perjury immediately after giving evidence for the accused was permissible,[927] as were the re-trial of the accused before a court that had earlier considered his application for bail[928] and the detention of a convicted person pending his appeal.[929] A procedure by which a person may plead guilty to an offence, with the proceedings being limited to sentencing, is not

---

[917] *Bullock v UK No 29102/95* hudoc (1996); 21 EHRR CD 85.

[918] *Klouvi v France* hudoc (2011) (allegation of rape).

[919] 6 YB 740 at 784 (1963) Com Rep; CM Res DH (63) 3. See also *Vilborg Yrsa Sigurdardotir v Iceland* hudoc (2000).   [920] See *Albert and Le Compte v Belgium* A 58 (1983); 5 EHRR 533 PC.

[921] *Albert and Le Compte v Belgium*.

[922] *Jalloh v Germany* 2006-IX; 44 EHRR 667 para 101 GC. See also *Austria v Italy* 6 YB 116 at 784 (1963) Com Rep; CM Res DH (63) 3. Cf *X v UK No 5076/71*, 40 CD 64 (pressure to plead guilty may be contrary to Article 6(2)). There is an overlap here with the general 'fair hearing' requirement in Article 6(1).

[923] *X v Austria No 2742/66*, 9 YB 550 (1966).

[924] *Austria v Italy* 6 YB 116 at 784 (1963) Com Rep; CM Res DH (63) 3. See also *Albert and Le Compte v Belgium* A 58 (1983); 5 EHRR 533 PC, and *Schenk v Switzerland* A 140 (1988); 13 EHRR 242 PC. Article 6(2) overlaps with Article 6(3)(d) in this respect.   [925] *X v Austria No 2291/64*, 24 CD 20 (1967).

[926] *Samoilă and Cionca v Romania* hudoc (2008)   [927] *X v Germany No 8744/79*, 5 EHRR 499 (1983).

[928] *X v Germany No 2646/65*, 9 YB 484 (1966).

[929] *Cuvillers and Da Luz v France No 55052/00* hudoc (2003) DA.

in breach of Article 6(2), provided that pressure has not been brought improperly to bear upon the accused to obtain the guilty plea.[930] However, a requirement that a tax surcharge be paid pending an appeal against its imposition may be in breach of Article 6(2) if it is not kept 'within reasonable limits that strike a fair balance between the interests involved', which include the financial consequences for the taxpayer and any effect upon the rights of the defence.[931]

The Court's jurisprudence considered so far has concerned the presumption of innocence as a procedural guarantee that applies in the course of a criminal prosecution. The presumption of innocence also has a second dimension, which is to protect individuals who have been acquitted of a criminal charge, or against whom criminal proceedings have been discontinued, 'from being treated by public officials and authorities as though they are in fact guilty of the offence charged'; this second dimension counters the risk that the fair trial guarantees in Article 6 may be 'theoretical and illusory' only and serves to protect the individual's reputation.[932] The Court first spelt out this second dimension to the presumption of innocence in *Minelli v Switzerland*.[933] In that case, a private prosecution against the applicant was discontinued because it had become statute-barred. A Swiss court thereupon ordered the applicant to pay part of the private prosecutor's and court costs on the basis that the applicant would 'very probably' have been convicted had the case gone to trial. The European Court held that Article 6(2) had been infringed. Although there was no formal decision as to guilt, the court's judgment as to costs 'showed that it was satisfied' that the accused was guilty, and this was sufficient.[934]

Following the *Minelli* case, the Court has applied this second dimension of the presumption of innocence to several other kinds of cases. These include cases in which individuals who have been acquitted or against whom criminal proceeding have been discontinued have claimed defence costs[935] or compensation for their detention on remand[936] or for wrongful prosecution,[937] or have been the subject of disciplinary proceedings,[938] and cases in which victims of crime have sought compensation.[939] In these cases, the Court has drawn a distinction between statements by courts indicating guilt and statements by them that merely voice suspicion. The latter have been held permissible where no final decision in the accused's trial has been taken. Thus the voicing just of suspicion by a court when ruling on claims for compensation for detention on remand and/or costs in cases in which the prosecution has been discontinued,[940] or when ruling on claims for provisional measures,[941] is not a breach of Article 6(2). The position is different following acquittal. Court statements voicing continuing suspicion (and *a fortiori* guilt)[942] after the accused has been acquitted have been held to be in reach of Article 6(2).[943]

---

[930] *X v UK* No 5076/71, 40 CD 69 (1972). See also *Duhs v Sweden* No 12995/87, 67 DR 204 (out of court car-parking fines). See also *Panarisi v Italy* hudoc *(2007)*.

[931] *Janosevic v Sweden* 2002-VII; 38 EHRR 473 para 106.

[932] *Allen v UK* hudoc 2013- para 94 GC. The term 'public offical' includes judges.

[933] A 62 (1983); 5 EHRR 554. See also *Adolf v Austria* A 49 (1982); 4 EHRR 313.

[934] Cf *Yassar Hussain v UK* hudoc (2006) and *Ashendon and Jones v UK* hudoc (2011). See also *Poncelet v Belgium* hudoc (2010).   [935] Eg *Lutz v Germany* A 123 (1987); 10 EHRR 182 PC.

[936] Eg *Sekanina v Austria* A 266-A (1993); 17 EHRR 221.

[937] Eg *Grabchuk v Ukraine* No 8599/02 hudoc (2006) DA.   [938] Eg *Sikić v Croatia* hudoc (2010).

[939] Eg *Lagardère v France* hudoc (2012).

[940] Eg *Lutz v Germany* A 123 (1987); 10 EHRR 182 PC.   [941] *Gökçeli v Turkey* hudoc (2003).

[942] *Del Latte v Netherlands* hudoc (2004); 41 EHRR 176 and *Geerings v Netherlands* hudoc (2007); 46 EHRR 1212.

[943] *Sekanina v Austria* A 266-A (1993); 17 EHRR 221 and *Rushiti v Austria* hudoc (2000); 33 EHRR 1331. Adverse comments short of suspicion are not a breach: *Fashanu v UK* No 38440/97 hudoc (1998); 26 EHRR CD 217 DA.

But statements of suspicion by a court following acquittal in proceedings for compensation for detention on remand when there was reasonable suspicion at the time of the arrest have not.[944]

The Grand Chamber reviewed its jurisprudence on this second dimension of the presumption of innocence in *Allen v UK*.[945] In that case, the applicant's conviction for manslaughter of her son as a case of 'shaken baby syndrome' was quashed, and the accused formally acquitted, by the English Court of Appeal as 'unsafe' in the light of new evidence indicating that there could have been another cause of death. The applicant's claim for compensation on the statutory ground that a new or newly discovered fact had shown 'beyond reasonable doubt' that there had been a 'miscarriage of justice' was, however, rejected by the Secretary of State. Her application for judicial review of this decision was dismissed by the High Court and the Court of Appeal because the conviction had been quashed on the basis that the new evidence created the *possibility* that a jury might acquit, not that there was no case to answer: so the 'miscarriage of justice' requirement had not been met. The Strasbourg Court held that the judgments of the English courts when dismissing the applicant's claim for compensation did not violate Article 6(2). This was because in considering whether there was a 'miscarriage of justice' the courts were not called upon to comment, and did not comment, on the applicant's guilt or innocence.

The cases just discussed concern statements made following an acquittal or discontinuance of the case in judicial decisions that directly concern the applicant. Article 6(2) may also be infringed in criminal proceedings against another person when the court refers in its judgment to the involvement of the applicant in the same offence.[946] In addition, although civil proceedings are not directly subject to it,[947] Article 6(2) requires that a civil court act in accordance with an acquittal of an accused who is later party to the proceeding before it arising out of the same facts.[948] But the mere suspension of civil proceedings pending the outcome of a criminal case is not a breach.[949]

The rule in the *Minelli* case concerns statements made in judicial decisions. Article 6(2) has also been applied to statements made by judges while a case is pending, whether in or outside of court proceedings. Thus in *Kyprianou v Cyprus*,[950] the trial court stated in the course of exchanges with defence counsel during a court hearing, that his conduct in court amounted to criminal contempt. After a short adjournment, the court sentenced counsel to five days' imprisonment without giving him an opportunity to defend himself on the charge of contempt. The Strasbourg Court held that the statements indicating contempt were a breach both of the requirement that an accused be tried by an impartial tribunal in Article 6(1) and of the presumption of innocence in Article 6(2). As to statements made outside of court proceedings, in *Lavents v Latvia*[951] there was a breach of both Article 6(1) (partial tribunal) and Article 6(2) when the trial judge stated in press interviews which she gave during the trial that she was not sure whether to convict the accused on all or only some counts, and expressed her astonishment that he totally denied his guilt. As well as statements by judges, prejudicial comment by counsel or witnesses may raise a question under Article 6(2) if the court's failure to control it shows judicial

---

[944] *Hibbert v Netherlands No 38087/97* hudoc (1999) DA.   [945] 2013- GC.

[946] *Vulakh and Others v Russia* hudoc (2012).   [947] *X v Germany No 6062/73*, 2 DR 54 (1974).

[948] *X v Austria No 9295/81*, 30 DR 227 (1982) and *Diamantides v Greece (No 2)* hudoc (2005). But civil liability may be found on the same facts using a lower standard of proof, provided that the civil court does not question the acquittal in so doing: see *Ringvold v Norway* 2003-II and *Y v Norway* 2003-II; 41 EHRR 87.

[949] *Farragut v France No 10103/82*, 39 DR 186 (1984).   [950] 2005-XIII; 44 EHRR 565 GC.

[951] Hudoc (2002).

bias.[952] With regard to these cases, although it is possible to see a presumption of innocence element in them, it might be simpler and more natural to treat them just under the 'impartial tribunal' requirement in Article 6(1).[953]

The approach in the *Minelli* case applies not only to judicial statements, but also to statements by other public officials. In *Allenet de Ribemont v France*,[954] a senior police officer, flanked by other officials who made supporting remarks, stated at a press conference that the applicant was one of the 'instigators' of a murder. The Court stated that this 'was clearly a declaration of the applicant's guilt which, firstly, encouraged the public to believe him guilty and, secondly, prejudged the assessment of the facts by the competent judicial authority'.

A breach of Article 6(2) was also found in *Butkevicius v Lithuania*,[955] when statements by the Chairman of the Lithuanian Parliament were made to the press shortly after the applicant, who was the Lithuanian Minister of Defence, had been apprehended in a hotel lobby accepting an envelope full of US dollars. The Chairman said that he 'had no doubt' that the applicant, who was later convicted of attempting to obtain property by deception, had accepted a bribe and that he was a 'bribe-taker'. In the Court's view, these remarks amounted to declarations by a public official of the applicant's guilt in breach of Article 6(2). In contrast, in *Daktaras v Lithuania*,[956] the Court found no breach of Article 6(2) when a prosecutor indicated that the applicant was guilty in his decision to refuse an application for discontinuance of the prosecution. The Strasbourg Court drew a distinction between public statements made in a context, such as a press conference, that was separate from the court proceedings concerning the applicant and statements, such as that by the prosecutor, that were a part of those proceedings. It is probable that the Court would have reached a different conclusion had the statement been made not by the prosecutor but by the judge in the case, as in *Lavents v Latvia*.[957] In a different kind of case, the dismissal of a customs officer from his employment because he was in pre-trial detention for a customs offence, but not yet convicted, was not a violation of the presumption of innocence.[958]

The Court has recognized that, as well as statements by judges or other public officials, a 'virulent press campaign' may raise issues under Article 6(2), so that the state has an obligation to take steps to control them. Although some of the Strasbourg jurisprudence might be read as suggesting that prejudicial publicity in the press or other media[959] may be a breach of Article 6 even in trials before judges alone,[960] this is obviously less likely to be so than in cases in which juries (or lay assessors) are involved.[961] This was confirmed in

---

[952] See *Austria v Italy* 6 YB 740 Com Rep; CM Res DH (63) 3; *Nielsen v Denmark No 343/57*, 2 YB 412; *X, Y, Z v Austria No 7950/77*, 4 EHRR 270 at 274 (1980). In determining whether proceedings have been allowed to get out of hand to the prejudice of the accused, allowance may be made for different national temperaments and legal traditions: *Austria v Italy*.   [953] As in *Buscemi v Italy* 1999-VI.

[954] A 308 (1995); 20 EHRR 557 paras 37, 41. Cf *GCP v Romania* hudoc (2011) (statements of guilt by public prosecutor and minister of the interior).

[955] 2002-II. Cf *Kuzmin v Russia* hudoc (2010) (statement of guilt by political election candidate: breach). In *Mustafa (Abu Hamza) v UK No 31411/07* hudoc (2011) DA, the Secretary of State had stated that the reason for withdrawing the applicant's citizenship was that he had provided support and advice to terrorist groups; this statement was held not to be sufficiently closely linked to the offences for which he would later be prosecuted to be in breach of Article 6(2).

[956] 2000-X; 34 EHRR 1466. See also *Hentrich v France* A 296-A (1994); 18 EHRR 440. Contrast *Fatullayev v Azerbijan* hudoc (2010); 52 EHRR 58 and *Virabyan v Armenia* hudoc (2012). See also *Teodor v Romania* hudoc (2013).   [957] Hudoc (2002).

[958] *Tripon v Romania* hudoc (2012).

[959] *Ninn-Hansen v Denmark No 28972/95*, 1999-V (television).

[960] See, eg, *Anguelov v Bulgaria, No 45963/99* hudoc (2004) DA.

[961] See, eg, *Priebke v Italy No 48799/99* hudoc (2001) DA.

Craxi v Italy,[962] in which the Court, when finding that the trial of a former First Minister, which attracted a great deal of media coverage, was not a breach of the presumption of innocence, emphasized that the case was decided entirely by professional judges. However, several limits to possible breaches of Article 6 on a 'virulent campaign' basis have been set, which together help to explain why, despite the great publicity that sometimes attends trials, no case of a violation of Article 6 has yet been found on this ground. Thus the Court has stressed that, in accordance with freedom of expression, some press comment on a trial involving a matter of public interest must be expected,[963] and that its impact is likely to be limited where the trial takes place a considerable time later.[964] In addition, the test is not 'the subjective apprehensions' of the suspect as to the impact of the comment, but whether 'his fears can be held to be objectively justified'.[965] Moreover, in a jury case, the effect of prejudicial comment may be countered by the judge's direction to the jury to discount it.[966] There are also statements suggesting that state involvement in the generation of the publicity is necessary for the state to be responsible for any resulting prejudice,[967] although in the theory of the Convention, the simple failure of the court, a state organ, to counter the possible prejudicial effect should be sufficient to engage responsibility under the Convention.

Finally, it should be noted that where a national appeal court does not consider that the trial has been unfair on this ground, it is unlikely that a breach will be found at Strasbourg.[968]

A violation of the presumption of innocence by a lower court may be made good by a higher court on appeal.[969] It may be, however, that 'the failure of the lower court to observe the principle of presumption of innocence has so distorted the general course of proceedings' that this is not possible.[970]

5. ARTICLE 6(3): FURTHER GUARANTEES IN CRIMINAL CASES

I. ARTICLE 6(3): GENERALLY

Article 6(3) guarantees certain rights that are necessary to the preparation and conduct of the defence and to ensure that the accused is able to defend himself on equal terms with the prosecution. The rights listed are 'minimum rights'. They are elements of the wider concept of the right to a fair trial in Article 6(1). Because of this, the Court commonly decides cases on the basis of Article 6(1) *and* the relevant specific right in Article 6(3) or even on the basis of Article 6 as a whole.[971]

---

[962] Hudoc (2002). Cf *GCP v Romania* hudoc (2011) and *Priebke v Italy No 48799/99* hudoc (2001) DA.

[963] See, eg, *Papon v France (No 2) No 54210/00* hudoc (2001) DA. See also *Sunday Times v UK (No 1)* A 30 (1979); 2 EHRR 245, in which a conviction for criminal contempt for comment on pending civil litigation was contrary to the guarantee of freedom of speech in Article 10.

[964] *GCP v Romania* hudoc (2011).   [965] *GCP v Romania*, para 46.

[966] *Noye v UK No 4491/02* hudoc (2003); 36 EHRR CD 231 DA. Cf *Pullicino v Malta No 45441/99* hudoc (2000) DA and *Mustafa (Abu Hamza) v UK No 31411/07* hudoc (2011) DA.

[967] See *Ensslin, Baader and Raspe v Germany Nos 7572/76, 7586/76 and 7587/76*, 14 DR 64 at 112 (1978) and *Wloch v Poland* No 27785/95 hudoc (2000).   [968] See, eg, *X v UK No 3860/68*, 30 CD 70 (1969).

[969] *Adolf v Austria* A 49 (1982); 4 EHRR 313 and *Arrigo and Vella v Malta* hudoc (2005) DA.

[970] *Austria v Italy* 6 YB 740 at 784 (1963) Com Rep; CM Res DH (63) 3.

[971] For an 'Article 6 as a whole' case, see *Vidal v Belgium* A 235-B (1992).

The rights in Article 6(3) are guaranteed only to persons 'charged with a criminal offence'. This wording is identical to that in Article 6(2) and has the same autonomous Convention meaning as it has in that paragraph and in the equivalent wording in Article 6(1).[972] Accordingly, a person is charged with a criminal offence for the purposes of Article 6(3) from the moment that he is 'substantially affected' by the steps taken against him as a suspect. Article 6(3) does not protect a person who is suspected of a criminal offence but not yet charged with it in this sense. Nor does it benefit a person who is being extradited for prosecution in another jurisdiction.[973]

However, the fact that a person is 'charged with a criminal offence' does not mean that each of the rights in Article 6(3) extends to him from the very moment of his being so charged.[974] Whether Article 6(3) applies at all to the pre-trial stage of criminal proceedings was formerly a matter of dispute, with a number of civil law contracting parties questioning whether it did. This argument was expressly rejected by the Court in *Imbrioscia v Switzerland*.[975] Noting that the reasonable time guarantee in Article 6(1) applied at the pre-trial stage, the Court stated:

> Other requirements of Article 6—especially of paragraph 3—may also be relevant before a case is sent for trial if and insofar as the fairness of the trial is likely to be seriously prejudiced by the initial failure to comply with them.

Article 6(3) applies to appeal proceedings, although its requirements at this stage are shaped by the function of the appellate court concerned and its place in the proceedings as a whole.[976]

II. ARTICLE 6(3)(A): THE RIGHT TO BE INFORMED OF THE ACCUSATION

Article 6(3)(a) requires that a person charged with a criminal offence 'be informed promptly, in a language which he understands and in detail, of the nature and cause of the accusation against him'. It overlaps with Article 5(2), which provides a similarly worded guarantee for persons detained pending trial.[977] Although both provisions respond to the legitimate claim of an individual to know why the state has acted against him, the purpose of the two guarantees is essentially different. Whereas Article 5(2) seeks to assist the arrested person in challenging his detention, Article 6(3)(a) is intended to give the accused person the information he needs to answer the accusation against him. For this reason, the information required by Article 6(3)(a) is to be understood in the light of the accused's right to prepare his defence that is guaranteed in Article 6(3)(b).[978]

---

[972] See *Adolf v Austria* A 49 (1982); 4 EHRR 313.

[973] But see the *Soering v UK* A 161 (1989); 11 EHRR 439 PC exception.

[974] Thus Article 6(3)(d) does not generally apply at the pre-trial stage.

[975] A 275 (1993); 17 EHRR 441 para 36. Cf *Öcalan v Turkey* 2005-VI para 131; 41 EHRR 985 GC.

[976] See, eg, *Artico v Italy* A 37 (1980); 7 EHRR 528 and *Kremzow v Austria* A 268-B (1993); 17 EHRR 322 para 58.

[977] But, unlike Article 5(2), Article 6(3)(a) may apply to unarrested persons concerning whom a preliminary investigation has commenced, provided they are 'substantially affected': see *Brozicek v Italy* A 167 (1989); 12 EHRR 371 PC. For cases in which Article 6(3)(a) claims did not meet this requirement, see *C v Italy* No 10889/84, 56 DR 40 (1988) and *Padin Gestoso v Spain* No 39519/98 1999-II DA.

[978] *Pélissier and Sassi v France* 1999-II; 30 EHRR 715 para 54 GC. Compliance with Article 6(3)(a) is a condition of compliance with Article 6(3)(b): *Ofner v Austria* No 524/59, 3 YB 322 at 344 (1960).

The requirement in Article 6(3)(a) that persons 'charged with a criminal offence' be given the necessary information 'promptly' has not been strictly interpreted. In *Kaminski v Austria*,[979] it was met when the information, in the civil law system concerned, was given at the time of the indictment hearing, some eleven days after the accused's arrest. In other cases, no breach has been found where the accused has had sufficient time to prepare his defence despite the delay in informing him of the investigation against him.[980] 'Promptly' has been interpreted more strictly than this in Article 5(2).

The accused must be informed of the 'nature and cause of the accusation against him'. The 'nature' of the accusation is the offence with which the accused is charged. This may be altered as the case proceeds provided that the accused is given the opportunity to prepare his defence to the new charge in 'a practical and effective manner and, in particular, in good time'.[981] Article 6(3)(a) was infringed when the applicant was only informed of the new charge on the final day of the trial[982] and where a court of appeal convicted the applicants of a new offence of which they only learnt when that court's judgment was delivered.[983] There was no breach, however, where the accused could reasonably have anticipated that an aggravating factor which was present on the facts, but not argued, would be taken into account in sentencing.[984] Nor was there a breach where the accused had sufficient opportunity to respond at the appeal stage to a reformulated charge on the basis of which he had been convicted at first instance.[985]

The 'cause' of an accusation consists of the 'acts he is alleged to have committed and on which the accusation is based'.[986] What needs to be communicated to the accused will depend upon what he can be taken to know from the questioning he has undergone and from the other circumstances of the case.[987] The accused must take advantage of what opportunities exist to learn of the accusation against him; if a prisoner fails to attend a hearing at which he could have obtained further information, this will count against his claim of a breach of Article 6(3)(a).[988]

The words 'in detail' clearly suggest that the information to which an accused is entitled under Article 6(3)(a) is 'more specific and more detailed' than that which an accused must receive under Article 5(2).[989] In *Mattoccia v Italy*,[990] the Court stated that the accused must be told of the 'material facts' that form the basis of the accusation against him: the level of detail may vary with the circumstances, but the accused 'must at any rate be provided with sufficient information as is necessary to understand fully the extent of the charges against him with a view to preparing an adequate defence'. There was clearly a breach of Article 6(3)(a) in *Kyprianou v Cyprus*,[991] where a lawyer was held guilty of

---

[979] A 168 (1989); 13 EHRR 36. But a delay of almost ten years was a breach: *Casse v Luxembourg* hudoc (2006).

[980] See *Padin Gestoso v Spain No 39519/98* 1999-II DA.

[981] *Péllisier and Sassi v France* 1999-II; 30 EHRR 715 para 62 GC. See also *Mattoccia v Italy* 2000-IX; 36 EHRR 825 and *Varela Geis v Spain* hudoc (2013).

[982] *Sadak v Turkey (No 1)* 2001-VIII; 36 EHRR 431. Cf *Chichlian and Ekindjian v France* A 162-B (1989); 13 EHRR 553 Com Rep (F Sett before Court).

[983] *Péllisier and Sassi v France* 1999-II; 30 EHRR 715 GC. See also *Mattoccia v Italy* 2000-IX 89; 36 EHRR 825 and *Sipavičius v Lithuania* hudoc (2002).

[984] *Gea Catalan v Spain* A 309 (1995); 20 EHRR 266 and *De Salvador Torres v Spain* 1996-V; 23 EHRR 601.

[985] *Dallos v Hungary* 2001-II; 37 EHRR 524.

[986] *Péllisier and Sassi v France* 1999-II; 30 EHRR 715 para 51 GC.

[987] *Kamasinski v Austria* A 168(1989); 13 EHRR 36.

[988] *Campbell and Fell v UK* A 80 (1984); 7 EHRR 165.

[989] *Neilsen v Denmark No 343/57*, 2 YB 412 at 462 (1959).

[990] 2000-IX; 36 EHRR 825 paras 59–60. See also *Brozicek v Italy* A 167 (1989); 12 EHRR 371.

[991] Hudoc (2004). Chamber decision. The Grand Chamber did not consider Article 6(3)(a).

contempt in the face of the court following a ten-minute recess after an outburst by him in court. The transcript of the proceedings indicated that the court had already decided on his guilt before informing the accused of the nature and cause of the accusation against him and the lawyer only learnt of the 'material facts' on which the charge was based when a sentence of five days' imprisonment was imposed following his conviction.

Article 6(3)(a) does not impose any special formal requirement as to the manner in which the information is to be given. Although the importance of the required information is such that it should normally be given in writing, this is not essential in all cases: depending on the facts, the accused may be given the information orally or he may have waived his right to a written communication. In *Kamasinski v Austria*,[992] sufficient information was given orally to the applicant during the questioning sessions following his arrest. Where the information is sent in writing by post, proof of delivery is generally required.[993] Where a person has mental difficulties, appropriate action must be taken to make sure that he is aware of the nature and cause of the accusation against him.[994]

The information must be given to the accused in a 'language which he understands'. Unless the authorities can prove or have reasonable grounds to believe that the accused has a sufficient command of the language in which the information is given to him, they must provide him with an appropriate translation if he requests it.[995] Since the right is that of the defence as a whole, Article 6(3)(a) is complied with if the required information is given in a language that the accused *or* his lawyer understands.[996] The cost of any translation must be met by the state under Article 6(3)(e).

III. ARTICLE 6(3)(B): THE RIGHT TO ADEQUATE TIME AND FACILITIES

Article 6(3)(b) guarantees a person charged with a criminal offence 'adequate time and facilities for the preparation of his defence'. This right was explained by the Commission in *Can v Austria*[997] as requiring that the accused has 'the opportunity to organise his defence in an appropriate way and without restriction as to the possibility to put all relevant defence arguments before the trial court, and thus to influence the proceedings'.

a. Adequate time

The guarantee in Article 6(3)(b) of 'adequate time' to prepare a defence, which protects the accused against a 'hasty trial',[998] is the counterpoise to that in Article 6(1) by which an accused must be tried within a reasonable time. The guarantee begins to run from the moment that a person is subject to a criminal charge, ie from the moment that he is

---

[992] A 168 (1989); 13 EHRR 36.

[993] *C v Italy No 10889/84*, 56 DR 40 (1988). But the accused may be shown to have avoided delivery of a warrant with the required information: *Erdogan v Turkey No 14723/89*, 73 DR 81.

[994] *Vaudelle v France* 2001-I; 37 EHRR 397.

[995] *Brozicek v Italy* A 167 (1989); 12 EHRR 371 PC. The case for a written translation of a key document such as an indictment is particularly strong: *Kamasinski v Austria* A 168 (1989); 13 EHRR 36. And see *Hermi v Italy* 2006-XII; 46 EHRR 1115 GC.

[996] *X v Austria No 6185/73*, 2 DR 68 (1975). The question was not ruled on in *Kamasinski v Austria* A 168 (1989); 13 EHRR 36, the applicant having requested that the indictment be sent to his lawyer. For the view that the information should be given in a language that the accused understands so that he can control his defence, see Stavros, p 174.

[997] A 96 (1985); 8 EHRR 14 Com Rep para 53 (F Sett before Court). Cf *Galstyan v Armenia* hudoc (2007); 50 EHRR 618.

[998] *Kröcher and Müller v Switzerland No 8463/78*, 26 DR 24 at 53 (1981).

arrested or otherwise 'substantially affected'. Generally, the adequacy of the time allowed will depend upon the particular facts of the case.[999] Relevant considerations are the complexity of the case,[1000] the stage of proceedings,[1001] the fact that the accused is defending himself in person,[1002] and the accused's lawyer's workload.[1003] A legal aid lawyer must be appointed,[1004] or the accused allowed to appoint his own lawyer,[1005] in good time before the hearing.[1006] If a lawyer is replaced for good reason, additional time must be allowed for the new lawyer to prepare the case.[1007] Any breach of Article 6(3)(b) that results from the brevity of the time allowed for a lawyer to prepare a case may be rectified in appeal proceedings.[1008]

As to what is 'adequate time', in cases at the trial stage, two weeks for the accused's lawyers to examine a case file of 17,000 pages were insufficient,[1009] as were, in a different kind of case, just a few hours for an accused who was defending himself in person in a minor public order case 'to enable him to familiarise himself properly with and to assess adequately the charge and evidence against him, and to develop a viable legal strategy for his defence'.[1010] In contrast, a period of seventeen days' notice of the hearing before a criminal court in a 'fairly complicated' case of misappropriation was 'adequate',[1011] as was five days' notice of a prison disciplinary hearing.[1012] Generally, less time will be needed to prepare for an appeal than for a trial.[1013] An accused who considers that the time allowed is inadequate should, as a matter of local remedies, seek an adjournment or postponement of the hearing,[1014] but there may be exceptional circumstances which make this unnecessary.[1015] The reclassification on the final day of a trial of the offence with which the accused was charged gave him inadequate time to consult with his lawyer to prepare his defence and was a breach of both Article 6(3)(a) and (b).[1016]

In *Artico v Italy*,[1017] the Court recognized that proof of actual prejudice caused by the absence of a lawyer—which might be 'impossible' to show—was not required to establish a breach of Article 6(3)(c), and this, it is submitted, should apply also to the failure to appoint a lawyer in sufficient time in breach of Article 6(3)(b).[1018]

---

[999] *Mattick v Germany No 62116/00* hudoc (2005) DA.

[1000] *Albert and Le Compte v Belgium* A 58 (1983) PC and *Oao Neftyanaya Kompaniya Yukos v Russia* hudoc (2011); 54 EHRR 599.   [1001] *Huber v Austria No 5523/72*, 17 YB 314 (1974); 46 CD 99 (1974).

[1002] *X v Austria No 2370/64*, 22 CD 96 (1967).

[1003] *X and Y v Austria No 7909/77*, 15 DR 160 (1978) and *Berlinski v Poland* hudoc (2002).

[1004] *X and Y v Austria* and *Galstyan v Armenia* hudoc (2007).

[1005] *Perez Mahia v Spain No 11022/84*, 9 EHRR 145 (1985).

[1006] An accused cannot complain if he or she is responsible for the delay: *X v Austria No 8251/78*, 17 DR 166 (1979).

[1007] See *Goddi v Italy* A 76 (1984) (Article 6(3)(c) decision) and *Samer v Germany No 4319/69*, 14 YB 322 (1971).   [1008] *Twalib v Greece* 1998-IV; 33 EHRR 584.

[1009] *Öcalan v Turkey* 2005 IV; 41 EHRR 985 GC. Cf *Kremzow v Austria* A 268-B; 17 EHRR 322 (twenty-one days to examine forty-nine-page document sufficient). See also *GB v France* 2001-X; 35 EHRR 1233.

[1010] *Galstryan v Armenia* hudoc (2007). But see *X v UK No 4042/69*, 13 YB 690 (1970). Fast-track procedures are permissible if the defence is not prejudiced: *Galstryan v Armenia*. Cf *Borisova v Bulgaria* hudoc (2006).   [1011] *X and Y v Austria No 7909/77*, 15 DR 160 (1978).

[1012] *Campbell and Fell v UK* A 80 (1984); 7 EHRR 165. Cf *Albert and Le Compte v Belgium* A 58 (1983); 5 EHRR 533 PC.   [1013] *Huber v Austria No 5523/72*, 17 YB 314 (1974); 46 CD 99 (1974).

[1014] *Campbell and Fell v UK* A 80 (1984) 7 EHRR 165. In *Murphy v UK No 4681/70*, 43 CD 1 (1972), in which a legal aid barrister was allocated to the accused just minutes before a hearing, the application was refused because an adjournment would have been granted if requested. See also *Craxi v Italy* hudoc (2002) and *Backstrom and Andersson v Sweden No 67830/01* hudoc (2006) DA.

[1015] *Goddi v Italy* A 76 (1984). Cf *Mattei v France* hudoc (2006).

[1016] *Sadak v Turkey (No 1)* 2001-VIII; 36 EHRR 431.

[1017] A 37 (1980); 3 EHRR 1, discussed later. But see *Twalib v Greece* 1998-IV; 33 EHRR 584 para 40.

[1018] Cf *Korellis v Cyprus* hudoc (2003), discussed in the next section (adequate facilities).

b. Adequate facilities

Adequate facilities include the accused's right of access to a lawyer at the pre-trial stage and later to the extent necessary to prepare his or her defence.[1019] There is an overlap here between Article 6(3)(b) and the right to legal assistance in Article 6(3)(c).[1020] The following paragraphs are based on the jurisprudence of the Court and the Commission under Article 6(3)(b).[1021]

The right of access to a lawyer has particular significance for persons in detention on remand pending the hearing. A prisoner must be allowed to receive a visit from his lawyer out of the hearing of prison officers or other officials in order to convey instructions or to pass or receive confidential information relating to the preparation of his defence.[1022] Restrictions upon visits by lawyers may be imposed if they can be justified in the public interest (eg to prevent escape or the obstruction of justice).[1023] A restriction by which a lawyer may not discuss certain evidence with his client may be permissible to protect the identity of an informer.[1024] In early decisions, the Commission held that a refusal to allow a prisoner to take his notes and annotated documents to an interview with his lawyer,[1025] and that an accused's lack of opportunity to discuss his appeal with his legal aid lawyer in person because the lawyer lived too far away,[1026] were not a breach of the Convention. It is for the accused who appoints his own lawyer to ensure that the lawyer speaks a language that the accused understands or to arrange for an interpreter; the state is under no obligation to provide an interpreter in such circumstances.[1027] The right to communicate with one's lawyer extends to written as well as oral communication. In practice, questions concerning prison correspondence, in respect of which most problems of correspondence between accused persons and their lawyers concerning criminal proceedings[1028] are likely to arise, have generally been considered under Article 8 (the right to respect for correspondence).[1029]

Apart from access to a lawyer, Article 6(3)(b) 'recognises the right of the accused to have at his disposal, for the purpose of exonerating himself or of obtaining a reduction in his sentence, all relevant elements that have been or could be collected by the authorities', including any document that 'concerns acts of which the defendant is accused, the credibility of testimony, etc'.[1030] In any criminal case, the prosecution will have at its disposal the results of the police investigation or, in a civil law system, the case file prepared during the preliminary investigation.[1031] This will include both documents and other evidence

---

[1019]   *Campbell and Fell v UK* A 80 (1984) 7 EHRR 165 and *Goddi v Italy* A 76 (1984).

[1020]   See *Goddi v Italy* A 76 (1984) para 31.

[1021]   The right of access to a lawyer is now usually dealt with by the Court under Article 6(3)(c), not under Article 6(3)(b): see, eg, *Öcalan v Turkey* 2005-IV; 41 EHRR 985 GC.

[1022]   *Can v Austria* A 96 (1985); 8 EHRR 14 paras 51–2 Com Rep (F Sett before Court); *Campbell and Fell v UK* A 80 (1984); 7 EHRR 165 para 113; and *Öcalan v Turkey* 2005-IV; 41 EHRR 985 GC. The restrictions permitted in the pre-*Can* case of *Kröcher and Möller v Switzerland* No 8463/78, 34 DR 25 (1982) Com Rep CM Res DH (83) 15, would not now be accepted, even in a terrorist context.

[1023]   See *Can v Austria* A 96 (1985); 8 EHRR 14 and *Campbell and Fell v UK* A 80 (1984); 7 EHRR 165.

[1024]   *Kurup v Denmark* No 11219/84, 42 DR 287 (1985).

[1025]   *Koplinger v Austria* No 1850/63, 12 YB 438 (1968). See also *Moiseyev v Russia* hudoc (2008); 53 EHRR 306.

[1026]   *X v Austria* No 1135/61, 6 YB 194 (1963) (correspondence was possible).

[1027]   *X v Austria* No 6185/73, 2 DR 68 (1975).

[1028]   As to prisoners' correspondence in civil proceedings, see section 3.I.a.

[1029]   See, eg, *Schönenberger and Durmaz v Switzerland* A 137 (1988). See also *McComb v UK* No 10621/83, 50 DR 81 (1986) (Article 6(3)(c)). Article 6(3)(c) may be infringed by delays caused by monitoring correspondence with a lawyer: *Domenchini v Italy* 1996-V; 32 EHRR 68.

[1030]   *Jespers v Belgium* No 8403/78, 27 DR 61 at 88 (1981) Com Rep; CM Res DH (82) 3. Cf *Khodorkovskiy and Lebedev v Russia* hudoc (2013). See also *CGP v Netherlands* No 29835/96 hudoc (1997) DA

[1031]   As to access in a civil law system to the complete case-file, see Stavros, pp 181–3. See also *Foucher v France* 1997-II; 25 EHRR 234. Article 6(3)(b) requires that the accused by given sufficient personal access

obtained by questioning or searches backed by the power of the state or by the use of forensic resources which the defence may well lack.[1032] In this context, the primary purpose of Article 6(3)(b) is to achieve 'equality of arms' between the prosecution and the defence by requiring that the accused be allowed 'the opportunity to acquaint himself, for the purposes of preparing his defence, with the results of investigations carried out throughout the proceedings'.[1033] Article 6(1) requires that the prosecution disclose to the defence all material evidence in its possession for or against the accused, and this obligation must apply also under Article 6(3)(b).[1034] Access to documents may, however, be restricted for national security reasons.[1035] As well as access to documents, an accused in pre-trial detention requires conditions of detention that allow him to concentrate on preparing his defence.[1036]

Article 6(3)(b) also extends to 'facilities' that the defence requires at the trial in order to plead its case so that, for example, defence counsel must be allowed sufficient time to present the defence[1037] and to call expert witnesses,[1038] or be allowed an adjournment.[1039] But Article 6(3)(b) does not imply a right to attend a pre-trial hearing by an investigating judge of witnesses abroad who may give evidence later at the trial.[1040]

If there is a right of appeal against the trial court decision, Article 6(3)(b) requires that the applicant be allowed sufficient facilities to prepare his appeal. Thus the applicant must be informed of the reasons for the decision against him or her[1041] and given a copy of the pleadings[1042] in good time.[1043] If the applicant is detained, the prison authorities must take reasonable steps to supply him or her with the legal and other materials needed to prepare an appeal.[1044]

It would appear from *Korellis v Cyprus*[1045] that the accused does not have to show 'actual prejudice' to the defence resulting from the state's failure to allow access to documents or other 'facilities': the test instead is one of 'relevance' to the preparation of the defence.

to the documents in the case file to allow his defence to be prepared properly: *Öcalan v Turkey* 2005-IV; 41 EHRR 985 GC. See also *Kremzow v Austria* A 268-B (1993); 17 EHRR 322. In some circumstances it may be sufficient that the accused's lawyer has access: *Kamasinksi v Austria* A 168 (1989); 13 EHRR 36 para 88.

[1032] Under the 'equality of arms' requirement, the defence must have access to relevant evidence to conduct a forensic examination.

[1033] *Jespers v Belgium* No 8403/78, 27 DR 61 at 87 (1981) Com Rep; CM Res DH (82) 3. See also *Öcalan v Turkey* 2005-IV; 41 EHRR 985 para 140 GC.

[1034] *Edwards v UK* A 247-B (1992); 15 EHRR 417. Claims of non-disclosure of evidence to the defence are now generally dealt with not under Article 6(3), but the 'fair hearing' guarantee in Article 6(1). On the late introduction of prosecution witnesses, see *X v UK No 5327/71*, 43 CD 85 (1972).

[1035] *Moiseyev v Russia* hudoc (2008); 53 EHRR 306.   [1036] *Moiseyev v Russia*.

[1037] *X v Germany* No 7085/75, 2 Digest 809 (1976) (no breach).

[1038] *GB v France* 2001-X; 35 EHRR 123.

[1039] *X v UK* No 6404/73, 2 Digest 895 (1975) (no breach).

[1040] *X v Germany* No 6566/74, 1 DR 84 (1974). See also *Crociani v Italy* No 8603/79, 22 DR 147 (1980).

[1041] *Hadjianastassiou v Greece* A 252 (1992). An abridged (not a full) copy of the trial court judgment will be sufficient if the applicant's defence rights are not 'unduly affected': *Zoon v Netherlands* 2000-XII; 36 EHRR 380.   [1042] *Kremzow v Austria* A 268-B (1993).

[1043] As to the need to give notice of the date of the hearing, see *Goddi v Italy*, A 76 (1984) and *Vacher v France* 1996-V; 24 EHRR 482.   [1044] *Ross v UK* No 11396/85, 50 DR 179 (1986).

[1045] Hudoc (2003) (access to evidence for forensic examination; decided under Article 6(1), but relevant to Article 6(3)(b)). But see the earlier Commission cases of *Koplinger v Austria* No 1850/63, 12 YB 438 (1968); *X v Germany* No 8770/79, 2 Digest 405 (1981); and *F v UK* No 11058/84, 47 DR 230 (1986).

IV. ARTICLE 6(3)(C): THE RIGHT TO DEFEND ONESELF IN PERSON OR THROUGH LEGAL ASSISTANCE

The purpose of this guarantee is to ensure that proceedings against an accused 'will not take place without an adequate representation of the case for the defence'.[1046] The accused's lawyer may also serve as the 'watchdog of procedural regularity',[1047] both in the public interest and for his client.

Article 6(3)(c) protects any person subject to a criminal charge. It applies to all stages of the criminal process, including the pre-trial phase. '[A]s a rule, access to a lawyer should be provided as from the first interrogation of a suspect by the police... The rights of the defence will in principle be irretrievably prejudiced when incriminating statements made during police interrogation without access to a lawyer are used for a conviction.'[1048] Thus in Öcalan v Turkey,[1049] the applicant was interrogated by the security forces, a public prosecutor, and a judge over a period of almost seven days after his forced return to Turkey, during which time his lawyer was refused permission to visit him. Under interrogation, the applicant made incriminating statements that proved to be a 'major contributing factor in his conviction'. The Court held that 'to deny access to a lawyer over such a long period and in a situation in which the rights of the defence might well be irretrievably prejudiced' was a breach of Article 6(3)(c). In Dayanan v Turkey,[1050] the applicant did not have legal assistance while in police custody because it was not allowed under the law then in force. The Court held that 'a systematic restriction of this kind...is sufficient in itself for a violation of Article 6 to be found, notwithstanding the fact that the applicant remained silent when questioned in police custody', and hence was not prejudiced by the absence of a lawyer.

In Murray (John) v UK,[1051] the Court stated that access to a lawyer at the pre-trial stage 'may be subject to restrictions for good cause. The question, in each case, is whether the restriction, in the light of the entirety of the proceedings, has deprived the accused of a fair hearing'. In that case, the applicant terrorist suspect was denied access to his lawyer during the first forty-eight hours following his arrest under emergency legislation. During this time he was questioned by the police, but refused to answer any questions. The Court held that the forty-eight hours' restriction was a breach of Article 6(3)(c). Crucial to this decision was the fact that under the legislation, an adverse inference could be drawn by the trial court if the accused exercised his right to silence during police questioning. Whereas the government justified the denial of access on the ground that it would prejudice the gathering of information about acts of terrorism, the Court held that the concept of 'fairness' in Article 6 meant that to 'deny access to a lawyer for the first 48 hours of police questioning, in a situation where the rights of the defence may well be irretrievably prejudiced, is—whatever the

---

[1046] Pakelli v Germany A 64 (1983); 6 EHRR 1 para 84 Com Rep.

[1047] Ensslin, Baader and Raspe v Germany Nos 7572/76, 7586/76 and 7587/76, 14 DR 64 at 114 (1978).

[1048] Salduz v Turkey 2008-; 49 EHRR 421 para 55. GC. In their concurring opinion, Judge Zagrebelsky, Casadevall, and Turmen understood the Court to mean that it is 'at the very beginning of police custody or pre-trial detention that a person accused of an offence must have the possibility of being assisted by a lawyer, and not only while being questioned.' Cf the concurring opinion of Judge Bratza. This interpretation was adopted in Dayanan v Turkey hudoc (2009). The right of access to a lawyer did not apply to police questioning at a road check prior to arrest: Aleksandr Zaichenko v Russia hudoc (2010).

[1049] 2005-IV; 41 EHRR 985 para 131 GC. Cf Imbrioscia v Switzerland A 275 (1993); 17 EHRR 441 and Quaranta v Switzerland A 205 (1991). See also Adamkiewicz v Poland hudoc (2010) (access to a lawyer for a juvenile).   [1050] Hudoc (2009).

[1051] 1996-I; 22 EHRR 29 para 63 GC. See also Magee v UK 2000-VI; 31 EHRR 822 and Brennan v UK 2001-X; 34 EHRR 507. Cf Averill v UK 2000-VI; 31 EHRR 839. The Youth, Justice and Criminal Evidence Act 1999, s 58 now provides that inferences may not be drawn from silence if the accused has been denied access to legal advice. See also Berlinski v Poland hudoc (2002) and Salduz v Turkey 2008- GC.

justification for such denial—incompatible with the rights of the accused under Article 6'.[1052] A delay of over a year in appointing a lawyer for remand prisoners, during which period they were questioned by the prosecutor and medically examined, was also a breach of Article 6(3)(c).[1053] But there was no breach where the applicant was not allowed access to a lawyer during detention on remand, when no statements he made to the investigating judge or *procureur* during that period were relied on in court.[1054] The rights of private access to a lawyer and to sufficient visits by a lawyer (sub-section d below), which are treated by the Court as aspects of the right to effective legal assistance in Article 6(3)(c), also apply at the pre-trial stage.

The question whether an accused's lawyer is entitled to be present during pre-trial questioning was raised in *Imbrioscia v Switzerland*.[1055] There the applicant was questioned by the police and later the district prosecutor in the absence of his lawyer. The lawyer had neither been invited to attend the initial interrogation sessions nor asked to attend. When the lawyer later complained that he had not been given notice of the sessions, he was invited to attend the remaining one. The Court held that Articles 6(1) and 6(3)(c) had not been infringed. What emerges from the case is that Article 6(3)(c) does not require a state to take the initiative to invite an accused's lawyer to be present during questioning in the course of the investigation. However, although the Court does not say this in so many words, it would appear from the tenor of its judgment that if the accused or his lawyer requests the latter's attendance, this must be allowed if, as is likely, there is a risk the information obtained will prejudice the accused person's defence. The question whether the accused must be asked if he wishes to have his lawyer present during questioning was not considered in the Court's judgment. Referring to *Miranda v Arizona*,[1056] Judge De Meyer, dissenting, suggested that he should. The *Imbrioscia* case concerned a civil law system. The Court's approach can be taken to apply to police questioning in a common law system also.[1057] In *Brennan v UK*,[1058] a Court Chamber agreed that both the attendance of the suspect's lawyer and video or taped recordings of police interviews were safeguards against police misconduct, but was 'not persuaded that these were an indispensable precondition of fairness': the facts of each case had to be considered as a whole. However, the admission as evidence at trial of statements obtained by police questioning in breach of Article 3 in the absence of a lawyer has been a factor in ruling that the trial has been unfair in breach of Article 6: see the cases at note 500 above.

As far as other stages of proceedings are concerned, Article 6(3)(c) applies to the trial and to any appeal proceedings following the accused's conviction, although when assessing its requirements at the appellate level, regard must be had to the special features of the appeal proceedings concerned and the part they play in the case as a whole.[1059] Thus the appointment of a legal aid lawyer for the hearing of an appeal will not remedy the absence

---

[1052] *Murray (John) v UK*, para 66. The Court found a breach of Articles 6(1) and 6(3)(c) by a majority of twelve votes to seven. The minority dissented on the basis that the Court should have decided the case not the *possibility* of 'irretrievable prejudice', but on its facts and the applicant had failed to show that the drawing of an adverse inference at his trial had rendered it unfair as a whole.

[1053] *Berlinski v Poland* hudoc (2002).   [1054] *Yurttas v Turkey* hudoc (2004).

[1055] A 275 (1993); 17 EHRR 441.

[1056] 384 US 436 (1966). As to the *Miranda* requirement to inform an arrested person of his rights, see *Brusco v France* hudoc (2010).

[1057] In English law, an arrested person is entitled to have his lawyer present during police questioning and must be so informed: Code C, para 6.8, issued under s 67, PACE 1984.

[1058] 2001-X; 34 EHRR 507 para 53. The question whether an accused's lawyer is entitled to be present during questioning was left unanswered in the *Murray (John)* case.

[1059] *Meftah and Others v France* 2002-VII para 41 GC. See also *Granger v UK* A 174 (1990); 12 EHRR 469.

of a lawyer at the trial stage where the appeal court lacks jurisdiction to consider the case again fully on the law and the facts.[1060] With regard to leave to appeal applications, in *Monnell and Morris v UK*,[1061] a hearing of the applicants in person was not required; it was sufficient that they could present written submissions to the Court of Appeal.

a. Defence in person

Article 6(3)(c) guarantees the right of the accused to defend himself in person.[1062] However, this is not an absolute right. The law of a number of Convention parties provides that in certain kinds of cases the accused must be represented by a lawyer at the trial stage[1063] or on appeal[1064] in the interests of justice. In *Correia de Matos v Portugal*,[1065] the Court confirmed that this approach was consistent with Article 6(3)(c), the interests of justice being a 'relevant and sufficient' reason for insisting upon legal representation. A 'margin of appreciation' applies, as the contracting states are 'better placed than the [Strasbourg] Court' to decide whether the interests of justice require that the defence be conducted by a legal representative, rather than the accused, in a particular case or kind of case.[1066]

Where the accused does defend himself, his manner of conducting his defence may bear upon a state's liability under Article 6(3)(c). In *Melin v France*,[1067] the Court held that an accused who elects to defend himself in person, having 'thus deliberately waived his right to be assisted by a lawyer', is 'under a duty to show diligence'. Accordingly, there will be no breach of Article 6 by the state because of a deficiency in the proceedings that results from a lack of diligence that may reasonably be expected of the accused, given his capabilities and knowledge.[1068]

In contrast, a state may be in breach of Article 6(3)(c) if it impedes the exercise of the accused's legal right to defend himself. In *Brandstetter v Austria*,[1069] the accused had been convicted of defamation on the basis of allegedly false statements made by him when defending himself at an earlier trial for another offence. While finding no breach of Article 6(3)(c) on the facts, the Court accepted that 'the position might be different if it were established that, as a consequence of national law or practice in this respect being unduly severe, the risk of subsequent prosecution is such that the defendant is genuinely inhibited from freely exercising' his rights of defence, including defending himself in person.

b. Legal assistance

Article 6(3)(c) provides that an accused who does not defend himself in person is entitled to have legal assistance through his own lawyer or, subject to certain conditions, by means of free legal assistance provided by the state.[1070] The state thus cannot require an

---

[1060] *Quaranta v Switzerland* A 205 (1991).   [1061] A 115 (1987); 10 EHRR 205.

[1062] *Foucher v France* 1997-II; 25 EHRR 234.

[1063] See *Croissant v Germany* A 237-B (1992); 16 EHRR 135.

[1064] See *Philis v Greece* No 16598/90, 66 DR 260 (1990) and *Meftah v France* 2002-VII GC.

[1065] *No 48188/99* hudoc (2001) DA (lawyer denied the right to defend himself on a charge of insulting the court: no breach). Contrast the contrary ruling by the UN Human Rights Committee in *Correia de Matos v Portugal (1123/02)*, 13 IHRR 38 (2006). See O'Boyle, in Breitenmoser *et al*, eds, *Human Rights, Democracy and the Rule of Law: Liber Amicorum Lucius Wildhaber*, 2007, p 329 and Treschel, *Human Rights in Criminal Proceedings*, 2005, p 263.   [1066] *Correia de Matos v Portugal*.

[1067] A 261-A (1993); 17 EHRR 1 para 25.

[1068] However, there is a duty to intervene where the accused's lawyer is not diligent.

[1069] A 211 (1991); 15 EHRR 378 paras 51, 53.

[1070] Legal assistance refers to advice and representation, both in and out of court.

accused to defend himself in person.[1071] 'Although not absolute, the right of everyone charged with a criminal offence to be effectively defended by a lawyer, assigned officially if need be, is one of the fundamental features of a fair trial'.[1072] In view of its importance, an accused must be informed of his right to consult a lawyer before police questioning, especially, but not only, when he is a minor.[1073]

Where an accused is represented by a lawyer, Article 6(3)(c) guarantees the accused's right to be present at the trial as well.[1074] However, the right to legal representation is not dependent upon the accused's presence.[1075] Thus in *Campbell and Fell v UK*,[1076] the Court held that Article 6(3)(c) had been infringed by the United Kingdom because a prisoner, who had refused to attend in person, was, like prisoners who attended, denied legal representation at a Board of Visitors hearing of a disciplinary charge against him. Other cases in which the Court has also found a breach have concerned an accused who absconds, in which context the refusal to allow the proceedings to continue with the accused being represented by his lawyer is to deter or punish.[1077] Such a penalty is in breach of Article 6(3)(c); although a state must be able to impose sanctions to discourage the unjustified absence of an accused from appearing in court, it is 'disproportionate' to deny the accused the legal representation needed for his or her defence.

Article 6(3)(c) guarantees an accused the right to legal assistance 'of his own choosing', ie assistance by a lawyer whom the accused appoints and pays for. As a general rule, the accused's choice of lawyer should be respected.[1078] However, the state may refuse to recognize it for 'relevant and sufficient' reasons.[1079] Rules limiting the accused's choice of lawyer to members of a specialist bar when appealing to a Court of Cassation or other appeal court are permissible.[1080] Regulations governing the qualifications and conduct of lawyers authorized to practise law in a state's legal system are obviously permissible, as are regulations concerning the practice in its courts of lawyers qualified in another legal system. A lawyer may be excluded for failure to comply with professional ethics,[1081] for refusal to wear robes,[1082] for showing disrespect to the court,[1083] or because he or she is appearing as a witness for the defence[1084] or has a personal interest in the case.[1085] A restriction upon the number of lawyers appointed by the accused is permissible, so long as the defence is able to present its case on an equal footing with the prosecution.[1086] Nor is a state liable if an accused is unable to find a lawyer who will act for him, provided that this failure is not the result of 'pressure or manoeuvres' by the state.[1087] Although the state

---

[1071] *Pakelli v Germany* A 64 (1983); 6 EHRR 1.

[1072] *Poitrimol v France* A 277-A (1993); 18 EHRR 130 para 34. See also *Yaremenko v Ukraine* hudoc (2008).

[1073] *Panovits v Cyprus* hudoc (2008).

[1074] *FCB v Italy* A 208-B (1991); 14 EHRR 909 and *Ezeh and Connors v UK* 2003-X; 39 EHRR 1 GC.

[1075] *Poitrimol v France* A 277-A (1993); 18 EHRR 130.

[1076] A 80 (1984); 7 EHRR 165. See further *Ezeh and Connors v UK* 2003-X; 39 EHRR 1 GC.

[1077] *Van Geyseghem v Belgium* 1999-I; 32 EHRR 554. This so though even though the accused violates a legal obligation by not attending (*Poitrimol v France* A 277-A (1993); 18 EHRR 130) and a conviction *in absentia* may be set aside in later proceedings (*Van Geyseghem* case). See also *Lala v Netherlands* A 297-A (1994); 18 EHRR 586 and *Pietiläinen v Finland* hudoc (2009).

[1078] *Goddi v Italy* B 61 (1982) p. 5.

[1079] See *Croissant v Germany* A 237-B (1992); 16 EHRR 135 para 30.

[1080] *Meftah and Others v France* 2002-VII GC.

[1081] *Ensslin, Baader and Raspe v Germany* Nos 7572/76, 7586/76 and 7587/76, 14 DR 64 (1978).

[1082] *X and Y v Germany* Nos 5217/71 and 5367/72, 42 CD 139 (1972).

[1083] *X v UK* No 6298/73, 2 Digest 831 (1975). [1084] *K v Denmark* No 19524/92 (1993) unreported.

[1085] *X v UK* No 8295/78, 15 DR 242 (1978) (prosecution of barrister's father).

[1086] *Ensslin, Baader and Raspe v Germany* Nos 7572/76, 7586/76 and 7587/76, 14 DR 64 (1978).

[1087] *X and Y v Belgium* No 1420/62 et al, 6 YB 590 at 628 (1963).

thus has a general regulatory power, the Strasbourg Court retains the capacity to intervene if it is used improperly, eg by excluding a lawyer simply because of his willingness to represent an 'unpopular accused' or his opposition to the government.

Article 6(3)(c) refers to 'legal' assistance. This can be taken to allow assistance by a person chosen by the accused who is not a qualified lawyer,[1088] although the state must have a regulatory power to control representation by such persons too. The drafting history[1089] and the object and purpose of Article 6(3)(c) suggest that professional qualifications are not necessary so long as the legal assistance provided is 'effective' in fact.[1090]

The right to legal representation may be waived. As stated in *Pishchalnikov v Russia*,[1091] a waiver of the right must be established in 'an unequivocal manner and be attended by minimum safeguards commensurate with its importance'. It must 'not only be voluntary but must also constitute a knowing and intelligent relinquishment' of the right. An accused may waive the right expressly or implicitly, but in the case of a waiver implied from conduct, it must be 'shown that he could reasonably have foreseen what the consequences of his conduct would be'.[1092] A valid waiver occurred when an accused signed a form in which he was informed of his right to a lawyer and did not respond by requesting one.[1093] However, waiver could not be inferred from the fact that the accused answered police questions in the absence of his lawyer after earlier invoking his right to be assisted by a lawyer during interrogation.[1094]

c. Legal aid

In practice, most accused persons are indigent so that the guarantee of legal aid in Article 6(3)(c) is of particular importance. Although an assessment of whether legal aid is required is in the first instance for the national authorities to make and a 'margin of appreciation' may apply,[1095] the Strasbourg Court is competent to review and disagree with their assessment, applying the terms of Article 6(3)(c).[1096]

The right to legal aid in Article 6(3)(c) is subject to two conditions. First, the accused must lack 'sufficient means' to pay for legal assistance. The Convention contains no definition of 'sufficient means' and there is no case law indicating the level or kind of private means that may be taken into account when deciding whether to award legal aid. When seeking to establish a breach of Article 6(3)(c), the onus is on the accused to show that he lacks 'sufficient means'. The accused need not, however, do so 'beyond all doubt'; it is sufficient that there are 'some indications' that this is so. This test was formulated and satisfied on the facts in *Pakelli v Germany*,[1097] on the basis that the applicant had spent two years in

---

[1088] See *Engel v Netherlands* A 22 (1976); 1 EHRR 647 PC and *Morris v UK* 2002-I; 34 EHRR 1253 (representation by non-lawyers in army disciplinary proceedings).

[1089] In the drafting of Article 14, ICCPR, upon which Article 6 is based, the words 'qualified representative' were replaced by 'legal assistance' so that they 'did not necessarily mean a lawyer, but merely assistance in the legal conduct of a case': UN Doc E/CN.4/SR 107, p 6.

[1090] See *X v Germany No 509/59*, 3 YB 174 (1960) (probationary lawyer).

[1091] Hudoc (2009) para 77. Cf the rules on waiver of other Article 6 rights.

[1092] See *Saman v Turkey* hudoc (2011) (poor command of Turkish impeded understanding of consequences).

[1093] *Yoldas v Turkey* hudoc (2010). Cf *Salduz v Turkey* hudoc (2008) (no waiver on facts).

[1094] *Pishchalnikov v Russia* hudoc (2009).

[1095] Cf *Correia de Matos v Portugal No 48188/99* hudoc (2001) DA, mentioned earlier.

[1096] The question whether the right to legal aid is a 'civil right' so that it should be determined by a tribunal complying with Article 6 was raised but not decided in *Gutfreund v France* hudoc 2003-VII; 42 EHRR 1076.

[1097] A 64 (1983); 6 EHRR 1 para 34. The fact that the accused has been granted legal aid at another stage in the national proceedings is relevant: *Twalib v Greece* 1998-IV; 33 EHRR 584 and *RD v Poland* hudoc (2001); 39 EHRR 240. See also *Morris v UK* 2002-I; 34 EHRR 1253.

custody shortly before the case, had presented a statement of means to the Commission that led it to award him legal aid in bringing his Strasbourg application, and had offered to prove lack of means to the West German Federal Court.

The Commission took the view that Article 6(3)(c) does not prohibit a contracting party from requiring an accused upon conviction to pay the costs of any free legal assistance that he has been allowed if he then has the necessary means to do so.[1098] The point was left open by the Court in *Luedicke, Belkacem and Koç v Germany*,[1099] in which it held that there was such a prohibition under Article 6(3)(e) with regard to the costs of an interpreter. The text of Article 6 supports the Commission's interpretation in that, in contrast with the right in Article 6(3)(e), the right to legal aid in Article 6(3)(c) is made conditional upon the accused's means. Nonetheless, the possibility that an accused might have to repay the cost of legal aid could, as was recognized in the *Luedicke* case, cause him to defend himself in person rather than apply for legal aid in a case in which legal representation would be in the interests of a fair trial and hence of the object and purpose of the Convention. Moreover, the word 'given' in the English text can be read as meaning an irrevocable grant of free legal aid where the accused is without means at the time that the grant is made.

Second, legal aid need only be provided 'where the interests of justice so require'. This is to be judged by reference to the facts of the case as a whole, including those that may materialize after the competent national authority has taken its decision. Thus in *Granger v UK*,[1100] the refusal of legal aid should have been reviewed when it was proved during the appeal proceedings that the case was more complicated than appeared earlier.

A number of criteria have been identified by the Court as being relevant when determining whether the 'interests of justice' call for legal assistance. First, what is 'at stake' for the applicant in terms of the seriousness of the offence and hence the possible sentence that could result is of great importance.[1101] In *Benham v UK*,[1102] it was stated that where any 'deprivation of liberty is at stake, the interests of justice in principle call for legal representation'. In *Quaranta v Switzerland*,[1103] the 'mere fact' that the possible sentence that could be imposed upon the accused for drugs offences was three years' imprisonment meant that legal aid should have been provided.[1104] In contrast, in *Gutfreund v France*,[1105] the 'interests of justice' did not require legal aid where the maximum possible sentence on a minor assault charge was not imprisonment but a modest fine (FF5,000) and where the procedure was 'simple'. Secondly, as the *Gutfreund* case suggests, the more complicated the case on the law or the facts, the more likely that legal assistance is required.[1106] Third, regard must be had to the contribution that the accused would be able to make if he defended himself; in this connection, the test is the capacity of the

---

[1098] *Croissant v Germany* A 237-B (1992) Com Rep.

[1099] A 29 (1978); 2 EHRR 149. Also left open by the Court in *Croissant v Germany*.

[1100] A 174 (1990); 12 EHRR 469.   [1101] See, eg, *Twalib v Greece* 1998-IV; 33 EHRR 584.

[1102] 1996-III; 22 EHRR 293 para 61 GC (possible three months' imprisonment for non-payment of community charge).   [1103] A 205 para 33 (1991).

[1104] The Court emphasized the possible, rather than the likely, penalty. Cf *Pham Hoang v France* A 243 (1992). In appeal proceedings the actual sentence imposed takes over: see, eg, *Boner v UK* A 300-B para 41 and *Maxwell v UK* A 300-C para 38 (1994), although any possibility of the sentence being increased must be relevant.

[1105] 2003-VII; 42 EHRR 1076 para 39. Cf *Barsom and Varli v Sweden* hudoc (2008). In contrast, a heavy fine without imprisonment is a relevant factor: *Pham Hoang v France* A 243 (1992).

[1106] See also *Granger v UK* A 174 (1990); 12 EHRR 469; *Quaranta v Switzerland* A 205 (1991); and *Pham Hoang v France* A 243 (1992).

particular accused to present his case.[1107] Legal representation may be required 'in the interests of justice' when the applicant's hearing is impaired so that he cannot follow the proceedings.[1108]

In appeal cases, it does not matter that the accused's chances of success are negligible.[1109] To the extent that the accused is granted a right of appeal by national law, he must be provided with legal aid if this is required for him to exercise it effectively. Thus in *Boner v UK*,[1110] the applicant was refused legal aid on the statutory ground that he did not have 'substantial grounds for making the appeal'. In holding that there had been a breach of Article 6(3)(c), the European Court focused on the fact that the accused would need the services of a lawyer in order to argue the point he wished to raise, as well as the importance of what was at stake for him (an eight-year sentence).

When applying the 'interests of justice' requirement, the test is not whether the absence of legal aid has caused 'actual prejudice' to the presentation of the defence. In *Artico v Italy*,[1111] the Court stated that the test is a less stringent one, *viz* whether 'it appears plausible in the particular circumstances' that the lawyer would be of assistance, as was true on the facts of that case. There the Court noted that a lawyer would have been more likely than the applicant to have emphasized a statute of limitations argument in the applicant's favour before the Court of Cassation and that only a lawyer was competent to request a hearing at which the defence could have replied to the Public Prosecutor's arguments against the appeal. On this basis, legal aid comes close to being generally required, because a lawyer will nearly always, by virtue of his professional expertise, be able to add to the accused's defence.[1112]

Although the wishes of the accused must be taken into account, the choice of a lawyer is ultimately for the state. In *Lagerblom v Sweden*,[1113] the accused, whose mother tongue was Finnish and who was required by Swedish law to be legally represented in connection with assault and road traffic offences, wanted the lawyer chosen for him by the court to be replaced by a Finnish-speaking lawyer. The Strasbourg Court held that there had been no breach of Article 6(3)(c) because the appointed lawyer had already done a lot of work on the case and the accused had both sufficient knowledge of Swedish and an interpreter.

The funding of legal aid is an expensive item for states. In the context of legal aid in civil proceedings, it has been held that it must be provided in accordance with Article 6(1) irrespective of the economic cost.[1114] The same approach must apply to criminal cases under Article 6(3)(c), so that budgetary considerations should not prevent effective legal assistance for accused persons who otherwise qualify under Article 6(3)(c).[1115]

[1107] See the *Granger* and *Quaranta* cases discussed earlier; *Twalib v Greece* 1998-IV; 33 EHRR 584 (foreigner with no knowledge of the language or legal system); and *Vaudelle v France* 2001-I; 37 EHRR 397 (mental state).   [1108] *Timergaliyev v Russia* hudoc (2008).

[1109] The same must apply to the chances of acquittal at the trial stage.

[1110] A 300-B (1994); 19 EHRR 246 paras 41–4. Cf *Maxwell v UK* A 300-C (1994); 19 EHRR 97 paras 38–41.

[1111] A 37 (1980); 3 EHRR 1 para 35. Cf *Alimena v Italy* A 195-D (1991) and *Biondo v Italy* No 8821/79, 64 DR 5 (1983) Com Rep; CM Res DH (89) 30.

[1112] But for a case in which the 'interests of justice' did not require legal aid in respect of written appeal proceedings, see *X v Germany No 599/59*, 8 CD 12 (1961). See also *M v UK No 9728/82* 36 DR 155 (1983).

[1113] Hudoc (2003) para 54. See also *Croissant v Germany* A 237-B (1993); 16 EHRR 135. The state has a 'margin of appreciation' when deciding what the 'interests of justice' require: see *Correia de Matos v Portugal No 48188/99* hudoc (2001) DA.   [1114] See *Airey v Ireland* A 32 (1979); 2 EHRR 305.236.

[1115] But see *M v UK No 9728/82*, 36 DR 155 at 158 (1983) (number of consultations may be limited for reasons of cost).

d. Practical and effective legal assistance

The right in Article 6(3)(c) is to 'practical and effective' legal assistance.[1116] But a state cannot be held responsible for every shortcoming of a lawyer acting for the defence. As stated in *Kamasinski v Austria*,[1117] it 'follows from the independence of the legal profession of the state that the conduct of the defence is essentially a matter between the defendant and his counsel, whether counsel be appointed under a legal aid scheme or be privately financed'. Because of the state's lack of power to supervise or control his or her conduct, a lawyer, even though appointed by the state, is not an 'organ' of the state who can engage its direct responsibility under the Convention by his or her acts, in the way, for example, that a policeman or soldier may.[1118] Instead, the 'competent national authorities', who may be the courts or other state actors, 'are required by Article 6(3)(c) to intervene only if a failure by legal aid counsel to provide effective representation is manifest or sufficiently brought to their attention'.[1119] The state must also intervene 'in the interests of justice' in a case of the 'manifest failure' of a private lawyer, at least where the accused is a juvenile and the offence is serious: arguably in other cases too.[1120]

There may be liability on this *Kamasinski* basis where a lawyer simply fails to act for the accused. Thus in the leading case of *Artico v Italy*,[1121] the applicant was granted free legal aid under Italian law for his appeal to the Italian Court of Cassation. Unfortunately, the appointed lawyer never acted for the applicant, claiming other legal commitments and ill-health. Despite constant requests by the applicant, the Court of Cassation refused to appoint another lawyer to replace him. As a result, the applicant was forced to plead the case himself in circumstances in which legal assistance would have been likely to have been of value. Noting that the right in Article 6(3)(c) was to 'assistance', not 'nomination', the European Court rejected an Italian argument that by appointing a lawyer for the accused the Court of Cassation had done sufficient to comply with Article 6(3)(c).[1122]

There may also be liability on the *Kamasinski* basis where the lawyer fails to comply with a 'formal' but crucial procedural requirement. Thus in *Czekalla v Portugal*,[1123] the applicant's appeal to the Supreme Court had been dismissed because his legal aid lawyer had failed to include submissions in her pleadings. This failure to comply with a 'simple and purely formal rule' was a 'manifest failure' which 'called for positive measures on the part of the relevant authorities'. As to possible 'measures', the Strasbourg Court suggested that the Supreme Court could, in order to meet the requirements of Article 6(3)(c), have invited the lawyer to make submissions out of time, instead of declaring the appeal inadmissible. Whether an error of this kind will give rise to a violation of Article 6(3)(c) will depend on the facts. In the *Czekalla* case, the Court noted that the accused faced a lengthy prison sentence and—as a foreigner who did not know the language used in court—was utterly dependent on his lawyer.

[1116] *Artico v Italy* A 37 (1980); 3 EHRR 1 para 33.

[1117] A 168 (1989); 13 EHRR 36 para 65. Cf *Daud v Portugal* 1998-II; 30 EHRR 400 para 38.

[1118] *Alvarez Sanchez v Spain* No 50720/99 hudoc (2001) DA. Cf *Rudkowski v Poland* No 45995/99 hudoc (2000) DA. The state may have a positive obligation to ensure that the legal profession properly regulates itself. It might also be directly responsible if the lawyer were a 'public defender' in the employ of the state.

[1119] *Kamasinski v Austria* A 168 (1980); 13 EHRR 36 para 65. The obligation to intervene arises where the lawyer's failure has rendered the defence ineffective, 'taking the proceedings as a whole': *Rutkowski v Poland* No 44995/99 hudoc (2000) para 3 DA. Cf *Sannino v Italy* 2006-VI.

[1120] *Guvec v Turkey* hudoc (2009). But see *Tripodi v Italy* A 281-B (1994); 18 EHRR 295.

[1121] A 37 (1980); 3 EHRR 1.   [1122] Cf *Daud v Portugal* 1998-II; 30 EHRR 400.

[1123] 2002-VIII para 68. Contrast *Alvarez Sanchez v Spain* No 50720/99 2001-XI DA (no violation).

To be distinguished from a 'formal' or procedural error such as that in the *Czekalla* case, is 'an injudicious line of defence or a mere defect in argumentation'[1124] or any other professional error [1125] in presenting the accused's defence. In such cases, the state is unlikely to be liable for the lawyer's conduct of the case, whatever is 'at stake' for the accused and even though the lawyer is state appointed.[1126]

The right to effective legal assistance in Article 6(3)(c) includes a right of private access to a lawyer, both at the pre-trial stage and later. In *S v Switzerland*,[1127] Article 6(3)(c) was infringed when the accused, who was in detention on remand, was not allowed to consult with his lawyer out of the hearing of a prison officer. As the Court stated, 'if a lawyer were unable to confer with his client and receive confidential instructions from him without such surveillance, his assistance would lose much of its usefulness, whereas the Convention is intended to guarantee rights that are practical and effective'. It may also be a breach of Article 6(3)(c) to tap the telephone conversations between an accused and his lawyer[1128] or to search a lawyer's office without 'compelling reason'.[1129] The Article 6(3)(c) guarantee of access to a lawyer may be subject to restrictions in the public interest, but surveillance of 'the contacts of a detainee with his defence counsel is a serious interference with an accused's defence rights' so that 'very weighty reasons should be given for its justification'.[1130] The fear of collusion between the accused and the lawyer, resulting in the influencing of witnesses or the removal of documents, was insufficient to justify an investigating judge's order authorizing such surveillance in *Lanz v Austria*.[1131] In contrast, the need for confidentiality to catch other members of the accused's criminal gang was enough to justify surveillance in *Kempers v Austria*.[1132]

For access to be effective, the number and length of lawyers' visits to the accused must be sufficient. Thus in *Öcalan v Turkey*,[1133] after the first two visits, the accused was allowed only two one-hour visits a week from his lawyers. This was insufficient given the highly complex charges against the accused and the voluminous case-file that they had generated. Insofar as the frequency of visits was dictated by the times of ferries to the island on which the accused was detained, it was necessary for the state to provide other more adequate means of transport. In *Sakhnovskiy v Russia*,[1134] the fact that the applicant's legal aid lawyer on appeal was appointed at the last minute, combined with the fact that they had been given only fifteen minutes to communicate by video link (which presented concerns about privacy) meant that the applicant's access to a lawyer was not effective.

[1124] *Czekalla v Portugal* 2002-VIII para 60.

[1125] See *Tripodi v Italy* A 281-B (1994); 18 EHRR 295 (failure to ask for adjournment) and *Stanford v UK* A 282-A (1994) (failure to raise accused's hearing problem).

[1126] But see *Rutkowski v Poland No 45995/99* hudoc (2000) para 2 DA, in which the Court checked whether a legal aid lawyer was 'negligent or superficial' in deciding whether there were grounds for appeal.

[1127] A 220 (1991); 14 EHRR 670 para 48. See also *Brennan v UK* 2001-X; 34 EHRR 507; *Öcalan v Turkey* 2005-IV; 41 EHRR 985 GC; and *Khodorkovskiy and Lebedev v Russia* hudoc (2013).

[1128] *Zagaria v Italy* hudoc (2007) (breach). Cf *D v Austria No 16410/90* (1990) unreported. The right of access also includes access by correspondence, although such cases are most commonly dealt with under Article 8: see eg, *Campbell v UK* A 233 (1992); 15 EHRR 137. For an Article 6 case on correspondence with a lawyer in criminal proceedings, see *McComb v UK No 10621/83*, 50 DR 81 (1986) F Sett.

[1129] *Khodorkovskiy and Lebedev v Russia* hudoc (2013) para 634.

[1130] *Lanz v Austria* hudoc (2002) para 52. See also *Can v Austria* A 96 (1985); 8 EHRR 14 para 52 Com Rep (F Sett before Court); *Egue v France No 11256/84*, 57 DR 47 (1988); and *Castravet v Moldova* hudoc (2007).

[1131] Hudoc (2002).

[1132] *No 21842/93* hudoc (1997) DA. The limited period of surveillance was relevant.

[1133] 2005-IV; 41 EHRR 985 para 135 GC.

[1134] Hudoc (2010) GC. Cf *Bogumil v Portugal* hudoc (2008).

In guaranteeing a right of access to a lawyer, Article 6(3)(c) overlaps with Article 6(3)(b) which guarantees the accused 'adequate facilities' to prepare his defence, a phrase that has been interpreted to include the right of access. But Article 6(3)(c) is wider than Article 6(3)(b) since it 'is not especially tied to considerations relating to the preparation of the trial but gives the accused a more general right to assistance and support by a lawyer throughout the whole proceedings'.[1135]

The requirement that assistance be 'effective' has been considered in a variety of other contexts. A state will be in breach of it if it negligently fails to notify the accused's lawyer of the hearing with the result that the accused is not represented at it.[1136] To be 'effective' a lawyer appointed to defend an accused must be qualified to appear at the particular stage of proceedings for which his assistance is sought.[1137] Frequent changes of lawyers appointed for the defence may raise a problem of effectiveness,[1138] as may the allowance of inadequate time for a defendant's lawyer, whether a legal aid lawyer or not, to prepare his case.[1139] However, it is permissible to limit the role of the accused's lawyer, at least in army disciplinary proceedings, to the legal, as opposed to the factual, issues in the case where the facts are simple.[1140]

V. ARTICLE 6(3)(D): THE RIGHT TO CALL AND CROSS-EXAMINE WITNESSES

Article 6(3)(d) guarantees a person charged with a criminal offence the right:

> to examine or have examined witnesses against him and to obtain the attendance and examination of witnesses on his behalf under the same conditions as witnesses against him.

The right applies to the trial and any appeal proceedings. It does not generally apply at the pre-trial stage.[1141] Thus Article 6(3)(d) does not require that the accused be allowed to question a witness being interrogated by the police[1142] or by an investigating judge,[1143] although if the accused is permitted to cross-examine prosecution witnesses at the investigation stage this may satisfy the requirements of Article 6(3)(d) when the witness is justifiably excused from giving evidence at the trial.The refusal by an investigating judge to hear a defence witness who later gives evidence at the trial is not a breach of Article 6(3)(d).[1144]

With regard to trial proceedings, neither the accused's right to cross-examine witnesses against him in court nor his right to call defence witnesses is absolute or unlimited.[1145]

[1135] *Can v Austria* A 96 (1985); 8 EHRR 14 para 54 Com Rep (F Sett before Court). In *S v Switzerland* the Court focused on paragraph (c), not (b), seemingly because the restrictions on the applicant's communications with his lawyer were later lifted for a long enough period prior to the trial to permit the proper preparation of his defence, so that the facilities were 'adequate'.   [1136] *Goddi v Italy* A 76 (1984).

[1137] See *Biondo v Italy No 8821/79*, 64 DR 5 (1983) Com Rep; CM Res DH (89) 30. See also *Frexias v Spain No 53590/99* 2000-X DA (labour, not criminal, lawyer appointed; no breach on the facts).

[1138] See *Koplinger v Austria No 1850/63*, 9 YB 240 (1966).

[1139] Such cases have been considered under both Articles 6(3)(b) and 6(3)(c): see eg, *X v UK No 4042/69*, 32 CD 76 (1970): *Murphy v UK No 4681/70*, 43 CD 1 (1972).

[1140] *Engel v Netherlands* A 22 (1976); 1 EHRR 647 PC.

[1141] See *Can v Austria* A 96 (1985) para 47 Com Rep (F Sett before Court) and *Adolf v Austria* B 43 (1980) para 64 Com Rep.   [1142] *X v Germany No 8414/78*, 17 DR 231 (1979).

[1143] *Ferraro-Bravo v Italy No 9627/81*, 37 DR 15 (1984).

[1144] *Schertenlieb v Switzerland No 8339/78*, 17 DR 180 (1979).   [1145] *Gani v Spain* hudoc (2013).

However, any limitations must be consistent with the principle of 'equality of arms', the full realization of which is the 'essential aim' of Article 6(3)(d).[1146] There was a breach of Article 6(3)(d) when the accused was not allowed to examine or cross-examine any witnesses, either at the trial or on appeal.[1147] The right supposes that the examination of witnesses occurs before the judge who decides the case, so that if a judge is replaced after a witness is heard, generally the witness must be recalled.[1148]

The term 'witness' in Article 6(3)(d) has an autonomous Convention meaning. It is not limited to persons who give evidence at the trial; a person whose statements are introduced as evidence but who does not give oral evidence is also a 'witness' for the purposes of Article 6(3)(d).[1149] The term also includes expert witnesses called by the prosecution or the defence. An expert appointed by the court may be a 'witness against' the accused for the purposes of Article 6(3)(d) depending upon his evidence.[1150] A co-accused is a witness, so that depositions made by him during the investigation stage[1151] and statements made at his own separate trial[1152] that are introduced as evidence at the accused's trial are subject to Article 6(3)(d).

The right to call or cross-examine witnesses may be waived, but waiver must be established in an unequivocal manner and not run counter to any important public interest.[1153] There was no waiver of the right when the defence failed to challenge the admission of written statements by witnesses whom it had not been able to cross-examine when such a challenge was unlikely to succeed.[1154]

The right of the accused to 'examine... witnesses against him' 'enshrines the principle that, before an accused can be convicted, all evidence against him must normally be produced in his presence at a public hearing with a view to adversarial argument.'[1155] The right has been the subject of much case law at Strasbourg.[1156] The leading case is now the Grand Chamber judgment in *Al-Khawaja and Tahery v UK*,[1157] in which the Court considered certain exceptions to the hearsay rule in English criminal law. In that case the Court confirmed that, despite the unqualified wording of Article 6(3)(d), exceptions to it are permitted so that the evidence of a witness who does not attend may be admitted at the trial provided this does 'not infringe the rights of the defence which, as a rule, require that the accused should be given an adequate and proper opportunity to challenge and question a witness against him, either when that witness makes his statement or at a later stage of proceedings'.[1158] If the accused is given no such opportunity, the evidence of the missing witness may still be admitted at the trial if two requirements are met. First, there

---

[1146] *Engel v Netherlands* A 22 (1976); 1 EHRR 647 para 91 PC and *Bonisch v Austria* A 92 (1985); 9 EHRR 191 para 32. And see *Oyston v UK No 42011/98* hudoc (2002) DA (restrictions on questions to rape victim; no breach). But Article 6(3)(d) is not limited to 'equality of arms': *Vidal v Belgium* A 235-B (1992) para 33. See also *Al-Khawaja and Tahery v UK* 2011- ; 54 EHRR 807.

[1147] *Vaturi v France* hudoc (2006). On the forfeiture of the right to cross-examine witnesses by opting for an accelerated procedure leading to a reduced sentence, see *Panarisi v Italy* hudoc (2007).

[1148] *Graviano v Italy* hudoc (2005). See also the principle of immediacy discussed earlier.

[1149] *Kostovski v Netherlands* A 166 (1989); 12 EHRR 434 PC. Such statements have included statements to the police and depositions.

[1150] *Bonisch v Austria* A 92 (1985); 9 EHRR 191 and *Brandstetter v Austria* A 211 (1991); 15 EHRR 378. See also *Khodorkovskiy and Lebedev v Russia* hudoc (2013). [1151] *Luca v Italy* 2001-II; 36 EHRR 807.

[1152] *Cardot v France* A 200 (1991); 13 EHRR 853 para 51 Com Rep. See also *X v UK No 10083/82*, 6 EHRR 142 (1983).

[1153] *Craxi v Italy* hudoc (2002); 38 EHRR 995. See also *Rudnichenko v Ukraine* hudoc (2013).

[1154] *Craxi v Italy.* [1155] *Al-Khawaja and Tahery v UK* 2011- ; 54 EHRR 807, para 118 GC.

[1156] See Jackson and Summers, *The Internationalisation of Criminal Evidence*, 2012, pp 334ff and Maffei, *The Right to Confrontation in Europe*, 2nd edn, 2012, chap 4.

[1157] 2011-; 54 EHRR 807 GC. [1158] *Al-Khawaja and Tahery v UK*, para 118.

must be a good reason for non-attendance. In *Gani v Spain*,[1159] the Court identified three main contexts in which it has found there to be a good reason for a witness not giving evidence at the trial. These are (i) cases of 'anonymous witnesses', in which 'the identity of a witness is concealed in order, for instance, to protect him or her from intimidation or threats of reprisals';[1160] (ii) cases of 'absent witnesses', by whom the Court meant witnesses who have died,[1161] cannot be traced,[1162] or, although not anonymous, refuse to appear 'out of fear or for some other reason'; and (iii) cases of witnesses who invoke their privilege against self-incrimination.[1163] The Court has also recognized that the evidence of a non-attending witness may also be admitted at trial to excuse a victim of a sexual offence from having to confront the alleged offender;[1164] to excuse a witness from giving evidence against a family member[1165] or a co-accused;[1166] where a witness is ill;[1167] or where a foreigner resident abroad refuses to attend.[1168] As to cases where a witness fears reprisals (against himself or his family), the Court has drawn a distinction between fear generated by acts of the accused or a person acting for him and 'a more general fear of what will happen' if the witness gives evidence.[1169] In the former case, the accused can be taken to have waived his right to question the witness, so that there can be no breach of Article 6(3)(d). In the latter case, the *Al-Khawaja* requirements apply. However, 'any subjective fear' of the witness will not suffice; the court must enquire whether there are 'objective grounds' for the fear, supported by evidence.[1170] Moreover, where the reason is fear of reprisals, 'the trial court must be satisfied that all available alternatives, such as witness anonymity and other special measures, would be inappropriate or impracticable'.[1171] The Court has also emphasized in respect of all of the grounds that may be relied upon that 'when a witness has not been examined at any stage of the proceedings, allowing the admission of a witness statement in lieu of live evidence at trial must be a measure of last resort'.[1172] If there is no good reason to justify the non-appearance of the witness at the trial, there is a violation of Article 6 (3)(d) regardless of whether the second requirement is complied with.[1173]

The second requirement is that where a conviction is based 'solely or to a decisive degree' on the untested evidence in issue, the proceedings must be subjected 'to the most searching scrutiny' to establish that there 'are sufficient counterbalancing factors,

---

[1159] Hudoc (2013).

[1160] *Van Mechelen v Netherlands* 1997-III; 25 EHRR 647; *Doorson v Netherlands* 1996-II; 22 EHRR 330; and *Ludi v Switzerland* A 238 (1992); 15 EHRR 173.

[1161] *Ferrantelli and Santangelo v Italy* 1996-III; 23 EHRR 288.

[1162] *Isgro v Italy* A 194 (1991) and *Verdam v Netherlands* No 35253/97 hudoc (1999); 28 EHRR CD 161. The state must make sufficient efforts to find or bring to court a missing witness: *Calabro v Italy and Germany* No 59895/00 hudoc (2002) DA. The absence of a power in law to summon a witness whose whereabouts are known is not an excuse: *Mild and Virtanen v Finland* hudoc (2005). See also *Haas v Germany* No 73047/01 hudoc (2005) DA. On statements by witnesses abroad, see *X v Germany* No 11853/85, 53 DR 182 (1987);10 EHRR 521. On evidence from foreign court proceedings, see *S v Germany* No 8945/80, 39 DR 43 (1983).

[1163] *Vidgen v Netherlands* hudoc (2012).   [1164] *SN v Sweden* hudoc 2002-V; 39 EHRR 304.

[1165] *Unterpertinger v Austria* A 110 (1986); 13 EHRR 175 and *Asch v Austria* A 203 (1991); 15 EHRR 597 (unmarried partner).   [1166] *Luca v Italy* 2001-II; 36 EHRR 807.

[1167] *Bricmont v Belgium* A 158 (1989); 12 EHRR 217; *Kennedy v UK* No 36428/97 hudoc (1998); 27 EHRR CD 266; *Gani v Spain* hudoc (2013).   [1168] *Klimentyev v Russia* hudoc (2006); 49 EHRR 336.

[1169] *Al-Khawaja and Tahery v UK* 2011- ; 54 EHRR 807 para 122 GC.

[1170] *Al-Khawaja and Tahery v UK*, para 124. Cf *Visser v Netherlands* hudoc (2002).

[1171] *Al-Khawaja and Tahery v UK*, para 125.   [1172] *Al-Khawaja and Tahery v UK*, para 125.

[1173] *Rudnichenko v Ukraine* hudoc (2013) (non-attendance of co-conspirator was simply because the Court did not call him, as the accused had requested) and *Khodorkovskiy and Lebedev v Russia* hudoc (2013) (accused not allowed to call and cross-examine experts).

including the existence of strong procedural safeguards', that will ensure that any conviction is 'based on such evidence only if it is sufficiently reliable given its importance in the case'.[1174] In allowing this exception in 'sole or decisive' evidence cases, the Court rejected the absolute rule that a Chamber of the Court had adopted in *Doorson v Netherlands*,[1175] by which the admission of 'sole or decisive' evidence automatically and without exception was a breach of Article 6(3)(d). As the Grand Chamber stated, given that its role is to consider whether trials are 'fair', it would not be correct 'to apply this rule in an inflexible manner'.[1176] The Court added that, when applying Article 6(3)(d), it must not ignore the 'specificities of the particular legal system concerned, and in particular its rules of evidence'. 'To do so would transform the rule into a blunt and indiscriminate instrument that runs counter to the traditional way in which the Court approaches the issue of overall fairness of the proceedings, namely to weigh in the balance the competing interests of the defence, the victim, and witnesses, and the public interest in the effective administration of justice.'

Applying this approach to the facts of *Al-Khawaja and Tahery v UK*,[1177] the Grand Chamber held that the admission of hearsay evidence in English criminal proceedings, by which, in certain exceptional cases, the evidence of persons who do not give evidence in court may be admitted, 'will not automatically result in a breach of Article 6(1)'. Applying 'its searching scrutiny' test to the first applicant's case, the Court found that there was no breach of Article 6 (3)(d). In that case, the applicant had been convicted on two charges of indecent assault of female patients. One of the patients had died before the trial, but, as permitted by the hearsay rule, her witness statement was read out in court. Her statement, which was the decisive evidence, was corroborated by two friends in whom she had confided who were cross-examined at the trial, and the other patient victim gave a similar account. In addition, the judge had directed the jury that the witness statement should be given less weight in the absence of cross-examination. The Grand Chamber held that in these circumstances there were 'sufficient counterbalancing factors'. In contrast, there was a breach of Article 6 in the case of the second applicant. In that case, the applicant was convicted of a stabbing for which the decisive evidence was that of the only person who claimed to have seen the stabbing, who was a man whose written statement was read to the court but who was allowed under the hearsay rule not to appear as a witness for fear of reprisals. Although the applicant could cross examine other persons present when the stabbing occurred but who did not claim to have seen the stabbing, he could not cross-examine the only eye witness, and the judge's direction to the jury on untested evidence could not overcome this. The result of the *Al-Khawaja and Tahery* case is that the two hearsay rule exceptions in English law that were in issue survive,[1178] but their application may be in violation of Article 6 in some cases, particularly where the hearsay evidence is the 'sole or decisive' evidence.

The Court stated that its judgment concerned only absent witnesses whose statements are admitted in evidence at the trial, not 'testimony that is given at trial by witnesses

---

[1174] *Al-Khawaja and Tahery v UK* 2011-; 54 EHRR 807 para 147 GC.   [1175] 1996-II; 22 EHRR 330.
[1176] *Al-Khawaja and Tahery v UK* para 146.
[1177] *Al-Khawaja and Tahery v UK*, para 147. See De Wilde, 17 E & P 157 (2013); Doak and Huxley-Binns, 73 J Crim L 508 (2009); Wallace, 2010 EHRLR 408.
[1178] The Court stressed that it was ruling only on the permitted grounds for the admission of hearsay evidence—death and fear—in issue in the two cases, not on the English hearsay law generally. In *Trivedi v UK No 31700/96* hudoc (1997), the illness exception at common law was held not to be in breach of Article 6(3)(d). On the admission of exculpatory hearsay evidence, see *Blastland v UK No 12045/86*, 52 DR 273 and *Thomas v UK No 19354/02* hudoc (2005).

whose identity is concealed from the accused (anonymous testimony)'.[1179] The Court added, however, that although the problems present by absent and anonymous witnesses differ—with the lack of identity of the latter preventing the accused from challenging their probity and credibility and the absence of the former preventing questioning altogether—the two situations were subject to the same principle, *viz* that the accused should have 'an effective opportunity' to challenge the evidence against him. It would seem, therefore, that the two requirements in *Al-Khwaja* apply to anonymous witnesses as well as absent ones, but taking into account the differences between them.

The Court's judgment in *Al-Khawaja* applies to both civil law and common law jurisdictions. As far civil law jurisdictions are concerned,[1180] the necessary 'counterbalancing factors' include the possibility for cross-examination at the investigation stage of a witness who does not give evidence at the trial, provided that the procedure followed gives the accused 'an adequate and proper opportunity to challenge and question' the witness against him.[1181] No such opportunity was given in the following two pre-*Al-Khawaja* cases. In the *Kostovski* case,[1182] there was a breach of Article 6(3)(d) where the 'decisive evidence' against the accused consisted of statements made to the police and to an examining magistrate by private anonymous witnesses whom the defence was not allowed to confront at the pre-trial stage and who did not give evidence at the trial for fear of reprisals by organized crime. The second case concerned the evidence of anonymous witnesses who were police officers. In *Van Mechelen v Netherlands*,[1183] the Court stated that their position was different from that of a 'disinterested witness or a victim' who wished to remain anonymous for fear of reprisals.[1184] This was because of the links between the police and the state in the prosecution of offenders. With this in mind, the Court held that the special arrangements for the anonymous questioning by the investigating judge of police officers who then did not give evidence at the trial in the applicants' case did not sufficiently guarantee the rights of the defence to comply with Article 6(3)(d), given that the convictions of the applicants for attempted murder and robbery were 'to a decisive extent' based on the police evidence. In that case, the police officers were questioned in a separate room by the investigating judge, with the accused and their lawyers hearing the questions and answers by a sound link. The Court was concerned that in this situation, the defence was unaware of the demeanour of the witnesses under questioning, as well as their identity. The Court was also not satisfied that the claimed threat of reprisals had been shown on the facts or that there were not less extreme measures that could have been used.[1185]

Article 6(3)(d) may be violated post-*Al-Khawaja* even though the evidence of the non-appearing witness that is admitted at trial is not the 'sole or decisive' evidence leading to a conviction.[1186] In such a case, prior to *Al-Khawaja*, a balancing test applied, with the question being whether 'the handicaps under which the defence labours'

[1179] *Al-Khawaja and Tahery v UK* 2011- ; 54 EHRR 807 para 127 GC.

[1180] There is no opportunity for cross-examination at the investigation stage in common law systems.

[1181] *Al-Khawaja and Tahery v UK* 2011- ; 54 EHRR 807 para 118 GC.

[1182] A 166 (1989); 12 EHRR 434 PC.   [1183] 1997-III; 25 EHRR 647 paras 56, 63.

[1184] See, eg, *Windisch v Austria* A 186 (1990); 13 EHRR 281 and *Asch v Austria* A 203 (1991); 15 EHRR 597.

[1185] The Court suggested that it might have been sufficient just to disguise the police witnesses during the investigating judge's questioning. Cf *Ludi v Switzerland* A 238 (1992); 15 EHRR 173. On the screening of witnesses in a terrorist trial, see *X v UK* No 20657/92, 15 EHRR CD 113 (1992) DA. See also *R v Davis* [2008] UKHL 36 (special arrangements at trial to presere anonymity of a murder witness unacceptable).

[1186] *Rudnichenko v Ukraine* hudoc (2013). Jackson and Summers, *The Internationalisation of Criminal Evidence*, 2012, p 340, suggest that by 'decisive' the Court means 'evidence which is not supported by other independent evidence and which is therefore considered to be determinative to the conviction'.

were 'sufficiently counterbalanced by the procedures followed by the judicial authorities'.[1187] Thus in *Kok v Netherlands*,[1188] the Court reviewed the procedures that were followed at the pre-trial stage and concluded that they had been sufficient to comply with Article 6(3)(d). Relevant factors when applying a balancing test include whether an investigating judge knows the identity of an anonymous witness[1189] and whether the defence has taken advantage of opportunities of confrontation at the pre-trial stage or of other opportunities to counter-balance the lack of the ability to cross-examine the witness at the trial.[1190] Post-*Al-Khawaja*, there will be a breach of Article 6(3)(d) if there is no 'good reason' for the absence of the witness. If there is a good reason, it would seem that, as before *Al-Khawaja*, there will not be a breach if there are sufficient counter-balancing factors, but the level of scrutiny will be high, as in cases where the evidence is the 'sole or decisive' evidence.

In the pre-*Al-Khawaja* case of *SN v Sweden*,[1191] the Court accepted that special arrangements for the confrontation of a witness at the trial that would not normally comply with Article 6(3)(d) may suffice in cases involving sexual offences. In that case, the Court held that Article 6(3)(d) had to be interpreted as making some allowance for the 'special features' of criminal proceedings concerning such offences, because giving oral evidence at the trial in open court in such cases, particularly in cases involving children, may be an ordeal for the victim and may raise issues of respect for private life. In the *SN* case, the evidence of a ten-year-old child who had been sexually abused by his school teacher was 'virtually the sole evidence' on the basis of which the teacher was convicted. The child did not give evidence as a witness at the trial, but the videotape of his first police interview was shown during both the trial and appeal hearings, and the record of the second interview was read out at the trial and the audiotape played back at the appeal hearing. What was crucial for the Court was that the applicant's lawyer had been present during the police hearing (by a specially trained unit) and had been able to suggest lines of questioning. The Court considered that this was sufficient to enable the applicant to challenge the child's statements and his credibility. The Court also took into account that the 'necessary care' was taken by the national court in its evaluation of the child's statements.[1192] It seems likely that the same outcome would result post-*Al-Khawaja*, with there being both 'good reason' for the child's absence from the trial and 'sufficient counterbalancing factors'.

As to the calling of *witnesses for the defence*, it is for the national courts, 'as a general rule, to assess whether it is appropriate to call witnesses'.[1193] Although the national court's decision is subject to review under Article 6(3)(d), it will only be in exceptional circumstances that the Strasbourg Court will question a national court's exercise of its

---

[1187] *Doorson v Netherlands* 1996-II; 22 EHRR 330 para 76.

[1188] *No 43149/98* hudoc (2000) DA. Cf *Birutis and Others v Lithuania* hudoc (2002) and *Sapunarescu v Germany No 22007/03* hudoc (2006) DA.

[1189] *Isgro v Italy* (1991) A 194 and *Doorson v Netherlands* 1996-II; 22 EHRR 330.

[1190] *SN v Sweden* 2002-V; 39 EHRR 304; *Asch v Austria* A 203 (1991); 15 EHRR 597; *Baegen v Netherlands* A 327-B (1995) Com Rep; *PS v Germany* hudoc (2001); 36 EHRR 1139; *Solakov v Former Yugoslav Republic of Macedonia* 2001-X. See also *Pullar v UK* 1996-III; 22 EHRR 391.

[1191] 2002-V; 39 EHRR 304 para 46. For other sex offences cases, see *Baegen v Netherlands* A 327-B (1995) Com Rep (defence failure to use alternative options; no breach); *MK v Austria No 28867/95* hudoc (1997); 24 EHRR CD 59 (expert report sufficient; no breach); *PS v Germany* hudoc (2001) 36 EHRR 1139 (no special arrangements; breach); *VD v Romania* hudoc (2010) (accused of rape; not allowed a DNA test or opportunity to challenge the victim's statement); and *Mika v Sweden No 31243/06* hudoc (2009) DA. See also *Mayali v France* hudoc (2005) and *Bocos-Cuesta v Netherlands* hudoc (2005) (breaches).

[1192] Cf *Doorson v Netherlands* 1996-II; 22 EHRR 330 para 76.

[1193] *Vidal v Belgium* A 235-B (1992) para 33. Cf *Engel v Netherlands* A 22 (1976); 1 EHRR 647 PC; *Doorson v Netherlands* 1996-II; 22 EHRR 330; and *Perna v Italy* 2003-V; 39 EHRR 563 GC.

discretion in the assessment of the relevance of the proposed evidence.[1194] This 'hands off' approach may be justified on the ground that the text of Article 6(3)(d) refers to the calling of witnesses by the accused 'on his behalf' and not 'at his request'. It is also in accord with the 'fourth instance' doctrine,[1195] which the Strasbourg authorities generally apply when reviewing the decision of national courts. An exceptional case in which the Court did intervene was *Vidal v Belgium*.[1196] There the Court found a breach of Article 6 as a whole when the national court to which the accused's case had been remitted refused—without giving reasons—to hear the four witnesses requested by the accused and replaced a three-year suspended sentence by a four-year sentence that was not suspended, without any new evidence.

A state is not liable under Article 6(3)(d) for the failure of defence counsel to call a particular witness,[1197] but where witnesses are properly called by the defence, a court is under a positive obligation to take appropriate steps to ensure their appearance.[1198] There is no breach of Article 6(3)(d), however, if a defence witness fails to appear for reasons beyond the court's control[1199] or just because the witness is called by the court at a time other than that requested by the accused, unless this affects the presentation of the defence.[1200]

Article 6(3)(d) recognizes that at the trial court hearing it is 'in principle' essential that an accused is allowed to be present when witnesses are being heard in a case against him.[1201] Exceptionally, however, the interests of justice may permit the exclusion of the accused consistent with Article 6(3)(d) to ensure that a witness gives an unreserved statement, provided that the accused's lawyer is allowed to remain and conduct any cross-examination.[1202]

In *Luedicke, Belkacem and Koç v Germany*,[1203] the Court left open the question whether it would be a breach of Article 6(3)(d) for a state to require an accused to pay the costs associated with compliance with Article 6(3)(d) (eg interpreters' costs in questioning witnesses) if convicted.

VI. ARTICLE 6(3)(E): THE RIGHT TO AN INTERPRETER

Article 6(3)(e) guarantees the right of a person charged with a criminal offence 'to have the free assistance of an interpreter if he cannot understand or speak the language used in court'. As in the case of other Article 6(3) rights, the guarantee protects persons once they are 'charged with a criminal offence'.It does not benefit suspects being questioned by the police prior to their being 'charged' in the sense of Article 6(1); it does apply to the

---

[1194] See *L v Switzerland No 12609/86*, 68 DR 108 (1991) F Sett and *Wiechart v Germany* 7 YB 104 (1964). National courts are also permitted considerable discretion in controlling the accused's questioning of such defence witnesses as are called: see, eg, *Kok v Netherlands No 43149/98* hudoc (2000); 30 EHRR CD DA 273.

[1195] The Commission has also referred to the 'margin of appreciation' doctrine: see, eg, *Payot and Petit v Switzerland No 16596/90* hudoc (1991) DA.

[1196] A 235-B (1992). Cf *Popov v Russia* hudoc (2006). The refusal to order a psychological report requested by the applicant in a case of parental access to a child contributed to a breach of Article 6(1) in *Elsholz v Germany* 2000-VIII; 34 EHRR 1412 GC. Cf *Balsytė-Lideikiene v Lithuania* hudoc (2008) (refusal to call experts). Contrast *Sommerfeld v Germany* 2003-VIII; 38 EHRR 756 GC.

[1197] *F v UK No 18123/91* hudoc (1992) 15 EHRR CD 32.

[1198] *Sadak and Others v Turkey* 2001-VIII; 36 EHRR 431.

[1199] *Ubach Mortes v Andorra No 46253/99*, 2000-V DA (ill-health).

[1200] *X v UK No 5506/72*, 45 CD 59 (1973).

[1201] *Kurup v Denmark No 11219/84*, 42 DR 287 (1985). Cf *X v Denmark No 8395/78*, 27 DR 50 (1981).

[1202] *Kurup v Denmark* ibid. Cf *X v UK No 20657/92* hudoc (1992); 15 EHRR CD 113 (screening of witness from accused, but not his lawyer, permissible).   [1203] A 29 (1978); 2 EHRR 149.

pre-trial stage of proceedings thereafter. Thus in *Kamasinski v Austria*,[1204] an interpreter was required during police questioning following the accused's arrest and in the course of the civil law preliminary investigation in the case. As with Article 6 rights generally, Article 6(3)(e) applies during any appeal proceedings. The right to an interpreter may be waived,[1205] but it must be a decision of the accused, not his lawyer.[1206]

The obligation to provide 'free' assistance is unqualified. It does not depend upon the accused's means; the services of an interpreter for the accused are instead a part of the facilities required of a state in organizing its system of criminal justice.[1207] Nor can an accused be ordered to pay for the costs of interpretation if he is convicted, as was required by West German law in *Luedicke, Belkacem and Koç v Germany*.[1208] The language of Article 6(3)(e) indicates 'neither a conditional remission, nor a temporary exemption, nor a suspension, but a once and for all exemption or exoneration'. Any contrary interpretation would also be inconsistent with the object and purpose of Article 6, which is to ensure a fair trial for all accused persons, whether subsequently convicted or not, since an accused might forgo his right to an interpreter for fear of the financial consequences.[1209]

The 'assistance' required by Article 6(3)(e) applies to the translation of documents as well as the interpretation of oral statements; in both respects the obligation is to provide such assistance as is necessary to ensure a fair trial.[1210] Article 6(3)(e) does not require that every word of the oral proceedings is interpreted or that all documents are translated; the test is whether enough is done to allow the accused fully to understand and answer the case against him.[1211] Thus a written translation of the indictment may be unnecessary if sufficient oral information as to its contents is given to the accused, and it may be enough for an interpreter to summarize parts of the oral proceedings.[1212]

It is arguable that the state's obligation should extend to informing an accused who appears in need of assistance to his right to an interpreter.[1213] As to whether there is such a need, in *Cuscani v UK*,[1214] the Court stated that the onus was on the judge to reassure himself, following consultation with the applicant, that the latter was not prejudiced by the absence of an interpreter. In that case, the Court held that Article 6(3)(e) had been infringed when, although aware of the applicant's difficulty in following the proceedings and that his legal aid barrister had had problems in communicating with the applicant, the judge was persuaded by the barrister, without consulting the applicant, that it would be possible to 'make do and mend' with the assistance of the 'untested language skills' of the applicant's brother in a sentencing hearing that led to a four-year prison sentence and ten-year disqualification as a company director.

[1204] A 168 (1989); 13 EHRR 36. Cf *Diallo v Sweden* No 13205/07 hudoc (2010) DA and *Şaman v Turkey* hudoc (2011). Article 6(3)(e) extends to pre-trial appearances before a judge, remand hearings, and the translation of the indictment: *Luedicke, Belkacem and Koç v Germany* A 29 (1978); 2 EHRR 149.

[1205] See *Kamasinski v Austria* A 168 (1989); 13 EHRR 36 para 80.

[1206] *Cuscani v UK* hudoc (2002); 36 EHRR 11 and *Sardinas Alba v Italy* No 56271/00 hudoc (2004) DA.

[1207] See *Isyar v Bulgaria* hudoc (2008). But an accused may be charged for an interpreter provided for him at a hearing that he fails to attend: *Fedele v Germany* No 11311/84 hudoc (1987) DA.

[1208] A 29 (1978); 2 EHRR 149 para 40.   [1209] *Luedicke, Belkacem and Koç v Germany*, para 42.

[1210] *Kamsinski v Austria* A 168 (1989); 13 EHRR 36 para 74. As to whether written translation is required, see *Hermi v Italy* 2006-XII; 46 EHRR 1115 GC.   [1211] *Kamsinski v Austria*, paras 74, 83.

[1212] *Kamsinski v Austria*, paras 81, 83. An oral summary of the judgment may suffice to permit an appeal: *Kamsinski v Austria*. See also *Hayward v Sweden* No 14106/88 hudoc (1991) DA.

[1213] Cf Stavros, p 257.

[1214] Hudoc (2002); 36 EHRR 11 para 38. In *X v Austria* No 6185/73, 2 DR 68 (1975), the Commission ruled that Article 6(3)e) ('language in court') does not extend to communications between the accused and his lawyer.

Article 6(3)(e) only extends to the language used in court: an accused who understands that language cannot insist upon the services of an interpreter to allow him to conduct his defence in another language, including a language of an ethnic minority of which he is a member.[1215]

Where, as is usually the case, the accused does not defend himself in person but is represented by a lawyer, it will generally not be sufficient that the accused's lawyer (but not the accused) knows the language used in court. Interpretation of the proceedings is required, as the right to a fair trial, which includes the right to participate in the hearing, requires that the accused be able to understand the proceedings and to inform his lawyer of any point that should be made in his defence.[1216] A related question is whether the accused must be provided with an interpreter, where necessary, in order to communicate with his lawyer. In a legal aid case, the responsibility should lie with the state under Article 6(3)(c) to appoint a lawyer who can communicate with his client or to provide an interpreter.[1217] Where the accused appoints his own lawyer, it must be for him to appoint a lawyer who can communicate with him, if one is available.[1218]

Clearly, the interpreter who is provided must be competent. In this connection, the Court has stated that in order for the right guaranteed by Article 6(3)(e) to be 'practical and effective', the 'obligation of the competent authorities is not limited to the appointment of an interpreter but, if they are put on notice in the particular circumstances, may also extend to a degree of subsequent control over the adequacy of the interpretation provided'.[1219] Although there is no formal requirement that an interpreter be impartial or independent of the police or other authorities, the assistance provided must be 'effective' and 'not of such a nature as to impinge on the fairness of the proceedings'.[1220]

6. CONCLUSION

Although Article 6 cases do not generally catch the headlines as much as cases under some other articles of the Convention, they are the staple diet of the Convention system. As noted, the majority of cases decided at Strasbourg raise issues under Article 6, probably because it is in the administration of justice that the state is most likely to take decisions affecting individuals in the areas of conduct covered by the Convention.

Article 6 has been given an unexpectedly but commendably wide field of application. Although it does not yet extend to every situation in which an individual would benefit from a 'right to a court', Article 6 has acquired an extensive reach. It controls appellate as well as trial and some pre-trial proceedings. And it applies to certain disciplinary and other proceedings before special tribunals. While this is good for the individual, it presents problems for the uniform interpretation of a text that was devised with the classical court of law in mind. Article 6 also requires states to provide a right of appeal from, or

---

[1215] *K v France No 10210/82*, 35 DR 203 (1983) and *Bideault v France No 11261/84*, 48 DR 232 (1986). See also *Lagerblom v Sweden* hudoc (2003).

[1216] *Kamasinski v Austria* A 168 (1991); 13 EHRR 36 para 74 and *Cuscani v UK* hudoc (2002); 36 EHRR 11 para 38.

[1217] In *Lagerblom v Sweden* hudoc (2003), the accused sought to have his Swedish-speaking legal aid lawyer replaced by a Finnish speaking lawyer so that he could talk directly with him. The claim was rejected on the basis that an interpreter was provided and anyway the accused had sufficient Swedish.

[1218] *X v Germany No 1022/82*, 6 EHRR 353 (1983).

[1219] *Kamasinski v Austria* A 168 (1989) 13 EHRR 36 para 74. See also *Ucak v UK No 44234/98* hudoc (2002) DA.   [1220] *Ucak v UK No 44234/98* hudoc (2002) DA.

judicial review of, administrative decisions that are directly decisive for an individual's 'civil rights and obligations'. Should the Court's jurisprudence in this last regard appear confusing and in need of a coherent statement of principle, the result is still an extension of the rule of law into areas of administrative justice where it was sometimes lacking.

As to the meaning of a 'fair trial', Article 6 has been imaginatively interpreted. A right of access to a court has been read into the text, and understood to extend to the execution of judgments, as well of their attainment. The emphasis upon 'objective justice' has given more bite to the guarantees of an 'independent and impartial tribunal' and 'equality of arms', leading in some cases to changes in long-standing national practices.[1221] Issues of *res judicata* and the reversal of judgments and delays in their execution have been particular problems for post-Soviet states. The residual right to a 'fair hearing' has proved fertile ground for the addition of further nominate rights and has served as a means of dealing with cases on a flexible 'facts as a whole' basis.[1222] But the most striking feature of Article 6 cases has been the long line of decisions involving violations of the right to trial 'within a reasonable time'. If one feature of the administration of justice in European states has been highlighted by the working of the Convention, it is the delay that may occur before justice is delivered. Proceedings in some cases have lasted an almost unbelievable number of years.

As to the mechanics of the trial process, the Court has been far less intrusive. Given the great diversity of practice in European criminal justice systems concerning, for example, the rules of evidence, the Court has allowed considerable discretion as to means, requiring only that the outcome of the procedure followed is a fair trial. One issue in respect of which it has taken a stand is the admissibility of the hearsay evidence.This example demonstrates clearly the choice that the Court has between leading and following national in the administration of justice. Whereas Article 6, like the US Constitution, should not be seen as a 'uniform code of criminal procedure federally imposed',[1223] there are areas in which corrective action may properly be taken in respect of trial proceedings in the interests of human rights.

[1221] See *Piersack v Belgium* A 53 (1982); 5 EHRR 161.

[1222] See, eg, *Kraska v Switzerland*, A 254 (1983); 18 EHRR 188.

[1223] Frankfurter, *Law and Politics*, 1939, pp 192–3.

10

ARTICLE 7: FREEDOM FROM RETROACTIVE CRIMINAL OFFENCES AND PUNISHMENT

> **Article 7**
>
> 1. No one shall be held guilty of any criminal offence on account of any act or omission which did not constitute a criminal offence under national or international law at the time when it was committed. Nor shall a heavier penalty be imposed than the one that was applicable at the time the criminal offence was committed.
> 2. This article shall not prejudice the trial and punishment of any person for any act or omission which, at the time when it was committed, was criminal according to the general principles of law recognised by civilised nations.

Article 7 incorporates the principle of legality, by which, in the context of criminal law, a person should only be convicted and punished on a basis of law: *nullem crimen, nulla poena sine lege*.[1] The guarantee in Article 7 'is an essential element of the rule of law', which is mentioned in the Convention Preamble, and has as its object and purpose the provision of 'effective safeguards against arbitrary prosecution, conviction and punishment'.[2] The importance of the guarantee in Article 7(1) is recognized by the fact that it cannot be derogated from in time of war or public emergency.[3]

Given that Article 7 requires that national courts act on the basis of their national law and that they interpret and apply that law in accordance with Article 7, the Strasbourg Court may find itself reviewing the interpretation and application of national law by national courts. In accordance with the Court's general approach whereby it does not question the interpretation and application of national law by national courts, this supervisory function is undertaken with caution,[4] with the Court only exceptionally finding the interpretation and application of national law by the national courts to be in breach of Article 7.[5]

---

[1] *Kafkaris v Cyprus* 2008-; 49 EHRR 877 GC. On the principle of legality, see Hall, *General Principles of Criminal Law*, 2nd edn, 1960, pp 225 *et seq*.

[2] *Streletz, Kessler and Krenz v Germany* 2001-II; 33 EHRR 751 para 50 GC.

[3] See Article 15(2), Convention.

[4] *Streletz, Kessler and Krenz v Germany* 2001-II; 33 EHRR 751 GC.

[5] See, eg, *Başkaya and Okçuoğlu v Turkey* 1999-IV; 31 EHRR 292 GC and *EK v Turkey* hudoc (2002); 35 EHRR 1344.

1. *EX POST FACTO* CRIMINAL OFFENCES

The wording of Article 7(1) is limited to cases in which a person is ultimately 'held guilty' of a criminal offence.[6] A prosecution that does not lead to a conviction, or has not yet done so, cannot raise an issue under Article 7—at least not by means of an individual application.[7] A state application under Article 33 may question the compatibility with Article 7 of a law *in abstracto*, so that even a prosecution is not required. Thus in *Ireland v UK*,[8] Ireland challenged the consistency of the Northern Ireland Act 1972 with Article 7, insofar as it could be read as making it an offence retroactively to fail to comply with an order issued by the security forces. The application was withdrawn when the UK Attorney-General gave an undertaking that the Act would not be applied retroactively.

Article 7 does not prevent the retroactive application of laws in respect of such ancillary matters concerning criminal proceedings as detention on remand, the refusal of legal aid or of leave to appeal, or the entry of a conviction on a person's record, since they do not concern the characterization of the applicant's act or omission as an offence.[9] Similarly, a change in a statute of limitations rule to the detriment of an accused in pending proceedings is not a breach of Article 7, both for the above reason and because changes in procedural rules generally have immediate application in national law.[10] Likewise, an amendment to the rules of evidence to the detriment of the accused is not within Article 7.[11] Article 7, that is, applies only where a change in the *substantive* law has retroactive effect to the detriment of the accused.[12] It would appear from *Scoppola v Italy (No 2)*[13] that Article 7 also guarantees an accused the benefit of an amendment to the criminal law to his advantage, so that if his conduct ceases to be criminal after it occurs, it should no longer give rise to criminal responsibility. The *Scoppola* case concerned an amendment to the law concerning penalties, but can be taken to apply to the law concerning offences too. On other matters, Article 7 does not incorporate the principle *non bis in idem* (a person should not be tried twice for the same offence).[14] And since Article 7 applies only within the criminal justice system, decisions to deport or to extradite a person to another jurisdiction,[15] to order the preventive detention of a suspected terrorist,[16] or to detain a person as a vagrant[17] are also not controlled by it. Similarly, Article 7(1) does not apply to the imposition of a regime of civilian service upon a conscientious objector to military service[18] or to judicial decisions in non-criminal proceedings.[19]

---

[6] 'Guilty' has an autonomous Convention meaning: *X v Netherlands No 7512/76*, 6 DR 184 (1976).
[7] *Lukanov v Bulgaria No 21915/93*, 80-A DR 108 (1995).   [8] *No 5310/71*, 15 YB 76 (1972).
[9] See, eg, *X v Germany No 448/59*, 3 YB 254 (1960).
[10] *Coëme and Others v Belgium* 2000-VII. The question whether a new prosecution following the removal of an immunity from prosecution could lead to an infringement of Article 7 was left open. See also *Walczak v Poland No 77395/01* hudoc (2002) DA (appeal hearing abolished).
[11] See *X v UK No 6683/74*, 3 DR 95 (1975).   [12] See *G v France* A 325-B (1995); 21 EHRR 288.
[13] Hudoc (2009); 51 EHRR 323 GC.   [14] *X v Austria No 7720/76*, 3 Digest 32 (1978).
[15] *Moustaquim v Belgium* A 193 (1991); 13 EHRR 802; and *X v Netherlands No 7512/76*, 6 DR 184 (1976). *Quaere*, however, whether extradition to face a real risk of conviction contrary to Article 7 might be a breach of that Article: see *Soering v UK* A 161(1989); 11 EHRR 439 PC.
[16] *Lawless v Ireland* A 3 (1961); 1 EHRR 15.
[17] *De Wilde, Ooms and Versyp v Belgium* A 12 (1971); 1 EHRR 373 PC.
[18] *Johansen v Norway No 10600/83*, 44 DR 155 (1985).
[19] *X v Belgium No 8988/80*, 24 DR 198 (1981). *Quaere* whether Article 7 might control a non-criminal court ruling (eg, as to the presence of negligence) based upon an *ex post facto* law that would later be binding upon a criminal court when determining guilt.

Following *Engel v Netherlands*,[20] 'criminal' in Article 7(1) has an autonomous Convention meaning.[21] Hence a disciplinary offence that meets the requirements of the *Engel* case is a 'criminal' offence for the purposes of Article 7.[22] Likewise, offences that are classified as regulatory offences or are otherwise non-criminal offences in national law but are 'criminal' offences for the purposes of Article 6 may be regarded as 'criminal' for the purposes of Article 7 too.[23] As under Article 6, it is likely that an offence that is classified as a 'criminal' offence under the law of the state in which the person is found guilty is always to be regarded as such for the purposes of Article 7.

Article 7(1) refers to criminal offences that have a basis in 'law'. The term 'law' has the same autonomous meaning as it has elsewhere in the Convention, so that it includes, in terms of sources of law, judge-made law as well as legislation, whether primary or delegated.[24] It does not include 'state practice' that is inconsistent with a state's written or judge-made law and its international human rights obligations. This was ruled in *Streletz, Kessler and Krenz v Germany*.[25] There the three applicants had been convicted by a German court of offences of incitement to commit intentional homicide and sentenced to five to seven years' imprisonment under the criminal law of the German Democratic Republic (GDR), or East Germany, that applied in the GDR when they committed their offences (and which the courts of the new Germany continued to apply). The cases concerned the deaths of a large number of individuals who had been killed by GDR border guards by shooting or by mines as they tried to cross the border to West Germany at the time of the Berlin Wall. The applicants occupied senior positions in the GDR government and party apparatus that was responsible for orders to border guards to arrest or, if necessary, 'annihilate' border violators and to protect the border 'at all costs'. Whereas the applicants were tried under the GDR criminal law that existed when the deaths occurred, they argued that GDR 'state practice'—by way of the orders to border guards referred to above for which they shared responsibility—had superseded that law and justified their acts. The Court held that this 'state practice' was not 'law' for the purposes of Article 7, as it was contrary to both the fundamental right provisions of the GDR constitution and other GDR laws and the GDR's international human rights obligations. Accordingly, it did not replace the GDR criminal law existing at the time, which met the requirements of Article 7(1). The Court's judgment confirms that delegated legislation or administrative acts that are *ultra vires* in national law do not count as 'law' for the purposes of Article 7, whether to take away an otherwise valid legal basis for prosecution or to provide a basis for prosecution that otherwise does not exist. The case may also provide a basis for ruling that Article 7 is not complied with on the ground that a national 'law' which is valid within the national legal system is nonetheless contrary to the international human rights obligations of the state. In the companion case of *K-HW v Germany*,[26] no breach of Article 7 was also found where a young GDR border guard who shot and killed a border

---

[20] A 22 (1976); 1 EHRR 647 PC.

[21] *Brown v UK No 38644/97* hudoc (1998) DA. The drafting history of 'criminal' in Article 7 supports a wide reading: see Fawcett, *Application of the European Convention on Human Rights*, 2nd edn, 1987, pp 200–1.

[22] Army disciplinary offences did not meet these requirements in *Çelikateş v Turkey No 45824/99* hudoc (2000) DA.

[23] See *Harman v UK No 10038/82*, 38 DR 53 (1984); F Sett 46 DR 57 (1986) (whether civil contempt in English law 'criminal' under Article 7 left open).

[24] *Kafkaris v Cyprus* 2008-; 49 EHRR 877 GC.

[25] 2001-II; 33 EHRR 751 GC. See also *Glässner v Germany No 46362/99* 2001-VII DA.

[26] 2001-II; 36 EHRR 1081 paras 75–6 GC.

violator was convicted by a German court of intentional homicide. In this case, while acknowledging the great difficulties the border guard would have faced if he had not followed orders, the Court stated that the GDR constitution and criminal law under which he was prosecuted were accessible to him and that 'even a private soldier could not show total, blind obedience to orders which flagrantly infringed not only the GDR's own legal principles but also internationally recognised human rights, in particular the right to life, which is the supreme value in the hierarchy of human rights'. In support of this approach, it may be argued that the soldier's difficulties should be taken into account in sentencing rather than in determining guilt.[27] The same 'obedience to orders' defence was rejected in *Polednová v Czech Republic*,[28] in which the applicant had been convicted of murder for her involvement as a prosecutor in a number of political trials leading to death sentences in the former communist Czechoslovakia. In a striking passage, the Court noted that the applicant must have been aware that the outcome of these trials had been pre-determined by the political authorities and that they had 'completely flouted' the 'fundamental principles of justice.' To allow the applicant to rely on Article 7 would 'run counter to the object and purpose of that provision, namely to ensure that no one is subjected to arbitrary prosecution, conviction or punishment'.

The law under which a person is convicted must derive its authority from the state's lawful constitution. This can be problematic where an offence is committed in the course of a struggle for power as a new state emerges from its predecessor. In *Kuolelis, Bartosevicius and Burokevicius v Lithuania*,[29] the democratically elected government of the re-established state of Lithuania had in March 1990 declared its independence from the USSR and enacted new constitutional legislation. After strong opposition from the USSR, during the course of which it invaded Lithuania in January 1991, by September 1991 the new government achieved international recognition by other states, including the USSR. The applicants were leading members of the Communist Party of Lithuania opposed to independence who were convicted of criminal offences in connection with an attempted coup against the new government in January 1991. The offences were committed under laws enacted by the new government in November 1990 that applied prospectively to the applicant's conduct; the only question was whether they had legal force in Lithuania at the time. The Court held that by November 1990 the 'political will of the new Lithuanian Government was clearly established', that the applicants were convicted for offences under its laws that were 'sufficiently clear and foreseeable', and that the consequences of non-compliance were 'adequately predictable', both with legal advice and 'as a matter of common sense'.

As elsewhere in the Convention, the term 'law' also implies 'qualitative requirements, including those of accessibility and foreseeability'.[30] As to foreseeability, an individual must be able to know from the wording of the relevant law and the courts' interpretation of it, what acts and omissions will make him criminally liable and what penalty will be imposed.[31]

---

[27] Cf Article 8, Charter of the Nuremberg International Military Tribunal, 39 AJIL Supp 257 (1945). In the *K-HW* case, the sentence was one year ten months' imprisonment, suspended on probation.

[28] *No 2615/10* hudoc (2011) DA.   [29] Hudoc (2008) para 120.

[30] *Kafkaris v Cyprus* 2008-; 49 EHRR 877 para 140 GC; and *Korbely v Hungary* hudoc 2008-; 50 EHRR 1192 GC. This applies to offences and penalties. See also *Custers, Deveaux and Turk v Denmark* hudoc (2007); 47 EHRR 28 and *Camilleri v Malta* hudoc (2013). The requirements of accessibility and foreseeability overlap, with the former, which supposes, *inter alia*, that the 'law' is publicly available, see *G v France* A 325-B (1995); 21 EHRR 288, contributing to the latter.

[31] *Kafkaris v Cyprus, ibid*. As to the application of these qualitative requirements to case law, see the *CR* case, later in this section, and *Liivik v Estonia* hudoc (2009); 56 EHRR 1193. The applicant's technical

As indicated, for Article 7(1) to be infringed, the act or omission on the basis of which a person is convicted must not constitute a criminal offence 'at the time when it is committed'. This covers the position in which the offence of which the accused is convicted is introduced with retroactive effect by legislation or by the courts, after the accused's act or omission. In the case of a continuing offence, where the accused's conduct that is now an offence occurred both before and after it became an offence, there will be a breach of Article 7 unless it is shown that the conviction (and penalty) is based solely upon the accused's later conduct.[32] Article 7 also applies to the situation where a criminal offence has been abrogated or has ceased to apply by reason of desuetude.[33] In both cases, a person is convicted of an offence that does not exist at the time that his act or omission occurs.

Article 7 applies not only to the introduction of new offences but also to the situation in which the scope of the existing law is extended to acts or omissions that were previously not criminal, and lays down the principle that the 'criminal law must not be extensively construed to the accused's detriment'.[34] However, the application of an existing law may be extended by the courts by way of interpretation where its meaning has previously been unclear or, in some cases, where it is given a changed meaning by the courts in the applicant's case. As stated by the Court in *CR v UK*,[35] 'there will always be a need for elucidation of doubtful points and for adaptation to changed circumstances. Indeed...progressive development of the criminal law through judicial law-making is a well entrenched and necessary part of legal tradition' in Convention states, so that Article 7 'cannot be read as outlawing the gradual clarification of the rules of criminal liability through judicial interpretation from case to case, provided that the resultant development is consistent with the essence of the offence and could reasonably be foreseen'. As to the situation where the law is, at least initially, unclear, the Court has in several cases not found a breach of Article 7 despite some very generally worded or obscurely drafted laws.[36] This has been either because the national courts have already given it more precise meaning in their case law,[37] or because they have interpreted it for the first time in the applicant's case and given it a meaning that is both foreseeable and consistent with the essence of the offence.[38]

As to a changed interpretation of the law, in the *CR v UK*,[39] the applicant was found guilty of attempting to rape his wife when he attempted to have sexual intercourse with her without her consent after she had left the matrimonial home. The applicant relied during his trial on the long-established common law exception to rape whereby a husband

---

knowledge and background is relevant to foreseeability: *X v Austria No 8141/78*, 16 DR 141 (1978); and *Chauvy v France No 64915/01* hudoc (2003) DA. The applicant may be expected to have recourse to a lawyer, as far as is reasonable in the circumstances, to understand the law: *Cantoni v France* 1996-V GC.

[32] *Ecer and Zeyrek v Turkey* 2001-II; 35 EHRR 672; *Veeber v Estonia (No 2)* 2003-I; 39 EHRR 125; and *Puhk v Estonia* hudoc (2004). A substituted conviction for another pre-existing offence is not a breach of Article 7: *Garner v UK No 38330/97* hudoc (1999) DA.

[33] *X v Germany No 1169/61*, 6 YB 520 at 588 (1963). Cf *X v Netherlands No 7721/76*, 11 DR 209 at 211 (1977).

[34] *Kafkaris v Cyprus* 2008-; 49 EHRR 877 para 138 GC (a penalty case).

[35] A 335-C (1995); 21 EHRR 363 para 34. See also *SW v UK* A 335-B (1995); 21 EHRR 363 (companion case). Cf *Moiseyev v Russia* hudoc (2011); 53 EHRR 9.

[36] See, eg, *Radio France v France* hudoc (2004); 40 EHRR 29.

[37] *Kokkinakis v Greece* A 260-A (1993); 17 EHRR 397; *Larissis v Greece* 1998-I; 27 EHRR 329; *Başkaya and Okçuoğlu v Turkey* 1999-IV; 31 EHRR 292 GC; and *Schimanek v Austria No 32307/96* hudoc (2000) DA.

[38] *Jorgic v Germany* 2007-III; 47 EHRR 207 (interpretation of 'genocide' one of two predictable interpretations). See also *Custers, Devaux and Turk v Denmark* hudoc (2007); 47 EHRR 665; *Jobe v UK No 48279/09* hudoc (2011) DA; and *Khodorkovskiy and Lebedev v Russia* hudoc (2013).

[39] A 335-C (1995); 21 EHRR 363. See also *Kingston v UK No 27837/95* hudoc (1997) DA; and *Laskey, Jaggard and Brown v UK No 21627/93* hudoc (1995) DA.

could not be found guilty of raping his wife. The House of Lords held that this exception no longer applied, as it was inconsistent with the status of men and women in modern times, and English law had been moving in the direction of its abolition. Applying its foreseeability/essence of the offence approach, the Strasbourg Court held unanimously that Article 7(1) had not been infringed.[40] However, the Court's decision is open to criticism in respect of foreseeability. While the Court's argument that the exception was at variance with a 'civilised concept of marriage' and the 'fundamental objectives of the Convention', which concern 'human dignity and freedom',[41] was a very strong one, opportunities to change the law by legislation had not been taken by the time the applicant's offence was committed and, while some judicial erosion of the exception had been effected, the House of Lords decision can most easily be viewed as a direct reversal of the law that was not a foreseeable outcome of a process of gradual judicial development. In contrast with the CR case, the Court found that a changed interpretation of the law was not foreseeable when employees of a private bank were found guilty of accepting bribes under an offence which had previously been understood to apply only to public officials but which the court in their case had extended to private employees.[42]

A conviction that has no basis in national law, or results from its retroactive application, will not be in breach of Article 7 if the conduct upon which the conviction is based is a crime under 'international law' at the time of its commission.[43] This is particularly significant for a state if, and to the extent that, international law is not a part of its national law. The question then arises as to the meaning of crimes under 'international law'. In *Streletz, Kessler and Krenz v Germany*,[44] the Court held that it may include 'offences' under the international law of human rights. In that case, the guarantees of the right to life and freedom of movement in the International Covenant on Civil and Political Rights and the European Convention on Human Rights were infringed. Although these guarantees did not give rise to criminal responsibility on the part of individuals in international law, the GDR Criminal Code provided for individual criminal responsibility for those who violated the GDR's international obligations, so that, the Court considered, the applicant's acts constituted offences under the international law of human rights. Having reached this conclusion, the Court found it unnecessary to consider whether the applicants had committed crimes under international humanitarian law, notably crimes against humanity. The Court's ruling concerning violations of international human rights law is limited to the special case under the GDR constitution, and is not wholly convincing. As the Court acknowledged, international human rights law does not give rise to individual criminal responsibility. Such responsibility does exist under international humanitarian law—extending to genocide, war crimes, crimes against humanity, and aggression—and these have since been held to be crimes under international law for the purposes of Article 7.[45] As well as such crimes, it is likely that Article 7 refers to crimes in respect of which international law permits individuals to be prosecuted by states under their national criminal law on the basis solely of their custody of the alleged offender (universal jurisdiction). In *Ould Dah v France*,[46] the Court stated that a state's amnesty law

---

[40] In contrast, in *Pessino v France* hudoc (2006), the reversal of precedent was sudden and unforeseeable.
[41] *CR v UK* A 335-C (1995); 21 EHRR 363 para 42.
[42] *Dragotoniu and Militaru-Pidhorni v Romania* hudoc (2007).
[43] *Simsic v Bosnia and Herzegovina No 51552/10* hudoc (2012) DA (offence a crime against humanity in international law).   [44] 2001-II; 33 EHRR 751 GC.
[45] See *Van Anraat v Netherlands No 65389/09* hudoc (2010) DA (use of mustard gas). See also *Korbely v Hungary* 2008-; 50 EHRR 1192 GC and *Kononov v Latvia* 2010- GC; and *Jorgic v Germany* 2007-III; 47 EHRR 207 (genocide).
[46] *No 13113/03* hudoc (2009) DA.

could not prevent another state that was a party to the European Convention from prosecuting an offender for torture on a basis of universal jurisdiction in accordance with the UN Torture Convention: to rule otherwise would be to deprive the provision for universal jurisdiction in the Torture Convention of any meaning. In that case, the applicant qualified for amnesty under a Mauritian amnesty law for acts of torture committed by him as a member of the Mauritanian army. When he visited France he was arrested and convicted of torture by the French courts. The Strasbourg Court rejected the applicant's claim that his conviction involved the retrospective application of French criminal law contrary to Article 7 of the Convention because he could not have foreseen that the French courts would override the amnesty law. Other offences involving universal jurisdiction include piracy in customary international law and, for the states parties to the relevant treaties, drug trafficking and hijacking.[47]

2. *EX POST FACTO* CRIMINAL PENALTIES

Article 7(1) also provides that there shall not be imposed a 'heavier penalty…than the one that was applicable at the time the criminal offence was committed'. Article 7(1) applies to any 'penalty'. The meaning of 'penalty' was examined in *Welch v UK*.[48] The Court indicated that it had an autonomous Convention meaning. The measure in question must be one that is imposed following conviction for a criminal offence. Other factors that may be taken into account are 'the nature and purpose of the measure in question; its characterisation under national law; the procedures involved in the making and implementation of the measure; and its severity'. In the *Welch* case, the applicant was convicted of criminal offences involving drug trafficking. He was given a twenty-two-year prison sentence and a confiscation order was made under the Drug Trafficking Offences Act 1986. The order was for the payment of £59,000, in default of which he would receive a further two-year prison sentence. There was no doubt that the Act had been applied retroactively to an offence committed prior to it; the only question was whether the order made under it was a 'penalty' so that Article 7 applied. In deciding that it was, and that Article 7 had been infringed as a result, the Court noted that the order had been imposed following a conviction; that the measure had punitive as well as preventative and reparative aims;[49] and that there were indications of a regime of punishment in the fact that the amount of the order was related to the proceeds of drug dealing, not just the actual profits, and could be related to culpability; and that imprisonment might result in default of payment. The provision for preventive detention orders in Germany have been held to have sufficient punitive, as well as preventative, elements (and requires court action) to constitute a penalty.[50] Consequently the retrospective application of an amendment to the Criminal Code extending the applicant's detention was a breach of Article 7.[51]

In contrast, a statutory requirement that a convicted sex offender register with the police is not a penalty.[52] This is because the purpose is not to punish but to reduce the

---

[47] See Crawford, *Brownlie's Principles of Public International Law*, 8th edn, 2012, p 468.

[48] A 307-A (1995); 20 EHRR 247 paras 27–35. Cf *Jamil v France* A 317-B (1995); 21 EHRR 65.

[49] Contrast *M v Italy No 12386/86*, 70 DR 59 (1991), in which the confiscation of Mafia-owned property was preventive, not punitive, and did not follow a conviction.

[50] *M v Germany* hudoc (2009); 51 EHRR 976. Cf *OH v Germany* hudoc (2011); 54 EHRR 29.

[51] *M v Germany*.

[52] *Adamson v UK No 42293/98* hudoc (1999) DA. See also *Gardel v France* 2009- (registration on sex-offenders register was a preventive measure, not a penalty).

level of re-offending, the requirement does not result from a judicial process, and the obligation to register is not severe. The removal from the jurisdiction of an illegal immigrant as an administrative measure is also not a 'penalty' in the sense of Article 7.[53] In another case, the Commission left open the question whether Article 7 applies where a convicted person is sent to a mental institution as mentally disordered.[54] It would seem that it should not apply, since the purpose of committing a person to a mental institution is not to punish.

In *Scoppola v Italy (No 2)*,[55] the Grand Chamber held, by eleven votes to six, that 'Article 7 (1) guarantees not only the principle of non-retrospectiveness of more stringent criminal laws but also, and implicitly, the principle of retrospectiveness of the more lenient criminal law'. So, in the *Scoppola* case there was a breach of Article 7 because the accused had not, when sentenced,[56] benefited from an alteration in the law to the penalty applicable to his case that was introduced after he had committed his offence. This ruling reversed the Court's earlier interpretation of Article 7, by which it had held that an accused did not so benefit.[57] The Grand Chamber reversed its earlier interpretation on the basis that 'a consensus has gradually emerged in Europe and internationally around the view that the application of a criminal law providing for a more lenient penalty, even one enacted after the commission of the offence, has become a fundamental principle of criminal law'. The argument of the six dissenting judges that the Court's interpretation contradicted the clear meaning of the text and the *travaux préparatoires* has much force.

Article 7 applies only to the 'penalty' imposed, not to the manner of its execution. Hence it does not prevent any retroactive alteration in the law or practice concerning the parole or conditional release of a prisoner to his or her detriment.[58] or the place in which he is to serve his sentence.[59] However, in an early Commission decision, it was stated that Article 7 may apply to a retroactive change in the conditions of detention where the new conditions are 'essentially different' from those that would have applied previously.[60] The distinction between a penalty and the manner of its execution was in issue in *Kafkaris v Cyprus*.[61] In that case, the applicant was sentenced in 1989 to 'life imprisonment' for murder. At the time he committed the offence in 1987, under the prison regulations, life imprisonment meant twenty years' imprisonment, with the possibility of remission earlier. However, his trial court, following a later judicial decision, stated that life imprisonment meant imprisonment for the whole of an individual's life. The Strasbourg Court held that the change in the rule by which the applicant had lost the possibility of remission was not subject to Article 7, as it concerned the execution of a penalty, not the penalty itself, which remained life imprisonment. Nonetheless, the Court did find a breach of Article 7 for lack of foreseeability. At the time of the commission of the offence, the relevant Cypriot law 'as a whole' was not formulated with 'sufficient precision as to enable the applicant to discern, even with appropriate advice, the scope of the penalty of life imprisonment'.

---

[53] *Moustaquim v Belgium* A 193 (1991); 13 EHRR 802.

[54] *Dhoest v Belgium No 10448/83*, 55 DR 5 (1987).

[55] Hudoc (2009); 51 EHRR 323 paras 106, 109 GC.

[56] *Scoppola* does not apply to amendments to the law after 'a final judgment is rendered': *Scoppola*, para 109.   [57] See *Zaprianov v Bulgaria No 41171/98* hudoc (2003) DA.

[58] *Kafkaris v Cyprus* 2008-; 49 EHRR 877 GC. See also *Hogben v UK No 11653/85*, 46 DR 231 (1986); *Grava v Italy* hudoc (2003); and *Saccoccia v Austria No 69917/01* hudoc (2007) DA.

[59] *Müller v Czech Republic No 48058/09* hudoc (2011) DA (moved to a stricter regime abroad).

[60] *X v Austria No 7720/76*, 3 Digest 32 (1978).

[61] 2008-; 49 EHRR 877 para 150 GC. See also *Del Rio Prada v Spain* 2013- GC.

Much of what has been said earlier concerning *ex post facto* criminal offences applies to penalties also. As with such offences, an *ex post facto* 'penalty' is in breach of Article 7 where, as in the *Welch* case, a new penalty is applied to an offence committed before the penalty came into operation,[62] or where there is no legal basis for the penalty imposed,[63] or where an existing penalty is applied to the detriment of the convicted person in a way that is not reasonably foreseeable.[64] Foreseeability was in issue in *Achour v France*.[65] In that case, the French law for the punishment of recidivists was amended so as to double in some cases the sentence that would be given to persons convicted for a second time of a serious offence. The applicant complained of a breach of Article 7 when the amended law was applied to his detriment to increase his sentence to twelve years' imprisonment for a second drugs offence committed after the amended law came into force, when his first offence had been committed before it had done so. The Court ruled that there was no breach of Article 7; the doubling of his sentence was foreseeable because he knew of, or could have discovered, before he committed the second offence, the consequences of doing so and the long-established French judicial practice by which new laws on recidivism were applied with immediate effect.

The Court confirmed in the *Achour* case that a state is free to increase the penalties for an offence prospectively, without any issue arising under Article 7. Similarly the existence or harsh application of a tariff of possible penalties is not controlled by Article 7, unless it is applied retroactively.[66] Nor does Article 7 prevent a court from choosing to convict a person of an offence carrying a higher penalty instead of one carrying a lower one.[67] Generally, the nature and severity of a 'penalty' is a matter within a state's discretion; considerations of proportionality arise under Articles 2 and 3, not Article 7.

3. GENERAL PRINCIPLES OF LAW EXCEPTION

Article 7(2) provides that Article 7 'shall not prejudice the trial and punishment of any person for any act or omission which, at the time when it was committed, was criminal according to the general principles of law recognised by civilised nations'. The phrase 'general principles of law recognised by civilised nations' is taken word for word from Article 38, Statute of the International Court of Justice, in which it identifies a third formal source of public international law. In that context, and presumably in Article 7, 'general principles of law' are those found in municipal legal systems.

The *travaux préparatoires* indicate that Article 7(2) is intended 'to make it clear that Article 7 does not affect laws which, under the very exceptional circumstances at the end of the Second World War, were passed to punish, inter alia, war crimes',[68] and has been held to apply to laws punishing crimes against humanity committed then also.[69] In *Kolk*

---

[62] *Ecer and Zeyrek v Turkey* 2001-III; 35 EHRR 672. See also *Maktouf and Damjanovic v Bosnis and Herzegovina* hudoc (2013) GC (heavier penalty possible under new law). And see *Gurguchiani v Spain* hudoc (2009).

[63] See *Gabarri Moreno v Spain* hudoc (2003); 39 EHRR 885 (court applied the wrong sentencing rules, to the detriment of the accused: hence no legal basis for the sentence imposed).

[64] *Sud Fondi SRL v Italy* hudoc (2009).

[65] 2006-IV; 45 EHRR 9 GC. See also *Del Rio Prada v Spain* 2013- GC (change in case law on calculation of remission not reasonably foreseeable).

[66] See the facts of *Grant v UK No 12002/86*, 55 DR 218 (1988) (lawful increase in sentence on appeal).

[67] *X v UK No 6679/74*, 3 Digest 31 (1975). Cf *Gillies v UK No 14099/88* hudoc (1989) DA.

[68] *Kononov v Latvia* 2010-; 52 EHRR 663 GC para 186.

[69] *Touvier v France No 2940/95*, 88 DR-A 148 (1997); and *Papon v France (No 2) No 54210/00* 2001-XII DA.

and Kislyiy v Estonia,[70] Article 7(2) was extended to immediate post-war crimes that had a Second World War connection. The case was curious in that the Court held both that a crime against humanity contrary to international law had been committed (the 1949 deportation of civilians to the USSR), so that Article 7(1) applied, and that crimes against humanity fell within Article 7(2). Whereas it had been the Strasbourg practice to dispose of Second World War-related cases solely under Article 7(2), later in *Kononov v Latvia*,[71] the Court just applied Article 7(1). There the applicant was the commander of a Soviet 'Red Partisan' group that, as a reprisal, in 1944 killed Latvian villagers suspected of giving information to the German army, leading to the killing by the latter of the members of another such group. The applicant was convicted under a 1993 Latvian law for a war crime. The Court held, by fourteen votes to three, that the conviction was justified by the 'international law' limb of Article 7(1). On its interpretation of international humanitarian law, the killing of the villagers was a war crime. The three dissenting judges[72] argued, *inter alia*, that Article 7(1) had been infringed because in 1944 it had not been clearly established in international law that an individual could be prosecuted for war crimes, so that the applicant could not reasonably foresee this outcome. In contrast, the Court took the view that, 'having regard to the flagrantly unlawful nature' of the killing of the villagers, 'even the most cursory reflection by the applicant would have indicated that' they 'risked constituting war crimes for which, as commander, he could be held individually and criminally accountable'.[73]

In another recent case under Article 7, in *Korbely v Hungary*,[74] the applicant had been convicted of a crime against humanity by the Hungarian courts, for killing a 'non-combatant' during the 1956 uprising. Disagreeing with the national court's assessment of the facts—which turned upon what the victim intended when he drew a gun—the Grand Chamber held the conviction could not be justified under Article 7(1) as the victim was not a 'non-combatant', as required by international law. The Court did not apply Article 7(2), demonstrating its application to Second World War-related cases only. The case confirmed the Court's willingness to take issue with national courts. Whereas the Court may be at least as well qualified as a national court to interpret international (as opposed to national) law, the fourth instance doctrine may suggest a more cautious approach when it comes to findings of fact. The *Kononov*, *Korbely* and other recent cases show the Court, unavoidably, moving beyond human rights law into the field of international humanitarian law.

---

[70] *No 23052/04* 2006-I DA. See also *Penart v Estonia No 14685/04* hudoc (2006).

[71] Hudoc (2010); 52 EHRR 663 GC. See Malksoo, 105 AJIL 101 (2011). Unlike an ordinary criminal law prosecution, eg for murder, a prosecution under international humanitarian law is not statute barred: see *Kononov v Latvia*.   [72] Judge Costa, joined by Judges Kalaydjieva and Poalelungi.

[73] *Kononov v Latvia* 2010- GC; 52 EHRR 663 para 238 GC.

[74] 2008-; 50 EHRR 1192 GC. It was also 'open to question', para 85, whether there was a crime against humanity, as the national courts had not considered whether the killing was more than an isolated incident.

11

ARTICLES 8–11: GENERAL CONSIDERATIONS

1. INTRODUCTION

There are common features to and connections between Articles 8–11 which justify considering them together. Some of these are formal: Articles 8–11 are constructed in identical form, the first paragraph defining the protected rights, the second laying down the conditions upon which a state might legitimately interfere with the enjoyment of those rights. Others are substantive: Articles 9–11 protect 'freedoms', essentially liberties, against interference by the state with activities which an individual may or may not choose to engage in. However, the Articles are expressed in terms of 'rights' to the various freedoms, language which has enabled the Strasbourg authorities to interpret the protected rights beyond a mere guarantee of non-interference by the government. States have routinely, but unsuccessfully, argued that these are freedoms in the Hohfeldian sense of liberty, requiring only that the state not interfere with the exercise of the freedom by an individual.[1] Article 8 is unique in using the language 'right to respect' for various interests. It has sometimes been suggested that this formulation imposes a less onerous burden on the state but, again, the Strasbourg authorities have taken the opportunity to expand the obligations which flow from these words. The substantive rights protected are both multiple and complex. Four rights are set out in Article 8, three in Article 9, two in Article 11. Certain of the rights are said to 'include' particular rights. For instance, the right to freedom of association in Article 11 includes the right to form and join trade unions. As subsequent chapters show, in general, the Court has extended the content of the protected rights in Articles 8–11, such as including an element of activity in public spaces in 'private life' and regarding environmental protection as an aspect of Article 8 rights. This generous approach has, perhaps, been acceptable to states because of their powers to intervene with the enjoyment of human rights in the second paragraphs of these Articles, albeit powers subject to the supervision of the Court.

Further, as with other rights in the Convention, some of the rights in Articles 8–11 must be read in conjunction with those in other provisions. For instance, the right to respect for family life has, in some of its aspects, close relations with Article 12, on the right to marry and found a family, and with Article 5, Seventh Protocol, which protects the equality of spouses in private law. It may also overlap with the prohibition of inhuman or degrading treatment in Article 3. Finally, some of the language of Articles 8–11 is found elsewhere in the Convention—notions of 'law' in Article 7 or 'lawfulness' in Article 5, the understanding of proportionality in Article 14, for instance—and approaches to interpretation are

---

[1] See, eg, government arguments in *Lingens v Austria* A 103 (1986); 8 EHRR 407 para 37 PC and *Plattform 'Ärzte für das Leben' v Austria*, oral argument, 21 March 1988, Corr/Misc (88) 71, pp 15–17.

pervasive through the Convention provisions. There are, therefore, in some of what follows references to the Court's jurisprudence touching other articles of the Convention.

2. NEGATIVE AND POSITIVE OBLIGATIONS[2]

The classical conception of the fundamental right is that it imposes a duty on the state not to interfere with the enjoyment of the right. So the state must not torture anyone or, in the context of Articles 8–11, interfere, say, with a person's exercise of his freedom of expression by preventing the publication of his writing. Important though it is, this wholly negative view of a state's responsibility towards the enjoyment of civil liberties is inadequate to secure the effective exercise of the individual's freedoms. Thus freedom of expression, if it be restricted to requiring the state to tolerate the enunciation of certain opinions by an individual, will be of little practical consequence if the state is under no obligation to protect a speaker against a hostile group which wishes to prevent the dissemination of the message. The principle that the Convention protects the effective rather than the theoretical enjoyment of rights set out in *Golder v UK*[3] and *Airey v Ireland*[4] is of great importance here.

The Court has not determined any general theory of positive obligations[5] and, accordingly, it will be necessary to consider the question in relation to each particular right. However, it is worth noticing here what levels of positive obligation may be contained in each of the rights in Articles 8–11. In addition to the wholly negative obligation of non-interference already referred to, three other, inter-related, possibilities arise:

  (i)   the obligation of the authorities to take steps to make sure that the enjoyment of the right is effective;[6]

 (ii)   the obligation of the authorities to take steps to make sure that the enjoyment of the right is not interfered with by other private persons;[7] and

(iii)   the obligation of the authorities to take steps to make sure that private persons take steps to ensure the effective enjoyment by other individuals of the right.

It should be borne in mind that Article 13 will apply to positive obligations, so that the enjoyment of any right will be protected by minimum procedural guarantees, although in some cases more will be required of a state (eg, where the positive obligation touches a 'civil right' in the Article 6(1) sense), in some cases less, where the state successfully shows that its powers of interference would be prejudiced by a strict procedural duty.[8] It is a characteristic of positive obligations that the duties they impose are seldom absolute.

---

[2] On negative and positive obligations generally, see Mowbray, *The Development of Positive Obligations under the European Convention on Human Rights by the European Court of Human Rights*, 2004.

[3] A 18 (1975); 1 EHRR 524 para 28 PC.   [4] A 32 (1979); 2 EHRR 305 para 24.

[5] See *VgT Verein gegen Tierfabriken v Switzerland* 2001-VI; 34 EHRR 159 para 46.

[6] See *Golder v UK* A 18 (1975); 1 EHRR 524 PC. nd *Airey v Ireland* A 32 (1979); 2 EHRR 305 This general obligation includes the obligation to have in place laws that grant individuals the legal status, rights, and privileges required to ensure, for example, that their family and private life is properly respected. See, eg, the family law regime for children born out of wedlock required by *Marckx v Belgium* A 31 (1979); 2 EHRR 330 PC. The obligations in (ii) and (iii) can also be subsumed within the general obligation in (i), but are usually and helpfully separated out.

[7] *X and Y v Netherlands* A 91 (1985); 8 EHRR 235 para 32 and *Von Hannover v Germany* 2004-VI; 40 EHRR 1.   [8] Eg, *Leander v Sweden* A 116 (1987); 9 EHRR 433 para 84.

What is required of the state will vary according to the importance of the right and the resources required to be disbursed to meet any positive obligation. States have a 'margin of appreciation' in this regard. While the Strasbourg authorities have interpreted some positive obligations strictly, notably some of the state's obligations under Article 6,[9] more generally, they have considered only whether the state has taken reasonable measures to safeguard the individual's enjoyment of his right.[10] Nor is the state's obligation uniform with respect to the three categories of positive obligation listed above which may arise in connection with a single right. It is most likely that the state will be required to act to protect the exercise of the freedom against interference by other private groups.[11] In contrast, and hardly surprisingly, the obligation on the state to require one private person to provide facilities for another to exercise his right (see (iii) above) is little more than a suggestion in the practice of the Strasbourg authorities.[12]

The European Court deals with individual cases and the facts of each application loom large in the application of the law. In deciding whether or not an individual has the right he claims or whether state interference has justifiably interfered with an acknowledged right, both national decision-makers and the Court have some flexibility to pursue the just solution. As the Court has commonly noted, 'the boundaries between the State's positive and negative obligations under Article 8 do not lend themselves to precise definition',[13] so that the classification of a case as involving one or the other can be difficult. However, the Court has taken the view that this is not such a problem as might be supposed as the 'applicable principles are nonetheless similar. In particular, in both instances regard must be had to the fair balance to be struck between the competing interests.'[14] In view of this, the Court has in some cases proceeded to decide a case without determining on which side of the line the case falls.[15]

Nonetheless, 'bright-line' determinations are sometimes necessary and, at the margins, it may be impossible to avoid hardship in any particular instance.[16] This is especially so where the Court detects a clash of human rights and its solution must prefer one claim to the other.[17]

3. LIMITATIONS

The conditions upon which a state may interfere with the enjoyment of a protected right are set out in elaborate terms in the second paragraphs of Articles 8–11. These paragraphs have a common structure but differ in detail.[18] Limitations are allowed if they are 'in accordance with the law' or 'prescribed by law' and are 'necessary in a democratic society' for the protection of one of the objectives set out in the second paragraph.[19] The Court's

---

[9] See, eg, *Zimmermann and Steiner v Switzerland* A 66 (1983); 6 EHRR 17 para 29.

[10] See, eg, *Plattform 'Ärzte für das Leben' v Austria No 10126/82*, 44 DR 65 (1985) and *Rees v UK* A 106 (1986); 9 EHRR 56 paras 38–45 PC.

[11] Eg, *Young, James and Webster v UK* A 44 (1981); 4 EHRR 38 paras 55–6 PC and *Gustafsson v Sweden* 1996-II; 22 EHRR 409 GC.   [12] *X v UK No 4515/70*, 38 CD 86 at 88 (1971).

[13] *SH and Others v Austria* hudoc (2011) para 87 GC.   [14] *SH and Others v Austria*.

[15] See, eg, *Mouvement raëlien suisse v Switzerland* 2012-; 56 EHRR 482 GC.

[16] See, eg, *Pretty v UK* 2002-III; 35 EHRR 1 para 76 (blanket prohibition of assisted suicide not disproportionate interference with right to respect for private life).

[17] See, eg, *Evans v UK* 2007-I; 46 EHRR 728 GC.

[18] Eg, Article 8(2) alone permits restrictions for 'economic well-being'.

[19] There are further special powers of limitation in the final sentences of Articles 10(1) and 11(2).

usual practice is to consider those elements separately and in the order 'law', 'objective', and 'necessity'.

I. 'IN ACCORDANCE WITH THE LAW'/'PRESCRIBED BY LAW'

On the face of it, there is a significant difference between the formulation in Article 8(2), 'in accordance with the law' and the words used in Articles 9(2)–11(2), 'prescribed by law'. The first could carry the meaning 'not unlawful', whereas the second could imply that some specific authorization is required. However, it was established in *Malone v UK*[20] that both formulations are to be read in the same way.[21] They mean that, as a minimum, the respondent state must point to some specific legal rule or regime which authorizes the interfering act it seeks to justify.[22] The rule need not be a rule of domestic law but may be a rule of international law or Community law so long as it purports to authorize the interference.[23] It may consist of a whole legal regime regulating the area of activity, including rules made by a delegated rule-making authority[24] and rules from more than one legal order.[25] If a state does indicate the legal basis for its action, the Court is reluctant in the extreme to accede to arguments that the national law has not been properly interpreted or applied by the national courts.[26]

Domestic legality is a necessary condition but it is not sufficient. The Court has said that the notion of 'law' is autonomous.[27] The Court has taken a wide view of what delegated powers are capable of generating 'law'[28] in a Convention sense and has recognized that unwritten law, most importantly judge-made law, will satisfy its understanding of 'law'.[29] Reliance on the law of European Community[30] or international law[31] will be adequate, always assuming the rule in question otherwise satisfies the Convention notion of 'law'.

It is conceivable that the notion of 'law' here could include the element of propriety or absence of arbitrariness in terms of purpose which the Court has ascribed to it in

---

[20] B 67 (1983–5) paras 118–19 Com Rep. Cf oral argument, *Malone v UK*, pp 201–3.

[21] A 82 (1984); 7 EHRR 14 para 66 PC. The French text of each is identical: '*prévues par la loi*'.

[22] *Silver and Others v UK* A 61 (1983); 5 EHRR 347 para 86.

[23] *Groppera Radio AG and Others v Switzerland* A 173 (1990); 12 EHRR 321 para 68 PC; para 153 Com Rep.

[24] *Barthold v Germany* A 90 (1985); 7 EHRR 383 paras 45–6.

[25] *Groppera Radio AG and Others v Switzerland* A 173 (1990); 12 EHRR 321 paras 65–8 PC.

[26] *Bosphorus Airways v Ireland* 2005-VI; 42 EHRR 1 para 143 GC. But see *MM v Netherlands* hudoc (2003); 39 EHRR 414 para 45, where the domestic court was held to have misinterpreted 'interference by a public authority', so making a telephone-tap outside the authority of national law, and *Foxley v UK* hudoc (2000); 31 EHRR 637 para 35, where the Court held that a national official had acted beyond her powers under domestic law and so an interference with the applicant's Article 8 right was 'not in accordance with the law'. In *Malone v UK* A 82 (1984); 7 EHRR 14 para 69 PC, the Court preferred the judgment of the English High Court in *Malone v Commissioner of Police* [1979] 2 All ER 620 Ch D, to the government's account of the position in national law.   [27] *Sunday Times v UK (No 1)* A 30 (1979); 2 EHRR 245 para 49 PC.

[28] *Barthold v Germany* A 90 (1985); 7 EHRR 383 para 46. A professional association's rules were 'law', being traditionally regarded as made by 'parliamentary delegation' and monitored by the state.

[29] *Sunday Times v UK (No 1)* A 30 (1979); 2 EHRR 245 para 47 PC.

[30] *Bosphorus Airways v Ireland* 2005-VI; 42 EHRR 1 paras 143–8 GC (a case under Protocol 1, Article 1). The international law obligations of states may be relevant to the elaboration of states' duties under the Convention: eg, *Ignaccolo-Zenide v Romania* 2000-I; 31 EHRR 212 paras 95, 101–13 and *Iglesias Gil and AUI v Spain* 2003-V; 40 EHRR 55 paras 47–61, especially para 51, or the assessment of the legality of an interference with an individual's rights: eg, *Bianchi v Switzerland* hudoc (2006) (all referring to the Hague Convention on Civil Aspects of International Child Abduction).

[31] Eg, *Slivenko v Latvia* 2003-X; 39 EHRR 490 paras 104–9 GC.

other contexts, such as Article 5, but this is unlikely to be of consequence for it is hard to see how a manifestly arbitrary law could ever be 'necessary in a democratic society'. However, the Court has introduced the notion of arbitrariness in a different sense into its idea of 'law'. In *Sunday Times v UK (No 1)*,[32] the Court added two further criteria for a rule to be a 'law':

> Firstly, the law must be adequately accessible: the citizen must be able to have an indication that is adequate in the circumstances of the legal rules applicable to a given case. Secondly, a norm cannot be regarded as a 'law' unless it is formulated with sufficient precision to enable the citizen to regulate his conduct.

These are further guarantees against substantively arbitrary rules. Accessibility of course requires that the texts be available to an applicant,[33] but it is accepted that understanding of the texts may require access to appropriate advice.[34] If texts or rules are relied on to establish the foreseeability of the law, for instance, to supplement the wide language of the primary, published rule, then they also must be available to the applicant. In *Silver and Others v UK*,[35] the government conceded that some restrictions on prisoners' correspondence imposed on the basis of unpublished prison orders and instructions that supplemented the relevant delegated legislation could not be used to establish that interferences had been 'in accordance with law'. In *Autronic AG v Switzerland*,[36] the Court allowed that the horrendously complicated regime which regulated international broadcasting was sufficiently accessible to those whose activities as broadcasters were regulated by it, with proper advice. The same is true about the common law, the true purport of which is available only through the medium of legal advice.[37]

The meaning of 'sufficient precision' is more difficult to ascertain. Wholly general, unfettered discretion will not satisfy the Convention, no matter what the formal validity of the delegating rule, the more particularly if the exercise of the delegated powers may be secret. Good examples of this are the judgments of the Court in *Kruslin v France*[38] and *Huvig v France*.[39] The Court accepted that there was in French law a legal basis for secret telephone-tapping by the police to be found in the Code of Criminal Procedure and the case law interpreting it. However, the Court was not satisfied with the 'quality' of the French law. In the *Kruslin* case,[40] the Court said:

> Tapping and other forms of interception of telephone conversations represent a serious interference with private life and must accordingly be based on a 'law' that is particularly precise. It is essential to have clear, detailed rules on the subject, especially as the technology available for use is continually becoming more sophisticated.

---

[32] A 30 (1979); 2 EHRR 245 para 49 PC. See also *Rekvényi v Hungary* 1999-III; 30 EHRR 519 paras 34–8 GC, indicating that imprecision in constitutional rules may be compensated for by more detailed regulation at the level of ordinary law.

[33] *Silver and Others v UK* A 61 (1983); 5 EHRR 347 paras 87–8.

[34] *Sunday Times v UK (No 1)* A 30 (1979); 2 EHRR 245 PC and *Markt intern Verlag v Germany* A 165 (1989); 12 EHRR 161 para 30 PC ('commercial operators and their advisers').

[35] A 61 (1983); 5 EHRR 347 paras 87–8 and 91.

[36] A 178 (1990); 12 EHRR 485 paras 55 and 59 PC.

[37] The Court accepts that there may be a wide division of opinion about what the common law is without that resulting in inaccessibility of the law but that wholly new developments in the common law may not satisfy the test.

[38] A 176-A (1990); 12 EHRR 547. [39] A 176-B (1990); 12 EHRR 528.

[40] A 176-A (1990); 12 EHRR 547 para 33.

The Court was not satisfied that the Code of Criminal Procedure met this test. Amongst other deficiencies, the law neither identified the persons whose telephones might be tapped nor imposed any limits of time during which the process could be carried out. The test, the Court had said in *Silver and Others v UK*,[41] was that where a law conferred a discretion, it must also indicate with sufficient clarity the limits of that discretion. In *NF v Italy*,[42] the Court held that a national rule which provided for disciplinary measures against any judge 'who failed to fulfil his duties' did not make it foreseeable that membership of the freemasons was incompatible with the proper discharge of the judicial function and, accordingly, since action had been taken against the judge, there had been a breach of Article 11.

Other factors may serve to relax the degree of precision which is required of a national law. In *Müller v Switzerland*,[43] the Court acknowledged that obscenity laws could not be framed with 'absolute precision', not least because of the need to keep the law in accord with the prevailing views of society. It has taken a similar position about laws protecting against restraint of trade.[44] Since the exercise of the state's 'margin of appreciation' will often involve the promulgation of various kinds of legal rules, the Court takes a generous view about what regulations a state may rely on. In *Leyla Şahin v Turkey*,[45] the Court accepted that the phrase 'according to the law' could embrace both the constitution and the regulations of individual universities, as well as ordinary legislation—the case concerned dress codes as a condition for admission. The meaning of widely drawn legal texts and rules of common law may be worked out and developed by courts without affecting their quality as 'law'. Nonetheless, there is a limit to this process. In *Sunday Times v UK (No 1)*,[46] the applicants argued that the House of Lords had introduced a novel principle into the English common law of contempt, which they could not have anticipated and, accordingly, could not have based their conduct upon. The Court rejected this claim and held:

> the applicants were able to foresee, to a degree that was reasonable in the circumstances, a risk that publication of the draft article might fall foul of the principle.

The line between the reasonably foreseeable and the wholly novel is not an easy one to draw. The difficulties of the foreseeability test can be illustrated by reference to *Open Door and Dublin Well Women Centre v Ireland*.[47] Injunctions against the applicants had been issued by the national court forbidding them from circulating in Ireland information about the possibility of abortion outside Ireland. The injunctions had been issued to enforce a constitutional amendment which provided:

> The State acknowledges the right to life of the unborn and, with due regard to the equal right to life of the mother, guarantees in its laws to respect, and, as far as practicable, by its laws to defend and vindicate that right.

---

[41] A 61 (1983); 5 EHRR 347 para 80. See also *Leander v Sweden* A 116 (1987); 9 EHRR 433 paras 50–7.

[42] 2001-IX; 35 EHRR 106 para 31. For other Article 8 cases in which the 'precision' or foreseeability requirement was not met, see, eg, *Hasan v Bulgaria* hudoc (2007) and *MM v UK* hudoc (2012).

[43] A 133 (1988); 13 EHRR 212 para 29.

[44] *Barthold v Germany* A 90 (1985); 7 EHRR 383 para 47. See also *Markt intern Verlag v Germany* A 165 (1985); 12 EHRR 161 para 30 PC.   [45] 2005-XI; 44 EHRR 99 para 88 GC.

[46] A 30 (1979); 2 EHRR 245 para 52 PC. See also *Observer and Guardian v UK* A 216 (1991); 14 EHRR 153 para 53 PC. Cf *Kruslin v France* A 176-A (1990); 12 EHRR 547.

[47] A 246-A (1992); 15 EHRR 244 para 52 Com Rep.

The applicants argued that the language of the amendment did not clearly reach their activities and that it was in any case unforeseeable that the courts would issue injunctions to prevent the commission of constitutional torts. A majority of the Commission took the view that the 'prescribed by law' requirement had been infringed because a lawyer could reasonably have concluded that no illegal act was being committed, particularly because there had been no previous attempts to take enforcement action since the passing of the amendment. It said that 'in such a vital area' the law requires 'particular precision'. Although the Court conceded that these arguments were not without their cogency, it took the view that in the light of the very high threshold of protection given to the unborn in Irish law, it was foreseeable that the courts would use their powers against the applicants, a conclusion reinforced by legal advice given to one of the applicants to that effect.[48] An example of a national rule which was held to lack the substantive precision required by the Court for it to be 'law' was the power of an English magistrate to bind over a defendant to be of good behaviour. The Court said that the vagueness of what was required of the applicants during the period for which they were bound over did not satisfy the requirement of providing foreseeability about what was expected of them.[49] Furthermore, the Court will not allow the nature of the objective to which the interference is directed to justify unfettered executive discretion under the guise of a widely framed law. In *Al-Nashif v Bulgaria*,[50] a case involving deportation on national security grounds, the Court said that 'the law must indicate the scope of any such discretion conferred on the competent authorities and the manner of its exercise with sufficient clarity, having regard to the legitimate aim of the measure in question, to give the individual adequate protection against arbitrary interference'. The Court reaffirmed this case law in *Gorzelik and Others v Poland*.[51] The principles apply outside security cases. A discretionary power, unconfined in its terms, even if formally subject to judicial scrutiny, will not pass the foreseeability test.[52]

II. LEGITIMATE AIMS

A respondent state must identify the objective(s) of its interference with an individual's protected right. Applicants have frequently challenged the aims asserted by the state as being no more than rationalizations of limitations imposed for quite different and impermissible purposes.[53] However, the breadth of most of the grounds for interference is so wide—for example, 'the protection of public order', 'the interests of national security', 'the prevention of disorder or crime'[54]—that the state can usually make a plausible case

---

[48] *Open Door and Dublin Well Women Centre v Ireland*, para 60 PC.

[49] *Hashman and Harrup v UK* 1999-VIII; 30 EHRR 241 paras 36–42 GC. Cf *Steel and Others v UK* 1998-VII; 28 EHRR 603.

[50] Hudoc (2002); 36 EHRR 655 paras 119–23. And see *Association for European Integration and Human Rights and Ekimdzhiev v Bulgaria* hudoc (2007) paras 74–94.

[51] 2004-I; 40 EHRR 76 paras 64–71 GC.

[52] *Ostrovar v Moldova* hudoc (2005); 44 EHRR 378 paras 94 and 105–8.

[53] Eg, *Campbell v UK* A 233 (1992); 15 EHRR 137 paras 39–41, where the applicant prisoner alleged that the real reason for opening letters to him from his lawyer was to discover their contents. The Court accepted the government's claim that the interference was 'for the prevention of disorder or crime'. In *Vereinigung Bildender Künstler v Austria* hudoc (2007); 47 EHRR 189 para 31, the Court refused to accept the government's claim that an interference with the applicant's Article 10 right was for 'the protection of morals', rather than a politician's rights or interests.

[54] In *Groppera Radio AG and Others v Switzerland* A 173 (1990); 12 EHRR 321 para 70 PC and *Autronic AG v Switzerland* A 178 (1990); 12 EHRR 485 para 59 PC, the Court accepted that prevention of disorder in the telecommunications regime was a legitimate aim within Article 10(2).

that it did have a good reason for interfering with the right. The applicant's claim is thus essentially that the reason given is not the 'real' reason, an allegation tantamount to bad faith on the part of the government. Not surprisingly, the Strasbourg authorities have not been willing to accept such a claim easily, but there have been cases where it has succeeded.[55] Identification of the aim will be of importance, because an interference which might be appropriate to one aim will not necessarily be appropriate to another. There have been cases where the Court has not pursued this matter as vigorously as it might.[56] States sometimes cite more than one aim as the purpose for which they limit the enjoyment of a right. If the Court is satisfied that the measures are necessary for the protection of one of these aims, it has no need to go on and consider the others pleaded by the state, the absence of a violation having already been established. In the *Open Door* case,[57] the Court collapsed the alternative aims cited by the state—the protection of morals and the protection of the rights of others—into one enquiry: were the restrictions on the giving of advice about abortion necessary for the protection of morals? Although it found that the restrictions could properly be seen on the facts of the case as being for the protection of morals, it found a breach of Article 10 because they were disproportionate and hence not 'necessary'. Although this approach enabled the Court to avoid a difficult issue—was the unborn child an 'other' whose rights the state could protect?—it may be doubted whether the Court did full justice to the government's arguments.

III. 'NECESSARY IN A DEMOCRATIC SOCIETY': THE MARGIN OF APPRECIATION

It is not enough that a state has *some* reason for interfering with an individual's right under Articles 8(2)–11(2) for one of the appropriate aims. It must show that the interference is 'necessary in a democratic society', a phrase heavy with uncertainty. In *Handyside v UK*,[58] the Court explained the meaning of 'necessary' as follows:

> The Court notes...that, while the adjective 'necessary'...is not synonymous with 'indispensable', neither has it the flexibility of such expressions as 'admissible', 'ordinary', 'useful', 'reasonable' or 'desirable'.

Having thus excluded excessively strict or generous interpretations of the term 'necessary', the Court has since settled upon a requirement of proportionality. In *Olsson v Sweden (No 1)*,[59] it stated:

> According to the Court's established case-law, the notion of necessity implies that an interference corresponds to a pressing social need and, in particular, that it is proportionate to the legitimate aim pursued.

In assessing whether an interference is 'proportionate to the legitimate aim' to which the government claims that it responds, the Court and formerly the Commission have relied on the 'margin of appreciation' doctrine, which they concede to states when their

---

[55] Eg, *Moscow Branch of the Salvation Army v Russia* 2006-XI; 44 EHRR 912 para 97. In some cases the Court has left the question open: see, eg, *Tănase v Moldova* 2010-; 53 EHRR 744 para 170 GC (an Article 3, First Protocol case).

[56] *Barfod v Denmark* A 149 (1989); 13 EHRR 493 paras 30–6 and *Observer and Guardian v UK* A 216 (1991); 14 EHRR 153 paras 55–6, 69 PC.   [57] A 246-A (1992); 15 EHRR 244 para 67 PC.

[58] A 24 (1976); 1 EHRR 737 para 48 PC.   [59] A 130 (1988); 11 EHRR 259 para 67 PC.

institutions make the initial assessment of whether the interference is justified. The classic formulation of the doctrine is found in the passage from *Handyside v UK* in Chapter 1, section 4.VII quoted earlier.[60] It is worth emphasizing that the 'margin of appreciation' is a power conceded to the state.[61] It envisages that that power will be exercised in the first instance by organs of the states properly addressing the various elements of the Convention relevant to determining the content of a particular right and assessing the justification given for interfering with it. The function of the European Court is to see that the state has not exceeded its power of appreciation. In this connection, the Court will look for evidence that a process of balancing has taken place.[62] In principle, the doctrine of a 'margin of appreciation', which applies in other areas of the Convention too, is not a doctrine of judicial deference to the national decision, for the Convention authorities may carry out their own fact-finding and do apply the Convention law for themselves. Yet they have declined the role of a fully-fledged appeal mechanism from the national decision. Instead, the Court has said that the role of the Convention in protecting human rights is 'subsidiary' to the roles of the national legal systems.[63] This allows for a diversity of systems for the protection of human rights and even for different conceptions of the rights themselves and acknowledges the superiority of the organs of a state in fact-finding and in the assessment of what the local circumstances demand by way of limitation of rights.[64] However, the danger that excessive respect for national decision-making will result in the swamping of the individual right by national determinations of the public interest must be borne in mind.[65]

Putting the burden on the government to demonstrate a pressing social need for the interference preserves the superior character of the protected rights. On the other hand, it introduces a new dilemma for the Court: how is it to make its decisions in a principled manner so that its judgments do not appear to the states as the substitute of one discretion for another? The language of the Convention is so broad that the text alone will seldom dictate solutions, though it should be noticed that there are minor differences in the way Articles 8(2)–10(2) are drafted which allows differences of approach to particular questions.[66] The Court has adopted a variety of principles, which are considered in

---

[60] A 24 (1976); 1 EHRR 737 paras 48–50 PC. Cf *Sunday Times v UK (No 1)* A 30 (1979); 2 EHRR 245 para 59 PC. Both of these are Article 10 cases; the Court's pronouncements apply to Articles 8–11 generally.

[61] On the margin of appreciation doctrine, see the literature cited in Ch 1, section VII.

[62] See *Hirst v UK (No 2)* 2005-IX; 42 EHRR 849 GC (a case under Protocol 1, Article 3), where the Court noted that neither the UK Parliament (para 79) nor the UK courts (para 80) had carried out any balancing exercise between the prisoners' right to vote and the protection of any public interest. *Hirst (No 2)* was followed in *Dickson v UK* 2007-V; 46 EHRR 927 para 84 GC, finding a violation where the formulation of an executive policy (about access to artificial insemination for a prisoner and his wife) had not involved any serious balancing of the rights and competing interests, nor allowed for individuated decision-making where that could be done on a case-by-case basis.

[63] *Handyside v UK* A 24 (1976); 1 EHRR 737 para 48 PC.

[64] *Müller v Switzerland* A 133 (1988); 13 EHRR 212 para 35. There is a strong functional justification for the margin of appreciation as well. The Court could not, as a practical matter, take on the intensive review of all cases which might reach it—the margin of appreciation puts much of the fact-finding and the assessment of the factors within Articles 8(2)–11(2) in the hands of national decision-makers. For the argument that a distinction should be drawn between the substantive (identifying the protected rights) and the structural (determining the character of the judicial review to be exercised by the Court) uses of the 'margin of appreciation', see Letsas, *A Theory of Interpretation of the European Convention on Human Rights*, 2007, pp 80–98.

[65] Mahoney, 19 HRLJ 1 (1998).

[66] The language of Article 10(2) is more open-ended in ascribing powers to the state to interfere with the protected right than the other provisions—Article 8(2): 'There shall be no interference ... *except such as is* ...', Article 9(2): 'Freedom to manifest one's religion...shall be subject *only* to such limitations ...', Article 11(2): 'No restrictions shall be placed on the exercise of these rights *other than* ...' (emphasis added).

the following paragraphs, to give some structure to its judgments in which it considers the exercise of the margin of appreciation by states. For example, it looks to the law and practice of other states parties and will allow a greater margin of appreciation in the absence of consensus. While they supplement the general language of the Convention, it is important not to ascribe to these principles too great a weight: they are not rules and must be applied as a whole to each case with which the Court is faced.[67]

a. The importance of the protected right

When a state claims to be interfering with a right 'to protect the rights of others', those rights may be other human rights under the Convention. The Court has identified some human rights or some aspects of some human rights as being of more importance than others. For instance, in *Dudgeon v UK*,[68] which concerned the criminality of private, consensual, adult homosexual activity, the Court said:

> The present case concerns a most intimate aspect of private life. Accordingly, there must exist particularly serious reasons before interferences on the part of public authorities can be legitimate for the purposes of [Article 8(2)].

In *Lingens v Austria*,[69] the Court stressed the freedom of the press as a particularly significant aspect of the 'right to receive and impart information and ideas'. More generally concerning freedom of expression, the Court has allowed a wider margin of appreciation for interferences with commercial speech than it has for political speech.[70] In *Campbell v UK*,[71] the Court confirmed a line of authorities which determined that a prisoner's correspondence with his legal advisor was of such importance as to entitle it to greater protection against interference than his correspondence in general. Where a strong right is invoked by the applicant, there will be a demanding burden on the state to demonstrate the pressing social need for limiting his enjoyment of it. The Court has emphasized the importance of the right to respect for private life, including its social dimension, in the light of developments of technologies which allow for the collection and storage of information about individuals.[72]

b. The character of 'democratic society'

While an interference with a protected right may be 'necessary in a democratic society', the nature of democratic society may be a constraint on the justification of some forms of interference.[73] In *Dudgeon v UK*,[74] the Court spoke of 'tolerance and broad-mindedness' as two of the 'hallmarks' of democratic society, characteristics which inclined against the justifiability of interferences to protect the intolerance and narrow-mindedness of others, however widely and strongly felt. The importance of political expression derives from its role in a properly functioning democracy.[75] In *Klass and Others v Germany*,[76]

---

[67] See Delmas-Marty, in Delmas-Marty, ed, *The European Convention for the Protection of Human Rights: International Protection Versus National Restrictions*, 1992, p 319.

[68] A 45 (1981); 4 EHRR 149 para 52 PC.

[69] A 103 (1986); 8 EHRR 407 para 42 PC. Cf *Selistö v Finland* hudoc (2004); 42 EHRR 144 and *Bodrožić and Vujin v Serbia* hudoc (2009).

[70] *Mouvement raëlien suisse v Switzerland* 2012-; 56 EHRR 482 GC. See also *Animal Defenders International v UK* 2013-; 57 EHRR 607 GC.

[71] A 233 (1992); 15 EHRR 137 paras 46–7.

[72] *Von Hannover v Germany* 2004-VI; 40 EHRR 1 para 70.

[73] See Jacot-Guillarmod, in *Democracy and Human Rights*, Thessaloniki Colloquy Proc, 1990, pp 43–66, especially pp 57–63.   [74] A 45 (1981); 4 EHRR 149 para 53 PC.

[75] *Barthold v Germany* A 90 (1985); 7 EHRR 383 para 58.   [76] A 28 (1978); 2 EHRR 214 para 42 PC.

the Court referred to the dangers of destroying democracy under the guise of trying to preserve it, so requiring the strictest supervision of the justification for interferences with rights which removed the normal protections of the law against abuses of power by the authorities. Freedom of association, particularly for trade unions and professional bodies, was likewise important to democratic societies to protect plural centres of power and influence,[77] though it has to be said that until recently the Court had not given strong protection to the claims by trade unions to enjoy particular rights. These foundational features of the Court's conception of democratic society reinforce the special weight to be given to individual rights when assessing the legitimacy of an interference with a particular right. The Court has emphasized the significance of secularism as a condition for the tolerance which characterizes democratic societies[78] (though, at the same time its treatment of Article 9 rights to religious freedom within democratic societies has been quite favourable to those claiming such rights).[79] At the same time, given the 'wealth of historical, cultural and political differences within Europe…it is for each State to mould its own democratic vision' and accordingly be allowed 'some discretion' as to what the safeguarding of its particular democratic order requires.[80]

c. The European and international consensus

There might be little objection to the features isolated by the Court as characteristic of democratic society. However, that is in part because of their generality. If more precise guidance is to be obtained as to what is or is not necessary in a democratic society to interfere with protected rights, then the Court needs to look elsewhere for evidence one way or the other if it is not to be accused of simply substituting its judgment for the judgment of the state. One of the devices to which it has had recourse is to search for a 'European standard' among the national laws of the parties to the Convention.[81] It is an approach which requires some caution. Unless the case is particularly stark, the comparative investigation is likely to be complicated and will often be inconclusive.[82] Nonetheless, a European-wide standard of toleration may sometimes be established[83] and the burden on the state to justify its exceptional interference contrary to the consensus is increased. This may be particularly useful where a developing consensus indicates a clear trend to isolate the state maintaining an interference, the unacceptability of which has gradually become recognized elsewhere. An example of this is *Marckx v Belgium*,[84] where the Court found that the great majority of the Council of Europe states acknowledged the impermissibility of discrimination between the legitimate child and the illegitimate child in the law of affiliation. In the cases dealing with the criminalization of male homosexuality, the Court reinforced its findings that such an interference with an individual's right to respect for his private life may not be justified by noting 'the marked changes' in the laws of national states.[85] A strong consensus may also defeat an argument that a state, although

---

[77] *Le Compte, Van Leuven, De Meyere v Belgium* A 43 (1981); 4 EHRR 1 para 65 PC.

[78] *Refah Partisi (The Welfare Party) v Turkey* 2003-II; 37 EHRR 1 GC and *Leyla Şahin v Turkey* 2005-XI; 44 EHRR 99 GC.   [79] See Ch 10.

[80] *Animal Defenders International v UK* 2013-; 57 EHRR 607 para 111 GC. Cf *Ždanoka v Latvia* 2006-IV; 45 EHRR 478 GC.   [81] See the literature cited in Ch 1, section 4.IV.

[82] See, eg, *Evans v UK* 2007-I; 46 EHRR 728 GC (no 'uniform practice' on IVF treatment).

[83] See, eg, *Dudgeon v UK* A 45 (1981); 4 EHRR 149 PC (criminalization of homosexual acts). Sometimes the Court is presented with evidence of a consensus but finds no need to rely on it: *Lingens v Austria* A 103 (1986); 8 EHRR 407 PC. On the relevance of a lack of consensus in different jurisdictions within the respondent state, see the *Handyside* and *Dudgeon* cases.   [84] A 31 (1979); 2 EHRR 330 para 41 PC.

[85] See *Dudgeon v UK* A 45 (1981); 4 EHRR 149 PC.

alone, is in the vanguard in adopting new scientific techniques. Thus in *S and Marper v UK*,[86] the respondent state argued that it was leading the way in legislating for the indefinite retention of fingerprint and DNA material of any person of any age suspected of any recordable offence. However, the Court held that the legislation was an unjustified restriction on the right to respect for private life in Article 8: given that there was a 'strong consensus' among the Convention parties for setting limits on the retention of such data and the respondent state was alone in having no limitations at all, only a 'narrow' margin of appreciation applied.

Being able to rely on a consensus among the laws of the European states is especially valuable to the Court if it is confronted with a fundamental moral issue where a solution favouring one outcome over another will appear to the disappointed side to depend entirely on the premise from which the argument starts—abortion, euthanasia, recreational use of drugs, and homosexuality are among the questions of this kind. The Strasbourg authorities have shown themselves adept at avoiding taking them head-on. However, they cannot always be side-stepped. *Marckx v Belgium*, dealing with illegitimacy, and *Dudgeon v UK*, concerning adult homosexual relations, are examples where the Court has been able to rely on the consensus. To the contrary, where there is no consensus, the Court is the more likely to defer to the choice made by the state, unless there is a textual basis on which the Court may rely. It rejected an application of a woman that the national requirement of consent of both partners for the use of frozen gametes in IVF be dispensed with when the woman became unable to have natural children because of medical treatment some time after the partners had separated. One reason for this, despite the strong interest of the woman in being able to proceed without the man's consent, was the absence of a 'uniform European approach'.[87] On the other hand, the Court relied on a textual basis to find for the compatibility of Ireland's law excluding divorce, even in the face of a European standard to the contrary.[88] For some time, the Court had refused to interfere with the UK's position that it was under no obligation to issue a revised, post-operative birth certificate to a transsexual in his/her new gender, finding that there was no European consensus in the various applicants' favour. It abandoned this stance in *Goodwin (Christine) v UK*, in language suggesting that the 'consensus' which would be determinative could be sought on a wider basis than that which might (or might not) be found in Europe. It said:

> [It] attaches less importance to the lack of evidence of a common European approach to the resolution of the legal and practical problems posed, than to the clear and uncontested evidence of a continuing international trend in favour not only of increased social acceptance of transsexuals but of legal recognition of the new sexual identity of post-operative transsexuals.[89]

In similar vein, in *Demir and Baykara v Turkey*,[90] in the context of trade union rights, the Court stated:

> The Court, in defining the meaning of terms and notions in the text of the Convention, can and must take into account elements of international law other than the Convention, the interpretation of such elements by competent organs, and the practice of European

---

86 2008-; 48 EHRR 1169 para 112 GC.
87 *Evans v UK* 2007-I; 46 EHRR 728 paras 79, 90 GC.
88 *Johnston v Ireland* A 112 (1986); 9 EHRR 203 paras 51–4 PC.
89 *Goodwin (Christine) v UK* 2002-VI; 35 EHRR 447 para 85 GC.
90 2008-; 48 EHRR 1272 paras 85–6 GC.

States reflecting their common values. The consensus emerging from specialised international instruments and from the practice of Contracting States may constitute a relevant consideration for the Court when it interprets the provisions of the Convention in specific cases...In this context, it is not necessary for the respondent State to have ratified the entire collection of instruments that are applicable in respect of the precise subject matter of the case concerned. It will be sufficient for the Court that the relevant international instruments denote a continuous evolution in the norms and principles applied in international law or in the domestic law of the majority of member States of the Council of Europe and show, in a precise area, that there is common ground in modern societies.

This conclusion is not without its difficulties. It is hard to see how a 'clear and uncontested' international trend would not have a European component to it and, in every case, the inquiry required of applicants and states will be a demanding one, especially on applicants seeking to establish the international standard. Even establishing a European consensus is a formidable proposition in a Convention system of now nearly fifty states, the traditions of which are more diverse than they were when the Court first seized on the idea of a European standard as an element in the interpretation of the Convention. It has been suggested that the Court is less sympathetic to interferences based on what it perceives to be laws and practices influenced by the communist pasts of states admitted since 1989.[91] It may be, then, that it is easier to disregard certain deviations from the European consensus on the same grounds.

d. The interest to be protected by the interference

The weight of the interest to be protected

The reason for some interferences with rights is to protect the enjoyment of other rights protected by the Convention. This is a possibility which occurs with increased frequency as the Court's understanding of the content of rights expands. Freedom of expression may be limited in favour of the right to a fair trial[92] or to take into account the right of others to exercise their freedom of religion.[93] In these cases, the interest which is sought to be protected is a strong one and usually an accommodation must be reached between the two competing human rights, when the initial assessment by the state of how that accommodation should be made will carry great weight. The problem is a feature of disputes about rights to respect for family life, especially the resolution of conflicting claims between parents and children or between each parent about their children.[94]

In *Von Hannover v Germany (No 2)*,[95] the Court indicated the approach that should be followed in cases of conflict of rights (which, in one form or another, will always raise questions about the positive obligations of the state). The applicants in that case claimed that their right to respect for private life (Article 8) had been violated because the German courts had refused to grant an injunction to prevent intrusive press photography, whereas the publishers claimed to be acting in their right of freedom of expression (Article 10). German law and the German courts had addressed the conflict between the two human rights, seeking an appropriate balance between them, which, on the facts of the applicants'

---

[91] Sweeney, 21 Conn JIL 1 (2005).
[92] *Observer and Guardian v UK* A 216 (1991); 14 EHRR 153 PC.
[93] *Otto-Preminger-Institut v Austria* A 295-A (1994); 19 EHRR 34 para 47.
[94] Choudhry and Fenwick, 25 OJLS 453 (2005).
[95] Hudoc (2012); 55 EHRR 388 paras 106–7 GC. See also *Axel Springer AG v Germany* hudoc (2012); 55 EHRR 183 GC.

complaint, denied them protection in respect of one of the photographs. The fact that the protection of a countervailing right is the object of the state's interference is relevant to the application of the general principle that limitation powers (whether in this case those benefiting the press (Article 8(2)) or those restricting it (Article 10(2)) should be construed narrowly. Departing from this principle, the Court stated that in cases in which the right to respect for private life is to be balanced against the right to freedom of expression, 'the outcome of the application should not, in theory, vary according to whether it has been lodged' under Article 8 or Article 10. This was because 'as a matter of principle these rights deserve equal respect'. The Court then spelt out a list of criteria relevant to the balancing exercise and, referring to an approach which it now commonly uses, indicated that where 'the balancing exercise has been undertaken by the national authorities in conformity with' these criteria, 'the Court would require strong reasons to substitute its view for that of the domestic courts'.

Two further comments may be appropriate. If even some interferences in the interest of protecting fundamental rights, as the 'rights of others' may not always be within the margin of appreciation, then it would follow that no other of the interests set out in the second paragraphs of Articles 8–11 are of overwhelming weight, for, if that were the case, the rights protected by the Convention would lose their fundamental status. Finally, it should be noted that it is not so much the denominated interest but the actual situation in which it is invoked which is important[96]—action for the prevention of crime may be directed against homicide or parking offences: the weight of each compared with the right sought to be limited is not the same.

The objectivity of the interest

In *Sunday Times v UK (No 1)*,[97] the Court suggested that the greater the prospect of obtaining an objective understanding of the content of the interest sought to be protected, the narrower the state's margin to determine what interferences are necessary to protect it. The Court drew a contrast between the relative objectivity of 'maintaining the authority and impartiality of the judiciary' and the 'protection of morals'. The former, objectively ascertainable,[98] left a narrower margin to the state than the latter, which was subject to a wide notion of what 'morals' were and, therefore, what was necessary to protect them. The actual example chosen by the Court has been challenged,[99] but the principle seems well established. It has been made to carry considerable weight in upholding limitations of individual rights. *Müller v Switzerland*[100] is an example. The Court held that the idea of 'morals' might be determined by the opinions within even a narrow locality, let alone from state to state. However, it has not gone so far as accepting states' claims that questions of morals are so subjective that the Court should simply defer to their conclusions. The Court's jurisprudence on the standard of objectivity is weak. It has easily found ways of avoiding its consequences if it deems it desirable to do so.[101] The Court shows no inclination to abandon reliance on the objectivity standard as an indication of the reach of the

---

[96] *Handyside v UK* A 24 (1976); 1 EHRR 737 para 50 PC.   [97] A 30 (1979); 2 EHRR 245 PC.

[98] 'The domestic law and practice of the contracting states reveal a fairly substantial measure of common ground in this area': *Sunday Times v UK (No 1)*, para 59.

[99] *Weber v Switzerland* A 177 (1990), Swiss government, verbatim record, 23 January 1990, p 35.

[100] A 133 (1988); 13 EHRR 212 paras 35–6.

[101] In the homosexuality cases, eg *Dudgeon v UK* A 45 (1981); 4 EHRR 149 PC the Court struck down serious interferences with rights which it regarded as of high importance even though the states claimed to be acting to protect morals and brought evidence that the relevant prevailing moral climate was opposed to the toleration of private homosexual activity.

margin of appreciation with respect to different aims of interferences.[102] There are doubts, though, whether it adds anything to the calculations to be made about the necessity of interferences with protected rights.

The justiciability of the interest

In the *Greek* case,[103] the Commission rejected the argument that the assessment of the existence of an emergency within the terms of Article 15 was beyond its competence on grounds of non-justiciability. Given this ruling and the difficulty and the sensitivity of the issue with which the Commission was faced, it is hard to see why, in principle, the assessment of whether there is evidence that any of the interests listed in Articles 8(2)–11(2) is in jeopardy is not appropriate for the Strasbourg Court. Even when action is taken 'in the interests of national security', it may insist that the state produce some evidence that there is a national security interest to be protected by the interference.[104] The mere assertion of a national security interest is not sufficient.[105]

There are, however, two kinds of fact-finding and assessment involved. The first relates to the facts of the particular case, for example, what was the content of a proscribed publication and could access to it plausibly threaten moral standards?[106] The second is what is sometimes called 'constitutional fact-finding', ie establishing the factual accuracy of general claims about the protected interest, for example, that the perpetual or long-term confidentiality of security information as a whole is necessary to protect the integrity of the security services and the efficacy of its operations.[107] The Court took a view favourable to the government on the question of evidence about the economic effects of limiting night flights to Heathrow in *Hatton v UK*.[108] It said that 'it was reasonable to assume' that flights through Heathrow made some contribution to the general economy, so that complaints that the restrictions on night flights had not gone far enough to satisfy the right to respect for private life of residents in the neighbourhood were rejected as the restrictions were justifiable as being for the protection of the economy. *Hatton* has been criticized as lacking a coherent allocation of the burdens of proof between applicants and government,[109] but the Court put considerable weight on the procedures adopted by the United Kingdom to evaluate the competing rights and interests, which, given their length and complexity, were probably enough to persuade the Court that it could not repeat the exercise at the international level. Some of the questions which arise in the context of constitutional fact-finding are more intractable than others. They are questions which may arise about *any* protected interest, for example, whether the circulation of sexually explicit material

---

[102] *Otto-Preminger-Institut v Austria* A 295-A (1994); 19 EHRR 34 para 50.

[103] 12 YB (the *Greek* case) 1 at 72 (1969); CM Res DH (70) 1.

[104] *Observer and Guardian v UK* A 216 (1991); 14 EHRR 153 para 69 PC. In general, see Cameron, *National Security and the European Convention on Human Rights*, 2000.

[105] In *Observer and Guardian*, Judge Walsh, dissenting, para 4, suggested that the threat to national security was 'simply...an expression of opinion' and, therefore, inadequate to allow the state to rely on Article 10(2). See *Al-Nashif v Bulgaria* hudoc (2002); 36 EHRR 655, for rejection of the claim that matters of national security are wholly non-justiciable.

[106] See, eg, *Müller v Switzerland* A 133 (1988); 13 EHRR 212 para 36, where the inclusion of a description of the painting in the judgment, para 16, was insisted upon by the government and the Court sustained the state's assessment of the need to punish the artist for the protection of morals for exhibiting the painting.

[107] *Observer and Guardian v UK* A 216 (1991); 14 EHRR 153 paras 66–70 PC. In *Lustig-Prean and Beckett v UK* hudoc (1999); 29 EHRR 548, the Court dismissed scarcely evidenced claims by the UK that the recruitment of homosexuals into the armed services would adversely affect military efficiency.

[108] 2003-VIII; 37 EHRR 611 para 126 GC.

[109] Greer, *The European Convention on Human Rights*, 2006, pp 259–65.

has an impact on conduct, such that restrictions may be placed upon it to prevent crime or protect others, or whether immigration of aliens permitted in the exercise of the right to respect for family life may be limited because of the impact of such immigrants on the labour market and, hence, in the 'interests of…the economic well-being of the country'. The Court has used the existence of a European consensus as evidence that a factual claim made by a state is unfounded. In *Ünal Tekeli v Turkey*,[110] the Court used the widely established practice in the party states of allowing women to retain their maiden names after marriage to rebut the state's claim that such a possibility threatened family stability. In controversial matters, the Court has looked beyond mere assertions by the respondent state. For example, it has affirmed that legislation which differentiates against homosexuals on the basis of their asserted predatory character characteristics lacks a factual foundation.[111] The ascertainment of historical truth is a sub-set of constitutional fact. It has been an important element in cases involving 'Holocaust denial',[112] where the Court usually says that it will abstain 'from matters of purely historical fact'. However, its incidence is not restricted to this issue. In *Ždanoka v Latvia*, the Court said that such fact-finding is primarily for the national authorities. Its role is to 'satisfy itself that the national authorities based their decisions on an acceptable assessment of the relevant facts and did not reach arbitrary conclusions'.[113] While some interferences are of themselves more significant than others—a term of imprisonment rather than a fine, prior censorship rather than post-publication punishment—in other cases, the significance of the interference may be closely related to the particular facts. The forfeiture orders of the *Little Red School Book* in *Handyside v UK*[114] were of less significance to a publisher who could reproduce the publication elsewhere and modify it for publication in England than the forfeiture order of his paintings against the artist in *Müller v Switzerland*.[115] The weight of the interference, then, must be assessed by considering its effects in the circumstances of the particular application, conceding though that some interferences will have a great impact, whatever the situation. In *Dudgeon v UK*[116] and the other homosexuality cases, the Court put some weight on the criminalization of the applicants' private activities as an indication of the excessiveness of the interference. In *Observer and Guardian v UK*,[117] while rejecting the argument that Article 10 implied a complete proscription against prior censorship, the Court acknowledged that such an interference with freedom of expression called for 'the most careful scrutiny', especially for news media 'for news is a perishable commodity'. In finding a violation of Article 10 with respect to the freedom of expression of a politician in Turkey, in *Incal v Turkey*,[118] the Court took into account what it called the 'radical' nature of the consequences for the applicant—criminal punishments, including imprisonment, exclusion from the civil service and from participation in political and trade union activities. In *Connors v UK*,[119] the Court pointed to the seriousness of the consequences of the exercise of a summary power of eviction against gypsies who had lived on a site for fourteen years, in the absence of suitable alternative locations to which they could move. It held that there was a violation of Article 8.

---

[110] 2004-X; 42 EHRR 1185.   [111] *L and V v Austria* 2003-I; 36 EHRR 1022 paras 52–5.
[112] For instance, *Lehideux and Isorni v France* 1998-VII; 30 EHRR 665 GC and *Garaudy v France No 65831/01* hudoc (2003) DA.   [113] 2006-IV; 45 EHRR 478 para 96 GC.
[114] A 24 (1976); 1 EHRR 737 paras 19 and 22–3 PC.
[115] A 133 (1988); 13 EHRR 212 para 17. See also *Vereinigung Bildender Künstler v Austria* hudoc (2007); 47 EHRR 189 para 37, holding that an injunction against the exhibition of a controversial illustration which was 'unlimited in time and space' was an element in holding the interference disproportionate.
[116] A 45 (1981); 4 EHRR 149 paras 49 and 60 PC.   [117] A 216 (1991); 14 EHRR 153 para 60 PC.
[118] 1998-IV; 29 EHRR 449 paras 30–1 GC.   [119] Hudoc (2004); 40 EHRR 189 paras 85–95.

e. The resolution of the conflict between the different factors

The general approach

It will be appreciated now that the inquiry into the exercise of a state's margin of appreciation may be complex, involving a variety of factors, not merely a simple balance between the rights of the individual and the interests of the state, however convenient it might be to express it in these terms. The explanation of how the Court resolves the various forces is complicated by a difference between its rhetoric and practice in some judgments. The basic principle remains that explicated in the *Handyside* case,[120] that the word 'necessary' means neither 'indispensable' at the strict end nor 'reasonable' at the lenient end, so far as the state is concerned. What is 'necessary' in a particular case will fall along a spectrum between those two extremes and it is better to understand the Court's approach as being a multifaceted one, rather than try to demarcate its decisions into groups of 'strict scrutiny'/'rational basis' or other categories, on the American constitutional model.[121] If, after treating all the appropriate factors considered already, the Court finds that the interference might conceivably have been 'necessary in a democratic society', it reaches the final resolution of forces by asking whether the restriction of the applicant's rights was 'proportionate' to the interest sought to be protected.[122]

Assessing proportionality

Proportionality, it should be underlined, is the final factor the Strasbourg authorities take into account in determining whether an interference with a right is necessary[123]. The practice of the Court has isolated various factors which are to be taken into account in determining the proportionality issue. While the balance of factors in a close case may be difficult and, therefore, incline the Court to accept the balance struck by the state, manifest disproportionality will result in the Court finding that the measure of limitation is not necessary. An example of this may be seen in *Campbell v UK*,[124] where the government claimed the right to open and inspect incoming mail to prisoners from the European Commission to guard against the possibility that the Commission's envelopes might have been forged. The Court took the view that the eventuality was far-fetched and held the interference with the prisoner's right of correspondence unnecessary. Another way in which a lack of proportionality may be demonstrated is where there is an alternative, less intrusive way of protecting the public interest. The *Campbell* case also provides an example of this. The Court rejected a blanket right of the authorities to open and read a prisoner's letters to his legal advisors where they suspected that the letters contained illicit enclosures. The Court conceded only that a narrower rule, allowing inspection only on reasonable suspicion, with guarantees to the prisoner against abuse, such as opening letters in his presence, would satisfy the test of necessity.[125] In *Marckx v Belgium*,[126] though in a slightly different context, the Court pointed out that where there were alternative ways in which social policies might be pursued, the state was not entitled to choose a way which violated an individual's rights over one that did not.

Interference with an individual's rights is disproportionate where it is purposeless, that is, where the object cannot be achieved by the interference. It is not necessary to interfere

---

[120] *Handyside v UK* A 24 (1976); 1 EHRR 737 para 48 PC.   [121] See Gunther, 86 HLR 1 (1972).
[122] *Sunday Times v UK (No 1)* A 30 (1979); 2 EHRR 245 para 67 PC.
[123] On the principle of proportionality, see the literature cited in Ch 1, section 4.V.
[124] A 233 (1992); 15 EHRR 137 para 62.   [125] *Campbell v UK*, para 48.
[126] A 31 (1979); 2 EHRR 330 para 40 PC.

with freedom of expression on grounds of protecting confidential information where the confidence has been lost because of its publication elsewhere.[127] The proportionality requirement is not satisfied where the government does not provide evidence to show that the claim of necessity was made out. In *Kokkinakis v Greece*,[128] the government claimed the right to interfere with the applicant's right to freedom of religion because he had been attempting to convert others by 'improper means'. The Court held that because no evidence was presented to show that what he had done fell within 'improper means', the interference was not necessary.

Questions of proportionality involve some element of balancing one factor against another, but it is not a scientific process, despite the metaphor. The language is pervasive: the Court speaks of the 'fair balance' between the enjoyment of rights and the protection of other interests which runs through the Convention.[129] A state will be in a stronger position if the domestic institutions have themselves addressed the issue of proportionality of the interference with the applicant's right but, because of its ultimate responsibility, the Court will review, and may differ from, the results of even the most careful domestic scrutiny.[130]

Finally, questions of proportionality are dealt with in a particular way in cases concerning 'general measures'. The Court has allowed that a state may 'adopt general measures which apply to pre-defined situations regardless of the individual facts of each case even if this might result in individual hard cases'.[131] As the Court has recognized, such general measures may be 'more feasible means of achieving the legitimate aim than a provision allowing a case-by-case examination, when the latter would give rise to a risk of significant uncertainty'.[132] In cases within Articles 8–11, such measures have concerned, for example, a state's economic and social policy,[133] the destruction of frozen embryos,[134] and political advertising.[135] When determining the proportionality of such measures, the Court primarily assesses the 'legislative choices' that underlie them: in this connection, 'the quality of the parliamentary and judicial review of the necessity of the measure is of particular importance...including the operation of the relevant margin of appreciation'.[136] The Court also takes into account 'the risk of abuse if a general measure were to be relaxed', this being a matter primarily for the state to assess.[137] Following this approach, when ruling in *Animal Defenders International v UK* that a legislative prohibition of political advertising was, despite the impact it had on the work of the applicant campaigners against the use of animals in scientific experiments, proportionate to the aim of preventing the distortion of public interest debates and hence the democratic process, so that it was not in violation of Article 10, the Court gave 'considerable weight' to the 'exacting and pertinent reviews' of the legislation by both parliament and the courts.[138]

---

[127] *Weber v Switzerland* A 177 (1990); 12 EHRR 508 para 51 and *Observer and Guardian v UK* A 216 (1991); 14 EHRR 153 para 68 PC.   [128] A 260-A (1993); 17 EHRR 397 para 49.

[129] Eg, *Hatton v UK* 2003-VIII; 37 EHRR 611 para 122 GC.

[130] See, eg, *Beldjoudi v France* A 234-A (1992); 14 EHRR 801.

[131] *Animal Defenders International v UK* 2013-; 57 EHRR 607 para 106 GC.

[132] *Animal Defenders International v UK*, para 108.

[133] *Hatton v UK* 2003-VIII; 37 EHRR 611 GC.   [134] *Evans v UK* 2007-I; 46 EHRR 728 GC.

[135] *Animal Defenders International v UK* hudoc (2013); 57 EHRR 607 GC.

[136] *Animal Defenders International v UK*, para 108.

[137] *Animal Defenders International v UK*, para 108.

[138] *Animal Defenders International v UK*, para 116.

4. CONCLUSION

Cases alleging violations of Articles 8–11 will raise a variety of questions to be disposed of for their determination. In general, the Court has adopted the practice of taking each item in an application successively, no matter how simple some of them may be. The stages are:

 (i) the identification of the right, including positive aspects of the right;

 (ii) the identification of the interference;

 (iii) consideration of whether the interference is prescribed by law, including both the internal and external (Convention) understanding of 'law';

 (iv) determining what objectives are sought to be protected by the interference; and

 (v) deciding whether the interference is 'necessary in a democratic society', ie whether the state gives, and gives evidence for, relevant and sufficient reasons for the interference and those reasons are proportionate to the limitation of the applicant's enjoyment of his right, in which connection the margin of appreciation is most important.

While the Court has often used the same language in its judgments to explain what each of these various stages involves, the precedential value of previous judgments must be assessed against the changing social, technical, and economic conditions as reflected in national laws and decisions. In carrying out its task, the Court is conscious of its 'subsidiary' role. The states may adopt a variety of solutions to similar problems and all or several of them may be compatible with the Convention.[139] However hard the Court tries to establish clear rules of easy applicability, the reality is that it can often do no more than indicate the factors a decision-maker should take into account without being able to provide much guidance on the relative weight of each of them.[140] The result is that the processes of arguing and deciding cases brought under these articles are seldom simple and the outcome is difficult to anticipate.[141]

---

[139] Eg, *Buckley v UK* 1996-IV; 23 EHRR 101 para 75: 'It is not for the Court to substitute its own view of what would be the best policy in the planning sphere or the most appropriate individual measure in planning cases.'

[140] Eg, *Üner v Netherlands* 2006-XII; 45 EHRR 421 paras 57–9 GC.

[141] Macdonald, Matscher, and Petzold, eds, *The European System for the Protection of Human Rights*, 1993, Ch 6 at pp 160–1.

12

ARTICLE 8: THE RIGHT TO RESPECT FOR PRIVATE AND FAMILY LIFE, HOME, AND CORRESPONDENCE

Article 8

1. Everyone has the right to respect for his private and family life, his home and his correspondence.
2. There shall be no interference by a public authority with the exercise of this right except such as is in accordance with the law and is necessary in a democratic society in the interests of national security, public safety or the economic well-being of the country, for the prevention of disorder or crime, for the protection of health or morals, or for the protection of the rights and freedoms of others.

1. INTRODUCTION

Article 8 has been described as the 'least defined and most unruly of the rights enshrined in the Convention'.[1] It is hard to argue with this appraisal: Article 8 places on states the obligation to 'respect' a wide range of undefined personal interests which embrace a number of overlapping and inter-related areas. None of the four interests covered by Article 8(1)— private life, family life, home, and correspondence—is defined in the Convention and their content is a matter of interpretation. Like many other Convention expressions, each of these interests is an autonomous concept and the Court is not bound by the findings of domestic courts. It has tended to take a generous approach to the definition of the interests protected. As a result, the protection afforded by the provision continues to broaden in scope. A review of the Court's case law indicates that matters falling within the ambit of Article 8 include issues as diverse as gender identity, childcare proceedings, search and seizure powers, data protection, and environmental issues. While some have commented on the dangers of the Court's expansive approach,[2] the application of the Court's

---

[1] Per Mr Justice Stanley Burton in *Wright v Secretary of State for Health* [2006] EWHC 2886 (Admin) para 66.

[2] See, eg, Lady Hale *'Beanstalk or Living Instrument? How Tall Can the ECHR Grow?'* (Barnard's Inn Reading, 16 June 2011).

'living instrument' doctrine has had the advantage of facilitating the interpretation of Article 8(1) in line with social and technological developments.

The terms of Article 8(2) make it clear that the state must refrain from arbitrary interference with private and family life, home, and correspondence. This obligation is of the classic negative kind, described by the Court as 'the essential object' of Article 8.[3] However, the Court has not perceived the rights in Article 8(1) in wholly negative terms. Drawing on the language of Article 8(1)—which protects the right 'to respect for' each of the interests, and not the right to the interest itself—the Court has emphasized the need for states to act in a manner calculated to allow effective enjoyment of Article 8 rights. It has therefore explained that there are positive obligations inherent in Article 8 which require the state to take steps to provide particular rights or to protect people against the activities of other private individuals.[4] The 'margin of appreciation' plays an important role in Article 8 cases. Its width depends on a number of factors, some of which have been identified in the Court's case law.[5] Article 8 has also been found to give rise to procedural requirements which are intended to ensure that applicants' interests are adequately protected in domestic decision-making.

There is a complex interplay between Article 8(1) and the other Articles of the Convention. Many Article 8 rights are 'civil rights' in the sense of Article 6(1) and decisions concerning them must be taken by a procedure which satisfies the latter Article.[6] The extent to which the procedural rights under Article 8 reflect Article 6 guarantees is yet to be determined since the Court has not provided a comprehensive statement of the procedural rights arising under Article 8.[7] The effect of Article 8 may also be to impose a duty on the state to take measures which involve an interference with another Convention right, for example where the obligation under Article 8 to protect an individual's privacy or reputation comes into conflict with the freedom of expression enjoyed by the media pursuant to Article 10.[8] Where two qualified rights overlap, the Court seeks to strike a balance between the competing interests. In some cases, the treatment about which the applicant complains potentially falls within the scope of other Articles.[9] This has resulted in a certain amount of 'content creep' as the Court imports into Article 8—with varying degrees of explanation and justification—the standards and principles developed in the context of the other Articles.[10] Although historically the Court tended to examine an Article 8 complaint only where the similar Article 3 complaint had failed, more recently it has begun to examine complaints under both Articles and has found violations of both.[11] It is not clear what has prompted this change of practice: it does not appear to provide any significant legal or practical advantage.

---

[3] *Kroon and Others v Netherlands* A 297-C (1994); 19 EHRR 263 para 31.

[4] *Marckx v Belgium* A 31 (1979); 2 EHRR 330 PC.   [5] See Ch 11, pp 510–20.

[6] Eg, *Golder v UK* A 18 (1975); 1 EHRR 524 PC (prisoner's correspondence with lawyer); *Airey v Ireland* A 32 (1979); 2 EHRR 305 (access to legal procedure for terminating obligations of family life); and *Olsson v Sweden (No 1)* A 130 (1988); 11 EHRR 259 PC (proceedings concerning the care of children taken from natural parents).

[7] But for some examples see, eg, *Kay and Others v UK* hudoc (2010); 54 EHRR 1056 (eviction); *Raza v Bulgaria* hudoc (2010) (expulsion); and *YC v UK* hudoc (2012) (childcare proceedings).

[8] Eg, *Von Hannover v Germany* 2004-VI; 40 EHRR 1; *Mosley v UK* hudoc (2011); 53 EHRR 1011; *Von Hannover v Germany (No 2)* hudoc (2012); 55 EHRR 388 GC; and *Axel Springer AG v Germany* hudoc (2012); 55 EHRR 183 GC.

[9] Usually Articles 2 and 3: see, eg, *LCB v UK* 1998-III; 27 EHRR 212; *Z and Others v UK* 2001-V; 34 EHRR 97 GC; and *Georgel and Georgeta Stoicescu v Romania* hudoc (2011).

[10] Eg, *Georgel and Georgeta Stoicescu v Romania*.   [11] Eg, *MN v Bulgaria* hudoc (2012).

The first stage of the Court's examination of an Article 8 complaint requires it to decide whether the complaint falls within the scope of Article 8(1). If it does, the Court will consider whether the case should be assessed from the perspective of negative or positive obligations. The distinction between the two is not always easy to draw, a difficulty frequently acknowledged by the Court itself.[12] The second stage requires the Court to decide whether the state has complied with the requirements of Article 8(1). Where the case concerns a negative obligation, the Court must assess whether the interference was consistent with the requirements of Article 8(2), namely in accordance with the law, in pursuit of a legitimate aim, and necessary in a democratic society. In the case of a positive obligation, the Court considers whether the importance of the interest at stake requires the imposition of the positive obligation sought by the applicant, having regard to the fair balance which must be struck between the competing interests in the case.

2. THE FOUR INTERESTS PROTECTED BY ARTICLE 8(1)

In order to invoke Article 8(1), an applicant must show that his complaint falls within at least one of the four interests—private life, family life, home, and correspondence—identified in that Article. Some matters span more than one interest: laws governing assisted procreation, for example, may engage both private and family life;[13] complaints concerning telephone tapping usually give rise to an interference with both private life and correspondence, and sometimes also with the home.[14] The qualification of the interest in play appears to have no effect on the Court's approach to the questions of justification or the existence of positive obligations. This probably explains why the Court does not consider it necessary always to clarify which particular Article 8(1) interest is at stake.[15] While the primary responsibility lies on the applicant to characterize his complaint in a manner which fits within the Court's understanding of Article 8(1), the Court sometimes chooses to examine a complaint under Article 8 even where an applicant has not expressly invoked it.[16]

I. PRIVATE LIFE

The notion of private life is a broad concept,[17] and this makes an account of what it covers difficult.[18] The Court first considered the reach of Article 8 in a 1968 case concerning the right of parents of French-speaking children in Belgium to have their children educated in French.[19] It noted that Article 8 did not guarantee a right to education, explaining that

---

[12] Eg, *Evans v UK* 2007-I; 46 EHRR 728 GC and *SH and Others v Austria* hudoc (2011).

[13] *SH and Others v Austria* and *Costa and Pavan v Italy* hudoc (2012). Cf *Evans v UK* 2007-I; 46 EHRR 728 GC.

[14] *Klass and Others v Germany* A 28 (1978); 2 EHRR 214 PC and *Association for European Integration and Human Rights and Ekimdzhiev v Bulgaria* hudoc (2007).

[15] Eg, *A, B and C v Ireland* hudoc (2010); 53 EHRR 429 GC.

[16] Eg, *Mółka v Poland* No 56550/00 2006-IV DA; *MM v UK* hudoc (2012); and *Csoma v Romania* hudoc (2013).   [17] *EB v France* hudoc (2008); 47 EHRR 509 GC.

[18] See Moreham, EHRLR 44 (2008), for a discussion of the various threads covered by 'private life'.

[19] *Belgian Linguistics case* A 6 (1968).

its object was essentially that of protecting the individual against arbitrary interference by the public authorities in his private and family life. It continued:

> However, it is not to be excluded that measures taken in the field of education may affect the right to respect for private and family life or derogate from it; this would be the case, for instance, if their aim or result were to disturb private or family life in an unjustifiable manner, *inter alia* by separating children from their parents in an arbitrary way.

Thus from the beginning the Court eschewed a narrow approach, which would limit private life to notions of privacy and protection from publicity, in favour of a broader approach which emphasized the ability to live one's life without arbitrary disruption or interference. Similarly, in an early case concerning a complaint about a prohibition on keeping dogs in Reykjavik, the Commission explained that the right to respect for private life did not end with privacy but comprised the 'right to establish and to develop relationships with other human beings, especially in the emotional field for the development and fulfilment of one's own personality'.[20] This was an important moment in the interpretation of Article 8, opening the door to a whole new way of looking at the extent of the private life guarantee. The Court endorsed this understanding of 'private life' in its 1992 judgment in *Niemietz v Germany*,[21] where it said:

> [I]t would be too restrictive to limit the notion [of private life] to an 'inner circle' in which the individual may live his own personal life as he chooses and to exclude therefrom entirely the outside world not encompassed within that circle. Respect for private life must also comprise to a certain degree the right to establish and develop relationships with other human beings.

The relationships need not be of a personal nature: *Niemietz* itself concerned the search of a lawyer's office and Article 8 was found to be engaged notwithstanding the professional context. As a result, Article 8 potentially encapsulates any complaint where an applicant is able to show that his interaction with others is affected.[22] However, the Court has excluded the applicability of Article 8 in cases concerning interpersonal relations of 'such broad and indeterminate scope' that there is 'no conceivable direct link' between the actions of the state and a person's private life, explaining that the fact that an activity allows an individual to establish and develop relationships does not necessarily mean that it falls within the scope of Article 8.[23] But where the line is to be drawn is not obvious.

Several other threads to private life can be identified in the case law. In its 1981 decision in *X v Germany*,[24] the Commission found Article 8 to apply to a complaint regarding preservation of a police file, explaining that it raised an issue of data protection which came within the Article's broad scope. The applicability of Article 8 to issues of data protection

---

[20] *X v Iceland No 6825/74*, 5 DR 86 at 88 (1976). The Commission found that the ties between man and dog were not sufficient to give rise to 'private life'.   [21] A 251-B (1992); 16 EHRR 97 para 29.

[22] See the discussion of Article 8 applicability in *Mółka v Poland No 56550/00* 2006-IV DA.

[23] See *Friend and Others v UK Nos 16072/06 and 27809/08* hudoc (2009) DA (ban on hunting with dogs did not fall within private life). See also *Botta v Italy* 1998-I; 26 EHRR 241 (lack of disabled access to a public beach did not fall within private life) and *Zehnalová and Zehnal v Czech Republic No 38621/97* 2002-V DA (inaccessibility of public buildings to persons with impaired mobility did not fall within private life). However, recent references to the relevance of Article 8 to complaints about public funding to facilitate the mobility and quality of life of disabled applicants (see *Mółka v Poland No 56550/00* 2006-IV DA) suggest that the same conclusion might not be reached if *Botta* and *Zehnalová* were decided today.

[24] *No 8334/78*, 24 DR 103 (1981).

is now undisputed. The Court indicated for the first time that the concept of private life covered the physical and moral integrity of the person in *X and Y v Netherlands*,[25] concerning the sexual assault of a mentally disabled woman. Despite some initial reluctance,[26] a body of case law now recognizes the importance of physical and psychological integrity as part of 'private life'. The Court has also referred to 'personal autonomy' as an important principle underlying the interpretation of the private life guarantees in Article 8.[27] The principle was summarized in *Christine Goodwin v UK* as meaning that protection under Article 8 is given to the personal sphere of each individual, including the right to establish details of their identities as individual human beings.[28]

II. FAMILY LIFE

The development of the idea of 'family life' is one of the best examples of the way the Commission and Court have interpreted the Convention to take account of social changes.

Formal relationships represent the typical situation which will fall within Article 8. It is usually the case that formal marriages are accompanied by enough of substance for them to be regarded as constituting family life.[29] However, a marriage subsisting in form only, for example, a sham marriage entered into for the purposes only of avoiding immigration controls or obtaining nationality, is unlikely to satisfy the requirements for family life.[30] Where the union between partners has not been formalized by way of marriage, relevant factors for the establishment of family life include whether the couple lives together, the length of their relationship, and whether they have demonstrated their commitment to each other by having children together or by any other means.[31] Simply being engaged to be married, without more, is unlikely to be sufficient to establish family life.[32] Where a marriage has not been validly concluded, where, for example, a civil marriage is required and the parties have entered into a religious marriage only, the Court has looked to the substance of the relationship in order to conclude that family life existed.[33] The Commission and the Court accepted for a long time that the emotional and sexual relationship of a same-sex couple constituted 'private life' but did not consider it to fall within 'family life', even where a long-term relationship of cohabiting partners was at stake.[34] However, it is now clear that, following a rapid evolution of social attitudes towards same-sex couples in many member states, homosexual couples can enjoy family life.[35]

---

[25] A 91 (1985); 8 EHRR 235.   [26] Eg, *Costello-Roberts v UK* A 247-C (1993); 19 EHRR 112.

[27] *Pretty v UK* 2002-III; 35 EHRR 1 para 61. The term had already been used in the context of the balancing exercise under Article 8 in *Laskey, Jaggard and Brown v UK* 1997-I; 24 EHRR 39 para 44. See Marshall, EHRLR 337 (2008).   [28] 2002-VI; 35 EHRR 447 GC.

[29] *Abdulaziz, Cabales and Balkandali v UK* A 94 (1985); 7 EHRR 471 PC.

[30] See *Benes v Austria* No 18643/91, 72 DR 271 (1992) (annulment of marriage entered into for the sole purpose of obtaining spouse's nationality was examined as an interference with right to respect for private, and not family, life).

[31] *Van der Heijden v Netherlands* hudoc (2012); 57 EHRR 377 GC and *Şerife Yiğit v Turkey* hudoc (2010); 53 EHRR 872 GC.   [32] *Wakefield v UK* No 15817/89, 66 DR 251 at 255 (1990).

[33] See *Şerife Yiğit v Turkey* hudoc (2010); 53 EHRR 872 GC. See also *Abdulaziz, Cabales and Balkandali v UK* A 94 (1985); 7 EHRR 471 para 63 PC.

[34] *Mata Estevez v Spain* No 56501/00 2001-VI DA; *S v UK* No 11716/85, 47 DR 274 (1986); and *Kerkhoven, Hinke and Hinke v Netherlands* No 15666/89 hudoc (1992) DA.

[35] See *PB and JS v Austria* hudoc (2010); 55 EHRR 926; *Schalk and Kopf v Austria* hudoc (2010); 53 EHRR 683; *Gas and Dubois v France* hudoc (2012); *X and Others v Austria* hudoc (2013); 57 EHRR 405 GC; and

Children born to married parents are *ipso jure* part of that relationship and 'hence, from the moment of the child's birth and by the very fact of it, there exists between him and his parents a bond amounting to "family life".'[36] Where the parents cohabit but are unmarried, it will usually be the case that they enjoy family life together and with their children.[37] Where the parents are separated, the approach of the Court and the Commission has traditionally been more cautious. While the Court appears to take it for granted that the relationship between a single mother and her child constitutes family life from the moment of birth,[38] it has not given similar automatic recognition to the relationship between a child and his father.[39] Mere biological kinship, without any further legal or factual elements indicating the existence of a close personal relationship, does not give rise to 'family life'.[40] Relevant factors demonstrating family life include the nature of the relationship between the natural parents; the demonstrable interest in and commitment by the father to the child both before and after its birth;[41] the quality of the relationship between father and child, illustrated by arrangements regarding contact and maintenance; and formal recognition of paternity.[42] The importance of intent means that family life can extend to potential relationships that could have developed between a biological father and his child, even where the father has had no contact with the child after birth. In *Keegan v Ireland*,[43] where the child was born as a result of a conscious decision by the applicant and his girlfriend who were then in a loving relationship, the Court held family life to exist because at the material time their relationship had all the hallmarks of family life, even though it had broken down by the time the child was born and the father had met his child on only one occasion.[44] In *Ahrens v Germany*,[45] the Court was not convinced that family life existed in respect of the applicant and his biological daughter where conception had resulted from relations of a purely sexual nature and there was no evidence of an intention to found a family or of any commitment to the child before its birth. In any case the ramifications of failing to show that there is family life may not be significant: the Court accepts that proceedings concerning the establishment of paternity and access to biological children tend to concern private life.[46]

Unsurprisingly given its focus on the substance of relationships, a biological link is equally not necessary to show family life between parent and child. In *X, Y and Z v UK*,[47] delivered at a time when its approach to same-sex couples remained conservative, the Court confirmed that the reality of family arrangements between a transsexual male and the child born to his wife by artificial insemination by donor meant that their relationship constituted family life for the purposes of Article 8. Recently, in cases concerning second-parent adoption by the same-sex partner of the biological parent, the Court has confirmed that family life will exist provided that there is a *de facto* family situation.[48]

Vallianatos and Others v Greece hudoc (2013). For discussion of the evolution of the case law, see Hodson, 20 Intl J Child Rts 501 (2012).

[36] *Berrehab v Netherlands* A 138 (1988); 11 EHRR 322 para 21.

[37] *Johnston and Others v Ireland* A 112 (1986); 9 EHRR 203 PC.

[38] *Marckx v Belgium* A 31 (1979); 2 EHRR 330 PC and *Kearns v France* hudoc (2008); 50 EHRR 851.

[39] In contrast with the Court's case law, the *travaux préparatoires* reveal an emphasis on the father's right to family life: see Opsahl, in Robertson, ed, *Privacy and Human Rights*, 1973, pp 183–8. See now Seventh Protocol, Article 5, in Ch 24, p 974. For the right to marry, see Ch 16 on Article 12.

[40] *G v Netherlands No 16944/90*, 16 EHRR CD 38 (1993) and *Schneider v Germany* hudoc (2011); 54 EHRR 407.

[41] Eg, *Boughanemi v France* 1996-II; 22 EHRR 228 and *Ciliz v Netherlands* 2000-VIII.

[42] *Nylund v Finland No 27110/95* 1999-VI DA and *L v Netherlands* 2004-IV.

[43] A 290 (1994); 18 EHRR 342.   [44] See also *KAB v Spain* hudoc (2012).   [45] Hudoc (2012).

[46] *Ahrens v Germany*.   [47] 1997-II; 24 EHRR 143 GC.

[48] *Gas and Dubois v France* hudoc (2012) and *X and Others v Austria* hudoc (2013); 57 EHRR 405 GC. See also Hodson, 20 Intl J Child Rts 501 (2012).

Similarly, adoption creates family life between the adoptive parents and the adopted child.[49] Family life may also exist between foster-parent and foster-child.[50]

While the central relationships of family life are those of husband and wife and parent and child, relationships between siblings,[51] between uncle and nephew,[52] and between grandparents and grandchildren[53] are also covered by 'family life'. However, the remoteness of the relationship is likely to be relevant when assessing the proportionality of any interference under Article 8(2).[54]

Family life between husband and wife may be terminated by divorce, although as discussed earlier, this will not necessarily have the effect of terminating family life with children of the marriage.[55] The placement of a child in public care and the child's adoption do not sever the bond of family life.[56]

The Court's approach to whether the decision to have, or not to have, a family relates to 'family life' has not always been consistent. Although in *Evans v UK*,[57] the Court considered the decision to become a parent to give rise to an issue of 'private life', it has subsequently held that the right to respect for the decision to become genetic parents falls within the scope of both private and family life.[58] In cases brought by women complaining about restrictions on their access to abortion, the Court tends to examine the matter from the perspective of private life.[59] Similarly, it appears that the Court considers cases concerning access to adoption generally to raise issues relating to private, rather than family, life except where substantive family life exists.[60]

III. HOME

In general, 'home' is where one lives on a settled basis and 'will usually be the place, the physically defined area, where private and family life develops'.[61] The question is whether the applicant can demonstrate the existence of sufficient and continuous links with a specific place.[62] Applying this test, the Court has found Article 8 applicable in respect of a house where the applicants had formerly resided and to which they had returned after an absence of nineteen years, noting that they had originally sold up and moved family and furniture to the house, and had not established any other home in the meantime.[63]

---

[49] *X v France* No 9993/82, 31 DR 241 (1982); *Kurochkin v Ukraine* hudoc (2010); and *Ageyevy v Russia* hudoc (2013). This is the case even where the children have not been placed in the custody of their adoptive parents, provided they have formally been adopted: see *Pini and Others v Romania* 2004-V; 40 EHRR 312.

[50] *Gaskin v UK* A 160 (1989); 12 EHRR 36 PC and *Moretti and Benedetti v Italy* hudoc (2010).

[51] *Moustaquim v Belgium* A 193 (1991); 13 EHRR 802; *Olsson v Sweden (No 1)* A 130 (1988); 11 EHRR 259 PC; and *Mustafa and Armağan Akın v Turkey* hudoc (2010).

[52] *Boyle v UK* A 282-B (1994); 19 EHRR 179 Com Rep.

[53] *Marckx v Belgium* A 31 (1979); 2 EHRR 330 PC and *Price v UK* No 12402/86, 55 DR 224 at 237 (1988).

[54] See *Boyle v UK* A 282-B (1994); 19 EHRR 179 Com Rep (uncle–nephew).

[55] *Berrehab v Netherlands* A 138 (1988); 11 EHRR 322.

[56] *W v UK* A 121 (1987); 10 EHRR 29 PC and *Olsson v Sweden (No 1)* A 130 (1988); 11 EHRR 259 PC (placement in care); and *Kearns v France* hudoc (2008); 50 EHRR 851 and *AK and L v Croatia* hudoc (2013) (adoption).   [57] 2007-I; 46 EHRR 728 GC.

[58] *Dickson v UK* 2007-V; 46 EHRR 927 GC and *SH and Others v Austria* hudoc (2011).

[59] Eg, *Tysiąc v Poland* 2007-I; 45 EHRR 947; *RR v Poland* hudoc (2011); 53 EHRR 1047; and *A, B and C v Ireland* hudoc (2010); 53 EHRR 429 GC.

[60] See *Fretté v France* 2002-I; 38 EHRR 438 and *EB v France* hudoc (2008); 47 EHRR 509 GC.

[61] Eg, *Giacomelli v Italy* 2006-XII; 45 EHRR 871.

[62] *Gillow v UK* A 109 (1986); 11 EHRR 335; *Buckley v UK* 1996-IV; 23 EHRR 101; *Prokopovich v Russia* 2004-XI; 43 EHRR 167; and *Bjedov v Croatia* hudoc (2012).

[63] *Gillow v UK*. See also *Buckley v UK*; *Yordanova and Others v Bulgaria* hudoc (2012); and *Bjedov v Croatia*.

In *Demades v Turkey*,[64] the Court found that a house used as a holiday home and for providing hospitality to friends and work acquaintances qualified as a home, emphasizing that a person might divide his time between two houses or form strong emotional ties with a second house.[65] Probation and bail hostels, where the applicant's stay is of some duration, are likely to fall within the scope of 'home'.[66] In *Friend and Others v UK*,[67] the Court held that 'home' did not include land over which the owner permitted a sport to be conducted.

A person need not be the owner of his residence in order that it be considered his home. In a series of cases brought by tenants of state-owned property, the Court has found Article 8 to be applicable.[68] In *Pibernik v Croatia*,[69] it was uncontested that the applicant's flat which was owned by the Ministry for Defence was her 'home' within the meaning of Article 8.[70] In *O'Rourke v UK*,[71] the Court did not rule out that a hotel room used by a homeless man and paid for by the local authority could constitute his 'home' within the meaning of Article 8, provided that he had sufficient and continuing links with the place.

The applicant is not required to have a legal right to reside in the property in order for him to rely on Article 8. *Buckley v UK*[72] concerned a gypsy who moved her caravan onto her land but was then denied planning permission to use the caravan as her residence on that property. Because she had purchased the land to establish her residence there, she had lived there almost continuously for a number of years, and it had not been suggested that she had established another residence elsewhere, the Court found that the case concerned her right to respect for her 'home'.[73] In *Prokopovich v Russia*,[74] the Court held that a flat which the applicant shared informally with her partner, who had the tenancy, was her home within the meaning of Article 8, given that she shared the maintenance costs with her partner, received post at that address, and was regularly seen about the place. A number of recent cases have concerned eviction where the applicant's right to remain in the property has come to an end and the Court found that the properties constituted their 'homes'.[75] In *Yordanova and Others v Bulgaria*,[76] the applicants were gypsies who had occupied for a number of years land in respect of which they were not owners and on which they never had a right to reside. The Court nonetheless found that the buildings unlawfully constructed on the land constituted their homes for the purposes of Article 8.

In *Niemietz v Germany*,[77] the Court decided that 'home' could extend to a professional person's office. This, the Court said, was consonant with the object of Article 8 to protect against arbitrary interference by the authorities. Because 'activities which are related to a profession or business may well be conducted from a person's private residence and

[64] Hudoc (2003).

[65] See also *Fägerskiöld v Sweden No 37664/04* hudoc (2008) DA. In *Kanthak v Germany No 12474/86*, 58 DR 94 (1988), the question whether a camping van could be a 'home' was raised, but not answered.

[66] Although in *Brânduşe v Romania* hudoc (2009), concerning offensive smells emanating from waste tip in the vicinity of the applicant's prison cell, the Court did not discuss whether the cell constituted his home, preferring to find his private life engaged.

[67] *Nos 16072/06 and 27809/08* hudoc (2009) DA.

[68] Eg, *Larkos v Cyprus* 1999-I; 30 EHRR 597 GC; *McCann v UK* hudoc (2008); 47 EHRR 913; *Paulić v Croatia* hudoc (2009); *Zehentner v Austria* hudoc (2009); 52 EHRR 739; *Kay and Others v UK* hudoc (2010); 54 EHRR 1056; and *Bjedov v Croatia* hudoc (2012).   [69] Hudoc (2004); 40 EHRR 695.

[70] See also *Cvijetić v Croatia* hudoc (2004).   [71] *No 39022/97* hudoc (2001) DA.

[72] 1996-IV; 23 EHRR 101.

[73] See also *Connors v UK* hudoc (2004); 40 EHRR 189, where a case with similar facts was found to raise issues of 'private life', 'family life', and 'home'.   [74] 2004-XI; 43 EHRR 167.

[75] Eg, *Connors v UK* hudoc (2004); 40 EHRR 189; *McCann v UK* hudoc (2008); 47 EHRR 913; *Kay and Others v UK* hudoc (2010); 54 EHRR 1056; and *Gladysheva v Russia* hudoc (2011).

[76] Hudoc (2012).   [77] A 251-B (1992); 16 EHRR 97.

activities which are not so related may well be carried on in an office or commercial premises', it 'may not always be possible to draw precise distinctions'.[78] The Court subsequently held that 'home' was to be construed as including the business premises of a company owned and managed by the applicant and the business premises of an applicant company.[79]

IV. CORRESPONDENCE

The Court has recently explained that the right to respect for correspondence protects private communications whatever their form or content.[80] In keeping with developments in modern technology, the term correspondence covers telephone, facsimile, email and pager communication, and internet usage, as well as letters.[81] Other methods of communication may also fall within Article 8 in the future, although the appropriate level of protection required by 'respect' will have to take into account the techniques involved.

General papers or files which include correspondence are also covered by that term.[82] This adds a potentially significant protection in the business context since, as the Court has consistently pointed out, the term 'correspondence' is not limited to personal correspondence.[83]

V. CONCLUSION

While there has been criticism of the perceived absence of an adequate conceptual framework to the Court's approach to defining private life, the problem appears to be not so much the inadequacy of the framework as its sheer breadth. In developing its case law on the applicability of Article 8, the Court has made reference to notions of identity, physical and moral integrity, personal autonomy, and the development of relations with others, which it considers to be integral to the concept of private life. But these notions are vague and it is therefore unsurprising that it can be difficult to understand the rationale for the Court's decision in a given case. The frequent tendency of the Court, particularly in recent cases, to use formulaic language and to leave questions of applicability open has not helped bring clarity. However, arguably more than any other Article of the Convention, the Court's approach to Article 8 cases is often, of necessity, highly fact-specific. To the extent that the potential of Article 8 was not fully appreciated when the Convention was signed, this is perhaps attributable, at least in part, to unforeseen developments in the fields of ethics, social conditions, science, and technology, the greatest impact of which can be seen in the daily lives of individuals.

---

[78] *Niemietz v Germany*, para 30. See also *Petri Sallinen and Others v Finland* hudoc (2005); 44 EHRR 358 para 70.

[79] Eg, *Buck v Germany* 2005-IV; 42 EHRR 440; *Société Colas Est and Others v France* 2002-III; and *Saint-Paul Luxembourg SA v Luxembourg* hudoc (2013). See also *Chappell v UK* A 152-A (1989); 12 EHRR 1 Com Rep ('home' where part of premises used as residence and part for business purposes). A non-governmental organization can also claim a right to respect for the home: see *Association for European Integration and Human Rights and Ekimdzhiev v Bulgaria* hudoc (2007).   [80] *Michaud v France* hudoc (2012).

[81] *Halford v UK* 1997-III; 24 EHRR 523; *Taylor-Sabori v UK* hudoc (2002); 36 EHRR 248; *Copland v UK* 2007-I; 45 EHRR 858; and *Kennedy v UK* hudoc (2010); 52 EHRR 207.

[82] *Niemietz v Germany* A 251-B (1992); 16 EHRR 97.

[83] *Huvig v France* A 176-B (1990); 12 EHRR 528 and *Niemietz v Germany*.

By way of counterbalance to the Court's generous approach to applicability, while the scope of what falls within the four interests protected by Article 8 continues to increase, the second step of the Article 8 analysis—the justification for an interference or the existence of specific positive obligations—still presents a significant hurdle for applicants seeking redress for alleged violations.

3. NEGATIVE, POSITIVE, AND PROCEDURAL OBLIGATIONS

I. NEGATIVE OBLIGATION

Because of the wide scope of Article 8, states frequently take steps which interfere with Article 8 rights. Obvious examples are when a local authority takes a child into care;[84] when a person is dismissed from the armed services on account of his homosexuality;[85] when an immigrant is deported;[86] or when the state records and retains personal data.[87] Such cases involve the classic negative obligation of the state.[88]

It is for the applicant to establish the fact of an interference. The burden of proof is a high one: the Court has indicated that it requires facts to be proven 'beyond reasonable doubt',[89] a burden which applicants may not find easy to satisfy. In a number of applications concerning the alleged destruction of the applicants' homes by Turkish security forces, the Court found the allegations unproven and the applications were unsuccessful on that basis.[90]

Where a complaint can be construed as a challenge to the legislative or practical framework governing a particular area of activity, the applicant is not necessarily required to show that he has been affected by the application of the rule. In a series of telephone tapping cases,[91] alive to the difficulties of proving interception since the use of such powers is cloaked in secrecy, the Court accepted that the very existence of laws and practices permitting secret surveillance gave rise to an interference with Article 8 rights, explaining that '[i]n the mere existence of the legislation itself there is involved, for all those to whom the legislation could be applied, a menace of surveillance...'[92] In *Campbell v UK*,[93] the Court was satisfied that there had been an interference of the applicant prisoner's right to respect for his correspondence because the prevailing prison regime allowed for letters to be opened and read, even though he could not show that any particular letter had been opened. In *Dudgeon v UK*,[94] concerning a law which criminalized homosexuality, the

---

[84] Eg, *K and T v Finland* 2001-VII; 36 EHRR 255 GC.

[85] Eg, *Smith and Grady v UK* 1999-VI; 29 EHRR 493.

[86] Eg, *Boultif v Switzerland* 2001-IX; 33 EHRR 1179.

[87] Eg, *S and Marper v UK* hudoc (2008); 48 EHRR 1169 GC.

[88] Sometimes called 'the obligation to respect': see, eg, Nowak, *Introduction to the International Human Rights Regime*, 2003, pp 48–51.   [89] *Nuri Kurt v Turkey* hudoc (2005); 44 EHRR 752.

[90] Eg, *Nuri Kurt v Turkey*; *Çaçan v Turkey* hudoc (2004); and *Gündem v Turkey* 1998-III; 32 EHRR 350.

[91] *Klass and Others v Germany* A 28 (1978); 2 EHRR 214 PC and *Malone v UK* A 82 (1984); 7 EHRR 14 PC. Cf *Leander v Sweden* A 116 (1987); 9 EHRR 433.

[92] *Klass and Others v Germany*, para 41. In some cases the Court has indicated that the individual will have to establish some reason for explaining why the legal regime *might* be applied to him—see *Kennedy v UK* hudoc (2010); 52 EHRR 207.   [93] A 233 (1992); 15 EHRR 137.

[94] A 45 (1981); 4 EHRR 149 PC.

government argued that the applicant, a homosexual, had not been prosecuted for any offence and had therefore not suffered any interference. The Court considered that '[i]n the personal circumstances of the applicant, the very existence of this legislation continuously and directly affect[ed] his private life'.[95]

A different if more rare problem arises where the state maintains that the individual is directly responsible for the conditions about which he complains. In *McFeeley v UK*,[96] the Commission was faced with a wide variety of allegations of violations of the Convention during a prison protest in Northern Ireland by prisoners claiming political status and certain associated privileges. Parts of the protest took the form of refusing to wear prison clothes or to use lavatories, and the applicants argued that the resulting conditions interfered with their right to respect for their private life. Since the conditions resulted directly from the prisoners' own decisions, the Commission found that there were no interferences with their rights for which the state was responsible. The Court has taken a similar approach in cases where applicants complained about damage to their reputations as a consequence of a criminal conviction, where it has found the conviction to be a foreseeable consequence of the commission of a criminal offence.[97]

The finding that there has been an interference does not necessarily result in a violation of Article 8(1). The state has the power to interfere with Article 8(1) rights provided that the three conditions in Article 8(2) are met. The Court usually addresses each of these conditions in order. The conditions are cumulative: a failure to meet one is sufficient to result in a violation of Article 8. For this reason, the Court usually concludes its analysis when one condition has been breached, without considering whether the remaining conditions are satisfied.[98] The Court's approach to Article 8(2) in specific contexts is discussed more fully in section 4.[99]

II. POSITIVE OBLIGATIONS

If Article 8 imposed purely a negative obligation on states not to interfere arbitrarily with the rights guaranteed, this would absolve them of responsibility where, for example, the interference with private life was by a newspaper reporter or the complaint was one of an omission by the state, rather than action. Such a narrow reading was not acceptable to the Court. Accordingly, it set out the principle of positive obligations in *Marckx v Belgium*, which concerned the manner of establishing the maternal affiliation of an 'illegitimate' child, when it said:

> [T]he object of the Article is 'essentially' that of protecting the individual against arbitrary interference by the public authorities...Nevertheless it does not merely compel the state to abstain from such interference: in addition to this primarily negative undertaking, there may be positive obligations inherent in an effective 'respect' for family life.

---

[95] *Dudgeon v UK*, para 41. See also *Norris v Ireland* A 142 (1988); 13 EHRR 186 PC and *Modinos v Cyprus* A 259 (1993); 16 EHRR 485. Cf *Seven Individuals v Sweden* No 8811/79, 29 DR 104 at 113 (1982) (mere existence of legislation banning corporal punishment did not constitute an interference where it did not provide for sanctions).   [96] *No 8317/78*, 20 DR 44 (1980).

[97] See *Sidabras and Džiautas v Lithuania* 2004-VIII; 42 EHRR 105 and *Gillberg v Sweden* hudoc (2012) GC. See also the pending case of *Gough v UK No 49327/11*, where the applicant complains about convictions for being naked in public (communicated September 2012).

[98] *Malone v UK* A 82 (1984); 7 EHRR 14 PC and *Association for European Integration and Human Rights and Ekimdzhiev v Bulgaria* hudoc (2007). For a rare exception see *Juhnke v Turkey* hudoc (2008); 49 EHRR 534.

[99] A more general discussion of the Article 8(2) requirements can be found in Ch 11.

In the context of the case, respect for family life implied in particular the existence in domestic law of legal safeguards that rendered possible from the moment of birth the child's integration into his family.[100] This is the first aspect of the state's positive obligation: the obligation of the state to put in place a legislative and administrative framework to ensure the full realization of Article 8 rights.[101]

In *X and Y v Netherlands*,[102] the Court clarified that the positive obligations inherent in Article 8 might 'involve the adoption of measures designed to secure respect for private life even in the sphere of the relations of individuals between themselves'.[103] In this case, appropriate criminal law measures were required to enable the prosecution of a man who had raped a mentally disabled woman in a care home. This is the second aspect of the state's positive obligation: the obligation to prevent violations of Article 8 rights by third parties.[104] Where positive obligations on a state concern the conduct of private individuals, the case law presents the duty as one on the state to ensure individuals' compliance with the law.[105]

There is little clarity about the content of the states' positive obligations under Article 8. In *Abdulaziz, Cabales and Balkandali v UK*,[106] the applicants argued that the state had a positive obligation to admit their alien husbands to join them when these men had no independent right to be admitted under immigration law. The Court said:

> [E]specially as far as those positive obligations are concerned, the notion of 'respect' is not clear-cut: having regard to the diversity of practices followed and the situations obtaining in the Contracting states, the notion's requirements will vary considerably from case to case.

In *A, B and C v Ireland*,[107] the Court added some further guidance:

> [C]ertain factors have been considered relevant for the assessment of the content of those positive obligations on States. Some factors concern the applicant: the importance of the interest at stake and whether 'fundamental values' or 'essential aspects' of private life are in issue ... and the impact on an applicant of a discordance between the social reality and the law, the coherence of the administrative and legal practices within the domestic system being regarded as an important factor in the assessment carried out under Article 8 ... Some factors concern the position of the State: whether the alleged obligation is narrow and defined or broad and indeterminate ... and the extent of any burden the obligation would impose on the State.

As in the case of negative obligations, the state enjoys a certain margin of appreciation. This is important because the formulation of a positive obligation under Article 8 may

---

[100] *Marckx v Belgium* A 31 (1979); 2 EHRR 330 PC.

[101] Sometimes called 'the obligation to fulfil': see Nowak, *Introduction to the International Human Rights Regime*, 2003.

[102] A 91 (1985); 8 EHRR 235 para 23. See also eg, *Johnston and Others v Ireland* A 112 (1986); 9 EHRR 203 para 55 PC.

[103] See Clapham, *Human Rights in the Private Sphere*, 1993, pp 211–22, for a discussion of the early case law in this area.

[104] Sometimes called 'the obligation to protect': see Nowak, *Introduction to the International Human Rights Regime*, 2003.

[105] Eg, *Hokkanen v Finland* A 299-A (1994); 19 EHRR 139 and *Karadžić v Croatia* hudoc (2005); 44 EHRR 896.　　　　　　　　　　　　　　　　　　　　　　[106] A 94 (1985); 7 EHRR 471 para 67 PC.

[107] Hudoc (2010); 53 EHRR 429 para 248 GC.

impact negatively on other Convention rights. Where it finds a violation, the Court therefore rarely goes into detail as to what precise steps should have been taken to secure respect for Article 8 rights. However, in *X and Y v Netherlands*,[108] the Court held that the effective protection of Article 8 rights required criminal, and not merely civil, law provisions. There is an obvious tension between those fundamental values and essential interests of private life which require that the state desist from interference with a person's activities (for instance, the obligation not to criminalize adult, consensual homosexual activities in private)[109] and others, such as those that were present in *X and Y*, where the positive obligation demands that the state does interfere to the point of criminalizing private action. Where the activities are wholly consensual between adults, it might be expected that a state should be slow to intervene. However, cases involving actions which put the physical or moral integrity of children at risk appear to fall into the category of cases where the effective application of the criminal law is required to ensure adequate protection.[110] Outside this context, the Court would be unlikely to find positive obligations to criminalize conduct, where civil remedies exist.[111]

It can be difficult to identify whether positive or negative obligations are in play. Cases concerning a refusal by the state to take action itself to respect an applicant's Article 8 rights—such as a refusal to provide access to state records or the refusal to register a change of name—would appear to give rise to obligations of the classic negative kind. In both cases, the interference would be constituted by the refusal decision. However, perhaps surprisingly, the Court has often chosen to examine such cases from the perspective of the state's positive obligation to put in place an appropriate framework. In *Gaskin v UK*,[112] the refusal of the state to provide the applicant access to records it held about his time in local authority care as a child constituted a violation of its positive obligation. In *Stjerna v Finland*,[113] the refusal to register the applicant's desired change of surname could not 'necessarily' be considered an interference with his right to respect for his private life. The analysis of the case therefore followed the positive obligation approach. Similar challenges arise in cases involving civil disputes between two private parties that have been adjudicated by a court. As the matter concerns a dispute between individuals, this would point towards positive obligations being in play. However, in many cases the court order itself can be seen as an act of the state authorities which interferes with Article 8 rights. It seems that much will depend on the applicant's position in the domestic proceedings. If the applicant was the unsuccessful plaintiff, the case should properly fall within the positive obligation category: essentially, the applicant is complaining that the refusal to uphold his claim constitutes a failure by the state to protect his Article 8 rights as against a third party.[114] However, where the applicant was the unsuccessful defendant in domestic proceedings, the court order handed down against him can generally be construed as an interference with his Article 8 rights: here, the applicant's prior enjoyment of his Article 8 rights has been directly limited by the effect of the court's ruling.[115]

---

[108] A 91 (1985); 8 EHRR 235.

[109] Eg, *Dudgeon v UK* A 45 (1981); 4 EHRR 149 PC; *Laskey, Jaggard and Brown v UK* 1997-I; 24 EHRR 39; and *ADT v UK* 2000-IX; 31 EHRR 803.

[110] See also *KU v Finland* hudoc (2008); 48 EHRR 1237; *Remetin v Croatia* hudoc (2012) and *Söderman v Sweden* hudoc (2013) GC.

[111] But see *Sipoş v Romania* hudoc (2011), where the Court found a violation of the state's positive obligations following the acquittal of a broadcaster in criminal defamation proceedings.

[112] A 160 (1989); 12 EHRR 36 PC.   [113] A 299-B (1994); 24 EHRR 195.

[114] See *Evans v UK* 2007-I; 46 EHRR 728 GC and *Von Hannover v Germany* 2004-VI; 40 EHRR 1.

[115] See *Neulinger and Shuruk v Switzerland* hudoc (2010); 54 EHRR 1087 GC.

The difficulty in identifying whether a case gives rise to positive or negative obligations has few practical ramifications: as the Court has consistently said, the boundaries
between the state's positive and negative obligations under Article 8 'do not lend themselves to precise definition' and the applicable principles are in any event similar, with
the key question being whether a fair balance was struck between competing interests.[116]
However, aside from the unsatisfactory inconsistency in the Court's approach and the
lack of clear guidelines, the decision to analyse a case as giving rise to positive obligations,
instead of as an interference, has at least two concrete effects. The first is that there is
generally no separate examination of whether a measure is lawful or pursues a legitimate
aim, unlike Article 8(2) cases.[117] While this omission is appropriate where the applicant's
complaint is that there is no legal framework governing an area which impacts on his or
her Article 8 rights or that the state has failed altogether to act in circumstances where it
was obliged (under Article 8) to do so, the failure to assess legality in particular is unfortunate in cases which concern a refusal by the state—such as the refusal in *Gaskin* to grant
access to records—where the domestic legal framework may be of some importance. The
second impact of assessing a case in terms of positive obligations is that the absence of any
clear methodological approach in such cases frequently results in case-specific outcomes
with little in the way of guidance as to the scope and extent of the protection afforded by
Article 8.

III. PROCEDURAL OBLIGATIONS

Formerly, most Article 8 complaints concerned the substance of a decision taken at
domestic level. However, in *W v UK*,[118] the applicant complained about the procedures
applied by the local authority in reaching the decisions to restrict and then terminate his
access to his son, who was placed for adoption. On this basis, he contested the necessity of
the measure. The government disputed the relevance of procedural matters to the question of necessity. The Court acknowledged that Article 8 contained no explicit procedural
requirements, but said that this was not conclusive. Given the indisputable influence of
the decision-making process on the substance of the decision itself, the Court was entitled
to have regard to that process to determine whether it was fair and ensured due respect
to Article 8 rights. In *Connors v UK*,[119] a case concerning eviction, the existence of procedural safeguards was described as a 'crucial consideration' in the assessment of the
proportionality of the interference. Nowadays, applicants increasingly seek to challenge
decision-making procedures and the existence of procedural obligations under Article
8 is well-established in the case law, in particular in cases involving child abduction and
childcare proceedings,[120] eviction,[121] and environmental issues.[122]

---

[116] *Hokkanen v Finland* A 299-A (1994); 19 EHRR 139 para 55. See also *Dickson v UK* 2007-V; 46 EHRR
927 GC and *Hristozov and Others v Bulgaria* hudoc (2012). See *A, B and C v Ireland* hudoc (2010); 53 EHRR
429 GC and compare paras 216–42 (negative obligation) and paras 243–67 (positive obligation) for an example of where the Court has carefully turned its mind to the question of positive and negative obligations.

[117] Judge Wildhaber, concurring, in *Stjerna v Finland* A 299-B (1994); 24 EHRR 195, argued that, whether
negative or positive obligations are involved, the Court should consider whether there has been an interference with an Article 8(1) right and, if there has, whether it may be justified under Article 8(2). However, this
has not been the Court's approach.   [118] A 121 (1987); 10 EHRR 29 PC.

[119] Hudoc (2004); 40 EHRR 189 para 92.

[120] *Neulinger and Shuruk v Switzerland* hudoc (2010); 54 EHRR 1087 GC; and *YC v UK* hudoc (2012).

[121] *McCann v UK* hudoc (2008); 47 EHRR 913.

[122] *Guerra and Others v Italy* 1998-I; 26 EHRR 357 GC.

There is a clear practical benefit in holding that Article 8 imposes procedural require-ments. Deference to a decision made by a national body can be more readily accepted where the decision-making process is shown to have included the safeguards necessary to ensure the proper consideration of all relevant issues arising under Article 8 and the applicant's participation. Procedural safeguards under Article 8 overlap, to some extent, with the procedural guarantees of Article 6 and there is a tendency for the Court to con-sider the matter from the perspective of Article 8 only, importing the necessary aspects of Article 6. However, it can and sometimes does examine Article 6 complaints separately.[123] There is also an overlap between the procedural guarantees of Article 8 and the require-ment under Article 13 for an effective remedy. It is arguable that Article 8 procedural guarantees are relevant only to the first instance decision taken by the state authorities, with the guarantees offered by any appeal or review procedure being more appropriately examined from the standpoint of Article 13, but this is not a distinction which has gener-ally been made in the Court's case law.[124]

4. SUBJECT AREAS

There is no obvious manner of categorizing the Court's case law under Article 8. The following categorization offers a number of subject areas which seek to present the case law in some rational order, while recognizing that there are many overlaps between the different categories.

I. PERSONAL IDENTITY

a. Gender identification

It has long been accepted that the question of gender identification falls within the scope of private life. In *X v Germany*,[125] the applicant complained about the failure of the authorities to allow her to change her name and to amend her gender in the births register following a male-to-female sex change operation that she had undergone abroad. The Commission referred to medical evidence, which confirmed that the applicant felt and lived like a woman and that her transformation from a male to a female person had been completed. It also highlighted that the failure to amend her identity papers inevitably created various problems for her. It therefore considered that the refusal of the German authorities to give formal recognition to her situation seriously affected her private life.[126] The question of gender identification came before the Court in the case of *Rees v UK*.[127] The Court accepted that the question of official recognition of transsexuals fell within the scope of Article 8 without explicitly addressing the question.

The transsexual cases were examined from the perspective of the state's positive obliga-tions. In the early cases to come before the Court, the state had not forbidden the treatment

---

[123] See, eg, *RP and Others v UK* hudoc (2012), where the Court chose to examine complaints regarding safeguards in child care proceedings under Article 6. See also *Hoppe v Germany* hudoc (2002); 38 EHRR 285 and *Anghel v Italy* hudoc (2013).   [124] Eg, *Al-Nashif v Bulgaria* hudoc (2002); 36 EHRR 655.

[125] No 6699/74, 11 DR 16 (1977).

[126] Following the decision on admissibility, a friendly settlement was reached in the case: see Com Rep (31). See also *Van Oosterwijck v Belgium* B 36 (1979) para 52 Com Rep (later rejected by the Court for non-exhaustion of domestic remedies: A 40 (1980); 3 EHRR 557 PC).

[127] A 106 (1986); 9 EHRR 56 PC.

which brought about the applicant's gender reassignment. Indeed, in the United Kingdom cases,[128] the treatment was provided by the public health service. Rather, the applicants argued that the state had failed to respect their right to private life by refusing to amend their birth certificates. In considering the existence and extent of any positive obligation, the Court in *Rees* weighed the interest of the applicant in having the birth certificate altered against the burden on the state substantially to reassess the system for registering births.[129] It found the balance to be in favour of the state and held, therefore, that in light of the margin of appreciation enjoyed by the state in this area, it had not failed to respect the applicant's private life. The Court reached the same conclusion in 1990 in *Cossey v UK*[130] and again in 1998 in *Sheffield and Horsham v UK*.[131] The balance tipped the other way in *B v France*[132] in 1992 where the majority held that, compared with practice in the United Kingdom, the disadvantages resulting from the non-recognition for certain purposes of the applicant's new gender were greater in French law and practice while the consequences for the state in changing the system were less significant.

The Court broke new ground in the *Goodwin (Christine)* and *I* decisions in 2003,[133] when it concluded that as a result of the European and international consensus which had emerged around the legal recognition of transsexuals' acquired gender, states could no longer claim that the matter fell within their margin of appreciation, save as regards the appropriate means of achieving recognition of the right. Since there were no significant factors of public interest to weigh against the interest of the applicants in obtaining legal recognition of their gender reassignment, the balance had shifted in their favour. The decision that Article 8 had been violated was unanimous.[134]

The question of legal recognition resolved, more recent cases before the Court have concerned access to and reimbursement of the costs of gender reassignment surgery. In *Van Kück v Germany*,[135] the Court found a violation of Article 8 because in their approach to refusing the applicant's claim for reimbursement of the cost of gender reassignment surgery, the domestic courts had failed to strike a fair balance between the applicant's interests and the interests of her private health insurance company.[136] In *L v Lithuania*,[137] the failure of the state to put in place legal regulation governing access to reassignment surgery resulted in a violation of the state's positive obligation. The extent of the state's obligation to provide surgery is raised in the pending case of *YY v Turkey*,[138] where the applicant has complained about the refusal of the courts to grant her access to gender reassignment surgery. The Court's judgment may provide some helpful guidance as to where the boundaries of the state's positive obligations in this area lie.[139]

b. Information regarding one's origins

Gaskin v UK concerned access to records of the applicant's upbringing in foster care.[140] Some of the data contained in the records had been given on understandings of

---

[128] *Rees v UK; Cossey v UK* A 184 (1990); 13 EHRR 622 PC; and *Sheffield and Horsham v UK* 1998-V; 27 EHRR 163 GC.   [129] *Rees v UK*.

[130] A 184 (1990); 13 EHRR 622 PC.

[131] 1998-V; 27 EHRR 163 GC by eleven votes to nine with four separate dissenting opinions.

[132] A 232-C (1992); 16 EHRR 1 PC.

[133] *Christine Goodwin v UK* 2002-VI; 35 EHRR 447 GC and *I v UK* hudoc (2002); 36 EHRR 967 GC.

[134] See also *Grant v UK* 2006-VII; 44 EHRR 1.   [135] 2003-VII; 37 EHRR 973.

[136] See also *Schlumpf v Switzerland* hudoc (2009).   [137] 2007-VI; 46 EHRR 431.

[138] *No 14793/08* (communicated March 2010).

[139] See also *Hamalainen v Finland No 37359/09*, pending before the Grand Chamber, concerning a complaint under Articles 8 and 14 because full recognition of the applicant's new gender required her to transform her marriage into a civil partnership.   [140] A 160 (1989); 12 EHRR 36 PC.

confidentiality. As an adult, Gaskin sought access to the files held about him but the local authority would reveal only the data for which it had obtained a release from its obligation of confidentiality from the source of the information. The majority of the Court acknowledged the applicant's claim that the records of his upbringing were significant to him as part of what he was, as a substitute for the parental memory of children brought up within their own family. It therefore found that the records related to the applicant's private and family life in such a way that the question of his access to them fell within the ambit of Article 8.

Seeking to justify the restriction on access, the government in *Gaskin* emphasized the importance of confidential record-keeping for an effective system of public childcare and argued that if any positive obligation existed, it had been discharged by the measures the local authority had taken to obtain waivers of confidentiality. However, the Court found that persons in the applicant's position had a vital interest in receiving the information necessary to know and understand their childhood and early development. It concluded that the positive obligation on the state demanded independent adjudication to decide whether the continued confidentiality of information was really necessary where the contributor refused to waive confidentiality or could not be traced.[141] In *Godelli v Italy*,[142] the Court found a violation of Article 8 where the applicant had not had access to any relevant information about her origins and there was no attempt in the Italian system to balance the competing interests in the case. By contrast, the Court found no violation of Article 8 in *Odièvre v France*.[143] It explained that the applicant's vital interest in her personal development had to be balanced against her biological mother's interest in remaining anonymous in order to protect her health by giving birth in appropriate medical conditions. Having regard to the interests at play and the efforts made to provide some information, the state had not overstepped its margin of appreciation.[144]

A number of cases brought by (usually adult) children regarding establishment of paternity have been considered by the Court from the perspective of 'private life', and can properly be considered as giving rise to an interest in establishing one's origins. However, for the sake of coherence these are discussed later, together with paternity complaints lodged by fathers.[145]

c. Appearance

Aspects of physical appearance are rarely regulated by the state. Where there is some restriction imposed on, for example, dress, challenges tend to be made under Article 9 of the Convention.[146] As a consequence, there have been very few cases in which an applicant has complained of an interference with his right to respect for private life as a result of restrictions concerning appearance. However, intimate aspects like mode of dress and hairstyle are likely to fall within the ambit of private life and any attempt to regulate them will constitute an interference.[147] In the few Article 8 cases considered by them, the Commission

---

[141] See the dissenting opinion, which referred to concerns about the consequences for the child-care system of the possible revelation of information given in confidence. Judge Walsh thought Article 8 did not apply at all and instead found Article 10 relevant.   [142] Hudoc (2012).

[143] 2003-III; 38 EHRR 871 GC.

[144] See the discussion of the Article 8 interests at stake in Marshall, 71(2) CLJ 325 (2012).

[145] See section 4.X.a, at pp 564 et seq.

[146] See *Dahlab v Switzerland No 42393/98* 2001-V DA and *Eweida and Others v UK* hudoc (2013). However, *SAS v France No 43835/11*, concerning a law banning the wearing of the veil in public places, was communicated *inter alia* under Article 8 in February 2012 and is pending before the Grand Chamber.

[147] In *McFeeley v UK No 8317/78*, 20 DR 44 (1980) the Commission accepted that the requirement that the applicant wear prison uniform amounted to an interference with his right to respect for private life. In *Sutter*

and the Court have accepted that the interference was justified. In *Tiğ v Turkey*,[148] where the applicant complained about the refusal to allow him to enter a university campus because he had a beard, the Court said that even if Article 8 was engaged, the interference was justified. It noted that the regulation prohibiting beards was only applied to the applicant a year after it had come into force and that, in any event, after shaving off his beard, he was able to continue with his studies. Similarly, in *Popa v Romania*,[149] the requirement that the applicant prisoner have his hair cut upon entering prison was justified for reasons of hygiene and disease prevention.[150]

d. Names

The Court has dealt with a number of cases concerning various aspects of the regulation of names. In *Burghartz v Switzerland*,[151] it found that although the Convention did not contain any explicit provisions on names, as a means of personal identification and of linking to a family, a person's surname nonetheless concerned his private and family life.[152] In *Guillot v France*,[153] the Court said that, since forenames constituted a means of identifying persons within their families and the community, they also concerned private and family life.[154] The Court now appears to have accepted that disputes concerning forenames and surnames of a physical person, including their spelling, will *per se* fall within the scope of Article 8 under both private and family life.[155]

The Court's approach to whether such cases give rise to an interference with private life or whether they engage the state's positive obligations has varied. In *Stjerna v Finland*,[156] it explained that the refusal to allow the applicant to adopt a specific surname was not necessarily an interference with his right to respect for private life, as would have been an obligation on him to change surname. Referring to the state's positive obligations, it found that the level of inconvenience of which the applicant complained was insufficient to establish a failure on the part of the authorities.[157] Similarly in *Guillot*,[158] the Court examined whether the refusal to register the forename 'Fleur de Marie' constituted a failure to respect the applicants' private and family lives from the perspective of the state's positive obligations. It found that it did not, having regard to the degree of inconvenience suffered. In *Johansson v Finland*,[159] which also concerned the refusal of the authorities to register the chosen forename for a child, the Court distinguished the case from previous cases, noting that the applicants' choice of name ('Axl') was not whimsical like 'Fleur de Marie' (in *Guillot*), or likely to harm the child like 'Ainut Vain Marjaana' ('The One and Only Marjaana') in *Salonen v Finland*,[160] but was a name already accepted by the authorities in other cases and one which was not too different from other Finnish names, which the names policy was designed to

---

v Switzerland No 8209/78, 16 DR 177 (1979) the Commission had no doubt that the obligation for part-time soldiers to have their hair cut short might adversely affect the way in which the applicant expressed his personality. See also see also *Stevens v UK No 11674/85*, 46 DR 245 (1986) (school uniform: not applicable); and *Kara v UK No 36528/97* hudoc (1998) DA (transvestite: applicable).

[148] *No 8165/03* hudoc (2005) DA.   [149] *No 4233/09* hudoc (2013) DA.

[150] See also *Gough v UK No 49327/11* (communicated September 2012), where the applicant complains under, *inter alia*, Article 8 about convictions for being naked in public.

[151] A 280-B (1994); 18 EHRR 101.   [152] See also *Stjerna v Finland* A 299-B (1994); 24 EHRR 195.

[153] 1996-V.   [154] See also *Salonen v Finland No 27868/95* hudoc (1997) DA.

[155] Eg, *Mentzen alias Mencena v Latvia No 71074/01* 2004-XII DA; *Bulgakov v Ukraine* hudoc (2007); 52 EHRR 419; and *Kemal Taşkın and Others v Turkey* hudoc (2010).

[156] A 299-B (1994); 24 EHRR 195.

[157] But see *Henry Kismoun v France* hudoc (2013), where a violation was found.

[158] 1996-V.   [159] Hudoc (2007); 47 EHRR 369.   [160] *No 27868/95* hudoc (1997) DA.

preserve. Accordingly a fair balance was not struck in the case. There was also a breach of the state's positive obligations in *Garnaga v Ukraine*,[161] where the refusal to allow the applicant to change her patronymic to one based on the name of her step-father was not sufficiently reasoned, having regard to the authorities' flexible and generous approach to changes of forenames and surnames.

In contrast, cases where the spelling of names has been subject to regulation by the state's linguistic policy on transcription of names have generally been viewed as giving rise to an interference, described as a 'regulation of the use of the name'.[162] The Court has tended to view interferences as proportionate to the legitimate aim of protecting the rights and freedoms of others. In *Mentzen alias Mencena v Latvia*,[163] it found that the phonetic transcription of foreign names into Latvian enabled its accurate pronunciation in Latvia and that the difficulties encountered were not sufficiently serious to render the measure disproportionate, given that both forms of the surname were equivalent in law and both forms could appear in the applicant's passport.

e. Ethnic and religious identity

In *Ciubotaru v Moldova*,[164] the applicant complained about the refusal of the authorities to issue him with a new identity card confirming his ethnicity as Romanian and their insistence that he declare his ethnicity to be Moldovan. The Court found the facts to fall within the ambit of 'private life', noting that along with name, gender, religion, and sexual orientation, an individual's ethnic identity constituted an essential aspect of his private life and identity. This was particularly true in Moldova, where the problem of ethnic identity had been the subject matter of social tension and heated debate for a long time. The state's failure to enable the applicant to have his claim to belong to a certain ethnic group examined in the light of objectively verifiable evidence amounted to a violation of its positive obligations.

Cases concerning the inclusion of religious identity on identity cards tend to be brought under Article 9 of the Convention.[165] However, such cases could potentially be examined from the perspective of Article 8.

f. National identity

The Court has accepted that the arbitrary denial of citizenship might in certain circumstances raise an issue under Article 8 of the Convention because of the impact of such a denial on the private life of the individual.[166] In *Genovese v Malta*,[167] the Court explained that while there was no right to citizenship under the Convention, the impact of the denial of citizenship on the applicant's social identity was such as to bring it within the general scope and ambit of that Article.[168] However, as a result of the scarcity of cases on the point, the notion of national identity remains undeveloped in the case law.[169]

---

[161] Hudoc (2013).

[162] *Mentzen alias Mencena v Latvia No 71074/01* 2004-XII DA; *Kuharec alias Kuhareca v Latvia No 71557/01* hudoc (2004) DA; and *Kemal Taşkın and Others v Turkey* hudoc (2010). But contrast *Bulgakov v Ukraine* hudoc (2007); 52 EHRR 419.   [163] *Mentzen alias Mencena v Latvia*.

[164] Hudoc (2010).

[165] See *Sofianopoulos and Others v Greece Nos 1988/02, 1997/02 and 1977/02* 2002-X DA and *Sinan Işık v Turkey* hudoc (2010).   [166] See, eg, *Karassev v Finland No 31414/96* 1999-II DA.

[167] Hudoc (2011).   [168] The case was examined under Article 8 together with Article 14.

[169] But see *Kurić and Others v Slovenia* hudoc (2012); 56 EHRR 688 GC, concerning 'erased' ex-Yugoslavia nationals in Slovenia; and *M v Switzerland* hudoc (2011), concerning the refusal to provide a national with a passport.

II. MORAL, PHYSICAL, AND PSYCHOLOGICAL INTEGRITY

X and Y v Netherlands[170] showed that an unwelcome physical attack by one individual—in that case a sexual assault on a young woman—was capable of infringing private life because the concept of private life covers the physical and moral integrity of the person. In practice, Article 8 is often invoked where there is a complaint of ill-treatment which does not reach the Article 3 threshold. In the early case of *Costello-Roberts v UK*,[171] while the Court did not exclude that there might be circumstances in which Article 8 could offer protection which went beyond that given by Article 3, it found that the smacking of the applicant by his headmaster with a shoe did not reach the minimum level of severity under Article 8.[172] However, since then, the Court has embraced the application of Article 8 in this area, without necessarily delimiting with any clarity the extent of the protection afforded by Article 8 compared to that afforded by Article 3. In *X and Y*, it declined to consider the Article 3 complaint, having found a violation of Article 8. Given that Article 3 is the more serious allegation, the Court might justifiably be criticized for failing to examine it first.[173] However, in *MN v Bulgaria*,[174] which concerned an allegedly deficient investigation into a rape allegation made by a minor, the Court accepted at the outset that the allegation fell within the scope of Articles 3 and 8 and proceeded to examine the two simultaneously.[175] By contrast, in *IG v Moldova*,[176] also concerning an investigation into the rape of a minor, the Court examined first the Article 3 complaint and, a violation of that Article having been established, considered that no separate issue arose under Article 8. The Court's approach to these cases tends to suggest that it often views the sphere of protection under Articles 3 and 8 to be coterminous. This seems to be a regrettable blurring of important boundaries between two Articles with very different objectives and content. In most cases it is difficult to see any justification for analysing complaints under both Articles, and still less for finding a violation of both. In a case concerning the extent of a state's positive obligations, for example, then in the event of a non-violation of Article 3 on the ground that the positive obligation claimed does not arise under that Article, it is difficult to imagine how a violation of Article 8 could be established, given the emphasis on the margin of appreciation and the need to strike a fair balance in Article 8 cases which is not applied to cases under Article 3. Only in cases where the treatment of which the applicant complains does not fall within the scope of Article 3 does it make sense to examine the matter under Article 8.

Perhaps unusually given the injuries incurred in some cases, in domestic violence cases the Court often finds that the Article 3 threshold has not been met and instead examines the case under Article 8.[177] Despite this, the Court has consistently held that victims of domestic violence are of a particular vulnerability and has highlighted the need for active state involvement in their protection.[178] It has regularly found violations of the state's

---

[170] A 91 (1985); 8 EHRR 235.   [171] A 247-C (1993); 19 EHRR 112.

[172] Cf *Tyrer v UK* A 26 (1978); 2 EHRR 1.

[173] As it did in *Costello-Roberts v UK* A 247-C (1993); 19 EHRR 112.   [174] Hudoc (2012).

[175] See also *MC v Bulgaria* 2003-XII; 40 EHRR 459 and *M and C v Romania* hudoc (2011).

[176] Hudoc (2012).

[177] See *A v Croatia* hudoc (2010), where the applicant complained under Articles 2, 3, and 8 of a failure by the state to protect her from acts of violence committed by her husband. The violence was both verbal, including serious death threats, and physical, including hitting and kicking the applicant in the head, face, and body, causing her injuries. But in *B v Moldova* hudoc (2013), the Court accepted that the Article 3 threshold had been met.

[178] *Hajduová v Slovakia* hudoc (2010); 53 EHRR 292; *MT and ST v Slovakia No 59968/09* hudoc (2012) DA; and *Irene Wilson v UK No 10601/09* hudoc (2012) DA.

positive obligation in this area because of the absence of an effective and accessible remedy to protect one family member from the threats of violence of another or the failure to take appropriate measures to protect victims.[179] However, the Court has been slow to find a violation of Article 8 where criminal proceedings have been brought and pursued diligently by the authorities, even where the proceedings have resulted in acquittal or in a lenient sentence.[180]

In some cases concerning attacks on physical or psychological integrity, the Court has required criminal law measures to satisfy Article 8. In *X and Y v Netherlands*,[181] the Court held that the protection afforded by the civil law in the case of wrongdoing of the kind inflicted on the applicant was insufficient. In *KU v Finland*,[182] the Court found Article 8 applicable to a case in which an unknown person had placed an advertisement of a sexual nature concerning the applicant, a twelve-year-old boy, on the internet. It held that the practical and effective protection of the applicant required that effective steps be taken to identify and prosecute the person who placed the advertisement. In *Remetin v Croatia*,[183] a violation of Article 8 was found where the prosecution of a man alleged to have attacked the applicant, then a thirteen-year-old child, in the context of a playground dispute was time barred as a result of a lack of diligence by the authorities. So although there were appropriate criminal-law provisions, a violation of Article 8 had occurred because the manner in which the criminal-law mechanisms were implemented in the case was defective.[184] However, in *Söderman v Sweden*,[185] the Court—somewhat surprisingly—said that the attempted covert filming of a fourteen-year-old girl when naked by her step-father did not attain the seriousness of the grave acts of rape and sexual abuse of children, and that criminal law measures were therefore not necessary if the legal framework was otherwise adequate.[186]

The circumstances in which positive obligations arise in this area are not always easy to identify. In *Georgel and Georgeta Stoicescu v Romania*,[187] one of the applicants was attacked by a pack of stray dogs in Bucharest. The Court concluded that the lack of sufficient measures taken by the authorities in addressing the issue of stray dogs, despite their awareness of the problem, combined with their failure to provide appropriate redress to the applicant, amounted to a breach of the state's positive obligations.[188] However, despite knowledge on the part of the Turkish authorities of numerous indiscriminate attacks on teachers and civil servants in the region, the Court in *Ebcin v Turkey*[189] found no failure on the part of the authorities to take sufficient measures in a case where the applicant teacher sustained serious injuries as a result of an attack where acid was thrown in her face. The Court insisted on the need to show a specific risk, higher than that faced by the general population. It seems that the difference in result may come down to the fact that there were steps that could have been taken against the dogs in Romania, while in

---

[179] See, eg, *Airey v UK* A 32 (1979); 2 EHRR 305; *A v Croatia* hudoc (2010); *Hajduová v Slovakia*; *Kalucza v Hungary* hudoc (2012); *Eremia and Others v Moldova* hudoc (2013). and *B v Moldova* hudoc (2013).

[180] See *MT and ST v Slovakia* No 59968/09 hudoc (2012) DA; *Kowal v Poland* No 2912/11 hudoc (2012) DA; and *Irene Wilson v UK* No 10601/09 hudoc (2012) DA.   [181] A 91 (1985); 8 EHRR 235.

[182] Hudoc (2008); 48 EHRR 1237.   [183] Hudoc (2012).

[184] See also *M and C v Romania* hudoc (2011); and *MS v Croatia* hudoc (2013).

[185] Hudoc (2013) GC.

[186] There was a violation because it appeared that neither civil or criminal remedies were available.

[187] Hudoc (2011).

[188] The Court appeared to envisage a duty to take urgent operational measure, equivalent to the duty arising under Articles 2 and 3, where there is an immediate and identified to risk to the life or health of an identified individual. However, the justification for the radical extension of this duty to the Article 8 context is not explained and is not the basis of the Court's conclusion.   [189] Hudoc (2011).

Ebcin it was hard to see what specific measures the authorities could have taken against unknown attackers. But the reference in *Ebcin* to the need to demonstrate a specific risk was wholly absent in *Stoicescu*, leaving uncertainty as to the exact circumstances in which more extensive obligations will arise.

In some cases, the Court appears to expect state authorities to be particularly proactive in seeking to protect individuals from the acts of private parties; while in other apparently similar cases it reaches a different conclusion on the facts. In both *Đurđević v Croatia*[190] and *Đurđević v Croatia*,[191] the authorities were made aware of a problem of a campaign of bullying and harassment of the applicants. But while in *Đurđević* the authorities were expected to put in place relevant general measures to stop the harassment, in *Đurđević* they were not. It is true that in *Đurđević* the absence of specific details of the bullying was highlighted, but it is difficult to see what relevance this had to the need for general measures, given that it was not contested that sustained bullying had taken place.[192]

Article 8 is often invoked in the context of cases where applicants complain about measures restricting their legal capacity. The deprivation of legal capacity generally constitutes an interference with private life[193] and pursues the legitimate aim of protecting the interests of the person affected by the measure.[194] The key aspects to consider in the proportionality assessment are whether the measure has a drastic effect on personal autonomy, where stricter scrutiny will be applied by the Court; and the quality of the decision-making procedure.[195] Institution of proceedings to divest a person of legal capacity must be warranted on the facts.[196] The existence of a mental disorder, even a serious one, cannot in itself justify full incapacitation.[197] Full incapacitation will only be justified where the mental disorder is of a kind and degree warranting such a measure. In other circumstances, some form of lesser incapacitation only will be warranted.[198] As far as the procedural aspect is concerned, the Court has referred to the content of Article 6, and in particular the right of access to a court.[199] A measure depriving a person of legal capacity must be open to review, given that the situation of a person suffering from a mental illness is subject to change. Where there is neither automatic review nor direct access to court for an incapacitated person, there will be a violation of Article 8.[200]

III. MEDICAL CARE AND TREATMENT

a. Treatment without consent

Medical treatment administered with the consent of the patient does not give rise to an interference with the right to respect for private life.[201] However, the imposition of

---

[190] Hudoc (2012), concerning the harassment of a physically and mentally disabled man and his mother.

[191] Hudoc (2011), about persistent school bullying.

[192] See also *Whiteside v UK No 20357/92*, 76A DR 80 (1994), where the Commission found that persistent harassment by the applicant's ex-partner gave rise to a positive obligation to secure the applicant's rights by providing adequate protection against this type of deliberate persecution.

[193] *Matter v Slovakia* hudoc (1999); 31 EHRR 783; *Shtukaturov v Russia* hudoc (2008); 54 EHRR 962; and *X and Y v Croatia* hudoc (2011).

[194] *Lashin v Russia* hudoc (2013). But see *MS v Croatia* hudoc (2013).

[195] *Salontaji-Drobnjak v Serbia* hudoc (2009) and *Lashin v Russia*.

[196] *X and Y v Croatia* hudoc (2011).   [197] *Shtukaturov v Russia* hudoc (2008); 54 EHRR 962.

[198] *Lashin v Russia* hudoc (2013).

[199] *Lashin v Russia*. However, in *Stanev v Bulgaria* hudoc (2012); 55 EHRR 696 GC the Court looked at the issue of access to a court under Article 6(1) of the Convention. In *Salontaji-Drobnjak v Serbia* hudoc (2009) it considered the complaint under both Articles and found a violation of both.

[200] *Lashin v Russia*.   [201] See *Storck v Germany* 2005-V; 43 EHRR 96.

medical treatment without consent raises serious issues which fall within the scope of private life, however slight the intervention.[202] Although the Court formerly considered that treatment without consent did not constitute an interference when the patient was not capable of giving consent, it now appears to accept that there will be an interference in such cases and that the lack of capacity to consent is a matter pertinent to justification under Article 8(2).[203] A similar approach applies to cases concerning treatment without consent administered in an emergency.[204]

A number of cases have been brought by persons lacking capacity to consent. In *Matter v Slovakia*,[205] the Court found the interference caused by the applicant's forcible treatment to be proportionate given that the purpose of the medial examination was to determine whether his legal capacity should be restored.[206] In *Glass v UK*,[207] the applicant was treated in the face of opposition from his mother and legal guardian. The government argued that the doctors were confronted with an emergency and had to act quickly in the best interests of the applicant, but the Court emphasized the failure of the authorities to seek a court order authorizing treatment and found a violation of Article 8. The applicant in *Storck v Germany*[208] had been placed in a psychiatric institution against her will, where medical treatment had been administered by force. The Court found a violation of the state's positive obligation to protect the applicant because of the lack of state supervision and control over private psychiatric institutions at the time. It also found that the interference with the applicant's rights was not in accordance with the law, as the detention of a mentally insane person for the purpose of medical treatment necessitated a court order if the person concerned did not consent, and no such court order had been made. In *Shopov v Bulgaria*,[209] the applicant complained that for more than five years he had been forced to undergo psychiatric treatment at an outpatient clinic pursuant to a court order. The interference was not in accordance with the law because although the initial court order had a legal basis, there had been no regular judicial review of the need to continue the treatment, as required by domestic law.

There have been few cases concerning medical treatment administered without consent outside the context of applicants who lack legal capacity. Those which have come to the Court have tended to involve medical interventions which were relatively trivial and authorized by law or by court order;[210] or compulsory screening or vaccination programmes for dangerous diseases.[211] In these cases, the Court has found interferences justified under Article 8(2). However, in *MAK and RK v UK*,[212] blood tests were conducted on a nine-year-old girl who had been hospitalized, despite instructions from her parents that no further tests were to be carried out without speaking to her mother. Finding a violation of Article 8, the Court noted that the situation was not an emergency; that there was no evidence that the mother would have refused her consent; and that even if she had, a court

[202]   *Peters v Netherlands No 21132/93*, 77-A DR 75 (1994) (urine test) and *X v Finland* hudoc (2012) (forced administration of medication).

[203]   See *Herczegfalvy v Austria* A 244 (1992); 15 EHRR 457; *Matter v Slovakia* hudoc (1999); 31 EHRR 783; and *Glass v UK* 2004-II; 39 EHRR 341.   [204]   See *Glass v UK*.

[205]   Hudoc (1999); 31 EHRR 783.

[206]   The Court declined to consider the matter from the perspective of Article 3.

[207]   2004-II; 39 EHRR 341.   [208]   2005-V; 43 EHRR 96.   [209]   Hudoc (2010).

[210]   *X v Austria No 8278/78*, 18 DR 154 at 156 (1979) (blood test in paternity proceedings) and *Peters v Netherlands No 21132/93*, 77-A DR 75 (1994) (urine test in prison).

[211]   *Acmanne and Others v Belgium No 10435/83*, 40 DR 251 (1984) (compulsory screening for tuberculosis); *Boffa and Others v San Marino No 26536/95*, 92-B DR 27 (1998) (compulsory hepatitis B vaccination); and *Salvetti v Italy No 42197/98* hudoc (2002) DA (compulsory polio vaccination).

[212]   Hudoc (2010); 51 EHRR 396.

order could have been obtained.[213] In *Bogumil v Portugal*,[214] the Court found no violation of Article 8 where a drug trafficker underwent surgery to remove a packet of cocaine which he had swallowed. Although it was not clear that the applicant had consented to the surgery, the intervention was ordered by medical personnel to save the applicant's life rather than to collect evidence for use in criminal proceedings. Pending cases concerning the removal of tissue from deceased persons may provide an opportunity to explore the extent to which policies of 'presumed consent' are compatible with Article 8.[215]

A patient's consent to medical treatment must be free and informed in order to be valid for the purposes of Article 8. In *Trocellier v France*,[216] the applicant underwent a hysterectomy but after the procedure her leg was paralysed. She claimed that she had not been informed of the risks. The Court held that states were bound to adopt the necessary regulatory measures to ensure that doctors considered the foreseeable consequences of planned medical procedures on their patients' physical integrity and informed patients of those consequences to enable them to give informed consent. Here the applicant's paralysis was not a foreseeable consequence of the surgery and the complaint was manifestly ill-founded.[217] The applicant in *VC v Slovakia*[218] was of Roma ethnic origin who had been sterilized while giving birth. The authorities claimed that she had requested sterilization; the applicant claimed that she was pressured into agreeing during labour without understanding what was involved. As the Court had already found a violation of Article 3 on account of the sterilization which it held had been carried out without the applicant's full and informed consent, it declined to consider this complaint also under Article 8. However, the absence of safeguards giving special consideration to the reproductive health of the applicant as a Roma woman resulted in a failure by Slovakia to comply with its positive obligation to secure to her sufficient protection enabling her effectively to enjoy her right to respect for her private and family life. In *Juhnke v Turkey*,[219] the applicant's consent was not free and informed where she had agreed to a gynaecological examination after having been detained *incommunicado* for nine days and there were inadequate procedural safeguards. In *Csoma v Romania*,[220] the applicant was left permanently unable to have children after complications during an abortion. Finding a violation of Article 8, the Court attached weight to the fact that the doctor had failed to obtain the applicant's informed written consent and noted that he had also failed to perform the pre-operative checks required.

b. Medical negligence

The most serious cases of medical negligence resulting in death will fall within the scope of Article 2 of the Convention.[221] However, allegations of medical negligence may also fall within the scope of Article 8. The Court will usually defer to the findings of the national courts as to the extent of any responsibility under Article 8 for substandard medical care. In *Benderskiy v Ukraine*,[222] the applicant complained about a gauze compress left in his body during an operation. Holding that there was no violation of Article 8, the Court noted that in the domestic proceedings brought by the applicant, neither medical experts

---

[213] See also *Yuriy Volkov v Ukraine* hudoc (2013) where a violation was found because a blood sample was not taken by a medical specialist, as the law required.   [214] Hudoc (2008).

[215] *Petrova v Latvia* No 4605/09 (communicated November 2009) and *Elberte v Latvia* No 61243/08 (communicated April 2010).   [216] No 75725/01 2006-XIV DA.

[217] See also *Baytüre v Turkey* No 3270/09 hudoc (2013) DA.   [218] Hudoc (2011).

[219] Hudoc (2008); 49 EHRR 534.   [220] Hudoc (2013).

[221] Eg, *Calvelli and Ciglio v Italy* 2002-I GC and *Vo v France* 2004-VIII; 40 EHRR 259 GC.

[222] Hudoc (2007).

nor the courts had found the clinic responsible.[223] However, a violation of Article 8 arose in a case where a civil judgment against the doctor had been obtained but was not enforceable as a result of his insolvency.[224]

c. Availability of health care and treatment

While the Convention does not necessarily guarantee a right to free medical care or to specific medical treatment, Article 8 is relevant to complaints about insufficient availability of health care services.[225] The Court's general position is that matters of health care policy are in principle within the margin of appreciation of the domestic authorities, who are best placed to assess priorities, use of resources, and social needs.[226] In *Pentiacova and Others v Moldova*,[227] the Court rejected a complaint by applicants suffering from chronic renal failure about insufficient state financing of haemodialysis. Although it was prepared to accept that Article 8 applied, it considered that the applicants had enjoyed access to the standard of health care available to the general public, and Moldova had therefore struck a fair balance between the competing interests.[228] However, in *RR v Poland*,[229] a violation of Article 8 was found in a case where the applicant was denied access to prenatal genetic testing which she needed in order to obtain information relevant to her decision whether to have an abortion. In *Tysiąc v Poland*,[230] the Court found a violation of Article 8 because despite the need for safeguards where a disagreement arose as to whether the applicant was entitled to a legal abortion, Polish law did not contain any effective mechanisms capable of determining whether the conditions for obtaining a lawful abortion had been met. In *A, B and C v Ireland*,[231] the Court held that where abortion was available, the legal framework had to permit women to access abortion and to challenge the refusal to authorize an abortion.[232] *Ternovszky v Hungary*[233] concerned a complaint regarding ambiguous legislation which the applicant claimed dissuaded health professionals from assisting at home births. The Court found that the legal uncertainty caused by the lack of clarity in the legislation meant that the lawfulness requirement of Article 8(2) was not satisfied.[234]

In *Hristozov and Others v Bulgaria*,[235] the applicants, who were suffering from terminal cancer, complained about the refusal of the Bulgarian authorities to authorize the use of an experimental anti-cancer product after conventional treatments had failed. The Court

---

[223] See also *Spyra and Kranczkowski v Poland* hudoc (2012).

[224] *Codarcea v Romania* hudoc (2009). See also the communicated case of *Bulai v Moldova* (No 12740/09) where the applicant complains, *inter alia*, of a lack of sufficient reasons in a judgment absolving the doctor of criminal responsibility for an accidental sterilization during labour.

[225] *Zehnalová and Zehnal v Czech Republic* No 38621/97 2002-V DA; *Sentges v Netherlands* No 27677/02 hudoc (2003) DA; and *Pentiacova and Others v Moldova* No 14462/03 2005-I DA.

[226] *Shelley v UK* No 23800/06 hudoc (2008) DA and *Hristozov and Others v Bulgaria* hudoc (2012).

[227] No 14462/03 2005-I DA.

[228] See also the pending case of *McDonald v UK* No 4241/12 (communicated April 2012), concerning the provisions of incontinence pads to an applicant with limited mobility, instead of assistance to use the toilet.

[229] Hudoc (2011); 53 EHRR 1047.

[230] 2007-I; 45 EHRR 947. Cf *D v Ireland* No 26499/02 hudoc (2006) DA, where the Court found that absence of abortion services did not constitute a violation of Article 8.

[231] Hudoc (2010); 53 EHRR 429 GC.

[232] See also *P and S v Poland* hudoc (2012) para 111, where the Court referred to the 'striking discordance between the theoretical right to such an abortion on the grounds referred to in that provision and the reality of its practical implementation'.   [233] Hudoc (2010).

[234] See also the cases of *Kosaitė-Čypienė and Others v Lithuania* No 69489/12 (communicated December 2012) and *Krejzová and Dubská v Czech Republic* Nos 28473/12 and 28859/11 (communicated September 2012).   [235] Hudoc (2012).

identified the applicants' interest as their freedom to opt, as a measure of last resort, for an untested treatment which might carry risks but which they and their doctors considered appropriate to their circumstances in an attempt to save their lives. The countervailing public interest in regulating the access of terminally ill patients to experimental products was based on three premises: to protect them against action which might prove harmful to their health and life; to ensure that a statutory prohibition on, *inter alia*, the use of medication which had not been granted authorization would not be circumvented; and to ensure that the development of new medicinal products would not be compromised by diminished patient participation in clinical trials. Having noted a clear trend in the member states towards allowing, under certain exceptional conditions, the use of unauthorized medicinal products, the Court nonetheless considered there to be a wide margin of appreciation since the emerging consensus was not based on settled principles and did not extend to the precise manner in which that use should be regulated. The Bulgarian authorities' approach did not fall outside the margin of appreciation. As to the applicants' separate complaint that the system in place failed to allow individual circumstances to be taken into account, the Court said that it was not in itself contrary to the requirements of Article 8 for a state to regulate important aspects of private life without making provision for the weighing of competing interests in the circumstances of each individual case.[236] Having regard to the fact that the finding of no violation was by the slimmest of majorities,[237] this may not be the last word on this issue.[238]

d. Euthanasia

A number of cases brought before the Court have concerned access to treatment or assistance to allow an individual to end his or her life. In *Pretty v UK*,[239] the applicant complained that the refusal of the prosecuting authority to give an undertaking that her husband would not be prosecuted for assisting her death was a blanket and disproportionate interference with respect for her private life, especially given her state as a competent adult who had made a fully informed and voluntary decision concerning assisted suicide. The Court accepted that the applicant's complaint that the law prevented her from exercising her choice to avoid what she considered would be an undignified and distressing end to her life raised an issue of private life. However, it found no violation of Article 8, noting that the seriousness of the act for which immunity was claimed was such that the decision to refuse the undertaking could not be said to be arbitrary or unreasonable. The applicant in *Haas v Switzerland*[240] had suffered from a serious bipolar affective disorder for about twenty years and wanted to obtain sodium pentobarbital in order to end his life. In order to obtain the drug, a medical prescription based on a thorough psychiatric assessment was required. The applicant was unable to obtain medical assistance in light of his psychiatric condition. He submitted that, in an exceptional situation such as his, access to the necessary medical products for suicide ought to be guaranteed by the state. The case was different from the *Pretty* case in that the applicant was not in the terminal stages of disease requiring assistance to end his life, but instead argued that the failure to grant him access to the drug sought would strip the act of suicide of dignity. The Court acknowledged that an individual's right to decide in which way and at which time his life should end was one of the aspects of the right to respect for private life. However,

---

[236] See also *Evans v UK* 2007-I; 46 EHRR 728 GC. But compare *Dickson v UK* 2007-V; 46 EHRR 927 GC and *Sabanchiyeva and Others v Russia* hudoc (2013).   [237] The vote was four to three.

[238] Although the applicants' request for a rehearing before the Grand Chamber was refused.

[239] 2002-III; 35 EHRR 1.   [240] Hudoc (2011); 53 EHRR 1169.

considering the facts of the case to give rise to the question whether there was a positive obligation to take the necessary measures to permit a dignified suicide, the Court found that even if such an obligation existed, it had been satisfied here.[241] In its recent judgment in *Gross v Switzerland*,[242] the Court found a violation of Article 8 in the case of an elderly woman who was not suffering from a terminal illness but wished to end her life because of her advanced age and increasingly frailty. It held that Swiss law did not provide guidelines of sufficient clarity defining the extent of the right to obtain sodium pentobarbital.[243]

e. Assisted procreation

Technological advances in procreation have given rise to cases concerning access to and availability of assisted procreation. In *Evans v UK*,[244] the applicant sought to use frozen embryos created with her partner during an IVF procedure. Although he had initially consented to the fertilization, he later withdrew his consent. The applicant claimed that the law that permitted him to withdraw his consent violated her Article 8 rights. The Court accepted that Article 8 incorporated the right to respect for both the decisions to become and not to become a parent. The question was whether the UK law struck a fair balance between the competing public (legal certainty, the importance of consent) and private (Article 8 rights of both parents) interests involved. The Court referred to the complexity of the issue, the detailed consideration it had been given in Parliament and in the courts, and the fact that at the time of the procedure the rules were clear and had been made clear to the applicant. On this basis, the Court disagreed that the applicant's right to respect for her decision to become a parent in the genetic sense should be accorded greater weight than her ex-partner's right to respect for his decision not to have a genetically related child with her. Although detailed and well-reasoned, the judgment of the Grand Chamber was not unanimous, attesting to the sensitive and disputed nature of questions in this field.[245] *Dickson v UK*[246] concerned a complaint by a serving prisoner and his wife about the refusal of access to artificial insemination facilities pursuant to a policy which denied such rights to all prisoners unless there were exceptional circumstances. Given that access to artificial insemination facilities represented the applicants' only realistic opportunity to conceive a child, the failure of the policy to permit a proportionality assessment led to a violation of Article 8.[247]

The applicants in *SH and Others v Austria*[248] complained about the prohibition on the use of ova and sperm from donors for *in vitro* fertilization, the only medical techniques by which they could successfully conceive children. Given the sensitive moral and ethical questions in this area and the absence of any clear common ground among European states, the Court found that the margin of appreciation was a wide one. It concluded that, in 1999 when the matter was considered by the Austrian Constitutional Court, the prohibition of gamete donation did not exceed the margin allowed. The finding of no violation enjoyed a large majority,[249] but there was a clear signal by the Court that continuing developments in this area will be kept under review and that a different conclusion might be reached in a future case. *Costa and Pavan v Italy*[250] concerned

---

[241] See also *Koch v Germany* hudoc (2012); 56 EHRR 195, where the Court found a procedural violation of Article 8. It declined to make a ruling on the substantive complaint, noting that the majority of states did not allow any form of assistance to suicide and that, given the wide margin of appreciation, it was primarily for the domestic courts to examine the merits of the claim.   [242] Hudoc (2013).

[243] The judges were split four to three and the Grand Chamber has accepted a request to rehear the case.

[244] 2007-I; 46 EHRR 728 GC.   [245] The Court was divided thirteen to four.

[246] 2007-V; 46 EHRR 927 GC.   [247] The vote was twelve to five.   [248] Hudoc (2011) GC.

[249] Thirteen to four.   [250] Hudoc (2012).

a couple who were healthy carriers of cystic fibrosis. They had one child with cystic fibrosis and had aborted another when screening showed that the child was a carrier of the disease. They sought access to IVF in order that the embryo could be genetically screened prior to implantation. However, pre-implantation diagnosis was prohibited under Italian law and IVF was only allowed in limited cases. The government justified the prohibition by reference to the need to protect the health of the mother and child and the dignity and freedom of conscience of the medical professions; and to avoid the risk of eugenic practices. The Court was not persuaded by this argument, pointing out that legal abortion was available where pre-natal screening revealed the presence of cystic fibrosis. It found a violation because the Italian system lacked coherence and in order to have a healthy child, the applicants were forced to conceive normally and face the painful decision to have an abortion if the disease was detected in the foetus.

IV. SEXUAL ACTIVITIES

Sexual activity usually occurs in private places between two individuals, and practised in this way will generally fall within the scope of Article 8. In *Dudgeon v UK*,[251] concerning consensual homosexual relations between adult men in private, the Court described sexual life as 'a most intimate aspect' of private life. In *Stübing v Germany*,[252] the Court accepted that a conviction for incest interfered with the right to respect for his private life. *Laskey, Jaggard and Brown v UK*[253] concerned the prosecution of three men for assault and wounding as a result of sado-masochistic sexual activities in private. The Court said that not all sexual activity which took place in private was necessarily within the scope with Article 8, but did not examine the matter further in this case because there was no dispute between the parties on the applicability of Article 8.[254] Subsequently, in *ADT v UK*,[255] the Court rejected the government's argument that the prosecution of the applicant for gross indecency was not an interference with his private life given the number of people involved in the sexual activities and the fact that they were recorded on video tape.[256] In *Mosley v UK*,[257] the applicant's complaint arose in the context of an exposé in the press which disclosed his sado-masochistic sexual activities with five prostitutes and included photographs and video footage. The Court accepted that the publication of the articles, photographs, and video images of the applicant participating in sexual acts had had a significant impact on the applicant's right to respect for his private life.

Complaints arising from a criminal prosecution or threat of prosecution for certain sexual activities are examined from the perspective of the state's negative obligation. In *Dudgeon v UK*,[258] the applicant complained about the existence of laws which made certain homosexual acts between consenting adult males criminal offences. The Court considered that 'particularly serious reasons' were required to justify an interference. Holding that the criminalization of adult, private, consensual male homosexual relations was not necessary in a democratic society, the Court relied on the developing European consensus towards removing criminal sanctions and the absence of any evidence that the practice of the Northern Ireland authorities in refraining to implement the law had led to

---

[251] A 45 (1981); 4 EHRR 149 para 52 PC. [252] Hudoc (2012); 55 EHRR 768.
[253] 1997-I; 24 EHRR 39. [254] See also *KA and AD v Belgium* hudoc (2005).
[255] 2000-IX; 31 EHRR 803. [256] Cf *KA and AD v Belgium* hudoc (2005).
[257] Hudoc (2011); 53 EHRR 1011. [258] A 45 (1981); 4 EHRR 149 PC.

damage to moral standards.[259] In *Laskey, Jaggard and Brown v UK*,[260] on the other hand, the Court found that the applicants' prosecution and convictions for assault and wounding in the course of consensual sado-masochistic activities between adults did not violate Article 8, noting that the activities here involved a significant degree of injury or wounding, which could not be characterized as trifling or transient.[261] By contrast, in *ADT v UK*,[262] a violation of Article 8 was found in a case involving a conviction in respect of consensual homosexual activities between the applicant and more than one consenting male. The Court referred to the narrow margin of appreciation in the case, the absence of any public-health considerations, and the purely private nature of the behaviour. There are few cases concerning the criminalization of sexual activities outside the context of homosexual acts. In *Stübing v Germany*,[263] the Court found no violation of Article 8 where the applicant was convicted for having sexual intercourse with his sister, who was also the mother of his four children. It noted the absence of consensus among member states and the corresponding wide margin of appreciation, notwithstanding the intimate nature of the activities in question.[264] Publication by the press of intimate details concerning a person's sexual life, in the absence of a public interest, will give rise to a violation of the state's positive obligations under Article 8 if no adequate remedy is available.[265]

With the widespread acceptance of homosexuality, the challenge now is to ensure equality with heterosexuals and to prevent discrimination on the basis of homosexuality.[266] As a consequence, the cases are often considered from an Article 14 perspective.[267] In the employment context, a series of cases concerning discharge from the defence forces on the grounds of sexual orientation were addressed under Article 8 only.[268]

The Court has had little occasion to consider whether the reach of private life includes the manifestation of sexual relations in public places. In *Pay v UK*,[269] the applicant performed sexual acts in a nightclub and contended that the public performance aspect of his act was a fundamental part of his sexual expression. The Court expressed some reservations about whether Article 8 was applicable, but did not finally decide the point. The principle that some privacy rights at least may be enjoyed in public places where there is a reasonable expectation of privacy[270] suggests that Article 8 may well be capable of application in such a case. However, if Article 8 applies, the state is likely to enjoy a wide margin of appreciation in this area. In *Pay v UK*,[271] the Court held that the dismissal of

---

[259] See also *Norris v Ireland* A 142 (1988); 13 EHRR 186 PC and *Modinos v Cyprus* A 259 (1993); 16 EHRR 485 and note the development from earlier Commission decisions such as *X v Germany* No 5935/72, 3 DR 46 (1975) and *B v UK* No 9237/81, 34 DR 68 (1983).   [260] 1997-I; 24 EHRR 39.

[261] See also *KA and AD v Belgium* hudoc (2005).   [262] 2000-IX; 31 EHRR 803.

[263] Hudoc (2012); 55 EHRR 768.

[264] See the criticism of the judgment in Spencer, 72(1) CLJ 5-7 (2013), comparing the Court's approach here to that adopted in the homosexual cases.

[265] See *Biriuk v Lithuania* hudoc (2008); *Mosley v UK* hudoc (2011); 53 EHRR 1011 and section 4.V.a, pp 551 et seq.

[266] See Johnson, 10 HRLR 67 (2010) for an analysis of the continuing evolution of the case law on homosexuality.

[267] See *L and V v Austria* 2003-I; 36 EHRR 1022; *BB v UK* hudoc (2004); 39 EHRR 635; and compare *Santos Couto v Portugal* hudoc (2010) (challenge to the existence of different ages of consent for heterosexual and homosexual activities); and *Fretté v France* 2002-I; 38 EHRR 438; *EB v France* hudoc (2008); 47 EHRR 509 G; *Gas and Dubois v France* hudoc (2012); and *X and Others v Austria* hudoc (2013) (challenge to adoption rules).

[268] *Smith and Grady v UK* 1999-VI; 29 EHRR 493; *Perkins and R v UK* hudoc (2002); and *Beck, Copp and Bazeley v UK* hudoc (2002). See *Vallianatos and Others v Greece* hudoc (2013) where the Court lists at para 70 cases decided under Article 8 alone and together with Article 14.

[269] No 32792/05 hudoc (2008) DA.

[270] See *Von Hannover v Germany* 2004-VI; 40 EHRR 1; *Peck v UK* 2003-I; 36 EHRR 719.

[271] No 32792/05 hudoc (2008) DA.

the applicant from his employment because of his involvement in a company which sold BDSM supplies and his own participation in public BDSM sexual activities did not violate Article 8, referring to the sensitive nature of his work as a probation officer dealing with sex offenders.

V. PRESS PUBLICATIONS

a. Privacy

The Court has established the concept of a zone of privacy to which everyone—even those who live their lives in the public eye—is entitled. This zone of privacy also exists notwithstanding allegations of criminal wrongdoing or other notoriety.[272] The publication of private life details, usually by the press, will therefore engage Article 8. In *Von Hannover v Germany*,[273] the Court had no doubt that, despite the fact that the applicant was very well known, the publication of photographs of her in her daily life fell within the scope of her private life.[274] In this context, the Court often asks whether the applicant can rely on a reasonable or legitimate expectation of privacy.[275] No reasonable expectation was established where the applicant had freely divulged information in his own autobiography.[276] In *Alkaya v Turkey*,[277] the applicant, a well-known actress, complained about the publication of the full details of her address in a newspaper following a burglary at her house. The Court found that the home address of a person was personal information which was protected by Article 8.

The state has a positive obligation to respect private life by safeguarding against the intrusive activities of private persons, such as newspaper reporters. The precise content of the positive obligation is subject to a wide margin of appreciation, given the need to balance the Article 8 rights in play with competing interests of freedom of expression guaranteed by Article 10.[278] The question for the Court is whether a fair balance has been struck and recent guidance has been provided in *Von Hannover (No 2) v Germany*,[279] where the Court identified the relevant criteria as: the contribution of the publication to a debate of general interest; the role or function of the subject and what the report is about; the prior conduct of the subject; the content, form, and consequences of the publication; and the circumstances in which any photographs were taken. In respect of the latter criterion, the Court referred to the climate of continual harassment in which photographs appearing in the tabloid press are often taken. In *Von Hannover v Germany*,[280] the applicant had

---

[272] For private individuals see *Sciacca v Italy* 2005-I; 43 EHRR 400 (release of photograph to the media by the police); *Peck v UK* 2003-I; 36 EHRR 719 (CCTV footage broadcast on television without consent); and *Toma v Romania* hudoc (2009) (journalists invited to film applicant at police station after his arrest). For public figures see *Mosley v UK* hudoc (2011); 53 EHRR 1011 and *Von Hannover v Germany* 2004-VI; EHRR 1.

[273] 2004-VI; 40 EHRR 1.

[274] See also *Earl and Countess Spencer v UK Nos 28851/95 and 28852/95*, 92 DR 56 (1998) and *Von Hannover v Germany (No 2)* hudoc (2012); 55 EHRR 388 GC.

[275] See *Von Hannover v Germany* 2004-VI; 40 EHRR 1; *Von Hannover v Germany (No 2)* hudoc (2012); 55 EHRR 388 GC; and *Rothe v Austria* hudoc (2012).

[276] See *Hachette Filipacchi Associés (ICI PARIS) v France* hudoc (2009) and *Minelli v Switzerland No 14991/02* hudoc (2005) DA. See also *Axel Springer AG v Germany* hudoc (2012); 55 EHRR 183 GC (Article 10 case), where the subject had 'actively sought the limelight' and thus reduced his legitimate expectation that his private life would be effectively protected.   [277] Hudoc (2012).

[278] Compare, eg, *White v Sweden* hudoc (2006); 46 EHRR 23, concerning publication of details of the applicant's alleged criminal activities (no violation) and *Mitkus v Latvia* hudoc (2012), concerning publication of a prisoner's HIV-positive status (violation).   [279] Hudoc (2012); 55 EHRR 388 GC.

[280] 2004-VI; 40 EHRR 1.

complained about the lack of a remedy to prevent the paparazzi from taking photographs of her as she went about her daily life. The Court found that the publication of photos and articles whose sole purpose was to satisfy the curiosity of a particular readership regarding details of the applicant's private life did not satisfy the public interest test. Freedom of expression therefore required a narrower interpretation.[281] Because the German courts had interpreted domestic law to offer the applicant protection of her privacy only when in a 'secluded place', the Court considered this to be insufficient to satisfy the positive obligations to respect her private life under Article 8.[282] However, in *Von Hannover v Germany (No 2)*,[283] it found no violation in respect of similar facts because the domestic courts had carefully balanced the competing interests, taking into account the Court's case law.[284] In *Alkaya*,[285] the Court showed a willingness to conduct its own assessment of the various factors, holding that even assuming that there was a public interest in publishing the fact that the applicant had been burgled, there was no such interest in publishing the exact details of her address. The failure of the domestic courts properly to evaluate the interests at stake resulted in a breach of the state's positive obligation.[286] However, in its recent judgment in *Von Hannover v Germany (No 3)*,[287] the Court explained that only serious reasons would lead it to substitute its views for those of the national judge in this context, suggesting a more limited scope to the Court's supervisory role.

Even where an applicant has been successful before the domestic courts, he may still be able to establish a violation of Article 8 before the Strasbourg Court. *Armonienė v Lithuania*[288] concerned the publication by a newspaper of details of the applicant's husband's HIV-positive status. A derisory sum of damages was awarded by the domestic courts, as the ceiling for compensation was capped by law. The Court found that the severe legislative restrictions on judicial discretion in the award of compensation failed to provide the necessary protection for private life. In *Mosley v UK*,[289] the applicant was clandestinely filmed participating in sado-masochistic activities with five prostitutes. Articles and photographs were published by a newspaper in hard copy and on its website. That the publication had violated the applicant's right to respect for his privacy was accepted by the domestic courts and they awarded damages. Before the Strasbourg Court the applicant complained that the absence of a legal requirement for newspapers to give individuals prior notification of an intended publication, to allow them to apply for an injunction, violated the state's positive obligation. The Court appeared sympathetic to the applicant's case, noting that the facts revealed a 'flagrant and unjustified invasion' of the applicant's private life.[290] However, in assessing whether a positive obligation of the nature called for arose, the Court had to take into consideration the broader context. It found that there was a wide margin of appreciation in the case and expressed

---

[281] In *Armonienė v Lithuania* hudoc (2008); 48 EHRR 1252 and *Mosley v UK* hudoc (2011); 53 EHRR 1011, the Court referred to the narrow construction of freedom of expression required where the publication involved 'tawdry allegations about an individual's private life' concentrating on sensational news intended merely to titillate and entertain.

[282] Cf *White v Sweden* hudoc (2006); 46 EHRR 23, where details of the applicant's alleged criminal activities published in the media did not amount to a failure to respect his private life as there had been an appropriate balance reached between the interests of the applicant and the public interest in the information published.   [283] Hudoc (2012); 55 EHRR 388 GC.

[284] For a historical discussion of the case law on privacy and the taking of photographs, see Hughes, 1 JML 159 (2009).   [285] Hudoc (2012).

[286] Cf *Minelli v Switzerland No 14991/02* hudoc (2005) DA and *Schüssel v Austria No 42409/98* hudoc (2002) DA, where the Court found no flaw in the balancing exercise carried out at domestic level.

[287] Hudoc (2013).   [288] Hudoc (2008); 48 EHRR 1252.   [289] Hudoc (2011); 53 EHRR 1011.

[290] *Mosley v UK*, para 104.

concern about the effectiveness of any pre-notification requirement and the difficulties faced in enforcing such an obligation. There was therefore no violation of Article 8. It seems to have been of some relevance that the applicant's right to privacy was not wholly unprotected.[291] The Court has not yet been asked to consider whether protection of privacy rights requires removal of unlawfully published material from internet archives.[292]

b. Reputation

The extent to which reputation is protected by Article 8 is controversial. Although 'attacks upon...honour and reputation' are prohibited by Article 12 of the Universal Declaration of Human Rights, there is no mention of honour or reputation in Article 8 of the Convention. The Commission had shown reluctance to find that reputation fell within the scope of Article 8.[293] However, in the context of cases brought under Article 10, which under its second paragraph permits interferences with the right to freedom of expression in order to protect the reputation of others, a right to respect for reputation protected by Article 8 first began to emerge in the Court's case law. In *Chauvy and Others v France*,[294] the Court explained that a person's reputation, which was affected by the publication of a book, was protected by Article 8 as part of the right to respect for private life and had to be balanced against the right to freedom of expression.[295] In *Gunnarsson v Iceland*,[296] which involved an Article 8 complaint, the Court left open the question whether that Article encompassed a right to protection of reputation and honour. But its inclusion within the scope of Article 8 was later accepted in *Pfeifer v Austria*,[297] where the applicant complained that the Austrian courts had failed to protect his reputation against defamatory allegations made in a magazine. The Court found that a person's reputation formed part of his 'personal identity and psychological integrity' and so fell within the scope of his private life. Following *Pfeifer*, the right to reputation was recognized in a number of cases but the Court's approach to protection of reputation remained somewhat ambiguous.[298] While *Pfeifer* itself had expressed the right in broad terms, in later cases the Court explained that in order for Article 8 to come into play, the attack on personal honour and reputation had to attain a certain level of gravity and be made in a manner causing prejudice to personal enjoyment of the right to respect for private life.[299] In *Aksu v Turkey*,[300] the applicant complained about an interference with his right to respect for his 'reputation' by the publication of allegedly derogatory comments about his ethnic group (Roma). In such circumstances, the Court explained that attacks on reputation could be seen as attacks on his personal or group identity, thus engaging Article 8 of this broader 'identity' ground. It therefore seems that defamatory statements in themselves will not necessarily be sufficient to engage Article 8.[301]

---

[291] See also *Winer v UK No 10871/84*, 48 DR 154 at 170–1 (1986) and *Earl and Countess Spencer v UK Nos 28851/95 and 28852/95*, 92 DR 56 (1998).

[292] See the judgment of the Paris Tribunal de Grande Instance of 6 November 2013 ordering Google to delete the images or Mr Mosley. The Strasbourg Court has said that removal is not required in the context of protection of reputation: *Węgrzynowski and Smolczewski* hudoc (2013), but it is arguable that different considerations arise in the two kinds of cases.

[293] See, eg, *X v Germany No 2413/65* 23 CD (1966).   [294] 2004-VI; 41 EHRR 610.

[295] See also *Abeberry v France No 58729/00* hudoc (2004) DA and *Leempoel & SA ED Ciné Revue v Belgium* hudoc (2006).   [296] *No 4591/04* hudoc (2005) DA.

[297] Hudoc (2007); 48 EHRR 175.

[298] Cf, eg, *Petrina v Romania* hudoc (2008) and *Karakó v Hungary* hudoc (2009); 52 EHRR 1040.

[299] *A v Norway* hudoc (2009); *Polanco Torres and Movilla Polanco v Spain* hudoc (2010); *Mikolajová v Slovakia* hudoc (2011); *Roberts and Roberts v UK No 38681/08* hudoc (2011) DA; *Mater v Turkey* hudoc (2013) and *Pauliukienė and Pauliukas v Lithuania* (hudoc) 2013.   [300] Hudoc (2012); 56 EHRR 144 GC.

[301] But see *Putistin v Ukraine* (hudoc) 2013, concerning Article 8 protection for the reputation of a deceased family member.

In assessing whether a fair balance has been struck between the competing interests of reputation and freedom of expression, the Court will consider the nature of the comments made and the status of the person whom they concern: the degree of acceptable criticism is greater in respect of politicians or other public figures than in respect of private individuals.[302] Another important consideration is whether the impugned statements can be characterized as 'statements of fact', which can be proved, or whether they are 'value judgments', which must have sufficient factual basis in order to be compatible with Article 8.[303] In *Polanco Torres v Spain*,[304] concerning published allegations of the applicant's involvement in unlawful activities, the Court accepted that the journalist had used all 'effective' possibilities to verify his information and that the article contributed to a debate of general public interest. Although the journalist was not able to prove that the allegations were true, no violation arose. In *Petrenco v Moldova*,[305] the Court found that allegations in an article intended to imply that the applicant had collaborated with the Soviet secret services could not be considered mere value judgments, as whether an individual had collaborated was a historical fact, capable of being substantiated by relevant evidence. As the allegation had no sufficient factual basis, a violation of Article 8 had occurred.[306] In *A v Norway*,[307] the Court found a violation of Article 8 where the report consisted of factual information about a criminal investigation into the rape and murder of two young girls that was largely true but was presented in such a way as to convey wrongly the impression that the applicant could be considered a possible suspect. The applicants in *Roberts and Roberts v UK*,[308] who were members of the British National Party, claimed that the report of allegations that they were guilty of criminal offences damaged their reputations. The Court concluded that although the allegations were serious, they were published within the broader context of a debate on political divisions within the BNP at a time of heightened interest in that party. It also said that the author had not adopted the allegations as his own but had simply reported allegations made by others and had cited the source.[309] The case was declared inadmissible. In *Węgrzynowski and Smolczewski v Poland*,[310] the Court found no violation of Article 8 where the domestic courts upheld the applicants' defamation complaint but refused to order the deletion of the article from the newspaper's internet archives. It emphasized the importance of internet archives as a source of information and noted that the applicants had failed to request that the article be modified to include a reference to the defamation proceedings and their outcome.[311]

While the right to respect for reputation is most frequently invoked in press freedom cases, it may also arise in other circumstances. In *Sanchez Cardenas v Norway*,[312] the Court considered the applicant's reputation to be relevant to a complaint about the wording of a court judgment in family proceedings, which he claimed amounted to an affirmation of a suspicion that he had committed sexual abuse.[313]

---

[302] *Petrina v Romania* hudoc (2008) and *Petrenco v Moldova* hudoc (2010).
[303] *Pedersen and Baadsgaard v Denmark* 2004-XI; 42 EHRR 486 GC; *Timpul Info-Magazin and Anghel v Moldova* hudoc (2007); 52 EHRR 593; and *Petrina v Romania*.   [304] Hudoc (2010).
[305] Hudoc (2010).
[306] See also *Gurgenidze v Georgia* hudoc (2006), concerning allegations that the applicant had stolen a manuscript published in a newspaper together with photographs.   [307] Hudoc (2009).
[308] No 38681/08 hudoc (2011) DA.
[309] Compare *Lavric v Romania* hudoc (2014) (not yet final).   [310] Hudoc (2013).
[311] See also *Popovski v the Former Yugoslav Republic of Macedonia* hudoc (2013) (violation of Article 8 because criminal defamation proceedings were ineffective).
[312] Hudoc (2007); 49 EHRR 147. See also *Mikolajová v Slovakia* hudoc (2011) (disclosure of a police report indicating that the applicant was guilty of an offence for which she had never been convicted).
[313] See also Article 6(2).

VI. SECRET SURVEILLANCE

The term secret surveillance covers the observation and recording of a person's move-ments, the use of hidden listening devices and the interception of communications. The Court has recognized that surveillance will invade a person's private space, such as to bring it within the scope of 'private life'.[314] In most cases these activities will also engage the right to respect for the home and correspondence.

Cases involving allegations of interception of communication raise particular chal-lenges, as the very secrecy of these activities means that applicants are unlikely to be able to prove that their communications have, in fact, been intercepted. The Court generally accepts that an interference arises by virtue of the very existence of legislation allow-ing interception, where the applicants can demonstrate that they fell within the category of persons to whom the legislation could have been applied.[315] Secret surveillance cases tend to be analysed under the classic negative obligations test, with regard being had to whether the interference was justified under Article 8(2). They provide a good example of the important role played by the 'lawfulness' requirement in the Article 8 context.

While the Court has accepted the legitimate aims pursued by secret surveillance,[316] both legality and necessity have been found lacking in a number of interception cases. In *Klass and Others v Germany*,[317] the first case to be examined by the Court, it accepted that the existence of legislation granting powers of secret surveillance was, under excep-tional conditions, necessary in a democratic society. However, there had to be adequate and effective safeguards against abuse.[318] Having reviewed the German legislation, the Court found no violation of Article 8. Although the Court in *Klass* considered the ques-tion of safeguards in the context of the necessity of the measures, later cases tended to examine safeguards as part of the assessment of the quality of the law under the notion of 'legality', which requires that the law be sufficiently clear in its terms to give citizens an adequate indication of the conditions and circumstances in which the authorities are empowered to resort to secret surveillance.[319] In *Malone v UK*,[320] telephone tapping was regulated merely by administrative practice, the details of which were not published. The Court said that there was insufficient clarity about the scope or the manner in which the discretion of the authorities to listen secretly to telephone conversations was exercised.[321] In *Kruslin* and *Huvig*,[322] a general legal provision which had been interpreted by French

---

[314] But see *Peck v UK* 2003-I; 36 EHRR 719 (monitoring of the actions of an individual in a public place by CCTV did not itself give rise to an interference with private life, but recording and subsequent use of the data did).

[315] *Klass and Others v Germany* A 28 (1978); 2 EHRR 214 PC; *Association for European Integration and Human Rights and Ekimdzhiev v Bulgaria* hudoc (2007); *Iordachi and Others v Moldova* hudoc (2009); 54 EHRR 121; and *Kennedy v UK* hudoc (2010); 52 EHRR 207.

[316] Eg, national security or the prevention of disorder or crime.

[317] A 28 (1978); 2 EHRR 214 PC.

[318] For cases where the Commission held the procedural safeguards adequate and interferences in accord-ance with them 'necessary in a democratic society', see *Mersch v Luxembourg* No *10439/83*, 43 DR 34 (1985); *MS and PS v Switzerland* No *10628/83*, 44 DR 175 (1985); *Spillmann v Switzerland* No *11811/85*, 55 DR 182 (1988); and *L v Norway* No *13564/88*, 65 DR 210 (1990).

[319] In *Kvasnica v Slovakia* hudoc (2009) and *Kennedy v UK* hudoc (2010); 52 EHRR 207, the Court recog-nized the overlap between the requirements of foreseeability and necessity in the context of interception of communications and chose to examine these matters together.

[320] A 82 (1984); 7 EHRR 14 PC.

[321] See also *Halford v UK* 1997-III; 24 EHRR 523; *Hewitt and Harman v UK* No *12175/86*, 67 DR 88 at 99–101 (1989) Com Rep; CM Res DH (90) 36; *Christie v UK* No *21482/93*, 78-A DR 119, 133–135 (1994); *Valenzuela Contreras v Spain* 1998-V; 28 EHRR 483; and *Khan v UK* 2000-V; 31 EHRR 1016. For discussion of the case law in the UK context, see Esen, 76 JCL 164 (2012).

[322] *Kruslin v France* A 176-A (1990); 12 EHRR 547 and *Huvig v France* A 176-B (1990); 12 EHRR 528.

courts in extensive case law to include a power to order telephone tapping did not satisfy the legality requirement because the law failed to clarify the scope and the manner of the exercise of discretion conferred on the authorities. However, legality does not require that a person whose telephone might be tapped be provided with advance warning where to do so would threaten the object of the interception.[323]

To be deemed compatible with the legality requirement, telephone-tapping laws must identify: the categories of people liable to have their telephones tapped; the nature of the offences which could give rise to such an order;[324] the duration of telephone tapping; the procedure to be followed; the precautions to be taken; and the circumstances in which recordings are to be destroyed.[325] The arrangements for independent supervision of an interception regime are also relevant.[326] In cases where interception is ordered to discover journalistic sources, the Court has indicated that prior review by an independent body is essential.[327] The pending case of *Big Brother Watch and Others v UK*,[328] concerning extensive secret surveillance by the US and UK authorities, may provide further clarifications as to what is required here.

The Court has also considered the legality requirement in the context of the monitoring of emails[329] and the use of covert listening devices.[330] In *PG and JH v UK*,[331] the applicants complained about the recording of calls made in the police station. As there was no statutory system of regulating the matter at the relevant time, the interference was not in accordance with the law.[332] By contrast, in *Uzun v Germany*,[333] the Court found no violation of Article 8 in a case involving covert surveillance by GPS (satellite navigation). In particular, it considered that the strict standards as to safeguards developed in the context of secret surveillance cases were not appropriate for the lesser interference with private life occasioned by GPS surveillance of movement in a public place. The measure was both lawful and necessary.

There are few cases involving covert surveillance by non-state bodies. A recent example is *Köpke v Germany*.[334] The applicant was a supermarket cashier in the drinks department and her employer, suspecting her of theft, arranged for a private detective agency to put in place covert video surveillance of the supermarket's drinks department. Because the surveillance was carried out by a private body, the state's positive obligation was in play. Although the conditions under which an employer could arrange video surveillance

---

[323] *Mersch v Luxembourg* No 10439/83, 43 DR 34 (1985) and *Leander v Sweden* A 116 (1987); 9 EHRR 433.

[324] Although the law need not set out exhaustively by name the specific offences which might give rise to interception: *Kennedy v UK* hudoc (2010); 52 EHRR 207.

[325] See *Kopp v Switzerland* 1998-II; 27 EHRR 91; *Niedbała v Poland* hudoc (2000); *Lavents v Latvia* hudoc (2002); *Prado Bugallo v Spain* hudoc (2003); *Weber and Saravia v Germany* No 54934/00 2006-XI DA; *Association for European Integration and Human Rights and Ekimdzhiev v Bulgaria* hudoc (2007); *Liberty and Others v UK* hudoc (2008); 48 EHRR 1; *Iordachi and Others v Moldova* hudoc (2009); 54 EHRR 121; and *Kennedy v UK* hudoc (2010); 52 EHRR 207.

[326] See *Kopp*, *Association for European Integration and Human Rights* and *Kennedy*; *Dumitru Popescu v Romania (No 2)* hudoc (2007); and *Savovi v Bulgaria* hudoc (2012).

[327] *Telegraaf Media Nederland Landelijke Media BV and Others v Netherlands* hudoc (2012). The Court explained that independent review *post factum* could not restore the confidentiality of journalistic sources once it had been destroyed.   [328] No 58170/13 (communicated January 2014).

[329] See *Copland v UK* 2007-I; 45 EHRR 858 and *Narinen v Finland* Hudoc (2004).

[330] See *Khan v UK* 2000-V; 31 EHRR 1016 and *Bykov v Russia* hudoc (2009) GC.

[331] 2001-IX; 46 EHRR 1272.

[332] The Court added that the safeguards necessary to protect the applicants' rights would depend, to some extent at least, on the nature and extent of the interference in question. See also *Allan v UK* 2002-IX; 36 EHRR 143 (use of listening devices in prison) and *Perry v UK* 2003-IX; 39 EHRR 76 (use of CCTV footage for identification and prosecution purposes).   [333] Hudoc (2010); 53 EHRR 852.

[334] No 420/07 hudoc (2010) DA.

of an employee suspected of a criminal offence were not laid down in statute law, the courts had interpreted the scope of employees' fundamental right to privacy as guaranteed by law in a manner which developed important limits on video surveillance and so safeguarded employees' privacy rights against arbitrary interference. The Court found that the state's positive obligation did not require the establishment of a legislative framework. It noted that the measure in this case was limited in duration and space and was used for a restricted purpose. It also referred to the need to consider the shop owner's property right. It concluded that the domestic courts had weighed up the competing interests and that the state had not overstepped its margin of appreciation. The Court did, however, warn that the competing interests concerned might be given a different weight in the future, 'having regard to the extent to which intrusions into private life are made possible by new, more and more sophisticated technologies'.

VII. SEARCH AND SEIZURE POWERS

As with powers of surveillance, search and seizure powers may give rise to interferences with private or family life, the home, or correspondence. The Court accepts the legitimacy of using powers of search and seizure in the investigation of criminal activity. However, the exercise of such powers requires relevant and sufficient reasons and must be proportionate.[335] The relevant criteria are the circumstances in which the search order was issued, the content and scope of the warrant, the manner in which the search was carried out, including the presence of independent observers during the search, and the extent of possible repercussions on the work and reputation of the person affected by the search.[336] The absence of a prior judicial warrant may be counterbalanced by the availability of an *ex post factum* judicial review.[337] When assessing the necessity of the measure, the Court also examines whether domestic law and practice afforded adequate and effective safeguards against abuse and arbitrariness.[338]

In *Niemietz v Germany*,[339] the Court found that Article 8 applied to a search of the premises of a lawyer for documents to be used in criminal proceedings. The search was disproportionate to its purposes of preventing crime and protecting the rights of others, even though it took place under the authority of a warrant, because the warrant was drawn in terms that were too broad and the search impinged on the professional secrecy of some of the materials which had been inspected. There were, in German law, no special procedural safeguards attending the exercise of search powers on the premises of lawyers. In *Funke v France*, the Court said that in the absence of any requirement for a judicial warrant, the law governing the powers given to the customs authorities to institute searches of property appeared to be 'too lax and full of loopholes for the interferences with the applicant's rights to have been strictly proportionate to the legitimate aim pursued'.[340] The search and seizure was therefore not justified under Article 8(2).[341] In a

---

[335] In *Buck v Germany* 2005-IV; 42 EHRR 440, the Court expressed concern about the minor nature of the offence being investigated. See also *Saint-Paul Luxembourg SA v Luxembourg* hudoc (2013).

[336] *Niemietz v Germany* A 251-B (1992); 16 EHRR 97; *Camenzind v Switzerland* 1997-VIII; 28 EHRR 458; *Tamosius v UK No 62002/00* 2002-VIII DA; *Wieser and Bicos Beteiligungen v Austria No 74336/01* 2007-IV DA; and *Robathin v Austria* hudoc (2012).   [337] *Heino v Finland* hudoc (2011).

[338] See, eg, *Société Colas Est and Others v France* 2002-III; 39 EHRR 373 and *Robathin v Austria* hudoc (2012). Cf secret surveillance cases, where the question of safeguards tends to be examined in the context of the legality requirement: see section 4.VI, p 555.   [339] A 251-B (1992); 16 EHRR 97.

[340] A 256-A (1993); 16 EHRR 297 para 57. To the same effect, *Crémieux v France* A 256-B (1993); 16 EHRR 357 and *Miailhe v France* A 256-C (1993); 16 EHRR 332.

[341] See also *Elci and Others v Turkey* hudoc (2003), where no search warrants had been issued, the search and seizures were extensive, and privileged professional materials were taken without specific authorization

series of subsequent Russian cases, the Court found a violation of Article 8 where searches were conducted pursuant to broad powers under legislation and no individual warrants were obtained.[342] The applicant in *Robathin v Austria*[343] complained about the search and seizure of all his electronic data in the context of a police search of his law office under a judicial warrant. The Court accepted that the warrant was based on a reasonable suspicion, but considered that it was couched in very broad terms, authorizing in a general and unlimited manner the search and seizure of various documents and items. Despite the presence of a number of safeguards, the Court found a violation of Article 8 on the basis that the terms of the search warrant were simply too wide, having regard to the particular suspicions against the applicant.

In *Smirnova v Russia*,[344] the applicant complained about the withholding of her identity papers in the context of a criminal investigation in which she was a suspect. The Court did not appear to consider that the seizure of the documents was an interference *per se*. Instead, it based its finding of an interference on the basis of the need for Russians to prove their identities even to perform mundane daily tasks. As the government had failed to show that the refusal to return the identity papers had any basis in domestic law, there was a violation of Article 8. In *Knecht v Romania*,[345] the applicant complained about the seizure of embryos she had previously deposited in a clinic, after it became the subject of criminal investigations. The Court accepted that the seizure was in accordance with the law and pursued a legitimate aim. There was no evidence that the reasons for the seizure were arbitrary or unreasonable and no violation of Article 8 arose.

In some circumstances, search powers may be available in the context of civil proceedings. In *Chappell v UK*,[346] the applicant was sued in breach of copyright by the plaintiffs who obtained an order to search for pirate videos. An *ex parte* order was made authorizing the plaintiff to enter the applicant's premises to seize property that was the subject of the proceedings. The order was executed by five persons in premises that served as his offices and his home. At the same time, eleven policemen executed a separate criminal search warrant for obscene videos. The Court held that the resulting interference with the applicant's privacy and his home could be justified under Article 8(2) to protect the plaintiff's copyright. While the manner of execution was 'disturbing' and 'unfortunate and regrettable', with a large number of persons invading the applicant's privacy, the issue and execution of the order was not disproportionate. The Court reached the opposite conclusion in *McLeod v UK*.[347] Here the applicant's ex-husband entered her home in order to collect property that the court had ordered her to hand over to him. He was accompanied by the police, fearing a breach of the peace. On arrival, however, the applicant was not at home. The police officers entered anyway and the property was removed. According to the Court, the police did not take steps to verify whether the applicant's ex-husband was entitled to enter her home to remove property (in fact he had no such right) and moreover, they should not have entered the house upon being informed that the applicant was not present, since there was little risk of crime or disorder occurring. Accordingly, the interference was found to be disproportionate to the aim sought to be achieved.

More general powers of search are also likely to give rise to an interference with private life. In *McFeeley v UK*,[348] the Commission accepted that the search of prisoners in the

---

(violation); and *Smirnov v Russia* hudoc (2007); 51 EHRR 496, where the terms of the search warrant were very broad and open-ended and no provision was made for safeguarding privileged materials (violation).

[342] *Esmukhambetov and Others v Russia* hudoc (2011); *Imakayeva v Russia* 2006-XIII; 47 EHRR 139; and *Taziyeva and Others v Russia* hudoc (2013).   [343] Hudoc (2012).

[344] 2003-IX; 39 EHRR 450.   [345] Hudoc (2012).   [346] A 152-A (1989); 12 EHRR 1.

[347] 1998-VII; 27 EHRR 493.   [348] *No 8317/78*, 20 DR 44 at 91 (1980).

context of a large-scale protest campaign constituted an interference with the applicants' Article 8 rights. However, having regard to the real security threat posed and the previous disruptive behaviour of the prisoners, it was inevitable that close surveillance and thorough searching took place.[349] Invasive searches of those seeking to visit prisoners must also satisfy the requirements of Article 8.[350]

In *Gillan and Quinton v UK*,[351] the applicants complained about extensive powers of stop and search used against them by the police. The applicants had been stopped in the street and detained for less than twenty minutes under powers granted to police pursuant to anti-terrorism legislation. Nothing incriminating was found in either case, and both were allowed to leave. The Court explained that there were a number of elements relevant to a consideration of whether a person's private life was concerned in measures effected outside his home or private premises. Given the extent of the powers in this case (which included the power physically to search the person), the Court held that an interference with right to respect for private life had occurred notwithstanding the public nature of the search.[352] Unlike previous search power cases, the Court chose to examine the safeguards against abuse in the context of legality. It noted the breadth of the stop and search powers (which did not require the prior existence of a reasonable suspicion that a person had committed any offence) and the circumstances in which stop and search by uniformed officers could be authorized. It considered that the temporal and geographical limits provided by the legislature failed in practice to act as any real check on the exercise of stop and search powers. They were therefore neither sufficiently circumscribed nor subject to adequate legal safeguards against abuse. *Colon v Netherlands*[353] concerned powers granted to the public prosecutor, for up to twelve hours at a time, to order that any persons present in a part of Amsterdam city centre designated as a security risk area might be subjected to a search for the presence of weapons. The applicant complained that the powers allowed for invasion of his privacy without any form of prior judicial control. As in *Gillan and Quinton*, the Court found an interference with Article 8. However, it considered the powers to be justified: procedural safeguards existed, including the possibility of review, which meant that the powers were in accordance with the law. The existence of a robust legal framework as well as evidence that the preventive searches were having their intended effect of helping to reduce violent crime in Amsterdam meant that the measures could be seen as necessary.[354]

VIII. DATA COLLECTION, STORAGE, AND DISCLOSURE

The collection, storage, and disclosure of information by the state about an individual will interfere with his right to respect for his private life.[355] Thus Article 8 is engaged in respect of data collection by an official census;[356] fingerprinting and photography by the

---

[349] Where a prison search is carried out in a debasing manner, Article 3 may be engaged: see eg, *Valašinas v Lithuania* 2001 V-III.   [350] *Wainwright v UK* 2006-X; 44 EHRR 809.

[351] Hudoc (2010); 50 EHRR 1105.

[352] The Court remarked that the public nature of the search could compound the seriousness of the interference because of an element of humiliation and embarrassment.

[353] *No 49458/06* hudoc (2012) DA.

[354] See also the pending case of *Malik v UK* No 32968/11 (declared admissible May 2013), concerning UK powers of stop and search at airports.

[355] *Leander v Sweden* A 116 (1987); 9 EHRR 433; *Amann v Switzerland* 2000-II; 30 EHRR 843 GC; and *S and Marper v UK* hudoc (2008); 48 EHRR 1169 GC. Specific issues surrounding the collection of data via secret surveillance are considered in section 4.VI, pp 555–57.   [356] *X v UK No 9702/82*, 30 DR 239 (1982).

police;[357] the collection and storage of cellular samples and DNA profiles;[358] the collection of medical data and the maintenance of medical records;[359] and the collection and storage of GPS data.[360] Even public information can fall within the scope of private life where it is systematically collected and stored in files held by the authorities.[361] In *MM v UK*,[362] concerning information on a police caution, the Court explained that while criminal record data were public information, their systemic storing in central records meant that they were available for disclosure long after the event when everyone other than the person concerned was likely to have forgotten about it. As the caution itself receded into the past, it became part of a person's private life which had to be respected. The case law suggests that the mere capturing of images in public areas by state authorities will generally not amount to an interference with private life, but that there will be an interference if the image is recorded or used.[363]

As with other Article 8 interferences, lawfulness in this context means more than just the existence of a basis in domestic law for the measure. It requires that the law be adequately accessible and foreseeable. In *Dimitrov-Kazakov v Bulgaria*,[364] a violation was found where, after being questioned about a rape, the applicant's name was entered onto a police register as an offender on the basis of a law which was confidential and was therefore not accessible. In *S and Marper v UK*,[365] which concerned retention of biometric data, the Court explained that legality required the existence of clear, detailed rules governing the scope and application of measures, as well as minimum safeguards concerning, *inter alia*, duration, storage, usage, access of third parties, procedures for preserving the integrity and confidentiality of data, and procedures for destruction, thus providing sufficient guarantees against the risk of abuse and arbitrariness. However, it reached no conclusion as to whether the legislation in question met those requirements.[366] By contrast, legality was decisive in *MM v UK*.[367] While the Court recognized that there might be a need for a comprehensive record of all conviction data, it indicated that the indiscriminate and open-ended collection of such data was unlikely to comply with the 'legality' requirement in the absence of clear and detailed statutory regulations clarifying the applicable safeguards. It found a violation of Article 8 because of the absence of sufficient safeguards, noting the lack of a clear legislative framework for the collection and storage of data, and the lack of clarity as to the scope, extent, and restrictions of the common law powers of the police to retain and disclose caution data, the absence of any mechanism for independent review of a decision to retain or disclose data, and the limited filtering arrangements in respect of disclosures.[368]

---

[357] *Murray v UK* A 300-A (1994); 19 EHRR 191; *McVeigh v UK* No 8022/77, 25 DR 15 at 49 (1981); CM Res DH (82) 1; *S and Marper v UK* hudoc (2008); 48 EHRR 1169 GC; and *MK v France* hudoc (2013).

[358] *Van der Velden v Netherlands* hudoc (2012) and *S and Marper v UK*.

[359] *Chare née Jullien v France* No 14461/88, 71 DR 141 at 155 (1991).

[360] *Uzun v Germany* hudoc (2010); 53 EHRR 852.

[361] See *Rotaru v Romania* 2000-V GC; *PG and JH v UK* 2001-IX; 46 EHRR 1272; *Segerstedt-Wiberg and Others v Sweden* 2006-VII; 44 EHRR 14; and *Cemalettin Canlı v Turkey* hudoc (2008).

[362] Hudoc (2012).

[363] See *Peck v UK* 2003-I; 36 EHRR 719; *Perry v UK* 2003-IX; 39 EHRR 76; and *Khmel v Russia* hudoc (2013) (not yet final). See also *Herbecq and the Association 'Ligue des droits de l'homme' v Belgium* Nos 32200/96 and 32201/96, 92-B DR 92 (1998); and *Friedl v Austria* A 305-B (1995); 21 EHRR 83 Com Rep.

[364] Hudoc (2011).   [365] Hudoc (2008); 48 EHRR 1169 GC.

[366] A violation was found because the measures were not 'necessary'.   [367] Hudoc (2012).

[368] Cf *Bouchacourt v France* hudoc (2009), where the safeguards in French law regarding the inclusion of the applicant's name in a register of sex offenders (limit on duration, procedure for deletion, and strict limits on consultation) were deemed to be adequate. See also *Rotaru v Romania* 2000-V GC; *Amann v Switzerland*

In other cases, the Court's examination has focused on the necessity of the measures. In *Leander v Sweden*,[369] the applicant argued that there were insufficient guarantees against abuse where he was refused any possibility of challenging the correctness of the information concerning him contained in a secret dossier when he applied for employment in a sensitive job. The Court acknowledged the need for powers to collect and store secret personal information for use when assessing the suitability of candidates for employment in posts of importance for national security. A wide margin of appreciation was afforded to the state in this area. In finding no violation of Article 8, the Court accepted that the existence of several measures of control by bodies independent of government was sufficient to guard against abuse. In *S and Marper v UK*,[370] the Court found a violation of Article 8 where the blanket and indiscriminate nature of the powers of retention of the fingerprints, cellular samples, and DNA profiles of persons suspected but not convicted of offences failed to strike a fair balance between the competing public and private interests.[371] The margin of appreciation in the case had been narrowed by the strong consensus among member states as to the need for restrictions on the retention and use of DNA data.[372] However, in *Peruzzo and Martens v Germany*,[373] a complaint brought by two convicted applicants concerning retention of their DNA was declared inadmissible. The Court pointed out that DNA retention applied only to those convicted of offences of a certain gravity and that regular reviews of retention took place.

A number of cases have concerned the disclosure by the police of personal information obtained in the context of criminal investigations to third parties, including the media. In *Craxi v Italy (No 2)*,[374] there was a violation of Article 8 where the content of telephone conversations intercepted by the police was divulged to the media, because there were inadequate safeguards and no subsequent investigation into the disclosure took place. In *Doorson v Netherlands*,[375] a complaint about the decision of the police to show the applicant's photograph to third parties as a means of addressing drug-related crime in Amsterdam was declared inadmissible because the photograph was used solely for investigation purposes, it was not disclosed to the public generally, and it had been taken lawfully by the police during an earlier arrest. However, in *Sciacca v Italy*,[376] Article 8 was breached where a photograph of the applicant had been divulged by the police during a press conference, because the matter was not governed by a law that satisfied the Court's legality requirement.[377] In *Mikolajová v Slovakia*,[378] the disclosure to a private health insurer of a police decision to abandon criminal charges against the applicant, which noted nonetheless that the investigation had established that she had committed a criminal offence, resulted in a violation of Article 8 as there were insufficient safeguards to protect her rights. The measure was therefore not 'necessary'.

The disclosure without consent of an individual's medical information can also give rise to a violation of Article 8. In *TV v Finland*,[379] the Commission held that the disclosure to prison staff directly involved in a prisoner's custody that he was HIV-positive where they were subject to obligations of confidentiality was justified as being necessary for the

2000-II; 30 EHRR 843 GC; and *Shimovolos v Russia* hudoc (2011). For a discussion of Article 8 issues surrounding the sharing of criminal information, see Grace, 86(1) PJ 29 (2013).

[369] A 116 (1987); 9 EHRR 433.   [370] Hudoc (2008); 48 EHRR 1169 GC.
[371] See also *Khelili v Switzerland* Hudoc (2011).   [372] See Beattie, EHRLR 229 (2009).
[373] *Nos 7841/08 and 57900/12* hudoc (2013) DA.   [374] Hudoc (2003); 38 EHRR 995.
[375] *No 20524/92* hudoc (1993) DA.   [376] 2005-I; 43 EHRR 400.
[377] See also *Khuzhin and Others v Russia* hudoc (2008).   [378] Hudoc (2011).
[379] *No 21780/93*, 76A DR 140 at 150–1 (1994).

protection of the rights of others. In *Z v Finland*,[380] the applicant complained that her medical data, including details of her HIV status, had been disclosed and published during a criminal trial. According to the Court, '[i]n view of the highly intimate and sensitive nature of information concerning a person's HIV status, any state measures compelling communication or disclosure of such information without the consent of the patient call for the most careful scrutiny on the part of the Court, as do the safeguards designed to secure an effective protection'.[381] The Court accepted that the interest in protecting the confidentiality of medical data might be outweighed by the interest in investigating and prosecuting crime and publicizing court proceedings. On the facts of *Z v Finland*, the disclosure was 'necessary' for the purposes of the trial but the publication of the applicant's name and HIV-positive status in the appeal court judgment was not justified.[382] In *MS v Sweden*,[383] the Court found no violation where the applicant's confidential medical data were disclosed to another public authority, holding that there was a legitimate reason for the disclosure, which was furthermore subject to important limitations and was accompanied by effective and adequate safeguards against abuse.[384] In *LL v France*,[385] the applicant complained that the use by the judge in divorce proceedings of a document relating to his alcoholism violated his right to respect for his private life. While the Court acknowledged that it was not unusual for confidential information to be disclosed during divorce proceedings, any unavoidable interference had to be limited to that which was strictly necessary. Given that the document was relied upon as only a secondary and alternative basis for the conclusion reached in granting the divorce, its admissibility in the proceedings was found to be in breach of Article 8(2).

The Court has not yet been asked to consider the extent to which data concerning genetic testing, usually undergone to determine the presence of a gene mutation that causes or increases the risk of an inherited illness, is protected by Article 8. The evident private nature of such data would presumably mean that its collection, storage, or disclosure would fall within the scope of Article 8. But the Court is likely to face tricky questions as to the content of any legislative or regulatory regime for the protection of such data. While the evident advantages of sharing data for medical and research purposes suggest that some degree of disclosure is desirable, its highly sensitive nature militates in favour of limited access. Disclosure to insurers and employers, for example, could have significant adverse consequences on the individual concerned. The need to protect the privacy of such data would therefore likely require particularly robust provisions for collection, storage, and disclosure.

IX. ACCESS TO DATA

A right of access to personal data can be derived from the right to respect for private life in particular circumstances.[386] The Court has accepted the vital interest that a person has in

---

[380] 1997-I; 25 EHRR 371 paras 94–114. See also *MS v Sweden* 1997-IV; 28 EHRR 313 and *Panteleyenko v Ukraine* hudoc (2006) (use of psychiatric information).   [381] *Z v Finland*, para 96.

[382] See also *CC v Spain* hudoc (2009) (disclosure of HIV-positive status in civil proceedings: violation) and *Avilkina and Others v Russia* hudoc (2013) (disclosure of medical files following instructions from the prosecutor to report every refusal of transfusion of blood by Jehovah's Witnesses: violation).

[383] 1997-IV; 28 EHRR 313.

[384] See also *I v Finland* hudoc (2008) (failure to prevent unauthorized access to medical records of a nurse: violation).   [385] 2006-XI; 50 EHRR 834.

[386] On the right of access to information under Article 10, see *Kenedi v Hungary* hudoc (2009); *Társaság a Szabadságjogokért v Hungary* hudoc (2009); 53 EHRR 130 and *Österreichische Vereinigung zur Erhaltung,*

obtaining information on his origins.[387] A specific principle of access to information has also emerged in the context of information on risk to life or health. In *Guerra and Others v Italy*,[388] the Court was asked to consider a complaint about access to information on risks posed by the toxic emissions of a factory, brought by individuals residing nearby. It held that Article 8 was applicable and that the lengthy wait of the applicants for essential information that would have enabled them to assess the risks they might run if they continued to live in the town resulted in a violation of the positive obligation arising under that Article.[389] The case of *McGinley and Egan v UK*[390] concerned the applicants' exposure to nuclear tests on Christmas Island. They sought access to information which would have allowed them to assess the extent of the risk to which they had been exposed. The request was refused on grounds of national security. The Court found that, given the nature of the information sought, the issue of access to information was sufficiently closely linked to the applicants' private and family lives and that Article 8 was therefore applicable. It accepted that a positive obligation arose, and explained that where a government engaged in hazardous activities that might have hidden adverse consequences on the health of those involved in such activities, Article 8 required the establishment of an effective and accessible procedure which enabled individuals to seek all relevant and appropriate information. In *McGinley*, such a procedure existed in the context of litigation being pursued by the applicants, and no violation arose.[391]

Reflecting the shift in favour of access to information on risks to life and health, the Court has recently begun to appear more receptive to broader access to personal information claims brought under Article 8. In *KH and Others v Slovakia*,[392] the applicants sought photocopies of hospital medical records in order to confirm whether they had been sterilized during previous labour. The Court said that the complaint concerned the exercise by the applicants of their right of effective access to information concerning their health and reproductive status, which was linked to their private and family lives. The positive obligation inherent in Article 8 extended to making available to them copies of their files, and it was for the authorities to show that there were compelling reasons for refusing.

In *Haralambie v Romania*,[393] the Court found that the interest of the applicant in having access to a secret file on him compiled by the state authorities fell within the scope of private life.[394] Although domestic law had put in place a procedure granting a right of access to information held, the procedure was not effective, given the delay in allowing the applicant access to the file. The Court's broad approach in *Haralambie* provides some support for the argument that Article 8 now protects a general right of access to personal information, in the same way as it protects the collection, storage, and disclosure of such data.[395] This argument is further bolstered by the Court's conclusion in the recent case of *Joanna Szulc v Poland*,[396] where the applicant complained under Article 8 about her unsuccessful attempts to obtain access to all documents collected on her by

---

Stärkung und Schaffung eines wirtschaftlich gesunden land-und forstwirt-schaftlichen Grundbesitzes v Austria hudoc (2013); and McDonagh, 13 HRLR 25 (2013).

[387] *Gaskin v UK* A 160 (1989); 12 EHRR 36 PC and *Odièvre v France* 2003-III; 38 EHRR 871.

[388] 1998-I; 26 EHRR 357 GC.

[389] Access to information in the context of environmental risks is discussed more fully at section 4.XV, pp 582 et seq.

[390] 1998-III; 27 EHRR 1.

[391] See also *Roche v UK* 2005-X; 42 EHRR 600 GC, where the Court found a violation, emphasizing the need for structured disclosure: piecemeal release of some information was not sufficient; and *Vilnes and Others v Norway* hudoc (2013) where a violation was found in respect of a failure to provide information on the risks inherent in diving operations. [392] Hudoc (2009); 49 EHRR 857.

[393] Hudoc (2009). [394] Cf *Leander v Sweden* A 116 (1987); 9 EHRR 433.

[395] See also *Jarnea v Romania* hudoc (2011). [396] Hudoc (2012); 57 EHRR 161.

the communist-era secret services. The Court confirmed its finding in *Haralambie* as to the need for an effective and accessible procedure for accessing personal data, adding that the procedure should enable an interested party to have access to all relevant and appropriate information which would allow that party effectively to counter any allegations of his collaboration with the security services. It found a breach of the state's positive obligation. In *Antoneta Tudor v Romania*, the Court went even further, concluding that Article 8 guaranteed to the applicant the right of access to a secret file concerning her father, explaining that the document was important to allow her to establish the circumstances of her father death at a time when he was the subject of a secret services inquiry.[397]

X. FAMILY AND PERSONAL RELATIONSHIPS

One of the most important elements of the right to develop relationships with others is the formation of intimate relationships and family ties. The essential ingredient of family life is the right to live together so that family relationships may 'develop normally'[398] and members of the family may 'enjoy each other's company'.[399]

The Court has consistently reiterated that the obligation on the state under Article 8 is to respect existing family life. It has therefore previously found that Article 8 does not allow persons to claim a right to establish family life, eg the right to marry[400] or to found a family;[401] or a general right to formal termination of family life through divorce[402] or the revocation of an adoption at the request of the adoptive parents.[403] However, in practice, as societal values have evolved, the Court's approach to the content of Article 8 has become far more nuanced. While no right to marry can be discerned from Article 8, the Court has considered the right of homosexuals to marry or have access to registered partnership from the perspective of Article 8 taken together with Article 14.[404] It has held that Article 8 incorporates a right to respect for a decision to become genetic parents,[405] and more particularly a right for a couple to conceive a child and to make use of medically assisted procreation for that purpose.[406] A case brought today arguing for a right to divorce under Article 8, particularly in the case of an abusive husband or where divorce was necessary to allow formal recognition of a new family unit, might well be decided differently.

a. Recognition of parentage

Applicants frequently complain about legal recognition of the parentage of children. In *Marckx v Belgium*,[407] the Court held that the state had a positive obligation to provide a system of domestic law which safeguarded the integration of a child born outside

---

[397] Hudoc (2013).   [398] *Marckx v Belgium* A 31 (1979); 2 EHRR 330 para 31 PC.

[399] *Olsson v Sweden (No 1)* A 130 (1988); 11 EHRR 259 para 59 PC.   [400] But see Article 12.

[401] See *EB v France* hudoc (2008); 47 EHRR 509 GC.

[402] *Johnston and Others v Ireland* A 112 (1986); 9 EHRR 203 PC, where, unusually in the interpretation of Article 8, the Court set little store by social developments. But see *Airey v Ireland* A 32 (1979); 2 EHRR 305, where the Court found a violation because the remedy of judicial separation to relieve the wife of her duty to cohabit with an abusive husband was not accessible to her.

[403] *Goţia v Romania* No 24315/06 hudoc (2010) DA.

[404] See *Schalk and Kopf v Austria* hudoc (2010); 53 EHRR 683 (no violation) and *Vallianatos and Others v Greece* hudoc (2013) GC (violation).

[405] Eg, *Evans v UK* 2007-I; 46 EHRR 728 GC and *Dickson v UK* 2007-V; 46 EHRR 927 GC.

[406] See *SH and Others v Austria* hudoc (2011) GC.

[407] A 31 (1979); 2 EHRR 330 PC. See also *Johnston and Others v Ireland* A 112 (1986); 9 EHRR 203 PC.

marriage into its family. The situation in Belgian law which gave an unmarried mother the choice of either 'recognizing' her child with certain disadvantages in the succession of property between mother and child or avoiding these drawbacks at the expense of establishing a formal family tie between them was not consonant with Belgium's duty to respect mother and child's right to family life.

Cases have been brought both by children and by fathers seeking to establish paternity. Like cases brought by children seeking details of their origins,[408] despite the clear implications for family life the Court has generally categorized these cases as pertaining to private life. In *Rasmussen v Denmark*,[409] where the applicant father complained about limitations on his right to dispute paternity, the Court found that the determination of his legal relations with his 'daughter' undoubtedly concerned his private life.[410] In *Paulík v Slovakia*,[411] the applicant complained about the impossibility of challenging paternity after he had discovered, following a DNA test, that he was not the biological father. The Court found that the issue had direct implications for his private sphere and for his social identity in a broader sense. Article 8 was accordingly engaged in its private life head. In *Mikulić v Croatia*,[412] the applicant, a young girl, complained that her right to respect for private and family life had been violated because the domestic courts had been inefficient in deciding her paternity claim. The Court said that the facts of the case did not fall within the scope of 'family life' because no family tie had been established between the applicant and her alleged father; but in any case the applicant's private life was engaged.[413] However the Court may be more disposed to finding that family life exists where the applicant father seeks to have his paternity recognized. Thus in *Krušković v Croatia*,[414] the Court reiterated that the legal relationship between a child born out of wedlock and his natural father fell within the ambit of Article 8, and although it did not specify whether family life or private life was at stake, it appears to have considered both engaged. In *Shavdarov v Bulgaria*,[415] the Court noted that the applicant had lived with the children as their father for a number of years, and concluded that family life existed. Citing the right to know one's ascendants, the Court has also found Article 8 to be applicable to proceedings to establish grandpaternity.[416]

The first obligation on the state is to recognize paternity. In *Krušković v Croatia*,[417] the applicant, who had been divested of his legal capacity, complained about the fact that he was not permitted legally to recognize his paternity of his child. The Court found a violation of Article 8, as the authorities had ignored for over two years and for no apparent reason the claim by the applicant and the child's mother.[418] Where paternity is contested, there is an obligation to provide a procedure whereby the issue can be resolved.[419] A presumption of paternity of the husband to a formal marriage whose wife has a child does not, of itself, contravene the Convention. However, the Court established in *Kroon v*

---

[408] See section 4.I.b, pp 537–8.   [409] A 87 (1984); 7 EHRR 371.

[410] The complaint concerned a time limit on a father's right to challenge paternity which did not apply to the mother. The Court found no violation of Article 14 taken together with Article 8. See also *Różański v Poland* hudoc (2006); 45 EHRR 625 (father unable to establish paternity).

[411] 2006-XI; 46 EHRR 142.   [412] 2002-I.

[413] Cf *Haas v Netherlands* 2004-I; 39 EHRR 897 (where the applicant sought to have his paternity established in order to inherit and the Court said the complaint did not fall within the scope of Article 8) and *Pla and Puncernau v Andorra* 2004-VIII; 42 EHRR 522 (where the Court found family life in the context of an inheritance dispute). See also *Jäggi v Switzerland* 2006-X; 47 EHRR 702.   [414] Hudoc (2011).

[415] Hudoc (2010).   [416] *Menendez Garcia v Spain No 21046/07* hudoc (2009) DA.

[417] Hudoc (2011).

[418] See also *Znamenskaya v Russia* hudoc (2005); 44 EHRR 293 (paternity of a stillborn child).

[419] *Rasmussen v Denmark* A 87 (1984); 7 EHRR 371.

Netherlands[420] that biological and social reality should prevail over legal presumptions and the quest for legal certainty of relations, so that any presumption of paternity must be effectively capable of being rebutted and not amount to a *de facto* rule. Despite this conclusion, in *Shavdarov v Bulgaria*,[421] the Court effectively gave its blessing to a presumption of paternity of the husband which operated as a *de facto* rule, noting that the applicant could have taken steps to establish a parental link with his children even though he was not able to establish paternal filiation.

While the application of time limits for challenging presumptions is justifiable under Article 8(2), an inflexible system will be difficult to defend.[422] This is particularly so where the time limit continues to apply notwithstanding the fact that relevant circumstances may have become known only after its expiry[423] or where the application of a time limit precludes the possibility for the law to reflect the clearly established factual reality. In *Paulík v Slovakia*,[424] the applicant was precluded from challenging his paternity, despite conclusive DNA tests, by an inflexible time limit. The Court said that since his putative daughter was almost forty years old and was not dependent on him for maintenance, the general interest in protecting her rights had lost much of its importance compared to when she was a child. The lack of a procedure for bringing the legal position into line with the biological reality flew in the face of the wishes of those concerned and did not benefit anyone. There was therefore a breach of the state's positive obligation. In *Laakso v Finland*,[425] the Court found that the application of the limitation period, which the applicant (an adult) claimed had effectively prevented him from bringing proceedings after he discovered that his paternity had not previously been legally established, pursued the legitimate aim of protecting the interests of putative fathers from old claims.[426] In assessing whether a fair balance had been struck, a number of factors were relevant, including the particular point in time at which the applicant became aware of the biological reality and whether an alternative means of redress existed. The Court found that the rigid application of the time limit and the absence of an opportunity for the domestic courts to weight the competing interests in the particular case resulted in a violation of Article 8. It referred to the fact that a significant number of states set no limitation period for the bringing of paternity proceedings and to the tendency towards a greater protection of the rights of the child to have his paternal affiliation established.

In assessing claims brought by children, the Court has also considered the uncertainty created by unacknowledged paternity. In *Mikulić v Croatia*,[427] the only avenue available to the five-year-old applicant to have paternity established was to take a civil action against the putative father. However, he refused for over three years to have his DNA tested, after which time the first-instance court relied on his refusal and the evidence of the child's mother to conclude that he was the father. The appellate court subsequently found this evidence inconclusive and remitted the case for retrial, which led to further delay. The Strasbourg Court said that in paternity proceedings, courts were required to have regard to the basic principle of the child's interests. Here, the fact that there were no effective means of compelling the father to undergo DNA testing, together with the absence of alternative means available to the applicant to establish her identity, resulted in a violation of Article 8.[428] However, the balancing act might result in a

---

[420] A 297-C (1994); 19 EHRR 263. See also *Tavli v Turkey* hudoc (2006); 48 EHRR 225 and *Mizzi v Malta* 2006-I; 46 EHRR 529.   [421] Hudoc (2010).

[422] *Shofman v Russia* hudoc (2005); 44 EHRR 741, where no exceptions to the time limit were permitted.

[423] *Phinikaridou v Cyprus* hudoc (2007).   [424] 2006-XI; 46 EHRR 142.   [425] Hudoc (2013).

[426] This aim is not included in Article 8(2) itself, and should be understood as falling within the exception for protecting the rights and freedoms of others.   [427] 2002-I.

[428] See also *AMM v Romania* hudoc (2012).

different conclusion in the case of an adult child or where access to general information concerning parentage is concerned, rather than paternity proceedings against an identified individual.[429]

In *X, Y and Z v UK*,[430] the applicants were a female-to-male transsexual, a woman who was in a relationship with him, and the child born to the woman as a result of donor sperm. The parents wished to register the paternity of X, but the request was refused by the authorities. The Court accepted that *de facto* family ties linked the three applicants. However, it concluded that notwithstanding the inconveniences caused by the refusal, given that transsexuality raised complex scientific, legal, moral, and social issues, in respect of which there was no generally shared approach among the contracting states, Article 8 did not imply an obligation for the state formally to recognize as the father of a child a person who was not the biological father. The pending case of *Mennesson v France*[431] also raises the question of recognition of parentage of non-biological parents. It concerns the birth by a surrogate, using sperm donated by the second applicant father, of twin girls in the US. The second applicant and his wife, the first applicant, were recognized in the US as the legal father and mother of the children. They complain that on their return to France they were unable to obtain recognition of the fact—legally established abroad—of their parentage. The case may give the Court the opportunity to revise its approach to this question, having regard to the scientific and societal developments since the delivery of its judgment in *X, Y and Z*.

b. Adoption

The Convention does not guarantee the right to adopt as such and Article 8 does not oblige states to grant a person the status of adoptive parent or adopted child.[432] In *EB v France*,[433] the Court expressly left open the question whether the right to adopt fell within the scope of Article 8 of the Convention taken alone; but held that in any case an application for adoption fell within the ambit of Article 8 for the purposes of a complaint of discrimination under Article 14.[434] The Court has since had limited occasion to reconsider the extent to which adoption, entailing the need for procedural safeguards and relevant and sufficient reasons for a refusal, can now be said to fall within the remit of Article 8. In *Moretti and Benedetti v Italy*,[435] the applicants, who had acted as foster carers for A since she was four days old, complained under Article 8 about the failure of the authorities properly to evaluate their request to adopt her. As a result of the failure, A was placed with a new family by whom she was subsequently adopted. The Court reiterated that Article 8 did not guarantee a right to adopt, but added that this did not prevent an obligation arising on states to allow family ties to be formed. It criticized the failure of the authorities to examine the applicants' adoption request speedily, and in any case before declaring A free for adoption; and the fact that the request had eventually been dismissed with no reasons being given. The procedural shortcomings resulted in a failure to ensure respect for the applicants' family life. The case was not so much about the right of the applicants to adopt A as about the interference in the applicants' existing family life with A as a result of the refusal of the authorities to consider their adoption application properly. It therefore seems likely that the Court would be less willing to find a violation of family life where

---

[429] See eg, *Odièvre v France* 2003-III; 38 EHRR 871 GC.   [430] 1997-II; 24 EHRR 143 GC.

[431] *No 65192/11*, communicated February 2012.

[432] *X v Belgium and Netherlands No 6482/74*, 7 DR 75 (1975) and *Di Lazzaro v Italy No 31924/96* hudoc (1997) DA.   [433] Hudoc (2008); 47 EHRR 509 GC.

[434] See also *Fretté v France* 2002-I; 38 EHRR 438.   [435] Hudoc (2010).

the adoption application concerned a child who did not yet enjoy family life in substance with the applicants.[436]

Applicants have also complained under Article 8 about the failure to recognize adoptions. In *Wagner and JMWL v Luxembourg*,[437] the applicant, a Luxembourg national, had adopted a Peruvian girl and a judgment of full adoption was handed down by a court in Peru. The Luxembourg authorities refused to recognize the adoption because full adoption was not available to single women in Luxembourg. The Court found a violation of Article 8, holding that the child's best interests had to take precedence and that the Luxembourg courts could not reasonably disregard the legal status which had been created on a valid basis in Peru.[438] In *Negrepontis-Giannisis v Greece*,[439] the applicant, a Greek national, had been adopted by his uncle, a monk, while in the United States and an adoption order had been handed down by a US court. Upon his return to Greece some years later, his attempt to have the adoption order recognized failed as the domestic courts considered that monks were not capable of adopting. The Court found the refusal to be disproportionate and a violation of Article 8.

c. Other aspects of family relationships

The Court has explained that family life does not include only social, moral, or cultural relations but also comprises interests of a material kind. It therefore accepted in *Marckx* that the right of succession between children and parents, and between grandchildren and grandparents, was so closely related to family life that it came within the sphere of Article 8.[440] However, it should be noted that in *Marckx* the inheritance at issue was between mother and child, in respect of whom family life had been established. Similarly, in *Camp and Bourimi v Netherlands*,[441] the inheritance dispute concerned the impossibility of the child to inherit from his father because of the latter's death before the former's birth. However, the Court appears to have stretched the notion a little far in *Pla and Puncernau v Andorra*,[442] where it found Article 8 in its family life aspect applicable despite the fact that the testatrix—the applicant's adoptive grandmother—had died twenty years before the applicant's adoption into the family.[443]

The state's positive obligation stops short of support for the subsistence of family life. The Commission rejected an application demanding financial support from the state so that one parent could stay at home to look after the children, rather than the day-care offered so that both parents could work.[444] However, the Court found a violation of Article 8 taken together with Article 14 where there was an unjustified difference of treatment in the payment of child benefit of aliens with differing immigration statuses.[445]

A number of complaints have been lodged about the treatment of deceased family members. In *Hadri-Vionnet v Switzerland*,[446] the applicant complained about the burial of her stillborn child in a communal grave without her knowledge. The Court found

---

[436] See *Fretté v France* 2002-I; 38 EHRR 438; *EB v France* hudoc (2008); 47 EHRR 509 GC; and *Pini and Others v Romania* 2004-V; 40 EHRR 312.   [437] Hudoc (2007).

[438] See also *Harroudj v France* hudoc (2012), where no violation arose on account of the refusal of the French authorities to authorize the adoption of a child entrusted to the applicant in Algeria under the Islamic notion of 'kafala' (legal care).   [439] Hudoc (2011).

[440] *Marckx v Belgium* A 31 (1979) 2 EHRR 330 PC. See also *Velcea and Mazăre v Romania* hudoc (2009), concerning a complaint that the family of a murderer were able to inherit from the victim's estate.

[441] 2000-X; 34 EHRR 1446.   [442] 2004-VIII; 42 EHRR 522.

[443] Cf *Haas v Netherlands* 2004-I; 39 EHRR 897.

[444] *Andersson and Kullman v Sweden* No 11776/85, 46 DR 251 (1986).

[445] *Niedzwiecki v Germany* hudoc (2005); 42 EHRR 679.   [446] Hudoc (2008).

Article 8 applicable and held that the interference was not in accordance with the law as it failed to comply with domestic legislation. In *Pannullo and Forte v France*,[447] the Court found a violation of Article 8 on account of the authorities' delay in returning the body of the applicants' daughter to them for burial. In *Sabanchiyeva and Others v Russia*,[448] there was a violation where the authorities refused to return the bodies of suspected terrorists to relatives for burial. While the Court accepted that some restrictions might be justified in light of the activities of the deceased, it condemned the 'automatic' nature of the domestic legislation, which precluded a case-by-case assessment, pointing to the particularly severe interference in the case.[449]

In *Van der Heijden v Netherlands*,[450] the applicant complained about the national courts' refusal to exempt her from testifying against her long-term partner, who was suspected of killing someone. The Court accepted the government's argument that the applicant's relationship with her partner, although long-standing, was fundamentally different to that of a married couple or a couple in a registered partnership (who were entitled to exemptions). Although the applicant was not to be criticized for choosing not to formalize her union, she had to accept the consequences of her choice.

XI. CARE PROCEEDINGS, CUSTODY ISSUES AND CHILD ABDUCTION

a. Childcare proceedings

It is well established that removing children from the care of their parents to place them in the care of the state, decisions concerning contact with children in care, and decisions to place children for adoption constitute interferences with respect for family life that require justification under Article 8(2). Where a parent consents to adoption and later changes her mind, the Court has accepted that the refusal to return the child amounts to an interference.[451]

In *Olsson v Sweden (No 1)*,[452] the applicants argued that the test as to the risk of harm to the child that had to be established before intervention took place was too low and that the interference was not 'in accordance with the law'. The Swedish law at issue authorized the taking of children into care on various grounds including 'lack of care for him' or 'any other condition in the home'. While acknowledging its 'rather general' terms, the Court accepted that the provisions satisfied the notion of 'law' in Article 8. The circumstances in which social workers needed to be able to act were so various that a general power, including a pre-emptive authority, was necessary: to confine the authorities' entitlement to act to cases where there had already been actual harm to the child could unduly reduce the effectiveness of the protection which the child required.[453] The Court has clarified that a very wide margin of appreciation applies to decisions to take a child into care.[454]

---

[447] 2001-X; 36 EHRR 757.   [448] *No 38450/05* hudoc (2008) DA.

[449] See also *Elli Poluhas Dödsbo v Sweden* 2006-I; 45 EHRR 581 (refusal to authorize transfer of urn containing applicant's husband's ashes: no violation); and *Jovanović v Serbia* hudoc (2012) (failure to provide information about death of applicant's newborn son in hospital and inability to see his body: violation).

[450] Hudoc (2012); 57 EHRR 377 GC.

[451] *Kearns v France* hudoc (2008); 50 EHRR 851 (no violation where biological mother could not revoke her consent after the expiry of a two-month time period).   [452] A 130 (1988); 11 EHRR 259 PC.

[453] See also *Eriksson v Sweden* A 156 (1989); 12 EHRR 183 PC; *Olsson v Sweden (No 2)* A 250 (1992); 17 EHRR 134; and *TP and KM v UK* 2001-V; 34 EHRR 42 GC, where the Court rejected the claim of the applicant that the removal of her child into care was not in accordance with law because it was based on an erroneous assessment of the risk of harm to the child.

[454] *Scozzari and Giunta v Italy* 2000-VIII; 35 EHRR 243 GC; *Johansen v Norway* 1996-III; 23 EHRR 33; and *YC v UK* hudoc (2012).

When assessing the necessity of the measure, two aspects of the proceedings must be considered. First, it must be established that the decision to remove the child was supported by relevant and sufficient reasons pertaining to the welfare of the child.[455] This requires careful assessment of the impact of the proposed care measure prior to the implementation of a care measure.[456] The Court accepts that domestic authorities are in principle better placed to make such decisions,[457] and it follows that the Court's task is not to substitute itself for the domestic authorities here but to review the decisions that those authorities have taken. Once a child has been placed in care, stricter scrutiny is called for in respect of any further limitations, such as restrictions placed on parental rights of access or placement for adoption.[458]

In making decisions about the care of children, their best interests are paramount.[459] The Court has explained that it is in the child's best interests to maintain his ties with his or her family except in cases where the family has proved particularly unfit; and to ensure his or her development in a safe and secure environment.[460] Thus family ties may only be severed in very exceptional circumstances: it is not enough to show that a child could be placed in a more beneficial environment for his or her upbringing.[461] Everything must be done to preserve personal relations and, where appropriate, to rebuild the family. Relevant factors in identifying the best interests of a child and in assessing the relevancy and sufficiency of the reasons given include the age, maturity, and ascertained wishes of the child, the likely effect on the child of ceasing to be a member of his original family, and the relationship the child has with relatives.[462]

The Court has generally found a violation of Article 8 only in extreme cases, such as where the child has been removed from his mother at birth,[463] or where the failure of the authorities to take steps to preserve the family have been manifest.[464] It is also important in this context whether alternatives to draconian measures were considered[465] and whether the manner in which the measure was implemented was justified. In *Olsson v Sweden (No 1)*,[466] the Court found that although there were adequate explanations for the decision of the authorities placing the children in foster care, the manner in which that was undertaken, ie placing two of the children in care a great distance away from their parents and their brother, was inimical to the aim of reuniting the family.[467] In *Kurochkin*

---

[455] *Olsson v Sweden (No 1)* A 130 (1988); 11 EHRR 259 PC; *YC v UK*; and *AK and L v Croatia* hudoc (2013).
[456] *Venema v Netherlands* 2002-X; 39 EHRR 102 (violation). Cf *Couillard Maugery v France* hudoc (2004), where it was clear that the authorities had undertaken a careful and thorough examination of the case before reaching its decision.   [457] Eg, *Johansen v Norway* 1996-III; 23 EHRR 33.
[458] *Johansen v Norway*. The Court has emphasized that the decisions taken by the courts in this field are often irreversible: *B v UK* A 121 (1987); 10 EHRR 87; *X v Croatia* hudoc (2008); 51 EHRR 511; and *R and H v UK* hudoc (2011); 54 EHRR 28.
[459] *Johansen v Norway*; *Kearns v France* hudoc (2008); 50 EHRR 851; *R and H v UK*; and *YC v UK*.
[460] *R and H v UK* and *YC v UK*.
[461] *K and T v Finland* 2001-VII; 36 EHRR 255 GC; and *YC v UK*.   [462] *YC v UK*.
[463] *K and T v Finland* 2001-VII; 36 EHRR 255 GC; *P, C and S v UK* 2002-VI; 35 EHRR 1075; and *Haase v Germany* 2004-I; 39 EHRR 897.
[464] See *KAB v Spain* hudoc (2012), where the authorities' expulsion of the mother resulted in her baby being declared abandoned and placed for adoption, without sufficient assistance to the applicant father to be granted custody of his child. See also *RMS v Spain* hudoc (2013), where the applicant's young daughter was removed from her on account of her financial situation and the authorities failed to take into account a subsequent change of circumstances; and *KA v Finland* hudoc (2003).
[465] See *Wallová and Walla v Czech Republic* hudoc (2006), where the Court found that because the underlying reason for the children being taken into care was the housing difficulties faced by their parents, this decision was not proportionate. See also *Havelka and Others v Czech Republic* hudoc (2007) and *Saviny v Ukraine* hudoc (2008); 51 EHRR 780.   [466] A 130 (1988); 11 EHRR 259 PC.
[467] See also *Kutzner v Germany* 2002-I; 35 EHRR 653 and *AD and OD v UK* hudoc (2010); 51 EHRR 191.

v Ukraine,[468] the applicant complained about the annulment of an adoption order following his divorce from his wife, with whom he had jointly adopted a young boy. The Court found a violation of Article 8 on the basis that the authorities had failed properly to assess the impact of the annulment on the child and that they had not considered less far-reaching alternative measures. In *BB and FB v Germany*,[469] there was a violation because the court had relied solely on the children's uncorroborated allegations of violence when withdrawing parental authority. The automatic deprivation of parental rights, even following a criminal conviction for child neglect, is difficult to justify.[470] But where the domestic authorities have evidently weighed up the relevant considerations in proceedings in which the applicant has been fully involved, no violation will arise.[471] In *YC v UK*,[472] the Strasbourg Court was satisfied that although the judge who had made a placement order in respect of the applicant's child had not made express reference to Article 8 considerations, he had directed his mind to the child's best interests and to the possibility of rehabilitation of the child to his mother. No violation therefore arose.[473]

Harsh restrictions on contact will be justified only where they are motivated by an over-riding requirement pertaining to the best interests of the child.[474] In *Margareta and Roger Andersson v Sweden*,[475] the Court found a violation of Article 8 on the basis that the government had not shown that the conditions restricting access and communication between parent and child while the child was in care were necessary. They had to be supported by strong reasons. By contrast, in *RK and AK v UK*,[476] where steps had been taken to place the child within her extended family and in close proximity to the applicants' home so that they could easily and frequently visit, no breach was found.

The second aspect of the Court's review under the necessity requirement involves examination of whether the decision-making process was fair and afforded due respect to the applicant's rights under Article 8 of the Convention.[477] The Court has emphasized the need for the involvement of the parents in the decision-making process, to a degree sufficient to protect their interests and allow them fully to present their case.[478] In *W v UK*,[479] the applicants had not been informed of a decision which arranged the legal basis of their children's foster-care seriously to their disadvantage; they were not kept informed about the development of the long-term foster-care of their children and the possibility that it might lead to adoption; and they were not consulted about the decision to deny them access to the children. This was held not to be necessary for the protection of the rights of the child.[480] Subject to situations

---

[468] Hudoc (2010).   [469] Hudoc (2013).   [470] *MD and Others v Malta* hudoc (2012).

[471] See *Haase v Germany No 36106/05* hudoc (2008) DA; *Aune v Norway* hudoc (2010); 54 EHRR 1145; *R and H v UK* hudoc (2011); 54 EHRR 28; and *KS v UK No 62110/10* hudoc (2012) DA.

[472] Hudoc (2012).

[473] Since the case concerned the adoption of an eight-year-old boy the Court's willingness to accept—in the absence of clear evidence in the domestic judgments—that proper regard had been had to all relevant factors is surprising: see Judge De Gaetano's dissenting opinion.

[474] *Johansen v Norway* 1996-III; 23 EHRR 33 (decision to cut off contact resulted in a violation) and *Kutzner v Germany* 2002-I; 35 EHRR 653 (significant restrictions on contact with young children amounted to a violation). But compare *Gnahoré v France* 2000-IX; 34 EHRR 967 (no violation where the father had seen his son only three times in seven years).   [475] A 226-A (1992); 14 EHRR 615.

[476] Hudoc (2008); 48 EHRR 707. See also *Levin v Sweden* hudoc (2012).

[477] *K and T v Finland* 2001-VII; 36 EHRR 255 GC; *RK and AK v UK*; *AD and OD v UK* hudoc (2010); 51 EHRR 191; *R and H v UK* hudoc (2011); 54 EHRR 28; and *YC v UK* hudoc (2012). However, in some cases the Court examines procedural matters under Article 6: see *RP and Others v UK* hudoc (2012) on the role of the official solicitor in child care proceedings.

[478] *W v UK* A 121 (1987); 10 EHRR 29 PC; *R and H v UK*; and *YC v UK*.

[479] A 121 (1987); 10 EHRR 29 PC.

[480] See also *McMichael v UK* A 307-B (1995); 20 EHRR 205 and *Tsourlakis v Greece* hudoc (2009).

where disclosure would place the child at risk, all case material must be made available to the parents concerned, even in the absence of any request by them.[481] Involving parents may be problematic where urgent intervention in the family is required to protect a child from harm, and in such cases consultation may be neither possible nor advisable.[482] Full and open consultation may also be difficult where the child's parent or carer is alleged to be the child's abuser.[483] However, the Court has acknowledged the parent's interest in being informed of the nature and extent of the allegations of abuse made against them.[484] If there are doubts as to whether disclosure poses a risk to the welfare of the child, the domestic authorities should submit the matter to the court at the earliest possible stage in the proceedings for it to resolve the issues involved.[485]

The need to involve the parents fully in the decision-making process is all the greater where the proceedings may culminate in a child being placed for adoption.[486] In *Keegan v Ireland*,[487] the Court concluded that the failure to consult a natural father before placing his child for adoption did not respect his family life. In *AK and L v Croatia*,[488] the Court concluded that the applicant had not been sufficiently involved in the decision-making process where she was not legally represented in the proceedings whereby she was divested of parental responsibility and that she was not advised of the adoption proceedings.[489]

The Court has established that 'taking a child into care should normally be regarded as a temporary measure to be discontinued as soon as circumstances permit and that any measures of implementation of temporary care should be consistent with the ultimate aim of reuniting the natural parent and the child'.[490] Article 8 incorporates an obligation to undertake regular reviews to consider whether the conditions for maintaining the child in public care continue to be met.[491] In *RK and AK v UK*,[492] the child was taken into care following unexplained injuries sustained. In finding no violation of Article 8, the Court considered it of crucial significance that as soon as a further fracture occurred outwith the applicants' care, more tests were quickly ordered and the child was returned home within weeks.

b. Custody, contact disputes, and international child abduction

Where a court makes an order in the context of a dispute between private parties about custody of or contact with children, the order is likely to constitute an interference with Article 8 rights which will have to be justified.[493] In *Parviz v Sweden*,[494] an order preventing the applicant from having contact with his daughter had been made because he had previously unlawfully removed her to Iran. Even after the child had been returned, he had stayed in Iran for a further seven years. The case was declared inadmissible, as the Court found that the rupture of contact was the applicant's own fault, the child had expressed the wish not to have contact, and limited contact rights were eventually

---

[481] *TP and KM v UK* 2001-V; 34 EHRR 42 GC and *Venema v Netherlands* 2002-X; 39 EHRR 102.
[482] Eg, *K and T v Finland* 2001-VII; 36 EHRR 255 para 168 GC. Cf *HK v Finland* hudoc (2006); 46 EHRR 113, concerning an emergency measure where the applicant was involved.
[483] Eg, *TP and KM v UK* 2001-V; 34 EHRR 42 GC.
[484] See also *KA v Finland* hudoc (2003) and *Buchberger v Austria* hudoc (2001); 37 EHRR 356.
[485] *TP and KM v UK* 2001-V; 34 EHRR 42 GC.
[486] *R and H v UK* hudoc (2011); 54 EHRR 28 and *YC v UK* hudoc (2012).
[487] A 290 (1994); 18 EHRR 342.   [488] Hudoc (2013).
[489] See also *X v Croatia* hudoc (2008); 51 EHRR 511.
[490] *Olsson v Sweden (No 1)* A 130 (1988); 11 EHRR 259 para 81 PC.
[491] Eg, *KA v Finland* hudoc (2003) and *K and T v Finland* 2001-VII; 36 EHRR 255 GC.
[492] Hudoc (2008); 48 EHRR 707.   [493] *Parviz v Sweden No 8666/11* hudoc (2012) DA.
[494] Hudoc (2012) DA.

agreed. In *Hokkanen v Finland*,[495] the Court held that the transfer of custody rights from the father to the maternal grandparents was justifiable under Article 8(2), taking into account the girl's wishes and the length of time she had been in the *de facto* custody of her grandparents. This was so even though the authorities had previously failed to enforce court orders allowing the father custody and access against the recalcitrant grandparents. The interests of the child were elevated over those of the father and the Court emphasized the better position of national courts to assess the evidence upon which such decisions would be based. In *Mustafa and Armağan Akın v Turkey*,[496] the Court found a violation where the court had ordered the separation of siblings in the context of divorce proceedings, noting the lack of reasoning justifying the arrangement and the fact that the children's views had not been sought. In *Gluhaković v Croatia*,[497] a violation was found where the domestic courts had failed to take the applicant's personal circumstances, and in particular his work schedule, into account when arranging contact with his daughter.

Cases where an adoption order has been made outside the context of childcare proceedings initiated by the state are relatively rare. In *Söderbäck v Sweden*,[498] the applicant complained about an adoption order made in favour of his ex-partner's new husband without his consent, which had the effect of severing his ties with his daughter. The Court found no violation of Article 8, referring to the limited relations that he had enjoyed with his child prior to the adoption and the child's best interests.[499] The decision to base its findings on the limited contact enjoyed is open to criticism, given that the Court accepted that this was partly the result of the mother's continuing opposition to contact and since the adoption order was only sought when the applicant commenced domestic proceedings to obtain contact rights. However, as the adoptive father had taken part in the child's upbringing since she was eight months old and since she viewed him as her father, the Court's conclusion that the decision to make the order fell within the margin of appreciation appears justified.

Procedural rights have also played a significant role in cases involving disputes about contact and custody. In *Sahin v Germany*,[500] a dispute about an unmarried father's right to contact with his child, the Grand Chamber held that the national court's failure to hear the child did not lead to a violation of Article 8. It considered that it would be going too far to say that domestic courts were always required to hear a child on the issue of access and that it depended on the specific circumstances of each case having regard to the age and maturity of the child concerned.[501] Regular reviews of contact arrangements are required by Article 8. *Schaal v Luxembourg*[502] concerned a complaint about the courts' refusal to award access to the applicant father who had been accused of a sexual offence involving his daughter. The fact that the decision was reviewed promptly when circumstances changed meant that there was no violation of his Article 8 rights in the period following his acquittal.[503]

---

[495] A 299-A (1994); 19 EHRR 139.   [496] Hudoc (2010).   [497] Hudoc (2011).
[498] 1998-VII; 29 EHRR 95.
[499] See also *Kuijper v Netherlands No 64848/01* hudoc (2005) DA and *Eski v Austria* hudoc (2007).
[500] 2003-VIII para 73 GC, reversing the decision of the Chamber. On the wishes of the child see also *Zouhar v Czech Republic No 18923/04* hudoc (2005) DA; *C v Finland* hudoc (2006); 46 EHRR 485; and *Gobec v Slovenia* hudoc (2013).
[501] In *Sommerfeld v Germany* 2003-VIII; 38 EHRR 756 GC, it reached a similar conclusion on the need for psychological expert reports.   [502] Hudoc (2003); 41 EHRR 1071.
[503] However, a violation arose in the period before his acquittal because of delays in the criminal proceedings.

Where a court order has been made, the authorities are also under a positive obligation to ensure its enforcement. In contact cases, the key consideration is whether the authorities have taken all necessary steps to facilitate contact as can reasonably be demanded in the circumstances of each case.[504] In *Hokkanen v Finland*,[505] the non-enforcement of the father's right of access to his daughter against her grandparents did not respect his family life.[506] In *Santos Nunes v Portugal*,[507] the four-year delay in enforcing a decision to grant the father custody violated his Article 8 rights.

The non-enforcement of court orders is particularly complex where the child has been unlawfully abducted by one of its parents. In such cases, the positive obligations arising under Article 8 often have to be interpreted in light of the Hague Convention on Child Abduction.[508] In *Ignaccolo-Zenide v Romania*,[509] the applicant complained that the authorities had not taken sufficient steps to ensure rapid execution of court decisions granting her custody and to facilitate the return of her daughters who had been taken abroad by their father. According to the Court, the national authorities had a duty to facilitate reunion of the family but this was not absolute, since 'the reunion of a parent with children who have lived for some time with the other parent may not be able to take place immediately and may require preparatory measures to be taken'.[510] The adequacy of a measure was to be judged by the swiftness of its implementation, referring to Article 11 of the Hague Convention. Here, the total inaction of the Romanian authorities for more than one year and the failure to prepare the children for their return resulted in a violation of Article 8.[511] In finding violations of Article 8 in this context, the Court has held not only that the authorities had failed to take all the measures that could reasonably be expected to reunite parent and child, but that it did not do so 'without delay'.[512] It has found violations in several cases.[513]

In *Neulinger and Shuruk v Switzerland*,[514] the applicant mother unlawfully removed her son from Israel to Switzerland in 2005 after her ex-husband became involved in an ultra-orthodox, radical Jewish movement. In August 2007, the Swiss Federal Court ordered that the child be returned to Israel. The applicant lodged an application at the Strasbourg Court in September 2007 and the Court ordered that the return of the child not be enforced pending judgment. Following a Chamber judgment in 2009, the case was referred to the Grand Chamber. Handing down its judgment in July 2010, the Grand Chamber upheld the applicant's complaint. It noted that the Hague Convention only required the prompt return of an abducted child where there was no grave risk of physical or psychological harm. Article 8 therefore prohibited a child's automatic return where the Hague Convention was applicable. The Court explained that what was required was an assessment of:

> whether the domestic courts conducted an in-depth examination of the entire family situation and of a whole series of factors, in particular of a factual, emotional, psychological,

---

[504] See *Płaza v Poland* hudoc (2011) and *Cengiz Kılıç v Turkey* hudoc (2011).
[505] A 299-A (1994); 19 EHRR 139.
[506] See also *Eberhard and M v Slovenia* hudoc (2009) and *Nicolò Santilli v Italy* hudoc (2013).
[507] Hudoc (2012).
[508] Convention of 25 October 1980 on the Civil Aspects of International Child Abduction.
[509] 2000-I; 31 EHRR 212.   [510] *Ignaccolo-Zenide v Romania*, para 94.
[511] See also *Sylvester v Austria* hudoc (2003); 37 EHRR 417 and *Maumousseau and Washington v France* hudoc (2007); 51 EHRR 822.
[512] Eg, *Sylvester v Austria*. See also *Maire v Portugal* 2003-VII; 43 EHRR 231, where the Court emphasized the four-year delay returning the child who was particularly young at the time.
[513] *Macready v Czech Republic* hudoc (2010); *Šneersone and Kampanella v Italy* hudoc (2011); 57 EHRR 1180; and *Karrer v Romania* hudoc (2012).   [514] Hudoc (2010); 54 EHRR 1087 GC.

material and medical nature, and made a balanced and reasonable assessment of the respective interests of each person, with a constant concern for determining what the best solution would be for the abducted child in the context of an application for his return to his country of origin.[515]

Although the Grand Chamber accepted that the child's return when ordered by the domestic courts would not have breached Article 8, his return by the time of the Grand Chamber's judgment would, given the time that had passed.

This reference in *Neulinger and Shuruk* to the need for an in-depth examination has been criticized as being incompatible with the speedy return procedure envisaged by the Hague Convention and more appropriate to the determination of custody in the country of the child's habitual residence.[516] This was re-examined in *X v Latvia*,[517] where the Grand Chamber explained that a harmonious interpretation of the Hague Convention and Article 8 could be achieved if two conditions were observed, namely that the factors capable of constituting an exception to the child's immediate return under the Hague Convention be genuinely taken into account by the requested court and a reasoned decision provided; and that the factors be evaluated in the light of Article 8. A violation was found in the case, but at nine votes to eight and a unanimous dissenting opinion, this is hardly the decisive judgment hoped for.

Article 8 does not impose on domestic authorities any positive obligation to ensure the return of a child where the complaining parent only has the right of access.[518]

XII. IMMIGRATION

Although there is a distinction to be drawn between a decision refusing admission to a Convention state of a family member for reunification purposes and one ordering deportation of an individual already resident there, the net effect is the same in that it denies the individual the right to live in the state in question. Applicants argue that such decisions interfere with their respect for private and family lives.

In the context of deportation cases, family life has been interpreted more restrictively than in other areas of Article 8, with protection generally limited to an inner circle or the 'core family'. However, the Court tends to recognize family life with their parents of young adult children at risk of deportation, except where they have children of their own.[519] Where applicants have failed to establish family life, they are usually able to demonstrate that deportation or exclusion will interfere with private life. In *Slivenko v Latvia*,[520] the Grand Chamber recognized the applicant's ties with and in Latvia as an intrinsic part of private life. In light of the Court's restrictive approach to 'family life' in immigration cases, the importance of interpreting 'private life' to include links with community and society in general is clear.[521]

---

[515] *Neulinger and Shuruk v Switzerland*. Cf *B v Belgium* hudoc (2012).

[516] See Kuipers, EHRLR 397 at 403–05 (2012).   [517] Hudoc (2013).

[518] See *RR v Romania* hudoc (2009) and *Qama v Albania and Italy* hudoc (2013). The Court, however, found that there was an obligation to allow a person entitled to custody of a child unlawfully removed from her entry to a country to enable contact: *Polidario v Switzerland* hudoc (2013).

[519] *Bouchelkia v France* 1997-I; 25 EHRR 686; *Boujlifa v France* 1997-VI; 30 EHRR 419; *Maslov v Austria* hudoc (2008) GC; and *Bousarra v France* hudoc (2010). Cf *Slivenko v Latvia* 2003-X; 39 EHRR 490 GC; *Onur v UK* hudoc (2009); 49 EHRR 1057 paras 43–5; and *AW Khan v UK* hudoc (2010); 50 EHRR 1180 para 32, where the Court referred to the need for 'additional elements of dependence'.

[520] 2003-X; 39 EHRR 490 GC.   [521] See Thym, 57 ICLQ 87 at 91 (2008).

The position is less clear-cut where the case concerns the refusal to allow entry to a person outside the desired state of residence. The Convention does not protect the right to live in a contracting state. In *Abdulaziz, Cabales and Balkandali v UK*,[522] the Court explained that the duty imposed by Article 8 could not be considered as imposing a general obligation on the part of a contracting state to respect the choice by married couples of the country of their matrimonial residence and to accept the non-national spouses for settlement in that country. Such cases will only tend to fall within the scope of Article 8 where family life has been established.[523]

The state is entitled to refuse entry to or remove an alien for a good reason under Article 8(2), even where it might be difficult for him thereafter to enjoy his private or family life. In such cases, the issue is whether a fair balance has been struck between the applicant's interest and the public interest in deportation or exclusion. In the *Abdulaziz* case, no violation of Article 8 was found as the applicants had not shown that there were obstacles to establishing family life outside the UK.[524] However, in *Hasanbasic v Switzerland*,[525] the Court found a violation where the Swiss authorities refused family reunion in circumstances where the applicant, a Bosnian national, had formerly lived in Switzerland with his wife on the basis of a settlement permit for a number of years and was fully integrated into that country.[526] In *Berrehab v Netherlands*,[527] a previously married alien had lost his right to stay in the Netherlands after his divorce from his Dutch wife and the authorities proposed to deport him. What counted with the Court was the strength of the applicant's ties with his daughter and the importance to her of maintaining contact with him. Because refusal to grant him a residence permit seriously threatened those ties, the state had failed to strike a proper balance between their interests and those of the state.[528]

The extension of the principle established by these cases to cases involving immigrants involved in criminal activity has been more controversial. In *Moustaquim v Belgium*,[529] the applicant, a Moroccan national, had been brought to Belgium by his parents as a young child. As an adolescent, he had engaged in an intensive life of crime, much of it petty. Weighing up these considerations, the Court decided that his deportation would interfere with his family life in an unjustifiable manner. Perhaps even more remarkably, the Court took the same position in *Beldjoudi v France*,[530] where the applicant was a professional criminal who had spent about half of his adult life in prison. The Court found that it would be disproportionate to the aims of preventing crime or preserving public order if he were deported because, given the severe obstacles to his wife accompanying him, that 'might imperil the unity or even the existence of the marriage'. In recent years,

---

[522] A 94 (1985); 7 EHRR 471 PC.

[523] See *Gül v Switzerland* 1996 I; 22 EHRR 93; *Tuquabo-Tekle and Others v Netherlands* hudoc (2005); and *Sen v Netherlands* hudoc (2001); 36 EHRR 7. See also *IAA and Others v UK No 25960/13* (communicated January 2014).

[524] *Abdulaziz, Cabales and Balkandali v UK* A 94 (1985); 7 EHRR 471 PC. The Court found that there was a violation of Article 14 because men in the same position would have been entitled to have their wives join them. See also *Hode and Abdi v UK* hudoc (2012); 56 EHRR 960 (violation of Article 8 together with Article 14 because of discriminatory rules on admission of spouses); and *Gül v Switzerland* 1996 I; 22 EHRR 93 and *Tuquabo-Tekle and Others v Netherlands* hudoc (2005) (no violation).   [525] Hudoc (2013).

[526] See also *Sen v Netherlands* hudoc (2001); 36 EHRR 7 (violation of Article 8 because of refusal to allow child entry).   [527] A 138 (1988); 11 EHRR 322.

[528] But see *Berisha v Switzerland* hudoc (2013) and *Muradi and Alieva v Switzerland* hudoc (2013). On the separation of a minor child from his sole parent following an immigration measure, see *Nolan and K v Russia* hudoc (2009); 53 EHRR 977 and *Nunez v Norway* hudoc (2011).

[529] A 193 (1991); 13 EHRR 802.   [530] A 234-A (1992); 14 EHRR 801 para 78.

the Court has considered numerous applications regarding the compatibility with immigrants' right to respect for their private and family life of the decision to deport them. In most cases, the applicant was involved to some degree in criminal activity and this prompted the authorities to authorize his deportation,[531] although some cases concern applicants whose deportation was authorized on the grounds of their irregular immigration status.[532] While each case is different, the relevant criteria have been identified in *Üner v Netherlands*,[533] as the nature and seriousness of the offence; the length of the applicant's stay in the country; the time which had elapsed since the offence was committed and the applicant's conduct during that period; the nationalities of the various persons concerned; the applicant's family situation, such as the length of any marriage; whether the spouse knew about the offence before entering a family relationship; whether there are children of the marriage, and if so, their age and best interests; the seriousness of the difficulties which the spouse or children are likely to encounter in the foreign country; and the solidity of social, cultural and family ties with the host country and with the country of destination. Not all of the criteria are pertinent in every case, and the respective weight that they carry may vary from case to case. Where the appropriate balancing exercise has been conducted by the national authorities, their decision is likely to fall within the state's margin of appreciation. The case law shows that the Court is less sympathetic to applicants who do not have strong ties with the respondent state,[534] to applicants who have been less than honest with immigration officials,[535] and where the offences committed were serious, especially those involving drugs.[536] Where the exclusion is for a limited duration, or where there is a possibility of review, the measure is more likely to be compatible with Article 8.[537] Applicants are more likely to succeed where they have established long-term relationships or marriage with children in the Convention state,[538] have committed only minor offences,[539] or have committed the offences triggering the deportation proceedings as juveniles.[540] The deportation of children also requires special measures

---

[531] Eg, *Boughanemi v France* 1996-II; 22 EHRR 228 (no violation); *El Boujaïdi v France* 1997-VI; 30 EHRR 223 (no violation); *Baghli v France* 1999-VIII; 33 EHRR 799 (no violation); *Boultif v Switzerland* 2001-IX; 33 EHRR 1179 (violation); *Üner v Netherlands* 2006-XII; 45 EHRR 421 GC (no violation); *Omojudi v UK* hudoc (2009); 51 EHRR 289 (violation); *AW Khan v UK* hudoc (2010); 50 EHRR 1180 (violation); *Mutlag v Germany* hudoc (2010) (no violation); and *Samsonnikov v Estonia* hudoc (2012) (no violation).

[532] Eg, *Rodrigues da Silva and Hoogkamer v Netherlands* 2006-I; 44 EHRR 729 and *Darren Omoregie and Others v Norway* hudoc (2008).   [533] 2006-XII; 45 EHRR 421 GC.

[534] Eg, *Baghli v France* 1999-VIII; 33 EHRR 799 (applicant's links with France found to be tenuous even though his entire family lived there). See the dissenting judgment of Judges Costa and Tulkens.

[535] *Nsona v Netherlands* 1996-V; 32 EHRR 170.

[536] Eg, *C v Belgium* 1996-III; 32 EHRR 19 (applicant committed drugs offences and had some links with Morocco); *El Boujaidi v France* 1997-VI; 30 EHRR 223 (applicant had not lost all links with Algeria and had committed armed robbery and drugs offences); *Boujlifa v France* 1997-VI; 30 EHRR 419 (applicant lived in France since age five but was convicted of serious offences); and *Savasci v Germany No 45971/08* hudoc (2013) DA (applicant had lived in Germany for thirty years but was convicted of serious drugs offences). Contrast *AW Khan v UK* hudoc (2010); 50 EHRR 1180 (despite a conviction for a serious drug offence, applicant's deportation would violate Article 8) and *Udeh v Switzerland* hudoc (2013) (deportation after conviction for attempted importation of cocaine would violate Article 8).

[537] See *Emre v Switzerland* hudoc (2008) and *Vasquez v Switzerland* hudoc (2013).

[538] Eg, *Mehemi v France* 1997-VI; 30 EHRR 739 (applicant was father of three French children); *Ciliz v Netherlands* 2000-VIII (the deportation prejudged proceedings for access to his children); and *Udeh v Switzerland* hudoc (2013) (applicant had family life with young daughters who lived with their mother after divorce and so could not be expected to follow him).

[539] Eg, *Mokrani v France* hudoc (2003); 40 EHRR 123; *Sezen v Netherlands* hudoc (2006); 43 EHRR 621; and *Keles v Germany* hudoc (2005); 44 EHRR 249.

[540] *Maslov v Austria* Hudoc (2008) GC; *Yildiz v Austria* hudoc (2002); 36 EHRR 553; *Radovanovic v Austria* hudoc (2004); 41 EHRR 79; *Jakupovic v Austria* hudoc (2003); 38 EHRR 595; and *AA v UK* hudoc (2011).

designed to protect their family life from interference.[541] The case of *Jeunesse v Netherlands*, relinquished to the Grand Chamber in 2013, may bring some further clarity to the balancing exercise in this area.[542]

In more recent cases the legality and procedural propriety of immigrations measures have been the focus of the Court's attention. In *Liu and Liu v Russia*,[543] the Court held that domestic law which permitted the executive to choose between two different procedures for the deportation of a foreign national, one of which involved procedural safeguards and the other of which did not, did not meet the required standard to be 'in accordance with the law' under Article 8(2). A series of Bulgarian cases concerning deportation for reasons of national security established that pursuant to the lawfulness requirement, deportation measures must be subject to some form of adversarial proceedings involving effective scrutiny of the reasons for them and a review of the relevant evidence. Such proceedings must also allow for the Article 8 balancing act to be carried out.[544]

XIII. EMPLOYMENT AND POLITICAL ACTIVITIES

In *Niemietz v Germany*,[545] the Court found Article 8 to be applicable, in its private life head, in the context of a complaint about a search of the applicant's business premises, based on his right to establish and develop relationships with other human beings. Although the Court has continued to develop its case law in this area, the extent to which Article 8 applies in the professional sphere remains a matter for debate.

Article 8 does not guarantee a right of recruitment to the civil service[546] or a right to freedom of profession.[547] However, in *Sidabras and Džiautas v Lithuania*,[548] the Court concluded that the far-reaching ban on former KGB agents taking up private sector employment affected private life, noting that the ban had created serious difficulties for the applicants in terms of earning their living. The publicity caused by the ban and its application to them had also caused them to suffer constant embarrassment and had impeded their establishment of contacts with the outside world.[549] It found a violation of Article 14 together with Article 8 on account of the unjustified difference in treatment of former KGB officers.[550] By contrast, in *Calmanovici v Romania*,[551] the Court found Article 8 inapplicable to the applicant's complaint about his temporary suspension from

---

[541] See *Mubilanzila Mayeka and Kaniki Mitunga v Belgium* 2006-XI; 46 EHRR 449, where the Court found a violation of Article 8 because of the applicant child's detention separate from her mother prior to deportation.

[542] The case concerns the refusal to grant a residence permit to an illegal immigrant who had married a Dutch national and had two children with him.   [543] Hudoc (2007); 47 EHRR 751.

[544] *Al-Nashif v Bulgaria* hudoc (2002); 36 EHRR 655; *Musa and Others v Bulgaria* hudoc (2007); 49 EHRR 393; *Bashir and Others v Bulgaria* hudoc (2007); *CG and Others v Bulgaria* Hudoc (2008); *Raza v Bulgaria* hudoc (2010); and *Amie and Others v Bulgaria* hudoc (2013).

[545] A 251-B (1992); 16 EHRR 97 para 29.

[546] *Vogt v Germany* A 323 (1995); 21 EHRR 205 and *Vilho Eskelinen and Others v Finland* 2007-II; 45 EHRR 985 GC.   [547] *Thlimmenos v Greece* 2000-IV; 31 EHRR 411 GC.

[548] 2004-VIII; 42 EHRR 105.

[549] See also *Mateescu v Romania* hudoc (2014) (not yet final) (Article 8 applied to a condition that the applicant renounce his medical career if he wished to practise as a lawyer; and was violated since the condition was not in accordance with the law).

[550] See also the Court's judgment in *DMT and DKI v Bulgaria* hudoc (2012).

[551] Hudoc (2008).

his functions as a police officer, as he was not prevented from finding employment in the private sector.

Where the applicant's employment is affected by matters pertaining to his private life, Article 8 is likely to be engaged. In *Özpinar v Turkey*,[552] the applicant was removed from office as a judge in light of her close relationship with a lawyer and her personal appearance. The Court found that Article 8 applied and was violated because of the absence of procedural safeguards in the disciplinary proceedings.[553] In *Obst v Germany*,[554] and *Schüth v Germany*,[555] the Court found Article 8 applicable where the applicants had been dismissed from church employment for adultery. In doing so, it appears to have relied on the fact that the dismissal was for reasons relating to the applicants' sexual lives. In *Obst* the Court found no violation in light of the careful reasoning of the labour courts and the nature of the applicant's involvement in the Mormon church. It reached the contrary conclusion in *Schüth*, where the labour court's reasoning was not adequately detailed and the obligations accepted by the applicant when signing his contract of employment with the Catholic church were less evident.[556]

In the political sphere, the Commission in *Baškauskaitė v Lithuania*[557] examined a complaint by an individual about the refusal to register her candidacy in presidential elections. It considered that there had been no interference with her private life, noting that it was unable to detect what concrete restrictions were imposed on her or what other obligations the Lithuanian authorities had failed to meet which could have encroached upon her private life. However, in *Mółka v Poland*,[558] the Court of its own motion examined Article 8 in the context of facilities at a polling station not adapted to suit those in wheelchairs, which had prevented the applicant from exercising his right to vote. Although it did not decide on the applicability of Article 8 given that the case was inadmissible for other reasons, it considered it arguable that the situation at issue in the case touched on the applicant's possibility of developing social relations with other members of his community and the outside world, and was pertinent to his own personal development.[559] In *Misick v UK*,[560] the applicant complained under Article 8 about the dissolution of the Turks and Caicos House of Assembly, where he had been an elected representative. The Court found Article 8 to be inapplicable, noting that there was support in its case law for the idea that participation in politics was very much a matter of public life, to which Article 8 could have only limited application. The applicant here had failed to provide details of how the dissolution of the House of Assembly encroached upon his privacy or private life guarantees, including his ability to develop relationships with the outside world.

---

[552] Hudoc (2010).

[553] See also *Oleksandr Volkov v Ukraine* hudoc (2013), where a judge's dismissal was found not to be in accordance with the law.

[554] Hudoc (2010).   [555] Hudoc (2010).

[556] See *Fernández Martínez v Spain No 56030/07*, pending before the Grand Chamber, which concerns the refusal of a Catholic school to renew the applicant's employment contract after he publicly revealed his position as a married priest. See also cases concerning dismissal of homosexuals from the armed forces: *Smith and Grady v UK* 1999-VI; 29 EHRR 493; *Lustig-Prean and Beckett v UK* hudoc (1999); 29 EHRR 548; and *Beck, Copp and Bazeley v UK* hudoc (2002).   [557] *No 41090/98* hudoc (1998) DA.

[558] *No 56550/00* 2006-IV DA.

[559] This may, however, have been based on the importance given in other international texts to the importance of full participation of people with disabilities in society, and in particular in political and public life: see *Misick v UK No 10781/10* hudoc (2012) DA.   [560] Hudoc (2012) DA.

XIV. HOME AND HOUSING ISSUES

The core idea of protection of the home is one of sanctuary against intrusion by public authorities. The property right in houses is protected, if at all, by Article 1 of the First Protocol,[561] although the line is sometimes hard to draw.[562]

Numerous cases against Turkey established state responsibility for the destruction of applicants' homes and, finding that this was without any justification, the Court concluded that there had been a violation of Article 8.[563] In *Moldovan and Others v Romania (No 2)*,[564] the Court held that the failure to address the appalling conditions in which the applicants were forced to live following the destruction of their homes constituted a failure to put a stop to the continuing breaches of their right to respect for their homes. Similarly, in *Akdivar and Others v Turkey*,[565] the Court noted that the response of the authorities perpetuated the applicants' feelings of insecurity after the attack on their home and constituted in itself a hindrance of their rights to respect for their home. In *Surugiu v Romania*,[566] which concerned harassment by third parties who regularly entered the applicant's yard and dumped cartloads of manure in front of the door of the house, the Court found that the acts constituted repeated interference by third parties with the applicant's right to respect for his home and that Article 8 of the Convention was applicable. There was a violation in the case on account of the authorities' failure over a number of years to put a stop to the interference.

There is no right under Article 8 to be provided with a home.[567] This does not mean that complaints linked to homelessness automatically fall outside the scope of Article 8, but the extent of any positive obligation must be limited.[568] The Court has explained that an obligation to house particularly vulnerable individuals may flow from Article 8 in exceptional cases.[569] Where state accommodation is provided, it is arguable that complaints regarding its suitability or condition would engage the right to respect for the home, although the Court has preferred to consider the question from the perspective of 'private life'. In *Marzari v Italy*,[570] an applicant with a severe disability complained that the apartment he was allocated was inadequate for his needs and violated his right to respect for his home. The Court explained that a refusal by the authorities to provide assistance to an individual suffering from a severe disease might in certain circumstances raise an issue under Article 8 of the Convention. On the facts, the authorities were found to have taken reasonable measures to address the shortcomings of the applicant's accommodation and no violation of Article 8 was found.[571] However, in *Wallová and Walla v Czech Republic*,[572] a violation of the applicants' right to respect for family life was found where their children were taken into local authority care on account of the

---

[561] *James v UK* A 98 (1986); 8 EHRR 123 PC.

[562] In *Howard v UK No 10825/84*, 52 DR 198 (1987), the Commission decided that a compulsory purchase order potentially interfered with rights under Article 8 as well as under Article 1, First Protocol.

[563] Eg, *Akdivar and Others v Turkey* 1996-IV; 23 EHRR 143 GC; *Dulaş v Turkey* hudoc (2001); and *Altun v Turkey* hudoc (2004). In several other cases the Court found the applicants' allegations regarding the state authorities' destruction of their homes to be unsubstantiated: eg, *Gündem v Turkey* 1998-III; 32 EHRR 350 and *Çaçan v Turkey* hudoc (2004).   [564] Hudoc (2005); 44 EHRR 302.

[565] 1996-IV; 23 EHRR 143 GC.   [566] Hudoc (2004).

[567] *Chapman v UK* 2001-I; 33 EHRR 399 GC.

[568] *O'Rourke v UK No 39022/97* hudoc (2001) DA. For discussion of positive obligations see further Kenna, EHRLR 193 (2008).

[569] See *Yordanova and Others v Bulgaria* hudoc (2012). The Court also said that proportionality required the authorities to consider the risk that the Roma applicants, who had resided unlawfully on land for years, would become homeless as a result of their eviction.   [570] *No 36448/97*, 28 EHRR CD 175 (1999).

[571] See also *Costache v Romania No 25615/07* hudoc (2012) DA.   [572] Hudoc (2006).

poor quality of the family's accommodation. Given that the authorities had the power to monitor the applicants' living arrangement, advise them on how to improve the situation, and find a solution to their housing problem, the measure was disproportionate. While the Court was not asked to consider whether the failure to find a solution to their housing difficulties violated their right to respect for the home, its findings nonetheless support the argument that in exceptional circumstances, a positive obligation of this nature might well arise.[573]

Many aspects of private life will overlap with home life: the right to live one's life as one wishes or to adopt a particular lifestyle may have implications for the kind of home one wants and the level of protection to which one's home is entitled. This was raised as an issue in *Chapman v UK*,[574] concerning the interference with the applicant's Article 8 interests caused by the failure to grant her planning permission to live in a caravan on her land. The Grand Chamber noted that there was an emerging consensus in Council of Europe states 'recognising the special needs of minorities and an obligation to protect their security, identity and lifestyle'.[575] However, it did not consider this to be sufficiently concrete to offer any guidance as to the standards to be applied in cases of this kind and, accordingly, it concluded that its role was to ensure that such decisions were based on reasons that were relevant and sufficient. The majority found that they were in this case.[576] In *Connors v UK*,[577] the applicant gypsy complained that his family's eviction from the caravan site where he lawfully resided interfered with his 'private life', 'family life', and 'home'. Distinguishing *Chapman*, the Court held that a narrower margin of appreciation applied since the applicants had been lawfully resident on the site. It found that the weighty reasons of public interest required to justify the very severe interference with the applicant's rights—he was effectively rendered homeless with a detrimental impact on his and his family's health and education—did not exist in this case.[578]

While in *Connors* the Court had already spoken of the need for procedural safeguards under Article 8 in cases concerning eviction by local authorities, it was not until *McCann v UK*[579] that it spelled out more clearly what was required. The applicant had been a joint tenant of a local authority property together with his wife. His wife signed a notice to quit, which had the effect of ending the joint tenancy, and a possession order was made against the applicant. He sought judicial review of the order but his application was unsuccessful. The Court considered the possession proceedings to be in accordance with the law and to serve the twin aims of protecting the local authority's right to regain possession of the property from an individual who had no contractual or other right to be there; and ensuring that the statutory scheme for housing provision was properly applied, both of which fell within the notion of the rights and freedoms of others. However, it said that the loss of the home was a most extreme form of interference which required that the proportionality of the measure be determined by an independent tribunal in the light of the relevant principles under Article 8. In *McCann*, the court in the possession proceedings was not able to consider the proportionality of the order in the light of the applicant's personal circumstances. The lack of procedural safeguards led

---

[573] See also *Havelka and Others v Czech Republic* hudoc (2007) and *Saviny v Ukraine* hudoc (2008); 51 EHRR 780.

[574] 2001-I; 33 EHRR 399 GC. See also *Beard v UK* hudoc (2001); 33 EHRR 442 GC.

[575] *Chapman v UK*, para 93 GC.

[576] But see the joint dissenting opinion of Judges Pastor Ridruejo, Bonello, Tulkens, Strážnická, Lorenzen, Fischbach, and Casadevall, highlighting the vulnerability of the applicants as a minority group with a particular lifestyle directly related to their traditions and identity.

[577] Hudoc (2004); 40 EHRR 189.

[578] See also *Buckland v UK* hudoc (2012); 56 EHRR 557.   [579] Hudoc (2008); 47 EHRR 913.

to a violation of Article 8.[580] However, the Court explicitly said that it expected cases where such a review would lead to a finding that the making of a possession order would be disproportionate to be rare.[581] The Court has recently found a violation where the applicant was evicted by a private landlord, on the ground that the domestic court had considered only whether she had a legal entitlement to remain in the property and had not considered her other personal circumstances.[582] However, it is debatable whether cases involving two private parties require the same proportionality assessment, given the importance of the private owner's property rights.[583]

XV. ENVIRONMENTAL RIGHTS

Although the Court has frequently remarked that there is no explicit right in the Convention to a clean and quiet environment[584] or to preservation of the natural environment as such,[585] it has explained that breaches of the right to respect of the home are not confined to concrete or physical breaches, such as unauthorized entry into a person's home, but also include noise, emissions, smells, or other forms of interference.[586] This has led to a clear widening in the scope of Article 8 to cover environmental human rights.

Pollution must attain a minimum level if the complaints are to fall within the scope of Article 8,[587] although it is not necessary to show that the pollution seriously endangered health.[588] The assessment depends on all the circumstances of the case, such as the intensity and duration of the nuisance and its physical or mental effects.[589] There would be no arguable claim under Article 8 if the detriment complained of was negligible in comparison to the environmental hazards inherent to life in every modern city.[590]

In cases involving state decisions that affect environmental issues, there are two aspects to the Court's inquiry. The first is to assess the substantive merits of the decision. The Court's evaluation of the national authorities' decision to ensure that it is compatible with Article 8 requires careful examination of the legislative and regulatory

---

[580] See also *Kay and Others v UK* hudoc (2010); 54 EHRR 1056; *Ćosić v Croatia* hudoc (2009); 52 EHRR 1098; *Paulić v Croatia* hudoc (2009); *Zehentner v Austria* hudoc (2009); 52 EHRR 739; *Buckland v UK* hudoc (2012); 56 EHRR 557; *Bjedov v Croatia* hudoc (2012); *Yordanova and Others v Bulgaria* hudoc (2012); and *Winterstein and Others v France* hudoc (2013).

[581] It seems that such a case arose in *Yordanova v Bulgaria*. See also *Rousk v Sweden* hudoc (2013) (violation because applicant was evicted before the resolution of the issues underlying the eviction). For further reading, see Remiche, 12 HRLR 787 (2012).

[582] See *Brežec v Croatia* hudoc (2013). See also *Belchikova v Russia No 2408/06* hudoc (2010) DA (complaint about eviction from private property inadmissible because the domestic courts had weighed all factors in the balance).

[583] See the concurring opinion of Judge De Gaetano in *Buckland v UK* hudoc (2012); 56 EHRR 557. The case of *Brogan v UK No 74946/10* (communicated November 2011) may bring some clarity to this area.

[584] *Hatton v UK* 2003-VIII; 37 EHRR 611 GC; *Allen and Others v UK No 5591/07* hudoc (2009) DA; and *Greenpeace EV and Others v Germany No 18215/06* hudoc (2009) DA.

[585] *Kyrtatos v Greece* 2003-VI; 40 EHRR 390; *Ivan Atanasov v Bulgaria* hudoc (2010); and *Dubetska and Others v Ukraine* hudoc (2011).

[586] See Boyle, 23 EJIL 613 (2012) and Pedersen, 16 EPL 571 (2010).

[587] *López Ostra v Spain* A 303-C (1994); 20 EHRR 277; *Guerra and Others v Italy* 1998-I; 26 EHRR 357 GC; *Fadeyeva v Russia* 2005-IV; and *Dubetska and Others v Ukraine* hudoc (2011).

[588] *López Ostra v Spain*.

[589] See *Asselbourg and Others v Luxembourg No 29121/95* 1999-VI DA; *Fadeyeva v Russia* 2005-IV; and *Hardy and Maile v UK* hudoc (2012); 55 EHRR 841.

[590] *Dubetska and Others v Ukraine* hudoc (2011). See *Asselbourg and Others v Luxembourg* and *Gronuś v Poland No 39695/96* hudoc (1999) DA, for examples of where the applicants failed to provide evidence of damage such as to engage Article 8.

framework governing the activities in question. In this respect, the Court has consistently emphasized the wide margin of appreciation enjoyed by the authorities. The second aspect of the Court's review is to scrutinize the decision-making process to ensure it is fair and that due weight has been accorded to the interests of the individual. All procedural aspects must be considered, including the type of policy or decision involved, the extent to which the views of individuals were taken into account, and the procedural safeguards available. The decision-making process must involve appropriate investigations and studies so that the effects of activities that might damage the environment and infringe individuals' rights can be predicted and evaluated in advance and a fair balance struck between the various conflicting interests at stake. The Court has, however, been careful to clarify that this does not mean that the authorities can take decisions only if comprehensive and measurable data are available in relation to each and every aspect of the matter to be decided. Finally, there must be a possibility for individuals to appeal to the courts against any decision, act, or omission where they consider that their interests or their comments have not been given sufficient weight in the decision-making process.[591]

In *Hatton v UK*,[592] the applicants complained that the government's policy on night flights at a neighbouring airport violated their rights under Article 8. The Chamber found a breach of Article 8, but the case was subsequently referred to the Grand Chamber for reconsideration. The Grand Chamber viewed the central issue as being whether the appropriate balance had been struck between the relevant interests. In this regard, it remarked that economic interests were specifically enumerated as a legitimate aim under Article 8(2) and that the state could therefore take them into account in policy-making. It explained that while environmental protection should be taken into consideration, it would not be appropriate for the Court to adopt a special approach in this respect by reference to a special status of environmental human rights. Since the evidence regarding the noise generated by night flights, its impact on the applicants' rights, and the economic benefits of night flights were not conclusive, and measures had been taken to mitigate the effect of noise, the authorities had not overstepped their margin of appreciation. As regards the procedural aspect of the case, the Court did not find that there were fundamental flaws in the preparation of the government's policy in the area and concluded by twelve votes to five that there had been no violation of Article 8.[593]

In *Moreno Gómez v Spain*,[594] the applicant complained about the disruption to her home as a result of noise from bars and nightclubs. The level of noise and the authorities' failure over a number of years to address the night-time disturbances led the Court to conclude that there had been a violation of Article 8.[595] In *Deés v Hungary*,[596] the applicant complained that noise and vibrations as a result of heavy traffic in his street had made his home almost uninhabitable. The Court found a violation of Article 8 on the grounds that the measures which were taken by the authorities consistently proved to be insufficient,

---

[591] See *Giacomelli v Italy* 2006-XII; 45 EHRR 871; *Taşkın and Others v Turkey* 2004-X; 42 EHRR 1127; *Di Sarno and Others v Italy* hudoc (2012); and *Hardy and Maile v UK* hudoc (2012); 55 EHRR 841.

[592] 2003-VIII; 37 EHRR 611 GC.

[593] See also *Arrondelle v UK No 7889/77*, 19 DR 186 (1980); *Baggs v UK No 9310/81*, 44 DR 13 (1985); *Powell and Rayner v UK* A 172 (1990); 12 EHRR 355; and *Flamenbaum and Others v France* hudoc (2012).

[594] 2004-X; 41 EHRR 899.

[595] See also *Mileva and Others v Bulgaria* hudoc (2010), concerning noise caused by an office, an electronic games club and a computer club, and *Zammit Maempel v Malta* hudoc (2011), concerning fireworks. Cf *Kyrtatos v Greece* 2003-VI; 40 EHRR 390 (urban development) and *Fägerskiöld v Sweden No 37664/04* hudoc (2008) DA (wind turbines), where the Court found that the noise was not serious enough to engage Article 8.

[596] Hudoc (2010); 57 EHRR 370.

as a result of which the applicant was exposed to excessive noise disturbance over a substantial period of time.

Industrial pollution and hazardous industrial activities have generated a number of complaints under Article 8, both alone and together with Articles 2 and 3. In *López Ostra v Spain*,[597] which concerned hydrogen sulphide emission by a waste-treatment plant, the Court balanced the town's economic well being against the applicant's Article 8 interests and found that there had been a breach of Article 8(1). In *Guerra and Others v Italy*,[598] the key question for the Court, once it had decided that the highly toxic emissions from a nearby fertiliser factory had had a direct effect on the applicants' right to respect for their private and family life, was to consider whether the national authorities took the necessary steps to ensure effective protection of those rights. It decided on the facts that they had not, on the basis that the applicants had waited right up until the production of fertilisers ceased for essential information that would have enabled them to assess the risks they might run if they continued to live in their town.[599]

Cases involving serious risks to life as a result of hazardous activities will engage Article 2 of the Convention.[600] However, where the facts do not meet the Article 2 threshold, the Court has found Article 8 to apply in certain circumstances. Thus in *Taşkın and Others v Turkey*,[601] where the dangerous effects of mining activities using sodium cyanide leaching to which the applicants were likely to be exposed had been determined as part of an environmental impact assessment procedure in such a way as to establish a sufficiently close link with private and family life, Article 8 was applicable. Similarly in *Tătar v Romania*,[602] Article 8 was applicable in a case concerning a risk posed by the use of sodium cyanide at a mineral extraction plant. In that case, the absence of any internal decision or other official document indicating, in a sufficiently clear manner, the degree of risk posed to human health and the environment was held not to be fatal to the claim, given that the applicant had attempted to pursue domestic remedies and that a previous incident involving an accidental spillage had resulted in a higher than usual reading of certain toxic products in the vicinity. In *Hardy and Maile v UK*,[603] the applicant complained under Article 8 about the alleged inadequate regulation of the operation of liquefied natural gas terminals and the allegedly poor dissemination of relevant information. The Court was satisfied that the potential risks posed by the LNG terminals were such as to establish a sufficiently close link with the applicants' private lives and homes for the purposes of Article 8.[604]

There appears to be a stronger case that a violation has occurred where the applicants are able to show a failure by the national authorities to comply with some aspects of the domestic regime. In *López Ostra v Spain*,[605] the waste-treatment plant at issue was operating without the necessary licence, and was eventually closed down; and in *Guerra and Others v Italy*,[606] the violation was based on the fact that the applicants had been unable to obtain information that the state was under a statutory obligation to provide. In *Giacomelli v Italy*,[607] the Court found a violation where the authorities had failed to comply with domestic legislation and had not closed the hazardous waste treatment plant despite being ordered by the courts to do so. Similarly, in *Taşkın and Others v Turkey*,[608] a

---

[597] A 303-C (1994); 20 EHRR 277.   [598] 1998-I; 26 EHRR 357 GC.

[599] While the Court appears to have found a substantive breach in this case based on environmental pollution, it is more properly seen as a breach of the obligation to provide access to information.

[600] Eg, *Öneryıldız v Turkey* 2004-XII; 41 EHRR 325 GC.   [601] 2004-X; 42 EHRR 1127.

[602] Hudoc (2009).   [603] Hudoc (2012); 55 EHRR 841.

[604] See also *Fadeyeva v Russia* 2005-IV, regarding the operation of a steel plant, and *Brânduşe v Romania* hudoc (2009), regarding offensive smells emanating from a former refuse tip.

[605] A 303-C (1994); 20 EHRR 277.   [606] 1998-I; 26 EHRR 357 GC.

[607] 2006-XII; 45 EHRR 871.   [608] 2004-X; 42 EHRR 1127.

violation was found because although the decision to grant an operating permit for a gold mine had been annulled, its closure was ordered only ten months after the delivery of the judgment. By contrast, in *Martinez and Manzano v Spain*,[609] the Court found no violation of Article 8 where pollution was caused by an active stone quarry, but the applicants were living in an industrial zone not meant for residential use and pollution levels were tolerable. Similarly, in *Hardy and Maile v UK*,[610] there was no violation where there was no evidence that the operators had failed to comply with the requirements of domestic law.

Environmental cases frequently raise an issue of access to information, as part of the procedural aspect of the protection afforded by Article 8.[611] The need for provision of information on environmental and industrial hazards has long been recognized as an integral part of the state's positive obligations under Article 8. In *Guerra and Others v Italy*,[612] the violation found was based on the fact that the applicants had waited for some time to receive information of the risks posed. In *Taşkın and Others v Turkey*,[613] the Court said that the importance of access to the conclusions of relevant studies and to information which would enable members of the public to assess the danger to which they are exposed was beyond question. In *Hardy and Maile v UK*,[614] it explained that where a government engaged in hazardous activities which might have hidden adverse consequences on health and where no considerations of national security arose, an effective and accessible procedure of access to relevant and appropriate information had to be established.[615]

XVI. PRISONERS

The Court has acknowledged that detention, by its very nature, entails an interference with private and family life. Some measure of control over prisoners' contacts with the outside world is called for and is not in itself incompatible with the Convention.[616] At the same time, there is 'no question that a prisoner forfeits his Convention rights merely because of his status as a person detained following conviction'.[617] The guarantees of Article 8 therefore apply to prisoners, although when it comes to justification or the striking of a fair balance, specific considerations evidently arise in the prison context.

It is an essential part of a prisoner's right to respect for private and family life that the prison authorities assist him in establishing and maintaining contact with his family and the outside world while he is in detention.[618] Restrictions such as limitations on the number of family visits, supervision of those visits, and subjection of a detainee to a special prison regime or special visit arrangements constitute an interference with a prisoner's rights under Article 8.[619] The Court is unlikely to find a violation where there is no evidence that requests for visits were refused or where the applicant has not availed himself of all of his visiting entitlements.[620] But provisions restricting visits must indicate with reasonable clarity the

---

[609] Hudoc (2012). [610] Hudoc (2012); 55 EHRR 841.

[611] See also the information obligation at Article 5(1)(c) of the Aarhus Convention on Access to Information, Public Participation in Decision-making and Access to Justice in Environmental Matters, referred to in *Di Sarno and Others v Italy* hudoc (2012). [612] 1998-I; 26 EHRR 357 GC.

[613] 2004-X; 42 EHRR 1127. See also *Giacomelli v Italy* 2006-XII; 45 EHRR 871.

[614] Hudoc (2012); 55 EHRR 841.

[615] Access to information more generally is discussed at section 4.IX.

[616] See *Silver v UK* A 61 (1983); 5 EHRR 347; *Kalashnikov v Russia* No 47095/99 2001-XI DA; *Aliev v Ukraine* hudoc (2003); and *Ciorap v Moldova* hudoc (2007).

[617] *Hirst v UK (No 2)* 2005-IX; 42 EHRR 849 para 70 GC and *Dickson v UK* 2007-V; 46 EHRR 927 paras 67–8 GC.

[618] Eg, *Messina v Italy (No 2)* 2000-X; *Ciorap v Moldova* hudoc (2007); and *Piechowicz v Poland* hudoc (2012).

[619] *Piechowicz v Poland*. [620] *Epners-Gefners v Latvia* hudoc (2012).

scope and manner of the exercise of any discretion conferred on the relevant authorities to restrict visiting rights.[621] In *Sari and Colak v Turkey*,[622] the absence of a legal framework to facilitate prompt contact after arrest led to the violation of Article 8. An unreasoned refusal to grant permission for visits will not be in ' "accordance with the law".[623]

In assessing whether the authorities have struck a fair balance between the right of detainees to family contact and the legitimate aims provided for in Article 8(2), relevant factors include the duration and the nature of the restrictions on contact; the reasons given for the restrictions; the grounds for detention; the existence of the risk of collusion or other factors hampering the investigation or trial; other measures taken, such as the censorship of correspondence; and the authorities' consideration of alternative means, for example supervision of contact by a prison officer.[624] In a series of Italian Mafia cases, where there were significant restrictions on contact with family, the Court found that, given the specific nature of organized crime and the fact that family visits had frequently served as a means of conveying orders and instructions to the outside, the restrictions on visits and the accompanying controls could not be said to be disproportionate.[625] However, the Court found a violation of Article 8 in *Trosin v Ukraine*,[626] holding that restrictions regarding the frequency and length of family visits, the number of persons admitted per visit, and the manner of conducting the visits were not justified because there was no evidence that such far-reaching measures were necessary.[627] Restrictions must be kept under review. In *Piechowicz v Poland*,[628] a total prohibition of communication between the applicant and his common-law wife was justified at the initial stage of criminal proceedings where both were indicted in the same proceedings. However, the fact that for over two years and three months the applicant had only had one sixty-minute conversation with his wife and that no alternative measures were considered went beyond what was necessary in a democratic society.

While some prisoners have sought to rely on Article 8 to support their requests for prison transfers, the Commission consistently indicated that only in exceptional circumstances would the state's duty extend to transferring a prisoner from one jail to another.[629] However, it considered that an issue might arise where there was a court order granting a prisoner the right to see his child.[630] The Court has examined few cases on the subject, but it appears that this restrictive approach prevails today.[631] In *Plepi v Albania and Greece*,[632]

---

[621] *Gülmez v Turkey* hudoc (2008); *Wegera v Poland* hudoc (2010); and *Gradek v Poland* hudoc (2010).

[622] 2006-V.

[623] *Wegera v Poland* hudoc (2010); *Popenda v Poland* hudoc (2012); and *Kurkowski v Poland* hudoc (2013).

[624] For manifestly ill-founded and no violation cases, see *Kalashnikov v Russia No 47095/99* 2001-XI DA; *Aliev v Ukraine* hudoc (2003); *Rutecki v Poland No 18880/07* hudoc (2009) DA; and *Glinowiecki v Poland No 32540/07* hudoc (2010) DA. For violation cases, see *Klamecki v Poland (No 2)* hudoc (2003); 39 EHRR 137; *Kučera v Slovakia* hudoc (2007); *Ferla v Poland* hudoc (2008); and *Moiseyev v Russia* hudoc (2008); 53 EHRR 306.

[625] *Salvatore v Italy No 42285/98* hudoc (2002) DA; *Bastone v Italy No 59638/00* 2005-II DA; and *Enea v Italy* hudoc (2009); 51 EHRR 103 GC.   [626] Hudoc (2012).

[627] See also *Ciorap v Moldova* hudoc (2007) and *Kurkowski v Poland* hudoc (2013).

[628] Hudoc (2012).

[629] Eg, *Ouinas v France No 13756/88*, 65 DR 265 at 277 (1990); *PK, MK and BK v UK No 19085/01* hudoc (1992) DA; *McKenny v UK No 23956/94* hudoc (1994) DA; and *Hacisuleymanoğlu v Italy No 23241/94*, 79B DR 121 (1994). But see *Wakefield v UK No 15817/89*, 66 DR 251 (1990), where the Commission appears to have engaged in a more general proportionality assessment of the refusal.   [630] *Ouinas v France*.

[631] A number of cases in which the applicant prisoner raised a complaint of this nature were declared inadmissible by a Committee so it is not possible to scrutinize the reasons for the decisions: see *Midro v Poland No 43994/98*; *Bronk v Poland No 19394/06*; and *Kalinowski v Poland No 3761/07*.

[632] *Nos 11546/05, 33285/05*, and *33288/05* hudoc (2010) DA.

it declared a complaint about the refusal to authorize a transfer inadmissible as falling outside the scope of Article 8. However in *Khodorkovskiy and Lebedev v Russia*,[633] the applicants complained that the decision to send them to prisons in remote colonies interfered with their private and family lives. The Court concluded that the absence of clear and foreseeable rules for distributing convicts among penal colonies meant that there was inadequate legal protection against arbitrariness.[634]

The monitoring, interception, or censoring of correspondence will also interfere with Article 8. Prisoners have frequently alleged that such measures were not 'in accordance with the law'. The same basic principles apply here as with the cases on secret surveillance: the law must be sufficiently clear and precise, be accessible and foreseeable, and incorporate sufficient safeguards to prevent the arbitrary exercise of any discretion that the law conveys. In *Silver v UK*,[635] the applicant prisoner maintained that some of his letters had been stopped in accordance with directions to governors not having the force of law. The Court accepted that these instruments, which filled in some details of the necessarily wide legal authority to intercept prisoners' mail, could be taken into account to determine whether the legal regime satisfied the Convention standard of foreseeability. However, this was acceptable only to the extent that the directions were accessible to a prisoner, which in general they were not. The result was that the stopping of several of the applicant's letters had not been in accordance with the law.[636] In *Niedbała v Poland*,[637] the fact that Polish law permitted automatic censorship of all prison correspondence and did not set out any guidance on how this wide discretion should be exercised brought it in conflict with the legality requirement of Article 8(2). In a series of cases against Italy, Italian law was also found to be inadequate to satisfy the requirements of Article 8(2).[638] In *Aliev v Ukraine*,[639] a restriction on the number of parcels the applicant was allowed to receive from relatives was not in accordance with the law as he could not know with sufficient certainty whether the limits laid down in the applicable Code applied to him. In *Mehmet Nuri Özen and Others v Turkey*,[640] the refusal of the prison authorities to send letters written in Kurdish, rather than Turkish, was not in accordance with the law because there was no law governing the matter.

In the context of its assessment of the necessity of monitoring measures, the Court has emphasized that the opportunity to write and to receive letters is sometimes the prisoner's only link with the outside world.[641] Measures interfering with correspondence must be based on reasons that are relevant and sufficient and must be proportionate to the particular aim that they are designed to achieve.[642] Relevant factors in the proportionality assessment may include the type of offence which led to the detention,[643] the seriousness

---

[633] Hudoc (2013).

[634] See also *HS and Others v UK No 16477/09* hudoc (2010) DA (striking-out) and *Miler v Czech Republic No 56347/10* hudoc (2012) DA (both communicated but struck out or declared inadmissible for other reasons).

[635] A 61 (1983); 5 EHRR 347.

[636] See also *McCallum v UK* A 183 (1990); 13 EHRR 597 para 31, where 'management guidelines' were insufficient to supplement the generalities of the law.   [637] Hudoc (2000); 33 EHRR 1137.

[638] Eg, *Domenichini v Italy* 1996-V; 32 EHRR 68; *Labita v Italy* 2000-IV; 46 EHRR 1228 GC; *Ospina Vargas v Italy* hudoc (2004); *Salvatore (Manuele) v Italy* hudoc (2005); and *Enea v Italy* hudoc (2009); 51 EHRR 103 GC.

[639] Hudoc (2003).   [640] Hudoc (2011).

[641] Eg, *Campbell v UK No 7819/77*, 14 DR 186 (1978) and *Yefimenko v Russia* hudoc (2013).

[642] See *Van der Ven v Netherlands* 2003-II; 38 EHRR 967 (prevention of escape) and *Messina v Italy (No 2)* hudoc 2000-X (preventing use of Mafia contacts in prison).

[643] *Messina v Italy (No 2)* (Mafia crime) with *Płoski v Poland* hudoc (2002) (non-violent offences).

of what is at stake for the prisoner,[644] the nature of the correspondence concerned,[645] and the breadth or precise nature of the interference in a given case.[646] In *Puzinas v Lithuania (No 2)*,[647] disciplinary measures against an applicant who had sent his correspondence with a prisoner being released instead of sending it through official channels were held to be proportionate, as the applicant had failed to show a valid reason for circumventing the rule and the sanction imposed was minor. In *Aliev v Ukraine*,[648] the logistical problem involved in processing an unrestricted quantity of parcels arriving in a large penitentiary, here an establishment with over 3,000 inmates, had to be taken into account when assessing proportionality. In *Yefimenko v Russia*,[649] the applicable rules required all non-privileged correspondence to be processed by the prison administration and monitored as a matter of routine; no reasons were required to warrant monitoring. Monitoring was not limited as to its length or scope, the legal provisions did not specify the manner of exercise of monitoring powers, and there was no possibility of independent review of the scope and duration of the measure. As the government had failed to justify the routine monitoring of the correspondence or to show that sufficient safeguards were in place, it could not be considered necessary.[650]

The Court has accorded a particularly high priority to the protection of a prisoner's right to communicate with his legal advisors. In *Golder v UK*,[651] it rejected the government's claim that it was necessary 'for the prevention of disorder' to refuse to transmit a letter from a prisoner to his solicitor about the possibility of bringing a civil action against a prison officer. In *Campbell v UK*,[652] it held that the 'general interest' required that consultations with lawyers should be in conditions 'which favour full and uninhibited discussion'. Moreover, *all* letters to and from legal counsel were privileged, which meant that 'reasonable cause' had to be shown by the state for suspecting that a particular letter contained illicit material before it could be opened. Guarantees were required to ensure that any limited power to intercept and read correspondence was not being abused. *Erdem v Germany*[653] concerned the opening of the legal correspondence of a prisoner suspected of terrorist offences, which the state claimed was justified for the protection of national security and the prevention of crime and disorder.[654] Bearing in mind the applicant's right to prepare his defence, the Court said that legal correspondence could only be interfered with in exceptional circumstances. Given the precise wording of the law in question, and the safeguards involved in its application, an appropriate balance had been struck in this case. Although it was not explicit what the exceptional circumstances were in this case, the Court's reference to 'the threat posed by terrorism in all its forms' would suggest that the terrorism context provided the state with a greater margin of appreciation here.

The Court has staunchly defended the individual's right to communicate with it, and formerly the Commission, demonstrating something akin to a zero-tolerance approach to interference with and screening of its correspondence with those in detention, regardless

---

[644] *Płoski v Poland*, where the Court found that the refusal to grant the applicant temporary release to go to the funerals of his parents violated Article 8. See also *Marincola and Sestito v Italy No 42662/98* hudoc (1999) DA and *Georgiou v Greece No 45138/98* hudoc (2000) DA.

[645] *Yefimenko v Russia* hudoc (2013).

[646] *Jankauskas v Lithuania* hudoc (2005), where widespread censorship of the applicant's correspondence took place. See also *Yefimenko v Russia*; and *Szuluk v UK* hudoc (2009); 50 EHRR 227.

[647] Hudoc (2007).   [648] Hudoc (2003).   [649] Hudoc (2013).

[650] See also *Moiseyev v Russia* hudoc (2008); 53 EHRR 306 and *Petrov v Bulgaria* hudoc (2008).

[651] A 18 (1975); 1 EHRR 524 PC.   [652] A 233 (1992); 15 EHRR 137 paras 46–8.

[653] 2001-VII; 35 EHRR 383.

[654] See also *Messina v Italy (No 2)* 2000-X, concerning restrictions on the applicant's (an alleged Mafia member) contacts with his family and censorship of his correspondence.

of the offences with which they have been charged.[655] In *Sałapa v Poland*,[656] it examined *ex officio* a complaint about control of a prisoner's correspondence with the former Commission. It highlighted that it was of 'prime importance for the effective exercise of the right of individual petition under the Convention that the correspondence of prisoners with the Court not be subject to any form of control, which might hinder them in bringing their cases to the Court'. Because Polish law did not draw any distinction between the different categories of persons with whom the prisoners could correspond and the authorities were not obliged to give 'a reasoned decision specifying grounds on which the letter could be intercepted, opened and read', there was a violation of Article 8. In recent cases, the Court has begun to examine complaints regarding interference with correspondence addressed to it also under Article 34 of the Convention, as hindering the right of application to the Court.[657]

For prisoners, the possibility of corresponding with others will often depend on the provision of facilities by the authorities and there may be positive obligations inherent in Article 8 to provide such facilities. In *Boyle v UK*,[658] the Commission said that while the general principle was that the state did not have to pay for a prisoner's letters, an obligation might arise where the prisoner's inability to pay severely limited the possibility of correspondence. In *Boyle*, the applicant did not fall within the exception. However, in *Cotlet v Romania*,[659] the Court found a violation of Article 8 where the government had failed to show that the applicant had been provided with the envelopes to which he was entitled under the rules and where only envelopes for domestic correspondence were available. In *Grace v UK*,[660] the Commission said that there were positive obligations on the prison authorities where correspondence was routed through the prison administration to make sure that letters were posted and delivered, and that where there were difficulties with the postal service, the prisoner had a right to be informed.

Prisoners do not enjoy a right under Article 8 to make telephone calls, particularly where the facilities for contact by way of correspondence are available and adequate.[661] Where telephone facilities are provided, they may be subjected to legitimate restrictions, for example, in the light of the shared nature of the facilities with other prisoners and the requirements of the prevention of disorder and crime.[662]

Prisoners' ability to rely on Article 8 to claim entitlement to other privileges is limited. For example, Article 8 does not oblige states to put in place needle-exchange programmes in prison to reduce risks of infection.[663] As far as the right to conjugal visits is concerned, while the Court has expressed its approval for the evolution in several European countries towards allowing conjugal visits for prisoners, it has not yet interpreted the Convention as requiring contracting states to make provision for such visits.[664] It did, however, find a violation where the authorities failed to assess the applicant prisoner's request for access to artificial insemination facilities.[665]

---

[655] *Rehbock v Slovenia* 2000-XII; *Peers v Greece* 2001-III; 33 EHRR 1192; *AB v Netherlands* hudoc (2002); 37 EHRR 928; and *Karalevičius v Lithuania* hudoc (2005).   [656] Hudoc (2002) para 94, 97.

[657] *Yefimenko v Russia* hudoc (2013).   [658] *No 9659/82*, 41 DR 90 at 94 (1985).

[659] Hudoc (2003).   [660] *No 11523/85*, 62 DR 22 at 41 (1987) Com Rep; CM Res DH (89) 21.

[661] *AB v Netherlands* hudoc (2002); 37 EHRR 928; *Davison v UK No 52990/08* hudoc (2010) DA; and *Daniliuc v Romania No 7262/06* hudoc (2012) DA.

[662] *AB v Netherlands*; *Davison v UK*; and *Coşcodar v Romania No 36020/06* hudoc (2010) DA.

[663] *Shelley v UK No 23800/06* hudoc (2008) DA.

[664] *ELH and PBH v UK Nos 32094/96 and 32568/96*, 91 DR 61 (1997); *Kalashnikov v Russia No 47095/99* 2001-XI DA; *Aliev v Ukraine* hudoc (2003); *Dickson v UK* 2007-V; 46 EHRR 927 GC; and *Epners-Gefners v Latvia* hudoc (2012).   [665] *Dickson v UK*.

5. CONCLUSION

Article 8 is complex for several reasons. First, the formulation of the principles of applicability of Article 8 which are broad and vague has allowed the scope of protection of Article 8 to be extended to cover almost every aspect of a person's life. The interests that it protects are wide, ranging from press intrusion into privacy to claims of environmental pollution. Examples of recent cases where the Court has refused to find Article 8 applicable are rare, but provide welcome guidance as to where the limits of Article 8 might lie. On the other hand, there are certain areas where the Court appears dogmatically to apply case law which has become outdated as a result of the substantial developments which have occurred in Article 8 over the years.[666] The Court's failure sometimes to identify where developments are required can perhaps be explained by the sheer volume of cases which pass through the Court each year and its tendency as a result to continue to apply established principles where no well-structured challenge is made.

The wide scope of Article 8 protection presents further challenges when it comes to the content of the right and of the obligations it imposes on states. General statements formulated in the context of childcare cases cannot necessarily be easily applied to secret surveillance cases. Conversely, the failure to apply the same rules and principles to two different cases examined under Article 8 can cause confusion where it cannot properly be explained in Article 8 terms. A clear example of the ambiguity caused by the latter can be seen when one examines the Court's approach to the drawing of 'bright line' rules in legislation. It has generally acknowledged the need for such rules and in a number of cases in diverse areas it has accepted that the absolute rules at issue were not inconsistent with Article 8. However, in eviction cases, for example, the Court has held that it is insufficient for the legislation itself to balance the competing interests and that proportionality requires an individual judicial decision which takes account of the applicant's personal circumstances. While this difference in approach might be explained by the serious nature of the interference, it has not been adequately explained in the case law.[667]

The development of positive obligations has added to the complexity. On the one hand, there is the concern to control the state's capacity to interfere in central matters of inter-personal relationships, such as consensual sexual activities and parent and child relations, where the principal concern of the right-holder is keeping the state out. On the other hand, the state's assistance is called for to protect persons from harm inflicted by others, such as exploitative sexual conduct and children harmed or neglected by parents. The case law shows how hard the various balances are to strike. There is also a lack of coherent guidance as to when a negative or positive obligation is in play. As the Court itself has reiterated on numerous occasions, the boundaries between the two are not easy to draw. But while this could justify a refusal to decide the point in an occasional particularly complex case, it appears that the Court is these days more often than not happy to leave the question open.

---

[666] Eg, prisoner transfers.

[667] Cf *Evans v UK* 2007-I; 46 EHRR 728 GC and *Dickson v UK* 2007-V; 46 EHRR 927 GC, for example, both of which concerned the applicant's desire to conceive a child. In *Evans*, the Court considered that the absolute rules on consent in IVF cases were compatible with Article 8, whereas in *Dickson* a violation of Article 8 was found because the policy did not permit a proportionality assessment to be conducted in each individual case.

The notion of positive obligations has also given a great deal of freedom to the Court to interpret what is required to comply with Article 8. The challenges presented by positive obligations, in terms of trying to impose some order and coherence to the Court's case law in this area, continue to grow. Positive obligations are hardly ever absolute and the reach of obligations on states to secure rights themselves or to stand between private actors remains relatively unexplained by the Court. Once again, recourse is made to the 'balancing exercise', but the problem is deciding precisely what are the interests in play. More argument on the real nature of the individual's interest before embarking on a balancing exercise against the countervailing demands of the public interest would be welcome.

On Article 8 matters concerning issues whose principles are well-established and broadly applied by national courts, the Strasbourg Court generally defers to national decision-making bodies where no procedural defect has been identified. This is evident in childcare cases, where the Court appears most reluctant to interfere with the substantive decisions of local courts and other bodies. The former willingness of the Court to review substantive decisions of national authorities in the context of immigration cases appears now to have been replaced by more circumspection, with greater emphasis on the general principles and less evidence of the *à la carte* approach whereby each case was determined largely in isolation and on its merits. However, the practice is not uniform. The increasing emphasis on formal legality and procedural guarantees is a welcome development to enable the Court to deal flexibly with cases which fall within Article 8. If it seems a cautious conclusion that procedure will often prevail over substance, it is a reflection of the subsidiary role of the Convention in protecting rights. In principle, it should be only in exceptional cases that the Court rejects the conclusion of state authorities which have addressed themselves to the very question that comes before the Court and applied the relevant principles.

Finally, within the Article 8 context, more than any other Article, the Court is being asked to determine issues that are at the forefront of technology or which concern sensitive societal views and values. This inevitably presents challenges of its own. In this regard, Article 8 has passed the test as to its continuing relevance and application to modern legal dilemmas and human rights challenges with flying colours. It is one thing to get states to comply with obligations which affect only a few people and which are on the periphery of political concerns. It is much more of a test to secure the cooperation of the authorities on matters of such central and prominent interest. Yet it is against such threats to human rights that the Convention was originally designed.

13

ARTICLE 9: FREEDOM OF THOUGHT, CONSCIENCE, AND RELIGION

Article 9

1. Everyone has the right to freedom of thought, conscience and religion; this right includes freedom to change his religion or belief and freedom, either alone or in community with others and in public or private, to manifest his religion or belief, in worship, teaching, practice and observance.
2. Freedom to manifest one's religion or beliefs shall be subject only to such limitations as are prescribed by law and are necessary in a democratic society in the interests of public safety, for the protection of public order, health or morals, or for the protection of the rights and freedoms of others.

From complaints about curbs on religious dress and displays of religious symbols, to conflicts over faith at the workplace, few articles of the Convention have in recent years generated as much controversy as Article 9. After a slow start—because it was not until 1993 that the European Court examined Article 9 in any detail[1]—the Court has, in the last two decades, made important strides in formulating its own guidelines in relation to freedom of thought, conscience, and religion. Accordingly, the Court plays a key role today in regard to conflict resolution and standard setting in the field of religion and belief in contemporary Europe.

1. THE SCOPE OF ARTICLE 9

The scope of Article 9 is wide, in that it covers forms of both religious *and* non-religious belief.[2] This was originally made clear by the Court in *Kokkinakis v Greece*,[3] where it affirmed that the values of Article 9 were at the foundation of a democratic society:

It is, in its religious dimension, one of the most vital elements that go to make up the identity of believers and their conception of life, but it is also a precious asset for atheists, agnostics, sceptics and the unconcerned.

---

[1] See *Kokkinakis v Greece* A 260-A (1993); 17 EHRR 397, described by Judge Pettiti (p 425) in his partly concurring opinion as 'the first real case concerning freedom of religion to have come before the European Court'.
[2] Article 9 includes the 'freedom to hold or not to hold religious beliefs and to practice or not to practice a religion': *Grzelak v Poland* hudoc (2010) para 85.   [3] A 260-A (1993); 17 EHRR 397 para 31.

As a consequence, Article 9 of the ECHR is confined not merely to long-established religions (eg, Buddhism,[4] Christianity,[5] Hinduism,[6] Islam,[7] Judaism,[8] Sikhism[9]), but it has also afforded protection to relatively new religious organizations (eg, the Jehovah's Witnesses,[10] the Church of Scientology[11]), secularism,[12] and a wide range of other philosophical beliefs (eg, pacifism,[13] veganism,[14] and opposition to abortion[15]). Indeed, some previous rulings of the Commission appear to suggest that controversial political philosophies such as fascism,[16] communism,[17] and neo-Nazi principles[18] may even constitute beliefs for the purposes of Article 9.

By giving such a broad interpretation to Article 9,[19] the Convention organs have conspicuously avoided any determination of what is meant by the term 'religion'.[20] This approach is understandable, because any definition of 'religion' would need to be flexible enough to satisfy a broad cross-section of world faiths, as well as sufficiently precise for practical application in specific cases. Such a balance would be practically impossible to strike and echoes the approach of the Human Rights Committee, which has also refrained from seeking to define 'religion' under the International Covenant on Civil and Political Rights (1966).[21] Thus, the inclusion of the term 'belief' in Article 9(1) enables the Court to avoid having to grapple with the formidable problems associated with defining the word 'religion'.[22]

Even though 'belief' has been interpreted widely under Article 9, the meaning accorded to this term is not exhaustive. For example, an applicant's contention that his cremated ashes should be scattered over his land was held to be insufficiently 'coherent' to constitute a 'belief',[23] while the Court rejected the claim that Article 9 should encompass the notion of assisted suicide on the ground that 'not all opinions or convictions constitute beliefs in the sense protected by Article 9(1) of the Convention'.[24] Thus, it is generally recognized that in order to be afforded protection under the Convention, a belief must 'attain a certain level of cogency, seriousness, cohesion and importance',[25] and that once this threshold has been met the state may not 'determine whether religious beliefs...are legitimate'.[26]

---

[4] *X v UK No 5442/72*, 1 DR 41 (1975).   [5] *Stedman v UK No 29107/95*, 23 EHRR CD 168 (1997).

[6] *ISKCON v UK No 20490/92*, 18 EHRR CD 133 (1994).

[7] *X v UK No 8160/78*, 22 DR 27 (1981).   [8] *D v France No 10180/82*, 35 DR 201 (1983).

[9] *X v UK No 8231/78*, 28 DR 5 (1982).   [10] *Manoussakis v Greece* 1996-IV; 23 EHRR 387.

[11] *Church of Scientology Moscow v Russia* hudoc (2007); 46 EHRR 304 para 64.

[12] *Lautsi and Others v Italy* hudoc (2011); 54 EHRR 60 para 58 GC.

[13] *Arrowsmith v UK No 7050/75*, 19 DR 5 (1978) Com Rep; CM Res DH (79) 4.

[14] *H v UK No 18187/91*, 16 EHRR CD 44 (1993).

[15] *Knudsen v Norway No 11045/84*, 42 DR 247 (1985).   [16] *X v Italy No 6741/74*, 5 DR 83 (1976).

[17] *Hazar and Açik v Turkey Nos 16311/90, 16312/90 and 16311/93*, 72 DR 200 (1991).

[18] *X v Austria No 1747/62*, 13 CD 42 (1963).

[19] In *Chassagnou v France* 1999-III; 29 EHRR 615 GC, Judge Fischbach (p 72, in a separate opinion) even suggested 'that "environmentalist" or "ecological" beliefs come within the scope of Article 9 insofar as they are informed by what is a truly societal stance'.

[20] 'It is clearly not the Court's task to decide in abstracto whether or not a body of beliefs and related practices may be considered a "religion" within the meaning of Article 9 of the Convention': *Kimlya and Others v Russia* hudoc (2009) para 79.

[21] Human Rights Committee, General Comment 22, Article 18 (Forty-Eighth session, 1993) paras 1, 2.

[22] On this generally, see Gunn, 16 Harv HRJ 189 (2003).

[23] *X v Germany No 8741/79*, 24 DR 137 (1978).

[24] See *Pretty v UK* 2002-III; 35 EHRR 1 para 82, where the claim that assisted suicide constituted a belief for the purposes of Article 9(1) was rejected.

[25] *Campbell and Cosans v UK* A 48 (1982); 4 EHRR 293 para 36; and *Bayatyan v Armenia* hudoc (2011); 54 EHRR 467 para 110 GC.

[26] *Hasan and Chaush v Bulgaria* 2000-XI; 34 EHRR 1339 para 78 GC; and *Manoussakis v Greece* 1996-IV; 23 EHRR 387 para 47.

It is also important to bear in mind the structure of Article 9. The first part of Article 9(1) guarantees 'the right to freedom of thought, conscience and religion', whereas 'belief' is only mentioned in the next clause, which stipulates that 'this right includes freedom to change [one's] religion or belief'. Accordingly, it has been suggested that 'religion or belief' should be distinguished from 'thought and conscience' on the basis that Article 9 protects the manifestation of 'religion or belief', whereas expressions of one's 'thought and conscience' are protected by (and confined to) Article 10 of the Convention.[27] In this context Evans suggests that 'it is best to reserve the term "manifestation" to describe a particular form of expression which is only relevant to religion or belief [and that] there can be no question of manifesting or "actualizing" thought or conscience under Article 9'.[28]

2. FREEDOM OF THOUGHT, CONSCIENCE, AND RELIGION: THE RIGHT TO BELIEVE

There are two elements to Article 9(1). First, it has an 'internal' dimension (*forum internum*), in that it guarantees 'freedom of thought, conscience and religion'.[29] This right, which is 'largely exercised inside an individual's heart and mind',[30] falls beyond the jurisdiction of the state and must not be restricted.[31] Secondly, Article 9(1) has an 'external' element (*forum externum*) since it recognizes that everyone has the right to manifest a 'religion or belief' in 'worship, teaching, practice and observance'. Accordingly, subject to the 'prescribed by law' and 'necessary in a democratic society' criteria, the state may impose restrictions on the *manifestation* of religion or belief on the grounds of public safety, public order, health, or morals and 'for the protection of the rights and freedoms of others'.[32]

The distinction between this 'internal' and 'external' dimension is not clearly defined.[33] One view is that the scope of the *forum internum* is relatively narrow and that as long as 'individuals are able to continue in their beliefs',[34] Article 9(1) will not be violated, whereas a different (and broader) perspective is that there are more subtle ways in which the state may interfere with one's *forum internum*.[35] The jurisprudence of the Court tends to reflect the former rather than the latter approach.[36] For example, in *Buscarini*

---

[27] See M Evans, *Religious Liberty and International Law in Europe*, 1997, pp 284–6; and C Evans, *Freedom of Religion under the European Convention on Human Rights*, 2001, pp 52, 53. On Article 10 see Ch 14.

[28] M Evans, *Religious Liberty*, at p 285. See also *Ivanova v Bulgaria* hudoc (2007); 47 EHRR 1173 para 79, where the Court observed that '[u]nlike the second paragraphs of Articles 8, 10 and 11 of the Convention, which cover all the rights mentioned in the first paragraphs of those Articles, that of Article 9 of the Convention refers only to "freedom to manifest one's religion or belief"'.

[29] See Article 9(1) of the ECHR. Article 18 of the Universal Declaration of Human Rights (1948) and Article 18(1) and (3) of the International Covenant on Civil and Political Rights 1966 (ICCPR) are also drafted according to this model.

[30] Gomien, *Short Guide to the European Convention on Human Rights*, 1991, p 69.

[31] *Darby v Sweden* A 187 (1990); 13 EHRR 774 para 44 Com Rep.

[32] Article 9(2). Under Article 15 of the ECHR, a state may also derogate from its Article 9 obligations '[i]n time of war or other public emergency threatening the life of the nation'. This is in contrast to the ICCPR, whereby Article 4(2) precludes derogation from the principle of thought, conscience, and religion (Article 18) in such circumstances.

[33] See Petkoff, 7 Religion and Human Rights 183 at 185 (2012), who even poses the question 'whether this [forum internum and forum externum] divide does not weaken freedom of religion or belief as a right'.

[34] See M Evans, *Religious Liberty and International Law in Europe*, 1997, at p 295.

[35] See C Evans, *Freedom of Religion under the European Convention on Human Rights*, 2001, at pp 72–81.

[36] Indeed Carolyn Evans suggests that 'states have to act very repressively before the Court…will hold that they have interfered with the *forum internum*': *Freedom of Religion*, p 78.

and Others v San Marino[37]—where the applicants were required to swear an oath on the Christian Gospels in order to take their seats in the San Marino Parliament—the Court held that this legal obligation 'did indeed constitute a limitation within the meaning of the second paragraph of Article 9, since it required them to swear allegiance to a particular religion'.[38] Although some argue that on the facts of this case there was an interference with the *forum internum*[39]—which would have then precluded the imposition of restrictions on the applicants' rights—the Court refrained from considering such matters, and held instead that Article 9 had been violated because the obligation to swear an oath was not 'necessary in a democratic society' under Article 9(2).[40]

Whilst there is uncertainty at the margins, certain conduct is undoubtedly contrary to the *forum internum*. For example, the use of physical threats or sanctions that force people to deny or adhere to a particular religion or belief is forbidden.[41] Even though Article 9 does not outlaw such 'coercion' in express terms,[42] its inclusion of the right to change one's religion or belief is, in effect, a bulwark against 'indoctrination of religion by the state'.[43] Thus, as the Court observed in *Kosteski*—a case where the applicant claimed that his *forum internum* had been violated by being required to prove that he was a practising Muslim in order to secure time off work to attend a religious festival—'the notion of the State sitting in judgment on the state of a citizen's inner and personal beliefs is abhorrent'.[44]

Less draconian (albeit equally pervasive) state actions can also fall foul of Article 9. The state may, for example, neither dictate nor demand to know what an individual believes.[45] Although a legal obligation to complete a census form interferes with one's right to respect for a private life (Article 8(1)), and can be justified as being necessary for the economic well-being of the country under Article 8(2),[46] no such principle applies to Article 9. In contrast, however, because such a measure is seemingly incompatible with the *forum internum* under Article 9(1), a state's actions in seeking to compel an individual to reveal their beliefs cannot be justified under Article 9(2).

In recent years the Court has demonstrated its willingness to pay particularly close attention to national laws and policies which have the effect of requiring disclose of one's personal convictions. For example, in *Alexandridis v Greece*,[47] the Court held that Article 9 had been violated where the applicant had been required to divulge that he was not a member of the Orthodox Church when taking an oath to practise as a lawyer, and in *Dimitras v Greece*,[48] it ruled that witnesses and parties in legal proceedings, who had been unwilling to base their testimonies on religious oaths, should not have been forced

---

[37] 1999-I; 30 EHRR 208 GC.   [38] *Buscarini and Others v San Marino*, para 34.

[39] Evans, *Freedom of Religion under the European Convention on Human Rights*, 2001, at p 73; and Taylor, *Freedom of Religion: UN and European Human Rights Law and Practice*, 2005, p 130.

[40] *Buscarini and Others v San Marino* 1999-I; 30 EHRR 208 para 39 GC.

[41] See Tahzib, *Freedom of Religion or Belief: Ensuring Effective International Legal Protection*, 1996, p 26.

[42] This is in contrast to Article 18(2) of the ICCPR (1966) which provides that, '[n]o one shall be subject to coercion which would impair his freedom to have or to adopt a religion or belief of his choice'.

[43] *Angelini v Sweden No 10491/83*, 51 DR 41 at 48 (1986).

[44] *Kosteski v Former Yugoslav Republic of Macedonia* hudoc (2006); 45 EHRR 712 para 39. The applicant's claim failed on the basis that 'it is not oppressive to require some level of substantiation when the claim concerns a privilege or entitlement not commonly available': para 39.

[45] Eg, in *Folgerø and Others v Norway* 2007-III; 46 EHRR 1147 para 98 GC, the Court held that 'imposing an obligation on parents to disclose detailed information to the school authorities about their religious and philosophical convictions may constitute a violation of Article 8 of the Convention and possibly also of Article 9'.   [46] *X v UK No 8160/78*, 22 DR 27 at 36 (1981).

[47] Hudoc (2008).   [48] Hudoc (2010).

to reveal (according to court records) that they were 'atheists' or 'of the Jewish faith'. The Court has also been guided by this non-disclosure principle in areas beyond the taking or swearing of oaths. For example, in *Sinan Işık v Turkey*,[49] where the applicant alleged that he had been forced to disclose his religious beliefs, by being required to indicate his religion on his national identity card,[50] the Court, in finding a violation of Article 9, held that the state is forbidden from seeking to discover an individual's religious beliefs, or from obliging him/her to disclose such beliefs.[51] In this regard the Court also rejected the Turkish government's argument that the identity card contained a box which allowed the card's recipient to choose to declare (or not) their religious affiliation, on the basis that 'when identity cards have a religion box, leaving that box blank inevitably has a specific [negative] connotation',[52] especially for groups whose beliefs are different from those of the majority.

The importance of ensuring that minority communities are protected from the adverse consequences of having to reveal their beliefs (be they religious or not) has also been acknowledged by the Court. For example, in *Grzelak v Poland*,[53] the issue was whether a school, which had withdrawn a boy from its religious instruction lessons at the request of his agnostic parents, had in effect stigmatized the child as being different from his Catholic classmates, by failing to record a mark in successive school reports for a subject entitled 'religion/ethics'. The Court, in reiterating the principle that freedom to manifest one's religious beliefs includes the right not to reveal one's faith or equivalent beliefs, held that the absence of a mark for 'religion/ethics' constituted a violation of Article 14 (non-discrimination) taken in conjunction with Article 9, because the lack of any such mark 'inevitably has a specific connotation', particularly in a nation such as Poland 'where the great majority of the population owe allegiance to one particular religion'.[54]

There are, however, some very limited circumstances where a requirement to divulge one's religious affiliations may be consistent with Article 9. Thus, for example, in *Wasmuth v Germany*,[55] the Court rejected an applicant's contention that an obligation to disclose his non-affiliation with a church was contrary to Article 9. Under German tax law a small number of religions are entitled to church taxes from their members who pay income tax, and the applicant complained that, for the completion of his income tax card, he had been forced to reveal that he did not belong to one of the faith groups that could levy a church tax. In finding no violation of Article 9, the Court distinguished this case from its earlier rulings (ie, those in *Grzelak*, *Sinan Işık* and *Dimitras*) on the basis that Wasmuth had not been required to explain why he did not belong to any of the churches that could levy taxes, and that the purpose of the information requested by the state had merely been to ensure that he would only pay church taxes should he wish to do so.[56] The Court's less rigorous approach to the disclosure of religious affiliation in *Wasmuth*, in seeming contrast to that in *Sinan Işık*, may have much to do with its recognition of the practical difficulties of operating a system of religious taxation—an area synonymous with a wide margin of appreciation, given that there is 'no common

---

[49] Hudoc (2010).
[50] The Court observed that the applicant, who stated that he was a member of the Alevi religious community, was required to carry an identity card on which his religion was indicated as Islam: *Sinan Işık v Turkey*, para 39.   [51] *Sinan Işık v Turkey*, para 41.
[52] *Sinan Işık v Turkey*, para 51.   [53] Hudoc (2010).
[54] *Grzelak v Poland*, para 95. In *Sinan Işık v Turkey* hudoc (2010), the Court, having found a violation of Article 9, chose not to examine whether there had been a separate violation in relation to Articles 9 and 14.
[55] Hudoc (2011).   [56] *Wasmuth v Germany*, para 51.

European standard governing the financing of churches or religions'.[57] Yet, that said, there was agreement in both *Wasmuth* and *Sinan Işık* as to the general principle that the state must respect 'the right not to disclose one's religion or beliefs',[58] because such an obligation 'falls within the *forum internum* of each individual'.[59]

The Court's general approach in regard to the disclosure of personal convictions is perhaps hardly surprising. In essence, there are unlikely to be many good reasons why the state should need to have specific information about what an individual believes—but there are undoubtedly many bad ones, especially when one bears in mind the Inquisition and the coercive investigations of modern totalitarian regimes.

3. FREEDOM OF THOUGHT, CONSCIENCE, AND RELIGION: THE INDIVIDUAL, THE GROUP, AND THE STATE

I. CHURCH/STATE RELATIONS

A church or association with religious and philosophical objects is capable of exercising rights under Article 9.[60] Its interests, as well as those of its members, may be protected under the Convention,[61] a seeming legacy of the fact that Article 9(1) offers rights to '[e]veryone'. The Convention also affords protection to freedom *of*, as well as freedom *from*, a particular religion or belief, with the Court having held that Article 9 guarantees 'freedom to hold or not to hold religious beliefs and to practise or not to practise a religion'.[62]

Neutrality is evidently the watchword for the state's relationship with faith communities and individuals.[63] The Court has held that 'the believer's right to freedom of religion encompasses the expectation that the community will be allowed to function peacefully free from arbitrary State intervention',[64] and that the state's duty of neutrality and impartiality precludes it from having any power 'to assess the legitimacy of religious beliefs'[65] or the way in which such beliefs are expressed or manifested.[66] Moreover, the Court has emphasized that:

> the autonomous existence of religious communities is indispensable for pluralism in a democratic society and is thus an issue at the very heart of the protection which Article 9 affords.[67]

With this in mind, there are at least four areas where those in government must tread warily.

---

[57] *Wasmuth v Germany*, para 63. See also *Spampinato v Italy No 23123/04* hudoc (2007) DA.

[58] *Sinan Işık v Turkey* hudoc (2010) para 41; and *Wasmuth v Germany* hudoc (2011) para 50.

[59] *Sinan Işık v Turkey*, para 42. See also *Wasmuth v Germany*, para 51.

[60] *X and the Church of Scientology v Sweden No 7805/77*, 16 DR 68 (1979).

[61] *Cha'are Shalom Ve Tsedek v France* 2000-VII para 72 GC; and *Chappell v UK No 12587/86*, 53 DR 241 (1987).   [62] *Buscarini v San Marino* 1999-I; 30 EHRR 208 para 34 GC.

[63] *Hasan and Chaush v Bulgaria* 2000-XI; 34 EHRR 1339 para 78 GC.

[64] *Hasan and Chaush v Bulgaria*, para 62.

[65] *Hasan and Chaush v Bulgaria*, para 62; and *Jehovah's Witnesses of Moscow v Russia* hudoc (2010); 53 EHRR 141 para 99.   [66] *Hasan and Chaush v Bulgaria* 2000-XI; 34 EHRR 1339 para 78 GC.

[67] *Hasan and Chaush v Bulgaria*, para 62.

First, matters pertaining to the official recognition (or non-recognition) of certain faiths under national law may raise issues under Article 9.[68] For example, in *Metropolitan Church of Bessarabia and Others v Moldova*,[69] a faith group argued, successfully, that the government's refusal to recognize it as a registered church violated Article 9. In reiterating the need for the state 'to remain neutral and impartial' in such matters,[70] the Court rejected the government's submission that its refusal to recognize the Metropolitan Church was necessary to protect national security and Moldovan territorial integrity,[71] and accepted that whilst a religious organization's 'programme might conceal objectives and intentions different from the ones it proclaims', there was no evidence in this particular case to support such a claim.[72] However, there have been occasions where the Court has found that a state's refusal to grant official registration (or deny re-registration) to minority faith groups such as the Salvation Army,[73] the Church of Scientology,[74] and the Jehovah's Witnesses,[75] has contravened the state's duty of neutrality and impartiality.[76] Moreover, excessive *delays* in affording registration to religious bodies—including waiting periods of ten[77] and even fifteen[78] years before a group could apply for recognition as a religious society—have led to breaches of the Convention. In addition, the Court has upheld complaints of discrimination on the grounds of religion or belief where states have granted privileges, without any objective and reasonable justification, to some religious organizations but not to others.[79] And finally, the mere fact that a faith group is not officially registered does not justify the imposition of curbs on its members manifesting their beliefs (eg, praying) in public.[80]

Secondly, it is incumbent on the state not to ignore the communal nature of Article 9.[81] Given that 'religious communities traditionally and universally exist in the form of

---

[68] The adverse consequences of non-recognition for a religious group—such as not being able to own or rent property, maintain bank accounts, hire employees etc—were acknowledged by the Court in *Kimlya and Others v Russia* hudoc (2009) para 85.   [69] 2001-XII; 35 EHRR 306.

[70] *Metropolitan Church of Bessarabia and Others v Moldova*, para 116.

[71] The government argued that the applicant church posed a threat to national security and Moldovan territorial integrity because it was allegedly working towards the reunification of Moldova with Romania: *Metropolitan Church of Bessarabia and Others v Moldova*, para 120.

[72] *Metropolitan Church of Bessarabia and Others v Moldova*, para 125.

[73] See, eg, *Moscow Branch of the Salvation Army v Russia* 2006-XI; 44 EHRR 912.

[74] See, eg, *Church of Scientology Moscow v Russia* hudoc (2007); 46 EHRR 304.

[75] See, eg, *Jehovah's Witnesses of Moscow v Russia* hudoc (2010); 53 EHRR 141.

[76] See *Svyato-Mykhaylivska Parafiya v Ukraine* hudoc (2007); *Biserica Adevărat Ortodoxă din Moldova v Moldova* hudoc (2007); 48 EHRR 497; *Savez Crkava and Others v Croatia* hudoc (2010); 54 EHRR 1245; and *Fusu Arcadie and Others v Moldova* hudoc (2012).

[77] See *Religionsgemeinschaft der Zeugen Jehovas and Others v Austria* hudoc (2008); 48 EHRR 424 paras 79–80. See also *Verein der Freunde der Christengemeinschaft and Others v Austria* hudoc (2009), where a ten-year delay lacked any objective and reasonable justification, and violated Article 14 (the prohibition of discrimination) and Article 9.

[78] In *Kimlya and Others v Russia* hudoc (2009), a fifteen-year qualifying period for registration violated Article 9 read in the light of Article 11 (freedom of assembly and association).

[79] On such violations of Article 14 read together with Article 9 see, eg, *Savez Crkava and Others v Croatia* hudoc (2010); 54 EHRR 1245, where a number of reformist churches that had been denied legal status had, *inter alia*, been unable to obtain official recognition of their religious marriages; and *O'Donoghue and Others v UK* hudoc (2010); 53 EHRR 1, where, under UK immigration law, a scheme designed to prevent bogus marriages that required payment of an application fee from people wishing to marry, exempted those who wished to marry in accordance with the rites of the Church of England. See also *Ásatrúarfélagið v Iceland No 22897/08* hudoc (2012) DA, where a religious association's complaint that it had been discriminated against in comparison with the National Church of Iceland was declared inadmissible.

[80] See *Masaev v Moldova* hudoc (2009); 57 EHRR 185.

[81] The Court first recognized the collective dimension of manifestation in *Kokkinakis v Greece* A 260-A (1993); 17 EHRR 397 para 31, as did the Commission before that (*X v UK No 8160/78*, 22 DR 27 (1981)). See also *Jehovah's Witnesses of Moscow v Russia* hudoc (2010); 53 EHRR 141 para 99.

organised structures',[82] of which the 'collective dimension' is a key element,[83] the Court has been willing to interpret Article 9 in the light of Article 11 to ensure that believers can 'associate freely, without arbitrary state intervention'.[84] As a consequence, in *Barankevich v Russia*,[85] a ban on a group of Evangelical Christians holding a religious service in a public park was held to be contrary to Article 11 interpreted in the light of Article 9. In addition, the communal nature of Article 9 is demonstrated by the importance that the Court attaches to the relationship between believers and their places of worship. Thus, for example, in *Cyprus v Turkey*,[86] Article 9 was violated because Greek Cypriots living in Northern Cyprus did not have free access to their places of worship, whilst in *Manoussakis v Greece*,[87] a requirement that a group of Jehovah's Witnesses had to obtain prior authorization before they could use a meeting hall was held to contravene Article 9, because they had been waiting over a decade for such permission to be granted.[88] Furthermore, with states under a positive obligation to protect faith groups from harassment or physical attack,[89] and the Court having acknowledged the important role that religious organizations play in the democratic process,[90] there is little doubt that Article 9 has a collective, as well as an individual, dimension.

Thirdly, the state's duty of neutrality and impartiality may have significant consequences in terms of the way that it acts in relation to the appointment and dismissal of a faith group's office holders. For example, in *Hasan and Chaush v Bulgaria*,[91] following a dispute within the Bulgarian Muslim community as to who should be its national leader (Chief Mufti), the government effectively replaced the applicant who had been elected to this office (Hasan) with another candidate who had previously occupied the post. The Court held that, as a result of this decision, the state had been shown to 'favour one faction of the Muslim community...to the complete exclusion of the hitherto recognized leadership', and that Article 9 had been violated because of 'an interference with the internal organization of the Muslim community'.[92] This principle, that religious organizations must retain autonomy in relation to the selection of their own leaders,[93] has been re-affirmed in recent years by the Court.[94] Thus, even if a government contends that it has appointed the leader of a particular religious group with the (ostensibly) legitimate aim of avoiding intra faith strife, such a claim will almost certainly fail.[95]

---

[82] *Hasan and Chaush v Bulgaria* 2000-XI; 34 EHRR 1339 para 62 GC.

[83] *Metropolitan Church of Bessarabia and Others v Moldova* 2001-XII; 35 EHRR 306 para 118. See also *Moscow Branch of the Salvation Army v Russia* 2006-XI; 44 EHRR 912.

[84] *Jehovah's Witnesses of Moscow v Russia* hudoc (2010); 53 EHRR 141 para 99.

[85] Hudoc (2007); 47 EHRR 266.   [86] 2001-IV; 35 EHRR 731 para 245 GC.

[87] 1996-IV; 23 EHRR 387. See also *Pentidis v Greece* 1997-III; 23 EHRR CD 37.

[88] However, there may be circumstances where the need to protect the public interest by upholding planning provisions in respect of religious buildings or related public spaces will override the right to manifest one's religion or belief. See, eg, *Vergos v Greece* hudoc (2004); 41 EHRR 913 (planning permission rejected for a house of prayer); and *Johannische Kirche and Peters v Germany* No 41754/98 2001-VIII DA (planning permission rejected for a new cemetery).

[89] See *97 Members of the Gldani Congregation of Jehovah's Witnesses and 4 Others v Georgia* hudoc (2007); 46 EHRR 613.   [90] *Moscow Branch of the Salvation Army v Russia* 2006-XI; 44 EHRR 912 para 61.

[91] 2000-XI; 34 EHRR 1339 GC.   [92] *Hasan and Chaush v Bulgaria*, para 82.

[93] *Metropolitan Church of Bessarabia and Others v Moldova* 2001-XII; 35 EHRR 306 para 117.

[94] See *Holy Synod of the Bulgarian Orthodox Church (Metropolitan Inokentiy) v Bulgaria* hudoc (2009); 50 EHRR 41; and *Mirolubovs and Others v Latvia* hudoc (2009).

[95] See, eg, *Serif v Greece* 1999-IX; 31 EHRR 561 para 53, where, in acknowledging that community relations may be threatened by divisions between religious groups, the Court has nonetheless affirmed that the 'role of the authorities in such circumstances is not to remove the cause of tension by eliminating pluralism, but to ensure that the competing groups tolerate each other'.

By the same token, the concept of the autonomy of religious communities means that the state's power to intervene in disputes between religious organizations and their employees, under both Article 9[96] and other Articles,[97] has often been limited; and in cases where religious office holders have been dismissed for alleged breaches of church codes (eg, adultery), the Court has tended to consider such applications under Article 8 rather than Article 9.[98]

Fourthly, in the provision of education to children and young people, the state is under a duty to ensure 'that information or knowledge included in the curriculum is conveyed in an objective, critical and pluralistic manner'[99]—and is forbidden from pursuing 'an aim of indoctrination that might be considered as not respecting parents' religious and philosophical convictions'.[100] The Court has usually considered these matters under Article 2 of Protocol 1,[101] rather than Article 9,[102] although there is some degree of overlap between these two provisions. Thus, for example, in *Hasan and Eylem Zengin v Turkey*,[103] when the Court held that compulsory lessons in religious culture violated Article 2, Protocol 1, it added that a rule which required some parents (ie, those of the Christian and Jewish religion) to reveal their faith in order to exempt their children from such classes, 'may also raise a problem under Article 9'.[104] Moreover, in *Lautsi and Others v Italy*,[105] where the applicants claimed that the display of crucifixes in the classrooms of Italian state schools interfered with their freedom of thought and conscience, the Grand Chamber observed that 'in the area of education and teaching Article 2 of Protocol No.1 is in principle the *lex specialis* in relation to Article 9 of the Convention'.[106] On the facts of the case, the Grand Chamber held that there had been no violation of Article 2, Protocol No 1, because the crucifix on a wall was 'an essentially passive symbol', the display of which fell within the state's margin of appreciation.[107] However, in this regard, it declined to examine Article 9, so it is regrettable that the Court failed to elaborate on the relationship between these two Convention articles which often overlap in the areas of religion and education.

---

[96] See, eg, *Siebenhaar v Germany* hudoc (2011), where the Court held that there had been no violation of Article 9 following the dismissal of an employee of a children's nursery run by a Protestant church, on account of her active membership of another religious group

[97] See, eg, *Fernández Martínez v Spain* hudoc (2012), where there had been no violation of Article 8, following a Bishop's decision not to renew the teaching contract of a married priest who advocated optional celibacy. See also *Sindicatul 'Păstorul cel Bun' v Romania* hudoc (2013), where the Grand Chamber held that there had been no violation of Article 11 following a refusal to grant legal personality to a trade union which had been established by clergy and lay members of the Orthodox Church.

[98] See, eg, *Obst v Germany* hudoc (2010); and *Schüth v Germany* hudoc (2010); 52 EHRR 981.

[99] *Folgerø v Norway* 2007-III; 46 EHRR 1147 para 84 GC.   [100] *Folgerø v Norway*, para 84.

[101] Article 2 of Protocol 1 guarantees that '[n]o person shall be denied the right to education' and provides that 'the State shall respect the right of parents to ensure such education and teaching in conformity with their own religions and philosophical convictions.' See also Ch 22.

[102] In *Folgerø v Norway* 2007-III; 46 EHRR 1147 paras 78, 79 GC, the Court held there had been a violation of Article 2, Protocol 1 (rather than Article 9), following a complaint from humanist parents that they could only exempt their children from certain parts of a religion and philosophy course in a primary school. See also *Konrad v Germany No 35504/03* 2006-XIII DA, where the Court focused on Article 2, Protocol 1 (rather than Article 9) in refusing an application from Christian parents who wanted to educate their children at home. A similar approach was taken in rejecting challenges to mandatory school lessons on ethics and sex education (respectively) in *Appel-Irrgang and Others v Germany No 45216/07* hudoc (2009) DA; and *Dojan and Others v Germany No 319/08* hudoc (2011) DA.   [103] Hudoc (2007); 46 EHRR 1060.

[104] *Hasan and Eylem Zengin v Turkey*, para 73.   [105] Hudoc (2011); 54 EHRR 60 GC.

[106] *Lautsi and Others v Italy*, para 59.   [107] *Lautsi and Others v Italy*, para 72.

II. CONSCIENTIOUS OBJECTION

An issue which frequently generates conflict between the individual and the state is that of conscientious objection to military service. In the past Article 9 was interpreted restrictively in this area,[108] on the basis that Article 9 had to be read in conjunction with Article 4(3)(b) of the Convention.[109] However, today, such an approach has been expressly rejected by the Court. The catalyst for this sea-change was the Grand Chamber's ruling in *Bayatyan v Armenia*,[110] which established that conscientious objection, whilst not expressly guaranteed in Article 9, should be read as coming within the scope of this Article. In articulating its new approach, the Grand Chamber held that opposition to military service 'constitutes a conviction or belief of sufficient cogency, seriousness, cohesion and importance to attract the guarantees of Article 9'.[111] In so ruling the Grand Chamber was influenced primarily by the fact that, as a 'living instrument', the Convention should be interpreted in the light of prevailing conditions and ideas in contemporary Europe.[112] Thus, in view of the fact that the overwhelming majority of the Council of Europe's member states have recognized the right of conscientious objection, and that Armenia had failed to respect certain undertakings it had earlier given about its treatment of conscientious objectors,[113] the applicant's imprisonment for not having undertaken military service was contrary to Article 9.

In the wake of the Grand Chamber's ruling in *Bayatyan*, the Court has found violations of Article 9 in a number of cases. For example, in *Savda v Turkey*,[114] where a conscientious objector refused to serve in the armed forces, the state's failure to recognize alternative service or have in place an effective and accessible procedure wherein questions relating to conscientious objection might be examined, led to a violation of Article 9, on the basis that a proper balance had not been struck between the general interests of society and those of conscientious objectors.[115] Similarly, the system of compulsory military service in Turkey, and the lack of any equivalent civilian alternative to it, led to rulings in *Erçep v Turkey*[116] and *Feti Demirtaş v Turkey*[117] that the state had failed to comply with its Article 9 obligations in relation to the prosecution and imprisonment of Jehovah's Witnesses who had objected to military service. Thus, from having been criticized a decade ago for its 'slow development of the right to conscientious objection',[118] the Court has, in recent years, made important strides in terms of utilizing Article 9 more effectively in this area.[119]

The Court has also examined claims of religious discrimination in relation to conscientious objection.[120] A particularly emotive issue in this regard has been the extent to which the state is justified in differentiating between faith group leaders in regard to the obligation on such office holders to undertake civilian service in lieu of compulsory

---

[108] See, eg, *Grandrath v Germany No 2299/64*, 10 YB 626 at 674 (1966) Com Rep; CM Res (67) DH 1; and *Conscientious Objectors v Denmark No 7565/76*, 9 DR 117 (1978).

[109] Article 4(3)(b) provides that 'any service of a military character or, in the case of conscientious objectors in countries where they are recognised, service extracted instead of compulsory military service', is excluded from the Convention's prohibition of 'forced or compulsory labour'. On Article 4 see Ch 7.

[110] Hudoc (2011); 54 EHRR 467 GC.   [111] *Bayatyan v Armenia*, para 110.

[112] *Bayatyan v Armenia*, para 102.   [113] *Bayatyan v Armenia*, para 127.   [114] Hudoc (2012).

[115] See also *Tarhan v Turkey* hudoc (2012), where the non-recognition of a pacifist's right to conscientious objection led to a violation of Article 9.   [116] Hudoc (2011).

[117] Hudoc (2012).   [118] See Gilbert, EHRLR 554 (2001).

[119] See also *Bukharatyan v Armenia* hudoc (2012) para 36; and *Tsaturyan v Armenia* hudoc (2012), where the imprisonment of Armenian nationals for their refusal to undertake military service violated Article 9.

[120] See, eg, *Thlimmenos v Greece* 2000-IV; 31 EHRR 411 GC.

military service.[121] The Court's approach has been that the state, in according privileges to religious societies, must remain neutral, and that any difference of treatment between faith-group leaders in regard to their military service obligations risks being discriminatory, unless there is an 'objective and reasonable justification' for it.[122]

Today the Court's willingness to utilize Article 9, both alone and in conjunction with Article 14, stands in marked contrast to the Commission's earlier approach, under which applicants refusing to undertake military service had to look to other articles of the Convention for effective redress.[123] Of course, there are limits to the Court's new approach. As the Grand Chamber observed in *Bayatyan*, the extent to which an objection to military service falls within Article 9 'must be assessed in the light of the particular circumstances of the case',[124] while public policy constraints are likely to militate against any significant extension of the right to conscientious objectors in some politically controversial areas, such as the non-payment of certain forms of tax.[125] But, nonetheless, the recent tendency of the Court to refer to Article 9 when examining complaints in the field of conscientious objection is undoubtedly a very significant development.

4. MANIFESTING RELIGION OR BELIEF IN WORSHIP, TEACHING, PRACTICE, AND OBSERVANCE

I. THE NATURE OF MANIFESTATION

The second part of Article 9(1) protects the freedom 'to manifest' one's religion or belief, in public or in private, alone or with others. The manifestations to which Article 9(1) refers are 'worship, teaching, practice and observance',[126] and the term 'practice' in this list 'does not cover each act which is motivated or influenced by a religion or belief'.[127] Accordingly, for the purposes of Article 9, the word 'practice' would not include the

---

[121] See, eg, *Gütl v Austria* hudoc (2009); 52 EHRR 1018; *Löffelmann v Austria* hudoc (2009); 51 EHRR 876; and *Lang v Austria* hudoc (2009); 51 EHRR 700, where the Court found violations of Article 14 taken in conjunction with Article 9 in relation to the imposition of duties on the applicants, who were Jehovah's Witness religious leaders. However, in *Koppi v Austria* hudoc (2009); 52 EHRR 411, the Court rejected the charge of discrimination levelled by the applicant (a preacher who was applying for exemption from civilian service) on the basis that he had not been in an analogous position to that of a member of a recognized religious society.

[122] See *Religionsgemeinschaft der Zeugen Jehovas and Others v Austria* hudoc (2008); 48 EHRR 424 para 92; and *Löffelmann v Austria* hudoc (2009); 51 EHRR 876 para 53.

[123] See, eg, *Ülke v Turkey* hudoc (2006); 48 EHRR 1128 (Article 3); and *Tsirlis and Kouloumpas v Greece* 1997-III; 25 EHRR 198 (Article 5).

[124] *Bayatyan v Armenia* hudoc (2011); 54 EHRR 467 para 110 GC.

[125] For example, it is unlikely that the Court would seek to deviate from the Commission's ruling in *C v UK No 10358/83*, 37 DR 142 at 147 (1983), where it rejected the application of a Quaker who had objected to a proportion of his tax being used for military expenditure, on the basis that the distribution of tax revenue was a political matter which fell beyond the realm of any individual.

[126] The obligation under this part of Article 9(1) includes desisting from interference with acts of worship and from rites associated with worship. See *Chappell v UK No 12587/86*, 53 DR 241 (1987).

[127] *Arrowsmith v UK No 7050/75*, 19 DR 5 at 19 (1978) Com Rep; CM Res DH (79) 4. The Court has subsequently endorsed this formula. See *Metropolitan Church of Bessarabia and Others v Moldova* 2000-XI; 35 EHRR 306 para 117; and *Hasan and Chaush v Bulgaria* 2000-XI; 34 EHRR 1339 para 78 GC.

distribution of leaflets to soldiers advising them against serving in Northern Ireland,[128] nor would it cover the (religiously motivated) objections of pharmacists to selling contraceptive pills in their dispensary.[129]

A problem with this approach, which focuses on the nature of the *manifestation* of a religion or belief rather than its *motivation*, is that it can bring the Court dangerously close to adjudicating on whether a particular practice is formally required by a religion. Thus, for example, when a Jehovah's Witness child refused to attend a parade in her school commemorating an earlier war, the Court held that it was unable to discern anything 'either in the purpose of the parade or in the arrangements for it, which could offend the applicant's pacifist convictions'[130]—a ruling that has been criticized on the ground that the Court 'in effect substituted its judgment for the conscience of the persons involved, defining what was "reasonable" for them to believe'.[131]

Whereas the Commission in the past often questioned the 'necessity' of certain religious practices,[132] the Court has, in recent years, moved away from this approach.[133] Consequently, in determining what constitutes a 'manifestation' of religion or belief, the Court today not merely takes the view that 'the existence of a sufficiently close and direct nexus between the act and the underlying belief must be determined on the facts of each case', but that 'there is no requirement on the applicant to establish that he or she acted in fulfilment of a duty mandated by the religion in question'.[134] As a result, the Court, in *Jakóbski v Poland*, in holding that the state's failure to provide a vegetarian diet for a Buddhist prisoner violated Article 9, discounted the state's argument that vegetarianism was not 'an essential aspect of the practice of the applicant's religion'.[135] Similarly, in *Leyla Şahin v Turkey*,[136] the Court accepted the applicant's contention that she was manifesting her faith by wearing an Islamic headscarf at University, while in *Eweida and Others v UK*,[137] the Court held that an airline employee (Eweida) and a nurse (Chaplin), who both insisted on wearing a cross visibly at work, were manifesting their religious beliefs under Article 9(1).

The Court's rejection of the Commission's rigid 'necessity' approach is a positive development in at least three respects. First, it demonstrates an increasing willingness to take manifestations of 'worship, teaching, practice and observance' seriously under Article 9. Secondly, it frees the Court from having to examine the 'necessity' of a particular manifestation under Article 9—a task which, given the relevance of (often nebulous) doctrinal

---

[128] *Arrowsmith v UK*. On the facts the Commission held that this did not constitute the 'practice' of pacifist belief, in contrast to 'public declarations proclaiming generally the idea of pacifism and urging the acceptance of a commitment to non-violence…' that would fall within Article 9(1). See also *X and Church of Scientology v Sweden No 7805/77*, 16 DR 68 at 72 (1979), where a line was drawn between religious and commercial advertisements.

[129] *Pichon and Sajous v France No 49853/99* 2001-X DA. The Court's decision that there was no violation of Article 9(1) obviated it of the need to consider related matters such as 'health' and the 'rights and freedoms of others' under Article 9(2).

[130] *Valsamis v Greece* 1996-VI; 24 EHRR 294 para 32. See also *Efstratiou v Greece* 1996-VI; 24 EHRR 298.

[131] Martínez-Torrón and Navarro-Valls, 'Protection of Religious Freedom in the System of the Council of Europe', in Lindholm, Durham and Tahzib-Lie, eds, *Facilitating Freedom of Religion or Belief: A Deskbook*, 2004, p 234.

[132] Eg, in *X v Austria No 1753/63*, 8 YB ECHR 174 (1965), the Commission denied a prisoner access to a prayer chain on the ground that it was not 'an indispensable element in the proper exercise of the Buddhist religion'.

[133] See *Metropolitan Church of Bessarabia and Others v Moldova* 2001-XII; 35 EHRR 306 paras 96–8; and *Bayatyan v Armenia* hudoc (2011); 54 EHRR 467 para 111 GC.

[134] *Eweida and Others v UK* hudoc (2013) para 82.

[135] *Jakóbski v Poland* hudoc (2010); 55 EHRR 231 para 39.

[136] 2005-XI; 44 EHRR 99 para 78 GC.   [137] Hudoc (2013) paras 89 and 97.

or theological issues, its judges appear ill-equipped to handle. And thirdly, it is consistent with the Court's well-established principle that it is not for the state to determine how one manifests their religion or belief.[138]

II. THE PUBLIC MANIFESTATION OF RELIGION OR BELIEF

People often wish to exercise, share, or display their faith at the workplace so, perhaps unsurprisingly, this is an area that is frequently synonymous with controversy. But it is also an area in which the Court, in relation to manifestations of religion and belief, has recently displayed a fresh willingness to deviate from previous Convention jurisprudence.

In the past, the traditional approach of the Strasbourg organs was that there would be no interference with Article 9(1) if an employee could resign from their job and (by implication) find gainful new employment. Thus, for example, in *Stedman v UK*,[139] where a Christian working in a travel agency refused to work on Sundays, the Commission justified its rejection of her complaint on the basis that she 'was free to resign and did in effect resign from her employment'. Similarly, in *Ahmad v UK*,[140] the Commission rejected a Muslim teacher's request for an extended Friday lunch-break so that he could attend a Mosque for prayers, because the applicant 'remained free to resign if and when he found that his teaching obligations conflicted with his religious duties'. Moreover, this 'free to leave' test was used by the Commission in other fields of employment, including religious vocation,[141] and service in the armed forces.[142]

The Commission may once have referred to this test as 'the ultimate guarantee of…freedom of religion',[143] but reference to it has, however, waned in recent years. For example, in *Ivanova v Bulgaria*,[144] where Article 9 was violated following the applicant's dismissal from working at a school, due to her membership of an evangelical Christian group, the Court never considered the option of her moving to a less hostile working environment; nor was any such possibility explored in *Thlimmenos v Greece*,[145] where the Court held that a ban on a Jehovah's Witness working as a chartered accountant, because of an earlier criminal conviction for refusing to wear a military uniform, breached Article 14 (non-discrimination) taken in conjunction with Article 9. Indeed, most recently, in *Eweida and Others v UK*, the Court expressed the view that:

> Given 'the importance in a democratic society of freedom of religion', the Court considers that, where an individual complains of a restriction on freedom of religion in the workplace, rather than holding that the possibility of changing job would negate any interference with the right, the better approach would be to weigh that possibility in the overall balance when considering whether or not the restriction was proportionate.[146]

---

[138] See *Metropolitan Church of Bessarabia and Others v Moldova* 2001-XII; 35 EHRR 306 paras 97–8.

[139] No 29107/95, 23 EHRR CD 168 at 169 (1997).

[140] No 8160/78, 22 DR 27 (1981); 4 EHRR 126 at 135.

[141] See, eg, *Knudsen v Norway* No 11045/84, 42 DR 247 (1985), where it was held that a minister of religion had no claim against his religious organization under Article 9(1) in a dispute over doctrine, because in such circumstances he remained free to resign and leave the church.

[142] See, eg, *Kalaç v Turkey* 1997-IV; 27 EHRR 552 para 28, where, in relation to a senior air force officer who had been dismissed on account of his close ties with a controversial Muslim group, the Court held that Article 9(1) had not been breached on the basis of the contractual nature of his employment and his free choice to forgo certain rights by embarking on a career in the armed services. See also *Başpinar v Turkey* No 45631/99, 36 EHRR CD 1 (2003).   [143] *Konttinen v Finland* No 24949/94, 87A DR 68 at 75 (1996).

[144] Hudoc (2007); 47 EHRR 1173.   [145] 2000-IV; 31 EHRR 411 GC.

[146] *Eweida and Others v UK* hudoc (2013) para 83.

The Court's express repudiation of the 'free to resign' approach evidently applies to the field of employment, but it remains to be seen how far it extends to other areas. After all, the Court in *Eweida* conspicuously failed to disassociate itself from one of its previous rulings—*Cha'are Shalom Ve Tsedek v France*[147]—where a decision to refuse an Orthodox Jewish association a licence to carry out its form of ritual slaughter was not in breach of Article 9(1), because its members could obtain specially certified ('glatt') meat from other sources.[148] That said, whilst the Court has been criticized in the past for its reluctance to acknowledge 'the complete range of manifestations of religion or belief',[149] its ruling in *Eweida* displays a willingness to take a bolder and more imaginative approach towards the manifestation of religion and belief under Article 9.

There are certainly a number of reasons why the Court's recent rejection in *Eweida* of the 'free to resign' formula is a positive development. First, it ensures that there is consistency between Article 9 and other articles of the Convention (eg, Articles 8, 10, and 11[150]), where such a test has never been employed. Secondly, it is an acknowledgment of the fact that, with high rates of unemployment throughout Europe, the 'option' of choosing to resign to find fresh employment is an unrealistic one for many applicants. And thirdly, the Court's approach in *Eweida* may lead to the provision of more detailed guidance on the lawful parameters of manifestations of religion or belief, since it facilitates a shift from the narrow remit of Article 9(1), to the balancing of the competing factors that fall within Article 9(2)—the key elements of which are now examined in the paragraphs that follow.

5. JUSTIFIABLE INTERFERENCES

It is worth reiterating, as noted earlier, that the *forum internum* is inviolable, although the state can nonetheless interfere under Article 9(2) with the exercise of an Article 9(1) freedom. Under Article 9(2) a restriction on the manifestation of one's religion or belief may thus be justified if it is 'prescribed by law', has a legitimate aim, and is 'necessary in a democratic society'. These criteria, which resemble those in the second paragraphs of Articles 8, 10, and 11, will now be considered in more detail.

I. PRESCRIBED BY LAW

Under Article 9(2), a legitimate interference must be 'prescribed by law'. This has been taken to mean that such a law must be 'adequately accessible' and 'formulated with sufficient precision to enable the citizen to regulate his conduct'.[151] In the past the Court tended to avoid any serious discussion of this issue in the context of Article 9. As a consequence,

---

[147] 2000-VII para 81 GC.

[148] The rationale for the Court's decision in *Cha'are Shalom Ve Tsedek v France* was that 'the religious practice and observance at issue...was the consumption of meat only from animals that had been ritually slaughtered and certified to comply with religious dietary laws, rather than any personal involvement in the ritual slaughter and certification process itself': *Eweida and Others v UK* hudoc (2013) para 83.

[149] Taylor, *Freedom of Religion: UN and European Human Rights Law and Practice*, 2005, p 234.

[150] See, eg, *Smith and Grady v UK* 1999-VI; 29 EHRR 493 para 71 (Article 8); *Vogt v Germany* A 323 (1995); 21 EHRR 205 para 44 GC (Article 10); and *Young, James and Webster v UK* A 44 (1981); 4 EHRR 38 paras 54–5 (Article 11).

[151] *Sunday Times v UK* A 30 (1979); 2 EHRR 245 para 49 PC.

in both *Kokkinakis*[152] and *Larissis*,[153] the Court failed to examine critically the compatibility of a national law outlawing proselytism with the Convention. However, in *Hasan and Chaush v Bulgaria*,[154] the Court held for the first time that the 'prescribed by law' requirement in Article 9(2) had not been satisfied, following the decision of a government agency to replace the Chief Mufti and other senior Muslim clerics with the state's own preferred religious leaders. The Court reasoned that:

> the interference with the internal organisation of the Muslim community and the applicants' freedom of religion was not 'prescribed by law' in that it was arbitrary and was based on legal provisions which allowed an unfettered discretion to the executive and did not meet the required standards of clarity and foreseeability.[155]

This decision has paved the way for a number of decisions in recent years where the failure of states to comply with the 'prescribed by law' criterion has led to violations of Article 9. These include: a government's refusal to obey a court order and register a church as an official religious denomination;[156] the lack of any legal basis for refusing a prisoner awaiting execution access to a priest;[157] the absence of a law that would allow prison detainees to participate in religious ceremonies;[158] the use of an insufficiently precise law to tax gifts received by a religious association;[159] the actions of state officials in unlawfully disrupting meetings of religious groups;[160] and the use of a residence permit to prevent a non-national preacher from performing his religious activities.[161] As these cases indicate, the Court is increasingly willing to scrutinize the actions of state parties, so as to ensure that restrictions on the manifestation of religion or belief are 'prescribed by law'.[162]

II. LEGITIMATE AIM

Under Article 9(2), the state may interfere with the manifestation of religion or belief in 'the interests of public safety, for the protection of public order, health or morals, or for the protection of the rights and freedoms of others'. However, Article 9(2), unlike Articles 8(2), 10(2), and 11(2), does not sanction restrictions on the ground of national security—the rationale for this deliberate omission being that it 'reflects the primordial importance of religious pluralism ... and the fact that a State cannot dictate what a person believes or take coercive steps to make him change his beliefs'.[163]

---

[152] *Kokkinakis v Greece* A 260-A (1993); 17 EHRR 397 paras 40, 41.

[153] *Larissis v Greece* 1998-I; 27 EHRR 329 para 42.   [154] 2000-XI; 34 EHRR 1339 GC.

[155] *Hasan and Chaush v Bulgaria*, para 86.

[156] *Biserica Adevărat Ortodoxă din Moldova v Moldova* hudoc (2007); 48 EHRR 497 para 36. See also *Fusu Arcadie and Others v Moldova* hudoc (2012) para 38.

[157] *Poltoratskiy v Ukraine* 2003-V; 39 EHRR 916 para 170.

[158] *Igors Dmitrijevs v Latvia* hudoc (2006).

[159] *Association Les Témoins de Jéhovah v France* hudoc (2011). See also *Eglise Evangélique Missionnaire et Salaûn v France* hudoc (2013); and *Association des Chevaliers du Lotus d'Or v France* hudoc (2013), where the Court held that the requirement of the applicants to pay tax on certain gifts had violated Article 9.

[160] See, eg, *Kuznetsov v Russia* hudoc (2007); 49 EHRR 355, where agents of the state disrupted a meeting of Jehovah's Witnesses; and *Boychev and Others v Bulgaria* hudoc (2011), where the police unlawfully interrupted a religious meeting attended by members of the Unification Church.

[161] *Perry v Latvia* hudoc (2007) para 62.

[162] See, eg, *Svyato-Mykhaylivska Parafiya v Ukraine* hudoc (2007) para 139.

[163] *Nolan and K v Russia* hudoc (2009); 53 EHRR 977 para 73.

The Court has held that the state may be justified in imposing curbs on the manifestation of a religious belief on a range of different grounds.[164] More specifically, the need to maintain public order has been held to justify restrictions on access to a Druid summer solstice festival at Stonehenge,[165] a public protest against alcohol and pornography,[166] and the removal from a prisoner of a religious book containing a chapter on martial arts.[167] In addition, curbs may be imposed on the manifestation of religion or belief in order to protect public health[168] or public safety.[169] Thus, for example, a Christian nurse could be required to remove her cross for the protection of health and safety in a hospital ward,[170] a high caste Sikh prisoner made to clean the floor of his prison cell,[171] and a Sikh motor-cyclist obliged to wear a crash-helmet (rather than a turban) in order to protect public safety.[172] However, where a British Airways employee had been prevented from wearing a Christian cross around her neck at work because of the employer's wish to project a certain corporate image, the aim, whilst 'undoubtedly legitimate', had been afforded 'too much weight' by the national courts, on account of the need to take into account the applicant's desire to manifest her religious belief.[173]

The most nebulous of the Article 9(2) criteria are those whereby limits may be imposed on the manifestation of religion or belief for 'the protection of the rights and freedoms of others'. This is evidenced by two (of the four) applications considered by the Court in *Eweida and Others v UK*,[174] concerning allegations of religious discrimination made following the dismissals of a Council Registrar who objected to officiating at civil partnership ceremonies (Ladele), and a Relate Counsellor who objected to offering psycho-sexual counselling to same-sex couples (McFarlane), with both objecting on the basis that, as Christians, they disapproved of homosexual relationships. The Court, however, in rejecting these applications, held that the state had a wide margin of appreciation in striking a balance between the applicants' right to manifest their beliefs and the duty on employers to protect the rights of others;[175] and that, on the facts of the case, the right balance had been struck, on account of the employers' policies to promote equal opportunities, and the ban on employees from acting in a way that might discriminate against others.[176] Furthermore, other examples of measures that have been regarded as being necessary to protect 'the rights and freedoms of others' include controls on planning,[177] curbs

---

[164] *Dogru v France* hudoc (2008); 49 EHRR 179 para 64.

[165] *Chappell v UK No 12587/86*, 53 DR 241 (1987).

[166] *A v Sweden No 9820/82*, 5 EHRR CD 297 (1983).   [167] *X v UK No 6886/75*, 5 DR 100 (1976).

[168] See *Cha'are Shalom Ve Tsedek v France* 2000-VII para 84 GC.

[169] See *Metropolitan Church of Bessarabia and Others v Moldova* 2001-XII; 35 EHRR 306 para 113. See also *Leela Förderkreis eV and Others v Germany*, Hudoc (2008); 49 EHRR 117, where a government campaign aimed at drawing the public's attention to the potential dangers of 'sects', 'youth sects', 'youth religions', and 'psycho sects' was held to be a legitimate course of action for a democratic state to take for the protection of public safety and public order, as well as for the protection of the rights of others.

[170] For example, the application of Shirley Chaplin, considered by the Court with three other applications in *Eweida and Others v UK* hudoc (2013) para 99.

[171] *X v UK No 8231/78*, 28 DR 5 at 38 (1982).

[172] *X v UK No 7992/77*, 14 DR 234 (1978). The Commission so held even though, by the time of its ruling, national legislation had granted Sikh motor-cyclists the right to wear turbans rather than helmets.

[173] *Eweida and Others v UK* hudoc (2013) para 94, where the Court held that there had been a violation of Article 9 in relation to Eweida (a British Airways employee), on account of the state's failure to protect, sufficiently, her right to manifest her religion.   [174] Hudoc (2013).

[175] *Eweida and Others v UK*, para 105.   [176] *Eweida and Others v UK*, paras 106 and 109.

[177] *Vergos v Greece* hudoc (2004); 41 EHRR 913; *Johannische Kirche and Peters v Germany No 41754/98* 2001-VIII DA; and *ISKCON v UK No 20490/92*, 18 EHRR CD 133 (1994).

on religious dress,[178] compulsory motor insurance,[179] restrictions on religious rituals in prison,[180] and a refusal to adjourn a court hearing because of a lawyer's religious holiday.[181]

III. NECESSARY IN A DEMOCRATIC SOCIETY

The proportionality of a restriction on religion or belief and the extent to which it is 'necessary in a democratic society' is an issue that has often provoked controversy. Curbs on the manifestation of religion or belief must clearly be proportionate to their intended aim,[182] but states continue to enjoy a wide margin of appreciation in a number of areas.[183] Two of these will now be considered in more detail: the regulation of religious dress and the right to proselytize.

a. Religious dress

States have long been afforded considerable discretion in the often controversial area of religious dress.[184] For example, in *Dahlab v Switzerland*,[185] where the Court rejected a complaint from a female teacher in Switzerland who had failed to overturn a ban on wearing the Islamic veil in a primary school, the Court held that the state's actions were justified (under Article 9(2)) because they sought to guarantee religious neutrality in the classroom of a multi-faith society.

The issue of religious dress has also been examined by the Court in the context of state-sanctioned curbs on Islamic headscarves in Turkey. In *Leyla Şahin v Turkey*,[186] the applicant (Şahin), who considered it her religious duty to wear the Islamic headscarf, complained that a rule prohibiting students at Istanbul University from wearing such headscarves in class or during exams was contrary to Article 9. However, the Turkish government maintained that secularism was a key element in Turkey remaining a liberal democracy, and that because the Islamic headscarf was associated with extreme 'religious fundamentalist movements', its display posed a threat to Turkish secular values.[187] The government's argument was accepted by the Grand Chamber of the Court, which held (by sixteen votes to one) that the headscarf ban could be justified under Article 9(2).[188] In attaching considerable significance to the impact that the headscarf might have on those choosing not to wear it, the Court ruled that the relevant dress restrictions were proportionate to the legitimate aim of upholding public order and of protecting the 'rights and freedoms of others'.[189] Furthermore, in reaching the conclusion that the curbs on the headscarf were 'necessary in a democratic society', the Court accorded the state a wide margin of appreciation,[190] and focused on the need to protect two important principles: secularism and equality.

[178] *Dahlab v Switzerland* No 42393/98 2001-V DA.
[179] *X v Netherlands* No 2988/66, 10 YB 472 (1967).
[180] *Gatis Kovaļkovs v Latvia* No 35021/05 hudoc (2012) DA.
[181] *Francesco Sessa v Italy* hudoc (2012).
[182] *Manoussakis v Greece* 1996-IV; 23 EHRR 387 para 44.
[183] See *Cha'are Shalom Ve Tsedek v France* 2000-VII para 84 GC.
[184] See *Karaduman v Turkey* No 16278/90, 74 DR 93 (1993); and *Bulut v Turkey* No 18783/91 hudoc (1993) DA.
[185] No 42393/98 2001-V DA.   [186] 2005-XI; 44 EHRR 99 GC.
[187] *Leyla Şahin v Turkey*, paras 90–3.
[188] The Grand Chamber adopted a similar approach, and reached the same conclusion, as the Chamber: hudoc (2004); 41 EHRR 109.
[189] *Leyla Şahin v Turkey* 2005-XI; 44 EHRR 99 para 115 GC.
[190] This was because of the 'diversity of approaches' in Europe on the issue of religious dress: *Leyla Şahin v Turkey*, para 109.

With regard to secularism, the Court noted that this principle was not merely 'consistent with the values underpinning the Convention',[191] but was also 'the paramount consideration' for the headscarf ban.[192] Moreover, given the presence of 'extremist political movements' that wished to impose their values on Turkish society,[193] the Court found it 'understandable' that the state should 'wish to preserve the secular nature' of the university and thereby impose restrictions on the Islamic headscarf.[194]

In respect of equality, the Court was concerned about a link between the Islamic headscarf and women's rights. It cited (with apparent approval) a passage in *Dahlab*, which referred to the Islamic headscarf as a 'powerful external symbol' that 'appeared to be imposed on women by a religious precept that was hard to reconcile with the principle of gender equality' and which 'could not easily be reconciled with the message of tolerance, respect for others and, above all, equality and non-discrimination'.[195] But the Court's choice of words in this context was harshly criticized by Judge Tulkens (the sole dissenting judge), who suggested that it was 'not the Court's role to make an appraisal of this kind'[196] and, in questioning the majority's approach to gender equality and curbs on the Islamic headscarf, accused her fellow judges of '[p]aternalism'.[197]

Many of Judge Tulkens's criticisms of *Şahin* have been echoed by academics,[198] and the Court's (majority) decision has been attacked on a number of grounds, which include:

> Inadequate application of the margin of appreciation doctrine; narrow interpretation of the freedom of religion; imposition of 'fundamental secularism'; adverse implications of Muslim women's right to education; and promotion of the image of Islam as a threat to democracy.[199]

In spite of such criticism, the Court has subsequently used *Şahin* as the basis for upholding headscarf bans in Turkey on pupils attending public schools,[200] and on a University Professor prohibited from wearing the headscarf in the exercise of her functions.[201] However, in *Ahmet Arslan and Others v Turkey*,[202] where the conviction of members of a Muslim group for wearing distinctive religious dress in public violated Article 9, the Court distinguished it from *Şahin* on the basis that, unlike *Şahin*, the attire in *Arslan* was worn in a public street rather than in an official building, and that there was no risk of proselytism or any threat to public order.[203]

As with Turkey, France is a nation with a strong secular tradition, and the Court has taken account of these secular ties in affording France considerable discretion in the regulation of forms of religious dress. Thus, for example, a French public school's policy of not permitting a Muslim schoolgirl to wear an Islamic headscarf during physical education lessons was held to be necessary on health or safety grounds under Article 9,[204] while a Muslim woman, who had requested a visa to enter France to join her (French) husband, could, under Article 9(2), be required to lift her veil for an identity check, on

---

[191] *Leyla Şahin v Turkey*, para 114.   [192] *Leyla Şahin v Turkey*, para 116.
[193] *Leyla Şahin v Turkey*, para 115.   [194] *Leyla Şahin v Turkey*, para 116.
[195] *Leyla Şahin v Turkey*, para 111.
[196] *Leyla Şahin v Turkey*, dissenting opinion of Judge Tulkens, para 12.
[197] *Leyla Şahin v Turkey*.
[198] See, eg, Lewis, 56 ICLQ 395 (2007); and C Evans, 7 Melbourne JIL 52 (2006).
[199] Vakulenko, 16(2) S and LS 190 (2007).
[200] *Köse and Others v Turkey No 26625/02* 2006-II DA.
[201] *Kurtulmuş v Turkey No 65500/01* 2006-II DA.   [202] Hudoc (2010).
[203] *Ahmet Arslan and Others v Turkey*, paras 49 and 50.
[204] *Dogru v France* hudoc (2008); 49 EHRR 179; and *Kervanci v France* hudoc (2008).

the basis of a need to protect public safety and/or public order.[205] Similarly, male Sikhs have also been required to remove their turbans in order to comply with identification requirements for the renewal of a driving licence,[206] as well as to pass through airport security controls.[207] Indeed, more controversially, a challenge by Muslim and Sikh students to a French law and ministerial circular which banned pupils from wearing attire or symbols that visibly manifested a religious belief in school was rejected on the basis that it was intended solely to protect the constitutional principle of secularism and that, accordingly, the state had acted lawfully and within its margin of appreciation under Article 9.[208]

The former President of the Court, Sir Nicolas Bratza, has acknowledged that the Court pays 'close practice to the particular requirements of the society in question when examining complaints that a law or practice in that society violates the Convention',[209] and his comment seems particularly apposite given the Court's approach to the issue of religious dress. With some having argued that the 'structural concept of the margin of appreciation should be completely abandoned',[210] it is perhaps unsurprising that the Court's heavy reliance on this principle has been so controversial. But equally, given the close association of religious dress with the secular principles that are integral to the history and culture of many European states, and the fact that the structure of the 'European Convention system…is dependent upon the willful cooperation of Member States',[211] the Court's reliance on the margin of appreciation in the field of religious dress is perhaps not entirely surprising.

b. Proselytism

Another area synonymous with controversy, which raises issues under Article 9(2), is that of proselytism. In *Kokkinakis v Greece*,[212] the Court held that the application of a Greek law criminalizing the proselytizing activities of a Jehovah's Witness was not proportionate to the aim of protecting the rights of others. Even though the Greek anti-proselytism law was regarded as pursuing a legitimate aim ('the protection of the rights and freedoms of others'), it was held not to be 'necessary in a democratic society'. With this in mind, the Court contrasted 'true evangelism' and 'improper proselytism'.[213] Whilst the former was 'an essential mission and the responsibility of every Christian and every Church', 'improper proselytism' was 'a corruption or deformation of it', and could 'take the form of activities offering material or social advantage with a view to gaining new members for a Church or exerting improper pressure on people in distress or in need', possibly also entailing 'the use of violence or brainwashing'.[214] On the facts, the Court held that although the applicant had been persistent, he had done no more than try to persuade another person of the virtues of his faith and thus his criminal conviction could not be justified by a 'pressing social need'.

---

[205] *El Morsli v France No 15585/06* hudoc (2008) DA.
[206] *Mann Singh v France No 24479/07* hudoc (2008) DA.
[207] *Phull v France No 35753/03* 2005-I DA.
[208] *Aktas v France No 43563/08* hudoc (2009) DA; *Bayrak v France No 14308/08* hudoc (2009) DA; *Gamaleddyn v France No 18527/08* hudoc (2009) DA; *Ghazal v France No 29134/08* hudoc (2009) DA; *Jasvir Singh v France No 25463/08* hudoc (2009) DA; and *Ranjit Singh v France No 27561/08* hudoc (2009) DA.
[209] Bratza, EHRLR 505 (2011).
[210] Letsas, 26(4) OJLS 705 at 732 (2006). For a different view, in defence of the margin of appreciation, see Legg, *The Margin of Appreciation in International Human Rights Law: Deference and Proportionality*, 2012.
[211] Bakircioglu, 8 GLJ 711 at 712 (2007).   [212] A 260-A (1993); 17 EHRR 397.
[213] *Kokkinakis v Greece*, para 48.   [214] *Kokkinakis v Greece*.

The *Kokkinakis* case has attracted much criticism,[215] but the Court relied on it a short time later in *Larissis v Greece*.[216] In *Larissis* the issue was whether measures taken against three Pentecostal air force officers for seeking to win converts to their faith had been disproportionate. The Court distinguished between their attempts to proselytize other service personnel and those that related to civilians. With regard to service personnel, there was no violation of Article 9 because, in view of the 'particular characteristics of military life', it was necessary for the state to protect junior airmen from being put under 'improper pressure' by the more senior applicants.[217] However, in respect of the curbs on proselytizing civilians, Article 9(2) had been contravened because the civilians whom the applicants wished to convert 'were not subject to pressures and constraints of the same kind as the airmen'.[218]

It is significant that in *Larissis*, as in *Kokkinakis*, the Court's focus was narrow, in that it limited its analysis primarily to the facts of these two cases. A similarly narrow approach was evident more recently in *Jehovah's Witnesses of Moscow v Russia*,[219] where the Court, in finding a violation of Article 9 following the dissolution of a community of Jehovah's Witnesses on the basis of claims that they had (inter alia) used 'psychological pressure [and] "mind control" techniques' to win converts, held that there had been 'no evidence of improper methods of proselytising by members of the applicant community'.[220] In so doing, the Court noted that the 'doctrinal standards of behaviour' for Jehovah's Witnesses were similar to those of other religions,[221] and that although a person's 'arguments based on religious beliefs may be extremely persuasive and compelling, the right "to try and convince one's neighbour" is an essential element of religious freedom'.[222]

Whilst the Court referred briefly to the *Kokkinakis* test (mentioned earlier) of 'improper proselytism', and made a passing remark about there being 'no generally accepted and scientific definition of what constitutes "mind control"',[223] it focused primarily on the facts of the case in holding that the applicants in *Jehovah's Witnesses of Moscow* had not used improper pressure in sharing their faith with others. Thus, a regrettable characteristic of the Court's case law to date under Article 9 has been its general reluctance to offer detailed guidance on the limits of acceptable proselytism.[224]

6. CONCLUSION

Article 9 may have been criticized in the past for being of only 'limited importance',[225] but today such a characterization is no longer accurate. With matters pertaining to religion

---

[215] See Gunn, in Van der Vyver and Witte, eds, *Religious Human Rights in Global Perspective: Legal Perspectives*, 1996, p 329.   [216] 1998-I; 27 EHRR 329.

[217] *Larissis v Greece*, para 54.   [218] *Larissis v Greece*, para 59.

[219] Hudoc (2010); 53 EHRR 141.   [220] *Jehovah's Witnesses of Moscow v Russia*, para 122.

[221] *Jehovah's Witnesses of Moscow v Russia*, para 118.

[222] *Jehovah's Witnesses of Moscow v Russia*, para 139.

[223] *Jehovah's Witnesses of Moscow v Russia*, para 129.

[224] See also *Barankevich v Russia* hudoc (2007); 47 EHRR 266 para 34, where the Court, in rejecting the government's argument that it has been necessary to ban a religious meeting in a park to prevent the applicant (the pastor of an evangelical Christian Church) from allegedly trying to convert members of the public, merely mentioned that there had been no evidence of 'unlawful means of conversion' in this case. Similarly, in *Ahmet Arslan and Others v Turkey* hudoc (2010) para 51, the Court simply rejected, on the facts, the government's claims that members of a Muslim group, through their distinctive forms of dress, had attempted to put undue pressure on other members of the public.

[225] Skakkebaek, *Article 9 of the European Convention on Human Rights*, 1992, p 17.

and belief of increasing significance in European public life, the last two decades have witnessed the development of an influential and significant body of case law on Article 9. That said, in some areas the Court has seemingly been loath to make reference to Article 9. Thus, for example, on a range of issues, including the regulation of religious broadcasting,[226] the legal personality of churches,[227] conscientious objection to trade-union membership,[228] the legality of blasphemy laws,[229] and inter-faith child custody disputes,[230]the Strasbourg judges have chosen not to utilize Article 9, preferring instead to adjudicate on the basis of other Convention provisions. It is of course perfectly understandable that the Court, already burdened with a heavy case load, may quite simply wish to resolve the case before it as quickly as possible—and that this may be best achieved by avoiding having to examine an article that is as (frequently) controversial as Article 9. But, equally, such an approach is regrettable, for it may mean leaving some key issues unresolved, as well as potentially limiting the opportunities for Article 9 being interpreted in such a way as to realize its full potential.

Any criticism of the Court should perhaps be tempered by an acknowledgment of the fact that it continues to face a number of taxing challenges in relation to Article 9. To begin with, the Court has the invidious task of ensuring that the Convention affords proper respect to a variety of faiths and beliefs in a continent that is (simultaneously) increasingly secular yet ever more religiously diverse. In addition, there are the challenges presented by the accommodation of certain religious practices (eg dress codes, dietary rules, prayer times) which, until recent decades, were largely alien to Europe. And finally, there is the perennial problem of ensuring that the Convention sets appropriate standards for states which grant privileges to one particular church (eg the United Kingdom), as well as others that accord constitutional protection to secularism (eg France and Turkey).

Scholars differ as to the record of the Court in the area of religion and belief. For some 'Convention jurisprudence on freedom of religion has finally come of age',[231] whereas for others the Court has been 'overly deferential' to states, particularly in the area of religious dress.[232] However, what is clear is that, with disputes about religion and belief ever more commonplace in contemporary Europe, the case load of the Court under Article 9 seems set to increase.

---

[226] See *Murphy v Ireland* Hudoc (2003); 38 EHRR 212; and *Glas Nadezhda Eood and Elenkov v Bulgaria* Hudoc (2007); 48 EHRR 817 para 59.

[227] See *Canea Catholic Church v Greece* 1997-VIII; 27 EHRR 521.

[228] See *Young, James and Webster v UK* A 44 (1981); 4 EHRR 38 para 66.

[229] See *İA v Turkey* 2005-VIII; 45 EHRR 703; *Wingrove v UK*, 1996-V; 24 EHRR 1; and *Otto-Preminger-Institut v Austria*, A 295-A (1994); 19 EHRR 34.

[230] See *Hoffmann v Austria*, A 255-C (1993); 17 EHRR 293; *Palau-Martinez v France* 2003-XII; 41 EHRR 136; and *Deschomets v France*, No 31956/02 hudoc (2006) DA.

[231] Leigh and Ahdar, 75(6) MLR 1064 at 1064 (2012).

[232] Radačić, 7 Religion and Human Rights 133 at 149 (2012).

14

ARTICLE 10: FREEDOM OF EXPRESSION

> **Article 10**
>
> 1. Everyone has the right to freedom of expression. This right shall include freedom to hold opinions and to receive and impart information and ideas without interference by public authority and regardless of frontiers. This Article shall not prevent states from requiring the licensing of broadcasting, television or cinema enterprises.
> 2. The exercise of these freedoms, since it carries with it duties and responsibilities, may be subject to such formalities, conditions, restrictions or penalties as are prescribed by law and are necessary in a democratic society, in the interests of national security, territorial integrity or public safety, for the prevention of disorder or crime, for the protection of health or morals, for the protection of the reputation or rights of others, for preventing the disclosure of information received in confidence, or for maintaining the authority and impartiality of the judiciary.

1. INTRODUCTION

Article 10 guarantees freedom of expression,[1] one of the cardinal rights guaranteed under the Convention. The historical significance of this right is self-evident, as it has been dearly won after centuries of struggles. After the devastating turmoil of the two World Wars and the Holocaust, the drafters of the Convention reaffirmed it as one of the foundational values of the Council of Europe. The marked importance attached to this right is readily explicable by its close linkage to democracy's political process and its role as an indispensable vehicle for minorities, political opponents, and civil society to foster public debates. Such a constitutional underpinning of freedom of expression lends succour to the consistent assertion of the Court that interference with this right can be justified only by 'imperative necessities', and that exceptions to this right must be interpreted narrowly.[2] The 'constitutional' importance of freedom of expression is elaborated

---

[1] For analysis, see Macovei, *Freedom of Expression—A guide to the implementation of Article 10 of the European Convention on Human Rights, Human Rights Handbook* No 2, 2nd edn, 2004; Flauss, 84 Indiana Law Journal 809 (2009); and Casadevall, Bratza, Myjer, O'Boyle, and Austin (eds), *Freedom of Expression— Essays in Honour of Nicolas Bratza, President of the European Court of Human Rights*, 2012 (an extensive and comprehensive survey of the doctrines and case law on issues such as offensive speech, whistle-blowers, expression versus private life).

[2] *Vereinigung Demokratischer Soldaten Österreichs and Gubi v Austria* A 302 (1994); 20 EHRR 56 para 37. See also *Informationsverein Lentia v Austria* A 276 (1993); 17 EHRR 93 para 35.

in a steady stream of cases. The Court has explained its approach to the interpretation of Article 10 as follows:

> The Court's supervisory functions oblige it to pay the utmost attention to the principles characterising a 'democratic society'. Freedom of expression constitutes one of the essential foundations of such a society, one of the basic conditions for its progress and for the development of every man. Subject to paragraph 2 of Article 10, it is applicable not only to information or ideas that are favourably received or regarded as inoffensive or as a matter of indifference, but also to those that offend, shock or disturb the state or any sector of the population. Such are the demands of that pluralism, tolerance and broadmindedness without which there is no 'democratic society'. This means, amongst other things, that every 'formality', 'condition', 'restriction' or 'penalty' imposed in this sphere must be proportionate to the legitimate aim pursued.[3]

This approach has led to the development of a host of interpretive devices in the case law. As in the jurisprudence of Articles 8, 9, and 11, the Court initially examines whether there is an interference with freedom of expression under the first paragraph of Article 10, and, if so, whether such an interference can be justified under the second paragraph on the basis of the tripartite standards: (i) whether an impugned measure is 'prescribed by law'; (ii) whether it pursues a legitimate aim(s); and (iii) whether it is 'necessary in a democratic society'.

The first standard, 'prescribed by law' requires the state authorities to identify the basis in national law for restricting a person's right under Article 10. The second requirement of legitimate aim has rarely generated substantive discussion in the case law. Overall, the Court's analysis focuses on the third standard, which is the most demanding litmus test. The Court has taken the phrase 'necessary in a democratic society' as supposing a 'pressing social need', namely, a proportionate balance between a means chosen to satisfy a legitimate end and the degree of injury inflicted on expression rights. The Court engages itself in closely ascertaining whether the national authorities have adduced both 'relevant and sufficient reasons' to justify its measures of interference. While the subtest of relevance, which requires a measure to be suitable for attaining a legitimate goal, has hardly caused serious obstacles to respondent states,[4] the subtest of sufficiency of justificatory grounds has attracted the Court's rigorous assessment. For that purpose, the Court does not refrain from undertaking meticulous evaluations of specific factual circumstances of the case.

The inquiries in this chapter start with delineating the boundaries of protection of Article 10. The focus will then turn to different categories of expression, specific issues relating to the press and media licensing, the standard 'prescribed by law', legitimate aims, the notion of 'duties and responsibilities' of the bearers of expression rights, and some distinct methodologies advanced by the Court to deal with defamation cases.

2. THE SCOPE OF PROTECTION

I. GENERAL OVERVIEW

According to the consistent case law of the Strasbourg Court, the scope of expression rights must be broadly interpreted so as to encompass not only the substance of information and

---

[3] *Handyside v UK* A 24 (1976); 1 EHRR 737 para 49 PC.
[4] See, eg, *Roemen and Schmit v Luxembourg* 2003-IV para 59; *Ernst v Belgium* hudoc (2003); 37 EHRR 724 para 104. See also *Salov v Ukraine* hudoc (2005) para 116; and *Dammann v Switzerland* hudoc (2006).

ideas, but a diverse variety of forms and means in which they are manifested, transmitted, and received.[5] As regards the forms of expression safeguarded under Article 10, the broad construction suggests that persons exercising this right are entitled to choose the modality, free from state interference, which they consider most effective in reaching the widest possible audience.[6] A variety of forms recognized in the case law encompass handing out leaflets to the spectators of an official state ceremony and showing a poster above a demonstrator's rucksack,[7] a puppet show satirical of politicians,[8] use of a historical flag, which was also used as a symbol of Hungarian fascism,[9] a painting depicting crude sexual acts of far-right politicians at an exhibition,[10] and a planned workshop on women's reproductive rights on a boat in territorial water.[11] A press communiqué made in a gathering of many people was treated more as an issue of the expression right than that of a free assembly.[12] In some cases, what matters most is not necessarily the content of the ideas defended by the individuals or civil societies, but the forms of disseminating such ideas (seminars and workshops).[13]

Means of expression, as will be examined later in the chapter, certainly encompass the internet[14] and internet news portals.[15] Special importance is attached to the internet archives, which the Court considers vital in allowing the press to maintain previously reported information for educational and research purposes, the 'secondary role' of the press, in addition to its primary role as a 'public watchdog'.[16] In *Ashby Donald and Others v France*, the Court found that the publication of photographs on a website showing a line-up of fashion models, albeit taken in breach of copyright law, was protected under the scope of expression rights.[17]

In contrast, with regard to use of a particular language, Article 10 (and indeed the Convention as a whole) does not *per se* guarantee the right to employ a particular language in communications with public authorities or the right to receive information in a specific language.[18] In the Court's view, national authorities are accorded a margin of appreciation in formulating linguistic policies, taking into account particular historical and cultural circumstances.[19] That said, a state oversteps the bounds of acceptable margin if it forestalls use of an unofficial language by a politician to communicate with private persons. Such a measure is a disproportionate hindrance, when done in election settings.[20] Similarly, the refusal by a union of employees in education and science to delete reference to the use of its members' mother tongue from its constitution on the ground of

---

[5] *Nilsen and Johnsen v Norway* 1999-VIII; 30 EHRR 878 para 43 GC; and *Sokolowski v Poland* hudoc (2005) para 44. See also *Janowski v Poland* 1999-I; 29 EHRR 705 para 45 Com Rep.

[6] See, eg *Women on Waves and Others v Portugal* hudoc (2009) para 38.

[7] *Chorherr v Austria* A266-B (1993).   [8] *Alves da Silva v Portugal* hudoc (2009) paras 27–8.

[9] *Fáber v Hungary* hudoc (2012) paras 47 and 57 (holding that such an act, even though highly provocative, 'remains *prima facie* an act of freedom of expression'). See also *Vajnai (II) v Hungary* DA hudoc (2011).

[10] *Vereinigung Bildender Künstler v Austria* ECHR 2007-II, paras 33–4. See also *Tátar and Fáber v Hungary* hudoc (2012) paras 29, 38–9.   [11] *Women on Waves and Others v Portugal* hudoc (2009).

[12] *Karademirci and Others v Turkey* ECHR 2005-I para 26.

[13] *Women on Waves and Others v Portugal* hudoc (2009) para 39.

[14] *Times Newspapers Ltd (Nos 1 and 2) v UK* hudoc (2009); *Editorial Board of Pravoye Delo et Shktekel v Ukraine* Reports of Judgments and Decisions 2011; and *Ashby Donald and Others v France* hudoc (2013) para 34.   [15] See *Delfi AS v Estonia* hudoc (2013) para 75.

[16] *Times Newspapers Ltd (Nos 1 and 2) v UK* hudoc (2009) para 45.

[17] *Ashby Donald and Others v France* hudoc (2013) para 34 (though finding no violation of the restrictions imposed on the applicants).   [18] See *Mentzen v Latvia*, No. 71074/01, ECHR 2004-XII DA.

[19] *Şükran Aydin and Others v Turkey* hudoc (2013) para 51.

[20] *Şükran Aydin and Others v Turkey* hudoc (2013) para 52 (ban on using Kurdish language by a then local mayor before private citizens, many of whom could not understand Turkish).

its breach of the Turkish constitutional law, accompanied by the initiation of proceedings aimed at dissolving the union, was too categorical and disproportionate.[21]

On substantive matters, because of the demands of pluralism, tolerance, and broad-mindedness, the scope of protection under Article 10 is broadly construed as covering information or ideas that are unpalatable to the state, or offending or shocking to some people.[22] In the Court's view, such is the demand of pluralism in democracies. Article 10 as such does not forbid dissemination of information suspected of being false.[23]

Albeit sparse in the case law, Article 10 guarantees the negative aspect of the freedom of expression, namely, the right not to be compelled to express oneself.[24] One notable example is the right to remain silent. There is growing recognition of this implicit right in the practice of the Convention.[25] This right is of special importance to freedom from self-incrimination and the presumption of innocence.[26] Still, in *Gillberg v Sweden*,[27] the negative dimension of the expression right was not held to cover the 'right' claimed by a university researcher, a public employee, to refuse to disclose his research documents on child psychology. There was no statutory duty of secrecy on those documents. The judiciary authorized access to those documents by other researchers. The applicant's personal ethical ground on privacy was rejected as irrelevant. Any analogy that the applicant attempted to draw between journalists and researchers like him failed, because the source of information did not appertain to private persons. As such, Article 10 was *non-sequitur* and considered inapplicable to the instant case.

Although Article 10 is generally given a broad scope, the Court has held that it is not sufficient that a person's expression is in some way affected by a decision of the state. Where the impact on expression is collateral to the exercise by the state of its authority for other purposes, the Court has been reluctant to consider the matter as falling within Article 10. This has been an issue in respect of the duty of loyalty required of German civil servants, which may present problems for persons with certain political views. In two German cases, *Glasenapp* and *Kosiek*,[28] the Court found that a refusal to grant the applicants access to the civil service, which turned upon this requirement, was based essentially on the fact that the applicants did not possess one of the necessary qualifications for access, not on their political views, so that the complaints fell outside the scope of protection of Article 10. Subsequently, in *Vogt v Germany*,[29] a school teacher was dismissed because of her association with the German Communist Party. The Court distinguished this from those two earlier German cases on the ground that it concerned a permanent civil servant who was already employed. It was centrally about an 'interference' with her freedom

---

[21] *Eğitim Ve Bilim Emekçileri Sendikasi v Turkey* hudoc (2012) para 74 (the mere act of forcing the union to expurgate reference to the use of Kurdish language as such is sufficient to make the measure disproportionate).

[22] See, eg, *Handyside v UK* A 24 (1976); 1 EHRR 737 para 49 PC; *Müller and Others v Switzerland* A 133 (1988); 13 EHRR 212 para 33; *Jersild v Denmark* A 298 (1994); 19 EHRR 1 para 37; *Sokolowski v Poland* hudoc (2005) para 41; *Klein v Slovakia* hudoc (2006) para 47; and *Leroy v France* hudoc (2008) (a cartoon with a slogan that glorified the terrorist attacks on US on 11 September 2001 in a weekly paper).

[23] *Salov v Ukraine* hudoc (2005) para 113.

[24] *Strohal v Austria, No 20871/92* hudoc (1994) DA; and *Gillberg v Sweden* hudoc (2012) GC paras 85–5. See also *K v Austria, No 16002/90*, Com Rep hudoc (1992) para 45. Contrast these with *Ezelin v France* A 202 (1991) para 33 (finding that refusal to give evidence was not an issue within the scope of Article 10).

[25] *Funke v France* A 256-A (1993); 16 EHRR 297 para 44. See also *K v Austria* A 255-B (1993) para 46 Com Rep.

[26] See Article 6, Ch 9, section 3.II.h.   [27] *Gilberg v Sweden* hudoc (2012) GC paras 90–7.

[28] *Glasenapp v Germany* A 104 (1986); 9 EHRR 25 para 50 PC; and *Kosiek v Germany* A 105 (1986); 9 EHRR 328 para 36 PC.   [29] A 323 (1995); 21 EHRR 205 para 44 GC.

of expression, not the right of access to employment. Similarly, in *Otto v Germany*,[30] where a police officer was refused promotion to the position of chief inspector due to his membership of an extreme right-wing party, the Court found that the issue was not recruitment to the civil service, so that the refusal of promotion fell within the material scope of Article 10. In contrast, in *Harabin v Slovakia*,[31] the Court found that terminating the appointment of the President of the Supreme Court was concerned essentially with the right to hold a public post, a right not secured in the Convention. It was ruled that the removal of the judge was based largely on the appraisal of his professional qualifications. Even though the Minister's report, which prompted the removal, referred to the applicant's views on a constitutional amendment, it was not demonstrated that such views 'exclusively or preponderantly' served as the relevant factor to bring Article 10 into play.[32]

II. POSITIVE OBLIGATIONS

The positive obligation to protect an individual person's right to freedom of expression and to prevent encroachments on its guarantee by other private persons entails the horizontal application (*Drittwirkung*) of Article 10 rights in the relations of private persons. The Court has departed from its earlier approach of refraining from formulating a general theory on positive obligations and on the extent to which the Convention can be applied to relations between private persons.[33] It has gradually moved to the stance not dissimilar to that adopted in the context of Article 8. Nowadays, its consistent approach is to recognize that states must ensure that private individuals can effectively exercise their right of speech and communication among themselves.[34] There is full recognition that Article 10 rights apply equally to the relations between employers and employees that are governed by private law.[35] The doctrine of positive obligations that can be deployed to assess issues of access to information will be examined separately.

In determining whether a positive obligation exists in a particular situation, 'regard must be had to the fair balance that has to be struck between the general interest of the community and the interests of the individual'.[36] The ambit of the state's positive obligation varies, depending on considerations of distributive justice and the equitable allocation of resources required for different administrative tasks.[37] Relevant factors are: the kind of the expression rights at stake; their public interest nature; their capacity to contribute to public debates; the nature of restrictions on expression rights; the availability of alternative venues for expression; and the weight of countervailing rights of others or of the public.[38]

---

[30] *No 27574/02* hudoc (2005) DA.   [31] *No 62584/00* hudoc (2004) DA.

[32] *Harabin v Slovakia.* See also *Pitkevich v Russia No 47936/99* hudoc (2001) DA (dismissal of a judge because of her activities irreconcilable with the judicial post, rather than because of her expression of religious views).

[33] *VGT Verein gegen Tierfabriken v Switzerland* 2001-VI; 34 EHRR 159 para 46.

[34] *Fuentes Bobo v Spain* hudoc (2000) para 38; *Ozgür Gündem v Turkey No 23144/93* 2000-III paras 42–6; *Dink and Others v Turkey* hudoc (2010) para 106; and *Palomo Sánchez and Others v Spain* hudoc (2011) para 59 GC. See also Clapham, *Human Rights in the Private Sphere*, 1993, p 231. On positive obligations under the Convention, see Ch 1, p 00.

[35] See, for instance, *Fuentes Bobo v Spain* hudoc (2000) para 38; and *Heinisch v Germany* hudoc (2011) para 44.

[36] *Ozgur Gundem v Turkey* 2000-III; 31 EHRR 1082 para 43; and *Palomo Sánchez and Others v Spain* hudoc (2011) para 62 GC.   [37] *Appleby v UK* 2003-VI; 37 EHRR 783 para 40.

[38] *Appleby v UK*, paras 42–3, and 47–9.

A state's positive obligation has been held to apply in a variety of contexts. The require-ment that private employees must refrain from divulging information may be stipulated in an employment contract. If so, a breach of such a duty of loyalty may result in sus-pension or dismissal. According to the Commission, the enforcement of such legal con-sequences does not amount to 'interference by public authority' within the meaning of Article 10(1). In *Rommelfanger v Germany*,[39] a physician employed by a Catholic hospital was dismissed because of his views about abortion. The Commission considered that the requirement to refrain from making statements on abortion in conflict with the church's opinion was not unreasonable, as the issue of abortion was of crucial importance to the church. It found no interference within the meaning of Article 10(1) on the ground that the positive obligation imposed on the state did not go beyond the requirement of pro-tecting employees from any unreasonable compulsion impairing the very essence of their freedom of expression.

The case of *Rommelfanger* can be compared with the later case of *Fuentes Bobo v Spain*.[40] There, the applicant was laid off by the Spanish television company (TVE) because of his criticism of its management, which was made during a radio programme. TVE was a pri-vate legal person. Yet, the Court found that by virtue of its positive obligation, the Spanish government had to safeguard freedom of expression from threats stemming from pri-vate persons. The applicant's dismissal constituted an interference with his freedom of expression.

In *Palomo Sánchez and Others v Spain*,[41] the applicants, who were trade union mem-bers, were sacked by a private company after having distributed a newsletter among union members. This newsletter disparagingly depicted the director of human resources and two union members in a cartoon, and the latter members were denounced for testify-ing in favour of the company in proceedings, which the applicant had filed against their employer. The Grand Chamber confirmed in principle that the positive duty rested on state authorities to ensure union members could exercise free speech rights without being infringed by their employer. As regards the contents of the newsletter, the Court dis-tinguished between criticism and insult, considering that the latter would call for sanc-tions.[42] The International Labour Office has stated that 'in expressing their opinions, trade union organisations should respect the limits of propriety and refrain from the use of insulting language'.[43] The weight of public interests raised by that newsletter was insufficient to alter its nature, which was to attack the colleagues for having testified in proceedings, with little relevance to union activities.[44] The caricature was not a sponta-neous reaction, but published in written form.[45] Its reasoning was also influenced by the 'homogeneity of European legal systems' in respect of the balance between the employee's freedom of expression (and a state's positive duty) and the employer's rights.[46] Here, the 'European consensus' rationale was used to uphold the national courts' evaluations. The Grand Chamber was cautious about enlarging the potential of the doctrine of the positive

---

[39] *No 12242/86* hudoc (1989) DA. See also *Carrillo and Burgoa v Spain No 11142/84*, (1986) unreported.

[40] Hudoc (2000).

[41] Hudoc (2011) GC. Its Chamber judgment was *Aguilera Jimenez and Others v Spain* hudoc (2009) (referred to the Grand Chamber on 10 May 2010).

[42] *Skalka v Poland* hudoc (2003) para 34; and *Palomo Sánchez and Others v Spain*, para 67.

[43] Digest of decisions and principles of the Committee on Freedom of Association of the Governing Body of the International Labour Office, fifth edn (revised) para 154.

[44] *Palomo Sánchez and Others v Spain* hudoc (2011), paras 72 and 74, GC.

[45] *Palomo Sánchez and Others v Spain*, para 73.

[46] *Palomo Sánchez and Others v Spain*, para 75.

obligations under Article 10, holding that 'certain manifestations of the right to freedom of expression that may be legitimate in other contexts are not legitimate in that of labour relations'.[47]

One salient question is whether the expression rights under Article 10 entail positive duties on state authorities to ensure access to public forums (or even private premises that are quasi-public). The case law has yet to recognize any such freedom of forum for exercising expression rights to justify private persons' access to private property, or even, to publicly owned property.[48] In *Appleby v UK*,[49] the Court rejected a claim that Article 10 imposed a positive obligation to secure a 'freedom of forum' for the exercise of freedom of expression. The applicants, who were campaigners opposed to planning permission, set up stands at the entrance of a privately owned shopping mall, which was originally built by a public corporation. They displayed posters, warning the public of the likely loss of an open space. They were prevented by security guards from collecting signatures. The applicants contended that this shopping centre functioned as a town centre, providing venues for public services. According to the public forum doctrine in the United States, the authorities must allow individual persons access to privately owned shopping centres to enable them to exercise free speech rights. In the Court's view, Article 10 does not bestow any freedom of forum. In this case, the Court's reasoning was swayed by the limited nature of the restrictions, and alternative means, such as obtaining individual permission for a stand, distributing leaflets on public paths, or door-to-door calling. Still, the Court did not foreclose the possibility that a positive obligation may arise for a state to regulate property rights where the bar on access to property prevents any effective exercise of freedom of expression, as in the case of a corporate town.

It may be asked if the gamut of positive duties under Article 10 can be stretched to include the obligation of a state to provide private citizens or organizations a right of access to the media to disseminate their views. Unsurprisingly, the Court has been dissuaded from taking such far-reaching interpretation.[50] Similarly, the Court has rejected any claim that a state is obliged to ensure access of private citizens to publication of advertisements in privately owned media. In such cases, the essentially commercial nature of paid advertisement is an important consideration.[51] However, where a national court has already ordered a private citizen to be given access to media, but the national authorities have failed to enforce the order, clearly, their omission to take effective measures to assist the media journalists' expression rights amounts to a breach of their positive duty under Article 10.[52]

The concept of positive obligations under Article 10 assumes marked importance where private persons and the press are exposed to any violence or threats of violence directed by other private persons. This is particularly the case in situations of inter-ethnic conflict and against the background of violent nationalist agitations. In *Özgür Gündem v Turkey*,[53] the Court held that Turkey was under a positive obligation to undertake effective investigation and take protective measures where a pro-PKK newspaper was vulnerable to Turkish ultra-nationalists' campaign of intimidation and violence, including

---

[47] *Palomo Sánchez and Others v Spain*, para 76. The judgment was rendered by twelve votes to five. See also A 323 (1995); 21 EHRR 205, paras 51 and 59.

[48] Apart from *Appleby*, explained in the text, see also *Berladir and Others v Russia* hudoc (2012) para 58.

[49] 2003-VI; 37 EHRR 783.

[50] *Murphy v Ireland* 2003-IX; para 61; *Saliyev v Russia* hudoc (2010) para 52.

[51] *Remuszko v Poland* hudoc (2013), paras 79 and 81 (alleged right of access to paid advertisement).

[52] *Frăsilă and Ciocîrlan v Romania* hudoc (2012) paras 58–9, 65, and 71.

[53] 2000-III; 31 EHRR 1082 paras 42–6. See also *Fuentes Bobo v Spain* hudoc (2000) para 38.

killings. Despite the numerous requests for protection by the newspaper applicant, the government failed to take adequate or effective steps. Such an omission was considered to warrant the fear that the aggressive nationalist campaign was tolerated, if not approved, by state officials.[54] In the *Özgür Gündem* case, Turkey submitted that the applicant and its staff supported the PKK and acted as its propaganda tool. The Court held that even if this was proven to be true, this did not justify the omission to take necessary protective measures.

III. ACCESS TO INFORMATION

Unlike its counterparts in the International Covenant on Civil and Political Rights (ICCPR)[55] and EU law,[56] Article 10 has yet to be recognized by the Court as providing a basis for the right of access to information. It has consistently rejected the view that Article 10(1), which includes the phrase 'freedom...to receive...information', can be read to guarantee a *general* right of access to information possessed by public authorities. The freedom to receive information under Article 10 has yet to be translated into the national authorities' positive duty to disseminate information of their own motion.[57] Instead, the Court's approach has been to focus upon denial of access to information under Article 8.[58] However, where public access to information is recognized under national or EU law, the Court must apply the rigorous review of limitations on such right as in other expression cases.[59]

In *Leander v Sweden*,[60] the applicant applied for a temporary post of museum technician at the Naval Museum, which was adjacent to a Naval Base designated as a restricted military security zone, but he was denied the post for security reasons. He challenged the security procedure and sought to obtain reasons for the decision against him under, *inter alia*, Article 10. The Court held that: 'Article 10 does not, *in circumstances such as those of the present case*, confer on the individual a right of access to a register containing information on his personal position, nor does it embody an obligation on the Government to impart such information to the individual.' This reasoning was followed in *Gaskin v UK*,[61] which involved the refusal to grant an applicant access to his child-care records.

In *Guerra v Italy*,[62] the erstwhile Commission made a breakthrough in endorsing the right of access to information under Article 10, relying on teleological interpretation. There, the local authorities failed to provide residents with sufficient information on a potential health hazard arising from a chemical factory. The right to information under Article 10 was highlighted for preventing potential violations of the Convention rights in the event of serious environmental pollution. The scope of positive obligations

---

[54] *Özgür Gündem v Turkey*, para 41.

[55] Article 19 of the ICCPR clearly recognizes the right of the citizens to seek information.

[56] The right of access to documents has been established as a fundamental right: Case C-58/94, *Netherlands v Council*, [1996] ECR I-2169 paras 34–7; Case T-105/95, *WWF UK v Commission*, [1997] ECR II-313 para 55. See Peers, 21 YEL 385 (2002); and Arai-Takahashi, 24 YEL 27 at 53–69 (2005).

[57] See, eg, *Leander v Sweden* A 116 (1987); 9 EHRR 433 and *Gaskin v UK* A 160 (1989); 12 EHRR 36 PC.

[58] See, eg, *Gaskin v UK*, and *McGinley and Egan v UK* 1998-III; 27 EHRR 1 Com Rep; and *Roche v UK* hudoc (2005) para 172 GC (concerning access to information about the applicant's participation in tests on chemical weapons at Porton Down).

[59] See *Timpul Info-Magazin and Anghel v Moldova* hudoc (2007) para 31; *Times Newspaper Ltd (Nos 1 and 2) v UK* hudoc (2009) para 41; *Youth Initiative for Human Rights v Serbia* hudoc (2013) para 25.

[60] A 116 (1987); 9 EHRR 433 para 74 (emphasis added). See also paras 81 and 85 Com Rep; and *Roche v UK* hudoc (2005) para 172, GC.

[61] A 160 (1989); 12 EHRR 36 para 52 (finding of a violation of Article 8).

[62] 1998-I; 26 EHRR 357 para 43 Com Rep.

was interpreted as going beyond the general duty to make environmental information accessible to the public. It was considered to cover more *specific* duties, such as the duties 'to collect, process and disseminate information which…is not directly accessible and which cannot be known to the public unless the public authorities act accordingly'.[63] The Commission averred that the 'right of effective access' to information on environmental and health hazards must be recognized unless there is an overriding public interest in maintaining confidentiality of the information.[64] The Parliamentary Assembly of the Council of Europe recognized 'public access to clear and full information' as a 'basic human right'.[65] What can be inferred from the Commission's approach is that the general rule is open access to information, with the onus on a government to establish the necessity of confidentiality. The Commission's reasoning could be deployed to justify claims for access to information affecting national security, and information held by medical and welfare authorities.

However, the prospect of such dynamic interpretation was dampened by the Court in the same *Guerra* case when it followed the traditional understanding that the freedom to receive information is confined to the negative duty of the government not to interfere with communication of information among individuals *inter se*.[66] In *Sîrbu v Moldova*,[67] the Court held that the freedom to receive information under Article 10(1) '*basically* prohibits a government from restricting a person from receiving information that others wish or may be willing to impart to him', and that this freedom 'cannot be construed as imposing on a State, *in circumstances such as those of the present case*, positive obligations to disclose to the public any secret documents or information concerning its military, intelligence service or police'.

So far, the case law has yet to grapple with the positive duty of the states to disclose information unless national laws authorize public access to them. In *Kenedi v Hungary*,[68] a historian searching for records of security service during the communist era challenged a protracted reluctance to enforce a court order granting access to the relevant declassified documents. The right of access to information was specifically recognized by the Hungarian law and judicial orders. The Court found a breach of Article 10, as the case turned on hindrance to the right to receive public documents that should have been available.[69]

IV. ODIOUS EXPRESSION AND THE RELATIONSHIP BETWEEN ARTICLES 10 AND 17

The drafters of the Convention intended to provide an institutional framework based on liberal democratic values to overcome the extremism of Nazism and fascism and to set a counterbalance against a looming threat of Stalinist communism. In view of Europe's historical experiences in the first half of the twentieth century (in particular the Holocaust), some European states are sceptical of the ability of the democracy to resist the danger of racist propaganda leading to totalitarian dictatorships and massive abuses.[70] The case

---

[63] *Guerra v Italy*, para 49. [64] *Guerra v Italy*, para 51.
[65] Resolution 1087 (1996) of the Parliamentary Assembly of the Council of Europe, para 4; *Guerra v Italy*, para 44. [66] *Guerra v Italy*, para 53; and *Gillberg v Sweden* hudoc (2012) para 83.
[67] Hudoc (2004) para 18, emphasis added. [68] Hudoc (2009).
[69] *Kenedi v Hungary*, paras 43–5. See also *Társaság a Szabadságjogokért v Hungary* hudoc (2009) paras 35–9.
[70] Lester, in Macdonald, Matscher, and Petzold, eds, *The European System for the Protection of Human Rights*, 1993, Ch 18, p 474. See also Oetheimer, 17 Cardozo J Int'l L and Comp Law 427 (2009).

law reveals a variety of values which have been considered contrary to the 'constitutional paradigm' of the Convention. Apart from typical examples of (neo-)Nazism,[71] fascism, racism, anti-Semitism, and (Stalinist) communism, the Court has addressed variations of expression linked to Islamic 'fundamentalism'[72] and to aggressive forms of Kurdish nationalism, which involved discussions of hatred and an incitement to violence.[73] Indeed, the evolution of the case law reveals the Court's penchant to treat aggressive nationalism and hate speech against particular racial,[74] ethnic, or religious groups, or against homosexuals,[75] akin to ideology-based odious speech.

In an earlier case dealing with the dissolution of the German communist party, the Commission argued that the examinations of complaints under Article 17 would dispense with the need to analyse a case under Article 10(2).[76] This approach suggests that issues of restrictions on free speech could be subsumed under Article 17, so that some expression rights would fall outside the scope of protection of the Article 10 rights on the mere basis of their membership of a group espousing anti-Convention values. It would also corroborate the theory of inherent limitations, which must be rejected under Article 10. Still, such a methodology is squarely at variance with the entrenched status of free speech in the Convention's order.

Another feature emerging from the earlier case law of the Commission was that if national authorities justified the contested measures in their fight against racial discrimination or other anti-Convention values, a presumption operated in favour of their decisions.[77] As regards a criminal conviction of an applicant who participated in the publication of a work justifying the Nazi Holocaust against the Jewish population, the Commission was satisfied that the criminal conviction was proportionate to its legitimate purpose.[78]

However, the Court has come to develop a more finely tuned approach predicated on an appraisal of proportionality of specific measures to bolster press freedom. The essence is to ask if racist remarks are presented in an objective manner as part of news reporting and analysis—which supports a finding that there has not been a breach—or in a tendentious manner abetting the incitement of racial hatred.[79]

A sounder approach is to argue that all forms of free speech, however hideous and appalling, should be embraced within the scope of protection under Article 10(1), but that they may be lawfully restricted on the basis of the standards developed under Article 10(2).

---

[71] See, eg, *KPD v Germany No 250/57*, 1 YB 222 at 224 (1957); and *H, W, P and K v Austria No 12774/87*, 62 DR 216 at 220–1 (1989).

[72] See, eg, *Kalaç v Turkey* 1997-IV; 26 EHRR 552 para 28; *Refah Partisi (The Welfare Party) v Turkey* 2003-II paras 94 and 123 GC (incompatibility of sharia with democracy); *Yanasik v Turkey No 14524/89*, 74 DR 14 (1993); and *Erbakan v Turkey* hudoc (2006) paras 62 and 65.

[73] See, eg, *Sürek v Turkey (No 1)* 1999-IV paras 61–5 GC; *Gündüz v Turkey No 59745/00* hudoc (2003) DA; and *Medya FM Reha Radyo ve İletişim Hizmetleri AŞ v Turkey No 32842/02* hudoc (2006) DA.

[74] See, eg, *Féret v Belgium* hudoc (2009) paras 73 and 77 (holding that hate speech will 'risk raising among the public some reactions incompatible with a serene social climate and undermining the confidence in the democratic institutions').

[75] See, eg, *Vejdeland and Others v Sweden* hudoc (2009) para 55 (recognizing that 'discrimination based on sexual orientation is as serious as discrimination based on "race, origin or colour"').

[76] See *KPD v Germany No 250/57*, 1 YB 222 at 224 (1957).

[77] See, in particular, *H, W, P and K v Austria No 12774/87*, 62 DR 216 (1989) (neo-Nazi activities); and *Purcell v Ireland No 15404/89*, 70 DR 262 (1991) (ban on live interviews with spokespersons of a terrorist organization). See also the Danish argument in *Jersild v Denmark* A 298 (1994); 19 EHRR 1 para 29 GC.

[78] *T v Belgium No 9777/82*, 34 DR 158 at 170–1 (1983).

[79] *Jersild v Denmark*, A 298 (1994); 19 EHRR 1 para 37 GC.

This methodology prevents states from slipping into abusive recourse to Article 17 or to implied limitations based on 'duties and responsibilities' of bearers of expression rights.

As regards homophobic expression, the Court's approach is to follow the similar method of review. In *Vejdeland and Others v Sweden*,[80] the applicants were convicted of having distributed homophobic leaflets at a high school. The content of the leaflets, which described homosexuality as 'a deviant sexual proclivity', was offensive enough. This was aggravated by the fact that the leaflets were left in the lockers of teenagers of sensitive age.[81] These factors, combined with the modest nature of criminal sanction, readily persuaded the Court to find the interference proportionate.[82]

V. 'REVISIONIST' EXPRESSION

A vexed question is what coherent rationale can be found for balancing the expression rights of authors that cast revisionist light on generally accepted understandings of historical events (rather than on facts as such) on the one hand, and the rights and honour of victims of past atrocities on the other. In *Lehideux and Isorni v France*,[83] a political advertisement in a daily newspaper, *Le Monde*, sought to rehabilitate Marshal Pétain. The French courts convicted the applicants of the public defence of crimes of collaboration with the enemy during World War II, invoking the authors' failure to criticize Pétain's role in interning Jewish people and deporting them to extermination camps. The Court noted that it was 'morally reprehensible' of the applicants not to mention Pétain's involvement in the Holocaust. Still, this advertisement contained the expression 'Nazi atrocities and persecutions'. From this, the Court inferred that they defended the man, not the policies. Several decades after the tragedy, the advertisement was considered as part of the process of a country coming to reconcile with its 'painful' history. Even allowing for the margin of appreciation, the Court concluded that the criminal sanctions were disproportionate, as other lesser remedies, particularly civil remedies, were available.

Dissenting judges[84] considered the majority's decision insensitive to the victims of the Vichy regime and oblivious of the importance that the conviction could demonstrate a clear message against anti-Semitism and racism. It can be argued that sensitive historical subjects of a particular society cannot be 'objectively' or harmoniously determined. This case was decided in the country which, while historically very open to many immigrants from other European countries, saw the Vichy regime recognized by the National Assembly (albeit under coercive circumstances), and the extensive collaboration during World War II. Furthermore, as the dissenting judges noted, the penalty was limited to a symbolic payment of one franc to the civil parties and to publishing excerpts from the national judgment in *Le Monde*.[85]

Notwithstanding the conclusion reached in *Lehideux and Isorni*, what the Court at least agreed on is that in the light of Article 17 and the 'duties and responsibilities' in Article 10(2), the rejection of 'clearly established historical facts—such as the Holocaust', falls outside the scope of protection of Article 10,[86] the stance confirmed in the subsequent

---

[80] Hudoc (2009).   [81] *Vejdeland and Others v Sweden*, paras 54–6.

[82] *Vejdeland and Others v Sweden*, paras 58–9.   [83] 1998-VII; 30 EHRR 665 paras 53–5 GC.

[84] *Lehideux and Isorni v France*, joint dissenting opinion of Judges Foighel, Loizou, and Sir John Freeland. See also the dissenting opinion of Mrs S Trechsel joined by Mr C Bîrsan in the Commission's Report of 8 April 1997.

[85] *Lehideux and Isorni v France*.   [86] *Lehideux and Isorni v France*, para 51.

case law.[87] In *Garaudy v France*,[88] the applicant was a renowned academic and a former politician in France, who published a controversial book that not only criticized policies of the State of Israel but even denied the Nazi's genocide against the Jewish population. Relying partly on the Commission's case law,[89] the Court examined two related issues separately: (i) convicting the applicant for denying the crimes against humanity committed against the Jewish population; and (ii) his conviction for publishing defamatory statements and incitement to racial hatred based on his criticism against Israeli actions and the Jewish community. With regard to the first issue, the Court found that in view of Article 17, the complaint was incompatible *ratione materiae*. The book cast doubt on the existence and seriousness of the Holocaust, which 'are not the subject of debate between historians, but—on the contrary—are clearly established'.[90] Far from providing political criticisms of Zionism and an 'objective' study of the revisionist theories, the applicant was considered a subscriber to the kind of revisionist theorists that 'systematically' denied the fact of the crimes against humanity against the Jewish people. The purpose of the book was seen to rehabilitate the Nazi regime and to accuse the victims of falsifying history. The Court stressed that:

> Denying crimes against humanity constitutes one of the most serious forms of racial defamation of Jews and of incitement to hatred of them. The denial or rewriting of this type of historical fact undermines the values on which the fight against racism and anti-Semitism are based and constitutes a serious threat to public order. Such acts are incompatible with democracy and human rights because they infringe the rights of others. Its proponents indisputably have designs that fall into the category of aims prohibited by Article 17 of the Convention.[91]

As regards the second issue, the Court expressed 'serious doubt' over the protection of such opinion under Article 10, but appraised this under the second paragraph. The Court suggested that the generally sinister tenor of the book, buttressed by 'a proven racist aim', impaired any merits in the academic criticism of Zionism, rendering the conviction permissible under Article 10(2).

What emerges from the *Garaudy* case is that not only denying the existence of specific atrocities that are 'clearly established historical facts', but also minimizing their degree, fall outside the protection of Article 10.[92] This implication raises two issues. First, aside from the Holocaust, whose unprecedented nature in history is unassailable as an industrial genocide initiated in peacetime, to what extent will the Court expand the list of the 'clearly established historical facts', the negation or downplaying of which can be excluded from the ambit of protection under Article 10? Does it include other examples of genocide, such as the Nazi massacres of the Romani population and the genocide against the Tutsis in Rwanda? Second, even if the existence of a certain atrocity is well established in its historical context, its legal characterization (for instance, the denomination

---

[87] Apart from the *Garaudy* case cited in the text, see also *Chauvy and Others v France*, 2004-VI; 41 EHRR 610 para 69.

[88] No 65831/01, 2003-IX DA. And see *Chauvy and Others v France* 2004-VI; 41 EHRR 610 para 69.

[89] See, eg, *Glimmerveen and Hagenbeek v Netherlands* Nos 8345/78, 8406/79, 18 DR 187 (1979); *Pierre Marais v France* No 31159/96, 85 DR 184 (1996).   [90] *Garaudy v France* No 65831/01, 2003-IX DA.

[91] *Garaudy v France*.

[92] This is the approach followed by the Court in the *Garaudy* case in relation to the denial of the crimes against humanity.

of crimes against humanity or genocide) may be in dispute.[93] The proposal to apply the principle established in *Garaudy* to cases of crimes against humanity would entail the risk of extending it too far to the detriment of expression rights. The underlying offences stipulated under Article 7 of the Rome Statute of the International Criminal Court may be widened. It must be carefully examined whether and, if so, to what extent, such a principle can be applied by analogy to revisionist comments purported to shed different light on the magnitude and causes of atrocities. The Court has shrewdly abstained from dwelling on polemics over historical facts, stating that:

> it is an integral part of freedom of expression to seek historical truth and it is not the Court's role to arbitrate the underlying historical issues, which are part of a continuing debate between historians that shapes opinion as to the events which took place and their interpretation.[94]

Given the paramount importance of free speech, it may be preferable to carry out a specific contextual analysis, assessing impact of the impugned speech on surviving victims of atrocities in each case, rather than to take an 'across-the-board' approach of banning the speech as such. In *Fáber v Hungary*, the Court's approach is not to argue that such historical sensitivity would justify limiting the display of a historical flag of controversy (used also as a symbol of the fascist regime), but to underscore the specific contextual analysis (the place and timing of use of a controversial banner: at a site of massacre; and/ or on a day of remembrance, etc).[95] Nonetheless, in *Fáber*, the Court was quick to add that 'the display of a contextually ambiguous symbol at the specific site of mass murders may in certain circumstances express identification with the perpetrators of those crimes', and that 'even otherwise protected expression is *not equally permissible in all places and all times*'.[96]

Second, national authorities claiming to protect the 'objective' character of historical accounts may be suspected of verging on arbitrariness in favour of the 'official version'. If such 'objective' nature is invoked to downplay atrocities, this very label of 'objectivity' in historical analysis becomes of a very suspect kind. The case of *Monnat v Switzerland*[97] related to the broadcasting of a television programme, which shed critical light on the role of Switzerland during World War II, revealing details of collaboration by the Swiss government, banks, and insurance companies with Nazi Germany. Following public outcry, complaints that this reportage was biased against Switzerland were lodged before the Swiss media complaint authority. A journalist responsible for the programme complained of the surveillance envisaged by the Swiss legislature, and of the authority's decision to recognize the complaints on the ground that the programme did not deal with

---

[93] See the controversy over the use of the distinct term of art 'genocide' in relation to the Armenian massacres, Stalin's atrocities against various ethnic groups, the 'killing field' of the Khmer Rouge, and massacres in Srebrenica and in Darfur. On this matter, see Schabas, *Genocide in International Law—The Crime of Crimes*, 2nd edn, 2009, pp 19–26 (Armenian genocide); Schabas, 25 Fordham International Law Journal 23 (2001) (casting doubt on characterizing the Srebrenica massacre as 'genocide'); 'Report of the International Commission of Inquiry on violations of international humanitarian law and human rights law in Darfur', UN Doc S/2005/60 para 518, with International Criminal Court, *Bashir* (ICC-02/05-01/09), Decision on the Prosecution's Application for a Warrant of Arrest against Omar Hassan Ahmad Al Bashir, 4 March 2009 (reaching an opposing conclusion as to the legal characterization of the massacre in Darfur).

[94] *Chauvy and Others v France* 2004-VI; 41 EHRR 610 para 69. See also *Monnat v Switzerland* hudoc (2006) para 57.   [95] *Fáber v Hungary* hudoc (2012) para 58.

[96] *Fáber v Hungary*, para 58 (emphasis added).   [97] Hudoc (2006) para 57.

'an incontestable truth' but with an issue susceptible of different interpretations. The Court noted that determining the role of Switzerland during World War II was not its responsibility but a matter to be left to historians. The Court's inquiry focused on the question whether a proportionate balance was struck between the rights of audiences to receive objective information and freedom of expression.[98] It was held to be unreasonable to require the applicant to clarify that the reportage concerned 'subjective' points of view and not 'unique historical truth'.[99]

The term 'revisionist' is not confined to denial of historically uncontested atrocities, but it is certainly wide enough to be used in an innocuous context to indicate any historical analysis that challenges the conventional wisdom and the orthodox understanding of historical events.[100] Still, such an attempt to contest the widely believed thesis of particularly sensitive events may damage the reputation of individual persons. In *Chauvy and Others v France*,[101] a journalist tried to shed light on the question how the Resistance leaders were arrested in the outskirts of Lyon in 1943. His version of the analysis, which was built on the document submitted by Klaus Barbie, convicted of crimes against humanity, cast doubt, though not expressly, on the conduct of two Resistance members (Mr and Mrs Aubrac), as if they had betrayed their leaders. Following a private prosecution by direct summons instituted by Mr and Mrs Aubrac, the French courts held that this was defamation by innuendo and an infringement of their reputations. The courts ordered them to pay fines, as well as damages, together with the publishing company (third applicant) to Mr and Mrs Aubrac. They were also enjoined to publish a statement in periodicals and a warning in like terms in each copy of the book. It may be questioned whether the international judiciary is an appropriate organ that can authoritatively reconstruct an historical event which remains shrouded in mystery. In that light, understandably, the Court deferred to the findings of the national courts, noting that the domestic courts carried out 'a detailed and very thorough examination' of the impugned book to substantiate their verdict of public defamation.[102] Still, the Court did not abstain from its proportionality appraisal, stressing that there was no order to destroy the book or to ban its publication, and that the fines and damages were relatively modest.[103] One special feature of this case is that reference was made even to the publisher's 'duties and responsibilities' of a 'vicarious' nature.[104]

VI. INCITEMENT TO VIOLENCE

In a series of Turkish cases, the Grand Chamber was asked to examine criminal sanctions imposed on applicants of Kurdish origin for their virulent criticisms of the Turkish government. When confronted with remarks liable to incite to violence against an individual, a public official, or the population, the Court's methodology is, as in cases of other hate speeches, to recognize the generous protection of the expression rights under the first paragraph and to analyse the encroachments under the second paragraph. However, the Court has repeatedly stated that 'where... remarks constitute an incitement to violence against an individual or a public official or a sector of the population, the States

[98] *Monnat v Switzerland*, para 57.
[99] *Monnat v Switzerland*, paras 68–9. The Court suggested its scepticism of a 'unique historical truth' at the level of historical discussions: paras 68–9.
[100] For instance, Niall Ferguson is often labelled as a 'revisionist' historian for his unorthodox assessment of the British Empire and other historical events.   [101] 2004-VI; 41 EHRR 610.
[102] *Chauvy and Others v France*, paras 76–7.   [103] *Chauvy and Others v France*, para 78.
[104] *Chauvy and Others v France*, para 79.

authorities enjoy a wider margin of appreciation when examining the need for an inter-ference with freedom of expression'.[105]

In *Sürek v Turkey (No 1)*,[106] the applicant was the owner of a weekly review that pub-lished readers' letters that vehemently accused the Turkish military of brutality against the Kurds. Distinguishing the present case from the other Turkish cases, the majority of the Grand Chamber found that the criminal sanction, which was a relatively modest fine, did not upset the proportionate balance. What the majority considered serious was the accusation made by the letters that the Turkish army massacred the Kurds, and that the government connived in brutalities against the dissidents. The majority found that the labels such as 'the fascist Turkish army' and the reference to 'massacres' signalled 'a clear intention to stigmatise the other side to the conflict'. In their view, this amounted to 'an appeal to bloody revenge by stirring up base emotions and hardening already embedded prejudices which have manifested themselves in deadly violence'. Special importance was attached to the background of the security situations. Since 1985, serious fighting raged between the security forces and the PKK, resulting in heavy loss of lives and an emer-gency rule in the south-east region. Against such a violent background, the content of the letters was held to instil 'a deep-seated and irrational hatred' against perpetrators of the alleged atrocities, and to funnel a message to the reader that recourse to violence was jus-tified as a self-defence measure.[107] Further, that the letters specifically identified persons by name, stirred up hatred, and exposed them to possible risk of physical violence was considered an aggravating factor. The majority concluded that the protection of the ter-ritorial integrity against separatist propaganda constituted a both relevant and sufficient ground for the penal sanction.[108]

In *Sürek (No 1)*, it may be argued that the virulent and stigmatizing words employed in the publication reflected the partisan nature of the conflict. The applicant was not the author of the letters. Nor was he the editor of the review responsible for selecting the materials.[109] Further, he was not a prominent figure in Turkey, who could, as in *Zana v Turkey*,[110] have exerted an influence on the public.[111] The potentially disturbing fallout of *Sürek (No 1)* is to broaden the scope of vicarious responsibility on the basis of the 'duties and responsibilities' of editorial and journalist staff to inhibit press freedom seriously. This fear is all the stronger because the applicant did not personally associate himself with the contested views. Judge Bonello stated in his dissent that whether words encouraging violence deserved criminal sanction should be assessed on the basis of the US doctrine of 'a clear and present danger'. He suggested that where the invitation to violence remains in the abstract and removed in time and space from an actual or impending scene, the paramount interest of free speech should prevail.

In the parallel case of *Sürek and Özdemir v Turkey*,[112] the Grand Chamber, however, departed from *Sürek (No 1)* and presented a more finessed approach. The same appli-cant and the editor of the weekly complained of criminal sanctions imposed on them because they published interviews with a leading member of the PKK, an illegal organiza-tion, and a joint statement issued on behalf of other proscribed organizations committed to the Kurdish cause. One of the contested expressions included a message that '[t]he war will go on until there is only one single individual left on our side'. The majority confirmed

---

[105] *Surek v Turkey (No 1)* 1999-IV GC para 61.   [106] 1999-IV paras 60 and 62 GC.

[107] *Surek v Turkey*, para 62.

[108] By eleven votes to six, the Grand Chamber concluded that there was no violation of Article 10. The Commission also found no violation of Article 10 (by nineteen votes to thirteen).

[109] See the partly dissenting opinion of Judge Palm.   [110] 1997-VII; 27 EHRR 667 GC.

[111] 1999-IV GC, partly dissenting opinion of Judge Palm.   [112] Hudoc (1999) para 61 GC.

that the fact that the contested interviews were given by a leading figure of the banned organization could not in itself justify interference with the freedom of expression. What may be depicted as hard-hitting criticism was no sufficient ground to negate the guarantee under Article 10. The majority downplayed the virulent nature of some contested passages as an implacable resolve of the opposite side. The contents were not regarded as tantamount to an incitement to violence.[113] Another dimension was the right of the public to be informed of a different, albeit unpalatable, perspective on disturbances in the 'Kurdish region'.[114] In a stark contrast to the reasoning in the *Zana* case, the fact that the interviewed person was the key figure of the PKK, was invoked to highlight the newsworthiness of the information through which the public could gain an insight into the psychology of the political opponents. For the majority, the ground for the criminal sanction was insufficient.[115] The right of the public to receive information about different political ideas, even if considered hostile to national security and territorial integrity, has been highlighted in the subsequent case law.[116] This is true, even though the Court's review may end up endorsing a state's security measure.[117]

In manifold Turkish cases, the Court has scrutinized the contents of the contested statements,[118] focusing on specific elements criticized for encouraging, or even calling for, the use of violence, armed resistance, or insurrection.[119] Publishing a declaration made by a senior member of 'terrorist' or other illegal organizations alone is not sufficient to justify encroachments on press freedom.[120] In other cases, the contested words written in acerbic or derogatory terms were not considered an incitement to violence or hatred,[121] or even *liable* to incite to violence in the light of their content, tone, and context.[122]

Even if the impugned words fail to reach the threshold of incitement to violence, they may be curtailed to prevent serious public disturbance and inter-ethnic hatred in a volatile region.[123] However, that the interferences with free speech must be subject to the

---

[113] See also *Özgür Gündem v Turkey* 2000-III; 31 EHRR 1082 para 63.

[114] Hudoc (1999) para 61 GC.

[115] Further, the severity and nature of the penalties were considered particularly serious: *Sürek and Özdemir v Turkey*, para 62.   [116] *Kizilyaprak v Turkey* hudoc (2003) para 41.

[117] See, eg, *Halis Doğan v Turkey (No 3)* hudoc (2006), paras 32 and 34–6.

[118] See, *inter alia*, *Ceylan v Turkey* 1999-IV; 30 EHRR 73 para 36 GC; *Polat v Turkey* hudoc (1999) para 47 GC; *Erdal Taş v Turkey (No. 3)* hudoc (2007), paras 31–3; *Erdal Taş v Turkey (No 4)* hudoc (2007) paras 19–20. Compare these with *Karataş v Turkey* 1999-IV para 52 GC.

[119] See, eg, *Ceylan v Turkey* 1999-IV; 30 EHRR 73 para 36 GC; *Polat v Turkey* hudoc (1999) para 47 GC; *Kizilyaprak v Turkey* hudoc (2003) para 39; *Müslüm Gündüz v Turkey No 59745/01* hudoc (2003) DA; *Zana v Turkey* para 60; *Falakaoğlu and Saygili v Turkey Nos 11461/03*, Judgment, 19 December 2006, paras 27–8; *Erdal Taş v Turkey* hudoc (2006) para 38; *Erdal Taş v Turkey (No 3)* hudoc (2007), paras 31–3; *Erdal Taş v Turkey (No 4)* hudoc (2007) paras 19–20. Compare these with *Karataş v Turkey* 1999-IV para 52 GC; *Sürek v Turkey (No 1)*, ECHR 1999-IV para 62 GC; and *Gerger v Turkey*, 8 July 1999 para 50 GC.

[120] See, eg, *Erdal Taş v Turkey (No 3)* hudoc (2007), paras 31–3; *Erdal Taş v Turkey (No 4)* hudoc (2007), paras 19–20. Compare these with *Falakaoğlu and Saygili v Turkey* hudoc (2007) para 34 (publishing in a daily newspaper a declaration calling for a support for the unlimited hunger strike carried out by the 'terrorist' prisoners and calling on the public to demolish the prison). See also *Yalçinkaya and Others v Turkey* hudoc (2013) para 36.

[121] *Gerger v Turkey* hudoc (1999) para 50 GC; *Özgür Gündem v Turkey* 2000-III; 31 EHRR 1082 para 70; and *Halis Doğan v Turkey (No 3)* hudoc (2006) paras 34–6.

[122] See, eg, *Erdoğdu and İnce v Turkey* 1999-IV para 52 GC; *Başkaya and Okçuoğlu v Turkey* 1999-IV; 31 EHRR 292 para 64 GC; *Özgür Gündem v Turkey* 2000-III; 31 EHRR 1082 paras 60, 64. In *Özgür Gündem v Turkey*, however, the Court found that some passages of the impugned articles constituted the encouragement of the use of violence, and that the criminal measures were justified under Article 10(2): *Özgür Gündem v Turkey*, para 65.

[123] See, eg, *Incal v Turkey* 1998-IV; 49 EHRR 449 paras 54 and 58 GC; *Karataş v Turkey* 1999-IV para 51 GC.

Court's rigorous review can be borne out in some distinct ways. First, the Court has ascertained specific elements such as the position of the applicant, the tone, form, addressees of the contested statement,[124] and its impact on the public.[125] Still, when publishing or broadcasting an interview with representatives of organizations that espouse violence, media professionals must assume the 'duties and responsibilities' not to disseminate hate speech or glorification of violence.[126] Second, when scrutinizing the nature and severity of criminal sanctions imposed on bearers of free speech rights,[127] the Court does not baulk at requiring that the means be the least injurious for free speech rights and not entail a chilling effect.[128] Even when a criminal sentence is deferred or suspended, its mere threat may be sufficient to upset the fair balance.[129] Third, even if fiction or poetry actually calls for use of violence, regard should be had to its artistic nature. In *Karataş v Turkey*,[130] the contested poems included aggressive tones and the glorification of armed rebellions and martyrdom. Yet, given their limited adverse impact on the public, freedom of artistic expression held sway.[131]

Unsurprisingly, freedom of academic expression occupies a privileged status in the case law, even when the tenor of the expression is unpalatable to the government or the public. In *Başkaya and Okçuoğlu*,[132] a scholarly book referred to a 'racist policy of denial' vis-à-vis the Kurds and the annexation of 'Kurdistan' by Turkey as its 'colony'. The Turkish authorities viewed these words as supporting separatism against Turkey's territorial integrity. Nevertheless, the Court underscored that the incriminated book, far from being liable to incite to violence, was a serious academic work.

3. DIFFERENT CATEGORIES OF EXPRESSION

I. POLITICAL EXPRESSION

a. Overview

Freedom of political debate and free elections form 'the bedrock of any democratic system'.[133] Healthy democracy requires a government to be exposed to close scrutiny not only by the legislative and judicial authorities, but also by the general public and mass

---

[124] See, eg, *Ceylan v Turkey* 1999-IV; 30 EHRR 73 GC (an article in the weekly newspaper); *Karataş v Turkey* 1999-IV GC (poetry); *Başkaya and Okçuoğlu v Turkey* 1999-IV; 31 EHRR 292 para 64 GC (an academic book)   [125] See *Gerger v Turkey* hudoc (1999) para 50 GC.

[126] *Erdoğdu and İnce v Turkey* 1999-IV para 54 GC; and *Sürek v Turkey (No 1)* 1999-IV para 62 GC; and *Erdal Taş v Turkey (No 4)* hudoc (2007) para 18. See also *Stankov and United Macedonian Organisation Ilinden v Bulgaria*, 2002-IX para 103; and *Demirel and Ateş v Turkey* hudoc (2007) para 36.

[127] See, eg, *Ceylan v Turkey* 1999-IV; 30 EHRR 73 para 37 GC; *Karataş v Turkey* 1999-IV para 53 GC; *Polat v Turkey* hudoc (1999) para 48 GC; *Gerger v Turkey* hudoc (1999) para 51 GC.

[128] See, *inter alia*, *Ceylan v Turkey*, para 34; *Karataş v Turkey*, para 50; *Polat v Turkey*, para 45; *Erdoğdu and İnce v Turkey* 1999-IV para 50 GC; *Başkaya and Okçuoğlu v Turkey* 1999-IV; 31 EHRR 292 para 62 GC; *Sürek and Özdemir v Turkey* hudoc (1999) para 60 GC; *Özgür Gündem v Turkey* 2000-III; 31 EHRR 1082 para 60.   [129] *Erdoğdu and İnce v Turkey* 1999-IV para 53 GC.

[130] 1999-IV para 52 GC.

[131] See also *Kizilyaprak v Turkey* hudoc (2003) (a literature critical of Turkish policies in Kurdistan and based on memoirs of a soldier that served in Kurdistan).

[132] 1999-IV; 31 EHRR 292 paras 64–5 GC.

[133] *Mathieu-Mohin and Clerfayt v Belgium* A 113 (1987); 10 EHRR 1 para 47 PC; *Lingens v Austria* A 103 (1986); 8 EHRR 407 paras 41–2 PC; and *Bowman v UK* 1998-I para 42 GC.

media.[134] By virtue of its dominant power, government, both national and local,[135] must tolerate the greatest extent of criticisms against it. It must also be vigilant to avoid any chilling effect that any restrictive measures may have upon political expression.[136]

The nature of speech is crucial for the Court's standard of review. It is firmly established that restrictions on political discussions call for stringent review.[137] Political expression exercised by elected representatives or journalists is given a 'privileged' status because of its contribution to public debates on matters of general interest.[138] The Court has fleshed out distinct doctrines, such as the 'chilling effect' and the 'less restrictive alternative', bolstering the guarantee of political expression. In *Ahmet Sadik v Greece*,[139] a Greek parliamentarian, who circulated communiqués referring to Muslim minorities as 'Turkish', was convicted of the offence of deceiving an elector. The Commission considered such a measure clearly excessive because there was no indication of incitement to violence. Even a low amount of damages imposed on local councillors for libel or defamation in criticism against a public authority may entail a chilling effect on their political expression.[140] The onus may be imposed on a government to prove the overriding weight of a social end. Even statements perceived to threaten national security and public order or territorial integrity may not forestall the Court from ascertaining whether the contested measure is the least injurious.[141]

Immunity is often conferred upon parliamentarians to prevent their free speech being compromised by 'partisan complaints'.[142] Similarly, the national authorities are entitled to give immunity to statements made in the legislative chambers to safeguard the interests of Parliament as a whole.[143] In contrast, it would be excessive to accord senior politicians total immunity from accountability for their defamatory or insulting remarks against a prosecutor, as this may involve a breach of Article 6(1).[144]

While the requirement of free elections clashes with the freedom of political debate, this may warrant restrictions on the latter freedom to secure an equal opportunity for candidates in an election. In *Bowman v UK*,[145] an anti-abortion campaigner's leaflet showed candidates' voting records on abortion before parliamentary elections in the United Kingdom. She was charged with a statutory offence that forbad an unauthorized person expending more than £5 before an election when conveying information to electors to promote the election of a candidate. The restriction on expenditure was applicable only for a limited duration prior to the general election, and the applicant could have campaigned freely at any other time. However, the Grand Chamber noted that the distribution at other times would not have helped inform the electorate when the choice

---

[134] See, eg, *Sener v Turkey* hudoc (2000) para 40; *Lombardo v Malta* hudoc (2007) para 54; and *Vides Aizsardzības Klubs v Lithuania* hudoc (2004) para 46.

[135] *Lombardo v Malta* hudoc (2007), para 54.

[136] *Castells v Spain* A 236 (1992); 14 EHRR 445 para 46; and *Faruk Temel v Turkey* hudoc (2011) para 63.

[137] *Castells v Spain*, para 42; *Piermont v France* A 314 (1995); 20 EHRR 301 para 76; *Ceylan v Turkey* 1999-IV; 30 EHRR 73 para 34 GC.   [138] *Lombardo v Malta* hudoc (2007) para 53.

[139] 1996-V; 24 EHRR 323 Com Rep (non-exhaustion of the domestic remedies before the Court).

[140] *Lombardo v Malta* hudoc (2007) para 61. See also *Otegi Mondragon v Spain* hudoc (2011) para 59 (holding that 'the imposition of a prison sentence for an offence in the area of political speech will be compatible with freedom of expression as guaranteed by Article 10 of the Convention only in exceptional circumstances, notably where other fundamental rights have been seriously impaired, as, for example, in the case of hate speech or incitement to violence').   [141] *Incal v Turkey* 1998-IV; 49 EHRR 449 GC.

[142] *Cordova v Italy (No 1)* 2003-I; 40 EHRR 974 para 55; and *Karhuvaara and Iltalehti v Finland* 2004-X; 41 EHRR 1154 para 50.   [143] *Karhuvaara and Iltalehti v Finland*, para 50.

[144] *Cordova v Italy (No 1)* 2003-I; 40 EHRR 974; and *Cordova v Italy (No 2)* 2003-I. See also *Karhuvaara and Iltalehti v Finland* 2004-X; 41 EHRR 1154 para 52.

[145] 1998-I; 19 EHRR 179 para 45 GC.

of representatives was made. It rejected the effectiveness of alternative methods. It was not demonstrated that she could publish the material in a newspaper or broadcast it on radio or television. Further, contrast was made with the absence of restrictions upon the freedom of the press to support or oppose any candidate, or upon the right of political parties to advertise. In view of these, the Court found a violation of Article 10, ruling that the applicant was debarred from publishing information vital to political debates. Judge Freeland opined in his dissent that the Court was left a delicate task of examining how the funding of single-issue pressure groups at elections may be controlled to counter 'the risk of excessive diversion of the main electoral debates'.[146]

b. Political parties and the freedom of expression

The Court has recognized a crucial role of political parties in promoting pluralism[147] and ensuring the healthy function of democracy.[148] To the extent that their activities are considered a collective exercise of freedom of expression, political parties are fully entitled to the protection of the rights under Article 10.[149] In *United Communist Party of Turkey*,[150] the Court held that:

> one of the principal characteristics of democracy [is] the possibility it offers of resolving a country's problems through dialogue, without recourse to violence, even when they are irksome. Democracy thrives on freedom of expression. From that point of view, there can be no justification for hindering a political group solely because it seeks to debate in public the situation of part of the State's population and to take part in the nation's political life in order to find, according to democratic rules, solutions capable of satisfying everyone concerned.

A vexed question arises where leaders of political parties incite to violence, or craft policies flouting democratic principles. In the Court's view, such political parties 'cannot lay claims to the Convention's protection against penalties imposed on those grounds'.[151] Nevertheless, these parties may not inherently be divested of free speech rights. In *Stankov and the United Macedonian Organisation Ilinden v Bulgaria*,[152] the Court held:

> The essence of democracy is its capacity to resolve problems through open debate. Sweeping measures of a preventive nature to suppress freedom of assembly and expression other than in cases of incitement to violence or rejection of democratic principles—however shocking and unacceptable certain views or words used may appear to the authorities, and however illegitimate the demands made may be—do a disservice to democracy and often even endanger it.

Still, the preventive intervention associated with the concept of 'militant democracy'[153] must not end up dismantling the edifice of democracy through its corrosive impact.[154]

---

[146] *Bowman v UK*, para 13.

[147] The Court has stressed that there can be no democracy without the principle of pluralism: *Refah Partisi (The Welfare Party) v Turkey* 2003-II para 89 GC.

[148] *United Communist Party of Turkey v Turkey* 1998-I paras 42–3 GC; and *Refah Partisi (The Welfare Party) v Turkey* 2003-II para 88 GC.

[149] *Refah Partisi (The Welfare Party) v Turkey* 2003-II paras 43 and 89 GC.

[150] 1998-I para 57 GC.

[151] See, *inter alia*, *Socialist Party v Turkey* 1998-III paras 46-47 GC; *Yazar v Turkey* 2002-II para 49; and *Refar Partisi (The Welfare Party) v Turkey* 2003-II paras 98 and 110 GC.   [152] 2001-IX para 97.

[153] The term 'militant democracy' was coined by Karl Loewenstein, in 31 Am Pol Sci Rev 417 (1937).

[154] Macklem, 4 Int'l J Const L 488, at 514 (2006).

II. CIVIL EXPRESSION

The notion of public interest has an autonomous and broad meaning in the Convention. It has been liberally construed in the case law to encompass social, economic, cultural, or even commercial and religious aspects.[155] The edifice of healthy democracies is sustained by the dynamic interplay of a variety of civil societies, and without the broadest possible bounds of their free speech rights, their lively activities which are so fundamental in our democracies will be compromised.[156] The Court has recognized the role of civil societies as a 'public watchdog' akin to the press in safeguarding healthy democracies.[157]

Expression closely related to certain public interest can be described as 'civil expression'.[158] Broadcasting a programme that critically examined the Swiss collaboration with Nazi Germany during World War II was clearly of public interest.[159] The same applies to the planned seminars purported to discuss issues of women's reproductive rights.[160]

The Court has come to recognize that the meaning of civil expression should be construed broadly, and that obstacles to such expression be examined stringently.[161] In *Steel and Morris v UK*,[162] the Court considered the alleged responsibility of McDonald's, *inter alia*, for abusive farming, deforestation, cancer, and exploitation of children to be of public concern and worthy of a higher degree of protection. More controversial is the decision in *Paturel v France*.[163] A member of the Jehovah's Witnesses, who in his book compared deprogramming by an association aiding victims of religious sects to the methods used in Soviet internment camps, was found to have acted in the public interest in shedding light on methods of fight against sects.

III. ARTISTIC EXPRESSION

Needless to say, artistic freedom is vital to the enrichment of humanity and diversity of civilizations. The Court's dictum that the protection of Article 10 extends to expressions which 'offend, shock or disturb the state or any sector of the population'[164] is of special importance to artistic work. The fact that artistic expression is triggered by commercial incentives or profit-making purposes ought not to lessen its protection under Article 10. In democracy, artists should be encouraged freely to manifest their artistic conviction to challenge the orthodoxy as avant-gardes, and to create new and

---

[155] Compare *Hashman and Harrup v UK*, 25 November 1999 para 28 GC (protest against fox hunting by disrupting it through blowing a hunting horn found to be an expression of opinion).

[156] *Palomo Sánchez and Others v Spain* hudoc (2011) paras 56 and 72 GC. See also Inter-American Court of Human Rights, Advisory Opinion, OC-5/85193, paras 24 and 26.

[157] *Vides Aizsardzības Klubs v Latvia* hudoc (2004) para 42 (an environmental NGO).

[158] See Jacq and Teitgen, in Delmas-Marty, ed, *The European Convention for the Protection of Human Rights—International Protection versus National Restrictions*, 1992, p 64.

[159] *Monnat v Switzerland* hudoc (2006) para 58.

[160] See, eg, *Women on Waves and Others v Portugal* hudoc (2009), paras 41 and 43 (considering it 'radical' to send a warship to stop the arrival of a civil boat in territorial water, which was purported to hold a workshop on women's reproductive rights).

[161] See, however, the earlier case law, such as *Chorherr v Austria*, A266-B (1993); [1993] ECHR 36 para 32 (greater deference to the purpose of preventing disorder pleaded by the state with respect to the arrest and detention of the two protestors that distributed leaflets at an official ceremony, notwithstanding the Commission's finding of a violation of Article 10).   [162] 2005-II; 41 EHRR 403 para 88.

[163] Hudoc (2005) paras 41–2.   [164] *Handyside v UK* A 24 (1976); 1 EHRR 737 para 49 PC.

critical thinking.[165] The upshot of the constitutional significance of artistic expression has been stated as follows:

> Article 10 includes freedom of artistic expression—notably within freedom to receive and impart information and ideas—which affords the opportunity to take part in the public exchange of cultural, political and social information and ideas of all kinds... Those who create, perform, distribute or exhibit works of art contribute to the exchange of ideas and opinions which is essential for a democratic society. Hence there is an obligation on the State not to encroach unduly on the author's freedom of expression.[166]

Nevertheless, as compared with political expression, the decision-making policy of the Court is to accord a less privileged position to artistic expression. Still, what ought to be avoided is ready recourse to the notion 'duties and responsibilities' to mask oppressive measures, whose deterrent impact may stifle artistic imagination and creativity.

Some artistic work may be deemed offensive to religious or moral convictions of members of a particular religious faith. In such circumstances, the aims of protecting public morals or the rights of others may be invoked to justify restrictions on artistic expression. A more careful scrutiny is needed in the case of a clash with the reputation or honour of persons. Special regard must be had to the tone of accusation, the public status or otherwise of the persons recognizable in the artistic work, and its harmful impact.

Controversy arises where a hindrance to artistic activities is defended by the public interest in preventing crimes or disorder, or protecting national security. Arguably, novels and paintings may convey certain political messages considered an incitement to hatred, revolt, or even the use of violence. Nevertheless, in liberal democracies, it is unsustainable that artistic expression can be restricted on the alleged ground that it is of such a nature as to ignite the nationalistic or fundamentalist fervour of a minority and to incite to hatred and violence among rivalling religious or ethnic groups. In *Alinak v Turkey*,[167] the applicant, though formerly a member of parliament, was a private person when writing a novel which, although a work of fiction, recounted a real event, a massacre committed by Turkish security forces. National courts ordered the seizure of his book, ruling that its content incited to hatred and hostility by distinguishing Turkish citizens along ethnic or religious lines. The Court recognized that graphic details of fictional atrocities 'might be construed as inciting readers to hatred, revolt and the use of violence'.[168] Nevertheless, it quickly added that the novel was destined for a small public, and the applicant was then a private citizen. Further, an official involved in the massacre was not identified. The Court found that the seizure of the novel went too far. Indeed, even if the book had been addressed to a large readership *and* if the applicant had been a public figure, such factors *alone* should not justify inherently harsh measures such as the seizure of a novel. Presumptively privileged status is accorded to artistic expression. This requires the Court to examine specific factors such as the contents, nature, medium, and the impact of a contested artistic expression. In the subsequent case of *Lindon, Otchakovsky-Laurens and July v France*,[169] which concerned a novel based on real events, the Court distinguished this from *Alinak*. As will be examined in the context of defamation, in that case the Court highlighted the more serious nature

---

[165] Lester refers to 'the inherently subversive nature of the artistic impulse': Lester, in Macdonald, Matscher, and Petzold, eds, *The European System for the Protection of Human Rights*, 1993, Ch 18, at p 471, n 35.

[166] *Alinak v Turkey* hudoc (2005) para 42.   [167] *Alinak v Turkey*.

[168] *Alinak v Turkey*, para 41.   [169] Hudoc (2007) GC.

of accusations (complicity in racially motivated murder etc) and the identification of the person by name.

Reflecting cultural relativism, the boundaries between obscenity and art may vary from one society to another. The case of *Müller and Others v Switzerland*[170] involved the criminal conviction of an artist for publicly displaying pictures depicting sodomy and bestiality in crude forms, and the confiscation of his paintings. There was no public warning about the content of the exhibition, and entry was free of charge. The Commission's rigorous appraisal was commensurate with the approach followed in the assessment of political expression. It found that the order to confiscate his paintings violated Article 10, stressing the need to choose less onerous alternatives.[171] In contrast, the Court recognized the measures as necessary to protect morals. To justify this decision, the Court hastily invoked a margin of appreciation and the 'duties and responsibilities' of artists in selecting the means of expression.[172] Judge Spielmann, in his dissenting opinion, took issue with the lax approach followed by the majority, adverting to the historical struggle to obtain artistic freedom in liberal democracies.[173] In *Otto-Preminger-Institut v Austria*,[174] the Commission's robust review favouring artistic expression was once again reversed by the Court.[175] That case concerned the seizure and forfeiture of a film which provocatively portrayed God the Father, the Virgin Mary, and Jesus Christ. The Austrian courts considered it blasphemous for the predominantly Catholic population in Tyrol. The Court stressed the margin of appreciation in ensuring that religious beliefs of a pious population would not be offensively attacked.[176]

The inconsistency of the Court's approach becomes apparent when *Otto-Preminger-Institut* is compared with *Müller*. Whereas in *Müller* the applicants failed to warn the public of the content of the exhibition, which was free and open to the public, the *Otto-Preminger-Institut* informed the public of the content of the film and imposed an age limit for the admission. This point was emphasized by the minority in *Otto-Preminger-Institut*, who held that the applicant association ensured that no one would be faced with the film unwittingly.[177] They held that the contested action constituted prior restraint, disproportionate to the purpose of protecting religious sensitivities and detrimental to the principle of tolerance underpinning pluralist democracy.[178] It seems unreasonable that the (anticipatory) outrage of the people in a local region, however genuine, which was based only on the knowledge of the content of the film, was considered to outweigh artistic expression and to justify even prior restraint. The Court was aware that after the seizure of the film, the play on which the film was based was shown even in Innsbruck (the Tyrolean capital) without meeting criminal prosecution.[179] The Court's approach in *Müller* and *Otto-Preminger-Institut* must be criticized for overlooking the rational underpinnings of artistic expression in a pluralistic democracy.

---

[170] A 133 (1988); 13 EHRR 212 para 16.

[171] *Müller and Others v Switzerland*, para 70 Com Rep. See also *X Ltd and Y v UK No 8710/79* 28 DR 77 (1982).   [172] *Müller and Others v Switzerland*, para 34.

[173] *Müller and Others v Switzerland*, dissenting opinion of Judge Spielmann, para 10.

[174] A 295-A (1994); 19 EHRR 34 paras 72, 77 Com Rep.

[175] *Otto-Preminger-Institut v Austria*, paras 56–7.

[176] *Otto-Preminger-Institut v Austria*, para 56.

[177] *Otto-Preminger-Institut v Austria*, joint dissenting opinion of Judges Palm, Pekkanen, and Makarczyk, paras 8–9.   [178] *Otto-Preminger-Institut v Austria*, para 4.

[179] *Otto-Preminger-Institut v Austria*, para 19.

In contrast, the case law since then has clearly marked a turnaround bolstering artistic expression.[180] In *Vereinigung Bildender Künstler v Austria*,[181] an association of artists directed a gallery of contemporary arts. An exhibition it organized included a collage of public figures in sexual positions. Among the figures was the former general secretary of the extreme right-wing party, the Austrian Freedom Party (FPÖ), Mr Meischberger, who was shown naked, gripping the ejaculating penis of the former head of the FPÖ, Mr Haider, and ejaculating on Mother Teresa. Mr Meischberger was granted an injunction preventing the further exhibition of the painting on the ground that it was a debasement of his public standing. The Court found the depiction of Mr Meischberger 'somewhat outrageous' and accepted that the injunction aimed to protect the rights of others. But it held, by a narrow majority of four votes to three, that the injunction was disproportionate. The nature of the painting was considered 'satirical'. In the Court's view, 'satire is a form of artistic expression and social commentary and, by its inherent features of exaggeration and distortion of reality, naturally aims to provoke and agitate'.[182] Mr Meischberger was only one of over thirty public figures in the collage. This was found to diminish the attention drawn to him. Moreover, the offensive painting of his body had been completely covered by red paint, a result of vandalism by an exhibition visitor, so that he was not clearly recognizable. Further, the injunction was seen as being unduly broad, extending to all future exhibitions anywhere. In contrast, Judge Loucaides, in his dissent, placed special weight on the protection of the reputation of others, noting that:

> In the same way that we exclude insults from freedom of speech, so we must exclude from the legitimate expression of artists insulting pictures that undermine the reputation or dignity of others, especially if they are devoid of any meaningful message and contain nothing more than senseless, repugnant and disgusting images, as in the present case.[183]

Judge Loucaides also noted that the gallery was accessible even to the children.

IV. COMMERCIAL EXPRESSION

a. Overview

The identification of what constitutes commercial speech is not free from difficulty. In the EU law context, commercial expression is aptly defined as 'the dissemination of information, the expression of ideas or the dissemination of images in the course of the promotion of an economic activity and the corresponding right to receive such information'.[184] The principal aim of commercial expression is to enhance the economic interests of individuals and enterprises. Commercial advertising as a means of imparting information on characteristics of services and goods to consumers[185] is clearly the most salient form. Article 2(f) of the European Convention on Transfrontier Television 1989[186] defines

---

[180] Apart from *Vereinigung Bildender Künstler* hudoc (2007), see, eg, *Karataş v Turkey* 1999-IV para 49 GC (poems); *Yalçin Küçük v Turkey* hudoc (2002) (an interviewed book written in a literary and metaphorical style); *Kizilyaprak v Turkey* hudoc (2003) (memoirs) para 37; *Alinak v Turkey* hudoc (2005) para 41 (novel); *Dağtekin v Turkey* hudoc (2005) para 26 (novel). [181] Hudoc (2007) para 31.

[182] *Vereinigung Bildender Künstler v Austria*, para 33. See also *Eon v France* hudoc (2013) para 60.

[183] *Vereinigung Bildender Künstler v Austria*, dissenting opinion of Judge Loucaides.

[184] Case C-71/02, *Herbert Karner Industrie-Auktionen GmbH v Troostwijk GesmbH* para 75, *per* Albert AG.

[185] *Krone Verlag GmbH & Co. KG v Austria (No 3)* 2003-XII; 42 EHRR 578 para 31.

[186] ETS 132. In force 1993. Thirty-two parties.

advertisement as 'any public announcement in return for payment or similar consideration or for self-promotional purposes, which is intended to promote the sale, purchase
or rental of a product or service, to advance a cause or idea, or to bring about some other
effect desired by the advertiser or the broadcaster itself'.

A survey of the case law suggests that commercial expression remains less safeguarded
than political or artistic expression. As discussed later, the lax review based on a margin of appreciation[187] is marked by the absence of the distinct principles widely used in
cases involving political expression. Nevertheless, the fact that communicators pursue
a purely economic motive should not deprive them of the protection under Article 10.
Regard should be had to the interest of consumers in the free flow of commercial
information.[188]

b. Restrictions on commercial expression

Limitations on commercial advertising may be justified to prevent unfair competition
and misleading advertising. Such purposes can fall within the phrase 'the protection
of the reputation or rights of others'. The word 'others' can refer to both competitors
in the same market and consumers in general. The Court has recognized that even the
publication of objective and truthful advertisement may be restricted to ensure respect
for the rights of others, or because of the special interests of business activities and
professions.[189]

In *Markt Intern Verlag GmbH v Germany*,[190] the Court upheld an injunction against
a trade magazine, which was precluded from publishing information about a mail-order
firm dealing with chemist and beauty products. The article in the magazine described
one retailer complaining about the products and service of this mail-order firm, soliciting
information of similar experiences of dissatisfaction with this firm. The German courts
considered such statements to run counter to honest practices of competition. They held
that the contested article cast doubt on the reliability of the mail-order firm when the
latter promised to carry out an investigation of the reported case. The Court was equally
divided (seven votes to seven), with the casting vote of the President tipping the balance
in favour of the government. As an explanation for its curt examination and the application of a margin of appreciation, the Court referred to the 'complex and fluctuating'
nature of the issues involved.[191] It is doubtful whether the applicants (a small publishing
firm and its editor-in-chief) acted in a dishonest manner. Indeed, the majority of the
Court conceded that there lacked a competitive relationship between *Markt Intern* and
the mail-order firm, and that the applicant company intended 'legitimately' to safeguard
the interests of chemists and beauty product retailers.[192] Nevertheless, they were receptive to the government's formalistic argument that even in the absence of such a competitive relationship, the contested statements could, albeit *en passant*, provide objective
advantage to the specialized retail trade to the detriment of the mail-order firm which
was described as a competitor. They did so, even though the impact of the article reporting one incident and soliciting similar incidents was limited. Another striking element is
that while recognizing the truth contained in the impugned statements, the majority did

---

[187] See, eg, *Church of Scientology v Sweden No 7805/77*, 16 DR 68 at 73 (1979).
[188] See Lester, in Macdonald, Matscher, and Petzold, eds, *The European System for the Protection of Human Rights*, 1993, Ch 18, at p 480.
[189] *Krone Verlag GmbH & Co KG v Austria (No 3)* 2003-XII; 42 EHRR 578 para 31.
[190] A 164 (1989); 12 EHRR 161 PC.   [191] *Markt Intern Verlag GmbH v Germany*, para 33.
[192] *Markt Intern Verlag GmbH v Germany*, para 36.

not consider it sufficiently material. Overall, the commercial nature of the statements was considered preponderant for the Court's reasoning. The Court held that:

> even the publication of items which are true and describe real events may under certain circumstances be prohibited: the obligation to respect privacy of others [and] the duty to respect the confidentiality of certain commercial information are examples. In addition, a correct statement can be and often is qualified by additional remarks, by value-judgments, by suppositions or even insinuations.[193]

Oddly, none of these elements cited by the Court in this passage was relevant to the essence of the contested information, namely, the information on individual retailers' dissatisfaction with the product and the reimbursement of the mail-order firm. Without adducing any substantive justifications, the Court relied on the non-substitution principle, according to which it 'should not substitute its own evaluation for that of the national courts...where those courts, on reasonable grounds, had considered the restrictions to be necessary'.[194]

The restrained approach followed in *Markt Intern* may be criticized for lowering the standard of proportionality to the most lax level. It suggests that the Court would be required only to verify whether the contracting party exercised its discretion 'reasonably, carefully and in good faith'.[195] This reticent policy was boosted in *Jacubowski v Germany*,[196] which concerned the dismissal of an editor of a news agency. His employer issued a press release questioning his professional competence. In order to safeguard his reputation and career prospects, the applicant distributed a circular letter among news agency professionals, which criticized the management of the employer. Mainly because the circular contained his intention to set up a news agency, national courts found that its distribution amounted to an act of unfair competition against the interests of the employer, who would become his possible competitor. An injunction was granted, impeding the applicant from distributing the circular. In this case, the Commission's unanimous finding that Article 10 was breached was overturned by the Court.[197] The rationale adduced by the Court was essentially the same as in *Markt Intern*. The standard of review was confined only to the question 'whether the measures taken at national level are justifiable in principle and proportionate'.[198] As the minority judges pointed out, this judgment must be criticized for overlooking the applicant's main intention, which was to reply to the harsh criticism made by his employer in a press release and to secure his reputation. Further, the newspaper articles supporting his view were already circulated in the public domain.[199] On closer scrutiny, it is hard to read into the document an essentially competitive purpose and intention. The dissenting judges argued that to 'accept in this case a preponderance of the competitive element amounts to reducing the principle of freedom of expression to the level of an exception and to elevating the [German] Unfair Competition Act to the status of a rule'.[200]

---

[193] *Markt Intern Verlag GmbH v Germany*, para 35.

[194] *Markt Intern Verlag GmbH v Germany*, para 47. See also Eissen, in Macdonald, Matscher, and Petzold, eds, *The European System for the Protection of Human Rights*, 1993, Ch 7, at 145–6.

[195] See, however, the bolder approach of the Commission in *Markt Intern Verlag GmbH and Klaus Beermann v German* and in *Jacubowski v Germany*.   [196] A 291-A (1994); 19 EHRR 64.

[197] *Jacubowski v Germany*, para 28.

[198] *Jacubowski v Germany*, para 26. Clapham endorsed this approach based on non-substitution principle: Clapham, *Human Rights in the Private Sphere*, 1993, at p 224.

[199] *Jacubowski v Germany*, dissenting opinion of Judges Walsh, MacDonald, and Wildhaber.

[200] *Jacubowski v Germany*, in fine.

Many countries forbid comparative advertising or price comparison under their unfair competition laws. Even where such practice is recognized, rigorous requirements may effectively result in its denial. In *Krone Verlag GmbH & Co KG v Austria (No 3)*,[201] a court injunction prohibited the comparison of the sales prices of two regional newspapers without indicating the differences in their reporting styles on coverage of different issues. The Court found that the impact of the injunction was all the more excessive in view of a risk of fines for non-compliance with it.

Professional advertising and publicity has been treated as a genre of commercial expression in the case law. In *Casado Coca v Spain*,[202] where the Court was confronted with a regulatory power of a professional organization, it shied away from robust review.[203] There, a lawyer was subject to disciplinary proceedings after distributing advertisements. The Commission found a violation of Article 10, on the casting vote of the President. In contrast, the Court endorsed the measure, emphasizing a margin of appreciation owing to the absence of European consensus on professional advertising. It held that:

> [b]ecause of their direct, continuous contact with their members, the Bar authorities and the country's courts are in a better position than an international court to determine how, at a given time, the right balance can be struck between the various interests involved, namely the requirements of the proper administration of justice, the dignity of the profession, the right of everyone to receive information about legal assistance and affording members of the Bar the possibility of advertising their practices.[204]

In *Colman v UK*,[205] the British General Medical Council's guidance designed to protect patients from misleading or manipulative advertising prevented a doctor's advertisement in the press. This was considered compatible with Article 10(2), as the applicant's concern was purely commercial. In contrast, in *Stambuk v Germany*,[206] disciplinary punishment meted out to an ophthalmologist by a national medical court for disregarding the ban on advertising was found excessive. The publicity was considered a possible side effect of giving an interview on his laser operation technique, which was published in a local press with his photograph. Here, the photograph was closely connected to the contents of the article, so that this was not mere advertisement.[207]

The Court's general approach to limitations on commercial expression can be summarized here. As a consequence of lax review, its assessment of proportionality may not be attended by elaborate reasoning.[208] *Prima facie*, the compatibility of contested measures with Article 10 is presumed, so that the Court's review may be confined only to the question whether the measures are 'justifiable *in principle* and proportionate'.[209] As a justification for such a restrained stance, it has invoked its limited knowledge and expertise in assessing

---

[201] 2003-XII; 42 EHRR 578 paras 32–4.

[202] A 285-A (1994); 18 EHRR 1 para 66 Com Rep.

[203] As well as the *Casado Coca* case examined here, see also *Hempfing v Germany No 14622/89*, 69 DR 272 (1991).

[204] *Casado Coca v Spain*, para 55. See also *Colman v UK* A 258-D (1993); 18 EHRR 119 para 39 Com Rep.

[205] A 258-D (1993); 18 EHRR 119 para 39 Com Rep. In that case, the dissenting Commissioners questioned how a publicity containing only the name, qualifications, address, and telephone number of the applicant could pose a danger to public health: the dissenting opinion of Mr Martinez, joined by Messrs Nørgaard, Busuttil, Weitzel, Rozakis, and Loucaides. The case was settled before the Court.

[206] Hudoc (2002); 37 EHRR 845 para 50.   [207] *Stambuk v Germany*, para 48.

[208] Lester, in Macdonald, Matscher, and Petzold, eds, *The European System for the Protection of Human Rights*, 1993, Ch 18, at 478–80.

[209] *Markt Intern Verlag GmbH and Klaus Beermann v Germany* A 164 (1989); 12 EHRR 161 para 33 (emphasis added). See also *Jacubowski v Germany* A 291-A (1994); 19 EHRR 64 para 26.

complex details of commercial and competition regulations.[210] Yet, the cogency of this argument is challenged by the harmonization of European competition laws. Further, advertisement can be hybrid, comprised of both commercial and non-commercial (and public interest) elements.[211] As will be analysed later with respect to such category crossover, it may be argued that a more subtle calibration is required to assess what weight can be ascribed to non-commercial elements.[212]

c. Commercial expression and public interest

In contrast to the general tendency described earlier, where commercial expression is closely related to certain public interest understood broadly, the standard of review may be fine-tuned. In *Barthold v Germany*,[213] a local paper carried an opinion by a veterinary surgeon, who criticized the absence of veterinary service at night. He was interviewed by a local journalist who wrote about this problem, with his name and photograph. Barthold's fellow veterinarians filed an action against him under unfair competition law. The national court presumed that his intention was to act for commercial competition, unless this was entirely overridden by other motives. The injunction was ordered, withholding the applicant from repeating his criticisms. The Court rejected the claim that this case was about commercial advertising susceptible to greater restrictions. Instead, it considered that the statements contributed to public discussions of general interest and described the publicity effect as merely secondary. The German courts' presumption as to intention was considered too rigorous and hence disproportionate.

The nuanced approach in *Barthold* is followed in the subsequent case law. In *Hertel v Switzerland*,[214] the applicant was prevented from publishing views about allegedly hazardous effects of microwave ovens in a health journal. Again, the ground for interference was that his views would constitute an act of unfair competition and prejudice the interests of the manufacturers and suppliers. The Court deemed the ban out of proportion, as it amounted to a censorship that removed his opportunity to disseminate ideas of public concern. The disproportionate effect was aggravated by the risk of his imprisonment.[215]

In contrast, where contested publications do not contain any contribution to public debate, the discretionary power exercised by a professional body may be upheld. In *Hempfing v Germany*,[216] a reprimand was issued by a local bar association against a lawyer who sent circulars to collection agencies. The interference was found proportionate, because these were purely motivated by the intention of advertising.

4. DIFFERENT MEANS OF EXPRESSION

I. THE PRESS AND JOURNALISTIC FREEDOM

a. Overview

The Court has repeatedly emphasized that Article 10 safeguards not only the substance and contents of information and ideas, but also the means of transmitting it. The press

---

[210] *Markt Intern Verlag GmbH and Klaus Beermann v Germany*.

[211] See, eg, *Barthold v Germany* A 90 (1985) 7 EHRR 383 paras 54 and 58; and *Stambuk v Germany* hudoc (2002); 37 EHRR 845 para 42.

[212] Randall, 6 HRLR 53 at 65 (2006). See also Munro, 62 CLJ 134 at 149–50 (2003).

[213] A 90 (1985) 7 EHRR 383 para 58.   [214] 1998-VI; 28 EHRR 534 paras 47 *et seq.*

[215] *Hertel v Switzerland*, para 50.   [216] *No 14622/89*, 69 DR 272 (1991).

has been accorded the broadest scope of protection in the case law, which encompasses preparatory acts for publication, such as activities of research and inquiries carried out by journalists,[217] as well as the confidentiality of journalistic source as discussed in section 4.I.b. Prior restraints on the press are not in themselves incompatible with Article 10,[218] but must not provide a subterfuge for repressive measures against anti-governmental media. Indeed, prior restraints are the most serious threat to the free flow of information and to meaningful debate among the public. Accordingly, this is the area where not only the proportionality test,[219] but even the two standards 'prescribed by law'[220] and 'legitimate aims', may be stringently applied.

No doubt, the role of the press as a 'public watchdog' is vital to democracy's dynamic political process and interaction.[221] The press and investigative journalism guarantee the healthy operation of democracy, exposing actions or omissions of government to public scrutiny,[222] and facilitating the citizens' participation in the decision-making process. Such a democracy-fostering function of the press is significant when it operates in conjunction with the right of the public to receive information and ideas of public concern,[223] including those on divisive political issues.[224] The press furnishes the public with 'the best means of discovering an opinion of the ideas and attitudes of political leaders'.[225] Even outside the political process, the press helps shape an informed public opinion, and stimulates critical debate on issues of general public interest.[226] Further, news items are a 'perishable commodity'. For this reason, a *continued* injunction against the press must be subordinated to a stringent review as to the existence of 'compelling', countervailing interests.[227] As a corollary of its close linkage to democracy, the scope of press freedom must be construed broadly to permit a degree of exaggeration or even provocation,[228] with rigorous scrutiny of restrictions on press freedom.[229] The 'imposition of a prison sentence for a press offence will be compatible with journalists' freedom of expression...only in exceptional circumstances, notably where other fundamental rights have been seriously impaired, as in the case of hate speech or incitement to violence'.[230] Indeed, the Court has

---

[217] *Sunday Times v UK (No 2)* A 217 (1991); 14 EHRR 229 para 51 PC; and *Dammann v Switzerland* hudoc (2006) para 52.

[218] See, eg, *Krone Verlag GmbH & CoKG and MEDIAPRINT Zeitungs- und Zeitschriftenverlag GmbH & CoKG v Austria No 42429/98* hudoc (2003) DA; *Cumhuriyet Vakfı and Others v Turkey* hudoc (2013) para 60.

[219] See, eg, *Observer and Guardian v UK* A 216 (1991); 14 EHRR 153 para 60 PC; *Gaweda v Poland* 2002-II; 39 EHRR 90 para 35. [220] See, eg, *Gawęda v Poland*, para 40.

[221] See, *inter alia, Sunday Times v UK (No 1)* A 30 (1979); 2 EHRR 245 para 65 PC; *Sunday Times v UK (No 2)* A 217 (1991); 14 EHRR 229 para 50 PC; *Jersild v Denmark* A 298; 19 EHRR 1 para 35; *Goodwin v UK* 1996-II; 22 EHRR 123 para 39 GC; *Financial Times Ltd and Others v UK* hudoc (2009) para 59; and *Mackay and BBC Scotland v UK* hudoc (2010) para 32. See also *Vides Aizsardzības Klubs v Lithuania* hudoc (2004) para 42 (recognition of a similar 'public watchdog' function of NGOs).

[222] *Özgür Radyo-Ses Radyo Televizyon Yapim Ve Tanitim AŞ v Turkey* hudoc (2006) para 78. See also *Martin and Others v France* hudoc (2012) para 80.

[223] *News Verlags GmbH & CoKG v Austria* 2000-I; 31 EHRR 246 para 56.

[224] See, *inter alia, Lingens v Austria* A 103 (1986); 8 EHRR 407 paras 41-42 PC; *Erdoğdu and İnce v Turkey* 1999-IV para 48 GC; *Özgür Gündem v Turkey* 2000-III; 31 EHRR 1082 para 58.

[225] See, eg, *Lingens v Austria* A 103 (1986); 8 EHRR 407 paras 41-2 PC; and *Özgür Gündem v Turkey* 2000-III; 31 EHRR 1082 para 58.

[226] *Cumpǎnǎ and Mazǎre v Romania*, No 33348/96, Judgment, 17 December 2004, GC, 2004-XI; 41 EHRR 400 para 96.

[227] See, eg, *Editions Plon v France* 2004-IV; 42 EHRR 705 para 53; and *Stoll v Switzerland*, 2007-V; 44 EHRR 55 para 131 GC.

[228] *Radio France v France* 2004-II; 40 EHRR 706 para 37; and *Gaweda v Poland*, 2002-II para 34.

[229] *Observer and Guardian v UK* A 216 (1991); 14 EHRR 153 para 60 PC.

[230] *Cumpǎnǎ and Mazǎre v Romania* 2004-XI; 41 EHRR 400 para 115 GC.

stressed that the infliction of any criminal sanction, albeit minor in nature, may entail a chilling effect. What matters most is not the gravity of the penalty inflicted on journalists but the very fact that they are convicted.[231]

b. The protection of the confidentiality of journalistic sources

Clearly, the confidentiality of journalistic sources is indispensable for press freedom.[232] Without such protection, the role of the press as a public watchdog in providing accurate and reliable information to the public[233] and shaping a well-informed public may be jeopardized. Any encroachments on the confidentiality of journalistic sources require 'the most careful scrutiny'[234] and will not comply with Article 10 'unless it is justified by an overriding requirement in the public interest'.[235] In the *Goodwin* case,[236] an order for discovery served on a journalist to divulge the identity of his informant was considered excessive.[237] In *Financial Times Ltd and Others v UK*,[238] the judicial order of disclosure of journalistic sources was served for the primary purpose of averting a serious damage to the commercial interest of a claimant company.[239] The Court held that such a legitimate purpose, combined even with the malicious conduct and improper motives of the source of information, was insufficient to prevail over the countervailing interest in safeguarding journalists' sources, not least because this would entail a chilling effect on their expression rights.[240] Indeed, improper motives of the source are deemed irrelevant in examining the issues of confidentiality of journalists' sources.[241] Still in other cases, the Court noted that the conduct of the informant was one of the factors, crucial but not most decisive, to be taken into account when analysing whether a disclosure order should be made.[242]

As confirmed in the subsequent case law,[243] the disclosure order that entails chilling effect on sources and informants would risk compromising the role of the press as a public watchdog in disseminating the information that may be of vital public interest.[244] The tendency is that onus is imposed on a state to adduce any countervailing public interest of 'overriding' nature.[245]

In contrast, the requirement for journalists to supply some factual basis substantiating their statements contested as defamatory is not considered incompatible with Article 10. This is the case, insofar as such a duty does not go so far as to oblige the disclosure of the identity of sources.[246]

---

[231] *Dammann v Switzerland* hudoc (2006) para 57.
[232] *Goodwin v UK* 1996-II; 22 EHRR 123 GC; *Financial Times Ltd and Others v UK* hudoc (2009), paras 59–60.
[233] *Goodwin v UK.*   [234] *Goodwin v UK*, para 40.
[235] *Nordisk Film & TV A/S v Denmark No 40485/02* hudoc (2005) DA.
[236] *Goodwin v UK* 1996-II; 22 EHRR 123 GC.   [237] *Goodwin v UK.*   [238] Hudoc (2009).
[239] *Financial Times Ltd and Others v UK*, para 64. Clearly, there was an ancillary purpose of instituting proceedings against the source to recover possession of the leaked document, and unmasking the identity of a disloyal employee.   [240] *Financial Times Ltd and Others v UK*, paras 70–1.
[241] *Financial Times Ltd and Others v UK*, para 65. See also *Goodwin v UK* 1996-II; 22 EHRR 123, paras 15 and 38 GC.
[242] *Financial Times Ltd and Others v UK*, para 63. See also *Telegraaf Media Nederland Landelijke Media BV and Others v Netherlands* hudoc (2012) para 128.
[243] *Sanoma Uitgevers BV v Netherlands* hudoc (2010) para 51 GC; *Telegraaf Media Nederland Landelijke Media BV and Others v Netherlands* hudoc (2012) para 127.
[244] *Goodwin v UK* 1996-II; 22 EHRR 123 para 39 GC; *Voskuil v Netherlands* hudoc (2007) para 65; *Financial Times Ltd and Others v UK* hudoc (2009) para 59.
[245] *Telegraaf Media Nederland Landelijke Media B.V. and Others v Netherlands* hudoc (2012) para 127.
[246] *Katamadze v Georgia No 69857/01* hudoc (2006) DA.

A court order to disclose a journalist's research materials may be warranted for the purpose of preventing disorder or crimes. In *Nordisk Film & TV A/S v Denmark*,[247] a journalist went undercover and became involved in a paedophile association to produce a documentary on paedophilia. A court order was issued, compelling the applicant company to hand over the unedited footage and the notes that the undercover journalist wrote to produce evidence of a serious child abuse case. Since the majority of the programme's participants neither knowingly assisted the press nor gave consent to being filmed or recorded, they were not considered sources of journalistic information in the traditional sense. According to the Court, the applicant company was ordered not to divulge its journalistic source of information, but to hand over part of its own research material. The two situations differed in that the former involved the freedom of expression of both the journalist and the participants, whereas the latter concerned only the freedom of expression of the journalist. In the latter situation, where the persons filmed or recorded were unaware that this was happening, the chilling effect doctrine was considered inapplicable. This made it more likely that an order for disclosure—as opposed to something more intrusive such as a search—would be a proportionate interference with freedom of expression that was justifiable for the prevention of crime, particularly where the crime involved a breach of a Convention right, such as Article 3, as in the child abuse case. On the facts, the Court was satisfied with the proportionality of the court order.

When confronted with drastic measures aimed at identifying an individual, such as searches of the home or workplace of journalists and the seizure of materials, not surprisingly the Court's probing may start with the presumption that the reasonable balance is upset. In *Roemen and Schmit v Luxembourg*,[248] following the publication of a newspaper article concerning tax fraud by a government minister, a journalist's home and workplace were searched by the police. The searches were carried out not to seek evidence of any offence that the journalist had committed, but to identify the name of officials who allegedly had breached professional confidence. The applicant's home and workplace were raided unannounced by investigators armed with search warrants authorizing extensive investigations. This added up to an undue interference not corroborated by sufficient reasons. The exacting review was consistently followed in the subsequent case law.[249] The Court has consistently asserted that journalists' right not to divulge their sources 'is part and parcel of the right to information, to be treated with the utmost caution'.[250] Special regard should be had to any potential chilling effect that an order of source disclosure may produce, and to the effectiveness of judicial authorities examining the fair balance between the public interest of investigation and the journalists' right.[251]

In *Tillack v Belgium*,[252] the European Anti-Fraud Office (OLAF) lodged a complaint of a possible bribe paid by the applicant, a journalist, to a European civil servant to obtain confidential information on irregularities of the European institutions. The applicant's home and workplace were searched by the Belgian judicial authorities even though no charge was instituted against him. The allegation that he paid a bribe remained unsubstantiated rumour, and the European Ombudsman rebuked the OLAF for making allegations of bribery without a factual basis.[253] The Court confirmed that the right of journalists not to reveal their sources is part of the right to information which requires 'the utmost caution'.[254] In this case, the rationale for recognizing the paramount importance of the

---

[247] *No 40485/02* hudoc (2005) DA.

[248] 2003-IV paras 57 and 59. There was also a breach of Article 8.

[249] See, eg, *Ernst and Others v Belgium* hudoc (2003); 37 EHRR 724; and *Saint-Paul Luxembourg SA v Luxembourg* hudoc (2013) para 52. [250] *Nagla v Latvia* hudoc (2013) para 97.

[251] *Voskuil v Netherlands* hudoc (2007) para 65. See also *Nagla v Latvia* hudoc (2013) para 98.

[252] Hudoc (2007). [253] *Tillack v Belgium*, paras 12–13, 61.

[254] *Tillack v Belgium*, para 65.

confidentiality of journalistic source was reinforced by the disproportionate measure: the police seizure of a number of personal items without making an inventory and the loss of some of the items for several months.[255]

Where the information published by the journalist relates to matters of serious public concern, an onerous burden may be imposed on the national authorities to demonstrate the overriding nature of the countervailing public interest. It becomes clear that the less restrictive alternative doctrine can sit well with such an exacting review. The national authorities must establish that the measures other than searches of journalists' home and workplace, and seizure of materials, such as the interrogation of appropriate officials, would not have been effective in preventing disorder or crime.[256]

II. LICENSING FOR BROADCASTING

a. Overview

The free speech rights of mass media are fully covered by the first paragraph of Article 10.[257] There is specific recognition of the right of individual persons and the public at large to receive 'information and ideas…regardless of frontiers'. But the third sentence of Article 10(1) states that this provision does 'not prevent States from requiring the licensing of broadcasting, television or cinema enterprises'. Even though the third sentence refers to 'broadcasting', rather than to the reception or retransmission of broadcasts, this sentence has been interpreted as giving the state the general licensing power to regulate broadcasting and cinematographic activities within their territories, including the grant or refusal of a licence.[258] States have a variety of reasons to use their licensing power to impose content-based conditions on operators, such as the need to protect the press or national culture. At a time of globalization, there is a keenly felt need to ensure that, irrespective of the principle of market forces, the programme content is not only balanced but also diverse to promote cultural or linguistic pluralism in national societies.[259]

A question arises as to the interrelationship between the third sentence of Article 10(1), which is exclusive to broadcasting, and Article 10(2). The Court has recognized that there are distinct legitimate aims applicable to the licensing of broadcasting under the third sentence of Article 10(1). This suggests that interferences can be legitimated under that sentence, even if they do not accord with any of the aims exhaustively stipulated in Article 10(2).[260] In its earlier case law, the Commission considered a broad range of restrictions imposed in the exercise of the licensing and regulatory powers of states under the third sentence of Article 10(1) without subordinating them to examinations under Article 10(2).[261] However, such methodology, which would imply the doctrine of inherent limitations, was not consistent.[262] At any event, this methodology has been abandoned in the subsequent case law. It is now settled that measures based on the third sentence of the first

---

[255] *Tillack v Belgium*, para 66.

[256] *Roemen and Schmit v Luxembourg*, 2003-IV para 56; and *Ernst and Others v Belgium* hudoc (2003); 37 EHRR 724 para 102.   [257] See, eg, *Murphy v Ireland* 2003-IX; 38 EHRR 212 para 61.

[258] See, eg, *Hins and Hugenholtz v Netherlands No 25987/94* hudoc (1996) DA.

[259] See, eg, *X SA v Netherlands No 21472/93*, 76-A DR 129 (1994).

[260] *Informationsverein Lentia v Austria* A 276 (1993); 17 EHRR 93 para 32; and *Tele 1 Privatfernsehgesell schaft mbH v Austria* hudoc (2000); 34 EHRR 181 para 25.

[261] See, in this regard, *X and Association Z v UK No 4515/70* 38 CD 86 (1971); and *Radio X, S, W and A v Switzerland No 10799/84*, 37 DR 236 (1984).

[262] See, eg, *X v UK No 8266/78*, 16 DR 190 (1978); and *X and Y v Belgium No 8962/80*, 28 DR 120 (1982).

paragraph, including measures dealing with unlicensed operators, must be examined on the basis of the standards developed under Article 10(2).[263]

With respect to public monopolies of broadcasting which the national authorities considered necessary to ensure the impartiality and objectivity of reporting and the diversity of opinions, the Commission in its early decisions recognized the maintenance of such monopolies as compatible with the Convention.[264] Similarly, the Court found that the Austrian Broadcasting Corporation's monopoly in broadcasting through its supervisory powers over the media contributed to the quality and balance of programmes, and that this was compatible with the third sentence of Article 10(1).[265] Nevertheless, it concluded that as a result of technological progress, the public monopoly that prevented the establishment of a radio and television station was inconsistent with Article 10(2).[266] Reserving terrestrial television broadcasting to a state monopoly, while giving private broadcasters access only to cable broadcasting, was considered harmonious with the requirements of Article 10(2), because a high percentage of households could use cable television broadcasting as a viable alternative.[267] The fact that there were scarce frequencies available for terrestrial television broadcasting because of an alpine topography warranted the Austrian decision to assign most to a state monopoly while granting private broadcasters access only to cable and satellite broadcasting. Such a decision, taken at the time of a rapid technological change from analogue to digital transmission, was considered to fall within a margin of appreciation.[268] Further, when deciding the allocation of a given frequency, the primacy given to public broadcasting organizations over private organizations acting for commercial purposes may be justified in the light of the legitimate aim (efficient use of airwaves to safeguard pluralism in the media etc), and of the conditions under which it is implemented (the limited duration of such a priority right accorded to a local public broadcasting organization etc).[269]

Apart from technical aspects, the factors that need to be taken into account for assessing national decisions on the grant or refusal of a broadcasting licence include: (i) the nature and objectives of a proposed station; (ii) its potential audience, examined nationally, regionally, or locally; and (iii) the needs of a specific audience.[270] States may argue that the outer limits of their discretion in ascertaining commercial broadcasting should be broader, referring to such grounds as: (i) the technically complex and fluctuating nature of issues;[271] (ii) the need for equitable allocation of a limited range of transmitting spectrum;[272] and (iii) a policy-oriented concern to preserve diverse national media, a theme closely intertwined with cultural diversity and national identities. In *United Christian*

---

[263] *Groppera Radio AG v Switzerland* A 173 (1990); 12 EHRR 321 para 61 PC. See also *Autronic AG v Switzerland* A 178 (1990); 12 EHRR 485 paras 53 and 60-61 PC; *Informationsverein Lentia v Austria* A 276 (1993); 17 EHRR 93 paras 32, 39 and 43; and *Radio ABC v Austria* 1997-VI; 25 EHRR 185 para 28.

[264] *X v Sweden* No 3071/67 26 CD 71 (1968); and *Sacchi v Italy* No 6452/74 5 DR 43 at 50 (1976) (failure to exhaust domestic remedies).

[265] *Informationsverein Lentia v Austria* A 276 (1993); 17 EHRR 93 para 33; and *Radio ABC v Austria* 1997-VI; 25 EHRR 185 para 28.

[266] *Informationsverein Lentia v Austria* A 276 (1993); 17 EHRR 93 para 39.

[267] *Tele 1 Privatfernsehgesellschaft mbH v Austria* hudoc (2000); 34 EHRR 181 paras 36–41.

[268] *Tele 1 Privatfernsehgesellschaft mbH v Austria*, paras 33–4.

[269] *Hins and Hugenholtz v Netherlands* No 25987/94 hudoc (1996) DA.

[270] *Informationsverein Lentia v Austria* A 276 (1993); 17 EHRR 93 para 32.

[271] See, eg, *Demuth v Switzerland* 2002-IX; 38 EHRR 423 para 42.

[272] The rationale based on finite resources in broadcasting has, however, been increasingly challenged by technological advancements in satellite and cable: Lester, in Macdonald, Matscher, and Petzold, eds, *The European System for the Protection of Human Rights*, 1993, Ch 18, at pp 483–4, n 77.

Broadcasters Ltd v UK,[273] because of a statutory ban on awarding a *national* radio licence to a body whose objects were mainly of a religious nature, a charitable company was pre-empted from applying for a digital multiplex radio licence. The Court found the ban harmonious with Article 10(2), as it was based on the legitimate concern to forestall different religious groups from monopolizing limited national broadcasting resources with discriminatory results. The applicant company was also free to apply for licences for *local* radio broadcasting.

Patently, in case a broadcasting programme contains words of hatred or even incitement to violence and uprising, the national media supervisory body may employ necessary measures to stave off disorder or crime. In such a scenario, even a severe measure, such as suspending authorization of broadcasting for a year, may be justified to prevent the abuse.[274] The Court has been disposed to engage itself in close scrutiny of the contents, tenor, and context of the contested broadcasting. In *Nur Radyo Ve Televizyon Yayinciliği AŞ*,[275] the applicant company, linked to a religious group called Mihr, broadcast a programme in which the victims of a terrible earthquake that hit Turkey in 1999 was explained as the punishment of the Allah. The Court found an element of neither incitement to violence nor of hatred directed against persons who were not affiliated with the Mihr religious community, concluding that the 180-day suspension of the licence to broadcast was out of proportion.[276]

Despite the latitudes of national discretion over policy choices, the Court has gradually intensified the standard of reviewing the content of proposed broadcasting.[277] The Court's policy is no doubt prompted by the role of the media in shaping the informed public through the 'free flow of information' and contributing to 'open and free debate' in democracy.[278] As an indication of such a trend, the Council of Europe adopted the European Convention on Transfrontier Television.[279] As affirmed in *Centro Europa 7 Srl and Di Stefano v Italy*,[280] the Court has now come to highlight the positive obligation on the national authorities to adopt proper legislative and administrative measures to ensure 'effective pluralism' in the national audio-visual media.[281]

When exercising licensing and regulatory powers under the third sentence of Article 10(1), the national authorities may take into account factors other than technical or financial considerations, such as the nature and objectives of a proposed station, its potential audience, the needs of a specific audience, and obligations under international legal instruments.[282] The imposition of content-based conditions and regulations is hard to reconcile with the entrenched safeguard under Article 10. With respect to such content-based regulations, the case law reveals a clear policy shift from the reluctance in the earlier case law to challenge national decisions on licensing[283] to a willingness to appraise at

---

[273] *No 44802/98* hudoc (2000) DA.

[274] *Medya FM Reha Radyo ve İletişim Hizmetleri AŞ. v Turkey No 32842/02* hudoc (2006) DA.

[275] Hudoc (2007).   [276] *Nur Radyo Ve Televizyon Yayinciliği A.Ş. v Turkey*, paras 29–31.

[277] See, eg, *Demuth v Switzerland* 2002-IX; 38 EHRR 423 para 48.

[278] *Demuth v Switzerland*, para 40.

[279] See also the EU's Council Directive 89/552 concerning transfrontier television broadcasting: Council Directive 89/552 on the coordination of certain provisions laid down by law, regulation, or administrative action in Member States concerning the pursuit of television broadcasting activities [1989] OJ L298/23, as amended by Directive 97/36 of the European Parliament and of the Council [1997] OJ L202/60.

[280] Hudoc (2012) GC (the government's failure to allocate any frequencies of analogue terrestrial television broadcasting for nearly ten years).

[281] *Centro Europa 7 Srl and Di Stefano v Italy*, paras 134 and 138.

[282] *Demuth v Switzerland* 2002-IX; 38 EHRR 423 para 33.

[283] *X and Association Z v UK No 4515/70*, 38 CD 86 (1971).

length the exercise of regulatory powers in specific circumstances under Article 10(2). Because of the grave nature of content-based interference, rigorous review intervenes. In *Özgür Radyo-Ses Radyo Televizyon Yayin Yapim Ve Tanitim AŞ v Turkey*,[284] the applicant company had its operation suspended after broadcasting programmes criticizing capitalism, and the assassination and forced disappearance of the Kurds. The suspension was ordered on the ground that, under Turkish law, the media were not allowed to diffuse programmes which the authority considered to incite people to resort to violence, terrorism, or ethnic discrimination, or to provoke sentiments of hatred. After close examinations of the contents of the programmes, the Court concluded that none of such grounds were well-founded.

b. Broadcasting religious and political advertisement

In contrast to commercial or professional advertising primarily designed for financial gain and promotion purposes, many countries have prohibited the broadcasting of religious or political advertisement[285] which is essentially of a non-profit-making nature. This is mainly for the purpose of guaranteeing neutrality and fairness to all religious and political groups, irrespective of their financial resources. Yet this poses a serious question, and even a moral dilemma.[286] To what extent can a state's regulatory power meddle with religious and political advertising through a mechanism of content-based filtering without risking arbitrariness?

For the Chamber's approach until *Animal Defenders International v UK*,[287] a useful comparison can be made between *VgT Verein gegen Tierfabriken v Switzerland* and *Murphy v Ireland*. The former concerned the refusal of political advertisement in television while the latter involved the ban on religious advertisement in radio. In *VgT Verein gegen Tierfabriken*,[288] the applicant was an association for the protection of animals, which requested the broadcasting of an advertisement shedding critical light on the ways in which pigs were reared in commercial industries. The applicant's request was rejected on the basis of its political character, which was forbidden in the Swiss Federal Radio and Television Act. The Court was not receptive to the argument that because of its immediate impact, advertising in audio-visual media had to be neutral and free from any political character. It held that the ban on political advertising in audio-visual media, but not in other media such as the press, was discriminatory and not supported by both relevant and sufficient reasons. Moreover, the political nature of the advertisement dealing with a matter of public interest was such as to require stringent scrutiny.[289]

The scrupulous appraisal undertaken in the *VgT Verein gegen Tierfabriken* marks a contrast to the case of *Murphy v Ireland*,[290] which concerned religious advertising. There, a pastor requested an independent and commercial radio station to transmit an advertisement concerning a video-showing during Easter week, which was purported to provide evidence of the resurrection of Christ. The Independent Radio and Television Commission stopped the advertisement in accordance with the law banning

---

[284] Hudoc (2006) paras 81–5.

[285] For the earlier case law, see, eg, *X and Association Z v UK No 4515/70*, 38 CD 86 (1971).

[286] Eg, advertising for raising public awareness of gross human rights violations may be prohibited on political grounds, whilst the aggressive promotion of commercial projects are not. See, eg, *R v Radio Authority Ex p Bull* [1998] QB 294 (recognizing the ban on Amnesty International broadcasting a radio advertisement concerning genocide in Rwanda). See Lewis, EHRLR 290, at 290–1 (2005).

[287] *Animal Defenders International v UK* hudoc (2013) GC.

[288] 2001-VI; 34 EHRR 159 paras 70, 74–5 (unanimously finding a violation of Article 10).

[289] *VgT Verein gegen Tierfabriken*, para 70.   [290] 2003-IX; 38 EHRR 212 paras 67 and 81.

the broadcasting of religious and political advertising. The Court found no violation of Article 10. Decisive for the Court to recoil from a bold assessment of the national decision was the absence of European consensus on regulating the broadcasting of religious advertisements. Even then, on an empirical level, it is not clear whether common European standards on religious advertising were unverifiable.

The Court in *Murphy* was at pains to distinguish that case from *VgT Verein gegen Tierfabriken*. It argued that while the former involved religious expression[291] and an open-ended notion of respect for religious beliefs of others, the latter related to political expression and to a matter of public interest.[292] There is persuasive force in the argument that content-based restrictions through a mechanism of filtering excessive religious advertising on a case-by-case basis could entail the danger of arbitrariness.[293] Nevertheless, in the specific circumstances of *Murphy*, the content of the advertisement in question was essentially an announcement of a video-showing. In that light, it may be criticized that the Court's approach was rather categorical. In contrast, *VgT Verein gegen Tierfabriken* reveals its more fine-tuned approach. The Court carefully ascertained whether each of the legitimate objectives that would generally justify the ban on political advertisement was defensible in the *specific* circumstances of the case. The national authorities were required to adduce specific justifications for prohibiting political advertising. Merely invoking general and mundane grounds relating to the need for neutrality and independence of the media was insufficient.[294] In *Murphy*, the Court recognized the wariness of the respondent state as to the potential impact of the contested religious advertisement. This rationale is bolstered by the assumption that audio-visual media could have more immediate and pervasive impacts on passive recipients.[295] However, in *VgT Verein gegen Tierfabriken*, such a special impact of audio-visual media, though pleaded by Switzerland, was dismissed by the Court. Further, in *Murphy* the Court took the view that even a limited freedom to advertise would benefit a dominant religion more than smaller religions, breaching the principles of neutrality and equal participation of all religions.[296] If the Court's approach in *Murphy* is to be upheld, one may wonder whether the similar reasoning of equal opportunity could have been applied to political advertising examined in *VgT Verein gegen Tierfabriken*.

In *Animal Defenders International v UK*,[297] the Grand Chamber was given the occasion to reconsider the issue of paid political advertisement on radio and television and provide some element of consistency. In that case, the applicant non-governmental organization (NGO) sought to broadcast a campaign advertisement in television, which criticized the caging and other treatment of primates. The UK Broadcast Advertising Clearance Centre, however, refused to clear the advertisement on the ground that the applicant's objectives were entirely or principally of a political character. The then House of Lords unanimously dismissed the applicant's appeal based on a request for a declaration of incompatibility under section 4 of the Human Rights Act 1998.[298] It was not disputed that the ban was designed to provide political neutrality and impartiality in democracy, and pursuant to protecting 'rights of others' under Article 10(2).[299]

---

[291] *Murphy v Ireland*, paras 71 and 73.

[292] *Murphy v Ireland*, para 68.   [293] *Murphy v Ireland*, paras 76–7.

[294] *VgT Verein gegen Tierfabriken v Switzerland* 2001-VI; 34 EHRR 159 para 75.

[295] *Murphy v Ireland* 2003-IX; 38 EHRR 212 para 74.   [296] *Murphy v Ireland*, para 78.

[297] *Animal Defenders International v UK* hudoc (2013) GC.

[298] [2008] UKHL 15 (*per* Lord Bingham, Lord Scott, Baroness Hale, Lord Carswell, and Lord Neuberger). Note that Lord Bingham justified his cautious approach on the basis of absence of European consensus on how to regulate broadcasting of political advertisements: *Animal Defenders International v UK* hudoc (2013) GC para 26.

[299] *Animal Defenders International v UK* hudoc (2013) GC para 78.

The applicant claimed that the total ban on paid political advertising in audio-visual media by social advocacy groups was excessive in that it was not confined to pre-election periods. In response, the Grand Chamber ruled that the past case law did not bolster the argument that the positive obligation of a state to ensure effective pluralism in the audio-visual sector should be confined to a particular period.[300] The applicant also contended that confining the impugned ban only to audio-visual media was illogical in view of the ascending importance of the internet and social media. On this matter, the Grand Chamber nonetheless adhered to its consistent case law, according to which the broadcast media would produce a more immediate and powerful impact on society as a whole, together with its continuing role as the source of entertainment at home. In its view, using the internet and social media would generate comparatively less dramatic effect than the broadcast media, and there was no evidence to show a significant shift in the influences from the traditional broadcast media to newer media.[301] On reflection, the empirical basis of this contention may be debated. In contrast, the Grand Chamber's distinction between the old and newer media had a merit in one consideration: the expensive nature of paid broadcasted advertisements in old media, which would privilege financially more powerful political advocacy groups, to the detriment of smaller NGOs.[302] A further argument brought by the applicant relied specifically on the doctrine of less restrictive alternatives: the government should have opted for a less drastic measure, such as introducing financial caps on advertising to allow small social advocacy groups to channel their political views outside election periods. The Grand Chamber, however, endorsed the national finding that the objective of such financial caps could easily be circumvented by powerful NGOs and other social advocacy groups by creating similar interest groups to gain access to more advertisement slots. Moreover, the Ground Chamber dismissed the content-based, case-by-case distinction between advertisers and advertisements as too cumbersome and complex to be a feasible regulatory system, jeopardizing legal certainty.[303]

One of the decisive limbs of the Grand Chamber's argument was the lack of European consensus on how to regulate paid political advertisement in broadcast media. Diverse national approaches on this matter were explained by distinct cultural policies and different historical developments.[304] So far, the Committee of Ministers of the Council of Europe was unable to provide a common stance on paid political advertising. Another limb of the reasoning turned on other means of achieving the applicant's purported aim. The Court referred to the possibility of participating in radio or television discussion programmes, setting up its charitable arm to obtain access to advertisement on radio and television on a non-political basis, and relying on advertisement in non-broadcasting media (print media, the internet, etc).[305] The vote was close (nine to eight). Judge Ziemele and other four judges provided a criticism built on the less restrictive alternative doctrine, challenging the legality of the comprehensive ban (not limited in time and specific

---

[300] *Animal Defenders International v UK*, paras 81 and 111.
[301] *Animal Defenders International v UK*, paras 118–19.
[302] *Animal Defenders International v UK*, para 120.
[303] *Animal Defenders International v UK*, para 122.
[304] *Animal Defenders International v UK*, para 123. In this light, see also *Scoppola v Italy (No 3)* para 83 GC.
[305] *Animal Defenders International v UK*, para 124. In this respect, the Court's reasoning was somewhat contradictory. As discussed, earlier in its judgment, it considered the internet as entailing a less powerful influence than broadcast media, but here it admitted that the new media 'remain powerful communication tools'.

locality).[306] The five joint dissenting judges also noted that the impugned ban would exclude even the political advertisement purported to draw public attention to such events as the Rwandan genocide. To encompass such 'issue-advertising', they emphasized the importance of going beyond the rationale based on a financial consideration.[307]

5. PRESCRIBED BY LAW

With respect to the standard 'prescribed by law', the word 'law' has been extensively construed so as to include not only statutory laws but also unwritten laws to accommodate the legal cultures of common law countries.[308] It also encompasses the rules enacted by different administrative or professional bodies, to which the law-making and disciplinary authorities are delegated.[309] In some circumstances, rules of international law furnish a sufficient legal basis.[310]

The Court has identified two subtests that must be satisfied for a norm to be a 'law': accessibility; and foreseeability (or clarity).[311] The subtest of accessibility can be fulfilled if the citizen is 'able to have an indication that is adequate in the circumstances of the legal rules applicable to a given case'.[312] A more rigorous assessment is required for the subtest of foreseeability. Moreover, the development of the case law has added what may be considered the third subtest under the heading 'prescribed by law': availability of safeguards against abuse.[313]

The Court has elaborated the meaning of the subtest of foreseeability as follows:

> 'foreseeability' is one of the requirements inherent in the phrase 'prescribed by law' in Article 10§2 ... of the Convention. A norm cannot be regarded as a 'law' unless it is formulated with sufficient precision to enable the citizen—if need be, with appropriate advice—to foresee, to a degree that is reasonable in the circumstances, the consequences which a given action may entail.[314]

The case law has provided some guidelines for determining the foreseeability subtest, which is held to depend, in particular, on three specific factors: (i) the content of the contested statement; (ii) the field it is purported to cover; and (iii) the number and status of its addressees.[315] The subtest of foreseeability does not require the impossible task of

---

[306] *Animal Defenders International v UK*, joint dissenting opinion of Judges Ziemele, Sajó, Kalaydjieva, Vučinić, and de Gaetano para 8.   [307] *Animal Defenders International v UK*, paras 13 and 15.

[308] *Sunday Times v UK (No 1)* A 30 (1979); 2 EHRR 245 para 47 PC.

[309] Delegating rule-making powers to professional bodies by the general law does not prevent their rules being 'law' for the purposes of Article 10(2): *Barthold v Germany* A 90 (1985); 7 EHRR 383 para 46; and *Casado Coca v Spain* A 285-A (1994); 18 EHRR 1 paras 42–3.

[310] See *Groppera Radio AG v Switzerland* A 173 (1990); 12 EHRR 321 para 68 PC; and *Autronic v Switzerland* A 178 (1990); 12 EHRR 485 para 57.

[311] See, inter alia, *Sunday Times v UK (No 1)* A 30 (1979); 2 EHRR 245 para 49 PC; *Gawęda v Poland* 2002-II; 39 EHRR 90 para 39.

[312] *Sunday Times v UK (No 1)* A 30 (1979); 2 EHRR 245 para 49 PC.

[313] See, eg, *Weber and Saravia v Germany*, 2006-XI, paras 93–95 and 145; *Segerstedt-Wiberg and Others v Sweden*, 2006-VII para 76; *Liberty and Others v UK* hudoc (2008), paras 62–63; *Kennedy v UK* hudoc (2010) para 152; and *Editorial Board of Pravoye Delo and Shtekel v Ukraine* hudoc (2011) para 66.

[314] *Müller and Others v Switzerland* A 133 (1988); 13 EHRR 212 para 29. See also *Perrin v UK* hudoc (2005).

[315] See, eg, *Piroğlu and Karakaya v Turkey* hudoc (2008) para 51.

obtaining absolute precision in the framing of laws, especially in areas in which regulations change to reflect evolving perceptions in society. Such ambiguity may even be a
deliberate policy choice of the legislature, precisely for the purpose of proffering flexibility in the future decision-making policy of both the administrative and judicial organs.[316]
The Court has recognized that many laws are inevitably couched in flexible or even
vague terms to avoid excessive rigidity and to keep pace with changing circumstances.[317]
However, in case a failure to comply with a formal procedure for exercising a certain
form of expression brings about a criminal offence, Article 10, in tandem with Article 7,
requires that the relevant law must clearly define the circumstances in which it is applied,
and that the scope of restrictions must not be broadened at an accused person's expense,
for instance by analogy.[318]

In *Sunday Times v UK (No 1)*,[319] the Court had to examine whether the common law
concept of contempt of court was compatible with the forseeability subtest. The applicants submitted that the 'prejudgment principle' which required the domestic courts to
ascertain whether the proscribed article was liable to cause public prejudgment of an
issue in pending litigation, and contempt of court, was novel and inadequately indicated.
The Court expressed 'certain doubts' about the precision with which this principle was
formulated. Nevertheless, it quickly added that a risk that publishing the draft article
could be incompatible with the prejudgment principle was foreseeable 'to a degree that
was reasonable in the circumstances'.[320]

In the *Markt Intern* and *Barthold* cases,[321] the Court was satisfied that the relevant
provision of German Unfair Competition Law 1909, which required 'honest practices',
met the foreseeability subtest, despite a broad discretion given to the national courts in
assessing this imprecise wording. The impossibility of framing laws in absolutely precise
terms was considered all the more pertinent, as competition law governs 'a subject where
the relevant factors are in constant evolution in line with developments in the market
and in means of communication'. The availability of both 'clear and abundant' case law
and 'extensive' academic commentaries was considered sufficient to assist individuals
to obtain clarity over indefinite legal terms.[322] Similarly, in *Müller v Switzerland*,[323] the
Court found that the word 'obscene' under the Swiss Criminal Code satisfied the predictability subtest, as it was felt necessary to skirt excessive rigidity in legal terms to accommodate changing circumstances concerning obscenity laws.

The subtest of foreseeability must be applied in the light of the advice available to the
applicant. In *Open Door and Dublin Well Woman v Ireland*,[324] the Commission accepted
that the Irish law was insufficiently precise to allow the corporate applicants reasonably
to predict that their non-directive counselling service on abortion would be unlawful
and tantamount to an actionable, constitutional tort. But this argument was rejected
by the Court, which turned to two rationales: first, unlike the statutory laws, the case
law clarified the actionable nature of constitutional rights that were infringed even by

---

[316] See Shany, 16 EJIL 907 at 916 (2005).

[317] *Müller and Others v Switzerland* A 133 (1988); 13 EHRR 212 para 29.

[318] See, eg, *Karademirci v Turkey* 2005-I para 40.   [319] A 30 (1979); 2 EHRR 245 para 49 PC.

[320] *Sunday Times v UK (No 1)*, para 52. See also *Harman v UK No 10038/82* 38 DR 53 (1984): *Sunday Times
v UK* 46 DR 57 (1986) F Sett. In the *Goodwin case*, the Commission expressed 'some doubt' on the sufficient
precision with which s 10 of the Contempt of Court Act 1981 was implemented, but considered it unnecessary to deal with this issue: *Goodwin v UK* 1996-II; 22 EHRR 123 paras 56–7 Com Rep.

[321] *Barthold v Germany* A 90 (1985); 7 EHRR 383 para 47 and *Markt Intern Verlag v Germany* A 165 (1989);
12 EHRR 161 para 30 PC.   [322] *Markt Intern Verlag*, para 30.

[323] A 133 (1988); 13 EHRR 212 para 29.   [324] A 246-A (1992); 15 EHRR 244 paras 45–52 Com Rep.

private individuals; and second, one of the applicants was given legal advice as to a possible injunction against its counselling.[325]

The Court has tapped into the subtest of foreseeability to undertake a rigorous scrutiny over the precise nature of the national laws and case law.[326] In *Karademirci v Turkey*,[327] a group of individuals were convicted and sentenced under the Associations Act after making a statement to the press. According to relevant provisions of this act, associations were prohibited from publishing or distributing leaflets, written statements, or 'similar publications' without a prior resolution by their executive board. The failure to comply with this requirement was a criminal offence. The main question was whether a statement to the press could be categorized as a 'leaflet', 'written statement', or 'similar publication' to meet the foreseeability subtest. The Court answered in the negative. The fact that the applicants were sentenced to three months' imprisonment, albeit commuted to a suspended fine, was held to constitute an unacceptable extension of criminal sanction by analogy, which ran afoul of the foreseeability requirement.[328] In *Piroğlu and Karakaya v Turkey*,[329] the 'prescribed by law' standard came to the fore in relation to the conviction of executive members of a human rights association who participated in a collective press declaration. Under the Turkish Associations Act, associations could not form a legal entity other than federations and confederations. The Court found this wording insufficiently precise to allow members of the applicants' association to foresee that rallying to a movement would result in criminal sanctions. Merely supporting such a movement could not be equated to forming an organization.[330]

With respect to the third subtest of sufficient safeguards against arbitrary interference, any available procedure of judicial review must be effective in constraining a state authorities' abuse.[331] Surveillance measures directed against journalists would invite the Court's robust review, as they may adversely impinge upon the protection of journalistic sources.[332] In *Sanoma*,[333] the disclosure order of journalistic sources was issued by a public prosecutor. The Court considered the involvement of an investigating judge inadequate to forestall unmasking the identity of the sources. This was a *post-factum* intervention which had no basis in law, and the advice of the judge was not binding.[334] In *Telegraaf Media Nederland Landelijke Media BV*,[335] the targeted surveillance of journalists for the purpose of identifying the informants was not accompanied by any safeguard against risk of abuse. There was no prior review by an independent body that could prevent the use of special powers, as was crucial in the cases of *Klass and Others v Germany*,[336] *Weber and Saravia v Germany*,[337] and *Kennedy v UK*.[338]

---

[325] *Open Door and Dublin Well Woman v Ireland*, paras 59–60 PC.

[326] Apart from the Turkish cases discussed here, see also *RTBF v Belgium* hudoc (2011), paras 114–16.

[327] 2005-I para 42.   [328] *Karademirci v Turkey*, para 42.   [329] Hudoc (2008) para 54.

[330] See also *Hashman and Harrup v UK*, 1999-VIII para 41 GC (finding the binding over order to keep the peace and not to behave *contra bonos mores* to be imprecise).

[331] See, eg, *Altuğ Taner Akçam v Turkey* hudoc (2011) para 94 (application of the provisions of the Turkish Criminal Code (incitement to commit an offence, praising a crime and a criminal, and incitement to hatred and hostility among the people) in relation to a journalist's public defence of Hrant Dink, an Armenian Turkish who was prosecuted for 'denigrating Turkishness' under the same criminal code); and *Yildirim v Turkey* hudoc (2012) para 68 (a blocking order of a specific website).

[332] See, eg, *Weber and Saravia v Germany* 2006-XI paras 144–5 and 151 DA.

[333] Hudoc (2010).   [334] *Sanoma Uitgevers BV v Netherlands*, paras 96–9 GC.

[335] Hudoc (2012) para 97.   [336] *Klass and Others v Germany* A 28 (1978) paras 21 and 51.

[337] *Weber and Saravia v Germany* 2006-XI paras 25 and 117.

[338] *Kennedy v UK* hudoc (2008) para 56 (the interplay between the Investigatory Powers Tribunal and Interception of Communications Commission, both of which are composed of (former) high-ranking members of the judiciary).

Once an impugned measure is found to breach the legal basis test, the examination should terminate. Yet, in case the question relating to the subtest of foreseeability is inconclusive, the Court may turn to the standard 'necessary in a democratic society'.[339]

6. LEGITIMATE AIMS

I. OVERVIEW

The second paragraph of Article 10 lists nine legitimate purposes for which restrictions on the expression rights can be justified. These are:

   (i) the protection of national security;

  (ii) the protection of territorial integrity;

 (iii) the protection of public safety;

 (iv) the prevention of disorder or crime;

  (v) the protection of health;[340]

 (vi) the protection of morals;

 (vii) the protection of the reputation or rights of others;

(viii) the prevention of the disclosure of information received in confidence; and

 (ix) the maintenance of the authority and impartiality of the judiciary.

Among them, the following objectives are worthy of closer analysis: the protection of national security; the protection of morals; the protection of the reputation or rights of others; and the maintenance of the authority and impartiality of the judiciary. Moreover, the protection of copyrights features as part of the protection of the rights of others. As discussed earlier, with respect to licensing for broadcasting, the Court has acknowledged the possibility of other distinct legitimate aims in relation to the third sentence of the first paragraph.[341]

II. PROTECTION OF NATIONAL SECURITY

Clearly 'the interests of national security' under Article 10(2) constitutes one of the most solid grounds as a counterweight to freedom of expression. An expulsion order that prevented the leader of Sinn Fein from entering Great Britain to attend a political meeting was justified in view of a sensitive peace process in Northern Ireland, and of the real and continuous threat of renewed violence. Given that the expulsion order was lifted subsequent to the IRA's announcement of a ceasefire, the measure was justified.[342] In contrast, in *Çetin v Turkey*,[343] the interdiction on distributing a daily newspaper in an emergency

---

[339] See, eg, *Dammann v Switzerland* hudoc (2006) para 35.

[340] *Stambuk v Germany* hudoc (2002); 37 EHRR 845 para 30; *Verités Santé Pratique Sarl v France No 74766/01* hudoc (2005) DA. See also *Colman v UK* A 258-D (1993); 18 EHRR 119 Com Rep; and *J v Germany No 21554/93* hudoc (1994) Com Rep.

[341] *Informationsverein Lentia v Austria* A 276 (1993); 17 EHRR 93 para 32.

[342] *Adams and Benn v UK Nos 28979/95 and 30343/96* hudoc (1997) DA. See also, eg, *Medya FM Reha Radyo ve İletişim Hizmetleri AŞ v Turkey No 32842/02* hudoc (2006) DA.

[343] 2003-III paras 59–62, 66.

region was considered excessive, even seen against the fierce background of terrorism. The absence of sufficient safeguards against abuse, such as judicial review of administrative bans, was decisive for the finding.

When assessing constraints on the free expression of public officials dealing with delicate information on national security, the Court has invoked the 'duties and responsibilities' of those officials in sync with Article 10(2).[344] Considerations of national security may be reinforced by particular historical experience. In many former communist countries, civil servants' political expression and activities are constrained to safeguard national security and to prevent public disorder. It is against the background of peaceful transition to pluralistic democracies that the Court found pressing social needs for such restrictions in those transitional democracies.[345]

Nevertheless, when complaints relate to political or civil expression, the Court must scrutinize specific factual circumstances. Viewed in that way, the approach followed by the former Commission may be criticized for the brevity of its appraisal in many cases. The Commission upheld the conviction of a 'convinced pacifist' for distributing to troops leaflets dissuading service in Northern Ireland[346] and the ban on a civil servant revealing information on the establishment of atomic weapons.[347] In *Hadjianastassiou v Greece*,[348] the Court endorsed the conviction of an officer for disclosing secret military information of minor importance to a private company. In *Zana v Turkey*,[349] a former mayor of a city in south-eastern Turkey was imprisoned for his statements supporting the PKK. In an interview with a nationwide newspaper, he described the PKK as a 'national liberation movement', stating that the PKK would only kill women and children 'by mistake'. Yet he denounced the massacres. The Court's assessment focused on the question whether the tone of his criticism of terrorism reflected his genuine intention rather than a political gesture to avoid censure. The Court found no violation of Article 10, referring to the applicant's contradictory attitudes toward the terrorist organization and his influential political position. Nevertheless, as Judge Van Dijk stressed in his dissenting opinion, the Court failed to take into account the content of his controversial statements and personal background. When examining impacts of the statements on the 'explosive situation', the Court should have noted that when the interview took place, the applicant was in prison. Further, Turkey could have chosen a less harsh measure than two months' imprisonment.

In contrast, when confronted with a *prima facie* sweeping form of interference, the Court is prepared to apply a robust review, even if this is pleaded on national security ground.[350] The submission that national security is at stake does not in itself lessen the privileged status of political speech in democracy. In *Piermont v France*,[351] the Court endorsed the rights of a member of European Parliament who made public statements, supporting independence for Tahiti and New Caledonia and criticizing France's nuclear

---

[344] *Hadjianastassiou v Greece* A 252 (1992); 16 EHRR 219; *Rekvényi v Hungary* 1999-III para 43; and *B v UK No 10293/83*, 45 DR 41 (1985).

[345] *Rekvényi v Hungary* 1999-III paras 42–3, and 46–8. For analysis of the implications of cultural relativism linked to the former communist countries, see Sweeney, 54 ICLQ 459 (2005).

[346] *Arrowsmith v UK No 705075*, 19 DR 5 at 25 para 99 (1978). See also *X v UK No 6084/73* 3 DR 62 (1975).

[347] *B v UK No 10293/83* 45 DR 41 at 54 (1985). See also *Z v Switzerland No 10343/83* 35 DR 224 (1983) and *Brind v UK No 18714/91*, 77-A DR 42 (1994).

[348] A 252 (1992); 16 EHRR 219 para 47. See also *Steel v UK* 1998-VII; 28 EHRR 603 paras 101 and 105 *et seq.*

[349] 1997-VII; 27 EHRR 667 GC.

[350] See *Arslan v Turkey* hudoc (1999); 31 EHRR 264 paras 46–50 GC; and *Baskaya and Okçuoglu v Turkey* 1999-IV; 31 EHRR 292 paras 62–7 GC. See also *Vereinigung Demokratischer Soldaten Österreichs and Gubi v Austria* A 302 (1994); 20 EHRR 56 para 37.

[351] A 314 (1995); 20 EHRR 301 paras 77 and 85.

experiments in the southern Pacific. She was considered the beneficiary of a high stand-ard of protection, given that her speech contributed to a democratic debate. Likewise, even against pleas of national security, an enhanced protection may be accorded to civil expression raising 'matters of public interest', as in the case of a speech made by leading members of trade unions.[352]

Once the confidentiality of security information is lost, the question whether the information should continue to be withheld becomes moot. In the cases concerning contempt of court in the United Kingdom, a memoir of a former agent published else-where destroyed the confidentiality of the intelligence information, negating the ground to impose an injunction on the newspaper applicants.[353] The cogency of this rationale cannot be diminished even if security information has been revealed by illegal means. In *Bluf!*, despite the illegality of the applicants' disclosure of security information, with-drawing their periodicals from circulation was regarded as out of proportion.[354]

III. THE PREVENTION OF DISORDER OR CRIMES

Akin to the ground of national security, the objective of preventing disorder or crimes has been invoked by the national authorities in their fight against terrorism and other crimes. Again, this objective, set against a real threat of terrorism or insurrections, is closely linked to the rationale underpinning of Article 17. For all the pivotal nature of such an objective, the Court has stressed the importance of sufficient procedural safeguards against abuse. Faced with a political party whose ideas are considered to clash with the secular and pluralistic foundation of a member state, the Court's approach emerging from Turkish cases since the late 1990s is to examine at length whether impugned statements are likely to pose an 'immi-nent danger' to a society.[355] It has critically analysed whether and, if so, in what circum-stances, a newspaper publishing information about public officials, such as the identity of military personnel, has augmented the 'actual danger' of physical violence against them.[356]

In *Association Ekin v France*,[357] the Court partially endorsed the French argument that the ban on circulating a book concerning the Basque culture pursued the legitimate aim of preventing disorder, even though on a closer inspection, it did not find anything in the content suggesting incitement to violence or to separatism. However, the Court found a violation of Article 10. The content of the book was considered innocuous. The French Ministry was given wide discretionary power in proscribing publications classified as 'foreign origin'. Safeguards against such power were considered insufficient. Further, judicial review procedures were limited and ineffective.

The Danish cartoons that lampooned the Holy Prophet of Islam have generated much debate on the acceptable bounds of press freedom in relation to freedom of religion of others, the 'duties and responsibilities' of journalists, and on the propriety of state inter-vention in preventing possible public disorder and security.[358] A comparable issue arose

---

[352] *Ceylan v Turkey* 1999-IV; 30 EHRR 73 para 34 GC.

[353] *Observer and Guardian v UK* A 216 (1991); 14 EHRR 153 paras 66–70 PC; and *Sunday Times v UK (No 2)* A 217 (1991); 14 EHRR 229 paras 52–6 PC.

[354] *Vereniging Weekblad Bluf! v Netherlands* A 306-A (1995); 20 EHRR 189 para 44.

[355] *Erbakan v Turkey*, No 59405/00, Judgment, 6 July 2006 para 68. This can be contrasted to a Chamber's approach in *Aydin v Germany* hudoc (2011). See dissenting opinion of Judge Kalaydjieva in this case, who criticized the national courts' failure to examine the existence of a pressing social need.

[356] *Saygili and Falakaoğlu v Turkey* hudoc (2008) paras 26–7.

[357] 2001-VIII; 35 EHRR 1207 para 48.

[358] Dworkin, 'Even bigots and Holocaust deniers must have their say', *The Guardian*, 14 February 2006.

in *Leroy v France*, which concerned the publication of a cartoon in a regional left-wing newspaper, which symbolized the terrorist attacks on the twin towers in New York City on 11 September with the caption stating that 'We dreamed them all...Hamas did it'. In that case, the Court endorsed the French courts' conviction of the cartoonist of a complicity in apology of terrorism (and to convict the director of publication of apology of terrorism). It recognized that limitations on artistic expression called for robust scrutiny. Yet, the satirical nature of the work that allegedly criticized American imperialism was found to be *post factum*.[359] The timing of the publication was crucial. It was published only two days after the terrorist attacks in the United States. In view of these, the Court highlighted the 'duties and responsibilities' of artists. Further, the amount of penalty was modest.[360]

When confronted with the real or potential danger of terrorism, contracting parties are, without invoking far-reaching measures under Articles 15 and 17, fully entitled to take appropriate measures under Article 10(2), including a ban on broadcasting images or voices of proscribed organizations. Such measures are necessary to deny terrorist or other prohibited organizations unimpeded access to the broadcasting media, and to prevent them inciting to violence, or giving an impression of legitimacy through powerful audio-visual means. Still, the role of the press and media in exploring what they consider to be matters of public interest should be duly taken into account. In *Purcell v Ireland*,[361] a ministerial order prevented journalists from broadcasting an interview, or a report of an interview, with spokespersons of terrorist organizations such as the IRA and a political party such as Sinn Fein which, albeit not declared unlawful in Ireland, was part of such a terrorist organization. The ministerial order imposed a blanket ban on covering press conferences live, and even on reading out press statements afterwards. It was designed to prevent terrorist organizations from promoting or inciting crimes. The applicants claimed that, as a result, they were barred from providing a programme concerning political candidates' campaign manifesto. In view of the immediate impact of audio-visual media on the public, and of the need to prevent coded messages, the Commission found the order consistent with the objectives of protecting national security, and preventing disorder and crime. In *Brind v UK*,[362] the Commission was similarly sympathetic to notices restraining the broadcasting of any words spoken by a person representing or supporting the proscribed terrorist organizations such as the IRA. The applicants complained that an interview with Gerry Adams, President of Sinn Fein, could no longer be retransmitted, and that the notices, backed by the sanction, would generate a chilling effect, forcing broadcasters to err on the safe side. When finding no violation of Article 10, the Commission considered that the requirement that an actor's voice be used to broadcast interviews was interference of limited scope.

In *Purcell* and *Brind*, an impression cannot be effaced that the pivotal role of the media in informing the public of political extremists was underrated. Behind the semblance of the cogent rationales for shielding the edifice of democracy from terrorist violence, these decisions were marred by the failure finely to calibrate the scope of national discretion in favour of a robust review.

IV. THE PROTECTION OF MORALS

Among the legitimate aims enlisted under Article 10(2), it is the protection of morals which is arguably the most controversial. This is the area where the nebulous notion of

---

[359] *Leroy v France* hudoc (2008) paras 43–4.   [360] *Leroy v France*, paras 45–7.
[361] 15404/89, 70 DR 262 (1991).   [362] *No 18714/91*, 77-A DR 42 (1994).

margin of appreciation has 'thrived' to justify judicial self-restraint. There is no European consensus on the requirements of morals, whose variable nature can be seen even within a country.[363] The Court has also noted that national authorities, which have direct contact with national societies, are better suited than international judges to assess the requirements of local morals. The Court's position is aptly summarized in *Handyside v UK*,[364] where the Court held that:

> it is not possible to find in the domestic law of the various Contracting States a uniform European conception of morals. The view taken by their respective laws of the requirements of morals varies from time to time and from place to place, especially in our era which is characterised by a rapid and far-reaching evolution of opinions on the subject. By reason of their direct and continuous contact with the vital forces of their countries, State authorities are in principle in a better position than the international judge to give an opinion on the exact content of these requirements as well as on the 'necessity of a 'restriction' or 'penalty' intended to meet them.

In the area of freedom of expression, the Strasbourg organs have been confronted with diverse moral values, encompassing obscenity, abortion, and the significance of religion.[365] In the *Handyside* case, the Court recognized the seizure, forfeiture, and subsequent destruction of an allegedly obscene book (*Little Red Schoolbook*) as pursuant to the protection of morals. Further, reliance was made on safeguarding the rights of adolescent children, to whom the book was addressed. The Court noted as follows:

> despite the variety and the constant evolution in the United Kingdom of views on ethics and education, the competent English judges were entitled, in the exercise of their discretion, to think at the relevant time that the Schoolbook would have pernicious effects on the morals of many of the children and adolescents who would read it.[366]

The Court's approach in *Handyside* raises a serious doubt over whether the proportionality assessment was duly carried out. This concern was warranted in several ensuing cases.[367] In *Müller*, as examined previously, the Court found no violation of Article 10 with respect to the confiscation of paintings. The audience was not warned of the content of the exhibition, and the paintings crudely depicting homosexuality and bestiality were 'spontaneous'. The exhibition was free of charge, and without any age limit, and accessible even to small children.[368] Nevertheless, it is doubtful whether such a sweeping measure as confiscating the paintings struck a proportionate balance.

In *Scherer v Switzerland*,[369] the Commission averred that the conviction of the proprietor of a sex shop for showing explicit homosexual videos violated Article 10. Its reasoning was that no one was likely to be confronted with them against their will, and that only a

---

[363] See *Müller and Others v Switzerland* A 133 (1988); 13 EHRR 212 para 36; *Otto-Preminger-Institut v Austria* A 295-A (1994); 19 EHRR 34 para 56.

[364] A 24 (1976); 1 EHRR 737 para 48 PC. See also *X Company v UK No 9615/81*, 32 DR 231 at 234 (1983).

[365] As well as the cases cited here, see *X Company v UK No 9615/81*, 32 DR 231 at 234 (1983); and *X, Y and Z v Belgium Nos 6782-84/74*, 9 DR 13 at 20 (1977).

[366] *Handyside v UK* A 24 (1976); 1 EHRR 737 para 52 PC.

[367] See also *X Company v UK No 9615/81*, 32 DR 231 at 234 (1983), where the Commission endorsed the seizure and forfeiture of 'hard pornographic' magazines destined for export, partly on the ground of a legitimate concern to prevent the country from becoming a source of export trade of obscene materials.

[368] A 133 (1988); 13 EHRR 212 para 36.

[369] A 287 (1994); 18 EHRR 276 para 61 Com Rep. This was decisive for this case to be distinguished from the precedent in *W and K v Switzerland No 16564/90* hudoc (1991) DA.

limited number of consenting adults who paid the entrance fees would be admitted. This reasoning conformed to the Court's approach in *Müller*, even though it was shunned in *Otto-Preminger-Institut*. Turning back to the *Scherer* case, another factor was that the obscene videos were not visible from the street. *Scherer* was the missed opportunity to reset the Court's standard of review because, following the death of the applicant; the case was struck out of the list.[370] In *Wingrove v UK*,[371] the Court, however, confirmed its restrained stance in *Handyside*. The case arose from a short experimental video entitled 'Visions of Ecstasy', which depicted the mingling of religious ecstasy and sexual passion of St Teresa of Avila. The British Board of Film Classification rejected the application for a classification certificate lodged by a film director. The Commission submitted an argument similar to that advanced in *Scherer*, according to which the risk that any Christian would unwittingly view the contested video could have been averted if its distribution was limited to licensed sex shops. Because video boxes included a description of its content, only consenting adults would have been faced with those contents. However, the Court rejected this argument. It provided specious reasoning to the effect that, by their nature, videos, once available on the market, would easily escape the control of the authorities and be transmitted among audiences through copying, renting, etc.[372]

The rationale behind the application of a margin of appreciation is recognized in assessing obscenity in *Perrin v UK*.[373] There, the applicant was convicted under the Obscene Publications Act for publishing web pages full of hardcore pornographic photographs. The Court recognized the national state's broad margin of appreciation in choosing the measure to deal with issues of obscenity. The fact that the contested internet site was operated by a company based in the United States, and that disseminating the images was legal in other states, was found immaterial to the legitimacy of the British decision. The onus was shifted to the applicant to prove that an alternative measure that would be less injurious to his freedom of expression was '*more* effective'.[374] The burden imposed on the applicant was arguably greater than in *Handyside* and *Müller*. Nevertheless, it was critical in the *Perrin* case that, unlike in *Wingrove* (in the *Otto-Preminger-Institut* case), the applicant failed to impose an age limit and to block the impugned photographs on the free preview page.

In *Mouvement Raëlien Suisse v Switzerland*,[375] the Grand Chamber endorsed the Chamber's finding that the ban on displaying the applicant association's posters on public billboards did not breach Article 10 rights. The applicant, which was a non-profit-making association, planned to attract the public attention to its ideas with religious connotations, which included a message that it claimed to be transmitted by extra-terrestrials, with reference to its website address. The Grand Chamber considered that the nature of the expression rights in question was neither political nor commercial. Yet, in view of the proselytizing function, it considered the association's poster campaigns on public billboards akin to commercial speech. The Grand Chamber's methodology was to invoke such commercial nature of expression to justify 'broader' parameters of discretion of the local authorities in regulating the association's activities. In so doing, it felt able to

---

[370] Compare *Scherer* with *Hoare v UK No 31211/96* hudoc (1997) DA, where the Commission noted that despite the applicant's efforts to prevent the contested, pornographic video cassettes from accidentally falling into the hands of persons other than the purchasers, the cassettes, once distributed, could easily escape control.

[371] 1996-V; 24 EHRR 1 para 62. Contrast this with the Commission's Report of 10 January 1995, paras 65–9, where the Commission argued that any blasphemous effect of the video would be limited because it was a short experimental film destined for a smaller audience.   [372] *Wingrove v UK*, para 63.

[373] *No 5446/03* hudoc (2005) DA.   [374] *Perrin v UK* (emphasis added).   [375] Hudoc (2012).

deploy the bulk of the dictum developed in *Handyside*, and *Müller and Others*.[376] Relying on the notion of subsidiarity, the Grand Chamber ruled that different ways of responding to varying moral standards was recognizable in constituent parts of a federal state (so-called 'federal margin of appreciation'), as in Switzerland.[377] As regards proportionality, the availability of other means to propagate its ideas (use of website and distribution of leaflets)[378] exerted some influence on the conclusion.

On reflection, the Grand Chamber failed to ascertain the validity of the three main contested elements of the association: (i) promotion of human cloning; (ii) advocating 'geniocracy'; and (iii) the possibility that the applicant association's literature and ideas might lead some of its members to abuse children sexually. If proven true, no doubt, the third one would have been the most serious. Yet, the evidence shown by the national authorities was inconclusive. Some dissenting judges criticized the *ex post* justification of this rationale, noting that the original police ban did not include reference to the hyperlink whose content was deemed dangerous to minors. It was only two-and-a-half years after the original police ban that such a reference was invoked by a local court.[379] The controversial phrase 'privileged sexual object' in the applicant association's writing was considered to encourage paedophilia. However, there was little evidence that, statistically, the number of convictions among the applicant association's members was higher than in other denominations.[380]

This tightly voted conclusion (nine votes to eight) of the majority was criticized by dissenting judges for lack of rigour in examining the proportionality of the contested ban.[381] Several dissenting judges criticized it as contradictory that while a reference to the website on the posters was considered dangerous by enabling minors to have access to its website, that website was highlighted as an alternative means for exercising the applicant's expression right.[382] Furthermore, the majority's reasoning seemed to be predicated on the content not of the posters, but that of the association's website of the association, which was perceived as 'eccentric' to the general public. It may be seriously questioned whether the Grand Chamber's reasoning process was sound, as the impugned prohibition could be approximated to prior censorship.

V. PROTECTION OF REPUTATION AND HONOUR OF PRIVATE INDIVIDUALS

In a modern age of information, characterized by the paparazzi feeding the curiosity of the public about private lives of public figures, any sanction imposed on journalists for

---

[376] *Mouvement Raëlien Suisse v Switzerland*, paras 63–4 GC (holding that 'the national authorities are in principle, by reason of their direct and continuous contact with the vital forces of their countries, in a better position than the international judge to give an opinion on the "necessity"' of the interfering measures.

[377] *Mouvement Raëlien Suisse v Switzerland*, para 64.

[378] *Mouvement Raëlien Suisse v Switzerland*, para 75.

[379] *Mouvement Raëlien Suisse v Switzerland*, joint dissenting opinion of Judges Sajó, Lazarova Trajkovska, and Vučinić.

[380] *Mouvement Raëlien Suisse v Switzerland*, joint dissenting opinion of Judges Sajó, Lazarova Trajkovska, and Vučinić.

[381] See, *Mouvement Raëlien Suisse v Switzerland*, joint dissenting opinion of Judges Sajó, Lazarova Trajkovska, and Vučinić (criticizing reliance on what they call the 'mosaic theory', according to which some of the grounds invoked by the national authorities may not have been capable of justifying the impugned refusal, if taken separately, but may have been if taken as a whole).

[382] *Mouvement Raëlien Suisse v Switzerland*, joint dissenting opinion of Judges Tulkens, Sajö, Lazarova Trajkovska, Bianku, Power-Forde, Vučinić, and Yudkivska para 10.

intruding into privacy highlights an inevitable tension between the interest of journalists in imparting information to the public under Article 10 and the right of privacy under Article 8.[383]

Clearly, as compared with public figures, the permissible bounds of criticism of private persons are much narrower. Journalists must strictly adhere to their 'duties and responsibilities' and to professional ethics not to make disobliging references to the private life of individual persons.[384] Unless the protected reputation is essentially of the commercial interest of a corporation, which is devoid of moral dimension,[385] the presumption is that the reputation of private persons is prevalent. Publishing photographs and images containing intimate private aspects of individuals is a serious affront to their right to good reputation, honour,[386] and private and family life.[387] Even in relation to matters of special public concern, disclosing the identity of a child who is a victim of sexual abuse would overstep the boundaries of the ethics of journalism. In such a case, any *possible* public knowledge of the identity of the victim is immaterial, as compared with the identification of public figures or persons that have once entered the public sphere.[388]

Still, when confronted with a possible conflict between expression rights of private individuals other than journalists under Article 10 and the rights of privacy and honour under Article 8, the Court examines the sensitivities of the alleged victims of Article 8 rights in a specific context. This approach is followed even where a message contained in the expression may be of public interest. In *Peta Deutschland v Germany*,[389] an association for animal rights, which initiated an advertisement campaign comparing battery animal farming with extermination camp inmates with the head 'The Holocaust on your plate', was ordered to desist from the publication. Three senior figures of the German Central Jewish Council requested a civil injunction, contesting that this campaign, purported to shed light on animal suffering, was offensive in violation of the dignity and personal rights of one of their dead family victims. The reasoning of the German Federal Constitutional Court (*Bundesverfassungsgericht*) was less that this campaign violated the human dignity of either the depicted persons or the plaintiffs than the serious implication of trivializing the suffering of the Holocaust victims in breach of the plaintiffs' honour.[390] In this case, it can be argued that a major rationale for the margin of appreciation doctrine, if not the doctrine itself, operated, as the Court stressed the special sensitivity of the Jewish people living in Germany.[391]

When mediating the clash between the right of privacy under Article 8 and the expression rights of the press under Article 10, the Court has pointed out that the

---

[383] *Shabanov and Tren v Russia* hudoc (2006) para 46; and *Hachette Filipacchi Associés v France* hudoc (2007) para 43. [384] *Katamadze v Georgia No 69857/01* hudoc (2006) DA.

[385] See, eg, *UJ v Hungary* hudoc (2011) para 22. Note should also be taken of *Heinisch v Germany* hudoc (2011) para 90 (concerning the business reputation and interests of a limited liability company specializing in health care, geriatrics, and assistance to the elderly, as opposed to the expression right of a whistle-blower that criticized shortcomings in the provision of institutional care).

[386] Note that Article 17 of the ICCPR specifically recognizes the right to good reputation and honour.

[387] *Von Hannover v Germany* 2004-VI; 43 EHRR 1 para 59; and *Hachette Filipacchi Associés v France* hudoc (2007) para 42.

[388] *Kurier Zeitungsverlag und Druckerei Gmbh v Austria* hudoc (2012) para 52.

[389] Hudoc (2012).   [390] *Peta Deutschland v Germany*, para 48.

[391] The Court holds that: 'It observes that a reference to the Holocaust must also be seen in the specific context of the German past and respects the Government's stance that they deem themselves under a special obligation towards the Jews living in Germany ... the publication of the posters ... is not called into question by the fact that courts in other jurisdictions might address similar issues in a different way': *Peta Deutschland v Germany* para 49.

result of examinations should not vary, depending on whether the application has been brought under Article 10 or Article 8.[392] Whether this has been true in the Court's case law is, however, a matter of disagreement. According to the case law, the notion 'private life' under Article 8 is a wide concept encompassing the right to reputation of private citizens,[393] the persons' right to their image,[394] and any personal information that private individuals legitimately expect not to be disclosed without their consent.[395]

As regards the publication of articles or photos of private citizens, it must be examined whether they may, if at all, contribute to matters of general interest.[396] The celebrity of *private* persons claiming infringement of their privacy is a pertinent factor. Yet, the right of the public to be informed does not extend to detailed private aspects of non-public persons, however well-known they are.[397] Justifications for publishing private information or images may turn on the prior conduct of the persons challenging encroachment on their privacy, and on whether such information or image is published elsewhere.[398] Still, the fact that the persons concerned have cooperated with the press before is insufficient.[399] Moreover, it is crucial to appraise the method of obtaining the information and if its factual veracity is verified. Journalists must act in good faith and provide 'reliable and precise' information.[400] Clearly, the way in which reporting and photos are published is of special relevance.[401] In assessing the public impact of the publications, special regard should be had to the level of circulation and the number of readers.[402] Clearly, the nature and severity of the sanction imposed on journalists is germane to assessing proportionality of the restrictions.[403]

When the press and journalists bring their case before the Strasbourg Court after being condemned of defamation or intrusion into privacy rights, with the respondent government defending the decisions of the national courts which favoured rights of the private citizens concerned, this may give an impression that the press and journalists are victims of state interference. This may overlook the opposing rights of equal importance, which

---

[392] *Hachette Filipacchi Associés (ICI PARIS) v France* hudoc (2009) para 41; *Timciuc v Romania* hudoc (2010) para 144 DA; *Mosley v UK* hudoc (2011) para 111.

[393] *Chauvy and Others v France*, 2004-VI para 70; *Polanco Torres and Movilla Polanco v Spain* hudoc (2010) para 40; *Pfeifer v Bulgaria* hudoc (2011) para 35.

[394] *S and Marper v UK* 2008-; 48 EHRR 50 paras 66, 125-6 GC (finding of a violation of the Article 8 rights of the suspected, but not convicted, of offences in relation to the retention of fingerprints, cellular samples, and DNA profiles).

[395] *Flinkkilä and Others v Finland* hudoc (2010) para 75; *Saaristo and Others v Finland* hudoc (2010) para 61.

[396] *Von Hannover v Germany (No 2)* 2012- para 60 GC; *Leempoel & SA ED Ciné Revue v Belgium* hudoc (2006) para 68; and *Standard Verlags GmbH v Austria (No. 2)* hudoc (2009) para 46.

[397] *Von Hannover v Germany (No 2)* paras 63 and 65 GC (concerning Princess of Monaco); and *Standard Verlags GmbH v Austria (No 2)* hudoc (2009) paras 47 and 53; and *Axel Springer AG v Germany* hudoc (2012) para 91 GC.

[398] *Hachette Filipacchi Associés (ICI PARIS) v France* hudoc (2009) paras 52 and 53; and *Sapan v Turkey* hudoc (2010) para 34.   [399] *Egeland and Hanseid v Norway* hudoc (2009) para 62.

[400] *Fressoz and Roire v France*, 1999-I para 54 GC; *Pedersen and Baadsgaard v Denmark*, 2004-XI; 42 EHRR 486 para 78 GC; and *Stoll v Switzerland*, 2007-V; 44 EHRR 55 para 103 GC.

[401] *Wirtschafts-Trend Zeitschriften-Verlagsgesellschaft mbH v Austria (No 3)* hudoc (2005) para 47; *Reklos and Davourlis v Greece* hudoc (2009) para 42; *Jokitaipale and Others v Finland* hudoc (2010) para 68.

[402] *Karhuvaara and Iltalehti v Finland* 2004-X para 47; and *Gourguénidzé v Georgia* hudoc (2006) para 55.

[403] *Pedersen and Baadsgaard v Denmark*, 2004-XI para 93 GC; and *Jokitaipale and Others v Finland* hudoc (2010) para 77.

have been highlighted in domestic context (rights of privacy of private citizens).[404] This 'paradox' becomes salient in a serious case where the identity of a child or sex abuse is at stake.[405]

The Court's tendency to interpret the notion 'public interest' broadly has reinforced the press freedom under Article 10.[406] The nature of professional activity of private persons may be deemed of such a kind as to justify bringing them closer to the public figures that must assume greater bounds of acceptable criticism.[407] Such a method is an ingenious attempt to set the proper balance between the two countervailing rights under Articles 8 and 10. One implication of this method is that journalists may also be bound to tolerate greater criticisms. Still, when a journalist is the target of virulent criticism made by another journalist, the latter must at least establish that this is not a gratuitous personal attack, but that it entails a matter of public interest.[408]

There is no European consensus on appropriate responses to libellous opinions directed against private individuals.[409] Nevertheless, this does not handicap the Court's 'autonomous' decision-making policy in giving weight to press freedom.[410] The relevant factors include the amount of compensation or damages for libel or defamation, and the availability of 'adequate and effective safeguards' against an exorbitant award.[411] If a contested newspaper article does not relate to any matter of public interest, journalists have to establish that such information is not, by virtue of its nature and purpose, liable to constitute gratuitous personal attacks.

The media's intrusion into the privacy of individual persons who are international celebrities highlights the difficulty of adjusting the permissible bounds of expression rights exercised by the press, whose crude commercialism feeds the base curiosity of the public. On this matter again, the Court may recapitulate the general observation that neither Article 10 nor Article 8 enjoys a pre-eminence over the other.[412] On closer inspection, the Court's approach indicates a finessed method.

In *MGN Ltd v UK*, the company of a tabloid paper was found to have breached the common law tort of breach of confidentiality after having published articles about the drug addiction of a supermodel, Naomi Campbell. The photographs were also taken with a long-range lens outside her place of treatment for drug addiction. When weighing the balance between press freedom and the right to reputation of the supermodel, the Court took account of the duty of the press to act in good faith, and to provide 'reliable and precise' information consonant with the ethics of journalism.[413] In so doing, the Court displayed an approach more circumspect as to press freedom of the tabloid than in relation

---

[404] This is what some scholars call 'preferential framing'. According to Smet, before the Strasbourg Court, only the right invoked by the applicant comes to be highlighted, leaving 'the domestic defendant whose human rights are also at stake...to the background': Smet, 26 Am U Int'l L Rev 183, at 185 (2010).

[405] See, eg, *Kurier Zeitungsverlag und Druckerei Gmbh v Austria* hudoc (2012) para 52.

[406] See, eg, *Björk Eidósdóttir v Iceland* hudoc (2012) para 68.

[407] *Björk Eidósdóttir v Iceland*, para 68 (owner of a strip bar who was criticized for having tolerated prostitution and human trafficking of his employees).

[408] *Katamadze v Georgia No 69857/01* hudoc (2006) DA.

[409] *Tolstoy Miloslavsky v UK* A 316-B (1995); 2 EHRR 442 para 48.

[410] *Bergens Tidende v Norway* 2000-IV; 31 EHRR 430 para 52; and *Marônek v Slovakia* 2001-III paras 56–60.   [411] *Tolstoy Miloslavsky v UK* A 316-B (1995); 2 EHRR 442 para 50.

[412] *MGN Ltd v UK* hudoc (2011) para 145, referring to Resolution 1165/98 'Right to Privacy' of the Parliamentary Assembly of the Council of Europe; and *A v B plc* [2003] QB 195.

[413] *MGN Ltd v UK* hudoc (2011) para 141. See also *Pedersen and Baadsgaard v Denmark* 2004-XI para 78 GC.

to such freedom exercised by 'more respectable' newspapers. On this matter, the Court observed that 'the publication of the photographs and articles, the sole purpose of which is to satisfy the curiosity of a particular readership concerning the details of a public figure's private life, cannot be deemed to contribute to any debate of general interest to society despite the person being known to the public',[414] the dictum that can provide useful guideline for similar cases in the future. By way of this, the narrow interpretation of the scope of protection of expression rights was justified.[415] The intrusive nature of privacy rights was invoked as a factor tipping the balance. The Court noted that '[p]hotographs appearing in the tabloid press are often taken in a climate of continual harassment which induces in the person concerned a very strong sense of intrusion into their private life or even of persecution'.[416] Naomi Campbell herself accepted before the national courts that the information that, though having previously denied drug use, she was in therapeutic treatment with narcotic addiction, was tantamount to a matter of public interest. Yet, the public interest nature of the subject was not considered sufficient to warrant its disclosure in a mass-circulating tabloid. In the impugned reports, the aspects of the private information of the celebrity that she herself allowed to be made public had to be distinguished from the other elements of information that she kept confidential.[417] The Court endorsed the decision of the House of Lords, according to which the additional information disclosed concerned the supermodel's highly private aspects. Publishing such extra material was judged to be harmful to her therapeutic treatment. In this context, the application of the public figures doctrine (which will be discussed later) was rejected. The photographs in question were found distressing for a person of ordinary sensitivity,[418] and this favoured Ms Campbell's privacy rights. Finally, in the Court's view, since the public were already informed of the core facts of her drug addiction and treatment,[419] there was no compelling reason to publish the additional materials to satisfy its curiosity. Accordingly, there was no violation of Article 10 in respect of the British courts' finding of a breach of confidence against the applicant company.

In contrast, as regards the second issue raised by the applicant under Article 10, the success fees recoverable from an unsuccessful defendant, the Court came to the opposite conclusion. It accepted that these fees were in line with the protection of the rights of others, as being purported to secure the widest public access to legal services for civil litigations with funding from the private sector.[420] Nevertheless, it was quick to add that the flaws of this scheme, including its 'chilling effect' or 'ransom effect', were even recognized in the public consultation process and by the Ministry of Justice. Because of this, even having regard to a national margin of appreciation in assessing social and economic policy issues, the Court considered the imposition of the recoverable success fees to be disproportionate.[421]

In *Axel Springer AG v Germany*,[422] the court order forbad a publishing company of a mass-circulating tabloid from publishing the articles (and the photos) concerning the drug offence committed by one of the most popular television actors in Germany with a view to protecting his personality rights. The Court considered that the actor in issue was

---

[414] *MGN Ltd v UK* hudoc (2011) para 143.

[415] *Campmany y Diez de Revenga and Lopez Galiacho Perona v Spain*, No. 54224/00, ECHR 2000-XII DA; *Julio Bou Gibert and El Hogar Y La Moda J.A. v Spain* No 14929/02 hudoc (2003) DA; *Prisma Presse v France*, Nos 66910/01 and 71612/01 hudoc (2003) DA; and *Von Hannover v Germany*, 2004-V; 40 EHRR 1 paras 65–6.

[416] *Von Hannover v Germany* 2004-V; 40 EHRR 1 para 59; and *Hachette Filipacchi Associés v France* hudoc (2009) para 42. [417] *MGN Ltd v UK* hudoc (2011) para 147.

[418] *MGN Ltd v UK*, para 151. [419] *MGN Ltd v UK*, para 151. [420] *MGN Ltd v UK*, para 197.

[421] *MGN Ltd v UK*, paras 207, 217–19. [422] Hudoc (2012).

so widely known in the public that he was comparable to a public figure, strengthening the right of the public to be informed of the criminal proceedings against him.[423] The actor himself revealed details of his private life in several interviews. This provided the basis for reducing his 'legitimate expectation' of having his privacy rights effectively protected.[424] The applicant company, having obtained the contested information from the prosecuting authorities, believed that in view of the nature of the offence committed by the actor, his fame, and of the veracity of the information, there was no sufficient ground to preserve his anonymity. By the time the second article was published, the actor's conviction was already known to the public. In view of these, the Court found that the applicant company did not act in bad faith.[425] The articles in question did not contain any detail about the actor's private life, reporting only the arrest, criminal proceedings, and legal assessment of the offence. There was no disparaging expression or unsubstantiated allegation either.[426] These sanctions, though lenient, were considered to yield a chilling effect on the applicant company.[427]

Three cases relating to defamation against medical practitioners are worthy of detailed examinations for the purpose of assessing the Court's approach of balancing two countervailing rights (right of reputation of doctors and the press freedom engaged in reporting medical negligence). Investigative journalism which would intrude into the privacy and reputation of private citizens is set against the form of collegiality of elite members to defend their members. The Court's general principle is that given the paramount significance of the press freedom, journalists are allowed to rely on a certain degree of exaggeration or even provocation.[428] Journalists' assertiveness is salutary when the topics address matters of public interest such as health care and patient safety.[429] There is, however, a need to take into account the 'duties and responsibilities' of the journalists in verifying the accuracy and reliability of the information they report.[430]

In *Bergens Tidende and Others v Norway*,[431] a daily newspaper company and its journalists were found to have defamed a breast cosmetic surgeon and ordered to pay damages and costs to him. In several articles, the applicants reported accounts of dissatisfaction by many former patients with his post-surgical treatment and care after unsuccessful operations, stating that those women were 'disfigured' and 'ruined for life'. Among some 8,000 former patients, seventeen of them (with five later withdrawing) lodged an administrative complaint against the surgeon, but the Health Directorate found that he did not perform any improper surgery. The repercussions of the repeated articles was such that the surgeon lost patients and was forced to close down his clinic. The Court recognized that the grievances raised by several former patients were matters of general public interest.[432] Even the municipal courts found the allegations made by many women credible, and the contested information essentially accurate. As regards the question whether the ordinary readers of the newspaper would have interpreted the contested words 'disfigured' and 'ruined for life', as casting doubt on the plastic surgeon's surgical skills or post-surgery care, the Norwegian courts were divided. In contrast to the High Court, the Supreme Court held that the accusations undermined the plastic surgeon's competence, with the insinuation that he carried out his operation recklessly. Nevertheless, the Court objected

---

[423] *Axel Springer AG v Germany*, para 99 GC.
[424] *Axel Springer AG v Germany*, para 101.   [425] *Axel Springer AG v Germany*, para 107.
[426] *Axel Springer AG v Germany*, para 108.   [427] *Axel Springer AG v Germany*, para 109.
[428] *Prager and Oberschlick v Austria* A 313 (1995) para 38; *Bladet Tromsø and Stensaas* 1999-III (1999) para 59 GC.   [429] See, eg, *Selistö v Finland* hudoc (2004) para 51.
[430] *Fressoz and Roire v France* 1999-I para 54 GC.   [431] 2000-IV.
[432] *Bergens Tidende and Others v Norway* para 51.

that the Supreme Court's finding was based only on the inference from the general tenor of the articles,[433] and that the damage on the surgeon's professional reputation should have been seen 'inevitable'. Some 'justified criticisms' of his post-surgical care were invoked to support this conclusion.[434] For the Court, it was crucial that the newspaper gave the surgeon the opportunity of defence, and reported accounts of another plastic surgeon explaining the possibility of complications in breast operations and stories of other former patients that defended the surgeon.[435] Accordingly, no sufficient reason was found to override the press freedom. It should be noted that the national courts took some patients' criticisms as a ground for reducing the award for the defamation only to a third of damages. Moreover, the Court failed to analyse whether the contested expression was a statement of fact or value-judgment, even though the respondent government considered these as factual allegations, which remained unsubstantiated.[436] It is possible that the Court presumed these words to be value-judgments, as it noted that the contested expression reflected the women's emotional outcry.[437]

The case of *Kanellopoulou v Greece*[438] was another medical negligence case concerning a mastoplasty. Immediately after the operation at a cosmetic surgery's clinic, the applicant felt strong pain, with her breasts swollen. It turned out that the surgery was carried out despite the evidence of cancerous cells. The applicant had to undergo mastectomies and two further operations. She instituted a civil proceeding to obtain damages against the cosmetic surgeon. This was, however, followed by a counter-proceeding filed by that surgeon for the moral damage caused by the applicant's lawsuit. The tabloid, known for sensational articles, interviewed the applicant and published an article in which she reportedly noted, among others, that this surgeon slaughtered her like sheep. This time, a defamation proceeding ensued, and the applicant was convicted and sentenced to imprisonment with a reprieve. The Court held that even though the reputation of the surgeon might have been damaged by the contested article (unlike in *Bergens Tidende*, no evidence for this was adduced), this was because of his negligence. The legitimate aim of safeguarding his professional reputation was found insufficient to justify imposing such an onerous penalty as imprisonment.[439] This was especially the case, as the expression was understood as an emotional reaction.[440]

In *Selistö v Finland*,[441] a journalist of a daily newspaper published an article describing the allegedly unprofessional behaviour of an anonymous surgeon in an operation at a public hospital. The operation was purported to shorten the top rib that pressed on a patient's artery. Complications arose with the bursting of her subclavian vein, which resulted in her death. The widower of the patient filed a criminal complaint against the surgeon. The National Medico-Legal Board did not find it established that there was a causal link between her death and the surgeon's conduct. Nor did the regional prosecutor find the evidence that the surgeon was guilty of negligence or involuntary manslaughter. In her several articles, the applicant asserted that this surgeon conducted surgery 'with alcohol in his blood', and that he had alcohol-related problems, with a 'viable hangover'. The national court convicted the applicant of the offence of defamation. The Court found

---

[433] *Bergens Tidende and Others v Norway*, para 56.
[434] *Bergens Tidende and Others v Norway*, para 59.
[435] *Bergens Tidende and Others v Norway*, paras 15–16, 57–8.
[436] *Bergens Tidende and Others v Norway*, para 41.
[437] *Bergens Tidende and Others v Norway*, para 56.   [438] Hudoc (2007).
[439] *Kanellopoulou v Greece*, para 38. On this matter, see also *Ricci v Italy* hudoc (2013) para 59.
[440] *Kanellopoulou v Greece*, para 38. The Court rightly noted that the surgeon should have been satisfied with the civil proceeding only: para 38.   [441] Hudoc (2004).

that the impugned articles gave the impression that the surgeon operated on the patient while suffering from a hangover. The articles gave sufficient information to identify the unnamed surgeon.[442] There was consensus that the articles concerned factual statements and not value-judgments, so that the duties and responsibilities of journalists became of greater weight. The national courts did not contest the accuracy. Yet, they questioned the selective nature of the information conveyed: the omission to refer to some key facts (the public prosecutor's decision not to go ahead with charges; and the statement of the National Medico-Legal Board), and the tenor of the articles. The applicant was held by the national courts to have neglected her duty as a journalist when publishing further articles despite the decisions not to press charges against the surgeon.[443] Obviously, 'methods of objective and balanced reporting' vary, and the press should be allowed to choose the most appropriate techniques of reporting. The first article, which questioned 'how is it possible that a surgeon is allowed to conduct surgery with alcohol in his blood', use the expression of the widower of the deceased patient. This was found neither excessive nor misleading.[444] Of special import to the Court's reasoning was that the reported events drew on the police's pre-trial record, a public document. According to the established case law, no general duty is imposed on journalists to verify the veracity of public information.[445] In the Court's view, what may have been considered as the 'one-sided' nature of this pre-trial record (based only on a statement of one nurse present at the operation, but no quotations from other persons) was not important. The essence was that the reporting was predicated on information contained in an official document.[446] Some seven years after the prosecutor's decision not to press charges, and nine years after the death of the patient, the Deputy Parliamentary Ombudsman decided that it was preferable to have a court ruling, even though she refrained from bringing an action. The Court held that the expression rights outweighed the surgeon's right to professional reputation under Article 8, on the grounds that the applicant verified the contents of the articles, which were not essentially erroneous,[447] and that the information on patient safety was of serious public interest.[448] The Court found that the surgeon was given the chance to provide his comments *after* the publication of each of the contested articles, though not in advance.[449] However, in so deciding, the Court did not give due consideration to the surgeon's concern that his identity might have been disclosed if he published his rejoinder in the newspaper.[450] Further, the limited nature of the fine imposed on the applicant was dismissed as irrelevant.[451]

Sir Nicolas Bratza appended his dissenting opinion, highlighting that '[t]he more serious and damaging the allegation made, the stronger the obligation to confirm the truth of the information on which the allegation is based'.[452] As he noted, even though the national courts found the contents of the articles not erroneous, they found no reliable evidence to substantiate the allegation that the surgeon carried out the operation while under the influence of alcohol. In his view, the applicant selected from the police's pre-trial records those elements that supported her thesis, omitting to mention the waiver

---

[442] *Selistö v Finland*, para 57.   [443] *Selistö v Finland*, paras 55 and 57.
[444] *Selistö v Finland*, para 59.   [445] *Selistö v Finland*, para 60.
[446] *Selistö v Finland*, para 61.   [447] *Selistö v Finland*, paras 62–3.
[448] *Selistö v Finland*, para 63.   [449] *Selistö v Finland*, para 66.
[450] The Court was adamant that 'this circumstance in itself…cannot prevent the publication of matters of public interest, subject to the proviso that in the reporting of issues of general interest journalists act in good faith in order to provide accurate and reliable information in accordance with the ethics of journalism': *Selistö v Finland*, para 67.   [451] *Selistö v Finland*, para 70.
[452] *Selistö v Finland*, dissenting opinion of Sir Nicolas Bratza.

of charges against the surgeon. Judge Bratza distinguished the present case from the *Bergens Tidende* case, on the ground that in that case, the surgeon was approached by the newspaper prior to publishing the articles, with his comments invited on the interviews. In contrast, in *Selistö*, the surgeon was given an occasion to provide comments or to have a rejoinder published only after the appearance of the articles, namely, after the damage was already inflicted.

VI. PROTECTION OF THE PRIVACY, REPUTATION, AND HONOUR OF PUBLIC FIGURES

The phrase 'the protection of...rights of others' under Article 10(2) has been frequently invoked to ascertain the extent to which the privacy or reputation and honour of public figures can be guaranteed. As regards the protection of honour, the Court's approach is that giving heads of state (including monarchs) a robust shield from criticisms merely on the basis of their function or (hereditary) status is irreconcilable with the modern democratic ethos underlying the Convention's order.[453]

With respect to privacy, the Court has recognized that the public has the right to be informed even of private aspects of public figures.[454] Yet the condition under which public persons' privacy can be considered sufficiently related to their public function to justify their disclosure must be assessed in the specific context of the cases.[455] What must be taken into account is not limited to the well-established principles, such as the doctrine of chilling effect (which requires that a measure must not cause any deterrent effect on exercising expression rights) and the public figures doctrine (whereby the public figures in general must accept wider bounds of criticism against them). The Court's penchant for close review is discernible where criminal proceedings are imposed irrespective of the accuracy and subject matter of the divulged information.[456] The Court has highlighted the following specific factors: (i) impact of publication; (ii) public knowledge of the information or photograph, in case this has already been uncovered by other means;[457] and (iii) the degree of injuries to the personal feelings of (families of) individuals concerned.

According to the Court, 'the protection of the reputation...of others' within the meaning of Article 10(2) extends even to politicians who are *not* acting in their private capacity.[458] Such protection remains even where a politician is criticized by another in the 'privileged arena of Parliament'.[459] A politician who has levelled a defamatory or insulting criticism against a political opponent in a parliamentary debate is not exempted from proving the factual basis for the criticism, especially if this is classified as a serious allegation of fact. In *Keller v Hungary*,[460] a member of a parliament suggested at a parliamentary session that a cabinet minister had failed to investigate the practices of extreme right-wing

---

[453] *Otegi Mondragon v Spain* hudoc (2011) para 55. See also *Colombani and Others v France*, para 69.

[454] *Karhuvaara and Iltalehti v Finland* 2004-X; 41 EHRR 1154 para 45.

[455] *Von Hannover v Germany* 2004-VI; 43 EHRR 1; and *Hachette Filipacchi Associés v France* hudoc (2007). See also *Schüssel v Austria No 42409/98* hudoc (2002) DA.

[456] *Wizerkaniuk v Poland* hudoc (2011), paras 81-87 (criticizing the 'carte blanche' nature of the relevant provisions that debarred a journalist from publishing any interview that interviewees considered embarrassing).

[457] See, eg, *Karhuvaara and Iltalehti v Finland* 2004-X; 41 EHRR 1154 para 47; and *Édition Plon v France* 2004-IV; 42 EHRR 705 para 53.

[458] *Lingens v Austria* A 103 (1986); 8 EHRR 407 para 42 PC; and *Keller v Hungary No 33352/02* hudoc (2006) DA.   [459] *Keller v Hungary No 33352/02* hudoc (2006) DA.

[460] *No 33352/02* hudoc (2006) DA.

groups because the latter's father participated in the pro-Nazi *Hungarista* movement. The domestic courts ordered him to arrange a rectification in the press and pay damages for the infringement of the personality of the minister. According to the Court, the accusation that the cabinet minister deliberately neglected his ministerial duty for personal reasons was a serious allegation of fact, but this remained unproven.

In a Slovakian case, the Court did not baulk at challenging the national courts' finding that the recorded telephone conversations between high ranking governmental officials were private in nature.[461] The contested information was obtained illegally by a third person. Yet, this did not diminish the importance of the media in transmitting such information. The rights of journalists or the media was sustained by the finding that they were not responsible for illegally procuring the information, that no untrue or distorted information was made public, nor did they act in bad faith for any extraneous purpose.[462]

It is clear that once civil servants have resigned their post, they must be protected from the intrusive media coverage of their private life. In *Tammer v Estonia*,[463] a journalist made insulting remarks about the wife of a senior politician in a newspaper interview, referring to her role in destroying an earlier marriage of that politician and her act of deserting her child. By the time the interview was published, the woman in question had resigned from her post as a government official. Despite the fact that she was a public figure until six months before, and that she intended to publish her memoirs, the Court emphasized that, at the material time, she was a private person whose rights under Article 8 had to be specially protected, and that the offensive terms were not warranted by any public interest.

Two French cases deserve special analysis in highlighting the difficulty in striking a balance between the press rights and the privacy rights of public figures. In *Hachette Filipacchi Associés v France*,[464] *Paris-Match*, a popular magazine, published a photograph of the blood-covered and mutilated body of a prefect of Corsica. National courts ordered the publication of a notice acknowledging that the photograph was published without the consent of the prefect's bereaved family. The photograph appeared only ten days after the funeral of the prefect, and his family was expressly opposed to its publication. The publication of the photograph was considered to aggravate the trauma suffered by the family, and the Court found no violation of Article 10.[465] Judge Loucaides,[466] in his dissenting opinion, stressed that in view of the special importance of press freedom, an 'objective' appraisal had to be given to the *specific* circumstances of the case, rather than following a general approach favouring privacy rights. In his opinion, the photograph invited the public to show a sense of horror of the crime, and sympathy for the family. Further, the image of the assassinated body had already been broadcast on a television channel.

In *Éditions Plon v France*,[467] the applicant company published a book entitled *Le Grand Secret*, which described the secret medical history of the former French President Mitterrand. The book explained how the late President, who was diagnosed with cancer soon after his election in 1981, underwent his medical treatment while maintaining the confidentiality of this information. Upon Mitterrand's family complaining of a breach of medical confidentiality, damage to the late President's privacy, and of the injury to his

---

[461] *RADIO TWIST AS v Slovakia* hudoc (2006) para 58.

[462] *RADIO TWIST AS v Slovakia*, paras 60–63.   [463] 2001-I; 37 EHRR 857 paras 66–8.

[464] Hudoc (2007) paras 46–9.   [465] *Hachette Filipacchi Associés v France*, para 62.

[466] *Hachette Filipacchi Associés v France*, dissenting opinion of Judge Loucaides.

[467] 2004-IV; 42 EHRR 705 para 47. See also *Gubler v France* hudoc (2006) (no violation of Article 6(1) in response to the complaint, raised by the physician at issue, that the *conseil national de l'Ordre des médecins* lacked independence and impartiality).

family's feelings, an injunction was issued, preventing the distribution of the book and ordering the applicant to pay damages. The Court distinguished the interim injunction banning the distribution of the contested book, and the subsequent decision to maintain the ban on distributing the book. The interim injunction was upheld because of the timing of the publication and of the temporary nature of the injunction. The book was published barely ten days after Mitterrand's death, and this was considered to intensify the grief of his heirs while inflicting serious damage on his reputation. In contrast, no pressing social need was found for the continued ban on distribution. Unlike the interim measure issued only a day after the book's publication, the decision to maintain the injunction was made more than nine months afterwards. With the President's death becoming more distant in time, the interest of the deceased's family was considered of less consequence in contrast to the public interest in knowing the history of the President.

The judgment in *Éditions Plon* confirmed another established principle, according to which once confidentiality is breached, the need for maintaining a general ban becomes moot. In *Dupuis and Others*,[468] another case involving the former socialist President Mitterrand, the Court was asked to examine the offence of handling information obtained by breaching the secrecy of the criminal investigation or professional confidence. The first two applicants, who were journalists, published the information on criminal investigations into the illegal surveillance of journalists and lawyers, which was undertaken by the deputy director of Mitterrand's private office. That such information was partly disclosed to the public cast doubt on the need to maintain the ban on revealing the impugned information.[469]

In case a clash arises between the reputation of the press and the free speech right of a member of a small opposition political party, the general approach of according primacy to press freedom may be reset, with due regard to the context of the impugned statement and the power of the media. In *Andreas Wabl v Austria*, a member of the Green Party, who participated in a protest campaign against the stationing of interceptor fighter planes, got involved in an altercation with a member of the police during which scratches were made against him. The largest daily newspaper in Austria reported that this police officer was worried about infection with HIV positive as a result of this incident, and called on the applicant to take the AIDS test. The national court convicted the newspaper company of defamation. However, the court issued an injunction against the applicant preventing him from reproaching the company with the statement 'This is Nazi-journalism', which he made in an interview as a reaction against the media's sensational coverage. Finding no violation of Article 10, the Court endorsed the domestic courts' finding that the reproach of Nazi working methods was a serious allegation akin to a charge of criminal behaviour.[470] The controversial wording was uttered not in an immediate reaction, but a few days after a rectification appeared in that paper.[471] In the past, associating political opponents with an infectious disease was used by the Nazis to provoke fear against them. Still, it may be argued that this was an emotional reaction, which was a value-judgment, as found by the Supreme Court.[472] Yet, the Court failed to address this matter. One may wonder if the approach of the national courts was too formalistic. It may be suggested that accusing a powerful paper of the Nazi method was responded to by disproportionate

---

[468] Hudoc (2007).
[469] *Dupuis and Others v France*, para 45. See also *Mor v France* hudoc (2011), paras 61–3 (finding it disproportionate to condemn, even symbolically, a lawyer for having disclosed professional secret in the civil proceeding in which she was involved, and which concerned involuntary homicide of a child caused by vaccination against hepatitis B). [470] *Andreas Wabl v Austria* hudoc (2000) paras 40–1.
[471] *Andreas Wabl v Austria*, paras 42–3. [472] *Andreas Wabl v Austria*, para 37.

means (judicial injunction)[473] even in the country which has provided a fertile ground for far-right politicians. In his dissent, referring to the need to fight against a recurrence of Nazism, Judge Grevel noted that '[a] democratic political debate requires that where a politician is attacked, not for his political views but on a purely personal level, he should not be in a more disadvantageous position than the press, and that he should be allowed sufficient latitude to reply to press attacks'.[474]

VII. PROTECTION OF THE FREEDOM OF RELIGION OF OTHERS

The clash between free speech rights and the freedom of religion under Article 9 is another area where the phrase 'the protection of ... rights of others' has become the subject of disputes. Intimate religious beliefs and convictions of persons, which are specially guaranteed under Article 9, may be offended by a blasphemous expression in regard to objects of veneration. The notion 'duties and responsibilities' of those who exercise freedom of expression within the meaning of Article 10(2) encompasses 'a duty to avoid expressions that are gratuitously offensive to others and profane',[475] and 'which therefore do not contribute to any form of public debate capable of furthering progress in human affairs'.[476] As a corollary, the state authorities may punish improper attacks on objectives of religious veneration, or repress some form of expression, such as the imparting of information and ideas, which are incompatible with the rights guaranteed under Article 9.[477] The absence of European consensus on what is required for the protection of religious convictions may justify a broad margin of appreciation.[478] Yet it must always be remembered that it is for the Strasbourg Court to take the final decision.[479]

A survey of the case law reveals a clear evolution from the past jurisprudence, which was characterized by the timid stance,[480] to an assertive review. The Court has come to display readiness to analyse the allegedly offensive nature of the contested statements in the light of more 'objective' public sentiments, rather than the subjective feelings of specific individuals.

In *Otto-Preminger-Institut*,[481] the majority of the Court followed the reasoning in *Müller*, discussed earlier. It recognized the Austrian decisions to seize and order the forfeiture of a film as necessary for protecting the rights of others, especially adherents of Catholicism. The Court went so far as to state that the need to give due consideration to

---

[473] Compare *Sanocki v Poland* hudoc (2007) para 67 (a right-wing mayor convicted of having infringed the reputation of the editor of the local daily newspaper, after he published an article in a weekly paper, in response to the daily's allegation of his mishandling, and criticized the daily for using 'the Bolschevik's traditional method of denunciation associated with lies').

[474] *Andreas Wabl v Austria* hudoc (2000), dissenting opinion of Judge Greve.

[475] *Otto-Preminger-Institut v Austria* A 295-A (1994); 19 EHRR 34 para 49; *İA v Turkey* 2005-VIII; 45 EHRR 703 para 24; and *Wojtas-Kaleta v Poland* hudoc (2009) para 51.

[476] See, eg, *Gündüz v Turkey* 2003-XI; 41 EHRR 59 para 37; *Giniewski v France* 2006-I; 45 EHRR 589 para 43.   [477] *Otto-Preminger-Institut v Austria* A 295-A (1994); 19 EHRR 34 para 47.

[478] *Otto-Preminger-Institut v Austria*, para 50; *İA v Turkey* 2005-VIII; 45 EHRR 703 para 25.

[479] *Giniewski v France* 2006-I; 45 EHRR 589 para 44.

[480] See, *inter alia*, *Otto-Preminger-Institut v Austria* A 295-A (1994); 19 EHRR 34; *Wingrove v UK* 1996-V; 24 EHRR 1 and *Geerk v Switzerland No 7640/76*, 12 DR 103 (1978) (and 16 DR 56 (1979) F Sett); and *Gay News Ltd and Lemon v UK No 8710/79*, 28 DR 77 (1982); 5 EHRR 123 para 12. See, however, the Commission's finding of a violation of Article 10: *Otto-Preminger-Institute v Austria*, paras 75–8 Com Rep (nine votes to five as to the seizure of the film and thirteen votes to one with respect to the forfeiture of the film); and *Wingrove v UK*, paras 65–9 Com Rep (fourteen votes to two).

[481] A 295-A (1994); 19 EHRR 34 paras 56–7.

religious sensitivities constitutes a more potent ground than the protection of public morals. In *Wingrove v UK*,[482] the absence of European consensus on appropriate measures to balance the freedom of expression and the rights of third persons to religious faith was decisive for widening the ambit of margin of appreciation:

> as in the field of morals, and perhaps to an even greater degree, there is no uniform European conception of the requirements of 'the protection of the rights of others' in relation to attacks on their religious convictions. What is likely to cause substantial offence to persons of a particular religious persuasion will vary significantly from time to time and from place to place, especially in an era characterised by an ever growing array of faiths and denominations. By reason of their direct and continuous contact with the vital forces of their countries, State authorities are in principle in a better position than the international judge to give an opinion on the exact content of these requirements with regard to the rights of others as well as on the 'necessity' of a 'restriction' intended to protect from such material those whose deepest feelings and convictions would be seriously offended.[483]

In contrast, the Court's inclination for an exacting appraisal of national decisions is discernible by its emphasis on the principle of pluralism, tolerance, and open-mindedness. It has required persons exercising the right to manifest religion to tolerate and accept not only the rejection of their religious faith by others, but even the propagation of doctrines hostile to their own.[484] For fear of downgrading the standard of protection of free speech, the emphasis has now shifted from subjective feelings of pious followers of specific religious faith to a more 'objective' evaluation of the public sentiments, the approach that favours anti-conformist choice of individual persons.[485] A contrast should be made between *İA v Turkey*,[486] on the one hand, and *Giniewski v France* and *Klein v Slovakia* on the other. In *İA*, a philosophical novel contained the following controversial passage: 'God's messenger broke his fast through sexual intercourse, after dinner and before prayer. Muhammad did not forbid sexual intercourse with a dead person or a live animal.' The Istanbul public prosecutor lodged criminal proceedings against the applicant *proprio motu* on the basis of blasphemy against 'God, the Religion, the Prophet and the Holy Book' under the Turkish Criminal Code. The Court recognized that the above passage was an abusive attack on the Holy Prophet, and that this was so even in a secular society like Turkey, where there was 'a certain tolerance of criticism' of religious doctrine. The majority, by a close vote, endorsed the conviction of the applicant. The three dissenting judges, however, forcefully defended what they regarded as 'anti-conformist' perspectives. They considered that the book revealed the author's scepticism of any religious beliefs or atheism. They observed that Turkey was 'a highly religious society' with 'relatively few' atheists, and that materialist or atheist views were liable to shock the religious faith of the majority of the population. Even so, according to them, this did not provide 'sufficient' reasons for the criminal sanction.[487] The minority judges also stressed

---

[482] 1996-V; 24 EHRR 1 para 58.

[483] *Wingrove v UK*, para 58. See also *Murphy v Ireland* 2003-IX; 38 EHRR 212 para 67.

[484] *İA v Turkey* 2005-VIII; 45 EHRR 703 para 28; *Aydin Tatlav v Turkey* hudoc (2006) para 27. See also *Otto-Preminger-Institute v Austria* A 295-A (1994); 19 EHRR 34 para 47.

[485] *Aydin Tatlav v Turkey* hudoc (2006) paras 28 and 30; and *Klein v Slovakia* hudoc (2006) paras 51–2.

[486] 2005-VIII; 45 EHRR 703 paras 29–30.

[487] *İA v Turkey*, joint dissenting opinion of Judges Costa, Cabral Barreto, and Jungwiert, para 3.

the limited publicity impact, given that the book was never reprinted. While the penalty was relatively light, with the two-year prison sentence commuted to a modest fine, the dissenting judges underscored that any criminal sanction entailed 'a chilling effect', and that 'a risk of self-censorship' was perilous for free speech in democracy.[488] They specifically pleaded the need to depart from what they saw as a 'conformist' rationale behind the Court's application of the margin of appreciation.[489]

In contrast, the Court took a more audacious approach to favour expression rights in *Giniewski*.[490] There, a journalist published an article in a Parisian newspaper, accusing the papal encyclical 'The Splendour of Truth' ('Veritatis Splendor') of enshrining a theological doctrine of the 'fulfilment' of the Old Covenant in the New, which in his view led to anti-Semitism and ushered the way for Auschwitz. Following the proceedings launched by the General Alliance against Racism and for Respect for the French and Christian Identity, he was convicted of defamation. In the Court's opinion, the article was of the kind that could contribute to a wide-ranging debate as to the causes of the Holocaust, and this, in the light of the tenor of the article, 'without sparking off any controversy that was gratuitous or detached from the reality of contemporary thought'.[491] The article was not considered to incite to disrespect or hatred, or to 'cast doubt in any way on clearly established historical facts'.[492] In view of this, the Court unanimously found that the reasons for convicting the journalist of public defamation were insufficient.[493]

In *Klein v Slovakia*,[494] posters promoting a film 'The People vs. Larry Flynt' showed the main character 'crucified on a woman's pubic area dressed in a bikini'. The Archbishop of the Catholic Church in Slovakia considered the posters defamatory of the symbol of Christianity, calling for the withdrawal of the posters and the film. The applicant, a journalist, published an article in an intellectual weekly, sharply criticizing the moral integrity of the Archbishop, using slang and innuendo with sexual connotations, and calling him an 'ogre'. At the request of two religious associations, the applicant was convicted of defaming another person's belief. With regard to the contents of the controversial article, the Court did not consider that the applicant disparaged Catholics. It stressed the more objective test of assessing the allegedly offensive nature of expression:

> The fact that some members of the Catholic Church could have been offended by the applicant's criticism of the Archbishop and by his statement...cannot affect the position. The Court accepts the applicant's argument that the article neither unduly interfered with the right of believers to express and exercise their religion, nor did it denigrate the content of their religious faith.

The Court held that imposing the criminal offence of defaming another person's belief was misplaced, as the applicant's criticism was levelled exclusively at the person of the Archbishop.

---

[488] *İA v Turkey*, para 6.   [489] *İA v Turkey*, para 8.   [490] 2006-I; 45 EHRR 589 para 51.

[491] *Giniewski*, paras 50. On matters of historical controversy, it added that it is not supposed to 'arbitrate' the underlying historical issues: para 51. Compare *Chauvy v France* 2004-VI; 41 EHRR 610 para 69.

[492] *Giniewski*, para 52. See, *a contrario, Garaudy v France* No 65831/01, 2003-IX DA.

[493] The penalty imposed on the journalist at issue was very limited. Yet emphasis was placed on the fact that the notice mentioned the criminal offence of defamation, which was found to have a chilling effect: *Giniewski*, para 55.   [494] Hudoc (2006) paras 51–2.

VIII. PROTECTION OF THE COPYRIGHT LAW

In *Ashby Donald and Others v France*,[495] the Court examined whether restrictions imposed on the unauthorized use, on a commercial website, of photographs taken of a fashion show infringed Article 10. The applicants were fashion photographers who were invited to fashion shows. They published the photographs they took on the website of a fashion company without obtaining the permission of the French fashion houses. The applicants were convicted of infringing the copyright law and ordered to pay fines and damages to the French Federation of Dressmaking. With the right of property under Article 1 of the First Protocol interpreted broadly to cover intellectual property rights in the case law,[496] it was not disputed that the interference pursued the legitimate aim of protecting the rights of others. Still, the nature of the applicant's website was considered purely commercial in selling the photographs. Hence, restrictions on their activities were found receptive to a large measure of discretion of the national authorities. This consideration was further reinforced by the need to balance the expression right and the copyright of fashion creators.[497] The Court's approach was confined to confirming the national courts' findings, without undertaking its own finding of the factual circumstances.[498] Such a restrained stance was corroborated by the Court's scant regard to the onerous nature of the penalties and damages incurred by the applicants to the French Federation. The applicants were ordered to pay not only criminal penalties (8,000 euros each for two applicants, and 3,000 euros for the third applicant), but also a hefty sum of damages (approximately 100,000 euros for the two applicants, and 55,000 euros for the third), something that the applicants pleaded financially strangulated them. However, in the Court's view, this was not of such a nature as to upset the balance.[499]

IX. PREVENTION OF DISCLOSURE OF CONFIDENTIAL INFORMATION

The phrase 'the disclosure of information received in confidence' in Article 10(2) has been interpreted as encompassing the disclosure of confidential information by a person who has received the information subject to a duty of confidence, or by a third party, including a journalist, who has received it while subject to no such duty.[500] The right of journalists to engage in the free flow of information may be at odds with the legitimate aims of preventing the divulgence of confidential information. As discussed earlier, the fact that information has been obtained illegally by a third person, such as a journalist, does not divest that person of the protection of Article 10.[501] But ordering a journalist or the press to account for the profits and costs accruing from the publication of confidential material has been considered proportionate in view of the relatively minor nature of the interference and of the need to sanction the breach of confidence.[502] Similarly, the Court

---

[495] Hudoc (2013).

[496] *Anheuser-Busch Inc. v Portugal* 2007-I para 72 GC; and *Ashby Donald and Others v France* hudoc (2013) para 40.   [497] *Ashby Donald and Others v France*, para 39–41.

[498] *Ashby Donald and Others v France*, para 42.

[499] *Ashby Donald and Others v France*, para 43.

[500] *Stoll v Switzerland* 2007-V; 44 EHRR 55 para 61 GC. Faced with inconsistent English and French authentic texts, the Grand Chamber relied on Article 33(4) of the Vienna Convention on the Law of Treaties to interpret Article 10(2) as including third parties.

[501] *RADIO TWIST AS v Slovakia* hudoc (2006) para 62.

[502] *Times Newspapers Ltd and Neil v UK* No 14644/89 73 DR 41 (1991).

justified the measure to recover from a former government secret service agent the profits from publishing material in a book, which was done in breach of his undertaking to the government not to disclose information obtained in his employment. Even though the subject matter had ceased to be confidential, special note was taken of the fact that those profits derived from the notoriety and gravity of the applicant's criminal past.[503] As confirmed in the cases of *Sunday Times (Spycatcher)* (disclosure of national intelligence) and *Fressoz and Roire*[504] (use of confidential tax documents), once the contents of the confidential information have come to the public knowledge, it makes little sense to maintain sanctions against a journalist who has breached professional confidence.[505]

Despite the critical importance of political expression, the Commission endorsed the criminal conviction of an accredited parliamentary journalist who, while being aware of its confidential nature, published a parliamentary document.[506] Similarly, criminal sanction against a journalist who has breached the confidentiality of diplomatic correspondence may be warranted in view of the paramount national interest. In *Stoll v Switzerland*,[507] the Grand Chamber upheld the conviction of a journalist for publishing a confidential report written by the Swiss ambassador to the United States in preparation for the negotiations between Jewish organizations and Swiss banks concerning the unclaimed assets of the Holocaust victims deposited in Swiss banks. The journalist obtained a copy of the report from an unidentified person in breach of professional confidence. He published some of its extracts in a weekly newspaper, reporting that the ambassador insulted the Jewish representatives by calling them 'our adversaries...not to be trusted'. The Swiss courts found him culpable of making public 'secret official deliberations' within the meaning of the Swiss Criminal Code. The senior official position held by the author of the document was not considered to diminish the confidential nature of the diplomatic dossier.[508] Nor was the government's failure to establish that the applicant's articles prevented the Swiss government and banks from resolving issues of unclaimed assets deemed material. According to the Grand Chamber, what mattered was the *potentiality* that the revelation of the report might cause 'considerable damage' to the national interests.[509] In view of the ambassador's remarks, the Grand Chamber found that disclosing the extracts of the report at a delicate juncture could cause 'considerable damage' to those interests.[510] The applicant did not act unlawfully to obtain the document. The Swiss authorities could have opened an investigation to prosecute a staff member responsible for the leak of the document. Even so, according to the Grand Chamber, the duties and responsibilities of the applicant as a journalist held sway, countering the claim that he was unaware of the risk of criminal prosecution.

The Grand Chamber stressed that the articles isolated extracts from the impugned report, taken out of context. Given that one of the articles was placed on the front page, the applicant's intention was considered to make the ambassador's report 'the subject of needless scandal'.[511] When finding no violation of Article 10, the Grand Chamber ruled that the reductive form that the articles took was liable to mislead the reader concerning the ambassador's personality and abilities, and to lessen the worthiness of their contribution to the public debate. This is a curious line of reasoning. No action was taken to prosecute other journalists and the newspapers that published the contested document

---

[503] *Blake v UK No 68890/01* hudoc (2005) para 158 DA. Cf. *Blake v UK* hudoc (2006) (finding of a violation of Article 6(1)).   [504] *Fressoz and Roire v France*, hudoc (1999) GC.

[505] See also *Ressiot and Others v France* hudoc (2012) paras 116 and 122.

[506] *Z v Switzerland No 10343/83*, 35 DR 224 (1983).   [507] Hudoc (2007) para 16 GC.

[508] *Stoll v Switzerland*, para 114.   [509] *Stoll v Switzerland*, para 130.

[510] *Stoll v Switzerland*, paras 132–6.   [511] *Stoll v Switzerland*, para 151.

virtually *in full* the day after the applicant's articles appeared. As Judge Zagrebelsky noted in his dissent,[512] publishing only a few extracts from the document, albeit relating specifically to the manner in which the ambassador expressed himself, 'paradoxically' diminished the value of the press freedom, and the majority suggested that the applicant should have published the document in full.

Where divulging confidential information clashes with the right to privacy of a judge, it is crucial to examine the extent to which it can contribute to general public debate. In *Leempoel & SA ED Ciné Revue v Belgium*,[513] the Court found it reasonable to order the withdrawal of the sales of a magazine that published the confidential documents of a judge who was under parliamentary inquiry. An article in the magazine included a copy of the judge's private correspondence. The parliamentary inquiry was of great public interest, as it related to the judge's controversial handling of the case of kidnapped girls. The case turned on whether there was any reason to justify the publication of purely private material. The Court found that the applicants failed to demonstrate the overriding public interest in publishing the contested information, when to do so was harmful not only to the reputation and privacy of the judge under the inquiry but also to his fair trial rights.[514]

A trend emerging from the principle of transparency in Europe is that publication is the rule and prohibition of publication the exception.[515] This consideration has prompted the Court to recognize the divulgence of confidential information of vital public interest, which is obtained by journalists from whistle-blowers.[516] The corollary is that in case internal channels do not properly function, or are not expected to do so, external whistle-blowing is to be safeguarded. It is difficult to maintain the legitimacy of 'preventing the disclosure of information received in confidence', save in exceptional circumstances such as pending criminal investigations and a sensitive diplomatic document. As stressed earlier,[517] there would be no need to keep the confidentiality of the information held by a public prosecutor, once the information enters the public domain by different channels.[518] In *Dammann v Switzerland*,[519] a journalist was convicted of having instigated the violation of confidentiality of information after he obtained from the public prosecutor's office information concerning the criminal records of persons suspected of drug dealing. Given that the information could have been obtained by consulting reports of the judgments and the archives of newspapers, both the relevance and the sufficiency of the interference were deemed dubious. The information was considered to raise a matter of public interest. The applicant did not resort to a ruse, menace, or any other illegal means. Further, any alleged injury to the rights of persons, if at all, was held to have dissipated once the applicant himself decided not to publish the data in question. In these

---

[512] *Stoll v Switzerland*, dissenting opinion of Judge Zagrebelsky joined by Judges Lorenzen, Fura-Sandström, Jaeger, and Popović. [513] Hudoc (2006) para 79.

[514] *Leempoel & SA ED Ciné Revue v Belgium*, paras 74–80.

[515] See, eg, Committee of Ministers Resolution Res (2001) 6 of 12 June 2001 on access to Council of Europe documents; and Resolution 1551 (2007) of the Parliamentary Assembly of the Council of Europe on fair trial issues in criminal cases concerning espionage or divulging state secrets. See also I-A Ct HRts, *Claude Reyes and Others v Chile*, Judgment of 19 September 2006, Series C No 151 para 58.

[516] *Heinisch v Germany* hudoc (2011) para 73; and *Bucur and Toma v Romania* hudoc (2013) para 107. See also the Resolution 1729 of the Parliamentary Assembly of the Council of Europe (2010).

[517] See Ch 14, section 6.II.

[518] See, *inter alia*, *Fressoz v Roire v France* 1999-I GC; 31 EHRR 28 para 53 GC; *Observer and Guardian v UK* A 216 (1991); 14 EHRR 153 para 69 PC; and *Dammann v Switzerland* hudoc (2006) para 53.

[519] *Dammann v Switzerland* hudoc (2006).

circumstances, the imposition of the criminal sanction, albeit minor in nature, was found disproportionate.

X. MAINTENANCE OF THE AUTHORITY AND IMPARTIALITY OF THE JUDICIARY

a. Overview

Under Article 6(1), the Convention explicitly allows courts to hold criminal proceedings *in camera*, excluding journalists or the public in general. Such exclusion is aimed at protecting the privacy rights of juvenile offenders, preventing disorder or crime, maintaining the authority and impartiality of the judiciary, or protecting the rights of others.[520] The protection of privacy can be invoked together with the notion of 'maintenance of the authority and impartiality of the judiciary', or subsumed into the latter notion understood in a broader sense. The Court's general approach is that journalists and the press should be entitled to report pending court proceedings and provide critical comments on them, insofar as they inform the public of matters of special public interest, and provided that this is compatible with fair trial guarantees of the accused.[521]

Still, the interest of the media in reporting criminal proceedings may be outweighed by the need to maintain the 'authority and impartiality of the judiciary'. A court may order the exclusion of the public from the pending criminal proceedings involving highly sensitive matters, which, if disclosed to the public, may jeopardize the safety of third parties, including family members of those involved in organized crimes. The failure by a court to articulate the reasons for such an exclusion from criminal trials was deemed compatible with Article 10, where the senior judge of that court had offered to give the reasons in confidence to the chairperson of the association of journalists.[522]

A witness summons issued to a journalist or a media company to provide evidence in criminal proceedings belongs to a normal civil duty in democracy. This can be defended as being to 'maintain the authority and impartiality of the judiciary'. In *BBC v UK*,[523] the witness summons required the BBC to divulge recordings of riots for the purpose of a criminal proceeding. In contrast to the *Goodwin* case, where the disclosure order concerned information received on a confidential basis, this case related to information on events which took place in public, so that no duty of confidentially arose. The BBC challenged a disclosure obligation without being informed of the issues in the criminal trial. This argument was rejected by the Commission, which opined that witnesses often gave evidence without appreciating the impact of their evidence, and that its impact was the matter to be decided by a national court.

With respect to the live transmission of court proceedings by the media, there is a risk that journalists' subjectivity in filtering and editing may compromise the fair administration of justice. In *P4 Radio Helge Norge ASA v Norway*,[524] the Court recognized that a legal presumption against the live transmission of court hearings by radio was consistent with Article 10. Indeed, 'no common ground' was held to exist in European national legal systems to support the argument that live transmission by audiovisual means was vital for imparting information on criminal proceedings. Account was also taken of the fact that

---

[520] See Ch 9, section 3.III.a.

[521] *News Verlags GmbH & Co KG v Austria*, 2000-I para 56; *Dupuis and Others v France*, 2007-VII para 35; *Campos Dâmaso v Portugal* hudoc (2008) para 31.

[522] *Atkinson, Crook and The Independent v UK No13366/87*, 67 DR 244 1990.

[523] *No 25798/94* hudoc (1996) DA.   [524] *No 76682/01* hudoc (2003) DA.

the national authorities allowed the proceedings to be held in an open court, and even made arrangements for live transmission of 'picture and sound' to a press hall nearby to cater for the considerable media interest in a case that had attracted great public interest.

b. Criticisms levelled at the judiciary or at the prosecutors

It seems reasonable that according to the case law, among all public officials, judges are given the highest protection of their authority, and that the limit of acceptable criticism of them is the narrowest. This can be explained by their special role as guarantors of justice that must inspire confidence both in the accused in criminal proceedings and in the public at large.[525] Further, special regard must be had to their inability to reply to criticism.[526] Indeed, the Court has stressed the need to distinguish between criticism and insult. If the sole intention of any form of expression is to insult a court, or members of the court, an appropriate punishment can be justified under Article 10(2).[527] The authority of the judiciary needs to be safeguarded from any abusive or insulting language by the defence even in heated circumstances. In *Saday v Turkey,*[528] the defendant used virulent words, such as 'the State wish that we should be killed by the executioners wearing robes' and 'The fascist dictator...now wants to judge me before a security court of the State'. The Court accepted that such words could undermine the dignity of the judges by creating an atmosphere of insecurity to the detriment of the good administration of justice.

Clearly, for the purpose of safeguarding the authority of the judiciary and the dignity of the legal profession, many countries allow the legal professional bodies to take disciplinary measures. In *Schöpfer v Switzerland,*[529] a lawyer was subjected to disciplinary penalty for having criticized the administration of justice in pending proceedings at a press conference. He deliberately chose such a public venue before having resort to a legal remedy of appeal. The Court suggested that the applicant was under a special duty, as a member of the Bar, to contribute to the proper administration of justice and to maintain public confidence in it. In view of the tone of the accusation and of the modest amount of the fine, the Court concluded that a proper balance had been struck.

With respect to virulent criticisms or disparaging comments directed at judges, the approach followed by the Court in its early case law lacks both depth and rigour in its analysis.[530] In *Barfod v Denmark,*[531] a Danish citizen in Greenland criticized a judgment in a taxation case rendered by the High Court, which found in favour of the local government. The sitting judges of the High Court included two lay judges employed by the local government, namely the defendant of the case. The applicant wrote an article in a magazine, stating that these lay judges 'did their duty', implying that they cast vote as employees of the local government rather than as independent and impartial judges. He was convicted on the ground that his remarks were defamatory of the character of the judges. The Commission, by fourteen votes to one, found a violation of Article 10, recognizing that the contested remarks raised matters of public interest relating to the functioning of the public administration. This reasoning was upheld 'even if' the article in question could be interpreted as an attack on the integrity or reputation of the two lay

---

[525] See, *inter alia, Fey v Austria* A 255-A (1993); 6 EHRR 387 para 40; and *Skałka v Poland* hudoc (2003); 38 EHRR 1 para 40.   [526] *Prager and Oberschlick v Austria* A 313 (1995); 21 EHRR 1 para 34.
[527] *Skałka v Poland* hudoc (2003); 38 EHRR 1 para 34.
[528] Hudoc (2006) paras 35–6. Nevertheless, the severity of the criminal sanction was found disproportionate: para 36.   [529] 1998-III; 33 EHRR 845 paras 29 and 33.
[530] See, eg, *Hodgson, Woolf Productions Ltd, National Union of Journalists and Channel Four Television Co Ltd v UK Nos 11553/85 and 11658/85 (joined),* 51 DR 136 (1987); and *C Ltd v UK No 14132/88,* 61 DR 285 (1989).   [531] A 149 (1989); 13 EHRR 493.

judges'.[532] In contrast, the Court overturned the Commission's opinion by six votes to one, holding that the contested remarks did not entail any contribution to public debates. It did not find that his criminal conviction could entail any deterrent impact on his freedom of expression, referring to the possibility of criticizing the composition of the High Court without attacking the lay judges personally. It also rejected the argument that the applicant's critical remarks were made in a political context concerning a disputed tax levied in Greenland. According to the Court, the impugned remarks consisted of two elements: a criticism of the composition of the High Court in the tax case in question; and the statement that the two lay judges 'did their duty'.[533] The Court held that it was not demonstrated that these 'two elements of criticism... were so closely connected as to make the statement relating to the two lay judges legitimate'.[534] On closer scrutiny, this argument seems rather artificial. Indeed, the two elements concerned were inseparably intertwined. Further, even if these elements could have been disjoined, with the second element considered a personal attack, it would still be difficult to deem the tenor of the wording sufficiently offensive to amount to defamation.

The deference to the public end in safeguarding the authority of the judiciary was followed in *Prager and Obserschlick v Austria*.[535] There, a journalist and a publisher were convicted of defamation after the former wrote an article in a magazine, criticizing the judges of the Vienna Regional Criminal Court in virulent words. The article stated that the judges 'treat each accused at the outset as if he had already been convicted', and described Judge J as 'arrogant' and 'bullying'. Both the Commission[536] and the Court[537] found no violation of Article 10 by close votes. The Court recognized that these words were 'unnecessarily prejudicial' and defamatory, noting that this was true 'even in the absence of a sufficient factual basis'.[538] In his dissenting opinion, Judge Martens carefully examined the context in which the contested article was written. He noted that after months of research, the journalist considered that it was the personalities of judges at the Vienna Regional Criminal Court that explained why criminal justice in Vienna was more unduly harsh than elsewhere in Austria.[539] According to him, the article raised matters of crucial public interest, requiring special protection. Further, he cogently pointed out that while scathing criticism directed against Judge J was defamatory, other judges rebuked no less severely in the article did not institute defamation proceedings.

The Court's decision-making policy has, however, shifted to an approach that now gives more lengthy thought to the specific circumstances of the case (tenor and context of the contested statements), in tune with other defamation cases. In *De Haes and Gijsels v Belgium*,[540] journalists were found by the national courts to have defamed the judges in divorce proceedings, when criticizing them for bias and lack of independence in awarding child custody to a father accused of incest. The impugned statements were considered of special public interest because of the serious allegations concerning both the fate

---

[532] A 149 (1989); 13 EHRR 493 para 71 Com Rep (1987) (*B v Denmark No 11508/85*) (emphasis added).

[533] *Barfod v Denmark*, para 30.   [534] *Barfod v Denmark*, para 30.

[535] A 313 (1995); 21 EHRR 1.

[536] *Prager and Obserschlick v Austria*, Com Rep (fifteen votes to twelve).

[537] *Prager and Obserschlick v Austria* (five votes to four).

[538] *Prager and Obserschlick v Austria*, para 37. Instead of taking a critical stance, the Court deferred to the national authorities' classification of the contested passages in the article as value-judgments or allegations of fact: para 36.

[539] *Prager and Obserschlick v Austria*, dissenting opinion of Judge Martens, joined by Judges Pekkanen and Makarczyk.

[540] 1997-I; 25 EHRR 1 para 45. Compare this to *Falter Zeitschriften GmbH v Austria* para 45 (requiring rigorous standard of factual basis for serious criticism levelled at a judge in relation to a sensitive case).

of young children and the role of the local judiciary. The Court dissected different elements of the statements to ascertain whether they constituted facts or opinions. Some of the applicants' allegations, including the allusion to an extreme right-wing ideology espoused by a father of one judge as evidence of his political bias, were held to be irrelevant and deserving of penalty. Nevertheless, the Court was quick to stress that these were only part of the statements, and that it was essential not to overlook their *overall* tenor. In view of the special weight given to the role of the journalists in informing the public of a controversial decision in a child custody case, even an aggressive tone levelled at judges was found reasonable.

The Court's scrutiny may extend to the severity of a criminal sanction imposed, irrespective of whether the words used against judges were clearly offensive. In *Skałka v Poland*,[541] a prisoner wrote a letter to the President of the Katowice Regional Court, describing an unidentified judge, with whom he had made initial communication, as a 'small-time cretin' and 'some fool'. The Court found such wording clearly derogatory. Yet, this could not warrant a prison sentence of eight months, which was considered to upset the equilibrium. In *Amihalachioaie v Moldova*,[542] a lawyer was convicted of lack of regard for the Constitutional Court, after having stated in an interview given to a newspaper that the ruling of the Constitutional Court on compulsory membership of the Bar Council would cause anarchy in the legal profession. The Court found that the contested statements involved matters of public interest and should be grasped in the context of fierce debates among lawyers. Moreover, it was the press that reported the applicant's contested statement. Neither relevant nor sufficient reason was found to justify the interference in question.[543]

The similar rationales can be applied to the media reporting of proceedings that criticize the handling of prosecutors. Again, the Court is not prevented from giving primacy to the right of the press to inform the public of matters of special public interest.[544] The Court's close scrutiny turns on the context in which impugned reporting has taken place, and on the question whether the content of the reported information contains matters of public interest. In *Foglia v Switzerland*,[545] a lawyer was sanctioned after his criticism of the prosecutor's handling of the criminal cases of bank fraud was reported in a weekly newspaper together with the documents of the proceeding. The media had already informed the public of the death of the chief protagonist of the fraud well before the applicant gave interviews to the press. The applicant was representing the interest of his clients who were victims of this fraud.[546] The nature of the criticisms was considered mild. Even the domestic courts did not find it illegal to disclose the documents of the case to the media. In view of these, neither relevant nor sufficient ground to justify the impugned sanction was found.[547]

In *Guja v Moldova*,[548] the applicant, who was the head of the press department of the Prosecutor General's Office, was dismissed from his post after having disclosed to the press information concerning bribery committed by a Deputy-Speaker of the parliament. The applicant reacted to the call by the President to speak up to fight against corruption when his superior, the Prosecutor General, showed no sign of action against the Deputy-Speaker for half a year. The letter disclosed by the applicant contained such

---

[541] Hudoc (2003) 38 EHRR 1.   [542] *Amihalachioaie v Moldova* hudoc (2004) paras 34–9.
[543] *Amihalachioaie v Moldova*, paras 34–9.
[544] See, eg, *Foglia v Switzerland* hudoc (2007) para 83.   [545] Hudoc (2007).
[546] *Foglia v Switzerland*, paras 93–5.   [547] *Foglia v Switzerland*, paras 95–102.
[548] Hudoc (2008).

issues as the separation of powers, improper conduct of a high-ranking politician, and the government's attitude towards police brutality, all of which were considered of special public interest, and of which the public had the right to be informed.[549] The public interest in obtaining information on wrongdoing within the Prosecutor's Office was found to surpass the interest in maintaining public confidence in that Office.[550] In the Grand Chamber's view, this was bolstered by the right of civil servants to report any illegal conduct and wrongdoing at their workplace without fear of any sanction.[551] Despite the applicant's good faith in his action, which was never an issue, the severest sanction was imposed on the applicant.[552] All these features were decisive for convincing the Court to find a violation of Article 10.

c. Prevention of improper influence on trials

Maintaining the authority and impartiality of the judiciary is of special relevance to the doctrine of contempt of court in common law, according to which an injunction can be ordered to prevent the release of information on a pending trial to avoid any prejudgment or public pressure on the parties to the trial. In criminal proceedings, due account must be taken of the defendant's right to a fair trial and an impartial tribunal under Article 6 to hinder any deleterious impact of the publicity.

In *Sunday Times (No 1) v UK*,[553] the minority of the Commission and the government described the contempt of court doctrine as 'peculiar' to common-law countries. The same argument was taken up by the dissenting judges, who held that 'the notion of the authority of the judiciary was by no means divorced from national circumstances and could not be determined in a uniform way'.[554] This 'peculiar nature' of the doctrine was invoked by the dissenting judges to support a wide margin of appreciation. However, the majority of the Court did not follow this argument, stressing that the 'objective' nature of the doctrine of contempt of court required stringent scrutiny. It held that, in contrast to 'public morals', which were susceptible to diverse interpretation and standards, the notion of judicial authority was 'by far more objective' and capable of stringent review. Further, the fact that the case concerned restrictions on the press, one of the privileged means of expression, was pivotal. The contested newspaper articles related to the criticism of the pending settlement of the thalidomide tragedy, which was judged by the Court to be of 'undisputed public concern'.[555] The *Sunday Times (No 1)* case suggests that the Court's analysis of the clash between free speech and the doctrine of contempt of court may demonstrate a fine-tuning and relatively bold approach where the information concerns matters of considerable public interest.

Notwithstanding the seminal implication of *Sunday Times (No 1)*, the Commission endorsed a series of judicial measures, based on the contempt of court doctrine, which clashed with the rights of the media in reporting pending proceedings. In *C Ltd v UK*,[556] it defended the order of the Court of Appeal banning the TV broadcasting of a scheduled programme, which was a dramatic reconstruction of criminal proceedings based exclusively on the official shorthand transcripts. The dramatized re-enactment of criminal proceedings was distinguished from the reporting of such proceedings in the press,

---

[549] *Guja v Moldova*, paras 88 and 91 GC.   [550] *Guja v Moldova*, para 91.

[551] *Guja v Moldova*, para 97.   [552] *Guja v Moldova*, para 95.

[553] A 30 (1979); 2 EHRR 245 para 60 PC.

[554] *Sunday Times (No 1) v UK*, joint dissenting opinion of judges Wiarda, Cremona, Thor Vilhjalmsson, Ryssdal, Ganshof van der Meersch, Fitzmaurice, Bindschedler-Robert, Liesch, and Matscher, para 9.

[555] *Sunday Times (No 1) v UK*, para 67.   [556] *No 14132/88*, 61 DR 285 (1989).

because it was considered to entail the risk of subtly inviting the viewers to be placed in 'conditioned' settings. Similarly, in the *Hodgson Channel Four Television Co Ltd* cases,[557] a court order required the postponement of a programme 'Court Report', which was a rehearsal of a criminal trial concerning official secrets and highlighting the most dramatic parts of a hearing. The programme would consist of studio readings from a transcript of the proceedings, which were checked for accuracy and fairness. Actors were instructed to avoid any dramatic re-enactment of the proceedings. The Commission endorsed the court order to avoid 'a *real* risk of prejudice' to the jury, noting that imparting the same information could be effectuated in a revised programme. The Commission even rejected the argument that, short of prior restraint, there were other less injurious courses open to the trial judge, such as the instruction given to the jury not to watch the programme. In *Associated Newspapers Limited, Steven and Wolman v UK*,[558] the unauthorized disclosure of juries' deliberations for the purpose of research was found objectionable in jeopardizing the confidential deliberations of the jury trial.

On the basis of the doctrine of contempt of court, the Commission upheld the conviction of journalists to safeguard the fair trial rights of the accused and the right to privacy of victims or of witnesses. In *Crook and National Union of Journalists v UK*,[559] a court order withheld the publication of the name of a witness who was abducted for rape. Rather contradictorily, the order nonetheless allowed her name to be freely used in a public hearing so as not to prejudice the defence of the defendants. A request from journalists to reconsider the order was nevertheless rejected. The case was settled before the admissibility decision, following the United Kingdom government's proposal to amend the Criminal Justice Bill to allow an appeal to the Court of Appeal against orders of the kind raised in this case.

In *Kyprianou v Cyprus*,[560] the Court, in contrast to the Commission's earlier decisions, carried out scrupulous review of the rulings of contempt of court. In that case, a lawyer defending a person accused of murder made a mildly intemperate attack on judges. During heated debates, he used the Greek word which could mean both a love letter and a note, referring to a note exchanged between judges. Because of his remarks and conduct, he was convicted for contempt of court, and sentenced to five days' imprisonment in summary proceedings conducted by the same judges against whom his remarks were directed. The Grand Chamber found that the imposition of a custodial sentence would generate a chilling effect on the conduct of the applicant and lawyers in criminal proceedings. The penal sanction (five days' imprisonment) was considered excessive in response to his discourteous remarks. The applicant's status as a respected lawyer and the availability of less onerous alternatives[561] aggravated the disproportionate nature of the interference.

Clearly, civil law countries are equally well-equipped to deal with an affront to the authority and impartiality of the judiciary, even in the absence of a specific denomination of 'contempt of court'. A number of cases have arisen in relation to the improper influence exercised by the mass media on ongoing criminal trials. This is particularly true when press reporting concerns private individuals. In such circumstances, the protection of the rights of others (the right of privacy and reputation under Article 8 and the right to be

---

[557] *Hodgson, Woolf Productions Ltd and National Union of Journalists v UK and Channel Four Television Co Ltd v UK Nos 1553/85 and 11658/85*, 51 DR 136 (1987) (emphasis added). See also Commission's Report of 15 July 1988 (F Sett as to an alleged violation of Article 13).

[558] *No 24770/94* hudoc (1994) DA.   [559] *No 11552/85* hudoc (1988) DA.

[560] 2005-VIII para 150.

[561] The applicant referred to the possibility of an overnight adjournment of the trial: *Kyprianou v Cyprus*, para 79.

presumed innocent under Article 6) can be invoked in tandem with the purpose of safe-guarding judicial authority and impartiality to warrant limitations on press freedom. In *Egeland and Hanseid v Norway*, the editors of two national newspapers complained that their papers were ordered to pay fines due to the publication of the photographs taken, without consent, of one of the convicted persons of a major criminal case. In this case, the Court found applicable two rationales: preventing undue influence on pending criminal trials, as recognized in *P4 Radio Hele Norge ASA v Norway*;[562] and protecting personal information of the convicted in distress. The Court considered the second rationale more prevalent.[563] The photos concerned the convicted person in her emotional distress, and they were considered especially intrusive, as she was not a public figure. There was found no 'public interest' in publishing those photos. That her identity was already known to the public, or that she cooperated with the press previously,[564] was considered insufficient to lessen the protection of her privacy rights. Ancillary factors were the modest nature of fines imposed[565] and the absence of European consensus on this matter.[566]

If sanctions are imposed on the media reporting pending criminal proceedings of pub-lic figures, the 'public figures doctrine' (as examined later) may be deployed to lessen the significance of protecting the rights of others. Viewed in that light, the Court's approach in *Worm v Austria*[567] is a deviation from the general approach that favours journalists' expression rights over fair trial guarantees of defendants. In *Worm*, a journalist wrote an article commenting on pending criminal proceedings for tax evasion against a former Vice-Chancellor and Minister of Finance. He was convicted for having exercised prohib-ited influence on the criminal proceeding. The Commission considered that the incrimi-nated article had only raised a mere suspicion of the guilt of the defendant, and found that the imposition of conviction went too far. In contrast, the Court's assessment was that the article provided a clear opinion likely to affect the minds of the lay judges, contrary to the defendant's right to an impartial tribunal, so that there was no violation of Article 10. The balance between press freedom and the right to a fair trial was tipped in favour of the latter. The Court gave greater weight to the consideration invoked by the national judiciaries that the lay judges might be tempted to read the article in question, resulting in possible prejudgment. It may be commented that the majority of the Court departed from its approach in *Sunday Times (No 1)* and downplayed the emerging European consensus on the notion of the 'authority and impartiality of the judiciary'. The Court furnished the following explanations:

> With respect to the notion of the 'authority and impartiality of the judiciary', the Court has already noted its objective character and the fact that, in this area, the domestic law and practice of the Member States of the Council of Europe reveal a fairly substantial meas-ure of common ground... This does not mean that absolute uniformity is required and, indeed, since the Contracting States remain free to choose the measures which they con-sider appropriate, the Court cannot be oblivious of the substantive or procedural features of their respective domestic laws... It cannot thus hold that the applicant's conviction was

---

[562] *P4 Radio Hele Norge ASA v Norway, No 76682/01* (2009) hudoc.

[563] *Egeland and Hanseid v Norway* hudoc (2009) para 63. Compare this case with *Schweizerische Radio-und Fernsehgesellschaft SRG v Switzerland* hudoc (2012) (concerning refusal to obtain an authoriza-tion to enter a prison to film a portrait of a female prisoner serving a major criminal case, with her consent). In that case, the Court applied the less restrictive alternative doctrine to elevate the standard of proportion-ality scrutiny: *Egeland and Hanseid v Norway*, paras 61–5.

[564] *Egeland and Hanseid v Norway*, paras 60–3. See also *Axel Springer AG v Germany* hudoc (2012) para 92 GC.   [565] *Egeland and Hanseid v Norway* hudoc (2009) para 64.

[566] *Egeland and Hanseid v Norway*, paras 51–4.   [567] 1997-V; 25 EHRR 454 para 50.

contrary to Article 10 of the Convention simply because it might not have been obtained under a different legal system.[568]

It was not deemed decisive that this case concerned a highly influential politician, the factor that should have set the bounds of acceptable criticism wider. Further, the Court glossed over the argument raised by the applicant that the gist of the article was essentially a quotation of a statement made by the public prosecutor at the trial.

In the subsequent cases, the Court gave proper considerations to the argument that the press freedom and the right of the public to receive information on criminal proceedings that are of public interest should be accorded special protection. In *Du Roy and Malaurie v France*, the editor and the journalist of a weekly were convicted of having published information concerning criminal proceedings instituted on a civil-party application.[569] The problem was that under the then French Code of Criminal Procedure the ban of reporting pending criminal trials, derived from the principle of confidentiality of judicial investigations, was not, however, applicable to criminal proceedings instituted on an application by the public prosecutor's office, or on a complaint not so accompanied. In view of such a difference and of the right of the press to inform matters of public interest (socialist politicians' allegedly fraudulent actions as managers of a public company), the Court found that notwithstanding the objective of maintaining the proper administration of justice and safeguarding the right of the accused to be presumed innocent, the conviction of the journalist was out of proportion.

In *News Verlags GmbH & Co KG v Austria*,[570] the Court reasserted the primacy of press freedom and the right of the public to receive information on criminal proceedings that were of public interest. The case concerned injunctions prohibiting a magazine from printing photographs of a person suspected of sending letter bombs. The Court found that the injunctions pursued two legitimate aims: (i) the protection of the reputation or rights of the suspect in question; and (ii) the maintenance of the authority and impartiality of the judiciary. Nevertheless, it unanimously condemned the injunctions as disproportionate. The fact that the photographed person was a well-known right-wing extremist, whose views challenged the Convention's values, corroborated the argument that the suspect was a public figure, and that the photographs were of special public interest.

In *Tourancheau and July v France*,[571] a journalist was convicted for publishing an article on the investigation of a murder case. The article reproduced extracts from a declaration made by a girl under investigation, and the words of her fiancé. A photograph of the latter was published with a caption stating that he had been liberated while his fiancée stayed in prison. National courts held that the tenor of the article supported the story of one accused to the detriment of the other. This was considered to affect adversely the decisions of non-professional judges in pending criminal proceedings and to undermine the fair trial rights of the accused. The Court held that the ban on publication was minimal, as the applicant was free to comment on the investigation. The article was not deemed to raise public interest. According to the Court, it was up to the national courts to examine the probability of non-professional judges drawing adverse inferences. Primacy was given to the presumption of innocence and the interest in maintaining the authority and impartiality of the judiciary. The nature and severity of the penalty were not considered so excessive as to have a chilling effect. By a close vote of four to three, the Court concluded that Article 10 was not breached. The dissenting judges' opinions gave greater weight to

---

[568] *Worm v Austria*, para 50.
[569] *Du Roy and Malaurie v France* 2000-X paras 34–6.
[570] 2000-I; 31 EHRR 246 paras 54–8.   [571] Hudoc (2005) para 66.

the right of the public to receive information on pending trials. They considered that the present case departed from the more fine-tuned approach in *Worm*.[572] Given the lapse of almost twenty months between the publication of the article and the date of the hearing, it was difficult to detect any seriously adverse impact of publishing the article.

7. DUTIES AND RESPONSIBILITIES UNDER ARTICLE 10(2)

I. OVERVIEW

Article 10(2) refers to the 'duties and responsibilities' of persons exercising their freedom of expression. The inclusion of such duties and responsibilities is unusual for the Convention rights. However, to argue that the inclusion of such wording suggests an inherently greater limitation envisaged in the freedom of expression is untenable. Indeed, there is no room for implied limitations in Article 10. Even so, the Court has shrewdly parried the question whether individual persons are able to waive their right to freedom of expression,[573] confining itself to holding that the waiver of a right guaranteed under the Convention, if permissible, must satisfy three requirements: (i) this must not be incompatible with any significant public interest; (ii) it must be established in an unequivocal manner; and (iii) there must be minimum guarantees commensurate to the waiver's importance.[574]

The notion 'duties and responsibilities' has been invoked in relation to different bearers of expression rights, including politicians,[575] civil servants, lawyers,[576] the press, journalists, editors,[577] authors and publishers (vicariously),[578] and even artists such as novelists.[579] As regards journalists, the Court has repeatedly highlighted that they are to act in good faith to provide accurate and reliable information in accordance with the ethics of journalism,[580] as will be examined later.

The extent to which this notion occupies importance with regard to politicians is controversial. In *Willem v France*, a left-wing mayor of a small commune proposed the boycotting of Israeli products, in particular, fruit juice, as a protest against the policy of Ariel Sharon, the then Prime Minister of Israel, in the occupied Palestinian territories. The mayor's proposal was included in a local newspaper, which read that 'The Israeli people are not in question, [but] it is a man, Sharon, who is guilty of atrocities, [and] who does not respect any decision of the UN and continues to massacre'.[581] He also provided in the website of his commune more elaborate rationales for his proposal. He was convicted of provocation of discrimination. The interference was pursuant to the protection of rights

---

[572] Joint dissenting opinion of Judges Costa, Tulkens, and Lorenzen, paras 2 and 6. See also *Worm v Austria* hudoc (1997).   [573] See, eg, *Blake vUK No 68890/01* hudoc (2005) para 128 DA.

[574] *Håkansson and Sturesson v Sweden* A 171-A (1990); 13 EHRR 1 para 66; *Pfeifer and Plankl v Austria* A 227 (1992); 14 EHRR 692 para 37.

[575] *Willem v France No 10883/05* hudoc (2009) para 37 (a mayor of a small commune).

[576] *Steur v Netherlands* 2003-XI; 39 EHRR 706 paras 37–8.

[577] *Sürek v Turkey (No 1)* 1999-IV para 63 GC; and *Leempoel v SA. ED Ciné Revue v Belgium* hudoc (2006) para 66.   [578] *Édition Plon v France* 2004-IV; 42 EHRR 705 para 50.

[579] *Lindon, Otchakovsky-Laurens and July v France* hudoc (2007) para 51.

[580] For this principle, see, eg, *Bladet Tromsø and Stensaas v Norway* 1999-III; 29 EHRR 125 para 65 GC.

[581] *Willem v France No 10883/05* hudoc (2009) para 7 (translation into English by the author of this chapter).

of others, in this particular context, the rights of Israeli producers.[582] In the Court's view, by calling on the municipal services to boycott Israeli products, the mayor went too far, sending a message of discriminatory character. It held that while his intention was to denounce the nationalist policies of the then right-wing Prime Minister of Israel, the boycotting was tantamount to a discriminatory step. In this regard, special importance was attached to the fact that the mayor was not condemned for his political opinions as such.[583] Moreover, the applicant's 'duties and responsibilities' were spotlighted in relation to his negligence in ensuring open discussions of a matter of general interest, because his view was expressed in the municipal council without any vote.[584]

Setting aside the delicate political question of proposing such a boycott against a particular country's produce, it is conceivable that in case of any restriction on such a proposal made by a member of the civil society, the Court would be more likely to accord greater protection to free speech rights. Judge Jungwiert in his dissent defends robustness in safeguarding political expression, considering that the nature of the mayor's contested expression was political. He also noted the very limited effect of the boycott, which was purported to exclude fruit juice from the canteen of a small commune. In his view, 'one can easily imagine that in a similar situation, a mayor (who is almost always a member of a political party) appeals, for example, for the boycott of products coming from the United States to protest against the war in Iraq, of Russian products because of the conflict in Chechnya, or also of Chinese merchandise to support Tibet'.[585] Surely there is always the question of selectivity of countries targeted by any proposed boycott. One may wonder if democracies such as the United States and Israel have to meet a higher threshold of criticism than non-democracies notorious for more egregious records of human rights violations. It may be argued that both the doctrine of a 'margin of appreciation'[586] and the notion of 'duties and responsibilities' operated implicitly behind the Court's reasoning, so that the mayor was held to avoid being implicated in political controversies of the kind categorized as a 'political question' in the US constitutional law.[587]

The notion 'duties and responsibilities' assumes marked importance with respect to special categories of civil servants, such as diplomats, judges, intelligence agents, and police officers,[588] an issue that will be explored later. In relation to judges, it is considered reasonable to expect them to display a certain degree of discretion so as not to undermine their authority and impartiality. Even so, as demonstrated in *Wille v Liechtenstein*,[589] the question whether their statements have overstepped the acceptable bounds of freedom, flouting their professional ethics, is generally subject to the Court's rigorous assessment.

Members of civil society, such as representatives of professional bodies[590] and NGOs are also subject to the similar duties and responsibilities. In *Steel and Morris v UK*,[591] the Court held that the duty of journalists to act in good faith to provide accurate and reliable information in accordance with the ethics of journalism could apply by analogy to those that engage in public debate, such as campaigners of an NGO, who distributed leaflets.

---

[582] *Willem v France*, para 29.   [583] *Willem v France*, paras 35–8.

[584] *Willem v France*, paras 37–8. Further, when finding that there was no violation of Article 10, the Court endorsed the French prosecutor's argument that the mayor could not substitute the governmental authority to order a boycott of produce coming from a particular foreign country: paras 12, 22, and 39.

[585] *Willem v France*, dissenting opinion of Judge Jungwiert (translation into English by the author of this chapter).   [586] *Willem v France*, para 42.

[587] See *Baker v Carr* 369 US 186 (1962).

[588] With respect to secret agents, see, eg, *Blake v UK No 68890/01* hudoc (2005) paras 126 and 159.

[589] 1999-VII; 30 EHRR 558 GC.

[590] See, eg, *Nilsen and Johnsen v Norway* 1999-VIII; 30 EHRR 878 para 47 GC.

[591] 2005-II; 41 EHRR 403 para 90.

Even in an employment context, the notion 'duties and responsibilities' has been invoked to stress that employees must show some restraint in voicing their criticisms against their colleagues or employers. The bounds of criticisms may be overstepped if their contents are characterized more as personal accusations of specific individuals, devoid of public interest.[592] The application of the notion 'duties and responsibilities' to the employment context of journalists should, however, be treated with greater care. The Court has held that journalists are bound by the duty of loyalty, reserve, and discretion in relation to the public television broadcasters which are their employers.[593] Even so, the right of such employees to criticize publicly the conduct of their media corporations is likely to outweigh the interest in protecting good name or honour of such corporations, given the special importance of their role in imparting information and ideas of public interest.[594]

II. DUTIES AND RESPONSIBILITIES OF CIVIL SERVANTS

The notion 'duties and responsibilities' under Article 10(2) has been invoked to justify encroachments on civil servants' political speech and activities to ensure their neutrality and impartiality. The Court has found it compatible with this notion to impose obligations on special categories of public officials, including police officers, to refrain from political activities to ensure their 'politically neutral' views.[595] Moreover, in respect of disputes concerning employment relations of public officials, they should be, as in the case of private employees discussed earlier, expected to display certain restraint in not directing personal accusations against specific individuals by overstepping bounds of criticisms.[596]

The case of *Ahmed v UK*[597] concerned the ban on local government employees participating in political activities. In ruling against the applicant, the Court recognized the limitations on the free speech of public servants by widely interpreting the term 'duties and responsibilities'. It held that this term 'assume[s] a special significance, which justifies leaving to the authorities of the respondent State a certain margin of appreciation in determining whether the impugned interference is proportionate to the aim as stated'. In contrast, in the same case, the Commission had only moderately invoked the words 'duties and responsibilities'. It rejected any room for inherently wide restrictions on the rights of a public servant.[598] It called on the government to establish a less restrictive form of limitation than prior restraint.[599] The Commission's approach was more consonant with other cases revealing a rigorous standard of review.[600]

It must be examined whether and, if so, in what ways, the notion 'duties and responsibilities' under Article 10(2) is of special relevance to assessing anti-Convention values espoused by civil servants.[601] Several complaints have arisen in connection with the

---

[592] *De Diego Nafria v Spain* hudoc (2002) paras 37–41 (these features being aggravated by the fact that the criticisms and accusations were made in a written form rather than in a spontaneous oral reaction).

[593] *Wojtas-Kaleta v Poland* hudoc (2009) para 43. See also *Fuentes Bobo v Spain* hudoc (2000).

[594] *Wojtas-Kaleta v Poland* hudoc (2009) para 46.

[595] *Rekvényi v Hungary* 1999-III para 46 GC; and *Otto v Germany* No 27574/02 hudoc (2005) DA.

[596] *De Diego Nafria v Spain* hudoc (2002) para 37 (accusations made by a senior member of a central bank against his directors in a letter).

[597] 1998-VI para 61. Another decisive factor was that among the member states there existed diverse approaches to the regulations of local authorities: para 62.   [598] *Ahmed v UK*, para 76 Com Rep.

[599] *Ahmed v UK*, para 76.   [600] *Ahmed v UK*, paras 77 and 86.

[601] See, eg, *Vogt v Germany* A 323 (1995); 21 EHRR 205 para 53 GC.

German loyalty test for civil servants, which is premised on the constitutional safeguard called the *wehrhafte Demokratie* ('democracy capable of defending itself'[602] or 'militant democracy'). In view of the Nazi experience, the conscientious approach of post-World War II Germany is to ensure that all civil servants, irrespective of their job and rank, must swear to abide by the values incorporated in the Basic Law. Any connection to an organization whose aim is held unconstitutional may lead to 'wilful deceit' of this loyalty requirement. In the two German cases of *Glasenapp* and *Kosiek*, which concerned the dismissal of civil servants on probation, the Court evaded the question of conflict between the freedom of expression and the loyalty test. The Court's approach in *Glasenapp*,[603] which involved a school teacher associated with a proscribed communist party, may be described as 'a puzzling *non sequitur*'.[604] The Court considered that the essence of the complaint was the right of access to the civil service, a right not guaranteed under the Convention. In its view, the national authorities took account of the applicant's opinions only for the purpose of verifying her qualifications for the post. The Court took the same approach in *Kosiek v Germany*,[605] which concerned the dismissal of a probationary lecturer belonging to an extreme right-wing party. The potential repercussion of the non-application of Article 10 in respect of civil servants is disturbing.[606] By contrast, in both cases, the Commission considered that the freedom of expression was at issue. In *Glasenapp*, the Commission found that the categorical application of the loyalty test, which took no account of the rank, position, or nature of civil service, was excessive.[607] By contrast, in *Kosiek*, the Commission endorsed the national decision. The difference in the Commission's approach can be explained by the degree of the applicant's involvement in each extreme political group.

A distinction needs to be drawn between laying off civil servants who have a permanent contract, and dismissing those on probation. In *Vogt v Germany*,[608] this distinction was decisive. There, the Court considered it excessive to dismiss a secondary-school teacher on the ground of her political affiliation to a German communist party (DPK). Her discharge would make it almost impossible for her to find a teaching post, depriving her of her livelihood. She was a teacher of languages, a post which did not intrinsically pose any security threat. Further, the DPK was not prohibited by the Federal Constitutional Court. The German system of control was too categorical in applying to all civil servants irrespective of their function and rank, and disallowing separation between service and private life. Further, such a stringent duty of loyalty was not imposed in any other member states of the Council of Europe, including Austria. Nevertheless, the German system of loyalty control as such has yet to be called into question. Subsequently, in *Otto v Germany*,[609] where a police officer complained of the non-promotion to a senior position due to his active involvement in an extreme right-wing party, emphasis was placed again on the 'duties and responsibilities' of a civil servant. As compared with the more serious impact on the applicant in the *Vogt* case (loss of livelihood), in the *Otto* case the Court found the contested measure of non-promotion to be

---

[602] *Vogt v Germany*, para 51; and *Otto v Germany No 27574/02* hudoc (2005) DA.

[603] *Glasenapp v Germany* A 104 (1986); 9 EHRR 25 para 53 PC.

[604] Lester, in Macdonald, Matscher, and Petzold, eds, *The European System for the Protection of Human Rights*, 1993, Ch 18, at p 475.   [605] A 105 (1986); 9 EHRR 328 para 115 Com Rep.

[606] See dissenting opinion of Judge Spielmann in the *Glasenapp* case, paras 24 and 39, who stressed a more meticulous appraisal of such factors as the nature of the post held by the applicant, her behaviour, the circumstances in which the disputed opinion was made, and the nature of the opinion.

[607] *Glasenapp v Germany* A 104 (1986); 9 EHRR 25 PC paras 111 and 128 PC.

[608] A 323 (1995); 21 EHRR 205 para 61 GC.   [609] *No 27574/02* hudoc (2005) DA.

proportionate.[610] Clearly, the severity of the measure imposed on civil servants is crucial in cases of loyalty control.[611]

III. DUTIES AND RESPONSIBILITIES OF JOURNALISTS

a. Overview

With respect to journalists, the Court has consistently stressed their 'duties and responsibilities' to act in good faith to provide accurate and reliable information in accordance with ethics of journalism.[612] The ethics of journalists would require that their free speech right must not disseminate information and ideas inciting violence or hatred among the public,[613] or aggravate the tense climate through their gratuitously offensive expression in the context of inter-ethnic tension.[614]

The notion 'duties and responsibilities' of the press or of journalists has been invoked to reinforce the claim for protecting individual persons' honour and reputation, their right to private and family life,[615] and a public corporation's good name.[616] As will be analysed in the context of defamation, with regard to an affront to honour and reputation of individuals caused by allegedly defamatory statements, the Court has scrupulously appraised the nature and effect of such statements.

The Court has stressed that journalists' speech should not be subordinated to the requirement that they must systematically and formally distance themselves from the content of a quotation that might insult, provoke others, or damage their reputation. Such a rigorous requirement is at odds with the principle that the widest possible scope of protection must be accorded to the press and journalistic expression.[617] The *Verlagsgruppe News GmbH v Austria*[618] case arose from the forfeiture of a magazine. In his open letter, an artist criticized the politicians of the far-right political party, the Austrian Freedom Party (FPÖ), describing them as 'dastardly'. The applicant news company quoted this letter when reporting the FPÖ's defamation proceedings against the artist. The Court held that the mere reproduction of the controversial wording, coupled with sharp critical comments, did not provide sufficient basis for forfeiting the magazine. The requirement applied by the Austrian courts that journalists had systematically and formally to distance themselves from the content of a quoted passage, however insulting, was considered too formalistic to be proportionate.

b. The duty of journalists to provide accurate and reliable information

The concept 'duties and responsibilities' of journalists is closely linked to the requirement to act in good faith and 'provide accurate and reliable information in accordance with the ethics of journalism'.[619] Still, on the issue of accuracy of reporting, imposing criminal

---

[610] The Court noted that the applicant was promoted several times, and that the contested refusal of his non-promotion occurred at a very advanced stage of his career: *Otto v Germany* No 27574/02 hudoc (2005) DA.

[611] Apart from the cases of *Vogt* and *Otto*, see also *Wille v Liechtenstein* 1999-VII (refusal by the Prince to re-appoint the President of the Administrative Court because of his statement on a constitutional controversy).

[612] See, eg, *Bladet Tromsø and Stensaas v Norway* 1999-III; 29 EHRR 125 para 65 GC.

[613] *Sürek v Turkey (No 1) v Turkey* 1999-IV para 63 GC; and *Halis Doğan v Turkey (No 3)* hudoc (2006) para 36.   [614] See *Leroy v France* hudoc (2008) para 44.

[615] See *Von Hannover v Germany* 2004-VI; 43 EHRR 1 para 63.

[616] Compare *Wojtas-Kaleta v Poland* hudoc (2009) paras 43 and 48.

[617] *Thoma v Luxembourg* 2001-III; 36 EHRR 359 paras 58–63.   [618] Hudoc (2006) para 33.

[619] See *Goodwin v UK* 1996-II; 22 EHRR 123 para 39 GC; and *Fressoz and Roire* 1999-I; 31 EHRR 28 para 54 GC.

sanction on journalists for assisting in disseminating statements of an interviewee would go too far.[620] In the age of the internet, the Court has held that such duty and responsibility of the press and journalists in ensuring accuracy of information is more stringent with respect to historical information than as regards perishable information.[621]

In *Radio France and Others v France*,[622] the main question was whether the bounds of exaggeration or provocation were overstepped in reporting information originating from another source. The weekly magazine *Le Point* published an article stating that Michel Junot, a former deputy mayor of the Paris City Council, had supervised the maintenance of order during World War II in a town where a thousand Jewish people were interned before their deportation to Auschwitz. A journalist with *France Info*, a radio station of *Radio France*, reported that, according to *Le Point*, Mr Junot supervised the deportation of a thousand Jewish people in 1942. The French courts convicted the publishing director of *France Info* and a journalist for defaming Mr Junot. While *Le Point* mentioned the transport of Jews 'under Junot's responsibility', *France Info* went further in broadcasting that Mr Junot 'admits that he organised the departure of a transport of deportees to Drancy'.[623] The Court found that such a change in wording could not be justified on the basis of a 'degree of exaggeration' or 'provocation' because this constituted a dissemination of false information. When unanimously finding no violation of Article 10, the Court held that in view of the extremely grave allegations, the repeated form in which the information was broadcast and the immediate and powerful impact of audio-visuals, the journalists had to act with utmost care.

c. The duty of journalists to carry out independent research to corroborate veracity of the cited information

Aside from the question of accuracy, which is empirically ascertainable in the case of a quotation or citation from an original source, a more intriguing question would be the extent to which the press can reasonably regard its sources as reliable.[624] On this matter, a vexed question is to what extent the press is required, according to journalistic ethics and diligence, to carry out independent research to verify the accuracy or truthfulness of the information that it prints. The general approach is that the more serious the allegations are, the more stringent the obligation of the newspaper is to verify their accuracy by not automatically endorsing an allegation of one side of the dispute in question, but by hearing the other side's account.[625] The fact that matters of public interest are involved, such as issues of transparency, how public money is spent, and an allegation of abusive criminal proceedings, may give credence to the rights of journalists.[626] Yet, this does not dispense with the need for journalists and newspaper companies to verify the well-founded nature of the facts which they intend to report.[627] The ethics of journalism requires journalists and the press to act in good faith to verify the accuracy and reliability of the information

---

[620] *Björk Eidósdóttir v Iceland* hudoc (2012) para 80.

[621] *Times Newspapers Ltd (Nos 1 and 2) v UK* hudoc (2009) para 45.

[622] 2004-II; 40 EHRR 706 para 37.   [623] *Radio France and Others v France*, para 38.

[624] *McVicar v UK* 2002-III; 35 EHRR 566 para 84.

[625] *Europapress Holding DOO v Croatia* hudoc (2009) para 68.

[626] *Flux v Moldova (No 3)* hudoc (2007) para 24; *Flux v Moldova (No 4)* hudoc (2008) para 33; and *Flux v Moldova (No 5)* hudoc (2008) para 22.

[627] Compare *Flux v Moldova (No 6)* hudoc (2008) paras 30–2 (defamation brought by a principal of a high school based on the publication of a report on various issues of a high school, including bribery, all of which were derived from an anonymous letter without any journalist having visited the school or carried out investigations of its own) with *Flux v Moldova (No 7)* hudoc (2009) para 44 (at least an attempt made to prove the veracity of the report). See also *Rumyana Ivanova v Bulgaria* hudoc (2008) paras 55–71.

when there is a question of attacking the reputation of private individuals.[628] Publishing a report that charges specific individuals with criminal acts without giving them any opportunity to counter the accusations is a serious breach of the ethics of journalism, which cannot be remedied by the alleged public interest nature of the report.[629] Surely, the Court does not exclude other relevant factors: the difficulty in verifying the accuracy of the contested report in defamation proceedings brought long after its publication of the contested report; the fading away, with the passage of time, of the damage to the person allegedly defamed;[630] and fairness in defamation proceedings.[631]

In *Europapress Holding DOO*,[632] the biggest-selling national newspaper in Croatia reported that during their dispute, a journalist was allegedly threatened by a senior politician (Deputy Prime Minister) with a gun barrel pointed at her, only to be told that this was a joke. In this case, the Court endorsed the national courts' decisions, criticizing the applicant company for its negligence in its duties and responsibilities because of its failure to carry out sufficient verification of the information prior to publication. The omission to hear the other side's account[633] was considered fatal. No special ground was found to exempt the newspaper from verifying factual statements considered defamatory.[634]

d. Reliance on an 'official' report and the exemption of journalists from the duty to undertake independent research

The Court has conceded that the 'methods of objective and balanced reporting' is variable, depending, in particular, on the medium in question.[635] In this connection, it is of special import to compare *Bladet Tromsø and Stensaas v Norway*[636] and *Standard Verlagsgesellschaft mbH v Austria (No 2)*.[637] One can obtain crucial insight into the Court's method of absolving journalists of the duty to carry out independent research to ascertain the veracity of the information if they rely on an 'official' report.

In the former case, the issue arose from the publication of a minister-appointed inspector's report concerning seal-hunting in local newspaper articles, which highlighted acts of cruelty to seals committed by seal-hunters (including allegations of the flaying of seals alive) and an alleged assault on the inspector by the crew. The inspector's report accused the crew members of the seal-hunting vessel, without identifying the names of those allegedly implicated in the acts of cruelty. The Ministry of Fisheries issued an order, temporarily exempting the report from public disclosure to give the accused seal-hunters an opportunity to reply to the accusations. The independent Commission of Inquiries found that the serious accusations described were unproven. It also turned out that some crew members were not on board. The Norwegian courts held that the reproduction of the expert's report was damaging to the reputation and honour of the crew members of the vessel and convicted the newspaper company and its editor of defamation.

---

[628] *Savitchi v Moldova* hudoc (2005) para 46. See also *Flux v Moldova* hudoc (2007) para 30.

[629] *Flux v Moldova (No 6)* hudoc (2008) paras 31–2.

[630] *Flux v Moldova* hudoc (2007) paras 31–4.

[631] *Flux v Moldova (No 4)* hudoc (2008) para 41. Though not concerning defamation, see also *Stoll v Switzerland* 2007-V; 44 EHRR 55 para 137 GC.

[632] *Europapress Holding DOO v Croatia* hudoc (2009).

[633] *Europapress Holding DOO v Croatia*, para 68.

[634] According to the Court, such 'special grounds' depend on the nature and degree of the impugned defamation, and on the extent to which the media can reasonably believe that their sources as reliable:*Europapress Holding DOO v Croatia*.   [635] *Selistö v Finland* hudoc (2004) para 59.

[636] 1999-III; 29 EHRR 125 GC.   [637] Hudoc (2007).

The Grand Chamber considered that the allegations concerning the seals being flayed alive and hunters' assault on the inspector were serious. Nevertheless, it moderated their libellous effect, noting that they could be comprehended as an exaggerated presentation. In the majority's view, the applicants' decision not to publicize the names of the accused detracted from the defamatory impact. Paradoxically, some crew members of the vessel, who were not on board at the material time, argued that their reputation was infringed, because the articles mentioned the name of the vessel, so that the blame was laid on the entire crew members.

The gist of the question was whether the newspaper was required to undertake an independent research to establish factual basis for the allegations made in the inspector's report, or whether there were any special grounds that would exempt it from verifying factual statements that were defamatory of private individuals. The Norwegian courts found that by failing to establish the truth of the allegations, the applicants did not comply with the ethics of journalism. The Grand Chamber considered that the impugned report was an official one, with the expert appointed as an inspector by the Ministry of Fisheries, so that this was reliable. It held that, in the light of its public watchdog role, the press was normally entitled to rely on the contents of official reports without need to engage in independent research.[638]

In *Bladet Tromsø and Stensaas*, three dissenting judges[639] pointed out that the majority gave scant regard to the reputation of private individuals. Given the paramount interest of press freedom in democracy, it was essential, *as a general principle*, that the press should be exonerated from undertaking inquiries into the details of an official source to ascertain its veracity. However, it is questionable whether this general principle can be applied to *all* situations in which the reputation of private persons is at stake and where, as in this case, a newspaper has reproduced the contents of publicly inaccessible reports in disregard of a ministerial order explicitly banning such disclosure. Indeed, the three dissenting judges considered that the majority minimized the fact that the newspaper consciously took the risk of publishing the articles without checking the veracity of the contested claims.

In *Standard Verlagsgesellschaft mbH (No 2)*,[640] the applicant company, which was the owner of the daily newspaper 'Der Standard', published an article attributing administrative misconduct to Jörg Haider, a member of an extreme right-wing party, who was serving in a regional government. The Austrian courts found the contested statements to be incorrect factual statements and defamatory. They found that the applicant company had used an expert opinion in a one-sided manner. The article cited the expert opinion as reporting that Mr Haider deliberately deceived the regional government, even though that expert opinion did not contain such allegations. The applicant company argued that it relied on a press release of the Socialist Party, which summarized the expert opinion incorrectly. The Austrian courts ordered the forfeiture of the relevant issues of 'Der Standard', the publication of the judgment, and the revocation of the untrue statements. With respect to the 'duties and responsibilities' of journalists, the Strasbourg Court held that:

> special grounds are required before the media can be dispensed from their ordinary obligation to verify factual statements that are defamatory of private individuals. Whether such grounds exist depends in particular on the nature and degree of defamation in

---

[638] *Bladet Tromsø and Stensaas v Norway* 1999-III; 29 EHRR 125 para 68 GC.
[639] Joint dissenting opinion of Judges Palm, Fuhrmann, and Baka. [640] Hudoc (2007).

question and the extent to which the media can reasonably regard their sources as reliable with respect to the allegations.[641]

On the facts of the case, the Court held that the allegations in the article were false statements of fact and serious accusations of a defamatory nature, going beyond exaggerations or provocations. The Court distinguished the case from *Bladet Tromsø and Stensaas v Norway*. Statements by political opponents of Mr Haider were not considered comparable to the reports prepared by a government-appointed expert in the latter case. The lack of journalistic diligence was compounded by the failure to identify the press release as the source of citation and to verify the veracity of the information in the expert opinion even though this was available. By a close vote of four to three, the Court found no violation of Article 10. The three dissenting judges stressed journalists' entitlement to rely on press releases as a vital source of information for the media.[642] The applicant's misunderstanding of the expert opinion could have been corrected by the publication of a counter-statement, requested by Mr Haider. Because of the vital nature of journalistic freedom, it was crucial that such a less burdensome alternative should have been chosen at first.

One crucial principle emerging from the judgment of *Bladet Tromsø and Stensaas v Norway* is that journalists are absolved of the duty to undertake independent research to verify the veracity of the contents of their report if this relies on an official document.[643] This principle is confirmed in the subsequent case law.[644] In *Selistö v Finland*,[645] the Court confirmed this when assessing a journalist's articles, which were predicated on the police's pre-trial records to raise an allegation of medical negligence. Similarly, in *Gorelishvili v Georgia*,[646] the Court defended the approach of the journalist in drawing on the property declaration, an official document, to criticize the financial handling of an exiled parliamentarian without her own independent research. The principle can be applied by analogy to the information provided by the CEO of a formerly national plant, even though this is not an official document,[647] a finding that seems to depart from the Court's approach in *Standard Verlagsgesellschaft mbH (No 2)* as discussed earlier.

8. DISTINCT METHODOLOGIES AND PRINCIPLES DEVELOPED TO EXAMINE ISSUES OF DEFAMATION

I. OVERVIEW

No European minimum threshold below which it would be unjustifiable under Article 10 to impose a criminal sanction for defamatory expression has been established by the

---

[641] *Standard Verlagsgesellschaft mbH (No 2)*, para 38. See also *Pedersen and Baadgaard v Denmark* 2004-XI; 42 EHRR 486 para 78 GC.

[642] Joint dissenting opinion of Judges Rozakis, Vajić, and Spielmann, para 6.

[643] *Bladet Tromsø and Stensaas v Norway* 1999-III; 29 EHRR 125 para 68 GC.

[644] Apart from the cases cited in the text, see also *Colombani and Others v France* 2002-V para 65.

[645] *Selistö v Finland* hudoc (2004) para 60.   [646] *Gorelishvili v Georgia* hudoc (2007) para 41.

[647] *Flux v Moldova (No 2)* hudoc (2007) paras 42–3.

Court.[648] That said, from an abundance of cases on defamation, several salient doctrines and methods of review that are worthy of separate examination can be extrapolated. The first step of the Court is to examine whether the defamatory statement relates to an issue of general public interest, in which case any curtailment of it must be subject to stringent assessment. The notion of public interest has been broadly construed. It is also well-established in the case law that rulings that statements are defamatory of politicians invite a particularly stringent review.

In assessing the proportionate nature of a national measure adopted in response to a defamatory statement, the Court will examine: (i) the nature of the interference; (ii) the position of the applicant and the status of the alleged victim of defamation or insult in domestic proceedings; (iii) the subject matter of the contested statements; and (iv) the reasons for the interference, provided by the national authorities.[649] The Court has emphasized 'an objective link' between the contested statement and the person whose reputation is allegedly infringed.[650] Abstract criticism levelled at a political department or a regional government as such, which does not admit of identifying the specific persons targeted by that criticism, is not sufficient to constitute defamation.[651] There are numerous other factors, including the medium or form of the contested statement and the background against which it is made. With respect to the medium or form, clearly, audio-visual communications entail immediate and direct impact on the audience. Statements which could be described as offensive if expressed in a written form[652] may not overstep the boundaries of acceptable criticism if they are made orally, particularly in a spontaneous reaction in heated debates.[653] That there is little scope for reformulating or retracting oral words before publication can be invoked to lessen any negative impact of the impugned statement.[654] As regards the background against which the contested words need to be assessed, as affirmed in *Nilsen and Johnsen*,[655] special regard must be had to the question whether the allegedly defamatory statements have been made as a result of, or in response to, previous acerbic criticism, so as to counter what may be perceived as unfounded accusations.

The impact of publicity of the contested statement is a key to assessing the permissible reaction by the state.[656] In *Lindon, Otchakovsky-Laurens and July v France*,[657] it was not deemed objectionable that the mere act of reproducing a defamatory statement could result in criminal liability. One of the rationales for this was that the medium used was a national newspaper with broad public appeal. In contrast, in *Yankov v Bulgaria*,[658] it was disproportionate to impose a disciplinary punishment on a detainee who used insulting words to describe the personnel of the penitentiary and judiciary system in his private manuscript, which was far from being ready for publication. In *Grigoriades v Greece*,[659]

---

[648] Macdonald, in Matscher and Petzold, eds, *Protecting Human Rights: The European Dimension— Studies in Honour of Gérard J. Wiarda*, 1988, p 361 at 368.

[649] *Scharsach and News Verlagsgesellschaft GmbH v Austria* 2003-XI; 40 EHRR 569 para 31.

[650] *Dyuldin and Kislov v Russia* hudoc (2007) para 44.

[651] *Dyuldin and Kislov v Russia* hudoc (2007) para 44. Compare, however, *Thoma v Luxembourg* 2001-III para 56 (the Court acknowledging that due to the small size of the country, the unnamed claimants in the defamation action were readily identifiable).

[652] *De Diego Nafria v Spain* hudoc (2002) para 41. See also *Katamadze v Georgia No 69857/01* hudoc (2006) DA.

[653] See, eg, *Fuentes Bobo v Spain* hudoc (2000) para 48; and *Otegi Mondragon v Spain* hudoc (2011) para 54.

[654] *Nilsen and Johnsen v Norway* 1999-VIII; 30 EHRR 878 para 48 GC.

[655] 1999-VIII; 30 EHRR 878 para 52 GC.

[656] *Yankov v Bulgaria* 2003-XII; 40 EHRR 854. See also, eg, *Nikula v Finland* 2002-II; 38 EHRR 944 para 52.

[657] Hudoc (2007) para 66 GC.   [658] 2003-XII; 40 EHRR 854 paras 135–41.

[659] 1997-VII; 27 EHRR 464 para 47. Compare the dissenting opinion of Judge Sir John Freeland, joined by Judges Russo, Valticos, Loizou, and Morenilla, para 7.

an army officer was convicted of insulting the army, after writing a letter to his commanding officer in which the army was described as 'a criminal and terrorist apparatus'. Despite the harsh tone of his accusations, the Grand Chamber held in his favour, as the impugned letter was neither published nor disseminated to a wider audience.

Confronted with the conflict between press freedom and the honour of public figures, the Court generally accords the press a privileged status. It is well-established in case law that journalists' freedom of expression under Article 10 can encompass a degree of exaggeration, or even provocation, on their part.[660] This principle has been applied by analogy to members of civil society, such as NGO campaigners, who are also entitled to 'a certain degree of hyperbole and exaggeration'.[661] However, as already noted,[662] the Court has frequently made reference to the 'duties and responsibilities' of the press to act 'in good faith and on an accurate factual basis', and to provide 'reliable and precise' (or 'accurate and reliable') information in accordance with the ethics of journalism.[663] The press must not abuse its freedom of expression to make gratuitous personal attacks. Nevertheless, journalistic expression made in good faith does not forfeit its privileged status unless there lacks an element of truth underlying the words considered offensive and insulting.[664] With respect to the duty to act on an 'accurate factual basis', the extent to which journalists are expected to prove the veracity of information that they disclose has been analysed in relation to their duties and responsibilities.

A crucial question is whether on the facts of a particular case, the contested statements remain within the ambit of acceptable criticism on matters of public concern, or instead constitute abusive attacks on the personality of individuals. In some cases, the nature, content, tone, and context of the contested statements are clearly not such as to be considered insulting or defamatory.[665] For instance, a lawyer's critical comment that the decision of the Moldovan Constitutional Court would cause 'total anarchy in the legal profession' in encroaching on the independence of the legal profession was hardly insulting enough to overstep the limits of acceptable criticisms.[666] When assessing the boundary between acceptable criticism and gratuitous attacks, the Court distinguishes between factual elements and value-laden elements, the crucial question to which the examination will turn further in the paragraphs that follow.

II. PUBLIC PERSONS AND BROADER BOUNDS OF ACCEPTABLE CRITICISM

a. Political figures and public figures doctrine

According to the US 'public figures' doctrine, a successful claim for defamation by public officials will be consistent with freedom of expression only where malice is

---

[660] See, eg, *Prager and Oberschlick v Austria* A 313 (1995); 21 EHRR 1 para 38; *Perna v Italy* 2003-V; 39 EHRR 563 para 39 GC; and *Lindon, Otchakovsky-Laurens and July v France* hudoc (2007) para 62 GC.

[661] *Steel and Morris v UK* 2005-II; 41 EHRR 403 para 90.   [662] See section X.XX, p oo.

[663] *Bladet Tromsø and Stensaas v Norway* 1999-III; 29 EHRR 125 para 62 GC; *Colombani v France* 2002-V, para 65; *McVicar v UK* 2002-III; 35 EHRR 566 para 73; *Hachette Filipacchi Associés v France* hudoc (2007). See also *Shabanov and Tren v Russia* hudoc (2006) para 40.

[664] *Feldek v Slovakia* 2001-VIII paras 81 and 84.

[665] See, eg, *Reznik v Russia* hudoc (2013) para 49 (the word 'rummage' not considered going beyond the gamut of acceptable criticism in alleged defamation against a prison and prison warders).

[666] *Amihalachioaie v Moldova* 2004-III; 40 EHRR 833 para 36.

demonstrated.[667] The essence of this doctrine has been duly introduced in the Strasbourg Court's case law and developed into its own form.[668]

The consistent policy of the Court is that the permissible pale of criticism of politicians' deeds and words must be construed much more broadly than it is for private individuals.[669] The rationale is that, unlike private persons, politicians knowingly choose to become public figures exposed to close scrutiny by journalists and the general public.[670] Politicians must accordingly display greater tolerance of criticisms made by the press and the public.[671] If the contested expression is described as political or civil in nature, or based on press freedom,[672] robust review may intervene.[673] This is especially true when journalists or the press are accused of defamation of politicians,[674] an approach that can be strengthened when the disputed statement concerns issues of public interest understood in a wide sense. In such circumstances, assessment of any chilling effect on journalists or the press should be closely undertaken.[675] Even so, while the bounds of acceptable criticism against public figures are no doubt large, this does not mean that politicians who are under unfounded attack should be deprived of an opportunity to reply and defend their reputation in relation to any erroneous publications.[676]

However, it should be noted that once politicians withdraw from their political life, they regain the status of private persons entitled to a broader scope of privacy rights.[677] As will be analysed later, when applied to civil servants entrusted with administrative powers, the public figures doctrine requires modification, because most civil servants are not in a position to respond to criticisms in a way that politicians are able to do. Clearly, whether a certain public figure is actually known to the public is immaterial, as the essence is that he or she has entered the public arena voluntarily.[678]

A notable impact of the public figures doctrine was seen in the case where even the conditional discontinuation of criminal proceedings against a journalist convicted for defamation against a politician was considered a form of censorship, and hence unjustifiable, if a criminal record remained.[679] In *Dąbrowski v Poland*,[680] a journalist was convicted of defamation after publishing newspaper articles reporting criminal proceedings against a local politician. He described the allegedly defamed mayor as 'mayor burglar', but only after the trial court had found the mayor guilty of burglary. In finding a breach

---

[667] See *New York Times v Sullivan*, 376 US 254 (1964). See also Macdonald, in Matscher and Petzold, eds, *Protecting Human Rights: The European Dimension—Studies in Honour of Gérard J. Wiarda*, 1988, at p 369.

[668] See, *inter alia, Lingens v Austria* A 104 para 42; *Incal v Turkey* 1998-IV; 49 EHRR 449 para 54; *Brasilier v France* hudoc (2006) para 41; and *Vellutini and Michel v France* hudoc (2011) para 38.

[669] *Brasilier v France* hudoc (2006) para 41; and *Gorelishvili v Georgia* hudoc (2007) para 35.

[670] *Lingens v Austria* A 103 (1986); 8 EHRR 407 para 42 PC; *Oberschlick v Austria (No 1)* A 204 (1991); 19 EHRR 389 paras 57–9 PC; *Vereinigung Demokratischer Soldaten Österreichs and Gubi v Austria* A 302 (1994); 20 EHRR 56 para 37; *Oberschlick v Austria (No 2)* 1997-IV; 25 EHRR 357 para 29; *Incal v Turkey* 1998-IV; 49 EHRR 449 para 54 GC; *Hrico v Slovakia* hudoc (2004); 41 EHRR 300 para 40; *Turhan v Turkey* hudoc (2005) para 25; and *Brasilier v France* hudoc (2006) para 41.

[671] See, *inter alia, Dąbrowski v Poland* hudoc (2006) para 35.

[672] See, eg, *Lopes Gomes da Silva v Portugal*, 2000-X, paras 31 and 35 (a journalist convicted of libel for describing a lawyer standing for an election for Lisbon City Council for a conservative political party, known for his anti-Semitic speeches, as 'grotesque', 'buffoonish', and 'coarse').

[673] See, *inter alia, Dalban v Romania* 1999-VI GC paras 48–52; *Turham v Turkey* hudoc (2005) para 25; *Tara and Poiata v Moldova* hudoc (2007) paras 24–5.

[674] See, eg, *Lingens v Austria, Lingens v Austria* A 103 (1986); 8 EHRR 407 para 44.

[675] See, eg, *Krasulya v Russia* hudoc (2007), paras 44–5.

[676] *Gąsior v Poland* hudoc (2012) para 43.   [677] *Tammer v Estonia* 2001-I; 37 EHRR 857 para 68.

[678] *Krone Verlag GmbH & Co. KG v Austria* hudoc (2002) para 37.

[679] *Dąbrowski v Poland* hudoc (2006) para 3.   [680] Hudoc (2006) paras 33–5.

of Article 10, the Court gave special weight to the journalist's entitlement to a certain degree of exaggeration, and to the expectation that the mayor, as a public figure, should have displayed a greater degree of tolerance to criticism, some of which were classified as value-judgments not devoid of factual basis.[681] Where an issue of special public interest (such as public health) is involved, this can bolster a journalist's expression rights exercised in similarly harsh critical tones.[682]

The first *cause célèbre* in the field of defamation of politicians was the case of *Lingens v Austria*.[683] In this case, the Austrian Chancellor had described the Jewish Documentation Centre as a 'political mafia' when its President, Simon Wiesenthal, had reproached the President of the Austrian Liberal Party, with whom the Chancellor was seeking to arrange a post-election coalition, for having served in the SS during World War II. The applicant was convicted of criminal defamation when he accused the Chancellor of 'the basest opportunism' and of acting in an 'immoral' and 'undignified' manner. The Plenary Court held unanimously that the conviction was disproportionate, relying on the principle that political figures must tolerate a greater extent of criticism than private individuals. Against the background of heated political debates, the applicant's expressions, though offensive, were not deemed defamatory. The criminal sanction was all the more disproportionate because the applicant was required to prove the truth of his value-judgments relating to matters of political concern.

Similarly, in other cases involving defamation of politicians, the Court has boldly undertaken a critical examination of national decisions.[684] In the second *Oberschlick* case,[685] a journalist was convicted of defaming the then leader of the far-right political party, the Austrian Freedom Party, Jörg Haider, for describing him as an 'idiot'. Once again, the Commission and Court stressed the broad bounds of acceptable criticism of a politician.[686] The decisive factor was that the contested word was not classified as a 'gratuitous personal attack' in a polemical tone, but as an 'opinion' (hence value-judgment) worthy of protection under Article 10.[687] The emphasis was shifted to the *overall* context in which the expression was used.

As explained later, when participating in public debates, private persons must also tolerate greater extent of criticisms. In *Österreichischer Rundfunk v Austria*,[688] the applicant was a public law foundation which broadcast information on the release on parole of the head of a neo-Nazi organization in Austria. The news item also mentioned his deputy, S, who had been convicted and sentenced to a lengthy term of imprisonment for being a leading member of a neo-Nazi organization, but had been released on parole earlier. The broadcast showed S's picture for a couple of seconds, together with information about his conviction. At S's request, the national courts ordered the applicant to refrain from publishing S's picture without his consent following his release on parole. Holding that the injunction was a breach of Article 10, the Court stated that even though S was a private individual, the fact that he was a well-known neo-Nazi activist warranted the application of the public figures doctrine.

---

[681] See also *Tara and Poiata v Moldova* hudoc (2007) paras 28–31 (applying the broader notion of value-judgment to a newspaper and its journalist found to have defamed a politician for alleging abuses and nepotism).   [682] *Kaperzyński v Poland* hudoc (2012) paras 69–74.

[683] A 103 (1986); 8 EHRR 407 paras 42–3 PC, and also paras 74, 81–84 Com Rep.

[684] Apart from the second *Oberschlick* case discussed in the text, see, eg, *Turham v Turkey* hudoc (2005) paras 24–30.   [685] 1997-IV; 25 EHRR 357.

[686] *Oberschlick v Austria (No 2)*, para 29. See also *Turham v Turkey* hudoc (2005) paras 25–7.

[687] *Oberschlick v Austria (No 2)* 1997-IV; 25 EHRR 357 para 33.   [688] Hudoc (2006) para 65.

b. Civil servants and the public figures doctrine

Civil servants must be shielded from any abusive and defamatory attacks that are intended to impinge on their performance of duties and to damage public confidence in them.[689] The Court has suggested that the bounds of permissible criticism of civil servants under Article 10 hinge on the scope and nature of the public authorities concerned, and on the powers entrusted to them.[690] Unlike politicians, civil servants do not lay themselves open to public scrutiny. They also require public confidence in performing their duties.[691] According to the Court's case law, these principles apply with greater force to law-enforcement officers and prosecutors,[692] given the special importance of public confidence in them.

Nevertheless, the Court has held that the public figures doctrine can be applied by analogy to civil servants entrusted with certain administrative powers, so that they must tolerate criticism directed against their words and deeds.[693] When confronted with defamation proceedings filed by civil servants, the Court must closely ascertain whether there exists a real risk that an impugned remark may perturb public confidence in their performance. Even so, where the press freedom or political expression is at stake, and/or when alleged defamation impinges upon matters of public concern, such as alleged abuse of power by public officials in the sale of state-owned aircraft,[694] the protection of the environment, and public health,[695] the Court is disposed to dissect the substance of the case at length, in accordance with the methodology established in the case law, as will be examined later: the context in which the impugned statement was made; and the content of the statement, which may be considered a statement of alleged fact or a value-judgment accompanied by a reasonable factual basis.[696] In contrast, once civil servants or judges run for election, it is clear that they have entered the 'political arena' that requires them to endure greater bounds of public criticism.[697]

A case in which the parallel with politicians in applying the public figures doctrine was held not to apply in the same manner was *Janowski v Poland*.[698] In that case, a journalist was convicted for orally insulting 'municipal guards', who were civil servants, during a heated exchange in a public place about the exercise by the guards of their law-enforcement powers to move street traders on. The Court accepted that civil servants may need protection from offensive verbal attacks if they are successfully to perform their task. In its view, on the facts of the case, the requirements of such protection did 'not have to be weighed in relation to the interests of the freedom of the press or of open discussion of matters of public concern because the applicant's remarks were not uttered in such a context'.[699] Judge Bratza, in his dissenting opinion, persuasively argued that the applicant used virulent words as a spontaneous reaction in a heated exchange, rather than as a 'deliberate and gratuitous personal attack' on the guards.[700]

---

[689] *Busuioc v Moldova* hudoc (2004); 42 EHRR 252 para 64.

[690] *Busuioc v Moldova*, paras 64–5.   [691] *Raichinov v Bulgaria* hudoc (2006) para 48.

[692] See, eg, *Busuioc v Moldova* hudoc (2004) para 64.

[693] *Steur v Netherlands* 2003-XI; 39 EHRR 706 para 39.   [694] *Busuioc v Moldova* hudoc (2004).

[695] See, eg, *Mamère v France*, 2006-XIII (criticism of the public official that undermined the risk of radioactive contamination from Chernobyl); and *Desjardin v France* hudoc (2007) para 46 (another case concerning the French Green Party member who, during the election campaign, criticized the ancient mayor of a town for polluting the quality of communal water).

[696] *Busuioc v Moldova* hudoc (2004) paras 68, 74, 77–8, 84.

[697] *Hrico v Slovakia* hudoc (2004); 41 EHRR 300 para 46; and *Kwiecień v Poland* hudoc (2007) paras 52 and 54.   [698] 1999-I; 29 EHRR 705.

[699] *Janowski v Poland*, para 33.

[700] *Janowski v Poland*, dissenting opinion of Judge Sir Nicolas Bratza joined by Judge Rozakis. Cf the approach of the Commission, which stressed that the amount of the fine was excessive: Com Rep para 46.

In *Mamère v France*,[701] the case concerned a green party leader and a member of the European Parliament, who participated in a television programme in 1999, in which he mentioned that the then director of the now defunct official research organ (Central Service for Protection against Ionising Radiation) at the time of the Chernobyl nuclear disaster in 1986 was 'a sinister character', and that this expert 'kept on telling us that France was so strong—the Asterix complex—that the Chernobyl cloud had not crossed our borders'. The then director, who was already retired, filed a suit of public defamation of a civil servant, which the national courts endorsed. The Court found that the contested statement that criticized the insufficient information given by the authorities about levels of contamination related to issues of environment and public health, both of which were clearly of general public concern.[702] In view of his status as an elected representative committed to ecological issues, his statement was described as a political and 'militant' expression.[703] The impugned statements were considered to contain both value-judgments and factual allegations.[704] The applicant was precluded from relying on the defence of truth. He was time-barred, with the relevant event having occurred more than ten years before.[705] The Court found nothing insulting in respect of the contested expression 'sinister character', viewed against the background of the largest nuclear accident. With regard to the other contested words, 'Asterix complex', this was seen more as a caricature of the confident French authorities.[706] In this case, the Court has slightly qualified its approach in *Janowski* in the direction of greater protection of Article 10 rights. It asserted that 'while it cannot be said that civil servants knowingly lay themselves open to close scrutiny of their every word and deed to the extent to which politicians do, in certain cases civil servants acting in an official capacity are subject to wider limits of acceptable criticism than ordinary citizens'.[707] The Court was, however, quick to add a caveat that 'It would be going too far to extend the principle established in that judgment without reservation to all persons who are employed by the State, in any capacity whatsoever'.[708]

It is essential that the accountability of government-appointed experts, albeit non-elected, should be subject to constant scrutiny. Yet, the proposal that the public figures doctrine ought to be applied on the basis of their function *as such* was not taken up in *Nilsen and Johnsen v Norway*.[709] In that case, the Court held that it was not the activity of the government-designated expert that could justify treating him akin to a politician who had to tolerate close scrutiny. What was decisive for broadening the bounds of acceptable criticism of his work was his participation in public debates, which went beyond the remits of his duty as an appointed expert. As the expert in question himself contributed to a heated public discussion, he had to tolerate a greater degree of exaggeration.

III. DISTINCTION BETWEEN STATEMENTS OF FACT AND VALUE-JUDGMENTS

When confronted with statements that national courts have found defamatory, libellous, or insulting, the Court firstly examines whether such statements are to be categorized as factual assertions or value-judgments. Factual statements require proof of their truth,

---

[701] 2006-XIII. [702] *Mamère v France*, para 20. [703] *Mamère v France*, para 20.
[704] *Mamère v France*, para 23. [705] *Mamère v France*, para 24.
[706] *Mamère v France*, para 25. [707] *Mamère v France*, para 27.
[708] *Mamère v France*, para 27.
[709] This was the reasoning adopted by the Commission: 1999-VIII; 30 EHRR 878 Com Rep.

raising the questions of the burden of proof and of the evidentiary standard for applicants. On the other hand, value-judgments such as opinions and comments are regarded as not susceptible of proof.[710] This distinction is all the more important because statements described as value-judgments enjoy greater protection in terms of standard and onus of proof. The Court has rebuked national laws or courts for failing to make this important distinction utterly,[711] or for failing to differentiate properly those two elements within the impugned statements.[712] The Court has displayed a willingness to carry out its own evaluation of the impugned statements. In *Nikowitz and Verlagsgruppe News GmbH v Austria*, the newspaper article, which provided satirical comments by a rival skier upon the injury of his rival of international celebrity, was found defamatory. The Court considered that this finding was too formalistic in failing to appreciate its satirical and humorous feature.[713]

Still, the Court has acknowledged in several cases[714] that the distinction between value-judgments and statements of fact may be blurred, and that the issue needed to be resolved by examining the degree of factual proof. After all, such difficulty is inevitable, as 'rights are mediators between the domain of pure value judgements and the domain of factual judgements'.[715]

When classifying certain statements as value-judgments or as allegations of fact, the Court has desisted from succumbing to a margin of appreciation.[716] The case law suggests the Court's preparedness to examine scrupulously the contested statements to identify elements that can be described as value-judgments. This can often take the form of disaggregating the contested statement into different elements and appraising whether each of its components can amount to a value-judgment.[717] If such an approach had been applied to *Tolstoy Miloslavsky v UK*,[718] the applicant, who was a historian, could have successfully challenged the injunction preventing him from disseminating his research output, including the allegation of a war crime committed in the aftermath of World War II by a warden of a prestigious English 'public' school. In that case, when finding the balance to be upset, the Court focused instead on the absence of 'adequate and effective safeguards' against the award of an exorbitant sum for libel.

Generally, favouring freedom of expression, the Court has construed the notion 'value-judgment' generously, especially where the expression rights of a journalist or a politician are in issue. Using what may be commonly considered offensive expressions, such as 'fascist' or 'Nazi' (or arguably, 'communist') to describe a specific person does not in itself exceed the bounds of acceptable criticism under Article 10. Moreover, according to the Court's case law, such expressions, highly provocative as they may be, is not a factual statement that would require the proof that the persons targeted by the virulent

---

[710] See, *inter alia*, *De Haes and Gijsels v Belgium* 1997-I; 25 EHRR 1 para 47; *Nilsen and Johnsen v Norway* 1999-VIII; 30 EHRR 878 paras 49–50 GC; and *Hrico v Slovakia* hudoc (2004); 41 EHRR 300 para 40.

[711] *Gorelishvili v Georgia* hudoc (2007) para 38; *Flux v Moldova* hudoc (2007) para 29; and *Katrami v Greece* hudoc (2007) para 41.   [712] *Flux v Moldova (No 4)* hudoc (2008) paras 35–40.

[713] *Nikowitz and Verlagsgruppe News GmbH v Austria* hudoc (2007) paras 25–6. See also *Eon v France* hudoc (2013) paras 60–1.

[714] *Vides Aizsardzības Klubs v Latvia* hudoc (2004) para 43; *Krone Verlag GmbH & Co KG and MEDIAPRINT Zeitungs-und Zeitschriftenverlag GmbH & CoKG v Austria* No 42429/98 hudoc (2003) DA. See also *Katamadze v Georgia* No 69857/01 hudoc (2006) DA.

[715] Kennedy, *A Critique of Adjudication—fin de siècle*, 1997, p 305.

[716] *Amihalachioaie v Moldova* 2004-III; 40 EHRR 833 para 36.

[717] See, eg, *Busuioc v Moldova* hudoc (2004); 42 EHRR 252 paras 70–1, 74–5, 78–9, 81–5, 90–3.

[718] A 316-B (1995); 2 EHRR 442. The Court upheld the injunction: *Tolstoy Miloslavsky v UK*, paras 49–50 and 54.

criticisms are actual members of extremist political parties.[719] The evaluation must turn to the context in which such expressions are used, with the Court assessing whether or not the expression has been a spontaneous or emotional reaction.

In *Jerusalem*,[720] where a local politician remarked that sects shared totalitarian character and fascist tendencies, Austrian courts found her remark to be a statement of fact which was not proven true, so that it amounted to defamation. In contrast, the Court described it as a value-judgment and a fair comment on matters of general public interest, not requiring proof of its truth.[721] In *Hrico v Slovakia*,[722] a journalist published articles criticizing a decision of the Slovakian Supreme Court which found that a poet defamed a government minister when accusing the latter of having a fascist past. He described this decision as 'a legal farce', noting that it was explicable partly by the presiding judge's political candidacy for the Christian-Social Union party, which failed to condemn Slovakia's fascism during World War II. This led to legal proceedings against him, and he was ordered to make a public apology and to pay compensation. The Court classified the contested statement as an opinion, even if overblown, hence a value-judgment whose truth could not be proven. Even with respect to private persons, the Court's readiness to recognize elements of value-judgments can be seen. As discussed earlier, in *Paturel*,[723] a member of the Jehovah's Witnesses compared the method of 'deprogramming' proposed by an association assisting victims of religious sects to the Soviet psychological method against dissidents. Such a description may be staggering, yet the Court classified it as a value-judgment rather than as a statement of fact.

The broad interpretation of the notion of value-judgments can be reinforced by the public interest nature of the impugned article *taken as a whole*. In *Scharsach and News Verlagsgesellschaft GmbH v Austria*,[724] a magazine article described those persons who had an ambiguous relation to National Socialist ideas as 'closet Nazi', referring, among others, to Mrs Rosenkranz, an Austrian Freedom Party (FPÖ) politician. The Austrian courts considered the term 'closet Nazi' a statement of fact. They took a highly formalistic interpretation of this term, holding that it called for clandestine Nazi activities. They ruled that, in the absence of any proof of such activities by Mrs Rosenkranz, the use of this term went beyond the acceptable bounds of journalistic criticism. In contrast, the Court considered the contested term a value-judgment, which was supported by sufficient facts. In particular, Mrs Rosenkranz was an extreme right-wing politician, who publicly criticized the National Socialism Prohibition Act. The Court found that the degree of precision that the Austrian courts required for establishing the well-founded nature of a criminal charge was incompatible with the journalistic expression dealing with a matter of public interest.

In contrast, where the disparaging statements of fact voiced in a newspaper article are motivated by a competitive intention, this may weaken the claim that they are value-judgments. In *Krone Verlag GmbH & Co KG and MEDIAPRINT Zeitungs- und Zeitschriftenverlag GmbH & Co KG v Austria*,[725] an article published by the applicant

[719] *Feldek v Slovakia*, 2001-VIII para 86; *Gavrilovici v Moldova* hudoc (2009) para 56.

[720] *Jerusalem v Austria* 2001-II; 37 EHRR 567 para 44. The Court also found a sufficient factual basis for this: *Jerusalem v Austria*, para 45. See also *Sokolowski v Poland* hudoc (2005) para 47.

[721] The fact that the person claiming to be defamed is acting in the public domain was also of special relevance: *Jerusalem v Austria*, para 39. See also *Karman v Russia* hudoc (2006) para 35; and *Gavrilovici v Moldova* hudoc (2009), paras 55–6.

[722] Hudoc (2004); 41 EHRR 300 paras 40, and 45–6.

[723] *Paturel v France* hudoc (2005) para 37.   [724] 2003-XI; 40 EHRR 569 paras 39–43.

[725] Hudoc (2003) DA.

company virulently criticized an article of another newspaper which, written by a history professor, defended an exhibition of war crimes committed by the Wehrmacht during World War II. The applicant's article contained such statements as 'A Salzburg professor…—a Waldheim persecutor—praises this exhibition…anyone who…has been guilty of such criminal falsification…deserves our utter contempt.' The Austrian courts found the article not only to contain untrue and disparaging statements of fact, but also to be written with a competitive aim. The contents of the article, which related to the exhibition that caused public uproar in Salzburg, were surely of public interest. Yet, the Court, endorsing the national courts' decision, unanimously found that the public interest of the article was outweighed by what it saw as the defamatory statements aggravated by a competitive aim.

IV. 'SUFFICIENT FACTUAL BASIS'

Once the contested statements are found to include value-judgments, the next task is to ascertain whether there is a 'sufficient factual basis' to support them.[726] Even value-judgments necessitate at least some factual grounds.[727] Yet, the standard of proof required of applicants that have made impugned expression must not be rigorously precise. In *Dyuldin and Kislov*,[728] the open letter written by civil society groups to the President of the Russian Federation criticized a regional governor's policy as 'destructive'. The Russian courts required the applicants to show that such an allegation was supported by 'a scientifically sound comprehensive assessment of the social and economic development of the region'. The Court found such a precise requirement too onerous.[729]

When an applicant has made a *prima facie* case for some factual basis, the onus is shifted to the government to refute such a basis. Moreover, once the facts have come to the public knowledge, the requirement to adduce the facts on which a value-judgment is premised loses its importance.[730] In contrast, the absence of any factual basis for disputed allegations may undermine the presumptive protection given to value-judgments.[731] Serious allegations of corruption on the part of a prosecutor and a judge, made by an experienced lawyer with harsh words in a newspaper article, are unlikely to succeed under Article 10(2) if his allegations are not bolstered by factual evidence. One key consideration in such cases is the specially protected status of the judiciary who are not democratically elected and unable to respond to criticisms. In the Court's view, even those statements that can be described as emotional value-judgments in reaction may not be sufficient to lessen defamatory nature of the statements.[732] Similarly, allegations of political bias of the senior police management, written by a member of a trade union in its website, may call for corroboration of factual ground if made by a senior police officer. This is mainly because of the risk of insubordination that such writings may cause by discrediting the legitimacy of the police force.[733]

---

[726] See, eg, *Jerusalem v Austria* 2001-II; 37 EHRR 567 para 43; *Sokolowski v Poland* hudoc (2005) para 48; and *Lindon, Otchakovsky-Laurens and July v France* hudoc (2007) para 55.

[727] See, eg, *Turhan v Turkey* hudoc (2005) para 24; *Shabanov and Tren v Russia* hudoc (2006) para 41.

[728] Hudoc (2007).   [729] *Dyuldin and Kislov v Russia*, para 48.

[730] *Feldek v Slovakia* 2001-VIII para 86.

[731] *Karpetas v Greece* hudoc (2012) para 78. See also *De Diego Nafría v Spain* hudoc (2002) para 40.

[732] *Karpetas v Greece* hudoc (2012) paras 78–81 (the impugned statements recognized as a reaction to the decision to release a young man with a serious criminal record, who assaulted him physically).

[733] *Szima v Hungary* hudoc (2012) para 32.

The necessity of proving the degree of linkage between a value-judgment and its supporting facts may vary, depending on the specific circumstances of the case.[734] For instance, the fact that a mayor was examined by a national tribunal for fraudulent manoeuvres concerning a ballot was regarded as sufficient for the allegation that he stole the election.[735] Similarly, the revelations of false accusations of police brutalities, which cast doubt on the research methodology of a government-appointed expert, were held to constitute sufficient factual ground for harsh criticisms made by the representatives of police organizations against that expert to defend their reputation and honour.[736]

The rigour with which the subtest of sufficient factual basis is examined may vary, according to the close connection between the contested remarks and matters of public interest.[737] Special note must be taken of another sign of maturing methodology. The case law suggests that the evaluation of the public interest nature of the contested statements can be integrated into the process of examining the two stages (the distinction between factual allegations and value-judgments; and the sufficient factual basis for value-judgments).[738] In relation to markedly privileged expressions, such as political expression and journalistic or press freedom,[739] the Court has not recoiled from: (i) broadening the notion of public interest; and (ii) undertaking a detailed analysis of controversial statements to identify both value-judgments and some (even limited) factual basis for supporting them. With respect to journalists' expression rights, describing a local politician as 'burglar mayor' in newspaper articles was not considered devoid of any factual basis, if there was a finding by a trial court that he was guilty of burglary. In such cases, special regard must be had to the question whether the statements disclose any elements of gratuitous personal attacks or any intention to offend the criticized politician.

The assessment of the defamatory nature or otherwise of a reality novel, which, while using fictional characters, is based on real events, poses delicate questions as to the pertinence of the disjunction between value-judgments and facts, and the extent to which the factual basis needs to be established. The case of *Lindon, Otchakovsky-Laurens and July v France*[740] concerned a novel entitled 'Jean-Marie Le Pen on Trial', in which the ex-chairperson of the far-right political party was likened to the 'chief of a gang of killers' and portrayed as a 'vampire'. The book noted that he 'advocated' the murder of an immigrant, which was committed by a fictional character. The author of the book and the chairperson of the board of directors of the publishing company were convicted of defamation and complicity in defamation respectively. The French courts dismissed the defence of good faith because of the failure of the first two applicants to carry out sufficient investigations into the allegations and to use dispassionate language. The Grand Chamber held that the contested words revealed not only value-judgments but also allegations of fact, requiring investigations into the sufficient basis of the allegations. Special weight was placed on the virulent nature of the contested words, which were considered such as to indicate the intention of stigmatization and liable to stir up violence and hatred. These words were considered to exceed the limit of political debate. According to the Grand Chamber, even against the background of fierce political struggles, it was

---

[734] *Wirtschafts-Trend Zeitschriften-Verlags GmbH v Austria (No 3)* hudoc (2005) para 35.

[735] *Brasilier v France* hudoc (2006) paras 38 and 41.

[736] *Nilsen and Johnsen v Norway* 1999-VIII; 30 EHRR 878 paras 50–1 GC.

[737] *Amihalachioaie v Moldova* 2004-III; 40 EHRR 833 para 35. See also *Krasulya v Russia* hudoc (2007) para 41.

[738] For such an overall and synthesized approach, see *Kobenter and Standard Verlags GmbH v Austria* hudoc (2006) para 30.   [739] See, eg, *Dąbrowski v Poland* hudoc (2006) paras 33–5.

[740] Hudoc (2007) para 55.

legitimate for the French courts to ensure a minimum degree of moderation, 'especially as the reputation of a politician, even a controversial one, must benefit from the protection afforded by the Convention'.[741] The penalty imposed on the applicants was moderate.[742] The medium of the impugned expression was a fiction, rather than a news report. As the four dissenting judges noted,[743] it may be asked if the majority duly took account of these factors, so as not to stifle the role of artistic creation in political debates. The dissenting judges pointed out that the distinction between fact and value-judgment 'becomes *partly* pertinent when the novel and the reality coincide'.[744]

In *Lindon*, the publishing director of *Libération* (the third applicant) himself was convicted of defamation. The Grand Chamber accepted that his conviction was justified on the ground that *Libération* published a petition that reproduced extracts from the novel, which the domestic court found defamatory. Whether or not the bounds of acceptable 'provocation' had been transgressed was examined on the basis not only of the nature and the content of the impugned passages. Account was taken of other factors such as the potential impact of reproducing the defamatory passages in a widely circulated newspaper. The Grand Chamber noted that the 'duties and responsibilities' of the journalists to provide 'reliable and precise' information in accordance with the ethics of journalism was pivotal when assessing attacks of the reputation of a specific individual. The majority endorsed the national courts' finding, noting that '[w]hether such grounds exist depends in particular on the nature and degree of the defamation in question and the extent to which the media can reasonably regard their sources as reliable with respect to the allegations'.[745]

The implication of the majority's conclusion is to detract from the established principle that public figures, even though entitled to the protection of their reputation under Article 8, must endure greater extent of criticisms. As compared with the first two applicants, the blameworthiness imputable to the third applicant lay merely in publishing the extracts of the passages that the domestic courts found defamatory. He was not the author of the petition. As noted in dissent, imposing criminal sanctions, albeit moderate in nature, in itself, may yield chilling effects on journalists.[746]

V. PROOF OF THE TRUTH OF CONTESTED STATEMENT

Journalists accused of defamation are required to provide *prima facie* reliable evidence for supporting their claim, failing which the Court may demand the proof of the veracity of allegations.[747] For journalists, the duty of verifying the authenticity of the disclosed information should be embedded in their professional ethic. In contrast, such a duty should not be stringently applied to those individuals acting as whistle-blowers. Still, in case employees allege misdeeds of their employer in relations governed by private law, some further fine-tuning may be needed. Here, the criteria for ascertaining such cases include: (i) public interest of the disclosed information; (ii) authenticity of such

---

[741] *Lindon, Otchakovsky-Laurens and July v France*, para 57.

[742] *Lindon, Otchakovsky-Laurens and July v France*, para 59.

[743] Partly dissenting opinion of Judges Rozakis, Bratza, Tulkens, and Šikuta. They referred to *Vereinigung Bildender Künstler v Austria* hudoc (2007) para 33.

[744] *Lindon, Otchakovsky-Laurens and July v France*, para 5 (emphasis added).

[745] *Lindon, Otchakovsky-Laurens and July v France*, para 67.

[746] *Lindon, Otchakovsky-Laurens and July v France*, partly dissenting opinion of Judges Rozakis, Bratza, Tulkens, and Šikuta, paras 4 and 7.

[747] *McVicar v UK* 2002-III; 35 EHRR 566 para 86.

information; (iii) good faith of the whistle-blowers (which includes the examination of whether or not they have acted knowingly and frivolously to divulge incorrect information); (iv) any disadvantage to the employer; and (v) severity of the impugned sanction imposed on them.[748] The potency of element (iv) may be vitiated by the preponderance in element (i), as recognized by the Court in *Heinisch*,[749] where deficiencies in service provided by a state-owned company was in issue.

As stated in *Steel and Morris v UK*,[750] albeit not concerning press freedom, it is 'not in principle incompatible with Article 10 to place on a defendant in libel proceedings the onus of proving to the civil standard the truth of defamatory statements', namely that the statement is 'substantially true on the balance of probabilities'.[751] Nevertheless, as examined in the context of 'duties and responsibilities', the journalists are exempted from establishing the truth of *all* aspects of information. In *Thorgeir Thorgeirson v Iceland*,[752] the applicant was convicted of defaming the police by publishing articles stating that the Reykjavik police force was involved in serious assaults. His conviction was based on his failure to establish the truth of alleged police brutalities. The Court relieved him of establishing the accuracy of all the elements of the allegations, adducing several rationales. The applicant was reporting what was being said by others; he was not deemed responsible for the content of the allegations; nor was it established that the allegations were entirely false. The nature of the information disseminated in the press was of serious public concern. Further, the purpose of the applicant was not to damage the reputation of the police but essentially to urge the Minister of Justice to initiate an inquiry into alleged police brutalities.

Clearly, the onus and the standard of proof imposed on journalists and the press to establish the veracity of contested statements are keys to a proportionality appraisal. This can be demonstrated by *Dichand and Others v Austria*.[753] In a newspaper article, the applicants criticized a lawyer and the secretary-general of the Austrian People's Party, Mr Graff, stating that he violated 'moral concepts' in democracies by refusing to give up his job at a law firm when becoming a member of the government, and that he was involved in amending the law giving advantage to his clients. National courts found these statements to be an insult, granting an injunction ordering the retraction of certain statements. The Court considered that the contested statements were value-judgments related to public interest. It ruled that the criticisms, although harsh, remained within the bounds of acceptable criticism. The applicants were required under Austrian law to establish that the amendment to the law in question *exclusively* served the interests of Mr Graff's clients. Such an onerous burden of proof was decisive for the Court to find a violation of Article 10.[754]

In relation to statements considered false assertions of facts, the Court may take into account whether the applicants are responsible for the production or publication of such statements, and whether they intend to deceive other persons through such information. In *Salov v Ukraine*,[755] the applicant, one of the presidential candidates for Ukraine, was convicted and sentenced for having imparted false information. In an article disseminated in a copy of a 'forged newspaper', he noted that the incumbent president had died of an alcohol-related disease, and that a coup d'état by his 'criminal entourage' ensued. The Court recognized that the impugned article contained false factual statements.

---

[748] *Heinisch v Germany* hudoc (2011), paras 71–92.   [749] *Heinisch v Germany*, paras 89–90.
[750] 2005-II; 41 EHRR 403 para. 93.
[751] See also *McVicar v UK* 2002-III; 35 EHRR 566 para 87.
[752] A 239 (1992); 14 EHRR 843 para 65.   [753] Hudoc (2002) para 52.
[754] *Dichand and Others v Austria*, para 50.   [755] Hudoc (2005) para 113.

Nonetheless, the contested information was not produced by the applicant, and domestic courts failed to establish that he intended to deceive voters during the 1999 presidential elections. The impact of the information was minor, as he possessed only limited copies of the newspaper, which were addressed to a small number of persons. The Court emphasized that Article 10 safeguards even the information, which may be strongly suspected of being untrue. Further, the penalty was considered very severe. In the light of these, the reason for the interference was found not only insufficient but also irrelevant.

It should be noted, however, that where contested statements are manifestly insulting or defamatory of specially protected persons, such as judges or prosecutors, the Court's appraisal can be fixated on the question whether defendants have proved the veracity of their statements. In *Perna v Italy*,[756] the Grand Chamber was confronted with the conviction of a journalist for having defamed a public prosecutor, Mr Caselli. The latter brought proceedings against a well-known politician Mr Andreotti, who was accused of aiding and abetting the Mafia. In a newspaper article, the applicant suggested that Mr Caselli knowingly committed an abuse of authority in indicting Mr Andreotti, pursuant to the Italian Communist Party's partisan strategy, referring to Mr Caselli's 'ideological blinkers'. The applicant never established that the conduct that he attributed to Mr Caselli actually took place. The contested statements as a whole were considered factual assertions, and the whole text clearly besmirched Mr Caselli's honour and reputation. It may be argued that the disparaging tone was so manifest as to dispense with both the analysis of the contested article and the task of teasing out value-judgment elements.

In *Lešník v Slovakia*,[757] the applicant was convicted for insulting a public prosecutor by alleging that he unlawfully refused to uphold his criminal complaint, abused his power, and even got involved in bribery and the unlawful tapping of his telephone conversations. The Court considered the contested statements to be serious accusations which constituted statements of fact but remained unsubstantiated, and found the criminal proceedings proportionate.[758] Judges Bratza and Maruste, in their joint dissent, criticized that the majority downplayed the fact that the applicant raised the contested allegations only in his private correspondence to the public prosecutor, and that publication of their content in a newspaper was done by a third party, and this, after the criminal charge was filed against the applicant. They stressed that 'public servants must be prepared to tolerate such criticism, where it is personally addressed to them in private correspondence, even where such criticism is expressed in abusive, strong or intemperate terms and even where it consists of serious and unfounded allegations'. They added that in democracy, private citizens should be free to raise complaints against public officials without risk of prosecution for defamation or insult, even where allegations of a criminal offence prove to be groundless upon investigations.[759]

VI. SOME SALIENT APPROACHES DEVELOPED TO ESTABLISH THE VERACITY OF CONTESTED STATEMENTS

When ascertaining the truth of statements that national authorities have found defamatory, the Court may apply any of the following methodologies to retain the elevated standard of protection given to the freedom of expression: (i) the broad and liberal interpretation of the notion 'value-judgments'; (ii) the overall evaluation of the contested statements;

---

[756] 2003-V; 36 EHRR 563 paras 13 and 47.   [757] 2003-IV.
[758] *Lešník v Slovakia*, paras 58–9 and 64.
[759] *Lešník v Slovakia*, joint dissenting opinion of Judges Sir Nicolas Bratza and Maruste.

(iii) de-emphasizing the distinction between factual statements and value-judgments in relation to political expression; and (iv) side-stepping the question whether or not (part of) the impugned statement is defamatory, and focusing on a disproportionate element of the measures taken to sanction it.

The first such methodology was markedly demonstrated in *Unabhängige Initiative Informationsvielfalt v Austria*.[760] There, the applicant association published a periodical, which included a leaflet calling on readers to send the politicians of the extreme right-wing party (FPÖ) 'small gifts in response to their racist agitation'. The Austrian courts granted an injunction preventing the applicant from repeating the remark in question, describing the words 'racist agitation' as an insult to the reputation and honour of the then leader of FPÖ, Mr Haider. They characterized the words as statements of fact, demanding that their veracity had to be established in a manner akin to the proof of a criminal offence of incitement to hatred. In contrast, the Court classified the contested words not as a gratuitous personal attack, but as a value-judgment made in reaction to a political discussion on immigration controls. It held that the degree of precision required for establishing the well-founded nature of a criminal charge was irreconcilable with the duty of journalists to verify the sufficient basis of their opinions on a matter of public interest. No sufficient ground was found to justify the injunction.

In *Karman v Russia*,[761] the applicant, the editor-in-chief of a local newspaper, published an article in which he described the editor-in-chief of another newspaper who organized the meeting of an entrenched Russian nationalist movement as a 'local neo-fascist'. The Russian courts narrowly interpreted the term 'neo-fascist', which it linked to a designated membership in a neo-fascist party. Rejecting this interpretation, the Court rebuked the national courts' failure to distinguish between factual statement and value-judgments. The Court found that the expression 'local neo-fascist' was a value-judgment,[762] which was corroborated by the sufficient factual basis, as the applicant adduced the evidence that the editor-in-chief of the paper he criticized propagated hatred against Jewish people. The Court's approach was reinforced by the special role of the press in imparting information of public concern.[763] In *Desjardin v France*,[764] a Green Party member who stood for a cantonal election distributed a leaflet criticizing an ancient mayor for polluting the quality of the communal water. When examining the national courts' finding of defamation against this ecologist, the Court emphasized that the impugned statement was a value-judgment, and that its provocative wording was within the bounds of acceptable criticism, when understood in the heated context of an election campaign.[765]

The second methodology, based on an overall appraisal, is propitious where disparaging words appear isolated in the contested statements.[766] Focusing on the overall context in which such words are expressed enables the Court to treat the entire statements as value-judgments immune from the requirement of establishing their truth. In *Schwabe v Austria*,[767] a member of the Austrian People's Party was convicted of defamation. In a press release, he argued that a member of the Austrian Socialist Party had remained in public office even after committing a serious traffic accident whilst under the influence of alcohol. He added that this should have disentitled the Socialist's critical remarks against the applicant's colleague who remained in office despite his conviction for a similar offence.

---

[760] 2002-I; 37 EHRR 710 paras 9 and 41.   [761] Hudoc (2006).
[762] *Karman v Russia*, para 41.   [763] *Karman v Russia*, paras 28 and 40–2.
[764] Hudoc (2007).   [765] *Desjardin v France*, paras 42 and 48–9.
[766] *Nikula v Finland* 2002-II; 38 EHRR 944 para 44; *Skałka v Poland* hudoc (2003); 38 EHRR 1 para 35.
[767] A 242-B (1992) paras 14 and 34.

The Austrian courts held that the words 'while under the influence of alcohol' suggested the conviction of drunken driving after consuming more than the limit of alcohol, and that the applicant failed to prove the veracity of his statements along this casuistic line of interpretation. The Court, based on an overall evaluation, conflated facts and elements of value-judgments in Schwabe's statements and classified all of them as 'a value-judgment for which no proof of truth is possible'.[768] While salutary here, this conclusion leaves the question in what circumstances such an overall approach can be applied to expand the parameters of value-judgments. This question is of special merit because, unlike the First Amendment to the US Constitution, the Court has so far refrained from providing absolute protection to value-judgments.[769]

The third methodology is to minimize the importance of the distinction between factual statements and value-judgments in assessing political debates.[770] This methodology is discernible in cases of defamation against a politician.[771] In *Lombardo v Malta*,[772] elected members of a local council were convicted of defamation and libel against a mayor. The thrust of the Court's reasoning was that 'the distinction between statements of fact and value judgments is of less significance ... where the impugned statements are made in the course of a lively political debate at local level and where elected officials and journalists should enjoy a wide freedom to criticise the actions of a local authority, *even where the statements made may lack a clear basis in fact*'. It remains to be seen whether this suggests a *general* approach, so that the requirement to establish accuracy of factual statements can be dispensed with, every time the contested statements are judged to form part of political debates on matters of public interest.

According to the fourth methodology, even in the absence of proof of the veracity of serious allegations classified as statements of fact, the Court may focus on the nature and severity of sanction which may not strike the right balance, making the interference disproportionate. In *Steel and Morris v UK*,[773] two campaigners of London Greenpeace, who distributed leaflets containing serious allegations against McDonald's, ended up in defending themselves against the mighty multinational in defamation proceedings. The absence of legal aid for defamation resulted in a gross inequality of arms, disabling them from carrying out an effective defence of their case. This, together with the possible chilling effect that the substantial sum of damages awarded against them would have on their right freely to circulate information of public interest, led the Court to find a violation of Article 10. It is not, however, clear whether, if given sufficient legal aid, the applicants could have successfully established the veracity of their allegations that the Court classified as factual statements, such as their contention that McDonald's was accountable for health, environment, and labour problems. Nevertheless, such a question was immaterial for the Court's examination that spotlighted the disproportionate impact of the unfair proceedings on the applicants' free speech. This fourth methodology ingeniously bypasses difficult questions for the Court (and the applicant) concerning the establishment of the truth of allegations.

---

[768] *Schwabe v Austria*, para 34. Cf para 55 Com Rep.

[769] Macdonald, in Matscher and Petzold, eds, *Protecting Human Rights: The European Dimension—Studies in Honour of Gérard J. Wiarda*, 1988, at 367–8.

[770] Some authors consider this as 'an intermediate category: the remark that without a value determination cannot be likened stricto sensu to a factual declaration': Flauss, 84 Ind LJ 809 at 817 (2009).

[771] Apart from *Lombardo* discussed here, see also *Vides Aizsardzības Klubs v Latvia* hudoc (2004) para 46.

[772] Hudoc (2007) para 60 (emphasis added).

[773] 2005-II; 41 EHRR 403 paras 95–8.

VII. DENIAL OF THE OPPORTUNITY TO PROVE THE TRUTH OF ALLEGATIONS

Where a penal sanction is imposed on the basis that the factual statements are false, it is clear that denying the defendants the opportunity to prove the truth of the allegations contravenes Article 10.[774] In *Castells v Spain*,[775] the applicant was a senator and a member of a Basque nationalist party supporting the independence of the Basque Country. In newspaper articles, he contended that the police were responsible for the murder of Basque activists, and that the right-wing government in Madrid was behind the impunity of perpetrators. He was convicted of criminal offences involving serious insults to the government and public servants. He complained that he was denied the opportunity to establish the truth of his criticism. The Court held that because of 'the dominant position' held by the government, there was a special need to restrain recourse to criminal sanctions against a politician and to apply less burdensome measures in response to unjustified attacks or criticisms.[776] On close scrutiny, it did not matter whether the allegations were true or false. It was the denial of the opportunity to try to establish the truth of his allegations, combined with the chilling effect on political expression and press freedom, which was crucial.[777]

In *Colombani v France*,[778] the French daily newspaper *Le Monde* published an article that summarized the report commissioned by the European Commission. The article cited a report to assert that the Moroccan royal family assumed 'direct responsibility' for the lucrative business of drug trafficking. Upon the request of the King of Morocco, the public prosecutor took action against the editor-in-chief of *Le Monde* and the author of the article, and they were found guilty of the offence of publicly insulting a foreign head of state. The applicants' main contention was that under French law, unlike the position in the ordinary law of defamation, there was no defence of justification—that is to say proving the truth of the allegation—where the charge was insulting a foreign head of state. The Court considered the absence of such a defence disproportionate.

9. CONCLUSION

The foregoing survey suggests that an array of dynamic and refined methodologies and interpretive techniques have been devised by the Court to give enhanced effectiveness to the protection of freedom of expression. The nature and the form of expression, together with the position of persons exercising their right to free speech, will continue to be the lynchpin for assessing the standard of review and the choice of methodologies. Yet, these considerations are far from conclusive. Indeed, the interplay of numerous factors involved in free speech cases adds great complexity to an area in which the Court has already been experimenting with reasoning peculiar to Article 10 and with innovative interpretive devices. These make it difficult to draw general inferences from the case law and to present a coherent theoretical framework. Furthermore, the Court cannot be impervious to

---

[774] Apart from the cases discussed here, see also *Aquilina and Others v Malta* hudoc (2011) para 49.

[775] A 236 (1992); 14 EHRR 445 paras 12, 47–8.   [776] *Castells v Spain*, para 46.

[777] *Castells v Spain*, paras 48–50. Cf the concurring opinion of Judge Pekkanen, paras 3 and 4; and concurring opinion of Judge de Meyer, paras 3 and 4 (emphasis on the conviction of the applicant for having disseminated his political opinion).

[778] 2002-V para 66. See also *Otegi Mondragon v Spain* hudoc (2011) para 55 (albeit not concerning denial of an opportunity to establish the truth of alleged remarks).

such exogenous factors as changing social attitudes, technological developments, and the emergence of common European regulatory frameworks.

Despite the Court's robust decision-making policy, its case law leaves some questions unanswered. A general right of access to information held by public bodies has yet to be recognized under Article 10. Issues concerning defamation of public figures and the disclosure of their privacy by the press[779] will occupy ample space of the case law that pits free speech rights against privacy rights. It may be asked whether or to what extent the application of the public figures doctrine can be broadened to cover artists, celebrities in show business and sports, and popular newsreaders on television. One may attribute different weight to the privacy rights of those persons who possess certain public profiles and who are situated in the intermediate range between politicians and ordinary private individuals.[780] Further, there is a lack of European consensus on what weight can be ascribed to the free speech rights of the powerful entertainment press or tabloids of mass-circulation, which are primarily interested in increasing commercial gains by satisfying their readers' voyeuristic tendencies. This poses a delicate question whether it is necessary or legitimate for the international judicial organ in Strasbourg to categorize different types of national or local press on the basis of the news-worthiness of contents and their readership without being charged with arbitrariness and elitism.

Other questions concern the concept of 'public interest', which is crucial to the application of Article 10. For example, in the case of 'category crossover', such as hybrid expression that is essentially commercial in nature but can be seen as having a 'public interest' dimension also, the identification of a 'public interest' dimension will strengthen the standard of review that would otherwise be applied by the Court in a case of purely commercial expression.[781] Yet the Court has so far appeared content intuitively to invoke the notion of 'public interest' without formulating reasoned argument for determining what exactly amounts to such interest.[782] This approach entails a haze of vagueness. To what extent the notion of 'public interest' is autonomous under the Convention and broad enough to embrace diverse social needs cannot be uniformly diagnosed. Arguably, such amorphous nature has proven to be a practical advantage in enabling the Court to invoke this notion as a vehicle for providing semblance of explanation for the enhanced protection accorded to free speech in a variety of unexpected and convoluted cases in the near future.

Finally, in an overstated 'paradigm' of a post-September 11 world, an increasing securitization of societies faced with a perceived or real threat of terrorism has seen many European nations hastily rush to enact anti-terrorism laws with sweeping powers of stop, search, arrest, and detention. There is a legitimate fear that this may yield a corrosive effect on the Court's critical stance when assessing interferences with freedom of expression, as with other Convention rights. Rather than causing a stasis in the creativity of interpretational doctrines, a newly instituted form of 'militant democracy' within states may lead to a veiled attempt on their part to roll back the *acquis* of freedom of expression. Macklem cautions against the propensity of the militant democracy readily to resort to preventive intervention in an across-the-board fashion, which presents itself as an ad hoc exercise of interest balancing. He suggests that even confronted with terrorists or other subversive associations, their political agendas should be appraised not *ex ante* and in an abstract manner, but as close to the threshold between concrete proposal and policy as

---

[779] *Von Hannover v Germany* 2004-VI; 43 EHRR 1.
[780] See, eg, Sanderson, 6 EHRLR 631 at 636–7 (2004).   [781] See section 3.IV.c.
[782] Sanderson, 6 EHRLR 631, at 638 (2004).

possible, so that a close regard is had to disaggregated components such as timing, context,[783] and the probability of the harmful impact of their activities.

Another related element of controversy relates to hate speech or incitement to violence in the dimension of a secular Europe, at a time when its multicultural premise is challenged by the rise of the populist or far-right parties and terrorist organizations, both of which propagate hate speeches and even carry out violence. At what juncture can the exercising of free speech be said to run counter to the requirement of tolerance and pluralism? As the repercussions of the Danish cartoon case vividly illustrate, the risk of auto-censorship of the press faced with perceived threats of inter-religious or inter-ethnic violence cannot be brushed aside.

[783] Macklem, 4 Int'l J Const L 488, at 513–14 (2006).

15
ARTICLE 11: FREEDOM OF ASSEMBLY AND ASSOCIATION

Article 11

1. Everyone has the right to freedom of peaceful assembly and to freedom of association with others, including the right to form and to join trade unions for the protection of his interests.
2. No restrictions shall be placed on the exercise of these rights other than such as are prescribed by law and are necessary in a democratic society in the interests of national security or public safety, for the prevention of disorder or crime, for the protection of health or morals or for the protection of the rights and freedoms of others. This article shall not prevent the imposition of lawful restrictions on the exercise of these rights by members of the armed forces, of the police or of the administration of the state.

1. INTRODUCTION

Article 11 protects the two distinct, if sometimes connected, freedoms of peaceful assembly and association.[1] They are sufficiently different to be treated separately but they share the objective of allowing individuals to come together for the expression and protection of their common interests. Where those interests are political in the widest sense, the function of the Article 11 freedoms is central to the effective working of the democratic system. In particular, it provides for the creation and operation of political parties, interest groups, and trade unions which serve as diverse centres of power, and for the propagation of ideas and programmes, from among which others may choose and by which influence may be exerted on the holders of public power for the time being. Equally, Article 11 protects the right of individuals to assemble and to associate for the furtherance of their personal interests, be they economic, social, or cultural. Article 11 makes specific reference to trade unions, the roles of which overlap considerably between the political and the economic interests of their members.

---

[1] See Tomuschat, *European System*, Ch 19, pp 493–513 and Lewis-Anthony, in *Freedom of Association*, Rekjavik Seminar Proceedings, reprinted in 33A YB 27 (1994).

2. FREEDOM OF PEACEFUL ASSEMBLY

Article 11 protects the right to freedom of peaceful assembly as a 'fundamental right',[2] whether it is exercised for political,[3] religious or spiritual,[4] cultural,[5] social,[6] or other purposes. It covers private and public meetings,[7] including marches,[8] demonstrations,[9] pickets,[10] and sit-ins.[11] The holding of public meetings and the mounting of demonstrations through marches, picketing, and processions has played a significant part in the political history of European states. Events in Central and Eastern Europe in recent decades show the continued potency of these activities. It is true that much orthodox politics has moved to the private meeting and the orchestrated occasion, the impact of which depends upon transmission through the news media. However, public meetings and demonstrations are a tool for those outside the established parties, whose direct access to the media is limited but who may be able to gain attention by staging '*événements*' which capture the television and newspaper headlines,[12] while ritual and commemorative events continue to play a part in the expression of minority consciousness[13] and the manifestation of religious beliefs.[14]

The content of any message which the organizers of an assembly wish to project is not, of itself, a reason for regarding the occasion as being outside the scope of Article 11. The Court has said that the freedom of assembly guaranteed under Article 11 must be considered in the light of Article 10, the protection of opinions and the freedom to express them being one of the objectives of freedom of assembly.[15] Thus freedom of assembly under Article 11 protects an assembly that 'may annoy or give offence to persons opposed to the ideas or claims that it is seeking to promote'.[16] Nor is the form of the assembly of importance.[17] The only limitation is that the assembly must be 'peaceful'. Occupation of a building that in itself is peaceful, even though it is clearly in breach of domestic law, may be regarded as a 'peaceful' assembly.[18] Even disruption incidental to the holding of the assembly will not render it 'unpeaceful', whereas a meeting planned with the object of causing disturbances will not be protected by Article 11,[19] although the line between the two may not be clear.[20]

---

[2] *Djavit An v Turkey* 2003-III; 40 EHRR 1002 para 56.   [3] Eg, *Cissé v France* 2002-III.

[4] Eg, *Barankevich v Russia* hudoc (2007); 47 EHRR 266 and *Pendragon v UK No 31416/96* hudoc (1998); 27 EHRR CD 179.   [5] Eg, *Gypsy Council v UK No 66336/01* hudoc (2002); 35 EHRR CD 96.

[6] *Alekseyev v Russia* hudoc (2010).

[7] *Rassemblement Jurassien Unité Jurassienne v Switzerland No 8191/78*, 17 DR 93 at 119 (1979) and *Gün and Others v Turkey* hudoc (2013).

[8] *Christians against Racism and Fascism v UK No 8440/78*, 21 DR 138 at 148 (1980).

[9] *Oya Ataman v Turkey* 2006-XIV and *Alekseyev v Russia* hudoc (2010).

[10] *Sergey Kuznetsov v Russia* hudoc (2008).

[11] *G v Germany No 13079/87*, 60 DR 256 (1989). See also *Cissé v France* 2002-III (lengthy occupation of premises).   [12] Eg, *Cissé v France* 2002-III.

[13] Eg, *Stankov and The United Macedonian Organization Ilinden v Bulgaria* 2001-X; *United Macedonian Organization Ilinden and Ivanov v Bulgaria* hudoc (2005); 43 EHRR 119; and *Ivanov and Others v Bulgaria* hudoc (2005).   [14] *Barankevich v Russia* hudoc (2007); 47 EHRR 266.

[15] Eg, *Rai and Evans v UK Nos 26258/07 and 26255/07* hudoc (2009) DA and *Schwabe and MG v Germany* hudoc (2011) paras 98–101.

[16] See, eg, *Plattform 'Ärzte für das Leben' v Austria* 44 DR 65 (1985); 13 EHRR 204 para 32; *Stankov and The United Macedonian Organization Ilinden v Bulgaria* 2001-X paras 85–6; and *Alekseyev v Russia* hudoc (2010) para 80.   [17] *Djavit An v Turkey* 2003-III; 40 EHRR 1002 para 60.

[18] *Cissé v France* 2002-III.

[19] *Christians against Racism and Fascism v UK No 8440/78*, 21 DR 138 at 150 (1980); *Stankov and The United Macedonian Organization Ilinden v Bulgaria* 2001-X para 77; *Hyde Park and Others v Moldova (Nos 5 & 6)* hudoc (2010) para 49; and *Schwabe and MG v Germany* hudoc (2011) para 103.

[20] See, eg, *G v Germany No 13079/87*, 60 DR 256 at 263 (1989).

For the authorities, freedom of assembly raises a number of problems, especially where public meetings and marches are involved. These pose threats to public order through the disruption of communications and activities, the prospect of confrontation with the police, and the danger of violence with rivals, who themselves, of course, claim their own freedom to demonstrate. It is this last situation which raises particular difficulties under Article 11(1).

I. POSITIVE OBLIGATIONS

There is a positive duty on a state to protect those exercising their right of freedom of peaceful assembly from violent disturbance by counter-demonstrators.[21] This duty is imposed to ensure the right to freedom of assembly provided under Article 11 is effective.[22] Because both sides may claim to be exercising Article 11 rights, initially this may be a duty to hold the ring between rival meetings or processions, but if one of them is aimed at disruption of the activities of the other, the obligation of the authorities is to protect those exercising their right of peaceful assembly. In *United Macedonian Organization Ilinden and Ivanov v Bulgaria*[23] individual participants in a commemoration ceremony were physically attacked and their property damaged by counter-demonstrators. The police had formed a cordon to keep the two groups apart but failed to prevent the incidents. In the Court's view 'the authorities appeared somewhat reluctant' to protect the participants in the ceremony from the counter-demonstrators. In these circumstances the Court unanimously held that Article 11 had been violated because the authorities had failed to discharge their positive obligations to take 'reasonable and appropriate measures to enable lawful demonstrations to proceed peacefully'.[24] Presumably other measures that could be taken by the authorities in such a situation would be to give prior warnings to potential counter-demonstrators and/or proceed to arrest any perpetrators of the violence.[25] The threat of disorder from opponents does not of itself justify interference with the demonstration.[26] Indeed a failure to take preventative measures to neutralize the threat may weigh heavily against the necessity of a prohibition on the demonstration.[27] In order to enable the authorities to assess the risk posed by counter-demonstration, they 'must produce concrete estimates of the potential scale of the disturbance in order to evaluate the resources necessary for neutralising the threat of violent clashes'.[28] Nevertheless, the choice of means to enable the discharge of this positive duty leaves a good deal to the discretion of the authorities. The Court has said that the reasons given by the authorities for imposing an unconditional ban instead of taking preventative measures against counter-demonstrators will be subject to intense scrutiny,[29] otherwise the fact that action

---

[21] *Plattform 'Ärzte für das Leben' v Austria No 10126/82*, 44 DR 65 at 72 (1985) A 139 (1988); 13 EHRR 204 para 32; *United Macedonian Organization Ilinden and Ivanov v Bulgaria* hudoc (2005); 43 EHRR 1119 para 115; and *Barankevich v Russia* hudoc (2007); 47 EHRR 266 paras 32 and 33.

[22] *United Macedonian Organization Ilinden and Ivanov*, para 115; *Barankevich*, para 32; and *Alekseyev v Russia* hudoc (2010) para 81. See generally Mowbray, 1999 PL 703–25.

[23] Hudoc (2005); 43 EHRR 1119.

[24] *United Macedonian Organization Ilinden and Ivanov*, para 115.

[25] In *Alekseyev v Russia* hudoc (2010) para 76, the Court observed that states have an obligation to prosecute those who commit offences against demonstrators.

[26] *Christians against Racism and Fascism v UK No 8840/78*, 21 DR 138 at 148 (1980) and *Alekseyev v Russia*, para 77.

[27] *Barankevich v Russia* hudoc (2007); 47 EHRR 266 para 33 and *Alekseyev v Russia*, para 75. See also *Öllinger v Austria* 2006-IX; 46 EHRR 849 para 48.

[28] *Alekseyev v Russia*, para 75. See also *Barankevich v Russia*, para 33.

[29] *Öllinger v Austria* 2006-IX; 46 EHRR 849 paras 44 and 48.

may have to be taken in anticipation of possible disturbances or, in other cases, that policing measures must be taken at short notice, leaves a wide margin of appreciation to the state to decide what Article 11(1) requires in a particular case.[30]

One issue is whether there is a positive obligation on a state to require private individuals to allow the exercise of peaceful assembly by others on their property. As a freedom, in principle peaceful assembly confers no obligations on, say, owners of private halls, to make them available (on hire or not) to political groups for meetings. In *Anderson v UK*,[31] a commercial company which leased a shopping centre from the local council obtained an injunction forbidding the applicants, a group of young men, from entering the centre for an indefinite period on the grounds of their misconduct and disorderly behaviour at the centre. In finding that the exclusion of the applicants had not interfered with their rights under Article 11, the Commission said there was no support for the argument that freedom of assembly is 'intended to guarantee a right to pass or re-pass in public places, or to assemble for purely social purposes *anywhere* one wishes'. In the later case of *Appleby v UK*,[32] it was for the purposes of 'organized assembly', rather than for 'purely social purposes', that the applicants sought access to a shopping mall owned by a private company. The applicants contended that their rights to freedom of expression and assembly had been violated when the corporation refused them permission to distribute leaflets and collect signatures at the shopping mall in order to protest against the development of local playing fields. The issue before the Court was, therefore, whether the state had failed in any positive obligation to protect the exercise of those rights from interference by the owner of the property. The determination of this question, the Court reasoned, required a balance to be struck between the applicants' Convention rights and the property rights of the owner of the shopping centre under Article 1 of the First Protocol. It held that Article 10 rights, and by implication Article 11 rights, do not confer 'any freedom of forum' for the exercise of the right, nor do changing modes of social interaction require 'the automatic creation of rights of entry to private property'. However, while exclusion from quasi-public places is not itself a violation of Convention rights, the Court said a positive obligation to regulate property rights might arise in exceptional situations where a restriction on access to private property 'has the effect of preventing any effective exercise' of the right or when 'it can be said that the essence of the right has been destroyed'. The Court cited 'a corporate town where the entire municipality is controlled by a private body' as an example of when the positive obligation could arise. The decision in *Appleby* indicates that the Court will require proof of the negation of the core or 'essence' of an applicant's Convention rights before it will limit the owner's proprietorial right to exclude others. The circumstances in *Appleby* did not qualify, as there were alternative places for collecting signatures and alternative means of campaigning; the applicants could not claim that they were 'effectively prevented from communicating their views' to others.

II. RIGHTS OF THIRD PARTIES

An interesting issue arises where the exercise of the right of freedom of peaceful assembly impacts upon other Convention rights of third parties. In *Öllinger v Austria*,[33] the domestic authorities imposed a total ban on a small meeting organized by a member of

---

[30] *Plattform 'Arzte für das Leben' v Austria No 10126/82*, 44 DR 65 at 74 (1985); 13 EHRR 204. See also *Alekseyev v Russia* hudoc (2010) para 75.   [31] *No 33689/96* hudoc (1997); 25 EHRR CD 172.

[32] 2003-VI; 37 EHRR 38 para 47, in which the Court examined the case under Article 10, but said that 'largely identical considerations' arose under Article 11.

[33] 2006-IX; 46 EHRR 849 paras 46–8, by six votes to one. See generally Mead, 2 EHRLR 133–45 (2007).

parliament and planned for All Saint's Day at a Salzburg cemetery so as to coincide with a ceremony held by Comradeship IV to commemorate SS soldiers who were killed in World War II. The purpose of the applicant's meeting was to remember the crimes committed by the SS and to commemorate the Jews killed by SS members. The meeting was to be 'silent', conducted only by the use of messages attached to the garments of those assembled and without chants or banners. Previous similar meetings at Comradeship IV ceremonies had resulted in heated discussions between the groups. It was undisputed that there was no justification for banning the Comradeship IV meeting; rather the issue was characterized as one of balancing the interests of counter-demonstrators under Article 11 against the rights of others visiting the cemetery to manifest their religion under Article 9. The Austrian Constitutional Court had held that the unconditional prohibition of the meeting was justified in order to protect members of the public visiting the graves of their relatives in the exercise of their religion. The Strasbourg Court stressed that the Constitutional Court had failed to accord any weight to the far-reaching nature of the unconditional prohibition on the meeting when assessing the reasons for its imposition, particularly given its impact upon the expression of an opinion on a matter of public interest by a member of parliament. Further, the majority considered the subdued manner in which the counter-demonstration was to be conducted, the absence of the threat of violence, and the intended target of the counter-demonstration also to be relevant factors in determining the proportionality of the interference. The availability of policing measures to prevent disruption was a further reason for deciding that the prohibition failed to strike a fair balance between the interests, notwithstanding the state's wide margin of appreciation in this area.

III. INTERFERENCES WITH PEACEFUL ASSEMBLY

Because the threats to public order from the exercise of the freedom of peaceful assembly are real, the authorities may demand a variety of powers to meet or to mitigate them. These may include powers to impose requirements of prior notification, authorization, authorization subject to conditions, or complete bans. Requirements of notification or authorization for meetings in public places are permissible as 'an authorisation procedure does not normally encroach upon the essence of the right. Such a procedure is in keeping with the requirements of Article 11 § 1, if only in order that the authorities may be in a position to ensure the peaceful nature of a meeting, and accordingly does not as such constitute an interference with the exercise of the right.'[34] This is so provided that the requirement's purpose is to allow the authorities to take 'reasonable and appropriate measures' to ensure the peaceful conduct of the assembly[35] and that any formal requirements attaching to the procedure do 'not represent a hidden obstacle to the freedom of peaceful assembly' under Article 11.[36] Penalties may be imposed for participation in and organization of assemblies held in defiance of requirements[37] or for offences committed in the exercise of the right.[38]

---

[34] *Ziliberberg v Moldova No 61821/00* hudoc (2007) para 35 DA.

[35] *Sergey Kuznetson v Russia* hudoc (2008) para 42.

[36] *Oya Ataman v Turkey* 2006-XIV para 38; *Balçik v Turkey* hudoc (2007) para 49; and *Éva Molnár v Hungary* hudoc (2008) para 37.

[37] *Ziliberberg v Moldova No 61821/00* hudoc (2004) DA (administrative fine for participation in an unauthorized demonstration), and *Rai and Evans v UK Nos 26258/07 and 26255/09* hudoc (2009) DA (criminal sanction for organizing and participating in unauthorized demonstration). Cf *Çetinkaya v Turkey No 75569/01* hudoc (2006) (conviction and fine for being present at a press conference which was later labelled an unlawful assembly by the authorities).

[38] *Osmani v FYRM No 50841/99*, 2001-X DA and *Barraco v France* hudoc (2009).

The Court has given a broad interpretation to the term 'restrictions' contained in Article 11(2).[39] Thus post-demonstration penalties may amount to an interference with freedom of assembly,[40] and preventative arrest may also be an interference with the right.[41] Bans[42] and dispersals,[43] because of the seriousness of the restrictions that they impose, will similarly require justification under Article 11(2).

A refusal to authorize an assembly may be an interference with the freedom of assembly even where the assembly goes ahead. In *Bączkowski v Poland*,[44] a march and rallies organized to raise public awareness of discrimination against minorities, women, and disabled persons, were held on the days planned despite the mayor issuing refusals to give authorization eight and two days respectively before they were due to take place, and appeals against the refusals were still pending. Although the assemblies proceeded, the Court considered that there had been an interference with the applicant's freedom of assembly because a 'presumption of legality' constitutes 'a vital aspect of effective and unhindered exercise of the freedom of assembly and freedom of expression'. Holding an assembly with an official ban in force held its risks and, in particular, there was no guarantee of official protection. The potential for the refusals to give authorization to have a 'chilling effect' on the participants in the assemblies was clear.[45] Moreover, if a legal remedy is to ameliorate the negative effect of a ban, it must take effect before the date on which the assembly is planned to be held.[46] In *Bączkowski* the legal remedy was not effective as the decision to quash the refusals for being unlawful was not made until after the date on which the assemblies were held.

IV. LIMITATIONS ON INTERFERENCES

The Court has said that the 'only restriction capable of justifying an interference is one that may claim to spring from a democratic society'.[47] In accordance with the Court's standard formula, 'an interference will constitute a breach of Article 11 unless it is "prescribed by law", pursues one or more legitimate aims under paragraph 2 and is "necessary in a democratic society" for the achievement of those aims'.[48] In most cases the 'prescribed

---

[39] See, eg, *Kasparov and Others v Russia* hudoc (2013).

[40] *Ezelin v France* A 202 (1991); 14 EHRR 362 para 39 (disciplinary reprimand) and *Osmani v FYRM No 50841/01*, 2001-X DA (criminal sanction).

[41] *Schwabe & MG v Germany* 2011- (to ensure the applicants did not participate in demonstrations). See also *Djavit An v Turkey* 2003-III; 40 EHRR 1002 (refusal to grant a permit to travel to a place to participate in meetings was an interference with the right).

[42] *Christians against Racism and Fascism v UK*, No 8440/78 21 DR 138 at 150–1 (1980) (temporary general ban). Unconditional bans require 'particular justification': *Öllinger v Austria* 2006-IX; 46 EHRR 849 para 44. A legal framework that restricts the exercise of freedom of peaceful assembly within uncertain limits that depend on the national authorities' assessment of the aims and the memorandum of association of the association in question can amount to a general ban: *Çetinkaya v Turkey No 75569/01* hudoc (2006) DA. Cf *Rai and Evans v UK Nos 26258/07 and 26255/07* hudoc (2009) DA.

[43] See, eg, *Oya Ataman v Turkey* 2006-XIV paras 39, 41–2, *Bukta and Others v Hungary* hudoc 2007-III; 51 EHRR 25 para 36; *Balçik v Turkey* hudoc (2007) para 52, *Nurettin Aldemir and Others v Turkey Nos 32124/02 et al* hudoc (2007); *Saya and Others v Turkey* hudoc (2008); *Samüt Karabulut v Turkey* hudoc (2009); *Dısk and Kesk v Turkey* hudoc (2012) para 22; *İzcı v Turkey* hudoc (2013); and *Hyde Park and Others v Moldova (Nos 5 & 6)* hudoc (2010).

[43] See, eg, *Kasparov and Others v Russia* hudoc (2013).   [44] Hudoc (2007) para 57.

[45] For other interferences that may have a chilling effect on the exercise of the right, see *Nurettin Aldemir and Others v Turkey Nos 32124/02 et al* hudoc (2007) para 34 (unsuccessful prosecution of demonstrators) and *Patyi v Hungary* hudoc (2012) para 23 (lengthy and complicated judicial procedure).

[46] *Nurettin Aldemir and Others v Turkey*, para 68. See also *Éva Molnár v Hungary* hudoc (2008) para 40.

[47] *Sergey Kuznetsov v Russia* hudoc (2008) para 39.   [48] *Sergey Kuznetsov v Russia*, para 37. See Ch 11 above.

by law' requirement has been met. However, a violation of Article 11 was found in *Djavit An v Turkey*[49] because the government could not refer to any law or policy that applied to the refusals to issue permits to the applicant to allow him to cross the 'green line' into southern Cyprus to attend bi-communal meetings. Even when the interference is made with reference to law, if the decisions or provisions relied upon are shown to be unlawful by a national court or other body, the interference will offend the legality requirement.[50] In addition to the interference having a basis in domestic law, lawfulness requires that the law should be accessible and formulated with sufficient precision to enable those to whom it applies to foresee to a reasonable degree the consequences of their actions.[51] Laws conferring a discretion may be compatible with the foreseeability requirement provided the scope of the discretion and the manner of its exercise are indicated with sufficient clarity to give the individual protection against arbitrary interference.[52] The applicant in *Mkrtchyan v Armenia*[53] could not foresee his conviction and fine for holding a procession because there was no domestic legal provision or practice clearly stating whether the rules contained in the former laws of the Soviet Union, under which he was convicted, remained in force in Armenia. A finding of unlawfulness is sufficient to establish a violation of Article 11, so the Court will not need to proceed to examine the legitimacy of its aim or its necessity.[54]

The 'legitimate aims' in Article 11(2) are 'the interests of national security or public safety', 'the prevention of disorder or crime', 'the protection of health or morals', and 'the protection of the rights and freedoms of others'. They have been the subject of little analysis by the Strasbourg authorities and have given rise to no serious difficulties for states.[55]

Interferences with the right must also be 'necessary in a democratic society' to achieve a permitted aim.[56] The Court has allowed states the widest latitude in their assessment of the necessity of restrictions where the assembly intentionally causes disruption to activities.[57] However, if a peaceful assembly concerns the expression of opinions on a question

---

[49] 2003-III; 40 EHRR 1002. See also *Adali v Turkey* hudoc (2005) para 274.

[50] *Bączkowski v Poland* hudoc (2007); 48 EHRR 19 paras 70–1 and *Patyi v Hungary* hudoc (2012) para 25.

[51] *Galstyan v Armenia* hudoc (2007); 50 EHRR 25 paras 106–7 (public order offences sufficiently precise); *Ziliberberg v Moldova No 61821/00* hudoc (2004) DA (penalty for 'active participation' sufficiently clear); *Kakabadze and Others v Georgia* hudoc (2012) para 86 (definition of 'contempt of court' not sufficiently clear to enable its application to be foreseen). Cf *CS v Germany No 13858/88* hudoc (1989) DA.

[52] *Rai, Allmond and 'Negotiate Now' v UK No 25522/99* hudoc (1995); 19 EHRR CD 93 (broad statutory power to regulate the use of a public place for assemblies sufficiently precise).

[53] Hudoc (2007) para 43. See also *Vyerentsov v Ukraine* hudoc (2013) paras 54–5.

[54] See, eg, *Bączkowski v Poland* hudoc (2007); 48 EHRR 19 para 72. Cf *Kakabadze and Others v Georgia* hudoc (2012) para 86.

[55] Except in the *Greek* case, 12 YB (the *Greek* case) 1 at 171 (1969); CM Res DH (70)1. In *Ezelin v France* A 202 (1991); 14 EHRR 362 para 47, the applicant claimed that proceedings had been taken against him because of his opinions and trade union affiliation, but the Court was satisfied that the action was for 'the prevention of disorder'. For a generous application of the 'prevention of disorder' aim, see *Cissé v France* 2002-III, in which the Court applied the aim to an unlawful occupation of a church which had the consent of the church authorities and parishoners.

[56] For the Court's approach towards the justification of interferences with freedom of assembly, see *Makhmudov v Russia* hudoc (2007) paras 64–5.

[57] Eg, *Drieman v Norway No 33678/96* hudoc (2000) DA (fine and confiscation of property for obstruction of commercial whaling amounting 'to a form of coercion', declared inadmissible); *Nicol and Selvanayagam v UK No 32213/96* hudoc (2001) DA (two days' detention and twenty-one days' imprisonment for obstruction of leisure fishing: declared inadmissible); and *Barraco v France* hudoc (2009) (suspended three-month sentence and fine for obstructing motorway by stopping heavy goods vehicles during a traffic-slowing protest, not a violation). See also *Association Solidarité des Français v France No 26787/07* hudoc (2009) DA (discriminatory distribution of free meals considered by national authorities to be liable to cause public order: inadmissible).

of public interest the necessity for the restriction has been more closely examined in recent cases.[58] In both the early cases of *Rassemblement Jurassien Unite Jurassienne v Switzerland*[59] and *Christians against Racism and Fascism v UK*,[60] the Commission had found that total bans on marches were justified under Article 11(2). In the first case, it pointed to the relatively narrow area and short time for which the ban had been imposed, against the evidence of tension in the area and the government's expectation of trouble. In the second case, a general ban on processions in London was directed principally at marches by the National Front, a racist group whose demonstrations had frequently been attended by violence. The applicants, against whom no aspersions were made, were simply caught in a wide ban imposed on the whole of London for two months, which was framed in such terms to prevent its circumvention by the National Front. For the Commission, that was sufficient justification for the interference. Further, it said, the applicants were not precluded from holding meetings to press their point during the period of the ban on marches.

In the later case of *Stankov and United Macedonian Organization Ilinden v Bulgaria*,[61] the authorities placed total bans and then conditions, including prohibitions on speeches and the use of banners, on meetings organized by the applicants to commemorate events of historical importance to the Macedonian minority in Bulgaria. The Court accepted that there might be some tension caused by the meetings, but rejected as a rule that 'every probability of tension and heated exchange between opposing groups' during an assembly called for a 'wider margin of appreciation'. This was so even where sensitivities involving national symbols and identity were heightened. Moreover, states had an obligation to 'display particular vigilance to ensure that national public opinion is not protected at the expense of the assertion of minority views, no matter how unpopular they may be'. Nor was the reasonable prospect of separatist declarations or any expression of political ideas challenging the existing order sufficient justification for an automatic ban on assemblies.[62] In circumstances where, as on the facts of the case, there was 'no real foreseeable risk of violent action or of incitement to violence or any other form of rejection of democratic principles', the bans on the meetings were not justified under Article 11(2); the authorities had overstepped their margin of appreciation.[63] The rationale for the Court's approach is to be found in the possibility democracy offers of 'resolving a country's problems through dialogue, without recourse to violence, even when those problems are irksome'.[64] To do otherwise would be to 'do a disservice to democracy and often even endanger it'.[65]

The Court has adopted a similar approach to restrictions placed on religious assemblies as it has to assemblies involving the dissemination of political views. In *Barankevich*

---

[58] There is little scope for restrictions on political speech: see *Stankov and The United Macedonian Organization Ilinden v Bulgaria* 2001-X para 88, especially for the elected representative: see *Osmani v FYRM No 50841/99*, 2001-X DA.　　　　　　　　　　[59] *No 8191/78*, 17 DR 93 at 119 (1979).

[60] *No 8440/78*, 21 DR 138 at 150–1 (1980). See also *Rai, Allmond and 'Negotiate Now' v UK No 25522/94* hudoc (1995); 19 EHRR CD 93 (general ban on marches at high-profile location in London not disproportionate as alternative venues available).

[61] 2001-X para 107. See also *Christian Democratic People's Party v Moldova* 2006-II; 45 EHRR 13.

[62] *Stankov and United Macedonian Organization Ilinden v Bulgaria*, para 97. See also *United Macedonian Organization Ilinden and Ivanov v Bulgaria* hudoc (2005); 44 EHRR 75 para 115 and *Ivanov and Others v Bulgaria* hudoc (2005) para 64.

[63] *Stankov and United Macedonian Organization Ilinden v Bulgaria*, paras 111 and 112. See also *United Macedonian Organization Ilinden and Ivanov v Bulgaria* hudoc (2005); 44 EHRR 75 para 133 and *Singartiski and Others v Bulgaria* hudoc (2012) para 46.

[64] *Stankov and United Macedonian Organization Ilinden v Bulgaria*, para 88.

[65] *Stankov and United Macedonian Organization Ilinden v Bulgaria*, para 97. See also *Sergey Kuznetsov v Russia* hudoc (2008) para 45 and *Alekseyev v Russia* hudoc (2010) para 80.

v Russia,[66] the Court looked at the effect of restrictions on freedom of assembly when rejecting the government's argument that it was 'necessary in a democratic society' to deny authorization for an open-air religious service by an evangelical Christian church in order to avoid causing discontent amongst the population as the majority practised a different religion. The Court observed that it 'would be incompatible with the underlying values of the Convention if the exercise of Convention rights by a minority group were made conditional on its being accepted by the majority'. It considered that the role of the authorities in a democratic society where several religions co-exist was to be informed by 'pluralism, tolerance and broadmindedness'. These qualities required that the authorities act in a 'neutral and impartial' manner in order to ensure the competing groups tolerate each other, rather than removing the cause of tension by eliminating pluralism altogether. Consistent with the judgment in Stankov, the Court found that the ban was not justified under Article 11(2) in the light of Article 9 in the absence of evidence of incitement or resort to violence by those assembled or of the use of unlawful means of conversion of others.

The exercise of the right of assembly may be as important to the peaceful resolution of social issues as it is to overtly political ones such as those in Stankov. The case of Alekseyev v Russia[67] concerned marches with an estimated 2,000 participants called 'Pride March' and 'Gay Pride' proposed to be held in Moscow for two hours on 27 May in the three years from 2006 to 2008. The planned marches mirrored similar events held by LGBT communities in cities around the world. Through them the organizers sought to draw attention to discrimination against gay men and lesbians in Russia and to call for greater tolerance towards them on the part of the public and the authorities. However, the Mayor of Moscow banned the proposed marches and the pickets proposed in lieu of the marches and also imposed administrative sanctions on those who breached the bans. The government contended that the interferences were justified on the basis that the majority of Russians held religious and moral beliefs that were opposed to homosexuality and were not ready to accept the manifestation of individual and group homosexual identity beyond the private sphere into the public forum. It relied on a number of public petitions which the Moscow authorities had received from political, religious, governmental, and non-governmental organizations (NGOs) to support the argument that the events would generate such antipathy that there would be a high risk of violent clashes between the opposing groups if the marches went ahead. In these circumstances, the government claimed the measures taken by the authorities were appropriate to maintain public order and to protect morals, particularly for the benefit of children. The issue in Alekseyev was, therefore, whether the debate generated by the public expression of homosexual identity through marches and picketing would be a threat to public order and/or morals. First, the Court rejected the government's claim to a wide margin of appreciation in granting the right to freedom of assembly to gay men and lesbians by recounting that the Member States of the Council of Europe have in various ways recognized the right of individuals to openly identify themselves as gay or lesbian and to promote their rights and freedoms.[68] The Court then examined the basis for the government's exclusion of gay men and lesbians from public forums:

> There is no scientific evidence or sociological data at the Court's disposal suggesting that the mere mention of homosexuality, or open public debate about sexual minorities' social status, would adversely affect children or 'vulnerable adults'. On the contrary, it is only

---

[66] Hudoc (2007); 47 EHRR 266 para 31.   [67] Hudoc (2010).

[68] Alekseyev v Russia, para 84.

> through fair and public debate that society may address such complex issues as the one raised in the present case…This is exactly the kind of debate the applicant in the present case attempted to launch, and it could not be replaced by the officials spontaneously expressing uninformed views which they considered popular. In the circumstances of the present case the Court cannot but conclude that the authorities' decisions to ban the events in question were not based on an acceptable assessment of the relevant facts.

The Court concluded that the bans did not correspond to a pressing social need and were, therefore, not necessary in a democratic society. The judgment in *Alekseyev* is important because it demonstrates that the Court envisions a democratic society in which the right to freedom of assembly has an integrative social function by playing a distinct role in facilitating the resolution of complex and controversial social issues by peaceful dialogue.

Evidence of tolerance towards the peaceful and collective public expression of political opinions is a factor that will be taken into account by the Court when it considers whether measures taken by the authorities in response to assemblies that do not comply with notification and authorization requirements are proportionate. For example, in *Oya Ataman v Turkey*,[69] a group of fifty demonstrators against plans for 'F-type' prisons held a march in a park during rush hour without giving seventy-two hours' prior notification as required by law. After informing the demonstrators a number of times that their march was unlawful and would disrupt public order at a busy time of day, the police forcefully intervened to disperse the assembly by using pepper spray and arresting the demonstrators. In concluding that there had been a violation of the right to freedom of assembly, the Court took particular note of the fact that the police had intervened after only half an hour. The Court could find no evidence that the assembly was a danger to public order beyond the level of minor disturbance to be expected at an assembly in a public place. In concluding that the dispersal of the demonstrators was not necessary in a democratic society, the Court said:

> [W]here demonstrators do not engage in acts of violence, it is important for the public authorities to show a certain degree of tolerance towards peaceful gatherings if the freedom of assembly is not to be deprived of all its substance.[70]

Since *Oya Ataman* the Court has ruled in a series of cases that the speedy and forceful dispersal of peaceful but unlawful assemblies is a disproportionate interference with freedom of assembly.[71] In *Éva Molnár v Hungary* the Court considered that the interference

---

[69] 2006-XIV.

[70] *Oya Ataman*, para 42. See also *Bukta and Others v Hungary* 2007-III; 51 EHRR 25 para 37; *Éva Molnár v Hungary* hudoc (2008) para 36; *Nurettın Aldemır and Others v Turkey* hudoc (2007) para 46; *Akgöl and Göl v Turkey* hudoc (2011) para 43; *İzcı v Turkey* hudoc (2013) para 89; *Dısk and Kesk v Turkey* hudoc (2012) para 36; *Tahirova v Azerbaijan* hudoc (2013) para 74; and *Kasparov and Others v Russia* hudoc (2013) para 91.

[71] Typically the dispersal is alleged to pursue the aims of preventing disorder and protecting the rights of others. See, eg, *Nurettın Aldemır and Others v Turkey* hudoc (2007) (truncheons and tear gas); *Samüt Karabulut v Turkey* hudoc (2009) (beatings and arrest); *Balçik and Others v Turkey* hudoc (2009) (truncheons and tear gas); *Aytaş and Others v Turkey* hudoc (2009) (beatings); *Ekşi and Ocak v Turkey* hudoc (2010) (beatings); *Akgöl and Göl v Turkey* hudoc (2011) para 44 (eleven minutes not sufficient time to manifest views); *İzcı v Turkey* hudoc (2013) (beatings, truncheons, and tear gas); and *Dısk and Kesk v Turkey* hudoc (2012) (gas bombs, paint sprays, and pressurized water to disperse pre-march assembly). See also *Tahirova v Azerbaijan* hudoc (2013) (beatings and truncheons used against peaceful demonstrators for alleged delay in ending lawful demonstration protesting parliamentary election irregularities). Arrest of participants may amount to forceful intervention: see *Kasparov and Others v Russia* hudoc (2013) para 96.

with freedom of assembly was justified where the authorities were slow to disband the demonstration.[72] Restraint in the use of force against demonstrators is important if freedom of assembly is to be respected. Thus, while ruling in *İzcı v Turkey* that the heavy-handed use of force against demonstrators while they were dispersing of their own volition was not necessary for the prevention of disorder or crime, the Court also observed that 'the brutality of the dispersal had an inevitable dissuasive effect on people's willingness to demonstrate'.[73]

Tolerance towards the exercise of freedom of peaceful assembly was also the guiding principle in *Hyde Park & Others v Moldova (Nos 5 & 6)*,[74] where the Court found that the arrest of peaceful demonstrators for failing to obtain authorization for their assembly from the municipal authorities had the effect of breaking up the demonstration. It ruled that this effective dispersal of the assembly, together with the imposition of fines at the upper end of the statutory penalty scale, amounted to a disproportionate interference.[75] This was the case even though the Court considered that the applicants could have delayed their assembly to obtain the necessary authorization. The government relied on the case of *Rai and Evans v UK*,[76] in which the Court considered the applicants' prior knowledge of the time limit for applying for authorization and the clear opportunity to make an application, the limitation of the authorization requirement to designated security zones and then only to the imposition of defined conditions strictly referable to public interest objectives, the conduct of the police in allowing the applicants to continue with their demonstration and giving them the opportunity to disband without sanction, as well as the modest, albeit criminal, sanctions ultimately imposed, were reasons for finding the fines imposed on the applicants to be proportionate interferences with the freedom of assembly. When comparing the circumstances in *Hyde Park (Nos 5 & 6)* and those of *Rai and Evans*, however, the Court found critical differences. First, in *Hyde Park* the authorities disbanded the demonstration and, unlike *Rai and Evans*, the location of the demonstration could not be a relevant or sufficient reason for doing so. The Court observed that 'had the police asked the applicants to disperse and reassemble only where they had obtained authorization' then the lack of authorization might have been regarded as a 'relevant consideration' justifying the dispersal of the demonstration.[77] A most important difference, however, was that the level of fines imposed in *Rai and Evans* were at the lower end of the statutory scale; whereas in *Hyde Park* they were 80 per cent of the maximum fine.

An obligation to give prior notification of an assembly will be overridden where a delay in complying with it would render the assembly ineffective.[78] Thus the sudden nature of the events in *Bukta and Others v Hungary*[79] meant that the applicants did not have the opportunity to give the requisite prior notice of the demonstration to the authorities. By contrast, in *Éva Molnár v Hungary*,[80] the Court considered that there were no special circumstances to justify overriding the obligation to give notice of the demonstration and, therefore, the dispersal of the applicant's demonstration was necessary for the purposes of Article 11(2). In arriving at this conclusion, the Court took into account the procedural

---

[72] For a discussion, see later.

[73] Hudoc (2013) para 90 (beating with truncheons and weapons and use of tear gas).

[74] Hudoc (2010).

[75] See also *Kasparov and Others v Russia* hudoc (2013) (no pressing social need for arrest and administrative fines for particpation in unlawful demonstration).

[76] *Nos 26258/07 and 26255/07* hudoc (2009) DA. It relied also on *Skiba v Poland No 10659/03* hudoc (2009) DA.   [77] *Hyde Park & Others v Moldova (Nos 5 and 6)* hudoc (2010) para 47.

[78] *Bukta and Others v Hungary* 2007-III; 51 EHRR 25 para 38.

[79] The presence of the Prime Minister at an event leading to a demonstration was not known in time to give the required three days' notice.   [80] Hudoc (2008) paras 40–3.

safeguards available under national law that prevented unreasonable restrictions being imposed on public demonstrations by the authorities, the disruption to traffic and public order caused by the combination of events surrounding the demonstration, and the fact that the demonstration was allowed to proceed for several hours before being disbanded meant that the applicant had sufficient time to express her views and negated any chilling effect there may have been on spontaneous demonstrations as a result of the dispersal. Of primary importance, however, was that the Court was not persuaded that the demonstration, whose purpose was to protest against the dispersal by the police of an unauthorized assembly earlier that day, would have become ineffective had the demonstrators respected the notification rule.

As well as the effect of any delay, the availability of an alternative venue for staging public events may persuade the Court that an interference was a necessary response to a failure to observe authorization requirements. In *Berladir and Others v Russia*,[81] the applicants notified the Moscow authorities of their plan to hold an assembly in a square outside the Mayor's Office as it was against the decisions of that Office that they wished to protest. In response, the Office of the Mayor of Moscow proposed an alternative place for the demonstration on the grounds of 'security' and disruption to traffic. Nevertheless, the applicants proceeded with a gathering at the place of their choice. They were promptly arrested by a special security squad and administrative fines were imposed. In finding that the interference was proportionate and necessary the majority of the Court took into account the small amount of the penalty, but it also highlighted the fact that the authorities had proposed an alternative venue for the assembly.[82] The fact that the assembly was peaceful and that the dispersal was so prompt as to allow no opportunity for expression was not considered and it was only in the joint dissenting opinion of Judges Valić and Kolver that the question was raised as to how effective in fact the location chosen by the authorities would be for such an assembly. A judgment such as *Berladir* seems to allow little scope for the assessments organizers may make to ensure the most effective exercise of their right to freedom of assembly.

The limits to tolerance required by Article 11(2) were reached in *Cissé v France*,[83] where 200 illegal immigrants occupied a church for nearly two months. By occupying the church, with the consent of the church authorities and without disruption to religious services, the applicants had sought to draw attention to their plight under French immigration rules. In the Court's view, the state had acted within its 'wide margin of appreciation' when it forcibly evacuated the immigrants from the church because health conditions there had deteriorated. Furthermore, the 'symbolic and testimonial value of the applicant's and other immigrants' presence had been tolerated sufficiently long enough'.[84] While the heavy-handed method of evacuation used by the police 'went beyond what was reasonable' to curtail the assembly, the interference was nevertheless proportionate.[85]

In *Ezelin v France*,[86] it was established that the imposition of penalties for participation in lawful assemblies are only permissible under Article 11 where the person concerned

---

[81] Hudoc (2012). See also *Rai, Allmond and 'Negotiate Now' v UK No 25522/94* hudoc (1995); 19 EHRR CD 93 DA.   [82] *Berladir and Others v Russia*, paras 58, 60.

[83] 2002-III para 51.

[84] *Cissé v France*. See also *Friedl v Austria* A 305-B (1995); 21 EHRR 83 (sit-in located in a busy square continued day and night for one week, where there was evidence of disruption of the progress of passers-by, was inadmissible) and *Çiloğlu and Others v Turkey* hudoc (2007) (forceful dispersal of unlawful sit-in held every Saturday for over three years causing disruption to traffic and a breach of peace was within the state's margin of appreciation).   [85] *Cissé v France*.

[86] A 202 (1991); 14 EHRR 362 para 53 (disciplinary penalty). See also *Galstyan v Armenia* hudoc (2007); 50 EHRR 25 paras 116–17.

commits a 'reprehensible act on such an occasion'. The applicant had taken part in a demonstration in Basse-Terre (Guadeloupe) directed against the courts. Prior notice of the march had been given and the march was not prohibited. Ezelin attended in his capacity as lawyer and trade union official, carrying an inoffensive placard. The march disintegrated into violence. Ezelin did not leave the demonstration when this happened and he refused to answer police questions in an inquiry into the events. He was reprimanded by the Court of Appeal exercising its disciplinary function over lawyers for 'breach of discretion' in not disassociating himself from the march and for not cooperating with the police. No allegations of unlawful conduct during the march were made against Ezelin. The European Court held by six votes to three that there had been a lack of proportionality between the imposition of the sanction and the need to act in the interests of the prevention of disorder. A 'just balance' must not discourage persons from making their beliefs peacefully known. The judgment is a strong one in favour of freedom of assembly, given the relatively insignificant punishment imposed on the applicant.

In the case of unlawful assemblies (ie those for which notification and authorization procedures have not been complied with), administrative sanctions may generally be imposed for contravention of those procedures without offending Article 11. Thus in *Ziliberberg v Moldova*,[87] an administrative fine of €3—a penalty at the lower end of the statutory scale of penalties—imposed on the applicant for participating in a peaceful student demonstration held without authorization from the Municipal Council was not considered disproportionate to the aim of preventing disorder, despite the fact that it was 'heavy relative to the applicant's revenue'. However, more than a formal breach of a notification time limit is required if the imposition of administrative liability is to be justified as proportionate under Article 11(2).[88]

The Court has also sought 'relevant and sufficient reasons' to justify the imposition of administrative penalties where there is a dispute as to whether an assembly had in fact been authorized or existed at all. In *Sergey Kuznetsov v Russia*, the Court observed that the 'relatively small' amount of a fine of €35 did not detract from the fact that the administrative fine imposed on the applicant for allegedly breaching authorization procedures was not necessary in a democratic society.[89] In that case, the government contended that the applicant had held an assembly different to that which had been authorized. Similarly, in *Kasparov and Others v Russia*,[90] the Court considered that the fact that the alleged demonstration was unlawful was not sufficient to establish that there was a pressing social need for the arrests of the applicants for participating in an unauthorized assembly and the subsequent administrative fines of €25 imposed on them. The applicants argued that they were not staging a demonstration at the time of their arrests, but had been walking in the street on their way to participate in an assembly that the authorities had authorized, while the government contended that the applicants were engaging in an unlawful demonstration and posed such a threat to security that the heavy police presence in the streets was unable to maintain public order and safety without resorting to the interferences. Neither of the government's contentions were proved to the satisfaction of the Court and it concluded that 'the applicants were arrested and charged with administrative offences for the sole reason that the authorities perceived that their demonstration was unauthorized.'

---

[87] *No 61821/00* hudoc (2009) DA.

[88] *Sergey Kuznetsov v Russia* hudoc (2008) para 43 (picket notice submitted eight days before the event instead of the ten days as prescribed by law was not a relevant or sufficient reason for imposing an administrative fine).

[89] *Sergey Kuznetsov v Russia*, para 48.   [90] Hudoc (2013) para 95.

Criminal sanctions for the organization of or participation in unauthorized assemblies require 'particular justification'.[91] In *Rai and Evans v UK*,[92] the Court considered that criminal penalties, consisting of a fine of £350, an order to contribute to prosecution costs, and a suspended sentence imposed on the participants in an unauthorized demonstration, were proportionate to the aims of protecting national security and preventing disorder given that they 'were not severe'; the offences were confined to 'limited and security sensitive areas'; and that the police had given the applicants an opportunity to disband without sanction. Cases in which the Court has found a violation of Article 11 after the imposition of criminal sanctions following an unlawful assembly have involved severe criminal sanctions where the applicants are not personally involved in acts of violence. For instance, *Gün and Others v Turkey*[93] involved a public gathering in Cizre during which a press statement relating to the arrest of the political figure Abdullah Öcalan was read out. The assembly was not authorized but had remained peaceful except for a clash between the police and a small number of participants while the crowd was dispersing. In these circumstances, the Court found that there was no pressing social need for sentencing the organizers of the event to imprisonment for one year and six months and payment of criminal fines for leading an unauthorized gathering. Further, the Court observed that such excessive sentencing was liable to discourage persons belonging to an association or political party from exercising their right to assemble for fear of criminal sanctions.

However, if demonstrators resort to conduct which is independently criminal, like the sit-in blocking the entrance to American barracks in Germany in *G v Germany*,[94] even if it is done with the purpose of drawing attention to the cause, Article 11(2) is unlikely to protect them against prosecutions and conviction. A dramatic illustration of where Article 11 afforded no protection from sanctions following an assembly is to be found in *Osmani and Others v FYRM*.[95] The applicant had organized a public meeting entitled 'defending the official use of the national flag' and addressed it in his capacity as elected mayor of Gostivar. This occurred soon after the Constitutional Court had suspended the decision of the Gostivar local council to place the Albanian and Turkish flags alongside the Macedonian flag in front of the Town Hall. In the following weeks the applicant failed to execute the Constitutional Court's order, as his duty as mayor required. After a public riot following the meeting in which there was loss of life, injury, and damage to property, the applicant was charged and convicted with the offence of 'stirring up, as a public official, national, racial and religious hatred, disagreement and intolerance'. The European Court held that the prosecution and conviction served a 'pressing social need' and that sufficient reasons were given by the authorities to justify the conviction of the applicant. In particular, the applicant's speech at the public meeting and his other actions played a

---

[91] *Rai and Evans v UK* Nos 26258/07 and 26255/07 hudoc (2009) DA. Cf *Akgöl and Gol v Turkey* hudoc (2011) para 43 ('A peaceful demonstration should not, in principle, be made the subject to the threat of a penal sanction'). See also *Pekaslan v Turkey* hudoc (2012) para 81.

[92] *Nos 26258/07 and 26255/07* hudoc (2009) DA.

[93] Hudoc (2013). Similarly, see *İzmir Savaş Karşitlari Derneği v Turkey* hudoc (2006) (three months' imprisonment for not obtaining permission to leave the country in order to attend meetings a violation of freedom of assembly and association).

[94] *No 13079/87*, 60 DR 256 at 263 (1989). See also, eg, *Lucas v UK No 39013/02* hudoc (2003); 37 EHRR CD 86 (minor fine for breach of peace for sitting in a public road); *Nicol and Selvanayagam v UK No 32213/96* hudoc (2001) DA (two days' detention and twenty-one days' imprisonment for breach of peace for obstructing fishing); *Drieman v Norway No 33678/96* hudoc (2000) DA (fine and confiscation of boat for obstructing lawful whaling); and *McBride v UK No 27786/95* hudoc (2001) DA (arrest and detention for one-and-a-half hours for entering upon military land during a demonstration).   [95] *No 50841/99* 2001-X DA.

'substantial part in the subsequent violence'. Further, the Court considered that the applicant's imprisonment for one year and three months was proportionate to the numerous aims pursued in the light of the violent nature of the consequent events and the facts upon which his conviction was based, including the local council's decision to act in breach of the Constitution by displaying the flags.

3. FREEDOM OF ASSOCIATION

The existence of associations in which citizens can pursue common objectives collectively in the democratic process has been recognized by the Court as an important component of a healthy civil society.[96] Such an 'association' will have fundamental rights which must be respected and protected by the state[97] and will generally have rights against and owe duties to its members. An individual has no right to become a member of a particular association so that an association has no obligation to admit or continue the membership of an individual.[98] Equally, an individual cannot be compelled to become a member of an association nor disadvantaged if he chooses not to do so.[99] This last arrangement, the so-called 'negative' freedom of association, is not specifically spelled out in Article 11(1). Nonetheless, it is settled that this is the proper interpretation of Article 11(1).

I. MEANING OF ASSOCIATION

The notion of 'association' has an autonomous Convention meaning. As a result, the fact that a substantive coordination of activities of individuals is not recognized in the national law as an 'association' will not necessarily mean that freedom of association is not at stake under Article 11. Whereas association in the sense of the right to 'share the company' of others does not qualify as 'association' for the purposes of Article 11,[100] informal, if also stable and purposive, groupings will fall within its scope.[101] However, the mere existence of separate legal status for an institution beyond that of its individual members will not necessarily implicate Article 11(1). On several occasions, the Strasbourg authorities have decided that professional associations, established by law and requiring membership of all practising professionals, are not 'associations' within the meaning of Article 11(1).[102]

---

[96] *Sidiropoulos and Others v Greece* 1998-IV; 27 EHRR 633 para 44 and *Gorzelik and Others v Poland* 2004-I; 40 EHRR 76 para 93 GC.

[97] *Plattform 'Ärzte für das Leben' v Austria* No 10126/82, 44 DR 65 at 72 (1985); 13 EHRR 204. Eg, *İzmir Savaş Karşitlari Derneği v Turkey* hudoc (2006) (members of association imprisoned for failing to obtain permission to leave the country to attend meetings a violation); *Grande Oriente D'Italia Di Palazzo Guistiniani v Italy* 2001-VIII; 34 EHRR 629 (law barring freemasons from applying for public office that had a minimal impact on the association a violation); and *Grande Oriente D'Italia Di Palazzo Guistiniani v Italy (No 2)* hudoc (2007) (freemasons and members of secret associations required to declare their membership when applying for public office a breach of Article 14 in conjunction with Article 11); cf *Siveri and Chiellini v Italy* No 13148/04 hudoc (2008) DA (freemasons dismissed from public office for concealing membership in breach of rules requiring a declaration of membership inadmissible).

[98] *Cheall v UK* No 10550/83, 42 DR 178 at 185 (1985); 8 EHRR 74.

[99] *Young, James and Webster v UK* A 44 (1981); 4 EHRR 38 para 55 PC and *Chassagnou v France* 1999-III; 29 EHRR 615 para 117 GC.

[100] *McFeeley v UK* No 8317/78, 20 DR 44 at 98 (1980); 3 EHRR 161 (concerning contact between prisoners).

[101] See, however, Tomuschat, *European System*, Ch 19, p 494, requiring 'an organizational structure'.

[102] Eg, *Le Compte, Van Leuven and De Meyere v Belgium* A 43 (1981); 4 EHRR 1 paras 64–5 PC and *A v Spain* No 13750/88, 66 DR 188 (1990).

Amongst other things, this means that the issue of compulsory membership in such associations does not present a difficulty under the Convention. The autonomous meaning of 'association' is vital here too, because the question whether an institution is an association will not finally be decided by its classification in the national law.[103] Thus, the mere fact of incorporation under a general law mainly directed at facilitating economic enterprises is not enough to make the resulting corporate body an association; and the use of the corporate structure by associations whose principal purposes are the furtherance of the non-economic interests of their members will not take them outside Article 11. Elements used to determine whether an association is public or private are whether it was founded by individuals or by the legislature; whether it remained integrated within the structures of the state; whether it was invested with administrative, rule–making, and disciplinary power; and whether it pursued an aim in the general interest.[104]

II. LIMITATIONS UPON ASSOCIATIONS

As with freedom of assembly, interferences will be justified if they meet the conditions set out in Article 11(2), ie, are 'prescribed by law',[105] are for the protection of one of the objectives specified in the second paragraph, and are 'necessary in a democratic society'. These requirements will be examined in the following discussion on limitations on particular types of associations. Limitations on trade unions are considered separately in section 4.

a. Political parties

It is settled law that Article 11 on freedom of association applies to political parties.[106] The Court's conclusion on the applicability of Article 11 to political parties is based in part on the wording of Article 11(1), but is more compelled by the importance it attributes to the role of political parties in a 'democratic society', democracy itself being regarded as a fundamental feature of the Convention system and pluralism a precondition of that democracy.[107] The Court's conception of the relationship between political parties and the core democratic rights of freedom of expression, guaranteed in Article 10, and of free elections, guaranteed in Article 3 of the First Protocol, has also been a reason for construing the exceptions in Article 11(2) 'strictly' so that 'only convincing and compelling reasons' serve to justify restrictions on their freedom of association.[108] This narrow approach towards the exceptions to the rule of freedom of association is mitigated only by the state's power under Article 11(2) and its positive obligation under Article 1 of the Convention to impose restraint on an association's activities or intentions in order to secure the rights and freedoms of others.[109] As a 'power' granted to the state, the Court has said it must be

---

[103] *Sigurjonsson v Iceland* A 264 (1993); 16 EHRR 462 paras 30–1. See also *Chassagnou v France* 1999-III; 29 EHRR 615 para 101 GC (hunters' associations established by law and requiring the membership of private landowners fell within Article 11(1)).

[104] *Herrmann v Germany* hudoc (2011); 56 EHRR 7 para 76 (hunting associations regarded as public institutions and therefore outside Article 11).

[105] Eg, *Tebieti Mühafize Cemiyyeti and Israfilov v Azerbaijan* 2009-.

[106] *KPD v Germany* No 250/57, 1 YB 222 (1957) (*German Communist Party*); *United Communist Party of Turkey v Turkey* 1998-I; 26 EHRR 121 para 33 GC; and *Refah Partisi (The Welfare Party) v Turkey* 2003-II; 37 EHRR 1 GC.

[107] *United Communist Party of Turkey v Turkey* 1998-I; 26 EHRR 121 paras 25 and 45 GC and *Refah Partisi v Turkey*, para 89. On the Court's conception of democracy, see generally Marks, BYBIL 209 (1995) and Mowbray, PL 703 (1999). [108] *United Communist Party of Turkey v Turkey*, para 46.

[109] *Refah Partisi (The Welfare Party) v Turkey* 2003-II; 37 EHRR 1 para 103 GC and *Gorzelik and Others v Poland* 2004-I; 40 EHRR 76 para 94 GC.

used 'sparingly'.[110] The narrow ambit of the permitted limitations on the right to freedom of association for political parties was first articulated in *United Communist Party of Turkey v Turkey*.[111] In this case, the Turkish Constitutional Court dissolved the newly formed party and, by operation of law, a ban was placed on its founders and managers from holding similar office in any new political party because of the threat to the unity of the nation and the territorial integrity of Turkey that was allegedly created by, *inter alia*, the express recognition in the party's programme of a 'Kurdish nation' in Turkey and of a right to self-determination for the Kurdish people. This conclusion allows the state 'only a limited margin of appreciation' when determining whether the interference with the political party is 'necessary in a democratic society'.[112] Applied to the *United Communist Party* case,[113] the Grand Chamber reasoned that there could be no justification for restrictions on a political party 'solely because it seeks to debate in public the situation of part of the State's population...in order to find, according to democratic rules, solutions capable of satisfying everyone concerned'. Observing that the programme expressly strived for peaceful and democratic solutions, the Grand Chamber unanimously held that, despite the state's argument that what was at stake was the essential conditions for the state's existence, the penalties were disproportionate to the aim pursued and, therefore, constituted a violation of Article 11.[114] The same penalties were in issue in *Socialist Party v Turkey*, this time in response to statements made in party publications and by the party's chairman during an election campaign in which the establishment of a federal system of government as a solution to the 'Kurdish problem' in Turkey was advocated. The Grand Chamber accepted the government's argument that the statements were directed at the Kurdish population, but found no evidence of incitement to violence or otherwise of an infringement of the rules of democracy.[115] It also rejected the government's contention that a political programme that is incompatible with the current principles and structures of the state must be incompatible with the rules of democracy. The Grand Chamber reasoned:

> It is of the essence of democracy to allow diverse political programmes to be proposed and debated, even those that call into question the way a state is currently organised, provided that they do not harm democracy itself.[116]

---

[110] *Gorzelik and Others v Poland*, para 95. With the recognition of the positive obligation in the context of political party programmes, the Court has no longer found it necessary to examine complaints under Article 17; cf *WP v Poland No 42264/98* hudoc (2004) DA (prohibition on the formation of an association).

[111] 1998-I; 26 EHRR 121 GC.

[112] *Gorzelik and Others v Poland*, para 46; *Socialist Party v Turkey* 1998-III; 27 EHRR 51 para 50 GC; and *Christian Democratic People's Party v Moldova* 2006-II; 45 EHRR 392 para 68.

[113] 1998-I; 26 EHRR 121 para 57 GC. See also *Socialist Party v Turkey* 1998-III; 27 EHRR 51 para 45 GC and *Dicle on behalf of the DEP (Democratic Party) of Turkey v Turkey* hudoc (2002).

[114] An examination of the stated objectives of the programme sufficed as the party's limited period of existence meant that the Court could not, as a practical matter, look to the party's activities to discern the party's true intentions and responsibility for the terrorism situation in Turkey: *United Communist Party*, paras 58–9.

[115] *Socialist Party v Turkey* 1998-III; 27 EHRR 51 para 47 GC, although the Court suggests that had the statements encouraged secession from Turkey, then its conclusion may have differed. On the Court's conception of democracy advanced in the *United Communist Party* and the *Socialist Party* cases, see Mowbray, 1999 PL 703 at 703–6.

[116] *Socialist Party v Turkey* 1998-III; 27 EHRR 51 para 47 GC. See also, *Freedom and Democracy Party (ÖZDEP) v Turkey* 1999-III; 31 EHRR 674 para 41 GC (the Party's programme for government assumed there was a Kurdish people in Turkey with a separate language and culture and advocated the abolition of the Department of Religious Affairs) and *Democracy and Change Party v Turkey* hudoc (2005). In the context of non-governmental associations, see *United Macedonian Organization Ilinden and Others v Bulgaria* hudoc (2006) para 76 (demanding autonomy or secession not sufficient ground to refuse association's registration).

The Grand Chamber then found that the dissolution of the party was unnecessary in a democratic society for failing to meet the proportionality requirement.[117] The *Socialist Party* case illustrates that, where the Court is satisfied that an association does not question the need for compliance with democratic principles, vigorous demands by it for the fundamental reorganization of the structure of the state will not *per se* provide convincing and compelling reasons to justify restrictions on the exercise of the right to freedom of association under Article 11(2).

Such reasons were found to exist by the majority of the Grand Chamber in *Refah Partisi (The Welfare Party) v Turkey*.[118] Consolidating upon statements of principle articulated in the earlier cases, the Grand Chamber formulated two criteria to be satisfied in order to invoke the protection of Article 11 where a political party has promoted a change in the law or the legal and constitutional structures of the state:

> [F]irstly, the means used to that end must be legal and democratic; secondly, the change proposed must itself be compatible with fundamental democratic principles. It necessarily follows that a political party whose leaders incite violence or put forward a policy which fails to respect democracy or which is aimed at the destruction of democracy and the flouting of rights and freedoms recognised in a democracy cannot lay claim to the Convention's protection against penalties imposed on those grounds.[119]

Unlike the *United Communist Party* and *Socialist Party* cases, which raised concerns about separatism, *Refah* involved the principle of secularism. The earlier cases further differed from *Refah* in that they concerned the dissolution of fledgling political parties. In *Refah's* case, the Turkish Constitutional Court dissolved the largest political party in Turkey. The party had also held office in a coalition government for thirteen months (before it resigned under pressure from the military) and had been in existence for over fourteen years. Its assets were transferred to the state treasury and a five-year ban on participation in political activities was imposed on a number of its members, one of whom was the party's chairman (who had been Prime Minister during the time of the coalition government). The Constitutional Court did so on the ground that acts[120] and statements[121] imputable to the party disclosed that it had become a 'centre of activities contrary to the principle of secularism' guaranteed in the Turkish Constitution insofar as: (i) the party intended to set up a plurality of legal systems in the state; (ii) the party intended to apply

---

[117] *Socialist Party v Turkey*, para 49. See also *Freedom and Democracy Party (ÖZDEP)*, para 43 (no pressing social need); *Refah Partisi (The Welfare Party) v Turkey* hudoc (2001); 37 EHRR 1 para 104 GC (pressing social need); and *Democracy and Change Party v Turkey* hudoc (2005) (no pressing social need).

[118] Hudoc (2001); 37 EHRR 1 GC. See also *Partidul Comunistilor (Nepeceristi) and Ungureanu v Romania* hudoc (2005); 44 EHRR 340 para 48 (refusal to register a new political party a violation).

[119] *Refah Partisi v Turkey*, para 98. See also *Partidul Comunistilor (Nepeceristi) and Ungureanu v Romania* 2005-I; 44 EHRR 340 para 46 (refusing communists registration as a political party was a violation) and *United Macedonian Organization Ilinden-PIRIN v Bulgaria* hudoc (2005) (political party dissolved on grounds of national security because individual members held separatist views and sought autonomy of region a violation). In the context of political associations, see *Zhechev v Bulgaria* hudoc (2007) para 47 (NGO aiming for restoration of monarchy requiring amendment to Bulgarian constitution).

[120] Including the following conduct by the Prime Minister and Minister of Justice while in government: encouraging the wearing of Islamic headscarves in public and educational establishments; altering public service working hours to accommodate Ramadan fasting; visiting a Party member in prison awaiting trial for incitement to religious hatred; and hosting a reception for Islamic leaders at the Prime Minister's residence.

[121] The statements were made by some Refah members over a period of years prior to Refah holding government office.

Islamic principles and law (sharia) to the internal and external relations of the Muslim community within that framework; and (iii) statements had referred to the possible use of force as a political method. Relying on the same evidence as the Constitutional Court, the Grand Chamber emphasized the importance of the principle of secularism for the democratic system in Turkey.[122] It was satisfied that the penalties served the legitimate aims of protecting national security and public safety, prevention of disorder or crime, and protection of the rights and freedoms of others, and were prescribed by law. The issue was, therefore, whether the penalties were 'necessary in a democratic society'. Ruling that they were, the Grand Chamber first concluded that, at the time of its dissolution, Refah's standing in election polls indicated that it had the 'real potential to seize political power without being restricted by the compromises inherent in a coalition' and 'the real chances that Refah would implement its programme after gaining power' made the danger to Convention rights and freedoms posed by the party's proposed programme 'more tangible and more immediate'.[123] Second, the Grand Chamber found that the acts and statements of Refah's members were imputable to the whole party as it had not taken 'prompt practical steps', including disciplinary proceedings, to distance itself from those members.[124] Regarding the grounds for dissolving the party, the Grand Chamber held, agreeing with the majority of the Chamber,[125] that a plurality of legal systems, one of which would be religion based, is a societal system that is incompatible with the Convention because it removes the state's role as the impartial guarantor of human rights and neutral arbiter of beliefs, and infringes the principle of non-discrimination.[126] Furthermore, the Grand Chamber held that sharia is incompatible with the fundamental principles of democracy as contained in the Convention owing to its 'stable and invariable' nature and the divergence of its doctrines from Convention values in a number of respects, including the principle of pluralism.[127] The finding that sharia is incompatible with democracy was reinforced in *Refah* by the fact that Turkey had opted for secularism, confining religion to the private sphere, when the republican state was founded. The Court said that a state might oppose political movements based on 'religious fundamentalism' in the light of its own historical experience.[128] It also rejected the applicants' argument that prohibiting a plurality of private-law systems in the name of secularism constituted discrimination

---

[122] *Refah Partisi v Turkey* para 67.

[123] *Refah Partisi v Turkey*, paras 108–10. Cf *United Macedonian Organization Ilinden-PIRIN v Bulgaria* hudoc (2005); 43 EHRR 52 (no 'pressing social need' for party's dissolution where, *inter alia*, its public influence was negligible).

[124] *Refah Partisi v Turkey*, paras 113–15 and 131. This was so despite Refah's constitution and programme making no reference to a plurality of legal systems, to sharia or Islam, or the use of force as a political method: see paras 73, 117, and 131. The Court (para 101) said that, when determining a party's intentions and motives, the Court may go beyond the party's constitution and programme to consider the acts and stances of the party's leaders: *Refah Partisi v Turkey*, para 101. Nor had Refah sought during its period in office to introduce sharia.

[125] The Chamber held there was no violation of Article 11 by a slim majority of four votes to three.

[126] In his concurring opinion, Judge Kovler regretted the Chamber's failure to examine more closely the concept of plurality of legal systems.

[127] *Refah Partisi v Turkey*, para 123; cf, the concurring opinion of Judge Kovler. For a discussion of this finding, see Evans, in Ghanea, ed, *The Challenge of Religious Discrimination at the Dawn of the New Millennium*, 2004, pp 153–4. Although the Court observed, at para 100, that 'a political party animated by the moral values imposed by a religion cannot be regarded as intrinsically inimical to the fundamental principles of democracy, as set forth in the Convention'.

[128] *Refah Partisi v Turkey*, para 124. The Court noted (para 93) that 'the Convention institutions have expressed the view that the principle of secularism is certainly one of the fundamental principles of the state which are in harmony with the rule of law and respect for human rights and democracy'.

against Muslims. The Court observed that the right to freedom of religion as enshrined in the Convention is a matter of individual conscience that is separate from the field of private law, which is concerned with the organization of society as a whole. With regard to the possible use of force, it found that speeches made by several party members referred to the possible use of force as a political method to be used by Refah to gain and retain power.[129] It noted that the party did not exclude the use of force.[130] The Grand Chamber unanimously concluded that, despite the limited margin of appreciation, the penalties met a 'pressing social need' and could not be regarded as disproportionate. Refah had failed to meet the two conditions by which a political party may promote a change in the law and invoke the protection of Article 11. Accordingly, the penalties were 'necessary in a democratic society' and no violation of Article 11 had occurred.

The decision in *Refah* is controversial. It raises important questions about the relationships between secularism, religion, human rights, and democracy, and their connection within the framework of the Convention.[131] The joint dissenting opinion of Judges Fuhrmann, Loucaides, and Bratza in the Chamber provides a different approach towards the analysis of the issues posed in the *Refah* case. The minority found it unnecessary to examine the nature or effect of a plural legal system or to embark upon an assessment of sharia; rather their focus was on the standard of proof required to justify dissolution where a policy, not contained in the party's constitution or programme, is imputed. Indeed, the minority noted that Refah's constitution and programme for government expressly endorsed the principle of secularism contained in the Turkish constitution. In a case in which statements or acts of individual leaders or members are relied on to take the drastic measure of dissolving an entire party, the minority said that 'particularly convincing and compelling reasons' must be shown to justify the penalty, especially in *Refah*'s case where the representations were isolated events occurring in very different contexts over a period of six years, long before the party came to power. In the absence of reasons of that quality, a proportionate penalty would be the prosecution of the members responsible.

In *Herri Batasuna and Batasuna v Spain*,[132] a unanimous Chamber applied the criteria set out in *Refah* and ruled that the dissolution of two Basque political parties under Spain's 2002 Institutional Law on political parties met a 'pressing social need' and was proportionate to the legitimate aims of public safety, the prevention of disorder, and the protection of the rights of others.[133] In doing so the Court accepted the findings of the domestic courts that eighteen incidents during 2002, after the Law was enacted, established that the conduct of the parties, including their members and leaders, bore 'a strong resemblance to explicit support for violence and the commendation of people seemingly linked to terrorism' which was 'capable of provoking social conflict between supporters of the applicant parties and other political organizations, in particular those of the Basque country'. The Court noted in particular that the conduct had not ruled out the use of force to achieve the parties' aims.[134] Moreover, it concluded that the actions, taken as a whole, were 'part of a strategy adopted by the applicant parties to achieve a political aim essentially in breach of democratic principles enshrined in the Spanish Constitution'.[135] In the light of these findings, the Court considered that the domestic courts had arrived at the 'reasonable' conclusion that there was a link between the parties and the terrorist

---

[129] *Refah Partisi v Turkey*, para 130.   [130] *Refah Partisi v Turkey*, para 132.
[131] See Boyle, 1 EHRR 1 (2004) and McGoldrick, 5 HRLR 27 (2005) 52–3.   [132] 2009- para 83.
[133] *Herri Batasuna and Batasuna v Spain*, para 93.
[134] *Herri Batasuna and Batasuna v Spain*, para 86.
[135] *Herri Batasuna and Batasuna v Spain*, para 87.

organization ETA and 'that link may objectively be considered to constitute a threat to democracy'.[136]

By contrast, in *Republican Party of Russia v Russia*,[137] the Court unanimously ruled that the 'radical measure' of dissolution of a 'long-established and law abiding political party' on the 'formal ground' of failing to comply with statutory requirements regarding minimum membership numbers for political parties and regional branches was not 'necessary in a democratic society'. States have a 'certain margin of appreciation' in specifying formalities for the formation of a political party and also in refusing to allow 'serious defects in those steps to be cured subsequently'.[138] However, in the *Republican Party of Russia* case, the Court opined that a minimum membership requirement 'would be justified only if it allowed the unhindered establishment and functioning of a plurality of parties representing the interests of various population groups'.[139]

The Court observed that there was 'no common European approach' to minimum membership requirements for political parties but the number of members required in Russia was the highest in Europe. It considered that limiting the number of political parties, and thereby allowing the survival of large popular parties only, was a situation which could not be justified by reference to state budgetary considerations.[140] Nor was the prevention of excessive parliamentary fragmentation a persuasive reason for limiting the number of political parties entitled to participate in elections, given the introduction of an electoral threshold and the conditional entitlement of parties to participate in elections.[141] Moreover, the Court disagreed with the government's argument 'that only those associations that represent the interests of considerable portions of society are eligible for political party status'. On the contrary, it considered that 'small minority groups must also have an opportunity to establish political parties and participate in elections with the aim of obtaining parliamentary representation'.[142] Membership number restrictions for political parties may thus unacceptably reduce the variety of political parties and, therefore, the voters' choice at elections. The Court also considered that the government subjected political parties to 'intrusive' annual inspections concerning party activities and membership and, together with the 'uncertainty generated by changes in the minimum membership requirement in recent years', these obligations 'imposed a disproportionate burden on political parties' in Russia.[143] In light of the various electoral measures in Russia having an 'evident impact on the opportunities for various political forces to participate effectively in the political process and thus affect[ing] pluralism', the Court considered that the requirement that the government produce evidence to demonstrate that the amendments were justified to be 'all the more pressing'.[144] As to the statutory requirement that a political party should have regional branches in the majority of the Russian regions, the Court was prepared to depart from the practice of member states of the Council of Europe, which allows regional parties, in order to take into account 'special historical and political considerations' pertaining to Russia that may 'render a more restrictive practice necessary'.[145] However, the Court was not persuaded that what

---

[136] *Herri Batasuna and Batasuna v Spain*, para 89.   [137] Hudoc (2011).

[138] *United Macedonian Organization Ilinden-PIRIN and Others v Bulgaria (No 2)* hudoc (2011); 56 EHRR 29 para 92.   [139] *Republican Party of Russia v Russia* hudoc (2011) para 119.

[140] *Republican Party of Russia*, para 112.   [141] *Republican Party of Russia*, para 113.

[142] *Republican Party of Russia*, para 114.

[143] *Republican Party of Russia*, para 116, referring to the Venice Commission Explanatory Report on legislation on political parties and Code of Good Practice in Electoral Matters in support of the view that frequent changes to the conditions for obtaining and retaining political party status may be interpreted as an attempt to manipulate electoral laws to the advantage of the ruling party.

[144] *Republican Party of Russia*, paras 117–18.   [145] *Republican Party of Russia*, para 126.

was effectively a ban on establishing regional political parties was necessary to protect Russia's fragile democratic institutions, its unity, and its national security, as the government contended. The Court observed that, with the 'passage of time… [i]t becomes necessary to prefer a case-by-case assessment, to take account of the actual programme and conduct of each political party rather than a perceived threat posed by a certain category or types of parties'. Of significance was the fact that the ban on regional branches was not introduced in 1991 upon the collapse of the Soviet Union and the onset of democratic reform, but rather ten years after Russia had started its democratic transition. In those circumstances, the Court opined, there are sanctions, including dissolution of political parties in the 'most serious cases', which are more effective in protecting Russian laws, institutions, and national security than sweeping bans on regional parties.[146] Rather, the requirement for regional branches, the Court concluded, was 'illustrative of a potential for miscarriages inherent in the indiscriminate banning of regional parties', and it found incomprehensible the government's argument that the dissolution served to prevent disorder or to protect national security or the rights of others.[147]

b. Other associations

Political objectives may be pursued by associations other than those registered as political parties.[148] The Court has recognized that associations formed for other objectives, including protecting cultural or spiritual heritage, pursuing various socio-economic aims, proclaiming or teaching religion, seeking an ethnic identity, or asserting a minority consciousness, which may or may not have political objectives, also fall within Article 11, as they too are important for the 'proper functioning of democracy'.[149] Whatever the objective of the association, when determining whether an interference with the freedom of association is justified under Article 11(2) the stricter standard of review adopted in the political party cases, and transposed from Article 10, applies.

Applying this approach to associations asserting a minority consciousness, in *Sidiropoulos and Others v Greece*[150] the Court found there had been a violation of Article 11 when the Greek authorities refused to register an association purporting in its memorandum of association to preserve and develop the traditions and culture of the Macedonian minority of the region. The authorities considered that the true intent of the association was to undermine Greece's territorial integrity by disputing the Greek identity of the region. However, the Court was not persuaded that 'convincing and compelling reasons' for the refusal existed given the absence of a national system for review of associations prior to registration and the weak evidence relied on by the national courts that gave rise to no more than a 'mere suspicion' about the association's intention.[151] The Court observed that 'the inhabitants of a region in a country are entitled to form associations in order to promote the region's special characteristics, for historical as well as economic reasons'.[152] The Court also held the refusal was disproportionate because a national law

---

[146] *Republican Party of Russia*, para 129.   [147] *Republican Party of Russia*, paras 129–30.

[148] *Zhechev v Bulgaria* hudoc (2007).

[149] *Gorzelik and Others v Poland* 2004-I; 40 EHRR 76 para 92 GC. See also, eg, *Grande Oriente D'Italia Di Palazzo Guistiniani v Italy* 2001-VIII; 34 EHRR 629 (masonic association); *Koretskyy v Ukraine* hudoc (2008) (protection of the natural environment); and *Tebieti Mühafize Cemiyyeti and Israfilov v Azerbaijan* (2009) (environmental NGO).

[150] 1998-IV; 27 EHRR 633. See also *Association of Citizens Radko & Paunkovski v Former Yugoslav Republic of Macedonia* 2009- ; 49 EHRR 21 (dissolution of association debating Macedonian ethnicity).

[151] See also *Bozgan v Romania* hudoc (2007) (refusal to register association on basis of 'mere suspicion' that it intended to set up parallel structures to monitor the authorities a violation).

[152] *Bozgan v Romania*, para 44.

conferred power on the courts to dissolve an association once registered if it subsequently pursued aims contrary to those contained in its memorandum or the law.[153]

By contrast with the *Sidiropoulos* case, in *Gorzelik and Others v Poland*[154] the Court upheld the state's decision to refuse to register an association. In this case an association described itself in its memorandum of association as an 'organisation of the Silesian national minority'. The Polish court had found that the Silesian people did not constitute a 'national minority' under Polish law, a designation that would have given the association an entitlement to special privileges under electoral laws, including an exemption from the threshold of votes required to obtain seats in Parliament. Moreover, it was held that the registration itself set in motion a further train of events leading to the acquisition of privileges under electoral laws. The government sought to justify the interference by contending that the purpose of refusing the association's application for registration was to prevent it from acquiring those electoral benefits available to national minorities; while the association denied that it was interested in running for elections and argued the restriction was premature. When considering whether the refusal to register the association was justified, the Grand Chamber found that the interference sought to protect the existing democratic institutions and procedures in Poland by preventing an abuse of electoral law by the association itself, or other associations in similar situations. It accepted that once the association was registered, there was no national law capable of preventing the mischief the authorities perceived would occur. In other words, there was no way for the authorities to ensure the rights of others participating in parliamentary elections would not be infringed. In this circumstance, it held, the authorities had not overstepped their margin of appreciation in considering that there was a 'pressing social need' at the moment of registration to regulate the 'free choice of associations to call themselves an "organisation of a national minority"'.[155] Furthermore, the refusal to register the ethnic minority association owing to the threat of abuse of electoral laws was not disproportionate to the aim of protecting existing democratic institutions in Poland, as the refusal was not directed at the objectives of the association but rather the label it would use at law.[156] *Gorzelik* is a case where the Court clearly considered that the state had justifiably exercised the power, recognized in *Refah*, to restrain the freedom of association to protect its institutions.

The right to freedom of association of religious groups must be read in the light of Article 9 of the Convention. In *The Moscow Branch of the Salvation Army v Russia* the Court said:

> [T]he right of believers to freedom of religion [in Article 9], which includes the right to manifest one's religion in community with others, encompasses the expectation that believers will be able to associate freely, without arbitrary state intervention.[157]

The Court found that the refusal by the authorities to re-register the applicant's religious association after changes in the law on religious associations was not 'prescribed by law'

---

[153] *Bozgan v Romania*, paras 45–6. See also *United Macedonian Organization Ilinden and Others v Bulgaria* hudoc (2006) (alternative powers taken into account in finding no 'sufficient' ground for refusal to register association); *Bekir-Ousta v Greece* hudoc (2007) (refusal to register an association of a Muslim minority a violation); and *Bozgan v Romania* hudoc (2007) (refusal to register an association aiming at protecting citizens against organized crime a violation).

[154] 2004-I; 40 EHRR 76 GC. See also *Artyomov v Russia* No 17582/05 hudoc (2006) DA.

[155] *Gorzelik and Others v Poland*, para 103.   [156] *Gorzelik and Others v Poland*, para 105.

[157] 2006-XI; 44 EHRR 46 para 58. See also *Church of Scientology Moscow v Russia* hudoc (2007); 46 EHRR 16 para 72 and *Jehovah's Witnesses of Moscow and Others v Russia* hudoc (2010); 53 EHRR 4 para 99.

and lacked 'relevant and sufficient reasons'.[158] Moreover, the Court considered that where a religious community had operated as an independent and law abiding religious community for a number of years, the reasons for refusing re-registration should be 'particularly weighty and compelling'.[159] Not only had there been a violation of Article 11 read in the light of Article 9, but the Russian authorities 'did not act in good faith' and had 'neglected their duty of neutrality and impartiality' towards the religious community.[160]

The regulation of associations by law may raise an issue as to the 'quality of law'. The case of *Koretskyy v Ukraine*[161] illustrates how the question can arise as an aspect of the requirements contained in Article 11(2), ie, the interference must be lawful, as embodied in the expression 'prescribed by law',[162] and 'necessary in a democratic society'. In this case the authorities refused to register an environmental NGO on the basis that its articles of association did not comply with domestic law. The relevant law provided that an application for registration of an association may be refused if its articles of association 'contravene the legislation of Ukraine'. Relying on this provision, the authorities required, as a condition of the association's registration, *inter alia*, the exclusion of numerous activities from the applicant's articles of association, including distributing propaganda, lobbying authorities, involving volunteers in its work, publishing, and engaging its managing body in the everyday financial activities of the association, as well as a limitation restricting the association to acting within the region in respect of which it was registered. With respect to whether the lawfulness requirement was met, the Court said that the provision 'allowed a particularly broad interpretation'. In practice this would prohibit any departure from domestic legislation dealing with the activities of associations. In this circumstance, the Court found that the provision was 'too vague to be sufficiently "foreseeable"' for the persons concerned.[163] Nor could judicial review of a decision to refuse registration prevent arbitrary decision-making given the excessively wide discretion granted to the authorities by the provision. Regarding the question of whether the restrictions met a 'pressing social need' and, if so, whether they were proportionate, the Court held that the state had advanced no 'relevant and sufficient reasons' for the restrictions on the association's activities, and none could be found. Instead, an examination of the evidence satisfied the Court that the association intended to pursue peaceful and purely democratic aims and tasks. Thus, the refusal to register the association did not meet the requirement of lawfulness and was not necessary in a democratic society, constituting a violation of Article 11.

The Court has recognized that just as social organizations and movements contribute to the proper functioning of a democratic society,[164] they may also play a role in endangering it. *Vona v Hungary*[165] demonstrates how such a danger to democracy is to be assessed prior to a movement making an attempt to seize power and where the risk of

---

[158] *The Moscow Branch of the Salvation Army v Russia*, paras 86, 95, and 97. See also *Church of Scientology Moscow v Russia*, para 96 and *Jehovah's Witnesses of Moscow and Others v Russia*, para 180.

[159] *The Moscow Branch of the Salvation Army v Russia*, para 96.

[160] *The Moscow Branch of the Salvation Army v Russia*, para 97. See also *Church of Scientology Moscow* hudoc (2007); 46 EHRR 16 para 97 and *Jehovah's Witnesses of Moscow and Others v Russia* hudoc (2010); 53 EHRR 4 para 181. [161] Hudoc (2008).

[162] See also *NF v Italy* hudoc (2001); 35 EHRR 106 and *Maestri v Italy* hudoc (2004) GC (prohibition on membership of masonic association not foreseeable).

[163] *Koretskyy v Ukraine* hudoc (2008) para 48.

[164] Eg, in *Eğitim Ve Bilim Emekçileri Sendıkasi v Turkey* 2012-, the principle expressed in the applicant trade union's constitution that individuals in Turkish society should receive education in a mother tongue other than Turkish was not a 'relevant and sufficient reason' to justify the proceedings for dissolution of the association because it was not incompatible with the fundamental principles of democracy and the topic had been a matter of widespread public debate at the time. [165] Hudoc 2013.

its policy to democracy is not yet imminent. In *Vona* the Court established that the state is 'entitled to take preventative measures to protect democracy vis-à-vis such non-party entities, if a sufficiently imminent prejudice to the rights of others threatens to under-mine the fundamental values on the basis of which a democratic society exists and func-tions'. One such societal value the Court identified is 'the co-existence of members of society free from racial segregation, without which a democratic society would be incon-ceivable.'[166] The complaint concerned the dissolution of an association (the 'Hungarian Guard Association'), which was chaired by the applicant, and its associated movement (the 'Hungarian Guard Movement'). The stated aim of the Association was to preserve Hungarian traditions and culture; the objective of the Movement, which was established by the Association a couple of months after its founding, was defined as 'defending Hungary, defenceless physically, spiritually and intellectually'. Shortly after its creation the Movement swore in fifty-six 'guardsmen'. The authorities notified the Association that this and other activities it conducted were unlawful. After the Association noti-fied the authorities that it had ceased its unlawful activities, the Movement held rallies and demonstrations throughout Hungary, many in villages with large Roma popula-tions. At these assemblies the members wore uniforms with armbands displaying Arrow Cross-like symbols, issued commands and salutes, and paraded in military-like forma-tions. In one demonstration there were 200 members in a village of 1,800 inhabitants who called for the defence of 'ethnic Hungarians' against 'Gypsy criminality'. There, the police refused to allow the march to proceed down a street predominantly inhabited by Roma. In response, the authorities obtained a court order for the dissolution of the Association and, following further rallies, the order was expressed to extend to the Movement. In the view of the national courts, the activities of the Association and the Movement 'created an anti-Roma atmosphere through verbal and visual demonstrations of power', even though there was no actual violence at any of the events. The courts considered that the central theme of 'Gypsy criminality' was a racist concept and the Roma population subjected to such rallies was a 'captive audience'.[167] The national courts concluded that this activity 'amounted to creating a public menace by generating social tension and bringing about an atmosphere of impending violence.' The applicant contended before the domestic courts and at Strasbourg that the Association and the Movement were separate legal entities, but the Court found the conclusions of the domestic courts neither unreasonable nor arbi-trary on this and all other issues.[168] Rather, the Court shared the domestic courts' view that 'the activities and ideas expressed by the Movement relied on a race-based compari-son'.[169] The Court also disagreed with the applicant's contention that the Movement, as an association of individuals whose ideas and conduct might offend or shock, was protected under Article 11 interpreted in the light of Article 10. The Court noted the historical experience of the country in which the paramilitary formation used in the rallies 'was reminiscent of the Hungarian Nazi (Red Arrow) movement which was the backbone of the regime that was responsible...for the mass extermination of Roma in Hungary' and that the 'intimidating effect' of the rallies 'must have gained momentum' because of the established organizational links between the Movement whose activists were present and a registered association benefiting from legal recognition.[170] The Court held:

> [A] paramilitary march goes beyond the mere expression of a disturbing or offensive idea, since the message is accompanied by the physical presence of a threatening group

---

[166] *Vona v Hungary*, para 57.   [167] *Vona v Hungary*, para 61.   [168] *Vona v Hungary*, para 60.
[169] *Vona v Hungary*, para 62.   [170] *Vona v Hungary*, para 65.

of organized activists. Where the expression of ideas is accompanied by a form of conduct, the Court considers that the level of protection generally granted to the freedom of
expression may be reduced in the light of important public-order interests related to that
conduct.[171]

As to the timing of the authorities' intervention, the Court reasoned 'the authorities could
not be required to await further developments before intervening to secure the protection
of the rights of others, since the Movement had taken concrete steps in public life to implement a policy incompatible with the standards of the Convention and democracy.'[172]

In these circumstances, the Court identified 'the intimidating character of the rallies'
as the 'overriding consideration'. The fact that the rallies had not been banned and no
violent act or crime had occurred was irrelevant. The Court said:

[O]rganising a series of rallies allegedly in order to keep 'Gypsy criminality' at bay by
means of paramilitary parading can be regarded as implementing a policy of racial segregation. In fact, the intimidating marches can be seen as constituting the first steps in the
realization of a certain vision of 'law and order' which is racist in essence.

The Court concluded, in unequivocal terms:

Large-scale, coordinated intimidation—related to the advocacy of racially motivated policies which are incompatible with the fundamental values of democracy—may justify State
interference with freedom of association, even within the narrow margin of appreciation
applicable in the present case. The reason for this relates to the negative consequences
which such intimidation has on the political will of the people. While the incidental advocacy of anti-democratic ideas is not sufficient in itself to justify banning a political party
on grounds of compelling necessity . . . and even less so in the case of an association which
cannot make use of the special status granted to political parties, the circumstances taken
overall, and in particular any coordinated and planned actions, may constitute sufficient
and relevant reasons for such a measure, especially when other forms of expression of
otherwise shocking ideas are not directly affected.[173]

As to proportionality, the Court considered that the authorities chose the 'only reasonable' course of action. In particular, the authorities could have been perceived by the general public to have legitimized the Association's racist agenda had they 'acquiesced in
the continued activities of the Movement and the Association by upholding their legal
existence in the privileged form of an entity under the law on association' and 'thereby
have indirectly facilitated the orchestration of its campaign of rallies'.[174] The Court unanimously ruled that the dissolution of the Association and the Movement were not violations of the right to freedom of association under Article 11.

c. Interferences with freedom of association: the requirement of proportionality

The extent of the interference with an association's capacity to function can be decisive in
determining the necessity of the interference with the right to freedom of association.[175]
The immediate and permanent dissolution of a political party is a 'drastic measure' which

---

[171] *Vona v Hungary*, para 66. [172] *Vona v Hungary*, para 68.
[173] *Vona v Hungary*, para 69. [174] *Vona v Hungary*, para 71.
[175] *Parti Nationaliste Basque—Organisation Régionale D'Iparralde v France* 2007-II para 49. See also
Refah Partisi (The Welfare Party) v Turkey 2003-II; 37 EHRR 1 para 100 GC.

will be 'warranted only in the most serious cases'.[176] In order for the dissolution of an association to be considered proportionate, there must be no other means of achieving the same aims pursued by the authorities that would have interfered less seriously with the association's freedom of association.[177] Thus, in *Jehovah's Witnesses of Moscow and Others v Russia*,[178] the Court, observing that a 'blanket ban on the activities of a religious community belonging to a known Christian denomination is an extraordinary occurrence', ruled that the legislation empowering the authorities to impose the sanction constituted a 'drastic measure disproportionate to the legitimate aim pursued' and recommended that 'less radical alternative sanctions, such as a warning, a fine or withdrawal of tax benefits' would enable proportionate sanctions to be imposed in the event that an interference was warranted. In *Tebieti Mühafize Cemiyyeti and Israfilov v Azerbaijan*,[179] the Court held that states are entitled to insist on the observance of certain formalities in the internal management of associations, but 'the mere failure to respect certain legal requirements on internal management of non-governmental organizations cannot be considered such serious misconduct as to warrant outright dissolution'. The choice of name of an association does not in principle justify its dissolution.[180] Nor will a single speech made overseas in a foreign language by a former leader of a political party to an audience not directly concerned with the situation justify 'so general a penalty' as the dissolution of an entire party, despite the message of the speech amounting to a call to the use of force as a political tool.[181] In these circumstances, the impact of the speech on 'national security', public 'order', or 'territorial integrity' would be very limited.[182] Similarly, a temporary ban on a political party's activities will be justified only by very serious breaches such as 'those which endanger political pluralism or fundamental democratic principles'.[183] In *Refah's* case the Court considered the dissolution of the party and the temporary bar on its leaders from similar political activity to be a proportionate measure because the party's objectives and the means chosen to achieve them were found to be a threat to democratic principles.

The refusal to register an association is a 'radical measure' preventing, as it does, the association from commencing any activity.[184] Nevertheless, it has more limited consequences than the dissolution or ban of an association, and can be more easily remedied through a fresh application for registration.[185]

A refusal to amend an official register of legal entities to take into account changes in an association's organizational structure and functioning is a less radical interference, but nonetheless may 'severely' disrupt a political party's activities and will, therefore, amount

---

[176] In relation to political parties see, eg, *Refah Partisi (The Welfare Party) v Turkey* 2003-II; 37 EHRR 1 paras 100 and 133 GC and *United Macedonian Organization Ilinden-PIRIN and Others v Bulgaria* hudoc (2005); 43 EHRR 52 para 56. In relation to other associations, see *Association Rhino and Others v Switzerland* hudoc (2011) para 62.   [177] *Association Rhino and Others v Switzerland* hudoc (2012) para 65.

[178] Hudoc (2010) para 159 (the Court also found that there were no 'relevant and sufficient reasons for an interference').   [179] Hudoc (2009) paras 72-3, 82.

[180] *United Communist Party of Turkey v Turkey* 1998-I; 26 EHRR 121 para 54 GC (political party) and *Association of Citizens Radko & Paunkovski v The Former Yugoslav Republic of Macedonia* 2009- ; 49 EHRR 21 para 75.

[181] *Dicle on behalf of the DEP (Democratic Party) of Turkey v Turkey* hudoc (2002) (criminal proceedings had been taken against the maker of the speech).   [182] *Dicle v Turkey*.

[183] See *Christian Democratic People's Party v Moldova* 2006-II; 45 EHRR 392 para 76 (one month ban on the party's activities as a result of holding unauthorized but peaceful meetings outside Parliament buildings was a violation).

[184] *Gorzelik and Others v Poland* 2004-I; 40 EHRR 76 para 105 GC and *United Macedonian Organization Ilinden and Others v Bulgaria* hudoc (2006).

[185] *United Macedonian Organization Ilinden-PIRIN and Others v Bulgaria (No 2)* hudoc (2011) para 94.

to an interference requiring justification under Article 11(2).[186] In *Republican Party of Russia v Russia*, the government argued that breaches in the procedures prescribed in the Party's articles of association made it necessary for the authorities to refuse to register changes to the Party's representatives elected at the general conference where the irregularities occurred. While the Court accepted that 'in certain cases' it was within the state's margin of appreciation to 'interfere—subject to the condition of proportionality—with an association's internal organization and functioning' where the association fails to comply 'with reasonable legal formalities applying to its establishment, functioning or internal organizational structure', it also recognized that the authorities 'should not intervene' in effect in the internal organization of an association 'to ensure observance by an association of every single formality provided by its own charter'.[187] The manner in which conferences are organized fell into the latter category: enforcement of formalities 'should be primarily up to the association itself and its members', rather than the authorities taking it upon themselves to do so.[188] Thus, in the absence of complaints by the association's members and with no 'sufficiently clear legal basis' in domestic law, the authorities' refusal to amend the official register to reflect changes in the Party's representatives interfered with the Party's internal functioning in a manner that was unlawful and not 'necessary in a democratic society'.[189]

In *Parti Nationaliste Basque—Organisation Régionale D'Iparralde v France*,[190] the Court held that the prohibition on the funding of political parties by foreign political parties may have a significant impact on an association's financial resources and hence its ability to engage fully in its political activities. Moreover, the Court was not fully persuaded that funding of political parties by foreign political parties would undermine state sovereignty. However, the lack of consensus in member state practice and Article 7 of the Recommendation Rec(2003)4 of 8 April 2003 of the Committee of Ministers of the Council of Europe supporting the prohibition on funding of political parties from foreign sources were grounds for finding that the prohibition was not in itself incompatible with Article 11. Further, the interference was proportionate to the aim of the 'prevention of disorder' because the adverse impact on finances of the relevant political party placed it in a position that was no different from that of any small political party faced with a shortage of funds.

d. Legal recognition of associations

The first duty of a state is not to interfere either with individuals who seek to exercise their freedom of association or with the essential activities of any established association. However, although it is conceivable that informal associations will satisfy the aspirations of individuals, the effective exercise of their freedom will be enhanced by the provision of a legal basis for the formation and recognition of associations, both so that individuals may be certain of what is required of them to set up an association and also so that the resulting body has legal personality and is able to act in an independent way to further the interests of its members.[191] While an absolute, positive obligation on a state to institute a legal framework for every form of association that might be envisaged by groups

---

[186] *Republican Party of Russia v Russia* hudoc (2011) para 80.

[187] *Republican Party of Russia v Russia*, para 87.

[188] *Republican Party of Russia v Russia*, para 88. See also *Tebieti Mühafize Cemiyyeti and Israfilov v Azerbaijan* 2009- para 78 (formal requirement that public associations have certain governing bodies and periodically convene a general assembly of members is not in itself an undue interference with the right).

[189] *Republican Party of Russia v Russia*, paras 88–9.   [190] Hudoc (2007).

[191] *United Macedonian Organization Ilinden and Others v Bulgaria* hudoc (2006).

of individuals goes beyond what Article 11 demands,[192] the Convention states invariably do provide some options for associations which will lead to legal personality. Individuals have the right to avail themselves of the power to form associations and to have these actions recognized by the state.[193] Indeed the Court has said that the way in which a state legislates for the formation of associations and the law's practical application by the authorities is a measure of the 'state of democracy' in the state.[194] In *The Moscow Branch of the Salvation Army v Russia*,[195] the Court found there had been an interference with an established religious organization's freedom of association when it lost legal-entity status after the authorities refused to register it under new laws requiring the re-registration of all religious associations. As a consequence, the organization was liable to be dissolved by the courts, and its functioning and religious activities were adversely affected as, for example, lack of legal-entity status had been the ground relied upon by the authorities for refusing to register amendments to a religious association's charter and for staying the registration of a religious newspaper. In *Ramazanova v Azerbaijan*,[196] the Court held that there was a *de facto* refusal to register an association that triggered Article 11 when the authorities had delayed the registration process for almost four years. An association should not, however, be forced by the state to take on a legal shape it does not seek, as insurmountable requirements may be placed in its way and thus effectively obstruct freedom of association.[197]

III. POSITIVE OBLIGATIONS

Once the association is set up, the essential relationships are between itself and its members and non-members. There are indications from the trade union cases that members have a limited right to remain as members but, in general, neither they nor non-members may claim a right to membership over the objection of the association.[198] Because we are dealing here with the relationships between individuals or between individuals and the association, another aspect of the positive obligation of states intrudes: what is a state's duty to regulate these private relationships in the interest of the effective enjoyment of Article 11 rights? This is perhaps the most pressing context in which the question whether a state has a positive obligation under the Convention to control private action that infringes other individuals' rights arises.[199] Apart from important practice concerning

---

[192] Eg, it is not conceivable that the Convention protects the right to associate with limited liability or charitable status: *Association X v Sweden No 6094/73*, 9 DR 5 (1977).

[193] See *The Moscow Branch of the Salvation Army v Russia* 2006-XI; 44 EHRR 46 para 59. See also *Church of Scientology Moscow v Russia* hudoc (2007); 46 EHRR 16 and *Jehovah's Witnesses of Moscow and Others v Russia* hudoc (2010); 53 EHRR 4 para 170. In *Le Compte, Van Leuven and De Meyere v Belgium* A 43 (1981); 4 EHRR 1 para 65 PC, the Court emphasized that while medical practitioners were obliged to be members of the *public* association, they were quite free to establish private associations for the protection of their interests, so no violation of Article 11 had been demonstrated.

[194] *Sidiropoulos and Others v Greece* 1998-IV; 27 EHRR 633 para 40 and *Tebieti Mühafize Cemiyyeti and Israfilov v Azerbaijan* 2009- para 52.

[195] Hudoc (2007) 44 EHRR 46; para 74. Two other minority religions were refused registration in Russia see *Church of Scientology Moscow v Russia* hudoc (2007); 46 EHRR 16 and *Jehovah's Witnesses of Moscow and Others v Russia* hudoc (2010); 53 EHRR 4 para 172. See also *United Macedonian Organization Ilinden and Others v Bulgaria* hudoc (2006) (NGO representing ethnic minority refused registration).

[196] Hudoc (2007); 47 EHRR 407.

[197] *Zhechev v Bulgaria* hudoc (2007) para 56 (requiring an association with political aims to register as political party a violation) and *Republican Party of Russia v Russia* hudoc (2011) para 105 (requiring a political party to register as a public association). [198] See the *ASLEF* case in section 4.I.

[199] See Clapham, *Human Rights in the Private Sphere*, 1993, pp 232–40.

trade unions, which will be dealt with separately in section 4, one such case is *Redfearn v UK*.[200] In *Redfearn* the issue arose as to whether the state had a responsibility to protect employees against dismissal by private employers on the basis of affiliation with a political association. The applicant had been dismissed from his employment with a private transport company that provided services to vulnerable people. It was not disputed that the sole reason for the applicant's dismissal was his membership and election as a local councillor for the British National Party (BNP), a political party that, according to its constitution at the relevant time, opposed any integration between British and non-European persons. As the majority of the employer's customers were of Asian ethnicity, the employer and relevant workplace trade union raised concerns, when the applicant's political affiliation had become public knowledge, that his continued employment could raise health and safety risks among Asian passengers and carers and breach their rights, as well as damage the employer company's reputation, and on those grounds dismissed him. The applicant unsuccessfully brought a statutory claim in the Employment Tribunal for racial discrimination, but could not bring an action for unfair dismissal because the state's employment legislation provided a qualifying period of one-year's service before an employee could bring a claim. The issue before the Court was, therefore, whether the state took 'reasonable and appropriate measures' to protect the applicant's freedom of association in not extending the one-year qualifying period in unfair dismissal laws to include dismissal on the ground of political association or at least creating a free-standing cause of action covering the situation. The Court considered that the one-year qualifying period was a measure within the 'wide margin of appreciation' afforded to states 'in formulating and implementing social and economic policies' given that it was 'reasonable and appropriate' for the state to bolster the domestic labour market by preventing new employees from bringing unfair dismissal claims.[201] Nevertheless, by a slim majority of four votes to three, the Court ruled that there had been a violation of the right to freedom of association due to the existence of exceptions to the one-year qualifying period on the grounds of pregnancy, race, sex, and religion. It reasoned that the omission of an exception on the ground of political opinion or affiliation failed to take into account that associations in the form of political parties are essential to the democratic society envisaged by the Convention system. In order to determine the proper balance between the interests of the employer and the right of the employee to freedom of association under Article 11 in any particular circumstance, and regardless of length of employment, it considered that political affiliation should also be protected by judicial safeguards.[202]

The association will have rights of its own, for which the right to operate effectively provides a general rubric. Again, the trade union cases to one side, there is a duty on states to provide associations with suitable measures of protection against immediate threats of violence from acts of private individuals. In *Ouranio Toxo and Others v Greece*,[203] the Court held that where the authorities could reasonably foresee the danger of violence to members of an association and clear violations of freedom of association, they should take appropriate measures to prevent, or at least contain, the violence. A related positive obligation is the duty to undertake an effective investigation into complaints of interference with freedom of association by acts of private individuals.[204]

---

[200] Hudoc (2012); 57 EHRR 2.   [201] *Redfearn v UK*, para 53.

[202] *Redfearn v UK*, cf partly dissenting opinion of Judges Bratza, Hirvela, and Nicolaou, who noted that the current exceptions correspond to 'immutable characteristics' that have traditionally been treated by the Court as requiring 'weightier reasons in justification' for difference of treatment than those characteristics or status that contain 'an element of choice', such as freedom of political association.

[203] 2005-X; 45 EHRR 8 para 43.   [204] *Ouranio Toxo v Greece*.

4. FREEDOM TO FORM AND
JOIN TRADE UNIONS

The right to freedom to form and to join trade unions[205] is a sub-division of freedom of association, not a special and independent right.[206] Accordingly, the elements of freedom of association discussed earlier apply to trade unions as well as to other associations, so far as they are relevant.[207] There is no definition of a trade union in the Convention, beyond the indication in the text of Article 11(1) that they are organizations in the field of employment that have as their purpose the protection of their members' interests.[208]

'Everyone' has the right to form and join a trade union, which has been understood to mean everyone in employment, whether under a contract of employment or self-employed. However, a limitation was allowed in *Sindicatul 'Pastorul Cel Bun' v Romania*.[209] In this case, the Grand Chamber held that the state's refusal to register the applicant trade union, composed of priests and lay members of the Romanian Orthodox Church, was not in violation of Article 11. Although union members were held to be employees of the Church, the refusal was within the respondent state's margin of appreciation as being in the interest of preserving the 'autonomy of religious denominations' and the state's 'duty of neutrality' under Article 9 of the Convention. However, the exclusion of priests from the protection of Article 11 was particular to the facts of the case[210] and not an absolute one. Members of the armed forces, the police, and the administration of the state may have restrictions imposed on their freedom of association, but these must not take away the essence of the right; they have the basic right to form and join a trade union.[211]

Individuals must be free to form or join trade unions of their choice.[212] The state is not permitted to establish or to favour a single trade union in which membership of the appropriate individuals concerned is compulsory. In the professional association cases, the Court has made it clear that the right to set up these public law bodies must not be at the expense of the private right to establish other associations for the promotion of the interests of those professionals who elect to join and which can provide a different perspective to the government-required body.[213]

The right to freedom to form and join trade unions in Article 11 is complemented by similar guarantees in relevant International Labour Organization Conventions[214] and the European Social Charter.[215] The Court takes into account the guarantees in those

---

[205] See Forde, 31 AJCL 301 (1983); Hepple, in *Freedom of Association*, Rekjavik Seminar Proceedings, reprinted in 33A YB 27 (1994), p 162; and Morris, in Ewing *et al*, eds, *Human Rights and Labour Law: Essays for Paul O'Higgins*, 1994, pp 28–55.

[206] *National Union of Belgian Police* case A 19 (1975); 1 EHRR 578 PC.

[207] Eg, those concerning registration of associations in section 3.II.d.

[208] A works council is not an 'association' within Article 11: *Karakurt v Austria No 32441/96* hudoc (1999) DA.   [209] Hudoc (2013) para 148 GC.

[210] The union's members had not sought the permission of the Archbishop as required and had aims that were incompatible with the Church's Statute: *Sindicatul 'Pastorul Cel Bun' v Romania* 2013 GC, para 169.

[211] *Demir and Baykara v Turkey* 2008- GC.

[212] Individuals must also be free to hold a union office: *X v Ireland No 4125/69* 14 YB 198; 37 CD 42 (1971) (shop steward).

[213] *Le Compte, Van Leuven and De Meyere v Belgium* A 43 (1981); 4 EHRR 1 PC. See also *Young, James and Webster v UK* B 39 (1979) para 160 Com Rep—'a trade union monopoly is excluded'.

[214] Freedom of Association Convention 1948 (ILO 87), 68 UNTS 17 and Right to Organize and Collective Bargaining Convention 1949 (ILO 98), 96 UNTS 257.   [215] Article 5.

instruments as interpreted by the relevant enforcement bodies, and normally interprets the Convention consistently with them.[216]

Article 11 imposes both negative and positive obligations upon the state. The negative obligation of states not to interfere with individual and trade union freedom of association within Article 11(1) is qualified by Article 11(2), which, in its first sentence, permits restrictions on specified grounds, such as the 'protection of the rights of others', including employers, and, in its second sentence, permits restrictions on the exercise of Article 11 rights by members of the armed forces, the police, or the administration of the state.

Although the 'essential object' of Article 11 is to 'protect the individual against arbitrary interference by public authorities with the exercise of the rights protected, there may in addition be positive obligations on the state to secure the effective enjoyment of the rights protected'.[217] In the trade union context, there are positive obligations to secure the rights of individuals and trade unions against employers[218] and to protect the individual against abuse of power by a trade union.[219] The positive obligation to act to ensure that trade unions may protect their members' interests, or to protect individuals against trade union abuse, derives from Article 11(1). As with other similarly structured Convention articles, notably Articles 8–10, the Court has taken the view that in respect of both kinds of obligation, 'the criteria to be applied do not differ in substance': in both contexts, whether Article 11(1) or (2) is being applied, 'regard must be had to the fair balance to be struck between the competing interests of the individual and of the community as a whole'.[220] When deciding whether this 'fair balance' has been struck, 'in view of the sensitive character of the social and political issues involved in achieving a proper balance between the respective interests of labour and management, and given the wide degree of divergence between the domestic systems in this field, the Contracting States enjoy a wide margin of appreciation as to how the freedom of trade unions to protect the occupational interests of their members may be secured'.[221] In contrast, there is a narrower margin in cases concerning limitations on the right of individuals to form or join a trade union, or in 'closed shop' cases not to do so, 'as these run counter to the freedom of choice of the individual inherent in Article 11'.[222]

In the area of industrial relations, the state may appear in the guise of employer— of civil servants and others—rather than in a public capacity. The Court has rejected government arguments that Article 11 only applies to the state in its latter capacity.[223] Given that ruling, subjecting the 'state as employer' to Article 11, it would scarcely be consistent to regard the activities of private employers, who, vis-à-vis the individual worker, are hardly in a different case from the government, as not being subject to it. It is here that the state's positive obligations, referred to earlier, to ensure that private persons do not infringe the rights under Article 11 of other private persons becomes crucial.

---

[216] See *Demir and Baykara v Turkey* hudoc 2008- GC.

[217] *Demir and Baykara v Turkey*, para 97.   [218] *Demir and Baykara v Turkey*, para 110.

[219] *Cheall v UK* No 10550/83, 42 DR 178 at 186 (1985); 8 EHRR 74.

[220] *Sorensen and Rasmussen v Denmark* 2006-I; 46 EHRR 572 para 58 GC.

[221] *Sorensen and Rasmussen v Denmark*, para 58.

[222] *Sorensen and Rasmussen v Denmark*, para 58.

[223] *Swedish Engine Drivers' Union v Sweden* A 20 (1976); 1 EHRR 617 para 37. In view of this approach, in *Young, James and Webster v UK* A 44 (1981); 4 EHRR 38 PC, the Court stated that it did not have to decide whether the employer, British Rail, a nationalized industry, was a part of the state, in which case its acts would implicate the state directly.

I. THE TRADE UNION RIGHT TO REGULATE ITS INTERNAL AFFAIRS

In *Associated Society of Locomotive Engineers and Firemen (ASLEF) v UK*,[224] the Court stated that the right to form a trade union includes 'the right of trade unions to draw up their own rules and to administer their own affairs'. This right is subject, however, to the state's power to impose restrictions permitted by Article 11(2), coupled with its positive obligation under Article 11(1) 'to protect an individual against any abuse of a dominant position by trade unions'.[225] This is an area in which there may be difficult questions, given the tension between the individual and collective aspects of Article 11, when trade unions mobilize or discipline their members. In the *ASLEF* case, the Court stated that, as part of their right to regulate their internal affairs, '[p]rima facie trade unions enjoy the freedom to set up their own rules concerning conditions of membership, including administrative formalities and payment of fees, as well as more substantive criteria, such as the profession or trade exercised by the would-be member'.[226]

Whereas the state may interfere with a trade union's administration of its internal affairs to prevent abuse of a dominant position, there was no such abuse justifying or requiring interference in the *ASLEF* and *Cheall* cases respectively. In the *ASLEF* case, the applicant union had under its rules expelled a member because he was a member of the British National Party, a far right but lawful political party whose policies were diametrically opposed to the objects of the union. The expulsion was held to be illegal by the UK courts as being contrary to legislation which prohibited the expulsion of a union member because he was a 'member of a political party'. The Strasbourg Court upheld the applicant union's claim that the state's intervention limiting the union's freedom to expel a member for the reason given was an unjustified interference with its right to freedom of association. The Court ruled that the 'crucial question is whether the state has struck the right balance between Mr Lee's rights and those of the applicant trade union'.[227] Applying this text, the Court noted that the expulsion did not limit the former member's freedom of expression or lawful political activities and did not affect his employment or entitlement to benefits of union collective bargaining. At the same time, the Court noted that associations within Article 11 generally have the right to choose their members, and that where 'associations are formed by people, who, espousing particular values or ideals, intend to pursue common goals, it would run counter to the very effectiveness of the freedom at stake if they had no control over their membership'.[228] This, the Court stated, certainly was the case with trade unions, which 'are not bodies solely devoted to politically-neutral aspects of the well-being of their members, but are often ideological, with strongly-held views on social and political issues'.[229] Given that the expelled member's political values and ideals clashed fundamentally with those of the union and that there was nothing to suggest that the union had undertaken any responsibility to admit members to fulfil any wider role than the achievement of its own objectives, the state's intervention had failed to strike the 'right balance'.

Cheall v UK[230] involved an inter-union membership dispute in which the applicant had been expelled by his current union in response to a request from his previous union in implementation of a membership-protection agreement to which both unions were parties. The Commission said that, while matters of admission to membership and expulsion

---

[224] Hudoc (2007); 45 EHRR 793 para 38.   [225] *ASLEF v UK*, para 43.
[226] *ASLEF v UK*, para 43.   [227] *ASLEF v UK*, para 49.   [228] *ASLEF v UK*, para 39.
[229] *ASLEF v UK*, para 50.   [230] *No 10550/83*, 42 DR 178 at 186 (1985); 8 EHRR 74.

were generally a matter for the union and that there was no general right of an individual to be admitted nor not to be expelled:

> [n]onetheless for the right to join a union to be effective the state must protect the individual against any abuse of a dominant position by trade unions...such abuse might occur, for example, where exclusion or expulsion was not in accordance with union rules or where the results were wholly arbitrary or where the consequences of exclusion or expulsion resulted in exceptional hardship such as job loss because of a closed shop.

On the facts of the case, however, the Commission found nothing arbitrary about the decision, which was lawful under national law.

The question of alleged abuse by a trade union was also in issue in *Sibson v UK*.[231] The applicant argued that the decision of his employer to transfer him to another depot (in accordance with the terms of his contract and with the same pay) was arbitrary in the sense referred to by the Commission in the *Cheall* case because it had been motivated by a desire to appease a trade union from which the applicant had resigned after a dispute arising out of his conduct as its branch secretary. The employer's decision had been taken as a result of pressure by the trade union after the applicant had joined another trade union (as he was entitled to do under his contract). The members of his former union had refused to work with the applicant and voted for a closed shop in the union's favour, which was the reason for the offer of work at the other depot. The applicant argued that the government's failure to provide him with a remedy against the employer's decision was a violation of Article 11. The Court held against the applicant because he had not left his former union for reasons of personal conviction (and would have re-joined if given an apology) and, above all, was not threatened with the loss of his job: '[he] was not subjected to a form of treatment striking at the very substance of the freedom of association guaranteed by Article 11'.[232]

II. TRADE UNION ACTION AGAINST THIRD PARTIES

Trade union action in their members' interests may affect third parties adversely, sometime in breach of the third parties' freedom of association. This was the claim in *Gustafsson v Sweden*,[233] in which a trade union sought to have the applicant restaurant owner apply to his employees, some of whom were its members, a collective agreement that the union had negotiated with the relevant employers' associations. This could be achieved by the applicant becoming a member of one of the employers' associations concerned or negotiating a separate agreement with the union. The applicant declined to do either, as he was opposed in principle to participation in collective bargaining and argued that the resulting (lawful) union boycott of his restaurant, which eventually forced him to sell it, put pressure upon him to join an employers' association in breach of his negative right not to join an association.[234] The Grand Chamber rejected his claim, by twelve votes to

---

[231] A 258-A (1993); 17 EHRR 193. Cf *Roepstorff v Denmark No 32955/96* hudoc (2000) DA (dispute between union and member: no abuse) and *X v Ireland No 4125/69*, 14 YB 108; 37 CD 42 (1971) (pressure not to be shop steward may be abuse); *Johansson v Sweden No 13537/88*, 65 DR 202 at 205 (1990) (compulsory insurance: no abuse).

[232] A 258-A (1993); 17 EHRR 193 para 29. Cf *Kajanen and Tuomaala v Finland No 36401/97* hudoc (2000) DA; *Thorkelsson v Iceland No 35771/97* hudoc (2001) DA; *Evaldsson v Sweden No 75252/01* hudoc (2006) DA.

[233] 1996-II; 22 EHRR 409 GC. Cf, *Ab Kurt Kellermann v Sweden No 41579/98* hudoc (2003) DA.

[234] Although it is not clear if the Court regarded the employers' association as a trade union or an association otherwise within Article 11, the case is included in this section for convenience.

seven. It did so because the applicant was not legally compelled to join an association: he could have chosen to make a separate agreement. Moreover, the union pressure upon him did not raise an issue under the Convention, since Article 11 does not guarantee a right not to enter into a collective agreement. In this situation, the trade union pressure and the forced sale of the restaurant did not strike at the 'very substance' of the applicant's rights under Article 11. In reaching this decision, the Court stressed that a wide margin of appreciation applied, given the important role of collective agreements in labour relations in Sweden; the different approaches to their use across Europe; and the sensitive social and political issues involved in restricting trade union action.

In the related case of *Englund v Sweden*,[235] the Commission held inadmissible an application by employees of the restaurant owner who was the applicant in the *Gustafsson* case who were not members of the trade union taking action against him and who had not authorized the union to act on their behalf. They claimed that the union action interfered with their right to conclude employment contracts on terms agreed between them with their employer, and that, if the restaurant owner had acceded to the union's demand, there would have been an interference with their negative freedom of association because they would have been bound to accept the terms of the collective agreement. The Commission did not decide the government's main point that Article 11 did not apply at all, but, assuming that it did, said that it had not been violated because the employer's refusal to give in to the unions meant that the applicants did not have to join a union and the conditions of their employment were not affected. This last point may have seemed somewhat academic to the applicants because, as noted, the restaurant had been sold owing to the effectiveness of the industrial action and they had lost their jobs.

III. THE RIGHT NOT TO JOIN A TRADE UNION

The Court has recognized that Article 11 protects the negative right not join a union, as well as the positive right to do so. The negative right has been most significant in the context of 'closed shop' situations, in which an employer and a trade union or trade unions have agreed that employment is dependent upon trade union membership. This negative right applies both to the situation where an individual is refused employment or is 'continuously and directly running a risk of being prevented from obtaining a job' because of an existing closed shop agreement (pre-entry closed shop)[236] and to the situation where an individual is dismissed because of a closed shop agreement made after employment has commenced (post-entry closed shop). It is in these closed shop situations that the potential clash under Article 11 between the individual and collective aspects of the right to freedom of association is most noticeable.

The closed shop situation was first considered in *Young, James and Webster v UK*,[237] which concerned a post-entry closed shop. The Court rejected the government's arguments that the *travaux préparatoires* showed that the drafting states did not intend to protect the negative freedom of association at all and, in particular, did not intend to inhibit a state's right to impose or permit closed shops. The Court carefully avoided generalities. It was not prepared to endorse the position that compulsion to join a union was always prohibited by Article 11. The test was whether the compulsion 'strikes at the very substance of the freedom guaranteed by Article 11' on the facts of each case.[238] In *Young*,

---

[235] *No 15533/89*, 77-A DR 10 at 18–19 (1994).
[236] See *Hoffman Karlskov v Denmark No 62560/00* hudoc (2003) DA.
[237] A 44 (1981); 4 EHRR 38 para 52 PC.   [238] *Young, James and Webster v UK*, para 55.

James and Webster, the Court said that it did so because the closed shop was addressed to workers already in employment who had strong objections in principle to union membership (which touched interests under Articles 9 and 10) and the consequence of holding to their position was the very serious one of dismissal. Furthermore, in practice there was no choice open to the applicants as to which union to join and they were not in a position to form their own union.[239]

In *Young, James and Webster*, the government was not prepared to seek to justify the arrangements under Article 11(2)[240] but, as the case of *Sigurjonsson v Iceland*[241] shows, such justification will be difficult. In that case, the Court found that a requirement in law that a taxi licence holder be a member of an association of taxi drivers[242] was in violation of Article 11. The Court found that international legal developments were increasingly favouring the individual against closed shop arrangements and referred to a finding under the European Social Charter that Iceland's practice was not in accordance with the Charter. Again, what appeared to weigh most with the Court was that the consequences for the applicant were so severe, going to the very substance of the negative right: if he was not a member of the association, he could not earn his living as a taxi driver. Furthermore, the applicant had at all times objected to becoming a member of the association; had been allowed a licence before membership was required;[243] and had objections that were based on strongly held beliefs. When the Court turned to the government's case under Article 11(2), it found the reasons advanced, mainly that the arrangement facilitated the administration of the taxi service in the public interest, to be 'relevant but not sufficient'. The objective could have been achieved at not significantly greater cost whether membership was compulsory or not; the government could demonstrate expediency but not a pressing social need. In the Court's view, 'notwithstanding Iceland's margin of appreciation, the measures complained of were disproportionate to the legitimate aim pursued'.

In *Sorensen and Rasmussen v Denmark*,[244] the Grand Chamber had to consider a pre-entry closed shop. In that case the two applicants accepted employment in the knowledge that membership of the SID trade union, to which they were opposed because of the union's political views, was required by their different employers who had lawful closed shop agreements with the union under which membership was a condition of employment. The first applicant was dismissed when he indicated that he did not wish to pay the union's membership dues; the second applicant joined the union to gain employment but challenged the compulsion to do so as infringing Article 11. The Court first confirmed its earlier ruling that although the right not to join a trade union was not an absolute one, compulsion to join a union that 'strikes at the very substance' of the right is an interference with the guarantee of freedom of association in Article 11(1). Second, the Court declined to rule in the abstract on the question, which it had left open in earlier trade union cases, whether the positive and negative rights to join or not to join a trade union in Article 11 should be given the same level of protection, ie with equal weight being given to the individual and collective interests involved. Instead it ruled that this was a matter to be determined on the facts, weighing what was at stake for the individual and the union in the

---

[239] *Young, James and Webster v UK*, para 56.

[240] There had been a change of government during the progress of the application and the new Conservative government was not prepared to rely on Article 11(2). See Forde, 11 ILJ 1 (1982).

[241] A 264 (1993); 16 EHRR 462 paras 36, 37, 41.

[242] The Court said that it did not need to decide whether the association was a trade union.

[243] The Commission more explicitly makes the point that this was a post-entry closed shop case: *Sigurjonsson v Iceland*, para 57 Com Rep.　　　　　　[244] 2006-I; 46 EHRR 572 GC.

particular case. Third, the Court ruled that the negative right applied equally to both pre- and post-entry closed shops. The distinction between the two was only relevant when assessing the facts of each case: the 'very substance' of the right might be interfered with in pre-entry closed shop cases as well as post-entry cases, as was the case on the facts of the *Sorensen and Rasmussen* case. Although the applicants in that case knowingly took employment on the condition that they accepted SID membership, in the Court's view this did not 'significantly alter the element of compulsion inherent in having to join a trade union against their will'.[245] Moreover, the existence of the condition struck at the 'very substance' of the applicants' negative right not to join a trade union in that the first applicant was dismissed without notice when he indicated that he would not pay membership dues and the second applicant would have been dismissed, and probably have found it hard to gain employment elsewhere, if he had resigned his union membership. The Court then examined whether on the facts a 'fair balance' had been struck between the applicants' interests and those of the union in being able to protect its members' interests. Whereas under Article 11 the Court normally applies a 'wide margin of appreciation' in trade union cases, the Grand Chamber took the view that in this case that the 'margin of appreciation' was narrower in the case of closed shop agreements, 'as these run counter to the freedom of choice of the individual inherent in Article 11'.[246] It was also relevant that the dominant approach in Convention states parties was now not to regard closed shop agreements as an essential means for securing the interests of trade unions and their members: very few parties permitted such agreements in their law and Denmark itself had abandoned them in the public and much of the private sector.[247] Weighing these considerations against the impact upon the applicants of non-compliance with their right not to join a trade union,[248] the Grand Chamber found a violation of Article 11.[249]

In *Vordur Ólafsson v Iceland*,[250] the Court took its approach in closed shop cases a stage further. There the applicant was, as an employer, subject by law to an annual financial charge to an organization whose role was to promote Icelandic industry, when he was not a member of the organization and did not share some of its political views. The Court held that this was unjustifiable interferfence with the applicant's freedom of association in breach of Article 11 akin to making him join an organization against his wishes. Although the organization had a legitimate aim, there were insufficient safeguards by way of transparency and accountability to ensure that the organization did not use the charges to the disadvantage of non-members. In this connection, the Court referred to rulings by the ILO and the European Committee of Social Rights that the imposition of an obligation on a non-member to pay fees to a trade union could be incompatible with freedom of association.

---

[245] *Sorensen and Rasmussen v Denmark*, para 59.

[246] *Sorensen and Rasmussen v Denmark*, para 58.

[247] The Court also referred to the European Social Charter and EU human rights standards to the same effect.

[248] It was relevant that the applicants' objected to SID membership for reasons of principle; had they, as in *Sibson*, discussed earlier, just been in dispute with the union, their claim would have been weaker. Confirming its approach in *Young, James and Webster*, the Court stressed that 'the protection of personal opinions guaranteed by Articles 9 and 10 is one of the purposes of Article 11, and that such protection can only be effectively secured' by both a positive and negative Article 11 right: *Sorensen and Rasmussen v Denmark*, para 54.

[249] The five dissents concerned the first applicant, who was a student in temporary summer employment who could more easily have found other non-union work.   [250] Hudoc (2010).

IV. THE RIGHT TO PROTECT MEMBERS' INTERESTS

Article 11 imposes a positive obligation upon states to ensure that trade unions may function effectively. Until recently trade unions enjoyed little success in claims that they[251] or their members brought under Article 11 seeking to enforce this positive right. In a trio of cases in the 1970s, the Court gave little support to claims brought by unions or union members alleging that state restrictions upon trade union activities had infringed Article 11. In these cases the Court noted that Article 11 is phrased in very general terms and 'does not secure any particular treatment of trade unions, or their members'.[252] Article 11 demanded of states just that they protect rights 'that [are] indispensable for the effective enjoyment of trade union freedom'. Beyond those rights, what the Convention required was only that 'trade unions should be enabled, in conditions not at variance with Article 11, to strive for the protection of their members' interests',[253] leaving it to the discretion of states as to the particular measures that they adopted to this end.

In the 1970 cases, the Court took a very narrow view of what rights were 'indispensable'. In the *National Union of Belgian Police* case, the Court conceded that Article 11 did guarantee the right of a trade union to be heard by the employer on behalf of its members in order to function effectively. This did not, however, suppose a right to be consulted, which the applicants claimed and which in Belgium was allowed only to certain large trade unions. In the *Swedish Engine Drivers' Union* case,[254] the Court held that the right to be heard did not entail that the applicant trade union be allowed to have a right to collective bargaining or to enter into a collective agreement with an employer. In the Swedish system of industrial relations, the terms and conditions of work of state employees, including railway engine drivers, were governed by a collective agreement entered into with four large federations of trade unions to which the applicant union was not affiliated, the resulting agreement then being applied to its members. Although these arrangements limited the power of the applicant union to protect its members' interests, there was no breach of Article 11. In both cases, the Court stated that Article 11(1) allowed the state 'a free choice of means' as to how it ensured the right to be heard, and that these means might involve the right to bring claims or make representations rather than the specific right that was claimed.[255] Neither of the claimed rights were 'indispensable' or to be found generally in the 'national law and practice' of the states parties to the Convention.[256]

Finally, in *Schmidt and Dahlstrom v Sweden*,[257] the Court held that it was not a breach of Article 11 for the members of a striking trade union to be denied by the state as employer the retroactive benefit of a collective agreement, when the agreement was applied retroactively to the benefit of members of non-striking unions. The applicants had argued that this denial affected their right to strike, which was an 'organic' right in Article 11. In response, referring to the 'free choice of means' that states have when complying with their obligation to facilitate trade union action, the Court commented on the right to strike as follows:

> The grant of a right to strike represents without any doubt one of the most important of these means, but there are others. Such a right, which is not expressly enshrined in

---

[251] Trade unions, as well as individuals, may claim to be victims of a breach of their rights under Article 11: *National Union of Belgian Police v Belgium* A 9 (1975); 1 EHRR 578 para 39 PC.

[252] *National Union of Belgian Police v Belgium*, para 38.

[253] *National Union of Belgian Police v Belgium*, para 39.

[254] A 20 (1976); 1 EHRR 617. See also *Gustafsson v Sweden* 1996-II;-22 EHRR 409 GC.

[255] A 19 (1975); 1 EHRR 578 para 39 PC and A 20 (1976); 1 EHRR 617 para 40.

[256] A 19 (1975); 1 EHRR 578 para 38 PC and A 20 (1976); 1 EHRR 617 para 39.

[257] A 21 (1976) para 36; 1 EHRR 632.

> Article 11, may be subject under national law to regulation of a kind that limits its exercise in certain instances.

The Court held that the non-retroactivity clause did not deprive the applicants of their capacity through their trade union to strive for the protection of their occupational interests.

However, the Court has now become more sympathetic to claims by trade unions and their members. An early indication of this was the partially successful application in *Wilson, National Union of Journalists and Others v UK*.[258] There the applicant's employers decided not to renew their collective bargaining agreement with the applicant trade union. Withdrawing recognition from that (and any other) union, they adopted a policy of determining employees' salaries unilaterally. This was lawful under UK law, as both collective bargaining and the recognition of trade unions by employers were voluntary. The Strasbourg Court confirmed that there was no breach of Article 11 on these facts, as there was a positive obligation on states to ensure that trade unions could 'strive for the protection of their members or to union recognition'.[259] However, there was another dimension to the case. As allowed by UK law, in order to avoid possible union action aimed at preventing the employers' new policy being successfully implemented, the applicants' employers had offered their employees substantial pay rises if they signed personal contracts effectively renouncing their trade union rights. This was held by the Court to result in a breach of Article 11. The financial incentives were 'a disincentive or restraint on the use by employees of union membership to protect their interests' and, 'by permitting employers to use financial incentives to induce employees to surrender important trade union rights, the respondent state has failed in its positive obligation to secure the enjoyment of the rights under Article 11'.

This was followed by the breakthrough case of *Demir and Baykara v Turkey*,[260] in which the Grand Chamber explained its approach as follows:

> [T]he evolution of case law as to the substance of the right of association enshrined in Article 11 is marked by two guiding principles: firstly, the Court takes into consideration the totality of the measures taken by the state concerned in order to secure trade-union freedom, subject to its margin of appreciation; secondly, the Court does not accept restrictions that affect the essential elements of trade-union freedom, without which that freedom would become devoid of substance.

The Grand Chamber stated that the 'essential elements' that had been established in the Court's earlier jurisprudence were: (i) the right to form and join a trade union;[261] (ii) the prohibition of closed shops;[262] and 'the right for a trade union to seek to persuade the employer to hear what it has to say on behalf of its members'.[263] However, this was not a finite list: it was subject to evolution depending on developments in labour relations.

---

[258] 2002-IV; 35 EHRR 523 paras 47, 48. See Ewing, 32 ILJ 1 (2003). See also *Sanchez Navajas v Spain No 57442/00* hudoc (2001) DA (employee trade union representatives should 'enjoy appropriate facilities to enable them to perform their trade union functions rapidly and effectively', including an appropriate amount of paid leave during their hours of work; inadmissible on the facts).

[259] The Court took into account that in UK law, although collective bargaining and union recognition were not compulsory, there were other important means by which unions could protect their members, including the right to strike.   [260] 2008- para 144 GC. See Ewing and Hendy, 39 ILJ 1(2010).

[261] *Tum Haber Sen and Cinar v Turkey* 2006-II; 46 EHRR 374 was cited.

[262] *Sorensen and Rasmussen v Denmark* 2006-I; 46 EHRR 572 was cited.

[263] *Wilson, National Union of Journalists and Others v UK* 2002-IV; 35 EHRR 523 was cited. As noted earlier, the 'right to be heard' had earlier been recognized as 'indispensable' in the *National Union of Belgium Police* case.

Whereas the Grand Chamber's approach in the *Demir and Baykara* case is not dissimilar to that which the Court had adopted in the 1970s, what is important is that the Court in that case made two rulings favourable to the rights of trade unions and their members. First, it added the right to bargain collectively with an employer to its list of 'essential elements' of trade union freedom, or 'indispensable' rights. In doing so, it reversed the Court's earlier ruling in the *Swedish Engine Drivers Union* case, citing subsequent developments in international and national labour law and the current state practice of contracting parties. In *Demir and Baykara*, the applicant trade union[264] had entered into a collective agreement with a municipal council that for two years had governed all employer–employee relations within the municipality, but which was, in breach of Article 11, then annulled retrospectively as a result of a judicial decision ruling that the union was not competent to make collective agreements. Second, the Grand Chamber gave a restrictive meaning to the term 'administration of the state' in the second sentence of Article 11(2), so that the municipal civil servants in the case were not subject to restrictions that it might permit.

In another important development, the Court has, since *Demir and Baykara*, decided several cases in which it has held that a restriction on the right to strike was in breach of Article 11.[265] In *Enerji Yapi-Yol Sen v Turkey*[266] there was a breach of Article 11 when the government published a circular shortly before a one-day strike planned by a union of public servants working on land registration and similar matters to secure the right to enter into a collective bargaining agreement. The circular prohibited all public servants from taking part in the strike, and members of the trade union who did take part were later sanctioned on the basis of it. Referring to *Schmidt and Dahlstrom*, the Chamber stated that the right to strike was an important means of protecting members' interests. The restriction imposed by the circular could not be justified under the first sentence of Article 11(2) as it did not respond to a 'pressing social need' and was disproportionate in that it prohibited all public servants from striking. Although some categories of public servants might be prohibited from striking, not all could. In a separate group of Turkish cases, there was also a breach of Article 11 when school teachers in state schools were convicted of criminal offences[267] or disciplined[268] for being absent from their place of work to participate in a national one-day strike organized by their trade union. The Court held that these sanctions were an interference with the applicants' right to freedom of association by being likely to dissuade them from taking part in legitimate strike action or other action in defence of their occupational interests, and could not be justified under Article 11(2). Finally, in *Danilenkov and Others v Russia*,[269] there was a breach of Article 11 in conjunction with Article 14 when an employer discriminated against employees who had taken part in a strike by transferring them to less well paid work and later making them redundant. The Court held that the state had violated Articles 11 and 14 by not providing the applicants with a civil remedy for compensation for anti-union discrimination.

Although the Court did not in these cases add the right to strike to its list of 'essential elements' of trade union freedom,[270] it is clear from them that the Court does recognize its crucial importance for the effective use of collective bargaining and is now prepared to

---

[264] This was the civil servant trade union in the *Tum Haber Sen* case, discussed later.

[265] Another encouraging case was *Şişman and Others v Turkey* hudoc (2011) (ban on civil servant trade union members putting wall posters in their office advertising annual May Day meeting a violation of Article 11).

[266] Hudoc (2009).   [267] *Urcan v Turkey* hudoc (2008) and *Saime Özcan v Turkey* (2009)

[268] *Kaya and Seyhan v Turkey* (2009). Cf *Karaçay v Turkey* hudoc (2007).   [269] Hudoc (2009).

[270] In *Enerji Yapi-Yol Sen v Turkey* hudoc (2009) para 24, the Court noted that the right to strike was recognized by the ILO as an 'indissociable corollary' of freedom of association.

apply, and where appropriate to find unsatisfied, the 'necessity' and other requirements in the first sentence of Article 11(2) to any restriction imposed by the state upon the freedom of association of trade unions and their members. Whether this new rigour would cause it to reverse pre-*Demir and Baykara* decisions in which no breach of Article 11 had been found is unclear. For example, in *Federation of Offshore Workers' Trade Unions v Norway*,[271] there was no breach of Article 11 when the applicant federation and individual oil workers were banned from striking and their claim for a wage rise was referred to compulsory arbitration. Applying the 'free choice of means' approach followed in *Schmidt and Dahlstrom*, the Court noted that (i) the ban was implemented only when the trade union members concerned had been allowed to exercise their right to strike for thirty-six hours and the strike had been preceded by collective bargaining and compulsory mediation without success; and (ii) a strike would have had very serious economic implications for the respondent state's oil industry. In these circumstances, and in view of the wide margin of appreciation that states enjoyed, the Court held that the ban on striking was justified under Article 11(2) (although without identifying the particular public or other interest that applied). To the same effect, in *UNISON v UK*,[272] an injunction to prevent a strike against the likely conditions of employment of future employees of a private consortium taking over a hospital was justified to 'protect the rights of others'. Whereas the decision in the *Offshore Workers* case would be unlikely to be reversed, the decision in the *UNISON* case might be.

5. RESTRICTIONS ON PUBLIC SERVICE EMPLOYEES

The second sentence of Article 11(2) reads:

> This article shall not prevent the imposition of lawful restrictions on the exercise of these rights by members of the armed forces, of the police or of the administration of the state.

As in the case of 'restrictions' permitted by the first sentence of Article 11(2), restrictions allowed by the second sentence must be 'construed strictly and should therefore be confined to the 'exercise'of the rights in question'; they 'must not impair the very essence of the right to organise'. This was stated in *Demir and Baykara v Turkey*[273] in the context of a ban on civil servants forming and joining trade unions, and can be taken to apply to restrictions aimed at members of the armed forces and the police also. In the *Demir and Baykara* case,[274] the Court also held that 'municipal civil servants, who are not engaged in the administration of the state as such, cannot in principle be treated as "members of the administration of the state" upon whom restrictions permitted by Article 11(2) may be imposed'.

In *Tum Haber Sen and Cinar v Turkey*,[275] a trade union whose members were civil servants working in the communications field for the post office and the (non-national

---

[271] *No 38190/97* hudoc (2002) DA.

[272] 2002-I. See also *National Association of Teachers in Further and Higher Education v UK No 28910/95* hudoc (1998) DA (requirement that a union provide an employer with a list of members to be balloted on industrial action not an interference with Article 11 rights).

[273] 2008- para 97 GC. This overrules *Council of Civil Service Unions v UK No 11603/85*, 50 DR 228 (1987) DA.   [274] 2008-.

[275] 2006-II; 46 EHRR 374 para 35. Cf *Demir and Baykara v Turkey* in the preceding paragraph.

security) telecommunication service was dissolved by the state solely on the ground that civil servants were not allowed to form or join a trade union under Turkish law. When assessing the 'restriction', which, despite being a complete ban, it did not rule was in itself impermissible (but now see the *Demir and Baykara* case), the Court applied the 'prescribed by law'/'necessary in a democratic society' formula found in the first sentence of Article 11(2), taking the view that this formula governed restrictions justified by the second sentence also. As to the 'necessity' of the restriction, the Court held that a state needed to show 'convincing and compelling reasons' to 'justify restrictions on such parties freedom of association' and that 'only a limited margin of appreciation' applied.[276] In the absence from the respondent state of any 'concrete evidence' to suggest that the union represented a threat to Turkish society or the Turkish state or of any other credible public interest argument, the Court found that the absolute ban on the trade union was a breach of Article 11.

Other cases have involved participation by civil servants or the police in the activities of authorized trade unions. In *Metin Turan v Turkey*,[277] there was a breach of Article 11 when a civil servant who had engaged in such activities was transferred to another region. Although the terms of his employment allowed him to be moved from region to region, the reason for his transfer was his trade union activities, which was not a justifiable reason under Article 11(2). In contrast, there was no violation of Article 11, in the light of Article 10, in *Trade Union of the Police in the Slovak Republic and Others v Slovakia*.[278] In that case, the applicant police trade union had organized a public meeting protesting at the low pay and social security rights of their members at which participants had called for the resignation of the government and carried a banner stating that if the state did not pay the police properly, the mafia would. In response, the Minister of the Interior stated on television that this was conduct in violation of the duty of the police under their Ethics Code to be apolitical and impartial and that officers who violated this duty would be dismissed; trade union members involved in the meeting were later demoted or otherwise sanctioned. The Court ruled that the Minister's actions, which interfered with the freedom of association of the police, were a proportionate response to a 'pressing social need', *viz* the need to ensure that police officers acted 'in an impartial manner when expressing their views so that their reliability and trustworthiness in the eyes of the public' was maintained. Since the role of the police, as well as of civil servants and members of the armed forces, was to assist the government in discharging its functions, the duty of loyalty and reserve, which all employees owed to their employers, assumed special significance for them. In each of these cases, the Court's judgment does not indicate whether it is based on the first sentence or second sentence of Article 11(2).

As to whether members of the armed forces, the police, or the administration of the state may be prohibited under the second sentence of Article 11(2) from going on strike, in *Enerji Yapi-Yol Sen v Turkey*[279] the Court accepted that some categories of public servants might be prohibited from going on strike, but that others, who presumably would fall with one of the categories of public servants identified in the second sentence of Article 11(2), may not. In an early Commission decision, the Commission accepted that the long-standing prohibition on German civil servants (*beamte*) striking was not a breach of Article 11.[280]

---

[276] *Tum Haber Sen and Cinar v Turkey*, presumably those in the second sentence of Article 11(2).
[277] Hudoc (2006).   [278] Hudoc (2013) paras 69 and 70.   [279] Hudoc (2009).
[280] *S v Germany No 10365/83*, 39 DR 237 (1984)

6. CONCLUSION

The last decade has seen an abundance of cases on freedom of assembly and associa-tion with a high proportion of violations. Most of these cases have originated from the 'new democracies' of Central and Eastern Europe. The themes are tolerance of peace-ful dissent, pluralism in opinion, with some allowance for disturbance to others, and the lawfulness of government interference. Of general significance in the jurisprudence is the incorporation of the strict protection of the freedom to express opinions found in Article 10 into the freedoms of assembly and association in Article 11. Notable also is the development of positive obligations on the state to take preventative measures to protect assemblies and associations and an obligation to conduct effective investigations into interferences by private individuals with freedom of association. These are essential democratic standards that support the activities of civil society. Beyond these standards, the freedom of assembly cases concede a fairly broad margin of appreciation to states when deciding the necessity for an interference on the facts of a particular case. The limit to the ambit of the freedom is revealed in the direct action cases and in *Cissé v France*.[281] A further challenge to freedom of assembly is the increasing privatization of the public spaces available for its exercise.

Interferences with freedom of association have primarily involved the dissolution of political parties and the refusal to register associations. The limitations on freedom of association under Article 11(2) are strictly construed, following the approach taken to freedom of expression of political opinions in Article 10. The Court has allowed the curtailment of freedom of association where it is considered to be incompatible with Convention values, specifically political and religious pluralism, the prohibition on the use of violence and the 'co-existence of members of society free from racial segregation'.[282] However, as the *Refah* case[283] demonstrates, the circumstances in which the maintenance of democratic institutions and the rights of others demand limitation upon the right to freedom of association is debatable and the issue raises fundamental questions about the organization of European political democracy.

The unwillingness of the Court, and formerly the Commission, to find greater protec-tion for trade unions in the protection of their members' interests within Article 11 was the subject of criticism.[284] However, the Court is now demanding more of states, more closely in line with international labour law standards. The *Demir and Baykara* case and others that follow its lead in adopting a more interventionalist approach, particularly the *Enerji* case on the right to strike, have expanded the positive obligation of states in this regard and may signal a more general move away from the Court's unwillingness to use Article 11 as a vehicle for protecting trade union rights that was manifest in its 1970s judgments in the *National Union of Belgian Police* and other cases. But any such devel-opment will not affect the Court's clear stance in favour of the negative right not to join a trade union in the *Young, James and Webster* and later cases, in which the individual, as opposed to the collective, dimension of freedom of association has prevailed in the context of labour relations. In this respect the Court has not responded to arguments that it should take a more active role in protecting the collective interest and that there is

---

[281] 2002-III.
[282] See *Refah Partisi (The Welfare Party) v Turkey* 2003-II; 37 EHRR 1 GC; *Gorzelik and Others v Poland* hudoc (2004); 40 EHRR 76; and *Vona v Hungary* hudoc (2013).   [283] *Refah Partisi v Turkey*.
[284] Leader, 20 ILJ 39 at 57 (1991).

a danger that too great a concentration on the position of the dissenting individual will weaken the fundamental right of association of others and the effective capacity of the association to protect their interests.[285]

The references to standards of 'unreasonableness' and 'arbitrariness'[286] as those that are applicable when deciding whether the state's positive obligation to protect private persons from interferences with their Article 11 rights by others do not indicate a willingness by the Court, and formerly the Commission, to subject national laws and decisions to intensive scrutiny.[287] For some labour lawyers, this is an acceptable outcome.[288] Many of the conflicts are essentially between trade unions and members or non-members or between trade unions and employers. In the field of industrial relations, not only do the states adopt a variety of ways of managing these matters, they frequently acknowledge that considerable degrees of economic and social pressure are legitimate instruments in industrial conflict.[289] The Court has recognized this too. In a sense, this is a realistic attitude. The European Court cannot write a comprehensive trade union law on the narrow basis of Article 11. At the same time, there must be more that Article 11 can offer in the context of the protection by organized labour in the protection of members' interests than is to be found in the Court's early judgments, and, as suggested, the Court's recent judgments may indicate a new willingness to recognize this.

---

[285] Leader, 20 ILJ 39 at 57 (1991). See also the dissenting opinion of Judge Soerensen, joined by Judges Thór Vilhjálmsson and Lagergren in *Young, James and Webster v UK*.

[286] See *Cheall v UK No 10550/83*, 42 DR 178 at 185 (1985); 8 EHRR 74.

[287] But see Mr Busuttil, dissenting in *Sibson v UK* A 258-A (1993); 17 EHRR 193 Com Rep, who was effectively reviewing the judgment of the Court of Appeal.   [288] See Forde, 11 ILJ 1 (1982), pp 330–2.

[289] See Baglioni and Crouch, eds, *European Industrial Relations*, 1990, particularly Ch 1 by Baglioni.

16

ARTICLE 12: THE RIGHT TO MARRY AND TO FOUND A FAMILY

Article 12

Men and women of marriageable age have the right to marry and to found a family, according to the national laws governing the exercise of this right.

1. INTRODUCTION

The text of Article 12 asserts a relatively narrow right (or possibly rights) to marry and to found a family, subject to a wide power on the part of states to regulate the exercise of the right. The interpretation of Article 12 by the Strasbourg authorities has not greatly expanded its scope. Although closely connected with the notions of 'family life' and 'private life' in Article 8, which have been interpreted imaginatively, the Court, and formerly the Commission, has not been so receptive to developing the content of Article 12. This has had a particularly inhibiting effect on the right to found a family. The original understanding of Article 12 appears to have been, as its text suggests ('the right'), that it set out a single right of men and women to marry and found a family. Accordingly, although the right to marry has been held to be protected in circumstances where there is no intention or no possibility of procreation,[1] the Court has not been willing to admit that the right to found a family can arise under Article 12 in the absence of a marriage.[2]

If an unmarried couple do have a family, their various rights will be protected under Article 8, not under Article 12, and any differentiation that national law makes between married and unmarried couples in this respect will fall to be considered under Articles 8 and 14, not Articles 12 and 14.[3] In contrast, discrimination in national laws on marriage and the founding of a family within marriage do fall within Articles 12 and 14, for example in cases of discrimination between men and women.[4]

---

[1] See *Hamer v UK No 7114/75*, 24 DR 5 at 16 (1979) Com Rep; CM Res DH (81) 5.
[2] See *Rees v UK* A 106 (1986); 9 EHRR 56 para 49 PC and *Christine Goodwin v UK* 2002-VI; 35 EHRR 447 para 98 GC.
[3] See *KM v UK No 30309/96* hudoc (1997) DA and *McMichael v UK* A 308 (1995); 20 EHRR 205.
[4] *KM v UK No 30309/96* hudoc (1997) DA.

With regard to the relationship between Articles 12 and 8 in other respects, Article 12 does not apply to family life beyond the point of marriage, other than in respect of the founding of a family. For example, the taking of children into care is entirely a matter for Article 8.[5] Insofar as there is a potential overlap between the two Articles in respect of the founding of a family, the Court may deal with the case just under Article 8, as in its treatment of artificial insemination.[6]

Article 12 guarantees the right to marry and to found a family 'according to the national laws governing the exercise of this right'. While this wording provides a wide margin of appreciation for states, national 'laws' must satisfy a European standard as to the meaning of a 'law' and 'must not restrict or reduce the right in such a way or to such an extent that the very essence of the right is impaired'.[7] This interpretation is bolstered by the words 'governing the *exercise* of this right', which indicate that the national laws may regulate but not prohibit or exclude the right altogether.[8] Article 12 differs from Articles 8–11 in that it does not have a second paragraph that contains a list of permissible grounds for an interference with the protected right that are permitted provided that they are 'in accordance with the law' and 'necessary in a democratic society.' Instead, when deciding whether an interference, or limitation, to the right to marry or to found a family is permitted, the Court must 'determine whether, regard being had to the State's margin of appreciation, the impugned interference has been arbitrary or disproportionate'.[9]

2. THE RIGHT TO MARRY

I. GENERALLY

It is for the national law to regulate such matters as form and capacity to marry, but any procedural or substantive limitations that are adopted must not remove the very essence of the right.[10] As to procedural limitations, these 'relate mainly to publicity and the solemnization of marriage'.[11] A state may require a civil marriage, but is free in its discretion to recognize a religious marriage. In *Muñoz Díaz v Spain*,[12] there was no violation of Article 12 as read with Article 14 when the state recognized some religious marriages by virtue of agreements, but not the applicant's Roma marriage, for which there was no agreement with the state. As to substance, the state may impose limitations on such matters as marriageable age,[13] consanguinity,[14] the number of spouses,[15] consent,[16] and capacity.[17] The Court has yet to rule on limitations as to mental capacity. In *Lashin v*

---

[5] *P, C and S v UK* 2002-VI; 35 EHRR 1075.

[6] See *Dickson v UK* 2007-V; 46 EHRR 927 GC. An interference with family life that is justified under Article 8(2) cannot be a breach of Article 12: *Boso v Italy* No 50490/99 2002-VII DA.

[7] *Rees v UK* A 106 (1986); 9 EHRR 56 para 50 PC.

[8] *Hamer v UK* No 7114/75, 24 DR 5 (1979) Com Rep; CM Res DH (81) 5.

[9] *O'Donoghue and Others v UK* 2010-; 53 EHRR 1 para 84.

[10] *F v Switzerland* A 128 (1987); 10 EHRR 411 para 32 PC.   [11] *F v Switzerland*, para 32.

[12] Hudoc (2009); 50 EHRR 1244. Cf *Şerife Yiğit v Turkey* hudoc (2010); 53 EHRR 872 GC (Muslim marriage not recognized).

[13] See *Khan v UK* No 11579/85, 48 DR 252 (1986). Marriageable age varies within Europe.

[14] Cf *B and L v UK* hudoc (2005).

[15] See *X v UK* No 3898/68, 35 CD 102 (1970); 13 YBECHR 674 (1970) (bigamy). See also *Johnston and Others v Ireland* A 112 (1986); 9 EHRR 203 para 52 PC (Europe 'a society adhering to…monogamy').

[16] *F v Switzerland* A 128 (1987); 10 EHRR 411 para 32 PC. See also *Zu Leiningen v Germany* No 59624/00 2005-XIII DA (F Sett) (need for family approval of spouse).   [17] *F v Switzerland*.

Russia,[18] the decision by which a person suffering from schizophrenia was deprived of all legal capacity (including the right to marry) was held to violate Article 8: the Court did not rule on his claim that his inability to marry was a violation of Article 12. It is for the state to decide on the content of its conflict of law rules and their application.[19] The question of the recognition of foreign marriages, whether of a different kind to national ones[20] or not, will generally arise under Article 8 rather than Article 12.

Certain limitations have been found to be in breach of Article 12. In *F v Switzerland*,[21] a Swiss court ruled that the applicant could not marry again for three years after a divorce in which the court found him solely responsible for the breakdown of the marriage. After the divorce, the applicant was a single man and wanted to remarry. The European Court held, by just nine votes to eight, that the condition imposed by the Swiss court was 'unreasonable' because the reasons the government gave for it were inappropriate (to protect the future spouse) or its effects on others were disproportionate (the chance that children would be born out of wedlock). The majority judgment confirms that unreasonable state action or inaction that leads to delay in the exercise of the right to marry by two people who are ready to marry may be regarded as a serious infringement of their interests and a breach of Article 12.[22]

A state may impose limitations upon marriage between a national and a foreigner in order to prevent a marriage of convenience, or sham marriage, ie one 'entered solely for the purpose of securing an immigration advantage'.[23] Such limitations must be aimed at establishing the genuineness of the marriage and must not involve the payment of too high a fee. In *O'Donoghue and Others v UK*,[24] a Nigerian national who had sought asylum in the United Kingdom and had been granted discretionary leave to remain wished to marry a British national with whom he had been living in the United Kingdom for several years. As a person subject to immigrant control, he required a Certificate of Approval for the marriage, which he was refused because he did not have the required leave to remain for a sufficient time. The Court held that there had been a breach of Article 12 because the refusal was based not upon the genuineness of the marriage, but upon the first applicant's immigration status, and also because the fee for the Certificate was set at a level (£295) which a 'needy applicant' could not afford. In contrast, reasonable limitations requiring the provision of information that will establish the genuineness of the marriage are permissible, even though they may delay the marriage.[25]

Another substantive limitation was found to be in breach of Article 12 in *B and L v UK*.[26] This case concerned a statutory limitation prohibiting the marriage of X and the

---

[18] Hudoc (2013). The Court noted that in thirteen of twenty-five states parties whose law was reviewed, incapacitation decisions automatically led to the loss of the right to marry; in nine others, marriage was only possible with a guardian's consent.   [19] *X v Switzerland No 9057/80*, 26 DR 207 (1981).

[20] Eg, a state may recognize polygamous marriages celebrated lawfully abroad while not allowing them under its own law.

[21] A 128 (1987); 10 EHRR 411 paras 30–40 PC. See also *KM v UK No 30309/96* hudoc (1997) DA.

[22] See also the *Hamer* and *Draper* cases and the *Sanders* and *Klip and Krüger* cases, discussed later. Cf *Dadouch v Malta* hudoc 2010 (unjustified delay in registering the applicant's marriage: a violation of Article 8).

[23] *O'Donoghue and Others v UK* 2010-; 53 EHRR 1 para 83.

[24] 2010-; 53 EHRR 1.

[25] *Sanders v France No 31401/96*, 87-B DR 160 (1996) DA and *Klip and Krüger v Netherlands No 33257/96*, 91-A DR 66 (1997) DA.

[26] Hudoc (2005) paras 36, 37, 41. For other questionable restrictions, see *Selim v Cyprus* 2002-VI (F Sett) (civil marriage by Muslim Turkish Cypriots prohibited) and *Staiku v Greece No 35426/97* hudoc (1997) DA (woman dismissed from army for marrying within five years).

former wife of his son until after the death of both his son and X's former wife, the son's mother. The ban was aimed at protecting the integrity of the family (preventing sexual rivalry between parents and children) and preventing harm to the son's children. The Court noted that such a limitation, with the same 'legitimate aims', was present in the law of a 'large number of contracting states' (twenty-one). Nonetheless, the Court held unanimously that there was a breach of Article 12 'in the circumstances of the case'. First, the ban did not criminalize extra-marital relationships—indeed in this case the father and the former daughter-in-law were cohabiting, with the child of the latter's marriage living in their home. Second, the ban would not appear to be viewed as fundamental to society as it could be overcome by a personal act of parliament.

Prisoners do not forfeit their right to marry by virtue of their status as prisoners. The state 'may not restrict the right to marry unless there are important considerations flowing from such circumstances as danger to prison security or prevention of crime and disorder'.[27] Otherwise, what needs to be determined are the 'practical aspects of timing and making the necessary arrangements', concerning which the prison authorities may set conditions.[28] Generally, the 'authorities must strike a fair balance of proportionality among various public and individual interests at stake in a manner compatible with the Convention'.[29] It is permissible to require that a prisoner obtain prior leave from the prison authorities to marry,[30] but the authorities may not interfere with a prisoner's decision to marry a person of his choice, 'especially on the grounds that the relationship is not acceptable to them or deviates from prevailing social conventions and norms'.[31] In *Jaremowicz v Poland*,[32] there was a breach of Article 12 when the authorities refused a prisoner leave to marry when he and his intended wife had only become acquainted while both were in prison. In the words of the Court, 'the fact that the bond between a man and a woman developed when they were both detained does not automatically render their relationship "illegal", "superficial", having no rehabilitative value or not deserving respect', as the prison authorities had claimed.[33] In *Frasik v Poland*,[34] it was held that permission could not be refused in the belief that the reason for the marriage was that the wife would be excused giving evidence against the prisoner in court. As the Court noted, were he a free man, the prisoner would have been fully entitled to marry regardless of the consequences for testimonial privilege.

Where the national law requires that marriage be celebrated only in certain places outside of prison, the authorities must allow a prisoner temporary release to be married, or the law must be changed. In this regard, there is a positive obligation upon the state to facilitate a prisoner's marriage. Thus in *Hamer v UK*,[35] there was no specific rule of English law preventing prisoners from marrying but the Marriage Act 1949 required that marriages be celebrated only at certain places outside prisons and the prison authorities would not allow the applicant temporary release to be married outside the prison. The applicant's opportunity to be married would have been delayed for a period until he obtained parole. The Commission decided that there was a violation of Article 12, an assessment confirmed by the Committee of Ministers. Considerations of security did not preclude the state from making some arrangement which would have allowed the

---

[27] *Frasik v Poland* 2010- para 95.   [28] *Frasik v Poland*, para 95.
[29] *Frasik v Poland*, para 100.
[30] *Jaremowicz v Poland* hudoc (2010). Cf *Frasik v Poland* (offence to public opinion).
[31] *Jaremowicz v Poland*, para 59.   [32] Hudoc (2010) para 56.
[33] *Jaremowicz v Poland*, para 58.   [34] Hudoc (2010).
[35] No 7114/75, 24 DR 5 at 16 (1979) Com Rep; CM Res DH (81) 5. See also *Draper v UK No 8186/78*, 24 DR 72 at 81 (1980) Com Rep; CM Res DH (81) 4.

prisoner to marry. The effect of the law and the decision of the authorities was to cause such delay in the prisoner's opportunity to be married as to infringe the substance of his right to marry. As a result of the case, the government introduced legislation to allow prisoners to be married in prison.[36]

There is no positive duty on a state to provide the material conditions to make the right to marry effective. A state may foster marriage by granting benefits to married couples which it denies to single cohabitees but it is not obliged to do so.[37] Nor is it under a duty to guarantee that married couples are no worse off than cohabitees in a similar position to them.[38]

The right to marry does not 'in principle include the right to choose the geographic location of the marriage'.[39] Accordingly, a state is not obliged to admit an alien fiancé to its territory, or to allow him or her remain in it so that a marriage may be celebrated there, at least where the couple are able to marry elsewhere.[40] By implication, there may be an exception where one of the intended spouses is a national of the state concerned and the marriage may not be contracted elsewhere. Similarly, Article 12 does not require a state to admit an alien married to one of its nationals to enter or remain on its territory to establish or live in the marital home and found a family there; any such case would arise under Article 8 rather than Article 12.[41]

II. TRANSSEXUALS

The question whether marriage is limited to unions between a man and woman has arisen in two situations: marriages between a transsexual and another; and marriages of same-sex couples.

For the transsexual, the complaint is that a state which denies the transsexual the right to marry a person of the *now* opposite sex is inconsistent with his or her new status and the transsexual's possibilities for marriage. In its early jurisprudence, the Court rejected this complaint, but has since changed its mind. In *Rees v UK*,[42] the Court unanimously ruled against the applicant transsexual. It stated that 'the right to marry guaranteed by Article 12 refers to the traditional marriage between persons of opposite biological sex. This appears also from the wording of the Article which makes it clear that Article 12 is mainly concerned to protect marriage as the basis of the family'.

But in *Christine Goodwin v UK*,[43] the Court reversed *Rees*. It did so on the basis that the right to marry in Article 12 was distinct from the right to found a family in the same Article and that it could no longer be assumed that the wording 'men and women' in Article 12 referred to a 'determination of gender by purely biological criteria'. There had been 'major social changes in the institution of marriage since the adoption of the Convention', with now 'widespread acceptance of the marriage of transsexuals' to members of their new opposite sex in Council of Europe states. In addition, 'dramatic changes' had been brought about by developments in medicine and science in the field of transsexuality. While not so many states allowed in their law post-operative transsexuals to

---

[36] Marriage Act 1983, s 1, which also allows marriages for some mental patients in places of detention.

[37] *Marckx v Belgium* A 31 (1979); 2 EHRR 330 PC.

[38] *FPJM Kleine Staarman v Netherlands* No 10503/83, 42 DR 162 (1985) (loss of benefit on marriage) and *Lindsay and Lindsay v UK* No 11089/84, 49 DR 181 at 193 (1986) (married couple taxed more heavily than cohabitees).   [39] *Savoia and Bounegru v Italy* No 8407/05 hudoc (2006) DA.

[40] *Savoia and Bounegru v Italy*. Cf *X v Germany* No 7175/75, 6 DR 138 (1976).

[41] *Mahfaz v UK* No 20598/92 hudoc (1993) DA and *Schober v Austria* No 34891/97 hudoc (1999) DA.

[42] A 106 (1986); 9 EHRR 56 para 49 PC.   [43] 2002-VI; 35 EHRR 447 paras 100–3 GC.

marry members of their new opposite sex as gave full legal recognition to gender reassignment in other respects,[44] this did not support an argument for leaving the matter entirely within the contracting parties' margin of appreciation. While some discretion could be left to them on matters such as 'the conditions under which a person claiming legal recognition as a transsexual establishes that gender reassignment has been properly effected or under which past marriages cease to be valid and the formalities applicable to future marriages', not to allow a post-operative transsexual who was living as a member of his or her new sex the possibility in any circumstances of marrying a member of the new opposite sex was to deny him or her the very essence of the Article 12 right to marry. As to the validity of past marriages, in *Parry v UK*[45] it was held that it was within the margin of appreciation for a state to make the legal recognition of a transsexual's acquired gender contingent upon the dissolution of a marriage contracted with a person who was now of the same gender as the post-operation transsexual.

III. SAME-SEX MARRIAGES

The Court's ruling in the *Christine Goodwin* case that the right to marry is not limited to persons who are biologically of the opposite sex opens up the possibility that Article 12 might be extended to same-sex marriages. However, in *Schalk and Kopf v Austria*,[46] the Court held that Article 12 does not do so. This ruling was based not on the wording of Article 12 and the intention of the drafters of the Convention, but upon the fact that 'there is no European consensus regarding same sex marriage' and that 'no more than six out of forty seven Convention states allow same sex marriage'.[47] However, the Court signalled that it no longer considered that 'the right to marry enshrined in Article 12 must in all circumstances be limited to marriage between two persons of the opposite sex', but added that 'as matters stand, the question whether or not to allow same sex marriage is left to regulation by the national law of the contracting state'.[48] The phrase 'in all circumstances' allows for the situation where a state chooses to provide for same-sex marriages and requires that it comply with Article 12 if it does so. The phrase 'as matters stand' allows for the possibility that, in accordance with the Convention's character as a 'living instrument', Article 12 might be re-interpreted as requiring states to provide for same-sex marriages should there emerge the 'European consensus' that was lacking when the *Schalk and Kolf* case was decided. Given that the trend in European national law is towards the recognition of same-sex marriages,[49] it can be supposed that Article 12 will in due course be interpreted as requiring them. As generally on matters involving social *mores*, the Court is choosing to follow, not to lead.

---

[44] The Court had evidence (*Christine Goodwin v UK*, para 57) that twenty Convention parties allowed such marriages; Ireland and the United Kingdom did not and four had no legislation. The position in other parties was unclear. Where gender reassignment was publicly funded, only Ireland and the United Kingdom did not give full legal recognition to the new gender identity. See also *L v Lithuania* 2007-IV; 46 EHRR 431.

[45] No 42971/05 hudoc (2006) DA. Cf *R and F v UK No 35748/05* hudoc (2006) DA.

[46] 2010-; 53 EHRR 683. See Hodson, 11 HRLR 170 (2011). A claim of a violation of Article 8 (family life) and Article 14 (discrimination) was also unsuccessful.

[47] *Schalk and Kopf v Austria*, para 58.

[48] *Schalk and Kopf v Austria*, para 61. The Court referred to Article 9, EU Charter of Fundamental Rights, which is so worded (referring just to a 'right to marry' and not mentioning 'men and women') as to allow states to provide for same-sex marriages, but not to require them to do so.

[49] By 2014, the number of states parties providing for same-sex marriage had risen to ten; eleven others provided for some form of civil partnership.

IV. DIVORCE

There is no reference to the dissolution of marriage in Article 12. After a review of the *travaux préparatoires*, in *Johnston and Others v Ireland*,[50] the Court decided that the omission was deliberate: the drafting states did not intend the Convention to grant a right to divorce. The Court held that the prohibition on divorce in the Irish Constitution did not infringe the Convention and that a different conclusion would not be reached by taking into account developments in other European states which had established a very wide right to divorce, because 'the Court cannot, by means of an evolutive inter-pretation, derive from [the Convention and the Protocols] a right that was not included therein at the outset. This is particularly so here, where the omission was deliberate.'[51] The Court found that Article 5 of the Seventh Protocol also had been drafted in such a way as to avoid the implication that a right to divorce was contained in the Convention. The consequences of the judgment are less serious because of the requirement of a protective remedy between husband and wife under Article 8[52] and the steps the Court has taken to ameliorate the position of illegitimate children under the same Article,[53] but it does not sit happily with the importance the Court attached to the right to remarry to avoid children being born out of wedlock in its judgment in *F v Switzerland*.[54] However, if a state, in the exercise of its discretion, permits divorce, a divorce must be obtainable with reasonable expedition in order to allow re-marriage.[55]

3. THE RIGHT TO FOUND A FAMILY

The right to found a family exists only within marriage.[56] It does not apply to the many couples who now live together in European society without marrying. It also does not extend to having grandchildren, so that potential grandparents have no claim under Article 12 if their children take a vow of celibacy in holy orders.[57]

The Commission described the right to found a family as an 'absolute right' in the sense that Article 12 gives no grounds for the state to interfere with it.[58] The most obvious inter-ferences with the right to found a family are programmes of compulsory sterilization or abortion.[59] Voluntary sterilization or abortion by one partner to a marriage clearly has an impact on the interests of the other partner but, however serious this may be, it is hard to see that the Court would find a positive obligation on a state under Article 12 to regulate a private decision of such a kind except in circumstances where some other right under the Convention was more directly implicated, such as that in Article 2 or Article 8. In *Boso v Italy*,[60] an application by a husband who claimed that his wife's decision to have an abortion deprived him of his opportunity to have a family was declared inadmissible on

---

[50] A 112 (1986); 9 EHRR 203 PC.

[51] *Johnston and Others v Ireland*, para 53. Ireland legalized divorce in 1996. Malta is now the only Convention party that prohibits divorce.   [52] *Airey v Ireland* A 32 (1979); 3 EHRR 592.

[53] See *Marckx v Belgium* A 31 (1979); 2 EHRR 330 PC.

[54] A 128 (1987); 10 EHRR 411 para 36 PC.

[55] *Aresti Charalambous v Cyprus* hudoc (2007) and *VK v Croatia* hudoc (2012).

[56] *Christine Goodwin v UK* 2002-VI; 35 EHRR 447 para 98 GC.

[57] *Sijakova and Others v FYRM* No 67914/01 hudoc (2003) DA.

[58] *X v UK* No 6564/74, 2 DR 105 at 106 (1975).

[59] A claim of infertility resulting from nuclear tests was inadmissible *ratione temporis* in *McGinley and Egan v UK* Nos 21825/93 and 23414/94 hudoc (1995) DA.   [60] No 50490/99 2002-VII DA.

the ground that the abortion was to protect the wife's health, as allowed by national law and Article 2.

While states have the power to encourage the legitimate family, they have no positive obligation to do so. Article 12 cannot be made the vehicle for requiring positive social programmes from the state in support of the family.[61] We have already seen that couples have the right to marry even in the absence of a prospect of cohabitation. In these circumstances, the state has no duty to facilitate opportunities for the couple to found a family by allowing for consummation of the marriage.[62] Where couples are separated as the result of a deportation or an immigration order which prevents a party to a marriage or proposed marriage from entering a state, any Convention remedy will arise under Article 8, not Article 12.[63]

A further interference with the right to found a family exists for persons detained by the state. This can be remedied by conjugal visits, but, as yet, while noting that prisoners are allowed conjugal visits by their wives in more than half of the Convention parties,[64] the Court has held that such visits are not required by Article 12 or Article 8.[65]

While Article 12 protects married couples from interference by the state with their right to found a family, for some couples the chance will be an empty one because of their incapacity to procreate. Neither Article 12 nor any other Article of the Convention guarantees a right to adopt or otherwise integrate into a family a child which is not the natural child of the married couple concerned.[66] However, states do commonly provide for adoption and the adoption system that they have is subject to scrutiny by the Court, although a breach of Article 12 is likely to be found where adoption is refused only in an extreme case of substantive or procedural unfairness[67] or where discrimination brings Article 14 into play.[68]

More recently, attention has switched to artificial reproduction. The state may be implicated at two levels. It has to decide whether and what techniques of artificial reproduction may legally be used and to whom, if any, they should be made available by the state. Both questions were in issue, directly or indirectly, in *SH and Others v Austria*.[69] The case concerned an Austrian law which permitted artificial insemination in some cases, but prohibited the use of the sperm of a third party male donor for the purpose of *in vitro* fertilization and prohibited ovum donation by another woman entirely. The Court rejected the claims by the applicants, who were married,[70] that these limitations were a breach of Article 12 on the basis that Article 12 does not guarantee a right to procreation. Article 12, that is, is limited to the prohibition of interferences by the state with the having

---

[61] *Andersson and Kullmann v Sweden No 11776/85*, 46 DR 251 (1986).

[62] *X v UK No 6564/74*, 2 DR 105 (1975) and *X and Y v Switzerland No 8166/78*, 13 DR 241 (1978).

[63] See eg, *Beldjoudi v France* A 234-A (1992); 14 EHRR 801.

[64] *Dickson v UK* 2007-V; 46 EHRR 927 GC.

[65] *Dickson v UK* and *Aliev v Ukraine* hudoc (2003). See also *ELH and PBH v UK Nos 32094/96 and 32568/96* hudoc (1997) DA. On access to artificial insemination for a prisoner and spouse, see *Dickson v UK* (breach of Article 8).

[66] *Di Lazzaro v Italy No 31924/96* hudoc (1997) DA; *Akin v Netherlands No 34986/97* hudoc (1998) DA; *Fretté v France* 2002-I; 38 EHRR 438; and *EB v France* hudoc (2008); 47 EHRR 509 GC. A state is not obliged to recognize a foreign adoption: *X and Y v UK No 7229/75*, 12 DR 32 (1977).

[67] *X and Y v UK No 7229/75*, 12 DR 32 at 34 (1977) and *X v Netherlands No 8896/80*, 24 DR 176 at 177–8 (1981).

[68] See *Singh and Others v UK* hudoc (2006) (F Sett). See also *EB v France* hudoc (2008); 47 EHRR 509 GC (Article 8 case). Testamentary discrimination against adopted children falls within Article 8: *Pla and Puncernau v Andorra* 2004-VIII; 42 EHRR 522.   [69] *No 57813/00* hudoc (2007) DA.

[70] Artificial insemination claims by single women would fail under both Articles 12 and 14 on the Court's limited reading of the Article 12 right to found a family to the married state.

of children within marriage by natural means: there is no positive obligation to facilitate it by legislation to permit artificial insemination or, *a fortiori*, by providing for it through state-funded medical institutions. The decision is a disappointing one. Although there may be no right of procreation under Article 12, it is arguable that the right to found a family implies that where a couple can procreate by whatever means, the state should not impose unreasonable restrictions on their possibility of doing so.

4. NON-MARRIED PERSONS

In *Marckx v Belgium*,[71] the mother of an illegitimate child claimed a right 'not to marry', that is to say, that her right to found a family should not be inhibited by disadvantages which she and her child would suffer by reason only of the fact that the mother had chosen not to marry the father of the child. The Court held that there was no legal obstacle confronting the mother 'in the exercise of the freedom to marry or to remain single' and that the disadvantages to which she referred did not constitute an interference with that legal opportunity such as to violate Article 12, although issues might arise under Article 8. In *B, R and J v Germany*,[72] the Commission confirmed that a state could treat the legitimate family more favourably than the illegitimate one, provided that its treatment of the latter did not violate Article 8. The 'full protection' of German family law extended only to the legitimate family. Here, an unmarried father and mother were living in a stable relationship with their child. A parental link was recognized by German law between the father and his child but the law would not allow him to obtain custody of the child. Just as he could not rely on Article 8, the Commission said that he could not find the right to custody in Article 12, so long as the couple remained unmarried. This limited approach to the position of unmarried persons will only be broadened, as social changes in Europe suggest it should, through an alteration in the understanding of who can marry (homosexuals), and the ambit beyond marriage of the right to found a family, or by reliance upon of Article 8.

5. CONCLUSION

Article 12 has generated only a small number of Court judgments. One reason for this has been the limited textual scope of Article 12, which to its credit the Court has largely made good by its broad and dynamic interpretation of the rights to respect for private and family life in Article 8. Thus matters arguably pertinent to Article 12, such as having a family (outside the traditional marriage), child care, family support, and sustaining family life, have been dealt with under Article 8. A second reason has until recently been the Court's restriction in Article 12 of the right to marry to individuals of the biological opposite sex and of the right to found a family to married couples. The *Christine Goodwin* case concerning transsexuals marks an important departure in this regard and may presage other decisions that similarly reflect changing social values in personal relations in European states. What was particularly striking in the *Goodwin* case was the Grand Chamber's willingness to act on the basis of legal change in less than the 'great

---

[71] A 31 (1979); 2 EHRR 330 para 67 PC.
[72] No 9639/82, 36 DR 130 (1984). See also *X v Belgium and Netherlands* No 6482/74, 7 DR 75 (1975).

majority' of contracting parties. Other beneficial developments based on a similarly more dynamic approach to Article 12 would be the recognition of same-sex marriages and civil partnerships and adoption by same-sex couples; the extension of the right to found a family beyond marriage; and a wider guarantee of artificial insemination for childless couples. The recognition of conjugal visits for prisoners would also be in line with practice in many contracting parties, although the *Dickson* case may suggest a different (artificial insemination) approach to their right to found a family. Another approach to some of these matters would be their further development under Article 8, in some cases together with Article 14.

17

ARTICLE 13: THE RIGHT TO AN EFFECTIVE NATIONAL REMEDY

> **Article 13**
>
> Everyone whose rights and freedoms as set forth in this Convention are violated shall have an effective remedy before a national authority notwithstanding that the violation has been committed by persons acting in an official capacity.

1. INTRODUCTION

Article 13[1] requires the provision of effective national remedies for the breach of a Convention right. So, with Article 35 (addressing, *inter alia*, exhaustion of domestic remedies), this Article is central to the cooperative relationship between the Convention and national legal systems. Despite its importance, however, the language and precise objective of Article 13 are far from clear: two judges have called it the 'most obscure' provision of the Convention.[2] Some complex questions occur regarding its place within the scheme of the Strasbourg system of human rights control (see section 2). In the past, the approaches to the interpretation of Article 13 by the Strasbourg authorities have oscillated, sometimes demanding more of the state,[3] sometimes less,[4] as they have sought an understanding of it which fits into the whole structure of the Convention.

Over the last decade or so, the general trend of the jurisprudence has been to ask significantly more of the state in relation to Articles 2, 3, 5, and 6(1) (as regards trial within a reasonable time) of the Convention in particular. Indeed, Article 13 may be seen in the context of the sustainability of the Convention system overall during an era associated with a major overload of cases at Strasbourg, and the emphasis which the Interlaken, Izmir, and Brighton Declarations[5] have placed upon the shared responsibility of both the Court and the states parties to guarantee the viability of the Convention system of control. As was acknowledged in the Brighton Declaration,[6] if national remedies were more

---

[1] On Article 13, see Frowein in *Ryssdal Essays*.

[2] Judges Matscher and Pinheiro Farinha, partly dissenting in *Malone v UK* A 82 (1984); 7 EHRR 14 PC.

[3] Eg, *Plattform 'Ärzte für das Leben' v Austria* A 139 (1988); 13 EHRR 204.

[4] Eg, *Leander v Sweden* A 116 (1987); 9 EHRR 433.   [5] See Ch 3, section 7.

[6] See, eg, para 33. Reference should also be made to the 'pilot judgment' procedure, which has undergone a significant development at Strasbourg over the last decade, see Ch 3, section 3.VIII.

comprehensive there would be less need for applications to be made to the Court; consequently there would be less pressure of cases on that institution, which would be better able to deal with the cases reaching it; its case law could be more considered and so in turn it would be clearer to the national authorities what is required of them. Accordingly, via Article 13, the primary responsibility of the states to secure the enjoyment of human rights may be realized and the effective discharge of the subsidiary role of the institutions may be facilitated.[7] In this regard it is worth noting that, as of 2013, so-called 'repetitive' cases constitute the biggest single category of pending applications at Strasbourg (46,662, representing 41 per cent of the overall docket).[8]

2. ARTICLE 13 WITHIN THE GENERAL SCHEME OF THE CONVENTION

I. ARTICLE 13, INCORPORATION OF THE CONVENTION AND DISCRETION AVAILABLE TO THE STATE IN PROVIDING REMEDIES

Article 13 gives 'direct expression to the states' obligation to protect human rights first and foremost within their own legal system'.[9] It establishes 'an additional guarantee for an individual in order to ensure that he or she effectively enjoys those rights'.[10]

Article 13 cases will therefore involve the Court examining the domestic legal regime relevant to the applicant's Convention claim to see if it was possible for him or her to obtain relief at the national level. Generally speaking, the Court will be examining whether domestic law provided an 'effective remedy' in the sense that, if resorted to, it could have prevented the alleged violation occurring or continuing, or for any violation that had already occurred, the applicant could have achieved appropriate redress.[11]

The best way for a state to help to insulate itself from violating Article 13 in a Strasbourg case is, therefore, to effectively incorporate the Convention into domestic law. All states parties have incorporated the Convention in one form or another,[12] but this has not been through any legal obligation derived from Article 13 or the Convention generally. Indeed, Article 13 does not require incorporation of the Convention.[13] It is not even necessarily the case that it requires that the state be required to provide one single remedy, provided an aggregate of remedies suffices on the facts.[14] Nor does Article 13 guarantee a remedy to challenge domestic (primary) legislation[15] before a national authority on the basis of the Convention (secondary legislation is a different matter).[16] This position may be hard to reconcile with the effective protection of human rights, but it must be recalled that most states

---

[7] See Recommendation Rec(2004)6 of the Committee of Ministers to Member States on the Improvement of Domestic Remedies at Appendix para 4.

[8] See European Court of Human Rights, 'The Interlaken Process and the Court (2013 report)' (28 August 2013), at p 3. The same document noted that '92% of these cases come from seven countries: Italy (24%); Serbia (18.5%); Turkey (17%); Ukraine (14%); Romania (8.5%); United Kingdom (5%); Russia (5%)', at p 9.

[9] *Kudla v Poland* 2000-XI; 35 EHRR 198 para 152 GC.   [10] *Kudla v Poland*, para 152.

[11] Cf *Ramirez Sanchez v France* hudoc (2006); 45 EHRR 1099 para 160 GC.

[12] See Polakiewicz in Blackburn, ed, *Fundamental Rights in Europe: The ECHR and its Member States: 1950–2000*, 2001, ch 3.

[13] From many authorities see *Ireland v UK* A 25 (1978); 2 EHRR 25 para 239 PC and *PM v UK* hudoc (2005); 42 EHRR 1015 paras 32–4.   [14] See section 3.III.

[15] See *James v UK* A 98 (1986); 8 EHRR 123 para 85 PC and *A v UK* 2002-X; 36 EHRR 917 para 112.

[16] See *Abdulaziz, Cabales and Balkandali v UK* A 94 (1985); 7 EHRR 163 paras 92–3 PC.

parties to the Convention do not allow even their Supreme Courts to strike down legislation.[17] Similarly the unwillingness of a constitutional tribunal to exercise a discretion to undertake a review of the Convention question will not involve a violation of Article 13.[18]

Consistent with the fact that there is no requirement to incorporate the Convention, the exact way in which the states provide for Article 13 'relief at national level' is up to them; they are 'afforded a margin of appreciation in conforming with their obligations'.[19] It is not a requirement that the Convention be capable of being directly relied upon in the domestic courts; nonetheless, Article 13 requires that the legal remedies an applicant makes use of provide for the same remedy *in substance*. As the Grand Chamber put it in *Rotaru v Romania*:[20]

> Article 13 guarantees the availability at national level of a remedy to enforce the substance of the Convention rights and freedoms in whatever form they might happen to be secured in the domestic legal order. This Article therefore requires the provision of a domestic remedy allowing the 'competent national authority' both to deal with the substance of the relevant Convention complaint and to grant appropriate relief, although Contracting states are afforded some discretion as to the manner in which they conform to their obligation under this provision. The remedy must be 'effective' in practice as well as in law...

Although the requirement is that the applicant be able to put the substance of his Convention claim to the national decision-maker, there does not need to be a guarantee that that decision-maker will reach the right result on the Convention question in issue.[21]

The effectiveness of the remedy required by Article 13 may be conditioned by the character of the Convention right to which it is sought to attach it. More important rights require more stringent remedies,[22] but the effectiveness of any remedy that Article 13 requires may be limited by virtue of the nature of the state power—for example, those related to national security considerations—the exercise of which is being questioned.[23]

So the protection afforded by Article 13 'is not absolute'. The Court accepts that, '[t]he context in which an alleged violation—or category of violations—occurs may entail inherent limitations on the conceivable remedy'.[24] If so, Article 13 'is not treated as being inapplicable but its requirement of an "effective remedy" is to be read as meaning "a remedy" that is as effective as can be, having regard to the restricted scope for recourse inherent in [the particular context]'.[25]

II. A PRE-EMPTIVE REMEDY FOR 'ARGUABLE' CLAIMS

A literal reading of Article 13—'Everyone whose rights and freedoms...*are violated* shall have an effective remedy' (emphasis added)—might imply that it merely imposes

---

[17] See (for interesting comment) the separate opinions in *James v UK* A 98 (1986); 8 EHRR 123 PC.

[18] *VDSO and Gubi v Austria* A 302 (1994); 20 EHRR 56 paras 54–5.

[19] *Smith and Grady v UK* 1999-VI; 29 EHRR 493 para 135. See also *Kudla v Poland* 2000-XI; 35 EHRR 198 para 154.

[20] 2000-V para 67 GC. See also *Soering v UK* A 161 (1989); 11 EHRR 439 para 122 PC and *Vilvarajah v UK* A 215 (1991); 14 EHRR 248 paras 117–27.   [21] *Silver v UK* A 61 (1983); 13 EHRR 582 para 113.

[22] *Klass v Germany* A 28 (1979); 2 EHRR 214 para 55 PC.

[23] *Klass v Germany*, para 72 and *Leander v Sweden* A 116 (1987); 9 EHRR 433 para 84. In these cases the Court accepted that remedies against secret surveillance for national security reasons would inevitably be restricted.

[24] *Kudla v Poland* 2000-XI; 35 EHRR 198 para 151 GC (citing *Klass v Germany*, id, para 69).

[25] *Kudla v Poland*, para 151.

an obligation to establish a means of redress open to the individual in the domestic legal system to obtain the enforcement of a judgment he has *already* won at Strasbourg. This narrow view has been rejected,[26] the Court in *Klass v Germany* stating:[27]

> ...Article 13 requires that where an individual considers himself to have been prejudiced by a measure allegedly in breach of the Convention, he should have a remedy before a national authority in order both to have his claim decided and, if appropriate, to obtain redress. Thus, Article 13 must be interpreted as guaranteeing an 'effective remedy before a national authority' to everyone who *claims* that his rights and freedoms under the Convention have been violated. (emphasis added)

The Court sensibly qualified this statement ('everyone who claims' a violation) in *Silver v UK*,[28] such that the Article applies only to those with 'an arguable claim' that he or she is a victim of a violation of the Convention. Of course, there will be no violation of Article 13 if, for example, an applicant alleges a denial of his right to health care or to a passport, no matter how well-founded his claim on the facts, because no Convention right is implicated by the claim. But it is important to appreciate that a violation of Article 13 is not dependent on there actually being a violation of *another* Convention right. In *Leander v Sweden*,[29] the Court accepted that the applicant had had an arguable claim, even though it was eventually persuaded that no violation of another article had been made out. In *Bubbins v UK*,[30] the Court found no violation of Article 2 on the facts, but it acknowledged that the applicant's complaint under that Article had been 'arguable'. The case concerned a fatal police shooting and was brought by the deceased's sister. Examining the case under Article 13, the Court accepted that there had been an effective remedy as regards the procedural aspect of the Article 2 claim. However, it found a violation of Article 13 as the domestic legal regime was inadequate owing to lacunas in the compensatory regime. There had been no judicial determination as to the potential liability in damages of the police following their role and conduct in the death of the deceased. Furthermore, the applicant could not obtain compensation for non-pecuniary damage suffered as she was not a dependent of the deceased.[31]

No abstract definition of the notion of arguability has been provided. The Court insists that, arguability 'must be determined, in the light of the particular facts and the nature of the legal issue or issues raised, whether each individual claim of violation forming the basis of a complaint under Article 13 was arguable and, if so, whether the requirements of Article 13 were met in relation thereto'.[32]

III. AN AUXILIARY REMEDY, AND RELATIONSHIP WITH ARTICLE 35

In some instances the Convention text itself fixes on states a more stringent procedural obligation to provide a remedy in particular contexts than that required by Article 13: see Articles 5(4), 5(5), and 6. In such cases, and with the exception of Article 6(1) 'reasonable

---

[26] See Frowein in *Ryssdal Essays* 545 at 546.   [27] A 28 (1979); 2 EHRR 214 para 64 PC.
[28] A 61 (1983); 13 EHRR 582 para 113. See also *Verein Altenatives Lokalradio, Bern v Switzerland No 10746/84*, 49 DR 126 at 143 (1986).   [29] A 116 (1987); 9 EHRR 433 para 79.
[30] 2005-II; 41 EHRR 458 para 170. See also *Hatton v UK* 2003-VIII; 37 EHRR 611 GC.
[31] *Bubbins v UK*, para 172.
[32] *Boyle and Rice v UK* A 131 (1988); 10 EHRR 425 para 55 PC. See also *MA v Cyprus* hudoc (2013) para 117.

time' cases,[33] the 'context-specific' remedy required by the Article concerned is what the Convention requires, not the less rigorous Article 13 remedy. For example, any claim to an Article 13 remedy is absorbed by the claim that a detained person has the *habeas corpus* remedy required by Article 5(4).[34] The Court has also regarded Article 13 obligations as auxiliary in the sense that has narrowed the obligation to provide a remedy to claims of a violation which pass a threshold of 'arguability' (see section 2.II), a notion which is determined by Convention procedural standards and not by any independent substantive character of Article 13.[35]

Complex questions arise as to the inter-relationship between Article 13 and the rule in Article 35 that an applicant must exhaust local remedies before bringing an Article 34 application. As the Court has noted, there is a 'close affinity'[36] between these two Articles. The Court is obliged by Article 35 to determine whether an application is 'manifestly ill-founded', which can involve taking a position on the legal and/or factual merits of a claim.[37] In *Boyle and Rice v UK*,[38] the Court said that 'it is difficult to conceive how a claim that is "manifestly ill-founded" can nevertheless be "arguable", and *vice versa*'. Subsequently, in *Powell and Rayner v UK*,[39] it elaborated as follows:

> Article 13 and [Article 35(3)] are concerned within their respective spheres with the availability of remedies for the enforcement of the same Convention rights and freedoms. The coherence of this dual system of enforcement is at risk of being undermined if Article 13 is interpreted as requiring a national law to make available an 'effective remedy' for a grievance classified under [Article 35(3)] as being so weak as not to warrant examination on its merits at the international level.

Evidently a complaint that has been declared 'manifestly ill-founded' will not satisfy the threshold test for reliance on Article 13 and there will be no violation of that provision.[40] If there is a remedy that satisfies Article 13 then, of course, an individual will need to go on to Strasbourg only where the process has failed to reach a result satisfactory to him. If there is no remedy that complies with Article 13, then there can be no obligation to have recourse to it[41] for the purposes of Article 35 (although an individual may be advised to test whether a particular process satisfies Article 13, even if he has doubts whether it does).

3. ARTICLE 13: GENERAL PRINCIPLES/ REQUIREMENTS OF AN 'EFFECTIVE REMEDY'

The general principles which Article 13 embodies are set out in the paragraphs that follow. Their application to the facts of an individual case is not always easy; in particular,

---

[33] See below section 4.III.

[34] Eg, *Campbell and Fell v UK* A 80 (1984); 7 EHRR 165 para 123 (Article 6(1)) and *De Jong et al v Netherlands* A 77 (1984); 8 EHRR 20 para 60 (Article 5(4)).

[35] *Powell and Rayner v UK* A 172 (1990); 12 EHRR 355 para 33.

[36] *Kudla v Poland* 2000-XI; 35 EHRR 198 para 152 GC.   [37] See Ch 2, section 6.III.

[38] A 131 (1988); 10 EHRR 425 para 54 PC.

[39] A 172 (1990); 12 EHRR 355 para 33. See Hampson, 39 ICLQ 891 (1990).

[40] See *Conka v Belgium* 2002-I; 34 EHRR 1298 para 76.

[41] *Warwick v UK* No 9471/81, 60 DR 5 at 19 (1986) (no remedy to test parent's claim that lawful school beating of daughter violated Article 2, First Protocol).

the development of remedies in a national legal system over time may mean that previous Court judgments or decisions of the Commission finding them to be inadequate must be revised. This point is well illustrated by various Strasbourg cases which highlighted the inadequacies of UK law on judicial review but concerned facts occurring prior to the entry into force of the Human Rights Act 1998 in 2000.[42] It should also be noted that the Court's approach can be very context dependent, as is illustrated by the deferential standards set in some cases concerning national security and Article 13.[43] As the Court has noted, 'the scope of the obligation under Article 13 varies depending on the nature of the Convention right relied on'.[44]

I. SUBSTANTIVE REQUIREMENTS OF AN EFFECTIVE REMEDY

As noted, Article 13 requires the possibility of canvassing the substance of the Convention argument before a national authority and, if accepted, this should give rise to an *effective* remedy.[45] The remedy must be effective 'in practice as well as in law',[46] effectiveness encompassing a remedy that can prevent the alleged violation or its continuation, or one which can provide 'adequate redress for any violation that has already occurred'.[47]

As is noted later in this chapter, arguable claims of violations of Articles 2 and 3 by the direct actions of the state are treated as such an important issue that not only must compensation be paid to relatives, where appropriate,[48] but there must also be an effective investigation meeting certain standards elaborated by the Court.[49] In other cases, pecuniary compensation alone might suffice for the purposes of Article 13, though the Court has hinted that a compensatory award may be so derisory that it raises an issue as to the effectiveness of the redress.[50] Of course, if improper legal obstacles exist to the realization of such compensatory awards, then there may be a violation of Article 13.[51] The same applies if an individual has access to a commission, for example a press or media

[42] Eg, *Vilvarajah v UK* A 215 (1991); 14 EHRR 248; *Smith and Grady v UK* 1999-VI; 29 EHRR 493; and *Hatton v UK* 2003-VIII; 37 EHRR 611 GC.   [43] See section 4.II.

[44] *Hasan and Chaush v Bulgaria* 2000-XI; 34 EHRR 1339 para 98. This case concerned state interference in religious affairs, in particular the state's refusal to recognize a rival leadership to a religious group. The Court accepted that Article 13 was satisfied if representatives of the aggrieved religious community had access to a remedy, ie it was not necessary that every single member of the group should have such access, see paras 98–9.   [45] See *De Souza Ribeiro v France* ECHR-2012 paras 77–81 GC.

[46] *Kudla v Poland* 2000-XI; 35 EHRR 198 para 157 GC. The exercise of the effective remedy 'must not be unjustifiably hindered by the acts or omissions of the authorities of the respondent state', *Aksoy v Turkey* 1996-VI; 23 EHRR 553 para 95.

[47] *Kudla*, paras 157–8 GC. In *Petkov and Others v Bulgaria* hudoc (2009); 53 EHRR 950 the applicants' complaint concerned Article 3 of Protocol 1, as the electoral authorities failed to reinstate them on a party list (prior to an election) despite final judgments to that effect. The Court was robust in its insistence that the breach could not be made good through the mere payment of compensation (para 79), insisting that the situation could be rectified solely by means of a post-election remedy (para 80). In the specific circumstances of the case, Article 13 required 'a procedure by which the candidates could seek vindication of their right to stand for Parliament before a body capable of examining the effect which the alleged breach of their electoral rights had on the unfolding and outcome of the elections'. If the body 'deemed the breach serious enough to have prejudiced the outcome', ultimately 'it should have had the power to annul the election result, wholly or in part'.

[48] For Article 2, compensation for pecuniary and non-pecuniary damage should in principle be possible as part of the range of redress available, see, eg, *Edwards (Paul and Audrey) v UK* 2002-II; 35 EHRR 487 para 97.   [49] For full details see section 4.IV.

[50] See *Wainwright v UK* 2006-X; 44 EHRR 809 para 55. See also *Keenan v UK* 2001-III; 33 EHRR 913 para 129.

[51] See, eg, *Edwards (Paul and Audrey) v UK* 2002-II; 35 EHRR 487 (parents' inability to obtain compensation for death of son in prison); *Keenan v UK* 2001-III; 33 EHRR 913 (parents' inability to obtain

complaints commission, which does not have legal power to award damages to the person concerned.[52] Again the timely payment of a compensation award is an essential element of a remedy under Article 13.[53]

The prospect of a wholly discretionary response to the national authority's decision may raise issues under Article 13.[54] A remedy by dint of the exercise of political discretion will not suffice, so a petition to the Home Secretary by prisoners contesting the compatibility of Prison Rules with the Convention, rules made by him and amendable by him but only in the discharge of his political function, was not an effective remedy.[55] Nor will bodies whose powers are limited to advising the ultimate decision-maker of a remedially effective remedy for the purposes of Article 13:[56] some element of enforceability is generally required.[57] Of course, a judicial discretion will not undermine the effectiveness of proceedings before a court. However, no effective remedy will exist if the scope of review conducted by a domestic court or other authority is so weak that it is unable to properly address the key elements of whether there has been a violation of the Convention. On this basis the Court found violations of Article 13 with Article 8 of the Convention in *Smith and Grady v UK*[58] and *Hatton v UK*,[59] given the weak powers of judicial review exercised by the domestic courts in those pre-Human Rights Act 1998 cases. In *Murray v UK*,[60] the Court said that the 'feeble prospects of success' on the facts of a particular case did not detract from the effectiveness of a remedy for Article 13 purposes if it could, on stronger facts, have afforded the applicant relief.

It may be necessary for a respondent government which maintains that a particular remedy satisfies Article 13 to provide examples of the remedy's application so as to establish its effectiveness.[61] In this respect the Court will not regard an absence of judicial practice as decisive in relation to a law that has recently entered into force,[62] but it does require a remedy that has acquired a 'sufficient level of certainty'.[63]

In *Andersson (Margareta and Roger) v Sweden*,[64] the applicants were mother and son who claimed that the removal of the child to public care and the conditions of the care violated Article 8. Although there were remedies available in Swedish law to challenge the decisions, the child could take advantage of them only through his guardian, his mother. It was argued that the conditions of the separation of mother from child made it impossible for her to take effective action to protect the child's rights. By a narrow majority (five

---

compensation for ill-treatment of son in prison); and *Z v UK* 2001-V; 34 EHRR 97 GC (children's inability to sue local authority for its failure to prevent child abuse by parents).

[52] *Peck v UK* 2003-I; 36 EHRR 719 para 109.

[53] *Öneryıldız v Turkey* 2004-XII; 41 EHRR 325 para 152 GC (five-year delay in a case concerning loss of a close relative).

[54] Eg *Silver v UK* A 61 (1983); 13 EHRR 582 paras 54 and 115 and *Campbell and Fell v UK* A 80 (1984); 7 EHRR 165 paras 51 and 126.   [55] *Silver v UK*, para 116.

[56] Eg, the Unit Review Board and the Standing Committee on Difficult Prisoners: *McCallum v UK* A 183 (1990) para 80 Com Rep.

[57] In *Leander v Sweden* A 116 (1987); 9 EHRR 433 para 82 the Court conceded that the 'main weakness' of the Ombudsman/the Chancellor of Justice was that neither could make a binding decision. See also *Segerstedt-Wiberg v Sweden* 2006-VII; 44 EHRR 14 para 118.

[58] 1999-VI; 29 EHRR 493 (threshold of 'irrationality' set so high that there was no proper consideration by domestic courts of Article 8 issues).   [59] 2003-VIII; 37 EHRR 611 GC.

[60] A 300-A (1994); 19 EHRR 193 para 100.

[61] See *Kudla v Poland* 2000-XI; 35 EHRR 198 para 159 GC and *Segerstedt-Wiberg v Sweden* 2006-VII; 44 EHRR 14 para 120.   [62] *Krasuski v Poland* hudoc (2005); 44 EHRR 223 para 70.

[63] *Krasuski v Poland*, para 72. See also *Conka v Belgium* 2002-I; 34 EHRR 1298 para 83.

[64] A 226-A (1992); 14 EHRR 615 paras 98–103.

votes to four), the Court found that the claim was not made out on the facts. However, the principle is an important one for vulnerable or isolated individuals, such as prisoners and mental patients.

The Court's emphasis on a remedy needing to be practical and effective for the purposes of Article 13 is also illustrated by a case concerning public protest. Effective enjoyment of the right to freedom of assembly, the Court held, potentially entails that a demonstration be permitted to take place on or around a certain date relevant to the issue concerned, for outside that date the impact of the protest may be seriously diminished.[65] In other words, the speediness of the remedial action may be an important aspect of the Article 13 enquiry.[66] An effective, Article 13 remedy here must include a legal framework providing for reasonable time limits within which the authorities should act when taking decisions or giving permission for demonstrations.[67] *Post-hoc* decisions (ie made after the key date for the demonstration) cannot provide adequate redress in respect of alleged violations of Article 11.[68]

II. INSTITUTIONAL REQUIREMENTS OF AN EFFECTIVE REMEDY

In *Leander*,[69] the Court stated that it was a general principle that, 'the authority referred to in Article 13 need not be a judicial authority but, if it is not, the powers and the guarantees which it affords are relevant in determining whether the remedy before it is effective'. While the Court is prepared to be flexible in special cases, for instance *Klass* and *Leander*,[70] it is influenced by the judicial model in determining the question of the effectiveness of the remedy, and so will make a point of verifying the independence of the authority concerned and the procedural guarantees it offers.[71] In *Z v UK*,[72] although the Court did not address the applicants' suggestion that only court proceedings could have furnished effective redress on the facts of that case, it did acknowledge that 'judicial remedies indeed furnish strong guarantees of independence, access for the victim and family, and enforceability of awards in compliance with the requirements of Article 13'. In a case involving accountability for the prolonged detention of an applicant held in solitary confinement, the Grand Chamber had regard to the seriousness of the issues at stake before concluding that, on the facts, it was 'essential' that the Article 13 remedy be 'before a judicial body'.[73]

---

[65] *Bączkowski and Others v Poland* (hudoc) 2007 paras 81–3.
[66] See *De Souza Ribeiro v France* hudoc (2012) para 81 GC ('adequate nature of the remedy can be undermined by its excessive duration').   [67] *Bączkowski and Others v Poland* (hudoc) 2007 para 83.
[68] *Bączkowski and Others v Poland*.
[69] A 116 (1987); 9 EHRR 433 para 77. See also *Chahal v UK* 1996-V; 23 EHRR 413 para 152.
[70] See, eg, *Leander*, para 81 ('The Chancellor of Justice ... may likewise be regarded as being, *at least in practice*, independent of the government...' (emphasis added)).
[71] See *De Souza Ribeiro v France* ECHR-2012 para 79 GC (see paras 77–81 GC for a summary of general principles).
[72] 2001-V; 34 EHRR 97 para 110 GC (citing *Klass v Germany* A 28 (1979); 2 EHRR 214 para 67 PC). See also *Soering v UK* A 161 (1989); 11 EHRR 439 PC and *Andersson (M and R) v Sweden* A 226-A (1992); 14 EHRR 615.
[73] *Ramirez Sanchez v France* hudoc (2006); 45 EHRR 1099 para 165 GC. The Court indicated that judicial review would be required in a case concerning post-electoral law and the question of the attribution of a seat as a member of parliament: *Grosaru v Romania* hudoc (2010) para 62 (although it was not entirely clear on the point; see the separate opinion of Judge Ziemele).

If the national remedy need not always be judicial, still less does it need to satisfy all the criteria of Article 6(1).[74] In the past a variety of non-judicial authorities have been accepted as satisfying Article 13, including parliamentary and executive bodies.[75] As has been noted previously, the authority concerned must be able to produce a binding decision, so an ombudsman lacking this power will not usually suffice.

Institutional effectiveness requires that the decision-maker be 'sufficiently independent'[76] of the authority alleged to be responsible for the violation of the Convention.[77] In *Silver v UK*,[78] the Court accepted that a right of petition to the Home Secretary against a decision by the prison authorities applying his directives on the censorship of prisoners' correspondence could be an effective remedy. In *Khan v UK*,[79] the Court concluded that the avenues of complaints against the police available to the applicant did not 'meet the requisite standards of independence needed to constitute sufficient protection against the abuse of authority'. Of relevance here was that on the facts the local Chief Constable had a discretion to refer matters to the Police Complaints Authority, failing which the standard procedure was to appoint a member of his own force to carry out the investigation. Further, as regards the Police Complaints Authority itself, the Secretary of State had an important role in appointing, remunerating, and, in certain circumstances, dismissing its members, plus he had an influence on the withdrawal or referring of disciplinary charges and criminal proceedings.

In *Chahal v UK*,[80] which concerned the deportation of an alleged terrorist on national security grounds, the Court was critical of the fact that the advisory panel which reviewed the applicant's deportation order reached decisions which were not binding, plus it also suffered from a lack of 'sufficient procedural safeguards'. Amongst other things, the applicant had no right of legal representation and was only given an outline of the grounds for the notice of intention to deport. Furthermore, the details of the panel's decision were never disclosed.[81]

III. CUMULATION OF PROCEDURES MAY SUFFICE

A cumulation of possible channels of redress in the national legal system must be taken into account when deciding whether an applicant has an effective remedy for the purposes of Article 13, rather than examining any or each procedure in isolation. In *Leander*,[82] the Court stated that it was a general principle of Article 13 that, 'although no single remedy may itself entirely satisfy the requirements of Article 13, the aggregate of remedies

---

[74] Such a conclusion would absorb Article 13 within Article 6(1) and would have the effect of making all Convention rights 'civil rights' within its terms, an interpretation rejected by the Court in *Golder v UK* A 18 (1975); 1 EHRR 524 para 33 PC.

[75] See, eg, *Klass v Germany* A 28 (1979); 2 EHRR 214 para 21 PC ('G10 Commission' (parliamentary)) and *Silver v UK* A 61 (1983); 13 EHRR 582 para 53 (Home Secretary (executive)).

[76] *Silver v UK* A 61 (1983); 13 EHRR 582 para 116.

[77] *Leander v Sweden* A 116 (1987); 9 EHRR 433 para 81.

[78] A 61 (1983); 13 EHRR 582. If the appeal involved a challenge to the legality of his directions, the Home Secretary would not be sufficiently independent since he would in effect be a judge in his own cause: *Silver v UK*. A body which is independent for the purposes of Article 6(1), like Prison Boards of Visitors (*Campbell and Fell v UK* A 80 (1984); 7 EHRR 165 para 81) would be independent for the purposes of Article 13 also.

[79] 2000-V; 31 EHRR 1016 para 47. See also *PG and JH v UK* 2001-IX.

[80] 1996-V; 23 EHRR 413 para 154 GC.

[81] See also the discussion of Article 13 in the context of national security at section 4.II.

[82] A 116 (1987); 9 EHRR 433 para 77. See *Silver v UK* A 61 (1983); 13 EHRR 582 para 118 and, recently, *De Souza Ribeiro v France* ECHR-2012 para 79 GC.

provided for under domestic law may do so'. It falls to the respondent state to raise and substantiate a case here, otherwise the Court will not address it and will assume a violation of Article 13.[83]

So, where an appeal lies to a sufficiently independent body from the decisions of one which is not independent, then the applicant must use this opportunity, which will satisfy Article 13.[84] Additionally, where an applicant makes different kinds of complaint, the national remedies must be effective with respect to each kind. In *Silver v UK*,[85] the Court distinguished between complaints about the application of the Prison Rules (was it within the Rules to stop this letter?), for which the possibility of a petition to the Home Secretary was an effective remedy, and complaints about the Rules themselves (was a Rule which authorizes the stopping of letters to a legal advisor about litigation compatible with the Convention?), in which case a petition to the minister was not effective because he was not sufficiently detached to review his own rule-making.

The dangers of the Court's cumulative approach were made apparent in *Leander v Sweden*.[86] Four remedies in the national legal system were indicated by the Swedish government: appeal to the government from refusal to appoint to the post; request to the National Police Board for access to its secret register, with appeal to the courts in the event of refusal; complaint to the Chancellor of Justice; and complaint to the Ombudsman. The majority inclined to the view that the last two might have been effective remedies, even though neither the Chancellor nor the Ombudsman could give a binding decision, but held that, in any event, appeal to the government was capable of providing a remedy. The Court said:

> Even if, taken on its own, the complaint to the government was not considered sufficient to ensure compliance with Article 13, the Court finds that the aggregate of the remedies…satisfies the conditions of Article 13 in the particular circumstances of the instant case…[87]

It is not made clear how each of the remedies reinforces any other. If any of them individually was adequate to satisfy Article 13, then no reference need be made to the others. On the other hand, if none of them individually were sufficient, as the dissenting judges thought, and none were appeals from another, then aggregating the series of inadequate measures would not be satisfactory to an applicant in the absence of an explanation of how the deficiencies of one were made up by the advantages of another, which the Court did not give.[88] Until the Court is able to demonstrate the effective operation of the aggregation approach in an actual case, a degree of caution is appropriate in assessing a government's claim that this is the case.

The approach based on 'aggregate of remedies' may have been more defensible for sensitive cases such as *Leander* in the earlier years of the Court's 'life', when not all states had incorporated the Convention. But it is harder to justify it today and it is submitted the Court should be reluctant to employ it.[89]

[83] *Sürmeli v Germany* 2006-VII; 44 EHRR 438 para 115 GC.

[84] Eg, the possibility referred to in *Klass v Germany* A 28 (1979); 2 EHRR 214 para 70 PC of raising some questions before the Constitutional Court.

[85] A 61 (1983); 13 EHRR 582 para 118. See also *Lithgow v UK* A 102 (1986); 8 EHRR 329 paras 206–7 PC, where the Court talks about 'aggregate' remedies, when what was involved was different remedies for different claims.

[86] A 116 (1987); 9 EHRR 433 paras 80–2, on which see section 4.II below. See also the criticism of *Silver v UK* A 61 (1983); 13 EHRR 582 in the first edition of this book at p 457.   [87] *Leander v Sweden*, para 84.

[88] For further comment, see Drzemczewski and Warbrick, 7 YEL 364 (1987).

[89] Cf *Sürmeli v Germany* 2006-VII; 44 EHRR 438 para 115 GC.

4. ARTICLE 13: GENERAL PRINCIPLES/ REQUIREMENTS IN SPECIFIC CONTEXTS

I. ARTICLE 13 AND DEPORTATIONS

In deportation cases the effects of the violation of the Convention may be irreversible.[90] In this context the Court does not itself examine the immigration or asylum issue, rather Article 13 requires 'independent and rigorous scrutiny of a claim that there exist substantial grounds for fearing a real risk of treatment contrary to Article 3 and the possibility of suspending the implementation of the measure impugned'.[91]

With respect to deportation raising arguable issues under Articles 2, 3,[92] and 4 of the Fourth Protocol[93] (collective expulsion of aliens), given the possibility of irreversible consequences occurring, there must be a remedy which has automatic suspensive effect, and the Article 13 national authority must examine the Convention compatibility of the deportation order prior to its implementation.[94] The individuals concerned should also be provided with appropriate information about their situation so that they can make use of effective remedies, access to interpreters and legal assistance being of potential relevance.[95]

As to Article 8 ('private and family life') immigration issues that may arise in connection with deportations, the Grand Chamber held in *De Souza Ribeiro v France*[96] that automatic suspensive effect is not a requirement of Article 13. However, if there is 'an arguable claim' in respect of Article 8, the state 'must make available to the individual concerned the effective possibility of challenging the deportation or refusal-of-residence order and of having the relevant issues examined with sufficient procedural safeguards and thoroughness by an appropriate domestic forum offering adequate guarantees of independence and impartiality'.[97] In the context of *De Souza Ribeiro*, the Grand Chamber stated, rather vaguely, that 'there must be genuine intervention by the court or "national authority"'.[98] There had not been on the facts, as the applicant was deported within less than one hour of his submitting an appeal against such a measure (made the previous day, when he had been detained), circumstances which the Court described as 'extremely rapid, even perfunctory'.[99]

II. ARTICLE 13 AND NATIONAL SECURITY

Some of the most interesting Article 13 judgments have concerned cases in which the domestic legal position has been that there can be only very limited review of executive

---

[90] Even if measures are taken such that an applicant is no longer exposed to alleged violation(s) of Articles 2, 3 or 8, this does not necessarily render that complaint non-arguable or deprive an applicant of his victim status for the purposes of Article 13: see *MA v Cyprus* hudoc (2013) para 118.

[91] *Jabari v Turkey* 2000-VIII para 39.

[92] *Gebremedhin v France* hudoc (2007); 50 EHRR 745. See also *De Souza Ribeiro v France* ECHR-2012 para 82 GC.   [93] *Conka v Belgium* 2002-I; 34 EHRR 1298.

[94] *Conka v Belgium*, para 79.

[95] See *Hirsi Jamaa and Others v Italy* ECHR-2012; 55 EHRR 627 para 204 GC and *MSS v Belgium and Greece* ECHR 2011; 53 EHRR 28, paras 301-4 (and 294-322, generally) GC (and on access to appropriate legal advice (or legal aid) as a relevant factor, see para 319 and *Abdolkhani and Karimnia v Turkey* hudoc (2009) paras 114-15).

[96] ECHR-2012 para 83 GC. Cf the concurring opinions attached to the judgment (and also the Chamber judgment: hudoc (2011)) criticizing the Court on this point.

[97] *De Souza Ribeiro v France*, para 83.   [98] *De Souza Ribeiro v France*, para 93.

[99] *De Souza Ribeiro v France*, para 96. It did not matter that he was subsequently issued with a residence permit.

action because of national security considerations. In this context the Court has been prepared to accept significant limitations on the type of Article 13 remedy available with respect to Articles 8 and 10 in areas such as secret surveillance and secret checks on individuals for screening job candidates for sensitive posts. However, it has also demonstrated that it is not sufficient for a state simply to invoke the claim of 'national security' for the purposes of rebutting an Article 13 claim.

In *Klass v Germany*,[100] the Court held as compatible with Article 8 a German law allowing secret surveillance of individuals by the state, naturally without prior notification to the target but sometimes even without *ex post facto* notification. The applicants maintained that unless persons were told that their telephone calls had been intercepted, then they had no opportunity to challenge the surveillance as being contrary to their Convention rights and, accordingly, that there had been a breach of Article 13. Since there could be *no* remedy, *a fortiori* there could not be an effective one. If this argument had prevailed, there would have been an incompatibility with the Court's decision under Article 8 (which it determined had not been violated). The Court avoided this by saying:

> an effective remedy under Article 13 must mean a remedy that is as effective as can be having regard to the restricted scope for recourse inherent in any system of secret surveillance.[101]

It held on the facts that Article 13 was satisfied. In cases where there was later notification, the individual could go to the courts in the ordinary way. Where there was no notification, the process was supervised by an independent committee, which was, in the circumstances, the best that could be done. As the Court has since noted (citing *Klass*), 'where secret surveillance is concerned, objective supervisory machinery may be sufficient as long as the measures remain secret. It is only once the measures have been divulged that legal remedies must become available to the individual'.[102]

The Court found for the defendant state (by four votes to three) in much the same terms in *Leander v Sweden*,[103] where the applicant was unable to gain access to secret information contained on a national register which he might have wished to challenge in the context of an unsuccessful job application to a security-sensitive post. Again, in circumstances involving the protection of national security, the Court held that Article 13 could not guarantee a right to a remedy which undermined a state's rights to take action established elsewhere under the Convention.[104] Echoing *Klass*, the Court determined that, '[on the facts of *Leander*], an "effective remedy" under Article 13 must mean a remedy that is as effective as can be having regard to the restricted scope for recourse inherent in any system of secret checks on candidates for employment in posts of importance from a national security point of view'.[105] It may be pointed out that in both *Klass* and *Leander* there were still elements of procedural guarantees and independent review, albeit they were limited. The impact of the approach used in those two cases is limited because there is only a narrow range of situations where there will be a need to rely on wholly secret processes. Nonetheless, given the seriousness of what is at

---

[100] A 28 (1979); 2 EHRR 214 para 58 PC.   [101] *Klass v Germany*, para 69.

[102] *Rotaru v Romania* 2000-V para 69 GC.

[103] A 116 (1987); 9 EHRR 433 para 59. See also *Segerstedt-Wiberg v Sweden* 2006-VII; 44 EHRR 14 (storage of information on file and refusal to give advice as to its full extent).

[104] *Leander v Sweden*, paras 80–4.   [105] *Leander v Sweden*, para 78.

stake, the Court's conclusions are strong confirmations of the subsidiary character of the Article 13 obligation.[106]

The impression should not be gained, however, that the Court greatly dilutes Article 13 simply because the state claims that national security interests are involved. In *Smith and Grady v UK*,[107] the respondent government claimed that the ban on homosexuals serving in the armed forces, which entailed a violation of Article 8 on the facts, was justified by national security considerations. The Court nevertheless found a violation of Article 13, as the standard of judicial review operated by the domestic courts at the time (a modified irrationality test) had been too weak. It set such a high threshold that the domestic courts were 'effectively excluded' from addressing the key Article 8 aspects of the applicants' case.

Article 3 'deportation' cases have also highlighted the tension between the right to an effective remedy and 'national security' considerations. Here, however, the Court's stance is that national security considerations are immaterial so there is far less scope for the 'as effective as can be' in the circumstances doctrine as regards the remedies instituted to address the Article 3 claim.[108] In *Chahal v UK*, the claim was that neither judicial review under English law, nor a special advisory panel instituted to assess the applicant's claim regarding Article 3, constituted an effective remedy. The national security context entailed that the scope of judicial review operated by the domestic courts was too limited for an effective judicial evaluation of the Article 3 claim, whilst the aforementioned panel suffered from a number of procedural flaws. The Court highlighted the importance of Article 3 and made reference to 'the irreversible nature of the harm that might occur if the risk of ill-treatment materialised'.[109] This dictated that Article 13 requires 'independent scrutiny of the claim that there exist substantial grounds for fearing a real risk of treatment contrary to Article 3',[110] and that the scrutinizing body has sole regard to the issue of risk and not be influenced by national security assessments.

Al-Nashif v Bulgaria[111] also concerned expulsion on grounds of national security, though the Article 13 claim related to the lack of an effective remedy for the interference with the applicant's right to respect to family life that would result from his deportation. In essence, all the domestic proceedings brought by the applicant to challenge his deportation were rejected automatically as the government stated that the ground for expulsion was national security. There was, therefore, no effective possibility of challenging the deportation order in terms of 'having the relevant issues examined with sufficient procedural safeguards and thoroughness by an appropriate domestic forum offering adequate guarantees of independence and impartiality'.[112] The Court pointed out that, compared to *Klass* and *Leander*, it was easier to reconcile the interest of preserving sensitive information with the individual's right to an effective remedy, since in those two cases 'the system of secret surveillance or secret checks could only function if the individual remained unaware of the measures affecting him'.[113] It was accepted that in the deportation/national security context, the sensitivity of the material could justify 'procedural restrictions' on the presentation of evidence before the independent authority purportedly providing the

---

[106] See also *Amann v Switzerland* 2000-II; 30 EHRR 843 GC (telephone-tapping and storing of personal data in security card index); and *Rotaru v Romania* 2000-V GC (intelligence services' storage of secret information, some false). *Segerstedt-Wiberg v Sweden* 2006-VII; 44 EHRR 14 paras 120–1, highlights the Article 13 requirement that a legal remedy include procedures to secure the destruction of a secret file or its rectification in appropriate circumstances.   [107] 1999-VI; 29 EHRR 493 paras 137–9.

[108] See *Chahal v UK* 1996-V; 23 EHRR 413 para 150.   [109] *Chahal v UK*, para 151.

[110] *Chahal v UK*, para 151.

[111] Hudoc (2002); 36 EHRR 655. See also *CG v Bulgaria* hudoc (2008).

[112] *Al-Nashif v Bulgaria*, para 133.   [113] *Al-Nashif v Bulgaria*, para 137.

Article 13 remedy, which for its part 'may need to afford a wide margin of appreciation to the executive in matters of national security'.[114] However, there was no justification for 'doing away with remedies altogether'. As a minimum there had to be a 'competent independent appeals authority' hearing the reasons grounding the deportation decision (even if these were not made public), able to 'reject the executive's assertion that there is a threat to national security where it finds it arbitrary or unreasonable', and before which there has to be 'some form of adversarial proceedings, if need be through a special representative after a security clearance'. Additionally, the body in question should examine whether the deportation infringed the applicant's Article 8 rights.

III. ARTICLE 6(1) 'TRIAL WITHIN A REASONABLE TIME' AND ARTICLE 13

Over its history the Court has found more violations of the right to a trial within a reasonable time, as protected by Article 6(1), than any other provision of the Convention. In recent years a very high percentage of Strasbourg judgments on the merits have concerned unreasonable length of judicial proceedings. The problem seems to be endemic in a number of Convention states.

It is against this background that the Grand Chamber judgment in *Kudla v Poland*[115] marked a significant development in the Court's jurisprudence on Article 13. Before this ruling the Court's general position was that Article 6(1) was deemed to constitute a *lex specialis* in relation to Article 13, so the latter Article was not considered even when Article 6(1) was found to be violated. This was logical in most Article 6(1), cases as the standards set by that provision, encompassing as it did a range of due process safeguards, were more stringent than that required by Article 13. However, as the Court acknowledged in *Kudla*, for unreasonable length of judicial proceedings in particular, the Article 13 claim is not absorbed into that under Article 6(1) since:

> [t]he question of whether the applicant in a given case did benefit from trial within a reasonable time in the determination of civil rights and obligations or a criminal charge is a separate legal issue from that of whether there was available to the applicant under domestic law an effective remedy to ventilate a complaint on that ground.[116]

Indeed, in *Kudla*, the applicant's complaint was that the determination of fraud charges against him remained unresolved after nearly a decade, but it was only at Strasbourg that he was able to pursue a claim regarding the excessive length of proceedings. The Court in *Kudla* addressed the applicant's claim of excessive length not only under Article 6(1), but also under Article 13, finding a violation of both provisions. It rejected the Polish government's argument that requiring a remedy of unreasonable length of judicial proceedings would mean that domestic proceedings would be even more cumbersome and insisted that the new reading of Article 13 reinforced the requirements of Article 6(1).[117] It also proceeded to justify its stance by reference to the principle of subsidiarity, pointing out that if Articles 13 and 6(1) were not read in the way it suggested:

> individuals will systematically be forced to refer to the Court in Strasbourg complaints that would otherwise, and in the Court's opinion more appropriately, have to be addressed

---

[114] *Al-Nashif v Bulgaria.*   [115] 2000-XI; 35 EHRR 198 GC.   [116] *Kudla v Poland*, para 147.
[117] *Kudla v Poland*, para 152.

in the first place within the national legal system. In the long term the effective functioning, on both the national and international level, of the scheme of human rights protection
set up by the Convention is liable to be weakened.[118]

For unreasonable length of judicial proceedings under Article 6(1), Article 13 requires a
domestic remedy which would prevent the alleged violation or its continuation (ie expedite the determination of the applicant's legal proceedings), or provide 'adequate redress
for any violation that had already occurred'.[119] Damages alone would suffice, but, without
being prescriptive, the Court has also indicated its strong preference for a 'preventative'[120]
remedy, since this addresses the root cause of the problem and avoids 'a finding of successive violations in respect of the same set of proceedings and does not merely repair the
breach a posteriori, as does a compensatory remedy'.[121]

Following Kudla, a new statutory remedy was created in Poland which apparently provided applicants alleging a violation of the right to a hearing within a reasonable time in
judicial proceedings with an action for damages. This new law was subsequently in issue
in Krasuski v Poland,[122] where the Court held that since its entry into force an effective
remedy existed in Polish law for the purpose of Article 6(1) protracted legal proceedings.
However, it also indicated that it might review this conclusion if it transpired that the
functioning of a newly created statutory remedy proved not to be effective, sufficient,
and accessible.[123] Here it specifically referred to the adequacy of the level of compensation awarded and the Polish civil courts' ability to handle actions arising under the new
legislation with 'special diligence and attention, especially in terms of the length of time
taken for their determination'.[124]

Kudla may be seen as an attempt to use Article 13 of the Convention to repatriate
the problem of Article 6(1) unreasonable length of judicial proceedings to the member
states.[125] Those states that did not already have a right to an effective remedy in respect of a
complaint about the undue length of court proceedings will need to reform domestic law
or risk a double finding of a violation at Strasbourg. As and when appropriate applications
are made to it, the Court will also have to start to assess whether new laws put in place in
reaction to Kudla satisfy Article 13.

---

[118] Kudla v Poland, para 155. See, however, the partly dissenting opinion of Judge Casadevall who argued
passionately that the Court's new reading of Article 6(1) 'smack[ed] ... more of expediency than of law' and
would not necessarily benefit applicants at all.   [119] Kudla v Poland, para 158.
    [120] Sürmeli v Germany 2006-VII; 44 EHRR 438 para 100 GC. See also McFarlene v Ireland hudoc (2010)
para 108 GC.
    [121] Sürmeli (the Grand Chamber continued, '[s]ome states have understood the situation perfectly by
choosing to combine two types of remedy, one designed to expedite the proceedings and the other to afford
compensation' (citing Scordino v Italy (No 1) 2006-V; 45 EHRR 207 paras 183 and 186 GC). See also the comments at paras 138–9 made in connection with Article 46(1).   [122] 2005-V; 44 EHRR 223.
    [123] Krasuski v Poland. See also Sürmeli v Germany 2006-VII; 44 EHRR 438 para 101 GC.
    [124] Krasuski v Poland. See also, eg, the Court's consideration of the Italian 'Pinto' legislation in Scordino
v Italy (No 1) 2006-V; 45 EHRR 207 GC, including the important comments made in relation to obligations
arising under Article 46 of the Convention, at paras 229–40.
    [125] For further analysis see Directorate General of Human Rights and Legal Affairs, The improvement
of domestic remedies with particular emphasis on cases of unreasonable length of proceedings (Council of
Europe, 2006) and European Commission for Democracy through Law (Venice Commission), Study on The
Effectiveness of National Remedies in Respect of Excessive Length of Proceedings, CDL-AD(2006)036. As of
July 2013 pilot judgments concerning Article 6(1) length of proceedings (and Article 13) have been delivered
in respect of Germany, Turkey, Greece, and Bulgaria: see European Court of Human Rights Press Unit,
'Factsheet: Pilot Judgments', 2013.

IV. EFFECTIVE INVESTIGATIONS UNDER ARTICLE 13 FOR SERIOUS VIOLATION OF FUNDAMENTAL RIGHTS

In the context of cases concerning deaths or ill-treatment allegedly occurring under the responsibility of state agents, the Court has developed a number of 'effective investigation' principles for the application of Articles 2, 3, and 5.[126] Not only does this case law reinforce the subsidiary nature of the Convention, but there are clear practical reasons for this approach. In the case of *Aksoy v Turkey*,[127] where the Court found that the applicant had been tortured, in the context of its examination of Article 13 the Court stated, 'allegations of torture in police custody are extremely difficult for the victim to substantiate if he has been isolated from the outside world, without access to doctors, lawyers, family or friends who could provide support and assemble the necessary evidence. Furthermore, having been ill-treated in this way, an individual will often have had his capacity or will to pursue a complaint impaired'.[128] The Court emphasized that the nature of the right safeguarded under Article 3 had implications: both 'the fundamental importance of the prohibition of torture...and the especially vulnerable position of torture victims, [necessitated that] Article 13 imposes, without prejudice to any other remedy available under the domestic system, an obligation on states to carry out a thorough and effective investigation of incidents of torture'. The Court therefore ruled that where an individual has an arguable claim that he has been tortured by state agents—or in fact suffered any ill-treatment contrary to Article 3[129]—then Article 13 entails, 'in addition to the payment of compensation where appropriate, a thorough and effective investigation capable of leading to the identification and punishment of those responsible and including effective access for the complainant to the investigatory procedure'.[130] The Court saw this requirement as being implicit in Article 13.

In *Aksoy* itself the Court found that there had been a violation of Article 13 owing to the intransigence of the local prosecutor, who failed to investigate credible allegations of very serious of ill-treatment brought to him, despite a legal obligation to do so under domestic law. As the Court put it, 'such an attitude from a state official under a duty to investigate criminal offences was tantamount to undermining the effectiveness of any other remedies that may have existed'.[131] Hence, even if an Article 13 remedy may exist, if its exercise is unjustifiably hindered via the acts or omissions of the authorities of the respondent state, or if the investigation is otherwise generally incompetent and error-prone, then this will entail a violation of Article 13.[132]

---

[126] See Chs 5, 6, and 8.   [127] 1996-VI; 23 EHRR 553 para 97.

[128] For a similar point made in relation to Article 2, see, eg, *Makaratzis v Greece* 2004-XI; 41 EHRR 1092 para 73 GC.   [129] See *Assenov v Bulgaria* 1998-VIII; 28 EHRR 652 para 117.

[130] *Aksoy v Turkey* 1996-VI; 23 EHRR 553 para 98. Although the Court has also noted that Article 13 does not guarantee an applicant 'a right to secure the prosecution and conviction of a third party', see *Öneryıldız v Turkey* 2004-XII; 41 EHRR 325 para 147 GC. Nor has the Court explicitly developed Article 13 to establish the 'right to the truth', although one might argue that it is implicit in much of the jurisprudence. See the separate opinions attached to the Grand Chamber judgment in *El-Masri v the Former Yugoslav Republic of Macedonia* ECHR-2012; 57 EHRR 783 GC (extraordinary rendition).

[131] *Aksoy v Turkey* 1996-VI; 23 EHRR 553 para 99. See also *Hüseyin Esen v Turkey* hudoc (2006) (violation of Article 13 with Article 3 as police officers' conviction for torture so drawn out that it became discontinued under a statute of limitations).

[132] See also, eg, *Aydin v Turkey* 1997-V; 25 EHRR 251 para 107 (allegations of Article 3 ill-treatment by way of the victim's rape did not include the proper independent professional medical examination required by Article 13) and *Ilhan v Turkey* 2000-VII; 34 EHRR 869 para 103 (the domestic investigation into Article 3 ill-treatment was flawed on several grounds, eg inconsistencies in the gendarmes' reports and prosecutor's failure to interview important witnesses, so there was a violation of Article 13).

The approach to Articles 13 and 3 in *Aksoy* as regards a 'thorough investigation' etc has been extended to Article 2[133] and Article 5[134] with respect to deaths and 'disappearances' occurring at the hands of or with the connivance of the members of the security forces, plus also violations of Article 8 of the Convention occurring by virtue of the destruction of the applicant's home and possessions.[135]

The Court has stated that its willingness to find a violation of Article 13 in cases such as those concerning Article 2 was founded generally on the 'close procedural and practical relationship between the criminal investigation and the remedies available to those applicants in the legal system as a whole'.[136] A deficient investigation into a death or ill-treatment may have a negative 'knock-on' effect on the individual's access to any other available remedies relevant to Article 13, such as claims for compensation. It may be that without a criminal investigation by the authorities to establish liability for death, an applicant simply has no prospect of obtaining an effective remedy, but this will be dependent on the facts of each case.[137]

When examining an allegation under Article 13, the Court has on a number of occasions stated that 'the requirements' of that Article are 'broader' than the effective investigation duties respectively arising under Articles 2, 3, and 5. It has never really explained exactly why this is so, it not being clear in practical terms why an Article 13 remedy is more extensive than the procedural obligations which the Court has read in to Articles 2, 3, and 5, other than the possibility afforded by Article 13 of obtaining compensation.[138] In fact, the Court's general approach seems to be that it will not examine Article 13 separately once it has examined the procedural aspects of Articles 2 and/or 3.[139] The Court is prepared to make exceptions, however, as in cases raising very serious violations of Articles 2 and 3

---

[133] Eg, *Kaya v Turkey* 1998-I; 28 EHRR 1 para 107.

[134] Eg, *Kurt v Turkey* 1998-III; 27 EHRR 373 para 140.

[135] Eg, *Menteş v Turkey* 1997-VIII; 26 EHRR 595 para 89.

[136] See *Öneryıldiz v Turkey* 2004-XII; 41 EHRR 325 para 148 GC. The case concerned the responsibility of the state for the deaths and destruction of property occurring after an accidental explosion at a rubbish tip close to a shanty town. The Court stated, 'it does not inevitably follow ... that Article 13 will be violated if the criminal investigation or resultant trial in a particular case do not satisfy the State's procedural obligation under [the Court's] Article 2 [case law] ... What is important is the impact the State's failure to comply with its procedural obligation under Article 2 had on the deceased's family's access to other available and effective remedies for establishing liability on the part of State officials or bodies for acts or omissions entailing the breach of their rights under Article 2 and, as appropriate, obtaining compensation' (para 148).

[137] See *Kaya v Turkey* 1998-I; 28 EHRR 1 para 108. In *Cobzaru v Romania* hudoc (2007) para 83 the Court found a violation of Article 13 after the authorities had failed in their obligation to carry out an effective investigation into allegations of ill-treatment by police officers. The Court pointed out that the absence of a criminal investigation entailed that 'any other remedy available to the applicant, including a claim for damages, had limited chances of success and could be considered as theoretical and illusory, and not capable of affording redress to the applicant'. The Court acknowledged that the civil courts could independently assess the facts, but domestic case law evidenced that 'in practice the weight attached to a preceding criminal inquiry is so important that even the most convincing evidence to the contrary furnished by a plaintiff would often be discarded and such a remedy would prove to be only theoretical and illusory'. By contrast see *Öneryıldiz v Turkey* 2004-XII; 41 EHRR 325 para 151 GC, where the effectiveness of the administrative law remedy available to the applicants did not depend on the outcome of the pending criminal proceedings (although there was still a violation of Article 13 given the delay in payment of compensation).

[138] See Mowbray, *The Development of Positive Obligations Under the European Convention on Human Rights*, 2004, pp 212–13, and the partly dissenting opinion of Judge Zagrebelsky in *Khashiyev and Akayeva v Russia* hudoc (2005); 42 EHRR 397.

[139] See *Ramsahai v Netherlands* hudoc (2007); 43 EHRR 39 para 363 GC and *Makaratzis v Greece* 2004-XI; 41 EHRR 1092 para 86 GC.

emanating from the Chechnya region of Russia. The policy is that the Article 13 claim will be addressed when 'the criminal investigation into the deaths [for Article 2 claims] was ineffective and the effectiveness of any other remedy that may have existed, including...civil remedies...[are] consequently undermined'.[140]

The value of the additional protection afforded by Article 13 is also apparent in the context of claims under Article 8 and Article 1 of the First Protocol emanating from south-east Turkey and where applicants to Strasbourg alleged that they have been forcibly evicted from their homes, or that there has been deliberate destruction of their homes and property by the security forces. In accordance with its standard approach to assessing facts, the Court will only find a violation of Article 8 and Article 1 of the First Protocol here if it is satisfied beyond reasonable doubt that the events have occurred, ie the security forces are responsible. Sometimes the Court has found violations of one or both of these Articles; but sometimes doubts remain, it being simply unclear how the applicants' property was damaged, so no violation of the aforementioned Articles was found. However, Article 13 applies to 'arguable' claims. So, providing the claim as regards property destruction has been declared admissible and the Court accepts that the allegations 'could not be discarded as being *prima facie* untenable',[141] it is prepared to find a violation of Article 13 based on the ineffectiveness of the domestic enquiry into the allegations of property destruction.[142]

V. ARTICLE 2 AND 3 VIOLATIONS IN THE CONTEXT OF THE DUTY TO PROTECT FROM HARM

It is clear that Article 13 can have some applicability in cases involving the responsibility of the state arising out of its positive duties.[143] This is most relevant to the state's duty, in certain circumstances, to protect the individual from the harmful acts of others. In such circumstances, and where violations of Articles 2 and 3 have been found, 'Article 13 may not always require that the authorities undertake the responsibility for investigating the allegations'.[144] So it would seem that as regards the duties of investigation in this context, the requirements of Article 13 are not necessarily as stringent as they are in cases where the violation of Articles 2 or 3 occurred as a consequence of the direct action of state officials. Nonetheless, Article 13 still requires a domestic mechanism that is effectively accessible to an applicant and by which it may be established where responsibility for the harm to his or her relative lay.[145] Where Articles 2 and 3 are concerned then 'compensation for the non-pecuniary damage flowing from the breach should in principle be part of the

---

[140] See, eg, *Musayev v Russia* hudoc (2007) para 175.

[141] *Nuri Kurt v Turkey* hudoc (2005) para 117.

[142] *Nuri Kurt v Turkey*, paras 119–21. Cf *Soylu v Turkey* hudoc (2007) para 53 where the Court found no violation of Article 13 as the applicant was unable to lay the 'basis of a *prima facie* case of misconduct on the part of the security forces'.

[143] See Clapham, *The Human Rights Obligations of Non-State Actors*, 2006, pp 358 and 420.

[144] *Z v UK* 2001-V; 34 EHRR 97 para 109 GC. See also *Edwards (Paul and Audrey) v UK* 2002-II; 35 EHRR 487 para 97.

[145] *Z v UK* 2001-V; 34 EHRR 97 para 109 GC. See also *Keenan v UK* 2001-III; 33 EHRR 913 para 132, where the Court recognized that the inquest into the death of the applicant's child in prison was useful for establishing the facts surrounding the death, but did not properly go to the potential liability of the authorities for the same, and lacked compensatory powers.

range of available remedies'.[146] The administrative law remedies available to the applicant here should be effective in practice as well as in law.[147]

5. CONCLUSION

Article 13 is of autonomous but subsidiary character. While a breach of Article 13 does not depend on establishing a breach of another Article, what the obligations of a state are under Article 13 can be established only by taking the exact nature of each Convention claim into consideration. Nonetheless, this does not reduce the importance of Article 13 in securing cooperation between national legal systems and the Convention regime. The more effective and embracing the scheme of national remedies, particularly if the national authorities are sensitive to the developments in the Convention case law, the more likely it is that Convention cases may be decided without recourse to the Strasbourg authorities. This is, after all, one of the primary goals of the Convention system, a point which has been underlined by the Interlaken, Izmir, and Brighton Declarations. The Court should therefore continue its proactive interpretation of Article 13 to encourage the introduction of effective domestic remedies.

---

[146] A violation of Article 13 was found in *Keenan v UK*, paras 129–33, as the Court argued, *inter alia*, the civil claim for negligence that the applicants might have made would not have led to an award of 'adequate damages' (para 129) and legal aid was not available to pursue such a claim.

[147] See *Öneryıldız v Turkey* 2004-XII; 41 EHRR 325 paras 152–5 GC (ineffectiveness of the compensation proceedings and failure in practice to pay damages was a violation of Article 13).

18

ARTICLE 14 (FREEDOM FROM DISCRIMINATION IN RESPECT OF PROTECTED CONVENTION RIGHTS) AND PROTOCOL 12 (NON-DISCRIMINATION IN RESPECT OF 'ANY RIGHT SET FORTH BY LAW')

Article 14

The enjoyment of the rights and freedoms set forth in this Convention shall be secured without discrimination on any ground such as sex, race, colour, language, religion, political or other opinion, national or social origin, association with a national minority, property, birth or other status.

1. INTRODUCTION

Non-discrimination does not have the same, specific, foundational designation in the Statute of the Council of Europe or Preamble to the Convention as it does in the UN Charter.[1] Nor is there an equivalent in the main Convention text to Article 26 of the International Covenant on Civil and Political Rights, which provides comprehensive protection against discrimination in all those activities which the state chooses to regulate by law. Protocol 12[2] to the Convention, which entered into force in April 2005, has to some degree plugged this gap, but it has not been widely ratified to date.

---

[1] However, non-discrimination is central to the work of the Council of Europe, eg on equality between men and women see http://www.coe.int/t/DGHL/STANDARDSETTING/EQUALITY/ and on combating racial discrimination see http://www.coe.int/t/dghl/monitoring/ecri/default_en.asp. One should also note the important role of the European Union in the field of discrimination law as regards nationality, gender, and race equality in particular, but also religion or belief, sexual orientation, age, and disability, see http://europa.eu/pol/rights/index_en.htm and Chapter III of *The Charter of Fundamental Rights of the European Union*. See Bell, *Anti-Discrimination Law and the European Union*, 2002, and Ellis, *EU Anti-Discrimination Law*, 2005.

[2] See section 11 of this chapter. As of April 2014 it had been ratified by only eighteen contracting parties.

It follows that for the majority of states the key provision addressing discrimination within the Convention is Article 14,[3] which, as we shall see in this chapter, has a number of significant limitations. Above all, it is a 'parasitic' provision, ie it only applies to 'rights and freedoms set forth' in the Convention and its Protocols;[4] it 'only complements'[5] those other substantive provisions.

The main principles for the application of Article 14 were set out in one of the Court's first judgments, the so-called *Belgian Linguistic* case[6] of 1968, when it recognized that there could be a breach of Article 14 even if there is no breach of another Article. The Court soon established, however, that it would not always consider the Article 14 claim in such cases. As the Court has since put it, '[w]here a substantive Article of the Convention has been invoked, both on its own and together with Article 14, and a separate breach has been found of the substantive Article, it is not generally necessary...to consider the case under Article 14 also, though the position is otherwise if a clear inequality of treatment in the enjoyment of the right in question is a fundamental aspect of the case'.[7] Determining whether the centre of gravity of the complaint is Article 14 or another provision is not always straightforward.[8] Viewed overall the jurisprudence indicates that the Court has been disinclined to address Article 14 where another violation has been established (or even to consider whether the other violation precludes the Article 14 question).[9] Several examples of cases may be cited where one would have thought that the issue of discrimination was a 'fundamental aspect' of the case for the applicant, but where the Court did not address Article 14 in view of the fact that it had already found a breach of another Article.[10] In *Dudgeon v UK*,[11] for example, the Court decided that its ruling that the criminalization of adult, private homosexual acts was a breach of Article 8 absolved it from the need to adjudicate on the applicant's Article 14 allegations. It said that these concerned 'the same complaint, albeit seen from a different angle', as that underlying the

---

[3] On Article 14 generally, see *Handbook on European Non-Discrimination Law*, 2010 (hereafter *Handbook*) and *Handbook Case-law Update* (2012); Partsch, *European Supervision*, ch 23; Livingstone, 1 EHRLR 25 (1997) and Council of Europe, *Non-Discrimination: A Human Right*, Strasbourg, October 2005 available at http://www.coe.int/t/dghl/standardsetting/cddh/Publications/EN_Proceedings.pdf. Note that Article 16 (see Ch 20, section 1) and, by implication, Article 17 (Ch 20, section 2) allow discrimination. Also some provisions of the Convention have 'equality' obligations built into them, eg Article 5, Seventh Protocol.

[4] Cf Protocol 12 discussed in section 11 of this chapter.

[5] *EB v France* hudoc (2008) para 47 GC; 47 EHRR 509.   [6] A 6 (1968); 1 EHRR 252 PC.

[7] *Aziz v Cyprus* 2004-V; 41 EHRR 164 para 35. See also *Airey v Ireland* A 32 (1979); 2 EHRR 305 para 30. Cf *Dudgeon v UK* A 45 (1981); 4 EHRR 149 para 67; *Smith and Grady v UK* 1999 –VI; 29 EHRR 493; and *Chassagnou v France* 1999-III; 29 EHRR 615 para 89. In *Pla and Puncernau v Andorra* 2004-VIII; 42 EHRR 522, the Court considered that Article 14 (in conjunction with Article 1 of Protocol 1) to be at the heart of the complaint. In *SH v Austria* GC hudoc (2011); 52 EHRR 78, the Chamber examined the issues under Article 14, but the Grand Chamber limited its examination to Article 8; similarly in *Aksu v Turkey* paras 42–5 GC hudoc (2012), where the applicant had complained of statements in books which reflected an anti-Roma sentiment; cf *Opuz v Turkey* hudoc (2009); 50 EHRR 659.

[8] See, eg, *Eweida and Others v UK* GC hudoc (2013); 57 EHRR 21, where the Court examined some of the complaints under Article 8 and others under Article 14.

[9] See *Airey v Ireland* A 32 (1979); 2 EHRR 305 at paras 29–30.

[10] See *Anguelova v Bulgaria* 2002-IV and Judge Bonello's dissent concerning the death in custody of a young Roma man where the Court had declined to examine Article 14; also *Assenov v Bulgaria* 1998-III and *Velikova v Bulgaria* 2000-VI. For a recent objection to the Court's tendency to leave Article 14 unexplored, see the dissenting opinion of Judge Keller in *Şükran Aydin and Others v Turkey* hudoc (2013), concerning a prohibition of the use of Kurdish in election campaigns.

[11] A 45 (1981); 5 EHRR 573. See also *Goodwin (Christine) v UK* 2002-VI; 35 EHRR 447 para 108 GC; *Smith and Grady v UK* 1999-VI; 29 EHRR 493 para 115 and *X, Y and Z v UK* 1997-II; 24 EHRR 143.

Article 8 claim and that there was no useful legal purpose in deciding them.[12] *Chassagnou v France*[13] and *Aziz v Cyprus*[14] are relatively rare recent examples of the Court proceeding to address Article 14 even after finding a breach of other Articles (in fact, Article 11 and Article 1, First Protocol).[15]

The importance of Article 14 has nevertheless been brought out in a growing number of significant cases over the last decade, including important judgments and decisions concerning discrimination based on sexual orientation and allegations of racial discrimination against members of the Roma[16] community from countries in Central and Eastern Europe, for example, in the context of police violence and in the field of education. The Court has also developed its position on the notion of 'indirect discrimination' and the relevance of statistical evidence to claims of discrimination. In addition it has examined discrimination claims in a wider variety of settings and subjects including, *inter alia*, prisons, the military, immigration, and economic and social policies.

2. OVERVIEW OF THE APPLICATION OF ARTICLE 14

It is axiomatic that not every difference in treatment amounts to discrimination, but establishing clear principles for the application of Article 14 is not easy. The case in which the Court set out most clearly its approach to Article 14 is *Rasmussen v Denmark*.[17] A husband invoked Article 14 in combination with Articles 6 and 8 in relation to his complaint that he was subject to time limits to contest the paternity of a child born during the marriage, whereas his wife could institute paternity proceedings at any time. The Court decided that:

   (i) the allegations of a violation of Article 14 fell *'within the ambit'* of Articles 6 and 8 (see section 3 later in this chapter);

  (ii) there was *a difference of treatment* between a husband and a wife (and, since the list of categories of discrimination in Article 14 was not exhaustive, it was not necessary to determine the basis for this different treatment) (see section 4.I);

 (iii) it was not necessary in this case to decide whether the husband and the wife were in *'analogous situations'*, though the Court proceeded on the assumption that they were (see section 4.II); and

 (iv) there was an *'objective and reasonable' justification for the difference in treatment* of individuals in analogous positions, relying on the Danish state's margin of appreciation: in particular, the discrimination was proportionate to the legislator's aims of ensuring legal certainty and protecting the interests of the child, a conclusion reinforced by the absence of 'common [European] ground' as to how paternity proceedings should be regulated (on this fourth element to the Court's approach to Article 14, see section 5).

---

[12] *Dudgeon v UK*, para 69. However, note the dissent of Judge Matscher.
[13] 1999-III; 29 EHRR 615 GC. Cf *Hermann v Germany* hudoc (2012) GC concerning the same issue where the Grand Chamber, unlike the Chamber, did not consider it necessary to examine the matter under Article 14.   [14] 2004-V; 41 EHRR 164 para 35.
[15] For an earlier example, see *Marckx v Belgium* A31 (1979); 2 EHRR 330 PC (illegitimacy).
[16] On Article 14 in this context more generally, see Sandland, 8 HRLR 475 (2008).
[17] A 87 (1984); 7 EHRR 371.

As a result, the Court decided in the *Rasmussen* case that there was no violation of Article 14 of the Convention taken with another right.[18]

In more recent case law, the Court has simply stated that discrimination means 'treating differently, without an objective and reasonable justification, persons in relevantly similar situations'.[19] As the jurisprudence evidences, however, the relevance of Article 14 is not confined to discrimination on the state's part; the state also has a positive obligation to protect against private discrimination.[20] As regards indirect discrimination, the Court has accepted that 'a general policy or measure that has disproportionately prejudicial effects on a particular group may be considered discriminatory notwithstanding that it is not specifically aimed at that group ... and that discrimination potentially contrary to the Convention may result from a *de facto* situation'.[21] Furthermore, as regards affirmative action, the Court has also pointed out, 'Article 14 does not prohibit a member state from treating groups differently in order to correct "factual inequalities" between them; indeed in certain circumstances a failure to attempt to correct inequality through different treatment may in itself give rise to a breach of the Article'.[22]

3. PROTECTION FOR GUARANTEED RIGHTS ONLY AND THE AMBIT TEST

The 'reach' of Article 14 is restricted to discrimination *only with respect to the rights and freedoms set out elsewhere in the Convention*.[23] So, as a 'parasitic' provision Article 14 is not a general proscription against every kind of discrimination.[24] Where a right falls outside the Convention, such as the right of access to civil service employment,[25] a state has no obligation to avoid discrimination. In practice, this is a significant restriction because a great deal of discrimination law is concerned with the enjoyment of economic and social rights, such as rights to employment or to pay and working conditions or to housing, none of which are the direct concerns of the Convention.[26]

---

[18] For the UK courts' approach to the Article 14 tests and criticism thereof, see Baker, 2006 PL 476.

[19] *Zarb Adami v Malta* hudoc 2006 -VIII; 44 EHRR 49 para 71 (citing *Willis v UK* 2002-IV; 35 EHRR 547 para 48).

[20] See *97 members of the Gldani Congregation of Jehovah's Witnesses and 4 Others v Georgia* hudoc (2007) (failure to protect from attacks by extremist groups) and section 8.II of this chapter.

[21] *DH and Others v Czech Republic* 2007-VIII para 175 GC; also *Oršuš and Others v Croatia* hudoc (2010) GC; 52 EHRR 300; *Sampanis and Others v Greece* hudoc (2008).

[22] *DH and Others v Czech Republic*; *Thlimmenos v Greece* 2000-IV; 31 EHRR 411 para 44; and *Stec and Others v UK* GC hudoc (2006); 43 EHRR 1017 para 51.

[23] Those Protocols to the Convention which contain new substantive rights all provide that they shall be regarded as additional rights to the Convention itself and, accordingly, persons are protected by Article 14 in the enjoyment of them: see Article 5, First Protocol; Article 6(1), Fourth Protocol; Article 6, Sixth Protocol; Article 7(1), Seventh Protocol; Article 5, Thirteenth Protocol.

[24] Cf Protocol 12 considered in section 11 later in this chapter.

[25] *Glasenapp v Germany* A 104 (1986); 9 EHRR 25 para 53 PC and *Kosiek v Germany* A 105 (1986); 9 EHRR 328 para 39 PC.

[26] Such rights are protected by the European Social Charter 1961, which has a non-discrimination provision in its Preamble. See also Additional Protocol to the European Social Charter 1988, Article 1 (Right to equal opportunities and equal treatment in matters of employment and occupation without discrimination on the grounds of sex). Article 8 of the Convention has some application to housing. On the Convention and economic, social, and cultural rights see Warbrick, *Economic Social and Cultural Rights in Action*, 2007, ch 10. Cf *Andrejeva v Latvia* GC hudoc (2009) GC; 51 EHRR 650 and *Carson and Others v UK* hudoc (2010) GC, both concerning pension rights.

Subject to this limitation, the Court has generally approached the application and interpretation of Article 14 in an effective way. In particular, an applicant may establish a violation of Article 14, even though he cannot show or does not even claim a violation of another Article,[27] provided that the claim falls 'within the ambit' of a Convention right. This is possible as the Court has held that 'the notion of discrimination includes in general cases where a person or group is treated, without proper justification, less favourably than another, even though the more favourable treatment is not called for by the Convention'.[28] Put another way:

[t]he prohibition of discrimination enshrined in Article 14 ...extends beyond the enjoyment of the rights and freedoms which the Convention and the Protocols thereto require each State to guarantee. It applies also to those additional rights, falling within the general scope of any Convention Article, for which the State has voluntarily decided to provide.[29]

Hence in the *Belgian Linguistic* case,[30] where one of the complaints was about the right of access to language-based state education, it was accepted that the Convention does not require a state to provide *any* system of education but that, if it did, it may not restrict access to it on a discriminatory basis.[31] The principle then is that a state which goes beyond its obligations under a Convention right should do so in a non-discriminatory way. Thus, whilst the right to adopt is not covered by Article 8 taken alone,[32] French law permits adoption by single persons, so in *EB v France*[33] and *Fretté v France*,[34] the Court considered the ambit test satisfied, and went on to examine the claim of discrimination based on sexual orientation.[35] The practical significance of the Court's 'ambit test' approach is illustrated by case law on welfare benefits. For example, in *Stummer v Austria*,[36] the Court noted that Article 14 places no restriction on a state's freedom to decide whether to have a social security regime or to choose the level of benefits under such a scheme. But if the state has chosen to adopt legislation providing for welfare benefits, such legislation, irrespective of whether the scheme is a contributory one, generates a proprietary interest falling within the ambit of Article 1 Protocol 1.[37] The relevant test, in cases concerning property rights, is whether, but for the discriminatory ground about which the applicant complains, he would have an enforceable right under domestic law in respect of the asset or benefit in question.[38]

[27] See *Belgian Linguistic* case B 3 (1965) para 400 Com Rep. Cf the Court judgment: A 6 (1968); 1 EHRR 252 PC.

[28] *Zarb Adami v Malta* 2006-VIII; 44 EHRR 49 para 73 (citing *Abdulaziz, Cabales and Balkandali v UK* A 94 (1985); 7 EHRR 163 para 82 PC). See also *Delcourt v Belgium* A 11 (1970); 1 EHRR 355.

[29] *EB v France* hudoc (2008) para 48 GC.   [30] A 6 (1968); 1 EHRR 252 para 9 PC.

[31] *Belgian Linguistic* case, para 9. Cf *Skender v Former Yugoslav Republic of Macedonia* No 62059/00 hudoc (2001) DA.

[32] *EB v France* hudoc (2008) paras 41–6 GC. See, however, the dissenting opinion of Judge Mularoni.

[33] Hudoc (2008).   [34] 2002-I; 38 EHRR 438.

[35] See section 6.VI of this chapter. In *EB v France* the Grand Chamber held that the applicant's case 'undoubtedly' (para 49) fell within the ambit of Article 8 for the purposes of the Article 14 claim. The Court was clear that it was not called upon to decide whether the right to adopt fell 'within the ambit of Article 8...taken alone' (para 46); cf Judge Mularoni's dissenting opinion in *EB* and the earlier case of *Fretté v France* 2002-I; 38 EHRR 438 (especially the separate opinion of Sir Nicolas Bratza and Judges Fuhrman and Tulkens, and the partly concurring opinion of Judge Costa (joined by Judges Jungwiert and Traja)).

[36] Hudoc (2011) GC.   [37] *Stummer v Austria*, para 82, in the same vein.

[38] *Fabris v France* hudoc (2013) para 52 GC; also *Andrejeva v Latvia* hudoc (2009) paras 76–9 GC; *Stec v UK* hudoc (2005) GC; 41 EHRR 295 paras 54–5.

4. DIFFERENTIAL TREATMENT ON
A PROHIBITED GROUND

Assuming that the alleged ill-treatment falls within the ambit of a Convention right, the next issue to be considered is whether there has been a difference of treatment in fact and whether this has been on a ground prohibited by Article 14 of the Convention.

I. IDENTIFYING DIFFERENTIAL TREATMENT

In the typical discrimination case, the applicant will claim that he has been treated differently from others who, though in a similar position to him, are treated better.[39] However if, ordinarily, this question is not troublesome, there are circumstances where the applicant and the state are not in agreement as to whether or not there is differential treatment. In *Schmidt v Germany*,[40] for example, the applicant was a man who had had to pay a levy as an alternative obligation to serving in his local fire brigade. All men were potential firemen but women were not. Accordingly, women never had an obligation to pay the levy. Schmidt's complaint was that he was a victim of different treatment on the basis of his sex. But what was the different treatment? A majority of the Court, taking into account the fact that no man was ever obliged to serve in a fire brigade because the fire service was never short of volunteers, considered that the different treatment was the payment of the levy. There was no justification for taxing men and women differently by reason of their sex alone.[41] That being the case, it is somewhat surprising that these judges thought that Schmidt had been discriminated against with respect to Article 4(3)(d), work or service which forms part of normal civic obligations, rather than with respect to Article 1 of the First Protocol, which protects the right to property.[42] Two of the dissenting judges[43] said that the different treatment was with respect to the obligation to serve in the fire service. The distinction the state made was not primarily between men and women but between those who were fit to serve and those who were not.

The reasons given by the state for a difference of treatment by decision or in legislation may be challenged by the applicant as not being the 'real' reason for distinguishing him from others. Thus in *EB v France*,[44] it had been argued by the government that the applicant lesbian had been denied permission to adopt because the child would lack a father figure and not because of her sexual orientation. The Court decided otherwise after a detailed scrutiny of the domestic decisions which, taken in their entirety, revealed a difference of treatment based on her sexual lifestyle.[45]

---

[39] *Van der Mussele v Belgium* A 70 (1983); 6 EHRR 163 para 46 PC.

[40] A 291-B (1994); 1 EHRR 632 (cf the comments made about this case in the separate opinions annexed to *Zarb Adami v Malta* 2006-VIII; 44 EHRR 49). As another example, see *Dahlab v Switzerland No 42393/98*, 2001-V (inadmissible). Cf *Kara v UK No 36528/97* hudoc (1998) DA (concerning alleged discrimination regarding different dress codes for men and women at work imposed by a council; inadmissible).

[41] *Schmidt v Germany*, para 28.   [42] *Schmidt v Germany*, para 28.

[43] Judges Alphonse Spielmann and Gotchev, dissenting.   [44] Hudoc (2008) GC; 47 EHRR 21.

[45] *EB v France*, paras 80–9; cf *PV v Spain* hudoc (2010), where the Court considered that the real reasons for a custody decision was not the applicant's transsexualism but the court's assessment of the best interests of the child. Also *Bączkowski and Others v Poland* hudoc (2007), where the Court found that homophobia lay behind a decision to ban a march and not public order considerations. Also *Hoffman v Austria* A 255-C (1993); 14 EHRR 437 paras 33 and 36.

II. NO DISCRIMINATION IF SITUATIONS ARE NOT ANALOGOUS

The state only has to justify preferential treatment if situations are analogous, that is to say 'persons in relevantly similar situations'.[46] So an applicant will need to avoid the Court being able to conclude that his or her position (and the position of people like him or her) cannot be said to be similar to, that is 'analogous' to, the situation of people in the group he or she has identified as enjoying more favourable treatment. This was so in *Burden and Burden v UK*,[47] where two elderly (unmarried) sisters who had co-habited all their life and in the family home for the last thirty-one years claimed discrimination with respect to Article 1 of Protocol 1. Upon the death of one sister the survivor would have to pay inheritance tax (of 40 per cent) on their home, unlike married or Civil Partnership Act couples who benefited from exemptions. For the Court the relationship between siblings—based on consanguinity—was considered to be qualitatively different to that between married couples or homosexual civil partners. Moreover, the Court considered that marriage confers a special status to those who enter into it and gives rise to social, personal, and legal consequences. As the comparators were not analogous, the Grand Chamber did not go on to assess whether the difference of treatment could be justified.[48] Nor did the Court consider in *Carson* that non-residents in receipt of a UK pension were in a similar position to those resident in the UK who contributed to the UK economy and paid tax there.[49] However men seeking parental leave were in an analogous position to women, since the purpose of such leave was to enable parents to stay at home to look after the infant.[50] Similarly different categories of prisoners seeking release on parole were considered to be in comparable positions.[51]

The importance of this requirement is evident from such case law illustrating that, the Court will only examine complaints from applicants who are comparing like with like. However, this is another area of Article 14 that is difficult to apply[52] and which has given rise to conflicting views that determine the outcome.[53] Further, it has been noted that the

---

[46] *Zarb Adami v Malta* 2006-VIII; 44 EHRR 49 para 71.   [47] Hudoc (2008) GC paras 62–3.

[48] Cf the Chamber judgment which skipped over the analogous situation test yet found the difference of treatment justified, *Burden and Burden v UK* hudoc (2006); 44 EHRR 1023.

[49] Hudoc (2010) GC paras 86–9. The applicants complained that, unlike UK residents and pensioners living in countries with which the UK had concluded a bilateral agreement, their pensions were not index linked. On the latter point, the Court agreed with Lord Hoffmann that it would be extraordinary if the fact of entering into bilateral agreements in the social security sphere had the consequence of creating an obligation to confer the same advantages on all others living in all other countries: para 89. See also *Pichkur v Ukraine* hudoc (2013) (non-payment of pension because the applicant had left Ukraine; violation) and *Tarkoev v Estonia* hudoc (2010).

[50] *Konstantin Markin v Russia* hudoc (2012) GC para 132. The applicant soldier was denied parental leave. The Court found a violation of Article 14 in conjunction with Article 8. See also *Kiyutin v Russia* hudoc (2011) paras 59–61; 53 EHRR 897.

[51] *Clift v UK* hudoc (2010) paras 66–8. Prisoners sentenced to more than eighteen years required the approval of the Secretary of State before they could be released on parole. No such permission was required of those sentenced to less than fifteen years or those sentenced to life imprisonment. The Court found a violation of Article 14 in conjunction with Article 5; *Laduna v Slovakia* hudoc (2011) (distinctions between remand prisoners and convicted prisoners as regards visiting rights in prison). It also found a violation (no reasonable justification) where only convicted prisoners were entitled to conjugal visits but not remand prisoners: *Varnas v Lithuania* hudoc (2013). See, for a discussion of other cases, *Handbook*, pp 23–5.

[52] See Baker, PL 476 (2006).

[53] See, eg, the different approaches taken by the Commission and Court in *Stubbings v UK* 1996-IV; 23 EHRR 213 para 73. Also the dissenting opinions on this issue in *Burden and Burden v UK* and *Carson v UK* nn 48 and 49.

Court sometimes glosses over the analogous situation test and collapses it into the issue of whether there can be a *justification* for the differentiation.[54]

III. OBLIGATION TO TREAT DIFFERENTLY PERSONS WHOSE SITUATIONS ARE SIGNIFICANTLY DIFFERENT

In *Thlimmenos v Greece*,[55] the Grand Chamber stressed that '[t]he right not to be discriminated against in the enjoyment of the rights guaranteed under the Convention is also violated when states without an objective and reasonable justification fail to treat differently persons whose situations are significantly different'.[56] The Greek Institute of Chartered Accountants had refused to appoint the applicant, a Jehovah's Witness, on account of his prior conviction for insubordination (failing to wear military uniform). It was the applicant's case that the Institute should have distinguished his conviction from other convictions because it had stemmed from the exercise of his religious belief. The Court accepted this argument and concluded that the failure to treat the applicant differently was disproportionate and did not pursue a legitimate aim (leading to a violation of Article 9 in conjunction with Article 14). The principle has not been the subject of much Strasbourg case law, but it is of obvious relevance to those with particular physical handicaps, such as visual impairment or dyslexia, who can argue that their impairment should be taken into account when sitting examinations. It may also provide justification for special measures taken in respect of such persons or in respect of victims of past discrimination, such as minority groups or women.[57] The Court has indicated that Article 14 does not prohibit a state from treating groups differently in order to correct 'factual inequalities' between them and that in certain circumstances a failure to correct inequality through different treatment may give rise to a breach of this provision.[58] The exact scope of this principle, however, awaits elucidation in further cases.

IV. PROHIBITED GROUNDS (OR 'BADGES') OF DISCRIMINATION

Article 14 contains a long, and apparently non-exhaustive,[59] list of characteristics which might render differential treatment discriminatory, so identifying the 'badge' on the basis of which the differential treatment is made is not usually a problem. Furthermore these identified 'badges' are supplemented by an open-ended 'other status' category, which has

[54] Van Dijk and Van Hoof, p 1041.

[55] 2000-IV; 31 EHRR 411 GC; see also *Chapman v UK* 2001-I; 33 EHRR 399 para 129 GC.

[56] *Thlimmenos v Greece*, para 44. No indirect discrimination was found in *Chapman v UK* (applicants argued that domestic law failed to accommodate gypsies' traditional way of life as they were treated in the same way as the majority population) or *Pretty v UK* 2002-III; 35 EHRR 1 (applicant claimed blanket ban on assisted suicide was discriminatory on the facts given her particular disabilities; the application was rejected on this point on other grounds).

[57] See, eg, *Wintersberger v Austria* (friendly settlement) hudoc (2004), where the applicant complained unsuccessfully about the special employment protections afforded to those with disabilities. See the *Handbook*, pp 35–42 for a discussion of cases under EU law concerning reverse or positive discrimination.

[58] *Stummer v Austria* hudoc (2011) GC para 88 (citing *Andrejeva, Stec and Others* and *Thlimmenos*).

[59] The text reads 'any ground such as'. Article 14 may be compared to Article 21(1) of the Charter of Fundamental Rights of the European Union, which states 'Any discrimination based on any ground such as sex, race, colour, *ethnic* or social origin, *genetic features*, language, religion *or belief*, political or any other opinion, membership of a national minority, property, birth, *disability, age or sexual orientation* shall be prohibited' (emphasis added).

been held to include sexual orientation, marital status, illegitimacy, health, status as a trade union, military status, conscientious objection, professional status, and imprisonment. The Court has indicated that the words 'other status' will be given a wide meaning and may even include a distinction based on residence.[60] Financial status is a characteristic that has not been rejected peremptorily by the Court, but it did show some reluctance to address the claim in *Airey v Ireland*[61] that the applicant had been discriminated against by reason of her poverty. Article 14 forbids discrimination on the ground of 'property'. This is the most problematic of categories,[62] and a separate violation of Article 14 on this ground alone is rare.[63] In *Johnston v Ireland*,[64] the Court found that a lack of financial resources was not in fact the basis on which the applicants had been treated differently from others.

The Court has reiterated that Article 14 'is not concerned with all differences of treatment but only with differences having as their basis or reason a personal characteristic by which persons or group of persons are distinguishable from each other'.[65] So it may be argued that the term 'other status' should restrict the application of Article 14, as the specific grounds listed all relate to some sort of 'personal characteristic' of a potential victim.[66] But the case law suggests that this is too narrow an approach. In *Magee v UK*,[67] the applicant claimed a violation of Article 6(1) in conjunction with Article 14 regarding access to a lawyer. His point was that the different criminal regime operating in Northern Ireland entailed him obtaining access to his solicitor at a later stage than would have been the case on the UK mainland. The Court rejected the claim that there had been a violation of Article 14 read with Article 6, as the difference of treatment was 'not to be explained in terms of personal characteristics, such as national origin or association with a national minority, but on the geographical location where the individual is arrested and detained'.[68] The relevant legislation, the Court stated, took into account 'regional differences and characteristics of an objective and reasonable nature'. However the Court has subsequently indicated that 'status' is not limited to characteristics that are personal in the sense of being innate or inherently linked to the identity or personality of the individual, and in *Carson* the Court accepted that a place of residence constitutes an aspect of personal status for the purposes of Article 14. This is difficult to reconcile with the position taken by the Chamber in *Magee*,[69] although this case was distinguished in *Carson*.

Deciphering the limits to 'personal characteristic[s]' is thus not an easy exercise. In one case the Court implicitly accepted that the applicants' status as fisherman with rights to fish waters that became subject to fishing controls sufficed as a 'personal characteristic'.[70] In *Sidabras and Dziautas v Lithuania*,[71] the applicants' status as two former KGB agents

---

[60] *Carson v UK* hudoc (2010) GC para 70; *Topčić-Rosenberg v Croatia* hudoc (2013).

[61] A 32 (1979); 2 EHRR 305 paras 29–30.

[62] See Thornberry, 29 ICLQ 250 (1980) (on the *Airey* case). More generally, see Michelman, 83 Harv LR 7 (1969).

[63] Cf the rather different case of *Chassagnou and Others v France* 1999-III; 29 EHRR 615 and *Herrmann v Germany* hudoc (2012) GC.   [64] A 112 (1986); 27 EHRR 296 paras 59–61 PC.

[65] *Halis v Turkey No 30007/96* hudoc (2002) DA and *Jones v UK No 42639/04* hudoc (2005) DA (both citing *Kjeldsen, Busk Madsen and Pedersen v Denmark* A 23 (1976); 1 EHRR 711 para 56). For discussion of the matter of 'personal characteristic' before the UK courts, see *R v Secretary of State for Work and Pensions, ex p Carson* [2005] UKHL 37.

[66] *Dudgeon v UK* A 45 (1981); 4 EHRR 149 PC, see the separate opinion of Judge Matscher.

[67] 2000-VI; 31 EHRR 822.   [68] *Magee v UK*, para 50.

[69] *Carson v UK* hudoc (2010) GC. See also *Clift v UK* hudoc (2010). In *Stummer v Austria* hudoc (2011) GC para 90, the Court accepted that being a prisoner is an aspect of personal status for the purposes of Article 14.

[70] *Alatulkkila and Others v Finland* hudoc (2005) 43 EHRR 13.

[71] 2004-VIII; 42 EHRR 104; see also *Rainys and Gasparavičius v Lithuania* hudoc (2005).

seemed to suffice, as they complained that they had suffered discrimination (Article 8 with Article 14) since the law excluded them from certain private sector jobs.[72] As is noted later in this chapter, certain personal characteristics, such as race, sex, or birth status, ie those specifically mentioned in Article 14, will be treated more seriously than others ('other status') in the broader assessment of whether there has been discrimination in fact.

5. DIFFERENTIAL TREATMENT MAY BE JUSTIFIED ON OBJECTIVE AND REASONABLE GROUNDS

If there is differential treatment within the ambit of a protected right on a prohibited ground for the purposes of Article 14, the central issue becomes whether it can be justified or whether it should be stigmatized as discrimination. As the Court has put it in *Zarb Adami v Malta*,[73] 'Article 14 does not prohibit distinctions in treatment which are founded on an objective assessment of essentially different factual circumstances and which, being based on the public interest, strike a fair balance between the protection of the interests of the community and respect for the rights and freedoms safeguarded by the Convention'.[74]

I. THE TESTS SET IN THE *BELGIAN LINGUISTIC* CASE

The tests to be applied by the Court were set out in one of its earliest judgments: the *Belgian Linguistic* case.[75] First, the Court easily rejected the argument made on the basis of the French text that every difference of treatment in the exercise of Convention rights is excluded. It recognized the existence of a wide variety of national legislative and administrative regimes based on differential treatment which could well be seen to be for a good reason. As a result, a test had to be formulated to allow the distinction to be drawn between permissible differentiation and unlawful discrimination.[76] The resulting test embraces two elements: the identification of a legitimate aim for the different treatment, which is the obligation of the state; and an assessment of whether there is a 'reasonable relationship of proportionality' between the different treatment and the aim pursued, where it is for the applicant to 'clearly establish' the lack of proportionality.[77] In the *Belgian Linguistic* case, the Court also noted[78] that its role was not to put itself in the place of the national law-maker, but to exercise its subsidiary role of ensuring that national determinations were not incompatible with the Convention. Accordingly, it conceded to states a 'margin of appreciation' in making their assessments of what different treatment was proportionate to the legitimate objective they had chosen.

---

[72] See also the partial dissents of Judges Loucaides and Thomassen.

[73] 2006-VIII; 44 EHRR 49.   [74] *Zarb Adami v Malta*, para 73.

[75] A 6 (1968); 1 EHRR 252 PC. See Verhoeven, 23 RBDI 353 (1990).

[76] *Belgian Linguistic* case, para 10.   [77] See Eissen, *European Supervision*, ch 7, p 141.

[78] A 6 (1968); 1 EHRR 252 para 10 PC. For the most recent application of these principles, see *Fabris v France* hudoc (2013) GC; 57 EHRR 563 (differences in succession laws between legitimate and illegitimate children).

II. 'DIFFERENCE OF TREATMENT IN THE EXERCISE OF A RIGHT LAID DOWN IN THE CONVENTION MUST . . . PURSUE A LEGITIMATE AIM'

When the Court scrutinizes the differential treatment before it, if the government does not plead any justification for alleged discrimination then, other than exceptional circumstances, the applicant's claim of a violation will be made out.[79] If the government suggests an explanation, the justification which it gives must have a rational basis and an evidential foundation.

There is a tendency in the case law to accept the policy aims submitted by the government as legitimate. This is rarely a ground for disagreement between the parties, although in some cases the Court is half-hearted and tentative about its endorsement of the aim as being legitimate where there are question marks about its basis in fact or its discriminatory impact.[80] Needless to say, the fact that an aim is deemed by the Court to be legitimate does not mean that the Court considers that the difference in treatment can necessarily be justified. As it indicated in *Sedjić and Finci v Bosnia and Herzegovina*,[81] the exclusion of 'non-constituent peoples' from standing for election pursued at least one aim that was compatible with the Convention, namely the restoration of peace. Such an aim could explain, without necessarily justifying, the exclusion of the other communities such as the Jewish or Roma communities.[82]

Legitimate aims have included: in the *Belgian Linguistic* case, to achieve the effective implementation of the policy of developing linguistic unity of the two large language regions;[83] in the *Marckx v Belgium* case, to support and encourage the traditional family;[84] and in the *Fabris v France* case, to ensure the stability of completed inheritance arrangements.[85] In *Karner v Austria*,[86] which concerned differential treatment for homosexuals regarding succession to tenancies, again there were detailed submissions from both sides, but the Court accepted that protection of the family in the traditional sense is, in principle, a weighty and legitimate reason which might justify a difference in treatment.

It may be necessary for the state to demonstrate the proper link between the legitimate aim pursued and the differential treatment being challenged by the applicant.[87] Furthermore, the applicant may contest the authenticity of the government's

---

[79] *Darby v Sweden* is an example, A 187 (1990); 13 EHRR 774 para 33. The explanation for treating resident and non-resident non-nationals differently for the purposes of religious tax was administrative convenience, which the state declined to put by way of excuse to the Court. See also *Zarb Adami v Malta* 2006-VIII; 44 EHRR 49 para 82. By contrast see *Petrovic v Austria* 1998-II; 33 EHRR 307, where the Court conveniently avoided the legitimate aim test, proceeding to conclude that there was no Article 14 discrimination based on the proportionality test.

[80] See, eg, *Oršuš and Others v Croatia* hudoc (2010) GC para 157. The Court considered that temporary placement of children in separate classes on the grounds that they lack an adequate command of language could pass muster as a legitimate aim 'in certain circumstances' as an adaptation of the education system to the specific needs of the children.   [81] Hudoc (2009) GC para 45.

[82] *Sedjić and Finci v Bosnia and Herzegovina*, para 45. The applicants, of Jewish and Roma origin, could not stand as candidates for election to the House of Peoples (the second Chamber of the state parliament) and the Presidency (the collective Head of State). See the dissenting opinion of Judge Bonnello and, for a strong criticism of this judgment, McCrudden and O'Leary, *Courts and Consociations: Human Rights versus Power-Sharing*, 2013.   [83] A 6 (1968); 1 EHRR 252 para 7 PC.

[84] A 31 (1979); 2 EHRR 330 para 40 PC.

[85] Hudoc (2013) paras 64–6 GC. The Court did not accept, however, that denying the inheritance rights of family members could contribute to strengthening peaceful relations within a family: para 66.

[86] 2003-IX para 40; although the Court went on to find a violation.

[87] *Larkos v Cyprus* 1999-I; 30 EHRR 597.

explanation, so requiring the Court to adjudicate upon the argument.[88] In the *Abdulaziz* case, the applicants were able to show that the supposed reason for distinguishing between men and women, that they had a different effect on the labour market, was without factual basis.[89] The Court has made it clear that 'Contracting states enjoy a margin of appreciation in assessing whether and to what extent difference in otherwise similar situations justify a difference in treatment'.[90] However, as is noted later, the Court has identified certain types of differences of treatment, for example discrimination based exclusively on sex, that it will find justified only if 'very weighty reasons' have been put forward.

III. PROPORTIONALITY

As the Court stated in the *Belgian Linguistic* case,[91] differences in treatment between the members of the groups 'strike a fair balance between the protection of the interests of the community and respect for the rights and freedoms safeguarded by the Convention'. The test is whether it is established that there is in fact no reasonable relationship of proportionality between the means employed by the state and the legitimate aim that it is attempting to realize. In other words, this is an area where the Court will condemn arbitrary distinctions, but in their absence the public interest may provide a justification for some forms of differential treatment. Moreover, in assessing the issue of public interest, the Court will take account of the subsidiary nature of the Convention system of protection and pay due deference to the task of the domestic authorities: it 'cannot disregard those legal and factual features which characterise the life of the society in the state which, as a Contracting Party, has to answer for the measure in dispute'.[92]

As regards the margin of appreciation, in the context of Article 14 the Court has stated that its 'scope . . . will vary according to the circumstances, the subject matter and its background; in this respect, one of the relevant factors may be the existence or non-existence of common ground between the laws of the Contracting states'.[93] When 'general measures of economic or social strategy'[94] are in issue, the Court will grant a wide margin of appreciation. This has been so in some notable cases which have related to national taxation policy, where the Court has indicated that 'it is primarily for the state to decide how best to strike the balance between raising revenue and pursuing social objectives'.[95] The national authorities, because of their direct knowledge of their society and its needs are 'in principle better placed than the international judge to appreciate what is in the public

---

[88] In *Abdulaziz, Cabales and Balkandali v UK* A 94 (1985); 7 EHRR 163 PC.

[89] *Abdulaziz, Cabales and Balkandali v UK*, paras 74–83. But the Court rejected the applicant's argument that the immigration rules were racially motivated, paras 85–6.

[90] See, as recent examples, *L and V v Austria* 2003-I; 36 EHRR 1022 para 44; *Chassagnou v France* 1999-III; 29 EHRR 615 para 91 and *Stec and Others v UK* 2006-VI; 43 EHRR 1017 para 51 GC.

[91] A 6 (1968); 1 EHRR 252 para 7 PC. See also *G v Netherlands No 11850/85*, 51 DR 180 (1987), upholding a longer period of compulsory service for conscientious objectors than the period of military service for conscripts, to avoid too much opting out.   [92] *Belgian Linguistic* case, para 10.

[93] *Petrovic v Austria* 1998-II, 33 EHRR 307.

[94] *Burden v UK* hudoc (2008) para 60 GC (unmarried cohabiting family members' claimed discrimination (Article 1, First Protocol with Article 14) as they were liable to pay inheritance tax, unlike survivors of a marriage or a civil partnership).

[95] *Burden v UK* hudoc (2006); 44 EHRR 1023 para 60 (Chamber judgment). See also *Stec and Others v UK* (hudoc) 2006; 43 EHRR 1017 para 52 GC (differential regime between men and women for industrial injuries social security benefits).

interest on social or economic grounds and the Court will generally respect the legislature's policy choice unless it is "manifestly without reasonable foundation".[96]

As a general rule, the less evidence there is that the state's differential treatment departs from a common standard in the Convention states, the less likely the Court is to condemn it. For example, in *Rasmussen v Denmark*,[97] there was evidence that a Danish law distinguishing between husbands and wives in the matter of time limits applicable to paternity proceedings was not different to that in some other European states. Accordingly, the Court found that making the distinction fell within the state's margin of appreciation.[98] On the other hand in *Glor v Switzerland*,[99] the applicant whose disability had been assessed at 40 per cent was obliged to pay a tax for not serving in the army, whereas those with disabilities assessed at a higher level were exempted. The Court attached weight to the fact that the payment of such tax was uncommon in Europe and that there had been no possibility of challenging its proportionality in the light of his earnings or of doing alternative service. It found that there was a lack of fair balance between the public and private interests involved.[100] In the *Belgian Linguistic* case, with a single exception,[101] the Court found that the policies adopted by Belgium for promoting the language regions could be justified and did not impinge excessively on the rights of individuals.

One factor in assessing proportionality is the possibility of alternative means for achieving the same end. However, as the Court frequently asserts that it is not its function to substitute itself for the national decision-maker, the identification of an alternative will not be decisive. According to the Court in the *Rasmussen*[102] case, a state's margin of appreciation extends to choosing between alternatives. The fact that some schemes will have even a marked disparity in their impact on separate individuals will not be conclusive that the arrangements are disproportionate if the overall effect is achieved with reasonable tolerance.[103] In *James v UK*,[104] a scheme of leasehold enfranchisement aimed at protecting disadvantaged leaseholders in general produced windfall benefits for some tenants and large losses for some landlords, but these exceptional cases were not sufficient for the Court to condemn the whole deal. If a generous margin of appreciation is granted to the state (whether expressly or otherwise),[105] the impression may be gained that Strasbourg merely endorses the state's own conclusion in Article 14 case law.[106]

[96] *Carson and Others v UK* hudoc (2010) para 61 GC; also *Andrejeva v Latvia* hudoc (2009) para 83 GC; *Burden v UK* hudoc (2008) para 60 GC.

[97] A 87 (1984); 7 EHRR 371 para 41. See Helfer, 65 NYULR 1044 at 1075 (1990). On discrimination in contesting paternity and the need for proportionality, see also *Paulík v Slovakia* 2006-XI; 46 EHRR 142.

[98] See also *Petrovic v Austria* 1998-II; 33 EHRR 307.   [99] Hudoc (2009).

[100] *Glor v Switzerland*, paras 83–94.

[101] The Court held that there was no objective and reasonable justification for allowing Dutch-speaking children resident in the French language region to have access to Dutch language schools in the bilingual zone while French-speaking children resident in the Dutch language area were denied access to French language schools in the same zone: *Belgian Linguistic* case A 6 (1968); 1 EHRR 252 PC.

[102] A 87 (1984); 7 EHRR 371 para 41.

[103] See, eg, *Stubbings and Others v UK* Reports 1996 – IV paras 74–6, concerning different limitation periods for negligently inflicted injury and intentionally inflicted injury. Cf *Altinay v Turkey* hudoc (2013), where the Court found a change in the rules for access to university without any provision for transitional measures to be disproportionate to the aim of securing higher educational standards.

[104] A 98 (1986); 8 EHRR 123 para 77 PC.

[105] In recent years the Court has shown some inconsistency here.

[106] Eg *Gillow v UK* A 109 (1986); 11 EHRR 335 (concerning housing policy on a small island) and *National and Provincial Building Society and Others v UK* 1997-VII; 25 EHRR 127 (wide margin of appreciation for taxation policy).

However, recent Grand Chamber judgments demonstrate that the Court is prepared to find violations even when the margin is deemed to be a wide one.[107]

6. INTENSIVE SCRUTINY OF DIFFERENTIAL TREATMENT FOR 'SUSPECT CATEGORIES'

The notion of proportionality implies that the more serious the difference of treatment is deemed to be then the greater the reasons required from the state to justify it must be. Where (potentially) serious discrimination is at stake, usually the margin of appreciation owing to a state will be narrower and the disproportionality of the state's chosen means more easily condemned by evidence of practical alternatives.

The Court has identified differential treatment on the basis of certain badges as particularly serious, making them equivalent to 'suspect categories' in United States constitutional law.[108] In fact, the European Court has never used this terminology, but it has stated that certain types of differences of treatment can only to be justified if 'very strong or weighty reasons' or 'particularly serious reasons' have been put forward. This statement has been made in connection with differential treatment based on race, religion, sex (gender), nationality, sexual orientation, and illegitimacy.[109] In addition, 'very weighty reasons' have also to be shown by the state to justify differences of treatment of vulnerable members of society who have previously been the victims of discrimination, such as, *inter alios*, the disabled.[110]

These categories generally relate to those specifically set out in the text of Article 14 and to what might be broadly termed the 'right to respect for the individuality of a human being'.[111] They are issues that go to the core of the notion of equal treatment and so may be distinguished from other grounds as, for example, differentiation based on residence in a country or abroad,[112] and where considerations of general social policy may have a greater role in justifying differential treatment.

One might compare the 'suspect category' under Article 14 with the special weight given to interests (eg privacy in sexual matters) falling within the sphere of a protected Convention right.[113] Certainly there is a heavy burden on the state to justify differential treatment on such grounds. Yet there are some cases when the margin of appreciation doctrine has provided protection for the state, especially when no European consensus can be found or when 'general measures of economic or social strategy' are concerned.

I. RACE (OR ETHNIC ORIGIN)

As early as 1973, the Commission expressed the view that publicly to single out a group of persons for differential treatment on the basis of race might, in certain circumstances,[114]

---

[107] Eg *Kiyutin v Russia* hudoc (2011) GC; *Stummer v Austria* hudoc (2011) hudoc GC; *X and Others v Austria* hudoc (2013) GC; *Konstantin Markin v Russia* hudoc (2012) GC, *Fabris v France* hudoc (2013) GC; 51 EHRR 563   [108] Ely, *Democracy and Distrust: A Theory of Judicial Review*, 1980, pp 145–70.
[109] See also *Sahin v Germany*, section 6.VII of this chapter, regarding certain fathers' access to their children.   [110] *Alajos Kiss v Hungary* hudoc (2010) para 42.
[111] Lord Hoffmann in *R v Secretary of State for Work and Pensions, ex p Carson* [2005] UKHL 37 at para 17.
[112] Cf *R v Secretary of State for Work and Pensions, ex p Carson* [2005] UKHL 37, the same issues eventually being examined by the Court in *Carson v UK* hudoc (2010) GC.   [113] See Ch 12, section 4.IV.
[114] An indication of the general circumstances was given in *Abdulaziz, Cabales and Balkandali v UK* A 94 (1985); 7 EHRR 163 PC. In that case the immigration rules did not lead to a violation of Article 3 as '... the

constitute a special affront to human dignity amounting to degrading treatment in violation of Article 3.[115] Consistent with this, the Strasbourg jurisprudence indicates that a special importance should be attached to discrimination based on race[116] (or ethnic or national origin),[117] which the Court describes as 'a particularly invidious kind of discrimination … [that], in view of its perilous consequences, requires from the authorities special vigilance and a vigorous reaction'.[118] For this reason, the Court states, 'the authorities must use all available means to combat racism, thereby reinforcing democracy's vision of a society in which diversity is not perceived as a threat but as a source of enrichment'.[119]

Where a difference in treatment concerning the enjoyment of a Convention right is based on 'race, colour or ethnic origin', the Grand Chamber has stated that 'the notion of objective and reasonable justification must be interpreted as strictly as possible'.[120] In *Sejdić and Finci v Bosnia and Herzegovina*,[121] concerning a difference in treatment between the 'constituent peoples' and persons of Jewish and Roma origin, the Court expressed the view that 'no difference in treatment which is based exclusively or to a decisive extent on a person's ethnic origin is capable of being objectively justified in a contemporary democratic society built on the principles of pluralism and respect for different cultures'.[122] It might be asked whether such a broad principle could also apply to discrimination under other heads, for example religious belief?

Finally as is noted later,[123] there have been some important judgments regarding Article 14 with Articles 2 and 3 and concerning death and serious ill-treatment allegedly motivated by racial prejudice. The race context has also been important for key case law concerning indirect discrimination, for example in the field of education.[124]

II. NATIONALITY

As regards discrimination based on national origin, in *Gaygusuz v Austria*,[125] the Court made reference to a state's margin of appreciation but added that very weighty reasons

difference in treatment … did not denote any contempt or lack of respect for the personality of the applicants … it was not designed to, and did not, humiliate or debase them', para 91.

[115] See Ch 6, section 5.II.

[116] As regards race discrimination in Europe generally, see Goldston, 5 EHRLR 462 (1999). Details of the Council of Europe's '*European Commission against Racism and Intolerance*' can be found at http://www.coe.int/DefaultEN.asp.

[117] For the Court's understanding of these terms see *Timishev v Russia* hudoc (2005); 44 EHRR 776 para 55.

[118] *DH and Others v Czech Republic* hudoc (2007) para 176 GC. Also *Oršuš and Others v Croatia* hudoc (2010) para 149 GC; *Sampanis and others v Greece* hudoc (2008); all concerning discrimination against Roma in the area of schooling. [119] *DH and Others v Czech Republic* para 176.

[120] *DH and Others v Czech Republic*, para 196. [121] Hudoc (2009) GC.

[122] *Sejdić and Finci v Bosnia and Herzegovina*, para 44; also *Timishev v Russia* hudoc (2005) 44 EHRR 776 para 58, concerning a diffence of treatment between persons of Chechen and non-Chechen ethnic origin as regards the enjoyment of their right to liberty of movement; see also *Paraskeva Todorova v Bulgaria* hudoc (2010) (discrimination against a Roma accused by a sentencing judge); *Epstein and Others v Belgium* dec hudoc (2008) (special measures in favour of Jewish and Roma victims of World War II; inadmissible); *DH and Others v Czech Republic* hudoc 2007-IV GC; *Moldovan and Others v Romania (No 2)* hudoc (2005); 44 EHRR 302; *Cisse v France* No 51346/99, 2001-I DA (whether a system of identity checks in which only dark-skinned occupants are stopped and subsequently detained, may raise issues under Article 5 in conjunction with Article 14); *Gregory v UK* 1997-I; 25 EHRR 577 (alleged racial bias in the context of the right to a fair trial); *Reid v UK No 32350/96* hudoc (1997) DA (allegedly racist summing up remarks of judge in civil action;inadmissible); and *Čonka v Belgium No 51564/99* hudoc (2001) DA (Court rejected allegations of racial discrimination in the context of collective expulsion (Article 4 of the Fourth Protocol with Article 14).

[123] See section 8.I of this chapter. [124] See section 9 of this chapter.

[125] 1996-IV; 23 EHRR 364 para 42 (refusal to grant emergency social security assistance to non-national-violation). See also *Koua Poirrez v France* 2003-X 40 EHRR 2, where the applicant was denied

would have to be put forward to justify a difference of treatment based exclusively on the ground of nationality as compatible with the Convention.[126]

The leading case is *Andrejeva v Latvia*.[127] The applicant resided in Latvia since 1950 but was not a national. During the Soviet period she had worked for a state enterprise outside of Latvia. In calculating her retirement pension after Latvia had gained independence, the authorities refused to take account of her work outside Latvia and awarded her a considerably reduced pension. It was not disputed that a Latvian citizen in the same position as the applicant would be paid a full pension which took into account the periods worked in the USSR. The Court considered that the applicant was a victim of discrimination on the grounds of nationality and that there was no relationship of proportionality between the aim of protecting the country's economic system and the impugned difference in treatment, notwithstanding the state's wide margin of appreciation. The Court also rejected the argument that it was open to the applicant to become a naturalized citizen and receive the full pension. For the Court the prohibition of discrimination is meaningful only if, in each particular case, the applicant's personal situation is taken into account exactly as it stands. To proceed otherwise would, in the Court's view, render Article 14 devoid of substance.[128]

III. SEX (GENDER)

The Court established that discrimination based on 'sex' is a 'suspect category' in the *Abdulaziz* case.[129] In *Opuz v Turkey*,[130] the Court, in a landmark Chamber judgment, found a violation of Article 14 in conjunction with Articles 2 and 3 on the grounds that the criminal law system (the general attitude of the police when confronted with allegations of domestic violence and judicial passivity in providing effective protection to victims) did not provide sufficient protection to the applicant's mother who had been killed by a violent husband. It cited with approval the statement by the UN Committee on the Elimination of Discrimination against Women (CEDAW) that 'violence against women, including domestic violence is a form of discrimination against women'.[131] In *Eremia v Moldova*,[132] the Court also considered the reactions of the authorities to be discriminatory against the first applicant who drew repeated abuse to the attention of the authorities to little avail. The Court held that the authorities' reactions to repeated violence against

---

a disability allowance on the ground that he was not a French national or the national of a state with which the government had concluded a reciprocal agreement. The Court found a violation of Article 14 in conjunction with Article 1 Protocol 1.

[126] However, note Article 16 of the Convention and its implications. Of course, virtually all states make certain distinctions based on nationality concerning certain rights or entitlements to benefits in the immigration context, and the Court will frequently find that such complaints will not pass the analogous situation test: *Moustaqium v Belgium* A 193 (1991); 13 EHRR 802 para 49 (Belgian juveniles could not legally be deported whilst the Moroccan juvenile applicant could); cf *C v Belgium* 1996-III; 32 EHRR 19 para 38 (preferential treatment of EC nationals compared to non-EC nationals deemed objective and reasonable for purposes of Article 14). Cf *Biao v Denmark* hudoc (2014). The Court accepted the nationality requirement as regards entry to the legal profession: *Bigaeva v Greece* hudoc (2009). [127] Hudoc (2009) GC.

[128] *Andrejeva v Latvia*, paras 88–91. Latvia was the only state that could assume responsibility for her for purposes of social security. See also *Weller v Hungary* hudoc (2009) (where the applicants could not benefit from a maternity allowance since their father was a Hungarian and their mother a foreigner), the Court found a violation of Article 14 in conjunction with Article 8; also *Luczak v Poland* hudoc (2007); *Zeïbek v Greece* hudoc (2009); *Fawsie v Greece* hudoc (2010): all violations of Article 14.

[129] A 94 (1985); 7 EHRR 163 para 78 PC. [130] Hudoc (2009); 50 EHRR 659.

[131] *Opuz v Turkey*, paras 74, 187 and 199. See Ch 6, section 7. [132] Hudoc (2013).

the applicant was not a simple failure or delay in dealing with violence, but amounted to repeatedly condoning such violence and reflected a discriminatory attitude towards the first applicant as a woman.[133]

In *Ünal Tekeli v Turkey*,[134] the Court noted the emergence of a consensus among the contracting states of the Council of Europe in favour of allowing a spouse to choose whether her family name should remain her maiden name or be changed to that of her new husband. There had been a violation of Article 14 read with Article 8 in this case insofar as under Turkish law a woman could not bear her maiden name alone after marriage whereas married men could. The Court stated that the objective of reflecting family unity through a joint family name could not provide a justification for the gender-based difference in treatment complained of.

That the Court has found discrimination on the ground of 'sex' against women[135] and men[136] is illustrated by case law concerning lack of equality regarding financial benefits where Article 1 of the First Protocol usually has been in issue.[137] Here the Court reassures states that they have a margin of appreciation, but the principle is that exemptions or benefits should be applied even-handedly to both men and women unless 'compelling reasons' are adduced to justify a difference of treatment.[138] In *Stec v UK*,[139] the difference in state pensionable age between men and women in the UK, which was at the root of the applicants' claims concerning differences in the entitlement for men and women to certain industrial social security benefits, did not entail a violation of Article 1 of the First Protocol when read with Article 14. The difference of treatment was reasonably and objectively justified in that it was intended to correct the disadvantaged economic position of women. Also, whilst measures were being taken to remove the difference in treatment, the state concerned benefited from a wide margin of appreciation given that, amongst other things, general measures of economic or social strategy were concerned and in many European states there remained a difference in the ages at which men and women become eligible for the state retirement pension.[140] *Petrovic v Austria*[141] illustrates the potential problems that could be associated with an insistence on even-handedness in all circumstances, as well as the speed of societal developments in this area. It concerned parental leave allowances which were paid only to mothers, not fathers. The Court stressed that the margin of appreciation was broad in this case, such that there was no violation of Article 14

---

[133] *Eremia v Moldova*, paras 85–91.   [134] Hudoc (2004); 42 EHRR 1185 para 61.

[135] Eg *Wessels-Bergervoet v Netherlands* 2002-IV; 38 EHRR 793 (differential treatment of married women under pension legislation).

[136] Eg *Schmidt v Germany* A 291-B (1994); 18 EHRR 523; *Burghartz v Switzerland* A 280-B (1994); 18 EHRR 101 paras 25–30; and *Zarb Adami v Malta* hudoc (2006), concerning the negligible number of women called for jury service; 44 EHRR 49; also *Spöttl v Austria No 22956/93* hudoc (1996); 22 EHRR 88 DA.

[137] Eg *Van Raalte v Netherlands* 1997-I; 24 EHRR 503. There have been many UK-originated complaints both before the domestic courts (post the Human Rights Act 1998) and before Strasbourg regarding discrimination and social security provision; see, eg, *Willis v UK* 2002-IV; 35 EHRR 547 (sex discrimination in connection with claim for Widow's Payment Allowance). An application alleging sex discrimination given the differing retirement ages of men and women in the UK was declared inadmissible for lack of victim status on the basis that the applicant received the same amount in state benefits as would a woman of the same age in his position: *Bland v UK No 52301/99* hudoc (2002) DA. A friendly settlement was reached in a case when sex discrimination had been alleged because the applicant had been denied an elderly person's bus permit when aged sixty-four even though a women could obtain the same at sixty: *Matthews v UK No 40302/98* hudoc (2002) (F Sett).   [138] *Van Raalte v Netherlands* 1997-I; 24 EHRR 503 para 42.

[139] *Stec and Others v UK* hudoc (2006); 43 EHRR 1017 GC. See also *Andrle v Czech Republic* hudoc (2011) concerning a similar issue.   [140] *Stec and Others v UK*, paras 61–5.

[141] 1998-II; 33 EHRR 307. *Spöttl v Austria No 22956/93* hudoc (1996); 22 EHRR 88 DA, concerning military service being confined to men only (Article 4 with Article 14; inadmissible)

read with Article 8, given the absence at the material time of a 'common standard in this field, as the majority of Contracting states did not provide for parental leave allowances to be paid to fathers'[142] (indeed there was 'a very great disparity between the legal systems of the Contracting states in this field').[143] It is doubtful whether this is still good law today given the social progress that has been made in this area throughout Europe, as the Court has noted in *Konstantin Markin v Russia*,[144] which concerned a complaint by a soldier that, unlike women recruits, he was not entitled to parental leave. The Court observed that a majority of European countries, including Russia, provide that parental leave may be taken by civilian men and women.[145] The Court considered that the difference in question had the effect of perpetuating gender stereotypes and is disadvantageous both to women's careers and to men's family life.[146] It was not impressed by the argument that Russian society was not yet ready to accept equality between men and women serving in the armed forces or that there would be a risk to the operational effectiveness of the army if parental leave was granted to men—the argument not having been substantiated by specific examples.[147] It accepted, however, that it may be justified to exclude 'any personnel, male or female, who may not easily be replaced in their duties owing to such factors as, for example, their hierarchical position, rare technical qualifications or involvement in active military actions'.[148]

IV. BIRTH

Another suspect category is discrimination based on birth status, in particular 'illegitimacy'. Here, with respect to succession matters such as the exclusion of illegitimate children on an intestacy, the principle that children should be treated equally regardless of their descent has been firmly established in the Strasbourg jurisprudence.[149]

In the *Marckx* case[150] the Court found that the reasons for treating the 'illegitimate' mother and child differently from the legitimate mother and child were not sufficiently supported in fact or, even if generally true, imposed too big a burden on those 'illegitimate' mothers and children which did not fit the state's stereotype. In relation to the different processes by which legitimate and 'illegitimate' mothers had to establish the affiliation of their children, the government said, *inter alia*, that they were justified because legitimate mothers were more likely to accept the responsibilities of motherhood than 'illegitimate' mothers. The Court found this unsustainable. The government had provided no evidence to support its general assertions and it clearly was not true that all 'illegitimate' mothers were susceptible to abandoning their children.[151]

---

[142] *Petrovic v Austria*, para 39.   [143] *Petrovic v Austria*, para 42.   [144] Hudoc (2012) GC.

[145] *Konstantin Markin v Russia*, para 140.   [146] *Konstantin Markin v Russia*, para 141.

[147] *Konstantin Markin v Russia*, paras 142–3. The Court added that 'gender stereotypes, such as the perception of women as primary child-carers and men as primary breadwinners, cannot, by themselves, be considered to amount to sufficient justification for a difference in treatment, any more than similar stereotypes based on race, origin colour or sexual orientation: para 143. It also indicated that further restrictions on grounds of national security may be justified provided they were not discriminatory: para 147.

[148] See Malksoo, 106 AJIL 4 at 836–42 (2012).

[149] *Inze v Austria* A 126 (1987); 10 EHRR 394 para 41. Reference was made to the 1975 European Convention on the Legal Status of Children born out of Wedlock. ETS 85; UKTS 43 (1981), Cmnd 8287.

[150] *Marckx v Belgium* A 31 (1979); 2 EHRR 330 PC.

[151] *Marckx v Belgium*, paras 38–9. See also the later case of *Vermeire v Belgium* A 214-C (1991) and *Johnston and Others v Ireland* A 112 (1986); 15 EHRR 313. As regards the exclusion of an adopted child from inheritance, see *Pla and Puncernau v Andorra* 2004-VIII; 42 EHRR 522.

The leading cases on illegitimacy and succession remain the 'old court' judgments in *Inze v Austria* and, before that, *Marckx v Belgium*,[152] but even in the new millennium the Court has still been addressing cases of discrimination under this head from long-standing Convention member states.[153] *Pla and Puncernau v Andorra*[154] is notable, as the violation of Article 14 stemmed not from domestic legislation but the domestic court's interpretation of a will dating from 1939. This had stipulated that the estate was to pass to a son or grandson of a lawful and canonical marriage. The domestic courts had assessed the intention of the testatrix and interpreted the clause in question so as to exclude application to the applicant adopted child. The Court emphasized the Convention's character as a living instrument and the importance attached to eradicating discrimination based on birth out of wedlock.

In the Grand Chamber case of *Fabris v France*,[155] the Court examined the Law of 2001 (which had been introduced to give effect to the *Mazurek* judgment). However this law restricted application of the new inheritance rights of 'children born of adultery' to successions opened prior to 4 December 2001 that had not given rise to division before that date. The Court found a violation of Article 14 in conjunction with Article 1 Protocol 1, holding that protecting the legitimate expectation of the deceased and their families must be subordinated to the imperative of equal treatment between legitimate and illegitimate children. It should be noted that this judgment turns on its rather particular facts. It suggests that had the applicant's half-brother and sister not been aware of his existence or had his filiation only been established after the division of the property, a reasonable relationship of proportionality would have existed.[156]

V. RELIGION

Hoffman v Austria[157] concerned parental rights with respect to children, the Court stating that '[n]otwithstanding any possible arguments to the contrary, a distinction based essentially on a difference in religion alone is not acceptable'. As noted earlier,[158] this case had concerned alleged discrimination against the applicant who was a Jehovah's Witness. In *Vojnity v Austria*,[159] the Court found that the withdrawal of all access rights from a father on the grounds that he sought to communicate his religious beliefs to his child was disproportionate. It noted that Article 2 of Protocol 1 conveyed on parents the right

---

[152] A 126 (1987) and A 31 (1979); 2 EHRR 330 PC.

[153] See *Mazurek v France* 2000-II; 42 EHRR 170; *Merger and Cros v France* hudoc (2004); 43 EHRR 1103; and *Camp and Bourimi v Netherlands* 2000-X; 34 EHRR 1446. Cf *Haas v Netherlands* 2004-I; 39 EHRR 897; *Genovese v Malta* hudoc (2011) (denial of citizenship on ground of illegitimacy; violation); *Brauer v Germany* hudoc (2009); 51 EHRR 574 (legislation recognizing the inheritance rights of illegitimate children did not apply to children born before 1949; violation); *Zaunegger v Germany* hudoc (2009) (father of illegitimate child needing consent of mother before joint custody can be granted; violation).

[154] 2004-VIII; 42 EHRR 522. See the cogent dissent by Judges Bratza and Garlicki.

[155] Hudoc (2013) GC; 57 EHRR 563.

[156] See, in this connection, the inadmissibility decision in *Alboize-Barthes and Alboize-Montzume v France* dec hudoc (2008), where the estate had been wound up long before filiation was established. However, the Court indicated that an issue could arise concerning the relevant legislation and Protocol 12 which France has not ratified.

[157] A 255-C (1993); 14 EHRR 437 para 36 (the Court was split five votes to four in this judgment and several dissenting opinions were attached). See also *Palau-Martinez v France* 2003-XII; 41 EHRR 136 and *Ismailova v Russia* hudoc (2007). [158] See Ch 13, section 7.

[159] Hudoc (2013).

to communicate and promote their religious convictions in their children's upbringing. Such a right would be uncontested in the case of two married parents sharing the same religious ideas or worldview and promoting them to their child unless it exposed them to dangerous practices or physical or psychological harm. The Court saw no reason why the position of a separated or divorced parent who did not have custody of his or her child should be different.[160]

The right to freedom of religion is protected by Article 9 of the Convention and there is of course a potential distinction to be made between discrimination with respect to the enjoyment of a Convention right based on religion[161] and discrimination regarding the enjoyment of the right to freedom of religion itself.[162] As regards the latter, the establishment of delicate relations between the Church and state may bring a margin of appreciation into play.[163] When those relations involve preferential treatment to one religion over another, the Court has tended to find a violation.[164] In the recent case of *Eweida and Others v UK*,[165] the Court endorsed the right to wear religious symbols (such as crosses) where they did not give rise to health or safety concerns. In the case of one applicant, it found that too much weight had been attached to the projection of a certain corporate image by the employer (British Airways) to the detriment of the applicant's religious beliefs. On the other hand, it found no violation of Article 14 in conjunction with Article 9 in the case of a Registrar of marriages who lost her job because she refused to officiate in same-sex marriages, finding that the local authority's policy of prioritizing the rights of others to marry fell within the margin of appreciation. A similar finding was recorded in respect of an applicant who had refused to provide counselling to same-sex couples. Of particular interest in this judgment is the finding that the decision to enter into a contract of employment and to undertake responsibilities which the person knows will have an impact on his religious beliefs is not determinative of the question whether there has been an interference with the right to freedom of religion or the right not to be discriminated against.[166]

---

[160] *Vojnity v Austria*, paras 36–9; there was no evidence of psychological harm.

[161] Eg *Canea Catholic Church v Greece* 1997-VIII; 27 EHRR 521; also *Sâmbata Bihor Greek Catholic Parish v Romania* hudoc (2010).

[162] The need to identify a claim as one of genuine discrimination regarding enjoyment of Article 9 can be important, as is illustrated by *Dahlab v Switzerland* 2001-V, discussed in Ch 13, section 5.III.a; also *Stedman v UK No 29107/95* hudoc (1997); 23 EHRR CD 168. Further, the limited scope of Article 9 and the fact that an applicant is not actually treated any differently from others may be fatal to Article 9 discrimination applications. Hence, Article 9 does not cover the right to take certain days off work in order to worship for religious reasons and this has meant that certain applications have failed at admissibility: eg, *Ahmad v UK No 8160/78*, 22 DR 27 (1981); 4 EHRR 126 and *Konttinen v Finland No 24949/94*, 87-A DR 68 (1996). If the state were to grant time off for one religion but not others, then Article 9 in conjunction with Article 14 could come into play. But provided all are treated the same there is no discrimination.

[163] See, eg, *Cha'are Shalom ve Tsedek v France* 2000-VII GC. Also *Mouvement Raëlien v Switzerland* hudoc GC (2012).

[164] See *Manzanas Martin v Spain* hudoc (2012), where the state afforded rights to Catholic priests to have a full pension but not to members of the Evangelical church (violation); also *O'Donoghue v UK* hudoc (2010), where persons subject to immigration control who wished to marry but were not able or not willing to do so under the Church of England rites had to apply for a certificate of approval from the Secretary of State for which a fee had to be paid (violation); *Religionsgemeinschaft der Zeugen Jehovas and Others v Austria* hudoc (2008); 48 EHRR 424, discrimination against Jehovah's Witnesses who were required to wait ten years for registration as a religious society (violation).   [165] Hudoc (2013); 50 EHRR 213.

[166] *Eweida and Others v UK*, paras 94–5, 98, 105–6, 109.

VI. SEXUAL ORIENTATION

There have been considerable advances in the Strasbourg jurisprudence in this field, which has undergone a significant evolution.[167] *Smith and Grady v UK*,[168] the so-called 'gays in the military' case, where the Court found a violation of Article 8, arguably marked the start of a fresh approach, even though the Court did not address Article 14 issues in that case.[169]

It is perhaps surprising that it was not until 1999 and the case of *Salgueiro da Silva Mouta v Portugal*[170] that the Court found a violation of Article 14 in conjunction with another Article (Article 8) in a case concerning sexual orientation. The applicant's homosexuality was a decisive factor in the domestic court's decision to award parental responsibility for his daughter to his ex-wife rather than to himself, a distinction which the Court stated was 'not acceptable under the Convention'.[171] Before this, in 1997, the Convention's quality as 'a living instrument' was cited when the Commission for the first time condemned differences in the criminal law as regards the age of consent to enter sexual relations for homosexuals as opposed to heterosexuals.[172] The Court showed its approval of this authority in *L and V v Austria*[173] in 2003 when it stated that '[j]ust like differences based on sex... differences based on sexual orientation require particularly serious reasons by way of justification'[174] for the purposes of Article 14. It warned that if the laws permitting differing age of consent 'embodied a predisposed bias on the part of a heterosexual majority against a homosexual minority, these negative attitudes cannot of themselves be considered by [the Court] to amount to sufficient justification for the differential treatment any more than similar negative attitudes towards those of a different race, origin or colour'.[175]

Karner v Austria,[176] which concerned the housing rights of same-sex partnerships, was also delivered in 2003.[177] The domestic courts had denied the homosexual applicant the status of 'life companion' with respect to his late partner, thereby preventing him from succeeding to his tenancy. After noting that there was an emerging European consensus in favour of the applicant, the Court concluded that insufficient reasons had been advanced by the respondent state and found a violation of Article 8 in conjunction with Article 14.[178]

---

[167] See Johnston, *Homosexuality and the European Court of Human Rights*, 2012; Commissioner for Human Rights, *Discrimination on Grounds of Sexual Orientation and Gender Identity in Europe*, 2nd edn, 2011. Helfer 95 AJIL 422 (2001). It is clear that 'sexual orientation' is covered by Article 14, though not whether it is always to be so through the label of 'sex' (cf the UN Human Rights Committee, in *Toonen v Australia* decision of 4 April 1994) or 'other status' (as employed by European Commission of Human Rights, *Sutherland v UK* hudoc (1997) para 51 Com Rep).

[168] 1999-VI; 29 EHRR 493, see Ch 12, section 4.IV.

[169] *Smith and Grady v UK*, para 121. Other leading judgments concerning human rights and homosexuality, when Article 14 has not necessarily been addressed by the Court, include *Dudgeon v UK* A 45 (1981); 4 EHRR 149 PC; *Norris v Ireland* A 142; 13 EHRR 186 PC; *Modinos v Cyprus* A 259; 16 EHRR 485; *Laskey, Jaggard and Brown v UK* 1997-I; 24 EHRR 39; and *ADT v UK* 2000-IX; 31 EHRR 803.

[170] 1999-IX; 31 EHRR 1055.   [171] *Salgueiro da Silva Mouta v Portugal*, para 36.

[172] *Sutherland v UK* hudoc (1997) Com Rep, and judgment (striking off list) hudoc (2001). Cf *BB v UK* hudoc (2004); 39 EHRR 635.

[173] 2003-I; 36 EHRR 1022. The Court noted that it was not contested that there was 'an ever growing European consensus to apply equal ages of consent for heterosexual, lesbian and homosexual relations', para 50.   [174] *L and V v Austria*, para 45.

[175] *L and V v Austria*, para 52; also *EB and Others v Austria* hudoc (2013) (refusal to amend the criminal record of person convicted under the impugned age of consent legislation; violation).

[176] 2003-IX; 38 EHRR 528. See also *PB and JS v Austria No 18984/02* hudoc 2008 DA (judgment pending) (allegations of discrimination as homosexual partner excluded from insurance cover for 'dependants').

[177] Cf *Mendoza v Ghaidan* [2004] UKHL 30.

[178] *Karner v Austria* 2003-IX; 38 EHRR 528 para 41.

The Grand Chamber's ruling in *EB v France*[179] is probably the most significant case yet in the field of Article 14 and sexual orientation. The applicant, who was in a lesbian relationship, had been refused authorization to adopt as a single person; she claimed she had been discriminated against on grounds of her sexuality. Crucially, French law permitted adoption by single persons, so the case fell within the ambit of Article 8 for the purposes of an Article 14 claim.[180] As sexual orientation was 'in issue' in this context, the Court called for 'particularly convincing and weighty reasons to justify a difference in treatment regarding rights falling within Article 8'.[181] Citing the Convention's character as a living instrument,[182] it stated that there would be discrimination if the reasons advanced for a difference in treatment 'were based solely on considerations regarding the applicant's sexual orientation'.[183] The Court proceeded to hold that the applicant's sexuality had been 'a decisive factor leading to the decision to refuse her authorization to adopt',[184] and found a violation of Article 8 read with Article 14. The judgment is notable for the bold stance taken by the majority in scrutinizing, indeed reassessing, the negative decisions taken by the domestic authorities and concluding that they were decisively influenced by the applicant's sexuality.[185]

There have also been important developments in cases concerning the right of same-sex couples to marry and the issue of second-parent adoption. In *Schalk and Kopf v Austria* the Court accepted that in light of the rapid evolution of social attitudes towards same-sex couples in many member states a cohabiting same-sex couple living in a stable *de facto* partnership falls within the notion of family life just as a different–sex couple in the same situation would.[186] In previous cases this relationship had been seen as amounting to private life only.[187] However, the Court was not prepared to find that the Convention granted a right for same-sex couples to marry either under Article 12 or under Article 14 in conjunction with Article 8.[188] Of interest, the Court held that it would no longer consider that the right to marry in Article 12 must in all circumstances be limited to marriage between two persons of the opposite sex.[189] As regards Article 14, it noted that although there was an emerging European consensus towards legal recognition of same-sex couples, there was only a minority of states who had provided for it. Accordingly the matter was to be regarded as one of evolving rights with no established

---

[179] Hudoc (2008) GC; 47 EHRR 509.

[180] *EB v France*, para 49.   [181] *EB v France*, para 91.   [182] *EB v France*, para 92.

[183] *EB v France*, para 93.   [184] *EB v France*, para 89.

[185] *EB v France* therefore overturned *Fretté v France* 2002-I; 38 EHRR 438, which had been decided by a Chamber of the Court just five years earlier. In that judgment the Court had found (albeit by four votes to three) that there had been a difference of treatment based on sexuality in the (single) applicant's application for adoption, but that it pursued a legitimate aim (protecting the health and rights of children who could be involved in an adoption procedure). Judges Bratza, Fuhrmann, and Tulkens argued that there had been a violation on the facts.

[186] Hudoc (2010) paras 93–4; 53 EHRR 683. The Court noted that a considerable number of member states have afforded legal recognition to same-sex couples and that certain provisions of EU law reflected a growing tendency to include same-sex couples in the notion of 'family'. In view of this evolution it was thought artificial to maintain the view that, in contrast to a different-sex couple, a same-sex couple cannot enjoy 'family life' for the purposes of Article 8. Consequently the relationship of a cohabiting same-sex couple living in a stable *de facto* partnership, falls within the notion of 'family life', just as the relationship of a different-sex couple in the same situation would: see paras 93–4.   [187] See Ch 12, section 2.I and II.

[188] See *Vallianatos and Others v Greece* hudoc (2013) GC. The case concerns the application of civil partnerships to same-sex couples only. This was found to be in breach of Article 14 in conjection with Article 8. Hamilton 1 EHRLR (2013) pp 47–55.

[189] *Vallianatos and Others v Greece*, paras 60–1. The Court was influenced by Article 9 of the EU Charter of Fundamental Rights, where the reference to marriage being a union between men and women had been dropped.

consensus. Thus the states must enjoy a margin of appreciation in the timing of the introduction of legislative changes.[190] In *Gas and Dubois v France*,[191] the Court did not consider that there was a violation of Article 14 because of a refusal to grant an adoption order in favour of the homosexual partner of the biological mother of the child. The couple had been living in a civil partnership. The Court, however, did not consider that their legal situation could be compared to that of a married couple, marriage conferring a special status on those who enter into it. In addition, the legal consequences of simple adoption would be contrary to the child's interests, given that the adoption would entail the transfer of parental responsibility to the adoptive parent while depriving the child's biological mother of her rights, despite the fact that she intended to continue bringing up her child.[192] Of decisive importance for the Court's finding, it was noted that any heterosexual couple in a comparable legal situation would also have their request for an adoption order refused for the same reasons.[193]

The Court has recently revisited the area of second-parent adoption in the Grand Chamber case of *X v Austria* where adoption by a homosexual partner was also not possible under the law.[194] However, there was a vital difference with *Gas and Dubois* in that Austrian law permitted second-parent adoption where the unmarried couple were of a different sex. For the Court, the government had not provided any evidence to show that it would be detrimental to a child to be brought up by a same-sex couple or to have two mothers or two fathers for legal purposes. Moreover, under domestic law, adoption by one person, including one homosexual, was possible. If he or she had a registered partner, the latter had to consent to the adoption. The legislature had thus accepted that a child might grow up in a family based on a same-sex couple and that this was not detrimental to the child.[195] The government had failed to give convincing reasons to show that excluding second-parent adoption in a same-sex couple, while allowing that possibility in an unmarried different-sex couple, was necessary for the protection of the family in the traditional sense or for the protection of the interests of the child. The distinction was therefore discriminatory.[196]

Finally, *Baczkowski v Poland*[197] provides another example of the Court's progressive approach to Article 14 and sexual orientation in an altogether different context. The applicants claimed they had been refused permission to organize an assembly on a commemorative date important to them in Warsaw, the aim of which was to draw attention to discrimination against various minorities, including homosexuals. Their point was that a number of other groups, for example one against homosexual adoption, had been permitted to protest on the same day. The decisions in this regard had all been taken at the same time by administrative authorities who acted in the name of the mayor. There was nothing in the texts of the decision refusing the applicants permission to indicate discrimination, but at the relevant time the mayor had publicly expressed strong personal opinions against homosexuality. A striking feature of the judgment was that the Court was of the view that 'it may be reasonably surmised that [the mayor's] opinions could have affected the decision-making process in the present case and, as a result, impinged on the

---

[190] *Vallianatos and Others v Greece*, para 105.   [191] Hudoc (2012).

[192] *Gas and Dubois v France*, paras 62 and 68.   [193] *Gas and Dubois v France*, para 69.

[194] Hudoc (2013) GC.   [195] *X v Austria*, para 142 and 144.

[196] *X v Austria*, paras 151–3. As the Court pointed out, the question was not whether the adoption request should have been granted, but whether the applicants were discriminated against on account of the fact that the courts had no opportunity to examine whether the adoption was in the child's best interests, given that it was legally impossible: para 152.   [197] Hudoc (2007).

applicants' right to freedom of assembly in a discriminatory manner'.[198] The Court found a violation of Article 14 with Article 11.

EB, Baczkowski, and *X v Austria* demonstrate the Court's heightened awareness of the unacceptability of discrimination on grounds of sexual orientation and its greater readiness to scrutinize cases coming before it in this regard. *EB* is especially significant for the Grand Chamber's endorsement of the principle that distinctions based solely or decisively on sexual orientation are unacceptable under the Convention. Having said this, Article 14's inherent limitations as a parasitic provision entail that its impact and potential in this field should not be exaggerated. *EB*'s claim would have failed if French law had not allowed single persons to adopt.[199] Furthermore, in *Karner*[200] the Court addressed Article 8 in conjunction with Article 14 through the specific (and more discrete) notion of respect for 'home', not the broader notion of right to respect for 'private' or 'family life', although, as noted earlier, *Shalk and Kopf* has developed the law in this respect. Furthermore, even when Article 8 family life issues are relevant, an Article 14 claim is not bound to succeed since even the more recent cases such as *X v Austria, Schalk and Kopf*, and *Gas and Dubois* have not gone so far as to equate same-sex couples with married couples. One important question that arises from these cases is whether former decisions of the Court rejecting complaints concerning the payment of survivor's pensions to married couples only are still good law.[201] A key question will be whether the law treats unmarried heterosexual couples and same-sex couples in an even-handed manner. Indeed, as legislation enabling same-sex couples to get married becomes more widespread, issues relating to the equality of their marital status with that of heterosexual couples as regards adoption and reproductive rights will undoubtedly be raised before the Court.

VII. UNMARRIED FATHERS' ACCESS TO CHILDREN AND ISSUES RELATING TO MARITAL STATUS

As a general rule unmarried fathers who have established family life with their children can claim equal rights of contact and custody with married fathers. In *Sahin v Germany*,[202] domestic law gave divorced fathers a legal right of access to their child, whereas unmarried fathers had no such automatic right. The Grand Chamber stated that 'very weighty reasons' will be required to justify a 'difference in the treatment of the father of a child born of a relationship *where the parties were living together out of wedlock* as compared with the father of a child born of a marriage-based relationship'[203] (emphasis added). Also in *Zaunegger v Germany*,[204] the father of a child born out of wedlock needed the mother's consent before joint custody could be awarded. The applicant had lived with the mother for five years. The Court was not prepared to agree that joint custody against the will of the mother could be assumed to be in the best interests of the child. However, the fact that the father was prevented from seeking a judicial ruling on the issue of whether

---

[198] *Baczkowski v Poland*, para 100 (see also paras 97–9 for the Court's comments on the importance attached by it to the notion that elected politicians exercise their powers of freedom of expression responsibly); also *Alexseyev v Russia* hudoc (2010).

[199] See discussion of the 'ambit' test at section 3 of this chapter.

[200] 2003–IX; 38 EHRR 24 para 33.   [201] See, eg, *Estevez v Spain No 56501/00* 2001-VI DA.

[202] 2003-VIII; 44 EHRR 99 GC. See also *PM v UK* hudoc (2005); 42 EHRR 1015 para 28 (different tax regime for maintenance payments applicable for unmarried and married fathers subsequently divorced and separated violated Article 14).

[203] *Sahin v Germany*, para 94. See also *Elsholz v Germany* 2000-VIII; 34 EHRR 1412 GC.

[204] Hudoc (2009).

joint parental custody served the child's best interest was disproportionate to the aim of protecting the child.[205]

More generally, however, the Court has found that differences in treatment on the basis of marital status can have objective and reasonable justification.[206] Furthermore, unmarried partners are not generally considered by the Court to be in an analogous position to spouses for the purpose of Article 14, 'marriage continu[ing] to be characterised by a corpus of rights and obligations that differentiate it markedly from the situation of a man and woman who cohabit'.[207] This statement was made in *Nylund v Finland*, which is one example of several applications that have been declared inadmissible on this basis.[208] The applicant claimed to be the father of a child and had lived with its mother, but he was unable to obtain a paternity test because the mother blocked the application for this. She had given birth after marrying another man and domestic law then presumed the husband to be the father. The applicant complained of preferential treatment for the mother compared to him, as she could block the paternity claim now she was married. The Court questioned whether the 'analogous situation' test was passed but took the view that in any case the domestic law pursued the legitimate aim of 'securing or reconciling the rights of the child and its family' and was not disproportionate.

The Court is therefore prepared to allow some differential treatment on the basis of the promotion of marriage which, in its words, 'remains an institution that is widely accepted as conferring a particular status on those who enter it and, indeed,...is singled out for special treatment under Article 12 of the Convention'.[209] *Saucedo Gómez v Spain*[210] demonstrates this. It concerned a former cohabiter who complained about the legal arrangements regarding property entitlement put in place following her relationship break up, claiming that there had been discrimination based on her status as a non-married woman as compared to a married one. Declaring the application inadmissible,[211] the Chamber indicated that it had doubts whether this was a case of discrimination at all. But it made it clear that, even if there had been differential treatment, it was justifiable (protection of the traditional family) and not disproportionate (especially as the applicant had been able to marry her former partner but had declined to do so). This was an area, the Court stated, where a margin of appreciation applied and it was not for it to dictate or indicate to states the measures that they should take with regard to the existence of stable, non-married, relationships between men and women.

Accordingly, even when the Court has been prepared to accept that in a case concerning unmarried applicants it is faced with an analogous situation to married couples, it has recognized that states 'may be allowed a certain margin of appreciation to treat differently married and unmarried couples in the fields of, for instance, taxation, social security or

---

[205] *Zaunegger v Germany*, paras 58–63.

[206] See *McMichael v UK* A 307-B (1995); 20 EHRR 205. This concerned legislation which did not grant automatic parental responsibility to unmarried fathers since they varied in their commitment to and interest in, or even knowledge of, their children. There was no violation of Article 14 with Article 8 as the relevant legislation pursued a legitimate aim—identifying meritorious fathers—and the conditions imposed upon the applicant were proportionate.

[207] *Nylund v Finland No 27110/95*, 1999-VI DA. See also *Burden v UK* hudoc (2008) at para 63 GC ('marriage remains an institution which is widely accepted as conferring a particular status on those who enter it').

[208] Eg *Lindsay v UK No 11089/84*, 49 DR 181 (1986); 9 EHRR 555 (different tax rules for married and unmarried couples) and *Shackell v UK No 45851/99* hudoc (2000) DA (widow different to unmarried partner upon death of husband/partner for purpose of entitlement to social security benefits).

[209] *Shackell v UK No 45851/99* hudoc (2000) DA.   [210] *No 37784/97* hudoc (1999) DA.

[211] This was a majority decision.

social policy'.[212] There are, however, limits to this. Article 8 read with Article 14 was violated in a case[213] concerning contact telephone calls for individuals held in custody. The law allowed married partners to call each other in such circumstances but not unmarried partners, even when they had established family life in the sense required by Article 8. The disparate treatment was unjustified.

VIII. DISABILITY AND HEALTH

It might be thought that the European Court would require 'very weighty reasons' to be put forward before it regarded a difference of treatment based exclusively on the ground of disability as compatible with the Convention. In fact, no statements to this effect can be found in the jurisprudence and there is little Article 14 case law directly addressing the rights of disabled people.[214] This may be a reflection, above all, of the weakness of that Article as a parasitic right and the Court's approach to interpreting Article 8 in relevant case law.[215] However, in some recent judgments the Court has indicated that the margin of appreciation will be reduced in cases concerning discrimination on the basis of disability.[216]

On the other hand, the Court has indicated in *Kiyutin v Russia* that very weighty reasons had to be adduced to justify treating those with HIV in a different manner.[217] Such groups were a particularly vulnerable and had been subject to discrimination in the past with lasting consequences, resulting in their social exclusion. The applicant was a foreign national who had been living for many years with his Russian wife in Russia. He was denied a residence permit because he tested HIV-positive. The Court considered that he was in an analogous position with other foreign nationals who had applied for a residence permit. It considered that the mere presence of an HIV-positive person in the country was not in itself a threat to public health and noted that restrictions were not imposed on tourists or short-term visitors. It did not accept the argument that the applicant could become a burden on the health system since foreigners had no entitlement to free medical assistance. It also noted that travel and residence restrictions might also damage public health if migrants chose to remain illegally to avoid HIV screening or if the local population were to come to view HIV as solely a 'foreign problem'. A further concern was the indiscriminate nature of the measure that left no room for an individualized assessment on the facts of the case. The Court considered that the applicant had been a victim of discrimination on account of his health status in breach of Article 14 in conjunction with Article 8.[218]

Finally in *GN and Others v Italy*,[219] the Court found a violation of Article 14 combined with Article 2 in respect of a compensation scheme for those who had contracted HIV from blood transfusions, but which had made a distinction between those who were

---

[212] *Petrov v Bulgaria* hudoc (2008) para 55, citing *Shackell* and *Lindsay*, n 212; *McMichael v UK* A 307-B (1995); 20 EHRR 205 and *Sahin v Germany* 2003-VIII; 44 EHRR 99 GC.

[213] *Petrov v Bulgaria* hudoc (2008).

[214] Although this is not to say that the Convention does not have relevance in this field: see, eg, *Price v UK* 2001-VII; 34 EHRR 1285. See generally Clements, *Disability and European Human Rights*, 2003. See also Article 26 of the Charter of Fundamental Rights of the European Union, available at http://eur-lex.europa.eu/LexUriServ/LexUriServ.do?uri=OJ:C:2010:083:0389:0403:en:PDF.

[215] The most notable cases have been *Botta v Italy* 1998-I; 26 EHRR 241 (no violation of Article 8 with Article 14) and *Zehnalová and Zehnal v Czech Republic No 38621/97* hudoc (2002) DA; inadmissible. See also *Malone v UK No 25290/94* hudoc (1996) DA; inadmissible.

[216] See *Glor v Switzerland* hudoc (2009) and *GN and Others v Italy* hudoc (2009).

[217] Hudoc (2011); 53 EHRR 897. See also *IB v Greece* hudoc (2013).

[218] *Kiyutin v Russia*, paras 62–74.   [219] Hudoc (2009) and (2011).

transfused because they suffered from haemophilia and thalassaemia (hereditary blood disorder) sufferers, the latter receiving no compensation. While accepting that the state was not obliged to pay compensation under the Convention, once it chose to do so it was required by Article 14 not to discriminate. The Court rejected the argument that the state had chosen to save money and found that the distinctions operated were arbitrary.[220]

7. ARTICLE 14, THE BURDEN OF PROOF AND THE PROTECTION OF MINORITIES

I. BURDEN OF PROOF AND STATISTICS

In many of the cases discussed so far, the applicant will be able to point to a particular law, rule, or decision and describe its impact on him or her in order to establish the necessary *prima facie* evidence of discrimination required for Article 14. It will then fall to the state to discharge the burden placed upon it and justify the difference of treatment. However, even when discrimination is rife, it may be very difficult for an applicant to establish a *prima facie* case of this on the facts of his or her case. The law or regulation in issue may not be explicitly racist or sexist, but in practice it may be applied by public officials in discriminatory ways. This may be particularly so if there is so-called 'institutional' discrimination.

As regards what constitutes *prima facie* evidence capable of placing a burden of proof on the respondent state for Article 14, the Grand Chamber has indicated that the distribution of the burden of proof is intrinsically linked to the specificity of the facts, the nature of the allegation made, and the Convention right at stake.[221]

This is particularly relevant to the examples detailed in the paragraphs that follow concerning indirect discrimination and allegations of violence motivated by discrimination, ie situations where it may be practically difficult for applicants to establish a *prima facie* of discrimination. In these cases it has been argued that where credible statistics are overwhelming in the disproportionate (and discriminatory) impact they reveal, then they should shift the burden of proof to the respondent state so as to require it to rebut a finding of discrimination.[222] Initially this argument was rejected,[223] however the Court's case law evolved in 2006[224] and in the highly significant Grand Chamber judgment in *DH v Czech Republic*,[225] the Court confirmed that it had modified its position with respect to indirect discrimination (a concept which is discussed further later).[226] The Court stated that 'less strict evidential rules' should apply to this field of discrimination in order to guarantee those concerned 'the effective protection of their rights'.[227]

---

[220] *GN and Others v Italy* (friendly settlement).

[221] *DH and Others v Czech Republic* (hudoc) 2007 paras 178 and 179.

[222] See the third party intervention of Interights and Human Rights Watch in *DH*, para 163.

[223] See *Hugh Jordan v UK* 2001-III; 37 EHRR 52, where the Court rejected arguments that statistics concerning civilian deaths in Northern Ireland exhibited discrimination against the Catholic community. See also *Ireland v UK* A 25 (1978); 2 EHRR 225 paras 224–9 PC. See further *DH and Others v Czech Republic* hudoc (2007); 43 EHRR 923 para 46 (this Chamber ruling was reversed by the GC: *DH v Czech Republic*) and *Zarb Adami v Malta* hudoc 2006-VII; 44 EHRR 49 para 76.

[224] See *Zarb Adami*, paras 78 and 82–3 (violation of Article 14 as civic obligation of jury service fell predominantly on males not females).

[225] Hudoc (2007); 43 EHRR 923. Also *Sampanis and Others v Greece* hudoc (2008).

[226] Section 9 of this chapter.   [227] *DH v Czech Republic*, para 186. See also para 189.

The Grand Chamber cited an earlier admissibility decision[228] which had placed a burden on the state to account for statistics which apparently evidenced discrimination. It also cited relevant EC law[229] concerning the burden of proof and referred generally to the equivalent practice of domestic courts as well as the supervisory bodies of UN human rights treaties before concluding that, 'when it comes to assessing the impact of a measure or practice on an individual or group, statistics which appear on critical examination to be reliable and significant will be sufficient to constitute the *prima facie* evidence the applicant is required to produce [to place the burden on the respondent state to justify a difference of treatment]'.[230]

As shall be seen later, the issue of the burden of proof and the use that may be made of statistical evidence has been highly relevant to cases concerning racism against Roma. The European Commissioner on Human Rights has acknowledged that there is a serious problem in many Council of Europe states regarding widespread and deep-rooted racial discrimination against Roma.[231]

II. THE CONVENTION AND THE PROTECTION OF MINORITIES

At first sight it would seem that there is little role for Article 14 here. Many minorities' concerns fall outside the Convention altogether, so neither as individual rights nor as an aspect of Article 14 protection do they fall within the competence of the Strasbourg authorities.[232] Article 14 cites 'association with a national minority' as a specific 'badge' of forbidden discrimination, but the Convention provides only partial and indirect obligations in favour of minorities.[233] States may insist, indeed may have a duty to insist, that minorities respect the rights of others guaranteed by the Convention.[234] The thrust of the Convention is the securing of individual rather than group rights,[235] so generally

---

[228] *DH v Czech Republic*, para 180, citing *Hoogendijk v Netherlands No 58641/00* hudoc (2005) DA.

[229] *DH v Czech Republic*, para 187 and paras 81–91. The European Union's Race Directive (Directive 2000/43/EC implementing the principle of equal treatment between persons irrespective of racial or ethnic origin), which applies to limited fields including education, training, and employment, provides for the reversal of the burden of proof, see Article 8. As regards sex discrimination, see Directive 97/80/EC (Article 4(1)) and Directive 2000/78/EC.

[230] *DH v Czech Republic*, para 188 GC (it added, '[t]his does not, however, mean that indirect discrimination cannot be proved without statistical evidence'). In *Orsus and Others v Croatia* hudoc (2010) paras 153–5 GC, the Court found that the statistics submitted did not suffice to establish that there was *prima facie* evidence of discrimination. It relied on uncontested evidence that Roma children were placed in separate classes allegedly on the basis of their insufficient command of the Croatian language and that this measure was applied exclusively to this ethnic group.

[231] See especially Council of Europe Human Rights Commissioner, *Final report on the human rights situation of the Roma, Sinti and Travellers in Europe*, CommDH(2006)1. For Council of Europe documentation relevant to the situation of 'Roma and Travellers' see http://www.coe.int/T/DG3/RomaTravellers/Default_en.asp. The Court has adopted some important statements of principle regarding the need to afford particular protection to Roma/gypsies, see *Chapman v UK* 2001-I; 33 EHRR 399 para 96 GC; *Connors v UK* hudoc (2004); 40 EHRR 189 para 84; and *DH and Others v Czech Republic* hudoc (2007) para 181 GC; *Orsus and Others v Croatia* hudoc (2010) para 147 GC.

[232] This includes economic and social rights, where the prospects of oblique protection, relying on *Airey v Ireland* A 32 (1979); 2 EHRR 305, are not encouraging. See, eg, *X v UK No 8160/78*, 22 DR 27 (1981).

[233] Gilbert, 23 NYIL 67 at 81–93 (1992) and 24 HRQ 736 (2002).

[234] Poulter, 36 ICLQ 589 at 614–15 (1987). Although making a strong plea for tolerance and pluralism, the author accepts the limits imposed by international human rights obligations.

[235] See *48 Kalderas Gypsies v Germany and Netherlands Nos 7823/77 and 7824/77*, 11 DR 221 (1977) (the applicants were *individual* gypsies).

speaking minority organizations may assert rights of their own only if they are, *mutatis mutandis*, like individual rights. Of key importance will be rights such as the right of a political party to a free and fair election, plus the rights of freedom of expression, assembly, association, and religion. Some compensation may be found in the development of positive obligations for states so that individual members of a minority may enjoy their rights effectively, for instance in matters of religion, education, or right to respect for Article 8 rights.[236] However, it is difficult to demonstrate the existence of such obligations and relatively easy for a state to show that it has satisfied them[237]—hence the importance of the burden of proof in such cases.

Past plans to create a new Protocol to the Convention addressing minorities' protection have not progressed to completion.[238] However the Council of Europe has adopted a number of measures in this field,[239] the most notable of which is the Framework Convention for the Protection of National Minorities,[240] the first ever legally binding multilateral instrument devoted to the protection of *national* minorities in general.

8. ARTICLE 14 AND VIOLENCE MOTIVATED BY DISCRIMINATION

I. *NACHOVA V BULGARIA*: ARTICLE 14 AND RACIAL VIOLENCE IN THE CONTEXT OF POLICING AND CRIMINAL JUSTICE

The Court's abhorrence of racial discrimination generally is clear.[241] As regards racial violence, the Grand Chamber has stated that this:

> is a particular affront to human dignity and, in view of its perilous consequences, requires from the authorities special vigilance and a vigorous reaction. It is for this reason that the authorities must use all available means to combat racism and racist violence, thereby reinforcing democracy's vision of a society in which diversity is not perceived as a threat but as a source of its enrichment.[242]

The Court has nonetheless acknowledged that 'proving racial motivation [for Article 14 claims] will often be extremely difficult'[243] on the facts of a case. Indeed the Court has

---

[236] In this connection, see the joint dissenting opinion of Judges Pastor Ridruejo *et al* in *Chapman v UK* 2001-I; 33 EHRR 399 GC and *Connors v UK* hudoc (2004); 40 EHRR 189 para 84.

[237] As demonstrated by the almost complete lack of success of the applicants in the *Belgian Linguistic* case A 6 (1968); 1 EHRR 252 PC.   [238] As to the proposals see Malinverni, 12 HRLJ 265 (1991).

[239] See Council of Europe ((DH-MIN), Activities of the Council of Europe in the Field of the Protection of National Minorities, DH-MIN(2005)003; see also generally http://www.coe.int/t/dghl/monitoring/minorities/default_en.asp.

[240] ETS 157. On this Convention, see Wheatley, 6 EHRLR 583 (1996); Keller, 18 OJLS 29 (1998) and Weller, The Rights of Minorities: A Commentary on the European Framework Convention for the Protection of National Minorities 2006. For general information and reports consult http://www.coe.int/t/dghl/monitoring/minorities/default_en.asp.   [241] See section 6.I of this chapter.

[242] *Nachova and Others v Bulgaria* 2005-VII; 42 EHRR 933 para 145 GC.

[243] *Nachova v Bulgaria* hudoc (2004); 39 EHRR 793 para 159 (Chamber judgment). The violations of Article 14 found in *Moldovan and Others v Romania* 2005-VII; 44 EHRR 302 and *Timishev v Russia* 2005-XII; 44 EHRR 776 were exceptional for their factual circumstances in that the racial discrimination occurring was blatant.

been strongly criticized[244] as it has repeatedly found violations of Articles 2 and 3 in cases of violence against Roma, but has apparently been very reluctant to find that such violence was inflicted for racial reasons so as to contravene Article 14. The leading case is *Nachova v Bulgaria*,[245] which was heard by both the Chamber and the Grand Chamber. Two unarmed Roma conscripts were shot dead by the police who, it was claimed, had acted in a racially motivated way (there was excessive use of force and witness evidence of racist verbal abuse by one officer who shot the deceased). It was further claimed that the investigation that followed failed to properly pursue and unmask this racial abuse. Violations of Article 2 were found under two heads—unlawful death and the failure to effectively investigate the same—and it was claimed that there were corresponding violations of Article 14 too. The case proceeded against the backdrop of substantial *general* evidence of the existence of widespread discrimination against Roma in Bulgaria, reference being made in the judgment to previous cases examined by the Court raising similar issues and a body of germane reports and opinions authored by institutions within the Council of Europe and the UN, some of which had not been contested by the Bulgarian authorities.[246]

a. Article 14 and state responsibility for racial violence committed by the authorities (the substantive question)

As regards Article 14, the most controversial issue in *Nachova* was whether the individuals had been killed as a result of racism. The Grand Chamber departed from the novel approach set by the Chamber[247] and followed the Court's standard approach to the substantive question relevant to Articles 2 and 14. That is the Court undertakes a free assessment of all the evidence before it,[248] and will conclude that Article 2 or 3 ill-treatment has been racially motivated (in violation of Article 14) if it is established beyond reasonable doubt that racist attitudes played a role in the applicants' treatment by the police.[249] This approach had been adopted in earlier cases concerning police violence against Roma in Bulgaria,[250] when no violation of Article 14 read with Article 2 was found, and in *Nachova* it was concluded once again that, on the facts, there was no violation under this head.[251] In reaching its conclusion, the Grand Chamber acknowledged to some extent the general situation of Roma in Bulgaria—'a number of organisations, including intergovernmental bodies, have expressed concern about the occurrence of such incidents [of racial violence]'—but it emphasized that 'its sole concern [was] to ascertain whether in the case at hand the killing of [the deceased] was motivated by racism'.[252] *Interights* had argued that the beyond reasonable doubt standard of proof was 'inappropriate in a human rights

---

[244] See Goldston, 5 EHRLR 462 (1999) and the separate opinions of Judge Bonello in *Anguelova v Bulgaria* 2002-IV; 38 EHRR 659 and *Nachova and Others* hudoc (2004); 39 EHRR 793 (Chamber judgment).

[245] Hudoc (2004); 39 EHRR 793 and 2005-VII; 42 EHRR 933 GC.

[246] *Nachova v Bulgaria*, paras 173–4 (Chamber judgment).

[247] The Chamber considered that the burden of proof could be reversed if there was evidence of a culture of impunity as regards treatment of the racial issue in the ensuing police investigation and by general background circumstances: *Nachova v Bulgaria*, paras 168–9.

[248] See the Court's elaboration at *Nachova and Others v Bulgaria* 2005-VII; 42 EHRR 933 para 155 GC. See also *DH v Czech Republic* hudoc (2007) para 178 GC.

[249] See also *Bekos and Koutropoulos v Greece* hudoc (2005); 43 EHRR 22 paras 47 and 67 (allegations of Article 3 ill-treatment motivated by racial prejudices) and *Moldovan and Others v Romania* 2005-VII; 44 EHRR 302 (racist attitudes clearly influencing enjoyment of Article 6 and Article 8 rights).

[250] See *Velikova v Bulgaria* 2000-VII and *Anguelova v Bulgaria* 2002-IV; 38 EHRR 659.

[251] *Nachova v Bulgaria* 2005-VII; 42 EHRR 933 para 155 GC. See also *Ognyanova and Choban v Bulgaria* hudoc (2006); 44 EHRR 169.   [252] *Nachova v Bulgaria*, para 155.

context and provides too great an evidentiary obstacle for applicants'.[253] However, the Grand Chamber was not persuaded that it should reverse the burden of proof. It stated that it would not 'exclude the possibility that in certain cases of alleged discrimination it may require the respondent Government to disprove an arguable allegation of discrimination and—if they fail to do so—find a violation of Article 14 of the Convention on that basis'.[254] But it then highlighted the evidentiary difficulties that would face a respondent state in discharging a burden placed upon it in cases where there were allegations that individual police officers used lethal force in a racially motivated way. To reverse the burden for violent acts motivated by racial prejudice, the Court stated, 'would amount to requiring the respondent Government to prove the absence of a particular subjective attitude on the part of the person concerned'.[255]

It nevertheless left open the possibility of doing so, and indeed, in *Stoica v Romania*,[256] a Chamber did just this. The case concerned a serious assault on the applicant which occurred in the context of a day of racist confrontations between the police and members of a Roma village. From the general facts, including various statements made by the police on the day (eg, assaulting an individual after having asked him whether he was 'Gypsy or Romanian'), the Court concluded that there was 'clear'[257] evidence that individuals such as the applicant had been deliberately targeted on the basis of their ethnic origin. The burden was therefore placed on the respondent government to establish that the particular attack on the applicant, which violated Article 3 on its own, was not racially motivated. The Court found a violation of Article 3 read with Article 14.

b. Article 14 and effective domestic investigations into racial violence (the procedural question)

As to the (less controversial) procedural aspect of Article 14, the Grand Chamber in *Nachova* took into account general indications of a culture of impunity as regards racial violence. It held that Article 14 with Article 2 had been violated with respect to the positive obligation to investigate allegations of racially-motivated violence. In particular, the authorities had failed to carry out a thorough examination of the wider circumstances of the deaths in order to uncover possible racist motives. They should have done so as they had 'plausible information'[258] before them in the form of witness evidence of racist verbal abuse by the shooting officer; furthermore that had to be 'seen against the background of the many published accounts of the existence in Bulgaria of prejudice and hostility against Roma'.[259] The Court insisted that where 'there is suspicion that racial attitudes induced a violent act it is particularly important that the official investigation is pursued with vigour and impartiality, having regard to the need to reassert continuously society's condemnation of racism and ethnic hatred and to maintain the confidence of minorities in the ability of the authorities to protect them from the threat of racist violence'.[260] The duty to investigate under Article 2 had to be conducted

---

[253] Third Party Intervention of Interights in *Nachova v Bulgaria*, para 27.

[254] *Nachova v Bulgaria*, para 157; cf the comments made by the Chamber at para 165. See the concurring opinion of Judge Bratza who provided examples of when reversal of the burden would be appropriate in his view. [255] *Nachova v Bulgaria*, para 157.

[256] Hudoc (2008). [257] *Stoica v Romania*, para 131 (see generally paras 117–33).

[258] *Nachova v Bulgaria* 2005-VII; 42 EHRR 933 GC para 166. [259] *Nachova v Bulgaria*, para 163.

[260] *Nachova v Bulgaria*, para 157 (Chamber judgment), endorsed by the GC at para 160. The Chamber also emphasized that acts motivated by ethnic hatred and that lead to deprivation of life undermine the foundations of democratic society, para 155.

without discrimination and the domestic legal system had to 'demonstrate its capacity to enforce [the] criminal law against those who unlawfully took the life of another, irrespective of the victim's racial or ethnic origin'.[261] Investigations into violent incidents and, in particular, deaths at the hands of state agents, the Court stated, placed the state authorities under an additional duty to take 'all reasonable steps to unmask any racist motive and to establish whether or not ethnic hatred or prejudice may have played a role in the events', failing which a breach of Article 14 with Article 2 might ensue. In order to maintain 'public confidence in their law enforcement machinery', states had to ensure that in the investigation of incidents involving the use of force, 'a distinction is made both in their legal systems and in practice between cases of excessive use of force and of racist killing'.[262]

This duty to investigate will be triggered by the facts of the case which suggest that the death or ill-treatment was actually the result of racial prejudice. In some cases it may be enough that there is general recognition in published accounts of a pattern of prejudice and hostility against the minority concerned in the respondent state.[263] Equivalent standards apply to Article 3 ill-treatment purportedly inspired by racism or even political reasons.[264] The special investigative duties upon the state will also apply when the actual treatment contrary to Article 3 or 2 of the Convention was inflicted by private individuals.[265]

In summary, the Court will no doubt remain open to criticism as regards the issue of the burden of proof in connection with 'the substantive question'. However, as regards 'the procedural question' there is a clear message in the jurisprudence which should encourage states acting in good faith to put procedures in place which start to end impunity in the field of racial violence.

II. STATE TOLERATION OF VIOLENCE MOTIVATED BY DISCRIMINATION

The Court found a violation of Article 14 with Article 9 (as well, in fact, of Article 3) in the case of 97 *Members of the Gldani Congregation of Jehovah's Witnesses and 4 Others v Georgia*.[266] The case concerned an extremely violent physical attack on a congregation of Jehovah's Witnesses by an extremist Orthodox religious group, the applicants' complaint being that the authorities' comments and attitudes upon being notified of the same evidenced official toleration of what had occurred. The Court accepted that the authorities had refused to intervene to stop the continuation of the attack and had shown indifference toward the perpetrators' prosecution to an extent that was incompatible 'with the principle of equality of

---

[261] *Nachova v Bulgaria*, para 157 (Chamber judgment), endorsed by the GC at para 160.

[262] *Nachova v Bulgaria*, para 158 (Chamber judgment), endorsed by the GC at para 160. See also *Stoica v Romania* hudoc (2008) paras 119 and 124. Also *Abdu v Bulgaria* hudoc (2014).

[263] See *Cobzaru v Romania* hudoc (2007) para 97 (although the violation found there apparently owed much to the tendentious remarks made by the prosecutor, see paras 98–101); see also *Ognyanova and Choban v Bulgaria* hudoc (2006); 44 EHRR 7 para 148 (authorities not sufficiently on notice by virtue of general reports of racism).

[264] See *Bekos and Koutropoulos v Greece* hudoc (2005); 43 EHRR 22 para 73; *BS v Spain* hudoc (2012) (failure of a court to examine a claim of racist violence by the police against a prostitute); *Virabyan v Armenia* hudoc (2012) (failure of the authorities to investigate whether the applicant was the victim of political violence due to his membership of the opposition party); *Cakir v Turkey* hudoc (2009) (failure to investigate racist motives behind police violence).   [265] See, eg, *Šečić v Croatia* hudoc (2007) para 67.

[266] Hudoc (2007); 46 EHRR 613 para 140. See also *Milanovic v Serbia* hudoc (2010) (*pro forma* investigation into religiously motivated violence against a member of the Hare Krishna community).

every person before the law'[267] and even raised objective doubts as to whether the authorities could be regarded as complicit.[268] The applicants were 'victims of a violation of Article 14 in conjunction with Articles 3 and 9 of the Convention'.[269]

9. INDIRECT DISCRIMINATION

Indirect discrimination results from a rule or practice that in itself does not involve impermissible discrimination but that disproportionately and adversely affects members of a particular group.[270] There does not necessarily have to be discriminatory intent for indirect discrimination.

Article 14 potentially covers indirect discrimination, the Court stating that 'a difference in treatment may take the form of disproportionately prejudicial effects of a general policy or measure which, though couched in neutral terms, discriminates against a group'.[271] It has accepted that discrimination contrary to the Convention may arise not only from the direct actions of the state, but also from 'a *de facto* situation'.[272]

In *DH v Czech Republic*,[273] the eighteen applicants claimed that they had been victims of indirect discrimination with respect to the right to education. They were all members of the Roma community and pointed to the significantly disproportionate numbers of Roma children living in their area of the Czech Republic who were educated in ordinary schools. As in the case of the applicants, Roma children tended to be placed in 'special schools' for intellectually less able children, and so received an inferior education with inevitable consequences for their life chances thereafter. Amongst other things, the applicants produced a survey which revealed that in their region 1.8 per cent of non-Roma children were placed in special schools compared to 50.3 per cent of Roma children.[274] Their claim was not that the regime governing school selection and allocation was explicitly and deliberately discriminatory in terms of requiring, in effect, separate schooling arrangements. However, they insisted that the way the system worked entailed that a disproportionate number of Roma children—including themselves—had been placed in special schools without justification, this being due to the manner in which the relevant legislation was applied in practice.

The Court upheld the applicants' claim. Critical to this outcome was the stance it took on statistics and the reversal of the burden of proof.[275] Relying on statistics found in documentation[276] authored by Council of Europe bodies and the (UN) Committee on the Elimination of Racial Discrimination, the Grand Chamber concluded that the relevant statutory education provisions in the Czech Republic had 'had considerably more impact in practice on Roma children than on non-Roma children and resulted in statistically disproportionate numbers of placements of the former in special schools'.[277] With the burden of proof placed upon it, the Czech government was not able to persuade the Court that

---

[267] *Jehovah's Witnesses v Georgia*, para 141.   [268] *Jehovah's Witnesses v Georgia*, para 142.

[269] *Jehovah's Witnesses v Georgia*, para 143.

[270] The legal origin of this concept is *Griggs v Duke Power Co* 401 US 424 (1971). See Article 2 (1)(b) of the EU's Race Directive, n 233, for a definition of indirect discrimination.

[271] *DH v Czech Republic* hudoc (2007) para 184 GC (citing, *inter alia* relevant EU law (Council Directives 97/80/EC and 2000/43/EC) and documentation authored by the European Commission against Racism and Intolerance). The case of *Thlimmenos v Greece* 2000-IV; 31 EHRR 411 GC, discussed in this chapter at section 4.III., might also be considered one of indirect discrimination.

[272] *Zarb Adami v Malta* hudoc (2006); 44 EHRR 49 para 76.   [273] Hudoc (2007) GC.

[274] *DH v Czech Republic*, para 190.   [275] See section 7.I of this chapter.

[276] *DH v Czech Republic* hudoc (2007) para 192 GC.   [277] *DH v Czech Republic*, para 193.

there was an objective and reasonable justification for this situation. The Court refused to accept that the educational tests employed to decide on schooling were not unbiased in their impact on Roma children.[278] It also rejected the argument that each parent had consented to their child's placement in a special school, taking the view that there could be no waiver of the right in question and that the parents themselves were ill-equipped to make an informed and responsible decision on the matter.[279]

The Grand Chamber was clear that it did not need to examine the individual applicants' cases.[280] It saw no need to do so as it regarded it as established that 'the relevant legislation as applied in practice at the material time had a disproportionately prejudicial effect *on the Roma community*'[281] (emphasis added), which the applicants formed part of. The Court acknowledged that the Czech authorities had a margin of appreciation in the field under consideration, ie education provision and curriculum design etc. However, they had failed to institute schooling arrangements for Roma children that were attended by 'safeguards...that would ensure that...the state took into account their special needs as members of a disadvantaged class'.[282] It was therefore the state's fault that the applicant children had 'received an education which compounded their difficulties and compromised their subsequent personal development instead of tackling their real problems or helping them to integrate into the ordinary schools and develop the skills that would facilitate life among the majority population'.[283]

In *Oršuš and Others v Croatia*,[284] the issue concerned the transfer of Roma children to separate classes on the grounds of their inadequate command of language. Unlike the *DH* case, the Court was not satisfied that the statistics demonstrated that there was *prima facie* evidence that the effect of the measure was discriminatory since the percentage of Roma children in schools other than those of the applicants was not as high as in that case.[285] The case was nevertheless considered to be one of indirect discrimination since the measure was applied to Roma children only.[286] For the Grand Chamber, where measures impacted disproportionately on a particular ethnic group, safeguards had to be put in place to ensure that the applicant's made speedy progress in their grasp of the language and were reintegrated into mixed classes as soon as possible. The Court was not satisfied that such safeguards existed and noted that the applicants' placement in separate classes with an adapted curriculum had lasted for substantial periods of time and in some cases during their entire primary schooling. In particular, no monitoring procedure had been put in place to provide individual reports of the child's progress or to identify problem areas. Nor had it been shown that the applicants had been provided with any specific programme in order to address their alleged linguistic deficiencies. There was thus no reasonable relationship of proportionality between the means used and the legitimate aim (improvement of language skills) pursued.[287]

In the recent judgment of *Horváth and Kiss v Hungary*,[288] the Court noted the high and uncontested number of Roma children who had been placed in schools for the mentally

---

[278] *DH v Czech Republic*, paras 200–1 and 204.
[279] *DH v Czech Republic*, para 203; cf the dissenting opinion of Judge Borrego Borrego at paras 14–16.
[280] *DH v Czech Republic*,para 209.   [281] *DH v Czech* Republic, para 209.
[282] *DH v Czech Republic*, para 207, cf para 181.   [283] *DH v Czech Republic*, para 207.
[284] Hudoc (2010); see *Sampanis and Others v Greece* hudoc (2008) also concerning discrimination against Roma children in the area of education.   [285] *Oršuš and Others v Croatia*, para 152.
[286] *Oršuš and Others v Croatia*, paras 153–6. The Court accepted that indirect discrimination could be demonstrated without statistical evidence. It took into account the ECRI report on Croatia.
[287] *Oršuš and Others v Croatia*, paras 158–84. See also the dissenting opinions of Judges Zupancic, Borrego Borrego, and Jungwiert.   [288] Hudoc (2013).

disabled. It accepted that such different, and potentially disadvantageous, treatment applied much more often in the case of Roma than for others. The burden thus fell on the government to justify such differential treatment.[289] The Court found that the schooling arrangements for Roma with an alleged 'mild mental disability' had not been attended by adequate safeguards that would have ensured that their special needs as members of a disadvantaged group were taken into account.[290]

The situation identified as a violation of Article 14 in *DH*, *Oršuš*, and *Horváth and Kiss* is a reflection of a wider problem in Europe. In a general report concerning the human rights of Roma in Europe, the Council of Europe's Commissioner of Human Rights raised a 'particular concern' relating to 'segregation in education, which, in one form or another, is a common feature in many Council of Europe member states'.[291] He referred to the fact that there are '[i]n some countries…segregated schools in segregated settlements'. The rulings in these cases are important instances of the Court coming to the assistance of an historically disadvantaged and vulnerable minority in need of special protection by stressing the obligations on the state to take positive measures to improve their lot and to correct discriminatory practices.[292]

10. POSITIVE OBLIGATIONS TO PROTECT AGAINST DISCRIMINATION AND REVERSE DISCRIMINATION

I. POSITIVE OBLIGATION TO PROTECT AGAINST PRIVATE DISCRIMINATION

According to Article 14, the enjoyment of the rights and freedoms in the Convention 'shall be secured' without discrimination. This replicates the language of the guarantee in Article 1[293] and emphasizes that states may have positive obligations under Article 14, as well as the negative obligation not to discriminate in their official acts.[294]

The obligation of the state to take action to protect against private acts of discrimination which affect the enjoyment of Convention rights could embrace matters like membership of private associations or the right to be freed from privately imposed discriminatory fetters, like restrictive covenants on property rights. The inference to be drawn from *Young, James and Webster v UK*[295] and *Sigurjonsson v Iceland*[296] is that a state does have a duty to prevent private action which compels a person to be a member of an association. On the other hand, there cannot, in general, be a duty to compel a private club to accept a member because that would violate the freedom of association of the club. Yet, if the reason for the exclusion were motivated by race or religion, it is arguable that the state should have a positive duty to disallow it. Like other positive obligations, that duty will be qualified. The egregiousness of the badge of differentiation, the 'closeness' of the society, the impact of the decision on the

---

[289] *Horváth and Kiss v Hungary*, para 110.   [290] *Horváth and Kiss v Hungary*, paras 114–28.

[291] See n 231, para 46. For the work done by the Council of Europe in this field see the reports and speeches contained in the Roma rights website accessible at http://hub.coe.int/web/coe-portal/roma.

[292] See the remarks in *Oršuš and Others v Croatia* hudoc (2010) para 147, concerning the specific vulnerable position of the Roma population.

[293] On this Article, see Ch 1, section 5 and Ch 2, section 7.IV.

[294] See *Belgian Linguistic* case B 3 (1965) para 400.   [295] A 44 (1981); 4 EHRR 38 para 57 PC.

[296] A 264 (1993); 16 EHRR 462 para 37.

individual (membership of a trade union might be more important than participation in a social club), and the rationality of the exclusion (restricting political associations to supporters, churches to believers) will all weigh in assessing the compliance with a positive duty with respect to private action once one is established. It has been considered already that a state might justify as having an objective and reasonable justification action taken against some kinds of expression or some kinds of association (without necessarily relying on Article 14 or Article 17).[297] It is doubtful whether the Convention imposes a positive obligations on states to take action against expression which gratuitously insults religious feelings.[298] Religions can be expected to bear a considerable degree of criticism, provided it does not amount to incitement to religious hatred or incitement to anti-Semitism. It remains to be seen whether a like obligation can be found in other substantive articles to restrain racially inflammatory speech or associations.[299] As a strong European consensus about the unacceptability of such opinions or activities develops, it cannot be ruled out that the Court could read into Article 14 a positive obligation on the state to take action against private speech or action to ensure the effective enjoyment of other Convention rights of those against whom the sentiments were directed.[300]

As was noted earlier, the state may be under specific positive obligations to investigate racial elements to violent crime[301] and cases of indirect discrimination may imply a corresponding positive obligation upon states under Article 14 where the state fails to introduce appropriate exceptions to general rules to deal with persons whose situation requires being treated differently.[302] One should also keep in mind the operation of Article 8 insofar as it may impact on the position of minorities such as the Roma[303] and on cases concerning difference of treatment on grounds of health conditions, such as the dismissal of an employee on the grounds that he is HIV positive.[304]

II. REVERSE DISCRIMINATION

Reverse discrimination involves 'programmes designed to favour or promote the interests of disadvantaged groups'.[305] A state may engage in reverse discrimination within the ambit of Convention rights without being in breach of Article 14. The Court acknowledged this in the *Belgian Linguistic* case,[306] when it noted generally that not all instances of differential treatment are unacceptable and that 'certain legal inequalities tend only to correct factual inequalities'. Thus a protected quota of university student places for members of a particular racial group would amount to different treatment within the ambit of

---

[297] On Article 17, see Ch 20.

[298] *Otto-Preminger-Institut v Austria* A 295-A (1994); 19 EHRR 34 para 49. See Ch 14, section 3.III.

[299] Cf Article 20(1), ICCPR and Article 4, Racial Discrimination Convention.

[300] Such other Convention rights include the rights in Articles 10 and 11.

[301] See section 8.b of this chapter.

[302] *Thlimmenos v Greece* 2000-IV; 31 EHRR 411 para 48. See also the separate opinion of Judge Greve in *Price v UK* 2001-VII; 35 EHRR 1285. On indirect discrimination see section 9 of this chapter.

[303] See n 235. In *Chapman v UK* 2001-I, 33 EHRR 399, the Court noted that there could be said to be an emerging international consensus amongst the Member States of the Council of Europe recognizing the special needs of minorities and an obligation to protect their security, identity, and lifestyle, not only for the purpose of safeguarding the interests of the minorities themselves, but also to preserve a cultural diversity of value to the whole community: at para 93.

[304] See the Chamber judgment in *IB v Greece* hudoc (2012) (dismissal of employee who was HIV positive because the staff refused to work with him; violation of Article 14 in conjunction with Article 8).

[305] Parekh, in Hepple and Szyszczak, eds, *Discrimination: The Limits of Law*, 1992, ch 15, p 261. See also *Handbook*, ch 2, n 3.

[306] A 6 (1968); 1 EHRR 252 para 10 PC. See also *Stec v UK* (hudoc) 2006; 43 EHRR 1017 para 51.

a Convention right (the right to education, Article 2 of the First Protocol), but would not be in breach of Article 14 if it had the 'objective and reasonable justification' of increasing the disproportionately low percentage of members of that disadvantaged group in the university student population.[307] However, given the parasitic nature of Article 14, there can be no *legal obligation* on the part of states derived from that Article to engage in a policy or act of reverse discrimination; any such obligation would stem from a positive obligation in another Article guaranteeing a Convention right. As noted earlier, in the *Airey* case the Court held that the applicant was entitled to legal aid on the basis of Article 6 and did not examine her Article 14 claim. If there was an Article 14 claim on the facts of that case, it stemmed from the positive obligation in Article 6 to provide 'access to court' coupled with Article 14, not from any reverse discrimination claim based upon Article 14 by itself.

11. PROTOCOL 12

Article 1—General prohibition of discrimination

1. The enjoyment of any right set forth by law shall be secured without discrimination on any ground such as sex, race, colour, language, religion, political or other opinion, national or social origin, association with a national minority, property, birth or other status.
2. No one shall be discriminated against by any public authority on any ground such as those mentioned in paragraph 1.

Protocol 12[308] was drafted in recognition of the deficiencies of Article 14, but it is a weaker text than Article 26 of the International Covenant on Civil and Political Rights (ICCPR).[309] It was opened for signature on 4 November 2000 and entered into force on 1 April 2005. Many states have been reluctant to ratify the Protocol as they consider that it contains too many uncertainties and that its application is potentially too wide. The United Kingdom, for example, has stated that it will 'wait and see' how the Court interprets and applies Protocol 12 before ratifying it.[310] However, to date there have been few cases where the Court has interpreted this provision.[311] The Explanatory Report provides some detailed (if non-binding) comments on the Protocol's expected application.

---

[307] Cf *DG and DW Lindsay v UK No 11089/84*, 49 DR 181 at 190–1 (1986); 9 EHRR CD 555 at 559 (a tax advantage for married women, which fell within the ambit of the right to property, Article 1, First Protocol, had 'an objective and reasonable justification in the aim of providing positive discrimination' to encourage married women back to work).

[308] ETS 177. See Explanatory Report to Protocol 12 (herafter Explanatory Report), available at http://conventions.coe.int/; Grief, 27 (HR Supp) ELR 3 (2002); Khaliq, 2001 PL 458; Council of Europe, *Non-Discrimination: a Human Right*, 2005; Danish Institute for Human Rights in Lagoutte, ed, *Prohibition of Discrimination in the Nordic Countries: The Complicated Fate of Protocol No 12 to the European Convention on Human Rights*, 2005.

[309] All Convention states are parties to the ICCPR and almost all (though not the UK) have accepted the Optional Protocol to that instrument allowing individuals to bring complaints before the Human Rights Committee.

[310] See Kissane, in Council of Europe, *Non-Discrimination: A Human Right*, 2005, p 87 and Grief, 27 (HR Supp) ELR 3 (2002).

[311] See the examples set out later on in this section.

The Protocol does not prevent all differential treatment. The notion of 'discrimination' is to be understood in the same way as that already existing under Article 14. Differences of treatment that can be justified by objective and reasonable grounds should be compatible with Protocol 12.[312] Also the list of non-discrimination grounds remains the same as for Article 14, it being understood that it was not necessary to add new badges of discrimination to the list given its non-exhaustive nature, the Court's capacity to do this in any case, and for fear that the inclusion of any particular additional ground might give rise to unwarranted *a contrario* interpretations as regards discrimination based on grounds not so included.[313]

The advance offered by the Protocol is that the narrow field to which Article 14 currently restricts non-discrimination standards is extended to 'any right set forth by law'. However, the essential question is, what does this terminology potentially cover? For example, do the words relate to existing domestic law or do they extend to international law? Some governments apparently fear that if the scope of Protocol 12 is extended to the latter, then significant new commitments could be introduced into domestic law.[314] According to the Explanatory Report, the additional scope of protection under Article 1 concerns cases where a person is discriminated against: '(i) in the enjoyment of any right specifically granted to an individual under national law; (ii) in the enjoyment of a right which may be inferred from a clear obligation of a public authority under national law, that is, where a public authority is under an obligation under national law to behave in a particular manner; (iii) by a public authority in the exercise of discretionary power (for example, granting certain subsidies); and (iv) by any other act or omission by a public authority (for example, the behaviour of law enforcement officers when controlling a riot)'.[315]

The extent to which the Protocol might place positive obligations upon the state to prevent discrimination, even between private individuals, is also debatable. The Explanatory Report states that 'the prime objective of Article 1 is to embody a negative obligation for the Parties: the obligation not to discriminate against individuals'.[316] In this respect the Protocol is 'not intended to impose a general positive obligation on the Parties to take measures to prevent or remedy all instances of discrimination in relations between private persons'. This is because '[a]n additional protocol to the Convention, which typically contains justiciable individual rights formulated in concise provisions, would not be a suitable instrument for defining the various elements of such a wide-ranging obligation of a programmatic character'.[317] However the Explanatory Report suggests that positive obligations could arise if there is a clear lacuna in domestic law protection from discrimination. In particular, as regards private persons, 'a failure to provide protection from discrimination in such relations might be so clear-cut and grave that it might engage clearly the responsibility of the state and then Article 1 of the Protocol could come into play' in accordance with the stance taken by the Court in *X and Y v Netherlands*.[318] The Explanatory Report specifically states that:

any positive obligation in the area of relations between private persons would concern, at the most, relations in the public sphere normally regulated by law, for which the state

---

[312] Explanatory Report para 16. See also the Preamble to the Protocol.

[313] Explanatory Report para 20.

[314] For discussion see Grief, 27 (HR Supp) ELR 3 (2002) and Khaliq, 2001 PL 458. The Protocol is not to be construed as limiting or derogating from domestic or treaty provisions which provide further protection from discrimination, such as those found under the Convention on Elimination of All Forms of Racial Discrimination and the Convention on the Elimination of All Forms of Discrimination against Women.

[315] Explanatory Report para 22.   [316] Explanatory Report para 24.

[317] Explanatory Report para 25.   [318] A 91 (1985); 8 EHRR 235 paras 23–4, 27, and 30.

has a certain responsibility (for example, arbitrary denial of access to work, access to restaurants, or to services which private persons may make available to the public such as medical care or utilities such as water and electricity, etc). The precise form of the response which the state should take will vary according to the circumstances. It is understood that purely private matters would not be affected. Regulation of such matters would also be likely to interfere with the individual's right to respect for his private and family life, his home and his correspondence, as guaranteed by Article 8 of the Convention.[319]

In *Sejdić and Finci v Bosnia and Herzegovina*,[320] the Court applied Article 1 of Protocol 12 for the first time in respect of the complaint that the applicants (members of the Jewish and Roma communities) could not stand in elections for the Presidency, not being members of the 'constituent peoples'. This complaint could not be examined under Article 14 in conjunction Article 3 of Protocol 1 since it did not fall within the ambit of the latter provision that only concerned elections to the 'legislature'. The Court saw no reason to depart from the settled interpretation of discrimination developed in its case law under Article 14. It found a violation of this provision for the same reasons as it had found a violation of Article 14 as regards the bar of standing for elections to the House of Peoples.[321] The Court also considered Protocol 12 to be applicable in *Savez cravka 'Riječ života' and Others v Croatia*,[322] which concerned a refusal to register the applicant churches as religious communities to enable them to provide *inter alia* religious education. The Court had found a violation of Article 14 in conjunction with Article 9 and, although it found Article 1 of Protocol 12 to be applicable, it found it unnecessary to examine it.

12. CONCLUSION

By envisaging very early on in its career that there could be a violation of Article 14 when read with a main Convention right, even though that main right had not itself been violated on its own, the Court ensured that the Convention's non-discrimination provision would not remain the dead letter that it might otherwise have been. Part of the problem is that Article 14 can be seen as a specific corner of all Convention articles and thus most complaints have a discrimination dimension to them. Whether such complaints deserve to be singled out for separate examination may depend on how the case is pleaded or whether the pith and substance of the complaint can be easily identified as discrimination. However, through the 1970s and into the 1990s, the Court often opted not to resolve Article 14 questions in some apparently key cases and it is certainly striking that, for example, only in 1999 did it find a violation of Article 14 in conjunction with another Article in respect of a 'homosexual' case.[323] There is still a tendency in the Court today to leave Article 14 issues unexplored where a breach of another substantive article has been found.[324] It is open to debate whether the apparent early reluctance to address Article 14

[319] Explanatory Report para 28.
[320] Hudoc (2009) GC. Also *Maktouf and Damjanović v Bosnia and Herzegovina* hudoc (2013) GC paras 78–83.
[321] *Sejdić and Finci v Bosnia and Herzegovina*, paras 55–6. The Court had found it unnecessary to examine the complaint of discrimination in respect of election to the House of Peoples under Article 1 of Protocol 12, para 51. See also Ch 23, section 2.   [322] Hudoc (2010) paras 113–15.
[323] *Salgueiro da Silva Mouta v Portugal* 1999-IX; 31 EHRR 1055.
[324] See, eg, Judge Keller's dissent in *Sukran Aydin v Turkey* hudoc (2013).

properly reflected the parasitic nature of that provision or was evidence that the Court was not taking Article 14 as seriously as it should have. Either way, since the late 1990s, cases such as *EB v France*, *DH v Czech Republic*, *X v Austria*, *Kiyutin v Russia*, *Schalk and Kopf v Austria*, *Konstantin Markin v Russia*, and *Thlimmenos v Greece* illustrate a strong positive approach to Article 14, and more discrimination cases have since been addressed by the Court. Areas of Convention jurisprudence such as discrimination based on 'birth' have been re-applied to new contexts, and there is now in place a richer jurisprudence on discrimination in the field of, for example, 'sex (gender)' and 'sexual orientation'.

It will be appreciated that advances in Convention jurisprudence with respect to the main substantive rights have served to heighten the potential impact that Article 14 may have. For example, the Grand Chamber's admissibility decision in *Stec v UK*, which determined that Article 1 of the First Protocol applied to individuals who have 'an assertable right under domestic law to a welfare benefit',[325] has entailed that, in effect, Article 14 will apply to a great proportion of social security provisions in the member states. It remains to be seen how the Court will interpret and apply Protocol 12, how this will strengthen the effectiveness of the Convention in the field of anti-discrimination, and if this will have an impact on the application of Article 14 itself. The Protocol has the long-term potential to establish a much more robust anti-discrimination basis for the Convention, allowing it, to some extent at least, to catch up with EU law in this field. It may therefore be especially significant for non-EU states.

The Court's judgments have also been criticized, at least in the past, for being too favourable to states. National non-discrimination law is often more elaborate than the brief language of Article 14. However, when reading cases such as *Stec*, *Petrovic*, and *Carson*, it is necessary to keep in mind that it is not for the Strasbourg Court to seek to impose equality standards on the forty-seven sovereign member states to the Convention in areas such as social security where national policies will inevitably be very different.[326]

Finally, case law from several of the member states that ratified the Convention in the 1990s and concerning allegations of severe discrimination against Roma has presented major new challenges for the Court. It has made some strong comments condemning racism and ethnic hatred, and set new standards for Article 14 as regards, for example, the procedural obligation to investigate police violence motivated by race. The Grand Chamber ruling in *DH v Czech Republic* is arguably one of the most important Article 14 judgments ever. It remains to be seen what contribution Article 14, and indeed Protocol 12, will make to the plight of minorities such as the Roma in the future.

---

[325] *Stec v UK Nos 65731/01* and *65900/01* hudoc (2005); 41 EHRR SE 295 para 34 GC. Also *Gaygusuz v Austria* hudoc (1996).

[326] Cf *Topčić-Rosenberg v Croatia* hudoc (2013). See Dembour, 12 HRLR 689–721 (2012).

19

ARTICLE 15: DEROGATION IN TIME OF WAR OR OTHER PUBLIC EMERGENCY THREATENING THE LIFE OF THE NATION

Article 15

1. In time of war or other public emergency threatening the life of the nation any High Contracting Party may take measures derogating from its obligations under this Convention to the extent strictly required by the exigencies of the situation, provided that such measures are not inconsistent with its other obligations under international law.
2. No derogation from Article 2, except in respect of deaths resulting from lawful acts of war, or from Articles 3, 4 (paragraph 1) and 7 shall be made under this provision.
3. Any High Contracting Party availing itself of this right of derogation shall keep the Secretary General of the Council of Europe fully informed of the measures which it has taken and the reasons therefor. It shall also inform the Secretary General of the Council of Europe when such measures have ceased to operate and the provisions of the Convention are again being fully executed.

1. INTRODUCTION

Article 15[1] enables a state to unilaterally derogate from some of its substantive Convention obligations in certain exceptional circumstances. The provision is therefore of great importance to the Convention's general integrity and, in practice, the protection of human rights in situations where individuals may be especially vulnerable to the authoritarian actions of the state. Accordingly, Article 15 subjects the measure of derogation to a specific regime of safeguards that may be monitored by the Court, although only in applications reaching it.

---

[1] See Ergec, *Les Droits de l'homme à l'épreuve des circonstances exceptionelles: Etude sur l'article 15 de la Convention Européenne des droits de l'homme*, 1987; Chowdhury, *Rule of Law in State of Emergency: The Paris Minimum Standards of Human Rights Norms in a State of Emergency*, 1989; Doswald-Beck, *Human Rights in Times of Conflict and Terrorism*, 2011, ch 3; Oraa, *Human Rights in States of Emergency in International Law*, 1992; Fitzpatrick, *Human Rights in Conflict: the International System for Protecting Human Rights during States of Emergency*, 1994; Svensson-McCarthy, *The International Law of Human Rights and States of Exception*, 1998.

At the international level, instruments for the general protection of civil and political rights usually[2] have a derogation clause. They are very similar in their terms, and the practice of international institutions under other international human rights treaties[3] is potentially more useful in the interpretation of Article 15 than anywhere else in the European Convention. The dilemma posed by derogation clauses is as easy to state as it is hard to resolve. Once the necessity for derogation is conceded, it becomes difficult to control abusive recourse to the power of suspending rights that the provision permits. In many cases, the effective use of the power will require expedition. The evidence on which recourse to the power is based may be extensive but at the same time sensitive. The determination of the propriety of particular measures of derogation, once the existence of an emergency has been established or conceded, is a matter of practical judgment rather than refined analysis. Any review, especially by an international court, is inevitably open to the criticism that fraught decisions made at a time of crisis are being subjected to considered re-evaluation with the comfort of hindsight. It has been suggested that the value of judicial intervention in the exercise of what is essentially a political power is limited—and that the more narrowly the power of derogation is confined, that is to say, the more serious the circumstances must be before it may be relied upon, the less the room for judicial review.[4] However, the experience of abusive recourse to the derogation power is extensive enough for an abstentionist approach to be highly undesirable. In the nature of things, the national judicial means of redress will often have been undermined, so the responsibility of international institutions is the more compelling.

The Strasbourg authorities have rejected the claims of states that questions arising under Article 15 are beyond their competence altogether, but they have approached cases before them rather cautiously, some say too cautiously. Happily, the number of occasions when states have relied on Article 15 has been small. Details of the notices of derogation submitted by member states can be found in the respective editions of the *Yearbook of the European Convention*.[5] The great majority of states have never derogated from the Convention at any time. As of 31 July 2013, no state had entered a notice of derogation. However, only in March 2005 did the United Kingdom withdraw a derogation made soon after the events of 'September 11th'.[6] The Grand Chamber examined this derogation in *A v UK*.[7]

Other examples of derogations that have been addressed by the Strasbourg organs in the context of cases reaching them include: the British derogation in the second half of the 1950s concerning the governance of Cyprus (*Greece v UK*);[8] the derogation entered by Ireland in 1957 following terrorist violence connected to Northern Ireland (*Lawless v*

---

[2] The African Charter of Human and Peoples' Rights does not have an express emergency clause.

[3] See Oraa, *Human Rights in States of Emergency in International Law*, 1992 and Svensson-McCarthy, *The International Law of Human Rights and States of Exception*, 1998. The equivalent Article under the ICCPR is Article 4; see General Comment No 29 CCPR/C/21/Rev.1/Add.11, 31 August 2001; and Joseph, 2 HRLR 81 (2002).

[4] Alexander, 5 HRLJ 1 (1984).   [5] See also http://conventions.coe.int.

[6] Russia never derogated with respect to Chechnya, cf *Isayeva v Russia* hudoc (2005); 41 EHRR 791 paras 133 and 191. Albania entered a derogation, referring to a constitutional and public order crisis, covering the period 10 March 1997 until 24 July 1997. Armenia appears to have briefly derogated from the Convention in March 2008, concerning 'the state of emergency in the city of Yerevan'. Georgia entered a derogation for a thirteen-day period in March 2006 aimed at preventing the further spread of bird flu. For details consult http://conventions.coe.int.

[7] *A v UK* ECHR 2009; 49 EHRR 625 GC, see sections 4 and 5. See Shah, 9 HRLR 473 (2009) and Elliott, 8 IJCL 131 (2010).

[8] *No 176/56*, 2 YB 176 (1958) Com Rep, fully reported at 18 HRLJ 348 (1997); CM Res (59) 12. See especially Simpson, *Human Rights and the End of Empire*, 2001.

Ireland);[9] the derogation submitted by the Greek government in 1967 connected to the *coup d'état* occurring in that country (the *Greek* case);[10] the derogation entered by the United Kingdom in respect of terrorism in Northern Ireland in the early 1970s (*Ireland v UK*)[11] and which was renewed on a number of occasions; a further derogation submitted by the United Kingdom in 1989 in respect of Northern Ireland terrorism (*Brannigan and McBride v UK*);[12] and derogations made by the Turkish government in respect of south-east Turkey (Kurdish separatist violence/terrorism) and which have been examined in various cases (including *Aksoy v Turkey*).[13] It is worth noticing that some of these authorities are now many years old.

2. THE NEED TO RESORT TO ARTICLE 15 (SOME COMMENTS ON THE COURT'S GENERAL APPROACH TO 'TERRORISM CASES')

The Strasbourg jurisprudence reveals that states have some leeway within the Convention itself before having to contemplate invoking Article 15 in the context of there being a 'public emergency threatening the life of the nation'.[14] Hence it has been suggested that part of the explanation why states other than the United Kingdom did not derogate from the Convention given the apparent threat of terrorism[15] after 'September 11th' was that such states had 'found quite enough flexibility in the Convention standards to accommodate any special provisions for counter-terrorist purposes'.[16] The following paragraphs briefly comment on the approach adopted by the Court to cases involving terrorism when Article 15 has not been relied upon.

In general, states will wish to avoid relying on Article 15, especially in cases of internal disorder, where there is a risk that the government's opponents will use the emergency derogation as evidence of the effectiveness of their campaign against the authorities. Article 15(2) makes it clear that some measures of derogation are impermissible whatever the emergency, so some options that the state might wish to take advantage of are absolutely forbidden to it. Article 3, for example, is an absolute non-derogable right, so it provides for no exceptions, even if they are purportedly justified by the fight against terrorism and organized crime.[17] The British government was therefore unable to derogate

---

[9] A 3 (1961); 1 EHRR 15. See Doolan, *Lawless v Ireland (1957–1961): The First Case Before the European Court of Human Rights*, 2001.

[10] 12 YB (the *Greek* case) 1 (1969) CM Res (70) DH 1 and 17 YB 618 (1974); CM Res (74) DH 2. See Coleman, 2 IYHR 121 (1972).   [11] A 25 (1978); 2 EHRR 25 PC. See O'Boyle, 71 AJIL 674 (1977).

[12] A 258-B (1993); 17 EHRR 539 PC. See Marks, 15 OJLS 69 (1995).   [13] 1996-VI; 23 EHRR 553.

[14] On the European response to terrorism and protection of human rights see Warbrick, 15 EJIL 989 (2004) and 3 EHRLR 287 (2002); Hedigan, 28 Fordham 2005 Int'l L J 392; Doswald-Beck, *Human Rights in Times of Conflict and Terrorism*, 2011; and Myjer in María Salinas de Frías, Samuel, and White (eds), *Counter-Terrorism International Law and Practice*, 2012, ch 28. See also European Court of Human Rights, *Factsheet—Terrorism*, available at http://www.echr.coe.int. See also *The Guidelines of the Committee of Ministers of the Council of Europe on human rights and the fight against terrorism* ('CoE Terrorism Guidelines') (11 July 2002).

[15] On the definition of terrorism by Council of Europe bodies, see Parliamentary Assembly Recommendation 1426 (1999), *European Democracies Facing Up to Terrorism* (23 September 1999), para 5. See also *CoE Terrorism Guidelines* at 16–17.   [16] Warbrick, 3 EHRLR 287 (2002) at p 311.

[17] *Chahal v UK* 1996-V; 23 EHRR 413 paras 78–80.

from Article 3 in December 2001, so as to permit it to expel certain suspected international terrorists in circumstances that might otherwise have breached that provision.[18]

In contrast to Article 3, the majority of the Articles of the Convention have express limitation clauses in them that allow restriction on rights in most of the circumstances that fall within a 'public emergency'. So it may be 'necessary in a democratic society' for a state to interfere with, say, freedom of expression to preserve public order to a greater extent in time of emergency than it would be in more settled conditions.[19] A similar comment may be made, for example, as regards certain potential restrictions on the right to respect for private life when there is an identifiable need to conduct secret surveillance of terrorist suspects.[20] As early as 1978 the Court stated that:

> some compromise between the requirements for defending democratic society and individual rights is inherent in the system of the Convention...As the Preamble to the Convention states, 'Fundamental Freedoms...are best maintained on the one hand by an effective political democracy and on the other by a common understanding and observance of the Human Rights upon which (the Contracting States) depend'. In the context of Article 8, this means that a balance must be sought between the exercise by the individual of the right guaranteed to him under paragraph 1 and the necessity under paragraph 2 to impose secret surveillance for the protection of the democratic society as a whole.[21]

It follows that, in practice, the measures of derogation most likely to be implemented under the authority of Article 15 will be ones that involve derogation from those Articles which are not qualified in the same way as, for example, Articles 8–11. Here states have argued that special regimes to meet emergency circumstances, while deviating from the ordinary standards of domestic law, do not violate the Convention because the ordinary rules are above the minimum standards of Articles 5 and 6 and the exceptional measures do not fall below these levels.[22]

In 1990, in the context of a case concerning arrest and detention under criminal legislation enacted to deal with acts of terrorism connected with the affairs of Northern Ireland, the Court explained that its 'general approach' was to take into account 'the need, inherent in the Convention system, for a proper balance between the defence of the institutions of democracy in the common interest and the protection of individual rights'. It would therefore 'take into account the special nature of terrorist crime and the exigencies of dealing with it, as far as is compatible with the applicable provisions of the Convention in the light of their particular wording and its overall object and purpose'.[23] Accordingly, when a state has not derogated under Article 15, the Court will proceed on the basis that the Articles of the Convention in respect of which complaints have been made are fully applicable.[24] However, this does preclude proper account being taken of the background circumstances[25] of the

---

[18] It derogated from Article 5(1)(f) instead.

[19] Eg, *Brind v UK No18714/91*, 77-A DR 42 (1994); 18 EHRR CD 76. Cf, *Çetin v Turkey* 2003-III.

[20] Eg, *Klass v Germany* A 28 (1978); 2 EHRR 214 PC and *Erdem v Germany* 2001-VII; 35 EHRR 383 (monitoring of prison correspondence).   [21] *Klass v Germany*, para 59.

[22] This was the argument in *Klass*.

[23] *Fox, Campbell and Hartley v UK* A 182 (1990); 13 EHRR 157 para 28.

[24] See *Isayeva v Russia* hudoc (2005); 41 EHRR 791 para 191 (no derogation; so 'judged against a normal legal background').

[25] *Brogan v UK* A 145-B (1988); 11 EHRR 117 para 48 PC. See also *A v UK* ECHR 2009; 49 EHRR 29 paras 216–17 GC, and the statement made by the Commission in *McVeigh, O'Neill and Evans v UK Nos 8022/77, 8025/77 and 8027/77*, 25 DR 15 at 39 (1981); 5 EHRR 71 para 157.

case, ie 'problems linked to the prevention of terrorism',[26] and the balancing exercise referred to earlier is undertaken in that context. Nevertheless, there are limits as the Article 5 and 6 jurisprudence demonstrates.

As will be seen from the cases noted in this chapter, typically emergency legislation is directed to extending the powers of the executive to arrest and detain persons suspected of engagement in forbidden activities, who would normally rely on Articles 5 and 6 to protect them. A number of applications involving these Articles against the backdrop of terrorist situations have reached the Court's attention when the particular right in issue has not been derogated from. Several of these cases reveal that, even in the context of terrorism and defence of national security, certain interpretations of Articles 5 and 6 cannot be accepted. Hence, in *Lawless v Ireland*,[27] the Court declined to interpret Article 5(1)(c) in a manner wide enough to embrace the measures of preventative detention used in Ireland at the time. In *Incal v Turkey*,[28] the Court found that a National Security Court, which included a military legal officer as one of its three judges, did not satisfy standards of independence and objective impartiality for the purposes of Article 6.

Other cases indicate that whilst the Court is prepared to take into account the terrorism or national security context, consistent with the fact that the state has not derogated, it will not allow the very essence of the safeguard in issue to be impaired. For example, the Court evidently did take notice of the background of terrorism in *Fox, Campbell and Hartley v UK*,[29] when it said:

> Certainly Article 5(1)(c) of the Convention should not be applied in such a manner as to put disproportionate difficulties in the way of the police authorities of the Contracting States in taking effective measures to counter organised terrorism...

Nonetheless, *some* evidence of 'reasonable suspicion' to justify an arrest has to be produced to satisfy Article 5(1)(c). In the *Fox* case, the Court held that there had been a breach because no evidence had been produced. In contrast, in *Murray v UK*[30] and *O'Hara v UK*,[31] there was sufficient evidence from national court proceedings to satisfy the Court's discounted 'reasonable suspicion' test in terrorist cases. As the Court has acknowledged on several occasions, 'the investigation of terrorist offences undoubtedly presents the authorities with special problems',[32] but this does not mean 'that the investigating authorities have *carte blanche* under Article 5 to arrest suspects for questioning, free from effective control by the domestic courts and, ultimately, by the Convention supervisory institutions, whenever they choose to assert that terrorism is involved'.[33]

---

[26] *Incal v Turkey* 1998-IV; 29 EHRR 449 para 58. See also *Ireland v UK* A 25 (1978); 2 EHRR 25 PC; *Aksoy v Turkey* 1996-VI; 23 EHRR 553 paras 70 and 84; *Zana v Turkey* 1997-VII; 27 EHRR 667 paras 59–60; *United Communist Party of Turkey and Others v Turkey* 1998-I; 26 EHRR 121 para 59. See also *Chraidi v Germany* 2006-XII; 47 EHRR 47 para 37 (regarding 'international terrorism').

[27] A 3 (1961); 1 EHRR 15 para 15.   [28] 1998-IV; 29 EHRR 449.

[29] A 182 (1990); 13 EHRR 157 para 34. See also para 32.

[30] A 300-A (1994); 19 EHRR 191 paras 47 and 63 GC (by thirteen votes to five).

[31] 2001-X; 34 EHRR 812.

[32] See *Murray v UK* A 300-A (1994); 19 EHRR 193 para 58; *Aksoy v Turkey* 1996-VI; 23 EHRR 553 para 78; *Sakık v Turkey* 1997-VII; 26 EHRR 662 para 44; *Demir v Turkey* 1998-VI; 33 EHHR1056 para 41; *Dikme v Turkey* 2000-VII para 64.

[33] *Murray v UK*, para 58. See also *El-Masri v the Former Yugoslav Republic of Macedonia* ECHR-2012; 57 EHRR 783 para 232 GC. See also *Medvedyev v France* ECHR-2010; 51 EHRR 899 para 126 GC (fight against drug trafficking).

In *Brogan v UK*,[34] a majority of the Court was not persuaded that the background of terrorism justified, on the facts before them, the extended periods of post-arrest detention in the absence of judicial supervision under Article 5(3). However, the Court did accept that 'subject to the existence of adequate safeguards, the context of terrorism in Northern Ireland has the effect of prolonging the period during which the authorities may, without violating Article 5 para 3, keep a person suspected of serious terrorist offences in custody before bringing him before a judge or other judicial officer'.[35]

A not dissimilar approach was evident in *Chahal v UK*[36] and *A v UK*[37] as regards the operation of Article 5(4) in the context of national security. The Court refused to accept that legitimate security concerns about the nature and sources of information identifying the applicants as a security threat was a justification for denying them a substantial measure of procedural justice under Article 5(4). As we have observed,[38] it required a balance to be struck between procedural fairness and the demands of national security, one that did not require that all information against the detainee be disclosed, but that appropriate and sufficient information be provided to him in the context of the special court regime in operation (which included the role of special advocates).[39]

As to Article 5(1)(f), which was relevant to *A v UK*, the Court refused to accept British arguments to the effect that, as the individuals concerned were suspected terrorists, the standards of protection under the relevant provision should be diluted on the basis that this would strike an appropriate balance between the individual's right to liberty and the state's interest in protecting its population from terrorist threat, particularly in the post-'September 11th' era.[40] Similar arguments were put to the Court, and rejected by it, in case law concerning Article 3 and the deportation of (suspected) terrorists. The British government failed to persuade Strasbourg that its established case law on this aspect of that Article should be modified (in fact, diluted) so as to allow the deporting state to balance the risk of harm an individual may suffer in the receiving state against the dangers that person poses to the community as a whole in the host (Convention) state.[41] However, the Grand Chamber has accepted that appropriately robust and effective Memoranda of Understanding may negate the (otherwise existing) 'real risk' of treatment contrary to Article 3 so as to permit deportation.[42]

It will be observed, therefore, that the Court has acknowledged the relevance of exceptional circumstances of disorder to the interpretation of Articles 5 and 6, although it has been generally reluctant to give decisive weight to them given the importance of the (non-derogated from) right at stake. The jurisprudence is in keeping with the general principle that '[w]hen a measure restricts human rights, restrictions must be defined as precisely as possible and be necessary and proportionate to the aim pursued'.[43]

---

[34] A 145-B (1988); 11 EHRR 117 paras 55–62 PC (twelve votes to seven).

[35] *Brogan v UK*, para 61. See Judge Evans' strong dissent. There was no support for Judge Martens' dissenting opinion, which sought to establish a wider margin of appreciation for states faced with terrorist campaigns. Although not expressly, his opinion seeks to introduce the *Klass* principle (see earlier in the main text of this section) into the interpretation of Article 5.

[36] 1996-V; 23 EHRR 413 GC. See also *Al-Nashif v Bulgaria* hudoc (2002); 36 EHRR 655 para 94.

[37] ECHR 2009; 49 EHRR 29 GC.   [38] See the analysis of Article 5(4) in Ch 8, section 8.II.c.

[39] *A v UK* ECHR 2009; 49 EHRR 625 paras 216–20 GC.

[40] *A v UK*, para 171 (British submissions at para 148), and see Ch 8, section 5.VI.b.

[41] *Saadi v Italy* ECHR 2008; 49 EHRR 30 paras 137–41 GC (the UK intervened in this case). See Moeckli, 8(3) HRLR 534 (2008).

[42] See *Othman v United Kingdom* ECHR-2012; 55 EHRR 1, and see generally Ch 6, section 3.IV.

[43] *CoE Terrorism Guidelines* III (2).

Arguably, therefore, some of the judgments noted so far, and the Strasbourg jurisprudence generally, go some way towards sparing a state from having to make an Article 15 declaration in the face of a terrorist campaign. It must be made clear, however, that the fight against terrorism alone is not enough to justify derogation from the Convention. A state may only legally take this highly significant step when the fight against terrorism takes place in the context of 'a public emergency threatening the life of the nation', and then the other qualifying requirements set out by Article 15 must be satisfied too.

3. THE GENERAL PATTERN OF ARTICLE 15

The language of Article 15 seeks to balance the formidable power given to states by subjecting its exercise to various kinds of limitation. The first are textual limitations, confining the power to 'time of war or other public emergency threatening the life of the nation' and allowing states to take only such action as is 'strictly required by the exigencies of the situation'. Next, the power to derogate is subject to substantive restrictions: no derogation is permitted in the case of the specific Articles of the Convention referred to in Article 15(2),[44] nor those covered by the Sixth[45] and Thirteenth[46] Protocols, and the derogating state must not contravene other international law obligations (Article 15(1)).[47] Finally, there are procedural conditions in Article 15(3) which attend recourse to the derogation power, which have the important consequence of drawing attention to these special situations and which are also a source of information which will be useful in the pursuit of any applications in Strasbourg.

4. 'IN TIME OF WAR OR OTHER PUBLIC EMERGENCY THREATENING THE LIFE OF THE NATION'

It is for the Court to interpret each element in Article 15, including what can constitute a 'public emergency'.[48] It will be appreciated, nonetheless, that it is a very delicate task for the European Court to assess whether a respondent state acting in good faith was correct in identifying the existence of a 'public emergency' under Article 15. Hence the case law is strongly associated with the granting to the respondent state of a generous margin of appreciation[49] which has led some to question the effectiveness of Strasbourg review in this important context.[50] Only in one instance, the *Greek* case, has a Strasbourg

---

[44] These are 'Article 2, except in respect of deaths resulting from lawful acts of war ... Articles 3, 4 (paragraph 1), and 7'. [45] Article 3, Sixth Protocol.

[46] Article 2, Thirteenth Protocol.

[47] It has been argued that there are other Articles of the Convention which operate as substantive restrictions on the power of derogation. Cf, *Habeas Corpus in Emergency Situations* (Articles 27(2), 25(1), ACHR), I-A Ct HRts Rep, Series A 8 (1987); 9 HRLJ 94 (1988) advisory opinion.

[48] *Greece v UK No 176/56*, 2 YB 176 (1958) Com Rep, 18 HRLJ 348 (1997); CM Res (59) 12 and *Lawless v Ireland* A 3 (1961); 1 EHRR 15 para 28.

[49] On the evolution of this doctrine in the Article 15 context see O'Boyle, 19 HRLJ 23 (1998). For a highly critical appraisal see Gross and Ní Aoláin, 23 HRQ 625 (2001).

[50] Van Dijk and Van Hoof *et al* (eds), *Theory and Practice of the European Convention on Human Rights*, 2006. at p 1059 and pp 1071–5.

institution (in fact, the Commission—the case did not reach the Court) disagreed with a respondent state as to the very existence of a 'public emergency'. In that case it was strongly arguable that the derogation was made in bad faith by the military Greek government and the Commission refused to extend to the respondent state any margin of appreciation.[51]

I. INTERPRETATION OF ARTICLE 15(1): CIRCUMSTANCES REPRESENTING 'A PUBLIC EMERGENCY THREATENING THE LIFE OF THE NATION'

The jurisprudence on precisely what is covered by the notion of 'public emergency threatening the life of the nation', notably in terms of the severity of the situation concerned (level of violence, harm or threat required), and how 'imminent' a potential emergency must be, is far from comprehensive. All cases reaching the Court have concerned terrorism, something that the drafters of the Convention almost certainly did not have specifically in mind in 1949–50.

a. Basic definition

As to what suffices for a 'war'[52] or other public emergency threatening the life of the nation' within the meaning of Article 15(1), in *Lawless v Ireland*,[53] the Court adopted the language of the Commission in holding that:

> in the general context of Article 15 of the Convention, the natural and customary meaning of the words 'other public emergency threatening the life of the nation' is sufficiently clear;[54] ... *they refer to an exceptional situation of crisis or emergency which affects the whole population and constitutes a threat to the organised life of the community of which the State is composed*. (emphasis added)

In the *Greek* case,[55] the Commission noted that the French text of the *Lawless* judgment was authentic and that it had additionally referred to the notion that an emergency may be not just actual but also 'imminent'. It described the qualifying features of such an emergency as follows:

(1) It must be actual or imminent.

(2) Its effects must involve the whole nation.

(3) The continuance of the organized life of the community must be threatened.

(4) The crisis or danger must be exceptional, in that the normal measures or restrictions, permitted by the Convention for the maintenance of public safety, health and order, are plainly inadequate.[56]

---

[51] See section 4.II.

[52] To date there has been no case before the Strasbourg organs when a respondent state has claimed that it has derogated from the Convention on the basis that a state of war exists. Neither Russia nor Georgia derogated in the context of the armed conflict between both states of 2008. On 'war' in the context of Article 15, see Costa and O'Boyle, 'The European Court of Human Rights and International Humanitarian Law' in *Rozakis Essays* 107 at 115–20.   [53] A3 (1961); 1 EHRR 15 para 28.

[54] The Court did not, therefore, consult the Convention's *travaux préparatoires*.

[55] 12 YB (the *Greek* case) 1 (1969) Com Rep; CM Res (70) DH 1.   [56] The *Greek* case, para 153.

b. *A and others v UK*

The Grand Chamber confirmed its approval of these standards in *A v UK*, concerning the British derogation[57] from the Convention submitted in late 2001. A point of contention then was whether Article 15(1) applied to the uncertainty of a situation apparently represented by the purported *threat* posed to the United Kingdom by a highly organized and secretive terrorist organization (al'Qaeda) supposedly capable and willing to perpetrate atrocities like those witnessed in the United States on 'September 11th' (2001).[58] No other Council of Europe state had derogated from the Convention, even though others were also subject to al'Qaeda threats,[59] although the British government referred to its close links with the United States, making it a particular target.[60] At the time the derogation was made there had been no (al'Qaeda) terrorist attack on the United Kingdom, although the London bombings of July 2005 preceded Strasbourg's hearing of the case by some time. Its conclusion that there was a public emergency threatening the life of the nation did not follow from its independent examination of the issues, or the application of the definitions mentioned earlier. Instead it owed much to the approach it took. The Court stated that the wide margin of appreciation owing to the national authorities included the domestic courts, and that it would not disagree with the conclusions reached by the highest domestic court unless it had 'misinterpreted or misapplied Article 15 or the Court's jurisprudence under that Article or reached a conclusion which was manifestly unreasonable'.[61] The Court went on to state that it 'share[d]' the view of the House of Lords[62] that there was a 'public emergency threatening the life of the nation' at the relevant time, the Law Lords being better 'placed to assess the evidence relating to the existence of an emergency', such that 'significant weight'[63] had to be accorded to their views. In reality it appeared that the Court relied to a large extent on the House of Lords' conclusions. Although that approach accords with the principle of subsidiarity, a significant problem with its application in *A v UK* was that the House of Lords itself had been highly deferential to the executive and Parliament.[64] It had not seen the closed evidence underpinning the existence of a threat, and some of the Law Lords were evidently unsure on the Article 15(1) threshold question.[65]

Nonetheless, *A v UK* did develop the Court's Article 15(1) jurisprudence in some ways. The Grand Chamber refused to endorse the approach adopted by Lord Hoffmann in his judgment. He took Strasbourg's stipulation that there be 'a threat to the organised life of the community' (*Lawless*) to require more than a threat of serious physical damage

---

[57] On which see Doswald-Beck, *Human Rights in Times of Conflict and Terrorism*, 2011, at pp 86–8.

[58] The British government contended that the events of 11 September 2001 demonstrated that al'Qaeda-inspired international terrorists 'had the intention and capacity to mount attacks against civilian targets on an unprecedented scale', and that 'their fanaticism, ruthlessness and determination' made it difficult for the state to prevent such attacks: *A v UK* ECHR 2009; 49 EHRR 625 para 10 GC.

[59] Cf the Court's statement, *A v UK*, para 180 GC.   [60] *A v UK*, para 10 GC.

[61] *A v UK* ECHR 2009; 49 EHRR 625 para 174 GC, and see also para 180.

[62] *A and Others v Secretary of State for the Home Department* [2004] UKHL 56.

[63] *A v UK* ECHR 2009; 49 EHRR 625 para 180 GC (weight was also given to the assessments made by the United Kingdom's executive and Parliament).

[64] For criticism see Shah, 9 HRLR 473 (2009) at p 480 and Doswald-Beck, *Human Rights in Times of Conflict and Terrorism*, 2011 at p 88.

[65] *A and Others v Secretary of State for the Home Department* [2004] UKHL 56. The majority showed considerable deference to the executive in its capacity to take what was regarded as a primarily 'political' decision that verged on being 'non-justiciable' (Lord Bingham, para 29, but see also doubts expressed at para 26, Lord Rodger (para 165) and Lord Scott (para 154)). Lords Bingham and Rodger expressed some sympathy with Lord Hoffmann's view, on which see the paragraph that follows.

and loss of life. Accepting that there was credible evidence of a threat of serious terrorist attack, he saw Article 15(1) as requiring a threat to 'our institutions of government or our existence as a civil community'. Rejecting this high threshold test, the Grand Chamber referred to its previous Article 15(1) jurisprudence—discussed later—which did not require the threat posed to rise to the level of imperiling the institutions of the state.[66]

So it was accepted, at least on the facts, that it was feasible for a derogation to be made on the basis that a major terrorist atrocity might be committed without warning at any time, and on that basis was 'imminent' (all previous Article 15(1) cases reaching the Court had concerned on-going terrorism). As the Court put it: '[t]he requirement of imminence cannot be interpreted so narrowly as to require a State to wait for disaster to strike before taking measures to deal with it',[67] stating that 'the purpose of Article 15 is to permit States to take derogating measures to protect their populations from future risks'. The Court observed that evidence purportedly sustaining the threat had been adduced before the domestic courts and accepted by them as credible. It added that the existence of the threat to the life of the nation 'must be assessed primarily with reference to those facts which were known at the time of the derogation'.[68] However, it was 'not precluded... from having regard to information which comes to light subsequently', noting that the London bombings of July 2005 occurred after the British derogation was withdrawn.

c. Earlier case law: intensity of violence; temporariness; geographical aspects

These comments on *A v UK* demonstrate that Article 15(1) has been read flexibly by the Court, the threshold for reliance on Article 15(1) being set at a considerably lower level than a strict or literal reading of the text might require. The trend was in evidence from the beginning of the Court's Article 15 jurisprudence. In *Lawless*[69] (1960) the Court found the existence of the emergency to be 'reasonably deduced' from a combination of three factors: the violent operations of a secret army (the IRA); the fact that its cross-border activities threatened Ireland's relations with the United Kingdom; and the escalation of terrorist activities during the period under review, culminating in a particularly serious incident which triggered the introduction of emergency legislation. The Court's acceptance that there was a public emergency seemed to be owed as much to the very existence of the IRA and the fact that its cross-border raids could seriously jeopardize relations between Ireland and the United Kingdom, as to the actual level of the violence occurring (which was minimal) and *anticipated* at the time the emergency was declared. It is certainly arguable that *Lawless* sets the threshold for the application of Article 15 at a rather low level,[70] given the critical nature of the provision in question. The case is nearly fifty years old and was the first ever judgment on the merits delivered by the Court, so the question remains whether the Court would take a stricter approach were it presented with similar facts today.

Article 15(1) has been interpreted generously in other ways too, notably as regards the duration of the public emergency and its geographical reach. On the first point, prior to *A v UK*, and apart from *Lawless*, the Court's Article 15 case law concerned ongoing terrorism jeopardizing the entire infrastructure of, in fact, Northern Ireland or the south-east of Turkey. It suggested that Article 15 allowed a state to derogate from its Convention obligations in the face of relatively low-intensity, irregular terrorist violence stretching over a number of years. This prompted questions as to whether the derogation power could only

---

[66]   *A v UK* ECHR 2009; 49 EHRR 625 para 178 GC.   [67]   *A v UK*, para 177.

[68]   *A v UK*, para 177.   [69]   A 3 (1961); 1 EHRR 15.

[70]   The low threshold set in *Lawless* was influential to the outcome of *A and Others v Secretary of State for the Home Department* [2004] UKHL 56.

be a temporary expedient, as commentators have argued,[71] and the UN Human Rights Committee has required should be the case in respect of the equivalent provisions of the International Covenant on Civil and Political Rights (ICCPR). In *A v UK*, however, the Grand Chamber cited the view of the Human Rights Committee, commenting that 'the Court's case law has never, to date, explicitly incorporated the requirement that the emergency be temporary', although, it added, 'the question of the proportionality of the response may be linked to the duration of the emergency'. Noting that the derogations in respect of Northern Ireland had lasted 'many years', the Court concluded that it did not consider 'that derogating measures put in place in the immediate aftermath of the al'Qaeda attacks in the United States of America, and reviewed on an annual basis by Parliament, can be said to be invalid on the ground that they were not "temporary"'.[72] The Court's position on whether an emergency must be 'temporary' was, therefore, equivocal;[73] it indicated that it did not see the length of an emergency as a factor that *automatically* deprived it of validity, but also stressed the importance of regular review.

As to the geographical reach of derogations, in *Lawless* the Court referred to 'an exceptional situation of crisis or emergency *which affects the whole population*'[74] (emphasis added). In practice this standard has been relaxed or, put another way, it has been accepted that the whole population may be affected by events in only part of a state and that the derogation may be restricted to that part. Hence, derogation notices submitted by Turkey have, in the past, confined the territorial applicability of the notice to the south-east region of that country and the Court has not questioned the validity of the notice on this ground.[75] The Court will, however, construe such territorial limitations strictly. In *Sakik v Turkey*,[76] the applicant was arrested in Ankara (an area not specified as being covered by the derogation). The respondent government argued that the terrorist threat concerned was not confined to any particular part of Turkish territory and that the applicant's detention had to be seen in the context of the prolongation of a terrorist campaign being conducted from inside the area where the state of emergency had been proclaimed. However, the Court did not accept this. It noted the requirement under Article 15(1) that derogations be confined 'to the extent strictly required by the exigencies of the situation'. It stated that the very object and purpose of Article 15 would be undermined if a respondent government were able to extend the effects of derogation to an area not explicitly named in the notice.[77]

II. EXISTENCE OF PUBLIC EMERGENCY AND MARGIN OF APPRECIATION

The flexible stance taken with respect to Article 15(1) is also manifested in the overall approach the Court takes, in terms of the *standard of review* it operates. On this it stated in *Brannigan and McBride v UK*:[78]

> The Court recalls that it falls to each Contracting State, with its responsibility for 'the life of [its] nation', to determine whether that life is threatened by a 'public emergency' and,

---

[71] On public emergencies as a temporary phenomenon, see Human Rights Committee General Comment No 29, paras 1 and 2; *CoE Terrorism Guidelines* XV(1) and (3); the materials set out in *A v UK* ECHR 2009; 49 EHRR 625 at paras 109–10 GC, and Judge Makarczyk, dissenting in *Brannigan and McBride v UK* A 258-B (1993); 17 EHRR 539 PC. See also Gross, 23 Yale JIL 437 (1998).

[72] *A v UK* ECHR 2009; 49 EHRR 625 para 178 GC.

[73] See Doswald-Beck, *Human Rights in Times of Conflict and Terrorism*, 2011 at p 87.

[74] See section 4.I.a.   [75] Eg, *Aksoy v Turkey* 1996-VI; 23 EHRR 553.

[76] 1997-VII; 26 EHRR 662.   [77] *Sakik v Turkey*, para 39.

[78] A 258-B (1993); 17 EHRR 539 para 43 PC.

if so, how far it is necessary to go in attempting to overcome the emergency. By reason of their direct and continuous contact with the pressing needs of the moment, the national authorities are in principle in a better position than the international judge to decide both on the presence of such an emergency and on the nature and scope of derogations necessary to avert it. Accordingly, in this matter a wide margin of appreciation should be left to the national authorities...

Nevertheless, Contracting Parties do not enjoy an unlimited power of appreciation. It is for the Court to rule on whether *inter alia* the States have gone beyond the 'extent strictly required by the exigencies' of the crisis. The domestic margin of appreciation is thus accompanied by a European supervision... At the same time, in exercising its supervision the Court must give appropriate weight to such relevant factors as the nature of the rights affected by the derogation, the circumstances leading to, and the duration of, the emergency situation.

The Grand Chamber approved these passages—including the reference to a 'wide'[79] margin of appreciation - in *A v UK*.[80] As noted earlier,[81] its approach to the Article 15 issues arising in that case placed significant reliance upon the fact that the House of Lords had already examined the issues relating to the derogation, concluding there was a public emergency threatening the life of the nation (although the House of Lords concluded the measures taken in response were not strictly required by the exigencies of the situation).

Putting to one side the *Greek* case,[82] the application of a margin of appreciation to respondent states has been important[83] in other cases too. That said, in the leading judgments the existence of a public emergency has not been hotly disputed. *Ireland v UK*,[84] concerned terrorist violence that amounted to 'a particularly far-reaching and acute danger for the territorial integrity of the United Kingdom, the institutions of the six counties and the lives of the province's inhabitants'.[85] The Irish government accepted that conditions in the province were sufficiently exceptional for Article 15 to apply. The period involved was from 1970 to 1976, which included the most violent period in the continuing disturbances from Northern Ireland. From August 1971 to March 1972, more than 200 people were killed and nearly 30,000 injured in over 3,000 bombing and shooting incidents.[86] Even so, it has been questioned whether the Court was correct to endorse the applicant government's assessment that there was a public emergency without making its own inquiries and assessment. That there ought to be this obligation on the Court is explained by the nature of the rights in the Convention: since they are the rights of individuals, they ought not to be capable of being diminished by the unilateral act of a state.

---

[79] The extension of a '*wide* margin of appreciation' (emphasis added) in *Brannigan and McBride v UK* was controversial; see Judge Martens' separate opinion ('no justification for leaving them a wide margin of appreciation' the Court being 'the "last-resort" protector of the fundamental rights and freedoms guaranteed under the Convention', so it had to 'strictly scrutinise every derogation'). See also Judge Makarczyk's separate opinion.

[80] *A v UK* ECHR 2009; 49 EHRR 625 para 173 GC.   [81] See section 4.I.b.

[82] 12 YB (the *Greek* case) 1 (1969); CM Res DH (70) 1. Regarding the margin of appreciation the case may best be viewed in the light of the fact that the respondent government was a revolutionary (military) one, which resorted to Article 15 in highly questionable, bad faith, circumstances. It was a matter of dispute amongst the members of the Commission as to whether any margin of appreciation at all was owing to the respondent government. The Commission's report expressed the view that there had been a catalogue of very serious human rights violations and, furthermore, shortly after the report was produced, Greece denounced its membership of the Council of Europe. On this case see the second edition of this book at p 626.

[83] The Court did not refer to a margin of appreciation in the *Lawless* case (A 3 (1961); 1 EHRR 15 para 28); it concluded that the existence of an emergency had been 'reasonably deduced' by the Irish government.

[84] A 25 (1978); 1 EHRR 15 paras 20–77 PC.   [85] *Ireland v UK*, para 212.

[86] *Ireland v UK*, para 48.

While it is not suggested that an independent inquiry by the Court would have resulted in a different outcome in *Ireland v UK*, the possibility of unjustifiable reliance on Article 15 increases as the level of violence diminishes. In *Brannigan and McBride v UK*,[87] concerning the continuing security situation in Northern Ireland, the applicants accepted that there was a public emergency in Northern Ireland, but the Commission said that it had to make its own assessment of the situation, 'albeit [a] limited [one]'. It was very limited, the Commission concluding on the basis of cumulative government statistics[88] that the situation remained 'very serious'.[89] The brief of one of the intervening parties, the non-governmental organization (NGO) 'Liberty', argued that there was not an emergency of sufficient seriousness for Article 15 to be relied upon.[90] The Court briefly endorsed the Commission's conclusion:

> ...making its own assessment, in the light of all the material before it as to the extent and impact of terrorist violence in Northern Ireland and elsewhere in the United Kingdom..., the Court considers there can be no doubt that such a public emergency existed at the relevant time.[91]

This degree of scrutiny is hardly different from accepting the parties' own view of the situation. Similar comments may be made regarding the assessment of the existence of a public emergency in the case of *Aksoy v Turkey*. In that judgment the Court simply stated that it considered that 'in the light of all the material before it, that the particular extent and impact of PKK terrorist activity in south-east Turkey has undoubtedly created, in the region concerned' a 'public emergency'.[92]

As *A v UK* suggests, the Court may allow for some flexibility on the state's part as regards the timing of the decision to derogate. In the *Lawless* case the President of the Commission put it to the Court that it may be consistent with the goal of Article 15 to allow a state acting in good faith to derogate from the Convention before a 'public emergency' fully erupts and in order to 'nip trouble in the bud'.[93] Clearly there are dangers to guard against if this is so—the examination of whether the measures are strictly required becomes crucial.

As regards the timing of the withdrawal of a derogation, the admissibility decision in *Marshall v UK*,[94] a very similar case to *Brannigan and McBride*, suggests that, against the backdrop of a prolonged terrorist campaign satisfying Article 15(1), the Strasbourg Court is prepared to afford a state a considerable benefit of doubt. This is so if there is reason to believe that there is a genuine risk of a return to serious violence of an Article 15(1) order in contrast to the relative calm that may exist when an application is made.

Marshall, decided in 2001, was one of a series of cases concerning the public emergency declared in relation to terrorism connected with the affairs of Northern Ireland. The relevant derogation dated from December 1988[95] until withdrawal in February 2001 (it was renewed annually at the domestic level). The derogation from Article 5(3) was originally made in 1988 in reaction to the Court's judgment in *Brogan v UK*, and it was in issue in *Brannigan and McBride* when the Court accepted its legality and the proportionality of

---

[87] A 258-B (1993); 17 EHRR 539 PC. [88] *Brannigan and McBride v UK*, paras 26–7.
[89] *Brannigan and McBride v UK*, para 49. [90] *Brannigan and McBride v UK*, para 45 PC.
[91] *Brannigan and McBride v UK*, para 47. [92] 1996-VI; 23 EHRR 553 para 70.
[93] See O'Boyle, 19 HRLJ 23 (1998) at 26; cf, the Court's statement in *Refah Partisi (The Welfare Party) v Turkey* 2003-II; 37 EHRR 1 paras 98–9 GC, regarding the timing for the dissolution of a political party with an anti-democratic agenda. [94] *Marshall v UK* No 41571/98 hudoc (2001) DA.
[95] Derogations had applied to the territory before 1984 too.

the measures taken pursuant to it. Through the derogation the UK government sought to curtail the full application of Article 5(3) by enabling an individual terrorist suspect to be detained on the authority of the state (ie without the judicial intervention required by Article 5(3)) for up to seven days. The existence of a public emergency had not been fully contested by the applicants in *Brannigan and McBride*, which related to events taking place in 1989, a time of heightened terrorist activity in Northern Ireland. However, after the major paramilitary groups declared a ceasefire in 1994, the derogation remained in place because of ongoing terrorist activity and the threat posed by dissident groups that was confirmed by annual, independent reviews. The applicant in *Marshall* questioned the continuing validity of the derogation, having been detained in 1998 in circumstances which, but for derogation, would normally infringe Article 5(3). He argued that by this stage there was no longer a genuine 'public emergency' for the purposes of Article 15(1), given the significant improvement in the security situation in Northern Ireland at the time. The application was refused at the admissibility stage by a Chamber of the Court. It stated that it was required to address 'with special vigilance the fact that almost nine years separate the prolonged administrative detention of the applicants in *Brannigan and McBride* from that of the applicant in the case before it'. Although the decision referred in some detail to the factual situation existing in Northern Ireland at the relevant time, as regards the question of the existence of a 'public emergency' the Court stated that it: '[did] not agree with the applicant's submission that the security situation in Northern Ireland at the time of his detention had improved to the point where it was no longer justified to refer to it as a public emergency "threatening the life of the nation"'.[96] The Court also refused to accept submissions to the effect that the authorities had failed to conduct meaningful reviews of the continuing necessity for the derogation to Article 5(3). It was satisfied that the matter had been addressed with sufficient frequency given the annual renewal debate that took place in Parliament. More generally it was stated that 'the authorities have approached the operation of the 1989 Act with an eye to developments in the political and security situation in Northern Ireland'. It seems that a significant benefit of doubt was granted to the state on the facts of this case and, as the peace process progressed, the Court was unwilling to intrude into what undoubtedly was a very delicate state of affairs. Perhaps the Court was comforted by the fact that by the time it delivered its admissibility decision, in 2001, the UK had in fact withdrawn the derogation in issue.

III. SUMMARY

Putting *A v UK* to one side, cases such as *Marshall*, plus the Court's apparent general reliance in the Article 15 jurisprudence on cumulative figures relating to deaths, casualties, and property destruction, which necessarily do not give an accurate picture of the seriousness of the circumstances at a particular time, provide an indication that the Strasbourg authorities accept a view of some emergencies as 'campaigns' or continuing events. Where there is an organized campaign of violence resulting in deaths at a relatively low level among the security forces and civilians, it remains hard to see how the Court could avoid confirming a state's claim that there is a public emergency within Article 15, assuming there is no evidence of bad faith on the latter's part. The case law indicates that derogations will not be condemned by the Court simply because of their

---

[96] The authorities 'continued to be confronted with the threat of terrorist violence' notwithstanding its reduction; an 'outbreak of deadly violence' preceded the applicant's detention which confirmed 'there had been no return to normality'.

prolonged effect. It is not necessarily the case, therefore, that the notion of 'emergency' implies a requirement of temporariness as regards the derogation, something which *A v UK* confirmed. However, the longer the derogation subsists then the greater the need is for the Court to effectively address whether there are sufficient and effective safeguards in place domestically to ensure that the public emergency is not perpetuated indefinitely.[97] Throughout their duration the measures must be 'strictly required by the exigencies of the situation'.

5. 'MEASURES . . . TO THE EXTENT STRICTLY REQUIRED BY THE EXIGENCIES OF THE SITUATION . . .'

As regards derogable rights, the extent to which their normal operation may be curtailed must be proportionate to the nature of the emergency existing: the measures taken must be 'to the extent strictly required by the exigencies of the situation . . .'. Essentially, the issue here is whether the actual measures resorted to, and which in normal circumstances would infringe the Convention, are proportional to the actual crisis facing the governing authorities at the time. Here the Court asserts a right of review and states must carefully justify their actions, but this is again an area where a margin of appreciation will be available to them.[98] In this connection we are reminded of the limitations on the role that is feasible for an international court in the conduct of such a review, and the deferential approach Strasbourg will adopt if the domestic courts have examined the matter from the perspective of Article 15(1), concluding that measures taken were not strictly required.[99]

As was noted in the *Marshall*[100] case, it is not the Court's role to 'substitute its view as to what measures were most appropriate or expedient at the relevant time in dealing with an emergency situation for that of the Government which have direct responsibility for establishing the balance between the taking of effective measures to combat terrorism on the one hand, and respecting individual rights on the other'. The Court has stated that 'in exercising its supervision [it] must give appropriate weight to such relevant factors as the nature of the rights affected by the derogation, the circumstances leading to, and the duration of, the emergency situation'.[101] It has also stressed the great importance of the existence of safeguards against abuse of power that may serve to reduce the chance that an individual will be the subject of serious human rights violations whilst the emergency situation and modified legal regime associated with it subsists.

---

[97] The *CoE Terrorism Guidelines* state: 'The circumstances which led to the adoption of such derogations need to be reassessed on a regular basis with the purpose of lifting these derogations as soon as these circumstances no longer exist', XV(3). In *Brannigan and McBride* the interveners, *Liberty, Interights* and the *Committee of the Administration of Justice* had argued that the margin of appreciation available to a state should become narrower the more permanent the emergency becomes, A 258-B (1993), 17 EHRR 539 para 42 PC.

[98] See the extract from *Brannigan and McBride v UK* cited in section II and at para 66 (judgment). For criticism of the Court's approach see Marks, 15 OJLS (1995) 85; Gross, 23 YJIL (1998) 437; Gross and Ní Aoláin, 23(1) HRQ (2001); and Campbell, 54 ICLQ 321 (2005).

[99] See *A v UK* ECHR 2009; 49 EHRR 625 GC paras 182–90.

[100] *Marshall v UK No 41571/98* hudoc (2001) p 12 DA.

[101] *Brannigan and McBride v UK* A 258-B (1993); 17 EHRR 539 para 43 PC.

I. 'STRICTLY REQUIRED . . .'

'[S]trictly required' suggests a test more demanding than 'necessary' in, for example, Article 10(2), which requires that the state show a 'pressing social need' for its measures of limitation. The Court has worked out a series of factors to be taken into account to determine whether measures are strictly required.

The first inquiry is into the necessity for the measures at all by examining why the ordinary law or action otherwise compatible with the Convention is not adequate to meet the emergency and why the exceptional measures are. In *Lawless v Ireland*,[102] the Court accepted that neither ordinary nor special courts in Ireland were able to meet the dangers to public order occasioned by the secret, terrorist character of the IRA, in particular the near impossibility of obtaining evidence necessary to convict suspects by judicial proceedings. Internment or detention without trial did have the effect of meeting this problem. In *Ireland v UK*,[103] the Court held that 'the British government was reasonably entitled to consider' that the ordinary criminal procedure was inadequate to meet the 'far-reaching and acute danger' presented by the 'massive wave of violence and intimidation' characterizing the IRA's activities in Northern Ireland. Extrajudicial deprivation of liberty, even for the purposes of interrogating witnesses—otherwise contrary to Article 5(1)—and the removal of procedural guarantees to regulate deprivation of liberty—otherwise in violation of Article 5(4)—were necessary to meet the emergency situation.[104] In *Brannigan and McBride v UK*,[105] the Court acceded to the government's argument that, in a common law system, it was not feasible to introduce a judicial element into the detention process at an early stage. It accepted also that extended detention was necessary to successfully investigate terrorist crimes when some of the suspects would have been given training in resisting interrogation and where extensive forensic checks might be required.[106] The Court therefore held that the UK government had not exceeded its margin of appreciation by derogating from obligations under Article 5(3) of the Convention to the extent that individuals suspected of terrorist offences were allowed to be held for up to seven days without judicial control. In reaching this conclusion, it is important to note that the Court expressed the view that it was satisfied that there were effective safeguards in operation in Northern Ireland which, in the Court's view, provided a significant measure of protection against the dangers of arbitrary behaviour and *incommunicado* detention. Such basic safeguards included the fact that the actual arrest remained challengeable by *habeas corpus* in the ordinary courts. Also there was a right to see a solicitor after forty-eight hours of detention, and a detainee was entitled to have other persons informed about his detention and have access to a doctor.

The continuing presence of such safeguards appears to have been an important factor in the dismissal of the application in *Marshall v UK* where the applicant disputed the effectiveness of *habeas corpus* as an effective remedy but did not claim an actual violation of Article 5(4). In fact, the jurisprudence of the UN Human Rights Committee and the Inter-American Court suggests that the suspension of *habeas corpus* may never be justified given the fundamental nature of the guarantee in a democracy and the importance

---

[102]   A 3 (1961); 1 EHRR 15 para 36.   [103]   A 25 (1978); 2 EHRR 25 para 212 PC.
[104]   *Ireland v UK*, paras 214–20.   [105]   A 258-B (1993), 17 EHRR 539 PC.
[106]   The Court found that the government's position had been supported by the various independent inquiries into the situation in Northern Ireland, but there was little analysis of the evidence or assessment of its worth in the judgment. See Marks, 15 OJLS 69 (1995).

attached to the provision of safeguards against abuse of exceptional powers.[107] Strasbourg has not gone as far as this, and, in *Ireland v UK* (dating from the 1970s) it accepted that the derogation from Article 5(4) was strictly required on the facts. In *A v UK* there was no derogation from Article 5(4), and, although the Court took into account the terrorist context to the case, having in mind the length of the detention (which appeared to be indefinite at one stage), it insisted that individuals know enough of the case against them to enable them to rebut it.[108] It remains open to debate, then, how Strasbourg would have treated a derogation from Article 5(4).[109]

The judgment in the *Brannigan* case was open to the criticism that it did not answer sufficiently the concerns of Amnesty International in its intervention that, in particular circumstances, safeguards were necessary not only to protect against unnecessarily prolonged detentions but also to protect detainees who might be detained *incommunicado* during the first forty-eight hours of detention. The evidence of worldwide abuse of persons detained without supervision during interrogation is strong[110] and in *Aksoy v Turkey*,[111] the first case in which the Court found a state to have tortured an individual, it stressed the fact that prompt judicial intervention may lead to the detection and prevention of serious ill-treatment. In *Aksoy*, laws were in place that potentially permitted detention of an individual without being brought before a judge or other officer (Article 5(3)) for up to thirty days. The government sought to justify this by reference to the particular demands of police investigations in a geographically vast area and as it was faced with a terrorist organization receiving outside support (although generally the Court criticized the fact that the government had not adduced any detailed reasons before it as to why the fight against terrorism in south-east Turkey rendered judicial intervention impracticable). The applicant was in fact detained in the way identified for at least fourteen days, a period described by the Court as 'exceptionally long'[112] and which gave rise to a situation which 'left the applicant vulnerable not only to arbitrary interference with his right to liberty but also to torture'. The Court went on to condemn the insufficient nature of the safeguards available to the applicant: 'the denial of access to a lawyer, doctor, relative or friend and the absence of any realistic possibility of being brought before a court to test the legality of the detention meant that he was left completely at the mercy of those holding him'.[113] On the one hand, the Court was prepared to take account of 'the unquestionably serious problem of terrorism in south-east Turkey and the difficulties faced by the State in taking effective measures against it'.[114] On the other hand, it was 'not persuaded that the exigencies of the situation necessitated the holding of the applicant on suspicion of involvement in terrorist offences for fourteen days or more in *incommunicado* detention without access to a judge or other judicial officer'. The Court therefore held that there had been a violation of Article 5(3), the first time that it had concluded that measures taken by a state pursuant to a 'public emergency' were not 'strictly required by the exigencies of the situation'. In subsequent judgments,[115] the Court has indicated that in cases of

---

[107] Cf *Habeas Corpus in Emergency Situations* (Articles 27(2), 25(1), ACHR), I-A Ct HRts Rep, Series A 8 (1987); 9 HRLJ 94 (1988) advisory opinion. See Doswald-Beck, *Human Rights in Times of Conflict and Terrorism*, 2011 at 90–3.   [108] See Ch 8, section 8.II.c.

[109] See Doswald-Beck, *Human Rights in Times of Conflict and Terrorism*, 2011 at p 97.

[110] See Amnesty International in *Brannigan and McBride v UK* A 258-B (1993), 17 EHRR 539 para 61 PC. See also Judge Pettiti dissenting, *Brannigan and McBride v UK*; *Ireland v UK* A 25 (1978); 2 EHRR 25 paras 165–8 PC; *Tomasi v France* A241-A (1992); 15 EHRR 1 paras 114–15 and *Tomasi v France*, paras 99–100 Com Rep.   [111] 1996-VI; 23 EHRR 553.

[112] *Aksoy v Turkey*, para 78.   [113] *Aksoy v Turkey*, para 83.   [114] *Aksoy v Turkey*, para 84.

[115] See also *Nuray Şen v Turkey* hudoc (2003) (eleven days' incommunicado detention).

prolonged extra-judicial detention under Article 5(3), it will expect to be furnished with 'precise reasons relating to the actual facts'[116] of the case before it which demonstrate that 'judicial scrutiny of the applicants' detention [would] have prejudiced the progress of the investigation' in process. It will not be sufficient for the respondent state 'to refer in a general way to the difficulties caused by terrorism and the number of people involved in the inquiries'.[117]

As indicated earlier, in practice most of the emergency situations that have reached the Court's attention have involved continuing campaigns of irregular, terrorist violence. Inevitably the question arises whether a state can justify the continuance of measures, which may be a proper response to the most intense periods of violence and disorder, during periods of relative calm, albeit possibly temporary ones. The exact point has not been fully addressed on the merits by the Court, but the admissibility decision in *Marshall v UK*[118] throws some light on this. The decision suggests that at a later, less violent stage of a public emergency, it may be difficult to persuade the Court to condemn measures which it has accepted as justified at the beginning of that emergency, provided that the state can muster evidence to the effect that its belief that the campaign was at least dormant (with real potential to revive) was not an unreasonable one. In *Marshall*, the Court accepted that the UK authorities had not 'overstepp[ed] their margin of appreciation' by maintaining the extended period of pre-trial detention that had been in issue in *Brannigan and McBride*. The justifications provided by the UK for such measures in *Marshall* were the same as those in *Brannigan and McBride*, and the Court accepted that they remained 'relevant and sufficient'. Although the peace process was well underway, the Court pointed out that, as of 1998, 'the threat of terrorist outrage was still real and...the paramilitary groups in Northern Ireland retained the organisational capacity to kill and maim on a wide scale'.[119] The applicant had argued that, in fact, the level of violence in Northern Ireland in 1998 was little different to that which had existed at other times in other parts of the UK, but where there had been no recourse to derogation under Article 5(3). To this the Court stated that it 'consider[ed] that the applicant's reasoning does not take sufficient account of the specific nature of the violence which has beset Northern Ireland, less so the political and historical considerations which form the backdrop to the emergency situation'.

In *Ireland v UK*,[120] the Irish government maintained that the measures adopted by the authorities in Northern Ireland had manifestly failed in their purpose because the period during which they had been in operation had seen an increase in terrorist violence and, eventually, the UK government had abandoned administrative detention. In principle, the argument about effectiveness has much to recommend it: how can an interference with human rights which does not contribute to some other good end be 'strictly required'? Indeed, one might go further and argue that, because of what is at stake, the government should be called upon to demonstrate the effectiveness of the measures it has introduced. However, the difficulty is not of principle and desirability but of practicability and justiciability. Hence the Court refused to accept the Irish government's argument as noted immediately above, emphasizing that its function was confined not to assessing what was the most prudent or most expedient policy

---

[116] *Demir v Turkey* 1998-VI; 33 EHRR 1056 para 52.
[117] *Demir v Turkey*. The subsequent conviction of the detainee for a 'terrorist' offence is not a relevant factor for the purpose of Article 5(3), para 53.   [118] *Marshall v UK No 41571/98* hudoc (2001) DA.
[119] *Marshall v UK*, para 12.
[120] A 25 (1978); 2 EHRR 25 para 214 PC. See also Judge Makarczyk, dissenting, in *Brannigan and McBride v UK* A 258-B (1993); 17 EHRR 539 PC.

to combat terrorism, rather it had to do no more than review the lawfulness, under the Convention, of the measures adopted. In this the margin of appreciation applied and the Court had to look to the conditions and circumstances reigning when the measures were originally taken and subsequently applied, and so avoid 'a purely retrospective examination of the efficacy of those measures'.[121] It follows that the simple fact that a government modifies and mitigates the measures on which it relies under Article 15 during the course of a campaign against the authorities is not, of itself, evidence that the measures were not 'strictly required' at some earlier stage.[122] The interpretation of Article 15 'must leave a place for progressive adaptations'[123] and '[w]hen a State is struggling against a public emergency threatening the life of the nation, it would be rendered defenceless if it were required to accomplish everything at once, to furnish from the outset each of its chosen means of action with each of the safeguards reconcilable with the priority requirements for the proper functioning of the authorities and for restoring peace within the community'.[124]

Establishing the necessity for having some emergency measures will not always be sufficient to demonstrate that the particular measures employed are 'strictly required'. The Strasbourg authorities may go on to inquire into the proportionality between the need and the response.[125] The greater the need—eg, the 'very exceptional situation' in Northern Ireland, acknowledged by the Court in *Ireland v UK*[126]—the greater the permissible derogation—eg, detention of a person not suspected of an offence for the purposes of the investigation. Proportionality does not imply some arithmetic calibration. Instead, the Court takes into account whether the measure is less draconian than others which might have been contemplated. In the *Lawless* case,[127] the Court considered that one alternative—sealing the border between Ireland and Northern Ireland as a means of combating cross-border raids—would have gone beyond the exigencies of the emergency in Ireland, thus reinforcing the proportionality of the government's lesser reaction. Many of the contested measures of derogation have involved the removal of safeguards against abuse of powers of arrest or detention, usually the removal of the judicial element. In establishing the proportionality of the response, the Court also looks at the alternative mechanisms of supervision introduced by the state. Thus the system of administrative detention examined in the *Lawless* case was accompanied by detailed and continuous supervision by Parliament and a detainee could make representations to a tribunal, the 'Detention Commission'.[128] In *Ireland v UK*,[129] the judicial control of detention was replaced by non-judicial advisory committees and there remained a residuary and, in the view of the Court, not a wholly illusory possibility of access to the courts. In *Brannigan and McBride v UK*,[130] as well as *Marshall v UK*,[131] though not in *Aksoy v Turkey*,[132] the respondent government succeeded in rebutting the claim that there were no effective safeguards against abuse of the extended period of pre-trial detention in issue.

In *Brannigan and McBride v UK*,[133] the applicants argued that the extended period of pre-trial detention could not be strictly required because the government had previously withdrawn its derogation notice. That was because, the government responded, it

---

[121] *Ireland v UK*, para 214.　　[122] *Ireland v UK*, para 213.　　[123] *Ireland v UK*, para 220.
[124] *Ireland v UK*, para 220.
[125] *De Becker v Belgium* B 4 (1962) ; 1 EHRR 43 para 271 Com Rep.
[126] A 25 (1978); 2 EHRR 25 para 212 PC.　　[127] A 3 (1961); 1 EHRR 15 para 36.
[128] *Lawless v Ireland*, para 67.　　[129] A 25 (1978); 2 EHRR 25 paras 218–19 PC.
[130] A 258-B (1993); 17 EHRR 539 paras 61–5 PC.　　[131] *No 41571/98* hudoc (2001) DA (at p 13).
[132] 1996-VI; 23 EHRR 553.　　[133] A 258-B (1993); 17 EHRR 539 paras 47 and 51 PC.

had taken the view that the detention power was compatible with Article 5 and that no derogation was necessary. The withdrawal of the notice did not show that there was no emergency, nor that it was not one for which the power was strictly required. The Court agreed. It rejected by a majority the arguments that because there had been no increase in the intensity of the emergency in the time between the withdrawal of the notice and the judgment in *Brogan* there was no power to rely on Article 15, and so the real purpose of the British government had been to avoid the effect of the *Brogan* judgment.[134] The British government's claim was that the *power* of extended detention had always been necessary and that the dispute hinged only on the appropriate legal basis for it.

II. MARGIN OF APPRECIATION

The Court accepts that the state has a wide margin of appreciation in assessing whether the measures which it has taken were 'strictly required'.[135] The practical effect is that the decision about what measures to adopt, whether to modify them, whether to continue or discontinue them, so long as they otherwise satisfy Article 15, is principally for the state. Matters of prudence or expediency are not for the Court.[136] While the Court did not refer explicitly to the margin of appreciation in the *Lawless* case, it did rely on the idea in *Ireland v UK*,[137] when it said, in somewhat curious language, that internment could 'reasonably have been considered strictly required' by the emergency. The words used in *Brannigan and McBride v UK*,[138] couched in the negative, further underline the primacy of the state's assessment of what is strictly required. At one stage, the Court noted that, 'The Commission was of the opinion that the government had *not overstepped* their margin of appreciation...' and it said that, 'it *cannot be said* that the government *have exceeded* their margin of appreciation...'[139] and again, 'the Court takes the view that the government have *not exceeded* their margin of appreciation...'[140] This essentially negative review, which takes into account matters of evidence, necessity, proportionality, adequacy of safeguards, individually and together, does not amount to a particularly intrusive form of review, despite the strong words of Article 15(1).[141] What it does do is force the state into a public justification for its actions but there are some doubts whether this is enough.[142] Too generous an employment of a margin of appreciation avoids a rigorous review by the Court of alternative, less authoritarian, methods that might have been employed by the respondent state. This would not accord with the notion of real and effective protection, a principle that has been at the heart of so much Strasbourg jurisprudence.

The Council of Europe's Commissioner for Human Rights has argued that national authorities enjoy a large margin of appreciation in respect of derogations 'precisely because the Convention presupposes domestic controls in the form of a preventive

---

[134] Van Dijk and Van Hoof *et al* (eds), *Theory and Practice of the European Convention on Human Rights*, 2006, at p 1073, maintain that the events demonstrated the bad faith of the British government.

[135] *Brannigan and McBride v UK* A 258-B (1993); 17 EHRR 539 paras 57 and 43 PC, emphasis added.

[136] *Ireland v UK* A 25 (1978); 2 EHRR 25 paras 207 and 214 PC.   [137] At para 213.

[138] A 258-B (1993); 17 EHRR 539 para 57 PC (emphasis added).

[139] *Brannigan and McBride v UK*, para 60 (emphasis added).

[140] *Brannigan and McBride v UK*, para 66 (emphasis added). Cf *Marshall v UK* No 41571/98 hudoc (2001) DA, at p 12.

[141] The Court's approach is endorsed by Merrills, *The Development of International Law by the European Court of Human Rights*, 2nd edn, 1993, pp 139–40.

[142] *Brannigan and McBride v UK* A 258-B (1993); 17 EHRR 539 PC, Judge Martens, concurring, Judges Pettiti and Walsh dissenting. See also Marks, 15 OJLS 69, 84–95 (1995).

parliamentary scrutiny and posterior judicial review'.[143] In the *A and Others* case,[144] the House of Lords refused to follow the Strasbourg jurisprudence to the extent that the government was not afforded the equivalent of a 'wide' or 'large' margin of appreciation on the issue of whether the measures taken by the state in response to the derogation made were 'strictly required'. Given the importance of the right at stake, several of the Law Lords emphasized the duty of a national court, in distinction to an international one, to scrutinize the actions of the executive with close attention. In particular, it was more appropriate for a domestic court, rather than an international one,[145] to assess the relative effectiveness of competing alternative measures that might be less harmful to the rights of the individuals concerned so as to establish the disproportionate nature of the existing measures. By eight votes to one, the Law Lords held that the special detention regime was, *inter alia*, disproportional (and, in fact, discriminatory) for a combination of reasons. These included the fact that the Secretary of State had not established that the special detention arrangements were 'strictly required' by the public emergency in that he had not shown that monitoring arrangements or movement restrictions less severe than incarceration in prison would have sufficed. The Court upheld these conclusions in *A v UK*, holding that there had been violations of Article 5(1) in respect of several applicants.[146] Its approach was somewhat parasitic to that adopted by the House of Lords, and does not necessarily mark a willingness on the Court's part to undertake a more exacting review than has previously been the case.[147]

6. OTHER INTERNATIONAL LAW OBLIGATIONS

Even if measures of derogation can be justified under Article 15, a state is precluded from relying on them if their introduction would breach other international law obligations of the state.[148] This specific provision reinforces the general principle of Article 53.[149] The obvious sources of treaty obligations are the ICCPR[150] and the Geneva Red Cross

---

[143] *Opinion of the Commissioner for Human Rights, Mr Alvaro Gil-Robes on certain aspects of the UK 2001 derogation from Article 5 par. 1 of the European Convention on Human Rights*, CommDH (2002)7/28 August 2002 (hereafter '*Opinion of the Commissioner for Human Rights*') para 9.

[144] [2004] UKHL 56.

[145] See, eg, Lord Rodger ([2004] UKHL 56) at para 176, Lord Hope, para 114 and paras 108, 130–1 and Lord Bingham at para 40.   [146] *A v UK* ECHR 2009; 49 EHRR 625 paras 184–90 GC.

[147] At Strasbourg the British government challenged the House of Lords' conclusion that the Article 15(1) derogation had been disproportionate in that it was discriminatory, arguing that the latter should have applied a wider margin of appreciation. The Court was highly supportive of the stance adopted by the House of Lords, namely that issues of proportionality were ultimately a judicial matter ('especially', it noted, in a case when individuals had been deprived of their liberty for a long time, para 184). As noted, the Court's approach was deferential to the national court, whose decision it agreed with (paras 185–90), although it was prepared to hear some new arguments as pleaded by the UK. As to the margin of appreciation doctrine, the Court stated that this 'has always been meant as a tool to define relations between the domestic authorities [which includes the domestic courts] and the Court', but that it could not have 'the same application to the relations between the organs of State at the domestic level', para 184. For criticism, see Elliott, 8 IJCL 131 (2010) at p 136–7.   [148] See Allain, 5 EHRLR (2005) 480.

[149] Article 53: 'Nothing in this Convention shall be construed as limiting or derogating from any of the human rights and fundamental freedoms which may be ensured under the laws of any High Contracting Party or *under any other agreement to which it is a Party*' (emphasis added).

[150] All the Convention member states are parties to the ICCPR.

Conventions.[151] It is conceivable that the European Union treaties could contain obligations which would be relevant to emergency measures, especially if the emergency were economic or industrial in character. While the terms of Article 15(1) do not preclude obligations under customary international law, these are unlikely to raise any questions in practice because of the wide participation of the European states in the Covenant and the Conventions. In all these cases, it will be necessary for the European Court to interpret the other treaty to identify the state's obligation. In practice, this provision has been of little significance. In *Lawless v Ireland*[152] and *Ireland v UK*,[153] the Court decided that the measures of derogation did not conflict with the defendant state's obligations, if any, under international law. In *Brannigan and McBride v UK*,[154] it was argued that the more stringent provisions of Article 4 of the ICCPR—that the existence of the emergency be 'officially proclaimed'—had not been satisfied. There was a dispute between the applicants and the government about what Article 4 required. The Court disclaimed any responsibility to resolve it authoritatively but was satisfied that parliamentary statements by a British minister were sufficient in terms of their certainty and publicity to comply with Article 4.[155] The Court said that it was obliged to examine the applicants' argument, but it found it was without 'any plausible basis'.[156] The Court in *Marshall* was quick to dismiss the ICCPR's Human Rights Committee's adverse comments regarding the measures taken pursuant to the emergency situation in Northern Ireland in 1996.

According to Article 4(1) ICCPR, one of the conditions for the justifiability of any derogation from the Covenant is that the measures taken do not involve discrimination solely on the ground of race, colour, sex, language, religion, or social origin.[157] Article 4 contains a longer list of non-derogable provisions than Article 15(2). It is a convincing argument that a state which is a party to the Convention and the ICCPR is precluded from derogating under the Convention from those rights listed in Article 4 that are not in Article 15(2), *viz* the right not be imprisoned for the non-fulfilment of a contractual obligation, the right to be recognized as a person before the law, and the right to freedom of thought, etc.[158]

7. ARTICLE 15(2): THE
NON-DEROGABLE PROVISIONS

Whatever the seriousness of the emergency and however convincing the case a state might make that a derogation was strictly required, in no circumstances may a state depart from

---

[151] The great majority of Convention member states are parties to the 1949 Geneva Conventions.
[152] A 3 (1961); 1 EHRR 15 para 41. The Court undertook this inquiry *proprio motu*.
[153] A 25 (1978); 2 EHRR 25 para 222 PC (Geneva Conventions).
[154] A 258-B (1993); 17 EHRR 539 para 68 PC.   [155] *Brannigan and McBride v UK*, paras 73–4.
[156] *Brannigan and McBride v UK*, para 72.
[157] In the *A and Others* case Lord Bingham ruled that the measures applied by the British government had been discriminatory in violation of Article 14 of the Convention and also Article 26 of the ICCPR which he argued applied by virtue of the 'other obligations under international law' clause of Article 15, *A and Others v Secretary of State for the Home Department* [2004] UKHL 56, Lord Bingham para 68.
[158] Van Dijk and Van Hoof *et al* (eds), *Theory and Practice of the European Convention on Human Rights*, 2006, at p 1067. In 2001 the Human Rights Committee produced a detailed General Comment regarding the operation of Article 4 ICCPR. In this it pointed out that in addition to those rights specifically listed under Article 4, in its view, there were certain other obligations under the ICCPR (and, in fact, international law generally) that were non-derogable. Human Rights Committee *General Comment No 29* CCPR/C/21/Rev.1/Add.11, 31 August 2001, see especially para 13 and also para 16.

its obligations under Articles 2, 3, 4(1), and 7 of the main Convention, Protocol 6, Article 4 of Protocol 7, and Protocol 13. These limitations are not the absolute prohibitions they might at first appear. Article 15(2) itself makes an exception for deaths resulting from lawful acts of war and Article 2 contains exceptions, some of which, such as the right to use force resulting in death to suppress an insurrection, are clearly relevant to some kinds of emergency.[159] Article 7(2) of the Convention provides an exception to the proscription against retrospective criminal penalties, which may be applicable in some emergency situations, notably international armed conflicts. There are no limitations in Articles 3 and 4(1) and these, it has been pointed out, are the only true absolute obligations in the Convention.[160]

Although there is no specific reference to them in Article 15, there are other provisions of the Convention which may have an impact on the legality of measures of derogation. One example is Article 14.[161] In *Ireland v UK*,[162] the Court examined the Irish government's complaint that internment had been applied discriminatorily to republican/nationalist suspects in conjunction with Article 5. It held that there were objective and reasonable differences between republican/nationalist and loyalist/unionist violence, notably the much greater extent of the former. Furthermore, the authorities had found it easier to proceed in the ordinary courts against loyalist/unionist defendants. There was, accordingly, no breach of Article 14 combined with Article 5 and, thus, no need to consider the matter separately under Article 15. Judge Matscher, who dissented on this matter, raised but did not answer the question whether a breach of Article 14 could be strictly necessary within the terms of Article 15(1). He alluded to this again in *Brannigan and McBride v UK*.[163] In the *A and Others*[164] case, a majority of the House of Lords held that even in the context of the subsisting public emergency, there had been a violation of Article 14 read with Article 5 given the discriminatory treatment existing (on grounds of nationality) between suspected international terrorists and UK nationals who were also suspected of terrorism.

The American Convention on Human Rights prohibits the suspension of a list of numerated substantive rights and also 'the judicial guarantees essential for the protection of such rights' (Article 27(2)).[165] Relying on these words, the Inter-American Court has advised that states may not suspend the rights to a judicial remedy to test the lawfulness of detention (Article 7(6)) and the general right of judicial protection (Article 25). The Inter-American Court recognized that the right of emergency derogation was not unlimited and that, both in the scope and application of emergency measures, national courts had a role to play in guaranteeing that the emergency powers were not exceeded.[166] While this argument cannot be made in precisely the same terms, given the language of Article 15 of the European Convention, it does enhance the position taken by the Court that the proportionality of derogation measures will ordinarily require a process for their supervision to prevent or reduce the possibility of abuse.

---

[159] Cases involving the use of force which has resulted in death in Northern Ireland have been argued under Article 2, see Ch 5.

[160] Higgins, 48 BYIL 281 (1976–77) p 306.

[161] There is also conceivably room for the application of Articles 17 and 18 as limitations on a state's powers under Article 15. [162] A 25 (1978); 2 EHRR 25 paras 225–32 PC.

[163] A 258-B (1993); 17 EHRR 539 PC. [164] [2004] UKHL 56.

[165] See Fitzpatrick, in Harris and Livingstone, eds, *The Inter-American System of Human Rights*, 1998.

[166] See *Habeas Corpus in Emergency Situations* (Articles 27(2), 25(1), ACHR), I-A Ct HRts Rep, Series A 8 (1987); 9 HRLJ 94 (1988) advisory opinion.

8. ARTICLE 15(3): THE PROCEDURAL REQUIREMENTS

The Convention does not expressly require an effective domestic parliamentary scrutiny of the decision to enter a derogation under Article 15; however, the Court has said that Article 15(3) implies an obligation to keep the need for emergency measures under permanent review, an obligation implicit in the proportionality of any measures of derogation.[167]

The specific requirement of Article 15(3) is that a state relying on the right of derogation shall keep the Secretary General fully informed of the measures it has taken and the reasons for doing so. The importance of this safeguard is that the Secretary General informs the other parties to the Convention about the notice of derogation.[168] If the idea that the Convention contains a collective guarantee is to mean anything at all, it surely ought to apply when exceptional measures of interference with human rights are introduced. The other parties to the Convention are thus put on notice that there is a situation which demands their consideration. As mentioned already, Article 4 of the ICCPR requires a public proclamation of the emergency. In *Cyprus v Turkey*,[169] the Commission said that some formal and public declaration of the state of emergency (unless special circumstances prevented it) was a precondition for reliance on Article 15(1).

The obligation under Article 15(3) is not necessarily one of prior notification, that is to say, prior to the date from which the state wishes to execute the measures of derogation, at least if the state can give reasons why this should be so. In *Ireland v UK*,[170] the British government explained that its notifications (communicated on 20 August 1971) had been delayed until after the implementation of internment (9 August 1971) so that no persons whom it was desired to detain might have notice and escape. In accepting the adequacy of this justification,[171] the Court relied on the *Lawless* case,[172] where a twelve-day delay in notification was accepted as having been made 'without delay'. In the *Greek* case,[173] the Commission concluded that Greece had 'not fully met the requirements of Article 15(3)'. In particular, while the Commission did not find that Article 15(3) required the state to identify the provisions from which it was derogating, the respondent government had failed to communicate to the Secretary General the texts of some of its emergency legislation and had not provided full information on the administrative measures taken, especially measures for the detention of persons without a court order; the provision of information to the Commission in the course of the proceedings in the application brought against the state was not a substitute for its obligation to communicate the required information to the Secretary General. In addition, it had not informed the Secretary General of the reasons for the measures of derogation for more than four months after they had been taken. Since the *Greek* case, notices of derogation have generally appeared adequate for the purpose of Article 15(3) and to have been delivered without delay.[174] The exception

---

[167]   *Brannigan and McBride v UK* A 258-B (1993); 17 EHRR 539 para 54 PC.

[168]   The Secretary General circulates notices of derogation to other member states: CM Res (56) 16. See also the *Greek* case, 12 YB (the *Greek* case) 1 at 42 (1969).

[169]   4 EHRR 482 (1976) para 527 Com Rep; CM Res DH (79)1. But note the dissent of Mr Sperduti in *Cyprus v Turkey* and the judgment of the Court in *Lawless v Ireland* A 3 (1961); 1 EHRR 15 para 47.

[170]   A 25 (1978); 2 EHRR 25 para 80 PC.   [171]   *Ireland v UK*, para 223.

[172]   A 3 (1961); 1 EHRR 15 para 47.

[173]   12 YB (the *Greek* case) 1 at 41–2 (1969); CM Res DH (70) 1.

[174]   Oraa, *Human Rights in States of Emergency in International Law*, 1992, p 85.

has been Turkey's unwillingness to accept responsibility under the Convention for the acts of its forces in northern Cyprus, which has led it not to make any formal declaration applicable there.[175] Turkey maintained that it had no jurisdiction over any part of Cyprus, which was exercised in the northern part of the island by the Turkish Cypriot authorities.[176] The Commission took the view that Turkey is responsible under the Convention for acts which can be attributed to its armed forces, wherever they may be.[177]

Because the Commission found that there was no emergency in the *Greek* case, it had no need to consider what were the legal consequences of a violation of Article 15(3). While it might be salutary if the Strasbourg authorities regarded a deficiency in notification as rendering the declaration a nullity, the seriousness of what is at stake if the state demonstrates the existence of an emergency at the appropriate time may equally make it appear too draconian a sanction and one which is likely to be of little efficacy.

Article 15(3) requires that the Secretary General be notified when the derogation measures have been terminated. Action taken under measures justified only by the emergency may not be continued after the emergency has ended.[178]

9. PROPOSALS FOR REFORM

It has been said that, '[a]n emergency or crisis situation challenging a state Party is also a test for Convention system as a whole... If the Convention system can function only when times are good, but fails to respond to a real emergency, then its authority and legitimacy in all situations is undermined.'[179] Some strong arguments have been made for the case that the institutions of the Council of Europe should have a more proactive role in the supervision of derogations made under Article 15 (as opposed to the merely reactive role performed by the European Court after an application reaches it).[180]

It is a major weakness of Article 15 that once a derogation has been entered, it is necessary for an individual or inter-state application to be made before the Court can address the derogation's validity and the proportionality of the measures taken in accordance with it. As has been the case in the past, even when such an application has been made, the ensuing judgment from the Court is delivered a number of years after the declaration of the emergency. This entails the real risk that the existence of the emergency and the measures taken pursuant to it remain wholly unsupervised for a considerable period of time, and perhaps at the very time when supervision, guidance, and, quite possibly, condemnation are required. In this connection it has been proposed that the powers of the Secretary General of the Council of Europe under Articles 15(3) and 52 be widened so as to enable requests for further information on derogations as and when necessary and assuming that the initial information provision (required by Article 15(3)) is regarded as inadequate. More effective would be the implementation

---

[175] *Cyprus v Turkey* 4 EHRR (1976) 482 at 555–556; CM Res DH (79) 1 and id, *No 8007/77*, para 67, 72 DR 5 at 24 (1992).

[176] *Cyprus v Turkey Nos 6780/74 and 6950/74*, 2 DR 125 at 130 (1975). See Necatigil, *The Cyprus Question and the Turkish Position in International Law*, 1989, pp 94–100.

[177] *Cyprus v Turkey* 4 EHRR 482 at 509 (1982); CM Res DH (79) 1 and id, *No 8077/77*, 72 DR 5 at 23 (1992). The Commission declined also to accept Turkey's argument that its Article 15 declaration for parts of its national territory could be taken into account with respect to its treatment of Greek Cypriots taken to Turkey. See now *Loizidou v Turkey* A 310 (1995); 20 EHRR 99 GC and *Cyprus v Turkey* 2001-IV; 35 EHRR 731 GC. [178] *De Becker v Belgium*, B 4 (1962); 1 EHRR 43 para 271 Com Rep.

[179] Macdonald, in *Ryssdal Melanges* p 817. [180] See especially, Macdonald.

of a requirement for states to submit periodic reports to the Secretary General regarding the ongoing existence of the emergency and the proportionality of the measures taken. Similarly, the Committee of Ministers might be given some sort of monitoring role once a derogation notice has been submitted to the Secretary General. A role for this institution might be regarded as particularly appropriate in some instances, given the political attributes of that body and the power it has to impose sanctions such as expulsion from the Council of Europe.

The Commissioner for Human Rights of the Council of Europe[181] may 'identify possible shortcomings in the law and practice of member states concerning the compliance with human rights as embodied in the instruments of the Council of Europe'.[182] He may 'issue recommendations, opinions and reports',[183] though he must not take up individual complaints and must 'respect the competence of, and perform functions other than those fulfilled by, the supervisory bodies set up under the European Convention of Human Rights'.[184] There is some scope therefore for the monitoring of derogations; indeed in 2002 the Commissioner for Human Rights issued an opinion on certain aspects of the United Kingdom's 2001 derogation from Article 5(1) of the European Convention on Human Rights.[185]

10. CONCLUSION

Article 15 occupies a very important position in the Convention.[186] It might be intolerable for a state faced by an extraordinary crisis not to be able to derogate from certain of the international obligations the Convention provides for. One justification for suspension of full enjoyment of derogable rights in the circumstances covered by Article 15 is that without such drastic measures it could transpire that there would be an even greater threat to the liberty and freedom of a population, and perhaps even the existence of the state itself. In other words, derogations can be justified upon the basis of preserving democracy and maintaining the fabric of the state.

Derogation from the Convention is and has been an exceptional event. It must be anticipated that a democratic state will usually think hard before resort to Article 15 because of the political consequences of acknowledging there to be a 'public emergency'. However, although it is notable how few states have resorted to Article 15 in the past, one wonders what message the Article 15 jurisprudence might communicate to them for the future. The *Aksoy* judgment revealed that the Court has indicated that there are limits beyond which a state may not proceed even during an emergency. In the more borderline cases, the Court has been content to employ a wide margin of appreciation so as to favour the

---

[181] See http://www.coe.int/web/commissioner.

[182] Articles 3(e) of Resolution (99) 50 of the Committee of Ministers on the Commissioner for Human Rights.

[183] Article 8(1) of Resolution (99) 50 of the Committee of Ministers on the Commissioner for Human Rights.

[184] Article 1(2) of Resolution (99) 50 of the Committee of Ministers on the Commissioner for Human Rights.

[185] *Opinion of the Commissioner for Human Rights, Mr Alvaro Gil-Robes on certain aspects of the UK 2001 derogation from Article 5 par. 1 of the European Convention on Human Rights*, CommDH (2002)7/28 August 2002.

[186] On issues related to the French reservation to Article 15, see the second edition of this book at p 642.

state when it finds the reassurance provided by safeguards against abuse (*Brannigan and McBride*). Does this jurisprudence, in particular the reliance on a wide margin of appreciation, convey the message that Strasbourg scrutiny of Article 15 issues will not be particularly rigorous?[187]

With respect to Article 15 in particular, one sees a real tension between the status of the Court as an international institution and as a human rights tribunal interpreting a Convention, which, as it has stated on many occasions, is designed to protect rights that are not theoretical and illusory but which are real and effective.

On the one hand, it may be observed that the Strasbourg Court is an international Court and the Convention system as a whole is founded on the principle of subsidiarity. From *that* perspective, in assessing the fair balance to be struck between the rights of individuals and the general interest of the community, a respondent government that has derogated in *good faith* and is seen to be democratic should surely be given a significant benefit of doubt, assuming there has been proper domestic review of the emergency and its associated measures. If this entails a risk that in practice the absolute minimum interference with rights does not occur, this might be accepted for several reasons. First, restricting rights to the absolute minimum required by the circumstances in emergency scenarios is not an exact science. Furthermore, an international institution of control should be reluctant to second-guess governmental actions growing out of Article 15. Indeed, the Court risks being accused of adjudicating too much with the luxury of hindsight, perhaps meddling too deeply in affairs about which it has little practical expertise, detached from the true realities and politics of a highly complex situation, and precisely at a time of great sensitivity for the respondent state concerned. This would appear to be one of the rationales for the application of a margin of appreciation by the Court in the case law, a point which seems to have been reinforced by Strasbourg's approach to the domestic court's examination of the Article 15 issues in *A v UK*.[188] The Court's willingness in that case to find that the derogating measures were disproportionate owed much, it seems, to its readiness to agree with the conclusions already reached by the House of Lords to that effect.

On the other hand, it may be observed that practice has demonstrated that it is precisely during emergency situations that some of the greatest threats to the human rights of individuals arise. Arguably, therefore, it is inappropriate for the Court's power of review to be confined in effect to assessing essentially not much more than the general good faith nature of declarations of public emergency and the measures taken in connection with it, especially when that 'emergency' has existed for some time. From this perspective the Court has been sharply criticized for being too deferential in its approach to Article 15, especially its examination of whether the measures taken in accordance with a derogation are 'strictly required'.[189] It has been argued that the deference employed 'inject[s] a strong subjective element into the interpretation of the European Convention, weakening the Court's authoritative position vis-à-vis national Governments', which may 'in turn, undermine any hope of effective regional supervision and enforcement of rights protected by the European Convention'.[190] In particular, it has been said that the Court has wrongly condoned entrenched public emergencies.[191]

---

[187] Cf the points made by Judges Martens and Makarczyk in *Brannigan and McBride*, see section 4.II.
[188] See section 4.I.b.
[189] Marks, 15 OJLS (1995) 85; Gross and Ní Aoláin, 23(1) HRQ (2001); Gross, 23 YJIL (1998) 437; and Campbell, 54 ICLQ (2005) 321. [190] Gross and Ní Aoláin, pp 628–9.
[191] Gross, 23 Yale JIL 437 (1998) and Marks, 15 OJLS (1995) 85.

It may be argued that the use of a wide margin of appreciation as regards the existence of a 'public emergency' may be compensated for by a more stringent examination by the Court under the second limb of Article 15(1), 'exigencies of the situation'. However, one commentator has requested that the Court provide 'a more principled approach' to the application of that doctrine in the context of Article 15.[192]

---

[192] O'Boyle, 19 HRLJ 23 (1998) at 29, although see now the Court's statements in *A v UK*, discussed in section 4.I.b.

20

ARTICLES 16–18: OTHER RESTRICTIONS UPON THE RIGHTS PROTECTED

1. ARTICLE 16: RESTRICTIONS ON THE POLITICAL RIGHTS OF ALIENS

> **Article 16**
>
> Nothing in Articles 10, 11 and 14 shall be regarded as preventing the High Contracting Parties from imposing restrictions on the political activities of aliens.

Article 16 allows potentially wide-ranging interference with the political rights of aliens. It runs counter to the basic principle of Article 1 that rights in the Convention are to be enjoyed by 'everyone within [the state's] jurisdiction'.[1] It applies specifically to Articles 10 and 11, but there is no indication that the reference to Article 14 is confined to restrictions imposed on aliens' rights under those articles. Rather, it appears that the state may take advantage of Article 16 with respect to discriminatory rules within the ambit of any of the Convention's provisions. This includes rights under Article 3 of the First Protocol involving the right to vote.[2] Draconian though such a power would be, it must not be forgotten that a state has the ultimate remedy of deportation against an alien to whose activities it objects and the Convention provides no direct protection[3] against the use of that power, even if it is because of the political activities of the person expelled.[4] The right to vote in national law is frequently confined to citizens. Article 25 of the International Covenant on Civil and Political Rights (ICCPR) also protects the right to vote expressly for citizens only and the United Nations Declaration on the Human Rights of Individuals who are not Nationals of the Country in which They Live[5] does not afford any protection for the political rights of aliens.

Piermont v France[6] was the first case in which the Court had to give serious consideration to Article 16. The applicant was an environmental activist who was a member of the European Parliament, elected in Germany, and had been invited to French overseas territories

---

[1] Distinctions are drawn between nationals and aliens with respect to freedom of movement, see Articles 3 and 4 of the Fourth Protocol, Ch 24, and, formally at least, there is different protection for national and alien-owned property under Article 1 of the First Protocol: see Ch 21.

[2] *Mathieu-Mohin v Belgium* A 113 (1987); 10 EHRR 1 para 54 PC.

[3] Indirect protection may be provided by Article 3 (likely treatment in destination state), see Ch 6 or Article 8 (family ties in expelling state), see Ch 12.　　　　　[4] See *Agee v UK* No 7729/76, 7 DR 164 (1976).

[5] GA Res 40/53.　　　[6] A 314 (1995); 20 EHRR 301.

in the South Pacific by groups opposed to the French government's nuclear testing policy. She went to French Polynesia and took part in peaceful demonstrations against the government, but was formally expelled from the territory and forbidden to re-enter. One of her claims was that the action violated her rights of expression under Article 10, either alone or in conjunction with Article 14. For its part, the respondent government argued that the interference, if not otherwise justified under the Convention, could be excused by relying on Article 16. However, the Court refused to accept this, the majority maintaining that Article 16 could not be raised against Mrs Piermont to restrict her Article 10 rights as she was a national of an EU state and a member of the European Parliament, and this 'especially as the people of the [Overseas Territories] take part in the European Parliament elections'.[7] The case was therefore considered under Article 10 alone, with a narrow majority of the Court finding that the interference with the applicant's rights was disproportionate to the protection of any interest under Article 10(2). Even if Article 16 does have relevance to a case, this would not necessarily mean that the host state has an unfettered right to restrict the exercise of Articles 10 and 11 by an 'alien'.[8]

The Court in *Piermont* refused to accept the applicant's argument that Article 16 did not apply on the simple basis that she was a European citizen, since 'the Community treaties did not at the time [of the facts] recognise any such citizenship'.[9] If European Union citizens were not considered to be 'aliens' for the purposes of Article 16,[10] this would be an important re-reading of the text.

2. ARTICLE 17: RESTRICTIONS ON ACTIVITIES SUBVERSIVE OF CONVENTION RIGHTS

Article 17

Nothing in this Convention may be interpreted as implying for any state, group or person any right to engage in any activity or perform any act aimed at the destruction of any of the rights and freedoms set forth herein or at their limitation to a greater extent than is provided for in the Convention.

I. INTRODUCTION

The main objective of Article 17,[11] which is a prohibition on abuse of rights,[12] is 'to prevent totalitarian or extremist groups from justifying their activities by referring to the Convention',[13] for example by relying on Article 10 to advocate violent racist programmes.

---

[7] *Piermont v France*, para 64.
[8] *Piermont v France*, joint partly dissenting opinion of Judges Ryssdal, Matscher, Sir John Freeland, and Jungwiert.   [9] *Piermont v France*, para 64.
[10] Cf European Union citizenship now recognized under EC Treaty Articles 17–18(1).
[11] On Article 17 see Cannie and Voorhoof, 29 NQHR 54 (2011); Villiger in *Bratza Essays* p 321, and Tulkens in *Bratza Essays* p 279 at pp 282–7.
[12] Cf Articles 29(3) and 30 of the UDHR, Article 5(1) ICCPR, and Article 5(1) ICESCR.
[13] *Zdanoka v Latvia* hudoc (2004); 41 EHRR 659 para 109 (Chamber judgment). Article 17 may therefore be seen in the context of the emphasis placed by the Court on the protection of democracy, in particular Strasbourg jurisprudence expounding the notion of 'a democracy capable of defending itself', see *Zdanoka v Latvia* hudoc (2006); 45 EHRR 478 paras 98–101 GC. The notion that the Convention's provisions may not be relied upon to weaken or destroy the ideals and values of a democratic society has been at the heart of key

Article 17, the so-called 'abuse clause', therefore allows action to be taken against an individual where he seeks to use his Convention rights in a subversive way. It may defeat a Strasbourg claim, but it does not mean that such a person is deprived of *all* Convention rights.[14]

So, Article 17 covers 'essentially [*only*] those rights which, if invoked, will facilitate the attempt to derive therefrom a right to engage personally in activities aimed at the destruction of any of the rights and freedoms set forth in the Convention'.[15] The result is that it is most likely to be called in aid by a state when it acts to restrict an individual who is seeking to rely on his or her Article 9, 10, and 11, and perhaps Article 3 of the First Protocol, rights to achieve outcomes that destroy another person's Convention rights. It does not come into play when other interests are in issue. Hence, the Court refused the Turkish government's argument that Article 17 applied to a series of cases concerning political parties which had been banned for reasons such as acting contrary to the unity of the Turkish nation[16] (ie an interest that the Convention did not directly protect).

II. ARTICLE 17 PLEADED BY THE STATE

The original threat to which Article 17 was directed was communist manipulation of political rights, especially in circumstances where the threat has not reached such proportions that the state could rely on Article 15, and where there might be difficulties in showing that an interference with an individual's rights was otherwise justified under the Convention. Hence, in a very early decision,[17] the Commission held that an order banning the German Communist Party could be founded on Article 17 because the programme of the party inevitably envisaged a period of dictatorship by the proletariat in which rights under the Convention would be destroyed. The realm of Article 17 was identified as being 'to protect the rights enshrined in the Convention by safeguarding the free functioning of democratic institutions'.[18]

However, as commentators have noted,[19] Article 17's sphere of application has broadened. It potentially covers the protection of the fundamental values of democracy and human rights, the case law mainly concerning Articles 10 and 11, with Article 17 being of potential relevance to extremist material or groups identified by the Court with an agenda that is 'contrary to the text and spirit of the Convention'.[20] Cases have concerned communism, groups with profoundly anti-democratic ambitions, Holocaust denial, justification for Nazi-like policies, and hate speech (racial, religious, and ethnic). In such cases the state will often claim that censorship of some sort or, as the case may be, the banning of a political party or association, is a necessary measure as the ambition of the applicant is to destroy the rights of others (broadly defined). It will maintain that Article 17 applies such that the applicant should not be able to rely on a Convention right. The effect of the application of Article 17 is therefore very significant, for it potentially negates the

---

judgments such as *Refah Partisi (The Welfare Party) v Turkey*, 2003-II; 37 EHRR 1 paras 98–9 GC. See also *Kasymakhunov and Saybatalov v Russia* hudoc (2013), and the references at paras 99, and 104–5.

[14] See, eg, *Lawless v Ireland* A 3 (1961); 1 EHRR 15 para 7. See also *Kasymakhunov and Saybatalov v Russia* hudoc (2013) (violation of Article 7, Court also holding that neither applicant could rely on Article 9, 10, or 11). [15] *WP v Poland No 42264/98* ECHR 2004-VII DA.

[16] See, eg, *United Communist Party of Turkey v Turkey* 1998-I; 26 EHRR 121 para 60 GC. Cf *WP v Poland* (Article 17 applied; banned association whose memorandum of association included statements that could revive anti-Semitism (inadmissible)). [17] *KPD v Germany No 250/57*, 1 YB 222 (1957).

[18] *KPD v Germany* at 223 (1957). [19] Cannie and Voorhoof, 29 NQHR 54 (2011) at 62–3.

[20] Cf *Paksas v Lithuania* ECHR-2011 para 88 GC, summarizing relevant case law. See also *Lehideux and Isorni v France* 1998-VII; 30 EHRR 665, concurring opinion of Judge Jambrek para 2.

exercise of a particular right(s) by a group or individual. It is important therefore that Article 17 is strictly scrutinized by the Court, it being possible to apply it at the admissibility stage, or to do so on the merits of a case via the qualification clause to a Convention right, for example Article 10(2).[21] The former option terminates the case, immediately concluding the matter—hence references to Article 17 as a 'guillotine' provision—with potentially little rights-based analysis, and so this is one reason why the Court has been encouraged to directly apply Article 17 only with moderation and consider cases on the merits, unless there is a very clear case for dismissal at the admissibility stage. To that end, perhaps, a recent Grand Chamber judgment has highlighted that Article 17 be applied only 'on an exceptional basis and in extreme cases'.[22] Looking to recent case law, the Court is still prepared to dismiss applications at the admissibility stage in the most serious cases,[23] thereby underlining its repugnance of the matter before it as not being worthy of a rights-balancing exercise (Articles 10(2) or 11(2)). More usually, however, and particularly in hate speech cases,[24] it is prepared to examine matters on the merits and apply Article 17 then, if necessary, although resort to that Article is not always required given the qualifications Article 10(2) affords.

In cases when Article 17 has been directly applied at the admissibility stage the Court has made reference to the notion of Article 10 or 11 being 'deflect[ed] from its real purpose'.[25] Article 17 has been applied in this way to Islamaphobic or anti-semitic[26] freedom of expression. As to the former, in *Norwood v UK*,[27] the applicant was a regional organizer of the British National Party (in the words of the Court, 'an extreme right wing political party') and, following complaints, had had a poster removed by the police from his window, the display of which led to a conviction. As described by the Court, the poster 'contained a photograph of the Twin Towers in flame, the words "Islam out of Britain—Protect the British People" and a symbol of a crescent and star in a prohibition sign'. A chamber of the Court rejected the applicant's complaint of a violation of Article 10, refusing the application as incompatible *ratione materiae* with the Convention, for the display of the poster was an 'act' within the meaning of Article 17 which was not protected by Article 10 or Article 14. The Court stated that it agreed with the domestic courts' assessment of the poster as 'a public expression of attack on all Muslims' in the UK. It was clear that '[s]uch a general, vehement attack against a religious group, linking the group as a whole with a grave act of terrorism, [was] incompatible with the values proclaimed and guaranteed by the Convention, notably tolerance, social peace and non-discrimination'.

Article 17 has also been applied in cases concerning justification for Nazi-like policies. For example, in *Garaudy v France*,[28] the Court applied Article 17 at the admissibility

---

[21] For the various approaches—which are not always easy to decispher or predict—and for analysis, see Villiger in *Bratza Essays* at pp 342–7.   [22] *Paksas v Lithuania* ECHR-2011 para 87 GC.

[23] See *Hizb ut-Tahrir and Others v Germany* No 31098/08 hudoc (2012) DA and *Kasymakhunov and Saybatalov v Russia* hudoc (2013).   [24] On which see Tulkens in *Bratza Essays* p 279.

[25] *Paksas v Lithuania* ECHR-2011 para 88 GC, summarizing preceding case law.

[26] See also *Pavel Ivanov v Russia* No 35222/04 hudoc (2007) DA (articles portraying the Jews as the source of evil in Russia; declared inadmissible, using Article 10(2)) and *WP v Poland* No 42264/98 ECHR 2004-VII DA.

[27] *No 23131/03* hudoc (2004); 40 EHRR SE 111, cf *Jersild v Denmark* A 298 (1994); 19 EHRR 1 para 35. See also *Glimmerveen and Hagenback v Netherlands* Nos 8348/78 and 8406/78, 18 DR 187 (1979); 4 EHRR 260 (1982).

[28] *No 65831/01* ECHR 2003-IX DA. See also *Witzsch v Germany* No 7485/03 hudoc (2005) DA ('disdain towards the victims of the Holocaust') and *Schimanek v Austria* No 32307/96 hudoc (2000) DA (inadmissible, applying Article 10(2): 'National Socialism is a totalitarian doctrine incompatible with democracy and human rights and its adherents undoubtedly pursue aims of the kind referred to in Article 17 of the Convention').

stage in a case concerning a book which resulted in the applicant's criminal conviction for Holocaust denial. The Court agreed that the book's 'real purpose [was] to rehabilitate the National-Socialist regime and [so] accuse the victims themselves of falsifying history'. It was not deserving of protection as a serious historical analysis of matters such as the Holocaust and the Nuremberg Trials. Denying crimes against humanity[29] was 'one of the most serious forms of racial defamation of Jews and of incitement to hatred of them'. Negationist speech, such as Holocaust denial, was unacceptable and racist: it was a denial of or an attempt to rewrite 'historical fact', so it 'undermine[d] the values on which the fight against racism and anti-Semitism are based and constitute[d] a serious threat to public order'. Such acts were 'incompatible with democracy and human rights because they infringe the rights of others'.

As noted, there are also cases when the Court has made reference to Article 17 during its consideration on the merits of whether one of the rights pleaded by an applicant has been infringed. In *Lehideux and Isorni*,[30] for example, in the context of its consideration of Article 10, the Court indicated that Holocaust deniers could not rely on that Article. It referred to categories of certain 'clearly established historical facts—such as the Holocaust—whose negation or revision would be removed from the protection of Article 10 by Article 17'.[31] The Court was nevertheless clear that Article 17 would not be employed to suppress genuine historical debate, and that the facts of the case before it fell into this category. It examined the case under Article 10, found a violation of this provision, and then stated that it considered that it was inappropriate to apply Article 17 on the facts.[32]

Article 17 has also been applied at the admissibility stage in connection with Article 11 in cases when an association sought to rely on the latter as a basis to engage in activities which were contrary to the text and spirit of the Convention and aimed at the destruction of the rights and freedoms it sets forth.[33] For example, a banned organization was unable to rely on Article 11, or indeed Articles 9 and 10, at Strasbourg given its anti-Semitic and pro-violence statements, notably those justifying suicide attacks and calling for the violent destruction of Israel. Interestingly, when applying Article 17 with reference to the organization's agenda, the Court referred rather broadly to a clash with 'the values of the Convention, notably the commitment to the peaceful settlement of international conflicts and to the sanctity of human life'.[34] By contrast, the Court refused to apply Article 17 at the admissibility stage in *Vona v Hungary*,[35] concerning the dissolution of an association (of which the applicant were members) after it had had involvement with anti-Roma rallies and had undertaken intimidatory para-military rallies in the vicinity of a Roma-populated village. On the facts, those actions formed part of the Court's basis for concluding that there had been no violation of Article 11, in what was an important case for that provision. As to the government's plea for the application of Article 17 at the admissibility stage, this was rejected by the Court, which emphasized the need for a link

---

[29] See also *Orban v France No 20985/05* hudoc (2005) DA, the Court noting that statements unequivocally seeking to justify war crimes such as torture or summary executions would not be protected by Article 10.

[30] 1998-VII; 30 EHRR 665 (conviction as applicants had procured an advert in a national newspaper which, it was claimed, showed their support for Nazi collaborators during the war (in particular, Philippe Pétain)).   [31] *Lehideux and Isorni*, para 47.

[32] Cf *Purcell v Ireland No 15404/89*, 70 DR 262 at 278 (1991). The Commission used Article 17 in the *Purcell* case and in *Kühnen v Germany No 12194/86*, 56 DR 205 (1988), to reinforce its conclusion that an interference with freedom of expression is justified under Article 10(2).

[33] See, eg, *WP v Poland No 42264/98* ECHR 2004-VII DA (inadmissible by application of Article 17: association with anti-Semitic agenda).

[34] *Hizb ut-Tahrir and Others v Germany No 31098/08* hudoc (2012) DA para 74. See also, concerning the same organization, *Kasymakhunov and Saybatalov v Russia* hudoc (2013).   [35] Hudoc (2013).

between the activity in question and 'totalitarian oppression' of some sort. The government had not argued that the association in question had 'totalitarian ambitions', or had 'expressed contempt for the victims of a totalitarian regime',[36] and there was no 'prima facie'[37] indication of that on the facts.

III. ARTICLE 17 PLEADED AGAINST THE STATE

Article 17 is unusual in the Convention in that it may be invoked both by an individual against a state and by a state to justify its interference with the rights of an individual. The Article serves to control the powers of the state, as well as to enhance them in the manner just discussed. The nature of the complaint by an applicant will be that the state has used its powers to interfere with rights for a purpose or in a manner beyond those permitted by the Convention. It is essentially an allegation of bad faith against the state because it is hardly conceivable that a limitation of a right which, on its face, could otherwise be justified under the Convention, would be excluded by Article 17.[38] Thus, when relied on by an individual, the applicant frequently couples his complaint that Article 17 has been violated with an allegation that there has been a breach of Article 18 also. Bad faith to one side—and there are always the greatest difficulties in demonstrating this—Article 17 thus becomes subsidiary to the determination that interferences with Convention rights by the state are, in any event, not compatible with the Convention. It explains why, even in the relatively few cases in which it has been called upon to consider Article 17 as applied against a state, the Court has found no need to deal with the question.

In the *Greek* case,[39] the applicant states argued that the government of Greece could not under Article 17 limit the exercise of individual rights in order to consolidate its hold on power. They said that Article 17 was directed against 'totalitarian conspiracies' and that the Greek government was one of these. The majority of the Commission found no need to decide this question because it had already decided that the government could not base its actions on Article 15, there being no emergency. Mr Ermacora found the derogation to be impermissible under Article 17, accepting the applicants' argument and pointing out that the government had shown no inclination to comply with its obligation to hold free and fair elections.[40] Mr Busuttil allowed that there might be circumstances when a revolutionary government might have to rely on Article 17 while it set about restoring democracy; it was entitled to a 'reasonable period' to prove that this was its objective, an obligation manifestly not met by the Greek regime.[41]

Allegations that Article 17 should be applied to state activities have been rare and, even where the Commission was prepared to look at them, the Court has managed to avoid reaching a decision.[42] Article 17 confers a power on states to act,[43] not a positive duty.[44] On the one hand, in what will be a narrow range of circumstances, Article 17 legitimates action by a state which, as a matter of routine, cannot be brought within any of the ordinary exceptions of the Convention when circumstances sufficient to give a wider power to

---

[36] *Vona v Hungary*, para 37.　　[37] *Vona v Hungary*, para 38.

[38] See *Engel v Netherlands* A 22 (1976); 1 EHRR 647 para 108 PC and *Lithgow v UK* A 102 (1986) para 448 Com Rep (the Article 17 point was not argued before the Court).

[39] 12 YB (the *Greek* case) 1 at 111–12 (1969); CM Res DH (70) 1.　　[40] The *Greek* case, pp 102–3.

[41] The *Greek* case, p 119.

[42] Eg, *Sporrong and Lönnroth v Sweden* A 52 (1982); 5 EHRR 35 para 76 PC. For the Commission, see id, B 46 (1980) paras 122–3 Com Rep.　　[43] Warbrick, 32 ICLQ 82 at 91–3 (1983).

[44] But see Fawcett, pp 275–6, suggesting that in some circumstances there may be a positive obligation to discriminate against a group whose activities are covered by Article 17.

derogate under Article 15 have not arisen. On the other hand, it provides some protection against states, where the individual shows that the state is interfering with his rights other than for the good (in Convention terms) reason it claims.

3. ARTICLE 18: PROHIBITION OF THE USE OF RESTRICTIONS FOR AN IMPROPER PURPOSE

Article 18

The restrictions permitted under this Convention to the said rights and freedoms shall not be applied for any purpose other than those for which they have been prescribed.

Article 18 concerns misuse of powers or breaches of the principle of good faith, and must be applied in conjunction with another Convention's Article(s). A violation may be found[45] even when the main Convention Article is not violated on its own. It can only arise where the right or freedom concerned is subject to restrictions permitted under the Convention.

I. SPECIFIC VIOLATIONS OF ARTICLE 18 READ WITH ANOTHER ARTICLE

There was a violation of Article 18 taken with Article 5(1)(c) in *Gusinskiy v Russia*.[46] The applicant was a businessman involved in a commercial dispute with 'Gazprom', a company controlled by the state. He was arrested and detained for several weeks in connection with a completely separate matter relating to his media business. So, on the face of it, there was a valid basis for detention: Article 5(1)(c) in connection with the media business investigations. Indeed, the Court held that this provision was not breached. However, during the detention period, a deal had been struck. The applicant agreed to sell certain interests to Gazprom at a favourable rate, a state minister signed the agreement off, and in return the investigation against him was dropped. The Court concluded these facts 'strongly suggest[ed] that the applicant's prosecution was used to intimidate him', insisting that 'it is not the purpose of such public-law matters as criminal proceedings and detention on remand to be used as part of commercial bargaining strategies'.[47] The restriction of the applicant's liberty permitted under Article 5(1)(c) was applied 'not only for the purpose of bringing him before the competent legal authority on reasonable suspicion of having committed an offence, but also for other reasons'.[48]

Similar violations of Article 5(1)(c) in conjunction with Article 18 were found in two recent Ukrainian cases. In *Lutsenko v Ukraine*[49] and *Tymoshenko v Ukraine*,[50] both applicants were politicians prosecuted for alleged misdemeanours during office. *Lutsenko* concerned a former minister prosecuted on grounds of abuse of office (in relation to work-related benefits for his driver), the Court assessing that, on the facts, the real reason for detaining the applicant prior to and during trial was not to bring him before the

---

[45] *Gusinskiy v Russia* 2004-IV; 41 EHRR 281 para 73.
[46] 2004-IV; 41 EHRR 281. See also *Cebotari v Moldova* hudoc (2007). For earlier Article 18 case law see the second edition of this book at p 653.   [47] *Gusinskiy v Russia*, para 76.
[48] *Gusinskiy v Russia*, para 77.   [49] Hudoc (2012).   [50] Hudoc (2013).

domestic court on Article 5(1)(c) 'reasonable suspicion' grounds, but was retribution for his speaking out against the accusations made against him, and proclaiming his innocence, which he was entitled to do. *Tymoshenko* concerned Yulia Tymoshenko, a leader of the 'Orange Revolution', a former Prime Minister, and, at the time of her trial, 'the most visible opposition politician and the head of one of the strongest opposition parties in Ukraine'.[51] She was prosecuted for abuse of power during her time in office related to enormous losses incurred by the state in relation to an international contract for the supply of gas. Focusing specifically on Article 5(1)(c), the Court looked to the factual context and the specific reasoning advanced by the authorities when restricting liberty during the trial, concluding that the 'actual purpose' of the detention had been to punish the applicant, this time 'for a lack of respect towards the court which it was claimed she had been manifesting by her behaviour during the proceedings'.[52]

II. POLITICALLY MOTIVATED PROSECUTIONS AND ARTICLE 18

In fact, the Article 18 arguments put to the Court by the applicants in *Lutsenko* and *Tymoshenko* were of a broader and far more serious nature than the specific Article 5(1)(c) aspects upheld by the Court. In essence, each claimed that, as leading opposition politicians, they were prosecuted to exclude them from political life ahead of parliamentary elections. As the Court noted, '[m]any national and international observers, including various non-governmental organisations, media outlets, those in diplomatic circles and individual public figures',[53] expressed some support for these claims.

Certain high-profile Russian applicants have also argued that their criminal prosecution and punishment—for tax evasion and fraud—were driven by political ends, in their case to appropriate company assets. *Khodorkovskiy v Russia (No 1)*[54] and *Khodorkovskiy and Lebedev v Russia*[55] concerned an extremely wealthy businessman, Mikhail Khodorkovskiy, who had promised to dedicate significant funds to an opposition party, and who had been a critic of alleged anti-democratic trends in Russian internal policy. His and Platon Lebedev's (co-accused) plight attracted considerable attention domestically and abroad amidst broader claims of political influence in their trial,[56] and in 2011, after their conviction, Amnesty International declared them prisoners of conscience.

How should the Court approach such claims? Politically inspired prosecutions and punishments sanctioned by the state would amount to an abuse of power in blatant disregard for the core values of the Convention. Since the health of the relationship between human rights and democracy would be called into question—especially if opposition politicians are targeted in this way—any application properly raising Article 18 issues must be treated with exacting scrutiny by a court whose first role is to act as the 'conscience of Europe'. Then again, the gravity of the claim which Strasbourg is being asked to uphold as a court of law entails that there is a very heavy responsibility on it to ensure that its findings are correct. Moreover, it is clear that a state must be able to prosecute individuals who have a genuine case to answer, especially in respect of political corruption or major

---

[51] *Tymoshenko v Ukraine*, para 13.　　[52] *Tymoshenko v Ukraine*, para 299.
[53] *Tymoshenko v Ukraine*, para 296.
[54] Hudoc (2011); 53 EHRR 1103. The applicant was a major shareholder in 'Yukos'; see the separate case of *OAO Neftyanaya Kompaniya Yukos v Russia* hudoc (2011); 54 EHRR 599.　　[55] Hudoc (2013).
[56] Cf the Parliamentary Assembly and European Parliament documentation cited at paras 374–6 of the judgment, *Khodorkovskiy and Lebedev v Russia*.

misdemeanours, and the high status and/or wealth and influence of individuals should not be allowed to hinder or prevent that.

Against this background, the Ukrainian and Russian cases noted earlier have required the Court to carefully reflect upon[57] the approach it should take to Article 18. The evidential barrier has been a central issue posing something of a quandary for the Court. Accusations of corruption made by an individual may be false and exaggerated, so mere suspicions cannot suffice. Having said that, in genuine cases of foul play, individual applicants can be expected to face severe difficulties in actually establishing an Article 18 case, it being in the nature of matters that a malevolent agenda on the part of the authorities will, for obvious reasons, remain hidden and secretive. Hard proof of an abuse of power is unlikely, knowledge about 'hidden agendas' being 'within the sphere of the authorities' and so inaccessible to an applicant. Given these considerations, might the Court look at and draw inferences from the broader context to a case? Might it have regard to the resolutions of political institutions, non-governmental organizations (NGOs), and statements of various public figures?

As to the last point, the Court has noted that it is unlikely that such material will carry much (if any) weight, the 'political process and adjudicative process' being 'fundamentally different', judges having to decide matters 'only on evidence in the legal sense'.[58] Nor has the Court accepted arguments[59] that the applicant's disadvantaged position and problems associated with establishing proof 'inconvertibly'[60] should mean that he or she should merely have to establish a strong *prima facie* case of improper purpose, it then being for the respondent state to rebut it. Its position on this is based on policy reasons. Firstly: 'the whole structure of the Convention rests on the general assumption that public authorities in the member States act in good faith'. [61] Secondly, the Court has also argued that reversal of the burden of proof would lead to Strasbourg finding 'violations in every high-profile case where the applicant's status, wealth, reputation, etc. gives rise to a suspicion that the driving force behind his or her prosecution was improper', making it 'impossible' for the legitimate prosecution of such figures to be carried out.[62] It maintains that, 'high political status does not grant immunity',[63] observing that the prosecution of any high-profile, political figure will inevitably have political consequences, and this should not prevent prosecution if there are serious charges against such a figure.

The Court accepts that the assumption of good faith on the part of the national authorities 'is rebuttable in theory, but [that] it is difficult to overcome in practice'.[64] The onus is therefore on the applicant alleging that his rights and freedoms were limited for an improper reason to 'convincingly show that the real aim of the authorities was not the same as that proclaimed (or as can be reasonably inferred from the context)'.[65] This very exacting standard of proof entails that the burden of proof rests with the applicant in

---

[57] Cf the joint concurring opinion of Judges Jungwiert, Nußberger, and Potocki in *Tymoshenko v Ukraine* hudoc (2013).

[58] *Khodorkovskiy v Russia (No 1)* hudoc (2011); 53 EHRR 1103 para 259; as to the evidential value of domestic court cases, for example, concerning extradition, the standard of proof was likely to be different to Article 18, ECHR, see para 260.

[59] See the reference to the applicants' submissions in *Khodorkovskiy and Lebedev v Russia* hudoc (2013) at para 892.   [60] *Khodorkovskiy and Lebedev v Russia* hudoc (2013) para 892.

[61] *Khodorkovskiy and Lebedev v Russia*, para 899.

[62] *Khodorkovskiy and Lebedev v Russia*, para 903. The Court maintained that this would be a result that the drafters of Article 18 would have opposed.

[63] *Khodorkovskiy v Russia (No 1)* hudoc (2011); 53 EHRR 1103 para 258.

[64] *Khodorkovskiy and Lebedev v Russia* hudoc (2013) para 899.

[65] *Khodorkovskiy and Lebedev v Russia*, para 899.

Article 18 cases, 'even where the appearances speak in favour of [an applicant's] claim of improper motives'.[66] As noted earlier, *specific* violations of Article 5(1)(c) with Article 18 were found in certain cases when the Court had particular evidence to do so, such as the actual reasoning employed by the domestic courts when detaining the person concerned. In *Lutsenko* and *Tymoshenko* it saw the applicants' arrest and detention as 'distinguishable' or 'specific' features which allowed it to address that aspect 'separately from the more general context of politically motivated prosecution of the opposition leader'.[67] No violations of Article 18 were found in *Khodorkovskiy and Lebedev*, when the Court saw the broader allegations made as an attempt to persuade it 'that everything in their case was contrary to the Convention, and that their conviction was therefore invalid'. That assailed the 'general presumption of good faith on the part of the public authorities', requiring 'particularly weighty evidence in support'.[68] Indeed, it was striking that, on the facts of the case, the Court did not 'exclude that in limiting some of the applicants' rights throughout the proceedings some of the authorities or State officials might have had a "hidden agenda"'. However, it did not agree that 'their whole case was a travesty of justice', noting that the domestic case against them did not concern 'their political activities *stricto sensu*, even remotely', the applicants not being 'opposition leaders or public officials'.[69] This suggests that the Court is prepared to accept that a prosecution might not be completely free from a political agenda, but that such corrupting influence, if it exists, needs to have a decisive effect on matters, which it would not if the fundamental intention of the authorities had been legitimate, it being sufficient that the case against the applicants had a 'healthy core'.[70]

As we have seen, the Court's approach appears to be based on policy reasons which assume good faith on the part of the state, but it may be asked whether applicants are left facing an overwhelming obstacle when it comes to establishing Article 18 claims. In that regard, it is interesting to note that in *Tymoshenko* three judges were prepared to uphold the applicant's broader claim that the aim of the authorities had been to exclude the applicant from active political life and to prevent her standing in forthcoming parliamentary elections. They agreed that a very exacting standard of proof was required, but argued that that requirement 'must not, however, be such as to render it impossible for the applicant to prove a violation of Article 18'. Noting the difficulties facing applicants trying to establish their case, the judges pointed out that to maintain the effective application of Article 18, the Court should 'accept evidence of the authorities' improper motives which relies on inferences drawn from the concrete circumstances and the context of the case'.[71] They then pointed to the applicant's indefinite pre-trial detention, which was hard to justify in itself and commenced within a time frame proximate to the preparations for the relevant election campaign. Moreover, the way in which the authorities acted—the frequent requirement to attend questioning and then hearings almost every day at

---

[66] *Khodorkovskiy and Lebedev v Russia*, para 903. In *Gusinskiy v Russia* 2004-IV; 41 EHRR 281, there was strong evidence of foul play on the part of the authorities.

[67] *Lutsenko v Ukraine* hudoc (2012); 56 EHRR 802 paras 108-109 (arrest and detention was for 'other reasons' than Article 5(1) permitted) and *Tymoshenko v Ukraine* hudoc (2013) paras 298–300 (same phraseology).   [68] *Khodorkovskiy and Lebedev v Russia* hudoc (2013) para 905.

[69] *Khodorkovskiy and Lebedev v Russia*, para 906.

[70] *Khodorkovskiy and Lebedev v Russia*, para 908, and see this para more generally for the high threshold the Court sets for a violation of Article 18 in this context. See also *Khodorkovskiy v Russia* hudoc (2011); 53 EHRR 1103 para 260.

[71] Cf *Khodorkovskiy and Lebedev v Russia*, para 899, the Court accepting that 'improper reason' might be 'reasonably inferred from the context'.

trial—completely hindered her ability to continue political activity. Also of note was the fact that criminal charges had been brought against more than eight high-level members of her government.

4 CONCLUSION

The Article 18 cases heard by the Court in recent years (2012–2013) clearly raise issues of considerable concern, their political backdrop and sensitivity being obvious. With the Court's approach so heavily dependent on the policy issues noted in this chapter, a Grand Chamber ruling on Article 18 would be welcome.

21

ARTICLE 1, FIRST PROTOCOL: THE RIGHT TO PROPERTY

> **Article 1, First Protocol**
>
> Every natural or legal person is entitled to the peaceful enjoyment of his possessions. No one shall be deprived of his possessions except in the public interest and subject to the conditions provided for by law and by the general principles of international law.
>
> The preceding provisions shall not, however, in any way impair the right of a state to enforce such laws as it deems necessary to control the use of property in accordance with the general interest or to secure the payment of taxes or other contributions or penalties.

1. INTRODUCTION

It proved exceedingly difficult to reach agreement on a formulation of the right to property when the European Convention was being drafted.[1] Eventually, it was one of the provisions left over until the First Protocol. Even then, the differences between states were considerable and the provision finally adopted guarantees only a much qualified right, allowing the state a wide power to interfere with property.[2] The United Kingdom and Sweden in particular were concerned that no substantial fetter be placed on the power of states to implement programmes of nationalization of industries for political and social purposes.[3] In its final form, Article 1 of the First Protocol contains no express reference to a right to compensation at any level in the event of interference with property, save any that might be found in the reference to 'the general principles of international law'. The Court has made frequent reference to the drafting history of Article 1 and its influence has been substantial in confirming the wide latitude states have in interfering with the right.

The right of '[e]very natural or legal person' is protected, wording which provides specific recognition of the general position that corporate bodies have rights under the Convention.

---

[1] See Robertson, 28 BYIL 359 (1951); Peukert, 2 HRLJ 37 at 38–42 (1981) and Allen, *Property and the Human Rights Act 1998*, 2005 (hereafter 'Allen, *Property*'), pp 17–33. On Article 1 generally, see Sermet, *La Convention européenne des droits de l'homme et le droit de propriété*, Dossiers sur les droits de l'homme, 1998; Frowein, *European System*, ch 20; Windisdoerffer, 19 HRLR 18 (1998); Çoban, *Protection of Property Rights within the European Convention on Human Rights*, 2004; and Allen, *Property*.

[2] For the main items in the preparatory work, see 3 TP 92–6, 106–8 (Consultative Assembly) and 134–6 (Secretary General's Memorandum). The text was eventually approved by the Consultative Assembly: 8 TP 168. 　　　　　　　　　　　　　　　　　　　　　　　　　　　　　　　　[3] 6 TP 140, 200.

It is necessary that the applicant be the real 'victim', ie, the corporation if its rights are affected, the shareholder if their rights have been interfered with.[4]

I. POSSESSIONS

The English language text uses the word 'possessions' to describe the protected interest but any suggestion that it should be read narrowly is refuted by the word '*biens*' in the French text which indicates that a wide range of proprietorial interests were intended to be protected. The essential characteristic of a 'possession' is the acquired economic value of the individual interest.[5] A 'possession' embraces immoveable and moveable property[6] and corporal and incorporeal interests, such as company shares[7] and intellectual property.[8] Contractual rights,[9] including leases,[10] and monies due under court judgments (sometimes referred to by the Court as judgment debts)[11] are possessions. Pension rights are also possessions,[12] as are other welfare benefits.[13]

Various other rulings demonstrate the wide-ranging meaning given to 'possessions'. Thus the term includes wrongly paid tax,[14] and permission to occupy a dwelling[15] or to

[4] *Olczak v Poland No 30417/96* 2002-X DA. A company's legal personality will be disregarded only in 'exceptional circumstances', see, eg, *Pine Valley Developments Ltd and Others v Ireland* A 222 (1991); 14 EHRR 319 (managing director and sole shareholder 'victim' of interference with company land as company was a 'vehicle' for applicant); *Ankarcrona v Sweden No 35178/97*, 2000-VI DA (sole shareholder 'victim' as company injured was his 'vehicle'); *Eugenia Michaelidou Developments Ltd and Michael Tymvios v Turkey* hudoc (2003) (sole director and substantial majority shareholder 'victim' when company and applicant 'so closely identified with each other'); and *Khamidov v Russia* hudoc (2007) (co-owner of family company issued with general power of attorney by other owner a 'victim' of interference with company's property). For cases in which shareholders were not 'victims', see *Agrotexim and Others v Greece* A 330-A (1995); 21 EHRR 250; *Lebedev v Russia* hudoc (2007); *TW Computeranimation GmbH and Others v Austria No 53818/00* hudoc (2005) DA ; *Bayramov v Azerbaijan No 23055/03* hudoc (2006) DA; and *Družstevní záložna Pria and Others v Czech Republic* hudoc (2008). See generally Emberland, *The Human Rights of Companies— Exploring the Structure of ECHR Protection*, 2006, pp 65–109.

[5] See, eg, *De la Cierva Osorio de Moscoso and Others v Spain Nos 41127/98 et al* 1999-VII DA (peerage not a 'possession' where title has no economic value). There was an economic value in *Anheuser-Busch Inc v Portugal* 2007-I; 45 EHRR 830 GC (application for registration of trade mark) and *Paeffgen GmbH v Germany Nos 25379/04 et al* hudoc (2007) DA (exclusive right to use internet domain names).

[6] *Wiggins v UK No 7456/76*, 13 DR 40 (1978).

[7] *Bramelid and Malmström v Sweden Nos 8588/79 and 8589/79*, 29 DR 64 (1982); 5 EHRR 249 and *Sovtransavto Holding v Ukraine* 2002-VII; 34 EHRR 44. It includes the corresponding rights that the holder of a share in a company possesses: see *Olczak v Poland No 30417/96*, 2002-X DA. Whether influence and power as a majority shareholder constitutes a 'possession' remains an open question: *Türk Ticaret Bankasi Munzam Sosyal Güvenlik Emekli Ve Yardim Sandiği Vakfi v Turkey Nos 48925/99 and 36109/04* hudoc (2006) DA.

[8] *Anheuser-Busch Inc v Portugal* 2007-I; 45 EHRR 830 GC. Eg, *Smith Kline and French Laboratories Ltd v Netherlands No 12633/87*, 66 DR 70 (1990) (patent); *Lenzing AG v UK No 38817/97* hudoc (1998) DA (patent); *Anheuser-Busch Inc v Portugal* 2007-I; 45 EHRR 830 GC (application for registration of trade mark); *Melnychuk v Ukraine No 28743/03* 2005-IX DA (copyright). See Helfer, 49 HILJ 1 (2008).

[9] See, eg, *Gasus Dosier und Fördertechnik GmbH v Netherlands* A 306-B (1995); 20 EHRR 403.

[10] *Mellacher and Others v Austria* A 169 (1989); 12 EHRR 391 PC. Cf *JLS v Spain No 41917/98*, 1999-V DA (occupier of premises under an arrangement with authorities). Claims for rent are not 'possessions': *Xenodochiaki SA v Greece No 49213/99* hudoc (2001) DA.

[11] *Stran Greek Refineries and Stratis Andreadis v Greece* A 301-B (1994); 19 EHRR 293 (arbitral award); *Burdov v Russia* 2002-III; 38 EHRR 639; and *Kotov v Russia* hudoc (2012) GC.

[12] *Carson and Others v UK* hudoc 2010 GC and *Valkov and Others v Bulgaria* hudoc (2011).

[13] *Stec v UK* 2006-VI; 43 EHRR 1017 GC. See generally, Leijten 13 HRLR 309 (2013). A mistakenly paid benefit may be a possession: *Moskal v Poland* hudoc (2009). See also *NKM v Hungary* hudoc (2013) (severance pay).

[14] *Iovioni and Others v Romania Nos 57873/10 et al* hudoc (2012) DA.

[15] *Saghinadze and Others v Georgia* hudoc (2010).

build on land.[16] In *Oneryildiz v Turkey*,[17] the respondent state's tolerance for five years of the applicant's illegally erected dwelling gave him a sufficient proprietary interest in it for the dwelling to be his 'possession'. At the same time, a 'possession' must be owned by the applicant in their private, not public, capacity.[18]

'Legitimate expectations' may also give rise to 'possessions'.[19] In *Gratzinger and Gratzinger v Czech Republic*,[20] the Grand Chamber stated: '"Possessions" within the meaning of Article 1 of Protocol No 1 can be either "existing possessions" or assets, including claims, in respect of which an applicant can argue that he has at least a "legitimate expectation" that they will be realised'. In the case of both kinds of 'possession', there is a sufficient proprietary interest to bring Article 1 into play. Where the proprietary interest is in the nature of a claim,[21] the person in whom it is vested may be regarded as having a 'legitimate expectation' if there is a sufficient basis for the interest in national law, for example where there is settled case law of the domestic courts confirming its existence.[22] In contrast, where there is uncertainty as to the interpretation of the law to be applied in the applicant's claim, or where the applicant's interpretation is rejected by the courts, there is no 'legitimate expectation'.[23] In *Pressos Compania Naviera SA and Others v Belgium*,[24] the applicants argued that Article 1 was breached when their pending claims against the state for negligence in the provision of piloting services to the applicants' ships were extinguished by legislation that took effect retrospectively. The government contended that the applicants' claims did not constitute 'possessions' as none of them had been recognized and determined by a judicial decision having final effect. The Court found that the claims constituted an 'asset' for the purposes of Article 1 because under the national law of negligence the claims for compensation came into existence as soon as the

---

[16] *Consorts Richet et Le Ber v France* hudoc (2010).   [17] 2004-XII; 41 EHRR 325 GC.

[18] *The Former King of Greece and Others v Greece* 2000-XII; 33 EHRR 516 GC

[19] On 'legitimate expectations', see Allen, *Property*, pp 46–57 and Popelier, 10 EHRLR 10 at 12–20 (2006).

[20] No 39794/98 2002-VII; 35 EHRR CD 202 para 69 GC.

[21] Conditional claims are discussed later.

[22] *NKM v Hungary* hudoc (2013) para 35. Regarding the stage of proceedings that the claim must reach in order to constitute a 'possession', see *Stran Greek Refineries and Stratis Andreadis v Greece* A 301-B (1994); 19 EHRR 293 (final judgment); *Smokovitis and Others v Greece* hudoc (2002) (first instance decision); and *SA Dangeville v France* 2002-III; 38 EHRR 699 (first instance decision in line with authority). Cf *Arvanitaki-Robati v Greece* hudoc (2006) (no 'possession' where claim not established by final court decision).

[23] See *Kopecký v Slovakia* 2004-XI; 41 EHRR 944 para 50 GC; *Anheuser-Busch Inc v Portugal* hudoc 2007-I; 45 EHRR 830 para 65 GC; and *Iovioni and Others v Romania Nos 57583/10 et al* hudoc (2012) DA. See also *Optim and Industerre v Belgium No 23819/06* hudoc (2012) DA 9 (no 'legitimate expectation' because the amount of tax liability unknown). And see *Ramaer and Van Willigen v Netherlands No 34880/12* hudoc (2012) DA.

[24] A 332 (1995); 21 EHRR 301. For other cases of pending claims in which there was a 'legitimate expectation' of success, see *Draon v France* hudoc (2005); 42 EHRR 807 GC; *Maurice v France* 2005-IX; 42 EHRR 885 GC; and *Smokovitis and Others v Greece* hudoc (2002). And see *SA Dangeville v France* 2002-III; 38 EHRR 699 ('legitimate expectation' generated by European Community Directive). In *National & Provincial Building Society, Leeds Permanent Building Society and Yorkshire Building Society v UK* 1997-VII; 25 EHRR 127, there was no 'legitimate expectation' that a pending claim would succeed owing to foreshadowed legislative intervention. For cases in which a public authority acted beyond its powers, see *Pine Valley Developments Ltd and Others v Ireland* A 222 (1991); 14 EHRR 319 (outline planning permission gave rise to 'legitimate expectation' before it was held to be *ultra vires*) and *Stretch v UK* hudoc (2003); 38 EHRR 196 (local authority acting in excess of powers, by granting an option to renew a lease, created 'legitimate expectation' that the applicant could exercise the option). See also *Bozcaada Kimisis Teodoku Rum Ortodoks Kilisesi Vakfi v Turkey (No 2)* hudoc (2009) (legitimate grounds to believe that title had been obtained by adverse possession).

damage occurred, and the applicants had a 'legitimate expectation' that their claims would be determined in accordance with the general law of tort in which the highest national court, following early case law, had recognized the liability of public authorities in negligence.

Initially, the ascription and identification of property rights is for the national legal system[25] and it is incumbent on an applicant to establish the precise nature of the right in the national law and his entitlement to enjoy it.[26] However, the concept of 'possession' is autonomous.[27] The mere fact that the national law does not acknowledge as a legal right a particular interest or does so in terms which do not result in it being recognized as a property right does not conclusively determine that the interest is not a 'possession' for the purposes of Article 1.[28] In *Anheuser-Busch Inc v Portugal*,[29] the Court stated, that when deciding whether Article 1 applied, it would examine 'whether the circumstances of the case, considered as a whole, conferred on the applicant title to a substantive interest protected by Article 1 of the First Protocol'. In that case, the Court noted that the 'bundle of financial rights and interests that arise upon an application for the registration of a trade mark [such as a right to sell or license for consideration] ... possess—or are capable of possessing—a substantial financial value', so that 'the applicant company's legal position as an applicant for the registration of a trade mark came within Article 1 of Protocol No. 1, as it gave rise to interests of a proprietary nature'.[30] The fact that the rights attached to the application were conditional, becoming final only if the trademark was registered, made no difference.

The demonstration of an established economic interest by an applicant may by itself be sufficient to establish that Article 1 applies. Thus in *Tre Traktörer Aktiebolag v Sweden*,[31] the Court rejected the government's argument that because a liquor licence conferred no rights in national law, it could not be a 'possession' for the purposes of Article 1. It was essential to the successful conduct of the applicant's restaurant and its withdrawal had adverse effects on the goodwill and value of the business. The Court may also be prepared to undertake a broader examination of the circumstances of a case where property is held in possession contrary to national law or under a contract having no legal effect. For instance, in *Beyeler v Italy*,[32] a contract for the purchase of a painting was 'null and void'

---

[25] There are few restrictions upon what a state may regard as capable of being owned—perhaps only individuals because of freedom from slavery in Article 4. But the fact that something is capable of being owned in one legal system (eg, human blood or organs) is not a reason why it must be capable of being owned in another.

[26] See, eg, *Agneessens v Belgium No 12164/86*, 58 DR 63 (1988) ; *Kopecký v Slovakia* 2004-XI; 41 EHRR 944 GC (claim for restitution of land rejected by court not a 'possession'); and *Zhigalev v Russia* hudoc (2006) (claim to sole ownership of farm not upheld by courts not a 'possession').

[27] Eg, *Gasus Dosier und Fördertechnik GmbH v Netherlands* A 306-B (1995); 20 EHRR 403 and *Broniowski v Poland* 2004-V; 40 EHRR 495 GC.

[28] *Depalle v France* 2010- GC (title not recognized in French law, but length of occupancy of land gave rise to a propriety interest for the purposes of Article 1). Cf *Öneryildiz v Turkey* 2004-XII; 41 EHRR 325, see section 1.IV, and *Doğan and Others v Turkey* 2004-VI; 41 EHRR 231.

[29] 2007-I; 45 EHRR 830 para 75 GC.   [30] *Anheuser-Busch Inc v Portugal*, paras 76–8.

[31] A 159 (1989); 13 EHRR 309. See also *Van Marle and Others v Netherlands* A 101 (1986); 8 EHRR 483 PC and *Iatridis v Greece* 1999-II; 30 EHRR 97 GC (clientele built up by the applicants' efforts an 'asset' (cf business goodwill) that qualified as a 'possession'); *Buzescu v Romania* hudoc (2005) (legal practice and its goodwill an 'asset' that qualified as a 'possession') and *Megadat.com SRL v Moldova* 2008- (licence to conduct a business a 'possession'). Cf *Bauquel v France No 71120/01* hudoc (2004) DA (no possession where no established professional practice).

[32] 2000-I; 33 EHRR 1225 GC. See also *Matos e Silva, Lda and Others v Portugal* 1996-IV; 24 EHRR 573; *The Synod College of the Evangelical Reformed Church of Lithuania v Lithuania No 44548/98* hudoc (2002); 36 EHRR CD 94; and *Öneryildiz v Turkey* 2004-XII; 41 EHRR 325 GC. Cf *Kötterl and Schittily v Austria No 32957/96* hudoc (2003); 37 EHRR CD 205, in which the Court based its assessment of the facts on the determination of the national courts that the contract was void.

under national law yet the Court found an interest protected by Article 1 on the basis that the applicant had been in possession of the property for several years and the authorities had, for some purposes, treated the applicant as having a proprietary interest it.

As indicated in Chapter 9,[33] the right to a fair trial in Article 6 applies to the determination of 'civil rights and obligations'. This is a term with an autonomous Convention meaning that has been interpreted as including pecuniary rights. The coherence of the Convention as a whole demands that the autonomous concept of 'possessions' in Article 1 be no less a category than the concept of pecuniary rights for the purposes of Article 6: the reasoning about the essence of the interest measured by its nature and importance to an individual should apply to its formal protection (Article 6(1)) and its substance (Article 1 of the First Protocol) alike.[34] The minimum in each case is that the applicant shows that he is entitled to some real, if yet unattributed, economic benefit. This is relevant to the treatment of welfare benefits as property. While the Court has consistently said that there is no general right to welfare benefits to be derived from Article 1, it has allowed that a welfare right under domestic law is a possession for the purposes of Article 1. What is required is that the applicant demonstrates that he has a legal right in domestic law to some benefit if he satisfies certain conditions, rather than that he seeks to ensure that a discretion is exercised in his favour.[35]

In this connection there is no distinction to be drawn between benefits to which the applicant has made contributions and those to which no direct contribution has been made.[36] However, while he may be entitled under Article 6(1) to a fair hearing to determine whether any conditions for their payment are satisfied, if they are not, the applicant will have no right to the benefit and the state will not be put to justifying why the benefit does not accrue, except where the conditions comprise a discriminatory ground under Article 14, in which case there will be a breach of Article 1 of the First Protocol and Article 14 taken together: a right to receive the benefit will exist notwithstanding a failure to fulfil the conditions.[37]

---

[33] See, eg, *Beaumartin v France* A 296-B (1994); 19 EHRR 485, discussed previously (compensation agreement negotiated by France for its nationals concerned the applicant's pecuniary rights so that Article 6 applied even though there was no legal right in French law; right to compensation was likewise treated as a 'possession' under Article 1).

[34] *Feldbrugge v Netherlands* A 99 (1986); 8 EHRR 425 PC; *Salesi v Italy* A 257-E (1993); 26 EHRR 187; and *Stec and Others v UK Nos 65731/01 and 65900/01* 2005-X, 41 EHRR SE 295 GC DA (welfare rights cases). To similar effect, see Rosas, in Rosas and Helgesen, eds, *The Strength of Diversity: Human Rights and Pluralist Democracy*, 1992, pp 150–1.

[35] *Stec and Others v UK Nos 65731/01 and 65900/01* 2005-X, 41 EHRR SE 295 GC DA, para 51. See also *Gaygusuz v Austria* 1996-IV; 23 EHRR 364. There is no right to a benefit of a particular amount under Article 1: *Kjartan Ásmundsson v Iceland* 2004-IX; 41 EHRR 927 or to pension increases in line with inflation: *Carson and Others v UK* 2010-GC. See Allen, 28 MJIL 287 at 310–1 (2007).

[36] The Court sought to adopt an interpretation of the concept of 'possessions' that promoted consistency with the concept of pecuniary rights under Article 6(1), reflected 'the variety of funding methods and the interlocking nature of benefits under most welfare systems' within member states, and recognized the social function of welfare benefits: *Stec and Others v UK*, para 50.

[37] *Stec and Others v UK* (eligibility for reduced earnings allowance based on difference in UK pensionable ages between men and women not a violation of Article 14 with Article 1 of the First Protocol; Cf Judge Loucaides dissenting). See also *Runkee and White v UK* hudoc (2007) (non-payment of widow's pension to male widowers not a violation of Article 14 with Article 1 of the First Protocol). Cf *Gaygusuz v Austria* 1996-IV; 23 EHRR 364 (eligibility for work-related welfare benefits based on nationality a violation of Article 14 with Article 1 of the First Protocol) and *Luczak v Poland* hudoc (2007) (eligibility for farmers' social-security scheme based on nationality a violation of Article 14 with Article 1 of the First Protocol).

The Convention protects an applicant's existing possessions against interference. It does not provide a right to be put into the possession of things he does not already have, however strong the individual's interest in this happening may be.[38] In *Marckx v Belgium*,[39] the Court said that Article 1 'does not guarantee the right to acquire possessions whether on intestacy or through voluntary dispositions'. There is also no right to have food or to have shelter, however destitute, under this provision.[40] However, its affiliation with civil rights need not severely circumscribe the reach of Article 1 for, as the Grand Chamber in *Stec v UK*[41] observed in the context of welfare rights, there is no 'water-tight division' separating the sphere of economic and social rights from that of civil and political rights set forth in the Convention.

Property rights constituting possessions may cease to do so if they have 'long been impossible to exercise effectively'.[42] The principle appears in cases dealing with the restoration of property rights in the aftermath of World War II and upon the fall of the former communist governments in Central and Eastern Europe. In this context the Court has granted states wide latitude in the determination of claims for restitution and compensation.[43] In *Malhous v Czech Republic*,[44] a right of ownership in land held by the applicant's father was extinguished when the land was expropriated, without compensation, under legislation enacted in 1948 by the communist regime. While legislation passed after the collapse of the communist government provided for restitution of land taken under the 1948 legislation, this entitlement was expressed to exclude land that had been transferred under the 1948 legislation to natural persons, as had the applicant's land. In the case of *Von Maltzan and Others v Germany*,[45] the political framework established for the reunification of the communist German Democratic Republic with the democratic Federal Republic of Germany expressly excluded the right to restitution of land, such as the applicants' land, expropriated between 1945 and 1949 in the Soviet occupied zone in Germany. In neither case did the applicant's interest in property survive in a form that was recognized as a possession: the 'mere hope of restitution' lacked a sufficient basis in law to qualify for protection under Article 1.[46] The position will differ where rights not able to be exercised have nevertheless had 'a continuing legal basis in domestic law'. Such a case was *Broniowski v Poland*,[47] where the applicants held 'a right to credit'[48] under Polish law in lieu of restitution of real property lost as a result of repatriation from

---

[38] *Kopecký v Slovakia* 2004-XI; 41 EHRR 944 para 35 GC. Eg, future income not a possession until it has 'been earned or an enforceable claim to it exists': *Denimark Ltd and 11 Others v UK No 37660/97* hudoc (2000); 30 EHRR CD 144 (value of commercial business); *Xenodochiaki SA v Greece No 49213/99* hudoc (2001) DA (rent); *Ambruosi v Italy* hudoc (2000); 35 EHRR 125 (legal fees); and *Levänen and Others v Finland No 34600/03* hudoc (2006) DA (possible loss of future income and value of business assets, inadmissible).

[39] A 31 (1979); 2 EHRR 330 PC. Cf *Inze v Austria* A 126 (1987); 10 EHRR 394.

[40] See, eg, *Slivenko v Latvia* 2003-X; 39 EHRR 490 GC (housing); *Sardin v Russia No 69582/01*, 2004-II DA (medical and other social benefits); and *Kutepov and Anikeyenko v Russia* hudoc (2005) (ownership and control over resources necessary for basic subsistence). Cf Cassese, 1 EJIL 141 (1991) with discussion of *Van Volsem v Belgium No 14641/89* (1990), unreported. Insufficient state provision may raise an issue under Article 3: *Larioshina v Russia No 56869/00* hudoc (2002) DA. See Ch 6.

[41] *Nos 65731/01 and 65900/01* 2005-X; 41 EHRR SE 295 para 52 GC DA.

[42] *Mayer v Germany Nos 18890/91 et al*, 85 DR 5 (1996) Com Rep and *Von Maltzan and Others v Germany* 2005-V; 42 EHRR SE 93 para 74 GC DA. See Allen, 13 CJEL 1 at 17–22 (2006–7).

[43] *Von Maltzan*, para 74.   [44] *No 33071/96*, 2000-XII GC.

[45] 2005-V; 42 EHRR SE 11 GC.

[46] *Malhous v Czech Republic No 33071/96*, 2000-XII GC and *Von Maltzan v Germany* 2005-V; 42 EHRR SE 93 para 112 GC. See also *Myšáková v Czech Republic No 30021/03* hudoc (2006) DA.

[47] 2004-V; 43 EHRR 1 para 130 GC. Cf *Loizidou v Turkey* 1996-VI; 23 EHRR 513 GC.

[48] By this the value of the property was offset against the cost of buying land or a house from the state.

territories 'across the Bug River' when those territories ceased to be in Poland after World War II. Acknowledgement of the right in domestic law during the communist era and afterwards provided a basis for the Polish courts to define the right as a 'debt chargeable to the State Treasury which had a pecuniary and inheritable character', a right sufficiently concrete to constitute a 'possession' for the purposes of Article 1.

Another situation in which property rights may be lost is where a claim has been made conditional upon the fulfilment of statutory criteria such as time limits,[49] place of residence,[50] nationality,[51] or proof of location of the property.[52] In *Kopecký v Slovakia*,[53] the Grand Chamber confirmed the principle that a conditional claim which lapses as a result of non-fulfilment of the condition does not constitute a possession for the purposes of Article 1. A breach of Article 1 of the Protocol and Article 14 of the Convention may occur where the condition is discriminatory contrary to Article 14.[54]

In cases where property has been confiscated as a result of a criminal conviction, the Court has also rejected the idea that the right of ownership revives where the conviction and confiscation order are quashed with retrospective effect.[55] Nor will a claim for restitution constitute an 'asset' if the statutory requirements for restitution cannot be met, for there is no proprietary interest established in law to which a legitimate expectation may attach. This was the situation in *Kopecký*,[56] where the applicant claimed the return of coins taken in 1959 from his father by the authorities following a conviction. In 1992 the conviction and confiscation were quashed by judicial rehabilitation legislation. The legislation further provided that the state would restore movable property that had been confiscated on receiving a written request showing the location of the property. However, the applicant could not say where the coins were (nor could the authorities), and the domestic court found that he had not complied with the statutory requirements for restitution of the coins. The Grand Chamber held that in these circumstances the applicant's claim for restitution was not 'sufficiently established' to qualify as an 'asset'.[57] Thus, there was no longer a 'possession' for the purposes of Article 1.

II. PEACEFUL ENJOYMENT: THREE KINDS OF INTERFERENCE

The specific right protected by Article 1 is the right to the 'peaceful enjoyment' of possessions: the right to have, to use, to repair, to dispose of, to pledge, to lend, even to destroy one's possessions.[58] Enjoyment is protected principally against interference by the state.[59] Interference may be in the forms specifically referred to in Article 1—deprivation or control of use—but it is a wider category. So in *Sporrong and Lönnroth v Sweden*,[60] where

---

[49] *De Napoles Pacheco v Belgium No 7775/77*, 15 DR 143 (1979) Com Rep (reimbursement of proceeds of sale of shares).   [50] *Jantner v Slovakia* hudoc (2003).

[51] *Gratzinger and Gratzingerova v Czech Republic No 39794/98*, 2002-VII; 35 EHRR CD 202 GC and *Polacek and Polackova v Czech Republic No 38645/97* hudoc (2002) GC DA.

[52] *Kopecký v Slovakia* 2004-XI; 41 EHRR 944 GC.

[53] *Kopecký v Slovakia*, para 35. See also *Malhous v Czech Republic No 33071/96*, 2000-XII GC DA.

[54] See *Zeïbek v Greece* hudoc (2009). Cf the welfare benefits cases section 1.I above. See also *Gratzinger and Gratzingerova v Czech Republic No 39794/98*, 2002-VII; 35 EHRR CD 202 GC. See further Allen, 13 CJEL 1 at 23–4 (2006–7).   [55] *Polacek and Polackova v Czech Republic No 38645/97* hudoc (2002) GC.

[56] *Kopecký v Slovakia* 2004-XI; 41 EHRR 944 GC. See also *Glaser v Czech Republic* hudoc (2008).

[57] *Kopecký v Slovakia*, para 58.

[58] It includes the possibility of exercising those rights: *Sporrong and Lönnroth v Sweden* A 52 (1982); 5 EHRR 35 PC and *Loizidou v Turkey* 1996-VI; 23 EHRR 513 GC, see section 1.III.

[59] As to private interferences, see section 1.IV.

[60] A 52 (1982); 5 EHRR 35 PC. See also *Erkner and Hofauer v Austria* A 117 (1987); 9 EHRR 464; *Potomska and Potomski v Poland* hudoc (2011); and *Huseyin Kaplan v Turkey* hudoc (2013). In *Akkuş v Turkey* 1997-IV;

there was a long delay between an initial decision indicating that property was likely to be expropriated and its execution, the Court held that there had been an interference with the applicants' right to the enjoyment of their possessions, even though the interference was neither a seizure nor a measure of control. The imposition of financial liability that is not concerned with securing the payment of taxes also constitutes an interference with enjoyment of possessions.[61] The state will be responsible under Article 1 for interferences which affect the economic value of property.[62] Accordingly, claims about interferences with the aesthetic or environmental qualities of possessions are protected, if they be protected at all, elsewhere in the Convention.[63] In *S v France*,[64] the Commission looked at the effects on the value of property as a result of noise pollution, but did not consider amenity loss of the rural aspect from the property, resulting from industrial development nearby. Nevertheless, demonstration of economic loss sufficient to establish an interference with possessions may not always be necessary. In *Chassagnou and Others v France*,[65] there was an interference with property because of the personal impact of French laws allowing public entry onto the applicants' lands in order to pursue an activity—hunting—to which they held strong ethical objections.

III. ACCESS TO PROPERTY

In *Loizidou v Turkey*,[66] the Court had to deal with what it characterized as an issue of access to property in order that the property owner could exercise her rights. The facts of the case are complicated by the political background to the application, which concerns the Turkish occupation of northern Cyprus. The applicant claimed that the respondent state had interfered with her rights under Article 1 because, directly or indirectly, it had responsibility for her, a Greek Cypriot, being denied access to her real property in northern Cyprus. The Court noted that her complaint was not limited to the denial of physical access to her property; it was that the refusal of access 'has gradually, over the last 16 years affected the right of the applicant as a property owner'.[67] The Court considered that the applicant 'effectively lost all control over, as well as all possibilities to use and enjoy, her property. The continuous denial of access must therefore be regarded as an interference with her rights under Article 1 of the First Protocol.'[68] There is force in this argument: alien property owners may have no right of entry to a state to visit their property, but the rights they have in respect of their property which do not require their

---

30 EHRR 533 delay in payment of compensation for the expropriation of property constituted an interference with the enjoyment of property.

[61] Eg, *X v Netherlands* 14 YB 224 (1971) (social security contributions).

[62] See, eg, *Krickl v Austria* No 21752/93 hudoc (1997) DA; *Pitkänen v Finland* hudoc (2004) and *Ashworth and Others v UK No 39561/98* hudoc (2004) DA. Cf the position of shareholders where an interference with a possession held by the company results in a reduction in the value of their shares: *Agrotexim and Others v Greece* A 330-A (1995); 21 EHRR 250.

[63] Eg, *López Ostra v Spain* A 303-C (1994); 20 EHRR 277 (Article 8) and *Hatton and Others v UK* 2003-VIII; 37 EHRR 611 GC (Article 8).

[64] No 13728/88, 65 DR 250 (1990). Cf *Rayner v UK No 9310/81*, 47 DR 5 (1986) (Article 1 'does not, in principle, guarantee a right to the peaceful enjoyment of possessions in a pleasant environment').

[65] 1999-III; 29 EHRR 615 GC.   [66] 1996-VI; 23 EHRR 513 GC.

[67] *Loizidou v Turkey*, para 60. The Court has drawn a distinction between an instantaneous act and a continuing situation of deprivation of property, which is relevant to *ratione temporis* objections to jurisdiction: see *Chiragov v Armenia No 13216/15* hudoc (2011) GC DA.

[68] *Loizidou v Turkey*, paras 60, 61, and 63. See also *Cyprus v Turkey* 2001-IV; 35 EHRR 731 GC; *Eugenia Michaelidou Developments Ltd and Michael Tymvios v Turkey* hudoc (2003); and *Xenides-Arestis v Turkey* hudoc (2005); 44 EHRR SE 185.

presence should not be interfered with. Nor should they be deprived of their property by reason of their absence alone.

The finding of a violation of Article 1 on the basis of a denial of access to property has significant implications for the right of return for internally displaced persons. It was later applied in *Doğan and Others v Turkey*,[69] where the authorities cited terrorist-related incidents in the local area as the ground for the decision to refuse Turkish nationals access to their villages. The Court found that the measures 'deprived the applicants of all resources from which they derived their living' and 'affected the very substance of ownership' of the properties.[70] In the exercise of its powers to order 'just satisfaction', the Court stated that the most appropriate remedy for denial of access cases was for the national authorities to facilitate return of the applicants to their villages and pay compensation for the period during which they were denied access. In the *Doğan* case, 'just satisfaction' was an award of compensation only because the applicants no longer wished to return to their villages.[71]

IV. POSITIVE OBLIGATION TO PROTECT POSSESSIONS

That the state has a positive obligation to protect the enjoyment of possessions is implied in Article 1. In *Öneryildiz v Turkey*,[72] the Grand Chamber said of the protection afforded by Article 1:

> Genuine, effective exercise of the right protected by that provision does not depend merely on the state's duty not to interfere, but may require positive measures of protection, particularly where there is a direct link between the measures which an applicant may legitimately expect from the authorities and his effective enjoyment of his possessions.

The case concerned a methane explosion in a municipal refuse tip, which resulted in thirty-nine deaths and the destruction of ten homes in a surrounding illegal settlement. Two years before the explosion, the local council responsible for the tip and relevant government departments received an experts' report advising that the tip did not comply with health and safety regulations. Specifically, the report warned of the danger of a methane explosion to neighbouring dwellings due to the absence of a ventilation system to allow for the controlled release of accumulated gases. The applicant contended that the failure to inform the settlement's inhabitants of the danger posed by the tip together with the failure to install ventilation shafts violated Article 1. The Court held that the obligation to protect property required the authorities to 'take practical steps' to avoid the destruction of the applicant's house in the light of a risk of which they knew or ought to have known: an effective measure would have been 'the timely installation of a gas-extraction system' at the tip, since this would have complied with the relevant regulations and general practice in the area. Without a practical response of this kind, the mere provision of information to nearby residents enabling them to assess the risks they might run as a result of their choice to live near the tip would not have absolved the state of its

---

[69] 2004-VI; 41 EHRR 231, where, unlike the applicant in the *Loizidou* case, the applicants did not hold formal title, but derived economic benefit from the land.

[70] *Doğan and Others v Turkey*, para 143.

[71] *Doğan and Others v Turkey* hudoc (2006) (just satisfaction).

[72] 2004-XII; 41 EHRR 325 para 134 GC. Cf *Kolyadenko and Others v Russia* hudoc (2012) and *Hadzhiyska v Bulgaria No 20701/09* hudoc (2012) DA, both cases of failure to act to prevent flooding. On the right to life aspect of these cases, see Ch 5, section 2.

responsibilities.[73] The Court majority concluded that, as there was clearly a causal link between the state's 'negligence' and the destruction of the applicant's house, there was a breach of a positive obligation to protect property, which a mere award of compensation on generous terms could not remedy.[74]

The 'positive measures of protection' to which the Court refers in the Öneryildiz case are both preventive and remedial, and concern interferences with possessions by private persons and the state. The state must ensure that property rights are sufficiently protected by law and that adequate remedies are available to an injured party when they are violated.[75] However, in some contexts the state's obligations are less onerous where the interference is by a private person.[76] Thus with regard to the enforcement of judgments against the state, the Strasbourg Court 'usually insists on the State complying with the respective court decision both fully and timeously',[77] but when the judgment 'debtor is a private actor, the position is different since the State is not, as a general rule, directly liable for debts of private actors and its obligations under these Convention provisions are limited to providing the necessary assistance to the creditor in the enforcement of the respective court awards, for example, through a bailiff service or bankruptcy procedures.'[78] But state responsibility will be engaged (i) when a private interference with property is an outcome of the exercise of governmental authority;[79] or (ii) when private law rights in the law of tort and contract, etc, are not adequately secured[80] or the judicial or other remedies available are not adequate.[81] One positive obligation of a preventive kind extending to private interferences was indicated in *Zolatas v Greece*,[82] where it was held that states must require banks to inform the holders of dormant accounts that a limitation period, following which the account holders will in effect lose the money in the account, is due to expire. As to remedial action, there are many cases in which the state has been held not to have taken adequate measures to enforce judgment debts;[83] to ensure the restitution of property[84] or the payment of compensation for expropriation[85] or political repression;[86] or to enforce court orders for the repossession of dwellings.[87]

It is clear that the state is not obliged to act to prevent loss of value as a result of market factors.[88] Further, the scope of the positive obligation has not extended to protecting

---

[73] *Öneryildiz v Turkey*, paras 101, 107–8, and 136.

[74] *Öneryildiz v Turkey*, paras 135 and 137. Judge Mularoni opined that no positive obligation to protect a right of property should extend to buildings erected in breach of town planning regulations. Judge Türmen confined his dissent to the issue of whether there was a 'possession'.

[75] *Kotov v Russia* hudoc (2012) GC. As to remedies, see also *Shesti Mai Engineering OOD and Others v Bulgaria* hudoc (2011) and *Plechanow v Poland* hudoc (2009). Where interference leads to the determination of a civil right, the fair trial requirements of Article 6(1) apply.

[76] *Kotov v Russia*.   [77] See, eg, *Burdov v Russia* 2002-III; 38 EHRR 639.

[78] *Anokhin v Russia* No 25867/02 hudoc (2007) DA.

[79] Eg, *James and Others v UK* A 98 (1986); 8 EHRR 123 PC (enactment of legislation enabling long lease tenants to purchase the freehold interest in privately rented property).

[80] Although the extent of this obligation remains undeveloped, no doubt common European standards will be taken into account.   [81] *Kotov v Russia* hudoc (2012) paras 113–14 GC.

[82] Hudoc (2013).   [83] *Fuklev v Ukraine* hudoc (2005).   [84] *Păduraru v Romania* 2005-XII.

[85] *Almeida Garrett, Mascarenhas Falcão and Others v Portugal* 2000-I; 34 EHRR 642.

[86] *Klaus and Iouri Kiladzé v Georgia* hudoc (2010).

[87] *Immobiliare Saffi v Italy* 1999-V; 30 EHRR 756 GC, see further section 5.I, and *Prodan v Moldova* 2004-III (authorities failed to provide the means required by law to execute judgments for eviction of tenants and restitution of apartments).

[88] Nor to protect against the effects of inflation, *X v Germany* No 8724/79, 20 DR 226 (1980). Cf *Akkuş v Turkey* 1997-IV; 30 EHRR 533 (inflation may be relevant in determining the fair balance where there is delay by the state in the payment of a judgment debt) and *Solodyuk v Russia* hudoc (2005) (inflation relevant to the fair balance where there is delay in payment of pensions).

identifiable persons from economic loss that has been knowingly caused by the state in the reform of the economic sector. This is illustrated in *Gayduk and Others v Ukraine*,[89] where the state implemented a programme of monetary reform that, combined with high inflation, resulted in severe depreciation of the value of money deposited in savings accounts. In order to rectify the hardship caused to account holders, laws were passed that established an 'indexation-of-deposits' scheme to compensate savers for financial loss following devaluation and to maintain the real value of deposits. Payments under the scheme were subject to funds being made available in the state treasury, but the funds were never provided. The applicants contended that in establishing the scheme the state had assumed an obligation to pay the indexed amounts. The Court, however, applied a general principle regardless of the particular circumstances contended by the applicant: it held that Article 1 was not applicable because it 'does not impose any general obligation on states to maintain the purchasing power of sums deposited through the systematic indexation of savings'.[90]

In practice, whether an obligation is considered as a positive or negative obligation, the analysis will be the same. In *Broniowski v Poland*,[91] the Grand Chamber explained the approach to be taken:

> In both contexts regard must be had to the fair balance to be struck between the competing interests of the individual and the community as a whole. It also holds true that the aims mentioned in that provision may be of some relevance in assessing whether a balance between the demands of the public interest involved and the applicant's fundamental right of property has been struck. In both contexts the State enjoys a certain margin of appreciation in determining the steps to be taken to ensure compliance with the Convention.

It was the close inter-relation of the alleged omissions and acts that led the Court to decline to examine the facts under the head of positive obligations or negative duties in the *Broniowski* case. Instead, it simply proceeded to determine whether the conduct of the state had struck a fair balance after having decided Article 1 applied.

2. THE STRUCTURE OF ARTICLE 1, FIRST PROTOCOL, AND THE INTER-RELATIONSHIP OF ITS PROVISIONS

I. THE THREE RULES

The Court has broken down Article 1 into its component parts and has gradually established the relationship between them. Its language has become familiar by frequent repetition. In *Sporrong and Lönnroth v Sweden*,[92] the Court stated:

> [This provision] comprises three distinct rules. The first rule, which is of a general nature enounces the principle of peaceful enjoyment of property; it is set out in the first sentence of the first paragraph. The second rule covers deprivation of possessions and subjects it

---

[89] *Nos 45526/99 et al* 2002-VI DA.
[90] *Gayduk and Others v Ukraine*. Cf *Boyajyan v Armenia* hudoc (2011).
[91] 2004-V; 40 EHRR 495 para 144 GC. See also *Kotov v Russia* hudoc (2012) GC.
[92] A 52 (1982); 5 EHRR 35 para 61 PC.

> to certain conditions; it appears in the second sentence of the same paragraph. The third rule recognises that the [contracting] states are entitled, amongst other things, to control the use of property in accordance with the general interest, by enforcing such laws as they deem necessary for the purpose; it is contained in the second paragraph.

In *James and Others v UK*,[93] the Court explained the relationship between the three sentences:

> The three rules are not 'distinct' in the sense of being unconnected: the second and third rules are concerned with particular instances of interference with the right to peaceful enjoyment of property and should therefore be construed in the light of the general principle enunciated in the first rule.

The three sentences in Article 1 will henceforth be referred to as Article 1/1/1, Article 1/1/2, and Article 1/2.

It follows from the above passage from *James* that Article 1/1/1 is not only a statement of principle. It also provides a third, separate basis for regulating interferences with the 'peaceful enjoyment of possessions' that do not qualify as a deprivation of a person's possessions subject to Article 1/1/2 or a control of the use of property subject to Article 1/2.[94] For example, in the *Sporrong and Lönnroth* case itself, the Court found that the grant of expropriation permits, which did not fall within Article 1/1/2 or 1/2, was subject to control under Article 1/1/1 as an interference with the peaceful enjoyment of the houses concerned. The Court said that an analysis of the nature of an interference requires a consideration of the first sentence only after it is determined that the second and third sentences do not apply.

When considering whether Article 1/1/1 has been complied with, the Court applies a 'fair balance' test.[95] In the *Sporrong and Lönnroth* case,[96] the Court stated:

> For the purposes of [Article 1/1/1] . . . the Court must determine whether a fair balance was struck between the demands of the general interest of the community and the requirements of the protection of the individual's fundamental rights. The search for this balance is inherent in the whole of the Convention and is also reflected in the structure of Article 1.

The Court added that the requisite balance will not be struck if the person or persons concerned have had to bear an 'individual and excessive burden.'[97] On the facts of the *Sporrong and Lönnroth* case[98] the Court found that there had been a breach of Article 1/1/1 because the grant of the expropriation permits, which adversely affected the property rights of the applicants, did not involve a 'fair balance' between the public and the private interests concerned. In terms of the structure of Article 1, what is important to

---

[93] A 98 (1986); 8 EHRR 123 para 37 PC. See also, eg, *Anheuser-Busch Inc v Portugal* 2007-I; 45 EHRR 830 para 62 GC.

[94] Regarding the rationale for developing a residual category of interferences, see Allen, *Property*, pp 103–4; and Pellonpää, in Mahoney, Matscher, Petzold, and Wildhaber, eds, *Protecting Human Rights: The European Perspective*, 2000, pp 1088–92.

[95] The Court sometimes refers to a requirement of 'proportionality' instead of 'fair balance'. The interference must also have a legitimate aim and be lawful: see sections 2.II and III. The same three requirements govern the rules of Article 1/1/2 and Article 1/2.   [96] A 52 (1982); 5 EHRR 35, para 69 PC.

[97] *Sporrong and Lönnroth v Sweden*, para 73. Cf *James and Others v UK* A 98 (1986); 8 EHRR 123 para 50 PC.

[98] See further, section 3.

note is that the Court has since applied its 'fair balance' test—which was devised particularly to provide a criterion by which to assess compliance with Article 1/1/1—when deciding cases under Articles 1/1/2 and 1/2 also. Indeed, although cases may still be dealt with by reference to Article 1/1/2 or Article 1/2 separately, and may focus upon the particular language of these sentences when this is done, there is a tendency for the Court to decide cases simply by reference to its 'fair balance' test whatever sentence, if any, it identifies as being the one within which the case might technically fall.

When applying the 'fair balance' test, the Court generally leaves it to the state to identify the community interest: claims made by the state will seldom be reviewed.[99] The balancing process thereafter may be complex and involve acts of judgment of a political (or policy) kind. It is hardly surprising that the Court has conceded a wide margin of appreciation to a state in reaching its decision that the community interest outweighs the individual's claims. This is true whether the case falls within Article 1/1/1 or Article 1/1/2 or Article 1/2, although the language of these last two sentences indicates a little further what factors the state ought to take into account. To that extent, an applicant may enjoy a certain advantage if he is able to persuade the Court to consider the matter under these provisions rather than under the general principle, but the benefits will be marginal only. For instance, under Article 1/1/2, a foreign owner of property could always be assured of the minimum protection of general international law, even if a state were able to persuade the Court that the fair balance did not import equivalent protection for national owners. The language of Article 1/2 has also afforded states particularly wide latitude in respect of interferences that amount to a control of the use of property.[100]

The 'fair balance' test laid down in the *Sporrong and Lönnroth* case finds its authority in two complementary sources. The first is the general balance which the Court holds to be pervasive throughout the Convention between the enjoyment of individual rights and the protection of the public interest.[101] The second is in the substantive content of 'law' as understood by the Strasbourg authorities to include protection against the arbitrary and disproportionate effects of an otherwise formally valid national law.[102] The first provides the elements for the balancing equation. The second gives more precise guidance as to how the weight of the factors in the balance are to be assessed. One important aspect of the insistence that interferences with possessions be found in an identified legal source in the national legal system is that the law will generally provide an indication of the factors motivating the measures of interference and the application of the law will be evidence of how the state has assessed the competing interests. While the state's conclusions are not the last word, since the European Court claims the ultimate power of review,[103] they nonetheless carry great weight because the language of Article 1 suggests a wide measure of discretion for the state and because many factors have to be taken into account, some of which are not amenable to objective assessment.

The clear tendency in the jurisprudence has, as suggested, been to assimilate the assessment of all interferences with the peaceful enjoyment of possessions under the single principle of 'fair balance' set out in the *Sporrong and Lönnroth* case, this despite the language of Article 1 suggesting distinct standards for measures which deprive a person of his property and measures which seek to control property. There are two reasons for this. The first is, as already indicated, that the Court has isolated a third head of interference

---

[99] See section 2.II.   [100] See further, section 5.I.
[101] *Belgian Linguistic* case A 6 p 32 (1968); 9 EHRR 252.   [102] See Ch 11, section 3.I.
[103] *Sporrong and Lönnroth v Sweden* A 52 (1982); 5 EHRR 35 PC and *Broniowski v Poland* 2004-V; 43 EHRR 1 GC.

with the peaceful enjoyment of possessions in the *Sporrong and Lönnroth* case, a category which has assumed greater importance because of the reluctance of the Court to expand the notion of 'deprivation' to cover *de facto* deprivations of property beyond all but the most clear cases. The Court has subsumed other, extensive, but less absolute measures affecting property under the *Sporrong and Lönnroth* head. The second reason is that the Court has had to spell out the conditions upon which an interference in the sense of Article 1/1/1 could be properly exercised. These conditions are both substantive and procedural and are elaborated in such a way that has proved useful with respect to the express powers of interference in the second and third sentences of Article 1. The applicants succeeded in the *Sporrong and Lönnroth* case because there was no procedure by which they could challenge the long-continued application of the expropriation permits which were blighting their property, nor were they entitled to any compensation for the loss that this situation had brought about.[104] These matters are of general importance because neither of the express grounds of interference - deprivation or control of use - is expressly accompanied by either procedural conditions or compensatory obligations (save as may be required by 'the general principles of international law'[105]) for its use. The Court has relied on the *Sporrong and Lönnroth* principle to import similar considerations into cases falling under Article 1/1/2 or Article 1/2.[106] This is not to say that the detailed application of the 'fair balance' test will be the same in all circumstances,[107] but that it provides the framework for resolving issues whatever the characterization of the interference.[108] The protection the 'fair balance' test gives is that the burden of promoting a community interest should not fall excessively on a property owner. This was relevant, for example, in *Kjartan Ásmundsson v Iceland*,[109] where the Court found a violation of Article 1 because of the harsh impact on the individual of changes made to pension rules and the availability of an alternative method of securing the public interest. Property owners should also have some process to challenge whether this is the case, a process which can take into account not just the balance of advantage but which can consider whether the public good pursued could otherwise have been achieved than by trespassing on the individual rights of the property owner.[110] In the *Stran Greek Refineries* case,[111] the Court made reference to the position in public international law (even though it had no formal relevance because the case involved the government of Greece and two Greek nationals) as one element in deciding whether the state had struck a 'fair balance' between the rights of the applicants and the interests of the community.

---

[104] See also *Bruncrona v Finland* hudoc (2004); 41 EHRR 592. One of the factors which counted against the applicants in *Katte Klitsche de la Grange v Italy* A 293-B (1994); 19 EHRR 368 and *Phocas v France* 1996-II; 32 EHRR 221 was that they had not used a procedure available to them to remedy the interference.

[105] See section 4.II.

[106] Eg, deprivation of property (*Tre Traktörer Aktiebolag v Sweden* A 159 (1989); 13 EHRR 551 and *Hentrich v France* A 296-A (1994); 18 EHRR 440) and control of use of property (*Allan Jacobsson v Sweden (No 1)* A 163 (1989); 12 EHRR 56; *Immobiliare Saffi v Italy* 1999-V; 30 EHRR 756 GC; and *Megadat.com SRL v Moldova* 2008-).

[107] Eg, in *Gillow v UK* A 109 (1986); 11 EHRR 355 para 148 Com Rep, the Commission suggested that the application of the proportionality principle is different in cases involving deprivation and cases involving control of use. [108] Eg, *Stretch v UK* hudoc (2003); 38 EHRR 196.

[109] 2004-IX; 41 EHRR 927, where the Court considered a reduction, instead of a total deprivation, of entitlement would have amounted to an interference justified by legitimate community interests.

[110] Many interferences with the enjoyment of possessions will involve the 'determination of a civil right' and therefore the individual will be entitled to an Article 6(1) procedure: *Sporrong and Lönnroth v Sweden* A 52 (1982); 5 EHRR 35 PC. See, eg, *Katsoulis and Others v Greece* hudoc (2004). However, this will not always be the case, eg, for taxation.

[111] *Stran Greek Refineries and Stratis Andreadis v Greece* A 301-B (1994); 19 EHRR 293 para 72.

As will be apparent, it may be very difficult to determine within which sentence of Article 1 a particular case falls. It is perhaps for this reason that the Court does not always indicate under which sentence a case is being decided. This may be illustrated by reference to the treatment in *Papamichalopoulos and Others v Greece*[112] of the question whether there was a *de facto* deprivation of property that brought Article 1/1/2 into play. The applicants' land in Greece had been occupied by a public body for public purposes but without legal sanction. The Greek courts had upheld the applicants' title to the land but it, or land of equivalent value, had not been returned to them. The applicants had been denied access to the land and were effectively precluded from dealing with it in any way; even though they remained formally the owners, that situation had not been remedied.[113] What is remarkable, however, is that the Court did not identify the particular sentence within which the case fell. Although it concluded that the *de facto* interference was serious enough to amount to an expropriation of the property, which would suggest that technically Article 1/1/2 was the relevant sentence, the Court does not mention any particular sentence, merely deciding that there had been a breach of Article 1.[114] The Court's more recent disinclination in a number of cases[115] to specify the relevant sentence within which an interference falls to be considered, and use of earlier decisions to determine the fair balance regardless of the sentence under which they were decided, also suggests that the identification of the type of interference is less important to the outcome of a case than is the process involved in the application of the 'fair balance' test.

II. A LEGITIMATE AIM

As well as satisfying the 'fair balance' requirement, to comply with each of the three sentences of Article 1 an interference with the right to property must have a legitimate aim. This requirement has been read into Article 1/1/1,[116] and is expressly stated in the 'in the public interest' and 'in the general interest or to secure the payment of taxes and other contributions or penalties' requirements in Articles 1/1/2 and 1/2 respectively. There is no distinction to be made between the 'public interest' and the 'general interest'. Absence of a legitimate aim will entail a violation of Article 1 without more.[117]

The identification of the objective of an interference with property and its characterization as being for a legitimate aim is primarily for the state. Measures taken in compliance with European Community law pursue a legitimate aim.[118] Where the interference involves the implementation of social and economic policies by legislative action, it will be presumed that the interference has a legitimate aim, and the burden will rest with the applicant to demonstrate that the state's judgment is 'manifestly without reasonable

---

[112] A 260-B (1993); 16 EHRR 440 Com Rep. On *de facto* deprivation, see further section 4.I.

[113] *Papamichalopoulos and Others v Greece*, para 45.

[114] It is argued that in light of the treatment of the *Papamichalopoulos* case in *Matos e Silva, Lda v Portugal* 1996-IV; 24 EHRR 573, *de facto* expropriation should be regarded as governed by Article1/1/1: Pellonpää, in Mahoney, Matscher, Petzold, and Wildhaber, eds, *Protecting Human Rights: The European Perspective*, 2000, p 1100.

[115] Eg, *Öneryildiz v Turkey* 2004-XII; 41 EHRR 325 GC; *Stretch v UK* hudoc (2003); 38 EHRR 196; *SA Dangeville v France* 2002-III; 38 EHRR 699; and *Solodyuk v Russia* hudoc (2005).

[116] *Beyeler v Italy* 2000-I; 33 EHRR 1225 GC.   [117] *Burdov v Russia* 2002-III; 38 EHRR 639.

[118] *SA Dangeville v France* 2002-III; 38 EHRR 699 and *Bosphorus Hava Yolları Turizm ve Ticaret Anonim Şirketi v Ireland* 2005-VI; 42 EHRR 1 GC.

foundation'.[119] It is difficult to imagine circumstances in which the Court would dispute the purpose alleged by the government[120] or contest its assertion that the measure had a legitimate aim.[121] In *Lithgow v UK*,[122] the Court said that the 'public interest' factor in Article 1/1/2 'relates to the justification and motives for the actual taking'. In that case, the applicants strongly, but unsuccessfully, contested the desirability of measures for the nationalization of the ship-building industry. In *James and Others v UK*,[123] they challenged the characterization as being in the public interest of a legislative programme designed to transfer property rights from one individual to another for the purpose of enfranchising long lease-holders. The applicants relied on the French text—*'pour cause d'utilité publique'*—and the practice of some European states to narrow the notion of public interest to 'community interest'. The Court rejected this claim, maintaining that the object and purpose of Article 1 was to protect against *'arbitrary* confiscation of property'. Accordingly:

> The taking of property in pursuance of a policy calculated to enhance social justice within the community can properly be described as being 'in the public interest'.[124]

The Court's preparedness to describe the aim of an interference at a high level of abstraction means that even penal confiscations might be explained as being legitimate. In such a case, the most an applicant would be able to establish would be a lack of due process if the interference were decided to be in the determination of a criminal charge against him and the fair hearing obligation in Article 6 was not satisfied. In many cases, deprivations of property will be under acts of legislation by Parliament. Any 'civil' right that the applicant may have had will have been removed by the legislation and there will be no place for Article 6(1).[125] If, therefore, the expropriation is to be attacked successfully, it must be on the conditions that attach to it rather than for the reason for which it was done.

---

[119] *Broniowski v Poland* 2004-V; 43 EHRR 1 para 149 GC. See also *James and Others v UK* A 98 (1986); 8 EHRR 123 para 46 PC; *Pressos Compania Naviera SA and Others v Belgium* A 332 (1995); 21 EHRR 301 para 37; *Zvolský and Zvolská v Czech Republic* 2002-IX para 67; *Jahn and Others v Germany* 2005-VI; 42 EHRR 1084 para 91 GC; and *JA Pye (Oxford) Ltd and JA Pye (Oxford) Land Ltd v UK* 2007-III; 46 EHRR 1083 para 71 GC.

[120] The standard of proof is low: see, eg, *Ambruosi v Italy* hudoc (2000); 35 EHRR 125 para 28, where the state failed to indicate the purpose but the Court gleaned it from the 'elements of the case'. See also *Phocas v France* 1996-II; 32 EHRR 221.

[121] In *Hentrich v France* A 296-A (1994); 18 EHRR 440 para 39, the Court accepted the first (the prevention of tax evasion) of two reasons the state had given for interfering with the applicant's property and then found no need to consider the other (regulation of the property market). See also *The Former King of Greece and Others v Greece* 2000-XII; 33 EHRR 516 GC and *Chassagnou and Others v France* 1999-III; 29 EHRR 615 GC. The Court has found it sufficient to establish the legitimacy of the interference that the state 'considered it necessary to resolve this problem': *Zvolský and Zvolská v Czech Republic* 2002-IX para 68. The Court may, however, take international law into account: *Beyeler v Italy* 2000-I; 33 EHRR 1225 GC, and the practice of other member states: *Bäck v Finland* 2004-VIII; 40 EHRR 1184.

[122] A 102 (1986); 8 EHRR 329 PC. Cf *Rosenzweig and Bonded Warehouses Ltd v Poland* hudoc (2005); 43 EHRR 955.

[123] A 98 (1986); 8 EHRR 123 PC. See also *Holy Monasteries v Greece* A 301-A (1994); 20 EHRR 1 para 76 Com Rep. In most cases under Article 1/1/2, the public interest will be, in a wide sense, a planning objective. On the redistribution of property to private persons, see *Bramelid and Malmström v Sweden* Nos 8588/79 and 8589/79, 29 DR 64 (1982); 5 EHRR 249 and *Prötsch v Austria* 1996-V; 32 EHRR 255.

[124] *James and Others v UK* A 98 (1986); 8 EHRR 123 para 49 PC. See also *The Holy Monasteries v Greece* A 301-A (1994); 20 EHRR 1 paras 67–9.

[125] *The Holy Monasteries v Greece* A 301-A (1994); 20 EHRR 1 para 80.

III. THE PRINCIPLE OF LAWFULNESS

Each of the sentences of Article 1 also requires that the interference in question satisfies the test of lawfulness.[126] This requirement derives from the 'rule of law, one of the fundamental principles of a democratic society, inherent in all the Articles of the Convention'.[127] A finding that the requirement of lawfulness has been offended is conclusive of a violation of Article 1; the Court need not then proceed to determine the fair balance.[128] In the context of the Convention, the requirement of lawfulness means the state must have a basis in national law for its interference[129] and that the law concerned must be accessible, precise, and foreseeable.[130] The absence of a remedy to challenge the interference may also prevent compliance with the requirement of lawfulness.[131] The identification of the legal basis of interferences and the satisfaction of the criteria of accessibility and certainty have only occasionally posed difficulties for the Strasbourg authorities. An applicant's awareness of the way in which laws are publicized and an ability to seek information about the law will be relevant in determining whether laws are accessible and foreseeable. Where the applicant is a company, the Court has indicated that it will expect the company to obtain specialist advice on the requirements of domestic law.[132] Uncertainty in the law that is not sufficient to offend the lawfulness principle may be relevant in determining whether the fair balance has been upset. This is illustrated in *Beyeler v Italy* [133] in relation to the lack of clarity in the statutory time limits for the exercise of a right of pre-emption over cultural works and the considerable latitude the Court afforded the authorities in the exercise of that right.

The Court is unlikely to review the interpretation or the application of national law by national authorities unless it has been applied 'manifestly erroneously or so as to reach arbitrary conclusions'.[134] In this connection, the Court has recognized that the law may be developed by the courts by re-interpretation where this is reasonably foreseeable.[135] Decisions of courts and tribunals affecting property rights should therefore adequately

---

[126] Expressly stated in Article 1/1/2 ('provided by law') and Article 1/2 ('such laws'); implied in Article 1/1/1: see *Iatridis v Greece* 1999-II; 30 EHRR 97 para 58 GC.   [127] *Iatridis v Greece.*

[128] *Iatridis v Greece*, para 58 GC. Cf *Hentrich v France* A 296-A (1994); 18 EHRR 440. Sometimes the Court proceeds directly to the 'fair balance' requirement without ruling on lawfulness: see, eg, *Doğan and Others v Turkey* 2004-VI; 41 EHRR 231.

[129] Eg, *Iatridis v Greece* 1999-II; 30 EHRR 97 para 62 GC (refusal of the national authorities to reinstate the applicant in a cinema which he was licensed to operate, after the Athens High Court had quashed the order evicting him from the premises, was 'manifestly in breach of Greek law'). Cf *Saghinadze and Others v Georgia* hudoc (2010). Law means both statutory and case law: *Špaček, sro v Czech Republic* hudoc (1999); 30 EHRR 1010. European Community law will provide sufficient basis in national law where the interference results from compliance with its legal obligations: *Bosphorus Hava Yolları Turizm ve Ticaret Anonim Sirketi v Ireland* 2005-VI; 42 EHRR 1 GC.

[130] *Carbonara and Ventura v Italy* 2000-VI paras 91 and 107 and *Beyeler v Italy* 2000-I; 33 EHRR 1225 para 88 GC.   [131] See *Družstevní Záložna Pria and Others v Czech Republic*, hudoc (2008).

[132] *Špaček, sro v Czech Republic* hudoc (1999); 30 EHRR 1010 para 59.

[133] 2000-I; 33 EHRR 1225 GC.

[134] *Beyeler v Italy* 2000-I; 33 EHRR 1225 para 108 GC; Cf *Špaček, sro v Czech Republic* hudoc (1999); 30 EHRR 1010. In a case confined to the conduct of administrative authorities in the application of national law, the Court may prefer to consider the conduct when applying the fair balance test, where the conduct is not determinative of the complaint: see *Broniowski v Poland* 2004-V; 43 EHRR 1 para 154 GC (fair balance not struck where conduct had a basis in statutory law but failed to comply with judgments of the Polish courts declaring the provisions unconstitutional).

[135] *Hoare v UK No 16261/08* hudoc (2011) DA, applying *CR v UK* A 335-C (1995); 21 EHRR 363 in Ch 10, section 1, to Article 1. Cf *OAO Neftyanaya Kompaniya Yukos v Russia* hudoc (2011) (judicial re-interpretation of statutory time limit rules not foreseeable).

state the reasons on which they are based.[136] In *Baklanov v Russia*,[137] the Court held that the law was not formulated with sufficient precision to 'enable the applicant to foresee, to a degree that is reasonable in the circumstances, the consequences of his actions' because of the national courts' lack of reference in their decisions to any legal provision as a basis for the interference and the apparent inconsistencies between the case law applied by the national court compared to the relevant legislation.

The compatibility of the interpretation and application of domestic law with the principle of lawfulness was also in issue in *Carbonara and Ventura v Italy*.[138] In that case the local authorities took possession of the applicants' land and built a school without following the procedures for expropriation of land set down in legislation. At the time of the works there was a substantial divergence in the decisions of the Italian Court of Cassation as to the effect on the landowners' title where public works had been completed upon land unlawfully taken into possession by the authorities. Eleven years after completion of the works in *Carbonara*, the Court of Cassation developed a doctrine of 'constructive expropriation' whereby a landowner unlawfully dispossessed of land by the authorities in order to construct public works automatically lost ownership when the works were completed. Nine years after the Court of Cassation's decision, it was determined that the five-year limitation period for compensation claims commenced running from the date of completion of the works, whereas at the time of the works on the applicants' land the Court of Cassation had held that no limitation period applied. In a case brought by the applicant, the Court of Cassation held that the constructive expropriation rule and the limitation period applied retrospectively to the applicants' situation, effectively barring any claim to compensation for the expropriation, while the state derived a benefit from taking unlawful possession of the land. The European Court considered that the outcome for the applicants 'could not be regarded as "foreseeable" as it was only in the final decision, the judgment of the Court of Cassation, that the constructive expropriation rule could be regarded as being effectively applied'. The unpredictable nature of the evolution of the Court of Cassation's jurisprudence, taken with the state's evidence that the Italian courts are not bound to apply a case law rule, and the denial of any possibility for the applicants to obtain damages, led the Court to conclude that the effect of the application of the case law to the applicants' situation 'could only be described as arbitrary'.[139] The case highlights the value of uniformity in the interpretation and application of law by the highest domestic appeal court, but underlying the Court's findings is doubt about the lawfulness of a legal doctrine 'which, generally, enables the authorities to benefit from an unlawful situation in which the landowner is presented with a *fait accompli*'.[140]

The conferral under statute of wide powers to take exceptional measures may be lawful.[141] However, the Court in the *Hentrich* case[142] found that a right to take property by way of pre-emption, vested in the tax authorities but exercised by them according to an unexplained policy, did not satisfy the requirement of foreseeability.

The absence of procedural safeguards to prevent the unfair use of the power may also render an interference unlawful.[143] This was a further reason for the finding

---

[136] *Kushoglu v Bulgaria* hudoc (2007) para 52.   [137] Hudoc (2005) para 46.

[138] 2000-VI. Cf *Belvedere Alberghiera srl v Italy* 2000-VI and *Sud Fondi srl and Others v Italy* hudoc (2009).

[139] *Carbonara and Ventura v Italy*, paras 69 and 71–2.

[140] *Carbonara and Ventura v Italy*, para 66.

[141] Eg, *Air Canada v UK* A 316-A (1995); 20 EHRR 150 para 41 (forfeiture of aircraft).

[142] *Hentrich v France* A 296-A (1994); 18 EHRR 440 para 42.

[143] The absence of procedural safeguards may also be considered when applying the 'fair balance' test: see section 3, in which context it is just one of the totality of relevant considerations.

against the respondent state in the *Hentrich* case (mentioned earlier), as the applicant was not given the opportunity in domestic proceedings to make submissions on the underestimation of the price or the tax authorities' position.[144] The Court stated that 'a pre-emption decision cannot be legitimate in the absence of adversarial proceedings that comply with the principle of equality of arms, enabling argument to be presented on the issue of the underestimation of the price and, consequently, on the Revenue's position—all elements which were lacking in the present case'.[145] The absence of a remedy to challenge the exercise of administrative power was crucial in *Družstevní Záložna Pria and Others v Czech Republic*.[146] There the Court found that the exercise of a statutory power to place a credit union in receivership was not lawful for the purpose of Article 1 solely because of the absence of procedural safeguards accompanying the interference. What was required was a reasonable opportunity for the applicant credit union to present its case with a view to effectively challenging the decision to place it in receivership.[147] This entailed access by the credit union to its business documents and the availability of judicial review by an independent tribunal of any denial to grant access.

The principle of legal certainty may release the state from the requirement of lawfulness in situations involving either the continuing application of a law that has been held to be an unconstitutional 'for a limited, purely transitional, period of time' until a new law has been enacted, or the correction of legislative defects with only prospective effect, in order to avoid a 'substantial legal lacuna'.[148]

3. ARTICLE 1/1/1: INTERFERENCE WITH THE PEACEFUL ENJOYMENT OF POSSESSIONS

As noted, the origin of the Court's opinion that Article 1/1/1 provides a ground for regulating interferences with a person's peaceful enjoyment of his possessions that is separate from and additional to those in Articles 1/1/2 and 1/2 is the judgment in *Sporrong and Lönnroth v Sweden*.[149] There the applicants' properties had been affected by expropriation permits granted to the City of Stockholm for the purposes of redevelopment of the city centre. The expropriations had not been executed but, while the permits were in force, the owners were prohibited from construction on the sites and were subject to planning blight. The permits and prohibition orders remained in place in one case for twenty-three and twenty-five years and in the other for eight and twelve years. The prohibitions on construction were clearly measures of control of use within Article 1/2. However, the Court decided that neither the expropriation permits as a matter of form nor the consequential prohibitions on construction as a matter of substance amounted to a deprivation within Article 1/1/2.[150] It was their purpose as an initial step towards deprivation of property that

---

[144] See further section 4.I. Cf *Air Canada v UK* A 316-A (1995); 20 EHRR 150, where judicial review proceedings were available. See also *Saghinadze and Others v Georgia* hudoc (2010).

[145] *Hentrich v France* A 296-A (1994); 18 EHRR 440 para 42.

[146] Hudoc (2008) para 89. The Court distinguished *Fredin v Sweden (No 1)* A 192 (1991); 13 EHRR 784, in which the Court said that the absence of judicial review proceedings will not, in itself, constitute a violation of Article 1 of the First Protocol, although an issue under Article 6 may arise.

[147] *Družstevní Záložna Pria and Others v Czech Republic*, para 89.

[148] *Roshka v Russia No 63343/00* hudoc (2003) DA (tax legislation).

[149] A 52 (1982); 5 EHRR 35 PC.   [150] *Sporrong and Lönnroth v Sweden*, paras 62–5.

precluded their consideration as deprivations.[151] Instead, there had been an 'interference' with the applicants' enjoyment of their possessions under Article 1/1/1.

Even though the Court in *Sporrong and Lönnroth* was prepared to concede a wide margin to the state in 'complex and difficult' matters of city centre planning, when deciding whether a 'fair balance' had been struck, it did not find acceptable the 'inflexibility' of the Swedish arrangements which left the property owners in a state of great uncertainty over an extensive period, without any effective remedy for their concerns. The applicants, the Court said, had borne 'an individual and excessive burden which could have been rendered legitimate only if they had the possibility of seeking a reduction of the time-limits or of claiming compensation'.[152] What is interesting about this approach is the suggestion that the *way* in which the national authorities strike the balance may be a factor in deciding whether in *substance* they have struck the balance compatibly with the Convention's requirements.[153] Further, the provision of compensation as an element in striking the right balance can arise other than in cases of outright deprivation which would fall within Article 1/1/2.[154] Similar considerations motivated the Court in finding that the administration of a scheme for the consolidation of agricultural holdings in the interest of their economic exploitation was in violation of Article 1/1/1.[155] The scheme had not been brought to a conclusion sixteen years after it had been implemented against the applicants' land and there was no means of redress for their interim losses up to the time it was implemented.

Since the *Sporrong and Lönnroth* case, there have been many others involving an interference with the peaceful enjoyment of possessions against which Article 1/1/1 provides protection where there is neither a deprivation nor a control of property. Consequently, distinct types of Article 1/1/1 interferences have developed, although the jurisprudence does not establish a principle by which an interference within the first sentence may be discerned. In some cases the Court provides no reason for classifying a particular case under Article 1/1/1,[156] but in most a general approach by which such a classification may be arrived at is indicated.[157] The Court commonly uses a sequential analysis of an interference, by which it considers the application of the first sentence only after eliminating the applicability of the particular instances contained in the second and third sentences,[158] which enables it to maintain a clear definition of the ambit of Article 1/1/2 and Article 1/2

---

[151] See also *JA Pye (Oxford) Ltd and JA Pye (Oxford) Land Ltd v UK* 2007-III; 46 EHRR 1083 GC, where the purpose, rather than effect, of the interference was decisive in the determination that the measure was a 'control of use' of land not a 'deprivation of possessions'.

[152] *JA Pye (Oxford) Ltd and JA Pye (Oxford) Land Ltd v UK*, para 73. See also *Matos e Silva, Lda and Others v Portugal* 1996-IV; 24 EHRR 573 (measures taken preliminary to expropriation in place for thirteen years with the detriment to the applicant aggravated by uncertainty as to the fate of the property and compensation) and *Terazzi srl v Italy* hudoc (2002).

[153] See also *Bäck v Finland* 2004-VIII; 40 EHRR 1184, where the excessiveness of a court ordered irrevocable extinction of a creditor's debt depended on the procedure applied.

[154] *Sporrong and Lönnroth v Sweden* A 52 (1982); 5 EHRR 35 PC.

[155] *Erkner and Hofauer v Austria* A 117 (1987); 9 EHRR 464 and *Poiss v Austria* A 117 (1987); 10 EHRR 231. The cases are examples in which the Court did consider the facts in terms of each of the three particular sentences in Article 1. After concluding that the cases did not fall within either Article 1/1/2 or 1/2, it decided that there was a breach of Article 1/1/1.

[156] Eg, cases involving the delayed payment of compensation or inadequate compensation for the expropriation of land: see *Akkuş v Turkey* 1997-IV; 30 EHRR 365 para 27 and *Platakou v Greece* 2001-I para 54.

[157] Allen, *Property*, pp 108–10, argues for one conception of Article 1/1/1 that 'is concerned with the appropriation of resources for public use, where such appropriation is not in the form of a taking of a full ownership interest', although noting some important cases in which the Court has not adopted this approach. [158] See sections 4.I and 5.1.

while allowing the types of Article 1/1/1 interferences to otherwise remain open. For instance, cases involving measures taken with a view to the expropriation of property, as in the *Sporrong and Lönnroth* case, will fall within Article 1/1/1 for the reasons stated earlier.[159] For the same reasons, where the state denies access to property, this will amount to an interference with the peaceful enjoyment of possessions.[160]

The Court has found Article 1/1/1 applicable in various other situations. In *Iatridis v Greece*,[161] the Court indicated that an interference with a leasehold interest by the state that could amount to neither a deprivation, as the applicant held less than an ownership interest in the premises, nor a control of the use of property, nonetheless fell within Article 1/1/1. In *Bramelid and Malmström v Sweden*,[162] the Commission further circumscribed Article 1/1/2 when it considered that Article 1/1/1 was applicable to legislation permitting majority shareholders to buy out shares held by a minority on the basis that Article 1/1/2 should apply only to acquisitions by a public body. Extinction of a judgment debt by legislation may also fall within Article 1/1/1.[163] In *Stran Greek Refineries and Stratis Andreadis v Greece*,[164] the Court (somewhat surprisingly) decided that the making null and unenforceable by legislation of an arbitration award in the applicants' favour was an 'interference' within Article 1/1/1, rather than (as contended by the applicants) a *de facto* deprivation, or even a *de iure* deprivation within Article 1/1/2.[165]

The reduction or discontinuance of a person's pension or other social benefits is an interference with the peaceful enjoyment of his possessions in the sense of Article 1/1/1: it is not a deprivation or control of use within Article 1/1/2 or Article 1/2 [166] Such cases have mostly been decided by the application of the 'fair balance' test. In *Klein v Austria*,[167] the Court held that the 'fair balance' requirement was not met when a lawyer forfeited his entitlement to an old age pension, to which he had contributed for many years, when he

---

[159] See also *Erkner and Hofauer v Austria* A 117 (1987); 9 EHRR 464; *Poiss v Austria* A 117 (1987); 10 EHRR 231; *Prötsch v Austria* 1996-V; 32 EHRR 255 (transfers pending the completion of land consolidation schemes); *Pialopoulos v Greece* hudoc (2001); 33 EHRR 977; *Phocas v France* 1996-II; 32 EHRR 221; and *Matos e Silva, Lda and Others v Portugal* 1996-IV; 24 EHRR 573 (interferences with development of land pending expropriation).   [160] See *Loizidou v Turkey* 1996-VI; 23 EHRR 513 GC.

[161] 1999-II; 30 EHRR 97 GC. See also *Bruncrona v Finland* hudoc (2004); 41 EHRR 592.

[162] Nos 8588/79 and 8589/79, 29 DR 64 (1982); 5 EHRR 249. See also, *Bäck v Finland* No 37598/97 hudoc (2002) DA (debt adjustment legislation). Cf *James and Others v UK* A 98 (1986); 8 EHRR 123 PC, where legislation providing for the purchase of property by private persons was classified under Article 1/1/2.

[163] As may the simple non-payment by the state of monies awarded by a court: *De Luca v Italy* hudoc (2013).

[164] A 301-B (1994); 19 EHRR 293 para 67. See Sermet, *The European Court on Human Rights and Property Rights*, 1998, p 29. See also *Smokovitis and Others v Greece* hudoc (2002) (retrospective legislation extinguishing judgment debts) and *Mykhaylenky and Others v Ukraine* 2004-XII (failure to enforce court order for three to seven years).

[165] Regarding the extinction of civil claims by legislation, see, eg, *Pressos Compania Naviera SA and Others v Belgium* A 332 (1995); 21 EHRR 301 (extinction of civil claim a 'deprivation' within Article 1/1/2); *Draon v France* hudoc (2005); 42 EHRR 807 GC; and *Maurice v France* hudoc 2005-IX; 42 EHRR 885 GC (head of damage extinguished a 'deprivation' within Article 1/1/2); and *National & Provincial Building Society, Leeds Permanent Building Society and Yorkshire Building Society v UK* 1997-VII; 25 EHRR 127 (extinction of civil claims for the recovery of monies paid as taxes a control on the use of property to secure the payment of taxes within Article 1/2).   [166] See, eg, *Klein v Austria* hudoc (2011).

[167] Hudoc (2011). Cf *Apostolakis v Greece* hudoc (2009) (civil servant lost his pension and other social security benefits because of fraud conviction: breach). Contrast *Banfield v UK* 2005-XI (policeman's pension reduced by 65% after dismissal because of criminal convictions for sexual offences: no breach). For other cases of breach, see, eg, *Lakicevic and Others v Montenegro and Serbia* hudoc (2011) (pensioners lost their pensions because of a change in the law) and *Zeïbek v Greece* hudoc (2009) (mother refused large family pension because of national origins).

lost his right to practise law because of bankruptcy proceedings against him. However, in most cases it has been held that a 'fair balance' has been struck. For example, in *Koufaki and Adedy v Greece*,[168] the reduction in the size of state pensions as a part of an austerity programme adopted in response to the respondent state's economic crisis was held to comply with Article 1, as was the case in *Cichopek and Others v Poland*,[169] concerning a reduction in the pensions of former employees of the Soviet-style state security services to bring them into line with other pensions as the respondent state adapted its law and practice to its post-communist situation. In both cases, the Court took into account the respondent states' wide margin of appreciation. In another pension case,[170] the phasing out of the applicant's disability pension following a further medical examination was not a breach of Article 1.

Other kinds of cases of interference that have been considered under Article 1/1/1, and which likewise have mostly been decided by the application of the 'fair balance' test, include the following. A 'fair balance'under Article 1/1/1/ was held not to have been struck when the applicant's title to her flat was revoked because it had been obtained by fraud by a previous owner[171] and when the applicant was not allowed restitution of his flat after the civil war because of his ethnicity.[172] Nor was there a 'fair balance' when the applicant's severance pay was charged at a much higher rate of tax (52 per cent overall; 98 per cent in part) than normal.[173] In contrast, there was a 'fair balance' when the applicant, who had not complied with his bail conditions, forfeited his bail money even though he had been acquitted,[174] and when insurance companies were required to pay 8 per cent of their car insurance premiums for road safety purposes.[175]

The Court has also relied upon Article 1/1/1 in cases in which the 'complexity of the factual and legal position prevents it being classified in a precise legal category'.[176] In *Beyeler v Italy*,[177] the classification under Article 1/1/1 of an exercise by the state of a right of pre-emption over an art work purchased under a contract that was held to be void by the national authorities, released the Court from inquiring into the correctness of the decision of the national courts and the nature of the applicant's property interest under national law, which would have been required for a classification under Article 1/1/2 or Article 1/2. While in *Jokela v Finland*,[178] the 'interconnected factual and legal elements' of the case, involving a comparison between the valuation methods for the expropriation of land and the levying of tax with respect to it, led the Court to examine the nature of each interference and the effects of the interferences separately: the expropriation of the land, which clearly fell within Article 1/1/2, and the inheritance tax imposed on the land,

---

[168] *Nos 57665/12 and 57657/12* hudoc (2013) DA. Cf *Da Conceição Mateus and Santos Januário v Portugal Nos 62235/12 and 57725/12* hudoc (2013) DA (civil servants pensions reduced by 10% as an austerity measure: no breach) and *Aizpurua Ortiz and Others v Spain* hudoc (2010) (reduction in employees' pensions by new collective agreement to save company in financial difficulty: no breach).

[169] *Nos 15189/10 et al* hudoc (2013) DA. See also *Valkov and Others v Bulgaria* hudoc (2011) (cap on size of pensions as state moved to a market economy: no breach).   [170] *Wieczorek v Poland* hudoc (2009).

[171] *Gladysheva v Russia* hudoc (2011).   [172] *Đokić v Bosnia and Herzegovina* hudoc (2010).

[173] *NKM v Hungary* hudoc (2013).   [174] *Lavrechov v Czech Republic* 2013-.

[175] *Allianz-Slovenska Poistovna and Others v Slovakia* hudoc (2010).

[176] *Beyeler v Italy* 2000-I; 33 1225 para 106 GC. This is relevant where positive as well as negative obligations are engaged: *Broniowski v Poland* 2004-V; 43 EHRR 1 para 136 GC; *Öneryildiz v Turkey* 2004-XII; 41 EHRR 325 para 133 GC; and *Prodan v Moldova* 2004-III para 60.

[177] 2000-I; 33 EHRR 1225 GC. Cf *Hentrich v France* A 296-A (1996); 18 EHRR 440 and *Gladysheva v Russia* hudoc (2011). For criticism of the classification of the interference in *Beyeler* under Article 1/1/1 rather than Article 1/1/2, see Rudolf, 94 AJIL 736 at 739–40 (2000).

[178] 2002-IV; 37 EHRR 581 paras 55, 60, and 65.

within Article 1/2, were found to be proportionate and not in breach of Article 1; however, their combined effects, considered under Article 1/1/1, were excessive.

The Court has taken a number of factors into account when deciding whether a 'fair balance' has been struck. Among these, delay, unpredictability, and inconsistency in the exercise of the state's power to interfere with property rights have all been evidence that the measures adopted by the state and their implementation have led to a disproportionate interference with property rights. The obligation to safeguard these rights in a 'practical and effective' way requires the state to ensure that these features are not present when the power is exercised.[179]

Moreover, in *Broniowski v Poland*, the Grand Chamber[180] reasoned:

> [T]he imperative of maintaining citizen's legitimate confidence in the state and the law made by it, inherent in the rule of law, required the authorities to eliminate the dysfunctional provisions from the legal system and to rectify the extra-legal practices.

Uncertainty surrounding property rights that is generated by state action or inaction has been an influential factor in the decision that a fair balance has been upset in cases characterized under Article 1/1/2[181] and Article 1/2[182] as well, articulating a broader concern with the effects of the manner of exercise by national authorities of their powers of interference that goes beyond a consideration of the impact of the interference on the individual to an examination of the nature of the impact on the community.[183]

A 'fair balance' will sometimes require the payment of compensation for the interference with property rights under Article 1/1/1.[184] The *Sporrong and Lönnroth* case does not establish clearly the nature and extent of this obligation. While we know the extent of the 'just satisfaction' ordered by the Court, the judgment, typically, does not enunciate the principles upon which the award was made.[185] The identification and assessment of the loss endured by the applicants was difficult. Because a central element of their claim was that there had been no national process to make even a tentative evaluation of it, the Court was without any guidance from the national authorities, still less decisions, to which it could defer. It is not possible to discern whether the measures of 'just satisfaction' represent a different valuation of the loss suffered by the applicants or a proportion of the loss, the proportion required to satisfy the balance between the public interest in urban planning and the burden that should fall on any property owner. If the state had decided the question of compensation differently from that awarded by the Court

---

[179] *Broniowski v Poland* 2004-V; 43 EHRR 1 paras 151 and 184 GC. See also *Beyeler v Italy* 2000-I; 33 EHRR 1225 paras 114 and 120 GC. In *Erkner and Hofauer v Austria* A 117 (1987); 9 EHRR 464 para 76, the Court noted that the passing of time for the purposes of the balance in Article 1/1/1 was independent of the 'reasonable time' required by Article 6(1).   [180] 2004-V; 43 EHRR 1 para 184 GC.

[181] Eg, *Hentrich v France* A 296-A (1994); 18 EHRR 440 para 47 (power of pre-emption over land was exercised 'rarely and scarcely foreseeably').

[182] Eg, the series of eviction cases against Italy, eg, *Immobiliare Saffi v Italy* 1999-V; 30 EHRR 756 para 54 GC (inefficient enforcement of court orders); *Stere and Others v Romania* hudoc (2006); 45 EHRR 191 para 53; *Hutten-Czapska v Poland* 2006-VIII; 45 EHRR 52 para 168 GC; and *Megadat.com SRL v Moldova* 2008-para 71, a case decided as a 'control on use' under Article 1/2. See section 5.I.

[183] See generally Allen, *Property*, pp 155–62.   [184] See generally Allen, 28 MJIL 287 (2007).

[185] *Sporrong and Lönnroth v Sweden* A 88 (1984); 7 EHRR 293 (just satisfaction). In *Erkner and Hofauer v Austria* A 124-D (1987); 13 EHRR 413 (just satisfaction) and *Poiss v Austria* A 124-E (1987); 13 EHRR 414 (just satisfaction), the Court approved friendly settlements which involved elements of compensation. There is much more detail in *Pine Valley Developments Ltd and Others v Ireland* A 246-B (1993); 16 EHRR 379 (just satisfaction).

by way of satisfaction, it does not follow that the Court would have found a violation of Article 1/1/1, given the wide margin conceded to the state to fix the fair balance. The measure of compensation required by the fair balance test has been considered in cases concerning deprivations under Article 1/1/2 and measures of control under Article 1/2.[186]

Finally, the availability of remedies by which an interference with possessions may be challenged is an important factor when determining whether a 'fair balance' has been struck.[187] In *NKM v Hungary*,[188] the Court explained the position as follows:

> Although Article 1 of Protocol No. 1 contains no explicit procedural requirements, in order to assess the proportionality of the interference the Court looks at the degree of protection from arbitrariness that is afforded by the proceedings in the case (see *Hentrich v France* [section 2.III], para 46). In particular, the Court examines whether the proceedings concerning the interference with the applicants' right to the peaceful enjoyment of their possessions were attended by basic procedural safeguards. It has already held that an interference cannot be legitimate in the absence of adversarial proceedings that comply with the principle of equality of arms, enabling argument to be presented on the issues relevant for the outcome of a case (see *Hentrich*, para 42; and *Jokela v Finland*, para 45 [section 3].

Thus, one of the reasons for the absence of a 'fair balance' in *Sporrong and Lönnroth*[189] was the absence of a procedure by which the continued application of the permits could be challenged. Similarly, in *Bowler International Unit v France*,[190] a 'fair balance' was not struck when the applicant company's merchandise was seized while in transit upon being found to contain drugs, and whose good faith was acknowledged, because the company had not been allowed a reasonable opportunity of putting its case to the responsible authorities. In contrast, in *Friend and Others v UK*,[191] the thorough consideration given by the national courts to compliance with the Convention by the legislative ban on fox hunting was a factor when the ban was held to comply with Article 1.

4. ARTICLE 1/1/2: DEPRIVATION OF PROPERTY

I. WHAT IS A DEPRIVATION?

For there to have been a deprivation of property, the applicant must, of course, demonstrate that he or she had title to it.[192] In principle, there will be a deprivation of property only where all the legal rights of the owner are extinguished by operation of law[193] or

---

[186] See further section 4.III.

[187] The availability of procedural safeguards has also been treated as a part of the lawfulness requirement, as in fact it was in the *Hentrich* case, see section 2.III.

[188] Hudoc (2013) para 64. Cf *Anheuser-Busch Inc v Portugal* 2007-I; 45 EHRR 830 GC.

[189] Section 2.I.   [190] Hudoc (2009). See also *Zehentner v Austria* hudoc (2009).

[191] Nos *16072/06 and 27809/08* hudoc (2009) DA. The Court also noted the extensive public and parliamentary debate on the ban. Cf *Helly and Others v France No 28218/09* hudoc (2011) DA (applicants had full opportunity to present their case in court in expropriation proceedings); and *JA Pye (Oxford) Ltd & JA Pye (Oxford) Land Ltd v UK* and *AGOSI v UK*, in section 5.I.

[192] *The Holy Monasteries v Greece* A 301-A (1994); 20 EHRR 1.

[193] Eg, *Pressos Compania Naviera SA and Others v Belgium* A 332 (1995); 21 EHRR 301. In *Althoff and Others v Germany* hudoc (2011) the retrospective amendment of the law by which the applicants lost their entitlement after German reunification to the restitution or the proceeds of sale of property taken by the GDR was a deprivation under Article 1/1/2. Cf *Göbel v Germany* hudoc (2011).

by the exercise of a legal power to the same effect.[194] However, not all such incidents are deprivations. The Court has treated some seizures of property as an aspect of the control of property.[195] If ownership is seen as a bundle of rights, the fact that an owner has been deprived of one right will not usually be sufficient to say that he has been deprived of ownership: rather it is a control of the use of property.[196] In *The Holy Monasteries v Greece*,[197] the government argued that the creation of a presumption in favour of state ownership of disputed land was merely a procedural device to allow the settlement of such disputes and not an interference with established titles. In any event, no steps had been taken to implement the provisions of any law which might have transferred title from the applicants. The Court found that the presumption effectively vested an unchallengeable title in the state because the monasteries were not in a position to prove their own superior title, relying as they did on ancient, adverse possession. The Greek law was, the Court said, a substantive provision, the effect of which was to transfer ownership to the state. The fact that the law had not yet been implemented was no guarantee that it would not be. Taking both matters together, there had been a deprivation of the applicants' property.

In the absence of a formal extinction of the owner's rights, the Court has been very cautious about accepting that a *de facto* deprivation of property qualifies as a 'deprivation' for the purpose of Article 1/2.[198] *De facto* takings are generally understood to occur when the authorities interfere substantially with the enjoyment of possessions without formally divesting the owner of his title. In the *Sporrong and Lönnroth* case, the Court held that the facts did not amount to a *de facto* deprivation of property so that Article 1/1/2 did not apply.[199] It was in the *Papamichalopoulos* case[200] that the Court first conceded that the physical occupation of land was so extensive and the possibility of dealing with it in any way so remote that there was a *de facto* expropriation, though even here the Court did not say expressly that there had been a 'deprivation'. In *Hentrich v France*,[201] the applicant claimed that there had been a *de facto* expropriation, even though the effect of the national decision was to transfer ownership from the individual to the state. The act of

---

[194] Eg, *Lithgow and Others v UK* A 102 (1986); 8 EHRR 329 PC and *Moskal v Poland* hudoc (2009). Acts in accordance with the condition upon which property is held are not interferences and, *a fortiori*, not deprivations of property: *Fredin v Sweden (No 1)* A 192 (1991); 13 EHRR 784.

[195] The purpose, rather than the effect, of an interference will be important: eg, *Allgemeine Gold- und Silberscheideanstalt [AGOSI] v UK* A 108 (1986); 9 EHRR 1 and *Air Canada v UK* A 316-A (1995); 20 EHRR 150. See further section 5.I.

[196] *Banér v Sweden No 11763/85*, 60 DR 128 at 140 (1989) and *Hutten-Czapska v Poland* 2006-VIII; 45 EHRR 52 para 160 GC. See Pellonpää, in Mahoney, Matscher, Petzold, and Wildhaber, eds, *Protecting Human Rights: The European Perspective*, 2000, pp 1096–7. Where the operation of law transfers the beneficial ownership in registered land the interference is a 'control of the use' of property: see *JA Pye (Oxford) Ltd and JA Pye (Oxford) Land Ltd v UK* 2007-III; 46 EHRR 1083 GC.

[197] A 301-A (1994); 20 EHRR 1 para 66.

[198] Eg, *Stran Greek Refineries and Stratis Andreadis v Greece* A 301-B (1994); 19 EHRR 293 and *Hutten-Czapska v Poland* 2006-VIII; 45 EHRR 52 GC. The Court noted without comment that the treatment of the applicant was not regarded by the national law as a *de facto* expropriation (and that, therefore, he was not entitled to compensation) in *Katte Klitsche de la Grange v Italy* A 293-B (1994); 19 EHRR 368 para 47.

[199] *Stran Greek Refineries and Stratis Andreadis v Greece*, paras 62–3. For criticism of the judgment, see Higgins, 176 *Hague Recueil* 260 at 343–57 and 367–8 (1982). See also *Matos e Silva, Lda v Portugal* 1996-IV; 24 EHRR 573 (no *de facto* expropriation) and *Sarica and Dilaver v Turkey* hudoc (2010) (*de facto* expropriation). See also *Saliba and Others v Malta* hudoc (2011).

[200] *Papamichalopoulos and Others v Greece* A 260-B (1993); 16 EHRR 440. See section 2.I. The Court suggested in *Matos e Silva, Lda v Portugal* 1996-IV; 24 EHRR 573, that the *de facto* expropriation in *Papamichalopoulos* was governed by Article 1/1/2.

[201] A 296-A (1994); 18 EHRR 440. Cf *Beyeler v Italy* 2000-I; 33 EHRR 1225 GC (exercise of a right of pre-emption considered under Article 1/1/1).

interference complained of in the *Hentrich* case was the exercise of a right of pre-emption by the tax authorities over property bought by the applicant at a price the tax authorities considered to be below its market value. No allegation of fraud was necessary to trigger the right. An independent procedure to recover any lost tax revenue was available. If the right of pre-emption were exercised, the purchaser was paid his purchase price plus 10 per cent.[202] The Court did not explicitly endorse the applicant's claim that there had been a *de facto* taking, although it did agree that there had been a deprivation of property. Its treatment of the lawfulness of the deprivation entirely in terms of the substantive qualities of the French law indicates that the Court regarded the taking as *de iure*. Real instances of *de facto* takings will be rare and will be in breach of the Convention because they will not have been 'provided for by law'.[203] There has been little support so far for Professor Pellonpää's suggestion that the test should be whether the interference amounts to a taking under international law.[204]

It may be formally necessary to determine whether an interference is a deprivation of property or an extensive control of the use of property because, in principle, they are governed by different provisions. But in practice the classification is not so important[205] (and the Court sometimes does not make the distinction) because of the overriding importance and general and common application of the 'fair balance' test.

II. THE GENERAL PRINCIPLES OF INTERNATIONAL LAW

It is necessary to consider the reference in Article 1/1/2 to the 'general principles of international law'. General international law protects *alien* property against arbitrary expropriation without compensation.[206] Both the compensation standard[207] and the methods of valuation of property[208] taken are controversial and, arguably, they have changed considerably since the Convention was drafted.[209] The content of the 'general principles' to one side, reference to them in Article 1/1/2 allows two possible interpretations of their effect. The first is that the reference benefits only alien property holders, since they are, if only indirectly, the only beneficiaries under international law.[210] On this interpretation, what the Convention does is give such persons a tribunal where they, as individuals or legal persons, may bring claims against an expropriating state without the intervention of their governments.[211] The alternative is that the Convention incorporates the *standards* of general international law in this particular case for the benefit of all persons protected by the Convention, thereby establishing a right to compensation for all persons deprived of their property with the compensation payable being defined by the 'general principles of international law'.[212] In *James and Others v UK*,[213]

---

[202] *Hentrich v France*, paras 20–1.

[203] Eg, *Loizidou v Turkey* 1996-VI; 23 EHRR 513 GC; *Vasilescu v Romania* 1998-III; 28 EHRR 241; and *Carbonara and Ventura v Italy* 2000-VI (case law was arbitrary). See also *Brumărescu v Romania* 1999-VII; 33 EHRR 862 GC (the lawfulness of the interference was not decided).

[204] Concurring in *Papamichalopoulos v Greece* A 260-B (1993); 16 EHRR 440 Com Rep.

[205] But compensation is more likely to be required under Article 1/1/1: see section 4.III.

[206] Jennings and Watts, eds, *Oppenheim's International Law*, Vol I, 9th edn, pp 911–27.

[207] Western states insist on prompt, adequate, and effective compensation; developing states argue for a standard that is more favourable to the state.

[208] See Jennings and Watts, eds, *Oppenheim's International Law*, Vol I, 9th edn, pp 921–2.

[209] Christie, 38 BYIL 307 (1962); Aldrich, 88 AJIL 585 (1994); and *ELSI* case (*US v Italy*) (1989) ICJ Rep 15 at 67–71. [210] See *Beaumartin v France* A 296-B (1994); 19 EHRR 485.

[211] *James and Others v UK* A 98 (1986); 8 EHRR 123 para 62 PC.

[212] *James and Others v UK*, para 61. In the European context, these would probably mean 'prompt, adequate and effective compensation'.

[213] *James and Others v UK*, paras 58–66. See also *Lithgow and Others v UK* A 102 (1986); 8 EHRR 239 paras 111–19 PC.

relying on the *travaux*, the Court opted for the former interpretation, stating that it was not the intention of the drafting states to extend the protection of general international law to nationals. In fact, practically all cases arising under Article 1 have involved the property of nationals.

Whether reference to 'general principles of international law' will ever be given much effect for the compensation of aliens is doubtful if the view of the Commission in the *Gasus* case prevails.[214] A German company was deprived of its property which had been in the possession of a Dutch company, sold by the former to the latter under a reservation of title agreement by which title was not to pass to the purchaser until the final purchase price had been paid in full. On the bankruptcy of the Dutch company, the property had been seized by the Dutch authorities for the settlement of the company's tax debts. The Commission found no violation of Article 1/1/2, the seizure being in the public interest, according to Dutch law, and not disproportionate to the purpose of protecting creditors. This was a case where the nationality of the property owner might have been of consequence. However, the Commission said only:

> [T]he deprivation of property which occurred cannot be compared to these measures of confiscation, nationalisation or expropriation in regard to which international law provides special protection to foreign citizens and companies.[215]

Whether this really represents the condition of international law is open to doubt. Lump sum settlements commonly include isolated items of foreign property taken or destroyed by a state as well as those seized under nationalization programmes.[216] Still, if the former Commission's position prevails, even more attention will be focused on the 'fair balance' test, applying to the deprivation of some alien possessions as well as all national possessions, to establish the incidence and content of the obligation to provide compensation in the event of a deprivation of property.[217] In the *Gasus* case, the Court did not need to address this question because it found the case to be governed by Article 1/2 (to secure the payment of taxes) rather than Article 1/1/2.[218]

III. COMPENSATION

While it is clearly established under the Convention that nationals may not take advantage of the substance of 'the general principles of international law' to protect them against the consequences of deprivations of their property by their own state, the Court has not left such people bereft of protection. What it has said is that the need for a 'fair balance' between the public and the private interest that runs through Article 1 requires, in all

---

[214] *Gasus Dosier- und Fördertechnik GmbH v Netherlands* A 306-B (1995); 20 EHRR 403.

[215] *Gasus Dosier- und Fördertechnik GmbH v Netherlands*, para 63. The finding of no violation was only on the casting vote of the President but the dissenting opinions place practically no importance on the nationality of the applicant.

[216] Eg, *Yeager v Iran*, Iran-US Claims Tribunal, 17 Iran-US CTR92 (1987).

[217] A further reason why this is desirable is that it provides a proper standard of protection under the Convention for aliens, even if the development of the rules of general international law diminishes their entitlement: Frowein, *European System*, p 522.

[218] See section 5.I. See also *Beyeler v Italy* 2000-I; 33 EHRR 1225 GC. For criticism of the application of Article 1/1/1 to the exercise of a right of pre-emption in *Beyeler* as an attempt to circumvent the compensation standards applicable to aliens under the general principles of international law, see Rudolf, 91 AJIL 736 at 739 (2000).

but the exceptional case,[219] *some* compensation.[220] Even interferences in protection of strong public interests may require some compensation. In the *Stran Greek Refineries* case,[221] the Court was unanimously of the view that the cancellation of an arbitration award by legislation, rendering it unenforceable, in pursuit of the policy of rectifying distorted arrangements entered into by the former military dictatorship in Greece, was a disproportionate interference with the applicants' rights. The effect of the national law was that they had lost the entire award, which was an assessment of the compensation due to the applicants as a result of the termination of their contractual rights. The Court effectively deferred to the arbitration tribunal's judgment that this was the proportionate level of compensation by ordering the state to pay the full amount of the award plus interest as just satisfaction. The compensation requirement was also infringed in *The Holy Monasteries v Greece*, where there were strong public interest considerations as well.[222] The law which the Court found deprived the monasteries of their lands effectively made no provision for compensation, providing only a discretionary power for use by a public body if a monastery were left with insufficient land to support its monks. The law as a whole failed to provide a fair balance between the rights of the applicants and the public interest.

The level of compensation must be 'reasonably related' to the 'value' of the property taken.[223] The general measure of compensation for an expropriation is stated in *Pincová and Pinc v Czech Republic* as one that is 'reasonably related to its "market" value, as determined at the time of the expropriation'.[224] However, Article 1/1/2 requires neither full compensation[225] nor the same level of compensation for every category of deprivation.[226] In *James and Others v UK*,[227] the Court said that where the state was pursuing economic reform or social justice,

---

[219] Discussed later.

[220] *Lithgow and Others v UK* A 102 (1986); 8 EHRR 329 para 120 PC. The state will be vulnerable where there is *no* right to *any* compensation in national law: *Papastavrou and Others v Greece* 2003-IV; 40 EHRR 361. Moreover, compensation must be paid within a reasonable time: *Guillemin v France* 1997-I; 25 EHRR 435 and *Jucys v Lithuania* hudoc (2008) (a case decided under Article 1/2). This compensation requirement under the fair balance test will apply to non-nationals as well as nationals.

[221] *Stran Greek Refineries and Stratis Andreadis v Greece* A 301-B (1994); 19 EHRR 293.

[222] A 301-A (1994); 20 EHRR 1. The Court approved a friendly settlement. See also *Draon v France* hudoc (2005); 42 EHRR 807 GC and *Maurice v France* 2005-IX; 42 EHRR 885 GC, where ethical considerations, equitable treatment, and the proper organization of the health service did not justify extinguishing pending claims without compensation.

[223] Eg, *Draon v France* hudoc (2005); 42 EHRR 807 GC; *Maurice v France* 2005-IX; 42 EHRR 885 GC; and *Papachelas v Greece* 1999-II; 30 EHRR 923 para 48 GC. See also *Lallement v France* hudoc (2002) (the applicant's attachment to his family home was taken into account in deciding the adequacy of market value compensation paid for the expropriation of another portion of the applicant's farm) and *Kozacioğlu v Turkey* hudoc (2009) GC (compensation that failed to take into account the architectural and historical value of an expropriated building was a violation). See also the comparative survey of the level of compensation in member states in the *Kozacioğlu* case, para 34.

[224] 2002-VIII para 53. See also *Papamichalopoulos v Greece* A 330-B (1995) para 39 (just satisfaction) and *Hentrich v France* A 296-A (1994); 18 EHRR 440 para 71 ('current market value').

[225] See *Papachelas v Greece* 1999-II; 30 EHRR 923 GC and *JA Pye (Oxford) Ltd and JA Pye (Oxford) Land Ltd v UK* 2007-III; 46 EHRR 1083 para 54 GC.

[226] *Lithgow and Others v UK* A 102 (1986); 8 EHRR 329 PC, rejecting the applicants' claim that the measure of compensation in nationalization cases should be the same (ie market value) as for compulsory purchase of land. See also *Papamichalopoulos v Greece* A 330-B (1995), stating that the criteria for determining reparation for an unlawful deprivation of property will differ from that used for a lawful one.

[227] A 98 (1986); 8 EHRR 123 PC. In *The Former King of Greece and Others v Greece* hudoc (2002); 36 EHRR CD 43 para 78 GC (just satisfaction), it was accepted that less than full compensation may also be called for where the expropriation is with a view to achieving 'such fundamental changes of a country's constitutional system as the transition from monarchy to republic'. The onus is on the state to justify a departure from the

less reimbursement was due to the dispossessed owners than full market value. The state enjoys a wide margin in assessing the appropriate level of compensation and, indeed, in estimating the value of the property in the first place. Where the amounts are fixed by reference to objective standards, with the possibility of representation for those deprived of property in the process, intervention by the Court is unlikely.

The importance of valuation methods is demonstrated in a series of Greek cases in which the Court held that a standardized system of assessing compensation for land expropriated for the construction of roads imposed on the applicants 'an individual and excessive burden'. Greek legislation deemed that all land adjoining a major road derived a benefit from any road improvements, and provided for this presumed increase in value to be deducted from the compensation payable for the land expropriated to construct the road. While the Court considered it legitimate to take into account the benefit derived from the works by owners of expropriated land who retained ownership of land adjoining the road, it rejected the method of assessing compensation as 'too inflexible' so as to be 'manifestly without reasonable foundation' because the presumption of benefit could not be rebutted. What was required in order to respect the fair balance was a system that gave landowners an opportunity to make representation in the valuation proceedings[228] that the work had no, or less, benefit or caused varying degrees of loss.[229]

However, the Court has accepted that nationalization may require the application of a general scheme for assessing compensation. In *Lithgow and Others v UK*,[230] the legislation established alternative methods for valuing the ship building companies nationalized under the Aircraft and Shipbuilding Industries Act 1977, depending on the position of the companies to be nationalized. One method relied on the market value of the shares in quoted companies; the other, for shares in unquoted companies, was based on an assumed 'base value'. The value of all shares was assessed during a 'reference period' before the election after which the legislation was enacted, on the assumption that this was a period when the value would be influenced by market factors alone and not by political considerations, like the prospect of nationalization. Other methods of valuation, claimed by the applicants to be more appropriate, were nominated by them, but the Court held that those adopted by the government were not inconsistent with Article 1/1/2. The Court held to this conclusion even though the effects of the scheme in the legislation, both generally and in relation to individual firms, resulted in levels of compensation quite different from those claimed by the firms. Once the Court had accepted the rationality of the method itself, it was in no case persuaded that assessments were inconsistent with Article 1/1/2 by reason of the application of the general scheme.[231] Because the disparities between the companies' own valuations and the amounts of compensation awarded under the Act and approved by the Court were so great—for instance, one company received £1.8 million in compensation when its cash assets alone totalled £2.2 million—it would be a rare case for the Court to find a breach of Article 1 by reason of the level of compensation alone.

In *Hentrich v France*,[232] the government's interference took the form of the exercise of a right of pre-emption over the applicant's land. The Court measured the proportionality

---

market value standard: *Scordino v Italy (No 1)* 2006-V; 45 EHRR 207 GC. Less than the market value was justified in *Helly and Others v France No 28216/09* hudoc (2011) DA (expropriation of cave with prehistoric art work).

[228] *Efstathiou and Michailidis and Co Motel Amerika v Greece* 2003-IX; 43 EHRR 490.

[229] *Katikaridis and Others v Greece* 1996-V; 32 EHRR 113 para 49 and *Papachelas v Greece* 1999-II; 30 EHRR 923 para 53 GC.   [230] A 102 (1986); 8 EHRR 329 paras 125–36 PC.

[231] *Lithgow and Others v UK*, paras 137–51. For extensive comment, see Mendelson, 58 BYIL 33 at 52–63 (1987).   [232] A 296-A (1994); 18 EHRR 440 paras 47–9.

of the government's action against its objective: the prevention of tax evasion. *One element* in the equation was the level of compensation. The Court found that the action was arbitrary in that the right of pre-emption was not exercised systematically, that there were other methods available for dealing with tax evasion which were not so burdensome on the individual, *and* the level of compensation was inadequate. It was 'all these factors' which resulted in the conclusion that the applicant bore an 'individual and excessive burden'. While the judgment suggested that the matter might have been put right by procedural changes, it did not suggest that enhanced compensation would have done the same in the absence of procedural changes.[233] However, in *Beyeler v Italy*,[234] where the issue focused on delay, enhanced compensation might have ensured that the exercise of a right of pre-emption over a work of art struck a fair balance. Central to the Court's judgment was its finding that the state had 'derived an unjust enrichment' by delaying for six years the exercise of the pre-emption right and then basing compensation on the price the buyer earlier paid for the painting, effectively ensuring it acquired the property 'well below its market value'.[235]

A combination of the level of compensation and concerns about consistency in the conduct of the state led a unanimous Grand Chamber in *Broniowski v Poland*[236] to find a breach of Article 1. In that case, the state had provided compensation for property owners for real property lost by them following the redrawing of territorial boundaries after World War II.[237] For economic reasons, the compensation was capped at 15 per cent of the market value, with no entitlement to compensation even at this level where some compensation had been paid earlier under other arrangements. As the applicant fell within the exception, he received only the 2 per cent of the value of his expropriated property that he had been paid earlier. The Court affirmed the approach taken in *James* and *Lithgow* in allowing that gains and losses to particular persons may be an inevitable consequence of measures taken in the complex and wide-reaching reform of the state, justifying a wide margin of appreciation in the assessment of compensation.[238] Nevertheless, this margin was not without its limits: ascertaining the fair balance requires 'an overall assessment of the various interests in issue'.[239] In *Broniowski* this involved an assessment of the compensation terms and also the conduct of the parties. In deciding whether the amount of compensation was reasonably related to the value of the property taken, the Court once more examined the method for determining levels of compensation. By contrast with *James* and *Lithgow*, however, it rejected the rationality of the method adopted by the state, finding 'no cogent reason why such an insignificant amount should *per se* deprive the applicant of the possibility of at least a portion of his entitlement on an equal basis with other Bug River claimants'.[240] Nor had the authorities acted in a foreseeable

---

[233] *Hentrich v France*, para 49. Given the nature of the violation, the Court considered, at para 71, that return of the land was the best form of redress, failing which there must be compensation paid for pecuniary damage assessed on the 'current market value of the land'. See also *Papamichalopoulos v Greece* A 330-B (1995) (just satisfaction).

[234] 2000-I; 33 EHRR 1225 GC, a case characterized as an Article 1/1/1 interference.

[235] *Beyeler v Italy*, para 121. Compensation ordered on an 'equitable basis' also took into account the uncertainty and precariousness endured during the delay: *Beyeler v Italy* hudoc (2002) para 2 GC (just satisfaction).

[236] 2004-V; 43 EHRR 1 GC, where the interference is characterized under Article 1/1/1.

[237] For the facts, see further section 1.I.   [238] *Broniowski v Poland*, para 182.

[239] *Broniowski v Poland*, para 151.

[240] *Broniowski v Poland*, para 186. This reasoning suggests that 15% of the market value of the property would have sufficed to establish the fair balance, at least where other claimants were also receiving that level of compensation.

and consistent manner as required by the rule of law: administrative practices made the exercise of the applicant's legal entitlement unenforceable and legal provisions imposed continuing limitations on the applicant's assertion of his entitlement.[241]

In *Pincová and Pinc v Czech Republic*,[242] the level of compensation was central to the Court finding a breach of Article 1/1/2. In this case the Court focused on the impact on the individual of the method of assessing compensation. The unanimous view of the Court was that the applicants bore an 'excessive burden' as compensation payable under legislation that restored property wrongfully taken during the previous regime was based on the purchase price of the property paid by the applicants thirty years earlier. This amount did not enable the applicants to buy another home and, therefore, failed to take account of the applicants' consequent 'uncertain, and indeed difficult, social situation'.[243]

The circumstances surrounding the payment of compensation have been held to impose an 'excessive burden' in breach of Article 1 in a variety of other cases. Thus in *Yetis and Others v Turkey*,[244] there was a breach when the delay in the payment of compensation meant that the large difference between the value of the applicants' expropriated land when the compensation was assessed and when it was paid imposed an 'excessive burden' on them. There was also a breach in *Zaharievi v Bulgaria*,[245] when compensation by way of shares in a public company was changed to shares in another such company which were far less valuable. The late payment of 'Pinto' reparation has also been held to be a breach.[246] In *Perdigão v Portugal*,[247] it was not the level of compensation that was in issue, but the fact that the court fees in proceedings concerning the level of compensation were so large as to amount to the value of the compensation plus an additional €15,000, so that the applicants made a net loss on the expropriation of their land. This was held to place an 'excessive burden' upon them.

An exceptional circumstance justifying no payment of compensation may arise as a result of the manner in which property has been acquired. Thus *Jahn and Others v Germany*[248] involved a deprivation of property acquired during a transition period between two regimes. By land reform in the old German Democratic Republic (GDR), land was re-allocated to 'new farmers'. Their heirs could inherit the 'new farmers' rights to the land, which fell short of ownership under the communist GDR system, on condition that they kept the land in agricultural use; otherwise the land reverted to the state. The applicants in the *Jahn* case were heirs who did not meet this condition, but who, unlike other heirs in the same position, did not lose possession of their land owing to an administrative oversight. As a part of the process of transition to a system of private ownership of land in a capitalist system when the GDR became part of the new Germany, the GDR parliament enacted the 1990 Modrow law giving 'new farmers' and their heirs full ownership of their land (so that no limitation as to agricultural use applied), seemingly (their position was not mentioned) including persons such as the applicants who had benefited inadvertently. Following reunification, the German Parliament legislated in 1992, placing all heirs in the position they would have been in had the GDR land reform been properly applied, so that the applicants lost their land, without any compensation. It did so 'for reasons of fairness and social justice', seeking

---

[241] *Broniowski v Poland*, paras 184–5.   [242] 2002-VIII paras 61–2.
[243] *Pincová and Pinc v Czech Republic*, paras 61–2. Also relevant was the fact that the applicants had obtained the property in 'good faith' (para 59) and that costs reasonably incurred in the upkeep of the property, and required by law to be reimbursed, remained outstanding after seven years (para 63). Cf *Velikovi and Others v Bulgaria* hudoc (2007). See Allen, 13 CJEL 1 at 38–41 (2006–7).   [244] Hudoc (2010).
[245] Hudoc (2009).   [246] *Simaldone v Italy* hudoc (2009). On the Pinto law, see section 2.III.
[247] Hudoc (2010) GC.   [248] 2005-VI; 42 EHRR 1084 GC. See Allen, 13 CJEL 1 at 33–7 (2006–7).

to prevent heirs who had met the agricultural use condition having an 'unfair advantage' over others to whom the Modrow law properly applied.[249] The Grand Chamber [250] held that the deprivation of property without payment of compensation did not upset the fair balance to be struck between protection of property and the public interest. Three factors were decisive: the uncertainty of the applicants' legal position under the Modrow law, the fact that the German legislature intervened 'within a reasonable time' after reunification to correct the defect in the Modrow law, and the social justice objective of the legislation.[251] The Court considered that the fact that the interference with property rights was implemented without compensation did not render it disproportionate 'given the "windfall" from which the applicants undeniably benefited as a result of the Modrow Law'.[252]

The majority view in *Jahn's* case does find support elsewhere in the Court's jurisprudence. In *National & Provincial Building Society, Leeds Permanent Building Society and Yorkshire Building Society v UK*,[253] a similar approach towards applicants who exploit a situation of legal change to secure a property interest is evident. In *National & Provincial* the applicants claimed reimbursement of tax paid in the period mistakenly not covered by the relevant tax legislation between the end of a voluntary tax payment scheme and the commencement of a legally binding scheme for the payment of taxes, which applied retroactively. The Court unanimously decided that retrospective legislation extinguishing the applicants' claims to restitution of the unlawfully imposed tax without payment of compensation did not upset the fair balance. The 'windfall' feature of the case was relevant to both the strength of the public interest and the effect of the measure. The Court weighed 'the obvious and compelling public interest' to ensure private entities do not enjoy windfalls during transitional tax arrangements, particularly when they clearly understand it was Parliament's intention to include that period, against the fact that the applicants would have been obliged to pay the tax under the previous system of taxation.[254] More fundamentally, the Court viewed the case against the background of the public interest in creating legal certainty in the lawfulness of revenue collected and the applicant's 'attempts to frustrate by all legal means those efforts'.[255] However, the *National & Provincial* case differs materially from *Jahn* on the manner of acquisition of the property insofar as at the time the property right was acquired it was clear to the applicants that it was the legislature's intent that no property should be acquired; whereas in *Jahn* the legislative intent at the point of acquisition (under the Modrow law) did not address the applicants' situation.

In *Zvolský and Zvolská v Czech Republic*,[256] the Court said that 'the manner in which land was generally acquired' by individuals under a former communist regime—in violation of property rights—will constitute an exceptional circumstance justifying

---

[249] *Jahn and Others v Germany*, paras 107–8.

[250] By eleven votes to six, reversing the unanimous judgment of the Chamber.

[251] *Jahn and Others v Germany*, para 116. For a critique of the majority reasoning, see McCarthy, 3 EHRLR 295 at 300–2 (2007).

[252] *Jahn and Others v Germany*, para 116. See also *Vistiņš and Perepjolkins v Latvia* hudoc (2011), which also had a 'windfall' element.

[253] 1997-VII; 25 EHRR 127, a case considered under Article 1/2, see further section 5.II.

[254] *National & Provincial v UK*, para 81.

[255] *National & Provincial v UK*, para 82. See also *OGIS-Institut Stanislas, OGEC St Pie X and Blanche de Castille and Others v France* hudoc (2004).

[256] 2002-IX para 72. See also *Pincová and Pinc v Czech Republic*, discussed previously. See Allen, 13 CJEL 1 at 38–41 (2006–7).

the lack of compensation for a lawful expropriation carried out to redress such an infringement. However, the fair balance between protection of private property and the demands of the general interest may dictate that there be a mechanism by which the special circumstances of individual cases can be reviewed before government power to interfere with property rights is exercised. In *Zvolský and Zvolská* the applicants bore a 'disproportionate burden' when Czech legislation obliged them to return to previous owners, without compensation, land they had acquired in good faith under a deed that was freely entered into for good consideration during the communist era.[257]

The manner of acquisition of the property taken by the state may relate not only to conduct of the applicant but also to the source of the funding for the property. In *The Former King of Greece and Others v Greece*,[258] the state argued that there was no entitlement to compensation for the expropriation of property belonging to the deposed Greek royal family because the property benefited from considerable tax exemptions and other benefits that had been donated to the king acting in his public capacity. The Grand Chamber rejected the state's submission for three reasons. First, as a finding of fact, at least part of the property was paid for out of the Royal Family's private funds. Secondly, compensation had been paid when the property was previously expropriated, giving rise to a 'legitimate expectation to be compensated by the Greek legislation for the taking of their estates'. Thirdly, it was inappropriate that the state set off financial benefits granted against compensation, as benefits 'have no direct relevance to the issue of proportionality' of the interference.[259] This reasoning leaves open the question of the proper approach to be taken towards the payment of compensation where the property has been acquired or maintained by public funds. The first ground suggests that fairness requires the payment of compensation and counters the state's argument, as it is a rare case in which the state would have paid for the entire interest without contribution by the applicant. However, the second ground suggests that past practice establishing an expectation of compensation may qualify the operation of the principle contended and thus arguably upholds the principle's essential validity; while the third ground deals with the argument by an examination of the facts without determining the correctness of the principle asserted. In its just satisfaction judgment, the Court said that 'the manner of acquisition of the properties cannot deprive the first applicant of his right to compensation; it may, though, be taken into account for the determination of the level of compensation'.[260] While the Court was not prepared to take into account the benefits accruing from state financial support when determining whether the failure to pay compensation was disproportionate, it was prepared to reduce the amount of pecuniary damages by a substantial amount 'in view of the privileges and other benefits awarded in the past to the properties'.[261]

To summarize, in general the guiding principle remains the 'fair balance', reliance upon which is necessary to establish *any* right to compensation for nationals. It is also a principle that leaves a wide, though not unlimited, margin of appreciation to the state to determine what the level of compensation should be.

---

[257] *Zvolský and Zvolská v Czech Republic*, para 74.   [258] 2000-XII; 33 EHRR 516 GC.

[259] *The Former King of Greece and Others v Greece*, para 98.

[260] *Former King of Greece and Others v Greece* hudoc (2002); 36 EHRR CD 43 para 83 GC (just satisfaction).

[261] *The Former King of Greece and Others v Greece*, paras 96 and 98. The impact of this approach to the assessment of compensation was significant as the Court awarded a sum for pecuniary damage at £13.2 million, far below the state's estimate of the properties' value of approximately £70.6 million.

5. ARTICLE 1/2: CONTROL OF USE

I. CONTROL IN THE GENERAL INTEREST

If the provisions of Article 1/1 do not appear in practice to impose a substantial fetter on interference with property rights, the language of Article 1/2 is even more favourable to the state. Articles 1/1 and 1/1/1 are said 'not...in any way to impair' the right of a state to *control the use* of property. Instead, any protection for an individual must be found in the 'in accordance with the general interest' limitation in the text of Article 1/2.[262] The phrase 'as it [the state] deems necessary', suggests that the limitation which flows from the 'general interest' limitation in Article 1/2 is narrow, even giving the state an unfettered discretion. However, the Court has moved to the position that Article 1/2 is merely one of the three, not unconnected, rules in Article 1, that impose the same requirements. In consequence any 'control' of the use of property must have a legitimate aim (furthering the 'general interest'), be lawful, and comply with the 'fair balance' test.[263] Given the narrow reading ascribed to 'deprivation' of property in Article 1/1/2, the notion of 'control' of property in Article 1/2 is a correspondingly wider one[264] but, as the *Sporrong and Lönnroth* case shows, not every interference short of deprivation will be an act of controlling the use of property.[265]

The power of the state to intervene by 'control' that falls within Article 1/2 is a wide one. Moreover, the Court has been notably unsympathetic to those who have taken development risks and who have failed to make any gains as a result of action or inaction by the state.[266] In this situation, an applicant may be driven to seek protection of his property elsewhere in the Convention. Thus the powers of control under Article 1/2 may not be used discriminatorily,[267] and there may be specific guarantees that benefit some kinds of property, such as the guarantees of one's private life or home[268] or of the means of artistic communication.[269] There may also be procedural requirements under Article 6(1) or Article 13, which should accompany the exercise of Article 1/2 powers.[270]

---

[262] There is no significant difference between the way the Court regards 'general interest' in Article 1/2 and 'public interest' in Articles 1/1/1 and 1/1/2, see section 2.II.

[263] *Chassagnou and Others v France* 1999-III; 29 EHRR 615 GC and *OAO Neftyanaya Kompaniya Yukos v Russia* hudoc (2011).

[264] Eg, *Pine Valley Developments Ltd and Others v Ireland* A 222 (1991); 14 EHRR 319, where the Court held that the failure to re-validate a planning permission nullified by the courts, resulting in very substantial reduction in the value of land, was not a *de facto* deprivation but a control of use. See also *Housing Association of War Disabled and Victims of War of Attica v Greece* hudoc (2006) (prohibitions on construction on land). Moreover, 'control' refers not only to use of property, but also to the right to dispose of property: see *Marckx v Belgium* A 31 (1979); 2 EHRR 330 PC, and the right to possess property: see *Hutten-Czapska v Poland* 2006-VIII; 45 EHRR 52 GC.

[265] *Sporrong and Lönnroth v Sweden* A 52 (1982); 5 EHRR 35 PC. See also *Katte Klitsche de la Grange v Italy* A 293-B (1994); 19 EHRR 368, where a prohibition on construction imposed by a land use plan was characterized as an interference under Article 1/1/1.

[266] *Allan Jacobsson v Sweden (No 1)* A 163 (1989); 12 EHRR 56; *Pine Valley Developments Ltd and Others v Ireland* A 222 (1991); 14 EHRR 319; and *Håkansson and Sturesson v Sweden* A 171 (1990); 13 EHRR 1.

[267] *Pine Valley Developments Ltd and Others v Ireland* A 222 (1991); 14 EHRR 319 (Article 14).

[268] *Niemietz v Germany* A 251-B (1992); 16 EHRR 97 and *Gillow v UK* A 109 (1986); 11 EHRR 335 (Article 8).

[269] Cf *Müller and Others v Switzerland* A 133 (1988); 13 EHRR 212, where the Article 1 argument was not even put to the Court (although, in the end, the Article 10 claim failed).

[270] In *Allan Jacobsson v Sweden (No 1)* A 163 (1989); 12 EHRR 56 and *Webb v UK No 56054/00* hudoc (2004) DA, the Court found that there were adequate procedural avenues through which the applicants could have raised their complaints.

A state may effect 'control' by requiring positive action by individuals or legal persons,[271] as well as by imposing restrictions upon their activities. Such restrictions might result from planning controls,[272] environmental orders,[273] rent control,[274] import and export laws,[275] forfeiture[276] and confiscation orders,[277] economic regulation of professions,[278] the seizure of property for legal proceedings,[279] inheritance laws,[280] regulation of vehicle registration,[281] limitation periods for actions for recovery of land,[282] regulation of the use of materials in the course of business,[283] protection of trademarks,[284] sanctions regimes,[285] business licences,[286] or regulation of hunting.[287]

While the state must indicate what 'general interest' is being served by the interference, it is unlikely to have its claim that the measure is necessary to secure it successfully challenged.[288] As well as showing that the interference has a legitimate aim, Article 1/2 requires that it is lawful and involves a 'fair balance', ie, that, in the light of the public good underlying the control, the burden which falls on the individual is not excessive[289] and that the measures are not disproportionate.

JA Pye (Oxford) Ltd and JA Pye (Oxford) Land Ltd v UK [290] illustrates the wide scope of the margin of appreciation that may be enjoyed by the state when controlling the use of property. In the *Pye* case the Court considered the claim that the system of adverse possession as it applied to registered land in the United Kingdom did not strike a 'fair balance': it was a disproportionate interference with the registered owners' property rights under Article 1, in the form of a 'control of use' under Article 1/1/2, not a deprivation

---

[271] *Denev v Sweden No 12570/86*, 59 DR 127 (1989) (obligation on landowner to plant trees in interests of environmental protection).

[272] Eg, *Allan Jacobsson v Sweden (No 1)* A 163 (1989); 12 EHRR 56; *Pine Valley Developments Ltd and Others v Ireland* A 222 (1991); 14 EHRR 319; *Haider v Austria No 63413/00* hudoc (2004) DA; *Papastavrou and Others v Greece* 2003-IV; 40 EHRR 361; and *Saliba v Malta* hudoc (2005). See also *Depalle v France* 2010-GC (refusal to authorize continued occupancy of public land).

[273] Eg, *Fredin v Sweden (No 1)* A 192 (1991); 13 EHRR 784.

[274] Eg, *Mellacher and Others v Austria* A 169 (1989); 12 EHRR 391 PC; *Hutten-Czapska v Poland* 2006-VIII; 45 EHRR 52 GC; and *Lindheim and Others v Norway* hudoc (2012).

[275] Eg, *AGOSI v UK* A 108 (1986); 9 EHRR 1.

[276] Eg, *Air Canada v UK* A 316-A (1995); 20 EHRR 150 and *Butler v UK* 2002-VI DA.

[277] Eg, *Yildirim v Italy* 2003-IV DA. This will including restraint orders while criminal investigations and proceedings are in progress with a view to confiscation: eg, *Andrews v UK No 49584/99* hudoc (2002) DA.

[278] Eg, *Karni v Sweden No 11540/85*, 55 DR 157 (1988).

[279] Eg, *G, S and M v Austria No 9614/81*, 34 DR 119 (1983).

[280] Eg, *Inze v Austria* A 126 (1987); 10 EHRR 394.

[281] Eg, *Yaroslavtsev v Russia* hudoc (2004) and *Sildedzis v Poland* hudoc (2005); 44 EHRR 263.

[282] Eg, *JA Pye (Oxford) Ltd and JA Pye (Oxford) Land Ltd v UK* 2007-III; 46 EHRR 1083 GC.

[283] Eg, *Pinnacle Meat Processors Company and Others v UK No 33298/96* hudoc (1998); 27 EHRR CD 217 and *Denimark Ltd and Others v UK No 37660/97* hudoc (2000); 30 EHRR CD 144.

[284] *Paeffgen GmbH v Germany Nos 25379/04, et al* hudoc (2007) DA.

[285] *Bosphorus Hava Yolları Turizm ve Ticaret Anonim Sirketi v Ireland* 2005-VI; 42 EHRR 1 GC.

[286] *Megadat.com SRL v Moldova* 2008-.

[287] Eg, *Posti and Rahko v Finland* 2002-VIII; 37 EHRR 158 and *Alatulkkila and Others v Finland* hudoc (2005) (fishing rights).   [288] See section 2.II.

[289] Compensation may be less likely to be required for a fair balance under Article 1/2 than under Article 1/1/2: *JA Pye (Oxford) Ltd and JA Pye (Oxford) Land Ltd v UK* 2007-III); 46 EHRR 1083 para 79 GC. However, it may be a relevant factor in assessing proportionality: *Immobiliare Saffi v Italy* 1999-V; 30 EHRR 756; *Housing Association of War Disabled and Victims of War of Attica v Greece* hudoc (2006); *Islamic Republic of Iran Shipping Lines v Turkey* 2007-V, at least where the control is not in the nature of a penalty: *AGOSI v UK* A 108 (1986); 9 EHRR 1 and *Air Canada v UK* A 316-A (1995); 20 EHRR 150, or a limitation provision: *JA Pye (Oxford) Ltd and JA Pye (Oxford) Land Ltd v UK* 2007-III; 46 EHRR 1083 GC. Regarding compensation, see further section 4.III.   [290] 2007-III; 46 EHRR 1083 GC.

under Article 1/2. Under the UK legislation then in force, an action by a landowner for recovery of possession of registered land was prohibited after the land had been in adverse possession for a period of twelve years,[291] and the registered proprietor would be deemed to hold title to the land for the benefit of the adverse possessor, who therefore became the beneficial owner of the land.[292] The applicants in *Pye* were land development companies who, as the successive registered proprietors of agricultural land, entered into a grazing agreement with the Grahams, who were the owners of adjacent farmland. It was a term of the agreement that the Grahams were required to vacate the land when the agreement expired in 1983; however, the Grahams continued to use it for grazing even after their request for a further grazing agreement was refused and no response to their inquiries about their continued use of the land was received. In 1997 the Grahams registered cautions at the Land Registry Office indicating that they had obtained title to the land on the ground of adverse possession. In proceedings before the British courts, the applicants unsuccessfully sought to recover possession of the land by arguing that the Grahams had not been in 'adverse possession' as defined by domestic law. The applicants then took their complaints to the European Court where they argued, *inter alia*, that the absence of compensation for the loss of their right to ownership of the registered land upset the fair balance required by Article 1 The Grand Chamber disagreed: it held that there was no requirement to pay compensation for a loss resulting from the applicants' failure to observe a limitation period, as this would undermine the aim of legal certainty, ie to prevent landowners from pursuing legal actions after the passing of a certain period of time.[293] Moreover, the Grand Chamber observed that whereas there was generally a right to compensation for the deprivation of possessions under Article 1/1/2, this was not the case where possessions were taken by the control of their use under Article 1/2.[294] In *Friend and Others v UK*,[295] the Court stated that in the latter case compensation would be required only when interferences involving the control of the use of property were 'arbitrary or unreasonable'. There was no suggestion in the *Pye* case that the size of the economic loss could have a bearing on the question of the payment of compensation for an interference categorized under Article 1/2. Nor was the legislation disproportionate on the ground that the applicants' economic loss was substantial.[296] The Grand Chamber attributed importance to the purpose of statutory limitation periods, which it reasoned must apply regardless of size of the value of the land. Regarding the 'windfall profit' to the adverse possessor, the Grand Chamber stated:

> [T]he registered land regime in the United Kingdom is a reflection of a long established system in which a term of years' possession gave sufficient title to sell. Such arrangements fall within the State's margin of appreciation, unless they give rise to results which are so anomalous as to render the legislation unacceptable.[297]

---

[291] Section 15(1) of the Limitation Act 1980 (UK).

[292] Section 75(1) of the Land Registration Act 1920 (UK).

[293] Five of the dissentient judges agreed on this point. The Chamber had found the absence of compensation violated Article 1, but had categorized the interference as a deprivation under Article 1/1/2.

[294] However, while there may be no right to compensation, its presence or absence may be a relevant factor in assessing proportionality: *Immobiliare Saffi v Italy* 1999-V; 30 EHRR 756; *Housing Association of War Disabled and Victims of War of Attica v Greece* hudoc (2006); *Islamic Republic of Iran Shipping Lines v Turkey* 2007-V, at least where the control is not in the nature of a penalty: *AGOSI v UK* A 108 (1986); 9 EHRR 1 and *Air Canada v UK* A 316-A (1995); 20 EHRR 150, or a limitation provision: *JA Pye (Oxford) Ltd and JA Pye (Oxford) Land Ltd v UK* 2007-III; 46 EHRR 1083 GC.

[295] *Nos 16072/06 and 27809/08* hudoc (2009) DA.

[296] The government valued the land in 2002 at £2.5 million.

[297] *JA Pye (Oxford) Ltd and JA Pye (Oxford) Land Ltd v UK* 2007-III; 46 EHRR 1083 para 83 GC.

In this situation there was no anomaly as the acquisition of rights by the adverse possessor corresponded with the loss of property rights for the former owner. Any 'moral entitlement' to ownership of the land fell within the state's margin of appreciation in assessing what the fair balance required in a long-standing area of law that regulates private law matters between individuals. The Grand Chamber also rejected the applicants' argument that there were no adequate procedural safeguards for the registered proprietor.[298] The opportunity to take court action for repossession of the land within the twelve-year period would have stopped the limitation period from operating and, as they had done, it was open to the applicants to dispute before the domestic courts that there had been an adverse possession. The Grand Chamber concluded that the fair balance required by Article 1/2 was not upset by the operation of limitation periods in the land registration system in the United Kingdom.[299]

In a series of eviction cases brought against Italy, the Court initially considered that a fair balance had been struck in the administration of a temporary system for staggering the enforcement of court orders for the repossession of housing, given the strong community interest in protecting tenants on low incomes and avoiding the risk of prejudice to public order in a time of chronic housing shortage.[300] This was so despite the severe limitations placed on the landlords' disposition and use of the property by the resulting lengthy delays in repossession. It was only when the Court was presented with repeated petitions, evidencing the existence of a structural failure in the execution of court orders, that the need was identified for a national process capable of challenging the decision to delay enforcement action and to order compensation, to ensure that the impact of an otherwise acceptable system on the property owner is 'neither arbitrary nor unforeseeable'.[301]

The fact that a generally satisfactory scheme of control may impose greater costs on some individuals than others will not be an objection to it unless those suffering the greater burden can demonstrate an 'inappropriate or disproportionate' interference with the enjoyment of their possessions.[302] A scheme will not be satisfactory if it involves imposing a disproportionate and excessive shared social and financial burden on one particular group of individuals. This is illustrated in *Hutten-Czapska v Poland*,[303] which concerned a rent-control scheme that had operated for eleven years with the aim of radically reforming the Polish housing sector at the end of the communist regime. On several occasions the Polish Constitutional Court had declared the rent-control legislation to be incompatible with the constitutional principles of the right to property, the rule of law,

---

[298] Judges Rozakis, Bratza, Tsatsa-Nikolovska, Gyulumyan, and Šikuta dissented on the adequacy of the procedural safeguards against the loss of beneficial ownership of the land.

[299] By ten votes to seven, reversing the judgment of the Chamber, which was by a slim majority of four votes to three.

[300] Characterizing the interference under Article 1/2, see *Spadea and Scalabrino v Italy* A 315-B (1995); 21 EHRR 482. Cf *Scollo v Italy* A 315-C (1995); 22 EHRR 514. See also *Almeida Ferreira and Melo Ferreira v Portugal* hudoc (2010) (property owner unable to terminate lease if tenant has been in residence for twenty years: no breach).

[301] Eg, *Immobiliare Saffi v Italy* 1999-V; 30 EHRR 756 para 54 GC. See also Committee of Ministers, Interim Resolution ResDH (2004) 72, listing 156 other cases in which a violation of Article 1 was found on the same facts. When the state continued to fail to rectify the situation, the Court became more prescriptive, holding that delays of over four years and one month constitute a violation: see, eg, *Sorrentino Prota v Italy* hudoc (2004). See also *Prodan v Moldova* 2004-III, where the Court rejected the state's argument that lack of funds and alternative accommodation could justify the delay of four years in the execution of court orders for repossession of housing.

[302] *Mellacher and Others v Austria* A 169 (1989); 12 EHRR 391 para 55 PC.

[303] 2006-VIII; 45 EHRR 262 GC. See also *Ghigo v Malta* hudoc (2006). Cf *Spadea and Scalabrino v Italy* A 315-B (1995); 21 EHRR 482 and *Mellacher and Others v Austria* A 169 (1989); 12 EHRR 391 PC.

and social justice.[304] Before the Grand Chamber the issue was analysed in terms of the scheme's suitability for achieving the public good pursued. Notwithstanding the wide margin of appreciation granted to states in the choice of measures for securing the housing needs of the community, a unanimous Court found a violation of Article 1 based on the harsh impact of the scheme on landlords alone as a result of the combined effect of severe restrictions on their various entitlements: the right to derive income from their property,[305] and the right to use and to possess it. Striking a fair balance required securing the protection of the landlords' property rights and respecting the social rights of tenants. Material to the outcome of the case was the absence of a procedure that would reduce the economic impact of the scheme on landlords and thereby achieve a 'fair distribution' of the cost of the reform of housing throughout the community.[306]

The impact of a control may not be confined to economic loss when determining whether the fair balance has been upset. This is shown in *Chassagnou and Others v France*,[307] where the impact of the legislation requiring landowners to allow hunting on their property was assessed with reference to the personal beliefs of the landowners: the Court held that imposing on a landowner opposed to the hunt on ethical grounds the obligation to tolerate hunting on his or her property was a 'disproportionate burden' incompatible with Article 1.

While the last word remains with the Court, evidence that the substance of the 'fair balance' test has been applied by a national body will be helpful to a state in demonstrating that it has remained within the wide margin of appreciation conceded to it.[308] Moreover, measures taken in compliance with legal obligations arising from membership of an international organization are presumed to be justified as long as the organization provides 'equivalent protection' to that afforded human rights under the Convention.[309]

An important sub-set of measures which the Court has regarded as being for the control of property under Article 1/2 are forfeiture provisions for the enforcement of laws relating to the use or possession of property.[310] In *Handyside v UK*,[311] the Court said that the destruction of books after a finding of obscenity had been made was justified under Article 1/2. In *AGOSI v UK*,[312] gold Krugerrands (bullion coins) belonging to the applicants were confiscated by UK customs after third parties had tried unlawfully to import them into the country. The Court characterized the prohibition against importation as a control of the use of property and the forfeiture order as 'a constituent element of the procedure for the control of the use' of the Krugerrands, to be dealt with under Article 1/2 rather than as a deprivation of property within Article 1/1/2. The Court resorted again to

---

[304] The Court rejected the government's argument that the findings of the Constitutional Court regarding the general adequacy of the scheme could not be decisive in the individual applicant's case: *Hutten-Czapska v Poland*, para 201.

[305] The right to derive income from property includes profit, cf Judge Zupančič dissenting.

[306] *Hutten-Czapska v Poland*, para 225. It was on this basis that *Mellacher and Others v Austria* A 169 (1989); 12 EHRR 391 PC was distinguished: *Hutten-Czapska v Poland*, at para 202.

[307] 1999-III; 29 EHRR 615 (non-pecuniary damages of FF30,000 awarded). Cf *Herrmann v Germany* hudoc (2012) GC and *Schneider v Luxembourg* hudoc (2007).

[308] Eg, *ISKCON v UK* No 20490/92, 76-A DR 90 (1994); 18 EHRR CD 133. See also *Megadat.com srl v Moldova* 2008-.

[309] *Bosphorus Hava Yolları Turizm ve Ticaret Anonim Sirketi v Ireland* 2005-VI; 42 EHRR 1 GC, rebuttable in the case of 'manifest deficiency'. See Costello, 6 HRLR 87 (2006).

[310] But see *Allard v Sweden* 2003-VII; 39 EHRR 321 (destruction of the applicant's house in the enforcement of private law rules on joint ownership was held to be a deprivation of property under Article 1/1/2 with the agreement of the parties). For a discussion of the forfeiture and confiscation of property under Article 1, see Allen, *Property*, ch 9.

[311] A 24 (1976); 1 EHRR 737 PC.   [312] A 108 (1986); 9 EHRR 1.

the 'fair balance' test, the particular issue here being whether confiscation was justified as a measure of enforcement against an innocent owner. The 'fault' or otherwise of the owner was only one of the factors to be taken into account in reaching the fair balance, according to the Court. One other factor was the existence of a procedure by means of which the owner could put his case before seizure of his goods was confirmed. In UK law, the procedure was an administrative one before the Commissioners of Customs and Excise, whose decisions were subject to judicial review. These processes were sufficient. AGOSI had not established that reasonable account had not been taken of its behaviour in reaching the decision to order the forfeiture of its property.[313] The AGOSI case is further confirmation of the importance of procedural avenues to aggrieved parties in establishing the fair balance. Procedures must not only be effective to test an applicant's claims[314] but must be expeditious,[315] so that there is no unacceptable collateral impact on the enjoyment of his property while the exercise of the control measures takes place.[316]

In AGOSI the Court held that the forfeiture served the legitimate aim of prohibiting the importation of gold coins into the United Kingdom. If the general interest is strong enough, preventative seizures and confiscation may be even more readily justified. In Yildirim v Italy,[317] the applicant's bus was seized and destroyed as it had been used for the criminal offence of transporting 'clandestine' immigrants. The drivers of the bus had been convicted and, although no criminal prosecution against the owner was brought, the court in the confiscation proceedings expressed some doubt about his participation in the offence. Consequently, the 'vehicle's availability constituted a danger' to the general interest in preventing clandestine immigration and human trafficking. Before the European Court the applicant contended that he could not be held responsible for the offences for which the drivers had been convicted and, therefore, the domestic court's refusal to order the return of the vehicle violated his right to peaceful enjoyment of property under Article 1. The Court accepted that the confiscation served the legitimate aim of crime prevention and said that in this area states enjoy a wide margin of appreciation in choosing the means of enforcement and in ascertaining whether the consequences of enforcement are justified in the general interest. In determining the balance between the general interest and the individual's right, the Court confirmed its approach in AGOSI, that the property owner's behaviour is a relevant factor, and was satisfied in the applicant's case that the authorities 'had regard for the applicant's degree of fault or care' in a fair judicial procedure. Given the nature of the general interest and the state's wide margin of appreciation, the confiscation was not a disproportionate interference with the applicant's right to peaceful enjoyment of his possessions. In Raimondo v Italy,[318] confiscation orders were made against land and vehicles owned by the applicant at the same time as criminal proceedings were brought against him on suspicion of belonging to a 'mafia-type' group. The confiscation was ordered on the statutory ground that the property formed the proceeds from unlawful activities and was based on evidence of a discrepancy between his lifestyle

---

[313] See also Air Canada v UK A 316-A (1995); 20 EHRR 150 (after a series of incidents involving the importation of prohibited drugs using Air Canada aircraft, forfeiture of a 'jumbo jet' bringing drugs into the UK in its cargo was ordered, later returned to it on payment of £50,000 fine; held, by a narrow majority of five votes to four, that neither the seizure nor the fine were disproportionate; dissentient Judges Walsh, Martens, Russo, and Pekkanen, emphasized the relevance to the fair balance of the applicant's 'innocence' about the use of the aircraft).   [314] M v Italy No 12386/86, 70 DR 59 (1991).

[315] Preventative measures must be brought rapidly to an end when the need for them has ceased: Raimondo v Italy A 281-A (1994); 18 EHRR 237 and Vendittelli v Italy A 293-A (1994); 19 EHRR 464.

[316] Allan Jacobsson v Sweden (No 1) A 163 (1989); 12 EHRR 56.   [317] No 38602/02, 2003-IV DA.

[318] A 281-A (1994); 18 EHRR 237.

and his declared income. The Court agreed with the government that the order served the general interest in ensuring that the property acquired by 'unlawful activities' did not procure 'advantages to the detriment of the community' for the applicant or the criminal organization.[319] In concluding that the confiscation was proportionate to this aim, the Court considered the efficiency of the measure in securing the legitimate aim and the way in which organized crime operated by reinvesting proceeds of crime in the real property sector in the respondent state. It concluded that '[c]onfiscation, which is designed to block these movements of suspect capital, is an effective and necessary weapon in the combat against this cancer'.[320] Moreover, the preventative purpose of confiscation justified its immediate application before any appeal was determined. In *Arcuri v Italy*,[321] confiscation orders were made against the property of a number of members of the Arcuri family on the basis of the 'lifestyle discrepancy' of the first applicant. Unlike *Raimondo*, there were no criminal proceedings directly related to the confiscation order. The presumption that the family's fortune had been created by the proceeds of criminal offences committed by the first applicant was supported by the first applicant's long criminal history, which also indicated his involvement with organized crime. The Court found that the function of the confiscation order was to 'prevent the unlawful use, in a way dangerous to society, of possessions whose lawful origin has not been established'. As a crime prevention policy the Court accorded the state a 'wide margin of appreciation' in its implementation. In assessing the proportionality of the confiscation, the Court considered the rationale for the measure was sound taking into account the serious nature of organized crime and the threat it posed to the 'rule of law' in the state.[322] Further, the applicants' right to peaceful enjoyment of their possessions had not been infringed as the Italian courts had provided them with a 'reasonable opportunity of putting their case to the responsible authorities'.[323] In *Butler v UK*,[324] the Court allowed the state even greater latitude when ordering a preventative forfeiture. In *Butler* the applicant complained under Article 1 of the forfeiture of £240,000, which he had asked a friend to take abroad. After being seized by a Customs and Excise Officer, the domestic courts had ordered the forfeiture under the Drug Trafficking Act 1994 (UK) to prevent the money being used by an unidentified third party for the serious crime of drug trafficking. However, a criminal proceeding had not been brought against the applicant or anyone else; nor was there a finding that the applicant, or his friend, would be responsible for its use in drug trafficking. Further, unlike *Acuri's* case, the applicant did not have a serious criminal history. Nonetheless, in declaring the application inadmissible, the Court considered that the problems faced by states in combating the problem of drug trafficking justified the wide margin of appreciation accorded to them in this area and was satisfied that the applicant had had been given a fair hearing in his appeal challenging the forfeiture order.

II. PAYMENT OF TAXES, CONTRIBUTIONS, OR PENALTIES

Finally, Article 1/2 concedes a practically unlimited power to a state 'to enforce such laws as it deems necessary... to secure the payment of taxes or other contributions or penalties'. Because the powers of the state under this provision are very wide, it is a matter of significance whether an interference with the enjoyment of possessions falls within it or not. For example, in *Gasus Dosier- und Fördertechnik GmbH v Netherlands*,[325] the Court

---

[319] *Raimondo v Italy*, para 30.   [320] *Raimondo v Italy*, para 30.
[321] No 52024/99, 2001-VII DA. See also *Riela v Italy No 52439/99* hudoc (2001) DA.
[322] *Arcuri v Italy*.   [323] *Arcuri v Italy*.   [324] No 41661/98, 2002-VI DA.
[325] A 306-B (1995); 20 EHRR 403. See also *OAO Neftyanaya Kompaniya Yukos v Russia* hudoc (2011).

decided that the seizure by the tax authorities of property in the possession of a tax debtor in which title had been retained by the vendor was not a deprivation of the latter's possessions to be assessed under Article 1/1/2 but a measure for securing the payment of taxes falling within Article 1/2.

The power to secure the payment of taxes is not a separate matter but a specific aspect of the state's right to control the use of property. The 'fair balance' will require procedural guarantees to establish the applicant's liability to make the payments, but the state is largely unconstrained about the levels of taxation, the means of assessment, and the manner in which taxes are paid. Nevertheless, the formal power of the state to raise taxes is not totally unlimited. The Commission said that a taxation scheme may 'adversely affect the guarantee of ownership if it places an excessive burden on the taxpayer or fundamentally interferes with his financial position'.[326] However, the state's power of appreciation is wide and it will be an exceptional case where the Court declares a tax programme contrary to the Convention.[327] As far as the enforcement of the resulting tax obligations is concerned, the Court said in the *Gasus* case[328] that it 'will respect the legislature's assessment in such matters unless it is devoid of reasonable foundation'. In determining that the Dutch law was not beyond this considerable margin, the Court deferred to the legislature's position that security rights of the kind preserved by reservation of title clauses were not 'true' ownership. In the circumstances of this case, the applicant could not have expected otherwise than that the question would have been governed by this Dutch law and that, appreciating that there was some risk (hence the reservation of title clause), the applicant should have appreciated the risk of seizure of the property by the tax authorities and taken measures to protect itself against this eventuality. There had, then, been no failure of proportionality in the measures taken by the Netherlands to secure the payment of the tax debtor's obligations.[329]

In *National & Provincial Building Society, Leeds Permanent Building Society, and Yorkshire Building Society v UK*,[330] the Court said that there is a compelling public interest in the enactment of legislation imposing liability to pay tax with retrospective effect and without compensation where it is to ensure that private entities do not 'enjoy the benefit of a windfall in a changeover to a new tax-payment regime'. The fact that legislation had the incidental effect of extinguishing claims in restitution for taxes unlawfully imposed during the transition period did not create an excessive burden because the claims had arisen from a defect in the transitional law: the applicants had only paid that which would have been required of them to be paid under the old tax-payment regime.[331]

The state will be constrained by Article 6 insofar as it seeks to use the criminal process to enforce tax obligations.[332] The *Hentrich* case[333] shows that Article 1 itself imposes some

---

[326] *Svenska Managementgruppen AB v Sweden No 11036/84*, 45 DR 211 (1985) and *Wasa Liv Ömsesidigt v Sweden No 13013/87*, 58 DR 163 (1988).

[327] See, eg, *Di Belmonte v Italy* hudoc (2010) (tax liability resulting from undue delay in paying compensation for expropriation: breach) and *Darby v Sweden* A 187 (1990); 13 EHRR 774 (violation of Article 14 and Article 1). See also *Allianz–Slovenska Poistivna SA and Others v Slovakia* hudoc (2010).

[328] *Gasus Dosier- und Fördertechnik GmbH v Netherlands* A 306-B (1995); 20 EHRR 403 para 60.

[329] *Gasus Dosier- und Fördertechnik GmbH v Netherlands*, paras 65–74.

[330] 1997-VII; 25 EHRR 127 para 81 GC. For the facts, see further section 4.III.

[331] Cf *SA Dangeville v France* 2002-III; 38 EHRR 699 and *Stere and Others v Romania* hudoc (2006); 45 EHRR 191 (retrospective legislation quashing final court order for repayment of taxes).

[332] See *Funke v France* A 256-A (1993); 16 EHRR 297. Liability for tax does not constitute a civil right or obligation for the purposes of Article 6(1): *Ferrazzini v Italy* 2001-VII; 14 EHRR 45 GC.

[333] *Hentrich v France* A 296-A (1994); 18 EHRR 440.

limitations upon the methods a state may use to enforce its tax policies, and they arise under this part of Article 1/2[334] as well as under Article 1/1/1 and 1/1/2.

An order for the confiscation of property following a conviction for a criminal offence may constitute a 'penalty' for the purpose of the Convention.[335] In this case the order will fall within Article 1/2 to control the use of property to secure the payment of penalties. For example, in *Phillips v UK*,[336] the Court considered the compliance with Article 1 of the UK statutory regime for the confiscation of property under the Drug Trafficking Act 1994. Under section 4(2) and (3) of the Act, the court hearing the confiscation proceedings following the conviction of a defendant for a drug-trafficking offence was required to assume that any property held by the defendant six years prior to the date of the criminal proceedings, or since the conviction, was received in connection with drug trafficking unless the defendant established on the balance of probability that the property had been acquired by other means or there was a serious risk of injustice. In *Phillips* the applicant was ordered to pay £91,400 or be imprisoned for two years. In establishing whether the confiscation order was a 'penalty', what was significant was that the purpose of the confiscation procedure was not to convict or acquit the individual for any offence, but rather to assess the amount payable, if any, after the conviction. In finding that the confiscation regime was proportionate to the general interest in combating drug trafficking, the Court had regard to the function of the confiscation order and the procedural guarantees that operated to determine the defendant's liability. The Court construed the Act as having both a punitive function, in that it aimed to punish the offender against whom the order was made, and preventative functions, in that it aimed to deter others from engaging in crime and reduced the funds available for future drug trafficking.

6. CONCLUSION

Article 1 of the First Protocol both establishes the right to the peaceful enjoyment of one's possessions and expressly allows a state a wide power to interfere with the right in the public interest. While the Court has in some of its judgments confirmed the limited scope that its generous text suggests, it is nonetheless true that the Court has found violations of Article 1 in more than a few cases; Article 1 is by no means a dead letter. Since the late 1990s, the scope of Article 1 has generally been enhanced to embrace a greater variety of interests with the strengthening of the autonomous concept of possessions.[337] At the same time, the Court has developed the concept of positive obligations, as elsewhere under the Convention. The increasing awareness of the broad protection potentially afforded to property by Article 1 may, in part, account for the high rise in numbers of complaints received by the Court under this Article. However, the requirement that there be some recognition of a pecuniary right in national law or practice in order for there to be a 'possession' has placed limits on the application of Article 1, with the result that many of the numerous restitution cases, from Central and Eastern Europe that refer back to the communist era, have failed.

---

[334] Eg, *Jokela v Finland* 2002-IV; 37 EHRR 581.   [335] *Welch v UK* A 307-A (1995).

[336] 2001-VII. See also *Grifhorst v France* hudoc (2009) (confiscation of large sum of money plus a large fine following conviction for not declaring the money to customs was disproportionate).

[337] Eg, *Beyeler v Italy* 2001-I; 33 EHRR 1225 GC (null and void contract under national law); *Anheuser-Busch Inc v Portugal* 2007-I; 45 EHRR 830 GC (application for trade mark); and *Stec and Others v UK* 2005-X, 41 EHRR SE 295 GC DA (non-contributory welfare benefits).

Although there is specific language to regulate the deprivation and control of the use of property under Articles 1/1/2 and 1/2 respectively, these are not the only occasions when interference by the state may be justified. Nor does the different language of these two sentences indicate much substantial difference in the way the Court approaches claims that Article 1 has been violated. The 'fair balance' between the public interest identified by the state and the burden on the individual applicants affected by the interference set out in the *Sporrong and Lönnroth* case is pervasive throughout Article 1 cases. It is noticeable how more recent cases proceed straight to the application of the fair balance test, while earlier ones dissected the language of Article 1 in some detail.[338] When applying that test, the Court also makes reference to earlier cases decided by it under this Article, regardless of the particular issue before it and the issue considered in the other cases.[339]

The reference to a general 'fair balance' standard of protection against interference under Article 1/1/1 in the *Sporrong and Lönnroth* case avoids the need to break down and classify complex combinations of fact and laws which have had an impact on an applicant's enjoyment of his possessions. While there are factors that are to be taken into account in striking a fair balance—such as timeliness, predictability, and certainty in the exercise of state power; the impact of the interference on the individual; procedural safeguards; the payment of compensation; and alternative avenues of securing the legitimate aim—their justiciability is problematic and the Court has deferred extensively to the decisions of national bodies. This is seen in the lack of specificity in the Court's approach to compensation. The language of review here is not that of 'pressing social need' or 'strict necessity', but whether the applicant has shown that the state measures impose an 'individual and excessive burden' or are 'disproportionate'. In cases where the state has addressed the issues, either in establishing the legal basis for interference, which is always required to comply with Article 1, or in applying a general legislative scheme, the Court has generally confirmed that the state was acting within its powers under Article 1. Nevertheless, the Court has shown that it will be prepared to adopt a stricter approach in applying the fair balance test where there is evidence of systematic breach of the right to property by the state[340] or where the law is 'manifestly without reasonable foundation'.[341]

The recognition in *James and Others v UK* that states have a wide power to interfere with property rights in the general social and economic interest,[342] even where the benefits fall to the advantage of particular individuals,[343] has been of lasting significance. *Pye's* case[344] demonstrates that this is particularly so where the national law is a long-established and complex one which regulates private law between individuals. The breadth of the margin of appreciation also readily justifies the use of forfeiture and confiscation measures by

---

[338] Cf *James and Others v UK* A 98 (1986); 8 EHRR 123 PC and *Tre Traktörer Aktiebolag v Sweden* A 159 (1989); 13 EHRR 309. See further section 3.

[339] Eg, *Pine Valley Development Ltd and Others v Ireland* A 222 (1991); 14 EHRR 319 para 59, where the Court relied on *Håkansson and Sturesson v Sweden* A 171-A (1990) 13 EHRR 1, an Article 1/1/2 case, and *Fredin v Sweden (No 1)* A 192 (1991); 13 EHRR 784, an Article 1/2 case, for the same point.

[340] Eg, the long series of Italian eviction cases and *Hutten-Czapska v Poland* 2006-VIII; 45 EHRR 262 GC, regarding Polish rent control legislation, see section 5.I.

[341] Eg, the series of Greek cases on the standardized system of assessing compensation for land expropriated to construct roads, see section 4.III.

[342] A 98 (1986); 8 EHRR 123 PC. See also *National & Provincial Building Society, Leeds Permanent Building Society and Yorkshire Building Society v UK* 1997-VII; 25 EHRR 127 and *Jahn and Others v Germany* 2005-VI; 42 EHRR 1084 GC.

[343] See *JA Pye (Oxford) Ltd and JA Pye (Oxford) Land Ltd v UK* 2007-III; 46 EHRR 1083 GC.

[344] *JA Pye (Oxford) Ltd and JA Pye (Oxford) Land Ltd v UK* 2007-III; 46 EHRR 1083 GC.

states to control proscribed activity, such as terrorism, smuggling, drug trafficking, and crime generally.

Where the Court does find that a state has exceeded its powers under Article 1, the financial consequences can be severe. In the *Beyeler* case, the respondent state was ordered to pay approximately €1.3 million in compensation; in the *Housing Association of War Disabled and Victims of the War in Attica* case, it was €5 million; in *The Former King of Greece*, it was €13.2 million; in the *Pine Valley* case, it was approximately £1.25 million; and in *Stran Greek Refineries*, the order was for approximately £15 million plus £9 million interest.

22

ARTICLE 2, FIRST PROTOCOL: THE RIGHT TO EDUCATION

Article 2, First Protocol

No person shall be denied the right to education. In the exercise of any functions which it assumes in relation to education and teaching, the state shall respect the right of parents to ensure such education and teaching in conformity with their own religious and philosophical convictions.

1. INTRODUCTION

The right to education[1] had a 'stormy genesis'[2] in the drafting of the Convention. It was possible to reach an agreed text only in the First Protocol[3] and, even then, an unusually large number of states have appended reservations to Article 2 in their ratifications of the Protocol.[4] The Court has made reference to the preparatory work in its judgments. The text was transmuted from its original form—'every person has the right to education'—to its present one—'No person shall be denied the right to education'—to avoid what some states anticipated might be excessively burdensome, positive obligations.[5]

The result is that there is no obligation upon states parties to have a state system of education or to subsidize private schools or universities or other higher education institutions (hereafter universities). These are matters left to their discretion, with the prohibition of the denial of the right to education only extending to such educational institutions as states choose to provide or allow.[6]

---

[1] On Article 2, see Opsahl, in Robertson, ed, *Privacy and Human Rights*, 1973, pp 220–43 and Wildhaber, in Macdonald, Matscher, and Petzold, eds, *The European System for the Protection of Human Rights*, 1993, ch 21.   [2] Opsahl, in *Privacy and Human Rights* at p 221.

[3] Robertson, 28 BYIL 359 at 362–4 (1951).

[4] For the texts, see http://conventions.coe.int. For a summary, see Wildhaber, in Macdonald, Matscher, and Petzold, eds, *The European System for the Protection of Human Rights*, 1993, ch 21, at p 551. See also *Angeleni v Sweden No 10491/83*, 51 DR 41 at 46–47 (1986) (Swedish reservation valid). In *S.P. v UK No 28915/95* hudoc (1997) DA, the validity of the UK reservation was left undecided following *Belilos v Switzerland* A 132 (1988); 10 EHRR 466; the Court had not questioned it in *Campbell and Cosans v UK* A 48 (1982); 4 EHRR 293 (pre-*Belilos*).

[5] Robertson, 28 BYIL 359 at 362 (1951) and Clarke, 22 Ir Jur 28 at 34–41 (1987).

[6] *Belgian Linguistics* case *(No 2)* A 6 (1968), p 31; 1 EHRR 252, 280–1 PC.

Article 2 extends to all forms of education provided or permitted by the state—primary, secondary, and higher education.[7] Whereas there is jurisprudence suggesting that Article 2 concerns 'mainly elementary education',[8] there are many cases demonstrating that it applies to secondary education and in *Leyla Şahin v Turkey*,[9] the Court confirmed that it extends also to higher education. But individual rights with respect to one level of education may not be the same for another;[10] while a state, if it chooses to establish a state schooling system, may be obliged to provide *universal* primary and secondary education, it is permitted to restrict access to higher education to those with the ability to benefit from whatever it provides,[11] and to limit places in particular subject areas by reference to the resources and needs of society,[12] so that it is not strictly correct to speak about a *right* to higher education.

Article 2 extends to private schools and universities.[13] First, it guarantees a right to start and run a school (or university) in the private sector. Although the text of the first sentence of Article 2 does not make this clear, the Commission adopted this interpretation in the *Jordebo* case.[14] In doing so, it relied upon the Court's judgment in *Kjeldsen, Busk Madsen and Pedersen v Denmark*,[15] although that judgment refers to a 'freedom' to establish private schools, not a right. If there is not such a right, the requirements of the second sentence of Article 2, that the state respect the religious or philosophical convictions of parents, probably creates a practical imperative to permit the operation of *some* private schools.[16] If there is such a right, so that states must permit private schools to be established, then the corresponding right holder would appear to be the person seeking to establish the school.[17]

Second, the first and second sentences of Article 2 apply to 'existing' private schools whether they exist as of right under the Convention or not. Accordingly, the state has an obligation to regulate them to ensure the Convention is complied with; it cannot delegate this responsibility away to the private sector.[18] But, as with state schools, in its regulation of private schools the state cannot take away the essence of the right to education.[19] While a state is not obliged to fund or subsidize private schools,[20] any financial assistance that it gives must not discriminate between different schools in breach of Article 14.[21] In its regulation of private universities, the state may apply limitations on student numbers that it imposes on state institutions to private universities also in order to guarantee equality of treatment and to 'ensure that access to private institutions should not be available

---

[7] Article 2 does not apply to retraining programmes for prisoners: *Valašinas v Lithuania No 44558/98* hudoc (2000) DA.   [8] *Valašinas v Lithuania*.

[9] 2005-XI; 44 EHRR 99 GC.   [10] *Leyla Şahin v Turkey*.

[11] *Lukach v Russia No 48041/99* hudoc (1999) DA (admission requirements may be set).

[12] *Tarantino and Others v Italy* 2013- (limited numbers in medicine and dentistry).

[13] *Leyla Şahin v Turkey* 2005-XI; 44 EHRR 99 para 153 GC (Article 2 applies 'to pupils in state and independent schools without distinction').

[14] *Ingrid Jordebo Foundation of Christian Schools and Ingrid Jordebo v Sweden No 11533/85*, 51 DR 125 at 128 (1987).   [15] A 23 (1976); 1 EHRR 711 para 50.

[16] Cf Opsahl, in Robertson, ed, *Privacy and Human Rights*, 1973, at p 230.

[17] But see the *Jordebo* case, in which the foundation that ran the school was held not to be a 'victim' (the parent was). See also *Bachmann, Hofreiter and Gulyn v Austria No 19315/92* hudoc (1995) DA.

[18] *Kjeldsen, Busk Madsen and Pedersen v Denmark* A 23 (1976); 1 EHRR 711 and *Costello-Roberts v UK* A 247-C (1993); 19 EHRR 112.

[19] *Leyla Şahin v Turkey* 2005-XI; 44 EHRR 99 paras 153–4 GC.

[20] *Belgian Linguistic* case *(No 2)* A 6 (1968), p 31; 1 EHRR 252, 281 PC and *W and KL v Sweden No 10476/83*, 45 DR 143 at 148–9 (1985).

[21] *Bachmann, Hofreiter and Gulyn v Austria No 19315/92* hudoc (1995) DA.

purely on account of the financial ability of the candidates, irrespective of their qualifications and propensity for the profession'.[22]

The right to education consists of a variety of rights and freedoms for children and parents. These mostly belong to the pupil or student,[23] but parents do have certain rights of their own under Article 2 about the way in which their child is educated.[24] When the pupil is young, his or her right may have to be exercised by the parents,[25] but, as the child grows up, he or she will develop the capacity to act independently.[26] For higher education, the appropriate right holder will be the student.

'Education' and 'teaching' are differentiated in the text of Article 2. On this distinction the Court has said that 'the education of children is the whole process whereby, in any society, adults endeavour to transmit their beliefs, culture and other values to the young, whereas teaching or instruction refers in particular to the transmission of knowledge and to intellectual development'.[27] The implication of drawing the distinction this way appears to be that the state may not step between a child or student and a private provider of 'education' outside the school system, such as religious bodies or cultural institutions, lest otherwise a person be 'denied the right to education' in this wide sense. If it wished to intervene, the state would have to rely on its implied power to regulate educational activities.

The right to education in Article 2 is not to be interpreted restrictively. To do so would be inconsistent with its purpose given that in 'a democratic society, the right to education, which is indispensable to the furtherance of human rights, plays such a fundamental role'.[28] The right to education benefits from rules that govern the interpretation of the Convention generally, *viz* that Convention rights must be interpreted so as to render them 'practical and effective' and that the Convention is a 'living instrument which must be interpreted in the light of present day conditions'.[29] Since the provisions of the Convention must be read as a whole, 'the two sentences of Article 2 must be read not only in the light of each other but also, in particular, of Articles 8, 9 and 10', on private and family life, religion, and expression respectively.[30] Article 2 of the First Protocol is in principle the *lex specialis* in relation to education and teaching and religion, so that it should be applied rather than Article 9 of the Convention.[31] Article 2 should 'so far as possible be interpreted in harmony with other rules of international law of which it forms part', including the Convention on the Rights of the Child.[32]

---

[22] *Tarantino and Others v Italy* 2013- para 52 (state subsidies for private universities also a factor).

[23] See *Campbell and Cosans v UK* A 48 (1982); 4 EHRR 293 para 40 (right not to be denied education is 'a right of a child').

[24] A claim under the second sentence of Article 2 must normally be brought by the parent, as victim, not the child: *Simpson v UK No 14688/89*, 64 DR 188 (1989).

[25] Or grandparents: *Lee v UK* hudoc (2001); 33 EHRR 677 GC.

[26] See, eg, *Simpson v UK No 14688/89*, 64 DR 188 (1989). See also Mr Kellberg, in *Kjeldsen, Busk Madsen and Pedersen v Denmark* B 21 (1975), p 50.

[27] *Campbell and Cosans v UK* A 48 (1982); 4 EHRR 293 para 33. See Robertson, 28 BYIL 359 at 363 (1951), drawing attention to the French text of Article 2.

[28] *Leyla Şahin v Turkey* 2005-XI; 44 EHRR 99 para 137 GC.

[29] *Leyla Şahin v Turkey*, para 136.

[30] *Kjeldsen, Busk Madsen and Pedersen v Denmark* A 23 (1976); 1 EHRR 711 para 52.

[31] *Lautsi and Others v Italy* 2011-; 54 EHRR 60 para 59 GC.

[32] *Catan and Others v Moldova and Russia* 2012-; 57 EHRR 99 para 136 GC.

2. NO DENIAL OF THE RIGHT TO EDUCATION

The first sentence of Article 2 states: 'No person shall be denied the right to education'. As the Court stated in the *Belgian Linguistic* case *(No 2)*,[33] despite its negative formulation, this wording 'does enshrine a right', *viz* the right to education, albeit one that is limited in scope. Even in its limited form, it is not an absolute right. It may be regulated by the state, but any restriction must 'never injure the substance [or essence] of the right to education nor conflict with other rights enshrined in the Convention'.[34] When deciding whether restrictions are permissible, the Court will consider whether 'they are foreseeable for those concerned and pursue a legitimate aim' and whether the means employed to realize the intended aim are reasonably proportionate to its attainment.[35] The regulation of educational institutions 'may vary in time and in place, *inter alia*, according to the needs and resources of the community and the distinctive features of different levels of education'; accordingly, states enjoy a 'certain margin of appreciation' when regulating them.[36] The state enjoys a margin of appreciation when imposing restrictions upon the right to education in Article 2, a margin which increases in 'inverse proportion to the importance of that education for those concerned and for society at large'.[37] By this, the Court had in mind the distinction between primary, secondary, and higher education, with the margin of appreciation increasing from primary to higher education.

I. ACCESS TO EXISTING INSTITUTIONS OR EXCLUSION FROM THEM

As noted, the first sentence of Article 2 only guarantees 'a right of access to educational institutions existing at a given time'.[38] This guarantee applies fully to such state institutions as are in being; it also imposes an obligation upon states to regulate private institutions in some respects, for example, so as to prevent arbitrary admission or exclusion policies or practices,[39] although this is not an area in which the Strasbourg jurisprudence is well developed.

The Court has accepted several restrictions upon access to schools or universities, or exclusion from them, as not infringing Article 2. Thus it is permissible for a state to insist upon education occurring in school, whether state or private, instead of at home as the parents might wish,[40] or to exclude from school a disruptive child[41] or a child who is the subject of criminal investigation for causing a fire at school.[42] And the choice of state school for a child to attend will normally be one for the state, not the child or the parents.[43]

---

[33] A 6 (1968), p 31; 1 EHRR 252, 280 PC.

[34] *Belgian Linguistic* case *(No 2)*, p 32; 1 EHRR 252, 282 PC.

[35] *Belgian Linguistic* case *(No 2)*. Cf *Catan and Others v Moldova and Russia* 2012-; 57 EHRR 99 GC.

[36] *Leyla Şahin v Turkey* 2005-XI; 44 EHRR 99 para 154 GC.

[37] *Ponomaryovi v Bulgaria* 2011- para 56.

[38] *Belgian Linguistic* case *(No 2)* A 6 (1968); 1 EHRR 252.   [39] *Belgian Linguistic* case *(No 2)*.

[40] *Konrad v Germany* No 35504/03 hudoc (2006) DA. Necessary measures to enforce compulsory schooling are permissible: *Leuffen v Germany* No 19844/92 hudoc (1992) DA and *BN and SN v Sweden* No 17678/91 hudoc (1993) DA. If it allows home education, the state has both a right and a duty (to the child) to ensure that it is effective: see *Family H v UK* No 10233/83, 37 DR 105 (1984).

[41] *Kramelius v Sweden* No 21062/92 hudoc (1996) DA (lessons required at home). See also *Whitman v UK* No 13477/87 hudoc (1989) DA.   [42] *Ali v UK* hudoc (2011); 53 EHRR 413.

[43] *Cohen v UK* No 25959/94 hudoc (1996) DA. On single sex and selective schools see *W & DM and M & HI v UK* Nos 10228/82 and 10229/82, 37 DR 96 (1984); *X, Y and Z v Germany* No 9411/81, 29 DR 224 (1982); and further cases in Wildhaber, in Macdonald, Matscher, and Petzold, eds, *The European System for the Protection of Human Rights*, 1993, ch 21, at p 535, footnote 19.

On other matters, neither the fact that a prisoner cannot continue his education while in prison[44] nor that the deportation of a parent will terminate the attendance at school of a child who leaves the country with the parent[45] will infringe Article 2. The issue of school uniform requirements has not been ruled upon, but it is predictable that the Court will not normally intervene under Article 2.[46] The question whether school fees are permitted by Article 2 has not been fully resolved. In *Ponomaryovi v Bulgaria*,[47] the applicants had been charged school fees for secondary schooling because they were aliens. The Chamber held that the fees were in breach of Article 14 of the Convention in conjunction with Article 2. It did so because the circumstances were such that there was no suggestion that the applicants had come to the respondent state to benefit from the free secondary schooling that was offered to nationals—they had been brought there at a young age by their mother, an alien who had married a national. In these circumstances the discrimination was disproportionate in breach of Article 14. The Chamber emphasized that it was not deciding 'whether and to what extent it is permissible for the states to charge fees for secondary—or, indeed, any—education'. However, its judgment suggests that, in accordance with the Convention on the Rights of the Child, Article 28, school fees for primary education, whether for nationals or aliens, would not comply with Article 2, whereas states would be allowed a wide margin of appreciation when deciding whether to require fees for higher education, for both nationals and aliens. The permissibility of school fees for secondary education for nationals would be guided by any European consensus, and might be justified for aliens in some (immigration related) circumstances, even though discriminatory.

As to access to universities, in *Leyla Şahin v Turkey*[48] the exclusion of the applicant from her state university lectures and examinations for wearing the Islamic headscarf was held not to infringe Article 2. Applying the approach it had followed when ruling that the same facts did not amount to a breach of the applicant's right to religion in Article 9, the Grand Chamber held that the restriction had the legitimate aims of protecting the rights and freedoms of others and maintaining public order, having as its purpose the preservation of the secular character of educational institutions. It was also a proportionate restriction, since it did not hinder the applicant in performing the habitual duties of religious observance and was both imposed following an appropriate decision-making process and subject to various safeguards, including judicial review. By sixteen votes to one, the Grand Chamber held that the restriction did not impair the very essence of the right to education. More generally, the Grand Chamber stated in the *Şahin* case that the right to education 'does not exclude recourse to disciplinary measures, including suspension or expulsion from an educational institution in order to ensure compliance with its internal rules'.[49] Such measures must be proportionate. In *Irfan Temel and Others v Turkey*,[50] there was a disproportionate limitation on freedom of expression in breach of Article 2 when Kurdish university students were suspended for petitioning for optional Kurdish language courses. In contrast, in *Sulak v Turkey*,[51] it was held that a state university student could be expelled as a disciplinary measure for persistent cheating in examinations.

[44] *Arslan v Turkey* No 31320/02 hudoc (2006) DA.
[45] *Ebibomi and Others v UK* No 26922/95 hudoc (1995) DA.
[46] See *Stevens v UK* No 11674/85 hudoc (1986) DA.   [47] 2011- para 53.
[48] 2005-XI; 44 EHRR 99 GC.
[49] *Leyla Şahin v Turkey* 2005-XI; 44 EHRR 99 para 156 GC. Cf *Campbell and Cosans v UK* A 48 (1982); 4 EHRR 293 (suspension not justified).   [50] Hudoc (2009); 51 EHRR 154.
[51] No 24515/94 hudoc (1996) DA.

The Court has held certain other restrictions upon access to school or university to be contrary to Article 2. Thus a restriction excluding a child from school because her parent had been made to surrender his migrant card validating his residence was clearly a breach of Article 2 because it had no basis in national law.[52] The refusal to admit to a state university a student who had passed the entrance examination in the belief that his good results could not be explained was held to be a breach of Article 2 because it had no basis in national law and, in the absence of proof, was arbitrary.[53]

A number of cases have involved disagreement between the school authorities and parents on the allocation of children with special educational needs to mainstream schools or to suitable special schools. Recognizing the financial and staffing demands involved, the Court has allowed states 'a wide measure of discretion' in decision-making on this matter in order to make the 'best use possible of the resources available to them in the interests of disabled children generally'.[54]

Several cases have concerned the language of instruction in schools. In the *Belgian Linguistic* case *(No 2)*,[55] the issue of access by children to schools in which they would be instructed in their own language was resolved under Articles 14 of the Convention in conjunction with Article 2, on the basis of discrimination on grounds of language, not under Article 2 by itself.

In *Cyprus v Turkey*,[56] a somewhat similar issue was resolved just under Article 2. In that case, schooling in northern Cyprus had been provided with Greek as the language of instruction at the primary school level for Greek minority children, but secondary schooling was only provided for them in Turkish. The Court held that, 'having assumed responsibility for the provision of Greek-language primary schooling, the failure of the "TRNC" authorities to make continuing provision for it at the secondary school level must be considered in effect to be a denial of the substance of the right at issue'. Access to Greek language schooling in the south was not sufficient because of its impact on family life, as children who went to the south were not allowed by the TRNC to return north as adults.

The language of instruction in schools was also the key issue in *Catan and Others v Moldova and Russia*.[57] The case arose out of the breakup of the USSR, after which Moldova became an independent state, but with the territory of Transdniestria within it, with its large Russian/Ukrainian ethnic population, being controlled not by the Moldovan government but by Russia, which had troops based in it. After separatists had declared the 'Moldovan Republic of Transdniestria' (MRT), the MRT authorities closed schools in Transdniestria that taught in the Moldovan/Romanian language, which used the Latin alphabet and was the official language of Moldova. The schools were forced to move to premises that had inferior facilities and involved longer journeys for pupils. On their way to school, children were abused and had Latin script books seized by the police. The choice for members of the Moldovan community in the MRT was to tolerate this harassment or move their children to a school in the MRT in which the teaching would be in a language in the Cyrillic script (Russian, Ukrainian, or 'Moldovan'). The Grand Chamber held that the forced closure of the schools and the subsequent harassment of the children were interferences in breach of Article 2 with the children's 'rights of access to educational

---

[52] *Timishev v Russia* 2005-XII; 44 EHRR 776.

[53] *Mürsel Eren v Turkey* 2006-II; 44 EHRR 619. See also *Lukach v Russia No 48041/99* hudoc (1999) DA.

[54] *SP v UK No 28915/95* hudoc (1997) DA. Cf, eg, *Graeme v UK No 13887/88*, 64 DR 158 (1990) and *McIntyre v UK No 29046/95* hudoc (1998) DA.   [55] A 6 (1968); 1 EHRR 252 PC.

[56] 2001-IV; 35 EHRR 731 para 278 GC.   [57] 2012-; 57 EHRR 99 GC.

institutions existing at a given time and to be educated in their national language'.[58] The measures taken by the MRT authorities were 'intended to enforce the Russification of the language and culture of the Moldovan community living in Transdniestria, in accordance with the MRT's overall political objectives of uniting with Russia and separating from Moldova', and ran counter to the 'fundamental importance of primary and secondary education for each child's personal development and future success'.[59]

II. THE EFFECTIVENESS OF THE EDUCATION PROVIDED

In the *Belgian Linguistic* case *(No 2)*,[60] the Court stated that the right to education had to be 'effective'. Where the challenge to the effectiveness of education depends upon resources or the organization and pattern of the system set up by the state, the negative formulation of the right to education in the first sentence of Article 2 and the intended consequences of this, which were accepted by the Court in the *Belgian Linguistic* case *(No 2)*,[61] mean that a claim based upon such matters as the need for further funding, organizational or managerial change, the role of parents, school starting and leaving ages, the kind and choice of schools, and student loans at university are unlikely to succeed in the absence of clearly arbitrary action or the lack of a legal base.[62] Similarly, the 'setting and planning of the curriculum fall in principle within the competence of the contracting states', and involve 'questions of expediency on which it is not for the Court to rule and whose solution may legitimately vary according to the country and the era',[63] so that a challenge is unlikely to succeed outside of the application of the second sentence in Article 2 concerning the obligation to respect the convictions of parents.

However, in *Oršuš and Others v Croatia*,[64] in the course of finding a violation of Article 14 of the Convention in conjunction with Article 2, the Grand Chamber held that the poor attendance and high dropout rate of Roma children 'called for the implementation of positive measures' to improve the situation, particularly by 'active and structured involvement on the part of the relevant social services'. This is a ruling that could be applied so as to require the state to take other kinds of positive measures under Article 2 in both discrimination and non-discrimination contexts to improve access to education and its quality.

3. RESPECT FOR PARENTS' RELIGIOUS AND PHILOSOPHICAL CONVICTIONS[65]

The second sentence in Article 2 must be read together with the first sentence: it is to the fundamental right to education that the right of parents[66] for respect for their

---

[58] *Catan and Others v Moldova and Russia*, para 143.

[59] *Catan and Others v Moldova and Russia*, para 144. It was also a breach of the parents' Article 2 rights.

[60] A 6 (1968) p 31; 1 EHRR 252, 281 PC. Cf *Leyla Şahin v Turkey* 2005-XI; 44 EHRR 99 GC ('practical and effective').   [61] Cf more recently *Leyla Şahin v Turkey*, para 154.

[62] See eg, the special needs cases listed earlier, where a wide margin of appreciation was allowed.

[63] *Kjeldsen, Busk Madsen and Pedersen v Denmark* A 23 (1976); 1 EHRR 711 para 53. Insistence upon a qualification to take a course is permitted: *Çiftçi v Turkey No 71860/01* hudoc (2004) DA. On the recognition of studies abroad, see *Karus v Italy No 29043/95* hudoc (1998) DA.

[64] 2010-; 52 EHRR 300 para 177 GC.   [65] See Evans, 8 HRLR 449 (2008).

[66] The parent's right continues when the child is in care (*Aminoff v Sweden No 10554/83*, 43 DR 120 at 144 (1985)), but it will cease if the child is adopted (*X v UK No 7626/76*, 11 DR 160 (1977)). If the child is in the

religious and philosophical convictions is attached.[67] This right applies to both state and private systems of education. The state must 'respect' the parents' conviction in such state schools as it provides, and it has a positive obligation to ensure that private schools do likewise. This obligation extends to all the functions exercised in connection with education, whether academic or administrative.[68] It is principally a protection against indoctrination by the state[69] and teachers[70] in school lessons, but it covers administrative matters as well, such as the manner of maintaining discipline and 'the organization of the school environment',[71] insofar as they are capable of conflicting with parents' convictions.

If the parents' objection is sufficiently well founded on a religious or philosophical conviction, the state's duty is to 'respect' their right. This is far from providing an absolute guarantee that children must be educated in accordance with their parents' convictions: parents cannot require that a state provide an alternative course to one that is inconsistent with those convictions.[72] This is a conclusion reinforced by the limited nature of the duty in the first sentence upon which the second sentence is grafted: it is the state which determines and finances the provision of education.[73]

There are two further protections for the state against this potentially wide-ranging right of parental influence in the education system. These are, first, that the convictions which are to be taken into account are limited to religious and philosophical conviction and the burden on the parents to demonstrate their relevance to their stand is heavy. As to the meaning of 'convictions', in *Campbell and Cosans v UK*,[74] the Court stated that it was not synonymous with the words 'opinions' and 'ideas' in Article 10, but was more akin to the term 'beliefs' in Article 9 of the Convention and 'denoted views that attain a certain level of cogency, seriousness, cohesion and importance'. It is relatively easy to identify what is a 'religious' conviction. In *Hasan and Eylem Zengin v Turkey*,[75] it was held that the Alevi faith, which is an Islamic faith distinct from the Sunni faith, is a 'religious conviction': in the Court's words, it was 'certainly neither a sect nor a "belief" which did not attain the level of cogency', etc, required by *Campbell and Cosans*.[76] It is not so simple to set the limits of 'philosophical' convictions.[77] In *Campbell and Cosans*, the Court said that they comprehend 'such convictions as are worthy of respect in a "democratic society" and are not incompatible with human dignity; in addition, they must not conflict with the fundamental right of the child to education'.[78] In *Catan and Others v Moldova and Russia*,[79] the parents' wish that their children be educated in the official language of the country and mother tongue was held to be a philosophical conviction.

---

custody of one parent, it will cease for the other: *X v Sweden No 7911/77*, 12 DR 192 (1977). The right is that of parents; no mention is made of the convictions of the child, of whatever age.

[67] *Kjeldsen, Busk Madsen and Pedersen v Denmark* A 23 (1976); 1 EHRR 711 para 56.

[68] *Campbell and Cosans v UK* A 48 (1982); 4 EHRR 293 paras 33–6.

[69] *Kjeldsen, Busk Madsen and Pedersen v Denmark* A 23 (1976); 1 EHRR 711 para 53.

[70] Implied by *X v UK No 8010/77*, 16 DR 101 at 102 (1979).

[71] *Lautsi and Others v Italy* 2011-; 54 EHRR 60 para 63 GC (crucifix in classroom).

[72] *Bulski v Poland Nos 46254/99 and 31888/02* hudoc (2004) DA. Cf *Family H v UK No 10233/83*, 37 DR 105 (1984).   [73] *W & DM and M & HI v UK Nos 10228/82 and 10229/82*, 37 DR 96 (1984).

[74] A 48 (1982); 4 EHRR 293 para 36.

[75] Hudoc (2007); 46 EHRR 1060. Jehovah's Witnesses are a 'known' religion: *Valsamis v Greece* 1996-VI; 24 EHRR 294 para 26.   [76] *Hasan and Eylem Zengin v Turkey*, para 66.

[77] They do not include convictions as to the language of instruction: *Belgian Linguistic case (No 2)* A 6 (1968) p 35; 1 EHRR 252, 285 PC. See also Robertson, 28 BYIL 359 at 362 (1951).

[78] *Campbell and Cosans v UK* A 48 (1982); 4 EHRR 293 para 36.

[79] 2012-; 57 EHRR 99 GC.

As to the burden upon parents, they must show the basis for and the content of the belief;[80] that it is a belief they hold; that holding it is the reason for their objection to what the state is doing;[81] and that they have brought the reason for their objection to the attention of the authorities. The Court may reject an objection as not, in its view, offending the parents' convictions.[82]

Should the applicant be able to satisfy the above requirement, the second measure of protection for the state is that mere incidental treatment in lessons of matters about which religious and philosophical convictions may be held will not raise an issue under the second sentence of Article 2. As the Court said in *Kjeldsen, Busk Madsen and Pedersen v Denmark*,[83] this provision does not permit a parent to object to the integrated teaching of religious or philosophical information or knowledge, a right that would have disruptive consequences for the organization of teaching. All the parent is entitled to is that this information or knowledge, like any other, be conveyed 'in an objective, critical and pluralistic manner': the Convention, that is, demands only a negative quality, that students be not subjected to the indoctrination of a single point of view.[84]

As the *Kjeldsen* case showed, these are injunctions which are easier to articulate than to apply. There, Danish law required the teaching of sex education as an integral part of the curriculum for nine to eleven-year-olds. Children at state schools were not excused from the lessons. A claim by parents that this was a violation of their right to have their religious and philosophical convictions respected was rejected by six votes to one by the Court. For the majority, the crucial point was that the teaching programme was principally a matter of conveying information. There was no attempt to indoctrinate a particular moral attitude towards sexual activities, especially concerning contraception. Another factor that would appear to have influenced the Court in its decision was that the government provided 'substantial assistance to private schools' in which the parents could have their children educated in accordance with their beliefs; although recourse to such schools involved parents in 'sacrifices', the alternative solution that they provided was not to be 'disregarded in this case'.[85] The emphasis here appears to be on the provision of state subsidy. The Court would not appear to go as far as to say that a state can comply with Article 2 by allowing unsubsidized private schooling (or home education), with no need for it to modify the provision of education in its state schools so as to 'respect' the parents' convictions. The Court's more recent decision in *Jimenez Alonso and Jimenez Merino v Spain*[86] can be read as going this far, but private education in Spain is also heavily state subsidized and, although this is not mentioned, it may have been taken into account. The approach in the *Kjeldsen* case as regards subsidy is open to criticism; the better view is that Article 2 requires that if a state engages in schooling it should 'respect' the convictions of the parents, whatever subsidy it provides for private schools.

The Court has also applied its requirement that information or knowledge be conveyed in an 'objective, critical and pluralistic' way to courses in subjects such as religion, ethics, etc, that bear directly upon a parent's religious or philosophical convictions. In the leading

---

[80] *Campbell and Cosans v UK* B 42 (1980) para 93 Com Rep.

[81] *Warwick v UK* No 9471/81, 60 DR 5 at 18 (1986).

[82] *Valsamis v Greece* 1996-VI; 24 EHRR 294.   [83] A 23 (1976); 1 EHRR 711 para 53.

[84] The state will have the power under Article 17 to prohibit education in values which fall within its scope: Opsahl, in Robertson, ed, *Privacy and Human Rights*, 1973, at pp 235–7.

[85] *Opsahl*, para 50. Similarly, the permissibility of home education may be taken into account.

[86] No 51188/99 2000-VI DA (sex education). The UK also subsidizes some private schools.

case of *Folgerø and Others v Norway*,[87] the applicant parents were humanists who objected to state primary and lower secondary school lessons for their children in the compulsory subject 'Christianity, Religion and Philosophy'. The Court held that although the course focused on knowledge about Christianity to a greater extent than knowledge of other religions and philosophies, this was in itself not inconsistent with the requirements of objectivity and pluralism: in view of the place occupied by Christianity in the national history of the respondent state, which has a Lutheran established church, this choice fell within its margin of appreciation. However, the Court considered that the object of the course, which was to give pupils a Christian upbringing, and the *extent* of its focus upon Christianity were together so great as to make the difference in treatment a qualitative as well as a quantitative one, to the point where the objectivity and pluralism requirement in Article 2 was not met.

If the requirement is not met, the state will nonetheless have met its obligation to respect the parents' right if it allows the children to be exempted from the offending lessons.[88] But the exemption must be a sufficient one, which was not the case in the *Folgerø* case. Pupils could be granted a partial exemption, which meant that exemption would be granted only after the parents had given written reasons that were found to be reasonable. The Grand Chamber held, by just nine votes to eight, that this was not sufficient to remedy the situation. This was mainly because parents could have difficulty in discovering the details of the subject as actually taught and might feel compelled to give reasons that would impinge upon their right to privacy or engage them in controversy. In a collective dissent, the minority disagreed with the majority's finding of imbalance in the context of the course and concerns about requiring the parents to give reasons.

In reaching its decision in the *Folgerø* case, the Grand Chamber summarized and generally re-affirmed its earlier approach to the interpretation of Article 2 in *Kjeldsen* and other cases. It is noticeable, however, that the Grand Chamber both accepted that the requirements of objectivity and plurality do not prohibit a limited measure of imbalance in the content of a course that reflects a state's national traditions and also demonstrated a willingness to examine and evaluate more closely the details of the content of a challenged course than it had done before.[89]

If the *Folgerø* case shows the difficulty of deciding the acceptable limits of the parents' concern on the content of the curriculum, *Campbell and Cosans v UK*[90] raised the same problem about administrative matters, here school discipline maintained by corporal punishment over the parents' objections in breach of Article 2. The Court decided that the parents' objections were 'philosophical' because they attained the required 'level of cogency, seriousness, cohesion and importance'. It was surely not without significance that the practice complained about raised a serious question of the violation of a

---

[87] 2007-III; 46 EHRR 1147 GC. See also *Dojan and Others v Germany No 319/08* hudoc (2011) DA. The course syllabus in issue in *Folgerø* was an amended version of one that the UN Human Rights Committee had ruled infringed the Article 18 ICCPR guarantee of freedom of religion: *Leirvag v Norway* 15 IHRR 909 (2008).

[88] *Kjeldsen, Busk Madsen and Pedersen v Denmark* A 23 (1976); 1 EHRR 711. In the *Campbell and Cosans* case the Court suggested that a system of exemptions from corporal punishment might satisfy Article 2; the respondent government had argued that such differential treatment of pupils on matters of discipline would not be acceptable.

[89] The approach in the *Folgerø* case was followed in *Hasan and Eylem Zengin v Turkey* hudoc (2007); 46 EHRR 1060. Contrast *Appel-Irrgang and Others v Germany No 45216/07* hudoc (2009) DA (course on ethics was neutral; not contrary to secular beliefs; no need for exemption).

[90] A 48 (1982); 4 EHRR 293 para 36.

fundamental Convention provision—Article 3—even if on the facts the Court held that Article 3 had not been breached. It is less likely that the Court would reach the same conclusion about, say, obligations to wear school uniform or the fixing of the school starting and leaving ages, however strongly parents might feel about such things, unless another Convention right were implicated.

The organization of the 'school environment' in accordance with the 'philosophical convictions' of parents was in issue in *Lautsi and Others v Italy*,[91] in which the Grand Chamber held that the compulsory placing of crucifixes on classroom walls in state schools despite the objections of secular parents was not a breach of Article 2. The Court accepted that the crucifix was 'above all a religious symbol',[92] but stressed that a crucifix on a wall was 'an essentially passive symbol' which could not 'be deemed to have an influence on pupils comparable to that of didactic speech or participation in religious activities'.[93] While the presence of a crucifix undoubtedly gave Christianity 'greater visibility' than other beliefs, the Grand Chamber noted that it was not accompanied by compulsory teaching about Christianity and there was evidence that Italian state schools were tolerant of other religions, as, for example, by allowing Islamic headscarves to be worn and Ramadan to be celebrated. The Grand Chamber also accepted that it was not contrary to Article 2 to 'confer on a country's majority religion preponderant visibility in the school environment'.[94] At the same time, the Grand Chamber acknowledged that secular parents might well consider the presence of a crucifix as showing a lack of respect for their right to ensure that their children were educated and taught in conformity with their philosophical convictions. The obligation of the state under Article 2 was to reconcile the exercise of the educational functions they assumed with the parental right to respect for their convictions. In effecting this reconciliation, the state had a margin of appreciation, the existence of which in the present context was supported by the lack of any European consensus on the presence of religious symbols in state schools. The Grand Chamber had a duty in principle to respect the state's decisions in these matters provided they 'do not lead to a form of indoctrination'.[95] In exercising its margin of appreciation, the state could take into account that the presence of crucifixes in classrooms was a result of Italy's particular historical development. In this respect, the Grand Chamber took account of the fact that Europe was 'marked by a great diversity between the states of which it is composed, particularly in the sphere of cultural and historical development'.[96] The Grand Chamber's decision rejecting the applicants' claim, by fifteen votes to two, reversed a unanimous Chamber decision that had provoked considerable controversy. The Grand Chamber judgment is based centrally upon the margin of appreciation doctrine. Perhaps responding to the great outcry from many quarters against the Chamber's judgment, the Grand Chamber decided to leave such a sensitive matter to the state concerned.

4. DISCRIMINATION AND MINORITY RIGHTS

At the international level, discrimination with respect to educational provision has long been a matter of concern and claims for special treatment for minority education are

---

[91] 2011-; 54 EHRR 60 GC. See McGoldrick, 11 HRLR 451 (2011).
[92] *Lautsi and Others v Italy*, para 66.   [93] *Lautsi and Others v Italy*, para 72.
[94] *Lautsi and Others v Italy*, para 71. Cf its approach in the *Folgerø* case.
[95] *Lautsi and Others v Italy*, para 69.   [96] *Lautsi and Others v Italy*, para 68.

familiar.[97] The *Belgian Linguistic* case *(No 2)*[98] remains a core authority on Article 2 of the First Protocol, but it also addressed concerns of the applicants under Article 14 of the Convention. The parents of French-speaking children alleged that several of the schooling arrangements differentiated between their children and Dutch-speaking children and that, because there was no reasonable and objective justification for the differences, they constituted discrimination in breach of the Convention. The Court condemned only one, relatively minor, practice as contravening Article 14, where Dutch-speaking children in a particular area were allowed to be educated in Dutch-speaking schools in a bilingual district outside the neighbourhood, whereas French-speaking children in an equivalent Flemish area could not attend the French-speaking schools in the same bilingual district but were compelled to attend their local Dutch-language schools. The narrow effect the Court gave to Article 14 was in part because it endorsed as a legitimate policy the Belgian state's objective of securing unilingual regions in the bulk of the country. That this policy disadvantaged members of linguistic minorities was not discrimination and the children's rights had not been violated. Nor, because language, rather than religious or philosophical convictions, was the badge of distinction, could the parents find any protection in the second sentence of Article 2.[99]

The Court's approach to the Article 14 issue in the case has not escaped criticism.[100] The tolerance the judgment shows for assimilative policies, albeit in discrete regions, is out of line with its insistence on pluralism on other matters. The state, it is thought, may neither discriminate in the access to the educational system it provides nor establish segregated educational systems, although it may have to tolerate separate schools if that is necessary to respect the religious and philosophical convictions of parents.[101] To this extent, parents who are members of religious or philosophical minorities have the right to establish their own schools. Article 14 may then have a role where the state grants subsidies to *some* private schools established in respect of parents' religious and philosophical convictions. There may first be a question as to whether a state should be subsidizing denominational education at all. Since, in fact, several European states do so, here it may be argued that under Article 14 it may do so but that it may not discriminate between such groups by subsidizing some schools for some groups but not others. In a case from Northern Ireland,[102] the Commission held manifestly unfounded a claim by a parent that differential funding between state schools and 'maintained' schools in which private bodies could exercise a degree of control over the school violated Article 14 in conjunction with Article 2 of the First Protocol. The different treatment was justified because the amount of state subsidy to maintained schools was large (85 per cent of capital costs and 100 per cent of running costs) and the advantages to the private trusts were considerable (a controlling interest in the governors and the vesting of the school property in them).

Another dimension to the protection of minority education was in issue in *DH and Others v Czech Republic*, in which the respondent state was found to be in breach of Article 14 of the Convention in conjunction with Article 2 for a situation in which Roma children were allocated without justification and to their disadvantage to special schools for their education. The Grand Chamber's important judgment in this case is argued

---

[97] See Cullen, IJFL 143 at 146–51 (1993). See also the UNESCO Convention against Discrimination in Education 1960, 429 UNTS 93.   [98] A 6 (1968); 1 EHRR 252 PC.

[99] *Belgian Linguistic* case *(No 2)*. See also *Skender v FYRM No 62059/00* hudoc (2001) DA.

[100] See Cullen, IJFL 143 at 171–2 (1993).

[101] *Kjeldsen, Busk Madsen and Pedersen v Denmark* A 23 (1976); 1 EHRR 711 para 53 and *Karnell and Hardt v Sweden No 4733/71*, 14 YB 664 (1971). The *Karnell and Hardt* case was settled: *Council of Europe, Stock-Taking 1954–1984*, pp 149–50.   [102] *X v UK No 7782/77*, 14 DR 179 (1978).

entirely in terms of discrimination contrary to Articles 14 and is considered in Chapter 18 under that Article.

5. CONCLUSION

Article 2 of the First Protocol is far from the full guarantee of the right to education provided in some international human rights treaties protecting economic, social, and cultural rights.[103] There is no obligation upon the state to provide a state system of education, let alone to fund it appropriately or have it meet European standards as to such matters as course content or management. Its obligation is the more limited one of guaranteeing access to those state and private schools that the state chooses to provide or allow, coupled with a modest duty to secure their effective functioning in certain basic regards and to respect the religious and philosophical conviction of a child's parents in teaching and administration. The significance of the absence of an obligation to provide a state system of education is not so great as might appear for the reason that European states do in fact provide comprehensive systems of state education that are subject to Article 2, which extends to 'existing' institutions. At the same time, claims concerning 'existing' institutions in respect of such matters as the choice of school, the role of parents, school management generally, the curriculum and, above all, the funding of schools and universities are unlikely to succeed in the absence of clearly arbitrary or nationally illegal acts. The largely negative obligation that Article 2 contains leaves beyond its scope the proper funding and management of schools and universities, which is critical to the quality of the education which they provide.

While this situation accurately reflects the drafting history of Article 2, it would be open to the Court to adopt a more demanding interpretation of Article 2 by regarding the failure of the state to provide in its state schools or universities the requisite quality of education in a particular case (eg, special needs schooling)[104] as a 'denial' of the right to an effective education contrary to the first sentence of Article 2. This would be consistent with the Convention's character as a 'living instrument'[105] and would fill what is otherwise a gap in the protection afforded by the Convention to the right to education, which the Court has recognized as playing a 'fundamental role' in a democratic society.[106] It might even be argued that the obligation not to deny education in the first sentence of Article 2 should be read, contrary to the ruling in the *Belgian Linguistic* case, as imposing an obligation to provide a state education system. In *Kjeldsen, Busk Madsen and Pedersen v Denmark*,[107] the Court acknowledged that, given 'the power of the modern state, it is above all through state teaching' that the aim of safeguarding pluralism in education in the second sentence of Article 2 must be realized. The same might be said of the obligation not to deny an effective education in the first sentence of the same Article.

---

[103] See particularly Articles 13–14, International Covenant on Economic, Social and Cultural Rights 1966, 993 UNTS 3; Article 28, Convention on the Rights of the Child 1989, 1577 UNTS 3; and Article 17(2), Revised European Social Charter 1996, ETS 63.

[104] See *International Association Autism-Europe v France*, European Committee of Social Rights, Complaint No 13/2002 (2004) (insufficient educational provision made for autistic persons).

[105] *Leyla Şahin v Turkey* 2005-XI; 44 EHRR 99 para 136 GC.

[106] *Leyla Şahin v Turkey*, para 137.

[107] A 23 (1976); 1 EHRR 711 para 50. Cf *Konrad v Germany No 35504/03* hudoc (2006) DA.

The relationship of religion and education has been a contentious issue for the Court. In the *Şahin* and *Lautsi* cases, the Court relied upon the margin of appreciation doctrine to decide in favour of the state when resolving issues on which there were very strong views. In contrast with the *Lautsi* case, in the *Folgerø* case the Court held in favour of the right of parents to respect for their religious and philosophical convictions in the education of their children.

23

ARTICLE 3, FIRST PROTOCOL: THE RIGHT TO FREE ELECTIONS

The High Contracting Parties undertake to hold free elections at reasonable intervals by secret ballot, under conditions which will ensure the free expression of the opinion of the people in the choice of the legislature.

1. INTRODUCTION

Article 3 of the First Protocol[1] imposes a positive obligation on states to secure free elections.[2] The Court has read into this text individual rights to vote and to stand for election, reversing its technique of deriving positive obligations from the expressly articulated guarantees of individual rights contained in other Articles of the Convention.[3] This jurisprudence commenced in the 1987 judgment in *Mathieu-Mohin and Clerfayt v Belgium*.[4] Grand Chamber judgments have been given in a range of cases involving prisoner disenfranchisement;[5] the rights of expatriate voters;[6] state barriers to the electoral activity of former

---

[1] The guarantee of free elections was displaced from the main text of the treaty into the First Protocol because of a lack of consensus about the form and content of the proposed provision. There was disagreement between the states about the propriety of framing a human right to free elections, some states believing that this went 'outside the traditional domain of human rights': 4 TP 140. The *travaux préparatoires* are unclear as to whether the states intended to create an enforceable right to free elections or rather to stipulate a general—if unenforceable—obligation upon the states to maintain democratic structures.

[2] There are also a number of relevant 'soft law' instruments produced by Council of Europe organs. The Court frequently references approvingly the work of the European Commission for Democracy Through Law (the Venice Commission), such as its Code of Good Practice in Electoral Matters: http://www.venice. coe.int/WebForms/pages/default.aspx?p=01_main_reference_documents&lang=en.

[3] The Court maintains that the Article's 'unique phrasing was intended to give greater solemnity to the Contracting States' commitment and to emphasise that this was an area where they were required to take positive measures as opposed to merely refraining from interference': *Mathieu-Mohin and Clerfayt v Belgium* A 113 (1987); 10 EHRR 1 para 50.

[4] A 113 (1987); 10 EHRR 1. Early Commission decisions had held that Article 3, First Protocol did not confer rights on individuals: *X v Germany No 530/59*, 3 YB 184 at 190 (1960); see also *X v Belgium No 1065/61*, 4 YB 260 at 268 (1961): 'the right to vote is not, as such, guaranteed by Article 3'; *X v Belgium No 1028/61*, 4 YB 324 at 338 (1961): Article 3 'does not guarantee the right to vote, to stand for election or to be elected'. The Court in *Mathieu-Mohin*, at para 49, ruled that 'such a restrictive interpretation does not stand up to scrutiny'.

[5] *Hirst v UK (No 2)* 2005-IX; 42 EHRR 849 GC; *Scoppola v Italy (No 3)* hudoc (2012); 56 EHRR 19 GC.

[6] *Sitaropoulos and Giakoumopoulos v Greece* 2012-; 56 EHRR 9 GC.

communists;[7] rules prohibiting MPs from possessing dual nationality;[8] and laws requiring political parties to win a minimum vote share to qualify for seats in parliament.[9] The Court has recently given its first judgment concerning the application of Article 3 to the regulation of broadcasting in election campaigns.[10]

The Court's approach to the electoral rights protected by Article 3 correlates to its understanding of the political dimension of the rights to freedom of association (notably its Article 11 case law on freedom of political parties) and freedom of expression (and Article 10 case law on political debate in particular),[11] plus the Court's general vision of the state's role as the 'ultimate guarantor of pluralism'.[12] Although Article 3 of the First Protocol does not use the term 'democracy', the democratic ideal permeating all Convention jurisprudence underpins the Court's reading of the electoral rights. The Court is clear that '[d]emocracy constitutes a fundamental element of the "European public order"'[13] and that it 'is the only political model contemplated by the Convention and, accordingly, the only one compatible with it'.[14] This last point has been repeatedly made in Article 11 judgments concerning the banning of political parties,[15] the most prominent example being *Refah Partisi (The Welfare Party) and Others v Turkey*.[16] The connection between the right to free elections and 'effective political democracy' is often alluded to by the Court to stress the direct contribution which the right has to make to this goal.[17] Conceivably, preserving the conditions for the 'the free expression of the opinion of the people in the choice of the legislature', as protected by the Protocol, may on occasion foster election victories for a political party or candidate with anti-democratic aims or allegiances. In such circumstances the Court may endorse limited and strictly proportionate action by the state to protect its democracy, by finding that an interference with electoral rights is justified.[18] There is also the possibility of the Court finding Article 17 of the Convention applicable in such a case.[19]

2. GENERAL PRINCIPLES GOVERNING ARTICLE 3, FIRST PROTOCOL JURISPRUDENCE

The Court reads the positive obligation expressed in Article 3 as protecting a range of both 'active' and 'passive' electoral rights.[20] The former denotes the right to participate actively

---

[7] *Ždanoka v Latvia* 2006-IV; 45 EHRR 478 GC.

[8] *Tănase v Moldova* ECHR 2010; 53 EHRR 22 GC.

[9] *Yumak and Sadak v Turkey* 2008-III; 48 EHRR 4 GC.

[10] *Communist Party of Russia and Others v Russia* hudoc (2012).   [11] See Chs 15 and 14.

[12] *Yumak and Sadak v Turkey* 2008-III; 48 EHRR 4 GC para 106.

[13] *Ždanoka v Latvia* 2006-IV; 45 EHRR 478 para 98 GC.

[14] *Ždanoka v Latvia*, para 98 GC (citing *United Communist Party of Turkey and Others v Turkey* 1998-I; 26 EHRR 121 para 45 GC; *Refah Partisi (The Welfare Party) and Others v Turkey* 2003-II; 37 EHRR 1 GC; and *Gorzelik and Others v Poland* 2004-I; 40 EHRR 76 para 89 GC).   [15] See Ch 12.

[16] 2003-II; 37 EHRR 1 GC.

[17] See especially *Ždanoka v Latvia* 2006-IV; 45 EHRR 478 GC para 98; *Sadak and Others v Turkey (No 2)* 2002-IV; 36 EHRR 396 para 32; *Melnychenko v Ukraine* 2004-X; 42 EHRR 784 para 53; and *Hirst v UK (No 2)* 2005-IX; 42 EHRR 849 para 58 GC, 'the rights guaranteed under Article 3 ... are crucial to establishing and maintaining the foundations of an effective and meaningful democracy governed by the rule of law' (citation omitted).

[18] See *Ždanoka v Latvia* 2006-IV; 45 EHRR 478 GC, discussed in section 5.   [19] See Ch 20.

[20] See, eg, *Melnychenko v Ukraine* 2004-X; 42 EHRR 784 para 57 and *Ždanoka v Latvia* 2006-IV; 45 EHRR 478 paras 105–6 GC.

as a voter and the latter the right to offer oneself passively as a candidate for the position of elected representative. The rights have both a substantive and a procedural aspect. The former embraces, for example, entitlements to register and to cast a ballot;[21] the latter provides protection for procedural fairness in decision-making by domestic authorities about matters such as the disqualification of candidates and representatives, or the annulment of election results.[22] The Court affords the so-called passive electoral rights less protection than the active voting rights.[23] This doctrine derives from the Court's concern to respect the marked diversity of state laws governing candidature and the qualifications of representatives, and to acknowledge the special sensitivity surrounding the composition of national legislatures, determined by those laws. State laws governing candidature and the membership of legislatures tend not to display the same approximate consensus about the relevant democratic principles as do laws governing the franchise and other aspects of 'active' voting rights, which the Court consequently reviews more strictly.

The electoral rights are regarded in the Court's classification of rights as 'political' not 'civil'.[24] The guarantees of Article 6 therefore do not extend to them: there is thus no requirement under that Article that a state grant an individual a hearing prior to disenfranchisement or disqualification as a candidate or representative. Nor does Article 6 require that states which empower courts to make such determinations prescribe minimum standards to be observed by the judiciary in this task. This is an unfortunate doctrine, aptly criticized in the dissenting opinion of Judge De Meyer in *Pierre-Bloch v France*,[25] who observed—accurately—that 'in reality, "political" rights are a special category of "civil" rights. Indeed they are more "civil" than others in that they are more directly inherent in citizenship and, furthermore, are normally exclusive to citizens'. The limitations implied by the Court's contrary doctrine may be offset to some extent by its recent development of procedural protections under Article 3. In several judgments the Court has expanded its reading of Article 3 to provide substantially greater protection for procedural aspects of the processes governing the loss or qualification of voting and candidacy rights, and this to some extent meets the gap created by the Court's refusal to apply Article 6 to electoral matters.[26] The Court also employs a principle of legitimate expectations according to which unpredictable interpretations or applications of election laws and rules may be found to fall below the standards required by Article 3.[27] The Court has also found violations of Article 13 in cases involving inadequate state mechanisms for the resolution of electoral disputes.[28]

No grounds of restriction of the electoral rights are mentioned in Article 3.[29] However, 'the rights in question are not absolute';[30] they are subject to implied limitations. In the absence of a specific list of legitimate aims justifying restriction, such as

---

[21] See, eg, *Matthews v UK* 1999-I; 28 EHRR 361 GC; *Shindler v UK* hudoc (2013).

[22] See, eg, *Namat Aliyev v Azerbaijan* hudoc (2010); *Abil v Azerbaijan* hudoc (2012).

[23] See, eg, *Ždanoka v Latvia* 2006-IV; 45 EHRR 478 GC para 105.

[24] *Pierre-Bloch v France* 1997-VI; 26 EHRR 202. The Court has endorsed this ruling repeatedly in subsequent cases. See, eg, *Krasnov and Skuratov v Russia* hudoc (2007); *Boskoski v The Former Yugoslav Republic of Macedonia* No 11676/04 2004-VI DA; *Guliyev v Azerbaijan* No 35584/02 hudoc (2004) DA; *Gorizdra v Moldova* No 53180/99 hudoc (2002) DA; *Namat Aliyev v Azerbaijan* hudoc (2010); *Atakishi v Azerbaijan* hudoc (2012).   [25] 1997-VI; 26 EHRR 202.

[26] See, eg *Lykourezos v Greece* 2006-VIII; 46 EHRR 74 ; *Atakishi v Azerbaijan* hudoc (2012); and see section 6, and cases cited therein.

[27] See *Lykourezos v Greece*; *Communist Party of Russia and Others v Russia* hudoc (2012) paras 134–6.

[28] *Petkov and Others v Bulgaria* hudoc (2009); *Grosaru v Romania* hudoc (2010), both discussed later.

[29] Article 16 permits restrictions on the exercise of political activity by aliens, see Ch 20.

[30] *Mathieu-Mohin and Clerfayt v Belgium* A 113 (1987); 10 EHRR 1, para 52.

those stated in Articles 8–11, a Grand Chamber has held that the states are free to rely upon an aim not contained in the lists enumerated in Articles 8–11 to justify a restriction, 'provided that the compatibility of that aim with the principle of the rule of law and the general objectives of the Convention is proved in the particular circumstances of a case'.[31] Accordingly the familiar Articles 8–11 tests of 'necessity' or 'pressing social need' are not employed in the analysis of restrictions on the electoral rights,[32] and it is recognized too that, '[t]he standards to be applied for establishing compliance with Article 3 must ... be considered to be less stringent than those applied under Articles 8–11 of the Convention'.[33] The test applied by the Court in assessing whether Article 3 has been violated remains that originally set out in *Mathieu-Mohin and Clerfayt v Belgium*:[34]

> [The Court] has to satisfy itself that the conditions do not curtail the rights in question to such an extent as to impair their very essence and deprive them of their effectiveness; that they are imposed in pursuit of a legitimate aim; and that the means employed are not disproportionate. In particular, such conditions must not thwart the free expression of the opinion of the people in the choice of the legislature.

Any restrictions on electoral rights 'must reflect, or not run counter to, the concern to maintain the integrity and effectiveness of an electoral procedure aimed at identifying the will of the people through universal suffrage'.[35] In practice this means that the Court looks for arbitrariness or a lack of proportionality in the matter put before it.[36] Although Article 3 lacks any textual requirement that interferences with the rights be 'in accordance with the law' or 'prescribed by law', as mandated by Articles 8–11, the Court demands that election laws fulfill 'the requirements of lawfulness'.[37] This prompts the Court to consider whether legal requirements governing the exercise of electoral rights are sufficiently clear, accessible, and foreseeable to participants.[38] A law limiting electoral rights 'should satisfy certain minimum requirements as to its quality, such as the requirement of foreseeability ... a rule is "foreseeable" if it is formulated with sufficient precision to enable any individual—if need be with appropriate advice—to regulate his conduct'.[39]

Frequent or late changes to the rules governing polls can disadvantage voters, candidates and parties.[40] The Court has recently found a violation of Article 3 in a case where election regulations impacting negatively on potential candidates' ability to register to stand were created just two months prior to polling day.[41] This imports a principle of stability of election law into the Court's Article 3 jurisprudence, rendering all late changes to polling and campaigning rules potentially vulnerable to successful challenge under that provision.

Understandably the Court is conscious of the heightened political sensitivity of questions surrounding the design and implementation of electoral systems. It therefore affords

---

[31] *Ždanoka v Latvia* 2006-IV; 45 EHRR 478 GC, para 115(b) GC. See also *Yumak and Sadak v Turkey* 2008-III; 48 EHRR 4 GC para 109(iii).   [32] *Yumak and Sadak v Turkey*, para 115(c).

[33] *Yumak and Sadak v Turkey*, para 115(a).   [34] A 113 (1987); 10 EHRR 1 para 52.

[35] *Hirst v UK (No 2)* 2005-IX; 42 EHRR 849 para 62 GC; *Lykourezos v Greece* 2006-VIII; 46 EHRR 74 para 52.   [36] *Yumak and Sadak v Turkey* 2008-III; 48 EHRR 4 para 109(iii) GC.

[37] *Tănase v Moldova* ECHR 2010; 53 EHRR 22 GC para 162; *Paksas v Lithuania* hudoc (2011) para 97 GC; *Seyidzade v Azerbaijan* hudoc (2009) para 28.

[38] *Grosaru v Romania* hudoc (2010) paras 46–52.   [39] *Seyidzade v Azerbaijan* hudoc (2009) para 33.

[40] The Venice Commission Code of Good Practice in Electoral Matters, see n 2, para II.2, recommends that no changes be made to election law within one year prior to a poll.

[41] *Ekoglasnost v Bulgaria* hudoc (2012).

the states a wide margin of appreciation within which to manage their electoral affairs.[42] It acknowledges the consequent latitude granted to each state to fashion an electoral system reflecting its own constitutional traditions.[43] Article 3 jurisprudence thus demands flexibility: 'legislation must be assessed in the light of the political evolution of the country concerned, with the result that features unacceptable in the context of one system may be justified in the context of another'.[44] The margin tolerated by the Court may be reduced if the domestic measure restricting electoral rights has not been the subject of legislative scrutiny or debate.[45] The Court has consistently declined to read Article 3 as imposing any requirement that a state adopt a particular type of electoral system. It does not guarantee an entitlement to a system of proportional representation;[46] nor does it import a principle of equally weighted votes into Convention law.[47] This is because 'there are numerous ways of organising and running electoral systems and a wealth of differences, inter alia, in historical development, cultural diversity and political thought within Europe which it is for each Contracting State to mould into their own democratic vision'.[48]

3. THE SCOPE OF ELECTORAL RIGHTS: LEGISLATIVE AND OTHER ELECTIONS

Not all elections attract the protection of the Court's doctrine. Despite making the interpretative leap from the exclusively institutional obligation in the text of Article 3 to individual rights, the Court continues to tie the scope of those rights to the language of the clause prescribing 'the free expression of the opinion of the people in the choice of the legislature'. Presidential elections are thus presently excluded from the reach of the electoral rights.[49] The Court, however, has not ruled out entirely the possibility of so holding.[50] Referendums are similarly excluded from the scope of Article 3.[51] It is also worth noting in this context the Court's observation in a recent admissibility decision that 'there is nothing in the nature of the referendum at issue in the present case' that would lead the Court to revise its doctrine.[52] This may suggest perhaps that the Court does not reject entirely the possibility of extending the protection of Article 3 to referendums. As the case law stands, the exclusion of presidential polls and referendums from the Court's doctrine on electoral rights represents a significant limitation on the

---

[42] See, eg, *Mathieu-Mohin and Clerfayt v Belgium* A 113 (1987); 10 EHRR 1, para 52; *Hirst v UK (No 2)* 2005-IX; 42 EHRR 849, para 61 GC; *Podkolzina v Latvia* 2002-II para 33; *Yumak and Sadak v Turkey* 2008-III; 48 EHRR 5 para 109(ii) GC.

[43] See, eg, *Hirst v UK (No 2)* 2005-IX; 42 EHRR 849 para 61 GC.

[44] *Ždanoka v Latvia* 2006-IV; 45 EHRR 478 para 115 GC.

[45] See, eg *Alajos Kiss v Hungary* hudoc (2010) para 41; *Sukhovetskyy v Ukraine* 2006-VI; 44 EHRR 1185 para 65.   [46] *Liberal Party, R and P v UK No 8765/79*, 21 DR 211 (1980).

[47] *Bompard v France No 44081/02* 2006-IV DA.

[48] *Hirst v UK (No 2)* 2005-IX; 42 EHRR 849 para 61 GC.

[49] *Boškoski v FYRM No11676/04*, 2004-VI DA; *Guliyev v Azerbaijan No 35584/02* hudoc (2004) DA; *Baskauskaite v Lithuania No 41090/98* hudoc (1998); 27 EHRR CD 341; *Habsburg-Lothringen v Austria No 15344/89*, 64 DR 210 (1990); *Anchugov and Gladkov v Russia* hudoc (2013).

[50] See the rather cautious statement made in *Georgian Labour Party v Georgia* 2008-; 48 EHRR 288.

[51] *X v UK No 7096/75*, 3 DR 165 at 166 (1975); *Nurminen and Others v Finland No 27881/95* hudoc (1997) DA; *Castelli and Others v Italy Nos 35790/97 & 38438/97*, 94 DR 102 (1998).

[52] *McLean and Cole v UK* hudoc (2013) para 33, concerning the referendum on the proposed reform of the electoral system for Westminster Parliamentary elections from simple majority to an alternative vote system.

effectiveness of Article 3 as a mechanism for developing a robust and comprehensive Convention law on voting rights.

'The legislature' referred to in Article 3 is not synonymous with 'national parliament': the Court insists the term be interpreted in light of the constitutional structure of the state in question'.[53] So, in *Vito Sante Santoro v Italy*,[54] the Court accepted that regional councils formed part of 'the legislature' because they were 'competent to enact, within the territory of the region to which they belong, laws in a number of pivotal areas in a democratic society, such as administrative planning, local policy, public health care, education, town planning and agriculture'.[55] Article 3 does not, however, extend to elections to local governments which lack sufficient legislative authority—either in terms of the scope or strength of their powers—to be deemed to be performing a role as part of the legislature.[56] Uncertainties about the application of Article 3 to the European Parliament were removed by the Court's decision in *Matthews v UK*, in which it was deemed to be part of the legislature of Gibraltar.[57] Overturning the decision of the former Commission, the Grand Chamber concluded that Article 3 could be applicable to the European Parliament, even though it was an international organ,[58] and that in practice it had the characteristics of a 'legislature' for the people of Gibraltar. On the latter point, the Court had regard 'not solely to the strictly legislative powers which a body has, but also to that body's role in the overall legislative process'.[59] This landmark decision acknowledged the significant evolution of the European Parliament and its increased role in law-making.[60] The Court observed that, 'whatever its limitations, the European Parliament, which derives democratic legitimation from the direct elections by universal suffrage, must be seen as that part of the European Community structure which best reflects concerns as to "effective political democracy"'.[61]

Applicants in states bound by Protocol 12 may in certain circumstances use that provision to raise claims concerning elections falling outside the Court's current reading of the scope of Article 3. In cases in which a form of discrimination in the enjoyment of electoral rights is alleged, Protocol 12 may be employed to effectively extend the reach of Article 3. This is so because the former provision protects 'any right set forth by law'. This was read by the Grand Chamber in *Sejdić and Finci v Bosnia and Herzegovina*,[62] as protecting against discrimination in the enjoyment of any sort of voting rights set out in state law, regardless

---

[53] *Matthews v UK* 1999-I; 28 EHRR 361 GC para 40.

[54] 2004-VI; 42 EHRR 771 para 53. The Court's first decision on Article 3, *Mathieu-Mohin and Clerfayt v Belgium* A 113 (1987); 10 EHRR 1, accepted that the Flemish Council constituted part of the Belgian legislature by virtue of the range of its competence and powers. See also *X v Austria No 7008/75*, 6 DR 120 (1976); *X, Y and Z v Germany No 6850/74*, 5 DR 90 (1976) (Austrian and German *Lander* formed part of 'legislature') and *Py v France* 2005-I; 42 EHRR 548 (New Caledonian Congress was 'sufficiently involved' in the legislative process to count for Article 3).

[55] It follows that, for example, the Scottish Parliament qualifies as a part of the legislature of the United Kingdom, owing to its broad authority to legislate in devolved areas within that territory. See *R (Chester) v Secretary of State for Justice & McGeoch v Lord President of the Council* [2013] UKSC 63.

[56] *X v UK No 5155/71*, 6 DR 13 (1976); *Booth-Clibborn v UK No 11391/85*, 43 DR 236 (1985); *Gorizdra v Moldova No 53180/99* hudoc (2002) DA; *Cherepkov v Russia No 51501/99* ECHR 2000-I DA; *Salleras Llinares v Spain No 52226/99* 2000-XI DA.

[57] 1999-I; 28 EHRR 361 GC. See Myulle, 6 *EPL* 243 (2000).

[58] *Matthews v UK*, para 39. See also paras 40–4. Cf the dissenting opinion of Judges Freeland and Jungwiert.   [59] *Matthews v UK*, para 49.

[60] It was no longer merely 'advisory and supervisory' but had 'moved towards being a body with a decisive role to play in the legislative process of the European Community' (para 50) and in practice there were 'significant areas where Community activity has a direct impact in Gibraltar' (para 53).

[61] *Matthews v UK*, paras 51–2.   [62] Hudoc (2009) GC. Discussed further later in this chapter.

of the type of election at issue. In *Sejdić and Finci* the Court reasoned from this premise to find a violation of Protocol 12 in relation to voting rights in presidential elections. The same principle would extend to arguments about discrimination in the enjoyment of referendum voting rights.[63]

4. THE RIGHT TO VOTE

Universal suffrage is one of the '[t]he common principles of the European constitutional heritage, which form the basis of any genuinely democratic society, [and] frame the right to vote in terms of the possibility to cast a vote in universal, equal, free, secret and direct elections held at regular intervals'.[64] Any departure from the principle of universal suffrage 'risks undermining the democratic validity of the legislature thus elected and the laws it promulgates. Exclusion of any groups or categories of the general population must accordingly be reconcilable with the underlying purposes of Article 3'.[65]

I. VOTER QUALIFICATIONS: AGE, CITIZENSHIP, AND RESIDENCE LAWS

The Court has insisted since its first decision on Article 3 that the 'rights in question are not absolute' but subject to implied limitations that include franchise qualifications excluding some individuals from the electorate.[66] This reflects the ubiquitous use by all democracies, including those in the Council of Europe, of laws limiting the franchise on the basis of age, residence, and citizenship. Voter qualifications of this type are recognized by the Court as consistent in principle with Article 3.[67] A Grand Chamber has indicated that minimum voting age laws and residence rules may be justified restrictions on the right to vote.[68] They serve aims acknowledged as legitimate: age limits ensure 'the maturity of those participating in the electoral process';[69] residence requirements 'identify those with sufficiently continuous or close links to, or a stake in, the country concerned'.[70] Age laws are generally uncontentious politically, and have not generated any applications to the Court. There is less uniformity across states about the principles and practices relevant to the voting rights of non-resident citizens. The Court has decided two cases concerning expatriate voting rights. The Grand Chamber decision of *Sitaropoulos*

---

[63] On Protocol 12, see Ch 24.

[64] *Russian Conservative Party of Entrepreneurs and Others v Russia* hudoc (2007); 46 EHRR 863 para 70 (citing Resolution 1320 (2003) of the Parliamentary Assembly on the Code of Good Practice in Electoral Matters; the Declaration by the Committee of Ministers on the Code of Good Practice in Electoral Matters; and the Code of Good Practice in Electoral Matters adopted by the Venice Commission).

[65] *Hirst v UK (No 2)* 2005-IX; 42 EHRR 849 para 62 GC (citing *Aziz v Cyprus* 2004-V; 41 EHRR 164 para 28).

[66] *Mathieu-Mohin and Clerfayt v Belgium* A 113 (1987); 10 EHRR 1, para 52, cited with approval in every subsequent case involving voter qualifications.

[67] *X v Netherlands* No 6573/74, 1 DR 87 (1974); *X v UK* No 7566/76, 9 DR 121 (1976); *Luksch v Germany* No 35385/97, 89-B DR 175 (1997); *Hilbe v Liechtenstein* No 31981/96, 1999-IV DA; *Py v France* 2005-I; 42 EHRR 548; *Sevinger and Eman v Netherlands* Nos 17173/07 and 17180/07 hudoc (2007) DA; *Makuc v Slovenia* No 26828/06 hudoc (2007) paras 205–8 DA; *Doyle v UK* No 30158/06 hudoc (2006) DA.

[68] *Hirst v UK (No 2)* 2005-IX; 42 EHRR 849 para 62 GC (citing *Hilbe v Liechtenstein* No 31981/96, 1999-IV DA and *Melnychenko v Ukraine* 2004-X; 42 EHRR 784 para 56). See also *Doyle v UK* No 30158/06 hudoc (2006) DA.

[69] *Hirst v UK (No 2).*   [70] *Hirst v UK (No 2).*

and Giakoumopoulos v Greece[71] concerned two Greek citizens, living and working in Strasbourg—as employees of the Council of Europe—and wishing to cast votes in a general election in Greece. That country's constitution contains a commitment to the principle of the continued enjoyment of voting rights by overseas citizens, but leaves the matter to be regulated by statute. No statute has been passed, despite this authority to legislate being first incorporated into the constitution in 1975. Negotiating the sort of political compromise needed to produce such legislation has so far proved impossible. The issue is a pressing and contentious one as Greece has a huge diaspora (3.7 million people, compared with 11 million living in Greece).[72] Making statutory provision to facilitate practically the exercise of the theoretical voting rights enjoyed as a matter of constitutional law by citizens abroad would therefore have a potentially dramatic impact on the electoral landscape within Greece. In the absence of statutory provision enabling them to vote in their state of residence, the applicants only option to avoid *de facto* disenfranchisement was to travel home to Greece to cast their ballots. They argued that this constituted a disproportionate interference with their right to vote. The question for the Grand Chamber was whether it was a breach of Article 3 that Greek election statutes made no provision for voters overseas to vote from their place of residence. The principle of expatriate enfranchisement is conceded by the Greek constitution: did this require, too, that the state mandate absent voting to give practical effect to the rights? The Grand Chamber, reversing the decision of the Chamber, gave a unanimously negative answer to this question: states are under no obligation to enable citizens living abroad to exercise their right to vote.[73] The Court remained unconvinced that 'the disruption to the applicants' financial, family and professional lives...caused had they had to travel to Greece to exercise their right to vote would have been disproportionate to the point of impairing the very essence of the voting rights in question'. Although this decision is understandable in light of the margin afforded to states to make provision for voting facilities, the lack of European consensus on this matter, and the special sensitivity of the matter to Greece, it is disappointing that the unanimous ruling does not acknowledge—as the Chamber judgment did—the crippling impact on voting rights that the lack of absent voting facilities may have on expatriates unable to afford to travel to Greece to vote.[74] Where, as in this case, voting rights are granted by a constitution, the human right to vote offered by Article 3 ought to protect indigent expatriates who cannot afford to travel to vote. The Court would certainly not endorse a state law conditioning voting rights on payment of a fee nor, for example, would it condone election rules requiring rural inhabitants to pay to travel to a distant city to vote. Yet the *Sitaropoulos* ruling tolerates a comparable burdening of the voting rights of expatriates, at least in cases where the constitution conferring those rights merely authorizes but does not require legislative action to facilitate their exercise.

Expatriate voting rights were before the Court again in *Shindler v UK*,[75] a case concerning a challenge to the fifteen-year time limit on the enjoyment of voting rights by UK citizens living abroad. The applicant, a World War II veteran domiciled in Italy since 1982, when he retired there with his Italian wife, argued that the legislation depriving him of the right to vote in parliamentary elections after fifteen years' absence from the UK violated Article 3. The Court reviewed the practice across Europe, noting the various

[71] ECHR 2012; 56 EHRR 9 GC.   [72] *Sitaropoulos and Giakoumopoulos v Greece*, para 56.

[73] *Sitaropoulos and Giakoumopoulos v Greece*, para 75.

[74] See the Chamber judgment *Sitaropoulous and Others v Greece* hudoc (2010) para 43.

[75] Hudoc (2013). Cf *Doyle v UK No 30158/06* hudoc (2006) DA declaring inadmissible a similar complaint about the fifteen-year time bar on overseas voting rights.

models employed, ranged on a spectrum from deprivation of all voting rights, through measures permitting limited retention of rights by temporary absentees, to laws granting continuing and unlimited expatriate entitlement to vote.[76] The Court observed a clear trend across Council of Europe states in favour of allowing voting by non-residents.[77] Acknowledging that this was 'significant', the Court nonetheless concluded that 'the legislative trends are not sufficient to establish the existence of any common European approach concerning voting rights of non-residents'.[78] The Court supported this claim by referring to the Grand Chamber ruling in *Sitaropoulos* (mentioned earlier), and its observations in that case that there is no consensus within states offering expatriate voting rights about how the exercise of those rights should be facilitated. In *Shindler*, the Court supports its conclusion that expatriate voting rights may, consistently with Article 3, be time-limited by leaning on the absence of a European consensus on the provision of mechanisms facilitating the exercise of expatriate voting rights. But that is, as the *Sitaropoulos* judgment is at pains to stress, a distinct issue. The fact that there is no European consensus about how expatriates should exercise any rights to vote their home states may choose to grant (in person or by post or proxy) is irrelevant to the core question of how far, if at all, Article 3 should be read by the Court as extending to govern state choices about the prior decision to grant, restrict, or remove the right to vote from non-residents. In this respect its judgments in both *Sitaropoulos* and *Shindler* are disappointing: they offer a doctrine importing a very minimal supervision of state choices to limit the voting rights and opportunities of non-residents, and lack the sort of robust scrutiny of the relevant principles and arguments that the issue merits. Although in *Shindler*, the UK government had not expressly identified the purpose of the restriction, the Court deemed it to pursue 'the legitimate aim of confining the parliamentary franchise to those citizens with a close connection with the United Kingdom and who would be most directly affected by its laws'.[79] It is striking that the Court was willing to attribute, of its own motion, such a justifying purpose to the interference with voting rights. Given the significance of the rights at stake, it is regrettable that the Court did not insist that the UK government offer and defend its own specification of the aims asserted to justify limiting them.[80] Observing that fifteen years is 'not an unsubstantial period of time',[81] the *Shindler* Court approved the law as serving 'to promote legal certainty', especially given the 'significant burden which would be imposed if the respondent state were required to ascertain in every application to vote by a non-resident whether the individual had a sufficiently close connection to the country'.[82] The Court in *Shindler* noticed approvingly the legislative scrutiny given to this issue over a number of years, and that the law remained under review by the UK government.[83] These facts supported its conclusion that the fifteen-year cut-off point was within the government's margin of appreciation and proportionate to its hypothesized aim.

---

[76] *Shindler v UK*, paras 72–6.   [77] *Shindler v UK*, para 114.   [78] *Shindler v UK*, para 115.

[79] *Shindler v UK*, para 107, accepting the formulation of state aim advanced successfully as a justification by the UK government in domestic judicial review proceedings challenging the compatibility of the fifteen-year time-bar with EU law protections of freedom of movement: *Preston v Wandsworth Borough Council and Lord President of the Council* [2011] EWHC 3174 (Admin) and [2012] EWCA Civ 1378.

[80] The concurring opinion of Judge Kalaydjieva is critical of the Court's adoption, *proprio motu*, of a legitimate aim not specified by the UK government, and observes—correctly—that 'the grounds on which the majority found the restriction to be proportionate to an unknown aim remain unclear'.

[81] *Shindler v UK*, para 116.   [82] *Shindler v UK*, para 116.

[83] *Shindler v UK*, para 117, observing that 'there is…extensive evidence before the Court to demonstrate that Parliament has sought to weigh the competing interests and to assess the proportionality of the fifteen-year rule'.

II. DISENFRANCHISEMENT: PRISONER VOTING BANS AND OTHER DISQUALIFICATIONS

There is as yet no common European consensus on the question of how much inclusivity a state's franchise law ought to demonstrate to, for example, convicted prisoners, or persons with a mental incapacity. The matters are sensitive ones: claims concerning prisoner voting rights in particular have challenged the Court to reason to solutions sensitive to the acute political disagreements within some states on this question.[84] The marked lack of legal consensus across Council of Europe states on such questions has caused further difficulties for the Court, as it seeks to avoid rulings that prescribe common franchise principles for which there is no cross-democracy consensus. The resulting jurisprudence does provide, however, some brightline rules regarding the limits of a state's freedom to withdraw or withhold voting rights, whether temporarily or permanently.

A core principle concerning the compatibility of any disenfranchisement with Article 3 is that a state may not fence out of the electorate a 'cluster' of people on a randomized or unprincipled basis, such as, for example, where they happen to live within the territory for which the state is responsible for organizing elections.[85] The Court has repeatedly stressed that 'the exclusion of any groups or categories of the general population must accordingly be reconcilable with the underlying purposes of Article 3'.[86] Those purposes centre on the maintenance of an effective political democracy based on universal suffrage and 'the free expression of the opinion of the people in the choice of the legislature'. This recitation of the text of Article 3, commonly quoted by the Court, adds little doctrinally to its analysis: such language invokes the collective right of 'the people' as if it were a settled and fixed political institution, its composition agreed consensually, when that is the very matter being challenged by applicants seeking admission to the electorate. Perhaps this rather oracular language permits the Court to tread sensitively around the parameters of states' political and legislative decisions about disenfranchisement. Very few of its resultant judgments police prescriptively the boundaries of acceptable democratic descriptions of 'the people' by declaring certain types of disenfranchisement wholly illegitimate. A rare example is provided by the case law involving rules stripping bankrupts of the right to vote. These have been held to serve no purpose but to belittle those so disenfranchised. This is an illegitimate aim, and such laws thus violate Article 3.[87] All of the Court's other disenfranchisement decisions turn on arguments about the disproportionality of the restrictions.[88] So, for example, a state may, consistently with Article 3, deny the right to vote to electors with a mental incapacity. The Court considered such laws, still commonplace in democracies, for the first time in *Alajos Kiss v Hungary*,[89] holding that they do serve a legitimate aim. This is 'ensuring that only citizens capable of assessing the consequences of their decisions and making conscious and

---

[84] The leading cases are *Hirst v UK (No 2)* 2005-IX; 42 EHRR 849 GC; and *Scoppola v Italy (No 3)* hudoc (2012); 56 EHRR 19 GC, discussed later in this chapter. See too Fredman, PL 292 (2013); Briant, 70 Camb LJ 279 (2011).

[85] *Matthews v UK* 1999-I; 28 EHRR 361 GC; *Aziz v Cyprus* 2004-V; 41 EHRR 164.

[86] *Hirst v UK (No 2)* 2005-IX; 42 EHRR 849 para 62 GC (citing *Aziz v Cyprus* 2004-V; 41 EHRR 164 para 28).

[87] See, eg, *Vincenzo Taiani v Italy* hudoc (2006); *Chiumiento v Italy* hudoc (2006); *La Frazia v Italy* hudoc (2006); *Vertucci v Italy* hudoc (2006); *Campagnano v Italy* 2006-IV.

[88] For example, disenfranchisements of those with known criminal (Mafia) associations have been declared to violate Article 3 owing to the disproportionate nature of the restrictions. States are free to devise more proportionate laws conditioning electoral rights upon the absence of criminal contacts: *Labita v Italy* 2000-IV; 46 EHRR 1228 GC; *Vito Sante Santoro v Italy* 2004-VI.

[89] *No 38832/06* hudoc (2010).

judicious decisions should participate in public affairs'.[90] The Hungarian constitution disenfranchised any person subject to measures of guardianship, irrespective of their actual capacity to make political decisions. The Court adjudged this to be disproportionate: state legislatures must provide some means of tailoring such disenfranchisements to ensure that only the most severely mentally disabled are subject to the loss of voting rights.[91] In this case the Court also announced the principle that Article 3 claims involving the fundamental rights of vulnerable groups which have been subject historically to discrimination—such as those based on race, sex, or sexual orientation—generate a 'substantially' narrower margin of appreciation.[92] Likewise, the treatment as a single class of people with intellectual or mental disabilities is a 'questionable classification' requiring strict scrutiny of the challenged measure.[93] Such groups 'were historically subject to prejudice with lasting consequences, resulting in their social exclusion. Such prejudice may entail legislative stereotyping which prohibits the individualised evaluation of their capacities and needs'. States may still, consistently with Article 3, disenfranchise on the basis of mental incapacity, but need to demonstrate considerably more refinement than Hungary did in the legislative instruments they design to do so; and to show that the resultant law was the object of measured political reflection by legislators.[94]

The leading cases on prisoner disenfranchisement are *Hirst v UK (No 2)*[95] and *Scoppola v Italy (No 3)*.[96] Both are Grand Chamber judgments, the applicants in each serving life sentences for manslaughter and murder respectively. *Hirst* concerned the UK statute disenfranchising all convicted prisoners irrespective of the length of their sentence or nature of their crime. The Grand Chamber found a violation of Article 3. The critical weakness of the challenged law was that it effected a blanket removal of voting rights regardless of the seriousness of the offence committed or the length of sentence imposed. The Court's clear position is that 'such a general, automatic and indiscriminate restriction on a vitally important Convention right must be seen as falling outside any acceptable margin of appreciation'.[97] Further, 'the principle of proportionality require[d] a discernible and sufficient link between the sanction and the conduct and circumstances of the individual concerned'.[98] The Court recognized that prisoner disenfranchisement laws may serve legitimate aims. Those were described by the UK government as being connected to enhancing civic responsibility and respect for the rule of law; and imposing an ancillary punishment on offenders. The Grand Chamber endorsed those objectives, albeit rather unenthusiastically.[99]

As the Court's judgment indicates, there is no European consensus on the matter of prisoner disenfranchisement; and some states maintain bans more severe than that of the UK, where voting rights revive upon release from prison. Italy, the respondent state in

---

[90] *Alajos Kiss v Hungary*, para 38. This was the respondent state's formulation, and was accepted by the applicant.
[91] *Alajos Kiss v Hungary*, para 41. For example, by providing for individualized judicial determinations of capacity to vote (para 44).   [92] *Alajos Kiss v Hungary*, para 42.
[93] *Alajos Kiss v Hungary*, para 44.
[94] In this case there was 'no evidence that Hungarian legislature had ever sought to weigh the competing interests or to assess the proportionality of the restriction as it stands'; *Alajos Kiss v Hungary*, para 41.
[95] 2005-IX; 42 EHRR 849 GC. See Lewis, 209 PL (2006) and Easton, 69 MLR 443 (2006).
[96] Hudoc (2012) ; 56 EHRR 19 GC.
[97] *Hirst v UK (No 2)* 2005-IX; 42 EHRR 849 para 82 GC. In *Anchugov and Gladkov v Russia* hudoc (2013), the Court rejected an attempt by Russia to argue that locating a prisoner voting ban in the text of the constitution immunizes it from challenge under Article 3: a blanket disenfranchisement of all convicted prisoners was found to violate Article 3, applying the principles of *Hirst*.   [98] *Hirst v UK (No 2)*, para 71.
[99] *Hirst v UK (No 2)*, para 75.

the *Scoppola* case, maintains laws permanently disenfranchising offenders sentenced to more than five years' imprisonment; those sentenced to between three and five years are barred from voting for five years.[100] Scoppola was permanently disenfranchised by these provisions, and challenged them, employing the *Hirst* principles to argue that the Italian provisions constituted just the sort of general, automatic, indiscriminate ban condemned in *Hirst*. The Chamber judgment agreed, and ruled that Article 3 had been violated. The Grand Chamber, however, ruled that there had been no violation. It considered first whether it should confirm the principles established in *Hirst*. The UK Attorney General, as third-party intervener, had argued that the Grand Chamber should retract them and gift to states a margin to disenfranchise prisoners in any manner that was not manifestly arbitrary, such as, for example, attaching the loss of rights to any offending deemed serious enough to warrant a prison term.[101] The Grand Chamber declined to re-examine the *Hirst* principles, finding no developments at European or Convention level since that case to justify revisiting it.[102] It reiterated the proscription on any general, automatic, and indiscriminate disenfranchisement (a rule applicable to prisoners or to any other group), condemning as incompatible with Article 3 any laws 'based solely on the fact that they are serving a prison sentence, irrespective of the length of the sentence and irrespective of the nature or gravity of their offence and their individual circumstances'.[103]

The *Hirst* judgment offered states little guidance about framing prisoner disenfranchisement laws compatible with Article 3. The Grand Chamber in *Scoppola* took the opportunity to elaborate some. In particular, the Court considered and rejected the principle that the decision to disenfranchise prisoners needs to be taken by a court in order to be compatible with Article 3.[104] However, the use of such particularized judicial determinations 'is in principle likely to guarantee the proportionality of restrictions on prisoners' voting rights'.[105] Where this feature is absent, the law may instead supply the required element of proportionality by making disenfranchisement 'conditional on such factors as the nature or gravity of the offence committed'.[106]

Turning to Scoppola's case, the Court considered that Italy's legal scheme demonstrated the legislature's 'concern to adjust the application of the measure to the particular circumstances of the case ... taking into account such factors as the gravity of the offence

---

[100] *Scoppola v Italy (No 3)* hudoc (2012); 56 EHRR 19 paras 34-36 GC. The disenfranchisement is governed by a presidential decree which correlates the bar to a provision in the criminal code disqualifying such offenders from holding public office.

[101] The failure of the UK to amend its prisoner voting ban to comply with the *Hirst* judgment has placed the Convention's mechanisms under a degree of institutional stress: see *Firth and 2,353 Others v UK No 47784/09* hudoc (2013), adjourning consideration of pending cases while the draft Bill amending the law proceeds through the UK parliamentary process. See too *Greens and MT v UK* hudoc (2010).

[102] *Scoppola v Italy (No 3)*, para 95; and observing there that the European trend, if any, is towards a liberalization of restrictions on prisoners' voting rights.

[103] *Scoppola v Italy (No 3)*, para 96. The *Scoppola* principles were applied in *Cucu v Romania* hudoc (2012), in which a law performing an automatic disenfranchisement of prisoners was found to violate Article 3. See too *Calmanovici v Romania* hudoc (2008).

[104] This aspect of the *Scoppola* judgment, expressed in paras 97–102, overrules *Frodl v Austria* hudoc (2010), a Chamber judgment in which the Court (para 35) read into the *Hirst* judgment a stipulation that a Convention-compatible regime for disenfranchising prisoners contain some mechanism for particularized assessment of each prisoner's case by a judge. The Chamber judgment in *Scoppola* relied upon this aspect of the *Frodl* judgment in its ruling that Italy's law, lacking individualized judicial determinations, breached Article 3.   [105] *Scoppola v Italy (No 3)* hudoc (2012); 56 EHRR 19 para 99 GC.

[106] *Scoppola v Italy (No 3)*, although limiting disenfranchisement to offenders whose crimes were committed with intent was regarded by the Court as an insufficiently precise manner of achieiving proportionality in *Söyler v Turkey* hudoc (2013).

committed and the conduct of the offender'. The judgment describes the rule disenfranchising those sentenced to terms of more than three years as tying, proportionately, the loss of the right to vote to 'offences which the courts consider to warrant a particularly harsh sentence'.[107] It approved, too, of the sliding scale according to which only sentences of more than five years attracted permanent disenfranchisement.[108] In this respect it was determinative for the Court that Italian law contains provision for the formal rehabilitation of offenders. If successful in seeking this discretionary status, a prisoner regains the right to vote: 'In the Court's opinion this possibility shows that the Italian system is not excessively rigid.'[109]

There was a single dissent in *Scoppola*. Judge Thór Björgvinsson wrote of his regret that the Court 'has now stripped the *Hirst* judgment of all its bite as a landmark precedent for the protection of prisoners' voting rights in Europe'. This is so, he argues convincingly, because the Italian ban endorsed by the Grand Chamber is indistinguishable in principle from the UK law condemned in *Hirst*. It is 'just as blunt...albeit for slightly different reasons', in that it effects a permanent ban for those unsuccessful in seeking rehabilitation or ineligible to do so. The Grand Chamber judgment in *Scoppola* does seem to represent, as the dissent contends, ' a retreat from the main arguments advanced [in *Hirst*]'. It is arguably incoherent doctrinally for the Court to announce that blanket bans on voting by all convicted prisoners confined to the period of their sentences violate Article 3 but potentially permanent bans on some prisoners do not. The latter is saved in *Scoppola* only by the rather unpredictable and potentially remote possibility of reacquiring the rights through rehabilitation, whereas the former system failed to satisfy the Court despite containing a guaranteed mechanism for the automatic restoration of rights to all prisoners upon their release. The Italian law, tying permanent disenfranchisement to a minimum sentence period of five years, is not in the Court's view, indiscriminate, although its proportionality analysis of this feature of the law is perfunctory and ultimately unconvincing.[110]

The Italian law at issue in *Scoppola* tied the loss of voting rights to the disqualification of prisoners from holding public office. The disenfranchisement is part of a generalized loss of both voting and candidacy rights.[111] The Court's other case law establishes that the latter rights may be more heavily limited by states than the right to vote.[112] It should arguably follow that the Court ought to treat with heightened suspicion rules that disenfranchise any group, including prisoners, in pursuance of a broader policy presented primarily as being concerned with withdrawing candidacy rights. The integrated ban on voting and standing for office operated by Italian law makes disenfranchisement contingent on the basis of a person's loss of a related—and weaker—Convention right, namely to stand for office.[113] This method of disenfranchisement is thus arguably 'general, automatic and indiscriminate' in the sense that it captures all persons (in this case, convicted prisoners) subject to the law's relevant prohibition on standing for office. This argument was not put to the Court, which observed the derivative nature of the disenfranchising measure—as an ancillary consequence of the loss of the right to stand—but did not attach any doctrinal weight to this in its analysis of the compatibility of the measure with Article 3.

It is disappointing that the Court did not give more careful and critical scrutiny in either *Hirst* or *Scoppola* to the manner in which prisoner voting bans are argued to serve

---

[107] *Scoppola v Italy (No 3)*, para 106.   [108] *Scoppola v Italy (No 3)*, para 106.
[109] *Scoppola v Italy (No 3)*, para 109.   [110] *Scoppola v Italy (No 3)*, paras 105–8.
[111] *Scoppola v Italy (No 3)*, para 36.   [112] See section 3.
[113] As the dissent observes 'there is not necessarily any link between the right of an individual to hold public office and his right to vote in general elections'.

the sorts of aims asserted in their defence. These have been at best vaguely specified and poorly substantiated by states defending prisoner voting laws.[114] The Court's decision effectively to take on trust the legitimacy of the goals states assert for disenfranchising prisoners, and to default instead to proportionality analysis, is understandable given the acute political sensitivity of the question within many Council of Europe states. The Court's judgments on the issue provide rather cautious critiques of the practice. As further litigation follows, the Court will perhaps find an occasion to revisit and refine its reasons for regarding prisoner disenfranchisement as compatible with Convention law.[115]

5. THE RIGHT TO STAND FOR ELECTION

The passive aspect of the electoral rights protects the right to stand as a candidate and, if elected, to sit as a member of parliament.[116] These rights are intertwined with those of voters, as the availability of a plurality of candidates is necessary to preserve the 'free expression of the opinion of the people' as Article 3 requires. Candidacy rights are, however, subject to a potentially wider range of restrictions than voting rights. This is because, as the Court observes, each state has an 'incontestably legitimate' interest in ensuring 'the normal functioning of its own institutional system', especially its national parliament 'which is vested with legislative power and plays a primordial role in a democratic State'.[117] The Court is concerned to minimize its interventions into state law in this sphere. Hence it repeatedly emphasizes that contracting states enjoy considerable latitude in establishing constitutional rules on the status of members of parliament, including criteria governing eligibility to stand for election.[118]

In the 2009 Grand Chamber decision of *Sejdić and Finci v Bosnia and Herzegovina*,[119] the Court issued a highly controversial judgment involving the carefully crafted electoral arrangements made in that state as part of the Dayton Peace Accords of 1995.[120] In this ruling the Grand Chamber declared that the election rules prohibiting people of Roma and Jewish origin from standing for election to the House of Peoples and the Presidency of Bosnia and Herzegovina violated the protections against discrimination in the enjoyment of electoral rights provided by Articles 14 and Protocol 12.[121] This was contested vigorously by Judge Bonello in a scathing dissent. He condemned the majority for disrupting the arrangements designed to create checks and balances and promote the 'precarious

---

[114] The Grand Chamber judgment in *Scoppola* endorsed a further aim regarding the 'proper functioning and preservation of the democratic regime': paras 91–2. The dissent in that case correctly criticizies the Court for failing to indicate how prisoner voting bans promote this aim. See also *Anchugov and Gladkov v Russia* hudoc (2013) paras 88–90 and 102, elaborating (unsubstantiated) additional state aims connected to fears tht prisoners' votes would be 'negatively influenced by leaders of the criminal underworld' and flawed by a lack of political or campaign information. The Court (para 102) preferred to rely on the state's other asserted aims: 'enhancing civic responsibility and respect for the rule of law; and ensuring the proper functioning and preservation of civil society and the democratic regime'.

[115] It has recently rejected an attempt by Russia to argue that locating a prisoner voting ban in the text of the constitution immunizes it from challenge under Article 3: *Anchugov and Gladkov v Russia* hudoc (2013): the blanket ban on all convicted prisoners voting was found to violate Article 3, applying the principles of *Hirst*.   [116] See *Sadak and Others v Turkey (No 2)* 2002-IV; 36 EHRR 396 para 33.

[117] *Russian Conservative Party of Entrepreneurs and Others v Russia* hudoc (2007); 46 EHRR 863 para 62.

[118] See also *Podkolzina v Latvia* 2002-II para 33 and *Gitonas and Others v Greece* 1997-IV; 26 EHRR 691 para 39.   [119] 2009- GC. On Protocol 12, see Ch 18.

[120] See Claridge, 1 EHRLR 82 (2011); Milanovic, 104 Am J Int Law 636 (2010).

[121] *Sejdić and Finci v Bosnia and Herzegovina* 2009- paras 38–56 GC.

equilibrium that was laboriously reached' in the aftermath of the violent conflict.[122] It is difficult to resist his conclusion that the Grand Chamber in this case took an overly decontextualized approach to its reading of the relationship between the electoral rights and the non-discrimination guarantees of the Convention. While on its face, any law denying the right to stand on the basis of ethnicity seems clearly to violate Convention norms, the uniquely sensitive and fragile post-conflict political process in Bosnia and Herzegovina, of which these election laws formed part, arguably did deserve a degree of special deference that the Grand Chamber ruling was unwilling to afford it.[123]

I. CANDIDACY LAWS: AGE, CITIZENSHIP, AND RESIDENCE

The right to stand as a candidate may be limited on grounds of residence, citizenship, and age.[124] *Melnychenko v Ukraine*[125] concerned legislation establishing a minimum residence requirement[126] of five years as a condition on the right to stand. Melnychenko was unable to comply with this as he was seeking political asylum in the United States. The Court, deferring to the emergent democracy's choice to set the bar at five years, accepted that this lengthy period might be 'appropriate to enable candidates to acquire sufficient knowledge of the issues associated with the national parliament's tasks'[127] and so pursued a legitimate aim. This is a questionable premise, as any reasonably politically aware resident could surely acquire the relevant political knowledge in a much shorter time. Melnychenko's claim succeeded nonetheless: the Court considered that, given his peculiar circumstances, insistence upon continuous residence in Ukraine amounted to an arbitrary application of the law; Article 3 had been breached in this case because the residence law had been applied to him in a way that breached the principle that election law contain sufficient safeguards against such arbitrary decisions.[128] Protection against such arbitrariness is necessary to protect the general principle of Convention law that rights be 'not just theoretical or illusory but practical and effective'.[129] Melnychenko had sought asylum abroad due to fears of persecution. The Court observed that 'if he had stayed in Ukraine his personal safety or physical integrity may have been seriously endangered, rendering the exercise of any political rights impossible, whereas, in leaving the country, he was also prevented from exercising such rights'.[130] In light of those considerations, the Court considered that the Ukrainian authorities' refusal to register him as a candidate, although he maintained a residence in Ukraine and remained connected with politics there, constituted a violation of Article 3.

Dual nationality laws may impact on candidacy rights in a manner contestable under Article 3. The Grand Chamber judgment in *Tănase v Moldova*[131] concerned a

---

[122] See too the partly concurring and partly dissenting opinion of Judge Mijovic, joined by Judge Hajiyev, arguing that 'the Grand Chamber has failed to analyze both the historical background and the circumstances in which the Bosnia and Herzegovina Constitution was imposed'.

[123] See McCrudden and O'Leary, 24 EJIL 477 (2013).

[124] No challenges have been brought to age limits for standing for election. The Court's doctrine impliedly tolerates the imposition of higher age limits for candidates than for voters (a practice adopted in several states) as part of its broader principle that the passive rights may be more heavily burdened than voting rights. For an argument that this practice violates Article 3, see Emilianides, 5 EHRLR 670 (2009).

[125] 2004-X; 42 EHRR 784.

[126] On the broad acceptability of this see *Melnychenko v Ukraine*, para 56.

[127] *Melnychenko v Ukraine*, para 57.

[128] Judge Loucaides, dissenting, did not think it was arbitrary, and was critical of the weight given by the Court's judgment to the political circumstances.   [129] *Melnychenko v Ukraine*, para 59.

[130] *Melnychenko v Ukraine*, para 65.   [131] 2010-; 53 EHRR 22 GC.

law prohibiting dual nationals from becoming MPs. Moldova, a former Soviet republic, achieved independence in 1991. In 2002 it repealed a bar on Moldovans holding dual nationality. Tănase, a Moldovan citizen and opposition politician, then acquired Romanian nationality. In 2008 the government introduced changes to election law to require that candidates having dual nationality declare that when registering to stand. If successful in the election, the law required them to initiate steps to renounce their additional nationality in order to take up their seat in the legislature. Two general elections were held in 2009. In the first, twenty-one of 101 MPs elected held or were acquiring a second nationality, and were thus potentially barred from sitting in parliament. All twenty-one, including Tănase, were opposition MPs. Re-elected in the second poll that year, he was able to take his seat only after producing documents to prove he was in the process of renouncing his Romanian nationality. He argued that the law interfered with his rights to stand for election, and to sit in the legislature if elected. The Grand Chamber, agreeing with the Chamber ruling, found a violation of Article 3. The state asserted that the restriction served the legitimate aim of ensuring loyalty to the Moldovan state, by preventing people with potentially conflicting aspirations connected to their other nationality from sitting in parliament. The Grand Chamber was suspicious of the state's claim that the aim of the law was to sponsor loyalty to the state. Its judgment elaborates the need for care to distinguish such an aim, which it concedes is legitimate, from the goal of securing loyalty to a government, which is an aim inconsistent with pluralism and the proper functioning of democracy.[132] The Court noted that the bar was introduced as part of a package of electoral reforms that combined to substantially disadvantage opposition parties.[133] Leaving open the question whether the restriction did pursue the legitimate aim regarding state loyalty, the Grand Chamber proceeded to a proportionality analysis, which concluded in a finding that Article 3 had been violated.[134] This was based on a number of factors. First, the Court noted that there is a European consensus that where dual nationality is permitted by state law, dual nationals ought not to be deemed ineligible to sit in parliament:[135] 'However, notwithstanding this consensus, a different approach may be justified where special historical or political considerations exist which render a more restrictive practice necessary.'[136] Moldova has an unusually high proportion of dual nationals, a population subject to increase as Moldovans make use of rights to acquire citizenship of neighbouring Romania. It would therefore, the Court thinks, have been justified for Moldova to maintain a bar on dual nationals sitting in its parliament at the time of its first gaining independence in 1991. But 'with the passage of time, general restrictions on electoral rights become more difficult to justify'.[137] This ban was not put in place until seventeen years after independence, and five years after the state had relaxed its laws to allow dual citizenship.[138] Given its negative impact on the electoral prospects of opposition candidates, and on the right of dual citizens to be represented by people sharing their national affiliations and concerns,[139] the unanimous Grand Chamber

---

[132] *Tănase v Moldova*, paras 166–7.

[133] These included increasing the threshold for representation in parliament from 4 to 6% and a ban on electoral blocs or alliances between minority (opposition) parties.

[134] The Chamber ruling accepted that the law did serve the legitimate aim of protecting loyalty, but found that other means, such as the use of oaths for representatives, could achieve this: *Tănase and Chirtoacă v Moldova* hudoc (2008).

[135] *Tănase v Moldova*, para 172.   [136] *Tănase v Moldova*, para 172.

[137] *Tănase v Moldova*, para 175, citing *Ādamsons v Latvia* hudoc (2008).

[138] *Tănase v Moldova*, para 174.   [139] *Tănase v Moldova*, para 174.

found it to be a disproportionate interference with rights to stand and to sit.[140] This conclusion was supported also by the fact that the rule had been introduced shortly before elections, at a time when the governing party's share of the vote was in decline.[141] A vital broader principle emerging from the *Tǎnase* judgment is the Court's commitment to 'examine with particular care any measure which appears to operate solely, or principally, to the disadvantage of the opposition, especially where the nature of the measure is such that it affects the very prospect of opposition parties gaining power at some point in the future'.[142]

II. LEGAL DISQUALIFICATION OF REGISTERED CANDIDATES

Where a state seeks to disqualify a registered candidate on the basis of misconduct during election campaigning, proper process must be followed to ensure that the candidate is not arbitrarily deprived of the right to stand.[143] This proposition has been articulated in a number of cases brought following the 2005 general election in Azerbaijan.[144] These applications concerned claims of lack of procedural safeguards in the process for disqualifying candidates alleged to have been engaged in bribery of voters and other offences. All succeeded before the Court, its judgments making explicit the principle that Article 3 protects 'the right to effectively stand for election',[145] which implies safeguards against arbitrary disqualification by domestic authorities responding to allegations of electoral wrongdoing. A state may of course maintain laws excluding from candidacy people who seek to subvert the election process by fraudulent or other unethical means. The Court endorsed the relevant measures of Azerbaijan election law as pursuing 'the legitimate aim of ensuring fair and equal conditions for all candidates in an electoral campaign and protecting free expression of the opinion of the people in elections',[146] and 'ensuring that elections are held in accordance with democratic standards'.[147] In each case, however, the domestic authorities had failed to provide sufficient procedural safeguards for the candidates by, for example, failing to give them the opportunity to be heard before the electoral commission charged with determining the disqualification.[148] The Court ruled that 'relevant domestic procedures should contain sufficient safeguards protecting the candidates from abusive and unsubstantiated allegations of electoral misconduct and…decisions on disqualification should be based on sound, relevant and sufficient proof of such misconduct'.[149] Courts must also provide sufficient reasons for their decisions to endorse the disqualification of candidates.[150] The principles set out in these cases are important as they effectively establish candidates' rights to a fair hearing prior to disqualification,

---

[140] Although technically a bar on sitting only, the Court accepted that it impacted indirectly on candidacy rights too, as campaign success might be limited by voters doubting the intention or commitment of a dual national to renounce his or her other nationality if elected; or putative candidates with dual nationality might be deterred from standing entirely due to the need to renounce.

[141] *Tǎnase v Moldova*, para 179.

[142] *Tǎnase v Moldova*, para 179.   [143] *Krasnov and Skuratov v Russia* hudoc (2007).

[144] *Abil v Azerbaijan* hudoc (2012); *Atakishi v Azerbaijan* hudoc (2012); *Khanhuseyn Aliyev v Azerbaijan* No 19554/06 hudoc (2012); *Orujov v Azerbaijan* No 4508/06 hudoc (2012).

[145] *Abil v Azerbaijan*, para 31.   [146] *Abil v Azerbaijan*, para 31.

[147] *Atakishi v Azerbaijan* hudoc (2012) para 38.   [148] *Abil v Azerbaijan* hudoc (2012) para 39.

[149] *Orujov v Azerbaijan* hudoc (2012) para 46. See also *Khanhuseyn Aliyev v Azerbaijan* hudoc (2012).

[150] *Orujov v Azerbaijan*, paras 57–8, criticizing the Azerbaijan Court of Appeal for failing to provide any reasoning in its decision, and its Supreme Court for failing to detect and rectify the procedural failings of the lower courts.

filling at least part of the gap created by the Court's repeated refusal to extend the reach of Article 6 to the electoral rights.[151]

Although the right to stand is an individual right, issues may arise concerning the rights of a political party to offer itself collectively to the electorate in a party list system. In *Russian Conservative Party of Entrepreneurs and Others v Russia*,[152] a political party challenged the rejection of its party list by the electoral authorities for reasons related to an untrue financial declaration made by one of the party members on that list. This resulted, under Russian law, in the rejection of the entire list, prejudicing the political party and the candidates on its list who were innocent of any error or electoral offence. The Court acknowledged that the state had a legitimate aim in maintaining rules which regarded the party list as an integrated whole, especially as voters tend to make choices based on the names of the most prominent politicians near the top of that list. But where, as here, the second named candidate on the list has been disqualified, the culpability—or lack thereof—of the remaining candidates and the political party itself for the error or offence causing that disqualification is, in the Court's view, relevant to the proportionality of the state's decision to block the entire list.[153] As both the party and the other candidates were blameless, and the party had no obligation under state law to verify the truthfulness of statements made by individual candidates, their loss of the right to stand through the withdrawal of the entire list constituted a disproportionate interference with their right to stand.[154]

III. OTHER CONTROLS ON CANDIDACY

a. Election deposits

Incongruously, deposit laws condition the human right to stand for election on the ability to pay to the state a sum of money it stipulates as a precondition of entering the democratic contest. This can impact especially on the electoral chances of minor parties, as forfeiture of deposits for poor election results becomes very costly if many seats are contested and lost. The Court, though, has held that deposit laws serve a legitimate aim, namely 'guaranteeing the right to effective, streamlined representation by enhancing the responsibility of those standing for election and confining elections to serious candidates, while avoiding the unreasonable outlay of public funds'.[155] A state may, then, employ a proportionate deposit law. *Sukhovetskyy v Ukraine*[156] considered the limits of this proportionality in a challenge to Ukraine's requirement that candidates pay a sum greater than the applicant's annual income, forfeited if the seat was not won. The Chamber unanimously accepted that this stringent law was proportionate. It was influenced to do so by evidence that close parliamentary and judicial scrutiny had been given to the law domestically.[157] The Court concluded that in practice it was not 'excessive or such as to constitute an impenetrable administrative or financial barrier for a determined candidate wishing to enter

---

[151] The applicants in each of the cases against Azerbaijan, cited in n 144, raised Article 6 in their claims. In each case the Court adhered to its doctrine that it does not apply to the electoral rights.

[152] Hudoc (2007); 46 EHRR 863.

[153] *Russian Conservative Party of Entrepreneurs and Others v Russia* hudoc (2007); 46 EHRR 863, para 65.

[154] *Russian Conservative Party of Entrepreneurs and Others v Russia*, para 65.

[155] *Russian Conservative Party of Entrepreneurs and Others v Russia*, para 62. See also the former Commission's decisions in *Tete v France* No 11123/84, 54 DR 52 (1987) and *Desmeules v France* No 12897/87, 67 DR 166 (1990).

[156] 2006-VI; 44 EHRR 1185.   [157] *Sukhovetskyy v Ukraine*, para 67.

the electoral race'.[158] Although not an insuperable obstacle, the judgment concedes that the law represents a significant hurdle necessitating considerable financial sacrifice. This is clear from the Court's remark that the applicant 'could have taken out a bank loan or mortgaged an apartment that he owned to raise the required amount, if he had any faith in being elected'.[159] It is regrettable that this case was not heard by the Grand Chamber. Deposit laws place a wealth or property-based restriction on the right to stand. The margin left to the states by this case is arguably too wide, especially given the uniqueness and sensitivity of the issue of conditioning the enjoyment of a human right on payment of money.

b. Bars on candidature of public and religious office holders

Many European states limit the candidature of individuals who hold certain public offices. This may take the form of bars on standing while employed in such a role, or a requirement to take a leave of absence while campaigning and to resign if elected. In *Gitonas v Greece*,[160] the Court endorsed the legitimate aim of such a law as being to ensure that 'candidates of different political persuasions enjoy equal means of influence (since holders of public office may on occasion have an unfair advantage over other candidates) and protect[ed] the electorate from pressure from such officials who, because of their position, are called upon to take many—and sometimes important—decisions and enjoy substantial prestige in the eyes of the ordinary citizen, whose choice of candidate might be influenced'.[161]

In *Seyidzade v Azerbaijan*,[162] the Court considered a constitutional rule concerning the candidature of 'clergymen', and found a violation of Article 3 on the basis of its broad and poorly specified formulation.[163] The law barred 'clergy' and people undertaking 'professional religious activities' from elected office. The Court considered that this loose definition, which lacked any further statutory specification, allowed an excessively wide discretion to the electoral authorities and thus left too much room for arbitrariness in applying the restriction. This was so given the existence of a large variety of religious denominations within the state, with distinct organizational structures resulting in potential for uncertainty about who could be classed as a 'clergyman' in respect of each.[164] As the Court reiterates here, the core principle that states must not impair the 'very essence' or 'effectiveness' of the electoral rights demands that in relevant cases the Court address directly arguments about the adequacy of the law complained of. In addition to assessing laws for their compatibility with the principles governing the legitimacy of aims and proportionality, the Court will also consider whether the challenged law meets minimum requirements of certainty, clarity, and foreseeability.[165]

---

[158] *Sukhovetskyy v Ukraine*, para 73.   [159] 2006-VI; 44 EHRR 1185 para 48.
[160] 1997-IV; 26 EHRR 691.
[161] *Gitonas v Greece*, para 40. See also *Ahmed v UK* 1998-VI; 29 EHRR 1 (no violation of Article 3 that local authority officers had to resign before standing in an election); and the Court's comment in *Lykourezos v Greece* 2006-VIII; 46 EHRR 74 para 53 that a blanket prohibition on practising any profession in order to stand was something which was 'rarely encountered in other European States'.
[162] Hudoc (2009).
[163] It was unclear from the law whether it prohibited clergy from standing for election, or instead required only that they give up religious office in order to sit in the legislature if elected; *Seyidzade v Azerbaijan*, paras 34–5.
[164] *Seyidzade v Azerbaijan*, para 36.   [165] See n 37 and text thereto.

c. Language proficiency laws

States may, consistently with Article 3, prescribe language proficiency requirements for candidates seeking election to the national legislature. *Podkolzina v Latvia*[166] concerned a law which required prospective parliamentary candidates from Latvia's Russian-speaking minority to demonstrate proficiency in the Latvian language. This was deemed to serve the 'incontestably' legitimate aim of ensuring that the legislature could function properly. More generally, the matter of the national parliament's working language was 'in principle one which the State alone has the power to make' since this was 'determined by historical and political considerations specific to each country'.[167] Nonetheless, in this case the candidate's passive right had been breached by the unfair manner in which the law had been applied to her.[168] The authorities' assessment of her qualifications and language skills had not complied with principles of procedural fairness and legal certainty.[169] In this case the Court again highlighted the importance of proper processes being in place to ensure that removal of the right to stand was not arbitrary.[170]

d. Prior political affiliation as a bar to standing for election

Emergent democracies may face challenges in regulating the electoral participation of adherents of prior and oppressive regimes. The leading Article 3 case of *Ždanoka v Latvia*[171] is a Grand Chamber judgment involving this issue. Ždanoka sought to stand in parliamentary elections in 1998 and 2002 and was denied the right on the basis of her former involvement with the communist party. This pertained to events in 1991, the year of a failed coup which had threatened Latvia's early days as a democracy. The bar affecting her was enacted in 1995, and disqualified those who had 'actively participated' in the communist party after 1991 from standing. She retained legal rights to participate in other areas of Latvian democracy, which she exercised, being elected as a city councilor and as an MEP. The controls on standing for the national legislature were regarded by the Court as legitimate in principle. The legislation was not intended to punish; it was passed to 'protect the integrity of the democratic process by excluding from participation in the work of a democratic legislature those individuals who had taken an active and leading role in a party which was directly linked to the attempted violent overthrow of the newly-established democratic regime'.[172]

Turning to assess proportionality, the Grand Chamber announced that Article 3 did not require that the domestic authorities adjudicate separately on the entitlement of each aspiring candidate potentially affected by the disqualification law.[173] It was sufficient that the domestic courts establish 'whether a particular individual belongs to the impugned statutory category or group'. The critical issue remained whether the 'the statutory distinction itself [was] proportionate and not discriminatory as regards the whole category or group specified in the legislation'.[174] Applying these general tests, the Court noted that

---

[166] 2002-II. See F Hoffmeister, 97(3) Am J Int Law 664–9 (2003).

[167] *Podkolzina v Latvia*, para 34.   [168] *Podkolzina v Latvia*, para 36.

[169] *Podkolzina v Latvia*.   [170] *Podkolzina v Latvia*, para 35.

[171] 2006-IV; 45 EHRR 478 GC. See E Brems, 5 Int J Transitional Justice 282 (2011) , at 295–8.

[172] *Ždanoka v Latvia*, para 122.

[173] *Ždanoka v Latvia*, para 114. See also paras 115(d) and 125. The general principle was that, 'as long as the statutory distinction itself is proportionate and not discriminatory as regards the whole category or group specified in the legislation, the task of the domestic courts may be limited to establishing whether a particular individual belongs to the impugned statutory category or group' at para 114. There was no requirement, then, of 'individualization', for the right to stand under Article 3, at least in this case.

[174] *Ždanoka v Latvia*, para 144.

the ban applied only to those who had 'actively participated' in the communist party and not to its whole membership or support. This rendered it sufficiently precise.[175] Further, the ban was reasonably applied to Ždanoka, who had benefited from opportunities for satisfactory domestic judicial review of its extension to her.[176] The Grand Chamber therefore deemed the bar on standing acceptable under Article 3, notwithstanding Ždanoka's continued disqualification from candidature in 2006 (the year of judgment), some fifteen years on from the events of 1991.

Although the Court declined to find a violation of Article 3, it did effectively condemn the Latvian law as unsatisfactory and urged its imminent reform. The provisions that had been applied to Ždanoka, the Court made clear, would have been unacceptable if maintained by an established democracy.[177] Latvia had been granted special latitude in this case because of the country's 'very special historico-political context'.[178] Noting the 'greater stability which Latvia now enjoys, *inter alia*, by reason of its full European integration [ie membership of the EU]',[179] the Court issued a warning to the Latvian Parliament to 'keep the statutory restriction under constant review, with a view to bringing it to an early end'; failure to 'take active steps in this connection [could] result in a different finding by the Court' in the future.[180] This was not enough to placate four dissenting judges[181] who all considered, in effect, that the point had come to condemn the restrictions imposed on Ždanoka, as Latvia had now moved beyond the difficult times associated with the events of the early 1990s. Their argument reflects the majority in the Chamber judgment, which had found a violation. They argued that the measure had become effectively permanent and as such it was disproportionate.

Ždanoka was distinguished in *Ādamsons v Latvia*,[182] which concerned a law disqualifying former KGB officers from being elected to office and which was applied to the applicant who was barred from standing as a parliamentary candidate even though by then he had held public offices and had been an MP for several years previously. The Court held that at the general level, the prohibition may have been justifiable in principle on the basis of defending the democratic order. However, the prohibited group ('former KGB officers') was very generally defined. Accordingly, restrictions on the electoral rights of the members of that group needed a case-by-case approach which addressed the actual conduct of the person concerned. Indeed, the need for such an individualistic approach grew over time as the period when the impugned acts were supposed to have taken place grew more distant in the past. On the facts, the Court held that the restrictions as applied to the applicant breached Article 3. In particular, no facts had been adduced indicating that he opposed or expressed hostility to the recovery of Latvia's independence and democratic order or that he had been directly or indirectly involved in the misdeeds of the communist totalitarian regime. In fact, when the restriction was imposed on him he had already held important public offices and embarked on a parliamentary career in post-communist Latvia.

Access to the opportunity to stand as a representative of a political party is potentially protected by Article 3. *Kiliçgedik and Others v Turkey*[183] concerned a five-year ban on political party membership imposed on individuals formerly active in a political party

---

[175] *Ždanoka v Latvia*, para 126. [176] *Ždanoka v Latvia*, para 127–8.
[177] *Ždanoka v Latvia*, para 133. [178] *Ždanoka v Latvia*, para 121. See generally paras 119–21.
[179] *Ždanoka v Latvia*, para 135. [180] *Ždanoka v Latvia*, para 135.
[181] See the individual dissenting opinions of Judge Rozakis, and of Judge Zupančič (arguing strongly that the case was really about the Latvian majority's intolerance of a Russian-speaking minority) and the joint dissenting opinion of Judges Mijović and Gyulumyan.   [182] Hudoc (2008).
[183] Hudoc (2010).

dissolved by the state on the basis of allegations of illegal activity. The state argued in defence of this measure that it was a proportionate response to the state's need to prevent disorder and to protect national security, territorial integrity, and the rights of others.[184] While accepting those aims as legitimate in this context, the Court considered the sanction imposed on the applicants disproportionate in the circumstances, and was unconvinced by Turkey's argument that their electoral rights were adequately protected by the opportunity to stand as independent candidates at elections during the period of their ban from party candidatures.[185]

e. Political misconduct as a bar to candidacy

It is a general principle of Convention law that individuals should not be able to rely on Convention rights to destroy or weaken the ideals and values of the treaty, above all the notion of the democratic society.[186] In this regard the Court uses the concept of a 'democracy capable of defending itself',[187] which requires it to ensure that an appropriate balance is struck between the requirements of defending democratic society and defending individual rights.[188] Questions remain, however, as to what approach should be taken in assessing that balance in the context of Article 3, especially if the bar on standing is based on the anticipated subversive behaviour of the proposed candidate, and there has been no criminal conviction.[189]

The issue of past political misconduct was the subject of a Grand Chamber judgment in *Paksas v Lithuania*.[190] This involved a statutory provision barring permanently from candidacy for the national legislature anyone removed from office following impeachment proceedings. This law was enacted to target the impeached former president of Lithuania, who sought subsequently to stand for parliament. Paksas had been found by the Constitutional Court of Lithuania to have acted unlawfully and for personal ends by various unconstitutional means, including disclosing a state secret, and exploiting his official status to benefit acquaintances. The Court noted that in the majority of Council of Europe states, impeachment does not automatically trigger a general loss of electoral rights.[191] Lithuania's law was anomalous within Europe in its severe impact on electoral rights of impeached officials.[192] The issues of principle at stake concerned the balance between preserving the electorate's freedom to choose to re-elect an impeached official—in exercise of 'the free expression of the opinion of the people' guaranteed by

---

[184] *Kılıçgedik and Others v Turkey*, para 40.

[185] See also *Kavakçi v Turkey* hudoc (2007); *Silay v Turkey* hudoc (2007); and *Ilicak v Turkey* hudoc (2007).

[186] Relatedly, the case law of the former Commission indicates that war crimes and treasonous behaviour may justify a permanent bar on candidacy.See, eg, case law on Article 17 (Ch 17) and related case law such as *Refah Partisi (The Welfare Party) and Others v Turkey* 2003-II; 37 EHRR 1 para 86 GC. See also *Ždanoka v Latvia* 2006-IV; 45 EHRR 478 para 99 GC. See the comments made in *Ždanoka* at paras 109–10 and see, eg, *Glimmerveen and Hagenbeek v Netherlands* Nos 8348/78 and 8406/78, 18 DR 187 (1979). The applicants were leaders of a proscribed organization with racist and xenophobic traits and so had been denied the right to stand. The Commission declared the application inadmissible, reference being made to Article 17: the applicants 'intended to participate in these elections and to avail themselves of the right [concerned] for a purpose which the Commission [had] found to be unacceptable under Article 17'.

[187] *Vogt v Germany* A 323 (1995); 21 EHRR 205 GC. See *Ždanoka v Latvia* 2006-IV; 45 EHRR 478 para 99 GC.

[188] *Ždanoka v Latvia*, para 100 (with references to *Vogt*; *Refah Partisi (The Welfare Party) and Others v Turkey* 2003-II; 37 EHRR 1 GC; and *United Communist Party of Turkey and Others v Turkey* 1998-I; 26 EHRR 121).

[189] See the dissenting opinion of Judge Rozakis in *Ždanoka* [GC] and the references made to *Refah Partisi (The Welfare Party) and Others v Turkey* 2003-II; 37 EHRR 1 GC.   [190] Hudoc (2011) GC.

[191] *Paksas v Lithuania*, paras 62 and 106.   [192] *Paksas v Lithuania*, para 106.

Article 3—and restricting such candidatures to protect politics from the participation of persons found to have acted in an undemocratic manner. The Court referred approvingly to the latter as 'a self-protection mechanism for democracy',[193] affirming the principle established in *Ždanoka v Latvia* (discussed earlier) and accepting that the legitimate aim pursued by this candidacy restriction was 'to preserve the democratic order'.[194] However, the permanent and irreversible disqualification imposed here by a general statutory provision (rather than by a particularized measure such as a court order) was deemed to violate Article 3. It was a disproportionate restriction on his electoral rights because it created a lasting and insuperable obstacle to 'the free expression of the opinion of the people' being manifested later in the voters' choice to re-elect this disgraced politician. Paksas' individual right to stand for election, vindicated here, derives conceptually from the people's freedom to adjudge for themselves the credentials of officials previously censured for political wrongdoing. The proportionality of restrictions on such candidacies will turn, the Court states, on two factors: whether they are time-limited, and whether a mechanism exists for reviewing the measure.[195] In this case, the law was subject to no time limit and was 'set in constitutional stone'.[196] His disqualification 'carries a connotation of immutability that is hard to reconcile with Article 3 of Protocol No. 1'.[197] 'Additional indications' of disproportionality arose from the legislative process generating the law at issue: the very rapid enactment of the measure was triggered by a political desire to block Paksas' attempt to stand again for the presidency Although phrased as a general bar on the candidacies of impeached persons, the law's credentials were undermined, in the Court's view, by its provenance as a tool designed to achieve especially the applicant's exclusion from political life. The Grand Chamber distinguished *Ždanoka v Latvia*, observing that the threat posed to the democratic order in Lithuania by Paksas was not comparable to the risks to the emergent Latvian democracy raised by the political participation of former communist party members. The Court observed also that the disqualification law at issue in *Ždanoka* was—unlike this Lithuanian law—subject to periodic review by parliament.[198]

IV. RIGHTS OF REPRESENTATIVES

The passive rights embrace protection for the right to sit in parliament if elected. However, 'States enjoy considerable latitude to establish in their constitutional orders rules governing the status of parliamentarians including criteria for disqualification'.[199] In *Sadak and Others v Turkey (No 2)*,[200] the Democratic Party (DEP) was dissolved following the unconstitutional conduct of some party members. As a result, all the party representatives were ejected from parliament. This constituted a disproportionate interference with the electoral rights of the representatives and was 'incompatible with the very substance of the applicants' right to be elected and sit in parliament...and infringed the sovereign power of the electorate who elected them as members of parliament'.[201] In *Lykourezos v Greece*,[202] the Court denounced the application of a disqualification law to a sitting

---

[193] *Paksas v Lithuania*, para 100.   [194] *Paksas v Lithuania*, para 100.

[195] *Paksas v Lithuania*, para 109.   [196] *Paksas v Lithuania*, para 110.

[197] *Paksas v Lithuania*, para 110.   [198] *Paksas v Lithuania*, para 108.

[199] *Russian Conservative Party of Entrepreneurs and Others v Russia* hudoc (2007); 46 EHRR 863 para 49.

[200] 2002-IV; 36 EHRR 396.   [201] *Sadak and Others v Turkey (No 2)*, para 40.

[202] *Lykourezos v Greece* 2006-VIII; 46 EHRR 74.

representative who was properly elected before this law was passed and applied to him retrospectively. His expulsion from parliament was a breach of the principle of legitimate expectation, a doctrine introduced into Article 3 jurisprudence by this judgment. Both the representative and his electors had acted in the legitimate belief that he would represent them for a full parliamentary term.[203]

6. ELECTION ADMINISTRATION AND POST-ELECTORAL RIGHTS

The Court has given judgment in a series of recent cases concerning the application of Article 3 to the conduct of elections and their aftermath. Voters, candidates, and political parties have argued successfully in those cases that the guarantee of 'free elections' imports into the electoral rights certain minimum standards governing the practices and institutions designed to administer voting, counting, and the determination of election results. The Court has also begun to develop a branch of Article 3 jurisprudence concerning 'post-electoral rights', securing fairness and impartiality in the resolution of disputed elections.

I. CONDUCT OF ELECTIONS

Voter registration laws are vital to the free exercise of electoral rights. In *Georgian Labour Party v Georgia*,[204] the Court emphasized the importance of proper management of electoral rolls as a precondition to free and fair elections, and so the proper enjoyment of not only the right to vote but also the right to stand.[205] The Court refused to find a violation of Article 3 following the applicant party's complaint that, just one month before an election, the system of voter registration was changed by placing the onus on citizens to register to vote. For the unanimous Court, the system put in place had similarities to that used by some other West European states,[206] though it was recognized that as a matter of policy, electoral rules, such as those concerning voter registration, should not be changed in the lead-up to an election.[207]

In *Georgian Labour Party v Georgia*,[208] the Court also considered a complaint about a failure to hold a poll within two major electoral districts, resulting in approximately 60,000 registered voters (2.5 per cent of the national electorate) being disenfranchised. The Court approached the matter from the principle governing suffrage itself, that 'exclusion of any groups or categories of the general population must be reconcilable with the underlying principles of Article 3 of Protocol 1, including that of universal suffrage' and the notion that 'the democratic validity of the legislature' should not be undermined.[209]

---

[203] See also *Paschalidis, Koutmeridis and Zaharakis v Greece* hudoc (2008). In *McGuinness v UK No 39511/98* hudoc (1999) DA, a bar placed on an applicant's access to the facilities available in Parliament on account of his refusal to take the prescribed oath of office did not violate Article 3. An oath law for parliamentarians requiring a religious declaration which representatives had no option to waive was found to violate Article 9 in *Buscarini and Others v San Marino* 1999-I; 30 EHRR 208 GC.

[204] ECHR 2008; 48 EHRR 288.   [205] *Georgian Labour Party v Georgia*, paras 82–3.

[206] *Georgian Labour Party v Georgia*, para 91.   [207] *Georgian Labour Party v Georgia*, para 88.

[208] ECHR 2008; 48 EHRR 288.

[209] *Georgian Labour Party v Georgia*, para 119; see also para 123.

The essence of the government's defence of this clear interference with Article 3 was that the *de facto* disenfranchisement followed extreme political circumstances.[210] The first ballot had been voided because of electoral fraud and after this it was not possible to hold a subsequent vote within an appropriate time frame given the need to institute Parliament and bring closure to the nationwide election. The Court rejected each argument in turn and proceeded to find a violation of Article 3. It refused to absolve the respondent government of its responsibility to hold fresh elections in the districts.[211] There was a basic violation of Article 3 on the facts, as the two districts in question were excluded from the national vote following hasty decision-making processes that were essentially arbitrary and offensive to the rule of law.[212] The government's argument that the election needed to be brought to a close as quickly as it was, and so without the input of the two disenfranchised districts, was not accepted on the facts.

Democracies which use election commissions to administer elections are required by the principles governing Article 3 to ensure that the composition and functioning of those agencies guarantees their political impartiality. A complaint alleging political bias in the organization and operation of the election commissions was considered also by the Court in *Georgian Labour Party v Georgia*.[213] At all levels they were composed of a near majority of presidential appointees. Here the Court emphasized the importance of electoral administration functioning in a transparent manner that maintained independence and impartiality,[214] and the text of the judgment leaves no doubt as to the judges' view that the system in place was highly questionable.[215] In addition to insisting on the availability of impartial election commissions to resolve election disputes, the Court has also endorsed the use of domestic judicial review of the application of electoral rules. It has observed that only a few states still maintain purely political supervision of elections, and commented approvingly on the recommendation of the Venice Commission in its Code of Good Practice in Electoral Matters that judicial review be available in addition to any procedures available before election commissions or within parliaments.[216]

II. POST-ELECTION CHALLENGES TO THE CONDUCT OF ELECTIONS

The state's positive obligation to 'hold free elections' embraces a duty to institute mechanisms for the investigation of allegations of electoral wrongdoing and for remedying those which are established. *Namat Aliyev v Azerbaijan*[217] concerned a cocktail of alleged corrupt election practices which the authorities had failed to investigate. The Court

---

[210] The challenged election took place in 2004, in the aftermath of the revolution in Georgia in 2003, and was a re-run necessitated by the voiding of the earlier election following allegations of widespread electoral fraud and the subsequent resignation of the President.

[211] *Georgian Labour Party v Georgia*, paras 131–6.

[212] *Georgian Labour Party v Georgia*, para 141 (the commission which annulled the election in the controversial districts did so without proper analysis and investigation and exceeded its legal authority in doing so, see para 129).   [213] ECHR 2008; 48 EHRR 288.

[214] *Georgian Labour Party v Georgia*, paras 100–1; see also para 103 regarding lack of uniform European standards in this area.

[215] *Georgian Labour Party v Georgia*, paras 106–8. The commissions 'lacked sufficient checks and balances against the President's power' and 'could hardly [have] enjoy[ed] independence from…outside political pressure', at para 110. However, in the absence of proof put to it regarding actual electoral fraud committed by the commissions, the Court did not find a violation of Article 3.

[216] *Grosaru v Romania* hudoc (2010) paras 28 and 56.   [217] Hudoc (2010).

announced that 'the existence of a domestic system for effective examination of individual complaints and appeals...is one of the essential guarantees of free and fair elections'.[218] Finding a violation of Article 3, the Court noted that the 'conduct of the electoral commissions and courts revealed an appearance of lack of any genuine concern for the protection of the applicant's right to stand'.[219] In addition 'the state's compliance with its positive duty to hold free and fair elections was at stake'.[220]

The decision in *Grosaru v Romania*[221] subsequently established the principle that there must be some form of judicial process established to resolve election disputes. The absence of such here led to a finding that the Romanian system breached Article 3. The 'very essence' of the electoral rights was impaired by the lack of sufficient guarantees of an impartial appeals process.[222] This was found also to breach Article 13. This judicial process must not employ arbitrary methods. In *Kerimli and Alibeyli v Azerbaijan*,[223] the Court found a violation of Article 3 in response to a complaint about a Constitutional Court ruling invalidating election results. Two winning candidates deposed by this decision challenged it successfully, the Strasbourg Court finding that the Constitutional Court ruling lacked 'any degree of transparency' and followed proceedings from which the applicant had been unjustifiably excluded.

Where election commissions are charged with verifying election results and determining disputed outcomes, they must likewise act in a non-arbitrary manner to comply with Article 3. This has been established in a number of cases from Azerbaijan concerning the invalidation of constituency election results by election commissions. In *Hajili v Azerbaijan*,[224] for example, the Court found a violation of Article 3 because the election commission's decision to void results was arbitrary as it 'lacked any relevant and sufficient reasons and was in apparent breach of the procedures established by domestic electoral law'.[225] The decision of the election commission had prevented the applicant from exercising effectively his right to stand for election and thus violated Article 3.

In *Petkov and Others v Bulgaria*,[226] the Court considered the impact of a clash between the state electoral authorities and its Supreme Administrative Court on the electoral rights of individuals prevented from standing for election. The domestic court had ordered the reinstatement of certain disqualified candidates; the electoral commission refused to comply with this order. The Strasbourg Court concluded that this failure to give effect to the domestic court judgment had violated Article 3: 'the effective protection of the applicants' right to stand for Parliament presupposed an obligation on the electoral authorities' part to comply with the final judgments against them'.[227] This case is important also as it instances the Court's willingness to engage with arguments based on Article 13 in the area of election law. The applicants submitted that the state's failure to provide them with adequate post-election remedies violated that guarantee of effective remedies. The Court agreed.[228] This was so because the only remedy potentially available to the thwarted candidates was to seek monetary compensation. This the Court regarded as wholly inadequate to remedy the breach of their electoral rights, and as insufficient to protect the democratic

---

[218] *Namat Aliyev v Azerbaijan*, para 88.   [219] *Namat Aliyev v Azerbaijan*, para 90.
[220] *Namat Aliyev v Azerbaijan*, para 88.   [221] Hudoc (2010).
[222] *Grosaru v Romania*, para 57; The Court reviews comparative law models for handling post-electoral appeals at paras 26–35.   [223] Hudoc (2012).   [224] Hudoc (2012).
[225] *Hajili v Azerbaijan*, para 57. Violations were also established in cases with very similar facts in *Mammadov v Azerbaijan (No 2)* hudoc (2012) and *Kerimova v Azerbaijan* hudoc (2010). See too *Kovach v Ukraine* hudoc (2008).   [226] Hudoc (2009).   [227] *Petkov and Others v Bulgaria*, para 65.
[228] *Petkov and Others v Bulgaria*, paras 68–83.

process. Were the state able to simply to compensate disqualified candidates, elections would be susceptible to being rigged in this way. The Court concluded that:

> the requirements of Article 13 could be fulfilled only by a procedure by which the candidates could seek vindication of their right to stand for Parliament before a body capable of examining the effect which the alleged breach of their electoral rights had on the unfolding and outcome of the elections. If that body deemed the breach serious enough to have prejudiced the outcome, it should have had the power to annul the election result, wholly or in part.[229]

This principle establishes a strong protection for post-electoral rights of participants in elections, especially when coupled with the Court's willingness to find that Article 3 itself provides post-electoral guarantees of access to properly regulated and fair procedural mechanisms for the determination of complaints about the conduct of elections.[230]

7. ELECTORAL SYSTEMS

The Court's constant position is that states have a wide latitude to design their own electoral systems to suit the particularities of their respective democratic traditions and conditions.[231] Unsurprisingly, then, it approaches any assessment of electoral system design with caution, also recognizing that: 'electoral systems seek to fulfil objectives which are sometimes scarcely compatible with each other: on the one hand to reflect fairly faithfully the opinions of the people, and on the other, to channel currents of thought so as to promote the emergence of a sufficiently clear and coherent political will'.[232] It is clear that Article 3 does not demand that states implement proportional representation.[233] In the *Liberal Party* case,[234] the complaint was that the United Kingdom's ' first past the post' electoral system inevitably leads to a dissonance between the proportion of votes cast for a small national party and the proportion of seats it obtains in the legislature. The former Commission said that the UK system was overall an acceptable system for elections to the legislature and it did not become unfair by reason of the results obtained under it.[235]

The wide margin afforded states in the matter of electoral system design was affirmed again recently in the admissibility decision of *Saccomanno and Others v Italy*,[236] in which the Court declined to consider a complaint about the use of so-called closed party lists in

---

[229] *Petkov and Others v Bulgaria*, para 80. The Court goes on to state that 'while this option should undoubtedly have been reserved for the most serious cases, the competent authority should have been able to resort to it if necessary'.

[230] See *Namat Aliyev v Azerbaijan* hudoc (2010); See also *Atakishi v Azerbaijan* hudoc (2012); *Orujov v Azerbaijan* hudoc (2011); *Abil v Azerbaijan* hudoc (2012); *Mammadov v Azerbaijan (No 2)* hudoc (2012); *Kerimli and Alibeyli v Azerbaijan* hudoc (2012).

[231] See, eg, *Hirst v UK (No 2)* 2005-IX; 42 EHRR 849 para 61 GC.

[232] *Yumak and Sadak v Turkey* 2008- para 112 GC.

[233] *Yumak and Sadak v Turkey*, para 110; *Mathieu-Mohin and Clerfayt v Belgium* A 113 (1987); 10 EHRR 1 para 54 PC; *X v Iceland No 8941/80*, 27 DR 145 (1981); nor is proportional representation incompatible with Article 3: *Lindsay and Others v UK No 8364/78* hudoc (1979) 4 EHRR 106 DA. Various drafts of Article 3 were rejected because of, for example, concerns that their wording might imply a commitment to some form of proportional representation: 7 TP 128–30; 8 TP 150–1. The earlier drafts are reproduced in 5 TP 184–6; 7 TP 130, 150–2; 8 TP 12–14.   [234] *Liberal Party, R and P v UK No 8765/79*, 21 DR 211 at 225 (1980).

[235] *Liberal Party v UK*, pp 224–5.   [236] Hudoc (2012) DA.

an electoral system.[237] In *Bompard v France*,[238] the applicant claimed a violation of Article 3 as the state had failed to review constituency boundaries prior to an election. The Court declared the application inadmissible, citing the wide margin of appreciation owed to states in this regard and accepting a plea that it was proper that boundary reviews should not be rushed but must follow comprehensive studies and consultations. Irrespective of the sort of electoral system a state employs, it must specify the legal principles governing its operation with sufficient clarity in order to meet the requirements of lawfulness stipulated by the Court's Article 3 doctrine. In *Grosaru v Romania*,[239] the Court concluded that Romanian election rules regarding the allocation of seats to special representatives of national minorities violated Article 3 on the basis of a lack of such specificity. This was because the rules stipulated merely that the candidate winning the 'largest number of votes' was entitled to take up the seat set aside in Parliament for the relevant national minority group. It was unclear whether this meant the winner of the largest number of votes at a national or at a constituency level, a detail that could prove determinative of the electoral fate of candidates.[240]

Laws requiring political parties to achieve a certain proportion of the total vote before becoming entitled to any seats in the legislature may be compatible with Article 3. A number of such 'threshold' cases have reached the former Commission[241] and Court[242] in the past and none have involved a violation of Article 3. However, it is evident from *Yumak and Sadak v Turkey*[243] that high thresholds may breach Article 3. The case saw a challenge to a law which required a political party to obtain 10 per cent of the national vote before it could obtain parliamentary seats. This had a devastating effect on the applicants in 2002 when they stood for election for a party promoting Kurdish concerns. Even though they had obtained almost 46 per cent of the total vote in their (south-eastern) province,[244] nationally their party's share of the vote was just 6.22 per cent. Accordingly they were barred from taking positions in the National Assembly.

The Grand Chamber rejected the argument that the 10 per cent threshold interfered excessively with the free expression of the people for the purposes of Article 3. Thresholds like the one in question were acceptable in principle since they served a legitimate aim: they were 'intended in the main to promote the emergence of sufficiently representative currents of thought within the country'; they avoided 'excessive and debilitating parliamentary fragmentation' and so 'strengthen[ed] governmental stability'.[245] Article 3 nevertheless delineated certain boundaries. On the one hand, it did not go so far as to oblige contracting states to adopt a system whereby parties with an essentially regional

---

[237] The unsuccessful argument was that this system violated Article 3 by restricting the electoral choices of voters who have no influence over the order in which party candidates are preferred.

[238] *No 44081/02* 2006-IV DA.   [239] Hudoc (2010).

[240] The finding of a violation was based also on the lack of impartiality in the bodies responsible for examining Grosaru's challenges to the system: paras 54–6.

[241] *Silvius Magnago and Südtiroler Volkspartei v Italy No 25035/94*, 85-A DR 116 (1996) (4% threshold required for the election of the remaining 25% of the members of the Chamber of Deputies; no violation as covered by wide margin of appreciation left to states in the matter). See also *Etienne Tête v France No 11123/84*, 54 DR 68 (1987).

[242] *Federación nacionalista Canaria v Spain No 56618/00*, 2001 VI DA (proportional representation in the Canary Islands) and *Partija 'Jaunie Demokrati' and Partija 'Musu Zeme' v Latvia Nos 10547/07 and 34049/07* hudoc (2007) DA (5% threshold for parliamentary elections accepted as it encouraged sufficiently representative currents of thought and made it possible to avoid an excessive fragmentation of parliament).

[243] Hudoc (2008) GC. Chamber judgment: hudoc (2007). See Zimbron, 49 Harv ILJ Online (2007) 10.

[244] In fact, that year as a result of the threshold, approximately 45% of people who voted nationally were not represented in Parliament, see para 19.

[245] *Yumak and Sadak v Turkey*, para 125 (citations omitted).

base were guaranteed parliamentary representation irrespective of the national vote.[246] On the other hand, issues could arise if the system 'tended to deprive such parties of parliamentary representation'.[247] So it was not in itself 'decisive' that a high threshold deprived 'part of the electorate of representation'.[248] The Court's task was:

> to determine whether the effect of the rules governing parliamentary elections is to exclude some persons or groups of persons from participating in the political life of the country...and whether the discrepancies created by a particular electoral system can be considered arbitrary or abusive or whether the system tends to favour one political party or candidate by giving them an electoral advantage at the expense of others.[249]

The Court's finding, by thirteen votes to four, that there was no breach of Article 3 reflected this very minimal level of protection. It would seem, too, that it was a result of a diplomatic choice from a Grand Chamber prepared to see the best in the Turkish electoral system whilst indicating to the respondent state that it raised serious concerns such that reform would be welcomed. Indeed the Court labelled the 10 per cent threshold as 'excessive'[250] and concurred with the Parliamentary Assembly's view that the 'exceptionally high level...[should] be lowered'.[251] The Turkish threshold was the highest in Europe, where a 5 per cent threshold was typical.[252] In the majority's view, however, an election system that was otherwise dubious under Article 3 was saved as the political parties that were affected by the threshold had managed in practice to 'develop strategies whereby they can attenuate some of its effects'.[253] That is, there existed 'correctives' and 'other safeguards' associated with the electoral system that made it tolerable from the perspective of Article 3. For example, the applicants could have stood as independent candidates (freeing themselves from the threshold requirement) and formed a parliamentary group once elected. The Court emphasized, too, the safeguarding role played by the Turkish Constitutional Court, which had ruled upon the threshold question in 1995: it had proven its ability to exercise 'vigilance to prevent any excessive effects of the impugned electoral threshold by seeking the point of equilibrium between the principles of fair representation and governmental stability' and it provided 'a guarantee calculated to stop the threshold concerned impairing the essence of the right enshrined in Article 3 of Protocol No 1'.[254]

The Court's reasoning in failing to find a violation in *Yumak and Sadak v Turkey* is certainly open to strong criticism, as was demonstrated by the joint dissenting opinion of Judges Tulkens, Vajić, Jaeger, and Šikuta.[255] It is difficult to disagree with their observation that the very essence of Article 3 was impaired in that the threshold deprived 'a large proportion of the population of the possibility of being represented in parliament', and that it had a profoundly negative effect on the fortunes of political parties with a regional

---

[246] *Yumak and Sadak v Turkey*, para 124.   [247] *Yumak and Sadak v Turkey* (emphasis added).

[248] As the Court explained, such a threshold could 'work as a necessary corrective adjustment to the proportional system, which has always been accepted as allowing for the free expression of the opinion of the people even though it may operate to the detriment of small parties when accompanied by a high threshold', para 122 (citing *Liberal Party, R and P v UK No 8765/79*, 21 DR 225 (1980)).

[249] *Yumak and Sadak v Turkey*, para 121 (citing *Aziz v Cyprus* 2004-V; 41 EHRR 164 para 28 and *X v Iceland No 8941/80*, 27 DR 156).   [250] *Yumak and Sadak v Turkey*, para 147.

[251] *Yumak and Sadak v Turkey*, see also para 130.   [252] *Yumak and Sadak v Turkey*, para 129.

[253] *Yumak and Sadak v Turkey*, para 143. The Chamber judgment had rejected such arguments, see paras 70–3.   [254] *Yumak and Sadak v Turkey*, para 146.

[255] See also, in the Chamber judgment, the joint dissenting opinion of Judges Cabral Barreto and Mularoni, arguing that the 10% rule did exceed the margin of appreciation permitted to Turkey.

focus, something which was hard to reconcile with the need for pluralism in a democratic society, which the Court frequently emphasizes in its Article 11 case law.[256] They also took issue with the validity of the so-called correctives. At the general level, they questioned how an improperly functioning system could be saved by what were in effect 'stratagems' used by smaller parties, especially as these were dependent on the vagaries of politics, they had no guaranteed place in the system, and relied on the candidates to circumvent the existing electoral rules. More specifically, they thought it dubious that smaller parties had to find political allies or disappear (in the sense that individual members had to stand as independents to achieve a parliamentary presence).

The Court considered a threshold law of a different sort in *Özgürlük ve Dayanişma Partisi (ÖDP) v Turkey*.[257] This concerned a Turkish provision limiting state financial assistance to political parties polling at least 7 per cent of the votes cast at the last elections. The ÖDP did not qualify, and argued that this violated Article 3 taken in conjunction with Article 14. The Court disagreed, considering that the system of public funding of political parties 'pursues the legitimate aim of enhancing democratic pluralism while preventing the excessive and dysfunctional fragmentation of candidacies, thereby strengthening the expression of the opinion of the people in the choice of the legislature'.[258] The Court was influenced in its finding that this rule was proportionate by the fact that the 7 per cent vote-share requirement was lower than the 10 per cent threshold stipulated for parliamentary representation.[259] Thus state financial support was not being monopolized by those parties which had already secured parliamentary seats. Further, the ÖDP did not convince the Court that it enjoyed a level of electoral support sufficient to render it representative of a significant portion of the Turkish electorate.[260] The Court concluded that there had therefore been no violation of Article 14 and Article 3. In a joint opinion dissenting on this point, Judges Tulkens and Sajo offer a convincing critique of the Court's decision. They observe that the 7 per cent threshold for state funding is the highest in Europe (all other states using figures between 0.5 per cent and 5 per cent of vote-share). They note too that, whereas in *Yumak and Sadak* (discussed earlier) the Court endorsed the 10 per cent electoral threshold for reasons related to preserving governmental stability, the same consideration does not apply to the state funding rule. Further, as the dissenters remark, it is not the Court's proper role to adjudge the electoral credentials of minor political parties such as ÖDP. The dissenters' assessment is that the effect of the law 'is damaging to small parties and, accordingly, to political pluralism', and discriminatory, in violation of Article 14 taken with Article 3.

8. MEDIA REPORTING OF ELECTION CAMPAIGNS

The Court considered this issue under Article 3 for the first time in *Communist Party of Russia and Others v Russia*.[261] The case concerned a complaint by opposition candidates of biased and unequal media coverage of the 2003 Russian general election campaign by the major TV stations. This was alleged to have favoured disproportionately the

---

[256] See Ch 15.   [257] Hudoc (2012).

[258] *Özgürlük ve Dayanişma Partisi (ÖDP) v Turkey*, para 42, citing *Fournier v France* No 11406/85; DR 55; and *Cheminade v France* No 31559/96 1999-III DA.   [259] *ÖDP v Turkey*, para 44.

[260] *ÖDP v Turkey*, para 45.   [261] Hudoc (2012).

candidates of the pro-government United Russia Party. The Court considered that this complaint fell within the scope of Article 3, rejecting the government's claim that the Article was inapplicable because media coverage was effectively an aspect of electoral system design immune from Court supervision under the Article.[262] Ruling to the contrary, the Court asserted its competence to examine complaints about unequal media coverage. This authority derives from the core principle of Article 3 that the state act as 'ultimate guarantor of pluralism', protecting the free expression of the opinion of the people not only at the polls, but during the campaigns that precede them.[263] The Communist Party's complaint was essentially that the unequal coverage meant that the elections were not 'free'. In response, the Court announced the following principles: the guarantee of 'the free expression of the opinion of the people' in Article 3 contains also an implied commitment to the principle of equality of treatment, and this extends to media coverage of elections.[264] The intimate interrelationship of free expression and free elections, intensified during the campaigning period, is stressed by the Court.[265] There is a wide margin of appreciation for states to set and apply media coverage rules for elections, but this margin is not 'all-embracing';[266] the rights at stake are the passive rights of candidacy of opposition party members and as such may be more heavily restricted than voting rights, producing a diminished entitlement to strictly equal media coverage.

Turning to the facts of this case, the Court considered the applicants' claim that the pro-government propaganda broadcast on the major TV channels during the 2003 parliamentary election campaign far outweighed the airtime devoted to opposition party policies. This, it was argued, prevented voters making a properly informed choice;[267] they further argued that Article 3 required the government to adopt positive measures to ensure equal coverage.[268] The Court declined to prescribe a principle requiring equality of coverage for opposition parties, ruling instead that, considered in context, the state had met its positive obligation to provide 'at least minimum visibility' on TV to opposition parties.[269] This is a rather cautious conclusion, especially when matched against the relative boldness of the Court's decision to articulate new principles to govern future cases concerning state obligations in this sphere.

9. CONCLUSION

As the Court has observed, Article 3, First Protocol 'was not conceived as a code on electoral matters, designed to regulate all aspects of the electoral process.'[270] Nonetheless, the expanding jurisprudence of the Court involving Article 3 reaches into many corners of election law: in addition to the long-established protection offered to voting and

---

[262] *Communist Party of Russia and Others v Russia*, para 79.

[263] *Communist Party of Russia and Others v Russia*, para 79.

[264] *Communist Party of Russia and Others v Russia*, para 108, referring to the Venice Commission's promotion of the principle of equality of opportunity for electoral participants; see too para 51.

[265] *Communist Party of Russia and Others v Russia*, para 107.

[266] *Communist Party of Russia and Others v Russia*, para 110.

[267] *Communist Party of Russia and Others v Russia*, para 103.

[268] *Communist Party of Russia and Others v Russia*, para 104.

[269] *Communist Party of Russia and Others v Russia*, para 126. The applicants also argued that the government had been manipulating the media to ensure prominence was given to its views in the election coverage. The Court regarded these claims as insufficiently substantiated, paras 111–22.

[270] *Communist Party of Russia and Others v Russia*, para 108.

candidacy rights, its doctrine now offers guarantees of procedural protections for individuals seeking to challenge the conduct or outcomes of elections.[271] These procedural and post-electoral rights enhance significantly the effectiveness of Article 3, facilitating claims from individuals aggrieved by lapses in impartiality or fair process by domestic authorities charged with administering polls. The recent application of Article 3 to the issue of state regulation of broadcast election coverage is also notable.[272] Overall, the Court is employing Article 3 to positive effect in decisions in which it polices the openness and impartiality of state electoral structures. Its contribution to Convention law on the right to vote is, however, weakened substantially by limitations in its judgments on the critical issue of disenfranchisement. Its doctrine prohibits states from fencing out of the electorate unpopular minorities on the basis of laws that effect a 'general, automatic and indiscriminate' disenfranchisement. But this minimum standard is easily met, as evidenced by the Court's deferential proportionality analysis of prisoner disenfranchisement in the *Scoppola* decision.[273] It is understandable that the Court is reluctant to stipulate binding substantive principles governing the distribution of suffrage within states; but nonetheless disappointing that on this core question it has declined to do more to scrutinize the justifications given by democracies for denying the fundamental human right to vote to disenfranchised populations.

---

[271] See section 6 of this chapter.

[272] *Communist Party of Russia and Others v Russia* hudoc (2012).

[273] See too the Court's endorsement of the restrictions on voting rights in *Sitaropoulos and Giakoumopoulos v Greece* ECHR 2012; 56 EHRR 9 GC and *Shindler v UK* hudoc (2013).

24

THE FOURTH, SIXTH, SEVENTH, AND THIRTEENTH PROTOCOLS

Protocols 4 and 7 protect a selection of civil and political rights not covered by the main Convention text and which in part[1] make up for the substantive deficiencies of the Convention when compared to the International Covenant on Civil and Political Rights (ICCPR). Protocol 4 has been ratified by forty-three states (31 October 2013),[2] as has Protocol 7 (31 October 2013).[3] Protocols 6 (forty-six ratifications)[4] and 13 (forty-three ratifications)[5] both concern the abolition of the death penalty.[6]

1. ARTICLE 1, FOURTH PROTOCOL: FREEDOM FROM IMPRISONMENT FOR NON-FULFILMENT OF A CONTRACTUAL OBLIGATION

Article 1 of the Fourth Protocol reads:

> No one shall be deprived of his liberty merely on the ground of inability to fulfil a contractual obligation.

It extends to a failure to fulfil a contractual obligation of any kind. It may thus include non-delivery, non-performance, and non-forbearance, as well as the non-payment of debts.[7] Article 1 is limited in its application by the words 'merely on the ground of inability to fulfil' an obligation. So it 'prohibits imprisonment for debt solely when the debt arises under a contractual obligation'.[8] That is, deprivation of liberty is not forbidden if there is

---

[1] For examples of the (still more) extensive coverage provided by the ICCPR compared to the Convention and its Protocols, see Articles 10, 14(3)(g), 24–5 and 27 ICCPR.

[2] Turkey and the UK have signed but not ratified; Greece and Switzerland have never signed the instrument.

[3] Germany, Netherlands, and Turkey have signed but not ratified; the UK has never signed.

[4] All except Russia, which signed the instrument in 1997.

[5] Armenia and Poland have signed but not ratified. Azerbaijan and Russia have not signed.

[6] On Protocol 12, see Ch 18.

[7] Explanatory Report to Protocol 4 (hereafter 'Explanatory Report to P4') available at http://conventions. coe.int/ para 3. Explanatory Reports or Memoranda accompanying Council of Europe treaties provide guidance as to their meaning but are not an authoritative source of interpretation.

[8] *Göktan v France* 2002-V; 37 EHRR 320 para 51. See also *Gatt v Malta* ECHR 2010; 58 EHRR 32 para 39.

some other factor present, as where the detention is because the debtor acts fraudulently or negligently or for some other reason refuses to honour an obligation that he is able to comply with. Thus, where a person was detained on the request of a creditor for refusing to make an affidavit in respect of his property, Article 1 of the Fourth Protocol did not apply.[9] Other examples given in the Explanatory Report to the Protocol[10] are where a person, knowing that he does not have the money to pay, orders food in a restaurant; through negligence, fails to supply goods under contract; or is preparing to leave the country in order to avoid his contractual obligations.

The term 'deprivation of liberty' is that found in Article 5 of the Convention and can be taken to have the meaning that it has there.[11] Under Article 5(1)(b) of the Convention, a person may be deprived of his liberty for 'non-compliance with a lawful order of a court'. This could include a court order that results from the failure to fulfil a contractual obligation. The effect of Article 1 is that, for parties to the Fourth Protocol, the detention of a person for failure to comply with such a court order merely because that person is unable to comply with the contractual obligation concerned is prohibited.

2. ARTICLE 2, FOURTH PROTOCOL: FREEDOM OF MOVEMENT WITHIN A STATE AND FREEDOM TO LEAVE ITS TERRITORY

Article 2 of the Fourth Protocol reads:

1. Everyone lawfully within the territory of a state shall, within that territory, have the right to liberty of movement and freedom to choose his residence.
2. Everyone shall be free to leave any country, including his own.
3. No restrictions shall be placed on the exercise of these rights other than such as are in accordance with law and are necessary in a democratic society in the interests of national security or public safety, for the maintenance of *ordre public*, for the prevention of crime, for the protection of health or morals, or for the protection of the rights and freedoms of others.
4. The rights set forth in paragraph 1 may also be subject, in particular areas, to restrictions imposed in accordance with law and justified by the public interest in a democratic society.

For the purposes of Article 2 as a whole, a territory to which the Fourth Protocol is extended by declaration upon ratification is a separate territory from a state's metropolitan territory, so that freedom of movement, etc applies only within the non-metropolitan territory concerned (Article 5(1), Fourth Protocol).[12] A state's embassy abroad is not a part of its territory for the purposes of the Fourth Protocol generally.[13]

---

[9] *X v Germany No 5025/71*, 14 YB 692 (1971).   [10] Explanatory Report to P4 para 6.
[11] See Ch 8, section 2, and see *Gatt v Malta* ECHR 2010.
[12] See *Piermont v France* A 314 (1995); 20 EHRR 301 (French Polynesia considered by the Court as a separate territory to metropolitan France).
[13] *WM v Denmark No 17392/90* hudoc (1992); 15 EHRR CD 28.

I. FREEDOM OF MOVEMENT WITHIN A STATE'S TERRITORY

Article 2(1) of the Fourth Protocol provides that 'everyone lawfully within the territory of a state shall, within that territory, have the right to liberty of movement and freedom to choose his residence'. 'Everyone' includes aliens, ie nationals of other states and stateless persons,[14] although, as is well established, 'the Convention does not guarantee the right of an alien to enter or to reside in a particular country and...Contracting States have the right, as a matter of well-established international law and subject to their treaty obligations including the Convention, to control the entry, residence and expulsion of aliens'.[15] Moreover, the term 'lawfully' was inserted to take into account the sovereign power of states to control the entry of aliens.[16] Article 2 does not apply to an illegal entrant, whilst an alien who infringes the conditions attaching to his entry into a state's territory is not 'lawfully' within it,[17] and an individual will no longer be 'lawfully' present once an effective expulsion order has been served.[18] *Piermont v France*[19] established that an applicant is not necessarily 'lawfully' present simply because they have passed passport control at an airport. In that case the applicant was detained by the authorities before leaving the airport perimeter and served with an effective exclusion order. Article 2 of the Fourth Protocol did not apply.

A person's right to 'liberty of movement' has to be distinguished from the right not to be 'deprived of his liberty', which is protected by Article 5, Convention. The latter involves a severe form of restriction on freedom of movement.[20] The distinction can be critical as Article 5(1) provides for an exhaustive list of circumstances potentially justifying a deprivation of liberty whilst restrictions on the right to freedom of movement are subject to the (much more) general qualifications found within Article 2(3)–(4) (Fourth Protocol).

The Court is clear that 'special supervision accompanied by an order for compulsory residence in a specified district does not of itself come within Article 5'.[21] It has also held that Article 5 did not apply to cases concerning preventive regimes whereby an individual has been subjected to curfews periods of ten to twelve hours stretching over long periods.[22] Individuals subject to such regimes, which clearly represent a profound interference with their freedom, will have to argue (if they can)[23] that they have been the subject of an unjustified interference with their right to freedom of movement.[24]

[14] See Explanatory Report to P4, p 4.

[15] *Sisojeva v Latvia* hudoc (2005); 43 EHRR 694 para 99. See also *Chahal v UK* 1996-V; 23 EHRR 413 para 73.   [16] Explanatory Report to P4 para 8.

[17] *Paramanathan v Germany* No 12068/86, 51 DR 237 (1986); 10 EHRR CD 157. See also *Omwenyeke v Germany* No 44294/04 hudoc (2007) DA.

[18] *Piermont v France* A 314 (1995); 20 EHRR 301 para 44. On the 'lawful' requirement see also *Tatishvili v Russia* 2007-I; 45 EHRR 1246.

[19] *Piermont*, para 49. The case concerned an MEP who claimed, *inter alia*, that her expulsion from the Republic of French Polynesia, which she had entered lawfully, for speaking out against nuclear tests there, restricted her freedom of movement between Tahiti and another island within the Republic where she was to address another meeting. Although the Court found no violation of Article 1 of the Fourth Protocol, it did find a violation of Article 10 of the Convention.

[20] See Ch 8, section 2. On the relationship between the 'distinct' provisions of Article 5 and Article 2, Fourth Protocol, see *Austin v UK* ECHR-2012; 55 EHRR 359 para 55 GC.

[21] *Guzzardi v Italy* A 39 (1980); 3 EHRR 333 para 94 PC. See also *Raimondo v Italy* A 281-A (1994); 18 EHRR 237 para 39, and *Labita v Italy* 2000-IV; 46 EHRR 1228 GC.

[22] See *Raimondo* and *Labita* (Mafia suspects subjected to ten-hour curfews living at home (inviolable) and subject to reporting restrictions). Also see *Trijonis v Lithuania* No2333/02 hudoc (2005) DA (twelve-hour curfew for weekdays and all weekend; Article 5 not engaged as applicant was 'allowed to spend time at work as well as at home' during the (almost) sixteen-month period applicable).

[23] Not all states have ratified Protocol 4, see the introduction to this chapter.

[24] The point at which Article 5 applies is of great relevance to (non-derogating) anti-terrorism control orders in the UK (since replaced by Terrorism Prevention and Investigation Measures), which is not a state party to the Fourth Protocol.

Preventing someone from leaving their house and/or stopping them from leaving a certain area are clear examples of interferences with freedom of movement. What counts is the fact that an individual needs to seek permission to leave, so it is irrelevant if he or she is consistently granted such permission.[25] The Court has also found Article 2 applicable when individuals are required to report to the police every time they change their place of residence or visit family and friends.[26] An interference with the right to freedom of movement can also occur when an individual is excluded from a specified public area, for example a city centre district.[27] Article 2 can also apply to what the Court has referred to as 'restrictions on [an individual's] movements', as in a Cypriot case where the authorities closely monitored the applicants' movements between the northern part of the island and the south, and within the south. They were not allowed to move freely in the south and had to report to the police every time they wanted to go to the north to visit their families or friends or upon their entry into the south.[28]

The restrictions contained in Articles 2(3) and (4) are similar to Articles 8–11.[29] Article 2(4) adds to them a further ground for restriction that is not found in Articles 8–11, *viz* 'public interest'.[30] This would appear to allow the state a broader basis upon which to justify interference with the rights protected by Article 2(1) when the case is confined to 'particular areas', although case law is lacking.[31] The Explanatory Report[32] indicates that paragraph (4) was included because the majority of the committee drafting the Protocol was against including under paragraph (3) a restriction permitting restrictions on the ground of economic welfare. Paragraph (4) was therefore inserted because of the possibility that *in particular areas* it might be necessary, for legitimate reasons, and solely in the 'public interest in a democratic society' (Article 2(4)), to impose restrictions (such as those based on economic welfare) which it might not always be possible to bring within the concept of '*ordre public*'.[33] The intention was not to limit the 'particular area' to any definite geographical or administrative area; any 'well defined area' would qualify.

Both Articles 2(3) and (4) require that a restriction be 'in accordance with law'.[34] The requirement was infringed in *Raimondo v Italy*,[35] when a person who was suspected of Mafia activities was made the subject of a court supervision order by which, *inter alia*, he was required not to leave his home without informing the police. The Court found that the case fell within Article 2 of the Fourth Protocol—not Article 5 of the Convention— and that the restriction upon the applicant's freedom of movement could be justified under Article 2(3) as being necessary 'for the maintenance of "*ordre public*"' for the 'prevention of crime'. However, the applicant was not informed of the judicial revocation of the order for eighteen days, during which time he continued to be restricted in his movements.[36]

---

[25] See *Ivanov v Ukraine* hudoc (2006) para 85.

[26] *Denizci v Cyprus* 2001-V; and *Bolat v Russia* 2006-XI; 46 EHRR 18.

[27] *Olivieira v Netherlands* 2002-IV 1990; 37 EHRR 693.

[28] *Denizci v Cyprus* 2001-V para 404. It may also have been relevant that they were expelled to the northern part of the island. See also *Bolat v Russia* 2006-XI; 46 EHRR 18.   [29] See Ch 11.

[30] Note also that Article 2(4) requires that a restriction be 'justified', but not 'necessary' in a democratic society, which is the standard and seemingly stricter formula in Article 2(3). The proportionality test still applies for both paragraphs of the Article.

[31] Though it was relevant to *Olivieira v Netherlands* 2002-IV; 37 EHRR 693.

[32] Explanatory Report to P4 para 15.

[33] The notion of '*ordre public*' is to be understood in the broad sense in general use in continental countries.

[34] See *Gochev v Bulgaria* hudoc (2009) para 46.

[35] A281 (1994); 18 EHRR 237 paras 39–40. See also *Tatishvili v Russia* 2007-I; 45 EHRR 1246 (authorities' refusal to register applicant as resident at her home address).

[36] See also *Vito Sante Santoro v Italy* 2004-VI; *Timishev v Russia* 2005-XII; 44 EHRR 776; and *Bolat v Russia* 2006-XI; 46 EHRR 18. See also *Olivieira v Netherlands* 2002-IV; 37 EHRR 693 (municipal order

Restrictions on freedom of movement may be imposed upon an accused person released on bail,[37] or a person suspected of Mafia activities on the ground of 'prevention of crime',[38] or for national security reasons if it is feared an individual will disclose state secrets.[39] The withdrawal of a liquor licence (following a person's conviction for running a disorderly house) that affects his place of 'residence'[40] can be justified as being both 'for the prevention of crime' and 'protection of health or morals'.[41] The *ordre public* restriction has also been used to justify the removal of families from one mobile site to another.[42]

The restrictions permitted by Articles 2(3) and (4) are subject to the principle of proportionality. In *Labita v Italy*,[43] the applicant was suspected of being a member of the Mafia and subjected to a preventive regime supposedly directed at impeding his involvement in serious criminal activity. For three years he was under daily ten-hour curfews plus he had to inform the police on leaving home and on Sunday mornings. He could not associate with others subject to similar preventative measures or with criminal records, nor visit bars, nor attend public meetings. The grounds relied on by the domestic courts for imposing this regime were informer evidence and because the applicant's deceased brother-in-law was in the Mafia. In the Court's view this was insufficient. Whilst it acknowledged the 'threat posed by the Mafia',[44] it refused to accept the serious interference with Article 2(1) that had occurred was necessary in the absence of 'concrete evidence to show that there was a real risk that [Labita] would offend'.[45] The Court did maintain, nevertheless, that it considered it legitimate for preventive measures, including special supervision, to be taken against persons suspected of being members of the Mafia, 'even prior to conviction, as they are intended to prevent crimes being committed'.[46] Furthermore, restriction of freedom of movement might conceivably be justified even if there was an acquittal, as 'concrete evidence gathered at trial, though insufficient to secure a conviction, may nonetheless justify reasonable fears that the person concerned may in the future commit criminal offences'.[47]

More moderate restrictions on freedom of movement than those just described may violate Article 2, especially when imposed for long periods. In *Rosengren v Romania*,[48] the applicant was required to remain in Bucharest as he was the subject of a fraud investigation. It dragged on for over five years (when it became time-barred), though even then the restriction remained in place for another eighteen months. The Court suggested that the duration of the restriction alone (six years and three months) was capable of constituting a violation of Article 2,[49] but also referred to the delay in cancelling the order once the criminal prosecution was dropped and the domestic courts' failure to properly justify the measures when the applicant contested them.[50]

---

prohibiting drug addict from entering specified area for fourteen days; Court divided by four votes to three on the 'in accordance with the law' test).

[37] *Schmid v Austria* No 10670/83, 44 DR 195 (1985). See also *Rosengren v Romania* hudoc (2008) para 33.

[38] *Raimondo v Italy* A 281-A (1994); 18 EHRR 237 and *Ciancimino v Italy* No12541/86, 70 DR 103 (1991).

[39] *Bartik v Russia* 2006-XV para 43.

[40] On residence, see *Gillow v UK* A 109 (1986); 11 EHRR 335 para 42 (breach of Article 8, UK had not ratified Protocol 4). See also *Lacko v Slovakia* No 47237/99 hudoc (2002) DA (allegations of discrimination regarding ability of Slovak nationals of Roma origin to settle in a place where they had been granted permanent residence).   [41] *X v Belgium* No 8901/80, 23 DR 237 (1980).

[42] *Van de Vin v Netherlands* No 13628/88 hudoc (1992) DA.   [43] 2000-IV; 46 EHRR 1228 GC.

[44] *Labita v Italy*, para 197.   [45] *Labita v Italy*, para 196.   [46] *Labita v Italy*, para 195.

[47] *Labita v Italy*, para 195.   [48] Hudoc (2008).

[49] *Rosengren v Romania*, para 38. See also *Ivanov v Ukraine* hudoc (2006) (violation: eleven-year order (nine years of which was in Court's jurisdiction)); *Fedorov and Fedorova v Russia* hudoc (2005); 43 EHRR 943; and *Antonenkov v Ukraine* hudoc (2006).   [50] *Rosengren v Romania*, para 39.

An 'automatic' travel ban imposed for debt or unpaid tax may be initially justifiable, but risks falling foul of the proportionality principle over time.[51] The restriction must not become 'a *de facto* punishment for inability to pay'; it must exist for the genuine purpose of recovering the debt.[52] Proportionality here requires periodic reassessment of the restrictions 'in the light of factors such as whether or not the fiscal authorities had made reasonable efforts to collect the debt through other means and the likelihood that the debtor's leaving the country might undermine the chances to collect the money'.[53]

Restrictions imposed under Article 2 must be justified and proportionate throughout their duration. Hence national authorities should be alive to the reality that the actual need for restriction on movement may diminish with the passage of time. If the restriction exists for a long period, the individual circumstances of the applicant must be reviewed regularly so as to ensure its continued need.[54] So a condition that a bankrupt should not absent himself from the district without prior authorization can be acceptable as a legitimate aim on the grounds of '*ordre public*' and the protection of the rights and freedoms of others (ie creditors). Nevertheless, a point may be reached where the length of the bankruptcy proceedings, and so the restrictions on movement, result in the imposition of an excessive burden on the applicant given the balance to be maintained between the general interest in payment of a bankrupt's creditors and the applicant's individual interest in freedom of movement.[55]

Proportionality assessments also apply to exclusions from public areas. *Olivieira v Netherlands*[56] concerned an 'emergency' zone in Amsterdam blighted by trafficking in and abuse of hard drugs. The applicant had been convicted for breaching a fourteen-day order prohibiting his entry into this area, given his own consistent (and proven) record of drug-related misdemeanours within it. Accepting the proportionality of the measures imposed, the Court acknowledged the margin of appreciation allowed to the domestic court and took into account the fact that the applicant had already been issued with several eight-hour prohibition orders (flouting them by returning and openly using hard drugs in the area), and had been warned that a fourteen-day prohibition order might ensue. It also noted that he did not live or work in the area in question and did not have a post office box there for collection of mail.[57] The authorities may therefore take special measures to overcome an emergency situation related to drugs in certain areas concerned at the relevant time, it being arguable that the Court could exercise some power of review on the issue of whether it was necessary to establish the emergency restriction area in the first place.[58]

---

[51] See *Riener v Bulgaria* hudoc (2006); 45 EHRR 723; *Földes and Földesné Hajlik v Hungary* hudoc (2007); 47 EHRR 316; and *Khlyustov v Russia* hudoc (2013) (travel restriction on judgment debtor).

[52] *Riener v Bulgaria*, paras 122–3.   [53] *Riener v Bulgaria*, para 124.

[54] See *Bartik v Russia* 2006-XV (violation in case of lengthy and absolute foreign travel ban for person with past access to 'state secrets'; see also *Soltysyak v Russia* hudoc (2011)).

[55] See *Luordo v Italy* 2003-IX; 41 EHRR 547 and *Bottaro v Italy* hudoc (2003) (breach was found even though in neither case did the files show that the applicants had wished to leave their place of residence, or that they had been refused permission; bankruptcy proceedings had lasted approximately fourteen and twelve years respectively, so the very duration made the restriction disproportionate). See also *Goffi v Italy* hudoc (2005) and *Bassani v Italy* hudoc (2003). Cf *Fedorov and Fedorova v Russia* hudoc (2006); 43 EHRR 943 (context (criminal proceedings) and duration ('significantly shorter', para 43) was a basis to distinguish from *Luordo*, hence necessary to ascertain 'whether the applicants actually sought to leave the area of their residence and, if so, whether permission to do so was refused', para 44).

[56] 2002-IV; 37 EHRR 693.

[57] *Olivieira v Netherlands*, para 65. See also *Landvreugd v Netherlands* hudoc (2002); 36 EHRR 1039 (applicant could enter area with impunity to collect social-security etc).

[58] *Olivieira v Netherlands*, para. 64. In *Landvreugd* the applicant had argued, unsuccessfully, that in practice the emergency areas were not necessary either for crime prevention or other policy reasons, para 69.

II. FREEDOM TO LEAVE A STATE'S TERRITORY

Freedom to leave a country (Article 2(2)) is a personal right which does not imply a right to transfer one's possessions out of it.[59] The freedom extends to nationals and aliens, with Articles 2(3) and (4) applying. As far as Article 2(3) restrictions are concerned, an accused may be detained in prison[60] or refused a passport[61] in connection with pending criminal proceedings on grounds of 'ordre public' or 'the prevention of crime'.

The Court views Articles 2(1) and (2) as part of one general right, in some contexts at least. Both provisions imply 'a right to leave for such country of the person's choice to which he may be admitted'.[62] There will be an interference with the exercise of liberty of movement in terms of Article 2(2) if an individual is dispossessed of an identity document such as, for example, a passport.[63] Such a measure must be proportionate,[64] as must a refusal to issue a passport, for example as a measure to ensure performance of military service.[65]

Travel bans imposed for various reasons[66] (pending criminal or bankruptcy proceedings, enforcement of criminal sentences, failure or refusal to pay penalties or taxes, or judgment debts to private persons, failure to comply with military service obligations, or knowledge of 'State secrets')[67] will raise issues. In *Riener v Bulgaria*[68] the applicant, whose family was in Austria, had been banned from leaving Bulgaria for nine years owing to unpaid taxes. In principle this was a valid reason to prevent exit from the country; however, the principle of proportionality demanded that the aim of securing the unpaid debt could only be justified whilst it served its aim. The initial travel restriction was justified, but was automatically renewed over the years with little or no reference to the specific facts, including whether the fiscal authorities were still trying to obtain the outstanding money, whether the prospects of obtaining the money would have been reduced if the applicant had left the country, and the fact that the applicants' family was abroad. There was a violation of Article 2(2) of the Fourth Protocol.[69] In another case concerning refusal to leave a country, this time due to a pending criminal case, the Court placed weight upon the fact that the (French) applicant was in a foreign country (Poland) and not allowed to leave even for a short period of time. The preventive measure lasted over five years and the applicant's family life, business, and medical care opportunities etc were based in France.[70]

---

[59] *S v Sweden No 10653/83*, 42 DR 224 (1985).   [60] *X v Germany No 7680/76*, 9 DR 190 (1977).

[61] See *Schmid v Austria No 10670/83*, 44 DR 195 (1985) and *M v Germany No 10307/83*, 37 DR 113 (1984).

[62] *Baumann v France* 2001-V; 34 EHRR 1041 para 61. See also *Peltonen v Finland No 19583/92*, 80-A DR 38, para 31.

[63] *Baumann v France*, para 62. See also *M v Germany No 10307/83*, 37 DR 113. The same applies to an arbitrary entry in a passport that prohibits the individual leaving, *Sissanis v Romania* hudoc (2007).

[64] *Napijalo v Croatia* hudoc (2003); 40 EHRR 735 para 82. See also *Baumann v France* 2001-V; 34 EHRR 1041.   [65] *Peltonen v Finland No 19583/92*, 80-A DR 38.

[66] See *Khlyustov v Russia* hudoc (2013) paras 85–91.

[67] See *Stamose v Bulgaria* ECHR 2012 para 29. *Stamose* concerned a blanket (two-year) ban on leaving Bulgaria, on account of breaches of the immigration laws of the US. Despite its relatively short duration, and the fact that the ban may have been imposed in the context of measures designed to allay fears amongst EU member states of illegal emigration from Bulgaria, the automatic imposition of such a measure without any regard to the individual circumstances of the person concerned breached Article 2.

[68] Hudoc (2006); 45 EHRR 723. See also *Prescher v Bulgaria* hudoc (2011).

[69] *Riener v Bulgaria*, paras 127–8.

[70] *Miażdżyk v Poland* hudoc (2012) (no fair balance; notable that preventive measure was eventually lifted and, with the agreement of the domestic court concerned, the proceedings then proceeded without his presence).

Travel restrictions imposed upon convicted offenders may be justified by the need to prevent re-engagement in crime, but only 'if there are clear indications of a genuine public interest which outweigh the individual's right to freedom of movement'.[71] There must be 'concrete elements which are truly indicative of the continued existence of the risk that such measures seek to forestall'. So, imposition of restrictions on freedom to leave a country cannot be imposed merely because of an earlier criminal conviction and as the individual has not yet been rehabilitated.

Any interference with an individual's right to leave his or her country must 'from the outset and throughout its duration, [be] justified and proportionate in view of the circumstances'.[72] Measures lasting long periods must be subject to 'regular re-examination of their justification', and review 'should normally be carried out, at least in the final instance, by the courts, since they offer the best guarantees of the independence, impartiality and lawfulness of the procedures'. The review 'should enable the court to take account of all the factors involved, including those concerning the proportionality of the restrictive measure'.

When the inability to leave a country stems from the applicant's insistence upon remaining in an airport transit area (refusing to enter its territory to complete reasonable administrative documentation and checks), this may be an obstacle preventing enjoyment of the right in question that is not imputable to the respondent state.[73] An order temporarily prohibiting a spouse from taking her children with her when travelling abroad (and aimed at preventing removal of the children from her estranged husband) interferes with Article 2(2), but can be justified under Article 2(3).[74]

3. ARTICLE 3, FOURTH PROTOCOL: THE RIGHT OF A NATIONAL NOT TO BE EXPELLED FROM AND TO ENTER A STATE'S TERRITORY

Article 3 of the Fourth Protocol reads:

1. No one shall be expelled, by means either of an individual or of a collective measure, from the territory of the state of which he is a national.
2. No one shall be deprived of the right to enter the territory[75] of the state of which he is a national.

An expulsion occurs when a person is 'obliged permanently to leave the territory[76] of a state of which he is a national without being left the possibility of returning later'.[77]

---

[71] *Nalbantski v Bulgaria* hudoc (2011) para 65. See also *Hajibeyli v Azerbaijan* hudoc (2008) para 63.

[72] *Gochev v Bulgaria* hudoc (2009) para 50 (violation as ban was automatic and unlimited in practice).

[73] *Mogos v Romania* No 20420/02 hudoc (2004) DA.

[74] *Roldan Texeira v Italy* No 40655/98 hudoc (2000) DA.

[75] Article 3 issues may be raised potentially, see the *East African Asians* cases 3 EHRR 76 (1973) Com Rep para 242 (Mr Fawcett separate opinion); CM Res DH (77) 2.

[76] A person who is required to leave his national state's embassy abroad is not expelled from its 'territory', as an embassy is not territory for the purposes of the Fourth Protocol, *V v Denmark* No 17392/90 hudoc (1992); 15 EHRR CD 28.

[77] *X v Austria and Germany* No 6189/73, 46 CD 214 (1974). As with Article 2 of the Fourth Protocol, a non-metropolitan territory to which the Fourth Protocol is extended is a separate unit for the purposes of Article 3 (see Article 5(1), Fourth Protocol).

According to the Explanatory Report to the Fourth Protocol, which is not authoritative, extradition of nationals is outside the scope of Article 3. A request from the East German authorities for the extradition of a West German national from West Germany was not covered by Article 3, Fourth Protocol.[78] Article 3 only protects nationals of the expelling state.[79] The fact that a person has an application for the nationality of the expelling state under consideration by its authorities is not sufficient for Article 3 to apply; if he is granted nationality later, he will be able to return as a national.[80]

Article 3 of the Fourth Protocol secures an absolute and unconditional freedom from expulsion[81] of 'a national', so the meaning and scope of that term can be crucial. It is not explored in the Explanatory Report to the Protocol, but was highly relevant to *Slivenko v Latvia*,[82] a case of considerable political significance which concerned a Russian soldier, his wife, and child. All had been resident in Latvia for many years but were removed to Russia following Latvian independence in 1991 and a 1994 Russo-Latvian agreement regarding the withdrawal of Russian troops. The wife and child had never been 'nationals' of independent Latvia, but until 1991 they had been nationals of the Latvian SSR and stated that they had not lived in or had citizenship of another country. They, and the Russian government as third party interveners, argued that they should be regarded as Latvian 'nationals' given the autonomous Convention meaning of that term within Article 3 of the Fourth Protocol, and that their removal from Latvia breached that provision. However, in a Grand Chamber admissibility decision, the Court rejected this argument. It stated that ' "nationality" must be determined, in principle, by reference to the national law,' [83] and noted that a 'right to nationality' similar to that in Article 15 of the Universal Declaration of Human Rights was not guaranteed by the Convention or its Protocols. The Court accepted that an arbitrary denial of nationality could under certain circumstances amount to an interference with the rights under Article 8 of the Convention.[84] In determining what is 'arbitrary' it is suggested that the Court would at least take into account the limited controls general international law subjects states to when granting or withdrawing nationality.[85] The Court ultimately determined that as the mother and child in *Slivenko* had not been nationals of Latvia since it had ratified the Convention in 1997, and, as it appeared that neither had been arbitrarily denied Latvian citizenship, then their complaints were manifestly ill-founded.[86]

4. ARTICLE 4, FOURTH PROTOCOL: FREEDOM OF ALIENS FROM COLLECTIVE EXPULSION

Article 4 of the Fourth Protocol reads:

Collective expulsion of aliens is prohibited.

---

[78] *Brückmann v Germany No 6242/73*, 17 YB 458 (1974). As to extradition under Article 3 of the Convention, see Ch 6.   [79] See eg, *X v Sweden No 3916/69*, 32 CD 51 (1969).

[80] *L v Germany No 10564/83*, 40 DR 262 (1984). See also *X v Germany No 3745/68*, 31 CD 107 (1969).

[81] Cf the qualified nature of Article 8, which may have relevance in expulsion proceedings when the rights protected in para 8(1) are interfered with.   [82] 2003-X; 39 EHRR 490 GC.

[83] *No 48321/99* hudoc (2002) para 77 GC.

[84] *Slivenko v Latvia*. See also *Karassev and Family v Finland No 31414/96*, 1999-II DA.

[85] On this see Explanatory Report to P4 paras 21–3.

[86] *Slivenko v Latvia* 2003-X; 39 EHRR 490 paras 78–9 GC.

The core purpose is 'to prevent States being able to remove certain aliens without examining their personal circumstances and, consequently, without enabling them to put forward their arguments against the measure taken by the relevant authority'.[87]

Article 4 applies regardless of whether the individual has entered the state lawfully or remains a lawful entrant,[88] although, as is noted later in this section, entrance to the physical territory of the state concerned may not be required. Aliens are understood to include stateless persons.[89] 'Expulsion' can be taken to have the same meaning as it has under Article 3, Fourth Protocol. Article 4 does not prohibit individual cases of expulsion; this is a matter dealt with by Article 1 of the Seventh Protocol instead.

'[C]ollective expulsion' concerns 'any measure compelling aliens, as a group, to leave a country, except where such a measure is taken on the basis of a reasonable and objective examination of the particular case of each individual alien of the group'.[90] The fact that a number of aliens 'receive similar decisions does not lead to the conclusion that there is a collective expulsion when each person concerned has been given the opportunity to put arguments against his expulsion to the competent authorities on an individual basis'.[91]

In *Conka v Belgium*,[92] some Slovakian nationals of Romany origin had exhausted legal channels regarding their asylum requests—in which the Court duly recognized that each individual's circumstances were addressed—and had been properly served with orders requiring them to leave Belgium. Those orders were ignored. A short period of time after this, the unsuspecting applicants were tricked into attending a police station along with around seventy other individuals of the same status and nationality. They received a notice informing them that their presence was required in order to proceed with further aspects of their asylum claim. On arrival they were detained[93] and then deported after having been served with 'fresh' expulsion orders which identified them as illegal immigrants and which did not indicate that they had been formulated with regard to individual personal circumstances. The Court's (four to three) division stemmed from the influence these background circumstances had on the Article 4 claim. The majority of four, finding a violation, cited the deficiency associated with the fresh expulsion order and appear to have been influenced by the nature of what was evidently a pre-planned operation to execute group repatriation. They could not 'eliminate all doubt that the expulsion might have been collective' [94] and criticized the fact that the personal circumstances of each applicant had not been 'genuinely and individually' taken into account in the period following when they were encouraged to attend the police station via the misleading notice'.[95] The minority of three took a less formalistic approach to the 'fresh' expulsion order given the completeness of the legal procedures that had been concluded before, albeit some time before, the applicants went to the police station. They emphasized the freedom for a state to repatriate as a group (after a reasonable and objective examination of the particular

---

[87] *Hirsi Jamaa and Others v Italy* ECHR-2012; 55 EHRR 627 para 177 GC.

[88] Cf Article 2 applies to those 'lawfully' within a territory.

[89] Explanatory Report to P4 para 32.   [90] *Andric v Sweden No 45917/99* hudoc (1999) DA.

[91] *Andric v Sweden*; see also *Hirsi Jamaa and Others v Italy* ECHR-2012; 55 EHRR 627 para 184 GC; *MA v Cyprus* hudoc (2013) (mistake made processing numerous cases did not indicate a collective expulsion, para 254); *Berisha and Haljiti v the former Yugoslav Republic of Macedonia No 18670/03* (2005) DA (single common decision, applicants having made a joint asylum claim) and *Dritsas v Italy No 2344/02* hudoc (2011) DA (expulsion orders not in the applicants' names as they refused to submit identify papers).

[92] 2002-I; 34 EHRR 1298. See also *Sultani v France* hudoc (2007).

[93] Which was also a violation of Article 5(1)(f), see Ch 8, section 5.VI.b.

[94] *Conka v Belgium* 2002-I; 34 EHRR 1298 para 61. See also the reasoning at para 62 explaining why doubt existed on the facts.   [95] *Conka v Belgium*, para 63.

case of each individual alien of the group),[96] an option the national authorities were free to choose for reasons of efficiency and economy, and one which clearly could not take place without prior preparation.

The second ever violation of Article 4 was found in *Hirsi Jamaa and Others v Italy*.[97] The applicants, eleven Somali nationals and thirteen Eritrean nationals, formed part of a group of some 200 people intent on irregular migration in Italy. They were intercepted by official Italian ships thirty-five miles off an Italian island which was proximate to the Libyan and Tunisian coast, embarked onto official Italian ships (possessions and documents being confiscated), returned to Libya, and (according to the applicants) forced to disembark. The merits of the case were straightforward in that there were no identification procedures and so no attempt to examine the personal circumstances of the applicants. Rather, the crucial question was whether Article 4 applied in the first place, it being argued by the Italian government that what occurred was a refusal to authorize entry, and so not (collective) 'expulsion', as the applicants had not entered Italian territory or gained illegal entry. Rejecting this, the unanimous Grand Chamber took the principled stance that:

> the removal of aliens carried out in the context of interceptions on the high seas by the authorities of a State in the exercise of their sovereign authority, the effect of which is to prevent migrants from reaching the borders of the State or even to push them back to another State, constitutes an exercise of jurisdiction within the meaning of Article 1 of the Convention which engages the responsibility of the State in question under Article 4 of Protocol No. 4.[98]

On the facts, the Court was satisfied that the operation had been carried out with the intention of preventing irregular migrants reaching Italian soil.[99]

The stance taken by the Grand Chamber with respect to Article 4 was justified in part by the need to apply it against the background of the Convention as a 'living instrument'.[100] In effect, the Court ruled that it was necessary for Article 4 to apply were the level of protection it was intended to afford not to fall away given a new environment, it being noted that since Protocol 4 had been drafted 'migratory flows in Europe have continued to intensify, with increasing use being made of the sea, although the interception of migrants on the high seas and their removal to countries of transit or origin are now a means of migratory control, in so far as they constitute tools for States to combat irregular immigration'.[101] Article 4 had to apply otherwise:

> a significant component of contemporary migratory patterns would not fall within the ambit of that provision, notwithstanding the fact that the conduct it is intended to prohibit can occur outside national territory and in particular, as in the instant case, on the high seas. Article 4 would thus be ineffective in practice with regard to such situations,

---

[96] On group repatriation see also *Sulejmanovic v Italy* hudoc (2002) F Sett.

[97] ECHR-2012; 55 EHRR 627 GC. Two violations of Article 3 (main Convention) were also found.

[98] *Hirsi Jamaa and Others v Italy*, para 180.

[99] *Hirsi Jamaa and Others v Italy*, para 181 (referring to a press conference in which an Italian minister cited the push back operation as a success in the struggle against illegal migration and referred to an Italian-Libyan agreement secured earlier in the year).

[100] For the Court's approach to this important question of interpretation, see paras 166–81. The *travaux préparatoires* did not preclude the Court's interpretation, and Article 4 did not refer to 'territory', unlike Article 3 of Protocol 4 and Article 1 of Protocol 7.

[101] *Hirsi Jamaa and Others v Italy* ECHR-2012; 55 EHRR 627 para 176 GC.

which, however, are on the increase. The consequence of that would be that migrants having taken to the sea, often risking their lives, and not having managed to reach the borders of a State, would not be entitled to an examination of their personal circumstances before being expelled, unlike those travelling by land.[102]

Finally, Article 3 of the main Convention may be relevant to collective expulsion in certain circumstances.[103]

5. THE SIXTH AND THIRTEENTH PROTOCOLS: THE DEATH PENALTY

In the 1990s, abolition of the death penalty became a precondition for membership of the Council of Europe and today the Sixth and Thirteenth Protocols have been ratified by the great majority of Convention states.[104] No execution has taken place in the Council of Europe's member states since 1997,[105] and it has been claimed that Europe has become a *de facto* 'death penalty free area', since all Convention states have either abolished this sentence or at least have instituted a moratorium on executions.

The text of Article 2(1) of the Convention envisages the death penalty. Article 1 of the Sixth Protocol (opened for signature in 1983) states '[t]he death penalty shall be abolished. No-one shall be condemned to such penalty or executed', although Article 2 of this Protocol allowed use of the death penalty in time of war. This exception was removed by the Thirteenth Protocol (opened for signature in 2002) through which ratifying states express their resolve to 'take the final step in order to abolish the death penalty in all circumstances' (Preamble to Thirteenth Protocol).[106] Parties to the Protocols must abolish the death penalty, if it still exists in its law, and must not reintroduce it. The Protocols create a 'subjective right', ie one that a person is able to enforce in the national courts.[107] No reservations are allowed to either Protocol, nor may either instrument be the subject of a derogation.

The case law on the relationship between Articles 2(1) and 3 (main Convention) and Protocols 6 and 13 provide an interesting example of the Court's approach to evolutive interpretation. It has long been established that issues may arise under Article 3 of the Convention in respect of a state which proposes to deport an individual to a country where there is a real risk of Article 3 ill-treatment, and that issues relating to the employment of the death penalty may be of relevance.[108] *Soering v United Kingdom*[109] (1989) was a seminal case here, although at that stage the Court clearly concluded that Article 3 could not be interpreted as generally prohibiting the death penalty. With respect to Article 2(1) of the main Convention, which permitted use of the death penalty, the Court noted that, by creating Protocol 6, the states had demonstrated their intention to use a normal method of amendment of the text in order to introduce a new obligation, here to abolish capital punishment in time of peace.

---

[102] *Hirsi Jamaa and Others v Italy*, para 177.   [103] See Ch 6.

[104] See the introduction to this chapter.

[105] For further information consult http://hub.coe.int/what-we-do/human-rights/death-penalty.

[106] Article 2(2) of the EU Charter of Fundamental Rights states: 'No one shall be condemned to the death penalty, or executed'. There are no qualifications.

[107] Explanatory Report to the Sixth Protocol, CE Doc H (83) 3, p 6.   [108] See Ch 6.

[109] A161 (1989); 11 EHRR 439.

However, in the subsequent cases of *Öcalan v Turkey*[110] and *Al-Saadoon v UK*,[111] the Court modified its position, looking in particular at state acceptance of Protocols 6 and 13. In 2003, via its Chamber judgment in *Öcalan v Turkey*, the Court, citing the 'living instrument' doctrine, suggested that the states might have agreed to abrogate or modify Article 2(1) of the main Convention. It had regard to the Convention states' practice as regards abolition of the death penalty and the near universal ratification of the Sixth Protocol (which, at that stage all states had signed, and all but three ratified) to conclude that capital punishment *in peacetime* had 'come to be regarded as an unacceptable, if not inhuman, form of punishment which is no longer permissible under Article 2'.[112] Having said this, both the Chamber and Grand Chamber avoided a firm conclusion as to whether the death penalty was incompatible *per se* with Article 3 of the Convention.[113] Seven years later in *Al-Saadoon v UK* (2010), the Court observed that matters had evolved since *Öcalan*: Protocol 13 had been ratified by forty-two member states, and signed but not ratified by a further three, there being just two states which had not signed it. Such 'figures, together with consistent State practice in observing the moratorium on capital punishment, [were] strongly indicative that Article 2 ha[d] been amended so as to prohibit the death penalty in all circumstances'.[114] On that basis, the Court did not consider that the wording of Article 2(1) 'continue[d] to act as a bar to its interpreting the words "inhuman or degrading treatment or punishment" in Article 3 as including the death penalty'.

The Court has therefore *indicated* that the use of the death penalty will breach Article 2(1) of the Convention, and that there is *no bar* (under Article 2(1)) to its holding the death penalty is contrary to Article 3 *per se*. In fact, however, it has not held so. In *Öcalan*, when the applicant had had his death sentence commuted to life imprisonment, the Court concluded that the *imposition* of the death sentence on the applicant *following an unfair trial* amounted to inhuman treatment in violation of Article 3.[115] As to *Al-Saadoon*, the Court considered it unnecessary to decide whether there had been violations of the applicants' rights under Article 2 (main Convention) and Article 1 of Protocol 13. This was because it held that the transfer of the detainee applicants to the Iraqi authorities violated Article 3, *the fear of execution* by the Iraqi authorities giving rise to psychological suffering breaching that provision. *Al-Saadoon* nevertheless established that Article 2(1) (main Convention) and Article 1 of Protocol 13 'prohibit the extradition or deportation of an individual to another State where substantial grounds have been shown for believing that he or she would face a real risk of being subjected to the death penalty

---

[110] Hudoc (2003); 37 EHRR 238 (Chamber judgment); see also *Öcalan v Turkey* 2005-IV; 41 EHRR 985 GC.   [111] ECHR-2010; 51 EHRR 9.

[112] *Öcalan v Turkey* hudoc (2003)at paras 196 and 198. The Grand Chamber stated that it agreed with the relevant passages of the judgment expressed by the Chamber, *Öcalan v Turkey*, para 163. Cf, the statement in the (Chamber) judgment in *Shamayev v Georgia and Russia* 2005-III para 333.

[113] The Chamber stated that state practice regarding Sixth and Thirteenth Protocols entailed that 'it can also be argued that *the implementation of the death penalty* can be regarded as inhuman and degrading treatment contrary to Article 3' (emphasis added *Öcalan v Turkey*, para 198 (see however the dissenting judgment of Judge Türmen)). The Grand Chamber was more cautious, implying that it was probably not possible to say that the death penalty was contrary to Article 3 *per se* until all states had ratified the Thirteenth Protocol, though it would not commit itself to a definitive statement on the point: *Öcalan v Turkey* 2005-IV; 41 EHRR 985 para 165 GC. In *GB v Bulgaria* hudoc (2004) para 72 the Court cited European state practice and stated that 'capital punishment, . . . is no longer seen as having any legitimate place in democratic society'.

[114] *Al-Saadoon v UK* ECHR-2010; 51 EHRR 9 para 120.

[115] The imposition of the death penalty in certain other circumstances can violate Article 3, see *Shamayev v Georgia and Russia* 2005-III para 333 and *Ilaşcu v Moldova and Russia* 2004-VII; 40 EHRR 1030 paras 431 and 440 GC.

there'.[116] In such situations, in order for the removal to proceed it will be necessary to obtain 'sufficient and binding assurances...from the responsible authorities of the requesting State'.[117] The Court will examine the quality of such assurances and whether in light of the requesting state's practices they can be relied upon.[118]

6. ARTICLE 1, SEVENTH PROTOCOL: FREEDOM FROM EXPULSION OF INDIVIDUAL ALIENS

Article 1 of the Seventh Protocol reads:

1. An alien lawfully resident in the territory of a state shall not be expelled therefrom except in pursuance of a decision reached in accordance with law and shall be allowed:
   a. to submit reasons against his expulsion,
   b. to have his case reviewed, and
   c. to be represented for these purposes before the competent authority or a person or persons designated by that authority.

2. An alien may be expelled before the exercise of his rights under paragraph 1, a, b and c of this Article, when such expulsion is necessary in the interests of public order or is grounded on reasons of national security.

In contrast with Article 4 of the Fourth Protocol, this concerns cases of individual, rather than collective, expulsion;[119] however, unlike Article 4, it requires only that the rule of law be complied with (an obvious breach occurring when an applicant is served with a deportation notice and immediately deported).

Article 1 is not a prohibition on expulsion and applies only to aliens who are 'lawfully resident' in a state's territory, so it does not apply to illegal entrants. It does not protect aliens who have not passed through immigration, those in transit, those admitted for a non-residential purpose, those awaiting a decision on residence,[120] or those whose visa or residence permit has expired.[121] A person will not be lawfully resident if he has gained admission illegally or has infringed other conditions of his permit.[122] The term 'lawful'

---

[116] *Al-Saadoon v UK* ECHR-2010; 51 EHRR 9 para 123. See paras 124–5 as to its approach; as to conflicting international obligations, see paras 126–8. Article 19(2) of the EU Charter of Fundamental Rights states 'No one may be removed, expelled or extradited to a state where there is a serious risk that he or she would be subjected to the death penalty.'

[117] *Rrapo v Albania* hudoc (2012) para 70. A 'diplomatic note' from the United States Embassy sufficed on the facts of this case. See also *Babar Ahmad and Others v the United Kingdom No 24027/07* hudoc (2010) DA.

[118] *Rrapo v Albania* hudoc (2012) para 72 (no potential breach: assurances provided by US were 'specific, clear and unequivocal', and binding upon the US Department of Justice, there being no reported breaches of an assurance given by the US government to a contracting state; the US's 'long-term interest in honouring its extradition commitments alone would be sufficient to give rise to a presumption of good faith against any risk of a breach of [the] assurances' (para 73)).

[119] Expulsion cases may also raise issues under Articles 3, 5(1)(f), 8, and 13 of the Convention and Article 4 of the Fourth Protocol.

[120] Explanatory Report on the Seventh Protocol ('Explanatory Report P7'), CE Doc H (83) 3, para 9. An alien in this context can be taken to include a stateless person. The Court has compared the notion of 'residence' to 'home' under Article 8 of the Convention, in that 'both are not limited to physical presence but depend on the existence of sufficient and continuous links with a specific place', *Nolan and K v Russia* hudoc (2009); 53 EHRR 977 para 110.

[121] *Bolat v Russia* 2006-XI; 46 EHRR 18 para 76 (citing *Voulfovitch and Oulianova v Sweden No 19373/92* hudoc (1993) DA). [122] *Bolat v Russia*.

refers to national law, which must therefore be followed.[123] 'Expulsion' is an autonomous concept[124] and can be taken *mutatis mutandis* to have the meaning that it has under Article 3 of the Fourth Protocol,[125] so that, *inter alia*, it does not include extradition. The requirement that the expulsion be 'in accordance with law' can likewise be taken to have the autonomous meaning that it has in other Convention provisions,[126] so it addresses matters such as the quality of the law.[127]

Exceptionally, an alien may be expelled before he has exercised the procedural rights set out in Article 1(1)(a)–(c), where the expulsion is 'necessary in the interests of public order or is grounded on reasons of national security' (Article 1(2)).[128] If so, these exceptions should be applied taking into account the principle of proportionality[129] plus the rights set out in Article 1(1) should be available after expulsion.[130]

According to the Explanatory Report for Protocol Seven, an alien's right to submit reasons against his expulsion applies 'even before being able to have his case reviewed'.[131] As to the right to have the expulsion decision 'reviewed', this 'does not necessarily require a two-stage procedure before different authorities'; it would be sufficient for the 'competent authority' that took the decision to consider the matter again.[132] The 'competent authority' does not have to give the alien or his representative an oral hearing; a written procedure would suffice. Nor does it have to have a power of decision; it is enough that it may make a recommendation to the body that does take the final decision. Clearly, the 'competent authority' does not itself have to be a judicial body that complies with Article 6, Convention.[133] Although, therefore, Article 1 offers an alien at least the possibility of having his arguments against expulsion taken into account by the executive, it offers only a modest guarantee of procedural due process. Having said this, as regards the nature of the review process itself, the Court has referred to the principle of effectiveness and found a violation of this provision when the review itself was a pure formality such that 'the applicant was not genuinely able to have his case examined in the light of reasons militating against his deportation'.[134]

7. ARTICLE 2, SEVENTH PROTOCOL: THE RIGHT TO REVIEW IN CRIMINAL CASES

Article 2 of the Seventh Protocol reads:

> 1. Everyone convicted of a criminal offence by a tribunal shall have the right to have his conviction or sentence reviewed by a higher tribunal. The exercise of this right, including the grounds on which it may be exercised, shall be governed by law.

[123] It was not in *Bolat v Russia* 2006-XI; 46 EHRR 18.

[124] *Bolat v Russia*, para 79. Issuing a decision to bar someone from returning to the country following his next trip abroad would count, *Nolan and K v Russia* hudoc (2009) para 112.

[125] See Ch 24, section III.   [126] See Ch 11.

[127] See *Lupsa v Romania* 2006-VII; 46 EHRR 810 para 55 and *CG v Bulgaria* hudoc (2008).

[128] See, eg, *Al-Dabbagh v Sweden* No 36765/97 hudoc (1997) DA.

[129] *CG v Bulgaria* hudoc (2008) paras 77–8 (Court concluded that expedited expulsion was not necessary on national security grounds or otherwise proportionate).

[130] *Lupsa v Romania* 2006-VII; 46 EHRR 810 para 53.   [131] Explanatory Report, p 7.

[132] Explanatory Report, p 7.

[133] *Maaouia v France* 2000-X; 33 EHRR 1037 para 37 GC (by 'adopting Article 1 of Protocol 7 containing guarantees specifically concerning proceedings for the expulsion of aliens the states clearly intimated their intention not to include such proceedings within the scope of Article 6(1) of the Convention').

[134] *Lupsa v Romania* 2006-VII; 46 EHRR 810 para 60 (expulsion for 'national security' reasons). See also *CG v Bulgaria* hudoc (2008) para 74 and *Kaushal and Others v Bulgaria* hudoc (2010).

> 2. This right may be subject to exceptions in regard to offences of a minor character, as prescribed by law, or in cases in which the person concerned was tried in the first instance by the highest tribunal or was convicted following an appeal against acquittal.

Article 2 of the Seventh Protocol guarantees a right to 'review' for a conviction or sentence by a higher tribunal. It does not provide for a right to appeal on the 'merits' of a judgment, and this is not protected by Article 6 of the main Convention either, although that provision has been interpreted as controlling any right of appeal in criminal cases that a state in its discretion may provide under its law.

In *Krombach v France*,[135] the Court stated that the contracting states had a 'wide margin of appreciation' to determine how the right secured by Article 2 of the Seventh Protocol was to be exercised. It acknowledged (as is confirmed in the Explanatory Report) that the review by a higher court of a conviction or sentence may concern both points of fact and points of law or be confined solely to points of law. Procedural limitations, such as the requirement to seek leave to appeal, are compatible with Article 2, but the right to review must be directly available to those concerned and 'independent of any discretionary action by the authorities'.[136] Restrictions on the right to a review have to pursue a legitimate aim and not infringe the very essence of the right.[137] This is analogous with the right of access to a court embodied in Article 6(1) of the Convention[138] and consistent with the exception authorized by paragraph 2 of Article 2.

The term 'tribunal' within Article 2(1) is capable of an autonomous interpretation and has the same meaning as 'tribunal' within Article 6(1) of the main Convention text.[139] Still, the condition that Article 2(1) only applies to offences tried by a 'tribunal' is restrictive. Hence, on the face of it, someone who is the subject of a disciplinary offence which qualifies as a 'criminal offence' for the purposes of Article 2 has no right to review of that decision under Article 2 if it was not made by a 'tribunal'.[140] It is submitted that the fair trial requirements in Article 6 of the Convention, as they apply to appeal proceedings,[141] must be respected by the 'higher tribunal' when it conducts its review of the tribunal decision for Article 2 to be complied with.

The guarantee in Article 2(1) of the Seventh Protocol is in certain respects limited in its impact by Article 2(2). This provides that the right of appeal 'may be subject to exceptions in regard to offences of a minor character, as prescribed by law, or in cases in which the person concerned was tried in the first instance by the highest tribunal or was convicted following an appeal against acquittal'. As to the meaning of 'minor' offences, the Court has followed the Explanatory Report which suggests that 'an important criterion is whether

---

[135] 2001-II para 96 (French law denied a right of appeal on points of law to an applicant convicted in his absence). See also *Papon v France* 2002-VII; 39 EHRR 217; *Pesti and Frodl v Austria* Nos 27618–27619/95, 2000-I DA; *Zaicevs v Latvia* hudoc 2007; and *Galstyan v Armenia* hudoc (2007).

[136] *Gurepka v Ukraine* hudoc (2005); 43 EHRR 1004 paras 59–60 (the relevant procedure was not a sufficiently effective remedy as it was not directly accessible to a party to the proceedings and did not depend on his or her motion and arguments, para 60; further the mere fact that the review initiated by the Prosecutor's Office suspended the sentence was insufficient to make the remedy effective, para 61)

[137] *Krombach v France* 2001-II para 96.   [138] See Ch 9.

[139] *Didier v France* No 58188/00, 2002-VII DA. See also Explanatory Report P7 para 17.

[140] Of course, if the offence is a 'criminal' one in the sense of Article 6, that provision requires at least an appeal to an Article 6 tribunal. In that case, Article 2 of the Seventh Protocol requires a right of review of the second, Article 6 tribunal, decision. See further Van Dijk and Van Hoof *et al* (eds), *Theory and Practice of the European Convention on Human Rights*, 2006, p 972.

[141] For the application of Article 6 to appeal proceedings, see Ch 9.

the offence is punishable by imprisonment or not'.[142] The Report also suggests that where a person pleads guilty at his trial, his right of review is limited to his sentence. The same Report also states that the same right is satisfied by leave to appeal proceedings where leave is not given and that, as case law has confirmed,[143] it is not necessary for the appeal to be on points of fact and law; the state concerned may decide to limit it to one or the other.

8. ARTICLE 3, SEVENTH PROTOCOL: RIGHT TO COMPENSATION FOR MISCARRIAGES OF JUSTICE

Article 3 of the Seventh Protocol reads:

> When a person has by a final decision been convicted of a criminal offence and when subsequently his conviction has been reversed, or he has been pardoned, on the ground that a new or newly discovered fact shows conclusively that there has been a miscarriage of justice, the person who has suffered punishment as a result of such conviction shall be compensated according to the law or the practice of the state concerned, unless it proved that the non-disclosure of the unknown fact in time is wholly or partly attributable to him.

Article 3 provides for a right to compensation for miscarriages of justice in the circumstances and subject to the conditions that are set out. The person must have been convicted of a criminal offence by a final decision and suffered consequential punishment. A decision will be final when it is *res judicata*. The Explanatory Report states that this will be the case where it 'is irrevocable, that is to say when no further ordinary remedies are available or when the parties have exhausted such remedies or have permitted the time-limit to expire without availing themselves of them'.[144] Article 3 does not apply where a charge has been dismissed or an accused person is acquitted by the trial court or by a higher court on appeal.[145]

The conviction must have been overturned or a pardon granted because of 'new or newly discovered *fact[s]*'.[146] The Court has followed this narrow formula carefully,[147] such that quashing of convictions on other grounds will not suffice. Thus a conviction that was quashed due to a review court's reassessment of the evidence used in the original trial did not suffice.[148] What would be required, it seems, is an overturning based on 'omission or

---

[142] Explanatory Report P7 para 21. As to relevant case law see, *Luchaninova v Ukraine* hudoc (2011) ('minor' as petty theft and was not punishable by imprisonment, para 72); *Zaicevs v Latvia* ECHR 2007 IX ('an offence for which the law prescribes a custodial sentence as the main punishment cannot be described as "minor"', para 55) and *Kakabadze and Others v Georgia* hudoc (2012) (thirty days' detention was not regarded as 'minor', para 97).

[143] *NW v Luxembourg No 19715/92* hudoc (1992) DA; 15 EHRR CD 107 and *Loewenguth v France No 53183/99* hudoc (2000) DA.

[144] Explanatory Report P7 para 22. The Report is quoting the Explanatory Report of the European Convention on the International Validity of Criminal Judgments 1970, p 22.

[145] It clearly does not apply when an applicant is detained on remand, *Nakov v the Former Yugoslav Republic of Macedonia No 68286/01* hudoc (2002) DA.

[146] According to the Explanatory Report for Protocol 7, the new facts should show conclusively that there has been a miscarriage of justice, by which is meant 'some serious failure in the judicial process involving grave prejudice to the convicted person', Explanatory Report P7 para 23.

[147] In accordance with the intention of the drafters of Protocol 7, see comments made in *Bachowski v Poland No 32463/06* hudoc DA.   [148] *Matveyev v Russia No 26601/02* hudoc DA.

concealment of facts which could or should have been known' to the convicting court, or the subsequent 'coming to light of new facts' of such a nature as 'cast fundamental doubt on the soundness of the criminal conviction'.[149] So, the overturning of an earlier conviction on the basis that it was politically motivated (under a previous governmental regime) would not on its own be a basis for Article 3 to apply.[150] It may also be noted that Article 3 provides that there is no right to compensation if the non-disclosure of the unknown fact in time is wholly or partly attributable to the person convicted.

The Explanatory Report states that the procedure to be followed to establish a miscarriage of justice is a matter for national law.[151] It is for the state concerned to determine the compensation to be paid in accordance with its law and practice, although presumably the Strasbourg authorities are competent to ensure that it is not totally insufficient. A violation (the first ever of this Article) was found in *Poghosyan and Baghdasaryan v Armenia*,[152] when national law made no provision for compensation and the applicant, who had spent approximately five-and-a-half years in detention before being considered to have been acquitted, had merely received an apology from the state and pecuniary damages. The Court stated that, 'the purpose of Article 3 of Protocol No. 7 is not merely to recover any pecuniary loss caused by a wrongful conviction but also to provide a person convicted as a result of a miscarriage of justice with compensation for any non-pecuniary damage such as distress, anxiety, inconvenience and loss of enjoyment of life'.[153]

The Explanatory Report indicates that Article 3 should oblige states to compensate persons 'only in clear cases of miscarriage of justice, in the sense that there would be acknowledgement that the person concerned was clearly innocent'. Thus only if all the conditions mentioned in Article 3 are satisfied should compensation be paid. So there would be no automatic violation of this provision where no compensation is awarded after an appellate court had quashed a conviction because it had discovered some fact which introduced a reasonable doubt as to the guilt of the accused which had been overlooked by the trial judge.[154]

Article 3 of Protocol 7 is a derogable right. As regards the right to compensation for illegal detention under Article 5, reference should be made to Article 5(5).[155]

9. ARTICLE 4, SEVENTH PROTOCOL: *NE BIS IN IDEM*

Article 4 of the Seventh Protocol reads:

> 1. No one shall be liable to be tried or punished again in criminal proceedings under the jurisdiction of the same state for an offence for which he has already been finally acquitted or convicted in accordance with the law and penal procedure of that state.

---

[149] *Bachowski v Poland No 32463/06* hudoc DA (1959 judgment overturned as applicable substantive criminal law had been seriously distorted and misapplied; however, Article 3 did not apply as the acquittal was based on a reassessment of evidence already used and known to the court in the original proceedings).
[150] *Bachowski v Poland No 32463/06* hudoc DA.   [151] Explanatory Report P7 para 25.
[152] Hudoc (2012).   [153] *Poghosyan and Baghdasaryan v Armenia* ECHR 2012 para 51.
[154] Explanatory Report P7, para 25.
[155] See Ch 8, although, for reasons that are not easy to decipher, the Court stated that it was not necessary to examine Article 5(5) in *Poghosyan and Baghdasaryan v Armenia* ECHR 2012 as it had found a violation of Article 3 Protocol 7, para 54.

2. The provisions of the preceding paragraph shall not prevent the re-opening of the case in accordance with the law and penal procedure of the state concerned, if there is evidence of new or newly discovered facts, or if there has been a fundamental defect in the previous proceedings, which could affect the outcome of the case.

Article 4 of the Seventh Protocol incorporates the principle *ne bis in idem*.[156] In other terms it protects freedom from double jeopardy. The protection against duplication of criminal proceedings is one of the specific safeguards associated with the general guarantee of a fair hearing in criminal proceedings. Nevertheless, in the Convention system in principle *ne bis in idem* is protected under Article 4 of the Seventh Protocol and not Article 6 of the main Convention. Accordingly, if the respondent state concerned has not ratified the Protocol, those parts of applications raising a *ne bis in idem* claim will be rejected at the admissibility stage.[157]

The first point to note is that Article 4 only applies to duplication of criminal proceedings. So it does not prevent an individual being subject to criminal proceedings and then, for the same act, to action of a different character (for example, disciplinary action in the case of an official),[158] or subject to an administrative sanction followed by criminal proceedings.[159] The notion of 'criminal' is an autonomous one.[160] Here the Court looks to the general principles concerning the corresponding words 'criminal charge' and 'penalty' respectively in Articles 6 and 7 of the Convention, and applies the so-called '*Engel* criteria'.[161]

It does not matter whether or not the person was actually acquitted in the first set of proceedings, or the second, or both, Article 4 being broader than the right not to be *punished* twice, or a prohibition on a second conviction. Rather the Article 4 guarantee provides for three distinct elements: no one should be '(i) liable to be tried, (ii) tried or (iii) punished for the same offence'.[162] The aim of Article 4 is therefore to prohibit the repetition of a prosecution or trial—which may involve being remanded in custody, participation in an investigation, and standing in a trial lasting a substantial period of time—that has been concluded by a 'final' acquittal or conviction. It becomes 'relevant on commencement of a new prosecution, where a prior acquittal or conviction has already acquired the force of *res judicata*'.[163]

---

[156] For a useful survey of relevant comparative and international law, see *Sergey Zolotukhin v Russia* ECHR 2009; 54 EHRR 503 paras 31-44 GC.

[157] *Blokker v Netherlands* No 45282/99 hudoc (2000) DA.

[158] See *RT v Switzerland* No 31982/96 hudoc (2000) DA and Explanatory Report P7 para 32.

[159] *Kurdov and Ivanov v Bulgaria* hudoc (2011).

[160] See *Sergey Zolotukhin v Russia* ECHR 2009; 54 EHRR 503 paras 52-54 GC and *Storbråten v Norway* No 12277/04 hudoc (2007) DA; 44 EHRR SE 289 (citing authorities including *Rosenquist v Sweden* No 60619/00 hudoc (2004) DA; 40 EHRR SE 222; *Manasson v Sweden* No 41265/98 (2003) DA; and *Göktan v France* 2002-V; 37 EHRR 320 para 48).

[161] *Sergey Zolotukhin v Russia* ECHR 2009; 54 EHRR 503 para 53 GC, on the '*Engel* criteria' see Ch 9, section 2.I.a.

[162] *Sergey Zolotukhin v Russia*, para 110 GC.

[163] *Sergey Zolotukhin v Russia*, para 83 GC. The Grand Chamber adopted (para 107) the wording of the Explanatory Report to the Seventh Protocol, which itself referred back to the European Convention on the International Validity of Criminal Judgments, to the effect that a 'decision is final "if, according to the traditional expression, it has acquired the force of *res judicata*. This is the case when it is irrevocable, that is to say when no further ordinary remedies are available or when the parties have exhausted such remedies or have permitted the time-limit to expire without availing themselves of them" ', Explanatory Report P7 para 22. In *Marguš v Croatia* hudoc (2012); 56 EHRR 1085 (GC judgment awaited), on which see further analysis later in this section, the first prosecution of the applicant was terminated by the application of an amnesty law.

Two points may be made here. Firstly, valid (within time) prosecution rights of appeal are compatible with Article 4.[164] However, extraordinary remedies are not taken into account in the assessment of finality, even if they represent a continuation of proceedings, since the final nature of the decision does not depend on their being used.[165]

The second point concerns instances when a second prosecution is brought, but then retracted by the authorities in acknowledgement of the *non bis in idem* principle and offering appropriate redress (notably by terminating the second proceedings and effacing its effects).[166] Here the Court accepts that there will be a loss of 'victim' status.

It may be the case that what the applicant alleges is a new set of proceedings is not viewed that way by the Court. For example, one application declared inadmissible concerned an individual convicted for drink driving and who, as a result of a subsequent administrative decision, had his licence taken away. The Court agreed that the latter penalty was 'criminal' for the purposes of Article 4; however, there was 'a sufficiently close connection...in substance and in time' between the conviction and penalty such that the withdrawal was viewed as part of the sanctions under domestic law for the offences in issue.[167]

It is clear that, subject to Article 4(2), Article 4(1) prohibits a further prosecution for exactly the same offence. However, a matter that has troubled the Court is how Article 4 might be relevant to a single criminal act or, one might say, episode, which is capable of being separated out into more than one criminal 'offence', for example a driving offence which may be caught by various statutory definitions. In principle, Article 4 does not preclude separate offences being tried by the same[168] or even different courts[169] if they were part of a single criminal act. But whilst in some cases identifying what are separate offences will be a straightforward exercise,[170] in others the issue is very complicated.[171]

As the Grand Chamber acknowledged in 2009 in *Sergey Zolotukhin v Russia*,[172] its preceding jurisprudence had demonstrated 'several approaches to the question whether the offences for which an applicant was prosecuted were the same'. The relevant cases were *Gradinger*, *Oliveira*, and *Franz Fischer*, and they will be mentioned briefly here to provide context to *Sergey Zolotukhin*.

The chamber doubted (para 67) whether what occurred had been an assessment of the applicant's guilt, and so whether there had been a 'final acquittal or conviction' for the purposes of Article 4 of Protocol 7, but it was prepared to leave open that question.

[164] *Sergey Zolotukhin v Russia* ECHR 2009; 54 EHRR 503 para 108 GC.

[165] *Sergey Zolotukhin v Russia*, para 108 (referring to requests to reopen proceedings or for an extension of the expired time limit).

[166] *Sergey Zolotukhin v Russia*, para 115, referring to earlier case law, including *Zigarella v Italy No 48154/99* 2002-IX DA (Italian authorities brought prosecution in ignorance of earlier proceedings and immediately closed them when their mistake was realized; this was adequate redress).

[167] *Nilsson v Sweden No 73661/01* hudoc (2005) DA.

[168] *Goktan v France* 2002-V; 37 EHRR 320 (dealing in illegally imported drugs as an offence under the general criminal law and as a customs offence resulting in a fine which when not paid resulted in further imprisonment; no violation of Article 4).   [169] *Oliveira v Switzerland* 1998-V; 28 EHRR 289.

[170] Convictions for speeding eight times in the course of one journey will not attract the applicability of Article 4 when the offences are treated as separate events involving different speed limit zones, *Kantner v Austria No 29990/96* hudoc (1999) DA. See also *Aşci v Austria No 4483/02* hudoc (2006) DA.

[171] Applications rejected at the admissibility stage of proceedings because separate offences were in issue include: *Ponsetti and Chesnel v France No 36855/97* and *No 41731/98*, 1999-VI DA (criminal as well as administrative penalties imposed for failure to complete tax declarations) and *Isaksen v Norway No 13596/02* hudoc (2003) DA (conviction for tax fraud and imposition of a tax surcharge were two distinct legal entities).

[172] ECHR 2009; 54 EHRR 503 para 70 GC, and see paras 71–7 for an overview of its case law.

In *Gradinger v Austria*,[173] the Court found Article 4 of the Seventh Protocol violated as the applicant had been punished twice, by two different courts, on formally different accusations, though both for causing death by negligence while driving under the influence of alcohol. It was critical that 'both impugned [domestic court] decisions were based on *the same conduct*'.[174] By contrast, in *Oliveira v Switzerland*,[175] the Court, distinguishing the case from *Gradinger*, found that there had been a single act constituting multiple offences (*concours idéal d'infractions*), holding that there had been no violation of Article 4. That Article, the Court stressed, 'prohibits people being tried twice for the same offence whereas in cases concerning a single act constituting various offences (*concours idéal d'infractions*) one criminal act constitutes two separate offences [which could be tried by different courts]'.[176] *Oliveira* concerned one driving event leading to two separate criminal convictions based on (i) the failure to control a vehicle; and (ii) the negligent causing of physical injury (as a consequence of (i)). The conclusion that Article 4 had not been violated was reinforced, the Court noted, by the fact that the penalties in the two sets of proceedings were *not* 'cumulative' as the lesser was absorbed by the greater.[177] In *Franz Fischer v Austria*,[178] the Court placed emphasis on the 'essential elements' of two offences as a condition for the application of Article 4. Following one event, the applicant was first convicted by an administrative authority for drunken driving then convicted by a domestic court of causing death by negligence. The Court held that there was a violation of Article 4(1) as the two offences did not differ 'in their essential elements'.[179]

In *Sergey Zolotukhin*,[180] the Grand Chamber endeavoured to harmonize its approach to the application of Article 4.[181] A focus on 'the legal characterisation of the two offences' (as well as, it would seem, the 'essential elements' criteria) was rejected, this being too restrictive and contrary to the principle of practical and effective protection. Article 4 had to be understood as 'prohibiting the prosecution or trial of a second "offence" in so far as it *arises from identical facts or facts which are substantially the same*'.[182] That assessment would be made by the Court in the light of the documentary evidence before it, which would include materials related to the new prosecution and charges, and 'the decision by which the first "penal procedure" [Article 4] was concluded'.[183] The Court would look to 'those facts which constitute a set of concrete factual circumstances involving the same defendant and inextricably linked together in time and space, the existence of which must be demonstrated in order to secure a conviction or institute criminal proceedings'.[184] Proceeding on this basis, the offences for which the applicant was prosecuted in *Sergey Zolotukhin* were regarded as the same for the purposes of Article 4. The first proceedings—which were administrative under domestic law, but viewed as

---

[173] A 328-C (1995).   [174] *Gradinger v Austria*, para 55 (emphasis added).
[175] 1998-V; 28 EHRR 289 para 26.   [176] *Oliveira v Switzerland*, para 26.
[177] *Oliveira v Switzerland*, para 27 (and see *Nikitin v Russia* 2004-VIII; 41 EHRR 149 para 35). See, however, the strong dissenting opinion of Judge Repik.   [178] Hudoc (2001) para 23.
[179] *Franz Fischer v Austria*, para 29.   [180] ECHR 2009; 54 EHRR 503 para 70 GC.
[181] It noted (and appeared to follow) the approach adopted by the Court of Justice of the European Communities and the Inter-American Court of Human Rights, *Sergey Zolotukhin v Russia*, para 79, and seemed to link this to the idea of the Convention as a 'living instrument', para 80.
[182] *Sergey Zolotukhin v Russia*, para 82, emphasis added. The principle was applied in *Ruotsalainen v Finland* hudoc (2009); 56 EHRR 10, concerning the imposition of a fuel-fee debit after a conviction for minor tax fraud (violation as substantially the same facts).
[183] *Sergey Zolotukhin v Russia*, para 83 GC. See also *Asadbeyli and Others v Azerbaijan* hudoc (2012).
[184] *Sergey Zolotukhin v Russia*, para 84 GC.

criminal by the Court—had concerned breach of public order (swearing at public officials and physically pushing away an official), resulted in conviction, and had become final. This was substantially the same in terms of conduct and facts for the purposes of Article 4 as one aspect of the second proceedings (breaching public order by uttering obscenities and threatening an official with violence, whilst resisting him), for which the applicant was, in fact, acquitted. It was not relevant that the offences were distinct in terms of the penalty they entailed.[185]

Article 4(2) specifically envisages the resumption of a trial ('re-opening of the case'), perhaps involving prosecution on exactly the same counts, in relatively exceptional circumstances. Such resumption must be 'in accordance with the law and penal procedure of the state concerned', a qualification that evidently prevents arbitrary decisions to re-try individuals. Moreover, the re-opening of the case may only occur, 'if there is evidence of new or newly discovered facts, or if there has been a fundamental defect in the previous proceedings'. Article 4(2) requires that the new facts or defect be significant enough that they 'could affect the outcome of the case', suggesting a significant level of caution is required from the authorities before re-opening a case lest this provision be breached (as does the word 'fundamental', as in 'fundamental defect'). The Court adopted a broad reading of Article 4(2), 'fundamental defect in the previous proceedings' in *Marguš v Croatia*.[186] In that case the applicant's prosecution in a first set of proceedings had been terminated by legislation granting an amnesty,[187] but this was followed by a conviction in respect of some of the same events, subsequently characterized as war crimes. The Court noted that amnesties in respect of 'international crimes' were 'increasingly considered prohibited by international law', referring to 'a growing tendency for international, regional and national courts to overturn general amnesties enacted by Governments'.[188] It regarded the application of the amnesty as 'a fundamental defect in the [earlier] proceedings', such that the conditions set out under paragraph 2 of Article 4 of Protocol 7 for the reopening of proceedings were met.[189] Those proceedings did not therefore breach Article 4; the reopening of proceedings could be justified.

According to the Explanatory Report the words 'new or newly discovered facts' can encompass new means of proof relating to previously existing facts.[190] Precisely what is meant by this is not clear, but it will presumably be particularly relevant given scientific advances for example in the field of DNA analysis. The Explanatory Report to the Seventh Protocol states that Article 4(2) 'does not prevent a reopening of the proceedings in favour of the convicted person and any other changing of the judgment to the benefit of the convicted person'.[191]

Finally, the words 'under the jurisdiction of the same state' also limit the application of Article 4(2) to the national level only. That is, the principle *ne bis in idem* does not apply to where a person has been or will be tried or punished by the courts of different states.[192] Article 4 may not be derogated from under Article 15 of the Convention in time of war or other public emergency threatening the life of the nation.

---

[185] *Sergey Zolotukhin v Russia*, para 97.   [186] Hudoc (2012) (GC judgment awaited).
[187] See the analysis earlier in this section (re 'final acquittal or conviction').
[188] *Marguš v Croatia* hudoc (2012); 56 EHRR 1085 (GC judgment awaited) para 74.
[189] *Marguš v Croatia*, para 76.   [190] Explanatory Report P7 para 31.
[191] Explanatory Report P7 para 31.
[192] *Amrollahi v Denmark No 56811/00* hudoc (2001) DA. Cf, Article 50 of the EU Charter of Fundamental Rights.

10. ARTICLE 5, SEVENTH PROTOCOL:
EQUALITY OF RIGHTS OF SPOUSES

Article 5 of the Seventh Protocol reads:

> Spouses shall enjoy equality of rights and responsibilities of a private law character between them, and in their relations with their children, as to marriage, during marriage, and in the event of its dissolution. This Article shall not prevent states from taking such measures as are necessary in the interests of the children.

This provision relates to the rights and responsibilities of spouses (as opposed between the sexes more generally) under private law only. The Explanatory Report[193] states that it 'does not apply to other fields of law, such as administrative, fiscal, criminal, social, ecclesiastical or labour law'. Accordingly, the state's obligation under Article 5 involves essentially a positive obligation to provide a satisfactory framework of law by which spouses have equal rights and obligations concerning such matters as property rights and their relations with their children.[194] Article 5 does not protect the partners to any relationship outside marriage,[195] and specifically excludes the period preceding marriage. Article 5 does not concern the 'conditions of capacity to enter into marriage provided by national law'; the words 'as to marriage' relate instead to the 'legal effects connected with the conclusion of marriage'.[196] Although Article 5 refers to the 'dissolution of marriage', the Explanatory Report states that this does not 'imply any obligation on a state to provide for dissolution of marriage'.[197] The Report also suggests that Article 5 does not prevent the national authorities 'from taking due account of all relevant factors when reaching decisions with regard to the division of property in the event of dissolution of marriage'.[198] The final sentence of Article 5 enters the caveat that Article 5 does not prevent state legislative or administrative action that results in the spouses not having equal private law rights and responsibilities in their relations with their children where this is necessary in the 'interests of the children'.

The case law indicates an understandable reluctance on the part of the Court to question a final domestic judgment based on the interests of the child unless it is manifestly unreasonable. Such decisions are likely to be in the margin of appreciation of the national authorities.[199] At the general level, Article 5 of the Seventh Protocol is not violated by a law which excludes the possibility of joint custody after divorce whilst providing access and information rights to the parent not having custody.[200] Although this would be an interference with one of the former spouse's right to equality, it would not be disproportionate to the aim of protecting the children by providing a clear solution for custody and would fall within the respondent state's margin of appreciation.[201]

---

[193] Explanatory Report P7, para 35. See also *Klöpper v Switzerland No 25053/94* hudoc (1996) DA and *Konstantin Markin v Russia* (Chamber judgment) hudoc 2010; 55 EHRR 1099 para 61.

[194] See *Iosub Caras v Romania* hudoc (2006) para 56 and *Purtonen v Finland No 32700/96* hudoc (1998) DA.

[195] See *Kaijalainen v Finland No 24671/94* (1996) DA.

[196] Explanatory Report P7 para 37. As to the capacity to marry, see Article 12, Convention, Ch 16.

[197] Explanatory Report P7 para 37.

[198] Explanatory Report P7 para 38. In *EP v Slovak Republic No 33706/96* hudoc (1998) DA, the Commission exercised a power of review over the decision of the domestic court but found that decision 'neither unfair nor arbitrary'.

[199] See *Purtonen v Finland No 32700/96* hudoc (1998) DA and *Heckl v Austria No 32012/96* hudoc (1999) DA.

[200] See *Cernecki v Austria No 31061/96* hudoc (2000) DA.   [201] *Cernecki v Austria*.

As the Explanatory Report[202] notes, the need to take the interests of the children into account is already reflected in the Strasbourg jurisprudence under Articles 8 and 14, as is the basic principle of equality of treatment between spouses. Citing this aspect of the Explanatory Report, the Court has stated that the necessity clause contained in Article 5 should be interpreted in the same way as the necessity clauses contained in other provisions of the Convention.[203]

---

[202] Explanatory Report P7 para 36.   [203] See *Cernecki v Austria No 31061/96* hudoc (2000) DA.

INDEX

References to ECHR refer to European Convention on Human Rights, while ECtHR refers to European Court of Human Rights.

abortion
  involuntary 220–221
  and other harmful acts 221
  positive obligations of
    states 618
  voluntary 219–220
access
  to children, by unmarried
    fathers 806–808
  to court
    Golder case 398–399
    immunity 405–407
    and 'law' 496
    relationship with
      Article 13 408
    restrictions upon right of
      access 402–408
    right of effective
      access 399–402
    waiver of right of
      access 408
  to data 562–564
  of EU to ECHR 171–176
  to information 620–621
  to property 869–870
  review of lawfulness
    354–355
Accession Agreement
  (accession of EU to ECHR)
  admissibility of
    applications 174
  co-respondents 173, 174–175
  general philosophy 173
  reform of ECtHR 171–176
accountability
  pre-trial detention,
    during 338–351
administrative decisions
  application of Article 6(1)
    in 392–395
  categories 393–394
admissibility of applications
  Accession Agreement
    (accession of EU to
    ECHR) 174

burden of proof 147
communication of
  application 43
exhaustion of domestic
  remedies 47–61, 73, 74
general approach to 43–45
grounds, other 72–81
  abuse of right of petition
    provision 79–81
  anonymity 73
  another procedure
    of international
    investigation or
    settlement 74–78
  manifestly ill-founded
    provision 43, 44, 45,
    78–79
  matter already examined
    by the Court 74
  substantially the
    same 73–78
incompatibility and
  competence of the court
  competence *ratione
    materiae* 44, 95–96
  competence *ratione
    personae* 81–95
  competence *ratione
    temporis* 97–99
inter-state cases, application
  of requirements to 45–47
no significant disadvantage
  criterion 67–72
phases to be considered 43–44
prima facie evidence of
  administrative practice
  only required 46
six-month rule 44, 47, 61–67,
  73, 169
see also ARTICLE 35
  (ADMISSIBILITY
  CRITERIA)
admissibility of evidence
  fair hearing, right
    to 418–420

adoption
  Article 8 567–568, 571, 573
  orders 571, 573
adverse inferences
  freedom from self-
    incrimination 423–424
advertising
  and commercial
    expression 635–636
  comparative, forbidden
    under unfair competition
    laws 638
  religious and political
    advertisement,
    broadcasting 646–649
advisory opinions
  Protocol 16169–171
  requested by Committee of
    Ministers 135–136
Advisory Panel
  and organization of
    ECtHR 107–109
**African Charter on Human
  and People's Rights 1981**
  ECHR comparable to 5
'alcoholics'
  detention grounds
    322–324
aliens
  entry, conditions of stay and
    removal of 385–386,
    576
  freedom from collective
    expulsion 960–963
  freedom from individual
    expulsion 965–966
  restrictions on political
    rights of 851–852
**American Convention on
  Human Rights 1969**
  and Article 15 845
  ECHR comparable to 5
amnesties
  Article 2 205–206
  Article 6 377

anonymity provision
  admissibility of
    applications 73
  ECtHR procedure 136
  prosecution witnesses 217
anti-Semitism
  and freedom of
    expression 622, 623
appeal proceedings
  Article 6(1), application
    to 459–460
  Constitutional Court (Spain),
    amparo appeals 49
  exhaustion rule 55–58
  'settled legal opinion' 56
appearance
  personal identity 538–539
arbitrariness
  protection from 304–306
arguability
  pre-emptive remedy
    (Article 13) 766–767
arrest
  bringing promptly before
    judge/other authorized
    officer following 338–343
  exception to prohibition
    of taking of life by
    force 231–232
  force, use of 243
  meaning 289–296
  'reasonable suspicion' to
    justify 827
  reasons to be given promptly
    general issues 334–335
    information, level
      required 335–338
**Article 1 (obligation to respect
  human rights)**
  application of ECHR by
    national courts 26
  and Article 16 851
  competence *ratione
    personae* 83
  concept of 'jurisdiction'
    in 99–100
  negative and positive
    obligations 21, 24
  procedural obligation to
    investigate 214
Article 2 (right to life)
  amnesties 205–206
  basic values of democratic
    societies 203
  competence *ratione
    temporis* 98
  criminal sanctions,
    requirement of 215
  death by state agent 222, 223
  euthanasia 204–205

execution of Court
    judgments 187
  force, prohibition of taking
    of life by
    disappeared persons
      223–224
    exceptions permitted
      225–233
    general rule 221–224
  hazardous activities 584
  health care and other social
    services 212–214
  interim measures 142
  interpretation of ECHR 19
  law enforcement
    machinery 206–207
  laws prohibiting taking of
    life 204
  legal and administrative
    framework 204–206
  legal obligation to protect
    life 203–207
  margin of appreciation
    doctrine 208, 213
  medical negligence 213–214,
    545
  non-fatal cases, application
    of obligation to protect life
    to 218
  positive obligations 22
  preventive action 207–212
  priority policy for dealing
    with cases 120
  procedural obligation to
    investigate 214–218
  regulation of activities and
    situations posing risk to
    life 206
  relationships with other
    Articles
    Article 3 236, 276
    Article 8 584
    Article 13 769, 780–781
    Article 14 812, 813–814
    Article 15 845
  right to die, not
    guaranteeing 205
  standard of proof 148
  text 203, 204
  threats to life by criminal
    acts of another 209
  unborn child,
    protection 219–221
  victim status of relatives 92
  violation in context of
    duty to protect from
    harm 779–781
**Article 3 (freedom from torture
  or inhuman or degrading
  treatment or punishment)**

absolute guarantee contained
    in 235
  basic values of democratic
    societies 203
  burden of proof 147
  competence *ratione
    temporis* 98
  complaints 277
  corporal punishment, whether
    consistent with 9
  and death penalty
    245–246
  degrading punishment
    271–273
  degrading treatment
    see DEGRADING
    TREATMENT
  dynamic or broad
    interpretation 278
  inhuman punishment
    259–260
  inhuman treatment
    see INHUMAN
    TREATMENT
  interim measures 142
  interpretation of ECHR 9, 13
  negative obligations 21
  physical assault by state
    agent 222
  positive obligations 22, 23
  priority policy for dealing
    with cases 120
  proportionality principle
    13
  proscribed ill-treatment,
    obligation to protect
    individuals from
    investigation and
      enforcement 275–277
    prevention 274–275
  relationships with other
    Articles
    Article 2 236, 276
    Article 8 238, 523, 541
    Article 13 769, 776, 779,
      780–781
    Article 14 812, 813
    Article 15 825, 826, 845
    Article 46 162
  remedies, adequacy and
    effectiveness 54
  scope of application 235
  standard of proof 148
  state responsibility 24
  text 277
  torture *see* torture
  unqualified terms, expressed
    in 235–236
  victim status of
    relatives 92–93

violation in context of
duty to protect from
harm 779–781
see also COMMITTEE FOR
THE PREVENTION
OF TORTURE
AND INHUMAN
OR DEGRADING
TREATMENT OR
PUNISHMENT (CPT)
**Article 4 (freedom from
slavery, servitude or forced
or compulsory labour)**
and Article 15 845
deportation or extradition to
another state 286
freedom from forced
or compulsory
labour 280–284
freedom from slavery or
servitude 279–280
human trafficking 284–286
infringements/violations 36
positive obligations 284–286
priority policy for dealing
with cases 120
text 279
**Article 5 (right to liberty and
security of the person)**
arrest
exception to prohibition
of taking of life by
force 231–232
meaning 289–296
reasons to be given
promptly 334–338
bail
conditions (including
amount) 348–350
grounds for refusing
346–348
compensation, right to for
illegal detention under
Article 5(5) 366–368
continuing remedy at
reasonable intervals
363–365
death of applicant 95
detention *see* DETENTION
domestic law
quality of 302–304
review of compliance
with 301–302
execution of judgments 29
generally 288–289
implied procedural
safeguards under Article
5(1) 300
infringements/violations 36
interpretation of ECHR 15, 18

legal certainty 302–304
loss of liberty
conditions of detention 298
disappeared persons 300
engaging the
responsibility of the
state, and positive
obligations 297
meaning of 'deprivation of
liberty' 289–294
physical detention at
hands of police or state
officials 292
public protection
motives 296
transfer across borders,
extradition and
expulsion' 298–300
no significant disadvantage
criterion 69–70
notion of 'liberty' 288
overall purpose 288
overarching
principles 301–306
priority policy for dealing
with cases 120
procedural guarantees on
review of detention
adversarial proceedings
356
decision to be taken
'speedily' 362–363
equality of arms 356–357
fairness 357, 358, 359
legal assistance 360–361
oral hearing and presence
of detainee 359–360
terrorism 358
time and facilities
to prepare an
application 361
relationships with other
Articles
Article 8 288
Article 13 767, 768, 780
Article 15 826, 827, 828,
836, 843
Article 18 857–858
security of the person 300
structure of Article 5(1) 289
text 287
trial
bringing promptly before
judge/other authorized
officer 338–339
characteristics of judicial
officer 341–342
function of officer and
procedure to be
followed 342–343

pre-trial, accountability
during 338–351
within a reasonable
time 350–351
right to release pending,
in reasonable
circumstances 343–350
victim status 95
see also DETENTION
Article 6 (right to fair trial)
administrative decisions,
application of Article 6(1)
in 392–395
appeal proceedings,
application of Article 6(1)
to 459–460
application, problems created
by 371
breaches, non-pecuniary
awards 156
civil rights and obligations
autonomous Convention
meaning 379–380
commercial activity, right
to engage in 381–382
'contestation' or dispute
concerning 390
entry, conditions of
stay and removal of
aliens 385–386
illegal state action, right
to compensation
for 382–383
meaning 378–388
non-pecuniary 383–384
pecuniary rights 381
political 385
private law 378–379, 380
private persons, relations
between 380
profession, right to
practise 381–382
property right 381
public law 384–385, 387
public service
employment 386–387
social security/assistance,
right to 383
state action determining
private law rights and
obligations 380
tax, obligation to pay 385
when determined
391–392
criminal charge,
determination
meaning of
charge 376–378
meaning of criminal
373–376

Article 6 (right to fair trial) (*Cont.*)
criminal offences for purposes of 374, 495
execution of Court judgments 187
and expulsion 299
fair hearing, right to *see* FAIR HEARING, RIGHT TO
field of application 373–398
fourth instance (*quatrième instance*) doctrine 17
generally 370–373
guarantees
adequate facilities, right to 472–473
adequate time, right to 470–471
appeal proceedings, application of Article 6(1) to 459–460
in criminal and non-criminal cases, under Article 6(1) 398–460
defending oneself in person/through legal assistance 474–483
fair hearing, right to 409–433
further guarantees in criminal cases under Article 6(3) 467–491
independent and impartial tribunal, right to 446–458
interpreters, right to 489–491
presumption of innocence 421, 460–467
public hearing, right to 433–438
public pronouncement of judgment, right to 438–439
right of access to a court 398–408
right to be informed of accusation 468–470
trial, right to within a reasonable time 439–446
witnesses, right to call and cross-examine 483–489
infringements/violations 36
interim measures 142
interpretation of ECHR 7, 8, 12, 16, 17, 18–19
language texts 7

'manifestly contrary' to provisions of 307, 308
margin of appreciation doctrine 16, 371, 402
no significant disadvantage criterion 68, 71
pecuniary damage 159
positive obligations 22
presumption of innocence 421, 460–467
public hearing, right to 433–438
public pronouncement of judgment, right to 438–439
reach of 491–492
relationships with other Articles
Article 8 523
Article 10 681
Article 13 767–768, 777–778
Article 14 785, 791, 819
Article 15 826, 827
in Protocol 1 866
reservations 25
right of access to a court
Golder case 398–399
relationship with Article 13 408
restrictions upon right of access 402–408
right of effective access 399–402
waiver of right of access 408
rights and obligations
civil *see above*
meaning 389–390
scope, Swiss reservation concerning 25
silent, right to remain 423
stages of proceedings covered by Article 6(1) 395–398
striking out cases 131
text 370
trial within reasonable time 350–351, 439–446
tribunal, independent and impartial 446–458
victim status 93
violations 187
see also TRIAL

Article 7 (freedom from retroactive criminal offences and punishment)
ancillary matters 494
and Article 15 845
autonomous Convention meaning 495

crimes against humanity 498, 502
ex post facto criminal offences 494–499
ex post facto criminal penalties 499–501
'law'
and Articles 8–11 503
existing law 497
general principles of law exception 501–502
'international law' 498, 502
law deriving authority from state's lawful constitution 496
relevant, application to 494
substantive law, application only to 494
national courts in breach of 493
post-war crimes with Second World War connection 502
sex offenders 499–500
text 493
unilateral declarations 130
war crimes 498, 502

Article 8 (right to respect for private and family life, home and correspondence)
adoption orders 573
child abduction, international 572–575
childcare proceedings 569–572
contact disputes 572–575
correspondence 530
court orders, non-enforcement 574
custody 572–575
data
access 562–564
collection, storage and disclosure 559–562
protection of 525–526
deceased family members 568
definition issues 522
degrading treatment 271
deportation 575
email monitoring 556
employment and political activities 578–579
environmental rights 582–585
essential object 523
evidence obtained in breach of 419

family and personal
   relationships
      adoption 567–568
      other aspects 568–569
      parentage, recognition
         564–567
family life 526–528
four interests protected by
   Article 8(1)
      correspondence 530
      definition issues 522
      family life 526–528
      home 528–530
      private life 524–526, 555
home and housing
   issues 528–530, 580–582
immigration 575–578
infringements/violations 36
interference with rights 531,
   532
interplay between Article
   8(1) and other Convention
   Articles 523
interpretation of ECHR 9
language 503
margin of appreciation
   doctrine 533
medical care and treatment
   see MEDICAL CARE
   AND TREATMENT
moral, physical and
   psychological
   integrity 541–543
negative obligation 531–532,
   533
non-transferability of
   rights 93
personal identity
   appearance 538–539
   ethnic and religious 540
   gender
      identification 536–537
   information regarding
      one's origins 537–538
   names 539–540
   national 540
positive obligations 22, 23,
   532–535, 542
press publications 551–554
prisoners 585–589
private life 524–526, 555, 581
procedural
   obligations 535–536
procedural rights 573
relationships with other
   Articles
   Article 2 584
   Article 3 238, 523, 541
   Article 5 288
   Article 6 523

Article 9 606
Article 10 524, 551, 614,
   659–660
Article 12 754, 755, 756,
   760, 762
Article 13 770, 775, 781
Article 14 785, 787, 803,
   804, 808
in Protocol 1 908
search and seizure
   powers 557–559
secret surveillance 555–557
sexual activities 549–551
subject areas 536–589
   personal identity 536–540
substantive rights 503
telephone-tapping 507, 556
text 522
victim status 93
wide scope of protection 522,
   531, 590
see also ARTICLES 8–11
Articles 8–11
   'in accordance with the
      law'/'prescribed by
      law' 506–509
   ECtHR procedure 521
   and First Protocol,
      Article 3 923
   force, deaths resulting
      from use for permitted
      purposes 227
   general
      considerations 503–521
   interest to be protected by
      interference
      justiciability of
         interest 517–518
      objectivity of
         interest 516–517
      weight of interest to be
         protected 515–516
   interpretation of ECHR 15
   language 503
   limitations
      'in accordance with the
         law'/'prescribed by
         law' 506–509
      legitimate aims 509–510
      necessary in a democratic
         society 510–520
      where permitted 505
   margin of appreciation
      doctrine 15, 511
   'necessary in a democratic
      society' requirement see
      under DEMOCRACY
   'necessity' of interference
      with Convention rights,
      demonstration of 148

negative and positive
   obligations 504–505
public hearing, right to 434
resolution of conflict between
   different factors
   general approach 519
   proportionality
      assessment 519–520
violations of 521
see also ARTICLE 8 (RIGHT
   TO RESPECT FOR
   PRIVATE AND FAMILY
   LIFE, HOME AND
   CORRESPONDENCE);
   ARTICLE 9 (FREEDOM
   OF THOUGHT,
   CONSCIENCE AND
   RELIGION); ARTICLE
   10 (FREEDOM OF
   EXPRESSION); ARTICLE
   11 (FREEDOM OF
   ASSEMBLY AND
   ASSOCIATION)
Article 9 (freedom of thought,
   conscience and religion)
   broad interpretation 593
   church/state relations
      597–600
   coercion forbidden by 595
   communal nature 598–599
   conscientious
      objection 601–602
   external dimension (forum
      externum) 594
   identity cards 540
   internal dimension (forum
      internum) 594, 595, 597,
      605
   justifiable interferences
      legitimate aim 606–608
      necessary in a democratic
         society 608–611
      prescribed by
         law 605–606
   manifesting religion or belief
      see under RELIGION OR
      BELIEF
   'necessary in a democratic
      society' requirement
      proselytism 610–611
      religious dress 603,
         608–610
   proselytism 610–611
   relationships with other
      Articles
      Article 8 606
      Article 10 606, 614, 669
      Article 11 606, 714, 732, 740
      Article 14 790, 802
      in Protocol 1 908, 913

Article 9 (freedom of thought, conscience and religion) (*Cont.*)
religious dress 603, 608–610
right to believe 594–597
scope 592–594
structure 594
substantive rights 503
text 592
victim status 93
see also ARTICLES 8–11;
RELIGION OR BELIEF
Article 10 (freedom of expression)
access to public forums or
media 619
categories of expression
artistic 632–635
civil 632
commercial 635–639
political 629–631
defamation *see*
DEFAMATION
duties and responsibilities
under Article10(2)
civil servants 685–687
journalists 683, 687–691
overview 683–685
politicians 683–684
execution of Court
judgments regarding
violations 192, 193
foreseeability
subtest 649–651
friendly settlement 127
infringements/violations 36
interference by public
authority 618
interpretation 14, 15, 614
language 615
legitimate aims for which
restrictions can be
justified
copyright law, protecting
672
crime prevention 654–655
disclosure of confidential
information,
preventing 672–675
disorder, prevention
654–655
freedom of religion of others,
protecting 669–671
judiciary, maintenance
of authority and
impartiality 675–683
morals, protecting
655–658
national security,
protecting 652–654

overview 652
public figures, protecting
privacy, reputation and
honour 666–669
reputation and honour
of private individuals,
protecting 658–666
licensing for broadcasting
643–649
margin of appreciation
doctrine 15
means of expression 615,
639–649
negative obligations 21
positive obligations 617–620
'prescribed by law' 614,
649–652
press and journalistic
freedom 639–643
protection and
confidentiality of
sources 640, 641–643
relationships with other
Articles
Article 6 681
Article 8 523, 551, 614,
659–660
Article 9 606, 614, 669
Article 11 614, 713, 725, 751
Article 15 655
Article 16 851
Article 17 621–623, 624,
655, 852, 853
in Protocol 1 908, 921
'revisionist' expression
623–626
scope of protection
access to
information 620–621
general overview 614–617
incitement to
violence 626–629
positive obligations
617–620
'revisionist' expression
623–626
substantive matters 616
text 613
victim status 93
violations 192, 193
see also ARTICLES 8–11
**Article 11 (freedom of assembly
and association)**
essential object 741
freedom of association
see FREEDOM OF
ASSOCIATION
freedom of peaceful assembly
see FREEDOM OF
PEACEFUL ASSEMBLY

positive obligations 712–713,
738–739
relationships with other
Articles
Article 9 606, 714, 732, 740
Article 10 614, 713, 725,
751
Article 13 771
Article 14 749
Article 16 851
Article 17 853
in Protocol 1 921
substantive rights 503
text 710
trade unions *see* TRADE
UNIONS
unilateral declarations 130
victim status 93
see also ARTICLES 8–11
**Article 12 (right to marry and
found a family)**
breach/violations 36,
756–757
non-married persons 762
relationships with other
Articles
Article 8 754, 755, 756,
760, 762, 803
Articles 8–11 503
Article 14 754, 761
right to found a
family 760–762
right to marry *see under*
MARRIAGE
text 754
**Article 13 (right to an effective
national remedy)**
application of ECHR by
national courts 28
cumulation of procedures
to be taken into
account 772–773
and deportations 774
effective remedy
general principles/
requirements 768–773
institutional
requirements 771–772
substantive requirements
769–771
effectiveness of remedy
required by 766
exhaustion rule 47
general principles/
requirements
effective remedy 768–773
specific contexts 774–782
general principles/
requirements in specific
contexts 774–782

within general scheme of
Convention 765–768
incorporation of Convention
and discretion available
to state in providing
remedies 765–766
and national
security 774–777
positive obligations 504
pre-emptive remedy, for
'arguable' claims 766–767
relationships with other
Articles
Article 2 769, 780–781
Article 3 769, 776, 779,
780–781
Article 5 767, 768, 780
Article 6 767–768,
777–778
Article 8 770, 775, 781
Article 11 771
Article 35 764, 767–768
in Protocol 1 781
and right of access to a court
(under Article 6) 408
serious violations
of fundamental
rights, effective
investigations 779–781
text 764
trial within reasonable
time 777–778
**Article 14 (freedom from
discrimination)**
Belgian Linguistic case
784–785, 787, 792, 793,
794, 795
burden of proof 148
and death penalty 226
differential treatment
see DIFFERENTIAL
TREATMENT
exhaustion rule 49
indirect discrimination 785,
815–817
interpretation of ECHR 13, 16
overview of
application 785–786
as 'parasitic' provision 784,
786
principles for
application 784–785
private discrimination,
positive obligation to
protect against 817–818
proportionality principle 13
protection for guaranteed
rights only and ambit
test 786–787
and Protocol 12 819–821

racial discrimination 270
relationships with other
Articles
Article 2 812, 813–814
Article 3 812, 813
Article 4 788
Article 6 785, 791, 819
Article 8 785, 787, 803,
804, 808
Article 9 790, 802
Article 11 749
Article 12 754, 761
Article 15 845
in Protocol 1 787, 789,
866, 907
violence motivated by
discrimination 811–814
racial, in context of
policing and criminal
justice 811–814
state toleration 814–815
see also DISCRIMINATION
**Article 15 (derogation in time
of emergency)**
derogation clauses, dilemma
posed by 824
examples of
derogations 824–825
existence of public
emergency 833–836
general approach of Court to
terrorism cases 825–829
general pattern 829
international law obligations,
other 843–844
interpretation of ECHR 13, 16
margin of appreciation
doctrine 16, 842–843,
848
measures strictly required
by exigencies of the
situation 837–843
margin of appreciation
doctrine 842–843
'strictly required',
meaning 838–842
need to resort to 825–829
non-derogable provisions
under Article 15(2)
844–845
procedural
requirements under
Article15(3) 846–847
proportionality principle 13
'public emergency
threatening life of the
nation' *see under* PUBLIC
EMERGENCY
purpose 823
reform proposals 847–848

relationships with other
Articles
Article 2 845
Article 3 825, 826, 845
Article 4 845
Article 5 826, 827, 828,
836, 843
Article 6 826, 827
Article 7 845
Article 10 655
Article 14 845
text 823
'in time of war or other
public emergency
threatening the life of the
nation' 829–837
**Article 16 (restrictions on the
political rights of aliens)**
case law 851–852
**Article 17 (restrictions on
activities subversive of
Convention rights)** 852–857
'abuse clause' 853
pleaded against
state 856–857
pleaded by state 853–856
relationship with Article
10 621–623, 624, 655,
852
**Article 18 (prohibition of the
use of restrictions for an
improper purpose)**
politically motivated
prosecutions 858–861
specific violations of,
read with another
Article 857–858
Article 20 (number of judges)
composition of
ECtHR 104–105
Article 21 (criteria for office)
ad hoc and common interest
judges 110
composition of ECtHR 105
election of judges and
Advisory Panel 107,
108, 109
ineligibility to sit 109
**Article 22 (election of
judges)**
Parliamentary Assembly
of Council of Europe
(PACE) 107, 108
**Article 23 (terms of office
and dismissal)**
composition of ECtHR
105
**Article 24 (Registry and
rapporteurs)**
provisions of 112

Article 26 (single judges,
   Committees, Chambers
   and Grand Chamber)
   plenary Court 111
Article 27 (competence of
   single judges)
   ad hoc and common interest
      judges 110
Article 28 (competence of
   Committees)
   ad hoc and common interest
      judges 110
   Committee procedure 121, 122
Article 29 (decisions by
   Chambers on admissibility
   and merits)
   Chamber procedure 123
   just satisfaction 158
Article 30 (relinquishment
   of jurisdiction to Grand
   Chamber)
   appropriate
      circumstances 123
   procedure 124
Article 33 (inter-state cases)
   application of admissibility
      to inter-state cases 45–47
   enforcement 6
   inter-state complaints versus
      individual complaints 116
   provisions of 115
Article 34 (individual
   applications)
   admissibility of
      applications 44, 72
   competence *ratione
      materiae* 96
   competence *ratione personae*
      81, 84
   enforcement 6
   individual complaints 113
   inter-state complaints 117
   procedure before
      ECtHR 113, 114
   reservations 25
Article 35 (admissibility
   criteria)
   abuse of the right of petition
      provision 79–81
   advisory opinions 135
   anonymity provision 73
   application of admissibility
      to inter-state cases 45
   and auxiliary
      remedy 767–768
   burden of proof 51
   exhaustion rule 47, 50
   final decision 62
   general approach to
      admissibility 44

inadmissibility grounds 72
   manifestly ill-founded
      provision 78–79
   no significant disadvantage
      criterion 43, 67–72
      cases considered 68–70
      duly considered
         by a domestic
         tribunal 71–72
      examination of application
         on the merits
         requirement 70–71
      Protocol 15 reforms 169
   relationship with Article
      13 764, 767
   six-month rule 61
   substantially the same
      provision 73–78
      another procedure
         of international
         investigation or
         settlement 74–78
      matter already examined
         by the Court 74
   see also ADMISSIBILITY OF
      APPLICATIONS
Article 36 (third party
   intervention)
   interim measures 143
   oral hearings 138
   provisions of 152
Article 37 (striking out
   applications)
   conditions for striking
      out 131
   death of applicant 94
   no significant disadvantage
      criterion 70
   procedure before
      ECtHR 130–132
Article 38 (examination of
   the case)
   competence *ratione
      materiae* 96
   investigations and
      fact-finding 146
Article 39 (friendly
   settlements)
   provisions of 127, 128
Article 41 (just satisfaction)
   Chamber procedure 122
   costs and expenses 157,
      158–159
   European Court of Human
      Rights (ECrHR) 155–162
   execution of judgments 29,
      184
   pecuniary and
      non-pecuniary
      damage 157, 159–162

referral to Grand
   Chamber 124
   text 155
Article 43 (referral to the
   Grand Chamber)
   admissibility of
      applications 44
   appropriate circumstances 123
   procedure 124
Article 46 (binding force and
   execution of judgments)
   and Article 14 788
   and Committee of
      Ministers 180, 181, 198
   competence *ratione
      materiae* 96
   consequential orders 162
   contracting party in
      violation of obligations
      under 193–194
   Court practice 162–165
   and Protocol 14 196–198
   provisions of 162
   State obligations under 193
Article 47 (advisory opinions)
   provisions of 135
Article 51 (privileges and
   immunities of judges)
   composition of ECtHR 105
Article 53 (safeguarding of
   existing human rights)
   and Article 15 843
Article 56 (territorial
   application)
   as 'colonial clause' 100
   competence *ratione loci*
      100–102
   jurisdiction concept in
      Article 1 99
   'logical requirements' 101
   purpose 101
Article 57 (reservations)
   competence *ratione loci* 102
   competence *ratione
      materiae* 96
   provisions of 24
   and Switzerland 26
   text 25
artificial reproduction *see*
   ASSISTED PROCREATION
artistic expression
   Article 10 632–635
assaults
   inhuman treatment 241–243
assembly, freedom of *see*
   FREEDOM OF PEACEFUL
   ASSEMBLY
assisted procreation
   Article 8 548–549
   Article 12 761–762

associations
interferences with,
proportionality
requirement 735–737
legal recognition 737–738
limitations upon
associations other than
political 731–735
political parties 725–731
meaning of
association 724–725
regulation raising issue of
'quality of law' 733
religious groups 732–733
see also ARTICLE 11
(FREEDOM OF
ASSEMBLY AND
ASSOCIATION)

bail
conditions (including
amount) 348–350
grounds for refusing
crime prevention 348
danger of
absconding 346–347
interference with course of
justice 347
public order 348
**Bank for International
Settlements (BIS)**
failed mediation by 75
belief *see* RELIGION OR
BELIEF
beyond reasonable doubt
standard of proof 148
birth
differential treatment,
scrutiny 800–801
borders, transfer across
loss of liberty 298–300
'bright-line rule'
and exhaustion rule 49
**Brighton Conference and
Declaration (2012)**
advisory opinions 170
and Article 13 764–765, 782
case law, ensuring
consistency of 126
election of judges and
Advisory Panel 107
execution of Court
judgments 190
interim measures 143
reform of ECtHR 39, 104,
167, 170
broadcasting, licensing for
overview 643–646
programmes inciting hatred
or violence 645

public monopolies 644
religious and political
advertisement 646–649
**Broadcasting Advertising
Clearance Centre, UK**
and licensing of
broadcasting 647
burden of proof
differential
treatment 809–810
ECtHR procedure 146–148
exhaustion rule 51–52
presumption of
innocence 462

case law
ensuring consistency
of 126–127
**Case Law Conflict Prevention
Unit (CLCP)**
case law, ensuring
consistency of 126
celebrities *see* PUBLIC
FIGURES
**Central and East European
states**
non-compliance with
judgments 31
Chambers, ECtHR
and composition of
ECtHR 111, 112
interpretation of ECHR 12,
20, 21
legal aid 137
procedure 122–123
referral to Grand
Chamber 123
**Charter of Fundamental
Rights**
European Union (EU) 32
Charter of United Nations
non-discrimination 783
children
abduction 572–575
access to by unmarried
fathers 806–808
adoption 567–568, 573
childcare
proceedings 569–572
custody 572–575
family life 527
parentage, recognition
564–567
see also EDUCATION,
RIGHT TO (FIRST
PROTOCOL)
church/state relations
freedom of thought,
conscience and
religion 597–600

civil and political rights
negative obligations 21–22
in Universal Declaration of
Human Rights 5
civil expression
Article 10 632
civil litigation
right to trial within
reasonable time 441
civil rights and obligations
Article 4 283–284
autonomous Convention
meaning 379–380
character of the right 379–380
commercial activity, right to
engage in 381–382
'contestation' or dispute
concerning 390
entry, conditions of stay
and removal of
aliens 385–386, 576
illegal state action, right to
compensation for 382–383
meaning 378–388
non-pecuniary
rights 383–384
pecuniary rights 381
political 385
private law 378–379, 380
private persons, relations
between 380
profession, right to
practise 381–382
property rights 381
public law 384–385, 387
public service employment
386–387
social security/assistance,
right to 383
state action determining
private law rights and
obligations 380
tax, obligation to pay 385
when determined 391–392
civil servants
Article 10(2), duties and
responsibilities under
685–687
loyalty duty, in Germany 616
media coverage 667
and public figures
doctrine 696–697
civil societies
as 'public watchdog' 632
closed shop cases
gradualist approach 9
members' interests, right to
protect 748
trade unions, right not to
join 745

commercial activity
right to engage in 381–382
commercial expression
Article 10 635–639
and public interest 639
restrictions on 636–639
Commission on Human Rights
and international
investigation or
settlement, another
procedure 76
Commissioner for Human Rights
Council of Europe 842–843,
848
Committee for the Prevention of Torture and Inhuman or Degrading Treatment or Punishment (CPT)
admissibility of
applications 75
detainees, conditions
of detention and
treatment 262
and ECtHR 145, 147
Committee of Legal Experts (CDDH)
Council of Europe 172
Committee of Ministers
advisory opinions requested
by 135–136
Advisory Panel set up by
(2010) 107
Annual Reports
(2007–2012) 188
competence 183
Court encroaching upon
jurisdiction of 193
EU participation 176
Group of Wise Persons set up
by 104
and interpretative role of
European Court 20
meetings 182
pilot judgment
procedure 150
whether possessing
exclusive competence in
enforcement 191–192
role in execution of
judgments 180, 181, 198
supervision of execution of
judgments 31
Committee on Legal Affairs and Human Rights (CLAHR)
Parliamentary Assembly
of Council of Europe
(PACE) 31, 189, 194, 195,
196, 198

Committees, ECtHR
and composition of
ECtHR 111, 112
procedure 121–122
community service in a public emergency
freedom from forced or
compulsory labour 283
compensation
breach of Article 1,
Protocol 1 29
deprivation of
property 888–894
illegal detention 366–368
illegal state action 382–383
miscarriages of
justice 968–969
victim status 91
competence
of Committee of
Ministers 191–192
ratione materiae see
COMPETENCE
RATIONE MATERIAE
ratione personae see
COMPETENCE
RATIONE PERSONAE
ratione temporis see
COMPETENCE
RATIONE TEMPORIS
competence *ratione loci*
Article 56 100–102
concept of 'jurisdiction' in
Article 1 99–100
competence *ratione materiae*
admissibility 44, 95–96
competence *ratione personae*
death of applicant 94–95
indirect victims 91–94
inter-state cases 45
loss of victim status
after lodging of an
application 90–91
respondent state 81–84
victim status 81, 84–91
competence *ratione temporis*
facts giving rise to the
application 97–98
scope of Convention
right 98–99
complaints, European Court of Human Rights
Article 3 277
individual complaints 113
inter-state
complaints 115–117
inter-state complaints versus
individual complaints 116
national security
protection 653

confidentiality
of journalistic sources 640,
641–643
preventing disclosure
of confidential
information 672–675
conscience, freedom of *see*
ARTICLE 9 (FREEDOM OF
THOUGHT, CONSCIENCE
AND RELIGION);
FREEDOM OF THOUGHT,
CONSCIENCE AND
RELIGION
conscientious objection
Article 9 601–602
consent
medical treatment
without 543–545
contempt of court doctrine
and trials, prevention of
improper influence
on 679, 680
continuing situations
six-month rule 47, 64–65
Convention on Human Rights *see* EUROPEAN
CONVENTION ON
HUMAN RIGHTS
AND FUNDAMENTAL
FREEDOMS 1950 (ECHR)
conviction, detention following
'causal connection' 308–310
by competent court 306–310
copyright law, protecting
restrictions upon freedom of
expression 672
corporal punishment
abolition 30
Article 3, consistent with
9, 273
Article 46 162
state responsibility 24
correspondence rights, under Article 8
prisoners 587, 589
provisions of Article 8 530
costs
just satisfaction 158–159
Council of Europe
Commissioner for Human
Rights 842–843, 848
Committee for the
Prevention of Torture 75,
145, 147, 262
Committee of Legal
Experts 172
Directorate General of
Human Rights and Legal
Affairs 182
ECHR drafted within 3

foundational values 613
Framework Convention for
the Protection of National
Minorities 811
human rights guarantee,
continuing need for states
of 278
Parliamentary Assembly
see PARLIAMENTARY
ASSEMBLY OF
COUNCIL OF EUROPE
(PACE)
penal policy of member
states 9
Registry of ECtHR recruited
by 113
Secretary General 847, 848
Sixth Protocol to General
Agreement on Privileges
and Immunities 105, 106
Statute 181, 783
Steering Committee for
Human Rights 165
Venice Commission 144
Court of Human Rights *see*
EUROPEAN COURT OF
HUMAN RIGHTS (ECRHR)
court orders
non-compliance 310–311
non-enforcement 574
crime prevention
bail, grounds for
refusing 348
restrictions upon freedom of
expression 633, 654–655
crimes against humanity
and amnesties 205
Article 7 498, 502
against Jewish people 624
criminal offence
Article 6, application 374, 495
basis in 'law' 495
detention on
suspicion of having
committed 314–319
lawfulness 318–319
'offence' 315
purpose of
detention 315–316
reasonable
suspicion 316–318
determination of a criminal
charge
meaning of
charge 376–378
meaning of
criminal 373–376
ex post facto 494–499
immigrants, involvement
of 576

inhuman punishment 259
post-war crimes with
Second World War
connection 502
professional misconduct
375
and right to review in
criminal cases (Seventh
Protocol, Article 2)
966–968
see also ARTICLE 7
(FREEDOM FROM
RETROACTIVE
CRIMINAL OFFENCES
AND PUNISHMENT)
custody
children 572–575
preventive purposes 313–314
Cyprus
exhaustion rule,
application 49, 51
just satisfaction
case 184–185
UN Committee of Missing
Persons in 75

data
access 562–564
collection, storage and
disclosure 559–562
protection 525–526
de minimis non curat praetor
principle
no significant disadvantage
criterion 67
death
of applicant
(competence *ratione
personae*) 94–95
force, use for permitted
purposes 227–229
medical negligence resulting
in 545
right to die, Article 2 not
guaranteeing 205
by state agent 222, 223
see also SUICIDE
death penalty
and breach of Article 3
245–246
exception to prohibition
of taking of life by
force 225–227
Sixth and Thirteenth
Protocols 963–965
defamation
contested statements
establishing
veracity 704–706
proof 702–704

denial of opportunity to prove
truth of allegations 707
distinction between
statements of fact and
value judgments 697–700
and ECtHR 691–692
medical practitioners
663–666
methodologies and
principles developed to
examine 691–707
overview 691–693
private individuals,
protection of reputation
and honour 660
public figures and broader
bounds of acceptable
criticism 693–697
civil servants and
public figures
doctrine 696–697
political figures and
public figures
doctrine 693–695
'sufficient factual
basis' 700–702
defending oneself
legal aid 478–480
legal assistance 476–478
in person 476
right under Article 6(3)(c)
474–483
degrading punishment
Article 3 271–273
degrading treatment
defined 261
detention 261–269
discrimination 269–270
forced shaving off of hair 263
health care and other social
services 213
other kinds 270–271
psychiatric care 266
strip searches of
prisoners 263
delay
assemblies 720–721
registration of religious
bodies 598
right to trial within
reasonable time 441–442
democracy
character 512–513
and electoral rights 921
freedom of thought,
conscience and
religion 608–611
limitations of Articles
8–11 510–520
'militant democracy' 631

democracy (*Cont.*)
  'necessary in a
    democratic society'
    requirement 510–520
  character of 'democratic
    society' 512–513
  derogation in time of
    war/other public
    emergency 826
  European and
    international
    consensus 513–515
  freedom of expression 614
  freedom of peaceful
    assembly 716–717
  importance of protected
    right 512
  interest to be protected by
    interference 515–518
  meaning of
    'necessary' 510
  proselytism 610–611
  religious dress 603,
    608–610
  political expression 629–631,
    673
Denmark
  cartoons lampooning
    Prophet of Islam 654
deportation
  action being taken with view
    to 330–334
  Article 4 286
  Article 8 575
  Article 13 774
  detention pending 330–334
  inhuman treatment 247–256
  Soering v UK decision 247
Deputy Section Registrar
  assistance by 112
detention
  'alcoholics' and 'drug
    addicts' 322–324
  arbitrariness, protection
    from 304–306
  Article 5, controlled by 288
  classic case 290
  compulsory medical
    intervention 267–268
  conditions 244, 298
  continued 29
  custody for preventive
    purposes 313–314
  degrading treatment 261–269
  following conviction by
    competent court 306–310
    'causal connection'
    308–310
  fulfilment of any obligation
    prescribed by law 311–313

custody for preventive
    purposes 313–314
  generally 261
  grounds for
    following conviction
      by competent
      court 306–310
    fulfilment of any
      obligation prescribed by
      law 311–314
    infectious diseases,
      prevention of
      spreading 321–322
    minors, acts by 319–321
    non-compliance
      with lawful court
      order 310–311
    pending deportation
      and extradition,
      etc 330–334
    persons of unsound mind,
      alcoholics, vagrants,
      etc 322–328
    on suspicion of having
      committed a criminal
      offence 314–319
    'unauthorized entry',
      preventing 328–330
  handcuffing/other
    restraints 268–269
  illegal, right to compensation
    under Article
    5(5) 366–368
  infectious diseases,
    prevention of
    spreading 321–322
  inhuman treatment 244
  lawfulness of
    generally 318–319
    overarching principles of
      Article 5 301, 302, 303
    review 352–366
  legality, remedy to
    challenge under Article
    5(4) 352–366
  continuing remedy
    at reasonable
    interviews 363–365
  importance of Article
    5(4) 352–353
  judicial character of
    review body 355–363
  procedural guarantees
    on review of
    detention 356–363
  qualities and procedures
    required of Article 5(4)
    court 354–363
  scope of Article 5(4)
    application 365–366

meaning 289–296
  medical assistance 265–267
  of minors 319–321
  Osman obligation 211
  'persons of unsound
    mind' 324–328
  pre-trial, accountability
    during 338–351
  prolonged, more
    than 'reasonable
    suspicion' required to
    sustain 344–346
  review of lawfulness
    352–366
    effective access to 354–355
    judicial character of
      review body 355–363
    procedural guarantees
      required 356–363
  social care, context
    of 294–296
  solitary confinement
    264–265
  United Nations Working
    Group on Arbitrary
    Detention 76, 78
  'vagrants' 322
  work during 282–283
  see also ARTICLE 5 (RIGHT
    TO LIBERTY AND
    SECURITY OF THE
    PERSON)
differential treatment
  birth 800–801
  burden of proof and
    statistics 809–810
  identifying 788
  intensive scrutiny
    of, for 'suspect
    categories' 796–809
    birth 800–801
    disability and
      health 808–809
    nationality 797–798
    race (or ethnic
      origin) 796–797
    religion 801–802
    sex (gender) 798–800
    sexual orientation
      803–806
    unmarried fathers
      806–808
  justified on objective
    and reasonable
    grounds 792–796
  legitimate aims 793–794
  proportionality
    principle 794–796
  minorities, protection
    810–811

nationality 797–798
obligation where situations
  are significantly
  different 790
'other status'
  category 790–791
on prohibited grounds 790–792
sex (gender) 798–800
sexual orientation 803–806
tests in *Belgian Linguistics*
  case 784–785, 787, 792,
  793, 794, 795
see also FREEDOM FROM
  DISCRIMINATION
disability and health
  differential treatment,
  scrutiny 808–809
disappeared persons
  force, prohibition of taking of
  life by 223–224
  inhuman treatment 257
  loss of liberty 300
  mental suffering caused to
  family member as breach
  of Article 3 258
disclosure
  of confidential information,
  preventing 672–675
  of data 559–562
  of evidence 421
discrimination
  'badges' of 790–792
  defined 786
  detainees,
  treatment 269–270
  education, right to (First
  Protocol, Article 2)
  916–918
  indirect 785, 815–817
  institutional 809
  non-existent if situations not
  analogous 789–790
  private, positive obligation to
  protect against 817–818
  racial 270
  religious 601–602
  reverse 818–819
  Roma, against 810
  violence motivated
  by 811–814
  see also ARTICLE 14
  (FREEDOM FROM
  DISCRIMINATION);
  FREEDOM FROM
  DISCRIMINATION
disorder, prevention
  restrictions upon freedom of
  expression 654–655
divorce
  Article 12 760

DNA material
  destruction or retention 11
domestic law
  exhaustion of domestic
  remedies *see*
  EXHAUSTION RULE
  no significant disadvantage
  criterion considered by
  domestic tribunal 71–72
  quality of 302–304
  review of compliance
  with 301–302
domestic violence
  positive obligations 23
Drittwirkung concept (reliance
  upon national bill of rights
  to bring claim against
  private individuals)
  Article 10 rights 617
  context of ECHR 23
'drug addicts'
  detention grounds 322–324
drug trafficking
  ex post facto criminal
  penalties 499
dual nationality
  right to stand for
  election 934–935

ECHR *see* EUROPEAN
  CONVENTION ON
  HUMAN RIGHTS
  AND FUNDAMENTAL
  FREEDOMS 1950
  (ECHR)
economic, social and cultural
  rights
  in Universal Declaration of
  Human Rights 5
ECtHR *see* EUROPEAN
  COURT OF HUMAN
  RIGHTS (ECRHR)
education, right to (First
  Protocol)
  access to existing institutions
  and exclusions
  from 909–912
  discrimination and minority
  rights 916–918
  education versus
  teaching 908
  effectiveness of education
  provided 912
  negative and positive
  obligations 24
  no denial of right to 909–912
  parents' religious and
  philosophical convictions,
  respect for 801–802,
  912–916

relationships with other
  Articles
  Article 8 524–525
  Article 9 600
  scope of protection 907
  sex education 914
  text 906
  see also CHILDREN
elections, free (First
  Protocol) 920–951
  age laws 926
  and Article 16 851
  associations, limitations
  upon 725
  candidacy controls
  bars on candidature of
  public and religious
  office holders 938
  election deposits 937–938
  language proficiency
  laws 939
  political misconduct as bar
  to candidacy 941–942
  prior political affiliation
  as bar to standing for
  election 939–941
  citizenship 926–927
  conduct of
  elections 943–946
  disenfranchisement of
  prisoners 929–933
  election
  administration 943–946
  electoral systems 946–949
  expatriates 927–928
  general principles governing
  jurisprudence of Article 3
  921–924
  media reporting of election
  campaigns 949–950
  non-residents, voting
  rights 928
  political rights 922
  post-election challenges
  to conduct of
  elections 944–946
  right to stand for
  election 933–943
  candidacy laws 934–936
  controls of candidacy
  937–942
  dual nationality 934–935
  legal disqualification
  of registered
  candidates 936–937
  political misconduct as bar
  to candidacy 941–942
  prior political affiliation
  as bar to standing for
  election 939–941

elections, free (First Protocol) (*Cont.*)
  representatives, rights 942–943
  residence 934
  rules governing polls, changes to 923
  scope of electoral rights 924–926
  voter qualifications 926–928
  voting rights 926–933
emergency *see* PUBLIC EMERGENCY
employment
  'free to resign' formula and public manifestation of religion or belief 604, 605
  political activities 578–579
  public service 386–387
    trade union activity restrictions 750–751
  state as employer 741
enforcement
  Committee of Ministers, whether possessing exclusive competence 191–192
  context of ECHR 6–7
  court orders, non-enforcement 574
  inter-state complaints 115
  proscribed ill-treatment, obligation to protect individuals from 275–277
  right to life 206–207
entrapment
  fair hearing, right to 427–428
environmental rights
  Article 8 582–585
  industrial pollution 584
  noise 583
equality of arms
  fair hearing, right to 413–416
  procedural guarantees on review of detention 356–357
escape, preventing
  exception to prohibition of taking of life by force 231–232
European Commission against Racism and Intolerance (ECRI)
  investigations and fact-finding 145
European Commission of Human Rights
  and setting up of new Court 103

European Convention on Human Rights and Fundamental Freedoms 1950 (ECHR)
  access of EU to (Accession Agreement) 171–176
  achievements
    contribution to international law of human rights 34
    impact on protection of human rights in Europe 34–37
    remedy for individuals 35–37
  background 3–5
  civil and political rights protected in 5
  context 3–40
  'Convention values' clause 99
  enforcement machinery 6–7, 38
  and European Union 31–34
  functions 3–4
  interpretation *see* INTERPRETATION OF ECHR
  language *see below under* 'terminology, autonomous meaning'
  in national law 26–31
  numbers of applications 38–39
  prospects 37–40
  purpose 3, 7–8, 9, 18, 19, 37
  subsidiary role in protecting human rights 17
  substantive guarantee 5–6
  terminology, autonomous meaning 19, 379–380, 495, 506
European Court of Human Rights (ECtHR)
  ad hoc and common interest judges 110–111
  adoption 3
  application 117–118
  Article 46
    contracting party in violation of obligations under 193–194
    procedure 162–165
    state obligations under 193
  backlog of cases 38, 39, 444
  binding precedent doctrine, lack of 21
  Bureau, composition 127
  Chambers 12, 20, 21, 111, 112, 137

  procedure (communication and joint procedure) 122–123
  Committees 111, 112
    procedure 121–122
  composition 104–107
  constitutional role, strengthening 178
  defamation 691–692
  election of judges and Advisory Panel 107–109
  execution of judgments 180–199
  exhaustion rule, application 48
  Filtering Division 112
  formations 111–112
  friendly settlement and unilateral declarations 127–130
  future 176–179
  Grand Chamber *see* GRAND CHAMBER, ECTHR
  hindering effective exercise of right of individual petition 113–115
  individual complaints 113
  ineligibility to sit 109–110
  internal mechanisms for ensuring consistency of case law 126–127
  interpretation, requests for (Rule 79) 132, 133
  interpretive role 20–21
  inter-state complaints 115–117
  judgments, execution 180–199
  judicial work 111
  Jurisconsult 112, 126
  just satisfaction 155–162
  languages, official 117
  lowest common denominator approach of 11
  misleading 79
  organization 103–113
  pilot judgments 149–151
  plenary Court 111
  presentation 118–119
  President 106, 111, 117, 126
  priority policy for dealing with cases 119–120
  procedure before 113–155
    application 117–118
    Article 46 162–165
    burden and standard of proof 146–148
    Chamber procedure (communication and joint procedure) 122–123

Committee of Ministers,
advisory opinions
requested by 135–136
Committee procedure
121–122
friendly settlement
and unilateral
declarations 127–130
Grand Chamber 123–126
individual complaints 113
interim measures 138–143
internal mechanisms for
ensuring consistency of
case law 126–127
inter-state
complaints 115–117
investigations and
fact-finding 143–146
legal aid 137
legal representation
136–137
oral hearings 137–138
pilot judgments 149–151
presentation of
application 118–119
priority policy for dealing
with cases 119–120
Protocol 14 165–166
publicity 136
single judge
procedure 120–121
striking out cases 130–132
third party interventions
152–155
purpose 3
ratio decidendi and *obiter
dicta*, no common law
distinction 20
rectification of errors,
requests for 132–133
reform 166–176
access of EU to
Convention 171–176
advisory opinions,
requests for 169–171
Protocol 15 168–169
Registry 66, 112–113
revision, requests for
(Rule 80) 132, 133–134
Rules of Court
ad hoc and common
interest judges 110
admissibility of
applications 66, 79
advisory opinions 135
composition of
ECtHR 105, 106–107
execution of judgments
182, 183, 185
friendly settlement 128

ineligibility to sit 109, 110
interim measures 142
interpretation, requests
for 132, 133
inter-state complaints 117
just satisfaction 157, 159
presentation of application
under Rule 47 118–119
rectification of errors,
requests for 132–133
referral to Grand
Chamber 124
revision, requests for 132,
133–134
third party
interventions 152, 154
Sections 111, 112, 126
setting up of new
Court 103–104
single judges 111, 112
procedure 120–121
striking out cases
(Article 37) 130–132
terrorism, general approach
to 825–829
time limits 119
WECL (well-established case
law) 112, 121, 165, 177
withdrawal of judges 109
workload 38, 39, 181, 444, 445
European Social Charter
trade unions, freedom to
form and join 740
European Union (EU)
access to European
Convention (Accession
Agreement) 171–176
challenged action inconsistent
with ECHR 32
Charter of Fundamental
Rights 32
Charter on Human Rights
and Fundamental
Freedoms 172
Committee of Ministers,
participation in 176
complaints against 83
and context of ECHR 31–34
Court of Justice 172
emergency measures 844
impact of ECHR on
protection of rights
in 34–37
individual member
states 32–33
information, access to 620
Legal Service of EU
Commission 172
euthanasia
active 205

medical care and
treatment 547–548
passive 204
and right to life 204–205
evangelism
and proselytism 610
evidence
admissibility of 418–420
assessment 421
disclosure 421
rules of 418–421
ex post facto **criminal offences**
Article 7 494–499
ex post facto **criminal penalties**
Article 7 499–501
exhaustion rule
adequacy and effectiveness of
remedies 52–54
admissibility of
applications 47–61
appeals to higher
courts 55–58
Article 35 73
basic requirements
appropriate domestic
body 49–51
compliance with formal
requirements and time
limits 50–51
in substance 48–49
burden of proof 51–52
and exceptions 46
extraordinary or
discretionary
remedies 54–55
inter-state cases 46
matter already examined by
the Court 74
purpose and crux 47–48
several remedies 54
special circumstances
and exemptions
from obligation to
exhaust 58–61
waiver 46
see also ADMISSIBILITY
OF APPLICATIONS;
REMEDIES
expenses
just satisfaction 158–159
expression, freedom of *see*
ARTICLE 10 (FREEDOM OF
EXPRESSION); FREEDOM
OF EXPRESSION
expulsion
loss of liberty 298–300
extradition
action being taken with view
to 330–334
Article 4 286

extradition (*Cont.*)
humanitarian
considerations 254
inhuman treatment 244–256
loss of liberty 298–300
Soering v UK decision 245,
246, 247
extraordinary rendition
inhuman treatment 256

fact-finding
ECtHR procedure 143–146
justiciability of interest 517
fair balance
interpretation of ECHR 14
property, right to 873–874,
875, 876, 882, 884, 885
fair hearing, right to
adversarial trial, right
to 416–418
under Article 6 409–433
entrapment 427–428
equality of arms 413–416
evidence, rules of 418–421
freedom from self-
incrimination 422–426
hearing in one's
presence 410–412
immediacy principle 421
interpretation of ECHR 12
legal certainty
principle 431–432
meaning 492
other issues 432–433
prejudicial media
publicity 428–429
presumption of
innocence 421, 429
reasoned judgment 430–431
retroactive legislation
designed to defeat a
litigant's claim 429
right to have one's case
properly examined 429
right to participate effectively
at hearing 412–413
see also ARTICLE 6 (RIGHT
TO FAIR TRIAL); TRIAL
fairness
procedural guarantees on
review of detention 357,
358, 359
**family and personal
relationships**
adoption 567–568, 573
biological factors, relative
importance 527
deceased family
members 568–569
intentionality 527

non-married persons 762
other aspects 568–569
parentage,
recognition 564–567
prisoners 585–586
relevant factors 527
right to found a
family 760–762
right to marry
divorce 760
generally 755–758
same-sex marriages 758,
759, 804
transsexuals 758–759
termination by divorce 528
unmarried fathers
and differential
treatment 806–808
see also ARTICLE 8 (RIGHT
TO RESPECT FOR
PRIVATE AND FAMILY
LIFE, HOME AND
CORRESPONDENCE)
fascism
and freedom of
expression 622
First Protocol
Article 1 (right to property)
access to property
869–870
and Article 11 713
and Article 13 781
and Article 14 787, 789
breach 29
compensation for
deprivation 888–894
competence *ratione
temporis* 98
control of use 895–903
deprivation of
property 885–894
exhaustion rule 49
fair balance test 873–874,
875, 876, 882, 884, 885
final form 862
financial benefits, lack of
equality 799
interpretation of
ECHR 10–11, 15
just satisfaction 184
lawfulness 878–880
legitimate aim 876–877
peaceful enjoyment,
interference with
868–869, 880–885
positive obligation
to protect
possessions 870–872
possessions 863–868,
870–872

structure 872–880
three rules 872–876
victim status 93
violation by Ireland 33
Article 2 (right to
education) 906–919
access to existing
institutions
and exclusions
from 909–912
and Article 8 524–525
and Article 9 600
discrimination
and minority
rights 916–918
drafting history 918
education versus
teaching 908
effectiveness of education
provided 912
negative and positive
obligations 24
no denial of right to
education 909–912
parents' religious
and philosophical
convictions, respect
for 801–802, 912–916
scope of protection 907
sex education 914
Article 3 (right to free
elections) 920–951
age laws 926
and Article 16 851
associations, limitations
upon 725
breach by UK 33–34
citizenship 926–927
conduct of
elections 943–946
disenfranchisement 929–933
election administration
and post-electoral
rights 943–946
expatriates 927–928
general principles
governing
jurisprudence 921–924
Gibraltar 83
interpretation of
ECHR 12
non-residents, voting
rights 928
political rights 922
positive obligations 22
post-election challenges
to conduct of
elections 944–946
representatives,
rights 942–943

right to stand for
    election 933–943
rules governing polls,
    changes to 923
scope of electoral
    rights 924–926
victim status 93
violations 189–190
voter
    qualifications 926–928
voting rights 926–933
force, prohibition of taking of
life by
disappeared
    persons 223–224
exceptions permitted
    capital
        punishment 225–227
    deaths resulting from use
        of force for permitted
        purposes 227–229
    to effect arrest or prevent
        escape 231–232
    self-defence/defence of
        another 229–231
general rule 221–224
insurrection 230, 232–233
permitted purposes 227–229
riot, quelling 232–233
force feeding
    Article 2 212
forced or compulsory
labour see FREEDOM
    FROM FORCED OR
    COMPULSORY LABOUR
foreseeability
and 'law' 496
and novelty 508
as subtest under freedom of
    expression 649–651
fourth instance (quatrième
instance) doctrine
interpretation of
    ECHR 17–18
Fourth Protocol
Article 1 (freedom
    from imprisonment
    for non-fulfilment
    of contractual
    obligations) 952–953
Article 2 (freedom of
    movement within a
    state and freedom to
    leave its territory)
    953–959
    freedom of movement
        within a state's
        territory 954–957
    freedom to leave a state's
        territory 958–959

Article 3 (right of national
    not be expelled
    from/to enter state's
    territory) 959–960
France
Code of Criminal
    Procedure 507, 508
religious dress, and Article 9
    609–610
telephone-tapping 507
freedom from discrimination
differential treatment
    burden of proof and
        statistics 809–810
    identifying 788
    intensive scrutiny
        of, for 'suspect
        categories' 796–809
    justified on objective
        and reasonable
        grounds 792–796
    minorities, protection
        810–811
    no discrimination
        if situations not
        analogous 789–790
    obligation where situations
        are significantly
        different 790
    'other status'
        category 790–791
    on prohibited grounds
        790–792
indirect discrimination
    815–817
private discrimination,
    positive obligation to
    protect against 817–818
protection for guaranteed rights
    only and ambit test 786–787
and Protocol 12 819–821
violence motivated by
    discrimination 811–814
    racial, in context of
        policing and criminal
        justice 811–814
    state toleration 814–815
see also ARTICLE 14
    (FREEDOM FROM
    DISCRIMINATION);
    DISCRIMINATION
freedom from forced or
compulsory labour
community service in a
    public emergency 283
ILO Forced Labour
    Convention (1930) 280
meaning of forced
    or compulsory
    labour 280–281

military service or substitute
    civilian service 283
normal civic obligations
    283–284
permitted work or
    services 282
work during
    detention 282–283
freedom from
self-incrimination
fair hearing, right
    to 422–426
freedom of association
interferences with 735–737
legal recognition of
    associations 737–738
limitations upon associations
    associations other than
        political 731–735
    interferences,
        proportionality
        requirement 735–737
    legal recognition of
        associations 737–738
    political parties 725–731
meaning of
    association 724–725
minorities,
    protection 731–732
positive obligations 738–739
regulation of associations
    raising issue of 'quality of
    law' 733
religious groups 732
freedom of expression
access to public forums or
    media 619
and Article 8 523
categories of expression
    artistic 632–635
    civil 632
    commercial 635–639
    political 629–631
    'constitutional'
        importance 613–614
defamation
    methodologies and
        principles developed to
        examine 691–707
    overview 691–693
    public figures and
        broader bounds
        of acceptable
        criticism 693–697
'democratic society' 512
duties and responsibilities
    under Article10(2)
    civil servants 685–687
    journalists 687–691
    overview 683–685

freedom of expression (*Cont.*)
and elections 630–631
   see also ELECTIONS,
      FREE (FIRST
      PROTOCOL)
foreseeability subtest
   649–651
as foundational value of
   Council of Europe 613
homophobia 623
interests to be protected by
   interference 515
interference by public
   authority 618
language 615
legitimate aims for which
   restrictions can be
   justified 652–683
   copyright law, protecting 672
   crime prevention 654–655
   disclosure of confidential
      information, preventing
      672–675
   disorder, prevention
      654–655
   freedom of religion of
      others, protecting
      669–671
   judiciary, maintenance
      of authority and
      impartiality 675–683
   morals, protecting
      655–658
   national security,
      protecting 652–654
   overview 652
   public figures, protecting
      privacy, reputation and
      honour 666–669
   reputation and honour
      of private individuals,
      protecting 658–666
margin of appreciation
   doctrine 512
means of expression 615,
   639–649
odious expression and
   relationship between
   Articles 10 and 17 621–623
and political parties 631
prescribed by law 649–652
press and journalistic
   freedom 639–643
'revisionist'
   expression 623–626
scope of protection of
   Article 10 614–629
see also ARTICLE 10
   (FREEDOM OF
   EXPRESSION)

freedom of movement
arrest or detention
   (Article 5) 289
freedom to leave a state's
   territory 958–959
infringement 498
within a state's
   territory 954–957
freedom of peaceful assembly
bans on marches 717
counter-demonstrators,
   disturbance by 712–713
criminal conduct by
   demonstrators 723–724
as fundamental right 711
interferences with peaceful
   assembly 714–715
limitations on
   interferences 715–724
obligation to give prior
   notice of assembly,
   overriding 720–721
political opinions 719
positive obligations 712–713
religious assemblies 717–718
social issues 718–719
third party rights 713–714
tolerance 720, 721
unlawful/unauthorized
   assemblies 722, 723
see also ARTICLE 11
   (FREEDOM OF
   ASSEMBLY AND
   ASSOCIATION)
freedom of press *see under*
   PRESS
freedom of speech *see*
   ARTICLE 10 (FREEDOM OF
   EXPRESSION); FREEDOM
   OF EXPRESSION
**freedom of thought, conscience
   and religion**
interests to be protected by
   interference 515
justifiable interferences
   legitimate aim 606–608
   necessary in a democratic
      society 608–611
   prescribed by
      law 605–606
manifesting religion or belief
   nature of manifestation
      602–604
   'necessity' approach
      603–604
   public 604–605
   in worship, teaching,
      practice and
      observance 602–605
proselytism 610–611

religious dress 603, 608–610
right to believe 594–597
see also ARTICLE
   9 (FREEDOM
   OF THOUGHT,
   CONSCIENCE AND
   RELIGION)
friendly settlement
disclosure of terms of
   negotiations 79–80
ECtHR procedure 127–130
and unilateral
   declarations 129–130
fundamental rights
serious violations,
   investigating 779–781

genocide
and amnesties 205
Article 7 498
Germany
dissolution of communist
   party 622
and freedom of
   expression 616–617
German Democratic
   Republic (GDR)
   criminal law 495–496
   infringement of
      international
      obligations 498
Gibraltar
application of Article 3 of
   Protocol 1 to 83
***Golder* case**
right of access to a
   court 398–399
Grand Chamber, ECtHR
admissibility of
   applications 44
and composition of
   ECtHR 111, 112
contesting panel decision as
   to referral decision 125
on detention 292–293
interpretation of ECHR 12,
   20, 21
inter-state complaints 117
legal aid 137
oral hearings 138
procedure 123–126
guarantees
in criminal and non-criminal
   cases, under Article
   6(1) 398–460
   appeal proceedings,
      application of Article
      6(1) to 459–460
   fair hearing, right
      to 409–433

independent and impartial
tribunal, right
to 446–458
presumption of
innocence 421,
460–467
public hearing, right
to 433–438
public pronouncement
of judgment, right
to 438–439
right of access to a
court 398–408
trial, right to within
a reasonable
time 439–446
in criminal cases, under
Article 6(3)
adequate facilities, right
to 472–473
adequate time, right
to 470–471
defending oneself in
person/through legal
assistance 474–483
generally 467–468
interpreters, right
to 489–491
right to be informed of
accusation 468–470
witnesses, right to call and
cross-examine 483–489
international human rights,
enforceable in national
law 26
right of access to a court
Golder case 398–399
relationship with Article
13 408
restrictions upon right of
access 402–408
right of effective
access 399–402
waiver of right of
access 408

handcuffing/other restraints
treatment of
detainees 268–269
harm, duty to protect from
violations of Articles 2 and 3
779–781
health care
right to life 212–214
hearings
fair, right to
adversarial trial, right
to 416–418
entrapment 427–428
equality of arms 413–416

evidence, rules of 418–421
freedom from
lf-incrimination
422–426
hearing in one's
presence 410–412
immediacy principle 421
legal certainty
principle 431–432
other issues 432–433
prejudicial media
publicity 428–429
reasoned
judgment 430–431
retroactive legislation
designed to defeat a
litigant's claim 429
right to have one's case
properly examined 429
right to participate
effectively at
hearing 412–413
oral
before ECtHR 137–138
procedural guarantees
on review of
detention 359–360
public hearing, right
to 436–437
public, right to 433–438
oral 436–437
waiver 437–438
HIV status
discrimination 808–809
Holocaust
denial of 624
and freedom of
expression 621, 622, 623
home and housing issues
Article 8 528–530, 580–582
professional persons, office
of 529–530
residence and Article 8 529
same-sex partnerships 803
state-owned property,
relevance to Article 8 529
home curfew
as 'deprivation of
liberty' 290–291
homophobia
and freedom of
expression 623
homosexuality
acceptance 550
honour, protecting
private individuals 658–666
public figures 666–669
human rights
contribution of ECHR to
international law 34

impact of ECHR on
protection of rights in
Europe 34–37
obligation to respect
see ARTICLE 1
(OBLIGATION TO
RESPECT HUMAN
RIGHTS)
Human Rights Act 1998, UK
and application of ECHR by
national courts 27–28
declaration of
incompatibility under 55
Human Rights Committee
admissibility of
applications 75
Article 9 593
human trafficking
Article 4 284–286
Hungary
appeals to higher courts 58
crimes against humanity 502

identity
appearance 538–539
checks 313
ethnic and religious 540
gender 536–537
names 539–540
national 540
one's origins,
regarding 537–538
personal 536–540
ill-treatment
categories 237
minimum level of
severity requirement
to fall within
Article 3 236, 241
prisoners 239–240
proscribed, obligation to
protect individuals from
investigation and
enforcement 275–277
prevention 274–275
'real risk' requirement to fall
within Article 3 248
state responsibility 251,
252
see also ARTICLE 3
(FREEDOM FROM
TORTURE OR
INHUMAN OR
DEGRADING
TREATMENT OR
PUNISHMENT)
immediacy principle
fair hearing, right to 421
immigration
Article 8 575–578

immunity
  parliamentarians 630
  right of access to a
    court 405–407
impartiality
  judiciary 675–683
  juries 456, 456–457
  objective test 451, 452, 453,
    454–455
  state duty 598
  tribunals 450–457
imprisonment
  freedom from for
    non-fulfilment
    of contractual
    obligations 952–953
  possible versus actual
    punishment 376
  see also PRISONERS
independence
  tribunals 447–450
indirect discrimination
  Article 14 815–817
individuals, private
  ECHR as remedy for 35–37
  groups of individuals 82
  reputation and honour,
    protecting 658–666
industrial pollution
  and Article 8 584
infectious diseases, prevention
  of spreading
  detention grounds 321–322
information
  access to 620–621
  accurate and reliable, duties
    of journalists in relation
    to 687–688
  arrest, regarding 335–338
  confidential, preventing
    disclosure 672–675
  one's origins,
    regarding 537–538
inhuman punishment
  Article 3 259–260
inhuman treatment
  Article 3 241–258
  assaults 241–243
  conditions of detention
    and treatment of
    detainees 244
  deportation 244–256
  disappeared persons 257
  European Committee for the
    Prevention of Torture and
    Inhuman or Degrading
    Treatment or Punishment
    (CPT) 262
  experimental medical
    treatment as 258

extradition 244–256
extraordinary rendition 256
force not in breach of
  Article 3 242
other kinds 257–258
psychological interrogation
  techniques 244
see also ARTICLE 3
  (FREEDOM FROM
  TORTURE OR
  INHUMAN OR
  DEGRADING
  TREATMENT OR
  PUNISHMENT)
innocence *see* PRESUMPTION
  OF INNOCENCE
insurrection
  exception to prohibition of
    taking of life by force 230,
    232–233
integrity
  moral, physical and
    psychological 541–543
intellectual property rights
  restrictions upon freedom of
    expression 672
Inter-American Court of
  Human Rights
  and advisory opinions 171
interests of justice
  legal assistance 479
interim measures
  ECtHR procedure 138–143
  imminent risk of irreparable
    damage 141
  positive and negative 141
  scope 141–142
Interlaken Conference and
  Declaration (2010)
  and Article 13 764, 782
  case law, ensuring
    consistency of 126
  election of judges and
    Advisory Panel 107
  execution of Court
    judgments 190
  reform of ECtHR 104, 167
International Court of Justice
  (ICJ)
  and advisory opinions 171
International Covenant on
  Civil and Political Rights
  (ICCPR) 1966
  and Article 15 843, 844
  ECHR as regional
    counterpart to 5
  information, access to 620
  infringement 498
  non-discrimination 783
  Optional Protocol 76

and Protocol 12 819
religion or belief 593
substantive guarantee 6
voting rights 851
International Criminal Court
  (ICC)
  Rome Statute 625
International Labour
  Organization (ILO)
  Forced Labour Convention
    (1930) 280
  trade unions, freedom to
    form and join 740
international law
  and Article 15 843–844
  freedom from retroactive
    criminal offences and
    punishment 498
  general principles 887–888
International Law Commission
  draft Articles on the
    Responsibility
    of International
    Organizations 84
International Monetary Fund
  (IMF)
  failed arbitration by 75
international standards
  reliance upon 10–13
Internet
  and means of expression 615
Inter-Parliamentary Union
  Human Rights Committee 75
interpretation of ECHR
  autonomous meaning of
    Convention terms 19,
    379–380
  consistency of (Convention
    as a whole) 18
  Court of Human Rights,
    interpretive role 20–21
  dynamic or evolutive 9–10
  effective 18
  fair balance 14
  fourth instance (*quatrième
    instance*) doctrine 17–18
  general approach 7
  limits resulting from clear
    meaning of text 18–19
  margin of appreciation
    doctrine 11, 14–17
  object and purpose, emphasis
    upon 7–8, 9, 18, 19, 37, 43
  proportionality
    principle 13–14
  reliance upon national
    law and international
    standards 10–13
  travaux préparatoires,
    recourse to 19–20

see also EUROPEAN
CONVENTION ON
HUMAN RIGHTS
AND FUNDAMENTAL
FREEDOMS 1950
(ECHR); *individual
Articles*
interpretation requests
European Court of Human
Rights 132, 133
interpreters
right to 489–491
inter-state cases
admissibility requirements,
application to 45–47
complaints before
ECtHR 115–117
exhaustion rule and
exceptions 46
legislative measures 46
investigations
adequacy requirement 216, 217
ECtHR procedure 143–146
procedural obligation to
investigate and right to
life 214–218
promptness
requirement 217–218
proscribed ill-treatment,
obligation to protect
individuals from 275–277
racial violence 813–814
serious violations
of fundamental
rights 779–781
on-site 145
witnesses 145
involuntary abortion
Article 2 220–221
Ireland
and complaints against
EU 83
Islam
Danish cartoons lampooning
Prophet 654
Islamic fundamentalism, and
freedom of expression 622
Islamic headscarf, and
Article 9 603, 608, 609
**Izmir Conference and
Declaration (2011)**
and Article 13 764, 782
case law, ensuring
consistency of 126
election of judges and
Advisory Panel 107
execution of Court
judgments 190
interim measures 143
reform of ECtHR 104, 167

Jehovah's Witnesses
proselytizing activities 610
scope of Article 9 593
Jewish people
crimes against humanity
directed at 624
journalists
duties and responsibilities
687–691
accurate and reliable
information provision
687–688
and ethics of
journalism 683, 687
independent research
688–689
overview 687
exclusion from criminal
courts 675
exemption from duty to
undertake independent
research 689–691
journalistic
freedom 639–643
'official' report, reliance
on 689–691
protection and
confidentiality of
sources 640, 641–643
as witnesses 675
judges
bringing promptly before
following arrest 338–339
European Court of Human
Rights (ECrHR)
ad hoc and common
interest judges 110–111
composition 111, 112
election 107–109
interpretation of ECHR 13
single judge
procedure 120–121
withdrawal 109
Protocol 14 165–166
see also JUDICIARY,
MAINTENANCE OF
AUTHORITY AND
IMPARTIALITY
**judgments of Court,
execution** 180–199
Article 6, application 396
Committee of Ministers
Court encroaching upon
jurisdiction of 193
whether possessing
exclusive competence in
enforcement 191–192
role 180, 181
and Parliamentary
Assembly 194–196

procedure 181–191
general measures 188–191
individual measures
185–188
interim and final
resolutions 183
just satisfaction 184–185
Protocol 14 196–198
**judiciary, maintenance of
authority and impartiality**
criticisms of judiciary or
prosecutors 676–679
overview 675–676
trials, prevention of improper
influence on 679–683
see also JUDGES
juries
impartiality
requirement 456–457
jurisdiction
of Committee of Ministers,
Court encroaching
upon 193
concept in Article 1 99–100
just satisfaction
costs and expenses 157,
158–159
ECtHR procedure 155–162
execution of Court
judgments 29, 184–185
pecuniary and
non-pecuniary
damage 157, 159–162

Kurdish nationalism
and freedom of
expression 622, 627–628

labour, forced or compulsory
see FREEDOM
FROM FORCED OR
COMPULSORY LABOUR
language
Article 6 7
Article 8 503
Articles 8–11 503
Article 10 615, 618
autonomous Convention
meaning 19, 379–380,
495, 506
of instruction in
schools 911–912
offensive 79
official languages of
ECtHR 117
proficiency laws 939
'law'
Article 7 (freedom from
retroactive criminal
offences and punishment)

'law' (*Cont.*)
  existing law 497
  general principles of law
    exception 501–502
  'international law' 498,
    502
  law deriving authority
    from state's lawful
    constitution 496
  relevant, application
    to 494
  substantive law,
    application only to 494
  Articles 8–11
    'in accordance with the
      law'/'prescribed by
      law' 506–509
    language 503
  autonomous Convention
    meaning 495, 506
  binding over for good
    behaviour, in English
    law 509
  'prescribed by law'
    Articles 8–11 506–509
    freedom of
      expression 614,
      649–652
    freedom of thought,
      conscience and
      religion 605–606
'lawfulness'
  of detention 302, 303
    generally 318–319
    overarching principles of
      Article 5 301, 302, 303
  international law 498
  principle, and property
    rights 878–880
  review of lawfulness of
    detention 352–366
    effective access
      to 354–355
    judicial character of
      review body 355–363
    procedural guarantees
      required at
      review 356–363
legal aid
  ECtHR procedure 137
  funding of 480
  guarantees in criminal
    cases 478–480
  interests of justice 479
legal assistance
  practical and
    effective 481–483
  procedural guarantees
    on review of
    detention 360–361

right to defend oneself
  through 476–478
legal certainty
  Article 5 302–304
  fair hearing, right
    to 431–432
  res judicata principle 431
legal representation
  ECtHR procedure 136–137
legality principle
  incorporated in Article 7 493
legitimate aims
  Article 1, Protocol 1 876–877
  Article 6 402
  Article 8 586
  Articles 8–11 509–510
  Article 9 606–608
  Article 10 652–683
  Article 14 793–794
legitimate expectations
  possessions 864
lethal force
  security forces 147–148
liberty, right to
  implied procedural
    safeguards 300
  loss of liberty
    conditions of
      detention 298
    disappeared persons 300
    engaging the
      responsibility of the
      state, and positive
      obligations 297
    meaning of 'deprivation of
      liberty' 289–294
    physical detention at
      hands of police or state
      officials 292
    public protection
      motives 296
    by terrorists/kidnappers 23
    transfer across borders,
      extradition and
      expulsion' 298–300
  meaning of arrest or
    detention 289–296
  and security of the
    person 300
  see also ARTICLE 5 (RIGHT
    TO LIBERTY AND
    SECURITY OF THE
    PERSON); DETENTION
life, right to
  amnesties 205–206
  euthanasia 204–205
  hazardous activities 584
  infringement 498
  laws prohibiting taking of
    life 204

legal and administrative
  framework 204–206
obligation to protect by
  law 203–207
Osman obligation 209, 210,
  211, 212
regulation of activities and
  situations posing risk to
  life 206
right to die, Article 2 not
  guaranteeing 205
see also ARTICLE 2
  (RIGHT TO LIFE)
Lisbon Treaty (2009)
  accession of EU to
    ECHR 172
Lithuania
  re-established state of,
    Article 7 496

Malta
  list of judges to
    Parliamentary
    Assembly 108
margin of appreciation
  doctrine
  Article 2 208, 213
  Article 6 16, 371, 402
  Article 8 533, 551
  Articles 8–11 511
  Article 10 656, 657
  Article 14 799–800, 807–808
  Article 15 848
  differential application 16
  federal margin 658
  freedom of expression 512
  interpretation of ECHR 11,
    14–17
  morals, protecting 656, 657
  Protocol 1 909
  public emergency 842–843
  right of access to a court
    402
marriage
  capacity 755
  non-married persons 762
  physical location 758
  right to found a
    family 760–762
  right to marry
    divorce 760
    generally 755–758
    prisoners 757–758
    same-sex marriages 758,
      759, 804
    transsexuals 758–759
  unmarried fathers and
    marital status 806–808
mass media
  free speech rights 643

media
  live transmission of court
    proceedings by 675–676
  prejudicial
    publicity 428–429
  reporting of election
    campaigns 949–950
  see also BROADCASTING,
    LICENSING FOR;
    JOURNALISTS; PRESS
medical care and treatment
  assisted procreation 548–549
  availability 546–547
  compulsory medical
    intervention 267–268
  defamation actions
    against medical
    practitioners 663–666
  detainees, treatment 265–268
  disclosure without
    consent 561–562
  euthanasia 547–548
  experimental, as inhuman
    treatment 258
  medical negligence
    Article 2 213–214, 545
    Article 3 266
    Article 8 545–546
  treatment without
    consent 543–545
mental suffering
  as torture 240
mentally disordered persons
  detention grounds 324–328
military service or substitute
  civilian service
  freedom from forced or
    compulsory labour 283
minorities, protection
  education, right to (First
    Protocol, Article 2)
    916–918
  Framework Convention for
    the Protection of National
    Minorities 811
  freedom from
    discrimination 810–811
  revealing of beliefs 596
minors
  detention of 319–321
miscarriages of justice
  compensation 968–969
monopolies
  broadcasting 644
morals, protecting
  restrictions upon freedom of
    expression 655–658
movement, freedom of
  see FREEDOM OF
    MOVEMENT

murder
  amnesty for 205

Nachova v Bulgaria decision
  racial violence 811–814
names
  personal identity 539–540
national law
  and European Convention
    26–31
  application by national
    courts 26–29
  breach 27, 493
  execution of Strasbourg
    judgments 29–31
  increase in reliance on 28
  influence on national
    law 34–35
  'European standard' 513, 514
  local factors, influence
    of 27–28
  personal convictions,
    requiring disclosure
    595–596
  precision, degree of 508
  reliance upon 10–13
  ultra vires acts 495
national security protection
  Article 10 633, 652–654
  Article 13 774–777
  Article 15 828
nationality
  differential treatment,
    scrutiny 797–798
natural disasters
  Article 2 208
Nazism/neo-Nazism
  collaboration with
    Switzerland 632
  and freedom of
    expression 621, 622, 624
ne bis in idem principle
  Seventh Protocol (Article 4)
    969–973
negative obligations
  Article 2 234
  Article 8 531–532, 533
  Articles 8–11 504–505
  context of ECHR 21–22
negligence, medical
  Article 2 213–214, 545
  Article 3 266
  Article 8 545–546
neutrality
  state obligation 598, 599
NGOs see
  NON-GOVERNMENTAL
  ORGANIZATIONS (NGOs)
no significant disadvantage
  criterion

admissibility of
  applications 43, 67–72
  cases considered 68–70
  duly considered by a
    domestic tribunal 71–72
  examination of application
    on the merits
    requirement 70–71
noise
  environmental rights 583
non bis in idem (not tried twice
  for same offence)
  Article 7 494
non-governmental
  organizations (NGOs)
  broadcasting, licensing
    for 647, 648
  competence ratione
    personae 82
  and execution of
    judgments 182
  legal representation 137
non-pecuniary damages (moral
  damages)
  just satisfaction 160–161
non-retroactivity of treaties
  principle
  competence ratione
    temporis 97
non-retrospectiveness
  principle
  Article 7 500
'normal civic obligations'
  freedom from forced
    or compulsory
    labour 283–284
  public law rights and
    obligations under
    Article 6 387
Northern Ireland
  terrorist acts 826, 834, 835,
    836, 841
nullem crimen, nulla poena
  sine lege (conviction and
  punishment only on basis
  of law)
  Article 7 493

object and purpose of ECHR
  achievements 37
  admissibility of
    applications 43
  Article 8 523
  interpretation 7–8, 9, 18, 19
objectivity
  impartiality of tribunals 451,
    452, 453, 454–455
obscenity
  and artistic expression
    634

observance
    manifesting religion or belief
        in 602–605
offensive language
    abuse applications 79
ombudsmen
    complaints to 55
ordre public (European
    public order)
    ECHR as instrument of 8
origins
    differential treatment,
        intensive scrutiny
        796–797
    personal identity 537–538
Osman obligation
    life, right to 209, 210, 211,
        212

PACE *see* PARLIAMENTARY
    ASSEMBLY OF COUNCIL
    OF EUROPE (PACE)
parents
    recognition of
        parentage 564–567
    religious and philosophical
        convictions, respect
        for when educating
        children 801–802, 912–916
Parliamentary Assembly of
    Council of Europe (PACE)
    advisory opinions 135
    and Committee of
        Ministers 181
    Committee on Legal Affairs
        and Human Rights 31,
        189, 194, 195, 196, 198
    election of judges and
        Advisory Panel 107
    and execution of
        judgments 194–196
    investigations and
        fact-finding 145
    Resolution 1366 (2004) 108
    Resolution 1436 (2005) 108
    Resolution 1646 (2009) 109
    see also COUNCIL OF
        EUROPE
parliamentary immunity
    right of access to a court 405
peaceful assemblies *see*
    FREEDOM OF PEACEFUL
    ASSEMBLY
pecuniary damage
    civil rights and obligations 381
    just satisfaction 159–162
penalties
    distinction between
        penalty and manner of
        execution 500

ex post facto criminal
        penalties 499–501
    participation in lawful
        assemblies 721–722
personal identity *see*
    IDENTITY
'persons of unsound mind'
    detention grounds 324–328
petition
    abuse of right of 79–81
pilot judgments
    Article 46 164
    ECtHR procedure 149–151
    and execution of
        judgments 29–30
police
    disclosure of personal
        information by 561
    fingerprinting and
        photography 559–560
    physical detention at hands
        of 292
    search and seizure
        powers 557–559
    see also ARTICLE 5 (RIGHT
        TO LIBERTY AND
        SECURITY OF THE
        PERSON); DETENTION
political expression
    Article 10 629–631, 673
political issues
    civil rights and
        obligations 385
    defamation and
        politicians 695
    duties and responsibilities of
        politicians 683–684
    employment and political
        activities 578–579
    misconduct, as bar
        to standing for
        election 941–942
    political expression 629–631,
        673
    political figures and public
        figures doctrine 693–695
    politically motivated
        prosecutions 858–861
political parties
    associations, limitations
        upon 725–731
    and freedom of
        expression 631
positive obligations
    Article 1, Protocol 1 870–873
    Article 2 207
    Article 4 284–286
    Article 5 297
    Article 8 532–535, 542, 568
    Articles 8–11 504–505

Article 10 617–620
Article 11 712–713, 738–739
Article 14 817–818
    competence *ratione
        personae* 82
    context of ECHR 21, 22–23
    in Protocol 1 920
possessions
    under Article 1, First
        Protocol 863–868,
        870–873
    concept 863–864, 865
    essential characteristics 863
    established economic
        interest 865–866
    existing only protected under
        Protocol 1 867
    legitimate expectations 864
    positive obligation to
        protect 870–873
press
    balance between rights of
        and privacy rights of
        public figures 667
    democracy-fostering
        function 640
    freedom of 512, 640, 661
    and journalistic
        freedom 639–643
    primary and secondary
        role 615
    prior restraints on 640
    protection and
        confidentiality of
        sources 640, 641–643
    'public watchdog' role 615,
        632, 640, 641, 690
    publications
        privacy 551–553
        reputation 553–554
    see also ARTICLE 10
        (FREEDOM OF
        EXPRESSION);
        FREEDOM OF
        EXPRESSION
presumption of innocence
    burden of proof 462
    fair hearing, right to 421, 429
    right to be presumed
        innocent in criminal
        cases 460–467
    violation 467
pre-trial detention
    accountability
        during 338–351
price comparison
    forbidden under unfair
        competition laws 638
prisoners
    Article 8 585–589

of conscience 858
correspondence 587
detention, classic case 290
disenfranchisement 929–933
family, contact with 585–586
ill-treatment 239–240
legal advisors,
    communication with 588
restrictions on
    correspondence 507
right to marry 757–758
strip searches 263
telephone calls 589
privacy
press publications 551–553
of private individuals,
    protecting 660, 661
of public figures,
    protecting 666–669
see also PRIVATE LIFE
private conduct
context of ECHR 24
private discrimination
positive obligation to protect
    against 817–818
private law
civil rights and
    obligations 378–379
rights and obligations in
    relations between private
    persons 380
state action determining 380
private life
Article 8 protection 524–526,
    555
home life 581
secret surveillance 555
see also PRIVACY
Privy Council, UK
Judicial Committee 58
procedural guarantees on
review of detention
adversarial proceedings 356
'Belmarsh detainees'
    case 358
decision to be taken
    'speedily' 362–363
equality of arms 356–357
fairness 357, 358, 359
legal assistance 360–361
oral hearing and presence of
    detainee 359–360
terrorism 358
time and facilities to prepare
    an application 361
procedural obligations
Article 2 214–218
Article 8 535–536
profession
right to practise 381–382

professional advertising
and commercial expression
    638
professional misconduct
Article 6, application 375
promptness requirement
accountability
    during pre-trial
    detention 339–341
arrest, reasons to be given
    promptly
general issues 334–335
level of information
    required 335–338
investigations 217–218
trial within reasonable
    time 350–351
property, right to
access to property 869–870
Article 1, Protocol 1 see
    under FIRST PROTOCOL
under Article 6 381
control of use (Article 1/2)
in general
    interest 895–901
payment of taxes,
    contributions and
    penalties 901–903
deprivation of property
(Article 1/1/2)
compensation 888–894
definition of
    deprivation 885–887
general principles
    of international
    law 887–888
exhaustion rule 49
non-discrimination 791
peaceful enjoyment,
    interference with
Article 1/1/1 880–885
three kinds of
    interference 868–869
possessions 863–868
positive obligation to
    protect 870–872
proportionality principle
Article 2 204
Article 14 503
assessment under Articles
    8–11 519–520
differential treatment
    794–796
freedom of association,
    interferences with 735–737
gross disproportionality 259
interpretation of
    ECHR 13–14
margin of appreciation
    doctrine 658

'necessary in a democratic
    society' requirement 510
prosecutions
politically motivated
    858–861
proselytism
freedom of thought,
    conscience and
    religion 610–611
Protocols
First see FIRST PROTOCOL
Fourth 288–289, 952–963
Sixth 225, 963–965
Seventh
aliens, expulsion 386
divorce 760
equality of rights for
    spouses 974–975
freedom from expulsion
    of individual
    aliens 965–966
ne bis in idem
    principle 969–973
right to compensation
    for miscarriages of
    justice 968–969
right to review in criminal
    cases 966–968
Eighth 61
Eleventh
drafting history 124
enforcement machinery 6
setting up of new
    Court 103, 104
workload of ECtHR 38
Twelfth 783, 819–821,
    925–926
Thirteenth 963–965
Fourteenth
ad hoc and common
    interest judges 110
background 165
changes to ECHR 165–166
Committee procedure 121
drafting 104
execution of
    judgments 190,
    196–198
Explanatory Report 110,
    121, 196
formations of
    ECtHR 111–112
no significant
    disadvantage
    provision 67, 71
oral hearings 138
and procedure before
    ECtHR 165–166
prospects for ECHR 39
reform of ECtHR 166

Protocols (*Cont.*)
  Fifteenth
    case law, ensuring
      consistency of 127
    composition of
      ECtHR 105
    Explanatory Report 168
    no significant
      disadvantage
      criterion 71
    reform of ECtHR 168–169
    six-month rule 61
  Sixteenth
    advisory
      opinions 169–171
  Optional 6, 76, 171
pseudonyms
  inadmissibility grounds 73
psychiatric care
  degrading treatment 266
psychological interrogation
  techniques
  inhuman treatment 244
public emergency
  community service in 283
  duration 832–833
  existence 833–836
  proportionality principle 13
  threatening life of
    nation, circumstances
      representing 830–833
    basic definition 830
    duration of public
      emergency 832–833
    geographic aspects 832,
      833
    intensity of violence 832
    temporariness 833
    A v UK 828, 831–832, 843
    see also ARTICLE 15
      (DEROGATION IN TIME
      OF EMERGENCY)
public figures
  and broader bounds
    of acceptable
    criticism 693–697
  civil servants and public
    figures doctrine 696–697
  improper influence on trials,
    preventing 681
  political figures and public
    figures doctrine 693–695
  protection of privacy,
    reputation and
    honour 666–669
public hearing, right to
  Article 6 433–438
  oral 436–437
public interest
  commercial expression 639

defamation 708
press freedom 661, 662
public law
  rights and
    obligations 384–385
public order
  bail, grounds for
    refusing 348
public service, employment in
  civil rights and
    obligations 386–387
  restrictions upon
    employees 750–751
publicity
  defamation 692–693
  ECtHR procedure 136
  prejudicial media 428–429
  private individuals,
    protection of reputation
    and honour 660
punishment
  capital punishment *see*
    DEATH PENALTY
  degrading 271–273
  inhuman 259–260
  whole life sentences 259, 260

race
  differential treatment,
    intensive
    scrutiny 796–797
racial discrimination
  Article 3 270
racial violence
  committed by authorities,
    state responsibility
    for (substantive
    question) 812–813
  in context of policing and
    criminal justice (*Nachova
    v Bulgaria*) 811–814
  domestic investigation
    (procedural
    question) 813–814
racism
  and freedom of
    expression 622, 623
rape
  common law exception to
    497
ratione loci (competence/
  compatibility)
  Article 56 100–102
ratione materiae (competence)
  admissibility 44, 95–96
ratione personae (competence/
  compatibility)
  death of applicant 94–95
  inter-state cases 45
  respondent state 81–84

victim status 84–91
  indirect victims 91–94
  loss of following lodging
    of application 90–91
ratione temporis (competence/
  compatibility)
  facts giving rise to the
    application 97–98
  scope of Convention
    right 98–99
reciprocity principle
  inter-state complaints 115
rectification of errors, requests
  for
  European Court of Human
    Rights 132–133
reform of European
  Court 166–176
  access of EU to
    Convention 171–176
  advisory opinions, requests
    for 169–171
  Protocol 15 168–169
Registry, European Court of
  Human Rights
  Article 41 Unit 155
  organisation of
    ECtHR 112–113
religion or belief
  differential treatment,
    scrutiny 801–802
  manifesting
    nature of
      manifestation 602–604
    public 604–605
    in worship, teaching,
      practice and
      observance 602–605
  meaning of 'belief' 593
  minorities, protection 596
  parental, respect for
    when educating
    children 912–916
  personal convictions,
    requiring
    disclosure 595–596
  protection of freedom of
    religion of others 669–671
  religious assemblies 717–718
  religious dress 603, 608–610
  see also ARTICLE
    9 (FREEDOM
    OF THOUGHT,
    CONSCIENCE AND
    RELIGION); FREEDOM
    OF THOUGHT,
    CONSCIENCE AND
    RELIGION
religious dress
  Article 9 603, 608–610

remedies
  adequacy and
    effectiveness 52–54
  auxiliary, and relationship
    with Article 35 767–768
  cumulation of procedures
    to be taken into
    account 772–773
  domestic, exhaustion of see
    EXHAUSTION RULE
  effective
    general principles/
      requirements 768–773
    institutional
      requirements 771–772
    substantive
      requirements 769–771
  extraordinary or
    discretionary (exhaustion
    rule) 54–55
  general principles/
    requirements
    effective remedy 768–773
    specific contexts 774–782
  incorporation of Convention
    and discretion
    available to state in
    providing 765–766
  for individuals 35–37
  pre-emptive, for 'arguable'
    claims 766–767
  several (exhaustion rule) 54
  see also ARTICLE 13
    (RIGHT TO AN
    EFFECTIVE NATIONAL
    REMEDY)
rendu publiquement
  ('pronounced publicly')
  interpretation of ECHR 19
reputation
  press publications 553–554
  private individuals 658–666
  public figures 666–669
res judicata principle
  legal certainty principle 431
research, duties of journalists
  in relation to
  corroboration of cited
    information 688–689
  exemption from duty to
    undertake independent
    research 689–691
reservations
  context of ECHR 24–26
restitutio in integrum
  individual measures 185
  pecuniary damage 160
retroactive legislation
  designed to defeat litigant's
    claim 429

retrospectiveness principle
  Article 7 500
reverse discrimination
  Article 14 818–819
revision requests
  European Court of Human
    Rights 132, 133–134
riot, quelling
  exception to prohibition
    of taking of life by
    force 232–233
Roma
  discrimination against 810
  violence against 812

same-sex marriages
  right to marry 758, 759, 804
search and seizure powers
  Article 8 557–559
secret surveillance
  Article 8 555–557
  email monitoring 556
  non-state bodies 556–557
  telephone-tapping 507, 556
  terrorist suspects 826
Secretary General, Council of
  Europe
  and Article 15 847, 848
Section Registrar
  assistance by 112
  case law, ensuring
    consistency of 126
secularism
  scope of Article 9 593
security of the person
  Article 5 300
self-defence/defence of another
  exception to prohibition
    of taking of life by
    force 229–231
self-incrimination, freedom
  from
  fair hearing, right
    to 422–426
separation of powers
  impartiality 452
servitude
  freedom from 279–280
sex (gender)
  differential treatment,
    scrutiny 798–800
  personal identity 536–537
sexual activities
  Article 8 549–551
sexual orientation
  differential treatment,
    scrutiny 803–806
silent, right to remain
  freedom from
    self-incrimination 423

six-month rule
  admissibility of
    applications 44, 61–67
  aim 61–62
  amending the application 67
  Article 35 73
  continuing situations 47,
    64–65
  date of final decision 62–64
  date of introduction 66–67
  Protocol 15 reforms 169
slavery
  freedom from 279–280
social care
  detention in context
    of 294–296
social services
  right to life 212–214
  right to social security/
    assistance 383
Socialist Federal Republic of
  Yugoslavia
  foreign currency savings
    problem in successor
    states 75
solitary confinement
  detainees,
    treatment 264–265
Spain
  Constitutional Court,
    amparo appeals 49
  freedom of
    expression 618–619
special circumstances
  exhaustion rule 58–61
  six-month rule 65
Special Immigration Appeals
  Commission (SIAC)
  United Kingdom 358, 359
speech, freedom of see
  ARTICLE 10 (FREEDOM OF
  EXPRESSION); FREEDOM
  OF EXPRESSION
spouses
  equality of rights
    for 974–975
Stalinist communism
  and freedom of
    expression 621, 622
standard of proof
  ECtHR procedure 146–148
state immunity
  right of access to a court 405
statements of fact
  versus value
    judgments 697–700
states
  actions caught by Article 9 595
  Article 17 pleaded
    against 856–857

states (*Cont.*)
  Article 17 pleaded
    by 853–856
  breach of Article 3 251
  church/state
    relations 597–600
  deportation or extradition
    to 286
  as employers 741
  freedom of movement within
    territory of 954–957
  freedom to leave territory
    of 958–959
  illegal action by, right
    to compensation
    for 382–383
  ill-treatment, responsibility
    for 251, 252
  impartiality duty 598, 599
  inter-state cases
    admissibility requirements,
      application to 45–47
    complaints before
      ECtHR 115–117
    and enforcement 6
  medical negligence,
    responsibility for 213–214
  neutrality duty 598, 599
  obligations under
    Article 46 193
  positive obligations 618
    see also POSITIVE
      OBLIGATIONS
  racial violence committed by
    authorities, responsibility
    for 812–813
  respondent 81–84
  responsibility of, engaging in
    loss of liberty cases 297
  right of a national not to
    be expelled from or to
    enter 959–960
  state practice Article 7 495
  toleration of violence
    motivated by
    discrimination 814–815
  ultra vires acts, responsibility
    for 237–238
striking out cases
  conditions 131
  under European Court of
    Human Rights 130–132
strip searches
  prisoners 263
substantive guarantee
  context of ECHR 5–6
suicide
  assisted 205, 547
  Osman obligation 211
  see also DEATH

Supreme Court of United
  Kingdom
  Judicial Committee of Privy
    Council composed of
    Justices from 58
surveillance see SECRET
  SURVEILLANCE
Switzerland
  reservations 25–26

taking of life
  laws prohibiting 204
taxation, payment of
  civil rights and
    obligations 385
  property, control of
    use 901–903
teaching
  manifesting religion or belief
    in 602–605
television broadcasting
  terrestrial and cable 644
terrorism
  crime prevention 655
  detention on suspicion
    of having committed
    terrorist activities 315
  general approach of Court
    to 825–829
  Northern Ireland 826, 834,
    835, 836, 841
  post 9/11 era 825, 828
  and procedural guarantees on
    review of detention 358
third parties
  ECtHR procedure 152–155
  freedom of peaceful
    assembly 713–714
  trade union action
    against 743–744
thought, freedom of see
  ARTICLE 9 (FREEDOM OF
  THOUGHT, CONSCIENCE
  AND RELIGION);
  FREEDOM OF THOUGHT,
  CONSCIENCE AND
  RELIGION
time limits
  exhaustion rule 50–51
  presentation of
    applications 119
torture
  Article 3 provisions 238–240
  Committee for the
    Prevention of Torture
    (Council of Europe) 75,
    145, 147, 262
  defined 238
  and lesser kinds of
    ill-treatment 237

mental suffering 240
  of political detainees
    238–239
  UN Convention 499
  see also ARTICLE 3
    (FREEDOM FROM
    TORTURE OR
    INHUMAN OR
    DEGRADING
    TREATMENT OR
    PUNISHMENT)
totalitarian regimes
  and freedom of
    expression 621
trade unions
  action against third
    parties 743–744
  freedom of expression 618
  freedom to form and
    join 740–741
  members' interests, right to
    protect 747–750
  public service employees,
    restrictions on 750–751
  right not to join 744–746
  right to regulate internal
    affairs 742–743
  see also CLOSED SHOP
    CASES
trafficking, human
  Article 4 284–286
transsexuals
  gender identification
    536–537
  gender reassignment
    surgery 537
  interpretation of ECHR 10
  parentage, recognition 567
  right to marry 758–759
travaux préparatoires
  interpretation of
    ECHR 19–20
  trade unions, right not to
    join 744
treatment
  degrading
    conditions of detention
      and treatment of
      detainees 261–269
    defined 261
    discrimination 269–270
    forced shaving off of
      hair 263
    other kinds 270–271
    psychiatric care 266
    strip searches 263
  of detainees 244, 261–269
    compulsory medical
      intervention 267–268
    generally 261

handcuffing/other
restraints 268–269
medical assistance
265–267
solitary confinement
264–265
inhuman
Article 3 241–258
assaults 241–243
conditions of detention
and treatment of
detainees 244
deportation 244–256
disappeared persons 257
extradition 244–256
extraordinary
rendition 256
other kinds 257–258
psychological
interrogation
techniques 244
proscribed ill-treatment,
obligation to protect
individuals from
investigation and
enforcement 275–277
prevention 274–275
see also ARTICLE 3
(FREEDOM FROM
TORTURE OR
INHUMAN OR
DEGRADING
TREATMENT OR
PUNISHMENT)
Treaty on European Union
(TEU)
on EU and ECHR
relationship 32
trial
adversarial, right to 416–418
bringing promptly before
judge/other authorized
officer following
arrest 338–339
characteristics of judicial
officer 341–342
diligence in conduct of
proceedings, need
for 350–351
exclusion of public
from 675
function of officer and
procedure to be
followed 342–343
improper influence on,
preventing 679–683
more than 'reasonable
suspicion' required
to sustain prolonged
detention 344–346

pre-trial detention,
accountability
during 338–351
within a reasonable time
Article 5 350–351
Article 6 439–446
Article 13 777–778
right to release pending
trial in reasonable
circumstances 343–350
witnesses, right to call and
cross-examine 483–484
see also ARTICLE 5 (RIGHT
TO LIBERTY AND
SECURITY OF THE
PERSON); ARTICLE
6 (RIGHT TO FAIR
TRIAL); FAIR HEARING,
RIGHT TO
tribunal
defined 446–447
established by law 458
impartiality 450–457
independence 447–450
no significant disadvantage
criterion considered
by 71–72
Turkey
appeals to higher courts 57
criminal prosecution against
police in 143
destruction of homes, state
responsibility 580
just satisfaction
case 184–185
terrorism in 835
Twelfth Protocol
Article 14 819–821

Ukraine
list of judges to
Parliamentary
Assembly 109
ultra vires acts
Article 7 495
state responsibility 237–238
'unauthorized entry',
preventing
detention grounds 328–330
unborn child, protection
involuntary
abortion 220–221
other harmful acts 221
voluntary abortion 219–220
unilateral declarations
ECtHR procedure 129–130
United Kingdom
appeals to higher courts 58
breach of Article 3,
Protocol 1 33–34

extraordinary or
discretionary
remedies 54, 55
fingerprints and DNA
material, indefinite
retention 11
Human Rights Act 1998
and application of
ECHR by national
courts 27–28
declaration of
incompatibility
under 55
parliamentary
sovereignty 27
Special Immigration Appeals
Commission 358, 359
United Nations
Charter 783
High Commissioner for
Refugees 144
Interim Administration in
Kosovo (UNMIK) 84, 111
and international
investigation or
settlement, another
procedure 76
Security Council 84
Universal Declaration of
Human Rights (1948)
protection of rights spelt out
in 5
reputation, protection 553
unmarried fathers
differential treatment,
scrutiny 806–808
untrue facts
abuse applications 79

'vagrants'
detention grounds 322
value judgments
versus statements of
fact 697–700
Venice Commission
Council of Europe 144
vexatious application
abuse of the right of petition
provision 80
victim status
and compensation 91
competence ratione
personae 81, 84–91
concept of 'victim' 84
and criminal proceedings 87
deprivation of 87
indirect victims 91–94
loss of following lodging of
application 90–91
potential victims 85

Vienna Convention on the Law of Treaties (1969)
and interpretation of ECHR 7

violations
competence *ratione personae* 81
duty to protect from harm (Articles 2 and 3) 779–781
of fundamental rights, effective investigations 779–781
individuals, remedy for 36
just satisfaction 161
of obligations under Article 46 193–194
presumption of innocence 467
remedies, adequacy and effectiveness 53
'repetitive' 40
right to property guarantee under Article 1, Protocol 1 33
Second World War 3
specific violations of Article 18, read with another Article 857–858
standard of proof 148
see also specific Articles

violence
broadcasted programmes inciting 645
counter-demonstrators, disturbance by 712–713

discrimination, motivated by 811–814
state toleration 814–815
incitement to 626–629
intensity 832
lethal force, security forces 147–148
novels and paintings inciting 633
positive obligations under Article 10 619–620
racial, in context of policing and criminal justice 811–814
domestic investigation (procedural question) 813–814
state responsibility (substantive question) 812–813
see also TERRORISM; WAR OR OTHER EMERGENCY, DEROGATION IN TIME OF

voluntary abortion
Article 2 219–220

voting rights
expatriates 927–928
free elections, right to 926–933
International Covenant on Civil and Political Rights (ICCPR) 1966 851
and prisoners 929–933

war crimes
Article 7 205, 498

war or other public emergency threatening life of nation
Article 15
provisions 829–837
see also PUBLIC EMERGENCY

WECL (well-established case law)
European Court of Human Rights 112, 121, 165, 177

Wise Persons Group
Committee of Ministers, set up by 104
pilot judgment procedure 150

witnesses
investigations 145
right to call and cross-examine 483–489

Woolf Report
pilot judgment procedure 150

Working Group on Arbitrary Detention, UN
and international investigation or settlement, another procedure 76, 78

worship
manifesting religion or belief in 602–605

Zionism
criticism 624